The Thomas Guide®

Sacramento County
street guide

TELL US WHAT YOU THINK
comment card on last page

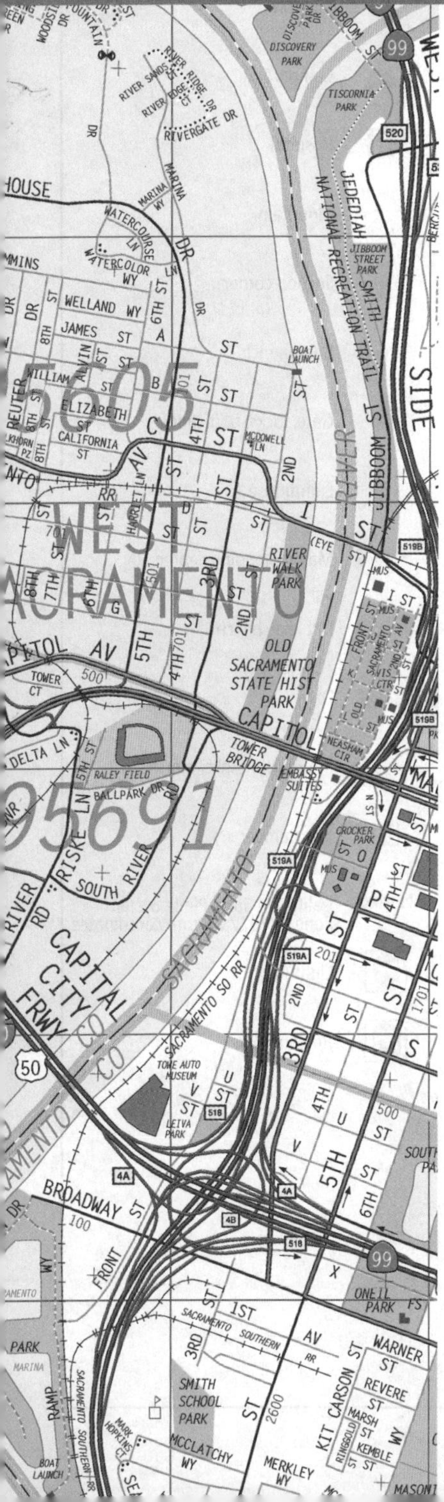

Contents

PageFinder™ Map U.S. Patent No. 5,419,586
Canadian Patent No. 2,116,425
Patente Mexicana No. 188186

RAND McNALLY
Rand McNally Consumer Affairs
P.O. Box 7600
Chicago, IL 60680-9915
randmcnally.com
For comments or suggestions, please call
(800) 777-MAPS (-6277)
or email us at:
consumeraffairs@randmcnally.com

Legend

- Freeway
- Interchange/ramp
- Highway
- Primary road
- Secondary road
- Minor road
- Restricted road
- Alley
- Unpaved road
- Tunnel
- Toll road
- High occupancy vehicle lane
- Stacked multiple roadways
- Proposed road
- Proposed freeway
- Freeway under construction
- One-way road
- Two-way road
- Trail, walkway
- Stairs
- Railroad
- Rapid transit
- Rapid transit, underground

- Ferry
- City boundary
- County boundary
- State boundary
- International boundary
- Military base, Indian reservation
- Township, range, rancho
- River, creek, shoreline
- 98607 ZIP code boundary, ZIP code
- Interstate
- Interstate (Business)
- U.S. highway
- State highways
- Carpool lane
- Street list marker
- Street name continuation
- Street name change
- Station (train, bus)
- Building (see List of Abbreviations page)
- Building footprint
- Public elementary school
- Public high school

- Private elementary school
- Private high school
- Fire station
- Library
- Mission
- Campground
- Hospital
- Mountain
- Section corner
- Boat launch
- Gate, locks, barricades
- Lighthouse
- Major shopping center
- Dry lake, beach
- Dam
- Intermittent lake, marsh
- 29 Exit number
- 2256000 California State Plane System Zone II (1927 Datum) coordinates
- Light Rail
- Regional Bus

Sacramento International Airport

Sacramento International Airport is conveniently close to surrounding communities of Auburn, Chico, Davis, Fairfield, Folsom, Lincoln, Lodi, Marysville, Oroville, Placerville, Roseville, Stockton, Vacaville, Woodland, Yuba City and Napa. There are over 20,000 public parking spaces at the airport, and four parking lots: Terminals A and B have Hourly and Daily lots, plus Economy parking. The maximum daily rates are $7.00 a day in the Economy lot, $12.00 a day for Daily lots and $26.00 a day for the close-in Hourly lots. The first 30 minutes are free in the hourly lots. The per hour rates for all lots are the same — $1.00 for the first hour and $2.00 for each additional hour or portion thereof. Parking rates are subject to change. Use the Hourly lots for pickup, drop-off, or quick visits to the airport. The hourly lots are located directly across the street from each terminal within easy walking distance. For more information visit www.sacairports.org.

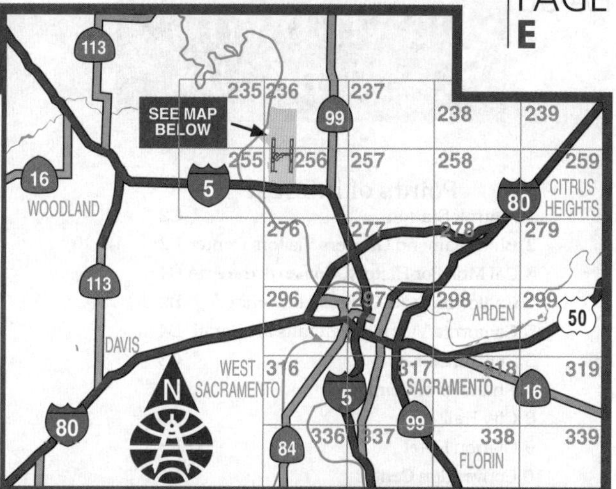

REFER TO MAP PAGE 256

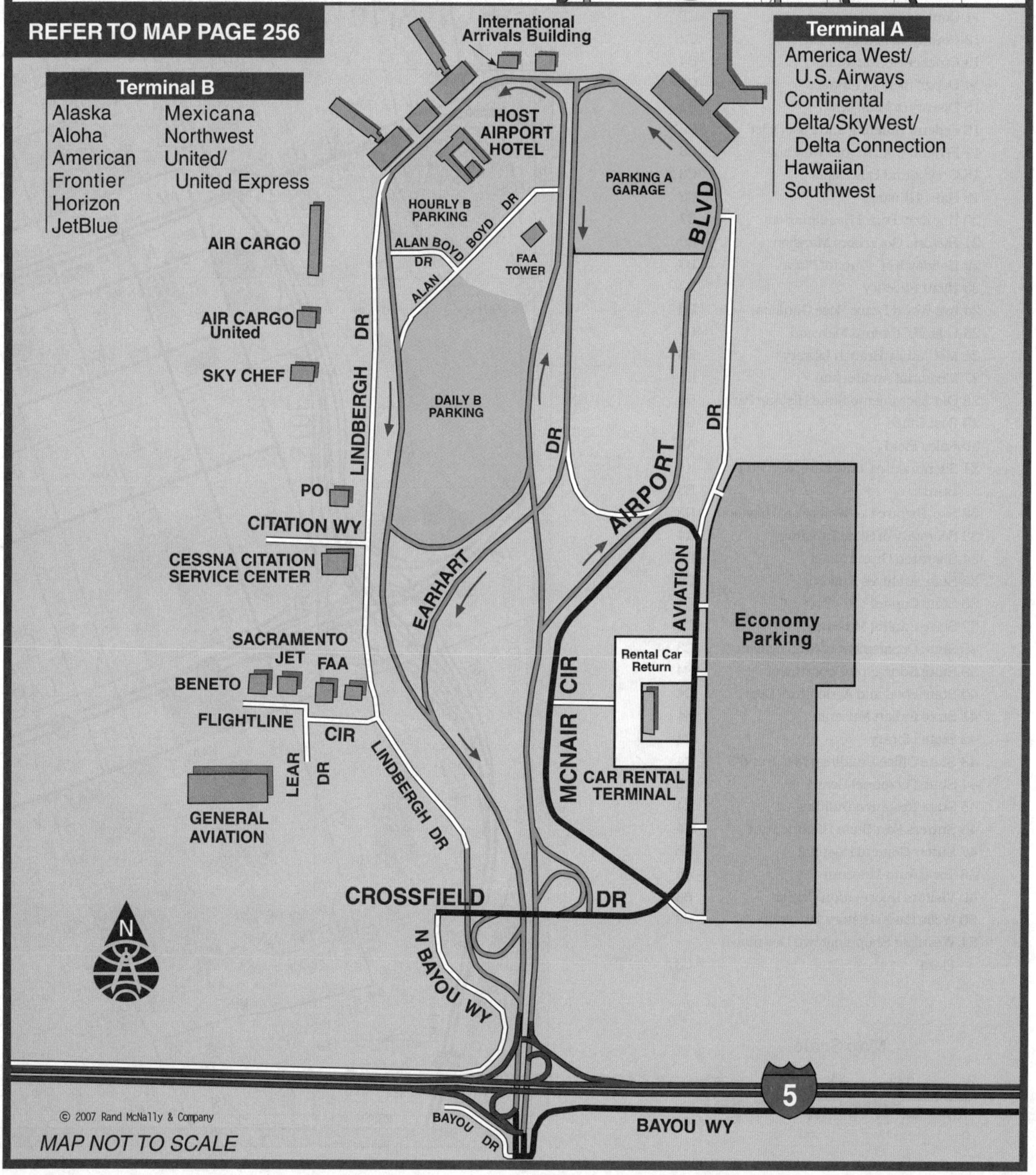

Downtown Sacramento

Points of Interest

1	Amtrak Station	C2
2	Blue Diamond Growers Visitors Center	E2
3	Cal Mus For History, Women & the Arts	C4
4	California State Railroad Museum	B2
5	California Vietnam Veterans Memorial	D4
6	Central Library	C3
7	Chamber of Commerce	C3
8	City Hall	C3
9	Clarion Hotel	E3
10	Convention Center	D3
11	County Administration	C3
12	County Courthouse	C2
13	Crocker Art Museum	B4
14	Department of Finance	C3
15	Discovery Museum	B2
16	Federal Building and Post Office	C3
17	Federal Courthouse Building	C3
18	Greyhound Bus Depot	C3
19	Hall of Justice	C3
20	Highway Patrol Headquarters	E7
21	Historic Governors Mansion	E3
22	Holiday Inn - Capitol Plaza	B3
23	Hyatt Regency	D4
24	Intl World Peace Rose Gardens	D4
25	Leland Stanford Mansion	C4
26	McClatchy Branch Library	E6
27	Memorial Auditorium	E3
28	Old Sacramento State Historic Park	B3
29	Post Office	G6
30	Raley Field	A3
31	Sacramento Convention & Visitors Bureau	E3
32	Sac Theatre Co/Wells Fargo Pavilion	D3
33	Secretary of State Building	C4
34	Sheraton Grand Hotel	D3
35	State Archives Building	C4
36	State Capitol	D4
37	State Capitol Museum	D4
38	State Department of Employment	C3
39	State Education Department	D4
40	State Food and Agriculture Dept	D4
41	State Indian Museum	F4
42	State Library	C4
43	State Office Buildings Nos. 8 and 9	C4
44	State Personnel Board	C3
45	State Resource Building	C4
46	Sutters Fort State Historic Park	F4
47	Sutter General Hospital	G5
48	Towe Auto Museum	A5
49	Visitors Information Center	B3
50	Wells Fargo History Museum	B3
51	Westfield Shoppingtown Downtown Plaza	C3

Map Scale

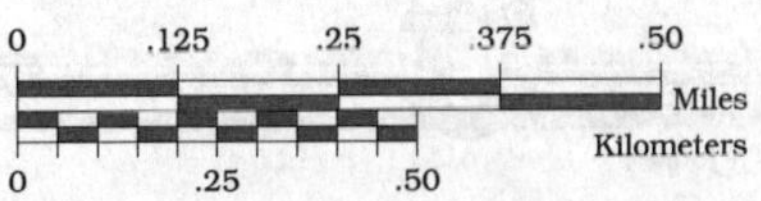

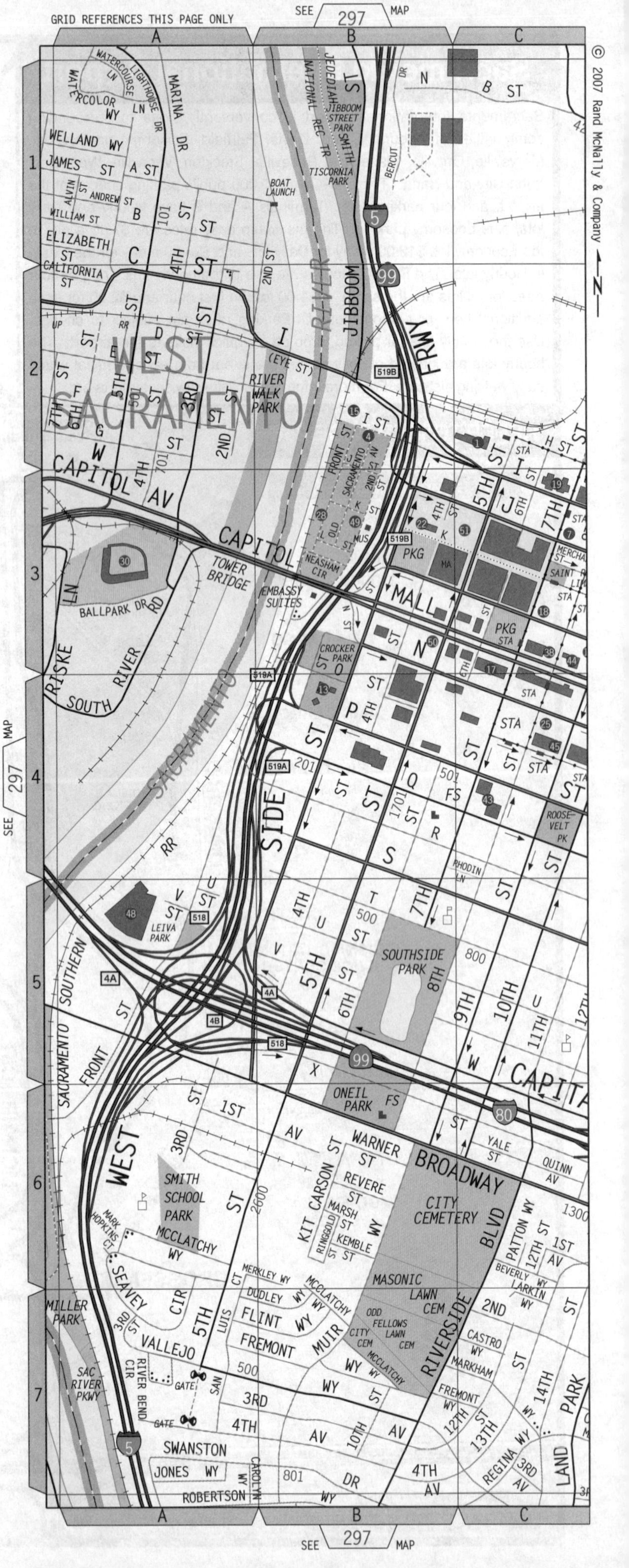

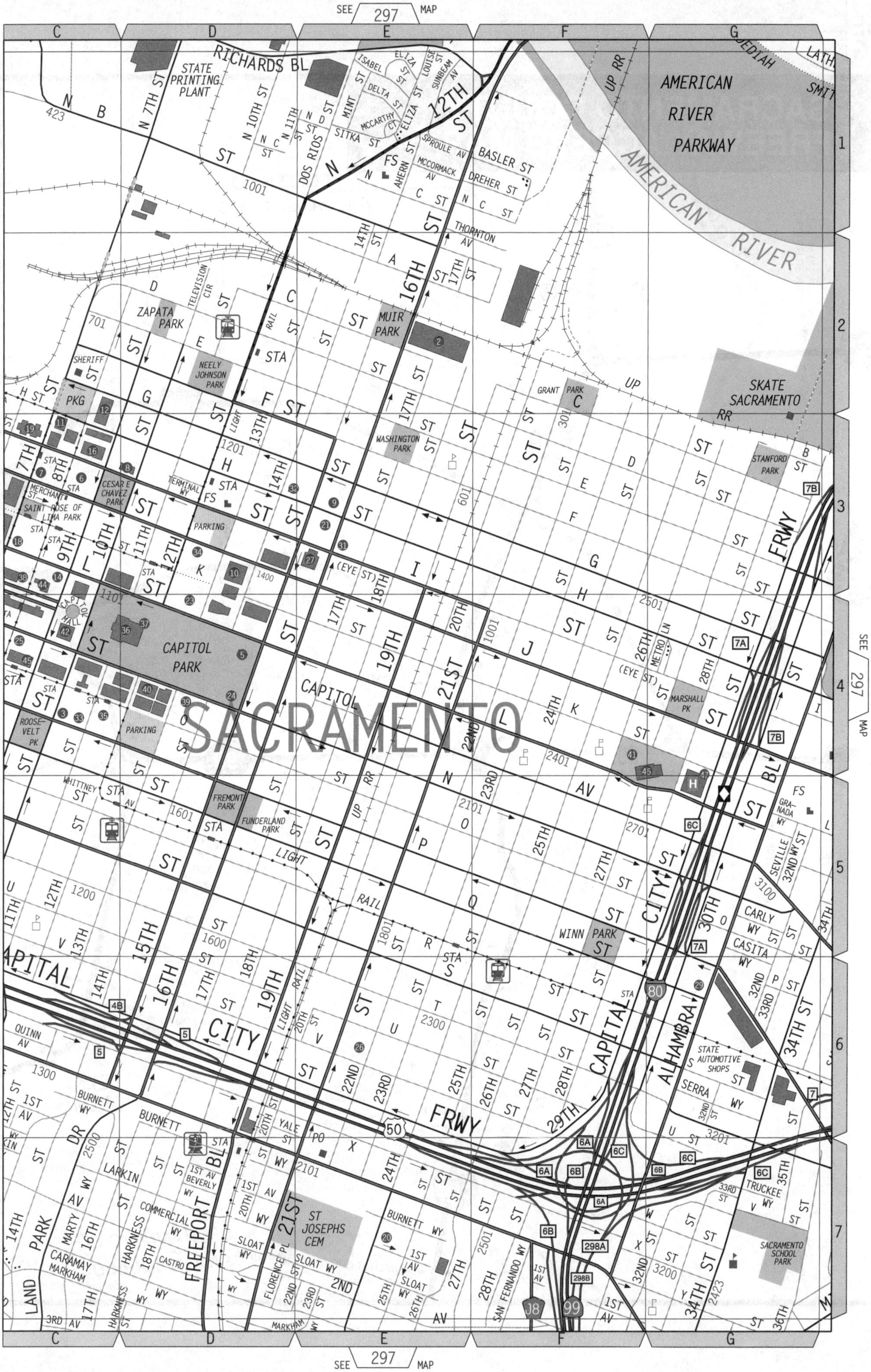
SEE 297 MAP
C
D
E
F
G
1
2
3
4
5
6
7
SEE 297 MAP
SACRAMENTO
AMERICAN RIVER PARKWAY
AMERICAN RIVER
RICHARDS BL
STATE PRINTING PLANT
N B ST
N 7TH ST
N 10TH ST
N 11TH ST
DOS RIOS ST
12TH ST
ISABEL ST
ELIZA ST
LOUISE ST
SUNBEAM AV
DELTA ST
MINT ST
MCCARTHY CT
SITKA ST
SPROULE AV
MCCORMACK AV
AHERN ST
BASLER ST
DREHER ST
THORNTON AV
UP RR
ZAPATA PARK
TELEVISION CIR
NEELY JOHNSON PARK
MUIR PARK
GRANT PARK
SKATE SACRAMENTO
SHERIFF
PKG
WASHINGTON PARK
STANFORD PARK
CESAR E CHAVEZ PARK
MERCHANT ST
SAINT ROSE OF LIMA PARK
TERMINAL WY
PARKING
CAPITOL PARK
CAPITOL MALL
(EYE ST)
CAPITOL AV
26TH ST
METRO LN
MARSHALL PK
ROOSEVELT PK
WHITNEY ST
FREMONT PARK
FUNDERLAND PARK
LIGHT RAIL
WINN PARK
GRANADA WY
SEVILLE WY
32ND WY ST
CARLY WY
CASITA WY
CAPITAL CITY FRWY
ALHAMBRA BL
STATE AUTOMOTIVE SHOPS
SERRA WY
34TH ST
QUINN AV
BURNETT WY
LAND PARK DR
LARKIN WY
COMMERCIAL WY
1ST AV
BEVERLY WY
FREEPORT BL
MARTY WY
CARAMAY WY
MARKHAM WY
HARKNESS ST
CASTRO WY
SLOAT WY
FLORENCE PL
ST JOSEPHS CEM
YALE ST
50 FRWY
80
99
J8
SAN FERNANDO WY
TRUCKEE WY
SACRAMENTO SCHOOL PARK
35TH ST
36TH ST
3RD AV
2ND AV

SACRAMENTO COUNTY FREEWAY ACCESS MAP

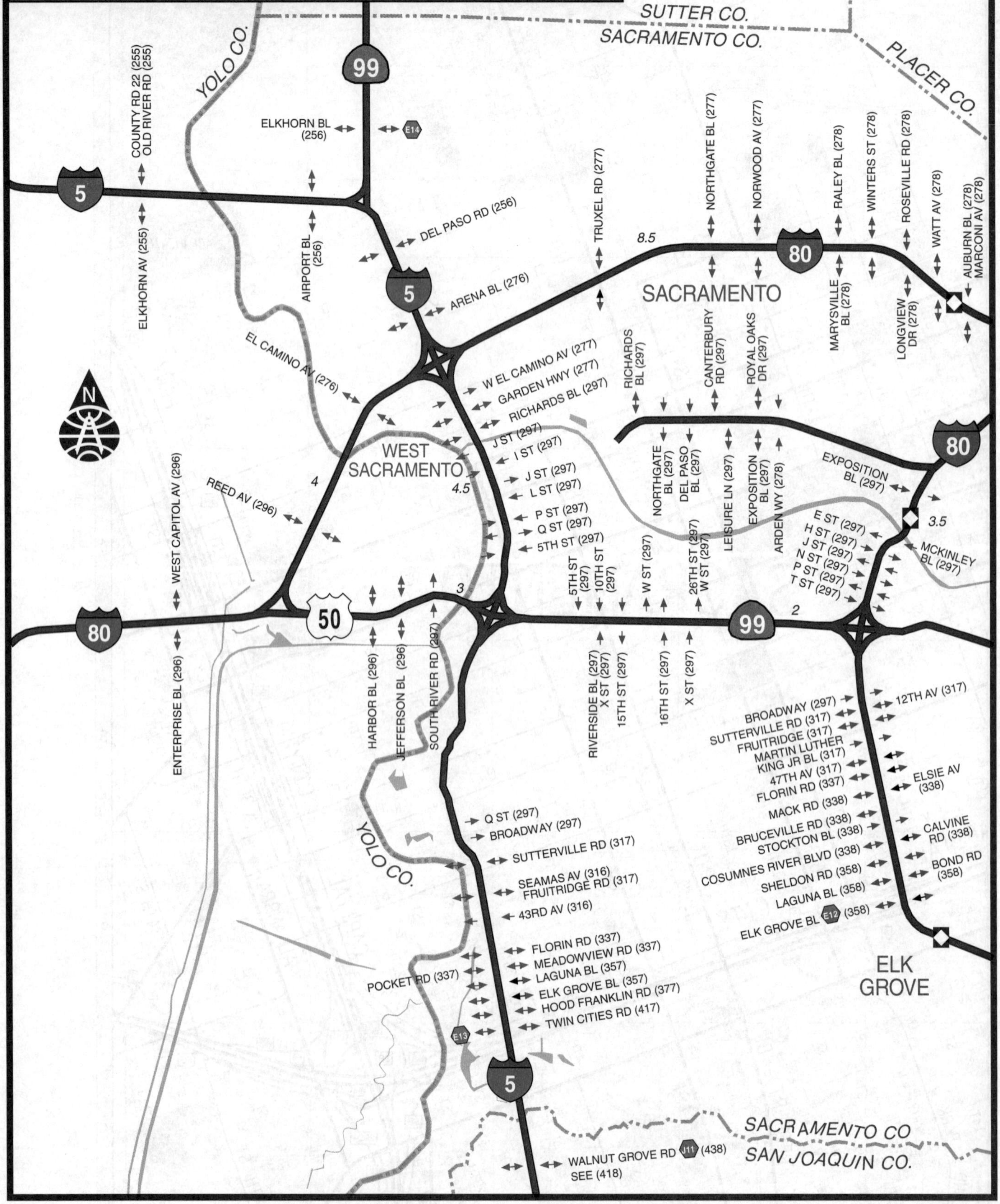
SUTTER CO.
SACRAMENTO CO.
PLACER CO.
YOLO CO.
99
5
80
50
ELKHORN BL (256)
E14
COUNTY RD 22 (255)
OLD RIVER RD (255)
ELKHORN AV (255)
AIRPORT BL (256)
DEL PASO RD (256)
ARENA BL (276)
EL CAMINO AV (276)
TRUXEL RD (277)
8.5
NORTHGATE BL (277)
NORWOOD AV (277)
RALEY BL (278)
WINTERS ST (278)
ROSEVILLE RD (278)
WATT AV (278)
AUBURN BL (278)
MARCONI AV (278)
SACRAMENTO
MARYSVILLE BL (278)
LONGVIEW DR (278)
CANTERBURY RD (297)
ROYAL OAKS DR (297)
RICHARDS BL (297)
W EL CAMINO AV (277)
GARDEN HWY (277)
RICHARDS BL (297)
J ST (297)
I ST (297)
J ST (297)
L ST (297)
P ST (297)
Q ST (297)
5TH ST (297)
WEST SACRAMENTO
4.5
4
3
REED AV (296)
WEST CAPITOL AV (296)
NORTHGATE BL (297)
DEL PASO BL (297)
LEISURE LN (297)
EXPOSITION BL (297)
ARDEN WY (278)
EXPOSITION BL (297)
3.5
E ST (297)
H ST (297)
J ST (297)
N ST (297)
P ST (297)
T ST (297)
MCKINLEY BL (297)
5TH ST (297)
10TH ST (297)
W ST (297)
26TH ST (297)
W ST (297)
2
ENTERPRISE BL (296)
HARBOR BL (296)
JEFFERSON BL (296)
SOUTH RIVER RD (297)
RIVERSIDE BL (297)
X ST (297)
15TH ST (297)
16TH ST (297)
X ST (297)
BROADWAY (297)
SUTTERVILLE RD (317)
FRUITRIDGE (317)
MARTIN LUTHER KING JR BL (317)
47TH AV (317)
FLORIN RD (337)
MACK RD (338)
BRUCEVILLE RD (338)
STOCKTON BL (338)
COSUMNES RIVER BLVD (338)
SHELDON RD (358)
LAGUNA BL (358)
ELK GROVE BL E12 (358)
12TH AV (317)
ELSIE AV (338)
CALVINE RD (338)
BOND RD (358)
ELK GROVE
Q ST (297)
BROADWAY (297)
SUTTERVILLE RD (317)
SEAMAS AV (316)
FRUITRIDGE RD (317)
43RD AV (316)
FLORIN RD (337)
MEADOWVIEW RD (337)
LAGUNA BL (357)
ELK GROVE BL (357)
HOOD FRANKLIN RD (377)
TWIN CITIES RD (417)
POCKET RD (337)
E13
SACRAMENTO CO
SAN JOAQUIN CO.
WALNUT GROVE RD J11 (438)
SEE (418)

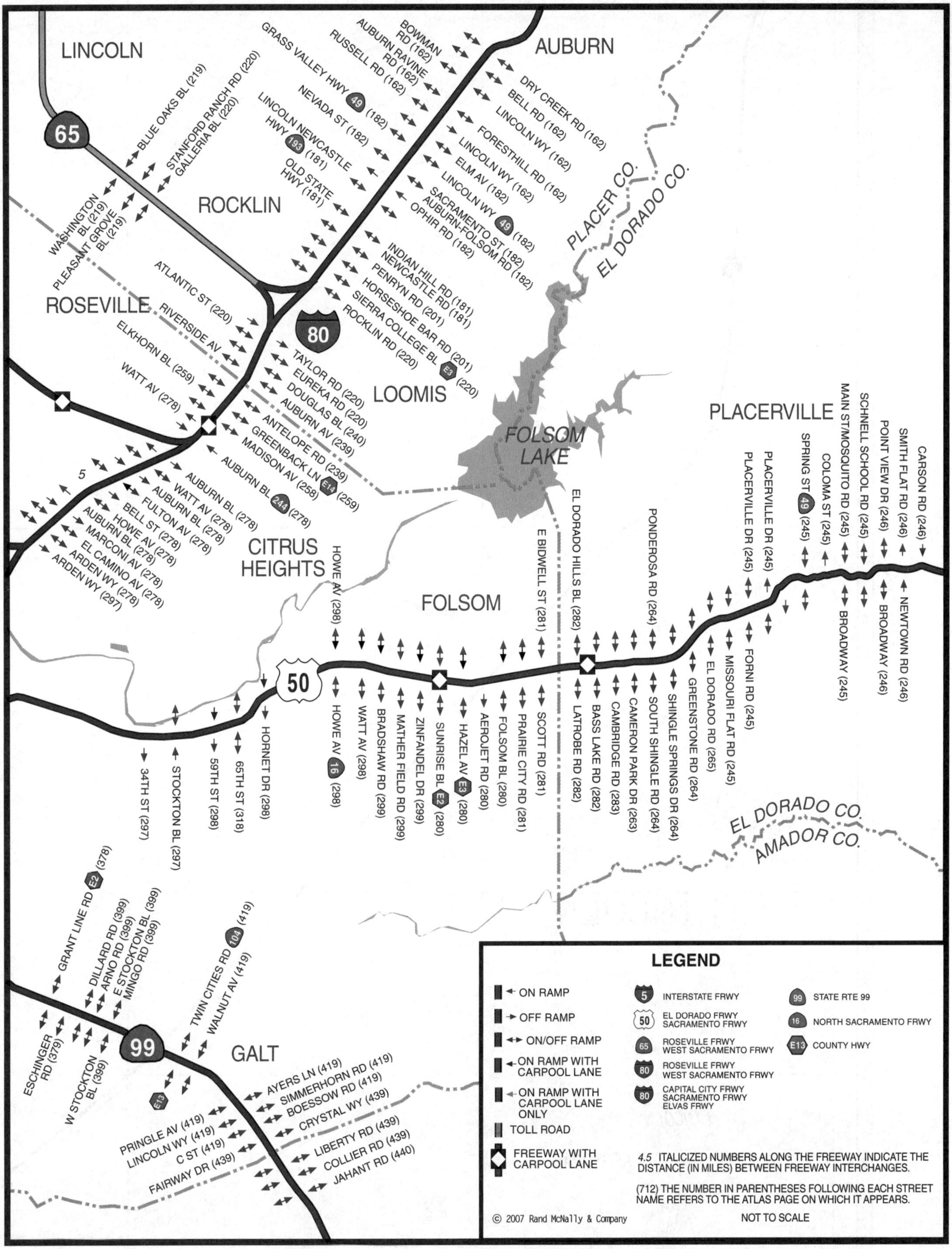
LINCOLN
AUBURN
ROCKLIN
ROSEVILLE
LOOMIS
CITRUS HEIGHTS
FOLSOM
FOLSOM LAKE
PLACERVILLE
GALT
PLACER CO.
EL DORADO CO.
AMADOR CO.
65
80
50
99
5
BOWMAN RD (162)
AUBURN RAVINE RD (162)
RUSSELL RD (162)
GRASS VALLEY HWY 49 (182)
NEVADA ST (182)
LINCOLN NEWCASTLE HWY 193 (181)
OLD STATE HWY (181)
DRY CREEK RD (162)
BELL RD (162)
LINCOLN WY (162)
FORESTHILL RD (162)
LINCOLN WY (162)
ELM AV (182)
LINCOLN WY 49 (182)
SACRAMENTO ST (182)
AUBURN-FOLSOM RD (182)
OPHIR RD (182)
BLUE OAKS BL (219)
STANFORD RANCH RD (220)
GALLERIA BL (220)
WASHINGTON BL (219)
PLEASANT GROVE BL (219)
ATLANTIC ST (220)
RIVERSIDE AV
ELKHORN BL (259)
WATT AV (278)
INDIAN HILL RD (181)
NEWCASTLE RD (181)
PENRYN RD (201)
HORSESHOE BAR RD (201)
SIERRA COLLEGE BL E3 (220)
ROCKLIN RD (220)
TAYLOR RD (220)
EUREKA RD (220)
DOUGLAS BL (240)
AUBURN AV (239)
ANTELOPE RD (239)
GREENBACK LN E14 (259)
MADISON AV (258)
AUBURN BL 244 (278)
AUBURN BL (278)
WATT AV (278)
AUBURN BL (278)
FULTON AV (278)
BELL ST (278)
HOWE AV (278)
AUBURN BL (278)
MARCONI AV (278)
EL CAMINO AV (278)
ARDEN WY (278)
ARDEN WY (297)
HOWE AV (298)
E BIDWELL ST (281)
EL DORADO HILLS BL (282)
PONDEROSA RD (264)
PLACERVILLE DR (245)
PLACERVILLE DR (245)
SPRING ST 49 (245)
COLOMA ST (245)
MAIN ST/MOSQUITO RD (245)
SCHNELL SCHOOL RD (245)
POINT VIEW DR (246)
SMITH FLAT RD (246)
CARSON RD (246)
34TH ST (297)
STOCKTON BL (297)
59TH ST (298)
65TH ST (318)
HORNET DR (298)
HOWE AV 16 (298)
WATT AV (298)
BRADSHAW RD (299)
MATHER FIELD RD (299)
ZINFANDEL DR (299)
SUNRISE BL E2 (280)
HAZEL AV E3 (280)
AEROJET RD (280)
FOLSOM BL (280)
PRAIRIE CITY RD (281)
SCOTT RD (281)
LATROBE RD (282)
BASS LAKE RD (282)
CAMBRIDGE RD (283)
CAMERON PARK DR (263)
SOUTH SHINGLE RD (264)
SHINGLE SPRINGS DR (264)
GREENSTONE RD (264)
EL DORADO RD (265)
MISSOURI FLAT RD (245)
FORNI RD (245)
BROADWAY (245)
BROADWAY (246)
NEWTOWN RD (246)
GRANT LINE RD E2 (378)
DILLARD RD (399)
ARNO RD (399)
E STOCKTON BL (399)
MINGO RD (399)
TWIN CITIES RD 104 (419)
WALNUT AV (419)
ESCHINGER RD (379)
W STOCKTON BL (399)
E13
AYERS LN (419)
SIMMERHORN RD (419)
BOESSOW RD (419)
CRYSTAL WY (439)
PRINGLE AV (419)
LINCOLN WY (419)
C ST (419)
FAIRWAY DR (439)
LIBERTY RD (439)
COLLIER RD (439)
JAHANT RD (440)
LEGEND
ON RAMP
OFF RAMP
ON/OFF RAMP
ON RAMP WITH CARPOOL LANE
ON RAMP WITH CARPOOL LANE ONLY
TOLL ROAD
FREEWAY WITH CARPOOL LANE
INTERSTATE FRWY
EL DORADO FRWY SACRAMENTO FRWY
ROSEVILLE FRWY WEST SACRAMENTO FRWY
ROSEVILLE FRWY WEST SACRAMENTO FRWY
CAPITAL CITY FRWY SACRAMENTO FRWY ELVAS FRWY
STATE RTE 99
NORTH SACRAMENTO FRWY
COUNTY HWY
4.5 ITALICIZED NUMBERS ALONG THE FREEWAY INDICATE THE DISTANCE (IN MILES) BETWEEN FREEWAY INTERCHANGES.
(712) THE NUMBER IN PARENTHESES FOLLOWING EACH STREET NAME REFERS TO THE ATLAS PAGE ON WHICH IT APPEARS.
NOT TO SCALE
© 2007 Rand McNally & Company

SACRAMENTO CO.

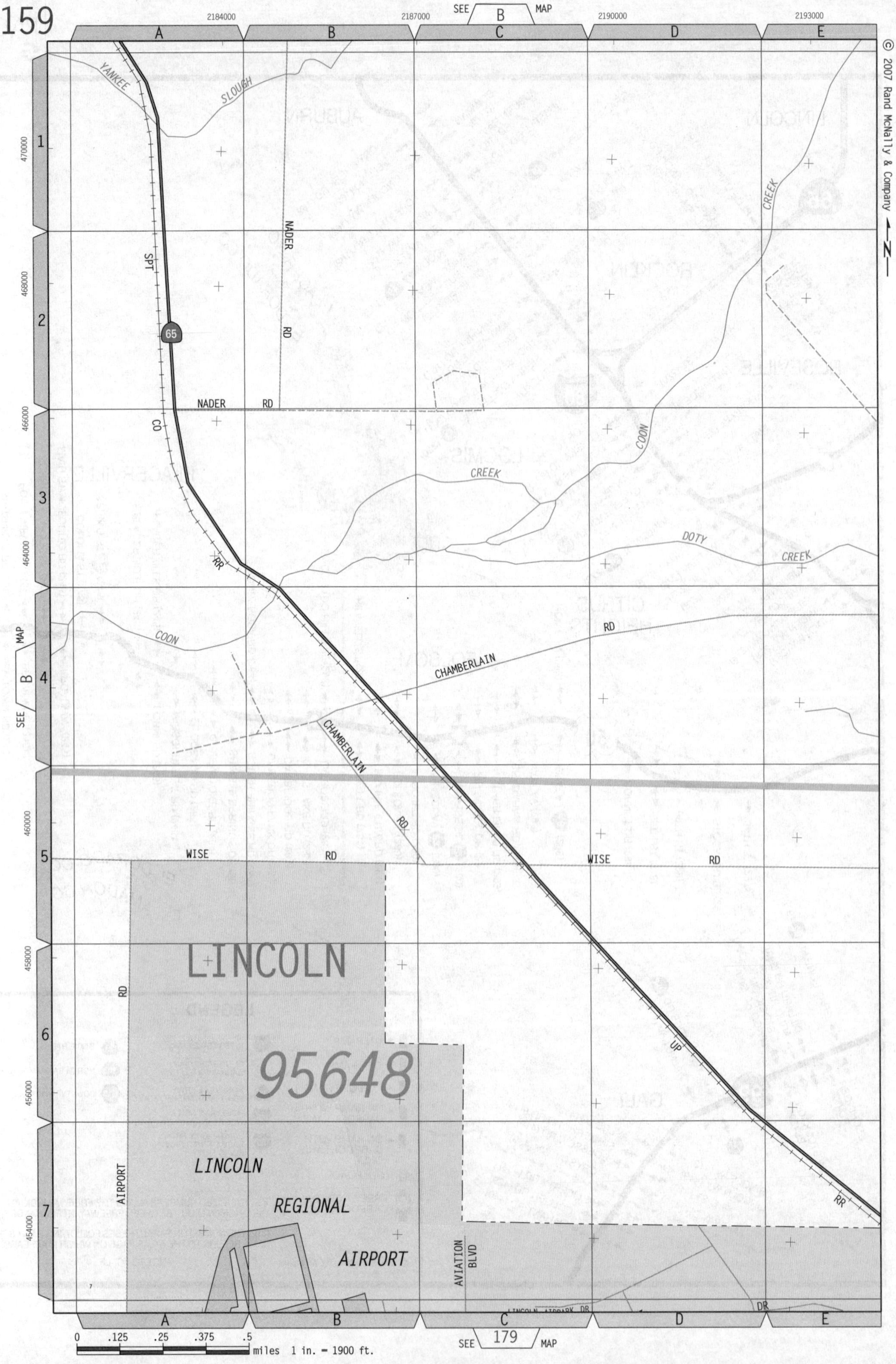
SEE B MAP
SEE B MAP
SEE 179 MAP
2184000
2187000
2190000
2193000
470000
468000
466000
464000
460000
458000
456000
454000
YANKEE SLOUGH
NADER RD
NADER RD
SPT CO RR
65
COON CREEK
COON
DOTY CREEK
CREEK
CHAMBERLAIN RD
CHAMBERLAIN RD
WISE RD
WISE RD
UP RR
LINCOLN
95648
AIRPORT RD
LINCOLN REGIONAL AIRPORT
AVIATION BLVD
LINCOLN AIRPARK DR
DR
0 .125 .25 .375 .5 miles 1 in. = 1900 ft.

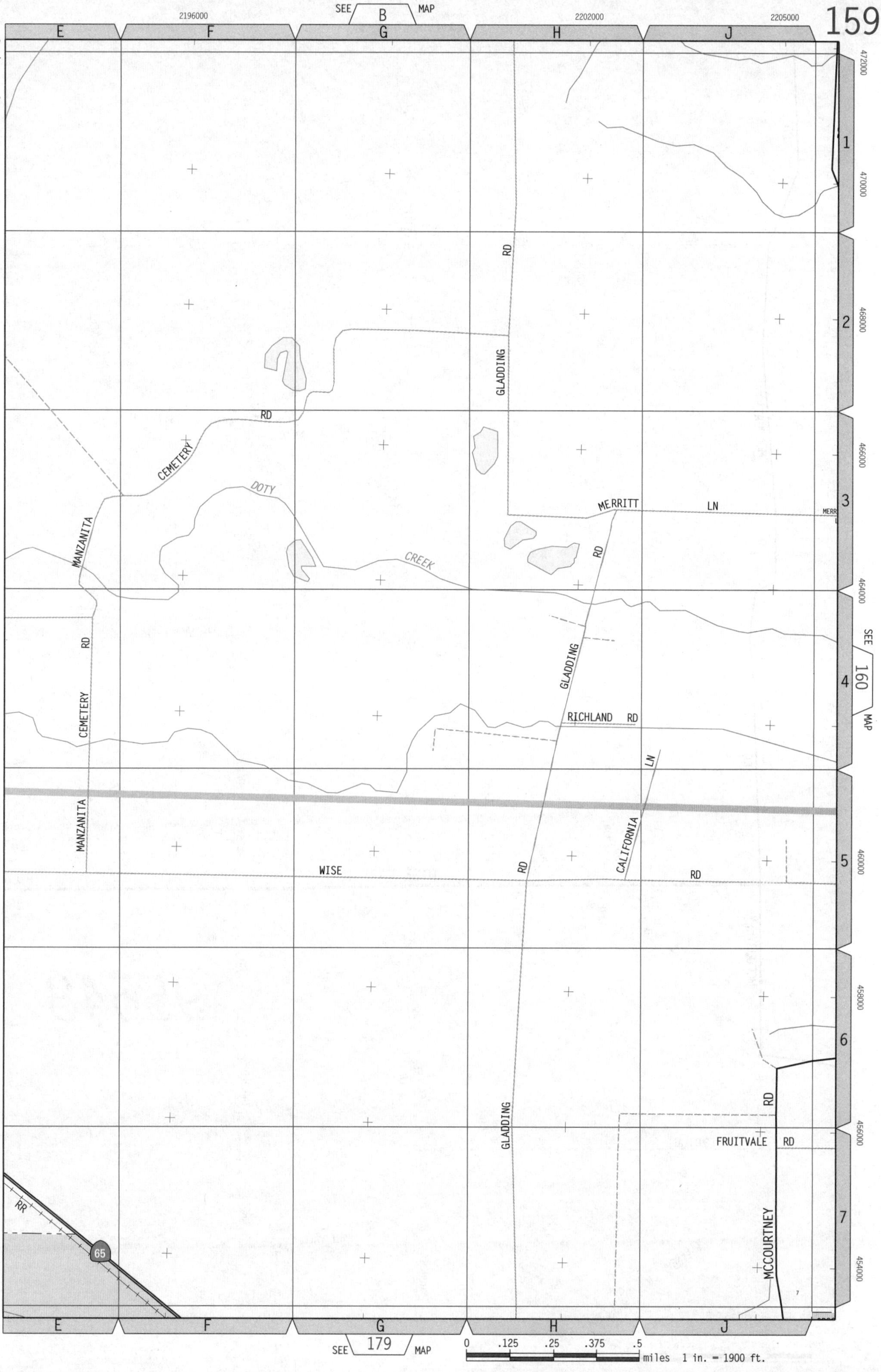
SEE B MAP
2196000
2202000
2205000
E
F
G
H
J
1
2
3
4
5
6
7
472000
470000
468000
466000
464000
460000
458000
456000
454000
CEMETERY RD
DOTY CREEK
MANZANITA
GLADDING RD
MERRITT LN
MERR
RICHLAND RD
CALIFORNIA LN
CEMETERY RD
MANZANITA
WISE RD
FRUITVALE RD
MCCOURTNEY RD
RR
65
SEE 160 MAP
SEE 179 MAP
0 .125 .25 .375 .5
miles 1 in. = 1900 ft.

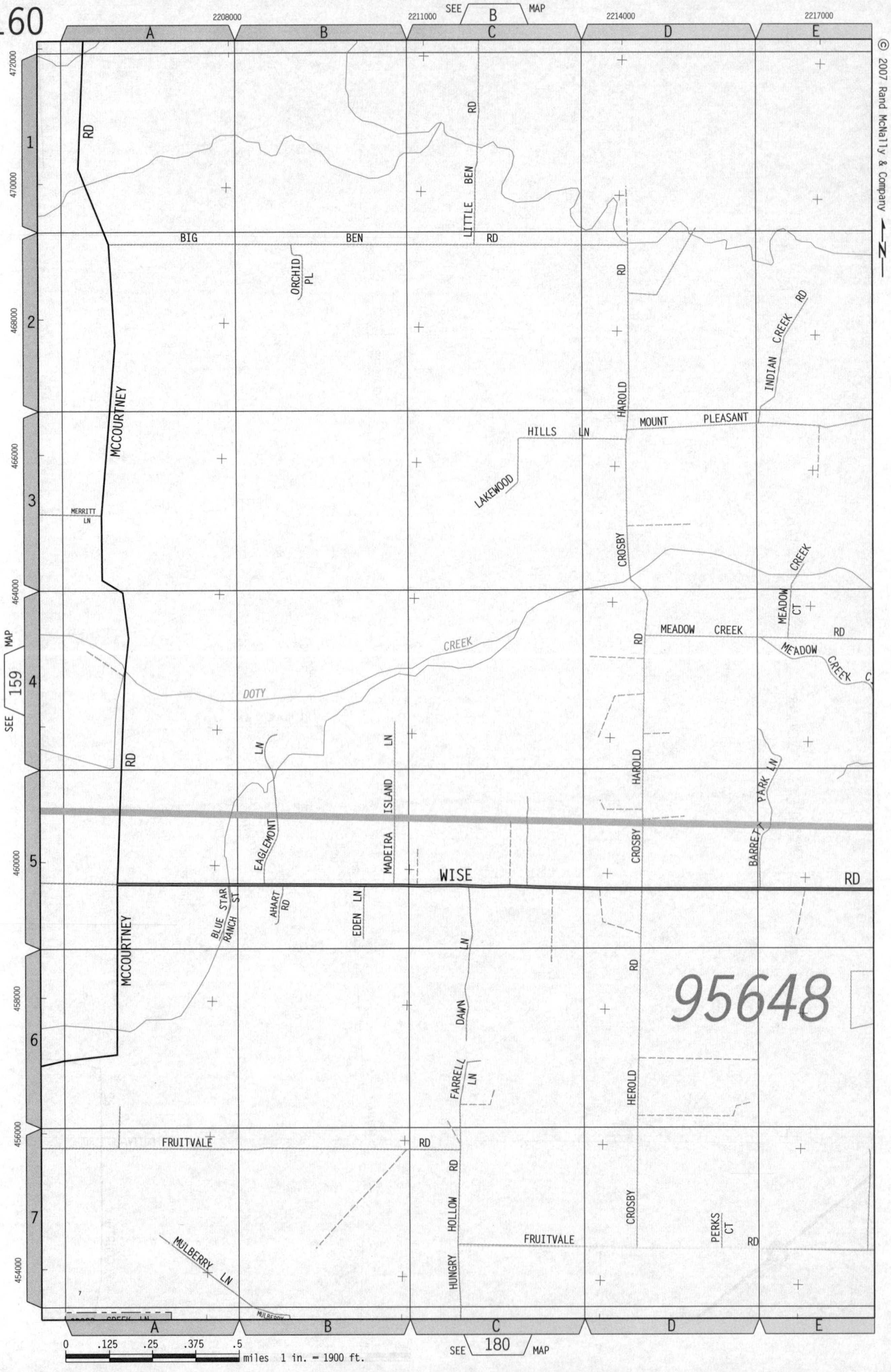
SEE B MAP
SEE 180 MAP
SEE 159 MAP
2208000
2211000
2214000
2217000
472000
470000
468000
466000
464000
460000
458000
456000
454000
A
B
C
D
E
1
2
3
4
5
6
7
MCCOURTNEY RD
BIG BEN RD
LITTLE BEN RD
ORCHID PL
HAROLD RD
INDIAN CREEK RD
MOUNT PLEASANT
HILLS LN
LAKEWOOD
MERRITT LN
CROSBY
MEADOW CREEK
MEADOW CT
MEADOW CREEK RD
MEADOW CREEK CT
DOTY CREEK
LN
EAGLEMONT
MADEIRA ISLAND LN
HAROLD
CROSBY
BARRETT PARK LN
WISE RD
BLUE STAR RANCH ST
AHART RD
EDEN LN
MCCOURTNEY
DAWN LN
RD
95648
FARRELL LN
HEROLD
FRUITVALE RD
HUNGRY HOLLOW RD
CROSBY
FRUITVALE
PERKS CT
RD
MULBERRY LN
0 .125 .25 .375 .5 miles 1 in. = 1900 ft.

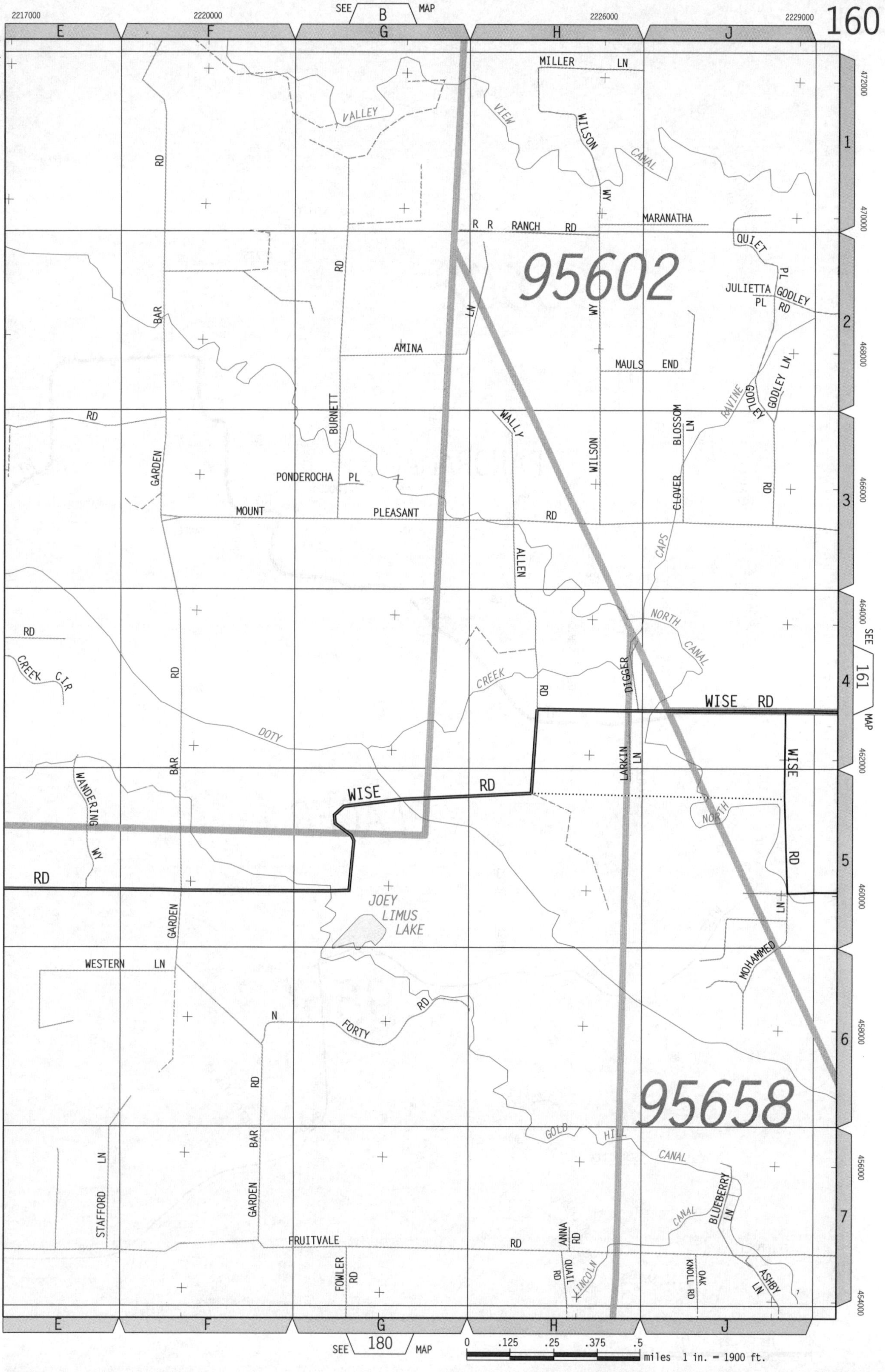
SEE B MAP
2217000
2220000
2226000
2229000
E
F
G
H
J
1
2
3
4
5
6
7
472000
470000
468000
466000
464000
462000
460000
458000
456000
454000
MILLER LN
VALLEY VIEW
WILSON WY
CANAL
R R RANCH RD
MARANATHA
95602
QUIET PL
JULIETTA PL
GODLEY RD
AMINA
MAULS END
GODLEY LN
RAVINE
BURNETT RD
WALLY LN
BLOSSOM LN
WILSON
PONDEROCHA PL
GARDEN BAR RD
MOUNT PLEASANT RD
CLOVER
CAPS
ALLEN RD
NORTH CANAL
DIGGER
SEE 161 MAP
WISE RD
CREEK CIR
DOTY CREEK
WANDERING WY
LARKIN LN
NORTH
JOEY LIMUS LAKE
MOHAMMED
WESTERN LN
N FORTY RD
95658
GOLD HILL CANAL
BLUEBERRY LN
STAFFORD LN
FRUITVALE RD
ANNA RD
QUAIL RD
LINCOLN
FOWLER RD
KNOLL OAK RD
ASHBY LN
SEE 180 MAP
0 .125 .25 .375 .5 miles 1 in. = 1900 ft.

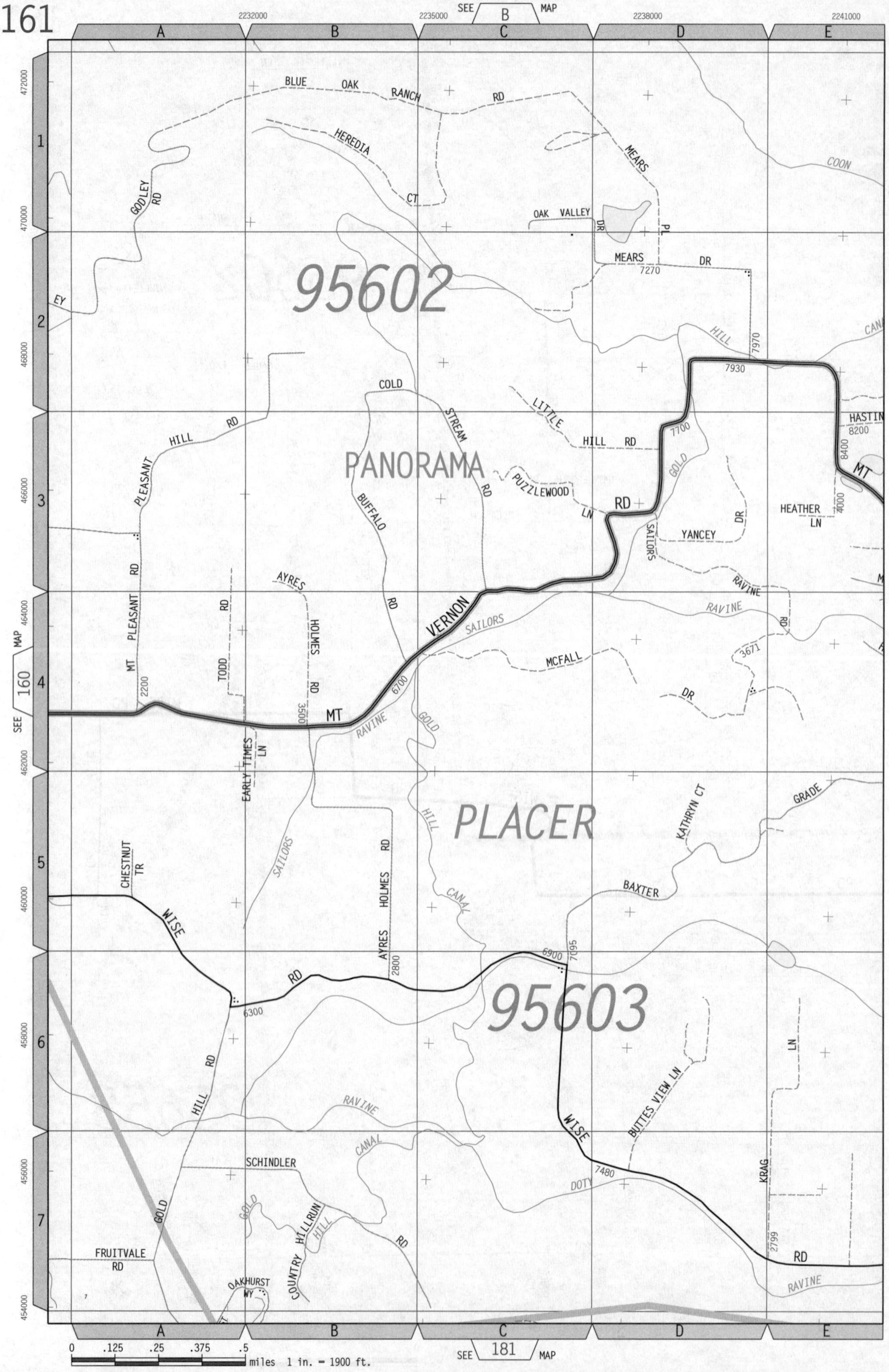
SEE B MAP
SEE 160 MAP
SEE 181 MAP
2232000
2235000
2238000
2241000
472000
470000
468000
466000
464000
462000
460000
458000
456000
454000
95602
95603
PANORAMA
PLACER
BLUE OAK RANCH RD
HEREDIA CT
GODLEY RD
MEARS PL
OAK VALLEY DR
MEARS DR
7270
COON
HILL
7970
7930
CANAL
COLD STREAM RD
LITTLE HILL RD
7700
HASTINGS
8200
8400
MT
PLEASANT HILL RD
PANORAMA
PUZZLEWOOD LN
RD
GOLD
YANCEY DR
HEATHER LN
4000
BUFFALO RD
SAILORS
RAVINE RD
MT PLEASANT RD
AYRES
TODD RD
HOLMES RD
VERNON
SAILORS
RAVINE
MCFALL DR
3671
2200
3500
MT
6700
RAVINE
GOLD
EARLY TIMES LN
HILL
KATHRYN CT
GRADE
CHESTNUT TR
SAILORS
HOLMES RD
AYRES
CANAL
BAXTER
WISE RD
6900
7095
2800
6300
HILL RD
RAVINE
BUTTES VIEW LN
LN
WISE
CANAL
SCHINDLER
GOLD
7480
DOTY
KRAG
GOLD
COUNTRY HILLRUN
HILL
RD
FRUITVALE RD
OAKHURST WY
2799
RD
RAVINE
miles 1 in. = 1900 ft.
0
.125
.25
.375
.5

SEE B MAP

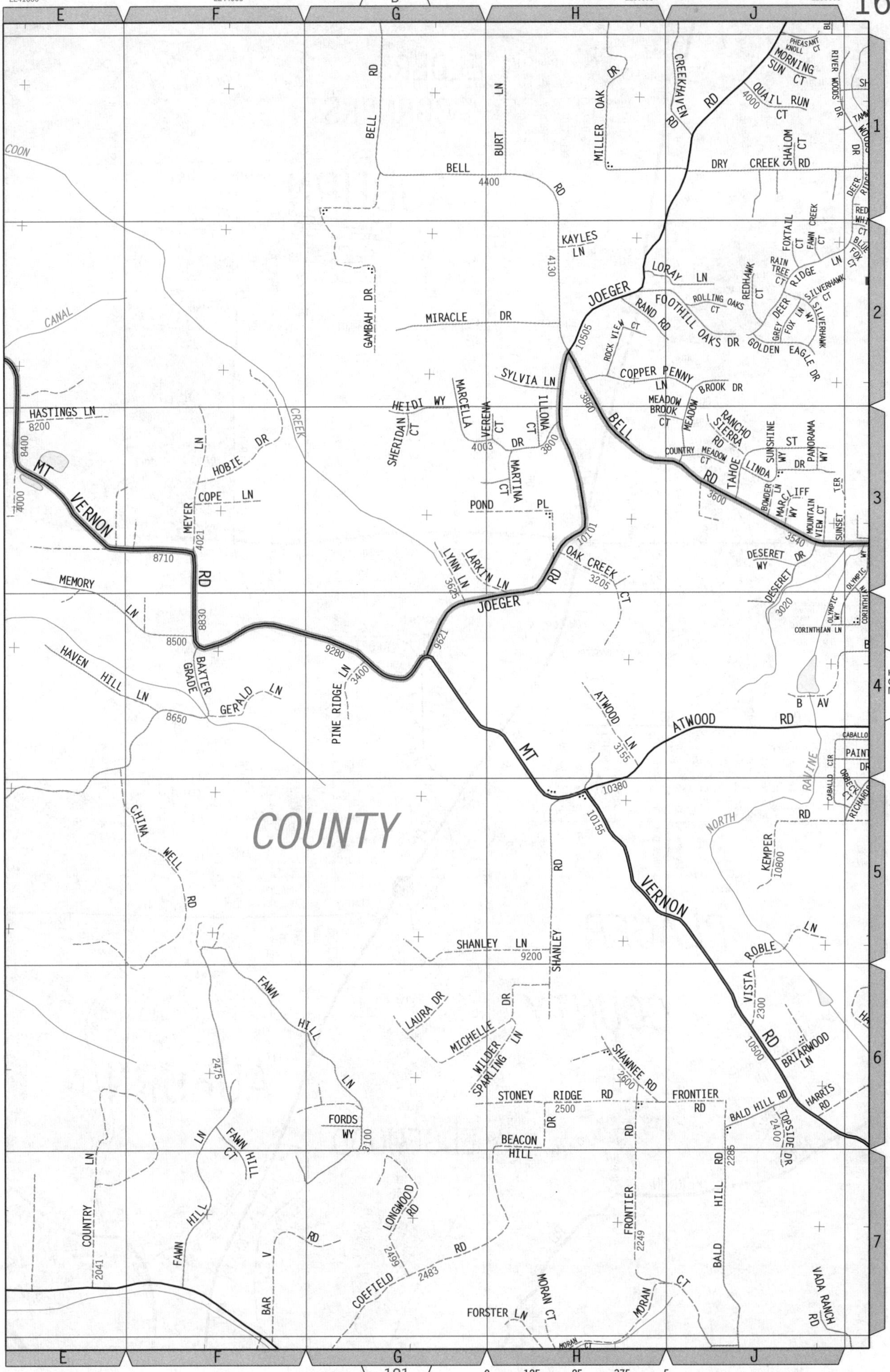
COUNTY
MT VERNON RD
JOEGER RD
BELL RD
ATWOOD RD
DRY CREEK RD
QUAIL RUN CT
MORNING SUN CT
PHEASANT KNOLL CT
RIVER WOODS DR
CREEKHAVEN RD
MILLER OAK DR
BURT LN
BELL RD
KAYLES LN
LORAY LN
ROLLING OAKS CT
FOOTHILL OAKS DR
RAND RD
ROCK VIEW CT
REDHAWK CT
RAIN TREE CT
FOXTAIL CT
FAWN CREEK CT
RIDGE LN
SILVERHAWK CT
GREY DEER WY
FOX LN
GOLDEN EAGLE DR
COPPER PENNY LN
BROOK DR
MEADOW BROOK CT
RANCHO SIERRA RD
COUNTRY MEADOW CT
TAHOE
SUNSHINE WY
ST
PANORAMA WY
LINDA DR
BOWDER LN
MARCLIFF WY
MOUNTAIN VIEW CT
SUNSET TER
DESERET WY
DESERET DR
OLYMPIC WY
CORINTHIAN LN
B AV
CABALLO CIR
RAVINE
NORTH
KEMPER RD
VISTA ROBLE LN
BRIARWOOD LN
HARRIS RD
BALD HILL RD
TOPSIDE DR
MIRACLE DR
GAMBAH DR
SYLVIA LN
HEIDI WY
MARCELLA
VERENA CT
ILLONA CT
SHERIDAN CT
MARTINA CT
POND PL
LYNN LN
LARKIN LN
OAK CREEK CT
ATWOOD LN
PINE RIDGE LN
HASTINGS LN
HOBIE DR
MEYER LN
COPE LN
MEMORY LN
HAVEN HILL LN
BAXTER GRADE
GERALD LN
CHINA WELL RD
COON CANAL
CREEK
SHANLEY LN
SHANLEY RD
LAURA DR
MICHELLE DR
WILDER LN
SPARLING LN
SHAWNEE RD
STONEY RIDGE RD
FRONTIER RD
BEACON HILL DR
FAWN HILL LN
FAWN HILL CT
FORDS WY
LONGWOOD RD
COEFIELD RD
BAR V RD
COUNTRY LN
FORSTER LN
MORAN CT
VADA RANCH RD
E F G H J
1 2 3 4 5 6 7
0 .125 .25 .375 .5 miles 1 in. = 1900 ft.

SEE 162 MAP
SEE 181 MAP

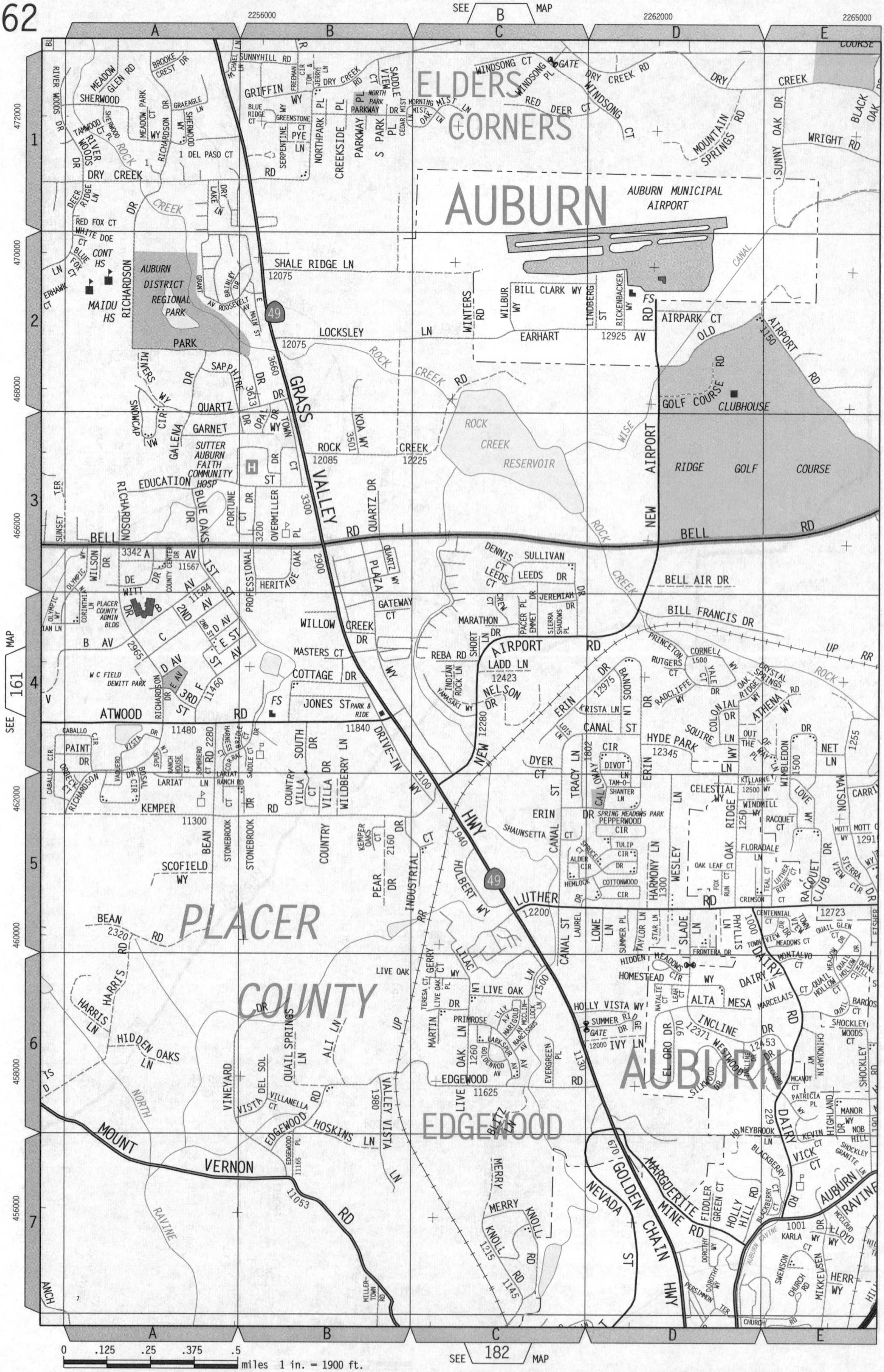
SEE B MAP
SEE 182 MAP
SEE 161 MAP
A
B
C
D
E
1
2
3
4
5
6
7
2256000
2262000
2265000
472000
470000
468000
466000
462000
460000
458000
456000
ELDERS CORNERS
AUBURN
AUBURN MUNICIPAL AIRPORT
PLACER COUNTY
EDGEWOOD
AUBURN
AUBURN DISTRICT REGIONAL PARK
MAIDU HS
CONT HS
SUTTER AUBURN FAITH COMMUNITY HOSP
PLACER COUNTY ADMIN BLDG
W C FIELD DEWITT PARK
ROCK CREEK RESERVOIR
RIDGE GOLF COURSE
CLUBHOUSE
SPRING MEADOWS PARK
GRASS VALLEY HWY
49
DRY CREEK RD
SHALE RIDGE LN
LOCKSLEY LN
ROCK CREEK RD
BELL RD
NEW AIRPORT RD
AIRPORT RD
BILL FRANCIS DR
BELL AIR DR
EDUCATION ST
RICHARDSON DR
ATWOOD RD
KEMPER RD
LUTHER RD
BEAN RD
HARRIS RD
HIDDEN OAKS LN
MOUNT VERNON RD
GOLDEN CHAIN HWY
NEVADA ST
MARGUERITE MINE RD
DAIRY RD
CANAL ST
INCLINE
AUBURN RAVINE
EDGEWOOD RD
HOSKINS LN
VALLEY VISTA LN
MERRY KNOLL RD
LIVE OAK LN
QUAIL SPRINGS LN
VINEYARD
ALI LN
INDUSTRIAL
HULBERT WY
WILLOW CREEK DR
GATEWAY CT
HERITAGE OAK
PROFESSIONAL
COUNTRY VILLA
WILDBERRY LN
DRIVE-IN WY
CELESTIAL WY
HYDE PARK
WESLEY
HARMONY LN
AIRPARK CT
OLD AIRPORT RD
GOLF COURSE RD
WINTERS RD
EARHART AV
BILL CLARK WY
WINDSONG CT
RED DEER CT
MOUNTAIN SPRINGS RD
SUNNY OAK DR
WRIGHT RD
BLACK OAK
GRIFFIN WY
SHERWOOD
MEADOW GLEN RD
SULLIVAN
LEEDS DR
MARATHON
NELSON DR
ERIN DR
TRACY LN
CALLOWAY
PEPPERWOOD CIR
COTTONWOOD CIR
HOLLY VISTA WY
SUMMER RIDGE DR
IVY LN
EL ORO DR
WESTWOOD
ALTA MESA
HOMESTEAD
SHOCKLEY
HIGHLAND
VICK CT
SWENSON
MIKKELSEN
HERR WY
CHURCH RD
SCOFIELD WY
STONEBROOK
PEAR DR
MASTERS CT
COTTAGE DR
JONES ST
PARK & RIDE
FS
UP RR
CANAL
WISE
ROCK CREEK
NORTH RAVINE
0 .125 .25 .375 .5
miles 1 in. = 1900 ft.

SEE B MAP

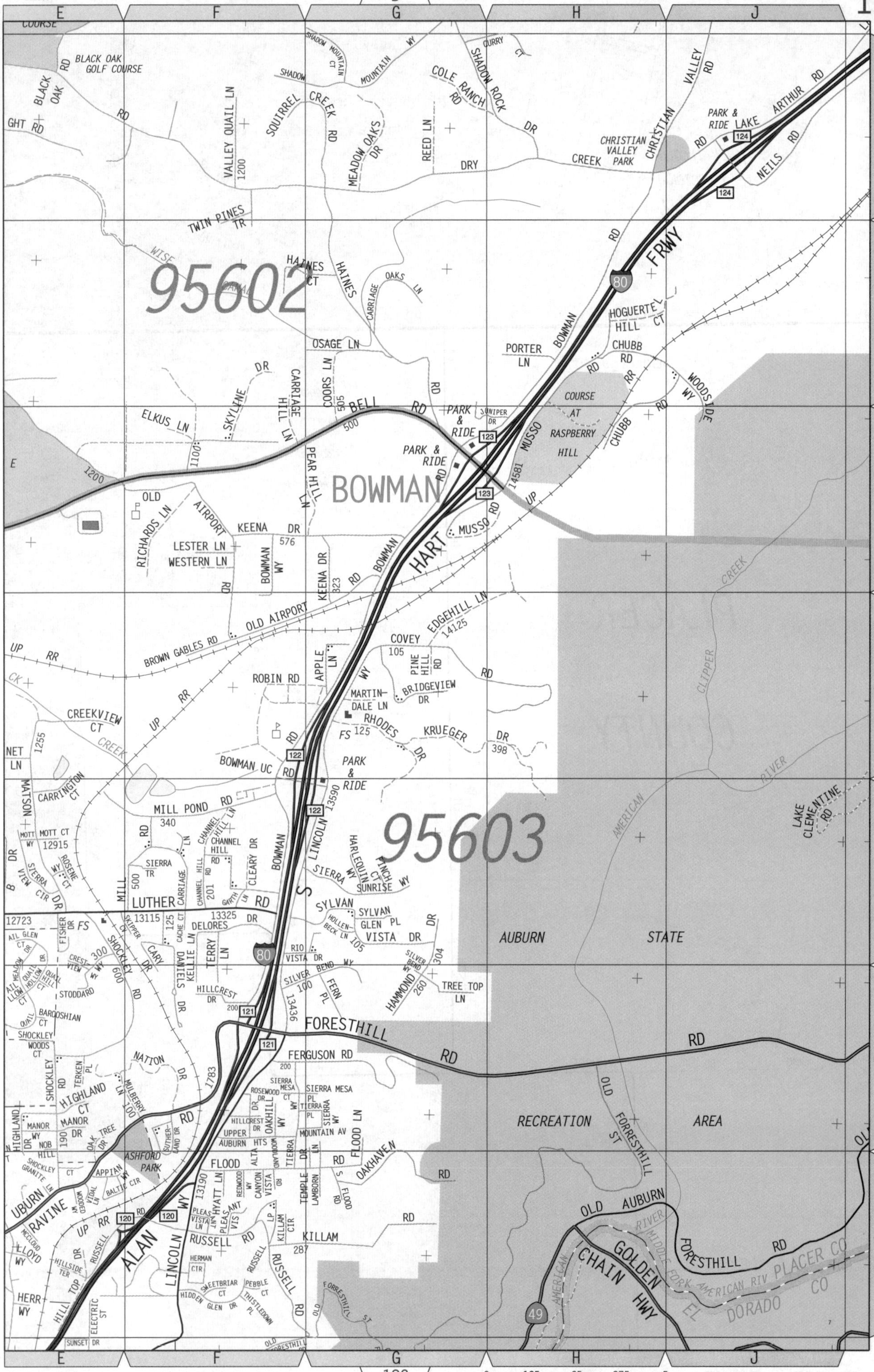
95602
95603
BOWMAN
AUBURN STATE RECREATION AREA
BLACK OAK GOLF COURSE
CHRISTIAN VALLEY PARK
COURSE AT RASPBERRY HILL
ASHFORD PARK
HART FRWY
FORESTHILL RD
OLD AUBURN FORESTHILL RD
GOLDEN CHAIN HWY
BELL RD
LUTHER RD
DRY CREEK RD
LAKE ARTHUR RD
PLACER CO
EL DORADO CO
MIDDLE FORK AMERICAN RIV
AMERICAN RIVER
CLIPPER CREEK
LAKE CLEMENTINE RD
UP RR
PARK & RIDE
2265000
2268000
2271000
2274000
472000
470000
468000
466000
462000
460000
458000
456000

SEE 182 MAP

0 .125 .25 .375 .5 miles 1 in. = 1900 ft.

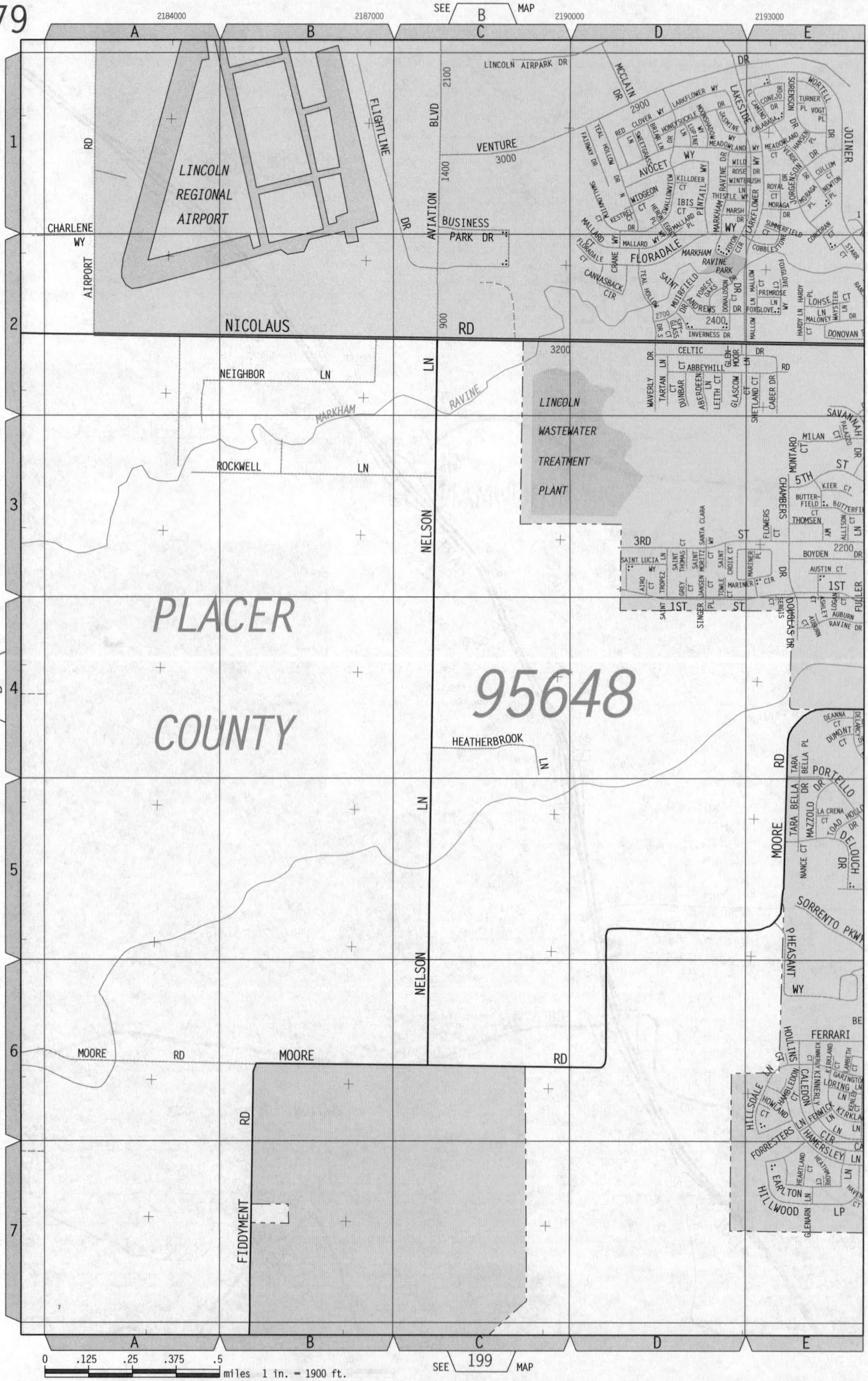
SEE B MAP
SEE 199 MAP
SEE B MAP
2184000
2187000
2190000
2193000
452000
450000
448000
446000
442000
440000
438000
436000
LINCOLN REGIONAL AIRPORT
LINCOLN WASTEWATER TREATMENT PLANT
PLACER COUNTY
95648
NICOLAUS RD
NELSON LN
MOORE RD
FIDDYMENT RD
AIRPORT RD
CHARLENE WY
FLIGHTLINE DR
AVIATION BLVD
BUSINESS PARK DR
VENTURE
LINCOLN AIRPARK DR
NEIGHBOR LN
ROCKWELL LN
MARKHAM RAVINE
HEATHERBROOK LN
MCCLAIN DR
LAKESIDE DR
FLORADALE
JOINER
3RD ST
1ST ST
5TH ST
SORRENTO PKWY
PHEASANT WY
FERRARI
HILLSDALE LN
HILLWOOD LP
DOUGLAS DR
0 .125 .25 .375 .5 miles 1 in. = 1900 ft.

SEE B MAP

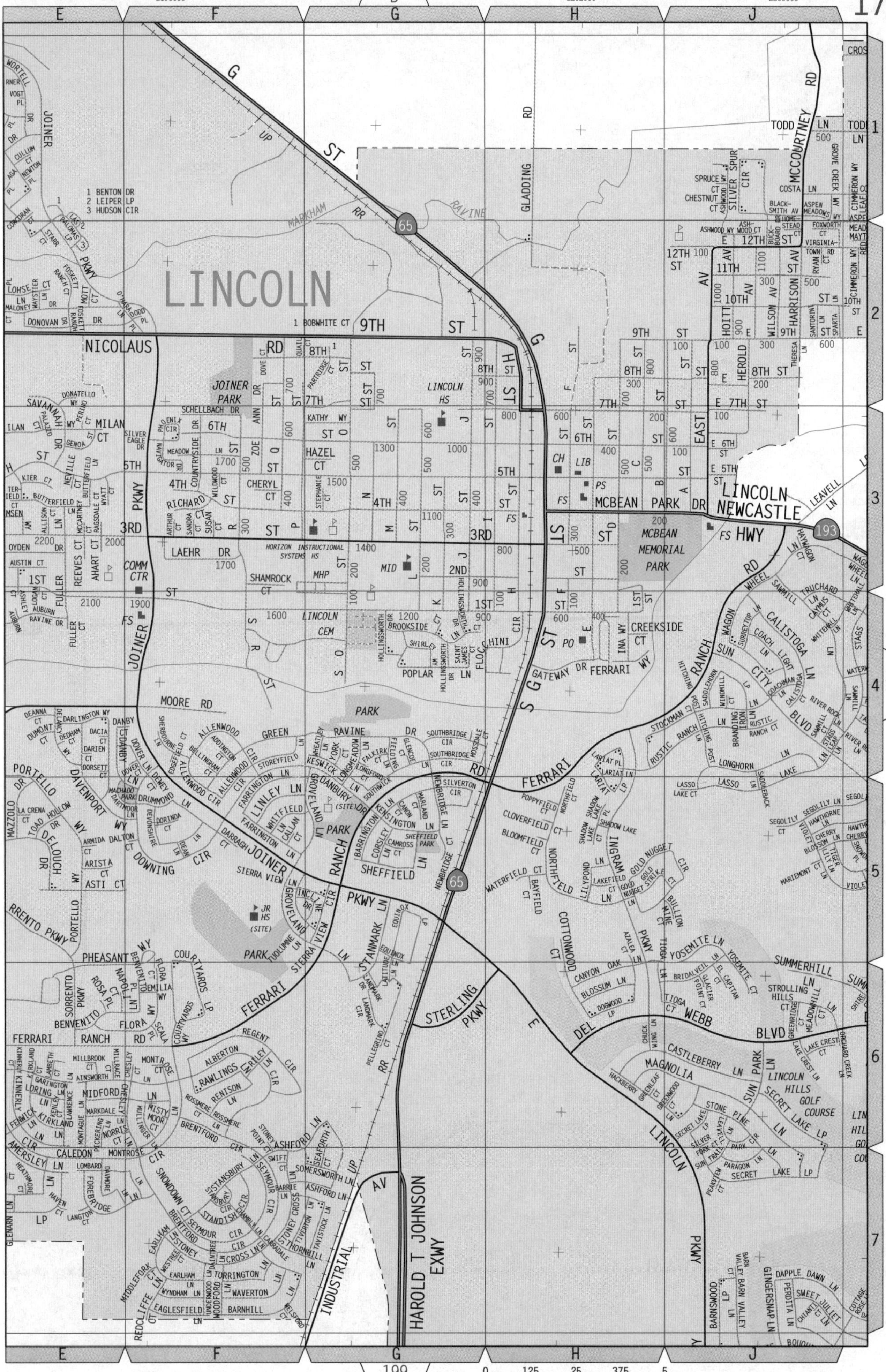
LINCOLN
G ST
MARKHAM RAVINE
GLADDING RD
MCCOURTNEY RD
TODD LN
JOINER PKWY
NICOLAUS RD
9TH ST
8TH ST
7TH ST
6TH ST
5TH ST
4TH ST
3RD ST
2ND ST
1ST ST
JOINER PARK
LINCOLN HS
LINCOLN CEM
MCBEAN PARK DR
LINCOLN NEWCASTLE HWY
MCBEAN MEMORIAL PARK
LEAVELL LN
CREEKSIDE CT
GATEWAY DR
FERRARI WY
MOORE RD
GREEN RAVINE DR
FERRARI RANCH RD
JOINER PKWY
SUN CITY BLVD
WAGON WHEEL RD
CALISTOGA LN
COACH LIGHT LN
INGRAM PKWY
SIERRA VIEW CIR
STERLING PKWY
DEL WEBB BLVD
E ST
LINCOLN PKWY
LINCOLN HILLS GOLF COURSE
SUMMERHILL LN
CASTLEBERRY LN
MAGNOLIA LN
STONE PINE LN
SECRET LAKE LP
SUN PARK LN
INDUSTRIAL AV
HAROLD T JOHNSON EXWY
G RR
MIDFORD LN
CALEDON CIR
SNOWDOWN CIR
DOWNING CIR
DAVENPORT WY
PORTELLO PKWY
SORRENTO PKWY
65
193
1 BENTON DR
2 LEIPER LP
3 HUDSON CIR
1 BOBWHITE CT
2196000
2202000
2205000
452000
450000
448000
446000
442000
440000
438000
436000
0 .125 .25 .375 .5
miles 1 in. = 1900 ft.

SEE 180 MAP

SEE 199 MAP

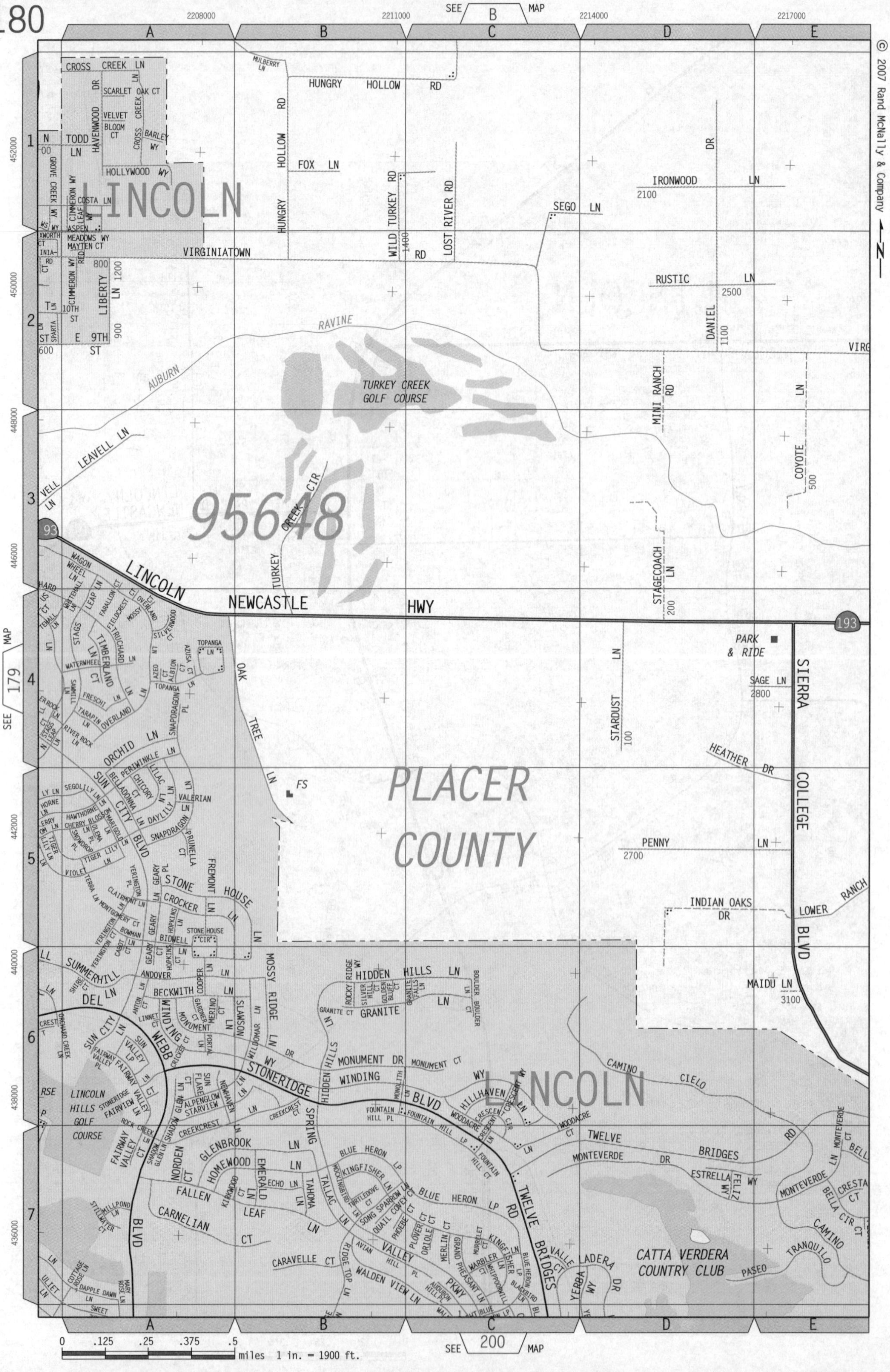

SEE B MAP
SEE 179 MAP
SEE 200 MAP
2208000
2211000
2214000
2217000
452000
450000
448000
446000
442000
440000
438000
436000
A
B
C
D
E
1
2
3
4
5
6
7
LINCOLN
95648
PLACER COUNTY
LINCOLN
TURKEY CREEK GOLF COURSE
CATTA VERDERA COUNTRY CLUB
LINCOLN HILLS GOLF COURSE
AUBURN RAVINE
LINCOLN NEWCASTLE HWY
193
VIRGINIATOWN RD
HUNGRY HOLLOW RD
HUNGRY HOLLOW RD
WILD TURKEY RD
LOST RIVER RD
FOX LN
SEGO LN
IRONWOOD LN
RUSTIC LN
DANIEL DR
MINI RANCH RD
STAGECOACH LN
COYOTE LN
STARDUST LN
SIERRA COLLEGE BLVD
PARK & RIDE
SAGE LN
HEATHER DR
PENNY LN
INDIAN OAKS DR
LOWER RANCH
MAIDU LN
OAK TREE LN
FS
LEAVELL LN
CROSS CREEK LN
SCARLET OAK CT
VELVET BLOOM CT
HOLLYWOOD WY
LIBERTY LN
E 9TH ST
10TH ST
ORCHID LN
SUN CITY BLVD
SNAPDRAGON
VALERIAN
STONE HOUSE
FREMONT LN
CROCKER LN
SUMMERHILL
DEL WEBB BLVD
BECKWITH
MOSSY RIDGE LN
HIDDEN HILLS LN
GRANITE LN
STONERIDGE BLVD
WINDING WY
MONUMENT DR
HILLHAVEN
CAMINO CIELO
TWELVE BRIDGES
MONTEVERDE DR
ESTRELLA WY
FELIZ WY
GLENBROOK LN
HOMEWOOD LN
EMERALD LN
BLUE HERON LP
KINGFISHER LN
FALLEN LEAF LN
CARNELIAN CT
CARAVELLE CT
SPRING VALLEY PKWY
TWELVE BRIDGES
YERBA WY
LADERA DR
TRANQUILO
PASEO
CAMINO
BELLA CIR
0 .125 .25 .375 .5 miles 1 in. = 1900 ft.

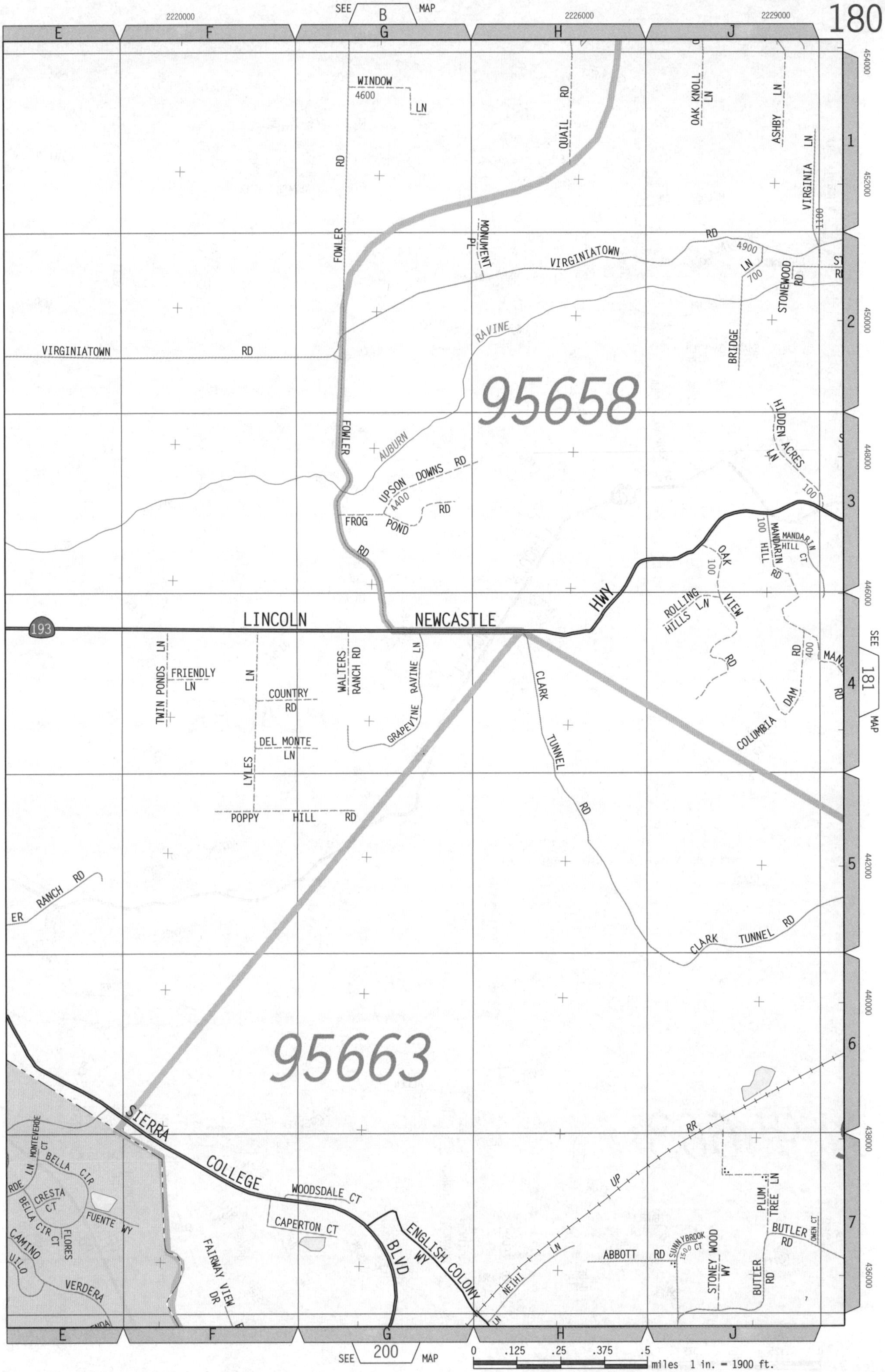
SEE B MAP
2220000
2226000
2229000
E
F
G
H
J
WINDOW
4600
LN
QUAIL RD
OAK KNOLL LN
ASHBY LN
VIRGINIA LN
1100
FOWLER RD
FOWLER
MONUMENT PL
VIRGINIATOWN
RD
4900
LN
700
STONEWOOD RD
BRIDGE
VIRGINIATOWN RD
RAVINE
95658
AUBURN
HIDDEN ACRES LN
100
UPSON DOWNS RD
4400
FROG POND RD
RD
MANDARIN HILL RD
MANDARIN HILL CT
OAK VIEW RD
193
LINCOLN
NEWCASTLE
HWY
ROLLING HILLS LN
TWIN PONDS LN
FRIENDLY LN
LN
COUNTRY RD
WALTERS RANCH RD
RAVINE LN
GRAPEVINE
CLARK TUNNEL RD
DEL MONTE LN
LYLES
POPPY HILL RD
400
COLUMBIA DAM RD
SEE 181 MAP
ER RANCH RD
CLARK TUNNEL RD
95663
SIERRA COLLEGE BLVD
RR
UP
MONTEVERDE CT
LN
BELLA CIR
CRESTA CT
BELLA CIR CT
FUENTE WY
FLORES
CAMINO
VERDERA
WOODSDALE CT
CAPERTON CT
ENGLISH COLONY WY
FAIRWAY VIEW DR
NEIHI LN
LN
ABBOTT RD
SUNNYBROOK CT
1500
STONEY WOOD WY
PLUM TREE LN
BUTLER RD
OWEN CT
BUTLER RD
454000
452000
450000
448000
446000
442000
440000
438000
436000
1
2
3
4
5
6
7
SEE 200 MAP
0 .125 .25 .375 .5 miles 1 in. = 1900 ft.

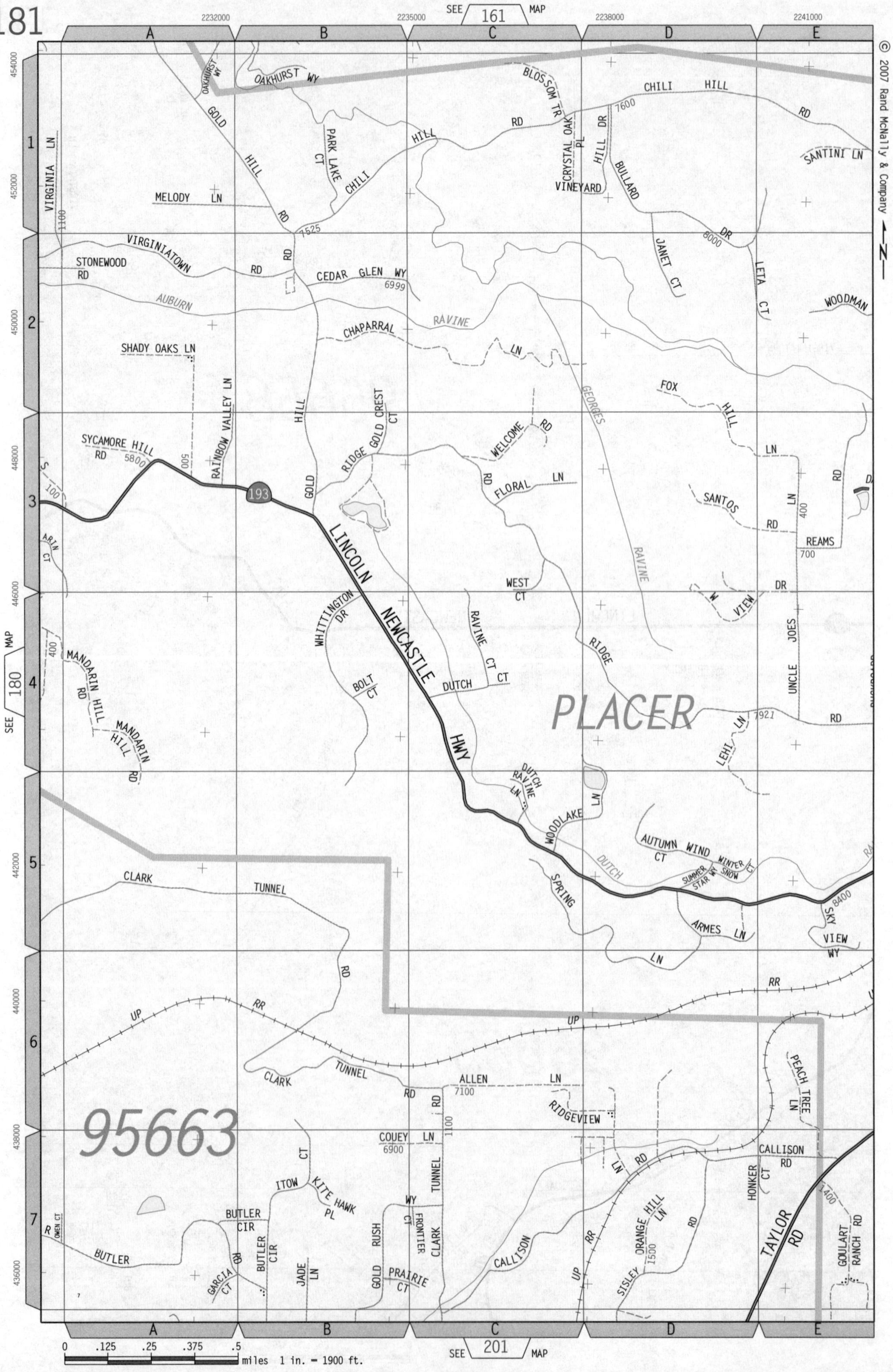
SEE 161 MAP
SEE 201 MAP
SEE 180 MAP
2232000
2235000
2238000
2241000
454000
452000
450000
448000
446000
442000
440000
438000
436000
A
B
C
D
E
1
2
3
4
5
6
7
PLACER
95663
OAKHURST WY
GOLD HILL RD
PARK LAKE CT
CHILI HILL RD
BLOSSOM TR
CRYSTAL OAK PL
HILL DR
BULLARD DR
VINEYARD
SANTINI LN
VIRGINIA LN
MELODY LN
VIRGINIATOWN RD
STONEWOOD RD
CEDAR GLEN WY
AUBURN RAVINE
CHAPARRAL LN
JANET CT
LETA CT
WOODMAN
SHADY OAKS LN
RAINBOW VALLEY LN
SYCAMORE HILL RD
GOLD RIDGE
GOLD CREST CT
WELCOME RD
FLORAL LN
GEORGES RAVINE
FOX HILL LN
SANTOS RD
REAMS
UNCLE JOES LN
ARIN CT
LINCOLN NEWCASTLE HWY
193
WHITTINGTON DR
WEST CT
W VIEW DR
RAVINE CT
DUTCH CT
BOLT CT
RIDGE
MANDARIN HILL RD
LEHI LN
DUTCH RAVINE LN
WOODLAKE LN
AUTUMN WIND CT
WINTER SNOW CT
SUMMER STAR WY
DUTCH RAVINE
SPRING LN
ARMES LN
SKY VIEW WY
CLARK TUNNEL RD
UP RR
ALLEN LN
RIDGEVIEW LN
PEACH TREE LN
COUEY LN
CALLISON RD
ITOW CT
KITE HAWK PL
BUTLER CIR
OWEN CT
BUTLER RD
GARCIA CT
JADE LN
GOLD RUSH WY
PRAIRIE CT
FRONTIER CT
CLARK TUNNEL
ORANGE HILL LN
SISLEY RD
HONKER CT
TAYLOR RD
GOULART RANCH RD
0 .125 .25 .375 .5 miles 1 in. = 1900 ft.

SEE 161 MAP
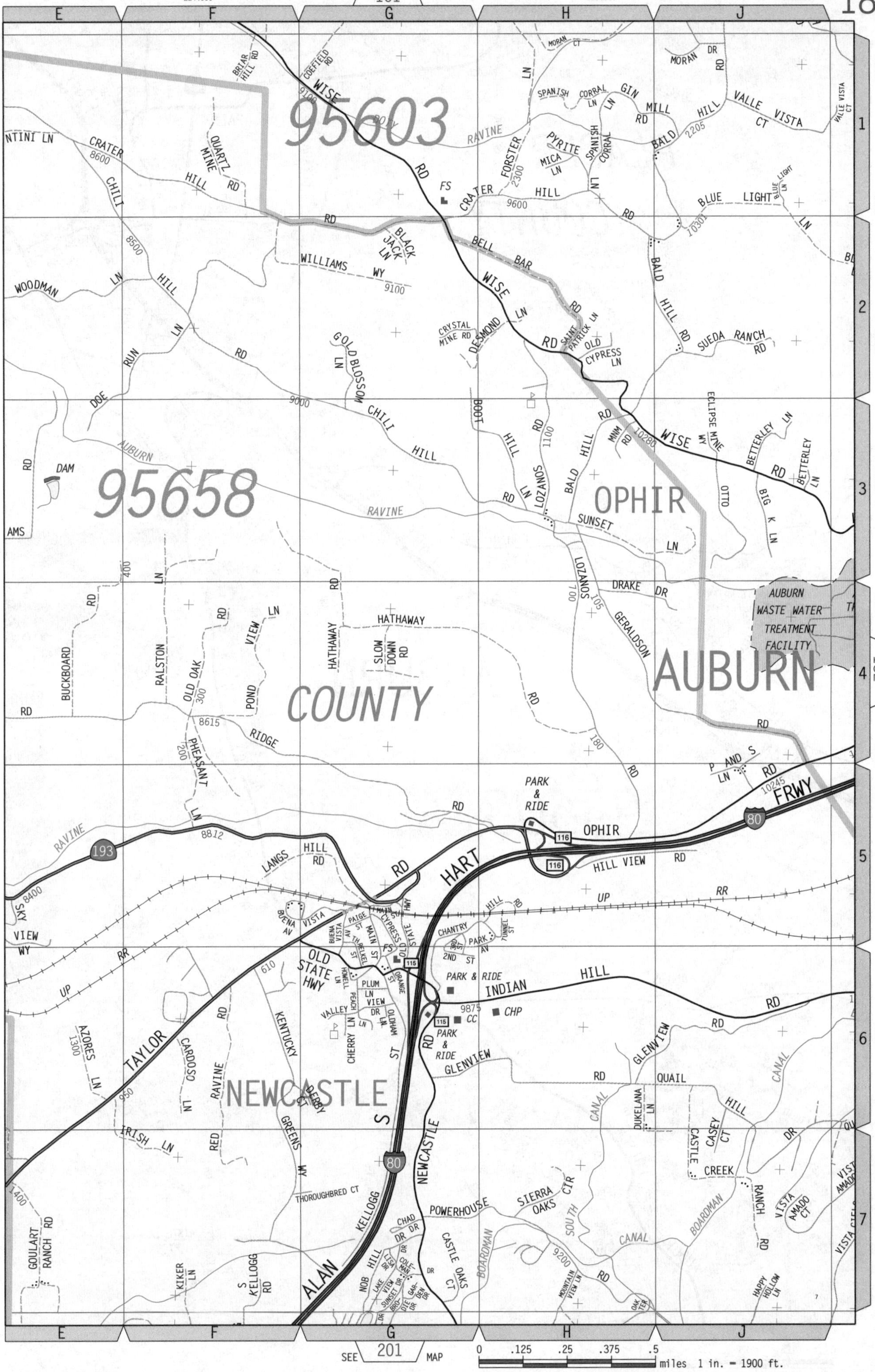
95603
95658
COUNTY
OPHIR
AUBURN
NEWCASTLE
AUBURN WASTE WATER TREATMENT FACILITY
WISE RD
CHILI HILL RD
CRATER HILL RD
BELL BAR RD
BALD HILL RD
BLUE LIGHT LN
SPANISH CORRAL LN
GIN MILL RD
VALLE VISTA CT
MORAN DR
MORAN CT
FORSTER LN
PYRITE LN
MICA LN
BLACK JACK LN
WILLIAMS WY
WOODMAN LN
DOE RUN LN
QUARTZ MINE RD
BRIAR HILL RD
COEFFELD RD
CRYSTAL MINE RD
DESMOND LN
SAINT PATRICK LN
OLD CYPRESS LN
SUEDA RANCH RD
GOLD BLOSSOM LN
BOOT HILL RD
LOZANOS RD
ECLIPSE MINE WY
BETTERLEY RD
BETTERLEY LN
OTTO
BIG K LN
SUNSET LN
DRAKE DR
GERALDSON RD
HATHAWAY RD
SLOW DOWN RD
BUCKBOARD RD
RALSTON LN
OLD OAK RD
POND VIEW LN
RIDGE RD
PHEASANT LN
AUBURN RAVINE
DAM
P AND S LN
PARK & RIDE
OPHIR RD
HILL VIEW RD
FRWY
LANGS HILL RD
HART HWY
UP RR
SKY VIEW WY
BUENA VISTA AV
OLD STATE HWY
MAIN ST
CYPRESS ST
STATE ST
CHANTRY HILL RD
TUNNEL ST
2ND ST
INDIAN HILL RD
FS
CC
CHP
PLUM LN
VALLEY VIEW DR
CHERRY LN
OLDHAM ST
GLENVIEW RD
QUAIL HILL DR
CANAL
TAYLOR RD
AZORES LN
CARDOSO LN
RAVINE RD
KENTUCKY GREENS WY
DERBY CT
IRISH LN
THOROUGHBRED CT
DUKELANA LN
CASTLE CREEK RD
CASEY CT
BOARDMAN RANCH RD
VISTA AMADO CT
NEWCASTLE RD
POWERHOUSE RD
SIERRA OAKS CIR
SOUTH CANAL
KELLOGG RD
S KELLOGG RD
ALAN RD
CHAD DR
NOB HILL DR
CASTLE OAKS CT
MOUNTAIN VIEW LN
OAK TER
HAPPY HOLLOW LN
GOULART RANCH RD
KIKER LN
0 .125 .25 .375 .5 miles 1 in. = 1900 ft.
SEE 182 MAP
SEE 201 MAP

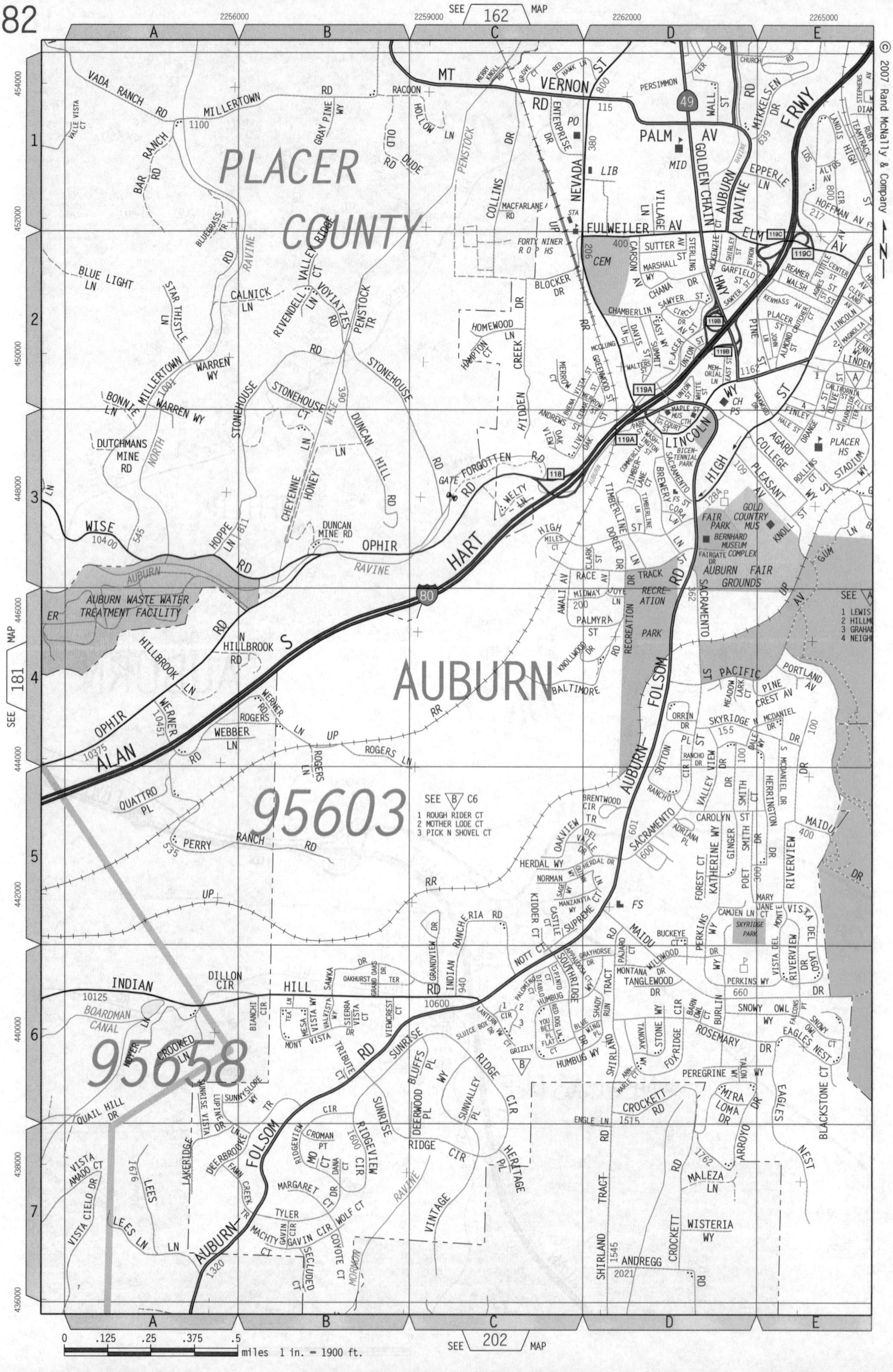
SEE 162 MAP
SEE 181 MAP
SEE 202 MAP
PLACER COUNTY
AUBURN
95603
95658
AUBURN WASTE WATER TREATMENT FACILITY
AUBURN FAIR GROUNDS
GOLD COUNTRY MUS
BERNHARD MUSEUM COMPLEX
PLACER HS
FORTY NINER R O P HS
RECREATION PARK
BICENTENNIAL PARK
SKYRIDGE PARK
CEM
MT VERNON RD
MILLERTOWN RD
VADA RANCH RD
BAR RANCH RD
BLUE LIGHT LN
STAR THISTLE LN
CALNICK LN
VOYIATZES RD
PENSTOCK TR
STONEHOUSE RD
STONEHOUSE CT
WARREN WY
DUTCHMANS MINE RD
DUNCAN HILL RD
DUNCAN MINE RD
CHEYENNE HONEY LN
OPHIR RD
WISE RD
HOPPE LN
HILLBROOK LN
N HILLBROOK RD
HART S
ALAN
WERNER RD
WEBBER LN
ROGERS LN
QUATTRO PL
PERRY RANCH RD
INDIAN HILL RD
DILLON CIR
BOARDMAN CANAL
CROOKED LN
QUAIL HILL DR
VISTA AMADO CT
VISTA CIELO DR
LEES LN
LAKERIDGE
AUBURN-FOLSOM RD
SUNRISE RIDGE CIR
BLUFFS PL
VINTAGE
HERITAGE PL
CROCKETT RD
ENGLE LN
SHIRLAND TRACT RD
ANDREGG
WISTERIA WY
MALEZA LN
ARROYO DR
MIRA LOMA DR
PEREGRINE WY
EAGLES NEST
BLACKSTONE CT
SNOWY OWL WY
ROSEMARY DR
MAIDU DR
RIVERVIEW DR
VISTA DEL LAGO DR
PERKINS WY
SKYRIDGE DR
PACIFIC ST
PORTLAND AV
HIGH ST
LINCOLN WY
PLEASANT AV
AGARD
COLLEGE
SACRAMENTO ST
PALM AV
GOLDEN CHAIN HWY
AUBURN RAVINE RD
FULWEILER AV
ELM AV
FRWY
NEVADA ST
COLLINS DR
HOMEWOOD LN
HIDDEN CREEK DR
FORGOTTEN RD
MELTY LN
TIMBERLINE
DORER DR
RACE TRACK ST
BALTIMORE
SEE B C6
1 ROUGH RIDER CT
2 MOTHER LODE CT
3 PICK N SHOVEL CT
SEE A
1 LEWIS
2 HILLM
3 GRAHA
4 NEIGH
0 .125 .25 .375 .5
miles 1 in. = 1900 ft.

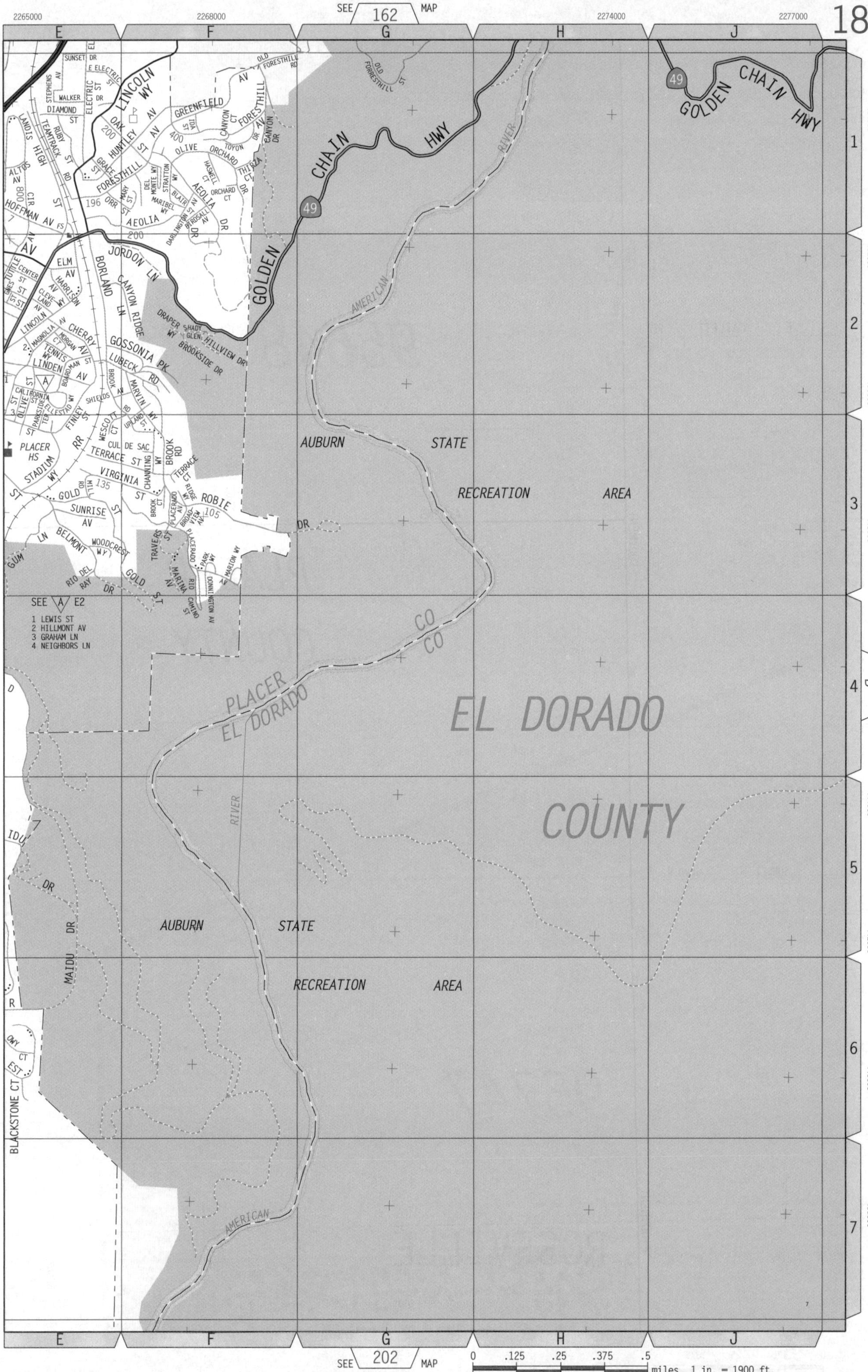
SEE 162 MAP
2265000
2268000
2274000
2277000
E
F
G
H
J
1
2
3
4
5
6
7
454000
452000
450000
448000
444000
442000
440000
438000
SEE B MAP
GOLDEN CHAIN HWY
49
LINCOLN WY
FORESTHILL
OLD FORESTHILL RD
GREENFIELD
OLIVE
ORCHARD
AEOLIA
AEOLIA DR
JORDON LN
BORLAND
CANYON RIDGE
GOSSONIA PK
LUBECK RD
DRAPER WY
SHADY GLEN
HILLVIEW DR
BROOKSIDE DR
PLACER HS STADIUM
TERRACE ST
VIRGINIA ST
ROBIE DR
SUNRISE AV
BELMONT
WOODCREST WY
RIO DEL RAY DR
GOLD ST
SEE A E2
1 LEWIS ST
2 HILLMONT AV
3 GRAHAM LN
4 NEIGHBORS LN
AUBURN STATE RECREATION AREA
AMERICAN RIVER
PLACER CO
EL DORADO CO
EL DORADO COUNTY
MAIDU DR
BLACKSTONE CT
SEE 202 MAP
0 .125 .25 .375 .5
miles 1 in. = 1900 ft.

SEE 179 MAP

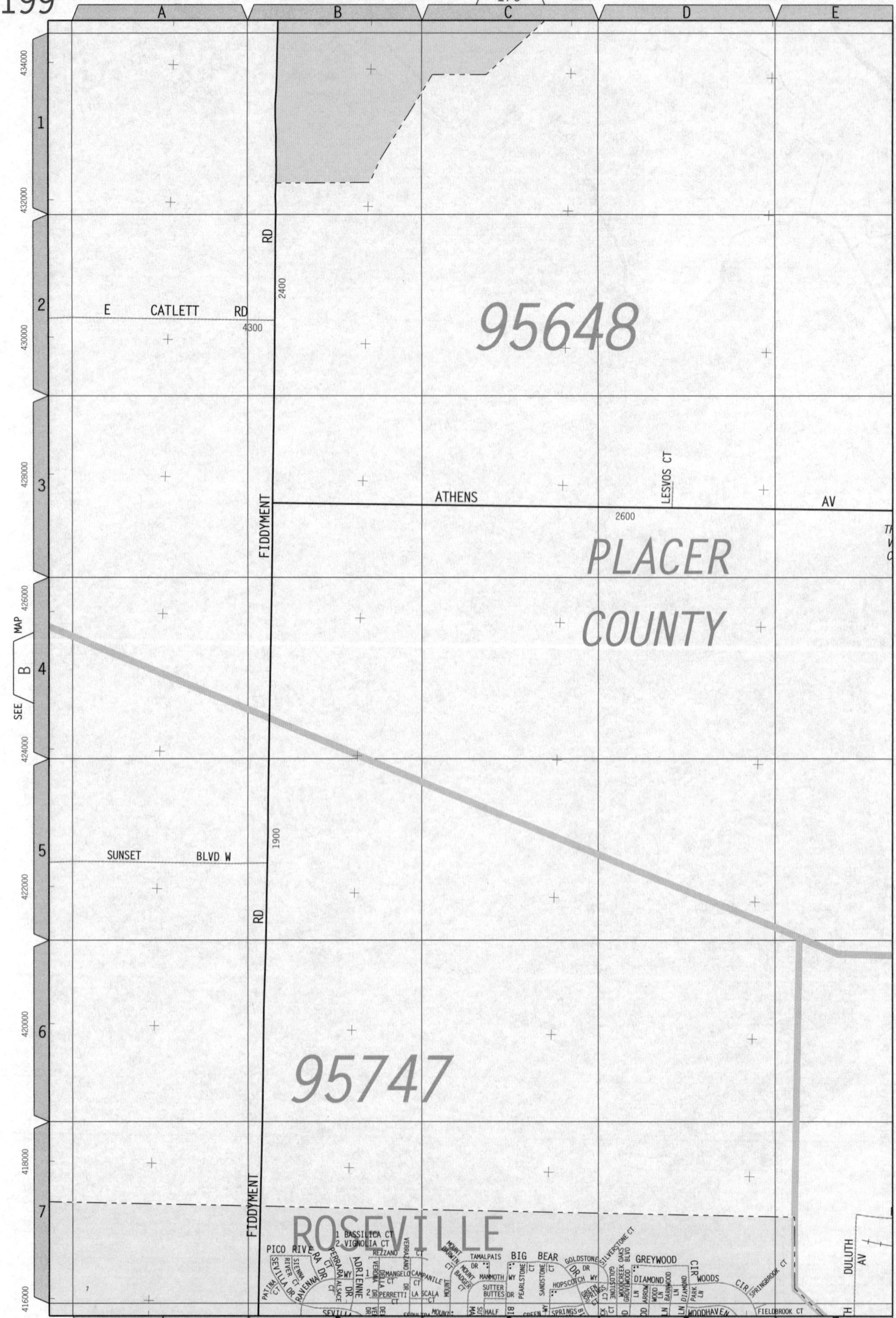

SEE B MAP

0 .125 .25 .375 .5 miles 1 in. = 1900 ft.

SEE 219 MAP

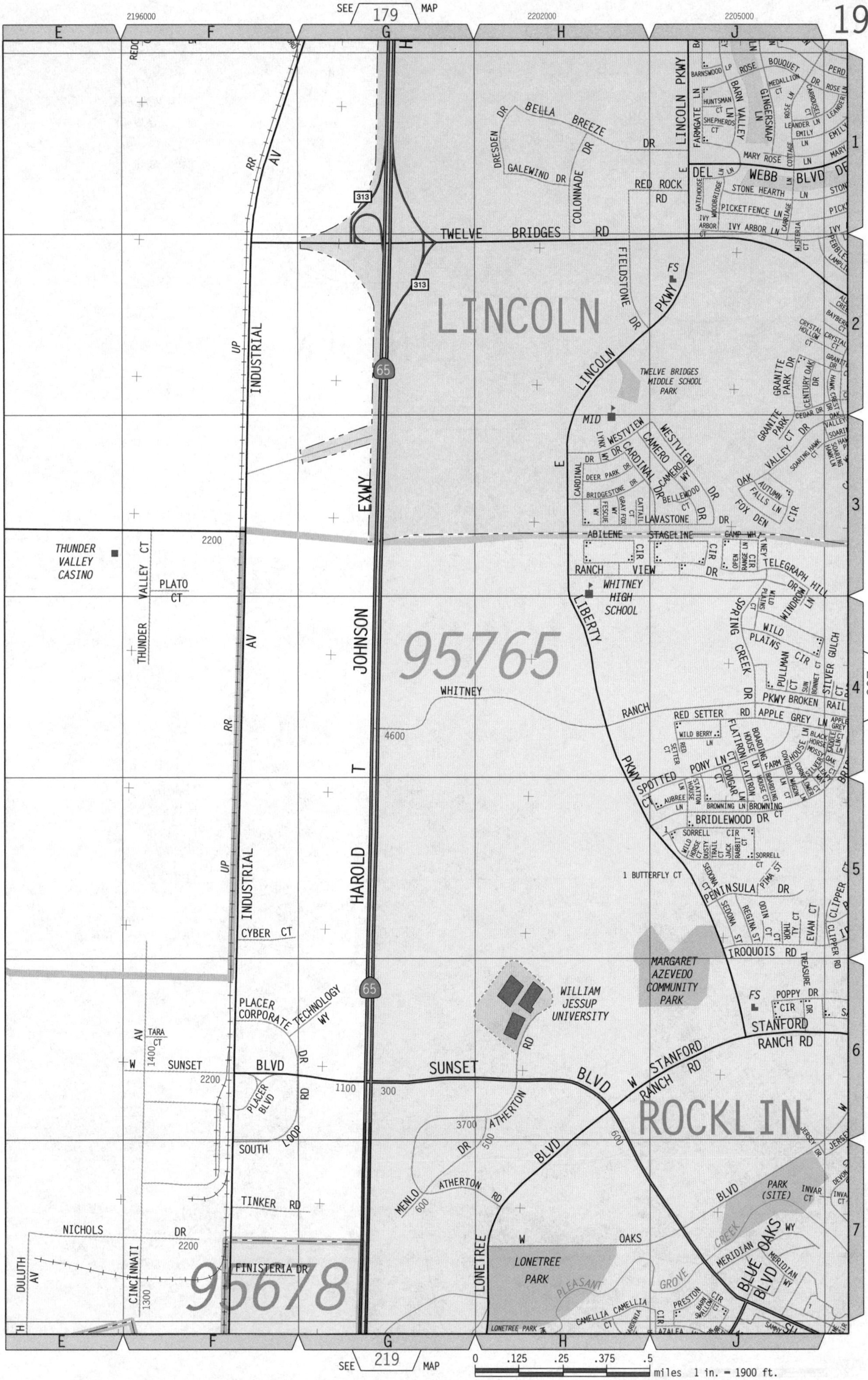
SEE 179 MAP
SEE 200 MAP
SEE 219 MAP
2196000
2202000
2205000
434000
432000
430000
428000
424000
422000
420000
418000
E
F
G
H
J
1
2
3
4
5
6
7
LINCOLN
95765
ROCKLIN
95678
LINCOLN PKWY
DEL WEBB BLVD
TWELVE BRIDGES RD
BELLA BREEZE DR
DRESDEN DR
GALEWIND DR
COLONNADE DR
RED ROCK RD
FIELDSTONE DR
FS
TWELVE BRIDGES MIDDLE SCHOOL PARK
MID
WESTVIEW DR
CAMERO WY
CARDINAL DR
BELLEWOOD CT
LAVASTONE DR
FOX DEN CIR
ABILENE
STAGELINE
RANCH VIEW DR
WHITNEY HIGH SCHOOL
LIBERTY
TELEGRAPH HILL
WINDROW LN
WILD PLAINS CIR
SPRING CREEK DR
PULLMAN CT
SILVER GULCH
WHITNEY RANCH PKWY
BROKEN RAIL
RED SETTER RD
APPLE GREY LN
SPOTTED PONY LN
BRIDLEWOOD DR
SORRELL CIR
1 BUTTERFLY CT
PENINSULA DR
IROQUOIS RD
MARGARET AZEVEDO COMMUNITY PARK
POPPY CIR
STANFORD RANCH RD
W STANFORD RANCH RD
WILLIAM JESSUP UNIVERSITY
THUNDER VALLEY CASINO
THUNDER VALLEY CT
PLATO CT
INDUSTRIAL AV
UP RR
HAROLD T JOHNSON EXWY
65
313
WHITNEY
4600
2200
CYBER CT
PLACER CORPORATE TECHNOLOGY WY
TARA CT
W SUNSET BLVD
SUNSET BLVD
PLACER BLVD
LOOP RD
SOUTH
TINKER RD
NICHOLS DR
ATHERTON RD
MENLO DR
LONETREE BLVD
W OAKS BLVD
LONETREE PARK
PLEASANT GROVE CREEK
PARK (SITE)
BLUE OAKS BLVD
MERIDIAN WY
PRESTON
CAMELLIA CT
FINISTERIA DR
CINCINNATI AV
DULUTH AV
1100
300
3700
500
600
1300
1400
0
.125
.25
.375
.5
miles 1 in. = 1900 ft.

SEE 180 MAP

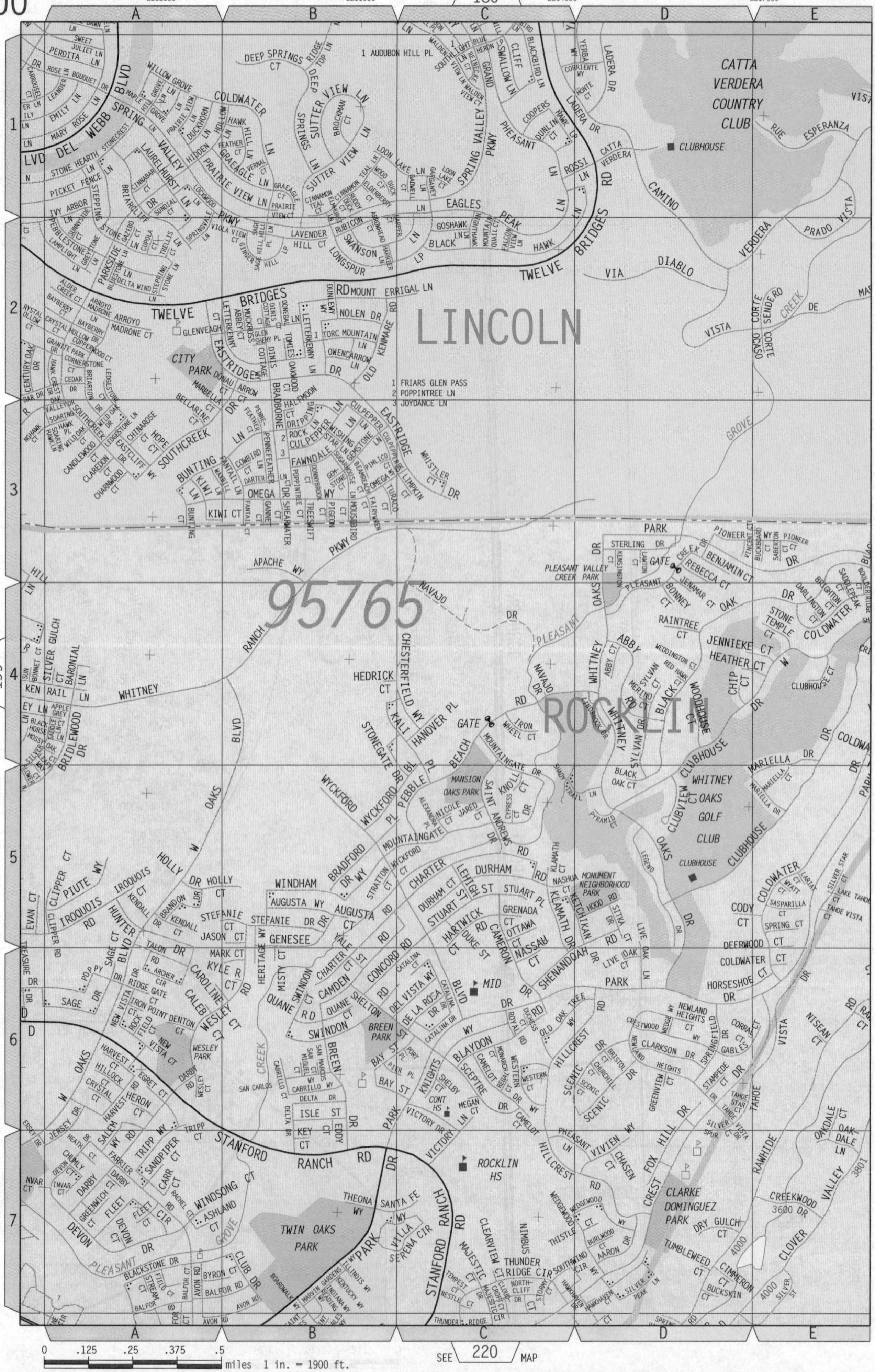

SEE 199 MAP

SEE 220 MAP

0 .125 .25 .375 .5 miles 1 in. = 1900 ft.

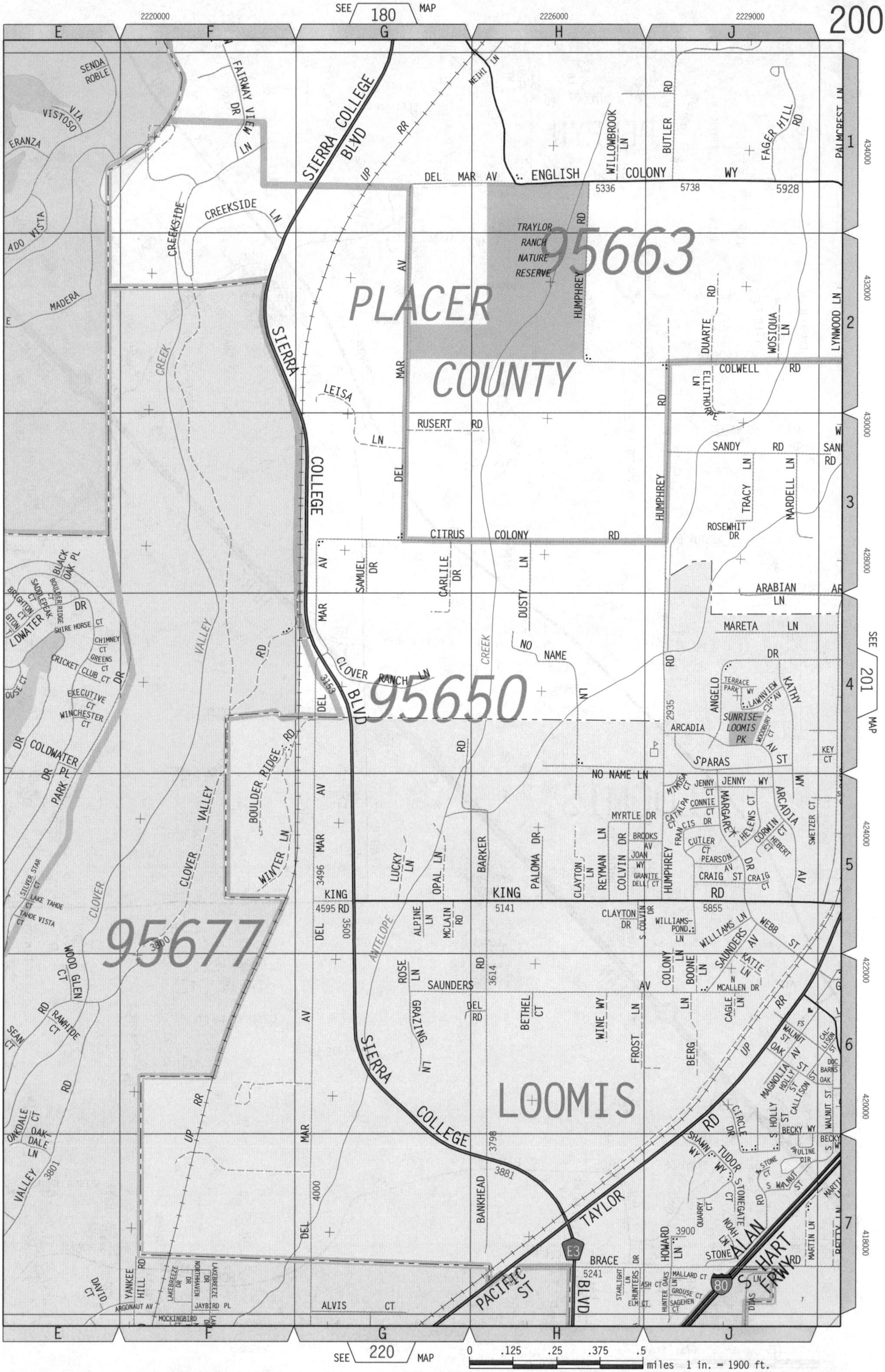
SEE 180 MAP
SEE 220 MAP
SEE 201 MAP
E
F
G
H
J
1
2
3
4
5
6
7
2220000
2226000
2229000
434000
432000
430000
428000
424000
422000
420000
418000
PLACER
COUNTY
LOOMIS
95663
95650
95677
TRAYLOR RANCH NATURE RESERVE
SUNRISE-LOOMIS PK
SIERRA COLLEGE BLVD
DEL MAR AV
ENGLISH COLONY WY
WILLOWBROOK LN
BUTLER RD
FAGER HILL RD
PALMCREST LN
FAIRWAY VIEW DR
CREEKSIDE LN
CREEKSIDE
SENDA ROBLE
VIA VISTOSO
MADERA
HUMPHREY RD
DUARTE RD
WOSIQUA LN
LYNWOOD LN
COLWELL RD
ELLITHORPE LN
LEISA LN
RUSERT RD
SANDY RD
TRACY LN
MARDELL LN
ROSEWHIT DR
CITRUS COLONY RD
SAMUEL DR
CARLILE DR
DUSTY LN
ARABIAN LN
MARETA LN
NO NAME LN
CLOVER RANCH LN
CLOVER VALLEY RD
BOULDER RIDGE RD
WINTER LN
KING RD
ARCADIA AV
SPARAS ST
KATHY DR
ANGELO DR
LAWNVIEW CT
TERRACE PARK WY
WOODBURY CT
KEY CT
JENNY WY
MIMOSA CT
CATALPA CT
CONNIE CT
FRANCIS DR
MARGARET DR
HELENS CT
CORWIN CT
HEBERT CT
SWETZER CT
MYRTLE DR
BROOKS AV
JOAN WY
GRANITE DELL CT
CUTLER CT
PEARSON AV
CRAIG ST
CRAIG CT
CLAYTON LN
REYMAN LN
COLVIN DR
LUCKY LN
OPAL LN
BARKER RD
PALOMA DR
ALPINE LN
MCLAIN RD
CLAYTON DR
S COLVIN DR
WILLIAMS-POND LN
WILLIAMS LN
WEBB ST
SAUNDERS AV
KATIE LN
N MCALLEN DR
BOONE LN
COLONY LN
ROSE LN
GRAZING LN
DEL RD
BETHEL CT
WINE WY
FROST LN
BERG LN
CAGLE LN
UP RR
WALNUT ST
OAK AV
MAGNOLIA ST
HOLLY ST
CALLISON ST
DOC BARNS OAK
CIRCLE DR
HOLLY ST
BECKY WY
PAULINE CIR
STONE CT
S WALNUT ST
MARTIN LN
BETTY LN
SHAWN WY
TUDOR WY
STONEGATE CT
QUARRY CT
NOAH LN
STONE
TAYLOR RD
BRACE DR
HOWARD LN
STARLIGHT LN
HUNTERS LN
ASH CT
ELM CT
HUNTER OAKS LN
MALLARD CT
GROUSE CT
SAGEHEN CT
S HART FRWY
ALAN RD
DIAS LN
PACIFIC ST
ALVIS CT
BANKHEAD RD
DEL MAR AV
YANKEE HILL RD
LAKEBREEZE DR
NORTHHAVEN DR
JAYBIRD PL
ARGONAUT AV
MOCKINGBIRD CT
DAVID CT
VALLEY DR
OAKDALE CT
OAK-DALE LN
SEAN CT
RAWHIDE CT
WOOD GLEN CT
COLDWATER PARK PL
SILVER STAR CT
LAKE TAHOE CT
TAHOE VISTA CT
CRICKET CLUB CT
EXECUTIVE CT
WINCHESTER CT
CHIMNEY CT
GREENS CT
SHIRE HORSE CT
BLACK OAK PL
SADDLEPEAK CT
BOULDER RIDGE DR
BRIGHTON CT
COLDWATER
CLOVER VALLEY CREEK
ANTELOPE CREEK
E3
80
0 .125 .25 .375 .5
miles 1 in. = 1900 ft.

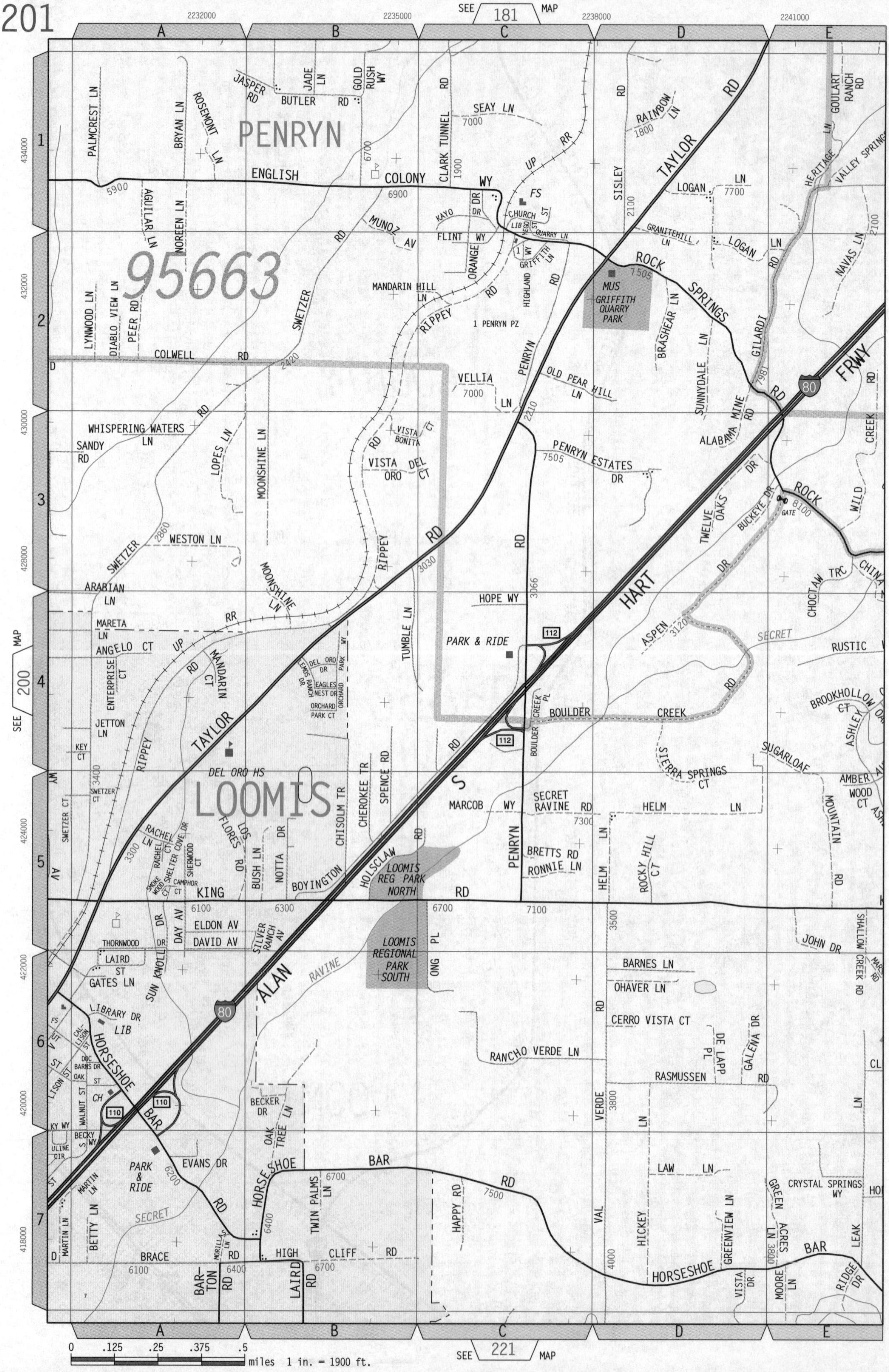
SEE 181 MAP
SEE 200 MAP
SEE 221 MAP
A
B
C
D
E
1
2
3
4
5
6
7
2232000
2235000
2238000
2241000
434000
432000
430000
428000
424000
422000
420000
418000
PENRYN
95663
LOOMIS
PALMCREST LN
BRYAN LN
ROSEMONT LN
JASPER RD
BUTLER RD
JADE LN
GOLD RUSH WY
CLARK TUNNEL RD
SEAY LN
UP RR
RAINBOW LN
SISLEY RD
TAYLOR RD
GOULART RANCH RD
HERITAGE LN
VALLEY SPRINGS
ENGLISH COLONY WY
AGUILAR LN
NOREEN LN
MUNOZ AV
KAYO DR
ORANGE DR
FLINT WY
CHURCH ST
LIB
QUARRY LN
GRIFFITH LN
FS
LOGAN LN
GRANITEHILL LN
ROCK SPRINGS RD
MUS
GRIFFITH QUARRY PARK
NAVAS LN
LYNWOOD LN
DIABLO VIEW LN
PEER RD
SWETZER RD
MANDARIN HILL LN
RIPPEY RD
HIGHLAND RD
1 PENRYN PZ
BRASHEAR LN
GILARDI RD
COLWELL RD
VELLIA LN
PENRYN RD
OLD PEAR HILL LN
SUNNYDALE LN
ALABAMA MINE RD
FRWY
80
WHISPERING WATERS LN
SANDY RD
LOPES LN
MOONSHINE LN
VISTA BONITA CT
VISTA DEL ORO CT
PENRYN ESTATES DR
TWELVE OAKS DR
BUCKEYE DR
GATE
WILD CREEK
WESTON LN
HART DR
CHOCTAW TRC
ARABIAN LN
HOPE WY
MARETA
ANGELO CT
ENTERPRISE CT
MANDARIN CT
LEWIS RANCH DR
DEL ORO DR
EAGLES NEST DR
ORCHARD PARK CT
TUMBLE LN
PARK & RIDE
112
ASPEN
SECRET
RUSTIC
BROOKHOLLOW CT
JETTON LN
KEY CT
BOULDER CREEK PL
BOULDER CREEK
ASHLEY
SUGARLOAF
DEL ORO HS
CHEROKEE TR
SPENCE RD
SIERRA SPRINGS CT
SWETZER CT
CHISOLM TR
MARCOB WY
SECRET RAVINE RD
HELM LN
AMBER WOOD CT
MOUNTAIN RD
RACHEL LN
RACHEL CT
SHELTER COVE DR
SHERWOOD CT
SMOKE WOOD CT
CAMPHOR CT
LOS FLORES RD
BUSH LN
NOTTA DR
BOYINGTON
HOLSCLAW RD
LOOMIS REG PARK NORTH
BRETTS RD
RONNIE LN
ROCKY HILL CT
KING RD
ELDON AV
DAVID AV
SILVER RANCH AV
SHALLOW CREEK RD
JOHN DR
THORNWOOD
LAIRD ST
GATES LN
SUN KNOLL DR
DAY AV
LOOMIS REGIONAL PARK SOUTH
ONG PL
BARNES LN
OHAVER LN
RAVINE
ALAN
LIBRARY DR
HORSESHOE BAR RD
CERRO VISTA CT
DE LAPP PL
GALENA DR
RANCHO VERDE LN
RASMUSSEN RD
LISON ST
WALNUT ST
BARNS DR
OAK ST
CH
110
BECKER DR
OAK TREE LN
VAL VERDE RD
KY WY
BECKY WY
ULINE CIR
EVANS DR
LAW LN
MARTIN LN
BETTY LN
TWIN PALMS LN
HAPPY RD
HICKEY LN
GREENVIEW LN
GREEN ACRES LN
CRYSTAL SPRINGS WY
LEAK RD
BRACE
MORILLAS LN
HIGH CLIFF RD
BARTON RD
LAIRD RD
VISTA DR
MOORE LN
RIDGE DR
0 .125 .25 .375 .5
miles 1 in. = 1900 ft.

SEE 181 MAP

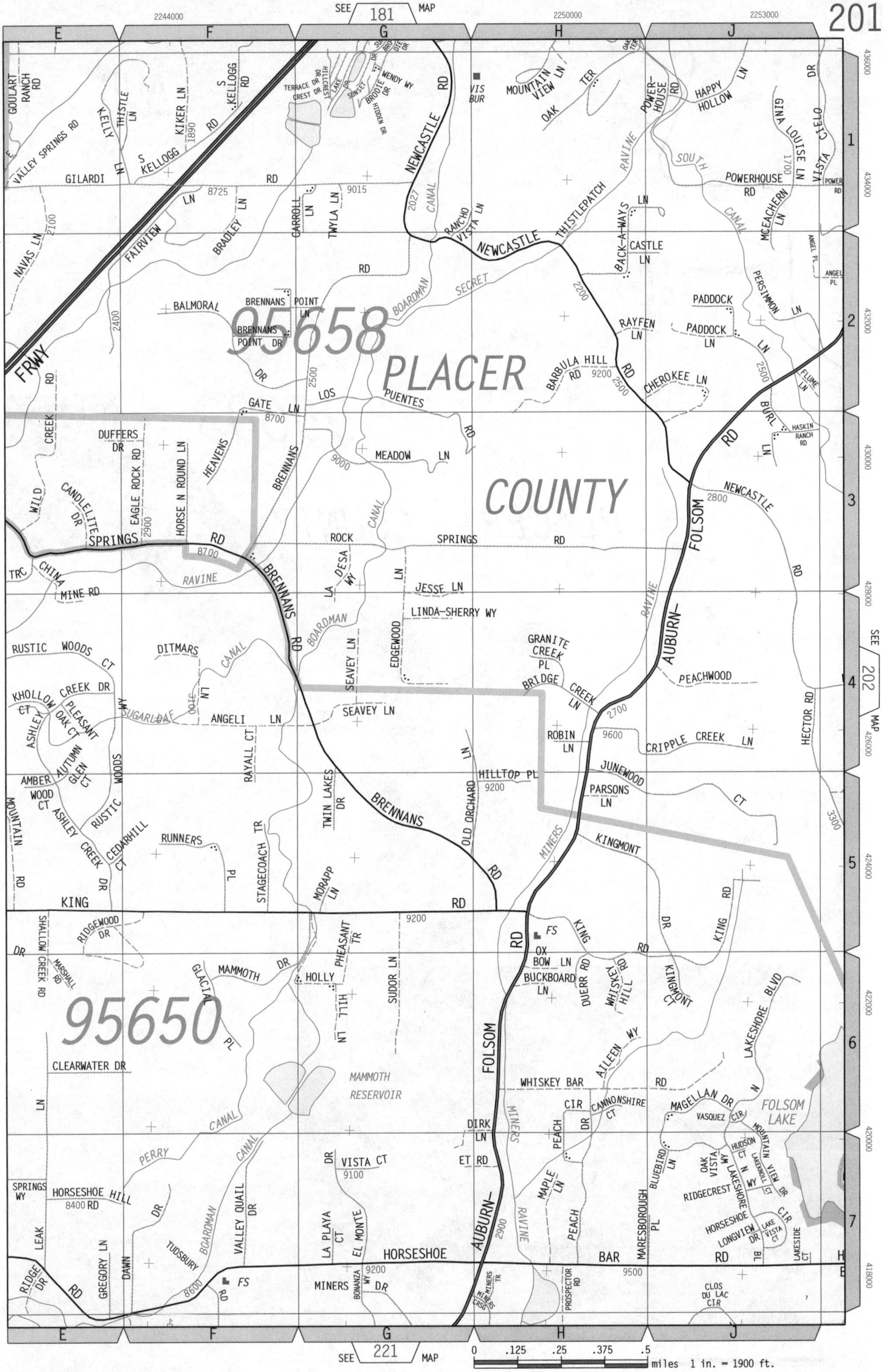

SEE 202 MAP
SEE 221 MAP

0 .125 .25 .375 .5 miles 1 in. = 1900 ft.

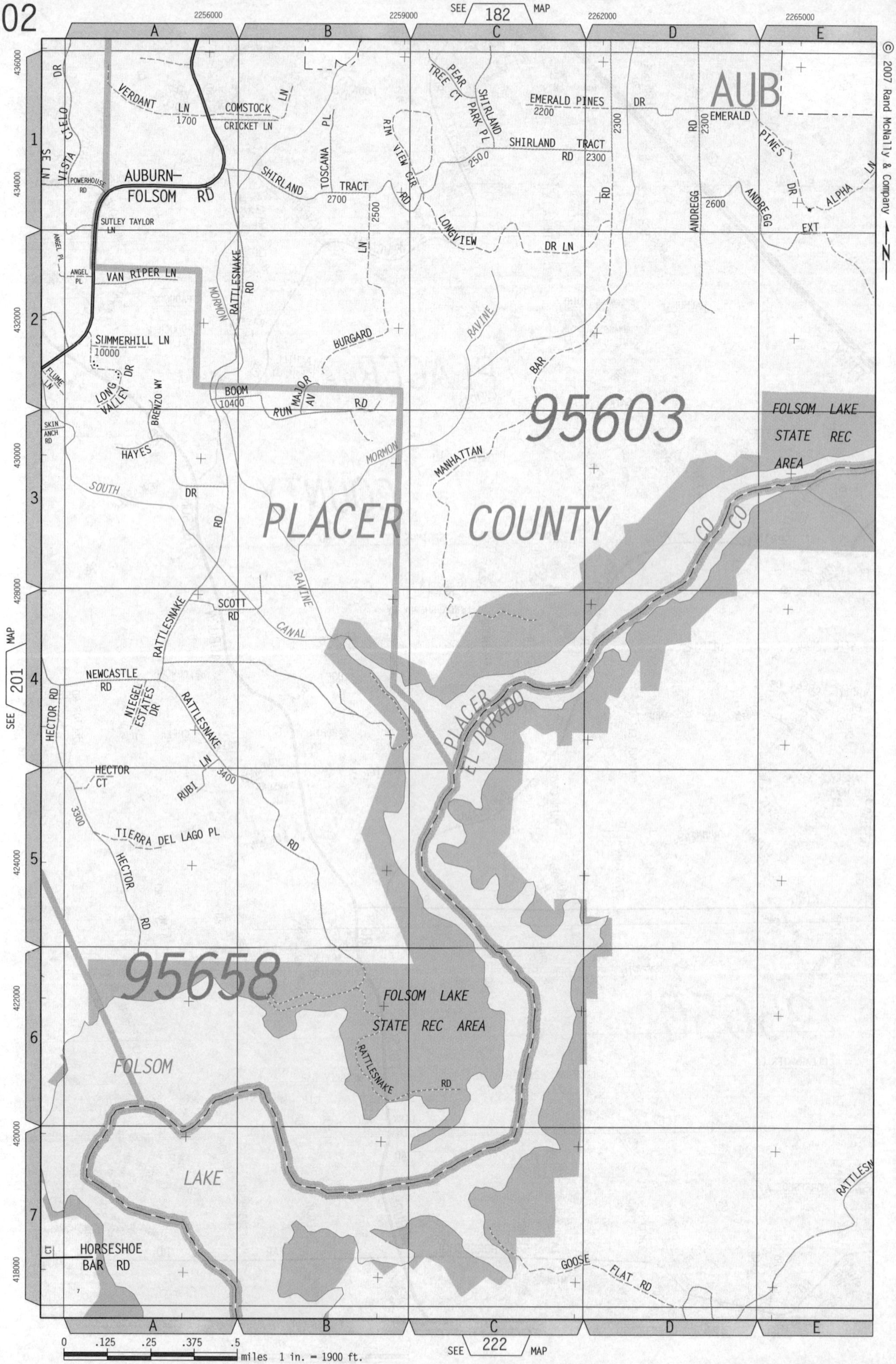
SEE 182 MAP
SEE 201 MAP
SEE 222 MAP
2256000
2259000
2262000
2265000
436000
434000
432000
430000
428000
424000
422000
420000
418000
A
B
C
D
E
1
2
3
4
5
6
7
AUB
VERDANT LN
1700
COMSTOCK LN
CRICKET LN
TOSCANA PL
PEAR TREE CT
SHIRLAND PARK PL
EMERALD PINES DR
2200
2300
EMERALD PINES DR
ALPHA LN
SHIRLAND TRACT RD
2500
2300
RIM VIEW CIR
VISTA CIELO DR
SE LN
POWERHOUSE RD
AUBURN-FOLSOM RD
SHIRLAND TRACT
2700
2500 LN
RD
ANDREGG RD
2600
ANDREGG EXT
SUTLEY TAYLOR LN
LONGVIEW DR LN
ANGEL PL
VAN RIPER LN
MORMON
RATTLESNAKE RD
RAVINE
BURGARD
BAR
SUMMERHILL LN
10000
FLUME LN
LONG VALLEY DR
BOOM RUN RD
10400
MAJOR AV
BRENZO WY
SKIN ANCH RD
HAYES DR
SOUTH
MORMON
MANHATTAN
95603
FOLSOM LAKE STATE REC AREA
PLACER COUNTY
RD
RAVINE
CO
CO
SCOTT RD
RATTLESNAKE
CANAL
NEWCASTLE RD
NIEGEL ESTATES DR
RATTLESNAKE
HECTOR RD
PLACER
EL DORADO
RUBI LN
3400
HECTOR CT
3300
TIERRA DEL LAGO PL
RD
HECTOR RD
95658
FOLSOM LAKE STATE REC AREA
FOLSOM
RATTLESNAKE RD
LAKE
HORSESHOE BAR RD
CT
GOOSE FLAT RD
RATTLESN
0
.125
.25
.375
.5
miles 1 in. = 1900 ft.

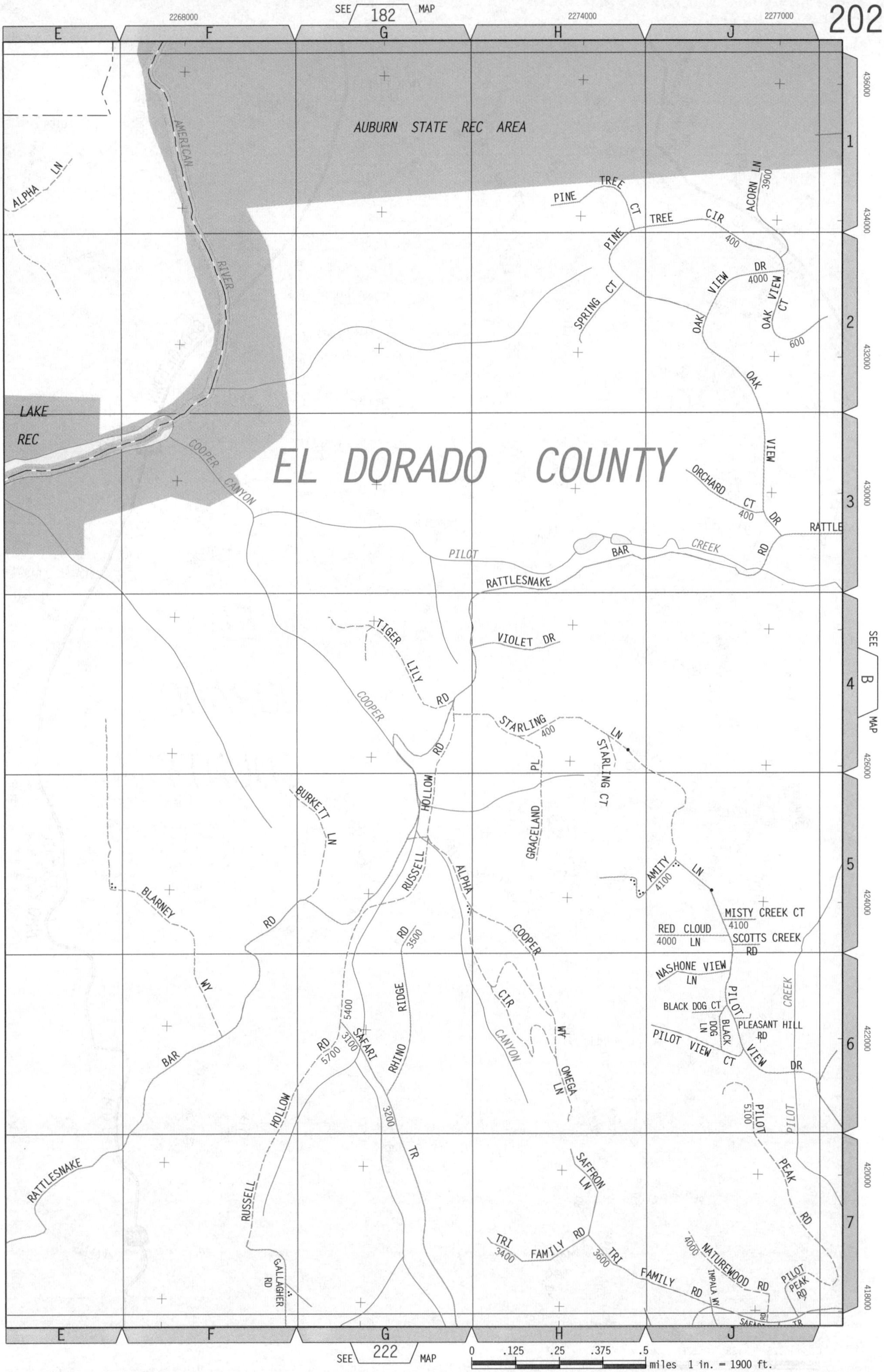
SEE 182 MAP
2268000
2274000
2277000
E
F
G
H
J
AUBURN STATE REC AREA
AMERICAN
RIVER
ALPHA LN
LAKE
REC
EL DORADO COUNTY
PINE
TREE
CT
PINE
TREE
CIR
400
ACORN LN
3900
SPRING CT
OAK
VIEW
DR
4000
OAK VIEW CT
600
OAK
VIEW
DR
ORCHARD
CT
400
RD
RATTLE
COOPER
CANYON
PILOT
CREEK
BAR
RATTLESNAKE
TIGER
LILY
RD
VIOLET DR
COOPER
RD
STARLING
400
LN
STARLING CT
GRACELAND PL
HOLLOW
BURKETT LN
RUSSELL
ALPHA
AMITY
4100
LN
MISTY CREEK CT
4100
RED CLOUD
4000 LN
SCOTTS CREEK
RD
BLARNEY
RD
RD
3500
COOPER
WY
NASHONE VIEW
LN
PILOT
BLACK DOG CT
DOG LN
BLACK
PLEASANT HILL
RD
CREEK
CIR
WY
PILOT VIEW CT
VIEW
DR
RIDGE
5400
SAFARI
3100
RD
5700
RHINO
CANYON
OMEGA LN
BAR
PILOT
5100
PILOT
HOLLOW
3200
TR
RATTLESNAKE
PEAK
SAFFRON
LN
RD
RUSSELL
TRI
3400
FAMILY RD
TRI
3600
FAMILY
RD
4000
NATUREWOOD RD
IMPALA WY
PILOT PEAK RD
GALLAGHER RD
SAFARI
TR
436000
434000
432000
430000
428000
426000
424000
422000
420000
418000
1
2
3
4
5
6
7
SEE B MAP
SEE 222 MAP
0 .125 .25 .375 .5
miles 1 in. = 1900 ft.

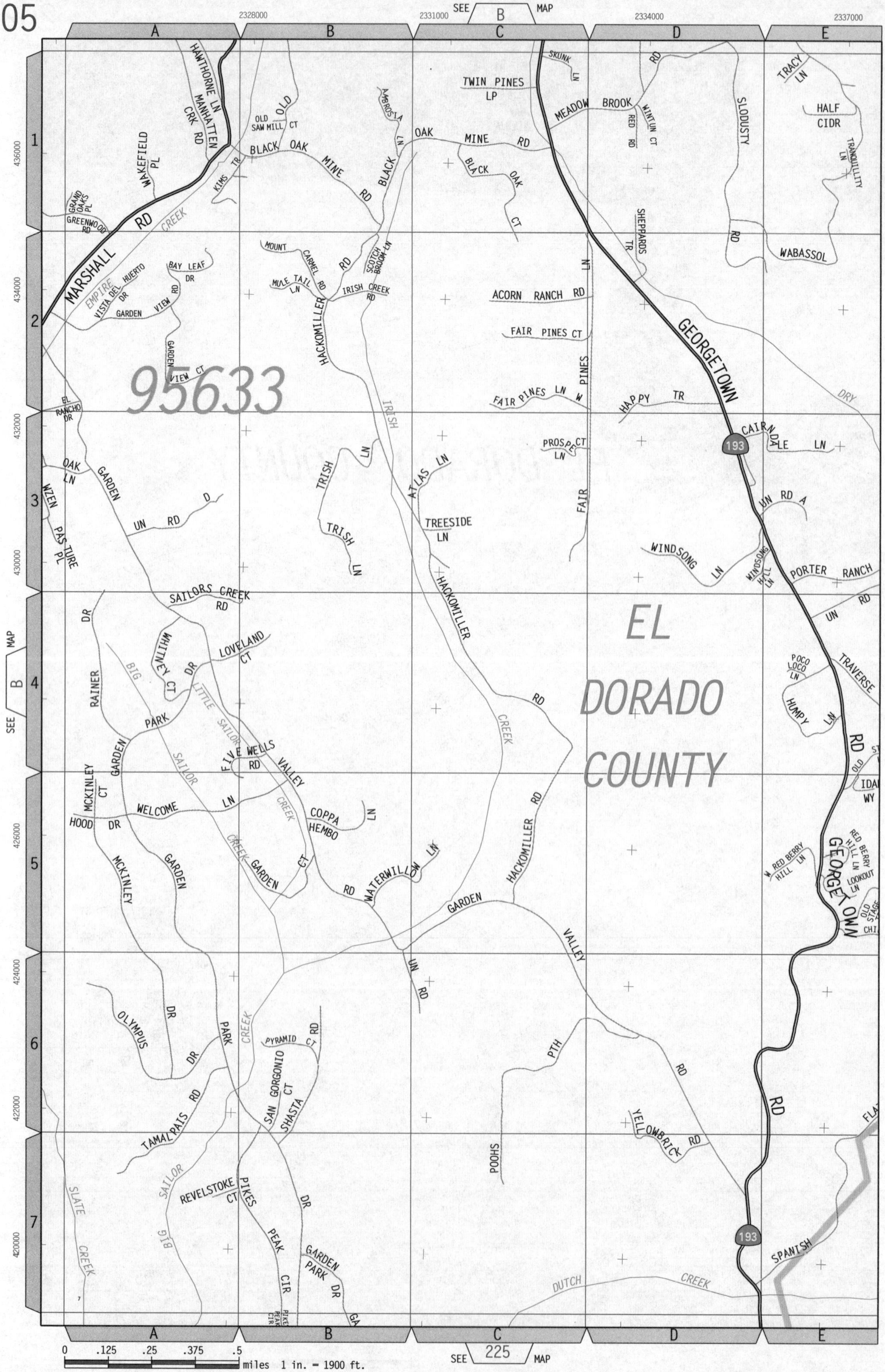
SEE B MAP
SEE B MAP
SEE 225 MAP
A
B
C
D
E
1
2
3
4
5
6
7
2328000
2331000
2334000
2337000
436000
434000
432000
430000
426000
424000
422000
420000
95633
EL DORADO COUNTY
MARSHALL RD
GEORGETOWN RD
193
HAWTHORNE LN
MANHATTEN CRK RD
WAKEFIELD PL
GRAND OAKS PL
GREENWOOD RD
EMPIRE CREEK
OLD SAW MILL CT
OLD
BLACK OAK MINE RD
KIMS TR
AMBROSIA LN
BLACK OAK MINE RD
BLACK OAK CT
SKUNK LN
TWIN PINES LP
MEADOW BROOK RD
RED RD
WINTUN CT
SLODUSTY RD
TRACY LN
HALF CIDR
TRANQUILITY LN
WABASSOL
SHEPPARDS TR
MOUNT CARMEL RD
MULE TAIL LN
SCOTCH BROOM LN
IRISH CREEK RD
HACKOMILLER
BAY LEAF DR
VISTA DEL HUERTO DR
GARDEN VIEW RD
GARDEN VIEW CT
ACORN RANCH RD
FAIR PINES CT
FAIR PINES LN
W PINES LN
HAPPY TR
CAIRNDALE LN
DRY
EL RANCHO DR
IRISH
TRISH LN
ATLAS LN
PROSPECT LN
FAIR
OAK LN
GARDEN
UN RD D
TREESIDE LN
UN RD A
WZEN
PASTURE PL
WINDSONG LN
WINDSONG HILL LN
PORTER RANCH
UN RD
SAILORS CREEK RD
HACKOMILLER RD
DR
WHITNEY CT
LOVELAND CT
DR
RAINER
BIG
LITTLE SAILOR
POCO LOCO LN
TRAVERSE
HUMPY LN
PARK
CREEK
FIVE WELLS RD
VALLEY
OLD ST
IDA WY
GARDEN
SAILOR
MCKINLEY CT
WELCOME LN
CREEK
COPPA HEMBO LN
HOOD DR
HACKOMILLER RD
RED BERRY HILL LN
W RED BERRY HILL LN
LOOKOUT LN
OLD STAGE
CHI
MCKINLEY
GARDEN
CREEK
GARDEN CT
WATERWILLOW LN
RD
GARDEN
VALLEY
UN RD
OLYMPUS DR
DR
PARK
CREEK
PYRAMID CT
RD
PTH
RD
TAMALPAIS RD
SAN GORGONIO CT
SHASTA
YELLOWBRICK RD
POOHS
FLA
SAILOR
REVELSTOKE CT
PIKES PEAK CIR
DR
SLATE CREEK
BIG
GARDEN PARK DR
SPANISH
DUTCH CREEK
PIKES PEAK CIR
GA
0
.125
.25
.375
.5
miles 1 in. = 1900 ft.
N

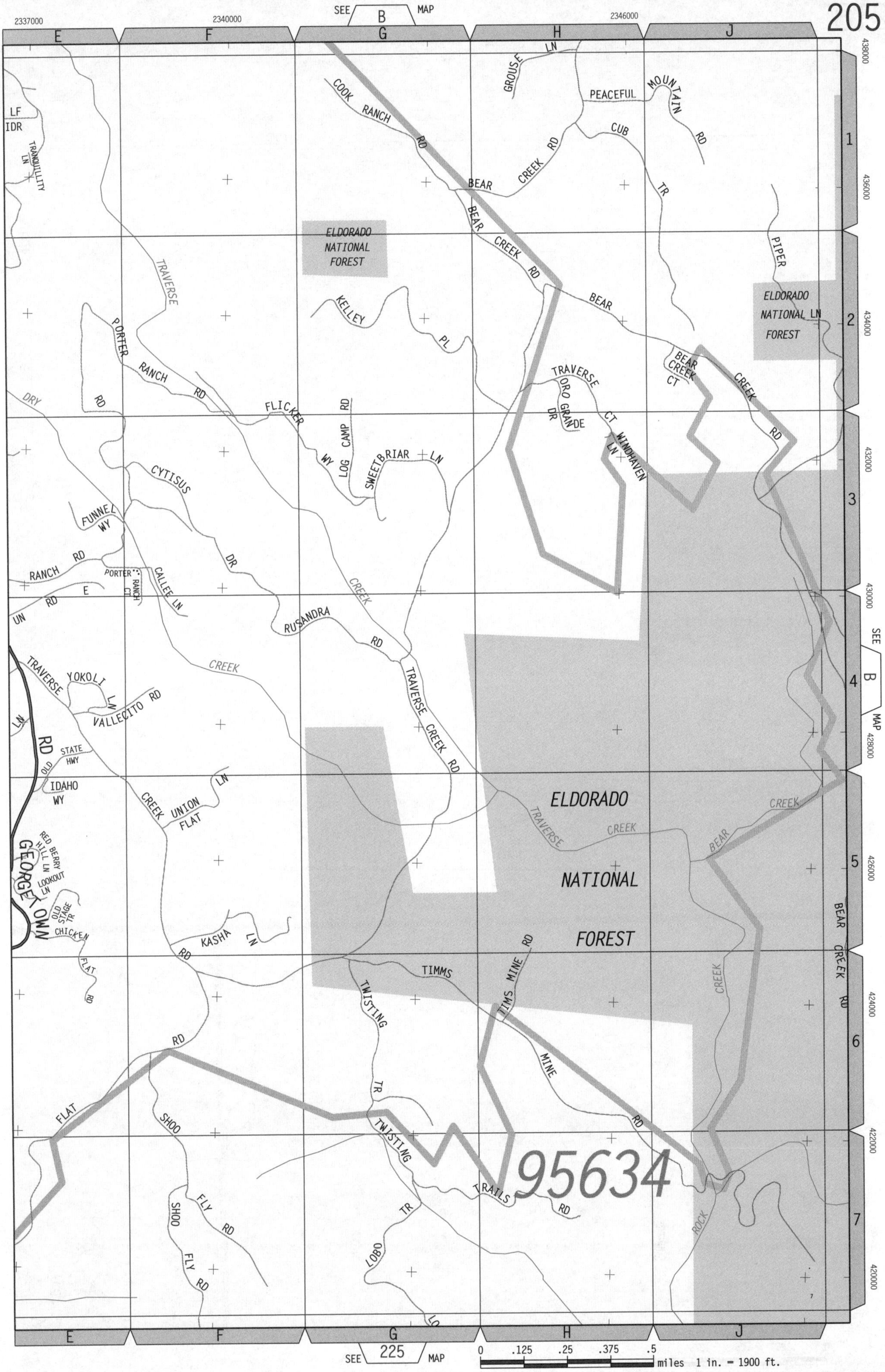
SEE B MAP
2337000
2340000
2346000
E
F
G
H
J
1
2
3
4
5
6
7
438000
436000
434000
432000
430000
428000
426000
424000
422000
420000
COOK RANCH RD
GROUSE LN
PEACEFUL MOUNTAIN RD
CUB TR
BEAR CREEK RD
LF
IDR
TRANQUILLITY LN
ELDORADO NATIONAL FOREST
TRAVERSE
PORTER RANCH RD
KELLEY PL
BEAR CREEK CT
PIPER
NATIONAL LN
CREEK
TRAVERSE CT
ORO GRANDE DR
WINDHAVEN LN
FLICKER WY
LOG CAMP RD
SWEETBRIAR LN
DRY
CYTISUS DR
FUNNEL WY
RANCH RD
PORTER RANCH CT
CALLEE LN
UN RD E
RUSANDRA RD
TRAVERSE CREEK RD
TRAVERSE
YOKOLI LN
VALLECITO RD
LN
RD
OLD STATE HWY
IDAHO WY
CREEK
UNION FLAT LN
RED BERRY HILL LN
LOOKOUT LN
GEORGETOWN
OLD STAGE TR
CHICKEN FLAT RD
KASHA LN
ELDORADO NATIONAL FOREST
TRAVERSE CREEK
BEAR CREEK
TIMMS
TIMS MINE RD
MINE RD
TWISTING TR
TWISTING TRAILS RD
FLAT RD
SHOO FLY RD
LOBO TR
LO
ROCK
BEAR CREEK RD
95634
SEE 225 MAP
0 .125 .25 .375 .5 miles 1 in. = 1900 ft.

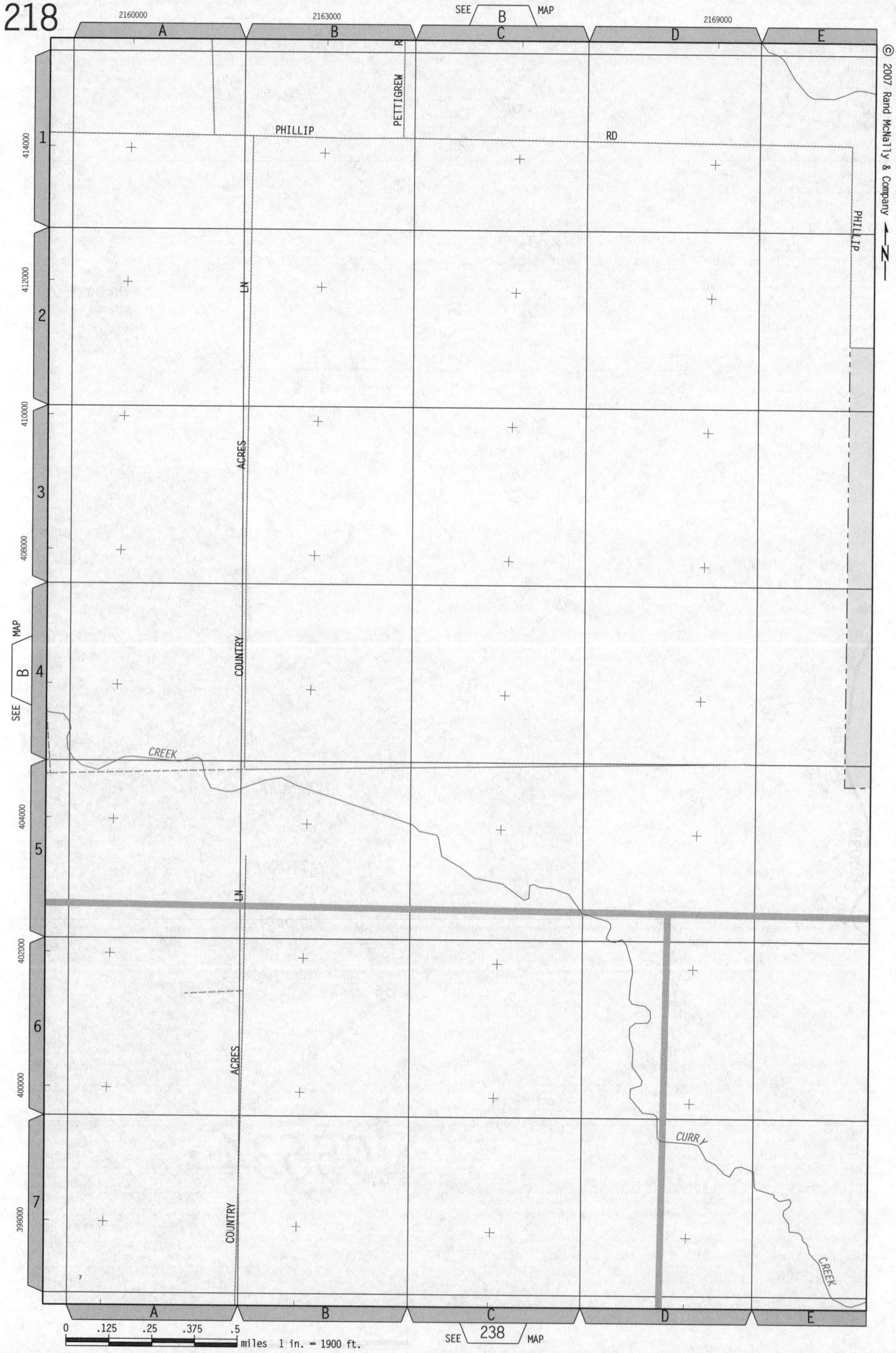
2160000
2163000
SEE B MAP
2169000
A
B
C
D
E
1
2
3
4
5
6
7
414000
412000
410000
408000
404000
402000
400000
398000
PHILLIP
RD
PETTIGREW
R
PHILLIP
COUNTRY
ACRES
LN
CREEK
CURRY
CREEK
SEE B MAP
SEE 238 MAP
0
.125
.25
.375
.5
miles 1 in. = 1900 ft.

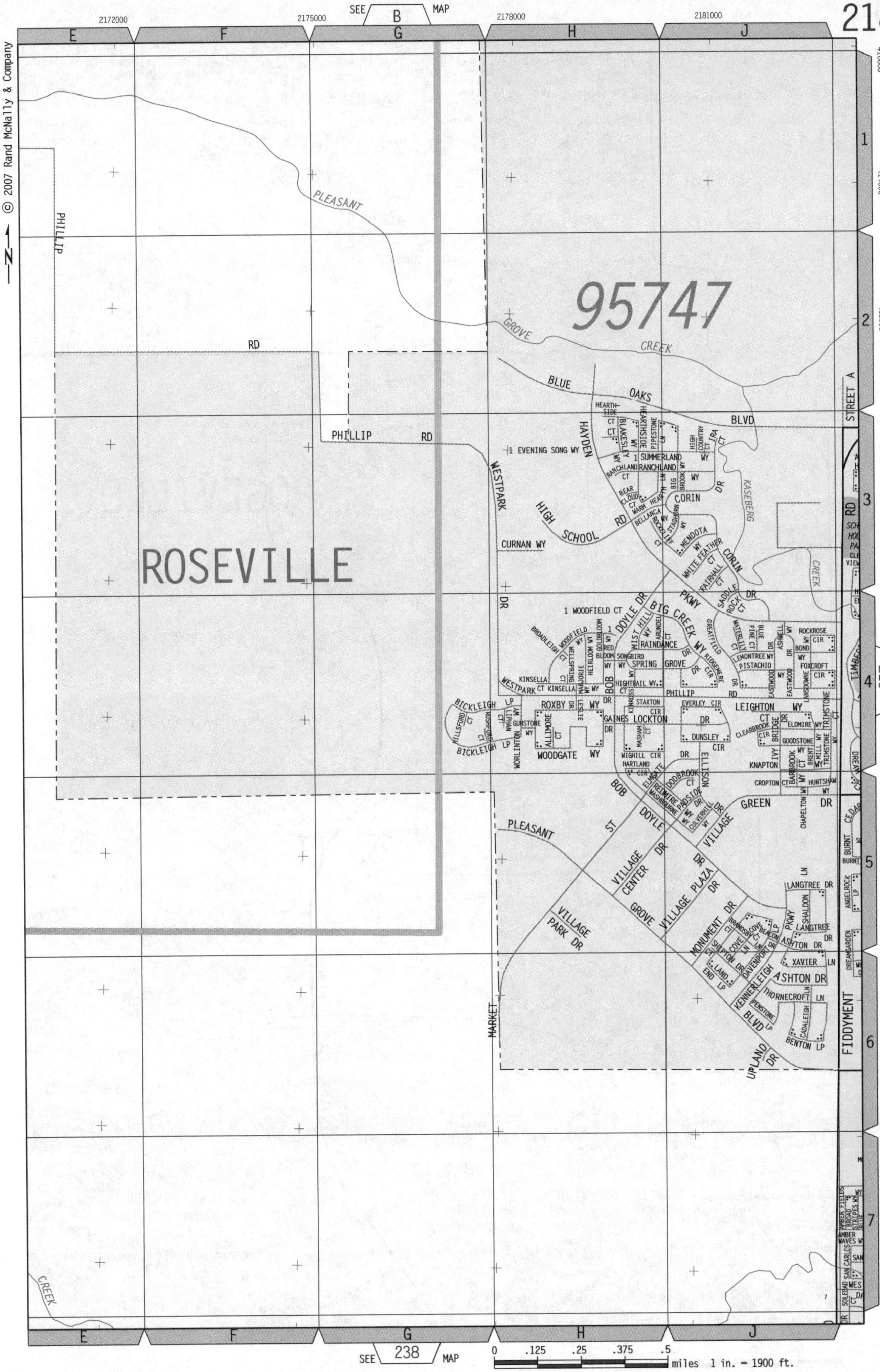
SEE B MAP
2172000
2175000
2178000
2181000
E
F
G
H
J
1
2
3
4
5
6
7
416000
414000
412000
410000
408000
404000
402000
400000
398000
95747
ROSEVILLE
PLEASANT
GROVE
CREEK
PHILLIP
RD
PHILLIP RD
BLUE OAKS BLVD
STREET A
HAYDEN
WESTPARK DR
HIGH SCHOOL RD
CURNAN WY
1 EVENING SONG WY
SUMMERLAND
RANCHLAND
CORIN DR
MENDOTA
WHITE FEATHER
FAIRHALL
SADDLE ROCK DR
KASEBERG
BIG CREEK WY
DOYLE DR
1 WOODFIELD CT
RAINDANCE
SPRING GROVE
SONGBIRD
HIGHTRAIL WY
KINSELLA
PHILLIP RD
LEIGHTON WY
EVERLEY CIR
STAXTON
LOCKTON
ROXBY WY
GAINES DR
BICKLEIGH LP
WOODGATE WY
ALLIMORE CT
DUNSLEY CIR
ELLISON
GREEN DR
PISTACHIO
LEMONTREE WY
ROCKROSE CIR
FOXCROFT
TRIMSTONE
KNAPTON
CROPTON CT
HUNTSHAW
BOB DOYLE DR
VILLAGE CENTER DR
VILLAGE PLAZA DR
GROVE VILLAGE DR
VILLAGE PARK DR
PLEASANT
MARKET ST
MONUMENT DR
LANGTREE DR
ASHTON DR
XAVIER LN
THORNECROFT LN
KENNERLEIGH BLVD
BENTON LP
UPLAND DR
FIDDYMENT
BURNT CEDAR
TIMBER
CREEK
SEE 219 MAP
SEE 238 MAP
0 .125 .25 .375 .5 miles 1 in. = 1900 ft.

SEE 199 MAP

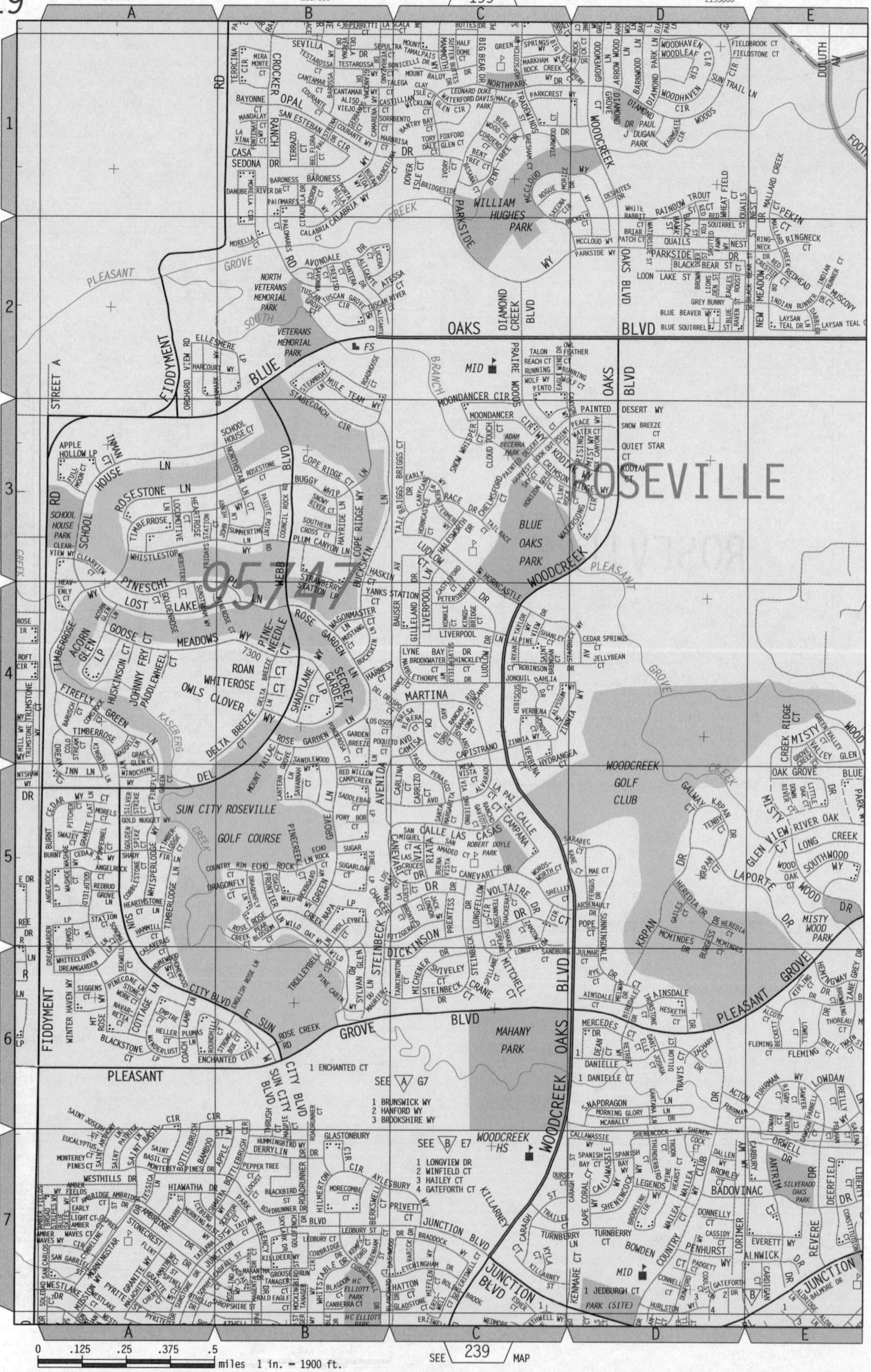

0 .125 .25 .375 .5 miles 1 in. = 1900 ft.

SEE 239 MAP

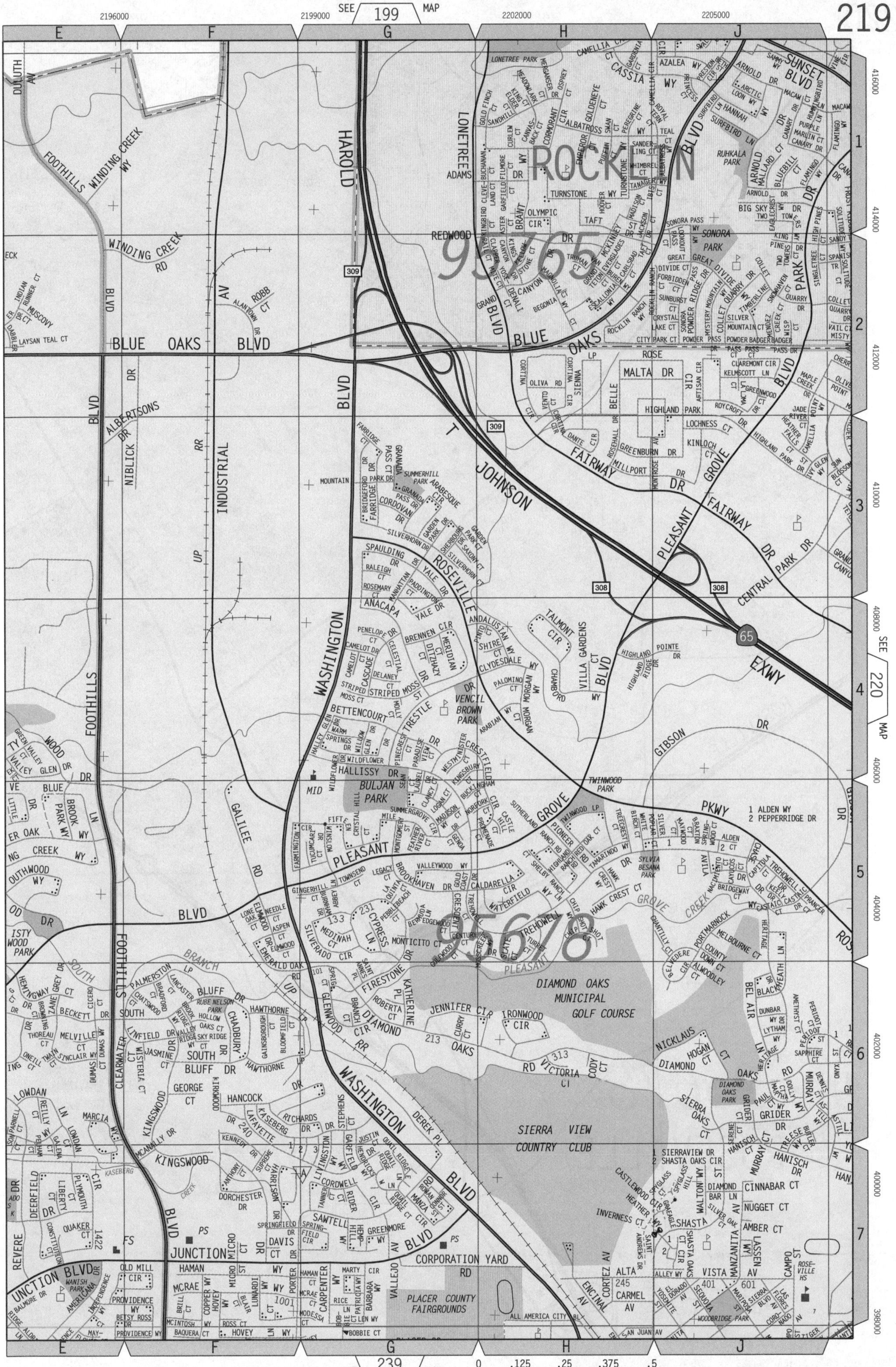
SEE 199 MAP
SEE 220 MAP
SEE 239 MAP
ROCKLIN
95765
95678
LONETREE PARK
RUHKALA PARK
SONORA PARK
VENCIL BROWN PARK
BULJAN PARK
TWINWOOD PARK
SYLVIA BESANA PARK
DIAMOND OAKS MUNICIPAL GOLF COURSE
SIERRA VIEW COUNTRY CLUB
DIAMOND OAKS PARK
CORPORATION YARD
PLACER COUNTY FAIRGROUNDS
WOODBRIDGE PARK
ROSEVILLE HS
BLUE OAKS BLVD
FOOTHILLS BLVD
WASHINGTON BLVD
HAROLD T JOHNSON EXWY
PLEASANT GROVE BLVD
FAIRWAY DR
SUNSET BLVD
PARK DR
INDUSTRIAL AV
UP RR
GALILEE RD
GIBSON DR
ROSEVILLE PKWY
JUNCTION BLVD
KINGSWOOD DR
DIAMOND OAKS RD
VICTORIA CT
CENTRAL PARK DR
WINDING CREEK RD
ALBERTSONS DR
NIBLICK DR
1 ALDEN WY
2 PEPPERRIDGE DR
1 SIERRAVIEW DR
2 SHASTA OAKS CIR
0 .125 .25 .375 .5 miles 1 in. = 1900 ft.

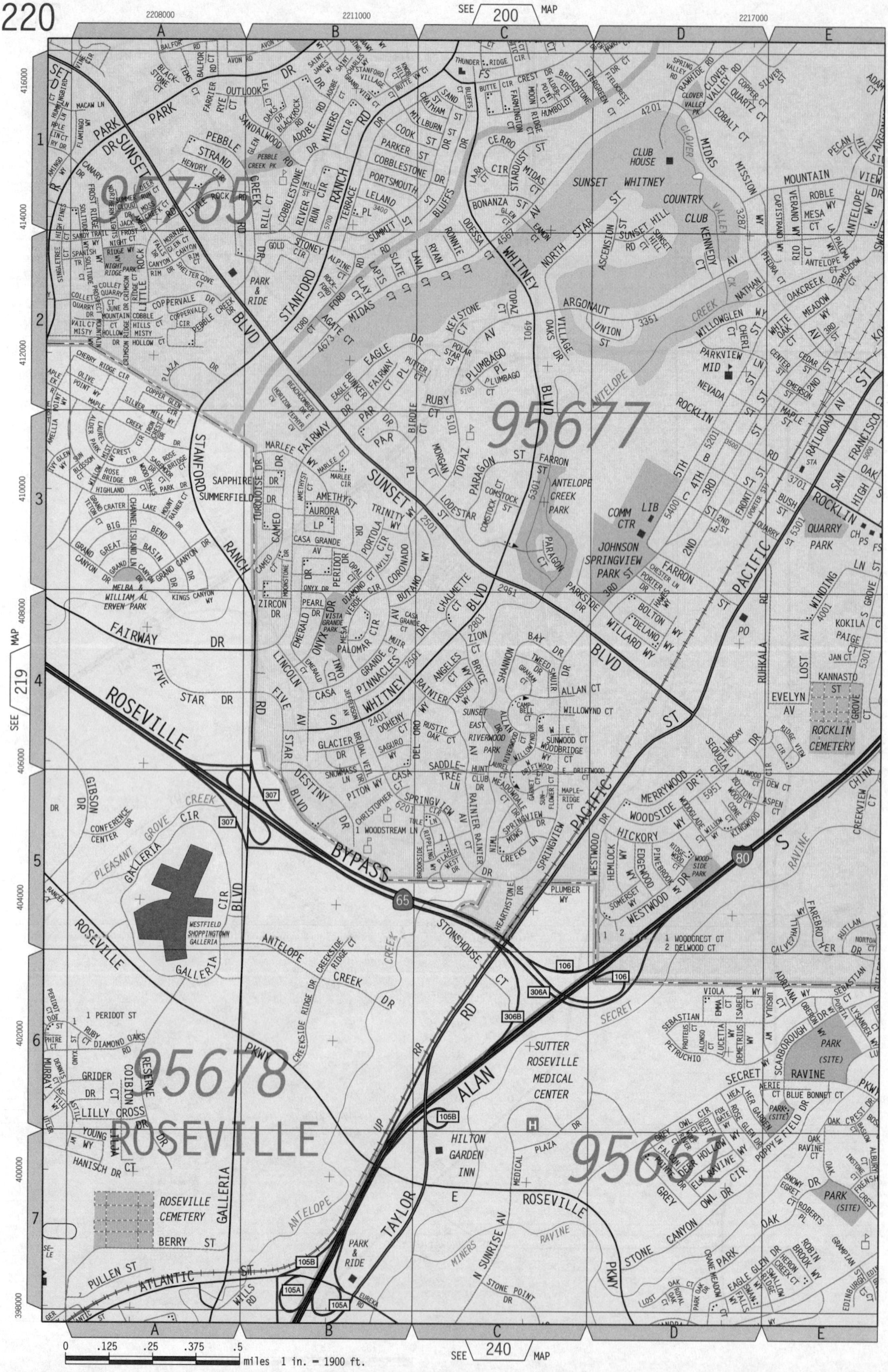
SEE 200 MAP
SEE 219 MAP
SEE 240 MAP
2208000
2211000
2217000
416000
414000
412000
410000
408000
406000
404000
402000
400000
398000
A
B
C
D
E
1
2
3
4
5
6
7
95765
95677
95678
95661
ROSEVILLE
SUNSET BLVD
PARK DR
STANFORD RANCH RD
WHITNEY BLVD
S WHITNEY BLVD
ROSEVILLE BYPASS
PACIFIC ST
ROCKLIN RD
SUNSET WHITNEY COUNTRY CLUB
CLUB HOUSE
ANTELOPE CREEK PARK
JOHNSON SPRINGVIEW PARK
COMM CTR
LIB
PARKVIEW MID
QUARRY PARK
ROCKLIN CEMETERY
MELBA & WILLIAM AL ERVEN PARK
FAIRWAY DR
FIVE STAR DR
GALLERIA BLVD
GALLERIA CIR
WESTFIELD SHOPPINGTOWN GALLERIA
ANTELOPE CREEK DR
PLEASANT GROVE CREEK
TAYLOR RD
ALAN
SUTTER ROSEVILLE MEDICAL CENTER
HILTON GARDEN INN
E ROSEVILLE PKWY
ROSEVILLE CEMETERY
ATLANTIC ST
PULLEN ST
BERRY ST
STONE CANYON
SECRET RAVINE
RAVINE PARK (SITE)
N SUNRISE AV
STONE POINT DR
EUREKA RD
PARK & RIDE
65
80
105A
105B
106
306A
306B
307
0 .125 .25 .375 .5 miles 1 in. = 1900 ft.

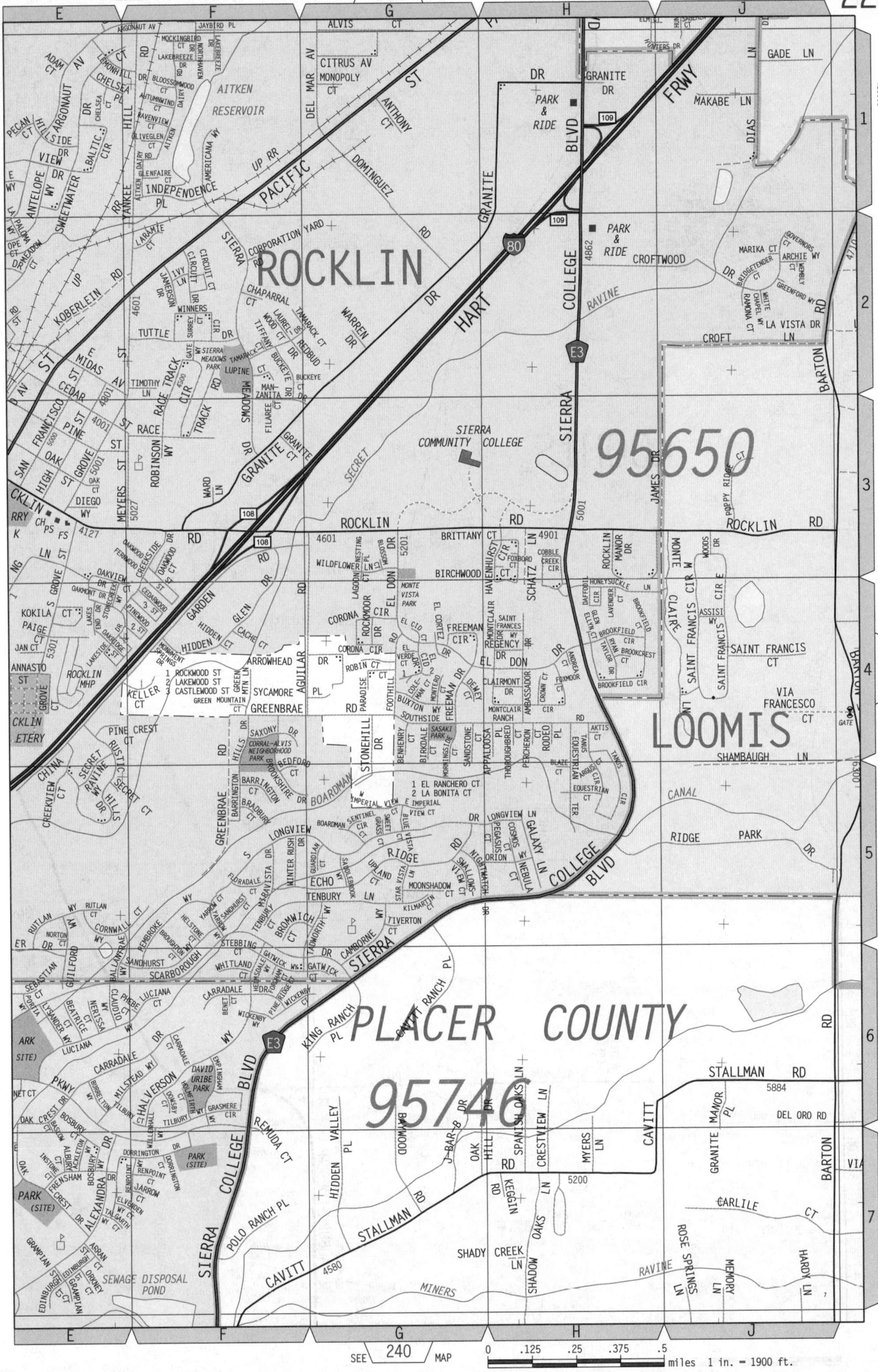

SEE 200 MAP
SEE 221 MAP
SEE 240 MAP
2220000
2223000
2226000
2229000
416000
414000
412000
410000
406000
404000
402000
400000
ROCKLIN
LOOMIS
PLACER COUNTY
95650
95746
AITKEN RESERVOIR
SIERRA COMMUNITY COLLEGE
PARK & RIDE
PACIFIC ST
UP RR
HART DR
GRANITE DR
SIERRA COLLEGE BLVD
ROCKLIN RD
KOBERLEIN RD
ARGONAUT AV
SWEETWATER
INDEPENDENCE PL
DOMINGUEZ RD
DEL MAR AV
CITRUS AV
MONOPOLY CT
ANTHONY CT
ALVIS CT
GADE LN
MAKABE LN
DIAS LN
CROFTWOOD DR
CROFT LN
BARTON RD
LA VISTA DR
SECRET RAVINE
RACE TRACK CIR
MEADOWS DR
WARREN DR
CHAPARRAL CT
TUTTLE DR
TIMOTHY LN
MIDAS AV
CEDAR
PINE ST
OAK ST
GROVE ST
HIGH ST
SAN FRANCISCO
DIEGO WY
ROBINSON WY
WARD LN
MEYERS ST
JAMES DR
POPPY RIDGE CT
ROCKLIN MANOR DR
MONTE CLAIRE
SAINT FRANCIS CIR
SAINT FRANCIS CT
VIA FRANCESCO CT
SHAMBAUGH LN
BIRCHWOOD
BRITTANY CT
WILDFLOWER LN
EL DON DR
CORONA CIR
FREEMAN CIR
REGENCY DR
SCHATZ LN
HAVENHURST CIR
ARROWHEAD DR
AGUILAR RD
SYCAMORE
GREENBRAE RD
HIDDEN GLEN
GARDEN DR
KELLER CT
1 ROCKWOOD ST
2 LAKEWOOD ST
3 CASTLEWOOD ST
GREEN MOUNTAIN
ROCKLIN MHP
PINE CREST CT
SECRET RAVINE HILLS DR
CHINA GARDEN
CREEKVIEW CT
BOARDMAN
BARRINGTON
BEDFORD CT
STONEHILL DR
1 EL RANCHERO CT
2 LA BONITA CT
W IMPERIAL VIEW
E IMPERIAL VIEW CT
LONGVIEW DR
APPALOOSA PL
THOROUGHBRED CT
PERCHERON CT
RODEO PL
EQUESTRIAN TER
GALAXY LN
ORION
NEBULA CT
CANAL
RIDGE PARK DR
S ECHO RIDGE
TENBURY LN
MOONSHADOW CT
TIVERTON
CAMBORNE
SIERRA COLLEGE BLVD
GUILFORD
SCARBOROUGH
WHITLAND
CARRADALE
LUCIANA
KING RANCH PL
CAVITT RANCH PL
STALLMAN RD
DEL ORO RD
GRANITE MANOR PL
CAVITT
MYERS LN
CRESTVIEW LN
SPANISH OAKS LN
OAK HILL RD
J-BAR-B DR
BAYWOOD
HIDDEN VALLEY PL
REMUDA CT
POLO RANCH PL
CAVITT STALLMAN RD
SHADY CREEK LN
SHADOW OAKS
ROSE SPRINGS LN
MEMORY LN
HARDY LN
CARLILE CT
MINERS RAVINE
SEWAGE DISPOSAL POND
DAVID URIBE PARK
PARK (SITE)
HALVERSON
ALEXANDRA DR
PKWY
E3
80
108
109
5884
5200
4580

0 .125 .25 .375 .5 miles 1 in. = 1900 ft.

SEE 201 MAP

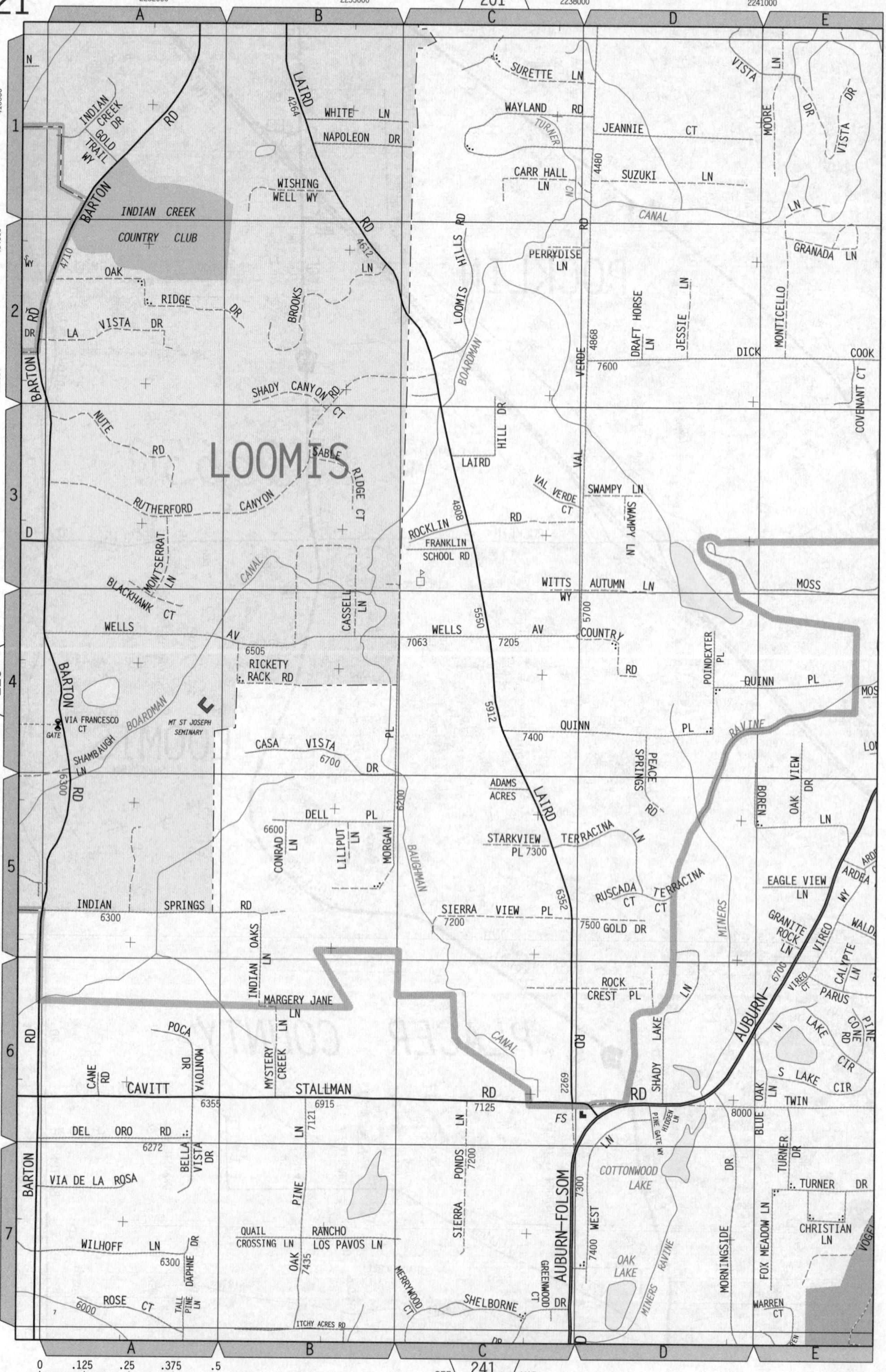

SEE 220 MAP
SEE 241 MAP

0 .125 .25 .375 .5 miles 1 in. = 1900 ft.

SEE 201 MAP
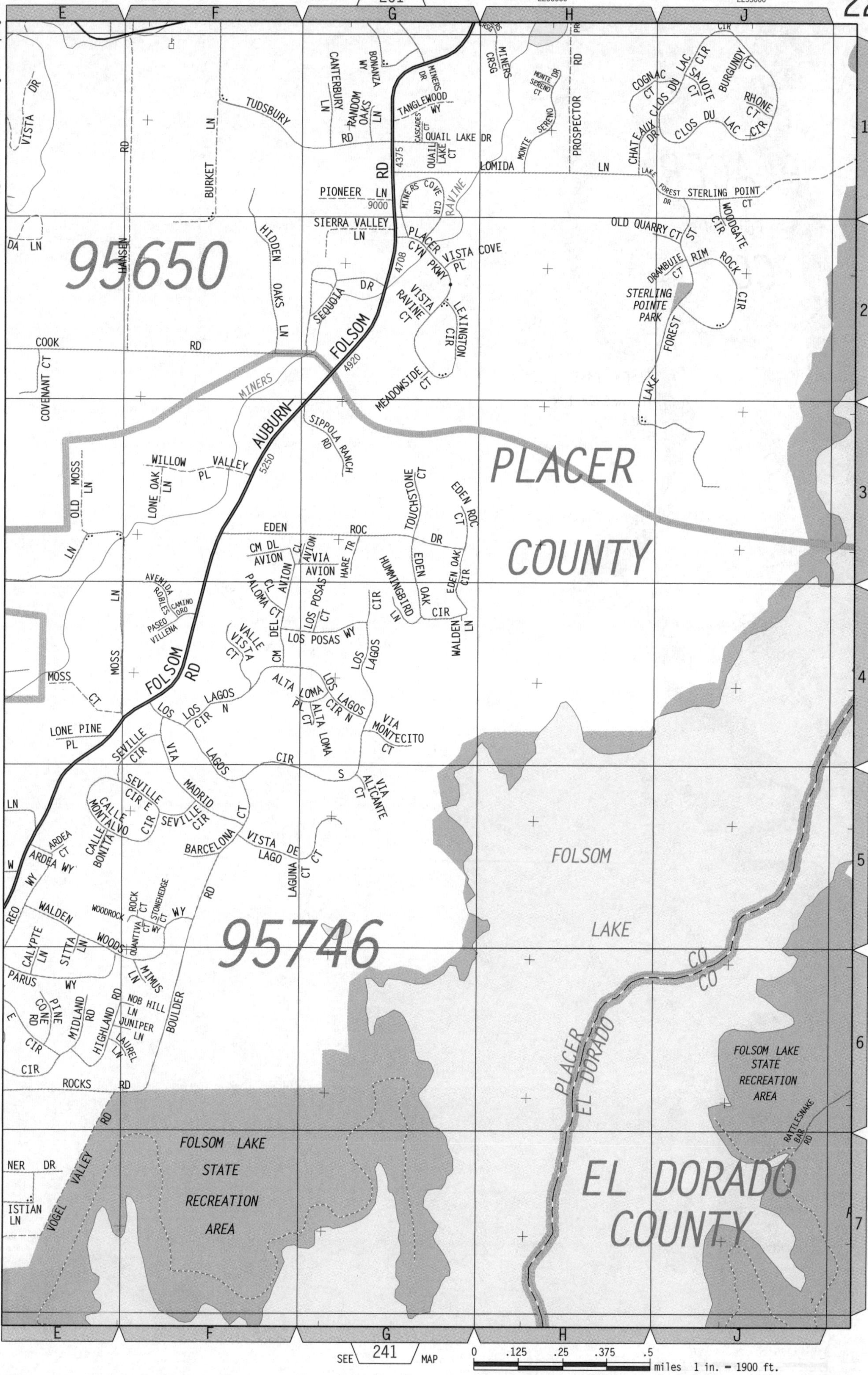

SEE 222 MAP
SEE 241 MAP
0 .125 .25 .375 .5 miles 1 in. = 1900 ft.

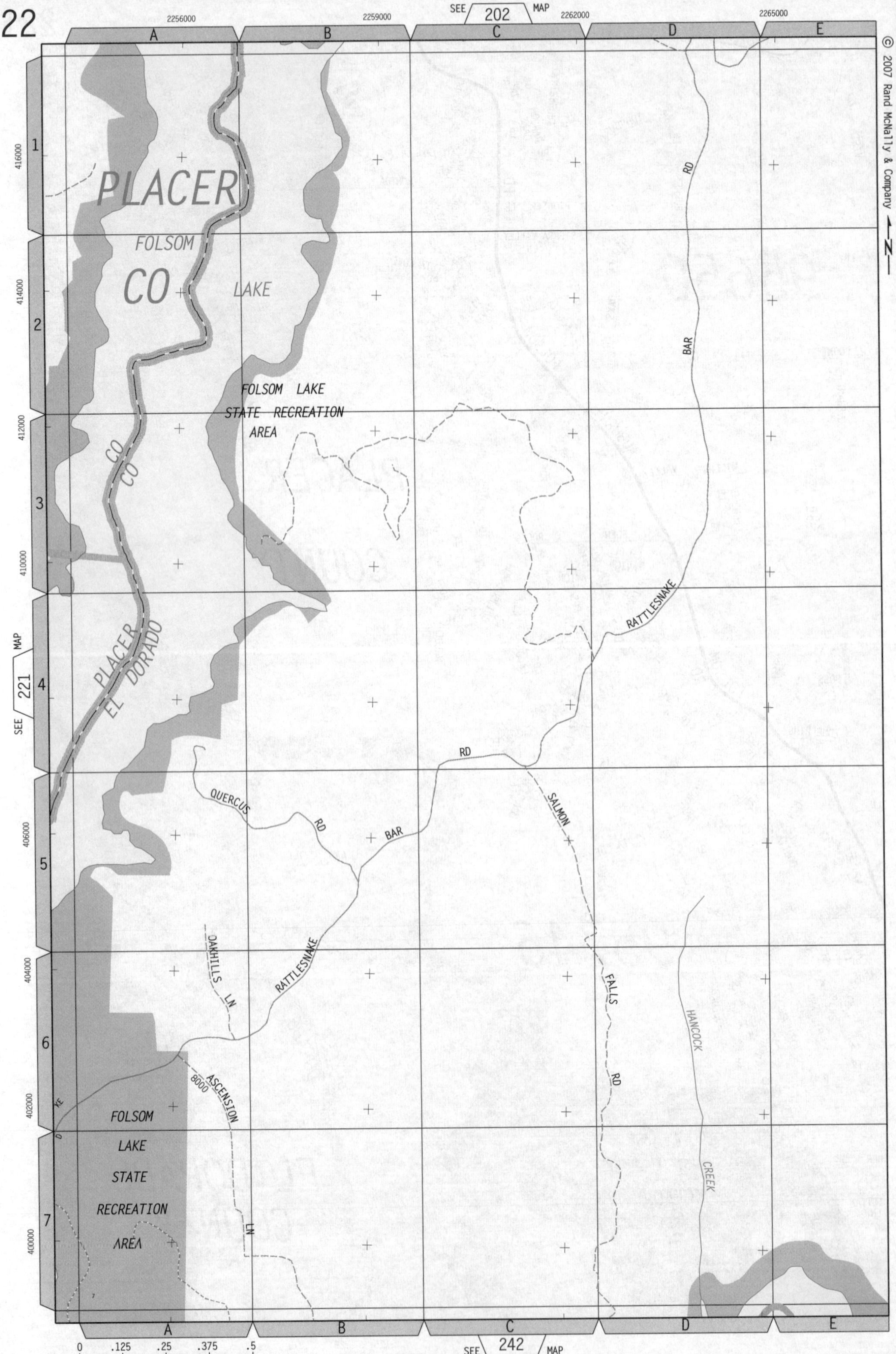
SEE 202 MAP
SEE 221 MAP
SEE 242 MAP
2256000
2259000
2262000
2265000
416000
414000
412000
410000
406000
404000
402000
400000
A
B
C
D
E
1
2
3
4
5
6
7
PLACER
CO
FOLSOM
LAKE
FOLSOM LAKE
STATE RECREATION
AREA
CO
CO
PLACER
EL DORADO
RATTLESNAKE
BAR
RD
QUERCUS
RD
SALMON
FALLS
RD
OAKHILLS
LN
ASCENSION
8000
LN
HANCOCK
CREEK
FOLSOM
LAKE
STATE
RECREATION
AREA
0
.125
.25
.375
.5
miles 1 in. = 1900 ft.

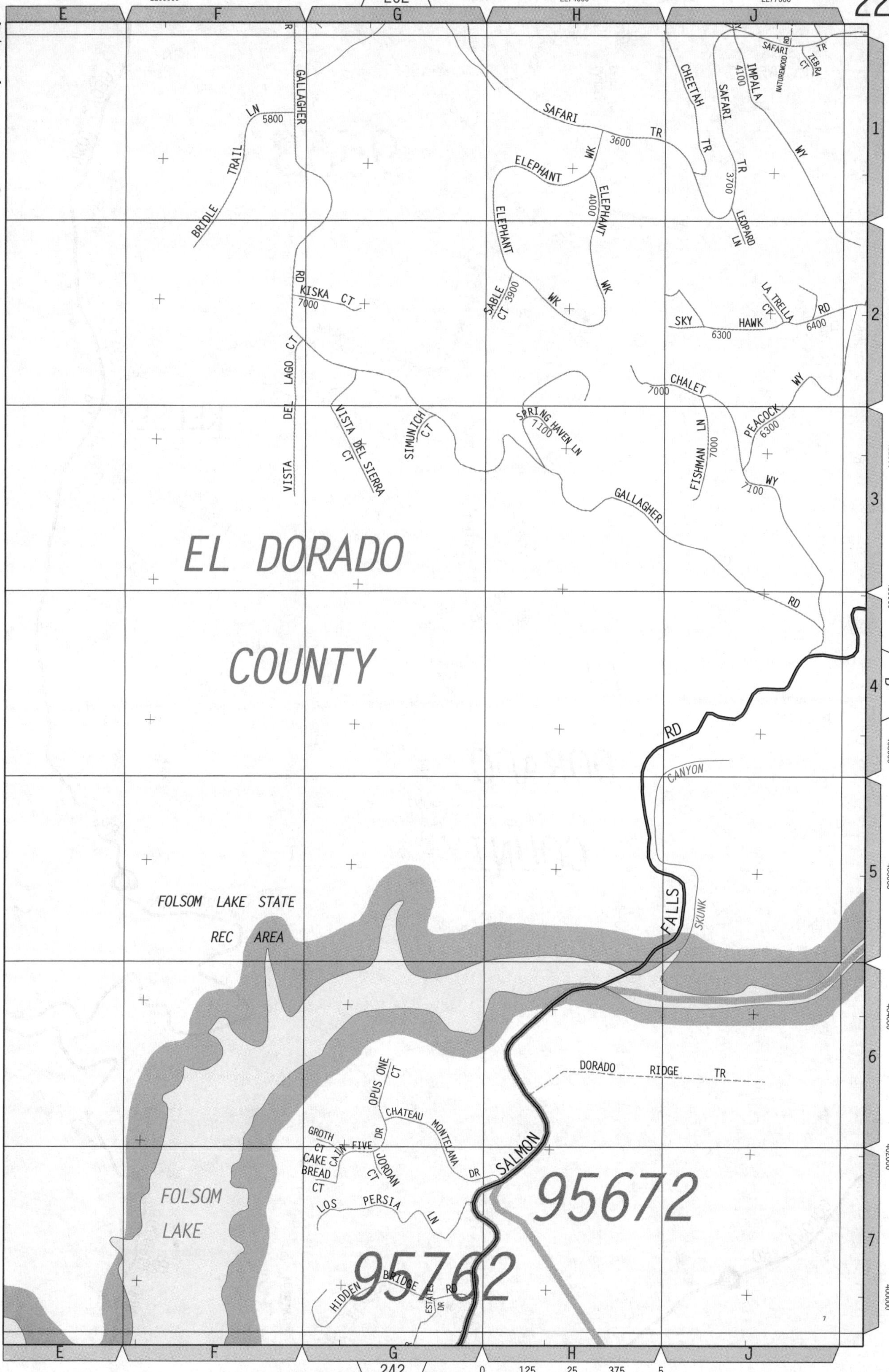
SEE 202 MAP
SEE B MAP
SEE 242 MAP
E
F
G
H
J
1
2
3
4
5
6
7
2268000
2274000
2277000
418000
416000
414000
412000
410000
408000
406000
404000
402000
400000
EL DORADO
COUNTY
FOLSOM LAKE STATE
REC AREA
FOLSOM
LAKE
95672
95762
GALLAGHER RD
BRIDLE TRAIL LN
5800
SAFARI TR
3600
ELEPHANT WK
4000
SABLE CT
3900
CHEETAH TR
SAFARI TR
4100
3700
IMPALA WY
NATUREWOOD RD
ZEBRA CT
LEOPARD LN
KISKA CT
7000
VISTA DEL LAGO CT
VISTA DEL SIERRA CT
SIMUNICH CT
SPRING HAVEN LN
1100
SKY HAWK RD
6300
6400
LA TRELLA CT
CHALET WY
7000
PEACOCK WY
6300
7100
FISHMAN LN
7000
GALLAGHER RD
SALMON FALLS RD
CANYON
SKUNK
DORADO RIDGE TR
OPUS ONE CT
CHATEAU MONTELANA DR
GROTH CT
CAIN FIVE DR
CAKE BREAD CT
JORDAN CT
LOS PERSIA LN
HIDDEN BRIDGE RD
ESTATES DR
0 .125 .25 .375 .5 miles 1 in. = 1900 ft.

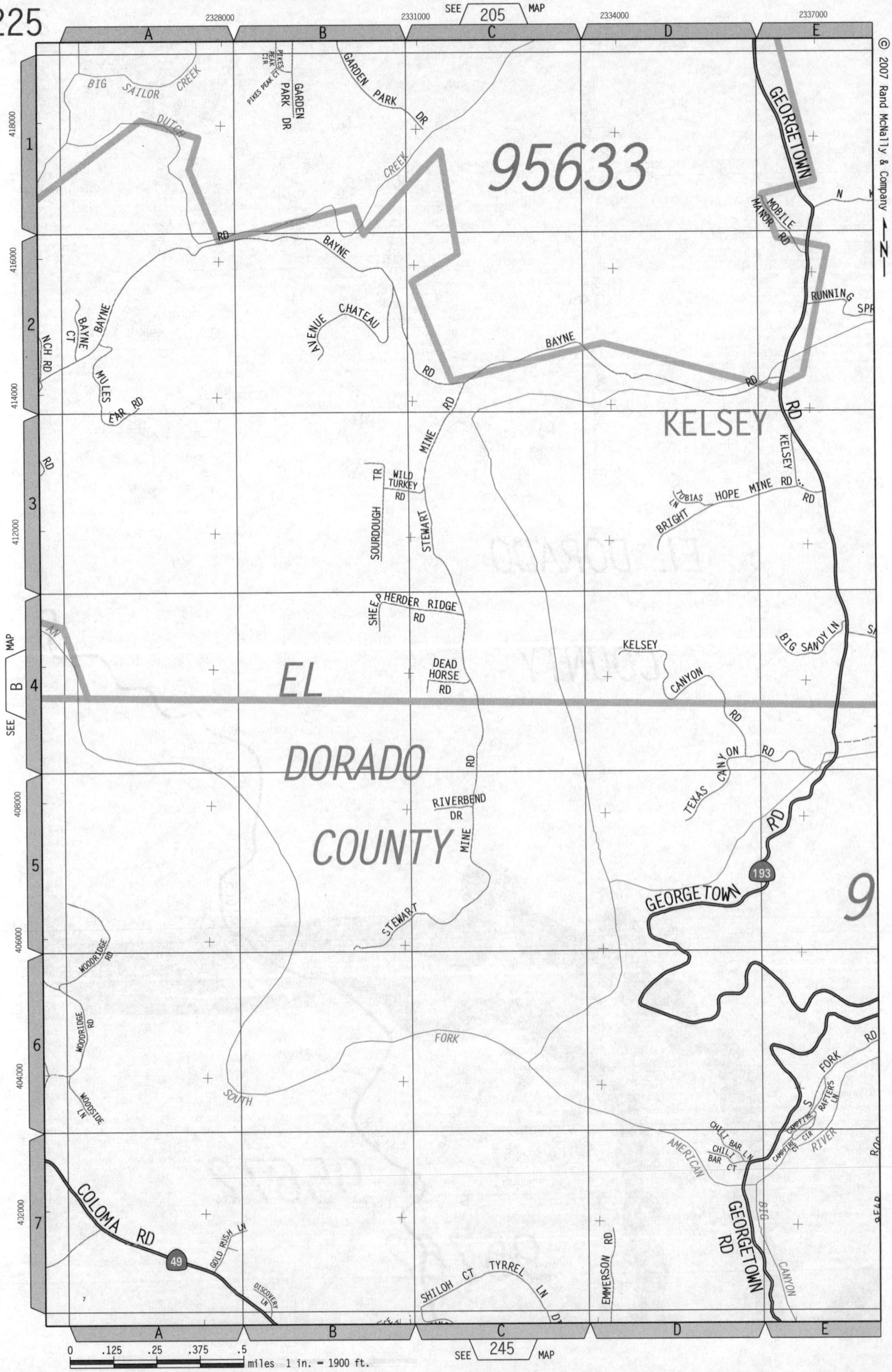
SEE 205 MAP
SEE 245 MAP
SEE B MAP
95633
KELSEY
EL DORADO COUNTY
GEORGETOWN RD
193
49
COLOMA RD
BIG SAILOR CREEK
DUTCH CREEK
GARDEN PARK DR
PIKES PEAK CT
PIKES PEAK CIR
BAYNE RD
BAYNE CT
CHATEAU AVENUE
MULES EAR RD
MINE RD
WILD TURKEY RD
SOURDOUGH TR
STEWART MINE RD
SHEEP HERDER RIDGE RD
DEAD HORSE RD
RIVERBEND DR
KELSEY CANYON RD
TEXAS CANYON RD
BIG SANDY LN
TOBIAS LN
BRIGHT HOPE MINE RD
KELSEY RD
MOBILE MANOR RD
RUNNING SPR
WOODRIDGE RD
WOODSIDE LN
SOUTH FORK AMERICAN
S FORK RD
RAFTERS LN
CAMPFIRE CT
CAMPFIRE CIR
CHILI BAR LN
CHILI BAR CT
BIG CANYON
RIVER
GOLD RUSH LN
DISCOVERY LN
SHILOH CT
TYRREL LN
EMMERSON RD
2328000
2331000
2334000
2337000
418000
416000
414000
412000
408000
406000
404300
402000
A B C D E
1 2 3 4 5 6 7
0 .125 .25 .375 .5 miles 1 in. = 1900 ft.

SEE 205 MAP

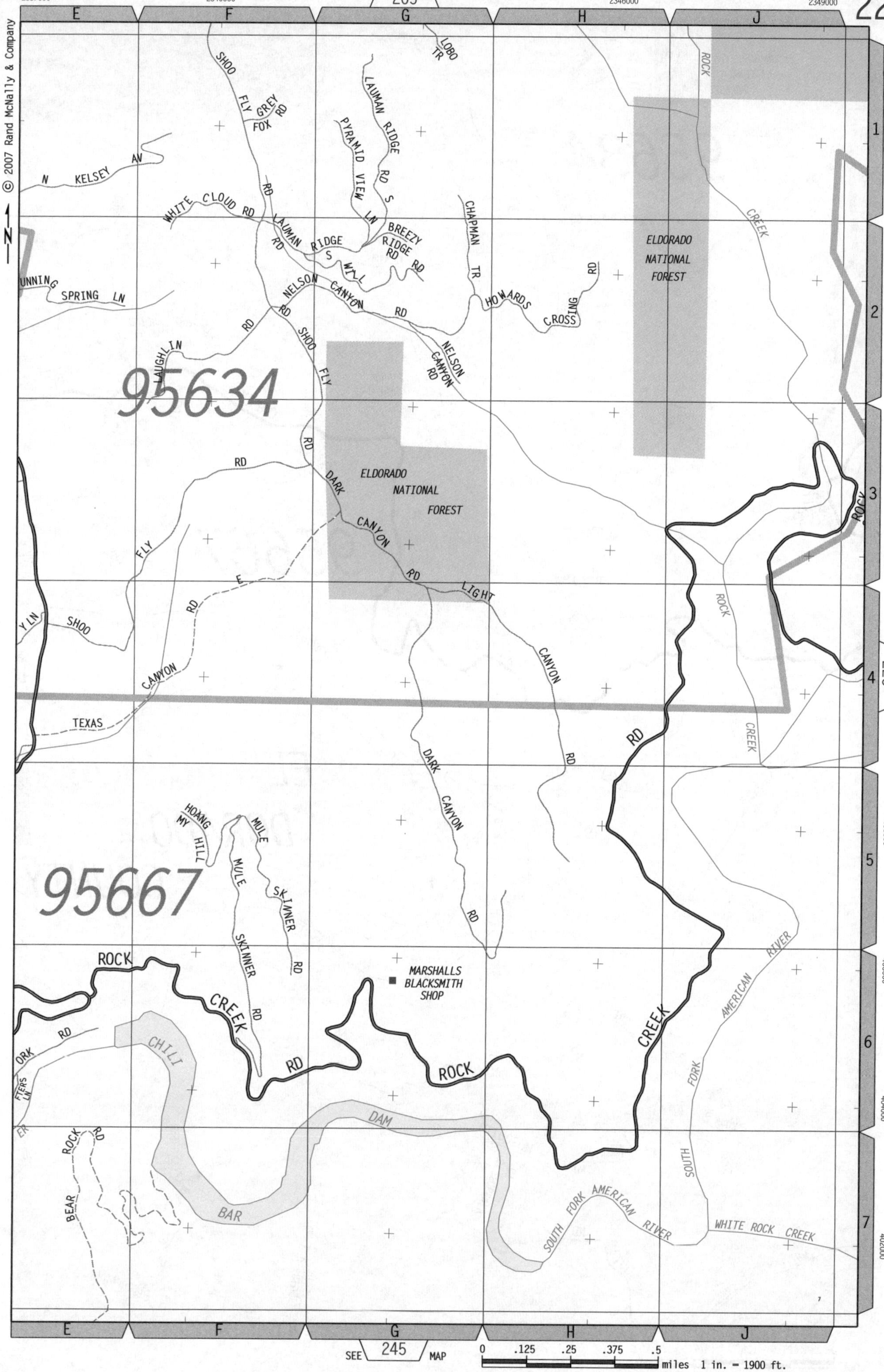

SEE 226 MAP

SEE 245 MAP

0 .125 .25 .375 .5 miles 1 in. = 1900 ft.

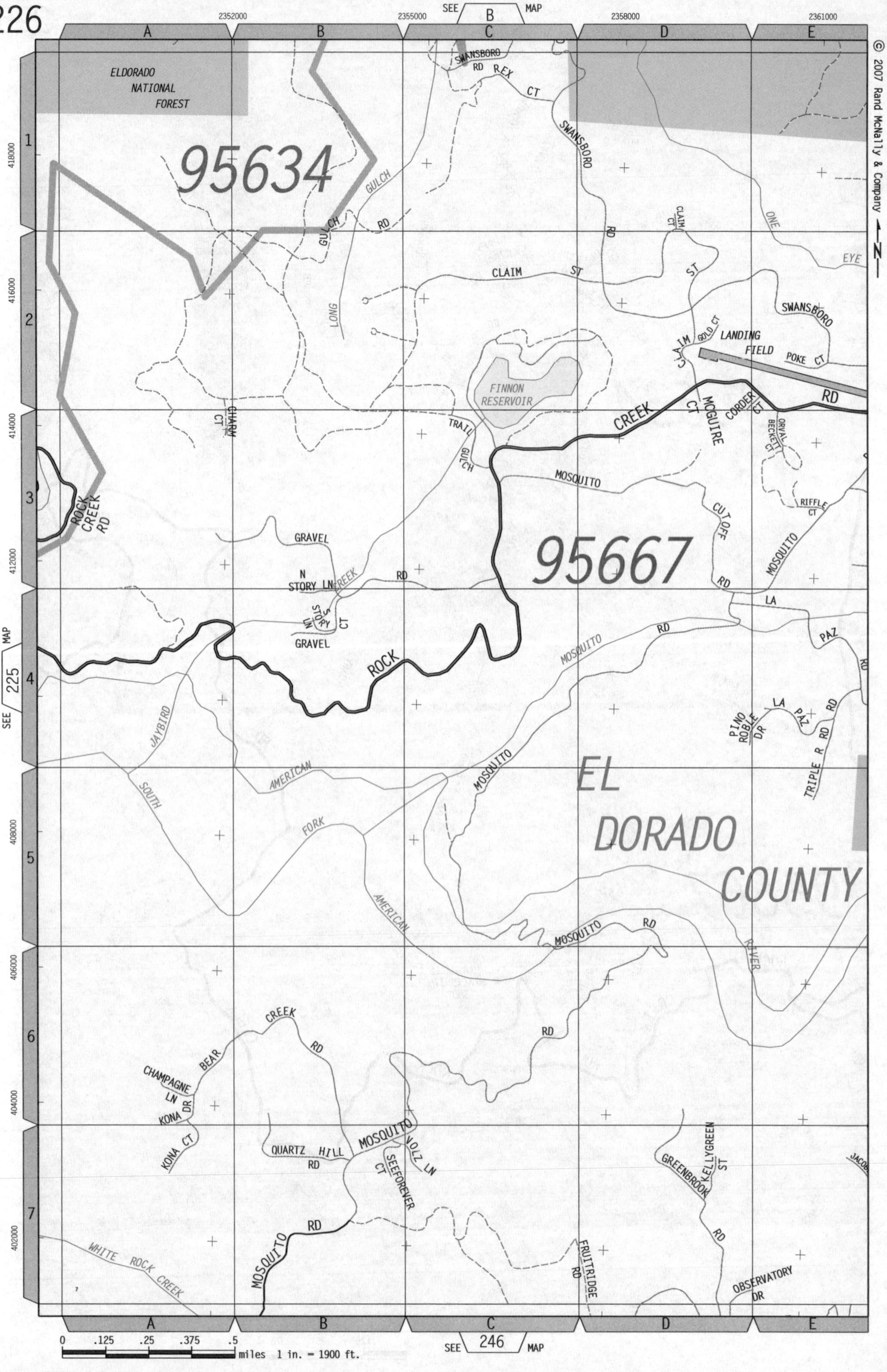
SEE B MAP
SEE 225 MAP
SEE 246 MAP
A
B
C
D
E
1
2
3
4
5
6
7
2352000
2355000
2358000
2361000
418000
416000
414000
412000
408000
406000
404000
402000
ELDORADO NATIONAL FOREST
95634
95667
EL DORADO COUNTY
SWANSBORO RD
REX CT
SWANSBORO RD
CLAIM CT
CLAIM ST
GOLD CT
CLAIM CT
LANDING FIELD
POKE CT
SWANSBORO
ONE EYE
LONG GULCH RD
GULCH
CHARM CT
FINNON RESERVOIR
TRAIL GULCH
CREEK RD
MCGUIRE CT
CORDER CT
ORVAL CT
BECKETT CT
RIFFLE CT
MOSQUITO
CUT OFF RD
MOSQUITO
LA PAZ RD
ROCK CREEK RD
GRAVEL
N STORY LN
CREEK
RD
S STORY LN
CT
GRAVEL
ROCK
MOSQUITO RD
PINO ROBLE DR
LA PAZ RD
TRIPLE R RD
JAYBIRD
SOUTH
AMERICAN
FORK
MOSQUITO
AMERICAN
RIVER
MOSQUITO RD
RD
BEAR CREEK RD
CHAMPAGNE LN
KONA DR
KONA CT
QUARTZ HILL RD
MOSQUITO
VOLZ LN
SEEFOREVER CT
GREENBROOK
KELLYGREEN ST
RD
JACOB
MOSQUITO RD
WHITE ROCK CREEK
FRUITRIDGE RD
OBSERVATORY DR
0 .125 .25 .375 .5 miles 1 in. = 1900 ft.

SEE B MAP

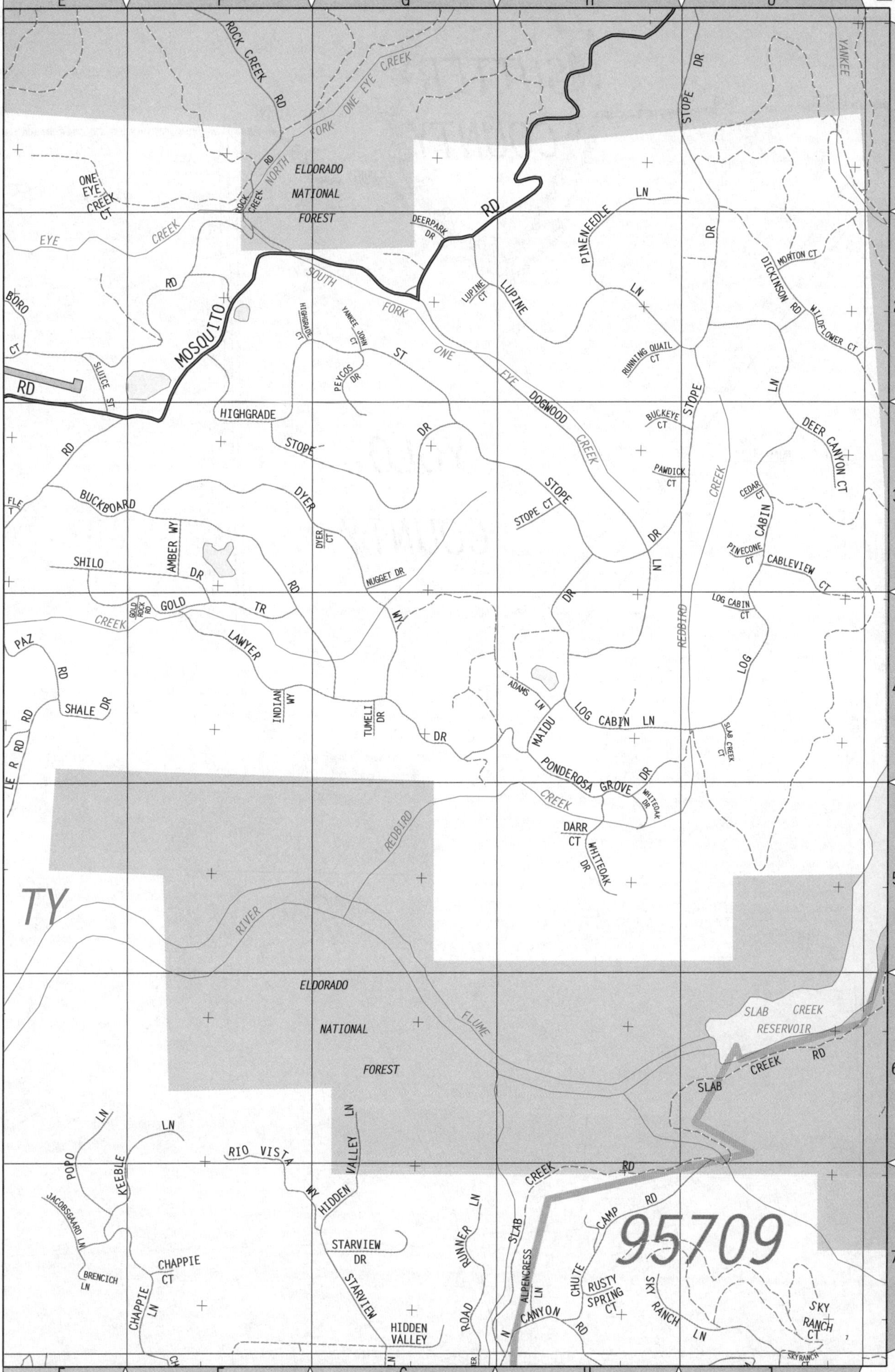
ROCK CREEK RD
NORTH FORK ONE EYE CREEK
ELDORADO
NATIONAL
FOREST
ONE EYE CREEK CT
EYE CREEK
DEERPARK DR
RD
STOPE DR
YANKEE
PINENEEDLE LN
MORTON CT
DICKINSON RD
WILDFLOWER CT
BORO CT
RD
MOSQUITO
SOUTH FORK ONE EYE CREEK
HIGHGRADE CT
YANKEE JOHN CT
ST
LUPINE CT
LUPINE
RUNNING QUAIL CT
SLUICE ST
PEYCOS DR
RD
HIGHGRADE
STOPE
DR
DOGWOOD
BUCKEYE CT
DEER CANYON CT
PAWDICK CT
RD
BUCKBOARD
DYER
STOPE
STOPE CT
CREEK
CEDAR CT
CABIN
DYER CT
AMBER WY
PINECONE CT
CABLEVIEW CT
SHILO
DR
NUGGET DR
RD
DR
LN
LOG CABIN CT
GOLD ROCK RD
GOLD TR
CREEK
WY
REDBIRD
PAZ
RD
LAWYER
LOG
ADAMS LN
SHALE DR
INDIAN WY
TUMELI DR
DR
MAIDU
LOG CABIN LN
SLAB CREEK CT
RD
LE R RD
PONDEROSA GROVE DR
WHITEOAK DR
CREEK
DARR CT
WHITEOAK DR
REDBIRD
TY
RIVER
ELDORADO
NATIONAL
FOREST
FLUME
SLAB CREEK RESERVOIR
CREEK RD
SLAB
POPO LN
LN
KEEBLE
RIO VISTA WY
HIDDEN VALLEY LN
CREEK RD
JACOBSGAARD LN
STARVIEW DR
RUNNER LN
SLAB
CAMP RD
95709
BRENCICH LN
CHAPPIE CT
CHAPPIE LN
STARVIEW
ALPENCRESS LN
CHUTE
RUSTY SPRING CT
SKY RANCH LN
SKY RANCH CT
CANYON RD
N
HIDDEN VALLEY
ROAD
SKYRANCH CT
361000
2364000
2370000
2373000
420000
418000
416000
414000
412000
410000
408000
406000
404000
402000
E F G H J
1 2 3 4 5 6 7
0 .125 .25 .375 .5
miles 1 in. = 1900 ft.

SEE B MAP

SEE 246 MAP

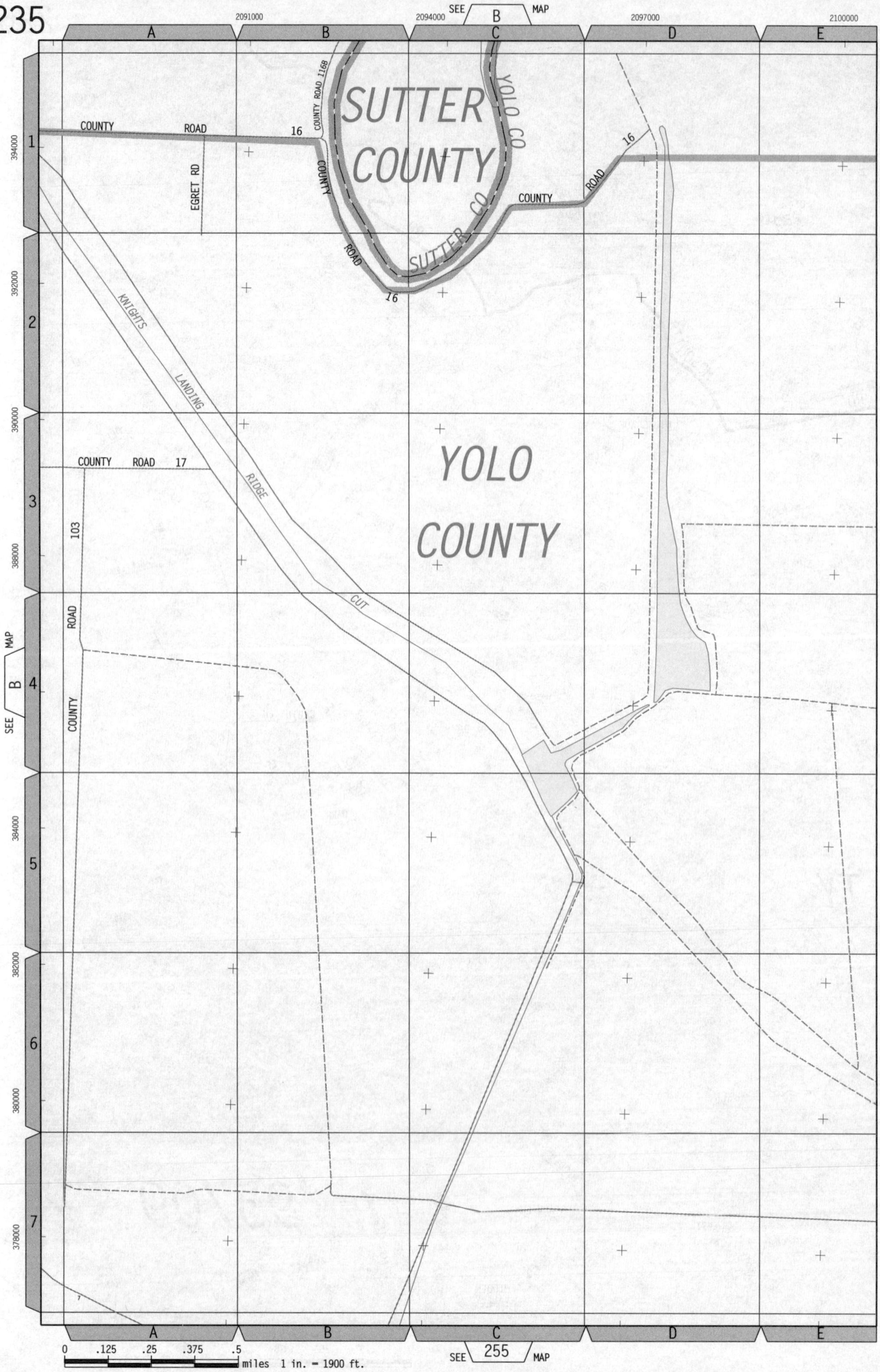
SEE B MAP
SEE B MAP
SEE 255 MAP
A
B
C
D
E
1
2
3
4
5
6
7
2091000
2094000
2097000
2100000
394000
392000
390000
388000
384000
382000
380000
378000
COUNTY ROAD 16
EGRET RD
COUNTY ROAD 116B
COUNTY ROAD 16
SUTTER COUNTY
YOLO CO
SUTTER CO
COUNTY ROAD 16
KNIGHTS LANDING RIDGE CUT
COUNTY ROAD 17
COUNTY ROAD 103
YOLO COUNTY
0 .125 .25 .375 .5 miles 1 in. = 1900 ft.

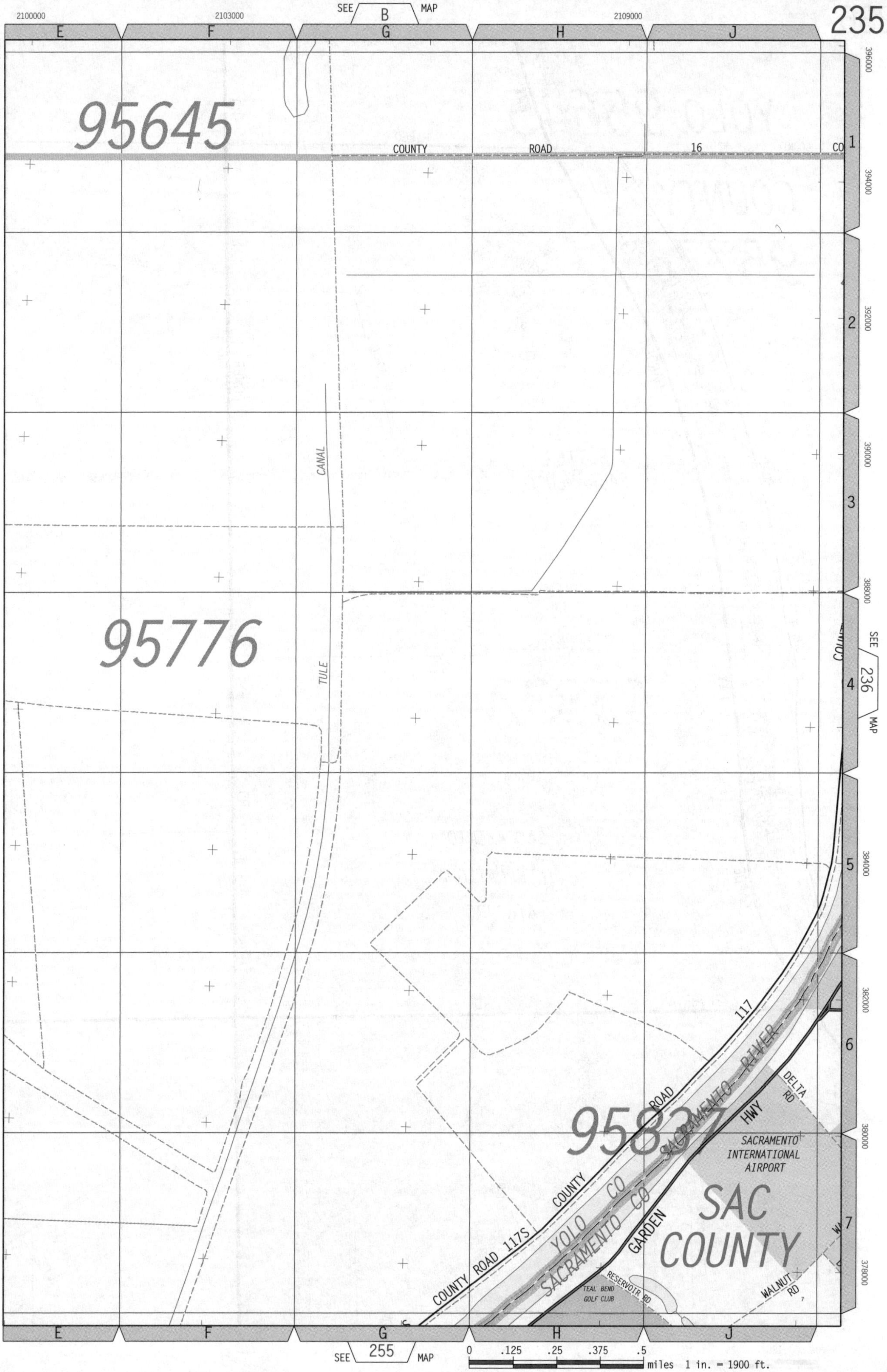

SEE B MAP
2100000
2103000
2109000
E
F
G
H
J
396000
394000
392000
390000
388000
384000
382000
380000
378000
1
2
3
4
5
6
7
95645
COUNTY ROAD 16
CO
CANAL
TULE
95776
SEE 236 MAP
COUN
117
COUNTY ROAD 117S
COUNTY ROAD
YOLO CO
SACRAMENTO CO
SACRAMENTO RIVER
95837
HWY
GARDEN
DELTA RD
SACRAMENTO INTERNATIONAL AIRPORT
SAC COUNTY
RESERVOIR RD
TEAL BEND GOLF CLUB
WALNUT RD
SEE 255 MAP
0 .125 .25 .375 .5
miles 1 in. = 1900 ft.

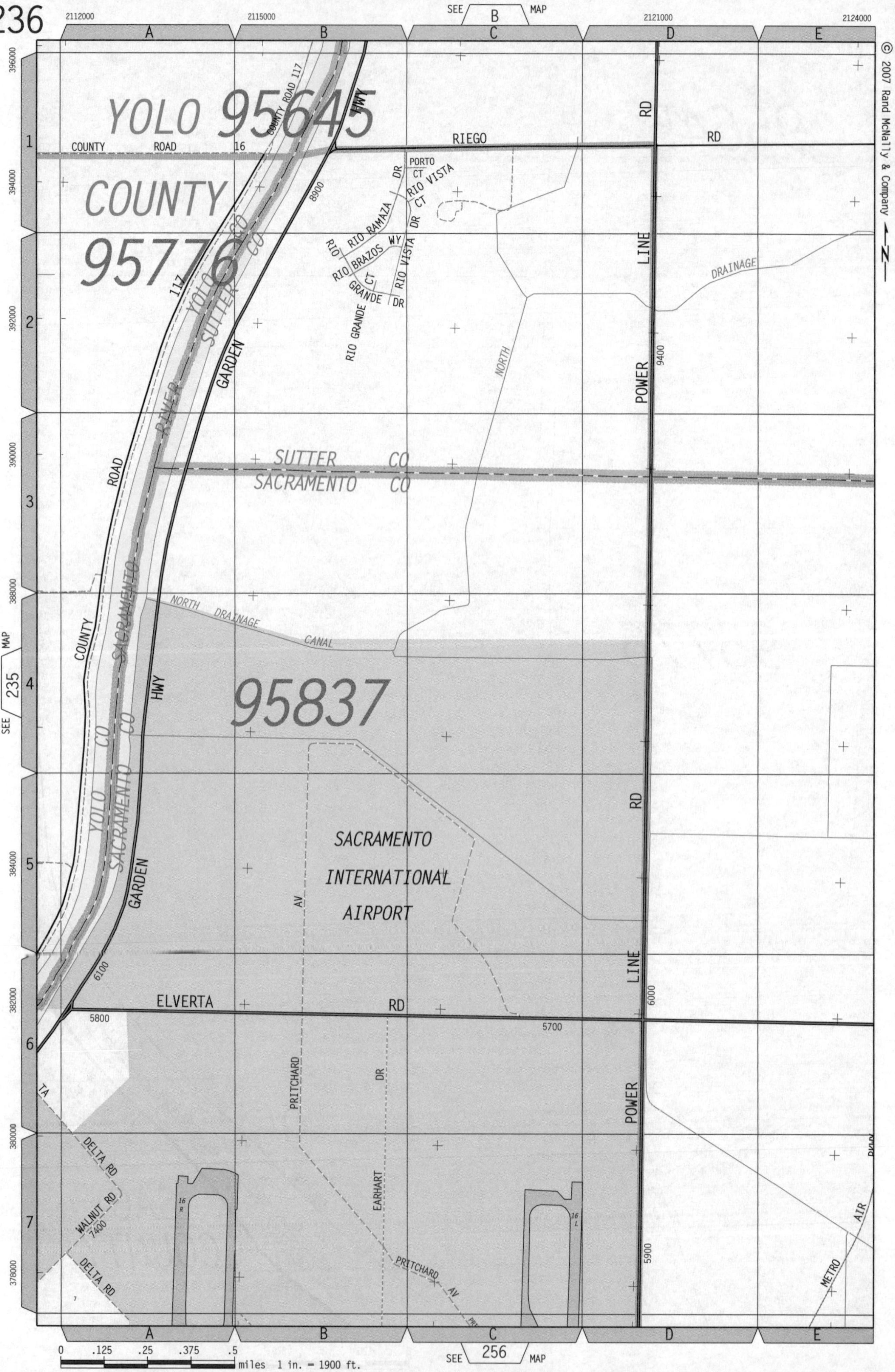

SEE B MAP
SEE 235 MAP
SEE 256 MAP
2112000
2115000
2121000
2124000
396000
394000
392000
390000
388000
384000
382000
380000
378000
YOLO 95645
COUNTY
95776
COUNTY ROAD 16
COUNTY ROAD 117
117
HWY
RIEGO RD
8900
PORTO CT
RIO VISTA CT
RIO VISTA DR
RIO RAMAZA DR
RIO BRAZOS WY
RIO GRANDE CT
GRANDE DR
RIO GRANDE
DRAINAGE
NORTH
POWER LINE RD
9400
YOLO CO
SUTTER CO
RIVER
GARDEN HWY
COUNTY ROAD
SUTTER CO
SACRAMENTO CO
NORTH DRAINAGE CANAL
SACRAMENTO
95837
SACRAMENTO INTERNATIONAL AIRPORT
AV
ELVERTA RD
5800
6100
5700
6000
PRITCHARD AV
EARHART DR
DELTA RD
WALNUT RD
7400
16 R
16 L
5900
METRO AIR PKWY
0 .125 .25 .375 .5 miles 1 in. = 1900 ft.

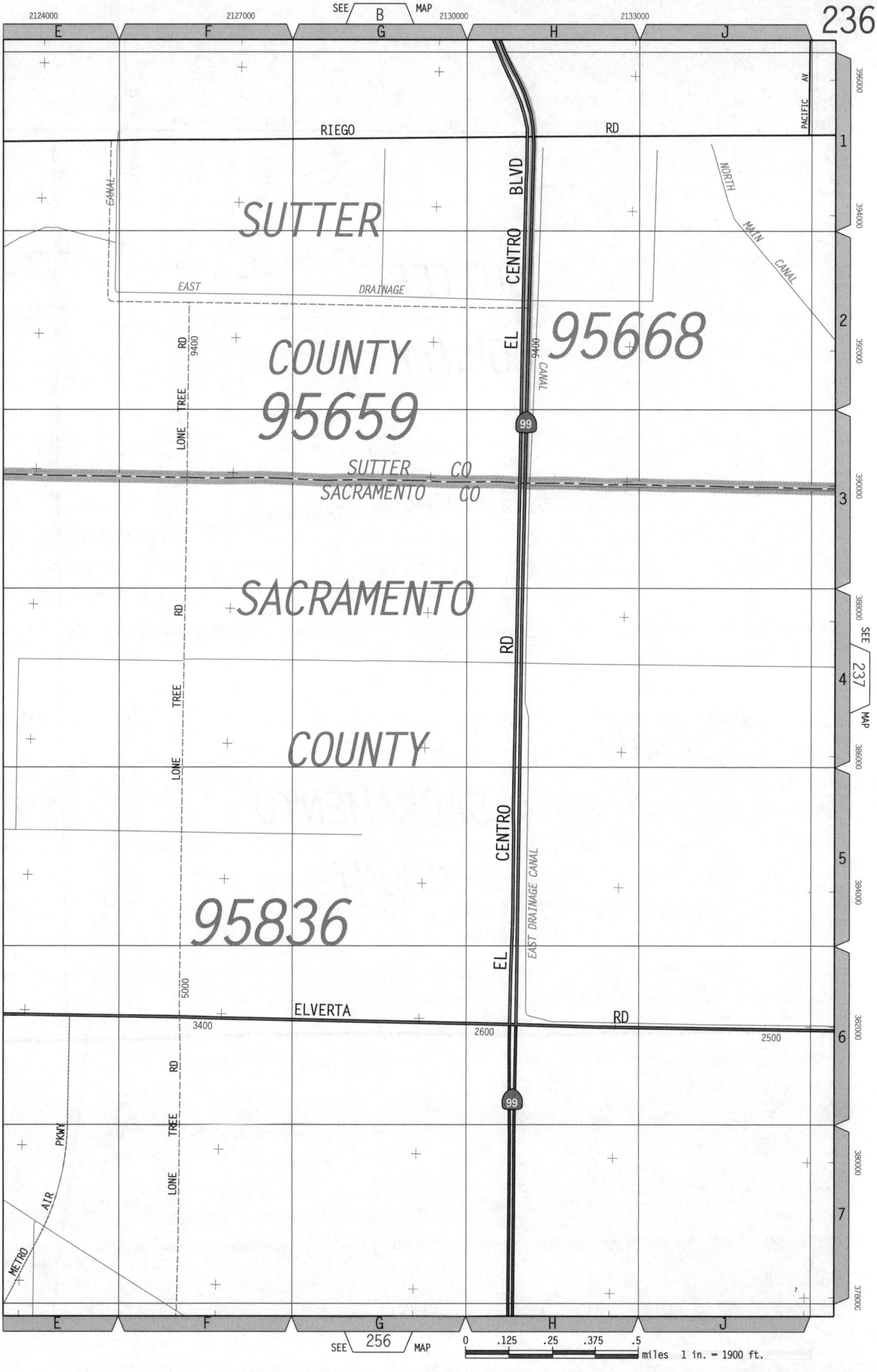
SEE B MAP
2124000
2127000
2130000
2133000
E
F
G
H
J
RIEGO
RD
PACIFIC AV
CANAL
EAST
DRAINAGE
SUTTER
COUNTY
95659
95668
NORTH
MAIN
CANAL
EL CENTRO BLVD
9400
CANAL
LONE TREE RD
99
SUTTER CO
SACRAMENTO CO
SACRAMENTO
COUNTY
95836
EL CENTRO RD
EAST DRAINAGE CANAL
SEE 237 MAP
ELVERTA
RD
3400
2600
2500
5000
METRO AIR PKWY
1
2
3
4
5
6
7
396000
394000
392000
390000
388000
386000
384000
382000
380000
378000
SEE 256 MAP
0 .125 .25 .375 .5
miles 1 in. = 1900 ft.

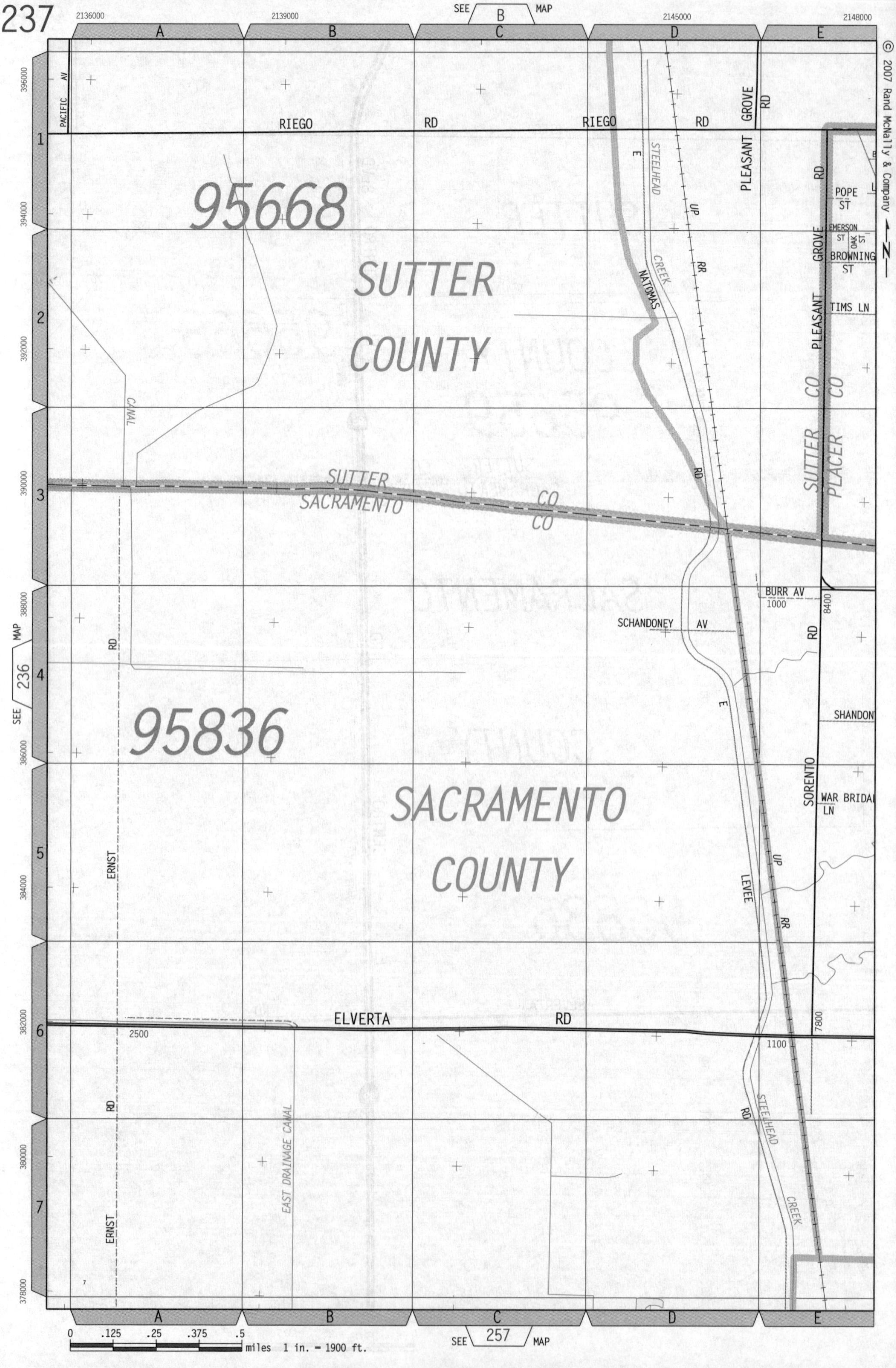
SEE B MAP
SEE 236 MAP
SEE 257 MAP
A
B
C
D
E
1
2
3
4
5
6
7
2136000
2139000
2145000
2148000
396000
394000
392000
390000
388000
386000
384000
382000
380000
378000
95668
SUTTER
COUNTY
95836
SACRAMENTO
COUNTY
RIEGO RD
PACIFIC AV
PLEASANT GROVE RD
STEELHEAD CREEK
NATOMAS E RD
UP RR
POPE ST
EMERSON ST
OAK ST
BROWNING ST
TIMS LN
SUTTER CO
PLACER CO
SUTTER SACRAMENTO CO CO
CANAL
BURR AV
1000
8400
SCHANDONEY AV
SHANDON
SORENTO RD
WAR BRIDAL LN
ERNST RD
LEVEE
ELVERTA RD
2500
1100
7800
EAST DRAINAGE CANAL
0 .125 .25 .375 .5
miles 1 in. = 1900 ft.

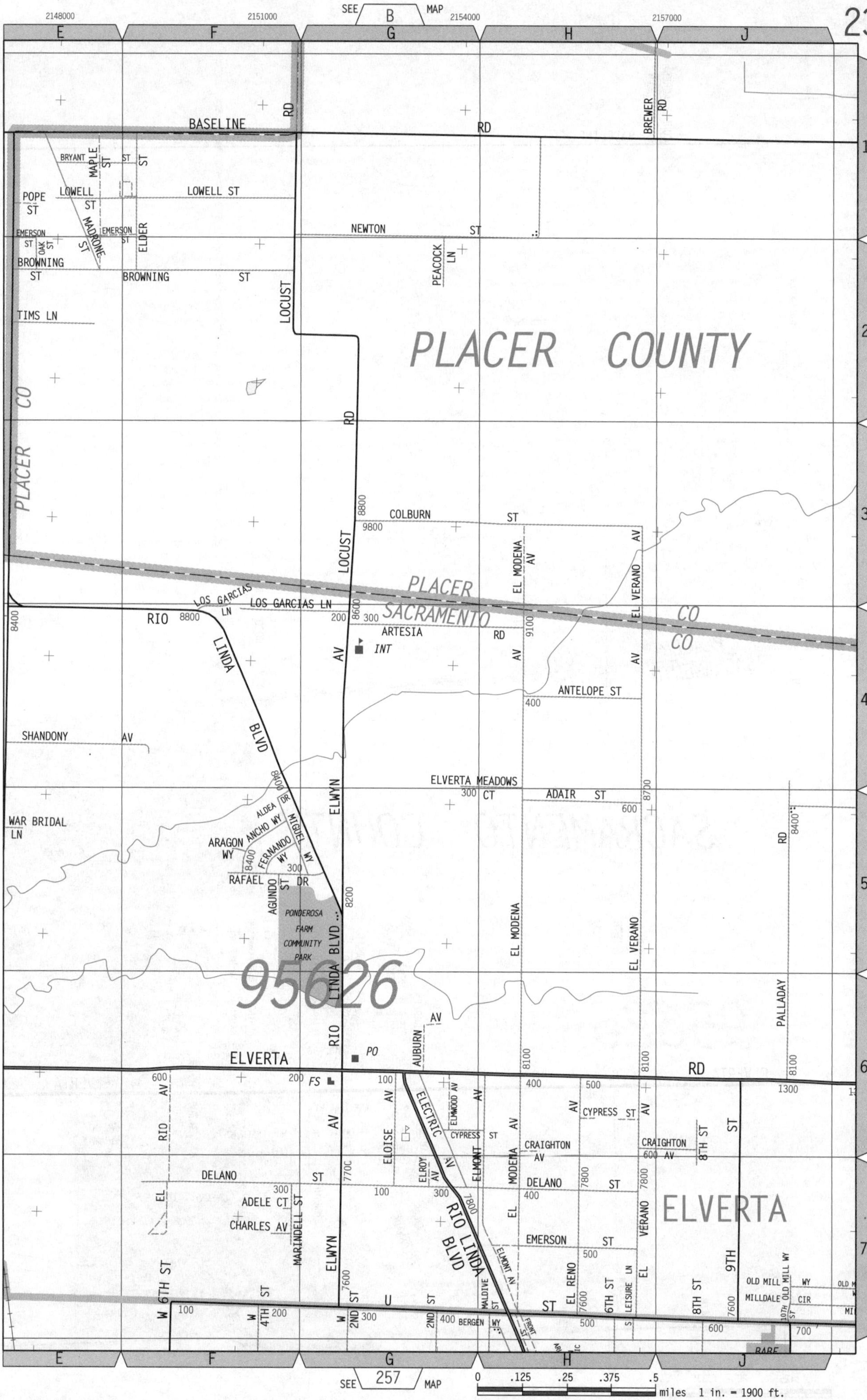
SEE B MAP
2148000
2151000
2154000
2157000
E
F
G
H
J
1
2
3
4
5
6
7
396000
394000
392000
390000
386000
384000
382000
380000
BASELINE
RD
BREWER RD
BRYANT
MAPLE ST
ST
ST
POPE ST
LOWELL
LOWELL ST
NEWTON
ST
EMERSON ST
OAK ST
MADRONE ST
EMERSON ST
ELDER
PEACOCK LN
BROWNING ST
BROWNING
ST
TIMS LN
LOCUST
PLACER COUNTY
PLACER CO
RD
8800
COLBURN
ST
9800
LOCUST
EL MODENA AV
EL VERANO
AV
PLACER
SACRAMENTO
CO
CO
LOS GARCIAS LN
LOS GARCIAS LN
RIO
8800
8400
200
8600
300
ARTESIA
RD
9100
INT
AV
LINDA
AV
AV
ANTELOPE ST
400
SEE 238 MAP
SHANDONY
AV
BLVD
ELVERTA MEADOWS
300 CT
ADAIR ST
600
8700
8400
ALDEA DR
WAR BRIDAL LN
ARAGON WY
ANCHO WY
MIGUEL WY
FERNANDO WY
8400
300
RAFAEL
ST
DR
AGUNDO
ELWYN
RD
8400
PONDEROSA FARM COMMUNITY PARK
8200
EL MODENA
EL VERANO
95626
RIO LINDA BLVD
AUBURN
AV
PALLADAY
ELVERTA
PO
8100
8100
8100
RD
600
200
FS
100
400
500
1300
RIO AV
AV
AV
ELECTRIC
ELMWOOD AV
AV
AV
AV
CYPRESS ST
AV
RIO
ELOISE
CYPRESS ST
ST
CRAIGHTON AV
CRAIGHTON
600 AV
8TH ST
DELANO
ST
770C
ELROY AV
ELMONT
MODENA
DELANO
7800
ST
7800
300
100
300
7800
400
EL
ADELE CT
CHARLES AV
MARINDELL ST
RIO LINDA BLVD
EL
VERANO
ELVERTA
EMERSON
ST
500
9TH
W 6TH ST
ELWYN
7600
ST
U
ST
ELKHORN AV
EL RENO
6TH ST
LEISURE LN
EL
8TH ST
OLD MILL
OLD MILL WY
WY
OLD M
MILLDALE
CIR
7600
7600
10TH ST
MI
100
W
4TH
200
W
2ND
300
2ND
400
BERGEN
WY
MALDIVE ST
ST
FRONT ST
ST
500
S
600
700
BARF
E
F
G
H
J
SEE 257 MAP
0
.125
.25
.375
.5
miles 1 in. = 1900 ft.

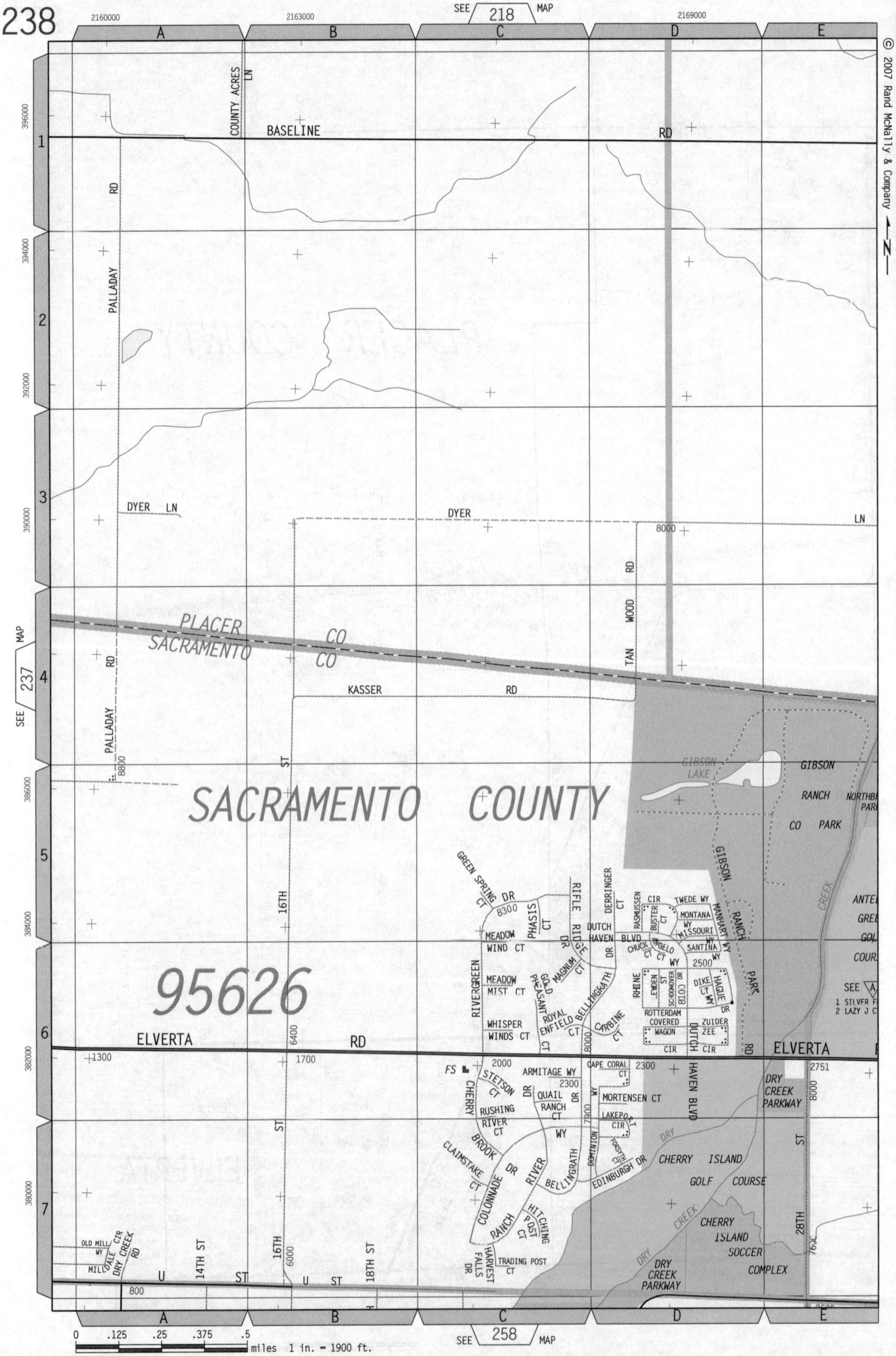
SEE 218 MAP
SEE 237 MAP
SEE 258 MAP
BASELINE RD
COUNTY ACRES LN
PALLADAY RD
DYER LN
DYER LN
TAN WOOD RD
PLACER CO
SACRAMENTO CO
KASSER RD
16TH ST
SACRAMENTO COUNTY
95626
GIBSON LAKE
GIBSON RANCH CO PARK
GIBSON RANCH PARK RD
ELVERTA RD
DRY CREEK PARKWAY
CHERRY ISLAND GOLF COURSE
CHERRY ISLAND SOCCER COMPLEX
DRY CREEK
DUTCH HAVEN BLVD
RIFLE RIDGE DR
DERRINGER CT
GREEN SPRING CT
PHASIS CT
MEADOW WIND CT
MEADOW MIST CT
RIVERGREEN CT
WHISPER WINDS CT
ROYAL ENFIELD CT
BELLINGRATH
CARBINE CT
MAGNUM CT
GOLD PHEASANT CT
CHERRY BROOK DR
STETSON CT
ARMITAGE WY
QUAIL RANCH CT
RUSHING RIVER CT
CLAIMSTAKE CT
COLONNADE RANCH
HITCHING POST CT
HARVEST FALLS DR
TRADING POST CT
CAPE CORAL CT
MORTENSEN CT
LAKEPORT CIR
EDINBURGH DR
DOMINION
FORSYTH CT
U ST
14TH ST
18TH ST
28TH ST
OLD MILL WY
MILLDALE CIR
DRY CREEK RD
RASMUSSEN
TWEDE WY
MONTANA WY
MISSOURI WY
SANTINA WY
MANHART WY
HAGUE WY
DIKE CT
RHINE
ROTTERDAM
COVERED WAGON CIR
ZUIDER ZEE CIR
ANTELOPE GREENS GOLF COURSE
© 2007 Rand McNally & Company
0 .125 .25 .375 .5 miles 1 in. = 1900 ft.

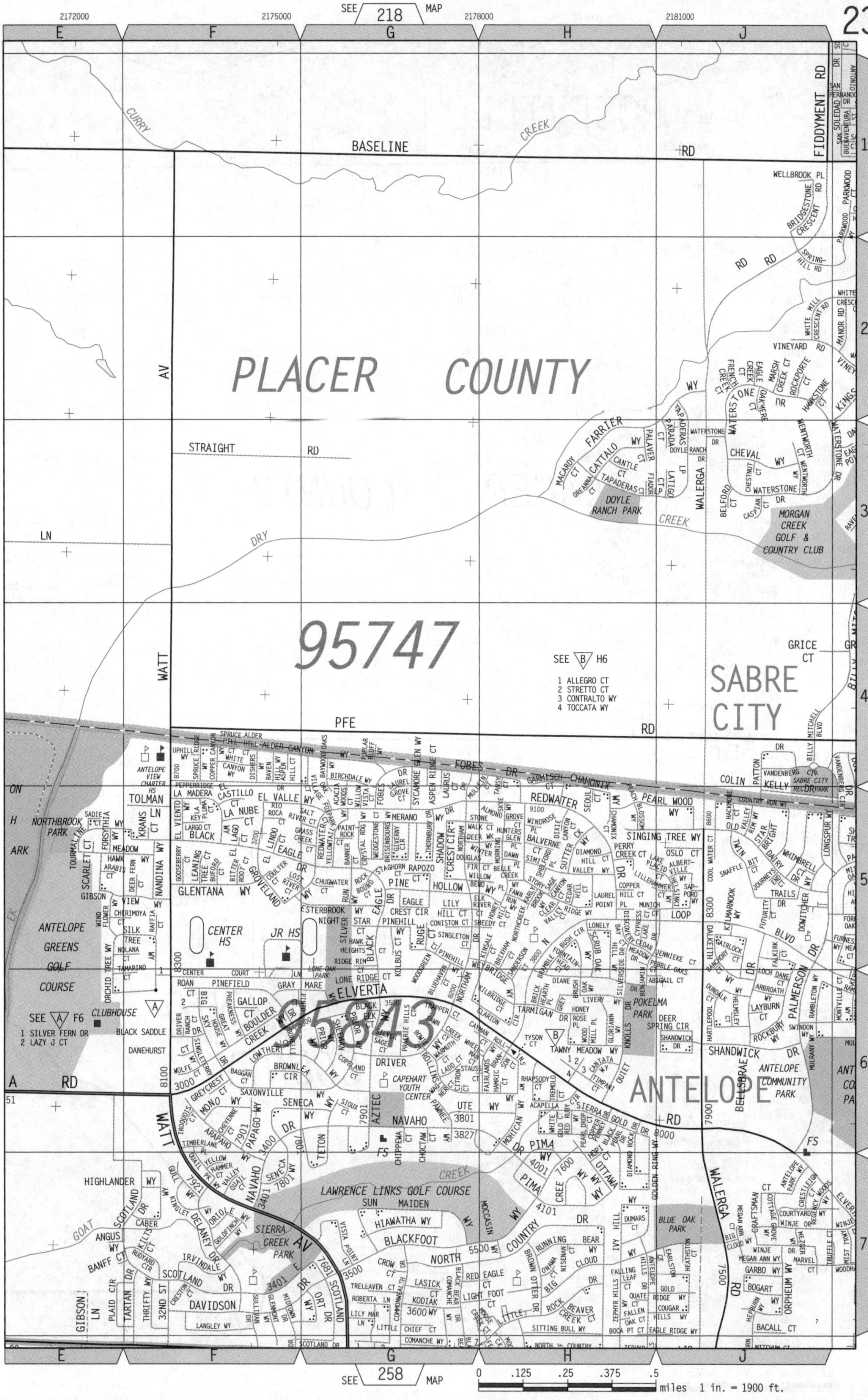
SEE 218 MAP
SEE 258 MAP
SEE 239 MAP
PLACER COUNTY
95747
95843
SABRE CITY
ANTELOPE
BASELINE RD
FIDDYMENT RD
WATT AV
STRAIGHT RD
PFE RD
ELVERTA RD
WALERGA RD
DRY CREEK
CURRY CREEK
DOYLE RANCH PARK
MORGAN CREEK GOLF & COUNTRY CLUB
ANTELOPE GREENS GOLF COURSE
NORTHBROOK PARK
ANTELOPE VIEW CHARTER HS
CENTER HS
JR HS
POKELMA PARK
ANTELOPE COMMUNITY PARK
CAPEHART YOUTH CENTER
LAWRENCE LINKS GOLF COURSE
SIERRA CREEK PARK
BLUE OAK PARK
SEE B H6
1 ALLEGRO CT
2 STRETTO CT
3 CONTRALTO WY
4 TOCCATA WY
SEE A F6
1 SILVER FERN DR
2 LAZY J CT
0 .125 .25 .375 .5 miles 1 in. = 1900 ft.

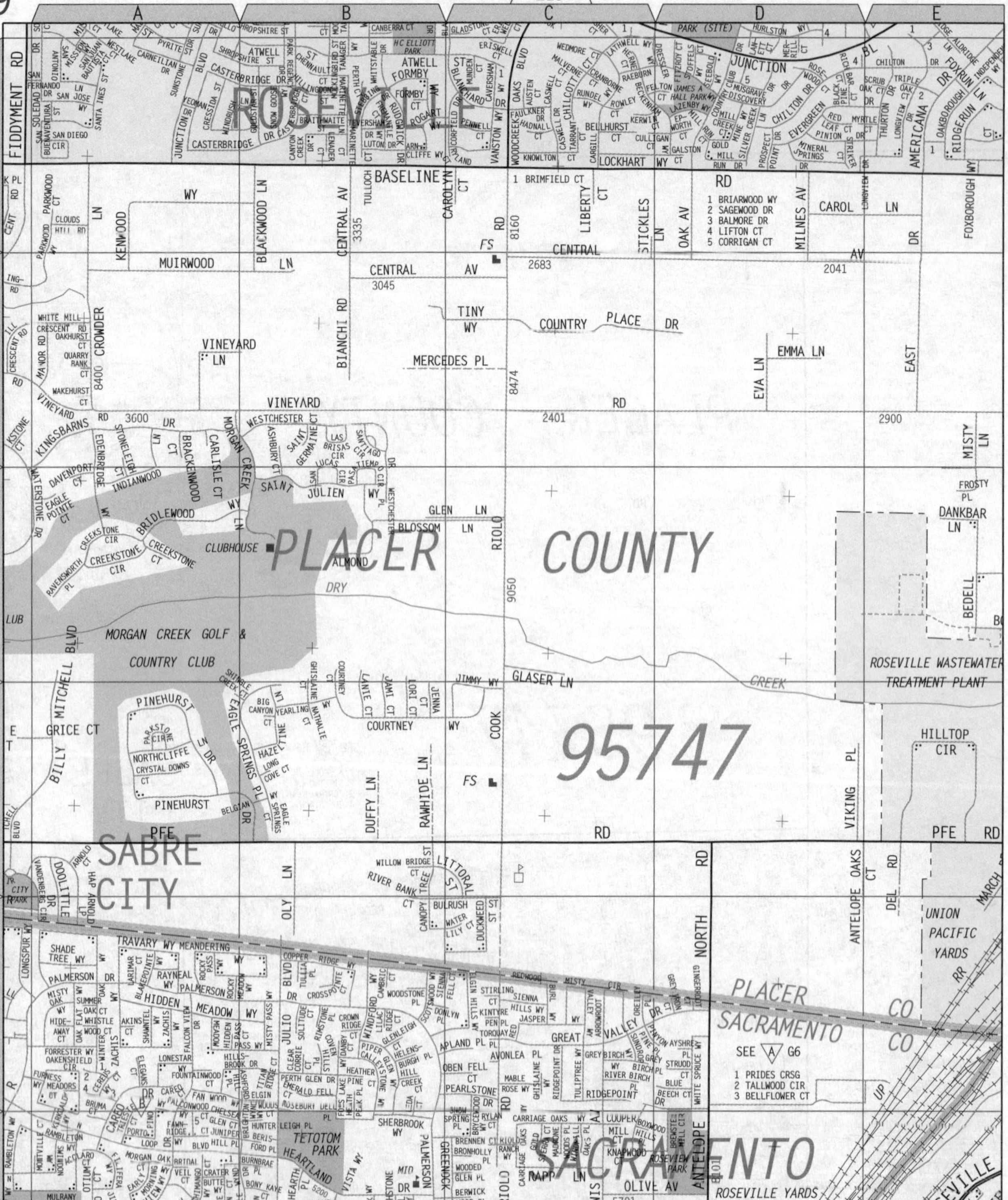
SEE 219 MAP
SEE 238 MAP
SEE 259 MAP
2184000
2187000
2193000
396000
394000
392000
390000
386000
384000
382000
380000
A
B
C
D
E
1
2
3
4
5
6
7
ROSEVILLE
PLACER COUNTY
95747
SABRE CITY
SACRAMENTO COUNTY
95843
PLACER CO
SACRAMENTO CO
MORGAN CREEK GOLF & COUNTRY CLUB
CLUBHOUSE
DRY CREEK
ROSEVILLE WASTEWATER TREATMENT PLANT
UNION PACIFIC YARDS
ROSEVILLE YARDS
TETOTOM PARK
ANTELOPE COMM PARK
ROSEVIEW PARK
NEW HARTFORD FIRESTONE PARK
HC ELLIOTT PARK
FIDDYMENT RD
BASELINE RD
CENTRAL AV
MUIRWOOD LN
VINEYARD RD
CROWDER LN
BIANCHI RD
BLACKWOOD LN
WALERGA RD
CAROLYN CT
TINY WY
COUNTRY PLACE DR
MERCEDES PL
LIBERTY CT
STICKLES LN
OAK AV
MILNES AV
CAROL LN
EMMA LN
EVA LN
EAST DR
RIOLO WY
GLEN LN
BLOSSOM LN
ALMOND
GLASER LN
COURTNEY WY
COOK RIOLO RD
DUFFY LN
RAWHIDE LN
VIKING PL
HILLTOP CIR
DANKBAR LN
MISTY LN
FROSTY PL
BEDELL
PFE RD
PINEHURST DR
EAGLE SPRINGS PL
BILLY MITCHELL BLVD
GRICE CT
LITTORAL ST
NORTH RD
ANTELOPE OAKS CT
DEL RD
PALMERSON DR
HIDDEN MEADOW WY
JULIO BLVD
GREAT VALLEY DR
APLAND PL
SHERBROOK WY
OLIVE AV
PRUITT LN
HAWKEYE LN
RICH LN
LEWIS LN
ANTELOPE RD
HUMP RD
PINE ST
BEACH ST
OAK ST
ASH ST
OLD ANTELOPE NORTH RD
SUNSET HILLS LN
POKER LN
DON JULIO BLVD
THOMASINO WY
SORENSON WY
ELVERTA WY
KATELLA AV
LEDGEWOOD WY
ROSEVILLE RD
SEE A G6
1 PRIDES CRSG
2 TALLWOOD CIR
3 BELLFLOWER CT
SEE B A5
1 GENERO WY
2 GENERO CT
3 HIEMO WY
4 MAGISTER CT
5 FOUNTAINARBOR WY
1 BRIARWOOD WY
2 SAGEWOOD DR
3 BALMORE DR
4 LIFTON CT
5 CORRIGAN CT
1 GAZELLE RUN WY
2 GRAYTREE WY
FS

0 .125 .25 .375 .5 miles 1 in. = 1900 ft.

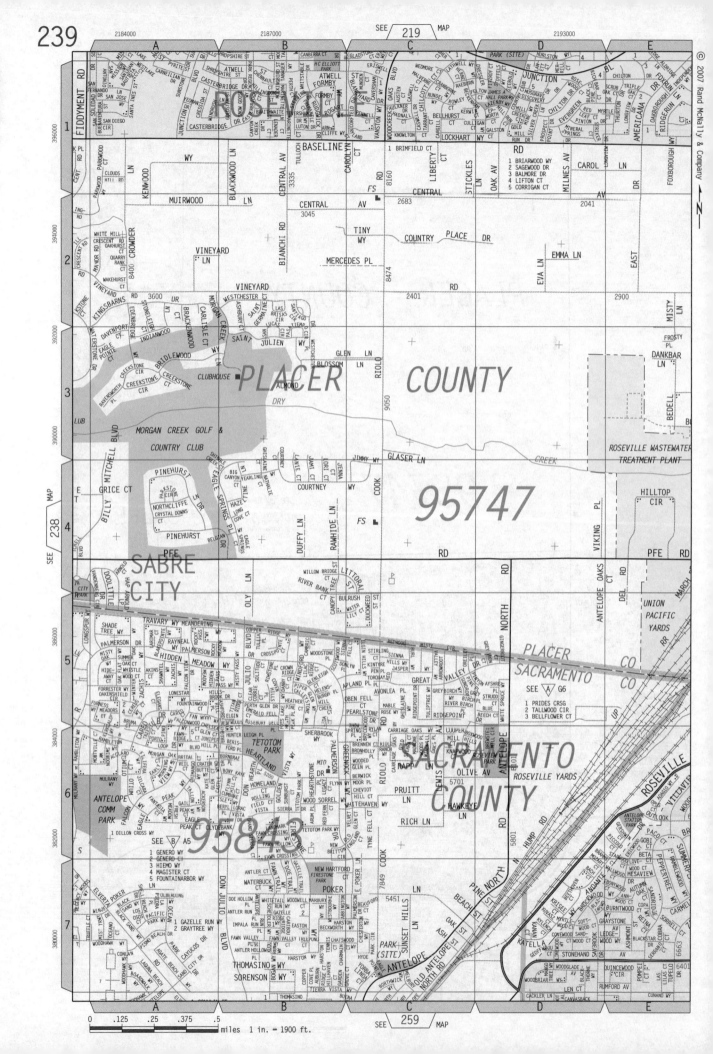

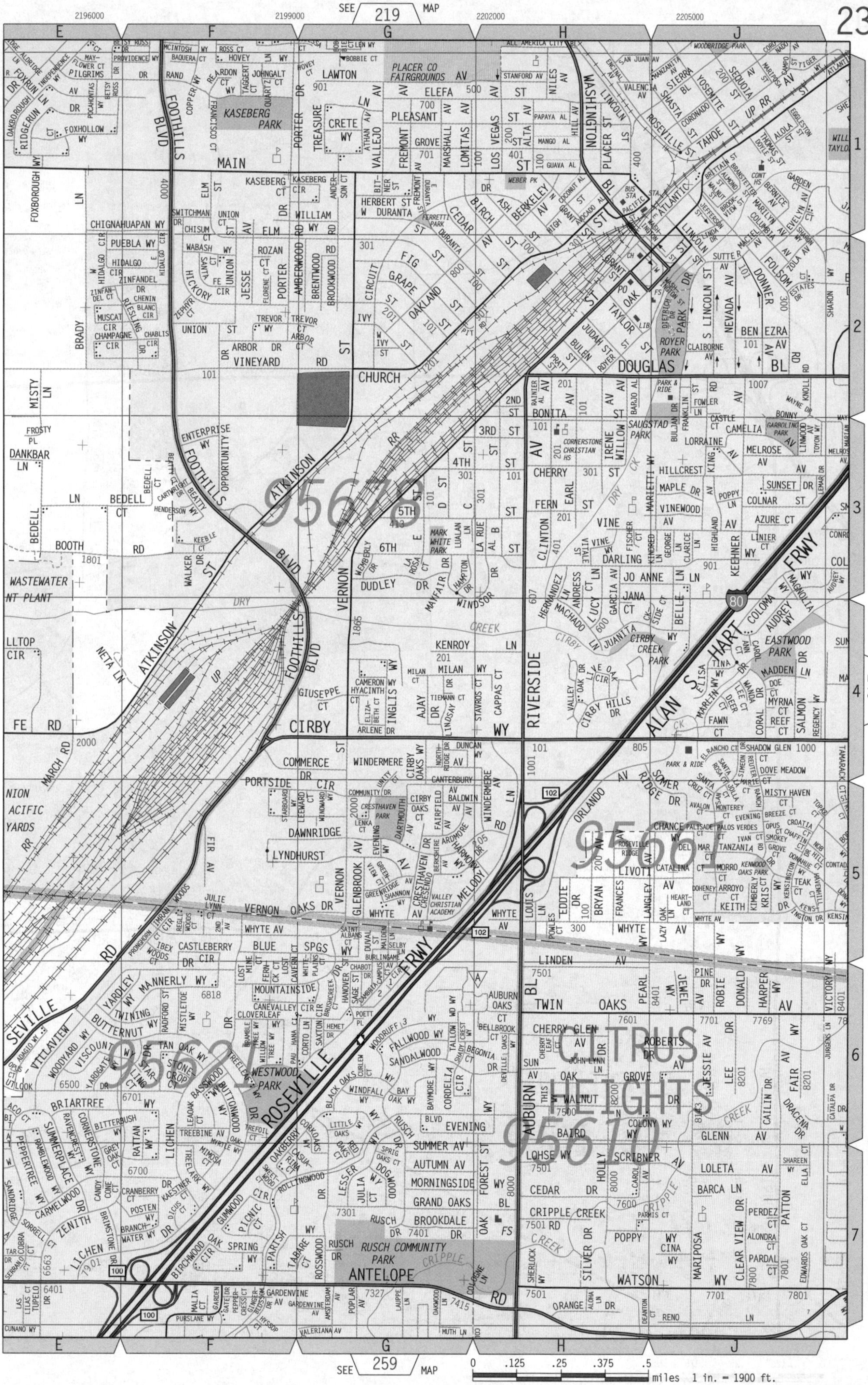
SEE 219 MAP
SEE 240 MAP
SEE 259 MAP
E
F
G
H
J
1
2
3
4
5
6
7
2196000
2199000
2202000
2205000
398000
396000
394000
392000
390000
386000
384000
382000
380000
95678
95661
95621
CITRUS HEIGHTS 95610
PLACER CO FAIRGROUNDS
KASEBERG PARK
WEBER PK
ROYER PARK
SAUGSTAD PARK
GARROLINO PARK
MARK WHITE PARK
CIRBY CREEK PARK
EASTWOOD PARK
CRESTHAVEN PARK
WESTWOOD PARK
RUSCH COMMUNITY PARK
WASTEWATER NT PLANT
UNION PACIFIC YARDS
FOOTHILLS BLVD
ATKINSON ST
WASHINGTON BL
DOUGLAS BL
CHURCH ST
CIRBY WY
RIVERSIDE AV
ALAN S HART FRWY
ROSEVILLE FRWY
VERNON ST
SUNRISE AV
AUBURN BL
ANTELOPE RD
WHYTE AV
LINDEN AV
TWIN OAKS AV
FOREST ST
DRY CREEK
CRIPPLE CREEK
80
102
100
0 .125 .25 .375 .5
miles 1 in. = 1900 ft.

SEE 220 MAP

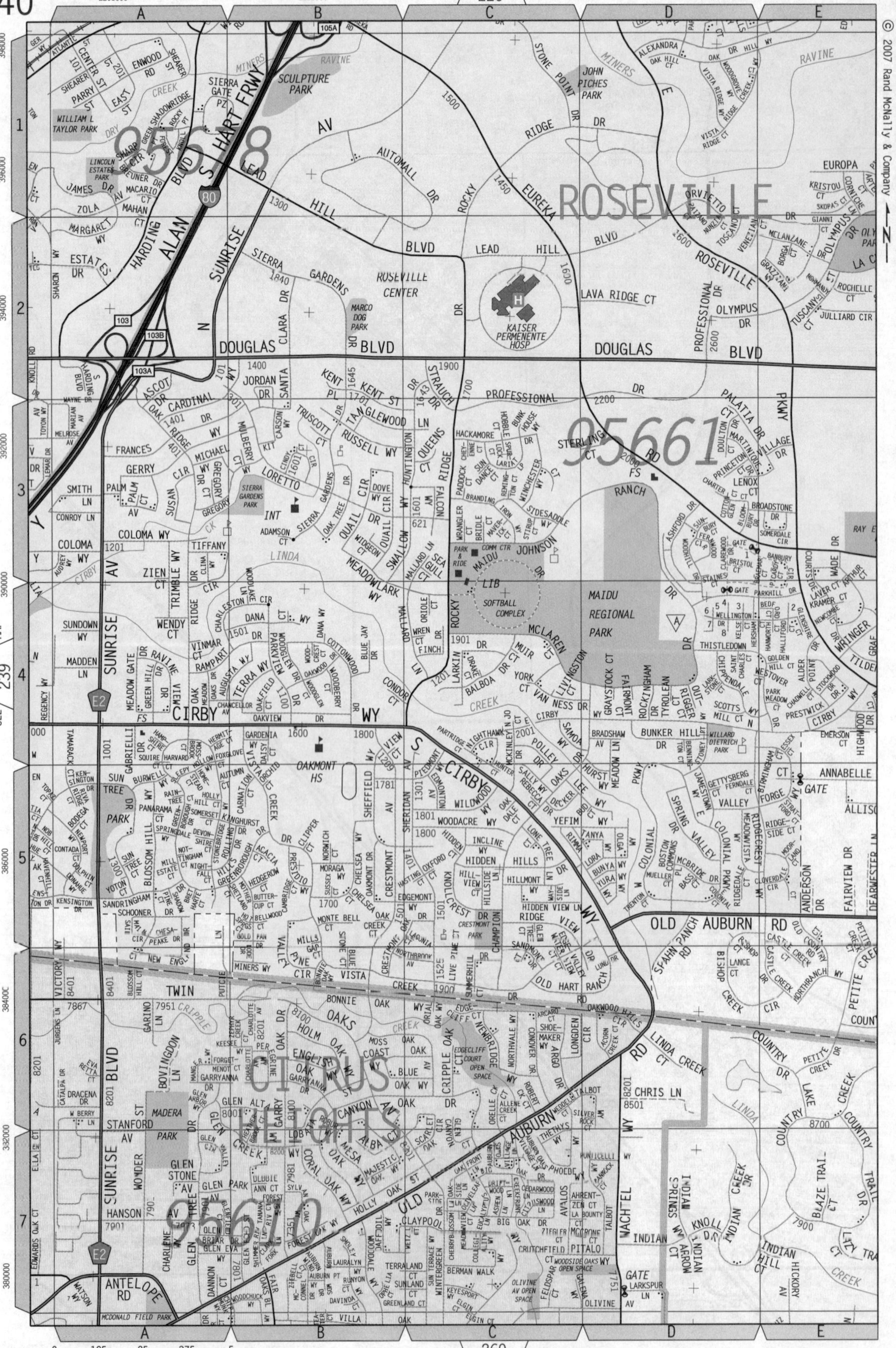

SEE 239 MAP

SEE 260 MAP

0 .125 .25 .375 .5 miles 1 in. = 1900 ft.

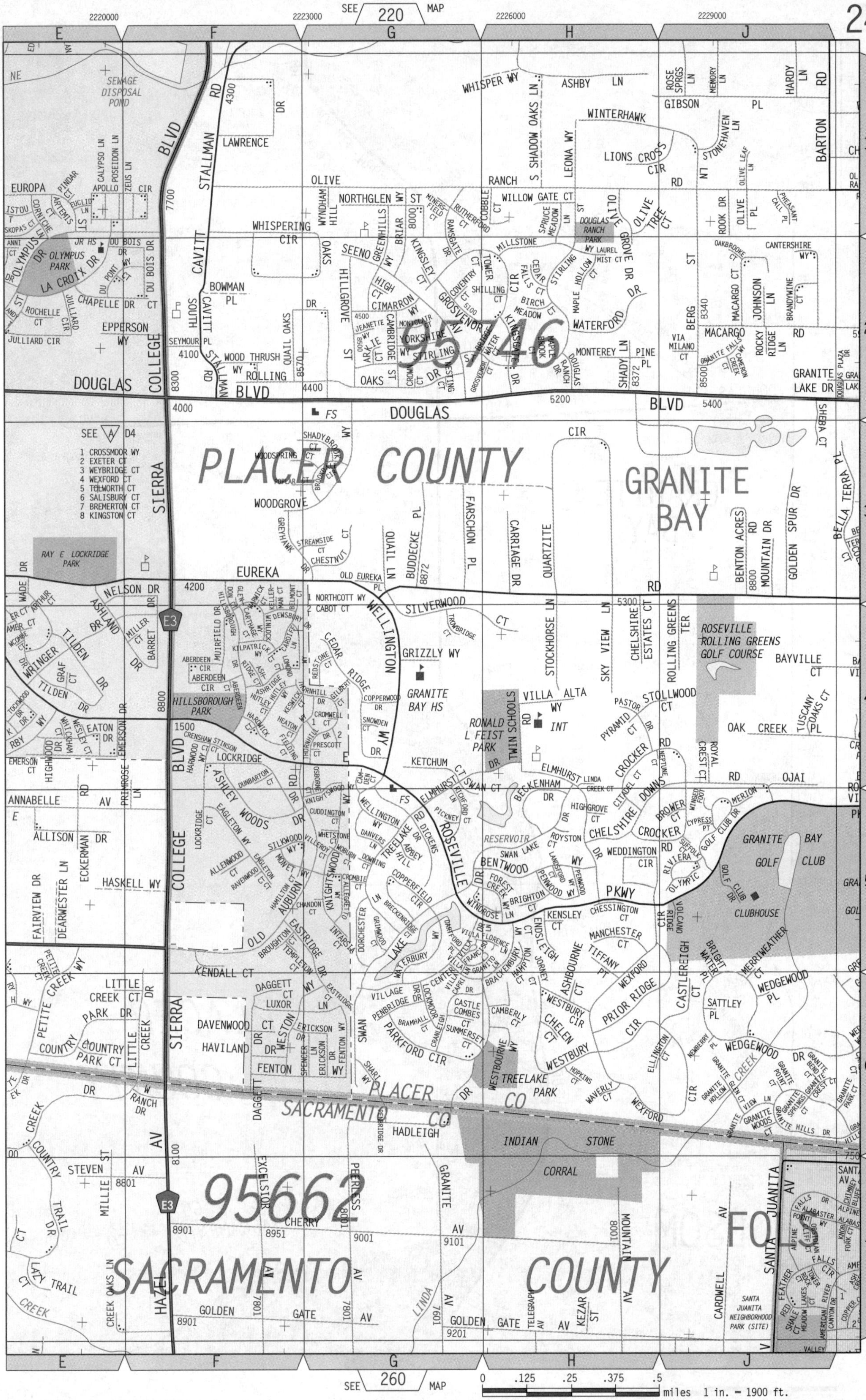
SEE 220 MAP
SEE 241 MAP
SEE 260 MAP
PLACER COUNTY
GRANITE BAY
SACRAMENTO COUNTY
95746
95662
PLACER CO
SACRAMENTO CO
SEWAGE DISPOSAL POND
OLYMPUS PARK
RAY E LOCKRIDGE PARK
HILLSBOROUGH PARK
GRANITE BAY HS
RONALD L FEIST PARK
TWIN SCHOOLS INT
RESERVOIR
ROSEVILLE ROLLING GREENS GOLF COURSE
GRANITE BAY GOLF CLUB
CLUBHOUSE
TREELAKE PARK
INDIAN STONE CORRAL
SANTA JUANITA NEIGHBORHOOD PARK (SITE)
DOUGLAS RANCH PARK
FS
SEE A D4
1 CROSSMOOR WY
2 EXETER CT
3 WEYBRIDGE CT
4 WEXFORD CT
5 TOLWORTH CT
6 SALISBURY CT
7 BREMERTON CT
8 KINGSTON CT
1 NORTHCOTT WY
2 CABOT CT
DOUGLAS BLVD
SIERRA COLLEGE BLVD
HAZEL AV
EUREKA RD
OLIVE RANCH RD
ROSEVILLE PKWY
WELLINGTON WY
AUBURN FOLSOM RD
CAVITT STALLMAN RD
SANTA JUANITA AV
GOLDEN GATE AV
CHERRY AV
ASHBY LN
WHISPER WY
WINTERHAWK
LIONS CROSS CIR
BARTON RD
GIBSON PL
MACARGO RD
GRANITE LAKE DR
CARRIAGE DR
QUARTZITE
FARSCHON PL
BUDDECKE PL
QUAIL LN
STOCKHORSE LN
SKY VIEW LN
CHELSHIRE DOWNS
CROCKER RD
ELMHURST
KETCHUM CT
BENTWOOD DR
PRIOR RIDGE CIR
WEDGEWOOD DR
WESTBURY
WEXFORD
COUNTRY PARK DR
PETITE CREEK WY
LITTLE CREEK
STEVEN AV
LACY TRAIL
CREEK OAKS LN
MOUNTAIN AV
CARDWELL
E3
miles 1 in. = 1900 ft.
0 .125 .25 .375 .5

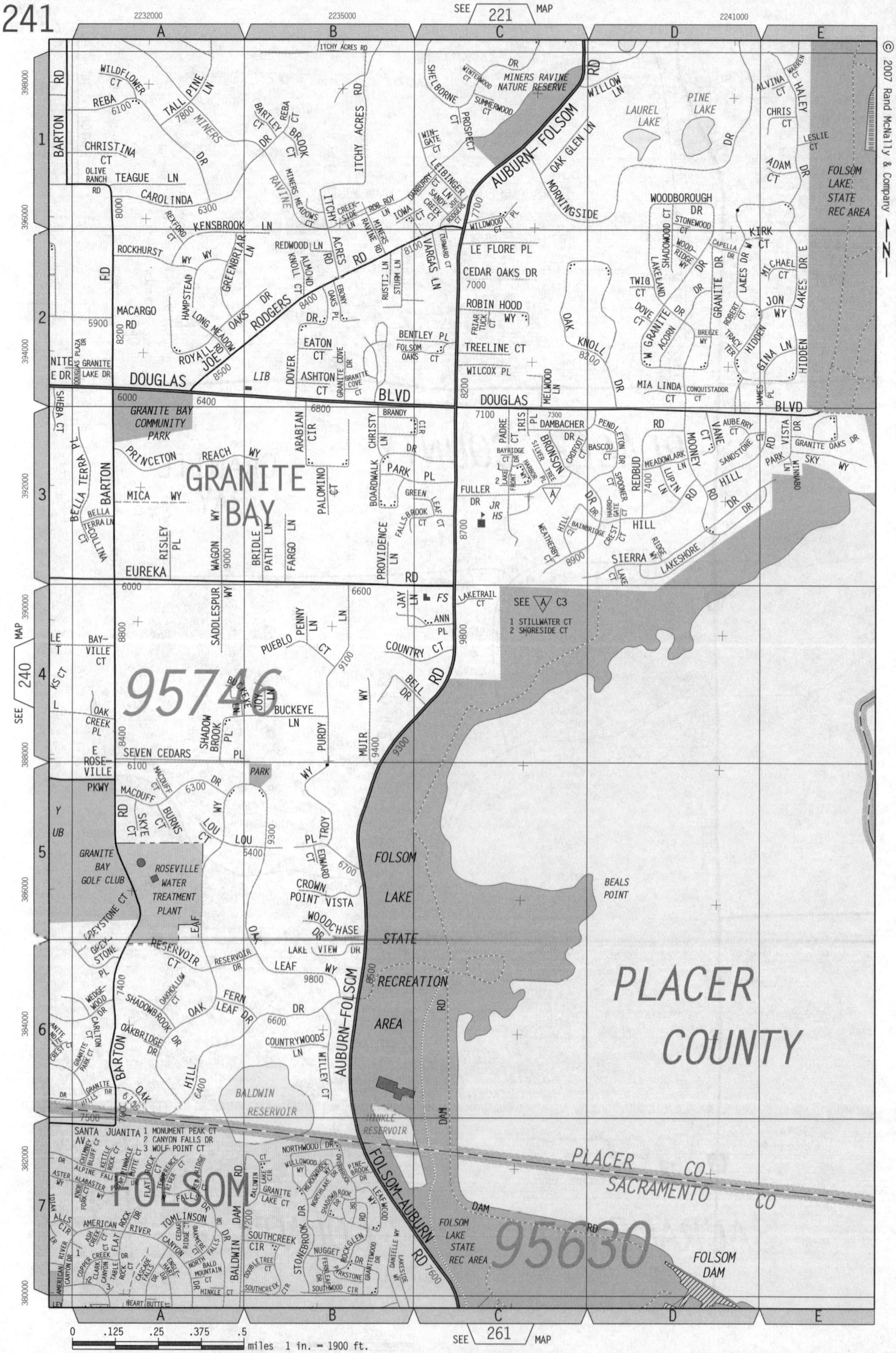
SEE 221 MAP
SEE 240 MAP
SEE 261 MAP
A
B
C
D
E
1
2
3
4
5
6
7
2232000
2235000
2241000
398000
396000
394000
392000
390000
388000
386000
384000
382000
380000
GRANITE BAY
95746
95630
FOLSOM
PLACER COUNTY
PLACER CO
SACRAMENTO CO
FOLSOM LAKE STATE RECREATION AREA
FOLSOM LAKE STATE REC AREA
FOLSOM DAM
BEALS POINT
BALDWIN RESERVOIR
HINKLE RESERVOIR
GRANITE BAY COMMUNITY PARK
GRANITE BAY GOLF CLUB
ROSEVILLE WATER TREATMENT PLANT
MINERS RAVINE NATURE RESERVE
LAUREL LAKE
PINE LAKE
PARK
LIB
FS
JR HS
AUBURN-FOLSOM RD
FOLSOM-AUBURN RD
DOUGLAS BLVD
BARTON RD
EUREKA RD
ITCHY ACRES RD
ITCHY ACRES LN
RODGERS RD
JOE RODGERS RD
DAM RD
SEE A C3
1 STILLWATER CT
2 SHORESIDE CT
1 MONUMENT PEAK CT
2 CANYON FALLS DR
3 WOLF POINT CT
0 .125 .25 .375 .5
miles 1 in. = 1900 ft.

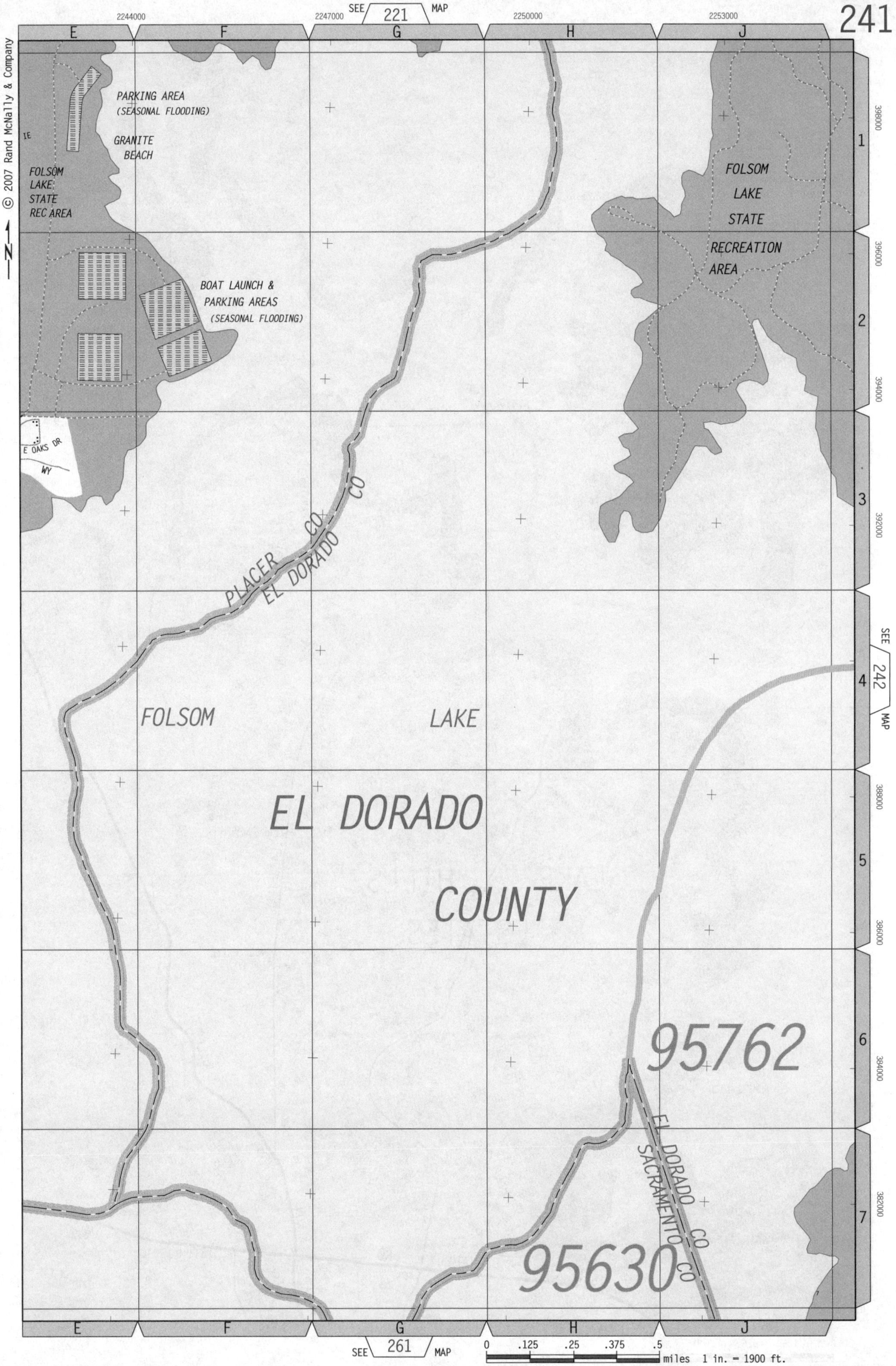
SEE 221 MAP
2244000
2247000
2250000
2253000
E
F
G
H
J
398000
396000
394000
392000
388000
386000
384000
382000
1
2
3
4
5
6
7
PARKING AREA
(SEASONAL FLOODING)
GRANITE
BEACH
FOLSOM
LAKE
STATE
REC AREA
BOAT LAUNCH &
PARKING AREAS
(SEASONAL FLOODING)
E OAKS DR
WY
FOLSOM
LAKE
STATE
RECREATION
AREA
PLACER CO
EL DORADO CO
FOLSOM
LAKE
EL DORADO
COUNTY
SEE 242 MAP
95762
95630
EL DORADO CO
SACRAMENTO CO
SEE 261 MAP
0 .125 .25 .375 .5
miles 1 in. = 1900 ft.

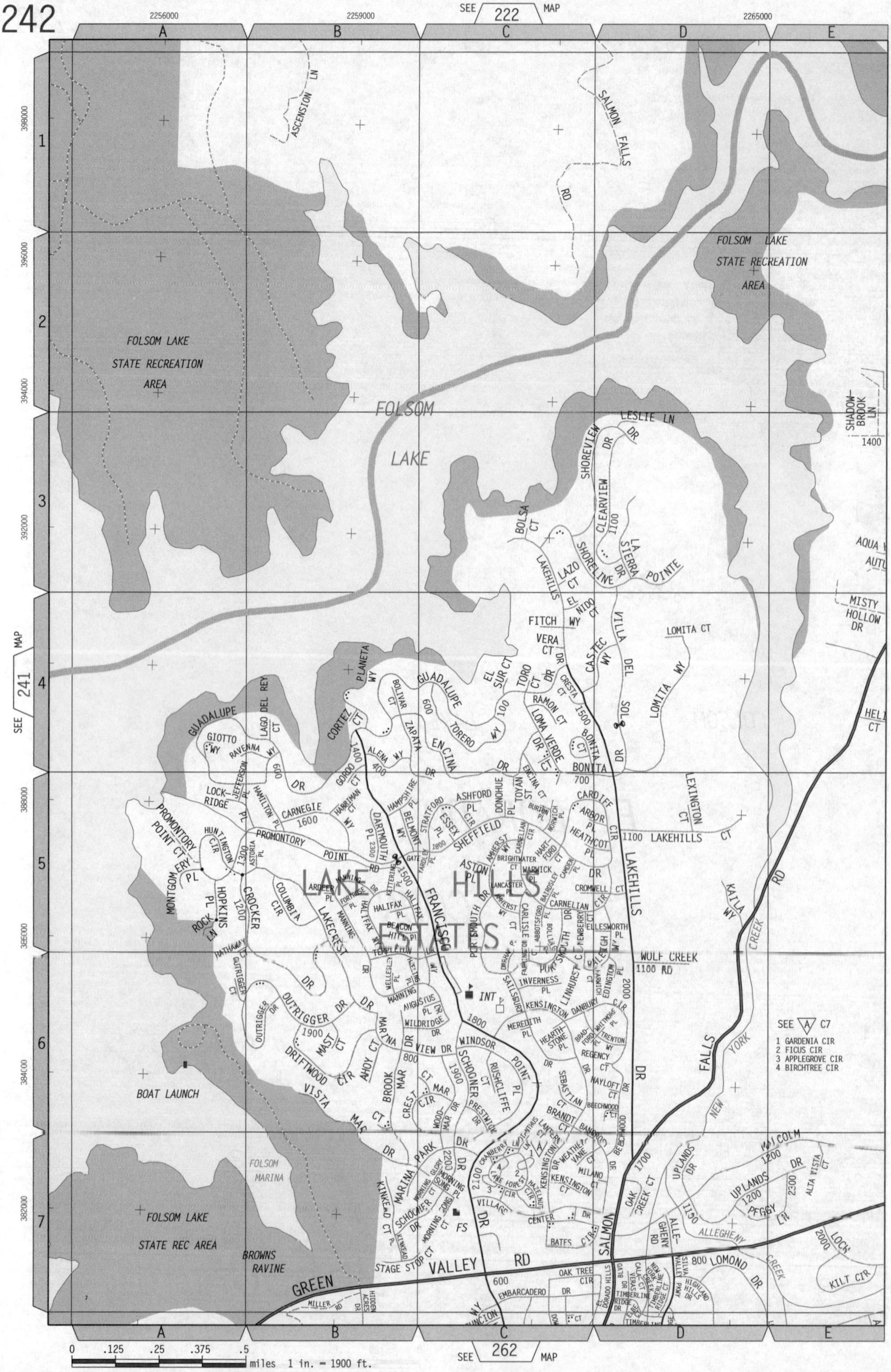
SEE 222 MAP
SEE 262 MAP
SEE 241 MAP
2256000
2259000
2265000
398000
396000
394000
392000
388000
384000
382000
A
B
C
D
E
1
2
3
4
5
6
7
FOLSOM LAKE STATE RECREATION AREA
FOLSOM LAKE
LAKE HILLS ESTATES
FOLSOM LAKE STATE REC AREA
BOAT LAUNCH
FOLSOM MARINA
BROWNS RAVINE
ASCENSION LN
SALMON FALLS RD
LESLIE LN
SHOREVIEW DR
CLEARVIEW
LA SIERRA POINTE
SHORELINE DR
BOLSA CT
LAZO CT
LAKEHILLS
EL NIDO CT
FITCH WY
VERA CT
VILLA DEL SOL
LOMITA CT
LOMITA WY
CASTEC WY
CRESTA
TORO CT
EL SUR CT
RAMON CT
LOMA VERDE
BONITA
GUADALUPE
PLANETA WY
CORTEZ CT
BOLIVAR CT
ZAPATA
TORERO WY
ENCINA DR
ALENA WY
GORDO
GIOTTO WY
RAVENNA WY
LAGO DEL REY CT
JEFFERSON PL
LOCKRIDGE PL
HAMILTON PL
CARNEGIE
HARRIMAN CT
HAMPSHIRE PL
DARTMOUTH PL
BELMONT WY
STRATFORD
ASHFORD PL
ESSEX
SHEFFIELD
DONOHUE
TOYAN ST
CARDIFF
ARBOR PL
HEATHCOT PL
LAKEHILLS CT
LEXINGTON CT
CROMWELL
CARNELIAN
ELLESWORTH PL
PROMONTORY POINT CT
PROMONTORY POINT RD
HUNTINGTON CIR
MONTGOMERY PL
ROCK LN
HOPKINS PL
CROCKER
COLUMBIA CIR
LAKECREST
ARDEER PL
HALIFAX
BEACON HILL PL
FRANCISCO
PORTSMOUTH DR
ASTON PL
AMHERST
HARTFORD
INVERNESS
KENSINGTON
DANBURY CIR
LINHURST
EDINGTON
WOLF CREEK RD
KAILA WY
FALLS DR
NEW YORK CREEK
MERIDETH PL
HEARTHSTONE PL
TRENTON WY
REGENCY CT
SEBASTIAN
HAYLOFT CT
BEECHWOOD
BRANDT CT
WINDSOR POINT
SCHOONER DR
RUSHCLIFFE PL
PRESTWICK
OUTRIGGER DR
OUTRIGGER CT
MAST CT
DRIFTWOOD CIR
VISTA
AHOY CT
MARINA VIEW DR
BROOK CT
MAR CREST
WOODMAR DR
WILDRIDGE
MARINA PARK DR
KINKEAD CT
SCHOONER DR
MORNING SONG PL
STAGE STOP CT
INT
FS
VILLAGE CENTER DR
BATES CIR
MILANO
KENSINGTON CT
SALMON FALLS
OAK CREEK CT
UPLANDS DR
MALCOLM DR
ALTA VISTA CT
PEGGY LN
ALLEGHENY
GREEN VALLEY RD
OAK TREE CIR
EMBARCADERO DR
MILLER RD
HIDDEN ACRES DR
LOMOND DR
KILT CIR
TIMBERLINE
EL DORADO HILLS
SHADOWBROOK LN
AQUA
MISTY HOLLOW DR
SEE A C7
1 GARDENIA CIR
2 FICUS CIR
3 APPLEGROVE CIR
4 BIRCHTREE CIR
0 .125 .25 .375 .5 miles 1 in. = 1900 ft.

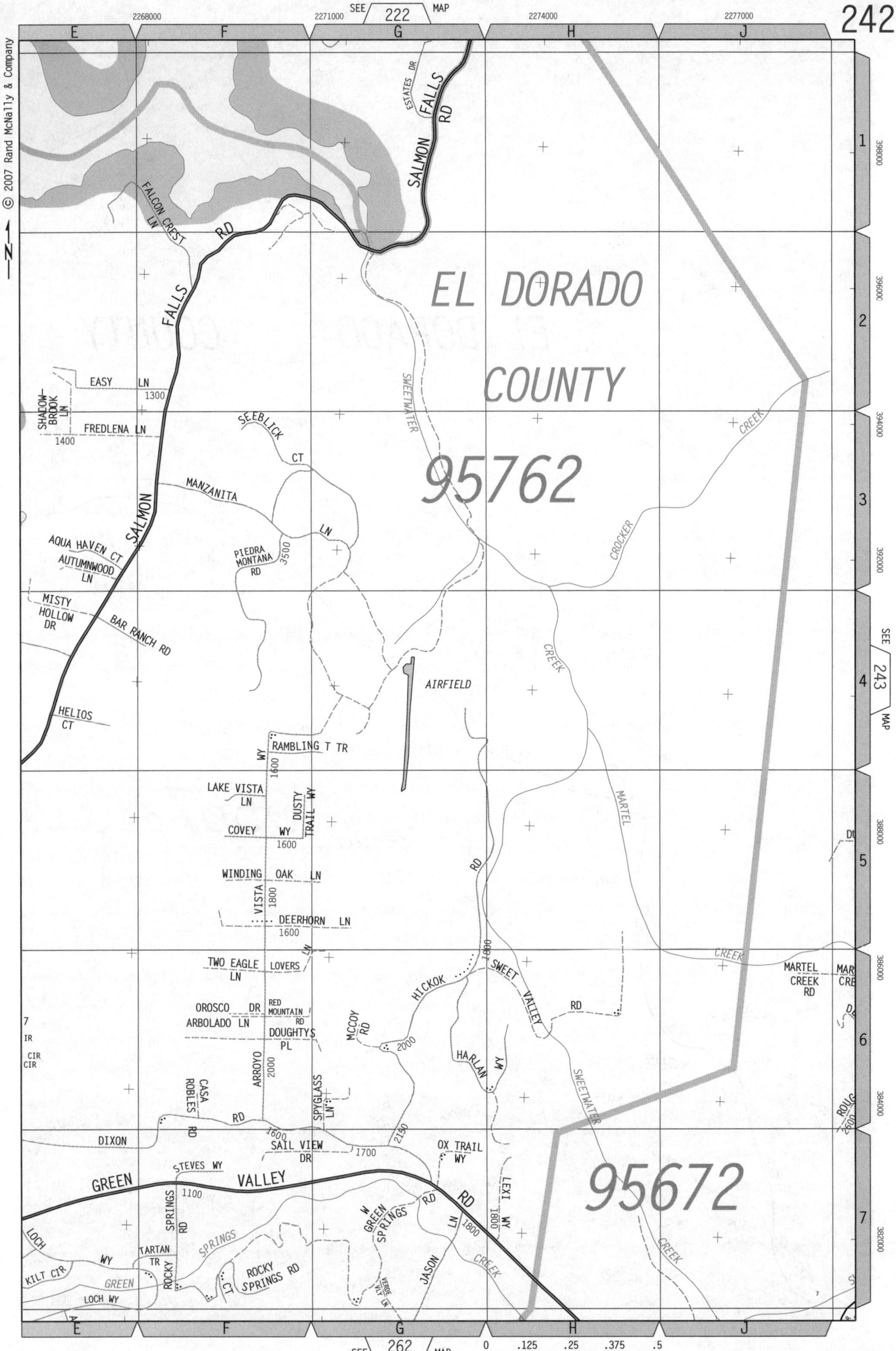
SEE 222 MAP
SEE 243 MAP
SEE 262 MAP
EL DORADO COUNTY
95762
95672
SALMON FALLS RD
ESTATES DR
FALCON CREST LN
EASY LN
SHADOW-BROOK LN
FREDLENA LN
SEEBLICK CT
MANZANITA LN
AQUA HAVEN CT
AUTUMNWOOD LN
PIEDRA MONTANA RD
MISTY HOLLOW DR
BAR RANCH RD
HELIOS CT
AIRFIELD
SWEETWATER RD
CROCKER CREEK
MARTEL CREEK
MARTEL CREEK RD
RAMBLING T TR
VISTA WY
LAKE VISTA LN
DUSTY TRAIL WY
COVEY WY
WINDING OAK LN
DEERHORN LN
TWO EAGLE LN
LOVERS LN
OROSCO DR
RED MOUNTAIN RD
ARBOLADO LN
DOUGHTYS PL
MCCOY RD
HICKOK
SWEET VALLEY RD
HARLAN WY
ARROYO
CASA ROBLES RD
SPYGLASS LN
DIXON RD
SAIL VIEW DR
OX TRAIL WY
STEVES WY
GREEN VALLEY RD
SPRINGS RD
LEXI WY
W GREEN SPRINGS RD
JASON LN
LOCH WY
KILT CIR
TARTAN TR
ROCKY
ROCKY SPRINGS RD
CT
VERDE VLY LN
LOCH WY
GREEN SPRINGS CREEK
0 .125 .25 .375 .5 miles 1 in. = 1900 ft.

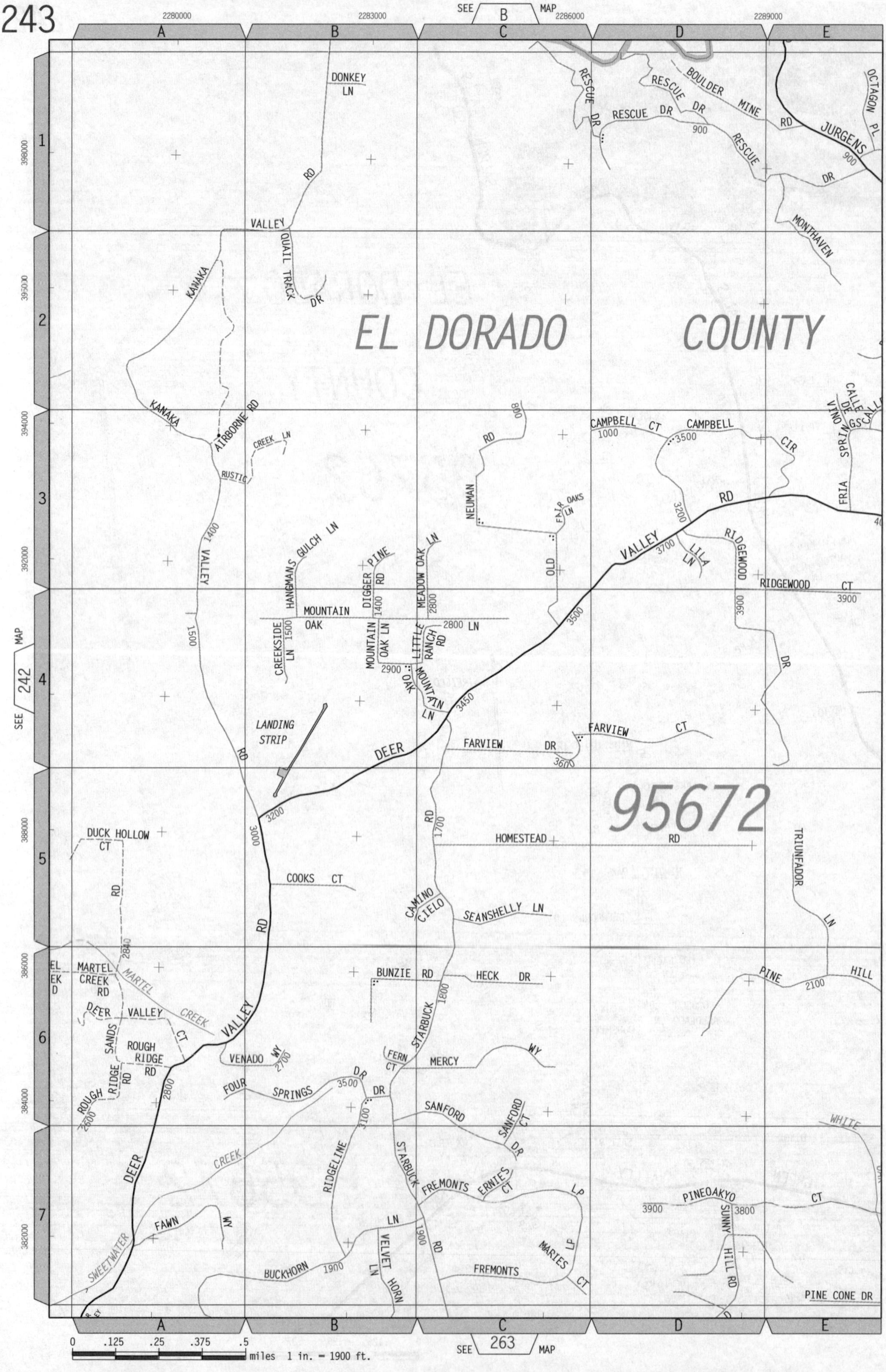

SEE B MAP
SEE 242 MAP
SEE 263 MAP
2280000
2283000
2286000
2289000
398000
395000
394000
392000
388000
386000
384000
382000
A
B
C
D
E
1
2
3
4
5
6
7
EL DORADO COUNTY
95672
DONKEY LN
VALLEY RD
QUAIL TRACK DR
KANAKA
AIRBORNE RD
CREEK LN
RUSTIC
VALLEY RD
HANGMANS GULCH LN
DIGGER PINE RD
MEADOW OAK LN
MOUNTAIN OAK
CREEKSIDE LN
MOUNTAIN OAK LN
LITTLE RANCH RD
OAK MOUNTAIN LN
2800 LN
NEUMAN RD
OLD FAIR OAKS LN
CAMPBELL CT
CAMPBELL CIR
RIDGEWOOD DR
RIDGEWOOD CT
LILA LN
VALLEY RD
DEER VALLEY RD
LANDING STRIP
FARVIEW DR
FARVIEW CT
HOMESTEAD RD
DUCK HOLLOW CT
COOKS CT
CAMINO CIELO
SEANSHELLY LN
TRIUNFADOR LN
PINE HILL
BUNZIE RD
HECK DR
STARBUCK RD
MARTEL CREEK RD
MARTEL CREEK
DEER VALLEY CT
SANDS
ROUGH RIDGE RD
VENADO WY
FERN CT
MERCY WY
FOUR SPRINGS DR
SANFORD
SANFORD CT
SANFORD DR
RIDGELINE LN
STARBUCK
FREMONTS
ERNIES CT
LP
MARIES CT
FAWN WY
SWEETWATER
CREEK
BUCKHORN
VELVET HORN LN
FREMONTS
PINEOAKYO CT
SUNNY HILL RD
PINE CONE DR
WHITE
RESCUE DR
RESCUE DR
BOULDER MINE RD
JURGENS DR
OCTAGON PL
MONTHAVEN
CALLE DE VINO
FRIA SPRINGS
0 .125 .25 .375 .5 miles 1 in. = 1900 ft.

SEE B MAP

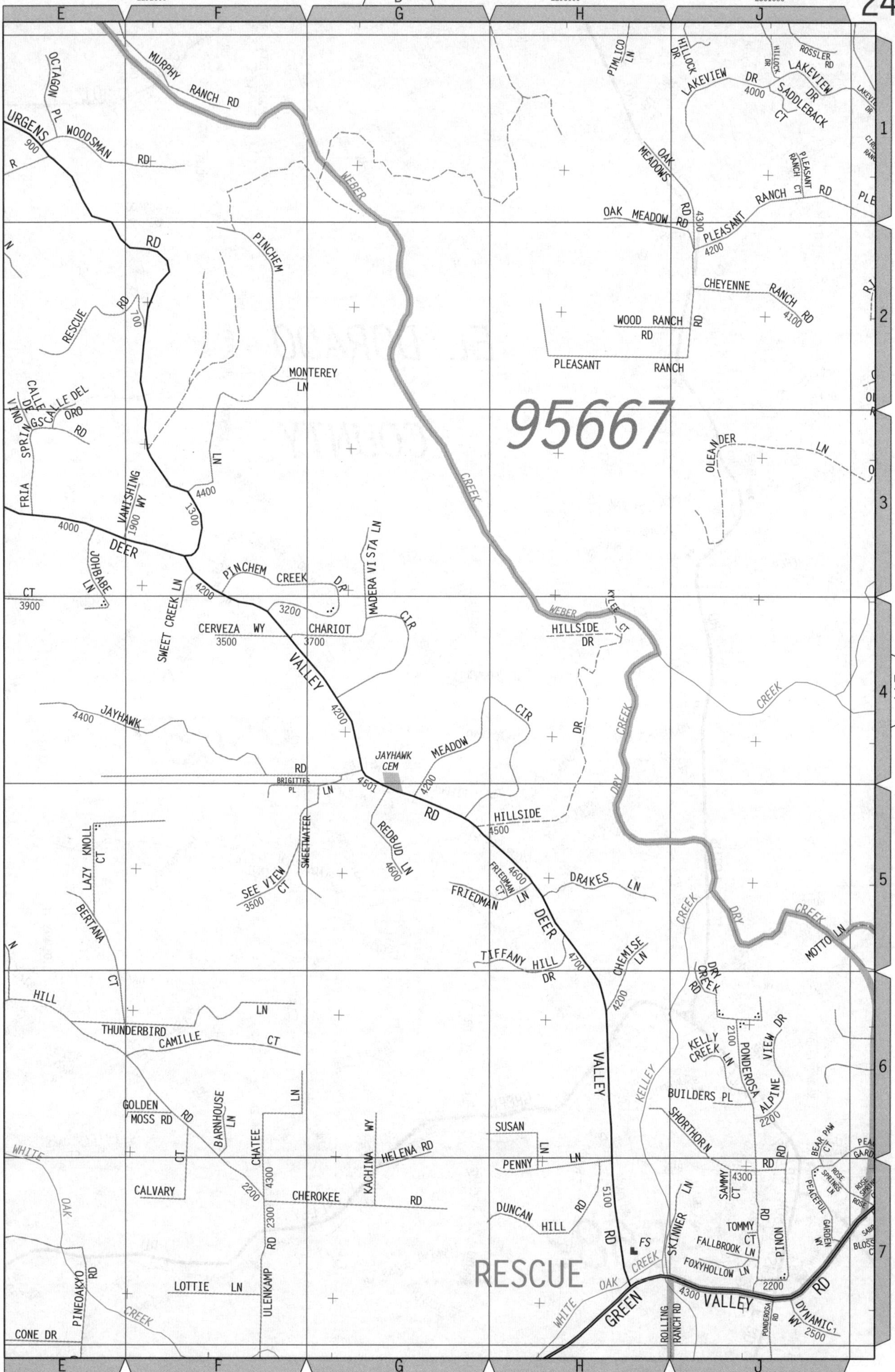
2292000
2298000
2301000
E
F
G
H
J
1
2
3
4
5
6
7
400000
398000
396000
394000
392000
390000
388000
386000
384000
382000
95667
RESCUE
MURPHY RANCH RD
OCTAGON PL
URGENS
900
WOODSMAN RD
RD
PINCHEM
RESCUE RD
700
MONTEREY LN
CALLE DE VINO
CALLE DEL ORO RD
SPRINGS
FRIA
VANISHING 1900 WY
LN
4400
1300
4000
DEER
JOHBABE LN
CT 3900
SWEET CREEK LN
4200
PINCHEM CREEK DR
MADERA VISTA LN
3200
CERVEZA WY 3500
CHARIOT 3700
CIR
VALLEY
4200
JAYHAWK 4400
JAYHAWK CEM
MEADOW
4200
CIR
DR
RD
BRIGITTES PL
LN
4501
RD
REDBUD LN 4600
HILLSIDE 4500
SWEETWATER
SEE VIEW CT 3500
LAZY KNOLL CT
BERTANA CT
N
HILL
THUNDERBIRD
CAMILLE CT
LN
GOLDEN MOSS RD
BARNHOUSE LN
CT
CHATEE LN
2200
4300
ULENKAMP RD 2300
CALVARY
CHEROKEE RD
KACHINA WY
HELENA RD
LN
SUSAN LN
PENNY LN
DUNCAN HILL RD
5100
RD
FS
WHITE OAK CREEK
PINEOAKYO RD
LOTTIE LN
CONE DR
CREEK
GREEN VALLEY RD 4300
ROLLING RANCH RD
PONDEROSA RD
DYNAMIC WY 2500
WEBER CREEK
PIMLICO LN
HILLOCK DR
ROSSLER RD
LAKEVIEW DR
4000
SADDLEBACK CT
LAKEVIEW DR
OAK MEADOWS RD
4300
OAK MEADOW RD
PLEASANT RANCH RD
4200
PLEASANT RANCH CT
CHEYENNE RANCH RD
4100
WOOD RANCH RD
RD
PLEASANT RANCH
OLEANDER LN
KYLEE CT
HILLSIDE DR
DRY CREEK
CREEK
FRIEDMAN CT
FRIEDMAN LN
4600
DRAKES LN
TIFFANY HILL DR
4700
CHEMISE LN
4200
MOTTO LN
DRY CREEK RD
2100
KELLY CREEK LN
PONDEROSA
VIEW DR
ALPINE
BUILDERS PL
SHORTHORN RD
2200
KELLEY
BEAR PAW CT
ROSE SPRINGS LN
PEACEFUL GARDEN WY
SAMMY CT
4300
TOMMY CT
PINON
SKINNER LN
FALLBROOK LN
FOXYHOLLOW LN
2200
SEE 244 MAP

SEE 263 MAP

0 .125 .25 .375 .5 miles 1 in. = 1900 ft.

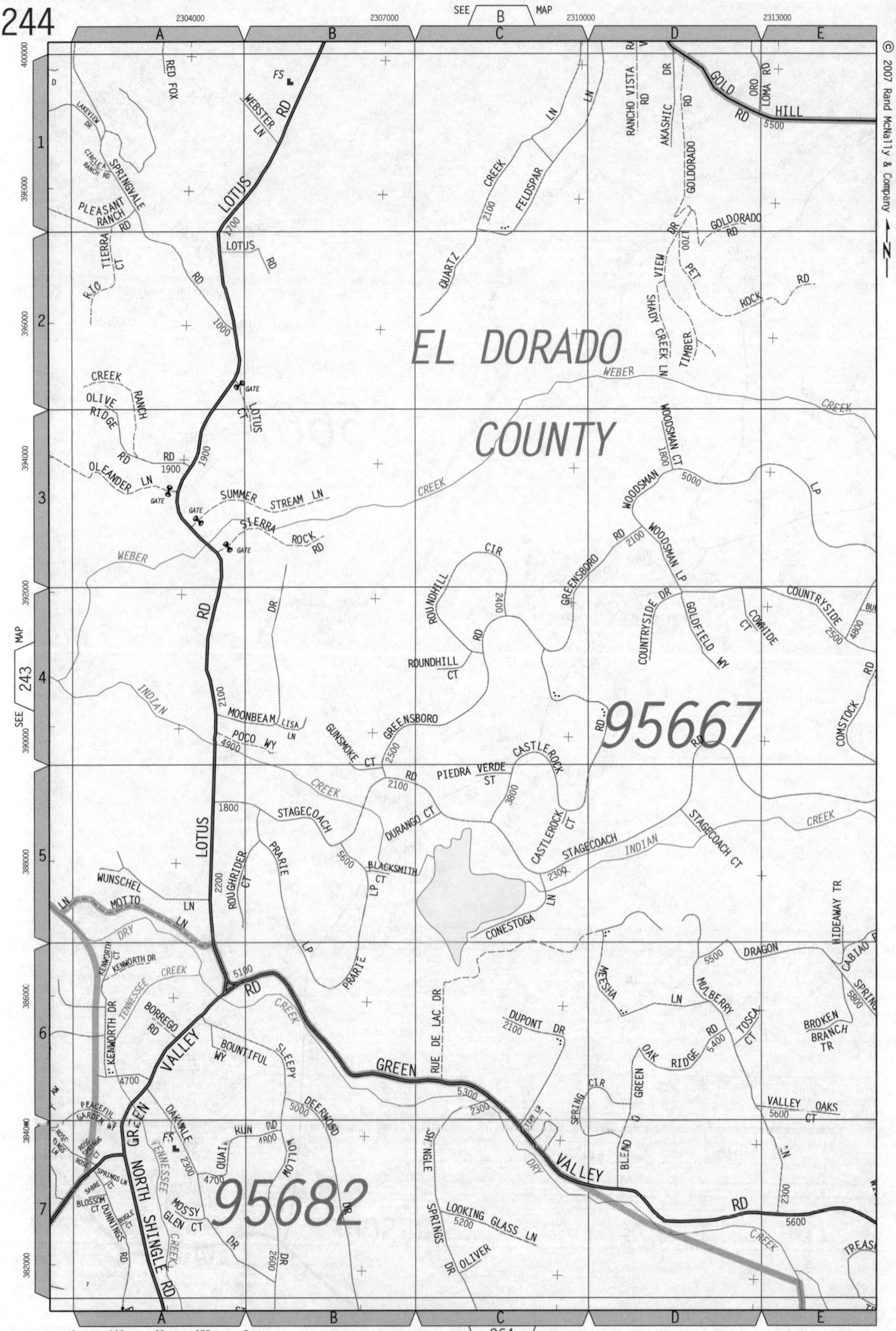
SEE B MAP
SEE 243 MAP
SEE 264 MAP
© 2007 Rand McNally & Company
EL DORADO
COUNTY
95667
95682
LOTUS RD
GREEN VALLEY RD
NORTH SHINGLE RD
GOLD HILL RD
WEBSTER LN
RED FOX
SPRINGVALE
PLEASANT RANCH RD
RIO TIERRA CT
OLIVE RIDGE RD
CREEK RANCH
OLEANDER LN
SUMMER STREAM LN
SIERRA ROCK RD
LOTUS CT
GATE
WEBER CREEK
INDIAN CREEK
MOONBEAM
LISA LN
POCO WY
GUNSMOKE CT
GREENSBORO RD
ROUNDHILL CIR
ROUNDHILL CT
PIEDRA VERDE ST
CASTLEROCK RD
CASTLEROCK CT
STAGECOACH
STAGECOACH CT
DURANGO CT
BLACKSMITH LP
PRARIE LP
ROUGHRIDER CT
WUNSCHEL LN
MOTTO LN
DRY CREEK
TENNESSEE CREEK
KENWORTH DR
KENWORTH CT
BORREGO RD
BOUNTIFUL WY
SLEEPY HOLLOW DR
DEERWOOD DR
QUAIL RUN RD
OAKDALE
MOSSY GLEN CT
DUNNINGS RD
BLOSSOM CT
BUGLE CT
PEACEFUL GARDEN
ROSE SPRINGS CT
SPRINGS LN
RUE DE LAC DR
CONESTOGA LN
DUPONT DR
SHINGLE SPRINGS DR
LOOKING GLASS LN
OLIVER
SPRING CIR
GREEN BLEND
OAK RIDGE RD
MESHA LN
MULBERRY
TOSCA CT
DRAGON
HIDEAWAY TR
BROKEN BRANCH TR
VALLEY OAKS CT
CABIAO
SPRINGS
TREAS
COMSTOCK RD
COUNTRYSIDE DR
COUNTRYSIDE
COWHIDE CT
GOLDFIELD WY
WOODSMAN CT
WOODSMAN LP
WOODSMAN
QUARTZ CREEK LN
FELDSPAR LN
RANCHO VISTA RD
AKASHIC DR
GOLDORADO VIEW DR
GOLDORADO RD
PET ROCK RD
SHADY CREEK LN
TIMBER
ORO LOMA RD
FS
miles 1 in. = 1900 ft.

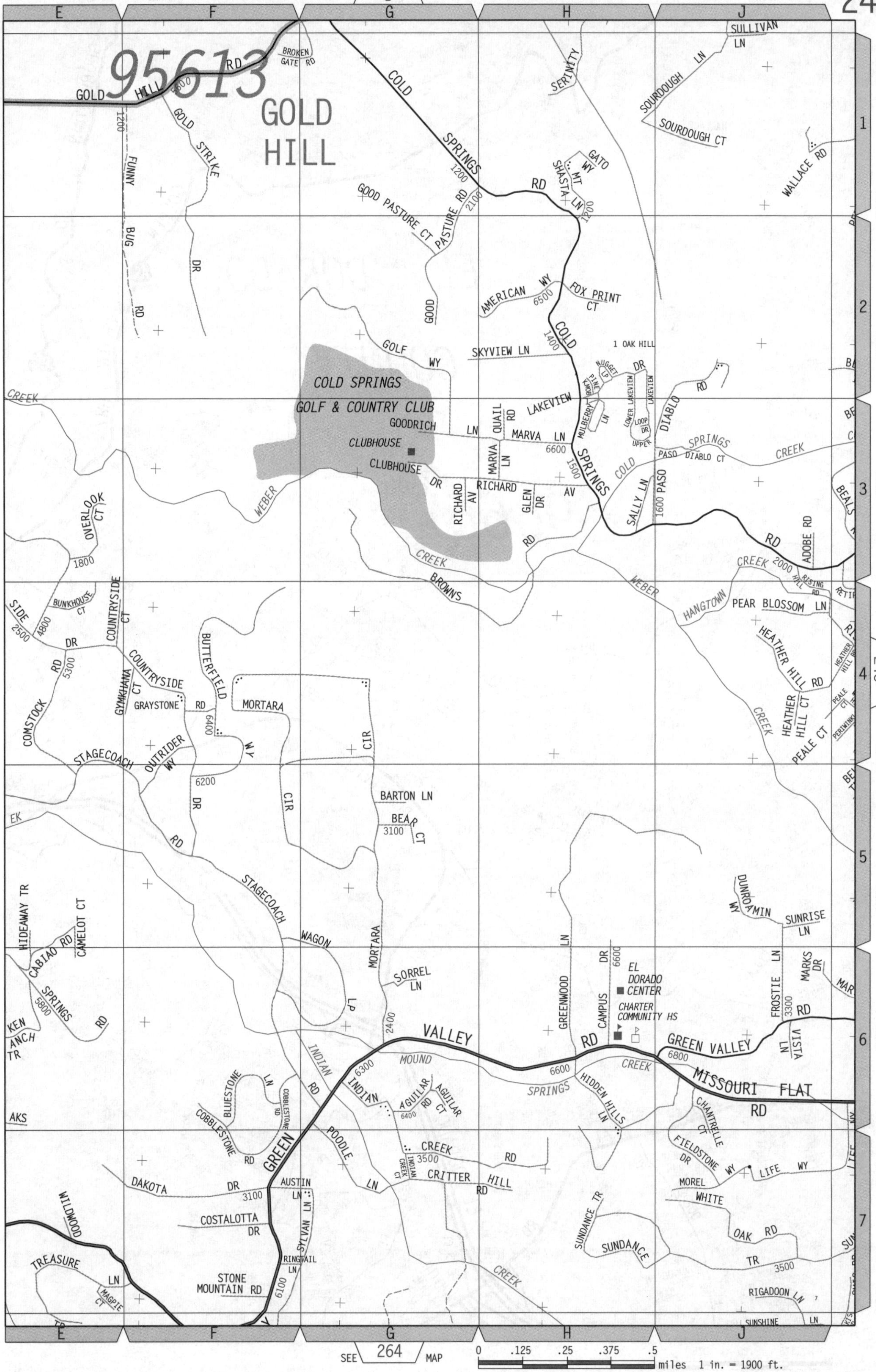
SEE B MAP
SEE 245 MAP
SEE 264 MAP
95613
GOLD HILL
COLD SPRINGS GOLF & COUNTRY CLUB
CLUBHOUSE
EL DORADO CENTER
CHARTER COMMUNITY HS
GOLD HILL RD
COLD SPRINGS RD
GREEN VALLEY RD
MISSOURI FLAT RD
STAGECOACH RD
MORTARA CIR
WEBER CREEK
HANGTOWN CREEK
MOUND SPRINGS CREEK
INDIAN CREEK
0 .125 .25 .375 .5 miles 1 in. = 1900 ft.

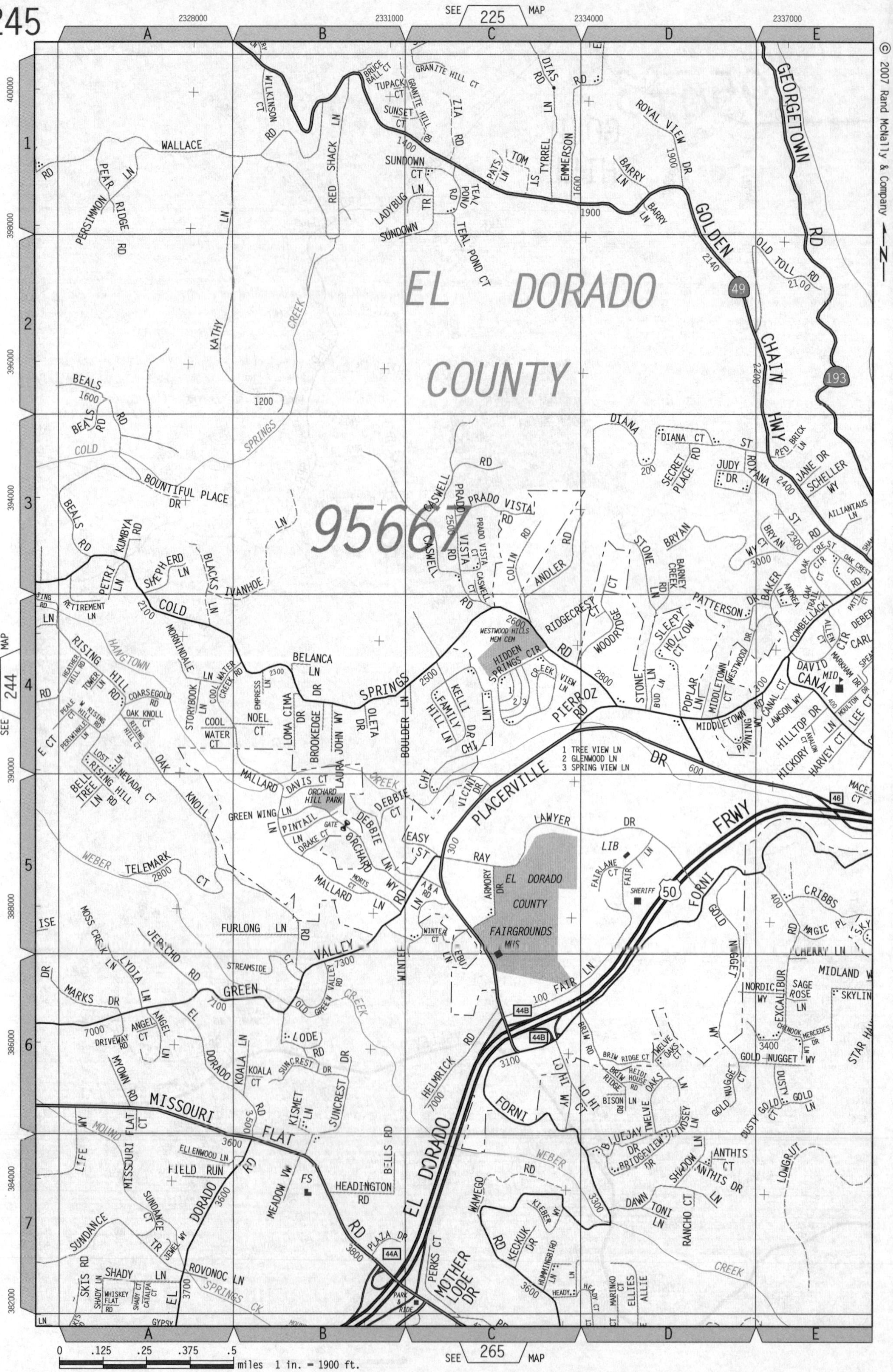
SEE 225 MAP
SEE 244 MAP
SEE 265 MAP
EL DORADO COUNTY
95667
GEORGETOWN RD
GOLDEN CHAIN HWY
49
193
50
44A
44B
46
ROYAL VIEW DR
BARRY LN
EMMERSON
TYRREL LN
DIAS RD
GRANITE HILL CT
TUPACK CT
SUNSET CT
BRUCE BALL CT
WILKINSON CT
RED SHACK LN
ZIA RD
SUNDOWN CT
LADYBUG LN
TEAL POND RD
TEAL POND CT
WALLACE RD
PEAR RIDGE LN
PERSIMMON RIDGE RD
KATHY LN
SPRINGS CREEK
BEALS RD
COLD SPRINGS RD
BOUNTIFUL PLACE DR
KUMBYA
PETRI LN
SHEPHERD LN
BLACKS LN
IVANHOE
OLD TOLL RD
DIANA ST
DIANA CT
SECRET PLACE RD
JUDY DR
ROXANA ST
RED BRICK LN
JANE DR
SCHELLER WY
ALLIANTAUS LN
BRYAN CT
CASWELL RD
PRADO VISTA RD
PRADO VISTA CT
COLIN RD
ANDLER RD
STONE LN
BARNEY CREEK RD
PATTERSON DR
BAKER
RIDGECREST CT
WOODRIDGE
SLEEPY HOLLOW CT
WESTWOOD HILLS MEM CEM
HIDDEN SPRINGS CIR
CREEK VIEW LN
PIERROZ RD
1 TREE VIEW LN
2 GLENWOOD LN
3 SPRING VIEW LN
POPLAR LN
MIDDLETOWN RD
PANNING WY
CANAL CT
LAWSON WY
HILLTOP DR
HICKORY LN
HARVEY CT
LEE CT
DAVID CANAL
MID
COMBELLACK
RETIREMENT LN
RISING HILL RD
HANGTOWN
MORNINDALE
STORYBOOK LN
COOL WATER CREEK RD
COOL WATER CT
EMPRESS CT
BELANCA LN
NOEL CT
LOMA CIMA DR
BROOKEDGE DR
AURA JOHN WY
OLETA DR
BOULDER LN
KELLI DR
FAMILY HILL LN
COARSEGOLD RD
OAK KNOLL CT
OAK KNOLL RD
NEVADA CT
BELL TREE LN
MALLARD LN
DAVIS CT
ORCHARD HILL PARK
GREEN WING LN
PINTAIL LN
DRAKE CT
ORCHARD
DEBBIE CT
EASY ST
PLACERVILLE DR
LAWYER DR
RAY
ARMORY DR
EL DORADO COUNTY FAIRGROUNDS
MUS
LIB
SHERIFF
FAIRLANE CT
FAIR LN
FRWY
FORNI RD
CRIBBS
MAGIC PL
CHERRY LN
MIDLAND
NORDIC WY
SAGE ROSE LN
EXCALIBUR RD
GOLD NUGGET WY
DUSTY GOLD CT
WEBER CREEK
TELEMARK CT
MOSS CREEK LN
JERICHO RD
LYDIA LN
FURLONG LN
GREEN VALLEY RD
STREAMSIDE CT
WINTER CT
MARKS DR
ANGEL CT
DRIVEWAY RD
EL DORADO RD
LODE RD
KOALA LN
KOALA CT
SUNCREST DR
MISSOURI FLAT RD
KISMET LN
HELMRICK RD
LO HI WY
BRIW RIDGE CT
TWELVE OAKS LN
HEIDI HOUSE RD
BISON LN
BLUEJAY DR
BRIDGEVIEW CT
ANTHIS CT
ANTHIS DR
LONGRUT
FIELD RUN
ELIENWOOD LN
MEADOW VW
FS
HEADINGTON RD
BELLS RD
PLAZA DR
PARK & RIDE
PERKS CT
MOTHER LODE DR
WAMEGO
KIEBER WY
KEOKUK DR
HUMMINGBIRD LN
HEADY
MARINKO CT
ELLIES
ALLIE
DAWN
TONI LN
RANCHO CT
SUNDANCE CT
JEWEL WY
ROVONOC LN
SHADY LN
WHISKEY FLAT RD
SKIS RD
CATALPA CT
GYPSY
LIFE WY
MISSOURI FLAT CT
0 .125 .25 .375 .5 miles 1 in. = 1900 ft.

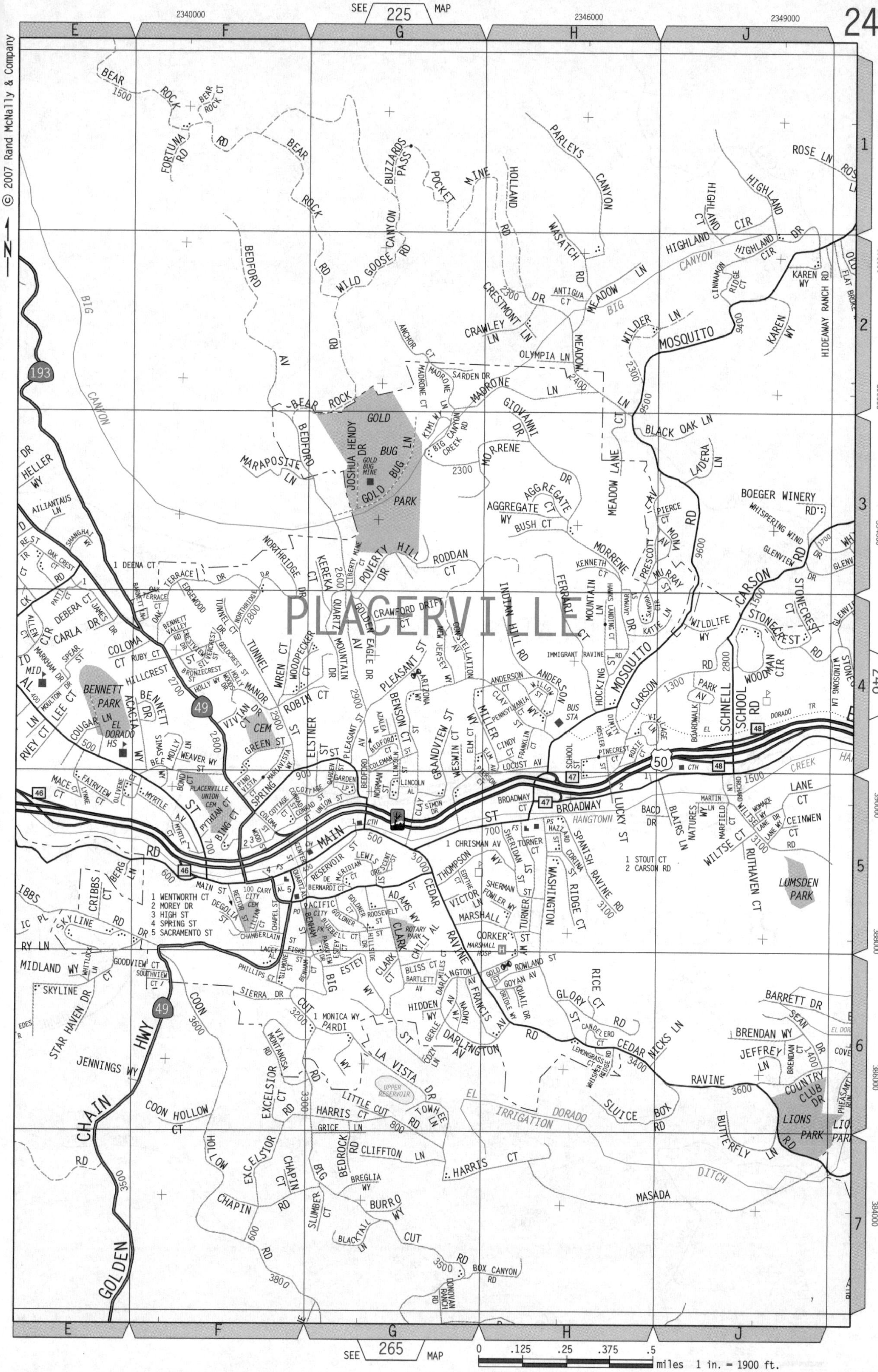
SEE 225 MAP
SEE 246 MAP
SEE 265 MAP
E
F
G
H
J
1
2
3
4
5
6
7
2340000
2346000
2349000
400000
398000
396000
394000
390000
388000
386000
384000
PLACERVILLE
BEAR ROCK RD
BEAR ROCK CT
FORTUNA RD
BUZZARDS PASS
POCKET MINE RD
HOLLAND RD
PARLEYS CANYON
WASATCH RD
HIGHLAND CT
HIGHLAND CIR
HIGHLAND DR
ROSE LN
BEDFORD AV
WILD GOOSE CANYON RD
CRESTMONT LN
CRAWLEY LN
ANTIGUA CT
MEADOW LN
BIG CANYON
WILDER LN
MOSQUITO RD
CINNAMON RIDGE CT
KAREN WY
HIDEAWAY RANCH RD
OLYMPIA LN
MADRONE LN
SARDEN DR
GIOVANNI DR
BLACK OAK LN
MEADOW LANE CT
GOLD BUG LN
GOLD BUG MINE
GOLD BUG PARK
JOSHUA HENDY DR
MARAPOSITE LN
BIG CANYON CREEK RD
MORRENE DR
AGGREGATE CT
AGGREGATE WY
BUSH CT
LADERA LN
BOEGER WINERY RD
WHISPERING WIND
GLENVIEW RD
PIERCE CT
MONA AV
PRESCOTT LN
MURRAY ST
HELLER WY
AILIANTAUS LN
SHANGHAI WY
DEENA CT
TERRACE DR
NORTHRIDGE DR
KEREKA CT
POVERTY HILL DR
RODDAN CT
QUARTZ MOUNTAIN DR
GOLDEN EAGLE DR
CRAWFORD DRIFT
INDIAN HILL RD
FERRARI CT
MOUNTAIN CT
KENNETH CT
CARSON RD
STONECREST CT
WILDLIFE WY
CARLA DR
COLOMA CT
HILLCREST ST
TUNNEL ST
WOODPECKER CT
PLEASANT ST
ARIZONA WY
CONSTELLATION
NEW JERSEY WY
ANDERSON CT
BUS STA
HOCKING ST
SCHNELL SCHOOL RD
WOODMAN CIR
BENNETT PARK
EL DORADO HS
ACACIA WY
BENNETT DR
COUGAR LN
ROBIN CT
ELSTNER ST
BENSON CT
GRANDVIEW ST
WESWIN CT
MILLER WY
VIVIAN DR
CEM
GREEN ST
WEAVER WY
FAIRVIEW CT
MYRTLE AV
PLACERVILLE UNION CEM
BING CT
PYTHIAN CT
SPRING ST
MAIN ST
BROADWAY
LUCKY ST
HANGTOWN CREEK
SPANISH RAVINE RD
BACO DR
NATURES WY
MARFIELD CT
WILTSE CT
CEINWEN CT
LANE CT
RUTHAVEN CT
LUMSDEN PARK
1 WENTWORTH CT
2 MOREY DR
3 HIGH ST
4 SPRING ST
5 SACRAMENTO ST
1 CHRISMAN AV
1 STOUT CT
2 CARSON RD
RESERVOIR ST
CEDAR RAVINE
THOMPSON WY
WASHINGTON
TURNER ST
RIDGE CT
CLARK ST
ADAMS WY
MARSHALL HOSP
CORKER ST
ROWLAND ST
CHILI AL
ESTEY WY
BIG CUT RD
SIERRA DR
SKYLINE DR
MIDLAND WY
STAR HAVEN DR
JENNINGS WY
COON HOLLOW RD
COON HOLLOW CT
CHAIN RD
GOLDEN CHAIN HWY
1 MONICA WY
PARDI ST
LA VISTA DR
DARLINGTON AV
HIDDEN WY
NAOMI AV
FRANCIS AV
GLORY ST
RICE CT
CEDAR RAVINE RD
NICKS LN
CANDLEWOOD
BARRETT DR
SEAN DR
BRENDAN WY
JEFFREY LN
COUNTRY CLUB DR
LIONS PARK
RAVINE
BUTTERFLY LN
EL DORADO IRRIGATION DITCH
SLUICE BOX RD
UPPER RESERVOIR
EXCELSIOR RD
EXCELSIOR CT
HARRIS CT
LITTLE CUT RD
TOWHEE LN
GRICE LN
BEDROCK RD
CLIFFTON LN
CHAPIN CT
CHAPIN RD
BREGLIA WY
BURRO WY
SLUMBER CT
BLACKTAIL LN
BOX CANYON RD
DONOVAN RANCH RD
MASADA
HOLLOW RD
0 .125 .25 .375 .5
miles 1 in. = 1900 ft.

SEE 226 MAP

SEE 245 MAP

SEE B MAP

0 .125 .25 .375 .5 miles 1 in. = 1900 ft.

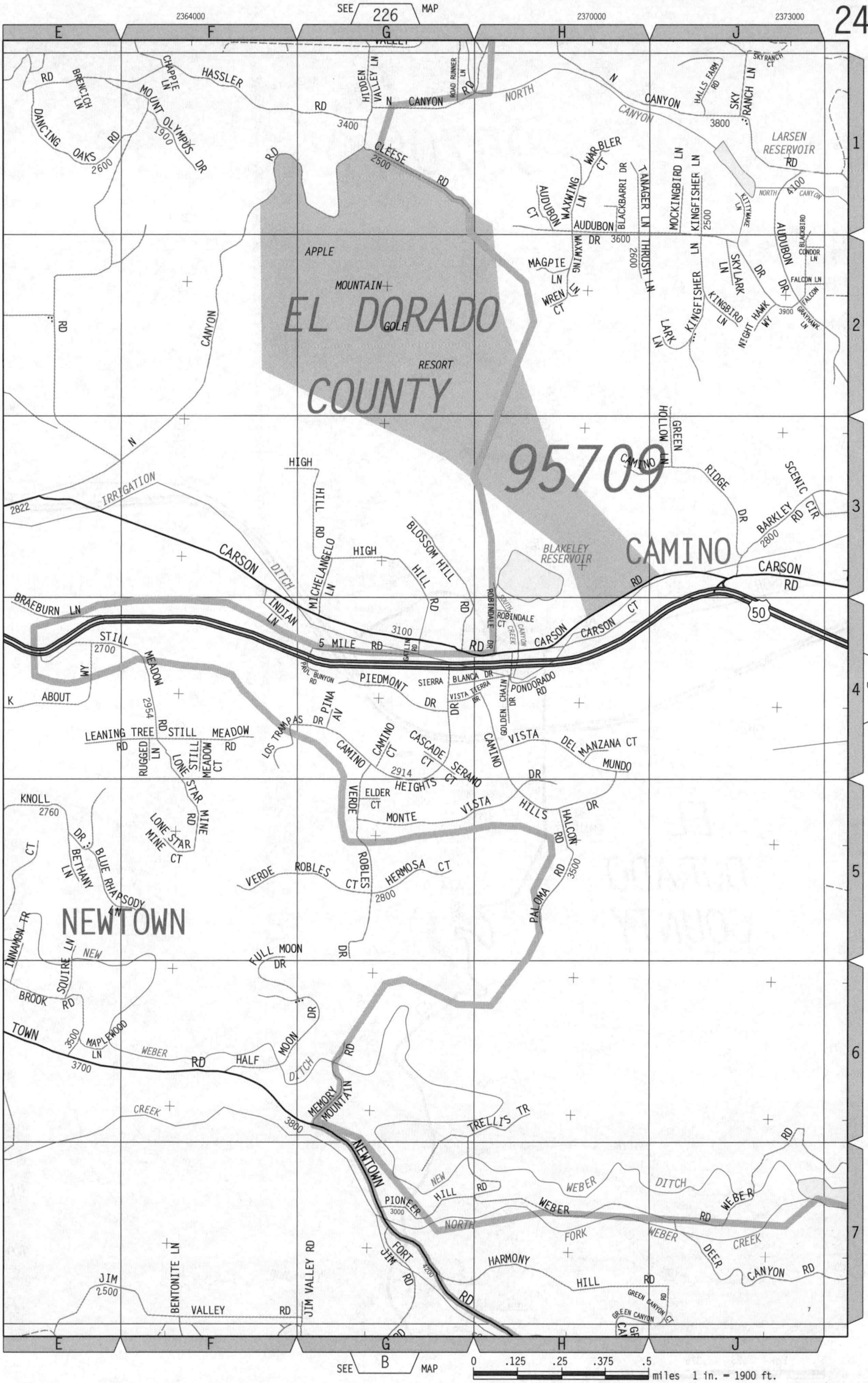
SEE 226 MAP
SEE B MAP
SEE B MAP
EL DORADO COUNTY
95709
CAMINO
NEWTOWN
APPLE MOUNTAIN GOLF RESORT
BLAKELEY RESERVOIR
LARSEN RESERVOIR
CARSON RD
5 MILE RD
50
N CANYON RD
NORTH CANYON
HASSLER RD
CHAPPIE LN
MOUNT OLYMPUS DR
DANCING OAKS RD
BRENCICH LN
HIDDEN VALLEY LN
ROAD RUNNER LN
CLEESE RD
AUDUBON DR
AUDUBON CT
WAXWING LN
WARBLER CT
BLACKBARRI DR
TANAGER LN
THRUSH LN
MOCKINGBIRD LN
KINGFISHER LN
SKY RANCH LN
SKYRANCH CT
HALLS FARM RD
KITTYHAWK LN
MAGPIE LN
WREN CT
SKYLARK LN
KINGBIRD LN
LARK LN
NIGHT HAWK WY
FALCON LN
CONDOR LN
GRAYHAWK LN
BLACKBIRD
GREEN HOLLOW LN
CAMINO RIDGE DR
SCENIC CIR
BARKLEY RD
N CANYON
IRRIGATION
CARSON DITCH
HIGH HILL RD
HIGH HILL RD
BLOSSOM HILL RD
MICHELANGELO LN
INDIAN LN
BRAEBURN LN
ROBINDALE DR
ROBINDALE CT
SOUTH CANYON CREEK
CARSON CT
GATLIN RD
STILL MEADOW RD
ABOUT
PAUL BUNYON RD
PIEDMONT DR
SIERRA BLANCA DR
VISTA TIERRA DR
GOLDEN CHAIN DR
PONDORADO RD
PINA AV
LOS TRAMPAS DR
CAMINO CT
CASCADE CT
SERANO CT
CAMINO HEIGHTS DR
VISTA DEL MUNDO
MANZANA CT
LEANING TREE RD
RUGGED LN
STILL MEADOW CT
LONE STAR MINE RD
LONE STAR MINE CT
KNOLL DR
BETHANY LN
BLUE RHAPSODY LN
VERDE ELDER CT
MONTE VISTA
HILLS DR
HALCON RD
PALOMA RD
VERDE ROBLES CT
HERMOSA CT
ROBLES DR
FULL MOON DR
HALF MOON DR
CINNAMON TR
SQUIRE LN
NEW BROOK RD
MAPLEWOOD LN
TOWN
WEBER RD
WEBER DITCH
CREEK
MEMORY MOUNTAIN RD
TRELLIS TR
NEWTOWN RD
NEW HILL RD
PIONEER
WEBER RD
WEBER DITCH
NORTH FORK WEBER CREEK
DEER CANYON RD
FORT JIM RD
HARMONY HILL RD
GREEN CANYON RD
GREEN CANYON CT
JIM VALLEY RD
BENTONITE LN
JIM VALLEY RD
0 .125 .25 .375 .5 miles 1 in. = 1900 ft.

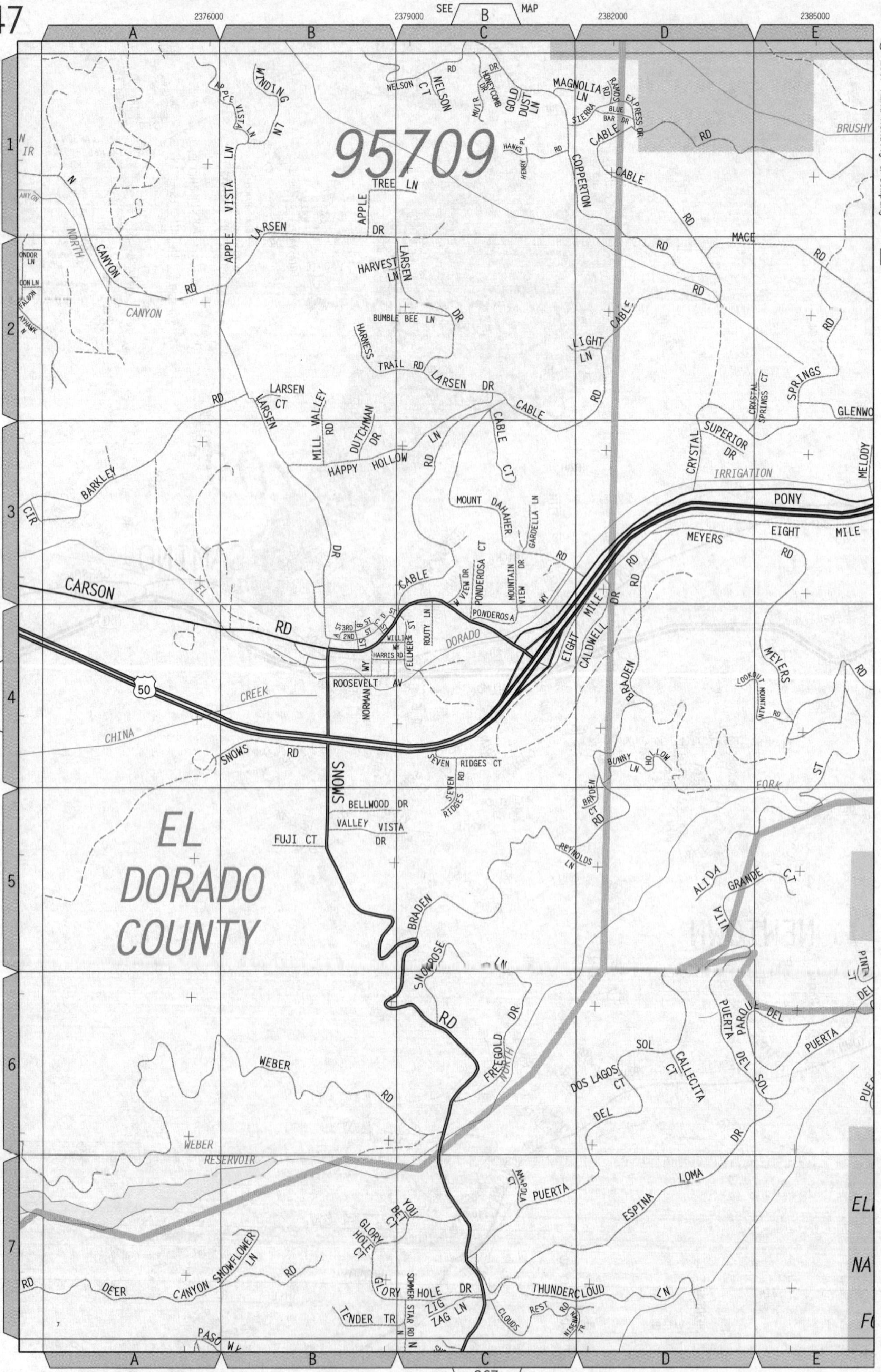
SEE B MAP
SEE 246 MAP
SEE 267 MAP
2376000
2379000
2382000
2385000
A
B
C
D
E
1
2
3
4
5
6
7
400000
398000
396000
394000
390000
388000
384000
95709
EL DORADO COUNTY
NELSON CT
RD
HONEYCOMB DR
MUIR DR
GOLD DUST LN
MAGNOLIA LN
RAMOS RD
SIERRA BLUE BAR DR
EXPRESS DR
CABLE RD
HANKS PL
HENRY RD
COPPERTON
BRUSHY
APPLE VISTA LN
WINDING LN
APPLE TREE LN
APPLE DR
LARSEN DR
NORTH CANYON RD
CANYON
HARVEST LN
LARSEN DR
MACE RD
BUMBLE BEE LN
HARNESS TRAIL RD
LIGHT LN
CABLE RD
CRYSTAL SPRINGS CT
SPRINGS
GLENWO
LARSEN CT
MILL VALLEY RD
DUTCHMAN DR
HAPPY HOLLOW RD
CABLE CT
SUPERIOR DR
CRYSTAL
IRRIGATION
MELODY
BARKLEY
CIR
MOUNT DAHAHER
GARDELLA LN
PONY
MEYERS
EIGHT MILE
CARSON RD
CABLE
PONDEROSA CT
MOUNTAIN VIEW DR
VIEW WY
PONDEROSA
3RD
2ND
A ST
B ST
C ST
D ST
WILLIAM WY
HARRIS RD
ELLMERA ST
ROUTY LN
DORADO
EL
ROOSEVELT AV
NORMAN WY
CREEK
CHINA
50
EIGHT MILE DR
CALDWELL
BRADEN RD
MEYERS
LOOKOUT MOUNTAIN RD
SNOWS RD
SEVEN RIDGES CT
SEVEN RIDGES RD
BUNNY HOLLOW LN
FORK
ST
SMONS
BELLWOOD DR
VALLEY VISTA DR
FUJI CT
BRADEN RD
REYNOLDS LN
ALIDA
GRANDE CT
VITA
NEWTOWN
BRADEN
SNOWROSE LN
RD
FREEGOLD DR
NORTH
SOL
CALLECITA CT
DOS LAGOS CT
PUERTA DEL SOL
PARQUE DEL
PUERTA
DEL
WEBER RD
WEBER RESERVOIR
DEL DR
LOMA
ESPINA
PUERTA
AMAPOLA CT
YOU BET CT
GLORY HOLE CT
CANYON SNOWFLOWER LN
RD
DEER
GLORY HOLE DR
SOMMER STAR RD N
ZIG ZAG LN
TENDER TR
PASO WY
THUNDERCLOUD LN
CLOUDS REST RD
NISENAN TR
EL
NA
FO

0 .125 .25 .375 .5 miles 1 in. = 1900 ft.

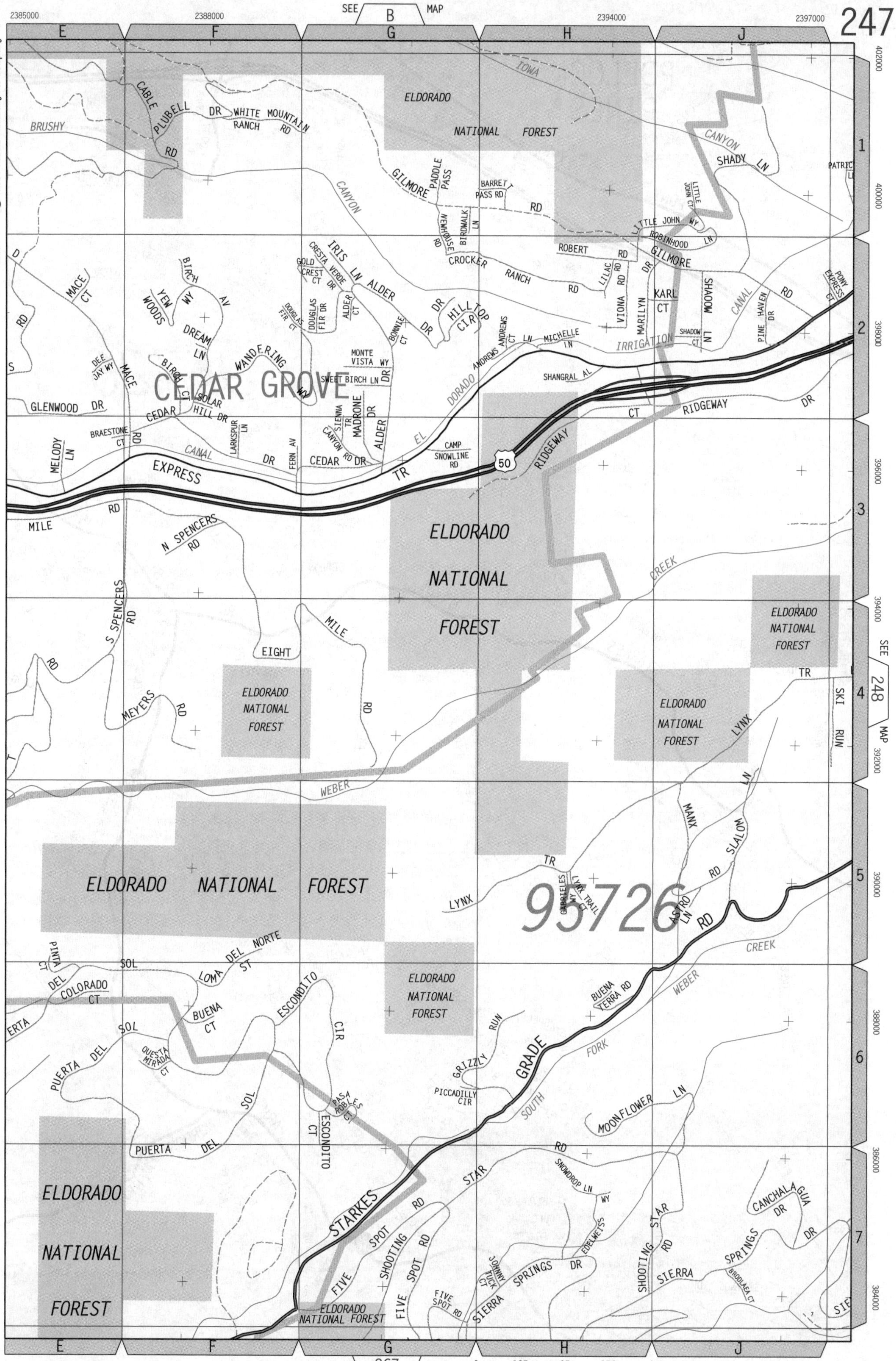
SEE B MAP
SEE 248 MAP
SEE 267 MAP
2385000
2388000
2394000
2397000
402000
400000
398000
396000
394000
392000
390000
388000
386000
384000
E
F
G
H
J
1
2
3
4
5
6
7
CEDAR GROVE
95726
ELDORADO NATIONAL FOREST
EXPRESS
MILE
RD
50
IOWA
CANYON
BRUSHY
CABLE
PLUBELL
DR
WHITE MOUNTAIN
RANCH
GILMORE
PADDLE PASS
BARRETT PASS RD
NEWHOUSE
BIRDWALK LN
LITTLE JOHN CT
LITTLE JOHN WY
ROBINHOOD LN
SHADY LN
ROBERT
CROCKER
RANCH
LILAC
VIONA
MARILYN
KARL CT
SHADOW CT
SHAOW LN
PINE HAVEN DR
PONY EXPRESS CT
CANAL
IRRIGATION
MACE CT
BIRCH
YEW WOODS
DREAM LN
WY
AV
IRIS LN
ALDER
GOLD CREST CT
CRESTA VERDE DR
DOUGLAS FIR CT
HILLTOP CIR
ANDREWS CT
ANDREWS LN
MICHELLE LN
BONNIE CT
MONTE VISTA WY
SWEET BIRCH LN
DORADO
EL
SHANGRAL AL
RIDGEWAY
DEE JAY WY
WANDERING
BIRCH CT
SOLAR
CEDAR HILL DR
GLENWOOD DR
BRAESTONE CT
MELODY LN
LARKSPUR LN
FERN AV
CEDAR
SIENNA TR
CANYON RD
MADRONE
CAMP SNOWLINE RD
TR
N SPENCERS
S SPENCERS
EIGHT
MEYERS
CREEK
WEBER
LYNX
SKI RUN
MANX
SLALOM
GABRIELES WY
LYNX TRAIL
ASTRO LN
PATRICK
PINTA CT
DEL SOL
COLORADO CT
LOMA DEL NORTE ST
ESCONDITO
CIR
BUENA CT
PUERTA DEL SOL
QUESTA MIRADA CT
PASA ROBLES CT
ESCONDITO CT
GRIZZLY RUN
PICCADILLY CIR
BUENA TERRA RD
GRADE
SOUTH
FORK
MOONFLOWER LN
STARKES
STAR
SNOWDROP LN
SHOOTING
FIVE SPOT RD
FIVE SPOT RD
JOHNNY TUCK CT
SIERRA SPRINGS DR
EDELWEISS
SHOOTING STAR RD
CANCHALAGUA DR
BRODLAEA CT
ELDORADO NATIONAL FOREST
0
.125
.25
.375
.5
miles 1 in. = 1900 ft.

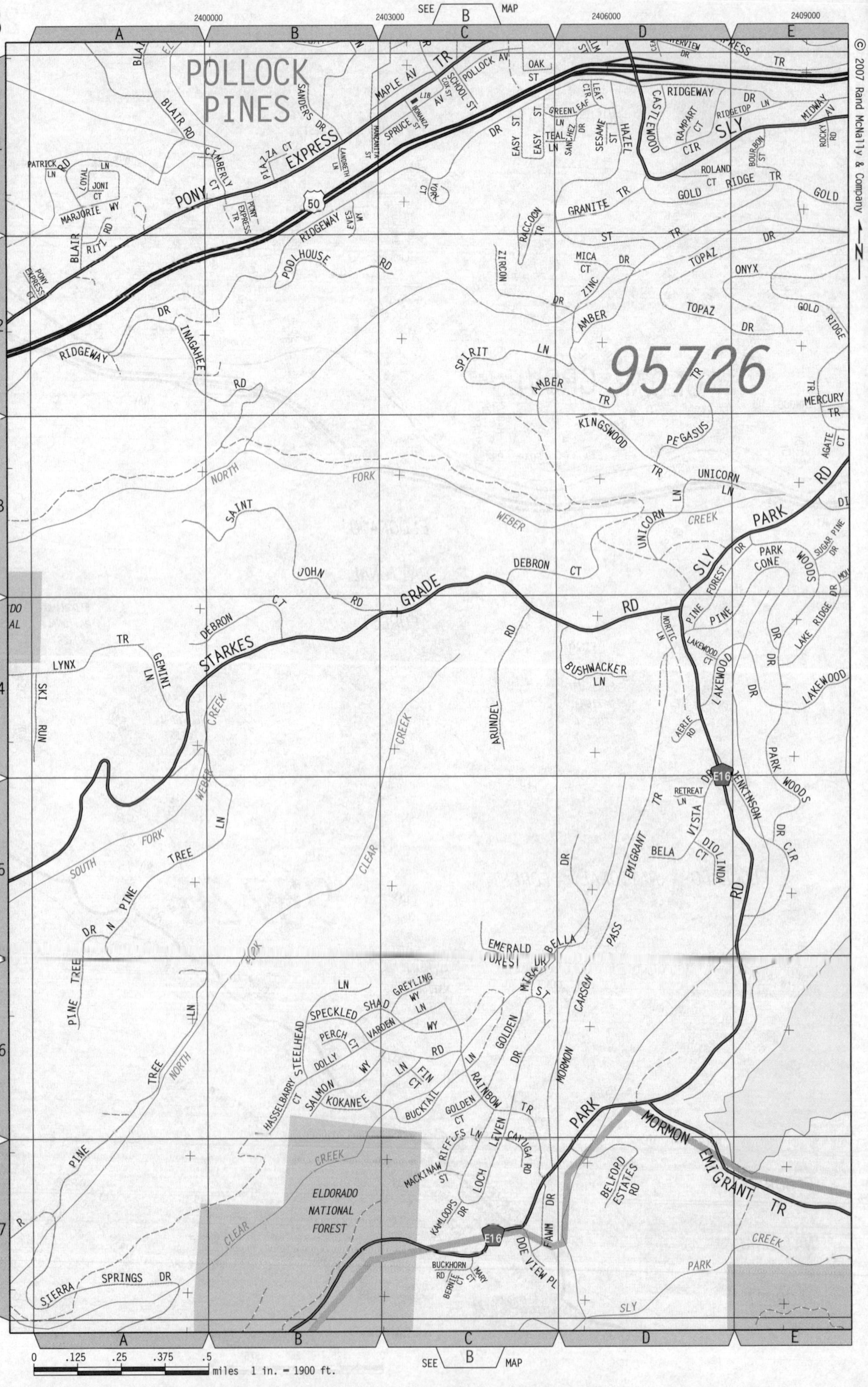
SEE B MAP
POLLOCK PINES
95726
PONY EXPRESS TR
RIDGEWAY DR
SLY PARK RD
STARKES GRADE RD
MORMON EMIGRANT TR
ELDORADO NATIONAL FOREST
SEE 247 MAP
SEE B MAP
miles 1 in. = 1900 ft.
© 2007 Rand McNally & Company

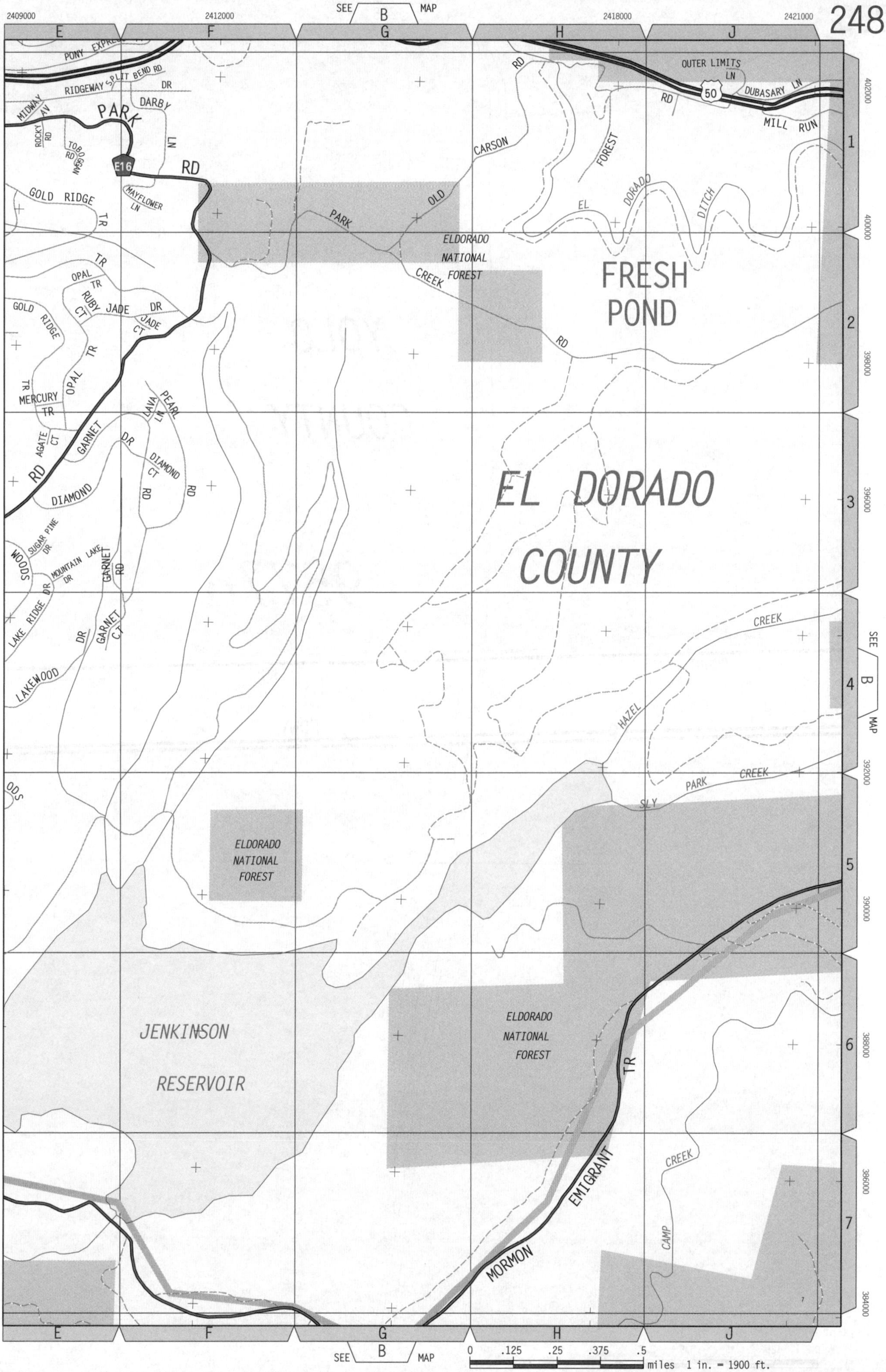
SEE B MAP
2409000
2412000
2418000
2421000
E
F
G
H
J
1
2
3
4
5
6
7
402000
400000
398000
396000
392000
390000
388000
386000
384000
PONY EXPRESS
RIDGEWAY
SPLIT BEND RD
DR
DARBY
MIDWAY AV
ROCKY RD
TOBOGGAN RD
PARK RD
E16
LN
MAYFLOWER LN
GOLD RIDGE TR
OPAL TR
RUBY CT
JADE DR
JADE CT
GOLD RIDGE
OPAL TR
MERCURY TR
AGATE CT
GARNET DR
LAVA LN
PEARL
DIAMOND CT
DIAMOND RD
RD
RD
SUGAR PINE DR
WOODS
MOUNTAIN LAKE DR
GARNET RD
LAKE RIDGE DR
GARNET CT
LAKEWOOD
OUTER LIMITS LN
50
DUBASARY LN
RD
RD
MILL RUN
CARSON
OLD
PARK
FOREST
EL DORADO DITCH
ELDORADO NATIONAL FOREST
CREEK
RD
FRESH POND
EL DORADO COUNTY
CREEK
HAZEL
SLY PARK CREEK
ELDORADO NATIONAL FOREST
JENKINSON RESERVOIR
ELDORADO NATIONAL FOREST
TR
EMIGRANT
MORMON
CREEK
CAMP
SEE B MAP
0 .125 .25 .375 .5
miles 1 in. = 1900 ft.

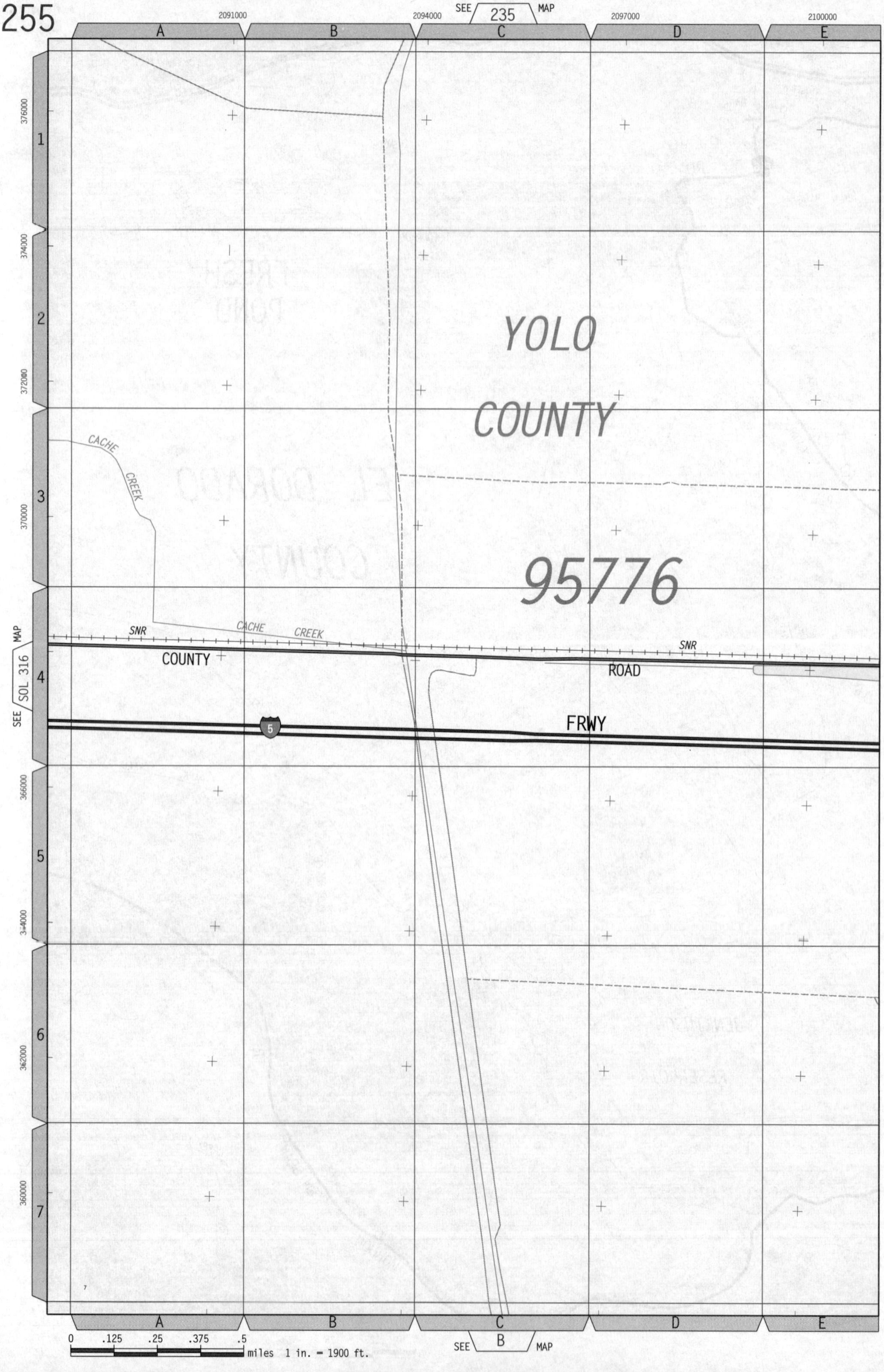
SEE 235 MAP
2091000
2094000
2097000
2100000
A
B
C
D
E
376000
374000
372000
370000
366000
362000
360000
1
2
3
4
5
6
7
YOLO
COUNTY
95776
CACHE
CREEK
SNR
CACHE
CREEK
COUNTY
ROAD
SNR
5
FRWY
SEE SOL 316 MAP
SEE B MAP
0 .125 .25 .375 .5
miles 1 in. = 1900 ft.

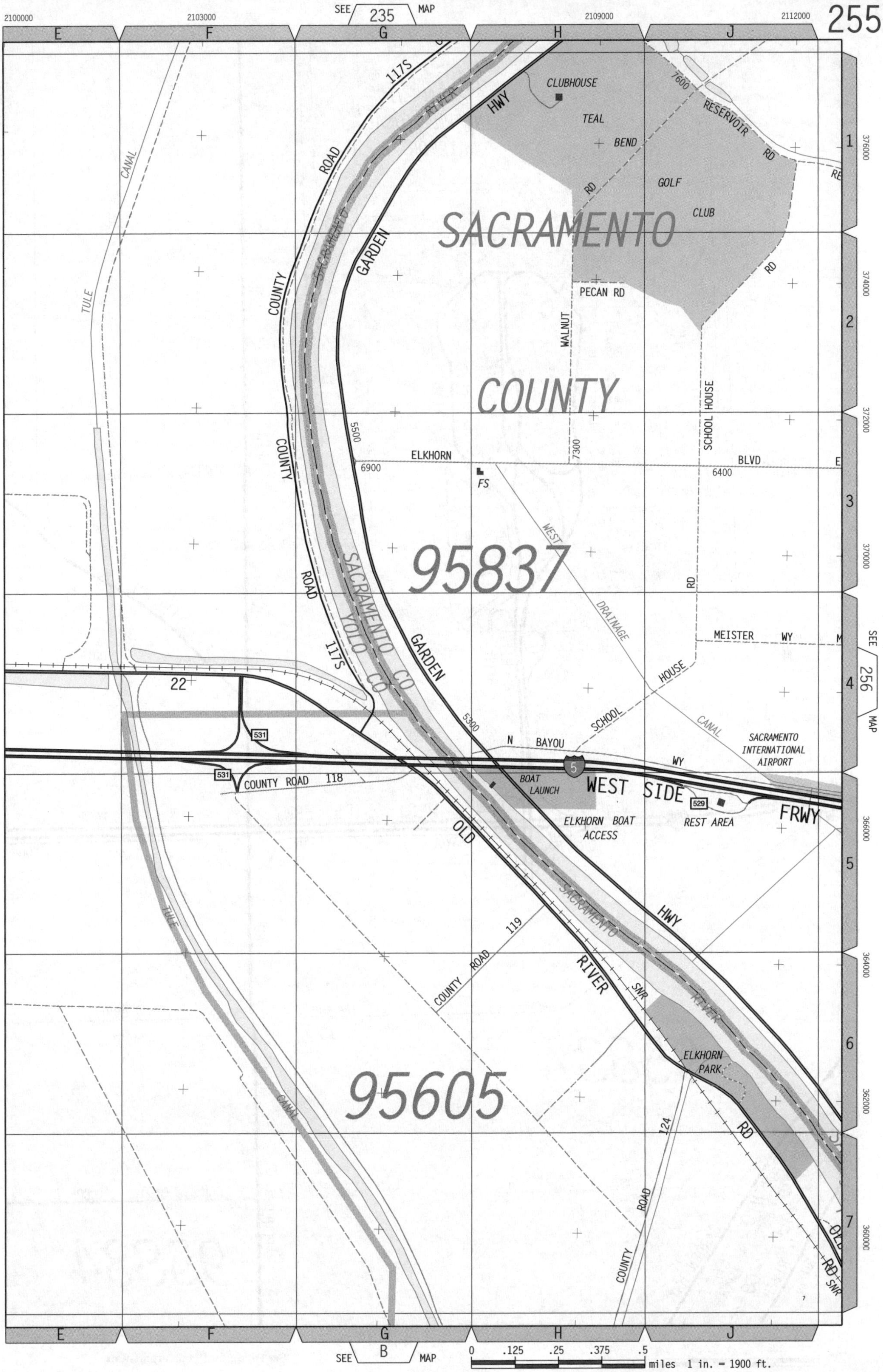
SEE 235 MAP
SEE 256 MAP
SEE B MAP
SACRAMENTO
COUNTY
95837
95605
CLUBHOUSE
TEAL BEND GOLF CLUB
7600 RESERVOIR RD
PECAN RD
WALNUT RD
7300
SCHOOL HOUSE RD
ELKHORN BLVD
6900
6400
FS
MEISTER WY
WEST DRAINAGE CANAL
SCHOOL HOUSE
N BAYOU WY
SACRAMENTO INTERNATIONAL AIRPORT
WEST SIDE FRWY
529
REST AREA
BOAT LAUNCH
ELKHORN BOAT ACCESS
5
531
22
COUNTY ROAD 118
COUNTY ROAD 117S
GARDEN HWY
5500
5300
SACRAMENTO RIVER
SACRAMENTO CO
YOLO CO
OLD RIVER RD
SNR
COUNTY ROAD 119
COUNTY ROAD 124
ELKHORN PARK
TULE CANAL
2100000
2103000
2109000
2112000
376000
374000
372000
370000
366000
364000
362000
360000
E F G H J
1 2 3 4 5 6 7
0 .125 .25 .375 .5 miles 1 in. = 1900 ft.

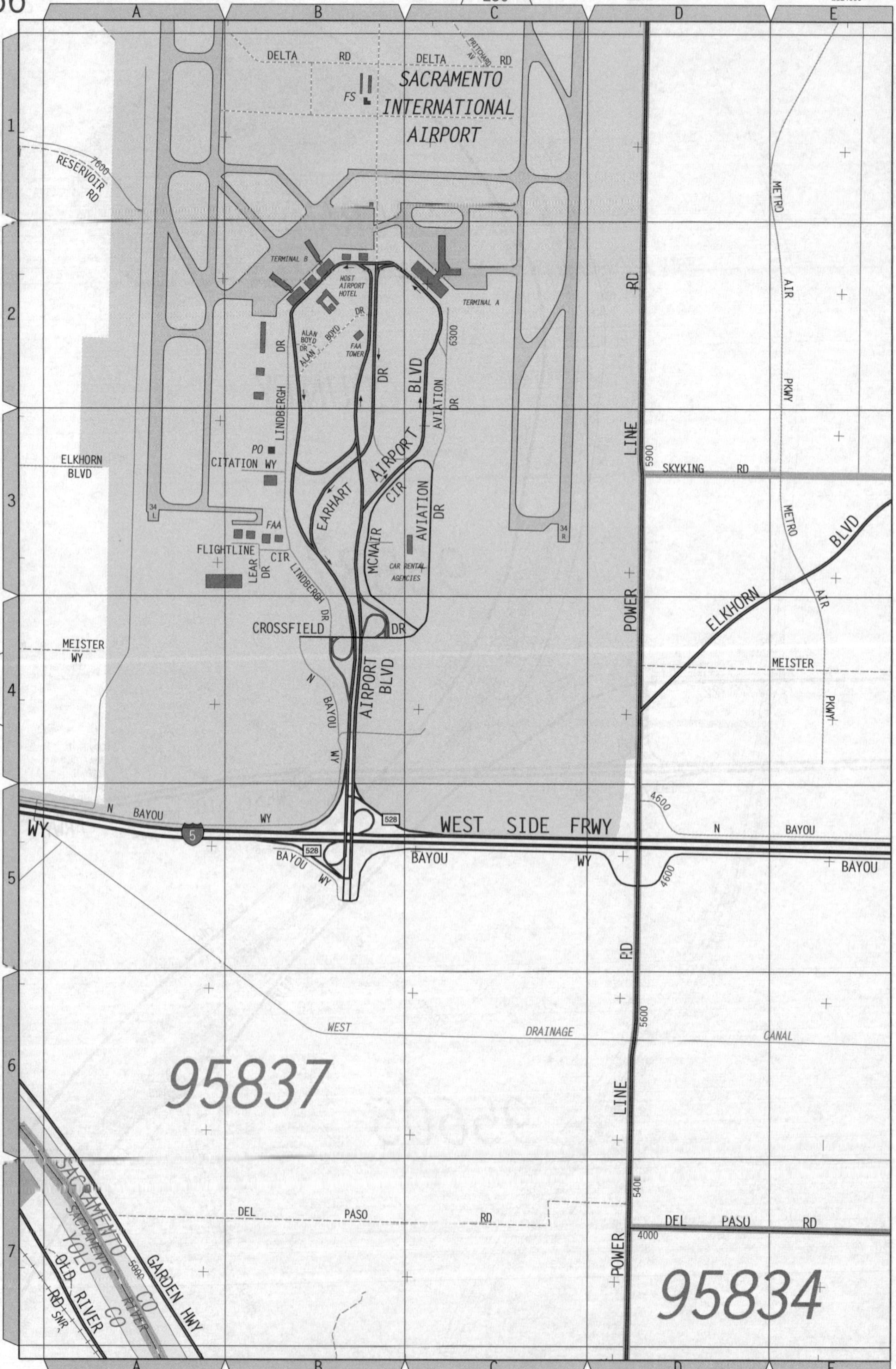
SEE 236 MAP
SACRAMENTO
INTERNATIONAL
AIRPORT
DELTA RD
DELTA RD
PRITCHARD AV
FS
RESERVOIR RD
7600
TERMINAL B
HOST AIRPORT HOTEL
ALAN BOYD DR
FAA TOWER
TERMINAL A
6300
LINDBERGH DR
AVIATION DR
AIRPORT BLVD
PO
CITATION WY
EARHART DR
AIRPORT CIR
MCNAIR
AVIATION DR
ELKHORN BLVD
FAA
FLIGHTLINE CIR
LEAR DR
LINDBERGH DR
CAR RENTAL AGENCIES
CROSSFIELD DR
MEISTER WY
SEE 255 MAP
N BAYOU WY
AIRPORT BLVD
POWER LINE RD
5900
SKYKING RD
METRO AIR PKWY
ELKHORN BLVD
MEISTER
N BAYOU WY
WEST SIDE FRWY
5
528
4600
BAYOU WY
BAYOU
WEST DRAINAGE CANAL
95837
5600
5400
DEL PASO RD
4000
95834
SACRAMENTO CO
YOLO CO
SACRAMENTO RIVER
5800
GARDEN HWY
OLD RIVER RD
SWR
A B C D E
1 2 3 4 5 6 7
2115000 2118000 2121000 2124000
376000 374000 372000 370000 366000 364000 362000 360000
0 .125 .25 .375 .5 miles 1 in. = 1900 ft.
SEE 276 MAP

See Page E for Detail Airport Map

SEE 236 MAP
2124000
2127000
2133000
2136000
E
F
G
H
J
378000
376000
374000
372000
370000
366000
364000
362000
360000
1
2
3
4
5
6
7
NORTH NATOMAS
95836
SACRAMENTO
COUNTY
95835
SACRAMENTO
EL CENTRO RD
LONE TREE RD
4200
4500
4400
ELKHORN BLVD
E14
307
99
5
306
525B
525A
PARK & RIDE
SEE A H4
1 AMAGANSETT PL
2 CRYSTAL COAST PL
3 N BEACH PL
4 HADDOCK PL
5 HALSEY PL
6 HERON CREST CT
7 STONY HILL PL
8 BEACHCOMBER PL
9 ENCLAVE PL
10 SEA HAWK PL
11 WESTHAMPTON BAY WY
12 GREAT PECONIC PL
13 SAG HARBOR PL
14 DIVINITY HILL PL
SEE B H4
1 DULCIBELLA PL
2 CREVALLE PL
3 POMPANO PL
4 BONACK PL
5 NARWAL PL
6 BELUGA PL
7 LONG WARF WY
8 HUBBARD CREEK PL
9 BELLOWS POND PL
10 PAINTED OCEAN PL
11 RUNAWAY BAY PL
WEST SIDE WY
BAYOU WY
E COMMERCE WY
COMMERCE PKWY
N PARK DR
FRWY
CLUB CENTER DR
MAYBROOK DR
MABRY DR
SANDPIPER WY
GRESHAM LN
HEBRON CIR
LANFRANCO CIR
CALLISON DR
EGRET PARK
DODSON LN
WESTLAKE CIR
SPARROW PARK
NATHAN CT
VISTA CREEK CIR
HAWKCREST CIR
VISTA COVE CIR
VERENA LN
WESTLAKE PKWY
CLUBSIDE LN
HAWKVIEW DR
WESTLAKE COMMUNITY PARK
COGNAC CIR
CANDELA CIR
WEST DRAINAGE CANAL
DEL PASO RD
4800
3100
2700
2900
MID
FISHERMANS LAKE
DUCKHORN DR
BONFAIR AV
QUAIL PARK
ADVANTAGE WY
BENEFIT WY
SPORTS PKWY
TOWN CENTER DR
NEW MARKET DR
NATOMAS REGIONAL PARK
KOKOMO PARK
KOKOMO
BROADWATER DR
QUINTER WY
HOLDREGE WY
LOGANSPORT DR
MAHASKA WY
DIORITE WY
TRAP ROCK WY
REDBUD PARK
ALLARD CT
BABCOCK WY
BANKSIDE WY
PICASSO CIR
KALAMER WY
LAWLER ST
MACON DR
HERITAGE LN
GREG THATCH CIR
LA CASA WY
CHANGO CIR
ALLAIRE CIR
LA CADENA WY
LOLET WY
VINCI WY
DA VINCI
PERAZUL
SAN MARIN
PELICAN BAY CIR
OKEEFE CT
SEE 257 MAP
SEE 276 MAP
0 .125 .25 .375 .5 miles 1 in. = 1900 ft.

SEE 237 MAP
SEE 277 MAP
SEE 256 MAP
SEE A B5
2139000
2145000
2148000
378000
376000
374000
372000
370000
366000
364000
362000
360000
A
B
C
D
E
1
2
3
4
5
6
7
95836
95835
95834
SACRAMENTO
1 MOUNT JUDAH PL
2 DEER PATH PL
3 KINGS BEACH PL
4 MOUNT PLUTO PL
5 COYOTE FORK PL
6 SERENE LAKE PL
ELKHORN BLVD
E14
MARNICE
3800
4000
ELKHORN STAGING AREA
CEMENT WY
BLACKTOP
SORENTO RD
E LEVEE RD
STEELHEAD CREEK
UP
7300
900
5800
5500
4900
BARROS
800
CAREY
KENMAR RD
EAST DRAINAGE CANAL
NATOMAS BLVD
BRIDGECROSS
REGENCY COMMUNITY PARK
REGENCY PARK CIR
CLUB CENTER DR
SYCAMORE PARK
HERON PARK
BURBERRY PARK
WILLOW PARK
AUTUMN MEADOW PARK
WHITE ALDER PARK
CALIFORNIA LILAC PARK
NORTH NATOMAS PARK NATURE CENTER
NORTH NATOMAS COMMUNITY PARK
1 JAMBOREE CT
2 ASHMEAD WY
DANBROOK DR
ARCHCREST
1 BABCOCK WY
2 ALLARD CT
NATOMAS REGIONAL PARK
N PARK DR
NORTHBOROUGH DR
FREDERICKSBURG
BANFIELD DR
N MARKET BLVD
N BEND DR
INDERKUM HS
LIB
PARK PLACE DR
COTTONWOOD PARK
NATOMAS CHARTER HS
BLACKROCK DR
DEL PASO RD
2200
1800
1400
1100
TRUXEL RD
EAST DRAINAGE PARKWAY DR
TERRACINA DR
GATEWAY
1 VAN BUREN WY
2 GRAND CANYON CT
3 ALLANO AV
SPORTS PKWY
PROFESSOR LN
NATIONAL DR
TOWN CENTER
LIBRARY ST
0 .125 .25 .375 .5
miles 1 in. = 1900 ft.

SEE 237 MAP

SEE 258 MAP

SEE 277 MAP

0 .125 .25 .375 .5 miles 1 in. = 1900 ft.

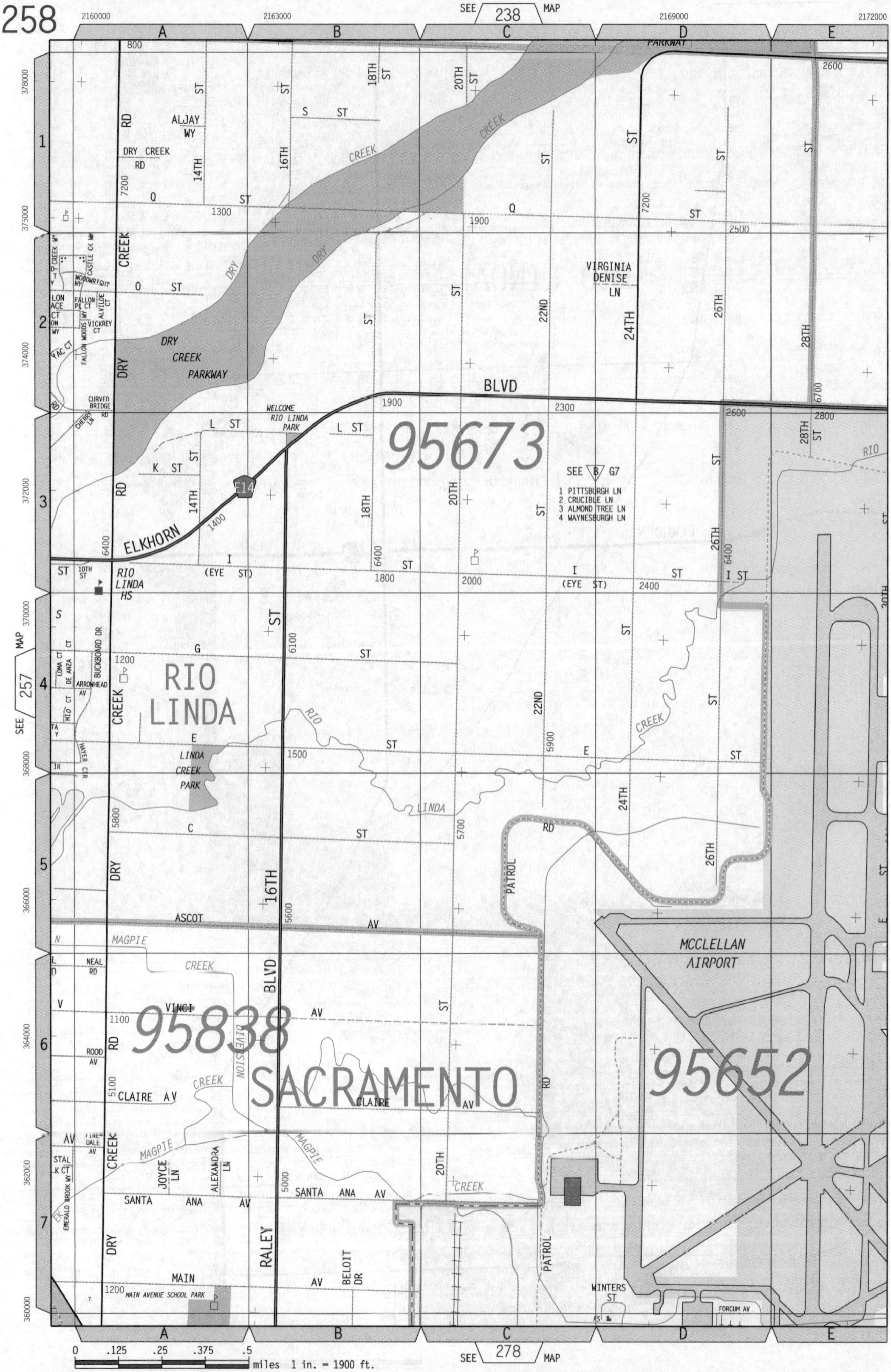
SEE 238 MAP
SEE 278 MAP
SEE 257 MAP
2160000
2163000
2169000
2172000
378000
375000
374000
372000
370000
368000
366000
364000
362000
360000
A
B
C
D
E
1
2
3
4
5
6
7
PARKWAY
800
18TH ST
20TH ST
2600
ALJAY WY
S ST
DRY CREEK RD
14TH
16TH
CREEK
7200
Q
ST
1300
1900
Q
2500
CREEK
CASTLE CK WY
WOODWRIGHT
O ST
VIRGINIA DENISE LN
DRY
LON ACE
FALLON PL CT
ALVILDE CT
VICKREY CT
FALLON WOODS WY
22ND
24TH
26TH
28TH
DRY CREEK PARKWAY
CURVED BRIDGE RD
CHERRY LN
BLVD
1900
2300
2600
2800
6700
WELCOME RIO LINDA PARK
L ST
L ST
95673
K ST
SEE B G7
1 PITTSBURGH LN
2 CRUCIBLE LN
3 ALMOND TREE LN
4 WAYNESBURGH LN
RIO
E14
ELKHORN
1400
6400
I (EYE ST)
1800
2000
I (EYE ST)
2400
I ST
10TH ST
RIO LINDA HS
LOMA CT
DE ANZA CT
BUCKBOARD DR
ARROWHEAD AV
MIO CT
1200
G ST
RIO LINDA
CREEK
E ST
LINDA CREEK PARK
1500
5900
WATER CIR
5800
C ST
LINDA
5700
PATROL RD
ASCOT AV
MAGPIE
CREEK
NEAL RD
MCCLELLAN AIRPORT
VINCI AV
1100
95838
DIVERSION
ROOD AV
5100
CLAIRE AV
SACRAMENTO
CLAIRE AV
95652
PINE DALE AV
MAGPIE
JOYCE LN
ALEXANDRA LN
5000
SANTA ANA AV
SANTA ANA AV
20TH
CREEK
EMERALD BROOK WY
RALEY BLVD
5600
6100
BELOIT DR
PATROL
MAIN AV
1200
MAIN AVENUE SCHOOL PARK
WINTERS ST
FORCUM AV
0 .125 .25 .375 .5
miles 1 in. = 1900 ft.

SEE 238 MAP

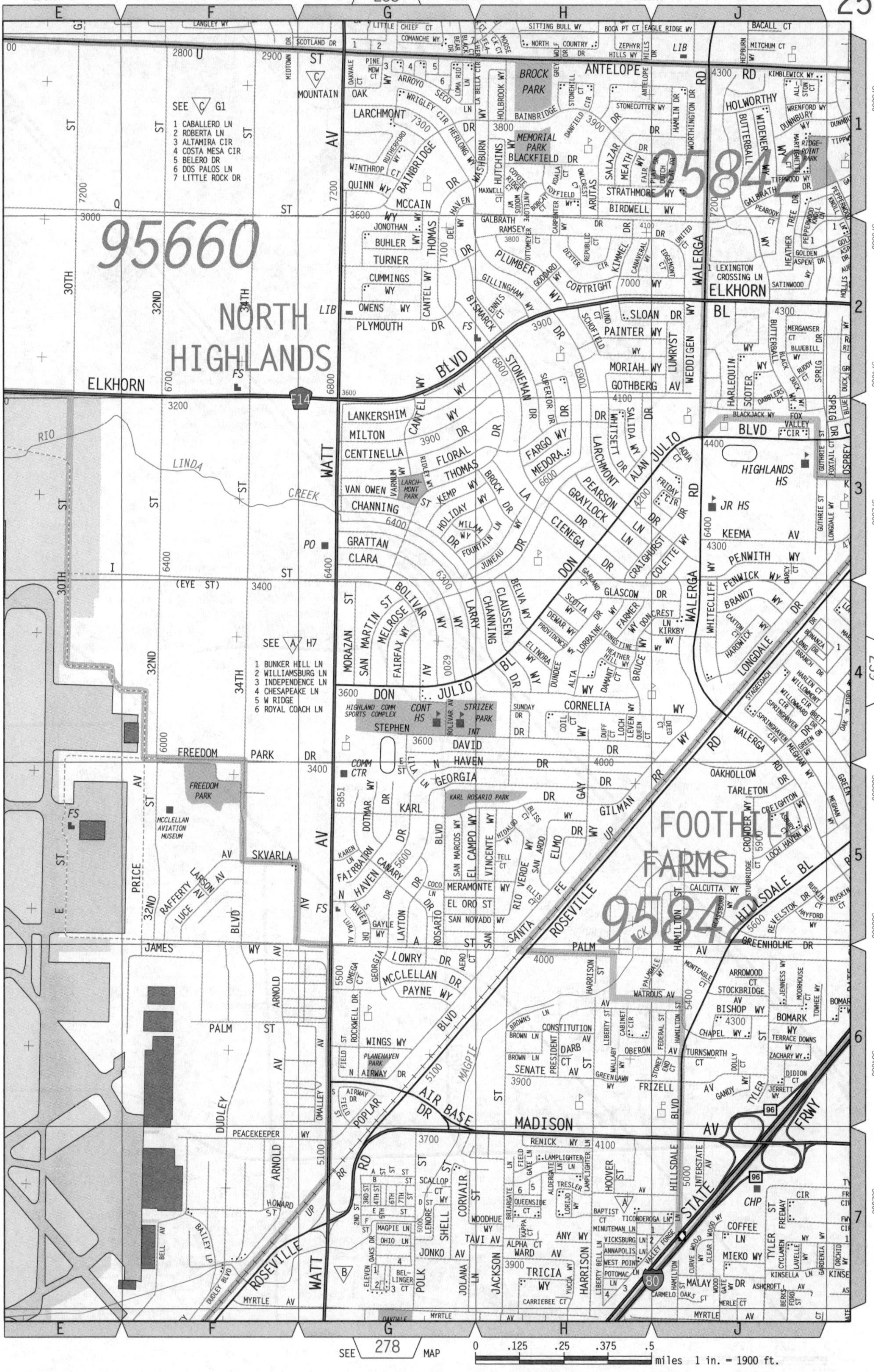
2172000
2175000
2178000
2181000
E
F
G
H
J
1
2
3
4
5
6
7
95660
NORTH
HIGHLANDS
95842
FOOTHILL
FARMS
SEE C G1
1 CABALLERO LN
2 ROBERTA LN
3 ALTAMIRA CIR
4 COSTA MESA CIR
5 BELERO DR
6 DOS PALOS LN
7 LITTLE ROCK DR
SEE A H7
1 BUNKER HILL LN
2 WILLIAMSBURG LN
3 INDEPENDENCE LN
4 CHESAPEAKE LN
5 W RIDGE
6 ROYAL COACH LN
1 LEXINGTON
CROSSING LN
BROCK PARK
MEMORIAL PARK
LARCHMONT PARK
FREEDOM PARK
MCCLELLAN AVIATION MUSEUM
KARL ROSARIO PARK
HIGHLAND COMM SPORTS COMPLEX
CONT HS
STRIZEK PARK
HIGHLANDS HS
JR HS
COMM CTR
PLANEHAVEN PARK
CHP
LIB
FS
PO
ELKHORN BLVD
WATT AV
ANTELOPE RD
WALERGA RD
DON JULIO BLVD
FREEDOM PARK DR
MADISON AV
ROSEVILLE RD
ROSEVILLE RD UP RR
AIR BASE DR
MYRTLE AV
PALM AV
SANTA FE
HILLSDALE BL
HILLSDALE BLVD
INTERSTATE AV
STATE
FRWY
MOUNTAIN
30TH ST
32ND ST
34TH ST
I ST
(EYE ST)
E ST
U ST
Q ST
JAMES WY
PALM ST
DUDLEY BLVD
PEACEKEEPER WY
ARNOLD AV
SKVARLA AV
PRICE AV
DAVID DR
HAVEN DR
GEORGIA DR
CORNELIA WY
LONGDALE DR
OAKHOLLOW
GREENHOLME DR
STOCKBRIDGE AV
BISHOP WY
BOMARK WY
COFFEE LN
MIEKO WY
TYLER
TRICIA WY
JONKO AV
JACKSON ST
HARRISON ST
96
80
E14
1 in. = 1900 ft.
miles
0
.125
.25
.375
.5

SEE 259 MAP

SEE 278 MAP

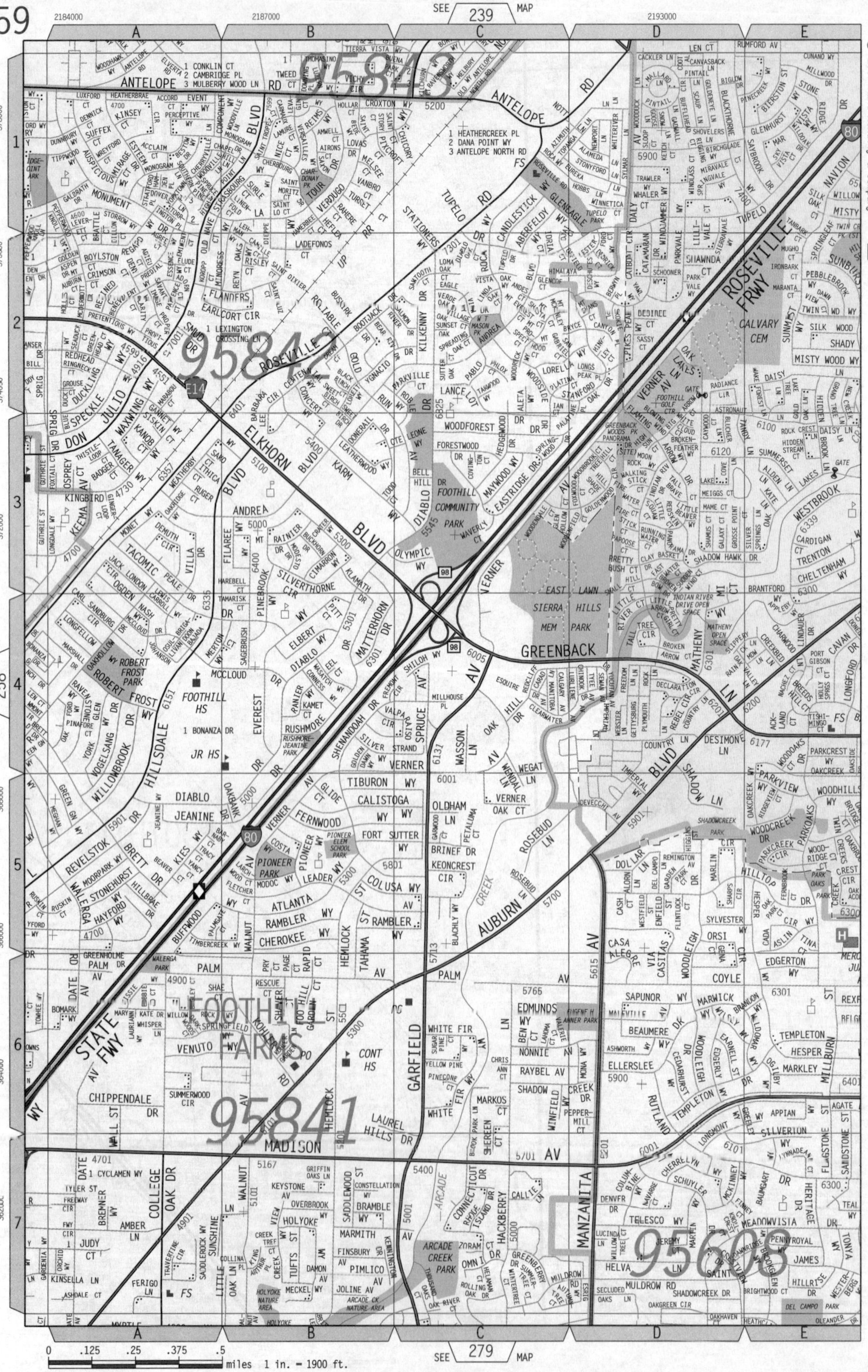
SEE 239 MAP
SEE 258 MAP
SEE 279 MAP
A
B
C
D
E
1
2
3
4
5
6
7
2184000
2187000
2193000
378000
376000
374000
372000
368000
366000
364000
362000
95843
95842
95841
95608
ANTELOPE RD
ANTELOPE NORTH RD
1 CONKLIN CT
2 CAMBRIDGE PL
3 MULBERRY WOOD LN
1 HEATHERCREEK PL
2 DANA POINT WY
3 ANTELOPE NORTH RD
1 LEXINGTON CROSSING LN
1 BONANZA DR
1 CYCLAMEN WY
ROSEVILLE RD
TUPELO DR
ROSEVILLE FRWY
STATE FWY
ELKHORN BLVD
WATT AV
DON JULIO BLVD
HILLSDALE BLVD
GREENBACK LN
AUBURN BLVD
MADISON AV
GARFIELD AV
MANZANITA AV
DIABLO DR
SHADOW LN
CALVARY CEM
FOOTHILL COMMUNITY PARK
EAST LAWN SIERRA HILLS MEM PARK
ROBERT FROST PARK
FOOTHILL HS
JR HS
CONT HS
FOOTHILL FARMS
PIONEER PARK
ARCADE CREEK PARK
HOLYOKE NATURE AREA
ARCADE CK NATURE AREA
DEL CAMPO PARK
SHADOWCREEK PARK
RUSHMORE-JEANINE PARK
WALERGA PARK
TUPELO PARK
GREENBACK WOODS PK PANORAMA (SITE)
FOOTHILL GOLF CTR
MATHENY OPEN SPACE
INDIAN RIVER DRIVE OPEN SPACE
0 .125 .25 .375 .5 miles 1 in. = 1900 ft.

SEE 239 MAP
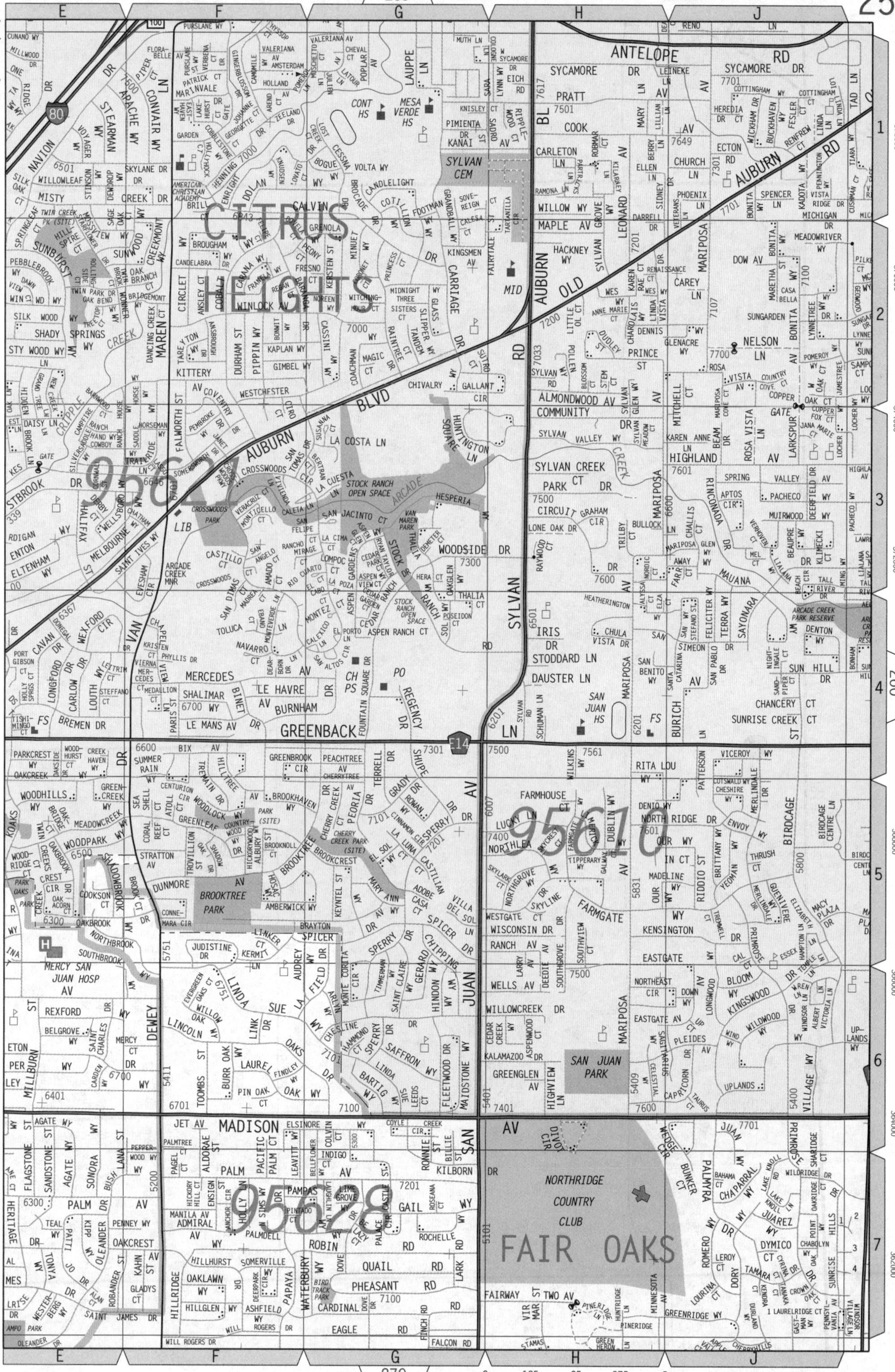

SEE 279 MAP
0 .125 .25 .375 .5 miles 1 in. = 1900 ft.

SEE 240 MAP

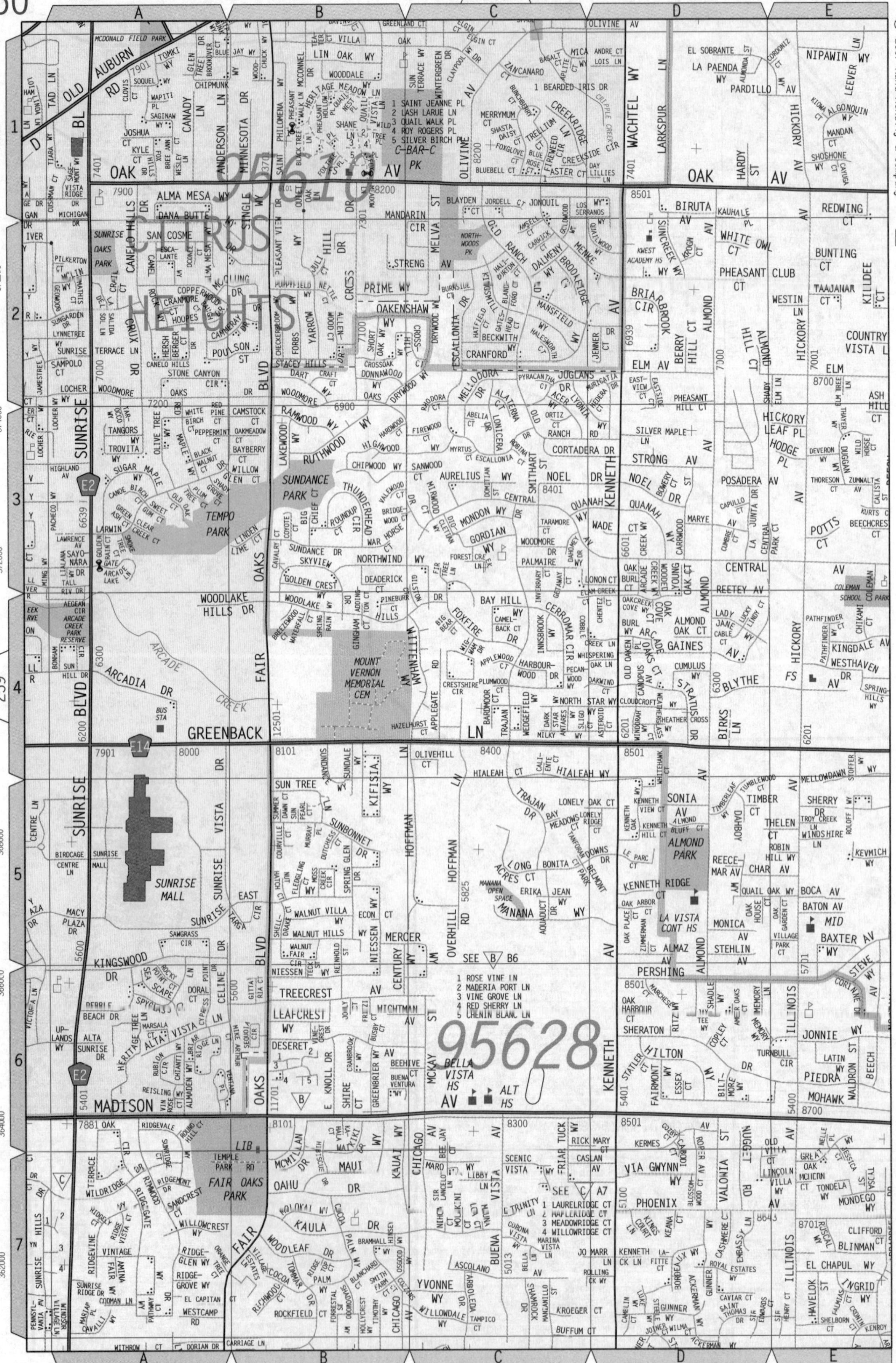

SEE 259 MAP

SEE 280 MAP

0 .125 .25 .375 .5 miles 1 in. = 1900 ft.

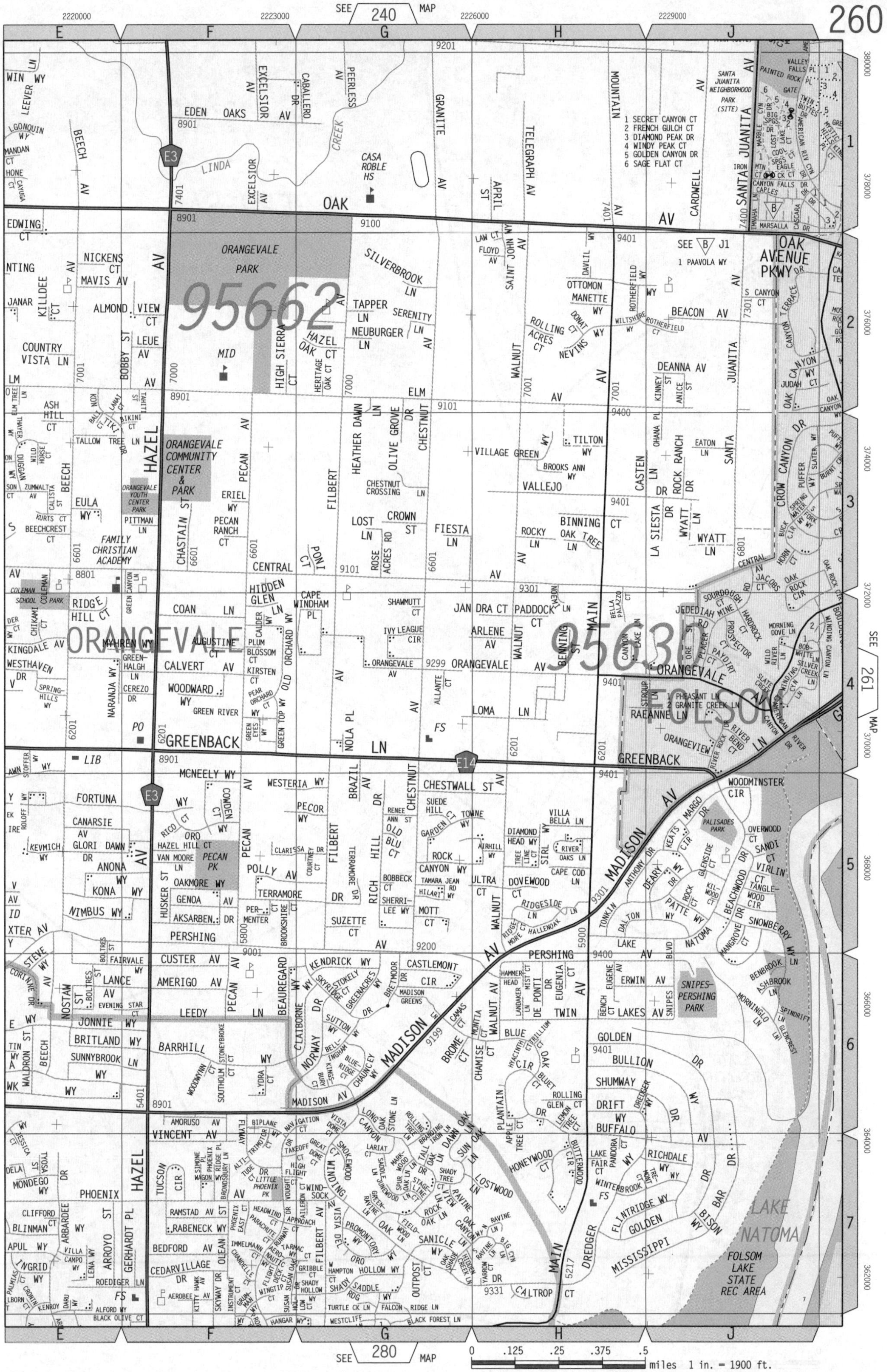
SEE 240 MAP
SEE 261 MAP
SEE 280 MAP
E
F
G
H
J
1
2
3
4
5
6
7
2220000
2223000
2226000
2229000
38000
37800
37600
37400
37200
37000
36800
36600
36400
36200
95662
95630
ORANGEVALE
FOLSOM
OAK AV
GREENBACK LN
MADISON AV
HAZEL AV
MAIN AV
SANTA JUANITA AV
CENTRAL AV
ORANGEVALE AV
ELM AV
PERSHING AV
WALNUT AV
FILBERT AV
CHESTNUT AV
PECAN AV
GRANITE AV
TELEGRAPH AV
MOUNTAIN AV
EDEN OAKS AV
LINDA CREEK
CASA ROBLE HS
ORANGEVALE PARK
ORANGEVALE COMMUNITY CENTER & PARK
ORANGEVALE YOUTH CENTER PARK
FAMILY CHRISTIAN ACADEMY
COLEMAN SCHOOL PARK
SANTA JUANITA NEIGHBORHOOD PARK (SITE)
PALISADES PARK
SNIPES-PERSHING PARK
PECAN PK
MID
PO
LIB
FS
E3
E14
OAK AVENUE PKWY
LAKE NATOMA
FOLSOM LAKE STATE REC AREA
1 SECRET CANYON CT
2 FRENCH GULCH CT
3 DIAMOND PEAK DR
4 WINDY PEAK CT
5 GOLDEN CANYON DR
6 SAGE FLAT CT
SEE B J1
1 PAAVOLA WY
1 PHEASANT LN
2 GRANITE CREEK LN
0 .125 .25 .375 .5
miles 1 in. = 1900 ft.

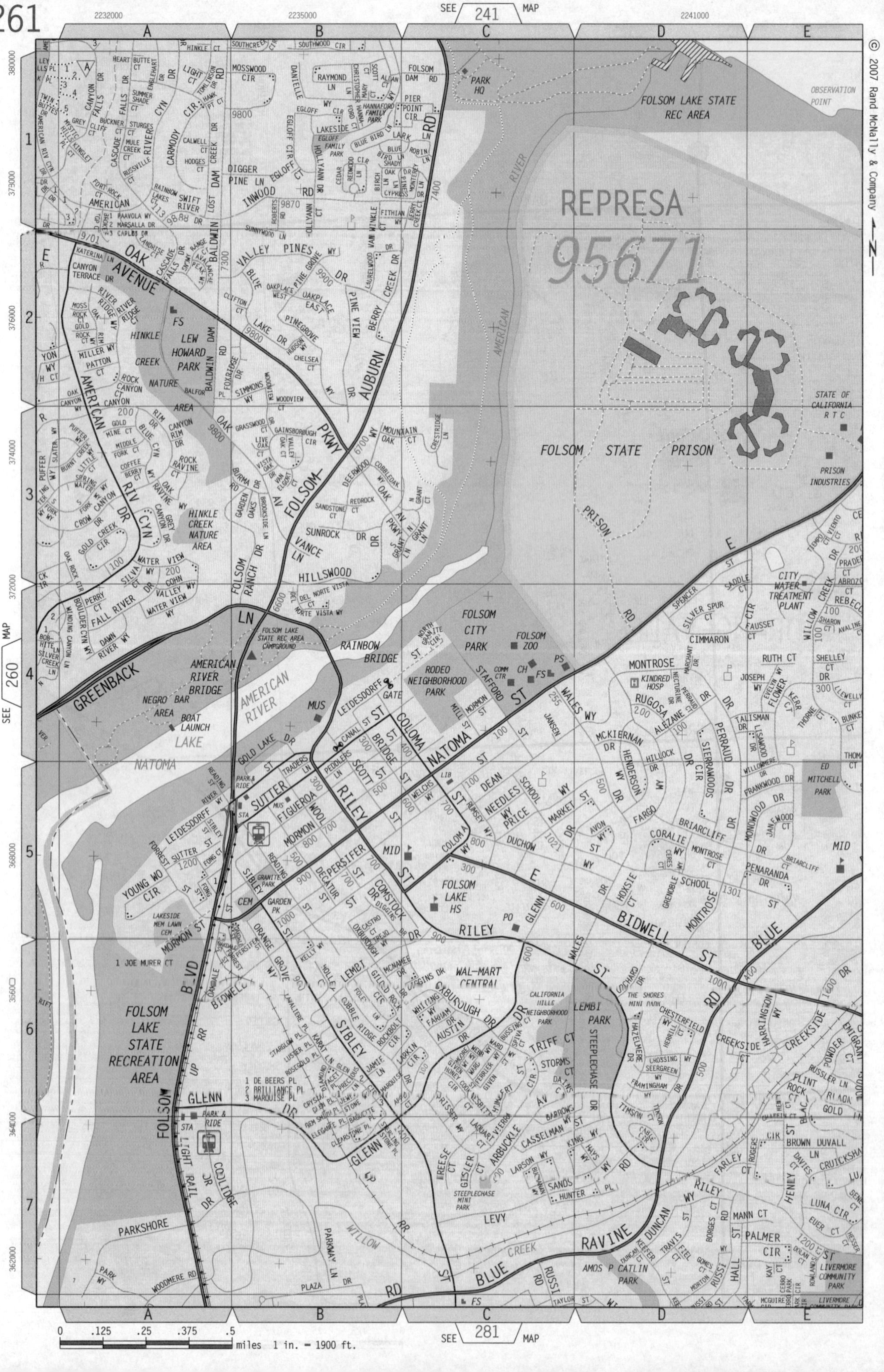
SEE 241 MAP
SEE 281 MAP
SEE 260 MAP
A
B
C
D
E
1
2
3
4
5
6
7
2232000
2235000
2241000
380000
378000
376000
374000
372000
370000
368000
366000
364000
362000
REPRESA
95671
FOLSOM LAKE STATE REC AREA
OBSERVATION POINT
PARK HQ
FOLSOM STATE PRISON
STATE OF CALIFORNIA R T C
PRISON INDUSTRIES
AMERICAN RIVER
FOLSOM CITY PARK
FOLSOM ZOO
RODEO NEIGHBORHOOD PARK
RAINBOW BRIDGE
AMERICAN RIVER BRIDGE
FOLSOM LAKE STATE REC AREA CAMPGROUND
NEGRO BAR AREA
BOAT LAUNCH
LAKE NATOMA
LEW HOWARD PARK
HINKLE CREEK NATURE AREA
EGLOFF FAMILY PARK
HANNAFORD FAMILY PARK
OAK AVENUE
FOLSOM-AUBURN RD
AUBURN PKWY
GREENBACK LN
NATOMA ST
SUTTER ST
RILEY ST
BIDWELL ST
E BIDWELL ST
BLUE RAVINE RD
GLENN DR
FOLSOM BLVD
FOLSOM LAKE HS
WAL-MART CENTRAL
CALIFORNIA HILLS NEIGHBORHOOD PARK
LEMBI PARK
THE SHORES MINI PARK
STEEPLECHASE MINI PARK
ED MITCHELL PARK
CITY WATER TREATMENT PLANT
KINDRED HOSP
FOLSOM LAKE STATE RECREATION AREA
AMOS P CATLIN PARK
LIVERMORE COMMUNITY PARK
PARK & RIDE
LIGHT RAIL
PARKSHORE
1 DE BEERS PL
2 BRILLIANCE PL
3 MARQUISE PL
1 JOE MURER CT
0 .125 .25 .375 .5 miles 1 in. = 1900 ft.

SEE 241 MAP

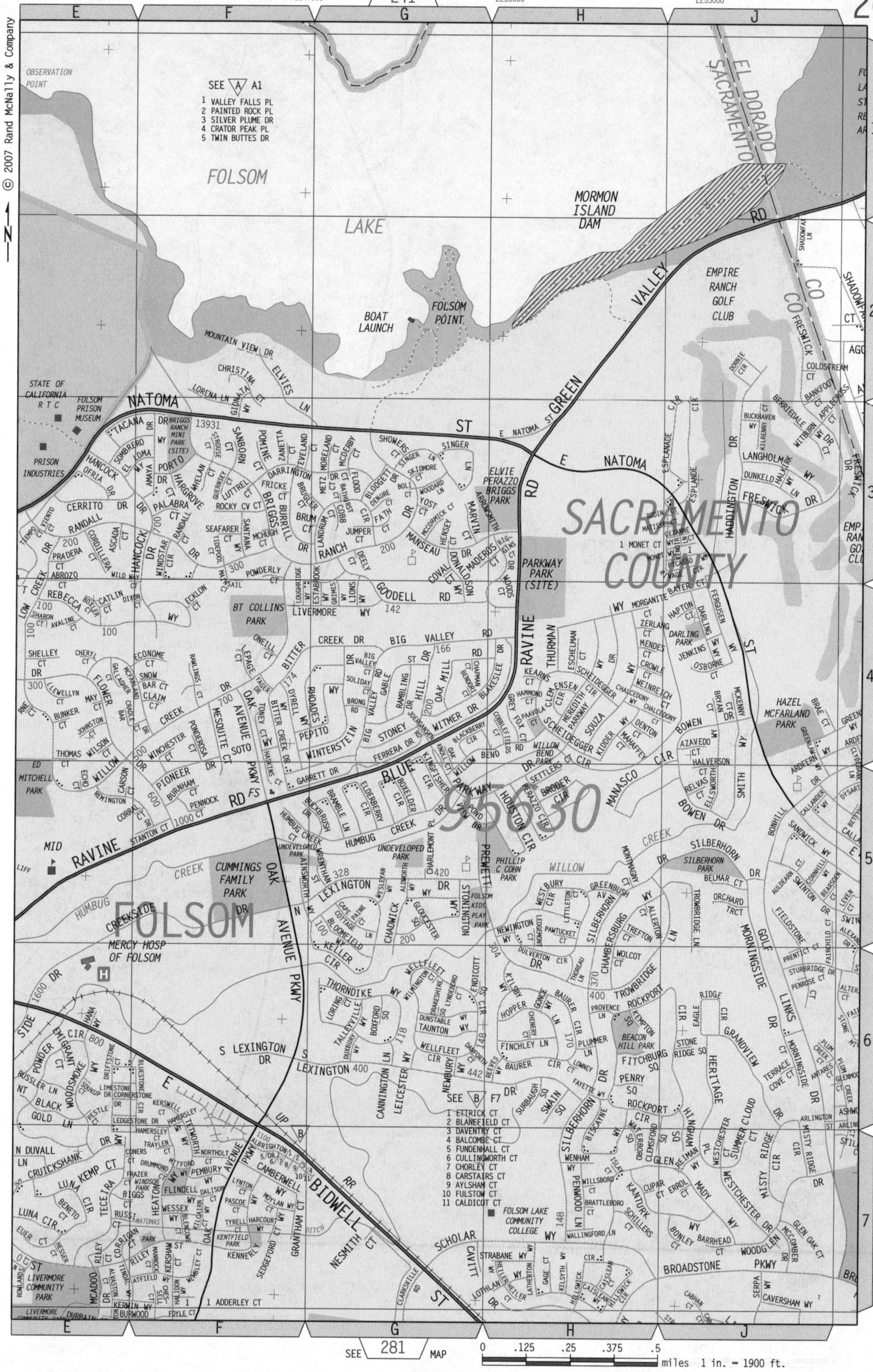

SEE 262 MAP

SEE 281 MAP

0 .125 .25 .375 .5 miles 1 in. = 1900 ft.

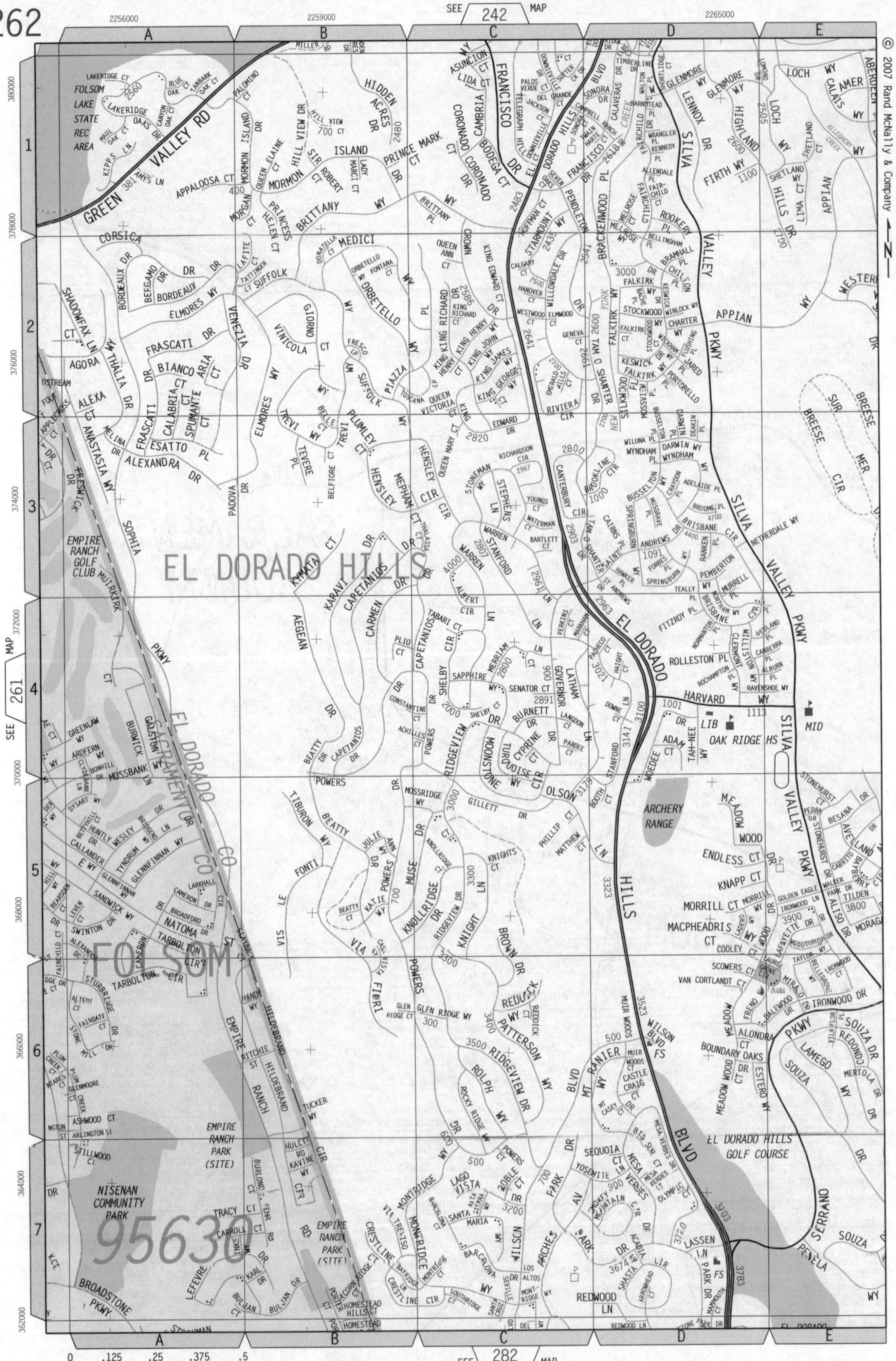
SEE 242 MAP
2256000
2259000
2265000
A
B
C
D
E
1
2
3
4
5
6
7
380000
378000
376000
374000
372000
370000
368000
366000
364000
362000
FOLSOM LAKE STATE REC AREA
LAKERIDGE CT
LAKERIDGE OAKS
BLUE OAK CT
TANBARK OAK CT
CANYON OAK DR
MAUI OAK CT
KIPPS LN
AMYS LN
GREEN VALLEY RD
MILLER RD
PALOMINO
HIDDEN ACRES DR
HILL VIEW DR
MORMON ISLAND DR
MORMON HILL VIEW DR
QUEEN ELAINE CT
SIR ROBERT CT
LADY MARCI CT
PRINCE MARK CT
APPALOOSA CT
MORGAN CT
PRINCESS HELEN CT
BRITTANY WY
BRITTANY PL
CORSICA
BORDEAUX DR
BERGAMO DR
ELMORES WY
LAFITE CT
TATTINGER CT
SUFFOLK
MEDICI
DONATELLA CT
ORBETELLO DR
FONTANA CT
SHADOWFAX LN
AGORA CT
THALIA DR
FRASCATI DR
BIANCO CT
ARIA CT
VENEZIA DR
VINICOLA CT
GIORNO
FRESCO LP
PIAZZA
TOSCANA LP
ALEXA CT
CALABRIA CT
SPUMANTE CT
ESATTO PL
ANASTASIA WY
ALEXANDRA DR
MELINA
SOPHIA
PADOVA DR
TREVI
TEVERE PL
BELFIORE CT
PLUMLEY CT
HENSLEY CIR
MEPHAM CT
QUEEN MARY CT
QUEEN VICTORIA
KING RICHARD
KING HENRY
KING JOHN
KING JAMES
KING GEORGE
KING EDWARD CT
QUEEN ANN CT
CROWN
ASUNCION
LIDA CT
CORONADO
CAMBRIA CT
BODEGA CT
FRANCISCO DR
EL DORADO HILLS BLVD
TELEGRAPH HILL
PALOS VERDE CT
JACKSON
DEL GRANDE
SONOMA
SONORA DR
CALAVERAS DR
CAMPBELL RANCH CT
FAIRCHILD
WALTON
BARNSTEAD
TIMBERLINE
WRANGLER PL
KENNEDY
ALLENDALE PL
SILVA VALLEY PKWY
GLENMORE WY
LENNOX DR
HIGHLAND
FIRTH WY
LOCH WY
LOCH HILLS DR
CALAIS WY
AMER
ABERDEEN
SHETLAND WY
LIMA CT
APPIAN WY
ALLEGHENY CREEK
HOFFMAN CT
STARMOUNT
PENDLETON
BRACKENWOOD PL
MELROSE
ROOKERY PL
BELLINGHAM
BRAMHALL
CHILLON
FALKIRK
BACHE
KESWICK
WINLOCK WY
STOCKWOOD
CHARTER
CALGARY CT
HANOVER CT
WILLOWDALE DR
WESTWOOD CT
ELMWOOD CT
GENEVA CT
TAM O SHANTER DR
EMERALD HILLS
RIVIERA CIR
NEW YORK CREEK
WICKHAM
FLUSHING
JARED
PORTORELLO
MOSSVIEW
EDWARD DR
BUSSELTON
DARWIN
DEAKIN
WILUNA PL
WYNDHAM
SUR
BREESE
MER CIR
RICHARDSON CIR
STONEMAN WY
STEPHENS LN
YOUNGS CT
WATERMAN
CANTERBURY
BROOKLINE CIR
SPRINGBURN
MUSGRAVE
CRAYDON
ADELAIDE PL
BROOME PL
BRISBANE CT
NETHERDALE WY
WARREN
STANFORD
BARTLETT CT
CAIRNS PL
SAINT ANDREWS
ANDREWS DR
FORBES
RANKEN
PEMBERTON
MURRELL
SPRINGBURN
HAWKER
EL DORADO HILLS
KYMATA CT
KARAVI
CAPETANIOS DR
AEGEAN
CARMEN
ALBERT CIR
TABARI CT
PLIO CT
PERKINS
MARKHAM
PACHECO
TEALLY
FITZROY PL
NORMANTON
WILLISTON
HEDLAND
CLERMONT
ROLLESTON PL
ROCHAMPTON PL
CANBERRA
ALBURN
RAVENSHOE WY
HARVARD WY
LIB
OAK RIDGE HS
MID
MERRIAM CT
SAPPHIRE
SHELBY CIR
SENATOR CT
LATHAM
GOVERNOR
HAIGHT CT
CONSTANTINE
ACHILLES
POWERS
RIDGEVIEW DR
BURNETT
LANGDON LN
PARDEE CT
DOWNE CT
MOONSTONE
TURQUOISE CIR
CYPRINE
ADAM CT
TAH-NEE WY
WOEDEE
BEATTY DR
TIBURON WY
MOSSRIDGE WY
GILLETT DR
OLSON
BOOTH CT
PHILLIP CT
MATTHEW CT
KNIGHTS CT
ARCHERY RANGE
MEADOW WOOD
ENDLESS CT
KNAPP CT
MORRILL CT
MACPHEADRIS CT
COOLEY
SCOWERS CT
VAN CORTLANDT CT
STONEHURST DR
BESANA
AVELLANO
TILDEN
ALISO DR
MORAGA
GOLDEN EAGLE
IRONWOOD LN
IRONWOOD DR
TAYLOR
LAUREL GROVE CIR
FONTI
VIS LE
JULIE ANN DR
POWERS
KATIE WY
MUSE
KNOLLRIDGE DR
KNIGHT LN
BROWN DR
VIA FIORI
CASA VISTA CT
REDDICK
PATTERSON WY
GLEN RIDGE WY
MUIR WOODS
WILSON BLVD
FS
MT RANIER DR
CASTLE CRAIG
ROLPH
RIDGEVIEW DR
ROCKY RIDGE DR
SEQUOIA CT
YOSEMITE
MESA VERDES
BIG SUR CT
OLYMPIC CT
ALONDRA CT
BOUNDARY OAKS
ESTERO WY
SOUZA DR
REDONDO
LAMEGO
MERTOLA
EL DORADO HILLS GOLF COURSE
SERRANO PKWY
PENELA
MONTRIDGE DR
LAGO VISTA
SANTA MARIA
ROBLE CT
ARCHES
CRESTLINE CIR
BAYRIDGE
SOUTHRIDGE
SANTA CRUZ
LOS ALTOS
SMOKEY MOUNTAIN CIR
ACADIA
LASSEN LN
SHASTA CIR
ARROWHEAD CT
REDWOOD LN
PARK DR
MAMMOTH
STONE PARK DR
EL DORADO
EMPIRE RANCH GOLF CLUB
MUIRKIRK
EMPIRE RANCH PKWY
SACRAMENTO CO
EL DORADO CO
GREENLAW WY
ARDFERN
BURWICK
GALSTON
MOSSBANK
DYSART WY
HUNTLY
WESLEY
TYNDRUM
GLENNFINNAN WY
CALLANDER
SANDWICK WY
CAMERON
BROADFORD
NATOMA ST
TARBOLTON CIR
FOLSOM
STURBRIDGE
FAIRGATE
STONE MILL DR
HANDY WY
HILDEBRAND
EMPIRE RANCH RD
RITCHIE ST
TUCKER WY
ASHWOOD CT
ARLINGTON ST
STILLWOOD
EMPIRE RANCH PARK (SITE)
HULETT RD
KAVINE WY
NISENAN COMMUNITY PARK
95630
TRACY CT
CARROLL CT
LEFEVRE
KARL DR
BULJAN DR
PORTER
HOMESTEAD HILLS CT
BROADSTONE PKWY
SEE 261 MAP
SEE 282 MAP
0 .125 .25 .375 .5 miles 1 in. = 1900 ft.
© 2007 Rand McNally & Company
N

SEE 242 MAP

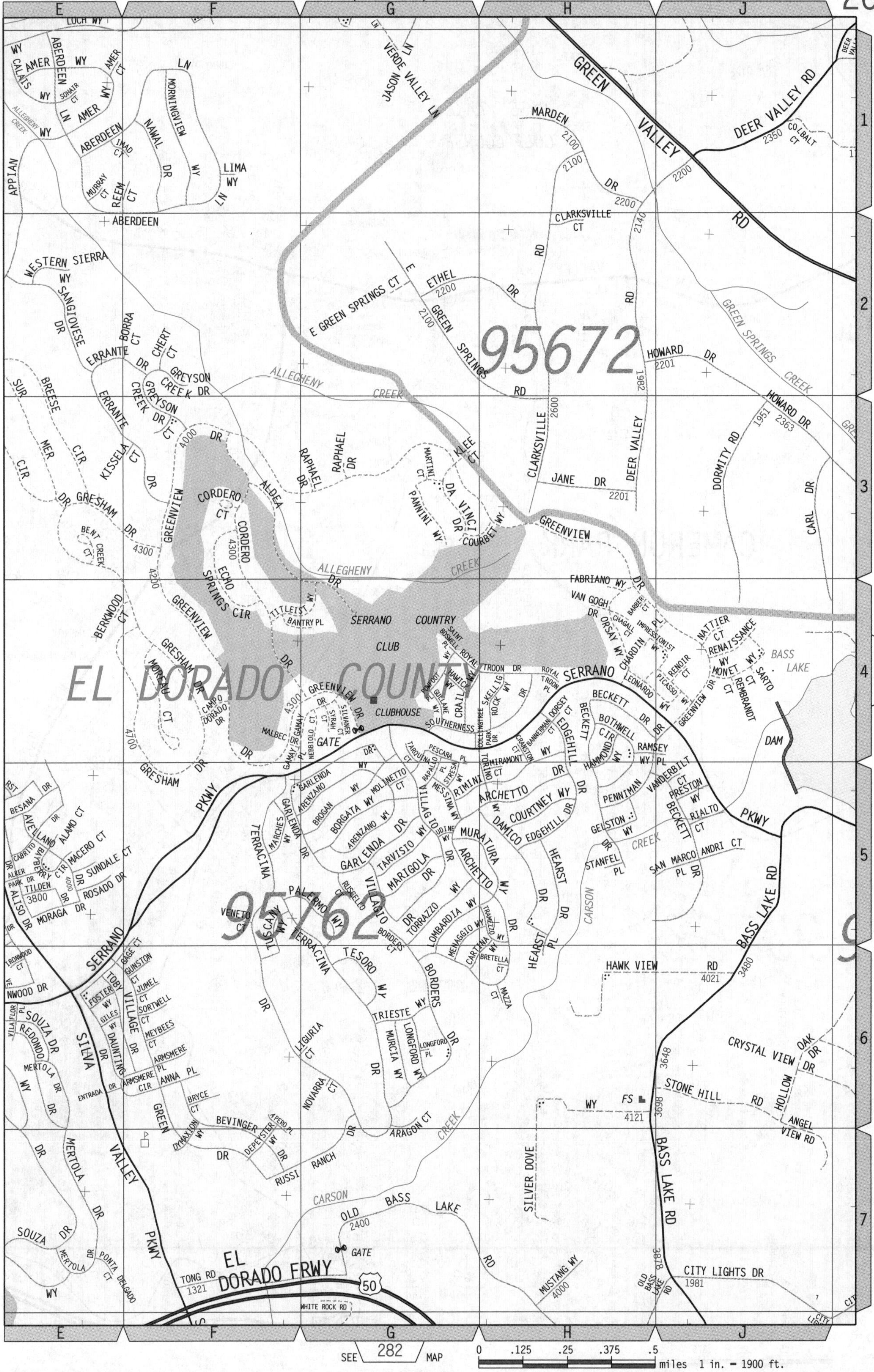
2268000
2271000
2274000
2277000
E
F
G
H
J
1
2
3
4
5
6
7
380000
378000
376000
374000
372000
370000
368000
366000
364000
95672
95762
EL DORADO COUNTY
SERRANO COUNTRY CLUB
CLUBHOUSE
GREEN VALLEY RD
DEER VALLEY RD
COLBALT CT
MARDEN DR
CLARKSVILLE CT
CLARKSVILLE RD
DEER VALLEY RD
E GREEN SPRINGS CT
ETHEL DR
GREEN SPRINGS RD
HOWARD DR
DORMITY RD
CARL DR
JANE DR
GREEN SPRINGS CREEK
ALLEGHENY CREEK
CARSON CREEK
BASS LAKE
DAM
VERDE VALLEY LN
JASON VALLEY LN
LOCH WY
AMER WY
ABERDEEN LN
CALAIS WY
SOHAIR CT
MORNINGVIEW WY
NAWAL DR
LIMA WY
IMAD CT
MURRAY CT
REEM CT
APPIAN WY
ABERDEEN
WESTERN SIERRA WY
SANGIOVESE DR
ERRANTE DR
BORRA CT
CHERT CT
GREYSON CREEK DR
BREESE CIR
SUR MER CIR
KISSELA CT
GRESHAM DR
BENT CREEK CT
GREENVIEW DR
CORDERO CT
ECHO SPRINGS CIR
ALDEA DR
RAPHAEL DR
MARTINI CT
PANNINI WY
DA VINCI DR
KLEE CT
COURBET WY
ALLEGHENY DR
TITLEIST WY
BANTRY PL
BERKWOOD CT
MOREAU CT
CAMPO DORADO CT
MALBEC DR
GAMAY PL
NEBBIOLO CT
SYRAH CT
SILVANER CT
GATE
SAINT BOSWELL PL
ROYAL TROON DR
HAMICK CT
CRAIL WY
SKELLIG ROCK WY
SOUTHERNESS
FABRIANO WY
VAN GOGH DR
ORSAY WY
CHAGALL CT
BARBERI CT
IMPRESSIONIST
CHARDIN PL
RENOIR CT
PICASSO CT
LEONARDO WY
NATTIER CT
RENAISSANCE WY
MONET CT
SARTO CT
REMBRANDT CT
SERRANO PKWY
BECKETT DR
DORSEY CT
EDGEHILL DR
BOTHWELL CIR
HAMMOND CT
RAMSEY WY
VANDERBILT PL
PRESTON CT
RIALTO CT
PENNIMAN WY
GELSTON CT
STANFEL PL
SAN MARCO PL
ANDRI CT
TARQUINI PL
PESCARA PL
RAPALLO CT
STRESA CT
TORINO DR
MIRAMONT CT
RIMINI WY
ARCHETTO DR
COURTNEY WY
DAMICO DR
MESSINA WY
VILLAGIO DR
GARLENDA DR
ARENZANO CT
BROGAN WY
BORGATA WY
MOLINETTO CT
TARVISIO WY
UDINE WY
MURATURA WY
MARIGOLA DR
RUSSELLO
TERRACINA DR
MARCHES WY
PALERMO WY
VENETO CT
ISCANY WY
TORRAZZO WY
LOMBARDIA WY
MENAGGIO WY
TRAMEZZO WY
CARTINA WY
BRETELLA CT
MAZIA CT
HEARST DR
HEARST PL
BORDERS DR
TESORO WY
TRIESTE WY
LIGURIA CT
MURCIA WY
LONGFORD WY
LONGFORD PL
NOVARRA CT
ARAGON CT
RUSSI RANCH DR
BEVINGER DR
DEPEYSTER WY
APERO PL
DYMAXION WY
BRYCE CT
HAWK VIEW RD
CRYSTAL VIEW DR
OAK HOLLOW DR
STONE HILL RD
ANGEL VIEW RD
FS
SILVER DOVE WY
BASS LAKE RD
OLD BASS LAKE RD
MUSTANG WY
CITY LIGHTS DR
GATE
EL DORADO FRWY
50
TONG RD
WHITE ROCK RD
SILVA VALLEY PKWY
BESANA DR
AVELLANO DR
ALAMO CT
CABRITO
BAYBERRY CIR
MACERO CT
SUNDALE CT
ALKER
PARK DR
TILDEN
ROSADO DR
ALISO DR
MORAGA DR
IRONWOOD CT
FOSTER WY
TOBY CT
BAGE CT
GUNSTON CT
JUMEL CT
SORTWELL CT
GILES WY
VILLAGE DR
MEYBEES CT
DAUNTING DR
ARMSMERE PL
ARMSMERE CIR
ANNA PL
ENTRADA DR
GREEN VALLEY
SOUZA DR
REDONDO DR
MERTOLA DR
PONTA DELGADO CT
1 in. = 1900 ft.
0 .125 .25 .375 .5 miles

SEE 263 MAP
SEE 282 MAP

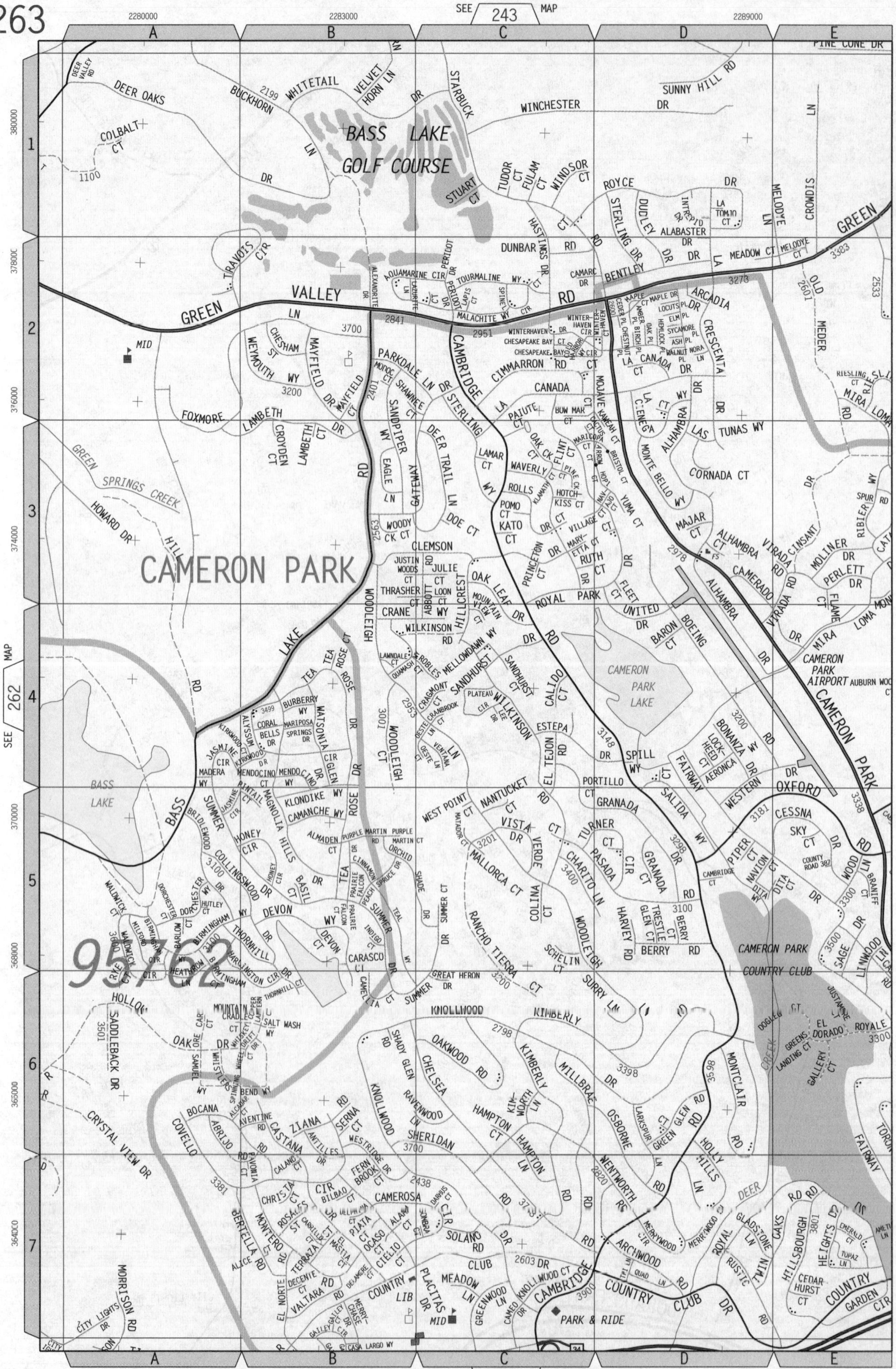
SEE 243 MAP
SEE 262 MAP
SEE 283 MAP
2280000
2283000
2289000
380000
378000
376000
374000
370000
368000
365000
364000
A
B
C
D
E
1
2
3
4
5
6
7
BASS LAKE GOLF COURSE
CAMERON PARK
95762
GREEN VALLEY RD
CAMBRIDGE RD
CAMERON PARK DR
BASS LAKE RD
COUNTRY CLUB DR
GREEN SPRINGS CREEK
BASS LAKE
CAMERON PARK LAKE
CAMERON PARK AIRPORT
CAMERON PARK COUNTRY CLUB
DEER CREEK
MID
LIB
FS
PARK & RIDE
DEER OAKS
BUCKHORN
WHITETAIL
VELVET HORN LN
STARBUCK
WINCHESTER
SUNNY HILL RD
ROYCE
DUNBAR RD
CIMMARRON RD
CANADA
PARKDALE LN
STERLING
DEER TRAIL LN
WOODLEIGH
KIMBERLY
KNOLLWOOD
OAKWOOD RD
HAMPTON
SHERIDAN
WENTWORTH
OSBORNE
MONTCLAIR
HOLLY HILLS
OXFORD
CESSNA
WESTERN
FAIRWAY
ALHAMBRA
MIRA LOMA
SADDLEBACK DR
CRYSTAL VIEW DR
MORRISON RD
CITY LIGHTS DR
COVELLO
BERTELLA DR
SOLANO RD
CAMEROSA
ARCHWOOD
TWIN OAKS
ROYAL PARK DR
UNITED DR
BOEING
PORTILLO
GRANADA
TURNER
MALLORCA CT
RANCHO TIERRA
DEVON
COLLINGSWOOD
SUMMER
HOLLOW
OAK DR
CAMELLIA

0 .125 .25 .375 .5 miles 1 in. = 1900 ft.

SEE 243 MAP

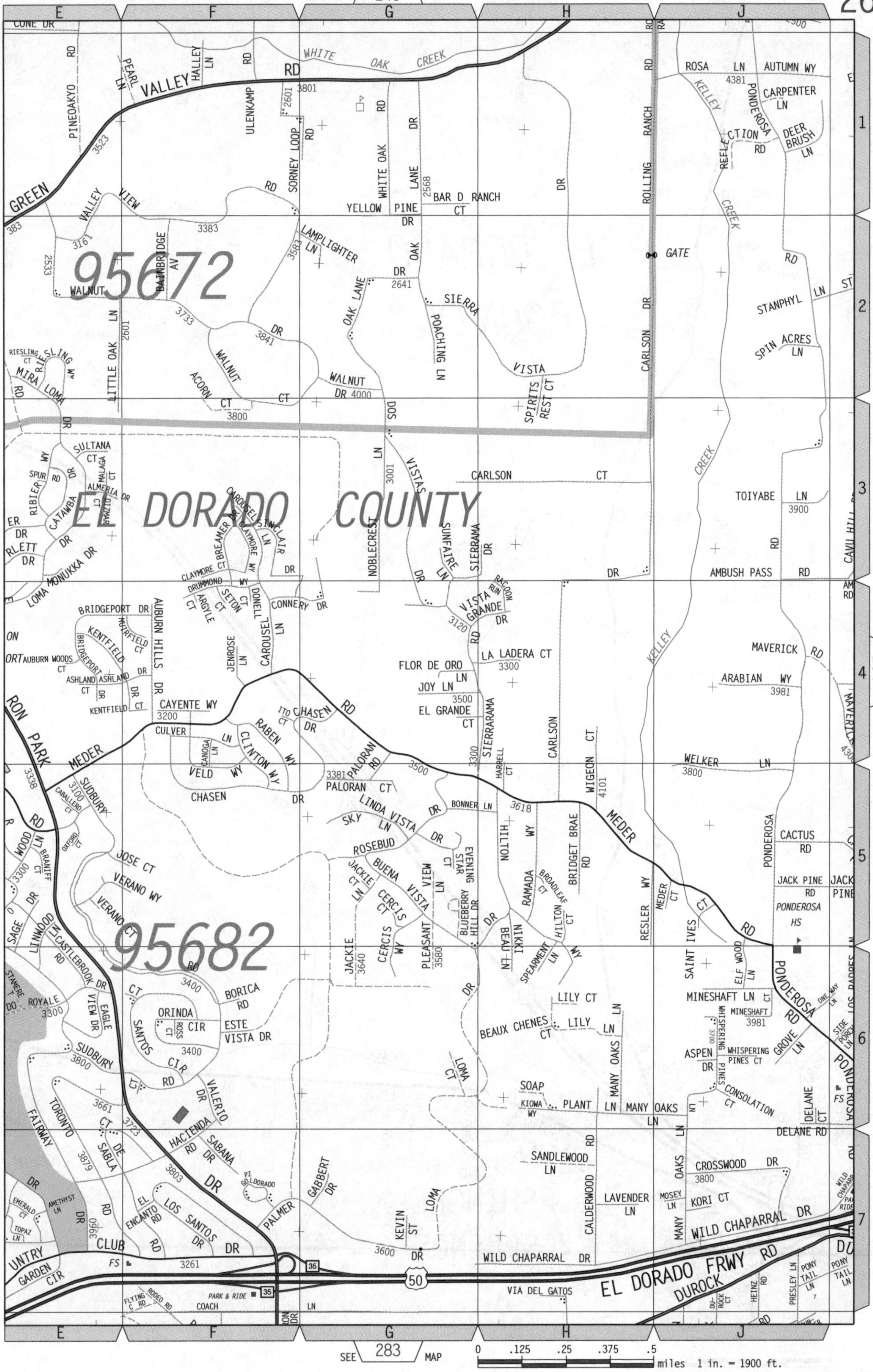

SEE 264 MAP

SEE 283 MAP

0 .125 .25 .375 .5 miles 1 in. = 1900 ft.

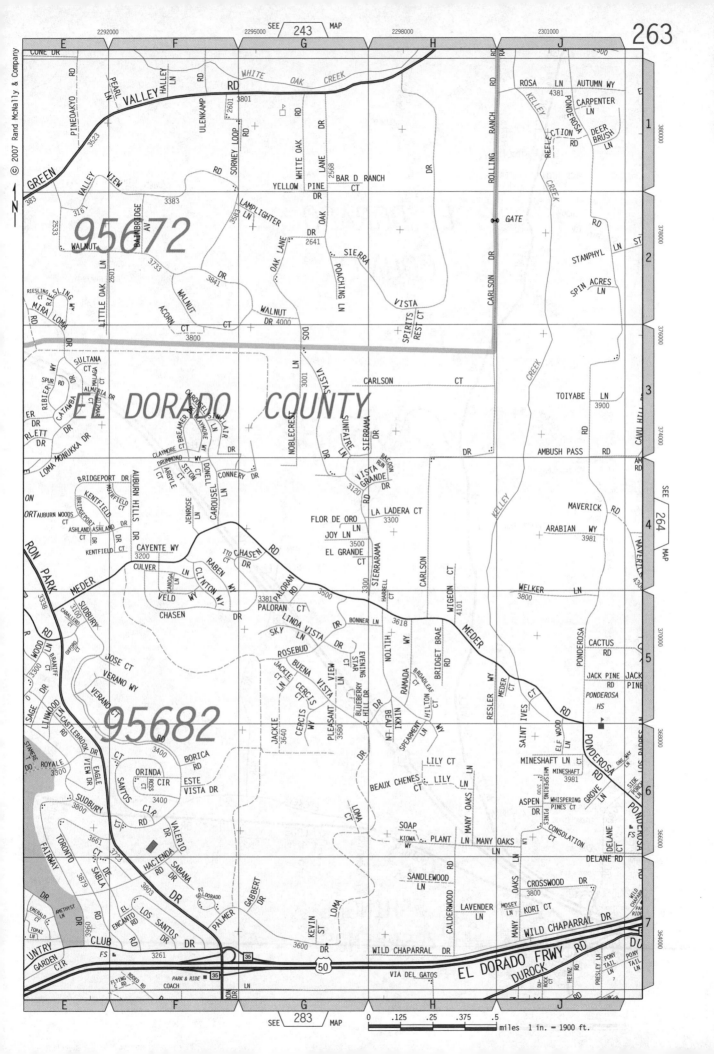

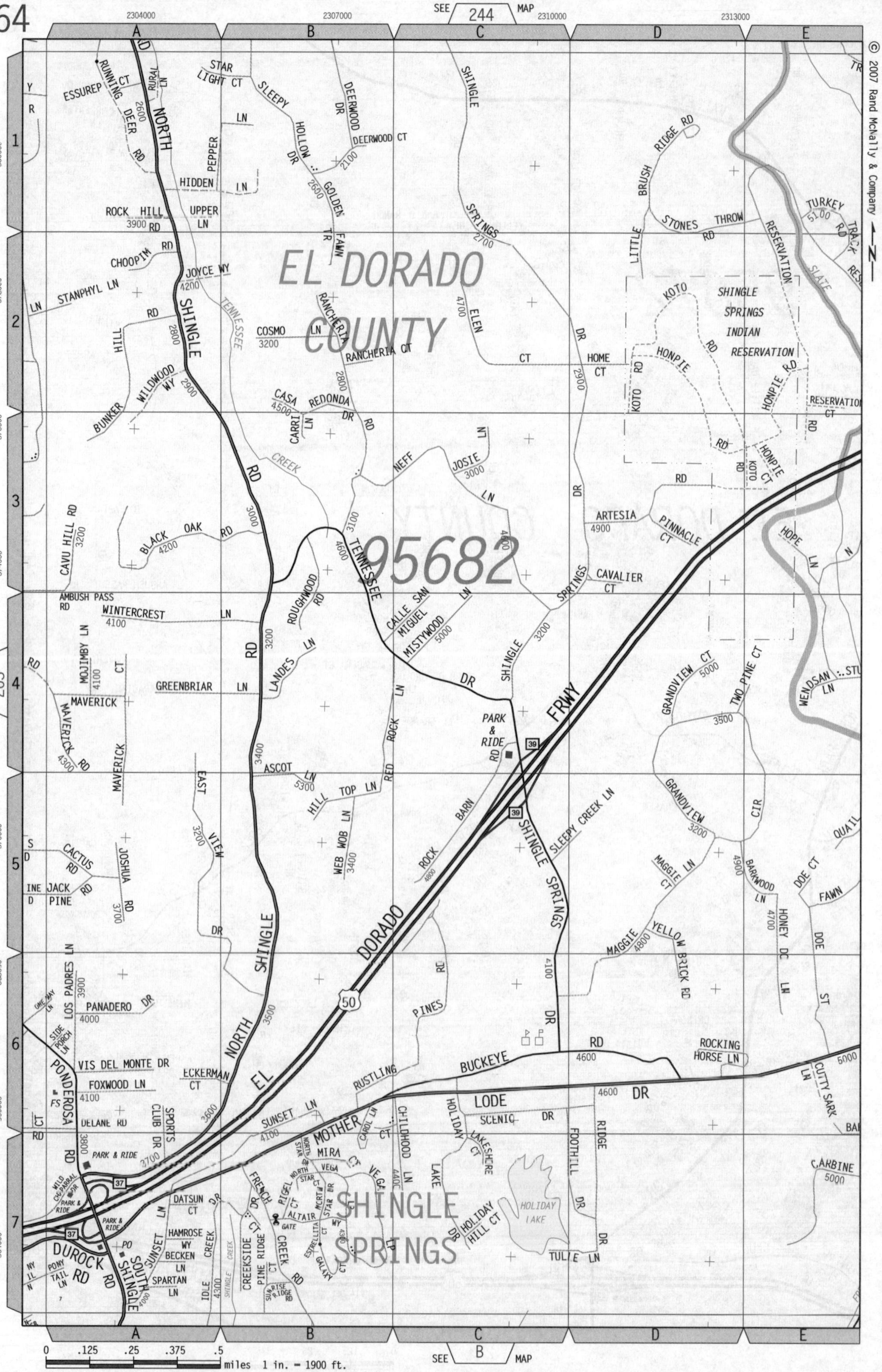
SEE 244 MAP
SEE 263 MAP
SEE B MAP
EL DORADO COUNTY
95682
SHINGLE SPRINGS
SHINGLE SPRINGS INDIAN RESERVATION
HOLIDAY LAKE
NORTH SHINGLE RD
SHINGLE SPRINGS DR
EL DORADO FRWY
MOTHER LODE DR
BUCKEYE RD
PONDEROSA RD
DUROCK RD
SOUTH SHINGLE RD
TENNESSEE DR
TENNESSEE CREEK
RANCHERIA CT
COSMO LN
ESSUREP CT
RUNNING DEER RD
RURAL LN
STAR LIGHT CT
SLEEPY HOLLOW DR
DEERWOOD DR
DEERWOOD CT
PEPPER LN
HIDDEN LN
GOLDEN FAWN TR
ROCK HILL RD
UPPER LN
CHOOPIM RD
JOYCE WY
STANPHYL LN
HILL RD
WILDWOOD WY
BUNKER
CASA REDONDA DR
CARRI LN
NEFF RD
JOSIE LN
ELEN CT
HOME CT
LITTLE BRUSH RIDGE RD
STONES THROW RD
TURKEY TRACK RD
RESERVATION RD
KOTO RD
HONPIE RD
HONPIE CT
KOTO CT
ARTESIA RD
PINNACLE CT
CAVALIER CT
HOPE LN
CAVU HILL RD
BLACK OAK RD
ROUGHWOOD RD
AMBUSH PASS RD
WINTERCREST LN
CALLE SAN MIGUEL
MISTYWOOD LN
MOJIMBY LN
MAVERICK CT
MAVERICK RD
GREENBRIAR LN
LANDES LN
RED ROCK LN
PARK & RIDE
GRANDVIEW CT
TWO PINE CT
GRANDVIEW CIR
WENDSAN LN
ASCOT LN
HILL TOP LN
EAST VIEW DR
WEB WOB LN
ROCK BARN RD
SLEEPY CREEK LN
CACTUS RD
JOSHUA RD
JACK PINE RD
MAGGIE LN
MAGGIE CT
BARTWOOD LN
HONEY DC LN
DOE CT
FAWN
DOE ST
QUAIL
YELLOW BRICK RD
PINES RD
LOS PADRES LN
PANADERO DR
SIDE PORCH LN
VIS DEL MONTE DR
FOXWOOD LN
ECKERMAN CT
RUSTLING
ROCKING HORSE LN
CUTTY SARK
DELANE RD
SPORTS CLUB DR
SUNSET LN
CAROL LN
CHILDHOOD LN
HOLIDAY CT
SCENIC DR
FOOTHILL DR
RIDGE DR
LAKESHORE CT
LAKE DR
HOLIDAY HILL CT
TULIE LN
CARBINE
MIRA CT
VEGA CT
STAR BR
ALTAIR
GALAXY
DATSUN CT
HAMROSE WY
BECKEN LN
SPARTAN LN
CREEK
IDLE CREEK
CREEKSIDE CT
PINE RIDGE CT
FRENCH CREEK RD
PONY TAIL LN
50
39
37
2304000
2307000
2310000
2313000
380000
378000
376000
374000
370000
368000
366000
364000
0 .125 .25 .375 .5 miles 1 in. = 1900 ft.

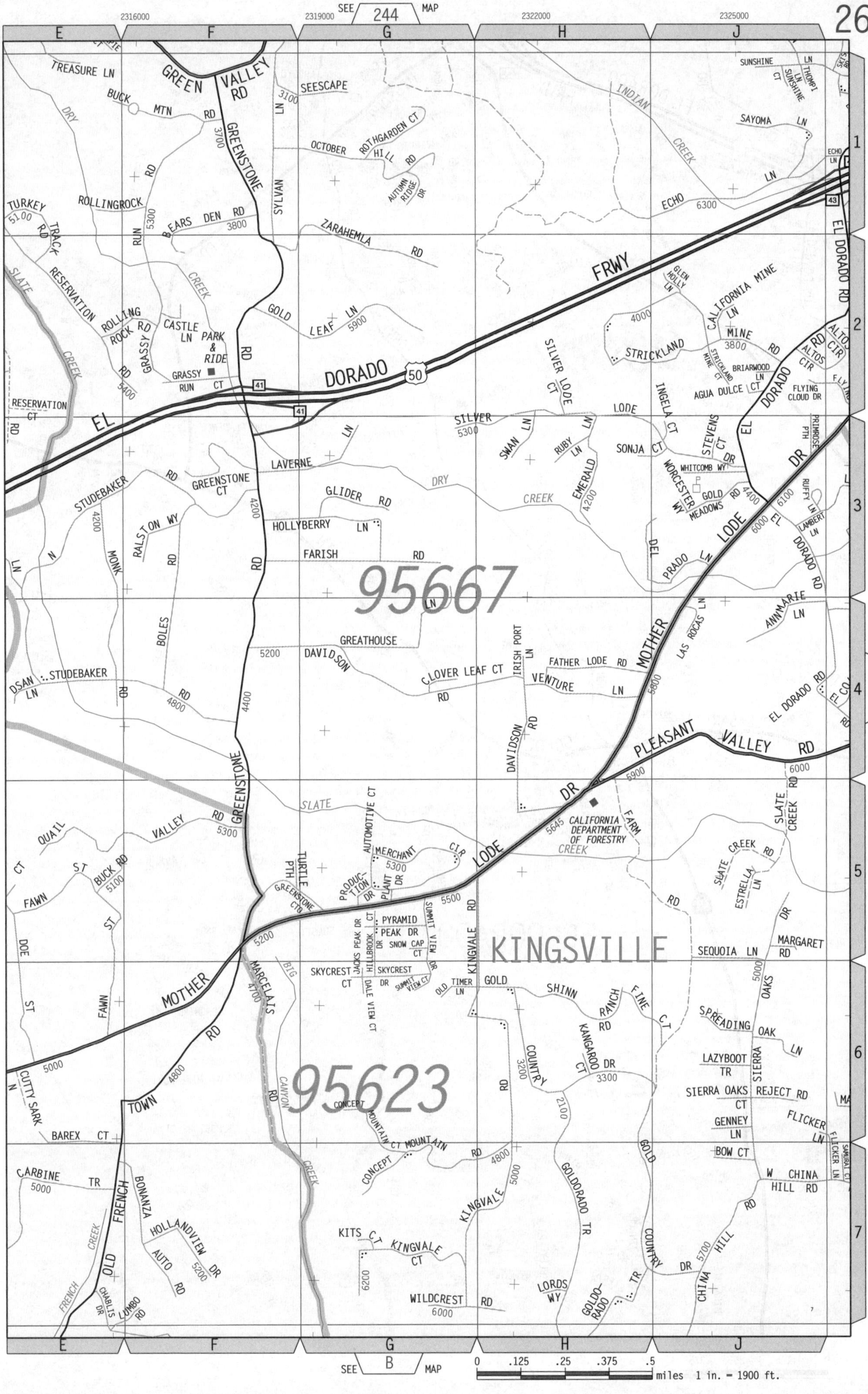
SEE 244 MAP
SEE B MAP
SEE 265 MAP
2316000
2319000
2322000
2325000
E
F
G
H
J
1
2
3
4
5
6
7
382000
380000
378000
376000
374000
372000
370000
368000
366000
364000
GREEN VALLEY RD
GREENSTONE RD
TREASURE LN
BUCK MTN RD
SEESCAPE
SYLVAN LN
OCTOBER
ROTHGARDEN CT
HILL RD
AUTUMN RIDGE DR
ROLLINGROCK
BEARS DEN RD
RUN RD
TURKEY TRACK RD
RESERVATION RD
ZARAHEMLA RD
INDIAN CREEK
SUNSHINE LN
THOMPI LN
SUNSHINE CT
SAYOMA LN
ECHO LN
ECHO 6300 LN
EL DORADO FRWY
EL DORADO RD
GOLD LEAF LN
ROLLING ROCK RD
GRASSY RD
CASTLE LN
PARK & RIDE
GRASSY RUN CT
RESERVATION CT
DRY CREEK
SLATE CREEK
GLEN HOLLY LN
CALIFORNIA MINE LN
MINE RD
STRICKLAND
STRICKLAND CT
BRIARWOOD CT
ALTOS CIR
ALTOS RD
AGUA DULCE CT
FLYING CLOUD DR
SILVER LODE CT
SILVER LODE
INGELA CT
SWAN LN
RUBY LN
EMERALD
SONJA CT
STEVENS CT
WHITCOMB WY
WORCESTER WY
GOLD MEADOWS RD
PRIMROSE PTH
RUFFY LN
LAMBERT LN
LAVERNE LN
STUDEBAKER RD
GREENSTONE CT
GLIDER RD
HOLLYBERRY LN
FARISH RD
RALSTON WY
MONK RD
DEL PRADO LN
MOTHER LODE DR
LAS ROCAS LN
ANNMARIE LN
95667
BOLES RD
GREATHOUSE LN
DAVIDSON
CLOVER LEAF CT
IRISH PORT LN
FATHER LODE RD
VENTURE LN
EL DORADO RD
DAVIDSON RD
PLEASANT VALLEY RD
SLATE CREEK RD
CALIFORNIA DEPARTMENT OF FORESTRY
FARM
QUAIL VALLEY RD
FAWN ST
BUCK RD
AUTOMOTIVE CT
MERCHANT CIR
TURTLE PTH
PRODUCTION DR
PLANT DR
GREENSTONE CT
SLATE CREEK RD
ESTRELLA LN
PYRAMID PEAK DR
JACKS PEAK DR
HILLBROOK CT
SNOW CAP CT
SUMMIT VIEW DR
KINGVALE RD
KINGSVILLE
SEQUOIA LN
MARGARET RD
SKYCREST CT
SKYCREST DR
DALE VIEW CT
OLD TIMER LN
GOLD SHINN RANCH RD
FINE CT
DOE ST
FAWN
MARCELAIS
BIG CANYON CREEK
SPREADING OAK LN
OAKS
LAZYBOOT TR
SIERRA OAKS REJECT RD
KANGAROO CT
KANGAROO DR
COUNTRY
CUTTY SARK
TOWN RD
95623
CONCEPT
MOUNTAIN CT
MOUNTAIN RD
GENNEY LN
FLICKER LN
BOW CT
BAREX CT
CARBINE TR
W CHINA HILL RD
BONANZA
OLD FRENCH
HOLLANDVIEW DR
AUTO RD
KINGVALE
GOLDORADO TR
GOLD COUNTRY DR
CHINA HILL RD
KITS CT
KINGVALE CT
WILDCREST RD
LORDS WY
GOLDORADO TR
FRENCH CREEK
CHABLIS DR
LUMBO RD
0
.125
.25
.375
.5
miles 1 in. = 1900 ft.

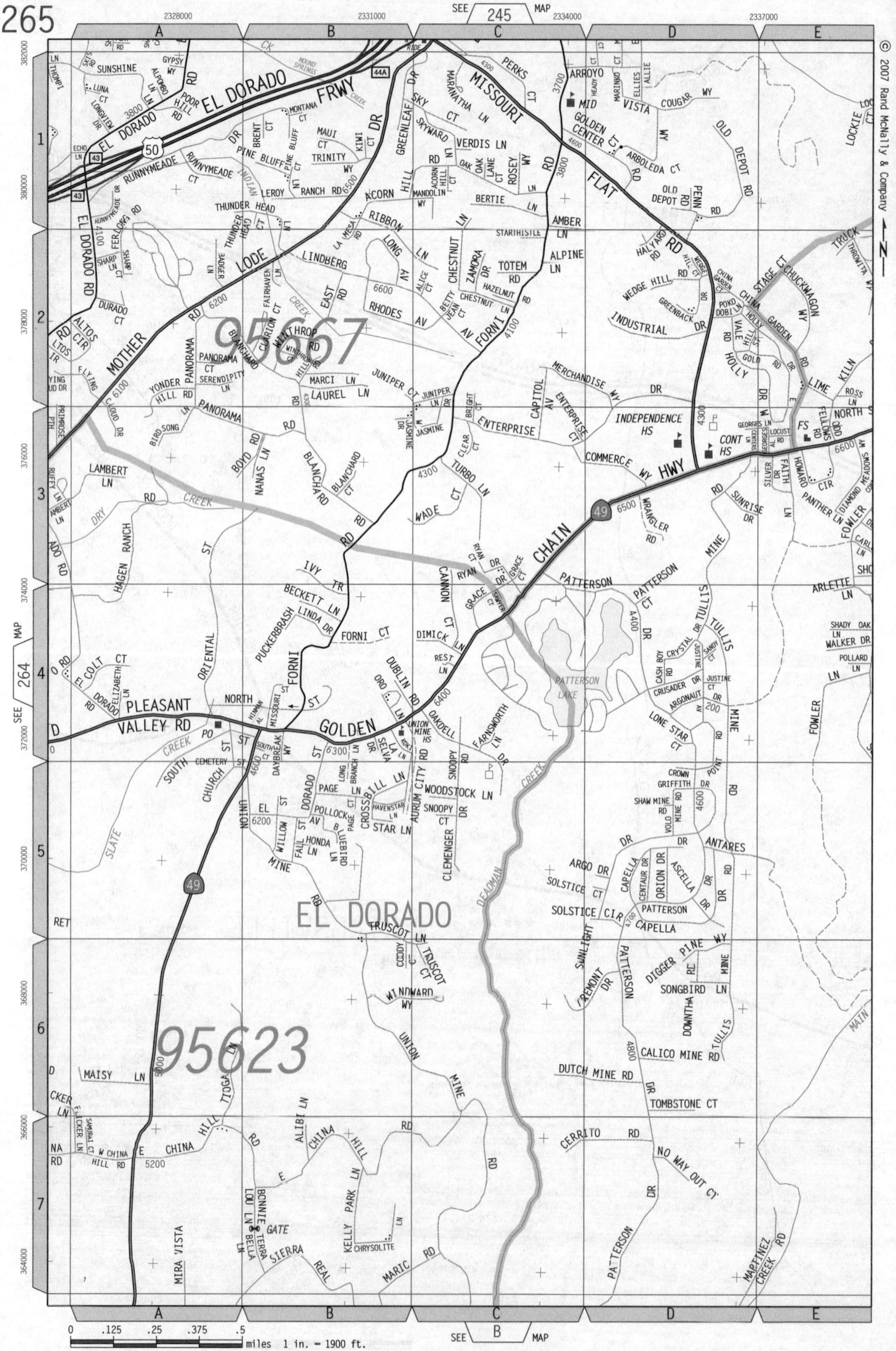

SEE 245 MAP
SEE 264 MAP
SEE B MAP
A B C D E
1 2 3 4 5 6 7
2328000 2331000 2334000 2337000
382000 380000 378000 376000 374000 372000 370000 368000 366000 364000
95667
95623
EL DORADO
EL DORADO FRWY
50
43
44A
49
MISSOURI FLAT RD
MOTHER LODE DR
EL DORADO RD
PLEASANT VALLEY RD
GOLDEN CHAIN HWY
FORNI RD
UNION MINE RD
CHINA HILL RD
MIRA VISTA
SIERRA
PATTERSON LAKE
PATTERSON DR
INDEPENDENCE HS
UNION MINE HS
CONT HS
MID
PO
FS
GATE
DRY CREEK
INDIAN CREEK
SLATE CREEK
DEADMAN CREEK
MOUND SPRINGS
SUNSHINE
GYPSY WY
ARROYO
GOLDEN CENTER CT
ARBOLEDA CT
OLD DEPOT RD
COUGAR WY
VISTA WY
LOCKIE
PERKS CT
MARANATHA LN
SKYWARD CT
VERDIS LN
ROSEY WY
BERTIE LN
AMBER LN
ALPINE LN
TOTEM RD
ZAMORA DR
CHESTNUT LN
HAZELNUT RD
RHODES AV
LINDBERG
RIBBON
ACORN
TRINITY WY
MAUI CT
MONTANA CT
PINE BLUFF
RUNNYMEADE CT
THUNDER HEAD
WINTHROP
BLANCHARD RD
PANORAMA RD
MARCI LN
LAUREL LN
JUNIPER CT
JASMINE
ENTERPRISE
CAPITOL AV
MERCHANDISE WY
INDUSTRIAL DR
WEDGE HILL RD
CHINA GARDEN RD
CHUCKWAGON WY
STAGE CT
HOLLY
LIME KILN
NORTH ST
COMMERCE WY
SUNRISE DR
WRANGLER RD
TURBO LN
WADE CT
LAMBERT LN
HAGEN RANCH
ORIENTAL ST
IVY TR
BECKETT LN
LINDA DR
PUCKERBRASH
FORNI CT
RYAN DR
GRACE CT
CANNON CT
DIMICK LN
PATTERSON CT
TULLIS MINE RD
CRYSTAL DR
CRUSADER DR
ARGONAUT DR
LONE STAR CT
GRIFFITH DR
POINT RD
ANTARES
ARGO DR
SOLSTICE CT
SOLSTICE CIR
CAPELLA
ORION DR
ASCELLA DR
DIGGER PINE WY
SONGBIRD LN
CALICO MINE RD
DUTCH MINE RD
TOMBSTONE CT
CERRITO RD
NO WAY OUT CT
MARTINEZ CREEK RD
ARLETTE LN
SHADY OAK LN
WALKER DR
POLLARD LN
FOWLER LN
COLT CT
ELIZABETH CT
NORTH ST
CHURCH ST
CEMETERY
SOUTH ST
DAYBREAK WY
DORADO
PAGE
POLLOCK AV
CROSSBILL LN
STAR LN
AURUM CITY RD
WOODSTOCK LN
SNOOPY CT
CLEMENGER DR
OAKDELL
FARNSWORTH LN
HONDA LN
BLUEBIRD LN
WILLOW
FAIL
TRUSCOT LN
WINDWARD WY
MAISY LN
TIOGA
ALIBI LN
KELLY PARK LN
CHRYSOLITE
REAL
MARIC RD
BONNIE
LOU LN
TERRA
BELLA
E CHINA

miles 1 in. = 1900 ft.

SEE 245 MAP

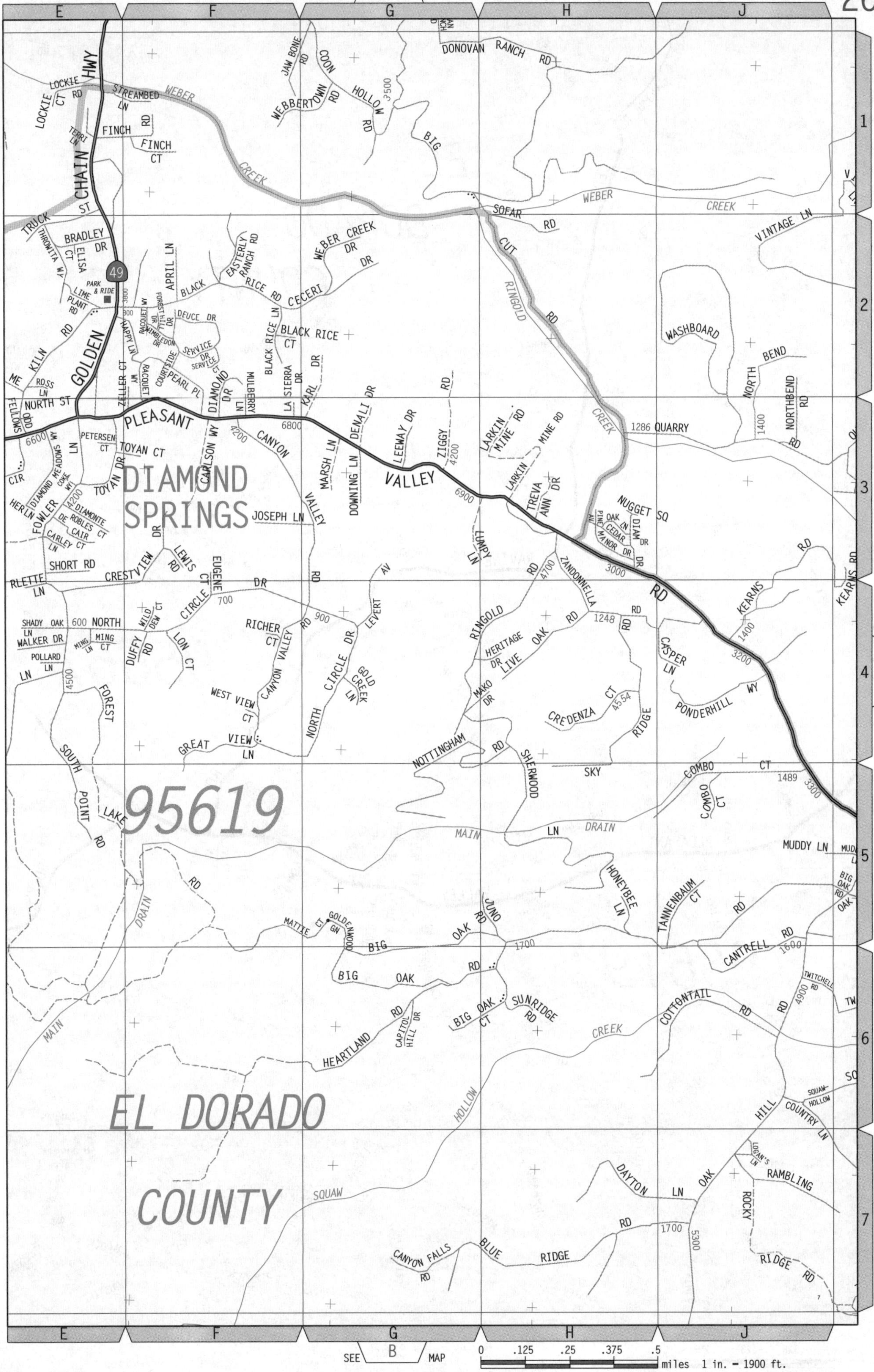

SEE 266 MAP
SEE B MAP
0 .125 .25 .375 .5 miles 1 in. = 1900 ft.

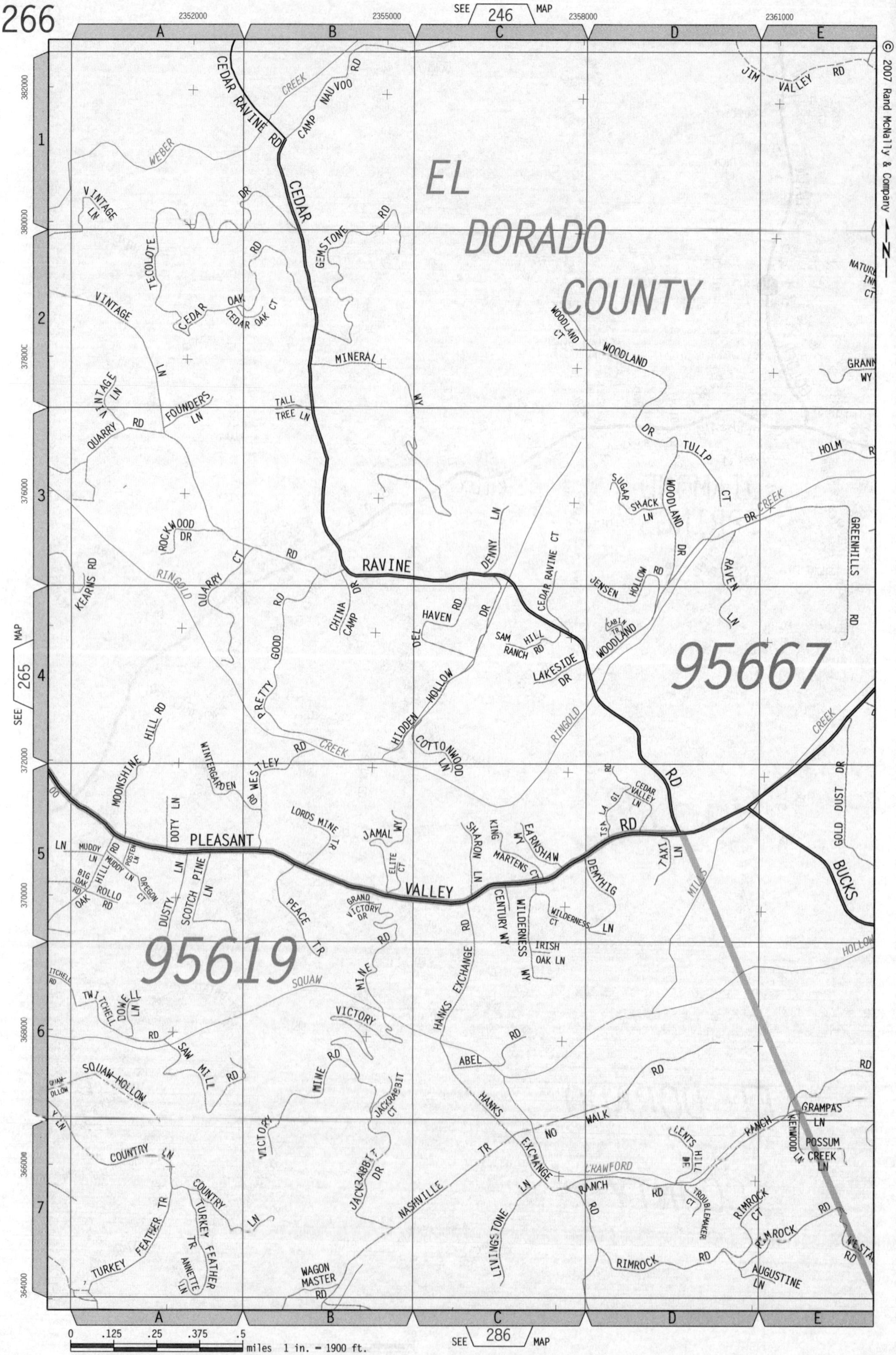
SEE 246 MAP
SEE 265 MAP
SEE 286 MAP
A
B
C
D
E
1
2
3
4
5
6
7
2352000
2355000
2358000
2361000
382000
380000
378000
376000
372000
370000
368000
366000
364000
EL DORADO COUNTY
95667
95619
CEDAR RAVINE RD
CAMP NAUVOO RD
WEBER CREEK
CEDAR RAVINE RD
VINTAGE LN
TECOLOTE DR
GEMSTONE RD
CEDAR OAK RD
CEDAR OAK CT
VINTAGE LN
MINERAL WY
TALL TREE LN
VINTAGE LN
FOUNDERS LN
QUARRY RD
ROCKWOOD DR
QUARRY CT
RD
RINGOLD CREEK
KEARNS RD
CHINA CAMP DR
PRETTY GOOD RD
DEL HAVEN RD
DENNY LN
CEDAR RAVINE CT
SAM HILL RANCH RD
LAKESIDE DR
HIDDEN HOLLOW DR
COTTONWOOD LN
MOONSHINE HILL RD
WINTERGARDEN RD
WESTLEY RD
CREEK
PLEASANT VALLEY RD
DOTY LN
MUDDY LN
MUDDY HILL RD
POSTEN LN
BIG OAK RD
ROLLO RD
OAK
OREGON CT
DUSTY LN
SCOTCH PINE LN
LORDS MINE TR
JAMAL WY
ELITE CT
PEACE TR
GRAND VICTORY DR
MINE RD
SHARON LN
KING MARTENS CT
EARNSHAW WY
CENTURY WY
WILDERNESS WY
WILDERNESS CT
WILDERNESS LN
IRISH OAK LN
DEMYHIG
ISA LA GI RD
CEDAR VALLEY LN
TAXI LN
MILLS
WOODLAND CT
WOODLAND DR
TULIP CT
SUGAR SHACK LN
WOODLAND DR
CREEK DR
JENSEN HOLLOW RD
CABIN TR
WOODLAND
RAVEN LN
GREENHILLS RD
HOLM RD
GRANN WY
NATURE INN CT
JIM VALLEY RD
GOLD DUST DR
BUCKS
CREEK
HOLLOW
SQUAW
TWITCHELL RD
DOWELL LN
SAW MILL RD
VICTORY
RD
HANKS EXCHANGE RD
ABEL RD
SQUAW HOLLOW
MINE RD
JACKRABBIT CT
VICTORY
NO WALK RD
LENTS HILL DE
RANCH
GRAMPAS LN
KENWOOD LN
POSSUM CREEK LN
COUNTRY LN
COUNTRY TR
TURKEY FEATHER TR
ANNETTE LN
JACKRABBIT DR
NASHVILLE TR
CRAWFORD
RANCH RD
TROUBLEMAKER CT
RIMROCK CT
RIMROCK RD
LIVINGSTONE LN
WAGON MASTER RD
AUGUSTINE LN
VESTA RD
0 .125 .25 .375 .5 miles 1 in. = 1900 ft.

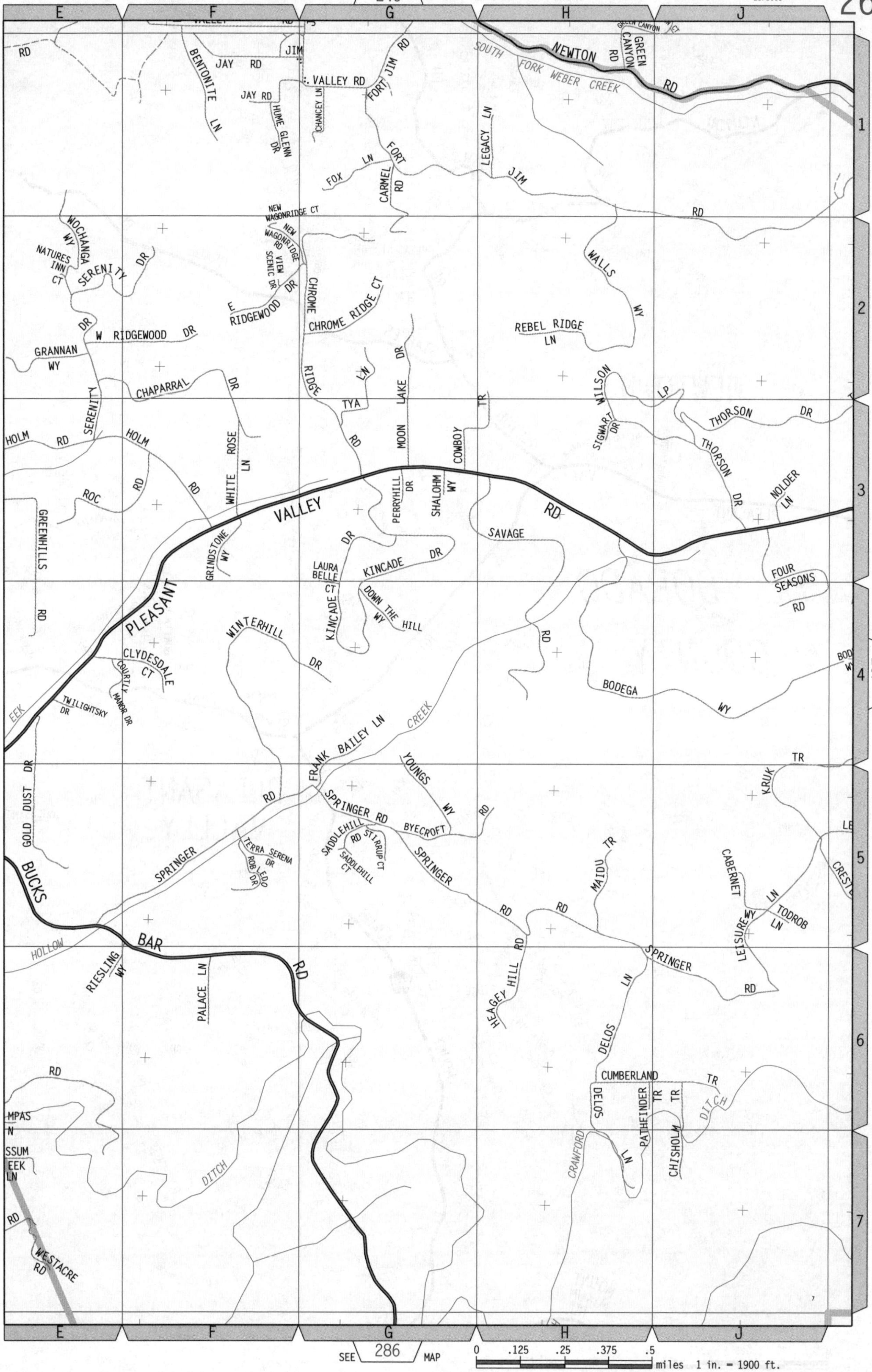
SEE 246 MAP
SEE 267 MAP
SEE 286 MAP
SACRAMENTO CO.
NEWTON RD
SOUTH FORK WEBER CREEK
GREEN CANYON RD
JAY RD
JIM
VALLEY RD
FORT JIM RD
BENTONITE LN
HUME GLENN DR
CHANCEY LN
LEGACY LN
FOX LN
CARMEL RD
JIM RD
WOCHANGA WY
NATURES INN CT
SERENITY DR
NEW WAGONRIDGE CT
NEW WAGONRIDGE RD
SCENIC VIEW DR
E RIDGEWOOD DR
CHROME RIDGE CT
CHROME RIDGE
W RIDGEWOOD DR
GRANNAN WY
WALLS WY
REBEL RIDGE LN
CHAPARRAL DR
WILSON LP
TYA LN
MOON LAKE DR
COWBOY TR
THORSON DR
SIGWART DR
HOLM RD
WHITE ROSE LN
ROC RD
GREENHILLS RD
PERRYHILL DR
SHALOHM WY
NOLDER LN
VALLEY RD
SAVAGE RD
GRINDSTONE WY
KINCADE DR
LAURA BELLE CT
KINCADE CT
DOWN THE HILL WY
FOUR SEASONS RD
PLEASANT
WINTERHILL DR
CLYDESDALE CT
COURTLY MANOR DR
TWILIGHTSKY DR
BODEGA WY
FRANK BAILEY LN
CREEK
YOUNGS WY
KRUK TR
GOLD DUST DR
SPRINGER RD
BYECROFT RD
SADDLEHILL RD
STIRRUP CT
SADDLEHILL CT
TERRA SERENA DR
ROBLEDO DR
MAIDU TR
CABERNET LN
CRESTE
BUCKS BAR RD
HOLLOW
LEISURE WY
TODROB LN
HEAGEY HILL RD
RIESLING WY
PALACE LN
DELOS LN
CUMBERLAND TR
PATHFINDER TR
CHISHOLM TR
DITCH
CRAWFORD
WESTACRE RD
E F G H J
1 2 3 4 5 6 7
2364000 2370000 2373000
382000 380000 378000 376000 372000 370000 368000 366000
0 .125 .25 .375 .5 miles 1 in. = 1900 ft.

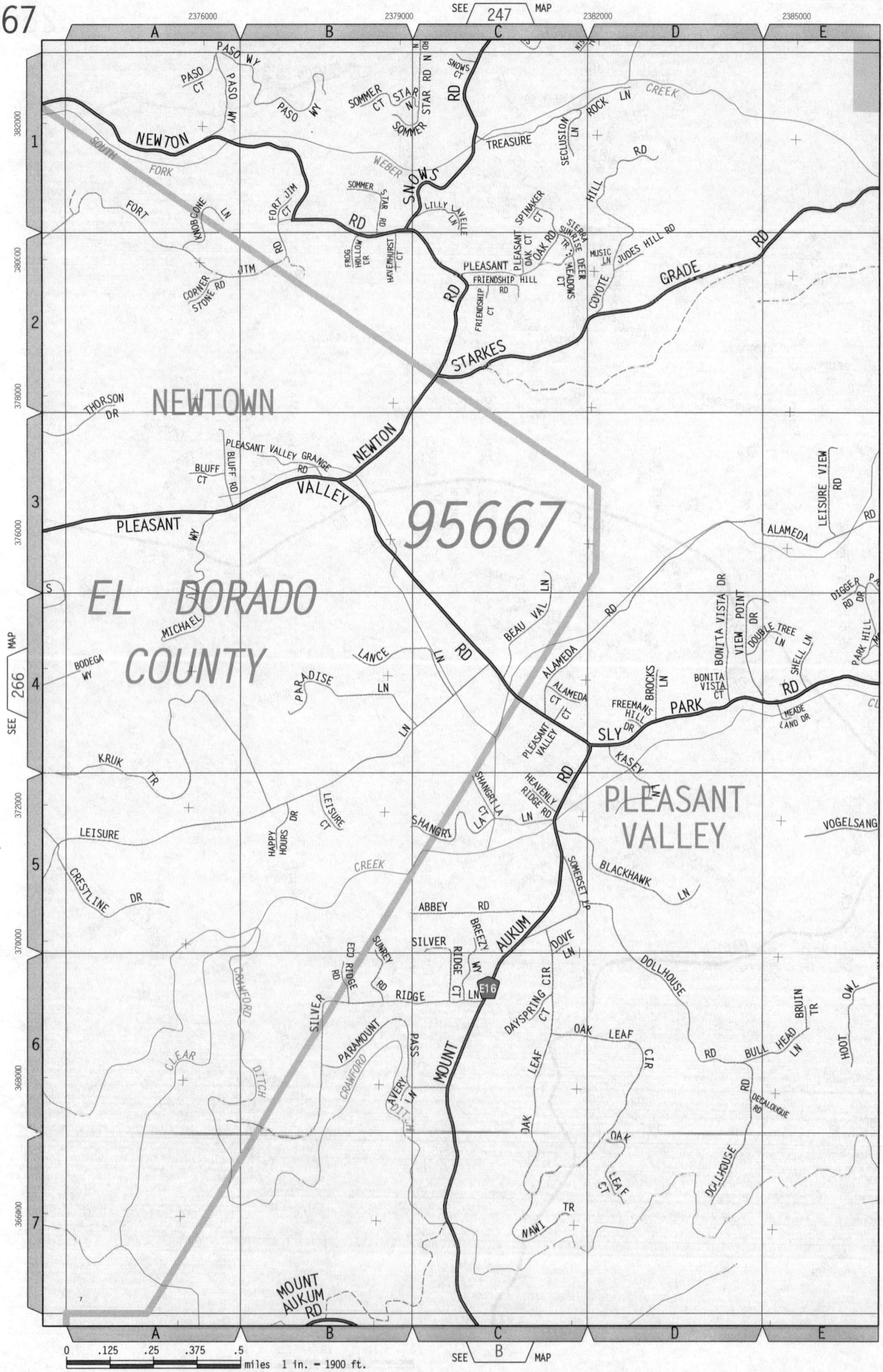
SEE 247 MAP
2376000
2379000
2382000
2385000
A
B
C
D
E
1
2
3
4
5
6
7
382000
380000
378000
376000
372000
370000
368000
366000
NEWTOWN
95667
EL DORADO
COUNTY
PLEASANT
VALLEY
NEWTON RD
SNOWS RD
STARKES GRADE RD
PLEASANT VALLEY RD
SLY PARK RD
MOUNT AUKUM RD
E16
PASO WY
PASO CT
SOMMER CT
STAR N
STAR RD N
SOMMER
SNOWS CT
TREASURE
SECLUSION LN
ROCK LN
CREEK
HILL RD
SOUTH FORK
WEBER
FORT JIM RD
KNOBCONE LN
FORT JIM CT
CORNER STONE RD
SOMMER
STAR RD
FROG HOLLOW CR
HAVENHURST CT
LILLY LAVELLE LN
PLEASANT OAK CT
SPINAKER CT
OAK RD
SIERRA SUNRISE TR
DEER MEADOWS CT
MUSIC LN
JUDES HILL RD
COYOTE
FRIENDSHIP HILL RD
FRIENDSHIP CT
THORSON DR
PLEASANT VALLEY GRANGE RD
BLUFF CT
BLUFF RD
WY
MICHAEL
BODEGA WY
LANCE LN
PARADISE LN
LN
BEAU VAL LN
ALAMEDA RD
ALAMEDA CT
BROCKS LN
FREEMANS HILL DR
BONITA VISTA DR
BONITA VISTA CT
VIEW POINT DR
DOUBLE TREE LN
SHELL LN
DIGGER RD
PARK HILL
MEADE LAND DR
LEISURE VIEW RD
ALAMEDA
RD
KASEY LN
KRUK TR
LEISURE
CRESTLINE DR
HAPPY HOURS DR
LEISURE CT
SHANGRI LA CT
SHANGRI LA LN
HEAVENLY RIDGE RD
PLEASANT VALLEY CT
VOGELSANG
BLACKHAWK LN
SOMERSET LP
CREEK
ABBEY RD
SILVER RIDGE CT
BREEZY WY
SUNREY RD
ECO RIDGE RD
RIDGE LN
DOVE LN
DAYSPRING CIR CT
DOLLHOUSE
SILVER
PARAMOUNT
PASS
CRAWFORD
CRAWFORD DITCH
DITCH
CLEAR
AVERY LN
OAK LEAF CIR
OAK LEAF CT
BULL HEAD LN
BRUIN TR
OWL
HOOT
DECALOUQUE RD
DOLLHOUSE
NAWI TR
MOUNT AUKUM RD
SEE 266 MAP
SEE B MAP
0 .125 .25 .375 .5
miles 1 in. = 1900 ft.

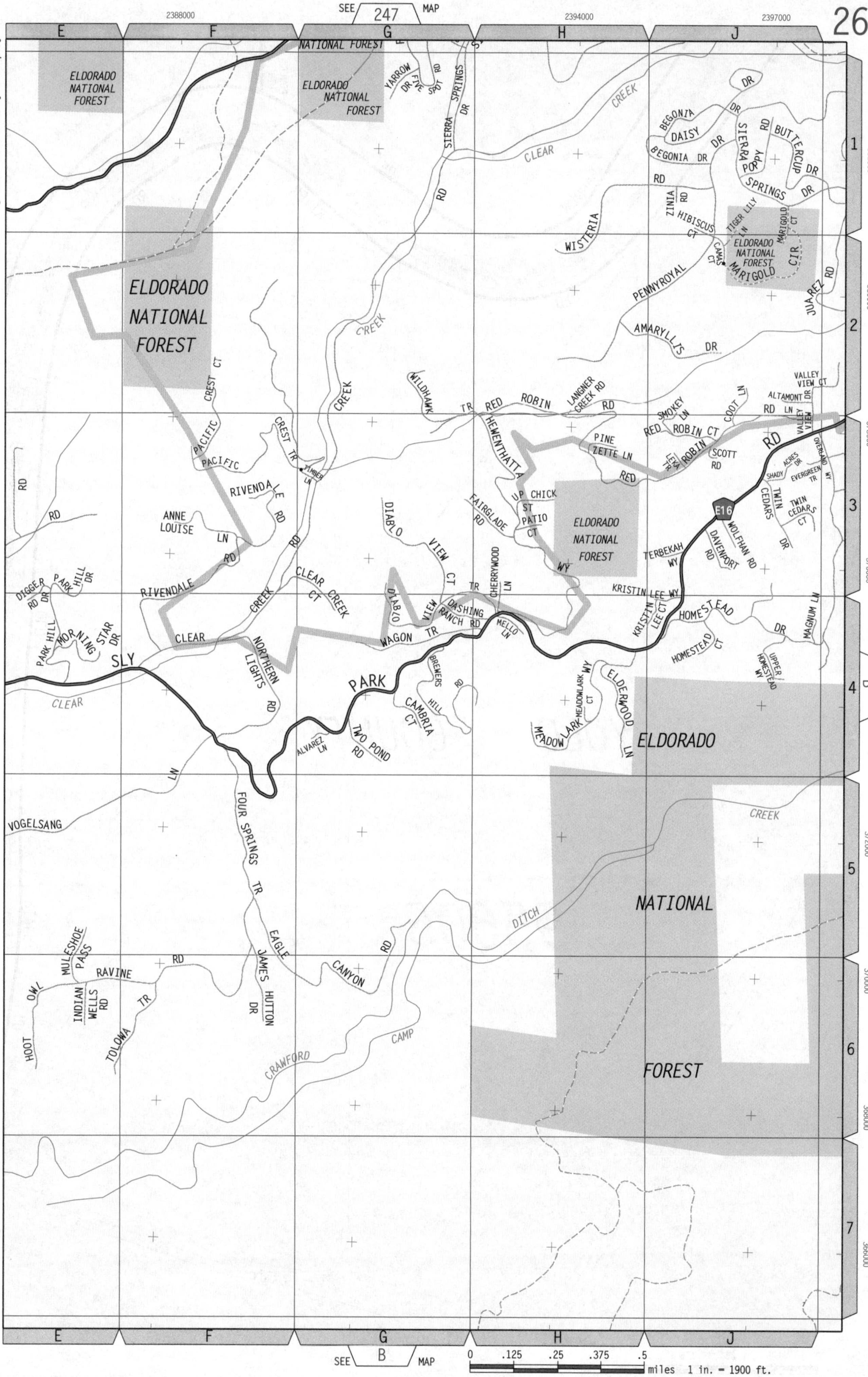
SEE 247 MAP
2388000
2394000
2397000
E
F
G
H
J
1
2
3
4
5
6
7
382000
380000
378000
376000
372000
370000
368000
366000
ELDORADO NATIONAL FOREST
ELDORADO NATIONAL FOREST
NATIONAL FOREST
ELDORADO NATIONAL FOREST
ELDORADO NATIONAL FOREST
ELDORADO NATIONAL FOREST
ELDORADO
NATIONAL
FOREST
YARROW DR
FIVE SPOT RD
SIERRA SPRINGS DR
SIERRA SPRINGS RD
CLEAR CREEK
CREEK
DAISY DR
BEGONIA
BEGONIA DR
DR
SIERRA POPPY RD
BUTTERCUP DR
SPRINGS DR
ZINIA RD
RD
HIBISCUS CT
TIGER LILY LN
CAMAS CT
MARIGOLD CT
MARIGOLD CIR
WISTERIA
PENNYROYAL
AMARYLLIS DR
JUAREZ RD
VALLEY VIEW CT
ALTAMONT DR
RD LN
VALLEY VIEW
WILDHAWK TR
RED ROBIN RD
LANGNER CREEK RD
SMOKEY LN
RED ROBIN CT
COOT LN
RD
PINE ZETTE LN
HEWENTHATTA
RED
LEXA TR
SCOTT RD
SHADY ACRES DR
EVERGREEN DR
OVERLAND WY
TWIN CEDARS DR
TWIN CEDARS CT
E16
WOLFHAN RD
DAVENPORT RD
TERBEKAH WY
UP CHICK ST
PATIO CT
FAIRGLADE RD
WY
CHERRYWOOD LN
DIABLO VIEW CT
DIABLO VIEW
DASHING RANCH RD
TR
MELLO LN
KRISTIN LEE WY
KRISTIN LEE CT
HOMESTEAD DR
HOMESTEAD CT
UPPER HOMESTEAD WY
MAGNUM LN
SEE B MAP
CREST CT
PACIFIC
PACIFIC
CREST TR
TIMBER LN
CREEK
RIVENDALE RD
ANNE LOUISE LN
RD
RD
RD
RIVENDALE
CLEAR CREEK CT
CLEAR CREEK
CLEAR
DIGGER RD DR
PARK HILL DR
PARK HILL
MORNING STAR DR
SLY
PARK
NORTHERN LIGHTS RD
WAGON TR
BREWERS HILL RD
CAMBRIA CT
TWO POND RD
ALVAREZ LN
MEADOWLARK WY
MEADOWLARK CT
MEADOWLARK
ELDERWOOD LN
CLEAR
LN
VOGELSANG
FOUR SPRINGS TR
EAGLE CANYON RD
DITCH
CREEK
MULESHOE PASS
RAVINE RD
HOOT OWL
INDIAN WELLS RD
TOLOWA TR
JAMES HUTTON DR
CAMP
CRAWFORD
SEE B MAP
0 .125 .25 .375 .5
miles 1 in. = 1900 ft.

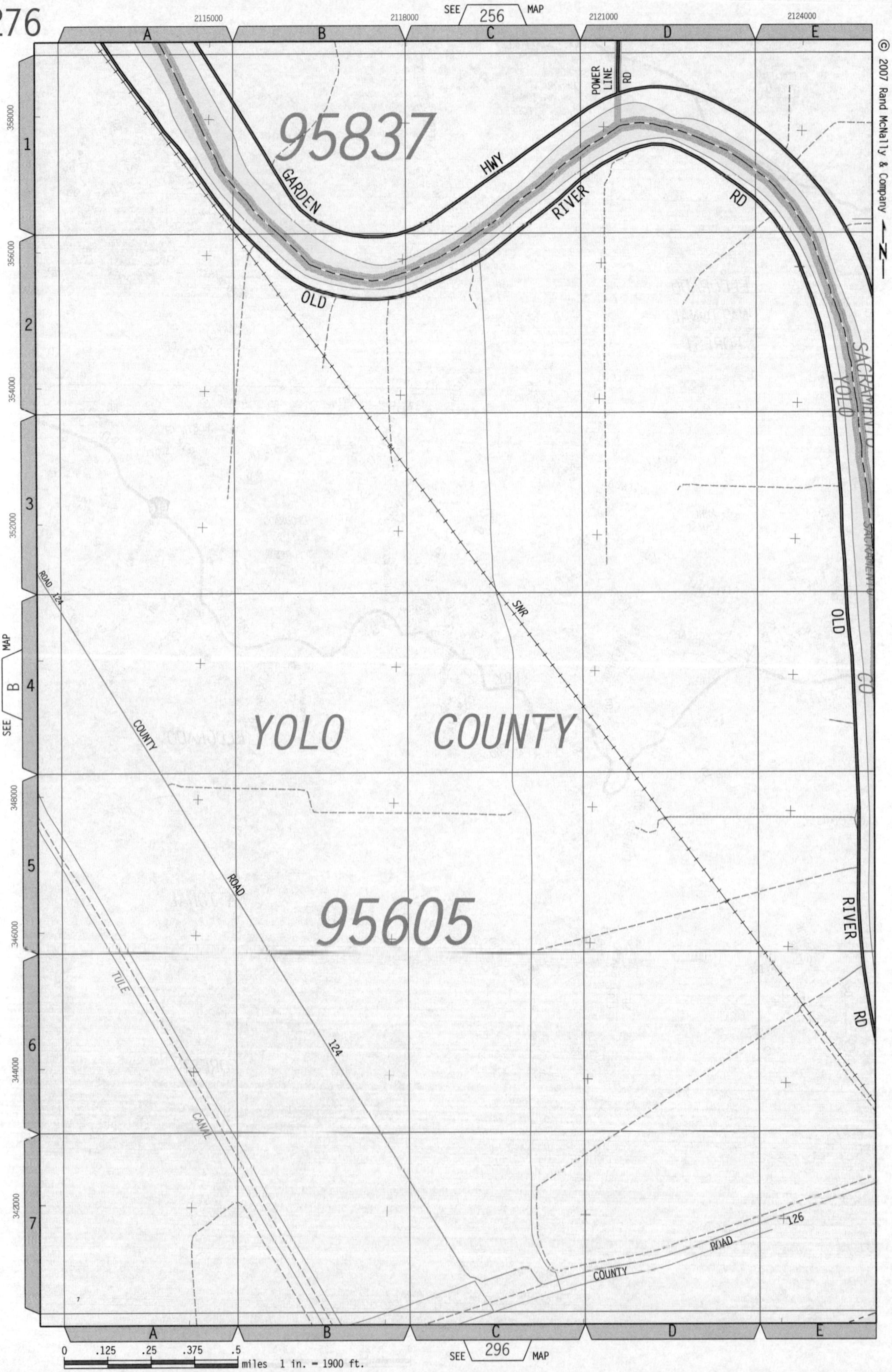
SEE 256 MAP
2115000
2118000
2121000
2124000
A
B
C
D
E
1
2
3
4
5
6
7
358000
356000
354000
352000
348000
346000
344000
342000
95837
GARDEN
HWY
POWER LINE
RD
RIVER
RD
OLD
YOLO
SACRAMENTO
OLD
CO
RIVER
RD
SNR
ROAD 124
COUNTY
YOLO COUNTY
ROAD
95605
TULE
CANAL
124
COUNTY
ROAD
126
SEE B MAP
SEE 296 MAP
0 .125 .25 .375 .5
miles 1 in. = 1900 ft.

SEE 256 MAP

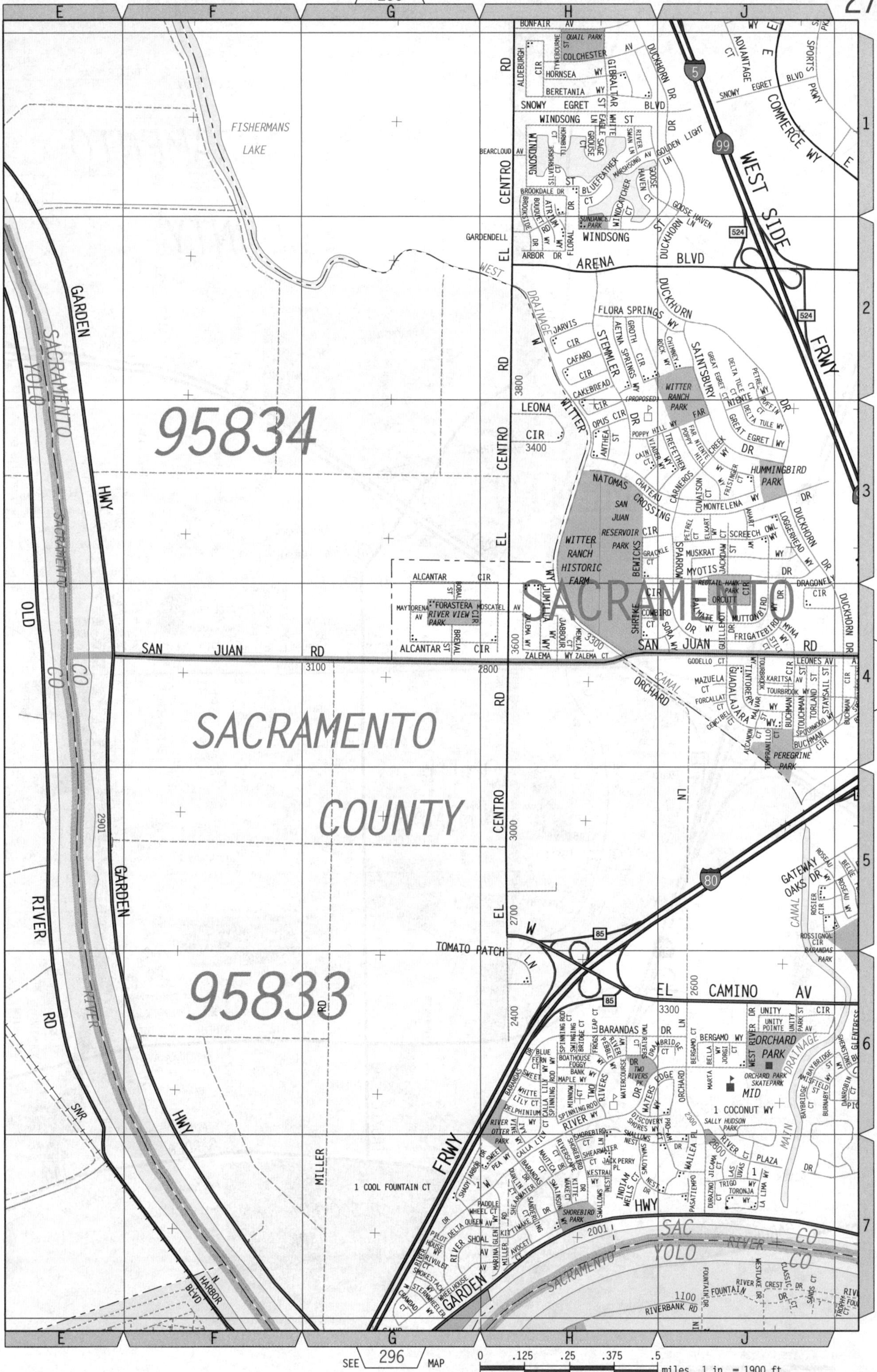

SEE 277 MAP

SEE 296 MAP

0 .125 .25 .375 .5 miles 1 in. = 1900 ft.

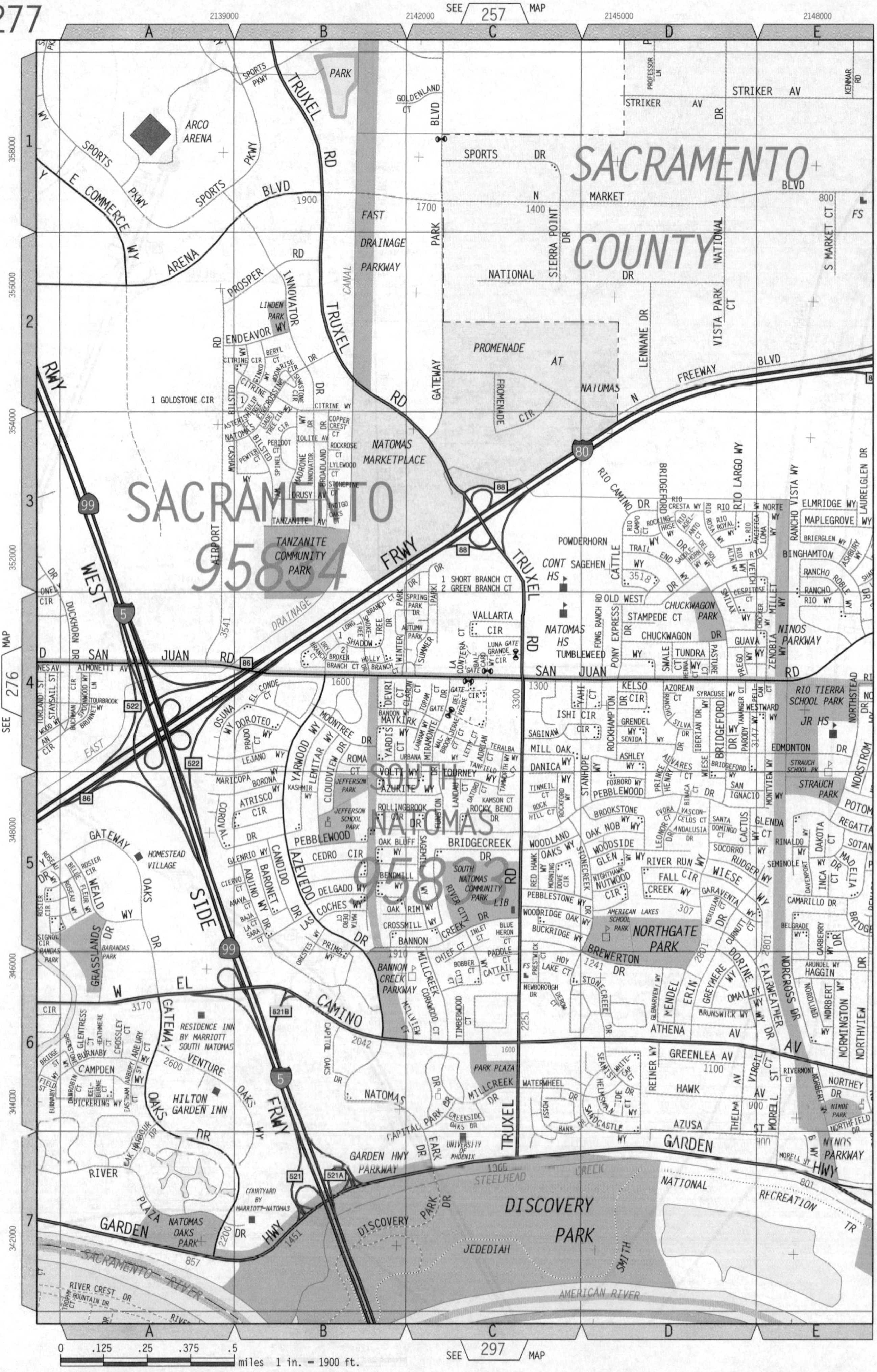
SEE 257 MAP
SEE 276 MAP
SEE 297 MAP
A
B
C
D
E
1
2
3
4
5
6
7
2139000
2142000
2145000
2148000
358000
356000
354000
352000
348000
346000
344000
342000
SACRAMENTO COUNTY
SACRAMENTO 95834
SOUTH NATOMAS 95833
ARCO ARENA
PARK
SPORTS PKWY
TRUXEL RD
GOLDENLAND CT
SPORTS DR
E COMMERCE WY
ARENA BLVD
N MARKET BLVD
EAST DRAINAGE CANAL PARKWAY
PROSPER RD
INNOVATOR DR
LINDEN PARK
ENDEAVOR WY
PROMENADE AT NATOMAS
GATEWAY PARK BLVD
SIERRA POINT DR
NATIONAL DR
LENNANE DR
VISTA PARK CT
STRIKER AV
PROFESSOR LN
KENMAR RD
S MARKET CT
FS
1 GOLDSTONE CIR
NATOMAS MARKETPLACE
N FREEWAY BLVD
80
88
99
5
86
522
WEST SIDE FRWY
TANZANITE COMMUNITY PARK
AIRPORT RD
DRAINAGE
POWDERHORN
CONT HS
NATOMAS HS
SAGEHEN
TUMBLEWEED
VALLARTA CIR
CHUCKWAGON PARK
RIO CAMINO DR
BRIDGEFORD DR
RIO LARGO WY
RANCHO VISTA WY
NINOS PARKWAY
ELMRIDGE WY
MAPLEGROVE
BINGHAMTON
SAN JUAN RD
DUCKHORN DR
RIO TIERRA SCHOOL PARK
JR HS
EDMONTON DR
STRAUCH PARK
NORSTROM
ISHI CIR
KELSO CIR
SAGINAW
MILL OAK
DANICA WY
PEBBLEWOOD
BROOKSTONE
JEFFERSON PARK
JEFFERSON SCHOOL PARK
CEDRO CIR
BRIDGECREEK DR
SOUTH NATOMAS COMMUNITY PARK
LIB
HOMESTEAD VILLAGE
GATEWAY OAKS DR
GRASSLANDS DR
WOODLAND
OAK NOB
WOODSIDE
RIVER RUN WY
FALL CREEK WY
WIESE WY
NORTHGATE PARK
AMERICAN LAKES SCHOOL PARK
BREWERTON DR
BANNON CREEK PARKWAY
W EL CAMINO AV
RESIDENCE INN BY MARRIOTT SOUTH NATOMAS
HILTON GARDEN INN
VENTURE OAKS WY
CAPITOL OAKS DR
NATOMAS PARK DR
PARK PLAZA
MILLCREEK DR
TRUXEL RD
GREENLEA AV
HAWK
AZUSA ST
ATHENA AV
NORCROSS DR
FAIRWEATHER DR
NORTHEY
NINOS PARK
NINOS PARKWAY
GARDEN HWY
GARDEN HWY PARKWAY
UNIVERSITY OF PHOENIX
COURTYARD BY MARRIOTT-NATOMAS
NATOMAS OAKS PARK
PLAZA
RIVER
STEELHEAD CREEK
DISCOVERY PARK
DISCOVERY PARK DR
JEDEDIAH SMITH
NATIONAL RECREATION TR
AMERICAN RIVER
SACRAMENTO RIVER
RIVER CREST DR
FOUNTAIN DR
521
521A
521B
0 .125 .25 .375 .5 miles 1 in. = 1900 ft.

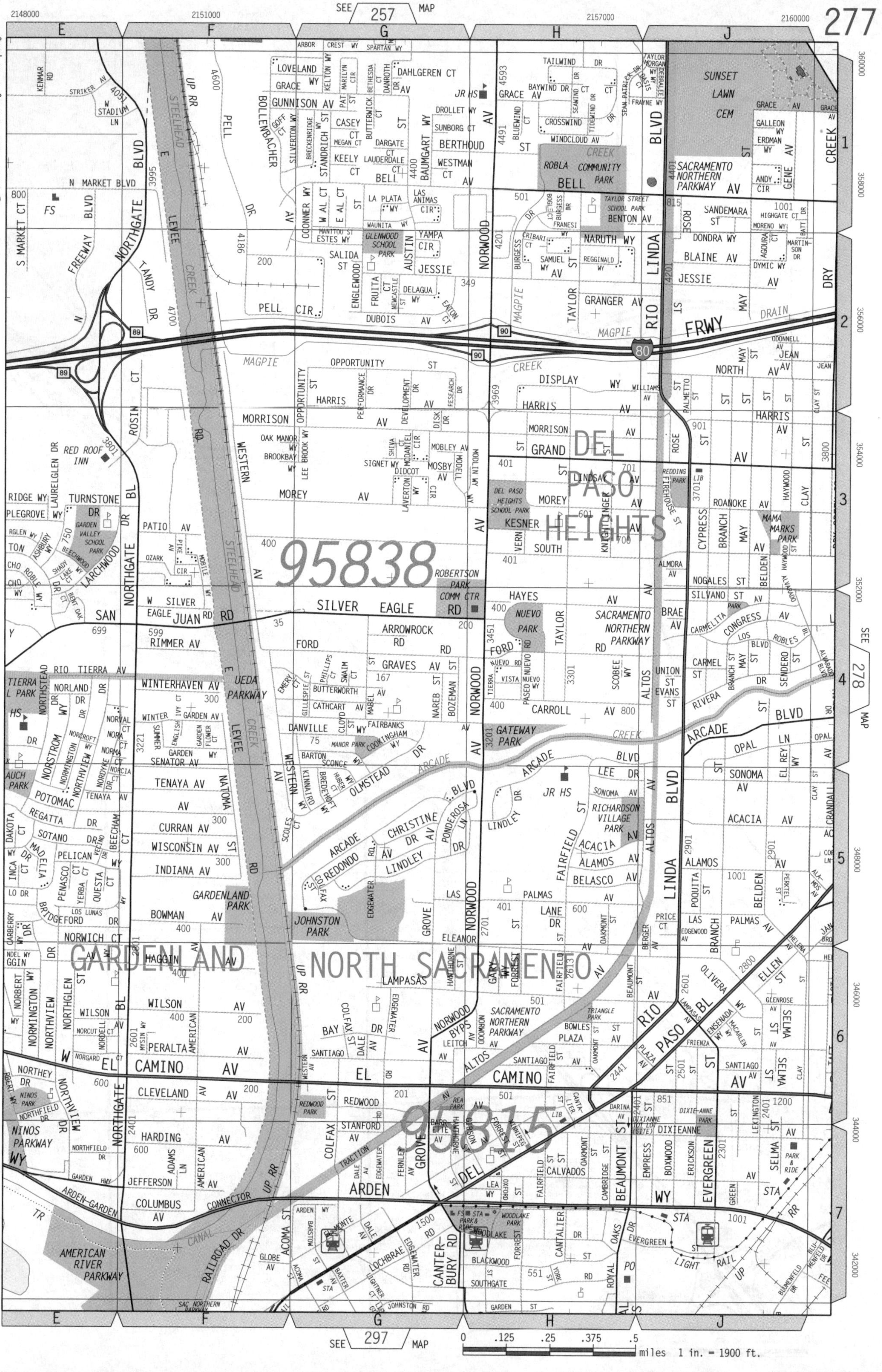
SEE 257 MAP
SEE 278 MAP
SEE 297 MAP
DEL PASO HEIGHTS
95838
95815
GARDENLAND
NORTH SACRAMENTO
SUNSET LAWN CEM
ROBLA CREEK COMMUNITY PARK
SACRAMENTO NORTHERN PARKWAY
TAYLOR STREET SCHOOL PARK
GLENWOOD SCHOOL PARK
DEL PASO HEIGHTS SCHOOL PARK
ROBERTSON PARK COMM CTR
NUEVO PARK
MAMA MARKS PARK
GARDEN VALLEY SCHOOL PARK
RED ROOF INN
TIERRA L PARK
UEDA PARKWAY
GATEWAY PARK
RICHARDSON VILLAGE PARK
JOHNSTON PARK
GARDENLAND PARK
TRIANGLE PARK
REDWOOD PARK
DIXIE-ANNE PARK
WOODLAKE PARK
NINOS PARKWAY
AMERICAN RIVER PARKWAY
FRWY
NORTHGATE BLVD
RIO LINDA BLVD
NORWOOD AV
ARCADE BLVD
EL CAMINO AV
DEL PASO BL
ARDEN WY
SILVER EAGLE RD
STEELHEAD CREEK
MAGPIE CREEK
DRY CREEK
0 .125 .25 .375 .5 miles 1 in. = 1900 ft.

SEE 258 MAP

SEE 277 MAP

0 .125 .25 .375 .5 miles 1 in. = 1900 ft.

SEE 298 MAP

SEE 258 MAP

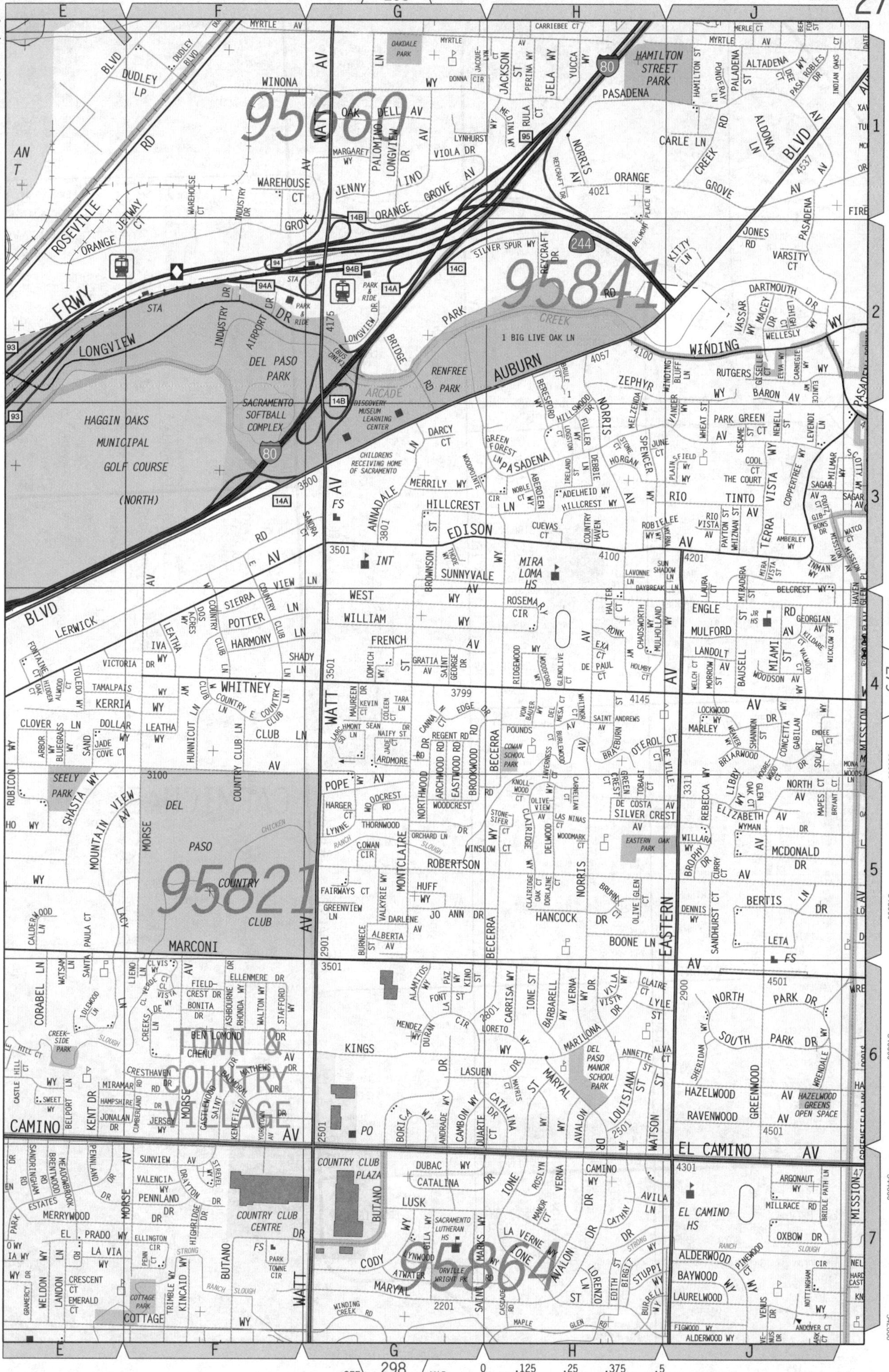

SEE 298 MAP

0 .125 .25 .375 .5
miles 1 in. = 1900 ft.

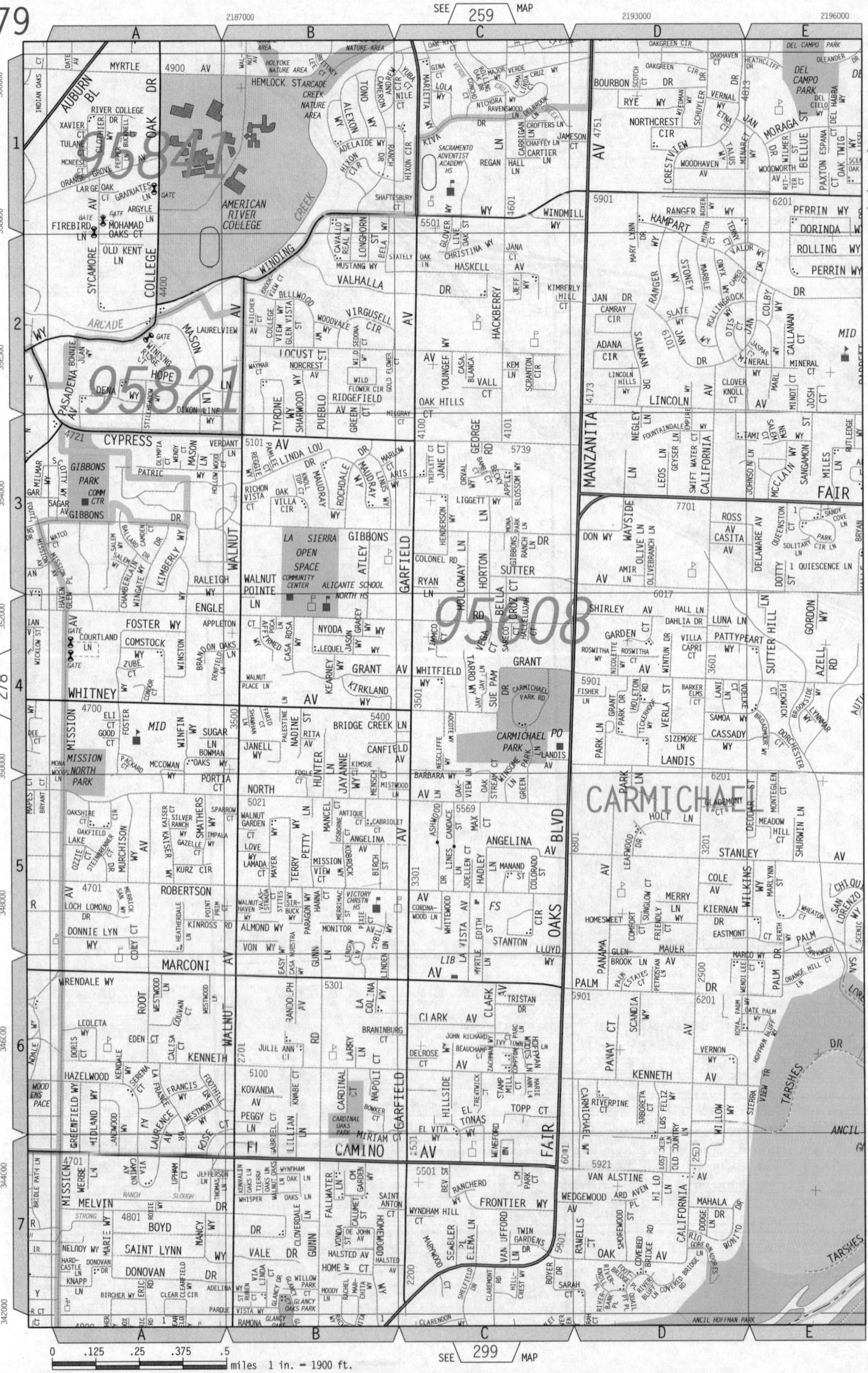
SEE 259 MAP
SEE 278 MAP
SEE 299 MAP
2187000
2193000
2196000
360000
358000
356000
354000
352000
350000
348000
346000
344000
342000
A
B
C
D
E
1
2
3
4
5
6
7
95841
95821
95608
CARMICHAEL
AMERICAN RIVER COLLEGE
ARCADE CREEK NATURE AREA
HOLYOKE NATURE AREA
SACRAMENTO ADVENTIST ACADEMY HS
DEL CAMPO PARK
GIBBONS PARK
COMM CTR
LA SIERRA OPEN SPACE
COMMUNITY CENTER
ALICANTE SCHOOL
NORTH HS
MISSION NORTH PARK
MID
CARMICHAEL PARK
PO
LIB
FS
VICTORY CHRSTN HS
CARDINAL OAKS PARK
GLANCY OAKS PARK
ANCIL HOFFMAN PARK
AUBURN BL
MYRTLE
4900 AV
HEMLOCK ST
COLLEGE OAK DR
WINDING WY
CYPRESS AV
WALNUT AV
GARFIELD AV
MANZANITA AV
FAIR OAKS BLVD
WINDMILL WY
VALHALLA DR
GIBBONS DR
WHITNEY AV
GRANT AV
NORTH AV
MARCONI AV
KENNETH AV
EL CAMINO AV
SAINT LYNN
DONOVAN
MISSION AV
MELVIN
RIDGEFIELD AV
LINDA LOU DR
ENGLE
FOSTER WY
PALM DR
LANDIS AV
STANLEY AV
MERRY LN
LINCOLN AV
SHIRLEY AV
FAIR
PERRIN WY
DORINDA
ROLLING WY
RAMPART
SUTTER AV
HOLLOWAY
ANGELINA AV
ROBERTSON
LOCH LOMOND
VAN ALSTINE AV
CALIFORNIA AV
COVERED BRIDGE RD
OAK AV
TARSHES DR
ANCIL
FRONTIER WY
MARIE WY
BOYD
VALE DR
ALMOND WY
VON WY
NORTHCREST CIR
BOURBON
RYE WY
MORAGA ST
WAYSIDE LN
SUTTER HILL LN
GORDON LN
AZELL RD
CARMICHAEL WY
WEDGEWOOD AV
MAHALA DR

miles 1 in. = 1900 ft.
0 .125 .25 .375 .5

SEE 259 MAP

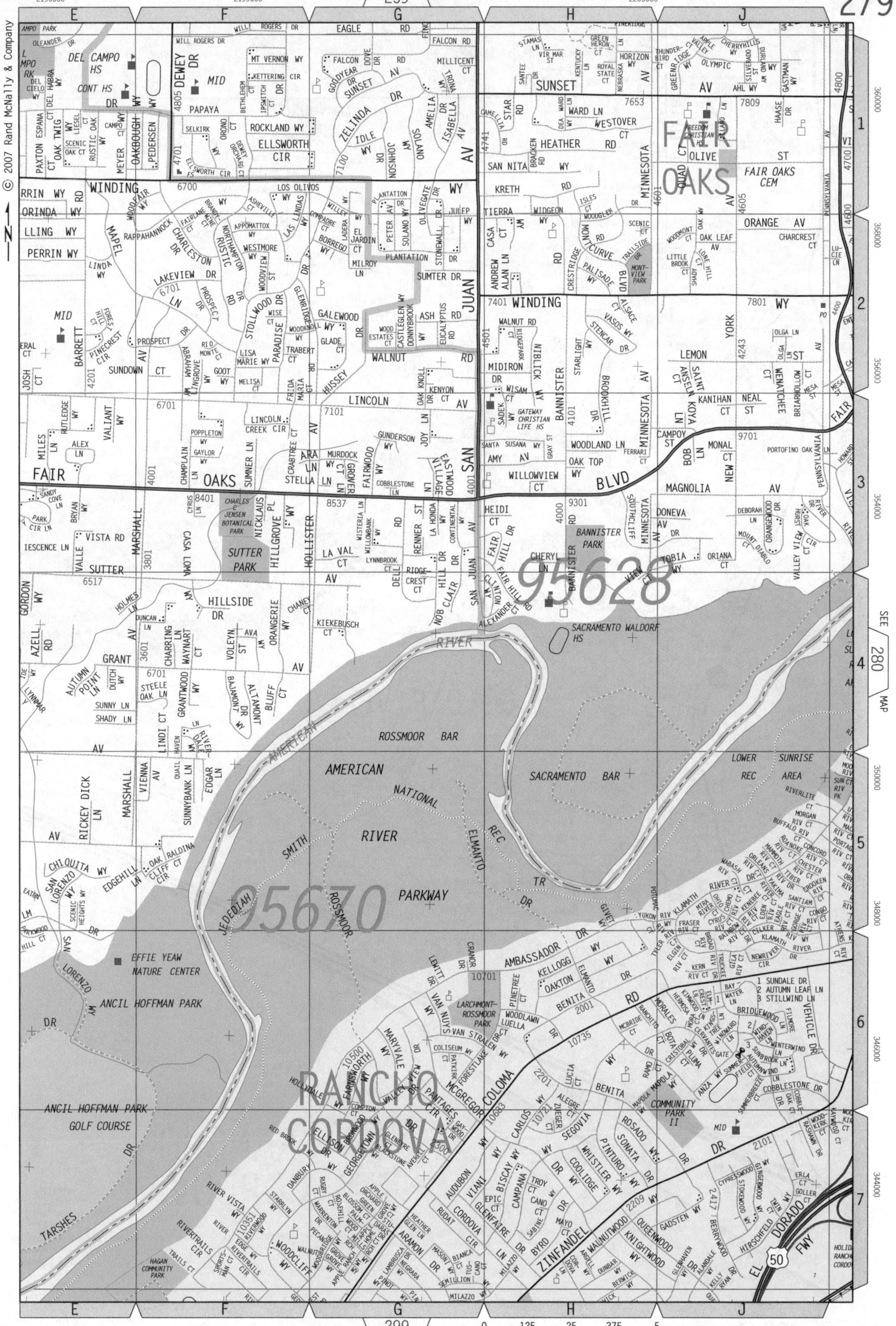
2196000
2199000
2205000
E
F
G
H
J
1
2
3
4
5
6
7
360000
358000
356000
354000
350000
348000
346000
344000
DEL CAMPO HS
CONT HS
MID
DEWEY DR
PAPAYA
PEDERSEN
OAKBOUGH
ELLSWORTH CIR
ROCKLAND WY
MT VERNON WY
EAGLE RD
FALCON RD
SUNSET AV
ZELINDA DR
IDLE WY
JOHNSON DR
SOLANO WY
AMELIA DR
ISABELLA AV
FAIR OAKS
FREEDOM CHRISTIAN HS
OLIVE ST
FAIR OAKS CEM
HEATHER RD
WESTOVER CT
WARD LN
KRETH RD
MINNESOTA AV
WINDING WY
PLANTATION
ORANGE AV
CHARCREST CT
MONTVIEW PARK
WALNUT RD
LEMON
YORK
SAINT ANSELM
LINCOLN AV
KANIHAN CT
NEAL ST
GATEWAY CHRISTIAN LIFE HS
BANNISTER RD
WOODLAND LN
FAIR OAKS BLVD
MAGNOLIA AV
SAN JUAN AV
CHARLES C. JENSEN BOTANICAL PARK
SUTTER PARK
SUTTER AV
HILLSIDE DR
BANNISTER PARK
95628
SACRAMENTO WALDORF HS
GRANT AV
RIVER
AMERICAN
ROSSMOOR BAR
SACRAMENTO BAR
LOWER SUNRISE REC AREA
AMERICAN NATIONAL RIVER PARKWAY
SMITH
ELMANTO
REC TR
JEDEDIAH
ROSSMOOR DR
95670
EFFIE YEAW NATURE CENTER
ANCIL HOFFMAN PARK
ANCIL HOFFMAN PARK GOLF COURSE
TARSHES DR
AMBASSADOR DR
LARCHMONT-ROSSMOOR PARK
COLOMA RD
RANCHO CORDOVA
BENITA DR
COMMUNITY PARK II
MID
ZINFANDEL DR
50
EL DORADO FWY
HAGAN COMMUNITY PARK
1 SUNDALE DR
2 AUTUMN LEAF LN
3 STILLWIND LN
SEE 280 MAP
SEE 299 MAP
0 .125 .25 .375 .5
miles 1 in. = 1900 ft.

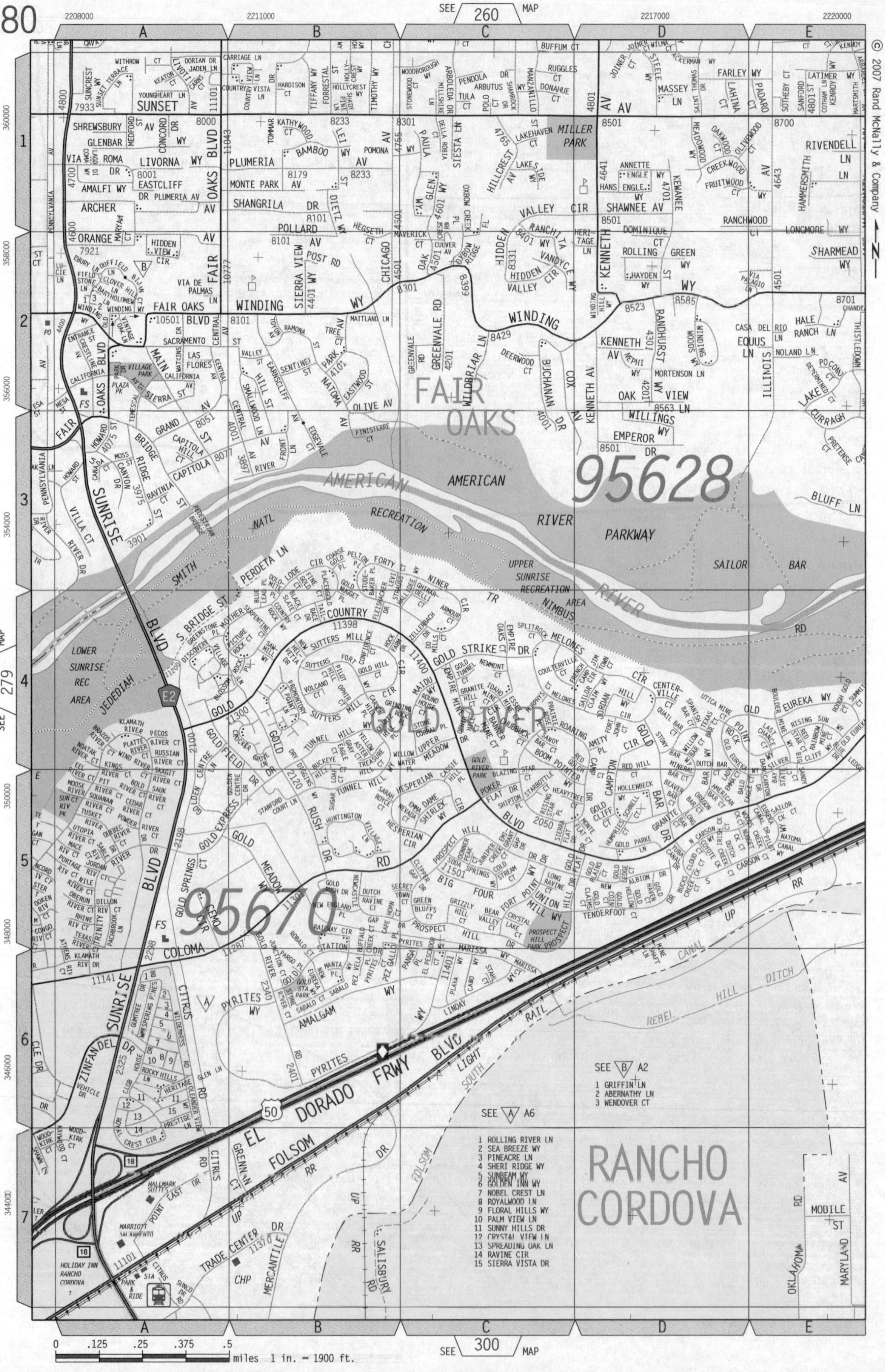
SEE 260 MAP
SEE 300 MAP
SEE 279 MAP
FAIR OAKS
95628
95670
GOLD RIVER
RANCHO CORDOVA
AMERICAN RIVER PARKWAY
AMERICAN RECREATION
UPPER SUNRISE RECREATION AREA
LOWER SUNRISE REC AREA
SAILOR BAR
SUNRISE BLVD
FAIR OAKS BLVD
WINDING WY
EL DORADO FRWY
FOLSOM BLVD
COLOMA RD
GOLD COUNTRY
GOLD EXPRESS DR
NIMBUS RD
MILLER PARK
GOLD RIVER PARK
PROSPECT HILL PARK
VILLAGE PARK
HALLMARK SUITES
MARRIOTT SACRAMENTO
HOLIDAY INN RANCHO CORDOVA
CHP
PARK & RIDE
SEE B A2
1 GRIFFIN LN
2 ABERNATHY LN
3 WENDOVER CT
SEE A A6
1 ROLLING RIVER LN
2 SEA BREEZE WY
3 PINEACRE LN
4 SHERI RIDGE WY
5 SUNBEAM WY
6 GOLDEN INN WY
7 NOBEL CREST LN
8 ROYALWOOD LN
9 FLORAL HILLS WY
10 PALM VIEW LN
11 SUNNY HILLS DR
12 CRYSTAL VIEW LN
13 SPREADING OAK LN
14 RAVINE CIR
15 SIERRA VISTA DR
0 .125 .25 .375 .5 miles 1 in. = 1900 ft.

SEE 260 MAP

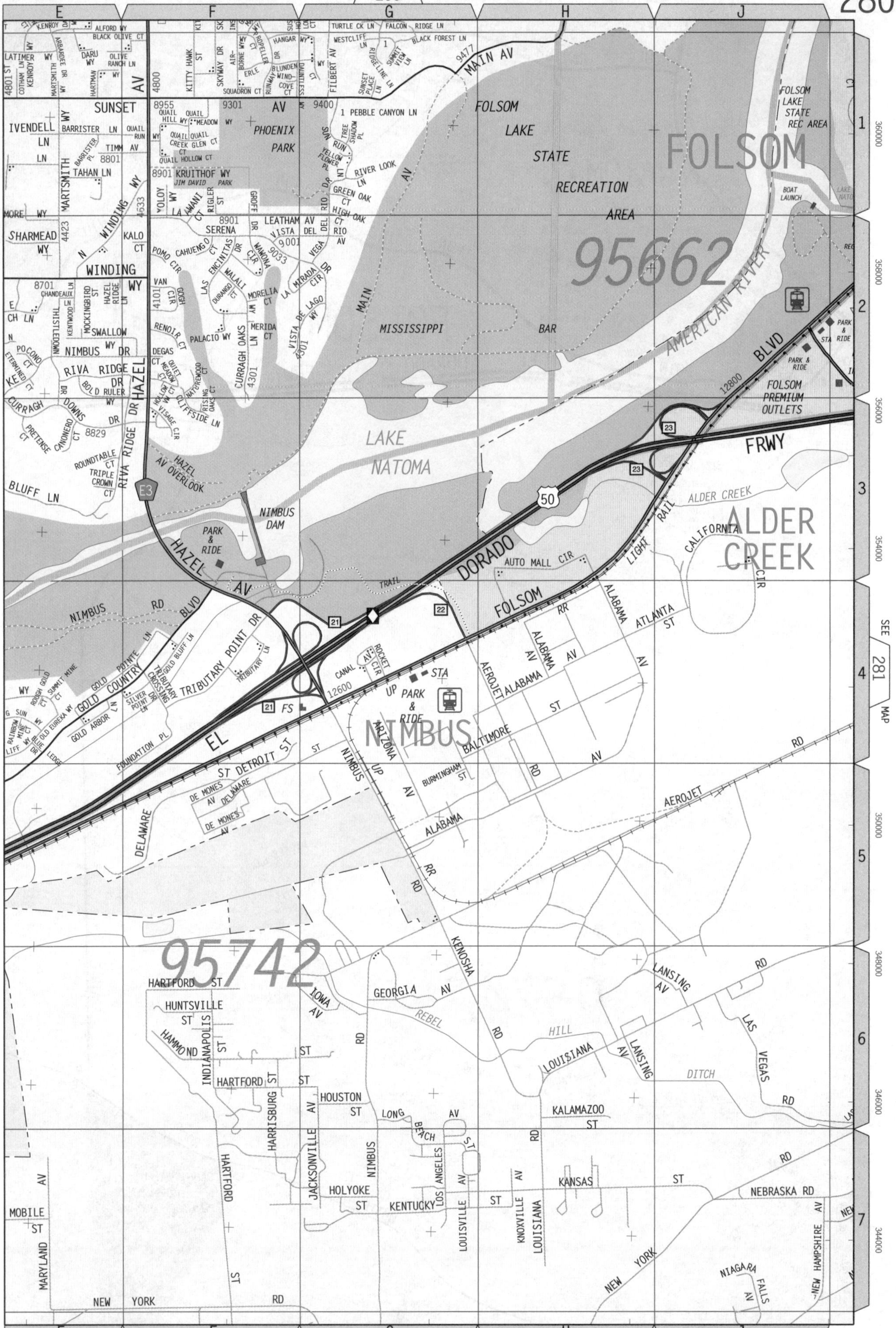

SEE 281 MAP

SEE 300 MAP

0 .125 .25 .375 .5 miles 1 in. = 1900 ft.

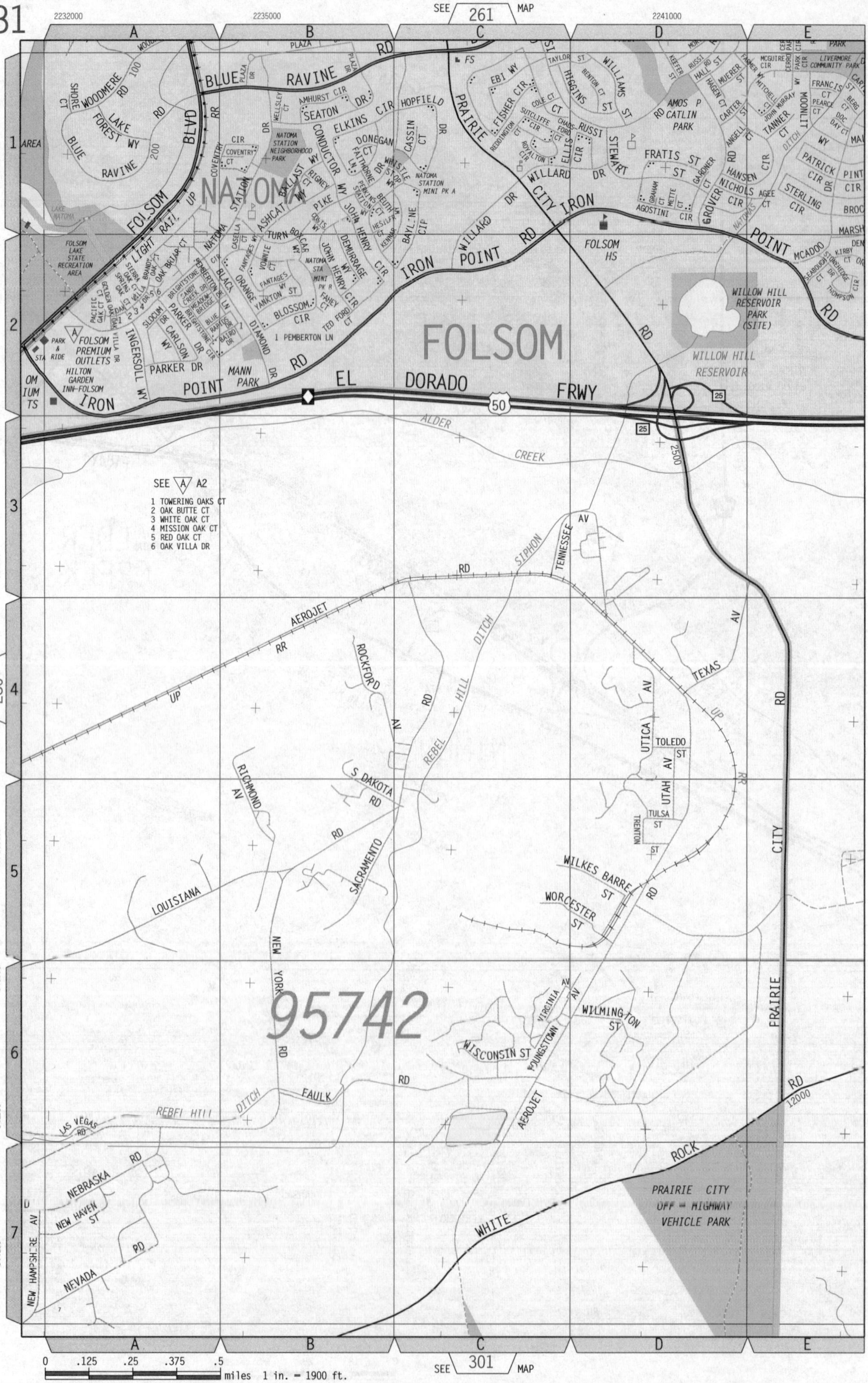
SEE 261 MAP
SEE 280 MAP
SEE 301 MAP
NATOMA
FOLSOM
95742
FOLSOM HS
WILLOW HILL RESERVOIR PARK (SITE)
WILLOW HILL RESERVOIR
AMOS P CATLIN PARK
NATOMA STATION NEIGHBORHOOD PARK
FOLSOM LAKE STATE RECREATION AREA
FOLSOM PREMIUM OUTLETS
HILTON GARDEN INN-FOLSOM
PARK & RIDE
1 PEMBERTON LN
EL DORADO FRWY
IRON POINT RD
BLUE RAVINE RD
FOLSOM BLVD
PRAIRIE CITY RD
WHITE ROCK RD
AEROJET RD
ALDER CREEK
REBEL HILL DITCH
SIPHON RD
UP RR
PRAIRIE CITY OFF – HIGHWAY VEHICLE PARK
SEE A A2
1 TOWERING OAKS CT
2 OAK BUTTE CT
3 WHITE OAK CT
4 MISSION OAK CT
5 RED OAK CT
6 OAK VILLA DR

0 .125 .25 .375 .5 miles 1 in. = 1900 ft.

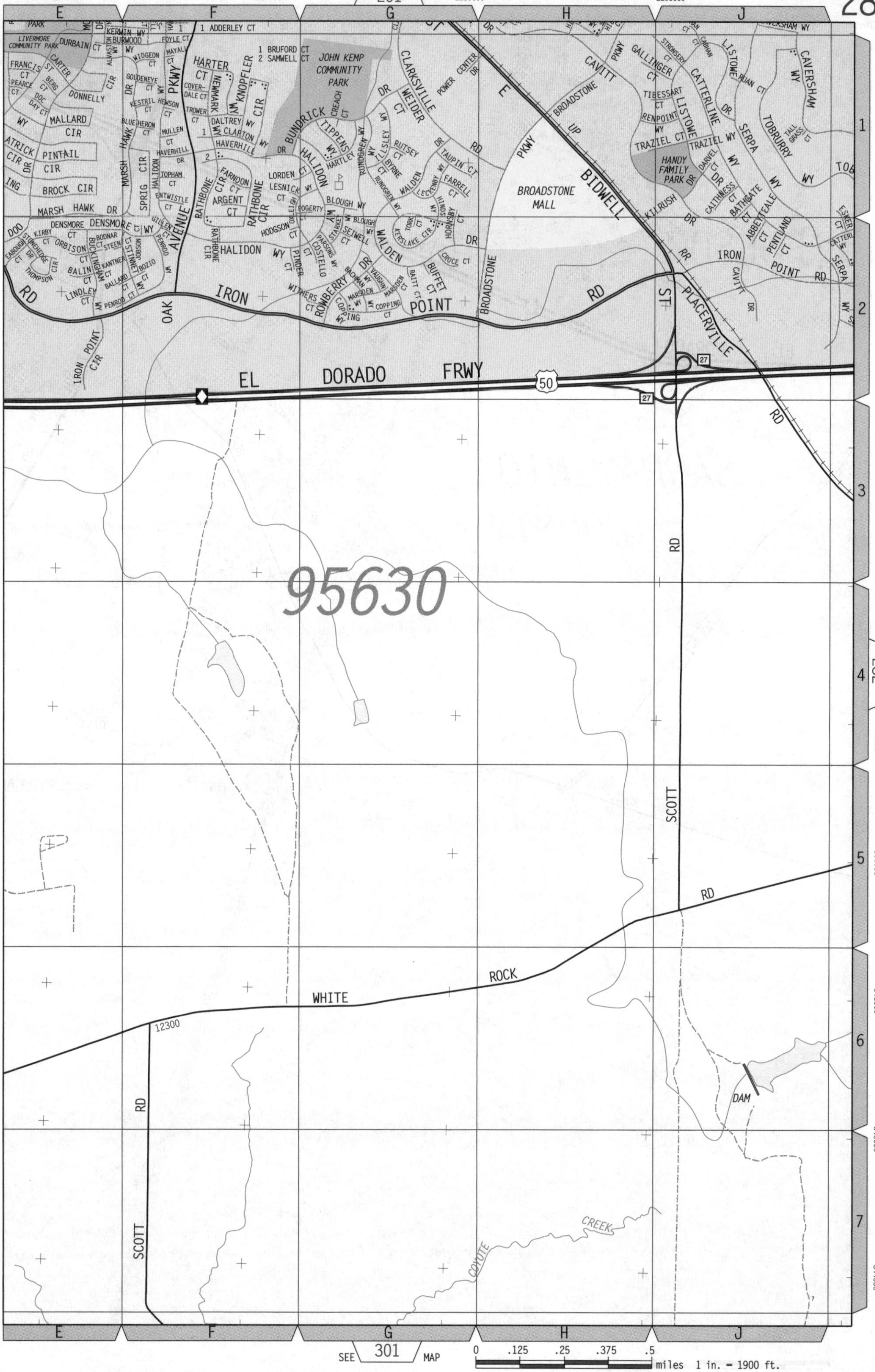
SEE 261 MAP
2244000
2247000
2250000
2253000
E
F
G
H
J
LIVERMORE COMMUNITY PARK
DURBAIN CT
KERWIN WY
BURWOOD
FOYLE CT
1 ADDERLEY CT
1 BRUFORD CT
2 SAMWELL CT
JOHN KEMP COMMUNITY PARK
FRANCIS CT
CARTER
PEARCE CT
BERG
DOC
DAY CT
DONNELLY
MALLARD CIR
ATRICK CIR
PINTAIL CIR
BROCK CIR
MARSH HAWK DR
DENSMORE
WIDGEON CT
GOLDENEYE CT
KESTRIL
BLUE HERON CT
HARTER CT
NEWMARK
KNOPFLER CIR
DALTREY WY
CLARTON
HAVERHILL
TOPHAM CT
ENTWISTLE CT
FARNOON CT
ARGENT CT
RATHBONE CIR
HALIDON WY
LORDEN CT
LESNICK CT
HODGSON CT
BUNDRICK
HALIDON
TIPPENS
HARTLEY
CLARKSVILLE
WEIDER CT
POWER CENTER DR
RUTSEY CT
BYRNE
TILSLEY
TAUPIN CT
FARRELL CT
WALDEN DR
BLOUGH WY
SEIWELL
COSTELLO
PINDER CT
ROWBERRY DR
BUFFET CT
CROCE CT
COPPING CT
OAK AVENUE PKWY
IRON POINT RD
IRON POINT CIR
BROADSTONE PKWY
BROADSTONE MALL
BIDWELL ST
E
UP RR
CAVITT
GALLINGER CT
STRONSERY CT
LISTOWE
CATTERLINE DR
TIBESSART CT
RENPOINT WY
TRAZIEL CT
TRAZIEL WY
HANDY FAMILY PARK
SERPA WY
TOBRURRY WY
CAVERSHAM WY
KILRUSH DR
BATHGATE CT
ABBEYFEALE CT
PENTLAND CT
IRON POINT RD
CAVITT DR
PLACERVILLE RD
EL DORADO FRWY
50
27
95630
SCOTT RD
WHITE ROCK RD
12300
SCOTT RD
DAM
COYOTE CREEK
362000
360000
358000
356000
354000
352000
350000
348000
346000
344000
1
2
3
4
5
6
7
SEE 282 MAP
SEE 301 MAP
0 .125 .25 .375 .5 miles 1 in. = 1900 ft.

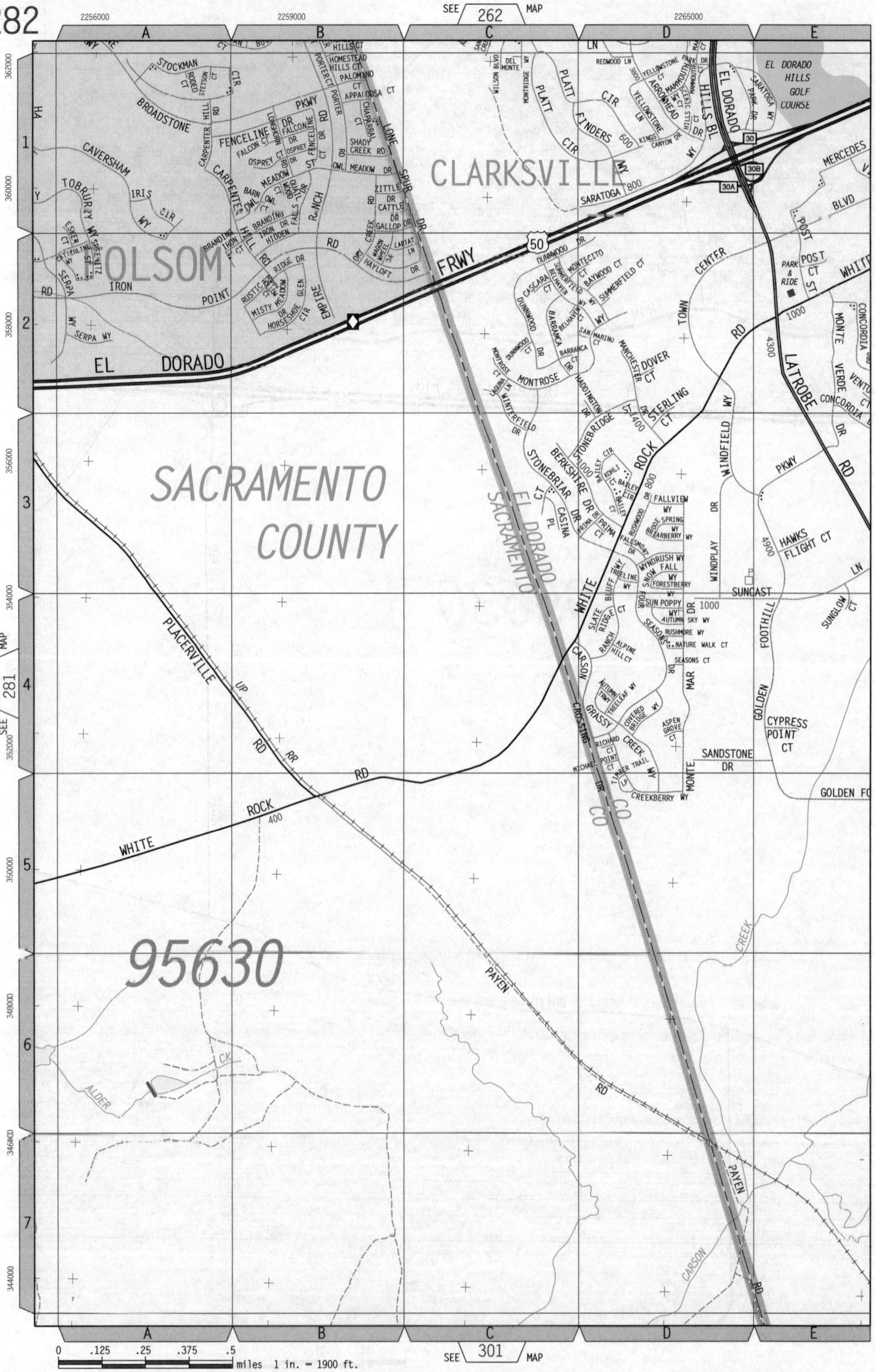
SEE 262 MAP
SEE 281 MAP
SEE 301 MAP
A
B
C
D
E
1
2
3
4
5
6
7
2256000
2259000
2265000
362000
360000
358000
356000
354000
352000
350000
348000
346000
344000
FOLSOM
CLARKSVILLE
SACRAMENTO COUNTY
95630
EL DORADO HILLS GOLF COURSE
STOCKMAN CIR
BROADSTONE PKWY
CAVERSHAM WY
TOBRURY WY
IRIS CIR
FENCELINE DR
CARPENTER HILL RD
MEADOW
EMPIRE RANCH RD
IRON POINT RD
SERPA WY
EL DORADO FRWY
50
LONE SPUR DR
SHADY CREEK RD
OWL MEADOW DR
HAYLOFT DR
PLATT CIR
FINDERS WY
SARATOGA 800
YELLOWSTONE LN
EL DORADO HILLS BL
30
30A
30B
MERCEDES
POST ST
PARK & RIDE
WHITE ROCK RD
TOWN CENTER
LATROBE RD
MONTE VERDE DR
CONCORDIA
DUNWOODY DR
MONTROSE DR
STONEBRIDGE ST
STONEBRIAR DR
BERKSHIRE DR
STERLING CT
DOVER CT
WINTERFIELD DR
EL DORADO
SACRAMENTO
CO
CO
FALLVIEW WY
WINDFIELD WY
WINDPLAY DR
PKWY
HAWKS FLIGHT CT
SUNCAST LN
SUNGLOW CT
FOOTHILL
GOLDEN
CYPRESS POINT CT
SANDSTONE DR
GOLDEN FO
FOUR SEASONS DR
MONTE MAR DR
CARSON CROSSING DR
GRASSY CREEK WY
CREEKBERRY WY
PLACERVILLE RD
UP RR
WHITE ROCK RD
400
1000
4300
4900
PAYEN RD
CREEK
CARSON
ALDER CK
0 .125 .25 .375 .5 miles 1 in. = 1900 ft.

SEE 262 MAP
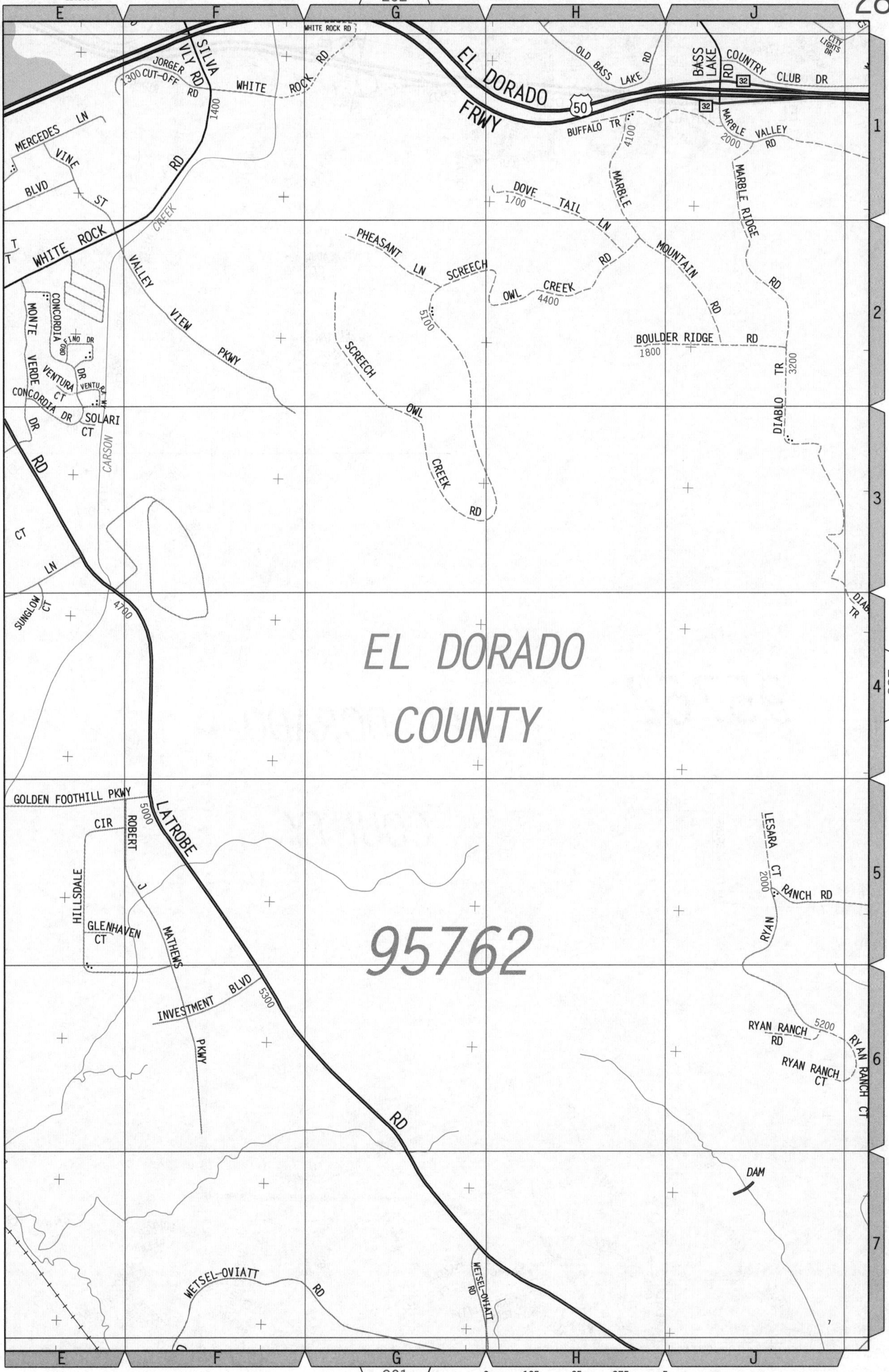
EL DORADO COUNTY
95762
EL DORADO FRWY
50
32
WHITE ROCK RD
SILVA VLY RD
JORGER RD
1300 CUT-OFF
1400
OLD BASS LAKE RD
BASS LAKE RD
COUNTRY CLUB DR
CITY LIGHTS DR
BUFFALO TR
4100
MARBLE VALLEY RD
2000
MARBLE RIDGE RD
MARBLE MOUNTAIN RD
DOVE TAIL LN
1700
PHEASANT LN
SCREECH OWL CREEK RD
4400
5100
BOULDER RIDGE RD
1800
DIABLO TR
3200
MERCEDES LN
VINE ST
BLVD
VALLEY VIEW PKWY
CARSON CREEK
MONTE VERDE DR
CONCORDIA CT
CINO DR
ORO
VENTURA CT
VENTURA DR
CONCORDIA DR
SOLARI CT
RD
CT
LN
SUNGLOW CT
4700
GOLDEN FOOTHILL PKWY
CIR
ROBERT J MATHEWS PKWY
5000
LATROBE RD
HILLSDALE
GLENHAVEN CT
INVESTMENT BLVD
5300
LESARA CT
2000
RYAN RANCH RD
RYAN RANCH RD
5200
RYAN RANCH CT
RYAN RANCH CT
DAM
WETSEL-OVIATT RD
WETSEL-OVIATT RD
E F G H J
1 2 3 4 5 6 7
2268000 2271000 2274000 2277000
362000 360000 358000 356000 352000 350000 348000 346000 344000
0 .125 .25 .375 .5 miles 1 in. = 1900 ft.
SEE 283 MAP
SEE 301 MAP

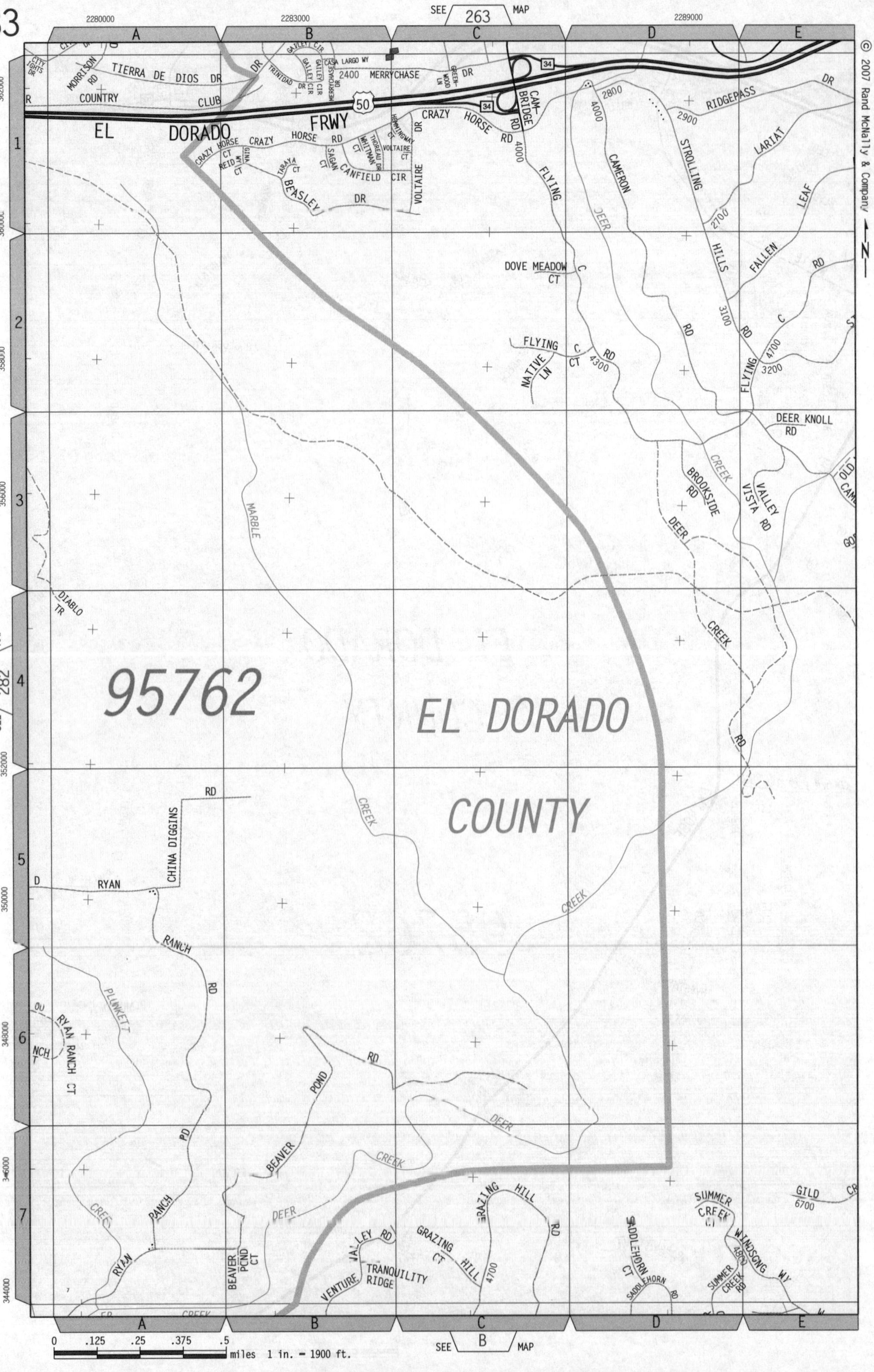
SEE 263 MAP
SEE 282 MAP
SEE B MAP
2280000
2283000
2289000
362000
360000
358000
356000
352000
350000
348000
346000
344000
A
B
C
D
E
1
2
3
4
5
6
7
95762
EL DORADO
COUNTY
EL DORADO FRWY
50
34
TIERRA DE DIOS DR
MORRISON RD
COUNTRY CLUB
CRAZY HORSE RD
CRAZY HORSE CT
CANFIELD CIR
BEASLEY DR
VOLTAIRE DR
MERRYCHASE
2400
CASA LARGO WY
GAILEY CIR
TRINIDAD DR
CAMBRIDGE RD
RIDGEPASS DR
FLYING C RD
CAMERON
STROLLING HILLS RD
LARIAT
FALLEN LEAF RD
DOVE MEADOW CT
FLYING C CT
NATIVE LN
DEER KNOLL RD
BROOKSIDE RD
VALLEY VISTA RD
DEER CREEK
DEER CREEK RD
MARBLE CREEK
DIABLO TR
CHINA DIGGINS RD
RYAN RANCH RD
RYAN RANCH CT
PLUNKETT
POND RD
BEAVER POND CT
VALLEY RD
TRANQUILITY RIDGE
VENTURE
GRAZING HILL RD
GRAZING HILL CT
SADDLEHORN CT
SADDLEHORN RD
SUMMER CREEK CT
SUMMER CREEK RD
WINDSONG WY
GILD
6700
0 .125 .25 .375 .5 miles 1 in. = 1900 ft.

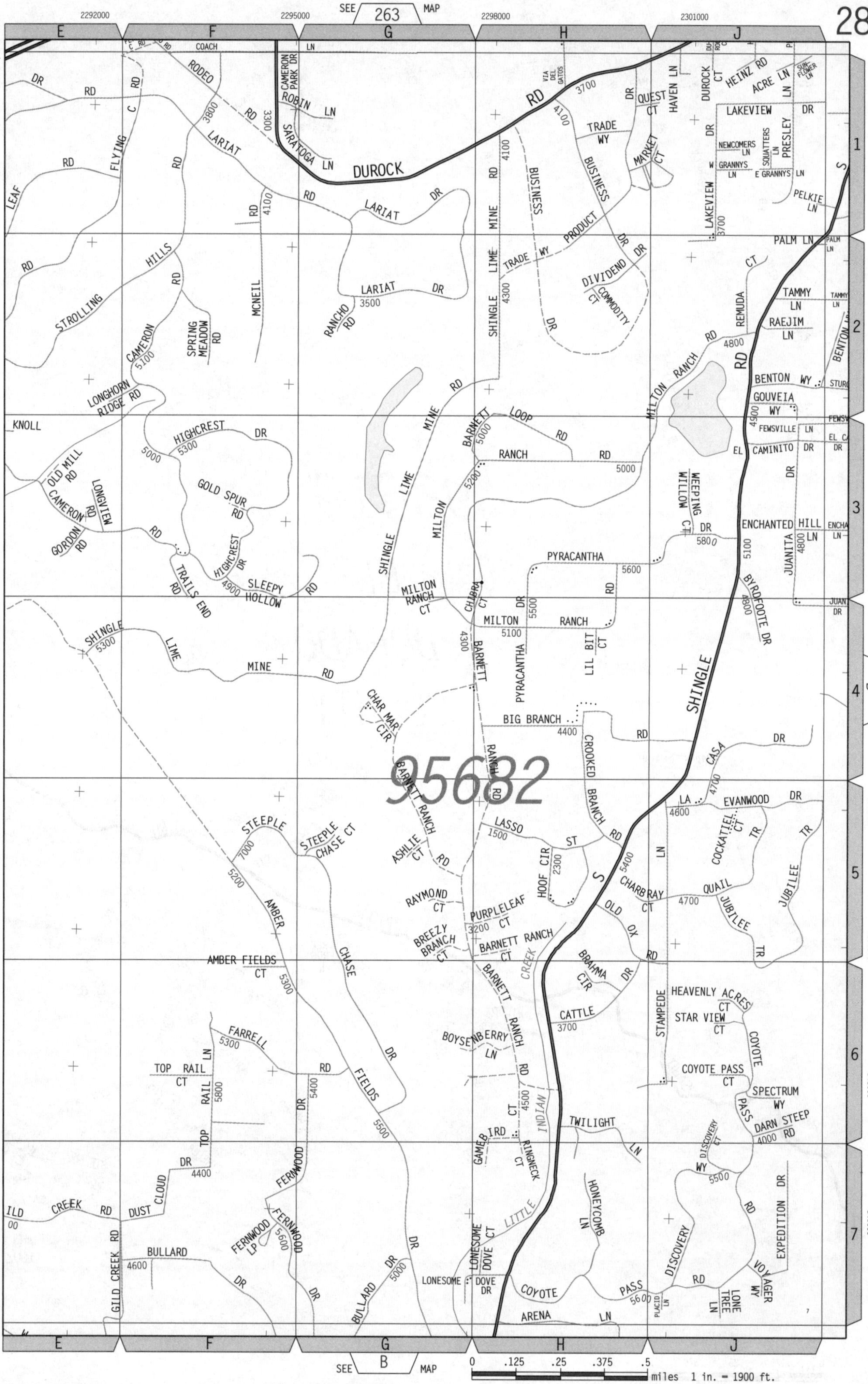
SEE 263 MAP
SEE B MAP
95682
2292000
2295000
2298000
2301000
362000
360000
358000
356000
352000
350000
348000
346000
E
F
G
H
J
1
2
3
4
5
6
7
DUROCK RD
COACH LN
RODEO RD
CAMERON PARK DR
ROBIN LN
SARATOGA LN
VIA DEL GATOS
QUEST CT
HAVEN LN
DUROCK CT
HEINZ RD
ACRE LN
SUNFLOWER LN
LAKEVIEW DR
NEWCOMERS LN
SQUATTERS LN
PRESLEY LN
W GRANNYS LN
E GRANNYS LN
PELKIE LN
LAKEVIEW DR
PALM LN
TRADE WY
MARKET CT
BUSINESS DR
PRODUCT DR
DIVIDEND DR
COMMODITY CT
LARIAT RD
LARIAT DR
FLYING C RD
LEAF RD
MCNEIL RD
SHINGLE LIME MINE RD
RANCHO RD
STROLLING HILLS RD
SPRING MEADOW RD
CAMERON RD
LONGHORN RIDGE RD
KNOLL
HIGHCREST DR
OLD MILL RD
LONGVIEW RD
GORDON RD
GOLD SPUR RD
TRAILS END RD
SLEEPY HOLLOW RD
MILTON RANCH RD
MILTON RANCH CT
BARNETT LOOP RD
RANCH RD
CHIBRA CT
PYRACANTHA DR
LIL BIT CT
WEEPING WILLOW CT
REMUDA CT
TAMMY LN
RAEJIM LN
BENTON WY
GOUVEIA WY
FEWSVILLE LN
EL CAMINITO DR
ENCHANTED HILL LN
JUANITA DR
BYRDFOOTE DR
SHINGLE RD
BIG BRANCH RD
CHAR MAR CIR
BARNETT RANCH RD
CROOKED BRANCH RD
CASA DR
LA
EVANWOOD DR
COCKATIEL CT
QUAIL TR
JUBILEE TR
LASSO ST
HOOF CIR
CHARBRAY CT
OLD OX RD
ASHLIE CT
RAYMOND CT
PURPLELEAF CT
BREEZY BRANCH CT
BARNETT RANCH CT
STEEPLE CHASE CT
STEEPLE CHASE DR
AMBER FIELDS DR
AMBER FIELDS CT
BRAHMA CIR
CATTLE DR
STAMPEDE LN
HEAVENLY ACRES CT
STAR VIEW CT
COYOTE PASS CT
COYOTE PASS
SPECTRUM WY
DARN STEEP RD
BOYSENBERRY LN
FARRELL RD
TOP RAIL LN
TOP RAIL CT
INDIAN CREEK
LITTLE INDIAN CREEK
TWILIGHT LN
GAMEBIRD CT
RINGNECK CT
DISCOVERY CT
DISCOVERY WY
EXPEDITION DR
HONEYCOMB LN
DUST CLOUD DR
WILD CREEK RD
GILD CREEK RD
FERNWOOD DR
FERNWOOD LP
BULLARD DR
LONESOME DOVE CT
LONESOME DOVE DR
COYOTE PASS
LONE TREE LN
VOYAGER WY
PLACID LN
ARENA LN
0 .125 .25 .375 .5
miles 1 in. = 1900 ft.

SEE 266 MAP

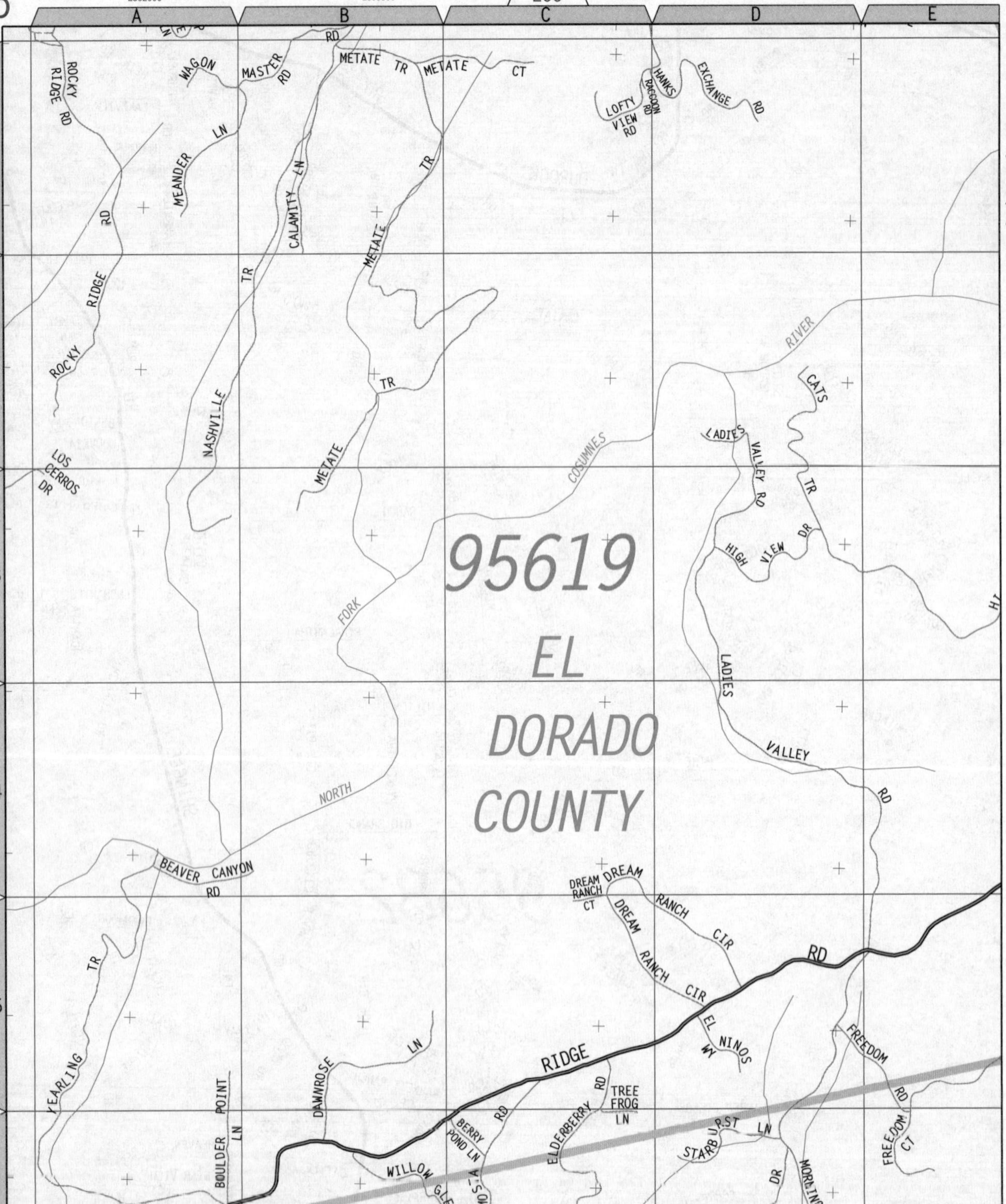
2352000
2355000
2358000
2361000
A
B
C
D
E
1
2
3
4
5
6
7
364000
362000
360000
358000
356000
354000
352000
350000
348000
346000
95619
EL DORADO COUNTY
ROCKY RIDGE RD
WAGON
MASTER RD
METATE TR
METATE CT
MEANDER LN
CALAMITY LN
LOFTY VIEW RD
RACCOON RD
HANKS
EXCHANGE RD
RIDGE
ROCKY
NASHVILLE TR
METATE TR
LOS CERROS DR
RIVER
CATS TR
LADIES VALLEY RD
COSUMNES
HIGH VIEW DR
FORK
NORTH
LADIES VALLEY RD
BEAVER CANYON RD
DREAM RANCH CT
DREAM RANCH CIR
DREAM RANCH CIR
RD
EL NINOS WY
YEARLING TR
DAWNROSE LN
BOULDER POINT LN
RIDGE
TREE FROG LN
ELDERBERRY RD
BERRY POND LN
RD
STARBURST LN
FREEDOM RD
FREEDOM CT
WILLOW GLEN RD
ALMOSTA
SAND
MONTES DR
MORLING
RANCHO
GORGE VIEW DR
CANYON
ETHELON PL
STREAM
VACATION
MIDDLE
WY
OU

SEE B MAP

0 .125 .25 .375 .5 miles 1 in. = 1900 ft.

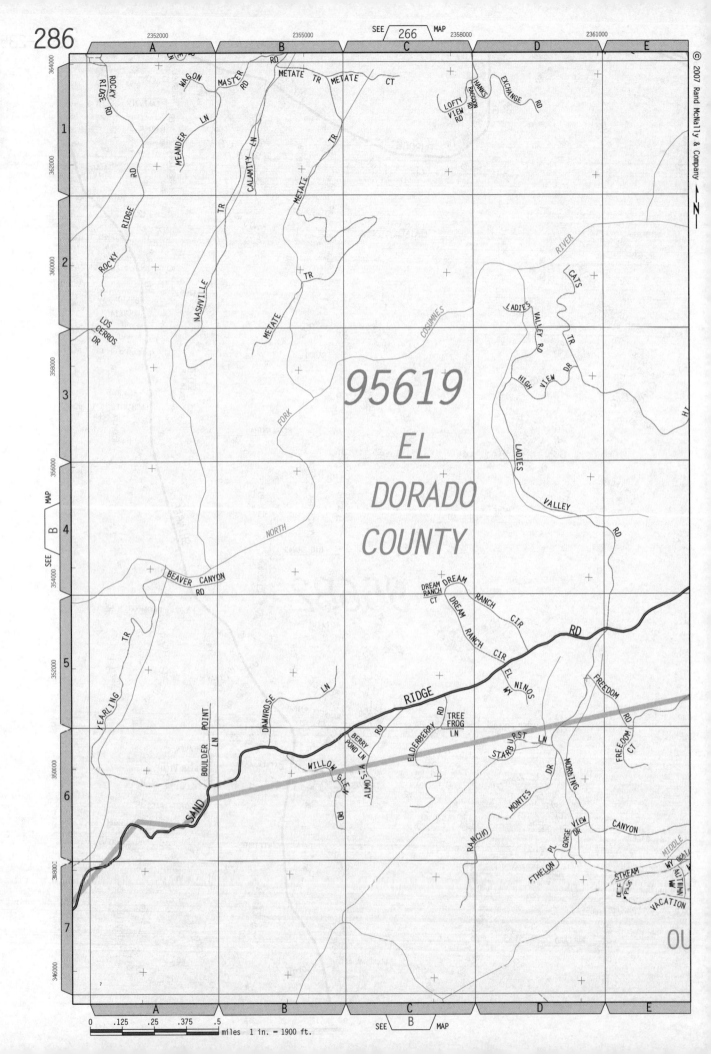

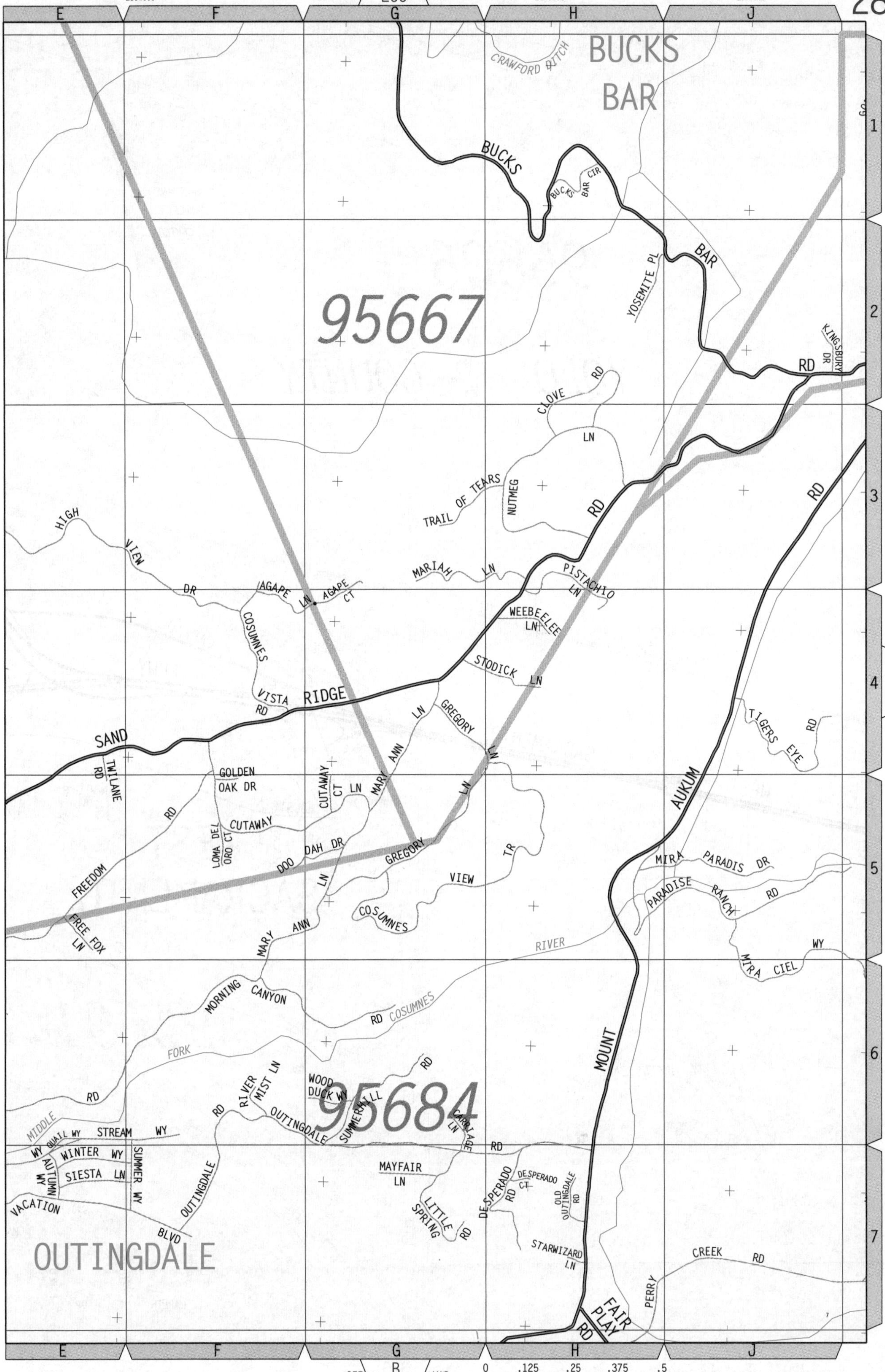
SEE 266 MAP
SEE B MAP
SEE B MAP
BUCKS BAR
95667
95684
OUTINGDALE
BUCKS BAR RD
BUCKS BAR CIR
YOSEMITE PL
KINGSBURY DR
CRAWFORD DITCH
CLOVE LN
CLOVE RD
TRAIL OF TEARS
NUTMEG
HIGH VIEW DR
MARIAH LN
PISTACHIO LN
AGAPE LN
AGAPE CT
COSUMNES
WEEBEELEE LN
STODICK LN
VISTA RD
SAND RIDGE RD
GREGORY LN
MARY ANN LN
TWILANE RD
GOLDEN OAK DR
CUTAWAY CT
CUTAWAY
LOMA DEL ORO CT
FREEDOM RD
DOO DAH DR
GREGORY
VIEW TR
COSUMNES
FREE FOX LN
MOUNT AUKUM RD
MIRA PARADIS DR
PARADISE RANCH RD
MIRA CIEL WY
RIVER
TIGERS EYE RD
MORNING CANYON RD
COSUMNES
FORK
MIDDLE
RD
RIVER MIST LN
WOOD DUCK WY
SUMMERHILL
OUTINGDALE RD
CARRIAGE LN
RD
QUAIL WY
STREAM WY
WINTER WY
AUTUMN WY
SIESTA LN
SUMMER WY
VACATION BLVD
OUTINGDALE
MAYFAIR LN
LITTLE SPRING RD
DESPERADO RD
DESPERADO CT
OLD OUTINGDALE RD
STARWIZARD LN
FAIR PLAY RD
PERRY CREEK RD
E F G H J
1 2 3 4 5 6 7
2364000 2370000 2373000
364000 362000 360000 358000 354000 352000 350000 348000 346000
0 .125 .25 .375 .5
miles 1 in. = 1900 ft.

SEE 276 MAP

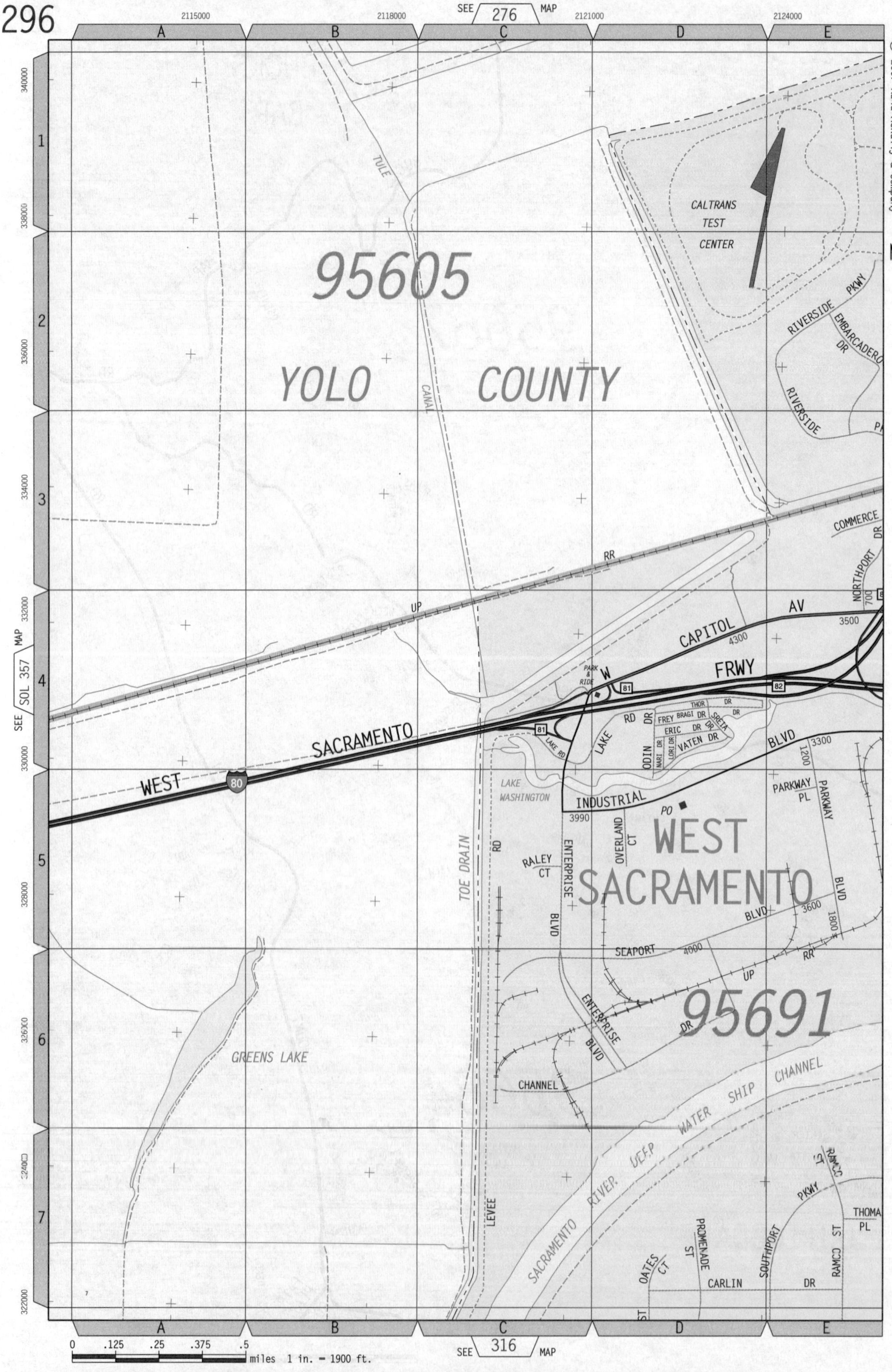
2115000
2118000
2121000
2124000
A
B
C
D
E
1
2
3
4
5
6
7
340000
338000
336000
334000
332000
330000
328000
322000
95605
YOLO
COUNTY
TULE
CANAL
CALTRANS
TEST
CENTER
RIVERSIDE
PKWY
EMBARCADERO
DR
RIVERSIDE
COMMERCE
DR
NORTHPORT
RR
UP
CAPITOL
AV
4300
3500
FRWY
PARK & RIDE
W
81
82
SACRAMENTO
WEST
80
LAKE
RD
DR
THOR
DR
FREY
BRAGI
DR
ERIC
DR
FREYA
VATEN
DR
ODIN
NARI DR
LORI DR
LAKE RD
BLVD
3300
1200
PARKWAY
PL
PARKWAY
LAKE
WASHINGTON
INDUSTRIAL
3990
PO
WEST
SACRAMENTO
OVERLAND
CT
TOE DRAIN
RD
RALEY
CT
ENTERPRISE
BLVD
BLVD
BLVD
3600
1800
SEAPORT
4900
RR
UP
95691
DR
ENTERPRISE
BLVD
GREENS LAKE
CHANNEL
CHANNEL
SHIP
WATER
LEVEE
SACRAMENTO
RIVER
PKWY
THOMA
PL
OATES
CT
ST
PROMENADE
SOUTHPORT
ST
RAMCO
CARLIN
DR
RAMCO
ST
0
.125
.25
.375
.5
miles 1 in. = 1900 ft.

SEE SOL 357 MAP

SEE 316 MAP

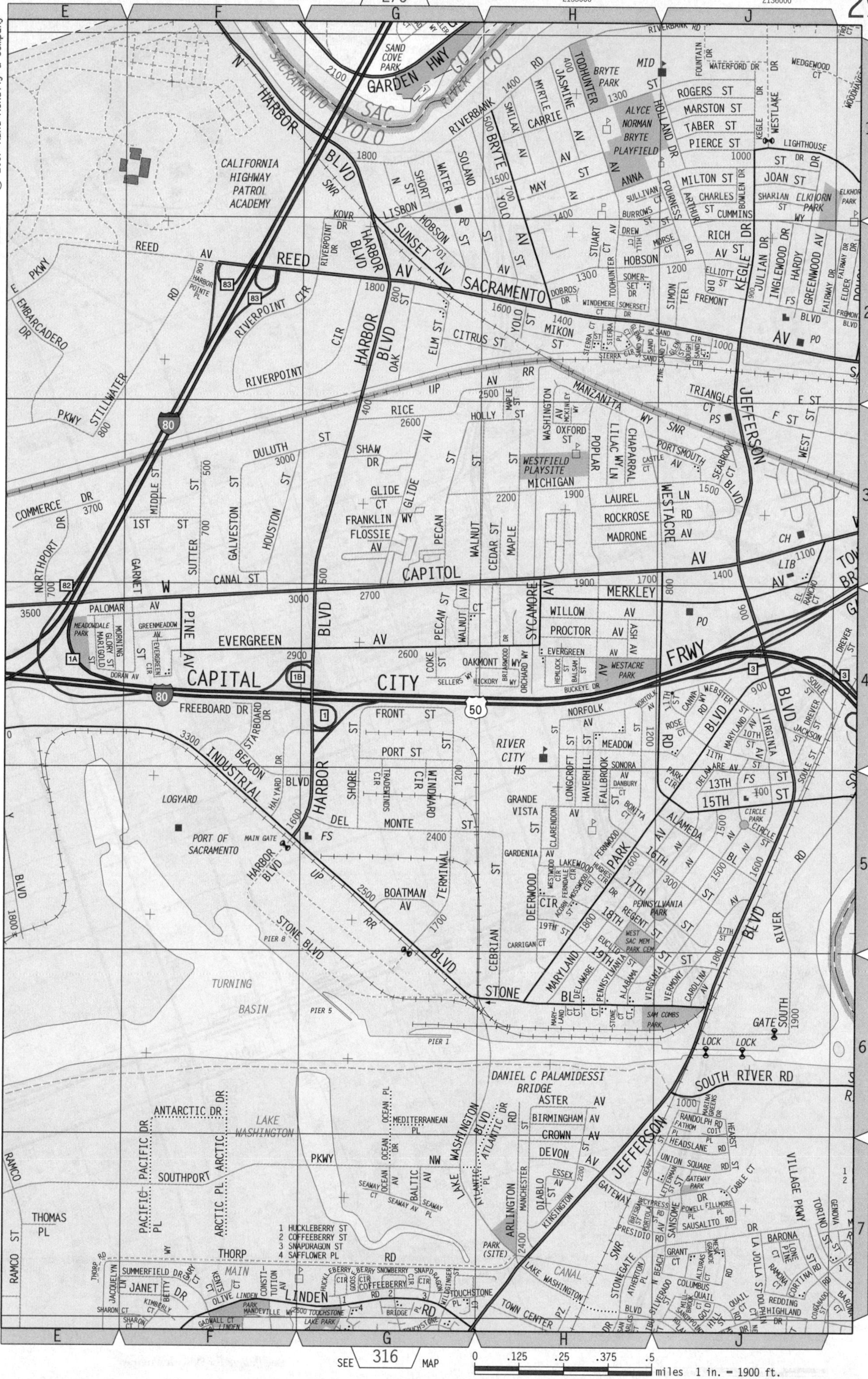
SEE 276 MAP
SEE 297 MAP
SEE 316 MAP
CALIFORNIA HIGHWAY PATROL ACADEMY
SACRAMENTO RIVER
YOLO CO
SAC CO
GARDEN HWY
SAND COVE PARK
BRYTE PARK
ALYCE NORMAN BRYTE PLAYFIELD
ELKHORN PARK
RIVERBANK RD
HARBOR BLVD
REED AV
SACRAMENTO AV
SUNSET AV
RIVERPOINT CIR
EMBARCADERO DR
STILLWATER PKWY
JEFFERSON BLVD
WESTFIELD PLAYSITE
MICHIGAN
CAPITOL AV
MERKLEY AV
EVERGREEN AV
MEADOWDALE PARK
WESTACRE PARK
CAPITAL CITY FRWY
FREEBOARD DR
INDUSTRIAL BLVD
LOGYARD
PORT OF SACRAMENTO
RIVER CITY HS
GRANDE VISTA
DEL MONTE ST
BOATMAN AV
STONE BLVD
PENNSYLVANIA PARK
WEST SAC MEM PARK CEM
SAM COMBS PARK
TURNING BASIN
PIER 1
PIER 5
PIER 8
LOCK
DANIEL C PALAMIDESSI BRIDGE
SOUTH RIVER RD
LAKE WASHINGTON
LAKE WASHINGTON BLVD
SOUTHPORT PKWY
VILLAGE PKWY
PARK (SITE)
MAIN CANAL
LINDEN RD
THORP RD
PARK MANDEVILLE
LAKE PARK
TOWN CENTER PZ
1 HUCKLEBERRY ST
2 COFFEEBERRY ST
3 SNAPDRAGON ST
4 SAFFLOWER PL

0 .125 .25 .375 .5 miles 1 in. = 1900 ft.

SEE 277 MAP

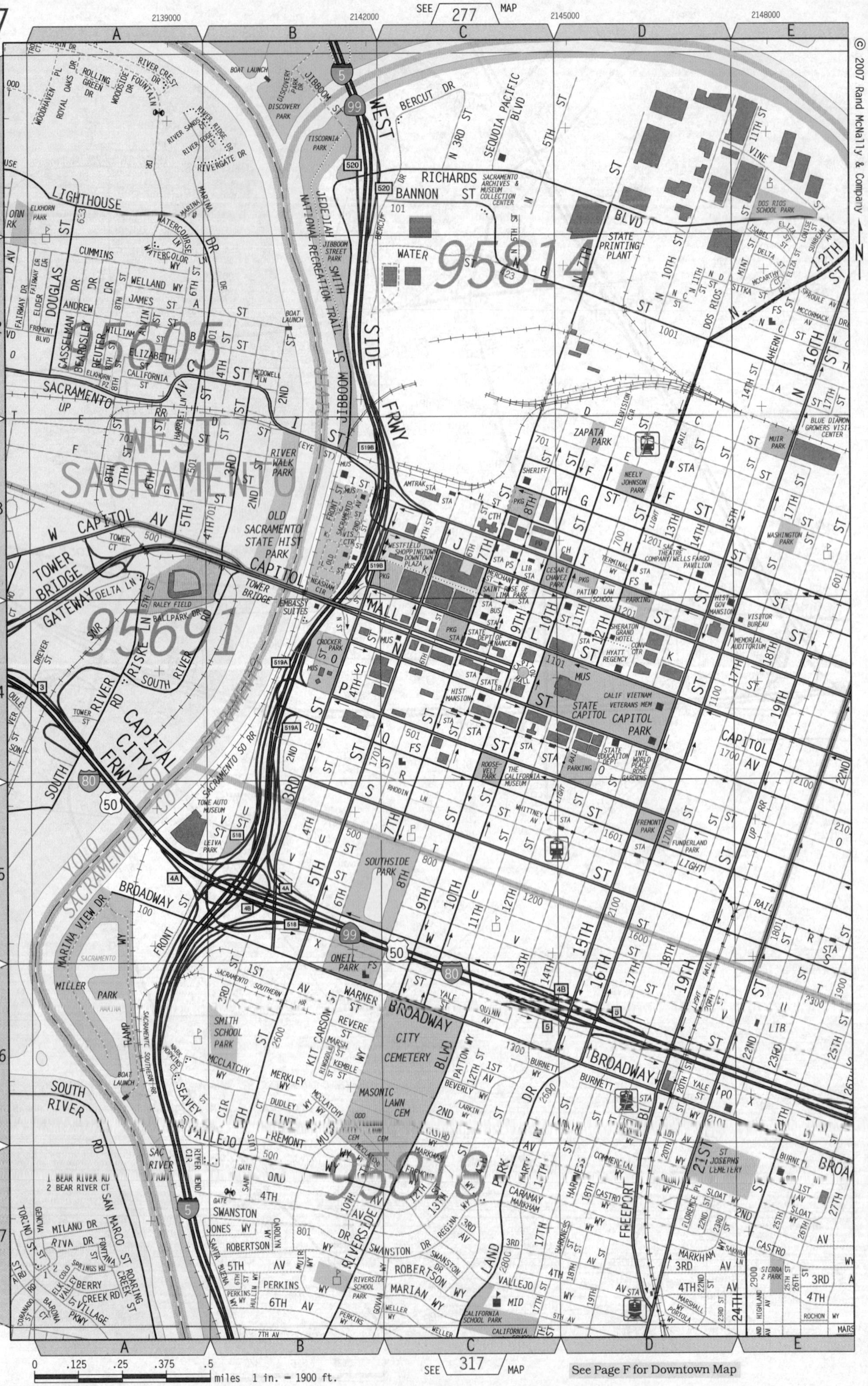

SEE 296 MAP

SEE 317 MAP

0 .125 .25 .375 .5 miles 1 in. = 1900 ft.

See Page F for Downtown Map

SEE 277 MAP

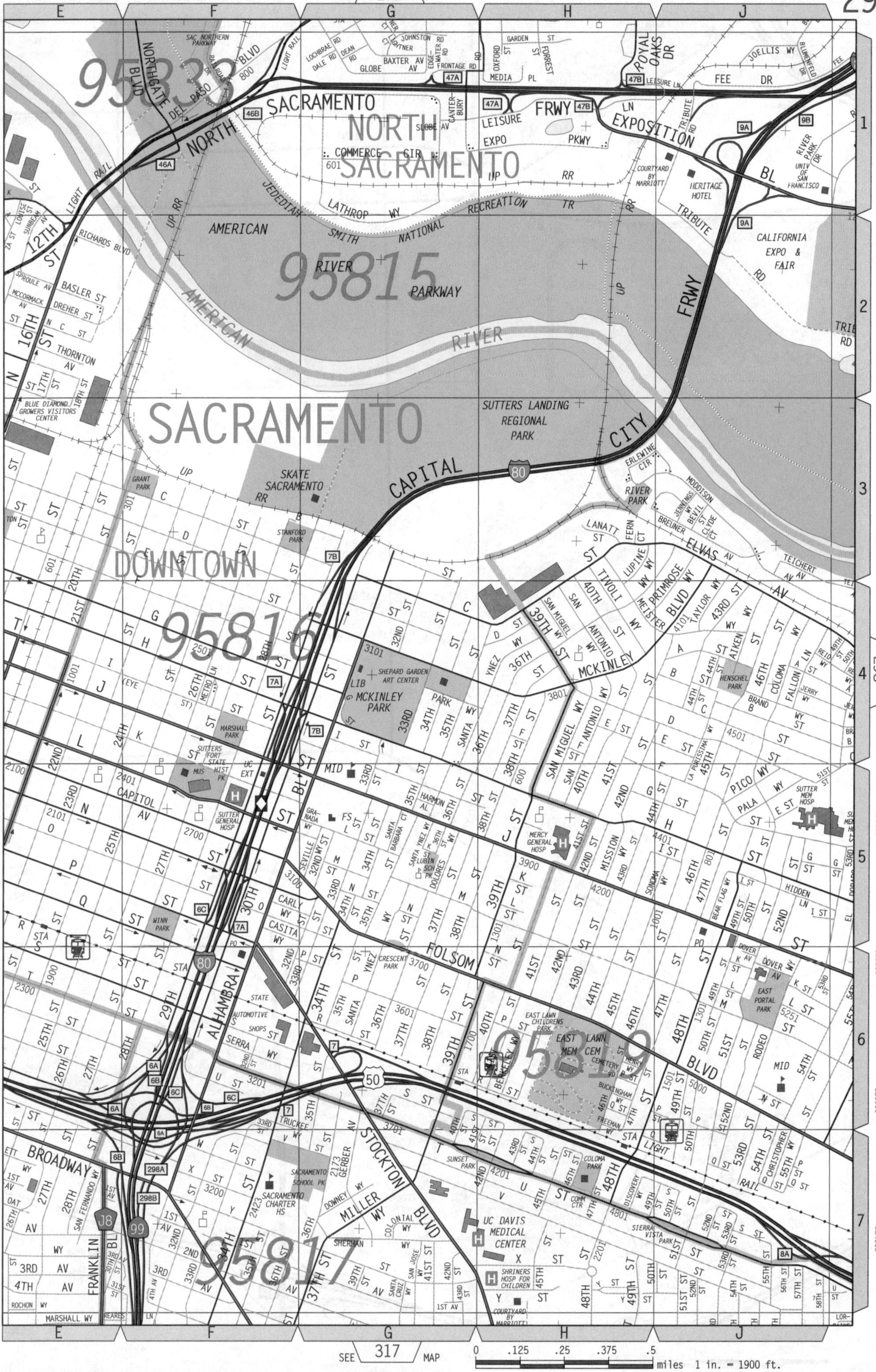
NORTH SACRAMENTO
SACRAMENTO
DOWNTOWN
95838
95815
95816
95819
95817
AMERICAN RIVER PARKWAY
JEDEDIAH SMITH NATIONAL RECREATION TR
AMERICAN RIVER
SUTTERS LANDING REGIONAL PARK
CAPITAL CITY FRWY
NORTH SACRAMENTO FRWY
EXPOSITION BL
LEISURE LN
EXPO PKWY
CALIFORNIA EXPO & FAIR
HERITAGE HOTEL
COURTYARD BY MARRIOTT
UNIV OF SAN FRANCISCO
RIVER PARK
SKATE SACRAMENTO
STANFORD PARK
GRANT PARK
BLUE DIAMOND GROWERS VISITORS CENTER
SHEPARD GARDEN ART CENTER
McKINLEY PARK
MARSHALL PARK
SUTTERS FORT STATE HIST PK
SUTTER GENERAL HOSP
MERCY GENERAL HOSP
SUTTER MEM HOSP
HENSCHEL PARK
EAST PORTAL PARK
CRESCENT PARK
WINN PARK
STATE AUTOMOTIVE SHOPS
EAST LAWN CHILDRENS PARK
EAST LAWN MEM CEM
COLOMA PARK
SUNSET PARK
SACRAMENTO SCHOOL PK
SACRAMENTO CHARTER HS
UC DAVIS MEDICAL CENTER
SHRINERS HOSP FOR CHILDREN
SIERRA VISTA PARK
CAPITOL AV
FOLSOM BLVD
ELVAS AV
McKINLEY BLVD
STOCKTON BLVD
BROADWAY
ALHAMBRA BL
FRANKLIN BL
MILLER WY
SAN MIGUEL WY
MARSHALL WY
2151000
2157000
2160000
340000
338000
336000
334000
332000
330000
328000
326000
324000
E
F
G
H
J
1
2
3
4
5
6
7
0 .125 .25 .375 .5 miles 1 in. = 1900 ft.

SEE 298 MAP

SEE 317 MAP

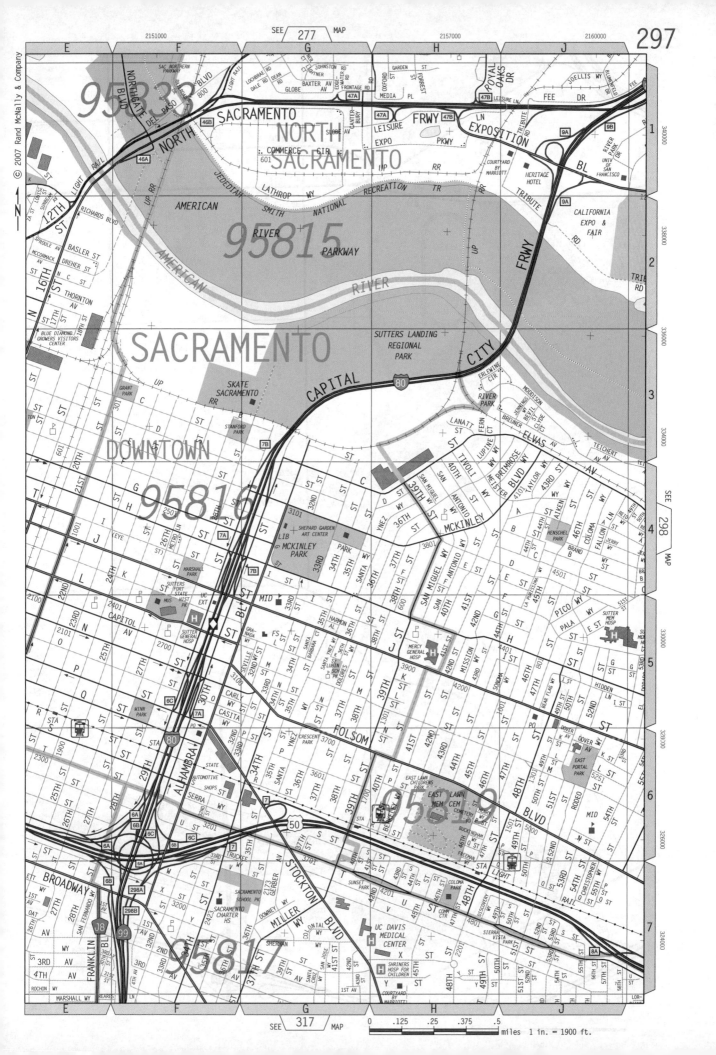

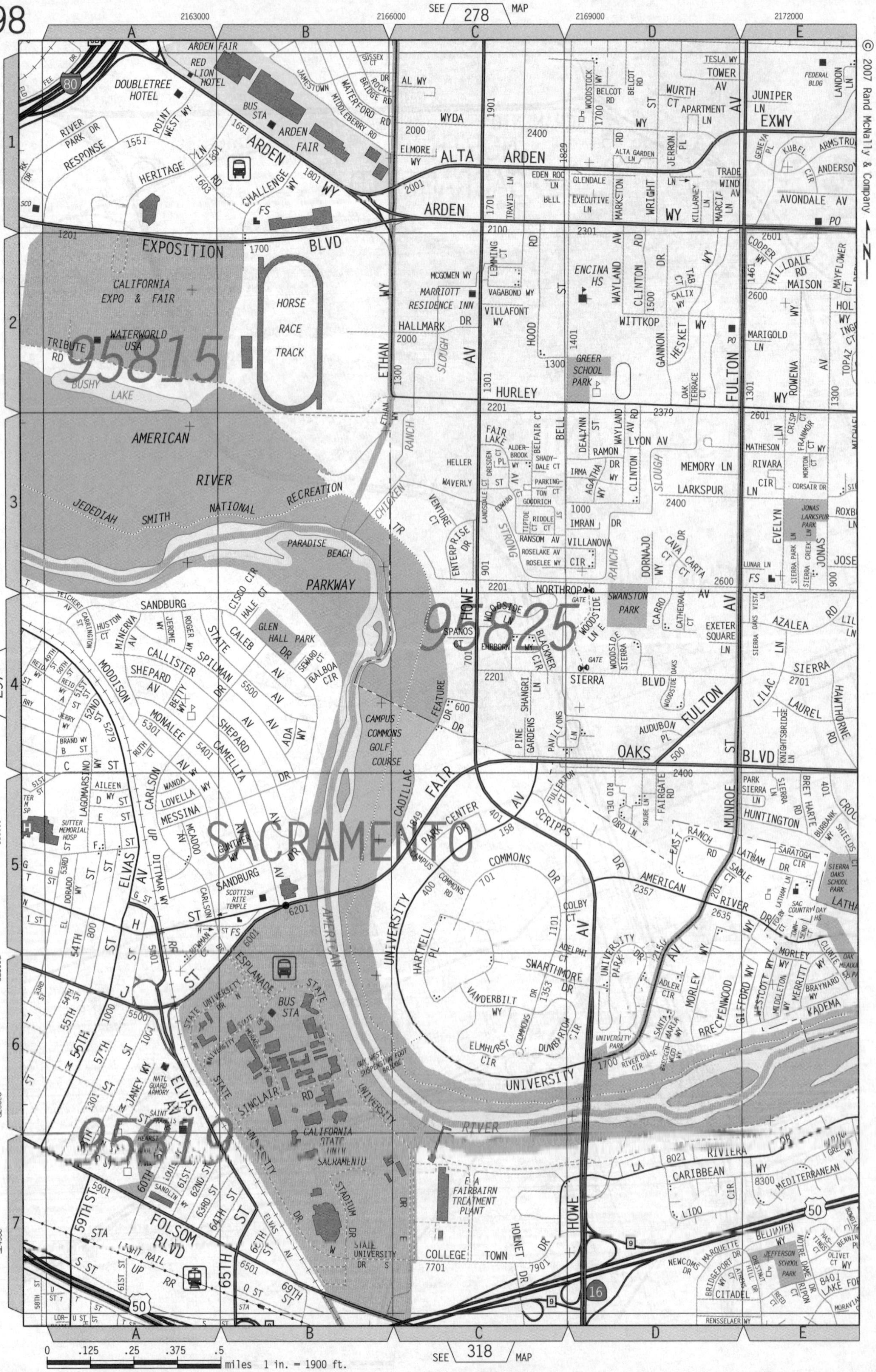
SEE 278 MAP
SEE 297 MAP
SEE 318 MAP
A
B
C
D
E
1
2
3
4
5
6
7
2163000
2166000
2169000
2172000
340000
338000
336000
334000
330000
95815
95825
95819
SACRAMENTO
DOUBLETREE HOTEL
RED LION HOTEL
ARDEN FAIR
BUS STA
ARDEN FAIR
ARDEN WY
ALTA ARDEN
EXPOSITION BLVD
CALIFORNIA EXPO & FAIR
WATERWORLD USA
HORSE RACE TRACK
BUSHY LAKE
TRIBUTE RD
AMERICAN RIVER
JEDEDIAH SMITH NATIONAL RECREATION
PARADISE BEACH
PARKWAY
MARRIOTT RESIDENCE INN
ENCINA HS
GREER SCHOOL PARK
ETHAN WY
HURLEY
FULTON AV
HOWE AV
SWANSTON PARK
GLEN HALL PARK
CAMPUS COMMONS GOLF COURSE
SIERRA BLVD
OAKS
FAIR OAKS BLVD
UNIVERSITY AV
AMERICAN RIVER DR
MUNROE ST
JONAS LARKSPUR PARK
SIERRA OAKS SCHOOL PARK
SUTTER MEMORIAL HOSP
ELVAS AV
SCOTTISH RITE TEMPLE
CALIFORNIA STATE UNIV SACRAMENTO
STATE UNIVERSITY DR
ESPLANADE
GUY WEST SUSPENSION FOOT BRIDGE
NATL GUARD ARMORY
E A FAIRBAIRN TREATMENT PLANT
COLLEGE TOWN DR
FOLSOM BLVD
65TH ST
LIGHT RAIL
RIVIERA DR
CARIBBEAN WY
MEDITERRANEAN
JEFFERSON SCHOOL PARK
CITADEL
LAKE FOREST
UNIVERSITY PARK
80
50
16
0 .125 .25 .375 .5 miles 1 in. = 1900 ft.

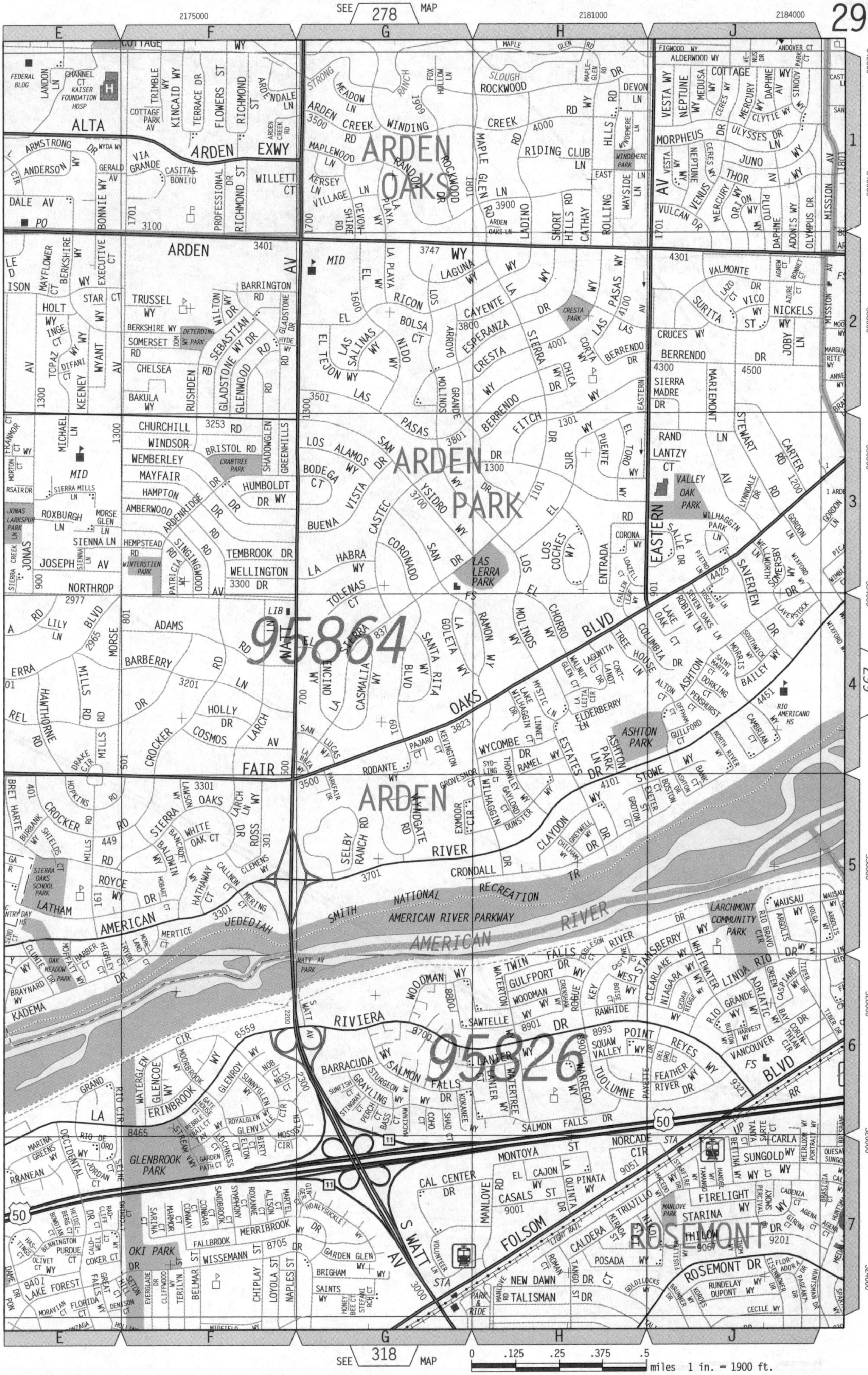
SEE 278 MAP
SEE 299 MAP
SEE 318 MAP
2175000
2181000
2184000
342000
340000
338000
336000
334000
330000
328000
326000
324000
E
F
G
H
J
1
2
3
4
5
6
7
ARDEN OAKS
ARDEN PARK
ARDEN
ROSEMONT
95864
95826
ALTA
ARDEN EXWY
ARDEN WY
WATT AV
FAIR OAKS BLVD
EASTERN AV
AMERICAN RIVER
SMITH NATIONAL RECREATION TR
AMERICAN RIVER PARKWAY
JEDEDIAH SMITH
RIVER DR
FOLSOM BLVD
S WATT AV
RIVIERA
LA RIVIERA DR
KIEFER BLVD
FEDERAL BLDG
KAISER FOUNDATION HOSP
CRESTA PARK
DETERDING PARK
CRABTREE PARK
WINTERSTIEN PARK
JONAS LARKSPUR PARK
LAS LERRA PARK
VALLEY OAK PARK
ASHTON PARK
WINDEMERE PARK
SIERRA OAKS SCHOOL PARK
LARCHMONT COMMUNITY PARK
WATT AV PARK
OAK MEADOW PARK
GLENBROOK PARK
OKI PARK
MANLOVE PARK
RIO AMERICANO HS
LIB
FS
PO
MID
STA
LIGHT RAIL
PARK & RIDE
UP RR
50
11
0 .125 .25 .375 .5
miles 1 in. = 1900 ft.

SEE 279 MAP
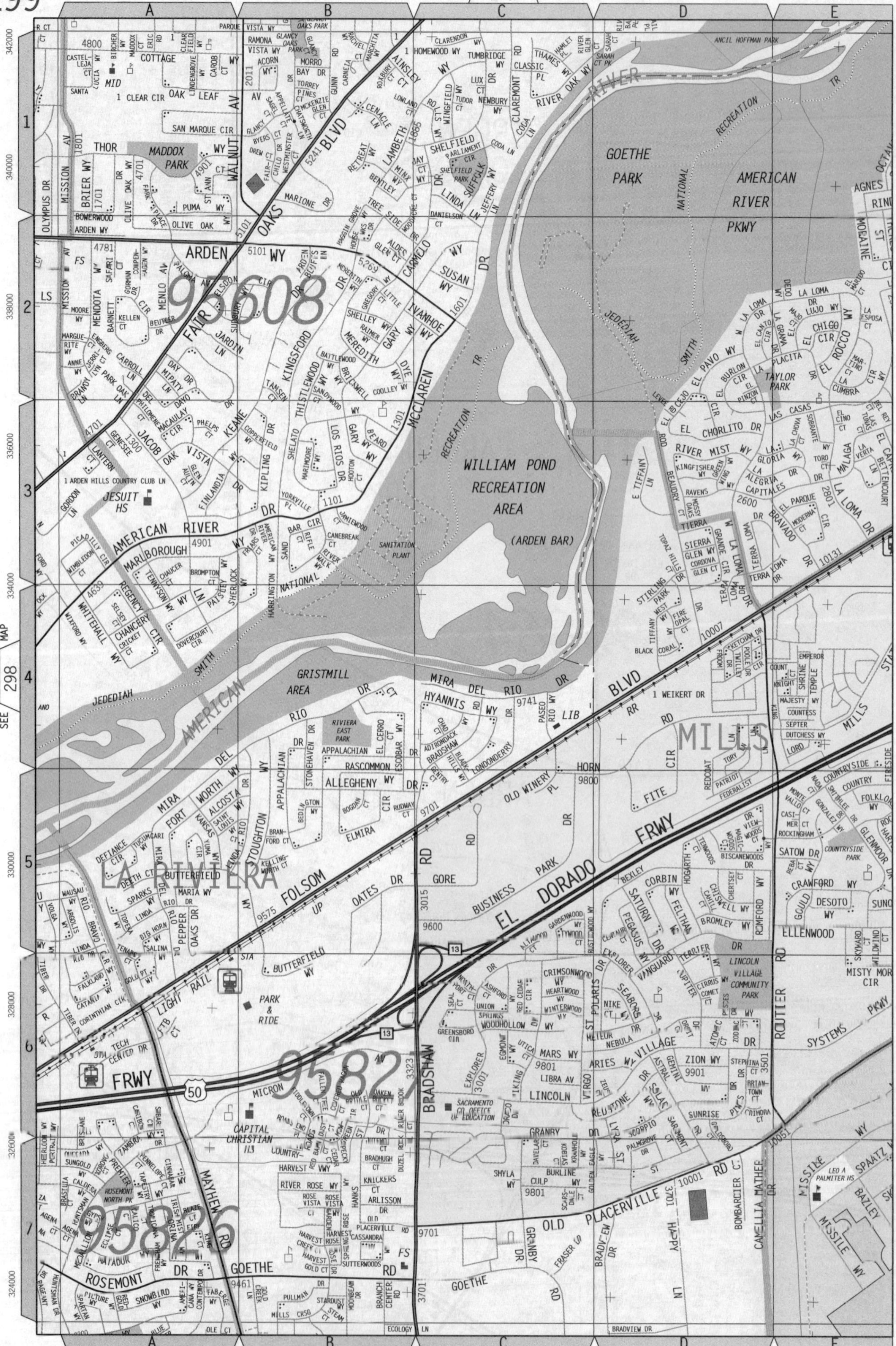

0 .125 .25 .375 .5 miles 1 in. = 1900 ft.

SEE 298 MAP
SEE 319 MAP

SEE 279 MAP

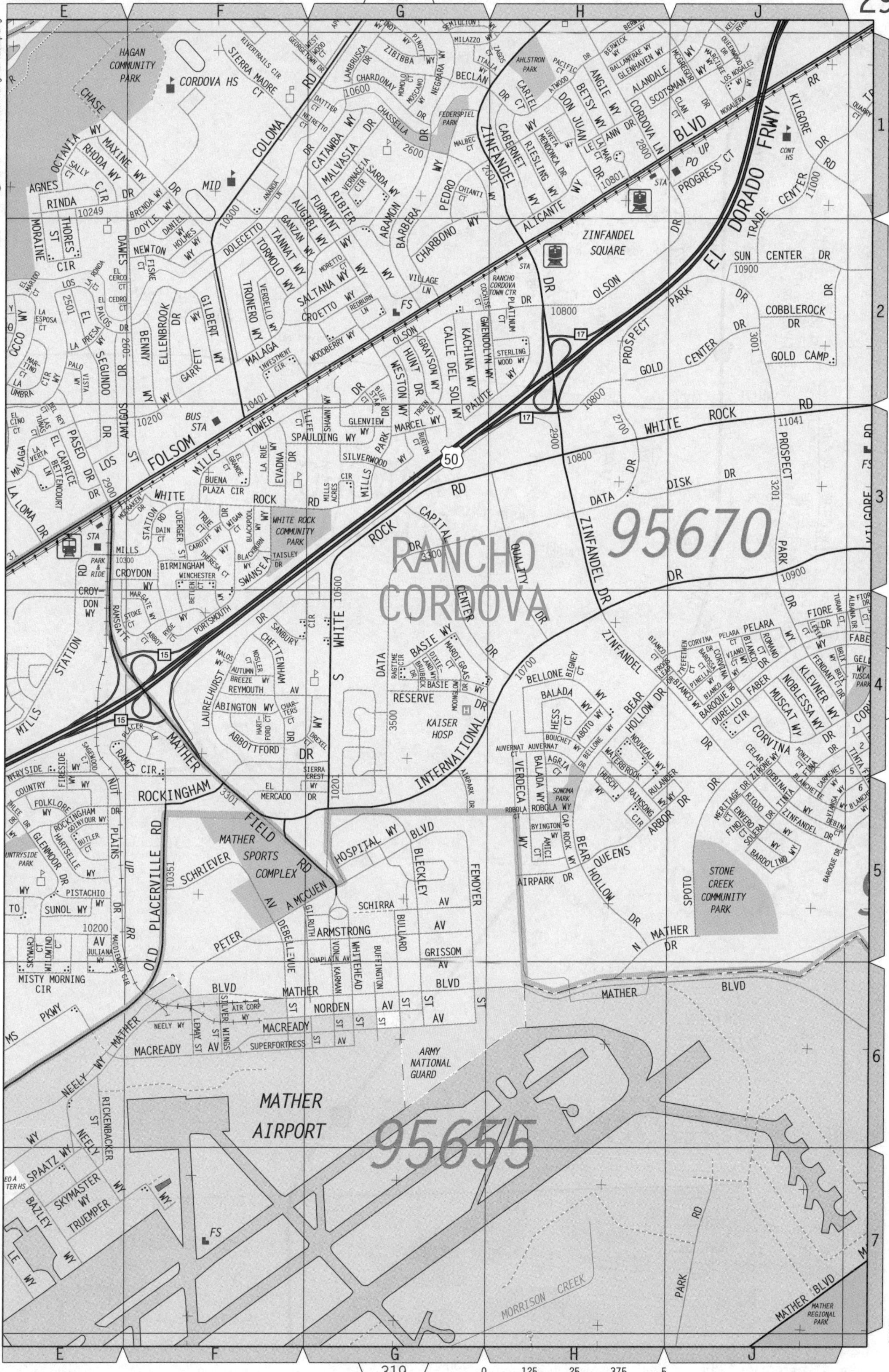
RANCHO
CORDOVA
95670
95655
MATHER
AIRPORT
HAGAN
COMMUNITY
PARK
CORDOVA HS
ZINFANDEL
SQUARE
WHITE ROCK
COMMUNITY
PARK
MATHER
SPORTS
COMPLEX
STONE
CREEK
COMMUNITY
PARK
KAISER
HOSP
ARMY
NATIONAL
GUARD
MATHER
REGIONAL
PARK
MORRISON CREEK
FOLSOM BLVD
WHITE ROCK RD
ZINFANDEL DR
EL DORADO FRWY
INTERNATIONAL DR
MATHER FIELD RD
S WHITE ROCK RD
OLD PLACERVILLE RD
MATHER BLVD
COLOMA RD
PROSPECT PARK DR
SUN CENTER DR
GOLD CENTER DR
CAPITAL CENTER DR
DATA DR
BEAR HOLLOW DR
ROCKINGHAM DR
KILGORE RD
TRADE CENTER DR
OLSON DR
NEELY WY
RICKENBACKER ST
MACREADY AV
ARMSTRONG AV
PETER A MCCUEN BLVD
HOSPITAL WY
AIRPARK DR
CORVINA DR
STATION DR
MILLS PARK DR
SCHRIEVER AV
FEMOYER ST
BLECKLEY ST
NORDEN AV
GRISSOM ST
BULLARD AV
WHITEHEAD ST
DATA DISK DR
RESERVE DR
QUALITY DR
VERDECA WY
SPOTO DR
N MATHER DR
COBBLEROCK DR
GOLD CAMP DR
EL SEGUNDO DR
PASEO DR
MILLS STATION RD
CROYDON WY
PLAINS DR
SUNOL WY
MISTY MORNING CIR
PISTACHIO DR
SPAATZ WY
SKYMASTER WY
TRUEMPER WY
BAZLEY ST
2196000
2199000
2205000
2208000
342000
340000
338000
336000
334000
332000
330000
328000
326000
324000
E
F
G
H
J
1
2
3
4
5
6
7
0
.125
.25
.375
.5
miles 1 in. = 1900 ft.

SEE 300 MAP

SEE 319 MAP

SEE 280 MAP

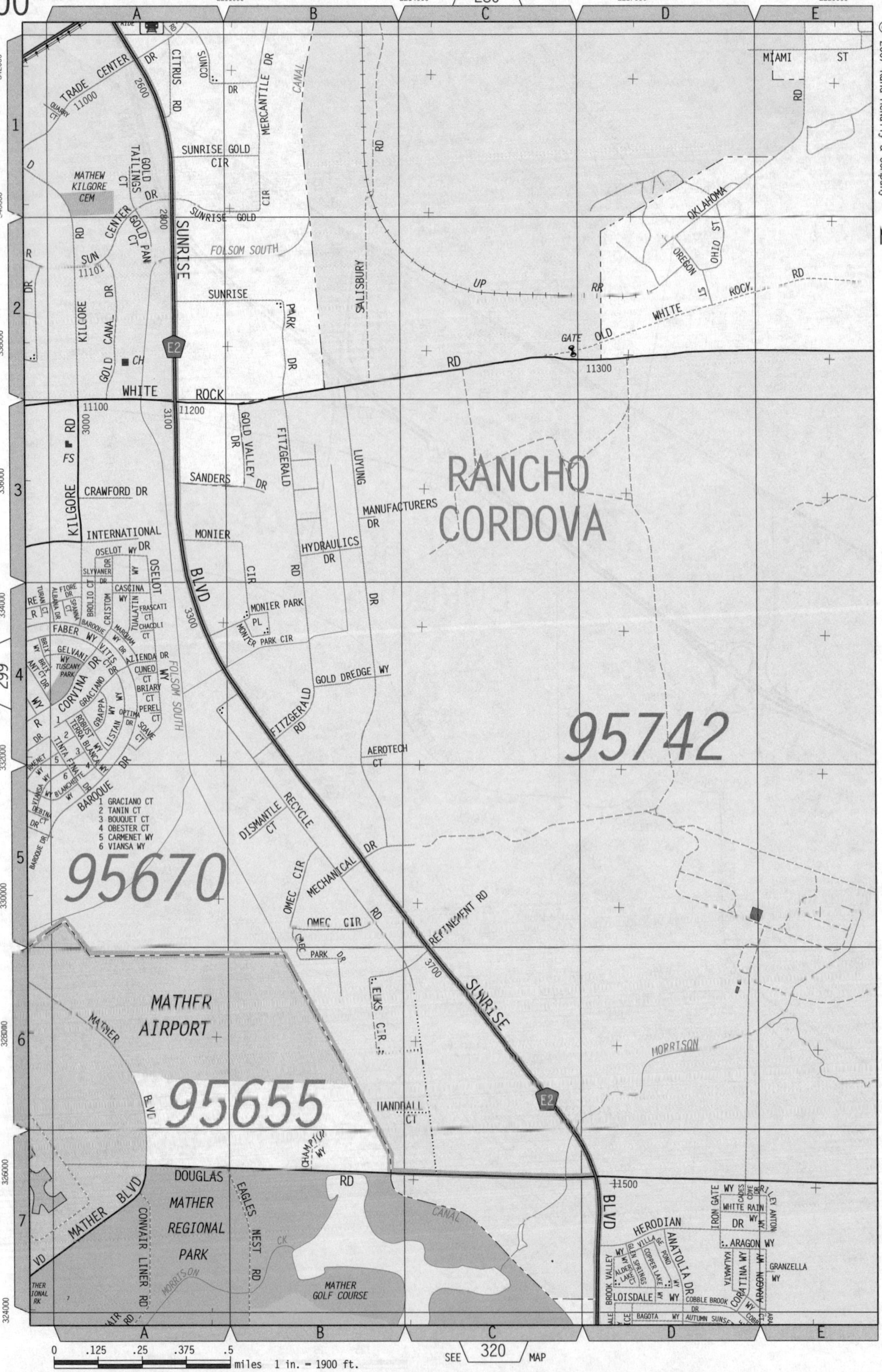

SEE 299 MAP

0 .125 .25 .375 .5
miles 1 in. = 1900 ft.

SEE 320 MAP

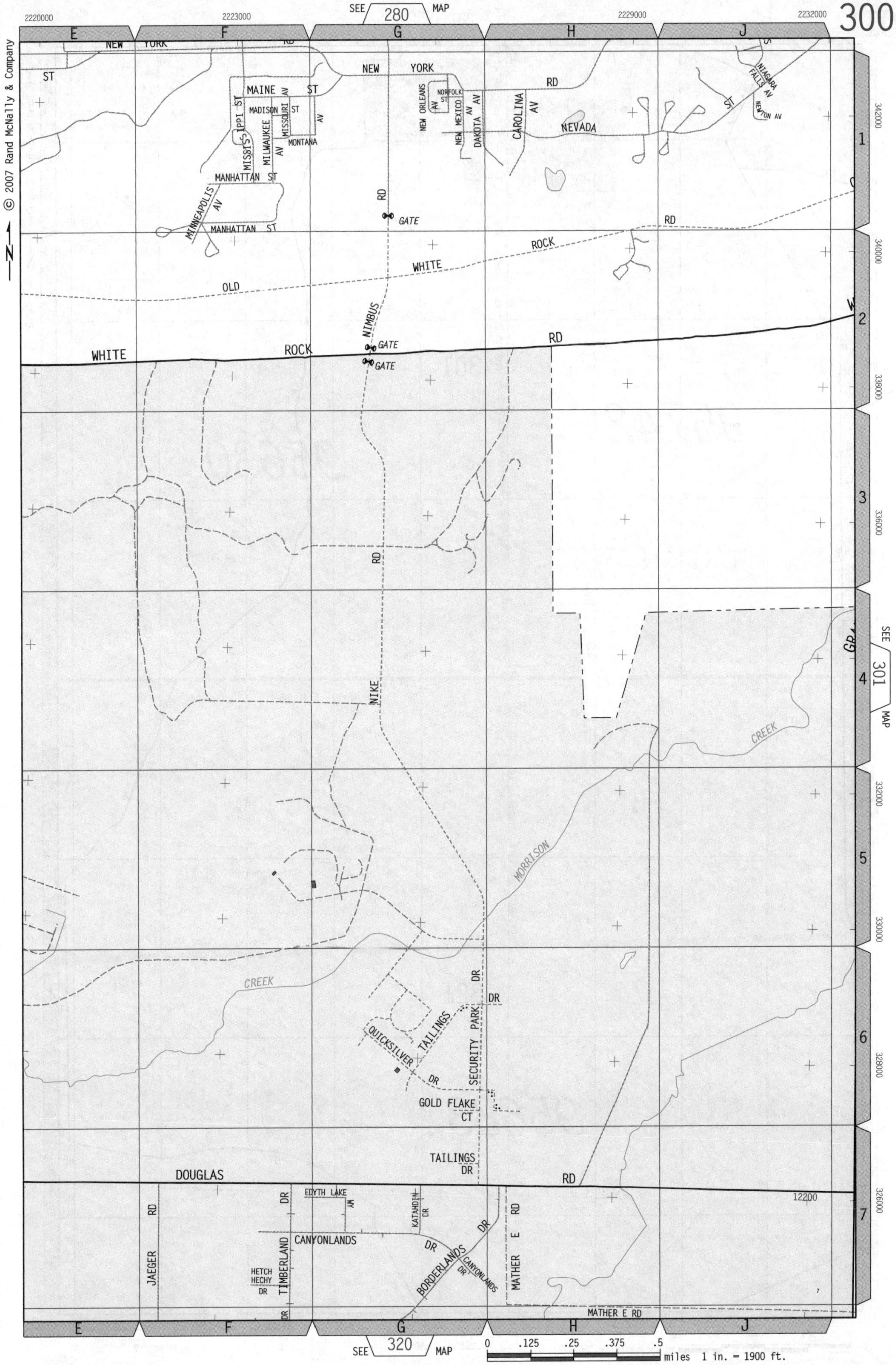
SEE 280 MAP
SEE 301 MAP
SEE 320 MAP
2220000
2223000
2229000
2232000
E
F
G
H
J
1
2
3
4
5
6
7
342000
340000
338000
336000
332000
330000
328000
326000
NEW YORK RD
NEW YORK ST
MAINE ST
MADISON
MISSISSIPPI ST
MILWAUKEE AV
MISSOURI ST
MONTANA
AV
MANHATTAN ST
MINNEAPOLIS AV
NEW ORLEANS AV
NORFOLK ST
NEW MEXICO AV
DAKOTA AV
CAROLINA AV
NEVADA
RD
NIAGARA FALLS AV
NEWTON AV
ST
GATE
OLD WHITE ROCK RD
WHITE ROCK RD
NIMBUS RD
NIKE RD
GRANT
CREEK
MORRISON
CREEK
DR
SECURITY PARK DR
TAILINGS DR
QUICKSILVER DR
GOLD FLAKE CT
TAILINGS DR
DOUGLAS RD
12200
JAEGER RD
EDYTH LAKE WY
TIMBERLAND DR
HETCH HECHY DR
CANYONLANDS DR
KATAHDIN DR
BORDERLANDS DR
CANYONLANDS DR
MATHER E RD
MATHER E RD
0
.125
.25
.375
.5
miles 1 in. = 1900 ft.

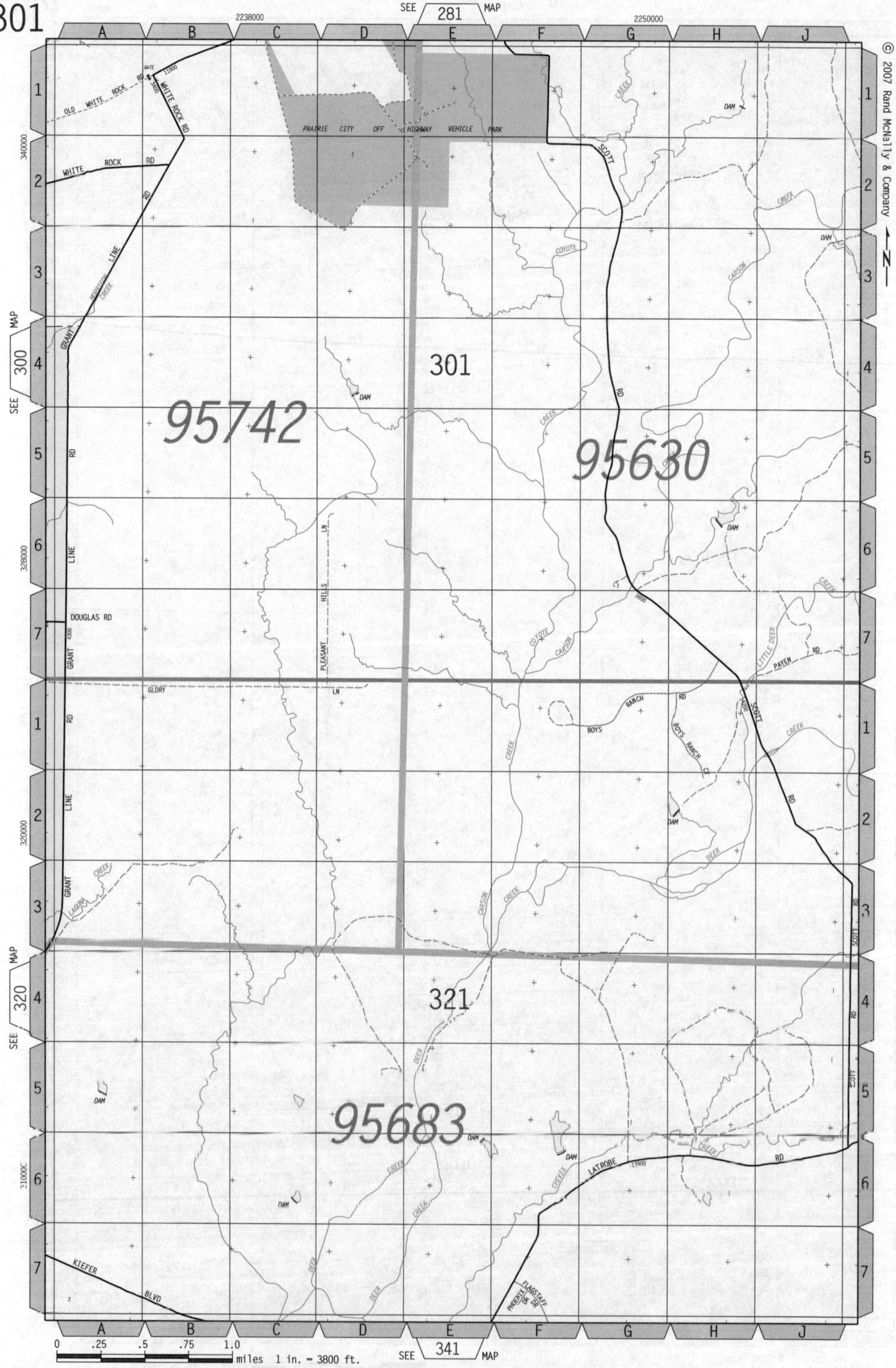
SEE 281 MAP
SEE 300 MAP
SEE 320 MAP
SEE 341 MAP
2238000
2250000
340000
328000
320000
310000
PRAIRIE CITY OFF HIGHWAY VEHICLE PARK
OLD WHITE ROCK RD
WHITE ROCK RD
MORRISON CREEK
GRANT LINE RD
DOUGLAS RD
GLORY LN
PLEASANT HILLS LN
SCOTT RD
COYOTE CREEK
CARSON CREEK
LITTLE DEER CREEK
PAYEN RD
BOYS RANCH RD
BOYS RANCH CT
DEER CREEK
LAGUNA CREEK
LATROBE RD
KIEFER BLVD
PHOENIX OK DR
FLAGSTAFF DR
DAM
95742
95630
95683
301
321
0 .25 .5 .75 1.0 miles 1 in. = 3800 ft.

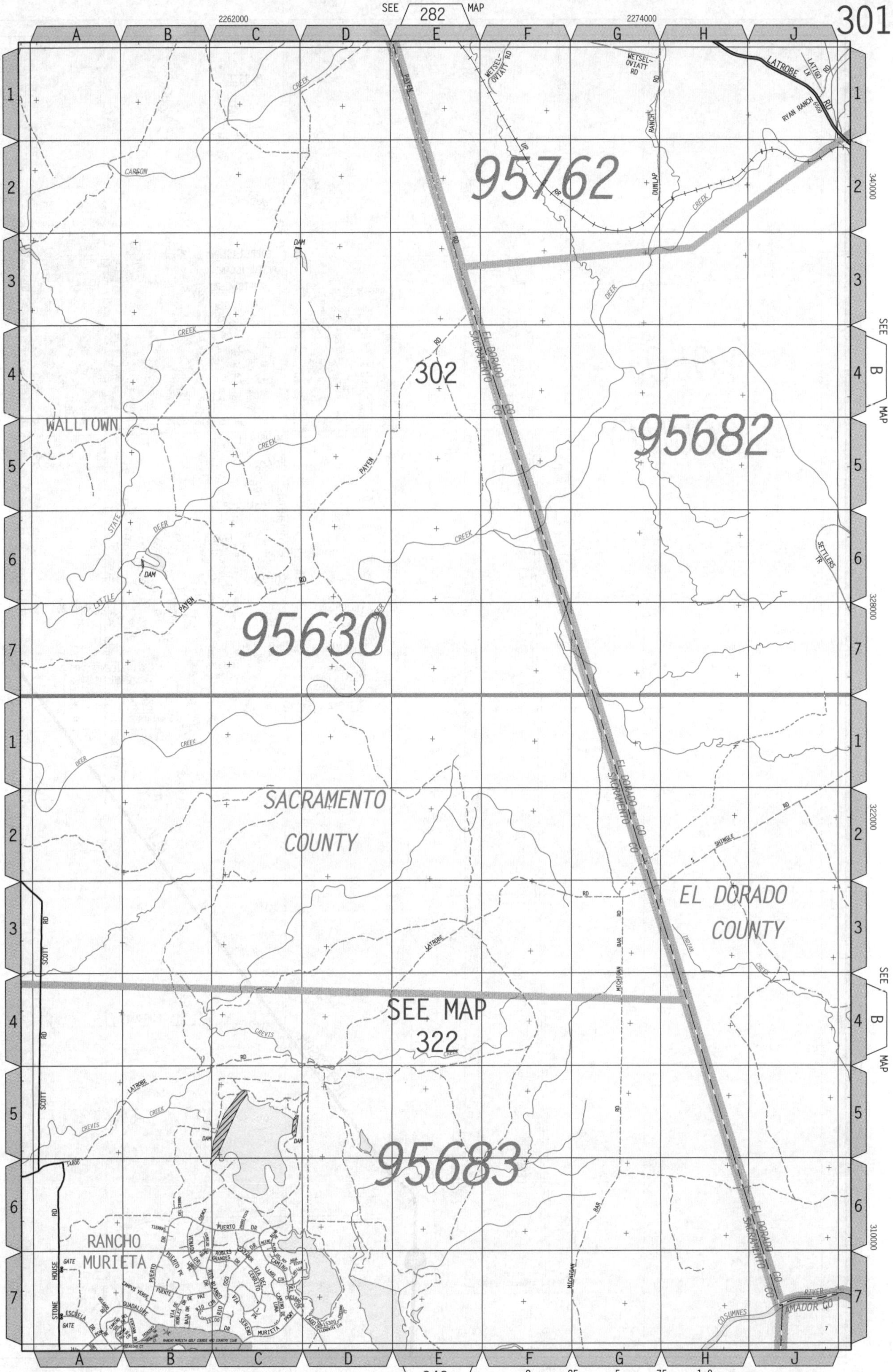
SEE 282 MAP
2262000
2274000
A
B
C
D
E
F
G
H
J
1
2
3
4
5
6
7
95762
95682
95630
95683
302
WALLTOWN
SACRAMENTO COUNTY
EL DORADO COUNTY
SEE MAP 322
RANCHO MURIETA
WETSEL-OVIATT RD
LATROBE RD
RYAN RANCH RD
LATIGO LN
RANCH RD
DUNLAP
PAYEN RD
EL DORADO SACRAMENTO CO
CARSON
DEER CREEK
STATE
LITTLE
DAM
SETTLERS TR
S SHINGLE RD
MICHIGAN BAR RD
INDIAN CREEK
LATROBE
SCOTT RD
STONE HOUSE RD
CREVIS CREEK
COSUMNES RIVER
AMADOR CO
GATE
SEE B MAP
340000
328000
322000
310000
SEE 342 MAP
0 .25 .5 .75 1.0
miles 1 in. = 3800 ft.

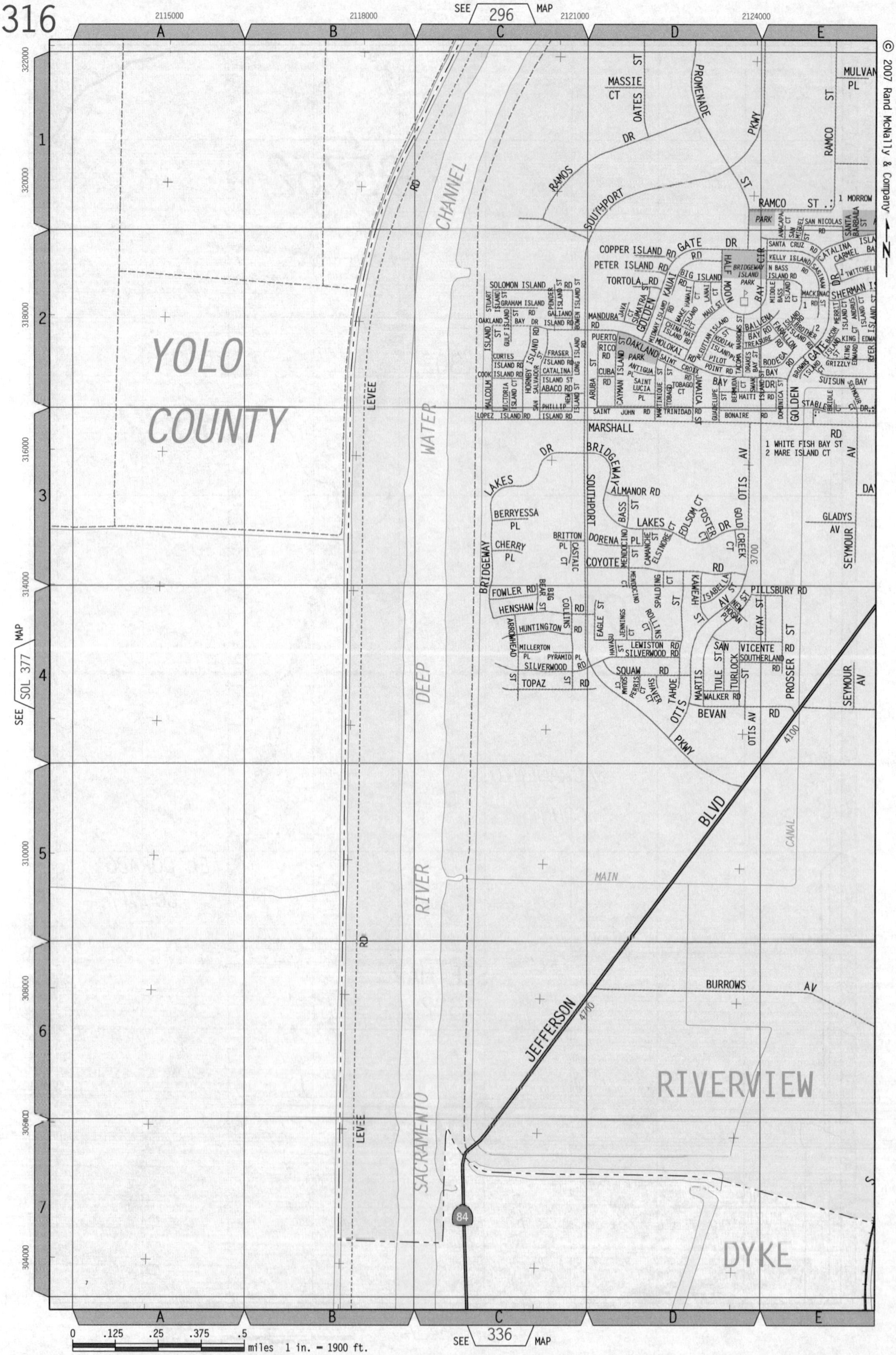
SEE 296 MAP
SEE 336 MAP
SEE SOL 377 MAP
YOLO COUNTY
RIVERVIEW
DYKE
SACRAMENTO RIVER DEEP WATER CHANNEL
LEVEE RD
JEFFERSON BLVD
SOUTHPORT PKWY
MARSHALL RD
BRIDGEWAY LAKES DR
OTIS AV
SEYMOUR AV
BURROWS AV
MAIN CANAL
GOLDEN GATE DR
RAMCO ST
PROMENADE PKWY
1 WHITE FISH BAY ST
2 MARE ISLAND CT
1 MORROW
0 .125 .25 .375 .5 miles 1 in. = 1900 ft.

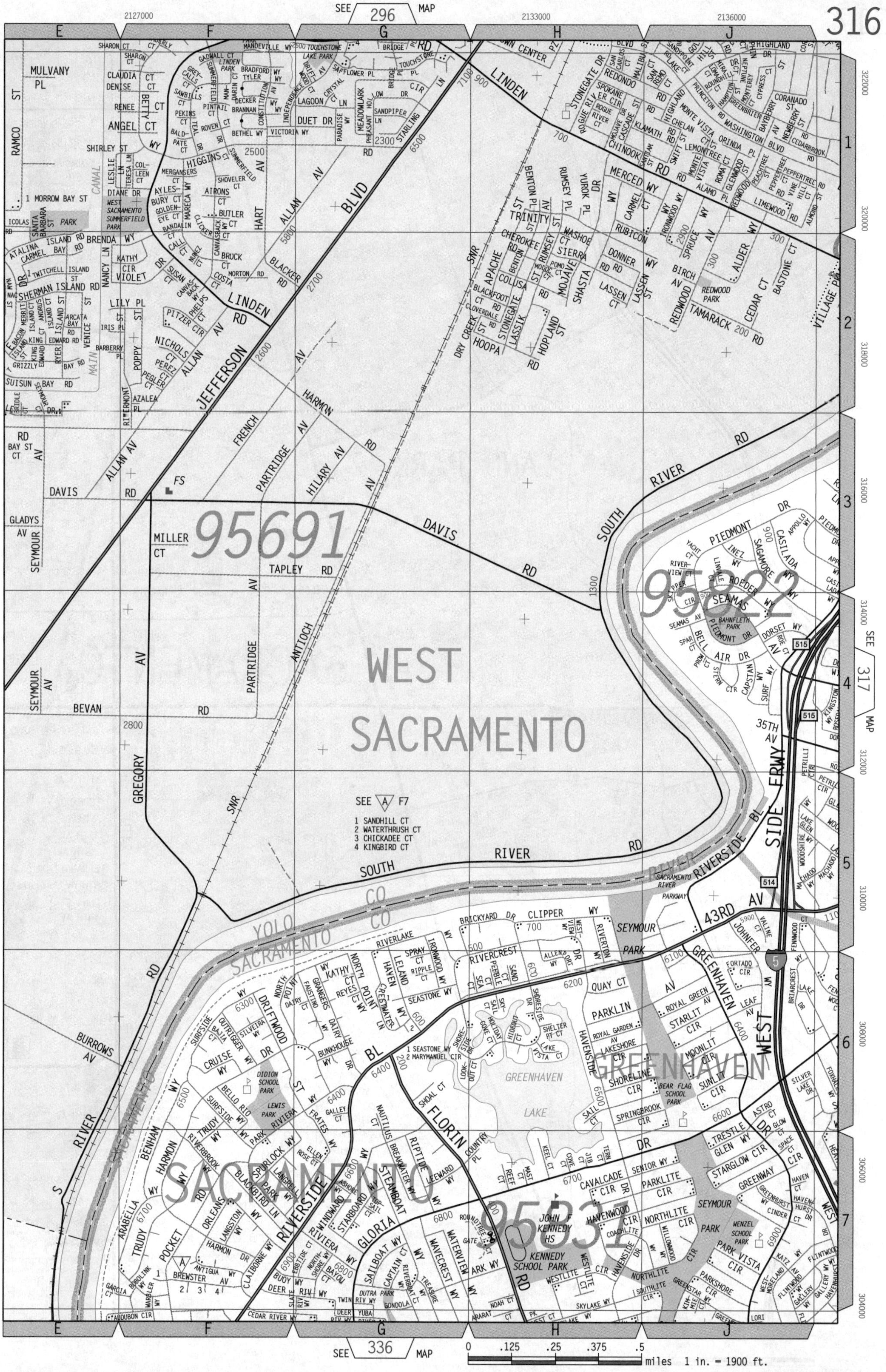
SEE 296 MAP
SEE 317 MAP
SEE 336 MAP
E
F
G
H
J
1
2
3
4
5
6
7
2127000
2133000
2136000
322000
320000
318000
316000
314000
312000
310000
308000
306000
304000
WEST SACRAMENTO
SACRAMENTO
GREENHAVEN
95691
95822
95831
JEFFERSON BLVD
LINDEN RD
SOUTH RIVER RD
DAVIS RD
GREGORY AV
SEYMOUR AV
BEVAN RD
TAPLEY RD
PARTRIDGE AV
ANTIOCH
HARMON
HILARY AV
FRENCH
MILLER CT
GLADYS AV
ALLAN AV
HART AV
BLACKER RD
BURROWS AV
S RIVER RD
YOLO CO
SACRAMENTO CO
SACRAMENTO RIVER
RIVERSIDE BL
43RD AV
WEST SIDE FRWY
GREENHAVEN DR
FLORIN RD
SEYMOUR PARK
DIDION SCHOOL PARK
LEWIS PARK
BEAR FLAG SCHOOL PARK
WENZEL SCHOOL PARK
JOHN F KENNEDY HS
KENNEDY SCHOOL PARK
GREENHAVEN LAKE
BAHNFLETH PARK
REDWOOD PARK
WEST SACRAMENTO SUMMERFIELD PARK
SANTA BARBARA ST PARK
SNR
FS
SEE A F7
1 SANDHILL CT
2 WATERTHRUSH CT
3 CHICKADEE CT
4 KINGBIRD CT
1 SEASTONE WY
2 MARYMANUEL CIR
0 .125 .25 .375 .5 miles 1 in. = 1900 ft.

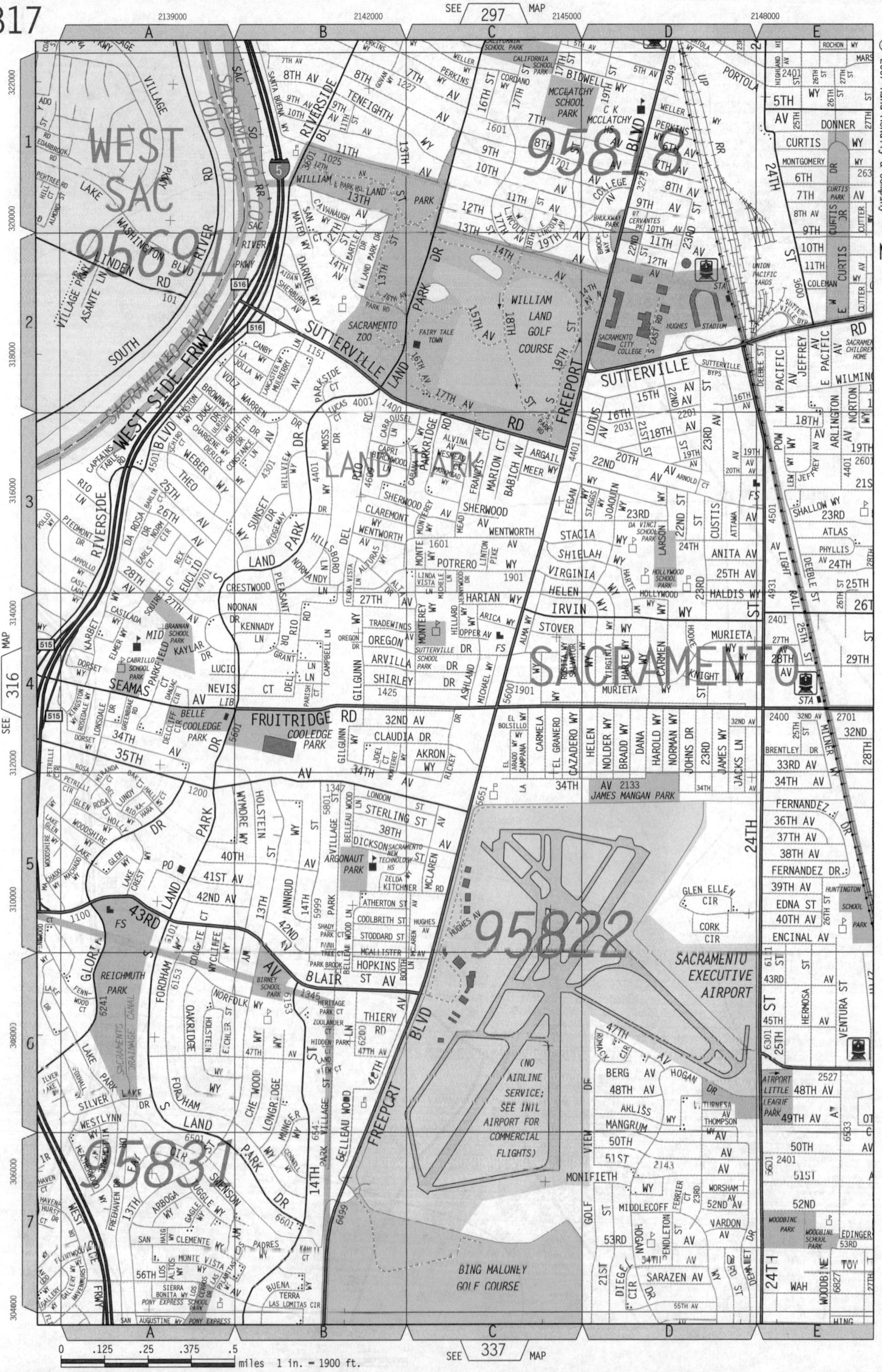
SEE 297 MAP
SEE 337 MAP
SEE 316 MAP
WEST SAC 95691
95818
95822
95831
SACRAMENTO
LAND PARK
WILLIAM LAND GOLF COURSE
SACRAMENTO ZOO
FAIRY TALE TOWN
SACRAMENTO CITY COLLEGE
HUGHES STADIUM
UNION PACIFIC YARDS
SACRAMENTO EXECUTIVE AIRPORT
(NO AIRLINE SERVICE; SEE INTL AIRPORT FOR COMMERCIAL FLIGHTS)
BING MALONEY GOLF COURSE
COOLEDGE PARK
BELLE COOLEDGE PARK
REICHMUTH PARK
JAMES MANGAN PARK
ARGONAUT PARK
MCCLATCHY SCHOOL PARK
AIRPORT LITTLE LEAGUE PARK
WOODBINE PARK
SACRAMENTO RIVER
WEST SIDE FRWY
SUTTERVILLE RD
FRUITRIDGE RD
FREEPORT BLVD
43RD AV
BLAIR AV
LAND PARK DR
RIVERSIDE BLVD
24TH ST
miles 1 in. = 1900 ft.
© 2007 Rand McNally & Company

SEE 297 MAP

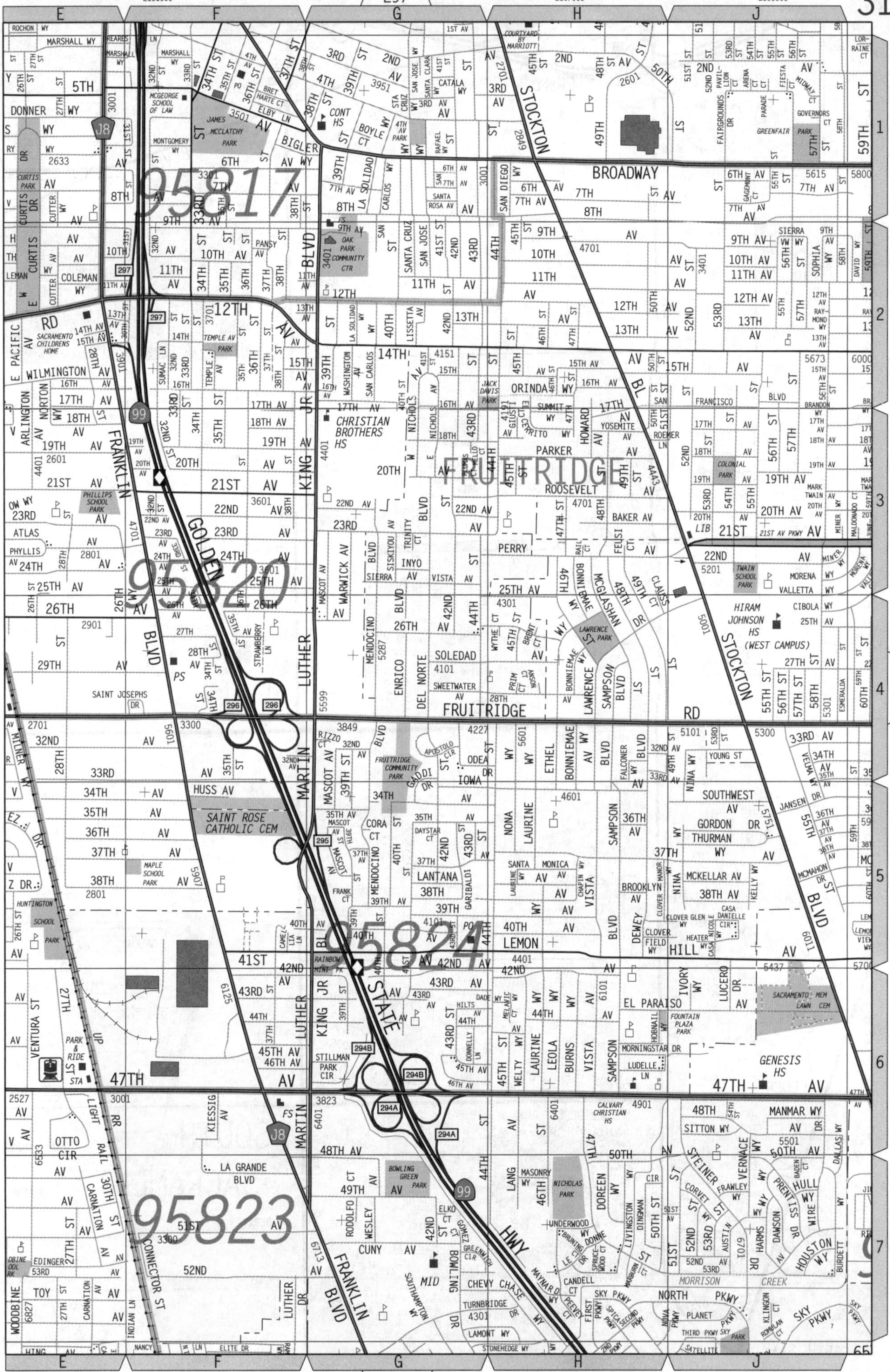
95817
95820
95824
95823
FRUITRIDGE
BROADWAY
STOCKTON BLVD
FRANKLIN BLVD
MARTIN LUTHER KING JR BLVD
GOLDEN STATE HWY
FRUITRIDGE RD
47TH AV
12TH AV
14TH AV
21ST AV
41ST AV
LEMON HILL AV
48TH AV
50TH AV
MORRISON CREEK
MCGEORGE SCHOOL OF LAW
JAMES MCCLATCHY PARK
CURTIS PARK
OAK PARK COMMUNITY CTR
SACRAMENTO CHILDRENS HOME
TEMPLE AV PARK
CHRISTIAN BROTHERS HS
JACK DAVIS PARK
COLONIAL PARK
PHILLIPS SCHOOL PARK
TWAIN SCHOOL PARK
HIRAM JOHNSON HS (WEST CAMPUS)
LAWRENCE PARK
FRUITRIDGE COMMUNITY PARK
SAINT ROSE CATHOLIC CEM
MAPLE SCHOOL PARK
HUNTINGTON SCHOOL PARK
SACRAMENTO MEM LAWN CEM
FOUNTAIN PLAZA PARK
GENESIS HS
CALVARY CHRISTIAN HS
BOWLING GREEN PARK
NICHOLAS PARK
SKY PARK
COURTYARD BY MARRIOTT
GREENFAIR PARK
CONT HS
PARK & RIDE
LA GRANDE BLVD
CONNECTOR ST
MILES 1 in. = 1900 ft.

SEE 318 MAP

SEE 337 MAP

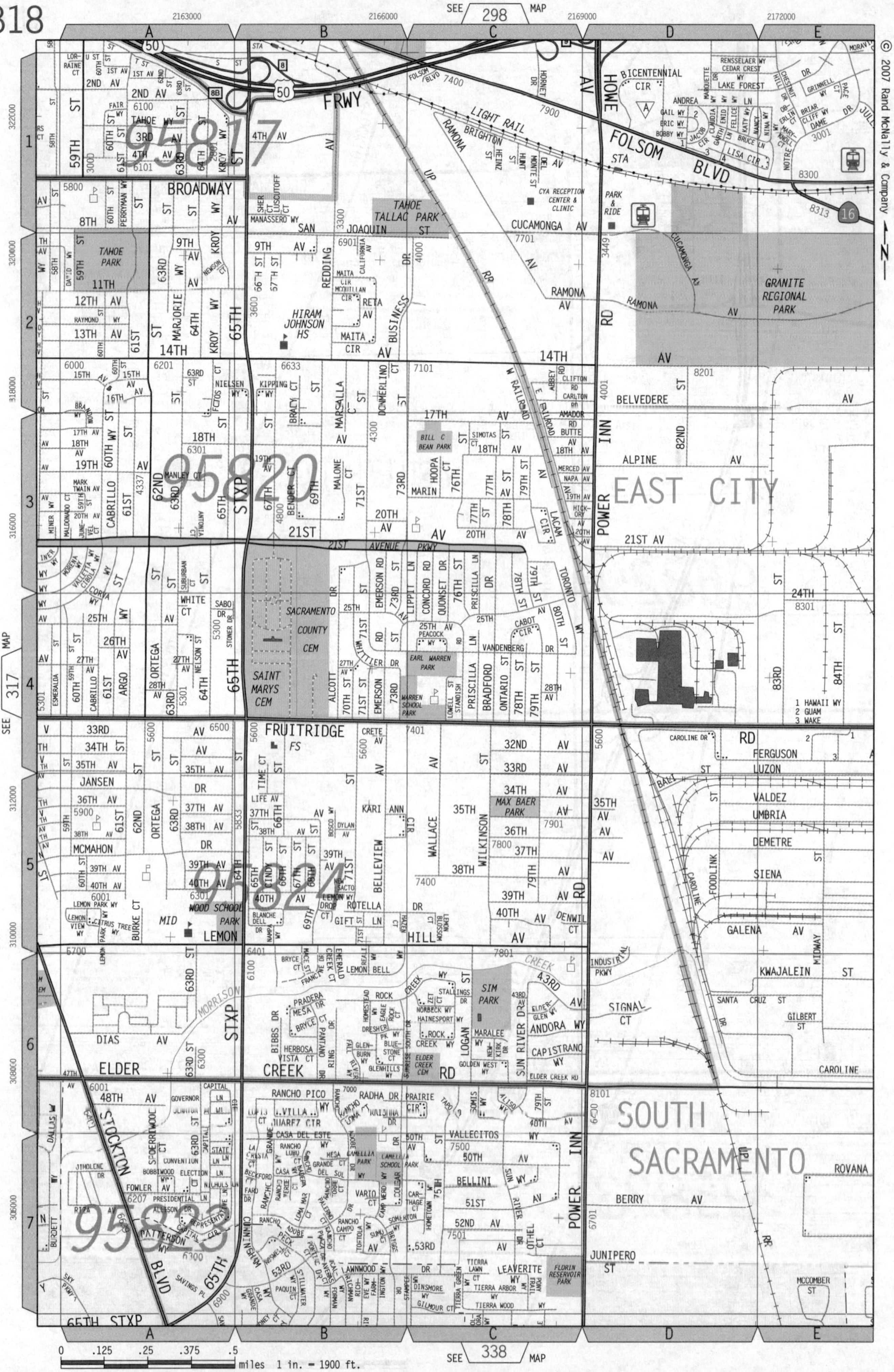
SEE 298 MAP
2163000
2166000
2169000
2172000
A
B
C
D
E
1
2
3
4
5
6
7
95817
95820
95824
95823
FOLSOM BLVD
FRWY
50
LIGHT RAIL
BROADWAY
SAN JOAQUIN ST
TAHOE TALLAC PARK
TAHOE PARK
HIRAM JOHNSON HS
CYA RECEPTION CENTER & CLINIC
PARK & RIDE
CUCAMONGA AV
RAMONA AV
GRANITE REGIONAL PARK
14TH AV
BELVEDERE
ALPINE AV
EAST CITY
POWER INN RD
HOWE AV
21ST AVENUE PKWY
21ST AV
BILL C BEAN PARK
SACRAMENTO COUNTY CEM
SAINT MARYS CEM
EARL WARREN PARK
WARREN SCHOOL PARK
65TH ST
STXP
FRUITRIDGE RD
FS
MAX BAER PARK
WOOD SCHOOL PARK
MID
LEMON HILL AV
SIM PARK
ELDER CREEK CEM
ELDER CREEK RD
MORRISON CREEK
DIAS AV
STOCKTON BLVD
CAMELLIA PARK
CAMELLIA SCHOOL PARK
FLORIN RESERVOIR PARK
SOUTH SACRAMENTO
BERRY AV
JUNIPERO ST
ROVANA
MCCOMBER ST
KWAJALEIN ST
FERGUSON
LUZON
VALDEZ
UMBRIA
DEMETRE
SIENA
GALENA AV
CAROLINE
UP RR
65TH STXP
1 HAWAII WY
2 GUAM
3 WAKE
SEE 317 MAP
SEE 338 MAP
0 .125 .25 .375 .5
miles 1 in. = 1900 ft.

SEE 298 MAP
SEE 338 MAP
SEE 319 MAP
E
F
G
H
J
1
2
3
4
5
6
7
2175000
2181000
2184000
PERKINS
95826
SACRAMENTO
ROSEMONT
95828
95829
FOLSOM BLVD
KIEFER BLVD
JACKSON RD
FRUITRIDGE RD
ELDER CREEK RD
FLORIN PERKINS RD
S WATT AV
SOUTH PORT DR
HEDGE AV
TOKAY LN
CENTRAL CALIF TRACTION RR
MORRISON CREEK
OKI PARK
PRIMROSE PARK
SEE A D1
1 GRACE LN
2 EDITH CIR
3 EDNA WY
4 MARGARET LN
FASHION DR
SUTTERS GOLD ST
IMPERIAL DR
ROSEWOOD DR
CONDESA
DONGSTON WY
LILIBET AV
NEWHALL DR
PLUMGROVE WY
BEATTY DR
SUNFIRE WY
IRISH GOLD WY
23RD AV
WAREHOUSE WY
DISTRICT CT
UNIVERSAL CT
UNSWORTH AV
OUTFALL CIR
THYS CT
YOUNGER CREEK DR
BLUE SKY CT
88TH ST
OSAGE AV
ALDER AV
WAYNE CT
43RD AV
TURNER RD
STAYNER CT
ROVANA CIR
MORRISON CREEK DR
SPECIALTY CIR
CAROLINE DR
OKINAWA ST
GARDNER AV
ASHER LN
0
.125
.25
.375
.5
miles 1 in. = 1900 ft.

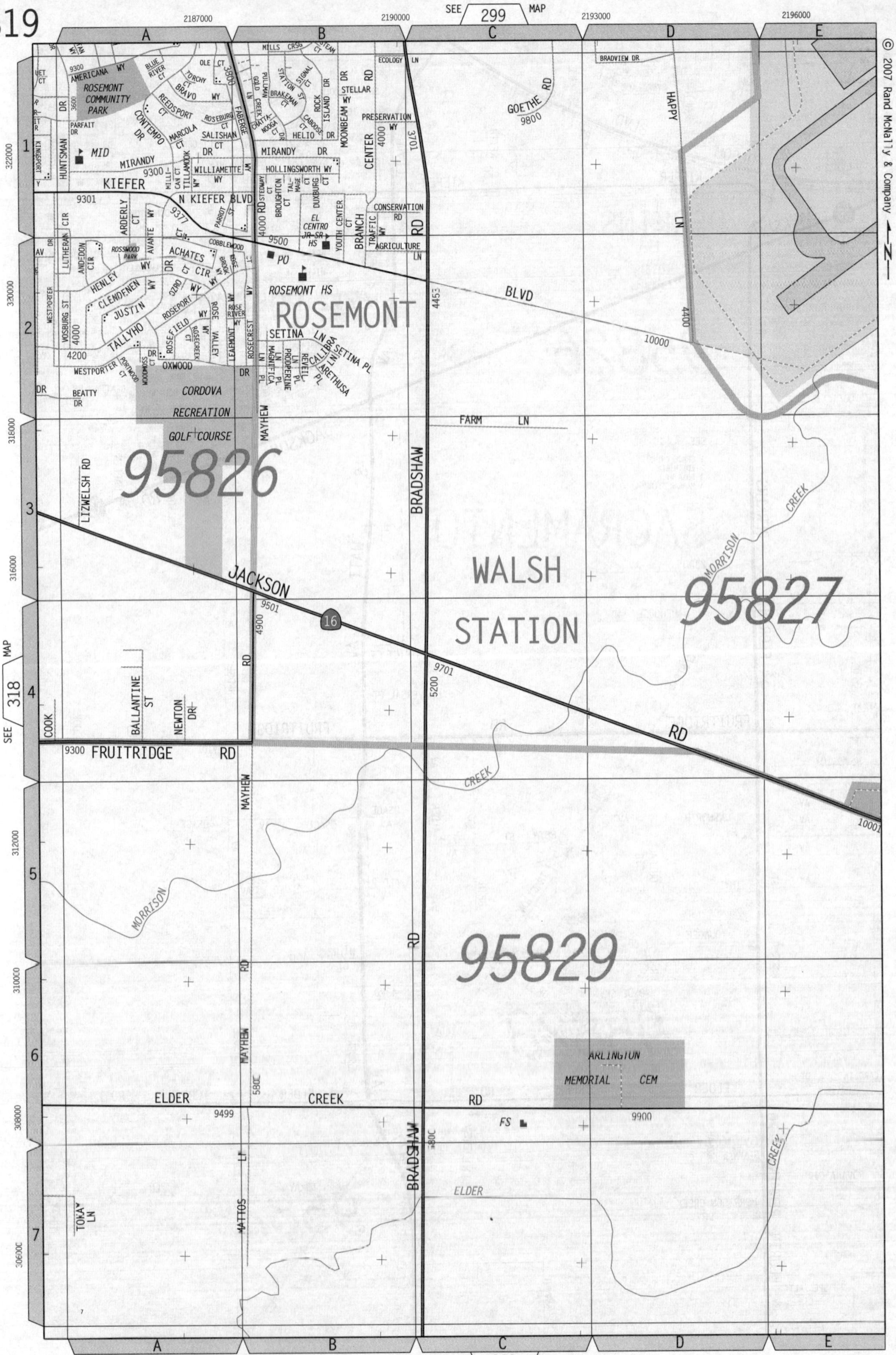
SEE 299 MAP
SEE 339 MAP
SEE 318 MAP
A
B
C
D
E
1
2
3
4
5
6
7
2187000
2190000
2193000
2196000
322000
320000
318000
316000
312000
310000
308000
306000
ROSEMONT
WALSH
STATION
95826
95827
95829
ROSEMONT COMMUNITY PARK
CORDOVA RECREATION
GOLF COURSE
ROSEMONT HS
EL CENTRO JR-SR HS
MID
PO
FS
ARLINGTON MEMORIAL CEM
KIEFER
N KIEFER BLVD
BLVD
BRADSHAW RD
JACKSON RD
16
FRUITRIDGE RD
ELDER CREEK RD
MAYHEW RD
LIZWELSH RD
BALLANTINE ST
NEWTON DR
COOK
FARM LN
HAPPY LN
GOETHE RD
BRADVIEW DR
ECOLOGY LN
STELLAR
PRESERVATION WY
CENTER RD
MOONBEAM WY
CONSERVATION RD
AGRICULTURE LN
TRAFFIC WY
BRANCH
YOUTH CENTER
MIRANDY DR
HOLLINGSWORTH WY
WILLIAMETTE WY
SALISHAN CT
MARCOLA CT
REEDSPORT CT
CONTEMPO DR
AMERICANA WY
BRAVO WY
FABERGE
ROSEMONT HS
SETINA LN
SETINA PL
CALIBRA LN
ARETHUSA PL
PROPERINE LN
OXWOOD DR
WESTPORTER DR
BEATTY DR
TALLYHO DR
JUSTIN WY
CLENDENEN WY
HENLEY WY
ACHATES CIR
ARDERLY CT
AVANTE WY
LUTHERAN CIR
VOSBURG ST
HUNTSMAN DR
KINGSPORT
PARFAIT DR
ROSE VALLEY WY
ROSEFIELD CT
ROSEPORT
LEAMONT WY
ROSECREST
MORRISON CREEK
ELDER CREEK
MATTOS
TOKAY LN
9300
9301
9377
9500
9501
9701
9499
9900
10000
10001
4000
4200
4400
4453
4900
5200
3701
3600
3800
9800
580C

0 .125 .25 .375 .5 miles 1 in. = 1900 ft.

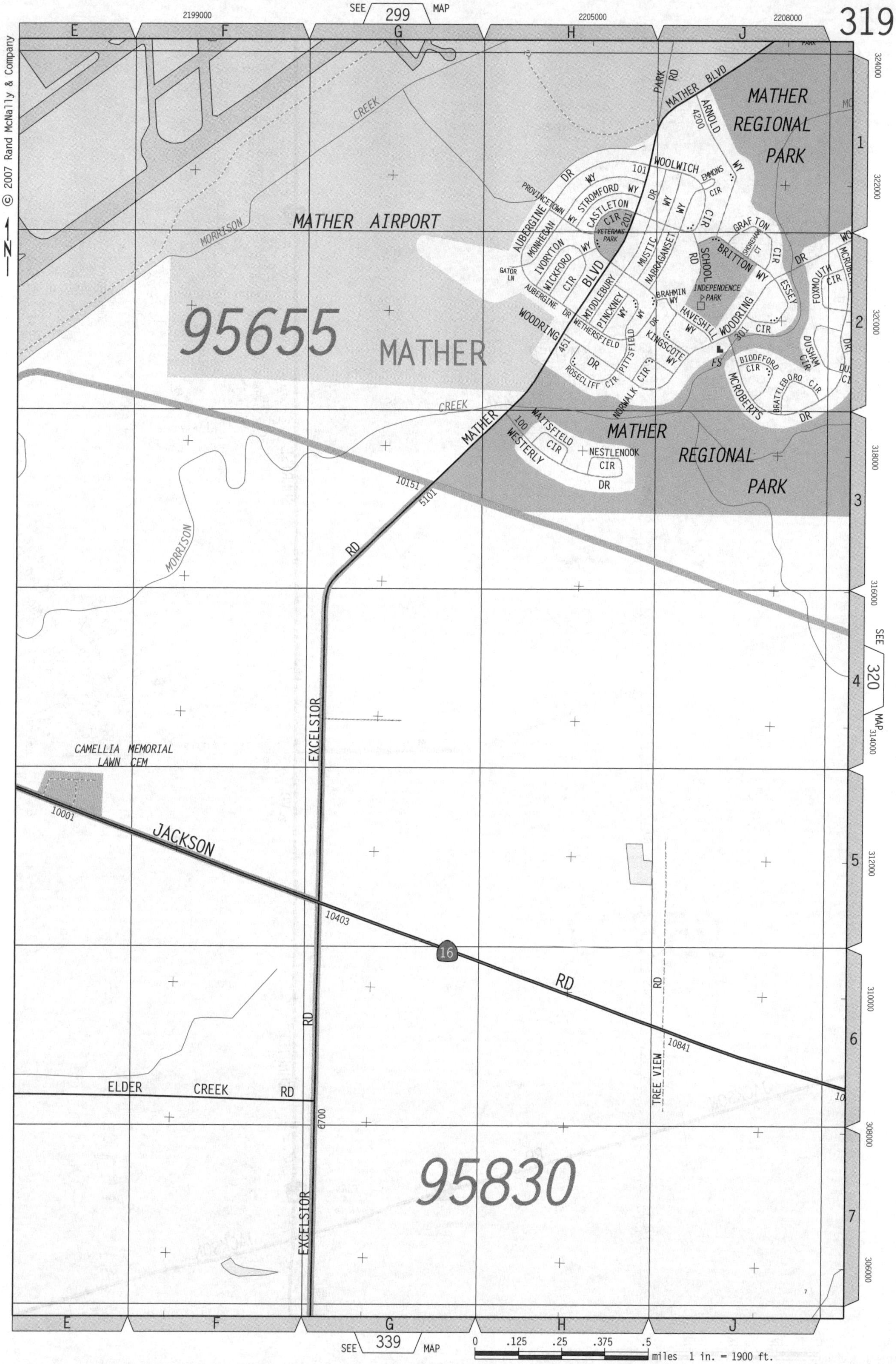
SEE 299 MAP
2199000
2205000
2208000
E
F
G
H
J
MATHER AIRPORT
MATHER REGIONAL PARK
95655
MATHER
MATHER BLVD
PARK RD
ARNOLD WY
WOOLWICH
EMMONS CIR
PROVINCETOWN WY
AUBERGINE DR
STROMFORD WY
CASTLETON CIR
VETERANS PARK
MONHEGAN
IVORYTON
WICKFORD CIR
GATOR LN
MIDDLEBURY
PINCKNEY WY
MUSTIC
NARRAGANSETT
SCHOOL RD
BRITTON WY
GRAFTON CIR
SHOREHAM CT
INDEPENDENCE PARK
BRAHMIN WY
HAVESHILL WY
WOODRING DR
KINGSCOTE WY
PITTSFIELD
WETHERSFIELD
ROSECLIFF CIR
NORWALK CIR
ESSEY
FOXMOUTH CIR
DUSHAM CIR
BIDDEFORD CIR
MCROBERTS DR
BRATTLEBORO CIR
FS
CREEK
MORRISON
WATTSFIELD CIR
WESTERLY
NESTLENOOK CIR
DR
MATHER RD
EXCELSIOR RD
CAMELLIA MEMORIAL LAWN CEM
JACKSON RD
16
TREE VIEW RD
ELDER CREEK RD
95830
SEE 320 MAP
1
2
3
4
5
6
7
SEE 339 MAP
0 .125 .25 .375 .5 miles 1 in. = 1900 ft.

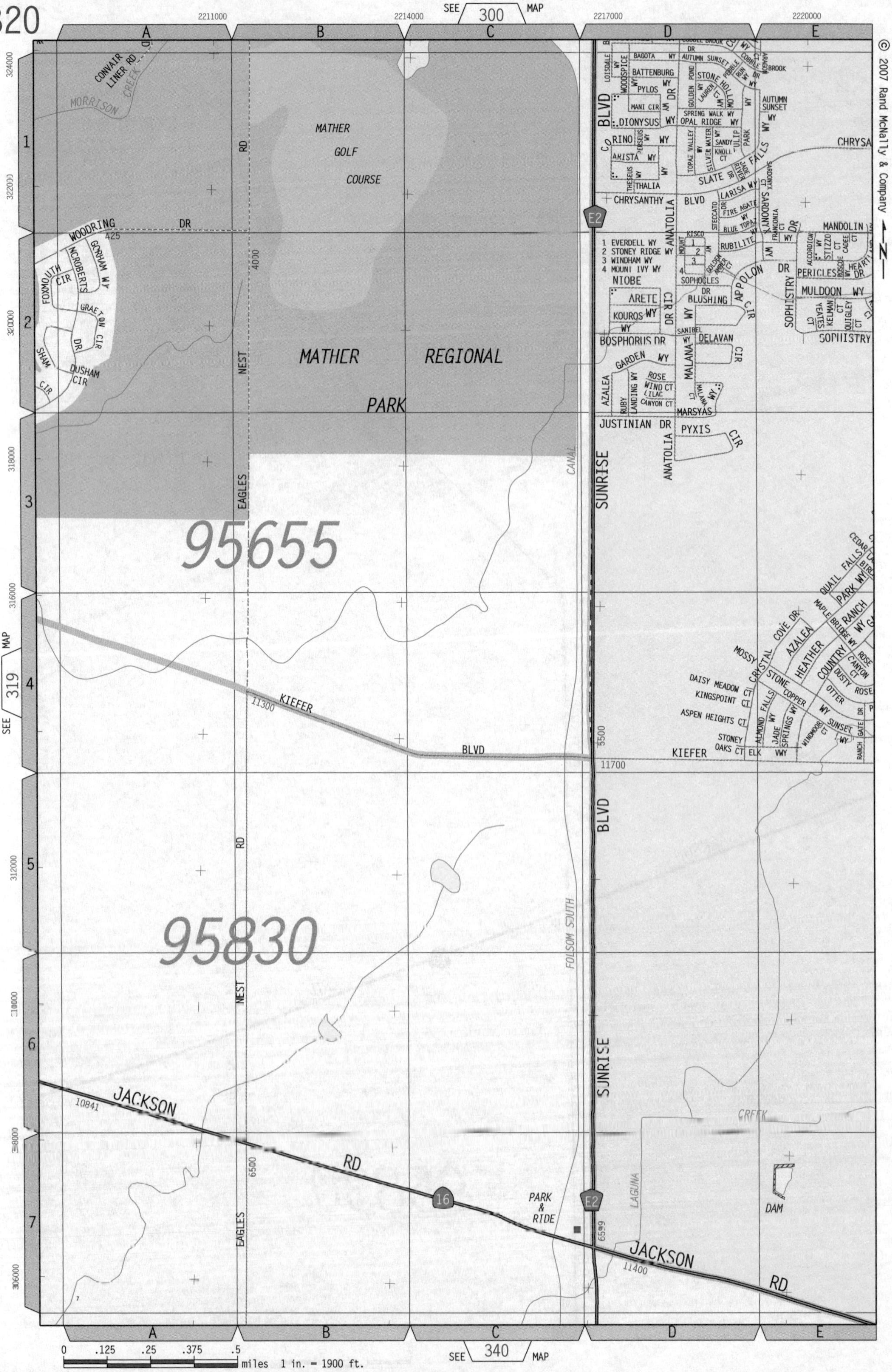
SEE 300 MAP
SEE 319 MAP
SEE 340 MAP
MATHER GOLF COURSE
MATHER REGIONAL PARK
95655
95830
MORRISON CREEK
CONVAIR LINER RD
WOODRING DR
FOXMOUTH CIR
MCROBERTS
GORHAM WY
GRAETON CIR
DUSHAM CIR
SHAM CIR
EAGLES NEST RD
KIEFER BLVD
SUNRISE BLVD
JACKSON RD
FOLSOM SOUTH CANAL
LAGUNA CREEK
PARK & RIDE
DAM
CHRYSANTHY BLVD
ANATOLIA DR
NIOBE
ARETE CIR
KOUROS WY
BOSPHORUS DR
GARDEN WY
AZALEA
DELAVAN CIR
MALANA WY
MARSYAS
JUSTINIAN DR
PYXIS CIR
APPOLON DR
BLUSHING
SOPHISTRY
MULDOON WY
PERICLES DR
MANDOLIN
SLATE FALLS
CORINO WY
ARISTA WY
THALIA
DIONYSUS WY
OPAL RIDGE WY
BATTENBURG
PYLOS WY
BAGOTA WY
AUTUMN SUNSET
1 EVERDELL WY
2 STONEY RIDGE WY
3 WINDHAM WY
4 MOUNT IVY WY
QUAIL FALLS
COUNTRY RANCH
HEATHER
CRYSTAL COVE DR
MOSSY
DAISY MEADOW CT
KINGSPOINT CT
ASPEN HEIGHTS CT
STONEY OAKS CT
KIEFER
ALMOND FALLS WY
JADE SPRINGS WY
A B C D E
1 2 3 4 5 6 7
0 .125 .25 .375 .5 miles 1 in. = 1900 ft.

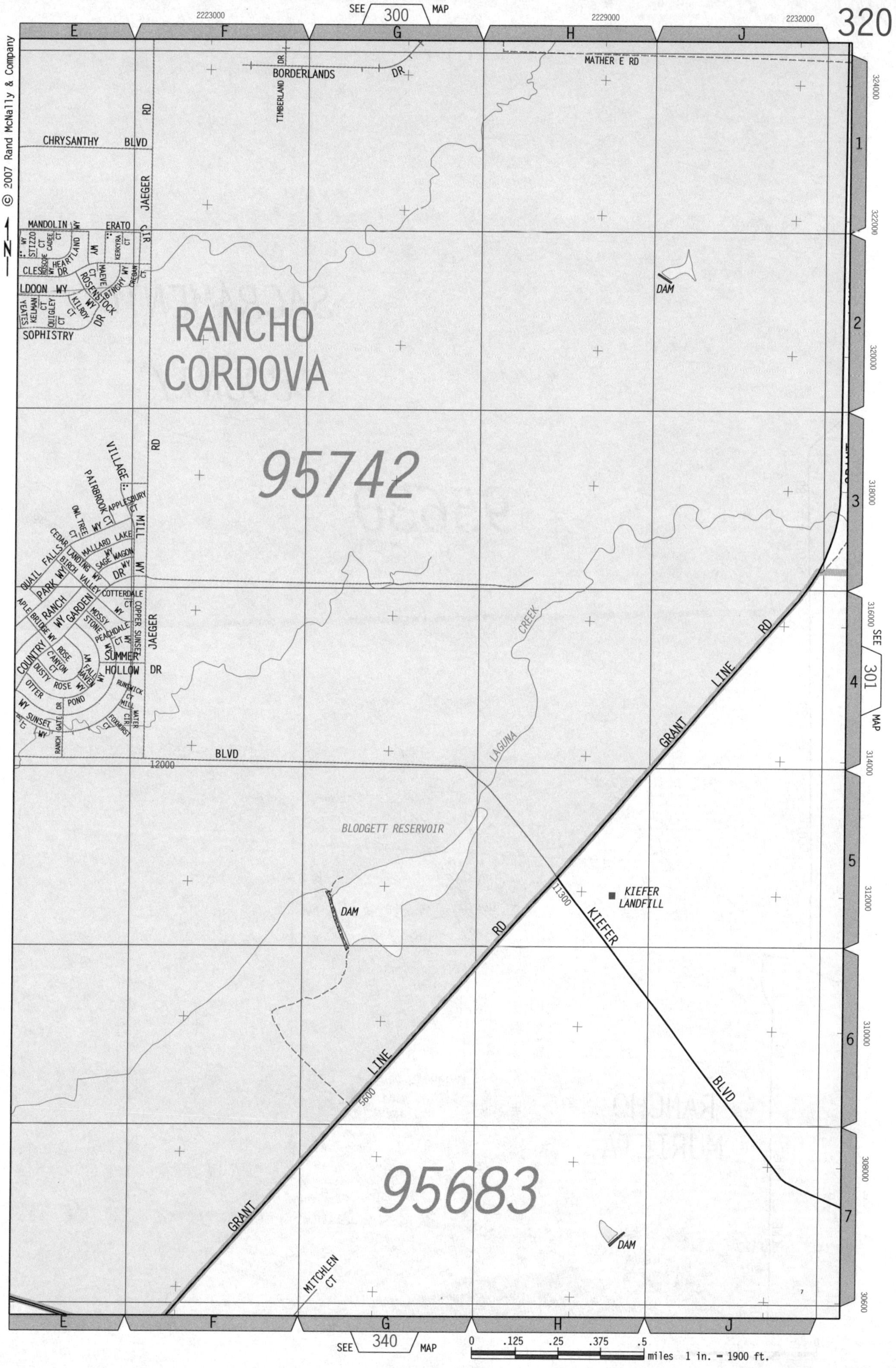
SEE 300 MAP
SEE 301 MAP
SEE 340 MAP
2223000
2229000
2232000
324000
322000
320000
318000
316000
314000
312000
310000
308000
30600
RANCHO CORDOVA
95742
95683
BORDERLANDS DR
TIMBERLAND DR
MATHER E RD
CHRYSANTHY BLVD
JAEGER RD
MANDOLIN
ERATO
STIZZO CT
ROSCOE WY
CADEE CT
HEARTLAND DR
KERKYRA CT
MAEVE CT
ROSENSTOCK WY
BINGHY WY
CREGAN CT
KILROY CT
QUIGLEY CT
KELMAN CT
YEATS
SOPHISTRY
LDOON WY
CLES
DAM
VILLAGE
PAIRBROOK CT
APPLESBURY
MILL WY
OWL TREE CT
CEDAR LANDING
MALLARD LAKE
SAGE WAGON
BIRCH VALLEY
QUAIL FALLS
PARK WY
RANCH WY
GARDEN DR
COTTERDALE CT
MOSSY STONE
PEACHDALE
COPPER SUNSET
SUMMER HOLLOW DR
COUNTRY
ROSE CANYON
DUSTY CT
OTTER
ROSE WY
POND
AM FALL HAVEN
RUNSWICK CT
MILL CIR
WATER
FOXHURST CT
SUNSET WY
RANCH GATE DR
12000
BLVD
CREEK
LAGUNA
BLODGETT RESERVOIR
GRANT LINE RD
KIEFER BLVD
KIEFER LANDFILL
11300
5600
MITCHLEN CT
0 .125 .25 .375 .5 miles 1 in. = 1900 ft.

SEE 301 MAP
SEE 342 MAP
SEE 301 MAP
A
B
C
D
E
1
2
3
4
5
6
7
2259000
2262000
2265000
2268000
324000
322000
320000
318000
314000
312000
310000
308000
SACRAMENTO
COUNTY
95630
DEER
CREEK
SCOTT
RD
LATROBE
CREVIS
CREEK
RD
DAM
DAM
14800
RANCHO
MURIETA
HOUSE
GATE
STONE
ESCUELA
GATE
DR
TIERRAS
DR
PUERTO
DR
DEL CERRO
CUESTA
CONEJO
PRADO VISTA
PUERTO PK
ROBLES
GRANDES
DR
CAZADOR
RIO BLANCO
OSO
VIA DEL
CERRITO
CAMINO
LAGO
CIR
DEL
CHESBRO
CIR
AGUA
VISTA
CAMPOS VERDE
FUENTE
GUADALUPE
VIA DE
ROBLES
BAJA DR
RIO CIR
15100
VIA
SERENO
MURIETA
PKWY
15300
CLEMENTIA CIR
LAGO
CHESBRO
CT
PERA
DR
CAMINO DEL SOL
DR
VENTANA DR
TRINIDAD
DR
TRINIDAD CT
RANCHO MURIETA GOLF COURSE AND COUNTRY CLUB
0
.125
.25
.375
.5
miles 1 in. = 1900 ft.

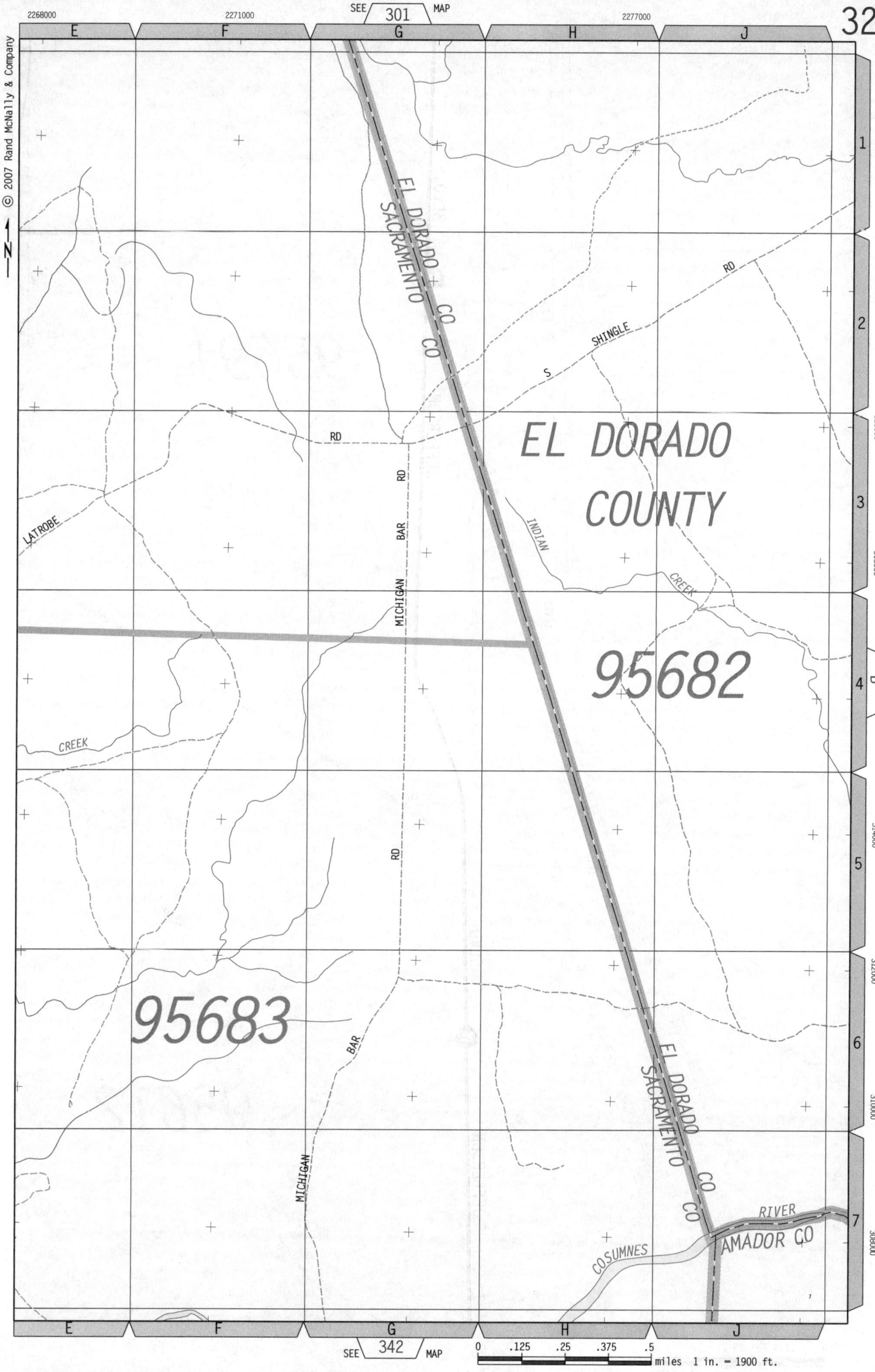
SEE 301 MAP
SEE B MAP
SEE 342 MAP
2268000
2271000
2277000
E
F
G
H
J
1
2
3
4
5
6
7
324000
322000
320000
318000
314000
312000
310000
308000
EL DORADO COUNTY
95682
95683
EL DORADO CO
SACRAMENTO CO
AMADOR CO
S SHINGLE RD
LATROBE RD
MICHIGAN BAR RD
INDIAN CREEK
CREEK
COSUMNES RIVER
0 .125 .25 .375 .5
miles 1 in. = 1900 ft.

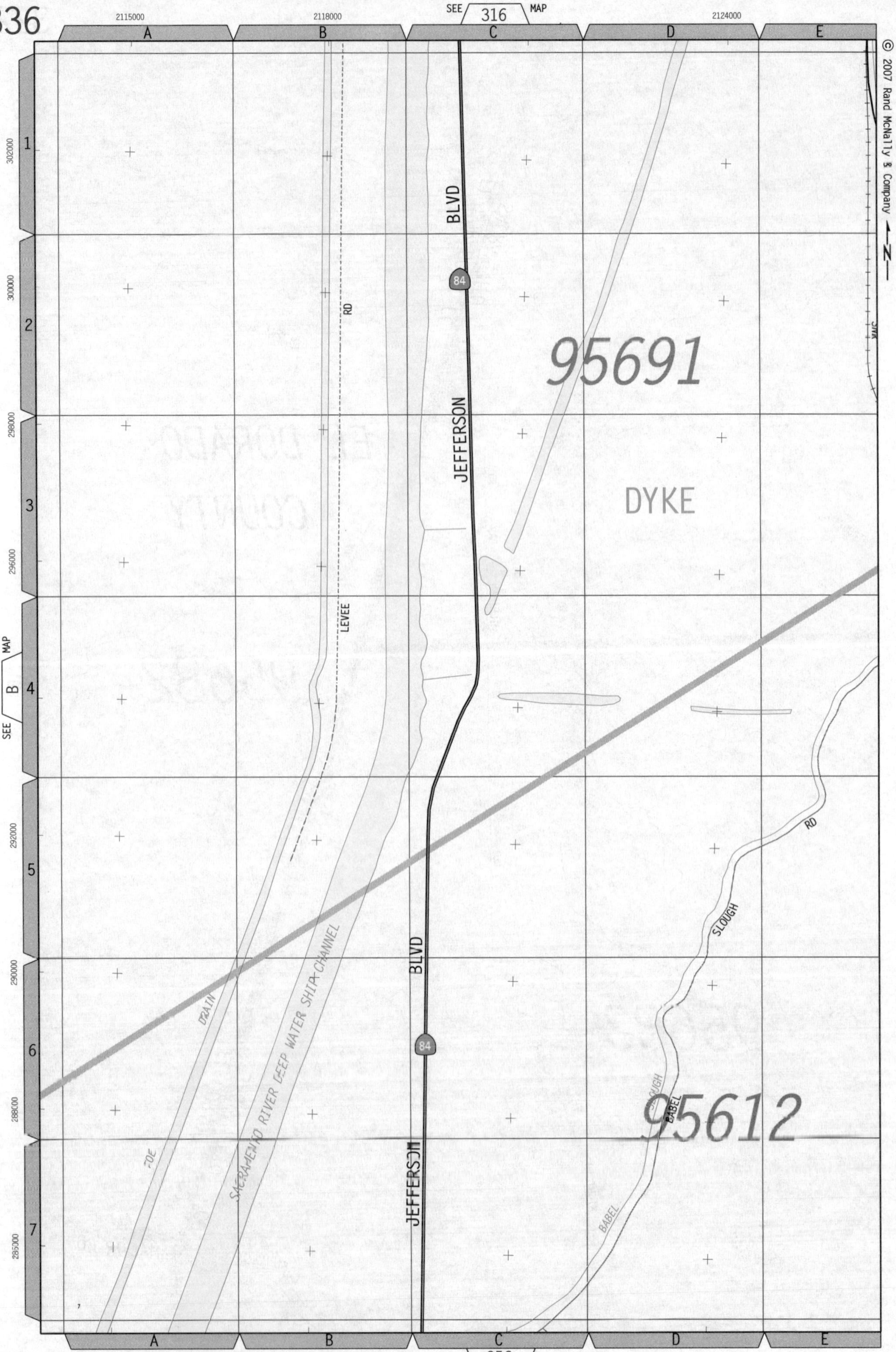
SEE 316 MAP
2115000
2118000
2124000
A
B
C
D
E
1
2
3
4
5
6
7
302000
300000
298000
296000
292000
290000
288000
285000
SEE B MAP
JEFFERSON BLVD
84
LEVEE RD
95691
DYKE
95612
SACRAMENTO RIVER DEEP WATER SHIP CHANNEL
TOE DRAIN
BABEL SLOUGH RD
BABEL SLOUGH
SEE 356 MAP
0 .125 .25 .375 .5 miles 1 in. = 1900 ft.

SEE 316 MAP

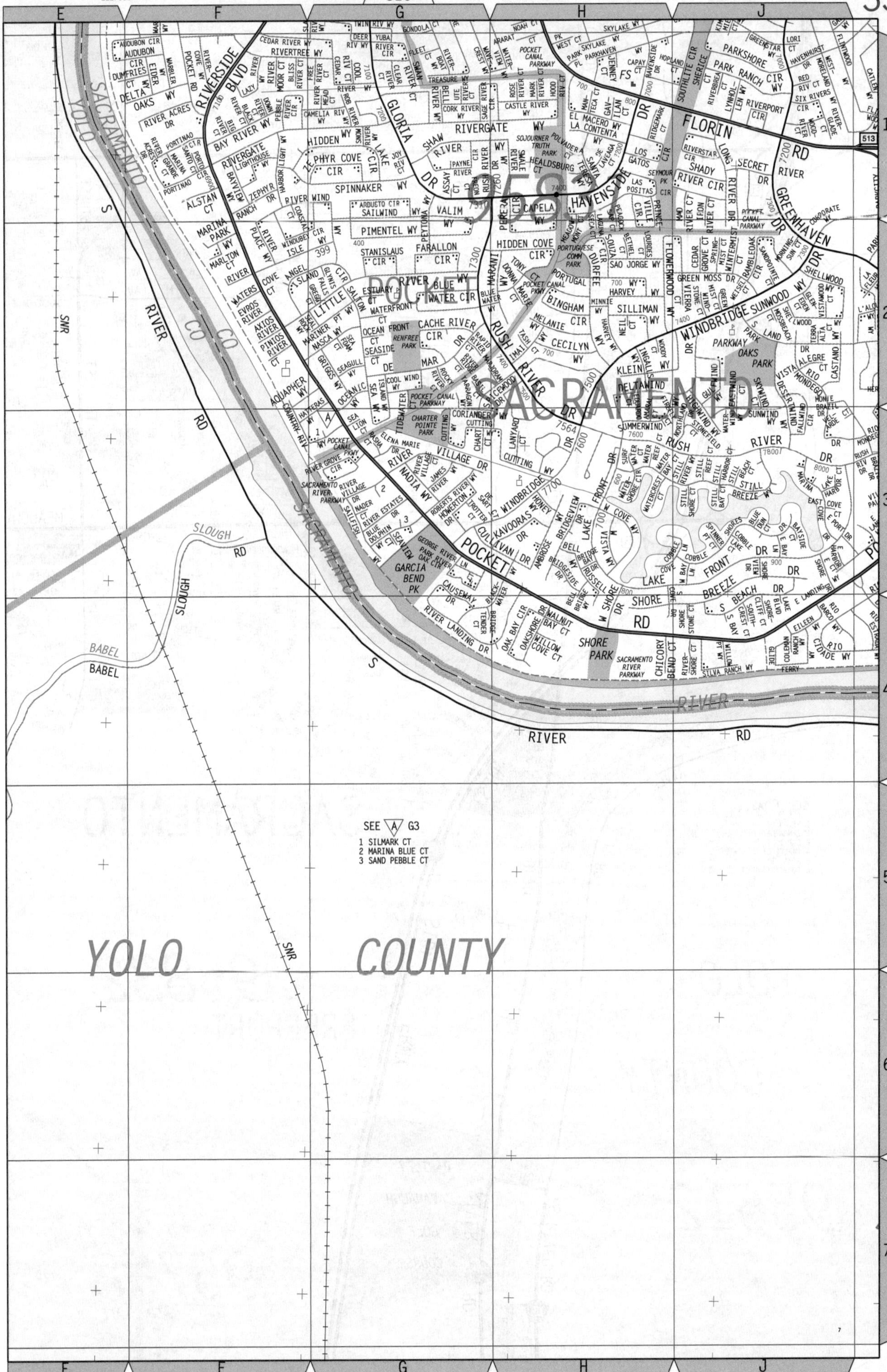
E F G H J
2127000 2130000 2133000 2136000
1 2 3 4 5 6 7
304000 302000 300000 298000 296000 294000 292000 290000 288000 286000
SACRAMENTO
POCKET
95831
YOLO COUNTY
SACRAMENTO RIVER
S RIVER RD
RIVER RD
SNR
SLOUGH RD
BABEL
FLORIN RD
GREENHAVEN DR
RIVERSIDE BLVD
GLORIA DR
RUSH RIVER DR
POCKET RD
WINDBRIDGE DR
SUNWOOD WY
LAKE FRONT DR
SHORE BREEZE DR
RIVERGATE WY
HAVENSIDE DR
RIVER VILLAGE DR
GARCIA BEND PK
SHORE PARK
RENFREE PARK
CHARTER POINTE PARK
PORTUGUESE COMM PARK
PARKWAY OAKS PARK
SOJOURNER TRUTH PARK
SACRAMENTO RIVER PARKWAY
POCKET CANAL PARKWAY
SEE A G3
1 SILMARK CT
2 MARINA BLUE CT
3 SAND PEBBLE CT
0 .125 .25 .375 .5 miles 1 in. = 1900 ft.

SEE 337 MAP

SEE 356 MAP

SEE 317 MAP
SEE 357 MAP
SEE 336 MAP
2139000
2142000
2148000
304000
302000
300000
298000
296000
292000
290000
286000
A
B
C
D
E
1
2
3
4
5
6
7
FLORIN RD
BING MALONEY GOLF COURSE
CHORLEY PARK
MORSE SCHOOL PARK
JOHN MORSE WALDORF HS
PONY EXPRESS SCHOOL PARK
WILLOW RANCHO PARK
FREEPORT BLVD
AMHERST ST
WAKEFIELD ST
MILFORD WY
17TH ST
CROMWELL AV
WAKEFIELD WY
NEWPORT AV
RIDWELL SCHOOL PARK
STRATFORD ST
68TH AV
TILDEN WY
WILLOWWICK WY
BENBOW ST
STOCKDALE ST
24TH ST
25TH ST
24TH STREET BYPASS PARK
BYPS LIB
FS
GOETHE SCHOOL PARK
MID
HOPKINS SCHOOL PARK
HOPKINS PARK
MATSON
MUIRFIELD
TROON
95822
95831
MEADOWVIEW
SLOAT SCHOOL PARK
CARELLA DR
HENRIETTA
21ST
WINKLEY
STEVE JONES PARK
MANUAL SILVA PARK
CASA LINDA DR
MEADOWVIEW RD
FERRAN AV
ARMINGTON AV
ANOKA AV
BELT WY
NEIHART AV
71ST AV
JANRICK AV
FREEPORT SCHOOL PARK
FREEPORT PARK
MEADOWGLEN
SAMUEL PANNEL COMMUNITY CENTER
STILL DR
STILL SCHOOL PARK
MEADOWVIEW PARK
HIGHFIELD
MANORSIDE DR
AMHERST EXPEDITION
RICHFIELD WY
CAVALIER
SACRAMENTO
GREENHAVEN
CORPORATE WY
S LAND PARK DR
POCKET RD
RIVER RANCH WY
MARRIOTT PARK
Z'BERG PARK
SACRAMENTO DRAINAGE CANAL
SACRAMENTO RIVER PARKWAY
SACRAMENTO RIVER
BILL CONLIN YOUTH SPORTS COMPLEX
WEST SIDE FRWY
5
160
513
512
E9
STONECREST AV
BEACH LAKE RD
SEE A A3
1 MILAN CT
2 GENOA CT
3 CAPRI CT
4 NAPLES CT
5 ROMA CT
6 CONSTANTINE CT
S RIVER RD
YOLO COUNTY
95832
FREEPORT
FREEPORT BRIDGE
S RIVER RD
RIVER RD
BARTLEY CAVANAUGH GOLF COURSE
95612
95758
MORRISON CREEK
BEACH LAKE
0 .125 .25 .375 .5 miles 1 in. = 1900 ft.

SEE 317 MAP

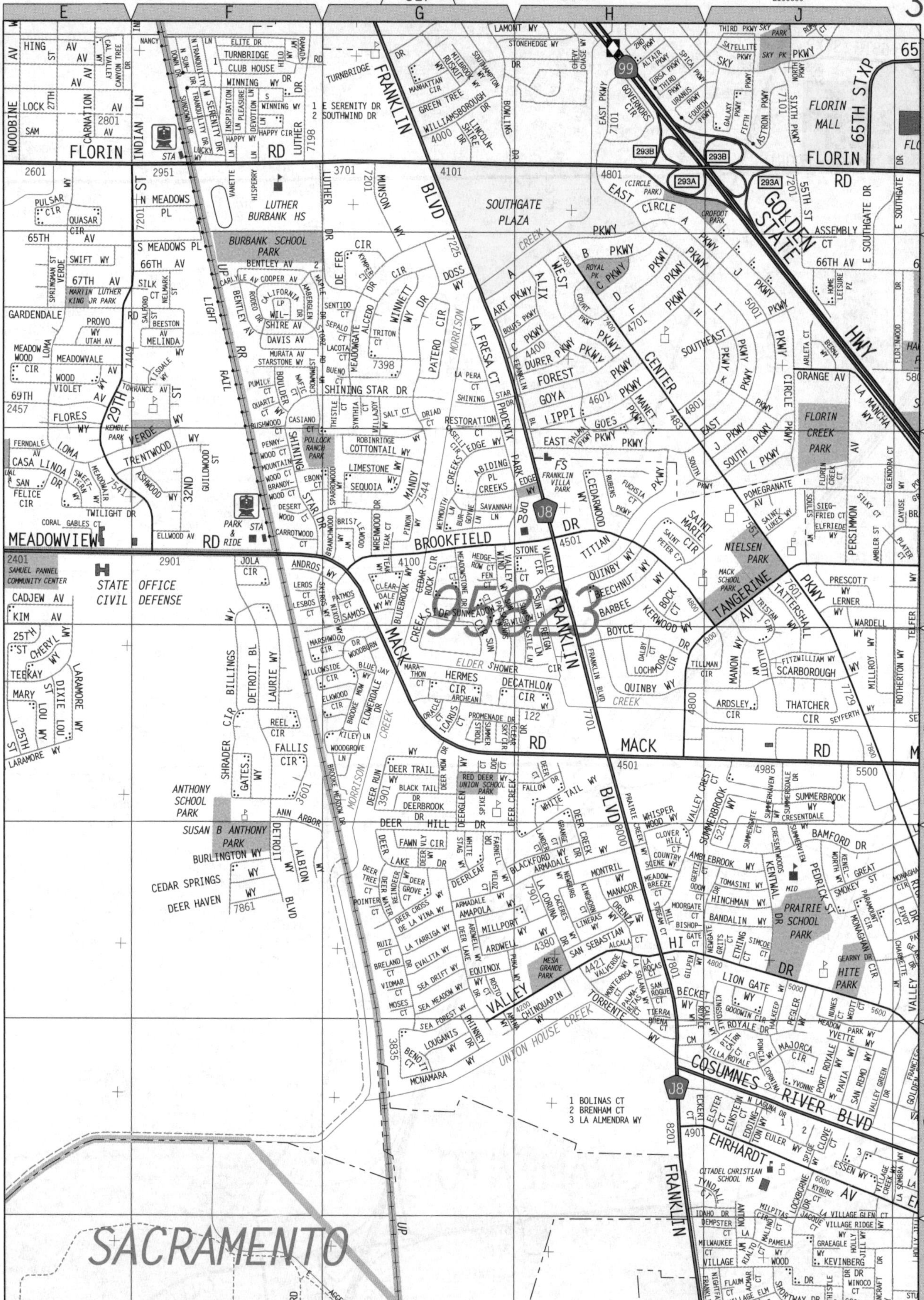

SEE 338 MAP

SEE 357 MAP

0 .125 .25 .375 .5 miles 1 in. = 1900 ft.

SEE 318 MAP

SEE 337 MAP

SEE 358 MAP

0 .125 .25 .375 .5 miles 1 in. = 1900 ft.

SEE 318 MAP

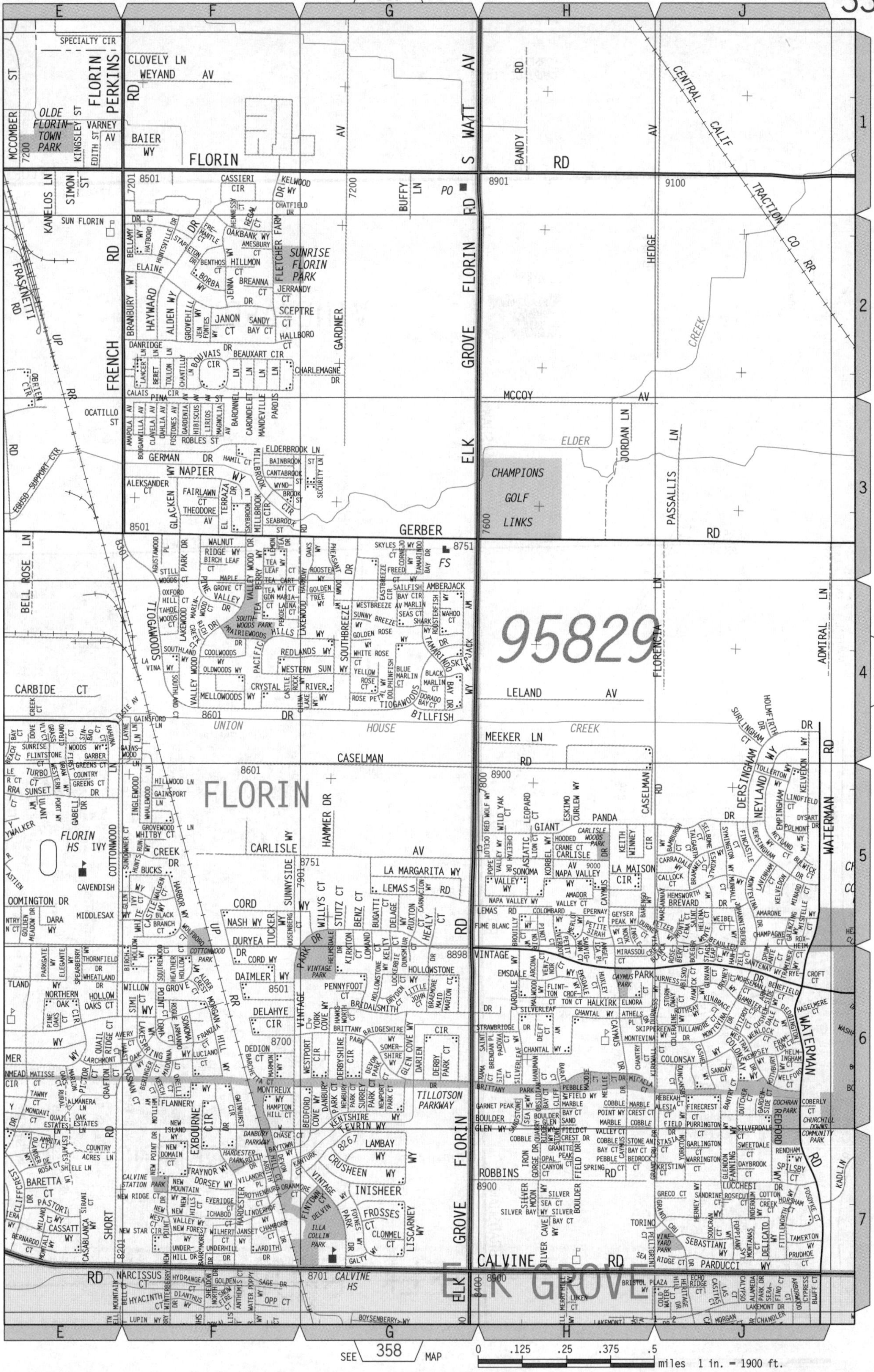

SEE 339 MAP

SEE 358 MAP

0 .125 .25 .375 .5 miles 1 in. = 1900 ft.

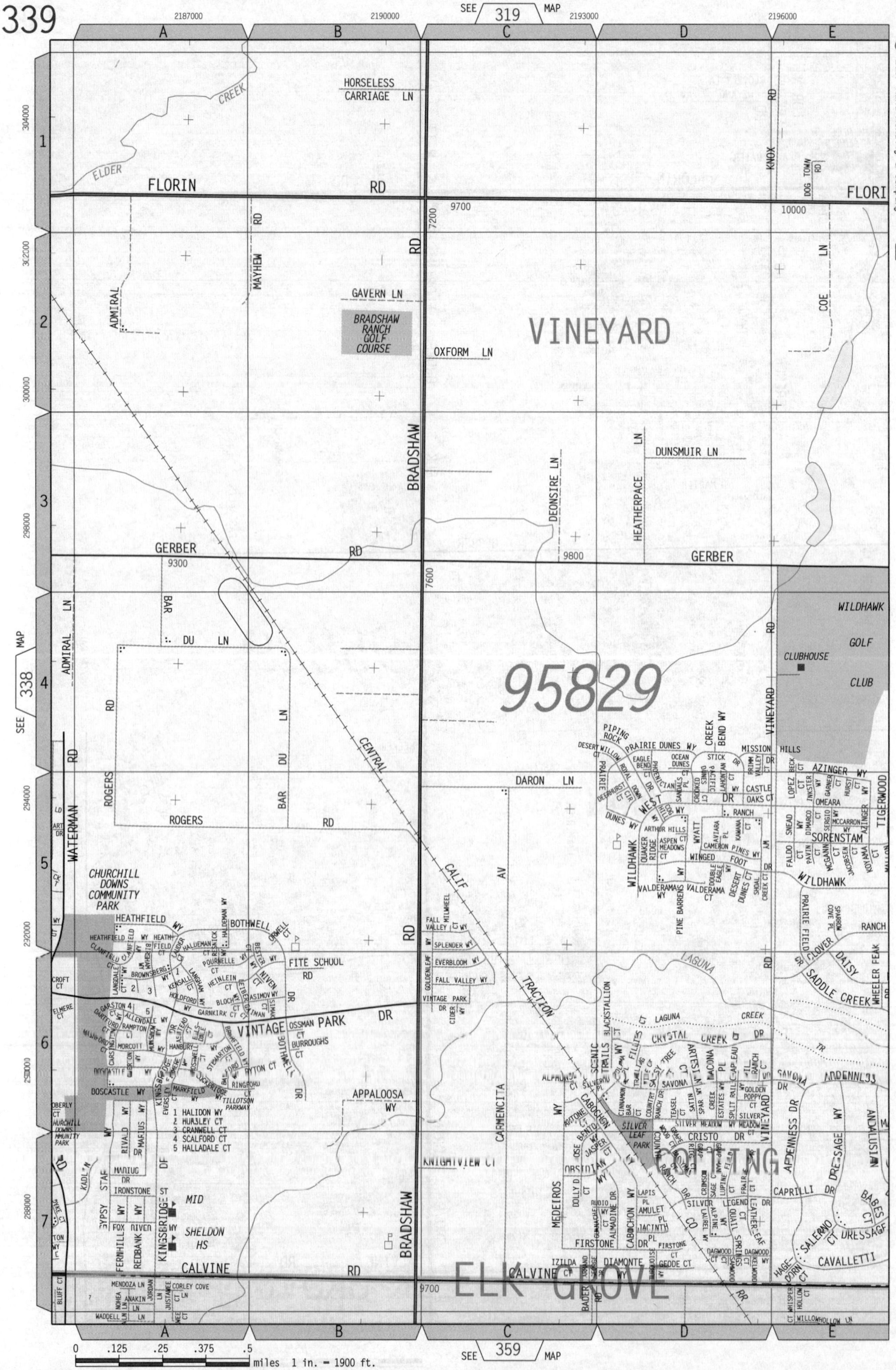
SEE 319 MAP
SEE 338 MAP
SEE 359 MAP
2187000
2190000
2193000
2196000
304000
302000
300000
298000
294000
292000
290000
288000
A
B
C
D
E
1
2
3
4
5
6
7
FLORIN
RD
FLORI
9700
10000
7200
7600
9300
9800
HORSELESS CARRIAGE LN
ELDER
CREEK
KNOX RD
DOG TOWN RD
COE LN
MAYHEW RD
ADMIRAL
GAVERN LN
BRADSHAW RANCH GOLF COURSE
OXFORM LN
VINEYARD
DUNSMUIR LN
HEATHERPACE LN
DEONSIRE LN
BRADSHAW
GERBER
RD
GERBER
BAR DU LN
ADMIRAL LN
WILDHAWK GOLF CLUB
CLUBHOUSE
95829
ROGERS RD
ROGERS
BAR DU LN
CENTRAL
CALIF
TRACTION
CO
RR
DARON LN
CARMENCITA AV
WATERMAN RD
CHURCHILL DOWNS COMMUNITY PARK
HEATHFIELD WY
BOTHWELL CT
FITE SCHOOL RD
VINTAGE PARK DR
OSSMAN PARK
BURROUGHS
TILLOTSON PARKWAY
APPALOOSA WY
KNIGHTVIEW CT
1 HALIDON WY
2 HUR3LEY CT
3 CRANWELL CT
4 SCALFORD CT
5 HALLADALE CT
BOSCASTLE WY
MID SHELDON HS
KINGSBRIDGE
FERNHILL
REDBANK
FOX RIVER
IRONSTONE
CALVINE RD
MENDOZA LN
BLUFF CT
WADDELL LN
PRAIRIE DUNES WY
WILDHAWK WEST DR
MISSION HILLS
AZINGER WY
TIGERWOOD
SORENSTAM
WILDHAWK
PRAIRIE FIELD
CLOVER
DAISY
SADDLE CREEK
WHEELER FEAK
LAGUNA
CREEK
CRYSTAL CREEK DR
SAVONA
ARDENNES DR
SILVER LEAF PARK
CRISTO DR
COTTING
DRESSAGE
CAPRILLI DR
CAVALLETTI
SALERNO CT
BABES CT
MEDEIROS
FIRSTONE
CABOCHON
DIAMONTE
IZILDA
CALVINE
ELK GROVE
WILLOWHOLLOW LN
0
.125
.25
.375
.5
miles 1 in. = 1900 ft.

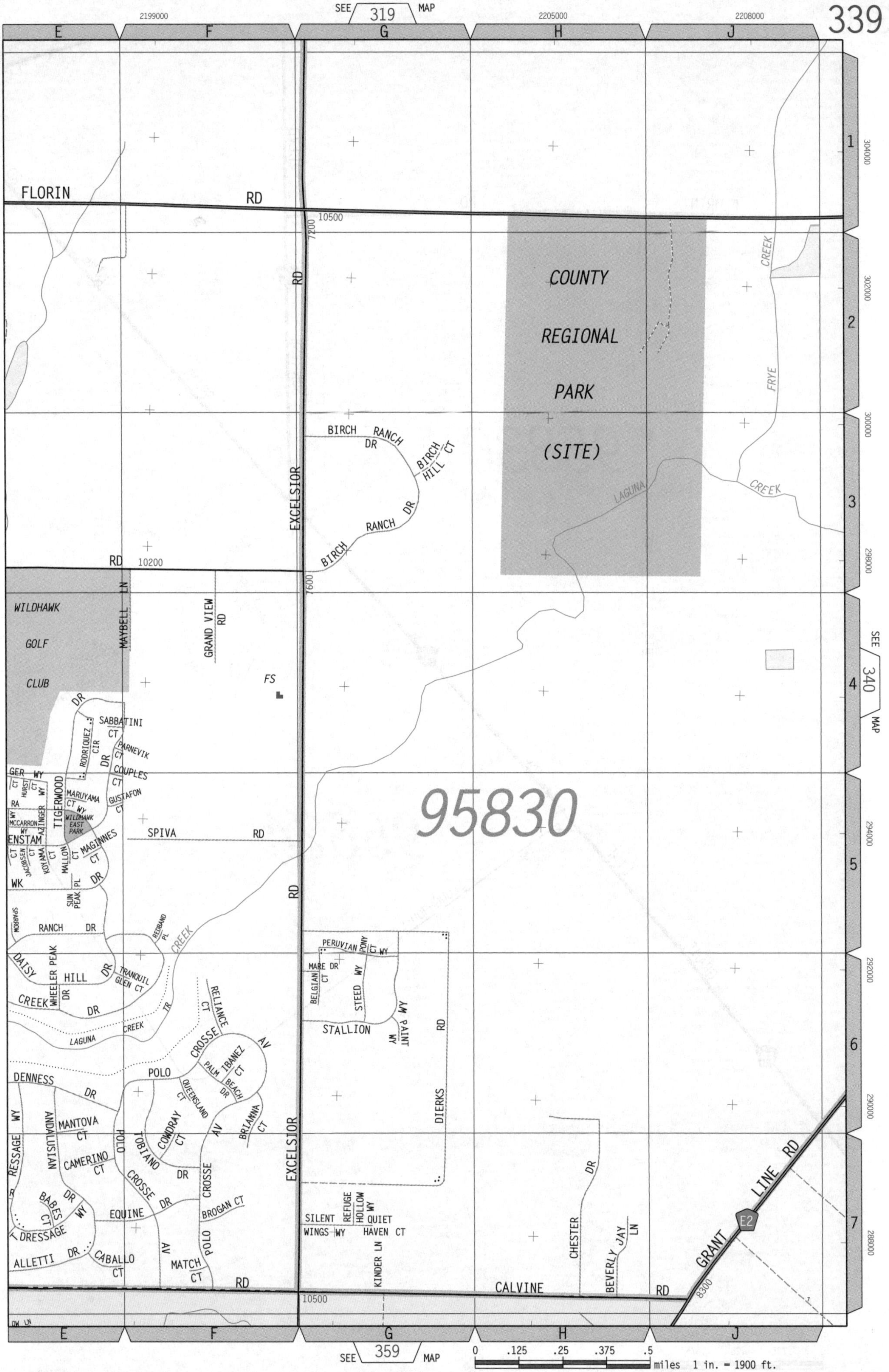
SEE 319 MAP
SACRAMENTO CO.
FLORIN RD
EXCELSIOR RD
COUNTY REGIONAL PARK (SITE)
FRYE CREEK
LAGUNA CREEK
BIRCH RANCH DR
BIRCH HILL CT
WILDHAWK GOLF CLUB
MAYBELL LN
GRAND VIEW RD
FS
SEE 340 MAP
95830
SPIVA RD
SABBATINI CT
PARNEVIK CT
COUPLES CT
GUSTAFON CT
MARUYAMA CT
TIGERWOOD
RODRIQUEZ CIR
WILDHAWK EAST PARK
MAGINNES CT
SUN PEAK PL
REDBAND PL
DAISY HILL DR
WHEELER PEAK DR
TRANQUIL GLEN CT
CREEK DR
RELIANCE CT
CROSSE AV
IBANEZ CT
PALM BEACH DR
POLO
DENNESS DR
MANTOVA CT
ANDALUSIAN
CAMERINO CT
DRESSAGE WY
BABES CT
EQUINE
ALLETTI DR
CABALLO CT
MATCH CT
BROGAN CT
QUEENSLAND CT
COWDRAY CT
TOBIANO
BRIANNA CT
PERUVIAN PONY CT WY
MARE DR
BELGIAN CT
STEED WY
STALLION
PAINT WY
DIERKS RD
SILENT WINGS WY
REFUGE HOLLOW WY
QUIET HAVEN CT
KINDER LN
CALVINE RD
CHESTER DR
BEVERLY JAY LN
GRANT LINE RD
E2
SEE 359 MAP
0 .125 .25 .375 .5 miles 1 in. = 1900 ft.

SEE 320 MAP

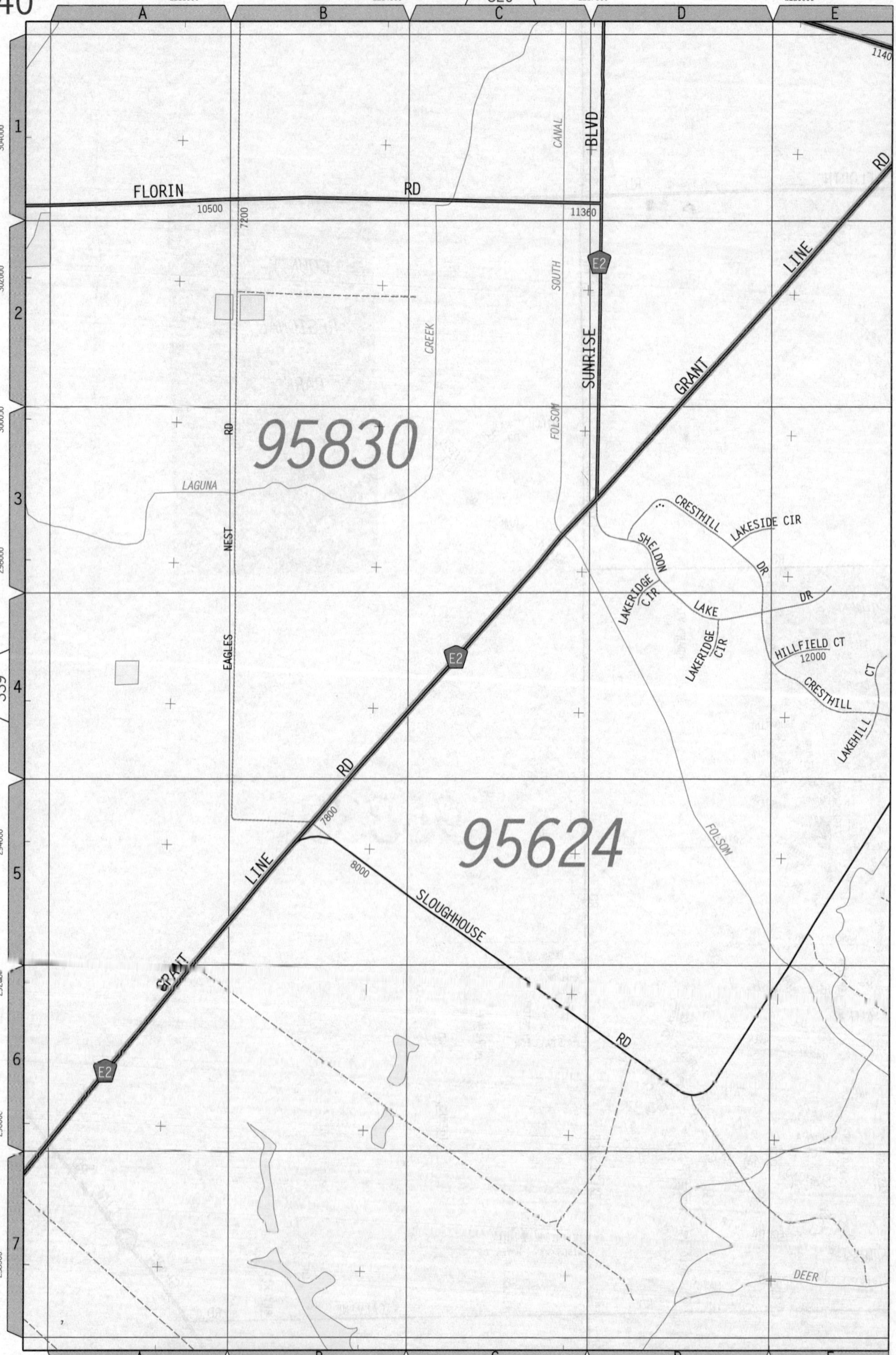

SEE 339 MAP

0 .125 .25 .375 .5 miles 1 in. = 1900 ft.

SEE 360 MAP

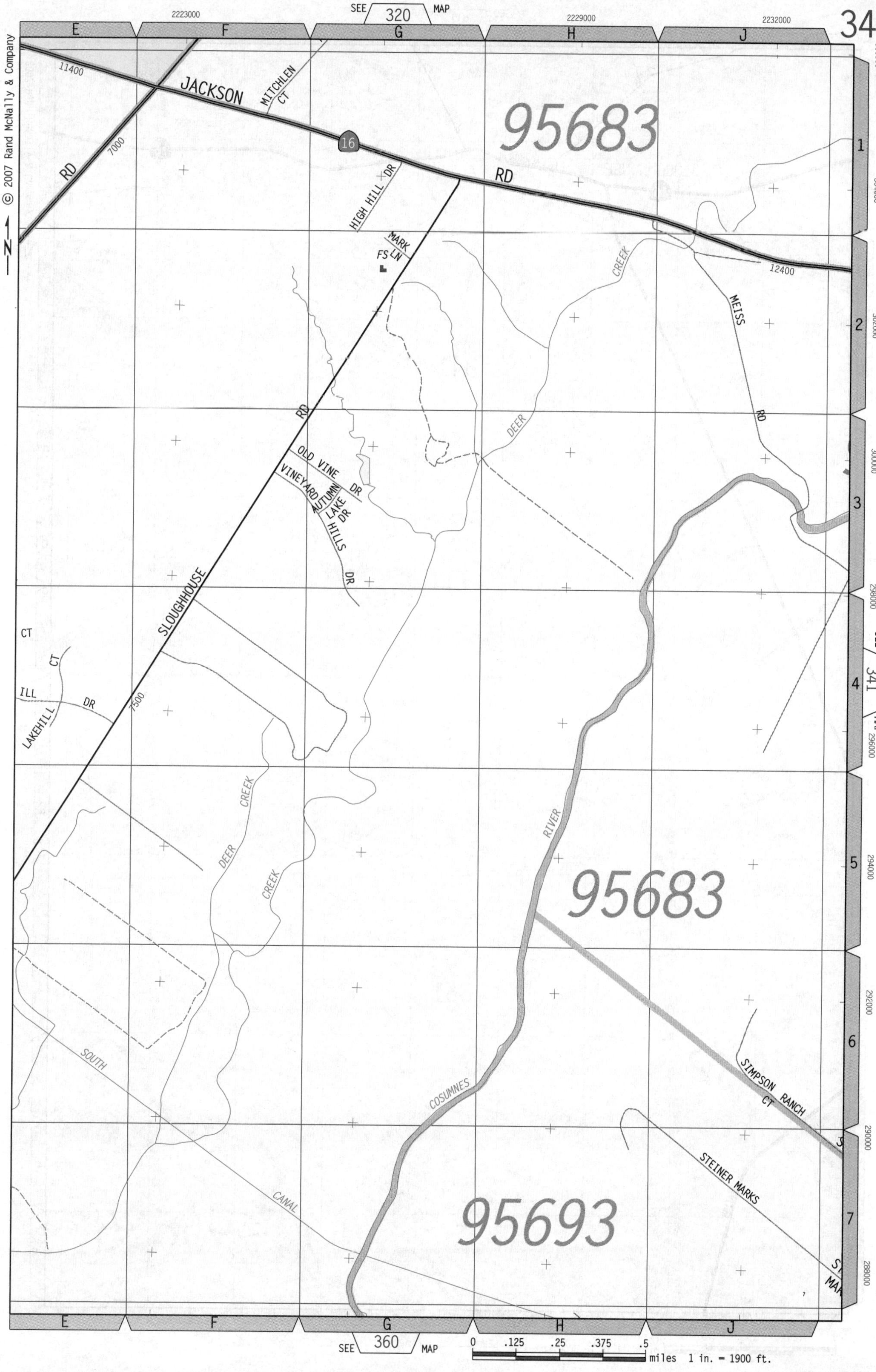
SEE 320 MAP
2223000
2229000
2232000
E
F
G
H
J
306000
304000
302000
300000
298000
296000
294000
292000
290000
288000
1
2
3
4
5
6
7
11400
JACKSON
RD
MITCHLEN CT
16
RD
7000
HIGH HILL DR
MARK LN
FS
12400
95683
CREEK
DEER
MEISS
RD
RD
OLD VINE DR
VINEYARD HILLS DR
AUTUMN LAKE DR
SLOUGHHOUSE
7500
CT
CT
ILL
DR
LAKEHILL
SEE 341 MAP
DEER CREEK
DEER CREEK
RIVER
95683
SOUTH
CANAL
COSUMNES
SIMPSON RANCH CT
STEINER MARKS
95693
SEE 360 MAP
0 .125 .25 .375 .5
miles 1 in. = 1900 ft.

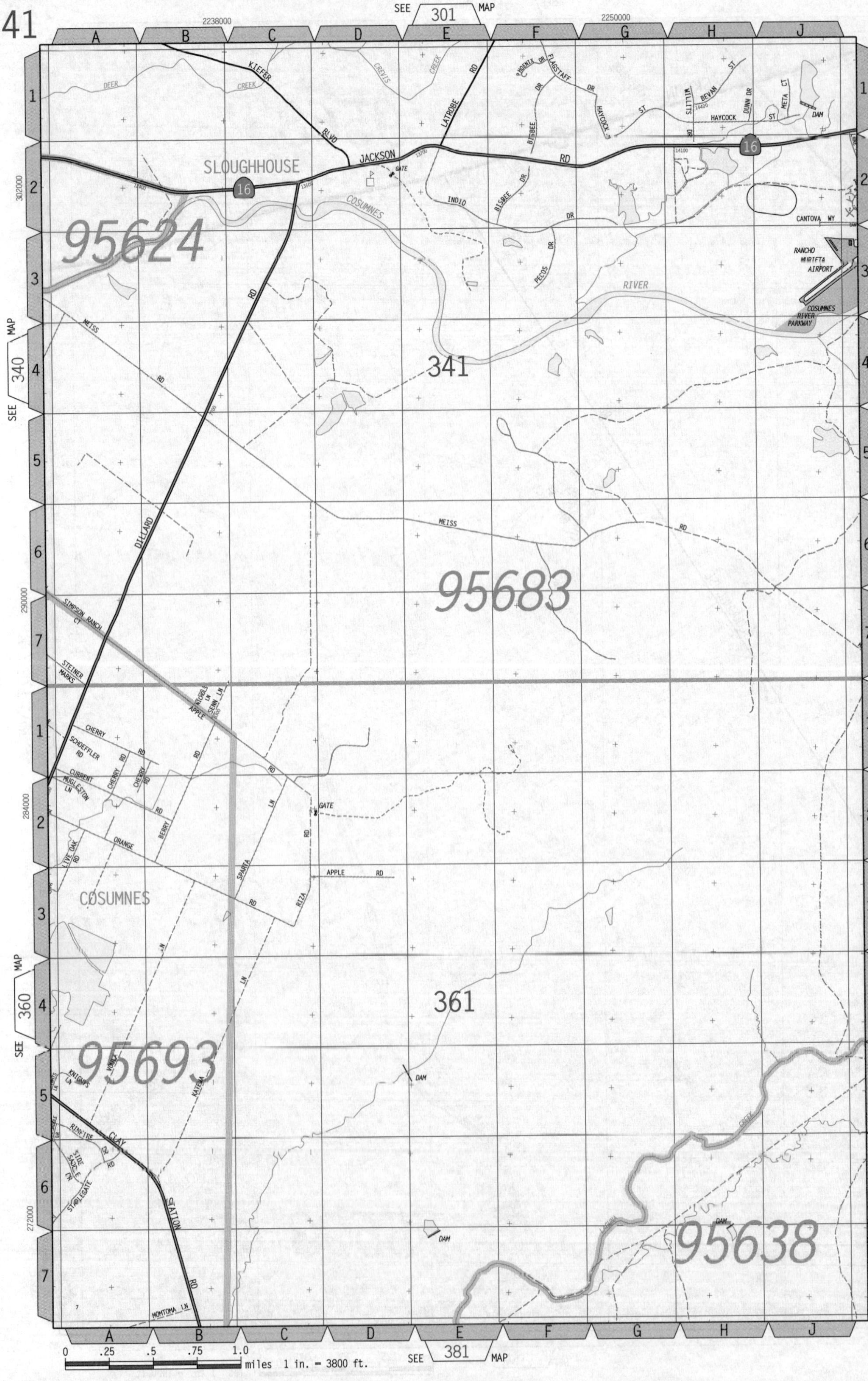
SEE 301 MAP
SEE 340 MAP
SEE 360 MAP
SEE 381 MAP
SLOUGHHOUSE
COSUMNES
95624
95683
95693
95638
341
361
KIEFER BLVD
JACKSON RD
LATROBE RD
DILLARD RD
MEISS RD
SIMPSON RANCH CT
STEINER
MARKS
CHERRY
SCHOEFFLER RD
CURRENT
MUGLESTON LN
CHERRY RD
BERRY
ORANGE
LIVE OAK RD
APPLE RD
SPARTA RD
RIZA
SENN LN
KATERA
KNIGHTS LN
CLAY STATION RD
RIMFIRE RD
SIDE SADDLE
STAGECOACH
MONTOMA LN
INDIO DR
BISBEE DR
PECOS DR
PHOENIX DR
FLAGSTAFF DR
HAYCOCK ST
WILLITS DR
BEVAN ST
DUNN DR
META CT
CANTOVA WY
RANCHO MURIETA AIRPORT
COSUMNES RIVER PARKWAY
COSUMNES RIVER
DEER CREEK
CREVIS CREEK
GATE
DAM
16
miles 1 in. = 3800 ft.

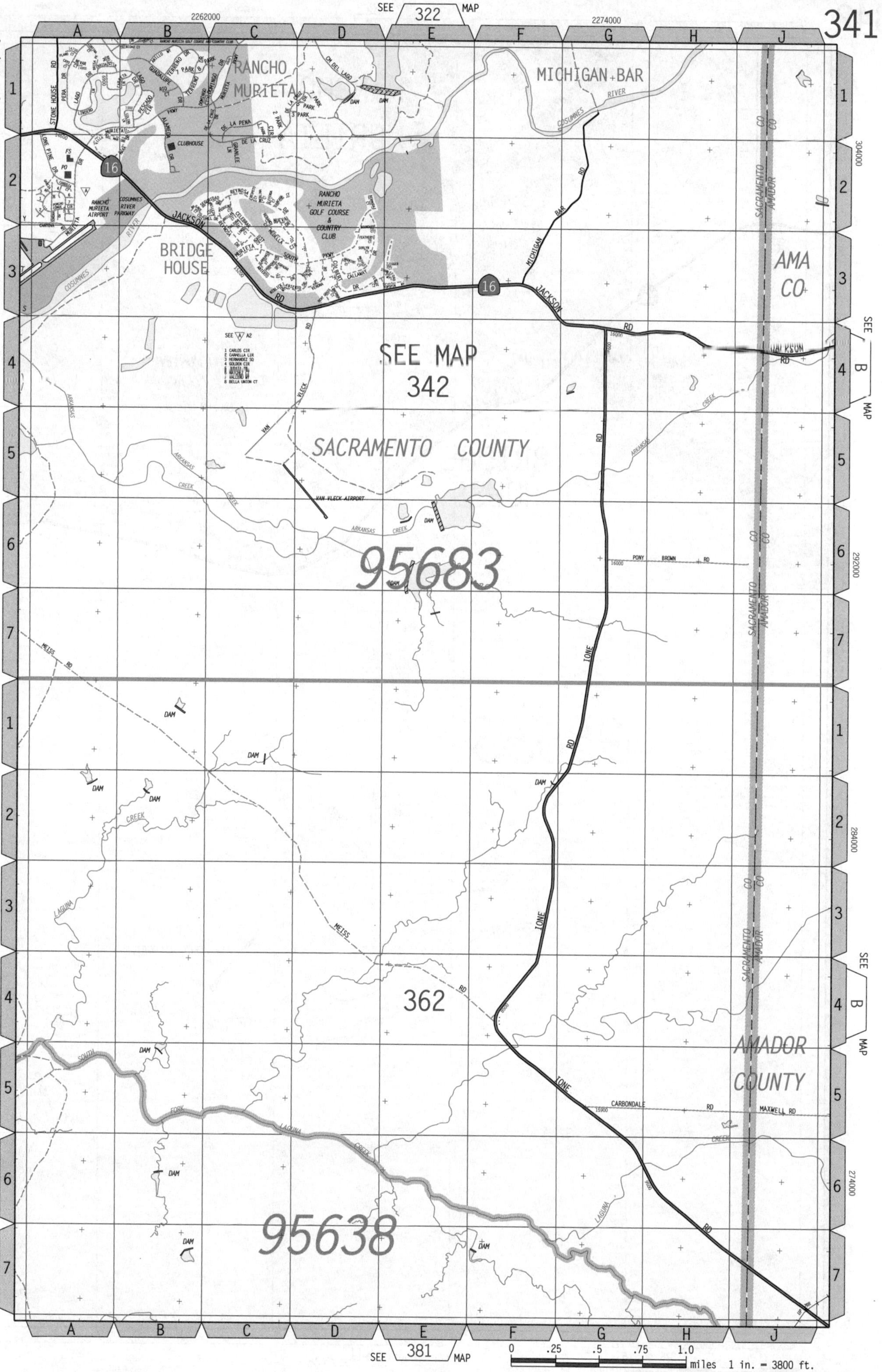
SEE 322 MAP
RANCHO MURIETA
MICHIGAN BAR
BRIDGE HOUSE
RANCHO MURIETA GOLF COURSE & COUNTRY CLUB
RANCHO MURIETA AIRPORT
COSUMNES RIVER PARKWAY
CLUBHOUSE
COSUMNES RIVER
JACKSON RD
16
MICHIGAN BAR RD
STONE HOUSE RD
LONE PINE DR
SEE MAP 342
SACRAMENTO COUNTY
VAN VLECK RD
VAN VLECK AIRPORT
ARKANSAS CREEK
95683
PONY BROWN RD
IONE RD
MEISS RD
AMA CO
SACRAMENTO CO
AMADOR CO
SEE B MAP
362
DAM
LAGUNA CREEK
SOUTH FORK LAGUNA CREEK
CARBONDALE RD
MAXWELL RD
AMADOR COUNTY
95638
SEE 381 MAP
0 .25 .5 .75 1.0 miles 1 in. = 3800 ft.

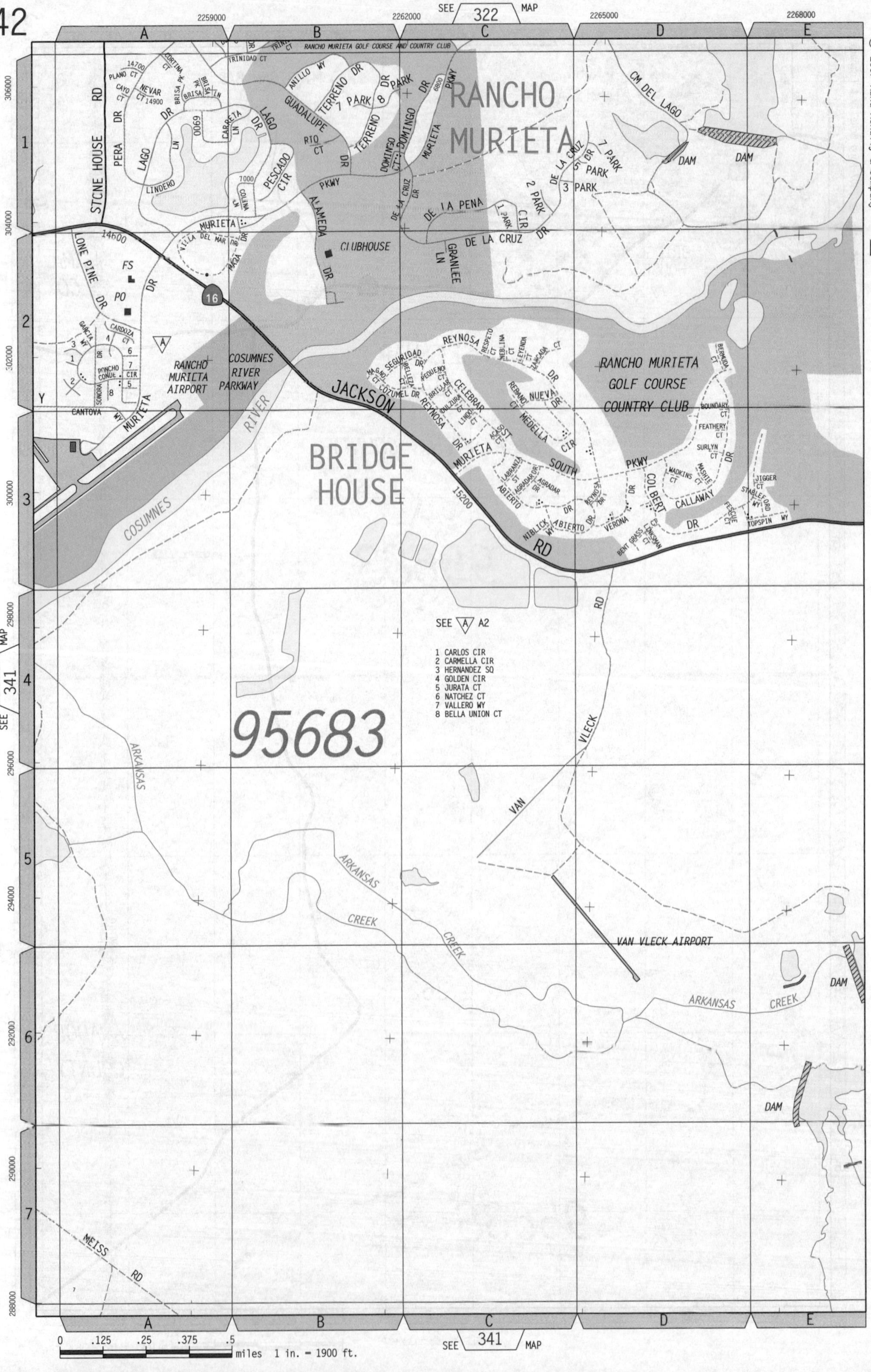
SEE 322 MAP
SEE 341 MAP
A
B
C
D
E
1
2
3
4
5
6
7
2259000
2262000
2265000
2268000
306000
304000
302000
300000
298000
296000
294000
292000
290000
288000
RANCHO MURIETA
BRIDGE HOUSE
95683
RANCHO MURIETA GOLF COURSE AND COUNTRY CLUB
RANCHO MURIETA GOLF COURSE COUNTRY CLUB
RANCHO MURIETA AIRPORT
COSUMNES RIVER PARKWAY
COSUMNES RIVER
CLUBHOUSE
FS
PO
JACKSON RD
16
14600
15200
STONE HOUSE RD
LONE PINE DR
MURIETA DR
MURIETA PKWY
MURIETA SOUTH PKWY
CANTOVA WY
PERA DR
LAGO LN
LINDERO
PLANO CT
CAYO CT
NEVAR CT
CORTINA CT
BRISA PK
BRISA LN
CARRETA LN
LAGO DR
GUADALUPE DR
PESCADO CIR
COLINA LN
ANILLO WY
TERRENO DR
7 PARK
8 PARK
RIO CT
DOMINGO DR
DOMINGO CT
ALAMEDA DR
DE LA CRUZ DR
DE LA PENA
GRANLEE LN
2 PARK CIR
3 PARK
5 PARK
7 PARK
CM DEL LAGO
DAM
REYNOSA CT
REYNOSA DR
SEGURIDAD DR
CELEBRAR
NUEVA DR
MEDELLA CIR
COZUMEL DR
ABIERTO DR
AGRADAR
COLBERT CT
CALLAWAY DR
TOPSPIN WY
STABLEFORD WY
JIGGER CT
BOUNDARY CT
FEATHERY CT
SURLYN CT
BERMUDA CT
VERONA
NIBLICK WY
BENT GRASS CT
VAN VLECK RD
VAN VLECK AIRPORT
ARKANSAS CREEK
MEISS RD
SEE A A2
1 CARLOS CIR
2 CARMELLA CIR
3 HERNANDEZ SQ
4 GOLDEN CIR
5 JURATA CT
6 NATCHEZ CT
7 VALLERO WY
8 BELLA UNION CT
0 .125 .25 .375 .5 miles 1 in. = 1900 ft.

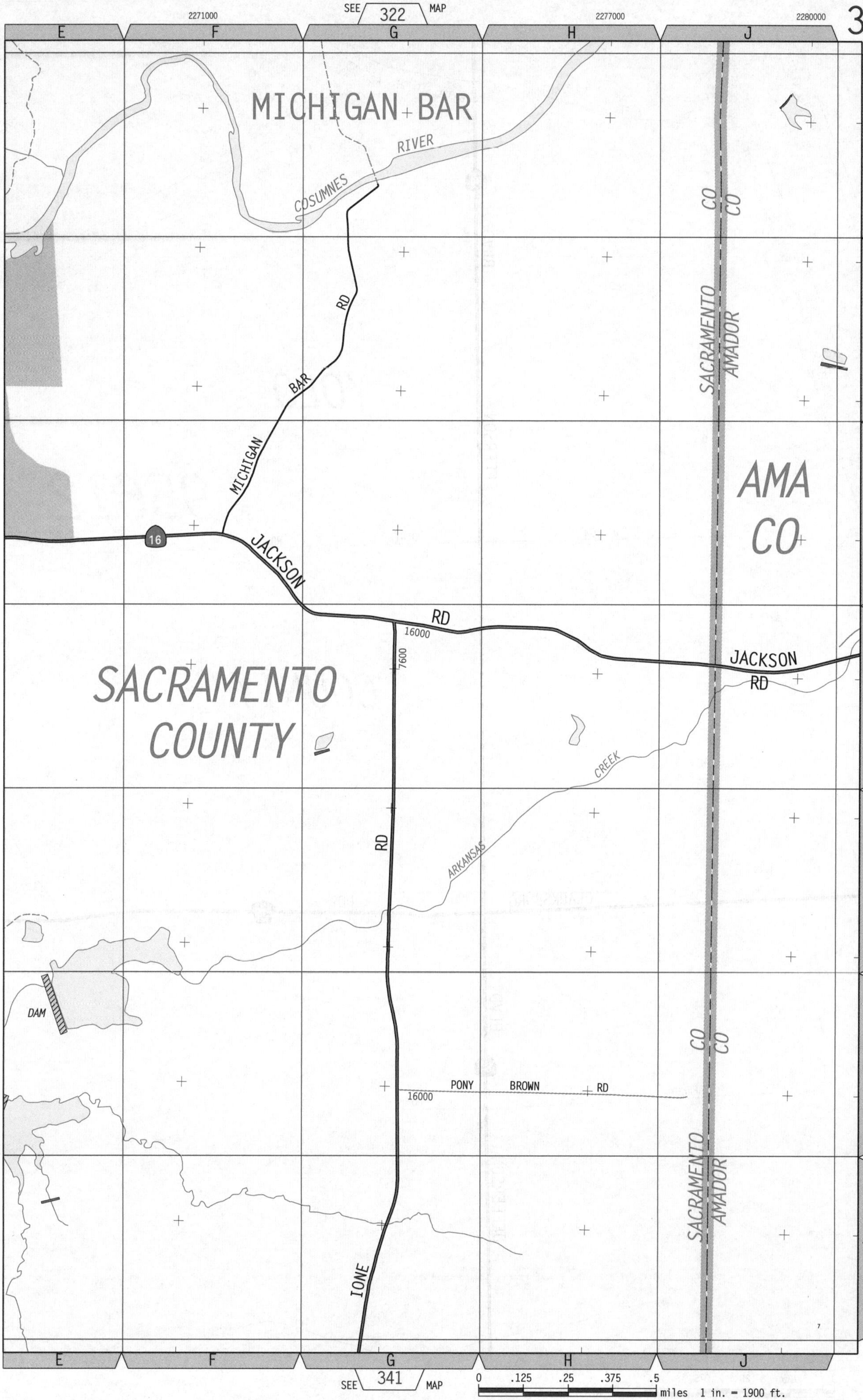
SEE 322 MAP
2271000
2277000
2280000
E
F
G
H
J
MICHIGAN BAR
COSUMNES
RIVER
CO
CO
SACRAMENTO
AMADOR
MICHIGAN
BAR
RD
AMA
CO
16
JACKSON
RD
16000
7600
JACKSON
RD
SEE B MAP
SACRAMENTO
COUNTY
CREEK
ARKANSAS
RD
DAM
PONY
BROWN
RD
16000
IONE
306000
304000
302000
300000
296000
294000
292000
290000
1
2
3
4
5
6
7
SEE 341 MAP
0
.125
.25
.375
.5
miles 1 in. = 1900 ft.

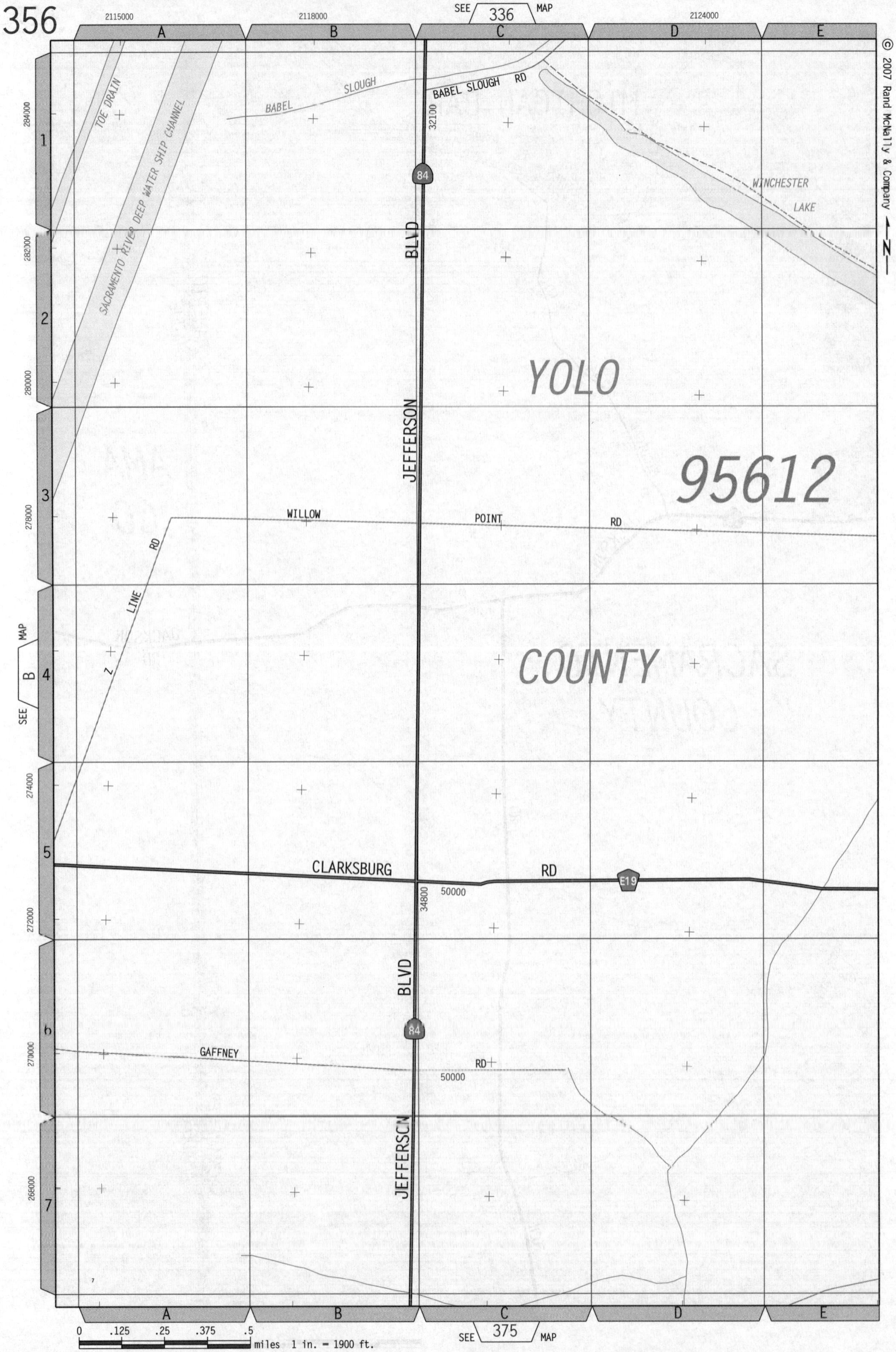
2115000
2118000
SEE 336 MAP
2124000
A
B
C
D
E
1
2
3
4
5
6
7
284000
282000
280000
278000
274000
272000
270000
268000
TOE DRAIN
SACRAMENTO RIVER DEEP WATER SHIP CHANNEL
BABEL SLOUGH
BABEL SLOUGH RD
32100
84
WINCHESTER LAKE
JEFFERSON BLVD
YOLO
95612
WILLOW POINT RD
Z LINE RD
SEE B MAP
COUNTY
CLARKSBURG RD
E19
50000
34800
GAFFNEY RD
50000
SEE 375 MAP
0 .125 .25 .375 .5
miles 1 in. = 1900 ft.

SEE 336 MAP
SEE 357 MAP
SEE 375 MAP
95832
SAC CO
CLARKSBURG
MERRITT ISLAND
SACRAMENTO RIVER
YOLO CO
PUMPHOUSE RD
S RIVER RD
RIVER RD
ROSE RD
WILLOW POINT RD
51000
CANAL
SNR
MAIN
WILLOW AV
ALEXANDRIA CT
LAUREL RD
DELTA BREEZE CT
FS
CLARKSBURG AV
SACRAMENTO ST
RIVERVIEW DR
CENTER PARK AV
SCHOOL
PEAR ST
ST
DELTA HS
CLARKSBURG RD
E19
E9
160
COUNTY ROAD 146B
NETHERLANDS AV
DAVID LN
ELK SLOUGH
WOOD DUCK LN (COUNTY ROAD 146A)
TULE RD
NETHERLANDS RD
CENTRAL AV
51500
141 ROAD
COUNTY ROAD 144
COUNTY
9100
2127000
2130000
2133000
2136000
284000
282000
280000
278000
274000
272000
270000
268000
E F G H J
1 2 3 4 5 6 7
0 .125 .25 .375 .5 miles 1 in. = 1900 ft.

SEE 337 MAP

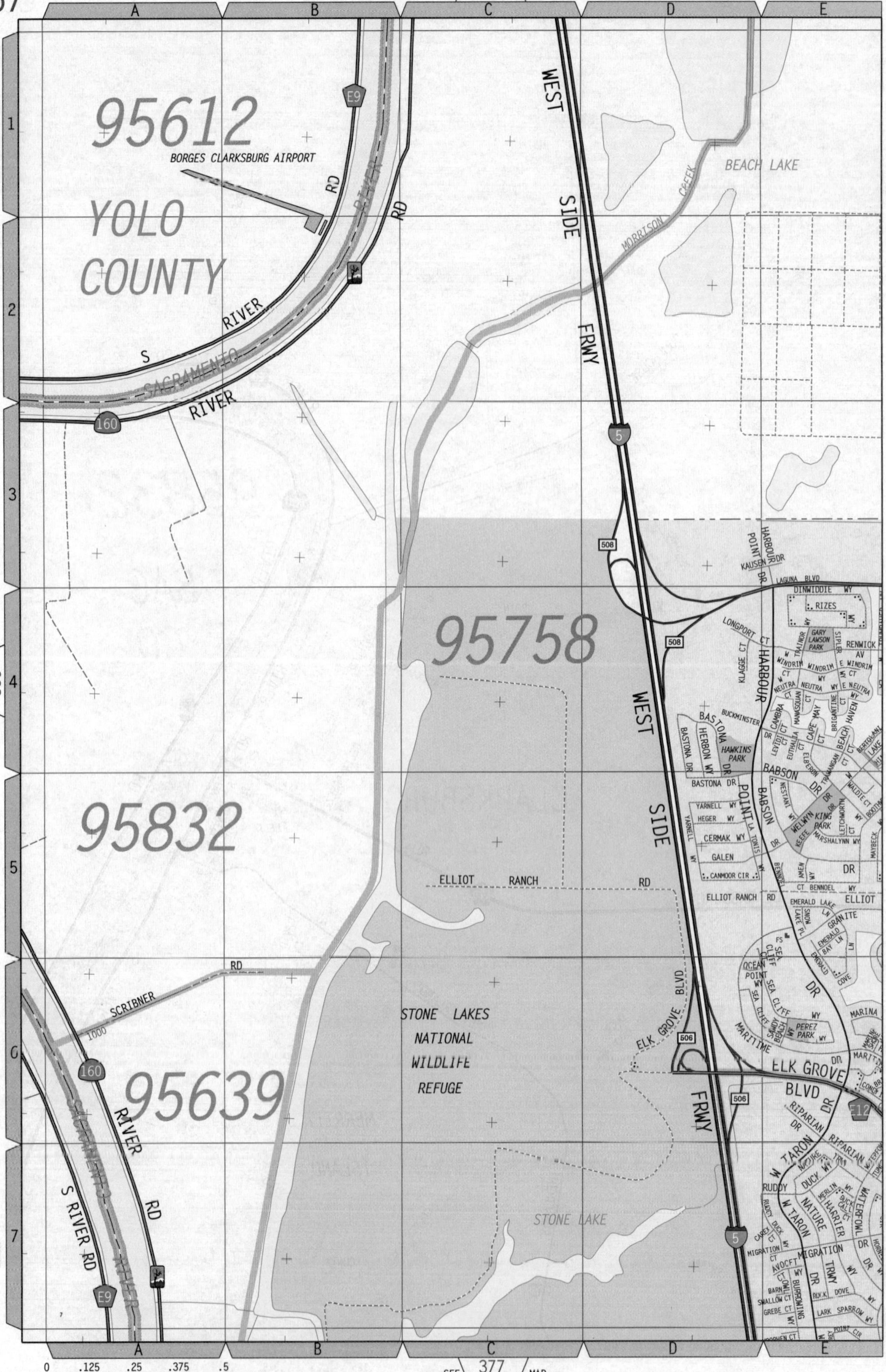
2139000
2142000
2148000
A
B
C
D
E
1
2
3
4
5
6
7
284000
282000
280000
278000
274000
272000
270000
268000
95612
BORGES CLARKSBURG AIRPORT
YOLO
COUNTY
S RIVER RD
SACRAMENTO
RIVER
160
E9
WEST SIDE FRWY
5
MORRISON CREEK
BEACH LAKE
508
HARBOUR POINT DR
KAUSEN DR
LAGUNA BLVD
DINWIDDIE WY
RIZES
LONGPORT CT
GARY LAWSON PARK
RENWICK AV
KLAGGE CT
HARBOUR
WINDRIM
NEUTRA
BUCKMINSTER
BASTONA DR
HERBON WY
HAWKINS PARK
CAMBRIA
CAPE MAY
BEACH HAVEN
BABSON DR
KING PARK
WELWYN
MARSHALYNN WY
MAYBECK
95758
95832
YARNELL WY
HEGER WY
CERMAK WY
GALEN
CANMOOR CIR
BENNOEL
CT BENNOEL WY
ELLIOT RANCH RD
ELLIOT
EMERALD LAKE
GRANITE
SEA CLIFF
OCEAN POINT WY
PEREZ PARK
MARITIME DR
MARINA
506
ELK GROVE BLVD
E12
RIPARIAN DR
W TARON
DUCK
RUDDY
MERLIN
HARRIER
NATURE
WATERFOWL
MIGRATION
AVOCET
BURROWING
BARN
SWALLOW CT
GREBE CT
DOVE
LARK SPARROW WY
SCRIBNER RD
1000
95639
STONE LAKES
NATIONAL
WILDLIFE
REFUGE
STONE LAKE
0
.125
.25
.375
.5
miles 1 in. = 1900 ft.

SEE 356 MAP

SEE 377 MAP

SEE 337 MAP

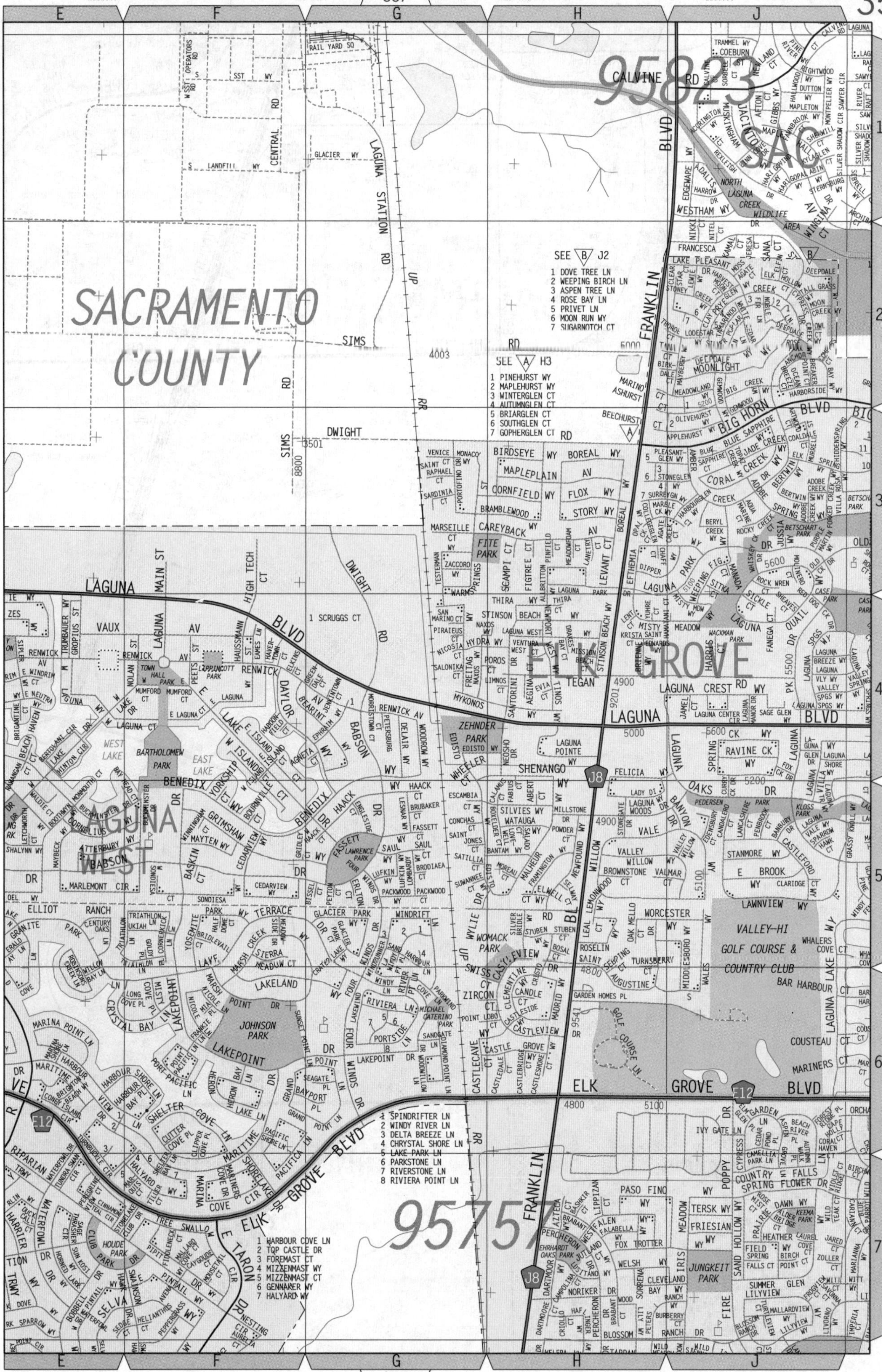
2151000
2154000
2157000
2160000
SACRAMENTO COUNTY
95823
SAC
CALVINE RD
FRANKLIN BLVD
LAGUNA STATION RD
SIMS RD
DWIGHT RD
LAGUNA BLVD
ELK GROVE
LAGUNA WEST
ELK GROVE BLVD
95757
VALLEY-HI GOLF COURSE & COUNTRY CLUB
JOHNSON PARK
NORTH LAGUNA CREEK WILDLIFE AREA
SEE B J2
1 DOVE TREE LN
2 WEEPING BIRCH LN
3 ASPEN TREE LN
4 ROSE BAY LN
5 PRIVET LN
6 MOON RUN WY
7 SUGARNOTCH CT
SEE A H3
1 PINEHURST WY
2 MAPLEHURST WY
3 WINTERGLEN CT
4 AUTUMNGLEN CT
5 BRIARGLEN CT
6 SOUTHGLEN CT
7 GOPHERGLEN CT
1 SCRUGGS CT
1 SPINDRIFTER LN
2 WINDY RIVER LN
3 DELTA BREEZE LN
4 CHRYSTAL SHORE LN
5 LAKE PARK LN
6 PARKSTONE LN
7 RIVERSTONE LN
8 RIVIERA POINT LN
1 HARBOUR COVE LN
2 TOP CASTLE DR
3 FOREMAST CT
4 MIZZENMAST WY
5 MIZZENMAST CT
6 GENNAKER WY
7 HALYARD WY
SEE 358 MAP
SEE 377 MAP
0 .125 .25 .375 .5 miles 1 in. = 1900 ft.

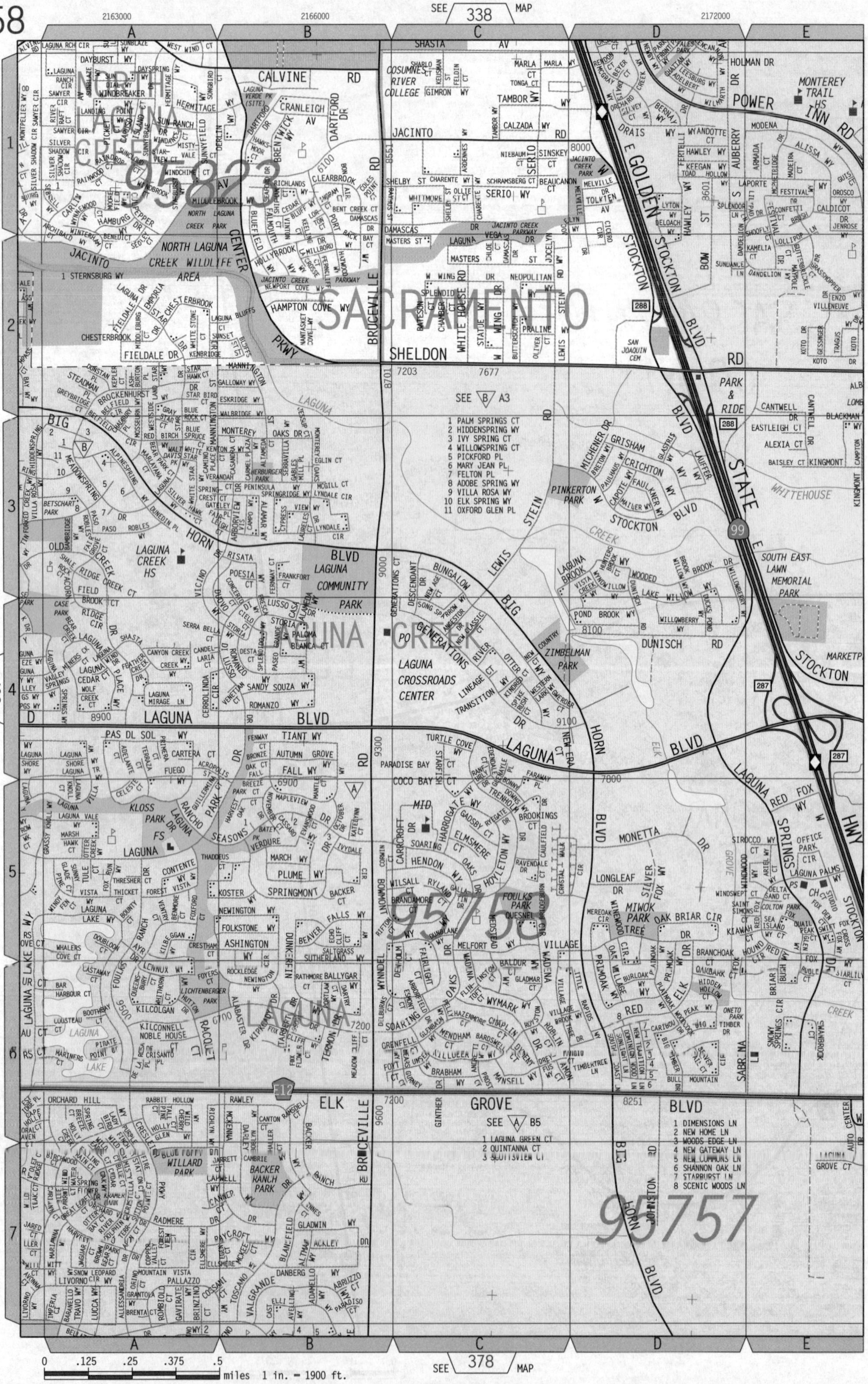
SEE 338 MAP
SEE 378 MAP
SEE 357 MAP
A
B
C
D
E
1
2
3
4
5
6
7
2163000
2166000
2172000
286000
284000
282000
280000
278000
274000
272000
270000
268000
CALVINE RD
SHASTA AV
JACINTO RD
NORTH LAGUNA CREEK
95823
95758
95757
SACRAMENTO
NORTH LAGUNA CREEK WILDLIFE AREA
COSUMNES RIVER COLLEGE
SHELDON RD
BRUCEVILLE RD
CENTER PKWY
E STOCKTON BLVD
STOCKTON BLVD
STATE HWY
99
288
287
E12
POWER INN RD
MONTEREY TRAIL HS
PARK & RIDE
PINKERTON PARK
BIG HORN BLVD
LAGUNA CREEK HS
LAGUNA COMMUNITY PARK
LAGUNA CREEK
LAGUNA CROSSROADS CENTER
ZIMBELMAN PARK
SOUTH EAST LAWN MEMORIAL PARK
LAGUNA BLVD
KLOSS PARK
LAGUNA PARK DR
FOULKS PARK
MIWOK PARK
LAGUNA SPRINGS
LAGUNA LAKE
ELK GROVE BLVD
WILLARD PARK
BACKER RANCH PARK
SEE B A3
1 PALM SPRINGS CT
2 HIDDENSPRING WY
3 IVY SPRING CT
4 WILLOWSPRING CT
5 PICKFORD PL
6 MARY JEAN PL
7 FELTON PL
8 ADOBE SPRING WY
9 VILLA ROSA WY
10 ELK SPRING WY
11 OXFORD GLEN PL
SEE A B5
1 LAGUNA GREEN CT
2 QUINTANNA CT
3 SCOTTSVIEW CT
1 DIMENSIONS LN
2 NEW HOME LN
3 WOODS EDGE LN
4 NEW GATEWAY LN
5 NEW COMMONS LN
6 SHANNON OAK LN
7 STARBURST LN
8 SCENIC WOODS LN
0 .125 .25 .375 .5 miles 1 in. = 1900 ft.

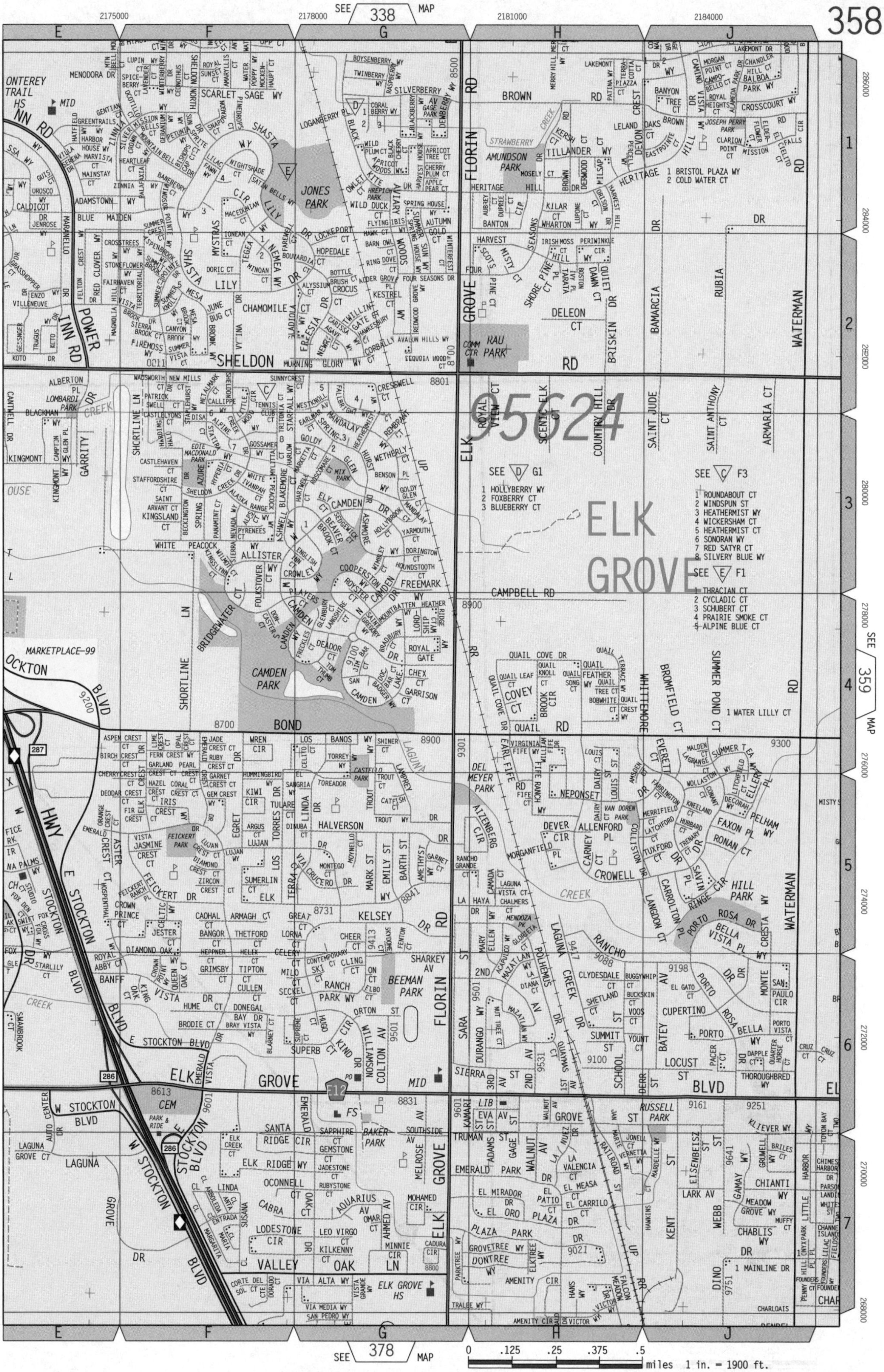
SEE 338 MAP
2175000
2178000
2181000
2184000
E
F
G
H
J
1
2
3
4
5
6
7
95624
ELK GROVE
JONES PARK
RAU PARK
COMM CTR
AMUNDSON PARK
CAMDEN PARK
MIX PARK
EDIE MACDONALD PARK
LOMBARDI PARK
DEL MEYER PARK
FEICKERT PARK
CASTELLO PARK
BEEMAN PARK
BAKER PARK
RUSSELL PARK
HILL PARK
MENDOZA PK
VAN DOREN PARK
ELK GROVE HS
CEM
LIB
MARKETPLACE-99
SHELDON RD
BOND RD
ELK GROVE BLVD
FLORIN RD
ELK GROVE FLORIN RD
WATERMAN RD
BROWN RD
CAMPBELL RD
BRISKIN DR
BAMARCIA DR
RUBIA
SHORTLINE LN
POWER INN RD
E STOCKTON BLVD
W STOCKTON BLVD
HWY 99
LAGUNA CREEK
LAGUNA BLVD
STRAWBERRY CREEK
SEE D G1
1 HOLLYBERRY WY
2 FOXBERRY CT
3 BLUEBERRY CT
SEE C F3
1 ROUNDABOUT CT
2 WINDSPUN ST
3 HEATHERMIST WY
4 WICKERSHAM CT
5 HEATHERMIST CT
6 SONORAN WY
7 RED SATYR CT
8 SILVERY BLUE WY
SEE E F1
1 THRACIAN CT
2 CYCLADIC CT
3 SCHUBERT CT
4 PRAIRIE SMOKE CT
5 ALPINE BLUE CT
1 BRISTOL PLAZA WY
2 COLD WATER CT
1 WATER LILLY CT
1 MAINLINE DR
SEE 359 MAP
SEE 378 MAP
0 .125 .25 .375 .5
miles 1 in. = 1900 ft.

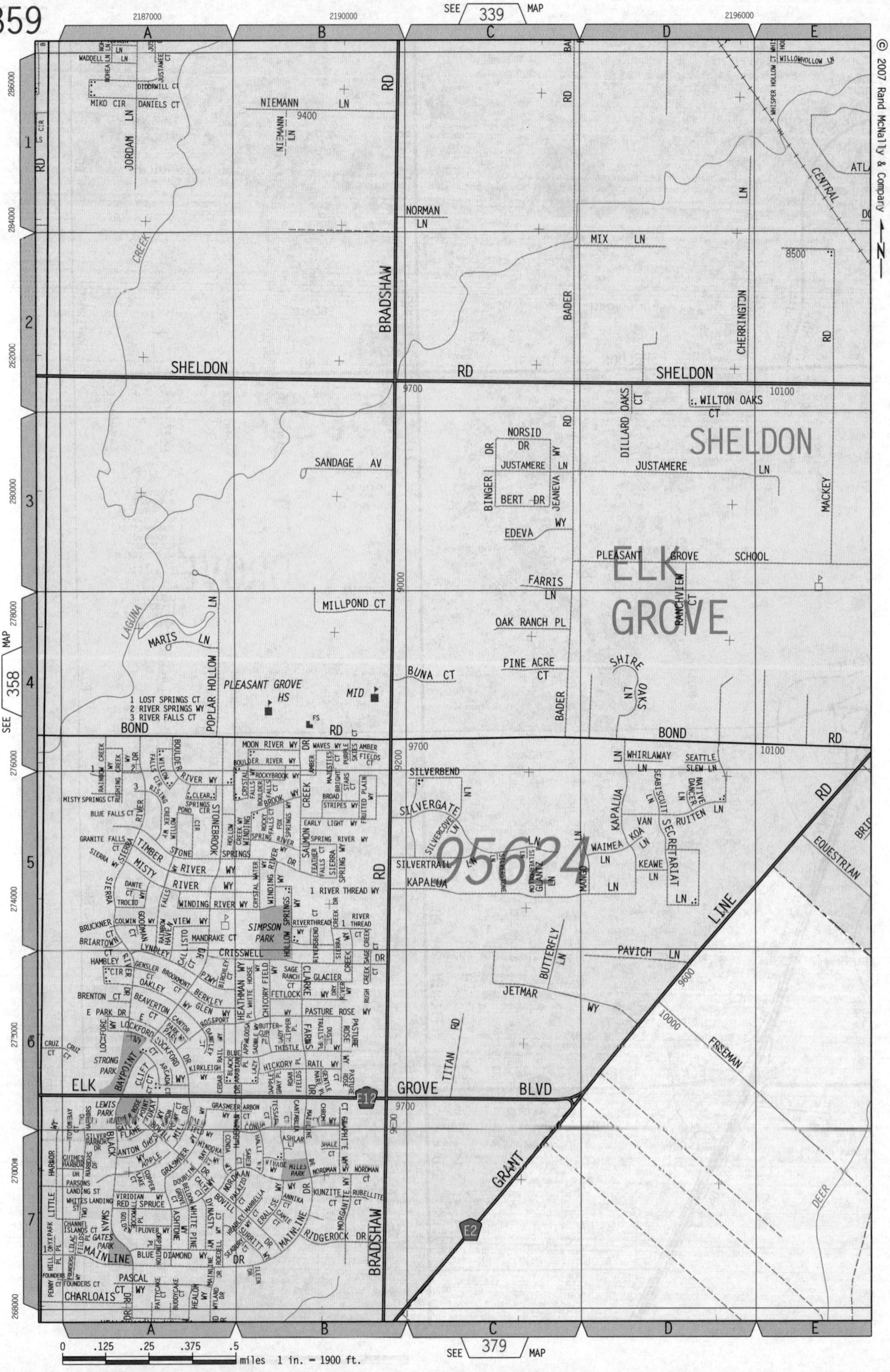
SEE 339 MAP
SEE 358 MAP
SEE 379 MAP
A
B
C
D
E
1
2
3
4
5
6
7
2187000
2190000
2196000
286000
284000
282000
280000
278000
276000
274000
272000
270000
268000
WADDELL LN
NOHEA LN
JUSTAMEE CT
DIDORWILL CT
MIKO CIR
DANIELS CT
JORDAN LN
NIEMANN LN
9400
BRADSHAW RD
NORMAN LN
MIX LN
BADER RD
CHERRINGTON LN
CENTRAL
WILLOWHOLLOW LN
WHISPER HOLLOW CT
8500
CREEK
SHELDON RD
SHELDON
9700
10100
WILTON OAKS CT
DILLARD OAKS CT
NORSID DR
BINGER DR
JUSTAMERE LN
JEANEVA WY
BERT DR
EDEVA WY
SANDAGE AV
MACKEY
PLEASANT GROVE SCHOOL
ELK GROVE
FARRIS LN
RANCHVIEW CT
MILLPOND CT
OAK RANCH PL
9000
LAGUNA
MARIS LN
POPLAR HOLLOW LN
BUNA CT
PINE ACRE CT
SHIRE OAKS LN
PLEASANT GROVE HS
MID
FS
1 LOST SPRINGS CT
2 RIVER SPRINGS WY
3 RIVER FALLS CT
BOND RD
9200
SILVERBEND
WHIRLAWAY LN
SEATTLE SLEW LN
SILVERGATE LN
KAPALUA LN
SEABISCUIT LN
NATIVE DANCER LN
RUITEN LN
VAN KOA LN
SECRETARIAT LN
WAIMEA LN
KEAWE LN
SILVERTRAIL
KAPALUA
95624
EQUESTRIAN
MOON RIVER WY
BOULDER RIVER WY
MISTY SPRINGS CT
BLUE FALLS CT
GRANITE FALLS CT
SIERRA WY
STONEBROOK CIR
SPRINGS
MISTY RIVER WY
WINDING RIVER WY
1 RIVER THREAD WY
SIMPSON PARK
HOLLOW SPRINGS
BRUCKNER CT
BRIARTOWN CT
CRISSWELL DR
HAMBLEY
MANDRAKE CT
PAVICH LN
BUTTERFLY LN
JETMAR WY
9600
LINE RD
10000
FREEMAN
TITAN RD
BRENTON CT
E PARK DR
LOCKFORD
STRONG PARK
CRUZ CT
BAYPOINT
ELK GROVE BLVD
E12
LEWIS PARK
GRANT
E2
DEER
GRASMEER
MILES PARK
NORDMAN
KUNZITE CT
RUBELLITE
MORGANITE DR
RIDGEROCK DR
MAINLINE DR
GATES PARK
MAINLINE
PASCAL WY
CHARLOAIS CT
FOUNDERS CT
BLUE DIAMOND WY
0 .125 .25 .375 .5 miles 1 in. = 1900 ft.

SEE 339 MAP

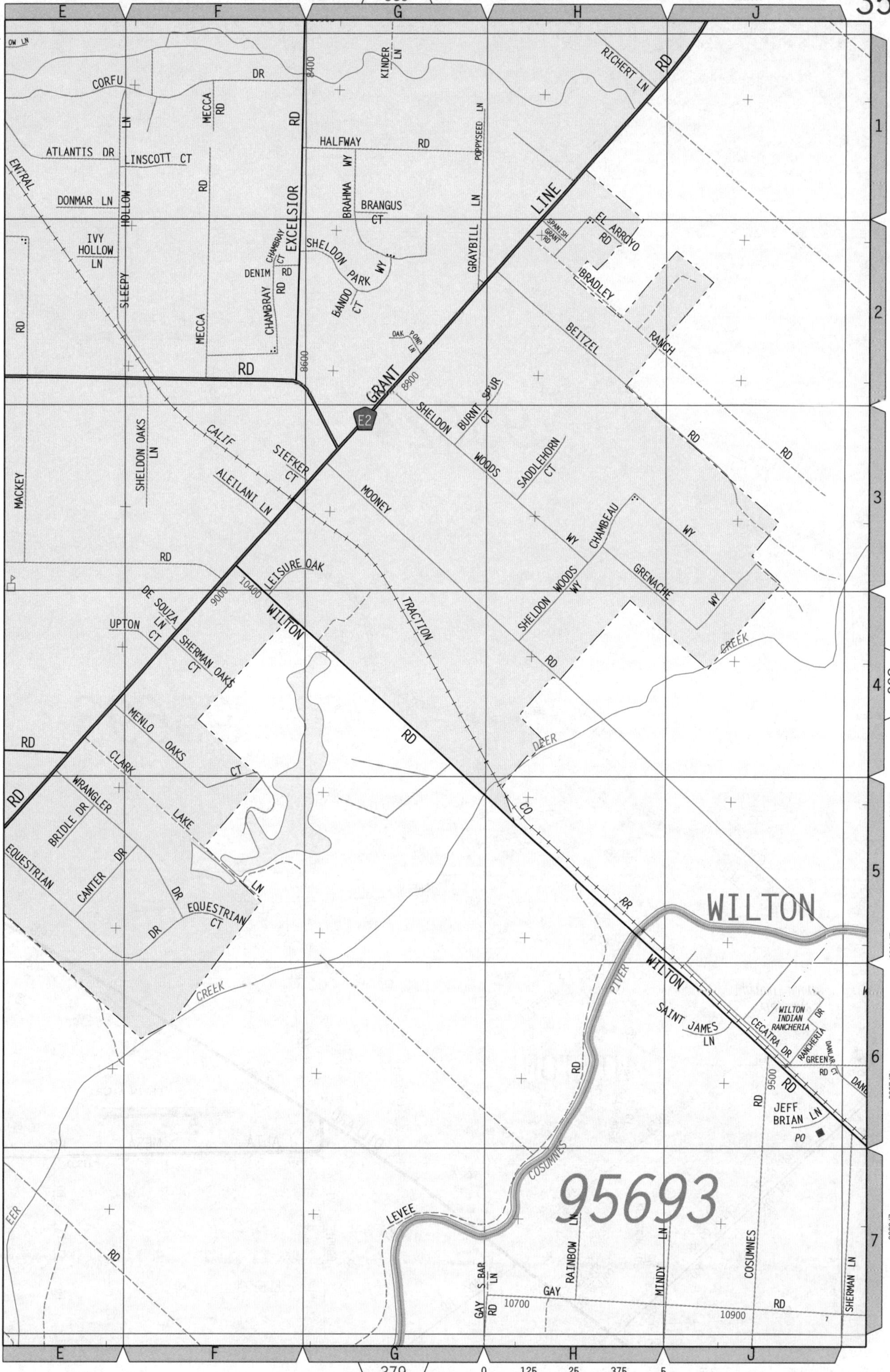

SEE 360 MAP

SEE 379 MAP

0 .125 .25 .375 .5 miles 1 in. = 1900 ft.

SEE 340 MAP
SEE 359 MAP
SEE 379 MAP
2211000
2214000
2217000
2220000
286000
284000
282000
280000
276000
274000
272000
270000
A
B
C
D
E
1
2
3
4
5
6
7
95624
95693
DEER CREEK
CREEK
DEER
COSUMNES RIVER
COSUMNES
RIVER
LEVEE RD
GREEN RD
11700
9300
SUNFLOWER RD
MAGOS RD
11500
9400
JEFFCOTT RD
WILTON INDIAN RANCHERIA
WILTON
GREEN
DANLAR CT
11200
RANDOLPH RD
OSTRANDER CT
RD
DILLARD RD
9500
ALTA MESA RD
11700
11800
9600
LANDING STRIP
MIWOK CT
11900
GREEN RD
CENTRAL CALIF TRACTION CO RR
WILTON RD
WILTON CHRISTIAN HS
9600
GERMANY RD
BONNIE VISTA RD
LA CLAIR RD
KETCHERSIDE LN
SILVER DOLLAR CT
COLONY RD
RINGWOOD RD
11700
SHERMAN LN
GAY RD
10800
ES

0 .125 .25 .375 .5 miles 1 in. = 1900 ft.

SEE 340 MAP
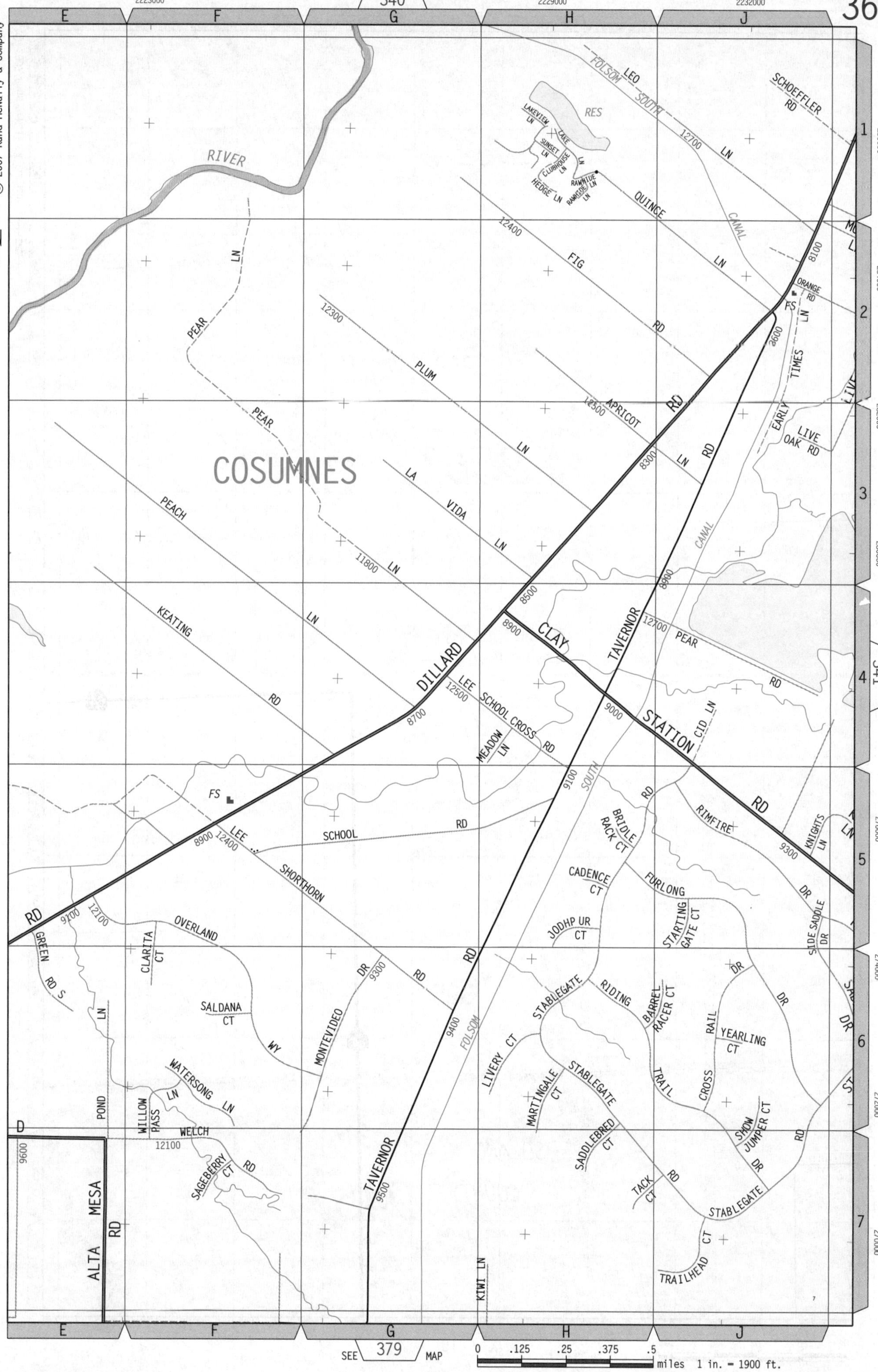

SEE 341 MAP
SEE 379 MAP
0 .125 .25 .375 .5 miles 1 in. = 1900 ft.

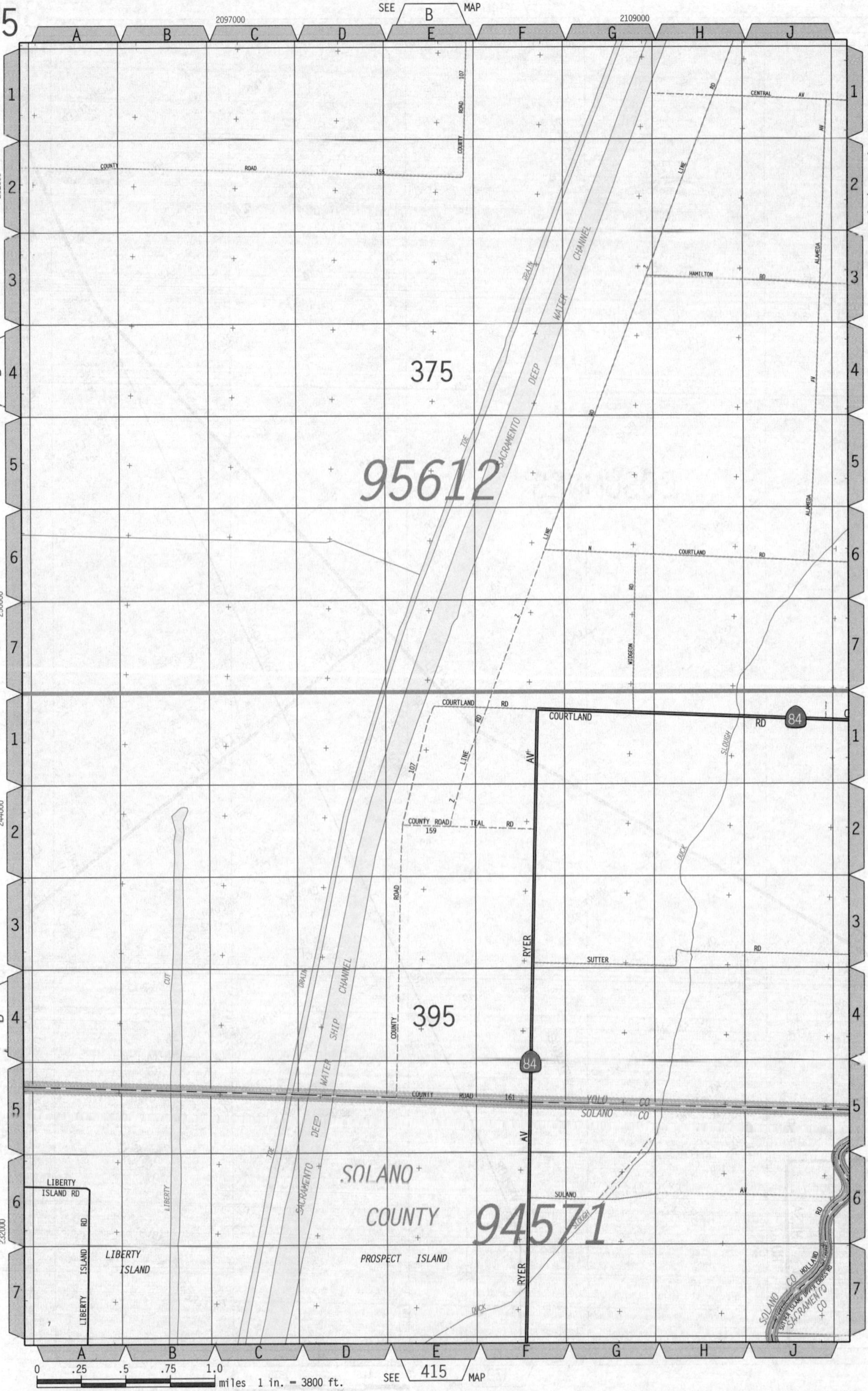
SEE B MAP
2097000
2109000
262000
250000
244000
232000
COUNTY ROAD 155
COUNTY ROAD 107
CENTRAL AV
HAMILTON RD
ALAMEDA AV
LINE RD
DRAIN
SACRAMENTO DEEP WATER CHANNEL
TOE
375
95612
N LINE
COURTLAND RD
WIDGEON RD
COURTLAND RD
COURTLAND RD
84
SLOUGH
RYER AV
COUNTY ROAD 159
TEAL RD
DUCK
SUTTER RD
395
COUNTY ROAD 161
YOLO CO
SOLANO CO
LIBERTY ISLAND RD
LIBERTY ISLAND RD
LIBERTY CUT
LIBERTY ISLAND
SOLANO COUNTY
94571
PROSPECT ISLAND
SOLANO AV
HOLLAND
SOLANO CO
SACRAMENTO CO
SEE 415 MAP
0 .25 .5 .75 1.0 miles 1 in. = 3800 ft.

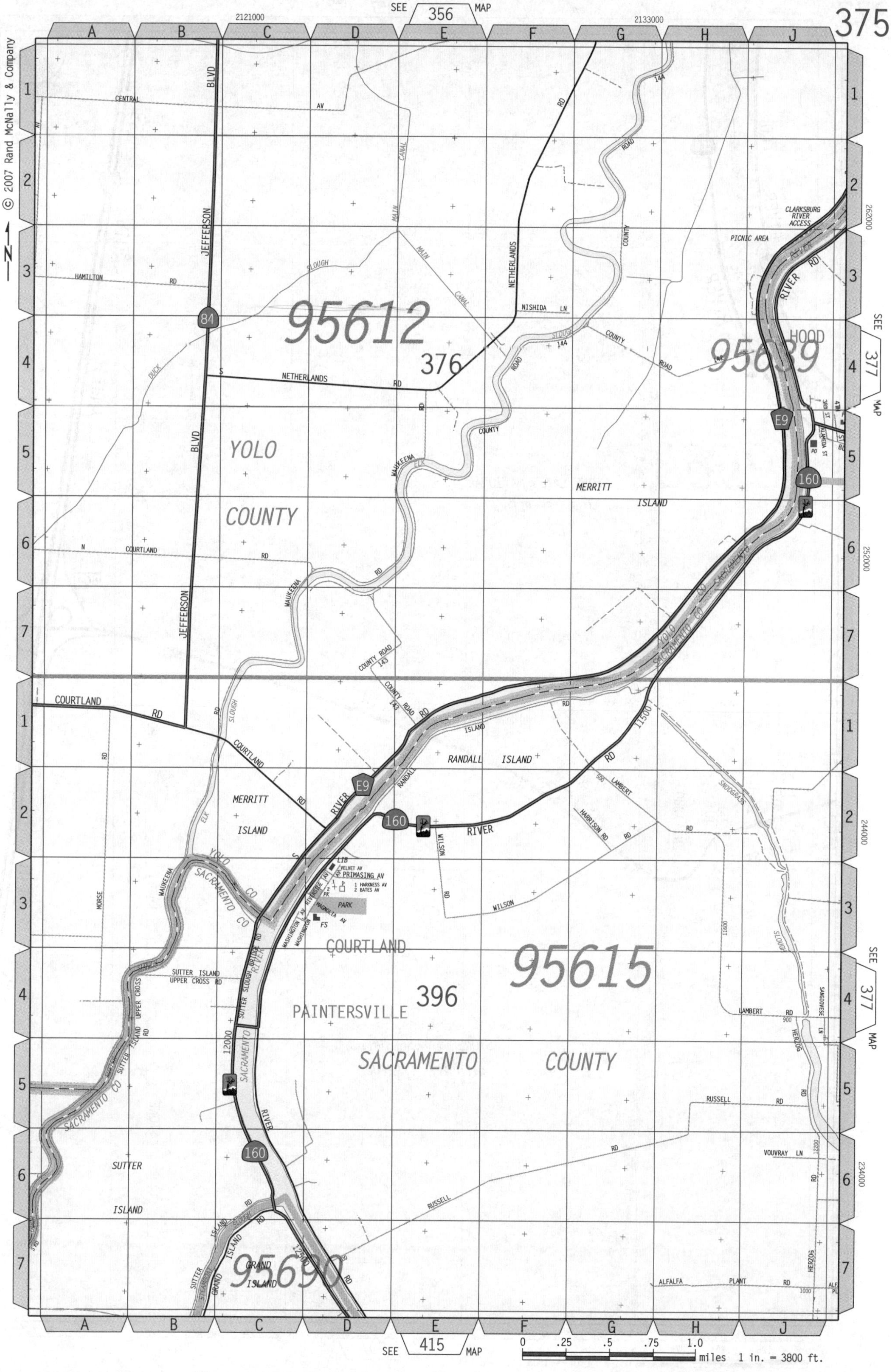
SEE 356 MAP
SEE 377 MAP
SEE 415 MAP
95612
376
95639
HOOD
YOLO
COUNTY
MERRITT
ISLAND
CLARKSBURG
RIVER
ACCESS
PICNIC AREA
JEFFERSON BLVD
CENTRAL AV
HAMILTON RD
NETHERLANDS RD
NISHIDA LN
N COURTLAND RD
COURTLAND RD
MAIN CANAL
DUCK SLOUGH
ELK SLOUGH
WAUKEENA
COUNTY ROAD 144
COUNTY ROAD 143
RIVER RD
YOLO CO
SACRAMENTO CO
RANDALL ISLAND RD
RANDALL ISLAND
LAMBERT RD
HARRISON RD
WILSON RD
SNODGRASS SLOUGH
MERRITT
ISLAND
COURTLAND
PARK
LIB
FS
PRIMASING AV
MAGNOLIA AV
WASHINGTON AV
95615
396
PAINTERSVILLE
SACRAMENTO
COUNTY
SUTTER ISLAND UPPER CROSS RD
SUTTER SLOUGH BRIDGE RD
MORSE RD
SUTTER
ISLAND
RUSSELL RD
VOUVRAY LN
HERZOG RD
SANGIOVESE LN
ALFALFA PLANT RD
GRAND ISLAND RD
95690
GRAND
ISLAND
STEAMBOAT SLOUGH
0 .25 .5 .75 1.0
miles 1 in. = 3800 ft.

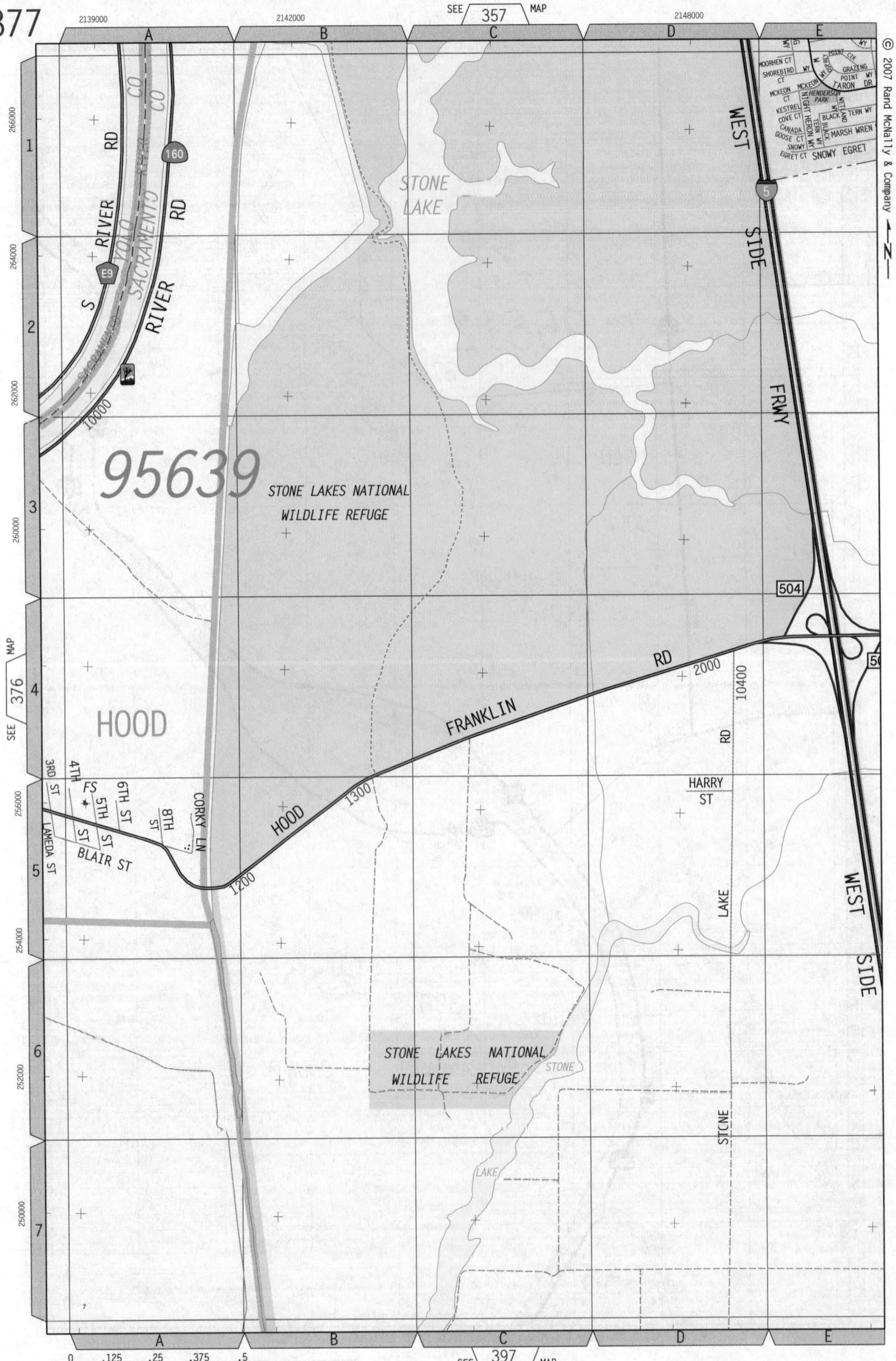
SEE 357 MAP
SEE 376 MAP
SEE 397 MAP
2139000
2142000
2148000
A
B
C
D
E
1
2
3
4
5
6
7
266000
264000
262000
260000
256000
254000
252000
250000
© 2007 Rand McNally & Company
95639
STONE LAKE
STONE LAKES NATIONAL WILDLIFE REFUGE
HOOD
S RIVER RD
RIVER RD
YOLO CO
SACRAMENTO CO
SACRAMENTO RIVER
160
E9
10000
WEST SIDE FRWY
5
504
FRANKLIN RD
HOOD FRANKLIN RD
2000
1300
1200
10400
RD
HARRY ST
LAKE
STONE
CORKY LN
3RD ST
4TH
5TH ST
6TH ST
8TH ST
FS
LAMEDA ST
BLAIR ST
MOORHEN CT
SHOREBIRD CT
MCKEON CT
KESTREL CT
COVE CT
CANADA GOOSE CT
SNOWY EGRET CT
SNOWY EGRET
NIGHT HERON WY
HENDERSON PARK
TERN WY
BLACK TERN WY
WETLAND
MARSH WREN
GRAZING
POINT WY
TARON DR

0 .125 .25 .375 .5 miles 1 in. = 1900 ft.

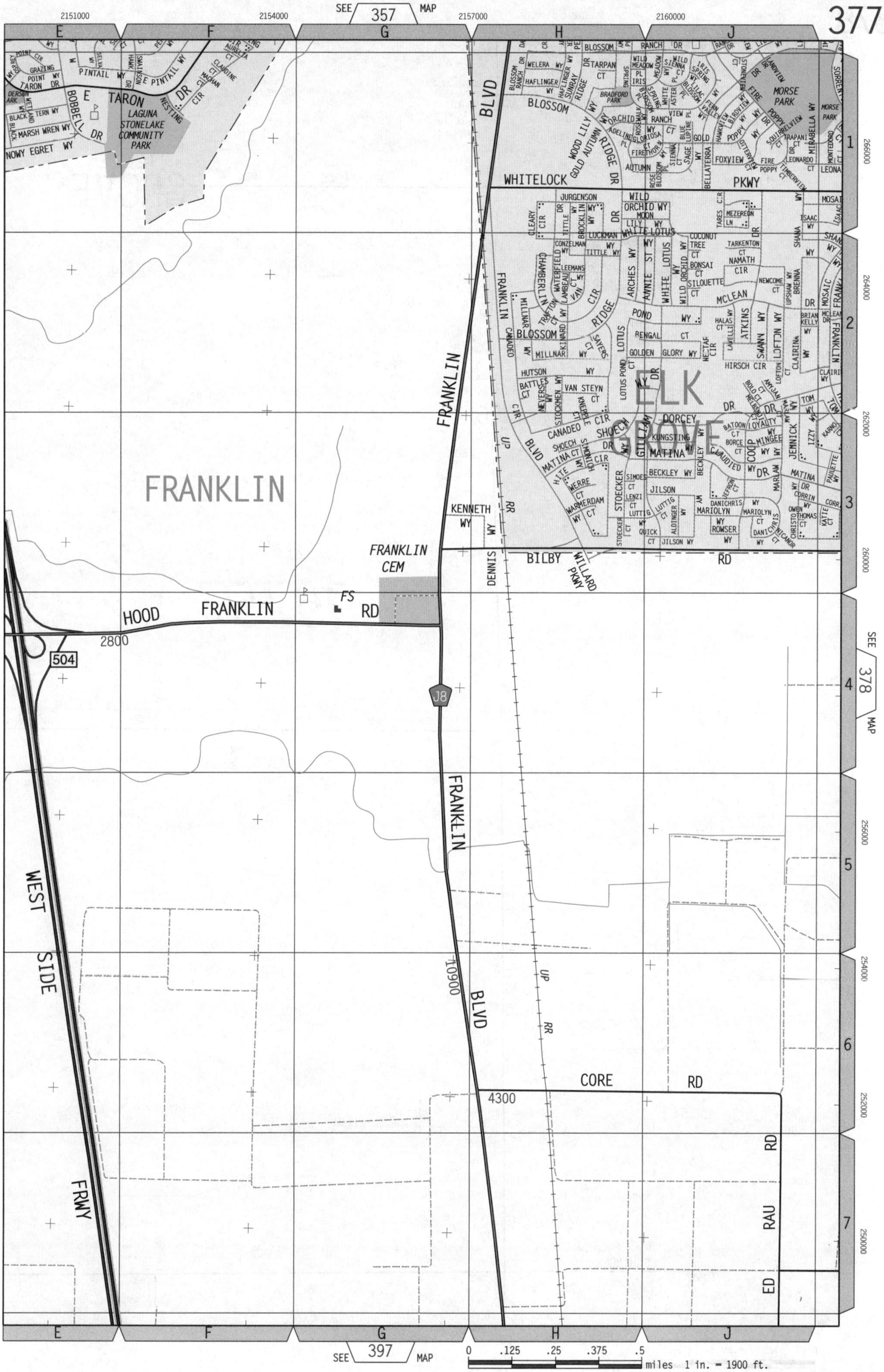
SEE 357 MAP
2151000
2154000
2157000
2160000
E
F
G
H
J
LAGUNA STONELAKE COMMUNITY PARK
E TARON DR
PINTAIL WY
BOBBELL DR
MARSH WREN WY
SNOWY EGRET WY
BLOSSOM RANCH DR
BRADFORD PARK
MORSE PARK
WHITELOCK PKWY
FOXVIEW
ELK GROVE
FRANKLIN
FRANKLIN BLVD
FRANKLIN CEM
FS
HOOD FRANKLIN RD
2800
504
J8
KENNETH WY
DENNIS WY
BILBY RD
WILLARD PKWY
UP RR
MCLEAN
POND
GOLDEN
DORCEY
MATINA
STOECKER
CANADEO
10900
WEST SIDE FRWY
CORE RD
4300
RAU RD
ED
SEE 378 MAP
266000
264000
262000
260000
256000
254000
252000
250000
1
2
3
4
5
6
7
SEE 397 MAP
0 .125 .25 .375 .5 miles 1 in. = 1900 ft.

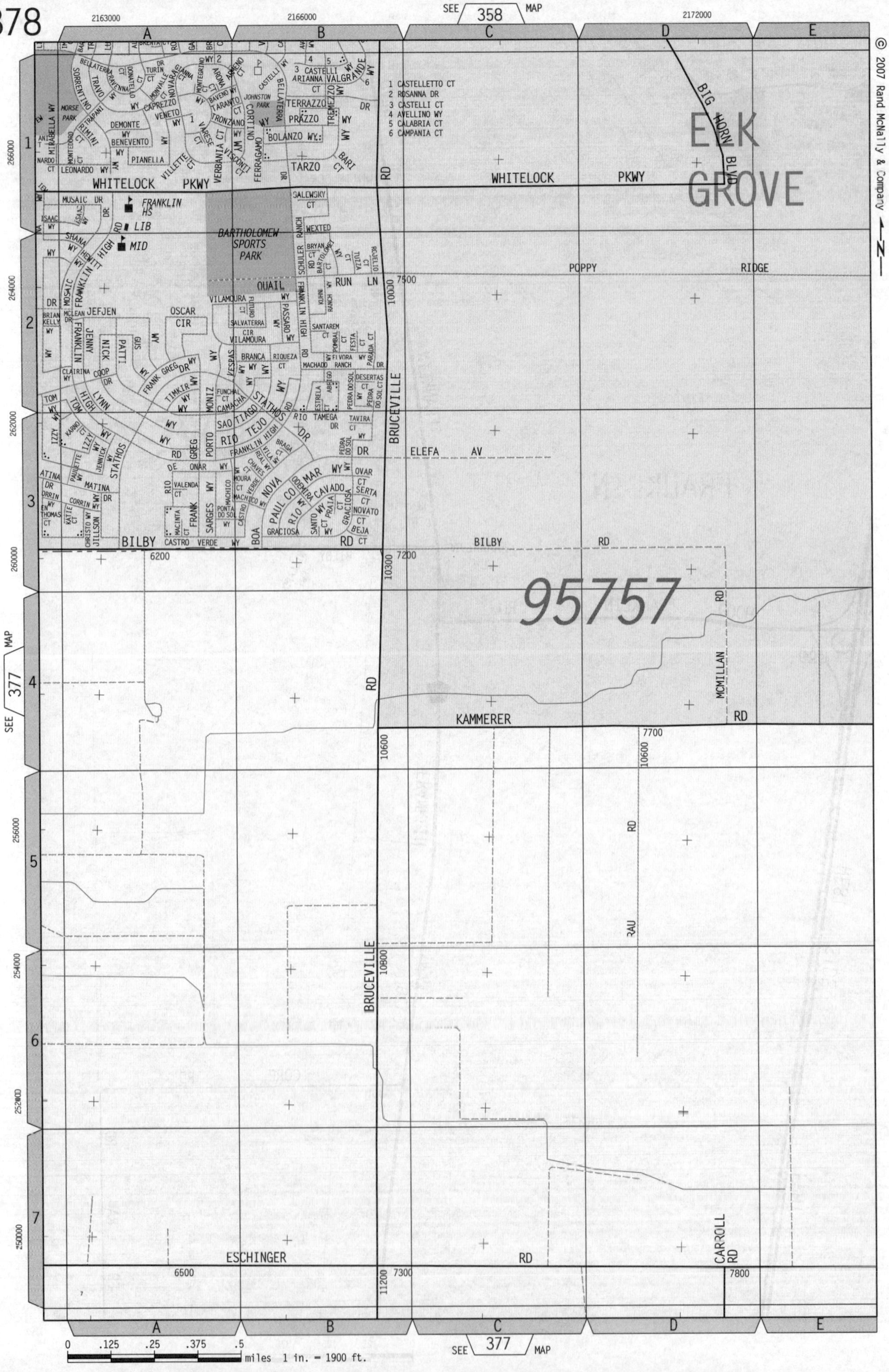
SEE 358 MAP
SEE 377 MAP
SEE 377 MAP
2163000
2166000
2172000
A
B
C
D
E
1
2
3
4
5
6
7
266000
264000
262000
260000
256000
254000
252000
250000
1 CASTELLETTO CT
2 ROSANNA DR
3 CASTELLI CT
4 AVELLINO WY
5 CALABRIA CT
6 CAMPANIA CT
ELK GROVE
95757
WHITELOCK PKWY
BIG HORN BLVD
MORSE PARK
JOHNSTON PARK
FRANKLIN HS
LIB
MID
BARTHOLOMEW SPORTS PARK
POPPY RIDGE
QUAIL RUN LN
BRUCEVILLE RD
ELEFA AV
BILBY RD
KAMMERER RD
MCMILLAN RD
RAU RD
CARROLL RD
ESCHINGER RD
FRANKLIN HIGH RD
STATHOS DR
OSCAR CIR
JEFJEN
RIO TEJO
SAO TIAGO
PAUL CO MAR WY
BOA NOVA
GRACIOSA
CASTRO VERDE WY
VILAMOURA CIR
SALVATERRA
TARZO
BOLANZO WY
PRAZZO
TERRAZZO
LEONARDO WY
PIANELLA
BENEVENTO
DEMONTE
7500
7200
6200
7700
10030
10300
10600
10800
11200
6500
7300
7800
0 .125 .25 .375 .5 miles 1 in. = 1900 ft.

SEE 358 MAP

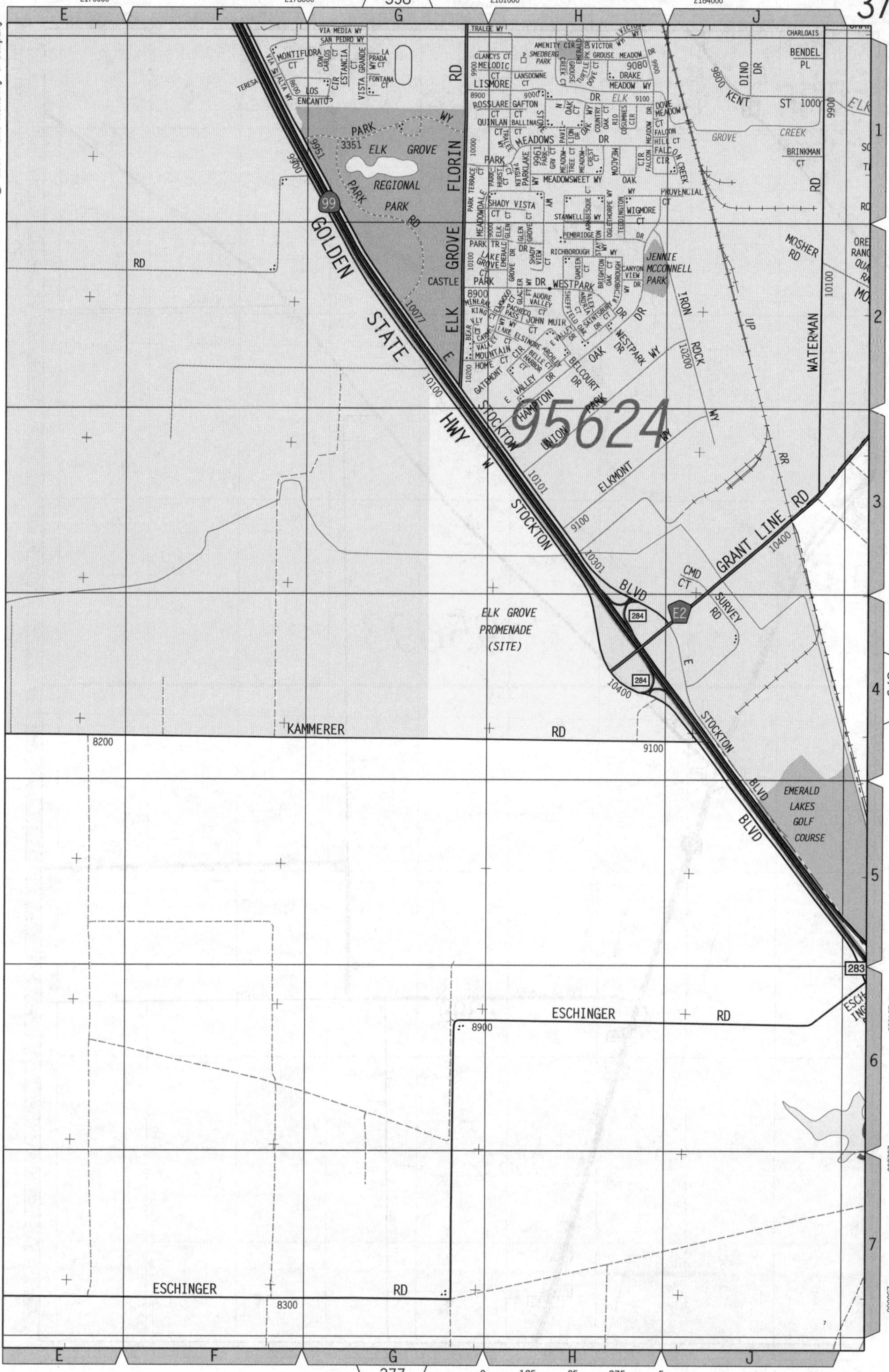

SEE 379 MAP
SEE 377 MAP

0 .125 .25 .375 .5 miles 1 in. = 1900 ft.

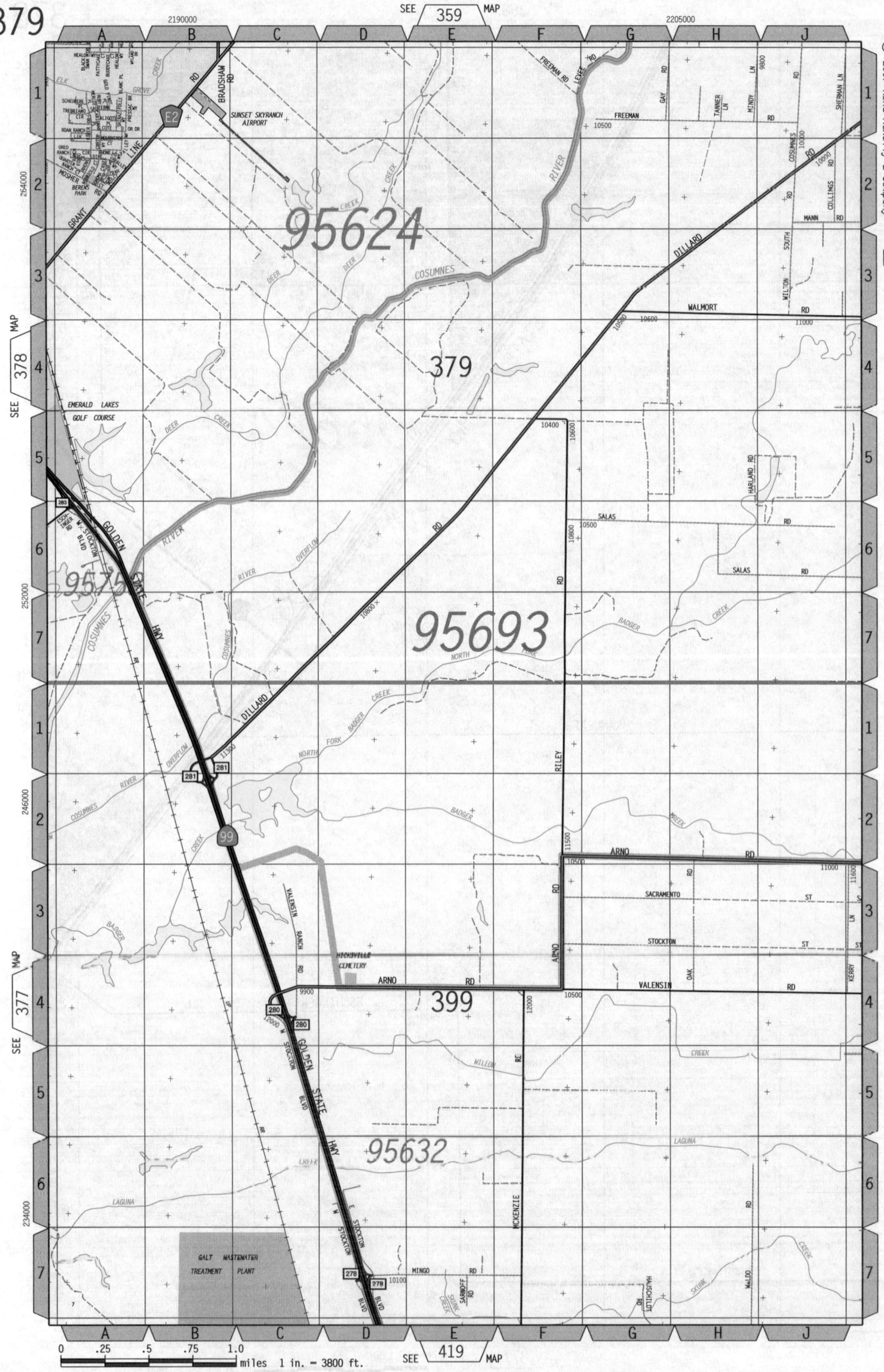
SEE 359 MAP
SEE 378 MAP
SEE 377 MAP
SEE 419 MAP
2190000
2205000
264000
252000
246000
234000
A B C D E F G H J
1 2 3 4 5 6 7 1 2 3 4 5 6 7
95624
95693
95632
9575
379
399
SUNSET SKYRANCH AIRPORT
BRADSHAW RD
GRANT LINE RD
E2
EMERALD LAKES GOLF COURSE
COSUMNES RIVER
DEER CREEK
ELK GROVE CREEK
FREEMAN RD
LEVEE RD
FREEMAN RD
GAY RD
TANNER LN
MINDY LN
SHERMAN LN
COSUMNES RD
COLLINGS RD
MANN RD
SOUTH WILTON RD
DILLARD RD
WALMORT RD
HARLAND RD
SALAS RD
RILEY RD
BADGER CREEK
NORTH FORK BADGER CREEK
OVERFLOW
GOLDEN STATE HWY
W. STOCKTON BLVD
ESCHINGER RD
283
281
99
280
279
278
ARNO RD
SACRAMENTO ST
STOCKTON ST
VALENSIN RD
OAK RD
KERRY LN
VALENSIN RANCH RD
HICKSVILLE CEMETERY
MCKENZIE RD
WILLOW CREEK
LAGUNA CREEK
GALT WASTEWATER TREATMENT PLANT
MINGO RD
SARNOFF RD
SKUNK CREEK
HAUSCHILDT RD
WALDO RD
E STOCKTON BLVD
W STOCKTON BLVD
10400 10500 10600 10800 11000 11300 11500 11600 9800 9900 10000 10100 12000
0 .25 .5 .75 1.0 miles 1 in. = 3800 ft.

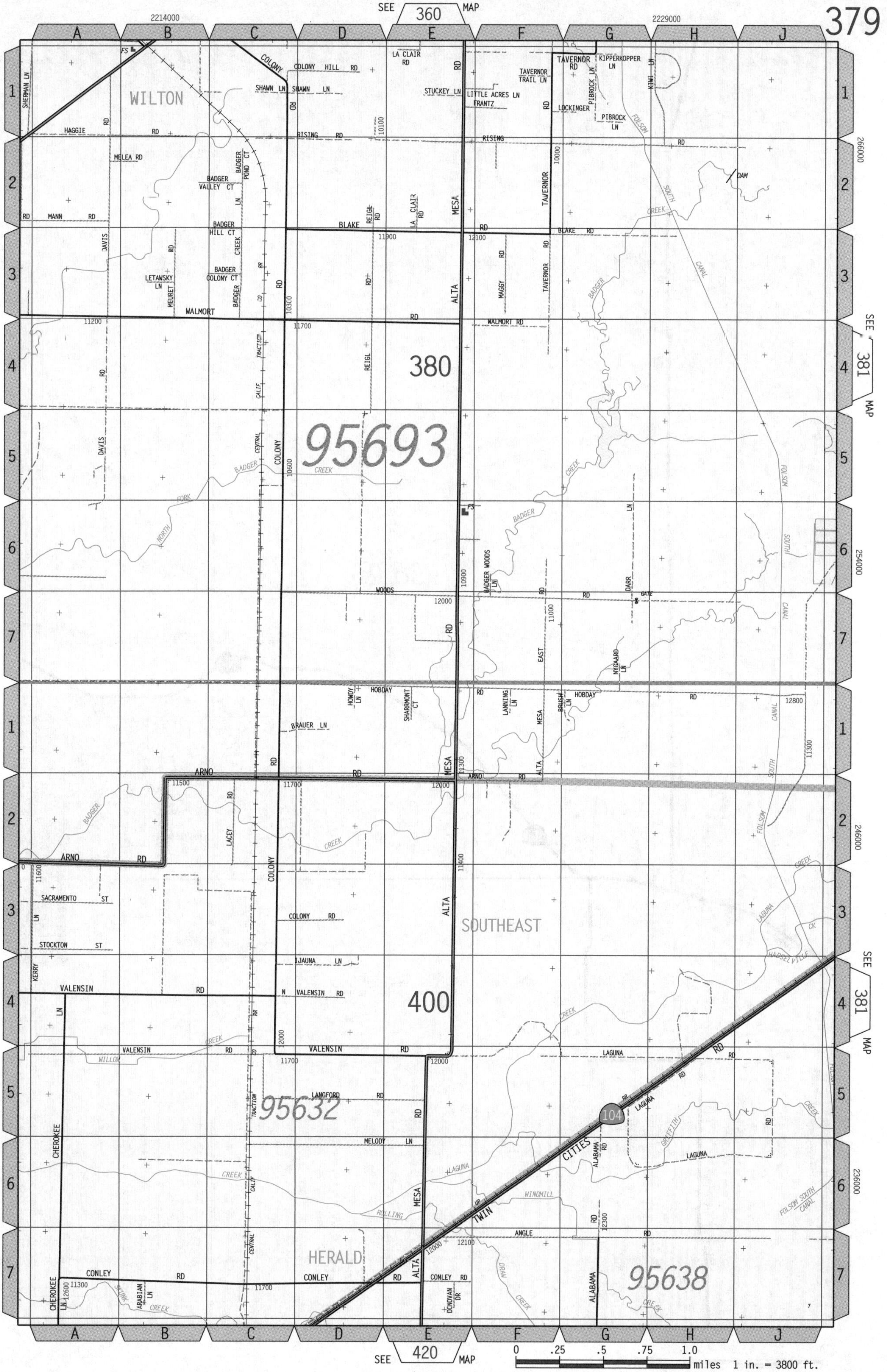
SEE 360 MAP
SEE 381 MAP
SEE 381 MAP
SEE 420 MAP
2214000
2229000
266000
254000
246000
236000
WILTON
SOUTHEAST
HERALD
95693
95632
95638
380
400
SHERMAN LN
HAGGIE RD
MELEA RD
MANN RD
DAVIS
BADGER VALLEY CT
BADGER POND CT
BADGER HILL CT
BADGER COLONY CT
CREEK
LETAWSKY LN
MEURET
WALMORT RD
COLONY HILL RD
SHAWN LN
RISING RD
BLAKE RD
REIGE RD
LA CLAIR RD
STUCKEY LN
LITTLE ACRES LN
FRANTZ
TAVERNOR TRAIL LN
TAVERNOR RD
KIPPERKOPPER LN
PIBROCK LN
LOCKINGER
KIWI LN
FOLSOM SOUTH CANAL
DAM
ALTA MESA RD
MAGGY
REIGL
CALIF CENTRAL TRACTION RR
BADGER CREEK
NORTH FORK
WOODS RD
BADGER WOODS LN
DARR LN
GATE
EAST
NYGAARD LN
HOBDAY RD
HOWDY LN
SHARMONT CT
LANNING LN
BRUSH
BRAUER LN
ARNO RD
LACEY
SACRAMENTO ST
STOCKTON ST
KERRY
COLONY RD
IJAUNA LN
VALENSIN RD
N VALENSIN RD
CHEROKEE LN
WILLOW CREEK
LAGUNA
LAGUNA CREEK
HARGSEL CK
TWIN CITIES RD
104
ALABAMA RD
GRIFFITH RD
LANGFORD RD
MELODY LN
ROLLING CREEK
WINDMILL
ANGLE RD
CONLEY RD
ARABIAN LN
DONOVAN DR
DRAW CREEK
SKUNK CREEK
11200
11700
11900
12100
10100
10000
10300
10600
10900
12000
11000
12800
11300
11500
11600
11400
11300
12600
12300
0
.25
.5
.75
1.0
miles 1 in. = 3800 ft.

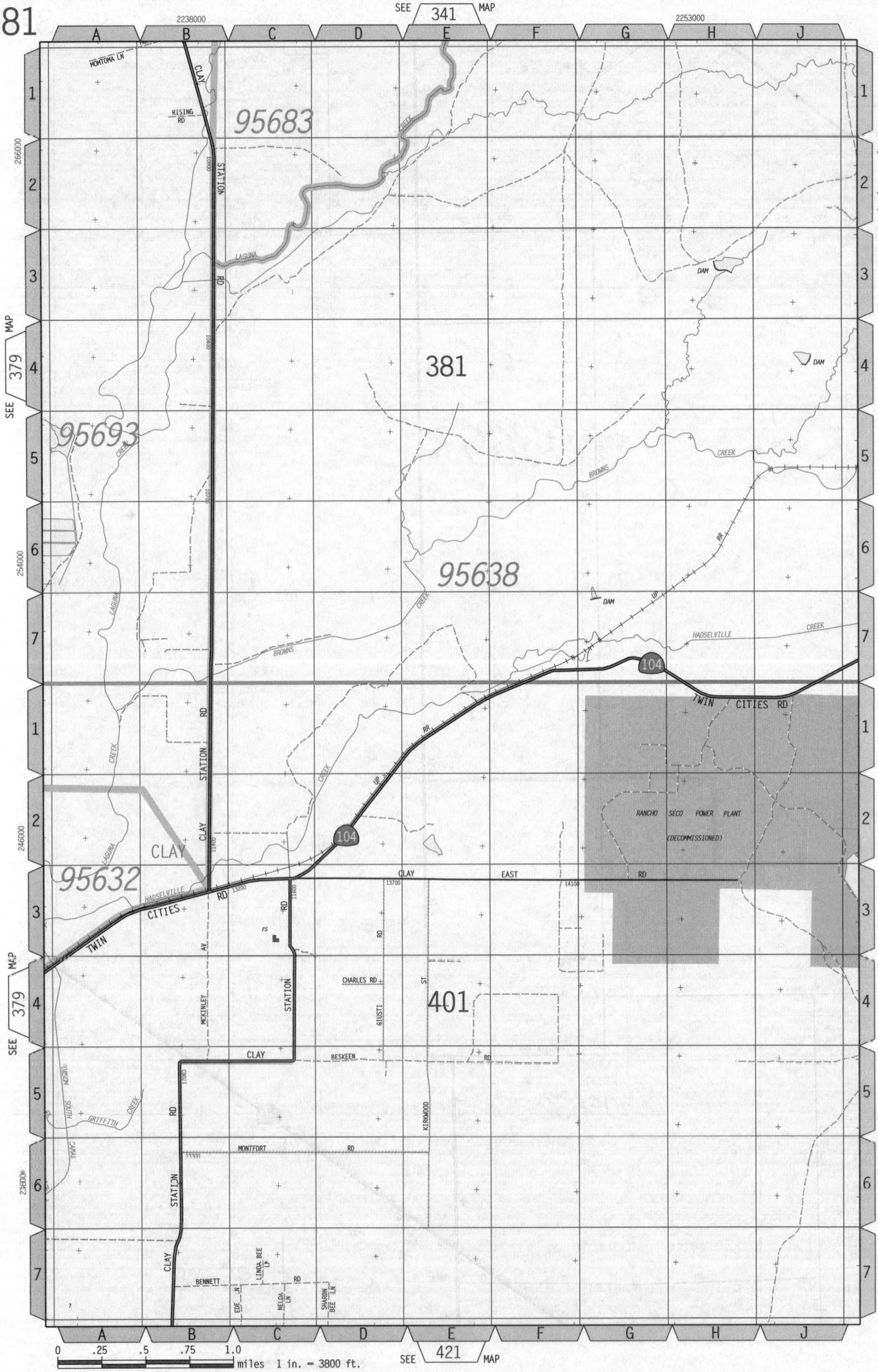
SEE 341 MAP
2238000
2253000
A
B
C
D
E
F
G
H
J
1
2
3
4
5
6
7
266000
254000
246000
236000
SEE 379 MAP
SEE 379 MAP
MONTOMA LN
RISING RD
CLAY STATION RD
95683
LAGUNA CREEK
DAM
DAM
381
95693
BROWNS CREEK
95638
UP RR
DAM
HADSELVILLE CREEK
104
TWIN CITIES RD
RANCHO SECO POWER PLANT
(DECOMMISSIONED)
CLAY
95632
HADSELVILLE
CLAY EAST RD
13200
13700
14100
11400
11600
10400
10700
MCKINLEY AV
FS
GIUSTI RD
CHARLES RD
ST
401
STATION RD
CLAY
BESKEEN
RD
KIRKWOOD
SOUTH CANAL
GRIFFITH CREEK
MONTFORT RD
CLAY STATION RD
LINDA BEE LN
BENNETT
RD
EDE LN
NELDA LN
SHARON BEE LN
0 .25 .5 .75 1.0 miles 1 in. = 3800 ft.
SEE 421 MAP

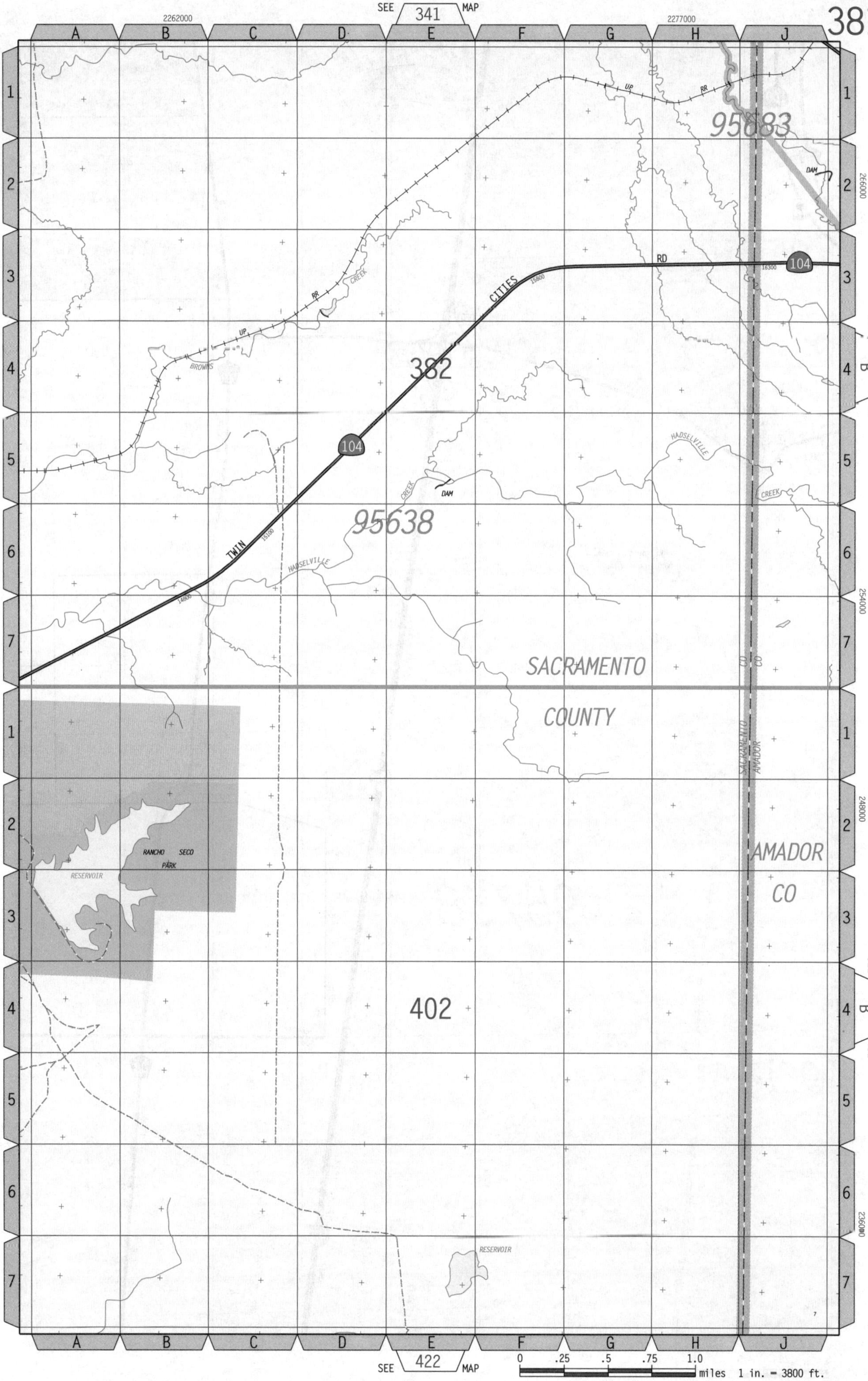
SEE 341 MAP
2262000
2277000
95683
UP RR
DAM
TWIN CITIES RD
104
CREEK
BROWNS
382
HADSELVILLE CREEK
DAM
95638
HADSELVILLE
SACRAMENTO COUNTY
SACRAMENTO CO
AMADOR CO
AMADOR CO
RANCHO SECO PARK
RESERVOIR
402
RESERVOIR
SEE B MAP
SEE B MAP
256000
254000
248000
236000
SEE 422 MAP
0 .25 .5 .75 1.0 miles 1 in. = 3800 ft.

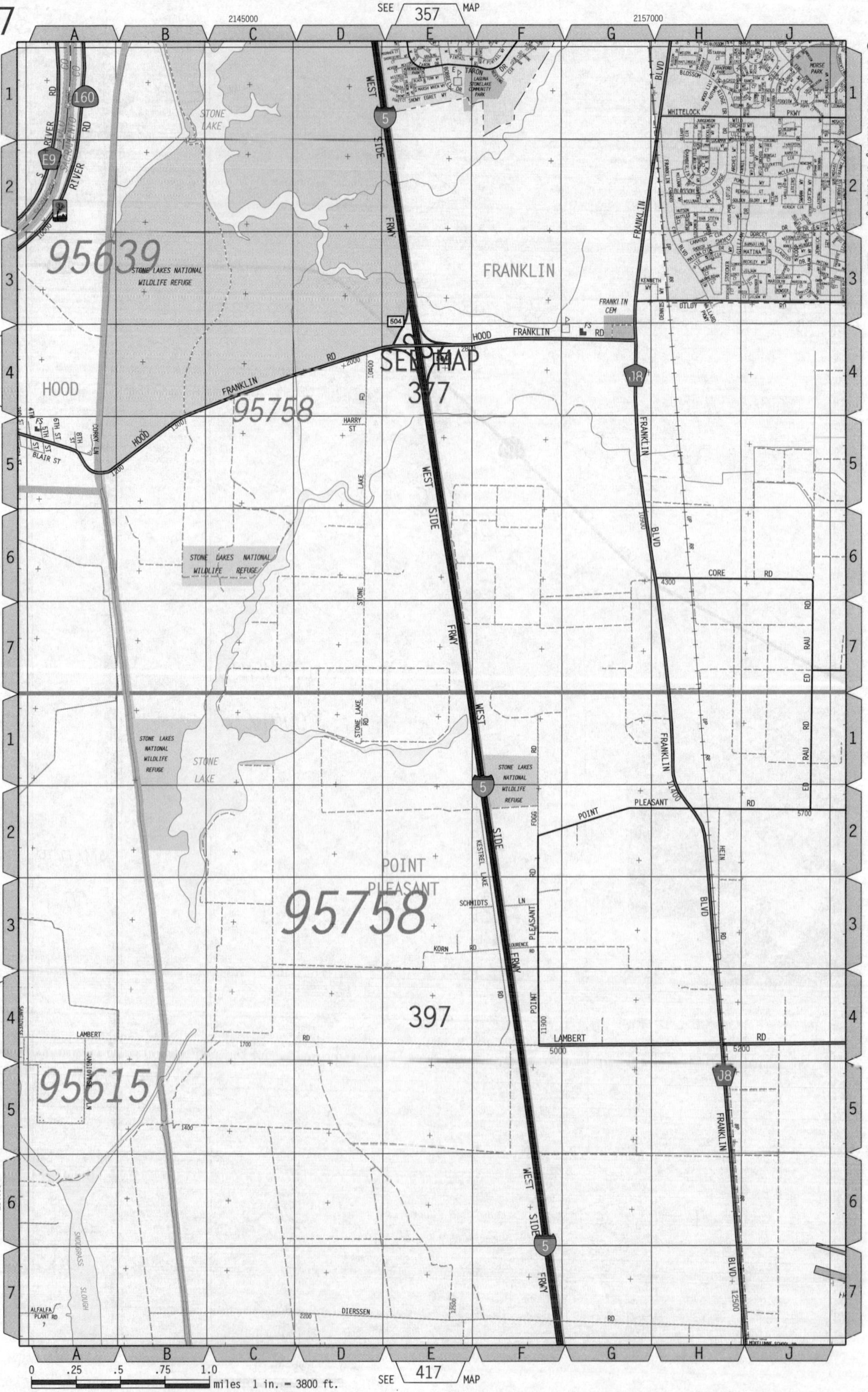
SEE 357 MAP
2145000
2157000
A B C D E F G H J
1 2 3 4 5 6 7
262000
252000
244000
234000
95639
STONE LAKES NATIONAL WILDLIFE REFUGE
STONE LAKE
WEST SIDE FRWY
5
160
E9
S RIVER RD
SACRAMENTO RIVER
LAGUNA STONELAKE COMMUNITY PARK
WHITELOCK PKWY
FRANKLIN BLVD
MORSE PARK
FRANKLIN
FRANKLIN CEM
HOOD FRANKLIN RD
504
SEE MAP 377
HOOD
95758
HARRY ST
BLAIR ST
CORKY LN
J8
SEE 375 MAP
STONE LAKES NATIONAL WILDLIFE REFUGE
STONE LAKE RD
CORE RD
ED RAU RD
POINT PLEASANT RD
FOGG RD
KESTREL LAKE
POINT PLEASANT
95758
SCHMIDTS LN
KORN RD
397
LAMBERT RD
95615
SNODGRASS SLOUGH
ALFALFA PLANT RD
DIERSSEN RD
MCKELUMNE SCHOOL RD
SEE 417 MAP
0 .25 .5 .75 1.0
miles 1 in. = 3800 ft.

SEE 358 MAP
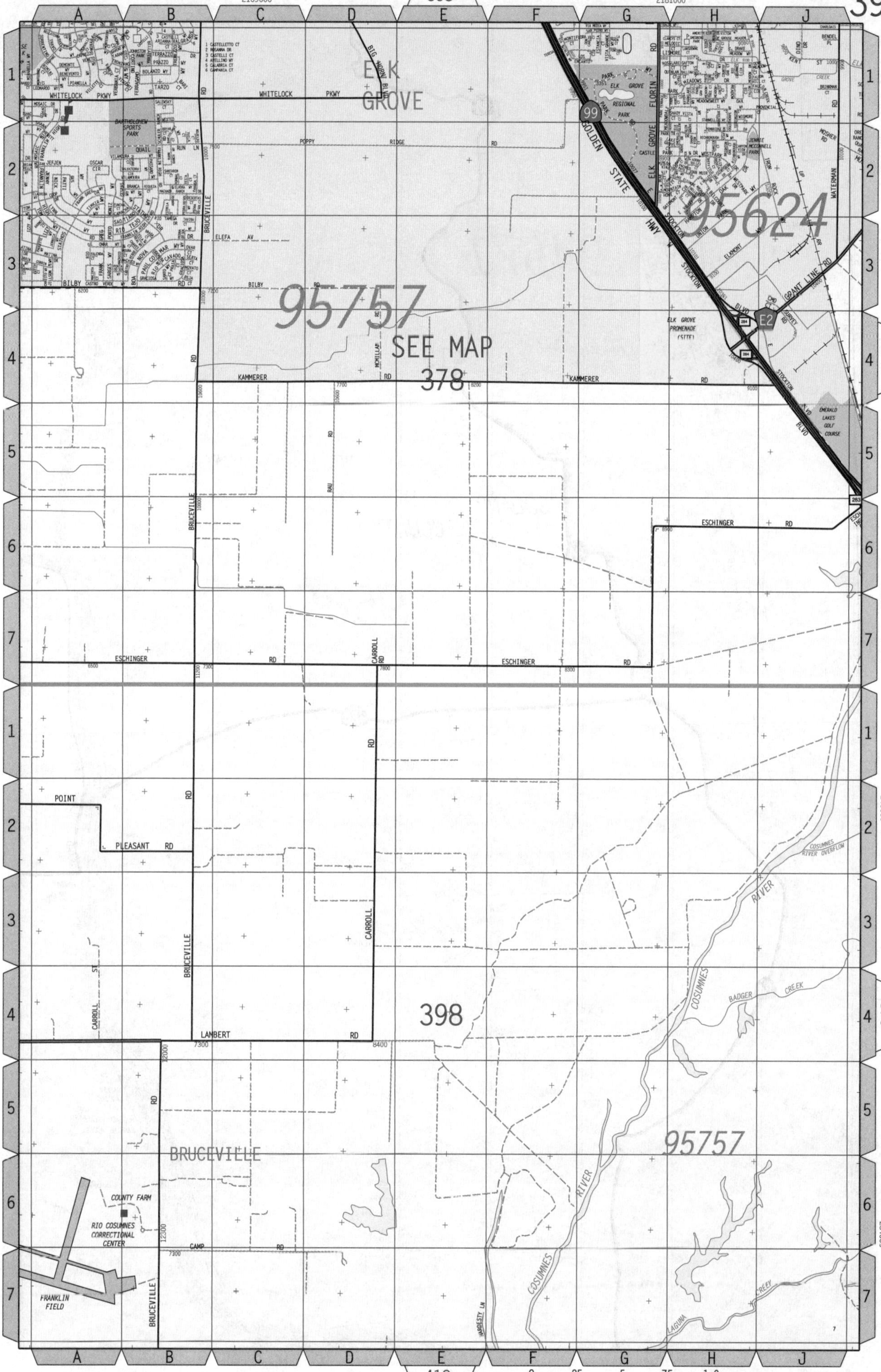
ELK GROVE
95757
SEE MAP 378
95624
WHITELOCK PKWY
POPPY RIDGE RD
BILBY RD
ELEFA AV
KAMMERER RD
ESCHINGER RD
BRUCEVILLE RD
CARROLL RD
POINT PLEASANT RD
LAMBERT RD
CAMP RD
BIG HORN BLVD
MCMILLAN RD
RAU RD
GOLDEN STATE HWY
STOCKTON BLVD
GRANT LINE RD
WATERMAN RD
MOSHER RD
BARTHOLOMEW SPORTS PARK
ELK GROVE REGIONAL PARK
JENNIE MCCONNELL PARK
ELK GROVE PROMENADE (SITE)
EMERALD LAKES GOLF COURSE
398
BRUCEVILLE
COUNTY FARM
RIO COSUMNES CORRECTIONAL CENTER
FRANKLIN FIELD
COSUMNES RIVER
COSUMNES RIVER OVERFLOW
BADGER CREEK
LAGUNA CREEK
HARDESTY LN
2169000
2181000
264000
252000
246000
234000
0 .25 .5 .75 1.0 miles 1 in. = 3800 ft.
SEE 379 MAP
SEE 379 MAP
SEE 418 MAP

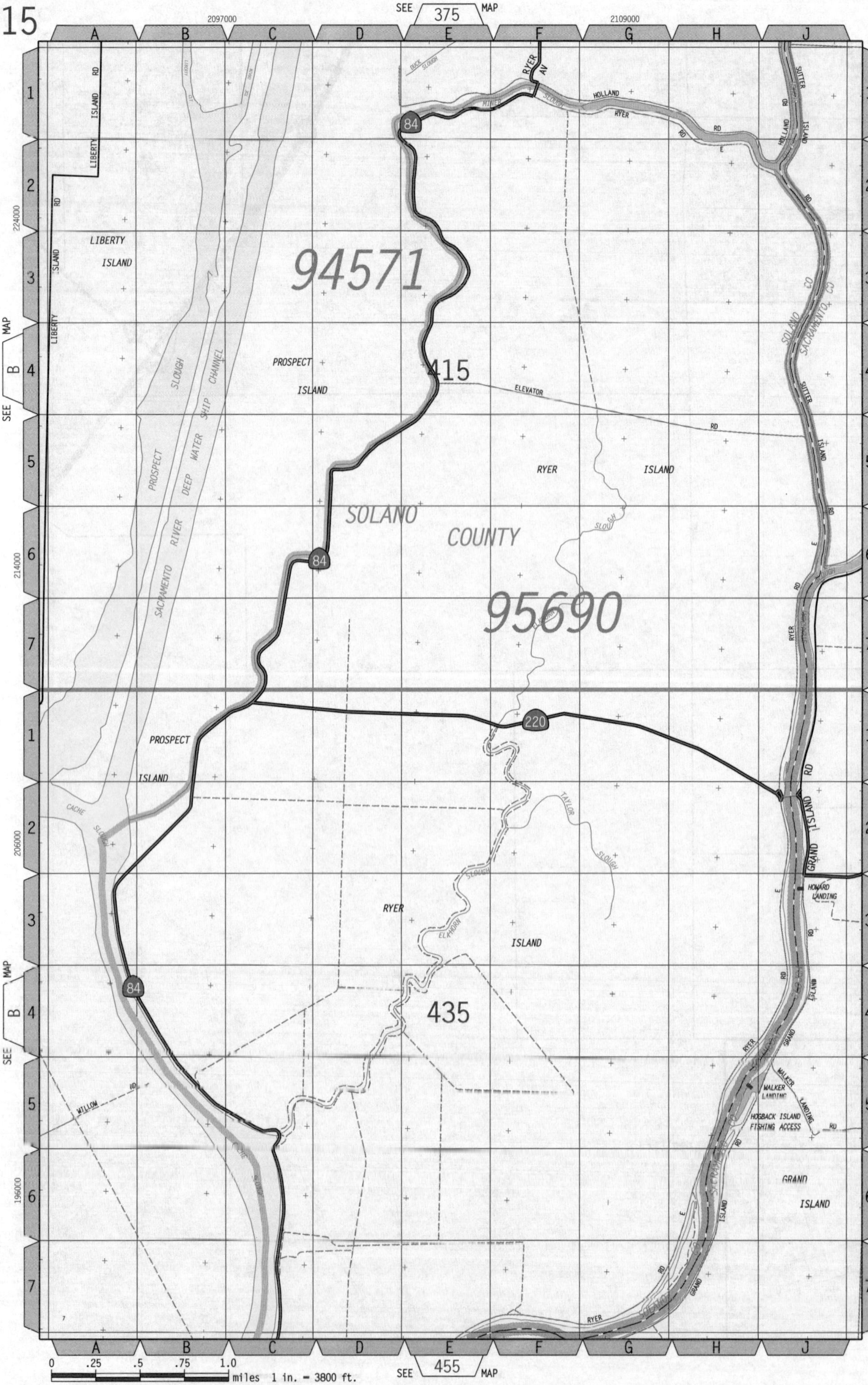
SEE 375 MAP
2097000
2109000
LIBERTY ISLAND RD
LIBERTY RD
LIBERTY ISLAND
94571
PROSPECT ISLAND
415
PROSPECT SLOUGH
SACRAMENTO RIVER DEEP WATER SHIP CHANNEL
RYER AV
MINER SLOUGH
HOLLAND RD
RYER RD
E RD
HOLLAND RD
SUTTER ISLAND RD
SOLANO CO
SACRAMENTO CO
ELEVATOR RD
RYER ISLAND
SOLANO COUNTY
95690
SLOUGH
ELKHORN
84
220
PROSPECT ISLAND
CACHE SLOUGH
TAYLOR SLOUGH
RYER ISLAND
ELKHORN SLOUGH
GRAND ISLAND RD
HOWARD LANDING
RYER ISLAND E RD
435
WILLOW RD
WALKER LANDING
WALKER LANDING RD
HOGBACK ISLAND FISHING ACCESS
GRAND ISLAND
SEE B MAP
224000
214000
206000
196000
0 .25 .5 .75 1.0 miles 1 in. = 3800 ft.
SEE 455 MAP

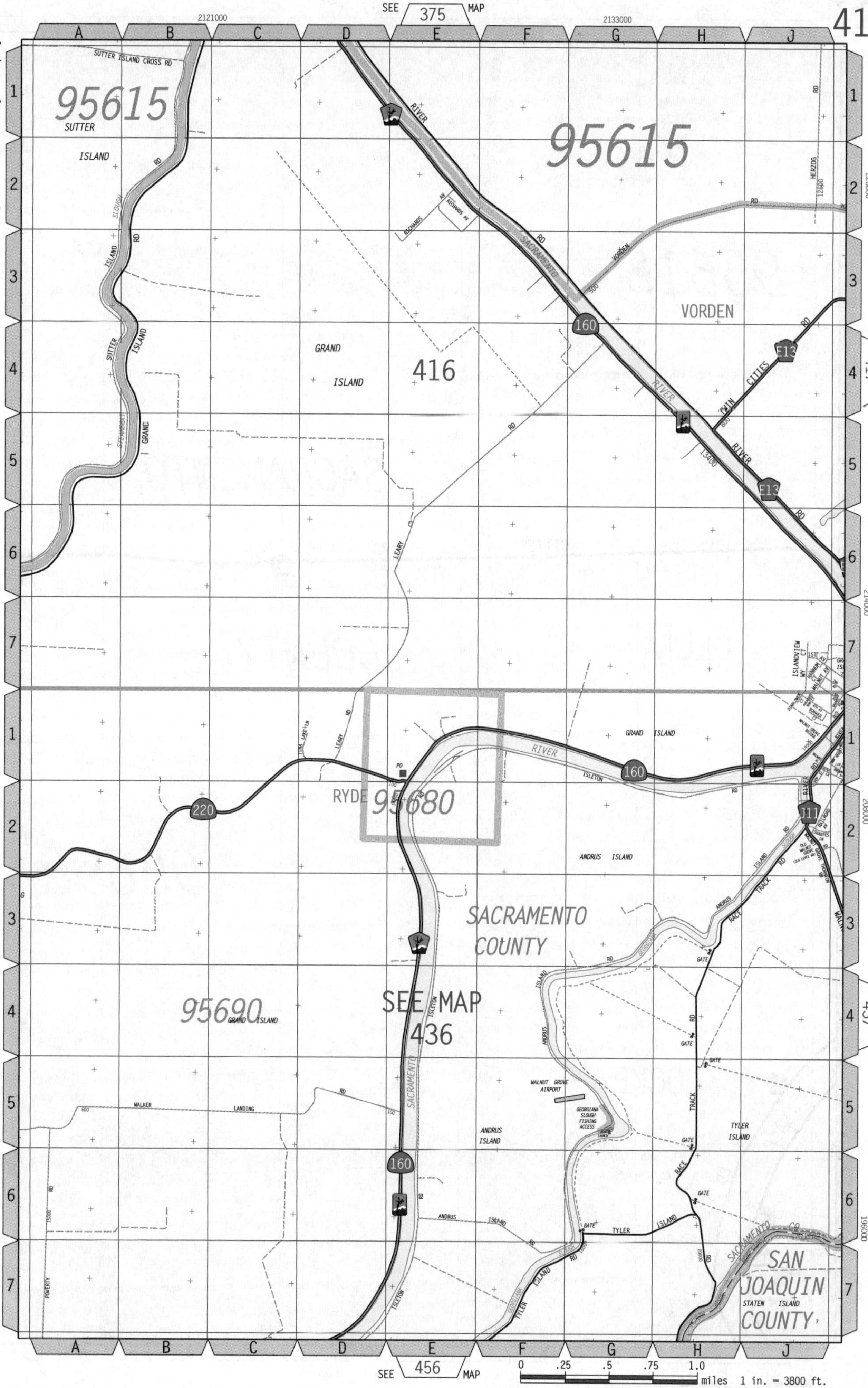
SEE 375 MAP
SEE 417 MAP
SEE 437 MAP
SEE 456 MAP
95615
SUTTER ISLAND CROSS RD
SUTTER
ISLAND
SUTTER ISLAND RD
SUTTER SLOUGH
STEAMBOAT
GRAND
GRAND ISLAND
416
RICHARDS AV
SACRAMENTO RIVER
RD
VORDEN RD
VORDEN
HERZOG RD
TWIN CITIES RD
RIVER RD
LEARY RD
LIMA LAKE LN
RYDE
95680
PO
GRAND ISLAND
ISLETON RD
ANDRUS ISLAND
SACRAMENTO COUNTY
SEE MAP 436
95690
WALKER LANDING RD
POVERTY RD
ANDRUS ISLAND RD
WALNUT GROVE AIRPORT
GEORGIANA SLOUGH FISHING ACCESS
GEORGIANA SLOUGH
TYLER ISLAND
TYLER ISLAND RD
RACE TRACK RD
GATE
SAN JOAQUIN COUNTY
STATEN ISLAND
SACRAMENTO CO
ISLANDVIEW WY
0 .25 .5 .75 1.0
miles 1 in. = 3800 ft.

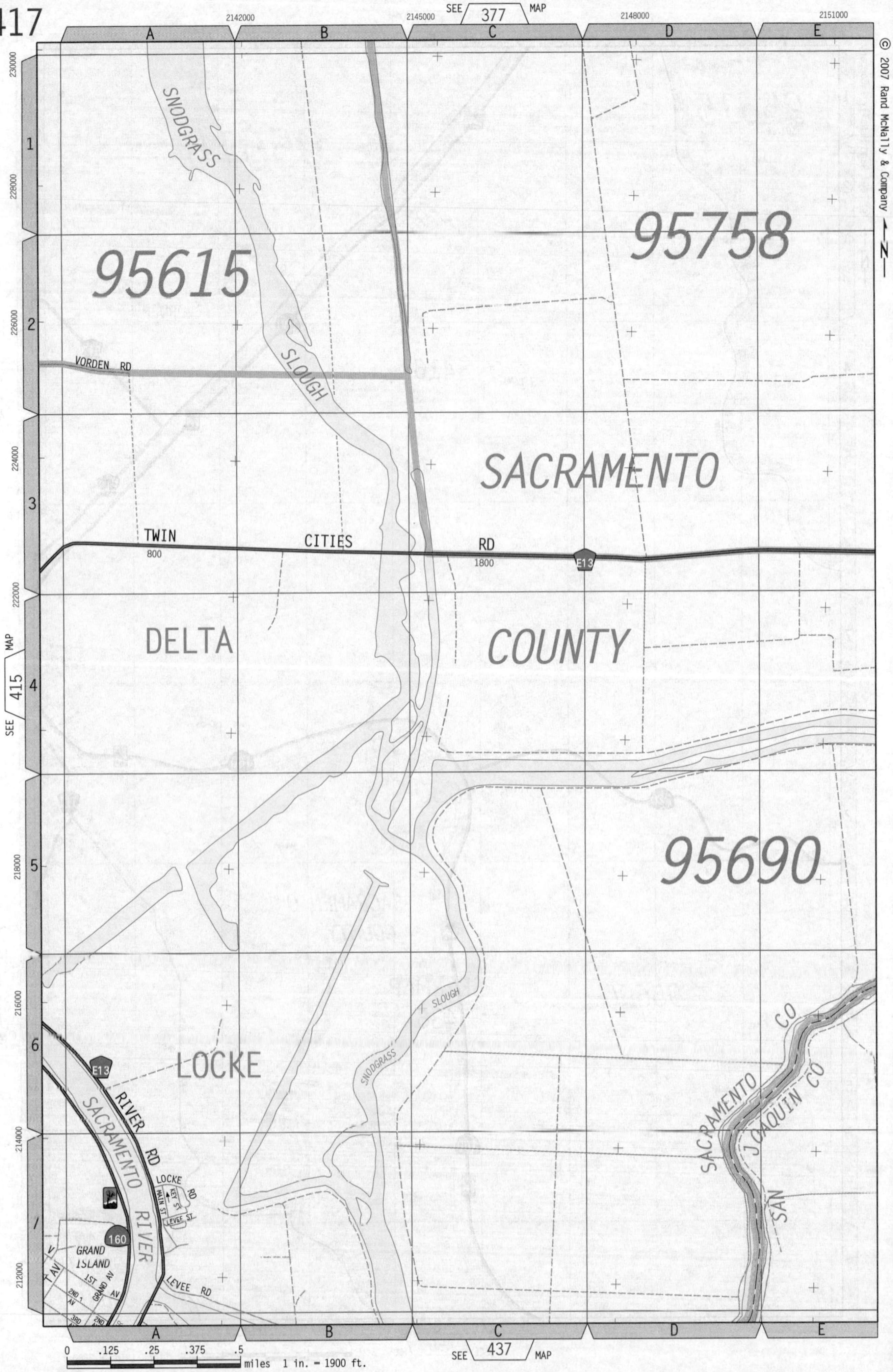
SEE 377 MAP
2142000
2145000
2148000
2151000
A
B
C
D
E
230000
228000
226000
224000
222000
218000
216000
214000
212000
1
2
3
4
5
6
7
SEE 415 MAP
SNODGRASS
SLOUGH
95615
95758
VORDEN RD
SACRAMENTO
TWIN
CITIES
RD
800
1800
E13
DELTA
COUNTY
95690
SNODGRASS
SLOUGH
LOCKE
E13
RIVER RD
SACRAMENTO RIVER
LOCKE RD
KEY ST
MAIN ST
LEVEE ST
160
GRAND ISLAND
V
T AV
1ST
GRAND AV
2ND AV
3RD
LEVEE RD
SACRAMENTO CO
SAN JOAQUIN CO
SEE 437 MAP
0 .125 .25 .375 .5
miles 1 in. = 1900 ft.

SEE 377 MAP
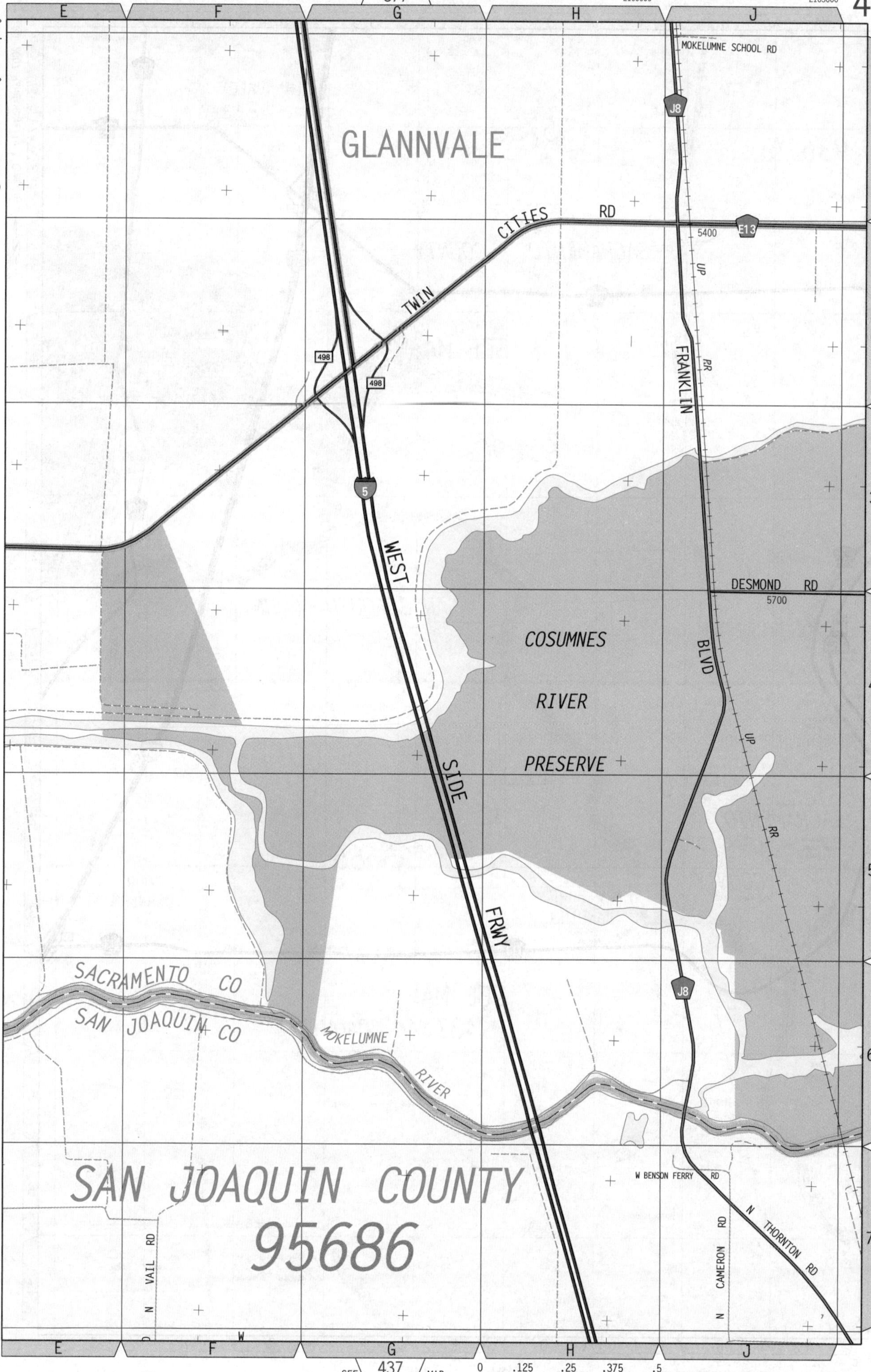
2151000
2154000
2160000
2163000
E
F
G
H
J
1
2
3
4
5
6
7
230000
228000
226000
224000
222000
220000
218000
216000
214000
212000
MOKELUMNE SCHOOL RD
J8
GLANNVALE
TWIN CITIES RD
E13
5400
UP RR
FRANKLIN BLVD
498
5
WEST SIDE FRWY
DESMOND RD
5700
COSUMNES RIVER PRESERVE
SACRAMENTO CO
SAN JOAQUIN CO
MOKELUMNE RIVER
W BENSON FERRY RD
N THORNTON RD
N CAMERON RD
N VAIL RD
W
SAN JOAQUIN COUNTY
95686
0 .125 .25 .375 .5 miles 1 in. = 1900 ft.
SEE 418 MAP
SEE 437 MAP

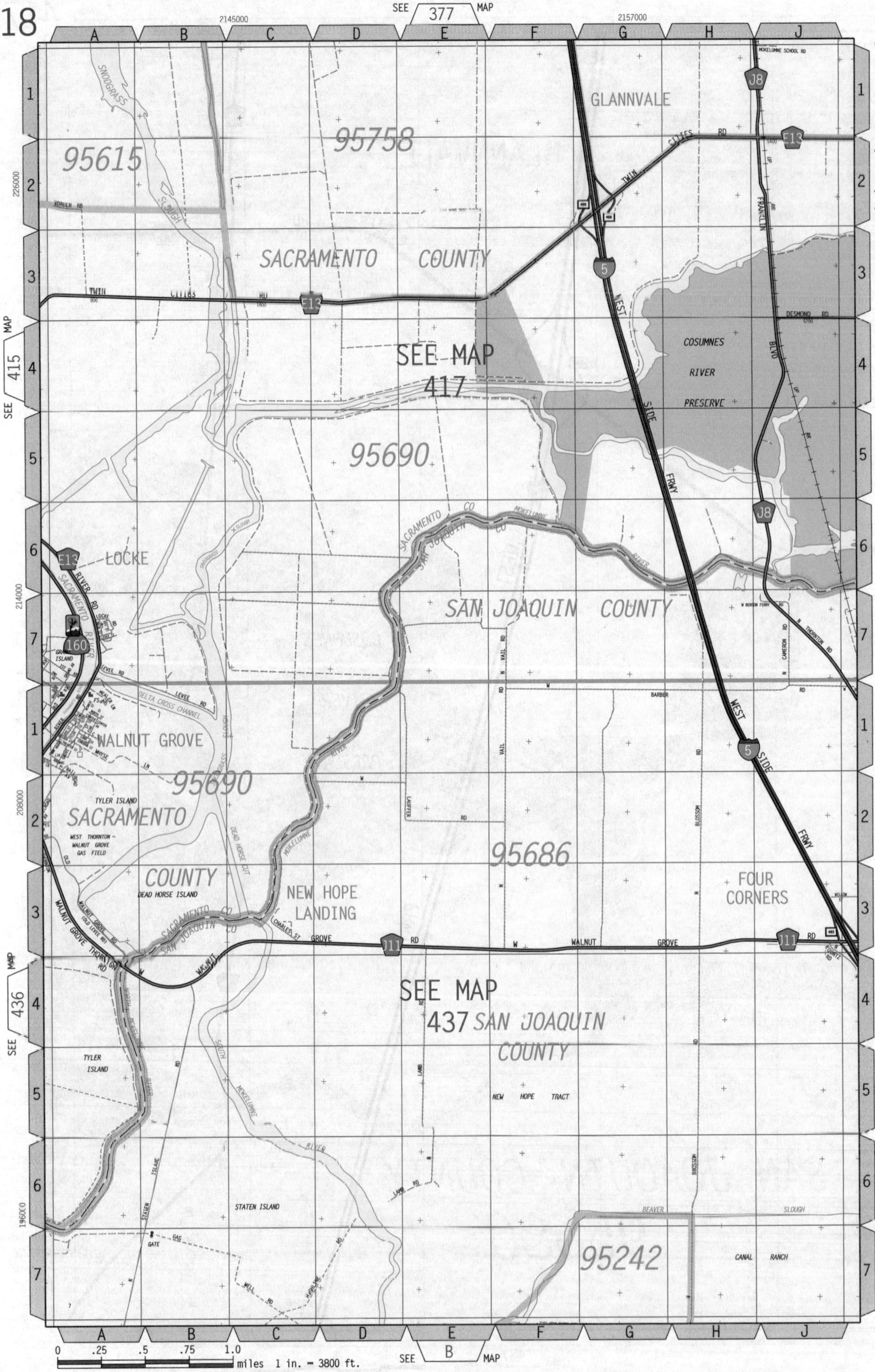
SEE 377 MAP
2145000
2157000
A
B
C
D
E
F
G
H
J
1
2
3
4
5
6
7
SNODGRASS
SLOUGH
GLANNVALE
95615
95758
TWIN CITIES RD
MOKELUMNE SCHOOL RD
FRANKLIN BLVD
E13
J8
226000
SACRAMENTO COUNTY
5
WEST SIDE FRWY
TWIN 800 CITIES RD 1800
DESMOND RD
SEE MAP 415
SEE MAP 417
COSUMNES RIVER PRESERVE
95690
SACRAMENTO CO
SAN JOAQUIN CO
MOKELUMNE RIVER
LOCKE
RIVER RD
SACRAMENTO RIVER
214000
160
GRAND ISLAND
SAN JOAQUIN COUNTY
W BENSON FERRY RD
N THORNTON RD
N CAMERON RD
LEVEE RD
DELTA CROSS CHANNEL
W BARBER RD
N VAIL RD
WALNUT GROVE
95690
208000
TYLER ISLAND
SACRAMENTO
WEST THORNTON - WALNUT GROVE GAS FIELD
LAUFFER RD
BLOSSOM RD
DEAD HORSE CUT
95686
COUNTY
DEAD HORSE ISLAND
NEW HOPE LANDING
FOUR CORNERS
WALNUT GROVE (OLD LEVEE RD)
WALNUT GROVE THORNTON RD
CHARLES ST
W WALNUT GROVE RD
J11
SEE MAP 436
SEE MAP 437
SAN JOAQUIN COUNTY
NORTH MOKELUMNE RIVER
SOUTH MOKELUMNE RIVER
TYLER ISLAND
LAMB RD
NEW HOPE TRACT
STATEN ISLAND
STATEN ISLAND RD
196000
BEAVER SLOUGH
GAS WELL RD
GATE
95242
CANAL RANCH
SEE B MAP
0 .25 .5 .75 1.0 miles 1 in. = 3800 ft.

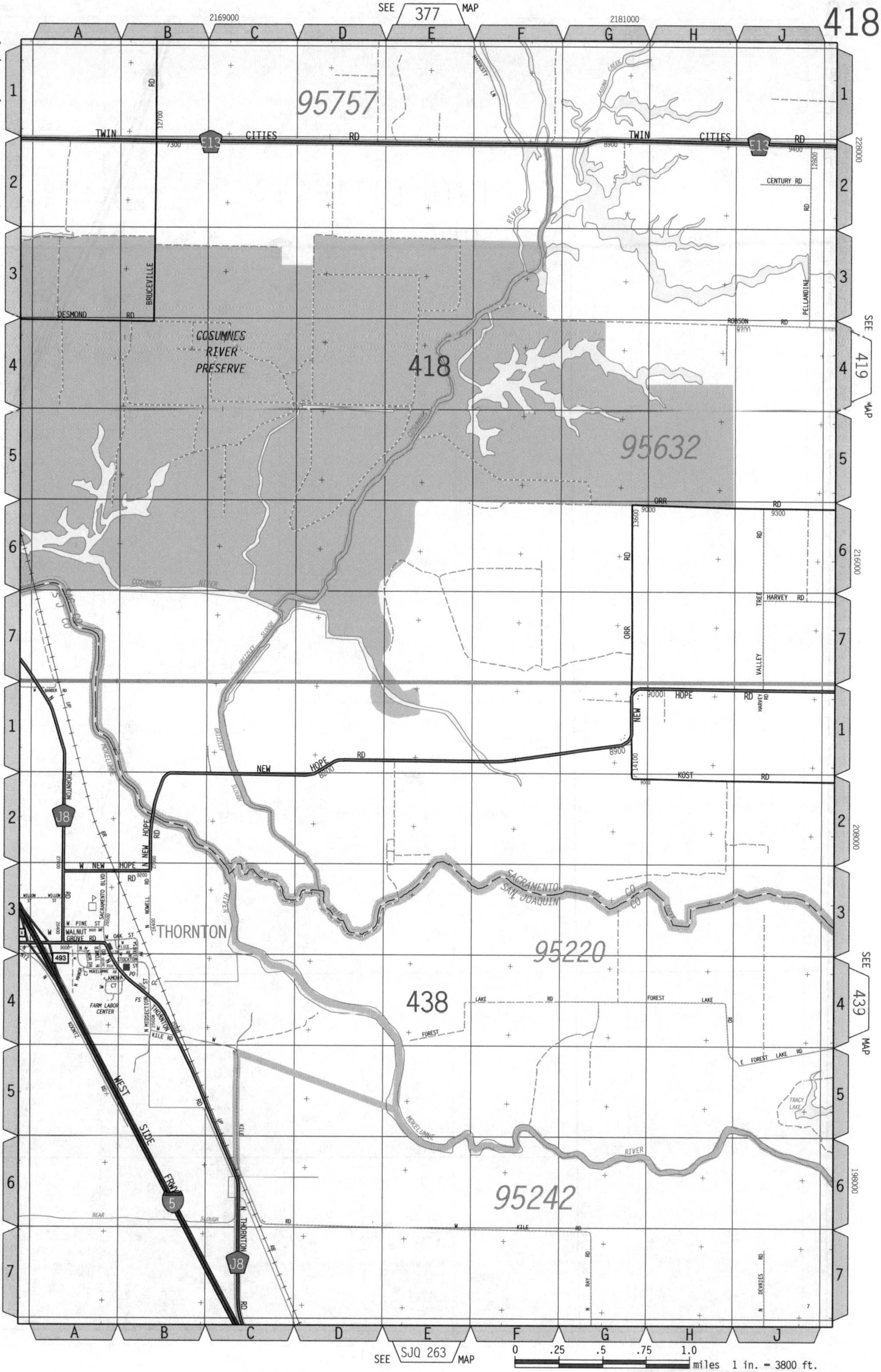
SEE 377 MAP
2169000
2181000
A B C D E F G H J
1 2 3 4 5 6 7 1 2 3 4 5 6 7
95757
TWIN CITIES RD
E13
12700
7300
8900
9400
22800
CENTURY RD
12800
RIVER
LAGUNA CREEK
HARDESTY LN
BRUCEVILLE RD
DESMOND RD
PELLANDINI
ROBSON RD
9700
COSUMNES RIVER PRESERVE
418
SEE 419 MAP
95632
COSUMNES
ORR RD
9000
9300
13600
216000
COSUMNES RIVER
HARVEY RD
TREE VALLEY RD
ORR RD
GRIZZLY SLOUGH
HOPE RD
9000
NEW
HARVEY RD
NEW HOPE RD
8200
8900
14100
KOST RD
MOKELUMNE
THORNTON
J8
208000
NEW HOPE RD
W NEW HOPE
SACRAMENTO BLVD
SACRAMENTO SAN JOAQUIN
CO
RIVER
W PINE ST
WALNUT GROVE RD
W OAK ST
THORNTON
95220
493
FARM LABOR CENTER
438
LAKE RD
FOREST LAKE RD
SEE 439 MAP
FOREST
E FOREST LAKE RD
WEST SIDE FRWY
TRACY LAKE
MOKELUMNE RIVER
KILE
198000
5
95242
BEAR SLOUGH
N THORNTON RD
W KILE RD
N RAY RD
N DEVRIES RD
J8

SEE SJQ 263 MAP

0 .25 .5 .75 1.0 miles 1 in. = 3800 ft.

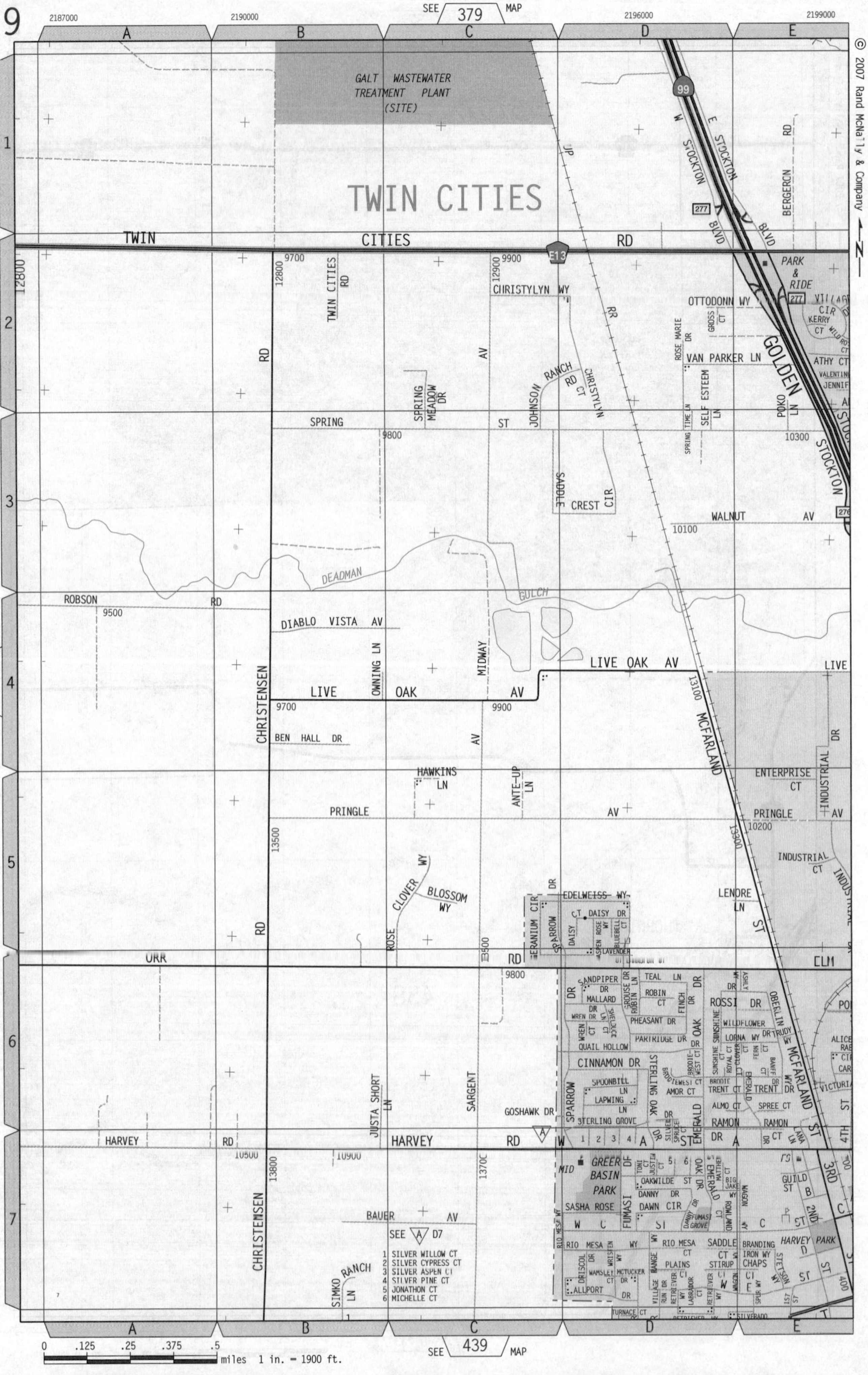
SEE 379 MAP
GALT WASTEWATER TREATMENT PLANT (SITE)
TWIN CITIES
TWIN CITIES RD
E13
99
W STOCKTON BLVD
E STOCKTON BLVD
BERGERON RD
PARK & RIDE
277
CHRISTYLYN WY
TWIN CITIES RD
OTTODONN WY
VILLAGE CIR
KERRY CT
ROSE MARIE DR
GROSS CT
VAN PARKER LN
GOLDEN STATE
ATHY CT
VALENTINE
JENNIFER
JOHNSON RANCH RD
CHRISTYLYN CT
CHRISTYLYN
SPRING MEADOW DR
SPRING ST
SELF ESTEEM LN
SPRING TIME LN
POKO LN
10300
STOCKTON
SADDLE CREST CIR
WALNUT AV
10100
276
DEADMAN GULCH
ROBSON RD
9500
DIABLO VISTA AV
OWNING LN
MIDWAY AV
LIVE OAK AV
9700
9900
CHRISTENSEN RD
BEN HALL DR
13100
MCFARLAND
HAWKINS LN
ANTE-UP LN
PRINGLE AV
ENTERPRISE CT
INDUSTRIAL DR
10200
13500
13300
CLOVER BLOSSOM WY
ROSE
INDUSTRIAL CT
LENORE LN
ST
EDELWEISS WY
GERANIUM CIR
SPARROW
DAISY CT
DAISY DR
BLUEBELL CT
LAVENDER
ORR RD
ELM
9800
SANDPIPER DR
MALLARD
TEAL LN
ROBIN CT
FINCH
ROSSI DR
OBERLIN
PHEASANT DR
PARTRIDGE DR
OAK
WILDFLOWER
LORNA WY
QUAIL HOLLOW
CINNAMON DR
STERLING OAK
SPOONBILL LN
LAPWING LN
AMOR CT
TRENT CT
ALMO CT
SPREE CT
RAMON DR
RAMON
VICTORIA
JUSTA SHORT LN
SARGENT
GOSHAWK DR
STERLING GROVE
EMERALD
MCFARLAND ST
4TH ST
HARVEY RD
10500
10900
13800
1370C
GREER BASIN PARK
OAKWILDE ST
DANNY DR
DAWN CIR
SASHA ROSE
FUMASI DR
GUILD ST
3RD
2ND
BAUER AV
SEE A D7
1 SILVER WILLOW CT
2 SILVER CYPRESS CT
3 SILVER ASPEN CT
4 SILVER PINE CT
5 JONATHON CT
6 MICHELLE CT
SIMKO RANCH LN
RIO MESA WY
RIO MESA CT
PLAINS CT
SADDLE STIRUP
BRANDING IRON WY
CHAPS CT
HARVEY PARK
DRISCOLL DR
WAMSLEY CT
MCTUCKER DR
ALLPORT DR
TURNACE CT
SILVERADO
SEE 418 MAP
SEE 439 MAP
0 .125 .25 .375 .5 miles 1 in. = 1900 ft.
© 2007 Rand McNally & Company

SEE 379 MAP

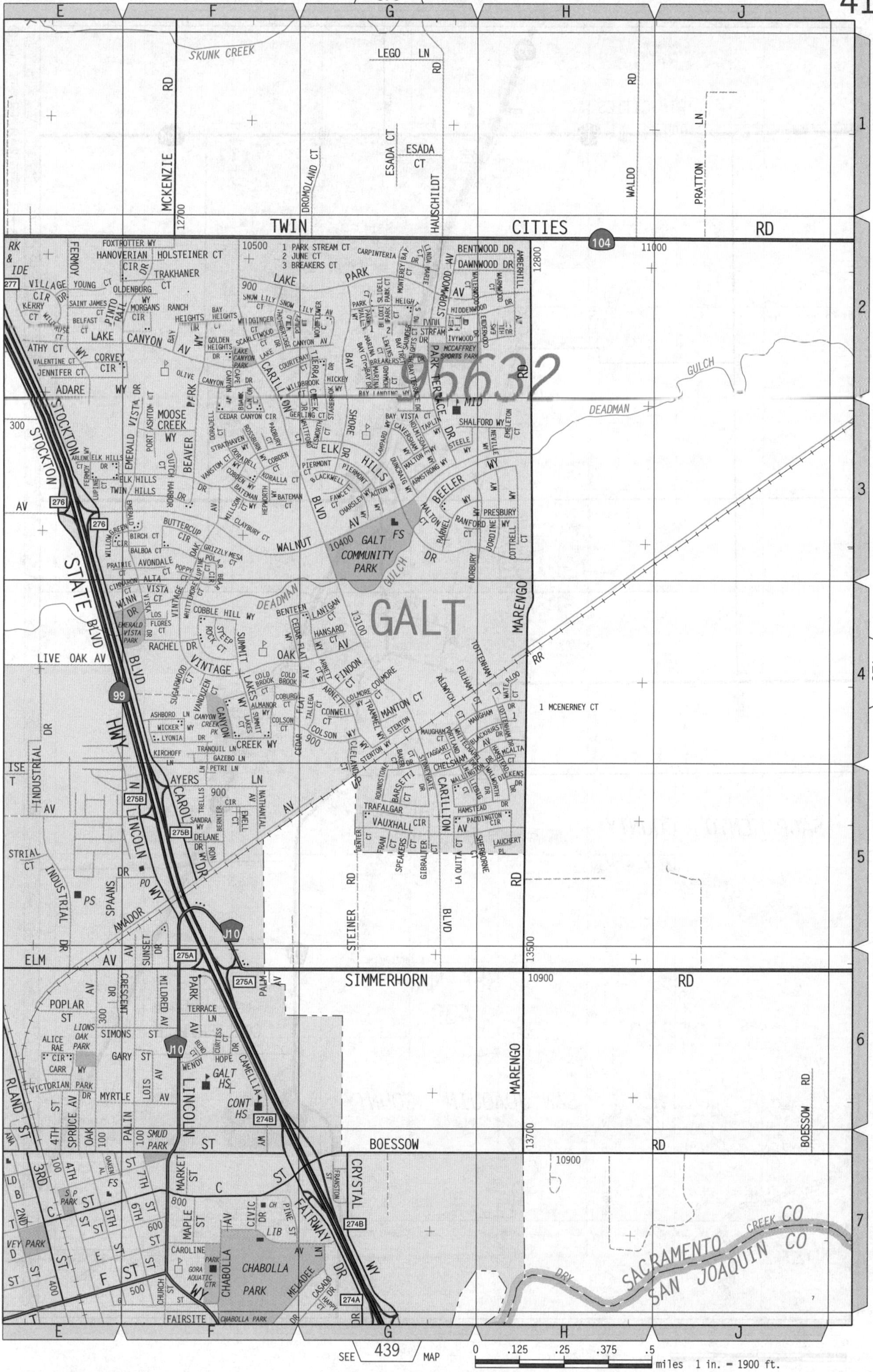

SEE 420 MAP

SEE 439 MAP

0 .125 .25 .375 .5 miles 1 in. = 1900 ft.

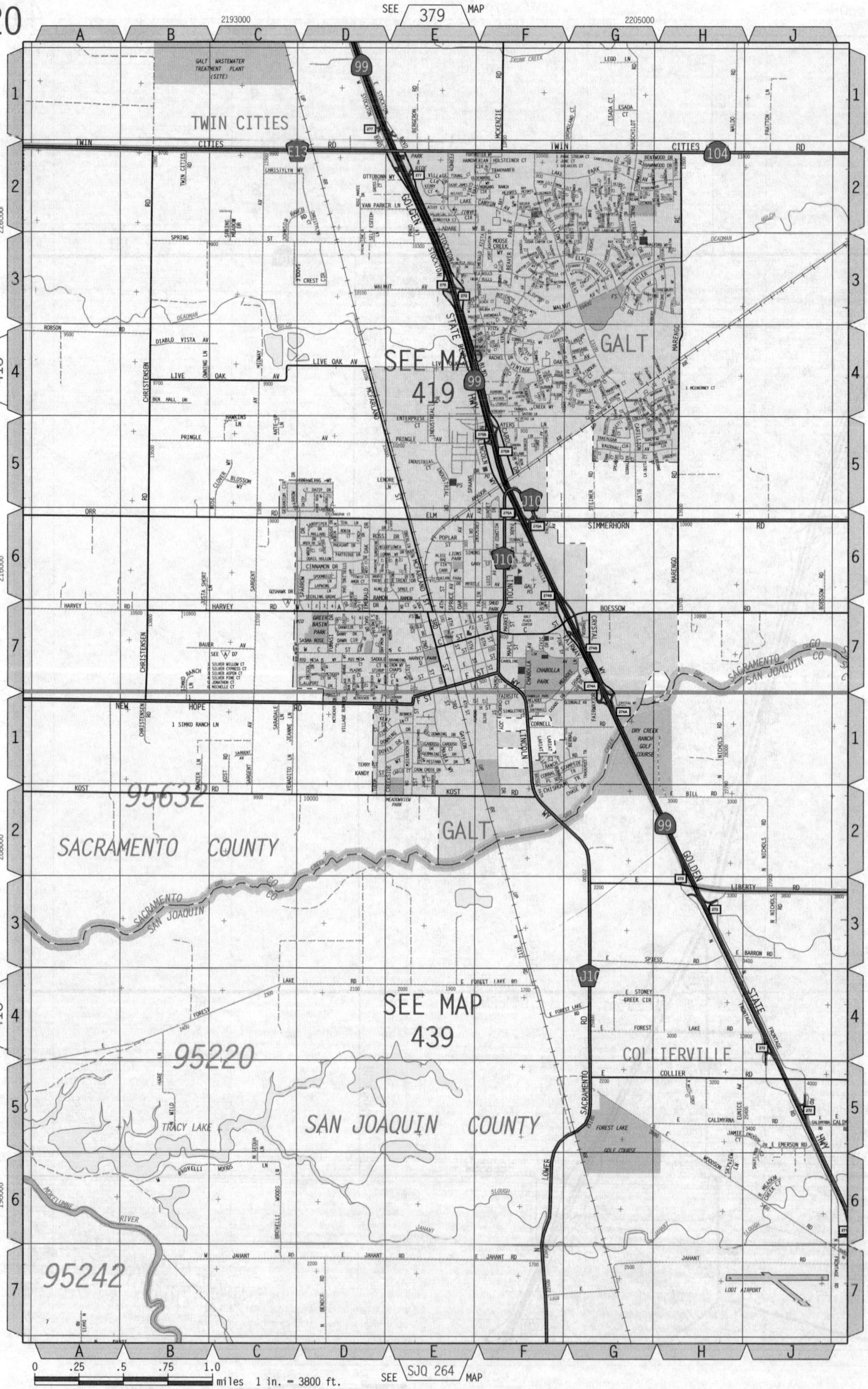
SEE 379 MAP
SEE 418 MAP
SEE SJQ 264 MAP
SEE MAP 419
SEE MAP 439
TWIN CITIES
GALT
GALT WASTEWATER TREATMENT PLANT (SITE)
COLLIERVILLE
SACRAMENTO COUNTY
SAN JOAQUIN COUNTY
95632
95220
95242
TWIN CITIES RD
SPRING ST
ROBSON RD
DIABLO VISTA AV
LIVE OAK AV
BEN HALL DR
PRINGLE AV
ORR RD
ELM AV
SIMMERHORN RD
HARVEY RD
BOESSOW RD
BAUER AV
NEW HOPE RD
KOST RD
E BILL RD
E LIBERTY RD
E SPIESS RD
E FOREST LAKE RD
E COLLIER RD
E CALIMYRNA RD
E JAHANT RD
WOODS LN
CHRISTENSEN RD
MARENGO RD
MCFARLAND ST
LINCOLN WY
GOLDEN STATE HWY
LOWER SACRAMENTO RD
N THORNTON RD
TRACY LAKE
DRY CREEK RANCH GOLF COURSE
FOREST LAKE GOLF COURSE
LODI AIRPORT
CHABOLLA PARK
GREENES BASIN PARK
DEADMAN GULCH
SKUNK CREEK
DRY CREEK
MOKELUMNE RIVER
2193000
2205000
226000
216000
208000
198000
0 .25 .5 .75 1.0 miles 1 in. = 3800 ft.

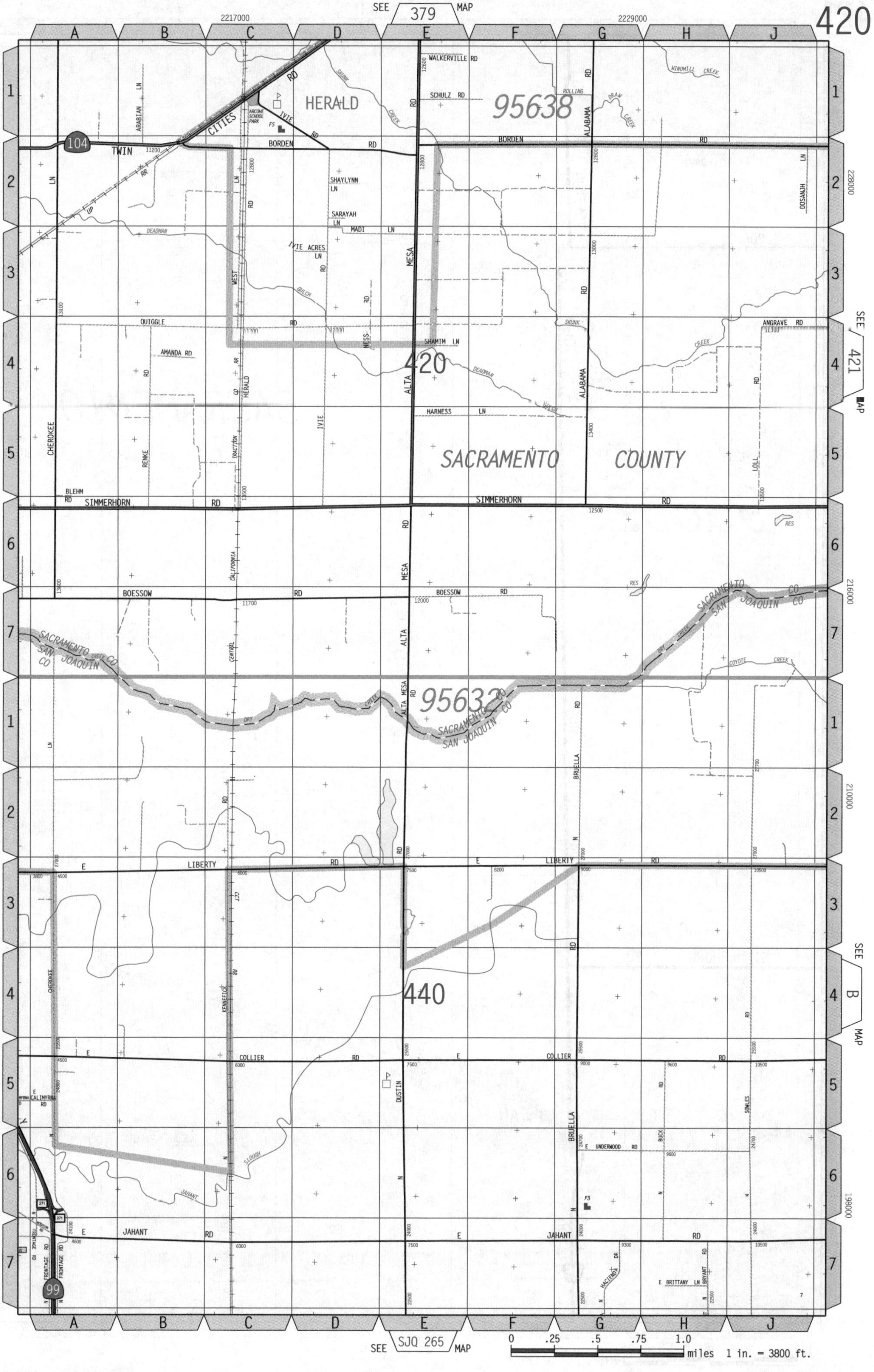
SEE 379 MAP
SEE 421 MAP
SEE B MAP
SEE SJQ 265 MAP
2217000
2229000
228000
216000
210000
198000
HERALD
95638
95632
420
440
SACRAMENTO COUNTY
SACRAMENTO CO
SAN JOAQUIN CO
WALKERVILLE RD
SCHULZ RD
BORDEN RD
TWIN CITIES RD
IVIE RD
ARCOHE SCHOOL PARK
ARABIAN LN
SHAYLYNN LN
SARAYAH LN
MADI LN
IVIE ACRES LN
DEADMAN GULCH
SKUNK CREEK
ROLLING
DRAW CREEK
WINDMILL CREEK
ALABAMA RD
WEST RD
MESA RD
ALTA MESA RD
QUIGGLE RD
AMANDA RD
SHAMIM LN
NESS RD
ANGRAVE RD
DOSANJH LN
HARNESS LN
CHEROKEE LN
RENKE RD
IVIE RD
HERALD RD
TRACTION RD
LOLL RD
BLEHM RD
SIMMERHORN RD
CALIFORNIA
CENTRAL
BOESSOW RD
RES
DRY CREEK
COYOTE CREEK
BRUELLA RD
E LIBERTY RD
KENNEFICK RD
CHEROKEE LN
DUSTIN RD
E COLLIER RD
CALIMYRNA RD
BUCK RD
SOWLES RD
E UNDERWOOD RD
SLOUGH
JAHANT
E JAHANT RD
FRONTAGE RD
HACIENDA DR
E BRITTANY LN
BRYANT RD
104
99
0 .25 .5 .75 1.0 miles 1 in. = 3800 ft.

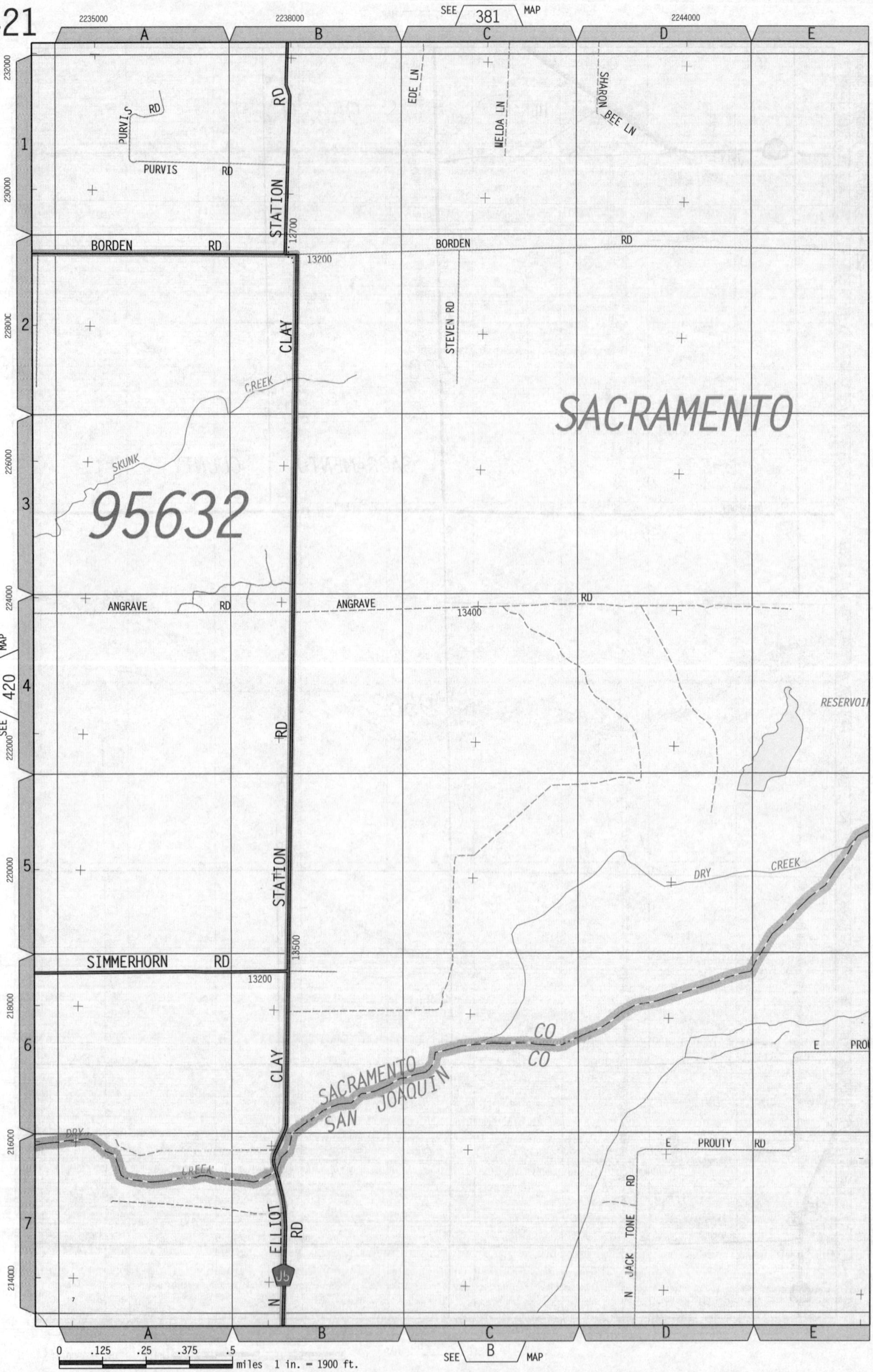
SEE 381 MAP
SEE 420 MAP
SEE B MAP
PURVIS RD
PURVIS RD
EDE LN
MELDA LN
SHARON BEE LN
STATION RD
CLAY STATION RD
BORDEN RD
BORDEN RD
STEVEN RD
SACRAMENTO
95632
SKUNK CREEK
ANGRAVE RD
ANGRAVE RD
RESERVOIR
DRY CREEK
SIMMERHORN RD
SACRAMENTO CO
SAN JOAQUIN CO
DRY CREEK
N ELLIOT RD
J5
N JACK TONE RD
E PROUTY RD
E PROU
0 .125 .25 .375 .5 miles 1 in. = 1900 ft.

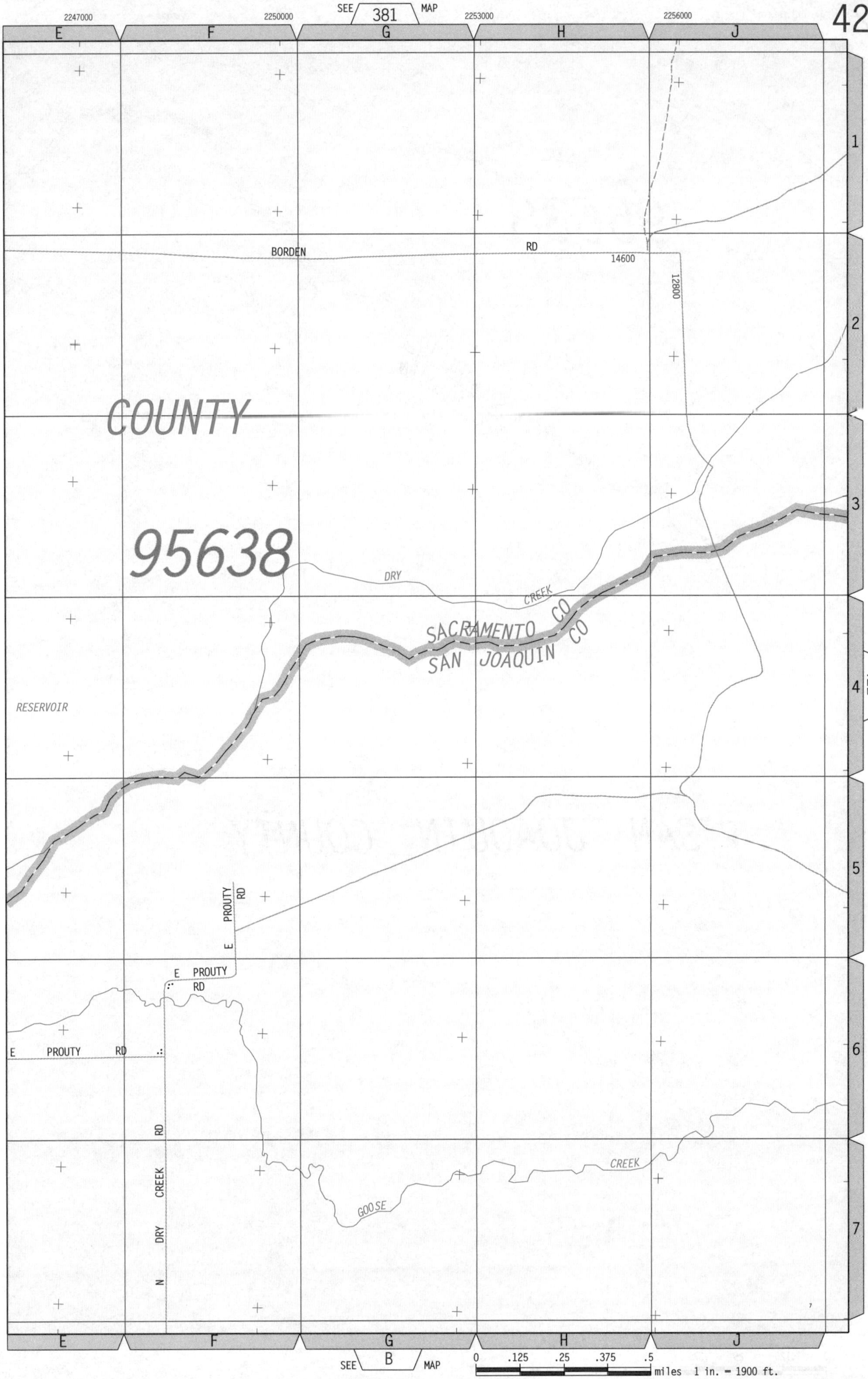
SEE 381 MAP
2247000
2250000
2253000
2256000
E
F
G
H
J
232000
230000
228000
226000
224000
222000
220000
218000
216000
214000
1
2
3
4
5
6
7
BORDEN
RD
14600
12800
COUNTY
95638
DRY
CREEK
SACRAMENTO CO
SAN JOAQUIN CO
RESERVOIR
SEE 422 MAP
E PROUTY RD
E PROUTY RD
E PROUTY RD
N DRY CREEK RD
GOOSE
CREEK
SEE B MAP
0 .125 .25 .375 .5 miles 1 in. = 1900 ft.

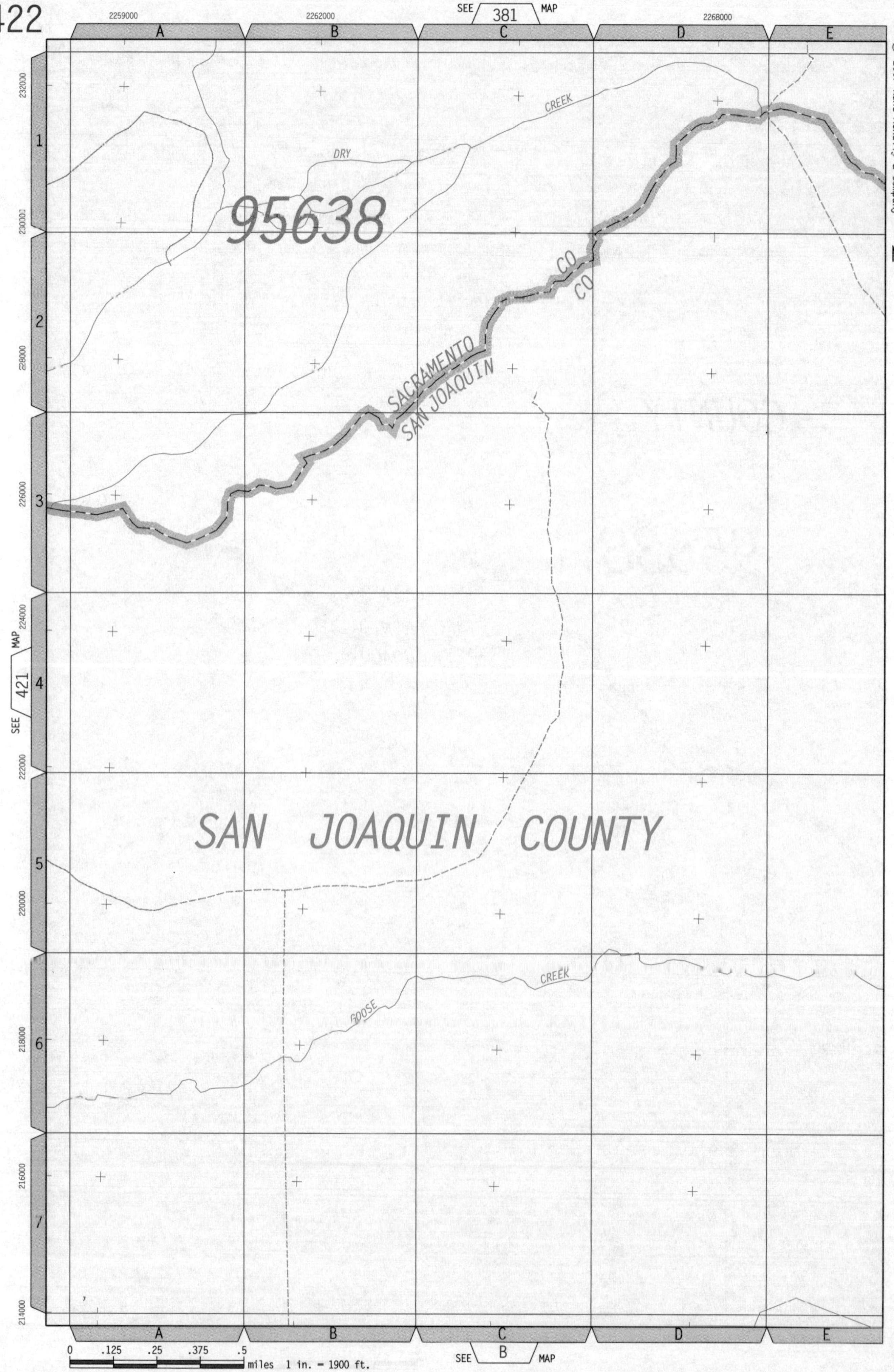
SEE 381 MAP
A
B
C
D
E
2259000
2262000
2268000
232000
230000
228000
226000
224000
222000
220000
218000
216000
214000
1
2
3
4
5
6
7
SEE 421 MAP
DRY
CREEK
95638
CO
CO
SACRAMENTO
SAN JOAQUIN
SAN JOAQUIN COUNTY
GOOSE
CREEK
SEE B MAP
0 .125 .25 .375 .5
miles 1 in. = 1900 ft.

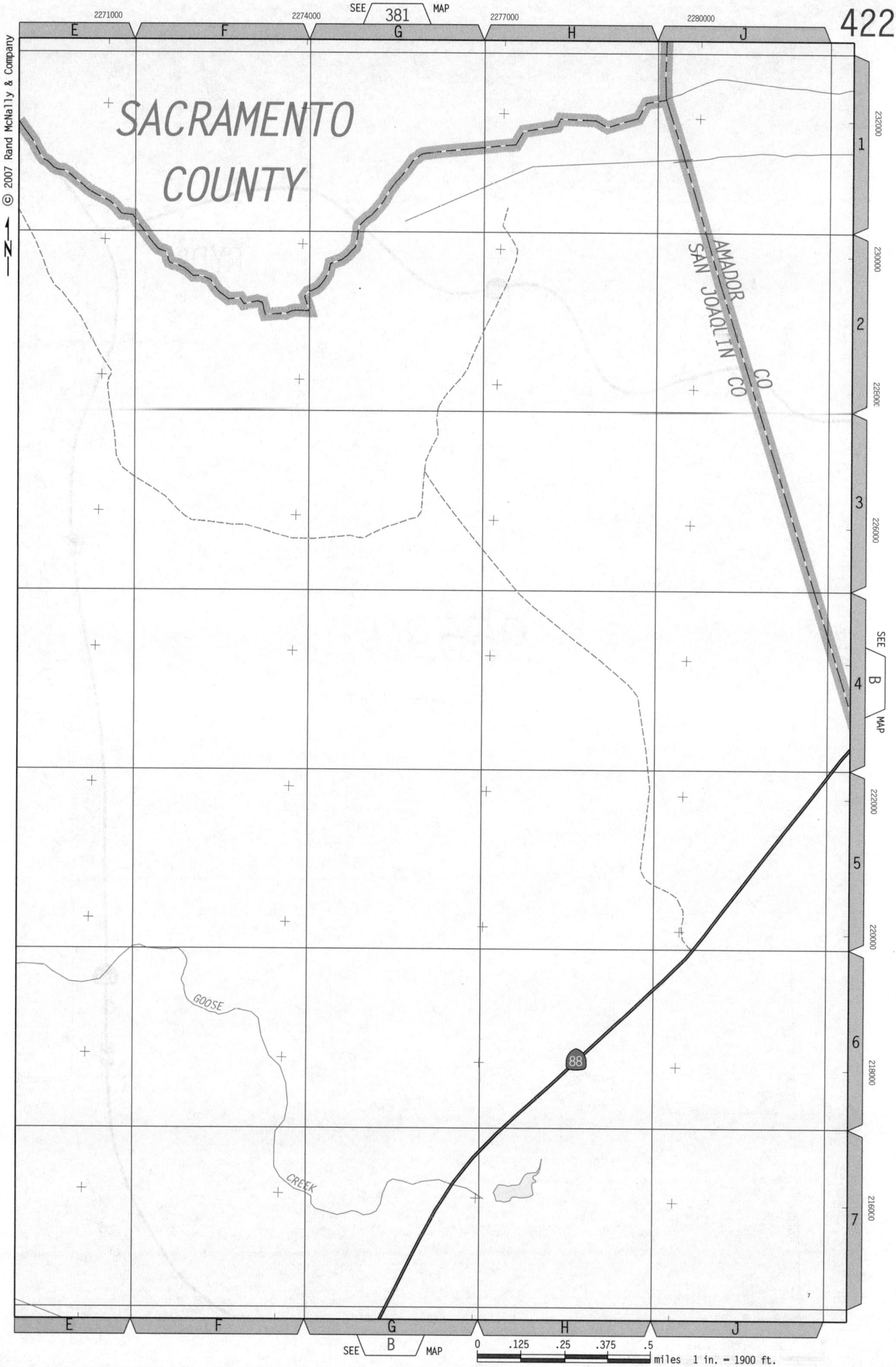
SEE 381 MAP
2271000
2274000
2277000
2280000
E
F
G
H
J
SACRAMENTO
COUNTY
AMADOR CO
SAN JOAQUIN CO
232000
230000
228000
226000
222000
220000
218000
216000
1
2
3
4
5
6
7
SEE B MAP
GOOSE
CREEK
88
N
SEE B MAP
0 .125 .25 .375 .5
miles 1 in. = 1900 ft.

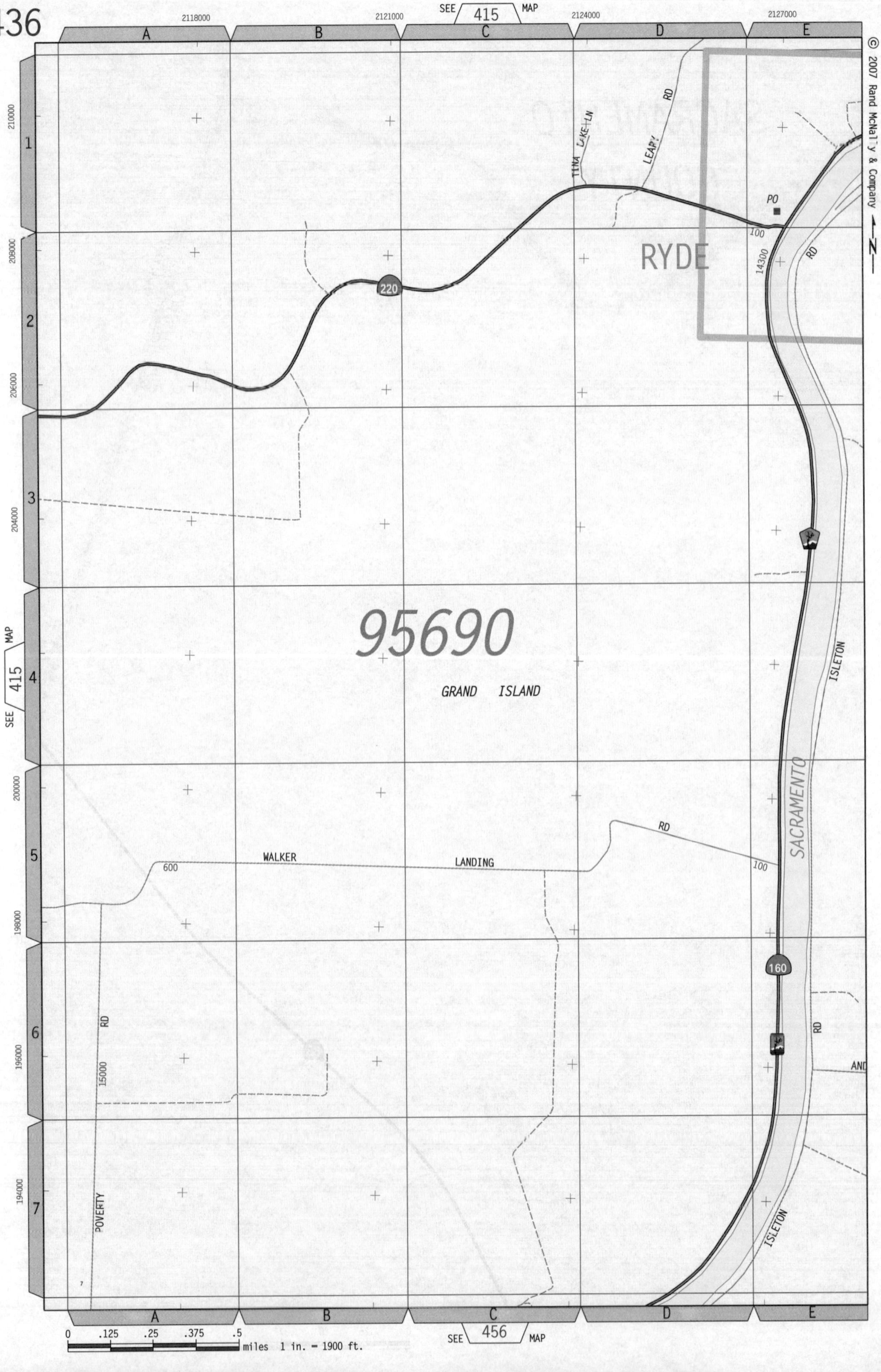
SEE 415 MAP
2118000
2121000
2124000
2127000
A
B
C
D
E
1
2
3
4
5
6
7
210000
208000
206000
204000
200000
198000
196000
194000
RYDE
PO
TINA LAKE LN
LEARY RD
100
14300
RD
220
95690
GRAND ISLAND
SEE 415 MAP
ISLETON
SACRAMENTO
WALKER
LANDING
RD
600
100
160
RD
AND
POVERTY
RD
15000
ISLETON
SEE 456 MAP
0 .125 .25 .375 .5
miles 1 in. = 1900 ft.

SEE 415 MAP

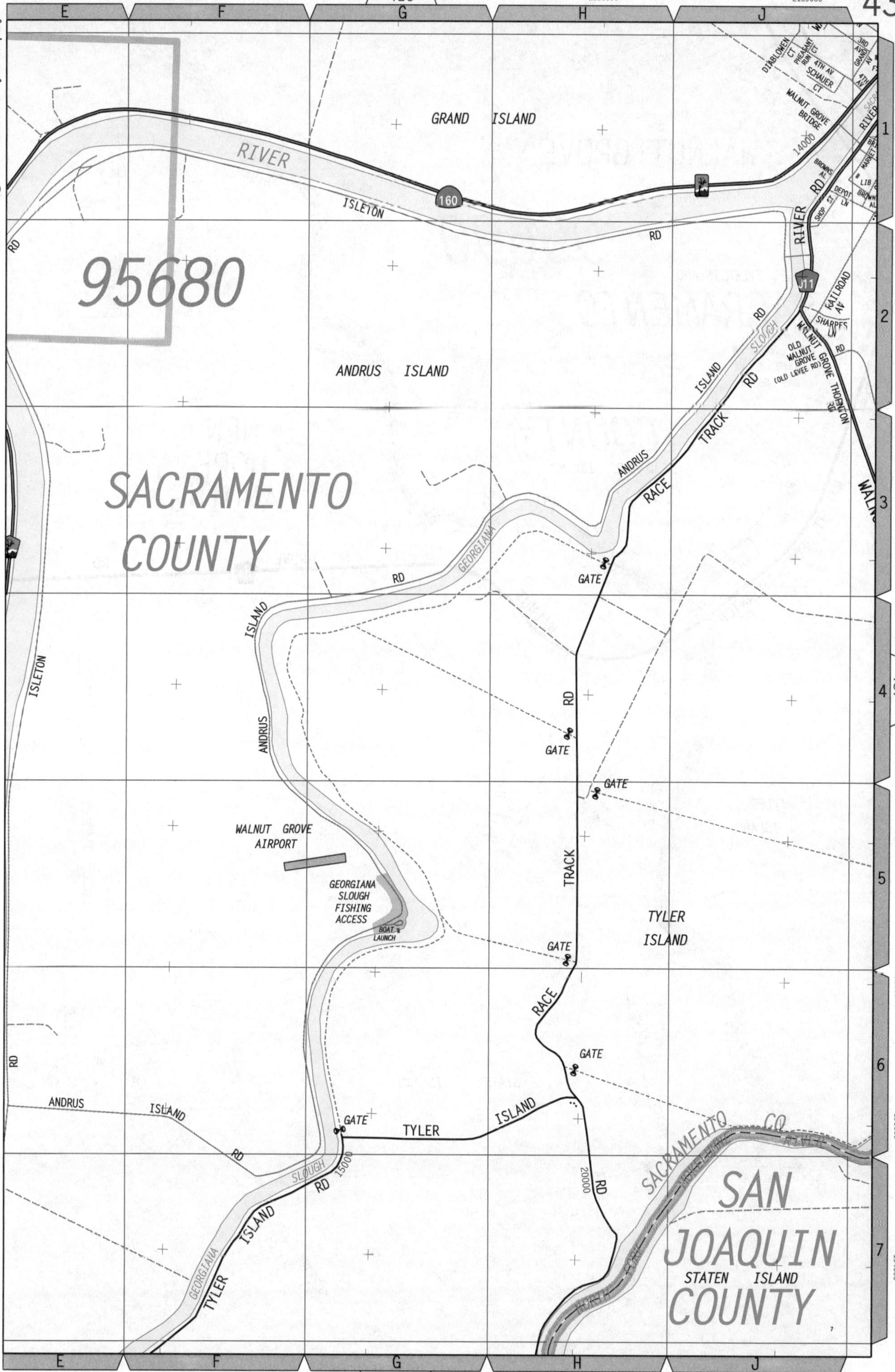

GRAND ISLAND
ANDRUS ISLAND
SACRAMENTO COUNTY
95680
RIVER
ISLETON RD
160
J11
WALNUT GROVE BRIDGE
DIABLOWEN CT
PHEASANT RUN CT
4TH AV
SCHAUER CT
RIVER RD
14000
BROWNS AL
DEPOT LN
SHOP ST
RAILROAD AV
SHARPES LN
OLD WALNUT GROVE (OLD LEVEE RD)
WALNUT GROVE THORNTON RD
ISLAND SLOUGH RD
ANDRUS ISLAND RD
RACE TRACK RD
GEORGIANA SLOUGH
GATE
ISLETON RD
WALNUT GROVE AIRPORT
GEORGIANA SLOUGH FISHING ACCESS
BOAT LAUNCH
TYLER ISLAND
TYLER ISLAND RD
15000
20000
SACRAMENTO CO
SAN JOAQUIN COUNTY
STATEN ISLAND
NORTH FORK
2130000
2136000
2139000
210000
208000
206000
204000
200000
198000
195000
194000
E F G H J
1 2 3 4 5 6 7
0 .125 .25 .375 .5 miles 1 in. = 1900 ft.

SEE 437 MAP
SEE 456 MAP

SEE 417 MAP
SEE 436 MAP
SEE B MAP
WALNUT GROVE
95690
SACRAMENTO
COUNTY
TYLER ISLAND
WEST THORNTON – WALNUT GROVE GAS FIELD
DEAD HORSE ISLAND
NEW HOPE LANDING
STATEN ISLAND
DELTA CROSS CHANNEL
LEVEE RD
SNODGRASS SLOUGH
DEAD HORSE CUT
MOKELUMNE RIVER
NORTH FORK MOKELUMNE RIVER
SOUTH FORK MOKELUMNE RIVER
SACRAMENTO CO
SAN JOAQUIN CO
WALNUT GROVE THORNTON RD
W WALNUT GROVE RD
J11
WALNUT GROVE RD (OLD LEVEE RD)
OLD THORNTON RD
CHARLES ST
LAUFFER
N LAMB RD
LAMB RD
STATEN ISLAND RD
N
GAS WELL RD
HIGHLINE RD
GATE
MEALER LN
WHYSE LN
RAILROAD AV
DEPOT LN
BROWNS AL
THEATER ST
BRIDGE ST
TYLER
GROVE
LIB
CORDOON ST
LORD ST
FS
miles 1 in. = 1900 ft.

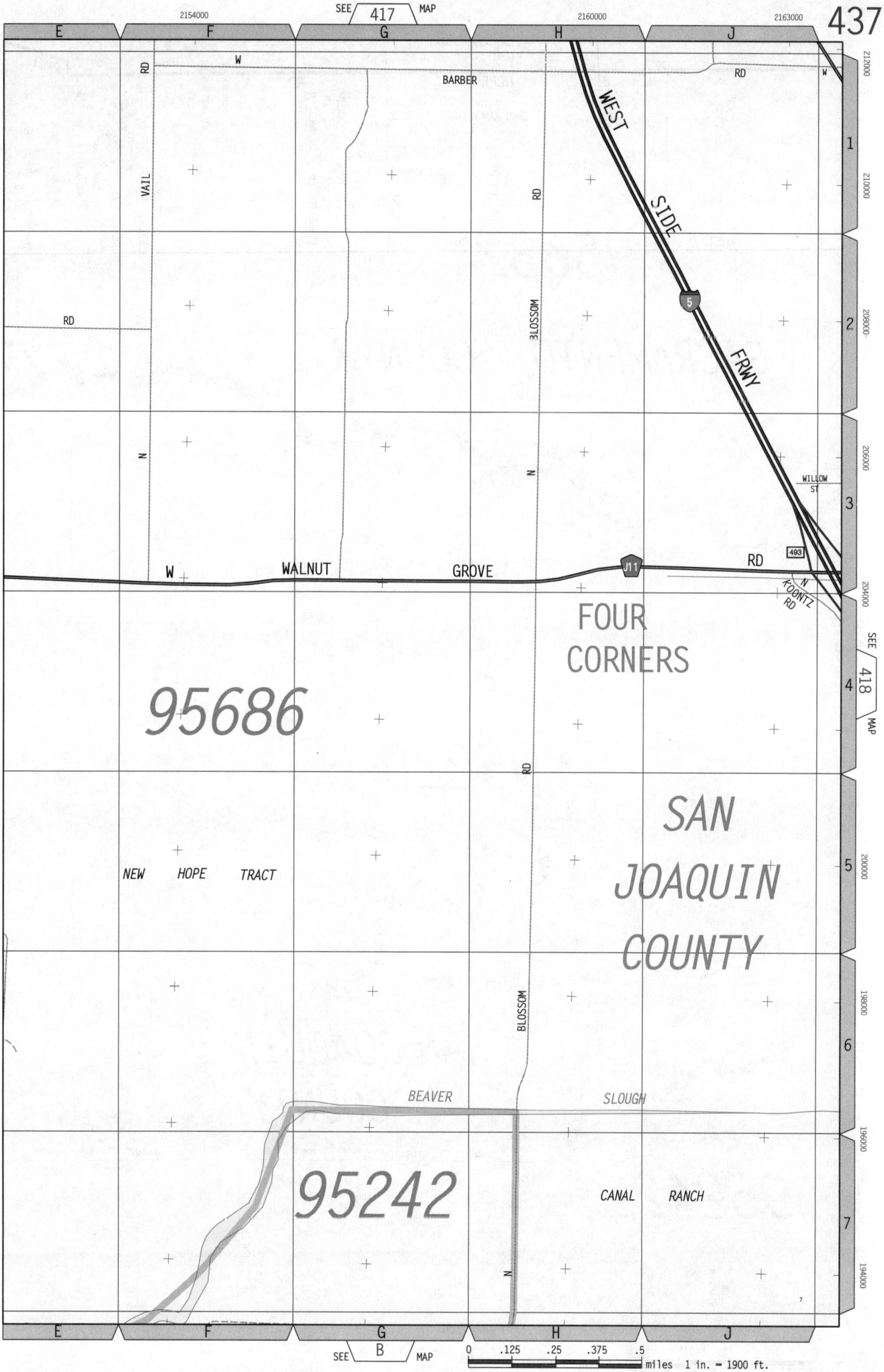
SEE 417 MAP
2154000
2160000
2163000
E
F
G
H
J
1
2
3
4
5
6
7
212000
210000
208000
206000
204000
200000
198000
196000
194000
W BARBER RD
W
VAIL RD
N
RD
WEST SIDE FRWY
5
N BLOSSOM RD
N BLOSSOM RD
WILLOW ST
493
W WALNUT GROVE RD
J11
N KOONTZ RD
FOUR CORNERS
SEE 418 MAP
95686
SAN JOAQUIN COUNTY
NEW HOPE TRACT
BEAVER SLOUGH
95242
CANAL RANCH
N
SEE B MAP
0 .125 .25 .375 .5 miles 1 in. = 1900 ft.

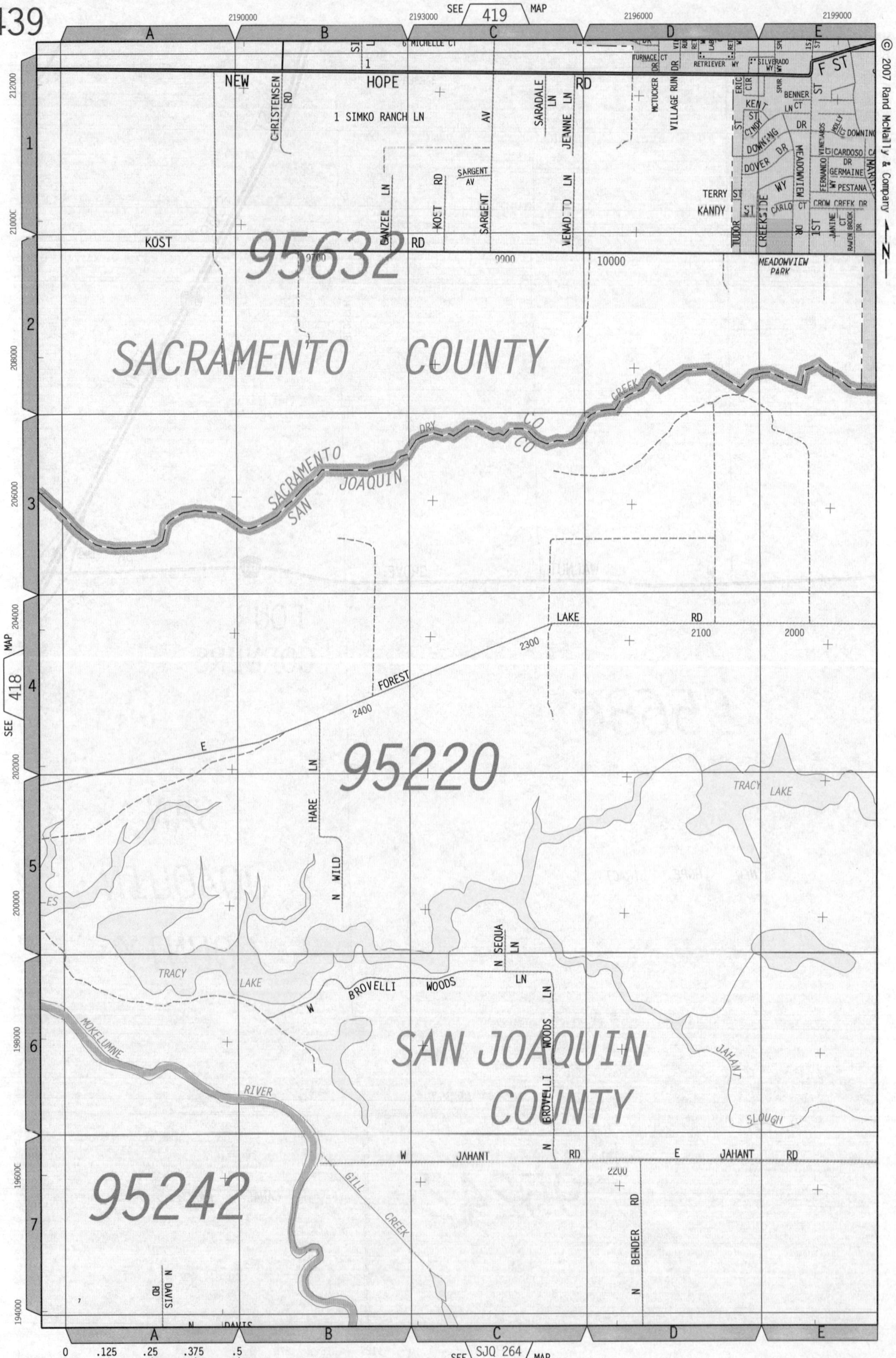
SEE 419 MAP
SEE 418 MAP
SEE SJQ 264 MAP
A
B
C
D
E
1
2
3
4
5
6
7
2190000
2193000
2196000
2199000
212000
210000
208000
206000
204000
202000
200000
198000
196000
194000
NEW HOPE RD
CHRISTENSEN RD
1 SIMKO RANCH LN
6 MICHELLE CT
SARADALE LN
JEANNE LN
MCTUCKER DR
VILLAGE RUN DR
TURNACE CT
RETRIEVER WY
SILVERADO WY
F ST
ERIC CIR
SPUR
BENNER ST
KENT LN CT
CINDY ST
DOWNING DR
DOVER DR
MEADOWVIEW DR
VINEYARDS
MOLLY CT
DOWNING
CARDOSO CT
FERNANDO WY
GERMAINE DR
PESTANA
CROW CREEK DR
CARLO CT
1ST
JANINE CT
RAVEN BROOK DR
TERRY ST
KANDY ST
TUDOR ST
CREEKSIDE WY
SARGENT AV
SARGENT
GANZER LN
KOST RD
VENADITO LN
KOST RD
9700
9900
10000
MEADOWVIEW PARK
95632
SACRAMENTO COUNTY
DRY CREEK
SACRAMENTO SAN JOAQUIN CO
LAKE RD
2100
2000
2300
E FOREST
2400
HARE LN
95220
TRACY LAKE
N WILD
N SEQUA LN
TRACY LAKE
W BROVELLI WOODS LN
N BROVELLI WOODS LN
MOKELUMNE RIVER
SAN JOAQUIN COUNTY
JAHANT SLOUGH
W JAHANT RD
E JAHANT RD
2200
GILL CREEK
95242
N BENDER RD
N DAVIS RD
N DAVIS
0 .125 .25 .375 .5 miles 1 in. = 1900 ft.

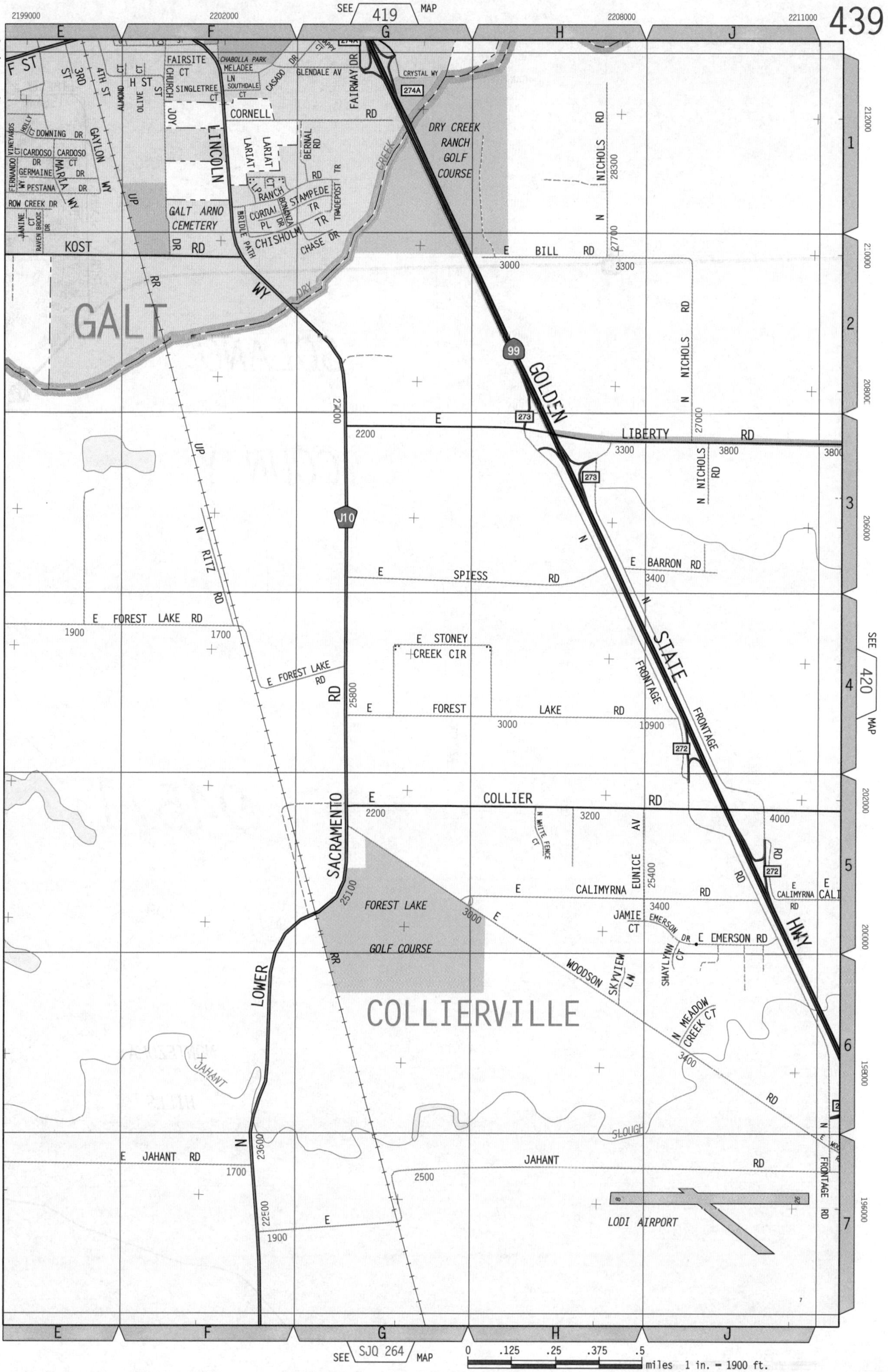
SEE 419 MAP
SEE 420 MAP
SEE SJQ 264 MAP
2199000
2202000
2208000
2211000
E
F
G
H
J
1
2
3
4
5
6
7
212000
210000
208000
206000
202000
200000
198000
196000
F ST
3RD ST
4TH ST
H ST
ALMOND
OLIVE ST
CHURCH
JOY
FAIRSITE CT
SINGLETREE CT
CHABOLLA PARK
MELADEE LN
SOUTHDALE CT
CASADO DR
CORNELL
GLENDALE AV
FAIRWAY DR
CRYSTAL WY
274A
RD
DOWNING DR
VINEYARDS CT
CARDOSO
CARDOSO CT
FERNANDO WY
GERMAINE DR
MARIA DR
PESTANA DR
GAYLON WY
ROW CREEK DR
JANINE CT
RAVEN BROOK DR
LINCOLN WY
LARIAT
LARIAT CT
LARIAT LP
BERNAL RD
RANCH
STAMPEDE TR
TRADEPOST TR
GALT ARNO CEMETERY
BRIDLE PATH
CORRAL PL
BONANZA DR
CHISHOLM TR
CHASE DR
KOST DR RD
UP RR
DRY CREEK RANCH GOLF COURSE
DRY CREEK
N NICHOLS RD
28300
27700
E BILL RD
3000
3300
GALT
99
GOLDEN STATE HWY
N NICHOLS RD
27000
2200
E LIBERTY RD
273
3300
3800
N NICHOLS RD
J10
N RITZ RD
N FRONTAGE
E BARRON RD
3400
E SPIESS RD
E FOREST LAKE RD
1900
1700
E STONEY CREEK CIR
E FOREST LAKE RD
25800
E FOREST LAKE RD
3000
10900
FRONTAGE
272
E COLLIER RD
2200
3200
4000
N WHITE FENCE CT
EUNICE AV
25400
SACRAMENTO RD
25100
E CALIMYRNA RD
3400
JAMIE CT
EMERSON DR
E EMERSON RD
E CALIMYRNA RD
FOREST LAKE GOLF COURSE
3800
E WOODSON RD
SKYVIEW LN
SHAYLYNN CT
COLLIERVILLE
N MEADOW CREEK CT
3400
LOWER
JAHANT
SLOUGH
N 23600
E JAHANT RD
1700
JAHANT RD
2500
N FRONTAGE RD
22600
E
1900
LODI AIRPORT
0 .125 .25 .375 .5
miles 1 in. = 1900 ft.

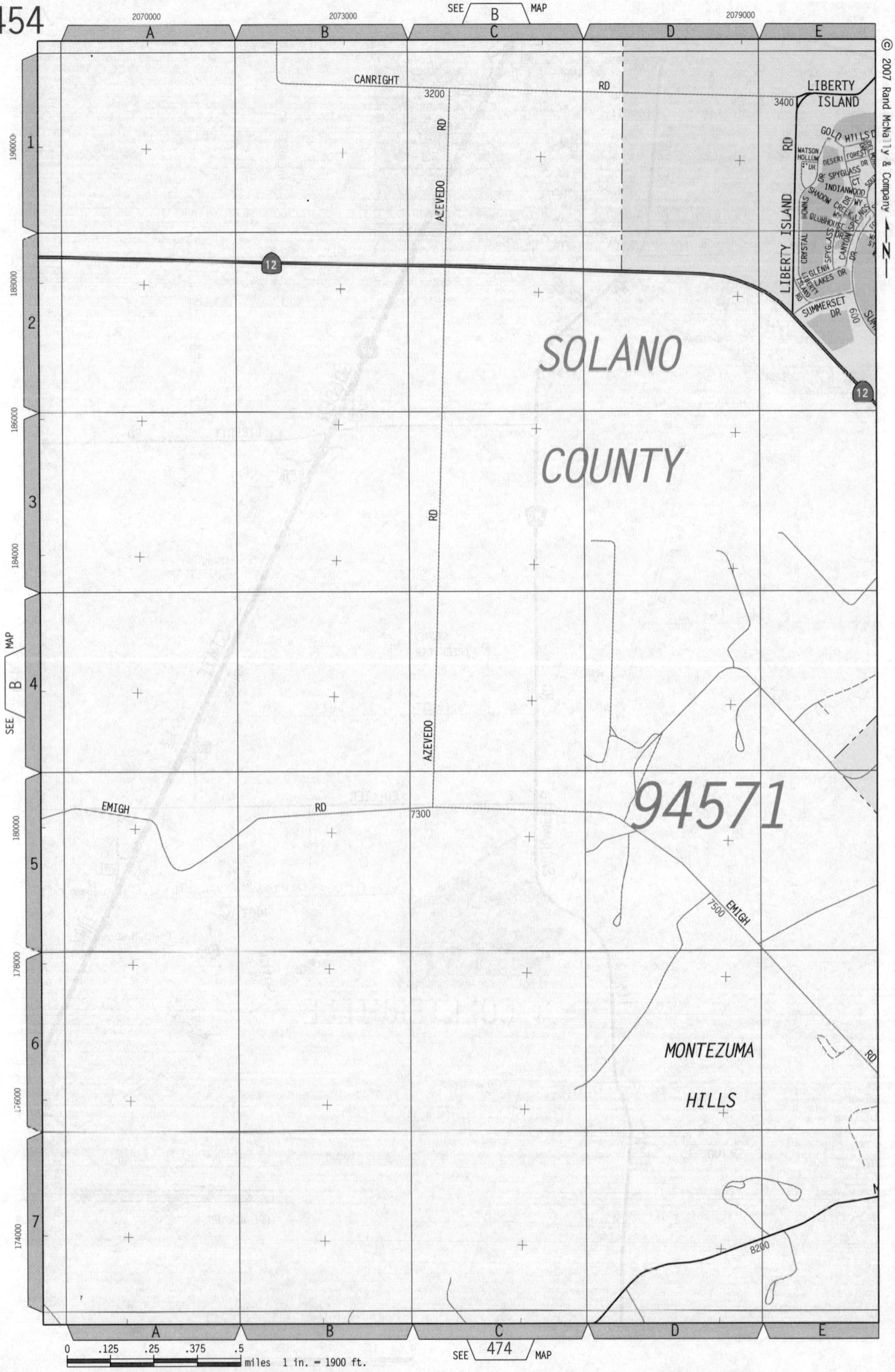
SACRAMENTO CO.
SEE B MAP
2070000
2073000
2079000
A
B
C
D
E
1
2
3
4
5
6
7
190000
188000
186000
184000
180000
178000
176000
174000
CANRIGHT
RD
3200
AZEVEDO
RD
LIBERTY
ISLAND
3400
LIBERTY ISLAND
RD
GOLD HILLS
WATSON
HOLLOW
DR
DESERT
FOREST
SPYGLASS
DR
CT
INDIANWOOD
SHADOW
CREEK
WY
CLUBHOUSE
CRYSTAL
SPYGLASS
CANYON
GLENN
LAKES DR
SUMMERSET
DR
600
12
SOLANO
COUNTY
RD
AZEVEDO
EMIGH
RD
7300
94571
7500
EMIGH
MONTEZUMA
HILLS
RD
8200
SEE 474 MAP
0
.125
.25
.375
.5
miles 1 in. = 1900 ft.

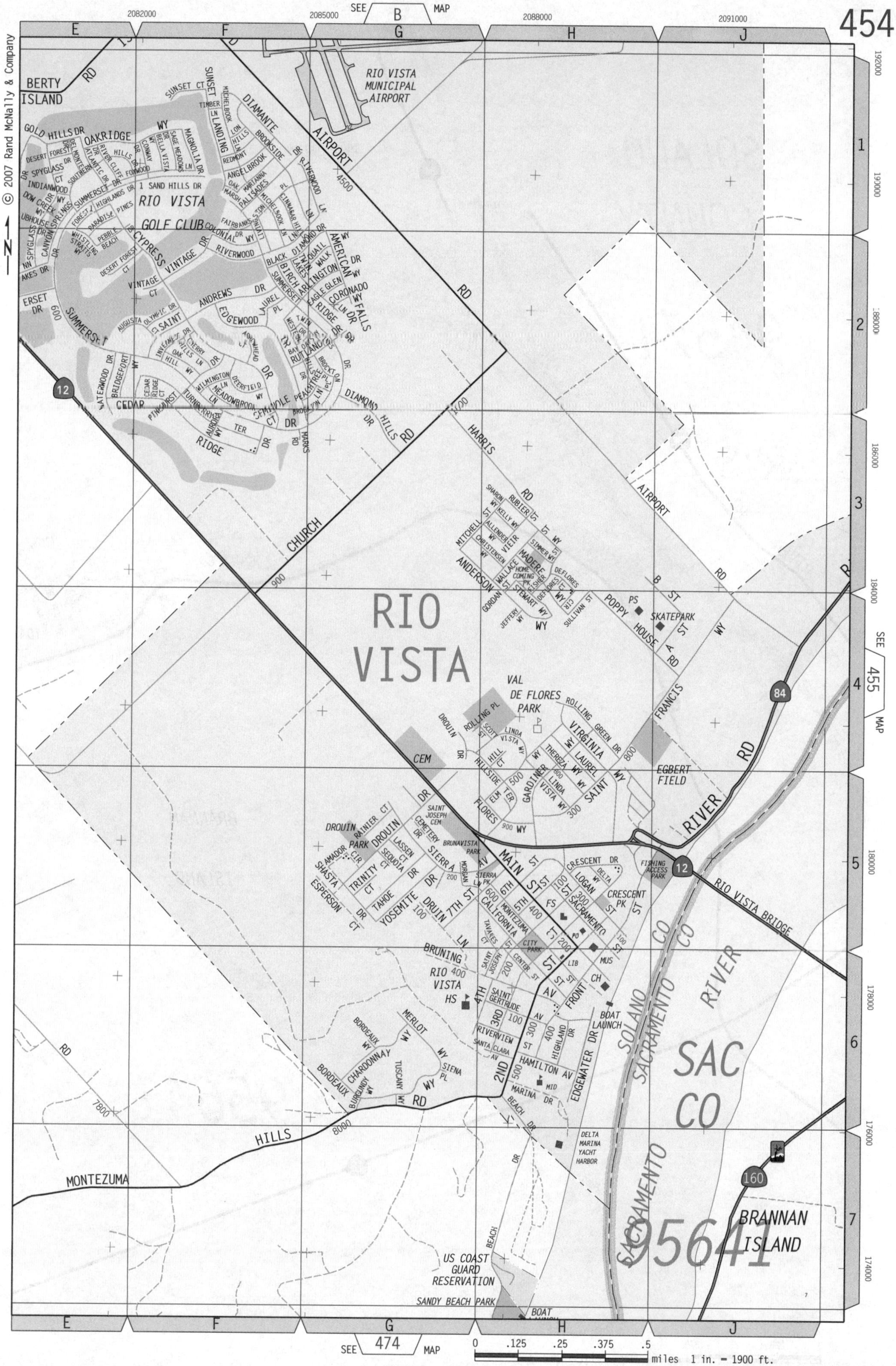
SEE B MAP
SEE 455 MAP
SEE 474 MAP
E
F
G
H
J
1
2
3
4
5
6
7
2082000
2085000
2088000
2091000
192000
190000
188000
186000
184000
180000
178000
176000
174000
RIO VISTA
RIO VISTA MUNICIPAL AIRPORT
RIO VISTA GOLF CLUB
VAL DE FLORES PARK
EGBERT FIELD
CEM
SAINT JOSEPH CEM
BRUNAVISTA PARK
DROUIN PARK
FISHING ACCESS PARK
CRESCENT PK
CITY PARK
SIERRA PK
RIO VISTA HS
PS
SKATEPARK
FS
PO
LIB
MUS
CH
MID
BOAT LAUNCH
DELTA MARINA YACHT HARBOR
US COAST GUARD RESERVATION
SANDY BEACH PARK
BRANNAN ISLAND
SAC CO
SOLANO CO
SACRAMENTO CO
SACRAMENTO RIVER
RIO VISTA BRIDGE
95641
12
84
160
AIRPORT RD
CHURCH RD
RIVER RD
MONTEZUMA HILLS RD
DIAMOND HILLS DR
HARRIS RD
BERTY ISLAND RD
FRANCIS
POPPY HOUSE RD
MAIN ST
FRONT ST
2ND ST
4TH ST
7TH ST
6TH ST
BRUNING LN
CALIFORNIA ST
SACRAMENTO ST
CRESCENT DR
EDGEWATER DR
HAMILTON AV
HIGHLAND DR
RIVERVIEW ST
MARINA DR
BEACH DR
SAINT GERTRUDE AV
SAINT JOSEPH
SANTA CLARA
LOGAN ST
DROUIN DR
YOSEMITE DR
TRINITY CT
LASSEN CT
SEQUOIA DR
SIERRA AV
CEMETERY DR
SHASTA
ESPERSON DR
TAHOE CT
AMADOR CIR
RAINIER CT
FLORES
HILLSIDE TER
GARDINER WY
LINDA VISTA WY
THEREZA WY
LAUREL WY
VIRGINIA WY
SAINT
ROLLING GREEN DR
ROLLING PL
ANDERSON
MITCHELL ST
CHRISTENSEN
MADERE
DEFLORES
SULLIVAN ST
B ST
A ST
BORDEAUX
CHARDONNAY
BURGUNDY
MERLOT WY
TUSCANY WY
SIENA PL
SUMMERSET
CYPRESS
VINTAGE DR
RIVERWOOD DR
ANDREWS DR
EDGEWOOD
SAINT
CEDAR RIDGE
OAKRIDGE
SUNSET CT
DIAMANTE
BROOKSIDE
AMERICAN
CORONADO
RUTLAND DR
PEACHTREE
900
800
500
300
100
200
400
600
4500
7800
8000
0
.125
.25
.375
.5
miles 1 in. = 1900 ft.

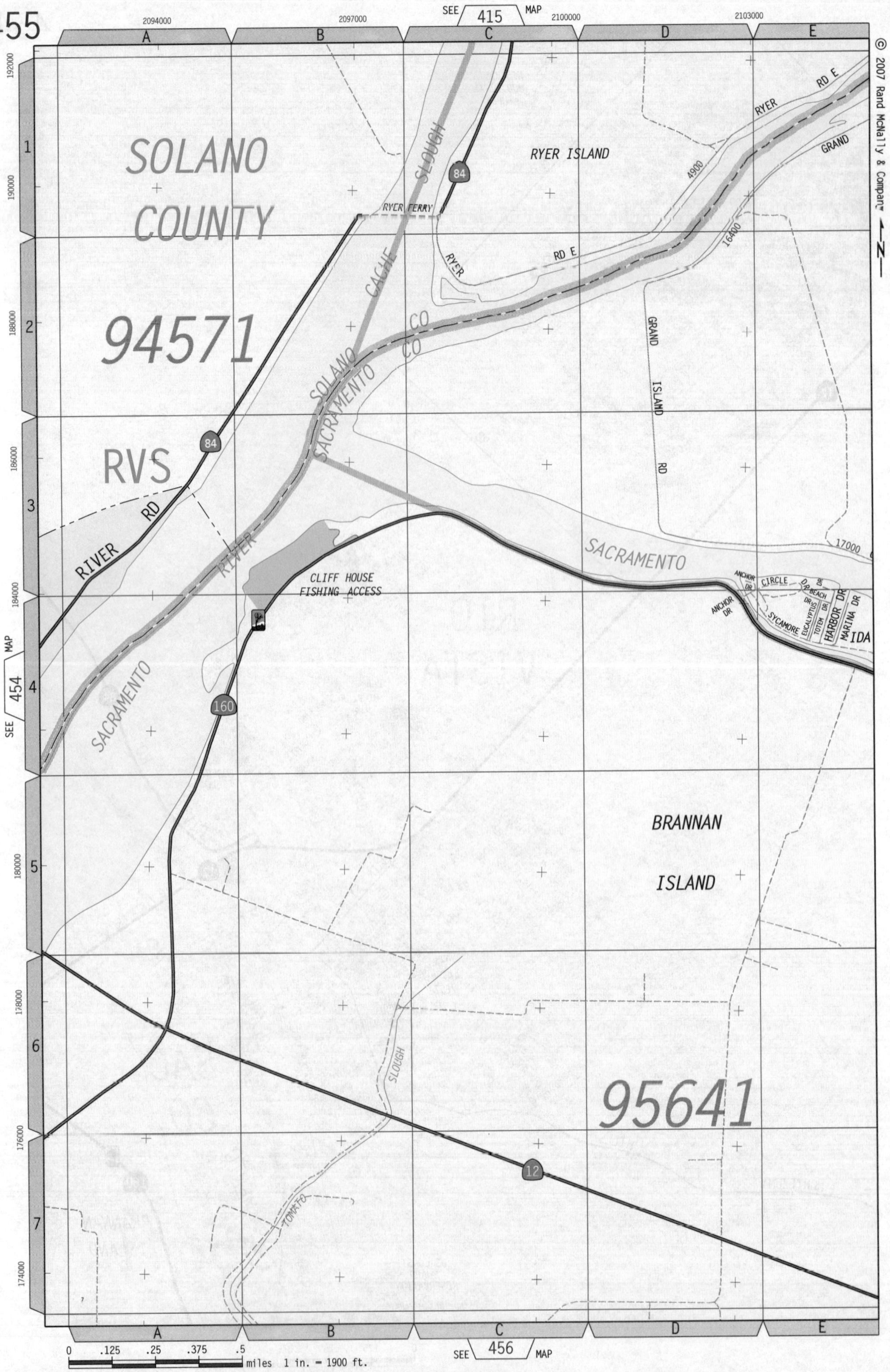
SEE 415 MAP
SEE 454 MAP
SEE 456 MAP
2094000
2097000
2100000
2103000
192000
190000
188000
186000
184000
180000
178000
176000
174000
A
B
C
D
E
1
2
3
4
5
6
7
SOLANO COUNTY
94571
RVS
95641
RYER ISLAND
BRANNAN ISLAND
CACHE SLOUGH
RYER FERRY
RYER RD E
GRAND ISLAND RD
RIVER RD
SACRAMENTO RIVER
SACRAMENTO
SOLANO CO
SACRAMENTO CO
CLIFF HOUSE FISHING ACCESS
TOMATO SLOUGH
ANCHOR DR
CIRCLE DR
BEACH DR
SYCAMORE
EUCALYPTUS DR
TOTEM DR
HARBOR DR
MARINA DR
IDA
4900
16400
17000
84
160
12
© 2007 Rand McNally & Company
N
0 .125 .25 .375 .5 miles 1 in. = 1900 ft.

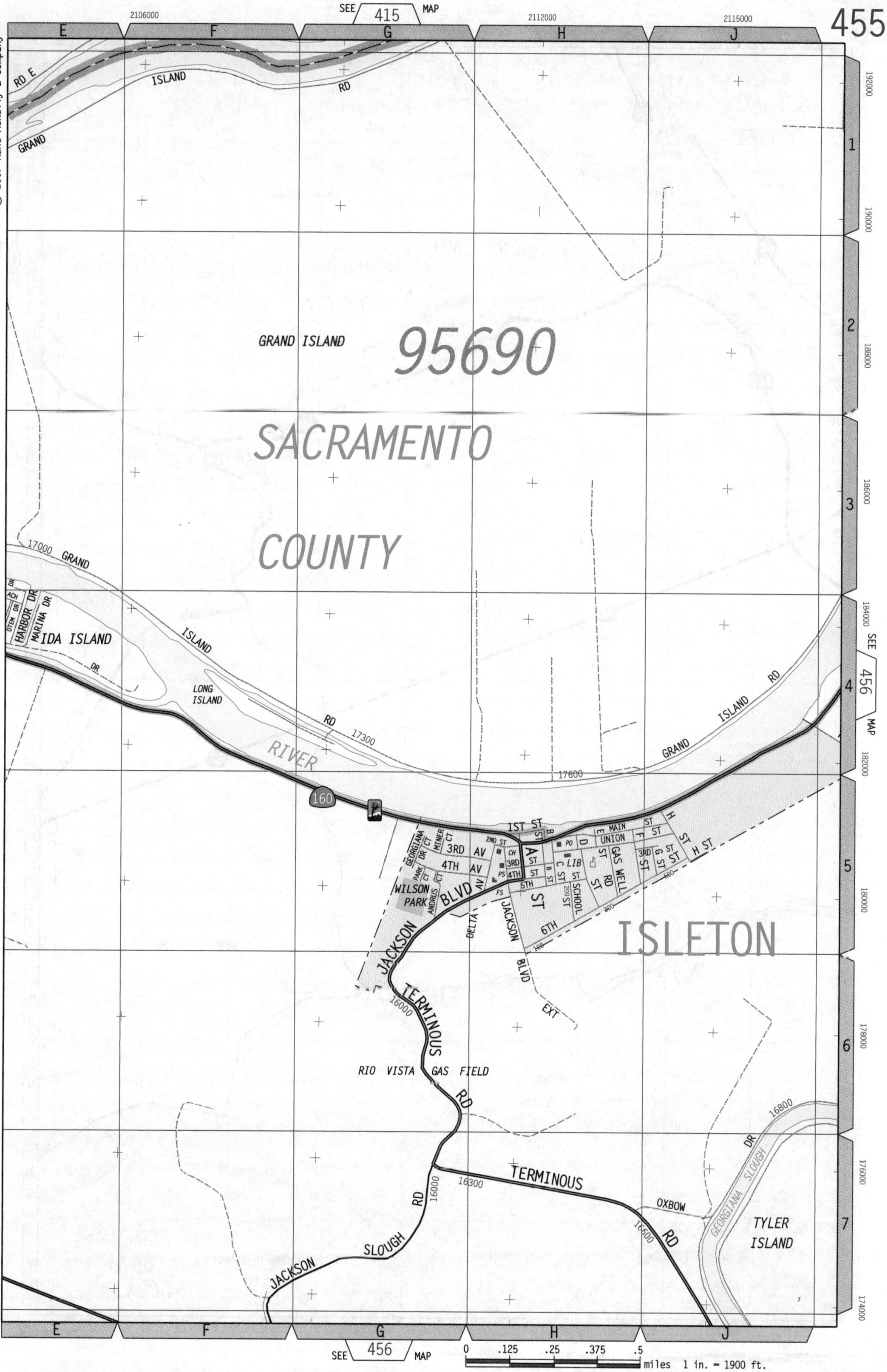
SEE 415 MAP
SEE 456 MAP
SEE 456 MAP
2106000
2112000
2115000
192000
190000
188000
186000
184000
182000
180000
178000
176000
174000
E
F
G
H
J
1
2
3
4
5
6
7
95690
SACRAMENTO
COUNTY
GRAND ISLAND
ISLETON
RIVER
GRAND ISLAND RD
RD E
17000
17300
17600
IDA ISLAND
LONG ISLAND
HARBOR DR
MARINA DR
DR
160
1ST ST
MAIN ST
UNION ST
GAS WELL RD
SCHOOL ST
H ST
2ND ST
3RD AV
4TH AV
MINER CT
GEORGIANA DR
PARK CT
WILSON PARK
ANDRUS CT
JACKSON BLVD
DELTA AV
JACKSON BLVD EXT
A ST
B ST
C ST
D ST
E ST
F ST
G ST
6TH ST
5TH
4TH
3RD
CH
PS
FS
PO
LIB
TERMINOUS RD
16000
16300
16500
16800
RIO VISTA GAS FIELD
TERMINOUS
OXBOW
JACKSON SLOUGH RD
GEORGIANA SLOUGH DR
TYLER ISLAND
0
.125
.25
.375
.5
miles 1 in. = 1900 ft.

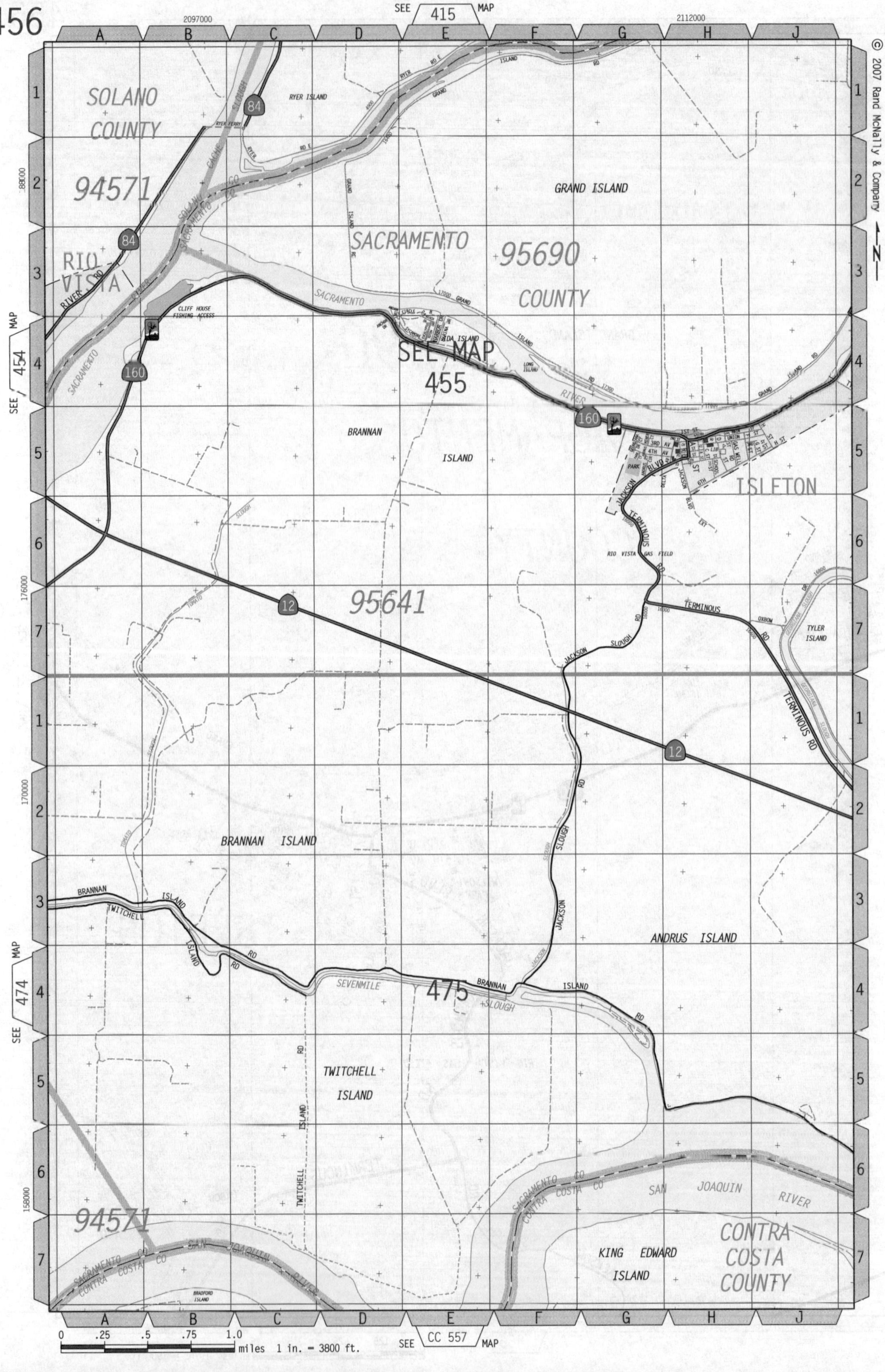
SEE 415 MAP
SEE 454 MAP
SEE 474 MAP
SEE CC 557 MAP
SEE MAP 455
475
2097000
2112000
188000
176000
170000
158000
SOLANO COUNTY
94571
RIO VISTA
RYER ISLAND
GRAND ISLAND
SACRAMENTO COUNTY
95690
CLIFF HOUSE FISHING ACCESS
BRANNAN ISLAND
ISLETON
RIO VISTA GAS FIELD
95641
TERMINOUS RD
JACKSON SLOUGH RD
TYLER ISLAND
OXBOW
ANDRUS ISLAND
SEVENMILE
BRANNAN SLOUGH
TWITCHELL ISLAND
TWITCHELL ISLAND RD
SAN JOAQUIN RIVER
KING EDWARD ISLAND
CONTRA COSTA COUNTY
BRADFORD ISLAND
SACRAMENTO RIVER
miles 1 in. = 3800 ft.
0 .25 .5 .75 1.0

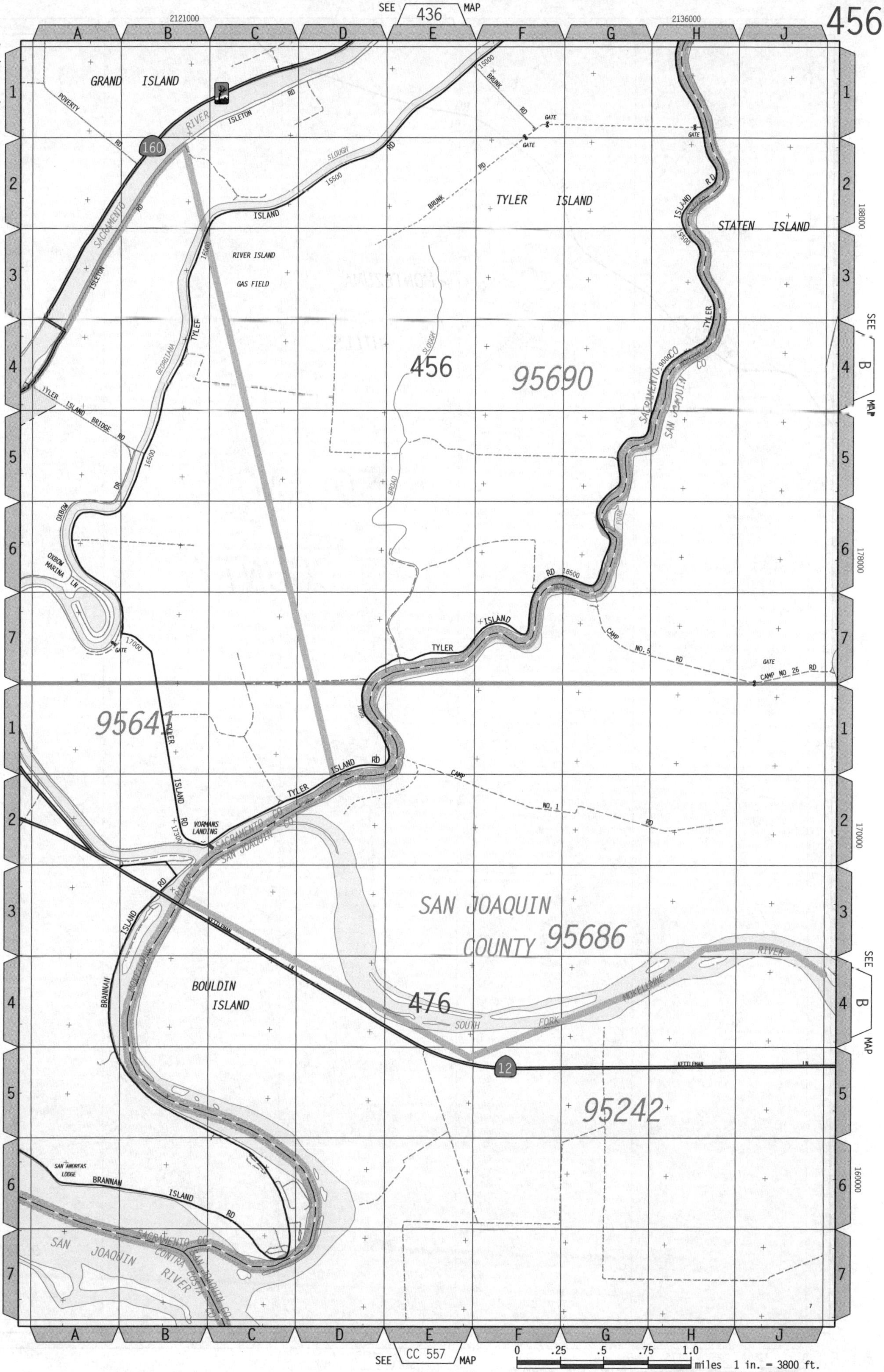
SEE 436 MAP
2121000
2136000
GRAND ISLAND
POVERTY RD
ISLETON RD
SACRAMENTO RIVER RD
160
SLOUGH
ISLAND
BRUNK RD
BRUNK PD
GATE
TYLER ISLAND
STATEN ISLAND
ISLAND RD
RIVER ISLAND
GAS FIELD
GEORGIANA
TYLER
SLOUGH
456
95690
SACRAMENTO CO
SAN JOAQUIN CO
TYLER ISLAND BRIDGE RD
OXBOW DR
OXBOW MARINA LN
BROAD
FORK
RD 18500
TYLER ISLAND
CAMP NO. 5 RD
CAMP NO. 26 RD
95641
TYLER ISLAND RD
CAMP NO. 1 RD
VORMANS LANDING
SACRAMENTO CO
SAN JOAQUIN CO
RIVER
SAN JOAQUIN COUNTY
95686
KETTLEMAN LN
BRANNAN ISLAND RD
BOULDIN ISLAND
476
SOUTH FORK
MOKELUMNE RIVER
12
95242
SAN ANDREAS LODGE
BRANNAN ISLAND RD
SAN JOAQUIN RIVER
SACRAMENTO CO
CONTRA COSTA CO
SAN JOAQUIN CO
SEE B MAP
188000
178000
170000
160000
SEE CC 557 MAP
0 .25 .5 .75 1.0 miles 1 in. = 3800 ft.

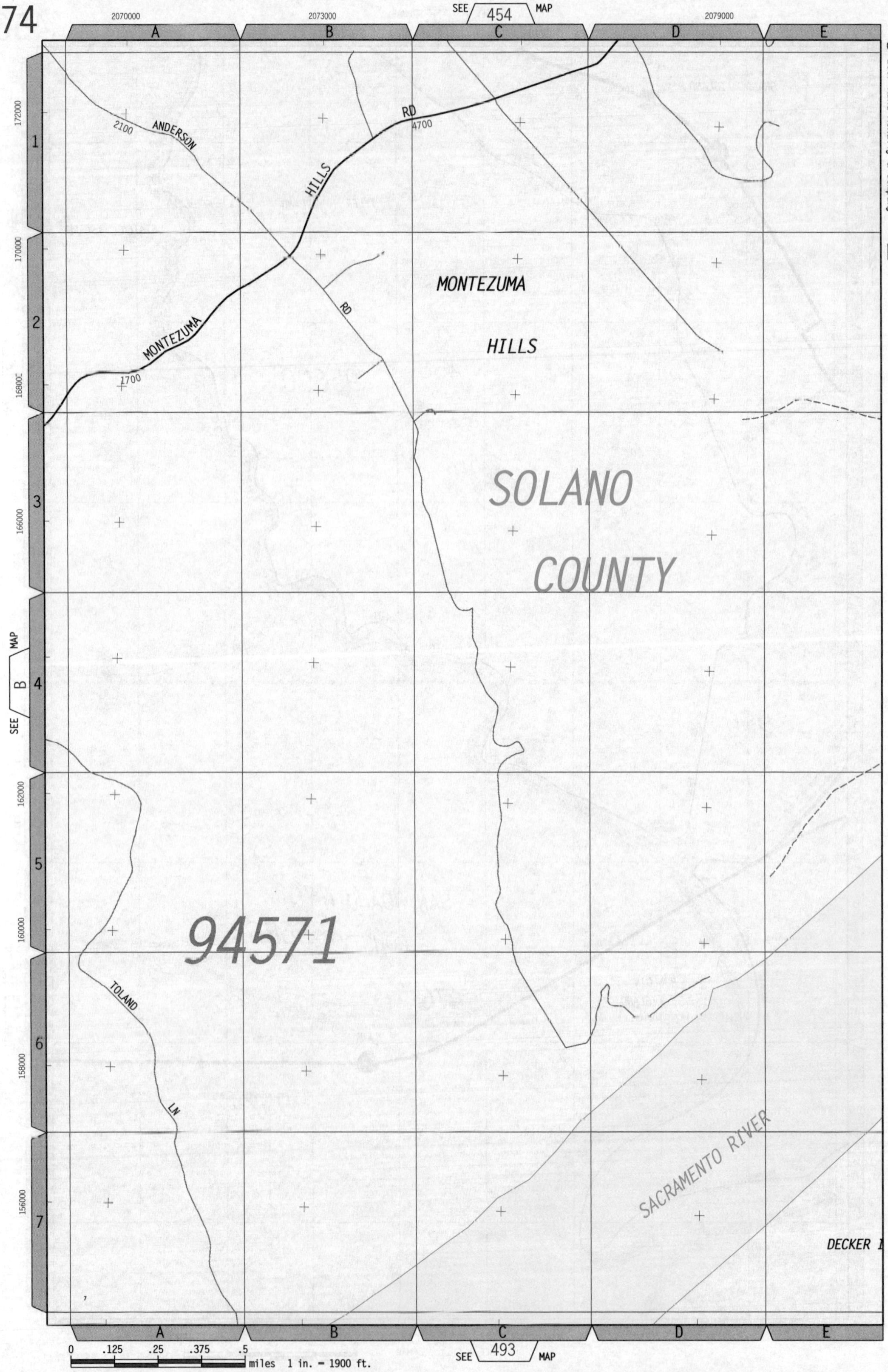
SEE 454 MAP
2070000
2073000
2079000
A
B
C
D
E
1
2
3
4
5
6
7
172000
170000
168000
166000
162000
160000
158000
156000
ANDERSON
2100
HILLS
RD
4700
MONTEZUMA
1700
MONTEZUMA
HILLS
SOLANO
COUNTY
SEE B MAP
94571
TOLAND
LN
SACRAMENTO RIVER
DECKER I
0 .125 .25 .375 .5 miles 1 in. = 1900 ft.
SEE 493 MAP

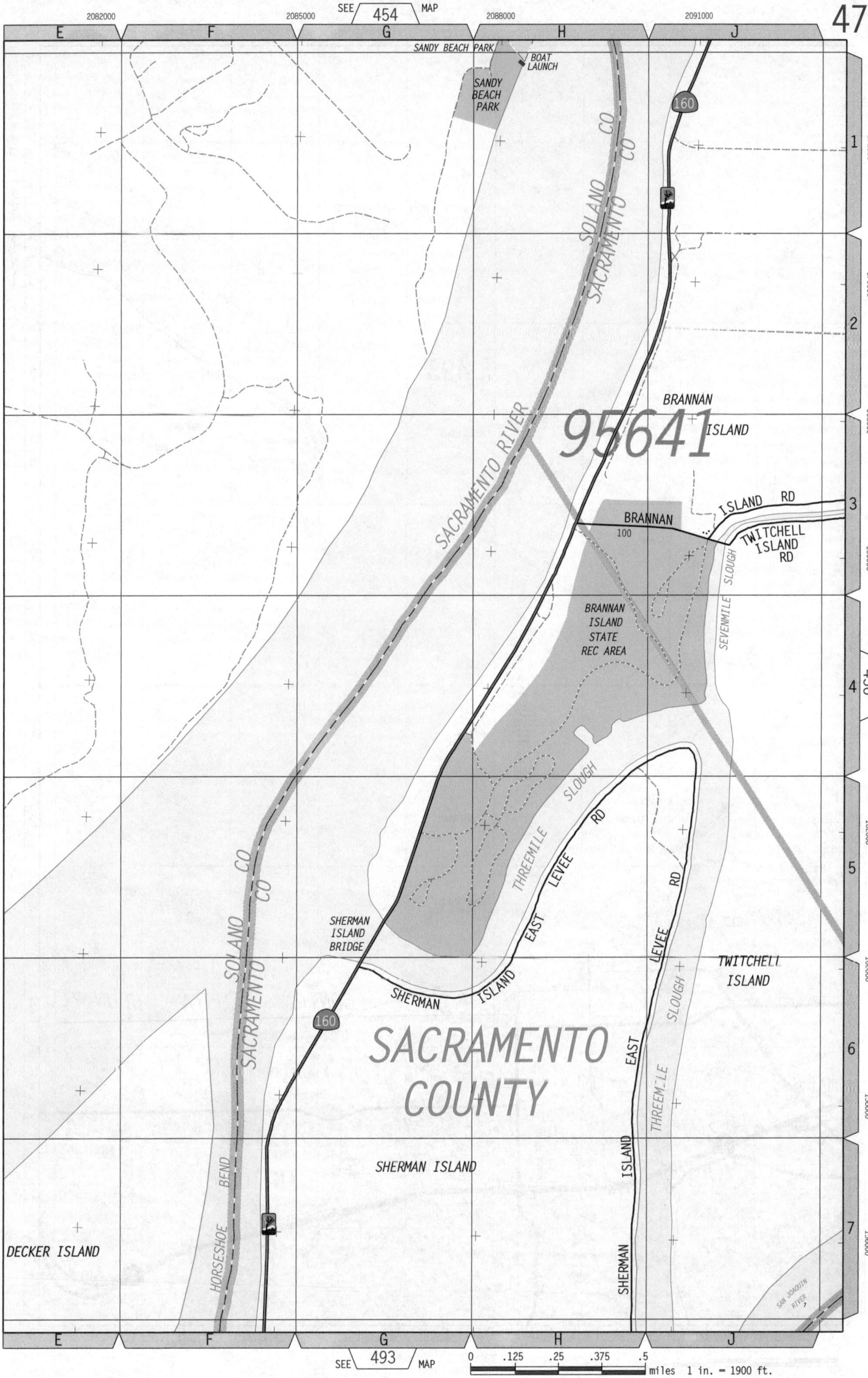

SEE 454 MAP
2082000
2085000
2088000
2091000
E
F
G
H
J
SANDY BEACH PARK
BOAT LAUNCH
SANDY BEACH PARK
160
SOLANO CO
SACRAMENTO CO
1
2
3
4
5
6
7
172000
170000
168000
166000
162000
160000
158000
156000
BRANNAN
ISLAND
95641
SACRAMENTO RIVER
BRANNAN
100
ISLAND RD
TWITCHELL ISLAND RD
BRANNAN ISLAND STATE REC AREA
SEVENMILE SLOUGH
SEE 456 MAP
THREEMILE SLOUGH
EAST LEVEE RD
SHERMAN ISLAND BRIDGE
SOLANO CO
SACRAMENTO CO
TWITCHELL ISLAND
SHERMAN ISLAND
SACRAMENTO COUNTY
EAST
THREEMILE SLOUGH
SHERMAN ISLAND
HORSESHOE BEND
DECKER ISLAND
SHERMAN ISLAND EAST LEVEE RD
SAN JOAQUIN RIVER
SEE 493 MAP
0 .125 .25 .375 .5
miles 1 in. = 1900 ft.

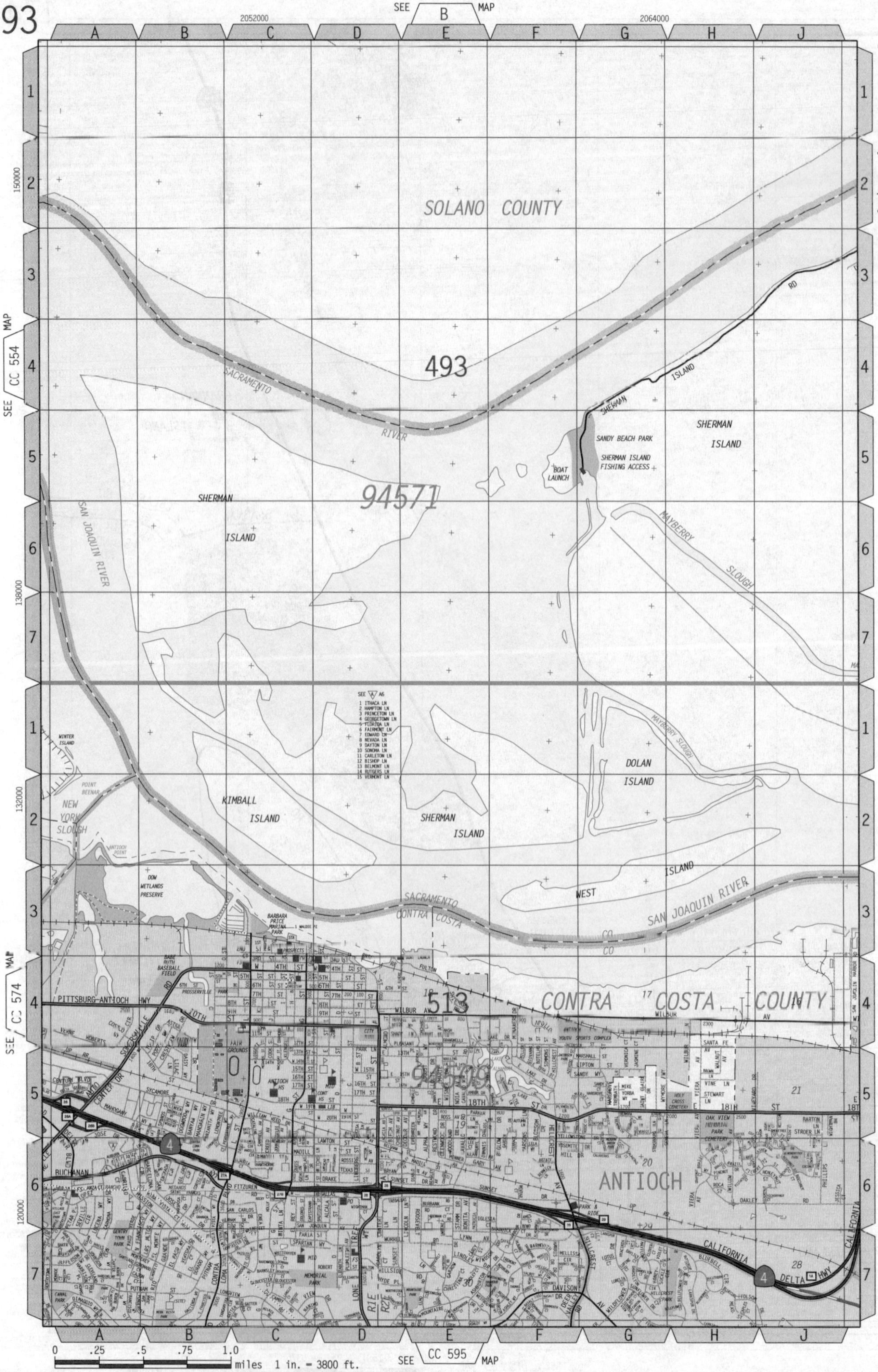
SEE B MAP
SEE CC 554 MAP
SEE CC 574 MAP
SEE CC 595 MAP
SOLANO COUNTY
CONTRA COSTA COUNTY
493
513
94571
94509
SACRAMENTO RIVER
SAN JOAQUIN RIVER
SHERMAN ISLAND
SANDY BEACH PARK
SHERMAN ISLAND FISHING ACCESS
BOAT LAUNCH
MAYBERRY SLOUGH
DOLAN ISLAND
KIMBALL ISLAND
WEST ISLAND
WINTER ISLAND
POINT BEENAR
NEW YORK SLOUGH
ANTIOCH POINT
DOW WETLANDS PRESERVE
BARBARA PRICE MARINA PARK
BABE RUTH BASEBALL FIELD
FAIR GROUNDS
PITTSBURG-ANTIOCH HWY
WILBUR AV
ANTIOCH
18TH ST
SUNSET DR
DELTA HWY
CALIFORNIA
BUCHANAN
HOLY CROSS CEMETERY
OAK VIEW MEMORIAL PARK CEMETERY
MEMORIAL PARK
ANTIOCH YOUTH SPORTS COMPLEX
SEE A6
1 ITHACA LN
2 HAMPTON LN
3 PRINCETON LN
4 GEORGETOWN LN
5 FLORIDA LN
6 FAIRMONT LN
7 EDWARD LN
8 NEVADA LN
9 DAYTON LN
10 SONOMA LN
11 CARLETON LN
12 BISHOP LN
13 BELMONT LN
14 RUTGERS LN
15 VERMONT LN
2052000
2064000
150000
138000
132000
120000
0 .25 .5 .75 1.0 miles 1 in. = 3800 ft.

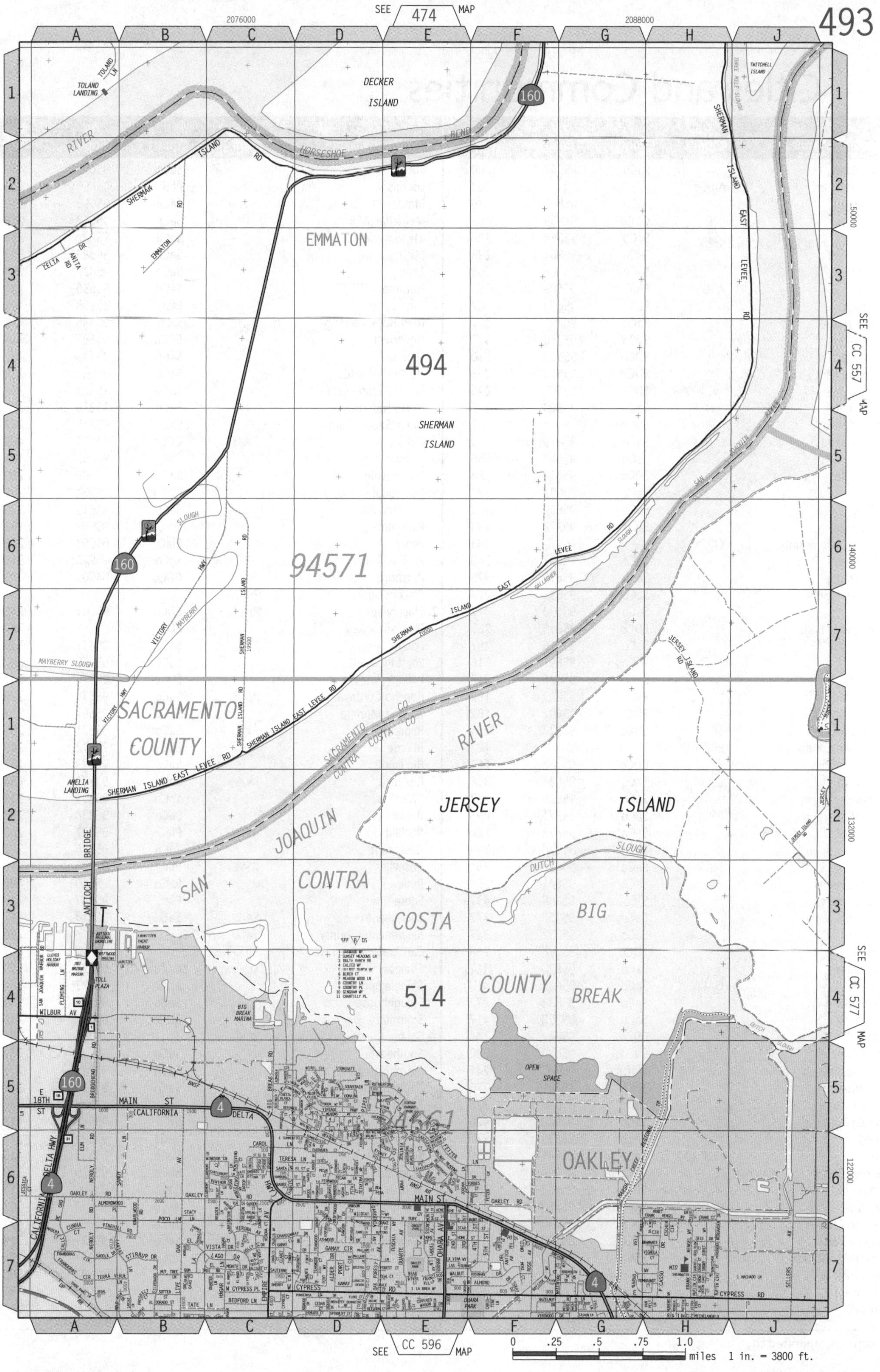
SEE 474 MAP
SEE CC 557 MAP
SEE CC 577 MAP
SEE CC 596 MAP
2076000
2088000
150000
140000
132000
122000
TOLAND LANDING
TOLAND LN
DECKER ISLAND
RIVER
HORSESHOE
BEND
160
SHERMAN ISLAND RD
EMMATON RD
EMMATON
EELTA DR
ANITA DR
THREE MILE SLOUGH
TWITCHELL ISLAND
SHERMAN ISLAND EAST LEVEE RD
494
SHERMAN ISLAND
SLOUGH
VICTORY HWY
MAYBERRY
MAYBERRY SLOUGH
SHERMAN ISLAND RD
94571
GALLAGHER SLOUGH
SAN JOAQUIN RIVER
JERSEY ISLAND RD
SACRAMENTO COUNTY
CONTRA COSTA CO
SACRAMENTO CO
AMELIA LANDING
ANTIOCH BRIDGE
JERSEY ISLAND
SAN JOAQUIN
DUTCH SLOUGH
CONTRA COSTA COUNTY
BIG BREAK
514
OPEN SPACE
BIG BREAK MARINA
TOLL PLAZA
WILBUR AV
BRIDGEHEAD RD
E 18TH ST
MAIN ST
(CALIFORNIA DELTA HWY)
BNSF
4
OAKLEY
CALIFORNIA DELTA HWY
OAKLEY RD
MAIN ST
CYPRESS RD
BIG BREAK RD
EMPIRE AV
OHARA AV
1.0 miles 1 in. = 3800 ft.

Cities and Communities

Community Name	Abbr.	County	ZIP Code	Map Page
Alder Creek		SaCo	95742	280
-- Amador County	AmCo			362
Antelope		SaCo	95843	238
* Antioch	ANT	CCCo	94509	493
Arden		SaCo	95864	298
Arden Oaks		SaCo	95864	298
Arden Park		SaCo	95864	298
* Auburn	AUB	PlaC	95603	182
Bowman		PlaC	95603	162
Bridge House		SaCo	95683	342
Bruceville		SaCo	95758	397
Bucks Bar		EDCo	95667	286
Cameron Park		EDCo	95672	263
Camino		EDCo	95709	246
Carmichael		SaCo	95608	279
Cedar Grove		EDCo		247
* Citrus Heights	CITH	SaCo	95610	259
Clarksburg		YoCo	95612	356
Clarksville		EDCo	95762	282
Clay		SaCo	95632	381
Coffing		SaCo	95829	339
Collierville		SJCo	95220	439
-- Contra Costa County	CCCo			493
Cosumnes		SaCo	95693	360
Courtland		SaCo	95615	375
Del Paso Heights		SaCo	95838	277
Delta		SaCo	95690	417
Diamond Springs		EDCo	95619	265
Downtown		SaCo	95816	297
Dyke		YoCo	95691	316
East City		SaCo	95826	318
Edgewood		PlaC	95603	162
Elders Corners		PlaC	95602	162
El Dorado		EDCo	95623	265
-- El Dorado County	EDCo			182
El Dorado Hills		EDCo	95762	262
* Elk Grove	ELKG	SaCo	95624	358
Elverta		SaCo	95626	237
Emmaton		SaCo	94571	493
Fair Oaks		SaCo	95628	280
Florin		SaCo	95828	338
* Folsom	FOLS	SaCo	95630	261
Foothill Farms		SaCo	95841	259
Four Corners		SJCo	95686	437
Franklin		SaCo	95758	377
Freeport		SaCo	95832	337
Fresh Pond		EDCo	95726	248
Fruitridge		SaCo	95820	317
* Galt	GALT	SaCo	95632	419
Gardenland		SaCo	95833	277
Glannvale		SaCo	95758	417
Gold Hill		EDCo	95667	244
Gold River		SaCo	95670	280
Granite Bay		PlaC	95746	241
Greenhaven		SaCo	95831	316
Hagginwood		SaCo	95838	278
Herald		SaCo	95638	420
Hood		SaCo	95639	377
* Isleton	ISLE	SaCo	95641	455
Kelsey		EDCo	95634	225
Kingsville		EDCo	95623	264
Laguna		SaCo	95758	358
Laguna Creek		SaCo	95758	358
Laguna West		SaCo	95758	357
Lake Hills Estates		EDCo	95762	242
Land Park		SaCo	95818	317
La Riviera		SaCo	95826	299
* Lincoln	LNCN	PlaC	95648	179
Locke		SaCo	95690	417
* Loomis	LMS	PlaC	95650	200
Mather		SaCo	95655	319
McClellan AFB		SaCo	95652	258
Meadowview		SaCo	95822	337
Michigan Bar		SaCo	95683	342
Mills		SaCo	95827	299
Natoma		SaCo	95630	281
Newcastle		PlaC	95658	181
New Hope Landing		SJCo	95686	437
Newtown		EDCo	95667	246
Nimbus		SaCo	95742	280
North Highlands		SaCo	95660	258
North Laguna Creek		SaCo	95823	358
North Natomas		SaCo	95836	256
North Sacramento		SaCo	95815	277
* Oakley	OAKL	CCCo	94561	493
Ophir		PlaC	95658	181
Orangevale		SaCo	95662	260
Outingdale		EDCo	95684	286
Paintersville		SaCo	95615	375
Panorama		PlaC	95602	161
Penryn		PlaC	95663	201
Perkins		SaCo	95826	318
* Pittsburg	PIT	CCCo	94565	493
-- Placer County	PlaC			161
* Placerville	PLCR	EDCo	95667	245
Pleasant Valley		EDCo		267
Pocket		SaCo	95831	336
Point Pleasant		SaCo	95758	397
Pollock Pines		EDCo	95726	248
* Rancho Cordova	RCCD	SaCo	95670	279
Rancho Murieta		SaCo	95683	322
Represa		SaCo	95671	261
Rescue		EDCo	95672	243
Rio Linda		SaCo	95673	257
* Rio Vista	RVIS	SolC	94571	454
Riverview		YoCo	95691	316
Robla		SaCo	95838	257
* Rocklin	RKLN	PlaC	95677	200
Rosemont		SaCo	95826	298
* Roseville	RSVL	PlaC	95678	219
Ryde		SaCo	95680	436
Sabre City		PlaC	95747	239
* Sacramento	SAC	SaCo	95814	297
-- Sacramento County	SaCo			236
-- San Joaquin County	SJCo			417
Sheldon		SaCo	95624	359
Shingle Springs		EDCo	95682	264
Sloughhouse		SaCo	95683	341
Smithflat		EDCo	92667	246
-- Solano County	SolC			454
Southeast		SaCo	95632	379
South Natomas		SaCo	95833	277
South Sacramento		SaCo	95828	318
-- Sutter County	SuCo			236
Thornton		SJCo	95686	418
Town & Country Village		SaCo	95821	278
Twin Cities		SaCo	95632	419
Vineyard		SaCo	95829	339
Vorden		SaCo	95690	415
Walltown		SaCo	95630	301
Walnut Grove		SaCo	95690	437
Walsh Station		SaCo	95827	319
* West Sacramento	WSAC	YoCo	95691	296
Wilton		SaCo	95693	360
-- Yolo County	YoCo			336

*Indicates incorporated city

List of Abbreviations

PREFIXES AND SUFFIXES	
AL	ALLEY
ARC	ARCADE
AV, AVE	AVENUE
AVCT	AVENUE COURT
AVD	AVENIDA
AVD D LA	AVENIDA DE LA
AVD D LOS	AVENIDA DE LOS
AVD DE	AVENIDA DE
AVD DE LAS	AVENIDA DE LAS
AVD DEL	AVENIDA DEL
AVDR	AVENUE DRIVE
AVEX	AVENUE EXTENSION
AV OF	AVENUE OF
AV OF THE	AVENUE OF THE
AVPL	AVENUE PLACE
BAY	BAY
BEND	BEND
BL, BLVD	BOULEVARD
BLCT	BOULEVARD COURT
BLEX	BOULEVARD EXTENSION
BRCH	BRANCH
BRDG	BRIDGE
BYPS	BYPASS
BYWY	BYWAY
CIDR	CIRCLE DRIVE
CIR	CIRCLE
CL	CALLE
CL DE	CALLE DE
CL DL	CALLE DEL
CL D LA	CALLE DE LA
CL D LAS	CALLE DE LAS
CL D LOS	CALLE DE LOS
CL EL	CALLE EL
CLJ	CALLEJON
CL LA	CALLE LA
CL LAS	CALLE LAS
CL LOS	CALLE LOS
CLTR	CLUSTER
CM	CAMINO
CM DE	CAMINO DE
CM DL	CAMINO DEL
CM D LA	CAMINO DE LA
CM D LAS	CAMINO DE LAS
CM D LOS	CAMINO DE LOS
CMTO	CAMINITO
CMTO DEL	CAMINITO DEL
CMTO D LA	CAMINITO DE LA
CMTO D LAS	CAMINITO DE LAS
CMTO D LOS	CAMINITO DE LOS
CNDR	CENTER DRIVE
COM	COMMON
COMS	COMMONS
CORR	CORRIDOR
CRES	CRESCENT
CRLO	CIRCULO
CRSG	CROSSING
CST	CIRCLE STREET
CSWY	CAUSEWAY
CT	COURT
CTAV	COURT AVENUE
CTE	CORTE
CTE D	CORTE DE
CTE DEL	CORTE DEL
CTE D LAS	CORTE DE LAS
CTO	CUT OFF
CTR	CENTER

CTST	COURT STREET
CUR	CURVE
CV	COVE
DE	DE
DIAG	DIAGONAL
DR	DRIVE
DRAV	DRIVE AVENUE
DRCT	DRIVE COURT
DRLP	DRIVE LOOP
DVDR	DIVISION DR
EXAV	EXTENSION AVENUE
EXBL	EXTENSION BOULEVARD
EXRD	EXTENSION ROAD
EXST	EXTENSION STREET
EXT	EXTENSION
EXWY	EXPRESSWAY
FOREST RT	FOREST ROUTE
FRWY	FREEWAY
FRY	FERRY
GDNS	GARDENS
GN, GLN	GLEN
GRN	GREEN
GRV	GROVE
HTS	HEIGHTS
HWY	HIGHWAY
ISL	ISLE
JCT	JUNCTION
LN	LANE
LNCR	LANE CIRCLE
LNDG	LANDING
LNDR	LAND DRIVE
LNLP	LANE LOOP
LP	LOOP
MNR	MANOR
MT	MOUNT
MTWY	MOTORWAY
MWCR	MEWS COURT
MWLN	MEWS LANE
NFD	NAT'L FOREST DEV
NK	NOOK
OH	OUTER HIGHWAY
OVL	OVAL
OVLK	OVERLOOK
OVPS	OVERPASS
PAS	PASEO
PAS DE	PASEO DE
PAS DE LA	PASEO DE LA
PAS DE LAS	PASEO DE LAS
PAS DE LOS	PASEO DE LOS
PAS DL	PASEO DEL
PASG	PASSAGE
PAS LA	PASEO LA
PAS LOS	PASEO LOS
PASS	PASS
PIKE	PIKE
PK	PARK
PKDR	PARK DRIVE
PKWY, PKY	PARKWAY
PL	PLACE
PLWY	PLACE WAY
PLZ, PZ	PLAZA
PT	POINT
PTAV	POINT AVENUE
PTH	PATH
PZ DE	PLAZA DE
PZ DEL	PLAZA DEL

PZ D LA	PLAZA DE LA
PZ D LAS	PLAZA DE LAS
PZWY	PLAZA WAY
RAMP	RAMP
RD	ROAD
RDAV	ROAD AVENUE
RDBP	ROAD BYPASS
RDCT	ROAD COURT
RDEX	ROAD EXTENSION
RDG	RIDGE
RDSP	ROAD SPUR
RDWY	ROAD WAY
RR	RAILROAD
RUE	RUE
RUE D	RUE D
RW	ROW
RY	RAILWAY
SKWY	SKYWAY
SQ	SQUARE
ST	STREET
STAV	STREET AVENUE
STCT	STREET COURT
STDR	STREET DRIVE
STEX	STREET EXTENSION
STLN	STREET LANE
STLP	STREET LOOP
ST OF	STREET OF
ST OF THE	STREET OF THE
STOV	STREET OVERPASS
STPL	STREET PLACE
STPM	STREET PROMENADE
STWY	STREET WAY
STXP	STREET EXPRESSWAY
TER	TERRACE
TFWY	TRAFFICWAY
THWY	THROUGHWAY
TKTR	TRUCK TRAIL
TPKE	TURNPIKE
TRC	TRACE
TRCT	TERRACE COURT
TR, TRL	TRAIL
TRWY	TRAIL WAY
TTSP	TRUCK TRAIL SPUR
TUN	TUNNEL
UNPS	UNDERPASS
VIA D	VIA DE
VIA DL	VIA DEL
VIA D LA	VIA DE LA
VIA D LAS	VIA DE LAS
VIA D LOS	VIA DE LOS
VIA LA	VIA LA
VW	VIEW
VWY	VIEW WAY
VIS	VISTA
VIS D	VISTA DE
VIS D L	VISTA DE LA
VIS D LAS	VISTA DE LAS
VIS DEL	VISTA DEL
WK	WALK
WY	WAY
WYCR	WAY CIRCLE
WYDR	WAY DRIVE
WYLN	WAY LANE
WYPL	WAY PLACE

DIRECTIONS	
E	EAST
KPN	KEY PENINSULA NORTH
KPS	KEY PENINSULA SOUTH
N	NORTH
NE	NORTHEAST
NW	NORTHWEST
S	SOUTH
SE	SOUTHEAST
SW	SOUTHWEST
W	WEST
BUILDINGS	
CH	CITY HALL
CHP	CALIFORNIA HIGHWAY PATROL
COMM CTR	COMMUNITY CENTER
CON CTR	CONVENTION CENTER
CONT HS	CONTINUATION HIGH SCHOOL
CTH	COURTHOUSE
FAA	FEDERAL AVIATION ADMIN
FS	FIRE STATION
HOSP	HOSPITAL
HS	HIGH SCHOOL
INT	INTERMEDIATE SCHOOL
JR HS	JUNIOR HIGH SCHOOL
LIB	LIBRARY
MID	MIDDLE SCHOOL
MUS	MUSEUM
PO	POST OFFICE
PS	POLICE STATION
SR CIT CTR	SENIOR CITIZENS CENTER
STA	STATION
THTR	THEATER
VIS BUR	VISITORS BUREAU
OTHER ABBREVIATIONS	
BCH	BEACH
BLDG	BUILDING
CEM	CEMETERY
CK	CREEK
CO	COUNTY
COMM	COMMUNITY
CTR	CENTER
EST	ESTATE
HIST	HISTORIC
HTS	HEIGHTS
LK	LAKE
MDW	MEADOW
MED	MEDICAL
MEM	MEMORIAL
MHP	MOBILE HOME PARK
MT	MOUNT
MTN	MOUNTAIN
NATL	NATIONAL
PKG	PARKING
PLGD	PLAYGROUND
RCH	RANCH
RCHO	RANCHO
REC	RECREATION
RES	RESERVOIR
RIV	RIVER
RR	RAILROAD
SPG	SPRING
STA	SANTA
VLG	VILLAGE
VLY	VALLEY
VW	VIEW

STREET
Block City ZIP Pg-Grid

A

A AV
11400 PlaC 95603 162-A3
A PKWY
4400 SaCo 95823 337-H1
A ST
- RVIS 94571 454-J4
- SaCo 95690 437-A1
- GALT 95632 419-E7
100 ISLE 95641 455-H5
200 WSAC 95605 297-A2
400 LNCN 95648 179-J3
600 ANT 94509 (513-D3 See Page 493)
1200 SAC 95814 297-E2
3500 SaCo 95660 258-G6
4100 SAC 95819 297-J4
4100 EDCo 95709 247-B4
4700 SAC 95819 298-A4
7300 SaCo 95823 338-A2
W A ST
9900 GALT 95632 419-D7
9900 SaCo 95632 419-D7
A&A RD
- PLCR 95667 245-C5
AARON DR
- RKLN 95765 200-D7
AARON WY
2100 SAC 95822 337-D1
ABACO RD
- WSAC 95691 316-C2
ABALINE WY
7700 SAC 95823 338-A4
ABBEY LN
- RSVL 95678 219-G5
ABBEY RD
- EDCo - 267-C5
3900 SAC 95826 318-C2
ABBEY HILL
4700 PlaC 95746 240-G5
ABBEYHILL RD
- LNCN 95648 179-D2
ABBEYTEALE CT
- FOLS 95630 281-J2
ABBEY WOOD CIR
- SAC 95823 338-B5
ABBINGTON WY
- SaCo 95843 239-B7
ABBOT CT
3000 RCCD 95670 299-F4
ABBOTSFORD PL
2300 EDCo 95762 242-C5
ABBOTT RD
2800 EDCo 95682 263-C4
5100 PlaC 95663 180-H7
5100 PlaC 95663 200-J1
ABBOTTFORD WY
10400 RCCD 95670 299-F4
ABBY CT
- RKLN 95765 200-D4
ABBY RD
- RKLN 95765 200-D4
ABEL RD
- EDCo 95619 266-C6
ABELIA CT
8300 SaCo 95662 260-C3
ABERDEEN CIR
1300 RSVL 95746 240-F4
ABERDEEN CT
100 RSVL 95746 240-F4
ABERDEEN LN
- LNCN 95648 179-D2
2400 EDCo 95762 262-E1
ABERDEEN WY
3800 SaCo 95821 278-H3
ABERFELDY WY
7200 SaCo 95842 259-C2
ABERNATHY LN
7900 SaCo 95628 280-D6
ABERT CT
9200 ELKG 95758 357-H5
ABIDING PL
7400 SAC 95823 337-G3
ABIERTO DR
15200 SaCo 95683 342-C3
ABIGAIL CT
4200 SaCo 95843 238-H6
ABILENE CIR
- RKLN 95765 199-H3
ABIN WY
5700 SAC 95823 357-J1
ABINGTON WY
10400 RCCD 95670 299-F4
ABISKO CT
8000 SaCo 95829 338-J6
ABLE CT
- SAC 95835 257-B6
ABLE WY
- SAC 95835 257-B6
ABOTO WY
3200 RCCD 95670 299-H4
ABRAHAM WY
4200 SaCo 95608 279-F2
ABRIGO WY
- ELKG 95757 378-B2
ABRIJO RD
4600 EDCo 95682 263-A6
ABROZO CT
100 FOLS 95630 261-E3
ABRUZZO CT
7200 ELKG 95757 358-B7
ACACIA AV
600 SAC 95815 277-H5
1200 SAC 95815 278-A5
1900 ANT 94509 (513-D5 See Page 493)
ACACIA CT
1300 RSVL 95661 240-B5
ACACIA WY
2800 PLCR 95667 245-E4
ACACIA WOODS CT
8600 SaCo 95843 238-G5
ACADEMY DR
- PLCR 95667 246-B5
ACADEMY WY
1700 SAC 95815 278-B4
ACADIA WY
3700 EDCo 95762 262-D7
ACAPELLA CIR
7900 SaCo 95843 238-H6
ACAPULCO WY
9300 ELKG 95624 358-H5
ACARI AV
1800 SAC 95835 257-C3
ACASO CT
7400 SaCo 95683 342-C3

E ACCESS RD
- SaCo 95758 337-G7
- SaCo 95758 357-G1
ACCLAIM CT
4800 SaCo 95842 259-A1
ACCLARO CT
4700 SaCo 95843 239-A6
ACCORD CT
4800 SaCo 95842 259-A1
ACCORDION WY
4300 RCCD 95742 320-E2
ACCRINGTON WY
- SAC 95823 357-J1
ACE CT
- SAC 95835 257-B5
ACER WY
6900 SaCo 95662 260-C2
ACERO CT
- SAC 95835 256-J5
- SAC 95835 257-A5
ACHATES CIR
9400 SaCo 95826 319-A2
ACHATES CT
9500 SaCo 95826 319-A1
ACHILLES CT
- EDCo 95762 262-B4
ACKERMAN WY
4800 SaCo 95628 260-D7
4800 SaCo 95628 280-D1
ACKERSON WY
8000 SaCo 95843 239-A6
ACKLAND CT
6200 CITH 95621 259-E4
ACKLETON WY
- RSVL 95661 220-E7
ACKLEY DR
- ELKG 95757 358-B7
ACMAR CT
- SAC 95823 337-J7
ACME AV
5200 SAC 95838 257-J6
E ACME ST
100 OAKL 94561 (514-E6 See Page 493)
W ACME ST
100 OAKL 94561 (514-E6 See Page 493)
ACOMA ST
2000 SAC 95815 277-G7
ACORN CT
3700 EDCo 95672 263-F2
ACORN DR
8200 PlaC 95746 241-D2
ACORN LN
100 EDCo 95630 202-J1
ACORN ST
1500 WSAC 95691 296-H5
ACORN WY
5200 SaCo 95608 299-B1
ACORN CREEK CT
8200 CITH 95610 240-D6
ACORN GLEN LN
7400 RSVL 95747 219-A4
ACORN GLEN LP
7200 RSVL 95747 219-A4
ACORN HILL CT
3900 EDCo 95667 265-C1
7200 SaCo 95673 257-H1
ACORN HILL RD
6600 EDCo 95667 265-B1
ACORN RANCH RD
- EDCo 95633 205-C2
ACORN RIDGE CIR
9000 ELKG 95758 358-A3
ACORN RIDGE CT
2200 FOLS 95630 262-B7
ACRE LN
3000 EDCo 95682 283-J1
ACROPOLIS ST
6400 ELKG 95758 358-A4
ACTON WY
900 GALT 95632 419-G3
3000 RSVL 95747 219-D6
ADA LN
5100 SAC 95838 257-J6
ADA WY
100 SAC 95819 298-B4
ADAGIO WY
7900 SaCo 95621 239-E6
ADAIR ST
400 SaCo 95626 237-H5
ADALIS DR
4900 SAC 95758 357-J1
ADAM CT
3300 EDCo 95762 262-D4
4700 RKLN 95677 220-E1
8000 PlaC 95746 241-E1
ADAMELLO WY
900 ELKG 95757 358-B7
ADAMS CT
- OAKL 94561 (514-E7 See Page 493)
3100 ANT 94509 (513-A7 See Page 493)
ADAMS DR
- RKLN 95765 219-G1
ADAMS LN
- EDCo 95667 266-H4
2200 SAC 95833 277-F7
ADAMS RD
3100 SaCo 95864 298-F4
ADAMS ST
9600 ELKG 95624 358-H6
ADAMS WY
900 PLCR 95667 245-G5
ADAMS ACRES
- PlaC 95650 221-C5
ADAMSON CT
1400 RSVL 95661 240-B3
ADAMSTOWN WY
8600 ELKG 95624 358-E1
ADAMSTOWNE WY
- SAC 95835 257-B5
ADANA CIR
5900 SaCo 95608 279-D2
ADARE WY
600 GALT 95632 419-E2
ADCOTE WY
- SaCo 95608 279-C4
ADDERLEY CT
100 FOLS 95630 261-F7
ADDIE AV
8100 SaCo 95828 338-D2
ADDINGTON CT
100 LNCN 95648 179-F4
6500 SaCo 95662 260-B4
ADDIS CT
- SAC 95835 257-C5

ADDISON WY
7500 SAC 95822 337-D3
7500 SAC 95832 337-D3
ADELAIDE PL
4600 EDCo 95762 262-D3
ADELAIDE WY
5200 SaCo 95841 279-B1
ADELANTE CT
9200 ELKG 95758 358-A4
ADELBERT WY
- ELKG 95624 358-D1
ADELE CT
7700 SaCo 95626 237-F7
ADELHEID WY
3900 SaCo 95821 278-H3
ADELINA WY
5100 SaCo 95608 279-A7
ADELINE PL
5100 ELKG 95757 377-H1
5100 ELKG 95757 397-H1
ADELPHI CT
- SAC 95825 298-C5
ADEN WY
8100 SaCo 95828 338-D6
ADIEU CT
4800 SaCo 95842 259-A2
ADIRONDACK WY
2800 SaCo 95827 299-C4
ADKINSON CT
- SAC 95835 257-A5
ADLER CIR
- SAC 95864 298-D6
ADMIRAL
7700 SaCo 95829 339-A2
ADMIRAL AV
6700 SaCo 95628 259-F7
ADMIRAL LN
7700 SaCo 95829 338-J4
ADOBE CT
2700 ANT 94509 (513-B6 See Page 493)
5500 RKLN 95765 220-B1
ADOBE RD
2000 EDCo 95667 244-J3
5500 RKLN 95765 220-B1
ADOBE CASA CT
7200 CITH 95621 259-G5
ADOBE CREEK WY
8900 ELKG 95758 357-J3
ADOBE SPRING WY
5500 ELKG 95758 357-J3
5800 ELKG 95758 358-A3
ADOBE VALLEY CT
8900 ELKG 95624 378-H2
ADONIS WY
1700 SaCo 95864 298-J1
ADORN CT
4900 SaCo 95842 259-A2
ADRIAN CT
- SAC 95833 277-C4
ADRIANA CT
- RSVL 95661 220-E6
ADRIANA PL
500 AUB 95603 182-D5
ADRIATIC WY
2700 SaCo 95826 298-J6
ADRIENNE CT
- RSVL 95747 199-B7
ADRIENNE DR
- RSVL 95747 199-B7
- RSVL 95747 219-B1
ADVANTAGE CT
- SAC 95834 256-J7
- SAC 95834 276-J1
ADVANTAGE WY
- SAC 95834 256-J7
AEGEAN CIR
7800 CITH 95610 259-J3
7800 CITH 95610 260-A4
AEGEAN DR
- EDCo 95762 262-B4
AEGINA CT
9100 ELKG 95758 357-H4
AEOLIA DR
100 AUB 95603 182-F1
AERIE CT
- RSVL 95661 220-D6
AERIE RD
- EDCo 95726 248-D4
AERO CT
3800 SaCo 95660 258-G6
AEROBEE AV
8900 SaCo 95628 260-F7
AEROJET RD
- FOLS 95742 280-H4
- SaCo 95742 281-B4
- SaCo 95742 280-H4
AERONAUTIC WY
9000 SaCo 95628 260-F7
AERONCA WY
3100 EDCo 95682 263-D4
AEROTECH CT
- RCCD 95742 300-B4
AETNA SPRINGS WY
- SAC 95834 276-H2
AFFIRMED WY
3600 SaCo 95608 279-B4
AFTON CT
- SAC 95823 357-J1
AGAPE CT
- EDCo 95667 286-G4
AGAPE LN
- EDCo 95619 286-F4
- EDCo 95667 286-F4
AGARD ST
- AUB 95603 182-E3
AGATE CT
4800 RKLN 95677 220-B2
4600 RKLN 95765 220-B2
5000 EDCo 95726 248-E3
AGATE WY
5300 SaCo 95608 259-E6
AGATE BEACH WY
- SaCo 95843 239-A7
- SaCo 95843 259-A1
AGATE CREEK CT
8900 ELKG 95758 357-H3
AGATHA WY
1000 SaCo 95825 298-D3
AGAVE WY
8700 ELKG 95624 358-G2
AGEE CT
- FOLS 95630 281-E1
AGENA CT
9200 SaCo 95826 298-J7
9200 SaCo 95826 299-A7
AGGREGATE CT
1100 PLCR 95667 245-H3

AGGREGATE WY
1100 PLCR 95667 245-H3
AGNELL CT
- SAC 95835 256-G6
AGNES CIR
10200 RCCD 95670 299-E1
AGNES ST
100 AUB 95603 182-E2
AGNETA CT
3600 ELKG 95758 357-F4
AGNEW CT
4500 SaCo 95864 298-J2
AGORA WY
- EDCo 95762 261-J2
- EDCo 95762 262-A2
AGOSTINI CIR
- FOLS 95630 281-D1
AGOURA CT
- SAC 95838 277-J2
AGRADAR DR
7400 SaCo 95683 342-C3
AGREE CT
4800 SaCo 95842 259-A2
AGRIA CT
10700 RCCD 95670 299-H4
AGRICULTURE LN
9600 SaCo 95827 319-B2
AGUA DULCE CT
4200 EDCo 95667 264-J2
AGUA VISTA
6400 SaCo 95683 322-C7
AGUILAR CT
3400 EDCo 95667 244-G6
AGUILAR LN
2100 PlaC 95663 201-A1
AGUILAR RD
5300 RKLN 95677 220-F4
5300 PlaC 95677 220-F4
6400 EDCo 95667 244-G6
AGUNDO ST
- SaCo 95626 237-F5
AGUSTAWOOD PL
7600 SaCo 95828 338-F3
AHART CT
300 LNCN 95648 179-E3
AHART RD
- PlaC 95648 160-B5
AHART WY
3500 SAC 95834 276-J3
AHERN ST
300 SAC 95814 297-E2
AHL WY
7800 SaCo 95628 279-J1
AHMED AV
8800 ELKG 95624 358-G7
AHOY CT
1900 EDCo 95762 242-B6
AHRENTZEN CT
8400 CITH 95610 240-C7
AIDAN WY
1000 SAC 95822 317-B2
AIKEN WY
- SAC 95819 297-J4
AILEEN WY
3600 PlaC 95650 201-H6
5300 SaCo 95819 298-A5
AILERON CT
5100 SaCo 95628 260-G7
AILIANTAUS LN
300 EDCo 95667 245-E3
AIMONETTI AV
2600 SAC 95833 277-A4
AIMWELL DR
- SAC 95835 257-D6
AINGER CIR
- SAC 95835 257-B6
AINSDALE CT
300 RSVL 95747 219-D6
AINSDALE DR
1600 RSVL 95747 219-D6
AINSLEY CT
2000 SaCo 95608 299-B1
AINSWORTH LN
- LNCN 95648 179-E6
AINSWORTH WY
- FOLS 95630 261-F5
AIR BASE DR
3600 SaCo 95660 258-G6
AIRBORNE RD
1400 EDCo 95672 243-A3
AIRBORNE WY
4800 SaCo 95628 280-F1
AIR CORP WY
8600 ELKG 95624 358-F3
AIRHILL WY
9200 SaCo 95662 260-H5
AIRO CT
- LNCN 95648 179-D3
AIRONS CT
2700 WSAC 95691 316-F1
5200 SaCo 95842 259-B1
AIRPARK CT
2000 PlaC 95602 162-D2
AIRPARK DR
- RCCD 95655 299-H5
- RCCD 95670 299-G4
AIRPORT BLVD
6700 SaCo 95837 256-B3
AIRPORT CT
1700 PLCR 95667 246-A5
AIRPORT DR
4300 SaCo 95660 278-F2
AIRPORT RD
300 PlaC 95648 159-A7
300 PlaC 95648 179-A2
300 LNCN 95648 159-A7
300 LNCN 95648 179-A2
1000 RVIS 94571 454-G1
1000 SolC 94571 454-H3
2100 PLCR 95667 246-B5
3100 EDCo 95667 246-B6
3400 SAC 95833 277-A3
3400 SAC 95834 277-A3
N AIRWAY DR
3600 SaCo 95660 258-G6
S AIRWAY DR
3600 SaCo 95660 258-G6
AITKEN DAIRY RD
- RKLN 95677 220-F1
AIZENBERG CIR
9300 ELKG 95624 358-G5
AJAY DR
- RSVL 95678 239-G4
AKASHIC DR
1400 EDCo 95667 244-D1
AKINS CT
4800 SaCo 95843 239-A5
AKRON WY
1500 SAC 95822 317-C4

AKSARBEN DR
8900 SaCo 95662 260-F5
AKTIS CT
- RKLN 95677 220-H4
E AL CT
- SAC 95838 277-G1
W AL CT
- SAC 95838 277-G1
AL WY
2000 SaCo 95825 298-C1
ALABAMA AV
- FOLS 95742 280-H4
1100 WSAC 95691 296-H6
1900 SaCo 95742 280-H4
ALABAMA CT
2000 WSAC 95691 296-H6
ALABAMA RD
12100 SaCo 95638 (400-G5 See Page 379)
12400 SaCo 95632 420-G4
12400 SaCo 95638 420-G1
ALABAMA MINE RD
2600 PlaC 95663 201-D3
ALABASTER DR
3200 EDCo 95672 263-D1
9500 ELKG 95758 358-B6
ALABASTER POINT WY
200 FOLS 95630 241-A7
200 FOLS 95630 240-J7
ALAMAR WY
6700 ELKG 95758 358-B3
ALAMEDA AV
39300 YoCo 95612 375-J1
ALAMEDA BLVD
- WSAC 95691 296-J5
ALAMEDA CT
- EDCo - 267-C4
ALAMEDA DR
7000 SaCo 95683 342-B1
ALAMEDA LN
5800 SaCo 95842 259-D1
ALAMEDA RD
- EDCo - 267-E3
ALAMEDA ST
- SaCo 95639 (376-J5 See Page 375)
ALAMEDA PARK DR
8400 ELKG 95624 338-J7
8400 SaCo 95624 338-J7
8400 ELKG 95624 358-J1
ALAMITOS WY
2800 SaCo 95821 278-G6
ALAMO CT
- EDCo 95762 262-E5
2700 ANT 94509 (513-B6 See Page 493)
ALAMO PL
- WSAC 95691 316-J1
ALAMOS AV
600 SAC 95815 277-H5
1200 SAC 95815 278-A5
ALAN CT
5000 SaCo 95608 259-E7
ALAN DR
4100 SaCo 95660 258-H3
ALANA CT
2600 EDCo 95682 263-B7
ALAN BOYD DR
5600 SaCo 95837 256-B2
ALANDALE WY
10800 RCCD 95670 299-H1
10900 RCCD 95670 279-J7
ALAN S HART FRWY
I-80
- AUB - 162-F7
- AUB - 182-A5
- LMS - 200-J7
- LMS - 201-B6
- LMS - 220-C6
- PlaC - 162-F7
- PlaC - 181-G7
- PlaC - 182-A5
- PlaC - 201-B6
- PlaC - 201-G1
- RKLN - 200-J7
- RKLN - 220-C6
- RSVL - 220-C6
- RSVL - 239-J4
- RSVL - 240-A2
ALANTOWN DR
- RSVL 95678 219-F2
ALASKA RANGE WY
8600 ELKG 95624 358-F3
ALATERNA CT
8300 SaCo 95662 260-C2
ALAZAR CT
- SAC 95835 257-A5
ALBA CT
8100 CITH 95610 240-B7
ALBANA DR
- RCCD 95670 300-A4
ALBANS CT
1100 ANT 94509 (513-F7 See Page 493)
ALBANY WY
3300 SAC 95838 278-B4
ALBATROSS WY
- RKLN 95765 219-H1
2300 SAC 95815 278-B6
ALBEMARLE AV
700 SaCo 95673 257-J2
ALBERT CIR
4000 EDCo 95762 262-C3
ALBERT LN
5600 CITH 95610 259-J6
ALBERTA AV
3600 SaCo 95821 278-G5
ALBERTON CIR
- LNCN 95648 179-F6
ALBERTON PL
- ELKG 95624 358-E2
ALBERTSONS DR
- RSVL 95678 219-E3
ALBERTVILLE WY
4300 SaCo 95843 238-J5
ALBEZZIA LN
7400 SaCo 95828 338-C3
ALBION CT
- LNCN 95648 180-A4
ALBION WY
7900 SAC 95832 337-F5
ALBION RIVER CT
8200 SaCo 95828 338-D7
ALBRIGHTON DR
- FOLS 95630 261-F7
ALBURN PL
1800 EDCo 95762 262-E4
ALBURY CT
- RSVL 95661 220-E7

ALBURY ST
6800 CITH 95621 259-F5
ALCADAR CT
4300 EDCo 95682 263-A6
ALCALA CT
- SAC 95823 337-H5
ALCALA ST
2700 ANT 94509 (513-D6 See Page 493)
ALCANON CT
- SAC 95833 276-J4
ALCANTAR CIR
300 SaCo 95834 276-G3
ALCEDO CIR
7200 SaCo 95823 337-G2
ALCOSTA WY
9400 SaCo 95827 299-A5
ALCOTT CT
- RSVL 95747 219-E6
ALCOTT DR
4900 SAC 95820 318-B4
6200 SAC 95824 318-B4
ALDEA DR
- EDCo 95762 262-F3
8500 SaCo 95626 237-F5
ALDEBURGH CIR
- SAC 95834 276-H1
ALDEN CT
- RSVL 95678 219-J5
ALDEN LN
6700 CITH 95621 259-E3
ALDEN WY
- RSVL 95678 219-J5
7300 SaCo 95828 338-F2
ALDER AV
5800 SAC 95828 318-G5
5900 SaCo 95828 318-H5
5900 SaCo 95829 318-H5
8900 SAC 95829 318-H5
ALDER CIR
1600 PlaC 95603 162-C5
ALDER CT
- EDCo - 247-G2
ALDER DR
1400 OAKL 94561 (514-D7 See Page 493)
2900 EDCo - 247-G2
ALDER ST
3800 SAC 95838 278-A3
ALDER WY
2900 WSAC 95691 316-J2
ALDERBERRY CT
- SAC 95835 257-A5
ALDERBERRY WY
- SAC 95835 256-J5
- SAC 95835 257-A5
ALDER BRIDGE CT
5700 ELKG 95757 357-J7
ALDERBROOK WY
1000 SaCo 95825 298-C3
ALDER CANYON WY
3300 SaCo 95843 238-F4
ALDER CREEK CT
- LNCN 95648 200-A2
ALDER CREST CT
8000 SaCo 95828 338-F6
ALDERGATE LN
5100 SaCo 95660 258-H7
ALDER GLEN CT
5400 SaCo 95608 299-B2
ALDER GROVE PL
- ELKG 95624 358-G2
ALDER HILL CT
3100 SaCo 95843 238-F4
ALDER LAKE CT
11700 RCCD 95742 300-D7
ALDER PARK CIR
- RSVL 95678 220-A3
ALDERPOINT CT
3500 RKLN 95765 220-C1
ALDER POINT DR
2800 RSVL 95661 240-E4
ALDERSON AV
8900 SaCo 95826 318-H2
ALDER TREE WY
1100 SaCo 95831 337-A3
ALDERWOOD WY
4300 SaCo 95864 278-J7
4400 SaCo 95864 298-J1
ALDINGER WY
10300 ELKG 95757 377-J3
10300 ELKG 95757 397-J3
ALDO ST
7400 SaCo 95823 338-B2
ALDONA LN
4600 SaCo 95841 278-J1
ALDORAE ST
5300 SaCo 95628 259-F7
ALDRIDGE LN
- RSVL 95747 239-E1
2300 RSVL 95747 219-E7
ALDWORTH WY
100 FOLS 95630 261-G5
ALDWYCH CT
600 GALT 95632 419-G4
ALEGRE CT
2200 RCCD 95670 279-H6
ALEILANI LN
10400 ELKG 95624 359-F3
ALEKSANDER CT
8500 SaCo 95828 338-F3
ALENA WY
400 EDCo 95762 242-B4
ALESIA CT
9100 SaCo 95829 338-J6
ALETA WY
6800 SaCo 95842 259-C2
ALEUTIAN ISLAND ST
- WSAC 95691 316-D2
ALEX LN
4000 SaCo 95608 279-E3
ALEXA CT
- EDCo 95762 262-A2
ALEXANDER CT
1800 EDCo 95667 246-C4
7400 SaCo 95628 279-G4
ALEXANDER DR
- FOLS 95630 261-J5
- FOLS 95630 262-A5
ALEXANDER LN
2000 EDCo 95667 246-C4
ALEXANDRA DR
- EDCo 95762 262-A3
- RSVL 95661 220-E7
- RSVL 95661 240-D1
ALEXANDRA LN
- SaCo 95838 258-A7
ALEXANDRA PL
- RKLN 95765 200-C5

ALEXANDRIA CT
- YoCo 95612 356-G4
10100 ELKG 95624 378-H2
ALEXANDRITE DR
3000 EDCo 95672 263-B2
ALEXIA CT
- ELKG 95624 358-E3
ALEXIS CT
1500 ANT 94509 (513-F7 See Page 493)
ALEXON WY
4800 SaCo 95841 279-B1
ALEZANE DR
100 FOLS 95630 261-D4
ALFALFA PLANT RD
800 SaCo 95615 (396-G7 See Page 375)
1100 SaCo 95615 397-A1
ALFORD WY
8800 SaCo 95628 260-E7
ALGONQUIN WY
8700 SaCo 95662 260-E1
ALHAMBRA BLVD
200 SAC 95816 297-F6
2000 SAC 95817 297-F6
ALHAMBRA CT
- ANT 94509 (513-F5 See Page 493)
2900 EDCo 95682 263-D3
ALHAMBRA DR
1700 ANT 94509 (513-F5 See Page 493)
2700 EDCo 95682 263-D3
ALI LN
2000 PlaC 95603 162-B6
ALIBI LN
5000 EDCo 95623 265-B7
ALICANTE CT
- RSVL 95747 219-B2
ALICANTE DR
- RSVL 95747 219-B2
ALICANTE WY
10700 RCCD 95670 299-H2
W ALICE AV
8400 SJCo 95686 (438-A3 See Page 418)
ALICE CT
2700 EDCo 95682 263-A7
4000 EDCo 95667 265-C2
ALICE RAE CIR
600 GALT 95632 419-E6
ALICIA WY
1500 SAC 95835 257-C3
ALIDA ST
- EDCo - 247-D5
ALIGOTE PL
9400 ELKG 95624 379-A1
ALII WY
5100 SaCo 95838 257-H6
ALISO DR
3700 EDCo 95762 262-E5
ALISO WY
6400 SaCo 95828 318-C6
ALISON CT
2800 SaCo 95826 298-F7
ALISO VIEJO CT
- RSVL 95747 219-B1
ALISSA WY
8500 ELKG 95624 358-E1
ALIX PKWY
7300 SaCo 95823 337-H2
ALJA WY
4700 SAC 95838 257-G7
ALJAY WY
1300 SaCo 95673 258-A1
ALLAIRE CIR
100 SAC 95835 256-H3
ALL AMERICA CITY BLVD
700 RSVL 95678 219-H7
ALLAN AV
2800 WSAC 95691 316-F1
ALLAN CT
- FOLS 95630 261-B1
5400 RKLN 95677 220-C4
ALLAN DR
5900 RKLN 95677 220-C4
ALLANO AV
- SAC 95835 257-C7
ALLANTE CT
6300 SaCo 95662 260-G4
ALLARD CT
- SAC 95035 256-J5
- SAC 95835 257-A5
ALLBRITTON WY
- ELKG 95758 357-H4
ALLEGHENY CT
- RSVL 95747 219-C1
ALLEGHENY DR
9500 SaCo 95827 299-B5
ALLEGHENY RD
2100 EDCo 95762 242-D7
ALLEGRETTO WY
- RSVL 95746 240-G5
ALLEGRO CT
3900 SaCo 95843 238-H4
ALLEN CT
600 PLCR 95667 245-E4
ALLEN LN
7000 PlaC 95663 181-C6
ALLENDALE PL
2400 EDCo 95762 262-D1
ALLENDALE WY
9300 SaCo 95829 339-A6
ALLENDER WY
- RVIS 94571 454-H3
ALLENE CREEK CT
8300 CITH 95610 240-C6
ALLENFORD PL
9000 ELKG 95624 358-H5
ALLENPORT WY
6100 SAC 95831 316-H6
ALLENWOOD CIR
1500 LNCN 95648 179-F4
ALLENWOOD CT
- RSVL 95746 240-F5
7000 CITH 95610 260-B2
ALLERTON CT
100 FOLS 95630 261-H5
ALLESSANDRIA DR
- ELKG 95757 358-A7
- ELKG 95757 378-A1
ALLEY WY
- RSVL 95678 219-J7
ALLIMORE CT
- RSVL 95747 218-H4
ALLISON CT
300 LNCN 95648 179-E3

STREET Block City ZIP Pg-Grid

ALLISON DR
3600 PlaC 95661 240-E5
6200 SAC 95828 318-A7
ALLISTER WY
8500 ELKG 95624 358-F3
ALLOTT WY
7600 SAC 95823 337-J4
ALLPORT DR
100 GALT 95632 419-D7
ALLSTON CT
7500 SaCo 95842 258-J1
ALMA WY
4900 SAC 95822 317-C4
ALMADEN CIR
900 OAKL 94561 (514-C5 See Page 493)
ALMADEN CT
100 OAKL 94561 (514-C5 See Page 493)
5100 EDCo 95762 263-B5
ALMADEN WY
5400 CITH 95610 260-A6
5400 CITH 95628 260-A6
ALMADINE DR
8300 SaCo 95829 339-D7
ALMA MESA WY
7900 CITH 95610 260-A1
ALMANERA LN
8200 SaCo 95828 338-E6
ALMANOR RD
- WSAC 95691 316-D3
ALMANOR WY
800 GALT 95632 419-F4
ALMA VISTA WY
7300 SAC 95831 337-B2
ALMAZ AV
8500 SaCo 95628 260-D5
8500 SaCo 95662 260-D5
ALMERIA DR
- EDCo 95682 263-E3
ALMO CT
- GALT 95632 419-D6
ALMOND AV
5700 SaCo 95628 260-D6
5700 SaCo 95662 260-D2
ALMOND CT
700 GALT 95632 439-F1
ALMOND DR
600 OAKL 94561 (514-F7 See Page 493)
ALMOND ST
- WSAC 95691 316-J1
- WSAC 95691 317-A1
100 AUB 95603 182-E2
100 RSVL 95678 239-J1
900 ANT 94509 (513-D4 See Page 493)
ALMOND WY
5100 SaCo 95608 279-B5
ALMONDA ST
8600 SaCo 95662 260-D1
ALMOND BLOSSOM LN
- PlaC 95747 239-B3
ALMOND BLUFF CT
8500 SaCo 95662 260-D5
ALMOND FALLS WY
5300 RCCD 95742 320-E4
ALMOND GROVE CT
3800 SaCo 95843 238-H5
ALMOND HILL CT
7000 SaCo 95662 260-D2
ALMOND KNOLL CT
6700 PlaC 95746 241-B2
ALMOND OAK CT
8500 SaCo 95662 260-D4
ALMONDRIDGE DR
2700 ANT 94509 (513-J6 See Page 493)
ALMOND TREE CT
3100 ANT 94509 (513-J6 See Page 493)
ALMOND TREE LN
4900 SaCo 95660 258-C3
ALMOND VIEW CT
7100 SaCo 95662 260-E2
ALMONDWOOD AV
7500 CITH 95610 259-H2
ALMONDWOOD DR
1200 ANT 94509 (513-F6 See Page 493)
ALMONDWOOD PL
2900 OAKL 94561 (514-A6 See Page 493)
ALMORA AV
800 SAC 95838 277-J3
ALMOSTA RD
- EDCo 95619 286-C6
- EDCo 95684 286-C6
ALNWICK DR
1600 RSVL 95747 219-E7
1600 RSVL 95747 239-E1
ALOHA LN
7700 CITH 95610 239-H7
ALOLA ST
500 RSVL 95678 239-J1
ALONDRA CT
4900 EDCo 95762 262-D6
7700 CITH 95610 239-J7
ALONSO CT
- RSVL 95661 220-D6
ALORN LN
5800 SaCo 95608 259-D5
ALPENA ST
- SAC 95835 257-A4
ALPENCRESS LN
- EDCo 95709 226-H7
ALPENGLOW LN
- LNCN 95648 180-A6
ALPHA CIR
5400 EDCo 95630 202-G5
ALPHA CT
3900 SaCo 95660 258-H7
ALPHA LN
11700 PlaC 95603 202-E1
ALPHA WY
1800 ANT 94509 (513-E5 See Page 493)
ALPHONSE CT
9800 SaCo 95829 339-C6
ALPINE AV
- SAC 95826 318-D3
ALPINE CT
3400 RKLN 95765 220-B2
ALPINE LN
100 EDCo 95667 265-C2
3500 LMS 95650 200-G5
ALPINE BLUE CT
8700 ELKG 95624 358-F2

ALPINE FALLS DR
200 FOLS 95630 240-J7
200 FOLS 95630 241-A7
ALPINE FROST DR
7200 SAC 95823 338-B6
ALPINE HILL CT
- EDCo 95762 282-D4
ALPINE LAUREL WY
8300 SaCo 95829 339-D7
ALPINESPRING WY
6000 ELKG 95758 358-A3
ALPINE VIEW DR
- RSVL 95747 219-C4
2100 EDCo 95672 243-J6
ALPINMEAD CIR
8300 SaCo 95828 338-E6
ALPOMBO LN
5000 EDCo 95667 265-A1
ALPS CT
8600 ELKG 95624 358-F3
ALSACE CT
- RSVL 95747 199-B7
4300 SaCo 95628 279-H2
ALSTAN CT
- SAC 95831 336-F1
ALTA AV
100 RSVL 95678 239-H1
ALTA DR
100 PlaC 95603 162-F7
4800 SAC 95822 317-B3
ALTA ARDEN EXWY
1800 SAC 95815 298-C1
1800 SaCo 95825 298-C1
1900 SAC 95825 298-C1
3400 SaCo 95864 298-E1
ALTADENA WY
4400 SaCo 95841 278-J1
ALTA GARDEN LN
2300 SaCo 95825 298-D1
ALTAIR PKWY
7000 SaCo 95823 337-H1
ALTAIR WY
4100 EDCo 95682 264-B7
ALTA LOMA CT
5900 PlaC 95746 221-G4
6100 SaCo 95673 257-J4
ALTA LOMA PL
6000 PlaC 95746 221-F4
ALTA LORRAINE WY
4000 SaCo 95660 258-H4
ALTAMEDA CT
- ELKG 95758 358-B3
ALTA MESA
12100 AUB 95603 162-D6
ALTA MESA RD
10800 SaCo 95693 (380-E1 See Page 379)
11700 SaCo 95693 360-E7
12500 SaCo 95693 (400-E1 See Page 379)
12700 SaCo 95632 (400-E2 See Page 379)
13100 SaCo 95638 (400-E7 See Page 379)
13200 SaCo 95638 420-E4
13500 SaCo 95632 420-E4
13800 SaCo 95632 (440-E1 See Page 420)
ALTA MESA EAST RD
10800 SaCo 95693 (380-F6 See Page 379)
11000 SaCo 95693 (400-F1 See Page 379)
ALTAMIRA CIR
7500 SaCo 95660 258-F1
ALTAMONT DR
3500 SaCo 95608 279-F4
ALTAMONT LN
- EDCo 95726 267-J2
ALTA SIERRA WY
4100 EDCo 95762 262-C7
ALTA SUNRISE DR
7800 CITH 95610 260-A6
ALTA VALLEY WY
7800 SAC 95823 338-B4
ALTA VISTA AV
100 RSVL 95678 219-H7
ALTA VISTA CT
- EDCo 95762 242-E7
700 GALT 95632 419-F4
ALTA VISTA LN
7900 CITH 95610 260-A6
ALTAWOOD CT
3200 RCCD 95827 299-C5
ALTERI CT
- FOLS 95630 262-A6
ALTERRA WY
- SAC 95835 257-D6
ALTITUDE CT
5200 SaCo 95628 260-F7
ALTMAN WY
- ELKG 95757 358-B7
ALTON CT
4200 SaCo 95864 298-J4
ALTOONA CT
6000 SaCo 95673 257-J4
ALTOS AV
2300 SAC 95815 277-J5
3200 SAC 95838 277-J4
ALTOS CIR
1900 EDCo 95667 264-J2
1900 EDCo 95667 265-A2
ALTURAS CT
- WSAC 95691 296-J7
ALTURAS WY
4800 SAC 95822 317-B3
ALVA CT
4200 SaCo 95821 278-H6
ALVARADO BLVD
3300 SAC 95838 277-J3
3300 SAC 95838 278-A4
ALVARES CT
- SAC 95833 277-D4
ALVAREZ LN
- EDCo - 267-G4
ALVASTON CT
- FOLS 95630 261-E7
ALVASTON WY
100 FOLS 95630 261-E7
100 FOLS 95630 281-E1
ALVERN WY
5900 SAC 95823 338-A5
ALVILDE CT
6900 SaCo 95673 258-A2
ALVIN ST
100 WSAC 95605 297-A2
ALVINA AV
1500 SAC 95822 317-C3

ALVINA CT
7900 PlaC 95746 241-E1
ALVIS CT
4000 RKLN 95677 200-G7
ALVOCA WY
- SAC 95835 257-C5
ALWOOD CT
3400 SaCo 95821 278-E4
ALWOODLEY CT
2100 SAC 95833 277-F6
ALYSSA CT
6500 CITH 95610 259-H4
ALYSSIUM CT
8700 ELKG 95624 358-G2
ALYSSUM CIR
3300 EDCo 95762 263-B4
ALYSSUM WY
1500 RSVL 95747 219-C4
AMADO CT
6500 CITH 95621 259-F3
AMADOR AV
- OAKL 94561 (514-E7 See Page 493)
500 GALT 95632 419-F5
AMADOR CIR
- RVIS 94571 454-G5
AMADOR RD
7900 SAC 95826 318-C3
AMADOR VALLEY CT
9000 SaCo 95829 338-H5
AMAGANSETT PL
- SAC 95835 256-G3
AMALFI WY
7900 SaCo 95628 280-A1
AMALGAM WY
11300 SaCo 95670 280-B6
AMANDA RD
- SaCo 95632 420-B4
AMANDA WY
2100 SAC 95822 337-D3
AMAPOLA AV
- SaCo 95828 338-F3
AMAPOLA CT
- EDCo - 247-C7
AMAPOLA WY
4100 SAC 95823 337-G5
AMARAL CT
- SAC 95831 336-H3
AMARILLO CT
- SAC 95835 257-B4
AMARONE WY
9200 SaCo 95829 338-J5
AMARYLLIS CT
8400 ELKG 95624 358-F1
AMARYLLIS DR
- EDCo 95726 267-H2
AMATRENE CT
- RSVL 95747 219-A7
AMAYA DR
100 FOLS 95630 261-F3
AMAZON AV
- SaCo 95835 257-D4
1500 SAC 95835 257-D4
AMBASSADOR DR
5600 RKLN 95677 220-H4
10200 RCCD 95670 279-H6
AMBER CT
600 RSVL 95678 219-J7
AMBER DR
500 ANT 94509 (513-E5 See Page 493)
AMBER LN
100 EDCo 95667 265-C1
4700 SaCo 95841 259-A7
AMBER PL
- EDCo 95682 263-D2
AMBER TR
2700 EDCo 95726 248-C2
AMBER WY
7000 EDCo 95667 226-F3
AMBER CREEK DR
8900 ELKG 95758 357-J3
AMBER FALLS DR
- RKLN 95765 220-A1
AMBER FIELDS CT
- ELKG 95624 359-B4
- RSVL 95747 219-A7
4400 EDCo 95682 283-F6
AMBER FIELDS DR
5200 EDCo 95682 283-F5
AMBER FIELDS WY
- RSVL 95747 219-A7
AMBERGLEN DR
100 SAC 95823 337-F2
AMBERHILL AV
1100 GALT 95632 419-H2
AMBERJACK WY
8800 SaCo 95828 338-G4
AMBER LEAF CT
- SAC 95838 257-G7
AMBER LEAF WY
4800 SAC 95838 257-G7
AMBERLEY WY
4500 SaCo 95821 278-J3
AMBER OAKS CT
8600 SaCo 95628 260-D6
AMBER WAVES CT
- RSVL 95747 219-A7
AMBER WAVES WY
- ELKG 95624 359-B5
- RSVL 95747 218-J7
- RSVL 95747 219-A7
AMBERWICK WY
6900 CITH 95621 259-F5
AMBER WOOD CT
- PlaC 95650 201-E5
AMBERWOOD RD
200 RSVL 95678 239-G2
900 SaCo 95864 298-F3
AMBLEBROOK WY
4700 SAC 95823 337-H5
AMBLER ST
5700 SaCo 95823 337-J3
5700 SaCo 95823 338-A3
AMBRIDGE CT
- RSVL 95747 219-A7
AMBRIDGE DR
- RSVL 95747 219-A7
AMBROSE WY
7600 SAC 95831 336-H3
AMBROSIA LN
- EDCo 95633 205-B1
AMBUSH PASS RD
3900 EDCo 95682 263-J3
3900 EDCo 95682 264-A4
AMELIA DR
4700 SaCo 95628 279-G1
AMEN WY
- ELKG 95758 357-E5

AMENITY CIR
9800 ELKG 95624 358-H7
9800 ELKG 95624 378-H1
AMER CT
3800 EDCo 95762 262-E1
AMER WY
3500 EDCo 95762 262-E1
AMERICAN AV
2100 SAC 95833 277-F6
AMERICAN WY
6400 EDCo 95667 244-H2
AMERICANA DR
1000 RSVL 95747 239-E1
1700 RSVL 95747 219-E7
AMERICANA WY
- RKLN 95677 220-F1
9300 SaCo 95826 299-A7
9300 SaCo 95826 319-A1
AMERICAN BAR CT
11800 SaCo 95670 280-D5
AMERICAN FALLS DR
- RVIS 94571 454-G2
AMERICAN RIVER DR
1000 SaCo 95608 299-A3
2300 SAC 95825 298-D5
2300 SAC 95864 298-D5
2600 SaCo 95864 298-E5
4500 SaCo 95864 299-A3
AMERICAN RIVER CANYON DR
- FOLS 95630 260-J1
FOLS 95662 280-J1
- FOLS 95630 261-A1
100 FOLS 95630 241-A7
200 FOLS 95630 240-J7
AMERIGO AV
8900 SaCo 95662 260-F6
AMES CT
- SAC 95823 338-A4
1100 ANT 94509 (513-F6 See Page 493)
AMESBURY CT
8600 SaCo 95828 338-F2
AMETHYST CT
100 RSVL 95678 219-J6
3500 RKLN 95677 220-B3
AMETHYST DR
3600 RKLN 95677 220-B3
AMETHYST LN
3200 EDCo 95682 263-E7
AMETHYST WY
9300 ELKG 95624 358-G5
AMHERST ST
7000 SAC 95822 337-B1
7500 SAC 95832 337-B4
AMHERST WY
- EDCo 95762 242-C5
AMHURST CIR
- FOLS 95630 281-B1
AMICI CT
3600 RCCD 95670 299-H5
AMINA LN
4600 PlaC - 160-G2
4600 PlaC 95602 160-G2
4600 PlaC 95648 160-G2
AMINA WY
8000 SAC 95823 337-G5
AMINA FAIR WY
5000 SaCo 95628 260-A7
AMIR LN
- SaCo 95608 279-D3
AMISFIELD ST
- SAC 95833 276-J6
AMITY LN
4100 EDCo 95630 202-J5
AMITY PL
11600 SaCo 95670 280-D4
AMNEST WY
5600 SAC 95835 257-D3
AMON CT
- ELKG 95758 358-C6
AMOR CT
100 GALT 95632 419-D6
AMORUSO AV
8900 SaCo 95628 260-F6
AMRITA CT
8400 SaCo 95828 338-E7
AMSDEN CT
9200 ELKG 95624 358-J4
AMSELL CT
8300 CITH 95610 260-C2
AMSTERDAM AV
7000 CITH 95621 259-F1
7200 CITH 95621 239-G7
AMULET PL
9900 SaCo 95829 339-D7
AMWELL CT
5200 SaCo 95842 259-B1
AMY AV
7400 SaCo 95628 279-H3
AMYJAN CT
10200 ELKG 95757 377-J2
10200 ELKG 95757 397-J2
AMYS LN
400 EDCo 95762 262-A1
ANACAPA CT
- WSAC 95691 316-E2
- SAC 95823 338-A4
ANACAPA DR
300 RSVL 95678 219-G4
ANAHEIM CT
2500 SaCo 95821 278-D5
ANAKIN LN
- ELKG 95624 339-A7
ANANDA LN
10400 RCCD 95670 299-F1
ANASTASIA WY
- EDCo 95762 262-A3
ANATOLIA DR
4100 RCCD 95742 300-D7
4100 RCCD 95742 320-D3
ANAVA CT
- SAC 95833 277-B5
ANCESTOR DR
- ELKG 95758 358-C3
ANCHO WY
8400 SaCo 95626 237-F5
ANCHOR CIR
6800 SaCo 95628 259-F7
ANCHOR CT
2200 EDCo 95667 245-G2
ANCHOR DR
- SaCo 95690 455-D3
ANCHOR BAY WY
- ELKG 95758 357-J2
ANDALUSIA DR
1100 SAC 95833 277-D5
ANDALUSIAN DR
8100 SaCo 95829 339-E6

ANDALUSIAN WY
- RSVL 95678 219-G4
ANDANTE DR
7800 SaCo 95621 239-D7
ANDEDON CIR
4000 SaCo 95826 319-A2
ANDERSON CT
- RSVL 95678 239-G1
300 SAC 95838 278-B1
1100 PLCR 95667 245-H4
ANDERSON DR
- PlaC 95661 240-E5
ANDERSON LN
7400 CITH 95610 260-A1
ANDERSON RD
2100 SolC 94571 474-A1
ANDERSON WY
- RVIS 94571 454-G3
1100 PLCR 95667 245-H4
2900 SaCo 95825 298-E1
ANDERSON WOOD WY
800 SaCo 95673 257-J2
ANDES CT
5600 SaCo 95842 259-C2
ANDLER RD
2500 EDCo 95667 245-C3
ANDORA WY
7900 SAC 95824 318-C6
ANDOVER CT
4500 SaCo 95864 278-J7
ANDOVER LN
- LNCN 95648 180-A6
ANDRADE WY
2400 SaCo 95864 278-G6
2500 SaCo 95821 278-G6
ANDRE CT
8400 CITH 95610 260-D1
ANDREA BLVD
4700 SaCo 95842 259-C2
ANDREA CT
5700 RKLN 95677 220-H4
ANDREA LN
2500 EDCo 95667 245-E3
2500 PLCR 95667 245-E3
8000 SAC 95826 318-D1
ANDREGG EXT
2600 PlaC 95603 202-D1
ANDREGG RD
2000 PlaC 95603 182-D7
2500 PlaC 95603 202-D1
ANDRESS CT
600 RSVL 95678 239-H4
ANDRETTI WY
- ELKG 95758 358-C6
ANDREW CIR
4800 SaCo 95841 279-B1
4900 SaCo 95841 259-C7
ANDREW ST
600 WSAC 95605 297-A2
ANDREW ALAN LN
4400 SaCo 95628 279-H2
ANDREWS CT
- EDCo - 247-H2
ANDREWS LN
- EDCo - 247-G2
ANDREWS ST
200 AUB 95603 182-C3
ANDREW-SARAH CT
7500 SaCo 95828 338-B3
ANDRI CT
- EDCo 95762 262-J5
ANDROS WY
3700 SAC 95823 337-F3
ANDRUS CT
100 ISLE 95641 455-G5
ANDRUS ISLAND CT
- WSAC 95691 316-E2
ANDRUS ISLAND RD
14700 SaCo 95690 436-H3
ANDY CIR
1000 SAC 95838 277-J1
ANGEL CT
1900 EDCo 95667 245-A6
2900 WSAC 95691 316-E1
ANGEL LN
3300 EDCo 95667 245-A6
ANGEL PL
9900 PlaC 95658 201-J2
9900 PlaC 95658 202-A2
ANGEL WY
- SaCo 95673 257-G2
ANGELBROOK
- RVIS 94571 454-F1
ANGELES CT
2600 RKLN 95677 220-C4
ANGELI LN
0700 PlaC 95650 201-F4
ANGELICA PL
8000 SaCo 95829 338-H6
ANGELINA AV
5300 SaCo 95608 279-B5
ANGEL ISLAND CIR
- SAC 95831 336-F2
ANGELL CT
- FOLS 95630 281-D1
ANGELO CT
6100 LMS 95650 201-A4
8200 SaCo 95626 238-D6
ANGELO DR
5500 LMS 95650 200-J4
5900 LMS 95650 201-A4
ANGELROCK CT
400 RSVL 95747 219-A5
ANGELROCK LP
5200 RSVL 95747 219-A5
ANGEL VIEW RD
2100 EDCo 95762 262-J6
ANGIE WY
2500 RCCD 95670 299-H1
ANGLE RD
12100 SaCo 95638 (400-G7 See Page 379)
ANGRAVE RD
12900 SaCo 95632 420-J4
12900 SaCo 95632 421-A4
13100 SaCo 95638 421-B4
ANGUS WY
3000 SaCo 95843 238-E7
ANICE ST
7000 SaCo 95662 260-J2
ANILLO WY
14900 SaCo 95683 342-B1
ANISTASIA CT
9100 SaCo 95829 338-H7
ANITA AV
2300 SAC 95822 317-D3
ANITA RD
18700 SaCo 94571 (494-A3 See Page 493)

ANJOU CIR
- SAC 95835 256-H6
ANN PL
- PlaC 95746 241-C4
ANNA PL
- EDCo 95762 262-F6
ANNA RD
- PlaC 95648 160-H7
ANNA ST
900 WSAC 95605 296-H1
ANNA WY
2500 SaCo 95821 278-C6
2500 SaCo 95825 278-C6
ANNABELLE AV
3500 PlaC 95661 240-E5
3700 RSVL 95661 240-E5
ANNABELLE CT
3500 RSVL 95661 240-E5
ANNADALE LN
3800 SaCo 95821 278-G3
ANNAPOLIS LN
4100 SaCo 95660 258-H7
ANN ARBOR WY
7800 SAC 95832 337-F4
ANNE WY
4700 SaCo 95608 299-A2
ANNELL CT
- SAC 95835 257-B5
ANNE LOUISE LN
- EDCo - 267-F3
ANNE MARIE CT
7600 CITH 95610 259-H2
ANNETTE LN
- EDCo 95619 266-A7
ANNETTE ST
4200 SaCo 95821 278-H6
ANNETTE ENGLE WY
8500 SaCo 95628 280-D1
ANNIE ST
10000 ELKG 95757 377-J2
10000 ELKG 95757 397-J2
ANNIKA CT
9500 ELKG 95624 359-B7
ANNMARIE CT
11000 AUB 95603 182-D6
ANNMARIE LN
- EDCo 95623 264-J4
- EDCo 95623 265-A4
ANNRUD WY
5800 SAC 95822 317-B5
ANNWOOD CT
6200 CITH 95621 239-E7
ANOKA AV
1500 SAC 95832 337-C3
ANONA WY
8800 SaCo 95662 260-E5
ANSBROUGH DR
7000 CITH 95621 259-F2
ANSLEY CT
7100 CITH 95621 259-F2
ANSON CT
5500 SaCo 95820 317-H4
ANTARCTIC DR
- WSAC 95691 296-F6
ANTARES
500 EDCo 95619 265-D5
ANTARES CT
1800 FOLS 95630 261-J6
ANTARES WY
6200 SaCo 95662 260-C4
ANTELL AV
- SAC 95835 257-C5
ANTELOPE CT
4200 RKLN 95677 220-E2
ANTELOPE RD
- SaCo 95843 239-G7
3500 SaCo 95660 258-H1
3500 SaCo 95843 258-H1
4300 SaCo 95842 258-H1
4300 SaCo 95842 259-C1
4300 SaCo 95843 259-A1
5500 SaCo 95842 239-G7
5900 CITH 95621 239-G7
5900 CITH 95842 239-G7
5900 SaCo 95621 239-G7
7400 CITH 95610 239-G7
7500 CITH 95610 239-J7
7700 CITH 95610 240-A7
8100 CITH 95610 260-A1
ANTELOPE ST
400 SaCo 95626 237-H4
ANTELOPE WY
3700 RKLN 95677 220-E1
ANTELOPE CREEK DR
- RSVL 95678 220-B5
ANTELOPE HILLS DR
7600 SaCo 95843 258-H1
7600 SaCo 95843 238-H7
ANTELOPE NORTH RD
4900 SaCo 95843 259-C1
5100 SaCo 95843 239-D6
8100 PlaC 95747 239-D6
ANTELOPE OAKS CT
9600 PlaC 95747 239-D5
ANTELOPE PARK WY
4400 SaCo 95843 238-J7
ANTELOPE RUN DR
7700 SaCo 95843 239-B7
ANTELOPE WOODS WY
7200 SaCo 95660 258-H1
ANTE-UP LN
13300 SaCo 95632 419-C5
ANTHEA ST
- SAC 95834 276-H3
ANTHEMIS CT
8400 ELKG 95624 338-F7
ANTHIS CT
100 EDCo 95667 245-D7
ANTHIS DR
3200 EDCo 95667 245-D7
ANTHONY CT
500 RSVL 95678 219-F7
4300 RKLN 95677 220-G1
ANTHONY DR
5900 SaCo 95662 260-H5
ANTIGUA CT
3000 EDCo 95667 245-H2
ANTIGUA PL
- WSAC 95691 316-D2
ANTIGUA WY
6800 SAC 95831 316-F7
ANTILLES DR
3700 EDCo 95682 263-B6
ANTIOCH AV
3500 WSAC 95691 316-G4
ANTIQUE CT
5300 SaCo 95608 279-B5
ANTLER CT
- SaCo 95843 239-B7

ANTLER HOLLOW PL
5100 SaCo 95843 239-B7
ANTLER RUN PL
5100 SaCo 95843 239-B7
ANTON CT
- LNCN 95648 180-A6
- SAC 95835 257-B5
ANTON LN
- LNCN 95648 180-A6
ANTON WY
- SAC 95835 257-B5
8200 SAC 95823 337-J6
ANTONE CT
9800 SaCo 95829 339-C6
ANTONIA CT
4700 SAC 95820 318-A3
ANTON OAKS WY
- ELKG 95624 359-A7
ANTRIM CT
1500 RSVL 95747 219-E7
ANTRIM DR
1300 RSVL 95747 219-E7
ANY WY
4000 SaCo 95660 258-H7
ANZA CT
2700 ANT 94509 (513-A6 See Page 493)
ANZA WY
2200 RCCD 95670 279-J6
APACHE ST
- WSAC 95691 316-H2
APACHE WY
- RKLN 95765 200-B3
7400 CITH 95621 259-E1
APARTMENT LN
1900 SaCo 95825 298-D1
APERO PL
900 EDCo 95762 262-F6
APLAND PL
5400 SaCo 95843 239-C5
APLITE CT
8400 CITH 95610 260-C1
APOLLO CIR
- RSVL 95661 240-E1
APOLLO CT
900 ANT 94509 (513-F4 See Page 493)
APOSTOLO CIR
4100 SaCo 95824 317-G4
APPALACHIAN DR
9400 SaCo 95827 299-B4
APPALOOSA CT
- AUB 95603 182-C6
400 EDCo 95762 262-A1
2100 FOLS 95630 282-B1
APPALOOSA PL
- ELKG 95624 359-B6
5800 RKLN 95677 220-H5
APPALOOSA WY
- SaCo 95829 339-B6
APPEL CT
100 FOLS 95630 261-B6
APPELLATE CT
5200 SaCo 95608 299-B1
APPIAN WY
3200 EDCo 95762 262-E1
6300 SaCo 95608 259-E6
12800 AUB 95603 162-E7
N APPLE CT
2900 ANT 94509 (513-A6 See Page 493)
APPLE LN
100 PlaC 95603 162-G4
APPLE RD
- SaCo 95683 (361-C1 See Page 341)
13000 SaCo 95693 341-A7
13000 SaCo 95693 (361-B1 See Page 341)
APPLE WY
- RSVL 95747 219-B7
APPLE BLOSSOM WY
3900 SaCo 95608 279-C3
APPLE BROOK WY
- ELKG 95624 338-D7
APPLEBY WY
6200 CITH 95621 259-E4
APPLE COVE CT
8200 SaCo 95828 338-D6
APPLECROSS CT
- FOLS 95630 261-J3
APPLEGARTH LN
2400 ANT 94509 (513-D6 See Page 493)
APPLEGATE DR
4100 SaCo 95826 318-J2
APPLEGATE RD
8200 SaCo 95662 260-C4
APPLE GREY CT
- RKLN 95765 200-A4
APPLE GREY LN
- RKLN 95765 199-J4
- RKLN 95765 200-A4
APPLEGROVE CIR
- EDCo 95762 242-E6
APPLE GROVE WY
10500 RCCD 95670 279-G7
APPLE HOLLOW LP
- RSVL 95747 219-A3
APPLEHURST WY
5200 ELKG 95758 357-J3
APPLE MILL DR
- ELKG 95624 359-A6
APPLE ORCHARD CT
2200 RCCD 95670 279-G7
APPLE PEAR CT
8800 ELKG 95624 358-G1
APPLE RANCH WY
- RCCD 95670 279-G7
APPLESBURY CT
12000 RCCD 95742 320-E3
APPLETON CT
5100 SaCo 95608 279-A4
APPLE TREE CT
5300 SaCo 95662 260-H7
APPLE TREE LN
- EDCo 95709 247-B1
APPLE VALLEY CT
7800 SaCo 95628 279-J1
APPLE VISTA LN
- EDCo 95709 247-A1
APPLEWOOD CT
8300 SaCo 95662 260-C4
APPOLLO WY
1000 SAC 95822 316-J3
1000 SAC 95822 317-A3
APPOLON DR
11800 RCCD 95742 320-D2

519 APPOMATTOX WY SACRAMENTO COUNTY STREET INDEX AURELIUS WY

SACRAMENTO CO.

STREET
Block City ZIP Pg-Grid

APPOMATTOX WY
6800 SaCo 95608 279-F2
APPROACH CT
9000 SaCo 95628 260-F7
APRICOT LN
12500 SaCo 95693 360-H3
APRICOT TREE CT
8800 ELKG 95624 358-G1
APRICOT WOODS WY
8700 ELKG 95624 358-G1
APRIL LN
4500 EDCo 95619 265-F2
APRIL ST
7400 SaCo 95662 260-H1
APTOS CIR
7700 CITH 95610 259-J3
AQUA CT
4300 SaCo 95660 258-J3
AQUADUCT DR
5800 SaCo 95628 260-C5
AQUA HAVEN CT
1000 EDCo 95762 242-E3
AQUAMARINE CIR
2800 EDCo 95672 263-B2
AQUA MARINE CT
8900 ELKG 95758 357-J3
AQUAMARINE CT
3200 EDCo 95672 263-C2
AQUAPHER WY
300 SAC 95831 336-F2
AQUARIUS AV
8700 ELKG 95624 358-G7
AQUINO DR
2800 SAC 95833 277-B5
ARA LN
- SaCo 95608 279-F3
ARABELLA WY
6700 SAC 95831 316-F7
ARABESQUE CIR
- RSVL 95678 219-G3
ARABESQUE CT
- ELKG 95624 378-H2
ARABIAN CIR
6500 PlaC 95746 241-B3
ARABIAN LN
5700 PlaC 95650 200-J3
5700 PlaC 95650 201-A3
12500 SaCo 95632 (400-B7 See Page 379)
12700 SaCo 95632 420-B1
ARABIAN WY
- RSVL 95678 219-H4
3800 EDCo 95682 263-J4
ARABIS CT
2900 SaCo 95843 238-E5
ARAGON CT
- EDCo 95762 262-G7
- RCCD 95742 300-E7
- RCCD 95742 320-E1
ARAGON WY
400 SaCo 95626 237-F5
4000 RCCD 95742 300-D7
ARAMON DR
2300 RCCD 95670 279-G7
2400 RCCD 95670 299-G2
ARAPAHO WY
3200 SaCo 95843 238-F6
ARARAT CT
- SAC 95831 316-H7
- SAC 95831 336-H1
ARBARDEE DR
4800 SaCo 95628 280-E1
4900 SaCo 95628 260-E7
ARBOGA WY
1300 SAC 95831 317-A7
ARBOLADO LN
1500 EDCo 95762 242-F6
ARBOLEDA CT
100 EDCo 95667 265-D1
ARBOLEDA DR
4800 SaCo 95628 280-C1
4900 SaCo 95628 260-C7
ARBON CT
9500 ELKG 95624 359-B6
ARBOR CT
1200 RSVL 95678 239-F2
ARBOR DR
1200 RSVL 95678 239-F2
4900 SAC 95834 276-H2
ARBOR PL
1100 EDCo 95762 242-C5
ARBOR WY
3300 SaCo 95821 278-E4
ARBOR CREST WY
200 SAC 95838 257-G7
ARBORETA CT
2600 SaCo 95608 279-D6
ARBORFIELD DR
9500 ELKG 95758 358-C6
ARBOR KNOLL CT
8300 SaCo 95828 338-E7
ARBORVIEW DR
8900 ELKG 95758 358-B3
ARBORWOOD CT
- ELKG 95624 338-J7
ARBROATH WY
4400 SaCo 95843 238-J6
ARBUCKLE AV
100 FOLS 95630 261-C7
ARBURY CT
- SAC 95833 277-A6
ARBURY ST
- SAC 95833 277-A6
ARBUSTO CIR
100 SAC 95831 336-G1
ARBUTUS WY
8400 SaCo 95628 280-C1
ARCADA CT
- ELKG 95624 359-A6
ARCADE BLVD
- SAC 95815 277-J4
1100 SAC 95815 278-A4
ARCADE CREEK MNR
6600 CITH 95621 259-F3
ARCADE CREEK WY
6500 SaCo 95662 260-D3
ARCADE LAKE LN
8000 CITH 95610 260-A3
ARCADE OAKS CT
8500 SaCo 95662 260-D4
ARCADIA AV
5500 LMS 95650 200-J4
ARCADIA DR
2700 EDCo 95672 263-D2
2700 EDCo 95682 263-D2
7900 CITH 95610 260-A4
ARCANO WY
200 SaCo 95673 257-G1

ARCARO CT
8400 CITH 95610 240-C6
ARCATA BAY RD
- WSAC 95691 316-E2
ARCHCREST WY
- SAC 95835 257-D6
ARCHEAN WY
4000 SAC 95823 337-G4
ARCHER AV
7900 SaCo 95628 280-A1
ARCHER CIR
2000 RKLN 95765 200-A6
ARCHES AV
200 EDCo 95762 262-C7
ARCHES CIR
- SAC 95835 257-B7
ARCHES WY
10000 ELKG 95757 377-H2
10000 ELKG 95757 397-H2
ARCHETTO DR
- EDCo 95762 262-G5
ARCHIBALD CT
- SAC 95823 357-J1
- SAC 95823 358-A1
ARCHIE WY
- RKLN 95677 220-J2
ARCHLEY CT
9100 ELKG 95624 378-H2
ARCHWAY AV
300 SaCo 95673 257-G2
ARCHWOOD RD
3200 SaCo 95821 278-G5
3700 EDCo 95682 263-D7
ARCOLA AV
- SAC 95835 257-D6
ARCONA CT
8000 SaCo 95829 338-H6
ARCTIC DR
- WSAC 95691 296-F7
ARCTIC PL
- WSAC 95691 296-F7
ARCTIC LOON WY
- RKLN 95765 219-J1
ARD AVEN PL
6000 SaCo 95608 279-D7
ARDEA CT
- PlaC 95746 221-E5
ARDEA PL
- SAC 95835 256-G6
ARDEA WY
- PlaC 95746 221-E5
ARDEER PL
2300 EDCo 95762 242-B5
ARDELLE WY
- ELKG 95624 338-D7
ARDEN WY
- SAC 95815 277-G7
1100 SAC 95815 278-A7
1500 SAC 95815 298-B1
1900 SAC 95825 298-C1
2200 SaCo 95825 298-C1
2600 SaCo 95864 298-F2
4500 SaCo 95608 299-A2
4500 SaCo 95864 299-A2
ARDEN BLUFFS LN
1600 SaCo 95608 299-B2
ARDEN CREEK RD
3400 SaCo 95825 298-F1
3400 SaCo 95864 298-G1
ARDENDALE LN
- SaCo 95825 298-F1
- SaCo 95864 298-F1
ARDEN-GARDEN CONNECTOR
- SAC 95815 277-E7
100 SAC 95833 277-E7
ARDEN HILLS COUNTRY CLUB LN
- SaCo 95864 298-J3
- SaCo 95864 299-A3
ARDENNES WY
8500 SAC 95758 358-C1
ARDENNESS DR
8000 SaCo 95829 339-E6
ARDEN OAKS LN
- SaCo 95864 298-H1
ARDENRIDGE DR
3100 SaCo 95864 298-F3
ARDERLY CT
3900 SaCo 95826 319-A1
ARDFERN WY
- FOLS 95630 261-J5
- FOLS 95630 262-A4
ARDITH DR
8600 SaCo 95828 338-F7
ARDMORE AV
200 RSVL 95678 239-G5
ARDMORE RD
3500 SaCo 95821 278-G4
ARDSLEY CIR
- SAC 95823 337-J4
ARDWELL WY
4100 SAC 95823 337-G5
ARENA BLVD
- SAC 95834 276-H2
1900 SAC 95834 277-A2
ARENA CT
- SAC 95817 317-J1
ARENA LN
6700 EDCo 95682 283-H7
AREND CT
7000 CITH 95621 259-F1
ARENZANO WY
- EDCo 95762 262-F5
ARETE WY
11700 RCCD 95742 320-D2
ARETHUSA PL
4400 SaCo 95827 319-B2
ARETZ CT
- SAC 95835 257-A5
ARGAIL WY
1900 SAC 95822 317-C3
ARGENT CT
- FOLS 95630 281-F1
ARGO DR
200 EDCo 95619 265-C5
8100 CITH 95610 240-C6
ARGO WY
5000 SAC 95820 318-A4
5200 SAC 95824 318-A4
ARGOLIS WY
2600 SaCo 95826 298-J5
2700 SaCo 95826 299-A5
ARGONAUT AV
2800 RKLN 95677 220-E1
3900 RKLN 95677 200-F7
4600 RKLN 95765 220-C2
ARGONAUT DR
100 EDCo 95619 265-D4

ARGONAUT WY
4500 SaCo 95864 278-J7
ARGUS CT
- RKLN 95765 220-H5
8600 ELKG 95624 358-F5
ARGYLE CT
- EDCo 95682 263-F4
ARGYLE LN
- SaCo 95841 279-A1
ARGYLL WY
10800 RCCD 95670 279-H7
ARIA CT
- EDCo 95762 262-A2
ARIANNA CT
6900 ELKG 95757 378-B1
ARICA WY
1900 SAC 95822 317-C4
ARIEL CT
9300 ELKG 95758 358-E5
ARIEL WY
9300 ELKG 95758 358-E5
ARIES WY
9900 RCCD 95827 299-D6
ARIS WY
5400 SaCo 95608 279-B3
ARISTA CT
- LNCN 95648 179-E5
ARISTA WY
11700 RCCD 95742 320-D1
ARIZONA AV
- SaCo 95742 280-G4
ARIZONA WY
- PLCR 95667 245-G4
ARK WY
500 SAC 95831 316-H7
ARKIE CT
8400 PlaC 95746 240-G2
ARLENE AV
9200 SaCo 95662 260-H4
ARLENE CT
600 GALT 95632 419-E3
ARLENE DR
500 RSVL 95678 239-G4
ARLETA CT
7300 SaCo 95823 337-J2
ARLETTE LN
500 EDCo 95619 265-E4
ARLINGDALE CIR
400 SaCo 95673 257-H1
ARLINGTON AV
4200 SAC 95820 317-E3
ARLINGTON DR
- RVIS 94571 454-F2
ARLINGTON RD
2100 WSAC 95691 296-H7
ARLINGTON ST
- FOLS 95630 261-J6
- FOLS 95630 262-A6
ARLISS WY
2000 SAC 95822 317-D6
ARLISSON DR
9600 SaCo 95827 299-B7
ARLYN WY
5600 SaCo 95628 259-G6
ARMADA CT
8500 ELKG 95624 358-E1
ARMADALE WY
4100 SAC 95823 337-G5
ARMAGH CT
9200 ELKG 95624 358-F5
ARMAND GEORGE DR
- ELKG 95624 339-C7
- ELKG 95829 339-C7
8300 SaCo 95829 339-C7
ARMANDO CT
8100 SaCo 95828 338-F6
ARMARIA CT
8800 ELKG 95624 358-J2
ARMENO CT
9800 ELKG 95757 378-A1
ARMES LN
7800 PlaC 95658 181-D5
ARMIDA CT
- LNCN 95648 179-E5
ARMINGTON AV
1700 SAC 95832 337-C3
ARMITAGE WY
2200 SaCo 95626 238-C6
ARMORY DR
100 PLCR 95667 245-C5
ARMOUR CT
11500 SaCo 95670 280-C4
ARMSMERE CIR
- EDCo 95762 262-E6
ARMSMERE PL
- EDCo 95762 262-F6
ARMSTRONG AV
- RCCD 95655 299-G5
ARMSTRONG DR
2600 SaCo 95825 298-E1
ARMSTRONG WY
- GALT 95632 419-G3
ARNCLIFFE WY
- RSVL 95747 239-B1
ARNETT CT
600 GALT 95632 419-G4
ARNETT WY
600 GALT 95632 419-G4
ARNO RD
9900 SaCo 95757 (399-C4 See Page 379)
9900 SaCo 95632 (399-F2 See Page 379)
9900 SaCo 95693 (399-D4 See Page 379)
10700 SaCo 95632 (400-B2 See Page 379)
11100 SaCo 95693 (400-B2 See Page 379)
ARNOLD AV
3300 SaCo 95652 260-F6
ARNOLD CT
- PlaC 95747 239-A4
2400 SAC 95822 317-D3
ARNOLD DR
- RKLN 95765 219-J1
ARNOLD WY
4200 SaCo 95655 319-J1
ARNOLD GAMBLE CIR
100 SAC 95835 257-B4
ARNSIDE WY
- SaCo 95829 338-J6
ARONA CT
9800 ELKG 95757 378-A1
ARRAN CT
- RSVL 95661 220-E7
ARRAN ST
- RSVL 95661 220-E7

ARRIBA WY
- SAC 95835 256-H3
ARROW CT
900 LNCN 95648 200-B2
2600 EDCo 95682 263-D3
ARROWBROOK AV
- SAC 95835 257-C6
ARROWHEAD AV
1000 SaCo 95673 257-J4
1100 SaCo 95673 258-A4
ARROWHEAD CT
- RVIS 94571 454-F2
100 LNCN 95648 200-B1
3700 EDCo 95762 263-D7
ARROWHEAD DR
3800 EDCo 95762 262-D7
3800 EDCo 95762 282-D1
4600 PlaC 95677 220-F4
ARROWHEAD ST
- WSAC 95691 316-C4
ARROWOOD CT
4400 SaCo 95842 258-J6
ARROW POINT WY
4900 SAC [illegible] 257-J7
ARROWROCK RD
100 SAC 95838 277-G4
ARROWROOT CIR
8400 SaCo 95843 239-C5
ARROWSMITH DR
100 FOLS 95630 261-G3
ARROW WOOD LN
- RSVL 95747 199-D7
- RSVL 95747 219-D1
ARROYO CT
1000 RSVL 95661 239-J5
ARROYO DR
1700 AUB 95603 182-D7
1700 PlaC 95603 182-D7
ARROYO ST
5000 SaCo 95628 260-E7
ARROYO GRANDE DR
1100 SaCo 95864 298-G2
ARROYO MADRONE CT
- LNCN 95648 200-A2
ARROYO MADRONE LN
- LNCN 95648 200-A2
ARROYO SECO LN
3600 SaCo 95660 258-G1
ARROYO VISTA DR
6600 SAC 95823 338-B5
ARROYO VISTA WY
- EDCo 95667 265-C1
1700 EDCo 95762 242-F6
ARSENAULT DR
- RSVL 95747 219-D5
ART PKWY
4400 SaCo 95823 337-G2
ARTEMIS CT
100 RSVL 95661 240-E1
ARTESIA RD
100 SaCo 95626 237-G4
4700 EDCo 95682 264-D3
ARTESIAN CT
- SaCo 95829 339-D6
ARTHUR CT
100 RSVL 95661 240-E4
300 LNCN 95648 179-F3
ARTHUR DR
800 WSAC 95605 296-J1
ARTHUR WY
3200 SaCo 95821 278-D5
ARTHUR HILLS CT
9900 SaCo 95829 339-D5
ARTISAN CIR
- RSVL 95678 219-J2
ARTWOOD CT
8800 ELKG 95758 357-J3
ARUBA CIR
- SAC 95823 338-B6
ARUBA ST
- WSAC 95691 316-D2
ARUM PL
- SaCo 95843 239-B6
ARUNDEL CT
- RSVL 95747 218-H4
ARUNDEL RD
- EDCo 95726 248-C4
ARUNDEL WY
800 SAC 95833 277-E6
ARUTAS DR
7100 SaCo 95660 258-H1
ARVADA CT
6900 SaCo 95828 338-B1
ARVILLA DR
1400 SAC 95822 317-B4
ARVIS CT
- SAC 95835 257-D6
ARZATE LN
2100 ANT 94509 (513-F6 See Page 493)
ASANTE LN
- WSAC 95691 317-A2
ASBURY CT
5900 SaCo 95842 258-J5
ASCADA CT
600 FOLS 95630 261-E3
ASCELLA DR
500 EDCo 95619 265-D5
ASCENSION LN
8000 EDCo 95630 222-A6
8000 EDCo 95630 242-B1
ASCENSION ST
4500 RKLN 95677 220-D2
ASCOLANO AV
8300 SaCo 95628 260-C7
ASCOT AV
300 SAC 95838 257-G5
300 SaCo 95673 257-G5
300 SaCo 95838 257-G5
300 SAC 95673 257-G5
1100 SaCo 95838 258-A5
1100 SAC 95838 258-A5
2000 SAC 95652 258-A5
2000 SaCo 95652 258-A5
W ASCOT AV
100 SaCo 95673 257-F5
100 SaCo 95838 257-F5
100 SAC 95673 257-F5
100 SAC 95838 257-F5
ASCOT DR
1400 RSVL 95661 240-A2
ASCOT LN
4200 EDCo 95682 264-B4
ASH AV
900 WSAC 95691 296-H4
ASH CT
5400 LMS 95650 200-H7
ASH PL
- EDCo 95682 263-D2

ASH RD
7200 SaCo 95628 279-G2
ASH ST
100 RSVL 95678 239-H1
7700 SaCo 95843 239-C7
ASHBORO LN
700 GALT 95632 419-F4
ASHBOURNE CT
9500 PlaC 95746 240-H6
ASHBOURNE DR
2800 SaCo 95821 278-F6
ASHBROOK LN
5700 SaCo 95662 260-J6
ASHBURTON DR
3000 ANT 94509 (513-F7 See Page 493)
ASHBURTON PL
8800 ELKG 95758 358-A2
ASHBURY CT
- PlaC 95747 239-B2
ASHBURY WY
3500 SAC 95834 277-E3
ASHBY LN
1500 PlaC 95658 160-J7
1500 PlaC 95658 180-J1
5200 PlaC 95746 240-H1
ASHCAT WY
100 FOLS 95630 281-B1
ASH CREEK CT
100 FOLS 95630 241-A7
ASHCROFT AV
4500 SaCo 95841 258-J7
ASHDALE CT
4600 SaCo 95841 259-A7
ASHER LN
6400 SAC 95828 318-G6
ASHEVILLE CT
4600 SaCo 95608 279-F1
ASHFIELD WY
6800 SaCo 95628 259-F7
ASHFORD CT
9700 RCCD 95827 299-C6
ASHFORD DR
1600 RSVL 95661 240-D3
ASHFORD LN
- LNCN 95648 179-F7
ASHFORD PL
2200 EDCo 95762 242-C5
ASHFORD HILL PL
8300 SaCo 95843 239-B5
ASHGROVE WY
3900 SaCo 95826 318-J2
ASH HILL CT
8700 SaCo 95662 260-E2
ASHINGTON WY
6700 ELKG 95758 358-A5
ASHLAND CT
- EDCo 95682 263-E4
- RKLN 95765 200-A7
ASHLAND DR
- EDCo 95682 263-E4
2700 RSVL 95661 240-E4
ASHLAND WY
5000 SAC 95822 317-C4
ASHLAR CT
9500 ELKG 95624 359-B7
ASHLEY CT
- LNCN 95648 179-E4
ASHLEY WY
3000 SAC 95833 277-D4
3100 ANT 94509 (513-F7 See Page 493)
ASHLEY CREEK CT
- PlaC 95650 201-E4
ASHLEY OAKS CT
- SAC 95815 278-A5
ASHLEY WOODS DR
- RSVL 95746 240-F4
ASHLIE CT
5000 EDCo 95682 283-G5
ASHLY WY
100 GALT 95632 419-E6
ASHMEAD WY
- SAC 95835 257-C5
ASHMONT ST
7800 CITH 95621 239-E7
ASHMORE WY
8900 ELKG 95624 358-G3
ASHORE WY
400 SAC 95831 316-G7
ASHRIDGE CT
- RSVL 95746 240-F4
ASHRIDGE WY
- RSVL 95746 240-F4
ASHTEAD CT
8100 SaCo 95829 339-A6
ASHTON CT
6500 PlaC 95746 241-B2
ASHTON DR
- RSVL 95747 218-J5
4100 SaCo 95864 298-J4
ASHTONE WY
9700 ELKG 95624 359-A7
ASHTON PARK LN
500 SaCo 95864 298-H4
ASHURST CT
5100 ELKG 95758 357-H2
ASHWELL CT
500 SaCo 95673 257-H4
ASHWELL WY
- RSVL 95747 218-J4
8900 ELKG 95624 358-G3
ASHWOOD CT
- LNCN 95648 179-J2
1800 FOLS 95630 261-J6
1800 FOLS 95630 262-A6
ASHWOOD DR
1400 OAKL 94561 (514-D7 See Page 493)
ASHWOOD LN
3200 SaCo 95608 279-C5
ASHWOOD WY
- LNCN 95648 179-J1
7500 SAC 95822 337-F3
ASHWORTH WY
5900 SaCo 95608 259-D6
ASIATIC LION CT
- SaCo 95829 338-H5
ASIMOV WY
- SaCo 95829 339-B6
ASLIN WY
6300 SaCo 95608 259-E5
ASPEN CT
- RSVL 95678 219-F5
5900 RKLN 95677 220-E5
ASPEN DR
3000 PlaC 95650 201-D4
3000 PlaC 95663 201-D4
3900 EDCo 95682 263-J6

ASPEN LN
8000 CITH 95610 240-C7
ASPENBROOK WY
8500 ELKG 95624 358-F2
ASPEN CREST CT
8500 ELKG 95624 358-E4
ASPEN GARDENS WY
- CITH 95621 259-G4
ASPEN GLEN CT
- CITH 95621 259-G3
ASPEN GROVE CT
- EDCo 95762 282-D4
ASPEN GROVE LN
5600 ELKG 95757 357-J6
ASPEN HEIGHTS CT
11800 RCCD 95742 320-D4
ASPEN HILL CT
- SaCo 95843 238-F4
ASPEN MEADOWS CT
9900 SaCo 95829 339-D5
ASPEN MEADOWS WY
- LNCN 95648 179-J1
- LNCN 95648 180-A2
ASPEN RANCH CT
- CITH 95621 259-G4
ASPEN RIDGE CT
8600 SaCo 95843 238-G5
ASPEN ROSE WY
300 GALT 95632 419-D6
ASPEN TREE LN
- ELKG 95758 357-H2
ASPEN VALLEY LN
100 SAC 95835 256-J4
2500 SAC 95835 257-A4
ASPEN VIEW CT
- CITH 95621 259-G3
ASPENWOOD CT
5500 CITH 95610 259-H6
ASSAY CT
- SAC 95831 336-G1
ASSEMBLY CT
6500 SaCo 95823 337-J1
ASSISI WY
5700 LMS 95650 220-J4
ASTER AV
1800 WSAC 95691 296-H6
ASTER CT
- RKLN 95765 219-H2
8400 CITH 95610 260-C1
ASTER DR
1300 ANT 94509 (513-B4 See Page 493)
ASTER CREST CT
9300 ELKG 95624 358-E5
ASTERISM CT
- SAC 95834 277-A3
ASTEROID CT
6200 SaCo 95662 260-D4
ASTI CT
- LNCN 95648 179-E5
ASTILL WY
600 RSVL 95678 219-J6
600 RSVL 95678 220-A6
ASTON PL
1700 EDCo 95762 242-C5
ASTORIA PL
1100 EDCo 95762 242-B5
ASTORIA ST
3500 SAC 95838 278-C2
ASTRAL DR
3500 RCCD 95827 299-D6
ASTRO CT
900 SAC 95831 316-J6
ASTRO LN
- EDCo 95726 247-J5
ASTRON PKWY
7000 SaCo 95823 337-J1
ASTRONAUT LN
6100 CITH 95621 259-D2
ASUNCION CT
- EDCo 95762 262-C1
ATESSA CT
- RSVL 95747 219-B2
ATFIELD WY
100 FOLS 95630 261-F7
ATHAN AV
100 RSVL 95678 239-G1
ATHELSON PL
9000 SaCo 95829 338-H6
ATHENA AV
1000 SAC 95833 277-D6
ATHENA WY
13100 PlaC 95603 162-D4
ATHENS AV
2300 PlaC 95648 199-C3
2400 PlaC 95765 199-C3
ATHENS CT
2600 SaCo 95826 298-D7
ATHENS LN
1800 ANT 94509 (513-G5 See Page 493)
ATHENS RIVER CT
2200 RCCD 95670 280-A5
ATHERTON PL
- WSAC 95691 296-H7
ATHERTON RD
3700 RKLN 95765 199-H6
ATHERTON ST
1400 SAC 95822 317-B5
ATHY CT
600 GALT 95632 419-E2
ATKINS DR
10000 ELKG 95757 377-J2
10000 ELKG 95757 397-J2
ATKINSON ST
100 RSVL 95678 239-F3
1500 RSVL 95747 239-F3
9100 PlaC 95747 239-F4
ATLANTA ST
- SaCo 95742 280-H4
ATLANTA WY
5100 SaCo 95841 259-B3
ATLANTIC DR
- RVIS 94571 454-E1
- WSAC 95691 296-H7
ATLANTIC PL
- WSAC 95691 296-H7
ATLANTIC ST
- RSVL 95678 239-J1
600 RSVL 95678 240-A1
800 RSVL 95678 220-A7
ATLANTIS DR
10200 ELKG 95624 359-E1
ATLAS AV
2500 SAC 95820 317-E3
ATLAS LN
- EDCo 95633 205-C3
ATLEY
- SaCo 95608 279-B3

ATOLL CT
6000 CITH 95621 259-F5
ATOMIC CT
10000 RCCD 95827 299-D6
ATRISCO CIR
2200 SAC 95833 277-B5
ATRIUM WY
4200 SAC 95834 276-H1
ATTAWA AV
3900 SaCo 95822 317-D3
ATTERBURY WY
- ELKG 95758 357-E5
ATWATER RD
3700 SaCo 95864 278-G7
ATWELL ST
1600 RSVL 95747 239-B1
ATWOOD DR
10600 RCCD 95670 299-H1
ATWOOD LN
3000 PlaC 95603 161-H4
ATWOOD RD
10200 PlaC 95603 161-J4
10900 PlaC 95603 162-A4
AUBERGINE DR
100 SaCo 95835 319-H2
AUBERRY CT
7700 PlaC 95746 241-D3
AUBERRY DR
- ELKG 95624 338-D7
- ELKG 95624 358-D1
8100 SaCo 95828 338-C6
8400 SaCo 95624 338-D7
S AUBERRY DR
- ELKG 95624 358-D1
AUBREE LN
- RKLN 95765 199-J5
AUBREY CT
8600 ELKG 95624 358-H1
AUBURN AV
8000 SaCo 95626 237-G6
AUBURN BLVD
1900 SAC 95815 278-A6
2000 SAC 95821 278-H2
2200 SaCo 95821 278-C5
4100 SAC 95841 278-H2
4400 SaCo 95841 278-H2
4700 SaCo 95841 259-C5
4700 SaCo 95841 279-A1
5900 CITH 95621 259-F3
5900 SaCo 95621 259-C5
5900 CITH 95841 259-C5
7000 CITH 95610 259-H2
7600 CITH 95610 239-H6
8500 RSVL 95661 239-H6
AUBURN CT
- LNCN 95648 179-E4
AUBURN LN
2500 ANT 94509 (513-B6 See Page 493)
AUBURN-FOLSOM RD
100 AUB 95603 182-D5
1600 PlaC 95603 182-A7
1600 PlaC 95603 202-A1
2100 PlaC 95658 202-A1
2300 PlaC 95658 201-J4
3000 PlaC 95650 221-F3
3200 PlaC 95650 201-H7
3500 PlaC 95746 221-F3
6900 PlaC 95746 241-C1
7600 FOLS 95630 241-B6
AUBURN HILLS DR
- EDCo 95682 263-F4
AUBURN OAKS CT
7400 CITH 95610 239-H6
7400 CITH 95621 239-H6
AUBURN OAKS VILLAGE LN
7900 CITH 95610 240-C7
AUBURN POINT WY
8100 CITH 95610 240-B7
AUBURN RAVINE DR
- LNCN 95648 179-E4
AUBURN RAVINE RD
200 AUB 95603 182-D1
600 AUB 95603 162-E7
1300 PlaC 95603 162-E7
AUBURN RIDGE CT
7600 SaCo 95843 239-B7
AUBURN WIND CT
7800 CITH 95610 240-B7
AUBURN WOODS CT
- EDCo 95682 263-E4
AUBURN WOODS DR
7700 CITH 95610 240-B7
AUDIA CIR
- SAC 95823 338-A3
AUDREY WY
900 RSVL 95661 239-J4
1000 RSVL 95661 240-A3
5700 SaCo 95628 259-F6
AUDUBON CIR
100 SAC 95831 336-E1
AUDUBON CT
3700 EDCo 95709 246-H1
AUDUBON DR
3600 EDCo 95709 246-H1
AUDUBON PL
500 SaCo 95825 298-D4
AUDUBON WY
10600 RCCD 95670 279-G7
AUDUBON HILL PL
- LNCN 95648 180-C7
- LNCN 95648 200-B1
AUGIBI WY
2500 RCCD 95670 299-F1
AUGUST WY
1200 ANT 94509 (513-E4 See Page 493)
AUGUSTA CT
- RKLN 95765 200-B5
900 RVIS 94571 454-E2
AUGUSTA WY
- RKLN 95765 200-B5
- SaCo 95828 338-D1
1100 RSVL 95661 240-A4
AUGUSTINE CT
8900 SaCo 95662 260-F4
AUGUSTINE LN
- EDCo 95619 266-D7
AUGUSTUS PL
2000 EDCo 95762 242-B6
AULDEARN CT
- FOLS 95630 261-J5
AURELIA CT
- ELKG 95757 357-F7
- ELKG 95757 377-F1
- ELKG 95757 397-F1
AURELIUS WY
6700 SaCo 95662 260-C3

© 2007 Rand McNally & Company

AURORA LP — SACRAMENTO COUNTY STREET INDEX — BASLER ST 520

(c) 2007 Rand McNally & Company

SACRAMENTO CO.

STREET Block City ZIP Pg-Grid

AURORA LP
3700 RKLN 95677 220-B3
AURORA WY
- RVIS 94571 454-F3
2800 SaCo 95821 278-C6
AURUM CITY RD
6400 EDCo 95623 265-C5
AUSPICIOUS WY
4600 SaCo 95842 259-A1
AUSTELL WY
8100 SaCo 95828 338-D3
AUSTEN CT
- RSVL 95747 239-C1
AUSTIN CT
- LNCN 95648 179-E3
AUSTIN DR
100 FOLS 95630 261-C6
AUSTIN LN
3300 EDCo 95667 244-F7
AUSTIN ST
4200 SAC 95838 277-G2
4700 SAC 95838 257-G7
AUSTIN WY
6600 SaCo 95823 317-J7
AUTO CENTER DR
1700 ANT 94509 (513-A5 See Page 493)
1700 PIT 94565 (513-A5 See Page 493)
9600 ELKG 95757 358-E6
AUTO MALL CIR
- FOLS 95742 280-H3
AUTOMALL DR
200 RSVL 95661 240-B1
AUTOMOTIVE CT
4500 EDCo 95667 264-G5
AUTUMN AV
7400 CITH 95621 239-G7
AUTUMN CT
1400 RSVL 95661 240-A5
AUTUMN LN
800 ANT 94509 (513-F5 See Page 493)
7700 PlaC 95650 221-D3
AUTUMN PK
1800 SAC 95834 277-B4
AUTUMN TRWY
- EDCo 95762 282-D4
AUTUMN WY
4400 EDCo 95682 263-J1
4400 EDCo 95682 264-A1
6500 EDCo 95684 286-E7
AUTUMN BREEZE WY
10400 RCCD 95670 299-F4
AUTUMN FALLS LN
- LNCN 95648 199-J3
AUTUMN GLEN CT
- PlaC 95650 201-E5
AUTUMNGLEN CT
- ELKG 95758 357-H3
AUTUMN GOLD CT
8800 ELKG 95624 358-G1
AUTUMN GROVE WY
6900 ELKG 95758 358-B4
AUTUMN LAKE DR
7400 SaCo 95624 340-G3
AUTUMN LEAF LN
2200 RCCD 95670 279-J6
AUTUMN MEADOW AV
- SAC 95835 257-A4
AUTUMN OAK CT
6300 CITH 95621 239-E7
AUTUMN OAK WY
1800 OAKL 94561 (514-D6 See Page 493)
AUTUMN POINT LN
3500 SaCo 95608 279-E4
AUTUMN RIDGE DR
3700 EDCo 95667 264-G1
AUTUMN SAGE WY
9900 ELKG 95757 377-H1
9900 ELKG 95757 397-H1
AUTUMN SKY WY
- EDCo 95762 282-D4
AUTUMN SUNSET WY
11800 RCCD 95742 320-D1
AUTUMNTREE CT
4900 SaCo 95841 259-C7
AUTUMN WALK PL
9600 ELKG 95757 357-J7
AUTUMN WIND CT
7500 PlaC 95658 181-D5
AUTUMNWIND CT
- RKLN 95677 220-F1
AUTUMNWIND LN
11000 RCCD 95670 279-J6
AUTUMNWOOD DR
8900 SaCo 95826 318-H1
AUTUMNWOOD LN
1100 EDCo 95762 242-E3
AUVERNAT CT
10700 RCCD 95670 299-H4
AUVERNAT DR
10700 RCCD 95670 299-H4
AVA WY
6900 SaCo 95608 279-F4
AVALANCHE PEAK WY
600 FOLS 95630 261-A2
AVALINE CT
100 FOLS 95630 261-E4
AVALON CT
- PLCR 95667 245-E4
900 RSVL 95661 239-J5
AVALON DR
2200 SaCo 95864 278-H7
2400 SaCo 95821 278-H6
AVALON HILLS WY
- ELKG 95624 358-G2
AVALOS WY
7900 CITH 95610 240-C7
AVANTE WY
3900 SaCo 95826 319-A2
AVELLANO DR
4000 EDCo 95762 262-E5
AVELLINO WY
9800 ELKG 95757 358-B7
9800 ELKG 95757 378-B1
AVENA WY
9800 ELKG 95757 357-F7
AVENIDA ALVARADO
1300 RSVL 95747 219-C5
AVENIDA CAMISA
1400 RSVL 95747 219-C4
AVENIDA MARTINA
1800 RSVL 95747 219-C4
AVENIDA ROBLES
- PlaC 95746 221-F4
AVENIDA SOLANO
1800 RSVL 95747 219-C4
AVENTINE RD
4400 EDCo 95682 263-B6
AVENUE CHATEAU
- EDCo 95634 225-B2
AVERELL CT
10600 RCCD 95670 279-G7
AVERY CT
8500 SaCo 95828 338-E6
AVERY LN
- EDCo - 267-B6
AVIAN HILL PL
- LNCN 95648 180-B7
AVIARA PL
7900 SaCo 95829 339-D5
AVIARY WOODS WY
8500 ELKG 95624 358-G1
AVIATION BLVD
1900 LNCN 95648 179-C1
1900 LNCN 95648 159-C7
AVIATION DR
6300 SaCo 95837 256-C3
AVIATOR CIR
- SAC 95835 257-B7
AVILA CT
5500 RKLN 95677 220-B3
AVILA DR
- RSVL 95678 219-J5
AVILA LN
- ANT 94509 (513-A6 See Page 493)
4200 SaCo 95864 278-H7
AVOCADO AL
- RSVL 95678 239-H1
AVOCET CT
- SAC 95833 276-H7
2300 ELKG 95757 357-E7
AVOCET WY
- LNCN 95648 179-D1
2400 ELKG 95757 357-E7
AVON RD
2900 RKLN 95765 200-A7
2900 RKLN 95765 220-A1
AVON WY
1100 FOLS 95630 261-D5
AVONDALE AV
1700 SaCo 95825 298-E1
1700 SaCo 95864 298-E1
AVONDALE CT
700 GALT 95632 419-F3
AVONDALE DR
- RSVL 95747 219-B2
AVONLEA PL
- SaCo 95843 239-C5
AWALI AV
100 AUB 95603 182-C4
AWANI CT
4600 SaCo 95628 280-F1
AWAY WY
7600 CITH 95610 259-J3
AXIOS RIVER
- SAC 95831 336-F2
AYALA WY
5600 SAC 95835 256-H4
AYERS LN
800 GALT 95632 419-F5
AYLESBURY CT
2800 WSAC 95691 316-F1
AYLESBURY WY
- RSVL 95747 219-B7
AYLSHAM CT
- FOLS 95630 261-G7
AYN RAND CT
8100 SaCo 95828 338-D5
AYR DR
6300 ELKG 95758 358-A5
AYRES HOLMES RD
3200 PlaC 95603 161-B6
3700 PlaC 95602 161-B3
AYSHRE PL
5800 SaCo 95843 239-D5
AZALEA CT
- LNCN 95648 179-H5
2800 ANT 94531 (513-G7 See Page 493)
AZALEA LN
2800 PLCR 95667 245-G4
AZALEA PL
- WSAC 95691 316-F2
AZALEA RD
2600 SaCo 95864 298-E4
AZALEA WY
- RKLN 95765 219-J1
AZALEA GARDEN WY
11700 RCCD 95742 320-D2
AZALEA PARK WY
4800 RCCD 95742 320-E4
AZAVEDO CT
- FOLS 95630 261-J4
AZELL RD
3600 SaCo 95608 279-E4
AZEO CT
- LNCN 95648 180-A4
AZEVEDO DR
2700 SAC 95833 277-B5
AZEVEDO RD
3000 SolC 94571 454-C1
AZEVEDO ST
1200 ANT 94509 (513-F5 See Page 493)
AZIENDA DR
- RCCD 95670 300-A4
AZIMUTH LN
7300 SaCo 95842 259-C1
AZINGER WY
10100 SaCo 95829 339-E5
AZOREAN CT
- SAC 95833 277-D4
AZORES LN
1200 PlaC 95658 181-E6
AZTEC LN
8200 SaCo 95828 338-D3
AZTEC WY
7800 SaCo 95843 238-G6
AZTECA CT
9700 ELKG 95757 357-H7
AZTECA WY
9700 ELKG 95757 357-H7
AZURE CT
1000 RSVL 95678 239-J3
4500 SaCo 95864 298-J2
AZURITE WY
1700 SAC 95833 277-B5
AZUSA CT
- LNCN 95648 180-A4
AZUSA ST
1000 SAC 95833 277-D6

B

B AV
11200 PlaC 95603 161-J4
11200 PlaC 95603 162-A4
B PKWY
4600 SaCo 95823 337-H2
B ST
- ISLE 95690 455-H5
- RVIS 94571 454-H3
- SaCo 95690 437-A1
100 ISLE 95641 455-H5
100 RSVL 95678 239-H3
200 WSAC 95605 297-A2
200 GALT 95632 419-E7
300 ANT 94509 (513-D4 See Page 493)
400 LNCN 95648 179-H3
2700 SAC 95816 297-G3
2800 EDCo 95709 247-B4
3500 RKLN 95677 220-D3
3500 SaCo 95660 258-G7
4100 SAC 95819 297-J4
4600 SAC 95819 298-A4
7300 SaCo 95823 338-A2
N B ST
400 SAC 95814 297-C2
B WY
2200 SAC 95833 277-E7
BABBE ST
1000 OAKL 94561 (514-C8 See Page 493)
BABCOCK WY
- SAC 95835 256-J5
- SAC 95835 257-A6
BABEL SLOUGH RD
50700 YoCo 95612 336-E4
50700 YoCo 95612 356-C1
BABES CT
10200 SaCo 95829 339-E7
BABETTE WY
2200 SAC 95832 337-D3
BABICH AV
4400 SAC 95822 317-C3
BABSON DR
3600 ELKG 95758 357-G4
BACALL CT
4400 SaCo 95843 238-J7
BACCHINI AV
7100 SaCo 95828 338-D1
BACCUS WY
5300 SAC 95835 257-A5
BACH CT
6100 SaCo 95621 239-D7
BACHE PL
3500 EDCo 95762 262-D2
BACHMAN WY
- FOLS 95630 281-G2
BACK CIR
3200 SaCo 95821 278-D4
BACK ST
- SAC 95821 278-C5
BACK-A-WAYS LN
2000 PlaC 95658 201-H2
BACK BAY CT
- SAC 95823 358-B1
BACKER CT
7100 ELKG 95758 358-B5
BACKER RANCH RD
- ELKG 95757 358-B6
BACO DR
3000 PLCR 95667 245-H5
BACON ISLAND ST
- WSAC 95691 316-E2
BADEN CT
6500 SaCo 95823 317-J7
BADER RD
8500 ELKG 95624 339-C7
5800 ELKG 95624 359-C2
BADGER CT
6600 SaCo 95842 259-A3
BADGER LN
4000 EDCo 95667 265-A2
BADGER COLONY CT
11500 SaCo 95693 (380-B3 See Page 379)
BADGER CREEK LN
10100 SaCo 95693 (380-C2 See Page 379)
BADGER HILL CT
10100 SaCo 95693 (380-B3 See Page 379)
BADGER HILL RD
2300 EDCo 95726 248-A1
BADGER PASS CT
- RKLN 95765 219-J2
BADGER PASS DR
- RKLN 95765 219-J2
BADGER POND CT
10000 SaCo 95693 (380-C2 See Page 379)
BADGER VALLEY CT
11400 SaCo 95693 (380-B2 See Page 379)
BADGER WOODS LN
10900 SaCo 95693 (380-F6 See Page 379)
BADOVINAC DR
1400 RSVL 95747 219-D7
BAGGAN CT
3200 SaCo 95843 238-F6
BAGLEY CT
5500 SaCo 95841 259-A6
BAGOTA WY
11700 RCCD 95742 320-D1
BAGUETTE PL
- FOLS 95630 261-B7
BAHAMA CT
7700 SaCo 95628 259-J7
BAIER WY
8500 SaCo 95828 338-F1
BAILEY CIR
- EDCo 95762 282-D3
BAILEY CT
- EDCo 95762 282-D3
BAILEY LP
5000 SaCo 95652 258-F7
BAILEY WY
4500 SaCo 95864 298-J4
BAINBRIDGE AV
3400 EDCo 95672 263-F2
BAINBRIDGE CT
7300 PlaC 95746 241-C3
BAINBRIDGE DR
3600 SaCo 95660 258-G1
4000 SaCo 95842 258-H1
BAINBROOK ST
- SaCo 95828 338-F3
BAINES AV
- SAC 95835 257-C6
BAIRD DR
300 FOLS 95630 281-B2
BAIRD WY
6500 CITH 95610 239-H6
BAIRDSLEY PL
2400 EDCo 95762 242-C5
BAIRNSDALE WY
3800 SaCo 95826 318-H2
BAISLEY CT
- ELKG 95624 358-E3
BAJA CT
- SAC 95833 277-B5
BAJA DR
- SaCo 95683 322-B7
BAJADA
6300 SaCo 95842 259-A4
BAJAMONT WY
3500 SaCo 95608 279-F4
BAJIA CT
- SAC 95831 316-F6
BAKER AV
4700 SaCo 95820 317-H3
BAKER CT
600 GALT 95632 419-G4
2200 ANT 94509 (513-A7 See Page 493)
BAKER RD
2500 EDCo 95667 245-E4
2500 PLCR 95667 245-E4
BAKULA WY
3100 SaCo 95864 298-F2
BALADA WY
3200 RCCD 95670 299-H4
BALBOA CIR
5600 SAC 95819 298-B4
BALBOA CT
700 GALT 95632 419-F3
2700 ANT 94509 (513-B6 See Page 493)
BALBOA DR
1800 RSVL 95661 240-C4
BALBOA PARK WY
- ELKG 95624 338-J7
- ELKG 95624 358-J1
BALCARO WY
100 SAC 95833 277-C4
100 SAC 95834 277-C4
BALCOMBE CT
- FOLS 95630 261-G7
BALD EAGLE CT
- RSVL 95747 219-B7
2100 SaCo 95670 280-D5
BALD HILL RD
1100 PlaC 95603 181-J1
1100 PlaC 95658 181-H3
2000 PlaC 95603 161-J6
BALD MOUNTAIN CT
100 FOLS 95630 241-A7
BALDPATE CT
2800 WSAC 95691 316-F1
BALDUR CT
7900 ELKG 95758 358-C6
BALDWIN AV
200 RSVL 95678 239-G5
BALDWIN WY
200 SaCo 95864 298-F5
BALDWIN DAM RD
7000 FOLS 95630 261-A2
7700 FOLS 95630 241-A7
BALDWIN LAKE CIR
100 FOLS 95630 241-B7
BALDWIN LAKE CT
100 FOLS 95630 241-B7
BALFOR CT
2800 RKLN 95765 200-A7
2800 RKLN 95765 220-A1
BALFOR PL
100 FOLS 95630 261-A2
BALFOR RD
5700 RKLN 95765 200-A7
5700 RKLN 95765 220-A1
BALFOUR WY
7400 SAC 95822 337-E2
BALI CT
6900 SaCo 95662 260-E3
BALI ST
- SAC 95828 318-D5
BALIN CT
- FOLS 95630 281-E2
BALL WY
2600 SaCo 95821 278-E4
BALLANTINE ST
5500 SaCo 95826 319-A4
5500 SaCo 95829 319-A4
BALLANTRAE WY
- RKLN 95677 220-E6
- RSVL 95661 220-E6
10800 RCCD 95670 279-H7
10800 RCCD 95670 299-H1
BALLARD CT
- FOLS 95630 281-E2
BALLARD DR
3800 SaCo 95608 279-A3
BALLAST WY
- FOLS 95630 281-B1
BALLENA BAY RD
- WSAC 95691 316-D2
BALLINA CT
8900 ELKG 95624 378-H1
BALLPARK DR
- WSAC 95691 297-A4
BALLYGAR WY
7100 ELKG 95758 358-B6
BALMORAL DR
3200 SaCo 95821 278-F6
8500 PlaC 95658 201-F2
BALMORE DR
- RSVL 95747 219-E7
- RSVL 95747 239-D1
BALSAM ST
1000 WSAC 95691 296-H4
3700 SaCo 95838 278-A2
BALTIC AV
- WSAC 95691 296-G7
BALTIC CIR
3800 RKLN 95677 220-E1
12800 AUB 95603 162-E7
BALTIMORE RD
300 AUB 95603 182-C4
BALTIMORE ST
- SaCo 95742 280-G4
BALVERNE CT
3900 SaCo 95843 238-H5
BAMA CT
7500 SaCo 95828 338-B2
BAMARCIA DR
8600 ELKG 95624 358-J1
BAMBI CT
3900 SaCo 95608 279-C3
BAMBOO ST
- RSVL 95747 219-A7
BAMBOO WY
4600 SaCo 95628 280-B1
BAMBRIDGE WY
8900 ELKG 95758 358-A3
BAMBURGH CT
7900 SaCo 95829 338-J5
BAMFORD DR
5200 SAC 95823 338-A5
5200 SAC 95823 337-J5
BANBRIDGE WY
1700 SAC 95832 337-C4
BANBURY CIR
2200 RSVL 95661 240-E3
BANBURY DR
9300 ELKG 95758 357-J5
BANCHORY CT
4300 SaCo 95843 238-J6
BANCROFT DR
4000 EDCo 95762 242-C6
BANCROFT WY
200 SaCo 95864 298-F5
BANDALIN CT
2800 WSAC 95691 316-F1
BANDALIN WY
- SAC 95823 337-J5
BANDERAS CT
- SAC 95835 257-A5
BANDERAS WY
- SAC 95835 257-A5
BANDO CT
8700 ELKG 95624 359-G2
BANDON WY
1700 SAC 95833 277-B4
BANDOS LN
1900 PlaC 95603 162-D4
BANDY RD
7100 SaCo 95829 338-H1
BANEBERRY CT
- ELKG 95624 358-F1
BANFF CT
100 GALT 95632 419-E6
3100 SaCo 95843 238-E7
BANFF VISTA DR
8500 ELKG 95624 358-E6
BANFIELD DR
- SAC 95835 257-B5
BANGOR CT
8600 ELKG 95624 358-F5
BANK CT
4200 SaCo 95864 298-J4
BANKFOOT CT
- FOLS 95630 261-J2
BANKHEAD RD
3500 LMS 95650 200-H7
BANKSIDE WY
- SAC 95835 256-J4
BANNER CT
8500 SaCo 95843 238-G5
BANNERMAN CT
- EDCo 95762 262-H4
BANNER MINE CT
2000 SaCo 95670 280-C4
BANNISTER RD
3700 SaCo 95628 279-H3
BANNOCK CT
8400 CITH 95610 240-D7
BANNON ST
200 SAC 95814 297-C1
BANNON CREEK DR
1600 SAC 95833 277-B5
BANTAM WY
4500 ELKG 95758 357-H5
BANTON CIR
8600 ELKG 95624 358-H1
BANTRY CT
8100 SaCo 95829 338-J6
BANTRY PL
- EDCo 95762 262-F4
BANTRY BAY CT
- RSVL 95747 219-C1
BANYAN WY
2100 ANT 94509 (513-B5 See Page 493)
BANYON DR
9300 ELKG 95758 357-J5
BANYON TREE CT
8400 ELKG 95624 358-J1
BAPTIST CT
4100 SaCo 95660 258-H7
BAQUERA CT
1000 RSVL 95678 239-F1
S BAR LN
9700 SaCo 95693 359-H7
BARANDAS DR
- SAC 95835 276-H6
BARANELLO WY
- ELKG 95757 358-A7
BARANGA DR
7000 CITH 95621 259-F2
BARAT CT
8100 SaCo 95829 338-H6
BARBARA ST
4000 SAC 95838 278-C2
BARBARA WY
600 RSVL 95678 219-G7
5500 SaCo 95608 279-C5
BARBARA LEE CIR
6800 SaCo 95842 259-B3
BARBARELL WY
2800 SaCo 95821 278-H6
BARBEE WY
4600 SAC 95823 337-H3
BARBER CT
- EDCo 95762 262-H4
W BARBER RD
9200 SJCo 95686 437-G1
9200 SJCo 95686 (438-A1 See Page 418)
BARBERA WY
2500 RCCD 95670 299-G2
BARBERRY LN
3000 SaCo 95864 298-F4
BARBERRY PL
- WSAC 95691 316-E2
BARBROOK CT
- RSVL 95747 218-J4
BARBROOK WY
- RSVL 95747 218-J5
BARBULA HILL RD
9200 PlaC 95658 201-H2
BARCA LN
7700 CITH 95610 239-J7
BARCELONA CIR
2700 ANT 94509 (513-B6 See Page 493)
BARCELONA CT
- RSVL 95747 219-B1
- EDCo 95762 262-C7
6000 PlaC 95746 221-F5
BARCELONA DR
1500 EDCo 95762 262-C7
BARCELONA WY
2300 SaCo 95825 278-C7
BARCHETTA CT
8600 SaCo 95828 338-F6
BARCON WY
3300 SAC 95838 278-A4
BARDMOOR CT
8300 SaCo 95662 260-C4
BARDOLINO WY
3500 RCCD 95670 299-J5
BAR D RANCH CT
2000 EDCo 95672 263-G1
BARDSWELL CT
7800 ELKG 95758 358-C6
BAR DU LN
- SaCo 95829 339-A4
BARENGO WY
8000 SaCo 95829 338-H5
BARETTA CT
8400 SaCo 95828 338-E7
BAREX CT
4900 EDCo 95682 264-E6
BAR HARBOUR CT
5900 ELKG 95758 357-J6
5900 ELKG 95758 358-A6
BARI CT
7100 ELKG 95757 378-B1
BARJO AL
- RSVL 95678 239-H2
BARKER RD
3200 LMS 95650 200-H5
BARKER ELMS CT
6100 SaCo 95608 279-D4
BARKLEY RD
2500 EDCo 95709 246-J3
2500 EDCo 95709 247-A3
BARKLEY WY
6500 SaCo 95828 338-B2
BARKWOOD LN
4800 EDCo 95682 264-E5
BARLEY WY
- LNCN 95648 180-A1
BARLIN CT
4600 SAC 95822 317-A3
BARLOW CT
3000 EDCo 95762 263-A5
BARMOUTH CT
900 ANT 94509 (513-F7 See Page 493)
BARMOUTH DR
3000 ANT 94509 (513-F7 See Page 493)
BARNABY CT
5000 SaCo 95842 259-A5
BARNES LN
7600 PlaC 95650 201-D6
BARNETT CIR
1500 SaCo 95608 299-A2
BARNETT LN
2600 EDCo 95667 245-F3
2600 PLCR 95667 245-F3
BARNETT LOOP RD
5000 EDCo 95682 283-G3
BARNETT RANCH CT
2500 EDCo 95682 283-H5
BARNETT RANCH RD
4300 EDCo 95682 283-G4
BARNEY CREEK RD
2600 EDCo 95667 245-D3
BARNHART CIR
- SAC 95835 257-A4
BARNHILL LN
- LNCN 95648 179-F7
BARNHOUSE LN
- EDCo 95672 243-F6
BARN OWL CT
300 FOLS 95630 282-B1
1800 AUB 95603 182-D6
8700 ELKG 95624 358-G2
BARNSLEY CT
900 ANT 94509 (513-C7 See Page 493)
BARNSTEAD PL
2700 EDCo 95762 262-D1
BARN SWALLOW CT
- RKLN 95765 199-J7
2300 ELKG 95757 357-E7
BARNSWOOD LP
- LNCN 95648 179-J7
- LNCN 95648 199-J1
BARNUM CT
6900 SaCo 95828 338-B1
BARN VALLEY CT
- LNCN 95648 179-J7
BARN VALLEY LN
- LNCN 95648 179-J7
- LNCN 95648 199-J1
BARNWOOD CT
- CITH 95621 259-E2
BARNWOOD LN
- RSVL 95747 199-D7
- RSVL 95747 219-D1
BARON AV
4400 SaCo 95821 278-J2
BARON CT
3200 EDCo 95682 263-D4
BARONA CT
- WSAC 95691 297-A7
BARONA ST
- WSAC 95691 296-J7
- WSAC 95691 297-A7
BARONESS CT
- RSVL 95747 219-B1
BARONESS WY
- RSVL 95747 219-B1
BARONET WY
2800 SAC 95833 277-B5
BARONIAL LN
- RKLN 95765 200-A4
BARONNEL LN
7400 SaCo 95828 338-F3
BAROOSHIAN CT
700 AUB 95603 162-E6
BAROQUE DR
- RCCD 95670 299-J4
- RCCD 95670 300-A4
BAROSSA CT
10900 RCCD 95670 299-J4
BAROSSA WY
- RSVL 95747 219-B1
BARR WY
7300 SAC 95831 337-A2
BARRACUDA WY
8700 SaCo 95826 298-G6
BARRAGAN CT
1000 EDCo 95667 246-D5
BARRANCA CT
- EDCo 95762 282-C2
BARRANCA DR
- EDCo 95762 282-C2
BAR RANCH RD
2200 EDCo 95762 242-E4
10400 PlaC 95603 182-A1
BARREL RACER CT
9400 SaCo 95693 360-H6
BARRET DR
2800 RSVL 95661 240-F4
BARRETT DR
1600 PLCR 95667 245-J6
1600 PLCR 95667 246-A6
BARRETT RD
4200 SaCo 95608 279-E2
BARRETTE AV
- SAC 95815 277-G7
BARRETT PARK LN
- PlaC - 160-D5
- PlaC 95648 160-D5
BARRETT PASS RD
- EDCo - 247-H1
BARRHEAD CT
1700 FOLS 95630 261-J7
BARRHILL WY
8900 SaCo 95628 260-F6
9000 SaCo 95662 260-F6
BARRIE LN
- LNCN 95648 179-F7
BARRINGTON CT
- RKLN 95677 220-F5
BARRINGTON LN
1100 LNCN 95648 179-G5
BARRINGTON RD
3300 SaCo 95864 298-F2
BARRINGTON HILLS DR
- RKLN 95677 220-F5
BARRISTER LN
8800 SaCo 95628 280-E1
BARRISTER PL
4700 SaCo 95628 280-E1
E BARRON RD
3400 SJCo 95220 439-J3
BARROS DR
700 SAC 95835 257-E6
BARROWS WY
100 FOLS 95630 261-C7
BARRY LN
1900 EDCo 95667 245-D1
BARRYMAN CT
8200 SaCo 95829 339-D7
BARRYMORE DR
- ELKG 95624 338-F7
- ELKG 95828 338-F7
- SaCo 95828 338-F7
BARSETTI CT
500 GALT 95632 419-G5
BARSTOW ST
2000 SAC 95815 277-G7
BART AV
100 ANT 94509 (513-E4 See Page 493)
BARTH ST
9300 ELKG 95624 358-G5
BARTHOLOMEW LN
7900 SaCo 95628 280-A2
BARTIG WY
- CITH 95621 259-G6
- CITH 95628 259-G6
BARTLETT AV
900 PLCR 95667 245-G6
BARTLETT CT
900 EDCo 95762 262-C3
BARTLEY CT
7800 PlaC 95746 241-B1
BARTLEY DR
3800 SAC 95822 317-B2
BARTOLOMEI CT
10000 ELKG 95757 378-B2
BARTON LN
3200 ANT 94509 (513-J5 See Page 493)
6400 EDCo 95667 244-G5
BARTON RD
4000 LMS 95650 201-A7
4000 LMS 95650 221-A1
5000 LMS 95650 220-J7
5000 RKLN 95650 220-J7
5000 RKLN 95650 221-A1
6300 PlaC 95746 220-J7
6300 PlaC 95650 220-J7
7000 FOLS 95630 241-A6
7000 PlaC 95746 241-A3
7500 PlaC 95746 240-J1
7600 RSVL 95746 241-A6
BARTON WY
100 SAC 95838 277-G4
BARUSCH CT
400 RSVL 95747 219-A4
BAR V RD
2100 PlaC 95603 161-F7
2100 PlaC 95603 181-F1
BASALT CT
900 ANT 94509 (513-F7 See Page 493)
8400 CITH 95610 260-C1
BASALT WY
800 ANT 94509 (513-F7 See Page 493)
BASCOM CT
- SAC 95835 257-A5
BASCOU CT
7400 PlaC 95746 241-D3
BASELINE RD
1300 RSVL 95747 239-B1
1500 PlaC 95747 239-B1
3900 RSVL 95747 238-G1
3900 PlaC 95747 238-G1
5900 PlaC 95626 238-B1
6300 PlaC 95626 237-F1
6300 SuCo 95626 237-F1
BASHKIR CT
9700 ELKG 95757 357-H7
BASIE WY
- RCCD 95670 299-G4
BASIL CT
- EDCo 95762 263-B5
- SAC 95831 336-G2
BASIN CT
- SAC 95758 358-C2
BASKIN CT
- ELKG 95758 357-F5
BASLER ST
1600 SAC 95814 297-E2

STREET	Block	City	ZIP	Pg-Grid
BASLOW CT	-	RSVL	95661	220-E6
BASS CT	100	RSVL	95661	240-D5
	2600	SaCo	95826	298-G6
BASS ST	-	WSAC	95691	316-D3
BASSETT WY	4900	SAC	95823	337-J7
BASSILICA CT	-	RSVL	95747	199-B7
N BASS ISLAND RD	-	WSAC	95691	316-E2
BASS LAKE RD	2300	EDCo	95672	263-A5
	2300	EDCo	95682	263-A5
	2600	EDCo	95762	262-J5
	2600	EDCo	95762	282-J1
	3400	EDCo	95762	263-A5
BASSWOOD WY	8100	CITH	95621	239-F6
BASTIEN CT	7900	SaCo	95828	338-E5
BASTONA DR	-	ELKG	95758	357-D4
BASTONE CT	-	WSAC	95691	316-J2
BATACAO LN	300	ANT	94509	(513-D6 See Page 493)
BATAVIA CT	-	SAC	95835	257-B6
BATEMAN CT	800	GALT	95632	419-F3
BATEMAN WY	800	GALT	95632	419-F3
BATES AV	-	SaCo	95615	(396-D3 See Page 375)
BATES CIR	2000	EDCo	95762	242-C7
BATESON CT	-	SAC	95758	358-C2
BATEY AV	9400	ELKG	95624	358-J6
BATHGATE CT	-	FOLS	95630	281-J2
BATHURST CT	100	FOLS	95630	261-G3
BATON AV	8700	SaCo	95662	260-E5
BATOON CT	5500	ELKG	95757	377-J3
	5500	ELKG	95757	397-J3
BATT DR	4300	SAC	95838	277-J1
BATTENBURG WY	11700	RCCD	95742	320-D1
BATTLECREEK CIR	100	SAC	95835	257-C4
BATTLES CT	4700	ELKG	95757	377-H2
	4700	ELKG	95757	397-H2
BATTLEWOOD WY	5300	SaCo	95608	299-B2
BAUER AV	-	SaCo	95632	419-B7
BAUGH CT	7100	CITH	95610	260-A2
BAUMGART WY	4400	SAC	95838	277-G1
	5300	SaCo	95608	259-E7
BAURER CIR	100	FOLS	95630	261-H6
BAUSELL ST	3500	SaCo	95821	278-J4
BAUSER AV	-	RSVL	95747	219-C4
BAUTISTA ST	2700	ANT	94509	(513-D6 See Page 493)
BAVENO WY	6600	ELKG	95757	378-A1
BAXTER AV	100	SAC	95815	277-G7
	100	SAC	95815	297-G1
BAXTER WY	8700	SaCo	95628	260-E5
	8700	SaCo	95662	260-E5
BAXTER GRADE	7100	PlaC	95603	161-F4
S BAY	900	SAC	95831	336-J4
BAY DR	-	SAC	95815	277-G6
E BAY LN	7600	SAC	95831	336-J3
W BAY LN	7600	SAC	95831	336-J3
BAY ST	5200	RKLN	95765	200-B6
BAY TRCT	-	GALT	95632	419-G2
BAYBERRY CIR	4100	EDCo	95762	262-E5
BAYBERRY CT	-	LNCN	95648	199-J2
	-	LNCN	95648	200-A2
	8000	CITH	95610	260-B3
BAYBERRY DR	-	LNCN	95648	200-A2
BAYBERRY ST	-	WSAC	95691	296-J7
	-	WSAC	95691	316-J1
BAYBRIDGE CT	-	SAC	95833	276-J6
BAYBRIDGE ST	-	SAC	95833	276-J6
	-	SAC	95833	277-A6
BAYER CT	-	FOLS	95630	261-J4
BAYFIELD CT	-	LNCN	95648	179-H5
BAYFORD WY	8100	SaCo	95829	339-A6
BAY HEAD CT	-	ELKG	95758	357-E4
BAY HEIGHTS CT	800	GALT	95632	419-F2
BAY HEIGHTS DR	700	GALT	95632	419-F2
BAY HILL WY	6400	SaCo	95662	260-C4
BAY HORSE LN	2200	SAC	95835	257-B3
BAY LANDING WY	-	GALT	95632	419-G2
BAY LEAF DR	-	EDCo	95633	205-A2
BAYLESS WY	2300	SAC	95835	257-A5
BAYLINE CIR	100	FOLS	95630	281-C2
BAY MEADOWS CT	8400	SaCo	95628	260-C5
BAYMORE WY	8200	CITH	95621	239-G6
BAYNE CT	-	EDCo	95634	225-A2
BAYNE RD	7200	EDCo	95634	225-A2
	7400	EDCo	95633	225-C2
BAY OAK WY	7300	CITH	95621	239-G6
BAY OAKS WY	-	RVIS	94571	454-G2
BAYONNE CT	-	RSVL	95747	219-B1
BAYOU CT	-	SAC	95831	316-G7
BAYOU WY	4800	SaCo	95835	256-E5
	4800	SaCo	95837	256-B5
N BAYOU WY	4600	SaCo	95835	256-E5
	5100	SaCo	95837	255-H4
	5100	SaCo	95837	256-B4
BAYPOINT WY	-	ELKG	95624	359-A6
BAYPORT PL	-	ELKG	95758	357-F6
BAYRIDGE CT	7100	PlaC	95746	241-C3
BAYRIDGE LN	1400	EDCo	95762	262-B7
BAY RIVER WY	300	SAC	95831	336-F1
BAY SHORE DR	1100	GALT	95632	419-G2
BAYSIDE CT	-	SAC	95831	336-J3
	200	OAKL	94561	(514-F7 See Page 493)
BAYSIDE WY	4600	OAKL	94561	(514-G7 See Page 493)
BAY STATE CT	2100	SaCo	95670	280-E5
BAY TERRACE DR	-	GALT	95632	419-G2
BAYTOWN WY	8600	SaCo	95828	338-F7
BAYVIEW DR	200	OAKL	94561	(514-G7 See Page 493)
BAYVIEW WY	7200	SAC	95831	336-F1
BAYVILLE CT	6000	PlaC	95746	240-J4
	6000	PlaC	95746	241-A4
BAY VISTA CT	-	GALT	95632	419-G3
BAYWATER LN	2200	RCCD	95670	279-J6
BAYWIND CT	4600	SAC	95838	277-H1
BAYWIND DR	4600	SAC	95838	277-H1
BAYWOOD CT	-	EDCo	95762	282-D2
BAYWOOD RD	7300	PlaC	95746	220-G6
BAYWOOD WY	4300	SaCo	95864	278-J7
BAYWOOD OAKS WY	8700	SaCo	95843	238-G4
BAZLEY WY	-	SaCo	95655	299-E7
N BEACH AV	-	WSAC	95691	296-J7
BEACH CIR	7700	CITH	95610	259-J3
BEACH DR	-	SaCo	95690	455-E4
	-	SolC	94571	454-H7
	700	RVIS	94571	454-H6
S BEACH DR	900	SAC	95831	336-J4
N BEACH PL	-	SAC	95835	256-G4
BEACH ST	7800	SaCo	95843	239-C7
BEACHCOMBER DR E	-	RKLN	95677	220-B2
BEACHCOMBER PL	-	SAC	95835	256-G4
BEACH HAVEN CT	-	ELKG	95758	357-E4
BEACH LAKE RD	7700	SAC	95832	337-C5
	7700	SaCo	95832	337-C5
BEACHMONT WY	8000	SaCo	95828	338-D6
BEACH RIVER PL	5700	ELKG	95757	357-J6
BEACHWOOD DR	9600	SaCo	95662	260-J5
BEACON AV	9500	SaCo	95662	260-J2
BEACON BLVD	3100	WSAC	95691	296-F4
BEACON DR	-	RSVL	95747	218-J5
BEACON HILL DR	7500	PlaC	95603	161-H6
BEACON HILL PL	2200	EDCo	95762	242-B5
BEADNELL WY	5700	SAC	95835	257-D4
BEALS RD	1700	EDCo	95667	244-J2
	1700	EDCo	95667	245-A2
BEAM DR	6800	CITH	95610	259-J3
BEAMER WY	6500	SaCo	95673	257-G3
BEAMREACH CT	-	LNCN	95648	200-B3
BEAN RD	2300	PlaC	95603	162-A5
BEAR CT	3200	EDCo	95667	244-G5
BEARCLOUD AV	-	SAC	95834	276-G1
BEAR CLOUD CT	-	RSVL	95747	218-H3
BEAR CREEK CT	-	EDCo	95634	205-J2
	6000	ELKG	95758	358-A4
BEAR CREEK RD	5200	EDCo	95634	205-G1
	5400	EDCo	95633	205-G1
	6700	EDCo	95667	226-A6
BEARD WY	1200	SaCo	95608	299-B3
BEARDED IRIS DR	7400	CITH	95610	260-C1
BEARDSLEY DR	700	WSAC	95605	297-A2
BEAR FLAG WY	000	SAC	95819	297-J5
BEAR HOLLOW DR	-	RCCD	95670	299-H4
BEARINT WY	-	ELKG	95758	357-F4
BEAR PARK CT	8900	ELKG	95758	358-A3
BEAR PAW CT	4200	EDCo	95672	243-J6
BEAR RIVER CT	-	WSAC	95691	297-A7
	4500	OAKL	94561	(514-E7 See Page 493)
BEAR RIVER DR	7000	SaCo	95842	259-B2
BEAR RIVER RD	-	WSAC	95691	297-A7
BEAR ROCK CT	-	EDCo	95667	245-F1
BEAR ROCK RD	-	PLCR	95667	245-F2
	1300	EDCo	95667	225-E7
	1300	EDCo	95667	245-E1
BEARSDEN CT	-	FOLS	95630	261-J5
BEARS DEN RD	5500	EDCo	95667	264-F1
BEAR VALLEY CT	10100	ELKG	95624	378-G2
	11500	SaCo	95670	280-C5
BEASLEY AV	2300	ANT	94509	(513-E6 See Page 493)
BEASLEY DR	-	EDCo	95682	283-B1
BEATRICE CT	-	RSVL	95661	220-E6
BEATTY CT	-	RSVL	95747	239-F3
	700	EDCo	95762	262-B5
BEATTY DR	3300	EDCo	95762	262-B4
	9200	SaCo	95826	318-J2
	9200	SaCo	95826	319-A2
BEATTY WY	-	RSVL	95747	239-F3
BEAUCANON CT	-	SAC	95758	358-C1
BEAUCHAMP CT	5600	SaCo	95608	279-C6
BEAUFORD CT	-	SaCo	95843	239-C7
BEAULIEU LN	400	OAKL	94561	(514-E5 See Page 493)
BEAULIEU WY	9100	SaCo	95829	338-J5
BEAUMERE WY	5900	SaCo	95608	259-D6
BEAUMONT ST	2200	SAC	95815	277-H6
BEAUPRE WY	7800	CITH	95610	259-J3
BEAUREGARD WY	5400	SaCo	95628	260-F6
	5400	SaCo	95662	260-F6
BEAU VAL LN	-	EDCo	95667	267-C4
BEAUXART CIR	7400	SaCo	95828	338-F2
BEAUX CHENES CT	2000	EDCo	95682	263-H6
BEAVER CT	5000	SaCo	95842	259-A5
BEAVER BAR CT	11700	SaCo	95670	280-D5
BEAVER BROOK CT	8900	ELKG	95624	358-G3
BEAVER CANYON RD	-	EDCo	95619	286-A4
BEAVER CREEK CT	4000	SaCo	95843	238-H7
BEAVER FALLS WY	6900	ELKG	95758	358-B5
BEAVER PARK WY	900	GALT	95632	419-F3
BEAVER POND CT	6000	EDCo	95762	283-B7
BEAVER POND RD	6700	EDCo	95762	283-B7
BEAVER TAIL CT	9500	ELKG	95758	358-D6
BEAVERTON CT	-	ELKG	95624	359-A6
BECERRA WY	2800	SaCo	95821	278-H4
BECK CT	7800	SaCo	95829	339-E5
BECKEN LN	4200	EDCo	95682	264-A7
BECKENHAM DR	-	PlaC	95746	240-H5
BECKENHAM WY	2100	RSVL	95747	239-C1
BECKER DR	6400	LMS	95650	201-B6
BECKET WY	4700	SAC	95823	337-H5
BECKETT DR	-	EDCo	95762	262-H4
	1200	RSVL	95747	219-E6
BECKETT LN	6000	SaCo	95623	265-B4
BECKFORD CT	-	SAC	95828	318-B7
BECKINGTON DR	8900	ELKG	95624	358-F3
BECKLEY WY	10300	ELKG	95757	377-J3
	10300	ELKG	95757	397-J3
BECKWITH LN	-	LNCN	95648	180-A6
BECKWITH WY	8300	CITH	95610	260-C2
BECKWORTH WY	-	SaCo	95843	239-B7
BECKY CT	3900	SaCo	95608	279-C3
BECKY WY	-	LMS	95650	200-J6
	-	LMS	95650	201-A7
BECLAN DR	10600	RCCD	95670	299-G1
BEDELL CT	1500	PlaC	95747	239-E3
BEDELL LN	1600	PlaC	95747	239-E3
BEDFORD AV	2200	PLCR	95667	245-F3
	2600	EDCo	95667	245-F2
	8900	SaCo	95628	260-F7
BEDFORD CT	-	PLCR	95667	245-G4
	-	RKLN	95677	220-F5
	500	RSVL	95661	240-E4
BEDFORD LN	500	OAKL	94561	(514-C7 See Page 493)
BEDFORD COVE WY	8200	SaCo	95828	338-G6
BEDINGTON WY	9500	SaCo	95827	299-B5
BEDROCK CT	9100	SaCo	95829	338-H7
BEDROCK DR	3300	EDCo	95667	245-G7
BEE ST	600	PLCR	95667	245-F4
BEECH AV	5500	SaCo	95628	260-E6
	5600	SaCo	95662	260-E1
BEECHAM CT	-	SAC	95833	277-E5
BEECHCREST CT	8700	SaCo	95662	260-E3
BEECHNUT CT	3000	ANT	94509	(513-J6 See Page 493)
BEECHNUT ST	3000	ANT	94509	(513-J6 See Page 493)
BEECHNUT WY	4500	SAC	95823	337-H3
BEECHURST CT	5100	ELKG	95758	357-H3
BEECHWOOD CT	5000	EDCo	95762	242-C6
BEECHWOOD DR	4500	EDCo	95762	242-D7
BEECHWOOD WY	700	SAC	95834	277-E3
BEEDE WY	-	ANT	94509	(513-D4 See Page 493)
BEEHIVE CT	8200	SaCo	95628	260-B6
BEE JAY CT	5300	SaCo	95628	260-C7
BEELER WY	-	GALT	95632	419-G3
BEESTON AV	6700	SAC	95822	337-F2
BEETHOVEN CT	7800	SaCo	95621	239-D7
BEGONIA CT	-	RKLN	95765	219-H2
	8300	CITH	95621	239-G6
BEGONIA DR	5400	EDCo	95726	267-J1
BEITZEL RD	-	ELKG	95624	359-H2
	-	SaCo	95624	359-H2
BEJA CT	7200	ELKG	95757	378-B3
BELA WY	4500	SaCo	95608	279-B2
BEL AIR LN	2100	RSVL	95678	219-J6
BELANCA LN	6300	EDCo	95667	245-B4
BELASCO AV	700	SAC	95815	277-H5
BELA VISTA DR	-	EDCo	95726	248-D5
BE LAZY CT	5100	SaCo	95628	259-G7
BELCAMP ST	7200	SaCo	95673	257-J1
BELCOT RD	1900	SaCo	95825	298-D1
	2000	SaCo	95825	278-D7
BELCOURT DR	9100	ELKG	95624	378-H2
BELCREST WY	4400	SaCo	95821	278-J4
BELDEN ST	2800	SAC	95815	277-J5
	3300	SAC	95838	277-J3
BELDIN LN	4800	OAKL	94561	(514-C6 See Page 493)
BELDON GROVE CT	9700	ELKG	95624	359-A7
BELERO DR	7500	SaCo	95660	258-F1
BELFAIR CT	1100	SaCo	95825	298-C3
BELFAST CT	-	GALT	95632	419-E2
BELFIELD CIR	6100	ELKG	95758	358-A2
BELFIORE CT	-	EDCo	95762	262-B3
BEL FLORA CT	-	RSVL	95747	219-B1
BELFONT CIR	-	SAC	95835	257-A4
BELFORD CT	-	PlaC	95747	238-J3
BELFORD ESTATES RD	-	EDCo		248-D7
	-	EDCo	95726	248-D7
BELGIAN CT	8000	SaCo	95830	339-G6
BELGIAN WY	-	PlaC	95747	239-A4
BELGRADE WY	2800	SAC	95833	277-E5
BELGROVE WY	6400	SaCo	95608	259-E6
BELHAVEN CT	-	EDCo	95762	282-C2
BELHAVEN WY	-	EDCo	95762	282-C2
	2500	SAC	95826	298-E7
BELINDA WY	1500	SAC	95822	337-C3
BELL AV	-	SAC	95838	277-G1
	1100	SAC	95838	278-A1
	2000	SaCo	95838	278-A1
	2100	SaCo	95652	278-A1
	2100	SAC	95652	278-A1
	5000	SaCo	95652	258-F7
BELL DR	6800	PlaC	95746	241-D4
BELL RD	500	PlaC	95603	162-A3
	500	PlaC	95602	162-A3
	3200	PlaC	95603	161-H3
	3200	PlaC	95602	161-G1
BELL ST	900	SaCo	95825	298-C3
	2000	SaCo	95825	278-D7
	2200	SaCo	95821	278-D5
BELLA CIR	1300	LNCN	95648	180-E7
BELLA LN	5100	SaCo	95628	260-C7
BELLA BREEZE DR	-	LNCN	95648	199-H1
BELLA CRUZ CT	3700	SaCo	95608	279-C4
BELLADONNA CT	-	SAC	95835	257-A6
BELLADONNA LN	-	LNCN	95648	180-A5
BELLADONNA WY	-	SAC	95835	257-A5
BELL AIR DR	800	SAC	95822	316-J4
	13000	PlaC	95603	162-D3
BELLAMY WY	8500	SaCo	95828	338-F2
BELLANCA WY	-	RSVL	95747	218-H3
BELLA PALAZZO CT	-	SaCo	95662	260-H4
BELLARINE CT	600	LNCN	95648	200-A3
BELLA ROSA CT	8300	SaCo	95828	338-E7
BELLATERRA DR	-	ELKG	95757	357-J7
	-	ELKG	95757	358-A7
	-	ELKG	95757	377-J1
	-	ELKG	95757	378-B1
	-	ELKG	95757	397-J1
BELLA TERRA LN	-	PlaC	95746	241-A3
BELLA TERRA PL	-	PlaC	95746	241-A3
BELLA UNION CT	7300	SaCo	95683	342-C4
BELLA VISTA DR	6200	PlaC	95746	221-A7
BELLA VISTA PL	9400	ELKG	95624	358-J5
BELLA VISTA WY	-	RVIS	94571	454-F1
	9200	ELKG	95624	358-J6
BELL BAR RD	9400	PlaC	95603	181-G2
	9400	PlaC	95658	181-G2
BELL BRIDGE WY	7700	SAC	95831	336-H4
BELLBROOK CT	7400	CITH	95621	239-H6
	7400	CITH	95610	239-H6
BELLE CT	-	EDCo	95762	262-B2
BELLE LN	600	RSVL	95678	239-J4
BELLEAU WOOD LN	5800	SAC	95822	317-B5
BELLE CREEK WY	3800	SaCo	95843	238-H5
BELLE FLEUR WY	-	SAC	95833	277-A5
BELLEGROVE WY	-	EDCo	95762	262-E6
BELLE HARBOR CT	9000	ELKG	95624	378-H2
BELLE ROSE CIR	-	RSVL	95678	219-H2
BELLEVIEW AV	5600	SAC	95824	318-B5
BELLEWOOD CT	-	LNCN	95648	199-J3
BELL EXECUTIVE LN	2300	SaCo	95825	298-C1
BELLEZA CT	7300	SaCo	95683	342-C2
BELLFLOWER CT	2900	ANT	94531	(513-H7 See Page 493)
	7300	CITH	95621	239-D5
BELLFLOWER DR	2800	ANT	94531	(513-H7 See Page 493)
BELLFLOWER WY	5300	SaCo	95628	259-G7
BELL HILL DR	5800	SaCo	95842	259-C3
BELLHURST CT	-	RSVL	95747	239-C1
BELLINGER CT	3600	SaCo	95660	258-G7
BELLINGHAM CT	200	LNCN	95648	179-F4
BELLINGHAM PL	3300	EDCo	95762	262-D2
BELLINGHAM WY	5500	SaCo	95662	260-G6
BELLINGRATH DR	7700	SaCo	95626	238-C6
BELLINI WY	7500	SAC	95828	318-C7
BELLONE WY	10700	RCCD	95670	299-H4
BELLO RIO WY	300	SAC	95831	316-F6
BELLOWS POND PL	-	SAC	95835	256-G5
BELL RIVER WY	7100	SAC	95831	336-G1
BELL ROSE LN	8600	SaCo	95828	338-E4
BELL RUSSELL WY	700	SAC	95831	336-H3
BELLS RD	3100	EDCo	95667	245-B7
BELLSBRAE DR	8100	SaCo	95843	238-J6
BELL TREE LN	2300	EDCo	95667	245-A5
BELLUE ST	4700	SaCo	95608	279-E1
BELLWOOD CT	1300	RSVL	95661	240-B5
BELLWOOD DR	-	EDCo	95709	247-B5
BELLWOOD WY	5100	SaCo	95608	279-B2
BELLWORT CT	2800	ANT	94531	(513-H7 See Page 493)
BELMAR CT	1800	FOLS	95630	261-J5
BELMAR ST	2800	SAC	95826	298-F7
	2900	SAC	95826	318-F1
BELMONT CT	-	RSVL	95746	240-F4
BELMONT DR	-	AUB	95603	182-E3
BELMONT LN	2600	ANT	94509	(513-B6 See Page 493)
BELMONT PK	5900	SaCo	95628	260-C5
BELMONT WY	2500	EDCo	95762	242-B5
	3200	SAC	95815	278-A4
BELMONT PLACE LN	4700	SaCo	95841	278-H2
BELOIT DR	4400	SAC	95838	278-B1
	4700	SAC	95838	258-B7
BELPORT LN	2500	SaCo	95821	278-E6
	2500	SaCo	95825	278-E6
BELSHAW ST	-	ANT	94509	(513-F5 See Page 493)
BELT WY	1600	SAC	95832	337-C3
BELUGA PL	-	SAC	95835	256-G5
BELVA WY	6200	SaCo	95660	258-H4
BELVEDERE AV	8100	SAC	95826	318-D2
BELVEDERE CIR	-	RSVL	95678	219-J6
BEN CT	5400	SaCo	95841	259-C6
BENBOW ST	7300	SAC	95822	337-D2
BENBROOK LN	5700	SaCo	95662	260-J6
BENCH CT	5600	SaCo	95662	260-H6
N BEND DR	-	SAC	95835	257-B6
BENDEL PL	9200	ELKG	95624	378-J1
BENDER CT	6700	SAC	95820	318-B3
N BENDER RD	22700	SJCo	95220	439-D7
BENDMILL WY	2900	SAC	95833	277-B5
BENDORI CT	100	FOLS	95630	261-G4
BENEDICT CT	-	SAC	95823	358-A2
BENEDIX WY	3600	ELKG	95758	357-F5
BENEFIELD CT	-	SaCo	95829	338-J6
BENEFIT WY	-	SAC	95834	256-J7
BENET CT	-	RSVL	95661	220-F6
BENETO CT	100	FOLS	95630	261-E7
BENEVENTO WY	-	ELKG	95757	378-A1
BENEVOLENT WY	7000	SaCo	95842	259-A2
BEN EZRA AV	100	RSVL	95678	239-J2
BENGAL CT	5100	ELKG	95757	377-H2
	5100	ELKG	95757	397-H2
BEN HALL DR	9700	SaCo	95632	419-B4
BENHAM CT	3100	PLCR	95667	245-F6
BENHAM ST	3000	PLCR	95667	245-F5
BENHAM WY	6500	SAC	95831	316-F7
BENHENRY CT	-	RKLN	95677	220-G4
BENITA DR	1900	RCCD	95670	279-H6
BENJAMIN CT	-	RKLN	95765	200-D3
BENJAMIN DR	8200	SaCo	95843	238-H6
BEN LOMOND DR	3200	SaCo	95821	278-F6
BENMORE CT	9400	ELKG	95758	358-A5
BENNER CT	100	GALT	95632	439-E1
BENNETT DR	2800	PLCR	95667	245-F4
BENNETT RD	13300	SaCo	95638	(401-D7 See Page 381)
BENNETT VALLEY RD	2800	PLCR	95667	245-F4
BENNING ST	6400	SaCo	95662	260-H4
BENNINGTON CT	1200	RSVL	95661	240-D4
BENNINGTON WY	8400	SaCo	95826	298-E7
BENNOEL CT	-	ELKG	95758	357-E5
BENNOEL WY	-	ELKG	95758	357-E5
BENNY WY	2600	RCCD	95670	299-F2
BENO CT	200	GALT	95632	419-F6
BENOIT CT	-	SAC	95823	337-G6
BENSON CT	2800	PLCR	95667	245-G4
BENSON PL	8800	ELKG	95624	358-G3
W BENSON FERRY RD	9700	SJCo	95686	417-H7
BENSTERMERE WY	-	RSVL	95747	219-C3
BENT CREEK CT	-	EDCo	95762	262-E3
	-	SAC	95823	358-B1
BENTEEN WY	700	GALT	95632	419-F4
BENT GRASS CT	15400	SaCo	95683	342-D3
BENTHOS CT	8600	SaCo	95828	338-F2
BENTLEY AV	-	SAC	95823	337-F2
BENTLEY DR	3100	EDCo	95672	263-D2
BENTLEY PL	6800	PlaC	95746	241-B2
BENTLEY WY	5400	SaCo	95608	299-B1
BENT OAK CT	-	SAC	95834	277-E4
BENTON AV	700	SAC	95838	277-H1
BENTON CT	-	FOLS	95630	281-D1
BENTON DR	-	LNCN	95648	179-E1
BENTON LP	-	RSVL	95747	218-J6
BENTON PL	-	WSAC	95691	316-H1
BENTON ST	-	WSAC	95691	316-H2
BENTON WY	4500	EDCo	95682	283-J2
BENTON ACRES RD	8600	PlaC	95746	240-J3
BENTONITE LN	3100	EDCo	95667	246-F7
	3100	EDCo	95667	266-F1
BENT TREE CT	-	RSVL	95747	219-C1
BENT TREE DR	-	RSVL	95747	219-C1
BENTWOOD DR	1200	GALT	95632	419-G2
BENTWOOD WY	4000	PlaC	95746	240-H5
BENVENITO LN	-	LNCN	95648	179-E6
BENVENITO PL	-	LNCN	95648	179-F5
BENZ CT	8000	SaCo	95828	338-G5
BERCUT DR	100	SAC	95814	297-C1
BERESFORD WY	4100	SaCo	95821	278-H2
BERET LN	7400	SaCo	95828	338-F2
BERETANIA WY	3200	SAC	95834	276-H1
BERG AV	2000	SAC	95822	317-D6
BERG CT	-	FOLS	95630	281-E1
BERG LN	-	EDCo	95667	245-E5
	3700	LMS	95650	200-J6
BERG ST	8000	PlaC	95746	240-J2
BERGAMO CT	-	SAC	95833	276-J6
BERGAMO DR	-	EDCo	95762	262-A2
BERGAMO WY	-	SAC	95833	276-J6
BERGEN WY	7500	SaCo	95673	237-G7
	7500	SaCo	95673	257-H1
BERGER AV	2700	SAC	95815	277-J5
BERGERON RD	12600	SaCo	95632	419-E1
BERGGREN WY	1200	SAC	95815	278-A6
BERGTHOLD WY	8300	SaCo	95828	338-E7
BERINGER CT	2000	OAKL	94561	(514-C5 See Page 493)
	8100	SaCo	95828	338-F6
BERINGER WY	-	OAKL	94561	(514-C5 See Page 493)
BERISFORD PL	5000	SaCo	95843	239-B6
BERKELEY AV	200	RSVL	95678	239-H1
BERKELEY WY	1600	SAC	95819	297-H6
BERKLEY GLEN WY	-	ELKG	95624	359-A6
BERKSFORD ST	4800	SaCo	95841	258-J7
	4800	SaCo	95841	278-J1
BERKSHIRE AV	1200	RSVL	95678	239-G5
BERKSHIRE DR	1000	EDCo	95762	282-C3
BERKSHIRE WY	7800	SaCo	95864	298-E2
BERKSWELL CT	-	RSVL	95747	219-B7
BERK WOOD CT	-	RSVL	95747	219-C1
BERKWOOD CT	4400	EDCo	95762	262-E4
BERMAN WALK WY	8300	CITH	95610	240-C7
BERMUDA CT	-	WSAC	95691	316-D2
	7300	SaCo	95683	342-D2
BERMUDA LN	100	RSVL	95678	219-G5
BERMUDA WY	1500	ANT	94509	(513-G5 See Page 493)
BERNA WY	7300	SaCo	95823	337-J2
BERNAL RD	800	GALT	95632	439-G1
BERNARD WY	2100	SAC	95822	337-D1

BERNARDO CT SACRAMENTO COUNTY STREET INDEX BLUE OAK RANCH RD 522

SACRAMENTO CO.

STREET
Block City ZIP Pg-Grid

BERNARDO CT
8400 SaCo 95828 338-E7
BERNAY WY
- ELKG 95624 358-D1
BERNICE AV
- RSVL 95678 239-J1
BERNIE CT
- EDCo - 248-C7
BERNIER CIR
500 GALT 95632 419-F5
BERRENDO DR
3800 SaCo 95864 298-H2
4600 SaCo 95608 299-A2
4600 SaCo 95864 299-A2
BERRIEDALE CT
- FOLS 95630 261-J3
BERRY AV
8100 SAC 95828 318-D7
BERRY CT
3900 EDCo 95682 263-D5
BERRY LN
7400 CITH 95610 259-H1
W BERRY LN
7900 CITH 95610 240-A6
BERRY RD
4000 EDCo 95682 263-D5
8400 SaCo 95693 (361-B1 See Page 341)
BERRY ST
100 RSVL 95678 219-J7
100 RSVL 95678 220-A7
100 RSVL 95678 239-J1
BERRY CREEK CT
200 FOLS 95630 261-C1
BERRY CREEK DR
100 FOLS 95630 261-B2
BERRY CREEK RD
- WSAC 95691 297-A7
BERRYESSA PL
- WSAC 95691 316-C3
BERRY HILL CT
7000 SaCo 95662 260-D2
BERRY OAK CT
200 SaCo 95673 257-G2
BERRY POND LN
- EDCo 95619 286-C6
BERRYWOOD DR
2400 RCCD 95670 279-J7
BERT DR
8200 ELKG 95624 359-C3
BERTANA CT
3100 EDCo 95672 243-E5
BERTELLA RD
2500 EDCo 95682 263-A7
BERTHOUD ST
300 SAC 95838 277-G1
BERTIE LN
6800 EDCo 95667 265-C1
BERTIS DR
3000 SaCo 95821 278-J5
3100 SaCo 95608 279-A5
3100 SaCo 95821 279-A5
BERTOLANI CIR
- ELKG 95758 357-E4
BERTRAN CT
6700 CITH 95621 259-G3
BERTWIN WY
8900 ELKG 95758 357-J3
BERWICK WY
10800 RCCD 95670 279-H7
10800 RCCD 95670 299-H1
BERWICK MOOR PL
5400 SaCo 95843 239-C6
BERWYN PL
7100 SaCo 95621 259-D2
BERYL CT
- SAC 95834 277-B2
BERYL PL
5000 SaCo 95843 239-B6
BERYL CREEK WY
8900 ELKG 95758 357-J3
BESANA CT
- RSVL 95747 219-C1
BESANA DR
3300 EDCo 95762 262-E5
BESKEEN RD
13300 SaCo 95638 (401-D5 See Page 381)
BESSEMER CT
- SAC 95835 257-A6
BESSEMER WY
- SAC 95835 257-A5
BESTER CT
- SaCo 95829 339-B5
BESTER WY
- SaCo 95829 339-B6
BESTOW WY
7400 SaCo 95842 259-A1
BETA CT
6300 CITH 95621 239-E6
BETH ST
- RKLN 95765 219-J1
7600 SAC 95832 337-D3
BETHANY CT
- SaCo 95823 338-B5
BETHANY LN
3200 EDCo 95667 246-E5
BETHEL CT
- LMS 95650 200-H6
- SAC 95831 336-H2
BETHEL WY
2600 WSAC 95691 316-F1
BETHESDA CT
- SAC 95838 277-G1
BETHLEHEM CT
4800 SaCo 95628 279-F1
BETLEN CT
2900 RCCD 95670 299-F4
BETSY WY
2500 RCCD 95670 299-H1
BETSY ROSS DR
1000 RSVL 95747 219-E7
1000 RSVL 95747 239-E1
BETTENCOURT DR
- RSVL 95678 219-G4
BETTENCOURT LN
2700 RCCD 95670 299-E3
BETTERLEY LN
600 PlaC 95603 181-J3
BETTINA WY
3000 SaCo 95826 298-J7
BETTY LN
3900 LMS 95650 201-A7
BETTY WY
2500 WSAC 95691 296-F7
2500 WSAC 95691 316-F1
5200 SAC 95819 298-A4
BETTYHILL CT
- FOLS 95630 262-A5

BETTY JEAN CT
4000 EDCo 95667 265-C2
BETTY LOU DR
7800 SaCo 95828 338-C1
BEUTH CT
100 FOLS 95630 281-B1
BEUTLER DR
4900 SaCo 95608 299-A2
BEV ST
2400 SaCo 95608 279-C7
BEVAN RD
2600 WSAC 95691 316-D4
BEVAN ST
14400 SaCo 95683 341-H1
BEVERLY ST
1200 ANT 94509 (513-E4 See Page 493)
BEVERLY WY
1100 SAC 95818 297-C6
BEVERLY JAY LN
8200 ELKG 95624 339-H7
8200 ELKG 95830 339-H7
8200 SaCo 95830 339-H7
BEVIL ST
5000 SAC 95819 297-J3
BEVINGER DR
- EDCo 95762 262-F6
BEWICKS CIR
100 SAC 95834 276-H3
BEXLEY DR
9800 RCCD 95827 299-D5
BEYER CT
- ELKG 95624 358-D1
BIANCA CT
2400 RCCD 95670 279-G7
BIANCHI CIR
- PlaC 95603 182-B6
BIANCHI RD
8300 PlaC 95747 239-B2
BIANCO CT
- EDCo 95762 262-A2
10800 RCCD 95670 299-H4
BIANCO WY
10800 RCCD 95670 299-J4
BIBBS DR
6200 SAC 95824 318-B6
6200 SAC 95828 318-B6
BICENTENNIAL CIR
200 SAC 95826 318-D1
BICKLEIGH LP
- RSVL 95747 218-G4
BIDDEFORD CIR
100 SaCo 95655 319-J2
BIDWELL LN
- LNCN 95648 180-A5
BIDWELL ST
700 FOLS 95630 261-A6
E BIDWELL ST
600 FOLS 95630 261-D5
1700 FOLS 95630 281-H1
BIDWELL WY
1700 SAC 95818 317-C1
BIERSTON ST
7600 CITH 95621 259-E1
7700 CITH 95621 239-E7
BIG ARROW CT
6900 CITH 95621 259-D3
BIG BARN CT
4000 EDCo 95667 246-D6
BIG BARN RD
3100 EDCo 95667 246-D6
BIG BEAR CT
- OAKL 94561 (514-G7 See Page 493)
6400 SaCo 95662 260-C4
BIG BEAR DR
- RSVL 95747 199-C7
- RSVL 95747 219-C1
BIG BEAR RD
- OAKL 94561 (514-G7 See Page 493)
BIG BEAR ST
- WSAC 95691 316-C4
BIG BEN RD
300 PlaC - 160-A2
BIG BEND DR
- RSVL 95678 220-A3
BIG BRANCH RD
4300 EDCo 95682 283-H4
BIG BREAK RD
- OAKL 94561 (514-C4 See Page 493)
BIG BROOK WY
- RSVL 95747 218-J3
BIG CANYON CT
- PlaC 95747 239-B4
BIG CANYON LN
5000 SaCo 95628 260-H7
BIG CANYON CREEK RD
2200 PLCR 95667 245-G3
BIG CHIEF CT
6600 SaCo 95662 260-B3
BIG CLOUD WY
3900 SaCo 95843 238-H7
BIG CREEK WY
- RSVL 95747 218-H4
5400 ELKG 95758 357-J2
BIG CUT RD
3100 PLCR 95667 245-G6
3300 EDCo 95667 245-E7
3500 EDCo 95667 265-G1
3700 EDCo 95619 265-G1
BIG FOUR WY
11500 SaCo 95670 280-C5
BIGGS CT
100 FOLS 95630 261-E7
BIG HORN BLVD
- ELKG 95757 358-D6
- ELKG 95757 378-D1
8900 ELKG 95758 357-J3
8900 ELKG 95758 358-D6
BIG HORN WY
9300 SaCo 95827 299-A5
BIG ISLAND RD
- WSAC 95691 316-D2
BIG JAKE WY
100 GALT 95632 419-D7
BIG K LN
- PlaC 95603 181-J3
BIGLER WY
3700 SAC 95817 317-F1
BIG LIVE OAK LN
- SaCo 95821 278-H2
BIGLOW DR
1800 ANT 94509 (513-F5 See Page 493)
6000 CITH 95621 259-D1
BIGNEY CT
3200 RCCD 95670 299-H4

BIG OAK CT
3000 EDCo 95619 265-G6
BIG OAK DR
8000 CITH 95610 240-C7
BIG OAK RD
1000 EDCo 95619 265-G6
1500 EDCo 95619 266-A5
BIG RIVER CT
- SAC 95831 336-F1
BIG SANDY CT
2100 SaCo 95670 280-E4
BIG SANDY LN
- EDCo 95634 225-E4
BIG SKY DR
- RKLN 95765 219-J1
8100 SaCo 95843 238-F6
BIG SPRINGS DR
100 FOLS 95630 260-J1
BIG SUR CT
900 EDCo 95762 262-D6
BIG TIMBER DR
9500 ELKG 95758 358-D6
BIG VALLEY CT
100 FOLS 95630 261-G4
BIG VALLEY RD
100 FOLS 95630 261-G4
BIJAN CT
4400 SaCo 95628 280-A2
BIKINI CT
8800 SaCo 95662 260-F3
BILBAO CT
3800 EDCo 95682 263-B7
BILBY RD
- SaCo 95757 378-A3
4200 ELKG 95757 377-H3
4200 ELKG 95757 397-H3
4200 SaCo 95757 377-H3
4200 SaCo 95757 397-H3
7400 ELKG 95757 378-A3
BILDAY CT
- SAC 95835 256-J5
- SAC 95835 257-A5
E BILL RD
2800 SJCo 95632 439-H2
BILLBEAN CIR
- SAC 95835 257-B4
BILL CLARK WY
12800 AUB 95602 162-C2
BILLFISH WY
8800 SaCo 95828 338-G4
BILL FRANCIS DR
13000 PlaC 95603 162-D4
BILLIE ST
5300 SaCo 95628 259-G7
BILLINGS WY
7700 SAC 95832 337-F4
BILLY MITCHELL BLVD
100 PlaC 95747 238-J4
9000 PlaC 95747 239-A4
BILOXI PARK CT
1100 GALT 95632 419-G2
BILSDALE CT
8100 SaCo 95829 339-A6
BILSTED WY
3600 SAC 95834 277-B3
BILTMORE WY
5400 SaCo 95628 260-D6
BIMINI CT
- SAC 95835 257-A5
BINACA CT
- SAC 95833 277-D5
BINCHY WY
4300 RCCD 95742 320-E2
BINET DR
6200 CITH 95621 259-F4
BING CT
700 PLCR 95667 245-F5
BINGER DR
8800 ELKG 95624 359-C3
BINGHAM CIR
- SAC 95831 336-H2
BINGHAMTON DR
3400 SAC 95834 277-E3
BINNING CT
9300 SaCo 95662 260-H3
BIPLANE WY
9000 SaCo 95628 260-F6
BIRCH AV
- EDCo - 247-F2
1700 WSAC 95691 316-J2
1900 ANT 94509 (513-D5 See Page 493)
BIRCH CT
- EDCo - 247-F2
- OAKL 94561 (514-D5 See Page 493)
700 GALT 95632 419-F3
BIRCH LN
- FOLS 95630 261-B1
BIRCH PL
- EDCo 95682 263-D2
BIRCH ST
100 RSVL 95678 239-G1
3100 SaCo 95608 279-B5
BIRCH CREST CT
8500 ELKG 95624 358-E4
BIRCHDALE WY
3400 SaCo 95843 238-G4
BIRCHER WY
2100 SaCo 95608 279-A7
2100 SaCo 95608 299-A1
BIRCHGLADE WY
5900 CITH 95621 259-D1
BIRCHGROVE WY
4000 SaCo 95826 318-J2
BIRCH HILL CT
- SaCo 95830 339-G3
BIRCH HOLLOW WY
8400 SaCo 95828 338-F6
BIRCH LEAF CT
8600 SaCo 95828 338-F3
BIRCHLEY CT
- ELKG 95624 359-A6
BIRCH MEADOW CT
- PlaC 95746 240-H2
BIRCH POINT CT
5700 ELKG 95757 357-J7
BIRCH RANCH DR
10500 SaCo 95830 339-G3
BIRCH RIDGE DR
- RVIS 94571 454-F2
BIRCHTREE CIR
- EDCo 95762 242-E6
BIRCH TREE WY
3400 SaCo 95826 318-H1
BIRCH VALLEY WY
4700 RCCD 95742 320-E3
BIRCHWOOD CIR
6900 CITH 95621 239-F7

BIRCHWOOD CT
5000 RKLN 95677 220-G3
5800 ELKG 95757 357-J7
5800 ELKG 95757 358-A7
BIRCHWOOD LN
1400 SAC 95822 317-B3
BIRDCAGE ST
5800 CITH 95610 259-J5
BIRDCAGE CENTRE LN
5900 CITH 95610 259-J5
5900 CITH 95610 260-A5
BIRDIE CT
5200 RKLN 95677 220-B3
7600 SaCo 95828 338-C3
BIRDSALL AV
- AUB 95603 182-F1
BIRDSEYE WY
4300 ELKG 95758 357-H3
BIRDSONG CT
9100 SaCo 95826 318-H2
BIRDSONG LN
6200 EDCo 95667 265-A3
BIRDVIEW WY
- ELKG 95757 377-J1
- ELKG 95757 397-J1
BIRDWALK LN
- EDCo - 247-G2
BIRDWELL WY
4100 SaCo 95660 258-H1
BIRGHAM WY
- SaCo 95829 339-A5
BIRGIT WY
4200 SaCo 95864 278-H7
BIRK WY
5300 SAC 95835 257-A5
BIRKDALE CT
- RKLN 95677 220-G4
5100 ELKG 95758 357-H2
6300 SAC 95823 338-A7
BIRKDALE DR
- RSVL 95747 219-D6
BIRKS LN
6200 SaCo 95662 260-D4
BIRMINGHAM AV
1900 WSAC 95691 296-H6
BIRMINGHAM CT
- EDCo 95762 263-A5
100 RSVL 95661 240-E5
BIRMINGHAM WY
3000 EDCo 95762 263-A5
10300 RCCD 95670 299-F3
BIRNAM ST
6600 SaCo 95673 257-G3
BIRTY CT
- SAC 95826 298-F7
BIRUTA AV
8500 SaCo 95662 260-D1
BISBEE DR
7300 SaCo 95683 341-F1
BISCANEWOODS WY
10000 RCCD 95827 299-D5
BISCAY WY
10600 RCCD 95670 279-H7
BISCAYNE WY
100 FOLS 95630 261-H7
BISHOP CT
- PlaC 95661 240-D5
BISHOP LN
2500 ANT 94509 (513-A6 See Page 493)
BISHOP WY
4300 SaCo 95842 258-J6
BISHOP CREEK CIR
- PlaC 95661 240-D6
BISHOPGATE CT
- SAC 95823 337-H5
BISHOPS CAP CT
- ELKG 95624 358-F1
BISMARCK DR
3900 SaCo 95660 258-G2
BISON LN
100 EDCo 95667 245-D6
BISON WY
9500 SaCo 95662 260-J7
BISSEL CT
9400 ELKG 95758 357-G5
BISSETT WY
- SAC 95835 257-C5
BITNER ST
300 RSVL 95678 239-G1
BITTERBUSH WY
6500 CITH 95621 239-E6
BITTER CREEK DR
100 FOLS 95630 261-F4
BITTER ROOT CT
8400 SaCo 95843 238-F5
BIX AV
6700 CITH 95621 259-F4
BIXBY CT
- SAC 95835 257-A5
BLACHLY WY
5700 SaCo 95841 259-C5
BLACK ARABIAN PL
- ELKG 95624 359-A6
BLACKBARRI DR
2500 EDCo 95709 246-H1
BLACK BEAR DR
7600 SaCo 95843 258-G1
7600 SaCo 95843 238-G7
BLACK BEAR ST
- RSVL 95747 219-D2
BLACKBERRY CIR
- FOLS 95630 261-G4
BLACKBERRY CT
100 AUB 95603 162-E7
BLACKBERRY WY
8500 ELKG 95624 358-G1
BLACKBERRY HILL
4200 PlaC 95602 161-J1
BLACK BIRCH CT
5200 SaCo 95842 259-B2
BLACKBIRD
2500 EDCo 95709 246-J2
BLACKBIRD LN
300 SAC 95831 316-F7
1700 LNCN 95648 180-C7
1700 LNCN 95648 200-C1
BLACKBIRD ST
- RSVL 95747 219-B7
BLACK BRANCH CT
8500 SaCo 95828 338-F5
BLACKBURN WY
10400 RCCD 95670 299-F3
BLACK CANYON CT
800 GALT 95632 419-F3
BLACK CHERRY CT
8500 ELKG 95624 358-G1
BLACK CORAL WY
2800 RCCD 95827 299-D4

BLACK DIAMOND DR
- RVIS 94571 454-F2
100 FOLS 95630 281-A2
BLACK DOG CT
4000 EDCo 95630 202-J6
BLACK DOG LN
4200 EDCo 95630 202-J6
BLACK DUCK WY
6800 SaCo 95842 258-J2
BLACK EAGLE DR
3000 SaCo 95843 238-F5
BLACK ELK CT
3500 SaCo 95843 238-G6
BLACKER RD
2600 WSAC 95691 316-F2
BLACKFIELD DR
3900 SaCo 95660 258-H1
BLACKFOOT CT
- WSAC 95691 316-H2
BLACKFOOT RD
- WSAC 95691 316-H2
BLACKFOOT WY
3500 SaCo 95843 238-G7
BLACKFORD WY
4200 SAC 95823 337-H5
BLACK FOREST LN
9100 SaCo 95628 260-G7
9100 SaCo 95628 280-G1
BLACK GOLD LN
100 FOLS 95630 261-E6
BLACKHAWK DR
7200 SaCo 95828 338-C2
BLACK HAWK LN
- LNCN 95648 200-C2
BLACKHAWK LN
- EDCo - 267-D5
BLACK HAWK ST
- RSVL 95747 219-D2
BLACKHEATH LN
2000 RSVL 95670 219-J6
BLACKHILLS WY
2800 SaCo 95827 299-C4
BLACK HORSE LN
- RKLN 95765 200-A4
BLACKHURST DR
1100 GALT 95632 419-G4
BLACK JACK LN
1600 PlaC 95658 181-G2
BLACKJACK WY
4300 SaCo 95842 258-J3
BLACK KITE DR
8500 ELKG 95624 358-G1
BLACKMAN WY
- ELKG 95624 358-E3
BLACK MARLIN CT
8800 SaCo 95828 338-G4
BLACKMER CIR
700 SaCo 95825 298-C4
BLACK OAK CT
- EDCo 95633 205-C1
- RKLN 95765 200-D5
BLACK OAK DR
- RKLN 95765 200-D4
BLACK OAK LN
2400 EDCo 95667 245-H3
BLACK OAK PL
- RKLN 95765 200-E3
BLACK OAK RD
2600 PlaC 95602 162-E1
4000 EDCo 95682 264-A3
BLACK OAK MINE RD
4900 EDCo 95633 205-B1
BLACK OAKS WY
7300 CITH 95621 239-G6
BLACK OLIVE CT
8800 SaCo 95628 280-E1
BLACK PEARL DR
- SaCo 95843 238-H6
BLACK PINE CT
100 RSVL 95747 239-D1
BLACKPOOL WY
3000 RCCD 95670 299-F3
BLACK POWDER CIR
100 FOLS 95630 261-E6
BLACK RICE CT
800 EDCo 95619 265-F2
BLACK RICE LN
800 EDCo 95619 265-F2
BLACK RICE RD
800 EDCo 95619 265-F2
BLACKRIDGE AV
- SAC 95835 257-B6
BLACK RIVER CT
- SAC 95831 336-F1
BLACKROCK DR
- SAC 95834 257-D7
- SAC 95835 257-D7
BLACKROCK RD
5600 RKLN 95765 220-B1
BLACKS LN
2500 EDCo 95667 245-A3
BLACK SADDLE DR
3100 SaCo 95843 238-E6
BLACK SAND WY
7700 SaCo 95843 239-A7
BLACK SLATE CT
1900 SaCo 95670 280-B4
BLACKSMITH AV
300 LNCN 95648 179-J1
BLACKSMITH CT
- EDCo 95667 244-B5
BLACKSTALLION CT
8100 SaCo 95829 339-D6
BLACKSTAR DR
6300 CITH 95621 239-E7
BLACKSTONE CT
600 RSVL 95747 219-A6
4000 AUB 95603 182-E7
5900 RKLN 95765 220-A1
BLACKSTONE DR
5900 RKLN 95765 200-A7
5900 RKLN 95765 220-A1
BLACKSTONE WY
2200 RCCD 95670 279-G7
BLACK SWAN DR
9600 ELKG 95624 359-A7
9700 ELKG 95624 379-A1
BLACK TAIL DR
4000 SAC 95823 337-G4
BLACKTAIL LN
3500 EDCo 95667 245-G7
BLACK TERN WY
2400 ELKG 95757 377-E1
2400 ELKG 95757 397-E1
BLACKTHORNE WY
7400 CITH 95621 259-D1
7600 CITH 95621 239-D7
BLACKTOP RD
5100 SaCo 95835 257-E4

BLACKTOP RD
5400 SaCo 95673 257-E4
BLACK TREE LN
7400 CITH 95610 260-B1
BLACK WALNUT CT
8000 CITH 95610 260-A3
BLACKWATER WY
7600 SAC 95831 336-G4
BLACKWELL CT
300 SaCo 95673 257-H2
BLACKWELL WY
- GALT 95632 419-G3
BLACKWOOD LN
8000 PlaC 95747 239-B2
BLACKWOOD ST
400 SAC 95815 277-H7
BLAGDON CT
- RSVL 95747 219-B7
BLAINE AV
800 SAC 95838 277-J2
BLAIR AV
1400 SAC 95822 317-B6
BLAIR CT
400 RSVL 95678 219-F7
BLAIR RD
2300 EDCo 95726 248-A1
BLAIR ST
100 AUB 95603 182-F1
1000 SaCo 95639 (376-J5 See Page 375)
1000 SaCo 95639 377-A5
1000 SaCo 95639 397-A5
BLAIRS LN
3000 PLCR 95667 245-J5
BLAKE RD
11700 SaCo 95693 (380-C3 See Page 379)
BLAKEMORE CT
8900 ELKG 95624 358-F3
BLAKEPOINTE WY
8500 SaCo 95843 239-A5
BLAKESLEE DR
100 FOLS 95630 261-G4
BLAKESLEY WY
- RSVL 95747 218-H3
BLAKESLY CT
- RSVL 95747 218-H3
BLANC CT
4400 OAKL 94561 (514-E7 See Page 493)
BLANCHARD CT
- SaCo 95628 260-B7
4400 EDCo 95667 265-B3
BLANCHARD DR
- RSVL 95747 219-C7
1600 RSVL 95747 239-C1
BLANCHARD RD
4200 EDCo 95667 265-A2
BLANCHE DELL DR
6500 SAC 95824 318-B5
BLANCHETTE WY
3500 RCCD 95670 299-J5
3500 RCCD 95670 300-A5
BLANDFORD CT
7100 CITH 95610 260-C2
BLANEFIELD CT
- FOLS 95630 261-G6
BLANSFIELD WY
- ELKG 95757 358-B7
BLARNEY CT
8700 ELKG 95624 358-F6
BLARNEY WY
- EDCo 95630 202-F5
BLAYDEN CT
8300 CITH 95610 260-C1
BLAYDON RD
- RKLN 95765 200-C6
BLAZE CT
5200 RKLN 95677 220-H5
9400 SaCo 95826 299-A7
BLAZE TRAIL CT
7900 SaCo 95662 240-E7
BLAZING STAR CT
11600 SaCo 95670 280-C5
BLAZINGWOOD
7900 CITH 95621 239-D7
BLECKLEY ST
- RCCD 95655 299-G5
BLEHM RD
11300 SaCo 95632 420-A5
BLENCOWE CT
100 FOLS 95630 261-F7
BLEND O GRN
1900 EDCo 95667 244-D7
BLINMAN WY
8700 SaCo 95628 260-E7
BLISS CT
900 PLCR 95667 245-G6
3900 SaCo 95660 258-H5
BLISS RIVER CT
- SAC 95831 336-F1
BLITZ LN
600 PlaC 95603 162-C6
BLOCH CT
- SaCo 95829 339-A6
BLOCKER DR
200 AUB 95603 182-C2
11500 PlaC 95603 182-C2
BLODGETT DR
100 FOLS 95630 261-G3
BLOOM WY
7700 CITH 95610 259-J6
BLOOMBURY DR
1900 RSVL 95661 240-D3
BLOOMFIELD CT
- LNCN 95648 179-H5
300 RSVL 95678 219-F6
BLOOMFIELD WY
100 FOLS 95630 261-G5
BLOOMINGTON DR
8300 SaCo 95828 338-E5
BLOOSSOMWOOD CT
- RKLN 95677 220-F1
BLOSSOM CT
3400 EDCo 95682 244-A7
5300 RKLN 95677 220-G3
6900 CITH 95610 259-H2
BLOSSOM DR
1800 ANT 94509 (513-F5 See Page 493)
N BLOSSOM RD
22500 SJCo 95242 437-H6
22500 SJCo 95686 437-H2
BLOSSOM TR
1000 PlaC 95658 181-C1
BLOSSOM WY
- SaCo 95632 419-C5
BLOSSOM HILL CT
8400 CITH 95610 240-A6

BLOSSOM HILL RD
3100 EDCo 95667 246-G3
BLOSSOM HILL WY
1300 RSVL 95661 240-A5
BLOSSOM RANCH DR
- ELKG 95757 357-H7
- ELKG 95757 377-H1
- ELKG 95757 397-H1
BLOSSOM RIDGE DR
- ELKG 95757 377-H1
- ELKG 95757 397-H1
BLOSSOM ROCK PL
1900 SaCo 95670 280-A4
BLOSSOMWOOD CT
5200 SaCo 95628 260-D7
BLOSSUM LN
- LNCN 95648 179-H6
BLOUGH WY
- FOLS 95630 281-G1
BLOWING WIND WY
6800 CITH 95621 259-D2
BLUCHER LN
6100 CITH 95621 259-D3
BLUE LN
1500 RSVL 95747 219-E5
BLUE BAR DR
- EDCo - 247-D1
- EDCo 95709 247-D1
BLUE BEAVER WY
- RSVL 95747 219-D2
BLUE BEECH CT
5800 SaCo 95843 239-D5
BLUEBELL CIR
2700 ANT 94531 (513-H7 See Page 493)
BLUEBELL CT
400 GALT 95632 419-D5
800 PLCR 95667 245-G5
8300 CITH 95610 260-C1
BLUEBERRY CT
8600 ELKG 95624 358-G1
BLUEBERRY LN
1500 PlaC 95658 160-J7
BLUEBERRY HILL DR
3600 EDCo 95682 263-G5
BLUEBILL CT
- RKLN 95765 219-J1
BLUEBILL WY
4500 SaCo 95842 258-J2
BLUE BIRD LN
200 FOLS 95630 261-B1
BLUEBIRD LN
- PlaC 95650 201-J7
2000 SaCo 95821 278-C6
4700 EDCo 95623 265-B5
BLUE BONNET CT
- RSVL 95661 220-E6
BLUEBONNET CT
2900 ANT 94531 (513-H7 See Page 493)
BLUEBROOK WY
7500 SAC 95823 337-G3
BLUE CANYON WY
100 FOLS 95630 261-A3
BLUECURL CT
2800 ANT 94531 (513-H7 See Page 493)
BLUE DIAMOND WY
9400 ELKG 95624 359-A7
BLUE DOLPHIN WY
400 SAC 95831 336-G3
BLUE DUCK WY
6700 SaCo 95842 259-A3
BLUE DUN CT
- SAC 95831 336-J3
BLUE FALLS CT
9400 ELKG 95624 359-A5
BLUEFEATHER CT
- SAC 95834 276-H1
BLUE FERN CT
- SAC 95833 276-H6
BLUEFIELD WY
6900 SAC 95823 358-B1
BLUE FOX CT
- PlaC 95602 162-A2
BLUEGATE CT
- SAC 95838 257-G7
BLUEGRASS TR
10500 PlaC 95603 182-A2
BLUEGRASS WY
3300 SaCo 95821 278-E4
BLUEHAVEN CT
8200 SaCo 95843 238-G6
BLUE HERON CT
- FOLS 95630 281-F1
- OAKL 94561 (514-H7 See Page 493)
- SAC 95833 277-C5
BLUE HERON LP
2100 LNCN 95648 180-B7
2800 LNCN 95648 200-C1
BLUE JAY DR
1800 RSVL 95661 240-B4
BLUEJAY DR
- EDCo 95667 245-D7
3300 ANT 94509 (513-F7 See Page 493)
BLUE JAY WY
- SAC 95823 337-G4
8600 CITH 95610 260-A1
BLUE LAKE DR
200 FOLS 95630 261-B2
BLUE LEAD PL
1900 SaCo 95670 280-B4
BLUE LEAF CT
- SAC 95838 257-G7
BLUE LEDGE DR
- SaCo 95670 280-E4
BLUE LIGHT LN
10200 PlaC 95603 181-J1
10200 PlaC 95603 182-A2
BLUE LUPINE PL
- ELKG 95757 377-J1
- ELKG 95757 397-J1
BLUE MAIDEN WY
8600 ELKG 95624 358-F1
BLUE MARLIN CT
8800 SaCo 95828 338-G4
BLUE OAK CT
500 EDCo 95762 262-A1
BLUE OAK DR
9200 SaCo 95662 260-H6
BLUE OAK LN
6900 PlaC 95746 221-E6
BLUE OAK WY
8200 CITH 95610 240-B6
BLUE OAK RANCH RD
- PlaC 95602 161-B1

STREET Block City ZIP Pg-Grid

BLUE OAKS BLVD
- RKLN 95765 199-J7
- RKLN 95765 219-H2
- RSVL 95747 218-H2
300 RSVL 95678 219-E2
2000 RSVL 95747 219-B2
BLUE OAKS DR
3200 PlaC 95602 162-A3
BLUE PARROT CT
- ELKG 95757 358-A7
BLUE PINE CT
- RSVL 95747 218-J4
BLUE POPPY DR
- ELKG 95757 358-A7
BLUE QUAIL CT
8300 SaCo 95828 338-E7
BLUE RAPIDS DR
200 FOLS 95630 281-A2
BLUE RAVEN ST
- RSVL 95747 219-D2
BLUE RAVINE RD
100 FOLS 95630 261-G5
100 FOLS 95630 281-A1
BLUE RHAPSODY LN
3200 EDCo 95667 246-E5
BLUE RIDGE CT
12200 PlaC 95602 162-B1
BLUERIDGE CT
5400 SaCo 95662 260-G6
BLUE RIDGE RD
1500 EDCo 95619 265-H7
BLUE RIVER CT
3500 SaCo 95826 299-A7
3500 SaCo 95826 319-A1
BLUE ROCK CT
6500 ELKG 95758 358-A3
BLUE ROSE CT
8300 CITH 95610 260-C1
BLUE SAPPHIRE CT
5200 ELKG 95758 357-J3
BLUE SAPPHIRE WY
5400 ELKG 95758 357-J3
BLUE SKIES WY
- RSVL 95747 219-A7
BLUE SKY CT
- SAC 95828 318-F6
BLUE SPRINGS WY
7000 CITH 95621 239-F5
7300 RSVL 95678 239-F5
BLUE SPRUCE CT
6500 ELKG 95758 358-A3
BLUE SQUIRREL ST
- RSVL 95747 219-D2
BLUE STAR CT
3000 RCCD 95670 299-G2
BLUE STAR RANCH ST
- PlaC 95648 160-A5
BLUESTONE CIR
700 FOLS 95630 261-F6
BLUE STONE CT
1500 RSVL 95661 240-B6
BLUESTONE CT
- SAC 95824 318-B6
BLUESTONE LN
- LNCN 95648 200-A2
6200 EDCo 95667 244-F6
BLUET CT
5400 SaCo 95662 260-H6
BLUE THISTLE WY
9600 ELKG 95624 359-A6
BLUE TOPAZ WY
11800 RCCD 95742 320-D2
BLUE VISTA
- RKLN 95677 220-G5
BLUE VISTA CT
- RKLN 95677 220-G5
BLUE WATER CIR
- SAC 95831 336-G2
BLUE WATER WY
600 SAC 95831 336-G2
BLUEWIND CT
- SAC 95838 277-H1
BLUE WING PL
- AUB 95603 182-C6
BLUFF CT
- EDCo 95667 267-A3
3500 SaCo 95608 279-F4
BLUFF LN
8700 SaCo 95628 280-E3
BLUFF RD
- EDCo 95667 267-A3
BLUFFS CT
5600 RKLN 95765 220-C1
BLUFFS DR
5600 RKLN 95765 220-C1
BLUFFS PL
1100 AUB 95603 182-C6
BLUMENFELD DR
1100 SAC 95815 297-J1
1100 SAC 95815 277-J7
1200 SAC 95815 278-A7
BLUSHING CIR
11800 RCCD 95742 320-D2
BLYTHE AV
8600 SaCo 95662 260-D4
BOA NOVA DR
6800 ELKG 95757 378-B3
6800 SaCo 95757 378-B3
BOARDING HOUSE CT
- RKLN 95765 199-J4
BOARDING HOUSE LN
- RKLN 95765 199-J4
BOARDMAN CT
6400 RKLN 95677 220-G5
BOARDMAN ST
200 AUB 95603 182-E2
BOARDWALK
2700 PLCR 95667 245-J4
BOARDWALK DR
6800 PlaC 95746 241-B3
BOARDWALK WY
- RKLN 95765 200-B7
- RKLN 95765 220-B1
- SaCo 95843 239-A7
- SaCo 95843 259-A1
BOATHOUSE WY
- SAC 95833 276-H6
BOATMAN AV
2400 WSAC 95691 296-G5
BOB LN
4000 SaCo 95628 279-J3
BOBAL ST
- SAC 95834 276-G4
BOBBECK CT
9100 SaCo 95662 260-G5
BOBBELL DR
9900 ELKG 95757 357-E7
9900 ELKG 95757 377-E1
9900 ELKG 95757 397-E1

BOBBER CT
- SAC 95833 277-C6
BOBBIE CT
500 RSVL 95678 219-G7
500 RSVL 95678 239-G1
BOBBIE JO CT
5500 SaCo 95841 259-A6
BOBBIWOOD WY
6200 SaCo 95828 318-A7
BOBBY ST
7000 SaCo 95662 260-F2
BOBBY WY
8000 SAC 95826 318-D1
BOBCAT CT
7200 SaCo 95660 258-H1
BOB DOYLE DR
- RSVL 95747 218-H4
BOBLYN WY
- ELKG 95757 358-B6
BOBOLINK WY
6900 SAC 95831 316-F7
6900 SAC 95831 336-F1
BOBWHITE CT
- ELKG 95624 358-H4
800 LNCN 95648 179-F2
BOBWHITE LN
- FOLS 95630 260-J4
- FOLS 95630 261-A4
BOCA AV
8700 SaCo 95662 260-E5
BOCANA RD
4400 EDCo 95682 263-A6
BOCA PT CT
4100 SaCo 95843 238-H7
BOCK CT
- SAC 95823 337-H3
BODEGA CT
- EDCo 95762 262-C1
1100 RSVL 95661 240-A5
2800 SaCo 95864 298-G7
BODEGA WY
- EDCo 95667 266-H4
- EDCo 95667 267-A4
BODEGA BAY RD
- WSAC 95691 316-E2
BODINE CIR
6700 SAC 95823 338-B5
BODNAR CT
- FOLS 95630 281-E2
BOEGER CT
8000 SaCo 95829 338-J6
BOEGER WINERY RD
- EDCo 95667 245-J3
BOEING RD
2900 EDCo 95682 263-D4
BOESSOW RD
10700 SaCo 95632 419-G7
10700 GALT 95632 419-G7
11200 SaCo 95632 420-B7
BOGAN WY
7600 SaCo 95843 239-B7
7600 SaCo 95843 259-B1
BOGART WY
4400 SaCo 95843 238-J7
BOGDAN CT
2800 SaCo 95827 299-B5
BOGEY CT
7600 SaCo 95828 338-C3
BOGLE CT
- SAC 95838 277-H1
BOGUE WY
7100 CITH 95621 259-G1
BOISE CT
9000 SaCo 95826 298-H6
BOLANZO WY
6800 ELKG 95757 378-B1
BOLD LN
7300 SaCo 95823 338-A2
BOLD RIVER CT
11200 RCCD 95670 280-A5
BOLD RULER WY
8800 SaCo 95628 280-E2
BOLES RD
4100 EDCo 95667 264-F4
BOLI CT
100 FOLS 95630 261-G3
BOLIN WY
6400 SaCo 95673 257-G3
BOLINAS CT
- SAC 95823 337-H6
BOLINGBROOK DR
- RSVL 95747 219-C7
BOLIVAR AV
3600 SaCo 95660 258-G4
BOLIVAR CT
1400 EDCo 95762 242-B4
BOLLENBACHER AV
- SAC 95838 277-F1
BOLLING PL
1800 EDCo 95762 242-C5
BOLO CT
10200 ELKG 95757 377-J2
10200 ELKG 95757 397-J2
BOLSA CT
700 EDCo 95762 242-C3
3700 SaCo 95864 298-G2
BOLT CT
- PlaC 95658 181-B4
9000 SaCo 95826 318-H2
BOLTON WY
5600 RKLN 95677 220-D4
BOLTRES ST
5600 SaCo 95662 260-E6
BOMARK WY
4500 SaCo 95842 258-J6
4500 SaCo 95842 259-A6
BOMBARDIER CT
- SaCo 95827 299-D7
BOMBAY CIR
100 SAC 95835 257-C4
BOMISE WY
2800 EDCo 95667 246-C4
BONACK PL
- SAC 95835 256-G5
BON AIR CT
- SAC 95823 358-B1
BONAIRE RD
- WSAC 95691 316-D3
BONANZA DR
900 GALT 95632 439-F1
3100 EDCo 95682 263-D4
6300 SaCo 95842 258-J4
6300 SaCo 95842 259-A4
BONANZA ST
2600 RKLN 95677 220-C1
2900 EDCo 95726 248-C1
BONANZA WY
4000 PlaC 95650 201-G7
4100 PlaC 95650 221-G1

BONANZA AUTO RD
4900 EDCo 95682 264-F7
BONAVENTURE CT
- SAC 95823 338-B6
BONAVISTA WY
1900 SAC 95832 337-C4
BOND CT
1100 ANT 94509 (513-F6 See Page 493)
2900 PLCR 95667 245-F5
BOND RD
8400 ELKG 95624 358-F4
9300 ELKG 95624 359-D4
BOND WY
- RSVL 95747 218-J4
BONELLI CT
8100 SaCo 95843 238-F6
BONFAIR AV
- SAC 95834 256-H7
BONFIELD WY
200 SAC 95838 257-G7
BONHAM CIR
6300 CITH 95610 260-A4
BONHILL DR
- FOLS 95630 261-J5
- FOLS 95630 262-A4
BONICELLI CT
- RSVL 95747 219-B1
BONITA AV
2700 ANT 94509 (513-E6 See Page 493)
BONITA CT
1300 WSAC 95691 296-H5
1500 EDCo 95762 242-C4
BONITA DR
700 EDCo 95762 242-C4
3200 SaCo 95821 278-F6
BONITA ST
100 RSVL 95678 239-H3
BONITA WY
7000 CITH 95610 259-J1
BONITA DOWNS DR
8400 SaCo 95628 260-C5
BONITA VISTA CT
- EDCo - 267-D4
BONITA VISTA DR
- EDCo - 267-D4
BONLEY CT
600 FOLS 95630 261-J7
BONNER LN
4000 EDCo 95682 263-G5
BONNET CT
4500 SaCo 95864 298-J2
BONNEY CT
- RKLN 95765 200-D4
BONNIE CT
- EDCo - 247-G2
BONNIE LN
1000 PlaC 95603 182-A2
BONNIE WY
1700 SaCo 95825 298-E1
1700 SaCo 95864 298-E1
BONNIE JEAN WY
4200 SaCo 95821 279-A2
BONNIE LOU LN
5300 EDCo 95623 265-B7
BONNIEMAE WY
4900 SAC 95820 317-H3
5600 SAC 95824 317-H4
BONNIE OAK WY
1600 RSVL 95661 240-B6
8100 CITH 95610 240-B6
BONNIE VISTA RD
9600 SaCo 95693 360-C7
9700 SaCo 95693 (380-C1 See Page 379)
BONNY DOWNS WY
7800 ELKG 95758 358-C4
BONNY KNOLL RD
100 RSVL 95678 239-J2
BONSAI CT
5300 ELKG 95757 377-J2
5300 ELKG 95757 397-J2
BONWIT WY
7000 CITH 95621 259-F2
BONY KAYE CT
5000 SaCo 95843 239-B6
BOOM POINTER WY
11600 SaCo 95670 280-C4
BOOM RUN RD
10200 PlaC 95658 202-A2
BOONE LN
3500 LMS 95650 200-J6
4100 SaCo 95821 278-H5
BOOTH CT
3100 EDCo 95762 262-D5
BOOTH LN
6200 SAC 95822 317-B6
BOOTH RD
1100 PlaC 95747 239-E3
1300 RSVL 95747 239-E3
BOOTHBAY CT
6100 ELKG 95758 358-A6
BOOT HILL LN
2100 PlaC 95658 181-G3
BOOTHWYN WY
- ELKG 95758 357-E5
BOOTJACK DR
5200 SaCo 95842 259-B2
BORBA WY
7300 SaCo 95828 338-F2
BORCE CT
5500 ELKG 95757 377-J3
5500 ELKG 95757 397-J3
BORDEAUX DR
- EDCo 95762 262-A2
4300 OAKL 94561 (514-E7 See Page 493)
BORDEAUX WY
- RVIS 94571 454-G6
8500 SaCo 95628 260-D7
BORDEN RD
11600 SaCo 95638 420-C2
11600 SaCo 95632 420-C2
12800 SaCo 95632 421-C2
12800 SaCo 95638 421-C2
BORDERLANDS DR
- RCCD 95742 300-G7
- RCCD 95742 320-F1
BORDERS CT
- EDCo 95762 262-G5
BORDERS DR
- EDCo 95762 262-G6
BOREAL WY
8800 ELKG 95758 357-H3
BOREN LN
7700 PlaC 95746 221-E5
BORGA CT
- RSVL 95661 240-E2

BORGATA WY
- EDCo 95762 262-G5
BORGES CT
- FOLS 95630 261-D7
BORICA RD
3500 EDCo 95682 263-F6
BORICA WY
2500 SaCo 95821 278-G6
2500 SaCo 95864 278-G6
BORLAND AV
100 AUB 95603 182-F2
BORON CT
- RSVL 95747 219-B1
BORON WY
8300 SaCo 95828 338-D6
BORONA WY
2100 SAC 95833 277-B5
BORRA CT
- EDCo 95762 262-F2
BORREGO RD
- EDCo 95682 244-A6
BORREGO WY
7100 SaCo 95608 279-G2
BORTHWICK WY
7700 SaCo 95843 239-C7
7700 SaCo 95843 259-C1
BOSAL CIR
- PlaC 95603 162-A5
BOSAL CT
4600 ELKG 95758 357-H5
BOSBURY CT
- RSVL 95661 220-E6
BOSBURY WY
- RSVL 95661 220-E7
BOSCASTLE WY
9200 SaCo 95829 339-A6
BOSCO WY
5800 SAC 95824 318-B5
BOSPHORUS DR
- RCCD 95742 320-D2
BOSTON CT
400 SaCo 95864 298-J5
BOSTON COMMONS PL
100 RSVL 95661 240-D5
BOSTON IVY PL
8600 ELKG 95624 358-H2
BOSWELL CT
- SAC 95835 257-B5
BOSWELL WY
- SAC 95835 257-B5
BOTA CT
2200 RCCD 95670 279-J6
BOTELHO ST
1200 ANT 94509 (513-F4 See Page 493)
BOTHWELL CIR
- EDCo 95762 262-H4
BOTHWELL DR
7700 SaCo 95829 339-A5
BOTTLEBRUSH CIR
- RSVL 95747 219-A7
BOTTLE BRUSH CT
8700 ELKG 95624 358-G2
BOUCHET WY
10700 RCCD 95670 299-H4
BOUGANVILLA AV
- SaCo 95828 338-F3
BOULDER CT
6200 EDCo 95682 263-F7
- LNCN 95648 180-C6
BOULDER LN
- LNCN 95648 180-C6
2700 EDCo 95667 245-C4
BOULDER RD
5300 PlaC 95746 221-F6
BOULDER WY
7400 SAC 95823 337-F2
BOULDER CANYON WY
100 FOLS 95630 261-A4
BOULDER CREEK PL
3100 PlaC 95650 201-C4
3100 PlaC 95663 201-C4
BOULDER CREEK RD
5700 PlaC 95650 201-C4
8400 PlaC 95663 201-C4
BOULDER CREEK WY
3100 SaCo 95843 238-F6
BOULDER FALLS CT
9200 ELKG 95624 359-B5
BOULDER FIELD DR
8200 SaCo 95829 338-H7
BOULDER GLEN WY
8900 SaCo 95829 338-H6
BOULDER MINE RD
800 EDCo 95672 243-D1
BOULDER MINE WY
2000 SaCo 95670 280-E4
BOULDER POINT LN
- EDCo 95619 286-A6
BOULDER RIDGE CT
- RKLN 95765 200-E3
BOULDER RIDGE RD
1800 EDCo 95762 282-H2
3300 LMS 95650 200-F5
BOULDER RIVER WY
9200 ELKG 95624 359-A4
BOULWARE CT
9100 SaCo 95826 318-J2
BOUNDARY CT
15400 SaCo 95683 342-D3
BOUNDARY OAKS DR
5000 EDCo 95762 262-D6
BOUNTIFUL WY
4300 EDCo 95682 244-A6
BOUNTIFUL PLACE DR
6600 EDCo 95667 245-A3
BOUNTY CT
- ELKG 95758 358-A5
BOUQUET CT
3400 RCCD 95670 300-A5
BOUQUET WY
4200 SAC 95834 276-H1
BOURBON DR
5900 SaCo 95608 279-D1
BOURBON ST
- EDCo 95726 248-E1
BOURNVILLE CT
- ELKG 95758 357-F5
BOURTON CT
800 ANT 94509 (513-C7 See Page 493)
BOUTS PKWY
4400 SaCo 95823 337-G2
BOUVAIS CIR
7400 SaCo 95828 338-F2
BOUVARDIA CT
8600 ELKG 95624 358-G2
BOVILL DR
9700 ELKG 95624 359-A7

BOVINGDON LN
8100 CITH 95610 240-A6
BOW CT
6000 EDCo 95623 264-J7
BOW ST
8600 ELKG 95624 358-D1
BOWDEN CT
200 RSVL 95747 219-D7
BOWDER LN
3300 PlaC 95602 161-J3
BOWDIAN CT
2600 SAC 95826 298-E7
BOWEN CIR
7500 SAC 95822 337-B3
BOWEN DR
- FOLS 95630 261-J4
BOWEN ISLAND ST
- WSAC 95691 316-C2
BOWERWOOD DR
4700 SaCo 95608 299-A2
BOWERY CT
8500 SaCo 95662 260-D3
BOWIE CT
3600 SaCo 95843 238-G6
BOWKER CT
2500 SaCo 95608 279-B6
BOWLEN DR
600 WSAC 95605 296-J1
BOWLES ST
600 SAC 95815 277-H6
BOWLING DR
6800 SaCo 95823 317-G7
6800 SaCo 95823 337-G1
BOWLING GREEN DR
1600 SAC 95815 278-B7
1900 SAC 95825 278-C7
2000 SaCo 95825 278-C7
BOWMAN AV
300 SAC 95833 277-F5
BOWMAN LN
- LNCN 95648 180-A5
BOWMAN PL
4100 PlaC 95746 240-F2
BOWMAN RD
13400 PlaC 95603 162-G3
14000 PlaC 95602 162-H2
BOWMAN WY
500 PlaC 95603 162-F3
BOWMAN OAKS WY
4900 SaCo 95608 279-A4
BOWMAN UC RD
- PlaC 95603 162-F4
BOW MAR CT
3300 EDCo 95682 263-C2
BOWMONT WY
9300 ELKG 95758 358-B5
BOX CANYON RD
1000 EDCo 95667 245-G7
BOX CANYON WY
- RSVL 95747 219-D3
BOXCAR WY
100 FOLS 95630 281-B2
BOXELDER CIR
- FOLS 95630 261-G5
BOXELDER WY
9300 ELKG 95758 357-H5
BOXER WY
4600 SaCo 95608 279-D1
BOXFORD SQ
100 FOLS 95630 261-G6
BOXLER CT
100 FOLS 95630 261-E4
BOXWOOD ST
2200 SAC 95815 277-J7
BOXWOOD HILLS PL
5700 SaCo 95843 239-C6
BOYCE DR
4600 SAC 95823 337-H4
BOYD DR
4800 SaCo 95608 279-A7
BOYD RD
4200 EDCo 95667 265-A3
BOYDEN DR
2100 LNCN 95648 179-E3
BOYER DR
2200 SaCo 95608 279-C7
BOYINGTON RD
3300 PlaC 95650 201-B5
3300 PlaC 95663 201-B5
3400 LMS 95650 201-B5
BOYLE CT
3900 SAC 95817 317-G1
BOYLSTON CT
4700 SaCo 95842 259-A2
BOYSENBERRY LN
4000 EDCo 95682 283-G6
BOYSENBERRY WY
- ELKG 95624 358-G1
BOYS RANCH CT
- SaCo 95630 (321-H1 See Page 301)
BOYS RANCH RD
- SaCo 95630 301-H7
- SaCo 95630 (321-H1 See Page 301)
BOYTON WY
5600 SAC 95823 337-J3
5600 SAC 95823 338-A3
BOZEMAN ST
3300 SAC 95838 277-G4
BOZIO CT
- FOLS 95630 281-F2
BRABANT CT
- ELKG 95757 357-H7
BRABANT WY
4700 ELKG 95757 357-H7
BRABHAM WY
- ELKG 95758 358-C6
BRACE RD
5200 LMS 95650 200-H7
5200 LMS 95677 200-H7
5200 RKLN 95650 200-H7
5200 RKLN 95677 200-H7
5600 LMS 95650 201-A7
BRACKEN RD
4600 SaCo 95628 279-H1
BRACKENBURY WY
- PlaC 95746 240-H6
BRACKENWOOD CT
8500 PlaC 95747 239-A2
BRACKENWOOD PL
3000 EDCo 95762 262-D2
BRADBORNE DR
- LNCN 95648 200-B2
BRADBURN DR
- SAC 95835 257-B4
BRADBURY CT
- RKLN 95677 220-F5
8800 ELKG 95624 358-G4

BRADD WY
5600 SAC 95822 317-D4
BRADDOCK WY
- RSVL 95747 219-C7
BRADEN CT
100 EDCo 95709 247-D5
BRADEN DR
3000 EDCo - 247-D4
3500 EDCo 95709 247-C5
BRADFORD CT
300 RSVL 95678 219-F6
BRADFORD DR
- RKLN 95765 200-B5
4500 SAC 95820 318-C4
5100 SAC 95824 318-C4
BRADFORD PL
- RKLN 95765 200-B5
3600 EDCo 95762 242-C6
BRADFORD WY
2600 WSAC 95691 316-F1
BRADHUGH CT
9600 SaCo 95827 299-B7
BRADLEY DR
3200 EDCo 95619 265-E2
BRADLEY LN
2100 PlaC 95658 201-F2
BRADLEY WY
300 SaCo 95673 257-H2
BRADLEY RANCH RD
10700 ELKG 95624 359-H2
10700 SaCo 95624 359-H2
BRADSHAW AV
2200 RSVL 95661 240-D4
BRADSHAW RD
2700 SaCo 95827 299-C4
2900 RCCD 95827 299-C6
3700 SaCo 95827 319-C3
5200 SaCo 95829 319-C7
6600 SaCo 95829 339-B7
9100 ELKG 95624 339-B7
8300 ELKG 95624 339-B7
8300 ELKG 95624 359-B2
9700 ELKG 95624 379-B1
9700 SaCo 95624 379-B1
BRADVIEW DR
3700 SaCo 95827 299-D7
3700 SaCo 95827 319-D1
BRADY CT
100 SAC 95820 318-B3
BRADY LN
8100 PlaC 95747 239-E2
8100 RSVL 95747 239-E2
BRAE AV
8000 SAC 95838 277-J4
BRAE CT
- FOLS 95630 261-J4
BRAEBURN LN
- EDCo 95667 246-E4
- EDCo 95709 246-E4
BRAEBURN ST
3300 SaCo 95821 278-H4
BRAEMAR CT
400 RSVL 95661 240-E3
BRAEMORE DR
8000 SaCo 95828 338-G6
BRAERIDGE WY
7400 SAC 95831 337-B2
BRAESTONE CT
- EDCo - 247-E3
BRAGA CT
10300 ELKG 95757 378-B3
BRAGI DR
- WSAC 95691 296-D4
BRAHMA CIR
3700 EDCo 95682 283-H5
BRAHMA WY
8500 ELKG 95624 359-G1
BRAHMIN WY
- SaCo 95655 319-J2
BRAHMS CT
6100 SaCo 95621 239-D6
BRAITHWAITE ST
- RSVL 95747 239-B1
BRAKEMAN CT
9500 SaCo 95827 319-B1
BRAMANTE CT
- OAKL 94561 (514-H7 See Page 493)
BRAMBLE LN
- FOLS 95630 261-G5
BRAMBLE WY
5300 SaCo 95841 259-B7
BRAMBLE BUSH CIR
8300 SaCo 95843 238-H6
BRAMBLE TRAIL WY
9000 SaCo 95826 318-H2
BRAMBLE TREE WY
8300 CITH 95621 239-F6
BRAMBLEWOOD WY
8900 ELKG 95758 357-G3
BRAMFIELD WY
8100 SaCo 95829 339-A6
BRAMHALL CT
9800 PlaC 95746 240-G6
BRAMHALL PL
3300 EDCo 95762 262-D2
BRAMHALL WY
- SaCo 95628 260-B7
BRAMPTON WY
5500 SAC 95835 257-A4
BRAMWELL WY
9100 SaCo 95829 338-J5
BRANBURY WY
7300 SaCo 95828 338-F2
BRANCA WY
6700 ELKG 95757 378-B2
BRANCH CT
- RSVL 95678 219-G6
BRANCH ST
2700 SAC 95815 277-J6
3000 SAC 95838 277-J3
BRANCH CENTER RD
3700 SaCo 95827 299-B7
3700 SaCo 95827 319-B2
BRANCHOAK CT
8200 ELKG 95758 358-D5
BRANCHWATER WY
6600 CITH 95621 239-F7
BRANCHWOOD WY
7500 SAC 95823 337-G3
BRAND WY
4500 SAC 95819 297-J4
4700 SAC 95819 298-A4
BRANDAMORE CT
7400 ELKG 95758 358-C5
BRANDING IRON CT
2000 FOLS 95630 282-A2
BRANDING IRON DR
- FOLS 95630 282-B1

BRANDING IRON LN
- LNCN 95648 179-J4
5300 SaCo 95662 260-G7
BRANDING IRON WY
100 GALT 95632 419-E7
1900 RSVL 95661 240-C3
BRANDON DR
- RKLN 95765 200-A5
BRANDON WY
5800 SAC 95820 317-J2
5800 SAC 95820 318-A2
6200 SaCo 95608 259-D6
BRANDON OAKS LN
- SaCo 95608 279-A4
BRANDSBY CT
- RSVL 95747 218-J5
BRANDSBY LN
- RSVL 95747 218-J5
BRANDT CT
3500 EDCo 95762 242-C6
BRANDT WY
4400 SaCo 95660 258-J4
BRANDY CIR
6900 PlaC 95746 241-B3
BRANDY LN
1300 SaCo 95608 299-A2
BRANDY OAK CT
200 FOLS 95630 281-A2
BRANDYWINE CT
4500 SaCo 95608 279-F1
5700 PlaC 95746 240-J2
BRANDYWOOD CT
- SAC 95823 337-F3
BRANFORD CT
9500 SaCo 95827 299-B5
BRANGUS CT
10500 ELKG 95624 359-G1
BRANIFF CT
3300 EDCo 95682 263-E5
BRANINBURG CT
5400 SaCo 95608 279-B6
BRANNAN WY
2600 WSAC 95691 316-F1
BRANNAN ISLAND RD
100 SaCo 94571 474-H3
100 SaCo 95641 474-H3
100 SaCo 95641 (475-B3 See Page 456)
100 SaCo 95641 (476-B2 See Page 456)
BRANSON CT
8000 SaCo 95843 238-H6
BRANSTETTER ST
200 RSVL 95678 239-J1
BRANT WY
- RKLN 95765 219-H1
BRANTFORD WY
6200 CITH 95621 259-E3
BRANWOOD WY
1200 SAC 95831 337-A2
BRASHEAR LN
2300 PlaC 95663 201-D2
BRASILIA CT
3100 SaCo 95826 299-A7
BRATTLE CT
7200 SaCo 95842 259-A2
BRATTLEBORO CIR
100 SaCo 95655 319-J2
BRATTLEBORO CT
500 FOLS 95630 261-H7
BRAUER LN
11700 SaCo 95693 (400-D1 See Page 379)
BRAVADO DR
2600 RCCD 95670 299-D3
2700 RCCD 95827 299-D3
BRAVO WY
9400 SaCo 95826 319-A1
BRAXTON CT
- RSVL 95678 219-J5
BRAYNARD WY
2700 SaCo 95864 298-E6
BRAYTON AV
6900 CITH 95621 259-F5
BRAY VISTA WY
8600 ELKG 95624 358-F6
BRAZIL AV
6100 SaCo 95662 260-G5
BRAZIL CT
2500 ANT 94509 (513-H6 See Page 493)
BRAZIL DR
2200 ANT 94509 (513-H6 See Page 493)
BRAZOS RIVER CT
11100 RCCD 95670 280-A4
BREAKER POINT CT
- ELKG 95758 357-J2
BREAKERS CT
- GALT 95632 419-F2
BREAKERS DR
- GALT 95632 419-G2
BREAKWATER WY
6600 SAC 95831 316-G7
BREAMER DR
- EDCo 95682 263-F3
BREANNA CT
7200 SaCo 95828 338-F2
BRECKENRIDGE CT
8400 PlaC 95746 240-G5
BRECKENRIDGE WY
4400 SAC 95838 277-G1
BRECKENWOOD WY
- SaCo 95864 298-D6
BREDEHOFT WY
3100 SAC 95838 277-G5
BREE ANN CT
- CITH 95610 260-A1
BREEDS HILL CT
6200 CITH 95621 259-E4
BREELAND CT
- SAC 95835 257-A5
BREEN DR
- RKLN 95765 200-B6
BREESE CIR
5100 EDCo 95762 262-E2
BREEZE WY
7600 PlaC 95746 241-D2
BREEZE WAY PL
- SAC 95835 256-H5
BREEZEWOOD CT
6400 SaCo 95662 260-B4
BREEZY WY
- EDCo - 267-C5
BREEZY BRANCH CT
3500 EDCo 95682 283-G5
BREEZY RIDGE RD
- EDCo 95634 225-G2

STREET
Block City ZIP Pg-Grid

BREGLIA WY
1100 EDCo 95667 245-G7
BRELAND CT
- SAC 95823 337-G5
BREMEN DR
6300 CITH 95621 259-E4
BREMERTON CT
400 RSVL 95661 240-E3
BREMNER WY
5000 SaCo 95841 259-A7
BRENCICH LN
- EDCo 95667 226-E7
BRENDA WY
2900 WSAC 95691 316-E2
10300 RCCD 95670 299-F1
BRENDAN CT
1600 PLCR 95667 245-J6
BRENDAN WY
1500 PLCR 95667 245-J6
BRENHAM CT
- SAC 95823 337-H6
BRENNA WY
- ELKG 95757 377-J2
- ELKG 95757 378-A2
- ELKG 95757 397-J2
BRENNAN CT
300 ANT 94509 (513-E6 See Page 493)
BRENNANS RD
2200 PlaC 95658 181-F3
2500 PlaC 95650 201-G5
2500 PlaC 95663 201-F3
BRENNANS POINT DR
- PlaC 95658 201-F2
BRENNANS POINT LN
- PlaC 95658 201-F2
BRENNEN CIR
300 RSVL 95678 219-G4
BRENNEN CT
- SaCo 95843 239-C6
BRENT CT
4100 EDCo 95667 265-B1
4500 SaCo 95820 317-H4
BRENTA CT
6300 ELKG 95757 358-A7
BRENTFORD CIR
- LNCN 95648 179-F6
6200 SAC 95823 338-A6
BRENTLEY DR
2400 SAC 95822 317-E4
BRENT MILL WY
- RSVL 95747 218-J4
BRENTON CT
- ELKG 95624 359-A6
BRENTWICK WY
8500 SaCo 95823 358-B1
BRENTWOOD CIR
10000 AUB 95603 182-D5
BRENTWOOD RD
300 RSVL 95678 239-G2
2400 SaCo 95825 278-E7
BRENZO WY
2600 PlaC 95658 202-A3
BRETELLA CT
- EDCo 95762 262-H6
BRET HARTE CT
1400 RSVL 95661 240-A5
3600 SAC 95817 317-F1
BRET HARTE RD
300 SaCo 95864 298-E5
BRETMOOR DR
5600 SaCo 95662 260-G6
BRETON WY
- ELKG 95758 358-D3
BRETT DR
5700 SaCo 95842 259-A5
6000 SaCo 95842 258-J4
BRETTS RD
3300 PlaC 95650 201-C5
BREUNER AV
3700 SAC 95819 297-J3
BREUNER DR
200 RSVL 95678 240-A1
BREVAL ST
- SAC 95833 276-G4
- SAC 95834 276-G4
BREVARD DR
9000 SaCo 95829 338-J5
BREWER RD
6800 PlaC 95626 237-H1
BREWERS HILL RD
- EDCo - 267-G4
BREWERTON DR
1200 SAC 95833 277-D6
BREWERY LN
100 AUB 95603 182-D3
BREWSTER AV
200 SAC 95831 316-F7
BREWSTER MILL CIR
8200 SaCo 95843 239-D6
BRIAN CT
9100 SaCo 95826 318-J2
BRIAN KELLY WY
- ELKG 95757 377-J2
- ELKG 95757 378-A2
- ELKG 95757 397-J2
BRIANNA CT
- SaCo 95829 339-F7
BRIANTOWN CT
10000 RCCD 95827 299-D6
BRIAR LN
- LNCN 95648 179-D1
BRIAR WY
8000 PlaC 95746 240-G2
BRIARBERRY WY
- EDCo 95762 282-D3
BRIARBROOK CIR
8500 SaCo 95662 260-D2
BRIAR BUSH WY
8300 ELKG 95758 358-E5
BRIARCLIFF CT
100 FOLS 95630 261-E5
BRIARCLIFF DR
100 FOLS 95630 261-D5
BRIARCLIFF LN
- LNCN 95648 200-A1
BRIAR CLIFF WY
8300 SAC 95826 318-E1
BRIAR CREEK CT
- SaCo 95838 257-J7
BRIARCREST WY
900 SAC 95831 316-J6
900 SAC 95831 317-A6
BRIARGATE LN
5000 SaCo 95660 258-H7
BRIARGLEN CT
5000 ELKG 95758 357-H3
BRIAR HILL RD
- PlaC 95603 161-F7
BRIAR HILL RD
- PlaC 95603 181-F1
BRIARHOLLOW CT
4100 SaCo 95628 279-J3
BRIAR PATCH CT
- RSVL 95747 219-D2
BRIAR RIDGE LN
8000 CITH 95610 260-A6
BRIARTON DR
- LNCN 95648 200-A2
BRIARTOWN CT
- ELKG 95624 359-A5
BRIARTREE WY
6400 CITH 95621 239-E6
BRIARWOOD CT
3500 ANT 94509 (513-E7 See Page 493)
BRIARWOOD DR
900 WSAC 95691 296-H4
4300 SaCo 95821 278-J4
BRIARWOOD LN
2700 PlaC 95603 161-J6
4200 EDCo 95667 264-J2
BRIARWOOD WY
- RSVL 95747 239-D1
BRIARY CT
11100 RCCD 95670 300-A4
BRICK HEARTH PL
8200 SaCo 95843 238-H6
BRICKWELL WY
1300 SaCo 95608 299-B2
BRICKYARD DR
600 SAC 95831 316-G5
BRIDALSMITH DR
8700 SaCo 95828 338-G6
8800 SaCo 95829 338-G6
BRIDAL VEIL CT
4800 SaCo 95843 239-A6
BRIDAL VEIL DR
6100 RKLN 95677 220-B4
BRIDALVEIL LN
- LNCN 95648 179-J6
BRIDE LN
700 PlaC 95658 180-J2
BRIDGE PL
300 WSAC 95691 296-G7
300 WSAC 95691 316-G1
BRIDGE RD
3600 SAC 95821 278-G2
3600 SAC 95841 278-G2
3600 SaCo 95821 278-G2
3600 SaCo 95841 278-G2
BRIDGE ST
- SaCo 95690 437-A1
200 FOLS 95630 261-B4
4000 SaCo 95628 280-A3
4000 SaCo 95670 280-A3
S BRIDGE ST
11200 SaCo 95670 280-A4
BRIDGE BAY DR
7600 SAC 95831 336-H3
BRIDGEBURN CT
- ELKG 95758 358-C5
BRIDGECREEK DR
1800 SAC 95833 277-C5
BRIDGE CREEK LN
5400 SaCo 95608 279-B4
9400 PlaC 95658 201-H4
9400 PlaC 95650 201-H4
BRIDGECROSS DR
5600 SAC 95835 257-C4
BRIDGEFORD DR
- RSVL 95678 219-G3
2700 SAC 95833 277-D4
3300 SAC 95834 277-D4
3500 SAC 95833 277-E5
BRIDGEFORD WY
3100 SAC 95833 277-D4
BRIDGEHEAD RD
5500 OAKL 94561 (514-A4 See Page 493)
5500 OAKL 94509 (514-A4 See Page 493)
5800 ANT 94509 (514-A4 See Page 493)
BRIDGEMONT WY
6600 CITH 95621 259-F2
BRIDGEND WY
- FOLS 95630 262-A5
BRIDGEPORT DR
- EDCo 95682 263-E4
BRIDGEPORT WY
- RVIS 94571 454-E2
2600 SAC 95826 298-D7
BRIDGESHIRE WY
8800 SaCo 95828 338-G6
BRIDGESIDE CT
- RSVL 95747 219-C1
BRIDGESIDE DR
- SAC 95831 336-H3
BRIDGESTONE DR
- LNCN 95648 199-H3
BRIDGESTONE CRESCENT RD
- PlaC 95747 238-J1
BRIDGET DR
- SaCo 95828 338-D7
BRIDGET BRAE RD
3300 EDCo 95682 263-H5
BRIDGETENDER CT
- RKLN 95677 220-J2
- SAC 95831 336-G4
BRIDGEVIEW DR
200 PlaC 95603 162-G4
1000 EDCo 95667 245-D7
7600 SAC 95831 336-H3
BRIDGEWATER CT
8400 PlaC 95746 240-H2
9000 ELKG 95624 358-F3
BRIDGEWAY CT
- RSVL 95678 219-J3
BRIDGEWAY LAKES DR
- WSAC 95691 316-C3
BRIDGEWOOD CT
8200 SaCo 95662 260-B3
BRIDLE CT
- WSAC 95691 316-E2
500 RSVL 95661 240-C3
1100 PlaC 95603 162-B4
BRIDLE DR
- ELKG 95624 359-E5
BRIDLE PTH
900 GALT 95632 439-F1
BRIDLE PATH LN
2300 SaCo 95864 278-J7
8800 PlaC 95746 241-B3
BRIDLE RACK CT
12700 SaCo 95693 360-H5
BRIDLE TRAIL LN
5800 EDCo 95630 222-F2
BRIDLE TRAIL WY
6900 SAC 95828 318-C7
6900 SAC 95828 338-C1
BRIDLEVAIL CT
- ELKG 95758 357-F5
BRIDLEWOOD DR
- RKLN 95765 199-J5
- RKLN 95765 200-A4
2200 RCCD 95670 279-J6
2900 EDCo 95762 263-A5
BRIDLEWOOD WY
100 PLCR 95667 245-D6
- PlaC 95747 239-A3
BRIENNE WY
9100 ELKG 95758 357-H4
BRIER WY
1700 SaCo 95608 299-A1
BRIERGLEN WY
800 SAC 95834 277-E3
BRIGADOON
6300 SaCo 95842 259-A4
BRIGANTINE CT
- ELKG 95758 357-E4
BRIGGS CT
- RSVL 95747 219-C3
BRIGGS DR
- RSVL 95747 219-C3
6700 SAC 95828 318-B7
6800 SaCo 95828 318-B7
6900 SaCo 95828 338-B1
BRIGGS RANCH DR
100 FOLS 95630 261-F3
BRIGHAM WY
8700 SAC 95826 298-G7
BRIGHT CT
800 SAC 95838 278-B1
3900 EDCo 95667 265-C3
BRIGHT HOPE MINE RD
- EDCo 95634 225-D3
BRIGHTON AV
7400 SAC 95826 318-C1
BRIGHTON CT
- RKLN 95765 200-E3
1000 ANT 94509 (513-F7 See Page 493)
4800 PlaC 95746 240-H5
BRIGHTON WY
3200 ANT 94509 (513-F7 See Page 493)
BRIGHTON BEACH WY
- ELKG 95758 357-E6
BRIGHTON OAK CT
10000 ELKG 95624 378-H2
BRIGHTON WYND WY
8200 SaCo 95843 239-B6
BRIGHTSIDE CT
8000 SaCo 95828 338-E5
BRIGHT STARS CT
- ELKG 95624 359-B5
BRIGHTSTONE CIR
100 FOLS 95630 281-A2
BRIGHTWATER CT
1600 EDCo 95762 242-C5
BRIGHT WATER PL
9700 PlaC 95746 240-J5
BRIGHTWOOD CT
4900 SaCo 95608 259-E7
BRIGITTES PL
1000 EDCo 95672 243-F4
BRILES CT
9200 ELKG 95624 358-J7
BRILL CT
100 RSVL 95678 219-F7
6800 CITH 95621 259-F1
BRILLAR CT
15100 SaCo 95683 342-C2
BRILLIANCE PL
1000 FOLS 95630 261-B6
BRIMFIELD CT
300 RSVL 95747 239-C1
BRIMSTONE DR
7900 CITH 95621 239-E7
BRINDLE CT
9600 ELKG 95757 358-A6
BRINEF DR
5500 SaCo 95841 259-C5
BRINKMAN CT
9200 ELKG 95624 378-J1
BRINZINO CT
9800 ELKG 95757 358-A7
BRISA LN
6800 SaCo 95683 342-A1
BRISA PK
6800 SaCo 95683 342-A1
BRISA RIBERA CT
400 RSVL 95747 219-C4
BRISBANE CIR
4000 EDCo 95762 262-D3
BRISBANE CT
3000 SaCo 95826 299-A7
BRISBANE ST
- WSAC 95691 296-H7
BRISDALE PL
- ANT 94509 (513-C5 See Page 493)
BRISENBOURG WY
8500 SaCo 95843 238-G5
BRISKIN DR
8700 ELKG 95624 358-H2
BRISTLEWOOD WY
3900 SAC 95823 337-G3
BRISTOL CT
400 OAKL 94561 (514-D7 See Page 493)
500 RSVL 95661 240-D3
2500 RKLN 95765 200-D6
3400 EDCo 95682 263-D3
BRISTOL RD
3200 SaCo 95864 298-F3
BRISTOL PLAZA WY
9000 ELKG 95624 338-J7
9000 ELKG 95624 358-H1
BRITLAND WY
8800 SaCo 95628 260-E6
BRITTAIN ST
100 RSVL 95678 239-J1
BRITTANY CT
4900 RKLN 95677 220-G3
E BRITTANY LN
9700 SJCo 95220 (440-H7 See Page 420)
BRITTANY PL
- EDCo 95762 262-C1
BRITTANY WY
- EDCo 95762 262-B1
5900 CITH 95610 259-J5
BRITTANY PARK DR
8700 SaCo 95828 338-G6
BRITTANY PARK DR
8700 SaCo 95829 338-H6
BRITTNEY LEE CT
4800 SaCo 95841 279-B1
BRITTON PL
- WSAC 95691 316-C3
BRITTON WY
- SaCo 95655 319-J2
BRIW RD
3000 PLCR 95667 245-C6
3000 EDCo 95667 245-C6
BRIW RIDGE CT
100 PLCR 95667 245-D6
BRIW RIDGE RD
3100 EDCo 95667 245-D6
BRIX CT
3300 RCCD 95670 299-J4
3300 RCCD 95670 300-A4
BRIX WY
3300 RCCD 95670 299-J4
BRIXHAM CT
8300 SaCo 95843 238-H5
BROADFORD DR
- FOLS 95630 262-A5
BROADGATE DR
- SAC 95834 256-G7
- SAC 95835 256-G7
BROADLAND ST
- SAC 95834 277-B3
BROADLEAF CT
3400 EDCo 95682 263-H5
BROADLEIGH CT
- RSVL 95747 218-H4
BROADMOOR WY
3400 SaCo 95608 279-E4
BROAD RIVER CT
2200 RCCD 95670 279-J6
BROADSTONE CT
3500 RKLN 95765 220-C1
BROADSTONE DR
2200 RSVL 95661 240-D3
BROADSTONE PKWY
- FOLS 95630 261-J7
- FOLS 95630 262-A7
- FOLS 95630 281-H1
- FOLS 95630 282-A1
BROAD STRIPES WY
- ELKG 95624 359-B5
- RSVL 95747 219-A7
BROADVIEW AV
100 AUB 95603 182-F3
BROADWATER DR
- SAC 95835 256-J6
BROADWAY
- SAC 95818 297-A5
1100 PLCR 95667 245-H5
1500 PLCR 95667 246-A5
1900 EDCo 95667 246-A5
2700 SAC 95817 297-E7
3500 SAC 95817 317-H1
4300 SAC 95820 317-H1
5800 SAC 95820 318-A1
6400 SAC 95817 318-A1
BROADWAY CT
- PLCR 95667 245-H5
BROCADE DR
7300 CITH 95621 259-G1
BROCK CIR
- FOLS 95630 281-E1
BROCK CT
2700 WSAC 95691 316-F2
BROCK DR
6500 SaCo 95660 258-H3
BROCK LN
100 OAKL 94561 (514-D6 See Page 493)
BROCKENHURST DR
6000 ELKG 95758 358-A2
BROCKMAN CT
- LNCN 95648 200-B1
BROCKS LN
- EDCo - 267-D4
BROCKTON PL
- RVIS 94571 454-G2
BROCKWAY CT
3500 SAC 95818 317-D2
BROCKWOOD WY
7800 CITH 95621 239-D7
BRODER CIR
- FOLS 95630 261-H5
BRODIAEA CT
4100 ELKG 95758 357-G5
BRODIE CT
8600 ELKG 95624 358-F6
BRODIE DR
- GALT 95632 419-D6
6200 PlaC 95658 181-G7
6200 PlaC 95658 201-G1
BRODIEWEST CT
- GALT 95632 419-D6
BRODLAEA CT
5400 EDCo 95726 247-J7
BROGAN CT
- SaCo 95829 339-F7
BROGAN WY
- EDCo 95762 262-G5
BROKEN ARROW CT
6000 CITH 95621 259-D4
BROKEN BOW DR
5900 CITH 95621 259-D3
BROKEN BRANCH CT
- SAC 95834 277-B4
BROKEN BRANCH TR
3300 EDCo 95667 244-E6
BROKENFEATHER WY
6000 CITH 95621 259-D3
BROKEN GATE RD
1100 EDCo 95667 244-F1
BROKEN RAIL LN
- RKLN 95765 199-J4
- RKLN 95765 200-A4
BROKEN TOP CT
500 FOLS 95630 261-A1
BROLIO CT
3300 RCCD 95670 300-A4
BROME CT
5500 SaCo 95662 260-G6
BROMFIELD CT
9200 ELKG 95624 358-J4
BROMLEY CT
500 RSVL 95747 219-D7
BROMLEY WY
10000 RCCD 95827 299-D5
BROMPTON CT
4800 SaCo 95608 299-A3
BROMWICH CT
- RKLN 95677 220-F5
BRONCO CREEK CT
- SAC 95835 256-J5
BRONCO CREEK WY
2700 SAC 95835 256-J4
BRONDSBURY LN
5100 SaCo 95628 260-F7
BRONG RD
100 FOLS 95630 261-G4
BRONHOLLY PL
5400 SaCo 95843 239-C6
BRONSON DR
8600 PlaC 95746 241-C3
BRONTE CT
600 RSVL 95747 219-C5
BRONWOOD WY
10500 RCCD 95670 279-G7
BRONZECREST ST
2800 PLCR 95667 245-F4
BRONZE OAK CT
6800 ELKG 95758 358-B4
BROOK CT
100 AUB 95603 182-F3
6600 SaCo 95628 259-F5
7900 PlaC 95746 241-B1
BROOK RD
100 AUB 95603 182-E2
E BROOK WY
5400 ELKG 95758 357-J5
BROOKBAY WY
- SAC 95838 277-F3
BROOKCREST CT
- RKLN 95677 220-H4
6900 CITH 95621 259-G5
BROOKDALE CIR
- PlaC 95746 240-G3
BROOKDALE CT
3500 ANT 94509 (513-E7 See Page 493)
BROOKDALE DR
4900 SAC 95834 276-H1
7400 CITH 95621 239-G7
BROOKE CREST DR
11600 PlaC 95602 162-A1
BROOKEDGE DR
2300 EDCo 95667 245-B4
BROOKE MEADOW DR
7700 SAC 95823 337-G4
BROOKFIELD CIR
- RKLN 95677 220-H4
BROOKFIELD CT
- RKLN 95677 220-H4
BROOKFIELD DR
4100 SAC 95823 337-G3
BROOKGLEN WY
4900 SaCo 95608 259-E7
4900 SaCo 95608 279-E1
BROOKHAVEN DR
100 RSVL 95678 219-G5
BROOKHAVEN WY
6900 CITH 95621 259-F5
BROOKHILL DR
4100 SaCo 95628 279-H2
BROOKHOLLOW CT
- PlaC 95650 201-E4
BROOKINGS CT
8000 ELKG 95758 358-C5
BROOKLINE CIR
1000 EDCo 95762 262-D3
1100 RSVL 95747 219-D7
BROOKLYN AV
4900 SaCo 95824 317-H5
BROOK MAR CT
2000 EDCo 95762 242-B6
BROOK MAR DR
1900 EDCo 95762 242-B6
BROOKMERE WY
- SAC 95835 256-J6
- SAC 95835 257-A5
BROOKMONT CT
- ELKG 95624 359-A6
BROOKNOLL CT
6800 CITH 95621 259-F5
BROOKOVER CT
7600 CITH 95610 240-A7
7600 CITH 95610 260-A1
BROOK PARK LN
- SaCo 95841 259-C7
BROOK PARK WY
1500 RSVL 95747 219-E5
BROOKRIDGE CT
7200 CITH 95610 260-C2
BROOK RIDGE WY
1500 RSVL 95678 219-F6
BROOKS AV
5500 LMS 95650 200-H5
BROOKS LN
6600 LMS 95650 221-B2
BROOKS ANN WY
9300 SaCo 95662 260-H3
BROOKSHIRE CT
5800 SaCo 95662 260-F3
BROOKSHIRE DR
- RKLN 95677 220-F4
BROOKSHIRE WY
100 RSVL 95678 219-B6
BROOKSIDE CIR
6000 RKLN 95677 220-C5
BROOKSIDE CT
1100 LNCN 95648 179-G4
BROOKSIDE DR
100 AUB 95603 182-F2
4200 SAC 95834 276-H1
BROOKSIDE LN
- FOLS 95630 261-B3
- RVIS 94571 454-F1
1100 LNCN 95648 179-G4
BROOKSIDE RD
4500 EDCo 95682 283-D3
BROOKSIDE WY
3400 SaCo 95608 279-E4
BROOKSTONE WY
7900 SAC 95833 277-D5
BROOKTREE DR
5900 CITH 95621 259-F5
BROOK VALLEY WY
11700 RCCD 95742 300-D7
BROOKVIEW CT
5100 SaCo 95608 279-B2
BROOKVIEW DR
300 OAKL 94561 (514-G7 See Page 493)
BROOKVIEW ST
100 RSVL 95678 239-J1
BROOKWATER CT
- RSVL 95747 219-C4
BROOK WILLOW WY
- ELKG 95758 358-D3
BROOKWOOD RD
200 RSVL 95678 239-G2
3200 SaCo 95821 278-G5
BROOME PL
4700 EDCo 95762 262-D3
BROPHY DR
3100 SaCo 95821 278-J5
BROTHER ISLAND RD
- WSAC 95691 316-E2
BROUGHAM WY
6800 CITH 95621 259-F2
BROUGHTON CT
- RKLN 95677 220-F5
200 RSVL 95746 240-F5
3900 SaCo 95827 319-B1
BROUILLY CT
8000 SaCo 95829 338-H5
N BROVELLI WOODS LN
- SJCo 95220 439-C6
W BROVELLI WOODS LN
- SJCo 95220 439-B6
BROWER CT
5000 PlaC 95746 240-J5
BROWN DR
700 EDCo 95762 262-C5
BROWN LN
1800 CCCo 94509 (513-H5 See Page 493)
3900 SaCo 95660 258-H6
BROWN RD
9000 ELKG 95624 358-G1
BROWN BEAR CT
9500 ELKG 95757 358-A7
BROWN DEER CT
- RSVL 95747 219-D2
BROWN DUVALL LN
- FOLS 95630 261-E7
BROWN GABLES RD
600 PlaC 95603 162-F4
BROWNING CT
- RKLN 95765 199-J5
300 RSVL 95747 219-E6
BROWNING DR
1200 SAC 95815 278-A5
BROWNING LN
- RKLN 95765 199-J5
BROWNING ST
10200 PlaC 95626 237-E2
BROWNLEA CIR
3300 SaCo 95843 238-F6
BROWN OTTER DR
7600 SaCo 95843 238-H7
BROWNS AL
1200 SaCo 95690 436-J1
1200 SaCo 95690 437-A1
BROWNS LN
5300 SaCo 95660 258-H6
BROWNS RD
6500 EDCo 95667 244-G4
BROWNSBERG WY
9300 SaCo 95829 339-A6
BROWNS ISLAND CT
- WSAC 95691 316-E2
BROWNSON ST
3700 SaCo 95821 278-G3
BROWNSTONE CT
4900 ELKG 95758 357-H5
BROWNWOOD WY
7500 SAC 95822 337-D3
BROWNWYK DR
1100 SAC 95822 317-A2
BRUBAKER CT
- ELKG 95758 357-G5
BRUBECK DR
- RCCD 95670 299-G4
BRUCE LN
8100 SAC 95826 318-D1
BRUCE ST
1600 ANT 94509 (513-E5 See Page 493)
BRUCE WY
4000 SaCo 95660 258-H4
BRUCE BALL CT
- EDCo 95667 245-B1
BRUCEVILLE RD
6600 SAC 95823 338-B5
8200 SAC 95758 338-B7
8300 SAC 95758 358-B1
8300 SAC 95823 358-B1
8500 ELKG 95758 358-B2
8500 ELKG 95823 358-B2
9300 ELKG 95757 358-B6
9400 ELKG 95757 378-B3
10200 ELKG 95757 378-B6
12400 SaCo 95757 418-B1
12700 SaCo 95690 418-B2
BRUCKNER CT
- ELKG 95624 359-A5
N BRUELLA RD
22500 SJCo 95220 (440-G6 See Page 420)
27000 SJCo 95632 (440-G2 See Page 420)
BRUFORD CT
2200 FOLS 95630 281-F1
BRUGLER CT
100 FOLS 95630 261-F3
BRUHN CT
4100 SaCo 95821 278-H5
BRUIN TR
- EDCo - 267-E6
BRULE CT
3900 SaCo 95821 278-H2
BRUM CT
100 FOLS 95630 261-F3
BRUMA CT
4700 SaCo 95843 239-A5
BRUNING AV
- RVIS 94571 454-G6
BRUNING CT
4600 SaCo 95823 317-H7
BRUNK RD
- SaCo 95690 456-E1
BRUNNER DR
3300 SaCo 95826 298-J7
3300 SaCo 95826 318-J1
BRUNNET LN
- SAC 95833 276-J4
- SAC 95833 277-A4
BRUNO WY
7300 SaCo 95828 338-C2
BRUNS WY
8200 SaCo 95828 338-D2
BRUNSWICK WY
100 RSVL 95678 219-B6
1100 SAC 95833 277-D6
BRUNTON WY
2200 SaCo 95825 278-D7
BRUSH LN
11200 SaCo 95693 (400-G1 See Page 379)
BRUSH WY
8600 ELKG 95624 358-E1
BRUSHCREEK CT
8200 CITH 95621 239-G6
BRUSH OAK WY
8200 SaCo 95843 238-H6
BRYAN AV
- ANT 94509 (513-D6 See Page 493)
100 PlaC 95661 239-H5
200 RSVL 95661 239-H5
BRYAN CT
- ELKG 95757 378-B2
- FOLS 95630 261-J4
3000 EDCo 95667 245-E3
BRYAN LN
1700 PlaC 95663 201-A1
BRYAN WY
2500 EDCo 95667 245-D3
3900 SaCo 95608 279-E3
BRYANT CT
3300 SaCo 95821 278-J5
N BRYANT RD
- SJCo 95220 (440-H7 See Page 420)
BRYANT ST
- PlaC 95626 237-E1
BRYCE CT
- EDCo 95762 262-F6
- SAC 95824 318-B6
BRYCE ST
2900 SaCo 95821 278-D5
BRYCE WY
5800 RKLN 95677 220-C4
BRYCE CANYON PL
5700 SaCo 95842 259-C2
BRYCEWOOD WY
5400 SaCo 95843 239-C6
BRYDON WY
8800 SaCo 95826 318-H2
BRYNMAR CT
- SAC 95835 257-A5
BRYTE AV
400 WSAC 95605 296-H1
BUCCANEER CIR
3400 SaCo 95826 318-J1
BUCHANAN CT
- RKLN 95765 219-H1
BUCHANAN DR
3900 SaCo 95628 280-C2
BUCHANAN RD
1100 ANT 94509 (513-B6 See Page 493)
BUCHANAN WY
- FOLS 95630 261-C7
BUCHMAN CIR
- SAC 95833 276-J4
- SAC 95833 277-A4
BUCK CIR
100 FOLS 95630 260-J3
100 FOLS 95630 261-A3
BUCK RD
5000 EDCo 95682 264-E5
N BUCK RD
24400 SJCo 95220 (440-H6 See Page 420)
BUCKBOARD CT
- RKLN 95765 200-E3
BUCKBOARD DR
1200 LNCN 95648 179-J2
6000 SaCo 95673 258-A4
BUCKBOARD LN
9300 PlaC 95650 201-H6
BUCKBOARD RD
- PlaC 95658 181-E4
2700 EDCo 95667 226-E3
BUCKBOARD WY
100 RSVL 95747 219-B5
BUCKBRUSH DR
- FOLS 95630 261-F5
BUCKELY CT
- RSVL 95747 219-C2
BUCKEYE CT
1300 AUB 95603 182-D5
2600 RKLN 95677 220-F2
3100 EDCo 95667 226-H3
BUCKEYE DR
1900 WSAC 95691 296-H4
2500 RKLN 95677 220-F2
2800 PlaC 95663 201-D3
BUCKEYE LN
6400 PlaC 95746 241-A4
BUCKEYE RD
4400 EDCo 95682 264-C6
BUCKEYE HILL CT
11300 SaCo 95670 280-B4
BUCKHAVEN WY
- FOLS 95630 261-J3
7500 CITH 95610 259-J1
BUCKHORN DR
6600 SaCo 95842 259-B3
BUCKHORN LN
1800 EDCo 95672 243-B7
2000 EDCo 95672 263-A1
BUCKHORN RD
- EDCo - 248-C7
BUCKINGHAM CT
- RSVL 95678 219-G5
BUCKINGHAM WY
- FOLS 95630 281-E2
4600 SAC 95819 297-H6
BUCKLEY WY
400 SAC 95838 278-B1
BUCKMINSTER DR
- ELKG 95758 357-D4
BUCK MOUNTAIN RD
5300 EDCo 95667 264-E1
BUCKNELL CT
4700 SaCo 95841 279-A1
BUCKNER CT
100 FOLS 95630 261-A1
BUCKRIDGE WY
1500 SAC 95833 277-C5
BUCKS BAR CIR
- EDCo 95667 286-H1
BUCKS BAR RD
3800 EDCo - 286-G1
3900 EDCo 95667 266-E5
3900 EDCo 95667 286-G1
BUCKS CREEK CT
2200 SaCo 95670 280-D5
BUCKS HARBOR WY
7900 SaCo 95828 338-F5
BUCKSKIN CT
3500 RKLN 95677 200-D7
9100 ELKG 95624 358-H6
BUCKSKIN LN
- RSVL 95747 219-B4

SACRAMENTO CO.

STREET / Block City ZIP Pg-Grid

BUCKTAIL LN
6100 EDCo 95726 248-C6
BUCKTHORN CT
2900 ANT 94531 (513-H7 See Page 493)
BUCKWOOD WY
5300 SAC 95835 257-C5
BUD CT
2200 RSVL 95661 240-D5
BUD LN
2800 PLCR 95667 245-D4
BUDDECKE PL
8700 PlaC 95746 240-G3
BUDDYLAKE CT
9800 ELKG 95624 359-A7
9800 ELKG 95624 379-A1
BUENA CT
- EDCo 95726 247-F6
BUENA PARK CT
5400 SaCo 95843 259-B1
BUENA PLAZA CIR
10300 RCCD 95670 299-F3
BUENA TERRA RD
- EDCo 95726 247-H6
BUENA TERRA WY
6800 SAC 95831 317-B7
6900 SAC 95831 337-B1
BUENA VENTURA WY
5400 SaCo 95628 260-B6
BUENA VIDA WY
- RSVL 95747 219-B1
BUENA VISTA AV
300 PlaC 95658 181-F5
4900 SaCo 95628 260-C7
4900 SaCo 95628 280-C1
BUENA VISTA CT
100 RSVL 95747 219-C5
BUENA VISTA DR
3400 EDCo 95682 263-G5
3500 SaCo 95864 298-G3
BUENA VISTA ST
100 AUB 95603 182-C3
BUENO CT
- SAC 95823 337-G2
BUENVANTE PL
- SAC 95835 257-A3
BUFFALO AV
9400 SaCo 95662 260-H6
BUFFALO RD
4200 PlaC 95602 161-B3
BUFFALO TR
1800 EDCo 95762 282-H1
BUFFALO CREEK CT
- SaCo 95670 280-B5
BUFFALO RIVER CT
11000 RCCD 95670 279-J5
BUFFET CT
- FOLS 95630 281-G2
BUFFINGTON ST
- RCCD 95655 299-G5
- SaCo 95655 299-G5
BUFFLEHEAD LN
7500 CITH 95621 259-D1
BUFFUM CT
8400 SaCo 95628 260-C7
8400 SaCo 95628 280-C1
BUFFWOOD WY
4800 SaCo 95841 259-A5
BUFFY LN
7200 SaCo 95828 338-G1
BUFORD CT
8400 SaCo 95843 238-F5
BUGATTI CT
8000 SaCo 95828 338-G5
BUGGYWHIP CT
9100 ELKG 95624 358-H6
BUGGY WHIP LN
- RSVL 95747 219-B3
BUGLE CT
2300 EDCo 95682 244-A7
8300 ELKG 95758 358-E6
BUHLER WY
3600 SaCo 95660 258-G2
BUHO
15000 SaCo 95683 322-B7
BUILDERS PL
3000 EDCo 95672 243-J6
BULEN ST
100 RSVL 95678 239-H2
BULJAN CT
2000 FOLS 95630 262-A7
BULJAN DR
- FOLS 95630 262-B7
100 RSVL 95678 239-J3
BULLARD DR
4500 EDCo 95682 283-F7
7400 PlaC 95658 181-D1
BULLARD ST
- RCCD 95655 299-G5
BULL HEAD LN
- EDCo - 267-D6
BULLION WY
9400 SaCo 95662 260-H6
BULLION MINE CT
- LNCN 95648 179-J5
BULL MOUNTAIN CIR
8200 ELKG 95758 358-D6
BULLOCK LN
6600 CITH 95610 259-H3
BULRUSH ST
- PlaC 95747 239-B3
BULWICK CT
- SaCo 95829 338-J5
BUMBLE BEE LN
- EDCo 95709 247-B2
BUMMER ST
6900 SaCo 95673 257-H2
BUNA CT
9700 ELKG 95624 359-C4
BUNCHBERRY CT
8300 CITH 95610 260-C1
BUNDRICK DR
- FOLS 95630 281-F1
BUNGALOW WY
7800 ELKG 95758 358-C3
BUNKER CT
100 FOLS 95630 261-E4
5300 SaCo 95628 259-J7
BUNKER DR
2300 RKLN 95677 220-B2
BUNKER HILL DR
1200 RSVL 95661 240-D4
BUNKER HILL LN
4200 SaCo 95660 258-F4
BUNKER HILL RD
3900 EDCo 95682 264-A3
BUNKHOUSE CT
1900 EDCo 95667 244-E4

BUNK HOUSE WY
1600 RSVL 95661 240-C3
BUNKHOUSE WY
400 SAC 95831 316-G6
BUNNY HOLLOW LN
- EDCo - 247-D4
- EDCo 95709 247-D4
BUNTING CT
- LNCN 95648 200-A3
8700 SaCo 95662 260-E2
BUNTING LN
- LNCN 95648 200-A3
BUNYA WY
100 RSVL 95661 240-D5
BUNZIE RD
400 EDCo 95672 243-B6
BUOY WY
300 SAC 95831 316-F7
BURBANK CT
300 ANT 94509 (513-E6 See Page 493)
BURBANK RD
300 ANT 94509 (513-E6 See Page 493)
BURBANK WY
400 SaCo 95864 298-F5
BURBERRY CT
- ELKG 95757 357-J7
BURBERRY WY
2400 SAC 95835 257-A4
3300 EDCo 95762 263-B4
BURDETT WY
5500 SAC 95823 317-J7
BURGARD LN
2600 PlaC 95603 202-B2
BURGESS DR
- RSVL 95747 219-D6
4300 SAC 95838 277-H1
BURGOYNE LN
7500 SAC 95823 337-G3
BURGUNDY CT
4200 PlaC 95650 221-J1
BURGUNDY DR
4500 OAKL 94561 (514-D7 See Page 493)
BURGUNDY WY
- RVIS 94571 454-G6
2400 SaCo 95825 278-D7
BURICH AV
6200 CITH 95610 259-J4
BURKE CT
6000 SAC 95824 318-A5
BURKET LN
4500 PlaC 95650 221-F1
BURKETT LN
4200 EDCo 95630 202-G5
BURL LN
2500 PlaC 95658 201-J2
BURL WY
8500 SaCo 95662 260-D4
BURLEWOOD CT
3400 SaCo 95821 278-H4
BURLIN WY
1400 AUB 95603 182-D6
BURLINE ST
9700 RCCD 95827 299-C7
BURLINGAME AV
- CITH 95621 239-G5
BURLINGTON WY
7800 SAC 95832 337-F5
BURLOAK WY
8200 ELKG 95758 358-D6
BURLOND CT
600 FOLS 95630 262-B7
BURLWOOD CT
- RKLN 95765 200-D7
BURMA RD
6800 FOLS 95630 261-B3
BURMINGHAM ST
- SaCo 95742 280-G5
BURNABY WY
- SAC 95833 276-J6
- SAC 95833 277-A6
BURNBRAE PL
- SaCo 95843 239-B6
BURNECE ST
2900 SaCo 95821 278-G5
BURNETT DR
2800 EDCo 95762 262-C4
BURNETT RD
4000 PlaC - 160-G3
BURNETT WY
1300 SAC 95818 297-C6
BURNEY WY
2200 SaCo 95821 278-C6
BURNHAM CT
100 FOLS 95630 261-F5
BURNHAM DR
200 RSVL 95678 219-G5
6900 CITH 95621 259-F4
BURNS CT
9400 PlaC 95746 241-A5
BURNS WY
6100 SaCo 95824 317-H6
6200 SaCo 95823 317-H6
BURNSIDE CT
8300 CITH 95610 260-C2
BURNT CEDAR CT
400 RSVL 95747 219-A5
BURNT CEDAR WY
6000 RSVL 95747 219-A5
BURNT CREEK WY
100 FOLS 95630 260-J3
100 FOLS 95630 261-A3
BURNT SPUR CT
8800 ELKG 95624 359-G3
BURNTWOOD WY
6100 CITH 95621 239-E7
BURR AV
1000 SaCo 95626 237-E4
BURRELL WY
4200 SaCo 95864 278-H7
4200 SaCo 95864 298-H1
BURRELTON WY
- RSVL 95661 220-E6
BURRILL DR
100 FOLS 95630 261-F3
BURRO WY
1000 EDCo 95667 245-G7
BURR OAK WY
5400 SaCo 95628 259-F6
BURROUGHS CT
5000 SaCo 95829 339-B6
BURROWING OWL WY
9800 ELKG 95757 357-E7
9800 ELKG 95757 377-E1
9800 ELKG 95757 397-E1
BURROWS AV
3000 WSAC 95691 316-D6

BURROWS ST
1200 WSAC 95605 296-H1
BURST CT
9000 SaCo 95826 318-H3
BURT LN
- PlaC 95602 161-H1
BURTON CT
3000 RCCD 95670 299-G3
BURTON PL
1900 EDCo 95762 242-C5
BURWELL WY
1200 RSVL 95661 240-A5
BURWICK LN
1100 FOLS 95630 262-A4
BURWOOD WY
100 FOLS 95630 281-E1
BUSBY CT
8200 SaCo 95628 260-B6
BUSH CT
1100 PLCR 95667 245-H3
BUSH LN
3400 LMS 95650 201-B5
BUSH ST
3700 RKLN 95677 220-E3
BUSH WY
6600 SaCo 95608 259-E7
BUSHWACKER LN
- EDCo 95726 248-D4
BUSHWOOD CT
- SAC 95823 337-F3
BUSINESS DR
3300 SAC 95820 318-B2
4100 EDCo 95682 283-H1
BUSINESS PARK DR
- LNCN 95648 179-C1
9600 RCCD 95827 299-C5
BUSKIRK DR
7000 SaCo 95842 259-B2
BUSSELTON PL
2500 EDCo 95762 262-D2
BUSSELTON WY
1100 EDCo 95762 262-D3
BUSSING CT
800 FOLS 95630 261-C6
BUSTER CT
8300 SaCo 95626 238-D5
BUTANO DR
2100 SaCo 95825 278-F7
2300 SaCo 95864 278-G7
2500 SaCo 95821 278-G7
BUTANO WY
5400 RKLN 95677 220-B4
BUTLER CIR
6300 PlaC 95663 181-A7
BUTLER CT
500 RSVL 95678 219-J6
2700 WSAC 95691 316-F1
3300 RCCD 95827 299-E5
BUTLER RD
5300 PlaC 95663 200-J1
5600 PlaC 95663 180-J7
5900 PlaC 95663 181-A7
6400 PlaC 95663 201-B1
BUTTE AV
7900 SAC 95826 318-C3
BUTTE CIR
5400 RKLN 95765 220-C1
BUTTERBALL WY
6800 SaCo 95842 258-J1
BUTTERBRICKLE CT
8600 ELKG 95624 358-E2
BUTTERCUP CIR
- GALT 95632 419-F3
BUTTERCUP CT
1300 RSVL 95661 240-B5
2800 ANT 94531 (513-H7 See Page 493)
BUTTERCUP DR
5300 EDCo 95726 267-J1
BUTTERCUP PL
- ELKG 95624 359-B6
BUTTERFIELD CT
- LNCN 95648 179-E3
BUTTERFIELD LN
- LNCN 95648 179-E3
BUTTERFIELD WY
6300 EDCo 95667 244-F4
9400 SaCo 95827 299-A5
BUTTERFLY CT
- RKLN 95765 199-H5
BUTTERFLY LN
3600 EDCo 95667 245-J6
3700 EDCo 95667 246-A7
9400 ELKG 95624 359-C6
BUTTERNUT DR
8000 CITH 95621 239-E6
8400 SaCo 95621 239-E6
BUTTERNUT ST
3000 ANT 94509 (513-J6 See Page 493)
BUTTERSCOTCH WY
- ELKG 95758 358-C2
8600 SAC 95758 358-C2
BUTTERWICK CT
- SAC 95838 277-G1
BUTTERWOOD CIR
5100 SaCo 95662 260-H7
BUTTERWORTH AV
- SAC 95838 277-G4
BUTTES VIEW LN
2400 PlaC 95603 161-D7
BUTTE VIEW CT
5500 RKLN 95765 220-B1
BUTTON CT
- SAC 95835 257-C4
BUTTONS CT
1400 OAKL 94561 (514-D7 See Page 493)
BUTTONWOOD WY
8000 CITH 95621 239-F6
BUXTON WY
2700 SaCo 95826 298-J6
4800 RKLN 95677 220-G4
BUZZARDS PASS
2000 EDCo 95667 245-G1
BYECROFT RD
- EDCo 95667 266-G5
BYERS CT
1800 SaCo 95608 299-B1
BYINGTON WY
10700 RCCD 95670 299-H5
BYNUM CT
600 OAKL 94561 (514-D5 See Page 493)
BYNUM WY
1300 OAKL 94561 (514-D5 See Page 493)
BYRD DR
2300 RCCD 95670 279-H7

BYRDFOOTE DR
4800 EDCo 95682 283-J3
BYRNE CT
- FOLS 95630 281-G1
BYRON CT
5700 RKLN 95765 200-A7
BYRON RD
2100 SaCo 95825 278-D7
BYRON ST
100 AUB 95603 182-D2

C

C AV
11400 PlaC 95603 162-A4
C PKWY
4400 SaCo 95823 337-H2
C ST
- SaCo 95690 437-A1
- GALT 95632 419-E7
100 ISLE 95641 455-H5
100 RSVL 95678 239-G3
200 WSAC 95605 297-A2
300 ANT 94509 (513-D4 See Page 493)
100 LNCN 95648 179-H3
1100 SAC 95814 297-D3
1200 SaCo 95632 419-F7
1400 SaCo 95673 258-A5
2000 SAC 95816 297-F3
2800 EDCo 95709 247-B4
3400 RKLN 95677 220-D3
3900 SAC 95819 297-J4
4700 SAC 95819 298-A4
7300 SaCo 95823 338-A2
N C ST
1000 SAC 95814 297-D2
W C ST
100 GALT 95632 419-D7
CABALLERO CT
3300 EDCo 95682 263-E5
CABALLERO DR
7600 SaCo 95662 260-G1
CABALLERO LN
3500 SaCo 95843 258-F1
CABALLO CIR
- PlaC 95603 161-J4
- PlaC 95603 162-A4
CABALLO CT
10200 SaCo 95829 339-E7
CABANA WY
4600 SAC 95822 317-C3
CABANA CLUB CT
8900 SaCo 95826 318-H1
CABER DR
- LNCN 95648 179-E2
CABER WY
7800 SaCo 95843 238-F7
CABERNET WY
- EDCo 95762 266-J5
2500 RCCD 95670 299-H1
CABHAN CT
- FOLS 95630 261-J7
- FOLS 95630 281-J1
CABIAO RD
2000 EDCo 95667 244-E6
CABIN TR
- EDCo 95667 266-D4
CABINET CIR
4100 SaCo 95660 258-H6
CABLE CIR
- FOLS 95630 261-D7
CABLE CT
- EDCo 95709 247-C2
- WSAC 95691 296-J7
6400 SaCo 95662 260-D4
CABLE RD
1200 EDCo - 247-F1
1700 EDCo 95709 247-D1
CABLEVIEW CT
3200 EDCo 95667 226-J3
CABO WY
2300 SaCo 95670 280-C6
CABOCHON WY
8200 SaCo 95829 339-C6
CABODI CT
5300 SaCo 95628 260-D6
CABOOSE CT
9500 SaCo 95827 319-B1
CABOT CIR
5100 SAC 95820 318-C4
CABOT CT
- LNCN 95648 180-A6
300 RSVL 95746 240-G4
CABRA CT
8700 ELKG 95624 338-F7
CABRILLO CT
- RKLN 95765 200-B6
2700 ANT 94509 (513-A6 See Page 493)
CABRILLO WY
- RKLN 95765 200-B6
4100 SAC 95820 318-A3
5500 SAC 95824 318-A4
CABRIOLET CT
3200 SaCo 95608 279-B5
CABRITO DR
3400 EDCo 95762 262-E5
CACERES WY
7900 SAC 95823 337-H5
CACHE CT
200 PlaC 95603 162-F5
4500 RKLN 95677 220-F4
CACHE RIVER CIR
- SAC 95831 336-G2
CACKLER LN
5900 CITH 95621 259-D1
CACTUS CT
2700 EDCo 95682 263-C3
CACTUS RD
4000 EDCo 95682 263-J6
4000 EDCo 95682 264-A5
CACTUS WY
- SAC 95833 277-D5
CADA CIR
5700 SaCo 95608 259-E5
CADALEIGH LN
- RSVL 95747 218-J6
CADBURY CT
- SAC 95835 257-D6
CADDINGTON WY
5500 SAC 95835 257-C3
CADEE CT
4300 RCCD 95742 320-E2
CADENCE CT
12700 SaCo 95693 360-H5
CADENZA CT
9200 SaCo 95826 298-J7

CADES COVE DR
- RCCD 95742 300-D7
CADFAEL CT
- RSVL 95747 219-B7
CADFAEL ST
- RSVL 95747 219-B7
CADILLAC DR
- SAC 95825 298-C5
- SaCo 95825 298-C5
CADIZ LN
- ANT 94509 (513-A6 See Page 493)
CADJEW AV
2500 SAC 95832 337-E3
CADMAN CT
- SAC 95835 257-D5
CADURA CIR
8800 ELKG 95624 358-G7
CAFARO CIR
- SAC 95834 276-H2
CAGLE LN
3600 LMS 95650 200-J6
CAGNEY CT
- SAC 95835 257-A5
CAGNEY DR
- SAC 95835 257-C6
CAHILL CT
3300 RCCD 95827 299-D5
CAHUENGO CT
4500 SaCo 95628 280-F2
CAILIN DR
- CITH 95610 239-J6
CAIN CT
- SAC 95834 276-H3
CAIN FIVE DR
- EDCo 95630 222-G7
CAIRNDALE LN
- EDCo 95633 205-D3
CAIRNS PL
3100 EDCo 95762 262-D3
CAISLEAN CT
- FOLS 95630 261-H7
CAISLEAN WY
- FOLS 95630 261-H7
CAITHNESS CT
1700 FOLS 95630 281-J1
CAJON CT
1500 ANT 94509 (513-A7 See Page 493)
CAKEBREAD CIR
- SAC 95834 276-H2
CAKE BREAD CT
- EDCo 95630 222-G7
CAL CT
5700 CITH 95610 259-J5
CALABASA DR
2200 LNCN 95648 179-E1
CALABRIA CT
- EDCo 95762 262-A3
- RSVL 95747 219-B2
9800 ELKG 95757 378-B1
CALABRIA WY
- RSVL 95747 219-B2
5300 SAC 95835 257-C4
CALAIS CIR
7400 SaCo 95828 338-F2
CALAIS WY
3800 EDCo 95762 262-E1
CALAMITY LN
- EDCo 95619 286-B1
CALAMUS CT
9200 ELKG 95758 357-H5
CALAND CT
4500 EDCo 95682 263-B7
CALAVERAS CIR
1900 ANT 94509 (513-G5 See Page 493)
CALAVERAS CT
- RSVL 95747 219-A6
1900 ANT 94509 (513-G6 See Page 493)
6900 SaCo 95828 318-B7
CALAVERAS DR
1700 EDCo 95762 262-D1
1700 EDCo 95762 242-D7
CAL CENTER DR
8800 SaCo 95826 298-G7
CALCUTTA WY
4300 SAC 95842 258-J5
CALDARELLA CIR
200 RSVL 95678 219-G5
CALDER WY
- SaCo 95662 260-F4
CALDERA WY
9000 SaCo 95826 298-H7
9200 SaCo 95826 299-A7
CALDERWOOD LN
2900 SaCo 95821 278-E5
CALDERWOOD RD
3700 EDCo 95682 263-H7
CALDICOT CT
- FOLS 95630 261-G7
CALDICOT DR
8400 ELKG 95624 358-E1
CALDONIA WY
7800 SAC 95832 337-C4
CALDWELL CT
2700 SaCo 95826 298-E7
CALDWELL DR
3000 EDCo 95709 247-D4
CALEB AV
5300 SAC 95819 298-B4
CALEB CT
- RKLN 95765 200-A6
CALEDON CIR
- LNCN 95648 179-E6
CALESA CT
7200 CITH 95621 259-G2
CALETA LN
6900 CITH 95621 259-F3
CALEXICO LN
7000 CITH 95621 259-G4
CALGARY AV
6200 SaCo 95841 259-C4
CALGARY CT
1000 EDCo 95762 262-C2
CALHOUN CT
900 SAC 95838 278-B2
CALIBRA LN
9500 SaCo 95827 319-B2
CALICO CT
3300 SaCo 95826 299-A7
CALICO WY
700 OAKL 94561 (514-D5 See Page 493)
CALICO MINE RD
1000 EDCo 95619 265-D6
CALIDO CT
2900 EDCo 95682 263-C4

CALIENTE CT
6100 SaCo 95628 260-C4
CALIFORNIA AV
- SAC 95820 318-B2
2300 SaCo 95608 279-D3
7900 SaCo 95628 280-A2
CALIFORNIA CIR
- SaCo 95742 280-J3
CALIFORNIA LN
3100 PlaC - 159-H5
3100 PlaC 95648 159-H5
CALIFORNIA LP
200 SAC 95823 337-F2
CALIFORNIA ST
- AUB 95603 182-E2
100 RVIS 94571 454-H5
600 WSAC 95605 297-A2
CALIFORNIA DELTA HWY Rt#-4
- ANT 94509 (513-A5 See Page 493)
- ANT 94531 (513-F6 See Page 493)
- ANT 94531 (514-A7 See Page 493)
600 OAKL 94561 (514-B5 See Page 493)
900 ANT 94509 (514-A5 See Page 493)
CALIFORNIA MINE LN
4100 EDCo 95667 264-J2
E CALIMYRNA RD
2800 SJCo 95220 439-H5
4200 SJCo 95220 (440-A5 See Page 420)
4200 SJCo 95632 (440-A5 See Page 420)
CALISA CT
2700 SaCo 95608 279-A6
CALISESI CT
- OAKL 94561 (514-C7 See Page 493)
CALISTA ST
6700 SaCo 95662 260-E3
CALISTOGA CT
400 LNCN 95648 179-J4
CALISTOGA LN
100 LNCN 95648 179-J4
CALISTOGA WY
5200 SaCo 95841 259-B5
CALL CT
2800 WSAC 95691 316-F2
CALLA WY
8200 SaCo 95828 338-D6
CALLA LILY CT
- SAC 95833 276-H7
CALLA LILY WY
- SAC 95833 276-H6
CALLAN CT
100 LNCN 95648 179-F5
CALLANAN CT
4200 SaCo 95608 279-E2
CALLANDER WY
- FOLS 95630 261-J5
- FOLS 95630 262-A5
CALLAWASSIE WY
1000 RSVL 95747 219-D7
CALLAWAY DR
7400 SaCo 95683 342-D3
CALLE ANTA
8700 ELKG 95624 358-F7
CALLE ARBOLEDA
- ELKG 95624 358-F7
CALLE AVION
- PlaC 95746 221-G3
CALLE BONITA
8800 PlaC 95746 221-E5
CALLE CAMPANA
1700 RSVL 95747 219-C5
CALLE CAMPANA CT
900 RSVL 95747 219-C5
CALLECITA CT
- EDCo - 247-D6
CALLECITA ST
3000 SAC 95815 278-A5
CALLE DEL ORO
- EDCo 95672 243-E3
CALLE DEL SOL WY
2900 RCCD 95670 299-G2
CALLE DE ORO
4800 OAKL 94561 (514-A6 See Page 493)
CALLE DE VINO
- EDCo 95672 243-E2
CALLEE LN
6000 EDCo 95633 205-F3
CALLE ENTRADA
- ELKG 95624 358-F7
CALLE LAS CASAS
1400 RSVL 95747 219-C5
CALLE LINDA
- ELKG 95624 358-F7
CALLE MARGARITA
- ELKG 95624 358-F7
CALLE MARIA
8700 ELKG 95624 358-F7
CALLE MONTALVO CIR
6200 PlaC 95746 221-E5
CALLE PALOMA CT
5600 PlaC 95746 221-F4
CALLE ROYALE WY
8000 SAC 95823 337-H5
CALLE SAN MIGUEL
3400 EDCo 95682 264-C4
CALLE SUSANA
- ELKG 95624 358-F7
CALLE VERDE CT
3100 SaCo 95821 278-F6
CALLE VISTA WY
2800 SaCo 95821 278-F6
CALLEYSTONE WY
8200 SaCo 95843 239-B5
CALLIA CT
200 OAKL 94561 (514-C7 See Page 493)
CALLIE LN
5700 SaCo 95841 259-C7
CALLIPPE WY
8600 ELKG 95624 358-F2
CALLISON DR
- SAC 95835 256-G5
CALLISON RD
1200 PlaC 95663 181-C7
7000 PlaC 95663 201-C1
7900 PlaC 95658 181-E7
CALLISON ST
3600 LMS 95650 201-A6
3700 LMS 95650 200-J6

CALLISTER AV
5200 SAC 95819 298-A4
CALLISTO CT
- ELKG 95624 359-A6
CALLNON CT
200 SaCo 95864 298-F5
CALLOCK CT
9100 SaCo 95829 338-J5
CALLOWAY CIR
1700 PlaC 95603 162-D5
CALMO WY
- SAC 95835 256-J6
CALNICK LN
10500 PlaC 95603 182-A2
CALTROP CT
9300 SaCo 95628 260-H7
CALUMET ST
2300 SaCo 95608 279-B7
CALVADOS AV
400 SAC 95815 277-H7
CAL VALLEY WY
6800 SAC 95822 337-E1
CALVARY CT
4500 EDCo 95672 243-F7
CALVERHALL WY
- RKLN 95677 220-E5
CALVERT AV
8900 SaCo 95662 260-F4
CALVIN DR
6800 CITH 95621 259-F1
CALVINE CT
5000 SAC 95823 357-J1
CALVINE RD
- SAC 95823 338-D7
5000 SAC 95823 357-H1
5600 SAC 95823 337-J7
6500 SAC 95823 358-A1
8100 SaCo 95828 338-D7
8100 SaCo 95624 338-D7
8500 ELKG 95624 338-D7
9300 SaCo 95624 339-A7
9700 ELKG 95624 339-C7
CALWELL CT
100 FOLS 95630 261-A1
CALYPSO CT
8400 ELKG 95624 338-J7
CALYPSO LN
- RSVL 95661 240-E1
CALYPTE LN
6500 PlaC 95746 221-E6
CALYX CT
9700 ELKG 95624 359-A7
CALZADA WY
- SAC 95758 358-C1
CAMACHA WY
6600 ELKG 95757 378-A3
CAMADA CT
9300 ELKG 95624 358-H5
CAMANCHE ST
- WSAC 95691 316-D3
CAMANCHE WY
5100 EDCo 95762 263-B5
CAMARC DR
- EDCo 95672 263-C2
CAMARENA WY
- RSVL 95747 219-B1
CAMARILLO DR
2800 SAC 95833 277-E5
CAMAS CT
- EDCo 95726 267-J2
5500 SaCo 95662 260-G6
CAMBERLY CT
9900 PlaC 95746 240-H6
CAMBERWELL WY
100 FOLS 95630 261-F7
CAMBLIN CT
4900 SaCo 95628 260-D7
CAMBON WY
2500 SaCo 95821 278-G6
2500 SaCo 95864 278-G6
CAMBORNE WY
- RKLN 95677 220-G6
CAMBRA CT
- ELKG 95758 357-E4
CAMBRIA CIR
- CITH 95621 239-G6
CAMBRIA CT
- EDCo - 267-G4
CAMBRIA WY
- EDCo 95762 242-C7
- EDCo 95762 262-C1
CAMBRIAN CT
600 SaCo 95864 298-J4
CAMBRIC CT
8500 SaCo 95843 239-B5
CAMBRIDGE CT
1600 RSVL 95661 240-B5
3100 EDCo 95682 263-D5
CAMBRIDGE PL
4900 SaCo 95842 259-A1
CAMBRIDGE RD
2600 EDCo 95672 263-C2
2600 EDCo 95682 263-C2
3900 EDCo 95682 283-C1
CAMBRIDGE ST
2100 SAC 95815 277-H7
8300 PlaC 95746 240-G2
CAMBRIE WY
- ELKG 95757 358-B7
CAMBY RD
2900 ANT 94509 (513-C7 See Page 493)
CAMDEN CT
4500 PlaC 95746 240-G4
4800 SaCo 95608 279-A3
N CAMDEN DR
- ELKG 95624 358-G3
W CAMDEN DR
8500 ELKG 95624 358-G3
CAMDEN PL
1300 EDCo 95762 242-C5
CAMDEN RD
- RKLN 95765 200-B6
S CAMDEN WY
9100 ELKG 95624 358-G4
CAMDEN LAKE WY
9000 ELKG 95624 358-G4
CAMELBACK CT
8300 SaCo 95662 260-C4
CAMELIA AV
900 RSVL 95678 239-J3
CAMELIA CT
1500 OAKL 94561 (514-D7 See Page 493)
CAMELIA RIVER WY
300 SAC 95831 336-G1
CAMELLIA AV
5300 SAC 95819 298-A4

STREET
Block City ZIP Pg-Grid

CAMELLIA CIR
- RKLN 95765 199-H7
- RKLN 95765 219-J1
CAMELLIA CT
- EDCo 95682 263-B6
- EDCo 95762 263-B6
- RKLN 95765 199-H7
CAMELLIA LN
2000 EDCo 95667 246-C4
6000 SaCo 95824 317-F5
CAMELLIA RD
4700 SaCo 95628 279-G1
CAMELLIA WY
200 GALT 95632 419-F6
CAMELLIA MATHER DR
3700 SaCo 95655 299-D7
CAMELLIA PARK LN
5500 ELKG 95757 357-J7
CAMELLIA POINT WY
- RSVL 95678 219-J3
CAMELOT CT
- RKLN 95765 200-C6
- RSVL 95678 219-G4
2000 EDCo 95667 244-E6
CAMELOT DR
- RKLN 95765 200-C6
- RSVL 95678 219-G4
CAMELOT ST
6400 SaCo 95673 257-H3
CAMEL ROCK WY
7100 CITH 95610 260-A2
CAMEO CT
3300 RKLN 95677 220-B3
6200 SaCo 95608 279-D2
CAMEO DR
2500 EDCo 95682 263-C7
2500 EDCo 95682 283-C1
6100 RKLN 95677 220-B3
CAMERADO DR
900 EDCo 95682 263-D3
CAMERINO CT
10200 SaCo 95829 339-E7
CAMERO DR
- LNCN 95648 199-H3
CAMERO WY
- LNCN 95648 199-J3
CAMERON DR
- FOLS 95630 262-A5
- RKLN 95765 200-C5
CAMERON RD
3700 SAC 95838 278-C3
4400 EDCo 95682 283-D1
N CAMERON RD
28500 SJCo 95686 417-J7
28500 SJCo 95686 437-J1
CAMERON WY
400 RSVL 95678 239-G4
CAMERON CREEK CT
- PlaC 95746 240-J2
CAMERON PARK DR
2600 EDCo 95682 263-E4
4000 EDCo 95682 283-F1
CAMERON PINES WY
10000 SaCo 95829 339-D5
CAMERON RANCH DR
4600 SaCo 95608 279-B1
4600 SaCo 95841 279-B1
4900 SaCo 95841 259-C7
CAMEROSA CIR
2900 EDCo 95682 263-B7
CAMIE CT
9500 ELKG 95624 359-B7
CAMILLE CT
2300 EDCo 95672 243-F6
5000 SaCo 95842 259-B2
CAMINO CT
3000 EDCo 95709 246-G4
CAMINO WY
4100 SaCo 95864 278-H7
CAMINO CAPISTRANO
1200 RSVL 95747 219-C4
CAMINO CIELO
- LNCN 95648 180-D6
400 EDCo 95672 243-C5
CAMINO DEL AVION
8900 PlaC 95746 221-F3
CAMINO DEL LAGO
6400 SaCo 95683 322-D7
15300 SaCo 95683 342-D1
CAMINO DEL REY
7200 SAC 95831 337-B1
CAMINO DEL SOL CIR
6700 SaCo 95683 322-B7
CAMINO DEL SOL DR
6600 SaCo 95683 322-A7
6600 SaCo 95683 342-A1
CAMINO DE LUNA
6500 SaCo 95683 322-C7
CAMINO GARDEN WY
2400 SaCo 95608 279-B7
CAMINO HEIGHTS DR
2900 EDCo 95709 246-G5
CAMINO HILLS DR
3500 EDCo 95709 246-H5
CAMINO ORO
- PlaC 95746 221-F4
CAMINO PARK CT
2400 SaCo 95608 279-C7
CAMINO PLACE CT
- ELKG 95758 358-A3
CAMINO RIDGE DR
- EDCo 95709 246-J3
CAMINO ROYALE DR
4700 SAC 95823 337-J6
CAMINO VERDERA
- LNCN 95648 180-E7
- LNCN 95648 200-D2
CAMINO VISTA WY
8400 ELKG 95624 338-J7
8400 ELKG 95624 358-J1
CAMJEN LN
11200 AUB 95603 182-D5
CAMMERAY DR
8000 CITH 95610 260-A2
CAMOMILE WY
7600 CITH 95621 259-F1
CAMPANA WY
10600 RCCD 95670 279-H7
CAMPANIA CT
7200 ELKG 95757 378-B1
CAMPANILE CT
- RSVL 95747 199-B7
CAMPANILE ST
6500 SaCo 95673 257-H3
CAMPBELL AV
100 ANT 94509 (513-C5 See Page 493)
CAMPBELL CIR
3200 EDCo 95672 243-D3

CAMPBELL CT
1000 EDCo 95672 243-D3
5500 RKLN 95677 220-C4
CAMPBELL LN
1300 SAC 95822 317-B4
CAMPBELL RD
9000 ELKG 95624 358-G4
CAMPBELL RANCH DR
2700 EDCo 95762 262-C1
CAMPCREEK LP
5200 RSVL 95747 219-B5
CAMPDEN WY
- SAC 95833 277-A6
CAMPFIRE CIR
- EDCo 95667 225-E7
CAMPFIRE CT
- EDCo 95667 225-E7
CAMPFIRE WY
- CITH 95621 259-E3
CAMPHOR CT
6100 LMS 95650 201-A5
CAMPHOR LN
7400 SaCo 95828 338-C3
CAMP NAUVOO RD
2200 EDCo 95667 246-C7
2200 EDCo 95667 266-B1
CAMP NO. 1 RD
- SJCo 95686 (476-E1 See Page 456)
CAMP NO 2G RD
- SJCo 95686 456-J7
CAMP NO 5 RD
- SaCo 95690 456-G6
- SJCo 95686 456-G6
CAMP NO. 5 RD
- SJCo 95686 456-G7
CAMPO CT
6500 SaCo 95608 279-E1
CAMPO ST
100 RSVL 95678 219-J7
100 RSVL 95678 239-J1
CAMPOBELLO CT
9100 ELKG 95624 358-J1
CAMPO DORADO DR
4500 EDCo 95762 262-F4
CAMPOLINA CT
- ELKG 95757 357-H7
CAMPOS VERDE
- SaCo 95683 322-B7
CAMPOY ST
7700 SaCo 95828 279-J3
CAMP SNOWLINE RD
- EDCo - 247-G3
CAMPTON CIR
2000 SaCo 95670 280-D5
CAMPTON GLEN PL
- ELKG 95624 358-E3
CAMPUS CT
100 CITH 95621 239-G6
CAMPUS DR
6600 EDCo 95667 244-H6
CAMPUS COMMONS RD
700 SAC 95825 298-C5
CAMP VERDE WY
6600 SAC 95828 318-B7
CAMP WHITNEY CIR
- RKLN 95765 199-J3
CAMRAY CIR
5900 SaCo 95608 279-D2
CAMROSA PL
- SAC 95835 257-A4
CAMROSE WY
7800 SaCo 95828 338-C2
CAMROSS CT
200 LNCN 95648 179-G5
CAMSTOCK CT
8000 CITH 95610 260-B3
CANADA GOOSE CT
2300 ELKG 95757 377-E1
2300 ELKG 95757 397-E1
CANADEO CIR
10100 ELKG 95757 377-H2
10100 ELKG 95757 397-H2
CANADY LN
7400 CITH 95610 260-A1
CANAL AV
- SaCo 95742 280-G4
CANAL CT
2800 PLCR 95667 245-E4
CANAL ST
300 PLCR 95667 245-E4
500 FOLS 95630 261-B4
1400 PlaC 95603 162-D4
3000 WSAC 95691 296-F4
CANARSIE AV
8800 SaCo 95662 260-E5
CANARY CT
- RKLN 95765 219-J1
CANARY DR
- RKLN 95765 219-J1
- RKLN 95765 220-A1
5600 SaCo 95660 258-G5
CANAVERAL WY
7100 SaCo 95660 258-H2
CANBERRA CT
- RSVL 95747 219-B7
8900 SaCo 95826 318-H2
CANBERRA DR
8900 SaCo 95826 318-H2
CANBERRA PL
1700 EDCo 95762 262-D4
CANBY WY
4100 SAC 95822 317-B2
CANCHALAGUA DR
- EDCo 95726 247-J7
CANDACE ST
3200 SaCo 95608 279-C5
CANDALERO CT
9300 ELKG 95758 357-J5
CANDELA CIR
100 SAC 95835 256-G7
CANDELABRA DR
6700 CITH 95621 259-F2
CANDELERO CT
1300 PLCR 95667 245-H6
CANDELL CT
4700 SaCo 95823 317-H7
CANDELLARIA CT
6600 ELKG 95758 358-B4
CANDICE CT
1800 ANT 94509 (513-G5 See Page 493)
CANDIDO DR
2800 SAC 95833 277-B5
CANDLE CT
4500 ELKG 95758 357-H6
CANDLELIGHT WY
7100 CITH 95621 259-G1

CANDLELITE DR
2800 PlaC 95650 201-E3
2800 PlaC 95650 201-E3
CANDLESTICK WY
7200 SaCo 95842 259-C2
CANDLEWOOD CT
100 LNCN 95648 200-A3
CANDLEWOOD WY
7300 SAC 95822 337-B3
CANDY CONE CT
8000 CITH 95621 239-E7
CANE RD
- PlaC 95746 221-A6
CANEBREAK CT
1100 SaCo 95608 299-B3
CANELO HILLS DR
7000 CITH 95610 260-A2
CANEVALLEY CIR
7000 CITH 95621 239-F6
CANEVARI DR
1200 RSVL 95747 219-C5
CANFIELD AV
5400 SaCo 95608 279-B4
CANFIELD CIR
- EDCo 95682 283-B1
CANMOOR CIR
- ELKG 95758 357-D5
CANNA CT
3700 SaCo 95821 278-G4
CANNA WY
1000 WSAC 95691 296-J4
CANNER CT
- ELKG 95757 358-B7
CANNINGTON LN
100 FOLS 95630 261-G6
CANNON CT
3000 EDCo 95623 265-C3
CANNON ST
1300 SAC 95815 278-A6
CANNONSHIRE CT
- PlaC 95650 201-H6
CANO CT
2300 RCCD 95670 279-H7
CANOE BIRCH CT
6700 CITH 95610 260-A3
CANOGA LN
3600 EDCo 95682 263-F4
CANON CT
200 LNCN 95648 179-G5
CANONERO CT
4000 SaCo 95628 280-E3
CANOPUS AV
6300 SaCo 95662 260-D4
CANOPY LN
4700 OAKL 94561 (514-C6 See Page 493)
CANOPY TREE ST
- PlaC 95747 239-B5
CANOVA WY
7700 SAC 95823 338-A4
CANRIGHT RD
2900 SolC 94571 454-B1
3500 RVIS 94571 454-B1
CANTABRIA CT
9600 ELKG 95624 359-B6
CANTABROOK ST
100 SaCo 95828 338-F3
CANTALIER ST
2100 SAC 95815 277-H6
CANTAMAR CT
- RSVL 95747 219-B1
CANTAMAR WY
- RSVL 95747 219-B1
CANTARA CT
- SAC 95835 257-A5
CANTARA WY
- SAC 95835 257-A5
CANTATA WY
8000 SaCo 95843 238-H6
CANTEL WY
3600 SaCo 95660 258-G2
CANTER DR
9300 ELKG 95624 359-E5
CANTERA CT
- RSVL 95747 219-B2
CANTERBURY AV
200 RSVL 95678 239-G5
CANTERBURY CIR
2800 EDCo 95762 262-C3
CANTERBURY LN
- PlaC 95650 221-G1
2200 OAKL 94561 (514-C6 See Page 493)
CANTERBURY RD
1900 SAC 95815 297-J1
2000 SAC 95815 277-G7
CANTERSHIRE WY
8100 PlaC 95746 240-J2
CANTINA CT
- SAC 95828 338-C1
CANTLE CT
- PlaC 95747 238-H3
CANTON CT
- ELKG 95757 358-B6
CANTOR PARK WY
- ELKG 95624 359-A6
CANTOVA WY
14600 SaCo 95683 341-J2
14600 SaCo 95683 342-A3
CANTRELL RD
1500 EDCo 95619 265-J6
CANTWELL DR
- ELKG 95624 358-E2
CANVASBACK CIR
- LNCN 95648 179-D2
CANVASBACK CT
- RKLN 95765 219-H1
CANVASBACK LN
6000 CITH 95621 259-D1
CANVASBACK WY
2800 WSAC 95691 316-F2
CANYCANE LN
- RSVL 95747 219-C3
CANYON CT
100 AUB 95603 182-F1
S CANYON CT
9500 FOLS 95630 260-J2
9500 SaCo 95630 260-J2
9500 SaCo 95662 260-J2
CANYON DR
500 AUB 95603 182-F1
500 PlaC 95603 182-F1
4000 SaCo 95628 280-A3
CANYON RD
- EDCo - 247-G3
N CANYON RD
2700 EDCo 95667 246-F2
3500 EDCo 95709 246-G1
3600 EDCo 95709 226-H7

N CANYON RD
3700 EDCo 95667 226-H7
4100 EDCo 95709 247-A2
CANYON BROOK WY
8500 ELKG 95624 358-F2
CANYON CREEK DR
- RSVL 95747 239-B1
CANYON CREEK WY
600 GALT 95632 419-F4
6300 ELKG 95758 358-A4
CANYON FALLS DR
300 FOLS 95630 241-A7
300 FOLS 95630 260-J1
300 FOLS 95630 261-A1
300 FOLS 95630 240-J7
CANYON FALLS RD
1400 EDCo 95619 265-G7
CANYON LAKE LN
- SaCo 95662 260-H4
CANYONLANDS DR
- RCCD 95742 300-F7
CANYON OAK CT
500 EDCo 95762 262-A1
CANYON OAK DR
8100 CITH 95610 240-B6
CANYON OAK LN
- LNCN 95648 179-H6
CANYON RIDGE LN
- AUB 95603 182-E2
CANYON RIM CT
- RKLN 95765 220-A2
CANYON RIM DR
- RKLN 95765 220-A2
100 FOLS 95630 261-A2
CANYON SPRINGS DR
- RVIS 94571 454-E2
CANYON TERRACE DR
- FOLS 95630 261-A2
200 FOLS 95630 260-J2
CANYON TREE DR
7000 SAC 95822 337-E1
CANYON VALLEY RD
4200 EDCo 95619 265-F3
CANYON VIEW CT
2900 ANT 94509 (513-G7 See Page 493)
CANYON VIEW DR
9100 ELKG 95624 378-H2
CANYON VISTA
300 PlaC 95603 162-F7
CANYON WOODS CT
7600 SaCo 95828 338-C4
CAOHAL CT
8600 ELKG 95624 358-F5
CAPAY CT
- SAC 95831 336-H1
CAPE CANYON WY
1000 GALT 95632 419-F2
CAPE COD LN
9300 SaCo 95662 260-H5
CAPE CORAL CT
300 RSVL 95747 219-D7
2200 SaCo 95626 238-D6
CAPE CORAL WY
1100 RSVL 95747 219-D7
CAPE COTTAGE LN
100 FOLS 95630 261-G5
CAPE HATTERAS PL
- SAC 95835 256-H5
CAPE HOLLY CT
5800 ELKG 95757 357-J6
5800 ELKG 95757 358-A6
CAPE HORN CT
2200 SaCo 95670 280-B5
CAPELA WY
600 SAC 95831 336-H1
CAPELLA DR
400 EDCo 95619 265-D5
7700 PlaC 95746 241-D2
CAPE MAY CT
- ELKG 95758 357-E4
CAPERTON CT
3000 PlaC 95663 180-F7
CAPETANIOS DR
- EDCo 95762 262-B4
CAPE WINDHAM PL
- SaCo 95662 260-G4
CAPISTRANO ST
2700 ANT 94509 (513-C6 See Page 493)
CAPISTRANO WY
3100 RKLN 95677 220-E1
7900 SAC 95824 318-C6
CAPITAL CIR
6300 SAC 95828 318-A6
CAPITAL DR
6300 SAC 95828 318-A7
CAPITAL CENTER DR
3300 RCCD 95670 299-G3
CAPITAL CITY FRWY
I-80
- SAC - 278-C5
- SAC - 297-G3
- SAC - 298-A1
- SaCo - 278-C5
CAPITAL CITY FRWY
U.S.-50
- SAC - 297-A4
- WSAC - 296-F4
- WSAC - 297-A4
CAPITALES DR
2500 RCCD 95670 299-D3
CAPITAL PARK DR
1700 SAC 95833 277-B7
CAPITOL AV
1700 SAC 95814 297-D4
2700 SAC 95816 297-E5
6300 EDCo 95667 265-C3
W CAPITOL AV
200 WSAC 95605 297-A3
200 WSAC 95691 297-A3
800 WSAC 95691 296-D4
CAPITOL MALL
900 SAC 95814 297-C4
CAPITOL MALL
Rt#-275
- WSAC 95691 297-B3
- SAC 95814 297-B3
CAPITOLA AV
4000 SaCo 95628 280-A3
CAPITOLA CT
- RSVL 95678 219-J5
CAPITOLA HILL CT
4000 SaCo 95628 280-A3
CAPITOL HILL DR
- EDCo 95619 265-G6
CAPITOL OAKS DR
- SAC 95833 277-B6

CAPLES CT
- ANT 94531 (513-H7 See Page 493)
CAPLES DR
- FOLS 95630 260-J1
- FOLS 95630 261-A2
CAPOTE WY
- ELKG 95758 358-D3
CAPPAS CT
- RSVL 95678 239-H4
CAPPS CROSSING RD
- EDCo 95720 248-J5
- EDCo 95726 248-J5
CAPPUCINO WY
200 SAC 95838 257-F7
CAPREZZO WY
6500 ELKG 95757 378-A1
CAPRI CT
- SAC 95831 337-A5
CAPRI WY
4400 SAC 95822 317-B3
CAPRICE CT
- SAC 95832 337-C4
CAPRICORN DR
7600 CITH 95610 259-J6
CAPRILLI DR
10100 SaCo 95829 339-E7
CAP ROCK WY
3500 RCCD 95670 299-H5
CAPSTAN WY
5600 SAC 95822 316-J4
CAPTAIN CT
- SAC 95831 316-G7
CAPTAINS TABLE RD
1000 SAC 95822 317-A3
CAPULET ST
6500 SaCo 95673 257-G3
CAPULLO CT
6700 SaCo 95662 260-D3
CAPWELL WY
- ELKG 95757 358-B7
CARAD LN
6200 SaCo 95841 259-C4
CARAGH ST
1000 RSVL 95747 219-C7
CARAMAY WY
1500 SAC 95818 297-C7
CARANA WY
7100 CITH 95621 259-F2
CARASCO CT
3800 EDCo 95762 263-B5
CARAVAGGIO CIR
100 SAC 95835 256-J4
CARAVELLE CT
1900 LNCN 95648 180-B7
CARBERRY WY
2800 SAC 95833 277-E5
CARBIDE CT
8300 SaCo 95828 338-E4
CARBINE CT
2200 SaCo 95626 238-D6
CARBINE TR
4900 EDCo 95682 264-E7
CARBONDALE RD
15900 AmCo 95683 (362-J5 See Page 341)
15900 SaCo 95683 (362-G5 See Page 341)
CARBURY WY
1500 RSVL 95747 219-E7
CARDALE WY
8000 SaCo 95829 338-H6
CARDEN WY
5400 SaCo 95608 259-E6
CARDENAS WY
7100 SaCo 95828 338-B2
CARDIFF CIR
2100 EDCo 95762 242-C5
CARDIFF CT
- RSVL 95746 240-F4
1100 ANT 94509 (513-F7 See Page 493)
CARDIFF LN
- RSVL 95746 240-F4
CARDIFF WY
10300 RCCD 95670 299-F3
CARDIGAN CT
600 RSVL 95747 219-E7
6200 CITH 95621 259-E3
CARDINAL CT
2600 SaCo 95608 279-B6
CARDINAL DR
- LNCN 95648 199-H3
1700 PLCR 95667 246-A4
CARDINAL RD
7000 SaCo 95628 259-G7
CARDINAL WY
1500 RSVL 95661 240-A3
CARDOSO CT
600 GALT 95632 439-E1
CARDOSO DR
600 GALT 95632 439-E1
CARDOSO LN
900 PlaC 95658 181-F6
CARDOZA CT
14700 SaCo 95683 342-A2
CARDWELL AV
- SaCo 95662 260-J1
7800 SaCo 95662 240-J7
CARELLA DR
7400 SAC 95822 337-B2
CAREO CT
4800 SaCo 95843 239-A5
CAREO DR
4700 SaCo 95843 239-A6
CAREX CT
2300 ELKG 95757 357-D7
CAREY LN
7600 CITH 95610 259-J2
CAREY RD
4900 SaCo 95835 257-E6
4900 SaCo 95834 257-E6
4900 SAC 95835 257-E6
CAREY ST
3000 ANT 94509 (513-E7 See Page 493)
CAREYBACK AV
4400 ELKG 95758 357-G3
CARGILL WY
2100 RSVL 95747 239-C1
CARIANN CT
- ELKG 95757 358-A7
CARIBBEAN WY
8000 SAC 95826 298-D7
CARIBOU CT
3000 SaCo 95826 299-A6
CARIBOU PEAK WY
8100 ELKG 95758 358-D6

CARIBOU RIDGE WY
7700 SaCo 95843 239-B7
CARIEL CT
2400 RCCD 95670 299-H1
CARIGNAN PL
10000 ELKG 95624 379-A1
CARILLION BLVD
12800 GALT 95632 419-F2
13400 SaCo 95632 419-G5
CARISSA WY
8700 ELKG 95624 358-G2
CARL DR
1700 EDCo 95672 262-J3
CARLA DR
2500 PLCR 95667 245-E4
CARLA WY
9200 SaCo 95826 298-J7
CARLE LN
4200 SaCo 95841 278-H1
CARLETON LN
2600 ANT 94509 (513-A6 See Page 493)
7400 CITH 95610 259-H1
CARLEY LN
- EDCo 95619 265-E3
CARLILE CT
5700 PlaC 95746 220-J7
CARLILE DR
3000 PlaC 95650 200-G3
CARLIN AV
8200 SAC 95823 338-A7
8400 SAC 95823 358-A1
CARLIN DR
- WSAC 95691 296-D7
CARLINA CT
300 RSVL 95747 219-C5
CARLISLE AV
8600 SaCo 95828 338-F5
8800 SaCo 95829 338-H5
CARLISLE CT
- PlaC 95747 239-A2
2300 EDCo 95762 242-C5
CARLO CT
200 GALT 95632 439-E1
CARLOS CIR
14700 SaCo 95683 342-C4
CARLOS WY
10700 RCCD 95670 279-H7
CARLOTTA DR
2100 SaCo 95825 278-D7
CARLOW DR
6200 CITH 95621 259-E4
CARL SANDBURG CIR
6100 SaCo 95842 259-A4
CARLSBAD AV
2300 SaCo 95821 278-D5
CARLSBAD CT
- RKLN 95765 219-H2
CARLSON CT
4100 EDCo 95682 263-G3
CARLSON DR
2600 EDCo 95672 263-H4
2600 EDCo 95682 263-H4
5300 SAC 95819 298-A5
CARLSON WY
400 FOLS 95630 281-A2
4200 EDCo 95619 265-F3
CARLTON CT
9800 PlaC 95746 240-J6
9800 PlaC 95746 241-A6
CARLTON RD
7900 SAC 95826 318-C2
CARLY WY
3100 SAC 95816 297-F5
CARLYLE AV
100 SAC 95823 337-F2
CARMAUX CT
7500 SaCo 95842 259-B1
CARMEL AV
100 RSVL 95678 219-H7
CARMEL CT
2900 WSAC 95691 316-H1
CARMEL RD
- EDCo 95667 266-G1
CARMEL ST
900 SAC 95838 277-J4
CARMELA WY
1900 SAC 95822 317-C4
CARMEL BAY RD
- WSAC 95691 316-E2
CARMELITA AV
800 SAC 95838 277-J4
CARMELLA CIR
7300 SaCo 95683 342-C4
CARMELO DR
1600 SaCo 95608 299-B2
CARMELO OAKS CT
4300 SaCo 95841 258-J7
CARMEL PLAZA WY
- ELKG 95758 358-B3
CARMEL VALLEY WY
8900 ELKG 95624 378-G2
CARMELWOOD DR
6400 CITH 95621 239-E7
CARMEN DR
- EDCo 95762 262-B4
CARMEN WY
4900 SAC 95822 317-D4
CARMENCITA AV
7800 SaCo 95829 339-C7
8000 ELKG 95624 339-C7
8000 ELKG 95829 339-C7
CARMENET WY
11000 RCCD 95670 299-J5
11000 RCCD 95670 300-A5
CARMI ST
7200 SaCo 95828 338-C2
CARMICHAEL WY
- SaCo 95608 279-D6
CARMICHAEL PARK RD
- SaCo 95608 279-C4
CARMODY CIR
100 FOLS 95630 261-A1
CARMONA WY
2800 ANT 94509 (513-A6 See Page 493)
CARNATION AV
6500 SAC 95822 317-E7
6600 SAC 95822 337-E1
CARNATION CT
1300 RSVL 95661 240-B5
CARNEGIE WY
1600 EDCo 95762 242-B5
4200 SaCo 95821 278-J2
CARNEIA CT
5300 SaCo 95608 299-B1
CARNEILIAN DR
- RSVL 95747 239-A1

CARNELIAN CIR
2500 EDCo 95762 242-C5
CARNELIAN CT
- LNCN 95648 180-A7
3200 SaCo 95821 278-H5
CARNEROS CREEK WY
- SAC 95834 276-J3
CARNEY CT
9300 ELKG 95624 358-H5
CARNIVAL CT
8400 ELKG 95624 358-E1
CARNS CT
8000 SaCo 95628 280-A1
CAROB CT
2000 SaCo 95608 299-A1
2700 ANT 94509 (513-H6 See Page 493)
CAROB ST
2700 ANT 94509 (513-J6 See Page 493)
CAROL AV
7600 CITH 95610 239-H7
CAROL DR
600 GALT 95632 419-F5
CAROL LN
100 OAKL 94561 (514-C6 See Page 493)
2000 PlaC 95747 239-D1
4500 EDCo 95682 264-B7
CAROL ANN CT
900 RSVL 95661 239-J4
CAROLINA AV
- SaCo 95742 300-H1
1900 WSAC 95691 296-J6
CAROLINDA DR
6000 PlaC 95746 241-A1
CAROLINE AV
800 GALT 95632 419-F7
CAROLINE CT
- RKLN 95765 200-A6
CAROLINE DR
- SAC 95828 318-D4
CAROLYN CT
2900 ANT 94509 (513-D7 See Page 493)
8000 PlaC 95747 239-C1
CAROLYN ST
- AUB 95603 182-D5
CAROLYN WY
2900 SAC 95818 297-B7
CARONDELET LN
7400 SaCo 95828 338-F3
CAROUSEL LN
2800 EDCo 95682 263-F3
CAROVA BEACH PL
- SAC 95835 256-H4
CARPENTER LN
3800 EDCo 95682 263-J1
CARPENTER WY
600 RSVL 95678 219-G7
7200 SaCo 95660 258-H2
CARPENTER HILL RD
300 FOLS 95630 282-A1
CARPINTERIA DR
1000 GALT 95632 419-G2
CARR CT
- RKLN 95765 200-A7
CARR WY
600 GALT 95632 419-E6
CARRADALE CT
- RSVL 95661 220-F6
CARRADALE DR
- RSVL 95661 220-E6
CARRADALE LN
- LNCN 95648 179-F7
CARRADALE WY
9100 SaCo 95829 338-J5
CARRCROFT DR
9300 ELKG 95758 358-C5
CARRETA LN
6900 SaCo 95683 342-B1
CARR HALL LN
7200 PlaC 95650 221-C1
CARRI LN
3000 EDCo 95682 264-B3
CARRIAGE DR
7000 CITH 95621 259-G2
8800 PlaC 95746 240-H3
CARRIAGE LN
- EDCo 95684 286-G6
- LNCN 95648 199-J1
- SaCo 95628 280-B1
200 PlaC 95603 162-F5
CARRIAGE HILL LN
13900 PlaC 95602 162-F2
CARRIAGE OAKS LN
14000 PlaC 95602 162-G2
CARRIAGE OAKS WY
- SaCo 95843 239-C6
CARRICK CT
8300 CITH 95610 260-C2
CARRIE ST
1100 WSAC 95605 296-H1
CARRIEBEE CT
4000 SaCo 95660 258-H7
CARRIERA WY
8300 SaCo 95828 338-E7
CARRIGAN CT
1900 WSAC 95691 296-H5
CARRIGAN LN
4600 SaCo 95608 279-C1
CARRILLO CT
2100 EDCo 95682 263-B7
CARRINGTON CT
12900 PlaC 95603 162-E5
CARRINGTON DR
4700 OAKL 94561 (514-C6 See Page 493)
CARRINGTON ST
5200 SAC 95819 298-A4
CARRISA WY
2800 SaCo 95821 278-H6
CARRIZO CT
200 RSVL 95747 219-C5
CARRO DR
700 SaCo 95825 298-D4
CARROLL AV
400 SAC 95838 277-H4
CARROLL CT
2000 FOLS 95630 262-A7
CARROLL DR
2000 FOLS 95630 262-B7
CARROLL LN
- PlaC 95658 201-G1
4800 SaCo 95608 299-A2
CARROLL RD
11200 SaCo 95757 378-D7
CARROLTON PL
9300 ELKG 95624 358-J5

STREET
Block City ZIP Pg-Grid

CARROTWOOD CT
- SAC 95823 337-F3
CARROUSEL CT
- LNCN 95648 199-J1
CARROUSEL LN
1400 SAC 95822 317-B3
CARRWOOD ST
6600 SaCo 95662 260-D3
CARSINGTON WY
8100 SaCo 95829 339-A6
CARSON AV
100 AUB 95603 182-D2
CARSON CT
100 FOLS 95630 261-E5
3800 EDCo 95709 246-H4
CARSON RD
1100 PLCR 95667 245-H4
1500 EDCo 95667 245-J4
1700 EDCo 95667 246-A3
3400 EDCo 95709 246-J3
3600 EDCo 95709 247-A3
CARSON WY
2500 SaCo 95821 278-D5
N CARSON WY
11600 SaCo 95670 280-D5
S CARSON WY
11700 SaCo 95670 280-D5
CARSON CROSSING DR
- EDCo 95762 282-C4
CARSON HILL PL
2000 SaCo 95670 280-B4
CARSTAIRS CT
- FOLS 95630 261-G7
CARTA CT
2400 SaCo 95825 298-D3
CARTER RD
1200 SaCo 95864 298-J3
CARTER ST
- FOLS 95630 281-D1
CARTER WY
2900 ANT 94509 (513-A7 See Page 493)
CARTERA CT
6500 ELKG 95758 358-A4
CARTHAGE CT
- RSVL 95746 240-F4
- SAC 95828 318-C7
CARTHY WY
7000 SaCo 95828 338-B1
CARTIER LN
5700 SaCo 95608 279-C1
CARTINA WY
- EDCo 95762 262-G6
CARTWRIGHT DR
- RSVL 95747 239-F3
CARUSO ISLAND CT
- SaCo 95823 358-A1
CARVEL PL
- SAC 95835 256-G6
CARVER CT
- SAC 95835 257-C7
CARY AL
700 PLCR 95667 245-F5
CARY DR
100 PlaC 95603 162-F5
CASA CT
4500 SaCo 95628 279-H2
CASA ALAMEDA WY
- ELKG 95758 358-B4
CASA ALEGRE
6000 SaCo 95608 259-D5
CASA BELLA WY
7800 CITH 95610 259-J2
CASA BLANCA
4200 SaCo 95608 279-C2
CASABLANCA WY
8500 SaCo 95828 338-E7
CASA DANIELLE CIR
5300 SaCo 95824 317-J5
CASA DEL ESTE WY
- SAC 95828 318-B7
CASA DEL ORO WY
2400 RKLN 95677 220-B5
CASA DEL RIO LN
- SaCo 95628 280-D2
CASA DEL SOL WY
6700 SAC 95828 318-B7
CASADO DR
900 GALT 95632 419-G7
900 GALT 95632 439-F1
CASA GRANDE AV
5500 RKLN 95677 220-B3
CASA GRANDE CT
2500 RKLN 95677 220-B4
CASA GRANDE WY
6900 SaCo 95828 318-B7
6900 SaCo 95828 338-B1
CASA LARGO WY
- EDCo 95682 283-B1
CASA LINDA CT
- SAC 95822 337-E3
CASA LINDA DR
2300 SAC 95822 337-D3
CASA LOMA WY
3700 SaCo 95608 279-F3
CASALS ST
900 SaCo 95826 298-H7
CASANDRA CT
- ELKG 95758 358-B3
CASA NICOLE WY
6000 SaCo 95824 317-J5
CASA NUESTRA WY
- SaCo 95608 279-B6
CASA REDONDA DR
4500 EDCo 95682 264-B2
CASA ROBLES RD
1400 EDCo 95762 242-F6
CASA ROSA WY
3600 SaCo 95608 279-B4
CASA SEDONA DR
1900 RSVL 95747 219-B1
CASA VISTA DR
6500 PlaC 95650 221-B4
CASA VISTA WY
- EDCo 95762 262-B5
CASCADE CT
3000 EDCo 95709 246-G4
CASCADE DR
- RSVL 95678 219-G4
CASCADE RD
2100 SaCo 95864 278-H7
CASCADE ST
- WSAC 95691 316-H1
CASCADE WY
6300 SaCo 95823 338-A3
CASCADE FALLS DR
100 FOLS 95630 261-A1
200 FOLS 95630 241-A7

CASCADES CT
9100 PlaC 95650 221-G1
CASCARA CT
- EDCo 95762 282-C2
CASCARA DR
- FOLS 95630 260-J1
CASCINA WY
11100 RCCD 95670 300-A4
CASELLA CT
100 FOLS 95630 281-B2
CASELLI CIR
- SAC 95823 337-G3
CASELMAN RD
8600 SaCo 95828 338-H5
8600 SaCo 95829 338-H5
CASEY CT
- SAC 95838 277-G1
1000 PlaC 95658 181-J7
CASH CT
5800 SaCo 95608 259-D5
CASHAW WY
- SAC 95834 277-A3
CASH BOY RD
3900 EDCo 95619 265-D4
CASHEL WY
8100 SaCo 95829 338-J6
CASHEW CT
2900 ANT 94509 (513-J6 See Page 493)
CASHEW ST
2800 ANT 94509 (513-J6 See Page 493)
CASHMAN CIR
- SAC 95835 257-C6
CASHMERE CT
5100 SaCo 95628 260-D7
CASIANO CT
- SAC 95823 337-F2
CASILADA WY
900 SAC 95822 316-J3
900 SAC 95822 317-A3
CASIMER CT
10100 RCCD 95827 299-E5
CASINA PL
5000 EDCo 95762 282-C3
CASITA AV
6200 SaCo 95608 279-D3
CASITA WY
3100 SaCo 95816 297-F5
CASITAS BONITO
3200 SaCo 95825 298-F1
CASLAN AV
8400 SaCo 95628 260-C7
CASMALIA WY
600 SaCo 95864 298-G4
CASPER CT
7700 SaCo 95828 338-D4
CASPER LN
1400 EDCo 95619 265-J4
CASPIAN CT
- PlaC 95747 238-J3
CASPIANE WY
9200 SaCo 95826 298-J6
CASSADY WY
6200 SaCo 95608 279-D4
CASSANDRA WY
9500 SaCo 95827 299-B7
CASSARO CT
9300 ELKG 95758 358-B5
CASSATT WY
8400 SaCo 95828 338-E7
CASSELL LN
5600 LMS 95650 221-B4
CASSELMAN DR
700 WSAC 95605 297-A2
CASSELMAN ST
100 FOLS 95630 261-C7
CASSIA WY
- RKLN 95765 199-H7
- RKLN 95765 219-H1
CASSIDY CT
300 RSVL 95747 219-D7
CASSIE HILL PL
2100 SaCo 95670 280-C5
CASSIERI CIR
8600 SaCo 95828 338-F1
CASSIN CT
100 FOLS 95630 281-C1
CASSINI WY
6900 CITH 95621 259-G2
CASTAIC CT
- RSVL 95678 219-J5
- WSAC 95691 316-C3
CASTAIC DR
- RSVL 95678 219-J5
CASTANA DR
4500 EDCo 95682 263-B6
CASTANO WY
7400 SAC 95831 336-J2
CASTAWAY CT
6100 ELKG 95758 358-A6
CASTEC DR
900 SaCo 95864 298-G3
CASTEC WY
700 EDCo 95762 242-C4
CASTELLEJA CT
2000 SaCo 95608 299-A1
CASTELLETTO CT
6500 ELKG 95757 378-B1
CASTELLI CT
9900 ELKG 95757 378-B1
CASTELLI WY
9800 ELKG 95757 358-B7
9800 ELKG 95757 378-B1
CASTEN LN
- SaCo 95662 260-H3
CASTERBRIDGE CT
- RSVL 95747 239-B1
CASTERBRIDGE DR
- RSVL 95747 239-A1
CASTILE CT
700 AUB 95603 182-C5
CASTILIAN CT
7200 CITH 95621 259-G5
CASTILLIAN CT
- RSVL 95747 219-B1
CASTILLO CT
6800 CITH 95621 259-F3
CASTINE CT
2700 SaCo 95826 298-H6
CASTLE CT
300 RSVL 95678 239-J3
1700 WSAC 95691 296-H3
CASTLE LN
- PlaC 95658 201-H2
5500 EDCo 95667 264-F2
CASTLE ST
5200 SaCo 95628 259-G7

CASTLEBAR WY
9100 SaCo 95826 318-H2
CASTLEBERRY CIR
6800 CITH 95621 239-F5
CASTLEBERRY LN
- LNCN 95648 179-J6
CASTLEBRIDGE CT
9500 ELKG 95758 357-H6
CASTLEBROOK RD
3400 EDCo 95682 263-E5
CASTLECAVE CT
9500 ELKG 95758 357-H6
CASTLECAVE WY
9500 ELKG 95758 357-G6
CASTLE COMBES CT
5000 PlaC 95746 240-G6
CASTLE CRAIG CT
1000 EDCo 95762 262-D6
CASTLE CREEK CT
- PlaC 95661 240-E5
CASTLE CREEK DR
- PlaC 95661 240-E6
CASTLE CREEK WY
7000 SaCo 95673 258-A2
7000 SaCo 95673 257-J2
CASTLE CREEK RANCH RD
1200 PlaC 95658 181-J7
CASTLEDALE CT
9500 ELKG 95758 357-H6
CASTLEFORD CT
- RSVL 95747 219-C4
CASTLEFORD DR
2800 ANT 94509 (513-C6 See Page 493)
CASTLEFORD WY
5400 ELKG 95758 357-J5
CASTLEGLEN WY
4300 SaCo 95628 279-G2
CASTLE GROVE WY
4400 ELKG 95758 357-H6
CASTLEHAVEN CT
- ELKG 95624 358-F3
CASTLE HILL CT
- RSVL 95678 219-H5
2700 SaCo 95821 278-E6
CASTLELYONS CT
- ELKG 95624 358-F3
CASTLEMONT CIR
9200 SaCo 95662 260-G6
CASTLE OAKS CT
- PlaC 95658 181-G7
10000 SaCo 95829 339-D5
CASTLE PARK DR
8900 ELKG 95624 378-G2
CASTLEREIGH CT
5200 PlaC 95746 240-J6
CASTLE RIVER WY
600 SAC 95831 336-H1
CASTLEROCK CT
2700 EDCo 95667 244-C5
CASTLEROCK RD
3500 EDCo 95667 244-C4
CASTLE ROCK WY
7700 SaCo 95828 338-F4
CASTLESHORE CT
9500 ELKG 95758 357-H6
CASTLESHORE WY
9500 ELKG 95758 357-H6
CASTLESIDE WY
- ELKG 95758 357-H6
CASTLETON CIR
100 SaCo 95655 319-H1
CASTLEVIEW DR
9200 ELKG 95758 357-H6
CASTLEWOOD CIR
200 RSVL 95678 219-H7
3000 EDCo 95726 248-D1
CASTLEWOOD DR
2500 SaCo 95821 278-F6
2500 SaCo 95825 278-F6
CASTLEWOOD ST
4200 RKLN 95677 220-F4
CASTLE WYND DR
8100 SaCo 95843 239-B6
CASTRO CT
- FOLS 95630 261-B5
CASTRO WY
1100 SAC 95818 297-C6
2700 SAC 95817 297-E7
CASTRO VERDE WY
6200 ELKG 95757 378-A3
CASUARINA CT
8000 CITH 95621 239-F7
CASWELL CT
- RSVL 95747 239-C1
- SAC 95838 257-J7
2700 EDCo 95667 245-C3
CASWELL DR
- RSVL 95747 239-C1
CASWELL RD
2400 EDCo 95667 245-C3
CATALA WY
4100 SAC 95817 317-G1
CATALINA CT
- RKLN 95765 200-C6
900 RSVL 95661 239-J5
CATALINA DR
- RKLN 95765 200-C6
2300 SaCo 95864 278-G7
2500 SaCo 95821 278-H6
CATALINA ISLAND RD
- WSAC 95691 316-C2
CATALINE AV
- ANT 94509 (513-C5 See Page 493)
CATALPA CT
3700 EDCo 95667 245-A7
5500 LMS 95650 200-J5
CATALPA DR
8200 CITH 95610 240-A6
CATAMARAN DR
7000 CITH 95621 259-D2
7000 SaCo 95621 259-D2
7000 SaCo 95842 259-D2
CATANIA WY
2700 SaCo 95826 299-A6
CATAWBA DR
3100 EDCo 95682 263-E3
CATAWBA WY
10500 RCCD 95670 299-G1
CATBOAT CIR
7200 CITH 95621 259-D2
CATECROFT LN
- EDCo 95630 202-J1
CATFISH CT
8800 ELKG 95624 358-G5
CATHAY WY
1700 SaCo 95864 298-H2

CATHAY WY
2300 SaCo 95864 278-H7
2500 SaCo 95821 278-H7
CATHCART AV
- SaCo 95838 277-G4
CATHEDRAL CT
800 SaCo 95825 298-D4
CATHERWOOD WY
- SAC 95835 257-B4
CATLEN WY
7000 SAC 95831 337-A1
E CATLETT RD
5600 PlaC 95648 199-A2
CATLIN CT
100 FOLS 95630 261-E4
CATS TR
- EDCo 95619 286-D2
CATSKILL WY
2100 SAC 95838 278-C4
CATTAIL CT
- LNCN 95648 199-H3
- SAC 95833 277-C6
CATTALO WY
- PlaC 95747 238-H3
CATTA VERDERA
- LNCN 95648 200-B1
CATTERLINE WY
200 FOLS 95630 282-A2
200 FOLS 95630 281-J1
CATTLE DR
2200 FOLS 95630 282-B1
3500 SAC 95834 277-D3
3700 EDCo 95682 283-H6
CAULFIELD DR
9200 ELKG 95758 358-C5
CAUSEWAY DR
500 SAC 95831 336-G3
CAVA CT
2400 SaCo 95825 298-D3
CAVALCADE CIR
- SAC 95831 316-H7
CAVALIER CT
4800 EDCo 95682 264-D3
CAVALIER DR
- SAC 95832 337-C4
CAVALIER WY
7800 SAC 95832 337-C4
CAVALLETTI DR
10100 SaCo 95829 339-E7
CAVALLI WY
7900 SaCo 95628 260-A7
CAVALLO RD
1100 ANT 94509 (513-E4 See Page 493)
CAVALLO REAL WY
4500 SaCo 95608 279-B2
CAVALRY CT
6600 SaCo 95662 260-B3
CAVAN DR
6200 CITH 95621 259-E4
CAVANAUGH WY
1000 SAC 95822 317-B1
CAVENDISH WY
8500 SaCo 95828 338-E5
CAVERSHAM WY
- GALT 95632 419-G3
1100 RSVL 95747 239-C1
1700 FOLS 95630 261-J7
1700 FOLS 95630 281-J1
1800 FOLS 95630 282-A1
CAVIAR CT
5000 SaCo 95628 260-D7
CAVITT DR
- FOLS 95630 261-G7
- FOLS 95630 281-H1
CAVITT RANCH PL
- PlaC 95746 220-G6
CAVITT STALLMAN RD
5900 PlaC 95746 240-F2
6100 PlaC 95746 220-H7
6800 PlaC 95746 221-A6
7200 PlaC 95650 221-A6
CAVITT STALLMAN SOUTH RD
5900 PlaC 95746 240-F2
CAVU HILL RD
3100 EDCo 95682 264-A3
CAXTON CT
4400 SaCo 95660 258-J4
CAYENTE WY
3000 EDCo 95682 263-F4
3800 SaCo 95864 298-G2
CAYES CT
1000 ANT 94509 (513-F7 See Page 493)
CAYGOUDE CT
9800 ELKG 95757 357-F7
CAYMAN CT
3800 SaCo 95843 238-G6
CAYMAN ISLAND ST
- WSAC 95691 316-D2
CAYMUS CT
- LNCN 95648 179-J4
CAYMUS DR
7900 SaCo 95829 338-H5
CAYO CT
14700 SaCo 95683 342-A1
CAYUCOS CT
- RSVL 95678 219-J5
CAYUCOS DR
- SaCo 95843 239-A7
CAYUGA CT
8700 SaCo 95662 260-E1
CAYUGA RD
5100 EDCo 95726 248-C6
CAYUGA ST
- OAKL 94561 (514-C6 See Page 493)
CAYUSE WY
7500 SaCo 95823 338-A3
CAYWOOD CT
6800 CITH 95621 259-D3
CAZADERO WY
5600 SAC 95822 317-C4
CAZADOR
6200 SaCo 95683 322-C7
CEBRIAN ST
1500 WSAC 95691 296-H6
CEBU LN
1200 EDCo 95667 245-C5
1200 PLCR 95667 245-C5
CECATRA DR
10900 SaCo 95693 359-J6
CECERI DR
6900 EDCo 95619 265-F2
CECILE WY
9100 SaCo 95826 298-J7
9100 SaCo 95826 318-J1

CECILYN WY
700 SAC 95831 336-H2
CEDAR CIR
- FOLS 95630 261-B1
CEDAR CT
- EDCo 95667 226-J3
1600 OAKL 94561 (514-D7 See Page 493)
3100 WSAC 95691 316-J2
CEDAR DR
- LNCN 95648 199-J3
- LNCN 95648 200-A2
4900 EDCo - 247-F3
7000 EDCo 95667 265-H3
7500 CITH 95610 239-H7
CEDAR ST
100 AUB 95603 182-C3
100 RSVL 95678 239-G1
2200 WSAC 95691 296-H3
3600 RKLN 95677 220-E2
CEDAR BLUFF WY
6800 SAC 95823 358-B1
CEDARBROOK RD
- WSAC 95691 316-J1
- WSAC 95691 317-A1
CEDAR BROOK WY
1200 SAC 95831 337-A3
CEDAR CANYON CIR
800 GALT 95632 419-F3
CEDAR CREEK WY
5500 CITH 95610 259-H6
CEDAR CREST WY
8200 SAC 95826 318-D1
CEDAR FALLS CT
- PlaC 95746 240-H2
CEDAR FLAT AV
600 GALT 95632 419-G4
CEDAR FLAT WY
700 GALT 95632 419-F4
CEDAR GARDEN CT
- CITH 95621 259-G4
CEDAR GLEN WY
6600 PlaC 95658 181-B2
CEDAR GROVE CT
- SAC 95831 336-J2
CEDAR GROVE DR
4100 SaCo 95826 318-J2
CEDAR HILL CT
8400 SaCo 95843 238-H5
CEDARHILL CT
- PlaC 95650 201-E5
CEDARHURST CT
3000 EDCo 95682 263-E7
CEDARHURST WY
5400 SaCo 95608 259-D6
CEDAR LANDING WY
4700 RCCD 95742 320-E3
CEDAR MEADOW DR
4100 SaCo 95843 238-H5
CEDAR MIST LN
12400 PlaC 95602 162-B1
CEDAR OAK CT
- EDCo 95667 266-A2
CEDAR OAK RD
- EDCo 95667 266-A2
CEDAR OAK WY
- ELKG 95757 358-A7
CEDAR OAKS DR
7000 PlaC 95746 241-C2
CEDAR PARK CT
- CITH 95621 259-G3
CEDAR POND PL
9600 ELKG 95757 357-J6
CEDAR RAIL WY
- ELKG 95624 359-A6
CEDAR RANCH DR
- CITH 95621 259-G4
CEDAR RAVINE CT
- EDCo 95667 266-C4
CEDAR RAVINE RD
3000 PLCR 95667 245-G5
3400 EDCo 95667 245-H6
3700 PLCR 95667 246-A7
3800 EDCo 95667 246-A7
4000 EDCo 95667 266-A1
CEDAR RIDGE CT
- RVIS 94571 454-F2
100 FOLS 95630 241-A7
CEDAR RIDGE DR
- PlaC 95746 240-G4
- RVIS 94571 454-E3
CEDAR RIDGE WY
2600 SaCo 95826 298-J6
CEDAR RIVER CT
11200 RCCD 95670 280-A5
CEDAR RIVER WY
300 SAC 95831 316-F7
300 SAC 95831 336-F1
CEDAR ROCK CIR
100 SAC 95823 337-G3
CEDAR SPRINGS CT
- RSVL 95747 219-D4
CEDAR SPRINGS WY
7800 SAC 95832 337-F5
CEDAR TREE WY
1100 SAC 95831 337-A3
CEDAR VALLEY LN
- EDCo 95667 266-D5
CEDARVIEW WY
9300 ELKG 95758 357-F5
CEDARVILLAGE DR
8900 SaCo 95628 260-F7
CEDARWOOD LN
8300 CITH 95610 240-C7
CEDARWOOD ST
4200 RKLN 95677 220-F4
CEDARWOOD WY
4500 SAC 95823 337-H3
CEDER PL
- EDCo 95682 263-D2
CEDRO CIR
- SAC 95833 277-B5
CEINWEN CT
3100 PLCR 95667 245-J5
CELAR CT
3400 RCCD 95670 299-J4
CELEBRAR ST
15100 SaCo 95683 342-C2
CELEBRATION ST
- SAC 95835 257-D4
CELEBRITY ST
7700 SAC 95832 337-C4
CELERY CT
8700 ELKG 95624 358-F6
CELESTE CT
6200 ELKG 95758 358-A5
CELESTIAL CT
- RSVL 95678 219-G4

CELESTIAL WY
5400 CITH 95610 259-H6
12400 AUB 95603 162-D5
12400 PlaC 95603 162-D5
CELIA AV
7100 SaCo 95828 338-C1
CELINE DR
5600 CITH 95610 260-A6
CELITO CT
9200 ELKG 95624 358-G4
CELTIC DR
- LNCN 95648 179-D2
CELTIC WY
9200 ELKG 95624 358-F5
CEMENT WY
- SaCo 95835 257-E4
CEMETERY DR
100 RVIS 94571 454-G5
CEMETERY RD
- SAC 95819 297-H6
CEMETERY ST
6200 EDCo 95623 265-A5
CEMO CIR
2200 SaCo 95670 280-A5
CENACLE LN
1900 SaCo 95608 299-B1
CENCIBEL CT
- SAC 95833 276-J4
CENTAUR CT
9900 RCCD 95827 299-D5
CENTAUR DR
200 EDCo 95619 265-D5
CENTENNIAL CT
- PLCR 95667 246-B4
900 AUB 95603 162-D5
2700 EDCo 95667 246-B4
CENTENNIAL WY
6900 SaCo 95842 259-B2
CENTER AV
- SaCo 95690 437-A1
CENTER LN
2700 ANT 94509 (513-D6 See Page 493)
CENTER PKWY
7200 SaCo 95823 337-H2
7500 SAC 95823 337-H2
7600 ELKG 95758 358-B2
7600 SAC 95758 358-B2
7600 SAC 95823 358-B1
7600 ELKG 95823 358-B2
7800 SAC 95823 338-A5
CENTER ST
- SaCo 95690 437-A1
- YoCo 95612 356-H5
100 AUB 95603 182-E2
100 RSVL 95678 240-A1
200 RVIS 94571 454-H6
3000 PLCR 95667 245-F5
3500 RKLN 95677 220-E2
CENTER COURT LN
- SaCo 95843 238-F6
CENTER MALL WY
6100 SaCo 95823 338-A2
CENTERS LN
- EDCo 95667 265-D3
CENTERVIEW CT
2900 EDCo 95726 248-D1
CENTERVILLE CT
11700 SaCo 95670 280-D4
CENTINELLA DR
3600 SaCo 95660 258-G3
CENTRAL AV
1700 SAC 95815 298-B1
2000 PlaC 95747 239-B1
3900 SaCo 95628 280-A2
8200 SaCo 95662 260-C3
9400 FOLS 95630 260-J3
9400 SaCo 95630 260-J3
48000 YoCo 95612 375-G1
48000 YoCo 95612 (376-E1 See Page 375)
49700 YoCo 95612 356-F7
CENTRAL RD
- SaCo 95758 337-F7
- SaCo 95758 357-F1
CENTRAL PARK CT
6600 SaCo 95662 260-D3
CENTRAL PARK DR
- RSVL 95678 219-J4
- RSVL 95678 220-A3
CENTURION CIR
6000 CITH 95621 259-F5
CENTURY BLVD
4600 PIT 94565 (513-A5 See Page 493)
CENTURY CT
- RSVL 95678 219-G5
CENTURY RD
- SaCo 95632 418-J2
CENTURY WY
- EDCo 95619 266-C5
- EDCo 95667 266-C5
5700 SaCo 95628 260-B6
CENTURY OAK DR
- LNCN 95648 199-J2
CENTURY OAKS LN
9400 ELKG 95758 357-E5
CEONOTHUS CT
- ELKG 95624 358-F1
CERCIS CT
- EDCo 95682 263-G5
CERCIS WY
3500 EDCo 95682 263-G6
CERES CT
100 FOLS 95630 261-D5
CERES WY
1800 SaCo 95864 298-J1
CEREUS CT
8300 SaCo 95843 239-A5
CEREUS WY
8300 SaCo 95843 239-A5
CEREZO DR
8800 SaCo 95662 260-F4
CERMAK WY
- ELKG 95758 357-D5
CERRITO DR
100 FOLS 95630 261-E3
CERRITO RD
5800 EDCo 95619 265-C7
CERRO CIR
3000 RKLN 95677 220-C1
CERROLINDA CIR
9200 ELKG 95758 358-B4
CERROMAR CIR
6300 SaCo 95662 260-C4
CERRO PARK CIR
- FOLS 95630 261-E7
- FOLS 95630 281-E1
CERRO VISTA CT
7500 PlaC 95650 201-D6

CERVANTES DR
2200 RCCD 95670 279-J6
CERVELLI WY
- ELKG 95757 357-J7
- ELKG 95757 358-A7
CERVEZA WY
3500 EDCo 95672 243-F4
CESA LN
- ANT 94509 (513-D5 See Page 493)
CESPITOSE CT
- SAC 95834 277-D4
CESSNA DR
3200 EDCo 95682 263-E5
7300 CITH 95621 259-G1
CEZANNE CT
300 FOLS 95630 261-J3
CEZANNE WY
100 FOLS 95630 261-J3
CHABLIS CIR
1200 RSVL 95747 239-F2
CHABLIS CT
4800 OAKL 94561 (514-C7 See Page 493)
CHABLIS DR
6000 EDCo 95682 264-E7
CHABLIS WY
4900 OAKL 94561 (514-C7 See Page 493)
9200 ELKG 95624 358-J7
CHABOLLA AV
600 GALT 95632 419-F7
600 GALT 95632 439-F1
CHABOLYN WY
7800 SaCo 95628 259-J7
CHABOT DR
- CITH 95621 239-G6
CHACOLI CT
11100 RCCD 95670 300-A4
CHAD CT
2800 SaCo 95827 299-C4
CHAD DR
6000 PlaC 95658 181-G7
CHADBURY DR
1500 RSVL 95678 219-F6
CHADBURY PL
8800 ELKG 95758 358-A3
CHADSFORD CT
100 FOLS 95630 281-C1
CHADSWORTH WY
3500 SaCo 95821 278-H4
CHADWELL CT
100 RSVL 95661 240-E4
CHADWICK WY
100 FOLS 95630 261-G5
CHAFF CT
9000 ELKG 95758 357-H3
CHAFFEY LN
5700 SaCo 95608 279-C1
CHAFFIN CT
- FOLS 95630 261-E7
1000 RSVL 95661 239-J5
CHAGALL CT
- EDCo 95762 262-H4
CHALCEDONY CT
- FOLS 95630 261-H4
CHALCEDONY WY
- FOLS 95630 261-H4
CHALET WY
7000 EDCo 95630 222-J2
CHALLENGE WY
CHALLIS CT
6600 CITH 95610 259-J3
CHALMERS CT
8900 ELKG 95624 358-H5
CHALMETTE CT
5600 RKLN 95677 220-C4
CHAMBEAU WY
10700 ELKG 95624 359-H3
CHAMBER CT
- SAC 95758 358-C2
CHAMBERLAIN RD
3500 PlaC - 159-B4
3500 PlaC 95648 159-B4
CHAMBERLAIN ST
700 PLCR 95667 245-F5
CHAMBERLAIN WY
3700 SaCo 95608 279-A4
CHAMBERLIN AV
200 AUB 95603 182-D2
CHAMBERLIN CIR
4500 ELKG 95757 377-H2
4500 ELKG 95757 397-H2
CHAMBERS DR
- LNCN 95648 179-E3
CHAMBERSBURG WY
100 FOLS 95630 261-H6
CHAMBLY LN
- LNCN 95648 179-F7
CHAMBORD CT
8600 SaCo 95828 338-F7
CHAMBORD WY
- RSVL 95678 219-H4
CHAMBRAY CT
- ELKG 95624 359-F2
CHAMBRAY RD
- ELKG 95624 359-F2
CHAMISE CT
5500 SaCo 95662 260-H6
CHAMOMILE CT
8700 ELKG 95624 358-G2
CHAMONIX CT
8600 SaCo 95843 238-H5
CHAMONIX WY
4000 SaCo 95843 238-H4
CHAMPAGNE CIR
1300 RSVL 95747 239-E2
CHAMPAGNE CT
9200 SaCo 95829 338-J5
CHAMPAGNE LN
- EDCo 95667 226-A6
CHAMPION WY
- SaCo 95655 300-B7
CHAMPION OAKS DR
1100 RSVL 95661 240-C6
CHAMPLAIN LN
4000 SaCo 95608 279-F3
CHANA DR
200 AUB 95603 182-D2
CHANCE WY
600 PlaC 95661 239-J5
600 RSVL 95661 239-J5
CHANCELLOR AV
1500 RSVL 95661 240-A4
CHANCERY CT
7700 CITH 95610 259-J4
CHANCERY WY
4600 SaCo 95608 299-A4

STREET
Block City ZIP Pg-Grid

CHANCERY WY
4600 SaCo 95864 299-A4
CHANCEY LN
- EDCo 95667 266-G1
CHANDEAUX LN
- SaCo 95628 280-E2
CHANDELLE CT
9000 SaCo 95628 260-F7
CHANDLER DR
6600 SaCo 95828 338-B2
CHANDLER HILL CT
- ELKG 95624 358-J1
CHANDON CT
- RSVL 95746 240-F5
600 OAKL 94561 (514-D5 See Page 493)
CHANDON WY
1700 OAKL 94561 (514-D5 See Page 493)
CHANEY CT
3700 SaCo 95608 279-F4
CHANGO CIR
100 SAC 95835 256-H3
CHANNEL CT
2900 SaCo 95825 298-E1
CHANNEL DR
1900 WSAC 95691 296-C6
CHANNEL HILL LN
200 PlaC 95603 162-F5
CHANNEL HILL RD
200 PlaC 95603 162-F5
CHANNEL ISLAND LN
- RSVL 95678 220-A3
CHANNEL ISLANDS ST
- ELKG 95624 358-J7
- ELKG 95624 359-A7
CHANNING DR
6000 SaCo 95660 258-G3
CHANNING WY
100 AUB 95603 182-F3
CHANTAL WY
8900 SaCo 95829 338-H6
CHANTILLY CT
- RSVL 95678 219-H5
CHANTILLY LN
7400 SaCo 95828 338-F2
CHANTILLY PL
- OAKL 94561 (514-D6 See Page 493)
CHANTRELLE CT
- EDCo 95667 244-J6
CHANTRY CT
8100 SaCo 95829 338-H6
CHANTRY HILL RD
9300 PlaC 95658 181-G5
CHAPARRAL CT
400 FOLS 95630 282-B1
2200 RKLN 95677 220-F2
CHAPARRAL DR
- EDCo 95667 266-F2
CHAPARRAL LN
6600 PlaC 95658 181-B2
CHAPARRAL WY
400 WSAC 95691 296-H3
7700 SaCo 95628 259-J7
CHAPEL ST
3000 PLCR 95667 245-F5
CHAPEL WY
4300 SaCo 95842 258-J6
CHAPEL HILL LN
- SaCo 95842 259-A1
CHAPELLE CT
100 RSVL 95661 240-F2
CHAPELLE DR
3300 RSVL 95661 240-E2
CHAPELTON WY
- RSVL 95747 218-J5
CHAPEL VIEW LN
6200 CITH 95621 259-F4
CHAPIN CT
3400 EDCo 95667 245-F7
CHAPIN RD
700 EDCo 95667 245-F7
CHAPIN WY
5900 SaCo 95824 317-H5
CHAPLAIN AV
- RCCD 95655 299-G6
CHAPLEAU CT
- SaCo 95829 339-D6
CHAPLIN CT
7800 ELKG 95758 358-C6
CHAPMAN CT
100 FOLS 95630 261-G4
CHAPMAN TR
- EDCo 95634 225-G1
CHAPPELET PL
- OAKL 94561 (514-E5 See Page 493)
CHAPPIE CT
- EDCo 95667 226-F7
CHAPPIE DR
- EDCo 95667 226-E7
CHAPPIE LN
5200 EDCo 95667 226-F7
5200 EDCo 95667 246-F1
CHAPS CT
100 GALT 95632 419-E7
CHAR AV
8600 SaCo 95662 260-D5
CHARBONO WY
10600 RCCD 95670 299-G2
CHARBRAY CT
3800 EDCo 95682 283-H5
CHARCREST CT
7900 SaCo 95628 279-J2
CHARDIN PL
- EDCo 95762 262-H4
CHARDON CT
7200 SaCo 95828 338-D2
CHARDONAY DR
10500 RCCD 95670 299-G1
CHARDONNAY CT
4900 OAKL 94561 (514-C7 See Page 493)
CHARDONNAY DR
1900 OAKL 94561 (514-D7 See Page 493)
CHARDONNAY WY
- RVIS 94571 454-G6
CHARENTE WY
8500 SAC 95758 358-C1
CHARGENE WY
1100 SAC 95822 317-A3
CHARIOT CIR
3700 EDCo 95672 243-G4
CHARITO LN
3300 EDCo 95682 263-C5
CHARLAURA CT
8200 SaCo 95828 338-D1
CHARLEMAGNE DR
- SaCo 95828 338-F2
CHARLEMONT PL
- FOLS 95630 261-G5
CHARLENE WY
4100 PlaC 95648 179-A2
7900 CITH 95610 240-A7
CHARLES AV
300 SaCo 95626 237-F7
CHARLES RD
- SaCo 95638 (401-D4 See Page 381)
CHARLES ST
1000 WSAC 95605 296-J1
13900 SJCo 95686 437-C3
CHARLES WY
5000 OAKL 94561 (514-C6 See Page 493)
CHARLESTON CIR
1000 RSVL 95661 240-A4
CHARLESTON DR
4500 SaCo 95608 279-F2
CHARLOAIS
9300 ELKG 95624 358-J7
9300 ELKG 95624 359-A7
CHARLOTTE AV
8200 CITH 95610 240-B6
CHARLOTTE LN
2500 SaCo 95821 278-D6
CHARM CT
- EDCo 95667 226-A2
CHARM WY
1500 SAC 95835 257-C4
CHARMAIN CT
7700 SaCo 95843 239-B7
CHAR MAR CIR
3300 EDCo 95682 283-G4
CHARMETTE WY
7800 SAC 95823 338-A5
CHARNWOOD CT
300 LNCN 95648 200-A3
CHAROLAIS WY
7000 CITH 95610 259-H2
CHARRING LN
3600 SaCo 95608 279-F4
CHARSLEY WY
- GALT 95632 419-G3
CHART CT
- SAC 95831 336-G3
CHARTER CT
- RKLN 95765 200-B6
2100 RSVL 95661 240-D3
CHARTER RD
- RKLN 95765 200-C5
CHARTER WY
3700 EDCo 95762 262-D2
CHARTERS CT
3200 RCCD 95670 299-F4
CHARWOOD LN
6100 CITH 95621 259-E4
W CHASE CT
8600 SaCo 95828 338-F7
CHASE DR
- GALT 95632 439-G2
- RSVL 95678 219-J5
1800 RCCD 95670 299-E1
CHASEN CT
- RKLN 95765 200-D7
CHASEN DR
- EDCo 95682 263-F4
CHASSELLA WY
2500 RCCD 95670 299-G1
CHASTAIN ST
6600 SaCo 95662 260-F3
CHATEAU CT
7500 SaCo 95828 338-C2
CHATEAU MONTELANA DR
- EDCo 95630 222-G6
CHATEAU MONTELENA WY
- SAC 95834 276-H3
CHATEAUX DR
- PlaC 95650 221-H1
CHATEE LN
4200 EDCo 95672 243-F7
CHATFIELD DR
8600 SaCo 95828 338-F1
CHATHAM ST
3400 RKLN 95765 220-C1
CHATHAM WY
6000 CITH 95621 259-F3
CHATSWOOD CT
200 RSVL 95678 219-F6
CHATSWOOD WY
5300 SaCo 95843 239-B7
CHATSWORTH LN
1900 SaCo 95608 299-B1
CHATTAN WY
- ELKG 95624 338-D7
- ELKG 95624 358-D1
CHATTANOOGA CT
9500 SaCo 95827 319-B1
CHAUCER CT
500 RSVL 95747 219-B5
1000 SaCo 95608 299-A3
CHAUNCEY WY
5400 SaCo 95662 260-G6
CHAVES CT
10300 ELKG 95757 378-B3
CHECKERBLOOM WY
7000 CITH 95610 260-B2
CHEER CT
8700 ELKG 95624 358-G5
CHEETAH DR
- SaCo 95829 338-H5
CHEETAH TR
- EDCo 95630 202-H7
- EDCo 95630 222-J1
CHELAN RD
- WSAC 95691 316-J1
CHELEN CT
9700 PlaC 95746 240-H6
CHELMSFORD CT
- RSVL 95747 219-C3
CHELSEA CT
100 FOLS 95630 261-B2
1200 ANT 94509 (513-F7 See Page 493)
1500 RSVL 95661 240-B5
3900 RKLN 95677 220-E1
CHELSEA PL
400 RKLN 95677 220-E1
CHELSEA RD
3100 SaCo 95864 298-F2
3400 EDCo 95682 263-C6
CHELSEA WY
1700 RSVL 95661 240-B5
CHELSEA GLEN CT
4900 SaCo 95843 239-A6
CHELSHAM AV
1100 GALT 95632 419-G5
CHELSHIRE DOWNS RD
5000 PlaC 95746 240-H5
CHELSHIRE ESTATES CT
- PlaC 95746 240-H4
CHELTENHAM WY
6300 CITH 95621 259-E3
CHEMISE LN
4200 EDCo 95672 243-H5
CHEMO RIVER CT
11000 RCCD 95670 279-J5
CHENERY CT
100 FOLS 95630 261-H6
CHENIN LN
4300 OAKL 94561 (514-E7 See Page 493)
CHENIN BLANC CIR
1200 RSVL 95747 239-F2
CHENIN BLANC LN
8100 SaCo 95628 260-C6
CHENNAULT CT
- RSVL 95747 239-B1
300 SAC 95838 278-B2
CHENTEZ CT
- SaCo 95662 260-D4
CHENU AV
3200 SaCo 95821 278-F6
CHERBOURG DR
5100 SaCo 95842 259-B1
CHERI CT
3500 RKLN 95677 220-D2
CHERIMOYA CT
2900 SaCo 95843 238-E5
CHERISH WY
9100 SaCo 95826 318-J3
CHEROKEE LN
9600 PlaC 95658 201-J2
12300 SaCo 95632 (400-A4 See Page 379)
12300 SaCo 95632 420-A5
N CHEROKEE LN
24100 SJCo 95220 (440-A4 See Page 420)
24600 SJCo 95632 (440-A4 See Page 420)
26300 SJCo 95632 420-A7
CHEROKEE RD
- WSAC 95691 316-H2
4100 EDCo 95672 243-F7
CHEROKEE TR
3200 PlaC 95650 201-B5
CHEROKEE WY
5100 SaCo 95841 259-B5
CHERRELYN WY
6000 SaCo 95608 259-D7
CHERRI LYNN AV
100 SaCo 95673 257-G3
CHERRINGTON LN
8500 ELKG 95624 359-D2
CHERRY AV
200 AUB 95603 182-E2
8900 SaCo 95662 240-F7
CHERRY LN
600 PlaC 95658 181-G6
700 EDCo 95667 245-E6
6400 SaCo 95673 257-J3
6400 SaCo 95673 258-A3
CHERRY PL
- WSAC 95691 316-C3
CHERRY RD
12900 SaCo 95693 (361-A1 See Page 341)
CHERRY ST
100 RSVL 95678 239-H3
CHERRY BLOSSOM LN
1100 LNCN 95648 180-A5
1200 LNCN 95648 179-J5
CHERRYBLOSSOM LN
7900 CITH 95610 240-C7
CHERRY BROOK DR
7800 SaCo 95626 238-C6
CHERRY CREEK CT
6000 CITH 95621 259-G5
CHERRY CREST CT
8500 ELKG 95624 358-E5
CHERRY GLEN AV
7500 CITH 95610 239-H6
CHERRY HILLS LN
700 RVIS 94571 454-F2
CHERRYHILLS WY
7800 SaCo 95628 279-J1
CHERRY LEAF CT
8300 CITH 95610 239-H6
CHERRY PLUM CT
8800 ELKG 95624 358-G1
CHERRY RIDGE CIR
- RSVL 95678 219-J2
- RSVL 95678 220-A2
CHERRYTREE AV
7000 CITH 95621 259-G5
CHERRYVILLE LN
- SaCo 95842 259-A1
CHERRYWOOD CIR
6700 SAC 95823 338-B6
CHERRYWOOD LN
- EDCo - 267-H4
- EDCo 95726 267-H4
CHERT CT
- EDCo 95762 262-F2
- RSVL 95747 219-A7
CHERTSEY CT
3300 RCCD 95827 299-D5
CHERYL CT
100 FOLS 95630 261-E4
1600 LNCN 95648 179-F3
CHERYL LN
7500 SaCo 95628 279-H3
CHERYL WY
2500 SaCo 95832 337-E4
CHESAPEAKE DR
1200 RSVL 95661 240-A5
CHESAPEAKE LN
4100 SaCo 95660 258-F4
CHESAPEAKE BAY CIR
- EDCo 95682 263-C2
CHESAPEAKE BAY CT
- EDCo 95682 263-C2
CHESBRO CIR
6300 SaCo 95683 322-C7
CHESBRO CT
- SaCo 95683 322-D7
CHESHAM ST
3300 EDCo 95672 263-B2
CHESHIRE WY
6000 CITH 95610 259-J5
CHESLEY CT
- LNCN 95648 179-F6
CHESLEY LN
- LNCN 95648 179-E6
CHESLINE DR
7000 SaCo 95628 259-G6
7100 CITH 95621 259-G6
7100 SaCo 95621 259-G6
7300 CITH 95610 259-G6
CHESNEY WY
700 SaCo 95673 257-J1
CHESSELL CT
100 FOLS 95630 261-F7
CHESSELL WY
100 FOLS 95630 261-F7
100 FOLS 95630 281-F1
CHESSINGTON CT
5200 PlaC 95746 240-H5
CHESTER DR
8100 ELKG 95624 339-H7
8100 ELKG 95830 339-H7
8100 SaCo 95830 339-H7
CHESTER LN
5500 RKLN 95677 220-D3
CHESTERBROOK DR
6300 SAC 95758 358-A2
CHESTERFIELD WY
- RKLN 95765 200-C4
100 FOLS 95630 261-D6
CHESTER RIVER CT
11100 RCCD 95670 279-J5
CHESTERTON WY
- SaCo 95843 239-C7
CHESTNUT AV
1900 ANT 94509 (513-D5 See Page 493)
5800 SaCo 95662 260-G3
CHESTNUT CT
- LNCN 95648 179-J1
- PlaC 95746 240-G3
- PlaC 95747 238-J3
CHESTNUT LN
4000 EDCo 95667 265-C2
CHESTNUT PL
- EDCo 95682 263-D2
CHESTNUT TR
- PlaC 95603 161-A5
CHESTNUT CROSSING LN
- SaCo 95662 260-G3
CHESTNUT HILL DR
2600 SAC 95826 298-E7
2700 SAC 95826 318-E1
CHESTWALL ST
9200 SaCo 95662 260-G5
CHETTENHAM DR
3100 RCCD 95670 299-F4
CHETWOOD WY
6200 SAC 95831 317-B6
CHEVAL CT
7200 CITH 95621 259-G1
CHEVAL WY
- PlaC 95747 238-J3
CHEVALIER WY
8300 SaCo 95828 338-E7
CHEVIOT HILL CT
5400 SaCo 95843 239-C6
CHEVY CHASE WY
6800 SaCo 95823 317-G7
6900 SaCo 95823 337-H1
CHEX CT
8800 ELKG 95624 358-G4
CHEYENNE CT
200 RSVL 95661 240-C3
7900 SaCo 95843 238-F6
CHEYENNE LN
100 PlaC 95603 182-B3
CHEYENNE RANCH RD
4000 EDCo 95667 243-J2
CHIANTI CT
- LNCN 95648 179-J7
10600 RCCD 95670 299-G1
CHIANTI WY
5500 CITH 95610 260-A6
9200 ELKG 95624 358-J7
CHIBRA CT
5000 EDCo 95682 283-G4
CHICA WY
1300 SaCo 95864 298-H2
CHICAGO AV
4300 SaCo 95628 280-B2
4800 SaCo 95628 260-B7
CHI CHI LN
2600 EDCo 95667 245-C4
2600 PLCR 95667 245-C4
CHICKADEE CT
- SAC 95831 316-G5
CHICKEN FLAT RD
- EDCo 95633 205-E5
CHICKPEA CT
3000 ANT 94509 (513-J6 See Page 493)
CHICORY CT
- LNCN 95648 180-A5
7500 SaCo 95842 259-C1
CHICORY BEND CT
- SAC 95831 336-H4
CHICORY FIELD WY
- ELKG 95624 359-B6
CHIEF CT
- SAC 95833 277-C6
CHIGNAHUAPAN WY
1300 RSVL 95747 239-E1
CHIKAMI CT
6400 SaCo 95662 260-E4
CHILCOTT CT
- RSVL 95747 239-C1
CHILDHOOD CT
4200 EDCo 95682 264-B7
CHILDHOOD LN
4300 EDCo 95682 264-C6
CHILHAM WY
400 SaCo 95864 298-H5
CHILI AL
900 PLCR 95667 245-G6
CHILI BAR CT
- EDCo 95667 225-D7
CHILI BAR LN
- EDCo 95667 225-D6
CHILI HILL RD
6700 PlaC 95658 181-B1
CHILTON DR
1600 RSVL 95747 239-D1
CHILTON PL
3200 EDCo 95762 262-D2
CHIMANGO CT
8100 SaCo 95843 239-A6
CHIMANGO WY
8100 SaCo 95843 239-A6
CHIMES HARBOR DR
- ELKG 95624 358-J7
- ELKG 95624 359-A7
CHIMNEY CT
- RKLN 95765 200-E4
CHIMNEY BLUFF CT
100 FOLS 95630 241-A7
CHIMNEY ROCK WY
- SAC 95834 276-J2
CHINA CAMP DR
- EDCo 95667 266-B4
CHINA DIGGINS RD
5800 EDCo 95762 283-A5
CHINA GARDEN CT
4100 EDCo 95667 265-D2
CHINA GARDEN RD
3700 EDCo 95619 265-D2
3800 EDCo 95667 265-D2
5200 RKLN 95677 220-E5
5200 PlaC 95677 220-E5
CHINA HAT ISLAND RD
- WSAC 95691 316-D2
CHINA HILL RD
5600 EDCo 95623 264-J7
E CHINA HILL RD
4800 EDCo 95623 265-A7
W CHINA HILL RD
5300 EDCo 95623 264-J7
5300 EDCo 95623 265-A7
CHINA LAKE WY
- SaCo 95828 338-G4
CHINA MINE RD
- PlaC 95650 201-E3
CHINAROSE CT
400 LNCN 95648 200-A3
CHINA WELL RD
2700 PlaC 95603 161-F5
CHINOOK AV
6200 SaCo 95841 259-D4
CHINOOK LN
500 EDCo 95667 245-E6
CHINOOK RD
- WSAC 95691 316-H1
CHINQUAPIN WY
500 PlaC 95603 162-E6
4200 SaCo 95823 337-H5
CHIP CT
- RKLN 95765 200-D4
CHIPLAY ST
2800 SAC 95826 298-F7
2900 SAC 95826 318-F1
CHIPMUNK WY
7500 CITH 95610 260-A1
7600 CITH 95610 240-A7
CHIPPENDALE DR
4700 SaCo 95841 259-A6
CHIPPENDALE WY
1000 RSVL 95661 240-D4
CHIPPEWA CT
7800 SaCo 95843 238-G7
CHIPPING WY
5600 CITH 95621 259-G5
CHIP SHOT CT
- RSVL 95678 219-H5
CHIP SHOT WY
- RSVL 95678 219-H5
CHIPWOOD WY
8000 SaCo 95662 260-B3
CHIQUITA WY
6500 SaCo 95608 279-E5
CHISHOLM TR
- EDCo 95667 266-J7
900 GALT 95632 439-F2
CHISOLM TR
3200 LMS 95650 201-B5
3200 PlaC 95650 201-B5
CHISUM AV
200 SaCo 95673 257-F4
CHISUM CT
1000 RSVL 95678 239-F1
CHISWELL WY
3300 RCCD 95827 299-D5
CHIVALRY WY
7300 CITH 95621 259-G2
CHLOE CT
- SAC 95758 358-C2
CHOCKER WY
- SAC 95834 277-E4
CHOCTAW CT
7800 SaCo 95843 238-G7
CHOCTAW TRC
- PlaC 95650 201-E4
CHOOPIM RD
4100 EDCo 95682 264-A2
CHORLEY CT
- FOLS 95630 261-G7
CHRIS AV
6900 SAC 95828 338-C1
6900 SaCo 95828 338-C1
CHRIS CT
8000 PlaC 95746 241-E1
CHRIS LN
8500 SaCo 95610 240-D6
CHRIS ANN CT
5600 SaCo 95841 259-C6
CHRISMAN AV
- PLCR 95667 245-G5
CHRISSE CT
3000 ANT 94509 (513-C7 See Page 493)
CHRISTA CT
3500 EDCo 95682 263-B7
CHRISTENSEN RD
12800 SaCo 95632 419-B4
13800 SaCo 95632 439-B1
CHRISTENSEN WY
- RVIS 94571 454-G3
CHRISTIAN LN
8100 PlaC 95746 221-E7
CHRISTIAN VALLEY RD
600 PlaC 95602 162-H1
CHRISTIE CT
3400 SAC 95838 278-B4
CHRISTINA CT
- FOLS 95630 261-E2
400 ANT 94509 (513-E7 See Page 493)
5900 PlaC 95746 240-J1
5900 PlaC 95746 241-A1
CHRISTINA WY
5500 SaCo 95608 279-C2
CHRISTINE DR
200 SAC 95815 277-G5
CHRISTINE LN
- OAKL 94561 (514-F7 See Page 493)
CHRISTO WY
- ELKG 95757 377-J3
- ELKG 95757 378-A3
- ELKG 95757 397-J3
CHRISTOPHER CT
2900 RKLN 95677 220-B5
CHRISTOPHER LN
400 FOLS 95630 261-B1
CHRISTOPHER WY
1500 SAC 95819 297-J7
CHRISTY LN
8500 PlaC 95746 241-B3
CHRISTYLYN CT
10100 SaCo 95632 419-D2
CHRISTYLYN WY
9900 SaCo 95632 419-C2
CHRISWOODS CT
8000 SaCo 95828 338-C4
CHROME CT
9600 ELKG 95624 359-B6
CHROME RIDGE CT
- EDCo 95667 266-G2
CHROME RIDGE RD
- EDCo 95667 266-G2
CHRYSANTHY BLVD
- RCCD 95742 320-D1
CHRYSOLITE LN
5800 EDCo 95623 265-B7
CHRYSTAL SHORE LN
- ELKG 95758 357-G6
CHUBB RD
100 PlaC 95602 162-H2
CHUBBUCK CT
11500 SaCo 95670 280-C4
CHUCK CT
2300 SaCo 95626 238-D6
CHUCKWAGON DR
1100 SAC 95834 277-D4
CHUCKWAGON WY
3600 EDCo 95619 265-E2
CHUCK WING LN
- LNCN 95648 179-H6
CHUGWATER CT
3400 SaCo 95843 238-G5
CHULA VISTA DR
7500 CITH 95610 259-H4
CHUMLY CT
- RKLN 95765 200-A7
CHURCH AV
2300 SaCo 95821 278-D5
CHURCH LN
7600 CITH 95610 259-J1
CHURCH RD
- AUB 95603 182-D1
300 AUB 95603 162-E7
900 RVIS 94571 454-F3
CHURCH ST
100 RSVL 95678 239-G2
600 GALT 95632 419-F7
700 GALT 95632 439-F1
4600 EDCo 95623 265-A5
7200 PlaC 95663 201-C1
CHURCHILL CT
2400 RKLN 95765 200-D6
CHURCHILL RD
3100 SaCo 95864 298-F3
CHURCH RANCH RD
1900 EDCo 95667 246-C2
CHUTE CAMP RD
- EDCo 95667 226-H7
1900 EDCo 95709 226-H7
CIBOLA WY
4800 SAC 95820 318-A3
5500 SAC 95820 317-J4
CICERO CIR
100 SAC 95758 358-D1
CICERO CT
200 RSVL 95747 219-E6
CID LN
9000 SaCo 95693 360-J4
CIDER WY
- SaCo 95829 339-C6
CIELIO CT
4200 EDCo 95682 263-B7
CIELO CT
6700 ELKG 95758 358-B4
CIERVO CT
- SAC 95833 277-A5
CILKER RIVER WY
11000 RCCD 95670 279-J6
CIMARRON WY
4500 PlaC 95746 240-G2
5100 SaCo 95842 259-B3
CIMBERLY CT
2900 EDCo 95726 248-A1
CIMMARON CIR
200 FOLS 95630 261-D4
CIMMARON CT
700 GALT 95632 419-E4
CIMMARRON CT
3300 EDCo 95682 263-C2
CIMMARRON RD
3200 EDCo 95682 263-C2
CIMMERON CT
3400 RKLN 95677 200-D7
CIMMERON WY
- LNCN 95648 180-A1
CINA WY
7600 CITH 95610 239-J7
CINCINNATI AV
1300 PlaC 95765 199-F7
1400 PlaC 95648 199-F7
CINDER CT
- SAC 95831 316-J7
CINDY CIR
1600 RSVL 95661 240-B3
CINDY CT
1000 PLCR 95667 245-H4
1600 RSVL 95661 240-B3
CINDY LN
100 GALT 95632 439-D1
CINDY ST
5900 SAC 95824 318-B5
CINNABAR CT
- LNCN 95648 200-A1
600 RSVL 95678 219-J7
3200 SaCo 95826 299-A7
CINNABAR HILLS
- RVIS 94571 454-F1
CINNAMON CIR
- CITH 95621 259-G5
CINNAMON DR
100 GALT 95632 419-D6
CINNAMON TR
3500 EDCo 95667 246-E6
CINNAMON BAR CT
- SaCo 95829 339-D6
CINNAMON RIDGE CT
1200 EDCo 95667 245-J2
CINNAMON TEAL CIR
2800 ELKG 95757 357-E7
CINNAMON TEAL CT
- LNCN 95648 200-B1
CINNAMON TEAL LN
- LNCN 95648 200-B1
CINNAMON TEAL WY
- EDCo 95682 263-B5
- EDCo 95762 263-B5
CINSANT DR
2900 EDCo 95682 263-E3
CIRANO CT
7800 SaCo 95828 338-E4
CIRBY WY
- RSVL 95678 239-G4
400 RSVL 95661 239-G4
1100 RSVL 95661 240-A4
E CIRBY WY
2000 RSVL 95661 240-C4
N CIRBY WY
1900 RSVL 95661 240-E4
2200 PlaC 95661 240-E4
S CIRBY WY
1800 RSVL 95661 240-C5
CIRBY HILLS DR
100 RSVL 95678 239-H4
CIRBY OAKS CT
400 RSVL 95678 239-G5
CIRBY OAKS WY
1000 RSVL 95678 239-G4
CIRCLE DR
- SaCo 95690 455-E3
100 AUB 95603 182-D2
3700 LMS 95650 200-J6
CIRCLE PKWY
- SaCo 95823 337-H1
CIRCLE ST
- WSAC 95691 296-J5
CIRCLE A RANCH RD
4400 EDCo 95667 244-A1
CIRCLET WY
7100 CITH 95621 259-F2
CIRCUIT CT
4400 RKLN 95677 220-F2
CIRCUIT DR
1000 RSVL 95678 239-G2
4200 RKLN 95677 220-F2
7500 CITH 95610 259-H3
CIRCUS CT
9100 SaCo 95826 318-J1
CIRO CT
6800 CITH 95621 259-F3
CIRRUS WY
10000 RCCD 95827 299-D6
CISCO CIR
5300 SAC 95819 298-B4
CISMONT CT
- SAC 95823 337-J7
CITADEL CT
5000 PlaC 95746 240-H5
CITADEL WY
8200 SAC 95826 298-D7
CITADELLA DR
- RSVL 95747 219-B2
CITATION WY
5700 SaCo 95837 256-A3
CITRINE CIR
- SAC 95834 277-A2
CITRINE WY
- SAC 95834 277-B2
CITRON CT
8000 SaCo 95843 238-G6
CITRUS AV
4100 RKLN 95677 200-G7
4100 RKLN 95677 220-G1
7400 SaCo 95823 338-A3
CITRUS RD
2300 RCCD 95670 280-A6
2300 SaCo 95670 280-A6
2300 RCCD 95742 280-A7
2300 SaCo 95742 280-A7
2600 SaCo 95742 300-A1
2700 RCCD 95742 300-A1
CITRUS ST
1600 WSAC 95605 296-G2
CITRUS COLONY RD
4700 PlaC 95650 200-G3
CITRUS TREE WY
5900 SAC 95824 318-A5
CITRUSWOOD LN
- CITH 95610 240-C7
CITY CT
- SAC 95833 277-C6
CITY LIGHTS DR
1900 EDCo 95762 262-J7
1900 EDCo 95762 263-A7
1900 EDCo 95762 282-J1
1900 EDCo 95762 283-A1
CIVIC DR
300 GALT 95632 419-F7
CLAIBORNE AV
100 RSVL 95678 239-J2
CLAIBORNE WY
5500 SaCo 95662 260-G6
6800 SAC 95831 316-F7
CLAIM CT
- EDCo 95667 226-D1
100 FOLS 95630 261-F4
CLAIM ST
6400 EDCo 95667 226-C2
CLAIMSTAKE CT
1900 SaCo 95626 238-C7
CLAIR DR
3700 SaCo 95608 279-G4
3800 SaCo 95628 279-G4
CLAIRE AV
400 SAC 95838 257-H6
1000 SAC 95838 258-A6
5000 SAC 95652 258-B6
CLAIRE CT
2800 SaCo 95821 278-H6
CLAIRIDGE WY
3100 SaCo 95821 278-H5
CLAIRIDGE OAK CT
3000 SaCo 95821 278-H5
CLAIRINA WY
- ELKG 95757 377-J2
- ELKG 95757 378-A2
- ELKG 95757 397-J2
CLAIRMONT DR
5000 RKLN 95677 220-H4
CLAIRMONT LN
- LNCN 95648 180-A5
CLAN CT
10800 RCCD 95670 299-J1
CLANCY CT
- RSVL 95678 219-G5
CLANCYS CT
9700 ELKG 95624 378-G1
CLANFIELD CT
9300 SaCo 95829 339-A5

STREET
Block City ZIP Pg-Grid

CLANFIELD WY
8000 SaCo 95829 339-A6
CLANTON CT
8100 SaCo 95828 338-D3
CLAPPER RAIL CT
- RKLN 95765 219-H2
CLAPTON WY
2200 FOLS 95630 281-F1
CLARA WY
6200 SaCo 95660 258-G3
CLARE CASTLE CT
4000 SaCo 95826 318-J2
CLAREDON CT
200 LNCN 95648 200-A3
CLAREMONT CIR
- RSVL 95678 219-J2
CLAREMONT CT
5000 OAKL 94561 (514-C6 See Page 493)
CLAREMONT LN
5100 OAKL 94561 (514-C6 See Page 493)
CLAREMONT RD
1800 SaCo 95609 299-C1
7100 SaCo 95608 279-C7
CLAREMONT WY
1400 SAC 95822 317-B3
CLARENDON ST
1000 WSAC 95691 296-H5
CLARENDON WY
5500 SaCo 95608 299-C1
CLARET CT
4800 OAKL 94561 (514-C7 See Page 493)
CLAREWOOD DR
1600 RSVL 95661 240-D3
CLAREWOOD WY
- SAC 95835 256-G7
CLARICE LN
600 RSVL 95678 239-J3
CLARIDGE CT
5800 ELKG 95758 357-J5
CLARINA WY
- ELKG 95757 377-J2
- ELKG 95757 397-J2
CLARION CIR
8100 SaCo 95843 238-H6
CLARION CT
5100 EDCo 95667 265-B2
CLARION POINT CT
- ELKG 95624 358-J1
CLARISSA DR
9000 SaCo 95662 260-F5
CLARITA CT
9300 SaCo 95693 360-F6
CLARITY CT
4800 SaCo 95842 259-A2
CLARK AV
2800 SaCo 95608 279-C6
CLARK CT
100 SAC 95838 278-B2
3100 PLCR 95667 245-G6
CLARK ST
100 AUB 95603 182-D3
3000 PLCR 95667 245-G5
3200 EDCo 95667 245-G5
CLARK CANYON CT
100 FOLS 95630 241-A7
CLARKE FARMS DR
9400 ELKG 95624 359-B6
CLARK FORK LN
- CITH 95610 240-B7
CLARK LAKE LN
10300 ELKG 95624 359-E4
10300 SaCo 95624 359-E4
CLARKSBURG AV Rt#-E19
48000 YoCo 95612 356-H5
CLARKSBURG RD Rt#-E19
48000 YoCo 95612 356-B5
CLARKSON CT
3600 SaCo 95838 278-A3
CLARKSON DR
- RKLN 95765 200-D6
CLARKSVILLE CT
- EDCo 95672 262-H2
CLARKSVILLE RD
- FOLS 95630 261-G7
- FOLS 95630 281-G1
2100 EDCo 95672 262-H3
CLARK TUNNEL RD
100 PlaC 95663 180-H4
1100 PlaC 95663 181-A5
1300 PlaC 95663 201-C1
CLARON CT
- SAC 95833 277-C4
CLASSIC CT
300 WSAC 95605 276-J7
CLASSIC PL
5700 SaCo 95608 299-C1
CLAUDIA CT
1000 ANT 94509 (513-C6 See Page 493)
2900 WSAC 95691 316-E1
CLAUDIA DR
1400 SAC 95822 317-B4
CLAUDIA WY
2900 SAC 95826 318-D1
CLAUDIED WY
5400 ELKG 95757 377-J3
5400 ELKG 95757 397-J3
CLAUDINE CT
- ELKG 95757 377-F1
- ELKG 95757 397-F1
CLAUDIO WY
- RSVL 95661 220-E6
CLAUSS CT
- SAC 95820 317-H3
CLAUSSEN WY
6200 SaCo 95660 258-H4
CLAVELA AV
- SaCo 95828 338-F3
CLAVELL CT
7900 SaCo 95828 338-D3
CLAY CT
4600 RKLN 95677 220-B2
CLAY ST
1100 PLCR 95667 245-H4
2400 SAC 95815 277-J6
3000 SAC 95815 278-A5
3600 SAC 95838 277-J3
3900 SAC 95838 278-A2
CLAY BASKET DR
5900 CITH 95621 259-D3
CLAYBURY CT
800 GALT 95632 419-F3
CLAYDON WY
300 SaCo 95864 298-H5

CLAY EAST RD
13500 SaCo 95638 (401-C3 See Page 381)
CLAY GLEN WY
8700 ELKG 95758 357-J2
CLAY ISLE CT
100 RSVL 95747 219-C1
CLAYMORE CT
- EDCo 95682 263-F3
CLAYMORE WY
- EDCo 95682 263-F3
CLAYPOOL WY
7700 CITH 95610 260-C1
7700 CITH 95610 240-C7
CLAY STATION RD
8900 SaCo 95693 360-H4
9300 SaCo 95693 (361-A5 See Page 341)
9800 SaCo 95693 381-B1
10000 SaCo 95683 381-B2
10300 SaCo 95638 381-B3
11100 SaCo 95638 (401-B1 See Page 381)
12700 SaCo 95638 421-B2
CLAYTON DR
3400 LMS 95650 200-H5
CLAYTON LN
3300 LMS 95650 200-H5
CLAYTON WY
- SAC 95835 257-C7
CLEAR CIR
4900 SaCo 95608 279-A7
4900 SaCo 95608 299-A1
CLEAR CT
4000 EDCo 95667 265-C3
CLEARBROOK CIR
- RSVL 95747 218-J4
CLEARBROOK WY
6900 SAC 95823 358-B1
CLEAR CORRIE CT
8300 SaCo 95843 239-B5
CLEAR CREEK CT
- EDCo 95726 267-F3
6600 CITH 95610 260-A3
CLEAR CREEK RD
4200 EDCo 267-F4
4200 EDCo 95726 267-F4
5400 EDCo 95726 247-H7
CLEARDALE WY
3800 SAC 95823 337-G3
CLEARFIELD WY
2000 SaCo 95608 279-A7
2000 SaCo 95608 299-A1
CLEARLAKE WY
2500 SaCo 95826 298-J6
CLEAR RIVER CT
- SAC 95831 336-G1
CLEAR SKY CIR
100 SAC 95823 337-G4
CLEAR SPRINGS CIR
9500 ELKG 95624 359-A5
CLEAR STAR CT
8700 ELKG 95758 357-J2
CLEARSTONE PL
- FOLS 95630 261-B7
CLEAR VALLEY CT
8400 SaCo 95843 238-H5
CLEARVIEW CT
200 RSVL 95747 219-A3
3300 RKLN 95765 200-C7
CLEAR VIEW DR
7800 CITH 95610 239-J7
CLEARVIEW DR
1100 EDCo 95762 242-D3
CLEARVIEW WY
7100 RSVL 95747 219-A3
CLEARWATER CT
100 RSVL 95678 219-E6
CLEARWATER DR
- PlaC 95650 201-E6
5700 SaCo 95841 259-C4
CLEAR WOOD WY
4900 SaCo 95841 258-J7
CLEARY CIR
- ELKG 95757 377-H2
- ELKG 95757 397-H2
CLEARY DR
200 PlaC 95603 162-F5
CLEESE RD
2500 EDCo 95667 246-G1
2500 EDCo 95709 246-G1
CLELAND CT
600 GALT 95632 419-G4
CLEMENGER DR
6500 EDCo 95623 265-C5
CLEMENS WY
3400 SaCo 95864 298-F5
CLEMENSEN CIR
- FOLS 95630 261-H4
CLEMENT CIR
7500 SaCo 95828 338-C3
CLEMENTIA CIR
15300 SaCo 95683 322-D7
CLEMENTINE WY
9400 ELKG 95758 357-H6
CLEMSFORD SQ
100 FOLS 95630 261-H7
CLEMSON DR
2800 EDCo 95682 263-C3
CLENDENEN WY
9100 SaCo 95826 319-A2
CLEO WY
2700 SaCo 95821 278-C6
CLERMONT WY
3000 EDCo 95762 262-D4
CLEVELAND AV
100 AUB 95603 182-E2
200 SAC 95833 277-F6
CLEVELAND CT
- RKLN 95765 219-H1
CLEVELAND PL
3000 ANT 94509 (513-A7 See Page 493)
CLEVELAND BAY WY
- ELKG 95757 357-H7
CLICKER CT
2700 WSAC 95691 316-F1
CLIFFCREST DR
8200 SaCo 95828 338-E7
8300 SaCo 95624 338-E7
CLIFFE WY
8100 SaCo 95828 338-D6
CLIFF HOUSE WY
5200 SAC 95835 256-H4
CLIFFORD CT
8700 SaCo 95628 260-E7
CLIFFSIDE LN
8900 SaCo 95628 280-F3

CLIFF SWALLOW LN
1700 LNCN 95648 200-C1
CLIFFTON LN
1000 EDCo 95667 245-G7
CLIFFWOOD WY
8500 SAC 95826 298-F7
8500 SAC 95826 318-F1
CLIFT CT
- ELKG 95624 359-A6
CLIFTON CT
100 FOLS 95630 261-A2
CLIFTON RD
7800 SAC 95826 318-C2
CLINA WY
800 RSVL 95661 240-A3
CLING CT
8700 ELKG 95624 358-G6
CLINGER CT
600 SAC 95838 278-B1
CLINTON AV
100 RSVL 95678 239-H3
CLINTON RD
1000 SaCo 95825 298-D2
CLINTON WY
3700 EDCo 95682 263-F4
3800 SaCo 95628 279-H4
CLIPPER CT
- RKLN 95765 200-A3
1500 RSVL 95661 240-B5
CLIPPER RD
- RKLN 95765 200-A5
CLIPPER WY
600 SAC 95831 316-H5
CLIPPER COVE PL
- ELKG 95758 357-F6
CLIPPER GAP DR
- SaCo 95670 280-C5
CLOE CT
- SAC 95835 257-B6
CLONMEL CT
8800 SaCo 95828 338-G7
CLOS DU LAC CIR
9600 PlaC 95650 221-J1
9700 PlaC 95650 201-J7
CLOTHIER WY
4700 SaCo 95841 279-A1
CLOUD CREEK CT
2200 SaCo 95670 280-D5
CLOUDCROFT CT
3400 RKLN 95765 200-C7
3400 RKLN 95765 220-C1
CLOUDCROFT WY
8500 SaCo 95662 260-D4
CLOUDS HILL RD
- PlaC 95747 239-A1
CLOUDS REST RD
- EDCo 247-C7
CLOUD TOUCH CT
- RSVL 95747 219-C3
CLOUDVIEW DR
3000 SAC 95833 277-B5
CLOVE CT
- SAC 95823 337-J6
CLOVE RD
- EDCo 95667 286-H3
CLOVELY LN
8500 SaCo 95828 338-F1
CLOVER CT
- GALT 95632 419-E6
2800 ANT 94531 (513-G7 See Page 493)
CLOVER LN
2700 SaCo 95821 278-E4
CLOVER BLOSSOM LN
4000 PlaC 95602 160-J3
CLOVERDALE CIR
1300 RSVL 95661 240-E5
CLOVERDALE CT
100 RSVL 95661 240-E5
CLOVERDALE LN
5200 SaCo 95608 279-B7
CLOVERDALE RD
- WSAC 95691 316-G2
CLOVERFIELD CT
- LNCN 95648 179-H5
CLOVER FIELD WY
5000 SaCo 95824 317-H5
CLOVER GLEN WY
5000 SaCo 95824 317-J5
CLOVER HILL CT
- SAC 95823 337-H5
CLOVER HILL LN
7900 SaCo 95628 280-A2
CLOVER KNOLL CT
4200 SaCo 95608 279-D2
CLOVER LEAF CT
5300 EDCo 95667 264-G4
CLOVERLEAF WY
7000 CITH 95621 239-F6
CLOVER MANOR WY
5900 SaCo 95824 317-H5
CLOVER RANCH DR
- SaCo 95829 339-E6
CLOVER RANCH LN
- PlaC 95650 200-G4
CLOVER VALLEY RD
3100 RKLN 95650 200-F5
3100 RKLN 95677 200-F5
3500 LMS 95650 200-F5
3500 LMS 95677 200-F5
4000 RKLN 95677 220-D1
CLOVER WOODS CT
7600 SaCo 95828 338-C3
CLOVIS CT
7500 CITH 95610 260-A1
CLOYD ST
200 SAC 95838 277-G4
CLUB DR
2800 RKLN 95765 200-B7
CLUB LN
3300 SaCo 95821 278-F4
CLUB CENTER DR
- SAC 95835 256-J5
- SAC 95835 257-A5
CLUBHOUSE CT
- RKLN 95765 200-E4
CLUB HOUSE DR
200 RCCD 95670 280-A6
3000 SAC 95823 337-F1
CLUBHOUSE DR
- RKLN 95765 200-D5
- RVIS 94571 454-E1
6500 EDCo 95667 244-G3
CLUBHOUSE DR W
- RKLN 95765 200-D5
CLUBHOUSE LN
8000 SaCo 95693 360-H1
CLUB PARK DR
9700 ELKG 95757 357-E7

CLUBSIDE LN
- SaCo 95835 256-G6
CLUBVIEW CT
- RKLN 95765 200-D5
CLUNIE DR
100 SaCo 95864 298-E5
CLYDE CT
4100 SAC 95819 297-J3
CLYDEBANK LN
- FOLS 95630 262-A4
CLYDEBANK WY
4800 SaCo 95843 239-A6
CLYDESDALE CT
- EDCo 95667 266-E4
9000 ELKG 95624 358-H6
CLYDESDALE WY
- RSVL 95678 219-H4
CLYTIE WY
4400 SaCo 95864 298-J1
CMD CT
- ELKG 95624 378-J3
COACH LN
3300 EDCo 95682 263-F7
3300 EDCo 95682 283-G1
COACH LAMP LN
4500 RSVL 95747 219-A6
COACH LIGHT LN
100 LNCN 95648 179-J4
COACHLITE WY
6700 SAC 95831 316-H7
COACHMAN LN
900 LNCN 95648 179-J4
COACHMAN WY
6900 CITH 95621 259-G2
COACH WHIP WY
100 RSVL 95747 219-B5
COALDALE CT
5700 ELKG 95758 357-J3
COAN LN
8900 SaCo 95662 260-F4
COARSE GOLD PL
1800 SaCo 95670 280-B3
COARSEGOLD RD
2000 EDCo 95667 245-A4
COASTAL CT
- SAC 95831 336-F1
COAST OAK WY
8200 CITH 95610 240-B6
COBALT CT
3200 RKLN 95677 220-D1
COBALT WY
6800 CITH 95621 259-F2
COBB CT
100 FOLS 95630 261-G3
COBBLE CT
8000 PlaC 95746 240-H1
COBBLE BAY CT
- SaCo 95829 338-H7
COBBLE BROOK DR
11800 RCCD 95742 300-D7
11800 RCCD 95742 320-D1
COBBLE COVE LN
800 SAC 95831 336-H3
COBBLE CREEK CIR
- RKLN 95677 220-H3
COBBLE CREEK LN
- SaCo 95662 260-C4
COBBLE CREST DR
9000 SaCo 95829 338-H7
COBBLE FIELD DR
9000 SaCo 95829 338-H6
COBBLEFIELDS CT
- FOLS 95630 261-H4
COBBLE HILL WY
700 GALT 95632 419-F4
COBBLE HILLS CT
- RKLN 95765 220-A2
COBBLE LAKE CT
- SAC 95831 336-J3
COBBLEOAK CT
2300 RCCD 95670 279-J6
COBBLEOAK WY
100 FOLS 95630 261-B3
COBBLE POINT WY
- SaCo 95829 338-H6
COBBLE RIDGE DR
100 FOLS 95630 261-B6
COBBLEROCK DR
- RCCD 95670 299-J2
COBBLE SHORES DR
900 SAC 95831 336-J3
COBBLESTONE CT
500 RSVL 95747 219-A5
COBBLESTONE DR
1200 LNCN 95648 179-E2
3400 RKLN 95765 220-B1
11000 RCCD 95670 279-J6
11000 RCCD 95670 280-A6
COBBLESTONE LN
4000 SaCo 95608 279-G3
COBBLESTONE RD
6100 EDCo 95667 244-F6
COBBLESTONE WY
6900 CITH 95621 259-F1
COBBLEWOOD CT
4100 SaCo 95826 319-A2
COBDEN CT
800 GALT 95632 419-F3
COBDEN WY
800 GALT 95632 419-F3
COBERLY CT
- SaCo 95829 338-J6
COBRA CT
7800 CITH 95621 239-E7
COBURG CT
900 GALT 95632 419-F4
COCHISE CT
2800 RCCD 95670 299-G2
COCKATIEL CT
- EDCo 95682 283-J5
COCKLEBUR DR
5600 SAC 95823 337-J7
COCO LN
3700 SaCo 95660 258-G5
COCOA PALM WY
5000 SaCo 95628 260-B7
COCO BAY CT
7700 ELKG 95758 358-C4
COCONUT AL
- RSVL 95678 239-H1
COCONUT CT
3000 ANT 94509 (513-J6 See Page 493)
COCONUT WY
2300 SAC 95833 276-J6
COCONUT TREE CT
5300 ELKG 95757 377-J2
5300 ELKG 95757 397-J2

CODA LN
5600 SaCo 95608 299-C1
CODMAN LN
- SaCo 95628 260-A7
CODY CT
300 RSVL 95678 219-H6
2400 RKLN 95765 200-D5
CODY WY
3500 SaCo 95864 278-G7
COE LN
7200 SaCo 95829 339-E2
COEBURN ST
8400 SAC 95823 337-J7
8400 SAC 95823 357-J1
COED LN
8100 SaCo 95828 338-D3
COEFIELD RD
2300 PlaC 95603 161-G7
2300 PlaC 95603 181-G1
COFFEE LN
4400 SaCo 95841 258-J7
COFFEE BERRY CT
100 FOLS 95630 261-A3
COFFEEBERRY RD
- WSAC 95691 296-G7
COFFEEBERRY ST
- WSAC 95691 296-F7
COFFEE TREE CT
2600 ANT 94509 (513-H6 See Page 493)
COFFEE TREE WY
2600 ANT 94509 (513-H6 See Page 493)
COG HILL WY
- SaCo 95829 339-D5
COGNAC CIR
- SAC 95835 256-G7
COGNAC CT
4300 PlaC 95650 221-H1
COHN VALLEY WY
100 FOLS 95630 261-A4
COHO CT
2600 SaCo 95826 298-G6
COIBION CT
- RSVL 95678 220-A6
COIL CT
6100 SaCo 95660 258-H4
COIT PL
- WSAC 95691 296-J6
COKE ST
900 WSAC 95691 296-G4
COKE WY
500 EDCo 95619 265-E3
COKER CT
8400 SAC 95826 298-E7
COLBALT CT
1000 EDCo 95672 262-J1
1000 EDCo 95672 263-A1
COLBERT DR
- SaCo 95683 342-D3
COLBURN ST
9800 PlaC 95626 237-G3
COLBY CT
- SAC 95825 298-D5
COLBY WY
4400 SaCo 95608 279-E2
COLCHESTER AV
- SAC 95834 276-H1
COLD BROOK CT
- GALT 95632 419-F4
COLD BROOK WY
900 GALT 95632 419-F4
COLD HARBOR WY
- EDCo 95682 263-C2
COLD SPRINGS RD
- WSAC 95691 297-A7
1100 EDCo 95667 244-G1
1900 EDCo 95667 245-A4
2500 PLCR 95667 245-A4
COLD STREAM CT
500 RSVL 95747 219-A4
2200 SaCo 95670 280-C5
COLDSTREAM CT
- FOLS 95630 261-J2
COLD STREAM RD
5800 PlaC 95602 161-B2
COLD WATER CT
8400 ELKG 95624 338-J7
8400 ELKG 95624 358-J1
COLDWATER CT
- RKLN 95765 200-D6
COLDWATER DR
- RKLN 95765 200-E4
COLDWATER LN
- LNCN 95648 200-A1
COLDWATER PL
- RKLN 95765 200-E4
COLE AV
6200 SaCo 95608 279-D5
COLE CT
- FOLS 95630 281-C1
COLEEN CT
3400 SaCo 95821 278-G4
COLEMAN
6500 SaCo 95662 260-E4
COLEMAN CT
5600 RKLN 95677 220-G4
COLEMAN DR
6000 PlaC 95658 181-G7
COLEMAN ST
900 PLCR 95667 245-G4
COLEMAN WY
2400 SAC 95818 317-E2
2600 SAC 95817 317-E2
COLEMAN RANCH WY
7700 SAC 95831 336-J4
COLERAINE WY
- SaCo 95829 338-J6
COLE RANCH RD
700 PlaC 95602 162-G1
COLES POINT CT
- SAC 95823 358-B1
COLETTE WY
6400 SaCo 95660 258-J3
COLFAX ST
100 SAC 95815 277-G5
COLGATE CT
6100 SAC 95822 317-A6
COLIN RD
- EDCo 95667 245-C3
- PLCR 95667 245-C3
COLINA CT
3300 EDCo 95682 263-C5
COLINA LN
7000 SaCo 95683 342-B1
COLIN KELLY DR
400 PlaC 95747 238-J4
400 PlaC 95747 239-A5

COLISEUM WY
10600 RCCD 95670 279-G6
COLLEEN CT
2900 WSAC 95691 316-F1
COLLEGE AV
3400 SAC 95818 317-D1
3700 SAC 95822 317-D1
COLLEGE WY
- AUB 95603 182-E3
COLLEGEGLEN WY
- ELKG 95758 357-H3
COLLEGE OAK DR
4500 SaCo 95841 279-A2
5000 SaCo 95841 259-A7
COLLEGE TOWN DR
7500 SAC 95826 298-C7
COLLEGE VIEW WY
4300 SaCo 95608 279-B2
COLLEGIALITY WY
7800 CITH 95610 240-C7
COLLET QUARRY CT
- RKLN 95765 220-A2
COLLET QUARRY DR
- RKLN 95765 219-J2
- RKLN 95765 220-A2
E COLLIER RD
2800 SJCo 95220 439-H3
4000 SJCo 95220 (440-C5 See Page 420)
4000 SJCo 95632 (440-C5 See Page 420)
COLLINA CT
- PlaC 95746 241-A3
COLLINA PL
5000 SaCo 95841 259-B7
COLLINGS RD
10000 SaCo 95693 379-J2
COLLINGSWOOD DR
3100 EDCo 95762 263-A5
COLLINGTREE PARK DR
100 EDCo 95762 262-H4
COLLINGWOOD ST
7500 SAC 95822 337-D3
7500 SAC 95832 337-D3
COLLINS DR
900 PlaC 95603 182-C1
900 AUB 95603 182-C1
COLLINS ST
- WSAC 95691 316-C4
COLLISTON DR
9300 ELKG 95624 358-H5
COLMORE CT
900 GALT 95632 419-G4
COLMORE WY
900 GALT 95632 419-G4
COLNAR ST
1000 RSVL 95678 239-J3
COLOGNE LN
7600 CITH 95621 239-H7
7600 CITH 95621 259-H1
COLOMA CT
2600 PLCR 95667 245-E4
COLOMA RD
10100 RCCD 95670 299-F1
10500 RCCD 95670 279-H6
11000 RCCD 95670 280-A6
11100 SaCo 95670 280-A6
COLOMA RD Rt#-49
2500 EDCo 95667 225-A7
COLOMA ST
300 FOLS 95630 261-B4
2900 PLCR 95667 245-F5
COLOMA WY
- SAC 95819 297-J4
900 FOLS 95630 261-C5
900 RSVL 95661 239-J4
1100 RSVL 95661 240-A3
COLOMBARD WY
8900 SaCo 95829 338-H5
COLONEL RD
5500 SaCo 95608 279-C3
E COLONIAL CT
100 RSVL 95661 240-D5
COLONIAL DR
100 PlaC 95603 162-D4
E COLONIAL PKWY
1400 RSVL 95661 240-D5
W COLONIAL PKWY
1400 RSVL 95661 240-D5
COLONIAL WY
- RVIS 94571 454-F1
3900 SAC 95817 297-G7
COLONNADE DR
- LNCN 95648 199-H1
COLONNADE WY
2000 SaCo 95626 238-C7
COLONSAY WY
9100 SaCo 95829 338-J6
COLONY CT
3500 EDCo 95667 246-E5
COLONY LN
3500 LMS 95650 200-J6
COLONY RD
9700 SaCo 95693 360-B7
9700 SaCo 95693 (380-C1 See Page 379)
11000 SaCo 95693 (400-C1 See Page 379)
11200 SaCo 95632 (400-C2 See Page 379)
N COLONY WY
7600 CITH 95610 239-H6
COLONY HILL RD
11700 SaCo 95693 (380-D1 See Page 379)
COLORADO CT
- EDCo 247-E6
- EDCo 95726 247-F6
COLORADO ST
3100 SaCo 95608 279-C5
COLSON CT
900 GALT 95632 419-F4
COLSON WY
900 GALT 95632 419-G4
COLT CT
3300 EDCo 95623 265-A4
COLTON AV
9500 ELKG 95624 358-G6
COLUMBIA AV
- RSVL 95678 239-J1
COLUMBIA CIR
1000 EDCo 95762 242-B5
COLUMBIA DR
- SaCo 95864 298-H4
COLUMBIA DAM RD
400 PlaC 95658 180-J4
COLUMBINE WY
5100 SaCo 95608 259-D7

COLUMBUS AV
500 SAC 95833 277-F7
COLUMBUS RD
- WSAC 95691 296-J7
COLUSA RD
- WSAC 95691 316-H2
COLUSA WY
5400 SaCo 95841 259-B5
COLVIN CT
5300 SaCo 95628 259-G6
COLVIN DR
3300 LMS 95650 200-H5
S COLVIN DR
3500 LMS 95650 200-J5
COLWELL RD
5500 PlaC 95650 200-J2
5900 PlaC 95650 201-A2
COLWIN WY
- ELKG 95624 359-A5
COMANCHE WY
3600 SaCo 95843 238-G7
3600 SaCo 95843 258-G1
COMBELLACK RD
- PLCR 95667 245-E4
COMBO CT
- EDCo 95619 265-J5
COMET CT
3400 RCCD 95827 299-D6
COMFORT CT
6000 SaCo 95608 279-D3
COMMERCE CIR
100 SAC 95815 297-G1
COMMERCE DR
600 RSVL 95678 239-F4
3700 WSAC 95691 296-E3
COMMERCE WY
6500 EDCo 95667 265-D3
E COMMERCE WY
- SAC 95834 256-J7
- SAC 95834 276-J1
- SAC 95834 277-A1
- SAC 95835 256-J4
- SAC 95835 256-J4
COMMERCIAL ST
300 AUB 95603 182-D3
COMMERCIAL WY
1800 SAC 95818 297-D7
COMMODITY CT
4400 EDCo 95682 283-H2
COMMODORE CT
- SAC 95838 278-B1
COMMODORE LN
- SAC 95838 278-B2
COMMONS DR
300 SAC 95825 298-C5
COMMONWEALTH DR
7600 SaCo 95843 258-G1
7600 SaCo 95843 238-G7
COMMUNITY DR
400 RSVL 95678 239-G5
7500 CITH 95610 259-H3
COMPADRE CT
7100 SaCo 95608 279-G2
COMPASS CT
- ELKG 95758 357-J2
COMPONENT WY
7500 SaCo 95842 259-B1
COMPTON CT
2000 RCCD 95670 279-G6
COMPTON PARC LN
2700 SaCo 95608 279-C6
COMSTOCK CT
300 RSVL 95747 219-A4
5300 RKLN 95677 220-C3
COMSTOCK DR
800 FOLS 95630 261-B5
COMSTOCK LN
10300 PlaC 95603 202-B1
COMSTOCK RD
5300 EDCo 95667 244-E4
COMSTOCK ST
3700 RKLN 95677 220-C3
COMSTOCK WY
3500 SaCo 95608 279-A4
CONANT CT
9200 ELKG 95624 358-J5
CONBAR CT
2800 SaCo 95826 298-F7
CONCANNON CT
- OAKL 94561 (514-C5 See Page 493)
CONCANNON DR
1700 OAKL 94561 (514-D5 See Page 493)
CONCEPT MOUNTAIN CT
3600 EDCo 95623 264-G6
CONCEPT MOUNTAIN RD
3600 EDCo 95623 264-G7
CONCERT WY
6800 SaCo 95842 259-B2
CONCERTO CT
9000 ELKG 95758 358-B3
CONCETTA WY
3400 SaCo 95821 278-J4
CONCHAS CT
4300 ELKG 95758 357-G5
CONCHO CT
4800 SaCo 95841 279-C1
CONCORD DR
4700 SaCo 95628 280-A1
CONCORD RD
- RKLN 95765 200-B6
4900 SAC 95820 318-C4
CONCORDIA DR
4700 EDCo 95762 282-E2
CONCORD RIVER CT
11100 RCCD 95670 279-J5
11100 RCCD 95670 280-A5
CONDA WY
9500 ELKG 95624 359-A7
CONDESA DR
9100 SaCo 95826 318-J1
CONDOR CT
1600 RSVL 95661 240-B4
3500 SaCo 95608 279-A4
CONDOR LN
4100 EDCo 95709 246-J2
CONDUCTOR WY
100 FOLS 95630 281-B1
CONE CT
3700 RKLN 95677 220-D5
CONEJO
6300 SaCo 95683 322-B6
CONEJO DR
- LNCN 95648 179-E1
CONERS CT
100 FOLS 95630 261-E7
CONESTOGA LN
3700 EDCo 95667 244-C5

CONEY ISLAND CIR
SACRAMENTO COUNTY STREET INDEX
COVENTRY CT 530
SACRAMENTO CO.

STREET
Block City ZIP Pg-Grid

CONEY ISLAND CIR
- ELKG 95758 357-E6
CONFERENCE CENTER DR
- RSVL 95678 220-A5
CONFETTI CT
8200 ELKG 95624 358-E1
CONFIDENCE CT
1900 SaCo 95670 280-B4
CONGO RIVER CT
11100 RCCD 95670 279-J5
CONGRESS AV
900 SAC 95838 277-J4
CONIFER WY
2200 SAC 95838 278-C3
CONISTON CT
3700 SaCo 95843 238-G5
CONKLIN CT
7600 SaCo 95843 259-A1
CONLAN WY
- SaCo 95843 239-A7
CONLEY RD
11500 SaCo 95632 (400-A7 See Page 379)
12000 SaCo 95638 (400-E7 See Page 379)
CONNECTICUT DR
5100 SaCo 95841 259-C7
CONNECTOR ST
6700 SaCo 95823 317-F7
CONNELL CT
900 RSVL 95747 219-D7
CONNEMARA CIR
6700 CITH 95621 259-F5
CONNERY DR
- EDCo 95682 263-F4
CONNESS WY
6200 SaCo 95842 259-B4
CONNIE CT
5700 LMS 95650 200-J5
CONNIE DR
2300 SAC 95815 278-C5
3100 SAC 95821 278-C5
CONNOR CIR
- SAC 95835 257-C6
CONNOR ST
- RSVL 95678 219-G7
CONOVER DR
8200 CITH 95610 240-C6
CONQUISTADOR CT
7600 PlaC 95746 241-D2
CONRAD CT
800 PLCR 95667 245-F5
CONRAD DR
6800 SaCo 95828 338-B1
CONRAD LN
- PlaC 95650 221-B5
CONRAD ST
2900 PLCR 95667 245-F5
CONROY LN
1100 RSVL 95661 239-J3
1100 RSVL 95661 240-A3
CONSERVATION RD
9600 SaCo 95827 319-B1
CONSOLATION CT
2500 EDCo 95682 263-J6
CONSTABLE CT
- SAC 95835 256-J3
CONSTANCE LN
4300 SAC 95822 317-A3
CONSTANTINE CT
- EDCo 95762 262-B4
- SAC 95831 337-A5
CONSTELLATION AV
3000 PLCR 95667 245-G4
CONSTELLATION WY
5300 SaCo 95841 259-B7
CONSTITUTION AV
2600 WSAC 95691 296-F7
2600 WSAC 95691 316-F1
3900 SaCo 95660 258-H6
CONSTITUTION CT
1200 RSVL 95747 219-E7
CONTADA CT
1100 RSVL 95661 240-A5
CONTEMPO DR
3500 SaCo 95826 299-A7
3500 SaCo 95826 319-A1
CONTEMPORARY CT
9300 ELKG 95624 358-G5
CONTENTE WY
6400 ELKG 95758 358-A5
CONTINENTAL WY
3900 SaCo 95608 279-G3
CONTRA LOMA BLVD
2500 ANT 94509 (513-C6 See Page 493)
CONTRALTO WY
4000 SaCo 95843 238-H4
CONVAIR WY
7400 CITH 95621 259-F1
CONVAIR LINER RD
- SaCo 95655 300-A7
- SaCo 95655 320-A1
CONVENTION LN
6300 SAC 95828 318-A7
CONVERSE CT
- SAC 95835 256-J4
CONWAY CT
2800 SAC 95826 298-F7
CONWAY DR
- RVIS 94571 454-F1
CONWELL CT
900 GALT 95632 419-G4
CONZELMAN WY
- ELKG 95757 377-H2
- ELKG 95757 397-H2
COODY CT
5100 EDCo 95623 265-B6
COOK
5500 SaCo 95826 318-J4
5500 SaCo 95829 318-J4
COOK AV
7500 CITH 95610 259-H1
COOK ST
1100 ANT 94509 (513-C4 See Page 493)
3400 RKLN 95765 220-B1
COOKINGHAM WY
200 SAC 95838 277-G4
COOK ISLAND RD
- WSAC 95691 316-C2
COOK RANCH RD
- EDCo 95633 205-G1
COOK RIOLO RD
7800 SaCo 95843 239-C7
8000 PlaC 95747 239-C4
COOKS CT
- EDCo 95672 243-B5

COOKSON CT
6500 SaCo 95621 259-E5
6500 SaCo 95628 259-E5
COOL CT
4400 SaCo 95821 278-J3
COOLBRITH ST
1400 SAC 95822 317-B5
COOLEY CT
- EDCo 95762 262-D5
COOLFIELDS WY
7600 SaCo 95828 338-D4
COOL FOUNTAIN CT
- SAC 95833 276-G7
COOLIDGE DR
- FOLS 95630 261-A7
COOLIDGE WY
2300 RCCD 95670 279-H7
COOLLEY WY
5500 SaCo 95608 299-B2
COOL RIVER CT
- SAC 95831 336-G1
COOL SPRINGS CT
100 FOLS 95630 260-J1
COOL WATER CT
3600 EDCo 95667 245-A4
8500 SaCo 95843 238-J5
COOL WATER CREEK RD
2300 EDCo 95667 245-A4
COOL WIND WY
400 SAC 95831 336-G2
COOLWOODS WY
8600 SaCo 95828 338-F4
COON HOLLOW CT
2100 EDCo 95667 245-F6
COON HOLLOW RD
3500 EDCo 95667 245-F6
3500 PLCR 95667 245-F6
3800 EDCo 95667 265-G1
COOP DR
- ELKG 95757 377-J3
- ELKG 95757 378-A2
- ELKG 95757 397-J3
COOPER AV
100 SAC 95823 337-F2
COOPER LN
- LNCN 95648 180-A6
COOPER WY
2600 SaCo 95864 298-E2
5700 EDCo 95630 202-H5
COOPER MILL CT
5700 SaCo 95843 239-C6
COOPERS HAWK LP
- LNCN 95648 200-C1
COOPERSTON WY
8700 ELKG 95624 358-G3
COORS LN
500 PlaC 95602 162-G2
COOT AL
7600 CITH 95621 259-D1
COOT LN
- EDCo 95726 267-J3
COPA CT
6300 CITH 95621 239-E7
COPE LN
9100 PlaC 95602 161-F3
COPELAND CT
3500 SaCo 95843 238-G6
COPE RIDGE CT
- RSVL 95747 219-B3
COPE RIDGE WY
- RSVL 95747 219-B3
COPLEY CT
8500 SaCo 95628 260-D6
COPPA HEMBO LN
- EDCo 95633 205-B5
COPPENHAGEN WY
1600 SaCo 95608 299-A2
COPPER CT
3200 RKLN 95677 220-D1
COPPER WY
600 RSVL 95678 219-F7
600 RSVL 95678 239-F1
COPPER CANYON WY
8600 SaCo 95843 238-F4
COPPER COVE PL
7600 SaCo 95843 239-B7
COPPER CREEK DR
100 FOLS 95630 241-A7
COPPER CREST CT
- SAC 95834 277-B3
COPPERFIELD CIR
4700 PlaC 95746 240-G5
COPPERFIELD WY
4900 SaCo 95608 299-B3
COPPER FOX CT
7800 CITH 95610 259-J3
COPPER GLEN CIR
- RSVL 95678 220-A2
COPPER HILL CT
4100 SaCo 95843 238-H5
COPPER ISLAND RD
- WSAC 95691 316-D2
COPPER LAKE CT
- ELKG 95624 359-A7
COPPER LAKE WY
4000 RCCD 95742 300-D7
COPPER LEAF WY
100 SAC 95838 257-G7
COPPER OAK CT
7800 CITH 95610 259-J2
COPPER PENNEY DR
- SaCo 95843 238-H6
COPPER PENNY LN
3700 PlaC 95602 161-H2
COPPER RIDGE WY
5100 SaCo 95843 239-B5
COPPERSMITH AV
5100 SAC 95838 257-H7
COPPER SUNSET WY
4800 RCCD 95742 320-F4
COPPERTON RD
- EDCo - 247-C1
- EDCo 95709 247-C1
COPPERTREE WY
3900 SaCo 95821 278-J3
COPPERVALE CIR
- RKLN 95765 220-A2
COPPERVALE DR
- RKLN 95765 220-A2
COPPER VALLEY CT
9700 ELKG 95757 358-A7
COPPERWOOD CT
- LNCN 95648 200-A2
COPPERWOOD DR
- PlaC 95746 240-G4
7900 CITH 95610 260-A2
COPPING CT
- FOLS 95630 281-G2

COPPING WY
- FOLS 95630 281-G2
CORA CT
5800 SaCo 95824 317-G5
CORA LN
1300 AUB 95603 182-D3
CORABEL LN
- SaCo 95821 278-E6
CORAL DR
1100 RSVL 95661 239-J4
CORAL LN
- SAC 95815 277-J5
- SAC 95815 278-A5
CORAL BELLS DR
3600 EDCo 95762 263-B4
CORAL BERRY WY
8700 ELKG 95624 358-G1
CORAL CREEK WY
5400 ELKG 95758 357-J3
CORAL CREST CT
8500 ELKG 95624 358-F5
CORAL GABLES CT
100 SAC 95822 337-E3
100 SAC 95832 337-E3
CORAL HAVEN CT
5800 ELKG 95757 357-J6
5800 ELKG 95757 358-A6
CORALIE WY
100 FOLS 95630 261-D5
CORAL OAK WY
7900 CITH 95610 240-B7
CORAL REEF CT
6600 CITH 95621 259-F5
CORAL SUN CT
600 SaCo 95673 257-H1
CORALWOOD WY
3500 SaCo 95826 318-H1
CORANADO ST
- WSAC 95691 296-J7
- WSAC 95691 297-A7
- WSAC 95691 316-J1
CORATINA WY
4100 RCCD 95742 300-D7
CORAZON CT
- SAC 95835 257-A5
CORAZON WY
- SAC 95835 257-A6
CORBALLY CT
8800 ELKG 95624 358-G2
CORBIN WY
3300 RCCD 95827 299-D5
CORBRIDGE DR
- RSVL 95747 219-B7
CORCORAN CT
- LNCN 95648 179-E2
CORD WY
8600 SaCo 95828 338-F5
CORDANO WY
1500 SAC 95818 317-C1
CORDELIA CIR
8200 CITH 95621 239-G6
CORDER CT
- EDCo 95667 226-D3
CORDERO CT
- RSVL 95747 219-C1
4400 EDCo 95762 262-F3
CORDERO DR
4200 EDCo 95762 262-F3
CORDILLERA CT
600 FOLS 95630 261-E3
CORDONIZ CT
8600 SaCo 95662 260-E1
CORDOVA LN
2300 RCCD 95670 279-G7
2400 RCCD 95670 299-H1
CORDOVA GLEN CT
10000 RCCD 95827 299-D3
CORDOVAN DR
- RSVL 95678 219-G3
CORDWELL CIR
800 RSVL 95678 219-G7
CORE RD
4900 SaCo 95757 377-H6
4900 SaCo 95757 397-H6
CORFIELD DR
1100 RSVL 95747 239-C1
CORFU DR
10200 ELKG 95624 359-E1
CORIANDER WY
- SAC 95831 336-G3
CORIN DR
- RSVL 95747 218-J3
CORINA ST
3100 PLCR 95667 245-H5
CORINNE DR
8700 SaCo 95628 260-E6
8700 SaCo 95662 260-E6
CORINO WY
11700 RCCD 95742 320-D1
CORINTHIAN CIR
9200 SaCo 95826 298-J6
9200 SaCo 95826 299-A6
CORINTHIAN LN
- PlaC 95603 161-J4
- PlaC 95603 162-A4
CORK CIR
2300 SAC 95822 317-D5
CORKER ST
1100 PLCR 95667 245-H5
CORKOAKS WY
8000 CITH 95621 239-G6
CORK RIVER WY
500 SAC 95831 336-G1
CORKWOOD CT
- SAC 95833 277-C6
CORKY LN
- SaCo 95639 377-A5
- SaCo 95639 397-A5
CORLEY COVE LN
9400 ELKG 95624 339-A7
CORMORANT CIR
- RKLN 95765 219-H1
CORMORANT WY
1600 SAC 95815 278-B7
CORNADA CT
2800 EDCo 95682 263-D3
CORNEJO WY
7600 SaCo 95828 338-G3
CORNELIA WY
4000 SaCo 95660 258-H4
CORNELIUS WY
- ELKG 95758 357-E5
CORNELL RD
10500 GALT 95632 439-F1
10500 SaCo 95632 439-F1
CORNELL WY
1300 SAC 95831 317-B7
1500 PlaC 95603 162-D4

CORNERKICK LN
- ELKG 95758 357-F5
CORNERKICK PL
- ELKG 95758 357-F5
CORNERSTONE CT
- LNCN 95648 200-A2
CORNERSTONE DR
1000 FOLS 95630 261-E6
CORNER STONE RD
- EDCo 95667 267-A2
CORNERSTONE WY
8000 CITH 95621 239-E6
CORNFIELD WY
4300 ELKG 95758 357-H3
CORNFLOWER LN
- RKLN 95765 199-J4
CORNHILL WY
- FOLS 95630 261-J5
CORNICHE LN
- RSVL 95661 240-E1
CORNINA CT
- SAC 95823 337-J6
CORNISH CT
400 OAKL 94561 (514-D7 See Page 493)
CORNWALL CT
- RKLN 95677 220-F5
CORNWALL ST
6500 CITH 95621 259-E3
CORNWALL WY
- RKLN 95677 220-E5
CORODON ST
- SaCo 95690 437-A1
CORONA CIR
4700 RKLN 95677 220-G4
CORONA WY
4200 SaCo 95864 298-H3
CORONADO AV
100 RSVL 95678 239-J1
500 RSVL 95678 219-J7
CORONADO BLVD
600 SaCo 95864 298-G3
CORONADO CT
- EDCo 95762 262-C1
1500 ANT 94509 (513-A7 See Page 493)
CORONADO DR
- EDCo 95762 262-C1
CORONADO WY
- RVIS 94571 454-G2
5400 RKLN 95677 220-B3
CORONATION CT
6900 SaCo 95673 257-H2
CORONA VISTA WY
8400 SaCo 95628 260-C7
CORONAWOOD LN
5500 SaCo 95608 279-C5
CORONET CT
7200 CITH 95621 259-G2
COROVAL DR
- SAC 95833 277-A5
CORPORATE WY
7300 SAC 95831 336-J2
7300 SAC 95831 337-A1
CORPORATION YARD RD
100 RSVL 95678 219-G7
2200 RKLN 95677 220-F2
CORRAL CT
- RKLN 95765 200-D6
100 FOLS 95630 261-E5
CORRAL DR
2200 PlaC 95603 162-A4
CORRAL PL
900 GALT 95632 439-F1
CORRIENTE WY
2900 LNCN 95648 200-C1
CORRIGAN CT
- RSVL 95747 239-D1
100 FOLS 95630 261-E7
CORRIN WY
- ELKG 95757 377-J3
- ELKG 95757 378-A3
- ELKG 95757 397-J3
CORSAIR DR
2700 SaCo 95864 298-E3
CORSICA DR
- EDCo 95762 262-A2
CORSLEY LN
600 LNCN 95648 179-G5
CORTA WY
1300 SaCo 95864 298-H2
CORTADERA DR
8400 SaCo 95662 260-C3
CORTE DEL SOL CT
8600 ELKG 95624 358-F7
CORTE DORADO CT
8700 ELKG 95624 358-F7
CORTE LEONE WY
5800 SaCo 95842 259-C3
CORTE OCASO
- LNCN 95648 200-E2
CORTE SENDERO
- LNCN 95648 200-E2
CORTES ISLAND RD
- WSAC 95691 316-C2
CORTEZ AV
600 RSVL 95678 219-H7
CORTEZ CT
300 EDCo 95762 242-B4
2700 ANT 94509 (513-B6 See Page 493)
CORTEZ LN
2100 SaCo 95825 278-D7
CORTINA CIR
- RSVL 95678 219-H2
CORTINA CT
14800 SaCo 95683 342-A1
CORTINA RD
- WSAC 95691 296-J7
CORTINO WY
9800 ELKG 95757 378-B1
CORTLANDT DR
700 SaCo 95864 298-H4
CORTNEY CT
- SAC 95832 337-D4
CORTO LN
200 CITH 95621 239-G6
CORTON WY
- ELKG 95624 379-A1
CORTRIGHT WY
4000 SaCo 95660 258-H2
CORVA WY
6000 SAC 95820 318-A4
CORVAIR ST
5000 SaCo 95660 258-G7
CORVET WY
5100 SaCo 95823 317-J7
CORVEY CIR
700 GALT 95632 419-E2

CORVINA DR
3300 RCCD 95670 299-J4
3500 RCCD 95670 300-A4
CORWIN CT
3400 LMS 95650 200-J5
9300 ELKG 95758 358-B5
CORY CT
4800 SaCo 95608 279-A5
COSGROVE WY
7400 SAC 95822 337-C2
COSMO LN
3200 EDCo 95682 264-B2
COSMOS AV
3300 SaCo 95864 298-F4
COSMOS CT
- RKLN 95677 220-H5
COSO CT
- SAC 95838 257-G7
COSSANI CT
6700 ELKG 95757 358-B7
COSTA CT
2700 WSAC 95691 316-F2
COSTA LN
- LNCN 95648 179-J1
- LNCN 95648 180-A1
COSTA WY
5100 SaCo 95841 259-B5
COSTA BRASE CT
- SAC 95838 257-G7
COSTALOTTA DR
3200 EDCo 95667 244-F7
COSTA MESA CIR
7500 SaCo 95660 258-F1
COSTCO WY
- ANT 94509 (513-A4 See Page 493)
COSTELLO CT
- FOLS 95630 281-G2
COSUMNES RD
9700 SaCo 95693 359-J7
9800 SaCo 95693 379-J1
COSUMNES RIVER BLVD
- SaCo 95758 338-C7
- SaCo 95828 338-C7
4800 SAC 95823 337-H6
4800 SAC 95823 338-A6
6800 SAC 95758 338-C7
COSUMNES VIEW TR
- EDCo 95684 286-G5
COSUMNES VISTA RD
- EDCo 95619 286-F4
COTATI CT
- OAKL 94561 (514-E6 See Page 493)
COTE D OR DR
- ELKG 95624 379-A1
COTHAM LN
- SaCo 95628 280-E1
COTILLION WY
7300 CITH 95621 259-G1
COTSWALD WY
7700 CITH 95610 259-J5
COTTAGE CT
700 PLCR 95667 245-F5
COTTAGE DR
2300 PlaC 95603 162-B4
COTTAGE LN
4700 RSVL 95747 219-A6
COTTAGE ST
800 PLCR 95667 245-F5
COTTAGE WY
2100 SaCo 95825 278-C7
3300 SaCo 95825 298-J1
3400 SaCo 95864 298-J1
4600 SaCo 95608 299-A1
4600 SaCo 95864 299-A1
COTTAGE GROVE WY
7800 SaCo 95843 238-J7
COTTAGE PARK AV
3100 SaCo 95825 298-F1
COTTAGE ROSE LN
- LNCN 95648 179-J7
- LNCN 95648 180-A7
- LNCN 95648 199-J1
COTTERDALE CT
12000 RCCD 95742 320-E4
COTTERDALE ALY
2300 SAC 95835 257-A3
COTTINGHAM CT
7800 CITH 95610 259-J1
COTTINGHAM WY
7700 CITH 95610 259-J1
COTTLE AV
800 SaCo 95673 257-J1
COTTON LN
7800 SAC 95758 338-C7
COTTONBALL WY
8200 SaCo 95828 338-D3
COTTON CREEK CT
9200 SaCo 95829 338-J7
COTTONFIELD WY
8200 SaCo 95828 338-D3
COTTONGIN WY
8200 SaCo 95828 338-D3
COTTONGLEN CT
700 RSVL 95661 240-D3
COTTONGLEN WY
8200 SaCo 95828 338-D3
COTTONLEAF WY
7900 SaCo 95828 338-C3
COTTONMILL CIR
8100 SaCo 95828 338-D3
COTTONRIDGE CIR
8100 SaCo 95828 338-D3
COTTONTAIL RD
- EDCo 95619 265-J6
COTTONTAIL WY
3900 SAC 95823 337-G3
COTTONTREE WY
7500 SaCo 95828 338-C3
COTTONWOOD CIR
1500 PlaC 95603 162-D5
COTTONWOOD CT
- LNCN 95648 179-H5
1900 FOLS 95630 282-A1
5900 RKLN 95677 220-D5
COTTONWOOD DR
800 RSVL 95661 240-B4
COTTONWOOD LN
- EDCo 95667 266-C4
7900 SaCo 95828 338-E5
COTTRELL CT
- GALT 95632 419-H3
COTTRELL WY
- GALT 95632 419-H3
COUEY LN
6800 PlaC 95663 181-B7
COUGAR CT
- RKLN 95765 199-J4

COUGAR DR
100 SAC 95828 318-B7
COUGAR LN
2800 PLCR 95667 245-E4
COUGAR WY
- EDCo 95667 265-D1
COUGAR HILLS WY
4200 SaCo 95843 238-J7
COULSTON CT
500 RSVL 95747 219-D7
COULTER CT
3200 SaCo 95843 238-F5
COULTERVILLE CT
11600 SaCo 95670 280-C4
COUNCIL ROCK RD
- RSVL 95747 219-B3
COUNT
- RCCD 95827 299-E4
COUNTESS
- RCCD 95827 299-E4
COUNTRY CT
6900 PlaC 95746 241-B4
COUNTRY LN
- EDCo 95619 266-A7
- OAKL 94561 (514-D5 See Page 493)
1600 EDCo 95619 265-J6
2000 PlaC 95603 161-E7
6000 CITH 95621 259-D4
COUNTRY PL
- SAC 95831 316-H7
OAKL 94561 (514-D5 See Page 493)
COUNTRY RD
4200 PlaC 95648 180-F4
7500 PlaC 95650 221-D4
COUNTRY WY
10100 RCCD 95827 299-E5
COUNTRY ACRES LN
5000 PlaC 218-B4
8200 SaCo 95828 338-E7
COUNTRY CLUB DR
1400 PLCR 95667 246-A6
1500 PLCR 95667 245-J6
2000 RSVL 95747 239-D1
2400 EDCo 95682 263-B7
2400 EDCo 95682 283-A1
2500 EDCo 95762 282-J1
2500 EDCo 95762 283-A1
2500 RSVL 95747 219-D7
COUNTRY CLUB LN
3300 SaCo 95821 278-F5
E COUNTRY CLUB LN
3400 SaCo 95821 278-F4
W COUNTRY CLUB LN
3400 SaCo 95821 278-F4
COUNTRY COVE CT
7700 CITH 95610 259-J2
COUNTRY CREEK DR
8600 SaCo 95662 240-E7
COUNTRY FALLS LN
9600 ELKG 95757 357-J7
COUNTRYFIELD DR
7600 SaCo 95828 338-D3
COUNTRY GARDEN DR
11800 RCCD 95742 320-E4
COUNTRY GLEN CT
8300 SaCo 95828 338-E5
COUNTRY GREENS CT
8400 SaCo 95828 338-E5
COUNTRY HAVEN CT
3800 SaCo 95821 278-H3
COUNTRY HILL DR
8800 ELKG 95624 358-H2
COUNTRY HILL RUN
- PlaC 95603 161-B7
COUNTRY LAKE DR
8200 SaCo 95662 240-D6
COUNTRY MANOR PL
5900 SAC 95835 257-A3
COUNTRY MEADOW CT
3600 PlaC 95602 161-J3
COUNTRY OAK CT
9900 ELKG 95624 378-H1
COUNTRY PARK CT
9800 PlaC 95661 240-E6
COUNTRY PARK DR
3700 PlaC 95661 240-E6
7600 SaCo 95828 338-D4
COUNTRY PLACE DR
2500 PlaC 95747 239-C2
COUNTRY RANCH DR
8200 SaCo 95829 339-D6
COUNTRY RIM CT
200 RSVL 95747 219-A5
COUNTRY RIVER WY
300 SAC 95831 336-F3
COUNTRYROADS DR
9400 SaCo 95827 299-B7
COUNTRY ROCK WY
- SaCo 95670 280-B4
COUNTRY RUN WY
4300 SaCo 95843 238-J5
COUNTRY SCENE WY
4600 SAC 95823 337-H5
COUNTRYSIDE CT
5100 EDCo 95667 244-E4
COUNTRYSIDE DR
400 LNCN 95648 179-F3
2300 EDCo 95667 244-D4
COUNTRYSIDE WY
10100 RCCD 95827 299-E5
COUNTRY TRAIL DR
7900 SaCo 95662 240-E6
COUNTRY VIEW LN
4900 SaCo 95628 280-B1
COUNTRY VILLA CT
2200 PlaC 95603 162-B5
COUNTRY VILLA DR
2000 PlaC 95603 162-B5
COUNTRY VISTA LN
8100 SaCo 95628 280-A1
8700 SaCo 95662 260-E2
COUNTRYWOOD DR
2700 ANT 94509 (513-F6 See Page 493)
COUNTRYWOOD WY
6800 CITH 95621 259-F5
COUNTRYWOODS LN
6500 PlaC 95746 241-B6
COUNTY ACRES LN
6300 PlaC 95626 238-A1
COUNTY CENTER DR
- PlaC 95603 162-A3
COUNTY DOWN CT
- RSVL 95678 219-J5
COUNTY ROAD 16
- YoCo 95645 236-A1
38400 YoCo 95645 235-A1

COUNTY ROAD 16
45100 YoCo 95776 235-B1
COUNTY ROAD 17
41400 YoCo 95776 235-A3
COUNTY ROAD 22
- YoCo 95605 255-A4
- YoCo 95776 255-A4
COUNTY ROAD 103
- YoCo 95776 235-A4
COUNTY ROAD 107
- YoCo 95612 375-E1
- YoCo 95612 (395-E1 See Page 375)
COUNTY ROAD 116B
35000 YoCo 95645 235-B1
COUNTY ROAD 117
- YoCo 95645 236-B1
- YoCo 95776 235-H7
- YoCo 95776 236-A4
COUNTY ROAD 117S
- YoCo 95605 255-F3
- YoCo 95776 235-G7
- YoCo 95776 255-F2
COUNTY ROAD 118
- YoCo 95605 255-F5
COUNTY ROAD 119
- YoCo 95605 255-G6
COUNTY ROAD 124
- YoCo 95605 255-H7
- YoCo 95605 276-A4
COUNTY ROAD 126
- YoCo 95605 276-D7
COUNTY ROAD 141
52600 YoCo 95612 356-H7
COUNTY ROAD 142
53000 YoCo 95612 (376-G4 See Page 375)
COUNTY ROAD 143
- YoCo 95612 (376-D7 See Page 375)
- YoCo 95612 (396-D1 See Page 375)
COUNTY ROAD 144
37100 YoCo 95612 356-G7
37300 YoCo 95612 (376-H1 See Page 375)
COUNTY ROAD 146B
- YoCo 95612 356-G5
COUNTY ROAD 155
44500 YoCo 95612 375-A2
COUNTY ROAD 159
- YoCo 95612 (395-E2 See Page 375)
COUNTY ROAD 161
- SolC 94571 (395-E5 See Page 375)
- YoCo 95612 (395-E5 See Page 375)
COUNTY ROAD 387
- EDCo 95682 263-E5
COUPLES CT
10200 SaCo 95829 339-E4
COURANTE CT
- RSVL 95747 219-B1
COURANTE WY
- RSVL 95747 219-B1
COURBET WY
- EDCo 95762 262-G3
COURT PKWY
7400 SaCo 95823 337-H2
COURT ST
100 AUB 95603 182-D3
COURTENAY CT
900 GALT 95632 419-F2
COURTLAND LN
- SaCo 95608 279-A4
COURTLAND RD
- YoCo 95612 (395-E1 See Page 375)
49400 YoCo 95612 (396-B1 See Page 375)
COURTLAND RD Rt#-84
48000 YoCo 95612 (395-F1 See Page 375)
48000 YoCo 95612 (396-A1 See Page 375)
N COURTLAND RD
47000 YoCo 95612 375-F6
49000 YoCo 95612 (376-A6 See Page 375)
COURTLY MANOR DR
- EDCo 95667 266-E4
COURTNEY CT
- PlaC 95747 239-B3
5900 SaCo 95662 260-G5
COURTNEY WY
- EDCo 95762 262-H5
- PlaC 95747 239-B4
COURTSIDE DR
600 EDCo 95619 265-F2
2700 RSVL 95661 240-E3
COURTYARD WY
4400 SaCo 95843 238-J7
COURTYARDS LP
- LNCN 95648 179-F5
COURTYARDS WY
- LNCN 95648 179-F6
COURVILLE CT
5900 SaCo 95628 260-B5
COUSTEAU CT
5900 ELKG 95758 357-J6
5900 ELKG 95758 358-A6
COUTS WY
100 FOLS 95630 281-B1
COVAL CT
100 FOLS 95630 261-G3
COVE CT
- RSVL 95747 218-J5
- SaCo 95683 322-D7
- SAC 95831 316-H7
S COVE DR
7700 SAC 95831 336-H3
COVE LN
- RSVL 95747 218-J6
W COVE WY
800 SAC 95831 336-H3
COVELLO CIR
3500 EDCo 95682 263-A6
COVENANT CT
- PlaC 95650 221-E3
COVEN HILLS PL
8300 SaCo 95843 239-B5
COVENTRY CIR
- FOLS 95630 281-A1
COVENTRY CT
- FOLS 95630 281-B1
- ANT 94509 (513-E6 See Page 493)
8300 PlaC 95746 240-G2

STREET	Block	City	ZIP	Pg-Grid
COVENTRY DR				
	6800	CITH	95621	259-F2
COVERDALE CT				
	2200	FOLS	95630	281-F1
COVERED BRIDGE RD				
	-	SaCo	95608	279-D7
COVERED BRIDGE WY				
	-	EDCo	95762	282-D4
COVERED WAGON CIR				
	2300	SaCo	95626	238-D6
COVERED WAGON CT				
	-	RKLN	95765	199-J5
	3300	SaCo	95827	299-B6
COVERED WAGON DR				
	1000	OAKL	94561	(514-E7 See Page 493)
COVERED WAGON LN				
	-	RKLN	95765	199-J4
COVEWOOD CT				
	6000	CITH	95621	239-D7
COVEY CT				
	-	ELKG	95624	358-H4
	-	PLCR	95667	246-A6
COVEY DR				
	-	PLCR	95667	246-A6
COVEY RD				
	100	PlaC	95603	162-D4
COVEY WY				
	1500	EDCo	95762	242-F5
COVEY CREEK WY				
	-	SAC	95823	338-B6
COVINA LN				
	8200	SaCo	95828	338-D3
COVINGTON CT				
	5500	SaCo	95842	259-C3
COWAN CIR				
	3100	SaCo	95821	278-G5
COWAN CT				
	500	RSVL	95747	219-E6
COWBIRD CT				
	-	LNCN	95648	200-B3
	-	SAC	95834	276-H4
COWBOY TR				
	-	EDCo	95667	266-G3
COWBOY WY				
	-	CITH	95621	259-E3
COWDEN CT				
	6000	SaCo	95662	260-F5
COWDRAY CT				
	-	SaCo	95829	339-F7
COWHIDE CT				
	5400	EDCo	95667	244-D4
COX AV				
	-	SaCo	95628	280-C2
COX ST				
	6100	EDCo	95726	248-C1
COYLE AV				
	5900	SaCo	95608	259-D6
COYLE CREEK CIR				
	-	SaCo	95628	259-G6
COYOTE CT				
	-	AUB	95603	182-B7
	6600	SaCo	95662	260-B3
COYOTE LN				
	500	PlaC	95648	180-E3
COYOTE RD				
	-	WSAC	95691	316-C3
COYOTE CREEK CT				
	2100	SaCo	95670	280-D5
COYOTE FORK PL				
	-	SAC	95835	257-A3
COYOTE HILL RD				
	-	EDCo	-	267-D2
COYOTE PASS CT				
	2200	EDCo	95682	283-J6
COYOTE PASS RD				
	5100	EDCo	95682	283-J6
COYOTE RIDGE CT				
	3900	SaCo	95660	258-H1
COZBY CT				
	5300	SaCo	95628	260-D6
COZUMEL DR				
	15000	SaCo	95683	342-B2
COZY LN				
	800	EDCo	95667	245-G6
COZZINS CT				
	-	SaCo	95628	260-B7
CRABTREE CT				
	4000	SaCo	95608	279-F3
CRADLE BAR CT				
	100	FOLS	95630	261-E4
CRADLE MOUNTAIN CT				
	-	EDCo	95762	263-A6
CRAFT CT				
	8100	SaCo	95662	260-B2
CRAFTON CT				
	8100	SaCo	95828	338-E6
CRAFTSMAN CT				
	7800	SaCo	95843	238-J7
CRAGMONT CT				
	-	EDCo	95682	263-C4
CRAIG AV				
	2200	SAC	95832	337-D4
CRAIG CT				
	5900	LMS	95650	200-J5
CRAIG ST				
	5800	LMS	95650	200-J5
CRAIGHTON AV				
	400	SaCo	95626	237-H6
CRAIGHURST DR				
	6400	SaCo	95660	258-H3
CRAIGMONT ST				
	1900	SAC	95815	278-B4
CRAIL CT				
	7100	CITH	95610	260-A2
CRAIL WY				
	5000	EDCo	95762	262-G4
CRANBERRY CT				
	6600	CITH	95621	239-F7
CRANBERRY LN				
	-	EDCo	95762	242-C7
CRANBORNE CT				
	500	RSVL	95747	239-C1
CRANBROOK CT				
	3100	EDCo	95682	263-C4
CRANBROOK WY				
	5500	SaCo	95628	260-B6
CRANDALL AV				
	3000	SAC	95815	278-A5
CRANE CT				
	-	OAKL	94561	(514-H6 See Page 493)
	200	RSVL	95747	219-C6
	2100	SaCo	95825	278-D7
CRANE WY				
	-	LNCN	95648	179-D2
	2600	EDCo	95682	263-B4
CRANE MEADOW CT				
	-	RSVL	95661	220-D7
CRANFORD WY				
	8300	CITH	95610	260-C2
CRANLEIGH AV				
	6900	SAC	95823	358-B1
CRANLEIGH DR				
	9800	PlaC	95746	240-G6
CRANMORE CT				
	7900	CITH	95610	260-A2
CRANOR DR				
	1900	RCCD	95670	279-G6
CRANSTON CT				
	-	EDCo	95762	262-H4
CRANSTON WY				
	7300	SAC	95822	337-C2
CRANWELL CT				
	8000	SaCo	95829	339-A7
CRATER WY				
	6600	SaCo	95842	259-B3
CRATER BUTTE WY				
	4900	SaCo	95843	239-A6
CRATER HILL RD				
	8400	PlaC	95658	181-E1
	9400	PlaC	95603	181-G1
CRATER LAKE DR				
	-	RSVL	95678	220-A3
CRATER LAKE WY				
	-	ELKG	95758	357-G6
CRATOR PEAK PL				
	-	FOLS	95630	261-F1
CRAWDAD CT				
	-	SAC	95833	276-G7
CRAWFORD DR				
	-	RCCD	95670	300-A3
CRAWFORD WY				
	10100	RCCD	95827	299-E5
CRAWFORD DRIFT CT				
	-	PLCR	95667	245 G4
CRAWLEY LN				
	2200	EDCo	95667	245-G2
CRAYDON PL				
	1300	EDCo	95762	262-D3
CRAZY HORSE CT				
	-	EDCo	95682	283-A1
CRAZY HORSE RD				
	-	EDCo	95682	283-B1
CREACH CT				
	-	FOLS	95630	281-G1
CREDENZA CT				
	4500	EDCo	95619	265-H4
CREE WY				
	4100	SaCo	95843	238-H7
CREED AV				
	100	ANT	94509	(513-C5 See Page 493)
CREEK RD				
	4600	SaCo	95841	278-J1
CREEKBED LN				
	6300	CITH	95621	259-E4
CREEK BEND WY				
	7700	SaCo	95829	339-D4
CREEKBERRY WY				
	-	EDCo	95762	282-D5
CREEK CENTRE CT				
	6400	SAC	95823	338-B4
CREEK CREST CIR				
	6300	CITH	95621	259-E5
CREEKCREST CT				
	-	LNCN	95648	180-B6
CREEKCREST LN				
	-	LNCN	95648	180-A7
CREEK ESTATES WY				
	-	SaCo	95829	339-D6
CREEKFRONT LN				
	8000	CITH	95610	240-C7
CREEKHAVEN RD				
	4000	PlaC	95602	161-J1
CREEK HAVEN WY				
	6500	CITH	95621	259-E4
CREEKMONT WY				
	6500	CITH	95621	259-F2
CREEK OAKS LN				
	8700	SaCo	95662	240-E7
CREEK RANCH RD				
	1800	EDCo	95667	244-A2
CREEK RIDGE CT				
	1100	RSVL	95747	219-E4
CREEKRIDGE LN				
	7500	CITH	95610	260-C1
CREEKS EDGE WY				
	-	SAC	95823	337-G3
CREEKSIDE CIR				
	100	SAC	95823	337-G4
	7500	CITH	95610	260-C1
CREEKSIDE CT				
	-	FOLS	95630	261-D6
	300	LNCN	95648	179-H4
	700	RSVL	95678	239-J4
	3900	EDCo	95682	264-B7
CREEKSIDE DR				
	1200	FOLS	95630	261-E5
	4000	EDCo	95682	264-B7
	4300	RKLN	95677	220-F3
CREEKSIDE LN				
	1500	EDCo	95672	243-B4
	1900	PlaC	95650	200-F1
	2000	PlaC	95663	200-F1
	2600	SaCo	95821	278-F6
	8000	PlaC	95746	241-B1
CREEKSIDE PL				
	3800	PlaC	95602	162-B1
CREEKSIDE WY				
	200	GALT	95632	439-E2
CREEKSIDE OAKS DR				
	1700	SAC	95833	277-C6
CREEKSIDE RIDGE CT				
	-	RSVL	95678	220-B6
CREEKSIDE RIDGE DR				
	-	RSVL	95678	220-B6
CREEKSTONE CIR				
	-	PlaC	95747	239-A3
CREEKSTONE CT				
	-	PlaC	95747	239-A3
CREEK TREE CT				
	5100	SaCo	95841	259-B7
CREEK VALLEY CIR				
	7800	SaCo	95828	338-D5
CREEKVIEW CT				
	4000	RKLN	95677	220-E5
	12900	PlaC	95603	162-E4
CREEK VIEW LN				
	2800	PLCR	95667	245-C4
CREEK VIEW WY				
	4900	SaCo	95841	259-B7
CREEKWOOD DR				
	3500	RKLN	95677	200-E7
CREEKWOOD WY				
	8500	SaCo	95628	280-D1
CREGAN CT				
	4300	RCCD	95742	320-F2
CREIGHTON WY				
	5900	SaCo	95842	258-J5
CRENSHAW CT				
	-	RSVL	95746	240-F4
CRENSHAW WY				
	2500	SaCo	95826	298-H6
CRESCENT CIR				
	-	LNCN	95648	180-C6
CRESCENT CT				
	2900	SaCo	95825	278-E7
CRESCENT DR				
	-	RSVL	95678	219-G5
	100	RVIS	94571	454-H5
	300	GALT	95632	419-E6
CRESCENT LN				
	-	LNCN	95648	180-C7
CRESCENT ST				
	900	PLCR	95667	245-G5
CRESCENT WY				
	-	LNCN	95648	180-C6
CRESENDO DR				
	1100	RSVL	95678	239-G5
CRESENTDALE WY				
	7800	SAC	95823	337-J4
CRESENTWOODS				
	5000	SAC	95823	337-J5
CRESLEIGH PKWY				
	-	ELKG	95757	358 A6
CRESSIDA ST				
	-	RSVL	95747	239-A1
CRESSWELL CT				
	8800	ELKG	95624	358-G2
CREST CT				
	8800	PlaC	95746	241-D3
CREST DR				
	-	RKLN	95677	200-D7
	-	SAC	95835	257-C6
	5300	RKLN	95765	220-C1
	5300	RKLN	95765	200-D7
	6500	PlaC	95658	201-G1
CREST RD				
	-	SaCo	95628	280-C2
CREST ST				
	200	ANT	94509	(513-E4 See Page 493)
CRESTA CT				
	100	LNCN	95648	180-E7
	700	EDCo	95762	242-C4
CRESTA WY				
	-	SaCo	95864	298-H2
CRESTA BLANCA CT				
	-	OAKL	94561	(514-C5 See Page 493)
	8000	SaCo	95829	338-H6
CRESTA VERDE DR				
	-	EDCo	-	247-G2
CRESTFIELD CIR				
	-	RSVL	95678	219-G4
CRESTHAM CT				
	6600	ELKG	95758	358-A5
CRESTHAVEN DR				
	1100	RSVL	95678	239-G5
	3000	SaCo	95821	278-F6
CRESTHILL DR				
	11700	SaCo	95624	340-D3
CRESTLEIGH CT				
	7800	SaCo	95843	238-J7
CRESTLINE AV				
	4100	SaCo	95628	280-A2
CRESTLINE CIR				
	1000	EDCo	95762	262-B7
CRESTLINE CT				
	1200	EDCo	95762	262-B7
CRESTLINE DR				
	-	EDCo	95667	266-J5
	-	EDCo	95667	267-A5
CREST MAR CIR				
	1900	EDCo	95762	242-B6
CREST MAR CT				
	2000	EDCo	95762	242-C6
CRESTMONT AV				
	1200	RSVL	95661	240-B5
	1600	CITH	95610	240-B5
CRESTMONT LN				
	2200	EDCo	95667	245-H2
CRESTMONT OAK DR				
	1500	RSVL	95661	240-B6
CRESTON CT				
	3200	SaCo	95843	238-F7
CRESTRIDGE LN				
	100	FOLS	95630	261-C3
CRESTRIDGE RD				
	4400	SaCo	95628	279-H2
CRESTSHIRE CIR				
	8200	SaCo	95662	260-C4
CRESTVIEW DR				
	500	EDCo	95619	265-E3
	1200	ANT	94509	(513-B4 See Page 493)
	2700	PLCR	95667	245-F4
	4700	SaCo	95608	279-D1
	4900	SaCo	95608	259-D7
CRESTVIEW LN				
	7100	PlaC	95746	220-H7
CRESTVIEW WY				
	300	PlaC	95603	162-F5
CRESTWATER LN				
	700	SAC	95831	316-G6
CRESTWOOD DR				
	1800	ANT	94509	(513-E5 See Page 493)
CRESTWOOD WY				
	-	RKLN	95765	200-D6
	4400	SAC	95822	317-A3
CRETE AV				
	7200	SAC	95824	318-B4
CRETE WY				
	1000	RSVL	95678	239-G1
CREVALLE PL				
	-	SAC	95835	256-G4
CREW CT				
	-	PlaC	95603	162-C4
CRIBARI CT				
	-	SAC	95838	277-H2
CRIBBS CT				
	3000	PLCR	95667	245-E5
CRIBBS RD				
	400	EDCo	95667	245-E5
	400	PLCR	95667	245-E5
CRICHTON WY				
	-	ELKG	95758	358-D3
CRICKET CT				
	-	LNCN	95648	180-A6
	600	SaCo	95864	299-A4
CRICKET LN				
	10200	PlaC	95603	202-A1
CRICKET CLUB CT				
	-	RKLN	95765	200-E4
CRIMORA CT				
	10000	RCCD	95827	299-D6
CRIMSON CT				
	4700	SaCo	95842	259-A2
	12500	AUB	95603	162-D5
CRIMSON RIDGE CT				
	-	RKLN	95765	220-A2
CRIMSON RIDGE DR				
	-	RKLN	95765	220-A2
CRIMSON RIDGE WY				
	-	RSVL	95747	219-C3
CRIMSON SAGE CT				
	8200	SaCo	95829	339-D7
CRIMSONWOOD WY				
	9800	RCCD	95827	299-C6
CRIOLLO CT				
	-	ELKG	95757	357-H7
CRIPPLE CREEK LN				
	9500	PlaC	95658	201-J4
CRIPPLE CREEK RD				
	7500	CITH	95610	239-H7
CRIPPLE OAK CT				
	8200	CITH	95610	240-C6
CRISP CT				
	1200	SaCo	95864	298-E3
CRISSWELL DR				
	9500	ELKG	95624	359-A6
CRISTALLA PL				
	-	SAC	95835	257-A3
CRISTELLA CT				
	-	ELKG	95757	358-A7
CRISTO DR				
	10000	SaCo	95829	339-D7
CRISTO WY				
	9400	ELKG	95758	357-H6
CRISTOBAL WY				
	10900	RCCD	95670	279-J6
CRISTOM DR				
	3300	RCCD	95670	300-A4
CRITTER HILL RD				
	5800	EDCo	95667	244-G7
CROATIA CT				
	1000	RSVL	95661	239-J5
CROCE CT				
	-	FOLS	95630	281-G2
CROCKER DR				
	1200	EDCo	95762	242-A5
CROCKER LN				
	-	LNCN	95648	180-A5
CROCKER RD				
	400	SaCo	95864	298-F4
	9300	PlaC	95746	240-H4
CROCKER GROVE LN				
	11200	SaCo	95670	280-B4
CROCKER RANCH RD				
	-	EDCo	-	247-G2
	-	RSVL	95747	219-B1
CROCKETT RD				
	1400	PlaC	95603	182-D6
CROCUS CT				
	8700	ELKG	95624	358-G2
CROETTO WY				
	10400	RCCD	95670	299-F2
CROFOOT CT				
	8600	PlaC	95746	241-C3
CROFT LN				
	5500	RKLN	95650	220-J2
	5500	LMS	95650	220-J2
CROFTERS LN				
	5700	SaCo	95608	279-C1
CROFTON CT				
	9000	SaCo	95829	338-H6
CROFTWOOD DR				
	-	RKLN	95677	220-H2
CROMAN PT				
	-	AUB	95603	182-B7
CROMBIE CT				
	4600	PlaC	95746	240-G5
CROMWELL CT				
	400	RSVL	95746	240-G4
	1300	EDCo	95762	242-C5
CROMWELL WY				
	7000	SAC	95822	337-C1
CRONDALL DR				
	3800	SaCo	95864	298-G5
CRONIN CT				
	4900	SaCo	95628	260-E7
CROOKED LN				
	700	PlaC	95658	182-A6
CROOKED BRANCH RD				
	3600	EDCo	95682	283-H4
CROOKED STICK DR				
	10000	SaCo	95829	339-D5
CROOKEN RIVER CT				
	11100	RCCD	95670	279-J5
	11100	RCCD	95670	280-A5
CROPTON CT				
	-	RSVL	95747	218-J5
CROSBY WY				
	2500	SAC	95815	278-B6
CROSBY HAROLD RD				
	2000	PlaC	-	160-D3
	2200	PlaC	95648	160-D5
CROSBY HEROLD RD				
	2000	PlaC	95648	160-D7
CROSS DR				
	6900	SaCo	95662	260-B2
	6900	CITH	95662	260-B2
	7100	CITH	95610	260-B2
	7100	SaCo	95610	260-B2
CROSSBILL LN				
	5500	EDCo	95623	265-B5
CROSSCOURT WY				
	9200	ELKG	95624	338-J7
	9200	ELKG	95624	358-J1
CROSS CREEK LN				
	-	LNCN	95648	180-A1
CROSSFIELD DR				
	-	SaCo	95837	256-B4
CROSS FOX WY				
	9400	ELKG	95758	358-E5
CROSSHILL CT				
	8200	SaCo	95610	260-C2
	8200	SaCo	95662	260-C2
CROSSING WY				
	100	FOLS	95630	261-D6
CROSSLEY CT				
	-	SAC	95833	277-A6
CROSSMILL WY				
	1700	SAC	95833	277-B5
CROSSMOOR WY				
	-	RSVL	95661	240-E3
CROSSOAK WY				
	8200	SaCo	95662	260-B2
CROSSON CT				
	6900	SaCo	95828	338-B2
CROSSPOINTE CT				
	8500	SaCo	95843	239-B5
CROSS RAIL DR				
	9300	SaCo	95693	360-J6
CROSSTREES WY				
	8500	ELKG	95624	358-E2
CROSSWELL CT				
	8100	SaCo	95829	339-A6
CROSSWIND CT				
	-	SAC	95838	277-H1
CROSSWIND DR				
	600	SAC	95838	277-H1
CROSSWOOD DR				
	3900	EDCo	95682	263-J7
CROSSWOODS CIR				
	6100	CITH	95621	259-F3
CROSSWOODS CT				
	6500	CITH	95621	259-F3
CROSSWOODS PKWY				
	6500	CITH	95621	259-F3
CROW CT				
	3600	SaCo	95843	238-G7
CROW CANYON DR				
	100	FOLS	95630	261-A3
	200	FOLS	95630	260-J3
CROW CREEK DR				
	600	GALT	95632	439-E1
CROWDER LN				
	8000	PlaC	95747	239-A2
CROWDER WY				
	5900	SaCo	95842	258-J5
CROWDIS LN				
	2500	EDCo	95672	263-E1
CROWELL DR				
	9200	ELKG	95624	358-J4
CROWLE CT				
	-	FOLS	95630	261-H4
CROWLEY WY				
	9000	ELKG	95624	358-F3
CROWN AV				
	1900	WSAC	95691	296-H7
CROWN CT				
	5700	RKLN	95677	220-H4
	8500	PlaC	95746	240-G2
CROWN DR				
	900	EDCo	95762	262-C2
CROWN ST				
	9100	SaCo	95662	260-G3
CROWN OAK CT				
	7800	SaCo	95628	259-J7
CROWN POINT RD				
	4500	EDCo	95619	265-D5
CROWN POINT WY				
	9400	ELKG	95624	358-F6
CROWN POINT VISTA				
	6500	PlaC	95746	241-B5
CROWN PRINCE CT				
	8500	ELKG	95624	358-E5
CROWN RIDGE CT				
	5200	SaCo	95843	239-B5
CROWNWEST WY				
	7400	SAC	95823	337-F2
CROXTON WY				
	5300	SaCo	95842	259-B1
CROYDEN CT				
	-	EDCo	95672	263-B3
CROYDON WY				
	10200	RCCD	95827	299-E4
	10200	RCCD	95670	299-E3
CRUCERO DR				
	8700	ELKG	95624	358-G5
CRUCIBLE LN				
	4900	SaCo	95660	258-C3
CRUICKSHANK DR				
	100	FOLS	95630	261-E7
CRUISE WY				
	200	SAC	95831	316-F6
CRUSADE CT				
	6400	SaCo	95673	257-G3
CRUSADER DR				
	100	EDCo	95619	265-D4
CRUSHEEN WY				
	8700	SaCo	95828	338-G7
CRUTCHER CT				
	100	AUB	95603	182-E2
CRUTCHFIELD CT				
	8400	CITH	95610	240-C7
CRUX DR				
	7000	CITH	95610	260-A2
CRUZ CT				
	9300	ELKG	95624	358-J6
	9300	ELKG	95624	359-A6
CRYSTAL CT				
	-	RKLN	95765	200-A6
	2600	WSAC	95691	316-G1
CRYSTAL DR				
	4400	EDCo	95619	265-D4
CRYSTAL RD				
	5700	SaCo	95673	257-H5
CRYSTAL WY				
	100	GALT	95632	419-G7
	400	GALT	95632	439-G1
CRYSTAL BAY LN				
	-	ELKG	95758	357-E6
CRYSTAL BROOK CT				
	-	SAC	95838	257-J7
CRYSTAL COAST PL				
	-	SAC	95835	256-G4
CRYSTAL COVE DR				
	5000	RCCD	95742	320-D4
CRYSTAL CREEK DR				
	9900	SaCo	95829	339-D6
CRYSTAL DOWNS CT				
	-	PlaC	95747	239-A4
CRYSTAL DOWNS DR				
	-	RVIS	94571	454-E2
CRYSTAL FALLS WY				
	-	ELKG	95624	359-B5
CRYSTAL GLEN PL				
	1000	FOLS	95630	261-B6
CRYSTAL HILL CT				
	-	RSVL	95678	219-G5
CRYSTAL HILL WY				
	5200	SAC	95823	337-J7
	5500	SAC	95823	357-J1
CRYSTAL HOLLOW CT				
	-	LNCN	95648	199-J2
	-	LNCN	95648	200-A2
CRYSTAL LAKE CT				
	-	RKLN	95765	219-J2
	11500	SaCo	95670	280-C5
CRYSTAL MINE RD				
	-	PlaC	95658	181-G2
CRYSTAL OAK PL				
	900	PlaC	95658	181-C1
CRYSTAL RIDGE WY				
	8500	SaCo	95843	238-G5
CRYSTAL RIVER WY				
	8600	SaCo	95828	338-F4
CRYSTAL SPRINGS CT				
	-	EDCo	-	247-E2
CRYSTAL SPRINGS RD				
	1400	PlaC	95603	162-D4
	2500	EDCo	-	247-D3
CRYSTAL SPRINGS WY				
	7900	PlaC	95650	201-E7
CRYSTAL VIEW DR				
	3000	EDCo	95762	262-J6
	3000	EDCo	95762	263-A6
CRYSTAL VIEW LN				
	300	RCCD	95670	280-C7
CRYSTAL WALK CIR				
	8100	ELKG	95758	358-C5
CRYSTAL WATER WY				
	-	ELKG	95624	359-B5
CUB TR				
	4200	EDCo	95634	205-H1
CUBA RD				
	-	WSAC	95691	316-D2
CUCAMONGA AV				
	-	SAC	95826	318-C1
CUDDINGTON CT				
	-	RSVL	95746	240-G5
CUENCA				
	-	SaCo	95683	322-B6
CUEVAS CT				
	4000	SaCo	95821	278-H3
CUL DE SAC				
	100	AUB	95603	182-E3
CULLEN CT				
	8700	ELKG	95624	358-F6
CULLIGAN CT				
	300	RSVL	95747	239-C1
CULLINGWORTH CT				
	-	FOLS	95630	261-G7
CULLIVAN DR				
	600	SAC	95831	336-G3
CULLUM CT				
	-	LNCN	95648	179-E1
CULP WY				
	9800	RCCD	95827	299-C7
CULPEPPER DR				
	8500	SAC	95823	358-A1
CULPEPPER LN				
	-	LNCN	95648	200-B3
CULPEPPER WY				
	-	LNCN	95648	200-B3
CULVER AV				
	8300	SaCo	95628	280-C2
CULVER LN				
	3500	EDCo	95682	263-F4
CULVERHILL WY				
	-	RSVL	95747	218-J5
CUMBERLAND RD				
	2500	SaCo	95821	278-F6
CUMBERLAND TR				
	-	EDCo	95667	266-H6
CUMBRAE ISLE WY				
	5000	SaCo	95843	239-B6
CUMBRE CT				
	8600	SaCo	95662	260-D3
CUMMINGS WY				
	3600	SaCo	95660	258-G2
CUMMINS WY				
	600	WSAC	95605	297-A2
	800	WSAC	95605	296-J1
CUMULUS WY				
	8500	SaCo	95662	260-D4
CUNANO WY				
	6300	CITH	95621	259-E1
CUNEO CT				
	11100	RCCD	95670	300-A4
CUNHA CT				
	-	OAKL	94561	(514-A7 See Page 493)
CUNNINGHAM WY				
	6400	SAC	95828	318-B7
	6800	SaCo	95828	318-B7
	6800	SaCo	95828	338-B1
CUNY AV				
	3900	SaCo	95823	317-G7
CUPAR CT				
	1600	FOLS	95630	261-H7
CUPERTINO DR				
	9100	ELKG	95624	358-J6
CUPOLA CT				
	-	LNCN	95648	200-A2
CURLEW CT				
	-	RKLN	95765	219-H1
	8300	CITH	95621	239-G6
CURNAN WY				
	-	RSVL	95747	218-H3
CURNUTT CT				
	-	SAC	95833	277-D5
CURRAGH DOWNS DR				
	8700	SaCo	95628	280-E3
CURRAGH OAKS LN				
	4300	SaCo	95628	280-F2
CURRAN AV				
	500	SAC	95833	277-F5
CURRENT RD				
	-	SaCo	95693	360-J1
	-	SaCo	95693	(361-A1 See Page 341)
CURRY CT				
	200	RSVL	95678	219-G6
	1500	PlaC	95602	162-H1
	3100	SaCo	95821	278-J5
CURRY CREEK DR				
	9200	ELKG	95758	357-J5
CURTIS DR				
	-	ANT	94509	(513-A7 See Page 493)
E CURTIS DR				
	3000	SAC	95818	317-E2
	3600	SAC	95820	317-E2
W CURTIS DR				
	3500	SAC	95818	317-E1
	3800	SAC	95820	317-E1
CURTIS WY				
	2400	SAC	95818	317-E1
	3000	SAC	95817	317-E1
CURTISS CT				
	200	GALT	95632	419-F6
CURVED BRIDGE RD				
	1100	SaCo	95673	257-J2
	1100	SaCo	95673	258-A2
CURVE WOOD WY				
	4900	SaCo	95841	259-J7
CUSHENDALL CT				
	-	SaCo	95829	338-J6
CUSHENDALL DR				
	-	RSVL	95747	219-B7
	-	RSVL	95747	239-B1
CUSHING WY				
	6300	SAC	95823	338-A5
CUSHMAN CT				
	7400	CITH	95610	259-J1
	7400	CITH	95610	260-A1
CUSTER AV				
	8900	SaCo	95662	260-F6
CUSTIS AV				
	4400	SAC	95822	317-D3
CUSTOM CT				
	9000	SaCo	95826	318-H2
CUTAWAY CT				
	-	EDCo	95619	286-G5
CUTAWAY LN				
	-	EDCo	95619	286-F5
CUTLER CT				
	5600	LMS	95650	200-J5
CUTLER WY				
	8300	SaCo	95828	338-E6
CUTTER WY				
	3200	SAC	95818	317-D1
	3600	SAC	95820	317-E2
CUTTER COVE PL				
	-	ELKG	95758	357-F6
CUTTING WY				
	600	SAC	95831	336-G3
CUTTY SARK LN				
	5100	EDCo	95682	264-E6
CUVAISON CT				
	-	SAC	95834	276-J3
CYBER CT				
	-	PlaC	95765	199-F5
CYCLADIC CT				
	8600	ELKG	95624	358-F2
CYCLAMEN WY				
	4500	SaCo	95841	258-J7
	4600	SaCo	95841	259-A7
CYMBELINE ST				
	-	RSVL	95747	219-A7
CYPRESS				
	-	PlaC	95658	181-G5
CYPRESS AV				
	4600	SaCo	95608	279-A3
CYPRESS CT				
	-	RKLN	95765	200-C5
	-	WSAC	95691	316-J1
	1900	OAKL	94561	(514-C7 See Page 493)
CYPRESS DR				
	100	FOLS	95630	261-B1
	2000	RVIS	94571	454-F2
CYPRESS LN				
	100	RSVL	95678	219-G5
W CYPRESS PL				
	-	OAKL	94561	(514-C7 See Page 493)
CYPRESS PT				
	-	PlaC	95746	240-J5
CYPRESS RD				
	-	WSAC	95691	296-H7
E CYPRESS RD				
	100	OAKL	94561	(514-G7 See Page 493)
W CYPRESS RD				
	100	OAKL	94561	(514-C7 See Page 493)
CYPRESS ST				
	200	SaCo	95626	237-G6
	3300	SAC	95838	277-J3
CYPRESS BLUFF CT				
	8400	ELKG	95624	338-J7
CYPRESS CREEK WY				
	-	ELKG	95758	357-J2
CYPRESS GARDEN LN				
	5500	ELKG	95757	357-J7
CYPRESS LAKE CT				
	8300	SaCo	95843	238-H5
CYPRESS POINT CT				
	-	EDCo	95762	282-E4
CYPRESS POINT DR				
	5600	CITH	95610	260-A6
CYPRESS VIEW WY				
	-	ELKG	95758	358-B3
CYPRESSWOOD WY				
	10900	RCCD	95670	279-J7
CYPRINE CT				
	1000	EDCo	95762	262-C4
CYRINA CT				
	5000	SaCo	95628	259-J7
CYRUS LN				
	3900	SaCo	95608	279-F3
CYRUS RIVER CT				
	11000	RCCD	95670	279-J5
CYTISUS DR				
	6000	EDCo	95633	205-F3
D				
D AV				
	11400	PlaC	95603	162-A4
D PKWY				
	4700	SaCo	95823	337-H2
D ST				
	100	ISLE	95641	455-H5
	100	LNCN	95648	179-H3
	100	RSVL	95678	239-G3
	100	WSAC	95605	297-B3
	200	ANT	94509	(513-D3 See Page 493)
	300	GALT	95632	419-E7
	700	SAC	95814	297-D3
	2000	SAC	95816	297-F3
	3500	SaCo	95660	258-G7
	3900	SAC	95819	297-J4
	4100	EDCo	95709	247-B4
	5300	SAC	95819	298-A5
	7300	SaCo	95823	338-A2
N D ST				
	100	SAC	95814	297-D2
DABBLER LN				
	-	RSVL	95747	219-E2
DABBLERS CT				
	4400	SaCo	95842	258-J3
DABNEY AV				
	700	SaCo	95673	257-J2
DACIA CT				
	-	LNCN	95648	179-E4
DADE WY				
	4400	SaCo	95824	317-G6
DAFFODIL CIR				
	-	RKLN	95677	220-H4
DAFFODIL WY				
	7800	CITH	95610	240-B7
DAGGETT CT				
	500	RSVL	95746	240-F6
DAGGETT DR				
	3000	RSVL	95746	240-F6
DAGGETT WY				
	1700	SAC	95835	257-C3
DAGWOOD CT				
	10000	SaCo	95829	339-D7
DAGWOOD WY				
	10000	SaCo	95829	339-D7

DAHBOY WY
SACRAMENTO COUNTY STREET INDEX
DEL PRADO WY 532
© 2007 Rand McNally & Company
SACRAMENTO CO.

STREET
Block City ZIP Pg-Grid

DAHBOY WY
5900 SaCo 95662 260-D5
DAHLGREN CT
- SAC 95838 277-G1
DAHLIA AV
- SaCo 95828 338-F3
DAHLIA CT
200 RSVL 95747 219-C4
DAHLIA DR
6100 SaCo 95608 279-D4
DAHOMEY DR
6500 SaCo 95662 260-C3
DAIMLER WY
8500 SaCo 95828 338-F6
DAIN CT
2900 RCCD 95670 299-F3
DAINS CT
100 FOLS 95630 261-C6
DAINTREE LN
- LNCN 95648 179-F7
DAIRY CT
6200 SAC 95831 316-F6
9200 ELKG 95624 358-H5
DAIRY LN
12400 AUB 95603 162-D6
DAIRY RD
200 AUB 95603 162-E6
1300 PlaC 95603 162-E6
DAIRY ST
9200 ELKG 95624 358-H5
DAISY CT
200 GALT 95632 419-D5
1300 RSVL 95661 240-B4
DAISY DR
200 GALT 95632 419-D5
5500 EDCo 95726 267-J1
DAISY LN
6200 CITH 95621 259-E2
DAISY WY
1500 ANT 94509 (513-B5 See Page 493)
DAISY FIELD WY
- ELKG 95624 359-A6
DAISY HILL DR
- SaCo 95829 339-E6
DAISY HOLLOW CT
8300 SaCo 95828 338-D5
DAISY MEADOW CT
11800 RCCD 95742 320-D4
DAKOTA AV
- SaCo 95742 300-G1
DAKOTA CT
- SAC 95833 277-E5
DAKOTA DR
3200 EDCo 95667 244-F7
S DAKOTA RD
- SaCo 95742 281-B5
DALBY CT
- SAC 95823 337-H4
DALE AV
2100 SAC 95815 277-G6
DALE RD
- SAC 95815 297-G1
DALE WY
100 AUB 95603 182-D4
DALEHURST CT
- SAC 95835 257-A5
DALE VIEW CT
4900 EDCo 95623 264-G6
DALEWOOD DR
4800 EDCo 95762 262-E6
DALEWOODS WY
7800 SaCo 95828 338-C4
DALHART WY
- SAC 95835 256-J4
- SAC 95835 257-A4
DALISON CT
100 FOLS 95630 261-F7
DALKEITH WY
8200 SaCo 95843 238-J5
DALLAS WY
6400 SaCo 95823 317-J7
DALLEN WY
1400 RSVL 95747 219-D7
DALMENY WY
8400 CITH 95610 260-C2
DALTON CT
200 LNCN 95648 179-E5
DALTON WY
9400 SaCo 95662 260-H5
DALTREY WY
2200 FOLS 95630 281-F1
DALY AV
7300 CITH 95621 259-D1
7300 SaCo 95621 259-D1
7500 SaCo 95842 239-D7
7500 SaCo 95842 259-D1
7500 CITH 95842 239-D7
7500 CITH 95842 259-D1
DAM RD
- FOLS 95630 241-C7
- PlaC 95746 241-C7
DAMANT CT
4000 SaCo 95660 258-H4
DAMASCAS DR
- SAC 95823 358-B1
7500 SAC 95758 358-C1
DAMBACHER DR
7200 PlaC 95746 241-C3
DAME SHIRLEY WY
2100 SaCo 95670 280-C5
DAMICO DR
- EDCo 95762 262-H5
DAMIEN CT
10000 ELKG 95624 378-H2
DAMON AV
5200 SaCo 95841 259-B7
DANA CT
- AUB 95603 182-B7
1500 RSVL 95661 240-B4
DANA WY
1500 RSVL 95661 240-B4
5100 SAC 95822 317-D4
DANA BUTTE WY
7900 CITH 95610 260-A1
DANA POINT WY
5400 SaCo 95843 259-C1
DANBERG WY
- ELKG 95757 358-B7
DANBERRY CT
1100 ANT 94509 (513-F7 See Page 493)
DANBROOK DR
- SAC 95835 257-C5
DANBURRY CT
7900 PlaC 95746 241-C1
DANBURY CIR
4700 EDCo 95762 242-C6
DANBURY CT
1300 WSAC 95691 296-H5
DANBURY DR
- LNCN 95648 179-G5
DANBURY WY
2100 RCCD 95670 279-F7
DANBURY PARK CT
8200 SaCo 95828 338-G6
DANBY CT
100 LNCN 95648 179-E4
8400 SaCo 95843 239-B5
DANBY LN
600 LNCN 95648 179-E4
DANCING CREEK CT
7100 CITH 95621 259-F2
DANCING OAKS RD
2600 EDCo 95667 246-E1
DANDELION CIR
2800 ANT 94531 (513-G7 See Page 493)
DANDELION CT
2800 ANT 94531 (513-G7 See Page 493)
DANDELION DR
8200 ELKG 95624 358-E2
DANEHURST CT
3000 SaCo 95843 238-F6
DANFIELD CIR
7300 SaCo 95660 258-H1
DANFORTH CT
100 FOLS 95630 261-G6
DANICA WY
1500 SAC 95833 277-C4
DANICHRIS WY
10300 ELKG 95757 377-J3
10300 ELKG 95757 397-J3
DANIEL DR
1100 PlaC 95648 180-D2
DANIEL WY
10300 RCCD 95670 299-F2
DANIELLE CT
500 RSVL 95747 219-D6
DANIELLE DR
1000 RSVL 95747 219-D6
DANIELLE WY
100 FOLS 95630 241-B7
100 FOLS 95630 261-B1
DANIELS CT
9400 ELKG 95624 359-A1
DANIELS DR
200 PlaC 95603 162-F5
DANIELSON CT
1700 SaCo 95608 299-C2
DANJAC CIR
5500 SaCo 95822 317-A4
DANKBAR LN
1600 PlaC 95747 239-E3
DANLAR CT
9500 SaCo 95693 359-J6
9500 SaCo 95693 360-A6
DANNON CT
7700 CITH 95610 240-A7
DANNY DR
100 GALT 95632 419-D7
DANRIDGE CT
- ANT 94509 (513-E7 See Page 493)
DANRIDGE DR
8500 SaCo 95828 338-F2
DANROBIN CT
- SAC 95833 277-A6
DANROTH DR
4600 SAC 95838 277-G1
DANSKE LN
2000 EDCo 95667 246-C2
DANTE CIR
- RSVL 95678 219-H3
DANTE CT
9400 ELKG 95624 359-A5
DANTLEY CT
- ELKG 95624 359-A6
DANUBE DR
2500 SaCo 95821 278-D6
DANUBE RIVER DR
- RSVL 95747 219-B1
DANVERS LN
4600 PlaC 95746 240-G5
DANVERS WY
1900 SAC 95832 337-C4
DANVILLE WY
- SAC 95838 277-G4
DAPHNE AV
1700 SaCo 95864 298-J1
DAPHNE DR
7300 PlaC 95746 221-A7
DAPPLE CT
9500 ELKG 95624 358-J6
DAPPLE DAWN LN
- LNCN 95648 179-J7
- LNCN 95648 180-A7
DAPPLE GRAY PL
- ELKG 95624 359-B6
DARA WY
8300 SaCo 95828 338-E5
DARB CT
4000 SaCo 95660 258-H6
DARBY CT
- RKLN 95765 200-A7
DARBY LN
3000 EDCo 95726 248-F1
DARBY RD
- RKLN 95765 200-A6
DARBY ST
- RSVL 95747 219-A7
DARCY CT
- SaCo 95821 278-G3
4500 SaCo 95660 258-J3
DARGATE CT
- SAC 95838 277-G1
DARHUS CT
2600 EDCo 95682 263-C7
DARIEL DR
- SAC 95838 257-J7
DARIEN CIR
8100 SaCo 95828 338-G6
DARIEN CT
- LNCN 95648 179-E4
DARINA AV
700 SAC 95815 277-H6
DARK CANYON DR
2100 SaCo 95670 280-E4
DARK CANYON RD
- EDCo 95634 225-G3
- EDCo 95667 225-G4
DARK STAR WY
6200 SaCo 95662 260-C4
DARKWOODS CT
5400 SaCo 95841 259-A6
DARLA WY
7600 SaCo 95828 338-D4
DARLENE AV
3600 SaCo 95821 278-G5
DARLEY WY
- ELKG 95757 358-B6
DARLING WY
- FOLS 95630 261-J4
- RSVL 95678 239-H3
DARLING RIDGE RD
- EDCo 95633 205-J4
- EDCo 95634 205-J4
DARLINGTON AV
100 AUB 95603 182-F2
800 PLCR 95667 245-G6
DARLINGTON CT
- RKLN 95765 200-E4
DARLINGTON WY
- LNCN 95648 179-E4
DARLINTON LN
- SAC 95835 256-G6
DARNEL WY
1000 SAC 95822 317-B2
DARN STEEP RD
4000 EDCo 95682 283-J6
DARON LN
- SaCo 95829 339-C5
DA ROSA DR
4700 SAC 95822 317-A3
DARR CT
2700 EDCo 95667 226-H5
DARR LN
9900 SaCo 95693 (380-G5 See Page 379)
DARRAGH CT
400 LNCN 95648 179-F5
DARRELL DR
7600 CITH 95610 259-H2
DARRINGTON DR
100 FOLS 95630 261-F3
DART WY
8100 SaCo 95662 260-B2
DARTER LN
- LNCN 95648 200-B3
DARTFORD CT
9300 SaCo 95829 339-A6
DARTFORD DR
8300 SAC 95823 358-B1
DARTFORD PL
4900 PlaC 95746 240-G5
DARTMOOR LN
- LNCN 95648 179-E5
DARTMOOR WY
- ELKG 95757 357-H7
DARTMOORE CT
- ELKG 95757 357-H7
DARTMOUTH AV
1100 RSVL 95678 239-G5
DARTMOUTH DR
4400 SaCo 95841 278-J2
DARTMOUTH PL
2200 EDCo 95762 242-B5
DARTRY CT
9400 ELKG 95758 358-B6
DARU WY
4900 SaCo 95628 260-E7
4900 SaCo 95628 280-E1
DARVEL CT
1700 FOLS 95630 281-J1
DARWIN PL
2600 EDCo 95762 262-D3
DARWIN ST
2300 SaCo 95825 278-C6
2400 SaCo 95821 278-C6
DARWIN WY
1700 EDCo 95762 262-D3
DASCO WY
5300 SAC 95835 257-C5
DASHING RANCH RD
- EDCo - 267-G4
- EDCo 95726 267-G4
DASHWOOD DR
- RSVL 95747 219-C7
DATA DR
3100 RCCD 95670 299-H3
DATE AV
- SaCo 95841 279-A1
4900 SaCo 95841 259-A7
5500 SaCo 95842 259-A6
DATE PALM WY
6300 SaCo 95608 279-E6
DATONI LN
- SAC 95835 256-G5
DATORO CT
- SAC 95833 277-C5
DATSUN CT
4100 EDCo 95682 284-A7
DATTIER CT
10400 RCCD 95670 299-G1
DAUNTING DR
- EDCo 95762 262-E6
DAUNTLESS WY
4800 SaCo 95628 280-G1
DAUSTER LN
7500 CITH 95610 259-H4
DAVE ST
7300 SaCo 95828 338-D2
DAVELAR CT
3500 RCCD 95827 299-C7
DAVENPORT CT
- PlaC 95747 239-A3
DAVENPORT LP
- RSVL 95747 218-J6
DAVENPORT RD
- EDCo - 267-J3
DAVENPORT WY
- LNCN 95648 179-E4
2900 SAC 95833 277-E5
DAVENTRY CT
- FOLS 95630 261-G7
DAVENWOOD CT
4000 RSVL 95746 240-F6
DAVID AV
6300 LMS 95650 201-A5
DAVID CIR
600 PLCR 95667 245-E4
DAVID CT
4700 RKLN 95677 200-E7
DAVID DR
3700 SaCo 95660 258-G4
DAVID LN
36500 YoCo 95612 356-H5
DAVID WY
3400 SAC 95820 318-A2
DAVIDSON DR
3200 SaCo 95843 238-F7
DAVIDSON RD
5000 EDCo 95667 264-G4
DAVIES CT
200 FOLS 95630 261-E7
DA VINCI CT
- OAKL 94561 (514-H6 See Page 493)
DA VINCI DR
- EDCo 95762 262-G3
DA VINCI WY
5600 SAC 95835 256-J3
DAVINDA CT
8100 CITH 95610 240-B7
DAVIS AV
100 SAC 95823 337-F2
DAVIS CT
100 RSVL 95678 219-F7
400 PLCR 95667 245-B5
DAVIS LN
100 AUB 95603 182-D2
2400 ANT 94509 (513-C6 See Page 493)
DAVIS RD
1900 WSAC 95691 316-E3
9900 SaCo 95693 (380-A1 See Page 379)
N DAVIS RD
23300 SJCo 95242 439-A7
DAVISON DR
700 ANT 94509 (513-F7 See Page 493)
DAVLIL WY
7300 SaCo 95662 260-H2
DAVMORE LN
- LNCN 95648 179-E7
DAWES ST
3300 RCCD 95670 [illegible]
DAWN CIR
100 GALT 95632 419-D7
DAWN DR
3900 PlaC 95650 201-F7
DAWN LN
PlaC 95648 160-C6
- EDCo 95667 245-D7
DAWN WY
2100 SaCo 95825 278-C7
DAWNELLE WY
1700 SAC 95835 257-C3
DAWN OAK LN
5300 SaCo 95628 260-G7
DAWNRIDGE RD
200 RSVL 95678 239-F5
DAWNRIDGE WY
6200 SaCo 95608 259-D7
DAWN RIVER WY
100 FOLS 95630 261-A4
DAWNROSE LN
- EDCo 95619 286-B6
DAWN VIEW CT
7100 CITH 95621 259-E2
DAWNWOOD DR
1200 GALT 95632 419-G2
DAWSON CT
300 RSVL 95747 219-E7
1600 OAKL 94561 (514-D6 See Page 493)
DAWSON DR
4800 OAKL 94561 (514-D6 See Page 493)
DAWSON WY
6500 SaCo 95823 317-J7
DAY AV
3500 LMS 95650 201-A5
DAY DR
1600 SaCo 95608 299-A2
DAYA WY
7600 SaCo 95828 338-D4
DAYBREAK LN
4200 SaCo 95821 278-H4
DAYBREAK WY
4500 EDCo 95623 265-B5
DAYBROOK CT
- SaCo 95829 338-J7
DAYBURST WY
6200 SAC 95823 358-A1
DAYLIGHT CT
8300 SaCo 95828 338-D5
DAY LILLIES LN
8400 CITH 95610 260-D1
DAYLILY CT
2800 ANT 94531 (513-G7 See Page 493)
DAYLILY LN
- LNCN 95648 180-A5
DAYLOR WY
9100 ELKG 95758 357-F4
DAYSPRING CT
- EDCo - 267-C6
DAYSPRING WY
6200 SAC 95823 358-A1
DAYSTAR CT
4100 SaCo 95824 317-G5
DAYTON LN
1400 EDCo 95619 265-H7
2600 ANT 94509 (513-A6 See Page 493)
DAYTON ST
3500 SAC 95838 278-C1
DEA WY
4700 SaCo 95628 279-H1
DEADERICK CT
6500 SaCo 95662 260-B3
DEAD HORSE RD
- EDCo 95634 225-C4
DEADOR CT
8700 ELKG 95624 358-G4
DEAKIN PL
2700 EDCo 95762 262-D3
DEALYNN ST
1100 SaCo 95825 298-D3
DEAN CT
700 RSVL 95747 219-D6
DEAN LN
- LNCN 95648 179-F5
DEAN RD
- SAC 95815 297-G1
DEAN ST
- SaCo 95652 278-C1
DEAN WY
- FOLS 95630 261-C5
DEANNA AV
9400 SaCo 95662 260-J2
DEANNA CT
- LNCN 95648 179-E4
DEANTON CT
7700 CITH 95610 239-H7
7700 CITH 95610 259-J1
DE ANZA CT
6100 SaCo 95673 257-J4
DEARBORN DR
6300 CITH 95621 259-F4
DEARWESTER LN
9500 PlaC 95661 240-E5
DEARY WY
5800 SaCo 95662 260-J5
DEBBIE CT
400 EDCo 95667 245-B5
DEBBIE LN
400 EDCo 95667 245-B5
400 PLCR 95667 245-B5
3900 SaCo 95821 278-H3
DEBBIE ANN CT
8000 CITH 95610 240-B7
DE BEERS PL
1000 FOLS 95630 261-B6
DEBELLEVUE ST
- RCCD 95655 299-F5
- SaCo 95655 299-F5
DEBENHAM CT
- RSVL 95747 219-B7
DEBENHAM ST
- RSVL 95747 219-B7
DEBERA CT
2600 PLCR 95667 245-E4
DE BERNARDI CT
800 PLCR 95667 245-G5
DEBERRY CT
- SAC 95835 257-A4
DEBINA CT
3500 RCCD 95670 299-J5
DEBINA WY
3500 RCCD 95670 300-J4
DEBORAH LN
7800 SaCo 95628 279-J3
DEBRALEE WY
4600 SAC 95838 277-J1
DEBRON CT
- EDCo 95726 248-C3
DEBUTANTE LN
7500 SaCo 95828 338-D3
DE CAIR CT
EDCo 95619 265-E3
DECALOUGUE RD
- EDCo - 267-D6
DECATHLON CIR
- SAC 95823 337-G4
DECATUR ST
300 FOLS 95630 261-B5
DECENTE CT
2100 EDCo 95682 263-B7
DECKER DR
1300 RSVL 95661 240-C5
DECKER WY
2600 WSAC 95691 316-F1
DECLARATION CIR
6000 CITH 95621 259-D4
DECORAH WY
9200 ELKG 95624 358-J5
DE COSTA AV
4100 SaCo 95821 278-H5
DE CRISANTO PL
6300 ELKG 95758 358-A6
DEDDINGTON WY
- SaCo 95829 338-J6
DEDHAM CT
- LNCN 95648 179-E4
DEDION CT
8600 SaCo 95828 338-F6
DEDO WY
2200 RCCD 95670 299-E2
DEDRICK CT
7200 SaCo 95842 259-D2
DEE CT
4400 SaCo 95841 278-J1
DEEBLE ST
4000 SAC 95820 317-E2
DEED CT
6100 SaCo 95660 258-J4
DEEDIE AV
5600 CITH 95610 259-H6
DEE JAY WY
- EDCo - 247-E2
DEELY CT
100 FOLS 95630 261-G3
DEENA CT
- PLCR 95667 245-E3
DEEPDALE WY
5200 ELKG 95758 357-J2
DEEP SPRINGS CT
- LNCN 95648 200-B1
DEEP SPRINGS LN
- LNCN 95648 200-B1
DEER CT
- SAC 95823 337-H4
900 RSVL 95661 239-J4
DEER PASS
5600 EDCo 95604 200-E7
DEERBROOK DR
3900 SAC 95823 337-G4
DEERBROOKE TR
- AUB 95603 182-A7
DEER BRUSH LN
2500 EDCo 95682 263-J1
DEER CANYON CT
6400 EDCo 95667 226-J3
DEER CANYON RD
- EDCo - 246-J7
- EDCo - 247-A7
DEER CREEK DR
7700 SAC 95823 337-H4
DEER CREEK RD
1200 EDCo 95682 283-D3
DEER CROSS WY
3900 SAC 95823 337-G5
DEER FERN CT
8400 SaCo 95843 238-F5
DEERFIELD CIR
1400 RSVL 95747 219-E7
DEERFIELD DR
6600 CITH 95610 259-J3
DEERFIELD WY
- RVIS 94571 454-F2
DEERGLEN WY
7800 SAC 95823 337-G4
DEER GROVE CT
- SAC 95823 337-G5
DEER HAVEN WY
7800 SAC 95832 337-F5
DEER HILL DR
3900 SAC 95823 337-G5
DEER HOLLOW WY
- RSVL 95661 220-D7
DEERHORN LN
1500 EDCo 95762 242-F5
DEERHURST CT
9900 SaCo 95829 339-D5
DEER KNOLL RD
3000 EDCo 95682 283-E3
DEER LAKE DR
7900 SAC 95823 337-G5
DEERLEAF DR
7800 SAC 95823 337-G5
DEER MEADOW DR
7800 SAC 95823 337-G4
DEER MEADOWS CT
- EDCo - 267-C2
DEER OAKS DR
2200 EDCo 95672 263-A1
DEERPARK CIR
5000 SaCo 95628 259-F7
DEERPARK CT
- OAKL 94561 (514-E6 See Page 493)
DEER PARK DR
- LNCN 95648 199-H3
DEERPARK DR
3400 EDCo 95667 226-G2
DEERPARK RD
1100 OAKL 94561 (514-E6 See Page 493)
DEERPARK WY
300 OAKL 94561 (514-E6 See Page 493)
DEER PATH PL
- SAC 95835 257-A3
DEER RIDGE LN
- PlaC 95602 161-J2
- PlaC 95602 162-A1
DEER RIVER WY
300 SAC 95831 316-F7
300 SAC 95831 336-G1
DEER RUN CT
- RKLN 95765 220-A1
DEER RUN WY
3900 SAC 95823 337-G4
DEER SPRING CIR
8100 SaCo 95843 238-J6
DEER TRAIL LN
2400 EDCo 95682 263-C3
DEER TRAIL WY
3900 SAC 95823 337-G4
DEER TREE CT
- SAC 95823 337-G5
DEER VALLEY CT
3400 EDCo 95672 243-A6
DEER VALLEY RD
1700 EDCo 95672 243-E3
2000 EDCo 95672 262-J1
2400 EDCo 95672 263-A1
3300 ANT 94509 (513-G7 See Page 493)
3300 ANT 94531 (513-G7 See Page 493)
DEER VALLEY WY
7900 SAC 95823 337-G5
DEER WALK WY
3700 SaCo 95843 238-G5
DEER WATER DR
7900 SAC 95823 337-G5
DEERWOOD CIR
1800 WSAC 95691 296-H5
DEERWOOD CT
- EDCo 95682 264-B1
- RKLN 95765 200-D6
8400 SaCo 95628 280-C2
DEERWOOD DR
5300 EDCo 95682 264-B6
5300 EDCo 95682 264-B1
DEERWOOD PL
1200 AUB 95603 182-C7
DEERWOOD ST
1500 WSAC 95691 296-H5
DEERWOOD WY
- FOLS 95630 261-B3
DEETH CT
9300 SaCo 95827 299-A5
DE FER CIR
- SAC 95823 337-G2
DEFIANCE CIR
9200 SaCo 95827 299-A5
DEFLORES CIR
- RVIS 94571 454-H3
DEFLORES CT
- RVIS 94571 454-H4
DEGAS CT
8900 SaCo 95628 280-F2
DEGOLIA ST
700 PLCR 95667 245-F5
DEJA CT
- SAC 95838 278-A2
DE JOHN AV
5300 SaCo 95608 279-B7
DEKALB CT
- SAC 95835 256-J6
DEL RD
4900 LMS 95650 200-H6
9500 PlaC 95747 239-E5
DE LA CRUZ DR
7100 SaCo 95683 342-C1
DELAFIELD WY
- SAC 95835 257-C6
DELAGE WY
8000 SaCo 95828 338-G5
DELAGUA WY
300 SAC 95838 277-G2
DELAHYE CIR
8500 SaCo 95828 338-F6
DELAIR WY
9200 ELKG 95758 357-G4
DELAMERE CT
3700 EDCo 95682 263-B7
DELANCY WY
- LNCN 95648 179-E4
DELANE CT
2800 EDCo 95682 263-J6
DELANE DR
800 GALT 95632 419-F5
DELANE RD
2800 EDCo 95682 264-A6
2800 EDCo 95682 263-J7
DELANEY CT
- RSVL 95678 219-G4
DELANEY DR
7600 SaCo 95843 238-F7
DELANO ST
100 SaCo 95626 237-F7
DELANO WY
5600 RKLN 95677 220-D4
DEL ANTICO AV
400 OAKL 94561 (514-F7 See Page 493)
DE LA PENA CIR
15100 SaCo 95683 342-C1
DE LAPP PL
3700 PlaC 95650 201-D6
DE LA ROSA DR
- RKLN 95765 200-C6
DE LA ROSA PL
9500 ELKG 95758 358-A6
DELAVAN CIR
11800 RCCD 95742 320-D2
DE LAVEAGA CT
- SAC 95831 336-H1
DE LA VINA WY
4000 SAC 95823 337-G5
DELAWARE AV
1100 WSAC 95691 296-J5
3800 SaCo 95608 279-E3
DELAWARE CT
2000 WSAC 95691 296-H6
DELAWARE ST
- SaCo 95742 280-F5
DELBROOK LN
5700 SaCo 95608 279-C1
DELBURNS CT
9500 ELKG 95758 358-B6
DEL CAMPO LN
5800 SaCo 95608 259-D5
DEL CERRO
- SaCo 95683 322-B6
DEL CIELO WY
6300 SaCo 95608 279-E1
DELCLIFF CIR
5600 SaCo 95822 317-A4
DEL CORONADO WY
7300 SaCo 95828 338-B2
DEL DAYO DR
1500 SaCo 95608 299-A2
DELFON CT
9000 ELKG 95624 358-H2
DELFT CT
8100 SaCo 95829 338-H6
DELGADO DR
- SaCo 95683 322-A7
DELGADO WY
1900 SAC 95833 277-B5
DEL GRANDE CT
1200 EDCo 95762 262-C1
DEL HABRA WY
4700 SaCo 95608 279-E1
DEL HAVEN RD
- EDCo 95667 266-C4
DEL HAVEN WY
7100 SaCo 95660 258-G2
DELICATO WY
8300 SaCo 95829 338-J7
DELL PL
6500 PlaC 95650 221-B5
DELL RD
3700 SaCo 95608 279-G4
DELLA CIR
7400 SaCo 95828 338-C2
DELLA ROBIA CT
4700 SaCo 95628 280-C1
DELLA VERONA DR
- RSVL 95747 199-B7
- RSVL 95747 219-B1
DEL LUNA CT
- SAC 95822 337-E3
DELMA WY
2000 SaCo 95825 278-C7
DEL MAR AV
1800 PlaC 95663 200-G1
2400 PlaC 95650 200-G4
3200 LMS 95650 200-G5
3200 PlaC 95677 200-G4
3900 LMS 95677 200-G7
3900 RKLN 95677 200-G7
4000 RKLN 95677 220-G1
DEL MAR CT
900 RSVL 95661 239-J5
DEL MAR WY
3200 SAC 95815 278-A4
DEL MESA CT
3400 SaCo 95821 278-H4
DEL MONTE
500 EDCo 95762 282-C1
DEL MONTE DR
- RVIS 94571 454-E1
DEL MONTE LN
4300 PlaC 95648 180-F4
DEL MONTE ST
2200 WSAC 95691 296-G5
2900 SAC 95826 318-C1
DEL MONTE WY
100 AUB 95603 182-F1
DEL NORTE BLVD
4600 SaCo 95820 317-G4
5500 SaCo 95824 317-G4
DEL NORTE VISTA CT
100 FOLS 95630 261-B4
DEL NORTE VISTA WY
100 FOLS 95630 261-B4
DELOACH WY
8200 ELKG 95624 358-D1
DEL OAK WY
7600 SAC 95831 337-A4
DEL OBISPO CT
- RSVL 95747 219-B4
DELORES DR
100 PlaC 95603 162-F5
DEL ORO CIR
2700 ANT 94509 (513-B6 See Page 493)
DEL ORO CT
2700 SaCo 95826 298-J6
DEL ORO DR
- LMS 95650 201-B4
DEL ORO RD
6100 PlaC 95746 220-J6
6100 PlaC 95746 221-A6
DELOS LN
- EDCo 95667 266-H6
DELOUCH DR
- LNCN 95648 179-E5
DEL PASO BLVD
500 SAC 95833 297-F1
700 SAC 95815 297-F1
900 SAC 95815 277-H7
2800 SAC 95815 278-B4
3400 SAC 95838 278-C4
DEL PASO CT
11700 PlaC 95602 162-A1
DEL PASO RD
700 SaCo 95834 257-C7
1300 SAC 95834 257-A7
2500 SaCo 95834 256-G7
3100 SaCo 95834 256-D7
3600 SaCo 95835 256-D7
3600 SAC 95837 256-B7
DELPHINA CT
1800 EDCo 95682 263-B7
DELPHINIUM WY
- SAC 95833 276-H6
DEL PRADO LN
4400 EDCo 95667 264-H3
DEL PRADO WY
7200 SaCo 95828 338-B2

STREET
Block City ZIP Pg-Grid

DEL REY CT
2600 RCCD 95670 299-E3
DEL RIO RD
4500 SAC 95822 317-B3
DELROSE CT
5500 SaCo 95608 279-C6
DEL SOL WY
3500 SAC 95834 277-D3
DELTA AV
100 ISLE 95641 455-H5
DELTA DR
- RKLN 95765 200-B6
DELTA LN
800 WSAC 95691 297-A4
DELTA RD
7600 SaCo 95837 235-J6
7600 SaCo 95837 236-A7
7600 SaCo 95837 256-B1
DELTA ST
1200 SAC 95814 297-E2
DELTA WY
100 RVIS 94571 454-H5
DELTA BREEZE CT
- YoCo 95612 336-H4
100 RSVL 95747 219-A4
DELTA BREEZE LN
- ELKG 95758 357-G6
7200 RSVL 95747 219-B4
DELTA FAIR BLVD
3000 ANT 94509 (513-A5 See Page 493)
DELTA GATEWAY BLVD
- PIT 94565 (513-A5 See Page 493)
DELTA LEAF WY
200 SAC 95838 257-G7
DELTA MEADOWS WY
1600 OAKL 94561 (514-D5 See Page 493)
DELTA OAKS WY
200 SAC 95831 336-F1
DELTA POINTE WY
7500 SaCo 95823 338-A3
DELTA QUEEN AV
3400 SAC 95833 276-G7
DELTA RANCH DR
5300 OAKL 94561 (514-D5 See Page 493)
DELTA SAND CT
8300 ELKG 95758 358-E5
DELTA SUNRISE CT
7800 SaCo 95828 338-E5
DELTA TULE CT
- SAC 95834 276-J2
DELTA TULE WY
3000 SAC 95834 276-J3
DELTAWIND DR
7400 SAC 95831 336-H2
DELTA WIND LN
- LNCN 95648 200-A2
DEL VALLE DR
800 AUB 95603 182-D5
DEL VERDE CIR
100 SAC 95833 277-C4
DELVIN WY
8700 SaCo 95828 338-G7
DEL VISTA CIR
- SAC 95823 338-A7
DEL VISTA WY
- RKLN 95765 200-C6
DEL WEBB BLVD
- LNCN 95648 179-H6
- LNCN 95648 180-A6
- LNCN 95648 199-J1
- LNCN 95648 200-A1
7000 RSVL 95747 219-A5
DEL WES LN
300 SaCo 95673 257-F1
DELWOOD CT
6500 RKLN 95677 220-D5
DELWOOD WY
3100 SaCo 95821 278-H5
DE MAR DR
400 SAC 95831 336-G2
DEMARET DR
6500 SAC 95822 317-D7
6800 SAC 95822 337-D1
DEMARTINI CT
- OAKL 94561 (514-D7 See Page 493)
DEMETER CT
7400 CITH 95621 259-G3
DEMETRE AV
- SAC 95828 318-D5
DEMETRIUS WY
- RSVL 95661 220-D6
DE MONES AV
- SaCo 95742 280-F5
DEMONTE WY
- ELKG 95757 378-A1
DEMPSTER CT
- SAC 95823 337-J7
DEMURRAGE WY
100 FOLS 95630 281-B2
DEMUTH CIR
6500 SaCo 95842 259-A3
DEMYHIG LN
- EDCo 95619 266-D5
- EDCo 95667 266-D5
DEN AV
6500 SaCo 95823 338-A2
DENA WY
4100 SaCo 95608 279-A2
4100 SaCo 95821 279-A2
DENALI CT
- RKLN 95765 219-H2
DENALI DR
4000 EDCo 95619 265-G3
DENFIELD LN
- SaCo 95608 279-A4
DENHOLM CT
9400 ELKG 95758 358-C5
DENIM CT
3700 EDCo 95667 246-A6
DENIM RD
- ELKG 95624 359-F2
DENIO WY
7600 CITH 95610 259-H5
DENISE CT
2900 WSAC 95691 316-E1
DENISE ST
7600 SAC 95832 337-E4
DENISON CT
8400 SAC 95826 298-E7
DENNICK CT
4600 SaCo 95842 259-A1
DENNIS CT
400 RSVL 95678 219-J6
12500 PlaC 95603 162-C3

DENNIS DR
2000 ANT 94509 (513-E5 See Page 493)
DENNIS WY
4300 SaCo 95821 278-J5
7600 CITH 95610 259-H2
10300 SaCo 95757 377-H3
10300 SaCo 95757 397-H3
DENNY LN
- EDCo 95667 266-C3
DENSLOW WY
6100 SaCo 95823 338-A5
DENSMORE CT
- FOLS 95630 281-E2
DENSMORE WY
- FOLS 95630 281-F2
DENTER CT
- GALT 95632 419-G5
DENTON CT
- FOLS 95630 261-H4
- RKLN 95765 200-A6
DENTON WY
6300 CITH 95610 259-J4
DENURE CT
100 FOLS 95630 281-D3
DENVER DR
5900 SaCo 95660 260-D7
DENWIL CT
- SAC 95824 318-C5
DENY CT
4800 SaCo 95842 259-A2
DEODAR AV
1900 ANT 94509 (513-E5 See Page 493)
DEODAR ST
3200 SaCo 95608 279-E5
DEODAR CREST CT
8500 ELKG 95624 358-E5
DEONSIRE LN
7400 SaCo 95829 339-C3
DE PAUL CT
4100 SaCo 95821 278-H4
DEPEYSTER WY
- EDCo 95762 262-F7
DE PONTI DR
5600 SaCo 95662 260-H6
DEPOT LN
- SaCo 95690 436-J1
- SaCo 95690 437-A1
DERBY CT
6600 CITH 95621 259-E3
8900 PlaC 95658 181-G6
DERBY PARK CT
8100 SaCo 95828 338-G6
DERBYSHIRE CIR
8100 SaCo 95828 338-G6
DEREK PL
100 RSVL 95678 219-G6
DERRICK WY
1100 SAC 95822 317-A3
DERLIN WY
8500 SAC 95823 358-B1
DE ROSA CT
8400 SaCo 95828 338-E7
DEROW CT
- SAC 95833 277-C6
DERR ST
9500 ELKG 95624 358-J6
DERRINGER CT
8300 SaCo 95626 238-D5
DERRYLIN DR
- RSVL 95747 219-B7
DERSINGHAM DR
7700 SaCo 95829 338-J5
DERWENT ALY
5700 SAC 95835 257-B3
DERWOOD CT
8500 ELKG 95624 358-H1
DE SABLA CT
3800 EDCo 95682 263-E6
DE SABLA RD
3700 EDCo 95682 263-E7
DE SART CT
- SAC 95831 336-G3
DESCENDANT DR
9000 ELKG 95758 358-C3
DESCHUTES WY
7100 SaCo 95621 259-D2
DESERET AV
8100 SaCo 95628 260-B6
DESERET DR
3100 PlaC 95603 161-J4
DESERET WY
3100 PlaC 95603 161-J3
DESERTAS CT
7200 ELKG 95757 378-B2
DESERT DUNES CT
- SaCo 95829 339-D5
DESERT FOREST CT
- RVIS 94571 454-E2
DESERT FOREST DR
- RVIS 94571 454-E1
DESERT WILLOW CT
9900 SaCo 95829 339-C4
DESERTWIND WY
7400 SAC 95831 336-J2
DESERT WOOD CT
- SAC 95823 337-F3
DESHUTES DR
- RSVL 95747 219-D1
DESIMONE LN
6100 CITH 95621 259-D4
DESIREE CT
5900 CITH 95621 259-D2
DESMOND LN
1400 PlaC 95658 181-H2
DESMOND RD
6900 SaCo 95690 417-J3
7100 SaCo 95690 418-A4
DESOTO WY
10100 RCCD 95827 299-E5
DE SOUZA LN
10300 ELKG 95624 359-F4
DESPERADO CT
- EDCo 95684 286-H7
DESPERADO RD
- EDCo 95684 286-H7
DESTA CT
6800 ELKG 95758 358-B4
DESTINY DR
- RKLN 95677 220-B5
DESTINY LN
8200 SaCo 95828 338-E3
DETERMINED CT
4100 SaCo 95628 280-E2
DETROIT BLVD
7600 SAC 95832 337-F4
DETROIT ST
- SaCo 95742 280-F5

DEUCE DR
- EDCo 95619 265-F2
DEVECCHI AV
- CITH 95621 259-D5
- SaCo 95621 259-D5
DEVELOPMENT DR
3900 SAC 95838 277-G3
DEVER CIR
9200 ELKG 95624 358-H5
DEVERON WY
8700 SaCo 95662 260-E3
DE VILLE CT
4200 SaCo 95821 278-H4
DEVILLE OAKS WY
8300 CITH 95621 239-H6
DEVON AV
1900 WSAC 95691 296-H7
DEVON CT
- RKLN 95765 200-A7
400 OAKL 94561 (514-D7 See Page 493)
3700 EDCo 95762 263-B5
DEVON DR
- RKLN 95765 200-A7
DEVON LN
4200 SaCo 95864 298-H1
DEVON WY
3500 EDCo 95762 263-B5
DEVON CREST WY
- ELKG 95624 358-J1
DEVON HILL CT
8200 SaCo 95828 338-F7
DEVON PARK CT
8100 SaCo 95828 338-G6
DEVONSHIRE CT
1200 RSVL 95661 240-A5
DEVONSHIRE LN
600 LNCN 95648 179-F5
DEVONSHIRE RD
1700 SaCo 95864 298-G1
DEVOTION LN
6900 SAC 95823 337-F1
DEVPAR CT
2400 ANT 94509 (513-F6 See Page 493)
DEVRI CT
- SAC 95833 277-B4
N DEVRIES RD
22500 SJCo 95242 (438-J7 See Page 418)
DEW CT
5800 RKLN 95677 220-E5
DEWAR WY
6200 SaCo 95660 258-H4
DEWBERRY WY
8500 ELKG 95624 358-G1
DEWDROP WY
7300 CITH 95621 259-E1
DEWEY BLVD
5600 SaCo 95824 317-H5
DEWEY CT
300 LNCN 95648 179-F4
4900 RKLN 95677 220-G4
DEWEY DR
4700 SaCo 95608 279-F1
4700 SaCo 95628 279-F1
4900 SaCo 95628 259-F6
5000 SaCo 95608 259-F6
5700 CITH 95621 259-F6
5700 CITH 95628 259-F6
5800 SaCo 95621 259-F6
DEWEY ORCHARD CT
4700 SaCo 95608 279-F1
4700 SaCo 95628 279-F1
DE WITT CT
200 SAC 95838 278-B2
DE WITT DR
- PlaC 95603 162-A3
DEWSBURY DR
- RSVL 95746 240-F4
DEXTER CIR
4000 SaCo 95660 258-H2
DIABLO AV
2300 ANT 94509 (513-E6 See Page 493)
DIABLO CT
- AUB 95603 182-C6
DIABLO DR
- SaCo 95842 259-C3
DIABLO ST
2300 WSAC 95691 296-H7
DIABLO TR
3200 EDCo 95762 282-J3
3200 EDCo 95762 283-A4
DIABLO OAK CT
7100 SaCo 95842 259-C2
DIABLO VIEW CT
- EDCo 95726 267-G3
DIABLO VIEW LN
- PlaC 95650 201-A2
- PlaC 95663 201-A2
DIABLO VIEW TR
- EDCo - 267-G3
- EDCo 95726 267-G3
DIABLO VISTA AV
9700 SaCo 95632 419-B4
DIABLOWEN CT
- SaCo 95690 436-J1
DIAM DR
- EDCo 95667 265-H3
DIAMANTE
- RVIS 94571 454-F1
DIAMOND AV
1300 SAC 95815 278-A4
DIAMOND CT
- RKLN 95677 220-B4
6800 EDCo 95726 248-F3
DIAMOND DR
4100 EDCo 95619 265-F3
6700 EDCo 95726 248-E3
DIAMOND ST
100 AUB 95603 182-E1
800 ANT 94509 (513-C4 See Page 493)
DIAMOND BAR LN
400 RSVL 95678 219-J7
DIAMOND CREEK BLVD
- RSVL 95747 219-C2
DIAMOND CREST CT
8600 ELKG 95624 358-F5
DIAMOND GLEN CIR
1000 FOLS 95630 261-B6
DIAMOND GROVE CT
- RSVL 95747 219-D1
DIAMOND HEAD WY
9300 SaCo 95662 260-H5
DIAMOND HILL CT
4000 SaCo 95843 238-H5

DIAMOND HILLS DR
- RVIS 94571 454-G2
DIAMOND MEADOWS WY
4200 EDCo 95619 265-E3
DIAMOND OAK WY
8500 ELKG 95624 358-F5
DIAMOND OAKS RD
100 RSVL 95678 219-G6
500 RSVL 95678 220-A6
DIAMOND PARK LN
- RSVL 95747 199-D7
- RSVL 95747 219-D1
DIAMOND PEAK DR
100 FOLS 95630 260-H1
DIAMOND POINT LN
- ELKG 95624 357-G6
DIAMOND ROCK DR
- SaCo 95843 238-H7
DIAMOND WOODS CIR
- RSVL 95747 199-D7
- RSVL 95747 219-D1
DIAMONTE WY
9900 SaCo 95829 339-D7
DIAMONTE ROBLES CT
1000 EDCo 95619 265-E3
DIANA CT
200 EDCo 95667 245-D3
DIANA ST
100 EDCo 95667 245-D3
DIANA WY
7200 SaCo 95828 338-D1
DIANE DR
2900 WSAC 95691 316-E1
3900 SaCo 95843 238-H6
DIANTHUS LN
- EDCo 95762 242-C7
DIANTHUS WY
- ELKG 95624 338-F7
DIAS AV
6000 SAC 95824 318-A6
DIAS LN
3900 LMS 95650 200-J7
3900 LMS 95650 220-J1
3900 LMS 95677 200-J7
3900 RKLN 95650 200-J7
3900 RKLN 95677 200-J7
3900 RKLN 95650 220-J1
5400 RKLN 95677 220-J1
DIAS RD
2100 EDCo 95667 245-C1
DICK COOK RD
7800 PlaC 95650 221-D2
8300 PlaC 95746 221-D2
DICKENS DR
1100 GALT 95632 419-H5
4600 PlaC 95746 240-G5
DICKINSON CT
1500 RSVL 95747 219-C5
DICKINSON DR
1500 RSVL 95747 219-C6
DICKINSON RD
6200 EDCo 95667 226-J2
DICKSON ST
1400 SAC 95822 317-B5
DICUS CT
8000 CITH 95621 239-F7
DIDCOT CIR
3700 SAC 95838 277-G3
DIDION CT
4500 SaCo 95842 258-J6
DIDORWILL CT
9400 ELKG 95624 359-A1
DIEGEL CIR
6800 SAC 95822 317-D7
DIEGO WY
4100 RKLN 95677 220-E3
DIEPPE WY
7200 SaCo 95842 259-B2
DIERKS RD
8200 SaCo 95830 339-G6
DIERSSEN RD
- SaCo 95615 397-D14
3000 SaCo 95757 397-D14
3000 SaCo 95758 397-D14
DIESEL DR
1800 SAC 95838 278-B1
DIETRICH DR
100 RSVL 95678 239-J2
DIETZ WY
4500 SaCo 95628 280-B1
DIFANI CT
1300 SaCo 95864 298-E2
DIGESTERS WY
- SaCo 95758 337-F7
DIGGER RD
- EDCo - 267-E4
3600 PlaC 95602 160-H4
3600 PlaC 95658 160-H4
DIGGER PINE LN
9800 FOLS 95630 261-B1
DIGGER PINE RD
1300 EDCo 95672 243-B4
DIGGER PINE WY
300 EDCo 95619 265-D6
DIGGINS DR
100 FOLS 95630 261-B5
DIGGS PARK DR
1600 SAC 95815 278-B4
DIKE CT
8100 SaCo 95626 238-D6
DILLARD RD
7400 SaCo 95683 341-C2
7800 SaCo 95693 341-A7
7800 SaCo 95693 (361-A1 See Page 341)
8400 SaCo 95693 360-G4
9700 SaCo 95693 (380-B1 See Page 379)
9800 SaCo 95693 379-J1
11100 SaCo 95693 (399-C1 See Page 379)
DILLARD OAKS CT
8800 ELKG 95624 359-D3
DILLON CIR
10400 PlaC 95603 182-A6
DILLON CT
300 RSVL 95747 219-D6
7200 SaCo 95842 259-A2
DILLON CROSS WY
4900 SaCo 95843 239-A6
DILLON RIVER CT
- RCCD 95670 280-A5
DI LUSSO DR
6200 ELKG 95758 358-B3
DIMAGGIO WY
3200 ANT 94509 (513-A7 See Page 493)
DIMARCO CT
7800 SaCo 95829 339-E5

DIMENSIONS LN
8200 ELKG 95758 358-D6
DIMICK LN
4700 EDCo 95623 265-C4
DIMITY LN
1300 PLCR 95667 245-H4
DINGMAN CIR
4900 SaCo 95823 317-H7
DINIS COTTAGE CT
- LNCN 95648 200-B2
DINIS COTTAGE WY
- LNCN 95648 200-B2
DINO DR
9700 ELKG 95624 358-J7
9700 ELKG 95624 378-J1
DINSMORE WY
7200 SaCo 95828 318-C7
DINUBA CT
8700 ELKG 95624 358-G5
DINWIDDIE WY
2200 ELKG 95758 357-E4
DIOCLETIAN WY
6600 SaCo 95662 260-C3
DIOLINDA CT
- EDCo 95726 248-D5
DION CT
4000 SaCo 95826 318-H2
DIONYSUS WY
11700 RCCD 95742 320-D1
DIORITE WY
- SAC 95835 256-J5
DIPPER WY
5100 ELKG 95758 357-H3
DIRK LN
9200 PlaC 95650 201-H6
DISA ALPINE WY
8600 ELKG 95624 358-F3
DISCOVERY CT
- EDCo 95682 283-J7
DISCOVERY DR
1800 RSVL 95747 239-D1
DISCOVERY LN
1300 EDCo 95667 225-B7
1300 EDCo 95667 245-B1
DISCOVERY WY
1900 SAC 95817 297-H7
1900 SAC 95819 297-H7
5500 EDCo 95682 283-J7
DISCOVERY BAY CT
8300 SaCo 95843 238-H5
DISCOVERY PARK DR
- SAC 95833 277-B7
- SAC 95833 297-B1
DISCOVERY SHORES WY
- SAC 95833 276-H6
DISCOVERY VILLAGE LN
1800 SaCo 95670 280-A4
DISHERS WY
8600 SaCo 95843 238-F4
DISK DR
- RCCD 95670 299-J3
- SAC 95838 277-G3
DISMANTLE CT
- RCCD 95670 300-B5
DISPLAY WY
500 SAC 95838 277-H2
DISTRICT CT
- SAC 95826 318-G4
DITA CT
3500 EDCo 95682 263-E5
DITA WY
3100 EDCo 95682 263-D5
DITMARS LN
3100 PlaC 95650 201-F4
DITTMAR WY
600 SAC 95819 298-A5
DITZHAZY CT
- RSVL 95678 219-G4
DIVIDEND DR
3800 EDCo 95682 283-H2
DIVINITY HILL PL
- SAC 95835 256-G4
DIVOT CIR
5300 SaCo 95628 259-H6
DIVOT LN
12400 PlaC 95603 162-D4
DIXIEANNE AV
600 SAC 95815 277-J7
1200 SAC 95815 278-A7
DIXIE CANYON CT
8600 SaCo 95843 238-H5
DIXIELAND WY
- RCCD 95670 299-G4
DIXIE LOU ST
7700 SAC 95832 337-E4
DIXON CT
100 FOLS 95630 261-E4
DIXON LINE WY
5000 SaCo 95608 279-A2
5000 SaCo 95821 279-A2
DIZMAR CT
- EDCo 95682 263-E3
DOBROS DR
1400 WSAC 95605 296-H2
DOC BAR CT
9100 ELKG 95624 358-G4
DOC BARNS DR
- LMS 95650 201-A6
DOC DAY CT
- FOLS 95630 281-E1
DODBROOK CT
- RSVL 95747 218-J5
DODD PL
- LNCN 95648 179-F3
DODGE LN
2300 SaCo 95608 279-D7
DODSON LN
- SAC 95835 256-G6
DODSON PL
- SAC 95835 256-G6
DOE CT
- SAC 95823 337-G4
1100 RSVL 95661 239-J4
3200 EDCo 95682 263-C3
4900 EDCo 95682 264-E5
DOE ST
4500 EDCo 95682 264-E5
DOE HOLLOW PL
5100 SaCo 95843 239-B7
DOE RUN LN
700 PlaC 95658 181-E3
DOE SPRING WY
- EDCo 95762 282-D3
DOE TRAIL WY
- SaCo 95843 239-B7
DOE VIEW PL
5200 EDCo - 248-C7
5200 EDCo 95726 248-C7

DOGLEG CT
3200 EDCo 95682 263-D6
DOG TOWN RD
- SaCo 95829 339-E1
DOGWOOD LN
3400 EDCo 95667 226-H2
DOGWOOD LP
- LNCN 95648 179-H6
DOGWOOD WY
2100 ANT 94509 (513-B5 See Page 493)
7900 CITH 95621 239-G7
DOHENEY CT
900 RSVL 95661 239-J5
DOHENY CT
2400 RKLN 95677 220-B4
DOLAN CT
900 FOLS 95630 261-E7
DOLAN WY
7000 CITH 95621 259-F1
DOLECETTO DR
10300 RCCD 95670 299-F2
DOLLAR LN
5900 SaCo 95608 259-D5
DOLLHOUSE RD
- EDCo - 267-D6
DOLLY CT
100 RSVL 95678 219-J6
4400 SaCo 95842 258-J6
DOLLY D CT
8300 SaCo 95829 339-C7
DOLLY VARDEN LN
6000 EDCo 95726 248-B6
DOLOMITE PL
1800 SaCo 95670 280-B3
DOLORES ST
2700 ANT 94509 (513-C6 See Page 493)
DOLORES WY
1000 SAC 95816 297-G5
DOLPHIN CT
- WSAC 95691 296-J7
1100 RSVL 95661 240-A5
DOLPHIN WY
100 SaCo 95673 257-G3
DOLPHINFISH WY
7700 SaCo 95828 338-G4
DOM WY
1400 SaCo 95864 298-F2
DOMAINE CT
700 OAKL 94561 (514-D5 See Page 493)
DOMAINE WY
1700 OAKL 94561 (514-D5 See Page 493)
DOMICH WY
3500 SaCo 95821 278-G4
DO MILLS CT
1900 SaCo 95670 280-C4
DOMINGO CT
- SaCo 95683 342-B1
DOMINGO DR
6800 SaCo 95683 342-C1
DOMINGUEZ RD
4200 RKLN 95677 220-G1
DOMINICA ST
- WSAC 95691 316-E3
DOMINION WY
7800 SaCo 95626 238-D7
DOMINION WOOD LN
9500 ELKG 95758 358-D6
DOMINIQUE CT
8500 SaCo 95628 280-D2
DOMINO AV
1500 SAC 95835 257-D4
DOMITIAN ST
6700 SaCo 95662 260-C3
DON WY
5900 SaCo 95608 279-D3
DONAHUE CT
8400 SaCo 95628 280-C1
DONAHUE WY
1200 RSVL 95661 239-J5
1200 RSVL 95661 240-A5
DONALD WY
8400 CITH 95610 239-J6
DONALDSON CT
900 LNCN 95648 179-D2
DONALDSON WY
100 FOLS 95630 261-G3
DONAT CT
9300 SaCo 95662 260-H2
DONATELLA CT
- EDCo 95762 262-B2
DONATELLO CT
- ELKG 95757 378-A1
DONATELLO WY
- LNCN 95648 179-E2
DONAU CT
800 LNCN 95648 200-A2
DON CARLOS CT
9800 ELKG 95624 378-G1
DONCASTER CT
9000 ELKG 95624 358-F4
DONCASTER DR
1000 ANT 94509 (513-C7 See Page 493)
DONCREST LN
6300 SaCo 95660 258-H4
DONDRA WY
900 SAC 95838 277-J2
DONEGAL CT
- LNCN 95648 200-B2
DONEGAL DR
6400 CITH 95621 259-E4
DONEGAL BAY DR
- ELKG 95624 358-F6
DONEGAN CT
100 FOLS 95630 281-B1
DONELL CT
- EDCo 95682 263-F4
DONERAIL DR
6700 SaCo 95842 259-B3
DONEVA AV
7700 SaCo 95628 279-J3
DONGSTON WY
9100 SaCo 95826 318-J1
DONHAM CT
800 ANT 94509 (513-C7 See Page 493)
DON JUAN DR
2500 RCCD 95670 299-H1
DON JULIO BLVD
3600 SaCo 95660 258-H3
4500 SaCo 95842 258-H3
4500 SaCo 95842 259-A3
7600 SaCo 95843 239-B6
7600 SaCo 95843 259-A3
8500 PlaC 95747 239-B6

DONKEY LN
- EDCo 95672 243-B1
DONLYN PL
5300 SaCo 95843 239-B5
DONMAR LN
10200 ELKG 95624 359-E1
DONMERLINO CT
- SAC 95820 318-B2
DONNA CIR
3800 SaCo 95660 278-G1
DONNA MARIE CT
- SAC 95831 336-H2
DONNAWOOD WY
8100 SaCo 95662 260-B2
DONNELLY CIR
- FOLS 95630 281-E1
DONNELLY CT
400 RSVL 95747 219-D7
DONNELLY LN
6200 SaCo 95824 317-G6
DONNER AV
100 RSVL 95678 239-J2
DONNER RD
- WSAC 95691 316-H2
DONNER TR
3900 EDCo 95667 246-B7
DONNER WY
2300 SAC 95818 317-E1
2700 SAC 95817 317-E1
DONNER PASS AV
- SAC 95835 257-A5
DONNER PEAK CT
2100 SaCo 95670 280-C5
DONNIE LYN WY
4700 SaCo 95608 279-A5
DONNINGTON AV
100 AUB 95603 182-F3
DONNYBROOK CT
- LNCN 95648 200-B3
DONNYBROOK WY
4300 SaCo 95628 279-G2
DONOHUE PL
2300 EDCo 95762 242-C5
DONOVAN DR
- LNCN 95648 179-E2
- SaCo 95638 (400-E7 See Page 379)
4700 SaCo 95608 279-A7
DONOVAN RANCH RD
2000 EDCo 95667 245-G7
2000 EDCo 95667 265-G1
DONTREE WY
8900 ELKG 95624 358-G7
DOO DAH DR
- EDCo 95619 286-F5
DOOLITTLE DR
200 PlaC 95747 239-A4
DOOLITTLE ST
100 SAC 95838 278-B2
DORADELL CT
900 GALT 95632 419-F3
DORADELL WY
900 GALT 95632 419-F3
DORADO ST
7200 SaCo 95673 257-H1
DORADO BAY CT
8800 SaCo 95828 338-G4
DORADO RIDGE TR
1700 EDCo 95672 222-H6
DORAL CT
8000 CITH 95610 260-A6
DORAN AV
3500 WSAC 95691 296-E4
DORCEY DR
5400 ELKG 95757 377-J3
5400 ELKG 95757 397-J3
DORCHESTER CT
3000 EDCo 95762 263-A5
6300 SaCo 95608 279-E4
DORCHESTER DR
1400 RSVL 95678 219-F7
DORCHESTER LN
4600 PlaC 95746 240-G5
DORCHESTER WY
3000 EDCo 95762 263-A5
DOREEN WY
6600 SaCo 95823 317-H7
DORENA PL
- WSAC 95691 316-D3
DORER DR
100 AUB 95603 182-D3
DORIAN DR
8000 SaCo 95628 280-A1
DORIC CT
8600 ELKG 95624 358-F2
DORINDA CT
300 LNCN 95648 179-F5
DORINDA WY
6400 SaCo 95608 279-E2
DORINE WY
2600 SAC 95833 277-D6
DORINGTON CT
8800 ELKG 95624 358-G3
DORIS CT
2700 SaCo 95608 279-A6
DORKING CT
4300 SaCo 95864 298-J4
DORLAINE CT
3000 SaCo 95821 278-H5
DORMITY RD
1700 EDCo 95672 262-J3
DORNAJO WY
- SaCo 95825 298-D3
DORNIE CIR
- FOLS 95630 261-J2
DOROTEO WY
3100 SAC 95833 277-B4
DOROTHY WY
600 AUB 95603 162-D7
DOROTHY JUNE WY
2200 SAC 95838 278-C2
DORRINGTON CT
- RSVL 95661 220-F7
DORRINGTON DR
- RSVL 95661 220-E7
DORSET WY
5400 SAC 95822 316-J4
5500 SAC 95822 317-A4
DORSETT CT
- LNCN 95648 179-E4
DORSEY CT
- EDCo 95762 262-H4
DORSEY WY
8600 SaCo 95828 338-F7
DORY WY
5000 SaCo 95628 259-J7
DOS ACRES WY
3600 SaCo 95821 278-F4

© 2007 Rand McNally & Company

STREET
Block City ZIP Pg-Grid

DOSANJH LN
- SaCo 95632 420-J2
DOS LAGOS CT
- EDCo - 247-C6
DOS PALOS LN
3600 SaCo 95660 258-F1
DOS RIOS ST
200 SAC 95814 297-D2
DOSS WY
4100 SAC 95823 337-G2
DOS VISTAS DR
2800 EDCo 95672 263-G3
2800 EDCo 95682 263-G3
DOTMAR WY
5800 SaCo 95660 258-G5
DOTTY ST
3800 SaCo 95608 279-E3
DOTY LN
- EDCo 95667 266-A5
DOUBLE EAGLE WY
- SaCo 95829 339-D5
DOUBLETREE CT
100 FOLS 95630 241-B7
DOUBLE TREE LN
- EDCo - 267-D4
DOUBLIN BAY CT
- ELKG 95624 359-A7
DOUBLOON CT
6100 ELKG 95758 358-A5
DOUGHTY'S PL
1700 EDCo 95762 242-F6
DOUGLAS BLVD
100 RSVL 95661 240-B2
100 RSVL 95678 239-H2
1100 RSVL 95678 240-B2
4000 PlaC 95746 240-G2
5600 PlaC 95746 241-A2
DOUGLAS DR
- LNCN 95648 179-E4
DOUGLAS RD
- RCCD 95655 300-A7
- SaCo 95655 300-A7
11400 RCCD 95742 300-F7
11700 RCCD 95742 301-A7
See Page 493
DOUGLAS ST
500 WSAC 95605 297-A2
3300 SAC 95838 278-B4
DOUGLAS FIR CT
- EDCo - 247-F2
3700 SaCo 95843 238-G5
DOUGLAS FIR DR
- EDCo - 247-G2
DOUGLAS PLAZA DR
- PlaC 95746 241-A2
DOUGLAS RANCH DR
- PlaC 95746 240-H2
DOULTON CT
200 RSVL 95661 240-D3
DOULTON DR
1500 RSVL 95661 240-D3
DOUVAN CT
4900 SaCo 95608 279-A6
DOVE CT
800 LNCN 95648 179-F2
7500 PlaC 95746 241-D2
DOVE DR
4900 SaCo 95628 279-G1
4900 SaCo 95628 259-G7
DOVE LN
- EDCo - 267-C5
DOVE WY
600 RSVL 95661 240-B3
DOVE CREEK CT
7800 SaCo 95828 338-E4
DOVELA CT
7300 CITH 95621 259-F2
DOVE MEADOW CT
- RSVL 95661 239-J4
2700 EDCo 95682 283-C2
9100 ELKG 95624 378-H1
DOVER AV
5000 SAC 95819 297-J6
DOVER CT
200 LNCN 95648 179-E4
800 EDCo 95762 282-D2
DOVER DR
200 GALT 95632 439-D1
8300 PlaC 95746 241-B2
DOVER LN
- SaCo 95842 259-A1
600 LNCN 95648 179-F4
DOVERCOURT CIR
4700 SaCo 95608 299-A4
DOVER ISLE CT
- RSVL 95747 219-C1
DOVE TAIL LN
1700 EDCo 95762 282-H1
DOVE TREE LN
- ELKG 95758 357-H2
DOVEWOOD CT
9300 SaCo 95662 260-H5
DOW AV
7700 CITH 95610 259-J2
DOWELL LN
- EDCo 95619 266-A6
DOWIE PL
2500 SaCo 95821 278-D6
DOWITCHER CT
- OAKL 94561 (514-H7
See Page 493)
DOWITCHER WY
8500 SaCo 95843 238-J5
DOWN WY
7600 CITH 95610 259-J6
DOWNAR WY
2200 SAC 95652 278-C2
2200 SAC 95838 278-C2
DOWNE CT
900 EDCo 95762 262-D4
DOWNEY WY
3600 SAC 95817 297-G7
DOWNIEVILLE CT
1600 EDCo 95762 262-C1
DOWNIEVILLE DR
1200 EDCo 95762 242-C7
1200 EDCo 95762 262-C1
DOWNING CIR
600 LNCN 95648 179-F5
DOWNING CT
4600 PlaC 95746 240-G5
DOWNING DR
100 GALT 95632 439-D1
DOWNING LN
4200 EDCo 95619 265-G3
DOWNING PL
7600 SaCo 95843 259-B1
DOWN RIVER CT
- SAC 95831 336-F1
1000 RSVL 95747 219-E5

DOWNTHA RD
4800 EDCo 95619 265-D6
DOWN THE HILL WY
- EDCo 95667 266-G4
DOWSBY CT
- RSVL 95661 220-F6
DOYLE ST
100 RSVL 95678 239-J1
DOYLE WY
10300 RCCD 95670 299-F2
DOYLE RANCH DR
- PlaC 95747 238-J3
DRACENA DR
7800 CITH 95610 240-A6
7800 CITH 95610 239-J6
DRACO DR
3400 RCCD 95827 299-C6
DRAFT HORSE LN
- PlaC 95650 221-D2
DRAGONFLY CIR
- SAC 95834 276-J4
- SAC 95834 277-A4
DRAGONFLY CT
200 RSVL 95747 219-A5
DRAGONFLY LN
100 RSVL 95747 219-B5
DRAGON SPRINGS RD
5500 EDCo 95667 244-D6
DRAIS CT
- ELKG 95624 358-D1
DRAIS WY
- ELKG 95624 358-D1
DRAKE CIR
400 SaCo 95864 298-E4
DRAKE CT
400 PLCR 95667 245-B5
1100 RSVL 95661 240-C4
1400 OAKL 94561 (514-D7
See Page 493)
DRAKE DR
800 PlaC 95658 181-H4
DRAKE ST
- ANT 94509 (513-C6
See Page 493)
DRAKE MEADOW WY
9000 ELKG 95624 378-H1
DRAKES LN
- EDCo 95672 243-H5
DRAKES BAY CT
9100 ELKG 95758 357-H4
DRAKES BAY ST
- WSAC 95691 316-D2
DRAKESHIRE SQ
100 FOLS 95630 261-G6
DRAMBUIE CT
- PlaC 95650 221-H2
DRAPER WY
1200 AUB 95603 182-F2
DRAWBRIDGE CT
- SAC 95833 276-H6
DRAYTON DR
2300 SaCo 95825 278-F7
DREAM CT
5100 SaCo 95842 259-B2
DREAM LN
- EDCo - 247-F2
- SAC 95821 278-C5
DREAMGARDEN LP
5000 RSVL 95747 219-A6
DREAM INN CT
- RSVL 95747 219-A5
DREAM INN LN
7000 RSVL 95747 219-A4
DREAM RANCH CIR
- EDCo 95619 286-C4
DREAM RANCH CT
- EDCo 95619 286-C4
DREAMY WY
1300 SAC 95835 257-C5
DREDGER WY
5000 SaCo 95662 260-H6
DREHER ST
1600 SAC 95814 297-E2
DRESDEN CT
2200 SaCo 95825 298-C3
DRESDEN DR
- LNCN 95648 199-H1
DRESHER PARK WY
7100 SAC 95824 318-B6
DRESSAGE WY
8200 SaCo 95829 339-E7
DRESSLER WY
2200 RSVL 95747 239-D1
2200 RSVL 95747 219-D7
DREVER ST
800 WSAC 95691 297-A4
900 WSAC 95691 296-J4
DREW CT
1800 SaCo 95608 299-B1
DREW ST
1100 WSAC 95605 296-H2
DREXEL CT
10400 RCCD 95670 299-G4
DREYFUS WY
- ELKG 95758 358-C6
DRIAD CT
- SAC 95823 337-G2
DRIFT WY
9400 SaCo 95662 260-H6
DRIFTSTONE CT
1000 FOLS 95630 261-E6
DRIFTWOOD
8300 CITH 95610 240-C7
DRIFTWOOD CIR
2000 EDCo 95762 242-B6
DRIFTWOOD CT
2600 WSAC 95691 316-G1
4900 OAKL 94561 (514-D6
See Page 493)
E DRIFTWOOD CT
5500 RKLN 95677 220-C5
W DRIFTWOOD CT
5600 RKLN 95677 220-C5
DRIFTWOOD ST
6300 SAC 95831 316-F6
DRIPPING ROCK LN
- LNCN 95648 200-B3
DRISCOL DR
800 GALT 95632 419-D7
DRIVE-IN WY
2000 PlaC 95603 162-C5
DRIVER WY
3500 SaCo 95843 238-G6
DRIVER RANCH CT
8100 SaCo 95843 238-F6
DRIVEWAY RD
3400 EDCo 95667 245-A6
DROLLET WY
300 SAC 95838 277-G1

DROMOLAND CT
12500 SaCo 95632 419-G1
DROUIN DR
100 RVIS 94571 454-G4
DRUIN LN
500 RVIS 94571 454-G5
DRUMMOND CT
100 FOLS 95630 261-F7
DRUMMOND LN
1400 LNCN 95648 179-F5
DRUMMOND WY
- EDCo 95682 263-F4
DRURY CT
9000 SaCo 95826 318-H2
DRUSY AV
- SAC 95834 277-B3
DRY BRANCH CT
- SAC 95834 277-B4
DRY CREEK RD
300 FOLS 95630 282-B2
3600 SAC 95838 278-A2
4600 EDCo 95672 243-J5
4600 SAC 95838 258-A7
5600 SaCo 95673 258-A1
5600 SaCo 95838 258-A5
7300 SaCo 95673 238-A7
7600 SaCo 95626 238-A7
11100 PlaC 95602 161-J1
11400 PlaC 95602 162-A1
N DRY CREEK RD
27700 SJCo 95638 421-F7
DRY CREEK ST
- WSAC 95691 316-G7
DRYDEN CT
8800 SaCo 95828 338-G6
DRY DIGGINS WY
2100 SaCo 95670 280-B4
DRY DOCK WY
4800 SAC 95838 257-H7
DRY GULCH CT
2900 RKLN 95677 200-D7
DRY LAKE LN
3800 PlaC 95602 162-A1
DRY RIVER WY
- ELKG 95624 359-B6
DRYWOOD WY
6900 SaCo 95662 260-B2
6900 SaCo 95610 260-C2
DUARTE AV
4500 OAKL 94561 (514-E6
See Page 493)
DUARTE CT
2500 SaCo 95821 278-G6
2500 SaCo 95864 278-G6
DUARTE RD
2200 PlaC 95650 200-J2
2200 PlaC 95663 200-J2
DUBAC WY
3700 SaCo 95864 278-G7
DUBASARY LN
- EDCo 95726 248-J1
DUBLIN RD
5100 EDCo 95623 265-B4
DUBLIN WY
6000 CITH 95610 259-H5
DUBOIS AV
100 SAC 95838 277-G2
DU BOIS DR
2500 RSVL 95661 240-E2
DUCHESS CT
- RKLN 95765 200-C6
DUCHOW WY
800 FOLS 95630 261-C5
DUCK CALL CT
2600 ELKG 95757 357-E7
DUCK HOLLOW CT
1500 EDCo 95672 242-J5
1500 EDCo 95672 243-A5
DUCKHORN CT
500 OAKL 94561 (514-D5
See Page 493)
DUCKHORN DR
- SAC 95833 277-A4
- SAC 95834 256-H7
- SAC 95834 276-H1
- SAC 95834 277-A4
DUCKHORN LN
- LNCN 95648 200-A1
DUCKHORN PL
500 OAKL 94561 (514-E5
See Page 493)
DUCKLING WY
6800 SaCo 95842 259-A2
DUCKS POND WY
- ELKG 95758 358-D3
DUCKWALK WY
5400 SAC 95835 256-H4
DUCKWEED ST
- PlaC 95747 239-C5
DUDEN DR
1600 PLCR 95667 246-A6
DUDLEY BLVD
- SaCo 95652 278-D1
5600 SaCo 95652 258-F7
5800 SaCo 95660 258-F7
DUDLEY DR
400 RSVL 95678 239-G3
2500 EDCo 95672 263-D1
DUDLEY LP
- SaCo 95652 278-F1
DUDLEY ST
7400 CITH 95610 259-H2
DUDLEY WY
600 SAC 95818 297-B6
DUERR RD
- PlaC 95650 201-H6
DUET CT
3500 SaCo 95826 318-J1
DUET DR
7500 WSAC 95691 316-G1
DUFF CT
6100 SaCo 95660 258-H4
DUFFERS DR
8300 PlaC 95663 201-E3
DUFFIELD LN
7900 SaCo 95628 280-A2
DUFFY LN
9300 PlaC 95747 239-B4
DUFFY RD
4500 EDCo 95619 265-F4
DUGGAN WY
6800 SaCo 95662 260-E3
DUKE DR
4300 SAC 95822 317-A3
DUKE ST
- RKLN 95765 200-C5
DUKELANA LN
1100 PlaC 95658 181-H6

DULCIBELLA PL
- SAC 95835 256-G4
DULUTH AV
- PlaC 95765 199-E7
- PlaC 95765 219-E1
- RSVL 95678 219-E1
- RSVL 95747 219-E1
DULUTH ST
2900 WSAC 95691 296-F3
DULVERTON CIR
100 FOLS 95630 261-H6
DULWICH WY
5800 SAC 95835 256-J3
DULZURA CT
15100 SaCo 95683 342-C3
DUMARS CT
4100 SaCo 95843 238-H7
DUMAS CT
400 RSVL 95747 219-E6
DUMAS WY
1100 RSVL 95747 219-E6
DU MAURIER CT
100 RSVL 95747 219-B6
DUMFRIES CT
- SAC 95831 336-E1
DUMONT CT
- LNCN 95648 179-E4
DUMONT LN
7300 SaCo 95823 338-A2
DUNBAR CT
- LNCN 95648 179-D2
DUNBAR RD
3400 EDCo 95672 263-C7
DUNBAR WY
2000 RSVL 95678 219-J6
10800 RCCD 95670 279-H7
10800 RCCD 95670 299-H1
DUNBARTON CIR
700 SAC 95825 298-C6
DUNBARTON CT
- RSVL 95746 240-F4
DUNBLANE WY
7600 ELKG 95758 358-C5
DUNCAN CT
- FOLS 95630 261-D7
DUNCAN LN
6700 SaCo 95608 279-F4
DUNCAN WY
- FOLS 95630 261-D7
100 RSVL 95678 239-G4
DUNCAN HILL RD
300 PlaC 95603 182-B3
4400 EDCo 95672 243-H7
DUNCAN MINE RD
100 PlaC 95603 182-B3
DUNCANSBY CT
8100 SaCo 95829 338-J6
DUNCRAIG WY
- GALT 95632 419-G3
DUNDALK CT
4300 SaCo 95843 238-J6
DUNDEE DR
6200 SaCo 95660 258-H4
DUNEDIN PL
6500 ELKG 95758 358-A3
DUNES CT
8100 SaCo 95828 338-D6
DUNFORD WY
- RSVL 95747 239-D1
1500 RSVL 95747 219-D7
DUNISCH RD
8100 ELKG 95758 358-D3
DUNKELD LN
- FOLS 95630 261-J3
DUNKERRIN WY
9400 ELKG 95758 358-B5
DUNLAP DR
2200 SaCo 95821 278-C5
DUNLAP RANCH RD
- EDCo 95762 (302-G1
See Page 301)
DUNLAY DR
- SAC 95835 257-A4
DUNLEWY WY
- LNCN 95648 200-B2
DUNLIN CT
- LNCN 95648 200-C1
- SAC 95833 276-H7
DUNMORE AV
6600 CITH 95621 259-F5
DUNN DR
- SaCo 95683 341-H1
DUNNBURY WY
4500 SaCo 95842 258-J1
4500 SaCo 95842 259-A1
DUNNINGS RD
2300 EDCo 95682 244-A7
2400 EDCo 95682 264-A1
DUNNWOOD CT
- EDCo 95762 282-C2
DUNNWOOD DR
- EDCo 95762 282-C2
DUNROAMIN WY
6800 EDCo 95667 244-J5
DUNSLEY CIR
- RSVL 95747 218-J4
DUNSMIUR CT
8000 SaCo 95828 338-G6
DUNSMUIR LN
8000 SaCo 95829 339-D3
DUNSTABLE WY
100 FOLS 95630 261-G6
DUNSTAN PL
6100 ELKG 95758 358-A2
DUNSTER WY
3900 SaCo 95864 298-H5
DUNSWOOD PL
- SAC 95835 256-J3
DUOVO WY
9000 ELKG 95758 358-D3
DU PONT CT
200 RSVL 95661 240-F2
DUPONT DR
2100 EDCo 95667 244-C6
DU PONT WY
2600 RSVL 95661 240-E2
DUPONT WY
9100 SaCo 95826 298-J7
DUPREE CT
8600 ELKG 95624 358-H1
DURADO CT
4200 EDCo 95667 265-A2
DURAN CIR
3700 SaCo 95821 278-G6
DURANGO CT
2600 EDCo 95667 244-B5
4400 SaCo 95628 280-F2
DURANGO WY
9400 ELKG 95624 358-H6

DURANTA ST
100 RSVL 95678 239-G2
E DURANTA ST
200 RSVL 95678 239-G1
W DURANTA ST
200 RSVL 95678 239-G1
DURAZNO CT
- SAC 95833 276-J7
DURBAIN CT
100 FOLS 95630 281-E1
DURELLO CIR
3400 RCCD 95670 299-J4
DURER PKWY
4400 SaCo 95823 337-H2
DURFEE WY
7300 SAC 95831 336-H2
DURHAM CT
- RKLN 95765 200-C5
DURHAM PL
1600 EDCo 95762 242-C6
DURHAM RD
- RKLN 95765 200-C5
DURHAM ST
7000 CITH 95621 259-F2
DURLAND WY
4900 SaCo 95628 259-J7
4900 SaCo 95628 279-J1
DURNESS WY
9000 SaCo 95829 338-J6
DURNEY CT
9000 SaCo 95829 338-H5
DUROCK CT
4100 EDCo 95682 263-J7
4100 EDCo 95682 283-J1
DUROCK RD
3300 EDCo 95682 263-J7
3300 EDCo 95682 283-G1
3800 EDCo 95682 264-A7
DURSEY CT
100 RSVL 95747 219-C7
DURWARD CT
8100 PlaC 95746 241-C2
DURYEA DR
8600 SaCo 95828 338-F5
DUSENBERG CT
8000 SaCo 95828 338-F5
DUSHAM CIR
100 SaCo 95655 319-J2
100 SaCo 95655 320-A2
DUST CLOUD DR
4500 EDCo 95682 283-F7
N DUSTIN RD
21900 SJCo 95220 (440-E5
See Page 420)
23400 SJCo 95632 (440-E5
See Page 420)
DUSTY CT
3300 SaCo 95827 299-B6
DUSTY LN
- EDCo 95619 266-A5
3000 PlaC 95650 200-H4
DUSTY GOLD CT
3300 EDCo 95667 245-D7
DUSTY GOLD LN
3300 EDCo 95667 245-E6
DUSTY ROSE WY
5100 RCCD 95742 320-E4
DUSTY TRAIL CT
- RKLN 95765 199-J5
DUSTY TRAIL WY
1700 EDCo 95762 242-F5
DUSTY TRAILS PL
9500 ELKG 95624 359-B6
DUTCH CT
7000 PlaC 95658 181-C4
DUTCH WY
- SaCo 95608 279-E4
DUTCH BAR CT
11800 SaCo 95670 280-D4
DUTCH CREEK CT
2100 SaCo 95670 280-D5
DUTCHER CT
- SaCo 95829 338-J6
DUTCHESS CT
5900 SaCo 95628 260-B5
DUTCHESS WY
100 RCCD 95827 299-E4
DUTCH FLAT DR
7200 SaCo 95660 258-J1
DUTCH HARBOR CT
900 GALT 95632 419-F3
DUTCH HAVEN BLVD
8100 SaCo 95626 238-D5
DUTCHMAN DR
- EDCo 95709 247-B3
DUTCHMANS MINE RD
10400 PlaC 95603 182-A3
DUTCH MINE RD
6500 EDCo 95619 265-C6
DUTCH RAVINE CT
11400 SaCo 95670 280-B5
DUTCH RAVINE LN
300 PlaC 95658 181-C5
DUTRA AV
800 SaCo 95673 257-J1
DUTRA BEND DR
1000 SAC 95831 337-A4
7700 SAC 95831 336-J3
DUTTON WY
5500 SAC 95823 357-J1
DUVAL ST
- CITH 95621 239-G5
DUXBURG CT
3900 SaCo 95827 319-B1
DUXBURY WY
100 FOLS 95630 261-G6
DUZEL ROCK PL
3400 SaCo 95827 299-B7
DWIGHT RD
- ELKG 95758 357-G3
- ELKG 95758 357-G4
3400 ELKG 95758 357-G3
3400 SaCo 95758 357-G3
DYE ST
- SaCo 95690 437-A1
DYE WY
5500 SaCo 95608 299-B2
DYER CT
2900 EDCo 95667 226-G3
7600 SaCo 95828 338-D3
12200 PlaC 95603 162-C4
DYER LN
5900 PlaC 95626 238-A3
5900 PlaC 95747 238-C3
DYER WY
2700 EDCo 95667 226-F3
DYLAN AV
7000 SAC 95824 318-B5

DYMAXION WY
- EDCo 95762 262-F7
DYMENT CT
7900 ELKG 95758 358-C6
DYMIC WY
4200 SAC 95838 277-J2
DYMICO CT
7800 SaCo 95628 259-J7
DYNAMIC WY
2500 EDCo 95682 243-J7
DYNASTY WY
- SAC 95835 257-C6
9700 ELKG 95624 359-A7
DYRELL WY
100 FOLS 95630 261-F4
DYSART DR
- SaCo 95829 338-J5
DYSART WY
- FOLS 95630 261-J5
- FOLS 95630 262-A5

E

E AV
11400 PlaC 95603 162-A4
E ST
100 ISLE 95641 455-H5
100 SaCo 95673 257-F4
100 LNCN 95648 179-H4
100 RSVL 95678 239-G3
100 WSAC 95605 297-A3
200 ANT 94509 (513-D3
See Page 493)
400 GALT 95632 419-E7
700 SAC 95814 297-D3
700 WSAC 95605 296-J3
1000 SaCo 95673 258-A4
2000 SAC 95816 297-F3
2600 SaCo 95652 258-E5
3500 SaCo 95660 258-G5
3900 SAC 95819 297-H4
5300 SAC 95819 298-A5
11500 PlaC 95603 162-A4
W E ST
100 GALT 95632 419-E7
EAGLE CT
2300 RKLN 95677 220-B2
EAGLE DR
2200 RKLN 95677 220-B2
EAGLE LN
2400 EDCo 95682 263-B3
EAGLE RD
7100 SaCo 95628 259-G7
EAGLE ST
- WSAC 95691 316-D4
EAGLE BEND CT
9900 SaCo 95829 339-D4
EAGLE CANYON RD
- EDCo - 267-F5
EAGLE CREEK CT
- PlaC 95747 238-J2
100 FOLS 95630 260-J1
EAGLE CREST CIR
3500 SaCo 95843 238-G5
EAGLECREST WY
- RKLN 95765 219-J1
EAGLE GLEN DR
- RSVL 95661 220-D7
- RSVL 95661 240-D1
EAGLE GLEN WY
- RVIS 94571 454-G2
EAGLEMONT LN
- PlaC - 160-B5
- PlaC 95648 160-B5
EAGLE PARK DR
7600 SaCo 95828 338-C4
EAGLE PEAK CT
4800 SaCo 95843 239-A6
EAGLE PEAK WY
7900 SaCo 95843 239-A6
EAGLE POINT WY
7600 SaCo 95843 239-C7
7600 SaCo 95843 259-C1
EAGLE POINTE CT
- PlaC 95747 239-A3
EAGLE RIDGE CIR
800 FOLS 95630 261-J6
EAGLE RIDGE WY
4200 SaCo 95843 238-H7
EAGLE RIVER CT
2200 RCCD 95670 279-J5
EAGLE ROCK CT
- SAC 95824 318-B6
EAGLE ROCK RD
2800 PlaC 95650 201-F3
2800 PlaC 95663 201-F3
EAGLESFIELD LN
- LNCN 95648 179-F7
EAGLES NEST
3000 AUB 95603 182-E6
EAGLES NEST DR
- LMS 95650 201-B4
EAGLES NEST RD
- SaCo 95655 300-B7
4000 SaCo 95655 320-B3
5600 SaCo 95830 320-B7
6300 SaCo 95830 340-B4
7100 SaCo 95624 340-B4
EAGLESON CT
8900 SaCo 95826 298-H6
EAGLES PEAK LN
- LNCN 95648 200-C1
EAGLE SPRINGS CT
- PlaC 95747 239-B4
EAGLE SPRINGS PL
- PlaC 95747 239-A4
EAGLES ROOST CT
- RSVL 95747 219-D2
EAGLETON CT
- RSVL 95746 240-F5
EAGLETON WY
- RSVL 95746 240-F5
EAGLE VIEW DR
3500 EDCo 95682 263-E6
EAGLE VIEW LN
7800 PlaC 95746 221-E5
EAGLE VIEW WY
5500 SaCo 95842 259-C2
EAGLE WIND DR
- RSVL 95747 219-C2
EAMES LN
- ELKG 95758 357-F4
EAMON CT
- RKLN 95677 220-C1
EARHART AV
12700 AUB 95602 162-C2
EARHART DR
6800 SAC 95837 256-B3
6900 SaCo 95837 236-B7

EARL AV
100 RSVL 95678 239-H3
EARLCORT CIR
4900 SaCo 95842 259-A2
EARL FIFE RD
9200 ELKG 95624 358-H4
EARLHAM LN
- LNCN 95648 179-F7
EARLMAR CT
8700 ELKG 95624 358-G3
EARLS CT
5100 SAC 95822 317-A3
EARLSTON CT
7700 SaCo 95843 238-J7
EARLTON LN
- LNCN 95648 179-E7
EARLY WY
- RSVL 95747 219-C3
EARLY LIGHT CT
- RSVL 95747 219-A7
EARLY LIGHT WY
- ELKG 95624 359-B5
EARLY MORNING WY
8100 SaCo 95843 239-A6
EARLY TIMES LN
3200 PlaC 95603 161-B5
8600 SaCo 95693 360-J3
EARNELL ST
5400 SaCo 95608 259-D6
EARNSCLIFF AV
4000 SaCo 95628 280-B2
EARNSHAW WY
- EDCo 95667 266-C5
EAST AV
400 LNCN 95648 179-J3
EAST DR
100 PlaC 95747 239-E2
EAST LN
4100 SaCo 95864 298-H1
EAST PKWY
7000 SaCo 95823 337-H1
EAST RD
4100 EDCo 95667 265-B2
S EAST RD
- SAC 95822 317-D2
EAST ST
100 AUB 95603 182-D2
100 RSVL 95678 220-A7
100 RSVL 95678 240-A1
EASTBREEZE CIR
7600 SaCo 95828 338-G4
EASTBROOK WY
- SAC 95835 257-A5
EASTCLIFF DR
8000 SaCo 95628 280-A1
EASTCLIFF WY
2700 LNCN 95648 200-A3
EAST COVE CT
- SAC 95831 336-J3
EASTERLY RANCH RD
900 EDCo 95619 265-F2
EASTERN AV
900 SaCo 95864 298-H2
2100 SaCo 95864 278-J5
2500 SaCo 95821 278-J5
EASTGATE AV
7500 CITH 95610 259-H5
EASTHAM CT
- SAC 95833 277-A6
EASTHAVEN WY
6800 CITH 95621 259-F1
EAST HILL CT
1100 GALT 95632 419-H2
EASTLEIGH CT
- ELKG 95624 358-E3
EASTMAN CT
7900 SaCo 95828 338-E5
EASTMONT CT
6200 SaCo 95608 279-D5
EASTON WY
5200 SaCo 95843 239-B7
EASTPOINTE CT
- ELKG 95624 358-H1
EAST RANCH RD
100 SAC 95825 298-D5
100 SAC 95864 298-D5
EASTRIDGE CT
400 RSVL 95746 240-G6
EASTRIDGE DR
- LNCN 95648 200-A2
400 RSVL 95746 240-F5
5500 SaCo 95842 259-C3
EASTSIDE CT
6900 SaCo 95662 260-D2
EASTVIEW CT
8500 SaCo 95662 260-D2
EAST VIEW DR
3200 EDCo 95682 264-A5
EASTWIND CT
- SAC 95831 336-J2
EASTWOOD DR
- RSVL 95747 218-J4
EASTWOOD RD
3200 SaCo 95821 278-G5
EASTWOOD ST
4100 SaCo 95628 280-B2
EASTWOOD VILLAGE LN
4000 SaCo 95608 279-G3
EASY LN
1300 EDCo 95762 242-E2
EASY ST
- EDCo 95726 248-C1
2800 EDCo 95667 245-C5
2800 PLCR 95667 245-C5
EASY WY
100 AUB 95603 182-D2
2900 SaCo 95608 279-B6
EATON CT
300 SAC 95838 277-G2
8500 PlaC 95746 241-D2
EATON DR
3300 RSVL 95661 240-E4
EATON LN
9500 SaCo 95662 260-J3
EBANO CT
6400 CITH 95621 259-F4
EBBTIDE CT
- SAC 95831 316-G7
EBE ST
3900 SaCo 95826 318-H2
EBI WY
- FOLS 95630 281-C1
EBONY CT
- SAC 95823 337-F3
EBONY OAKS PL
8300 PlaC 95746 241-B2
EBONYWOOD CT
6100 CITH 95621 239-E7

STREET / Block City ZIP Pg-Grid

EBURY LN
7900 SaCo 95628 280-A2
ECHO CT
100 FOLS 95630 261-E5
ECHO LN
1800 LNCN 95648 180-B7
6300 EDCo 95667 264-J1
6300 EDCo 95667 265-A1
ECHO WY
2600 SaCo 95821 278-E5
ECHO CLIFF CT
9400 ELKG 95758 358-B5
ECHO RIDGE CT
9100 ELKG 95624 338-J7
ECHO RIDGE RD
4600 RKLN 95677 220-G5
ECHO ROCK CT
100 RSVL 95747 219-B5
ECHO ROCK LN
200 RSVL 95747 219-B5
ECHO SPRINGS CIR
4500 EDCo 95762 262-F3
ECKARD WY
300 AUB 95603 162-E6
ECKERMAN CT
4200 EDCo 95682 264-A6
ECKERMAN RD
9300 PlaC 95661 240-E5
ECKERT CT
- SAC 95823 337-H6
ECKLON CT
100 FOLS 95630 261-F4
ECLIPSE CT
3300 SaCo 95826 299-A7
ECOLOGY LN
9600 SaCo 95827 319-B1
ECON CT
8200 SaCo 95628 260-B5
ECONOME CT
100 FOLS 95630 261-F4
ECO RIDGE RD
- EDCo - 267-B5
- EDCo 95667 267-B5
ECTON RD
7700 CITH 95610 259-J1
EDDIE DR
100 PlaC 95661 239-H5
EDDINGTON WY
8100 SAC 95823 337-J6
EDDY CT
- RKLN 95765 200-B6
EDDYLEE WY
7500 SAC 95822 337-D3
EDE LN
12500 SaCo 95638 (401-C7 See Page 381)
12500 SaCo 95638 421-C1
EDELWEISS WY
- EDCo 95726 247-H7
100 GALT 95632 419-D5
100 SaCo 95632 419-D5
EDEN CT
4900 SaCo 95608 279-A6
EDEN LN
- PlaC 95648 160-B5
7200 SaCo 95673 257-G1
EDENBRIDGE WY
- PlaC 95747 239-A2
EDENDALE CT
7800 ELKG 95758 358-C4
EDEN OAK CIR
9100 PlaC 95746 221-G3
EDEN OAKS AV
8900 SaCo 95662 260-F1
EDEN RIVER CT
2100 RCCD 95670 279-J5
EDEN ROC CT
9200 PlaC 95746 221-G3
EDEN ROC DR
5300 PlaC 95746 221-F3
EDEN ROC LN
2200 SaCo 95825 298-C1
EDENSBURY CT
9300 ELKG 95758 357-J5
EDEN VIEW DR
5200 SAC 95823 337-J7
EDENWOOD CT
7800 SaCo 95828 338-D4
EDEVA WY
9800 ELKG 95624 359-C3
EDGAR LN
3300 SaCo 95608 279-F5
N EDGE DR
3700 SaCo 95821 278-G4
EDGECLIFF CT
8400 CITH 95610 240-C6
EDGEFIELD CT
300 LNCN 95648 179-F4
EDGEHILL DR
- EDCo 95762 262-H4
EDGEHILL LN
3000 SaCo 95608 279-E5
14300 PlaC 95603 162-G4
EDGEMAR CT
- SAC 95835 257-A6
EDGEMONT CT
7100 SaCo 95660 258-J2
EDGEMONT WY
1700 RSVL 95661 240-B5
EDGEMORE AV
- SAC 95835 257-C6
EDGERLY WY
5400 SaCo 95608 259-D6
EDGERTON WY
6300 SaCo 95608 259-E6
EDGEVALE CT
3900 SaCo 95628 280-B3
EDGEWARE WY
8400 SAC 95758 357-J1
EDGEWATER CT
1500 RSVL 95661 240-C5
EDGEWATER DR
- RVIS 94571 454-H6
EDGEWATER RD
1900 SAC 95815 297-G1
1900 SAC 95815 277-G5
EDGEWOOD AV
800 SAC 95815 277-J5
EDGEWOOD CT
- RSVL 95678 219-G5
4800 OAKL 94561 (514-D7 See Page 493)
EDGEWOOD DR
- RVIS 94571 454-F2
1600 OAKL 94561 (514-D6 See Page 493)
2600 PLCR 95667 245-F3
EDGEWOOD LN
3000 PlaC 95658 201-G4
EDGEWOOD PL
11100 PlaC 95603 162-B7
EDGEWOOD RD
11100 PlaC 95603 162-C6
EDGEWOOD WY
6200 RKLN 95677 220-D5
EDINBURGH CT
- RSVL 95661 220-E7
EDINBURGH DR
2300 SaCo 95626 238-D7
EDINBURGH ST
- RSVL 95661 220-E7
EDINGER AV
2600 SAC 95822 317-E7
EDINGTON PL
2100 EDCo 95762 242-D6
EDISON AV
2000 SAC 95821 278-D4
2300 SaCo 95821 278-G3
EDISTO WY
9200 ELKG 95758 357-G4
EDITH CIR
8000 SAC 95826 318-F3
EDITH ST
2100 SaCo 95864 278-H7
2900 SaCo 95608 279-C5
7100 SaCo 95828 338-E1
EDMEADES CT
100 OAKL 94561 (514-E6 See Page 493)
EDMONTON AV
1300 RSVL 95661 240-C5
EDMONTON DR
800 SAC 95833 277-E4
EDMUNDS WY
5700 SaCo 95841 259-C6
EDNA ST
2400 SAC 95822 317-E5
EDNA WY
8000 SAC 95826 318-F3
ED RAU RD
11100 SaCo 95757 377-J7
11100 SaCo 95757 397-J7
EDUARDO CT
- SAC 95831 336-H2
EDUCATION ST
11700 PlaC 95602 162-A3
EDWARD CT
2200 SaCo 95825 298-C3
9500 PlaC 95746 241-B5
EDWARD LN
2500 ANT 94509 (513-A6 See Page 493)
EDWARDS OAK CT
7800 CITH 95610 239-J7
EDWIN WY
1900 SAC 95815 278-B7
1900 SAC 95825 278-B7
2000 SaCo 95825 278-B7
EDYTHE CT
3000 PLCR 95667 245-G5
EDYTH LAKE WY
- RCCD 95742 300-F7
EEL CT
6200 SaCo 95842 259-B4
EEL RIVER CT
11100 RCCD 95670 280-A4
EFTHEMIA WY
4900 ELKG 95758 357-H3
EGEN CT
- ELKG 95757 358-B7
EGGLESTON ST
100 RSVL 95678 239-J1
EGLIN CT
- ELKG 95758 358-B3
EGLOFF CIR
100 FOLS 95630 261-B1
EGLOFF CT
- FOLS 95630 261-B1
EGMONT WY
3300 RCCD 95827 299-C6
EGRET CT
- RKLN 95765 200-A6
EGRET DR
9200 ELKG 95624 358-F4
EGRET RD
- YoCo 95645 235-A1
- YoCo 95776 235-A1
EGRET WY
- LNCN 95648 179-D1
EGUSD SUPPORT CTR
- SaCo 95828 338-E3
EHRBORN WY
2200 SaCo 95825 298-C4
EHRHARDT AV
5100 SAC 95823 337-J6
5700 SAC 95823 338-A6
EICH RD
7400 CITH 95610 259-H1
7400 CITH 95621 259-H1
EICHLER ST
6300 SAC 95831 317-A6
EIDER WY
7000 SAC 95831 336-F1
EIGHT MILE RD
3900 EDCo 95709 247-C4
4500 EDCo - 247-E3
EILEEN WY
1000 SAC 95831 336-J4
EINSTEIN CT
- SAC 95823 337-J6
EISENBEISZ ST
9600 ELKG 95624 358-J6
EISENHOWER DR
3300 SaCo 95826 298-J7
3400 SaCo 95826 318-J1
3500 SaCo 95826 319-A1
ELAINE DR
7300 SaCo 95828 338-F2
ELAM CREEK CT
- SaCo 95662 260-C4
EL ARADO WY
5600 SAC 95822 317-C4
EL ARROYO RD
10800 ELKG 95624 359-H2
ELBE CT
2100 EDCo 95762 262-D1
ELBERON WY
- ELKG 95758 357-E4
ELBERT WY
5100 SaCo 95842 259-B4
ELBO CT
8800 ELKG 95624 358-G6
EL BOLSILLO WY
1900 SAC 95822 317-C4
EL BURLON CIR
2500 RCCD 95670 299-D2
ELBY LN
3700 SAC 95817 317-F1
EL CABO CT
6500 CITH 95621 259-G3
EL CAJON WY
9000 SaCo 95826 298-H7
EL CAMINITO DR
4400 EDCo 95682 283-J3
EL CAMINO AV
- SaCo 95821 278-D6
- SaCo 95864 279-B7
- SAC 95815 277-G6
1200 SAC 95815 278-A6
1900 SAC 95825 278-D6
1900 SaCo 95825 278-D6
3500 SaCo 95864 278-J7
4700 SaCo 95608 279-B7
W EL CAMINO AV
- SAC 95815 277-E6
- SAC 95833 277-A6
2400 SAC 95833 276-J6
3400 SaCo 95833 276-J6
EL CAMINO-80 PLAZA DR
1800 SAC 95815 278-B6
EL CAMINO VERDE DR
1500 LNCN 95648 179-D1
EL CAMPO WY
5700 SaCo 95660 258-G5
EL CANTO CIR
2200 RCCD 95670 299-D2
EL CAPITAN CT
- LNCN 95648 179-J6
8000 SaCo 95628 260-A7
EL CAPRICE DR
2700 RCCD 95670 299-E3
EL CARRILO CT
9000 ELKG 95624 358-H7
EL CASTILLO CT
3300 SaCo 95843 238-F5
EL CEDRO CT
2500 RCCD 95670 299-E2
EL CEJO CIR
2200 RCCD 95670 299-D3
EL CENTRO BLVD Rt#-99
2900 SuCo 95659 236-H2
2900 SuCo 95668 236-H2
4300 SaCo 95836 236-H2
EL CENTRO RD
2400 SaCo 95833 276-H5
3600 SAC 95833 276-H3
3600 SAC 95834 276-H2
3600 SAC 95834 276-H3
4800 SAC 95834 256-H7
4800 SAC 95835 256-H7
EL CENTRO RD Rt#-99
- SAC 95835 256-H2
2200 SaCo 95836 236-H6
2200 SaCo 95836 256-H2
EL CERCO CT
2500 RCCD 95670 299-E2
EL CERRITO WY
4400 SaCo 95820 317-H2
EL CERRO CT
2700 SaCo 95827 299-B4
EL CHAPUL WY
8700 SaCo 95628 260-E7
EL CHICO CIR
2400 RCCD 95670 299-E2
EL CHORLITO DR
9900 RCCD 95670 299-D3
EL CHORRO WY
800 SaCo 95864 298-H4
EL CID CT
4700 RKLN 95677 220-G4
EL CID DR
4700 RKLN 95677 220-G4
EL CIELITO CT
- ELKG 95624 358-J1
EL CINO CT
2600 RCCD 95670 299-E3
EL CONDE CT
- SAC 95833 277-B4
EL CORTEZ DR
4700 RKLN 95677 220-G4
ELDER CT
2900 EDCo 95709 246-G5
S ELDER CT
6400 SAC 95823 338-B4
ELDER DR
700 WSAC 95605 297-A2
ELDER ST
- SuCo 95626 237-F2
7200 SaCo 95673 257-J1
8100 PlaC 95626 237-F2
ELDERBERRY CIR
1300 FOLS 95630 261-G5
ELDERBERRY CT
- LNCN 95648 200-B1
ELDERBERRY LN
4100 SaCo 95864 298-H4
ELDERBERRY RD
- EDCo 95619 286-C6
- EDCo 95684 286-C6
ELDERBROOK LN
- SAC 95828 338-F3
ELDER CREEK RD
- SAC 95824 318-C6
6000 SAC 95828 318-F6
8900 SAC 95829 318-H6
9000 SaCo 95829 318-H6
9200 SaCo 95829 319-A6
9700 SaCo 95830 319-E6
ELDERDOWN WY
5300 SAC 95835 256-H4
ELDERFLOWER CT
- ELKG 95624 358-J1
ELDERGLEN WY
7900 SAC 95824 318-C6
ELDERWOOD DR
1100 GALT 95632 419-H2
ELDERWOOD LN
- EDCo - 267-H4
ELDMIRE WY
- RSVL 95747 218-J4
ELDON AV
6300 LMS 95650 201-A5
EL DON DR
4900 RKLN 95677 220-G4
EL DORADO AV
200 RSVL 95678 219-J7
EL DORADO FRWY U.S.-50
- EDCo - 245-C7
- EDCo - 246-A4
- EDCo - 262-F7
- EDCo - 263-H7
- EDCo - 264-B6
- EDCo - 264-E3
- EDCo - 265-A1
EL DORADO FRWY U.S.-50
- EDCo - 282-G1
- EDCo - 283-A1
- FOLS - 280-F4
- FOLS - 281-B2
- FOLS - 281-F2
- FOLS - 282-A2
- PLCR - 245-C7
- PLCR - 246-A4
- RCCD - 279-J7
- RCCD - 280-B7
- RCCD - 299-J1
- SaCo - 280-F4
- SaCo - 281-B2
- SaCo - 282-A2
EL DORADO RD
3300 EDCo 95667 245-A6
3600 EDCo 95667 265-A1
3900 EDCo 95667 264-J3
4100 EDCo 95623 264-J3
4200 EDCo 95623 265-A4
EL DORADO ST
- OAKL 94561 (514-B7 See Page 493)
6200 EDCo 95623 265-B5
EL DORADO WY
600 SAC 95819 298-A5
2900 ANT 94509 (513-B7 See Page 493)
EL DORADO HILLS BLVD
1700 EDCo 95762 242-D7
2600 EDCo 95762 262-C1
3700 EDCo 95762 282-D1
EL DORADO ROYALE DR
3200 EDCo 95682 263-E6
EL DOURO DR
7600 SAC 95831 337-A4
ELDRIDGE AV
1600 SAC 95815 278-B5
ELEANOR AV
200 SAC 95815 277-G5
ELECTION LN
6300 SAC 95828 318-A7
ELECTRIC AV
7800 SaCo 95626 237-G6
ELECTRIC ST
100 AUB 95603 182-E1
100 AUB 95603 162-E7
E ELECTRIC ST
100 AUB 95603 182-E1
ELEFA AV
7900 ELKG 95757 378-C3
ELEFA ST
100 RSVL 95678 239-G1
ELEGANCE PL
- FOLS 95630 261-B7
ELEGANS CT
8300 SaCo 95843 239-A5
ELEGANTE WY
8000 SaCo 95828 338-E6
ELEN CT
4700 EDCo 95682 264-C2
ELENA LN
2300 SaCo 95608 279-C7
ELENA MARIE DR
7700 SAC 95831 336-G3
EL ENCANTO RD
3200 EDCo 95682 263-F7
EL ENCANTO WY
1200 SAC 95831 337-A1
EL ENCINO WY
600 SaCo 95864 298-G4
ELEPHANT WK
3700 EDCo 95630 222-H1
ELEVATOR RD
- SolC 95690 415-E4
ELEVEN OAKS DR
4900 SaCo 95660 258-G7
EL FELIZ WY
2200 SaCo 95825 278-C7
ELFIN CT
- ELKG 95758 357-J2
ELFRIEDE WY
5400 SaCo 95823 337-J3
ELF WOOD LN
3600 EDCo 95682 263-J6
EL GATO CT
9100 ELKG 95624 358-J6
ELGIN CT
8300 CITH 95610 240-C7
8300 CITH 95610 260-C1
ELGIN HILLS WY
5200 SaCo 95843 239-C5
ELGIN RIVER CT
10000 RCCD 95670 279-J6
ELGIN WOODS CT
5000 SaCo 95843 239-B5
EL GRANDE CT
3500 EDCo 95682 263-G4
10300 RCCD 95670 299-F3
EL GRANERO WY
5600 SAC 95822 317-C4
ELI CT
4700 SaCo 95608 279-A4
ELINORA WY
6200 SaCo 95660 258-H4
ELISA CT
- EDCo 95619 265-E2
ELISA WY
800 RSVL 95661 239-J4
ELITE CT
- EDCo 95667 266-B5
ELITE DR
3300 SAC 95823 337-F1
ELIZA ST
300 SAC 95814 297-E1
ELIZABETH AV
4300 SaCo 95821 278-J5
ELIZABETH CT
300 ANT 94509 (513-D7 See Page 493)
400 RSVL 95678 239-G4
ELIZABETH LN
- EDCo 95623 265-A4
3000 ANT 94509 (513-D7 See Page 493)
5700 CITH 95610 259-J5
ELIZABETH ST
600 WSAC 95605 297-A2
EL JARDIN CT
7200 SaCo 95608 279-G2
ELK VWY
11800 RCCD 95742 320-D4
ELK WY
8700 ELKG 95624 358-G5
ELKART WY
3500 SAC 95834 276-J3
ELK CREEK CT
8600 ELKG 95624 358-F7
ELK CREST DR
9200 ELKG 95624 358-F4
ELK GLEN CT
10000 ELKG 95624 378-H2
ELK GROVE BLVD
- ELKG 95758 357-H5
- SaCo 95758 357-D6
ELK GROVE BLVD Rt#-E12
100 SaCo 95758 357-E6
2800 ELKG 95757 357-F7
2800 ELKG 95758 357-E6
5700 ELKG 95757 358-A6
5700 ELKG 95758 358-A6
8400 ELKG 95624 358-F6
9300 ELKG 95624 359-C6
9900 SaCo 95624 359-C6
ELK GROVE FLORIN RD
7400 SaCo 95829 338-G3
8300 SaCo 95624 338-G3
8400 ELKG 95624 338-G3
8400 ELKG 95624 358-G1
8900 SaCo 95624 378-G2
ELKHART ST
5500 SAC 95835 257-A4
ELK HILLS DR
700 GALT 95632 419-E3
ELK HOLLOW CT
- ELKG 95758 357-J2
ELKHORN BLVD
- SAC 95835 256-D4
3600 SaCo 95660 258-H2
5800 SaCo 95837 255-G3
6400 SaCo 95837 256-A3
ELKHORN BLVD Rt#-E14
100 SaCo 95673 257-A3
1100 SaCo 95673 258-A3
2400 SaCo 95652 258-E2
2800 SaCo 95660 258-E2
3000 SAC 95835 256-J3
3000 SaCo 95835 256-F3
3800 SAC 95673 257-A3
4100 SaCo 95835 257-A3
4100 SAC 95835 257-A3
4200 SaCo 95842 258-J2
4500 SaCo 95842 259-B3
ELKHORN PZ
700 WSAC 95605 297-A2
ELKHORN MANOR DR
6300 SaCo 95673 257-H4
ELKINS CIR
100 FOLS 95630 281-B1
ELKINS CT
- ELKG 95758 357-F4
ELKMONT WY
9100 ELKG 95624 378-H3
ELKO CT
4200 SaCo 95823 317-G7
ELK POINT CT
8300 SaCo 95828 338-E7
ELK RAVINE WY
- RSVL 95661 220-D7
ELK RIDGE WY
8600 ELKG 95624 358-F6
ELK RIVER CT
3700 SaCo 95843 238-G5
ELKS CIR
- RCCD 95670 300-B6
ELK SPRING WY
5600 ELKG 95758 357-J3
5900 ELKG 95758 358-A3
ELKTREE WY
9500 ELKG 95624 358-H7
ELKUS LN
1100 PlaC 95602 162-F3
ELK VALLEY ST
- WSAC 95691 297-A7
ELKWOOD CIR
- SAC 95823 337-G4
ELKWOOD CT
8900 ELKG 95624 378-H2
ELLA CT
8100 CITH 95610 239-J7
EL LAGO CT
4500 OAKL 94561 (514-C7 See Page 493)
8500 SaCo 95843 238-F5
EL LAGO DR
2100 OAKL 94561 (514-B7 See Page 493)
ELLEN LN
7600 CITH 95610 259-H1
ELLEN ST
2700 SAC 95815 277-J6
ELLENBROOK DR
2600 RCCD 95670 299-F2
ELLENMERE DR
3300 SaCo 95821 278-F6
ELLEN ROSE CT
- SAC 95831 316-G7
ELLENWOOD AV
10100 RCCD 95827 299-E5
ELLENWOOD LN
- EDCo 95667 245-A7
ELLERSLEE DR
5900 SaCo 95608 259-D6
ELLERTON PL
- SAC 95835 257-A3
ELLERY PL
9200 ELKG 95624 358-J5
ELLESMERE LP
- RSVL 95747 219-A2
ELLESTAD WY
- AUB 95603 182-E2
ELLESWORTH PL
2200 EDCo 95762 242-C5
ELLIES ALLIE
3700 EDCo 95667 265-D1
3700 EDCo 95667 245-D7
EL LINDO CT
8500 SaCo 95843 238-F5
ELLINGTON CIR
3100 SaCo 95825 278-F7
ELLINGTON CT
5100 PlaC 95746 240-H6
N ELLIOT RD Rt#-J5
27000 SJCo 95638 421-B7
29200 SaCo 95638 421-B7
ELLIOT RANCH RD
- SaCo 95758 357-C5
2600 ELKG 95758 357-D5
ELLIOTT ST
1000 WSAC 95605 296-J2
ELLIS CIR
- FOLS 95630 281-C1
ELLIS CT
5700 SaCo 95660 258-H5
ELLISON DR
- RSVL 95747 218-J4
2100 RCCD 95670 279-G7
ELLITHORPE LN
- PlaC 95650 200-J2
ELLMER ST
2800 EDCo 95709 247-C4
EL LOMA WY
100 FOLS 95630 261-E3
ELLSMERE WY
- ELKG 95757 358-A7
ELLSWORTH CIR
6700 SaCo 95628 279-F1
ELLSWORTH WY
- FOLS 95630 261-J5
EL LUJO WY
2400 RCCD 95670 299-E2
ELLWOOD AV
3000 SAC 95822 337-F3
ELM AV
100 AUB 95603 182-D2
500 GALT 95632 419-E6
1100 PLCR 95667 245-G4
6800 SaCo 95662 260-D2
10000 SaCo 95632 419-E6
ELM CT
1100 PLCR 95667 245-G4
5400 LMS 95650 200-H7
ELM LN
5200 OAKL 94561 (514-A5 See Page 493)
ELM PL
- EDCo 95682 263-D2
ELM ST
- EDCo 95726 248-D1
700 WSAC 95605 296-G2
1000 RSVL 95678 239-F1
3800 SAC 95838 278-A3
ELM WY
500 RVIS 94571 454-H5
EL MACERO WY
700 SAC 95831 336-H1
ELMANTO DR
2000 RCCD 95670 279-G5
2100 RCCD 95670 279-H6
EL MARIDO CT
2400 RCCD 95670 299-E2
EL MASITA CT
2300 EDCo 95682 263-B7
ELMCREST LN
2200 RCCD 95670 279-J6
EL MEASA CT
9000 ELKG 95624 358-H7
ELMER WY
5100 SAC 95822 317-A4
EL MERCADO DR
10400 RCCD 95670 299-F5
10400 RCCD 95827 299-F5
ELMGATE DR
- RSVL 95747 218-H5
ELM GLEN PL
5500 ELKG 95757 357-J6
ELMGROVE CT
9200 SaCo 95826 318-J2
ELMHURST CIR
200 SAC 95825 298-C6
ELMHURST DR
9700 PlaC 95746 240-H4
ELMHURST LN
- LNCN 95648 200-B1
ELMIRA CIR
9600 SaCo 95827 299-B5
EL MIRADOR DR
9600 ELKG 95624 358-H7
ELMO DR
5800 SaCo 95660 258-H5
ELMO RD
3000 ANT 94509 (513-E7 See Page 493)
EL MODENA AV
7600 SaCo 95626 237-H5
7600 SaCo 95673 237-H7
8900 PlaC 95626 237-H3
ELMONT AV
7600 SaCo 95626 237-H7
7600 SaCo 95673 237-H7
EL MONTE AV
1300 SAC 95815 277-G7
EL MONTE CT
3000 ANT 94509 (513-B7 See Page 493)
4500 OAKL 94561 (514-C7 See Page 493)
EL MONTE DR
2000 OAKL 94561 (514-C7 See Page 493)
3700 PlaC 95650 201-G7
EL MONTE WY
2900 ANT 94509 (513-B6 See Page 493)
ELMORE WY
2000 SaCo 95825 298-C1
ELMORES WY
- EDCo 95762 262-A2
EL MORRO CT
- SAC 95831 337-B4
ELMRIDGE WY
800 SAC 95834 277-E3
ELMSMERE CT
7700 ELKG 95758 358-C5
ELM TREE LN
6900 SaCo 95662 260-E2
ELMWOOD AV
7900 SaCo 95626 237-G6
ELMWOOD CT
- RSVL 95678 219-F5
1000 EDCo 95762 262-C2
5800 RKLN 95677 220-D5
ELMWOOD DR
- RSVL 95678 219-F5
EL NIDO CT
700 EDCo 95762 242-C4
EL NIDO WY
1300 SaCo 95864 298-G2
EL NINOS WY
- EDCo 95619 288-D3
ELNORA CT
9000 SaCo 95829 338-H6
EL NORTE RD
3900 EDCo 95682 263-B7
3900 EDCo 95682 283-B1
ELOAH WY
1300 SAC 95831 337-B3
ELOISE AV
7800 SaCo 95626 237-G7
EL ORO DR
800 AUB 95603 162-D6
EL ORO ST
3800 SaCo 95660 258-G5
EL ORO PLAZA DR
9000 ELKG 95624 358-H7
EL PARAISO AV
4900 SaCo 95824 317-H6
5200 SAC 95824 317-H6
EL PARQUE CIR
2600 RCCD 95670 299-E3
EL PASEO LN
2600 SaCo 95821 278-E5
EL PASO WY
2900 ANT 94509 (513-B7 See Page 493)
EL PATIO CT
9000 ELKG 95624 358-H7
EL PAVO WY
2400 RCCD 95670 299-D2
EL PESCADOR CT
- SaCo 95670 280-C6
EL PINZON CT
10000 RCCD 95670 299-D2
EL PORTO LN
6400 CITH 95621 259-G4
EL PRADO WY
2600 SaCo 95825 278-E7
EL RANCHERO CT
4700 RKLN 95677 220-G5
EL RANCHO CT
800 WSAC 95691 296-J4
900 RSVL 95661 239-J4
EL RANCHO DR
- EDCo 95633 205-A2
EL RENO AV
7600 SaCo 95626 237-H7
7600 SaCo 95673 237-H7
EL REY ST
2700 ANT 94509 (513-C6 See Page 493)
EL REY WY
3100 SAC 95815 277-J5
EL RICON WY
3500 SaCo 95864 298-G2
EL RIO AV
7800 SaCo 95626 237-F7
EL RITO WY
7600 SAC 95831 337-B4
EL ROCCO WY
2300 RCCD 95670 299-E2
ELROY AV
7800 SaCo 95626 237-G7
ELSDON CIR
1500 SaCo 95608 299-A2
EL SEGUNDO DR
2500 RCCD 95670 299-E2
EL SERENO CIR
7000 SAC 95831 337-A1
ELSIE AV
7500 SaCo 95828 338-C4
ELSINORE CT
- WSAC 95691 316-D3
ELSINORE WY
5300 SaCo 95628 259-F6
EL SOBRANTE WY
8600 SaCo 95662 260-D1
EL SOL WY
5900 CITH 95621 259-G5
ELSTER CT
- SaCo 95823 337-J6
ELSTNER ST
- PLCR 95667 245-G4
EL SUR CT
1500 EDCo 95762 242-C4
EL SUR WY
1000 SaCo 95864 298-H3
EL SUTTON LN
2500 SaCo 95821 278-D6
ELSWORTH CT
900 GALT 95632 419-G3
EL TEJON RD
3100 EDCo 95682 263-C4
EL TEJON WY
1400 SaCo 95864 298-G2
EL TERRAZA DR
7500 SaCo 95828 338-F3
ELTON CT
- SAC 95826 298-F7
EL TONAS WY
2500 SaCo 95608 279-C6
EL TOREADOR WY
8700 ELKG 95624 358-G4
EL TORO CT
- RSVL 95747 219-C4
EL TORO WY
1200 SaCo 95864 298-H3
ELUDE CT
4900 SaCo 95842 259-A2
ELVA WY
4200 SaCo 95821 278-J2
4200 SaCo 95841 278-J2
EL VADO CT
- SAC 95831 337-B4
EL VALLE WY
3200 SaCo 95843 238-F5
ELVAS AV
3400 SAC 95819 297-J3
4700 SAC 95819 298-A5
ELVENDEN CT
- RSVL 95661 220-E7
ELVENDEN WY
- RSVL 95661 220-E7
EL VERANO AV
7600 SaCo 95626 237-H5
7600 SaCo 95673 237-H7
8800 PlaC 95626 237-H4
EL VERDE CT
4800 RKLN 95677 220-G4
ELVERTA RD
- SaCo 95843 259-A1
300 SaCo 95626 237-F6
900 SaCo 95626 238-A6
1300 SaCo 95836 237-B6
2500 SaCo 95843 238-G6
3000 SaCo 95836 236-G6
4200 SaCo 95837 236-A6
4500 SaCo 95837 236-J6
8000 SaCo 95837 235-J6
ELVERTA MEADOWS CT
300 SaCo 95626 237-G4
ELVERTA RAIL WY
7200 SaCo 95673 257-H1
EL VIENTO WY
8500 SaCo 95843 238-F5
ELVIES LN
300 FOLS 95630 261-F2
EL VITA WY
2500 SaCo 95608 279-C6
ELVORA WY
6900 ELKG 95757 378-B2

STREET
Block City ZIP Pg-Grid

ELVYRA WY
2700 SaCo 95821 278-E6
ELWELL CT
4500 ELKG 95758 357-H5
ELWELL WY
4600 ELKG 95758 357-H5
ELWYN AV
7600 SaCo 95626 237-G5
7600 SaCo 95673 237-G7
ELY CT
8900 ELKG 95624 358-G3
ELYSIAN WY
3500 EDCo 95667 246-A7
ELZA CT
6500 CITH 95610 259-H4
EMBARCADERO DR
800 EDCo 95762 242-C7
800 WSAC 95605 296-E2
EMBASSY LN
- SaCo 95628 260-D7
EMDEE CT
4600 SaCo 95821 278-J4
EMELETON CT
- GALT 95632 419-H3
EMERALD CT
- GALT 95632 419-D6
2900 SaCo 95825 278-E7
3000 EDCo 95682 263-E7
6500 RKLN 95677 220-B4
EMERALD DR
100 GALT 95632 419-E6
6300 RKLN 95677 220-B4
EMERALD LN
- LNCN 95648 180-B7
4000 EDCo 95667 264-H3
EMERALD BAY LN
- ELKG 95758 357-E5
EMERALD BROOK WY
5000 SAC 95838 257-J7
EMERALD COVE LN
- ELKG 95758 357-E6
EMERALD CREEK CT
- SAC 95824 318-B5
EMERALD CREST DR
9200 ELKG 95624 358-F4
EMERALD FELL CT
5100 SaCo 95843 239-B5
EMERALD FOREST DR
- EDCo 95726 248-C5
EMERALD GROVE DR
9000 ELKG 95624 378-H2
EMERALD HILLS CT
1000 EDCo 95762 262-C2
EMERALD LAKE LN
- ELKG 95758 357-E5
EMERALD OAK DR
100 GALT 95632 419-D7
8700 ELKG 95624 358-G6
S EMERALD OAK DR
100 GALT 95632 419-D7
EMERALD OAK RD
- RSVL 95678 219-F5
EMERALD PARK DR
8900 ELKG 95624 358-G7
9800 ELKG 95624 378-H1
EMERALD PINES DR
2300 PlaC 95603 202-C1
EMERALD VISTA DR
800 GALT 95632 419-F3
8400 ELKG 95624 358-F5
EMERSON CT
300 RSVL 95661 240-E4
EMERSON DR
3300 RSVL 95661 240-F4
3500 SJCo 95220 439-J5
EMERSON RD
4800 SAC 95820 318-B4
5300 SAC 95824 318-B4
E EMERSON RD
3700 SJCo 95220 439-J5
EMERSON ST
- PlaC 95626 237-E1
300 SaCo 95626 237-H7
3600 RKLN 95677 220-E2
EMERY CT
3300 SAC 95838 277-F4
EMIGH RD
7700 SolC 94571 454-A5
EMIGRANT CT
100 FOLS 95630 261-E6
EMIGRANT GAP DR
2100 SaCo 95670 280-C5
EMILIA WY
- LNCN 95648 179-F6
EMILY LN
- LNCN 95648 199-J1
- LNCN 95648 200-A1
EMILY ST
9300 ELKG 95624 358-G5
EMINENT CT
7200 SaCo 95842 259-A2
EMMA CT
- RSVL 95661 220-D6
EMMA LN
- PlaC 95747 239-D2
EMMA NEVADA CT
11400 SaCo 95670 280-C5
EMMATON RD
- SaCo 94571 (494-B2 See Page 493)
EMMERSON RD
1600 EDCo 95667 225-D7
1600 EDCo 95667 245-C1
EMMET DR
2600 PlaC 95603 162-C4
EMMONS CIR
100 SaCo 95655 319-J1
EMMONS ST
300 SAC 95838 278-B2
EMPEROR
- RCCD 95827 299-E4
EMPEROR CT
- RKLN 95765 219-H1
EMPEROR DR
8500 SaCo 95628 280-D3
EMPINGHAM WY
- RSVL 95661 220-F6
7700 SaCo 95829 338-J5
EMPIRE AV
- OAKL 94561 (514-C6 See Page 493)
EMPIRE CT
500 RSVL 95747 219-A6
EMPIRE WY
4100 SaCo 95608 279-D3
EMPIRE MINE CIR
2000 SaCo 95670 280-C4
EMPIRE OAKS CT
- SaCo 95670 280-C4

EMPIRE RANCH RD
- FOLS 95630 262-A6
- FOLS 95630 282-B2
EMPORIA
- SAC 95758 358-A2
EMPRESS LN
2400 EDCo 95667 245-B4
EMPRESS ST
2200 SAC 95815 277-J7
EMSDALE WY
8900 SaCo 95829 338-H6
ENCHANTED CIR
4000 RSVL 95747 219-A6
ENCHANTED CT
4000 RSVL 95747 219-B6
ENCHANTED HILL LN
3000 EDCo 95682 283-J3
ENCINA CT
1100 ANT 94509 (513-B6 See Page 493)
1600 EDCo 95762 242-C4
ENCINA DR
400 EDCo 95762 242-C4
ENCINAL AV
400 RSVL 95678 239-H1
500 RSVL 95678 219-H7
2400 SAC 95822 317-E5
ENCLAVE PL
- SAC 95835 256-G4
ENCOMIUM CT
8000 SaCo 95828 338-D6
ENDEAVOR WY
- SAC 95834 277-A2
ENDICOTT SQ
100 FOLS 95630 261-G6
ENDLESS CT
- EDCo 95762 262-D5
ENDRES CT
1500 SAC 95822 337-B1
ENDSLEIGH CT
9600 PlaC 95746 240-H5
ENEA WY
2800 ANT 94509 (513-C6 See Page 493)
ENFIELD ST
5800 SaCo 95608 259-D5
ENGBERG CT
1600 SaCo 95608 299-A2
ENGLE LN
- PlaC 95603 182-C6
ENGLE RD
4200 SaCo 95821 278-J4
4600 SaCo 95821 279-A4
4600 SaCo 95608 279-A4
ENGLEHART DR
100 FOLS 95630 241-A7
100 FOLS 95630 261-A1
ENGLESIDE CT
9300 ELKG 95758 357-G5
ENGLEWOOD ST
4100 SAC 95838 277-G2
ENGLISH COLONY WY
1500 PlaC 95663 180-G7
3000 PlaC 95663 200-H1
5000 PlaC 95663 201-B1
ENGLISH INN CT
8700 ELKG 95624 358-F3
ENGLISH IVY CT
- SAC 95833 277-F4
ENGLISH OAK WY
8100 CITH 95610 240-B6
ENGLISH ROSE LN
- RSVL 95747 219-B6
ENID WY
3000 SAC 95826 318-D1
ENNIS CT
6900 SaCo 95660 258-H2
ENRICO BLVD
4900 SaCo 95820 317-G4
5400 SaCo 95824 317-G4
ENRIGHT DR
6900 CITH 95621 259-F1
ENSENADA WY
2600 SAC 95815 277-J6
ENSIGN ST
5700 SaCo 95628 259-F7
ENTERPRISE BLVD
1300 WSAC 95691 296-C5
ENTERPRISE CT
- GALT 95632 419-E5
3100 LMS 95650 201-A4
4200 EDCo 95667 265-C2
ENTERPRISE DR
900 SaCo 95825 298-C3
6300 EDCo 95667 265-C3
11700 AUB 95603 182-C1
ENTERPRISE WY
1000 RSVL 95678 239-F3
ENTRADA CIR
2700 ANT 94509 (513-B6 See Page 493)
ENTRADA DR
- EDCo 95762 262-E6
ENTRADA RD
900 SaCo 95864 298-H3
ENTRANCE ST
7900 SaCo 95628 280-A2
ENTWISTLE CT
100 FOLS 95630 281-F1
ENVERO WY
3500 RCCD 95670 299-J5
ENVOY WY
7700 CITH 95610 259-J5
ENWOOD RD
1000 RSVL 95678 240-A1
ENZO WY
8400 ELKG 95624 358-E2
EPERNAY CT
8900 SaCo 95829 338-H5
EPHRAIM WY
- ELKG 95758 357-G4
EPIC CT
10600 RCCD 95670 279-H7
EPPERLE LN
200 AUB 95603 182-D1
EPPERSON WY
3400 RSVL 95661 240-E2
EPWORTH CT
200 RSVL 95747 239-D1
EQUESTRIAN CT
5200 RKLN 95677 220-H5
10300 ELKG 95624 359-F5
EQUESTRIAN DR
10100 ELKG 95624 359-E5
EQUESTRIAN TER
6000 RKLN 95677 220-H4
EQUINE DR
10300 SaCo 95829 339-E7

EQUINOX LN
- LNCN 95648 179-G5
EQUINOX LP
- LNCN 95648 179-G5
EQUINOX WY
4100 SAC 95823 337-G5
EQUUS LN
8600 SaCo 95628 280-D2
ERALISE WY
9700 ELKG 95624 359-B7
ERATO CIR
11900 RCCD 95742 320-E1
ERDMAN WY
1000 SAC 95838 277-J1
ERIC CIR
200 GALT 95632 439-D1
ERIC DR
- WSAC 95691 296-D4
ERIC RD
2100 SaCo 95608 279-A7
2100 SaCo 95608 299-A1
ERIC WY
8000 SAC 95826 318-D1
ERICKSON DR
200 RSVL 95746 240-F6
ERICKSON ST
2200 SAC 95815 277-J7
ERICWOOD CT
8000 CITH 95621 239-E6
ERIEL WY
8900 SaCo 95662 260-F3
ERIKA JEAN WY
8400 SaCo 95628 260-C5
ERIN DR
2600 SAC 95833 277-D6
12300 PlaC 95603 162-C4
ERINBROOK WY
8500 SAC 95826 298-F6
ERISWELL CT
- RSVL 95747 219-C7
- RSVL 95747 239-C1
ERLA CT
11000 RCCD 95670 279-J7
ERLE BLUNDEN WY
9000 SaCo 95628 280-F1
ERLEWINE CIR
3700 SAC 95819 297-H3
ERLTON CT
9400 ELKG 95758 357-G5
ERMINA DR
3200 SAC 95815 278-A4
ERNEST WY
2000 SaCo 95825 278-C7
ERNESTINE WY
6300 SaCo 95660 258-H4
ERNIES CT
4700 EDCo 95672 243-C7
ERNST RD
- SaCo 95836 237-A5
ERRANTE DR
- EDCo 95762 262-E2
ERRIGAL PL
- LNCN 95648 200-B2
ERROL CT
1600 FOLS 95630 261-J7
ERWIN AV
9400 SaCo 95662 260-H6
ESADA CT
- SaCo 95632 419-G1
ESATTO PL
- EDCo 95762 262-A3
ESCALANTE WY
7200 CITH 95610 260-A2
ESCALLONIA DR
6800 SaCo 95662 260-C3
6900 CITH 95610 260-C2
6900 CITH 95662 260-C2
ESCALLONIA WY
- RKLN 95765 219-H2
ESCAMBIA CT
4300 ELKG 95758 357-G5
ESCHELMAN CT
- FOLS 95630 261-H4
ESCHER CIR
- OAKL 94561 (514-H6 See Page 493)
ESCHINGER RD
6000 SaCo 95757 377-J7
6000 SaCo 95757 378-H6
6000 SaCo 95757 397-J7
8900 SaCo 95757 379-A6
ESCOBAR WY
2600 SaCo 95827 299-B4
ESCONDITO CIR
- EDCo - 247-F6
- EDCo 95726 247-F6
ESCONDITO CT
- EDCo - 247-G6
ESCUELA DR
6700 SaCo 95683 322-A7
ESHER CT
200 RSVL 95747 219-C7
200 RSVL 95747 239-C1
ESKDALE CT
7900 SaCo 95829 338-J5
ESKER CT
1800 FOLS 95630 282-A1
ESKIMO CURLEW WY
- SaCo 95829 338-H5
ESKRIDGE WY
- ELKG 95758 358-B2
ESMERALDA ST
5100 SAC 95820 317-J4
5300 SAC 95824 317-J4
ESMONT CT
9500 ELKG 95758 358-C6
ESPANA CT
4700 SaCo 95608 279-E1
ESPERANZA DR
3700 SaCo 95864 298-G2
ESPERSON CT
- RVIS 94571 454-G5
ESPINA LOMA DR
- EDCo - 247-D7
ESPLANADE
1000 SAC 95819 298-B6
ESPLANADE CIR
- FOLS 95630 261-J3
ESPLANDE CIR
- FOLS 95630 261-J3
ESQUIRE DR
5700 SaCo 95841 259-C4
ESRIG WY
5800 SaCo 95841 259-D7
ESSEN WY
8100 SAC 95823 337-J6
ESSENCE WY
7100 SaCo 95842 259-A2

ESSEX AV
2300 WSAC 95691 296-H7
ESSEX CT
- RSVL 95661 240-E4
5400 SaCo 95628 260-D6
ESSEX LN
- CITH 95610 259-J5
ESSEX PL
2700 EDCo 95762 242-C5
ESSEX MINE CT
2000 SaCo 95670 280-C4
ESSEY CIR
200 SaCo 95655 319-J2
ESSUREP CT
3000 EDCo 95682 264-A1
ESTABROOK WY
100 FOLS 95630 261-G4
ESTANCIA CT
9800 ELKG 95624 378-G1
ESTATES CT
100 RSVL 95678 239-J2
ESTATES DR
- EDCo 95630 222-G7
- EDCo 95630 242-G1
100 RSVL 95678 239-J2
100 RSVL 95678 240-A2
300 SaCo 95864 298-H4
ESTEEM DR
7400 SaCo 95842 259-A1
ESTEPA DR
2900 EDCo 95682 263-C4
ESTERBROOK WY
3300 SaCo 95843 238-G5
ESTEREL WY
1900 SAC 95832 337-C4
ESTERO WY
- EDCo 95762 262-D6
ESTES WY
100 SAC 95838 277-G2
ESTE VISTA DR
3500 EDCo 95682 263-F6
ESTEY CT
1000 PLCR 95667 245-G6
ESTEY WY
800 PLCR 95667 245-G6
ESTRELA CT
10200 ELKG 95757 378-B3
ESTRELLA LN
4800 EDCo 95623 264-J5
ESTRELLA WY
100 LNCN 95648 180-D7
ESTRELLITA CT
4300 EDCo 95682 264-B7
ESTRELLITA WY
2300 SaCo 95825 278-C7
ESTUARY CT
- SAC 95831 336-G2
ET RD
9200 PlaC 95650 201-G7
ETCHINGHAM CT
- RSVL 95747 219-B7
ETCHINGHAM DR
- RSVL 95747 219-C7
ETHAN WY
1100 SAC 95825 298-B2
1100 SaCo 95825 298-B2
1200 SAC 95815 298-B2
2000 SAC 95825 278-C6
2000 SaCo 95825 278-C6
2500 SaCo 95821 278-C6
ETHEL DR
2200 EDCo 95672 262-G2
ETHEL WY
4700 SAC 95820 317-H4
4900 SAC 95824 317-H4
5600 SaCo 95824 317-H4
ETHELON PL
- EDCo 95684 286-D7
ETHING CT
- SAC 95823 337-J5
ETNA CT
4800 SaCo 95608 279-D1
ETTRICK CT
- FOLS 95630 261-G6
EUCALYPTUS CT
- RSVL 95747 219-A7
EUCALYPTUS DR
- SaCo 95690 455-E4
EUCALYPTUS LN
8000 CITH 95610 240-C7
EUCALYPTUS RD
4300 SaCo 95628 279-G2
EUCLID AV
4200 SAC 95822 317-A3
EUCLID LN
3200 RSVL 95661 240-E1
EUCLID ST
300 WSAC 95691 296-H5
EUER CT
300 FOLS 95630 261-E7
EUGENE AV
5600 SaCo 95662 260-H6
EUGENE CT
4300 EDCo 95619 265-F3
EUGENIA CT
5700 SaCo 95662 260-H6
EULA WY
8800 SaCo 95662 260-E3
EULER WY
5100 SAC 95823 337-J6
EUNICE AV
25100 SJCo 95220 439-H5
EUNICE WY
4100 SaCo 95821 278-J2
EUREKA LN
5800 SaCo 95842 259-C1
EUREKA RD
1200 RSVL 95678 220-B7
1200 RSVL 95661 220-B7
1400 RSVL 95661 240-C1
2800 RSVL 95746 240-F3
2800 PlaC 95746 240-F3
5700 PlaC 95746 241-A3
EUREKA ST
1800 EDCo 95667 246-B7
EUREKA CANAL DR
- SaCo 95670 280-E5
EUROPA ST
3200 RSVL 95661 240-E1
EUTHALIA CT
- ELKG 95758 357-E4
EVA AV
8900 ELKG 95624 358-H6
EVA LN
8400 PlaC 95747 239-D2
EVADNA DR
2900 RCCD 95670 299-F3
EVALITA WY
4100 SAC 95823 337-G5

EVAN CT
5100 RKLN 95765 199-J5
EVANS DR
6200 LMS 95650 201-A7
EVANS PL
1700 EDCo 95667 246-A4
EVANS ST
800 SAC 95838 277-J4
EVANSWOOD CT
9300 ELKG 95758 358-B5
EVANWOOD DR
4700 EDCo 95682 283-J5
EVA RETTA CT
8200 CITH 95610 240-A6
EVCAR WY
100 SaCo 95673 257-G3
EVELAND CT
100 FOLS 95630 261-F3
EVELYN AV
200 RSVL 95678 239-J1
300 RSVL 95678 240-A1
3900 RKLN 95677 220-E4
EVELYN CT
300 RSVL 95678 239-J1
EVELYN LN
900 SaCo 95864 298-E3
EVELYN WY
200 FOLS 95630 261-E4
EVENING WY
1200 RSVL 95678 239-G5
7400 CITH 95621 239-G6
EVENING BREEZE CT
- RSVL 95661 239-J5
EVENING SONG WY
- RSVL 95747 218-H3
EVENING STAR CT
3400 EDCo 95682 263-G5
8800 SaCo 95662 260-E6
EVENT WY
7500 SaCo 95842 259-A1
EVERBLOOM WY
9700 SaCo 95829 339-C6
EVERDELL WY
11800 RCCD 95742 320-D2
EVEREST WY
6100 SaCo 95842 259-B4
EVERETT CT
9200 ELKG 95624 358-J4
EVERETT WY
1400 RSVL 95747 219-E7
EVERGLADE DR
8400 SAC 95826 298-F7
8400 SAC 95826 318-F1
EVERGLADES CT
- RKLN 95765 219-H2
EVERGREEN AV
900 WSAC 95691 296-F4
1800 ANT 94509 (513-E5 See Page 493)
EVERGREEN CIR
3400 WSAC 95691 296-F4
EVERGREEN CT
3500 RKLN 95765 220-C1
EVERGREEN DR
1700 RSVL 95747 239-D1
EVERGREEN PL
1000 PlaC 95603 162-C6
EVERGREEN ST
2000 SAC 95815 277-H7
EVERGREEN TR
- EDCo - 267-J3
EVERGREEN OAKS CT
5600 SaCo 95628 259-F6
EVERIDGE CT
8600 SaCo 95828 338-F7
EVERLEY CIR
- RSVL 95747 218-J4
EVERSLEY CT
8200 SaCo 95829 339-A6
EVES WY
- EDCo 95726 248-B1
EVESHAM CIR
6500 CITH 95621 259-F4
EVIA CT
4600 ELKG 95758 357-H4
EVORA CT
- SAC 95833 277-D5
EVROS RIVER
- SAC 95831 336-F2
EWELL CT
500 GALT 95632 419-F5
EWING WY
6800 SaCo 95828 338-B2
EXA CT
4100 SaCo 95821 278-H4
EXBOURNE CIR
8200 SaCo 95828 338-F7
EXCALIBUR RD
3300 EDCo 95667 245-E6
EXCELSIOR AV
7400 SaCo 95662 260-F1
7600 SaCo 95662 240-F7
EXCELSIOR CT
3200 EDCo 95667 245-F6
EXCELSIOR RD
600 EDCo 95667 245-F7
4400 SaCo 95830 319-G4
6400 SaCo 95830 339-G3
8200 ELKG 95624 339-F7
8200 ELKG 95830 339-F7
8400 ELKG 95624 359-F2
EXCHANGE ST
400 SAC 95838 257-H7
EXECUTIVE CT
- RKLN 95765 200-E4
1600 SaCo 95864 298-E2
EXETER CT
500 RSVL 95661 240-E3
EXETER ST
600 SaCo 95864 298-H5
EXETER SQUARE LN
2500 SaCo 95825 298-D4
2500 SaCo 95864 298-D4
EXMOOR CIR
3800 SaCo 95864 298-G5
EXPEDITION DR
- EDCo 95682 283-J7
EXPEDITION WY
1900 SAC 95832 337-C4
EXPLORER DR
3000 RCCD 95827 299-C6
EXPO PKWY
- SAC 95815 297-H1
EXPOSITION BLVD
1300 SAC 95815 297-H1
1400 SAC 95815 298-A2
2000 SAC 95825 298-A2
2000 SaCo 95825 298-A2

EXPRESS CT
- SAC 95823 338-B6
EYE ST
100 SAC 95814 297-B3
100 WSAC 95605 297-B3
800 SAC 95819 297-E4
1400 SaCo 95673 258-A3
2100 SAC 95816 297-E4
2500 SaCo 95652 258-C3
3000 SaCo 95660 258-F4
5200 SAC 95819 298-A5

F

F AV
11400 PlaC 95603 162-B4
F PKWY
4800 SaCo 95823 337-H2
F ST
100 ISLE 95641 455-H5
100 ANT 94509 (513-D3 See Page 493)
100 GALT 95632 419-E7
100 GALT 95632 439-E1
100 LNCN 95648 179-H2
200 WSAC 95605 297-B3
700 SAC 95814 297-D3
800 WSAC 95605 296-J3
2000 SAC 95816 297-F4
3500 SaCo 95660 258-G7
3900 SAC 95819 297-H4
5200 SAC 95819 298-A5
7700 SAC 95823 338-A4
FABER WY
3600 RCCD 95670 299-J4
11000 RCCD 95670 300-A4
FABERGE WY
3500 SaCo 95826 299-A7
3500 SaCo 95826 319-B1
FABIUS CT
9200 ELKG 95758 357-H5
FABRIANO WY
- EDCo 95762 262-H4
FACET PL
- FOLS 95630 261-B6
FAGER HILL RD
1700 PlaC 95663 200-J1
FAHEY CT
100 FOLS 95630 281-B2
FAIR LN
- PLCR 95667 245-D5
100 EDCo 95667 245-C6
FAIR WY
6000 SAC 95817 318-A1
8200 CITH 95610 239-J6
8400 PlaC 95661 239-J6
8400 RSVL 95661 239-J6
FAIRBAIRN DR
5700 SaCo 95660 258-G5
FAIRBANKS AV
- SAC 95838 277-G4
FAIRBANKS DR
- RVIS 94571 454-F1
FAIRCHILD CT
- FOLS 95630 261-J6
2300 EDCo 95762 262-D1
FAIRCHILD DR
1800 SaCo 95608 299-B1
2900 EDCo 95762 262-D1
FAIRFAX WY
6200 SaCo 95660 258-G4
FAIRFIELD AV
1100 RSVL 95678 239-G5
FAIRFIELD ST
2100 SAC 95815 277-H5
FAIRGATE CT
- FOLS 95630 262-A6
FAIRGATE DR
200 AUB 95603 182-D3
FAIRGATE RD
200 SaCo 95825 298-D5
FAIRGLADE RD
- EDCo - 267-G3
- EDCo 95726 267-G3
FAIRGROUNDS DR
200 SAC 95817 317-J1
200 SAC 95820 317-J1
FAIR GROVE CT
9000 ELKG 95758 358-A3
FAIRHALL CT
- RSVL 95747 218-J3
FAIRHAVEN CT
1700 OAKL 94561 (514-D6 See Page 493)
8500 ELKG 95624 358-E2
FAIRHAVEN LN
4100 EDCo 95667 265-B2
FAIR HILL DR
3700 SaCo 95628 279-H3
FAIR HILL RD
3700 SaCo 95628 279-H4
FAIR LAKE AV
900 SaCo 95825 298-C3
FAIRLANDS WY
8000 SaCo 95843 238-H6
FAIRLANE CT
2800 PLCR 95667 245-D5
4500 SaCo 95608 279-F2
FAIRLAWN CT
8500 SaCo 95828 338-F3
FAIRLEIGH CT
6600 ELKG 95758 358-B3
FAIRLIGHT CT
9400 ELKG 95758 358-C5
FAIRMONT CT
400 RSVL 95661 240-D4
FAIRMONT LN
2600 ANT 94509 (513-A6 See Page 493)
FAIRMONT WY
8500 SaCo 95628 260-D6
FAIR OAKS BLVD
2100 SAC 95825 298-C5
2200 SaCo 95825 298-C5
2800 SaCo 95864 298-F4
4600 SaCo 95864 299-A2
4700 SaCo 95608 299-A2
5700 SaCo 95608 279-E3
9000 SaCo 95628 279-E3
9900 SaCo 95628 280-A2
11100 SaCo 95628 260-B7
11700 CITH 95628 260-B4
12600 CITH 95610 260-B4
12600 CITH 95662 260-B4
12600 SaCo 95610 260-B4
12600 SaCo 95662 260-B4
13900 CITH 95610 240-B7
FAIR OAKS LN
- EDCo 95672 243-C3

FAIROVER CT
1700 EDCo 95667 246-D7
FAIROVER DR
2600 EDCo 95667 246-D7
FAIR PINES CT
- EDCo 95633 205-C2
FAIR PINES LN
8000 EDCo 95633 205-C3
FAIR PINES LN W
- EDCo 95633 205-C2
FAIR PLAY DR
7200 SaCo 95660 258-H1
FAIR PLAY RD
7700 EDCo 95684 286-H7
FAIRSITE CT
700 GALT 95632 439-F1
FAIRVALE WY
5600 SaCo 95662 260-E6
FAIRVIEW CT
- LNCN 95648 180-A6
500 PLCR 95667 245-E5
3200 SaCo 95821 278-D4
FAIRVIEW DR
9500 PlaC 95661 240-E5
FAIRVIEW LN
2000 PlaC 95658 201-F2
FAIRWAY CT
5200 RKLN 95677 220-B2
FAIRWAY DR
- RSVL 95678 219-H3
- RSVL 95678 220-A4
400 GALT 95632 419-F7
500 GALT 95632 439-G1
700 WSAC 95605 296-J2
700 WSAC 95605 297-A2
900 LNCN 95648 179-D1
3100 EDCo 95682 263-D4
5300 RKLN 95677 220-B3
FAIRWAYS CT
3000 SaCo 95821 278-G5
FAIRWAY TWO AV
7400 SaCo 95628 259-G7
FAIRWAY VALLEY CT
- LNCN 95648 180-A7
FAIRWAY VALLEY LN
- LNCN 95648 180-A6
FAIRWAY VIEW DR
- PlaC 95650 200-F1
- PlaC 95663 180-F7
- PlaC 95663 200-F1
FAIRWEATHER DR
1000 SAC 95833 277-E6
FAIRWOOD WY
4000 SaCo 95608 279-G3
FAIRYTALE ST
7200 CITH 95621 259-H2
FAIRYWREN CT
- LNCN 95648 200-B3
FAITH LN
4200 EDCo 95619 265-E3
8200 SaCo 95828 338-D3
FAITHORNE LN
100 FOLS 95630 281-B1
FALABELLA WY
5000 ELKG 95757 357-H7
FALCON
4100 EDCo 95709 246-J2
FALCON CT
2100 FOLS 95630 282-B1
FALCON DR
2100 FOLS 95630 282-B1
FALCON LN
4100 EDCo 95709 246-J2
FALCON RD
7000 SaCo 95628 279-G1
FALCON WY
600 RSVL 95661 240-C3
FALCON CREEK CIR
9100 ELKG 95624 378-H1
FALCON CREST LN
500 EDCo 95762 242-F1
FALCONER WY
- SaCo 95824 317-H4
FALCON HILL CT
9100 ELKG 95624 378-H1
FALCON MEADOW DR
9700 ELKG 95624 358-H7
9700 ELKG 95624 378-H1
FALCON POINTE DR
- RSVL 95661 220-D7
FALCON RIDGE LN
9100 SaCo 95628 260-G7
FALCONS PT
2000 AUB 95603 182-E6
FALCON VIEW DR
7900 SaCo 95843 239-A5
FALCON VIEW LN
- LNCN 95648 200-C2
FALCONWOOD CT
4900 SaCo 95843 239-A6
FALCONWOOD WY
4900 SaCo 95843 239-A5
FALDO CT
7900 SaCo 95829 339-E5
FALETTO AV
1500 SAC 95835 257-D4
FALKIRK CT
300 LNCN 95648 179-G4
3700 EDCo 95762 262-D2
8300 SaCo 95843 238-J5
FALKIRK WY
3400 EDCo 95762 262-D2
FALKLAND WY
9200 SaCo 95826 299-A6
FALL LN
4400 OAKL 94561 (514-G7 See Page 493)
FALL ST
4800 EDCo 95623 265-B5
FALL WY
6900 ELKG 95758 358-B4
FALL BREEZE CT
6800 ELKG 95758 358-B4
FALLBRIGHT CT
8800 ELKG 95624 358-G3
FALLBRIGHT WY
8700 ELKG 95624 358-G2
FALLBROOK LN
2200 EDCo 95672 243-J7
FALLBROOK ST
1100 WSAC 95691 296-H5
FALLBROOK WY
8500 SAC 95826 298-F7
FALL CREEK WY
1200 SAC 95833 277-D5
FALLEN LEAF LN
1800 LNCN 95648 180-A7
FALLEN LEAF RD
2900 EDCo 95682 283-E2

STREET
Block City ZIP Pg-Grid

FALLEN LEAF WY
900 SaCo 95864 298-H4
FALLEN OAK CT
4100 SaCo 95843 238-H7
FALLEN TREE CT
3300 SaCo 95827 299-B6
FALL HAVEN WY
- RCCD 95742 320-E4
FALLING LEAF CT
4100 SaCo 95843 238-H7
FALLING RAIN CT
- ELKG 95757 358-A7
FALLIS CIR
3600 SAC 95832 337-F4
FALLON LN
- SAC 95819 297-J4
FALLON PLACE CT
1000 SaCo 95673 257-J2
1000 SaCo 95673 258-A2
FALLON WOODS WY
1000 SaCo 95673 257-J2
1000 SaCo 95673 258-A2
FALLOW DR
4300 SAC 95823 337-H4
FALL RIVER DR
100 FOLS 95630 261-A4
FALL RIVER WY
6300 SAC 95824 318-B6
6300 SAC 95828 318-B6
N FALLS DR
200 FOLS 95630 241-A7
FALLSBROOK CT
8800 PlaC 95746 241-B3
FALLSMONT DR
- EDCo 95762 282-D3
FALL TRAIL CT
2200 EDCo 95667 246-C4
FALL TRAIL RD
2100 EDCo 95667 246-C4
FALL VALLEY WY
9700 SaCo 95829 339-C5
FALLVIEW WY
- EDCo 95762 282-D3
FALLWATER LN
2300 SaCo 95608 279-B7
FALLWIND CIR
- SAC 95831 336-J3
FALLWOOD WY
7300 CITH 95621 239-G6
FALMOUTH WY
6800 SAC 95823 358-B1
FALWORTH ST
6800 CITH 95621 259-F3
FAMILY CT
3100 EDCo 95667 246-C6
FAMILY HILL LN
2600 EDCo 95667 245-C4
FANCY WY
5800 SAC 95835 257-C4
FANEGA CT
9000 ELKG 95758 357-J4
FANGIO CT
- ELKG 95758 358-C6
FANNING WY
- SaCo 95829 338-J7
FANTAGES WY
100 FOLS 95630 281-B2
FANTAIL CT
- LNCN 95648 200-B3
FANTAIL LN
- LNCN 95648 200-A3
FANTASIA CT
4800 SaCo 95843 239-A6
FAN WOOD WY
4900 SaCo 95843 239-A5
FARALLON CIR
- SAC 95831 336-G2
FARALLON CT
- LNCN 95648 180-A4
FARALLON RD
- WSAC 95691 316-E2
FARAWAY PL
9200 ELKG 95758 358-C4
FAREBROTHER DR
- RKLN 95677 220-E5
FAREWELL CT
8600 ELKG 95624 358-F1
FARGO LN
8800 PlaC 95746 241-B3
FARGO WY
100 FOLS 95630 261-D5
3900 SaCo 95660 258-H3
FARHAM DR
100 FOLS 95630 261-C6
FARIA ST
500 ANT 94509 (513-C7
See Page 493)
FARID CT
3400 SaCo 95608 279-B4
FARISH RD
5700 EDCo 95667 264-G3
FARLEY CT
- FOLS 95630 261-D7
FARLEY WY
8600 SaCo 95628 280-D1
FARM LN
9700 SaCo 95827 319-C3
FARM RD
4700 EDCo 95623 264-H5
FARM DALE WY
7200 SAC 95831 337-A1
FARMER WY
- FOLS 95630 261-D7
- FOLS 95630 281-D1
4000 SaCo 95660 258-H4
FARMGATE CIR
- RSVL 95747 219-D1
FARMGATE LN
- LNCN 95648 199-J1
FARMGATE WY
7400 CITH 95610 259-H5
FARM HOUSE CT
- RKLN 95765 199-J4
FARMHOUSE CT
7500 CITH 95610 259-H5
FARM HOUSE LN
- RKLN 95765 199-J4
FARMINGTON CIR
200 RSVL 95678 219-F5
FARMINGTON CT
1700 EDCo 95762 242-C6
3500 RKLN 95765 220-C1
FARMINGTON WY
6900 SaCo 95828 318-B7
6900 SaCo 95828 338-B1
FARNELL WY
7800 SAC 95823 337-G5
FAR NIENTE WY
- SAC 95834 276-J3

FARNOON CT
- FOLS 95630 281-F1
FARNSWORTH LN
4600 EDCo 95623 265-C4
FARNSWORTH WY
2000 RCCD 95670 279-G6
FARO DR
6800 SAC 95828 318-B7
FARR CT
6500 CITH 95610 259-J3
FARRELL CT
- FOLS 95630 281-G1
FARRELL LN
2200 PlaC 95648 160-C6
FARRELL RD
5300 EDCo 95682 283-F6
FARRIDGE CT
- RSVL 95678 219-G3
FARRIDGE DR
- RSVL 95678 219-G3
FARRIER RD
2200 RKLN 95765 200-A7
2200 RKLN 95765 220-A1
FARRIER WY
- PlaC 95747 238-H3
FARRINGTON CT
9100 ELKG 95624 358-J5
FARRINGTON LN
500 LNCN 95648 179-F5
FARRIS LN
9800 ELKG 95624 359-C3
FARRON ST
2800 RKLN 95677 220-C3
FARSCHON PL
8800 PlaC 95746 240-G3
FARVIEW CT
3500 EDCo 95672 243-C4
FARVIEW DR
3500 EDCo 95672 243-C4
FASCINATION CT
8100 SaCo 95828 338-D4
FASHION DR
8900 SaCo 95826 318-H1
FASSETT CT
- ELKG 95758 357-G5
FASSETT WY
9300 ELKG 95758 357-G5
FAST WATER CT
6500 CITH 95621 259-D3
FATH CT
100 FOLS 95630 261-G3
FATHER LODE RD
- EDCo 95667 264-H4
FATHOM PL
1700 WSAC 95691 296-J6
FAULK RD
- SaCo 95742 281-B6
FAULKNER DR
- RSVL 95747 239-C1
FAULKNER WY
- ELKG 95758 358-D3
FAUSSET CT
100 FOLS 95630 261-E4
FAUSTINO WY
6200 SAC 95831 316-G6
FAWCETT CT
- GALT 95632 419-G3
FAWN CIR
4000 SAC 95823 337-G5
FAWN CT
900 RSVL 95661 239-J4
FAWN DR
5100 EDCo - 248-C7
5100 EDCo 95726 248-C7
FAWN ST
4300 EDCo 95682 264-E5
FAWN WY
2600 EDCo 95672 243-A7
7200 SaCo 95823 338-A2
FAWNBROOK CT
- SAC 95823 357-J1
FAWN CREEK CT
- PlaC 95602 161-J2
3700 SaCo 95843 238-G6
FAWN CREEK TR
- AUB 95603 182-A7
FAWN CROSSING WY
- SaCo 95843 239-B6
FAWNDALE LN
- LNCN 95648 200-B3
FAWN HILL CT
8500 PlaC 95603 161-F6
FAWN HILL LN
2500 PlaC 95603 161-F6
FAWN HOLLOW WY
- SaCo 95843 239-B6
FAWNRIDGE CT
4900 SaCo 95843 239-A6
FAWNRIDGE WY
4900 SaCo 95843 239-A6
FAWN RUN WY
3900 SaCo 95843 238-H5
FAWN TRAIL WY
5300 SaCo 95843 239-B7
FAWN VALLEY CT
- SaCo 95843 239-B7
FAWN VALLEY PL
5100 SaCo 95843 239-B7
FAWN VALLEY WY
5100 SaCo 95843 239-B7
FAXON PL
9200 ELKG 95624 358-J5
FAY CIR
1100 SAC 95831 317-A7
FAYETTE WY
300 FOLS 95630 261-H6
FEATHER CT
- LNCN 95648 200-A1
7600 SaCo 95843 258-H1
FEATHER CREEK DR
- ELKG 95758 358-A4
FEATHER FALLS CIR
100 FOLS 95630 240-J7
100 FOLS 95630 241-A7
FEATHER FALLS CT
- ELKG 95624 359-B5
FEATHER RIVER CT
- RSVL 95678 219-G5
FEATHER RIVER WY
9000 SaCo 95826 298-J6
FEATHERY CT
15400 SaCo 95683 342-D3
FEATURE DR
600 SaCo 95825 298-C4
FEDERAL ST
5300 SaCo 95660 258-J6
FEDERALIST LN
3100 RCCD 95827 299-D5

FEE DR
900 SAC 95815 297-J1
1000 SAC 95815 277-J7
1000 SAC 95815 278-A7
1000 SAC 95815 298-A1
FEGAN WY
4600 SaCo 95822 317-C3
FEHR RD
500 FOLS 95630 262-B7
FEICKERT DR
9200 ELKG 95624 358-F5
FEICKERT RANCH PL
8400 ELKG 95624 358-F5
FELDIN CT
- SAC 95758 358-C1
FELDSPAR CT
7800 CITH 95610 240-C7
FELDSPAR LN
4600 EDCo 95667 244-C1
FELICE WY
2900 SAC 95826 318-D1
FELICIA WY
4900 ELKG 95758 357-H4
FELICITER WY
6400 CITH 95610 259-J4
FELIPE CT
7200 CITH 95621 259-F2
FELIZ WY
1300 LNCN 95648 180-D7
FELL ST
3800 SAC 95838 278-A2
FELTHAM WY
3300 RCCD 95827 299-D5
FELTON CT
500 RSVL 95747 239-C1
FELTON PL
6100 ELKG 95758 358-A3
FELTON CREST WY
8400 ELKG 95624 358-E1
FEMOYER ST
- RCCD 95655 299-G5
- SaCo 95655 299-G5
FEN CT
- SAC 95823 337-G3
FENCELINE CT
2200 FOLS 95630 282-B1
FENCELINE DR
2000 FOLS 95630 282-A1
FENDANT DR
3400 RCCD 95670 299-J4
3400 RCCD 95670 300-A4
FENMORE AV
- SAC 95835 257-B6
FENNWOOD CT
6100 SAC 95831 317-A6
6200 SAC 95831 316-J5
FENTON CT
8800 ELKG 95624 358-G5
FENTON WY
5200 RSVL 95746 240-F6
FENUGREEK WY
- SAC 95835 257-C7
FENWAY CT
6900 ELKG 95758 358-B4
FENWICK LN
- LNCN 95648 179-E6
FENWICK WY
4400 SaCo 95660 258-J4
FERGUS DR
- RSVL 95747 219-D5
FERGUSEN WY
- FOLS 95630 261-J4
FERGUSON AV
- SAC 95828 318-D4
FERGUSON RD
200 PlaC 95603 162-F6
FERIGO LN
4900 SaCo 95841 259-A7
4900 SaCo 95841 279-A1
FERLONG RD
4000 EDCo 95667 265-A2
FERMOY WY
1000 GALT 95632 419-E2
FERN AV
1900 EDCo - 247-F3
FERN CT
100 GALT 95632 419-E6
100 SAC 95819 297-H3
400 EDCo 95672 243-B6
FERN PL
- PlaC 95603 162-G6
FERN ST
100 RSVL 95678 239-H3
FERNANDEZ DR
2400 SAC 95822 317-E5
FERNANDO WY
900 GALT 95632 439-E1
8400 SaCo 95626 237-F5
FERN BROOK CT
3400 EDCo 95682 263-B7
FERNBROOK CT
5800 SaCo 95608 259-E5
FERNCLIFF CT
- SAC 95823 358-B2
FERNCREEK CT
8200 CITH 95621 239-F6
FERN CREST WY
8500 ELKG 95624 358-F4
FERNDALE AV
2500 SAC 95822 337-E3
FERNDALE CIR
1700 WSAC 95691 296-H5
FERNDALE CT
2100 PLCR 95667 246-B5
2300 RSVL 95661 240-D5
FERNGROVE WY
3000 ANT 94531 (513-G7
See Page 493)
FERNHILL WY
8300 SaCo 95829 339-A7
FERN LEAF DR
6300 PlaC 95746 241-A6
FERNLEAF DR
600 FOLS 95630 241-B7
FERNLEY AV
2200 SAC 95815 277-G7
FERNRIDGE DR
7400 SaCo 95828 338-D3
FERN VALLEY WY
- ELKG 95757 377-J1
- ELKG 95757 397-J1
FERNWAY CT
- ELKG 95758 358-B3
FERNWOOD CIR
2000 RSVL 95661 240-D3
5000 OAKL 94561 (514-D6
See Page 493)

FERNWOOD CT
5000 OAKL 94561 (514-D6
See Page 493)
FERNWOOD DR
1600 OAKL 94561 (514-D6
See Page 493)
5700 EDCo 95682 283-F7
FERNWOOD LP
5700 EDCo 95682 283-F7
FERNWOOD ST
1000 WSAC 95691 296-H5
4200 RKLN 95677 220-E3
FERNWOOD WY
5200 SaCo 95841 259-B5
FERRAGAMO WY
9900 ELKG 95757 378-B1
FERRAN AV
1500 SAC 95832 337-C3
FERRARI CT
- PLCR 95667 245-H3
7600 SaCo 95628 279-H3
FERRARI WY
300 LNCN 95648 179-H4
FERRARI RANCH RD
- LNCN 95648 179-H5
FERRERA DR
100 FOLS 95630 261-G4
FERRIER CT
6700 SAC 95822 317-D7
FERRIER WY
700 FOLS 95630 261-C6
FERTELLI DR
- ELKG 95624 358-D1
FESCUE CT
7500 SaCo 95683 342-D3
FESCUE WY
- LNCN 95648 199-H3
FESLER CT
7500 CITH 95610 259-J1
FESTA CT
10100 ELKG 95757 378-B2
FESTIVAL DR
8600 ELKG 95624 358-E1
FETLOCK WY
9400 ELKG 95624 359-B6
FETZER CT
800 OAKL 94561 (514-E6
See Page 493)
FETZER LN
1200 OAKL 94561 (514-E6
See Page 493)
FETZER WY
9100 SaCo 95829 338-J5
FEUSI CT
- SAC 95820 317-H3
FEWSVILLE LN
4500 EDCo 95682 283-J3
FIADOR CT
- PlaC 95747 238-H3
FICUS CIR
- EDCo 95762 242-E6
FIDDLENECK CT
9700 ELKG 95757 357-F7
FIDDLER GREEN CT
800 AUB 95603 162-D7
FIDDLETOWN CT
3300 SaCo 95827 299-B6
FIDDYMENT RD
1200 PlaC 95648 179-B7
1200 PlaC 95648 199-B3
1200 PlaC 95747 199-B3
1200 LNCN 95648 179-B7
1200 LNCN 95648 199-B3
3000 RSVL 95747 199-B3
3000 RSVL 95747 219-A2
5000 PlaC 95747 218-J6
5000 RSVL 95747 218-J6
6000 PlaC 95747 238-J1
6000 RSVL 95747 238-J1
FIEL CT
- FOLS 95630 261-D7
FIELD CT
2700 RKLN 95765 200-A7
FIELD RUN
7100 EDCo 95667 245-A7
FIELD ST
5200 SaCo 95660 258-G6
FIELDALE DR
6100 SAC 95758 358-A2
FIELD BROOK CT
6000 ELKG 95758 358-A3
FIELDBROOK CT
- RSVL 95747 219-D1
FIELDCREST CT
- LNCN 95648 180-A4
3500 RKLN 95765 220-D1
FIELDCREST DR
3200 SaCo 95821 278-F6
FIELD GATE LN
5100 SaCo 95660 258-H7
FIELDING CIR
3700 SaCo 95826 318-H1
FIELDING CT
900 RSVL 95746 240-F4
FIELDING LN
500 LNCN 95648 179-G4
FIELDPOPPY CIR
8200 SaCo 95828 338-D3
FIELDSTONE CT
- FOLS 95630 261-J5
- RSVL 95747 219-D1
FIELDSTONE DR
- EDCo 95667 244-J7
- LNCN 95648 199-H2
FIELD STONE LN
7900 SaCo 95628 280-A2
FIELDWOOD LN
9200 SaCo 95628 260-G7
FIELLEN CT
2300 SaCo 95825 278-D7
FIESTA CT
- SAC 95817 317-J1
FIESTA LN
6600 SaCo 95662 260-G3
FIFE CT
8900 ELKG 95624 358-H5
FIFE RANCH WY
9200 ELKG 95624 358-H4
FIFTEEN MILE DR
500 RSVL 95678 219-G5
FIFTH PKWY
6900 SaCo 95823 317-J7
6900 SaCo 95823 337-J1
FIG LN
4500 OAKL 94561 (514-E7
See Page 493)
FIG RD
12400 SaCo 95693 360-H2

FIG ST
100 RSVL 95678 239-G2
3600 SAC 95838 278-A3
FIG LEAF CT
- SAC 95838 257-G7
FIGTREE CT
9000 ELKG 95758 357-H3
FIGUEROA ST
- FOLS 95630 261-B5
FIGWOOD WY
4300 SaCo 95864 278-J7
FILAREE CT
2500 RKLN 95677 220-F3
FILAREE WY
6500 SaCo 95842 259-B3
FILBERT AV
5000 SaCo 95628 260-G7
5000 SaCo 95628 280-G1
5700 SaCo 95662 260-G3
FILBERT CT
300 OAKL 94561 (514-G7
See Page 493)
FILBERT ST
2600 ANT 94509 (513-H6
See Page 493)
FILIFERA WY
8100 SaCo 95843 239-A6
FILLIES CT
8100 SaCo 95829 339-D6
FILLMORE CT
2200 ANT 94509 (513-A7
See Page 493)
FILLMORE PL
- WSAC 95691 296-J7
FILMORE CT
- RKLN 95765 219-H1
FILMORE LN
2300 RCCD 95670 279-J6
FIN CT
4900 EDCo 95726 248-C6
FINCASTLE CT
- SaCo 95829 338-J5
FINCH CT
- PlaC 95603 162-G5
1000 EDCo 95619 265-F1
FINCH DR
200 GALT 95632 419-D6
1800 RSVL 95661 240-C4
FINCH RD
600 EDCo 95619 265-E1
4900 SaCo 95628 259-G7
4900 SaCo 95628 279-G1
FINCHLEY LN
100 FOLS 95630 261-H6
FINDERS WY
500 EDCo 95762 282-C1
FINDLEY WY
6900 SaCo 95628 259-F6
FINDON CT
900 GALT 95632 419-G4
FINE CT
- EDCo 95623 264-H6
FINE GOLD CT
1900 SaCo 95670 280-B3
FINE SAND CT
1000 WSAC 95605 296-J2
FINISTERIA DR
- RSVL 95678 199-F7
FINISTERRE CT
8200 SaCo 95628 280-B3
FINLANDIA WY
4800 SaCo 95608 299-A3
FINLEY ST
100 AUB 95603 182-E3
FINMERE WY
8100 SaCo 95829 339-A6
FINNEY CT
5100 SaCo 95608 259-D7
FINO CT
10900 RCCD 95670 299-J5
FINSBURY AV
5300 SaCo 95841 259-B7
FINTOWN CT
8300 SaCo 95828 338-G7
FIORE DR
11000 RCCD 95670 299-J4
11000 RCCD 95670 300-A4
FIR AV
- RSVL 95678 239-F5
FIR CREST CT
8500 ELKG 95624 358-F5
FIRE AGATE WY
11800 RCCD 95742 320-D1
FIREBIRD LN
- SaCo 95841 279-A1
FIRECREST CT
- SaCo 95829 338-J6
FIREFLY CT
- SAC 95831 336-H2
FIREFLY GREEN CT
- RSVL 95747 219-A5
FIREFLY GREEN LN
7000 RSVL 95747 219-A4
FIREHOUSE ST
3700 SAC 95838 277-J3
FIRE KING CT
9400 SaCo 95826 299-A7
FIRE LEAF CT
- SAC 95838 257-H7
FIRELIGHT WY
9100 SaCo 95826 298-J7
FIREMOSS WY
8500 ELKG 95624 358-F2
FIRE OPAL CT
10000 RCCD 95827 299-D4
FIRE POPPY DR
- ELKG 95757 377-J1
- ELKG 95757 397-J1
9700 ELKG 95757 357-J7
FIRESIDE WY
3200 RCCD 95827 299-E5
FIRE STATION CT
- ELKG 95757 358-A7
FIRE STICK CT
5900 CITH 95621 259-D3
FIRESTONE DR
200 RSVL 95678 219-G6
FIRESTONE WY
7700 SaCo 95843 239-B6
FIRETHORN WY
9900 ELKG 95757 377-H1
9900 ELKG 95757 397-H1
FIRE WATER CT
5900 CITH 95621 259-D3
FIREWEED CIR
7400 CITH 95610 260-C1
FIREWOOD CT
8200 SaCo 95662 260-C3

FIRGROVE CT
9200 SaCo 95826 318-J2
FIRST PKWY
7000 SaCo 95823 317-H7
7000 SaCo 95823 337-H1
FIRST DRAW WY
7800 SaCo 95828 338-E4
FIRSTONE CT
9900 SaCo 95829 339-D7
FIRSTONE DR
9900 SaCo 95829 339-C7
FIRTH WY
1100 EDCo 95762 262-D1
FIR TREE LN
6500 SaCo 95662 260-C3
FISCHER CT
500 RSVL 95678 239-H3
FISHER CIR
- FOLS 95630 261-C7
- FOLS 95630 281-C1
FISHER CT
- FOLS 95630 281-C1
FISHER DR
700 AUB 95603 162-E5
700 PlaC 95603 162-E5
FISHER LN
- SaCo 95608 279-D4
FISHER ST
- RVIS 94571 454-H3
FISHMAN LN
7000 EDCo 95630 222-J3
FISKE CT
10300 RCCD 95670 299-F2
FISKE ST
700 PLCR 95667 245-F6
FITCH WY
700 EDCo 95762 242-C4
1200 SaCo 95864 298-H3
FITCHBURG SQ
300 FOLS 95630 261-H6
FITE CIR
3100 RCCD 95827 299-D5
FITE SCHOOL RD
9500 SaCo 95829 339-B6
FITHIAN WY
100 FOLS 95630 261-B1
FITTLEWORTH WY
8300 SaCo 95829 338-J7
FITZGERALD RD
- RCCD 95670 300-B4
3100 RCCD 95742 300-B3
FITZGERALD WY
1500 RSVL 95747 219-C5
FITZROY CT
900 RSVL 95747 239-D1
8100 SaCo 95829 338-J6
FITZROY PL
1400 EDCo 95762 262-D4
FITZUREN RD
900 ANT 94509 (513-B6
See Page 493)
FITZWILLIAM WY
5100 SAC 95823 337-J4
FIVE SPOT RD
4600 EDCo - 247-G7
4600 EDCo 95726 247-G7
5000 EDCo 95726 267-G1
FIVE STAR BLVD
6700 RKLN 95765 220-B4
6800 RSVL 95678 220-B4
FIVE STAR DR
- RSVL 95678 220-A4
FIVE WELLS RD
7000 EDCo 95633 205-A4
FLAGSTAFF DR
14000 SaCo 95683 (321-F7
See Page 301)
14000 SaCo 95683 341-F1
FLAGSTONE ST
5200 SaCo 95608 259-E7
FLAME CT
3300 EDCo 95682 263-E3
FLAME TOKAY WY
- ELKG 95624 359-A7
FLAMING ARROW DR
6700 CITH 95621 259-D2
FLAMINGO WY
- RKLN 95765 219-J1
- RKLN 95765 220-A1
6600 SaCo 95828 338-B1
FLANDERS WY
6900 SaCo 95842 259-A2
FLANNERY WY
8500 SaCo 95828 338-F6
FLAT BROKE WY
2000 EDCo 95667 246-A2
FLATIRON CT
- RKLN 95765 199-J4
FLATIRON LN
- RKLN 95765 199-J4
FLAT ROCK CT
100 FOLS 95630 241-A7
FLAT ROCK DR
100 FOLS 95630 241-A7
FLAUM CT
- SAC 95823 337-J7
FLEDGLING CT
5800 SaCo 95628 260-B5
FLEET CIR
- RKLN 95765 200-A7
FLEET CT
- RKLN 95765 200-A7
- SAC 95831 336-G1
3100 EDCo 95682 263-D3
FLEETWOOD DR
100 ANT 94509 (513-D7
See Page 493)
5500 CITH 95621 259-G6
7300 CITH 95628 259-G6
FLEISHACKER DR
- SaCo 95670 280-B4
FLEMING AV
6800 SaCo 95828 338-B2
FLEMING CT
- RSVL 95747 219-E6
FLEMING DR
- RSVL 95747 219-E6
FLEMING LN
- CCCo 94509 (514-A4
See Page 493)
FLETCHER CT
5000 SaCo 95841 259-B5
FLETCHER FARM DR
7300 SaCo 95828 338-F2
FLICKER LN
5200 EDCo 95623 264-J6
5200 EDCo 95623 265-A6
FLICKER WY
- EDCo 95633 205-F2

FLIGHT DECK CT
5000 SaCo 95628 260-F7
FLIGHTLINE CIR
5800 SaCo 95837 256-A3
FLIGHTLINE DR
1900 LNCN 95648 179-B1
FLINDELL WY
100 FOLS 95630 261-F7
FLINT CT
2800 EDCo 95682 263-C3
FLINT ST
- RSVL 95747 219-A7
FLINT WY
600 SAC 95818 297-B6
7000 PlaC 95663 201-C2
FLINTLOCK CT
5800 SaCo 95608 259-D5
FLINTOFT CT
7800 ELKG 95758 358-C6
FLINTON CT
8900 SaCo 95829 338-H6
FLINTRIDGE WY
9500 SaCo 95662 260-H7
FLINT ROCK CT
- RSVL 95747 219-C3
100 FOLS 95630 261-E6
FLINTSTONE CT
8400 SaCo 95828 338-E4
FLINTWOOD WY
6800 SAC 95831 317-A7
6800 SAC 95831 316-J7
6900 SAC 95831 336-J1
6900 SAC 95831 337-A1
FLOCCHINI CIR
100 LNCN 95648 179-G4
FLOOD CT
100 FOLS 95630 261-G3
FLOOD LN
100 PlaC 95602 162-G7
FLOOD RD
- PlaC 95603 162-F7
S FLOOD RD
100 PlaC 95603 162-G7
FLORA CT
- LNCN 95648 179-F6
FLORA WY
- LNCN 95648 179-E6
FLORABELLE AV
6800 CITH 95621 259-F1
FLORADALE CT
- LNCN 95648 179-D2
- RKLN 95677 220-F5
FLORADALE LN
12500 AUB 95603 162-D5
FLORADALE WY
2300 LNCN 95648 179-D2
FLORADORA DR
9200 SaCo 95826 298-J7
FLORAL DR
3600 SaCo 95660 258-G3
4200 SAC 95834 276-H2
FLORAL LN
- PlaC 95658 181-C3
FLORAL HILLS WY
100 RCCD 95670 280-C7
FLORA SPRINGS WY
- SAC 95834 276-H2
FLORA VISTA LN
4800 SAC 95822 317-B4
FLOR DE ORO LN
3400 EDCo 95682 263-G4
FLORENCE CT
- SAC 95831 337-A3
FLORENCE PL
2700 SAC 95818 297-D7
FLORENCIA LN
7700 SaCo 95829 338-J4
FLORENE CT
300 RSVL 95678 239-F2
FLORES CT
300 LNCN 95648 180-E7
FLORES WY
800 RVIS 94571 454-G5
7300 SaCo 95822 337-E2
FLORI CT
- OAKL 94561 (514-D7
See Page 493)
FLORIDA CT
8400 SAC 95826 298-E7
FLORIDA LN
2500 ANT 94509 (513-A6
See Page 493)
FLORIN RD
200 SAC 95831 316-G6
500 SAC 95831 336-J1
1000 SAC 95831 337-B1
1400 SaCo 95822 337-E1
3100 SaCo 95823 337-E1
4100 SaCo 95823 337-J1
5700 SaCo 95823 338-A1
6500 SaCo 95828 338-F1
8800 SaCo 95828 338-F1
9200 SaCo 95829 339-A1
10100 SaCo 95830 339-E1
10500 SaCo 95830 340-A1
FLORIN CREEK CT
7400 SaCo 95823 337-J3
FLORINDA WY
7300 SaCo 95828 338-C2
FLORIN MALL DR
7200 SaCo 95823 338-A2
FLORIN PERKINS RD
3200 SAC 95826 318-F4
5000 SAC 95828 318-E7
6400 SaCo 95828 318-E7
6900 SaCo 95828 338-E1
6900 SAC 95828 338-E1
FLORINTOWN WY
8200 SaCo 95828 338-D2
FLORINWOOD DR
7300 SaCo 95823 338-A2
FLOSSIE AV
2600 WSAC 95691 296-G3
FLOWER DR
200 FOLS 95630 261-E4
FLOWERDALE DR
- SAC 95823 337-G4
FLOWERS CT
- LNCN 95648 179-E3
FLOWERS ST
1900 SaCo 95825 278-F7
1900 SaCo 95825 298-F1
FLOWERWOOD WY
7300 SAC 95831 336-H2
FLOX WY
4700 ELKG 95758 357-H3
FLOXTREE CT
8300 SaCo 95828 338-E5

STREET
Block City ZIP Pg-Grid

FLOYD AV
9200 SaCo 95662 260-H2
FLUME LN
2500 PlaC 95658 201-J2
FLUSHING PL
4200 EDCo 95762 262-D2
FLYING C CT
2900 EDCo 95682 283-C2
FLYING C RD
4100 EDCo 95682 283-C1
5000 EDCo 95682 263-F7
FLYING CLOUD DR
4100 EDCo 95667 264-J2
4100 EDCo 95667 265-A2
FLYING HAWK CT
- ELKG 95624 358-G1
FLYNN WY
5300 SaCo 95843 239-B6
FLYNN HILL CT
8100 SaCo 95843 239-B6
FLYWAY DR
5300 SaCo 95628 260-F6
FOBES DR
8600 SaCo 95843 238-G4
FOGERTY CT
- FOLS 95630 281-G1
FOGG RD
11200 SaCo 95757 397-F9
FOGGY BANK WY
- SAC 95833 276-H6
FOGLE CT
3300 SaCo 95608 279-B5
FOLEY CT
2600 SaCo 95864 298-E5
FOLEY LN
- FOLS 95630 261-B6
FOLKLORE WY
3200 RCCD 95827 299-E5
FOLKSTONE WY
6700 ELKG 95758 358-B5
FOLKSTOVER CT
9000 ELKG 95624 358-F3
FOLLE BLANC PL
9900 ELKG 95624 379-A1
FOLLETT CT
8100 SaCo 95828 338-D5
FOLSOM BLVD
100 FOLS 95630 261-A7
1700 FOLS 95670 280-H4
3200 SAC 95816 297-G6
3800 SAC 95819 297-G6
5600 SAC 95819 298-A7
6900 SAC 95826 298-A7
6900 SAC 95826 318-C1
8500 FOLS 95670 281-A1
8600 SaCo 95826 298-H7
8600 SaCo 95826 318-F1
9200 SaCo 95826 299-B5
9500 SaCo 95827 299-B5
9700 RCCD 95827 299-F3
10100 RCCD 95670 299-F3
10300 FOLS 95742 280-H4
10900 RCCD 95670 280-B7
10900 RCCD 95670 300-A1
11100 RCCD 95742 280-B7
11100 SaCo 95742 280-B7
13000 FOLS 95630 281-A1
FOLSOM BLVD Rt#-16
8000 SAC 95826 318-D1
FOLSOM CT
- WSAC 95691 316-D3
FOLSOM DR
3900 ANT 94531 (513-H7
See Page 493)
FOLSOM RD
100 RSVL 95678 239-J2
FOLSOM-AUBURN RD
6600 FOLS 95630 261-B3
7500 FOLS 95630 241-B7
FOLSOM DAM RD
- FOLS 95630 241-C7
200 FOLS 95630 261-C1
FOLSOM OAKS CT
6800 PlaC 95746 241-B2
FOLSOM RANCH DR
1000 FOLS 95630 261-B4
FONG CT
1100 FOLS 95630 261-A5
FONG ST
1300 FOLS 95630 261-A5
FONG RANCH RD
- SAC 95833 277-D4
- SAC 95834 277-D4
FONT ST
3700 SaCo 95821 278-G6
FONTAINE CT
3500 SaCo 95821 278-E4
FONTANA CT
- EDCo 95762 262-B2
8800 ELKG 95624 378-G1
FONTANA ST
- WSAC 95691 297-A7
FONTENAY WY
- RSVL 95747 219-B1
FONTES WY
1500 OAKL 94561 (514-D6
See Page 493)
FOODLINK ST
- SAC 95828 318-D5
FOOTBRIDGE PL
- SaCo 95608 279-D7
FOOTHILL DR
2600 SaCo 95608 279-A6
4500 EDCo 95682 264-D6
FOOTHILL RD
5500 RKLN 95677 220-G4
5500 PlaC 95677 220-G4
FOOTHILL GARDEN CT
5500 SaCo 95841 259-B6
FOOTHILL OAKS DR
3900 PlaC 95602 161-H2
FOOTHILLS BLVD
4200 RSVL 95747 219-E4
4200 RSVL 95678 219-E1
6200 RSVL 95747 239-F4
6200 RSVL 95678 239-F1
FOOTMAN WY
7300 CITH 95621 259-G1
FOPPIANO WY
8300 SaCo 95829 338-J7
FORASTERA CIR
- SAC 95834 276-G4
FORBES CT
- OAKL 94561 (514-E6
See Page 493)
FORBES PL
1100 EDCo 95762 262-D3
FORBIDDEN CT
- RKLN 95765 219-J2

FORBS WY
7000 CITH 95610 260-B2
FORCALLAT CT
- SAC 95833 276-J4
FORCUM AV
4500 SaCo 95652 278-D1
4700 SaCo 95652 258-D7
FORD CT
2800 ANT 94509 (513-A7
See Page 493)
5800 RKLN 95765 220-B2
FORD RD
- SAC 95838 277-G4
5800 RKLN 95765 220-B2
FORDHAM CT
- RKLN 95677 220-F6
FORDHAM WY
6100 SAC 95822 317-A6
6100 SAC 95831 317-A6
FORDS WY
- PlaC 95603 161-G6
FOREBRIDGE LN
- LNCN 95648 179-E7
FOREMAST CT
- ELKG 95758 357-F7
FOREST CT
200 AUB 95603 182-D5
1400 OAKL 94561 (514-D7
See Page 493)
FOREST PKWY
4400 SaCo 95823 337-H2
FOREST RD
2200 EDCo 95726 248-H1
FORESTBERRY WY
- EDCo 95762 282-D3
FOREST CREEK LN
8300 SaCo 95662 260-C3
FOREST CREEK WY
- PlaC 95746 240-H5
FOREST GLEN WY
8000 CITH 95610 240-B7
FOREST HIGHLANDS DR
- RVIS 94571 454-E1
FORESTHILL AV
100 AUB 95603 182-E1
600 PlaC 95603 182-F1
FOREST HILL CT
4300 SaCo 95608 279-E2
FOREST HILL DR
- EDCo 95619 265-F2
FORESTHILL RD
- PlaC 95603 162-G6
FOREST KNOLL
400 RSVL 95678 240-A1
FORESTLAKE DR
2100 RCCD 95670 279-G6
FOREST LAKE RD
3000 SJCo 95220 (438-G4
See Page 418)
5700 EDCo 95619 265-E4
E FOREST LAKE RD
1700 SJCo 95220 439-B4
2500 SJCo 95220 (438-J5
See Page 418)
FOREST OAK WY
8100 CITH 95610 240-B7
FOREST OAKS DR
2300 LNCN 95648 179-D2
FOREST RIDGE PL
5800 ELKG 95757 357-J6
FOREST VIEW CT
9700 ELKG 95757 358-A7
FOREST VISTA WY
9300 ELKG 95758 358-A5
FORESTWOOD DR
5500 SaCo 95842 259-C3
FORGETMENOT CT
8000 CITH 95610 240-A6
FORGOTTEN RD
- AUB 95603 182-C3
- PlaC 95603 182-C3
S FORK RD
- EDCo 95667 225-E6
S FORK WY
100 FOLS 95630 261-A3
100 FOLS 95630 260-J3
FORKED CREEK WY
8900 ELKG 95758 357-J3
FORMAN WY
6900 SaCo 95828 338-B1
6900 SaCo 95828 318-B7
FORMBY CT
- RSVL 95747 239-B1
FORMBY WY
- RSVL 95747 239-B1
FORNI CT
6300 EDCo 95623 265-B4
FORNI RD
300 EDCo 95667 245-D5
600 PLCR 95667 245-D5
3600 EDCo 95667 265-C2
4400 EDCo 95623 265-B4
FORREST ST
600 FOLS 95630 261-A5
1000 SAC 95815 297-H1
1200 SAC 95815 277-H6
FORRESTAL ST
4800 SaCo 95628 280-B1
4900 SaCo 95628 260-B7
FORRESTER WY
4600 SaCo 95843 238-J5
4600 SaCo 95843 239-A5
FORRESTERS LN
- LNCN 95648 179-E7
FORSTER LN
2200 PlaC 95603 161-G7
2200 PlaC 95603 181-H1
FORSYTH CT
7800 SaCo 95626 238-D7
FORSYTHIA WY
8500 SaCo 95843 238-E5
FORTADO CIR
100 SAC 95831 316-J6
FORT JIM CT
4800 EDCo - 267-B1
FORT JIM RD
2100 EDCo 95667 246-G7
2200 EDCo 95667 266-G1
3400 EDCo 95667 267-A1
3500 EDCo - 267-A1
FORT JOHN CT
2000 SaCo 95670 280-D4
FORT PITT WY
6800 SaCo 95828 338-B2
FORT POINT DR
2200 SaCo 95670 280-C5
FORT ROCK CT
500 FOLS 95630 261-A1

FORTROSE PL
2200 EDCo 95762 242-B5
FORT SUTTER WY
5300 SaCo 95841 259-B5
FORTUNA CT
2800 ANT 94509 (513-B6
See Page 493)
FORTUNA RD
2000 EDCo 95667 245-F1
FORTUNA WY
8800 SaCo 95662 260-E5
FORTUNE CT
3200 PlaC 95602 162-A3
FORT WORTH WY
9400 SaCo 95827 299-A5
N FORTY RD
- PlaC 95648 160-G6
FORTY NINER CIR
11400 SaCo 95670 280-B3
FOSDYKE CT
- SaCo 95829 338-J7
FOSKETT RANCH CT
- LNCN 95648 179-E2
FOSKETT RANCH DR
- LNCN 95648 179-E2
FOSS LAKE WY
8200 SaCo 95843 239-B6
FOSTER CT
- WSAC 95691 316-D3
FOSTER WY
- EDCo 95762 262-E6
4500 SaCo 95608 279-A4
FOSTONES AV
100 SaCo 95820 338-F2
FOTOS CT
3900 SAC 95820 318-A2
FOULKS RANCH DR
9400 ELKG 95758 358-A5
FOUNDATION PL
- SaCo 95670 280-E5
FOUNDERS CT
9800 ELKG 95624 358-J7
9800 ELKG 95624 359-A7
FOUNDERS LN
- EDCo 95667 266-A3
FOUNDERS WY
9700 ELKG 95624 359-A7
FOUNTAIN DR
500 WSAC 95605 297-A1
700 WSAC 95605 277-A7
900 WSAC 95605 276-J7
1000 WSAC 95605 296-J1
FOUNTAIN LN
6500 SaCo 95660 258-G3
FOUNTAINARBOR WY
8200 SaCo 95843 239-A7
FOUNTAINDALE WY
6100 SaCo 95608 279-D3
FOUNTAINHEAD CT
8300 SaCo 95843 238-H5
FOUNTAIN HILL CT
- LNCN 95648 180-C7
FOUNTAIN HILL LP
- LNCN 95648 180-C6
FOUNTAIN HILL PL
- LNCN 95648 180-B6
FOUNTAIN OAKS CIR
100 SAC 95831 337-A2
FOUNTAIN SPRINGS CIR
- SAC 95831 337-A2
FOUNTAIN SQUARE DR
6300 CITH 95621 259-G4
FOUNTAINWOOD CT
4900 SaCo 95843 239-A5
FOURNESS DR
700 WSAC 95605 296-J1
FOUR SEASONS DR
- EDCo 95762 282-D3
8900 ELKG 95624 358-H1
FOUR SEASONS RD
- EDCo 95667 266-J3
FOUR SPRINGS DR
3500 EDCo 95672 243-A6
FOUR SPRINGS TR
- EDCo - 267-F5
FOURTH PKWY
7000 SaCo 95823 337-H1
FOUR WINDS DR
- ELKG 95757 357-G6
- SaCo 95757 357-G6
9400 ELKG 95758 357-G5
FOUTZ CT
4600 SaCo 95608 278-J3
4600 SaCo 95821 278-J3
FOWLER AV
6200 SAC 95828 318-A7
FOWLER CT
6600 SAC 95828 318-A7
FOWLER LN
100 RSVL 95678 239-J2
4200 EDCo 95619 265-E3
FOWLER RD
- WSAC 95691 316-C4
400 PlaC 95648 180-G2
400 PlaC 95658 180-G3
1700 PlaC 95648 180-G7
FOWLER WY
1000 PLCR 95667 245-H5
FOX LN
- EDCo 95667 266-G1
1100 PlaC 95648 180-B1
FOXBERRY CT
8600 ELKG 95624 358-G1
FOXBORO CT
5000 RKLN 95677 220-H3
FOXBORO WY
1300 SAC 95833 277-D5
FOXBOROUGH WY
- RSVL 95747 239-E1
FOX CLIFF WY
6800 ELKG 95758 358-B6
FOX CREEK DR
5700 ELKG 95758 357-J4
FOXCROFT CIR
- RSVL 95747 218-J4
FOX DEN CIR
- LNCN 95648 199-J3
FOX DEN CT
9400 ELKG 95758 358-E5
FOXFIELD WY
7200 SaCo 95660 258-H1
FOXFIRE DR
8200 SaCo 95662 260-C4
FOX FLOWER CT
9500 ELKG 95758 358-B6
FOXFORD CT
9400 ELKG 95758 358-A5

FOXFORD GLEN CT
- RSVL 95747 219-C1
FOX GATE WY
- RSVL 95661 220-D6
FOX GLEN WY
8200 ELKG 95758 358-E5
FOXGLOVE CT
- LNCN 95648 179-E2
1400 RSVL 95661 240-A4
8300 CITH 95610 260-C1
FOXGLOVE WY
- LNCN 95648 179-E2
FOXHALL WY
1000 SAC 95831 317-A6
FOX HILL DR
- RKLN 95765 200-D7
FOX HILL LN
7700 PlaC 95658 181-D2
FOX HILLS DR
7400 CITH 95610 260-A1
FOXHOLLOW CT
500 RSVL 95747 239-E1
FOX HOLLOW LN
2000 SaCo 95864 298-G1
FOXHOLLOW WY
1300 RSVL 95747 239-E1
FOX HOUND CIR
8200 ELKG 95758 358-E5
FOX HUNT WY
400 SaCo 95673 257-H1
FOXHURST CT
5400 RCCD 95742 320-E4
FOX MEADOW LN
- CITH 95610 260-B1
8000 PlaC 95746 221-F7
FOX MEADOW PL
8200 CITH 95610 260-B1
FOXMOOR CT
5100 RKLN 95677 220-H4
FOXMORE LN
2400 EDCo 95672 263-A2
FOXMOUTH CIR
100 SaCo 95655 319-J2
100 SaCo 95655 320-A2
FOX OAK CT
- SAC 95831 337-A3
FOXPARK CT
8600 SaCo 95843 238-G5
FOX PRINT CT
6400 EDCo 95667 244-H2
FOXRIDGE CIR
1300 AUB 95603 182-D6
FOXRIDGE DR
100 FOLS 95630 261-A2
FOX RIVER WY
9300 SaCo 95829 339-A7
FOX RUN CT
1000 AUB 95603 162-D5
FOXRUN LN
- RSVL 95747 239-E1
FOX RUN WY
9300 ELKG 95758 358-A5
FOX SPRINGS WY
9200 ELKG 95624 359-B5
FOXTAIL CT
- PlaC 95602 161-J2
6600 SaCo 95660 259-A3
6600 SaCo 95842 259-A3
FOX TREE PL
7400 CITH 95610 260-B1
FOX TROTTER WY
5000 ELKG 95757 357-H7
FOXTROTTER WY
700 GALT 95632 419-E2
FOX VALLEY CIR
- SaCo 95660 258-J3
FOXVIEW WY
- ELKG 95757 377-J1
- ELKG 95757 397-J1
FOXWOOD CT
6600 CITH 95841 259-D3
FOXWOOD LN
- RVIS 94571 454-E1
4100 EDCo 95682 264-A6
FOXWORTH CT
600 LNCN 95648 179-J2
FOXYHOLLOW LN
4200 EDCo 95672 243-J7
FOYERS CT
6600 ELKG 95758 358-A6
FOYLE CT
100 FOLS 95630 281-F1
FOYNES WY
8300 SaCo 95828 338-G7
FOYT CT
- ELKG 95758 358-C6
FRAMINGHAM WY
100 FOLS 95630 261-D6
FRAMINGTON WY
9300 ELKG 95758 357-H5
FRAMTON CT
9200 SaCo 95829 338-J6
FRAN CT
- GALT 95632 419-G5
FRANCES AV
100 PlaC 95661 239-H5
200 RSVL 95661 239-H5
FRANCES DR
1200 RSVL 95661 240-A3
FRANCESCA ST
- ELKG 95758 357-J2
4900 SAC 95758 357-J2
FRANCINE DR
6100 SAC 95824 318-B6
FRANCIS AV
3100 PLCR 95667 245-G6
FRANCIS CT
- FOLS 95630 281-E1
100 OAKL 94561 (514-C7
See Page 493)
4400 SAC 95822 317-C3
FRANCIS DR
3400 LMS 95650 200-J5
FRANCIS WY
4800 SaCo 95608 279-A6
FRANCISCAN WY
5700 SAC 95823 337-J6
5700 SAC 95823 338-A6
FRANCISCO CT
500 RSVL 95678 239-F1
S FRANCISCO CT
1600 ANT 94509 (513-A7
See Page 493)
FRANCISCO DR
1500 EDCo 95762 242-C5
2300 EDCo 95762 262-C1
N FRANCISCO WY
2900 ANT 94509 (513-B6
See Page 493)

S FRANCISCO WY
3100 ANT 94509 (513-A7
See Page 493)
FRANCISCO VILLA DR
100 OAKL 94561 (514-E7
See Page 493)
FRANCO LN
2200 SaCo 95821 278-C6
FRANCONIA CT
4300 RCCD 95742 320-E2
FRANDORAS CIR
3000 OAKL 94561 (514-A7
See Page 493)
FRANELA WY
6900 CITH 95621 259-F2
FRANESI WY
500 SAC 95838 277-H1
FRANK CT
5900 SaCo 95824 317-G5
FRANK BAILEY LN
- EDCo 95667 266-G5
FRANKFORT CT
- ELKG 95758 358-B3
FRANK GREG WY
10300 ELKG 95757 378-A2
FRANK HENGEL WY
- OAKL 94561 (514-H6
See Page 493)
FRANKIE LN
- ELKG 95758 357-F6
FRANKLIN BLVD
- ELKG 95757 377-H2
- ELKG 95757 397-H2
7300 SaCo 95823 337-H2
7700 SAC 95823 337-H4
FRANKLIN BLVD Rt#-J8
2600 SAC 95817 297-E7
2900 SAC 95817 317-E3
3600 SAC 95820 317-E3
5400 SAC 95824 317-E3
5500 SAC 95824 317-E3
6300 SAC 95823 317-G7
6800 SAC 95823 337-H6
6800 SAC 95823 337-G1
8300 SaCo 95823 357-H2
8300 SAC 95823 357-H2
8500 SaCo 95758 357-H2
8500 SAC 95758 357-H2
8600 ELKG 95758 357-H2
9600 ELKG 95757 357-H7
9900 ELKG 95757 377-G3
9900 ELKG 95757 397-G3
9900 SaCo 95757 377-G3
9900 SaCo 95757 397-G3
12500 SaCo 95757 417-J2
12800 SaCo 95690 417-J2
FRANKLIN CT
1100 PLCR 95667 245-H4
FRANKLIN ST
100 RSVL 95678 239-J3
FRANKLIN WY
2600 WSAC 95691 296-G3
FRANKLIN HIGH RD
10000 ELKG 95757 378-A2
FRANKLIN SCHOOL RD
7000 PlaC 95650 221-C3
FRANK RICHARDSON CT
100 SAC 95823 338-C6
FRANKWOOD DR
200 FOLS 95630 261-E5
FRANMOR CT
1200 SaCo 95864 298-E3
FRANSTON ST
100 GALT 95632 419-G7
FRANTZ
12100 SaCo 95693 (380-E1
See Page 379)
FRANUSICH AV
7100 SaCo 95828 338-C1
FRANZIA CT
8600 SaCo 95828 338-F6
FRASCATI CT
11100 RCCD 95670 300-A4
FRASCATI DR
- EDCo 95762 262-A2
FRASER DR
- SaCo 95827 299-C7
FRASER ISLAND RD
- WSAC 95691 316-C2
FRASER RIVER CT
10000 RCCD 95670 279-J5
FRASINETTI RD
7200 SaCo 95828 338-E2
FRATES WY
6600 SAC 95831 316-G6
FRATIS ST
- FOLS 95630 281-D1
FRAWLEY WY
5400 SaCo 95823 317-J7
FRAYNE WY
700 SAC 95838 277-H1
FRAZER CT
100 FOLS 95630 261-E7
FRAZIER CT
2200 SaCo 95821 278-C5
FRECKLES CT
9100 ELKG 95624 358-G4
FREDERIC AV
8900 SaCo 95826 318-H1
FREDERICK WY
3200 SaCo 95821 278-D5
FREDERICKSBURG WY
- SAC 95835 257-A5
FREDLENA LN
1300 EDCo 95762 242-E3
FREEBOARD DR
3100 WSAC 95691 296-F4
FREED CT
8800 SaCo 95828 338-G4
FREED WY
8800 SaCo 95828 338-G3
FREEDOM CT
- EDCo 95684 286-E6
FREEDOM LN
6200 CITH 95621 259-D4
FREEDOM RD
- EDCo 95619 286-D5
- EDCo 95684 286-E5
FREEDOM PARK DR
3000 SaCo 95652 258-F4
3000 SaCo 95660 258-F4
FREE FOX LN
- EDCo 95619 286-E5
- EDCo 95684 286-E5
FREEGOLD DR
- EDCo 95709 247-C6
FREEHAVEN DR
6700 SAC 95831 317-A7

FREEMAN CIR
4100 PlaC 95602 162-B1
5500 RKLN 95677 220-G4
FREEMAN DR
5500 RKLN 95677 220-G4
FREEMAN RD
10100 SaCo 95624 359-D6
10100 SaCo 95624 379-F1
10500 SaCo 95693 379-G1
FREEMAN WY
4600 SAC 95819 297-H6
FREEMANS HILL DR
- EDCo - 267-D4
FREEMARK CT
- OAKL 94561 (514-D6
See Page 493)
FREEMARK LN
500 OAKL 94561 (514-D5
See Page 493)
FREEMARK WY
8800 ELKG 95624 358-G3
FREEPORT BLVD
2500 SAC 95818 297-D7
2900 SAC 95818 317-C3
3700 SAC 95822 317-C3
6500 SAC 95822 337-B2
6800 SAC 95832 337-B3
7400 SaCo 95832 337-B3
FREEPORT BRDG Rt#-E9
8000 SaCo 95832 337-B7
53900 YoCo 95612 337-B7
FREE RIVER CT
- SAC 95831 336-G1
FREESE CT
100 FOLS 95630 261-C7
FREESIA DR
8700 ELKG 95624 358-G2
FRWY I-5
- SAC - 277-A4
- SAC - 297-A5
- SAC - 297-B3
- SAC - 316-J4
- SAC - 337-B4
- SaCo - 377-E4
- SaCo - 397-E4
- SaCo - 417-H6
- SJCo - 417-H6
- YoCo - 255-A4
- YoCo - 255-F4
FRWY I-80
- SAC - 276-J5
- SAC - 277-B4
- SAC - 277-F2
- SAC - 278-A2
- SAC - 278-F2
- SAC - 296-G1
- SaCo - 276-J5
- SaCo - 277-E2
- SaCo - 278-H1
- SaCo - 296-G1
- WSAC - 296-F3
- WSAC - 296-G1
FRWY Rt#-99
- SAC - 256-H3
- SAC - 297-F6
- SaCo - 256-H3
- SaCo - 337-H1
FRWY Rt#-160
- ANT - (514-A4
See Page 493)
- CCCo - (514-A4
See Page 493)
- OAKL - (514-A4
See Page 493)
FRWY Rt#-244
- SAC - 278-H2
- SaCo - 278-H1
FRWY U.S.-50
- EDCo - 247-D3
- EDCo - 247-J2
- RCCD - 299-F4
- RCCD - 299-J1
- SAC - 297-F6
- SAC - 297-G6
- SAC - 298-A7
- SAC - 298-G7
- SAC - 318-A1
- SAC - 318-B1
- SAC - 318-C1
- SaCo - 298-J6
- SaCo - 299-A6
- SaCo - 299-C6
- EDCo - 248-F1
N FREEWAY BLVD
3600 SAC 95834 277-D2
3700 SaCo 95834 277-D2
FREEWAY CIR
4500 SaCo 95841 258-J7
4500 SaCo 95841 259-A7
FREITAG WY
4200 ELKG 95758 357-G4
FREMANTLE CT
- RSVL 95747 239-B1
8500 SaCo 95828 338-F2
FREMANTLE WY
- RSVL 95747 239-B1
FREMONT AV
100 RSVL 95678 239-G1
FREMONT BLVD
700 WSAC 95605 296-J2
700 WSAC 95605 297-A2
FREMONT CIR
4600 SaCo 95841 259-B4
FREMONT LN
- LNCN 95648 180-A5
FREMONT WY
500 SAC 95818 297-B6
FREMONTS LP
4200 EDCo 95672 243-C7
FRENCH AV
3000 WSAC 95691 316-F3
3600 SaCo 95821 278-G4
FRENCH RD
7200 SaCo 95828 338-E2
FRENCH CAMP CIR
1900 SaCo 95670 280-D4
FRENCH CREEK CT
- PlaC 95747 238-J2
FRENCH CREEK RD
4000 EDCo 95682 264-B7
FRENCH GULCH CT
100 FOLS 95630 260-H1
FRENO WY
4700 EDCo 95762 262-D6
FRENSHAM DR
- RSVL 95661 220-E7
FRENSHAM WY
3400 SaCo 95826 299-A7

FREON CT
- SAC 95831 336-G1
FRESCA WY
9000 ELKG 95758 358-B3
FRESCHI LN
- LNCN 95648 180-A4
FRESCO LP
- EDCo 95762 262-B2
FRESH MEADOW WY
8000 SaCo 95843 239-A6
FRESNO CT
7100 CITH 95621 259-F2
FRESWICK DR
- FOLS 95630 261-J2
- FOLS 95630 262-A3
FREY DR
- WSAC 95691 296-D4
FRIARS CT
800 SaCo 95608 299-B3
FRIARS GLEN PASS
- LNCN 95648 200-C2
FRIAR TUCK CT
8300 PlaC 95746 241-C2
FRIAR TUCK WY
8300 SaCo 95628 260-C7
FRIA SPRINGS RD
- EDCo 95672 243-E3
FRICKE CT
100 FOLS 95630 261-F3
FRIDA MARIA CT
4200 SaCo 95608 279-F3
FRIDAY CIR
6400 SaCo 95660 258-J3
FRIDAYS STATION CT
- RSVL 95747 219-A3
FRIEDMAN CT
4000 EDCo 95672 243-H5
FRIEDMAN LN
4000 EDCo 95672 243-G5
FRIENDLY CT
6100 SaCo 95608 279-D5
FRIENDLY LN
4100 PlaC 95648 180-F4
FRIENDSHIP CT
- EDCo - 267-C2
FRIENDSHIP HILL RD
- EDCo - 267-C2
FRIENZA AV
900 SAC 95815 277-J6
1200 SAC 95815 278-B6
FRIESIAN WY
5300 ELKG 95757 357-J7
FRIGATEBIRD DR
2800 SAC 95834 276-J4
FRISINGER CT
- SAC 95834 276-J3
FRITZI CT
5600 SaCo 95628 260-B6
FRIZELL AV
4200 SaCo 95660 258-H6
4200 SaCo 95842 258-H6
FROG HOLLOW DR
- EDCo - 267-B2
FROG POND RD
4500 PlaC 95658 180-G3
FROGS LEAP CT
- SAC 95833 276-H6
FROGS LEAP DR
- RCCD 95670 299-H4
FROGVIEW CT
- ELKG 95757 357-J7
FRONT ST
- RVIS 94571 454-H6
900 SAC 95814 297-B3
1600 SAC 95818 297-A5
2500 WSAC 95691 296-G4
5100 RKLN 95677 220-D3
6700 SaCo 95673 257-H1
7200 SaCo 95673 237-H7
FRONTAGE RD
- SAC 95815 297-G1
N FRONTAGE RD
21400 SJCo 95220 (440-A6
See Page 420)
24200 SJCo 95220 439-H4
FRONTERA DR
12300 PlaC 95603 162-D5
FRONTIER CT
1400 PlaC 95663 181-C7
FRONTIER LN
200 RSVL 95747 219-B5
FRONTIER RD
2500 PlaC 95603 161-J6
FRONTIER WY
5600 SaCo 95608 279-C7
FROOM CIR
9900 RCCD 95827 299-D4
FROSSES CT
8700 SaCo 95828 338-G7
FROST LN
3600 LMS 95650 200-H6
FROST WY
7700 SaCo 95828 338-C1
FROSTIE LN
3200 EDCo 95667 244-J6
FROST RIDGE WY
- RKLN 95765 220-A1
FROSTY PL
- PlaC 95747 239-E3
FROSTY FIR DR
2200 EDCo 95762 246-D2
FRUITA CT
4100 SAC 95838 277-G2
FRUITED PLAIN WY
- ELKG 95624 359-B5
FRUITRIDGE RD
1000 EDCo 95667 226-C7
1000 EDCo 95667 246-D1
1200 SAC 95822 317-B4
2000 SAC 95824 317-G4
3300 SaCo 95824 317-G4
5700 SAC 95824 318-B4
7900 SAC 95828 318-F4
8800 SAC 95829 318-H4
8900 SaCo 95829 318-H4
9100 SaCo 95829 319-A4
FRUITVALE RD
400 PlaC 95648 159-J7
400 PlaC 95648 160-A7
4900 PlaC 95658 160-F7
5700 PlaC 95658 161-A7
FRUITWOOD CT
8600 SaCo 95628 280-D1
FRYE CREEK DR
5200 ELKG 95758 357-J2
FTB CT
9600 SaCo 95827 299-A6
FUCHSIA CT
- SAC 95823 337-H3

STREET
Block City ZIP Pg-Grid

FUEGO WY
6300 ELKG 95758 358-A4
FUENTE WY
400 LNCN 95648 180-E7
FUENTE DE PAZ
14900 SaCo 95683 322-B7
FUHRMAN CT
1400 RSVL 95747 219-D6
FUHRMAN WY
1200 RSVL 95747 219-E6
FUJI CT
- EDCo 95709 247-B5
FULAM CT
2900 EDCo 95672 263-C1
FULBRIGHT WY
- SAC 95835 257-A5
FULHAM CT
600 GALT 95632 419-G4
FULLER CT
- LNCN 95648 179-E4
FULLER DR
7200 PlaC 95746 241-C3
FULLER LN
100 LNCN 95648 179-E4
FULLER WY
4000 SaCo 95821 278-H3
FULLERTON CT
- SAC 95825 298-C5
FULL MOON CT
- RSVL 95747 219-A3
FULL MOON DR
3300 EDCo 95667 246-F6
FULSTOW CT
- FOLS 95630 261-G7
FULTON AV
2300 SaCo 95825 298-D4
2400 SaCo 95864 298-D2
2900 SaCo 95825 278-E7
3000 SaCo 95821 278-E5
3600 SAC 95821 278-D3
FULTON SHIPYARD RD
200 ANT 94509 (513-E4 See Page 493)
200 CCCo 94509 (513-E4 See Page 493)
FULTON SQUARE LN
- SaCo 95821 278-D4
FULWEILER AV
100 AUB 95603 182-D2
FUMASI DR
100 GALT 95632 419-D7
FUME BLANC WY
8900 SaCo 95829 338-H5
FUNCHAL CT
10200 ELKG 95757 378-A2
FUNDENHALL CT
- FOLS 95630 261-G7
FUNNEL WY
- EDCo 95633 205-E3
FUNNY BUG RD
1100 EDCo 95667 244-F1
FUNSTON DR
3000 SAC 95833 277-C5
FURLONG DR
12700 SaCo 95693 360-H5
FURLONG LN
6500 EDCo 95667 245-A5
FURMINT WY
2500 RCCD 95670 299-G1
FURNESS WY
4600 SaCo 95843 238-J5
4600 SaCo 95843 239-A5
FUSCHIA WY
4800 OAKL 94561 (514-E6 See Page 493)
FUSILIER WY
3200 SaCo 95826 298-J7
FUTURITY CT
8400 SaCo 95843 238-J5
FUTURO CT
- ELKG 95757 378-B2

G

G ST
100 ANT 94509 (513-C3 See Page 493)
100 ISLE 95641 455-J5
400 SaCo 95673 257-H4
500 GALT 95632 419-F7
700 SAC 95814 297-D3
1000 SaCo 95673 258-A4
2000 SAC 95816 297-F4
4200 SAC 95819 297-H5
5200 SAC 95819 298-A5
G ST Rt#-65
- PlaC 95648 179-F1
100 LNCN 95648 179-H2
S G ST Rt#-65
- LNCN 95648 179-H4
GABBERT DR
3500 EDCo 95682 263-G7
GABELI DR
7900 SaCo 95820 338-E5
GABILAN WY
3400 SaCo 95821 278-J4
GABLE ST
100 FOLS 95630 261-G4
GABLES CT
- RKLN 95765 200-D6
GABLES MILL PL
- ELKG 95758 358-B3
GABRIEL CT
2500 SaCo 95608 279-B7
GABRIELES WY
- EDCo 95726 247-H5
GABRIELLI DR
1200 RSVL 95661 240-A5
GADDI DR
4100 SaCo 95824 317-G5
GADE LN
5800 LMS 95650 220-J1
GADSBY CT
7800 ELKG 95758 358-C5
GADSTEN WY
10600 RCCD 95670 279-J7
GADWALL CT
2800 WSAC 95691 316-F1
GADWALL LN
7500 CITH 95621 259-D1
GADWELL CT
- LNCN 95648 200-C1
GAFFNEY RD
50000 YoCo 95612 356-C6
GAFTON CT
8900 ELKG 95624 378-H1
GAGE CT
- EDCo 95762 262-F6
- FOLS 95630 261-H7

GAGE ST
9500 ELKG 95624 358-H6
GAGEMONT CT
5300 SAC 95820 317-J1
GAGLE WY
1300 SAC 95831 317-A7
GAIL WY
7100 SaCo 95628 259-G7
8000 SAC 95826 318-D1
GAILES CT
- RSVL 95747 219-D5
GAILEY CIR
4200 EDCo 95682 263-B7
4200 EDCo 95682 283-B1
GAILEY CT
4300 EDCo 95682 263-B7
GAIL PEAK CT
4800 SaCo 95843 239-A6
GAIMAN CT
- SaCo 95829 339-A6
GAINES AV
8500 SaCo 95662 260-D4
GAINES DR
- RSVL 95747 218-H4
GAINSBORO WY
8900 SaCo 95826 318-H2
GAINSBOROUGH CIR
100 FOLS 95630 261-B3
GAINSBOROUGH CT
200 RSVL 95678 219-F6
GAINSFORD LN
- SaCo 95828 338-F4
GAINSPORT LN
- SaCo 95828 338-F5
GAINSWOOD LN
- SaCo 95828 338-F4
GAIRLOCK CT
4300 SaCo 95843 238-J5
GALAXY CT
- EDCo 95682 264-B7
6600 CITH 95621 259-D3
GALAXY LN
- RKLN 95677 220-H5
GALAXY PKWY
5200 SaCo 95823 337-J1
GALBRATH DR
3800 SaCo 95660 258-H2
4100 SaCo 95842 258-J1
4500 SaCo 95842 259-A1
GALEN DR
- ELKG 95758 357-D5
GALENA AV
- SAC 95828 318-D5
GALENA CT
100 RSVL 95747 219-E6
GALENA DR
3500 PlaC 95602 162-A3
3700 PlaC 95650 201-D6
GALENA WY
7800 CITH 95610 240-C7
GALEWIND DR
- LNCN 95648 199-H1
GALEWOOD WY
4200 SaCo 95608 279-G2
GALIANO ISLAND RD
- WSAC 95691 316-C2
GALILEE RD
- RSVL 95678 219-F5
GALLAGHER CT
100 FOLS 95630 261-E4
GALLAGHER RD
4000 EDCo 95630 202-F7
6000 EDCo 95630 222-F1
GALLANT CIR
7400 CITH 95621 259-G2
GALLATIN DR
7700 ELKG 95758 358-C5
GALLEON WY
1000 SAC 95838 277-J1
GALLERIA BLVD
700 RSVL 95678 220-A7
GALLERIA CIR
- RSVL 95678 220-A5
GALLERON CT
- OAKL 94561 (514-E5 See Page 493)
GALLERY CT
2600 EDCo 95682 263-E6
GALLERY WY
6900 SAC 95831 316-J7
6900 SAC 95831 317-A7
GALLEY CT
- SAC 95831 316-G6
GALLINGER CT
1600 FOLS 95630 281-H1
GALLOP CT
3200 SaCo 95843 238-F6
GALLOP DR
2200 FOLS 95630 282-B1
GALLOWAY WY
6600 ELKG 95758 358-B2
GALSTON CT
- RSVL 95747 239-D1
GALSTON DR
1100 FOLS 95630 262-A4
GALTY WY
8700 SaCo 95828 338-G7
GALVESTON ST
600 WSAC 95691 296-F3
GALWAY CT
300 RSVL 95747 219-D5
7500 CITH 95610 259-H5
GAMAY CIR
1400 OAKL 94561 (514-D7 See Page 493)
GAMAY DR
- EDCo 95762 262-F4
1700 OAKL 94561 (514-C7 See Page 493)
GAMAY PL
- EDCo 95762 262-F5
GAMAY WY
9600 ELKG 95624 358-J7
GAMBAH DR
4300 PlaC 95602 161-G2
GAMBIER CT
9200 SaCo 95829 338-J6
GAMEBIRD CT
4500 EDCo 95682 283-H7
GANDY WY
4400 SaCo 95842 258-J6
GANDY DANCER WY
8100 SAC 95823 338-B6
GANNET CT
- LNCN 95648 200-B3
GANNET WY
4800 SaCo 95842 259-A2
GANNON DR
1300 SaCo 95825 298-D2

GANZAN WY
2500 RCCD 95670 299-F2
GANZER LN
- SaCo 95632 439-B2
GARAVENTA WY
1100 SAC 95833 277-D5
GARBER GREENS CT
11400 SaCo 95828 338-E4
GARBO WY
4400 SaCo 95843 238-J7
GARCIA AV
600 RSVL 95678 239-H4
GARCIA CT
- SAC 95831 316-E7
1400 PlaC 95663 181-A7
GARCIA WY
14700 SaCo 95683 342-A2
GARDELLA LN
2800 EDCo 95709 247-C3
GARDEN CIR
3100 EDCo 95682 263-E7
GARDEN CT
- EDCo 95633 205-B5
- ANT 94509 (513-F5 See Page 493)
300 RSVL 95678 239-J1
2000 OAKL 94561 (514-C6 See Page 493)
3600 SaCo 95608 279-D4
GARDEN DR
6000 PlaC 95658 181-G7
GARDEN HWY
500 SAC 95833 277-A7
1500 SAC 95833 276-G7
1700 SAC 95833 276-E5
1800 SAC 95833 296-G1
1800 SaCo 95833 296-G1
3200 SaCo 95834 276-E2
4300 SaCo 95837 255-G2
4300 SaCo 95837 256-A7
4300 SaCo 95837 276-B1
6500 SuCo 95659 236-A2
6900 SaCo 95837 235-H7
7700 SaCo 95837 236-A5
8100 SuCo 95837 236-A2
GARDEN LP
900 PLCR 95667 245-G5
GARDEN ST
500 SAC 95815 297-H1
2800 PLCR 95667 245-G5
GARDEN BAR RD
2400 PlaC - 160-F3
2500 PlaC 95648 160-F5
GARDEN BREEZE CT
400 RSVL 95747 219-B4
GARDENDALE RD
2500 SAC 95822 337-E2
GARDENDELL RD
4200 SAC 95834 276-G2
GARDEN FLOWER CT
- SAC 95833 277-F4
GARDEN GATE DR
7400 CITH 95621 259-F1
7600 CITH 95621 239-F7
GARDEN GLEN WY
8800 SAC 95826 298-G7
GARDEN GROVE CT
7600 SaCo 95843 239-B7
GARDEN HOMES PL
4800 ELKG 95758 357-H6
GARDENIA AV
- SaCo 95828 338-F3
1700 WSAC 95691 296-H5
4900 OAKL 94561 (514-D6 See Page 493)
GARDENIA CIR
- EDCo 95762 242-E6
GARDENIA CT
- RKLN 95765 219-H1
GARDENIA WY
1600 RSVL 95661 240-B4
4900 SaCo 95841 258-J7
GARDEN OAKS DR
6700 FOLS 95630 261-B3
GARDEN PARK CT
- RSVL 95678 219-G3
5800 SaCo 95608 259-D5
GARDEN PARK DR
- RSVL 95678 219-G3
5400 EDCo 95633 205-A5
5400 EDCo 95633 225-B1
GARDEN PATH CT
- SAC 95826 298-F7
GARDEN ROSE DR
3500 SaCo 95827 299-B7
GARDENSIDE CT
- SaCo 95829 338-J6
GARDEN TOWNE WY
6000 SaCo 95662 260-G5
GARDEN VALLEY RD
4900 EDCo 95633 205-A3
GARDEN VIEW CT
- EDCo 95633 205-A2
GARDEN VIEW RD
- EDCo 95633 205-A2
GARDEN VIEW WY
6100 SaCo 95823 338-A6
GARDENVINE AV
6900 CITH 95621 239-F7
GARDENWOOD WY
9800 RCCD 95827 299-C5
GARDINER WY
- RVIS 94571 454-H5
GARDNER AV
6800 SaCo 95828 318-G7
6800 SaCo 95828 338-G2
6800 SAC 95828 318-F7
GARDNER CT
- FOLS 95630 281-D1
- LNCN 95648 180-A6
GARFIELD AV
2000 SaCo 95608 279-C3
2000 SaCo 95608 299-C1
4700 SaCo 95841 279-C3
4800 SaCo 95841 259-C6
GARFIELD CT
- RKLN 95765 219-H1
GARFIELD PL
2900 ANT 94509 (513-A7 See Page 493)
GARFIELD ST
100 AUB 95603 182-D2
GARFIELD WY
300 RSVL 95678 219-G6
GARGANEY LN
- LNCN 95648 200-C1
GARIBALDI ST
5800 SaCo 95824 317-G5

GARINGTON LN
- LNCN 95648 179-E6
GARINO LN
8200 CITH 95610 240-A6
GARLAND CT
6300 SaCo 95660 258-H3
GARLAND CREST CT
8500 ELKG 95624 358-F4
GARLENDA DR
- EDCo 95762 262-F5
GARLINGTON CT
- SaCo 95829 338-J7
GARMISCH CT
3900 SaCo 95843 238-H4
GARNER CT
7800 SaCo 95829 339-E5
GARNET CT
- EDCo 95726 248-E4
5600 RKLN 95677 220-C5
9300 ELKG 95624 358-G5
GARNET RD
3700 EDCo 95726 248-E3
GARNET ST
800 WSAC 95691 296-F3
GARNET WY
11400 PlaC 95602 162-A3
GARNET CREST CT
8600 ELKG 95624 358-F5
GARNET PEAK WY
- SaCo 95829 338-G6
GARNKIRK CT
- SaCo 95829 339-A6
GARRETT DR
100 FOLS 95630 261-F5
GARRETT WY
2600 RCCD 95670 299-F2
GARRISON CT
8800 ELKG 95624 358-G4
GARRITY DR
- ELKG 95624 358-E2
GARROW DR
2700 ANT 94509 (513-E6 See Page 493)
GARRYANNA DR
8000 CITH 95610 240-A6
GARRY OAK DR
7800 CITH 95610 240-B6
GARSTON CT
9300 SaCo 95829 339-A6
GARTH LN
100 PlaC 95603 162-F5
3100 SAC 95826 318-D1
GARWOOD CT
5900 SaCo 95841 259-C5
GARY AV
500 ANT 94509 (513-E6 See Page 493)
GARY CT
2500 WSAC 95691 296-F7
GARY ST
700 GALT 95632 419-E6
GARY WY
1200 SaCo 95608 299-B2
2600 SAC 95815 277-H6
GASPAR CT
5000 OAKL 94561 (514-D6 See Page 493)
GASTMAN WY
4800 SaCo 95628 279-J1
4900 SaCo 95628 259-J7
GAS WELL RD
100 ISLE 95641 455-H5
21300 SJCo 95686 437-B7
GATE WY
4800 RKLN 95677 220-F2
GATEFORTH CT
- RSVL 95747 219-C7
- RSVL 95747 239-D1
GATEFORTH DR
1700 RSVL 95747 219-D7
GATE HOUSE CT
- SAC 95826 298-F6
GATEHOUSE LN
- LNCN 95648 199-J1
GATELEY PL
6600 ELKG 95758 358-A3
GATEMONT CIR
10100 ELKG 95624 378-G2
GATES LN
3600 LMS 95650 201-A6
GATES WY
3400 SAC 95832 337-F4
GATESHEAD CT
7100 CITH 95610 260-C2
GATEWAY CT
12200 PlaC 95603 162-B4
GATEWAY DR
- LNCN 95648 179-H4
- WSAC 95691 296-H7
3000 EDCo 95682 263-C3
GATEWAY OAKS DR
2200 SAC 95833 277-A5
2800 SAC 95833 276-J5
GATEWAY PARK BLVD
- SAC 95835 257-C7
3900 SAC 95834 277-C2
4000 SaCo 95834 277-C2
4000 SAC 95834 257-C7
GATLIN RD
2900 EDCo 95667 246-G4
2900 EDCo 95709 246-G4
GATO WY
1100 EDCo 95667 244-H1
GATOR LN
- SaCo 95655 319-H2
GATTER CT
800 ANT 94509 (513-C7 See Page 493)
GATTER DR
900 ANT 94509 (513-C7 See Page 493)
GATWICK WY
- RKLN 95677 220-F6
GAVERN LN
9600 SaCo 95829 339-B2
GAVILAN CT
- SAC 95831 336-H1
GAVIN CIR
- AUB 95603 182-B7
GAVIRATE WY
9800 ELKG 95757 358-A7
GAY RD
10500 SaCo 95693 359-H7
10500 SaCo 95693 379-H1
11000 SaCo 95693 360-A7
GAY WY
5900 SaCo 95660 258-H5
GAYLE WY
3600 SaCo 95660 258-G5

GAYLON WY
900 GALT 95632 439-E1
GAYLOR WY
8400 SaCo 95608 279-F3
GAYLORD CT
400 SaCo 95864 298-H5
GAYWOOD DR
2200 RCCD 95670 279-G7
GAZANIA CT
- SAC 95835 257-D5
GAZEBO CT
- LNCN 95648 200-A2
GAZEBO LN
800 GALT 95632 419-F4
GAZELLE CT
5000 SaCo 95608 279-A5
GAZELLE RIDGE WY
5100 SaCo 95843 239-B7
GAZELLE RUN WY
5100 SaCo 95843 239-A7
GAZELLE TRAIL WY
- SaCo 95843 239-D7
GEARNY DR
5600 SAC 95823 337-J5
5600 SAC 95823 338-A5
GEARY CT
- LNCN 95648 180-A6
GEARY LN
- LNCN 95648 180-A5
GEARY PL
- LNCN 95648 180-A5
GEARY ST
- WSAC 95691 296-H7
GELATO ST
300 SAC 95838 257-G7
GELSTON WY
- EDCo 95762 262-H5
GELVANI WY
11000 RCCD 95670 299-J4
11000 RCCD 95670 300-A4
GEM AV
7400 SaCo 95823 338-B2
GEM LN
2500 ANT 94509 (513-C6 See Page 493)
GEM CREST WY
9200 ELKG 95624 358-F5
GEMINI LN
- EDCo 95726 248-A4
GEMINI WY
3500 RCCD 95827 299-D6
GEM SMITH PL
- FOLS 95630 261-B7
GEMSTONE CT
- LNCN 95648 200-B3
8700 ELKG 95624 358-G7
GEMSTONE LN
- LNCN 95648 200-B3
GEMSTONE RD
- EDCo 95667 266-B2
GEMWOOD WY
8800 ELKG 95758 357-J2
GENA CT
6200 SaCo 95608 259-D5
GENE AV
4400 SAC 95838 277-J1
GENE MCKNIGHT CT
- SAC 95835 257-C4
GENERATIONS CT
9000 ELKG 95758 358-C3
GENERATIONS DR
7700 ELKG 95758 358-C4
GENERO CT
4700 SaCo 95843 239-A7
GENERO WY
4700 SaCo 95843 239-A6
GENESEE CT
1200 SaCo 95608 299-A3
GENESEE DR
- RKLN 95765 200-B5
GENESO ST
- OAKL 94561 (514-C6 See Page 493)
GENEVA CT
1000 EDCo 95762 262-C2
GENEVA LN
1800 ANT 94509 (513-G5 See Page 493)
GENEVA PL
1800 SaCo 95825 298-E1
GENEVA POINTE DR
8100 ELKG 95624 338-D7
GENNAKER WY
- ELKG 95758 357-F7
GENNEY LN
6000 EDCo 95623 264-J6
GENOA AV
8900 SaCo 95662 260-F5
GENOA CT
- RSVL 95678 219-G5
7500 SAC 95831 337-A5
GENOA ST
- LNCN 95648 179-E3
GENOVA ST
- WSAC 95691 297-A7
GENSLER CT
- ELKG 95624 359-A6
GENTIAN CT
- ELKG 95624 358-F1
GENTLE MARE PL
9500 ELKG 95624 359-B6
GENTRY CT
2800 SaCo 95827 299-C5
GENTRYTOWN DR
1400 ANT 94509 (513-A6 See Page 493)
GEODE CT
10000 SaCo 95829 339-D7
GEOFFWOOD CT
5900 CITH 95621 239-D7
GEORGE CT
600 RSVL 95678 219-F6
GEORGE LN
600 RSVL 95678 239-J3
GEORGE RD
4000 SaCo 95608 279-C3
GEORGE RIVER LN
7700 SAC 95831 336-G3
GEORGES AL
- EDCo 95667 265-E3
GEORGES LN
- EDCo 95667 265-D3
GEORGETOWN DR
10300 RCCD 95670 299-F1
10400 RCCD 95670 279-G7
GEORGETOWN LN
2500 ANT 94509 (513-A6 See Page 493)

GEORGETOWN RD Rt#-193
1700 EDCo 95667 245-E1
1700 PLCR 95667 245-E1
1700 EDCo 95667 225-D5
7300 EDCo 95633 205-E5
9300 EDCo 95633 225-E1
9300 EDCo 95634 225-E1
GEORGETTE CT
7400 CITH 95621 259-F1
GEORGIA AV
- SaCo 95742 280-G6
GEORGIA DR
5400 SaCo 95660 258-G5
GEORGIAN AV
4600 SaCo 95821 278-J4
GEORGIANA CT
100 ISLE 95641 455-G5
GEORGIANA DR
100 ISLE 95641 455-G5
GEOWOOD WY
7100 CITH 95610 260-A2
GERALD AV
3000 SaCo 95825 298-E1
GERALD LN
9100 PlaC 95603 161-F4
GERALDSON RD
- PlaC 95658 181-H4
400 PlaC 95603 181-H4
GERANIUM CIR
- GALT 95632 419-C6
GERANIUM WY
8500 ELKG 95624 358-F1
GERARD WY
5800 CITH 95621 259-G6
GERBER AV
1900 SAC 95816 297-G7
1900 SAC 95817 297-G7
GERBER RD
7100 SaCo 95828 338-C3
8800 SaCo 95829 338-G3
9400 SaCo 95829 339-A3
10400 SaCo 95830 339-D3
GERHARDT PL
5000 SaCo 95628 260-F7
GERLE AV
3100 PLCR 95667 245-G6
GERLING CT
- GALT 95632 419-F3
GERMAINE DR
600 GALT 95632 439-E1
GERMAN DR
8500 SaCo 95828 338-F3
GERMANY RD
11600 SaCo 95693 360-C7
GERRY CT
1600 PlaC 95603 162-C6
GERRY WY
1200 RSVL 95661 240-A3
GERSHWIN CT
6100 SaCo 95621 239-E6
GERTZ CT
- SAC 95823 337-H5
GESSNER DR
8400 ELKG 95624 358-E2
GESSNGER DR
8700 ELKG 95624 358-E2
GETAWAY CT
2500 SaCo 95662 260-C4
GETCHELL CT
- SAC 95835 257-A5
GETTA WY
5500 EDCo 95630 202-J6
GETTYSBERG CT
500 RSVL 95661 240-D5
GETTYSBURG LN
6200 CITH 95621 259-D4
GEYSER CIR
1600 ANT 94509 (513-G5 See Page 493)
GEYSER CT
1800 ANT 94509 (513-G5 See Page 493)
GEYSER LN
4100 SaCo 95608 279-D3
GEYSER PEAK WY
9000 SaCo 95829 338-H5
GHIRARDELLI CT
11400 SaCo 95670 280-C3
GHISLAINE CT
- PlaC 95747 239-B3
GHISLAINE WY
8300 SaCo 95843 239-C5
GIANCOMA DR
- RSVL 95747 219-B1
GIANNA CT
9800 ELKG 95757 378-A1
GIANNI CT
- RSVL 95661 240-E2
GIANT PANDA DR
9100 SaCo 95829 338-H5
GIBBONS DR
4600 SaCo 95608 278-J3
4600 SaCo 95821 278-J3
4600 SaCo 95608 279-B3
4900 SaCo 95821 279-A3
GIBBONS RANCH LN
- SaCo 95608 279-C3
GIBBS WY
8500 SaCo 95823 357-J1
GIBRALTAR ST
- SAC 95834 256-H7
- SAC 95834 276-H1
GIBRALTER CT
- GALT 95632 419-G5
GIBSON DR
- RSVL 95678 219-J4
- RSVL 95678 220-A5
GIBSON LN
7600 SaCo 95843 238-E7
7600 SaCo 95843 258-E1
GIBSON PL
5500 PlaC 95746 240-J1
GIBSON ST
2300 SAC 95815 277-H7
GIBSON RANCH PARK RD
- SaCo 95626 238-D5
GIBSON VIEW WY
2800 SaCo 95843 238-E5
GIFFORD WY
100 SAC 95864 298-E6
GIFT LN
5900 SAC 95824 318-B5
GIGI PL
7300 SaCo 95828 338-C2
GILA WY
2200 SaCo 95864 278-G7

GILARDI RD
2000 PlaC 95658 201-E1
7900 PlaC 95663 201-D2
GILA RIVER CT
2200 RCCD 95670 279-J6
GILBERT CT
500 RSVL 95746 240-G4
GILBERT ST
- SAC 95828 318-E6
GILBERT WY
2600 RCCD 95670 299-F2
GILCREST WY
1200 SAC 95831 337-A1
GILD CREEK RD
4500 EDCo 95682 283-E7
GILDED ROCK CIR
- FOLS 95630 261-B6
GILES WY
- EDCo 95762 262-E6
GILGUNN WY
5000 SAC 95822 317-B4
GILLELAND DR
- RSVL 95747 219-C4
GILLEN CT
- FOLS 95630 281-F2
GILLESPIE ST
3200 SAC 95838 277-G4
GILLETT DR
100 EDCo 95762 262-C5
GILLIAM DR
10300 ELKG 95757 377-J3
10300 ELKG 95757 397-J3
GILLINGHAM WY
6900 SaCo 95660 258-H2
GILMAN WY
5900 SaCo 95660 258-H3
GILMORE RD
- EDCo - 247-J2
5500 EDCo 95726 247-J2
GILMORE ST
1800 PLCR 95667 245-F6
GILMOUR CT
7200 SaCo 95828 318-C7
GILPEN WY
8000 SAC 95823 337-H5
GILRUTH ST
- RCCD 95655 299-G5
- SaCo 95655 299-G5
GILSTON CT
6500 SaCo 95662 260-C3
GIMBEL WY
6900 CITH 95621 259-F2
GIMRON WY
7800 SAC 95758 358-C1
GINA CT
5500 SaCo 95841 279-C1
GINA LN
8300 PlaC 95746 241-E2
GINA WY
- EDCo 95682 283-B1
GINA LOUISE LN
1800 PlaC 95658 201-J1
GINGER CT
2800 SAC 95826 298-G7
GINGER DR
100 AUB 95603 182-D5
GINGERBLOSSOM DR
7500 CITH 95621 259-F1
7600 CITH 95621 239-F7
GINGERHILL CT
- RSVL 95678 219-F5
GINGER HILL LP
- LNCN 95648 200-B2
GINGERLOOP CT
6600 SaCo 95842 259-A3
GINGERROOT CT
8500 SaCo 95843 239-D5
GINGERSNAP LN
- LNCN 95648 179-J7
- LNCN 95648 199-J1
GINGERWOOD WY
11000 RCCD 95670 279-J7
GINGHAM CT
3100 EDCo 95667 246-C6
6400 SaCo 95662 260-B4
GINGHAM WY
600 OAKL 94561 (514-D5 See Page 493)
GINGHAMTON WY
5000 SAC 95838 257-H7
GINKO WY
- SAC 95834 277-B2
GIN MILL RD
2100 PlaC 95603 181-H1
GINNY WY
300 SaCo 95673 257-H1
GINTHER DR
- ELKG 95758 358-C6
GIONATA WY
- FOLS 95630 261-F3
GIORNO WY
- EDCo 95762 262-B2
GIOTTO WY
- EDCo 95762 242-A4
GIOVANNI DR
2400 PLCR 95667 245-H2
GIOVANNI ST
1200 ANT 94509 (513-F4 See Page 493)
GIRONA CT
9200 SaCo 95826 298-J7
GIRVAN CT
8000 SaCo 95829 338-J6
GISELLE CT
- SaCo 95821 278-J2
GISLER CT
100 FOLS 95630 261-C7
GITTA RIA CT
5600 CITH 95610 260-B6
GIUSEPPE CT
500 RSVL 95678 239-G4
GIUSTI CT
4300 SaCo 95820 317-H3
GIUSTI RD
11800 SaCo 95638 (401-D3 See Page 381)
GIVEN ST
500 FOLS 95630 261-C6
GIVERNY CIR
8400 SaCo 95843 238-G5
GIVET WY
2800 RCCD 95670 279-H5
GLACIAL PL
8700 PlaC 95650 201-F6
GLACIER DR
2200 RKLN 95677 220-B4
GLACIER ST
2900 SaCo 95821 278-D5

STREET / Block City ZIP Pg-Grid

GLACIER WY
- SaCo 95758 357-G1
GLACIER CREEK WY
9600 ELKG 95624 359-B6
GLACIER PARK CT
- ELKG 95758 357-G5
GLACIER PARK WY
- ELKG 95758 357-G5
GLACIER POINT CT
- LNCN 95648 179-J6
GLACIER POINT WY
8900 ELKG 95624 378-H2
GLACKEN WY
7500 SaCo 95828 338-F3
GLADDING RD
900 LNCN 95648 179-H1
900 PlaC 95648 159-H7
1100 PlaC 95648 179-H1
3200 PlaC - 159-H2
GLADE CT
7100 SaCo 95608 279-G2
GLADEMONT CT
6200 SaCo 95608 279-D5
GLADIOLA WY
8700 ELKG 95624 358-G2
GLADMAR CT
8000 ELKG 95758 358-C6
GLADSTONE CT
- RSVL 95747 219-C7
GLADSTONE DR
1300 SaCo 95864 298-F2
GLADSTONE LN
2800 EDCo 95682 263-D7
GLADWIN WY
- ELKG 95757 358-B7
GLADYS AV
3100 WSAC 95691 316-F3
GLADYS CT
5000 SaCo 95608 259-F7
GLANCY CT
2100 SaCo 95608 279-B7
2100 SaCo 95608 299-B1
GLANCY DR
2200 SaCo 95608 279-B7
2700 SaCo 95608 299-B1
GLANTZ LN
- ELKG 95624 359-C5
GLASCOW CT
- LNCN 95648 179-D2
GLASCOW DR
4100 SaCo 95660 258-H4
GLASER LN
2800 PlaC 95747 239-C3
GLASSBORO WY
5700 SaCo 95842 258-J5
GLASS SLIPPER WY
7000 CITH 95621 259-G2
GLASTONBURY CIR
- RSVL 95747 219-B7
GLASTRIS WY
- ELKG 95758 358-D3
GLEN CT
2600 RKLN 95677 220-C1
GLEN DR
1600 EDCo 95667 244-H3
GLEN LN
- PlaC 95747 239-B3
GLEN ST
1000 WSAC 95605 296-J2
GLENACRE WY
7600 CITH 95610 259-J2
GLEN ALDER WY
8900 SaCo 95826 318-H1
GLEN ALTA WY
8000 CITH 95610 240-A6
GLEN ARBOR WY
7900 CITH 95610 240-A6
GLENARN LN
- LNCN 95648 179-E7
GLENARVEN WY
2700 SAC 95833 277-D6
GLEN AULIN CT
1100 SaCo 95608 299-A3
GLENAYLE PL
9200 ELKG 95758 358-C4
GLENBAIN WY
7600 ELKG 95758 358-C6
GLENBAR WY
7900 SaCo 95628 280-A1
GLEN BRIAR DR
8000 CITH 95610 240-A7
GLENBROOK AV
1200 RSVL 95678 239-G5
GLENBROOK LN
1800 LNCN 95648 180-A7
6000 SaCo 95608 279-D6
GLENBURN WY
7100 SAC 95824 318-B6
GLENBURY CT
9000 ELKG 95624 358-G4
GLENCANNON WY
- ELKG 95624 338-D7
- ELKG 95624 358-D1
GLEN CANYON CT
8100 CITH 95610 240-C6
GLENCOE CT
200 LNCN 95648 179-G4
5700 SaCo 95842 259-C2
GLENCOE WY
2200 SAC 95826 298-F6
GLEN COVE WY
8100 SaCo 95828 338-G6
GLEN CREEK WY
8000 CITH 95610 240-A6
GLENCREST LN
5600 SaCo 95662 260-J6
GLENDA CT
- SAC 95833 277-E5
GLENDALE AV
900 GALT 95632 439-G1
GLENDALE LN
2400 SaCo 95825 298-D1
GLENDON CT
- RSVL 95746 240-F3
GLENDON WY
8300 SaCo 95829 338-J7
GLENDORA CT
7500 SaCo 95823 337-J3
GLENEAGLE WY
7300 SaCo 95842 259-C1
GLEN ECHO ST
7800 CITH 95610 240-B7
GLENEDEN CT
- SAC 95831 336-J2
GLEN ELLEN CIR
2200 SAC 95822 317-D5
GLEN ELLEN CT
- OAKL 94561 (514-D5 See Page 493)

GLEN ELLYN CT
- RKLN 95677 220-H4
GLEN EVA WY
8000 CITH 95610 240-A7
GLENEYRE CT
2200 RCCD 95670 279-G7
GLENFAIRE CT
- RKLN 95677 220-F1
GLENFAIRE DR
2300 RCCD 95670 279-G7
GLENFIELD CT
7800 CITH 95610 240-A7
GLEN GROVE CT
10000 ELKG 95624 378-H2
GLENHAVEN CT
1200 EDCo 95762 282-E5
GLENHAVEN WY
10800 RCCD 95670 299-H1
10900 RCCD 95670 279-J7
GLENHILLS WY
6300 SAC 95824 318-B6
GLEN HOLLOW CT
6600 CITH 95841 259-C3
GLEN HOLLY LN
- EDCo 95667 264-J2
GLEN HOLLY WY
1000 SAC 95822 317-A5
GLENHURST WY
6100 CITH 95621 259-E1
GLEN INNES WY
4000 SaCo 95826 318-H2
GLEN IVY CT
8000 SaCo 95828 338-F5
GLENLEIGH CT
5300 SaCo 95843 239-B5
GLEN MADY WY
600 FOLS 95630 261-H7
GLENMARK WY
- RSVL 95747 219-B3
GLENMONT WY
7600 SaCo 95843 238-F7
7600 SaCo 95843 258-F1
GLENMOOR DR
3300 RCCD 95827 299-E5
GLENMOOR LN
- LNCN 95648 179-D2
GLENMOORE CT
1800 FOLS 95630 261-J6
1800 FOLS 95630 262-A6
GLENMORE WY
1100 EDCo 95762 262-D1
W GLENMORE WY
2400 EDCo 95762 262-D1
GLENN AV
7700 CITH 95610 239-J6
GLENN CT
1000 WSAC 95605 296-H2
GLENN DR
100 FOLS 95630 261-C5
GLENNFINNAN WY
- FOLS 95630 262-A5
GLENN LAKES DR
- RVIS 94571 454-E2
GLEN OAK CT
600 FOLS 95630 261-J7
4400 SaCo 95821 278-J5
GLEN OAKS DR
5600 RKLN 95765 220-B1
GLENOLIVE CT
4000 SaCo 95821 278-H4
GLEN PARK AV
8000 CITH 95610 240-A7
GLEN RACHAEL CT
7000 SaCo 95828 338-B3
GLEN RIDGE CT
300 EDCo 95762 262-B6
GLENRIDGE DR
4200 SaCo 95608 279-F2
GLEN RIDGE WY
200 EDCo 95762 262-C6
GLENRIO WY
2100 SAC 95833 277-A5
GLENROSE AV
1000 SAC 95815 278-B6
1000 SAC 95815 277-J6
GLENROY WY
8600 SAC 95826 298-F6
GLENSHIRE CT
400 RSVL 95661 240-E4
GLENSIDE CT
9500 SaCo 95662 260-J5
GLEN SPRINGS WY
4000 RCCD 95742 300-D7
GLEN STONE AV
7900 CITH 95610 240-A7
GLENTANA WY
3000 SaCo 95843 238-F5
GLEN TREE CT
1500 RSVL 95661 240-C5
GLEN TREE DR
7600 CITH 95610 260-A1
7600 CITH 95610 240-A7
GLENTRESS CT
- SAC 95833 277-A6
GLEN VALLEY CIR
8000 CITH 95610 240-A7
GLENVEAGH LN
- LNCN 95648 200-A2
GLEN VIEW CT
1400 RSVL 95747 219-E5
GLENVIEW DR
2700 EDCo 95667 246-A3
2700 PLCR 95667 246-A4
2700 EDCo 95667 245-J3
GLENVIEW RD
9500 PlaC 95658 181-G6
GLENVIEW WY
10500 RCCD 95670 299-G3
GLENVILLE CIR
- SAC 95826 298-F6
GLEN VISTA ST
4300 SaCo 95608 279-B2
GLENWOOD CIR
- RSVL 95678 219-G6
GLENWOOD DR
- EDCo - 247-E2
1900 ANT 94509 (513-E5 See Page 493)
GLENWOOD LN
2900 PLCR 95667 245-C4
GLENWOOD RD
1300 SaCo 95864 298-F2
GLENWOOD ST
- WSAC 95691 316-J1
GLIDDEN AV
1500 SAC 95822 337-C3
GLIDE AV
400 WSAC 95691 296-G3

GLIDE CT
500 WSAC 95691 296-G3
5200 SaCo 95841 259-B5
GLIDE FERRY WY
1000 SAC 95831 336-J4
GLIDER RD
4000 EDCo 95667 264-G3
GLIMMER WY
- EDCo 95726 248-C6
GLOBE AV
- SAC 95815 277-F7
100 SAC 95815 297-G1
GLORIA DR
5800 SAC 95822 317-A6
6100 SAC 95831 317-A6
6400 SAC 95831 316-G7
6900 SAC 95831 336-G1
GLORIANN WY
8100 SaCo 95843 238-H6
GLORI DAWN DR
8800 SaCo 95662 260-E5
GLORIETA CT
9000 ELKG 95624 358-H5
GLORIOSA CT
5200 ELKG 95757 377-H1
5200 ELKG 95757 397-H1
GLORY LN
13000 SaCo 95742 (321-A1 See Page 301)
GLORY RD
3100 PLCR 95667 245-H6
GLORY HOLE CT
- EDCo - 247-B7
GLORY HOLE DR
- EDCo - 247-D7
GLOUCESTER CT
900 ANT 94509 (513-C7 See Page 493)
GLOUCESTER SQ
100 FOLS 95630 261-G5
GLOUCESTER ST
800 ANT 94509 (513-C7 See Page 493)
GLOVER WY
4500 SaCo 95608 279-C2
GLOW CT
900 SAC 95831 316-J6
GLYNIS FALLS
- SAC 95831 336-G2
GOBERNADORES LN
- SaCo 95608 279-D7
GOBI CT
6300 CITH 95621 239-E6
GODDARD WY
3800 SaCo 95660 258-H2
GODELLO CT
- SAC 95833 276-J4
GODLEY LN
- PlaC 95602 160-J2
GODLEY RD
4000 PlaC 95602 160-J2
4200 PlaC 95602 161-A1
GOES PKWY
7600 SaCo 95823 337-H2
GOETHE RD
9400 SaCo 95827 299-B7
9900 SaCo 95827 319-C1
GOFF CT
- SAC 95838 277-F1
GOINYOUR WY
10100 RCCD 95827 299-E5
GOLD CIR
- RKLN 95765 220-B2
GOLD CT
- EDCo 95667 226-D2
2000 SAC 95821 278-C5
GOLD DR
7400 PlaC 95650 221-D5
GOLD RD
6700 EDCo 95667 265-D2
GOLD ST
- AUB 95603 182-E3
1000 PLCR 95667 245-H6
GOLD TR
- EDCo 95667 226-F4
GOLD ARBOR LN
- SaCo 95670 280-E4
GOLD AUTUMN WY
5000 ELKG 95757 377-H1
5000 ELKG 95757 397-H1
GOLD BAR DR
2000 SaCo 95670 280-D4
GOLDBLOOM WY
- RSVL 95747 218-H4
GOLD BLOSSOM LN
- PlaC 95658 181-G2
GOLD BLUFF LN
- SaCo 95670 280-F4
GOLD BUG LN
2500 EDCo 95667 245-G3
2500 PLCR 95667 245-G3
GOLD CAMP DR
3000 RCCD 95670 299-J2
GOLD CANAL DR
2900 RCCD 95670 300-A2
GOLD CENTER DR
10800 RCCD 95670 299-H2
GOLD CLAIMS CT
2100 SaCo 95670 280-D5
GOLD CLIFF CT
2100 SaCo 95670 280-D5
GOLD COAST DR
- RSVL 95678 219-G5
GOLD COIN CT
2100 SaCo 95670 280-D5
GOLD COUNTRY BLVD
11200 SaCo 95670 280-A4
GOLD COUNTRY DR
4900 EDCo 95623 264-H6
GOLD CREEK CIR
100 FOLS 95630 261-A3
GOLD CREEK CT
- WSAC 95691 316-D3
GOLD CREEK LN
- SaCo 95827 299-B7
3600 SaCo 95827 319-B1
4700 EDCo 95619 265-G4
GOLD CREST CT
- EDCo - 247-F2
200 PlaC 95658 181-B3
GOLDCREST ST
2800 PLCR 95667 245-F4
GOLD DREDGE WY
11400 RCCD 95742 300-B4
GOLD DUST DR
- EDCo 95667 266-E5
GOLD DUST LN
- EDCo 95709 247-C1

GOLDEN CIR
7300 SaCo 95683 342-C4
GOLDEN CT
5000 EDCo 95726 248-C6
GOLDEN DR
9500 SaCo 95662 260-H6
GOLDEN ST
- EDCo 95726 248-C6
GOLDEN AMBER CT
11800 RCCD 95742 320-D2
GOLDEN ASPEN DR
4600 SaCo 95842 258-J2
4600 SaCo 95842 259-A2
GOLDEN BLUFF CT
- LNCN 95648 180-B6
GOLDEN CANYON DR
100 FOLS 95630 260-H1
GOLDEN CENTER CT
6000 EDCo 95667 265-C1
GOLDEN CENTER RD
4300 EDCo 95667 265-D1
GOLDEN CENTRE DR
- SaCo 95670 280-B5
GOLDEN CENTRE LN
- SaCo 95670 280-A5
GOLDEN CHAIN DR
3000 EDCo 95709 246-H4
GOLDEN CHAIN HWY
Rt#-49
- EDCo 95630 162-H7
EDCo 95630 182-J1
100 AUB 95603 182-D1
100 PLCR 95667 245-D1
200 PlaC 95603 182-F2
400 PlaC 95603 162-D7
600 AUB 95603 162-D7
1500 EDCo 95667 245-D1
2600 EDCo 95667 225-A7
3800 EDCo 95619 265-E2
4600 EDCo 95623 265-B4
4700 EDCo 95667 265-E2
GOLDEN CREST WY
8100 SaCo 95662 260-B3
GOLDEN DAWN WY
6100 SaCo 95841 259-B4
GOLDEN EAGLE DR
- PlaC 95602 161-J2
2500 PLCR 95667 245-G4
GOLDEN EAGLE LN
3000 EDCo 95762 262-E5
GOLDEN EAGLE WY
3600 RCCD 95827 299-C7
GOLDENEYE CT
- FOLS 95630 281-F1
- RKLN 95765 219-H1
2800 WSAC 95691 316-F1
GOLDENEYE LN
7500 CITH 95621 259-D1
GOLDEN FAWN TR
2600 EDCo 95682 264-B1
GOLDEN FIELD WY
5800 SAC 95823 338-A5
GOLDEN FOOTHILL PKWY
4500 EDCo 95762 282-E4
GOLDEN GATE AV
8900 SaCo 95662 240-F7
GOLDEN GATE DR
- WSAC 95691 316-D2
GOLDEN GLORY WY
5100 ELKG 95757 377-H2
5100 ELKG 95757 397-H2
GOLDEN HEIGHTS DR
800 GALT 95632 419-F2
GOLDEN HILL CT
200 RSVL 95661 240-E4
GOLDEN INN WY
- RCCD 95670 280-C7
GOLDENLAND CT
- SAC 95834 277-B1
GOLDENLEAF WY
7900 SaCo 95829 339-C6
GOLDEN LIGHT LN
- SAC 95834 276-J1
GOLDEN MEADOW DR
8000 SaCo 95828 338-E5
GOLDEN MOSS RD
4100 EDCo 95672 243-F6
GOLDEN OAK CT
200 FOLS 95630 281-A2
GOLDEN OAK DR
- EDCo 95619 286-F5
GOLDEN OAK WY
7300 SAC 95831 337-A2
GOLDEN PARK CT
8200 SaCo 95828 338-D6
GOLDEN PLOVER WY
9400 ELKG 95624 359-A7
GOLDEN POND WY
4100 RCCD 95742 320-D1
GOLDEN POPPY CT
10000 SaCo 95829 339-D6
GOLDEN RAIN CT
6600 CITH 95610 260-A3
GOLDEN RING WY
- SaCo 95843 238-J7
GOLDENROD AV
- PlaC 95603 162-C6
GOLDEN ROD LN
7500 SaCo 95828 338-C3
GOLDENROSE CT
300 RSVL 95747 219-A4
GOLDEN ROSE WY
8700 SaCo 95828 338-G4
GOLDEN SAGE DR
8600 ELKG 95624 338-F7
GOLDEN SPIKE CT
- RSVL 95747 219-A5
GOLDEN SPUR DR
8700 PlaC 95746 240-J3
GOLDEN STATE HWY
Rt#-99
- ELKG - 358-D1
- ELKG - 378-G2
- ELKG - 379-A5
- ELKG - 378-G2
- ELKG - 358-D1
- GALT - 419-E2
- GALT - 439-H2
- SAC - 338-A3
- SAC - 358-D1
- SAC - 338-A3
- SAC - 358-D1
- SAC - 297-F6
- SAC - 317-F3
- SAC - 317-F3
- SAC - 338-A3
- SAC - 317-F3

GOLDEN STATE HWY
Rt#-99
- SAC - 338-A3
- SaCo - 338-A3
- SaCo - 378-G2
- SaCo - 379-A5
- SaCo - (399-C3 See Page 379)
- SaCo - 419-E2
- SaCo - 379-B7
- SaCo - (399-B1 See Page 379)
- SaCo - 378-G2
- SaCo - 379-A5
- SaCo - (399-B1 See Page 379)
- SaCo - 419-E2
- SaCo - 317-F3
- SaCo - 337-J1
- SaCo - 338-A3
- SaCo - 317-F3
- SaCo - 338-A3
- SJCo - 439-H2
- SJCo - (440-A6 See Page 420)
- SJCo - 439-H2
GOLDEN TREE WY
8700 SaCo 95828 338-G4
GOLDEN VISTA WY
9000 SaCo 95843 239-B6
GOLDEN WEST WY
7600 SAC 95824 318-C6
7700 SAC 95828 318-C6
GOLDENWOOD CIR
6600 CITH 95841 259-D3
GOLDENWOOD GN
1500 EDCo 95619 265-G5
GOLD EXPRESS DR
11200 SaCo 95670 280-A5
GOLD FIELD DR
2000 SaCo 95670 280-A4
GOLDFIELD WY
4900 EDCo 95667 244-D4
5000 RSVL 95747 219-A5
GOLD FINCH CT
- RKLN 95765 219-H1
GOLDFINCH DR
- RSVL 95747 219-B7
GOLDFINCH WY
7700 SaCo 95843 238-F7
GOLD FLAKE CT
- RCCD 95742 300-G6
GOLD FLAT DR
2100 SaCo 95670 280-C5
GOLD FLOWER CT
4200 SaCo 95608 279-B2
GOLD HAVEN CT
2100 SaCo 95670 280-D5
GOLD HILL CT
11400 SaCo 95670 280-B4
GOLD HILL RD
100 PlaC 95658 181-A1
1400 PlaC 95658 161-A7
2000 PlaC 95603 161-A7
5400 EDCo 95613 244-D1
5400 EDCo 95667 244-D1
6600 EDCo 95667 225-A7
GOLD HILL ST
- WSAC 95691 296-J7
- WSAC 95691 316-J1
GOLD HILLS DR
- RVIS 94571 454-E1
GOLD HOLLOW CT
2100 SaCo 95670 280-D5
GOLDILOCKS WY
9000 SaCo 95826 298-H7
GOLD LAKE DR
700 FOLS 95630 261-B5
GOLD LEAF LN
5600 EDCo 95667 264-F2
GOLD LEAF WY
8900 SaCo 95826 318-H1
GOLD LEDGE CT
2100 SaCo 95670 280-D5
GOLDMAN LN
1800 PLCR 95667 246-B5
GOLD MEADOW WY
2300 SaCo 95670 280-B5
GOLD MEADOWS RD
5900 EDCo 95667 264-J3
GOLD MINE CT
100 FOLS 95630 261-A3
GOLD MINE WY
2000 RSVL 95747 239-D1
GOLDNER CT
800 PLCR 95667 245-G5
GOLDNER ST
3000 PLCR 95667 245-G5
GOLD NUGGET CIR
- LNCN 95648 179-H5
GOLD NUGGET CT
3300 EDCo 95667 245-D6
GOLD NUGGET LN
- LNCN 95648 179-H5
GOLD NUGGET PL
1900 SaCo 95670 280-B3
GOLD NUGGET WY
- RSVL 95747 219-A5
3300 EDCo 95667 245-D6
3400 PLCR 95667 245-D5
GOLD OAK LN
6900 CITH 95621 259-E3
GOLDORADO RD
1400 EDCo 95667 244-D1
GOLDORADO TR
5200 EDCo 95623 264-H7
GOLD PAN CT
2900 RCCD 95670 300-A2
GOLD PAN DR
1200 RSVL 95661 240-B5
GOLD PARKE LN
11700 SaCo 95670 280-D5
GOLD PHEASANT CT
8000 SaCo 95626 238-C6
GOLD PLAINS CT
2100 SaCo 95670 280-D5
GOLD POINT WY
2700 SaCo 95827 299-A6
GOLD POINTE LN
- SaCo 95670 280-E4
GOLD POPPY WY
- ELKG 95757 377-J1
- ELKG 95757 397-J1
GOLD RIDGE TR
3100 EDCo 95726 248-D1
GOLD RIDGE WY
4200 SaCo 95843 238-J7
GOLD RIVER RD
2300 SaCo 95670 280-B5

GOLD ROCK CT
100 FOLS 95630 261-A2
GOLD ROCK RD
- EDCo 95667 226-F4
GOLD RUN AV
6600 SaCo 95842 259-B2
GOLD RUN DR
4400 OAKL 94561 (514-B7 See Page 493)
GOLD RUSH DR
2000 SaCo 95670 280-B4
GOLD RUSH LN
1200 EDCo 95667 225-A7
GOLD RUSH WY
1300 PlaC 95663 181-B7
1500 PlaC 95663 201-B1
GOLDSBORO CT
3600 RCCD 95827 299-D6
GOLD SIERRA CT
8200 SaCo 95843 239-C6
GOLDSMITH CT
4200 SaCo 95826 318-J2
GOLD SPRINGS CT
2200 SaCo 95670 280-A5
GOLD SPUR RD
4800 EDCo 95682 283-F3
GOLDSTAR ST
- RSVL 95747 239-B1
GOLD STATION DR
11300 SaCo 95670 280-B6
GOLDSTONE CIR
- SAC 95834 277-A2
GOLDSTONE CT
- RSVL 95747 199-D7
GOLDSTONE DR
- RSVL 95747 199-C7
GOLD STRIKE CT
- LNCN 95648 179-H5
GOLD STRIKE DR
- SaCo 95670 280-C4
1200 EDCo 95667 244-F1
GOLD TAILINGS CT
2800 RCCD 95670 300-A1
GOLD TRAIL WY
4300 LMS 95650 221-A1
GOLD TUNNEL CT
11500 SaCo 95670 280-C4
GOLD VALLEY DR
3100 RCCD 95742 300-B3
3100 SaCo 95742 300-B3
GOLDWOOD WY
7300 CITH 95610 260-C2
GOLDY PL
- ELKG 95758 357-F5
GOLDY GLEN CT
8800 ELKG 95624 358-G3
GOLDY GLEN WY
8700 ELKG 95624 358-F3
GOLF WY
1400 EDCo 95667 244-G2
GOLF CLUB CT
7400 SaCo 95828 338-C3
GOLF CLUB DR
9600 PlaC 95746 240-J5
GOLF COURSE LN
4900 ELKG 95758 357-H6
GOLF COURSE RD
- PlaC 95602 162-D2
GOLF LINKS DR
- FOLS 95630 261-J5
- FOLS 95630 262-A7
GOLF VIEW DR
6400 SAC 95822 317-D7
6700 SAC 95822 337-D1
GOLFWOOD CT
- RSVL 95678 219-G6
GOLLER CT
11000 RCCD 95670 279-J7
GOMES CT
- FOLS 95630 261-D7
GOMEZ CT
6700 SaCo 95823 317-G7
GONCE WY
100 FOLS 95630 261-H6
GONDOLA CT
- SAC 95831 316-G7
GONZAGA CT
8400 SAC 95826 318-E1
GONZALEZ WY
3300 RCCD 95827 299-E5
GOOD CT
4700 SaCo 95608 279-A4
GOODELL RD
100 FOLS 95630 261-G4
GOODMAN CT
- ELKG 95624 359-A5
GOOD PASTURE CT
1600 EDCo 95667 244-G1
GOOD PASTURE RD
2100 EDCo 95667 244-G2
GOODRICH LN
6400 EDCo 95667 244-G3
GOODRICH ST
2200 SaCo 95825 298-C3
GOODSTONE WY
- RSVL 95747 218-J4
GOODVIEW CT
600 EDCo 95667 245-E6
600 PLCR 95667 245-E6
GOODVIEW WY
6200 SAC 95823 338-A5
GOODWIN CIR
4900 SAC 95823 337-J5
GOODYEAR DR
7100 SaCo 95628 279-G1
GOOSEBERRY CIR
- WSAC 95691 296-G7
GOOSEBERRY CT
8400 SaCo 95843 238-F5
GOOSE FLAT RD
5800 EDCo 95630 202-C7
5800 EDCo 95630 222-D1
GOOSE HAVEN CT
- SAC 95834 276-H1
GOOSE HAVEN LN
- SAC 95834 276-J1
GOOSE MEADOWS WY
7300 RSVL 95747 219-A4
GOOT WY
6800 SaCo 95608 279-F2
GOPHERGLEN CT
5000 ELKG 95758 357-H3
GORDAN ST
- RVIS 94571 454-H4
GORDIAN WY
8300 SaCo 95662 260-C3
GORDO CT
300 EDCo 95762 242-B5

GORDON DR
5200 SaCo 95824 317-J5
GORDON LN
1200 SaCo 95864 298-J3
1200 SaCo 95864 299-A3
GORDON RD
5700 EDCo 95682 283-E3
GORDON WY
3700 SaCo 95608 279-E4
GORE RD
- RCCD 95827 299-C5
GORGE RIVER CT
2200 RCCD 95670 279-J5
GORGE VIEW DR
- EDCo 95684 286-D6
GORHAM CT
- SAC 95835 257-A6
GORHAM WY
- SAC 95835 257-A5
100 SaCo 95655 320-A2
GORMAN DR
1500 SaCo 95608 299-A2
GOSHAWK DR
100 GALT 95632 419-C6
GOSHAWK LN
- LNCN 95648 200-C2
GOSHEN WY
8000 SaCo 95828 338-D5
GOSS CT
- SaCo 95838 278-B2
GOSSAMER WY
8600 ELKG 95624 358-F3
GOSSONIA PK
100 AUB 95603 182-E2
GOTHAM CT
7200 SaCo 95828 338-B1
GOTHBERG AV
4000 SaCo 95660 258-H2
GOULART RANCH RD
1300 PlaC 95658 181-E7
1600 PlaC 95658 201-E1
GOULD WY
3200 RCCD 95827 299-E5
GOUVEIA WY
4500 EDCo 95682 283-J2
GOVAN WY
2900 SAC 95818 297-B7
3100 SAC 95818 317-B1
GOVERNOR DR
800 EDCo 95762 262-C4
GOVERNOR LN
6300 SAC 95828 318-A6
GOVERNORS CIR
7100 SaCo 95823 337-H1
GOVERNORS CT
- RKLN 95677 220-J2
- SAC 95817 317-J1
GOYA PKWY
4500 SaCo 95823 337-H2
GOYAN AV
1000 PLCR 95667 245-H6
GRACE AV
100 SAC 95838 277-F1
1100 SAC 95838 278-A1
GRACE CT
3200 EDCo 95667 265-C3
GRACE DR
3200 EDCo 95623 265-C4
3200 EDCo 95667 265-C4
GRACE LN
2900 SAC 95826 318-F3
GRACE ST
100 AUB 95603 182-E1
GRACE GLEN CT
200 RSVL 95747 219-A4
GRACELAND PL
1000 EDCo 95630 202-H5
GRACEN WY
- SAC 95835 257-B5
GRACEY WY
3600 SaCo 95608 279-B4
GRACIANO CT
11000 RCCD 95670 300-A5
GRACIANO DR
11000 RCCD 95670 300-A4
GRACIOSA WY
10300 ELKG 95757 378-B3
GRACKLE CT
- SAC 95834 276-H3
GRADUATES LN
- SaCo 95841 279-A1
GRADY DR
7100 CITH 95621 259-G5
GRAEAGLE
- RSVL 95678 219-J7
GRAEAGLE CT
- LNCN 95648 200-B1
GRAEAGLE LN
- LNCN 95648 200-B1
11600 PlaC 95602 162-A1
GRAEAGLE WY
- SaCo 95823 337-J7
GRAETON CIR
100 SaCo 95655 320-A2
GRAF CT
900 RSVL 95661 240-E4
GRAFF RIG CT
- SAC 95838 257-H7
GRAFTON CIR
100 SaCo 95655 319-J1
GRAHAM CIR
6600 CITH 95610 259-H3
GRAHAM CT
- FOLS 95630 281-D1
5500 RKLN 95677 220-C4
GRAHAM LN
- AUB 95603 182-E4
GRAHAM ISLAND RD
- WSAC 95691 316-C2
GRAMERCY DR
2100 SaCo 95825 278-E7
GRAMONT WY
7600 SAC 95823 338-A4
GRAMPAS LN
- EDCo 95619 266-E6
- EDCo 95667 266-E6
GRAMPIAN CT
- RSVL 95661 220-E7
GRAMPIAN ST
- RSVL 95661 220-E7
GRANADA CT
1100 ANT 94509 (513-B6 See Page 493)
3000 EDCo 95682 263-D5
GRANADA DR
3000 EDCo 95682 263-D5
GRANADA LN
8100 PlaC 95650 221-E2

STREET Block City ZIP Pg-Grid

GRANADA WY
3100 SAC 95816 297-G5
GRANADA PASS CT
- RSVL 95678 219-G3
GRANADA PASS DR
- RSVL 95678 219-G3
GRANBY DR
3400 RCCD 95827 299-C6
3600 SAC 95827 299-C7
GRAND AV
- SaCo 95690 417-A7
- SaCo 95690 436-J1
- SaCo 95690 437-A1
400 SAC 95838 277-H3
1200 SAC 95838 278-A3
8000 SaCo 95628 280-A3
GRANDBALL WY
7200 CITH 95621 259-G1
GRAND CANYON CT
- SAC 95835 257-C7
GRAND CANYON DR
- RKLN 95765 219-H2
- RSVL 95678 219-H2
- RSVL 95678 220-A3
GRAND CRU DR
8200 SaCo 95829 338-J7
8300 SaCo 95624 338-J7
GRANDE VISTA AV
1500 WSAC 95691 296-H5
GRAND ISLAND RD
12800 SaCo 95690 (396-C6 See Page 375)
12800 SaCo 95690 (416-B1 See Page 415)
14100 SaCo 95690 415-J6
14100 SaCo 95690 (435-J1 See Page 415)
15700 SaCo 95690 455-E1
17700 SaCo 95690 456-A3
GRAND ISLAND RD Rt#-220
- SaCo 95690 (435-J2 See Page 415)
GRAND OAKS BLVD
7300 CITH 95621 239-G7
7300 CITH 95610 239-G7
GRAND OAKS DR
- AUB 95603 182-B6
GRAND OAKS PL
- EDCo 95633 205-A1
GRAND PHEASANT LN
1500 LNCN 95648 180-C7
1600 LNCN 95648 200-C1
GRAND POINT LN
- ELKG 95758 357-F6
GRAND RIO CIR
- SAC 95826 298-E6
GRAND RIVER DR
1100 SAC 95831 337-A4
GRAND SIERRA CT
8000 SaCo 95843 239-B6
GRANDSTAFF DR
7800 SAC 95823 338-A5
GRAND TETON CT
- RKLN 95765 219-H2
- RSVL 95678 220-A3
GRAND TREE LN
6900 CITH 95621 259-E2
GRAND VICTORY DR
- EDCo 95619 266-B5
GRANDVIEW CIR
3200 EDCo 95682 264-D5
GRAND VIEW CT
5600 RKLN 95765 220-B1
GRANDVIEW CT
4900 EDCo 95682 264-D4
GRANDVIEW DR
- AUB 95603 182-C6
700 FOLS 95630 261-J6
GRAND VIEW RD
7600 SaCo 95829 339-F4
GRANDVIEW ST
2800 PLCR 95667 245-G4
GRANGE CT
- SAC 95823 337-H5
GRANGER AV
600 SAC 95838 277-H2
GRANGERS DAIRY DR
6200 SAC 95831 316-G6
GRANGNELLI AV
300 ANT 94509 (513-E4 See Page 493)
GRANITE AV
7500 SaCo 95662 240-G7
7500 SaCo 95662 260-G1
N GRANITE CIR
100 FOLS 95630 261-C4
GRANITE CT
- LNCN 95648 180-B6
- RKLN 95677 220-F3
GRANITE DR
400 RKLN 95677 220-H1
E GRANITE DR
8100 PlaC 95746 241-D2
W GRANITE DR
7600 PlaC 95746 241-D2
GRANITE LN
- LNCN 95648 180-B6
1200 AUB 95603 162-E7
GRANITE TR
6400 EDCo 95726 248-D1
GRANITE WY
- RSVL 95747 219-A7
2300 SaCo 95821 278-C6
GRANITE BAR WY
2000 SaCo 95670 280-D5
GRANITE BEND CT
- PlaC 95746 240-J6
GRANITE COVE CT
- PlaC 95746 241-B2
GRANITE COVE DR
- PlaC 95746 241-B2
GRANITE CREEK LN
100 FOLS 95630 260-J4
100 FOLS 95630 261-A4
GRANITE CREEK PL
3200 PlaC 95658 201-H4
GRANITE CREST CT
- PlaC 95746 240-J6
GRANITE DELL CT
5400 LMS 95650 200-H5
GRANITE FALLS CT
9300 ELKG 95624 359-A5
GRANITE FALLS LN
- LNCN 95648 180-C6
GRANITE FALLS WY
- PlaC 95746 240-J2
GRANITE FLAT LN
6100 RSVL 95747 219-A5

GRANITE GLEN CT
- PlaC 95746 240-J6
GRANITE HILL CT
2400 EDCo 95667 225-C7
2400 EDCo 95667 245-C1
11500 SaCo 95670 280-C4
GRANITEHILL LN
7600 PlaC 95663 201-D1
GRANITE HILL RD
1600 EDCo 95667 245-C1
GRANITE HILLS DR
- PlaC 95746 240-J6
- PlaC 95746 241-A6
GRANITE HOLLOW
- PlaC 95746 240-J6
GRANITE LAKE CT
100 FOLS 95630 241-B7
GRANITE LAKE DR
- PlaC 95746 240-J3
- PlaC 95746 241-A2
GRANITE MANOR PL
- PlaC 95746 220-J7
GRANITE OAKS DR
7900 PlaC 95746 241-E3
GRANITE PARK CT
- LNCN 95648 199-J3
- PlaC 95746 241-A6
GRANITE PARK DR
- LNCN 95648 199-J2
- LNCN 95648 200-A2
GRANITE PARK LN
2600 ELKG 95758 357-E5
GRANITE PEAK CT
9000 SaCo 95829 338-H7
GRANITE POINT CT
- PlaC 95746 240-J6
GRANITE ROCK LN
8000 PlaC 95746 221-E5
GRANITE SPRINGS CT
- PlaC 95746 240-J6
GRANITE VIEW LN
- PlaC 95746 240-J6
GRANITEWOOD DR
600 FOLS 95630 241-B7
GRANITE WOODS CT
- PlaC 95746 240-J6
GRANLEE LN
- SaCo 95683 342-C2
GRANNAN WY
- EDCo 95667 266-E2
E GRANNYS LN
4200 EDCo 95682 283-J1
W GRANNYS LN
4000 EDCo 95682 283-J1
GRANT AV
3500 SaCo 95608 279-B4
GRANT CT
- WSAC 95691 296-J7
N GRANT CT
100 FOLS 95630 261-C3
GRANT LN
1300 SAC 95822 317-B4
N GRANT LN
100 FOLS 95630 261-C3
S GRANT LN
100 FOLS 95630 261-B3
GRANT ST
- RSVL 95678 239-H2
N GRANT ST
100 RSVL 95678 239-H1
GRANTHAM CT
100 FOLS 95630 261-F7
GRANTLEY PL
- SAC 95835 257-A3
GRANT LINE RD
3000 RCCD 95742 301-A4
3000 SaCo 95742 301-B2
4000 RCCD 95742 (321-A1 See Page 301)
4000 SaCo 95742 (321-A1 See Page 301)
4400 RCCD 95742 320-J4
4400 SaCo 95683 320-J4
4400 SaCo 95742 320-J4
5400 SaCo 95624 340-D2
5400 SaCo 95683 340-D2
GRANT LINE RD Rt#-E2
6600 SaCo 95624 340-A6
7400 SaCo 95624 339-J7
7900 ELKG 95624 339-J7
8000 ELKG 95624 359-G2
8000 SaCo 95624 359-G2
9500 ELKG 95624 379-B1
9500 SaCo 95624 379-B1
10100 ELKG 95757 378-J3
10400 SaCo 95624 378-J3
10500 ELKG 95624 378-J3
GRANTOLA WY
6300 ELKG 95757 358-A7
GRANT PARK DR
3400 SaCo 95608 279-D4
GRANTWOOD WY
3500 SaCo 95608 279-F4
GRANVILLE CT
- SAC 95838 278-C2
GRANZELLA WY
- RCCD 95742 300-E7
GRAPE ST
100 RSVL 95678 239-G2
GRAPEMAN CT
8200 SaCo 95829 339-D7
GRAPENUT CT
2200 ANT 94509 (513-H6 See Page 493)
GRAPE RIDGE CT
8200 SaCo 95829 339-D7
GRAPEVINE RAVINE LN
- PlaC 95648 180-G4
GRAPE WOOD CT
8200 SaCo 95829 339-D7
GRAPHITE CT
9600 ELKG 95624 359-B6
GRAPHITE WY
9600 ELKG 95624 359-B6
GRAPPA WY
3400 RCCD 95670 300-A4
GRASMEER WY
9500 ELKG 95624 359-A6
GRASMERE CIR
- RSVL 95661 220-F6
GRASS CREEK CT
3300 SaCo 95843 238-F5
GRASSHOPPER CT
8700 ELKG 95624 358-E2
GRASSINGTON LN
5700 SAC 95835 257-A4
GRASSLANDS DR
2800 SAC 95833 277-A6

GRASS VALLEY CT
7800 SaCo 95828 338-E4
GRASS VALLEY HWY Rt#-49
800 PlaC 95603 162-B2
3000 PlaC 95602 162-B2
GRASSWOOD CT
100 FOLS 95630 261-B3
GRASSY CREEK WY
- EDCo 95762 282-D4
GRASSY KNOLL WY
9300 ELKG 95758 357-J5
9300 ELKG 95758 358-A5
GRASSY RUN CT
5500 EDCo 95667 264-F2
GRASSY RUN RD
5300 EDCo 95667 264-F2
GRATIA AV
3700 SaCo 95821 278-G4
GRATTAN WY
6200 SaCo 95660 258-G3
GRAVEL CT
- EDCo 95667 226-B4
GRAVEL RD
- EDCo 95667 226-B3
GRAVES AV
100 SAC 95838 277-G4
GRAY ST
4000 SaCo 95628 279-H3
GRAYBILL LN
8500 ELKG 95624 359-G2
GRAY EAGLE CT
2000 SaCo 95670 280-B4
GRAY FOX WY
- LNCN 95648 199-H3
GRAYHAWK LN
4100 EDCo 95709 246-J2
4100 EDCo 95709 247-A2
GRAYHORSE DR
- AUB 95603 182-D6
GRAYLING WY
8700 SaCo 95826 298-G6
GRAYLOCK LN
6400 SaCo 95660 258-H3
GRAYLODGE CT
7900 SaCo 95828 338-E5
GRAY MARE WY
3300 SaCo 95843 238-F6
GRAY PINE WY
11000 PlaC 95603 182-B1
GRAYSON WY
2900 RCCD 95670 299-G2
GRAY STAR CT
6100 ELKG 95758 358-A3
GRAYSTOCK CT
400 RSVL 95661 240-D4
GRAYSTONE AV
6100 CITH 95621 239-D7
GRAYSTONE RD
3100 EDCo 95682 244-F4
GRAYTREE WY
5200 SaCo 95843 239-A7
GRAYWOOD CT
8100 SAC 95823 338-B6
GRAZING LN
3600 LMS 95650 200-G6
GRAZING HILL CT
4600 EDCo 95682 283-C7
GRAZING HILL RD
5000 EDCo 95682 283-C7
GRAZING POINT WY
2600 ELKG 95757 377-E1
2600 ELKG 95757 397-E1
GRAZZIANI WY
- RSVL 95661 240-E2
GREAT CT
8700 ELKG 95624 358-F5
GREAT BASIN DR
- RSVL 95678 220-A3
GREAT DIVIDE CT
- RKLN 95765 219-J2
GREAT DIVIDE WY
- RKLN 95765 219-J2
GREAT DOME CT
9000 SaCo 95628 260-G7
GREAT EGRET CT
- SAC 95834 276-J2
9700 ELKG 95757 358-A7
GREAT EGRET WY
2900 SAC 95834 276-J3
GREAT FALLS WY
3000 SAC 95826 298-E7
3000 SAC 95826 318-E1
GREATFIELD DR
- RSVL 95747 218-J4
GREAT HERON DR
- EDCo 95682 263-C6
GREATHOUSE LN
5200 EDCo 95667 264-G4
GREAT HOUSE WY
8100 SaCo 95843 238-F6
GREAT OAK WY
8700 SaCo 95628 260-E7
GREAT PECONIC PL
- SAC 95835 256-G4
GREAT SMOKEY ST
- SAC 95823 337-J5
- SAC 95823 338-A5
GREAT VALLEY DR
5500 SaCo 95843 239-C5
GREAT VIEW LN
- EDCo 95619 265-F4
GREBE CT
2300 ELKG 95757 357-E7
GRECO CT
9100 SaCo 95829 338-J7
GREELEY WY
5300 SaCo 95608 259-D6
N GREEN CT
4100 SaCo 95608 279-B3
GREEN GRV
7400 SAC 95823 338-C3
GREEN RD
11000 SaCo 95693 359-J6
11100 SaCo 95693 360-C5
GREEN RD S
12000 SaCo 95693 360-E5
GREEN ST
800 PLCR 95667 245-F4
2200 SAC 95815 277-J7
GREEN ACRES LN
3800 PlaC 95650 201-E7
GREENACRES WY
5600 SaCo 95662 260-G6
GREEN ASH CT
6600 CITH 95610 260-A3
GREENBACK DR
4400 EDCo 95667 265-D2

GREENBACK LN
5500 SaCo 95842 259-C4
5600 SaCo 95841 259-C4
9600 FOLS 95630 260-F4
9600 FOLS 95630 261-B4
9600 FOLS 95662 260-F4
9600 SaCo 95662 260-F4
GREENBACK LN Rt#-E14
- CITH 95628 260-A4
5700 SaCo 95841 259-F4
5800 CITH 95621 259-F4
5800 CITH 95841 259-F4
7100 CITH 95610 259-F4
7800 CITH 95610 260-A4
8100 SaCo 95628 260-A4
8100 SaCo 95662 260-H4
9400 FOLS 95630 260-H4
9400 FOLS 95662 260-H4
9400 SaCo 95630 260-H4
GREEN BAY WY
2700 SaCo 95826 298-J6
GREENBERRY DR
5000 SaCo 95841 259-C7
GREEN BLOSSOM CT
2200 RCCD 95670 279-G7
GREEN BLUFFS CT
11400 SaCo 95670 280-C5
GREENBOROUGH DR
1300 RSVL 95661 240-A5
GREENBRAE RD
4100 RKLN 95677 220-F5
4100 PlaC 95677 220-F4
5600 SaCo 95822 317-A4
GREEN BRANCH CT
3300 SAC 95834 277-C3
GREENBRIAR LN
4100 EDCo 95682 264-A4
6300 PlaC 95746 241-A2
GREENBRIER RD
- WSAC 95691 316-J1
- WSAC 95691 317-A1
GREENBRIER WY
5400 SaCo 95628 260-B6
GREENBROOK CIR
6900 CITH 95621 259-F4
GREENBROOK RD
2700 EDCo 95667 226-D7
2700 EDCo 95667 246-D1
GREENBURN DR
- RSVL 95678 219-H3
GREENBUSH AV
200 FOLS 95630 261-H5
GREEN CANYON CT
4600 EDCo - 246-H7
GREEN CANYON LN
- SaCo 95662 260-F4
GREEN CANYON RD
4500 EDCo - 246-H7
4500 EDCo - 266-H1
4500 EDCo 95667 266-H1
GREENCREEK WY
6500 CITH 95621 259-E5
GREEN CREST CT
3200 SaCo 95821 278-H5
GREENDALE CT
- ELKG 95758 357-G4
GREEN EYES WY
6200 SaCo 95662 260-F4
GREENFIELD AV
100 AUB 95603 182-F1
200 PlaC 95603 182-F1
GREENFIELD WY
2500 SaCo 95608 279-A7
GREENFORD WY
- RKLN 95677 220-J2
GREEN FOREST LN
3900 SaCo 95821 278-H3
GREENGLEN AV
7500 CITH 95610 259-H6
GREEN GLEN CT
3500 EDCo 95682 263-D6
GREEN GLEN RD
2600 EDCo 95682 263-D6
GREEN GLEN WY
5900 SaCo 95842 258-J4
5900 SaCo 95842 259-A5
GREEN GROVE LN
5100 RSVL 95747 219-B5
GREENHALGH LN
8800 SaCo 95662 260-F4
GREENHALL WY
3000 ANT 94509 (513-C7 See Page 493)
GREENHAVEN DR
6100 SAC 95831 316-J6
6900 SAC 95831 336-J1
7300 SAC 95831 337-A2
GREENHEAD CT
6900 SaCo 95842 259-A2
GREEN HERON CT
7600 SaCo 95628 279-H1
GREEN HILL DR
1100 RSVL 95661 240-A4
GREENHILLS RD
- EDCo 95667 266-E3
1100 SaCo 95864 298-F3
GREENHILLS WY
8000 PlaC 95746 240-G2
GREEN HOLLOW LN
- EDCo 95709 246-J3
GREENHOLME DR
4300 SaCo 95842 258-J5
4400 SaCo 95842 259-A6
GREENHURST WY
900 SAC 95831 316-J7
GREENLAND CT
8200 CITH 95610 240-B7
GREENLAW WY
- FOLS 95630 261-J4
- FOLS 95630 262-A4
GREENLAWN WY
4100 SaCo 95660 258-H6
GREENLEA AV
1200 SAC 95833 277-D6
GREEN LEAF CT
6900 PlaC 95746 241-B3
GREENLEAF CT
- LNCN 95648 179-H6
GREENLEAF DR
6600 CITH 95621 259-F5
6700 EDCo 95667 245-C7
6700 EDCo 95667 265-B1
GREENLEAF LN
- EDCo 95726 248-C1
GREENMEADOW AV
3400 WSAC 95691 296-F4
GREEN MIST CT
- SAC 95831 336-J2

GREENMORE WY
300 RSVL 95678 219-G7
GREEN MOSS DR
800 SAC 95831 336-J2
GREEN MOUNTAIN CT
4400 PlaC 95677 220-F4
GREEN MOUNTAIN LN
5800 PlaC 95677 220-F4
GREEN OAK CT
9100 SaCo 95628 280-G1
GREENOCK WY
8000 SaCo 95843 239-B6
GREEN PARK LN
3300 SaCo 95608 279-C5
GREEN POINTE
400 RSVL 95678 240-A1
GREEN RAVINE DR
1100 LNCN 95648 179-E1
GREENRAVINE LN
9100 SaCo 95628 260-G7
GREENRIDGE AV
400 RSVL 95678 239-G5
GREENRIDGE CT
- LNCN 95648 179-J6
3100 ANT 94509 (513-E7 See Page 493)
GREENRIDGE WY
7600 SaCo 95628 259-J7
7700 SaCo 95628 279-J1
GREEN RIVER WY
9000 SaCo 95662 260-F4
GREENS CT
- RKLN 95765 200-E4
GREENSBORO CIR
9600 RCCD 95827 299-C6
GREENSBORO RD
2100 EDCo 95667 244-B4
GREENS LANDING CT
2500 EDCo 95682 263-E6
GREEN SPRING CT
1900 SaCo 95626 238-C5
GREEN SPRINGS CT
- RSVL 95747 199-C7
- RSVL 95747 219-C1
E GREEN SPRINGS CT
2300 EDCo 95672 262-G2
E GREEN SPRINGS RD
1900 EDCo 95672 262-G2
W GREEN SPRINGS RD
1800 EDCo 95672 242-G7
GREEN SPRINGS WY
- RSVL 95747 219-C1
GREENSTAR WY
- SAC 95831 336-J1
900 SAC 95831 316-J7
GREENSTONE CT
4100 PlaC 95602 162-B1
5500 EDCo 95667 264-F3
GREENSTONE CTO
1200 EDCo 95667 264-F5
GREENSTONE PL
11200 SaCo 95670 280-A4
GREENSTONE RD
3600 EDCo 95667 264-F1
4500 EDCo 95682 264-F5
GREEN TOP WY
6200 SaCo 95662 260-F4
GREENTRAILS CT
8400 ELKG 95624 358-E1
GREENTRAILS WY
8400 ELKG 95624 358-E1
GREEN TREE DR
4000 SaCo 95823 337-G1
GREENVALE RD
4200 SaCo 95628 280-C2
GREEN VALLEY CT
1300 RSVL 95747 219-E4
GREEN VALLEY RD
300 EDCo 95762 262-A1
400 EDCo 95762 242-B7
1500 EDCo 95672 262-H1
1700 EDCo 95672 242-E7
2800 EDCo 95672 263-E1
3000 EDCo 95682 263-E1
4100 EDCo 95672 243-H7
4200 EDCo 95682 243-H7
4500 EDCo 95682 244-A7
4500 EDCo 95672 244-A7
5100 EDCo 95667 244-B6
5900 EDCo 95667 264-F1
6900 EDCo 95667 245-A6
7300 PLCR 95667 245-A6
10900 FOLS 95630 261-H3
15100 EDCo 95762 261-H3
GREENVIEW CT
- RKLN 95765 200-D6
400 RSVL 95678 239-G5
GREENVIEW DR
4000 EDCo 95762 262-F3
GREENVIEW LN
3500 SaCo 95821 278-G5
3900 PlaC 95650 201-D7
GREENWAY CIR
- SAC 95831 316-J7
GREENWICH CIR
4300 SaCo 95823 317-G7
GREENWICH CT
- RKLN 95765 200-A7
GREEN WING LN
400 PLCR 95667 245-B5
GREEN WING WY
9900 RCCD 95670 299-D3
GREENWOOD AV
700 WSAC 95605 296-J2
2500 SaCo 95821 278-J6
2500 SaCo 95864 278-J6
GREENWOOD CT
- LNCN 95648 179-H6
- RSVL 95678 219-J2
7600 PlaC 95746 221-C7
GREENWOOD LN
2500 EDCo 95682 263-C7
2500 EDCo 95682 283-C1
3200 EDCo 95667 244-H6
GREENWOOD RD
4400 EDCo 95633 205-A1
GREENWOOD ST
100 AUB 95603 182-D2
GREGG CT
- SAC 95831 336-G2
GREGORY AV
3600 WSAC 95691 316-F5
GREGORY CT
600 RSVL 95661 240-A3
GREGORY LN
- EDCo 95667 286-G4
- EDCo 95684 286-G4
3900 PlaC 95650 201-E7
3900 PlaC 95650 221-E1

GREGORY WY
1400 RSVL 95661 240-A3
1500 SaCo 95608 299-B2
GREG THATCH CIR
100 SAC 95835 256-H4
GRENACHE WY
10800 ELKG 95624 359-H3
GRENADA CT
- RKLN 95765 200-C5
GRENDEL WY
1300 SAC 95833 277-D4
GRENFELL CT
7400 ELKG 95758 358-C6
GRENNAN CT
2500 SaCo 95742 280-B7
GRENOBLE WY
100 FOLS 95630 261-D5
3400 SaCo 95826 318-J1
GRENOLA WY
7200 CITH 95621 259-G2
GRESHAM CT
- RSVL 95747 219-C1
GRESHAM DR
4300 EDCo 95762 262-E3
GRESHAM LN
- SAC 95835 256-G5
GREY CT
- LNCN 95648 179-D3
GREY BIRCH PL
5700 SaCo 95843 239-C5
GREY BIRCH WY
5700 SaCo 95843 239-C5
GREYBRIDGE CT
6000 ELKG 95758 358-A2
GREY BUNNY DR
- RSVL 95747 219-D2
GREYCALLS CT
2800 WSAC 95691 316-F1
GREY CANYON DR
100 FOLS 95630 261-A3
GREY CLIFF CT
100 FOLS 95630 261-A1
GREYCREST CT
3100 SaCo 95843 238-F6
GREY FOX CT
- FOLS 95630 261-H4
GREY FOX LN
- PlaC 95602 161-J2
GREY FOX RD
- EDCo 95634 225-F1
GREYHAWK
4200 EDCo 95709 247-A2
GREYHAWK CT
7500 SaCo 95828 338-C2
GREYHAWK DR
- PlaC 95746 240-F3
GREY IRON CT
8500 SaCo 95843 239-D5
GREYLING WY
6200 EDCo 95726 248-C6
GREY LIVERY WY
3900 SaCo 95843 238-H6
GREYMERE WY
2700 SAC 95833 277-D6
GREY OAK CT
6500 CITH 95621 239-E7
GREY OWL CIR
- RSVL 95661 220-D7
GREYSON CREEK CT
- EDCo 95762 262-F3
GREYSON CREEK DR
- EDCo 95762 262-F2
GREYSTONE CT
9700 PlaC 95746 241-A5
GREYSTONE LN
- LNCN 95648 200-A2
GREYSTONE PL
9700 PlaC 95746 241-A6
9700 PlaC 95746 240-J6
GREYWELL WY
4000 SaCo 95864 298-H5
GREY WOLF DR
7600 SaCo 95843 258-H1
GREYWOOD CIR
- RSVL 95747 199-D7
GRIBBLE CT
9000 SaCo 95628 260-G7
GRICE CT
4100 PlaC 95747 238-J4
4100 PlaC 95747 239-A4
GRICE LN
800 EDCo 95667 245-G6
GRIDER CT
500 RSVL 95678 219-J6
GRIDER DR
500 RSVL 95678 219-J6
600 RSVL 95678 220-A6
GRIDLEY CT
3600 ELKG 95758 357-F5
GRIFFIN LN
7900 SaCo 95628 280-D6
GRIFFIN WY
12100 PlaC 95602 162-B1
GRIFFIN OAKS LN
5200 SaCo 95841 259-B7
GRIFFITH DR
200 EDCo 95619 265-D5
4300 SAC 95822 317-A3
GRIFFITH LN
2100 PlaC 95663 201-C2
GRIGGS WY
7400 SAC 95831 336-G2
GRIMES WY
100 FOLS 95630 261-G4
GRIMSBY CT
8600 ELKG 95624 358-F6
GRIMSHAW WY
3600 ELKG 95758 357-F5
GRIMWOOD CT
4700 PlaC 95746 240-G5
GRINDING ROCK PL
11400 SaCo 95670 280-B4
GRINDSTONE WY
- EDCo 95667 266-F3
GRINNELL WY
8300 SaCo 95826 318-E1
GRINZING WY
8000 SaCo 95829 338-J5
GRISHAM WY
- ELKG 95758 358-D3
GRISSOM AV
- RCCD 95655 299-G5
GRITS CT
- SAC 95823 337-J5
GRIZZLY CT
1900 ANT 94509 (513-G6 See Page 493)
GRIZZLY RUN
- EDCo 95726 247-G6

GRIZZLY WY
- PlaC 95746 240-G4
GRIZZLY BAY RD
- WSAC 95691 316-E2
GRIZZLY FLAT CT
1200 AUB 95603 182-C6
GRIZZLY HILL CT
2200 SaCo 95670 280-C5
GRIZZLY MESA CT
- GALT 95632 419-F3
GROFF DR
4500 SaCo 95628 280-F1
GROPIUS ST
- ELKG 95758 357-E4
GROSS CT
12800 SaCo 95632 419-D2
GROSSE POINT CT
6600 CITH 95621 259-D3
GROSVENOR CIR
4900 PlaC 95746 240-G2
GROSVENOR CT
8400 PlaC 95746 240-G2
GROTH CIR
- SAC 95834 276-H2
GROTH CT
- EDCo 95630 222-G6
GROTON CT
400 SaCo 95864 298-H5
GROUSE CT
- LMS 95650 200-J7
4600 SaCo 95842 259-A2
GROUSE DR
200 GALT 95632 419-D6
GROUSE LN
- EDCo 95634 205-H1
GROUSE CREEK CT
9800 ELKG 95624 378-H1
GROUSE MEADOW DR
9000 ELKG 95624 378-H1
GROUSE RUN CIR
- RSVL 95747 219-B7
GROVE AV
2200 SAC 95815 277-G5
GROVE CT
1200 AUB 95603 182-C1
5800 RKLN 95677 220-E4
GROVE LN
3900 EDCo 95682 263-J6
GROVE ST
- SaCo 95690 437-A1
100 RSVL 95678 239-G1
4600 RKLN 95677 220-E3
9000 ELKG 95624 358-H6
S GROVE ST
5300 RKLN 95677 220-E4
GROVE CREEK CT
1600 RSVL 95747 219-E4
GROVE CREEK WY
- LNCN 95648 179-J1
GROVEHILL WY
7300 SaCo 95828 338-F2
GROVELAND LN
600 LNCN 95648 179-F5
GROVELAND WY
3200 SaCo 95843 238-F5
GROVER CT
4000 SaCo 95608 279-G3
GROVER LN
- SaCo 95608 279-G3
GROVER RD
- FOLS 95630 281-D1
GROVESNOR CT
500 SaCo 95864 298-G5
GROVETREE WY
8900 ELKG 95624 358-G7
GROVEWOOD LN
- RSVL 95747 199-D7
- RSVL 95747 219-D1
- SaCo 95828 338-F5
GRUMMAN WY
9000 SaCo 95628 260-F7
9000 SaCo 95628 280-F1
GRUWELL WY
9600 ELKG 95624 358-J7
GUADALAJARA WY
3000 SaCo 95833 276-J4
GUADALUPE DR
- EDCo 95762 242-A4
14500 SaCo 95683 322-B7
14900 SaCo 95683 342-B1
GUADELUPE ST
- WSAC 95691 316-D3
GUALALA CT
8100 SaCo 95828 338-D7
GUAM
- SAC 95828 318-E4
GUANACHE CT
8300 SaCo 95829 339-D7
GUARDIAN CT
6500 RKLN 95677 220-G5
GUAVA AL
- RSVL 95678 239-H1
GUAVA WY
1000 SAC 95834 277-D4
GUENIVERE WY
7700 CITH 95610 259-J5
GUERNSEY CT
100 FOLS 95630 261-F3
GUILD ST
100 GALT 95632 419-E7
GUILDWOOD ST
7500 SAC 95822 337-F3
GUILFORD CT
4200 SaCo 95864 298-J4
GUILFORD WY
- RKLN 95677 220-E6
- RSVL 95661 220-E6
GUILLEMOT DR
- SAC 95833 276-J4
- SAC 95834 276-J4
GUILLERMINA CT
9200 ELKG 95758 358-B4
GUIS CT
8400 ELKG 95624 358-F1
GULCH RD
- EDCo 95667 226-B2
GULF ISLAND ST
- WSAC 95691 316-C2
GULFPORT WY
8900 SaCo 95826 298-H6
GULFWIND WY
800 SAC 95831 336-J2
GULL WY
7800 SaCo 95843 238-F7
GULLANE WY
7000 EDCo 95762 262-G4
GULL VIEW CT
- OAKL 94561 (514-H7 See Page 493)

STREET Block City ZIP Pg-Grid
GUM LN
- AUB 95603 182-E3
GUMTREE DR
100 RCCD 95670 280-A6
GUM TREE RD
2300 OAKL 94561 (514-B7
See Page 493)
GUMWOOD CIR
6900 CITH 95621 239-F7
GUNDERSON WY
7200 SaCo 95608 279-G3
GUNN LN
2900 SaCo 95608 279-B6
GUNN RD
2000 SaCo 95608 299-B1
2100 SaCo 95608 279-B7
GUNNER WY
8500 SaCo 95628 260-D7
GUNNISON AV
100 SAC 95838 277-F1
GUNSMOKE CT
2400 EDCo 95667 244-B4
GUNSTON CT
- EDCo 95762 262-F6
GUNSTONE WY
- RSVL 95747 218-H4
GUNTHER WY
300 SAC 95819 298-B5
GURNEY CT
- ELKG 95758 358-C6
GUS WY
- ELKG 95757 378-A2
GUSTAFON CT
10200 SaCo 95829 339-E5
GUSTINE WY
8100 SaCo 95828 338-D6
GUTHRIE ST
6400 SaCo 95660 258-J3
6600 SaCo 95842 258-J3
GUY WEST SUSPENSION FTBRDG
- SAC - 298-B6
- SAC - 298-C6
GWEN DR
2400 SaCo 95825 278-D7
GWENDOLYN WY
2900 RCCD 95670 299-G2
GWERDER CT
8100 ELKG 95758 358-C4
GWINHURST CIR
8200 SaCo 95828 338-F6
GYAN WY
7700 SaCo 95828 338-D4
GYMKHANA CT
5200 EDCo 95667 244-F4
GYPSY WY
3800 EDCo 95667 265-A1
9200 SaCo 95826 299-A7
GYPSY STAR WY
8200 SaCo 95829 339-A7

H

H PKWY
4800 SaCo 95823 337-H2
H ST
100 ISLE 95641 455-J5
100 LNCN 95648 179-H2
200 SaCo 95641 455-J5
300 ANT 94509 (513-C4
See Page 493)
400 GALT 95632 439-F1
600 SAC 95814 297-C3
2000 SAC 95816 297-F4
4000 SAC 95819 297-J5
5200 SAC 95819 298-A5
6100 SAC 95825 298-A5
HAACK CT
- ELKG 95758 357-G5
W HAACK CT
3600 ELKG 95758 357-G5
HAACK WY
3700 ELKG 95758 357-G5
HAASE DR
4700 SaCo 95628 279-J1
HAAST CT
8100 SaCo 95828 338-E6
N HACIENDA DR
23400 SJCo 95220 (440-G7
See Page 420)
HACIENDA RD
3200 EDCo 95682 263-F7
HACIENDA WY
2100 SaCo 95825 278-E7
3300 ANT 94509 (513-B7
See Page 493)
HACKAMORE DR
1900 RSVL 95661 240-C3
HACKBERRY LN
- LNCN 95648 179-H6
4200 SaCo 95608 279-C2
4700 SaCo 95841 279-C2
4800 SaCo 95841 259-C7
HACKMORE CT
8600 SaCo 95843 238-J5
HACKNEY WY
7500 CITH 95610 259-H2
HACKOMILLER RD
4900 EDCo 95633 205-B2
HADDINGTON DR
- FOLS 95630 261-J3
800 EDCo 95762 282-C2
HADDOCK PL
- SAC 95835 256-G4
HADDONFIELD CT
3500 ELKG 95758 357-F4
HADLEIGH DR
9900 PlaC 95746 240-G6
10000 SaCo 95662 240-G6
HADLEY LN
3100 SaCo 95608 279-C5
HADNALL CT
- RSVL 95747 239-C1
HAELING PL
2000 EDCo 95762 242-B6
HAFLINGER WY
- ELKG 95757 357-H7
- ELKG 95757 377-H1
- ELKG 95757 397-H1
HAGAR CT
4700 OAKL 94561 (514-C7
See Page 493)
HAGAR LN
4400 OAKL 94561 (514-C7
See Page 493)
HAGEDORN CT
8300 SaCo 95829 339-E7
HAGEN CT
- FOLS 95630 281-D1

STREET Block City ZIP Pg-Grid
HAGEN RANCH RD
- EDCo 95667 265-A4
6100 EDCo 95623 265-A4
HAGERMAN DR
9600 ELKG 95624 359-B7
HAGGIE RD
11100 SaCo 95693 379-J1
11100 SaCo 95693 (380-A1
See Page 379)
HAGGIN AV
300 SAC 95833 277-E6
HAGGIN GROVE WY
1700 SaCo 95608 299-B2
HAGUE WY
8100 SaCo 95626 238-D6
HAIG WY
6800 SAC 95831 317-A7
HAIGHT CT
900 EDCo 95762 262-D4
HAILEY CT
600 RSVL 95747 219-C7
HAINES CT
700 PlaC 95602 162-F2
HAINES RD
500 PlaC 95602 162-G2
HAINESPORT WY
7400 SAC 95824 318-C6
HAITI RD
- WSAC 95691 316-D2
HALAS CT
5400 ELKG 95757 377-J2
5400 ELKG 95757 397-J2
HALBRITE WY
7000 SaCo 95828 338-D4
HALCON RD
3500 EDCo 95709 246-H5
HALDEMAN CT
- SaCo 95829 339-A5
HALDEMAN WY
- SaCo 95829 339-A5
HALDIS WY
2300 SAC 95822 317-D4
HALE CT
5300 SAC 95819 298-B4
HALE ST
100 AUB 95603 182-E3
HALE RANCH LN
4300 SaCo 95628 280-E2
HALESWORTH CT
7000 CITH 95610 260-C2
HALESWORTH DR
- RSVL 95747 219-C3
HALESWOTH DR
- RSVL 95747 219-C3
HALEY DR
7600 PlaC 95746 241-E1
7900 PlaC 95746 221-E7
HALF CIDR
- EDCo 95633 205-E1
HALF DOME CT
- ELKG 95758 357-F5
- RSVL 95747 219-C1
HALF MOON CT
2100 SAC 95838 278-C4
HALFMOON CT
- LNCN 95648 200-B3
HALF MOON DR
3700 EDCo 95667 246-F6
HALF MOON BAY CIR
- WSAC 95691 316-D2
HALFWAY RD
10500 ELKG 95624 359-G1
HALIBURTON CT
8300 CITH 95610 260-C2
HALIDON WY
1300 FOLS 95630 261-F7
1300 FOLS 95630 281-F1
9400 SaCo 95829 339-A6
HALIFAX PL
2300 EDCo 95762 242-B5
HALIFAX ST
6500 CITH 95621 259-E3
HALIFAX WY
1500 EDCo 95762 242-B5
HALKEEP WY
6100 SAC 95823 337-J6
HALKIRK WY
- FOLS 95630 261-J3
9000 SaCo 95829 338-H6
HALL LN
6100 SaCo 95608 279-D4
HALL ST
- FOLS 95630 281-D1
100 OAKL 94561 (514-E6
See Page 493)
600 FOLS 95630 261-D7
HALLADALE CT
8100 SaCo 95829 339-A7
HALLBORO CT
8600 SaCo 95828 338-F2
HALLELUJAH CT
3600 SaCo 95608 279-C4
HALLENOAK LN
9300 SaCo 95662 260-H5
HALLER CT
- ELKG 95757 358-B7
HALLEY LN
1900 EDCo 95672 263-F1
HALLEY GLEN DR
- RSVL 95678 219-G4
HALLI WY
9600 ELKG 95624 359-D7
HALLIDEE WY
1900 SaCo 95670 280-C4
HALLIFORD CT
8100 RSVL 95661 240-E4
HALLISSY DR
- RSVL 95678 219-G4
HALLMARK DR
2000 SaCo 95825 298-C2
HALLS FARM RD
2200 EDCo 95709 246-J1
HALLWOOD CT
- SAC 95823 357-J1
HALO WY
1600 SAC 95835 257-C3
HALSEY PL
- SAC 95835 256-G4
HALSTED AV
5300 SaCo 95608 279-B7
HALTER CT
3600 SaCo 95821 278-H4
HALTON CT
- GALT 95632 419-G3
HALVERSON CT
- FOLS 95630 261-J5
HALVERSON DR
8700 ELKG 95624 358-G5

STREET Block City ZIP Pg-Grid
HALVERSON WY
- RSVL 95661 220-F6
HALYARD DR
1200 WSAC 95691 296-F5
HALYARD RD
3000 EDCo 95667 265-D2
HALYARD WY
- ELKG 95758 357-F7
HAMAN CT
- RSVL 95678 219-F7
HAMAN WY
1000 RSVL 95678 219-F7
HAMATANI CT
9000 ELKG 95758 357-J4
HAMBLEDON CT
- LNCN 95648 179-E6
HAMBLEY CIR
- ELKG 95624 359-A6
HAMBURG ST
1800 OAKL 94561 (514-C6
See Page 493)
HAMBURG WY
6000 SAC 95823 358-A1
HAMDEN PL
- SaCo 95842 259-A1
HAMERBEE CT
7300 SaCo 95842 259-B7
HAMERSLEY CT
100 FOLS 95630 261-F7
HAMERSLEY LN
- LNCN 95648 179-E6
HAMERSLEY WY
100 FOLS 95630 261-F6
HAMIL CT
7500 SaCo 95828 338-F3
HAMILTON AV
- RVIS 94571 454-H6
HAMILTON CT
- RSVL 95746 240-F5
HAMILTON PL
2100 EDCo 95762 242-B5
HAMILTON RD
48000 YoCo 95612 375-G3
48000 YoCo 95612 (376-A3
See Page 375)
HAMILTON ST
4700 SaCo 95841 278-J1
4900 SaCo 95841 258-J7
5400 SaCo 95660 258-J6
5400 SaCo 95842 258-J6
HAMLET PL
2100 SaCo 95608 299-C1
HAMLIN DR
7400 SaCo 95660 258-J1
HAMMER DR
- SaCo 95828 338-G5
HAMMERHEAD
4100 SaCo 95655 319-D1
HAMMERSMITH LN
8700 SaCo 95628 280-E1
HAMMILL CT
- RSVL 95747 219-A5
HAMMOND CT
- FOLS 95630 261-H4
5500 CITH 95621 259-G6
HAMMOND DR
200 PlaC 95603 162-G6
HAMMOND ST
- SaCo 95742 280-F6
HAMMOND WY
- EDCo 95762 262-H5
HAMPSHIRE CT
1200 RSVL 95661 240-A4
HAMPSHIRE DR
3000 SaCo 95821 278-E6
HAMPSHIRE PL
1800 EDCo 95762 242-B5
HAMPSTEAD WY
8100 PlaC 95746 241-A2
HAMPTON CT
200 AUB 95603 182-C2
3600 EDCo 95682 263-C6
5000 PlaC 95746 240-H6
W HAMPTON CT
9100 SaCo 95628 260-G7
HAMPTON DR
600 RSVL 95678 239-G3
HAMPTON LN
2500 ANT 94509 (513-A6
See Page 493)
3600 EDCo 95682 263-C6
5700 CITH 95610 259-J5
HAMPTON RD
900 SaCo 95864 298-F3
HAMPTON ST
- WSAC 95691 316-J1
HAMPTON COVE WY
6800 SAC 95823 358-B2
HAMPTON HILL CT
8600 SaCo 95828 338-F6
HAMPTON OAK DR
8900 ELKG 95624 378-H3
HAMRIC CT
8000 SaCo 95843 238-H6
HAMROSE WY
4300 EDCo 95682 264-A7
HAMSTEAD DR
500 GALT 95632 419-H4
HANA WY
700 FOLS 95630 261-E6
HANBURY WY
9400 SaCo 95829 339-A6
HANCE CT
- RSVL 95747 219-C4
HANCOCK DR
- RSVL 95678 219-F6
600 FOLS 95630 261-E3
3900 SaCo 95821 278-H5
HANDBALL CT
- RCCD 95670 300-B6
HANDEL WY
3000 SaCo 95826 298-J7
HANDLY WY
7500 SAC 95822 337-B3
HANDY WY
- FOLS 95630 262-B6
HANFORD WY
100 RSVL 95678 219-B6
7900 SAC 95823 338-A5
HANGAR CT
9300 SaCo 95628 280-G1
HANGAR WY
9000 SaCo 95628 280-F1
HANGMANS GULCH LN
1100 EDCo 95672 243-B4
HANISCH CT
300 RSVL 95678 219-J7
HANISCH DR
600 RSVL 95678 219-J7

STREET Block City ZIP Pg-Grid
HANISCH DR
600 RSVL 95678 220-A7
HANKS RD
- EDCo 95709 247-C1
HANKS ST
3300 SaCo 95827 299-B7
HANKS EXCHANGE RD
- EDCo 95619 266-C6
- EDCo 95619 286-D1
HANNA CT
3000 SaCo 95608 279-B5
HANNAFORD CT
100 FOLS 95630 261-B1
HANNAH WY
- RKLN 95765 219-J1
HANNUM CT
- SaCo 95690 (416-J7
See Page 415)
HANOVER CT
1000 EDCo 95762 262-C2
HANOVER PL
- RKLN 95765 200-C4
HANOVER ST
- CITH 95621 239-G6
HANOVERIAN CIR
700 GALT 95632 419-E2
HANS WY
9800 ELKG 95624 358-H7
9800 ELKG 95624 378-H1
HANSARD CT
900 GALT 95632 419-G4
HANSEN CIR
- FOLS 95630 281-D1
HANSEN PL
- LNCN 95648 179-E1
HANSEN RD
4500 PlaC 95650 221-F2
HANS ENGLE WY
8500 SaCo 95628 280-D1
HANSON AV
7900 CITH 95610 240-A7
HANUMAN CT
8100 SaCo 95829 338-H6
HANWORTH CT
400 RSVL 95661 240-E4
HANZELL CT
8000 SaCo 95829 338-J6
HAP ARNOLD LP
100 PlaC 95747 238-J4
100 PlaC 95747 239-A4
HAPPY CIR
3500 SAC 95823 337-F1
HAPPY CT
900 GALT 95632 419-G7
HAPPY LN
4000 EDCo 95619 265-E2
4100 SaCo 95655 319-D1
4100 SaCo 95827 299-D7
4100 SaCo 95827 319-D1
HAPPY RD
3900 PlaC 95650 201-C7
HAPPY WY
3300 SAC 95823 337-F1
HAPPY HOLLOW LN
- EDCo 95709 247-B3
9500 PlaC 95658 201-J1
9500 PlaC 95658 181-J7
HAPPY HOURS DR
- EDCo 95667 267-B5
HAPPY TRAILS LN
- EDCo 95633 205-D2
HAPTON CT
- FOLS 95630 261-J4
HARBER CT
100 SaCo 95864 298-E6
HARBOR BLVD
600 WSAC 95605 296-G2
800 WSAC 95691 296-F5
N HARBOR BLVD
- WSAC 95605 276-F7
- WSAC 95605 296-F1
E HARBOR CT
- SAC 95831 336-J3
HARBOR DR
16000 SaCo 95690 455-E4
HARBOR WY
7200 PlaC 95746 241-C3
HARBOR HOUSE CT
7400 ELKG 95624 358-E1
HARBOR HOUSE WY
8400 ELKG 95624 358-E1
HARBOR LIGHT WY
7200 SAC 95831 336-F1
HARBOR POINTE PL
- WSAC 95605 296-F2
HARBORSIDE WY
- ELKG 95758 357-J2
HARBOUR DR
2700 ANT 94509 (513-F6
See Page 493)
HARBOUR BAY PL
- ELKG 95758 357-E6
HARBOUR COVE LN
- ELKG 95758 357-F7
HARBOURGLEN WY
5200 ELKG 95758 357-J3
HARBOUR POINT DR
9100 ELKG 95758 357-D4
HARBOUR SHORE LN
- ELKG 95758 357-E6
HARBOUR VIEW LN
- ELKG 95758 357-E6
HARBOURWOOD DR
8400 SaCo 95662 260-C4
HARCOURT WY
- RSVL 95747 219-A2
100 FOLS 95630 261-F7
HARDCASTLE LN
4700 SaCo 95608 279-A7
HARDESTER DR
8200 SaCo 95828 338-F7
8500 ELKG 95624 338-F7
8500 ELKG 95828 338-F7
HARDESTY LN
- SaCo 95757 418-F1
HARDING AV
300 SaCo 95833 277-F7
HARDING BLVD
100 RSVL 95678 240-A2
300 RSVL 95678 220-A7
S HARDING BLVD
100 RSVL 95678 240-A2
HARDING CT
1800 ANT 94509 (513-A7
See Page 493)
HARDING WY
1700 ANT 94509 (513-A7
See Page 493)

STREET Block City ZIP Pg-Grid
HARDING HALL DR
- ELKG 95624 358-F2
HARDISON CT
4800 SaCo 95628 280-B1
HARDROCK CT
100 FOLS 95630 260-J4
HARDWICK CT
800 RSVL 95746 240-F4
HARDWICK WY
2000 RSVL 95746 240-F4
4400 SaCo 95660 258-J4
HARDWOOD CT
8100 SaCo 95662 260-B3
HARDY CT
- LNCN 95648 179-E2
HARDY DR
800 WSAC 95605 296-J2
HARDY LN
- LNCN 95648 179-E2
7600 PlaC 95746 220-J7
7600 PlaC 95746 240-J1
HARDY PL
- LNCN 95648 179-E2
HARDY ST
7400 SaCo 95662 260-D1
HARE TR
- PlaC 95746 221-G3
HAREBELL CT
4900 SaCo 95842 259-B3
HARGER CT
3400 SaCo 95821 278-G5
HARGROVE CT
100 FOLS 95630 261-F3
100 ANT 94509 (513-G5
See Page 493)
HARGROVE ST
1200 ANT 94509 (513-G5
See Page 493)
HARIAN WY
1700 SAC 95822 317-C4
HARI GOPAL WY
- SAC 95823 357-J1
HARI GOVIND WY
- SAC 95823 357-J1
HARKNESS AV
- SaCo 95615 (396-D3
See Page 375)
HARKNESS ST
2500 SAC 95818 297-D7
HARLAN WY
1900 EDCo 95762 242-G6
HARLAND RD
10800 SaCo 95693 379-H5
HARLEN CT
6100 SaCo 95842 258-J4
6100 SaCo 95842 259-A4
HARLEQUIN WY
- PlaC 95603 162-G5
6800 SaCo 95842 258-J3
HARLEY WY
6500 SaCo 95828 318-B7
6500 SaCo 95828 338-A1
HARLIN DR
4300 SaCo 95826 318-J3
HARLING CT
500 SaCo 95673 257-H3
HARLINGTON CIR
- EDCo 95762 263-A5
HARLOW CT
400 RSVL 95747 219-E6
8800 ELKG 95624 358-F3
HARLOW DR
400 ANT 94509 (513-E5
See Page 493)
HARMON AL
3500 SAC 95816 297-G5
HARMON DR
6300 SAC 95831 316-F7
HARMON RD
2300 WSAC 95691 316-G2
HARMONY LN
1200 PlaC 95603 162-D5
3300 SaCo 95821 278-F4
HARMONY WY
200 RSVL 95678 239-G5
HARMONY HILL RD
3000 EDCo - 246-H7
HARMONY OAKS WY
7600 SaCo 95828 338-G4
HARMS WY
6600 SaCo 95823 317-J7
HARNESS CT
- RSVL 95747 219-B4
1300 PlaC 95603 162-A4
HARNESS LN
12100 SaCo 95632 420-E5
HARNESS TRACT RD
4200 EDCo 95709 247-B2
HARNESS TRAIL RD
4200 EDCo 95709 247-C2
HAROLD WY
5600 SAC 95822 317-D4
HAROLD T JOHNSON EXWY Rt#-65
- PlaC - 199-G5
- RKLN - 199-G5
- RKLN - 199-G5
- RKLN - 199-G5
- RKLN - 219-G1
- RSVL - 199-G5
- RSVL - 219-G1
- RSVL - 220-A4
- LNCN - 199-G5
- LNCN - 179-G7
HARPER CT
200 LNCN 95648 200-B2
HARPER WY
8400 CITH 95610 239-J6
HARRELL CT
- EDCo 95682 263-H5
HARRIER LN
2300 LNCN 95648 200-B2
HARRIER WY
9700 ELKG 95757 357-E7
HARRIET LN
- WSAC 95605 297-A3
HARRIMAN CT
2200 EDCo 95762 242-B5
HARRINGTON WY
- FOLS 95630 261-E6
1000 SaCo 95608 299-B4
HARRIS AV
200 SAC 95838 277-G2
1100 SAC 95838 278-A3
HARRIS CT
1400 ANT 94509 (513-F7
See Page 493)
3200 EDCo 95667 245-G7
5100 ELKG 95758 357-J4

STREET Block City ZIP Pg-Grid
HARRIS DR
2800 ANT 94509 (513-F7
See Page 493)
HARRIS LN
2300 PlaC 95603 162-A6
HARRIS RD
- RVIS 94571 454-G3
800 EDCo 95667 245-G6
2300 PlaC 95603 162-A6
3900 EDCo 95709 247-B4
10500 PlaC 95603 161-J6
HARRISBURG ST
- SaCo 95742 280-F7
HARRISON AV
100 AUB 95603 182-E2
900 LNCN 95648 179-J2
HARRISON DR
1300 RSVL 95678 219-F7
HARRISON PL
3000 ANT 94509 (513-A7
See Page 493)
HARRISON RD
- SaCo 95615 (396-G2
See Page 375)
HARRISON ST
4900 SaCo 95660 258-H6
4900 SaCo 95660 278-H1
HARROGATE CT
8700 PlaC 95746 241-D3
HARROGATE WY
900 ANT 94509 (513-C7
See Page 493)
9100 ELKG 95758 358-C5
HARROW DR
4900 SAC 95758 357-J1
HARRY ST
- SaCo 95758 377-D5
- SaCo 95758 397-D5
HARSTON WY
5100 SaCo 95843 239-B7
HART AV
5000 WSAC 95691 316-F1
HARTE WY
4900 SAC 95822 317-D3
HARTER CT
2200 FOLS 95630 281-F1
HARTER WY
1100 FOLS 95630 281-F1
HARTFORD CT
2300 EDCo 95762 242-C5
10400 RCCD 95670 299-F4
HARTFORD ST
- SaCo 95742 280-F6
HARTLAND CIR
- RSVL 95747 218-H4
HARTLEPOOL WY
4200 SaCo 95843 238-J6
HARTLEY WY
- FOLS 95630 281-G1
HARTMAN WY
4800 SaCo 95628 280-E1
HARTNELL PL
300 SAC 95825 298-C6
HARTONA WY
5300 SAC 95835 257-C5
HARTSELLE WY
3300 RCCD 95827 299-E5
HARTWELL CT
8900 ELKG 95624 358-G3
HARTWICK CT
- RKLN 95765 200-C6
HARTWICK RD
- RKLN 95765 200-C5
HARTWICK WY
7800 SaCo 95828 338-C2
HARVARD CT
1200 RSVL 95661 240-A4
HARVARD ST
2300 SAC 95815 278-A6
HARVARD WY
1000 EDCo 95762 262-D4
HARVEST CT
- RKLN 95765 200-A6
HARVEST LN
- EDCo 95709 247-B2
HARVEST RD
- RKLN 95765 200-A6
HARVEST VWY
9500 SaCo 95827 299-B7
HARVEST WY
9100 SaCo 95826 298-J6
HARVEST CREEK CT
9500 SaCo 95827 299-B7
HARVEST FALLS DR
2100 SaCo 95626 238-C7
HARVEST GOLD CT
9500 SaCo 95827 299-B7
HARVEST HILL DR
- ELKG 95624 358-H1
HARVEST HILL WY
8800 ELKG 95624 358-H1
HARVEST HOUSE WY
8600 ELKG 95624 358-G1
HARVEST MOON CT
5300 ELKG 95758 357-J2
HARVEST OAK CT
6800 ELKG 95758 358-B5
HARVEST PARK DR
- ELKG 95757 358-A6
HARVEST ROSE WY
9500 SaCo 95827 299-B7
HARVEST SKY CT
- RSVL 95747 219-C3
HARVEST WOODS DR
7600 SaCo 95828 338-C4
HARVEY CT
400 PLCR 95667 245-E4
HARVEY RD
3700 EDCo 95682 263-D5
9300 SaCo 95632 418-J7
9300 SaCo 95632 419-A7
HARVEY WY
700 SAC 95831 336-H2
HARWICH CT
2000 EDCo 95762 242-D6
HARWOOD WY
- RSVL 95746 240-F4
- SAC 95835 257-C7
HASBRO CT
- SAC 95832 337-C4
HASELMERE CT
- SaCo 95829 338-J6
HASKELL AV
5500 SaCo 95608 279-C2
HASKELL WY
3700 PlaC 95661 240-E5
HASKIN CT
- RSVL 95747 219-B3

STREET Block City ZIP Pg-Grid
HASKIN RANCH RD
9900 PlaC 95658 201-J3
HASKINS CT
100 FOLS 95630 261-F4
HASSELBARRY CT
4000 EDCo 95726 248-B6
HASSLER RD
2100 EDCo 95667 246-D1
2600 EDCo 95667 226-D7
HASTING CT
1800 RSVL 95661 240-B5
HASTINGS CT
8400 SAC 95826 298-E7
HASTINGS DR
2500 EDCo 95672 263-C1
HASTINGS LN
8200 PlaC 95602 161-E3
HASWELL CT
100 AUB 95603 182-F1
HATBORO CT
7200 SaCo 95828 338-F2
HATFIELD CT
7000 CITH 95610 260-C2
HATFIELD WY
8500 ELKG 95624 358-E1
HATHAWAY CT
200 SaCo 95864 298-F5
1500 EDCo 95762 242-A6
HATHAWAY RD
9000 PlaC 95658 181-G4
HATTERAS WY
300 SAC 95831 336-F3
HATTON CT
- RSVL 95747 219-C7
HAUSCHILDT RD
12500 SaCo 95632 (399-G7
See Page 379)
12500 SaCo 95632 419-G2
HAUSSMANN ST
- ELKG 95758 357-F4
HAVASU ST
- WSAC 95691 316-D4
HAVELOK ST
5000 SaCo 95628 260-E7
HAVEN CT
- LNCN 95648 179-E7
- SAC 95831 316-J7
N HAVEN DR
5600 SaCo 95660 258-G5
S HAVEN DR
5600 SaCo 95660 258-G5
HAVEN LN
4000 EDCo 95682 263-J7
4000 EDCo 95682 283-J1
HAVEN GLEN PL
3700 SaCo 95821 279-A4
HAVENHILL CT
1200 RSVL 95661 239-J5
HAVEN HILL LN
8100 PlaC 95603 161-E4
HAVENHURST CIR
5400 RKLN 95677 220-H4
HAVENHURST CT
- EDCo - 267-B2
HAVENHURST DR
6700 SAC 95831 316-J7
6800 SAC 95831 317-A7
6900 SAC 95831 336-J1
6900 SAC 95831 337-A1
HAVENSIDE DR
6200 SAC 95831 316-H6
6800 SAC 95831 336-H1
HAVENSTAR LN
5800 EDCo 95623 265-B5
HAVENVIEW WY
- ELKG 95624 359-A5
HAVENWOOD CIR
- SAC 95831 316-H7
HAVENWOOD DR
- LNCN 95648 180-A1
HAVERHILL DR
- FOLS 95630 281-F1
HAVERHILL ST
1000 WSAC 95691 296-H5
HAVERTOWN CT
- ELKG 95758 357-F4
HAVESHILL WY
- SaCo 95655 319-J2
HAVILAND DR
4000 RSVL 95746 240-F6
HAWAII CT
- WSAC 95691 316-D2
HAWAII LN
8200 SaCo 95828 338-D3
HAWAII WY
- SaCo 95828 318-E4
HAWES WY
3500 RKLN 95677 220-D4
HAWICK WY
4000 EDCo 95762 262-G4
8000 SaCo 95829 338-J6
HAWK AV
900 SAC 95833 277-D6
HAWKCREST CIR
300 SAC 95835 256-G6
HAWK CREST CT
- RSVL 95678 219-H5
HAWK CREST DR
- LNCN 95648 200-A2
HAWK CREST WY
- RSVL 95678 219-H5
HAWKER PL
1000 EDCo 95762 262-D3
HAWKESBURY CT
8800 ELKG 95624 358-G2
HAWKEYE LN
5700 SaCo 95843 239-C6
HAWKHAVEN CT
5300 RKLN 95765 200-D7
HAWKHAVEN DR
3500 RKLN 95765 200-C7
3500 RKLN 95765 220-D1
HAWKHAVEN WY
- SAC 95835 257-C7
HAWK HEIGHTS CT
3400 SaCo 95843 238-G5
HAWK HILL LN
- LNCN 95648 200-B1
HAWKINS CT
9600 ELKG 95624 358-H7
HAWKINS LN
13300 SaCo 95632 419-C5
HAWK POINT CT
100 FOLS 95630 261-A1
HAWKS FLIGHT CT
1200 EDCo 95762 282-E3
HAWKS LANDING CT
2700 PLCR 95667 245-H3

STREET / Block City ZIP Pg-Grid

HAWKSMOOR CT
- SAC 95823 358-B1
HAWKSTONE CT
- PlaC 95747 238-J2
HAWKSWORTH CT
8100 SaCo 95828 338-G6
HAWKVIEW DR
- SAC 95835 256-H7
HAWK VIEW RD
4000 EDCo 95762 262-H6
HAWKVIEW WY
- ELKG 95757 377-J1
- ELKG 95757 397-J1
HAWLEY WY
8500 ELKG 95624 358-D1
HAWTHORNE AV
900 ANT 94509 (513-C6 See Page 493)
HAWTHORNE LN
1100 LNCN 95648 179-J3
1100 LNCN 95648 180-A5
6100 EDCo 95633 205-A1
HAWTHORNE LP
1100 RSVL 95678 219-F6
HAWTHORNE RD
500 SaCo 95864 298-E4
HAWTHORNE ST
2200 SAC 95815 277-G6
HAYCOCK ST
14300 SaCo 95683 341-J1
HAYDEN PKWY
- RSVL 95747 218-H3
- RSVL 95747 219-A4
HAYDEN WY
8500 SaCo 95628 280-D2
HAYER CIR
1000 SaCo 95673 257-J4
1000 SaCo 95673 258-A4
HAYES AV
400 SAC 95838 277-H4
HAYES DR
10000 PlaC 95658 202-A3
HAYES WY
2800 ANT 94509 (513-A7 See Page 493)
HAYFIELD CIR
8200 SaCo 95828 338-D4
HAYFORD WY
4500 SaCo 95842 258-J5
4500 SaCo 95842 259-A5
HAYGROUND WY
3200 SAC 95835 256-H4
HAYLOFT CT
4700 EDCo 95762 242-D6
HAYLOFT DR
2200 FOLS 95630 282-B2
HAYRIDE LN
- RSVL 95747 219-B3
HAYS WY
- FOLS 95630 261-D7
HAYSTACK DR
8100 SaCo 95828 338-D4
HAYWAGON CT
100 LNCN 95648 179-J3
HAYWARD DR
7100 SaCo 95828 338-F2
HAYWOOD ST
3600 SAC 95838 277-J3
HAZEL AV Rt#-E3
1900 SaCo 95628 280-F2
1900 SaCo 95670 280-F3
4900 SaCo 95628 260-F7
5600 SaCo 95662 260-F3
7500 SaCo 95662 240-F7
HAZEL CT
1500 LNCN 95648 179-G3
HAZEL ST
3000 EDCo 95726 248-D1
HAZEL AV OVLK
- SaCo 95628 280-F3
HAZEL CREST CT
8500 ELKG 95624 358-F5
HAZEL HILL CT
8900 SaCo 95662 260-F5
HAZELHURST CT
8200 SaCo 95662 260-B4
HAZELMERE DR
100 FOLS 95630 261-D6
HAZELNUT CIR
- EDCo 95762 242-C7
HAZELNUT CT
2400 ANT 94509 (513-H6 See Page 493)
HAZELNUT DR
400 OAKL 94561 (514-G7 See Page 493)
HAZELNUT LN
300 OAKL 94561 (514-G7 See Page 493)
7400 SaCo 95828 338-C3
HAZELNUT RD
6700 EDCo 95667 265-C2
HAZEL OAK CT
9000 SaCo 95662 260-G2
HAZEL RIDGE LN
8800 SaCo 95628 280-E2
HAZELTINE LN
- PlaC 95747 239-B4
HAZELWOOD AV
4300 SaCo 95821 278-J6
4600 SaCo 95608 279-A6
4600 SaCo 95821 279-A6
HAZEN CT
- SAC 95824 318-B5
HAZENMORE CT
7700 ELKG 95758 358-C6
HAZZARD ST
3000 PLCR 95667 245-H5
HEADINGTON RD
2400 EDCo 95667 245-B7
HEADLEY WY
9700 ELKG 95624 359-A7
HEADSLANE RD
- WSAC 95691 296-J7
HEADWIND CT
9000 SaCo 95628 260-F7
HEADY CT
3600 EDCo 95667 245-D7
3700 EDCo 95667 265-D1
HEADY LN
3600 EDCo 95667 245-C7
HEAGEY HILL RD
- EDCo 95667 266-H6
HEALDSBURG CT
- SAC 95831 336-H1
HEALON WY
9300 ELKG 95624 379-A1
9300 ELKG 95624 359-A7
HEALY CT
8000 SaCo 95828 338-G5
HEARST DR
- EDCo 95762 262-H5
HEARST PL
- EDCo 95762 262-H6
HEARST ST
- WSAC 95691 296-J6
HEART BUTTE CT
100 FOLS 95630 261-A1
HEARTH PL
8100 SaCo 95843 239-B6
HEARTHSIDE CT
- RSVL 95747 218-H2
HEARTHSIDE WY
- RSVL 95747 218-H2
HEARTHSTONE CT
- RSVL 95747 219-A5
HEARTHSTONE DR
- RKLN 95677 220-C5
HEARTHSTONE LN
- RSVL 95747 219-A5
HEARTHSTONE PL
4700 EDCo 95762 242-C6
8100 SaCo 95843 239-B6
HEARTLAND CT
- LNCN 95648 179-E7
600 PlaC 95661 239-J5
HEARTLAND DR
5100 SaCo 95843 239-B6
HEARTLAND RD
1000 EDCo 95619 265-G6
HEARTLAND WY
4200 RCCD 95742 320-E2
HEARTLEAF CT
- ELKG 95624 358-F1
HEARTROSE CT
- RSVL 95747 219-A3
HEARTWOOD WY
9800 RCCD 95827 299-C6
HEATER WY
- SaCo 95824 317-J5
HEATH CT
- RKLN 95765 200-A7
HEATH WY
6100 SAC 95823 338-A5
HEATHCLIFF DR
6200 SaCo 95608 279-E1
HEATHCOT PL
1200 EDCo 95762 242-C5
HEATHER CT
- RKLN 95765 200-D4
HEATHER DR
2700 PlaC 95648 180-D4
HEATHER LN
4000 PlaC 95603 161-E3
HEATHER RD
7400 SaCo 95628 279-H1
HEATHER WY
100 RSVL 95678 219-H7
HEATHERBRAE CIR
4800 SaCo 95842 259-A1
HEATHERBROOK CT
8100 CITH 95610 240-B7
HEATHERBROOK LN
2700 PlaC 95648 179-C4
HEATHERCREEK PL
5400 SaCo 95843 259-C1
HEATHER CROSS WY
8500 SaCo 95662 260-D4
HEATHERDALE LN
4900 SaCo 95608 279-A5
HEATHER DAWN LN
9100 SaCo 95662 260-G3
HEATHER FALLS CT
- RSVL 95678 219-J3
HEATHER FALLS ST
- RSVL 95678 219-J3
HEATHER FIELD WY
5500 ELKG 95757 357-J7
HEATHER GARDEN LN
- RSVL 95661 220-D6
HEATHER GATE WY
- ELKG 95624 359-A6
HEATHER GLEN LN
- RCCD 95670 279-G7
HEATHER GROVE CT
8100 SaCo 95828 338-D6
HEATHER HILL CT
2300 EDCo 95667 244-J4
HEATHER HILL RD
1800 EDCo 95667 244-J4
2200 EDCo 95667 245-A4
HEATHER HILL WY
4000 SaCo 95660 258-H4
HEATHER HOLLOW CT
8000 SaCo 95828 338-F6
HEATHER HTS CT
2800 ANT 94531 (513-G7 See Page 493)
HEATHERINGTON WY
7600 CITH 95610 259-H4
HEATHERMIST CT
8700 ELKG 95624 358-G2
HEATHERMIST WY
8700 ELKG 95624 358-G2
HEATHERMOOR WY
6300 SAC 95823 338-A7
HEATHERPACE LN
7400 SaCo 95829 339-D3
HEATHER PINE CT
5200 SaCo 95843 239-B5
HEATHER RANCH WY
4800 RCCD 95742 320-E4
HEATHER RIDGE CT
9000 ELKG 95624 358-G4
HEATHER TREE DR
7100 SaCo 95842 258-J2
HEATHERWOOD WY
6500 SAC 95831 317-A7
HEATHFIELD CT
9400 SaCo 95829 339-A5
HEATHFIELD WY
9300 SaCo 95829 339-A5
HEATHMAN WY
- ELKG 95624 359-B6
HEATHMERE CT
- SAC 95833 277-A6
HEATHMORE CT
- LNCN 95648 179-E7
HEATH PEAK PL
8200 SaCo 95843 239-B5
HEATHROW LN
3900 EDCo 95762 263-A6
HEATHSTON CT
7700 SaCo 95843 238-J7
HEATON CT
100 RSVL 95746 240-F4
HEATON WY
100 FOLS 95630 261-F7
HEAVENLY CT
100 RSVL 95747 219-A4
HEAVENLY ACRES CT
5500 EDCo 95682 283-J6
HEAVENLY RIDGE RD
12000 PlaC 95603 162-C5
- EDCo - 267-C5
HEAVENS GATE LN
8600 PlaC 95658 201-F3
8600 PlaC 95663 201-F3
HEAVYTREE CT
11600 SaCo 95670 280-C5
HEBERT CT
5800 LMS 95650 200-J5
HEBRON CIR
- SAC 95835 256-G5
HECK DR
3500 EDCo 95672 243-G6
HECTOR CT
3300 PlaC 95658 202-A5
HECTOR RD
3200 PlaC 95658 201-J4
3200 PlaC 95658 202-A5
HEDERA CT
8400 SaCo 95662 260-D3
HEDGE AV
4300 SaCo 95826 318-J3
4700 SaCo 95829 318-J6
6100 SAC 95829 318-J4
6500 SaCo 95829 338-J2
HEDGE LN
12500 SaCo 95693 360-H1
HEDGEROW CT
- SAC 95823 337-G3
1300 RSVL 95661 240-B5
HEDGEWOOD DR
6700 SaCo 95842 259-C3
HEDLAND PL
1600 EDCo 95762 262-D4
HEDMAN ST
- SAC 95820 318-F7
HEDRICK CT
- RKLN 95765 200-B4
HEFLEA CT
5200 SaCo 95842 259-B1
HEFLIN CT
8100 SaCo 95828 338-D3
HEGER WY
- ELKG 95758 357-D5
HEGSETH CT
8200 SaCo 95628 280-B1
HEIDELBERG CT
2600 SAC 95826 298-E7
HEIDI CT
7400 SaCo 95628 279-H3
HEIDI WY
9700 PlaC 95602 161-G3
HEIDI HOUSE RD
100 EDCo 95667 245-D6
HEIGHTS DR
3200 EDCo 95682 263-E7
HEILER CT
- FOLS 95630 261-H7
HEILER WY
- FOLS 95630 261-H7
HEIN RD
11500 SaCo 95757 397-H9
HEINLEIN CT
- SaCo 95829 339-A6
HEINLEIN WY
- SaCo 95829 339-B6
HEINZ RD
3900 EDCo 95682 263-J7
3900 EDCo 95682 283-J1
HEINZ ST
2800 SAC 95826 318-C1
HEIRLOOM WY
- RSVL 95747 218-H4
3000 SaCo 95826 298-J7
HELAMAN CT
4900 SaCo 95841 259-C7
HELEN WY
2100 SAC 95822 317-C4
HELENA AV
1100 SAC 95815 277-J5
1200 SAC 95815 278-A6
2000 SaCo 95821 278-C6
HELENA CT
300 OAKL 94561 (514-C7 See Page 493)
HELENA RD
4200 EDCo 95672 243-G7
HELENS CT
6200 LMS 95650 200-J5
HELENSBURGH PL
5300 SaCo 95843 239-B5
HELIANTHUS CT
2900 ELKG 95757 357-F7
HELIO DR
9500 SaCo 95827 319-B1
HELIOS CT
2200 EDCo 95762 242-E4
HELIOTROPE LN
7400 SaCo 95828 338-C3
HELIX CT
8700 ELKG 95624 358-F6
HELLER CT
400 RSVL 95747 219-A6
HELLER PL
2200 SaCo 95825 298-C3
HELM LN
3200 PlaC 95650 201-D5
HELMINGHAM CT
- SaCo 95829 338-J6
HELMRICK RD
7000 EDCo 95667 245-C6
HELMSDALE DR
8000 SaCo 95828 338-G6
HELMSDALE WY
- RKLN 95677 220-F6
- RSVL 95661 220-F6
HELMSLEY CT
8200 SaCo 95843 238-J6
HELMSMAN WY
1300 SAC 95833 277-D6
HELMUTH LN
- ANT 94509 (513-E5 See Page 493)
HELSINKI WY
8400 SaCo 95843 238-J5
HELSTONE CT
- RKLN 95677 220-F5
HELVA LN
5900 SaCo 95608 259-D7
HEMET DR
- CITH 95621 239-G6
HEMFORD CIR
100 SAC 95832 337-D4
HEMINGWAY CT
100 RSVL 95747 219-E6
HEMINGWAY DR
1200 RSVL 95747 219-E6
8100 SaCo 95828 338-D4
HEMLOCK DR
12000 PlaC 95603 162-C5
HEMLOCK PL
- EDCo 95682 263-D2
HEMLOCK ST
1900 WSAC 95691 296-H4
5100 SaCo 95841 279-B1
5200 SaCo 95841 259-B6
HEMLOCK WY
6200 RKLN 95677 220-D5
HEMMINGWAY CT
- EDCo 95682 283-C1
HEMPHILL WY
300 RSVL 95678 219-G7
HEMPSTEAD RD
3100 SaCo 95864 298-F3
HEMSWORTH WY
9100 SaCo 95829 338-J5
HENDERSON CT
- RSVL 95747 239-F3
HENDERSON WY
100 FOLS 95630 261-D4
3800 SaCo 95608 279-C3
HENDON WY
7400 ELKG 95758 358-C5
HENDRICKS WY
300 RSVL 95678 219-G7
HENDRY CIR
- RKLN 95765 220-A1
HENLEY WY
9200 SaCo 95826 318-J2
9200 SaCo 95826 319-A2
HENNA CT
- SAC 95834 277-D4
HENNESSY CT
7200 SaCo 95828 338-F2
HENNING DR
6900 CITH 95621 259-F1
HENRIETTA DR
7400 SAC 95822 337-C3
7500 SAC 95832 337-C3
HENRY CT
- FOLS 95630 261-E6
HENRY PL
- EDCo 95709 247-C1
HENRY ST
- FOLS 95630 261-E7
HENRY WY
4600 SAC 95819 297-H6
HENSEY CT
100 FOLS 95630 261-G3
HENSHAW CT
- SAC 95832 337-D4
HENSHAW RD
- WSAC 95691 316-C4
HENSLEY CIR
4000 EDCo 95762 262-B3
HEPBURN WY
7600 SaCo 95843 258-J1
7600 SaCo 95843 238-J7
HEPPNER CT
9300 ELKG 95624 358-F6
HEPWORTH WY
900 GALT 95632 419-F3
HERA CT
- CITH 95621 259-G3
HERALD RD
12700 SaCo 95638 420-C4
13300 SaCo 95632 420-C4
HERBAL WY
5700 SAC 95835 257-C4
HERBERT ST
800 RSVL 95678 239-G1
HERBERT WY
2700 SaCo 95821 278-D6
HERBON WY
- ELKG 95758 357-D4
HERBOSA VISTA CT
- SAC 95824 318-B6
HERDAL DR
12000 AUB 95603 182-D5
HERDAL WY
12200 AUB 95603 182-C5
HEREDIA CT
- PlaC 95602 161-B1
- RSVL 95747 219-D5
7700 CITH 95610 259-J1
HEREDIA DR
- RSVL 95747 219-D5
7700 CITH 95610 259-J1
HERITAGE DR
1000 EDCo 95619 265-H4
2000 RSVL 95678 219-J5
5100 SaCo 95608 259-E7
HERITAGE LN
- PlaC 95658 201-E1
- PlaC 95663 201-E1
1600 SAC 95815 298-A1
8400 SaCo 95628 280-D2
HERITAGE PL
700 FOLS 95630 261-J6
1000 AUB 95603 182-C7
1000 PlaC 95603 182-C7
HERITAGE WY
- RKLN 95765 200-B6
HERITAGE GLEN LN
200 RCCD 95670 280-A6
HERITAGE HILL DR
8400 ELKG 95624 338-J7
8400 SaCo 95624 338-J7
8400 ELKG 95624 358-J1
HERITAGE MEADOW LN
8000 CITH 95610 260-B1
HERITAGE MEADOW PL
7400 CITH 95610 260-B1
HERITAGE OAK CT
7000 SaCo 95662 260-G2
HERITAGE OAK PL
11900 PlaC 95603 162-B3
HERITAGE PARK CT
- SAC 95822 317-B6
- SAC 95831 317-B6
HERITAGE PARK LN
- SAC 95835 256-J4
- SAC 95835 257-A3
HERITAGE TREE LN
- CITH 95610 260-A6
- CITH 95628 260-A6
HERITAGE WOOD CIR
- SAC 95831 337-A2
HERLONG WY
7300 SaCo 95660 258-G1
HERMAN CIR
100 PlaC 95603 162-F7
HERMES CIR
- SAC 95823 337-G4
HERMITAGE CT
1400 RSVL 95661 240-A4
HERMITAGE WY
8400 SAC 95823 358-A1
HERMOSA
2200 RCCD 95670 279-J6
HERMOSA CT
2800 EDCo 95667 246-G5
HERMOSA ST
6100 SAC 95822 317-E6
HERNANDEZ LN
600 RSVL 95678 239-H4
HERNANDEZ SQ
14700 SaCo 95683 342-C4
HERNANDO RD
7300 SaCo 95826 278-D7
HERNDON CT
8300 SaCo 95828 338-E6
HERNE CT
800 RSVL 95747 239-C1
HERNEY WY
8300 SaCo 95829 338-J7
HERODIAN DR
11800 RCCD 95742 300-D7
HEROLD AV
600 LNCN 95648 179-J2
HERON CT
- RKLN 95765 200-A6
HERON LN
2700 EDCo 95709 247-A2
HERON PL
- LNCN 95648 179-D1
HERON WY
2800 SaCo 95821 278-C5
HERON BAY LN
- ELKG 95758 357-F6
HERON CREEK CT
- RSVL 95661 220-E7
HERON CREST CT
- SAC 95835 256-G4
HERON LAKE LN
- ELKG 95758 357-F6
HERON POINT CT
- ELKG 95624 359-A6
HERR WY
900 AUB 95603 162-E7
HERRILL CT
100 FOLS 95630 261-D6
HERRING AV
800 SaCo 95673 257-J1
HERRINGTON DR
100 AUB 95603 182-E5
HERSHAM CT
400 RSVL 95661 240-D4
HERSH BERGER CT
7000 CITH 95610 260-A2
HERZOG RD
12000 SaCo 95615 (396-J4 See Page 375)
12300 SaCo 95615 (416-J1 See Page 415)
12300 SaCo 95690 (416-J2 See Page 415)
HESBY WY
6100 SAC 95823 338-A5
HESILER CT
100 FOLS 95630 281-B1
HESKET WY
1400 SaCo 95825 298-D2
HESKETH CT
100 RSVL 95747 219-D6
HESPER WY
5300 SaCo 95608 259-E5
HESPERIA WY
6600 CITH 95621 259-G3
HESPERIAN CIR
11400 SaCo 95670 280-B5
HESS CT
3200 RCCD 95670 299-H4
HESSER CT
100 FOLS 95630 261-E7
HETCH HECHY DR
- RCCD 95742 300-F7
HEWENTHATTA WY
- EDCo 95726 267-H3
HEWITT WY
- ELKG 95757 378-A2
HEWSON CT
100 FOLS 95630 281-F1
HIALEAH CT
8400 SaCo 95628 260-C4
HIAWATHA DR
- RSVL 95747 219-A7
HIAWATHA WY
3500 SaCo 95843 238-G7
HIBISCUS AV
- SaCo 95828 338-F3
HIBISCUS CT
- EDCo 95726 267-J1
100 RSVL 95747 219-C4
HIBISCUS DR
5300 SaCo 95628 260-B6
HICKEY LN
3800 PlaC 95650 201-D7
HICKEY WY
- GALT 95632 419-G2
HICKOK RD
1800 EDCo 95762 242-G6
HICKORY AV
6200 SaCo 95662 260-E1
7600 SaCo 95662 240-E7
8000 SAC 95826 318-C3
HICKORY LN
2800 PLCR 95667 245-E5
HICKORY ST
1000 RSVL 95678 239-F2
HICKORY WY
2100 WSAC 95691 296-G4
3000 RKLN 95677 220-D5
HICKORY HILL CT
5200 SaCo 95628 259-F7
HICKORY LEAF PL
8600 SaCo 95662 260-E3
HICKORYNUT CT
- ANT 94509 (513-J6 See Page 493)
HICKORYNUT ST
- ANT 94509 (513-J6 See Page 493)
HICKORY RAIL WY
9600 ELKG 95624 359-B6
HICKORYWOOD WY
5900 CITH 95621 259-F5
HICKS LN
400 SaCo 95673 257-F1
HIDALGO CIR
1300 RSVL 95747 239-E2
E HIDALGO CIR
1400 RSVL 95747 239-F2
W HIDALGO CIR
1400 RSVL 95747 239-E2
HIDALGO WY
3900 SaCo 95660 258-H5
HIDDEN CT
1300 RSVL 95661 240-C5
4500 RKLN 95677 220-F4
HIDDEN DR
1900 PlaC 95658 201-G1
HIDDEN LN
4000 EDCo 95682 264-A1
4800 SAC 95819 297-J5
5200 SAC 95819 298-A5
7000 PlaC 95746 221-D6
HIDDEN WY
800 PLCR 95667 245-G6
HIDDEN ACRES DR
600 EDCo 95762 242-B7
600 EDCo 95762 262-B1
HIDDEN ACRES LN
100 PlaC 95658 180-J2
100 PlaC 95658 181-A3
HIDDEN BRIDGE RD
1400 EDCo 95630 222-G7
HIDDEN BROOK LN
6800 CITH 95621 259-E2
HIDDEN COVE CIR
- SAC 95831 336-H2
HIDDEN CREEK DR
- AUB 95603 182-C3
HIDDEN CREEK LN
5000 SaCo 95628 260-G7
HIDDEN FALLS DR
- FOLS 95630 282-B2
HIDDEN GLEN DR
- PlaC 95603 162-F7
5300 RKLN 95677 220-F4
5300 PlaC 95677 220-F4
HIDDEN GLEN LN
9000 SaCo 95662 260-F4
HIDDEN HILLS DR
1800 RSVL 95661 240-C5
HIDDEN HILLS LN
- LNCN 95648 180-B6
3300 EDCo 95667 244-H6
HIDDEN HOLLOW CT
9400 ELKG 95758 358-D6
HIDDEN HOLLOW DR
- EDCo 95667 266-B4
HIDDEN HOLLOW LN
- LNCN 95648 200-A1
HIDDEN LAKE CIR
- SAC 95831 336-G1
HIDDEN LAKES DR E
7900 PlaC 95746 241-E2
HIDDEN LAKES DR W
7900 PlaC 95746 241-D2
HIDDEN MEADOW WY
4800 SaCo 95843 239-A5
HIDDEN MEADOWS CIR
12300 AUB 95603 162-D6
HIDDEN OAK CT
3400 SaCo 95821 278-E4
HIDDEN OAKS LN
2400 PlaC 95603 162-A6
4700 PlaC 95650 221-F2
HIDDEN PARK CT
- SAC 95822 317-B6
- SAC 95831 317-B6
HIDDEN PASS CT
8400 SaCo 95843 239-A5
HIDDENSPRING WY
8800 ELKG 95758 357-J3
8800 ELKG 95758 358-A3
HIDDEN SPRINGS CIR
2700 PLCR 95667 245-C4
HIDDEN STREAM CT
6300 CITH 95621 259-E3
HIDDEN TRAIL LN
- SAC 95835 257-B3
HIDDEN VALLEY CIR
8300 SaCo 95628 280-C2
HIDDEN VALLEY LN
1900 EDCo 95667 226-G7
2100 EDCo 95667 246-G1
HIDDEN VALLEY PL
7000 PlaC 95746 220-G7
HIDDEN VIEW CIR
8000 SaCo 95628 280-A2
HIDDEN VIEW LN
1800 RSVL 95661 240-C5
HIDDENWOOD DR
1200 GALT 95632 419-G2
HIDEAWAY CT
4600 SaCo 95843 239-A5
HIDEAWAY TR
2000 EDCo 95667 244-E5
HIDEAWAY RANCH RD
2000 EDCo 95667 245-J2
HIDEOUT CT
- SAC 95831 316-H6
HIEMO WY
4700 SaCo 95843 239-A7
HIGGINS RD
2400 WSAC 95691 316-F1
HIGGINS ST
- FOLS 95630 281-C1
5900 SaCo 95608 259-D5
HIGH CT
4600 PlaC 95746 240-G2
HIGH ST
200 RSVL 95678 239-H1
400 AUB 95603 182-E1
800 PLCR 95667 245-F5
3100 SAC 95815 278-A5
3300 SAC 95838 278-A3
4800 RKLN 95677 220-E3
HIGHBRIDGE WY
1700 SAC 95832 337-C4
HIGH CLIFF RD
4100 LMS 95650 201-B7
HIGH COUNTRY CT
- RSVL 95747 218-J3
HIGHCREST DR
4900 EDCo 95682 283-F3
HIGHFIELD CIR
100 SAC 95832 337-D4
HIGH FLIGHT CT
- SaCo 95628 260-F7
HIGHGATE CT
- SAC 95838 277-J1
HIGHGRADE CT
- EDCo 95667 226-F2
HIGHGRADE ST
2800 EDCo 95667 226-F3
HIGHGROVE CT
5000 PlaC 95746 240-H5
HIGH HILL DR
7100 SaCo 95624 340-G1
HIGH HILL RD
2800 EDCo 95667 246-F3
HIGHLAND AV
400 RSVL 95678 239-J3
2900 SAC 95818 297-E7
2900 SAC 95818 317-E1
7600 CITH 95610 259-J3
7800 CITH 95610 260-A3
HIGHLAND CIR
1400 EDCo 95667 245-J2
HIGHLAND CT
1400 EDCo 95667 245-J1
12700 PlaC 95603 162-E6
HIGHLAND DR
- WSAC 95691 296-J7
- WSAC 95691 316-J1
- RVIS 94571 454-H6
1300 EDCo 95667 245-J1
12500 AUB 95603 162-E6
HIGHLAND RD
6700 PlaC 95746 221-E6
HIGHLAND WY
- PlaC 95663 201-C2
HIGHLANDER WY
2900 SaCo 95843 238-E7
HIGHLAND HILLS DR
2500 EDCo 95762 242-D7
2500 EDCo 95762 262-D1
HIGHLAND PARK DR
- RSVL 95678 219-H2
- RSVL 95678 220-A3
HIGHLAND POINTE DR
- RSVL 95678 219-H4
HIGHLAND RANCH RD
- RSVL 95678 219-H5
HIGHLAND RIDGE DR
- RSVL 95678 219-H4
HIGHLEY CT
100 SaCo 95864 298-E5
HIGHLINE RD
- SJCo 95686 437-C7
HIGH OAK CT
9100 SaCo 95628 280-G1
HIGH PINES CT
- RKLN 95765 219-J1
HIGH POINT LN
- SaCo 95842 259-A1
HIGHRIDGE DR
2300 SaCo 95825 278-F7
HIGH SCHOOL RD
- RSVL 95747 218-H3
HIGH SIERRA CT
7000 SaCo 95662 260-F2
HIGH SUN CT
6800 CITH 95621 259-D3
HIGH TECH CT
9200 ELKG 95758 357-F4
HIGHTRAIL CT
- RSVL 95747 218-H4
HIGHTRAIL WY
- RSVL 95747 218-H4
HIGH VIEW DR
- EDCo 95619 286-D3
HIGHVIEW LN
5400 CITH 95610 259-H6
5400 CITH 95628 259-H6
HIGHWAY Rt#-12
- RVIS 94571 454-D2
- SaCo 95641 454-J5
- SaCo 95641 455-A6
- SaCo 95641 (475-E1 See Page 456)
- SaCo 95641 (476-A2 See Page 456)
- SolC 94571 454-A2
HIGHWAY Rt#-65
600 PlaC - 159-A1
1400 PlaC 95648 159-C5
1600 LNCN 95648 159-E7
2700 LNCN 95648 179-H4
HIGHWAY Rt#-84
- RVIS 94571 455-A3
- SolC 94571 455-B1
3300 SolC 95690 415-F1
3300 SolC 95690 455-C1
3500 SolC 95690 (435-C1 See Page 415)
HIGHWAY Rt#-88
- SJCo 95638 422-J5
HIGHWAY Rt#-160
- CCCo 94509 (514-A3 See Page 493)
- ISLE 95641 455-J4
- OAKL 94509 (514-A3 See Page 493)
- SaCo 95641 455-B3
- SaCo 95641 456-A4
- SaCo 95680 436-F1
- SaCo 95690 455-D4
- SaCo 95690 456-D1
6800 SaCo 94571 (494-F1 See Page 493)
12000 SaCo 95615 (396-C4 See Page 375)
12400 SaCo 95690 (396-C6 See Page 375)
12400 SaCo 95690 (416-D1 See Page 415)
13400 SaCo 95690 417-A6
13700 SaCo 95690 437-A1
13700 SaCo 95690 436-J1
16700 SaCo 95641 454-J6
16700 SaCo 95641 474-J1
16800 SaCo 94571 474-H3
18100 SaCo 94571 (514-A1 See Page 493)
HIGHWAY Rt#-193
7900 PlaC 95658 181-H5
HIGHWAY Rt#-220
- SaCo 95690 (435-J2 See Page 415)
100 SaCo 95680 436-D1
100 SaCo 95690 436-D1
1000 SolC 95690 (435-C1 See Page 415)
HIGHWAY U.S.-50
- EDCo 95667 246-E4
- EDCo 95709 246-J3
- EDCo 95709 247-A4
HIGHWIND WY
7400 SAC 95831 336-J2
HIGHWOOD DR
2600 RSVL 95661 240-E4
HIGHWOOD WY
8000 SaCo 95662 260-B3
HILARI WY
9200 SaCo 95662 260-G5

HILARY AV SACRAMENTO COUNTY STREET INDEX HYDE PL 544

© 2007 Rand McNally & Company

SACRAMENTO CO.

STREET
Block City ZIP Pg-Grid

HILARY AV
3500 WSAC 95691 316-G3
HILDEBRAND CIR
500 FOLS 95630 262-B6
500 EDCo 95762 262-B6
HILL AV
300 RSVL 95678 239-H1
HILL CT
- RVIS 94571 454-H4
800 WSAC 95605 296-H2
HILL DR
1400 ANT 94509 (513-F6 See Page 493)
7200 PlaC 95746 241-C3
7700 CITH 95610 260-B2
HILL RD
2800 EDCo 95672 263-A3
2800 EDCo 95762 263-A3
6200 EDCo 95667 265-B2
7400 PlaC 95746 241-D3
HILL ST
4000 SaCo 95628 280-B2
4200 EDCo 95667 265-D2
HILLARD WY
5000 SAC 95822 317-C4
HILLBRAE DR
5700 SaCo 95842 259-A5
HILLBROOK CT
4700 EDCo 95623 264-G6
HILLBROOK DR
4800 EDCo 95623 264-G5
HILLBROOK LN
- PlaC 95603 182-A4
N HILLBROOK RD
200 PlaC 95603 182-A4
HILL CREEK CT
5300 SaCo 95843 239-B5
HILLCREST AV
700 RSVL 95678 239-J3
1200 ANT 94509 (513-F4 See Page 493)
3000 ANT 94531 (513-F6 See Page 493)
4700 SaCo 95628 280-C1
HILLCREST DR
100 PlaC 95603 162-F6
1900 PlaC 95658 201-G1
1900 PlaC 95658 181-G7
2600 EDCo 95682 263-C4
HILLCREST LN
3600 SaCo 95821 278-G3
HILLCREST RD
- RKLN 95765 200-C6
HILLCREST ST
800 PLCR 95667 245-E4
HILLCREST WY
2100 SaCo 95608 279-C7
4100 SaCo 95821 278-H3
HILLDALE RD
2600 SaCo 95864 298-E2
HILLFIELD CT
11900 SaCo 95624 340-E4
HILLGLEN WY
6700 SaCo 95628 259-F7
HILL GROVE LN
- LNCN 95648 200-A1
HILLGROVE ST
8200 PlaC 95746 240-G2
HILLGROVE WY
3800 SaCo 95608 279-F3
HILLHAVEN CT
7600 SaCo 95843 239-B7
HILLHAVEN LN
- LNCN 95648 180-C6
HILLHURST DR
4900 SaCo 95628 259-F7
HILLINGDON ST
- RSVL 95747 239-B1
HILLMON CT
8600 SaCo 95828 338-F2
HILLMONT AV
100 AUB 95603 182-E4
HILLMONT WY
1800 RSVL 95661 240-C5
HILLOCK CT
- RKLN 95765 200-A6
HILLOCK DR
100 FOLS 95630 261-D4
4200 EDCo 95667 243-J1
HILLRIDGE WY
4900 SaCo 95628 259-F7
4900 SaCo 95628 279-F1
HILLRISE DR
6300 SaCo 95608 259-E7
HILLS CT
200 SAC 95838 278-B2
3900 EDCo 95762 282-D1
HILLSBORO LN
4800 SAC 95822 317-B3
HILLSBOROUGH DR
8800 RSVL 95746 240-F4
HILLSBOURGH RD
3700 EDCo 95682 263-E7
HILLSBROOK DR
8300 SaCo 95843 239-A5
HILLSDALE BLVD
5100 SaCo 95842 258-J5
5600 SaCo 95842 259-A5
HILLSDALE CIR
- EDCo 95762 282-E5
HILLSDALE LN
- LNCN 95648 179-E6
- PlaC 95648 179-E6
HILLSFORD CT
- RSVL 95747 218-G4
HILL SHADE CT
5800 CITH 95841 259-D3
HILLSIDE CT
1700 PLCR 95667 246-B5
HILLSIDE DR
1700 PLCR 95667 245-G5
3600 RKLN 95677 220-E1
4500 EDCo 95672 243-H4
6800 SaCo 95608 279-F4
HILLSIDE LN
1400 RSVL 95661 240-C5
HILLSIDE RD
- ANT 94509 (513-D7 See Page 493)
HILLSIDE TER
100 PlaC 95603 162-E7
800 RVIS 94571 454-G4
HILLSIDE WY
2500 SaCo 95608 279-C6
HILLSPIRE CT
6400 CITH 95621 259-E2
HILLSWICK CIR
- FOLS 95630 261-H7
- FOLS 95630 281-H1

HILLSWOOD DR
100 FOLS 95630 261-B3
4000 SaCo 95821 278-H3
HILLTOP CIR
- EDCo - 247-G2
2000 RSVL 95747 239-E4
HILL TOP DR
500 AUB 95603 162-E7
500 PlaC 95603 162-E7
HILLTOP DR
2800 PLCR 95667 245-E4
5800 SaCo 95608 259-E5
HILL TOP LN
4300 EDCo 95682 264-B5
HILLTOP PL
9200 PlaC 95650 201-H5
HILLTREE AV
6100 CITH 95621 259-F4
HILL VIEW CT
600 EDCo 95762 262-B1
HILLVIEW CT
1300 RSVL 95661 240-C5
HILL VIEW DR
2200 EDCo 95762 262-B1
HILLVIEW DR
100 AUB 95603 182-F2
HILL VIEW RD
10100 PlaC 95658 181-H5
HILLVIEW WY
4400 SAC 95822 317-B3
HILLWOOD LN
- SaCo 95828 338-F6
HILLWOOD LP
- LNCN 95648 179-E7
HILMERTON CIR
- RSVL 95747 219-B7
HI LO LN
2400 SaCo 95608 279-D7
HILO WY
6800 SAC 95823 337-F1
HILTON CT
- EDCo 95682 263-H5
HILTON WY
3300 EDCo 95682 263-H5
8500 SaCo 95628 260-D6
HILTS AV
4300 SaCo 95824 317-G6
HIMALAYA WY
5700 SaCo 95621 259-C2
HINCHMAN WY
4800 SAC 95823 337-J5
HINCKLEY CT
- RSVL 95747 219-C4
7000 SaCo 95842 259-D2
HINDON WY
5600 CITH 95621 259-G6
HINDS WY
- FOLS 95630 281-G1
HING AV
2600 SAC 95822 337-E1
2800 SAC 95822 317-E7
HINGHAM SQ
100 FOLS 95630 261-J6
HINKLE CT
100 FOLS 95630 241-A7
HINMAN AL
4500 EDCo 95623 265-B4
HINSEY WY
8200 SaCo 95628 260-B7
HINTON CIR
- ELKG 95758 357-E4
HIRSCH CIR
5200 ELKG 95757 377-J2
5200 ELKG 95757 397-J2
HIRSCHFELD WY
10900 RCCD 95670 279-J7
HISPERRY LN
7100 SAC 95823 337-F1
HITCHCOCK WY
6400 SAC 95823 338-B6
HITCHING POST CT
- LNCN 95648 179-J4
2100 SaCo 95626 238-C7
HITCHING POST LN
- LNCN 95648 179-J4
HITE CIR
10300 ELKG 95757 377-H3
10300 ELKG 95757 397-H3
HIXON CIR
4600 SaCo 95841 279-B1
HOANG MY HILL
- EDCo 95667 225-F5
HOBART CT
3000 SaCo 95864 298-F5
HOBBLE CT
100 RSVL 95661 240-C3
HOBBS LN
5800 SaCo 95842 259-D1
HOBDAY RD
11700 SaCo 95693 (400-C1 See Page 379)
HOBIE DR
9100 PlaC 95602 161-F3
HOBNAIL WY
- SaCo 95824 317-H6
HOBSON AV
1000 WSAC 95605 296-H2
N HOBSON AV
600 WSAC 95605 296-G2
HOCK FARM DR
- SaCo 95670 280-B4
HOCKING ST
2800 PLCR 95667 245-H4
HODGE PL
8600 SaCo 95662 260-E3
HODGES CT
100 FOLS 95630 261-A1
HODGSON CT
- FOLS 95630 281-F2
HOFFMAN AV
100 AUB 95603 182-E1
HOFFMAN CT
2600 EDCo 95762 262-C1
HOFFMAN LN
5700 SaCo 95628 260-C5
HOFFMAN BLUFF WY
2800 SaCo 95608 279-E6
HOFFMAN WOODS LN
2700 SaCo 95608 279-C6
HOGAN CT
500 RSVL 95678 219-J6
HOGAN DR
6300 SAC 95822 317-D6
6900 SAC 95822 337-D1
HOGARTH DR
3100 RCCD 95827 299-D5
HOGUERTEL HILL CT
300 PlaC 95602 162-H2

HOITT AV
900 LNCN 95648 179-J2
HOLBROOK WY
7300 SaCo 95660 258-H1
HOLDEN CT
- SAC 95835 257-A6
HOLDFORD WY
9400 SaCo 95829 339-A6
HOLDREGE WY
- SAC 95835 256-J6
HOLETON RD
3500 SaCo 95608 279-D4
HOLIDAY WY
6500 SaCo 95660 258-G3
HOLIDAY COVE CT
- SAC 95831 316-H6
HOLIDAY HILL CT
4500 EDCo 95682 264-C7
HOLIDAY LAKE DR
4500 EDCo 95682 264-C6
HOLLAND AV
7000 CITH 95621 259-F1
HOLLAND DR
400 WSAC 95605 296-H1
2100 EDCo 95667 245-H1
HOLLAND RD
47500 SolC 94571 (395-J5 See Page 375)
47500 SolC 94571 415-F1
49000 SolC 94571 (396-A5 See Page 375)
HOLLANDVIEW DR
5100 EDCo 95682 264-F7
HOLLAR CT
5700 SaCo 95842 259-B1
HOLLENBECK LN
- PlaC 95603 162-G5
HOLLENBECK WY
11700 SaCo 95670 280-D5
HOLLEY CT
800 FOLS 95630 261-B6
HOLLINGSWORTH CT
900 LNCN 95648 179-G4
HOLLINGSWORTH DR
1000 LNCN 95648 179-G4
HOLLINGSWORTH WY
9500 SaCo 95827 319-B1
HOLLINS CT
- LNCN 95648 179-E6
8400 SAC 95826 318-E1
HOLLIS CT
7000 SaCo 95842 259-A2
HOLLISTER AV
3600 SaCo 95608 279-G3
HOLLOWAY LN
3700 SaCo 95608 279-C4
HOLLOW CREEK WY
9500 ELKG 95624 359-A5
HOLLOW OAK DR
3300 EDCo 95762 262-J6
3300 EDCo 95762 263-A6
HOLLOW OAKS CT
200 RSVL 95678 219-F6
8400 SaCo 95828 338-E6
HOLLOW SPRINGS WY
9400 ELKG 95624 359-B6
HOLLOWSTONE WY
8800 SaCo 95828 338-G6
HOLLOW VIEW CT
4100 SaCo 95628 280-F3
HOLLOW WOOD CT
4000 SaCo 95608 279-A3
HOLLY CT
- RKLN 95765 200-A5
600 GALT 95632 439-E1
1300 ANT 94509 (513-C6 See Page 493)
HOLLY DR
- RKLN 95765 200-A5
2100 OAKL 94561 (514-C7 See Page 493)
3300 SaCo 95864 298-F4
7900 CITH 95610 239-H7
HOLLY DR E
4200 EDCo 95667 265-D2
HOLLY DR W
300 EDCo 95667 265-D2
HOLLY LN
5200 SaCo 95628 259-F7
HOLLY ST
2200 WSAC 95691 296-G3
3700 LMS 95650 200-J6
S HOLLY ST
3800 LMS 95650 200-J6
HOLLY WY
800 PLCR 95667 245-F4
HOLLYANN CT
- FOLS 95630 261-B2
HOLLYANN DR
100 FOLS 95630 261-B1
HOLLYBERRY LN
5600 EDCo 95667 264-F3
HOLLYBERRY WY
8500 ELKG 95624 358-G1
HOLLY BRANCH CT
3300 SAC 95834 277-B4
HOLLYBROOK CT
8900 ELKG 95624 358-G3
HOLLYBROOK DR
6700 SAC 95823 358-B1
HOLLY CREEK CT
- ELKG 95757 358-A6
HOLLYCREST WY
4900 SaCo 95628 260-B7
4900 SaCo 95628 280-B1
HOLLYDALE WY
10400 RCCD 95670 279-F6
HOLLY GLEN WY
- ELKG 95757 358-A6
HOLLY GROVE CT
4000 SaCo 95826 318-J2
HOLLY HILL CT
1300 RSVL 95661 240-A5
HOLLY HILL LN
3500 PlaC 95650 201-G6
HOLLY HILL RD
800 AUB 95603 162-D7
HOLLY HILLS LN
2700 EDCo 95682 263-D6
HOLLYHOCK CT
7400 CITH 95621 259-F1
HOLLYHURST WY
5700 SAC 95823 337-J6
5700 SAC 95823 338-A6
HOLLY JILL WY
8200 SAC 95823 337-J7
8200 SAC 95823 338-A7
HOLLY OAK ST
8100 CITH 95610 240-B7

HOLLY SPRINGS CT
6200 CITH 95621 259-E4
HOLLY VISTA WY
12000 PlaC 95603 162-C6
HOLLYWOOD WY
- LNCN 95648 180-A1
2200 SAC 95822 317-D4
HOLLY WOODS DR
2700 PLCR 95667 245-F4
HOLM RD
- EDCo 95667 266-E3
HOLMAN DR
- ELKG 95624 358-D1
HOLMBY CT
4200 SaCo 95821 278-H4
HOLMES LN
6600 SaCo 95608 279-E4
HOLMES WY
10300 RCCD 95670 299-F2
HOLMFIRTH CT
- RSVL 95661 220-F6
HOLMFIRTH DR
7700 SaCo 95829 338-J4
HOLMISDALE WY
- GALT 95632 419-G3
HOLM OAK WY
8100 CITH 95610 240-B6
HOLSCLAW RD
3400 PlaC 95650 201-B5
HOLSTEIN WY
5700 SAC 95822 317-B5
6100 SAC 95831 317-A6
HOLSTEINER CT
700 GALT 95632 419-F2
HOLT LN
6000 SaCo 95608 279-D5
HOLT WY
2900 SaCo 95864 298-E2
HOLWORTHY WY
7200 SaCo 95842 258-J1
HOLYOKE ST
- SaCo 95742 280-G7
HOLYOKE WY
4800 SaCo 95841 259-B7
HOME CT
4800 EDCo 95682 264-D2
5400 SaCo 95608 279-B7
E HOME ST
200 OAKL 94561 (514-E7 See Page 493)
W HOME ST
100 OAKL 94561 (514-E7 See Page 493)
HOME COUNTRY WY
8200 SaCo 95828 338-D4
HOMEFIELD WY
8200 SaCo 95828 338-D4
HOMELAND CT
5100 SaCo 95843 239-B6
HOME LEISURE PZ
7300 SaCo 95823 337-J2
HOME RANCH CT
10500 RCCD 95670 279-G7
HOMESTEAD CT
- EDCo - 267-J4
400 LNCN 95648 179-J2
1300 RSVL 95661 240-A5
HOMESTEAD DR
- EDCo - 267-J4
HOMESTEAD RD
3600 EDCo 95672 243-C5
HOMESTEAD WY
6200 SAC 95824 318-B6
12100 AUB 95603 162-D6
HOMESTEAD HILLS CT
2200 FOLS 95630 282-B1
HOMESWEET WY
6000 SaCo 95608 279-D5
HOMETOWN WY
6600 SaCo 95828 318-C7
HOMEWOOD CT
- RSVL 95747 219-A6
HOMEWOOD LN
200 AUB 95603 182-C2
1800 LNCN 95648 180-A7
HOMEWOOD WY
- RSVL 95747 219-A6
2100 SaCo 95608 279-B7
2100 SaCo 95608 299-C1
HONDA LN
4800 EDCo 95623 265-B5
HONDO CT
- SAC 95823 338-A4
HONEY CIR
- EDCo 95762 263-B5
HONEY LN
200 PlaC 95603 182-B3
HONEY WY
600 SAC 95831 336-H3
HONEY BEE CT
- SAC 95826 298-G7
HONEYBEE LN
- EDCo 95619 265-H5
HONEYBROOK LN
12500 AUB 95603 162-D7
HONEYCOMB DR
- EDCo 95709 247-C1
HONEYCOMB LN
5600 EDCo 95682 283-H7
HONEYCOMB WY
8300 SaCo 95828 338-E7
HONEY COOK CIR
100 FOLS 95630 261-C6
HONEY DO LN
4600 EDCo 95682 264-E5
HONEY HILL CT
8400 SaCo 95843 238-H5
HONEYNUT ST
2900 ANT 94509 (513-J6 See Page 493)
HONEY ROSE PL
4000 SaCo 95843 238-H6
HONEYSUCKLE CIR
2800 ANT 94531 (513-G7 See Page 493)
HONEYSUCKLE CT
2900 ANT 94531 (513-G7 See Page 493)
HONEYSUCKLE DR
- LNCN 95648 179-D1
HONEYSUCKLE LN
- LMS 95650 220-H4
- RKLN 95650 220-H4
- RKLN 95677 220-H4
HONEYSUCKLE WY
2700 SAC 95826 298-G7
HONEYWOOD CT
9300 SaCo 95662 260-H7

HONKER CT
1200 PlaC 95663 181-D7
HONOR PKWY
- SAC 95835 257-C4
HONPIE CT
500 EDCo 95682 264-E3
HONPIE RD
5000 EDCo 95682 264-D2
HOOD DR
6800 EDCo 95633 205-A5
HOOD RD
- RKLN 95765 200-D5
1300 SaCo 95825 298-C2
HOODED CRANE CT
- SaCo 95829 338-H5
HOOD FRANKLIN RD
1000 SaCo 95639 (376-J5 See Page 375)
1000 SaCo 95639 377-B5
1000 SaCo 95639 397-B5
1200 SaCo 95758 377-B5
1200 SaCo 95758 397-B5
2500 SaCo 95757 377-F4
2500 SaCo 95757 397-F4
HOOD RIVER CT
600 SAC 95831 336-H1
HOOF CIR
1400 EDCo 95682 283-H5
HOOKE WY
2200 SAC 95822 317-D4
HOOPA CT
- SAC 95820 318-C3
HOOPA RD
- WSAC 95691 316-H2
HOOPES DR
7900 CITH 95610 260-A2
HOOTON CT
1200 SaCo 95608 299-B3
HOOT OWL RAVINE RD
- EDCo - 267-E6
HOOVER CT
- RKLN 95765 219-H1
HOOVER ST
5100 SaCo 95660 258-H7
HOPE CT
500 LNCN 95648 200-A3
HOPE LN
4400 EDCo 95667 264-E3
4800 SaCo 95821 279-A2
5000 SaCo 95608 279-A2
HOPE WY
7100 PlaC 95663 201-C4
HOPEDALE CT
8700 ELKG 95624 358-G2
HOPFIELD DR
- FOLS 95630 281-C1
HOPI CT
2600 EDCo 95682 263-D3
4200 SaCo 95843 238-H7
HOPKINS CT
- LNCN 95648 180-A6
5000 PlaC 95746 240-H6
HOPKINS LN
- LNCN 95648 180-A5
HOPKINS PL
3100 EDCo 95762 242-A5
HOPKINS RD
400 SaCo 95864 298-E5
HOPKINS ST
1300 SAC 95822 317-B6
HOPLAND CT
- SAC 95831 336-H1
HOPLAND ST
- WSAC 95691 316-H2
HOPPE LN
500 PlaC 95603 182-A3
HOPPER LN
100 FOLS 95630 261-H6
HOPSCOTCH WY
- RSVL 95747 199-C7
- RSVL 95747 219-C1
HORGAN WY
4100 SaCo 95821 278-H3
HORIZON CV
- RKLN 95677 220-B2
HORIZON LN
1900 ANT 94509 (513-B5 See Page 493)
HORIZON WY
7600 SaCo 95628 279-H1
HORIZON GOLD CT
- RSVL 95747 219-C3
HORN CT
100 FOLS 95630 260-J3
HORN RD
9800 RCCD 95827 299-C5
HORNBILL CT
- SAC 95834 276-H1
HORNBY ISLAND RD
- WSAC 95691 316-C2
HORNCASTLE AV
- RSVL 95747 219-C3
HORNCASTLE CT
- RSVL 95747 219-C3
HORNED LARK WY
9700 ELKG 95757 357-E7
HORNET DR
1100 SAC 95826 298-C7
1900 SAC 95826 318-C1
HORNSBY CT
- FOLS 95630 281-G2
HORNSEA WY
- SAC 95834 276-H1
HORSELESS CARRIAGE LN
9600 SaCo 95829 339-B1
HORSEMAN WY
- CITH 95621 259-F3
HORSE N ROUND LN
- PlaC 95663 201-F3
HORSESHOE CIR
3900 PlaC 95650 201-J7
HORSESHOE CT
- RKLN 95765 200-D6
HORSESHOE DR
3300 SaCo 95821 278-D4
HORSESHOE BAR RD
3600 LMS 95650 200-J6
3600 LMS 95650 201-A6
6500 PlaC 95650 201-D7
8000 PlaC 95650 221-F1
9800 PlaC 95650 202-A7
HORSESHOE GLEN CIR
1900 FOLS 95630 282-B2
HORSESHOE HILL RD
8400 PlaC 95650 201-E7
HORSHAM CT
- SaCo 95829 338-J7

HORTON LN
3700 SaCo 95608 279-C3
HOSAC WY
5800 CITH 95621 259-F5
HOSKINS LN
1800 PlaC 95603 162-B6
HOSPENTHAL WY
9300 ELKG 95624 358-E5
HOSPITAL DR
7900 SAC 95823 338-C6
HOSPITAL WY
- RCCD 95655 299-G5
HOTCHKISS CT
2800 EDCo 95682 263-C3
HOT SPRINGS CT
1200 RSVL 95661 240-B5
HOUNDSTOOTH CT
8800 ELKG 95624 358-G3
HOUSE WORKS DR
- SaCo 95608 299-B2
HOUSTON CIR
- FOLS 95630 261-H5
HOUSTON ST
- SaCo 95742 280-G6
500 WSAC 95691 296-F3
HOUSTON WY
5600 SaCo 95823 317-J7
HOVEY CT
- RSVL 95678 239-G1
HOVEY WY
500 RSVL 95678 219-F7
600 RSVL 95678 239-F1
HOWARD AV
4100 SaCo 95820 317-H3
HOWARD CIR
4200 EDCo 95619 265-E3
HOWARD CT
- GALT 95632 419-G2
HOWARD DR
2200 EDCo 95672 262-H2
2400 EDCo 95672 263-A3
HOWARD LN
3900 LMS 95650 200-J7
HOWARD ST
- SaCo 95652 258-F7
4000 SaCo 95628 279-J3
4100 SaCo 95628 280-A3
HOWARDS CROSSING RD
- EDCo 95634 225-G2
HOWDY LN
11200 SaCo 95693 (400-D1 See Page 379)
HOWE AV
- SAC 95825 298-C4
100 SAC 95826 298-C4
500 SaCo 95825 298-C4
1800 SaCo 95864 298-C4
1800 SaCo 95825 278-C7
2400 SaCo 95821 278-C5
2900 SAC 95821 278-C5
HOWE AV Rt#-16
1500 SAC 95826 298-D7
2200 SAC 95826 318-D1
HOWELL LN
500 PlaC 95658 181-G6
HOWERTON DR
7600 SAC 95831 336-G3
HOWLAND CT
- LNCN 95648 179-E6
HOXSIE CT
100 FOLS 95630 261-D5
HOYER LN
700 PlaC 95603 182-A6
700 PlaC 95658 182-A6
HOY LAKE CT
- SAC 95833 277-C6
HOYLETON WY
9300 ELKG 95758 358-C5
HOYT ST
- SAC 95835 256-J4
HUBBARD CT
9100 ELKG 95624 358-J5
HUBBARD CREEK PL
- SAC 95835 256-G5
HUBER CT
100 SAC 95838 277-G5
HUCKLEBERRY CIR
- WSAC 95691 296-G7
HUCKLEBERRY LN
7500 SaCo 95828 338-C3
HUCKLEBERRY ST
- WSAC 95691 296-F7
HUDSON CIR
- LNCN 95648 179-E1
HUDSON CT
9800 PlaC 95650 201-J7
HUDSON WY
200 FOLS 95630 261-B2
2000 SAC 95815 278-C4
HUFF WY
3700 SaCo 95821 278-G5
HUGHES AV
1500 SAC 95822 317-C5
HUGHES CIR
1600 WSAC 95691 296-H5
HUGO CT
9500 ELKG 95624 358-G6
HULBERT WY
- PlaC 95603 162-C5
HULETT RD
2100 FOLS 95630 262-B7
HULL WY
5700 SaCo 95823 317-J7
HULLIN WY
3000 SAC 95818 297-B7
HUMBERT ST
600 FOLS 95630 261-C6
HUMBOLDT CT
5300 RKLN 95765 220-D1
HUMBOLDT DR
5300 RKLN 95765 220-C1
HUMBOLDT WY
3400 SaCo 95864 298-F3
HUMBUG WY
1100 AUB 95603 182-C6
HUMBUG CREEK CT
- FOLS 95630 281-F5
HUMBUG CREEK DR
- FOLS 95630 261-G5
HUME CT
8600 ELKG 95624 358-F6
HUME GLENN DR
3100 EDCo 95667 266-F1
HUMMINGBIRD LN
- RKLN 95765 219-J1
3500 EDCo 95667 245-C7
9100 PlaC 95746 221-G3
HUMMINGBIRD WY
- RSVL 95747 219-B7

HUMMINGBIRD WY
8600 ELKG 95624 358-F5
N HUMP RD
- SaCo 95843 239-D6
HUMPHREY RD
2200 PlaC 95650 200-H2
2200 PlaC 95663 200-H2
2800 LMS 95650 200-J5
HUMPRIES CT
2100 SaCo 95670 280-D5
HUMPY LN
- EDCo 95633 205-E4
HUNGRY HOLLOW RD
1500 PlaC 95648 180-B1
1700 PlaC 95648 160-C7
HUNNICUT LN
3300 SaCo 95821 278-F4
HUNT DR
2900 RCCD 95670 299-G2
HUNT ST
- SAC 95826 318-C1
HUNT CLUB DR
3300 RKLN 95677 220-C4
HUNTER CT
100 RSVL 95661 240-C5
HUNTER DR
1900 RKLN 95765 200-A5
HUNTER LN
3300 SaCo 95608 279-B5
HUNTER PL
- FOLS 95630 261-C7
HUNTER LEIGH PL
5000 SaCo 95843 239-B6
HUNTER OAKS LN
- LMS 95650 200-J7
- LMS 95650 220-J1
HUNTERS DR
4000 LMS 95650 200-H7
4100 LMS 95650 220-H1
HUNTERS BROOK CT
- ELKG 95758 358-D3
HUNTERS CREEK DR
800 SAC 95838 257-J7
HUNTERS GLEN PL
3800 SaCo 95843 238-H5
HUNTINGTON CIR
2000 EDCo 95762 242-A5
HUNTINGTON DR
1600 RSVL 95661 240-C3
HUNTINGTON RD
- WSAC 95691 316-C4
2600 SaCo 95864 298-E5
HUNTINGTON SQUARE LN
7300 CITH 95610 259-G3
7300 CITH 95621 259-G3
HUNTINGTON VILLAGE LN
- SaCo 95670 280-B5
HUNTLEY AV
100 AUB 95603 182-E1
HUNTLY DR
- FOLS 95630 261-J5
- FOLS 95630 262-A5
HUNTRIDGE LN
4900 SaCo 95628 259-H7
HUNTSHAW WY
- RSVL 95747 218-J5
HUNTSMAN CT
- LNCN 95648 199-J1
HUNTSMAN DR
3100 SaCo 95826 299-A7
3100 SaCo 95827 299-A7
3300 SaCo 95826 298-J7
3300 SaCo 95826 319-A1
HUNTS RUN WY
7900 SaCo 95828 338-F5
HUNTSVILLE DR
7200 SaCo 95828 338-F2
HUNTSVILLE ST
- SaCo 95742 280-F6
HURLEY WY
2000 SaCo 95825 298-C2
2600 SaCo 95864 298-C2
HURLSTON WY
1400 RSVL 95747 219-D7
HURON ST
3800 SAC 95838 278-A2
HURSLEY CT
8000 SaCo 95829 339-A6
HURST CT
7800 SaCo 95829 339-E5
HURST WY
2200 RSVL 95661 240-D5
HUSCH WY
3500 RCCD 95670 299-H4
HUSKER ST
5800 SaCo 95662 260-F5
HUSKINSON CT
800 RSVL 95747 219-A4
HUSS AV
3400 SaCo 95824 317-F5
HUSSEY DR
4200 SaCo 95608 279-G2
4300 SaCo 95628 279-G2
HUST LN
300 SaCo 95673 257-H1
HUSTON CT
5200 SAC 95819 298-A4
HUTCHINS WY
7200 SaCo 95660 258-H1
HUTLEY CT
700 RSVL 95746 240-F4
2900 EDCo 95762 263-A5
HUTLEY WY
1000 RSVL 95746 240-F4
HUTSON WY
4600 ELKG 95757 377-H2
4600 ELKG 95757 397-H2
HUTTON DR
9500 ELKG 95758 358-A6
HUXLEY CT
8000 SaCo 95829 338-H6
HYACINTH CT
- ELKG 95624 338-F7
500 RSVL 95678 239-G4
2700 ANT 94531 (513-G7 See Page 493)
5500 SaCo 95662 260-H6
HYANNIS WY
2700 SaCo 95827 299-C4
HYANNIS PORT PL
- SAC 95835 256-H5
HYATT LN
100 PlaC 95603 162-F7
HYDE PL
100 ANT 94509 (513-E7 See Page 493)

STREET
Block City ZIP Pg-Grid

HYDE WY
3400 SaCo 95864 298-F2
HYDE PARK CIR
- SaCo 95843 239-C7
HYDE PARK LN
12400 AUB 95603 162-D4
12400 PlaC 95603 162-D4
HYDRA WY
4300 ELKG 95758 357-G4
HYDRANGEA CT
500 RSVL 95747 219-C4
8500 ELKG 95624 338-F7
HYDRAULICS DR
11400 RCCD 95742 300-B3
HYPERIA CT
8800 ELKG 95624 358-F3
HYSSOP CT
7700 CITH 95621 239-F7

I

I PKWY
4800 SaCo 95823 337-J2
I ST
100 SAC 95814 297-B3
100 WSAC 95605 297-B3
100 LNCN 95648 179-H3
100 ANT 94509 (513-C3
See Page 493)
800 SAC 95819 297-J5
1400 SaCo 95673 258-A3
2100 SAC 95816 297-E4
2500 SaCo 95652 258-D3
3000 SaCo 95660 258-E3
5200 SAC 95819 298-A5
IACOCCA WY
8000 SaCo 95828 338-D5
IAN CT
5700 SaCo 95842 259-C2
IBANEZ CT
- SaCo 95829 339-F6
IBERIAN DR
3100 SAC 95833 277-D4
IBEX WOODS CT
6600 CITH 95621 239-F5
IBIS CT
- LNCN 95648 179-D1
- RKLN 95765 219-J1
IBIS DR
- OAKL 94561 (514-H7
See Page 493)
IBIS WY
8600 ELKG 95624 358-G1
ICARUS CT
- SAC 95823 337-G4
ICEBERG LN
- RSVL 95747 219-A7
ICELAND CT
- SAC 95835 256-J5
ICHABOD CT
8600 SaCo 95828 338-F7
IDA ST
100 AUB 95603 182-F1
IDAHO DR
4800 SAC 95823 337-H6
IDAHO WY
- EDCo 95633 205-E5
IDAHO MINE CT
2000 SaCo 95670 280-C4
IDLE WY
7100 SaCo 95628 279-G1
IDLE CREEK DR
4200 EDCo 95682 264-A7
IDLE WILD ST
7300 SAC 95831 337-B2
IDLEWOOD LN
2700 SaCo 95821 278-E6
IDRIA CT
7200 SaCo 95842 259-C2
IGLESIA CT
600 ANT 94509 (513-E6
See Page 493)
IJAUNA LN
11800 SaCo 95632 (400-C4
See Page 379)
ILEEN DR
9800 ELKG 95624 359-B7
ILIFF CT
10400 RCCD 95670 299-F3
ILLINOIS AV
4300 SaCo 95628 280-E2
4900 SaCo 95628 260-E6
5700 SaCo 95662 260-E6
ILLINOIS WY
- RKLN 95765 200-B7
ILLONA CT
3800 PlaC 95602 161-H2
ILLSLEY WY
- FOLS 95630 281-G1
IMAD CT
- EDCo 95762 262-E1
IMAGE WY
4800 SaCo 95842 259-A2
IMAI WY
7400 SAC 95831 336-H2
IMMELMANN CT
9000 SaCo 95628 260-F7
IMMIGRANT RAVINE RD
- PLCR 95667 245-H4
IMNAHA LN
- FOLS 95630 260-J1
IMPALA WY
4000 EDCo 95630 202-J7
4000 EDCo 95630 222-J1
5000 SaCo 95608 279-A5
IMPALA RUN PL
5000 SaCo 95843 239-B7
IMPERIA CT
- ELKG 95757 358-A7
IMPERIAL LN
- CITH 95621 259-D4
- SaCo 95621 259-D4
IMPERIAL WY
3400 SaCo 95826 318-H1
5800 CITH 95621 259-D4
E IMPERIAL VIEW CT
- RKLN 95677 220-G5
W IMPERIAL VIEW CT
- PlaC 95677 220-G5
- RKLN 95677 220-G5
IMPRESSIONIST WY
- EDCo 95762 262-H4
IMRAN DR
2300 SaCo 95825 298-D3
IMRAN WOODS CIR
8500 CITH 95621 239-F5
8500 RSVL 95678 239-F5
IN CT
6000 CITH 95610 259-J5

INA WY
100 LNCN 95648 179-H4
INAGAHEE RD
5800 EDCo 95726 248-A2
INCA CT
- SAC 95833 277-E5
INCLINE DR
- LNCN 95648 179-F5
500 AUB 95603 162-D6
11700 PlaC 95603 162-D6
INCLINE WY
1800 RSVL 95661 240-C5
INDEPENDENCE AV
2600 WSAC 95691 296-G7
2600 WSAC 95691 316-F1
INDEPENDENCE CT
100 RSVL 95747 219-E7
INDEPENDENCE LN
4800 SaCo 95660 258-F4
INDEPENDENCE PL
- RKLN 95677 220-F1
INDEPENDENCE WY
2200 RSVL 95747 219-E7
2200 RSVL 95747 239-E1
INDERKUM WY
8300 SaCo 95829 338-J7
INDIAN LN
3200 EDCo 95667 246-F4
7000 SAC 95822 317-F7
7000 SAC 95822 337-F1
INDIAN WY
7100 EDCo 95667 226-F4
INDIANA AV
400 SAC 95833 277-F5
INDIANA WY
- RKLN 95765 200-B7
INDIANAPOLIS ST
- SaCo 95742 280-F6
INDIAN ARROW CT
7900 SaCo 95662 240-D7
INDIAN CREEK CT
3500 EDCo 95667 244-G7
INDIAN CREEK DR
4200 LMS 95650 221-A1
4300 RKLN 95650 221-A1
4300 RKLN 95677 221-A1
7900 SaCo 95662 240-D7
INDIAN CREEK RD
3400 EDCo 95667 244-G6
4100 PlaC - 160-E2
INDIAN HILL CT
8600 SaCo 95662 240-E7
INDIAN HILL RD
1100 PLCR 95667 245-H3
9800 PlaC 95658 181-H6
10300 PlaC 95603 182-A6
10300 PlaC 95658 182-A6
10500 AUB 95603 182-A6
INDIAN KNOLL DR
- SaCo 95610 240-D7
8500 SaCo 95662 240-D7
INDIAN OAKS CT
4900 SaCo 95841 278-J1
INDIAN OAKS DR
3000 PlaC 95648 180-D5
INDIAN OAKS LN
6500 PlaC 95650 221-B6
INDIAN RANCHERIA RD
800 AUB 95603 182-C6
INDIAN RIVER DR
6400 CITH 95621 259-D3
INDIAN ROCK LN
2100 PlaC 95603 162-C4
INDIAN RUNNER CT
- RSVL 95747 219-E2
INDIAN RUNNER DR
- RSVL 95747 219-E2
INDIAN SPRINGS RD
6100 LMS 95650 220-J5
6100 LMS 95650 221-A5
6100 PlaC 95650 220-J5
6100 PlaC 95650 221-A5
INDIAN SPRINGS WY
7900 SaCo 95662 240-D7
INDIAN WELLS CT
2200 SAC 95833 276-H7
INDIAN WELLS RD
- EDCo - 267-E6
INDIANWOOD LN
- PlaC 95747 239-A3
INDIANWOOD WY
- RVIS 94571 454-E1
INDIGO CT
- EDCo 95762 263-B5
7000 SaCo 95628 259-G7
INDIGO OAKS CT
- SAC 95834 277-B3
INDIO DR
13700 SaCo 95683 341-E2
INDUSTRIAL AV
1300 RSVL 95678 199-F5
1300 RSVL 95678 219-F2
1300 PlaC 95765 199-F5
1300 PlaC 95648 199-F2
2500 LNCN 95648 179-G7
2500 PlaC 95648 179-G7
INDUSTRIAL BLVD
2200 WSAC 95691 296-F4
INDUSTRIAL CT
- GALT 95632 419-E5
11800 PlaC 95603 162-C5
INDUSTRIAL DR
400 GALT 95632 419-E5
1500 PlaC 95603 162-C5
6500 EDCo 95667 265-D2
INDUSTRIAL PKWY
8100 SAC 95824 318-D6
INDUSTRY DR
4200 SaCo 95660 278-F1
4300 SAC 95660 278-F2
INEZ WY
900 SAC 95822 316-J3
INGALLS WY
7400 SAC 95831 336-H2
INGE CT
- SAC 95864 298-E2
INGELA CT
4300 EDCo 95667 264-J2
INGERSOLL WY
- FOLS 95630 281-A2
INGLENOOK CT
8000 SaCo 95829 338-H5
INGLESIDE WY
8000 SaCo 95828 338-D3
INGLETON LN
- SAC 95835 256-J3
2600 SAC 95835 257-A4
INGLEWOOD DR
700 WSAC 95605 296-J2

INGLEWOOD LN
7900 SaCo 95828 338-F5
INGLIS WY
1900 RSVL 95678 239-G4
INGRAM CT
- SAC 95823 358-B1
INGRAM PKWY
- LNCN 95648 179-H5
INGRID WY
8700 SaCo 95620 280-E7
INISHEER WY
8700 SaCo 95828 338-G7
INKS WY
- FOLS 95630 262-A7
INKSTER WY
7800 SaCo 95829 339-E5
INLAND CT
- ANT 94509 (513-E5
See Page 493)
INLET CT
- SAC 95833 277-C5
INMAN CT
- RSVL 95747 219-A3
INMAN WY
4600 SaCo 95821 278-J3
4600 SaCo 95821 279-A3
INNES CT
- ELKG 95757 358-B7
INNOVATOR DR
- SAC 95834 277-B2
INNSBROOK WY
6400 SaCo 95662 260-C4
INSKIP DR
8200 SaCo 95828 338-D6
INSPIRATION LN
6900 SAC 95823 337-F1
INSTONE CT
- RSVL 95661 220-E7
INSTOW CT
7800 ELKG 95758 358-C6
INSTRUMENT CT
4900 SaCo 95628 260-F7
4900 SaCo 95628 280-F1
INTARSIA CT
- RSVL 95746 240-G5
INTERNATIONAL DR
10400 RCCD 95670 299-G5
10900 RCCD 95670 300-A3
INTERSTATE AV
5100 SaCo 95842 258-J7
INTREPID DR
- EDCo 95672 263-D1
INVAR CT
- RKLN 95765 199-J7
- RKLN 95765 200-A7
INVERNESS CT
- RSVL 95678 219-H7
3300 SaCo 95821 278-H5
INVERNESS DR
1000 RVIS 94571 454-F2
2300 LNCN 95648 179-D2
INVERNESS PL
2300 EDCo 95762 242-C6
INVERRARY CT
6500 SaCo 95662 260-C4
INVESTMENT BLVD
- EDCo 95762 282-F6
INVESTMENT CIR
- RCCD 95670 299-F2
INWOOD RD
9800 FOLS 95630 261-B1
INYO AV
4000 SaCo 95820 317-G3
INYO CT
5800 RKLN 95677 220-B4
IOLITE AV
- SAC 95834 277-B3
IONA WY
7800 SaCo 95828 338-D5
IONE RD
7600 SaCo 95683 342-G7
8000 SaCo 95683 (362-G1
See Page 341)
8900 AmCo 95683 (362-J7
See Page 341)
IONE ST
2000 SaCo 95864 298-H1
2000 SaCo 95864 278-J7
2500 SaCo 95821 278-H6
IONEAN CT
8600 ELKG 95624 358-F2
IOWA AV
4200 SaCo 95742 280-G6
4200 SaCo 95824 317-G5
IOWA CT
6700 PlaC 95746 241-B1
IPSWITCH CT
4800 SaCo 95628 279-F1
IRA CT
- RSVL 95747 218-J3
IRELAND ST
3900 SaCo 95821 278-H3
IRENE AV
100 RSVL 95678 239-H3
IRIS AV
1700 SAC 95815 278-B5
IRIS CIR
300 FOLS 95630 282-A1
IRIS CT
2700 ANT 94531 (513-G7
See Page 493)
IRIS DR
7500 CITH 95610 259-H4
IRIS LN
- EDCo - 247-G2
IRIS PL
- WSAC 95691 316-E2
7100 PlaC 95746 241-C3
IRIS CREST WY
8500 ELKG 95624 358-F5
IRISH LN
8500 PlaC 95658 181-F7
IRISH CREEK CT
2100 SaCo 95670 280-D5
IRISH CREEK RD
- EDCo 95633 205-B2
IRISH GOLD WY
9100 SaCo 95826 318-J2
IRISH MIST WY
3300 SaCo 95826 299-A7
IRISH MOSS CT
8600 ELKG 95624 358-H2
IRISH OAK LN
- EDCo 95619 266-C6
IRISH PORT LN
4200 EDCo 95667 264-H4
IRIS MEADOW WY
9500 ELKG 95757 357-J7
9700 ELKG 95757 377-H1

IRIS MEADOW WY
9700 ELKG 95757 397-H1
IRIS SPRING WY
- ELKG 95757 377-J1
- ELKG 95757 397-J1
IRMA WY
2300 SaCo 95825 298-D3
IRONBARK CT
6200 CITH 95621 259-E2
IRON CREST DR
- RSVL 95678 220-A3
IRON GATE WY
3900 RCCD 95742 300-D7
IRONGATE WY
- SAC 95835 257-C7
IRON GORGE DR
- SaCo 95829 338-H7
IRON HORSE
8100 SAC 95823 338-B6
IRON MOUNTAIN CT
100 FOLS 95630 260-J1
IRON POINT CIR
- FOLS 95630 281-E2
IRON POINT CT
- RKLN 95765 200-A6
IRON POINT RD
- FOLS 95630 282-A2
- FOLS 95670 280-J2
500 FOLS 95630 281-C1
900 FOLS 95630 280-J2
IRON RIVER CT
- SAC 95831 336-J1
IRON ROCK WY
10200 ELKG 95624 378-J2
IRONSTONE CT
200 RSVL 95747 219-D6
IRONSTONE ST
9300 SaCo 95829 339-A7
IRON WHEEL CT
- RKLN 95765 200-C4
IRONWOOD CIR
200 RSVL 95678 219-H6
IRONWOOD CT
- EDCo 95762 262-E6
5200 OAKL 94561 (514-D6
See Page 493)
IRONWOOD DR
3900 EDCo 95762 262-E5
IRONWOOD LN
2100 PlaC 95648 180-D1
5200 OAKL 94561 (514-D6
See Page 493)
IRONWOOD WY
600 SAC 95831 316-G5
2900 WSAC 95691 316-J2
IROQUOIS CT
- RKLN 95765 200-A5
7900 SaCo 95843 238-F6
IROQUOIS RD
- RKLN 95765 200-A5
1600 RKLN 95765 199-J5
IRVIN WY
2100 SAC 95822 317-C4
IRVINDALE WY
3200 SaCo 95843 238-F7
IRVING AV
700 SAC 95838 257-H6
ISAAC WY
- ELKG 95757 377-J1
- ELKG 95757 378-A1
- ELKG 95757 397-J1
ISABEL ST
1200 SAC 95814 297-E1
ISABELLA AV
4700 SaCo 95628 279-G1
ISABELLA CT
- RSVL 95661 220-D6
ISABELLA ST
- WSAC 95691 316-D4
ISADOR LN
- SAC 95835 256-G5
ISHI CIR
- SAC 95833 277-C4
E ISLAND CT
3500 ELKG 95758 357-F4
W ISLAND CT
3500 ELKG 95758 357-F4
ISLAND WY
7400 SAC 95831 336-G2
ISLANDVIEW CT
- SaCo 95690 (416-J7
See Page 415)
ISLANDVIEW WY
- SaCo 95690 (416-J7
See Page 415)
- SaCo 95690 436-J1
ISLAY CT
1600 FOLS 95630 261-H7
ISLE ST
- RKLN 95765 200-B6
ISLES CT
7600 SaCo 95628 279-H1
ISLETON RD
13800 SaCo 95690 436-G1
14400 SaCo 95680 436-G1
15400 SaCo 95690 456-D1
16700 SaCo 95641 456-B2
ISTHMUS CT
6300 SaCo 95823 338-A3
ITALIA WY
10500 RCCD 95670 299-G1
ITASCA AV
- SAC 95835 257-C7
ITCHY ACRES RD
6400 PlaC 95746 221-B7
6400 PlaC 95746 241-B1
ITHACA LN
2600 ANT 94509 (513-A6
See Page 493)
ITHICA CT
4900 SaCo 95842 259-A3
ITO CT
- EDCo 95682 263-F4
ITOW CT
1000 PlaC 95663 181-B7
IVA WY
3100 SaCo 95821 278-F4
IVAN CT
- RSVL 95661 239-J5
IVANHOE LN
2000 EDCo 95667 245-A4
IVANHOE WY
5500 SaCo 95608 299-B2
IVANPAH CT
8600 ELKG 95624 358-F3
IVERSON WY
- SAC 95835 257-C7
IVES AV
- SAC 95835 257-C6

IVIE RD
11700 SaCo 95638 420-C1
13200 SaCo 95632 420-D5
IVIE ACRES LN
- SaCo 95638 420-C3
IVORY CT
- RSVL 95747 219-C1
IVORY WY
6100 SaCo 95824 317-J6
IVORYTON CIR
100 SaCo 95655 319-H2
IVY LN
4500 RKLN 95677 220-F2
12000 PlaC 95603 162-D6
IVY ST
100 RSVL 95678 239-G2
3300 SAC 95838 278-B3
W IVY ST
200 RSVL 95678 239-G2
IVY TR
6200 EDCo 95623 265-B3
IVY ARBOR CT
- LNCN 95648 199-J1
IVY ARBOR LN
- LNCN 95648 199-J1
- LNCN 95648 200-A2
IVY BRIDGE DR
- RSVL 95747 218-J4
IVY CREEK DR
8500 SaCo 95828 338-E5
IVYCREST WY
- SAC 95835 257-C7
IVYDALE CIR
- ELKG 95758 358-B5
IVY GATE LN
- ELKG 95757 357-J6
IVY GLEN WY
- RSVL 95678 219-J3
- RSVL 95678 220-A3
IVY HILL WY
7800 SaCo 95843 238-H7
IVY HOLLOW LN
10200 ELKG 95624 359-E2
IVY KNOLL CT
1300 EDCo 95667 246-E5
IVY KNOLL DR
2500 EDCo 95667 246-E5
IVY LEAGUE CIR
- SaCo 95662 260-G4
IVY SPRING CT
6000 ELKG 95758 358-A3
IVY TOWN LN
5700 SaCo 95608 279-C6
IVY VINE WY
- SAC 95833 276-H6
IVYWOOD DR
1200 GALT 95632 419-G2
IZILDA CT
9800 SaCo 95829 339-C7
IZZY WY
- ELKG 95757 377-J3
- ELKG 95757 378-A3
- ELKG 95757 397-J3

J

J PKWY
4800 SaCo 95823 337-J2
J ST
100 SAC 95814 297-B3
100 LNCN 95648 179-G3
200 ANT 94509 (513-C3
See Page 493)
2000 SAC 95816 297-E4
3800 SAC 95819 297-H5
5300 SAC 95819 298-A6
JABBOUR WY
- SAC 95833 276-H4
3400 SAC 95834 276-H4
JACARANDA CT
7600 SaCo 95828 338-C4
JACINTH PL
9900 SaCo 95829 339-D7
JACINTO AV
5200 SAC 95823 337-J7
5200 SAC 95823 357-J1
5800 SAC 95823 358-B1
JACINTO RD
7400 SAC 95758 358-B1
JACKDAW CT
- SAC 95834 276-J3
JACKDAW ST
- SAC 95834 276-J3
JACK FROST CT
- RKLN 95765 220-A1
JACKIE CT
3600 EDCo 95682 263-G5
JACKIE LN
3500 EDCo 95682 263-G6
JACK LONDON CIR
6100 SaCo 95842 259-A3
JACK LONDON CT
700 RSVL 95747 219-C5
JACK PERRY PL
- SAC 95833 276-H7
JACK PINE RD
3900 EDCo 95682 263-J5
3900 EDCo 95682 264-A5
JACK RABBIT CT
- RKLN 95765 199-J5
JACKRABBIT CT
- EDCo 95619 266-B6
JACKRABBIT DR
- EDCo 95619 266-B7
JACKS LN
5600 SAC 95822 317-D5
JACKSON BLVD
100 SaCo 95641 455-G6
100 ISLE 95641 455-G6
JACKSON CT
- RKLN 95765 219-J1
1400 EDCo 95762 262-C1
JACKSON DR
- RKLN 95765 219-H2
JACKSON OVPS
100 ISLE 95641 455-H5
100 SaCo 95641 455-H5
JACKSON PL
3100 ANT 94509 (513-A7
See Page 493)
JACKSON RD Rt#-16
8300 SAC 95826 318-E1
9000 SaCo 95826 318-H3
9200 SaCo 95826 319-A3
9200 SaCo 95827 319-F5
9800 SaCo 95829 319-F5
9800 SaCo 95830 319-F5
10700 SaCo 95830 320-A6
11000 SaCo 95624 340-F1

JACKSON RD Rt#-16
11000 SaCo 95830 340-F1
12200 SaCo 95624 341-A2
12800 SaCo 95683 341-J1
14500 SaCo 95683 342-B2
16000 AmCo 95683 342-J4
JACKSON ST
100 WSAC 95691 296-J4
4800 SaCo 95660 278-H1
4900 SaCo 95660 258-H7
JACKSON SLOUGH RD
16000 SaCo 95641 455-F7
16000 SaCo 95641 (475-F1
See Page 456)
JACKSONVILLE AV
- SaCo 95742 280-G7
JACKS PEAK DR
4800 EDCo 95623 264-G6
N JACK TONE RD
27000 SJCo 95638 421-D7
JACOB CIR
2900 SAC 95826 318-D1
JACOB LN
800 SaCo 95608 299-A3
JACOB WY
1700 PLCR 95667 246-A5
JACOBS CT
100 FOLS 95630 260-J3
JACOBSEN CT
7900 SaCo 95829 339-E5
JACOBSEN ST
900 ANT 94509 (513-F4
See Page 493)
JACOBSGAARD LN
- EDCo 95667 226-E7
JACQUELYN CT
4800 SaCo 95660 278-G1
JACQUELYN LN
2500 WSAC 95691 296-E7
JACQUIER CT
100 EDCo 95667 246-B3
JACQUIER RD
1900 EDCo 95667 246-B3
JADE CT
3600 SaCo 95821 278-G4
3900 EDCo 95726 248-F2
JADE DR
3400 EDCo 95726 248-E2
JADE LN
1300 PlaC 95663 181-B7
1300 PlaC 95663 201-B1
JADE COVE CT
2900 SaCo 95821 278-E4
JADE CREEK WY
5300 ELKG 95758 357-J3
JADE CREST CT
8600 ELKG 95624 358-F4
JADEN LN
8000 SaCo 95628 280-A1
JADE RIVER CT
- RSVL 95678 219-J2
JADE RIVER DR
- RCCD 95742 320-D1
JADE SPRINGS WY
5400 RCCD 95742 320-E4
JADESTONE CT
8700 ELKG 95624 358-G7
JADE TREE CIR
- SAC 95834 277-B3
JAEGER RD
- RCCD 95742 300-F7
4300 RCCD 95742 320-F1
JAGUAR CT
9500 ELKG 95757 358-A7
E JAHANT RD
100 SJCo 95220 439-D7
2500 SJCo 95220 (440-B7
See Page 420)
W JAHANT RD
100 SJCo 95220 439-C7
JAMAICA ST
- WSAC 95691 316-D2
JAMAL WY
- EDCo 95667 266-B5
JAMBOREE CT
- SAC 95835 257-C5
JAMEL CT
9100 ELKG 95758 357-J4
JAMERSON DR
4200 RKLN 95677 220-F2
JAMES DR
300 RSVL 95678 240-A1
600 PLCR 95667 245-F4
5100 LMS 95650 220-J3
5100 RKLN 95650 220-J3
JAMES PL
8500 PlaC 95746 241-E2
JAMES ST
600 WSAC 95605 297-A2
JAMES WY
2800 SaCo 95652 258-F6
3100 SaCo 95660 258-F6
5600 SAC 95822 317-D4
JAMES HUTTON DR
- EDCo - 267-F6
JAMESON CT
5800 SaCo 95608 279-C1
JAMESPORT WY
5400 SAC 95835 256-H4
JAMES RIVER WY
7700 SAC 95831 336-G3
JAMESTOWN DR
1800 SAC 95815 278-B7
1800 SAC 95815 298-B1
1900 SAC 95825 298-B1
JAMESTOWN WY
1300 RSVL 95661 240-D5
JAMESTREE WY
6900 CITH 95610 259-J2
JAMI CT
- PlaC 95747 239-B3
JAMIE CT
500 SaCo 95673 257-H3
3400 SJCo 95220 439-H5
JAMIE LN
100 FOLS 95630 261-B6
JAMIEWOOD CT
1100 SaCo 95608 299-B3
JAN CT
- RKLN 95677 220-E4
JAN DR
4200 SaCo 95608 279-E1
JANA CT
700 RSVL 95678 239-H4
5700 SaCo 95608 279-C2
JANA MARIE CT
7800 CITH 95610 259-J3
JAN DRA CT
9200 SaCo 95662 260-G4

JANE CT
4000 SaCo 95608 279-C3
JANE DR
300 EDCo 95667 245-E3
2200 EDCo 95672 262-H3
JANELL WY
5100 SaCo 95608 279-D4
JANERO WY
5300 SAC 95835 257-D5
JANET CT
600 PlaC 95658 181-D2
JANET DR
2800 WSAC 95691 296-F7
6700 CITH 95621 259-F3
JANETTE WY
2800 SAC 95815 [illegible]
2800 SAC 95815 278-A5
JANEWOOD CT
100 FOLS 95630 261-E5
JANEY WY
1100 SAC 95819 298-A6
JANICE AV
2000 SAC 95821 278-C5
JANINE CT
1000 GALT 95632 439-E2
JAN MARIE WY
9100 ELKG 95624 358-H6
JANON CT
8600 SaCo 95828 338-F2
JANRICK AV
1400 SAC 95832 337-C4
JANSEN
- FOLS 95630 261-C4
JANSEN CT
- LNCN 95648 179-D4
JANSEN DR
5400 SAC 95824 317-J5
5600 SAC 95824 318-A5
JANSET WY
- SaCo 95828 338-F7
JARDIN LN
5000 SaCo 95608 299-A2
JARED CT
- ELKG 95757 357-J7
- RKLN 95765 200-C5
JARED PL
4100 EDCo 95762 262-D2
JARRETT CT
- ELKG 95757 358-B7
JARROW CT
6300 RSVL 95661 220-F7
JARVIS CIR
- SAC 95834 276-H2
JARVIS LN
7700 SaCo 95828 338-B4
JASMINE AV
400 WSAC 95605 296-H1
JASMINE CIR
- EDCo 95762 263-A4
JASMINE CT
300 RSVL 95678 219-F6
1300 ANT 94509 (513-G5
See Page 493)
JASMINE DR
6700 EDCo 95667 265-C3
W JASMINE DR
6700 EDCo 95667 265-B3
JASMINE ST
3600 SAC 95838 278-B3
JASMINE WY
- LNCN 95648 179-D1
E JASMINE CREST CT
8500 ELKG 95624 358-F5
JASON CT
- RKLN 95765 200-A5
JASON LN
1900 EDCo 95762 242-G7
1900 EDCo 95762 262-G1
JASON WY
5300 SaCo 95608 279-B4
JASPAR CT
1400 SaCo 95608 279-E2
JASPER CT
9900 SaCo 95829 339-C7
JASPER RD
6300 PlaC 95663 201-A1
JAVA CT
- SAC 95835 257-A4
- WSAC 95691 316-D2
JAW BONE RD
4000 EDCo 95667 245-G7
4000 EDCo 95667 265-F1
JAY CT
1800 SaCo 95608 299-C1
JAY LN
- PlaC 95746 241-B4
JAY RD
2600 EDCo 95667 266-F1
JAYANNE WY
3300 SaCo 95608 279-B5
JAYBIRD PL
- RKLN 95677 200-F7
JAYHAWK RD
4000 EDCo 95672 243-E4
JAY JAY LN
3500 SaCo 95608 279-C4
JAYMAR ST
2800 PLCR 95667 245-H4
JAYTEE WY
8600 SaCo 95628 260-D6
J-BAR-B DR
7100 PlaC 95746 220-G7
JC CT
- SAC 95673 257-J2
JEAN AV
1000 SAC 95838 277-J2
1000 SAC 95838 278-A2
JEANETTE WY
8300 PlaC 95746 240-G2
JEANEVA WY
8800 ELKG 95624 359-C3
JEANINE DR
5900 SaCo 95842 259-A5
JEANINE WY
5900 SaCo 95842 259-A5
JEANNE CT
- ANT 94509 (513-E5
See Page 493)
JEANNE LN
14000 SaCo 95632 439-C1
JEANNIE CT
700 PlaC 95650 221-D1
JEANROSS CT
- SAC 95832 337-C4
JEBEL CT
- SAC 95835 257-A4
JEDBURGH CT
100 RSVL 95747 219-D7

STREET Block	City	ZIP	Pg-Grid
JEDEDIAH RD			
100	FOLS	95630	260-J4
JEFF WY			
5700	SaCo	95608	279-C2
JEFF BRIAN LN			
-	SaCo	95693	359-J6
JEFFCOTT RD			
9400	SaCo	95693	360-B6
JEFFERSON AV			
300	SAC	95833	277-F7
5900	RKLN	95677	220-B4
JEFFERSON BLVD			
500	WSAC	95605	296-J2
700	WSAC	95691	296-H7
1300	WSAC	95691	316-F3
JEFFERSON BLVD Rt#-84			
29700	WSAC	95691	316-C7
29700	YoCo	95612	336-C7
29700	YoCo	95612	356-B7
29700	YoCo	95691	316-C7
29700	YoCo	95691	336-C3
36500	YoCo	95612	(376-B1 See Page 375)
38600	YoCo	95612	(396-B1 See Page 375)
JEFFERSON LN			
5000	SaCo	95608	279-A7
JEFFERSON PL			
2400	EDCo	95762	242-A5
JEFFERSON ST			
-	RSVL	95678	239-J1
JEFFERSON WY			
2100	ANT	94509	(513-A7 See Page 493)
JEFFERY LN			
1700	SaCo	95608	299-C1
JEFFERY WY			
-	RVIS	94571	454-H4
JEFFREY AV			
3700	SAC	95820	317-E2
JEFFREY LN			
1500	PLCR	95667	245-J6
JEFJEN WY			
-	ELKG	95757	378-A2
JEFRON CT			
10300	ELKG	95757	377-J3
10300	ELKG	95757	397-J3
JELA WY			
4800	SaCo	95660	278-H1
JELLYBEAN CT			
-	RSVL	95747	219-D4
JENAMAR CT			
-	RKLN	95765	200-D3
JEN FONTES WY			
7300	SaCo	95828	338-F2
JENICH CT			
-	SAC	95823	337-J7
JENKINS WY			
-	FOLS	95630	261-J4
JENKINSON CIR			
-	EDCo	95726	248-D4
JENKINTOWN CT			
-	ELKG	95758	357-G4
JENNA CT			
-	PlaC	95747	239-B4
JENNA WY			
7200	SaCo	95828	338-F2
JENNER CT			
6900	CITH	95610	260-D2
JENNESS WY			
4500	SaCo	95842	258-J6
JENNEY CT			
-	SAC	95831	336-H1
JENNICK WY			
-	ELKG	95757	377-J3
-	ELKG	95757	378-A3
-	ELKG	95757	397-J3
JENNIEKE CT			
-	RKLN	95765	200-D4
4200	SaCo	95843	238-J5
JENNIFER CIR			
200	RSVL	95678	219-G6
JENNIFER CT			
600	GALT	95632	419-E2
JENNINGS CT			
-	WSAC	95691	316-D4
JENNINGS WY			
3600	EDCo	95667	245-E6
5000	SAC	95819	297-J3
JENNY CT			
5600	LMS	95650	200-J5
JENNY WY			
5700	LMS	95650	200-J5
JENNY LIND AV			
3500	SaCo	95660	278-G1
JENNY LYNN WY			
-	ELKG	95757	378-A2
JENNYWOOD DR			
4900	SAC	95822	317-C4
JENROSE LN			
1000	EDCo	95682	263-F4
JENROSE WY			
8600	ELKG	95624	358-E1
JENSEN HOLLOW RD			
-	EDCo	95667	266-D3
JERAE CT			
-	SAC	95833	277-C4
JEREMIAH DR			
12400	PlaC	95603	162-C4
JEREMY CT			
6000	SaCo	95608	259-D7
JERESA CT			
-	SAC	95758	357-J2
JERICHO RD			
3200	EDCo	95667	245-A5
JEROME WY			
5300	SAC	95819	298-A4
JERRANDY CT			
8600	SaCo	95828	338-F2
JERRETT WY			
5300	SaCo	95842	258-J6
JERRILYN CT			
1400	SaCo	95608	299-A2
JERRON PL			
1800	SaCo	95825	298-D1
JERRY WY			
5000	SAC	95819	297-J4
5000	SAC	95819	298-A4
7200	SaCo	95828	338-D2
JERRY LITELL WY			
-	SAC	95835	257-C4
JERSEY DR			
5700	RKLN	95765	199-J6
5700	RKLN	95765	200-A7
JERSEY WY			
3100	SaCo	95821	278-F6
JERSEY ISLAND RD			
5400	CCCo	94561	(514-J1 See Page 493)
5800	CCCo	94561	(494-J7 See Page 493)
JESSE AV			
300	RSVL	95678	239-F2
JESSE LN			
9200	PlaC	95658	201-G3
JESSICA CT			
-	ANT	94509	(513-J6 See Page 493)
5300	SaCo	95628	260-E7
JESSICA LN			
-	RSVL	95747	219-A7
JESSIE AV			
200	SAC	95838	277-G2
1400	SAC	95838	278-A2
7700	CITH	95610	239-J6
JESSIE LN			
4800	PlaC	95650	221-D2
JESSUP CT			
-	ELKG	95758	358-B3
JESTER CT			
8500	ELKG	95624	358-F5
JET AV			
6700	SaCo	95628	259-F6
JETMAR WY			
9800	ELKG	95624	359-C6
JETTON LN			
5900	LMS	95650	200-J4
5900	LMS	95650	201-A4
JETWAY CT			
4300	SaCo	95660	278-E2
JEWEL WY			
4200	EDCo	95667	245-A7
8400	CITH	95610	239-J6
JEWEL STONE WY			
1000	FOLS	95630	261-B6
JIB CT			
-	SAC	95831	316-H7
JIBBOOM ST			
-	SAC	95833	297-B1
100	SAC	95814	297-B2
JICAMA CT			
-	SAC	95833	276-J7
JIGGER CT			
15500	SaCo	95683	342-E3
JILCARA CT			
4700	SaCo	95843	239-A6
JILL WY			
2300	SaCo	95821	278-D5
JILLSON WY			
-	ELKG	95757	378-A3
JILSON WY			
5200	ELKG	95757	377-J3
5200	ELKG	95757	397-J3
JIM BAR CT			
9100	ELKG	95624	358-G4
JIM CASEBOLT WY			
1900	SAC	95835	257-C4
JIMMY WY			
-	PlaC	95747	239-C3
JIMOLENE DR			
5900	SAC	95823	318-A7
JIM TOWN CT			
1900	SaCo	95670	280-D4
JIM VALLEY RD			
2200	EDCo	95667	246-E7
2200	EDCo	95667	266-D1
N JO CT			
8600	RSVL	95661	240-C4
JOAN ST			
900	WSAC	95605	296-J1
JOAN WY			
1900	SAC	95815	278-B7
1900	SAC	95825	278-C7
2000	SaCo	95825	278-C7
5500	LMS	95650	200-H5
JO ANN DR			
3700	SaCo	95821	278-G5
JO ANNE LN			
600	RSVL	95678	239-H3
JOAQUIN WY			
4600	SAC	95822	317-D3
JOBSON CT			
-	FOLS	95630	281-F2
JOBY LN			
1400	SaCo	95864	298-J2
JOCELYN WY			
8600	SAC	95758	358-D1
JODHP UR CT			
12600	SaCo	95693	360-H5
JOEGER RD			
9600	PlaC	95602	161-H2
9600	PlaC	95603	161-G4
JOEL CT			
1400	SAC	95822	317-B4
JOELLEN CT			
3100	SaCo	95608	279-C5
JOELLIS WY			
1100	SAC	95815	297-J1
JOE MURER CT			
1100	FOLS	95630	261-A6
JOERGANSEN RD			
-	FOLS	95630	261-G4
JOERGER ST			
2900	RCCD	95670	299-F3
JOE RODGERS CT			
8000	PlaC	95746	241-C1
JOE RODGERS RD			
8100	PlaC	95746	241-A2
JOHANNE CT			
7500	CITH	95621	259-F1
JOHANNISBERG WY			
8000	SaCo	95829	338-J5
JOHANSON			
5300	SaCo	95842	259-A4
JOHBABE LN			
2200	EDCo	95672	243-E3
JOHN DR			
3600	PlaC	95650	201-E5
JOHN LN			
-	AUB	95603	182-E2
JOHNFER WY			
900	SAC	95831	316-J5
JOHNGALT CT			
200	RSVL	95678	239-F1
JOHN GILDI AV			
100	ANT	94509	(513-C5 See Page 493)
JOHN HENRY CIR			
100	FOLS	95630	281-B1
JOHN HENRY LN			
-	RSVL	95747	219-B3
JOHN LYNN LN			
-	CITH	95610	239-H6
JOHN MUIR CT			
8900	ELKG	95624	378-H2
JOHN MURRAY WY			
-	FOLS	95630	281-E1
JOHNNY FRY CT			
700	RSVL	95747	219-A4
JOHNNY TUCK CT			
-	EDCo	95726	247-H7
JOHN RICHARD CT			
3400	EDCo	95682	263-G4
JOHN RUNGE ST			
5700	SaCo	95608	279-C6
JOHNS CT			
5600	SAC	95835	257-C4
JOHNS DR			
5600	SAC	95822	317-D4
JOHNSON DR			
1800	ANT	94509	(513-A7 See Page 493)
4700	SaCo	95628	279-G1
JOHNSON LN			
4000	SaCo	95608	279-E3
8200	PlaC	95746	240-J2
JOHNSON RANCH DR			
1900	RSVL	95661	240-C3
JOHNSON RANCH RD			
12900	SaCo	95632	419-C3
JOHN STILL DR			
1900	SAC	95832	337-D4
JOHNSTON CT			
100	FOLS	95630	261-E4
JOHNSTON RD			
100	SAC	95815	297-G1
8100	ELKG	95757	358-D6
JOINER CT			
4900	SaCo	95628	260-D7
4900	SaCo	95628	280-D1
JOINER PKWY			
400	LNCN	95648	179-E1
JOLA CIR			
3400	SAC	95832	337-F7
JOLANA LN			
4900	SaCo	95660	258-G7
4900	SaCo	95660	278-G1
JOLINE AV			
5300	SaCo	95841	259-B7
JOLLY CT			
5600	SaCo	95628	260-B6
JO MARR LN			
8400	SaCo	95628	260-C7
JON WY			
7800	PlaC	95746	241-E2
JONALAN DR			
3000	SaCo	95821	278-E6
JONAS AV			
900	SaCo	95864	298-E3
JONATHON CT			
100	GALT	95632	419-C7
JONELL CT			
9100	ELKG	95624	358-H7
JONES RD			
4400	SaCo	95841	278-J2
JONES ST			
11700	PlaC	95603	162-B4
JONES WY			
500	SAC	95818	297-B7
JONESBORO WY			
-	SAC	95835	256-J4
-	SAC	95835	257-A4
JONES RANCH CT			
-	SAC	95838	257-J7
JONI CT			
5700	EDCo	95726	248-A1
JONKO AV			
3700	SaCo	95660	258-G7
JONNIE WY			
8700	SaCo	95628	260-E6
JONOTHAN WY			
3600	SaCo	95660	258-G2
JONQUIL CT			
300	RSVL	95747	219-C4
JONQUIL DR			
1600	RSVL	95747	219-C4
JONQUIL WY			
8400	CITH	95610	260-C1
JORDAN CT			
-	EDCo	95630	222-G7
-	OAKL	94561	(514-F6 See Page 493)
-	SAC	95826	298-E7
JORDAN DR			
1700	RSVL	95661	240-B2
JORDAN LN			
400	OAKL	94561	(514-E6 See Page 493)
7400	SaCo	95829	338-H3
8400	ELKG	95624	339-A7
8400	SaCo	95624	339-A7
8400	ELKG	95624	359-A1
JORDAN HILL WY			
2000	SaCo	95670	280-D4
JORDAN RIVER CT			
11100	RCCD	95670	280-A5
JORDELL CT			
8300	CITH	95610	260-C1
JORDINE WY			
-	GALT	95632	419-H3
JORDON LN			
-	AUB	95603	182-E2
JORGENSON DR			
-	LNCN	95648	179-E1
JORGER CUT-OFF RD			
1300	EDCo	95762	282-F1
JORGI CT			
-	SAC	95833	276-J6
JORNEY CT			
-	PlaC	95746	240-H5
JOSE CT			
3400	EDCo	95682	263-E5
JOSE BENTO WY			
8200	SaCo	95829	339-C7
JOSEPH AV			
1900	ANT	94509	(513-F5 See Page 493)
2800	SaCo	95864	298-E3
JOSEPH LN			
4300	EDCo	95619	265-F3
JOSEPH WY			
100	FOLS	95630	261-D4
JOSEPHINE CT			
8100	SAC	95828	338-D5
JOSH CT			
4200	SaCo	95608	279-E2
JOSHUA CT			
-	CITH	95610	260-A1
400	RSVL	95747	219-D6
JOSHUA RD			
3500	EDCo	95682	264-A5
JOSHUA HENDY DR			
2500	PLCR	95667	245-G3
JOSIE LN			
2900	EDCo	95682	264-C3
JOURNEYS END CT			
8500	SaCo	95843	238-J5
JOY DR			
14000	GALT	95632	439-F1
14000	SaCo	95632	439-F1
JOY LN			
3400	EDCo	95682	263-G4
4100	SaCo	95608	279-G3
9100	PlaC	95746	241-B4
JOYCE LN			
5000	SAC	95838	258-A7
JOYCE WY			
4100	EDCo	95682	264-A2
JOYDANCE LN			
-	LNCN	95648	200-C3
JOYE LN			
100	AUB	95603	182-D4
JOY RIVER CT			
-	SAC	95831	336-G1
JUAN WY			
7700	SaCo	95628	259-J6
JUANITA DR			
4700	EDCo	95682	283-J3
JUANITA LN			
2100	SaCo	95825	278-D7
JUANITA WY			
600	RSVL	95678	239-H4
JUAREZ RD			
5800	EDCo	95726	267-J2
JUAREZ WY			
7800	SaCo	95628	259-J7
JUBILEE TR			
4800	EDCo	95682	283-J5
JUBILEE WY			
200	SaCo	95673	257-G3
JUDAH CT			
100	FOLS	95630	260-J2
100	FOLS	95630	261-A2
JUDAH ST			
100	RSVL	95678	239-H2
3000	SAC	95815	278-B5
JUDETTE AV			
8100	SaCo	95828	338-D2
JUDISTINE DR			
6700	SaCo	95628	259-F5
JUDY CT			
4700	SaCo	95841	259-A7
JUDY DR			
100	EDCo	95667	245-D3
JUGLANS DR			
8300	SaCo	95662	260-C2
JULEP WY			
7300	SaCo	95628	279-G1
JULI CT			
8100	CITH	95610	260-B2
JULIA CT			
7900	CITH	95621	239-G7
JULIAN DR			
700	WSAC	95605	296-J2
JULIANA WY			
10200	RCCD	95827	299-E5
JULIE CT			
2600	EDCo	95682	263-C3
JULIE ANN CT			
2700	SaCo	95608	279-B6
JULIE ANN WY			
600	EDCo	95762	262-B5
JULIE LYNN CT			
6800	CITH	95621	239-F5
JULIEN LN			
7500	CITH	95621	259-G1
JULIESSE AV			
1500	SAC	95815	278-A5
2100	SAC	95821	278-C5
2200	SaCo	95821	278-C5
JULIETTA PL			
-	PlaC	95602	160-J2
JULLIARD CIR			
2400	RSVL	95661	240-E2
JULLIARD DR			
3000	SAC	95826	318-E1
JULMAR CT			
-	RSVL	95747	219-D6
JUMEL CT			
-	EDCo	95762	262-F6
JUMILLA WY			
3400	SAC	95834	276-H4
JUMP CT			
4200	SaCo	95826	318-J2
JUMPER CT			
100	FOLS	95630	261-G3
JUNCTION BLVD			
100	RSVL	95678	219-F7
300	RSVL	95747	219-A7
800	RSVL	95747	239-A1
JUNCTION CT			
2300	SaCo	95670	280-B5
JUNE CT			
-	GALT	95632	419-F2
3900	SaCo	95821	278-H3
JUNEAU WY			
6500	SaCo	95660	258-H3
JUNE BUG CT			
8600	ELKG	95624	358-F2
JUNE MOUNTAIN CT			
-	RKLN	95765	220-A2
JUNEVEL CT			
-	SAC	95820	318-A3
JUNEWOOD CT			
9400	PlaC	95658	201-H4
JUNEWOOD LN			
9100	SaCo	95628	260-G7
JUNIPER CT			
4100	EDCo	95667	265-B2
JUNIPER DR			
100	PlaC	95602	162-G3
JUNIPER LN			
2600	SaCo	95825	298-E1
6700	EDCo	95667	265-C2
8400	PlaC	95746	221-F6
JUNIPER CREEK CT			
2100	SaCo	95670	280-C5
JUNIPER HILL PL			
4900	SaCo	95843	239-A6
JUNIPERO ST			
8100	SAC	95828	318-D7
8100	SaCo	95828	318-D7
JUNO RD			
4700	EDCo	95619	265-H5
JUNO WY			
4400	SaCo	95864	298-J1
JUPITER DR			
3300	RCCD	95827	299-D6
JURATA CT			
14700	SaCo	95683	342-C4
JURGENS LN			
8300	CITH	95610	240-A6
JURGENS RD			
500	EDCo	95672	243-E1
JURGENSON WY			
-	ELKG	95757	377-H1
-	ELKG	95757	397-H1
JUSSIA WY			
-	ELKG	95758	357-J3
JUSTAMERE CT			
2400	EDCo	95682	263-E6
JUSTAMERE LN			
9800	ELKG	95624	359-C3
JUSTA SHORT LN			
13700	SaCo	95632	419-B7
JUSTAWEE CT			
8400	ELKG	95624	339-A7
8400	ELKG	95624	359-A1
JUSTICE ST			
4700	SAC	95838	257-G7
JUSTIN CT			
100	GALT	95632	419-D7
300	RSVL	95678	219-G6
JUSTIN WY			
4100	SaCo	95826	319-A2
JUSTINE AV			
4400	EDCo	95619	265-D4
JUSTINE CT			
200	EDCo	95619	265-D4
JUSTINIAN DR			
11700	RCCD	95742	320-D3
JUSTIN WOODS CT			
2700	EDCo	95682	263-B3
JUTEWOOD CT			
3400	SaCo	95827	299-B7
JUTLAND CT			
9700	ELKG	95757	357-H7
K			
K PKWY			
4900	SaCo	95823	337-J2
K ST			
100	LNCN	95648	179-G4
100	SAC	95814	297-B3
200	ANT	94509	(513-C3 See Page 493)
400	SaCo	95673	257-H3
1300	SaCo	95673	258-A3
2000	SAC	95816	297-F4
4900	SAC	95819	297-J6
5300	SAC	95819	298-A6
KACHINA WY			
2900	RCCD	95670	299-G2
4500	EDCo	95672	243-G7
KADEMA DR			
2500	SaCo	95864	298-E6
2500	SaCo	95864	298-E6
KADLIN DR			
-	SaCo	95829	338-J7
9300	SaCo	95829	339-A7
KADOTA WY			
7300	CITH	95610	259-J1
KAESTNER CT			
6600	CITH	95621	239-F7
KAHALA CT			
5300	SaCo	95628	260-B6
KAHARA CT			
5800	SAC	95822	317-A5
KAHLIA CT			
-	SAC	95831	317-B7
KAHN ST			
5000	SaCo	95608	259-F7
KAHUNA CT			
7800	SaCo	95828	338-E4
KAILA WY			
2000	EDCo	95762	242-D5
KAISER CT			
-	SaCo	95608	279-A5
KAISER WY			
3100	SaCo	95608	279-A5
KALAMATA WY			
-	RCCD	95742	300-D7
KALAMAZOO DR			
7400	CITH	95610	259-H6
KALAMAZOO ST			
-	SaCo	95742	280-H6
KALAMER WY			
-	SAC	95835	256-J4
KALE CT			
1400	OAKL	94561	(514-D7 See Page 493)
KALEY LN			
600	SaCo	95673	257-E3
KALI PL			
-	RKLN	95765	200-B4
KALISPELL WY			
-	SAC	95835	256-J4
-	SAC	95835	257-A4
KALLIE KAY LN			
7200	SaCo	95828	338-B4
KALMIA CT			
-	SAC	95835	257-A4
KALO CT			
8800	SaCo	95628	280-F2
KALWANI CIR			
7700	SaCo	95828	338-D4
KAM CT			
-	SAC	95838	257-G6
KAMAL CT			
-	SAC	95758	357-J2
KAMARI ST			
9600	ELKG	95624	358-H6
KAMELIA CT			
8300	ELKG	95624	358-E2
KAMET CT			
6200	SaCo	95842	259-B4
KAMLOOPS DR			
7000	EDCo	95726	248-C7
KAMMERER RD			
7300	SaCo	95757	378-C4
7300	ELKG	95757	378-C4
KAMSON CT			
-	SAC	95833	277-C5
KANAI AV			
7400	CITH	95610	259-G1
7400	CITH	95621	259-G1
KANAKA VALLEY RD			
500	EDCo	95672	243-A2
KANAN CT			
7800	SaCo	95621	239-D7
KANDAHAR			
-	SAC	95831	337-A2
KANDINSKY WY			
-	SAC	95835	256-J4
KANDY ST			
200	GALT	95632	439-D1
KANE AV			
-	SAC	95835	257-C6
KANE CT			
-	RSVL	95747	219-D5
KANELOS LN			
-	SaCo	95828	338-E2
KANGAROO CT			
3900	SaCo	95826	318-H2
5000	EDCo	95623	264-H6
KANIHAN CT			
7700	SaCo	95628	279-J3
KANKAKEE DR			
-	SaCo	95835	256-J5
KANNASTO ST			
4000	RKLN	95677	220-E4
KANOB CT			
4800	SaCo	95842	259-A3
KANSAS ST			
-	SaCo	95742	280-H7
KANSAS WY			
2500	SaCo	95827	299-A5
KANTNER CT			
-	FOLS	95630	281-E2
KANTURK CT			
8700	SaCo	95828	338-F7
KANTURK WY			
1700	FOLS	95630	261-H7
KAPALUA LN			
9700	ELKG	95624	359-C5
KAPLAN WY			
6900	CITH	95621	259-F2
KAPPA CT			
4900	SaCo	95660	258-H7
KARA DR			
7200	SaCo	95828	338-D2
KARAT LN			
1000	FOLS	95630	261-B6
KARAVI DR			
-	EDCo	95762	262-B4
KARBET WY			
4600	SAC	95822	317-A4
KAREN LN			
5700	SaCo	95660	258-G5
KAREN WY			
1700	EDCo	95667	245-J2
KAREN ANNE LN			
-	CITH	95610	259-H3
KAREN RAE CT			
7100	CITH	95610	259-H2
KARI ANN CIR			
7200	SAC	95824	318-B5
KARITSA AV			
2800	SAC	95833	276-J4
KARL CT			
-	EDCo	-	247-H2
-	EDCo	95726	247-H2
KARL DR			
-	FOLS	95630	262-B7
3600	SaCo	95660	258-G5
4100	EDCo	95619	265-G3
KARLA WY			
100	AUB	95603	162-E7
KARLY BROOK WY			
8400	SaCo	95843	238-H5
KARM WY			
5100	SaCo	95842	259-B3
KARNO CT			
-	ELKG	95757	378-A3
KASEBERG CIR			
1200	RSVL	95678	239-F1
KASEBERG CT			
1400	RSVL	95678	239-F1
KASEBERG DR			
-	RSVL	95678	219-F6
KASEY LN			
-	EDCo	-	267-D4
KASHA LN			
6800	EDCo	95633	205-F5
KASHMIR WY			
2100	SAC	95833	277-B5
KASSER RD			
1700	SaCo	95626	238-B4
KASTANIS WY			
-	SAC	95758	338-C7
KATAHDIN DR			
-	RCCD	95742	300-G7
KATE LN			
-	OAKL	94561	(514-C6 See Page 493)
6700	CITH	95621	259-E3
KATE GLEN CT			
8100	SaCo	95843	239-A6
KATELLA WY			
7700	SaCo	95621	239-D7
7700	SaCo	95842	239-D7
KATELYNN CT			
9300	ELKG	95758	358-B5
KATENA LN			
8900	SaCo	95683	(361-C3 See Page 341)
8900	SaCo	95693	(361-B4 See Page 341)
KATERINA LN			
200	FOLS	95630	261-A2
KATHARINE AV			
1400	SAC	95838	278-A2
KATHERINE PL			
2000	RSVL	95678	219-G6
KATHERINE WY			
200	AUB	95603	182-D5
KATHLEEN AV			
1500	SAC	95815	278-B5
KATHRYN CT			
-	PlaC	95603	161-D5
KATHRYN WY			
2000	SaCo	95821	278-C6
KATHY CIR			
2900	WSAC	95691	316-F2
KATHY CT			
-	SAC	95831	316-G6
KATHY LN			
1100	EDCo	95667	245-A2
KATHY WY			
1500	LNCN	95648	179-G3
3100	LMS	95650	200-J4
KATHYWOOD CT			
4700	SaCo	95628	280-B1
KATIE CT			
-	ELKG	95757	378-A3
KATIE LN			
1300	PLCR	95667	245-H4
N KATIE LN			
5800	LMS	95650	200-J6
KATIE WY			
800	EDCo	95762	262-B5
KATO CT			
2800	EDCo	95682	263-C3
KATY WY			
2900	SAC	95826	318-D1
KATZ AV			
1000	SAC	95831	316-J7
KAUAI RD			
-	WSAC	95691	316-D2
KAUAI WY			
5100	SaCo	95628	260-B7
KAUHALE PL			
8600	SaCo	95662	260-D1
KAULA DR			
8100	SaCo	95628	260-B7
KAUSEN DR			
-	ELKG	95758	357-D3
KAVINE WY			
2100	FOLS	95630	262-B7
KAVOORAS DR			
7600	SAC	95831	336-H3
KAWANA CT			
7900	SaCo	95829	339-D5
KAWEAH CT			
2700	EDCo	95682	263-D2
KAWEAH ST			
-	WSAC	95691	316-D3
KAY CT			
-	FOLS	95630	261-E7
KAYLAR DR			
1200	SAC	95822	317-A4
KAYLES LN			
10500	PlaC	95602	161-H2
KAYO DR			
6900	PlaC	95663	201-C1
KAYWOOD CT			
2400	RCCD	95670	280-A7
KEAN AV			
500	ANT	94509	(513-F6 See Page 493)
KEANA CT			
5100	SaCo	95628	260-D7
KEANE DR			
4800	SaCo	95608	299-A3
KEARNEY WY			
3600	SaCo	95608	279-B4
KEARNS CT			
-	FOLS	95630	261-H4
KEARNS RD			
1400	EDCo	95667	265-J4
1500	EDCo	95667	266-A4
KEATING RD			
12200	SaCo	95693	360-F4
KEATON CT			
8000	SaCo	95628	280-A1
KEATS CIR			
6000	SaCo	95662	260-J5
KEAWE LN			
-	ELKG	95624	359-D5
KEEBLE CT			
-	RSVL	95747	239-F3
KEEBLE LN			
-	EDCo	95667	226-F7
KEECH CT			
-	SaCo	95828	338-F6
KEEFE DR			
-	ELKG	95758	357-E5
KEEFER ST			
-	FOLS	95630	261-D7
-	FOLS	95630	281-D1
KEEGAN WY			
8200	ELKG	95624	358-D1
KEEHNER AV			
100	RSVL	95678	239-J3
KEEL CT			
-	SAC	95831	316-H7
KEELING CT			
-	SAC	95823	358-B1
KEELY CT			
-	SAC	95838	277-G1
KEELY DR			
-	RSVL	95678	219-J5
KEEMA AV			
4300	SaCo	95660	258-J3
4600	SaCo	95660	259-A3
4600	SaCo	95842	259-A3
KEENA DR			
300	PlaC	95603	162-F3
KEENAN CT			
8300	SaCo	95828	338-E7
KEENEY WY			
1300	SaCo	95864	298-E2
KEESEE WY			
8000	CITH	95610	240-A6
KEGAN LN			
5100	OAKL	94561	(514-C6 See Page 493)
KEGGIN RD			
7300	PlaC	95746	220-H7
KEGLE DR			
300	WSAC	95605	296-J1
KEITH DR			
900	RSVL	95661	239-J5
KEITH WY			
1700	SAC	95815	278-B7
1700	SAC	95815	298-B1
1900	SAC	95825	278-C7
2000	SaCo	95825	278-C7
KEITH WINNEY CIR			
-	SaCo	95829	338-H5
KELBURNE CT			
-	SAC	95833	277-A6
KELLEN CT			
1500	SaCo	95608	299-A2
KELLER CIR			
100	FOLS	95630	261-G6
KELLER CT			
5700	PlaC	95677	220-F4
KELLERMAN CT			
-	RSVL	95746	240-F3
KELLEY CT			
300	SAC	95838	278-B2
KELLEY PL			
-	EDCo	95633	205-G2
KELLI DR			
2600	EDCo	95667	245-C4
KELLIE LN			
100	PlaC	95603	162-F6
KELLINGWORTH CT			
9500	SaCo	95827	299-B5
S KELLOGG RD			
1800	PlaC	95650	201-F1
1800	PlaC	95658	181-F7
KELLOGG ST			
500	PlaC	95658	181-G7
KELLOGG WY			
1900	RCCD	95670	279-H6
KELLY LN			
1800	PlaC	95658	201-E1
KELLY WY			
-	RVIS	94571	454-H3
800	FOLS	95630	261-B6
5800	SaCo	95824	317-J5
KELLY CREEK LN			
2100	EDCo	95672	243-J6
KELLYGREEN ST			
-	EDCo	95667	226-D7
KELLY ISLAND RD			
-	WSAC	95691	316-E2

STREET Block City ZIP Pg-Grid

KELLY PARK LN
5200 EDCo 95623 265-B7
KELLY RYAN CT
10600 RCCD 95670 279-J7
10600 RCCD 95670 299-J1
KELMAN CT
4300 RCCD 95742 320-E2
KELMSCOTT LN
- RSVL 95678 219-J2
KELSE CT
400 RSVL 95661 240-D4
N KELSEY AV
- EDCo 95634 225-E1
KELSEY DR
8700 ELKG 95624 358-G5
KELSEY LN
5000 OAKL 94561 (514-C6 See Page 493)
KELSEY RD
- EDCo 95634 225-E3
KELSEY CANYON RD
- EDCo 95634 225-D4
- EDCo 95667 225-D4
KELSO CIR
- SAC 95833 277-D4
KELTON WY
4600 SAC 95838 277-G1
4600 SAC 95838 257-G7
KELTY CT
8000 SaCo 95828 338-G6
KELVEDON WY
7700 SaCo 95829 338-J5
KELWOOD CT
8300 SaCo 95829 339-D7
KELWOOD WY
8600 SaCo 95828 338-F1
KEM LN
5700 SaCo 95608 279-C2
KEMBLE ST
- SAC 95818 297-B6
KEMP CT
100 FOLS 95630 261-E7
KEMP WY
6500 SaCo 95660 258-G3
KEMPER RD
10600 PlaC 95603 161-J5
10600 PlaC 95603 162-A5
KEMPER OAKS CT
- PlaC 95603 162-B5
KEMPSEY WY
9200 SaCo 95829 338-J6
KEMPSFORD CT
- RSVL 95747 219-B7
KEMPTON SQ
400 FOLS 95630 261-H6
KENBRIDGE ST
- SAC 95758 358-A2
KENDALE WY
2600 SaCo 95608 279-A6
KENDALL CT
- RKLN 95765 200-A5
100 RSVL 95746 240-F6
KENDALL DR
- RKLN 95765 200-A5
KENDRA CT
5000 SaCo 95628 259-J7
KENDRICK WY
9100 SaCo 95662 260-G6
KENEBEE RIVER CT
11000 RCCD 95670 279-J5
KENELWORTH WY
7800 SAC 95823 337-J5
KENLEY CT
- LNCN 95648 179-E6
KENMAR RD
- SaCo 95834 277-E1
4800 SaCo 95834 257-E7
5100 SAC 95834 257-E7
5100 SAC 95835 257-E6
KENMARE CT
100 RSVL 95747 219-D7
KENMASS AV
100 AUB 95603 182-E2
KENMORE LN
7300 SaCo 95823 338-A2
KENNADY LN
1200 SAC 95822 317-B4
KENNAR WY
100 FOLS 95630 281-B2
KENNEDY CT
4700 RKLN 95677 220-D1
KENNEDY DR
1400 RSVL 95678 219-F6
KENNEDY PL
2500 EDCo 95762 262-D1
N KENNEFICK RD
23300 SJCo 95220 (440-C4 See Page 420)
24400 SJCo 95632 (440-C4 See Page 420)
KENNELFORD CIR
- SAC 95823 338-A6
KENNERLEIGH PKWY
- RSVL 95747 218-J6
KENNERLY WY
100 FOLS 95630 261-F7
KENNETH AV
4100 SaCo 95628 280-D2
4700 SaCo 95608 279-A6
4800 SaCo 95628 260-D6
6200 SaCo 95662 260-D3
7000 CITH 95662 260-D3
KENNETH CT
2700 PLCR 95667 245-H3
KENNETH WY
4400 SaCo 95757 377-G3
4400 SaCo 95757 397-G3
KENNETH CREEK LN
8500 SaCo 95628 260-D7
KENNETH HILL CT
8500 SaCo 95628 260-D5
KENNETH OAK WY
6000 SaCo 95628 260-D5
KENNETH RIDGE CT
8500 SaCo 95628 260-D5
KENNETH VIEW CT
8500 SaCo 95628 260-D5
KENNINGTON DR
4900 SaCo 95841 259-B7
KENORA ST
6600 SaCo 95673 257-G3
KENORA WY
6700 SaCo 95673 257-G2
KENOSHA RD
- SaCo 95742 280-G5
KENROY LN
200 RSVL 95678 239-G4
KENROY WY
4900 SaCo 95628 260-E7

KENROY WY
4900 SaCo 95628 280-E1
KENSALL CT
9400 SaCo 95829 339-A6
KENSBROOK LN
8100 PlaC 95746 241-A2
KENSINGTON CT
- RKLN 95765 200-D3
3400 EDCo 95762 242-C7
KENSINGTON DR
1000 RSVL 95661 240-A5
1000 RSVL 95661 239-J5
3100 EDCo 95762 242-C6
7600 CITH 95610 259-H5
KENSINGTON LN
1100 LNCN 95648 179-G5
KENSLEY CT
5100 PlaC 95746 240-H5
KENSTON WY
4300 SAC 95822 317-A3
KENT DR
2500 SaCo 95821 278-E6
2500 SaCo 95825 278-F6
KENT PL
1600 RSVL 95661 240-B2
KENT ST
100 GALT 95632 [illegible]
1700 RSVL 95661 240-B2
9600 ELKG 95624 358-J6
9700 ELKG 95624 378-J1
KENTFIELD CT
- EDCo 95682 263-E4
KENTFIELD DR
- EDCo 95682 263-E4
3200 SaCo 95821 278-F6
3200 SaCo 95825 278-F6
KENTON CT
2100 OAKL 94561 (514-C6 See Page 493)
KENTON WY
- ELKG 95758 358-A3
KENTS CT
2500 WSAC 95691 296-F7
KENTSHIRE WY
8700 SaCo 95828 338-G6
KENTUCKY LN
4800 SaCo 95628 279-H1
KENTUCKY ST
- SaCo 95742 280-G7
KENTUCKY WY
- RKLN 95765 200-B7
KENTUCKY GREENS WY
1000 PlaC 95658 181-F6
KENTWAL DR
7900 SAC 95823 337-J5
KENTWOOD LN
4300 SaCo 95628 280-E2
KENWOOD CT
- OAKL 94561 (514-D5 See Page 493)
KENWOOD LN
- EDCo 95619 266-E6
KENWOOD ST
1700 SAC 95815 278-B4
KENWOOD WY
3600 PlaC 95747 239-A2
KENWORTH CT
3000 EDCo 95682 244-A6
KENWORTH DR
4700 EDCo 95682 244-A6
KENWORTHY WY
2200 SAC 95832 337-D3
KENYON CT
4200 SaCo 95608 279-G2
KEOKE CT
- SAC 95838 257-G7
KEOKUK DR
3600 EDCo 95667 245-C7
KEONCREST CIR
5500 SaCo 95841 259-C5
KEPLER CT
8800 ELKG 95758 358-A2
KEREKA CT
4000 PLCR 95667 245-G3
KERKYRA CT
4300 RCCD 95742 320-E2
KERMES AV
8500 SaCo 95628 260-D6
KERMIT LN
6800 SaCo 95628 259-F5
6900 CITH 95621 259-F5
6900 CITH 95628 259-F5
KERN ST
3400 SAC 95838 278-B3
KERN RIVER CT
10000 RCCD 95670 279-J6
KERR CT
100 FOLS 95630 261-E4
KERRIA WY
2900 SaCo 95821 278-E4
KERRY CT
- GALT 95632 419-E2
KERRY LN
11600 SaCo 95632 (400-A2 See Page 379)
KERSEY LN
3500 SaCo 95864 298-G1
KERSH CT
9000 ELKG 95624 358-H1
KERSHAW CT
100 FOLS 95630 261-F7
KERSLAKE CIR
- FOLS 95630 281-G2
KERSTEN ST
7200 CITH 95621 259-G2
KERSWELL CT
100 FOLS 95630 261-F6
KERWIN CT
400 RSVL 95747 239-C1
KERWIN WY
100 FOLS 95630 261-E7
KERWOOD WY
4600 SAC 95823 337-H3
KESNER AV
400 SAC 95838 277-H3
KESTRAL WY
- SAC 95833 276-H7
KESTREL CT
- ELKG 95624 358-G2
- LNCN 95648 179-D1
KESTREL COVE CT
2300 ELKG 95757 377-E1
2300 ELKG 95757 397-E1
KESTREL LAKE RD
- SaCo 95758 397-F9
KESTRIL CT
- FOLS 95630 281-F1
KESWICK CT
600 RSVL 95746 240-F4

KESWICK DR
3400 EDCo 95762 262-D2
KESWICK LN
600 LNCN 95648 179-G4
KESWICK WY
3500 SaCo 95826 318-J1
KETCH CT
7500 CITH 95621 259-D1
KETCHAM DR
10000 RCCD 95827 299-D4
KETCHERSIDE LN
11300 SaCo 95693 360-B7
KETCHIKAN DR
- RKLN 95765 200-C5
KETCHUM CT
- PlaC 95746 240-G4
KETTERING CIR
6800 SaCo 95628 279-F1
KETTERING PL
2400 EDCo 95762 242-B5
KETTLEMAN LN Rt#-12
- SaCo 95641 (476-B3 See Page 456)
14900 SJCo 95242 (476-B3 See Page 456)
KETTLE ROCK CT
100 FOLS 95630 241-A7
KEUSMAN ST
8400 SAC 95758 338-C7
8400 SAC 95758 358-C1
KEVIN CT
300 AUB 95603 162-E7
3400 SaCo 95821 278-G4
KEVIN ST
3100 EDCo 95682 263-G7
KEVINBERG DR
5300 SAC 95823 337-J7
KEVINGTON CT
500 SaCo 95864 298-G4
KEVMICH WY
8700 SaCo 95662 260-E5
KEWANEE ST
4400 SaCo 95628 280-D1
KEY CT
- LMS 95650 200-B7
- LMS 95650 201-A4
- RKLN 95765 200-B7
KEY ST
13900 SaCo 95690 417-A7
KEYESPORT WY
8300 CITH 95610 240-C7
KEY LARGO CT
3100 SaCo 95843 238-F5
KEYNTEL ST
5800 CITH 95621 259-G5
KEYSTONE AV
5200 SaCo 95841 259-B7
KEYSTONE CT
4900 RKLN 95677 220-C2
KEY WEST WY
2500 SaCo 95826 298-H6
KEZAR ST
7800 SaCo 95662 240-H7
KIAWAH CT
8300 ELKG 95758 358-E5
KIDDER CT
900 AUB 95603 182-C5
KIDDER WY
- FOLS 95630 261-H4
KIEBER WY
3600 EDCo 95667 245-C7
KIEFER BLVD
8500 SAC 95826 318-F1
8500 SaCo 95826 318-G1
8700 SaCo 95826 318-H1
9200 SaCo 95826 319-A1
9300 SaCo 95827 319-A1
10000 SaCo 95655 319-A1
10100 SaCo 95830 319-A1
11300 RCCD 95742 320-D4
11300 SaCo 95830 320-B4
12300 SaCo 95830 320-H5
12400 SaCo 95683 (321-A7 See Page 301)
12400 SaCo 95683 341-B1
N KIEFER BLVD
- SaCo 95827 319-A1
9400 SaCo 95826 319-A1
KIEKEBUSCH CT
3600 SaCo 95608 279-G4
KIER CT
- LNCN 95648 179-E3
KIERNAN DR
6200 SaCo 95608 279-D5
KIES WY
5900 SaCo 95842 259-A5
KIESSIG AV
3300 SaCo 95823 317-F6
KIFISIA WY
6000 SaCo 95628 260-B5
KIKER LN
1700 PlaC 95658 181-F7
1700 PlaC 95658 201-F1
KILAR CT
9000 ELKG 95624 358-H1
KILARNEY LN
- CITH 95610 259-H1
KILBEGGAN WY
9300 ELKG 95758 358-A5
KILBORN DR
7300 SaCo 95628 259-G7
KILBRIDGE CT
3800 SaCo 95843 238-H6
KILCAIRN CT
100 FOLS 95630 261-F7
KILCAIRN WY
100 FOLS 95630 261-F7
KILCHER CT
4300 SaCo 95608 279-B2
KILCHURN CT
7700 SaCo 95843 259-C1
KILCOLGAN WY
9400 ELKG 95758 358-A5
KILCONNELL DR
6300 ELKG 95758 358-B6
KILDARE CT
4500 SaCo 95821 278-J4
W KILE RD
4500 SJCo 95242 (438-C5 See Page 418)
6800 SJCo 95686 (438-B4 See Page 418)
KILEY LN
- SAC 95823 337-G4
KILGORE RD
2700 RCCD 95670 299-J1
2700 RCCD 95670 300-A2
KILKENNY CT
8700 ELKG 95624 358-G7

KILKENNY DR
7000 SaCo 95842 259-C2
KILLAM CIR
- PlaC 95603 162-F7
KILLAM RD
200 PlaC 95603 162-F7
KILLARNEY CT
1100 RSVL 95747 219-C7
KILLARNEY LN
1700 SaCo 95825 298-D1
KILLARNEY ST
1000 RSVL 95747 219-C7
KILLARNEY WY
12500 AUB 95603 162-D5
12500 PlaC 95603 162-D5
KILLDEE CT
8700 SaCo 95662 260-E2
KILLDEER CT
- LNCN 95648 179-D1
KILLDEER WY
- RSVL 95747 219-B7
7500 ELKG 95758 358-C6
KILLEEN CIR
3400 SaCo 95821 278-D4
KILMARNOOK WY
8300 SaCo 95843 238-J5
KILMARTIN CT
- RKLN 95677 220-G5
KILMER CIR
8200 SaCo 95828 338-D4
KILPATRICK WY
- RSVL 95746 240-F4
KILRENNY CT
- FOLS 95630 261-J3
KILROY CT
4300 RCCD 95742 320-E2
KILRUSH DR
1700 FOLS 95630 281-H1
KILSBY WY
100 FOLS 95630 261-H6
KILSYTH WY
- FOLS 95630 261-H7
KILT CIR
4100 EDCo 95762 242-E7
KILTS CT
7700 SaCo 95843 238-F7
KILWOOD CT
9500 SaCo 95662 260-J5
KIM AV
2400 SAC 95832 337-E3
KIMBALL CT
- ANT 94509 (513-E5 See Page 493)
KIMBERLY CT
1100 RSVL 95661 239-J5
2800 WSAC 95691 296-F7
2800 WSAC 95691 316-F1
KIMBERLY RD
3300 EDCo 95682 263-C6
KIMBERLY WY
3700 SaCo 95608 279-A3
KIMBERLY HILL CT
5800 SaCo 95608 279-C2
KIMBLEWICK WY
7400 SaCo 95842 258-J1
KIMI WY
2300 PLCR 95667 245-G3
KIMMEL DR
7000 SaCo 95660 258-H2
KIMMIE CT
- SAC 95831 316-J7
- SAC 95831 336-J1
KIMS TR
- EDCo 95633 205-A1
KIMS WY
- EDCo 95633 205-A1
KIMSUE CT
5400 SaCo 95608 279-B4
KIMWOOD LN
2200 RCCD 95670 279-J6
KIMWORTH LN
3600 EDCo 95682 263-C6
KINARD WY
- ELKG 95757 377-H2
- ELKG 95757 397-H2
KINBRACE CT
9100 SaCo 95829 338-J6
KINCADE DR
- EDCo 95667 266-G3
KINCAID WY
1900 SaCo 95825 278-F7
1900 SaCo 95825 298-F1
KIND CT
9500 ELKG 95624 358-G6
KINDER LN
8400 ELKG 95624 339-G7
8400 ELKG 95624 359-G1
KINDRED CT
7900 ELKG 95758 358-C4
KINDRED LN
600 RSVL 95678 239-J3
KING
100 RCCD 95827 299-D4
KING RD
100 RSVL 95678 239-J3
4500 LMS 95650 200-G5
5900 LMS 95650 201-A5
6400 PlaC 95650 201-E5
KING WY
- FOLS 95630 261-C7
KING ARTHUR PL
4900 SaCo 95841 259-B7
KINGBIRD CT
- RKLN 95765 219-H2
- SAC 95831 316-G5
KINGBIRD LN
3800 EDCo 95709 246-J2
7100 RSVL 95747 219-A4
KINGBIRD WY
4700 SaCo 95660 258-J3
4700 SaCo 95660 259-A3
4700 SaCo 95842 259-A3
KINGDALE AV
8600 SaCo 95662 260-E4
KING EDWARD CT
- WSAC 95691 316-E2
2500 EDCo 95762 262-C2
KING EDWARD DR
2600 EDCo 95762 262-C2
KING EDWARD RD
- WSAC 95691 316-E2
KING ELDER CT
- RKLN 95765 219-H1
KINGFISHER CIR
- FOLS 95630 261-G4
KINGFISHER LN
2200 LNCN 95648 180-B7
2500 EDCo 95709 246-J1

KINGFISHER WY
10000 RCCD 95670 299-D3
KING GEORGE CT
2700 EDCo 95762 262-C2
KING GEORGE WY
900 EDCo 95762 262-C2
KING HENRY CT
900 EDCo 95762 262-C2
KING HENRY WY
900 EDCo 95762 262-C7
KINGHORN CT
- SAC 95823 337-H5
KINGHURST DR
1300 RSVL 95661 240-A5
KING JAMES WY
900 EDCo 95762 262-C2
KING JOHN WY
900 EDCo 95762 262-C2
KINGLET CT
400 FOLS 95630 261-A1
KINGLET WY
3000 SaCo 95843 238-F7
KINGMAN CT
- SAC 95835 257-C6
KING MARTENS CT
- EDCo 95667 [illegible]
KINGMONT CT
3600 PlaC 95650 201-J6
KINGMONT DR
3400 PlaC 95650 201-H5
KINGMONT WY
- ELKG 95624 358-E3
KING OAK CT
9500 ELKG 95624 358-F6
KING PINE DR
- RKLN 95765 219-J2
KING RANCH PL
- PlaC 95746 220-G6
KING RICHARD CT
900 EDCo 95762 262-C2
KING RICHARD DR
900 EDCo 95762 262-C2
KINGS WY
3700 SaCo 95821 278-G6
KINGSBARNS DR
- PlaC 95747 238-J3
- PlaC 95747 239-A2
KINGS BEACH PL
- SAC 95835 257-A3
KINGSBRIDGE CT
- RSVL 95747 219-C4
KINGSBRIDGE DR
8100 SaCo 95829 339-A6
8200 SaCo 95624 339-A6
KINGSBURY CT
- RSVL 95678 219-G5
5400 SaCo 95662 260-G6
KINGSBURY DR
- EDCo 286-J2
KINGS CANYON DR
- RKLN 95765 219-H2
900 EDCo 95762 282-D1
KINGS CANYON WY
- RSVL 95678 220-A4
KINGSCOTE WY
100 SaCo 95655 319-H2
KINGS COURT LN
5100 SaCo 95628 260-D7
KINGSDALE WY
4800 SAC 95823 337-J5
KINGSFORD DR
1100 SaCo 95608 299-B2
KINGSGATE DR
8500 PlaC 95746 240-H2
KINGSGATE RD
2300 EDCo 95667 246-A2
KINGSLAND CT
8400 ELKG 95624 358-F3
KINGSLEY CT
8200 PlaC 95746 240-G2
KINGSLEY ST
7100 SaCo 95828 338-E1
KINGSLYNN CT
8600 ELKG 95624 358-F3
KINGSMEN AV
7400 CITH 95621 259-G2
KINGSMILL WY
7000 CITH 95610 260-C2
KINGSPOINT CT
11800 RCCD 95742 320-D4
KINGSPORT WY
3600 SaCo 95826 318-J1
KINGS RIVER CT
11100 RCCD 95670 280-A4
KINGSTON CT
400 RSVL 95661 240-E3
KINGSTON WY
5600 SAC 95822 317-A4
KINGSTREE LN
2200 RCCD 95670 279-J6
KINGSWOOD DR
1300 RSVL 95678 219-F6
5400 CITH 95610 259-J6
7800 CITH 95610 260-A6
KINGSWOOD TR
4100 EDCo 95726 248-D3
KINGVALE CT
5400 EDCo 95623 264-G7
KINGVALE RD
4700 EDCo 95623 264-G6
KINGWOOD CIR
5900 RKLN 95677 220-D5
KINKEAD CT
- EDCo 95762 242-B7
KINKEAD PL
- EDCo 95762 242-B7
KINLOCH CT
- RSVL 95678 219-J3
KINNAIRD WY
3100 SAC 95838 277-G5
KINNERLY CT
- LNCN 95648 179-E6
KINNERLY LN
- LNCN 95648 179-E6
KINNEY ST
7000 SaCo 95662 260-J2
KINO ST
2800 SaCo 95821 278-G6
KINROSS RD
5000 SaCo 95608 279-A5
KINROSS WY
- RSVL 95747 218-H4
KINSALE CT
8300 SaCo 95843 238-H5
KINSELLA CT
- RSVL 95747 218-H4
KINSELLA LN
4500 SaCo 95841 258-J7
4600 SaCo 95841 259-A7

KINSELLA WY
- RSVL 95747 218-H4
KINSEY CT
4700 SaCo 95842 259-A1
KINSINGTON ST
2100 WSAC 95691 296-H7
KINTYRE PEN PL
- SaCo 95843 239-C5
KIOWA CT
8700 SaCo 95662 260-E1
KIOWA WY
2200 EDCo 95682 263-H6
KIPLING CT
- RSVL 95747 219-E6
KIPLING DR
4800 SaCo 95608 299-B3
KIPP WY
5100 SaCo 95608 259-E7
KIPPERKOPPER LN
12400 SaCo 95693 (380-G1 See Page 379)
KIPPING WY
6500 SAC 95820 318-B2
KIPPS LN
300 EDCo 95762 262-A1
KIRBY CT
1000 FOLS 95630 281-E2
KIRCHOFF LN
- GALT 95632 419-F4
KIRK CT
7800 PlaC 95746 241-D2
KIRK WY
1800 SAC 95822 337-C3
KIRKBY WY
4200 SaCo 95660 258-J4
KIRKCADY DR
9400 ELKG 95758 358-B6
KIRKCALDY WY
8200 SaCo 95843 239-A6
KIRKLAND CT
- LNCN 95648 179-E6
KIRKLAND LN
- LNCN 95648 179-E6
KIRKLAND WY
5300 SaCo 95608 279-B4
KIRKLEIGH WY
- ELKG 95624 359-A6
KIRKTON CT
8000 SaCo 95828 338-G6
KIRKWALL CT
8100 SaCo 95829 338-J6
KIRKWOOD CT
- EDCo 95762 263-A4
- LNCN 95648 180-A7
KIRKWOOD DR
- EDCo 95762 263-A4
200 RSVL 95678 219-F6
KIRKWOOD ST
11700 SaCo 95638 (401-E3 See Page 381)
KIRSTEN CT
9000 SaCo 95662 260-F4
KISKA CT
7000 EDCo 95630 222-G2
KISMET LN
3700 EDCo 95667 245-B6
KISSELA CT
- EDCo 95762 262-E3
KIT CT
- SAC 95838 278-B2
KIT LN
- SAC 95838 278-B2
KIT RD
- SAC 95838 278-B2
KIT WY
4700 SAC 95838 257-G7
KITAJ CT
- SAC 95835 256-J3
KIT CARSON ST
2500 SAC 95818 297-B6
KIT CARSON WY
1600 RSVL 95661 240-B3
KITCHNER RD
1400 SAC 95822 317-B5
KITE HAWK PL
- PlaC 95663 181-B7
KITS CT
5200 EDCo 95623 264-G7
KITTERY AV
6700 CITH 95621 259-F2
KITTIWAKE CT
- SAC 95833 276-H7
KITTIWAKE DR
- SAC 95833 276-H7
KITTY LN
4200 SaCo 95841 278-J2
KITTY HAWK ST
4800 SaCo 95628 280-F1
4900 SaCo 95628 260-F7
KITTYWAKE LN
2500 EDCo 95709 246-J1
KIVA DR
5500 SaCo 95608 279-C1
KIWI CIR
8600 ELKG 95624 358-F5
KIWI CT
- LNCN 95648 200-A3
5300 EDCo 95667 265-B1
KIWI LN
- LNCN 95648 200-A3
- SaCo 95693 360-H7
- SaCo 95693 (380-H1 See Page 379)
KLAGGE CT
- ELKG 95758 357-D4
KLAMATH CT
- EDCo 95682 263-C3
- RKLN 95765 200-C5
KLAMATH DR
- RKLN 95765 200-C5
5300 SaCo 95842 259-B3
KLAMATH RD
- WSAC 95691 316-H1
KLAMATH RIVER CT
- RCCD 95670 279-J5
KLAMATH RIVER DR
1400 RCCD 95670 280-A4
1400 RCCD 95670 279-J5
KLEE CT
- EDCo 95672 262-G3
- EDCo 95762 262-G3
KLEIN WY
700 SAC 95831 336-H2
KLENGEL ST
1100 ANT 94509 (513-C4 See Page 493)
KLEVNER WY
3400 RCCD 95670 299-J4

KLIEVER WY
9200 ELKG 95624 358-J6
KLIMECKI CT
6600 CITH 95610 259-J3
KLINGON CT
6800 SaCo 95823 317-J7
6800 SaCo 95823 337-J1
KLONDIKE CT
- SAC 95835 257-C7
KLONDIKE WY
5000 EDCo 95762 263-B5
KNABE CT
2600 SaCo 95608 279-B6
KNAKAKEE DR
- SAC 95835 256-J5
KNAPP CT
- EDCo 95762 262-D5
KNAPP LN
4700 SaCo 95608 279-A7
KNAPTON WY
- RSVL 95747 218-J4
KNAPWOOD CT
5700 SaCo 95843 239-C6
KNARLWOOD RD
4700 OAKL 94561 (514-B6 See Page 493)
KNEELAND CT
9100 ELKG 95624 358-J5
KNEPPLE CT
10200 ELKG 95757 377-H2
10200 ELKG 95757 397-H2
KNICKERS CT
9600 SaCo 95827 299-B7
KNIGHT
- RCCD 95827 299-E4
KNIGHT CT
- RCCD 95827 299-E4
KNIGHT LN
700 EDCo 95762 262-C5
KNIGHT WY
2200 SAC 95822 317-D4
KNIGHTLINGER ST
3600 SAC 95838 277-H3
KNIGHTS CT
3200 EDCo 95762 262-C5
KNIGHTS LN
9100 SaCo 95693 360-J5
9100 SaCo 95693 (361-A5 See Page 341)
KNIGHTS WY
- RKLN 95765 200-C6
KNIGHTSBRIDGE LN
500 SaCo 95864 298-E4
KNIGHTSWOOD WY
- RSVL 95746 240-G5
KNIGHTVIEW CT
9700 SaCo 95829 339-C7
KNIGHTWOOD WY
2400 RCCD 95670 279-H7
KNISLEY CT
7400 CITH 95621 259-G1
KNOBCONE LN
- EDCo 267-A2
- EDCo 95667 267-A2
KNOB FORK CT
100 FOLS 95630 241-A7
KNOB HILL CT
- RKLN 95765 220-B1
KNOLL CT
- RKLN 95765 200-C5
E KNOLL DR
5400 SaCo 95628 260-B6
KNOLL ST
100 AUB 95603 182-E3
2400 SAC 95815 278-A7
KNOLLCREST CT
6200 SaCo 95608 259-D7
KNOLLCREST DR
1400 RSVL 95661 240-C5
KNOLLRIDGE CT
3200 EDCo 95762 262-C5
KNOLLRIDGE DR
3200 EDCo 95762 262-B5
KNOLL TOP CT
4000 SaCo 95608 279-B3
KNOLLWOOD CT
2500 EDCo 95682 263-C7
3900 SaCo 95821 278-H5
KNOLLWOOD DR
400 AUB 95603 182-C4
2200 EDCo 95682 263-B6
KNOPFLER CIR
1100 FOLS 95630 281-F1
KNOTTY PINE WY
5300 SAC 95835 256-J5
KNOWLTON CT
- RSVL 95747 239-C1
KNOX RD
6900 SaCo 95829 339-E1
KNOXVILLE AV
- SaCo 95742 280-H7
KNUDSEN WY
7400 CITH 95621 259-F1
KOA LN
- ELKG 95624 359-D5
KOA WY
3500 PlaC 95602 162-B3
KOALA CT
2000 EDCo 95667 245-B6
7300 SaCo 95660 258-H1
KOALA LN
3300 EDCo 95667 245-B6
KOBERLEIN RD
4700 RKLN 95677 220-E2
KOBIAS CT
3600 RCCD 95827 299-C7
KOBROCK WY
3100 SaCo 95608 279-B5
KODIAK CT
- RSVL 95747 219-D3
KODIAK WY
- RSVL 95747 219-C3
3600 SaCo 95843 238-G7
KODIAK ISLAND PL
- WSAC 95691 316-D2
KOHLER RD
5400 SaCo 95841 259-B6
KOHLER GARDEN LN
5400 SaCo 95841 259-B6
KOHLI CT
- EDCo 95762 282-D3
KOKANEE LN
6000 EDCo 95726 248-B6
KOKANEE WY
2500 SaCo 95826 298-G6
KOKI LN
6400 EDCo 95623 265-B4
KOKILA CT
4000 RKLN 95677 220-E4

STREET Block City ZIP Pg-Grid

KOKOMO DR
4800 SAC 95835 256-J6
KOLBUS CT
8300 SaCo 95843 238-G6
KONA CT
- EDCo 95667 226-A7
KONA DR
- EDCo 95667 226-A7
KONA WY
8800 SaCo 95662 260-E5
KONKLE CT
- RSVL 95747 219-C4
KON TIKI DR
6900 SaCo 95662 260-E2
KONVALIN OAKS LN
2400 SaCo 95608 279-B7
N KOONTZ RD
25000 SJCo 95686 437-J3
25000 SJCo 95686 (438-A4 See Page 418)
KORALLA CT
800 GALT 95632 419-F3
KORBEL CT
- OAKL 94561 (514-D5 See Page 493)
KORBEL WY
7900 SaCo 95829 338-H5
KORDES WY
3300 SaCo 95826 298-J7
3300 SaCo 95826 318-J1
KORI CT
4200 EDCo 95682 263-J7
KORN RD
7800 SaCo 95758 [illegible]
KOROPP CT
7100 SaCo 95842 259-A2
KOROVO CT
3200 SaCo 95826 299-A7
KOST RD
8900 SaCo 95632 (438-G1 See Page 418)
9100 SaCo 95632 439-C1
10000 GALT 95632 439-E2
KOSTER WY
6600 ELKG 95758 358-B5
KOTO DR
8700 ELKG 95624 358-E2
KOTO RD
4600 EDCo 95682 264-D2
KOUROS WY
11700 RCCD 95742 320-D2
KOVANDA AV
5100 SaCo 95608 279-B6
KOVR DR
2700 WSAC 95605 296-G2
KOYA LN
4100 SaCo 95628 279-J3
KOYAMA CT
7700 SaCo 95829 339-E5
KRAG LN
2200 PlaC 95603 161-E7
KRAMER CT
500 RSVL 95661 240-E4
KRAMERIA AV
- SAC 95835 257-A4
KRANHOLD WY
3600 RCCD 95827 299-C7
KRANS CT
8500 SaCo 95843 238-F5
KRETH RD
7400 SaCo 95628 279-H1
KRIS WY
1100 RSVL 95661 239-J5
KRISEE CT
6000 SaCo 95621 239-D7
KRISHNA DR
6400 SAC 95828 318-B6
KRISTA CT
5000 ELKG 95758 357-H4
KRISTA LN
12300 PlaC 95603 162-C4
KRISTEN CT
6600 CITH 95621 259-F4
KRISTINA CT
9100 SaCo 95829 338-J7
KRISTIN LEE CT
- EDCo - 267-H4
KRISTIN LEE WY
- EDCo - 267-H3
KRISTOU CT
300 RSVL 95661 240-E1
KROEGER CT
8400 SaCo 95628 260-C7
KROGH CT
8500 SaCo 95662 260-D2
KROY WY
2700 SAC 95817 318-A1
2700 SAC 95820 318-A2
KRPAN CT
100 RSVL 95747 219-D5
KRPAN DR
1700 RSVL 95747 219-D5
KRUEGER DR
800 PlaC 95603 162-G4
KRUITHOF WY
8900 SaCo 95628 280-F1
KRUK TR
- EDCo 95667 266-J5
- EDCo 95667 267-A4
KUBEL CIR
1700 SaCo 95825 298-E1
KUDU RUN WY
5100 SaCo 95843 239-B7
KUHN RANCH WY
10100 ELKG 95757 378-B2
KUMBYA RD
6400 EDCo 95667 245-A3
KUNGSTING WY
5200 ELKG 95757 377-J3
5200 ELKG 95757 397-J3
KUNZITE CT
9600 ELKG 95624 359-B7
KURTS CT
8700 SaCo 95662 260-E3
KURZ CIR
4900 SaCo 95608 279-A5
KUVASZ CT
5900 SaCo 95621 239-D7
KWAJALEIN ST
- SAC 95828 318-E6
KYBURZ CT
- SAC 95823 337-J6
KYLA CT
200 RSVL 95747 219-C7
KYLAGLEN CT
- SAC 95823 357-J1
KYLE CT
- CITH 95610 260-A1
KYLEE CT
3000 EDCo 95667 243-H3
3000 EDCo 95672 243-H3
KYLENCH CT
5900 SaCo 95621 239-D7
KYLE R CT
- RKLN 95765 200-A6
KYMATA CT
- EDCo 95762 262-B3
KYMPER CT
- SAC 95823 337-G2

L

L PKWY
4800 SAC 95823 337-J3
L ST
100 SAC 95814 297-B3
100 LNCN 95648 179-G3
100 ANT 94509 (513-C3 See Page 493)
400 SaCo 95673 257-H3
1100 CCCo 94509 (513-C4 See Page 493)
1400 SaCo 95673 258-A3
2000 SAC 95816 297-E4
4900 SAC 95819 297-J6
LA ALEGRIA DR
10100 RCCD 95670 299-D3
LA ALMENDRA WY
6300 SAC 95823 338-A6
8100 SAC 95823 337-H6
LA BANDERA WY
7700 SaCo 95828 338-C4
LA BELLA CIR
7500 SaCo 95660 258-H1
LA BONITA CT
4900 RKLN 95677 220-G5
LA BOUNTY CT
8400 CITH 95610 240-C7
LABRADOR CT
800 GALT 95632 419-D7
LABRANZA ST
7400 SaCo 95683 342-C3
LA BREA WY
200 OAKL 94561 (514-E7 See Page 493)
3500 SaCo 95864 298-G4
LA CADENA WY
3300 SAC 95835 256-H3
LACAM CIR
- SAC 95820 318-C3
LA CAMPANA WY
5600 SAC 95822 317-C5
LA CANADA CT
2600 EDCo 95682 263-D2
4000 SaCo 95628 280-A3
LA CANADA DR
3200 EDCo 95682 263-C2
LA CARNACION WY
- SaCo 95828 338-G5
LA CASA CT
4500 OAKL 94561 (514-C7 See Page 493)
LA CASA DR
4600 EDCo 95682 283-J5
4600 OAKL 94561 (514-C7 See Page 493)
LA CASA WY
5600 SAC 95835 256-H4
LA CASTANA WY
5900 SAC 95823 338-A6
LACEY AL
- PLCR 95667 245-F6
LACEY RD
11400 SaCo 95632 (400-C2 See Page 379)
LA CHOVA CT
2700 RCCD 95670 299-E3
LA CIENEGA CT
2700 EDCo 95682 263-D2
LA CIENEGA DR
6200 SaCo 95660 258-H3
LA CIENEGA WY
3400 EDCo 95682 263-D2
LA CIMA CT
7000 CITH 95621 259-G3
LACKLAND WY
- SAC 95835 257-B4
LA CLAIR RD
9600 SaCo 95693 360-E7
9600 SaCo 95693 (380-E1 See Page 379)
LA COLINA WY
2800 SaCo 95608 279-B6
LACONIA CT
1800 RSVL 95661 240-C5
LA CONTENTA WY
700 SAC 95831 336-H1
LA CONTERA CT
- SAC 95834 277-C4
LA CORUNA DR
4400 SAC 95823 337-H5
LA COSTA LN
7000 CITH 95621 259-G3
LACOTA CT
- SAC 95823 337-G2
LA CRENA CT
- LNCN 95648 179-E5
LA CRESCENTA DR
2500 EDCo 95672 263-D2
2600 EDCo 95682 263-D2
LA CRESTA CT
- SAC 95828 318-B7
LA CROIX DR
2500 RSVL 95661 240-E2
LA CROSSE WY
8700 SAC 95823 358-B2
LA CUESTA CT
200 RSVL 95747 219-C5
LA CUESTA LN
7000 CITH 95621 259-G3
LA CUEVA WY
1300 SAC 95831 337-B4
LA CUMBRA CIR
2500 RCCD 95670 299-E2
LACY LN
2800 SaCo 95821 278-E5
LADD CT
8000 SaCo 95843 238-G6
LADD LN
12400 PlaC 95603 162-C4
LADEFONOS CT
5100 SaCo 95842 259-B2
LADERA DR
1900 LNCN 95648 200-C1
1900 LNCN 95648 180-D7
LADERA LN
2500 EDCo 95667 245-J3
LADERA WY
4600 SaCo 95608 279-G2
LADERO WY
- EDCo 95762 262-D5
LA DESA WY
3000 PlaC 95658 201-G3
LA DIANA CT
9300 ELKG 95624 358-H6
LADIES VALLEY RD
- EDCo 95619 286-D2
LADINO RD
1700 SaCo 95864 298-H2
LADY BIRD CT
- ELKG 95757 358-A6
LADYBUG LN
1800 EDCo 95667 245-B1
LADY DI WY
5000 ELKG 95758 357-H5
LADY EMMA CT
2100 SaCo 95670 280-D5
LADYHAWK CT
- SAC 95835 256-G7
LADY JANE WY
8600 SaCo 95662 260-D4
LADY MARCI CT
3100 EDCo 95762 262-B1
LADY SLIPPER PL
- ELKG 95624 359-B6
LAEHR DR
1700 LNCN 95648 179-F3
LA ESPOSA CT
2400 RCCD 95670 299-E2
LAFAYETTE DR
200 RSVL 95678 219-F6
2700 SaCo 95821 278-D5
4300 EDCo 95762 262-E5
LA FIELD DR
5600 SaCo 95628 259-F6
LA FIESTA WY
7700 SaCo 95828 338-C4
LAFITE CT
- EDCo 95762 262-B2
LAFITTE CT
8500 SaCo 95628 260-D7
LA FLEUR WY
1000 SAC 95831 337-A2
LA FRANCE DR
2500 SaCo 95608 279-A6
LA FRESA CT
- SAC 95823 337-G2
LA GAMA CT
- SAC 95835 256-H3
LA GLORIA WY
10100 RCCD 95670 299-D3
LAGO CIR
6400 SaCo 95683 322-C7
LAGO DR
14800 SaCo 95683 342-A1
LAGO DEL REY CT
- EDCo 95762 242-B4
LAGO DI COMA WY
4700 SaCo 95628 280-A1
LA GOLETA WY
700 SaCo 95864 298-G4
LAGOMARSINO WY
100 SAC 95819 298-A5
LAGOON CT
5400 RKLN 95677 220-G4
LAGOON LN
2400 WSAC 95691 316-G1
LAGO VISTA DR
3100 EDCo 95762 262-C7
LA GRAMA DR
2200 RCCD 95670 299-E2
LA GRANDE BLVD
3400 SaCo 95823 317-F7
LAGRANGE CT
9100 ELKG 95624 358-J4
LAGUNA BLVD
- ELKG 95624 358-E4
2500 ELKG 95758 357-E3
5600 ELKG 95758 358-E4
LAGUNA CT
6200 PlaC 95746 221-F5
E LAGUNA CT
- ELKG 95758 357-F4
W LAGUNA CT
- ELKG 95758 357-E4
N LAGUNA DR
4800 SAC 95823 337-J6
LAGUNA LN
- EDCo 95762 282-C2
LAGUNA RD
12300 SaCo 95632 (400-F5 See Page 379)
12300 SaCo 95638 (400-H5 See Page 379)
LAGUNA WY
3700 SaCo 95864 298-G2
E LAGUNA WY
9100 ELKG 95758 357-F4
W LAGUNA WY
- ELKG 95758 357-E4
LAGUNA BEACH WY
- SaCo 95843 239-A7
- SaCo 95843 259-A1
LAGUNA BLUFFS CT
8600 SAC 95758 358-A2
LAGUNA BREEZE WY
5800 ELKG 95758 357-J4
5800 ELKG 95758 358-A4
LAGUNA BROOK WY
- ELKG 95758 358-D3
LAGUNA CEDAR CT
6100 ELKG 95758 358-A4
LAGUNA CENTER CIR
9100 ELKG 95758 357-J4
LAGUNA CREEK DR
9400 ELKG 95624 358-H5
LAGUNA CREST WY
5200 ELKG 95758 357-H4
LAGUNA GLEN DR
- ELKG 95758 357-J4
LAGUNA GREEN CT
9200 ELKG 95758 358-B5
LAGUNA GROVE CT
8400 ELKG 95757 358-E7
LAGUNA GROVE DR
8500 ELKG 95757 358-E7
LAGUNA KNOLL CT
5800 ELKG 95758 358-A4
LAGUNA LAKE WY
7000 ELKG 95758 358-A5
9000 ELKG 95758 357-J5
LAGUNA MAIN ST
- ELKG 95758 357-F4
LAGUNA MANOR DR
- ELKG 95758 357-J4
LAGUNA MIRAGE LN
- ELKG 95758 358-A4
LAGUNA OAKS DR
5400 ELKG 95758 357-J4
LAGUNA PALMS WY
8300 ELKG 95758 358-E5
LAGUNA PARK DR
4800 ELKG 95758 357-H3
6000 ELKG 95758 358-B4
LAGUNA PLACE WY
8900 ELKG 95758 358-A4
LAGUNA POINTE WY
9400 ELKG 95758 357-H4
LAGUNA QUAIL WY
5600 ELKG 95758 357-J4
LAGUNA RANCH CIR
5900 SAC 95823 338-A7
5900 SAC 95823 358-A1
LAGUNA SECA CT
- SAC 95831 336-H1
LAGUNA SHORE WY
5800 ELKG 95758 357-J4
5800 ELKG 95758 358-A4
LAGUNA SPRINGS DR
9300 ELKG 95758 358-D4
LAGUNA SPRINGS WY
8900 ELKG 95758 357-J4
8900 ELKG 95758 358-A4
LAGUNA STAR DR
- SAC 95758 358-A2
6200 ELKG 95758 358-A2
LAGUNA STATION RD
- SaCo 95758 337-F7
8500 SaCo 95758 357-G1
LAGUNA TRAIL WY
5800 ELKG 95758 357-J4
5800 ELKG 95758 358-A4
LAGUNA VALE WY
5800 ELKG 95758 357-J5
5800 ELKG 95758 358-A5
LAGUNA VALLEY WY
5800 ELKG 95758 357-J4
5800 ELKG 95758 358-A4
LAGUNA VEGA DR
7700 SAC 95758 358-C2
LAGUNA VILLA WY
5800 ELKG 95758 357-J4
6100 ELKG 95758 358-A4
LAGUNA VISTA CT
8900 ELKG 95624 358-H5
LAGUNA WEST WY
4500 ELKG 95758 357-H4
LAGUNA WIND DR
6200 ELKG 95758 358-A4
LAGUNA WOODS DR
4900 ELKG 95758 357-H5
LAGUNITA CT
4100 SaCo 95864 298-H4
LA HABRA WY
3500 SaCo 95864 298-G3
LA HAYA DR
8900 ELKG 95624 358-G5
LAHINA CT
4800 SaCo 95628 280-D1
LAHOMA CT
5400 SaCo 95841 259-C6
LA HONDA WY
3900 SaCo 95608 279-G3
LAHONTAN CT
7800 SaCo 95829 339-D5
LAIRD CT
7200 SAC 95822 337-B1
LAIRD RD
4100 LMS 95650 201-B7
4100 LMS 95650 221-B1
4700 PlaC 95650 221-C5
5900 PlaC 95746 221-C5
LAIRD ST
3500 LMS 95650 201-A6
3600 LMS 95650 200-J6
LAIRD HILL DR
5000 PlaC 95650 221-C3
LA JACQUE CT
- SAC 95823 337-J6
LA JOLLA CT
1000 RSVL 95661 239-J5
LA JOLLA ST
- WSAC 95691 296-J7
LA JOLLA WY
1100 SAC 95822 317-B2
LA JUNTA DR
6600 SaCo 95662 260-D3
LAKE BLVD
- SAC 95831 336-J4
N LAKE CIR
- ANT 94509 (513-F4 See Page 493)
8000 PlaC 95746 221-E6
S LAKE CIR
7900 PlaC 95746 221-E6
LAKE CT
8900 PlaC 95746 241-D3
E LAKE CT
- ANT 94509 (513-F5 See Page 493)
S LAKE CT
- ANT 94509 (513-F5 See Page 493)
W LAKE CT
- ANT 94509 (513-E5 See Page 493)
LAKE DR
4700 SaCo 95608 279-A5
6200 PlaC 95658 201-G1
6400 PlaC 95658 181-G7
E LAKE DR
- ANT 94509 (513-F5 See Page 493)
3600 ELKG 95758 357-F4
N LAKE DR
- ANT 94509 (513-F4 See Page 493)
S LAKE DR
- ANT 94509 (513-F5 See Page 493)
W LAKE DR
- ELKG 95758 357-E4
- ANT 94509 (513-E5 See Page 493)
LAKE LN
12500 SaCo 95693 360-H1
E LAKE PL
- ANT 94509 (513-F5 See Page 493)
S LAKE PL
- ANT 94509 (513-F5 See Page 493)
W LAKE PL
100 ANT 94509 (513-E5 See Page 493)
LAKE RD
3900 WSAC 95691 296-C4
LAKE ARTHUR RD
14600 PlaC 95602 162-J1
LAKEBREEZE DR
- RKLN 95677 200-F7
- RKLN 95677 220-F1
LAKE CANYON AV
800 GALT 95632 419-E2
LAKE CLEMENTINE RD
- PlaC 95603 162-J5
LAKE COVE LN
6800 CITH 95621 259-D3
LAKE CREST CT
100 LNCN 95648 179-J6
LAKECREST DR
700 EDCo 95762 242-B5
LAKE CREST LN
900 LNCN 95648 179-J6
LAKE CREST WY
- SAC 95822 317-A5
LAKE ELSINORE CT
8900 ELKG 95624 378-H2
LAKE FAIR CT
5200 SaCo 95662 260-H7
LAKEFIELD CT
- LNCN 95648 179-H5
LAKE FOREST CIR
- EDCo 95762 242-C7
LAKE FOREST DR
8100 SAC 95826 318-D1
8300 SAC 95826 298-E7
9200 PlaC 95650 221-H1
LAKE FOREST ST
5000 PlaC 95650 221-H3
LAKE FOREST WY
100 FOLS 95630 281-A1
LAKE FRONT DR
600 SAC 95831 336-H3
8600 PlaC 95746 241-C3
LAKE GLEN WY
1000 SAC 95822 316-J5
1000 SAC 95822 317-A5
LAKE GROVE CT
8900 ELKG 95624 378-G2
LAKE HARBOR CT
- SAC 95831 336-J3
LAKEHAVEN CT
8400 SaCo 95628 280-C1
LAKEHILL CT
7500 SaCo 95624 340-E4
LAKEHILLS CT
1100 EDCo 95762 242-D5
LAKEHILLS DR
1300 EDCo 95762 242-C3
LAKEHURST CT
7500 CITH 95621 259-F1
LAKEKNOLL CT
3800 PlaC 95650 201-J7
LAKE KNOLL LN
5200 SaCo 95628 259-J7
LAKE KNOLL RD
5200 SaCo 95628 259-J7
LAKELAND DR
8000 PlaC 95746 241-D2
LAKELAND WY
- ELKG 95758 357-F6
LAKEMONT DR
9000 ELKG 95624 358-J1
9100 ELKG 95624 338-J7
LAKE NATOMA DR
9400 SaCo 95662 260-H5
LAKE NIMBUS DR
8700 SaCo 95628 280-E2
LAKE OAK CT
800 SaCo 95864 298-J4
LAKE PARK AV
900 GALT 95632 419-F2
LAKE PARK DR
6200 SAC 95831 316-J6
6200 SAC 95831 317-A6
LAKE PARK LN
- ELKG 95758 357-G7
LAKE PLACID CT
4100 SaCo 95843 238-H5
LAKE PLEASANT DR
5200 ELKG 95758 357-J2
LAKEPOINT DR
- ELKG 95758 357-F6
LAKEPORT CIR
7800 SaCo 95626 238-D6
LAKERIDGE CIR
7600 SaCo 95624 340-D4
LAKERIDGE CT
400 EDCo 95762 262-A1
LAKE RIDGE DR
4300 EDCo 95726 248-E4
LAKERIDGE DR
- AUB 95603 182-A7
LAKERIDGE OAKS DR
2500 EDCo 95762 262-A1
LAKES END DR
5400 RKLN 95677 220-E4
N LAKESHORE BLVD
3500 PlaC 95650 201-J6
LAKESHORE CIR
- SAC 95831 316-H6
LAKESHORE CT
4500 EDCo 95682 264-C7
LAKESHORE DR
7500 PlaC 95746 241-D3
LAKESIDE CIR
- SaCo 95624 340-D3
LAKESIDE CT
3900 PlaC 95650 201-J7
LAKESIDE DR
- EDCo 95667 266-C4
LNCN 95648 159-D7
- PlaC 95648 159-D7
1900 LNCN 95648 179-D1
4100 RKLN 95677 220-E4
LAKESIDE WY
400 FOLS 95630 261-B1
400 FOLS 95630 241-B7
4700 SaCo 95628 280-C1
LAKESPRING CT
- OAKL 94561 (514-E6 See Page 493)
LAKESPRING DR
5300 OAKL 94561 (514-E6 See Page 493)
LAKESPRING PL
300 OAKL 94561 (514-E6 See Page 493)
LAKESPRING WY
8100 SaCo 95828 338-F6
LAKE TAHOE CT
- RKLN 95677 200-E5
- RKLN 95765 200-E5
LAKE TERRACE DR
3700 ELKG 95758 357-F5
LAKETRAIL CT
7000 PlaC 95746 241-C4
LAKE TREE LN
6900 CITH 95621 259-E2
LAKE VIEW DR
1500 PlaC 95658 181-G7
6500 PlaC 95746 241-B6
LAKEVIEW DR
3700 EDCo 95682 283-J1
3800 EDCo 95667 243-J1
3800 EDCo 95667 244-A1
6700 SaCo 95608 279-F2
LAKEVIEW LN
- SaCo 95693 360-H1
LAKE VISTA CT
- SAC 95831 316-H6
3900 PlaC 95650 201-J7
LAKE VISTA LN
1500 EDCo 95762 242-F5
LAKE WASHINGTON BLVD
- WSAC 95691 316-J1
WSAC 95691 317-A1
2200 WSAC 95691 296-G7
LAKE WILHAGGIN DR
600 SaCo 95864 298-H4
LAKE WILLOW WY
8200 ELKG 95758 358-D3
LAKEWIND LN
9400 ELKG 95758 357-G6
LAKEWOOD CT
7000 EDCo 95726 248-D4
LAKEWOOD DR
1400 WSAC 95691 296-H5
6900 EDCo 95726 248-D4
LAKEWOOD RD
7600 SaCo 95828 338-G4
LAKEWOOD ST
4200 RKLN 95677 220-F4
LAKEWOOD WY
6700 SaCo 95662 260-B3
LAKEWOOD HILLS LN
- PlaC - 160-C3
LAKEWOOD PARK DR
7600 SaCo 95828 338-F4
LA LADERA CT
3300 EDCo 95682 263-H4
LA LEITA CIR
700 SaCo 95864 298-H4
LA LIMA WY
2300 SAC 95833 276-J7
LA LOMA CT
- RSVL 95678 219-J2
LA LOMA DR
2300 RCCD 95670 299-E2
2800 RCCD 95827 299-E3
W LA LOMA DR
2000 RCCD 95670 299-D2
2000 RCCD 95827 299-D3
L ALOUTTE WY
1000 SAC 95831 337-A2
LA LUNA CT
7200 CITH 95621 259-G5
LAMADA CT
3100 SaCo 95608 279-B5
LA MADERA WY
3000 SaCo 95843 238-F5
LA MAISON CIR
9000 SaCo 95829 338-H5
LA MANCHA WY
7400 SaCo 95823 337-J2
7400 SaCo 95823 338-A3
7600 SAC 95823 338-A3
LA MAR CT
2600 RCCD 95670 299-H1
LAMAR CT
3200 EDCo 95682 263-C3
LA MARGARITA WY
8700 SaCo 95828 338-G5
LAMB RD
23500 SJCo 95686 437-D6
N LAMB RD
24300 SJCo 95686 437-E5
LAMBAY WY
8700 SaCo 95828 338-G7
LAMBEAU CT
10100 ELKG 95757 377-H2
10100 ELKG 95757 397-H2
LAMBERT LN
6200 EDCo 95623 264-J3
6200 EDCo 95623 265-A3
LAMBERT RD
500 SaCo 95615 (396-G1 See Page 375)
1000 SaCo 95615 397-A11
1300 SaCo 95758 397-A11
4800 SaCo 95757 397-F11
LAMBERTON CIR
1200 SAC 95838 278-A1
LAMBETH CT
- EDCo 95672 263-B3
- LNCN 95648 179-E6
LAMBETH DR
2300 EDCo 95672 263-B3
LAMBETH WY
1700 SaCo 95608 299-B1
LAMBORN LN
13100 PlaC 95603 162-G7
LAMBRUSCA DR
10500 RCCD 95670 299-G1
10600 RCCD 95670 279-G7
LAMEGO WY
- EDCo 95762 262-E6
LAMER WY
7200 SaCo 95828 338-C1
LA MESA RD
5000 EDCo 95667 265-B2
LA MESA WY
2600 SaCo 95825 278-E7
LA MIRADA CIR
4400 SaCo 95628 280-F2
LAMONT WY
4300 SaCo 95823 317-G7
4300 SaCo 95823 337-H1
LAMPARD WY
2800 GALT 95632 419-G3
LAMPASAS AV
100 SAC 95815 277-G6
LAMPLIGHT LN
- LNCN 95648 199-J2
- LNCN 95648 200-A2
LAMPLIGHTER LN
2500 EDCo 95672 263-G2
3900 SaCo 95660 258-H7
LAMPREY DR
9200 ELKG 95624 358-G4
LAMURE CT
5100 SaCo 95842 259-B1
LANA LN
300 GALT 95632 419-E7
LANA ST
5300 SaCo 95608 259-F7
LANAI CT
- WSAC 95691 316-D2
6900 SaCo 95662 260-E2
LANATT ST
3200 SAC 95819 297-H3
LANCASHIRE CT
9300 ELKG 95758 357-J5
LANCASTER CT
300 RSVL 95678 219-F6
LANCASTER PL
1700 EDCo 95762 242-C5
LANCASTER WY
1100 SaCo 95822 317-B2
LANCE AV
8800 SaCo 95662 260-E6
LANCE CT
- PlaC 95661 240-D6
LANCE LN
- EDCo 95667 267-B4
LANCELOT DR
5500 SaCo 95842 259-C2
LANCER LN
7400 SaCo 95828 338-F2
LANCRAFT DR
8300 SAC 95823 337-J7
LAND AV
2800 SAC 95815 278-A6
LANDAKER LN
5600 SaCo 95662 260-H6
LANDAU CT
- SAC 95833 277-C5
LAND END LP
- RSVL 95747 218-J6
LANDER CT
- SAC 95823 337-H5
LANDES LN
- EDCo 95682 264-B4
S LANDFILL WY
- SaCo 95758 357-F1
E LANDING WY
1000 SAC 95831 336-J4
1000 SAC 95831 337-A3
LANDING POINT WY
5900 SAC 95823 358-A1
LANDIS AV
300 OAKL 94561 (514-E7 See Page 493)
5800 SaCo 95608 279-C4
LANDIS CIR
100 AUB 95603 182-E1
LANDMARK CIR
- LNCN 95648 179-G6
LANDMARK DR
- LNCN 95648 179-G6
LANDMARK PL
8000 SaCo 95843 239-B6
LANDOLT AV
4300 SaCo 95821 278-J4
LANDON LN
2000 SaCo 95825 278-E7
2000 SaCo 95825 298-E1
LAND PARK DR
2500 SAC 95818 297-C7
3000 SAC 95818 317-B2
3600 SAC 95822 317-B2
S LAND PARK DR
4100 SAC 95822 317-B3
6100 SAC 95831 317-A6
6900 SAC 95831 337-A2
7400 SAC 95831 336-J2
W LAND PARK DR
3800 SAC 95822 317-B2
LANDRETH LN
2900 EDCo 95726 248-B1
LANDRISE CT
6600 FOLS 95630 261-A2
LANDRUM CIR
100 FOLS 95630 261-G3
LANDSBOROUGH CT
7300 SaCo 95828 338-D2
LANDSDALE CT
1100 SaCo 95825 298-C3
LANDSFORD CT
9400 PlaC 95746 240-H5
LAND STAR WY
8700 ELKG 95758 358-A2
8700 SAC 95758 358-A2
LAND VIEW CT
- SAC 95822 317-B6
- SAC 95831 317-B6
LANDVIEW DR
- ELKG 95757 357-J7
- ELKG 95757 377-J1
- ELKG 95757 397-J1
LANDWOOD WY
2500 SaCo 95608 279-A7
LANE CT
1400 PLCR 95667 245-J5
1400 PLCR 95667 246-A5
LANE DR
500 SAC 95815 277-H5
1300 PLCR 95667 245-J5
LANE WY
1400 PLCR 95667 245-J5
LANETRY CT
9000 ELKG 95758 357-H3
LANETT CT
- RSVL 95747 219-D7
- RSVL 95747 239-D1
LANFRANCO CIR
- SAC 95835 256-G5
LANG AV
6400 SaCo 95823 317-H7
LANGDALE CT
8000 SaCo 95829 339-A6
LANGDALE WY
8000 SaCo 95829 339-A6
LANGDON CT
3800 EDCo 95762 262-C4
9300 ELKG 95624 358-H5
LANGFORD RD
11700 SaCo 95632 (400-C5 See Page 379)
LANGHAM WY
8000 SaCo 95829 339-A6
LANGHOLM WY
- FOLS 95630 261-J3
LANGLEY AV
100 PlaC 95661 239-J5

STREET
Block City ZIP Pg-Grid

LANGLEY CT
3000 ANT 94509 (513-C7
See Page 493)
LANGLEY WY
3200 SaCo 95843 238-F7
LANGNER CREEK RD
- EDCo 95726 267-H2
LANGRELL WY
6700 SAC 95831 316-F7
LANGS HILL RD
- PlaC 95658 181-F5
LANGSHIRE CT
9000 ELKG 95624 358-G4
LANGSTON WY
6700 SAC 95831 316-F7
LANGTON CT
- LNCN 95648 179-E7
LANGTREE DR
- RSVL 95747 218-J5
LANGTREE WY
8300 SAC 95823 338-A7
8300 SAC 95823 337-J7
LANHAM WY
3100 SAC 95833 277-C4
LANI LN
3500 SaCo 95608 279-D4
LANIE CT
- PlaC 95747 239-B3
LANIER CT
8900 SaCo 95826 298-H6
LANIER WY
8900 SaCo 95826 298-H6
LANIGAN CT
900 GALT 95632 419-G4
LANKERSHIM WY
3600 SaCo 95660 258-G3
LANNING LN
11200 SaCo 95693 (400-F1
See Page 379)
LANSDOWNE CT
8900 ELKG 95624 378-H1
LANSDOWNE LN
3000 EDCo 95667 246-C4
LANSDOWNE WY
- RSVL 95747 218-J4
LANSING AV
- SaCo 95742 280-H6
LANSING WY
2300 SaCo 95825 278-D7
LANTANA AV
4100 SaCo 95824 317-G5
LANTANA LN
- RSVL 95747 219-D6
LANTERN CT
1200 SaCo 95864 299-A3
3500 EDCo 95762 242-C6
LANTERN GROVE LN
5500 RSVL 95747 219-B5
LANTERN VIEW CT
1100 AUB 95603 182-C6
LANTERN VIEW DR
1100 AUB 95603 182-C6
LANTIS LN
1800 EDCo 95667 246-A4
1800 PLCR 95667 246-A4
LANTZY CT
4300 SaCo 95864 298-J3
LA NUBE CT
3300 SaCo 95843 238-F5
LA NUEZ DR
9000 ELKG 95624 358-H6
LANYARD CT
- SAC 95831 336-H3
LA PAENDA WY
8600 SaCo 95662 260-D1
LA PALOMA WY
2200 SaCo 95825 278-C7
3200 RKLN 95677 220-E1
LA PAMELA WY
5100 SAC 95823 337-J7
LA PAZ CT
100 RSVL 95747 219-C5
LA PAZ RD
- EDCo 95667 226-E4
LA PAZ WY
2800 SaCo 95821 278-G6
LA PERA CT
- SAC 95823 337-G2
LA PIEDRA PL
- SaCo 95843 239-A7
LAPIS CT
- SAC 95835 257-D5
3500 EDCo 95672 263-C2
4600 RKLN 95677 220-B2
LAPIS PL
9900 SaCo 95829 339-D7
LA PLACITA DR
10000 RCCD 95670 299-D2
LA PLATA WY
200 SAC 95838 277-G1
LA PLAYA CT
3900 PlaC 95650 201-G7
LA PLAYA WY
1600 SaCo 95864 298-G1
LA PLUMA CT
8600 SaCo 95843 238-F5
LAPORTE DR
1600 RSVL 95747 219-D5
LAPORTE WY
8300 ELKG 95624 358-D1
LA POZA CT
6500 CITH 95621 259-G3
LA PRADA CT
8800 ELKG 95624 378-G1
LA PRESA WY
10200 RCCD 95670 299-E2
LA PURISSIMA WY
100 SAC 95819 297-J5
LAPWING LN
100 GALT 95632 419-D6
LAQUART CT
100 FOLS 95630 261-C7
LA QUINTA CT
100 RSVL 95678 219-G5
LA QUINTA DR
2700 SaCo 95826 298-H7
LA QUITA CT
- GALT 95632 419-G5
LARA CT
2900 RKLN 95677 220-C1
LARAMIE CT
- RKLN 95677 220-F2
LARAMIE LN
2300 SAC 95815 278-B7
LARAMORE WY
7700 SAC 95832 337-E4
LARBRE WY
7300 SAC 95831 337-A2

LARCH LN
400 SaCo 95864 298-F4
LARCHMONT DR
6300 SaCo 95660 258-G1
LARCHMONT OAK WY
8400 SaCo 95828 338-E6
LARCHMONT SQUARE LN
3600 SaCo 95821 278-G4
LARCHWOOD CT
5000 SaCo 95841 259-B5
LARCHWOOD DR
3400 SAC 95834 277-E3
LAREDO RD
2300 SaCo 95825 278-D7
LA REINA WY
7700 SaCo 95828 338-C4
LARGE OAK CT
4700 SaCo 95841 279-A1
LARIAT CT
800 GALT 95632 439-F1
2700 RKLN 95765 200-E5
9100 SaCo 95628 260-G7
LARIAT DR
3500 EDCo 95682 283-G1
LARIAT LN
- LNCN 95648 179-H4
- PlaC 95603 162-A5
2200 FOLS 95630 282-B2
4400 OAKL 94561 (514-A7
See Page 493)
LARIAT LP
- LNCN 95648 179-H4
800 GALT 95632 439-F1
1500 RSVL 95661 240-C3
LARIAT PL
- LNCN 95648 179-H4
LARIAT RD
2700 EDCo 95682 283-E1
LARIAT RANCH RD
11400 PlaC 95603 162-A5
LARIMAR CT
8500 SaCo 95843 239-A5
LARISA WY
11800 RCCD 95742 320-D1
LA RIVIERA DR
7700 SAC 95826 298-E6
8600 SaCo 95826 298-E6
LARK AV
9100 ELKG 95624 358-J7
LARK LN
200 FOLS 95630 261-B1
3700 EDCo 95709 246-J2
LARK RD
5000 SaCo 95628 259-G7
LARKFLOWER WY
1200 LNCN 95648 179-D1
LARKHALL CIR
- FOLS 95630 262-A5
LARKIN CIR
100 FOLS 95630 261-C6
LARKIN DR
1800 RSVL 95661 240-C4
LARKIN LN
3200 PlaC 95658 160-H5
3600 PlaC 95602 161-G3
LARKIN WY
1100 SAC 95818 297-C6
LARKIN MINE RD
4300 EDCo 95619 265-H3
LARK SPARROW WY
2400 ELKG 95757 357-E7
LARKSPUR AV
- PlaC 95603 162-C6
6800 CITH 95610 259-J3
LARKSPUR CT
100 GALT 95632 419-D6
100 SaCo 95632 419-D6
LARKSPUR DR
2700 ANT 94531 (513-G7
See Page 493)
LARKSPUR LN
2400 SaCo 95825 298-D3
2400 SaCo 95864 298-D3
2800 EDCo - 247-F3
3500 EDCo 95682 263-D6
7600 SaCo 95610 240-D7
7600 SaCo 95662 240-D7
7600 SaCo 95662 260-D1
LARKSTONE CT
400 RSVL 95661 240-D4
LA ROCAS CT
- SAC 95823 337-H5
LA RONDA CT
10200 RCCD 95670 299-E2
LA ROSA CT
400 RSVL 95678 239-G3
LA ROSA RD
2800 SAC 95815 278-A5
LARRY AV
5700 CITH 95610 259-H6
LARRY LN
2700 SaCo 95608 279-B6
LARRY WY
5800 SaCo 95660 258-G4
LARSEN CT
- EDCo 95709 247-B2
LARSEN DR
2000 EDCo 95709 247-B2
LARSON AV
2200 SaCo 95652 258-F5
LARSON DR
2300 EDCo 95709 247-B2
LARSON WY
- FOLS 95630 261-C7
4600 SAC 95822 317-D3
LA RUE AL
200 RSVL 95678 239-H3
LA RUE WY
3000 RCCD 95670 299-F3
LARWIN DR
7900 CITH 95610 260-A3
LA SALIDA DEL SOL LN
7100 CITH 95610 260-A2
LA SALLE DR
1000 SaCo 95864 298-J3
LAS ANIMAS CIR
300 SAC 95838 277-G1
LA SARA CT
- SAC 95833 277-B5
LAS BRISAS CIR
- PlaC 95747 239-B2
LA SCALA CT
- RSVL 95747 199-B7
LAS CASAS WY
2500 RCCD 95670 299-E3
LAS CASITAS CT
8400 ELKG 95624 338-J7

LAS COCHES WY
1900 SAC 95833 277-B5
LAS CRUCES CT
600 RSVL 95747 219-C5
LAS CRUCES WY
1400 SaCo 95864 298-H2
LAS DUNAS AV
100 OAKL 94561 (514-F7
See Page 493)
LA SELVA DR
5400 EDCo 95623 265-B4
LAS ENCINITAS DR
4400 SaCo 95628 280-F2
LA SERENA DR
8900 SaCo 95628 280-F2
LAS FLORES
- SaCo 95628 280-A2
LAS FLORES AV
200 RSVL 95678 219-J7
LASH LARUE LN
8200 CITH 95610 260-C1
LASICK CT
3600 SaCo 95843 238-G7
LA SIERRA DR
500 SaCo 95864 298-H2
1000 EDCo 95762 242-D3
4100 EDCo 95619 265-F3
LA SIESTA DR
6700 SaCo 95662 260-J3
LAS LILAS CT
7700 CITH 95621 239-E7
7700 CITH 95621 259-E1
LAS LINDAS WY
4500 SaCo 95608 279-F2
LAS LOMITAS CIR
1300 SAC 95831 317-B7
1300 SAC 95831 337-B1
LAS MONTANAS CT
8300 SaCo 95829 338-J7
LAS NINAS CT
4000 SaCo 95821 278-H5
LA SOLANA WY
4500 SAC 95823 337-H5
LA SOLIDAD WY
2900 SAC 95817 317-G1
3700 SAC 95820 317-G2
LA SOMBRA WY
8200 SAC 95823 338-A6
LAS PALAMITAS WY
6800 SAC 95831 317-A7
LAS PALMAS AV
300 SAC 95815 277-G5
LAS PALOMAS LP
- LNCN 95648 179-E1
LAS PASAS WY
3500 SaCo 95864 298-G2
LAS POSITAS CIR
- SAC 95831 336-H1
LAS ROCAS LN
4700 EDCo 95623 264-J4
LAS SALINAS WY
1400 SaCo 95864 298-G2
LASSEN CT
- WSAC 95691 316-H2
100 RVIS 94571 454-G5
1800 ANT 94509 (513-F5
See Page 493)
LASSEN LN
900 EDCo 95762 262-D7
LASSEN ST
- WSAC 95691 316-H2
LASSEN WY
600 RSVL 95678 219-J7
2700 RKLN 95677 220-C4
3200 SaCo 95821 278-E5
LASSIK ST
- WSAC 95691 316-H2
LASSO CT
- CITH 95621 259-F3
LASSO ST
1400 EDCo 95682 283-H5
LASSO LAKE CT
100 LNCN 95648 179-J5
LASSO LAKE LN
1100 LNCN 95648 179-J5
LAST CHANCE CT
2000 SaCo 95670 280-E4
LAS TUNAS CT
10200 RCCD 95670 299-E3
LAS TUNAS WY
3500 EDCo 95682 263-D3
LASUEN DR
2600 SaCo 95821 278-G6
LAS UVAS CT
- SAC 95833 276-J7
LAS VEGAS RD
- SaCo 95742 280-J6
- SaCo 95742 281-A6
LA TARRIGA WY
4000 SAC 95823 337-G5
LATCHFORD CT
9100 ELKG 95624 358-J5
LATHAM DR
- SAC 95864 298-D5
2600 SaCo 95864 298-E5
LATHAM LN
- SAC 95864 298-E5
900 EDCo 95762 262-C4
LATHERTON WY
- FOLS 95630 261-H7
LATHROP WY
- SAC 95815 297-G1
LATHWELL WY
1500 RSVL 95747 219-C7
1500 RSVL 95747 239-C1
LATIGO CT
- PlaC 95747 238-J3
LATIGO LN
5800 EDCo 95762 (302-J1
See Page 301)
LATIMER WY
8700 SaCo 95628 280-E1
LATIN WY
5400 SaCo 95628 260-E6
LATITUDE LN
- LNCN 95648 179-G6
LA TOMJO CT
3200 EDCo 95672 263-D1
LA TONIS WY
- ELKG 95758 357-D5
LA TOUR DR
7200 SaCo 95842 259-B1
7600 SaCo 95843 259-B1
7600 SaCo 95843 239-B7
LATOUR LN
7500 CITH 95621 259-G1
LA TRELLA CT
8000 EDCo 95630 222-J2

LATROBE RD
4200 EDCo 95762 282-E2
5800 EDCo 95762 (302-H1
See Page 301)
6700 SaCo 95683 (321-H6
See Page 301)
6700 SaCo 95683 341-F1
14400 SaCo 95683 322-B5
15300 SaCo 95630 322-E3
LATTE WY
100 SAC 95838 257-G7
LAUCHERT PL
- GALT 95632 419-H5
LAUDER CT
9400 SaCo 95829 339-A6
LAUDERDALE CT
- SAC 95838 277-G1
W LAUFFER RD
12000 SJCo 95686 437-E2
LAUFFER WY
- ELKG 95758 358-D3
LAUGHLIN LN
5100 SaCo 95628 259-G7
LAUGHLIN RD
- EDCo 95634 225-F2
LAUMAN RIDGE RD S
- EDCo 95634 225-G1
LAUPPE LN
7600 CITH 95621 239-G7
7600 CITH 95621 259-G1
LAURA CT
3700 SaCo 95821 278-J4
LAURA DR
- PlaC 95603 161-G6
LAURA BELLE CT
- EDCo 95667 266-G3
LAURA JOHN WY
2300 EDCo 95667 245-B5
LAURALYN WY
8100 CITH 95610 240-B7
LAUREL CT
5600 RKLN 95677 220-C4
LAUREL DR
- RSVL 95678 219-G5
600 SaCo 95864 298-E4
2900 EDCo 95726 248-C1
12100 PlaC 95603 162-C5
LAUREL LN
1500 WSAC 95691 296-H3
6200 EDCo 95667 265-B2
8400 PlaC 95746 221-E6
LAUREL PL
- RVIS 94571 454-F2
LAUREL RD
- YoCo 95612 356-H4
LAUREL WY
700 RVIS 94571 454-H4
LAUREL COVE CT
5800 ELKG 95757 357-J7
LAUREL CREST CIR
- RSVL 95678 220-A3
LAURELES CT
- ELKG 95758 358-B3
LAURELGLEN DR
3600 SAC 95834 277-E3
LAUREL GROVE CIR
4500 EDCo 95762 262-E6
LAUREL GROVE CT
3600 SaCo 95843 238-G5
LAUREL HILLS DR
5300 SaCo 95841 259-B6
LAURELHURST DR
3000 RCCD 95670 299-F4
LAURELHURST LN
- LNCN 95648 200-A1
LAUREL MIST CT
- PlaC 95746 240-H2
LAUREL OAK WY
6900 SaCo 95628 259-F6
LAUREL POINT PL
4100 SaCo 95843 238-H5
LAURELRIDGE CT
7900 SaCo 95628 260-C7
7900 SaCo 95628 259-J7
LAURELVIEW AV
5100 SaCo 95608 279-A2
LAURELWOOD CT
800 ANT 94509 (513-F7
See Page 493)
2400 RKLN 95677 220-F2
LAURELWOOD DR
100 FOLS 95630 261-B2
LAURELWOOD WY
4300 SaCo 95864 278-J7
4500 SaCo 95608 279-A7
4500 SaCo 95864 279-A7
LAUREN CT
4100 RCCD 95742 320-D1
LAURENCE AV
2500 SaCo 95608 279-A7
LAURIANN WY
5400 SaCo 95841 259-A6
LAURIE WY
7700 SAC 95832 337-F4
LAURINE WY
5600 SaCo 95824 317-H5
6200 SaCo 95823 317-H6
LAURITZEN LN
- OAKL 94561 (514-A4
See Page 493)
LAURUS CT
8600 SaCo 95843 238-G5
LAVA CT
4600 RKLN 95677 220-B2
LAVA LN
3900 EDCo 95726 248-F3
LA VAL CT
7100 SaCo 95608 279-G3
LA VALENCIA CT
9000 ELKG 95624 358-H7
LAVALIERE PL
900 FOLS 95630 261-B6
LAVA RIDGE CT
- RSVL 95661 240-D2
LAVASTONE DR
- LNCN 95648 199-H3
LAVELLE WY
4900 SaCo 95841 258-J7
LAVELLI WY
10100 ELKG 95757 377-J2
10100 ELKG 95757 397-J2
LAVENDER CT
- ELKG 95624 358-F1
- RKLN 95677 220-H4
200 GALT 95632 419-D6
LAVENDER LN
- EDCo 95682 263-H7
LAVENDER HILL CT
- LNCN 95648 200-B2

LAVENHAM CT
- SaCo 95829 338-J5
LA VENTA WY
5600 SAC 95835 256-H4
LAVER CT
300 RSVL 95661 240-E4
LAVERNE LN
5600 EDCo 95667 264-F3
LA VERNE WY
3900 SaCo 95864 278-H7
LAVERSTOCK WY
800 SaCo 95864 298-J4
LA VERTA
2700 RCCD 95670 299-E3
LAVERTON WY
3700 SAC 95838 277-G3
LA VIA WY
2600 SaCo 95825 278-E7
LA VIDA LN
12300 SaCo 95693 360-G3
LA VINA CT
- RSVL 95747 219-B1
LA VINA WY
200 OAKL 94561 (514-E7
See Page 493)
8500 SaCo 95828 338-F4
LA VISTA AV
3000 SaCo 95608 279-G6
LA VISTA CT
4500 OAKL 94561 (514-C7
See Page 493)
LA VISTA DR
3300 EDCo 95667 245-G6
3300 PLCR 95667 245-G6
4600 OAKL 94561 (514-C7
See Page 493)
6000 LMS 95650 220-J2
6000 LMS 95650 221-A2
LAVONNE LN
4200 SaCo 95821 278-H3
LAW CT
7300 SaCo 95662 260-H2
LAW LN
7600 PlaC 95650 201-D7
LAWLER ST
- SAC 95835 256-J4
LAWNDALE CT
- EDCo 95682 263-B4
LAWNVIEW AV
3200 LMS 95650 200-J4
LAWNVIEW CT
- LMS 95650 200-J4
LAWNVIEW WY
5300 ELKG 95758 357-J5
LAWNWOOD DR
6900 SaCo 95828 318-B7
7400 SAC 95828 318-B7
LAWRENCE AV
- ANT 94509 (513-C5
See Page 493)
7800 CITH 95610 260-A3
LAWRENCE DR
4600 PlaC 95746 240-F1
5100 SAC 95820 317-H4
5300 SAC 95824 317-H4
LAWRENCE LN
- LNCN 95648 179-E6
LAWSON WY
400 SaCo 95864 298-F5
2800 PLCR 95667 245-E4
LAWTON AV
500 RSVL 95678 239-G1
LAWTON CT
- RKLN 95765 200-D3
LAWTON ST
200 ANT 94509 (513-C6
See Page 493)
LAWYER DR
2900 EDCo 95667 226-F4
LAYBURN CT
4400 SaCo 95843 238-J6
LAYNE LN
7900 SaCo 95828 338-F4
LAYSAN TEAL CT
- RSVL 95747 219-E2
LAYSAN TEAL DR
- RSVL 95747 219-E2
LAYTON DR
5600 SaCo 95660 258-G5
LAZENBY WY
1400 RSVL 95747 239-D1
LAZO CT
700 EDCo 95762 242-C3
1500 SaCo 95864 298-J2
LAZURITE LN
3100 EDCo 95672 263-B2
LAZYBOOT TR
6000 EDCo 95623 264-J6
LAZY J CT
3100 SaCo 95843 238-E6
LAZY KNOLL CT
3500 EDCo 95672 243-E5
LAZY OAK LN
100 PlaC 95661 239-J5
LAZY RIVER WY
7000 SAC 95831 336-F1
LAZY SADDLE WY
- ELKG 95624 359-B6
LAZY TRAIL CT
7800 SaCo 95662 240-E7
LEA CT
5500 RKLN 95765 220-B1
LEA WY
400 SAC 95815 277-H7
LEADER AV
5100 SaCo 95841 259-B5
LEAD HILL BLVD
- RSVL 95678 240-B1
1300 RSVL 95661 240-B1
LEAF AV
6300 SAC 95831 316-J6
LEAF CIR
- EDCo 95726 248-D1
LEAFCREST WY
8100 SaCo 95628 260-B6
LEAFMONT WY
4200 SaCo 95826 319-B2
LEAFWOOD DR
6000 SaCo 95608 279-D5
LEAFWOOD WY
100 FOLS 95630 241-B7
LEAFY WAY CT
- RKLN 95765 199-J4
LEAH CT
900 AUB 95603 162-D6
LEAK LN
3700 PlaC 95650 201-E7
LEAL CT
9400 ELKG 95758 357-H5

LEANDER LN
- LNCN 95648 199-J1
- LNCN 95648 200-A1
LEANING TREE CT
8400 SaCo 95843 238-F5
LEANING TREE RD
2600 EDCo 95667 246-E4
LE ANN DR
10600 RCCD 95670 299-H1
LEAOAK CT
6800 CITH 95621 239-F6
LEAR DR
6200 SaCo 95837 256-B3
LEARY RD
13500 SaCo 95690 (416-G4
See Page 415)
13800 SaCo 95690 436-D1
LEATHA WY
3300 SaCo 95821 278-F4
LEATHAM AV
8900 SaCo 95628 280-F2
LEATHERLEAF CT
8300 SaCo 95829 339-D7
LEATHERWOOD WY
6700 SaCo 95842 259-B3
LEAVELL LN
200 PlaC 95648 179-J3
200 PlaC 95648 180-A3
LEAVELL PARK CIR
- LNCN 95648 179-J6
LEAVERITE WY
7600 SAC 95828 318-C7
LEAVITT WY
5300 SaCo 95628 259-F7
LECKENBY WY
- FOLS 95630 281-G1
LEDA CT
8300 SaCo 95843 239-B5
LEDBURY CT
- RSVL 95747 219-B7
LEDBURY ST
- RSVL 95747 219-B7
LEDGEMONT CT
100 FOLS 95630 261-H5
LEDGESTONE CT
- LNCN 95648 200-A2
LEDGESTONE DR
1000 FOLS 95630 261-E6
LEDGESTONE LN
2700 LNCN 95648 200-A3
LEDGEWOOD WY
6100 CITH 95621 239-D7
LE DONNE DR
- SaCo 95823 317-H7
LEE CT
2800 PLCR 95667 245-E4
LEE DR
- EDCo 95682 263-C4
600 SAC 95815 277-H5
8200 CITH 95610 239-J6
LEE WY
2100 RSVL 95661 240-C5
LEE BROOK WY
3800 SAC 95838 277-G3
LEEDS CT
2800 PlaC 95603 162-C3
5400 CITH 95621 259-G6
LEEDS DR
12400 PlaC 95603 162-C3
LEEDY LN
8900 SaCo 95628 260-F6
8900 SaCo 95662 260-F6
LEEMANS WY
- ELKG 95757 377-H2
- ELKG 95757 397-H2
LEES LN
- PlaC 95658 182-A7
1500 PlaC 95603 182-A7
LEESBURG WY
- ELKG 95624 358-D1
LEE SCHOOL RD
12200 SaCo 95693 360-F5
LEE SCHOOL CROSS RD
12500 SaCo 95693 360-G4
LEEVER LN
7700 SaCo 95662 240-E7
7700 SaCo 95662 260-E1
LEEWARD CT
400 RSVL 95678 239-G5
LEEWARD WY
500 SAC 95831 316-G7
LEEWAY DR
4200 EDCo 95619 265-G3
LEEWILL AV
100 SaCo 95673 257-G2
LEFEVRE CT
700 FOLS 95630 262-B7
LEFEVRE DR
500 FOLS 95630 262-A7
LE FLORE PL
7100 PlaC 95746 241-C2
LEFORD WY
1900 SAC 95832 337-C4
LEGACY CT
- RSVL 95678 219-G5
8100 SaCo 95843 239-B6
LEGACY LN
- EDCo 95667 266-H1
LEGEND DR
- RKLN 95765 200-D5
LEGENDS WY
1400 RSVL 95747 219-D7
LEGGETT ST
1100 ANT 94509 (513-C4
See Page 493)
LEGO LN
- SaCo 95632 419-G1
LE HAVRE AV
6900 CITH 95621 259-F4
LEHI LN
100 PlaC 95658 181-D4
LEHIGH CT
4500 SaCo 95841 278-J2
LEHIGH ST
- RKLN 95765 200-C5
LEHMAN WY
5000 SaCo 95842 259-B1
LEI ST
4600 SaCo 95628 280-B1
LEIBER WY
- SaCo 95829 339-A6
LEIBINGER LN
6800 PlaC 95746 241-C1
LEICESTER WY
100 FOLS 95630 261-G6
LEIDESDORFF ST
200 FOLS 95630 261-B4
LEIGHTON CT
- RSVL 95747 218-J4

LEIGHTON WY
- RSVL 95747 218-J4
LEINEKE LN
7600 CITH 95610 259-H1
LEIPER LP
- LNCN 95648 179-E1
LEISA LN
4300 PlaC 95650 200-G2
4300 PlaC 95663 200-G2
LEISURE CT
- EDCo 95667 267-B5
LEISURE LN
400 SAC 95815 297-H1
3600 EDCo 95667 266-J6
3800 EDCo 95667 267-A5
S LEISURE LN
7500 SaCo 95673 237-H7
7500 SaCo 95673 257-H1
LEISURE OAK
8900 ELKG 95624 359-F3
LEISURE VIEW RD
- EDCo - 267-E3
LEITCH AV
300 SAC 95815 277-G6
LEITH CT
- LNCN 95648 179-D2
LEITRIM CT
6500 CITH 95621 259-E4
LEJANO WY
2100 SAC 95833 277-B4
LEKA TR
- EDCo - 267-J3
- EDCo 95726 267-J3
LELA WY
900 ANT 94509 (513-F6
See Page 493)
LELAND AV
9000 SaCo 95829 338-H4
LELAND ST
3400 RKLN 95765 220-B1
LELAND HAVEN WY
500 SAC 95831 316-G6
LELAND OAKS CT
- ELKG 95624 358-J1
LELIA DR
4200 SaCo 94571 (494-A2
See Page 493)
LE MANS AV
6700 CITH 95621 259-F4
LEMAR DR
400 RSVL 95678 239-J3
LEMARSH WY
7500 SAC 95822 337-D3
LEMAS RD
8700 SaCo 95828 338-G5
8800 SaCo 95829 338-H5
LEMAY ST
- SaCo 95655 299-F6
LEMBI DR
100 FOLS 95630 261-B6
LEMITAR WY
2900 SAC 95833 277-B5
LEMMING CT
2200 SaCo 95825 298-C2
LEMON ST
7700 SaCo 95628 279-J2
LEMON BELL WY
- SAC 95824 318-B6
LEMON BLOSSOM CT
- SAC 95824 318-C5
LEMON COVE CT
8100 SaCo 95828 338-D6
LEMON DROP CT
6900 SAC 95824 318-B5
LEMONGRASS CT
- PLCR 95667 245-H6
LEMON HILL AV
4400 SaCo 95824 317-H5
5400 SAC 95824 317-H5
5700 SAC 95824 318-A5
LEMONHILL DR
4600 RKLN 95677 220-E1
LEMON PARK WY
5800 SAC 95824 318-A5
LEMON TEA DR
7600 SaCo 95828 338-F3
LEMON TREE CT
5300 SaCo 95662 260-H6
LEMONTREE CT
2400 ANT 94509 (513-B6
See Page 493)
LEMONTREE RD
- WSAC 95691 316-J1
LEMONTREE WY
- RSVL 95747 218-J4
2100 ANT 94509 (513-B5
See Page 493)
LEMON VIEW WY
5500 SAC 95824 318-A5
LEMONWOOD WY
9300 ELKG 95758 357-H5
LEMOS RANCH DR
- LMS 95650 201-B4
LEN CT
6000 CITH 95621 239-D7
LEN WY
1300 RSVL 95678 219-G7
LENA WY
4900 SaCo 95628 260-E7
LENADER CT
- RSVL 95747 239-B1
LENGA WY
- SAC 95835 256-H3
LENHART RD
7700 SaCo 95828 338-C5
LENKA CT
300 RSVL 95678 239-G5
LENMAR CT
- SAC 95835 257-A5
LENNANE DR
- SaCo 95834 277-D2
LENNOX DR
3000 EDCo 95762 262-D1
LENNOX WY
6400 ELKG 95758 358-A5
LENORE LN
13400 SaCo 95632 419-D5
LENORE WY
3700 SaCo 95660 258-G7
LENOX CT
400 RSVL 95661 240-D3
LENT CT
5000 ELKG 95758 357-H4
LENTS HILL DR
- EDCo 95619 266-D7
LENZI CT
5100 ELKG 95757 377-H3
5100 ELKG 95757 397-H3

STREET Block City ZIP Pg-Grid

LEO LN
12600 SaCo 95693 360-H1
LEOLA WY
6100 SaCo 95824 317-H6
6200 SaCo 95823 317-H6
LEOLETA WY
2700 SaCo 95608 279-A6
LEONA CIR
3200 SaCo 95834 276-H3
LEONA WY
7800 PlaC 95746 240-H1
LEONARD AV
7200 CITH 95610 259-H2
LEONARDO CT
- ELKG 95757 377-J1
- ELKG 95757 397-J1
LEONARDO WY
- EDCo 95762 262-H4
- ELKG 95757 377-J1
- ELKG 95757 378-A1
- ELKG 95757 397-J1
LEONES AV
2700 SAC 95833 276-J4
2700 SAC 95833 277-A4
LEONOR DR
2900 SAC 95833 277-D5
LEOPARD CT
- SaCo 95829 338-H5
LEOPARD LN
4000 EDCo 95630 222-J1
LEOS LN
4000 SaCo 95608 279-D3
LEO VIRGO CT
8700 ELKG 95624 358-G7
LEPAGE CT
100 FOLS 95630 261-F4
LE PARC CT
8500 SaCo 95628 260-D5
LEQUEL WY
5200 SaCo 95608 279-B4
LERNER WY
5300 SAC 95823 337-J3
5600 SAC 95823 338-A3
LEROS CT
- SAC 95823 337-F3
LEROY CT
5000 SaCo 95628 259-J7
LEROY RANCH RD
5000 EDCo 95667 265-B1
LERWICK RD
2700 SaCo 95821 278-E4
LESARA CT
2000 EDCo 95762 282-J5
LESBOS CT
- SAC 95823 337-F3
LESLIE CT
- PlaC 95746 241-E1
LESLIE DR
- RSVL 95747 218-H4
LESLIE LN
2000 EDCo 95762 242-D3
2400 SaCo 95821 278-D6
2800 WSAC 95691 316-E1
LESNAR WY
- ELKG 95758 357-G5
LESNICK CT
- FOLS 95630 281-F1
LESSER WY
7900 CITH 95621 239-G7
LESTER LN
700 PlaC 95603 162-F3
LESTERFORD CT
7200 SaCo 95842 259-D2
LESVOS CT
2200 PlaC 95648 199-D3
LETA CT
600 PlaC 95658 181-D2
LETA LN
2900 SaCo 95821 278-J5
LETAWSKY LN
11300 SaCo 95693 (380-B3 See Page 379)
LETCHWORTH CT
- ELKG 95758 357-E5
LETITIA AV
2900 PLCR 95667 246-A5
LETIZIA CT
- SAC 95832 337-D4
LETTERKENNY CT
- LNCN 95648 200-B2
LETTERKENNY LN
- LNCN 95648 200-B2
LETTERMAN ST
- WSAC 95691 296-J7
LETTY CT
- SAC 95833 277-C4
LEUE AV
8800 SaCo 95662 260-F2
LEVAGIN CT
7500 SaCo 95842 259-B1
LEVANT CT
9000 ELKG 95758 357-H3
LEVEE RD
- SaCo 95690 417-A7
- SaCo 95690 437-B1
- WSAC 95691 296-C7
- WSAC 95691 316-B3
- YoCo 95691 316-B7
- YoCo 95691 336-B4
2900 RCCD 95670 299-D2
9000 SaCo 95624 359-G7
9300 SaCo 95624 379-G1
9400 SaCo 95693 360-A5
E LEVEE RD
2300 SAC 95833 277-F4
2500 SAC 95834 277-F1
3900 SAC 95834 257-E6
3900 SaCo 95834 277-F1
3900 SaCo 95834 257-E6
5300 SAC 95835 257-E6
5300 SaCo 95835 257-E4
6400 SaCo 95673 257-E2
6400 SaCo 95836 237-D5
6400 SaCo 95836 257-E2
LEVEE ST
1200 SaCo 95690 417-A7
LEVEN CT
- FOLS 95630 262-A5
LEVENDI LN
4100 SaCo 95821 278-J3
LEVERETT CT
4600 SaCo 95842 259-A1
LEVERING WY
8000 SAC 95823 338-A5
LEVERT AV
4300 EDCo 95619 265-G4
LEVIDI CT
- ELKG 95758 357-E4

LEVI STRAUSS CT
1800 SaCo 95670 280-B3
LEVY RD
100 FOLS 95630 261-C7
LEW WY
4500 SAC 95820 317-E3
LEWIE WY
8700 ELKG 95758 357-J2
LEWINS CT
- GALT 95632 419-G2
LEWIS AV
8100 SaCo 95843 239-C6
LEWIS RD
4400 EDCo 95619 265-F3
LEWIS ST
100 AUB 95603 182-E4
3000 PLCR 95667 245-G5
LEWIS CARROLL WY
4800 SaCo 95842 259-A4
LEWIS STEIN RD
- ELKG 95758 358-C3
- SAC 95758 358-C2
LEWISTON RD
- WSAC 95691 316-D4
LEWISTON WY
6900 SaCo 95828 338-B1
LEWITT DR
1900 RCCD 95670 279-G6
LEWROSA WY
5400 SAC 95835 257-D5
LEXI WY
1800 EDCo 95762 242-H7
LEXIA CT
3300 RCCD 95670 299-J4
LEXINGTON CIR
4800 PlaC 95650 221-G2
LEXINGTON CT
1200 EDCo 95762 242-D5
N LEXINGTON DR
300 FOLS 95630 261-G5
S LEXINGTON DR
300 FOLS 95630 261-F6
LEXINGTON ST
2200 SAC 95815 277-J7
LEXINGTON CROSSING LN
4600 SaCo 95842 258-J2
4600 SaCo 95842 259-A2
LEXUS WY
8000 SaCo 95828 338-D6
LEYDEN ST
8100 SaCo 95626 238-D6
LEYENDA CT
7300 SaCo 95683 342-C2
LIALANA WY
7700 CITH 95610 259-J3
7800 CITH 95610 260-A3
LIANI WY
1600 SAC 95835 257-C4
LIBBY LN
- SaCo 95628 260-C7
LIBBY WY
3200 SaCo 95821 278-J5
LIBERTY CT
1300 RSVL 95747 219-E7
2700 PlaC 95747 239-C1
LIBERTY LN
1000 LNCN 95648 180-A2
1000 PlaC 95648 180-A2
LIBERTY PKWY
- RKLN 95765 199-H4
E LIBERTY RD
2200 SJCo 95220 439-H3
3800 SJCo 95220 (440-B3 See Page 420)
4500 SJCo 95632 (440-B3 See Page 420)
LIBERTY ST
5300 SaCo 95660 258-H6
LIBERTY BELL LN
4800 SaCo 95660 258-H7
LIBERTY ISLAND RD
3200 RVIS 94571 454-E2
3900 SolC 94571 (395-A6 See Page 375)
3900 SolC 94571 415-A1
LIBERTY MINE CT
2600 PLCR 95667 245-G3
LIBRA AV
9800 RCCD 95827 299-C6
LIBRARY DR
- LMS 95650 201-A6
LIBRARY ST
- SAC 95834 257-A7
- SAC 95835 257-A7
LICHEN DR
7800 CITH 95621 239-E7
LIDA CT
- EDCo 95762 262-C1
LIDIA WY
7400 SaCo 95828 338-C2
LIDO CIR
- SAC 95826 298-D7
LIEBIG CT
500 GALT 95632 419-G5
LIENO LN
2800 SaCo 95821 278-F6
LIESEL CT
4700 SaCo 95608 279-E1
LIETO WY
4900 SAC 95835 256-J6
LIFE AV
6500 SAC 95824 318-B5
LIFE WY
3100 EDCo 95667 244-J7
3100 EDCo 95667 245-A7
LIFTON CT
100 RSVL 95747 239-D1
LIGGETT WY
5600 SaCo 95608 279-C3
LIGHT CT
100 FOLS 95630 261-A1
LIGHT LN
- EDCo 95709 247-C2
LIGHT CANYON RD
- EDCo 95634 225-G4
- EDCo 95667 225-G4
LIGHT FOOT CT
3700 SaCo 95843 238-G7
LIGHTHOUSE DR
400 WSAC 95605 297-A1
700 WSAC 95605 296-J1
LIGHTHOUSE WY
300 SAC 95831 336-F1
LIGHTNER CT
100 SAC 95815 277-G7
100 SAC 95815 297-G1
LIGHT RAIL
1700 SAC 95814 297-D5

LIGHT RAIL
2900 SAC 95816 297-D5
LIGHT SKY CT
- SAC 95828 318-G6
LIGURIA CT
- EDCo 95762 262-F6
LILA LN
1300 EDCo 95672 243-D3
5900 SaCo 95660 258-G4
LILAC LN
- LNCN 95648 180-A5
400 SaCo 95673 257-H3
400 WSAC 95691 296-H3
600 SaCo 95864 298-E4
1400 PlaC 95603 162-C6
1600 ANT 94509 (513-B5 See Page 493)
LILAC RD
2800 EDCo - 247-H2
LILAC BLOSSOM PL
5300 ELKG 95757 377-J1
5300 ELKG 95757 397-J1
LILAC CANYON CT
11700 RCCD 95742 320-D2
LILAC FAWN WY
8500 ELKG 95624 358-F1
LILAC FIELDS PL
9700 ELKG 95624 359-A7
LILAC RIDGE CT
8400 SaCo 95843 239-B5
LIL BIT CT
5200 EDCo 95682 283-H4
LILIAN CT
3000 PLCR 95667 245-F5
LILIBET AV
9200 SaCo 95826 318-J2
LILIPUT LN
6200 PlaC 95650 221-B5
LILJA CT
- RSVL 95678 220-A7
LILLEHAMMER CT
4100 SaCo 95843 238-H5
LILLIAN LN
2500 SaCo 95608 279-B7
7500 CITH 95610 259-H1
LILLIVALE CT
7200 CITH 95621 259-D2
LILLY CROSS DR
600 RSVL 95678 220-A6
LILLY LAVELLE LN
- EDCo - 267-C1
LILY AV
- PlaC 95603 162-C6
LILY CT
- EDCo 95682 263-H6
2700 ANT 94531 (513-G7 See Page 493)
LILY LN
2700 SaCo 95864 298-E4
3600 EDCo 95682 263-H6
LILY PL
- WSAC 95691 316-E2
LILY ST
3700 SAC 95838 278-B3
LILY HILL CT
3700 SaCo 95843 238-G5
LILY MAR LN
7600 SaCo 95843 238-G7
7600 SaCo 95843 258-G1
LILYPAD CT
8600 ELKG 95624 358-E1
LILYPAD LN
8600 ELKG 95624 358-E1
LILY POND CT
- SAC 95835 256-J4
LILYPOND LN
- LNCN 95648 179-H5
LILYVIEW WY
- ELKG 95757 357-J7
- ELKG 95757 377-J1
- ELKG 95757 397-J1
LIMA CT
- EDCo 95762 262-E1
LIMA WY
- EDCo 95762 262-F1
LIME COVE CT
8200 SaCo 95828 338-D6
LIME CREST CT
9200 ELKG 95624 358-F4
LIME GROVE WY
5200 SaCo 95608 259-G7
7000 SaCo 95628 259-G7
LIME KILN RD
600 EDCo 95619 265-E2
LIME PLANT RD
4000 EDCo 95619 265-E2
LIMERICK WY
7500 CITH 95610 259-H5
LIMESTONE DR
1000 FOLS 95630 261-E6
LIMESTONE WY
3800 SAC 95823 337-G3
LIMEWOOD DR
400 ANT 94509 (513-E7 See Page 493)
LIMEWOOD RD
- WSAC 95691 316-J1
LIMITED CT
- SAC 95823 338-B6
LIMNOS CT
4400 ELKG 95758 357-H4
LIMPKIN CT
- LNCN 95648 200-C3
LINCOLN AL
900 PLCR 95667 245-G5
LINCOLN AV
4100 SaCo 95608 279-D2
5800 RKLN 95677 220-B4
7300 SaCo 95628 279-G3
E LINCOLN AV
3600 SAC 95818 317-C2
W LINCOLN AV
3600 SAC 95818 317-C1
LINCOLN LN
2700 ANT 94509 (513-E6 See Page 493)
E LINCOLN PKWY
- LNCN 95648 179-H6
- LNCN 95648 199-J1
- RKLN 95648 199-H2
- RKLN 95765 199-H2
LINCOLN ST
100 RSVL 95678 239-H1
500 RSVL 95678 219-H7
900 PLCR 95667 245-G5
S LINCOLN ST
100 RSVL 95678 239-J2
LINCOLN WY
400 AUB 95603 182-F1

LINCOLN WY
6700 PlaC 95603 162-G5
6700 PlaC 95603 182-F1
6700 AUB 95603 162-F7
LINCOLN WY Rt#-J10
100 GALT 95632 419-F6
800 GALT 95632 439-F1
900 SaCo 95632 439-F1
LINCOLN AIRPARK DR
- LNCN 95648 159-D7
- LNCN 95648 179-C1
LINCOLN CREEK CIR
4000 SaCo 95608 279-F3
LINCOLN HILLS WY
5900 SaCo 95608 279-D2
LINCOLN NEWCASTLE HWY Rt#-193
1200 PlaC 95648 179-J3
1200 PlaC 95648 180-A3
1200 LNCN 95648 179-J3
1200 LNCN 95648 180-A3
4900 PlaC 95658 180-F4
6300 PlaC 95658 181-B3
LINCOLN OAKS DR
6700 SaCo 95628 259-F6
LINCOLNSHIRE DR
7100 SaCo 95823 337-G1
LINCOLN VILLA WY
5200 SaCo 95628 260-D7
LINCOLN VILLAGE DR
9700 RCCD 95827 299-C6
LINDA DR
100 RSVL 95678 239-J2
6200 EDCo 95623 265-B4
11100 PlaC 95602 161-J3
LINDA LN
- CITH 95610 259-J1
5500 SaCo 95608 299-C1
6300 SaCo 95673 257-H4
LINDA WY
6500 SaCo 95608 279-E2
LINDA BEE LN
12400 SaCo 95638 (401-C7 See Page 381)
LINDA CREEK CT
- PlaC 95746 240-H4
8500 SaCo 95610 240-D6
LINDALE DR
7100 SaCo 95828 338-A1
LINDA LOU DR
5100 SaCo 95608 279-B3
LINDA MARIE CT
1100 GALT 95632 419-G2
LINDA OAK CT
5600 SaCo 95842 259-C2
LINDA RIO CT
9500 SaCo 95827 299-A5
LINDA RIO DR
9100 SaCo 95826 298-J6
9200 SaCo 95826 299-A5
9300 SaCo 95827 299-A5
LINDA-SHERRY WY
9200 PlaC 95658 201-G4
LINDA SUE WY
6700 SaCo 95628 259-F6
7000 CITH 95621 259-G6
7000 SaCo 95621 259-G6
7200 CITH 95628 259-G6
LINDAUER DR
6200 CITH 95621 259-E4
LINDA VISTA DR
3400 EDCo 95682 263-G5
7100 CITH 95610 259-H2
LINDA VISTA LN
1500 SAC 95822 317-C3
LINDA VISTA WY
800 RVIS 94571 454-H4
LINDAY WY
11500 SaCo 95670 280-C6
LINDBERG AV
6500 EDCo 95667 265-B2
LINDBERG ST
2100 ANT 94509 (513-D6 See Page 493)
2300 AUB 95602 162-D2
LINDBERGH DR
6300 SaCo 95837 256-B3
LINDBROOK DR
- RKLN 95765 200-D4
LINDBROOK WY
6600 SAC 95823 338-B5
LINDEN AV
200 AUB 95603 182-E2
7600 CITH 95610 239-H6
LINDEN LN
2900 SaCo 95608 279-B6
LINDEN PL
1700 ANT 94509 (513-B5 See Page 493)
LINDEN RD
100 WSAC 95691 317-A2
200 WSAC 95691 316-H1
900 WSAC 95691 296-F7
LINDEN WY
1700 ANT 94509 (513-B5 See Page 493)
LINDENGROVE WY
2000 SaCo 95608 299-A1
LINDEN LIME CT
8000 CITH 95610 260-B3
8000 CITH 95662 260-B3
LINDENWOOD WY
3500 SaCo 95826 318-H1
LINDERHOF WY
8300 SaCo 95828 338-F7
LINDERO LN
6900 SaCo 95683 342-A1
LINDFIELD CT
9200 SaCo 95829 338-J5
LINDI CT
3400 SaCo 95608 279-F4
LINDLEY CT
- FOLS 95630 281-E2
3100 ANT 94509 (513-E7 See Page 493)
LINDLEY DR
100 SAC 95815 277-G5
400 ANT 94509 (513-E7 See Page 493)
LINDO CT
7300 SaCo 95683 342-C3
LINDSAY AV
400 SAC 95838 277-H3
LINDSAY CT
- RKLN 95677 220-D4
LINDSAY DR
- RSVL 95678 239-G4
LINDSEY LN
100 EDCo 95667 245-D7

LINEAGE CT
7700 ELKG 95758 358-C4
LINENFOLD CT
5000 SaCo 95842 259-B1
LINERAS WY
4400 SAC 95823 337-H5
LINES LN
3100 SaCo 95608 279-C5
LINFIELD DR
1300 RSVL 95678 219-F6
LINGROVE WY
4200 SaCo 95608 279-F2
LINHURST CT
1900 EDCo 95762 242-C6
LINIER CT
1000 RSVL 95678 239-J3
LINK DR
5500 SaCo 95628 259-F6
LINKER CT
6900 SaCo 95628 259-F5
LINKSMAN CT
7500 SaCo 95683 342-D3
LINLEY LN
600 LNCN 95648 179-F5
LINN WY
6400 SaCo 95673 257-G3
LINN COVE DR
- SAC 95823 357-J1
LINNET CT
- LNCN 95648 180-A6
4000 SaCo 95864 298-H4
LIN OAK WY
8100 CITH 95610 260-B1
LINSCOTT CT
10300 ELKG 95624 359-F1
LINTON PIKE
4800 SAC 95822 317-C3
LINUS WY
3900 SaCo 95608 279-B3
LINVALE CT
900 SAC 95822 316-J3
LINWOOD AV
300 RSVL 95678 239-J3
LINWOOD LN
3300 EDCo 95682 263-E6
LINWOOD WY
7000 SaCo 95828 338-B1
LIONEL CT
- SAC 95823 338-B6
LION GATE WY
4800 SAC 95823 337-J5
LION HEART CT
200 SaCo 95673 257-G3
LION HEART WY
200 SaCo 95673 257-F3
LIONS WY
100 FOLS 95630 261-G4
LIONS CROSS CIR
5400 PlaC 95746 240-H1
LIONS DEN ST
- RSVL 95747 219-D2
LIPHAN CT
- RSVL 95747 218-H4
LIPPI PKWY
4500 SaCo 95823 337-H2
LIPPIT LN
4900 SAC 95820 318-C4
LIPPIZAN CT
9700 ELKG 95757 357-H7
LIPTON ST
1500 ANT 94509 (513-F5 See Page 493)
1700 CCCo 94509 (513-G5 See Page 493)
LIRIOS AV
- SaCo 95828 338-F3
LISA CIR
8100 SAC 95826 318-D1
LISA CT
3100 ANT 94509 (513-E7 See Page 493)
LISA DR
1500 PlaC 95658 181-G7
LISA LN
3400 EDCo 95667 244-B4
LISA WY
7600 SAC 95832 337-E4
LISA ANN CT
7600 SaCo 95828 338-C4
LISA MARIE WY
6900 SaCo 95608 279-F2
LISAWOOD DR
200 FOLS 95630 261-E4
LISBON AV
1300 WSAC 95605 296-G1
LISBON WY
8100 SAC 95823 338-A6
LISCARNEY WY
8400 SaCo 95828 338-G7
LISMORE DR
8900 ELKG 95624 378-G1
LISSETTA AV
3700 SAC 95820 317-G2
LISTAN WY
3400 RCCD 95670 300-A4
LISTOWE DR
300 FOLS 95630 281-J1
LITCHFIELD CT
9200 ELKG 95624 358-J5
LITTLE CT
100 FOLS 95630 261-A3
1500 SaCo 95608 299-B2
LITTLE ACORN WY
7300 SaCo 95673 257-H1
LITTLE ACRES LN
12100 SaCo 95693 (380-E1 See Page 379)
LITTLE ARROW CT
5900 CITH 95621 259-D4
LITTLE BEAVER WY
6000 CITH 95621 259-D3
LITTLE BEN RD
- PlaC - 160-C2
LITTLE BROOK CT
4400 SaCo 95628 279-J2
LITTLE BRUSH RIDGE RD
5100 EDCo 95682 264-D2
LITTLE CHIEF CT
3600 SaCo 95843 238-G7
LITTLE CREEK CT
3900 PlaC 95661 240-E6
LITTLE CREEK DR
8800 PlaC 95661 240-F6
8800 SaCo 95662 240-F6
LITTLE CUT CT
800 EDCo 95667 245-G6
LITTLE HARBOR CT
- ELKG 95624 358-J6

LITTLE HARBOR WY
- ELKG 95624 358-J7
LITTLE HILL RD
7100 PlaC 95602 161-C2
LITTLE JOHN CT
- EDCo - 247-J1
8800 SaCo 95828 338-G6
LITTLE JOHN WY
- EDCo - 247-H1
- EDCo 95726 247-H1
LITTLE OAK CT
1000 RSVL 95747 219-E5
LITTLE OAK LN
2600 EDCo 95672 263-E2
4900 SaCo 95841 259-B7
4900 SaCo 95841 279-B1
LITTLE OAKS WY
7300 CITH 95621 239-G6
LITTLE OL CT
7100 CITH 95610 259-H2
LITTLE RANCH RD
3300 EDCo 95672 243-C4
LITTLE RAPIDS WY
9400 ELKG 95758 358-C6
LITTLE RIVER CT
6400 CITH 95621 259-D4
LITTLE RIVER WY
300 SAC 95831 336-G2
LITTLE ROCK DR
3800 SaCo 95843 258-F1
3800 SaCo 95843 238-H7
LITTLE ROCK RD
- RKLN 95765 220-A1
LITTLE SPRING RD
- EDCo 95684 286-G7
LITTLE SQUAW CT
5900 CITH 95621 259-D3
LITTLETON CT
200 FOLS 95630 261-H5
LITTLE WOOD CIR
8800 ELKG 95624 358-F2
LITTORAL ST
- PlaC 95747 239-B4
LIVE OAK AV
4300 OAKL 94561 (514-B5 See Page 493)
9900 SaCo 95632 419-B4
10200 GALT 95632 419-D4
LIVE OAK CIR
200 RSVL 95678 239-H4
LIVE OAK CT
- RKLN 95765 200-D6
100 FOLS 95630 261-B3
LIVE OAK LN
- RKLN 95765 200-D5
1200 PlaC 95603 162-C6
LIVE OAK PL
1500 PlaC 95603 162-C6
LIVE OAK RD
4600 EDCo 95619 265-H4
8600 SaCo 95693 360-J3
8600 SaCo 95693 (361-A2 See Page 341)
LIVE OAK ST
100 AUB 95603 182-C3
4500 SaCo 95608 279-C2
LIVE OAK WY
800 PlaC 95603 162-C6
LIVE PINE CT
1700 RSVL 95661 240-C6
LIVERMORE WY
100 FOLS 95630 261-F4
LIVERPOOL LN
- RSVL 95747 219-C4
LIVERY CT
9600 SaCo 95693 360-H6
LIVINGSTON CT
300 RSVL 95661 240-C4
LIVINGSTON PL
- RVIS 94571 454-F2
LIVINGSTON WY
100 RSVL 95678 219-G7
4300 SaCo 95823 317-H7
LIVINGSTONE LN
- EDCo 95619 266-C7
LIVORNA WY
8000 SaCo 95628 280-A1
LIVORNO WY
- ELKG 95757 357-J7
- ELKG 95757 358-A7
- ELKG 95757 378-A1
LIVOTI AV
200 PlaC 95661 239-H5
200 RSVL 95661 239-H5
4800 SaCo 95628 280-A1
4900 SaCo 95628 260-A7
LIZWELSH RD
4400 SaCo 95826 319-A3
LLANO LN
4700 SaCo 95628 279-J1
LLANOVISTA DR
- SaCo 95828 338-D7
LLEWELLYN CT
100 FOLS 95630 261-E4
LLOYD LN
2200 SaCo 95825 278-D7
LLOYD WY
100 AUB 95603 162-E7
5700 SaCo 95608 279-C5
LOAZELL CT
4200 SaCo 95864 298-H3
LOBATA ST
8100 CITH 95610 240-B7
LOBELIA CT
2700 ANT 94531 (513-G7 See Page 493)
LOBO
6400 SaCo 95683 322-B7
LOBO TR
- EDCo 95634 205-G7
- EDCo 95634 225-G1
LOCH WY
2000 EDCo 95762 242-E7
2100 EDCo 95762 262-E1
LOCHBRAE RD
1000 SAC 95815 277-G7
1000 SAC 95815 297-G1
LOCH DANE CT
4100 SaCo 95843 238-J6
LOCHER WY
7700 CITH 95610 259-J3
7700 CITH 95610 260-A2
LOCH HAVEN WY
4500 SaCo 95842 258-J5
LOCHINVAR WY
- SAC 95823 338-A6
LOCH LEVEN DR
4800 EDCo 95726 248-C7

LOCH LEVEN WY
6100 SaCo 95660 258-H4
LOCH LOMOND DR
4700 SaCo 95608 279-A5
LOCHMOOR CIR
- SAC 95823 337-H4
LOCHNESS CT
- RSVL 95678 219-J3
- SAC 95826 298-F7
LOCK AV
2600 SAC 95822 337-E1
LOCKBORNE DR
5300 SAC 95823 337-J6
LOCKE RD
1200 SaCo 95690 417-A7
LOCKEPORT CT
8700 ELKG 95624 358-G2
LOCKERBIE CT
8000 SaCo 95828 338-G6
LOCKERIDGE WY
9400 SaCo 95829 339-A6
LOCKFORD CT
- ELKG 95624 359-A6
LOCKFORD WY
9400 ELKG 95624 359-A6
LOCKHART WY
1400 RSVL 95747 239-C1
LOCKHEED CT
3100 EDCo 95682 263-D4
LOCKIE CT
500 EDCo 95667 265-E1
LOCKIE RD
500 EDCo 95667 265-E1
LOCKINGER
12300 SaCo 95693 (380-F1 See Page 379)
LOCKMOOR DR
5100 PlaC 95746 240-G6
LOCKRIDGE DR
- RSVL 95746 240-F4
LOCKRIDGE PL
2000 EDCo 95762 242-A5
LOCKSLEY LN
12000 PlaC 95602 162-B2
12600 AUB 95602 162-B2
LOCKTON DR
- RSVL 95747 218-H4
LOCKWOOD LN
- LNCN 95648 200-A1
LOCKWOOD WY
4300 SaCo 95821 278-J4
LOCOMOTIVE LN
- RSVL 95747 219-A3
LOCUST AV
1000 PLCR 95667 245-H4
5100 SaCo 95608 279-B2
LOCUST CT
- RSVL 95747 219-B7
LOCUST RD
1000 PlaC 95626 237-F2
1000 SuCo 95626 237-F2
6600 EDCo 95667 265-E3
9000 SaCo 95626 237-G3
LOCUST ST
9000 ELKG 95624 358-H6
LOCUTS PL
- EDCo 95682 263-D2
LODE RD
3400 EDCo 95667 245-B6
LODESTAR ST
2500 RKLN 95677 220-C3
LODESTAR WY
5200 ELKG 95758 357-J2
LODESTONE CIR
8600 ELKG 95624 358-G7
LOFTON CT
10100 ELKG 95757 377-J2
10100 ELKG 95757 397-J2
LOFTON WY
10100 ELKG 95757 377-J2
10100 ELKG 95757 397-J2
LOFTY VIEW RD
- EDCo 95619 286-C1
LOGAN CT
- LNCN 95648 179-E4
- RSVL 95678 219-G5
LOGAN LN
7600 PlaC 95663 201-D1
LOGAN ST
100 RVIS 94571 454-H5
6100 SAC 95824 318-C6
6300 SAC 95828 318-C6
LOGANBERRY CT
- SAC 95835 257-A6
LOGANBERRY PL
- ELKG 95624 358-G1
LOGAN'S LN
4900 EDCo 95619 265-J7
LOGANSPORT DR
- SAC 95835 256-J6
LOG CABIN CT
3100 EDCo 95667 226-J4
LOG CABIN LN
6200 EDCo 95667 226-H4
LOG CAMP RD
- EDCo 95633 205-G3
LOGGERHEAD WY
3400 SAC 95834 276-J3
LOGSTON CT
4000 SaCo 95821 278-H3
LOHEIT WY
6900 SaCo 95842 259-B2
LO HI CT
3100 EDCo 95667 245-C6
LO HI WY
3000 EDCo 95667 245-C6
3000 PLCR 95667 245-C6
LOHSE CT
- LNCN 95648 179-E2
LOHSE LN
- LNCN 95648 179-E2
LOHSE WY
7500 CITH 95610 239-H7
LOI LINDA LN
7500 CITH 95610 259-J1
LOIRE VALLEY WY
- ELKG 95624 379-A2
LOIS AV
200 GALT 95632 419-F6
LOIS LN
600 OAKL 94561 (514-D7 See Page 493)
1800 PLCR 95667 246-B5
7400 CITH 95610 260-D1
12300 PlaC 95603 162-C4
LOISDALE WY
11700 RCCD 95742 300-D7
11700 RCCD 95742 320-D1

STREET
Block City ZIP Pg-Grid

LOLA WY
4800 SaCo 95608 279-C1
4800 SaCo 95841 279-C1
LOLET WY
5600 SAC 95835 256-H4
LOLETA AV
7700 CITH 95610 239-J7
LOLL RD
13500 SaCo 95632 420-J5
LOLLIPOP LN
8300 ELKG 95624 358-E2
LOMA CT
3700 EDCo 95682 263-G6
LOMA DR
3600 EDCo 95682 263-G7
LOMA LN
700 ANT 94509 (513-C4 See Page 493)
9200 SaCo 95662 260-H4
LOMA CIMA DR
2300 EDCo 95667 245 B4
LOMA DEL NORTE ST
- EDCo 95726 247-F6
LOMA DEL ORO CT
- EDCo 95619 286-F5
LOMA LINDA CT
5700 SaCo 95841 279-C1
LOMA MAR CT
- SAC 95828 318-B7
LOMAND CT
8000 SaCo 95828 338-G6
LOMA OAK CT
5500 SaCo 95842 259-C2
LOMA RIO LN
7500 SaCo 95660 258-G1
LOMAS WY
1400 SAC 95822 337-B2
LOMA VERDE CT
600 EDCo 95762 242-C4
LOMA VERDE DR
1500 EDCo 95762 242-C4
LOMA VERDE WY
2900 SAC 95822 337-E2
LOMA VISTA DR
2200 SaCo 95825 278-E7
LOMBARD CT
700 SAC 95838 278-B1
LOMBARD LN
- LNCN 95648 179-E7
LOMBARDIA WY
- EDCo 95762 262-G6
LOMBARDY WY
9300 ELKG 95758 357-G5
LOMIDA LN
9200 PlaC 95650 221-H1
LOMITA CT
1300 EDCo 95762 242-D4
LOMITA WY
800 EDCo 95762 242-D4
1000 SaCo 95673 257-J4
1000 SaCo 95673 258-A4
LOMITAS AV
100 RSVL 95678 239-G1
LOMOND CT
- RSVL 95746 240-F4
LOMOND DR
1000 EDCo 95762 242-D7
1000 EDCo 95762 262-E1
LOMPOC CT
7000 CITH 95621 259-G3
LON CT
4400 EDCo 95619 265-F4
LONDON ST
1400 SaCo 95822 317-B5
LONDONDERRY DR
2800 SaCo 95827 299-C5
LONE HILL CT
4400 SaCo 95628 279-J2
LONE LEAF DR
- SAC 95838 257-G7
LONELY HILL WY
8200 SaCo 95843 238-H5
LONELY OAK CT
8400 SaCo 95628 260-C5
LONELY RIDGE CT
- SaCo 95628 260-C5
LONE OAK CT
- RSVL 95678 219-F5
LONE OAK DR
7500 CITH 95610 259-H3
LONE OAK LN
5300 PlaC 95746 221-F3
LONE PINE CT
- WSAC 95691 296-J7
LONE PINE DR
7200 SaCo 95683 342-A2
LONE PINE PL
8100 PlaC 95746 221-E4
LONE RIDGE CT
3500 SaCo 95843 238-G6
LONESOME DOVE CT
4600 EDCo 95682 283-H7
LONESOME DOVE DR
4700 EDCo 95682 283-G7
LONE SPUR DR
200 FOLS 95630 282-B1
LONE STAR CT
100 EDCo 95619 265-D4
LONESTAR WY
4800 SaCo 95843 239-A5
LONE STAR MINE CT
3200 EDCo 95667 246-F5
LONE STAR MINE RD
3200 EDCo 95667 246-F4
LONETREE BLVD
- RKLN 95765 199-H7
- RKLN 95765 219-G1
- RSVL 95678 219-G1
LONE TREE CT
1400 RSVL 95661 240-C5
LONE TREE LN
1400 RSVL 95661 240-C5
5700 EDCo 95682 283-J7
LONE TREE RD
5900 SaCo 95835 256-F4
6500 SaCo 95836 256-F3
6500 SaCo 95836 256-F2
8100 SuCo 95659 236-F3
LONE TREE WY
1800 ANT 94509 (513-D6 See Page 493)
LONEWOOD WY
7800 CITH 95621 239-D7
LONG AV
6700 EDCo 95667 265-B2
LONG ACRES CT
5900 SaCo 95628 260-C5
LONG BAR CT
11700 SaCo 95670 280-D5

LONG BEACH ST
- SaCo 95742 280-G6
LONG BRANCH CT
3300 SAC 95834 277-B4
LONG BRANCH DR
4600 SaCo 95842 258-J4
4600 SaCo 95842 259-A4
LONG BRANCH LN
4500 EDCo 95623 265-B5
LONG CANYON DR
5100 SaCo 95628 260-G6
LONG COVE CT
- PlaC 95747 239-B4
LONG COVE PL
- ELKG 95758 357-F6
LONG CREEK WY
1400 RSVL 95747 219-E5
LONGCROFT ST
1000 WSAC 95691 296-H5
LONGDALE DR
6200 SaCo 95660 258-J4
6400 SaCo 95660 259-A3
LONGDEN CIR
8200 CITH 95610 240-C6
LONGFELLOW CIR
1300 RSVL 95747 219-C5
LONGFELLOW WY
6100 SaCo 95842 259-A4
LONGFORD CT
400 LNCN 95648 179-G4
LONGFORD DR
6200 CITH 95621 259-E4
LONGFORD PL
- EDCo 95762 262-G6
LONGFORD WY
- EDCo 95762 262-G6
LONGHORN LN
1000 LNCN 95648 179-J4
LONGHORN RD
300 FOLS 95630 282-B1
LONGHORN ST
4500 SaCo 95608 279-B2
LONGHORN RIDGE RD
3200 EDCo 95682 283-E2
LONG ISLAND RD
- WSAC 95691 316-C2
LONGLEAF DR
- ELKG 95758 358-D5
LONGMEADOW LN
500 LNCN 95648 179-G5
LONG MEADOW RD
6300 PlaC 95746 241-A2
LONGMONT WY
6100 SaCo 95608 259-D7
LONGMORE WY
8700 SaCo 95628 280-E2
LONGPORT CT
- ELKG 95758 357-D4
LONG RAVINE CT
11600 SaCo 95670 280-C5
LONGRIDGE WY
6300 SAC 95831 317-B6
LONG RIVER DR
7200 SAC 95831 336-J1
LONGRUT RD
3500 EDCo 95667 245-E7
LONGSHORE CT
1300 SAC 95838 278-A2
LONGSHORE DR
1200 SAC 95838 278-A2
LONGS PEAK PL
5800 SaCo 95842 259-D2
LONGSPUR LP
2100 LNCN 95648 200-B2
LONGSPUR WY
8500 SaCo 95843 238-J5
8700 SaCo 95843 239-A5
LONG VALLEY DR
2300 PlaC 95658 202-A2
LONGVIEW DR
2200 RSVL 95747 239-E1
2200 RSVL 95747 219-C7
2800 SaCo 95660 278-E2
2800 SaCo 95660 278-G1
6200 EDCo 95667 265-A1
9700 PlaC 95650 201-J7
S LONGVIEW DR
1800 RKLN 95677 220-F5
LONGVIEW LN
- RKLN 95677 220-H5
10800 PlaC 95603 202-C1
LONGVIEW RD
2700 ANT 94509 (513-B7 See Page 493)
4600 EDCo 95682 283-E3
LONG WARF WY
- SAC 95835 256-G5
LONGWOOD RD
2400 PlaC 95603 161-G7
LONGWOOD WY
5600 CITH 95610 259-J6
LON HILLS
- RVIS 94571 454-F1
LONICERA DR
6800 SaCo 95662 260-C3
LONON CT
8400 SaCo 95662 260-C3
LONSDALE DR
5600 SAC 95822 317-A4
LOOKING GLASS LN
5200 EDCo 95682 244-C7
LOOKOUT CT
- SAC 95831 316-G6
LOOKOUT LN
- EDCo 95633 205-E5
LOOKOUT MOUNTAIN RD
- EDCo - 247-D4
LOOKOUT PASS CT
- RKLN 95765 219-J1
LOOK OUT POINT CT
- RSVL 95747 219-C3
LOOMIS HILLS RD
- PlaC 95650 221-C2
LOON CT
2800 EDCo 95682 263-C3
LOON LAKE CT
- LNCN 95648 200-C1
LOON LAKE LN
- LNCN 95648 200-B1
LOON LAKE ST
- RSVL 95747 219-D2
N LOOP BLVD
3700 SaCo 95843 238-J5
4500 SaCo 95843 239-A6
LOOP DR
- EDCo 95667 244-H3
LOORZ CT
- SAC 95823 338-A5

LOPES LN
2800 PlaC 95650 201-A3
LOPEZ CT
7800 SaCo 95829 339-E5
LOPEZ DR
1900 ANT 94509 (513-A6 See Page 493)
LOPEZ ISLAND RD
- WSAC 95691 316-C3
LOPIS CT
- SAC 95828 318-B6
LORA WY
- RSVL 95661 240-D5
LORAC VISTA DR
5000 SaCo 95843 239-B6
LORAY LN
3800 PlaC 95602 161-H2
LORD
100 RCCD 95827 299-E4
LORD ST
- SaCo 95690 437-A1
LORDEN CT
- FOLS 95630 281-F1
LORDS WY
5500 EDCo 95623 264-H7
LORDSHIP WY
9000 ELKG 95624 358-G4
LORDS MINE TR
- EDCo 95667 266-B5
LORELLA WY
5700 SaCo 95842 259-C2
LORENA LN
- FOLS 95630 261-F2
LORENZETTI DR
4300 OAKL 94561 (514-D7 See Page 493)
LORENZO LN
2100 SaCo 95864 278-H7
LORETO WY
3900 SaCo 95821 278-H6
LORETTO DR
200 RSVL 95661 240-B3
LORI CT
- PlaC 95747 239-B4
- SAC 95831 336-J1
LORI DR
- WSAC 95691 296-D4
LORIJO WY
5000 SaCo 95660 258-H7
LORIMER WY
1300 RSVL 95747 219-D7
LORIN AV
8000 SaCo 95828 338-C1
LORING CT
100 FOLS 95630 261-G6
LORING LN
- LNCN 95648 179-E6
LORNA CT
9200 ELKG 95624 358-F5
LORNA WY
- GALT 95632 419-D6
LORRAINE AV
200 RSVL 95678 239-J3
LORRAINE CT
5800 SAC 95817 318-A1
LORTON CT
- SAC 95823 358-B1
LOS ALAMOS WY
3500 SaCo 95864 298-G3
LOS ALTOS
1500 EDCo 95762 262-C7
LOS ALTOS AV
400 AUB 95603 182-E1
LOS ALTOS WY
2900 ANT 94509 (513-B6 See Page 493)
6800 SAC 95831 317-A7
LOS AMIGOS DR
2600 RCCD 95670 299-E3
LOS ANGELES AV
- SaCo 95742 280-G7
LOS BANOS WY
8700 ELKG 95624 358-G4
LOS CERROS DR
- EDCo 95619 286-A2
6900 SAC 95831 317-A7
6900 SAC 95831 337-A1
LOS COCHES WY
4100 SaCo 95864 298-H3
LOS ENCANTOS CIR
8700 ELKG 95624 378-G1
LOS FELIZ WY
2500 SaCo 95608 279-D6
LOS FLORES CT
700 GALT 95632 419-F4
LOS FLORES RD
3400 LMS 95650 201-A5
LOS GARCIAS LN
200 SaCo 95626 237-F4
LOS GATOS CIR
- SAC 95831 336-H1
LOS LAGOS CIR
- PlaC 95746 221-G4
LOS LAGOS CIR N
5900 PlaC 95746 221-F4
LOS LAGOS CIR S
8500 PlaC 95746 221-F4
LOS LUNAS WY
600 SAC 95833 277-E5
LOS MOLINOS WY
800 SaCo 95864 298-G2
LOS NOGALES WY
2600 RCCD 95670 299-J1
LOS OLIVOS WY
6900 SaCo 95608 279-F1
LOS OSOS CT
- RSVL 95747 219-B4
4700 SaCo 95843 239-A7
LOS PADRES LN
3900 EDCo 95682 264-A6
LOS PADRES WY
1400 SAC 95831 317-B7
LOS PALOS DR
10200 RCCD 95670 299-E2
LOS PERSIA LN
- EDCo 95630 222-G7
LOS POSAS CT
- PlaC 95746 221-G4
LOS POSAS WY
- PlaC 95746 221-F4
LOS PUEBLOS WY
- SAC 95835 256-H4
LOS PUENTES RD
9000 PlaC 95658 201-G2
LOS RAMBLAS CT
300 RSVL 95747 219-B5
LOS RANCHO WY
7700 SAC 95831 337-B4

LOS RIOS DR
1100 SaCo 95608 299-B3
LOS ROBLES BLVD
900 SAC 95838 277-J4
1200 SAC 95838 278-A4
LOS SANTOS DR
3700 EDCo 95682 263-F7
LOS SERRANOS WY
8400 CITH 95610 260-C1
LOST AV
5400 RKLN 95677 220-E4
LOST LN
2200 EDCo 95667 245-A4
6600 SaCo 95662 260-G3
LOST CAVERN CT
8400 CITH 95621 239-F6
LOST CREEK CT
7500 CITH 95621 259-G1
LOST CREEK DR
100 FOLS 95630 261-A1
LOST DEER LN
2500 SaCo 95608 279-D7
LOST LAKE CT
100 FOLS 95630 260-J1
LOST LAKE LN
7000 RSVL 95747 219-A4
LOST MINE CT
8400 CITH 95621 239-F6
LOST OAK CT
- RSVL 95661 220-D7
LOS TORRES DR
8600 ELKG 95624 358-F5
LOS TRAMPAS DR
2800 EDCo 95667 246-F4
2800 EDCo 95709 246-F4
LOST RIVER CT
8400 SaCo 95843 238-F5
LOST RIVER RD
1300 PlaC 95648 180-C2
LOST SPRINGS CT
9300 ELKG 95624 359-A4
LOSTWOOD LN
9200 SaCo 95628 260-H7
LOS VEGAS AV
100 RSVL 95678 239-H1
400 RSVL 95678 219-H7
LOTHLAN WY
- FOLS 95630 261-G7
LOTTIE LN
4200 EDCo 95672 243-F7
LOTUS AV
4100 SAC 95822 317-D3
LOTUS CT
2700 ANT 94531 (513-G7 See Page 493)
4800 EDCo 95667 244-B2
LOTUS RD
1600 EDCo 95667 244-A1
2200 EDCo 95682 244-A5
LOTUS POND CT
4900 ELKG 95757 377-H2
4900 ELKG 95757 397-H2
LOTUS POND WY
4900 ELKG 95757 377-H2
4900 ELKG 95757 397-H2
LOU CT
6200 PlaC 95746 241-A5
LOU PL
6300 PlaC 95746 241-A5
LOUCRETA DR
7600 SaCo 95828 338-C2
LOUGANIS WY
4000 SaCo 95823 337-G6
LOUGHRIDGE WY
100 FOLS 95630 261-F4
LOUIS CT
9200 ELKG 95624 358-H4
LOUIS DR
1300 ANT 94509 (513-E5 See Page 493)
LOUIS LN
100 RSVL 95661 239-H5
LOUIS ST
9200 ELKG 95624 358-H5
LOUIS WY
1200 SAC 95819 298-A7
N LOUISA AV
26200 SJCo 95686 (438-B3 See Page 418)
LOUISE ST
500 SAC 95814 297-E2
LOUISIANA RD
- SaCo 95742 280-H6
- SaCo 95742 281-A5
LOUISIANA ST
2600 SaCo 95821 278-H6
LOUISVILLE AV
- SaCo 95742 280-G7
LOURDES CT
- SAC 95831 336-H2
LOURENCE RD
3000 SaCo 95757 397-F10
LOURINA CT
5000 SaCo 95628 259-J7
LOUTH WY
6200 CITH 95621 259-E4
LOVAS DR
5200 SaCo 95842 259-B1
LOVATO CT
7400 CITH 95621 259-F1
LOVE WY
1400 PlaC 95603 162-E5
5100 SaCo 95608 279-B5
LOVELAND CT
- EDCo 95633 205-A4
LOVELAND WY
100 SAC 95838 277-F1
LOVELLA WY
400 SAC 95819 298-A5
LOVERS LN
1600 EDCo 95762 242-F6
LOVEWELL CT
9300 ELKG 95758 357-H5
LOVEWOOD CT
6200 CITH 95621 239-E7
LOWDAN CT
4000 RSVL 95747 219-E6
LOWDAN LN
4000 RSVL 95747 219-E6
LOWE LN
1400 PlaC 95603 162-D5
LOWELL CT
- RSVL 95747 219-E6
LOWELL ST
5500 SAC 95820 318-C4
5500 SAC 95824 318-C4
10200 PlaC 95626 237-E1
LOWER LAKEVIEW
- EDCo 95667 244-H3

LOWER RANCH RD
- PlaC 95648 180-E5
N LOWER SACRAMENTO RD Rt#-J10
22500 SJCo 95220 439-F6
LOWLAND CT
1900 SaCo 95608 299-B1
LOWNEY CT
100 FOLS 95630 261-H6
LOWRY DR
3600 SaCo 95660 258-G6
LOWTHER WY
3200 SaCo 95843 238-F6
LOYAL LN
2800 EDCo 95726 248-A1
LOYALTY WY
5600 ELKG 95757 377-J3
5600 ELKG 95757 397-J3
LOYOLA ST
2900 SAC 95826 298-F7
2900 SAC 95826 318-F1
LOZANOS RD
100 PlaC 95658 181-H3
LUALAN LN
200 RSVL 95678 239-G3
LUBECK RD
100 AUB 95603 182-E2
LUCAS CT
4100 SAC 95822 317-B2
LUCCA WY
- ELKG 95757 358-A7
- ELKG 95757 378-A1
LUCCHESI CT
4700 OAKL 94561 (514-C7 See Page 493)
LUCCHESI DR
5100 SaCo 95829 338-J7
LUCE AV
5600 SaCo 95652 258-F5
LUCENA WY
2700 ANT 94509 (513-A6 See Page 493)
LUCERA CT
- RSVL 95747 219-B2
LUCERO DR
6100 SaCo 95824 317-J6
LUCETTA WY
- RSVL 95661 220-D6
LUCIA CT
2200 RCCD 95670 279-H6
LUCIANA CT
- RSVL 95661 220-F6
LUCIANA WY
- RSVL 95661 220-E6
LUCIANO CT
8600 SaCo 95828 338-F6
LUCIE LN
7900 SaCo 95628 279-J2
7900 SaCo 95628 280-A2
LUCILE WY
800 SaCo 95673 257-J1
LUCINDA LN
5900 SaCo 95608 259-D7
LUCIO LN
1200 SAC 95822 317-A4
LUCKMAN WY
- ELKG 95757 377-H2
- ELKG 95757 397-H2
LUCKY LN
3300 LMS 95650 200-G5
7400 CITH 95610 259-H5
LUCKY ST
- PLCR 95667 245-H5
LUCKY WY
3100 SAC 95823 337-F1
LUCKY LINDY CT
6400 SaCo 95662 260-D4
LUCY LN
600 RSVL 95678 239-H4
LUDELLE LN
4900 SaCo 95824 317-H6
LUDLOW CT
- RSVL 95747 219-C3
LUDLOW DR
- RSVL 95747 219-C3
LUELLA CT
10700 RCCD 95670 279-H6
LUFKIN WY
9300 ELKG 95758 357-G5
LUJAN DR
9100 ELKG 95624 358-F5
LUJAN WY
9100 ELKG 95624 358-F5
LUJAN CREST CT
9200 ELKG 95624 358-F5
LUKE WY
5000 SaCo 95628 260-D7
LUKEN CT
- ELKG 95624 338-H7
LUMBO RD
5300 EDCo 95682 264-F7
LUMPY LN
4200 EDCo 95619 265-G3
LUMRY ST
6800 SaCo 95660 258-J2
LUNA CIR
200 FOLS 95630 261-E7
LUNA CT
3800 EDCo 95667 265-A1
LUNA LN
6200 SaCo 95608 279-D4
LUNA GRANDE CIR
- SAC 95834 277-C4
LUNAR LN
2600 SaCo 95864 298-E3
LUNARDI CT
400 RSVL 95678 219-F7
LUNARDI WY
400 RSVL 95678 219-F7
LUND CT
4100 SaCo 95660 258-H2
LUND DR
1900 RSVL 95661 240-D6
LUNDY CT
- SAC 95822 317-A5
LUPIN CT
- ELKG 95624 358 F1
LUPIN LN
8700 PlaC 95746 241-D3
LUPIN WY
- ELKG 95624 358-F1
LUPINE CT
- GALT 95632 419-E3
2700 RKLN 95677 220-F2
2800 ANT 94531 (513-G7 See Page 493)
6500 EDCo 95667 226-G2
LUPINE LN
- AUB 95603 182-A6

LUPINE LN
- LNCN 95648 179-D1
3100 EDCo 95667 226-H2
LUPINE WY
- SAC 95819 297-H3
LUPINE FIELD CT
8200 SaCo 95829 339-D7
LUPONE CT
- ELKG 95624 358-H1
LURA AL
5600 SaCo 95660 258-G5
LURLIENE AV
6200 SaCo 95841 259-D4
LUSCUTOFF CT
3200 SAC 95820 318-B1
LUSITANO WY
- ELKG 95757 357-H7
LUSK DR
3600 SaCo 95864 278-G7
LUSTER PL
1000 FOLS 95630 261-B6
LUTHER DR
- SaCo 95823 317-F7
6900 SAC 95823 317-F7
6900 SAC 95823 337-F1
LUTHER RD
12000 PlaC 95603 162-C5
12400 AUB 95603 162-C5
LUTHERAN CIR
3900 SaCo 95826 318-J1
3900 SaCo 95826 319-A2
LUTHER RIDGE CT
12600 AUB 95603 162-E5
LUTON DR
- RSVL 95747 239-B1
LUTTIG CT
5200 ELKG 95757 377-J3
5200 ELKG 95757 397-J3
LUTTIG WY
5100 ELKG 95757 377-H3
5100 ELKG 95757 397-H3
LUTTREL CT
100 FOLS 95630 261-F3
LUVETA WY
2600 RCCD 95670 299-H1
LUX CT
2000 SaCo 95608 299-C1
LUXFORD CT
4600 SaCo 95842 259-A1
LUXOR LN
4000 RSVL 95746 240-F6
LUYUNG DR
3100 RCCD 95742 300-B3
LUZERN WY
7600 SaCo 95843 259-B1
LUZON AV
- SAC 95828 318-D4
LYCOMING CT
2600 SAC 95826 298-F7
LYDIA LN
1000 EDCo 95667 245-A6
LYLE ST
4200 SaCo 95821 278-H6
LYLES LN
- PlaC 95648 180-F5
LYLEWOOD CT
- SAC 95834 277-B3
LYMAN CIR
- SAC 95835 257-C6
LYNDALE CIR
- ELKG 95758 358-B3
LYNDEBORO CT
100 FOLS 95630 261-G6
LYNDHURST AV
400 RSVL 95678 239-F5
LYNDLEY PZWY
- ELKG 95624 359-A6
LYNE BAY DR
- RSVL 95747 219-C4
LYNETTE WY
1300 SAC 95831 337-B3
LYNHOLLEN WY
7100 SAC 95831 336-J1
LYNHURST WY
3700 SaCo 95660 278-G1
LYNN AV
400 ANT 94509 (513-E7 See Page 493)
LYNN LN
3600 PlaC 95602 161-G3
LYNNADEANE CT
5200 SaCo 95608 259-E7
LYNNBROOK CT
7200 SaCo 95608 279-G3
LYNNDALE DR
1100 SaCo 95864 298-J3
LYNNE CT
400 PLCR 95667 245-E5
LYNNE WY
3300 SaCo 95821 278-G5
LYNNETREE WY
7000 CITH 95610 259-J2
7000 CITH 95610 260-A2
LYNNMAR WY
3500 SaCo 95608 279-E4
LYNTON CT
100 FOLS 95630 261-F7
LYNWOOD LN
2300 PlaC 95650 201-A2
2300 PlaC 95663 201-A2
LYNWOOD WY
3700 SaCo 95864 278-G7
LYNX TR
- EDCo 95726 247-J4
- EDCo 95726 248-A4
LYNX WY
- LNCN 95648 199-H3
LYNX TRAIL CT
- EDCo 95726 247-H5
LYON AV
2300 SaCo 95825 298-D3
LYONIA DR
700 GALT 95632 419-F4
LYONIA WY
6900 SaCo 95662 260-C2
LYRA ST
3500 RCCD 95827 299-D6
LYSANDER WY
- RSVL 95661 220-E6
LYTHAM WY
2000 RSVL 95678 219-J6
LYTLE ST
7600 SAC 95832 337-C4
LYTON WY
8200 ELKG 95624 358-D1

M

M ST
100 SaCo 95673 257-F2
300 LNCN 95648 179-G3
400 ANT 94509 (513-C4 See Page 493)
3200 SaCo 95816 297-G5
3900 SAC 95819 297-J6
5400 SAC 95819 298-A6
MABEL ST
3200 SAC 95838 277-G4
MABLE ROSE WY
5500 SaCo 95843 239-C5
MABRY DR
2100 SAC 95835 257-A4
2600 SAC 95835 256-J4
MACADAMIA LN
4400 OAKL 94561 (514-G7 See Page 493)
MACARDY CT
- PlaC 95747 238-H3
MACARGO CT
- PlaC 95746 240-J2
MACARGO RD
5600 PlaC 95746 240-J2
5800 PlaC 95746 241-A2
MACARIO CT
200 RSVL 95678 240-A1
MACARLEN WY
1000 SAC 95815 277-J6
MACARTHUR ST
100 SAC 95838 278-B2
MACAULAY CIR
1200 SaCo 95608 299-A3
MACAULAY ST
1100 ANT 94509 (513-C4 See Page 493)
MACAW LN
- RKLN 95765 219-J1
- RKLN 95765 220-A1
MACCAN CT
- SAC 95832 337-C4
MACDUFF CT
9300 PlaC 95746 241-A5
MACDUFF DR
6200 PlaC 95746 241-A5
MACE CT
- EDCo - 247-E2
400 PLCR 95667 245-E5
MACE RD
2500 EDCo - 247-D2
MACE ST
6100 SAC 95824 318-B5
MACEDO WY
3000 SaCo 95826 298-J7
MACEDONIAN CT
8600 ELKG 95624 358-F1
MACE RIVER CT
11100 RCCD 95670 280-A5
MACERO CT
- EDCo 95762 262-E5
MACERO ST
- RSVL 95747 219-C1
MACEY DR
4200 SaCo 95841 278-J2
MACFADDEN DR
7700 SaCo 95828 338-C3
MACFARLANE RD
- PlaC 95603 182-C1
MACFINLEY WY
7500 SaCo 95828 338-C3
MACHADO LN
700 RSVL 95678 239-H4
4200 OAKL 94561 (514-J7 See Page 493)
MACHADO WY
6000 SAC 95822 316-J5
6000 SAC 95822 317-A5
MACHADO RANCH DR
- ELKG 95757 378-B2
MACHAN CT
- ELKG 95757 377-F1
- ELKG 95757 397-F1
MACHICO WY
10300 ELKG 95757 378-A3
MACHTY CT
- AUB 95603 182-B7
MACIEL AV
100 RSVL 95678 239-J2
MACINTA CT
10300 ELKG 95757 378-A3
MACK RD
3900 SAC 95823 337-G4
6000 SAC 95823 338-A4
MACKEY RD
8500 ELKG 95624 359-E3
MACKINAC RD
- WSAC 95691 316-E2
MACKINAW ST
6200 EDCo 95726 248-C7
MACKINAW WY
2500 SaCo 95826 298-G6
MACON DR
- SAC 95835 257-A4
2900 SAC 95835 256-J4
MACPHEADRIS CT
- EDCo 95762 262-D5
MACPHEADRIS WY
- EDCo 95762 262-D5
MACREADY AV
- RCCD 95655 299-F6
- SaCo 95655 299-F6
MACY PLAZA DR
7800 CITH 95610 259-J5
7800 CITH 95610 260-A5
MADAMIN WY
- SAC 95835 256-J6
MADDEN LN
1000 RSVL 95661 239-J4
1000 RSVL 95661 240-A4
1400 EDCo 95667 246-B2
MADDIE CT
- SaCo 95829 338-H6
MADDIEWOOD CIR
3500 RCCD 95827 299-E5
MADDOX CT
2100 SaCo 95608 299-A1
MADEIRA CT
8500 ELKG 95624 358-E1
MADEIRA ISLAND LN
- PlaC - 160-B5
- PlaC 95648 160-B5
MADELIA DR
2900 SAC 95833 277-E5
MADELINE WY
7600 CITH 95610 259-H5

STREET
Block City ZIP Pg-Grid

MADERA CT
- OAKL 94561 (514-A7 See Page 493)
MADERA RD
2100 SaCo 95825 278-D7
MADERA WY
- EDCo 95762 263-A4
MADERA VISTA LN
- EDCo 95672 243-G4
MADERE WY
- RVIS 94571 454-H3
MADERIA PORT LN
8100 SaCo 95628 260-C6
MADEROS CT
100 FOLS 95630 261-G3
MADI LN
- SaCo 95638 420-D3
MADILL CIR
- ANT 94509 (513-C6 See Page 493)
MADILL CT
- ANT 94509 (513-D6 See Page 493)
MADILL ST
- ANT 94509 (513-C6 See Page 493)
E MADILL ST
- ANT 94509 (513-D6 See Page 493)
MADISON AV
- FOLS 95662 260-H5
3600 SaCo 95660 258-H7
4200 SaCo 95842 258-H7
4500 SaCo 95841 258-H7
4600 SaCo 95841 259-B7
5700 SaCo 95608 259-F6
6700 SaCo 95628 259-F6
7000 CITH 95628 259-F6
7800 CITH 95628 260-A6
7800 SaCo 95628 260-A6
9000 SaCo 95662 260-H5
MADISON CT
- RKLN 95765 219-H1
800 RSVL 95678 219-H1
3000 ANT 94509 (513-A7 See Page 493)
MADISON ST
- SaCo 95742 300-F1
MADISON WY
800 RSVL 95678 219-G5
MADISON GREENS LN
9100 SaCo 95662 260-G6
MADONNA CT
8100 SaCo 95828 338-F6
MADREA CT
6800 CITH 95621 259-F4
MADRID LN
- ANT 94509 (513-A6 See Page 493)
MADRID WY
9500 ELKG 95758 357-H6
MAD RIVER CT
- SAC 95831 336-J1
MADRONE AV
1500 WSAC 95691 296-H3
MADRONE CT
1000 EDCo 95667 245-G2
1000 PLCR 95667 245-G2
MADRONE DR
2800 EDCo - 247-G3
MADRONE LN
1000 EDCo 95667 245-G2
1000 PLCR 95667 245-G2
MADRONE ST
- PlaC 95626 237-E1
MADRONE WY
- SAC 95834 277-B3
MADRONE WOODS PL
8200 SaCo 95843 239-C6
MAE CT
- RSVL 95747 219-D5
MAEVE CT
4300 RCCD 95742 320-E2
MAFIC CT
- SAC 95823 337-F2
MAGDELINA ST
6000 SaCo 95673 257-G4
MAGELLAN DR
9700 PlaC 95650 201-J6
MAGENTA CT
- RSVL 95747 219-B7
MAGENTA DR
- RSVL 95747 219-B7
MAGGIE CT
- EDCo 95682 264-D5
MAGGIE LN
4600 EDCo 95682 264-D6
MAGGY RD
10200 SaCo 95693 (380-F3 See Page 379)
MAGIC CT
7000 CITH 95621 259-G2
MAGIC PL
400 EDCo 95667 245-E5
MAGICWOODS CT
3200 RCCD 95827 299-D5
MAGINNES CT
10200 SaCo 95829 339-E5
MAGISTER CT
4700 SaCo 95843 239-A7
MAGNIFICA LN
4300 SaCo 95827 319-B2
MAGNIFICA PL
4400 SaCo 95827 319-B2
MAGNO CT
15000 SaCo 95683 342-B2
MAGNOLIA AV
- SaCo 95615 (396-D3 See Page 375)
100 AUB 95603 182-E2
100 SaCo 95828 338-F3
3600 LMS 95650 200-J6
3600 LMS 95650 201-A6
7700 SaCo 95628 279-J3
MAGNOLIA CT
- RKLN 95765 219-H2
MAGNOLIA DR
- RVIS 94571 454-F1
MAGNOLIA LN
- EDCo 95709 247-C1
- LNCN 95648 179-H6
MAGNOLIA WY
- RKLN 95765 219-H2
1000 RSVL 95661 239-J3
1700 ANT 94509 (513-B5 See Page 493)
MAGNOLIA HILL WY
8600 ELKG 95624 358-E1
MAGNOLIA HILLS DR
3800 EDCo 95672 263-B5
3800 EDCo 95762 263-B5
MAGNUM CT
2100 SaCo 95626 238-C6
MAGNUM LN
- EDCo - 267-J4
MAGOS RD
9300 SaCo 95693 360-D6
MAGPIE CT
- RSVL 95747 219-B7
3500 EDCo 95667 244-E7
MAGPIE LN
3500 EDCo 95709 246-H2
3600 SaCo 95660 258-G7
MAGUITTE CT
3100 SAC 95835 256-J3
MAHAFFEY CT
- FOLS 95630 261-H4
MAHALA DR
6200 SaCo 95608 279-D7
MAHAN CT
200 RSVL 95678 240-A1
MAHASKA WY
- SAC 95835 256-J6
MAHOGANY ST
3500 SAC 95838 278-B3
MAHOGANY WY
1700 ANT 94509 (513-A5 See Page 493)
MAHONIA CIR
100 SAC 95835 257-B4
MAIDEN LN
- CITH 95621 239-G5
- RSVL 95678 239-G5
MAID MARION CT
8100 SaCo 95828 338-G6
MAIDSTONE WY
5400 CITH 95621 259-G6
MAIDU DR
400 AUB 95603 182-D5
400 PlaC 95603 182-E6
1500 RSVL 95661 240-C3
7000 EDCo 95667 226-H4
MAIDU LN
3100 PlaC 95648 180-E6
MAIDU TR
- EDCo 95667 266-H5
MAIDU WY
2000 SaCo 95670 280-C4
MAILER WY
- ELKG 95758 358-D3
MAIN AV
- SAC 95834 257-F7
- SAC 95838 257-F7
700 SaCo 95834 257-F7
1000 SAC 95838 258-A7
1800 SAC 95652 258-A7
1800 SaCo 95652 258-A7
4000 SaCo 95628 280-G1
4000 SaCo 95662 280-G1
4500 SaCo 95662 260-H4
MAIN ST
- PLCR 95667 245-F5
- RVIS 94571 454-H5
- SAC 95821 278-C5
100 ISLE 95641 455-H5
100 RSVL 95678 239-F1
400 PlaC 95658 181-G5
3900 SaCo 95628 280-A2
13000 SaCo 95690 417-A7
MAIN ST Rt#-4
600 OAKL 94561 (514-B5 See Page 493)
900 ANT 94509 (514-A5 See Page 493)
900 OAKL 94509 (514-A5 See Page 493)
MAINE ST
- SaCo 95742 300-F1
MAINLINE DR
9300 ELKG 95624 358-J7
9300 ELKG 95624 359-B6
MAIN SAIL CIR
1100 RSVL 95661 240-A5
MAINSAIL CT
100 FOLS 95630 261-F3
MAINSTAY CT
8400 ELKG 95624 358-E1
MAISON WY
2600 SaCo 95864 298-E2
MAISY LN
6100 EDCo 95623 265-A6
MAITA CIR
6900 SAC 95820 318-B2
MAITLAND LN
8200 SaCo 95628 280-B2
MAJAR CT
3400 EDCo 95682 263-D3
MAJESTIC CT
3300 RKLN 95765 200-C7
MAJESTIC DR
3400 RKLN 95765 220-C1
3400 RKLN 95765 200-C7
MAJESTIC LN
200 SAC 95838 278-B2
MAJESTIC RD
200 SAC 95838 278-B2
MAJESTIC OAK WY
8200 CITH 95610 240-B7
MAJESTIES CT
- ELKG 95624 359-B5
MAJESTY WY
- RCCD 95827 299-E4
MAJO CT
10100 RCCD 95670 299-E2
MAJOR AV
- PlaC 95603 202-B2
- PlaC 95658 202-B2
MAJOR WY
5600 SaCo 95841 279-C1
MAJORCA CIR
200 SAC 95823 337-J6
MAKABE LN
5500 RKLN 95650 220-J1
5500 RKLN 95677 220-J1
MAKO DR
1100 EDCo 95619 265-H4
MALACHITE WY
- RSVL 95747 219-A7
- RSVL 95747 239-A1
3700 EDCo 95672 263-C2
MALAGA CT
- EDCo 95682 263-E3
MALAGA WY
10100 RCCD 95670 299-F2
MALANA CT
4400 RCCD 95742 320-D2
MALANA WY
4300 RCCD 95742 320-D2
MALAY DR
4300 SaCo 95841 258-J7
MALBEC CT
2500 RCCD 95670 299-G1
MALBEC DR
- EDCo 95762 262-F4
MALCOLM DIXON RD
1000 EDCo 95762 242-D7
MALCOLM ISLAND ST
- WSAC 95691 316-C2
MALDEN CT
9100 ELKG 95624 358-J4
MALDIVE ST
7500 SaCo 95673 237-H7
7500 SaCo 95673 257-H1
MALDONADO CT
- SAC 95820 318-A3
MALEVILLE AV
5900 SaCo 95608 259-D6
MALEZA LN
11200 PlaC 95603 182-D7
MALHEUR WY
9200 ELKG 95758 357-H5
MALIA CT
7700 CITH 95621 239-F7
MALIBU CT
- WSAC 95691 316-H1
MALINO CT
- SAC 95823 337-J7
MALLARD CIR
- FOLS 95630 281-E1
MALLARD CT
- LMS 95650 200-J7
- LNCN 95648 179-D1
- RKLN 95765 219-J1
4800 OAKL 94561 (514-D7 See Page 493)
MALLARD DR
100 GALT 95632 419-D6
MALLARD LN
1200 RSVL 95661 240-C3
1400 OAKL 94561 (514-D7 See Page 493)
2300 PLCR 95667 245-B5
5900 CITH 95621 259-D1
MALLARD PL
- LNCN 95648 179-D1
MALLARD WY
- LNCN 95648 179-D2
MALLARD COVE CT
9800 ELKG 95757 357-F7
MALLARD CREEK CT
- RSVL 95747 219-E1
MALLARD CREEK DR
- RSVL 95747 219-E2
MALLARD LAKE WY
12000 RCCD 95742 320-E3
MALLARDVIEW WY
- ELKG 95757 357-J7
MALLON CT
7700 SaCo 95829 339-E5
MALLORCA CT
3100 EDCo 95682 263-C5
MALLOW CT
- LNCN 95648 179-E2
MALLOW LN
- LNCN 95648 179-E2
MALONE CT
- SAC 95820 318-B3
MALONEY DR
- LNCN 95648 179-E2
MALORY CT
7700 SaCo 95828 338-C3
MALOS WY
- RCCD 95670 299-F4
MALT CT
7600 SaCo 95828 338-D4
MALTA DR
- RSVL 95678 219-H2
MALTON WY
- GALT 95632 419-G3
MALVAR ST
- SAC 95833 276-J4
MALVASIA DR
10500 RCCD 95670 299-G1
MALVERNE CT
400 RSVL 95747 239-C1
MALWOOD WY
- SaCo 95829 338-H6
MAME CT
6100 CITH 95621 259-D3
MAMMOTH DR
3500 PlaC 95650 201-F6
MAMMOTH WY
- RSVL 95747 199-C7
- RSVL 95747 219-C1
MAMMOTH RIVER CT
11000 RCCD 95670 279-J5
MAMMOUTH CT
- EDCo 95762 262-D7
- EDCo 95762 282-D1
MAMMOUTH LN
- OAKL 94561 (514-G7 See Page 493)
MAMMOUTH WY
900 EDCo 95762 282-D1
MANACOR DR
4500 SAC 95823 337-H5
MANADA CT
5500 ELKG 95758 357-J3
MANANA WY
8300 SaCo 95628 260-C5
MANAND ST
3100 SaCo 95608 279-C5
MANASCO CIR
- FOLS 95630 261-H5
MANASQUAN CT
- ELKG 95758 357-E4
MANASSERO WY
6500 SAC 95820 318-B1
MANCEL CT
3200 SaCo 95608 279-B5
MANCHESTER CT
5000 PlaC 95746 240-H5
MANCHESTER DR
1300 EDCo 95762 282-D2
MANCHESTER RD
1900 SAC 95815 278-B7
1900 SAC 95825 278-B7
MANCHESTER ST
2100 WSAC 95691 296-H7
MANDALAY CT
- RSVL 95747 219-B1
8900 ELKG 95624 358-G3
MANDALAY WY
8700 ELKG 95624 358-G2
MANDAN CT
8700 SaCo 95662 260-E1
MANDARIN CIR
7200 CITH 95610 260-B1
MANDARIN CT
2600 WSAC 95691 316-F1
3500 LMS 95650 201-A4
MANDARIN WY
2100 ANT 94509 (513-B5 See Page 493)
MANDARIN HILL CT
- PlaC 95658 180-J3
- PlaC 95658 181-A3
MANDARIN HILL LN
2300 PlaC 95663 201-B2
MANDARIN HILL RD
100 PlaC 95658 180-J3
100 PlaC 95658 181-A4
MANDEL ST
- SAC 95835 257-A5
MANDEVILLE LN
7400 SaCo 95828 338-F3
MANDEVILLE WY
2600 WSAC 95691 296-F7
2600 WSAC 95691 316-F1
MANDOLIN WY
- EDCo 95667 265-C1
11900 RCCD 95742 320-E1
MANDRAKE CT
- ELKG 95624 359-A5
MANDURA RD
- WSAC 95691 316-D2
MANDY DR
- SAC 95823 337-G3
MANET PKWY
7700 SaCo 95823 337-H2
MANETTE WY
9300 SaCo 95662 260-H2
MANGELO CT
- RSVL 95747 199-B7
MANGER WY
8200 CITH 95610 240-A6
MANGO AL
- RSVL 95678 239-H1
MANGO LN
- ELKG 95624 359-D5
MANGO TREE WY
7700 CITH 95621 239-D7
MANGROVE CT
5700 SaCo 95662 260-J5
MANGRUM AV
2000 SAC 95822 317-D6
MANHART WY
8200 SaCo 95626 238-D5
MANHATTAN CIR
3900 SaCo 95823 337-G1
MANHATTAN DR
500 RSVL 95678 219-G3
MANHATTAN ST
- SaCo 95742 300-F1
MANHATTAN BAR RD
2100 PlaC 95603 202-C3
MANHATTEN CRK RD
6100 EDCo 95623 205-A1
MANI CIR
11700 RCCD 95742 320-D1
MANILA AV
6700 SaCo 95628 259-F7
MANITOBA AV
6200 SaCo 95841 259-C4
MANITOU ST
100 SAC 95838 277-G2
MANKATO CT
- SAC 95835 256-J6
MANLEY CT
- SAC 95820 318-A3
MANLOVE RD
2800 SaCo 95826 298-H7
3100 SaCo 95826 318-H1
MANMAR WY
5600 SaCo 95823 317-J6
MANN CT
1100 FOLS 95630 261-D7
MANN RD
10900 SaCo 95693 379-J2
11000 SaCo 95693 (380-A2 See Page 379)
MANNERLY WY
6700 CITH 95621 239-F6
MANNING DR
1000 EDCo 95762 242-B5
MANNING ST
2300 SAC 95815 278-A7
MANNINGTON ST
8700 ELKG 95758 358-B2
MANNOCK CT
100 FOLS 95630 261-F7
MANON WY
7600 SAC 95823 337-J4
MANOR CT
2400 SaCo 95864 278-H7
N MANOR CT
26000 SJCo 95686 (438-A4 See Page 418)
MANOR DR
2800 PLCR 95667 245-F4
4100 EDCo 95667 265-H3
12700 PlaC 95603 162-E6
N MANOR DR
2200 SAC 95822 337-D1
26100 SJCo 95686 (438-A3 See Page 418)
S MANOR DR
2200 SAC 95822 337-D2
MANOR RD
- PlaC 95747 239-A2
MANOR WY
12600 AUB 95603 162-E6
MANORCREST WY
7600 SAC 95832 337-D4
MANORSIDE DR
7600 SAC 95832 337-D4
MANSEAU DR
100 FOLS 95630 261-G3
MANSELL WY
- ELKG 95758 358-C6
MANSFIELD DR
8400 CITH 95610 260-C2
8400 CITH 95662 260-C2
MANTA PL
11300 SaCo 95670 280-B6
MANTAUK POINT PL
- SAC 95835 256-H4
MANTECA CT
- SAC 95831 336-H1
MANTLE CT
9200 ELKG 95758 358-B4
MANTON CT
900 GALT 95632 419-G4
MANTOVA CT
10200 SaCo 95829 339-E6
MANUEL ST
7200 SaCo 95673 257-J1
MANUFACTURERS DR
- RCCD 95742 300-B3
MANX RD
- EDCo 95726 247-J5
MANY OAKS LN
3600 EDCo 95682 263-H6
MANZA CIR
- RSVL 95678 219-G7
MANZANA CT
3500 EDCo 95709 246-H4
MANZANILLO ST
4800 SaCo 95628 260-C7
4800 SaCo 95628 280-C1
MANZANITA AV
200 RSVL 95678 239-J1
300 RSVL 95678 219-J7
5400 SaCo 95608 259-D7
5400 SaCo 95841 259-D7
5800 CITH 95608 259-D7
5800 CITH 95841 259-D7
6200 SaCo 95608 279-D3
MANZANITA DR
2600 RKLN 95677 220-F2
MANZANITA LN
- EDCo 95762 242-F3
MANZANITA ST
2900 EDCo 95726 248-B1
MANZANITA WY
1700 WSAC 95691 296-H2
2100 ANT 94509 (513-B5 See Page 493)
13000 AUB 95603 182-C5
MANZANITA CEMETERY RD
3000 PlaC - 159-E3
3500 PlaC 95648 159-E5
MANZANO WY
1300 SAC 95831 337-A4
MAPEL LN
4200 SaCo 95608 279-E2
MAPES CT
3200 SaCo 95821 278-J5
MAPLE AV
2900 EDCo 95726 248-C1
7500 CITH 95610 259-H2
MAPLE CT
- EDCo 95682 263-D2
MAPLE DR
- EDCo 95682 263-D2
100 SAC 95823 337-F2
700 RSVL 95678 239-J3
MAPLE LN
3900 PlaC 95650 201-H7
MAPLE ST
- PlaC 95626 237-E1
100 AUB 95603 182-D3
300 GALT 95632 419-F7
400 WSAC 95691 296-H3
3600 RKLN 95677 220-E3
MAPLE BRIDGE WY
- RCCD 95742 320-E4
MAPLE BROOK CT
- PlaC 95746 240-H2
MAPLE CREEK DR
- RSVL 95678 219-J2
- RSVL 95678 220-A2
MAPLE GLEN RD
1700 SaCo 95864 298-H1
1900 SaCo 95864 278-H7
MAPLE GROVE CT
8600 SaCo 95828 338-F4
MAPLE GROVE LN
- LNCN 95648 200-A1
MAPLEGROVE WY
800 SAC 95834 277-E3
MAPLE HALL DR
8500 SAC 95823 357-J1
MAPLE HOLLOW CT
- PlaC 95746 240-H2
MAPLEHURST WY
- ELKG 95758 357-H2
MAPLE LEAF LN
7500 SaCo 95828 338-C3
MAPLEPLAIN AV
4400 ELKG 95758 357-H3
MAPLERIDGE CT
5100 SaCo 95628 260-C7
5600 RKLN 95677 220-C5
MAPLETON WY
5300 SAC 95823 357-J1
MAPLE TRAILS WY
8300 SaCo 95828 338-E7
MAPLE TREE WY
1100 SAC 95831 337-A3
MAPLEVIEW WY
7000 ELKG 95758 358-B4
MAPLEWOOD LN
3500 SaCo 95864 298-G1
3800 EDCo 95667 246-E6
MAPOLA WY
10300 RCCD 95670 279-H6
MARA DR
- SaCo 95683 342-B2
MARABOU CT
6800 SaCo 95842 259-A2
MARALEE WY
7600 SAC 95824 318-C6
MARANATHA
- PlaC 95602 160-H1
MARANATHA LN
6700 EDCo 95667 265-C1
MARANELLO DR
8600 ELKG 95624 358-E1
MARANI WY
7300 SAC 95831 336-H2
MARANTA CT
6300 CITH 95621 259-E2
MARANTHA DR
- RSVL 95747 219-B7
MARAPOSITE LN
900 EDCo 95667 245-F3
MARATHON CT
- SAC 95823 337-G4
MARATHON DR
- PlaC 95603 162-C4
MARBELLA CT
700 LNCN 95648 200-A2
MARBLE CT
9700 ELKG 95624 359-B7
MARBLE WY
4400 SaCo 95608 279-D2
MARBLE BAY CT
- SaCo 95829 338-H6
MARBLE CANYON DR
100 FOLS 95630 260-J1
MARBLE CREEK CT
5200 ELKG 95758 357-J3
MARBLE CREEK WY
5100 ELKG 95758 357-H3
MARBLE CREST CT
9000 SaCo 95829 338-H6
MARBLE MOUNTAIN RD
4000 EDCo 95762 282-H1
MARBLE RIDGE RD
4000 EDCo 95762 282-J1
MARBLETHORPE DR
- RSVL 95747 219-C4
MARBLE VALLEY CT
- SaCo 95829 338-H6
MARBLE VALLEY RD
2000 EDCo 95762 282-J1
MARBRISA CT
- RSVL 95747 219-B1
MARBURN CT
5000 SaCo 95823 317-H7
MARBURY WY
- SaCo 95843 239-B7
MARCEL WY
10500 RCCD 95670 299-G3
MARCELAIS CT
- AUB 95603 162-E6
MARCELAIS RD
4700 EDCo 95623 264-F6
4700 EDCo 95682 264-F6
MARCELLA DR
3700 PlaC 95602 161-G2
MARCH RD
2100 RSVL 95747 239-E5
MARCH WY
6900 ELKG 95758 358-B5
MARCHANT DR
100 FOLS 95630 261-D4
MARCHES WY
- EDCo 95762 262-F5
MARCHESE CT
5600 SaCo 95628 260-D6
MARCHITA WY
2100 SaCo 95608 279-B7
2100 SaCo 95608 299-B1
MARCI LN
- EDCo 95667 265-B2
MARCIA LN
1700 SaCo 95825 298-D1
MARCIA WY
- RSVL 95747 219-E6
MARCILEE WY
2600 RCCD 95670 299-J1
MARCLIFF WY
3300 PlaC 95602 161-J3
MARCO WY
2900 SaCo 95608 279-D6
MARCOB WY
7100 PlaC 95650 201-C5
MARCOLA CT
9400 SaCo 95826 319-A1
MARCONI AV
2100 SAC 95821 278-B5
2100 SAC 95821 278-F5
2600 SAC 95815 278-B5
4600 SaCo 95821 279-A6
4600 SaCo 95608 279-A6
MARCONI CIR
1900 SAC 95815 278-B5
1900 SAC 95821 278-B5
MARCUS CT
1200 ANT 94509 (513-F7 See Page 493)
2100 SAC 95821 278-C5
MARDELL LN
2800 PlaC 95650 200-J3
MARDELLE WY
9100 ELKG 95624 358-J6
MARDEN DR
2000 EDCo 95672 262-H1
MARDI GRAS CT
- RCCD 95670 299-G4
MARE DR
- SaCo 95830 339-G6
MARECA WY
2800 WSAC 95691 316-F1
MARE ISLAND CT
- WSAC 95691 316-E3
MARENGO RD
12800 SaCo 95632 419-H6
12800 GALT 95632 419-H4
MARESBOROUGH PL
3900 PlaC 95650 201-H7
MARETA LN
5800 LMS 95650 200-J4
5800 LMS 95650 201-A4
MARETHA ST
7100 CITH 95610 259-J2
MARFIELD CT
- PLCR 95667 245-J5
MARGARET CT
- AUB 95603 182-B7
MARGARET DR
3300 LMS 95650 200-J5
MARGARET LN
3000 SAC 95826 318-F3
MARGARET RD
6100 EDCo 95623 264-J5
MARGARET WY
300 RSVL 95678 239-J2
300 RSVL 95678 240-A2
3500 SaCo 95660 278-G1
MARGATE WY
3000 RCCD 95670 299-F4
MARGERY JANE LN
- PlaC 95650 221-B6
- PlaC 95746 221-B6
MARGO DR
6000 SaCo 95662 260-J5
MARGUERITE WY
4700 SaCo 95608 299-A2
MARGUERITE MINE RD
800 AUB 95603 162-D7
800 PlaC 95603 162-D7
MARIA WY
800 GALT 95632 439-E1
9400 SaCo 95827 299-A5
MARIAH LN
- EDCo 95667 286-G3
MARIAH PL
4900 SaCo 95628 260-A7
MARIALAINA CT
8600 SaCo 95828 338-F4
MARIAN AV
300 RSVL 95678 240-A3
MARIAN WY
1100 SAC 95818 297-C7
MARIANNA
- RVIS 94571 454-F1
MARIANNA WY
- ELKG 95757 358-A7
MARIAVISTA WY
800 PLCR 95667 245-F5
MARIBEL WY
100 AUB 95603 182-F1
MARIC RD
5600 EDCo 95623 265-B7
MARICOPA CT
3300 EDCo 95682 263-C3
MARICOPA WY
2100 SAC 95833 277-A5
MARIE AV
900 ANT 94509 (513-E4 See Page 493)
MARIE CT
- RSVL 95661 239-J5
MARIE WY
2200 SaCo 95608 279-A7
MARIE ANN LN
2600 SaCo 95608 279-C6
MARIELLA CT
- RKLN 95765 200-E5
MARIELLA DR
- RKLN 95765 200-D5
MARIEMONT AV
1100 SaCo 95864 298-J2
MARIEMONT CT
200 LNCN 95648 179-J5
MARIES CT
- EDCo 95672 243-C7
MARIETTA WY
4800 SaCo 95608 279-C1
4800 SaCo 95841 279-C1
MARIETTI WY
400 RSVL 95678 239-J3
MARIGOLA DR
- EDCo 95762 262-G5
MARIGOLD AV
100 PlaC 95603 162-C6
MARIGOLD CIR
- EDCo 95726 267-J2
MARIGOLD CT
- EDCo 95726 267-J2
MARIGOLD LN
- SaCo 95864 298-E2
200 LNCN 95648 180-A5
MARIGOLD ST
800 WSAC 95691 296-E4
MARIKA CT
- RKLN 95677 220-J2
MARILLA CT
- SAC 95835 256-H3
MARILONA DR
2700 SaCo 95821 278-H6
MARILYN AV
- RSVL 95678 239-J1
MARILYN CIR
- SAC 95838 277-G1
MARILYN DR
- EDCo - 247-H2
MARIMOORE WY
5300 SaCo 95608 299-B3
MARIN AV
7300 SAC 95820 318-C3
MARINA AV
100 AUB 95603 182-F3
MARINA DR
- RVIS 94571 454-H6
- SaCo 95690 455-E4
400 WSAC 95605 297-A1
MARINA WY
500 WSAC 95605 297-A1
MARINA BAY CT
- GALT 95632 419-G2
MARINA BAY DR
- GALT 95632 419-G2
MARINA BLUE CT
- SAC 95831 336-G5
MARINA COVE CIR
- ELKG 95758 357-F7
MARINA COVE DR
- SAC 95831 336-J3
MARINA DUNES WY
- SAC 95835 256-H4
MARINA GLEN WY
- SAC 95833 276-H7
MARINA GRANDE CT
- SAC 95831 336-F1
MARINA GREENS DR
- WSAC 95691 296-J6
MARINA GREENS WY
8300 SaCo 95826 298-E7
MARINA PARK DR
700 EDCo 95762 242-B7
MARINA PARK WY
200 SAC 95831 336-F2
MARINA POINT LN
- ELKG 95758 357-E6
MARINA SHORE LN
- ELKG 95758 357-E6
MARINA VIEW DR
700 EDCo 95762 242-B6
2700 SAC 95818 297-A5
MARINA VISTA LN
8400 SaCo 95628 260-C7
MARINDELL ST
7600 SaCo 95626 237-G7
MARINER CIR
- LNCN 95648 179-D3
MARINER PL
- LNCN 95648 179-E3
MARINER POINT WY
300 SAC 95831 336-G2
MARINERS CT
5900 ELKG 95758 357-J6
5900 ELKG 95758 358-A6
MARINERS COVE DR
- ELKG 95758 357-F7
MARINETTE CT
- RSVL 95747 239-B1
MARINETTE LN
- RSVL 95747 239-B1
MARING WY
- SAC 95835 257-C4
MARINKO CT
3700 EDCo 95667 245-D7
3700 EDCo 95667 265-D1
MARINO CT
5100 ELKG 95758 357-H2
MARINVALE DR
6800 CITH 95621 259-F1
MARINWOOD CT
7600 SaCo 95828 338-F4
MARIOLYN CT
5600 ELKG 95757 377-J3
5600 ELKG 95757 397-J3
MARIOLYN WY
5400 ELKG 95757 377-J3

STREET
Block City ZIP Pg-Grid

MARIOLYN WY
5400 ELKG 95757 397-J3
MARION CT
4400 SAC 95822 317-C3
MARION WY
100 AUB 95603 182-F3
100 PlaC 95603 182-F3
MARIONE DR
5200 SaCo 95608 299-B1
MARION OAKS CT
8100 SJCo 95828 338-E6
MARIPOSA AV
100 PlaC 95661 239-J7
100 RSVL 95661 239-J7
5400 CITH 95610 259-J2
5400 CITH 95628 259-H6
7700 CITH 95610 239-J7
MARIPOSA CT
2800 ANT 94509 (513-B6
See Page 493)
MARIPOSA ST
100 RSVL 95678 239-J1
200 RSVL 95678 219-J7
MARIPOSA COVE CT
6900 CITH 95610 259-J3
MARIPOSA GLEN WY
7600 CITH 95610 259-J3
MARIPOSA SPRINGS DR
3700 EDCo 95762 263-B4
MARIS LN
9400 ELKG 95624 359-A4
MARISSA CT
11500 SaCo 95670 280-C6
MARISSA WY
11500 SaCo 95670 280-C6
MARITIME DR
- ELKG 95758 357-D6
MARIUS DR
9300 SaCo 95829 339-A7
MARIUS WY
9400 SaCo 95829 339-A7
MARJON WY
8000 SaCo 95828 338-D5
MARJORAM
- SAC 95831 336-G2
MARJORIE WY
- RSVL 95747 218-H4
3500 SAC 95820 318-A2
5700 EDCo 95726 248-A1
MARK CT
- RKLN 95765 200-A6
MARK LN
7100 SaCo 95624 340-G2
MARK ST
9300 ELKG 95624 358-G5
MARKDALE LN
- LNCN 95648 179-E6
N MARKET BLVD
600 SaCo 95834 277-D1
1300 SAC 95834 277-D1
MARKET CT
3800 EDCo 95682 283-H1
S MARKET CT
4200 SaCo 95834 277-E2
MARKET ST
- PlaC 95747 218-H6
- RSVL 95747 218-H6
- SaCo 95690 436-J1
- SaCo 95690 437-A1
100 FOLS 95630 261-C5
200 GALT 95632 419-F7
MARKETTA CT
8800 ELKG 95624 358-G3
MARKFIELD WY
9400 SaCo 95829 339-A6
MARKHAM CT
900 EDCo 95762 262-C4
MARKHAM DR
- PLCR 95667 245-E4
MARKHAM WY
- RSVL 95747 219-C1
1100 SAC 95818 297-C7
MARKHAM RAVINE DR
1200 LNCN 95648 179-D1
MARK HOPKINS CT
- SAC 95818 297-A6
MARKLEY WY
6300 SaCo 95608 259-E6
MARKOS CT
5600 SaCo 95841 259-C6
MARK RIVER CT
- SAC 95831 336-H1
MARKS DR
7000 EDCo 95667 244-J6
7000 EDCo 95667 245-A6
MARKS RD
- RVIS 94571 454-F3
MARKSTON RD
1700 SaCo 95825 298-D1
MARK TWAIN AV
5800 SAC 95820 317-J3
5800 SAC 95820 318-A3
MARKWOOD LN
5300 SaCo 95628 260-G7
MARL WY
4200 SaCo 95608 279-E2
MARLA CT
- SAC 95758 358-C1
MARLA WY
- SAC 95758 358-D1
MARLAND CT
100 LNCN 95648 179-G5
MARLAW CT
10200 ELKG 95757 377-J2
10200 ELKG 95757 397-J2
MARLAW WY
10200 ELKG 95757 377-J3
10200 ELKG 95757 397-J3
MARLAYANA CT
6000 ELKG 95758 358-A3
MARLBOROUGH WY
4700 SaCo 95608 299-A3
MARLEE CIR
- RKLN 95677 220-B3
MARLEE CT
- RKLN 95677 220-B3
MARLEE WY
3400 RKLN 95677 220-B3
MARLEMONT CIR
- ELKG 95758 357-E5
MARLENE DR
3300 SaCo 95821 278-D4
MARLEY DR
4300 SaCo 95821 278-J4
MARLIN CIR
5900 SaCo 95608 259-D5
MARLIN DR
1100 RSVL 95661 239-J4
MARLIN SEAS CT
8800 SaCo 95828 338-G4
MARLIN SPIKE WY
400 SAC 95838 257-H7
MARLOW CT
4000 SaCo 95608 279-B3
MARLTON CT
- SAC 95831 336-F2
MARLYNN ST
3000 SaCo 95608 279-E5
MARMITH AV
5300 SaCo 95841 259-B7
MARMON WY
8600 SaCo 95828 338-F6
MARMOR CT
2800 SAC 95826 298-F7
MARNICE RD
600 SaCo 95673 257-E3
MARO WY
8300 SaCo 95628 260-C7
MAROSO WY
- SAC 95835 257-C4
MARQUAM WY
3300 RCCD 95670 300-A4
MARQUETTE DR
2600 SAC 95826 298-D7
2700 SAC 95826 318-D1
MARQUIS CT
- ELKG 95758 357-F7
MARQUISE PL
1000 FOLS 95630 261-B6
MARS WY
9700 RCCD 95827 299-C6
MARSALA CT
7900 CITH 95610 260-A6
MARSALLA CT
3900 SAC 95820 318-B3
MARSALLA DR
- FOLS 95630 260-J1
- FOLS 95630 261-A1
MARSANNAY WY
7900 SaCo 95829 338-J5
MARSDEN CT
- FOLS 95630 281-G2
MARSDEN WY
- FOLS 95630 281-G2
MARSEILLE CT
4100 ELKG 95758 357-G3
MARSH DR
2300 LNCN 95648 179-D1
MARSH LN
4200 EDCo 95619 265-G3
MARSH ST
700 SAC 95818 297-B6
MARSHALL AV
100 RSVL 95678 239-G1
3200 SaCo 95608 279-F3
MARSHALL DR
6300 SaCo 95842 258-J4
6300 SaCo 95842 259-A4
MARSHALL RD
2800 WSAC 95691 316-D3
3500 PlaC 95650 201-E6
4600 EDCo 95633 205-A2
MARSHALL ST
1500 ANT 94509 (513-F5
See Page 493)
MARSHALL WY
200 AUB 95603 182-D2
1000 PLCR 95667 245-G5
2100 SAC 95818 297-D7
2200 SAC 95818 317-E1
2700 SAC 95817 317-E1
MARSHALYNN WY
- ELKG 95758 357-E5
MARSH CREEK CT
- PlaC 95747 238-J2
MARSH CREEK DR
800 SAC 95838 257-J7
MARSH CREEK WY
- ELKG 95758 357-F6
MARSH HAWK CT
6000 ELKG 95758 358-A5
MARSH HAWK DR
- FOLS 95630 281-E1
MARSH POINT DR
- ELKG 95758 357-F6
MARSHSONG AV
- SAC 95834 276-H1
MARSHWOOD CIR
- SAC 95823 337-F4
MARSH WREN WY
2500 ELKG 95757 377-E1
2500 ELKG 95757 397-E1
MARSTON ST
1000 WSAC 95605 296-J1
MARSYAS WY
11800 RCCD 95742 320-D3
MARTA BELLA WY
- SAC 95833 276-J6
MARTEL CT
2800 SAC 95826 298-F7
MARTEL CREEK RD
2800 EDCo 95672 242-J6
2800 EDCo 95672 243-A6
MARTHA WY
600 RSVL 95678 219-J6
MARTIGNETTI CT
7400 SaCo 95842 258-J1
MARTIN DR
1200 PlaC 95603 162-C6
MARTIN LN
1300 PLCR 95667 245-J5
3800 LMS 95650 200-J7
3800 LMS 95650 201-A7
MARTIN ST
5000 OAKL 94561 (514-D6
See Page 493)
MARTIN WY
5000 SaCo 95608 259-D7
MARTINA CT
3700 PlaC 95602 161-H3
MARTINDALE LN
100 PlaC 95603 162-G4
MARTINEZ CREEK RD
- EDCo 95619 265-D7
MARTINGALE CT
9600 SaCo 95693 360-H6
MARTINI CT
- EDCo 95762 262-G3
MARTINIQUE DR
1500 RSVL 95661 240-D3
MARTINIQUE ST
- WSAC 95691 316-D3
MARTIN LUTHER KING JR BLVD
3000 SAC 95817 317-G5
3600 SAC 95820 317-G5
4700 SaCo 95820 317-G5
MARTIN LUTHER KING JR BLVD
5100 SAC 95824 317-G5
5600 SaCo 95824 317-G5
6300 SaCo 95823 317-F6
MARTINO CT
2500 RCCD 95670 299-E2
MARTINSON DR
- SaCo 95838 277-J2
MARTIS ST
- WSAC 95691 316-D4
MARTIS VALLEY CIR
100 SAC 95835 257-A5
MARTSMITH WY
4400 SaCo 95628 280-E1
MARTY CIR
1200 RSVL 95678 219-G7
MARTY WY
2500 SAC 95818 297-C7
MARUYAMA CT
10200 SaCo 95829 339-E5
MARVA LN
6500 EDCo 95667 244-H3
MARVEL CT
4400 SaCo 95843 238-J7
MARVIN CT
100 FOLS 95630 261-G3
MARVIN WY
100 AUB 95603 182-F2
MARVIN GARDENS WY
- RKLN 95765 200-B7
MARVISTA CT
8400 ELKG 95624 358-E1
MAR VISTA WY
7400 CITH 95621 259-E1
MARWICK WY
6100 SaCo 95608 259-D6
MARWOODS CT
7800 SaCo 95828 338-C4
MARY CT
- EDCo - 248-C7
- FOLS 95630 261-B1
1800 PLCR 95667 246-B5
MARY LN
7500 CITH 95610 259-H1
MARY ST
100 AUB 95603 182-F1
MARYAL DR
1800 SaCo 95864 278-G7
2500 SaCo 95821 278-H6
MARYAM CT
4500 SaCo 95628 280-A2
MARY ANN LN
- EDCo 95619 286-G5
- EDCo 95667 286-G5
- EDCo 95684 286-F5
MARY ANN WY
7100 CITH 95621 259-G5
MARYE AV
8500 SaCo 95662 260-D3
MARY ELLEN WY
9300 ELKG 95624 358-H5
MARYETTA CT
2800 EDCo 95682 263-C3
MARY JANE CT
1500 AUB 95603 182-E5
MARY JEAN PL
6200 ELKG 95758 358-A3
MARY KATE DR
4700 SaCo 95841 259-A6
MARY KNOLL CT
3100 SAC 95826 318-E1
MARYLAND AV
- SaCo 95742 280-E7
1000 WSAC 95691 296-J4
MARYLAND CT
2000 WSAC 95691 296-H6
MARY LOU WY
7700 SAC 95832 337-E4
MARY LYNN LN
4500 SaCo 95608 279-D2
MARYMANUEL CIR
800 SAC 95831 316-G6
MARY ROSE LN
- LNCN 95648 180-A7
- LNCN 95648 199-J1
- LNCN 95648 200-A1
MARYSVILLE BLVD
2800 SAC 95815 278-A4
3200 SaCo 95838 278-A1
4700 SAC 95838 257-J7
4700 SAC 95838 277-J1
5800 SaCo 95673 257-F2
MARYVALE WY
2000 RCCD 95670 279-G6
MARYWOOD CT
2200 SaCo 95608 279-C7
MASADA
- EDCo 95667 245-H7
MASADA CT
3600 PLCR 95667 246-A7
MAS AMILOS WY
3300 SAC 95835 256-H3
MASCOT AV
4900 SAC 95820 317-G4
5700 SaCo 95824 317-G5
MASHAM CT
- RSVL 95747 218-H4
MASHIE CT
7400 SaCo 95683 342-D3
MASON LN
4000 SaCo 95608 279-A3
4100 SaCo 95821 279-A2
MASONI WY
2400 RCCD 95670 279-G7
MASONRY WY
4700 SaCo 95823 317-H7
MASSEY LN
4800 SaCo 95628 280-D1
MASSIE CT
- WSAC 95691 316-D1
3200 SAC 95823 338-B4
7600 SaCo 95823 338-B4
MAST CT
- SAC 95831 316-H7
700 EDCo 95762 242-B6
MASTERS CT
11900 PlaC 95603 162-B4
MASTERS ST
7600 SAC 95758 358-B2
MASTERSON CT
- SAC 95835 257-A5
MATA DERO CT
- SAC 95833 277-B5
MATADOR CT
3100 EDCo 95682 263-C5
MATADOR WY
9300 SaCo 95826 299-A7
MATCH CT
- SaCo 95829 339-F7
MATEO CT
6100 SaCo 95673 257-J4
MATHENY WY
6400 CITH 95621 259-D4
MATHER BLVD
- RCCD 95655 299-F6
- SaCo 95655 299-E6
- SaCo 95655 300-A6
- SaCo 95830 319-G3
100 SaCo 95655 319-J1
N MATHER DR
- RCCD 95655 299-H5
- RCCD 95670 299-H5
MATHER E RD
- RCCD 95742 300-H7
- RCCD 95742 320-H1
- RCCD 95742 (321-A1
See Page 301)
MATHER FIELD RD
2900 RCCD 95670 299-F4
3000 RCCD 95827 299-F4
3500 RCCD 95655 299-F4
MATHESON WY
2600 SaCo 95864 298-E3
MATHEWS WY
1400 SAC 95822 337-B2
MATHIS CT
7100 CITH 95610 260-A2
MATINA DR
- ELKG 95757 378-A3
5200 ELKG 95757 377-H3
5200 ELKG 95757 397-H3
MATISSE CT
- OAKL 94561 (514-H7
See Page 493)
100 FOLS 95630 261-H3
8400 SaCo 95828 338-E6
MATSON DR
800 PlaC 95603 162-E5
1700 SAC 95822 337-D2
MATTERHORN DR
6500 SaCo 95842 259-B4
MATTHEW CT
100 GALT 95632 419-D7
800 EDCo 95762 262-C5
MATTIE CT
1500 EDCo 95619 265-F5
MATTOS LN
6500 SaCo 95829 319-B7
MAUANA WY
6400 CITH 95610 259-J3
MAUDRAY WY
3800 SaCo 95608 279-B3
MAUER AV
6000 SaCo 95608 279-D5
MAUGHAM CT
1000 GALT 95632 419-G4
MAUGHAM DR
1100 GALT 95632 419-G4
MAUI CT
6500 EDCo 95667 265-B1
MAUI ST
- WSAC 95691 316-D2
MAUI WY
5200 SaCo 95628 260-B7
MAUL OAK CT
300 EDCo 95762 262-A1
MAULS END
4200 PlaC 95602 160-H2
MAUNA LOA CT
5100 SaCo 95628 260-C7
MAUREEN DR
3400 SaCo 95821 278-G4
MAVERICK
- EDCo 95682 264-A4
MAVERICK CT
400 RSVL 95661 240-C3
3200 EDCo 95682 264-A5
8300 SaCo 95628 280-B2
MAVERICK RD
4000 EDCo 95682 263-J4
4000 EDCo 95682 264-A4
MAVIS AV
8800 SaCo 95662 260-E2
MAX CT
3200 SaCo 95608 279-C5
MAXINE WY
2200 RCCD 95670 299-E1
MAXWELL CT
7200 SaCo 95660 258-H1
MAXWELL RD
16000 AmCo 95683 (362-J5
See Page 341)
MAY CT
100 FOLS 95630 261-E4
MAY ST
1300 WSAC 95605 296-H1
3300 SAC 95838 277-J2
MAYALL CT
100 FOLS 95630 281-F1
MAYBECK WY
- ELKG 95758 357-E5
MAYBELL LN
7600 SaCo 95829 339-F4
MAYBELLINE WY
7900 SAC 95823 338-A5
MAYBERRY RD
2900 ANT 94509 (513-E7
See Page 493)
MAYBERRY WY
5100 ELKG 95758 357-J2
MAYBROOK DR
- SAC 95835 256-J4
- SAC 95835 257-A5
MAYER WY
3100 SaCo 95608 279-B5
MAYFAIR DR
600 RSVL 95678 239-G4
3200 SaCo 95864 298-F3
MAYFAIR LN
- EDCo 95684 286-G7
MAYFIELD CT
3500 EDCo 95672 263-B2
MAYFIELD DR
3300 EDCo 95672 263-B2
MAYFIELD ST
- SAC 95835 257-D6
MAYFLOWER CT
1000 RSVL 95747 239-E1
1500 SaCo 95864 298-E2
MAYFLOWER DR
2700 ANT 94531 (513-G7
See Page 493)
MAYFLOWER LN
- EDCo 95726 248-F1
MAYHEW RD
3000 SaCo 95827 299-A7
MAYHEW RD
3700 SaCo 95827 319-B3
5400 SaCo 95829 319-B5
6100 SaCo 95829 339-B2
MAYKIRK WY
1800 SAC 95833 277-B4
MAYNARD WY
6900 SaCo 95823 317-H7
MAYO CT
2300 RCCD 95670 279-H7
MAYPOLE WY
- ELKG 95624 358-E2
MAYRIS CT
2600 SaCo 95821 278-H6
MAYTEN CT
700 LNCN 95648 180-A2
MAYTEN WY
- ELKG 95758 357-F5
MAYTORENA AV
- SAC 95834 276-G4
MAYWOOD CT
- RSVL 95678 219-J5
MAYWOOD WY
6700 SaCo 95842 259-C3
MAZATLAN WY
9100 ELKG 95624 358-H6
MAZUELA CT
- SAC 95833 276-J4
MAZZA CT
- EDCo 95762 262-H6
MAZZOLO DR
- LNCN 95648 179-E5
MCADOO AV
5600 SAC 95819 298-A5
MCADOO DR
- FOLS 95630 261-E7
- FOLS 95630 281-E2
N MCALLEN DR
5700 LMS 95650 200-J6
MCALLISTER AV
1400 SAC 95822 317-B6
MCALTA CT
1100 GALT 95632 419-H4
MCANALLY DR
1200 RSVL 95678 219-F7
1300 RSVL 95747 219-D6
MCAVOY CT
12600 AUB 95603 162-E6
MCBEAN PARK DR
Rt#-193
- LNCN 95648 179-H3
MCBETH WY
7700 SaCo 95828 338-C3
MCBRIDE CT
10800 RCCD 95670 279-H6
MCBRIDE DR
1400 RSVL 95661 240-D5
MCBRIDE WY
7700 SAC 95832 337-C4
MCCAIN WY
3600 SaCo 95660 258-G1
MCCARRON WY
10100 SaCo 95829 339-E5
MCCARTHY CT
- SAC 95814 297-E2
MCCARTNEY CT
300 LNCN 95648 179-E3
MCCLAIN DR
- LNCN 95648 159-D7
- LNCN 95648 179-D1
MCCLAIN WY
4000 SaCo 95608 279-E3
MCCLAREN DR
1000 SaCo 95608 299-C3
MCCLATCHY WY
400 SAC 95818 297-B6
MCCLELLAN DR
3500 SaCo 95660 258-G6
MCCLINLOCK LN
1300 PlaC 95603 162-C6
MCCLINTOCK WY
7700 SaCo 95828 338-C3
MCCLOUD
1100 AUB 95603 162-E7
MCCLOUD DR
4800 SaCo 95842 259-A4
MCCLOUD WY
- RSVL 95747 219-C1
MCCLUNG DR
8000 CITH 95610 260-A2
MCCLUNG ST
100 AUB 95603 182-D2
MCCLURE CT
7100 SaCo 95828 338-C1
MCCOMBER DR
- FOLS 95630 261-J7
MCCOMBER ST
7000 SaCo 95828 318-E7
7000 SaCo 95828 338-E1
MCCONNEL DR
7600 CITH 95610 260-B1
7700 CITH 95610 240-B7
MCCORMACK AV
1400 SAC 95814 297-E2
MCCORMICK CT
100 FOLS 95630 261-G3
MCCOURTNEY RD
1300 LNCN 95648 179-J1
1600 PlaC 95648 179-J1
1900 PlaC 95648 159-J7
2400 PlaC 95648 160-A6
3000 PlaC - 160-A3
MCCOWAN WY
3300 SaCo 95608 279-A4
MCCOY AV
9000 SaCo 95829 338-H3
MCCOY RD
1700 EDCo 95762 242-G6
MCCRAKEN DR
10200 RCCD 95670 299-E3
MCCRONE CT
8400 CITH 95610 240-C7
MCCURDY LN
7100 SaCo 95828 338-D1
MCDANIEL CIR
- SAC 95838 277-G3
N MCDANIEL DR
200 AUB 95603 182-E4
S MCDANIEL DR
100 AUB 95603 182-E4
MCDERBY CT
100 FOLS 95630 261-G3
MCDERMOTT DR
7000 SaCo 95842 259-A2
MCDONALD DR
4500 SaCo 95608 279-A5
4500 SaCo 95821 278-J5
4500 SaCo 95821 279-A5
MCDOWELL LN
- WSAC 95605 297-B2
MCEACHERN LN
2000 PlaC 95658 201-J2
MC ELHENY RD
200 ANT 94509 (513-E4
See Page 493)
MCENERNEY CT
1100 GALT 95632 419-H4
MCFALL DR
6900 PlaC 95603 161-C4
MCFARLAND DR
100 FOLS 95630 261-E4
MCFARLAND ST
100 GALT 95632 419-E6
13200 SaCo 95632 419-D4
MCFERGUS CT
7600 SaCo 95828 338-C2
MCGANN CT
7900 SaCo 95829 339-E5
MCGILL CT
- ELKG 95758 358-B3
MCGINLEY AV
2300 ANT 94509 (513-E6
See Page 493)
MCGLASHAN ST
4900 SAC 95820 317-H3
5300 SaCo 95824 317-H3
MCGOWEN WY
1400 SaCo 95825 298-C2
MCGRAY WY
- ELKG 95624 338-D7
- ELKG 95624 358-D1
MCGREGOR DR
2000 RCCD 95670 279-G6
2500 RCCD 95670 299-J1
MCGUIRE CIR
- FOLS 95630 281-E1
MCGUIRE CT
- EDCo 95667 226-D2
MCHERN CT
8700 SaCo 95628 260-E7
MCHUGH CT
100 FOLS 95630 261-F3
MCINTOSH WY
1200 RSVL 95678 219-F7
MCKAY ST
5400 SaCo 95628 260-C6
MCKEE CT
- ELKG 95757 358-B7
MCKELLAR AV
5100 SaCo 95824 317-J5
MCKENNA DR
- ELKG 95757 358-B6
MCKENNY CT
- FOLS 95630 261-J4
MCKENZIE CT
100 AUB 95603 182-D2
MCKENZIE RD
11900 SaCo 95632 (399-F4
See Page 379)
12200 SaCo 95632 419-F1
MCKENZIE GLEN CT
5200 SaCo 95608 299-B1
MCKEON CT
2300 ELKG 95757 377-E1
2300 ELKG 95757 397-E1
MCKEON WY
2400 ELKG 95757 377-E1
2400 ELKG 95757 397-E1
MCKIERNAN DR
100 FOLS 95630 261-D4
MCKILT CT
- SAC 95835 257-A5
MCKINLEY AV
11600 SaCo 95638 (401-B3
See Page 381)
MCKINLEY BLVD
3100 SAC 95816 297-H4
3900 SAC 95819 297-H4
MCKINLEY CT
5600 EDCo 95633 205-A5
MCKINLEY DR
1200 RSVL 95661 240-C4
5700 EDCo 95633 205-A5
MCKINLEY ST
- RKLN 95765 219-H2
MCKINLEY WY
1900 WSAC 95691 296-H3
MCKINNEY WY
5100 SaCo 95608 259-D7
MCLAIN RD
3500 LMS 95650 200-G5
MCLAREN AV
5800 SAC 95822 317-C5
MCLAREN CT
100 RSVL 95661 240-C4
MCLAREN DR
1900 RSVL 95661 240-C4
MCLEAN DR
- ELKG 95757 378-A2
5400 ELKG 95757 377-J2
5400 ELKG 95757 397-J2
MCLIN WY
7800 CITH 95610 260-A2
MCMAHON DR
5400 SaCo 95824 317-J5
5600 SaCo 95824 318-A5
MCMILLAN DR
5300 SaCo 95628 260-B7
MCMILLAN RD
10400 ELKG 95757 378-D4
MCMINDES CT
- RSVL 95747 219-D5
MCMINDES DR
- RSVL 95747 219-D5
MCMULLEN WY
7500 SaCo 95828 338-C3
MCNAIR CIR
6100 SaCo 95837 256-B3
MCNAMARA WY
4000 SAC 95823 337-G6
MCNAMEE DR
100 FOLS 95630 261-B6
MCNEELY WY
6000 SaCo 95662 260-F5
MCNEESE CT
4700 SaCo 95841 279-A1
MCNEIL RD
4100 EDCo 95682 283-F2
MCNIE AV
8300 SaCo 95828 338-E1
MCPHETRIDGE DR
8500 ELKG 95624 358-E1
MCQUILLAN CIR
6900 SAC 95820 318-B2
MCRAE CT
- RSVL 95678 219-F7
MCRAE WY
1000 RSVL 95678 219-F7
MCROBERTS DR
- SaCo 95655 319-J2
100 SaCo 95655 320-A2
MCTAVISH CIR
7500 SaCo 95828 338-C3
MCTUCKER DR
800 GALT 95632 419-D7
800 GALT 95632 439-D1
MEAD AV
4400 SAC 95822 317-C3
MEAD ST
- ANT 94531 (513-H7
See Page 493)
MEADE LAND DR
- EDCo - 267-E4
MEADER AV
6500 SaCo 95823 338-B2
MEADORS CT
4000 SaCo 95843 239-A5
MEADOW CIR
4300 EDCo 95672 243-G4
MEADOW CT
3200 RKLN 95677 220-E2
3300 EDCo 95672 263-D2
MEADOW LN
1200 RSVL 95661 240-D5
1700 LNCN 95648 179-F3
2100 EDCo 95667 245-H2
2300 PLCR 95667 245-H2
2500 EDCo 95682 263-C7
3600 SaCo 95864 298-G1
8900 PlaC 95658 201-G3
9100 SaCo 95693 360-H4
MEADOW RD
1000 WSAC 95691 296-H4
MEADOW VW
3500 EDCo 95667 245-B7
MEADOW WY
3300 RKLN 95677 220-E2
MEADOWAIR WY
7500 SAC 95822 337-E3
MEADOWBREEZE CT
- SAC 95823 337-H5
MEADOWBRIDGE DR
200 FOLS 95630 281-A2
MEADOW BROOK CT
3700 PlaC 95602 161-H2
MEADOW BROOK DR
3700 PlaC 95602 161-J3
MEADOWBROOK LN
- RVIS 94571 454-F2
MEADOW BROOK RD
4500 EDCo 95633 205-C1
MEADOWBROOK RD
2200 SaCo 95825 278-E7
MEADOW CLIFF CT
9500 ELKG 95758 358-B6
MEADOW CREEK CIR
- PlaC - 160-E4
MEADOW CREEK CT
2200 PlaC - 160-E4
N MEADOW CREEK CT
24500 SJCo 95220 439-J6
MEADOW CREEK RD
2700 PlaC - 160-D4
MEADOWCREEK WY
6400 CITH 95621 259-E5
MEADOWCREST CT
9900 ELKG 95624 378-H1
MEADOWDALE CT
5800 RKLN 95677 220-C5
MEADOWDALE DR
5800 RKLN 95677 220-C5
MEADOWDALE WY
9000 ELKG 95624 378-G2
MEADOWFOAM CT
9000 ELKG 95758 357-H3
MEADOW GATE DR
1100 RSVL 95661 240-A4
MEADOWGATE DR
7200 SAC 95823 337-G2
MEADOWGLEN AV
2100 SAC 95832 337-D3
MEADOW GLEN RD
4200 PlaC 95602 162-A1
MEADOWGREEN CIR
9500 SAC 95827 299-B6
MEADOW GROVE WY
9200 ELKG 95624 358-J7
MEADOWHAVEN DR
8200 SaCo 95828 338-D6
MEADOW HAWK WY
2800 SaCo 95843 238-E5
MEADOW HILL CT
6400 SaCo 95608 279-E5
MEADOWHILL CT
- LNCN 95648 179-J6
MEADOW LAKE ST
4100 ANT 94531 (513-J7
See Page 493)
MEADOW LAKES CT
100 FOLS 95630 240-J7
MEADOWLAND CT
2200 LNCN 95648 179-E1
MEADOWLAND WY
- LNCN 95648 179-D1
5100 ELKG 95758 357-J2
MEADOW LANE CT
1000 EDCo 95667 245-H3
1000 PLCR 95667 245-H3
MEADOWLARK CIR
- WSAC 95691 316-G1
MEADOW LARK CT
100 AUB 95603 182-D4
MEADOWLARK CT
- EDCo - 267-H4
- RKLN 95765 219-H1
MEADOWLARK LN
2100 SaCo 95821 278-C6
7500 PlaC 95746 241-D3
MEADOWLARK WY
- EDCo - 267-H4
1500 RSVL 95661 240-B3
MEADOW MIST CT
2000 SaCo 95626 238-C6
MEADOWMONT CT
- SAC 95831 336-H2
MEADOW OAK CIR
9900 ELKG 95624 378-H1
MEADOW OAK LN
2700 EDCo 95672 243-C4
MEADOW OAKS DR
900 PlaC 95602 162-G1
1100 RSVL 95661 240-A4
MEADOWOOD WY
4700 SaCo 95628 280-D1

STREET Block City ZIP Pg-Grid

MEADOW PARK CT
4100 PlaC 95602 162-A1
MEADOW PARK WY
- SAC 95823 337-J6
- SAC 95823 338-A5
MEADOW PASS WY
4800 SaCo 95843 239-A5
MEADOWRIDGE CT
7900 SaCo 95628 259-J7
7900 SaCo 95628 260-C7
MEADOWRIVER WY
7800 CITH 95610 259-J2
7800 CITH 95610 260-A2
MEADOWROCK WY
200 FOLS 95630 241-B7
MEADOWS CT
- AUB 95603 162-E5
N MEADOWS PL
2900 SAC 95822 337-F1
S MEADOWS PL
7200 SAC 95822 337-F2
MEADOWSIDE CT
9200 PlaC 95650 221-G3
MEADOWSIDE DR
- ELKG 95758 357-F5
MEADOWSPRING DR
8800 ELKG 95758 358-A3
MEADOWSTONE CT
- SAC 95823 337-G3
MEADOWSTONE DR
7600 SAC 95823 337-G3
MEADOWSWEET WY
9000 ELKG 95624 378-H1
MEADOWTREE CT
9900 ELKG 95624 378-H1
MEADOWVALE AV
2600 SAC 95822 337-E2
MEADOWVIEW CT
7900 CITH 95610 240-C7
MEADOWVIEW DR
800 GALT 95632 439-E1
MEADOWVIEW RD
1400 SAC 95832 337-B3
3500 SAC 95823 337-E3
MEADOWVISTA DR
6200 SaCo 95608 259-E7
MEADOWVISTA WY
1300 RSVL 95661 240-D5
MEADOW WIND CT
2000 SaCo 95626 238-C5
MEADOW WOOD CIR
2500 SAC 95822 337-E2
MEADOW WOOD CT
- EDCo 95762 262-D6
MEADOW WOOD DR
4000 EDCo 95762 262-D5
MEADOW WOOD LN
5300 OAKL 94561 (514-D5 See Page 493)
MEALER LN
- SaCo 95690 437-A1
MEANDER LN
- EDCo 95619 286-A1
MEANDERING WY
8500 SaCo 95843 239-A5
MEARS DR
7000 PlaC 95602 161-D2
MEARS PL
- PlaC 95602 161-D1
MEARS WY
- ELKG 95758 358-C6
MEATH WY
7200 SaCo 95660 258-H1
MECCA RD
8500 ELKG 95624 359-F1
MECHANICAL DR
- RCCD 95670 300-B5
- RCCD 95742 300-B5
MECKEL WY
5100 SaCo 95841 259-B7
MEDALLION CT
- LNCN 95648 199-J1
6600 CITH 95621 259-F4
MEDALLION WY
9200 SaCo 95826 299-A7
MEDANOS ST
1100 ANT 94509 (513-C4 See Page 493)
MEDEIROS WY
8100 SaCo 95829 339-C7
MEDELLA CIR
15200 SaCo 95683 342-C3
MEDER CT
3600 EDCo 95682 263-J5
MEDER RD
3000 EDCo 95682 263-E5
MEDFORD ST
4700 SaCo 95628 280-A1
MEDIA PL
500 SAC 95815 297-H1
MEDICAL PLAZA DR
- RSVL 95661 220-C7
MEDICI WY
- EDCo 95762 262-B2
MEDINA WY
4700 SaCo 95660 278-H1
MEDINAH CT
100 RSVL 95678 219-G5
MEDITERRANEAN PL
- WSAC 95691 296-G6
MEDITERRANEAN WY
8200 SAC 95826 298-E7
MEDOC WY
- ELKG 95624 379-A2
MEDORA DR
6600 SaCo 95660 258-H3
MEDSTEAD WY
9400 ELKG 95758 358-C5
MEDUSA WY
2000 SaCo 95864 298-J1
MEEKER LN
- SaCo 95829 338-H4
MEEKS WY
5900 SAC 95835 257-C3
MEER WY
2000 SAC 95822 317-C3
MEESHA LN
5500 EDCo 95667 244-D6
MEGAN CT
- RKLN 95765 200-C6
- SAC 95838 277-G1
MEGAN ANN CT
7800 SaCo 95843 238-J7
MEGAN ANN WY
7700 SaCo 95843 238-J7
MEGHAN WY
5800 SaCo 95842 258-J4
5800 SaCo 95842 259-A5

MEHAFFEY WY
4200 OAKL 94561 (514-D7 See Page 493)
MEIGGS CT
6100 CITH 95621 259-D3
MEISS RD
12300 SaCo 95624 340-J2
12700 SaCo 95683 340-J2
12700 SaCo 95683 341-A3
14300 SaCo 95683 342-A7
14600 SaCo 95683 (362-A1 See Page 341)
MEISTER WY
- SaCo 95837 255-J4
- SaCo 95837 256-A4
100 SAC 95819 297-H4
4500 SaCo 95835 256-E4
MEL CT
6500 CITH 95610 259-J3
MELADEE LN
800 GALT 95632 439-F1
900 GALT 95632 419-F7
MELANIE WY
700 SAC 95831 336-H2
MELANZANE DR
- RSVL 95661 240-E2
MELAVIC CT
6200 SaCo 95824 317-H6
MELAVIC WY
6100 SaCo 95824 317-H6
MELBENJI CT
10200 ELKG 95757 377-J2
10200 ELKG 95757 397-J2
MELBOURNE CT
- RSVL 95678 219-J5
MELBOURNE WY
6500 CITH 95621 259-E3
MELBURY WY
5500 SaCo 95843 259-C1
5500 SaCo 95843 239-C7
MELEA RD
11100 SaCo 95693 (380-B2 See Page 379)
MELFORT WY
7800 ELKG 95758 358-C5
MELINA DR
- EDCo 95762 262-A3
MELINDA WY
2900 SAC 95822 337-F2
MELISA CT
4200 SaCo 95608 279-F2
MELLIE CT
- SaCo 95829 338-H6
MELLISSA CIR
1400 ANT 94509 (513-F7 See Page 493)
MELLISSA CT
1500 ANT 94509 (513-F7 See Page 493)
MELLO CT
4400 SaCo 95820 317-G3
MELLO LN
- EDCo - 267-H4
MELLODORA DR
6800 SaCo 95662 260-C2
MELLOWDAWN WY
2400 EDCo 95682 263-C4
8700 SaCo 95662 260-E5
MELLOWOOD DR
4000 OAKL 94561 (514-G7 See Page 493)
MELLOWOODS WY
8600 SaCo 95828 338-F4
MELODIC CT
9700 ELKG 95624 378-G1
MELODY LN
- PlaC 95658 181-A1
- SaCo 95632 (400-C6 See Page 379)
1100 RSVL 95678 239-G5
2800 EDCo - 247-E3
MELODYE CT
3300 EDCo 95672 263-E2
MELODYE LN
2600 EDCo 95672 263-E1
MELONES CIR
11600 SaCo 95670 280-C4
MELROSE AV
1000 RSVL 95678 239-J3
1100 RSVL 95678 240-A3
8800 ELKG 95624 358-G6
MELROSE CT
3000 EDCo 95762 262-D1
MELROSE DR
6200 SaCo 95660 258-G4
MELROSE WY
3100 EDCo 95762 262-D1
MELSEE CT
5300 SaCo 95842 259-B1
MELTON LN
1900 ANT 94509 (513-J5 See Page 493)
MELVA ST
6900 CITH 95610 260-C2
MELVILLE CT
300 RSVL 95747 219-E6
MELVILLE DR
300 SAC 95758 358-D1
MELVIN DR
4700 SaCo 95608 279-A7
MELWAY DR
- RSVL 95747 219-D6
MELWOOD LN
8400 PlaC 95746 241-C2
MELZENDA WY
4000 SaCo 95821 278-H3
MEMORIAL LN
100 AUB 95603 182-D2
MEMORY LN
2500 SaCo 95825 298-D3
2500 SaCo 95864 298-D3
5600 SaCo 95628 260-D6
7600 PlaC 95746 220-J7
7600 PlaC 95746 240-J1
8200 PlaC 95603 161-E3
MEMORY WY
5600 SaCo 95628 260-D6
MEMORY MOUNTAIN RD
3800 EDCo 95667 246-G6
3800 EDCo 95709 246-G6
MENAGGIO WY
- EDCo 95762 262-G6
MENARD CIR
- SAC 95835 257-C6
MENCIA CT
- SAC 95834 276-H4
MENDEL WY
2700 SAC 95833 277-D6

MENDES CT
- FOLS 95630 261-H4
MENDEZ WY
3700 SaCo 95821 278-G6
MENDEZ CREEK CT
- RKLN 95765 219-J2
MENDHAM CT
7600 ELKG 95758 358-C6
MENDOCINO BLVD
4600 SAC 95820 317-G4
4700 SAC 95820 317-G4
5400 SaCo 95824 317-G5
5400 SAC 95824 317-G4
MENDOCINO CT
- WSAC 95691 316-D3
4000 EDCo 95762 263-B4
MENDOCINO ST
- WSAC 95691 316-D3
MENDOCINO WY
5000 EDCo 95762 263-B4
MENDONCA DR
2700 RCCD 95670 299-H1
MENDOTA WY
- RSVL 95747 218-J3
1400 SaCo 95608 299-A2
MENDOZA LN
9300 ELKG 95624 339-A7
MENKE WY
8400 CITH 95610 260-C2
8400 CITH 95662 260-C2
8500 SaCo 95662 260-C2
MENLO AV
1500 SaCo 95608 299-A2
MENLO DR
600 RKLN 95765 199-G7
MENLO OAKS CT
10300 ELKG 95624 359-F4
10300 SaCo 95624 359-F4
MENODORA DR
- ELKG 95624 358-E1
MENSCH CT
- SaCo 95608 279-B5
MEPHAM CT
4200 EDCo 95762 262-B3
MERAMONTE WY
3800 SaCo 95660 258-G5
MERANO WY
3500 SaCo 95843 238-G5
MERCANTILE DR
2600 SaCo 95742 280-B7
2600 SaCo 95742 300-B1
MERCED AV
7900 SaCo 95826 318-C3
MERCED WY
1700 WSAC 95691 316-H1
MERCEDES AV
6600 CITH 95621 259-F4
MERCEDES CT
600 RSVL 95747 219-D6
6500 CITH 95621 259-F4
MERCEDES DR
200 EDCo 95667 245-E6
1200 RSVL 95747 219-D6
MERCEDES LN
- EDCo 95762 282-E1
MERCEDES PL
3100 PlaC 95747 239-B2
MERCER WY
8200 SaCo 95628 260-B5
MERCHANDISE WY
6300 EDCo 95667 265-C2
MERCHANT CIR
5200 EDCo 95667 264-G5
MERCHANT ST
700 SAC 95814 297-C3
MERCURY TR
3300 EDCo 95726 248-E2
MERCURY WY
1700 SaCo 95864 298-J1
MERCY CT
6600 SaCo 95608 259-E6
MERCY WY
3500 EDCo 95672 243-C6
MEREDITH PL
2500 EDCo 95762 242-C6
MEREDITH WY
- FOLS 95630 261-H4
1200 SaCo 95608 299-B2
MEREOAK CIR
- ELKG 95758 358-D5
MERGANSER CT
- OAKL 94561 (514-H7 See Page 493)
- RKLN 95765 219-H1
4500 SaCo 95842 258-J2
MERGANSER DR
- OAKL 94561 (514-H6 See Page 493)
MERGANSERS CT
2800 WSAC 95691 316-F1
MERIDA CT
4300 SaCo 95628 280-F2
MERIDIAN CT
- SAC 95833 277-D5
- RSVL 95678 219-G4
3000 PLCR 95667 245-G5
MERIDIAN WY
- RKLN 95765 199-J7
MERING CT
100 SaCo 95864 298-F5
MERINO CT
- LNCN 95648 180-A6
- RKLN 95765 200-D4
MERION
- PlaC 95746 240-J5
MERITAGE CT
10900 RCCD 95670 299-J5
MERITAGE DR
10900 RCCD 95670 299-J5
MERIWEATHER WY
- SaCo 95843 259-A1
MERKLEY AV
800 WSAC 95691 296-H4
MERKLEY WY
500 SAC 95818 297-B6
MERLE CT
4800 SaCo 95841 258-J7
4800 SaCo 95841 278-J1
MERLIN CT
600 LNCN 95648 180-C7
MERLIN WY
2500 ELKG 95757 357-E7
MERLINDALE DR
5800 CITH 95610 259-J5
MERLOT CT
- OAKL 94561 (514-E5 See Page 493)

MERLOT LN
200 OAKL 94561 (514-E5 See Page 493)
MERLOT WY
- RVIS 94571 454-G6
8000 SaCo 95829 338-H5
MERRIAM LN
2800 EDCo 95762 262-C4
MERRIBROOK DR
8500 SaCo 95826 298-F7
MERRICK SAN WY
3000 SaCo 95608 279-A5
MERRIFIELD CT
9100 ELKG 95624 358-J5
MERRILL CT
700 RSVL 95747 219-D7
700 RSVL 95747 239-D1
MERRILL DR
100 ANT 94509 (513-D4 See Page 493)
MERRILY WY
3700 SaCo 95821 278-G3
MERRIMAC ST
3000 SaCo 95608 279-B5
MERRIT ISLAND CT
- WSAC 95691 316-E2
MERRITT LN
- PlaC - 159-H3
- PlaC - 160-A3
MERRITT WY
100 SaCo 95864 298-E6
MERRIVALE WY
- SAC 95835 257-A5
MERRIWEATHER CT
9700 PlaC 95746 240-J5
MERROW CT
200 AUB 95603 182-C2
MERROW ST
100 AUB 95603 182-D2
MERRY LN
6100 SaCo 95608 279-D5
MERRYCHASE DR
2400 EDCo 95682 263-B7
2400 EDCo 95682 283-B1
MERRY HILL WY
- ELKG 95624 338-H7
- ELKG 95624 358-H1
- SaCo 95624 338-H7
MERRY KNOLL RD
1000 PlaC 95603 182-C1
1100 PlaC 95603 162-C7
1200 AUB 95603 162-C7
MERRYMUM CT
8300 CITH 95610 260-C1
MERRYWOOD CIR
2800 EDCo 95682 263-D7
MERRYWOOD CT
6900 PlaC 95746 221-C7
MERRYWOOD DR
2800 SaCo 95825 278-E7
5900 RKLN 95677 220-D5
MERRYWOOD LN
3600 EDCo 95682 263-D7
MERTICE CT
3200 SaCo 95864 298-F5
MERTOLA DR
- EDCo 95762 262-E6
MERTON CT
6300 SaCo 95842 259-B4
MERTON WY
6300 SaCo 95842 259-A4
MESA CT
4000 RKLN 95677 220-E1
MESA ST
7900 SaCo 95628 279-J2
7900 SaCo 95628 280-A2
MESA BROOK CT
8800 ELKG 95624 358-F2
MESA BROOK WY
8500 ELKG 95624 358-F2
MESA GRANDE
- WSAC 95691 296-J7
MESA GRANDE CT
6900 SAC 95828 318-B7
MESA OAK WY
8000 CITH 95610 240-B7
MESA VERDE CIR
5600 RKLN 95677 220-B4
MESA VERDES CT
3400 EDCo 95762 262-D7
MESA VERDES DR
3300 EDCo 95762 262-D6
MESAVIEW DR
6200 CITH 95621 239-E7
MESA VISTA CT
400 RSVL 95747 219-C5
MESA VISTA WY
800 AUB 95603 182-B6
MESQUITE CT
100 FOLS 95630 261-F4
MESSINA DR
200 SAC 95819 298-A5
MESSINA WY
- EDCo 95762 262-G5
META CT
7000 SaCo 95683 341-J1
METALMARK CT
8800 ELKG 95624 358-F2
METATE CT
100 EDCo 95619 286-B1
METATE TR
- EDCo 95619 286-B1
METEOR DR
9800 RCCD 95827 299-C6
METRO LN
- SAC 95816 297-F4
METRO AIR PKWY
- SaCo 95835 256-E3
- SaCo 95836 236-E7
- SaCo 95836 256-E1
METTE CT
- FOLS 95630 281-D1
METZ CT
100 FOLS 95630 261-G3
MEURET RD
10200 SaCo 95693 (380-B3 See Page 379)
MEYBEES CT
- EDCo 95762 262-F6
MEYER LN
4000 PlaC 95602 161-F3
MEYER WY
4600 SaCo 95608 279-E1
MEYERS RD
3000 EDCo - 247-D3
MEYERS ST
5000 RKLN 95677 220-E3
MEZEREON LN
5500 ELKG 95757 377-J1

MEZEREON LN
5500 ELKG 95757 397-J1
MEZGER WY
7800 SaCo 95843 238-J7
MI CT
6500 CITH 95621 259-D3
MIA PL
- ELKG 95758 357-F6
MIA LINDA CT
7500 PlaC 95746 241-D2
MIAMI ST
- RCCD 95742 300-E1
- SaCo 95742 280-E7
- SaCo 95742 300-E1
3500 SaCo 95821 278-J4
MICA CT
6400 EDCo 95726 248-D2
MICA LN
- PlaC 95603 181-H1
MICA WY
6000 PlaC 95746 241-A3
8400 CITH 95610 240-C7
8400 CITH 95610 260-C1
MICAELA CT
- SaCo 95829 338-H6
MICHAEL CT
7800 PlaC 95746 241-E2
MICHAEL LN
1200 SaCo 95864 298-E3
4200 PlaC 95602 162-A1
MICHAEL WY
- EDCo 95667 267-A4
1400 RSVL 95661 240-A3
5300 SaCo 95822 317-C4
MICHAEL POINT CT
- EDCo 95762 282-C4
MICHELANGELO LN
- EDCo 95667 246-G4
MICHELBOOK LN
- RVIS 94571 454-F1
MICHELE LN
4900 SAC 95822 317-C4
MICHELLE CT
100 GALT 95632 419-C7
MICHELLE DR
2400 SaCo 95821 278-D5
9300 PlaC 95603 161-G6
MICHELLE LN
- EDCo - 247-H2
MICHELSON CT
- SAC 95835 257-A5
MICHENER DR
- ELKG 95758 358-D3
1500 RSVL 95747 219-C6
MICHIGAN BLVD
1400 WSAC 95691 296-H3
MICHIGAN DR
7800 CITH 95610 259-J1
7800 CITH 95610 260-A1
MICHIGAN BAR RD
7100 SaCo 95630 322-G4
7100 SaCo 95683 322-F7
7100 SaCo 95683 342-F3
MICRO CT
800 RSVL 95678 219-F7
MICRO ST
800 RSVL 95678 219-F7
MICRON AV
9600 SaCo 95827 299-B6
MIDAS AV
3100 RKLN 95677 220-D1
E MIDAS AV
3800 RKLN 95677 220-E2
MIDAS CT
2800 RKLN 95677 220-C1
MIDDLE ST
500 WSAC 95691 296-F3
MIDDLE BASS ISLAND CT
- WSAC 95691 316-E2
MIDDLEBERRY RD
1900 SAC 95815 298-B1
1900 SaCo 95825 298-B1
2000 SAC 95815 278-B7
MIDDLEBROOK WY
6600 SAC 95823 358-B1
MIDDLEBURG CT
- SAC 95758 358-A2
MIDDLEBURY DR
100 SaCo 95655 319-H2
MIDDLECOFF WY
6700 SAC 95822 317-D7
6900 SAC 95822 337-D1
MIDDLE FORK CT
100 FOLS 95630 261-A3
MIDDLEFORK CT
- LNCN 95648 179-F7
MIDDLE RIVER CT
8300 SaCo 95828 338-E5
MIDDLESAX WY
8500 SaCo 95828 338-E5
MIDDLESBORO WY
9400 ELKG 95758 357-J6
MIDDLETON WY
100 SaCo 95864 298-E6
MIDDLETOWN CT
2800 EDCo 95667 245-D4
MIDDLETOWN RD
100 EDCo 95667 245-D4
100 PLCR 95667 245-D4
MIDFIELD WY
8600 SAC 95826 318-F1
MIDFORD LN
- LNCN 95648 179-E6
MIDIRON DR
7400 SaCo 95628 279-H2
MIDLAND RD
8300 PlaC 95746 221-E6
MIDLAND WY
500 EDCo 95667 245-E6
2500 SaCo 95608 279-A7
MIDNIGHT WY
7200 CITH 95621 259-G2
N MIDSECTION ST
25600 SJCo 95686 (438-B4 See Page 418)
MIDSUMMER WY
8200 SaCo 95823 338-A7
MIDTOWN DR
7600 SaCo 95843 258-F1
7600 SaCo 95843 238-F7
MIDWAY AV
100 AUB 95603 182-C4
3300 EDCo 95726 248-E1
12800 SaCo 95632 419-C4
MIDWAY CT
- SAC 95817 317-J1
MIDWAY ST
- SAC 95828 318-E6

MIDWAY ISLAND RD
- WSAC 95691 316-D2
MIEKO WY
4400 SaCo 95841 258-J7
MIFFLEN CT
- RSVL 95747 219-C7
MIFFLEN WY
- RSVL 95747 219-C7
MIGNON ST
3500 SaCo 95826 318-J1
MIGRATION CT
2300 ELKG 95757 357-D7
MIGRATION DR
2400 ELKG 95757 357-E7
MIGUEL DR
5000 OAKL 94561 (514-D6 See Page 493)
MIGUEL WY
8400 SaCo 95626 237-F5
MIJA MADISON CT
- SAC 95835 256-H3
MIKE ARTHUR CT
5500 CITH 95610 260-B6
MIKE GARTRELL CIR
100 SAC 95835 257-B4
MIKE WALDRON DR
3200 SAC 95835 256-H3
MIKE YORBA WY
- CCCo 94509 (513-G5 See Page 493)
MIKKELSEN DR
600 AUB 95603 182-E1
700 AUB 95603 162-E7
MIKO CIR
9300 ELKG 95624 359-A1
MIKON ST
1400 WSAC 95605 296-H2
MILAM WY
6500 SaCo 95660 258-G3
MILAN CT
- LNCN 95648 179-E3
- RSVL 95678 239-G4
6500 SAC 95831 337-A5
MILAN WY
- LNCN 95648 179-E3
- RSVL 95678 239-G4
MILANO CT
4100 EDCo 95762 242-C7
8300 SaCo 95828 338-E7
MILANO DR
- WSAC 95691 296-J7
- WSAC 95691 297-A7
MILAZZO WY
10500 RCCD 95670 299-G1
10600 RCCD 95670 279-H7
MILBROOK WY
6900 SaCo 95823 337-G1
MILDRED AV
300 GALT 95632 419-F6
MILES CT
- AUB 95603 182-C3
3000 PLCR 95667 245-G6
MILES LN
6400 SaCo 95608 279-E3
MILFORD CIR
3500 EDCo 95762 263-A5
MILFORD ST
7200 SAC 95822 337-C1
MILGRAY CT
5400 SaCo 95608 279-B3
MILKEN RD
- EDCo 95667 246-B3
MILKY WY
8400 SaCo 95662 260-C4
MILL RD
100 PlaC 95603 162-F5
500 AUB 95603 182-E3
MILL RUN
7900 EDCo 95726 248-J1
MILL ST
- RKLN 95765 220-B1
400 FOLS 95630 261-C4
MILLBORO WY
6900 SAC 95823 358-B2
MILLBRAE RD
3600 EDCo 95682 263-C6
MILL BRANCH CT
- SaCo 95829 339-D6
MILLBROOK CIR
- SaCo 95828 338-F3
MILLBROOK CT
- LNCN 95648 179-E6
- WSAC 95691 296-J7
MILLBURN ST
3400 RKLN 95765 220-B1
5300 SaCo 95608 259-E6
MILL CREEK CT
500 RSVL 95747 239-D1
MILLCREEK DR
2500 SAC 95833 277-C6
MILLDALE CIR
7600 SaCo 95626 237-J7
7600 SaCo 95626 238-A7
MILLER CT
- WSAC 95691 316-F3
100 RSVL 95661 240-F4
MILLER LN
- PlaC 95602 160-H1
MILLER RD
- SaCo 95833 276-G7
- SaCo 95833 296-G1
600 EDCo 95762 242-B7
600 EDCo 95762 262-B1
1800 SAC 95833 276-H7
MILLER ST
1200 ANT 94509 (513-F4 See Page 493)
MILLER WY
100 FOLS 95630 261-A2
2400 SAC 95817 297-G7
2900 PLCR 95667 245-G4
MILLER OAK DR
4300 PlaC 95602 161-H1
MILLERTON PL
- WSAC 95691 316-C4
MILLERTOWN RD
200 PlaC 95603 182-A1
1800 PlaC 95603 162-B7
MILL ESTATE CT
1100 RSVL 95661 240-A5
MILLET WY
1000 SAC 95834 277-E4
MILLHOUSE PL
5500 SaCo 95841 259-C4
MILLICAN CT
3900 SaCo 95826 319-A1
MILLICENT CT
7300 SaCo 95628 279-G1

MILLIE ST
8000 SaCo 95662 240-E7
MILLNAR WY
4500 ELKG 95757 377-H2
4500 ELKG 95757 397-H2
MILL OAK WY
3000 SAC 95833 277-C4
MILLPOND CT
9500 ELKG 95624 359-B4
MILLPOND LN
- LNCN 95648 180-A7
MILL POND RD
300 PlaC 95603 162-F5
MILLPORT DR
- RSVL 95678 219-H3
MILLPORT WY
4200 SAC 95823 337-G5
MILLRACE CT
- LNCN 95648 179-E6
MILLRACE RD
4500 SaCo 95864 278-J7
MILLROY WY
7600 SAC 95823 337-J4
7600 SAC 95823 338-A4
MILL RUN CT
600 RSVL 95747 239-D1
MILL RUN DR
1500 RSVL 95747 239-D1
MILLS CRSG
9500 SaCo 95827 299-B7
MILLS PL
1100 OAKL 94561 (514-E7 See Page 493)
MILLS RD
100 SaCo 95864 298-E4
MILLS ACRES CIR
10500 RCCD 95670 299-G3
MILLS GAP CT
300 RSVL 95661 240-B5
MILLS GAP WY
8100 SaCo 95828 338-D2
MILLS GROVE CT
7400 SaCo 95828 338-D2
MILLSHIRE LN
- SaCo 95628 280-C1
MILLSON CT
800 GALT 95632 419-F3
MILLS PARK DR
2700 RCCD 95670 299-G3
MILLS RANCH WY
2300 RCCD 95670 279-G7
MILLS STATION RD
10000 RCCD 95827 299-E4
10200 RCCD 95670 299-E3
MILLSTONE DR
4700 ELKG 95758 357-H5
MILLSTONE WY
5000 PlaC 95746 240-H2
MILLS TOWER DR
10300 RCCD 95670 299-F3
MILL STREAM CT
- SAC 95823 337-H5
MILL VALLEY CIR N
100 SAC 95835 257-A4
MILL VALLEY CIR S
100 SAC 95835 257-B4
MILL VALLEY RD
- EDCo 95709 247-B3
MILLVIEW CT
- SAC 95833 277-B6
MILL WATER CIR
5400 RCCD 95742 320-E4
MILLWOOD DR
6300 CITH 95621 259-E1
MILMAR WY
3900 SaCo 95821 278-J3
MILNER RD
3100 ANT 94509 (513-C7 See Page 493)
MILNER WY
5600 SAC 95822 317-E4
MILNES AV
8000 PlaC 95747 239-D1
MILO CT
8700 ELKG 95624 358-G6
MILPITAS CIR
- SAC 95823 337-J6
MILROY LN
4400 SaCo 95608 279-G2
MILSAP CT
8500 ELKG 95624 358-H1
MILSTEAD WY
- RSVL 95661 220-E6
MILTON ST
1000 WSAC 95605 296-J1
MILTON WY
3600 SaCo 95660 258-G3
MILTON RANCH CT
6000 EDCo 95682 283-G3
MILTON RANCH RD
5300 EDCo 95682 283-J2
MILWAUKEE AV
- SaCo 95742 300-F1
MILWAUKEE CT
- SAC 95823 337-H7
MILWHEEL CT
7900 SaCo 95829 339-C5
MIMOSA CT
5500 LMS 95650 200-J5
8000 CITH 95621 239-F7
MIMOSA WY
7400 SaCo 95828 338-B4
MIMUS LN
6500 PlaC 95746 221-F6
MINAKER DR
900 ANT 94509 (513-F4 See Page 493)
MINARD CT
- SaCo 95829 338-J5
MINARET WY
4700 SaCo 95608 279-E1
MINDEN CT
- SAC 95835 257-A5
MINDEN WY
- SAC 95835 257-A5
MINDOKA WY
- ELKG 95624 359-A7
MINDT CT
4100 SaCo 95608 279-E2
MINDY LN
9700 SaCo 95693 359-J7
9700 SaCo 95693 379-J1
MINER CT
100 ISLE 95641 455-G5
MINER WY
4800 SAC 95820 317-J3
MINERAL CT
6300 SaCo 95608 279-E2

STREET
Block City ZIP Pg-Grid

MINERAL WY
- EDCo 95667 266-B2
6200 SaCo 95608 279-D2
MINERAL BAR CT
11700 SaCo 95670 280-D4
MINERAL KING CT
8900 ELKG 95624 378-G2
MINERAL SPRINGS DR
2000 RSVL 95747 239-D1
MINERS CIR
3000 RKLN 95765 220-B1
MINERS CRSG
9300 PlaC 95650 201-H7
9300 PlaC 95650 221-H1
MINERS CT
3900 EDCo 95667 246-B7
MINERS DR
4000 PlaC 95650 201-G7
4000 PlaC 95650 221-G1
MINERS TR
4000 PlaC 95650 201-H7
MINERS WY
1200 RSVL 95661 240-B6
11200 PlaC 95602 162-A2
MINERS COVE CIR
4600 PlaC 95650 221-G1
MINERS CREEK CT
9100 ELKG 95758 358-A4
MINERSFIELD CT
4800 PlaC 95746 240-G1
MINERS MEADOWS CT
8100 PlaC 95746 241-B1
MINER SP RD
- EDCo 95667 225-D7
MINERS RAVINE RD
6700 PlaC 95746 241-B1
MINERVA AV
5200 SAC 95819 298-A4
MINESHAFT CT
3900 EDCo 95682 263-J6
MINE SHAFT LN
- SaCo 95742 280-D5
MINESHAFT LN
3800 EDCo 95682 263-J6
MING CT
- EDCo 95619 265-E4
MING LN
- EDCo 95619 265-E4
MING WY
6500 CITH 95610 259-J3
MINGEE WY
5600 ELKG 95757 377-J3
5600 ELKG 95757 397-J3
MINGO RD
10200 SaCo 95632 (399-D7 See Page 379)
MINING BROOK CT
4900 EDCo 95667 246-E5
MINING BROOK RD
3400 EDCo 95667 246-E6
MINI RANCH RD
700 PlaC 95648 180-D3
MINNEAPOLIS AV
- SaCo 95742 300-F2
MINNER AV
300 ANT 94509 (513-E6 See Page 493)
MINNESOTA AV
3900 SaCo 95628 279-H1
4900 SaCo 95628 259-H7
MINNESOTA DR
7400 CITH 95610 260-B1
MINNIE CIR
8800 ELKG 95624 358-G7
MINNIE WY
700 SAC 95831 336-H2
MINNOW CT
- SAC 95833 276-H6
MINOAN CT
8600 ELKG 95624 358-F2
MINORESS WY
7100 SaCo 95842 259-B2
MINT ST
300 SAC 95814 297-E2
MINTA LN
2700 ANT 94509 (513-C6 See Page 493)
MINT LEAF WY
100 SAC 95838 257-G7
MINTON CT
6100 SaCo 95608 279-D2
MINUET WY
7200 CITH 95621 259-G2
MINUTEMAN LN
4100 SaCo 95660 258-H7
MINX WY
5400 SaCo 95608 299-B1
MIO CT
6000 SaCo 95673 257-J4
MIPATY LN
1400 SaCo 95608 299-A2
MIRA CT
3600 EDCo 95682 264-B7
6800 SaCo 95828 338-B1
MIRA BELLA DR
- EDCo 95726 248-C6
MIRABELLA WY
- ELKG 95757 377-J1
- ELKG 95757 397-J1
MIRA CIEL WY
- EDCo 95684 286-J5
MIRACLE DR
- PlaC 95602 161-G2
MIRACLE MOUNTAIN DR
2300 EDCo 95667 246-C2
MIRADA ST
3000 SaCo 95826 298-H7
MIRA DEL RIO CT
9600 SaCo 95827 299-B4
MIRA DEL RIO DR
9300 SaCo 95827 299-C4
MIRADERA ST
3700 SaCo 95821 278-J4
MIRADOR WY
6900 SaCo 95828 338-B2
MIRAGE CT
7300 SaCo 95842 259-A1
MIRALO DR
4600 EDCo 95762 262-E6
MIRA LOMA CT
- WSAC 95691 316-J1
MIRA LOMA DR
- EDCo 95672 263-E2
3300 EDCo 95682 263-E4
11200 AUB 95603 182-D6
MIRAMAR RD
3000 SaCo 95821 278-E6
MIRAMONT CT
- EDCo 95762 262-H5

MIRA MONTE CT
- RSVL 95747 219-B1
MIRAMONTE DR
3100 SAC 95833 277-C4
MIRANDA CT
- SaCo 95822 317-A5
MIRANDY DR
9300 SaCo 95826 319-A1
9400 SaCo 95827 319-B1
MIRA PARADIS DR
- EDCo 95684 286-H5
MIRA RIVER CT
10900 RCCD 95670 279-J5
MIRASSOU CT
9000 SaCo 95829 338-H6
MIRAVALE CT
6100 CITH 95621 259-D1
MIRA VISTA
5200 EDCo 95623 265 A7
MIRA VISTA CT
1300 ANT 94509 (513 B6 See Page 493)
MIRAVISTA DR
- RKLN 95677 220-F5
MIRA VISTA ST
3700 SaCo 95821 278-J3
MIRIAM CT
5400 SaCo 95608 279-B7
MIRWOOD CT
6600 SaCo 95662 260-C3
MISSIE WY
5500 SaCo 95841 259-A6
MISSILE WY
- SaCo 95655 299-E7
MISSION AV
1200 SaCo 95608 299-A2
1200 SaCo 95864 299-A1
3500 SaCo 95608 279-A3
3800 SaCo 95608 278-J3
3800 SaCo 95821 278-J3
3800 SaCo 95821 279-A3
MISSION DR
1000 ANT 94509 (513-A6 See Page 493)
MISSION WY
- RSVL 95747 219-A7
- RSVL 95747 239-A1
800 SAC 95819 297-H5
3200 RKLN 95677 220-D1
MISSION BEACH CT
4800 ELKG 95758 357-H4
MISSION BELLS CT
- ELKG 95624 358-F1
MISSION FALLS CIR
8400 ELKG 95624 358-J1
MISSION HILLS DR
10000 SaCo 95829 339-D4
MISSION OAK CT
200 FOLS 95630 281-A3
MISSION VIEW CT
5200 SaCo 95608 279-B5
MISSISSIPPI ST
- SaCo 95742 300-F1
MISSISSIPPI BAR DR
5100 SaCo 95662 260-H7
MISSOURI AV
- SaCo 95742 300-F1
MISSOURI ST
4500 EDCo 95623 265-B4
MISSOURI WY
2300 SaCo 95626 238-D5
MISSOURI FLAT CT
3600 EDCo 95667 245-A7
MISSOURI FLAT RD
3200 EDCo 95667 244-J6
3500 EDCo 95667 245-A6
4000 EDCo 95667 265-C1
MIST CT
5700 SaCo 95662 260-H6
MIST TRWY
7700 SaCo 95843 239-A7
MISTELLE CT
8000 SaCo 95829 338-J5
MIST HILL WY
- RSVL 95747 218-H4
MISTLETOE WY
8300 CITH 95621 239-F6
MISTWOOD LN
5400 SaCo 95608 279-B5
MISTY CT
- RKLN 95765 200-B6
8600 ELKG 95624 358-H2
MISTY LN
1500 PlaC 95747 239-E2
MISTY BLUE CT
- ELKG 95757 358-A7
MISTY COVE PL
- ELKG 95758 357-F6
MISTY CREEK CT
4100 EDCo 95630 202-J5
MISTY CREEK DR
6500 CITH 95621 259-E1
MISTY HAVEN CT
- RSVL 95661 320 J5
MISTY HOLLOW CT
- RKLN 95765 220-A2
MISTY HOLLOW DR
- RKLN 95765 219-J2
- RKLN 95765 220-A2
1100 EDCo 95762 242-E4
MISTY MEADOW DR
1900 FOLS 95630 282-B2
MISTY MEADOW WY
5100 ELKG 95758 357-H4
MISTY MOOR CT
- LNCN 95648 179 F6
MISTY MORNING CIR
3400 RCCD 95827 299-E6
MISTY OAK WY
8400 SaCo 95843 239-A5
MISTY PASS WY
8400 SaCo 95843 239-B5
MISTY RIDGE CIR
600 FOLS 95630 261-J6
MISTY RIVER WY
9300 ELKG 95624 359-A5
MISTY SPRINGS CT
9300 ELKG 95624 359-A5
MISTYVALE CT
- SAC 95823 358-A1
MISTY VALLEY WY
8400 SaCo 95843 239-C5
MISTY WOOD DR
1500 RSVL 95747 219-E4
MISTYWOOD LN
4900 EDCo 95682 264-C4
MISTY WOOD WY
6300 CITH 95621 259-E2

MITCHELL CT
- FOLS 95630 281-E1
800 RSVL 95747 219-C6
6900 CITH 95621 259-J3
MITCHELL ST
- RVIS 94571 454-G3
MITCHLEN CT
6900 SaCo 95624 340-F1
6900 SaCo 95683 320-G7
8300 SaCo 95683 340-F1
MITCHS LN
2400 ANT 94509 (513-D6 See Page 493)
MITCHUM CT
4400 SaCo 95843 258-J1
MITFORD WY
- FOLS 95630 261-F7
MIWOK CT
11900 SaCo 95693 360-E6
MIX LN
9900 ELKG 95624 359-D2
MIZZENMAST CT
- ELKG 95758 357-F7
MIZZENMAST WY
- ELKG 95758 357-F7
MNM RD
- PlaC 95603 181-H3
- PlaC 95658 181-H3
MO CT
- AUB 95603 182-B7
MOBILE ST
- SaCo 95742 280-E7
MOBILE WY
3500 SaCo 95834 277-F3
MOBILE MANOR RD
- EDCo 95633 225-E1
- EDCo 95634 225-E1
MOBLEY AV
300 SaCo 95838 277-G3
MOCCASIN WY
7700 SaCo 95843 238-H7
MOCKENHAUPT CT
8400 ELKG 95624 358-F1
MOCKINGBIRD CT
- RKLN 95677 220-F1
MOCKINGBIRD LN
1300 LNCN 95648 180-B7
2400 EDCo 95709 246-J1
MOCKINGBIRD ST
- RSVL 95747 219-B7
- RSVL 95747 239-B1
4200 SaCo 95628 280-E2
MODDISON AV
3700 SAC 95819 297-J3
5000 SAC 95819 298-A4
MODELL WY
3700 SAC 95838 277-G3
MODENA PL
- SAC 95835 257-A4
MODENA WY
8400 ELKG 95624 358-E1
MODERNA CT
2600 RCCD 95670 299-E3
MODESSA CT
- RSVL 95678 219-F7
MODESTO DR
6600 SaCo 95842 259-B3
MODLIN WY
3700 SAC 95838 277-H3
MODOC CT
- WSAC 95691 316-H2
1800 ANT 94509 (513-G5 See Page 493)
3100 EDCo 95682 263-B2
MODOC WY
5100 SaCo 95841 259-B5
MOFFATT WY
100 SaCo 95864 298-E5
MOGAN AV
2300 SAC 95652 278-C2
2300 SAC 95838 278-C2
MOHAMAD OAKS CT
- SaCo 95841 279-A1
MOHAMED CIR
8800 ELKG 95624 358-G7
MOHAMMED LN
2500 PlaC 95603 160-J6
2500 PlaC 95658 160-J6
MOHAWK WY
8700 SaCo 95628 260-E6
MOHICAN WY
7800 SaCo 95843 238-H6
MOJAVE CT
2700 EDCo 95682 263-D2
MOJAVE DR
2900 WSAC 95691 316-H1
9000 SaCo 95826 318-H1
MOJIMBY LN
4100 EDCo 95682 264-A4
W MOKELUMNE AV
8500 SJCo 95686 (438-A3 See Page 418)
MOKELUMNE SCHOOL RD
- SaCo 95757 417-J1
MOLAKINI CT
5100 SaCo 95628 260-C7
MOLINER DR
3000 EDCo 95682 263-E3
MOLINERO CT
9000 ELKG 95758 357-J3
MOLINETTO CT
- EDCo 95762 262-G5
MOLITOR CT
7400 SaCo 95673 257-H1
MOLLY CT
- RSVL 95678 219-G4
MOLLY LN
2800 PLCR 95667 245-F4
MOLOKAI RD
- WSAC 95691 316-D2
MOLOKAI WY
8100 SaCo 95628 260-B7
MOMOLO CT
10600 RCCD 95670 299-G1
MOMTOMA LN
13000 SaCo 95693 (361-B7 See Page 341)
13000 SaCo 95693 381-B1
MONA AV
2600 EDCo 95667 245-J3
2600 PLCR 95667 245-J3
MONA WY
5400 SaCo 95841 259-D6
MONACO WY
- ELKG 95758 357-G3
MONAGHAN CIR
- SAC 95823 337-J5
- SAC 95823 338-A5

MONAL CT
7700 SaCo 95628 279-J3
MONALEE AV
5300 SAC 95819 298-A4
MONA PARK LN
- SaCo 95608 279-C3
MONARCH AV
1900 SAC 95832 337-C4
MONARCH CT
- RKLN 95765 200-C6
MONA WOODS LN
4600 SaCo 95608 279-A4
4600 SaCo 95821 279-A4
MONDAVI CT
- OAKL 94561 (514-D5 See Page 493)
8400 SaCo 95828 338-E6
MONDEGO WY
8700 SaCo 95628 260-E7
MONDON WY
8300 SaCo 95662 260-C3
MONET CT
300 FOLS 95630 261-H3
MONET DR
- OAKL 94561 (514-G6 See Page 493)
MONET WY
- EDCo 95762 262-J4
- RSVL 95746 240-F5
100 FOLS 95630 261-H3
4700 SaCo 95842 259-A3
MONETTA DR
- ELKG 95758 358-D5
MONETTA LN
- SAC 95835 256-G6
MONHEGAN WY
100 SaCo 95655 319-H2
MONICA AV
8600 SaCo 95662 260-D5
MONICA WY
- PLCR 95667 245-G6
MONIER CIR
3100 RCCD 95742 300-A3
MONIER PARK CIR
- RCCD 95742 300-B4
MONIER PARK PL
11300 RCCD 95742 300-B4
MONIFIETH WY
2000 SAC 95822 317-C7
MONITOR AV
5200 SaCo 95608 279-B5
MONK RD
4100 EDCo 95667 264-E3
MONMOUTH CT
- ELKG 95758 357-E5
MONO WY
3300 SaCo 95843 238-F6
MONOGRAM DR
7300 SaCo 95842 259-A1
MONOLITH LN
- LNCN 95648 180-B6
MONOPOLY CT
4000 RKLN 95677 220-G1
MONOWOOD DR
100 FOLS 95630 261-E5
MONROE CT
3000 ANT 94509 (513-A7 See Page 493)
MONTAGUE AV
4800 OAKL 94561 (514-D6 See Page 493)
MONTAGUE LN
- LNCN 95648 179-E6
MONTAGUE WY
300 SaCo 95673 257-G3
MONTALI WY
- SaCo 95828 338-E7
MONTALVO CT
- AUB 95603 162-E6
MONTANA AV
- SaCo 95742 300-F1
MONTANA CT
6400 EDCo 95667 265-B1
MONTANA DR
- AUB 95603 182-D6
MONTANA WY
2300 SaCo 95626 238-D5
MONTARA AV
- SAC 95835 257-C6
MONTARO CT
- LNCN 95648 179-E3
MONTAZUMA CIR
3400 SaCo 95826 318-H1
MONTCLAIR CIR
5600 RKLN 95677 220-H4
MONTCLAIR CT
4600 PlaC 95746 240-G2
MONTCLAIR DR
5500 RKLN 95677 220-H4
MONTCLAIR RD
3700 EDCo 95682 263-D6
MONTCLAIRE ST
2900 SaCo 95821 278-G5
MONTCURVE BLVD
4400 SaCo 95628 279-H2
MONTE CT
10 LNCN 95648 200-D1
MONTE WY
4800 SAC 95822 317-C3
MONTEAGLE CT
5500 SaCo 95842 258-J6
MONTE BELL CT
1700 RSVL 95661 240-B5
MONTE BELLO WY
2800 EDCo 95682 263-D3
MONTE BRAZIL DR
7500 SAC 95831 336-J2
7500 SAC 95831 337-A3
MONTE CASINO WY
6900 SaCo 95828 338-B1
MONTECITO CT
- EDCo 95762 282-C2
MONTECITO WY
2100 SAC 95822 337-D2
MONTE CLAIRE LN
5600 LMS 95650 220-J3
MONTE CORITA CIR
5600 CITH 95621 259-G6
MONTE CRESTA WY
9400 ELKG 95624 358-J5
MONTEDORO CT
- ELKG 95757 378-A1
MONTE FLAT CT
11600 SaCo 95670 280-D5
MONTEGLEN CT
3300 SaCo 95608 279-E5
MONTEGO CT
8700 ELKG 95624 358-G5

MONTEGRINO CT
9800 ELKG 95757 378-A1
MONTELENA CT
8000 SaCo 95829 338-J5
MONTE MAR DR
- EDCo 95762 282-D5
MONTE PARK AV
8100 SaCo 95628 280-B1
MONTEREY CT
- WSAC 95691 316-J1
1000 RSVL 95661 239-J5
MONTEREY DR
1000 ANT 94509 (513-A7 See Page 493)
MONTEREY LN
- EDCo 95672 243-F2
100 FOLS 95630 261-C1
MONTEREY RD
3000 EDCo 95667 246-B5
3000 PLCR 95667 246-B5
MONTEREY WY
4700 SAC 95822 317-C3
MONTEREY BAY CT
1100 GALT 95632 419-G2
MONTEREY OAKS DR
8900 ELKG 95758 358-B3
MONTEREY PINE PL
8400 PlaC 95746 240-H2
MONTEREY PINES CT
- RSVL 95747 219-A7
MONTEREY PINES DR
- RSVL 95747 219-A7
MONTERO CT
5600 RKLN 95677 220-G4
MONTERO RD
3400 EDCo 95682 263-B7
MONTEROSA CT
- SAC 95823 337-H5
MONTE SERENO CT
- PlaC 95650 221-H1
MONTE SERENO DR
- PlaC 95650 221-H1
MONTE VALLO CT
10100 RCCD 95827 299-E5
MONTEVERDE CT
200 LNCN 95648 180-E7
MONTE VERDE DR
4000 EDCo 95762 282-E2
MONTEVERDE DR
3400 LNCN 95648 180-C7
MONTEVERDE LN
3300 LNCN 95648 180-E7
6300 CITH 95621 259-F4
MONTEVIDEO DR
9400 SaCo 95693 360-G6
MONTEVINA DR
7900 SaCo 95829 338-J5
MONTEVINO CT
- OAKL 94561 (514-C6 See Page 493)
MONTEVINO WY
- OAKL 94561 (514-C6 See Page 493)
MONTE VISTA CT
- WSAC 95691 316-J1
MONTE VISTA DR
4600 EDCo 95709 246-G5
MONTE VISTA ST
- WSAC 95691 316-J1
MONTE VISTA WY
- EDCo 247-G2
1100 SAC 95831 317-A7
MONTEZ CT
6400 CITH 95621 259-G4
MONTEZUMA ST
100 RVIS 94571 454-H5
MONTEZUMA HILLS RD
1700 SolC 94571 474-A2
5200 SolC 94571 454-E7
8000 RVIS 94571 454-E7
MONTFORT RD
13600 SaCo 95638 (401-B6 See Page 381)
MONTGOMERY CT
- LNCN 95648 180-A5
MONTGOMERY LN
- SAC 95821 278-C5
MONTGOMERY PL
2500 EDCo 95762 242-A5
MONTGOMERY ST
100 RSVL 95678 219-G5
MONTGOMERY WY
2400 SAC 95818 317-E1
2600 SAC 95817 317-F1
MONTHAVEN
- EDCo 95672 243-E1
MONTIA CT
5500 SaCo 95662 260-H6
MONTICELLO AV
100 SaCo 95673 257-G3
MONTICELLO CT
- CITH 95621 259-F3
1000 OAKL 94561 (514-C5 See Page 493)
MONTICELLO LN
4500 PlaC 95650 221-E2
MONTICITO CT
100 RSVL 95678 219-G5
MONTIFLORA CT
8700 ELKG 95624 378-F1
MONTILLA CIR
- SAC 95835 257-B4
MONTMAGNY CT
400 FOLS 95630 261-H5
MONTOYA ST
8900 SaCo 95826 298-H7
MONTPELIER WY
8400 SaCo 95823 357-J1
MONTREUX WY
8100 SaCo 95828 338-F6
MONTRIDGE CT
1300 EDCo 95762 262-C7
MONTRIDGE WY
500 EDCo 95762 262-B7
600 EDCo 95762 282-C1
MONTRIL WY
4500 SAC 95823 337-H5
MONTROSE AV
- RSVL 95678 219-J3
MONTROSE CT
- EDCo 95762 282-C2
- LNCN 95648 179-F6
100 FOLS 95630 261-D5
MONTROSE DR
- FOLS 95630 261-D4
MONTROSE LN
- LNCN 95648 179-E7
MONTROSE ST
3300 SAC 95838 278-B4

MONTROSE WY
- EDCo 95762 282-C2
MONTVIEW WY
3000 SAC 95833 277-E5
MONTVILLE CT
8200 SaCo 95843 239-A6
MONT VISTA DR
12000 AUB 95603 182-B6
MONUKKA DR
3200 EDCo 95682 263-E4
MONUMENT CT
- LNCN 95648 180-C6
MONUMENT DR
- LNCN 95648 180-A6
- RSVL 95747 218-J6
4600 SaCo 95842 259-A1
MONUMENT PL
1100 PlaC 95658 180-H1
MONUMENT PEAK CT
100 FOLS 95630 240-J7
100 FOLS 95630 241-A7
MONUMENT SPRINGS DR
- PlaC 95677 220-F4
- RKLN 95677 220-F4
MONVALLE CT
- ELKG 95757 378-A1
MOODY LN
5300 SaCo 95608 279-B7
MOON AV
1400 SAC 95822 337-B2
MOONBEAM DR
2000 EDCo 95667 244-A4
3600 SaCo 95827 299-B7
3700 SaCo 95827 319-B1
MOON CREEK WY
- ELKG 95758 357-J2
MOONCREST WY
7400 SAC 95831 337-B2
MOONDANCER CIR
- RSVL 95747 219-C3
MOONEY RD
8500 PlaC 95746 241-D3
8900 ELKG 95624 359-G3
8900 SaCo 95624 359-G3
MOONFLOWER LN
- EDCo 95726 247-H6
MOONGLOW DR
- RCCD 95670 299-G4
MOON LAKE DR
- EDCo 95667 266-G3
MOONLIGHT WY
5200 ELKG 95758 357-J2
MOON LILY WY
5100 ELKG 95757 377-H1
5100 ELKG 95757 397-H1
MOONLIT CIR
- SAC 95831 316-J6
MOONLIT WY
- FOLS 95630 281-E1
MOONLIT BAY WY
5200 SAC 95835 256-J4
MOON RIDGE CT
3500 RKLN 95765 220-C1
MOONRISE CIR
- SAC 95834 277-B2
MOON RIVER WY
9500 ELKG 95624 359-B4
MOON ROCK WY
5900 CITH 95621 259-D3
MOON RUN WY
5100 ELKG 95758 357-H2
MOONSHADOW CT
- RKLN 95677 220-G5
MOONSHADOW WY
- LNCN 95648 179-D1
MOONSHINE LN
3100 PlaC 95650 201-B3
MOONSHINE HILL RD
- EDCo 95667 266-A5
MOONSTONE CIR
2000 EDCo 95762 262-C4
MOONSTONE DR
6300 RKLN 95677 220-B4
MOONSTONE WY
- SAC 95835 257-B6
MOONTREE DR
1900 SAC 95833 277-B4
MOORBROOK WY
2200 SAC 95826 298-F6
MOORE LN
4000 PlaC 95650 201-E7
4000 PlaC 95650 221-E1
MOORE RD
1000 LNCN 95648 179-F4
1100 PlaC 95648 179-E5
MOORE WY
700 FOLS 95630 261-C6
4700 SaCo 95608 299-A2
MOOREFIELD WY
8600 SAC 95823 358-A1
MOOREWOOD CT
3300 SaCo 95821 278-J5
MOORGATE CT
- SAC 95823 337-H5
MOORHAVEN WY
8100 SaCo 95828 338-D2
MOORHEN CT
2300 ELKG 95757 377-D1
2300 ELKG 95757 397-D1
MOORHOUSE CT
4500 SaCo 95842 258-J6
MOORLAND CT
100 RSVL 95661 240-E5
MOORPARK WY
4700 SaCo 95842 259-A5
MOOSE CREEK CT
7600 SaCo 95843 238-H7
7600 SaCo 95843 258-H1
MOOSE CREEK WY
800 GALT 95632 419-F3
MOOSE RIVER CT
11100 RCCD 95670 280-A5
MORA CT
2200 RCCD 95670 279-J6
MORAGA DR
2200 LNCN 95648 179-E1
3900 EDCo 95762 262-E5
6300 SaCo 95608 279-E1
6400 SaCo 95628 279-E1
MORAGA PL
- LNCN 95648 179-E1
MORAGA WY
- SAC 95819 298-B6
1700 RSVL 95661 240-B5
MORAINE CIR
2400 RCCD 95670 299-E2
MORALES
2200 RCCD 95670 279-J6

MORAN CT
10100 PlaC 95603 161-H7
10100 PlaC 95603 181-J1
MORAN DR
10100 PlaC 95603 181-J1
MORAPP LN
3400 PlaC 95650 201-G5
MORAVIAN ST
8400 SaCo 95826 298-E7
MORAZAN ST
6200 SaCo 95660 258-G4
MORCOTT WY
9300 SaCo 95829 339-A6
MOREAU CT
4500 ELKG 95758 357-H5
4800 EDCo 95762 262-F4
MORECOMBE CT
- RSVL 95747 219-B7
MOREL WY
3100 EDCo 95667 244-J7
MORELAND CT
100 FOLS 95630 261-G3
3100 SaCo 95864 298-F5
MORELIA CT
4300 SaCo 95628 280-F2
MORELL ST
2100 SAC 95833 277-E6
MORELLA CIR
- RSVL 95747 219-B1
MORELLA CT
- RSVL 95747 219-B2
MORELS CT
300 RSVL 95747 219-A5
MORENA WY
4800 SAC 95820 317-J3
4800 SAC 95820 318-A3
MORENO WY
1000 SAC 95838 277-J1
MORETTI WY
2500 SaCo 95821 278-C6
2500 SaCo 95825 278-C6
MORETTO CT
2600 RCCD 95670 299-G2
MOREY AV
100 SAC 95838 277-F3
MOREY DR
800 PLCR 95667 245-F5
MORGAN CT
- RSVL 95678 219-H4
100 AUB 95603 182-E2
400 EDCo 95762 262-B1
2500 RKLN 95677 220-C3
4700 OAKL 94561 (514-B7 See Page 493)
MORGAN LN
800 RVIS 94571 454-G5
MORGAN PL
5800 LMS 95650 221-B5
5800 PlaC 95650 221-B5
MORGAN WY
- RSVL 95678 219-H4
MORGAN CREEK LN
- PlaC 95747 239-A2
MORGANFIELD PL
9000 ELKG 95624 358-H5
MORGAN HILL WY
8100 SaCo 95828 338-F6
MORGANITE CT
- FOLS 95630 261-H4
MORGANITE WY
9700 ELKG 95624 359-B7
MORGAN OAK CT
4700 SaCo 95843 239-A6
MORGAN OAK WY
4800 SaCo 95843 239-A6
MORGAN POINT CT
9100 ELKG 95624 358-J1
MORGAN RIVER CT
11100 RCCD 95670 279-J5
MORGANS RANCH CIR
700 GALT 95632 419-F2
MORI CT
- OAKL 94561 (514-F7 See Page 493)
MORIAH WY
4100 SaCo 95660 258-H2
MORICE DR
- RSVL 95747 219-C1
MORILLAS LN
3900 LMS 95650 201-A7
MORISOT CT
- SAC 95835 256-J4
MORLEY WY
2000 SAC 95864 298-D6
2600 SaCo 95864 298-E6
MORMON ST
100 FOLS 95630 261-C4
MORMON CARSON PASS EMIGRANT TR
- EDCo 95726 248-D6
MORMON EMIGRANT TR
- EDCo 248-H7
- EDCo 95726 248-D6
MORMON ISLAND DR
2300 EDCo 95762 262-B1
MORNINDALE LN
2100 EDCo 95667 245-A4
MORNING CANYON RD
- EDCo 95619 286-D6
- EDCo 95684 286-D6
MORNING DOVE CIR
- SAC 95833 277-C5
MORNING DOVE LN
100 FOLS 95630 260-J4
MORNING GLEN CT
- RKLN 95765 220-A2
MORNING GLORY CT
1000 EDCo 95762 242-C7
MORNING GLORY LN
- RSVL 95747 219-D6
MORNING GLORY ST
800 WSAC 95691 296-E4
MORNING GLORY WY
8700 ELKG 95624 358-F2
MORNINGLO LN
5600 SaCo 95662 260-J6
MORNING MIST LN
12400 PlaC 95602 162-C1
MORNING MIST WY
- RSVL 95747 219-A7
MORNINGSIDE CT
- RKLN 95677 220-G5
600 FOLS 95630 261-J6
MORNINGSIDE DR
700 FOLS 95630 261-J5
7000 PlaC 95746 221-D7
7000 PlaC 95746 241-C1
MORNINGSIDE WY
7400 CITH 95621 239-G7

© 2007 Rand McNally & Company

MORNING SKYE WY SACRAMENTO COUNTY STREET INDEX NEVADA RD 556
© 2007 Rand McNally & Company
SACRAMENTO CO.

STREET Block City ZIP Pg-Grid

MORNING SKYE WY
8400 SaCo 95843 238-H5
MORNING SONG CT
1200 EDCo 95762 242-C7
MORNING SONG PL
1200 EDCo 95762 242-C7
MORNING STAR DR
- EDCo - 267-E4
MORNINGSTAR DR
- RSVL 95747 219-A7
4900 SaCo 95824 317-H6
MORNING SUN CT
4000 PlaC 95602 161-J1
MORNINGSUN CT
- SAC 95831 336-J2
MORNINGVIEW WY
- EDCo 95762 262-F1
MORPHEUS LN
4300 SaCo 95864 298-J1
MORRENE DR
2300 PLCR 95667 245-H3
MORRILL CT
- EDCo 95762 262-D5
MORRILL WY
- EDCo 95762 262-D5
MORRIS WY
500 SaCo 95864 298-J4
MORRISON AV
- SAC 95838 277-F3
MORRISON RD
3400 EDCo 95762 263-A7
3400 EDCo 95762 283-A1
MORRISON CREEK DR
8500 SAC 95828 318-F7
MORRISTOWN CT
9100 ELKG 95758 357-G4
MORRO CT
1000 RSVL 95661 239-J5
MORRO BAY DR
5200 SaCo 95608 299-B1
MORROW ST
3400 SaCo 95821 278-J4
MORROW BAY ST
- WSAC 95691 316-E1
MORSE AV
500 SaCo 95864 298-E4
1700 SaCo 95825 298-E4
1800 SaCo 95825 278-F7
2500 SaCo 95821 278-F5
MORSE CT
1100 WSAC 95605 296-H2
MORSE RD
41000 YoCo 95612 (396-A1 See Page 375)
MORSE GLEN LN
2800 SaCo 95864 298-E3
MORTAR CT
3300 EDCo 95667 246-D5
MORTARA CIR
2400 EDCo 95667 244-F4
MORTENSEN CT
2300 SaCo 95626 238-D6
MORTENSON LN
8500 SaCo 95628 280-D2
MORTON CT
1100 SaCo 95864 298-E3
3200 EDCo 95667 226-J2
MORTON RD
- WSAC 95691 316-F2
MORTON WY
- FOLS 95630 261-D7
- FOLS 95630 281-D1
2100 ANT 94509 (513-A7 See Page 493)
MORTONO ST
- SAC 95838 318-E6
MORTS CT
2700 PLCR 95667 245-B5
MOSAIC DR
- ELKG 95757 377-J1
- ELKG 95757 378-A1
- ELKG 95757 397-J1
MOSBY AV
300 SAC 95838 277-G3
MOSCANO WY
2500 RCCD 95670 299-G1
MOSCATEL AV
- SAC 95834 276-H4
MOSELY CT
9000 ELKG 95624 358-H1
MOSES CT
- SAC 95823 337-G5
MOSEY LN
- EDCo 95682 263-J7
MOSHER RD
10000 ELKG 95624 378-J2
10000 ELKG 95624 379-A2
10000 SaCo 95624 379-A2
MOSQUITO RD
1800 EDCo 95667 226-F2
8800 EDCo 95667 246-A1
9200 EDCo 95667 245-J2
9600 PLCR 95667 245-H4
MOSQUITO CUTOFF RD
2300 EDCo 95667 226-C3
MOSS CT
8300 PlaC 95746 221-E4
MOSS DR
4100 SAC 95822 317-B3
MOSS LN
5000 PlaC 95746 221-E3
MOSS ST
7900 SaCo 95628 280-A3
MOSS AGATE CT
8600 ELKG 95758 357-J2
MOSSBANK WY
- FOLS 95630 262-A5
MOSSBEACH CT
- SAC 95831 336-J2
MOSSBROOK CT
1300 RSVL 95661 240-A4
MOSSBURN WY
6200 ELKG 95758 358-A2
MOSS CREEK CIR
5900 SaCo 95628 260-B5
MOSS CREEK CT
- RKLN 95765 220-A1
MOSS CREEK LN
- EDCo 95667 245-A5
MOSSCREEK WY
- RSVL 95678 219-H6
MOSSDALE CT
100 LNCN 95648 179-G4
MOSSGLEN CIR
- SAC 95826 298-F7
MOSS OAK AV
8200 CITH 95610 240-B6
MOSSRIDGE WY
3700 EDCo 95762 262-B5
MOSS ROCK CT
100 FOLS 95630 261-A2
MOSSVIEW PL
3900 EDCo 95762 262-D3
MOSSVIEW WY
6500 CITH 95621 259-E2
MOSSWOOD CIR
1700 WSAC 95691 296-H5
9800 FOLS 95630 261-B1
MOSSY CT
- LNCN 95648 180-A4
MOSSY BANK DR
- SAC 95833 277-C6
MOSSY GLEN CT
4600 EDCo 95682 244-A7
MOSSY OAK CT
- RKLN 95765 199-J4
- RKLN 95765 200-A4
MOSSY OAKS CT
2500 RCCD 95670 299-D3
MOSSY RIDGE LN
- LNCN 95648 180-B6
MOSSY STONE WY
5000 RCCD 95742 320-E4
MOTHER LODE CIR
11300 SaCo 95670 280-A4
MOTHER LODE CT
1100 AUB 95603 182-C5
MOTHER LODE DR
1400 RSVL 95661 240-B5
4000 EDCo 95682 264-F6
5300 EDCo 95667 264-H4
5300 EDCo 95623 264-H4
6000 EDCo 95623 265-A2
6000 EDCo 95667 265-A2
6500 EDCo 95667 245-C7
MOTT CT
- LNCN 95648 179-E2
9200 SaCo 95662 260-G5
12900 PlaC 95603 162-E5
MOTT WY
12800 PlaC 95603 162-E5
MOTTO LN
4600 EDCo 95667 244-A5
4600 EDCo 95682 244-A5
4600 EDCo 95667 243-J5
4600 EDCo 95682 243-J5
MOULTON DR
2800 PLCR 95667 245-E4
MOUNTAIN AV
100 PlaC 95603 162-F6
7500 SaCo 95662 240-H7
7500 SaCo 95662 260-H1
MOUNTAIN DR
8800 PlaC 95746 240-J3
MOUNTAIN LN
2700 PLCR 95667 245-H4
MOUNTAIN WY
1900 EDCo 95667 246-C1
MOUNTAIN BELL CT
- ELKG 95624 338-E7
- ELKG 95624 358-E1
MOUNTAIN BELL DR
- ELKG 95624 358-E1
MOUNTAINGATE DR
- RKLN 95765 200-C4
MOUNTAIN HOME CT
8900 ELKG 95624 378-G2
MOUNTAIN LAKE DR
3200 EDCo 95726 248-E3
MOUNTAIN OAK CT
100 FOLS 95630 261-B3
MOUNTAIN OAK LN
2600 EDCo 95672 243-B4
MOUNTAIN OAK WY
7500 SaCo 95660 258-G1
MOUNTAIN PARK DR
- RSVL 95678 219-G3
MOUNTAIN QUAIL CT
- LNCN 95648 200-C2
MOUNTAINSIDE DR
7000 CITH 95621 239-F6
MOUNTAIN SPRINGS RD
2000 PlaC 95602 162-D1
MOUNTAIN VIEW AV
3100 SaCo 95821 278-E5
MOUNTAIN VIEW CT
2000 PlaC 95602 161-J3
2900 EDCo 95682 263-C3
MOUNTAIN VIEW DR
300 FOLS 95630 261-F2
2800 EDCo 95709 247-C3
3500 RKLN 95677 220-E1
3700 PlaC 95650 201-J6
MOUNTAIN VIEW LN
1500 PlaC 95658 181-H7
1500 PlaC 95658 201-H1
MOUNTAIN VISTA CIR
9700 ELKG 95757 358-A7
MOUNTAINWOOD CT
- SAC 95823 337-F3
MOUNTAIRE DR
3100 ANT 94509 (513-E7 See Page 493)
MOUNT AUBURN CT
4600 SaCo 95842 259-A2
MOUNT AUKUM RD Rt#-E16
3800 EDCo - 267-C5
5300 EDCo 95684 286-J5
MOUNT BADGER CT
- RSVL 95747 199-C7
MOUNT BALDY DR
- RSVL 95747 219-C1
MOUNTBATTEN WY
8800 ELKG 95624 358-G4
MOUNT CARMEL RD
- EDCo 95633 205-B2
MOUNT CASEY CT
900 EDCo 95762 262-D6
MOUNT DAHAHER RD
2900 EDCo 95709 247-C3
MOUNT DARWIN CT
- RSVL 95747 199-C7
MOUNT DIABLO CT
7800 SaCo 95628 279-J3
MOUNT EVANS CT
5800 SaCo 95842 259-D2
MOUNT EVEREST CT
5600 SaCo 95842 259-C2
MOUNT HOOD CT
5700 SaCo 95842 259-C2
MOUNT IVY WY
4300 RCCD 95742 320-D2
MOUNT JUDAH PL
- SAC 95835 257-A3
MOUNT KISCO WY
4300 RCCD 95742 320-D2
MOUNT MCKINLEY CT
5700 SaCo 95842 259-C2
MOUNT OLYMPUS DR
1800 EDCo 95667 246-F1
MOUNT PLEASANT RD
2200 PlaC 95602 161-A4
2400 PlaC 95602 160-G3
2700 PlaC - 160-D3
2900 PlaC 95648 160-G3
MOUNT PLUTO PL
- SAC 95835 257-A3
MOUNT PROSPECT CT
5600 SaCo 95842 259-C2
MOUNT RAINER CT
- RSVL 95678 220-A3
MOUNT RAINIER DR
5100 SaCo 95842 259-B3
MOUNT RANIER WY
700 EDCo 95762 262-D6
MOUNT ROSE WY
4700 RSVL 95747 219-A6
MOUNT SHASTA CT
5700 SaCo 95842 259-C2
MOUNT SHASTA LN
1100 EDCo 95667 244-H1
MOUNT STEPHENS CT
- SAC 95835 256-J5
- SAC 95835 257-A5
MOUNT TAILAC CT
500 RSVL 95747 219-B5
MOUNT TAMALPAIS DR
- RSVL 95747 199-C7
- RSVL 95747 219-C1
MOUNT VERNON RD
5200 PlaC 95648 160-J4
5200 PlaC 95658 160-J4
5200 PlaC 95603 160-J4
5800 PlaC 95602 161-E3
5800 PlaC 95603 161-H5
10700 PlaC 95603 162-A7
11400 PlaC 95603 182-C1
11400 AUB 95603 182-C1
MOUNT VERNON WY
6800 SaCo 95628 279-F1
MOURA CT
10300 ELKG 95757 378-B3
MOURVERDE CT
- ELKG 95624 379-A2
MOUSEBIRD CT
- LNCN 95648 200-B3
MOUSETAIL CT
9800 ELKG 95757 357-F7
MOYLAN CT
100 FOLS 95630 261-F7
MOYLAN WY
100 FOLS 95630 261-F7
MOYNELLO CT
9300 ELKG 95624 358-G5
MOZART CT
6100 SaCo 95621 239-D6
MUA MACALL CT
- SAC 95835 256-H3
MUCKROSS ABBEY CT
- LNCN 95648 200-B2
MUDDY LN
1700 EDCo 95619 265-J5
1700 EDCo 95619 266-A5
MUELLER CT
100 RSVL 95661 240-D5
MUERER ST
- FOLS 95630 281-D1
MUFFY CT
9200 ELKG 95624 358-J7
MUGHO CT
6300 CITH 95621 259-E2
MUGLESTON LN
12900 SaCo 95693 360-J1
12900 SaCo 95693 (361-A2 See Page 341)
MUIR CT
1100 RSVL 95661 240-C4
2500 RKLN 95677 220-B4
MUIR DR
- EDCo 95709 247-C1
MUIR WY
2500 SAC 95818 297-B6
9100 PlaC 95746 241-B4
MUIRFIELD CT
- EDCo 95682 263-E4
MUIRFIELD DR
1100 RSVL 95746 240-F4
2500 LNCN 95648 179-D2
MUIRFIELD WY
7400 SAC 95822 337-D2
MUIRKIRK CT
1200 FOLS 95630 262-A3
MUIRWOOD LN
3500 PlaC 95747 239-A2
MUIRWOOD WY
7700 CITH 95610 259-J3
MUIR WOODS CT
900 EDCo 95762 262-D6
MUIR WOODS DR
3000 EDCo 95762 262-D6
MULBERRY CT
500 RSVL 95661 240-B3
MULBERRY LN
100 PlaC 95603 162-F6
400 PlaC 95648 160-A7
400 PlaC 95648 180-B1
1800 EDCo 95667 244-H3
4000 SAC 95822 317-B2
4100 EDCo 95619 265-F2
MULBERRY WOOD LN
- SAC 95842 259-A1
MULDOON WY
11900 RCCD 95742 320-E2
MULDROW RD
5700 SaCo 95841 259-C7
5800 SaCo 95608 259-D7
MULE CREEK CT
100 FOLS 95630 261-A1
MULES EAR RD
- EDCo 95634 225-A2
MULESHOE PASS
- EDCo - 267-E6
MULE SKINNER RD
- EDCo 95667 225-F5
MULE TAIL LN
- EDCo 95633 205-B2
MULE TEAM WY
- RSVL 95747 219-B2
MULFORD AV
4300 SaCo 95821 278-J4
MULHOLLAND WY
3500 SaCo 95821 278-H4
MULLEIN CT
8600 SaCo 95843 238-G5
MULLEN CT
100 FOLS 95630 281-F1
MULLINGER LN
- LNCN 95648 179-F6
MULRANY WY
8100 SaCo 95843 238-J6
8100 SaCo 95843 239-A6
MULVANY PL
- WSAC 95691 316-E1
E MUMFORD CT
- ELKG 95758 357-F4
W MUMFORD CT
- ELKG 95758 357-F4
MUNDEN CT
400 RSVL 95747 239-C1
MUNGER WY
1300 SAC 95831 317-B7
MUNHALL CT
7900 SaCo 95829 338-J5
MUNICH CT
4100 SaCo 95843 238-H5
MUNICIPAL DR
300 SAC 95838 257-G7
MUNOZ AV
6800 PlaC 95663 201-B1
MUNROE ST
200 SAC 95864 298-D5
200 SaCo 95864 298-D5
MUNSLOW WY
8100 SaCo 95829 339-A6
MUNSON WY
7200 SAC 95823 337-G1
MUO BRODY CT
- SAC 95835 256-H3
MURATA AV
- SAC 95823 337-F2
MURATURA WY
- EDCo 95762 262-G5
MURCHISON WY
3100 SaCo 95608 279-A5
MURCIA WY
- EDCo 95762 262-G6
MURDOCK WY
7000 SaCo 95608 279-G3
MURICATIA DR
6900 SaCo 95662 260-D2
MURIETA DR
7100 SaCo 95683 342-A3
MURIETA PKWY
7100 SaCo 95683 322-C7
7100 SaCo 95683 342-A1
MURIETA WY
1900 SAC 95822 317-D4
MURIETA SOUTH PKWY
15200 SaCo 95683 342-C3
MURILLO CT
- OAKL 94561 (514-H6 See Page 493)
MURPHY RANCH RD
- EDCo 95667 243-F1
MURPHYS CT
2000 SaCo 95670 280-C4
MURRAY CT
- EDCo 95762 262-E1
400 RSVL 95678 219-J7
MURRAY PL
5900 SaCo 95628 260-B5
MURRAY ST
1100 PLCR 95667 245-J3
MURRAY WY
700 RSVL 95678 219-J6
MURRELET CT
100 LNCN 95648 180-C7
MURRELL PL
1600 EDCo 95762 262-D3
MURRELL ST
5600 ELKG 95758 357-J3
MUSCAT CIR
1300 RSVL 95747 239-E2
MUSCAT WY
3400 RCCD 95670 299-J4
MUSCHETTO CT
7600 CITH 95621 259-G1
MUSCOVY CT
- RSVL 95747 219-E2
MUSE DR
300 EDCo 95762 262-C5
MUSGRAVE DR
- RSVL 95747 239-D1
MUSGRAVE PL
2600 EDCo 95762 262-D3
MUSIC LN
- EDCo - 267-D2
MUSKINGHAM WY
- SAC 95823 357-J1
MUSKRAT WY
2800 SAC 95834 276-J3
MUSSO RD
14000 PlaC 95603 162-G3
14100 PlaC 95602 162-H3
MUSTANG CT
- RSVL 95747 219-B4
MUSTANG WY
3900 EDCo 95762 262-H7
5300 SaCo 95608 279-B2
MUSTIC WY
100 SaCo 95655 319-H2
MUTH LN
7400 CITH 95621 259-G1
MUTTONBIRD WY
2900 SAC 95834 276-J4
MYERS LN
7100 PlaC 95746 220-H7
MYHREN WY
8800 SaCo 95662 260-E4
MYKONOS WY
4300 ELKG 95758 357-G4
MYLITTA CT
8800 ELKG 95624 358-F3
MYNA WY
3300 SAC 95833 276-J4
3300 SAC 95834 276-J4
MYOTIS DR
2800 SAC 95834 276-J3
MYOWN RD
3400 EDCo 95667 245-A6
MYRNA CT
1100 RSVL 95661 239-J4
MYRNA WY
3800 SaCo 95821 278-H3
MYRTLE AV
500 PLCR 95667 245-F5
500 WSAC 95605 296-H1
600 GALT 95632 419-E6
3300 SaCo 95660 258-F7
3500 SaCo 95660 278-G1
4200 SaCo 95841 278-J1
4600 SaCo 95841 279-A1
MYRTLE CT
200 RSVL 95747 239-D1
600 PLCR 95667 245-F5
MYRTLE DR
3300 LMS 95650 200-H5
MYRTLE LN
2900 SaCo 95608 279-C6
MYRTLE VISTA AV
7400 SAC 95831 337-A2
MYRTLEWOOD CT
6000 CITH 95621 239-D7
MYRTUS CT
8300 SaCo 95662 260-C3
MYSIN WY
- SAC 95833 277-D6
MYSTERY CREEK LN
6500 PlaC 95746 221-B6
MYSTERY MOUNTAIN WY
- RKLN 95765 219-J2
MYSTIC LN
- SaCo 95864 298-H4
MYSTIC HILLS PL
- FOLS 95630 261-A1
MYSTRAS CIR
- ELKG 95624 358-F1

N

N ST
200 SAC 95814 297-B4
300 LNCN 95648 179-G3
400 ANT 94509 (513-B4 See Page 493)
400 SaCo 95673 257-H2
1900 SAC 95816 297-E5
5300 SAC 95819 297-J6
5800 SAC 95819 298-A7
6300 SaCo 95823 338-A2
NACHEZ CT
6300 CITH 95621 259-E4
NACIMIENTO CT
- RSVL 95678 219-J5
NACONA PL
- SaCo 95829 339-D6
NADA CT
10100 RCCD 95827 299-E5
NADER CT
- SAC 95831 336-G3
NADER RD
200 PlaC - 159-B1
NADIA WY
7500 SAC 95831 336-G3
NADINE ST
3400 SaCo 95608 279-B4
NAIFY ST
3600 SaCo 95821 278-G4
NAMATH CIR
- ELKG 95757 377-J2
- ELKG 95757 397-J2
NAMPA WY
- SAC 95824 318-B5
NANAS LN
4200 EDCo 95667 265-B3
NANCE CT
- LNCN 95648 179-E5
NANCY LN
2900 WSAC 95691 316-E2
3000 SAC 95823 337-F1
3000 SaCo 95823 337-F1
NANCY WY
2200 SaCo 95608 279-A7
2900 SAC 95826 318-E1
NANDINA WY
8400 SaCo 95843 238-F5
NANIMO CT
100 ANT 94509 (513-D7 See Page 493)
NANTASKET COVE WY
8800 SAC 95823 358-B2
NANTUCKET CT
3300 EDCo 95682 263-C5
NANTUCKET WY
- SAC 95835 257-C5
NAOMI WY
1900 SAC 95815 278-B5
3200 PLCR 95667 245-G6
NAPA AV
7900 SaCo 95826 318-C3
NAPA LP
- RSVL 95747 219-B5
NAPA VALLEY WY
8900 SaCo 95829 338-H5
NAPIER WY
8500 SaCo 95828 338-F3
NAPLES CT
- SAC 95831 337-A5
NAPLES ST
2900 SAC 95826 298-F7
2900 SAC 95826 318-F1
NAPOLEON DR
6700 LMS 95650 221-B1
NAPOLI CT
- LNCN 95648 179-E6
2600 SaCo 95608 279-B6
NAPONEE CT
- SAC 95835 256-J6
NARANJA WY
6300 SaCo 95662 260-E4
NARCISSUS AV
- PlaC 95603 162-C6
NARCISSUS CT
8500 ELKG 95624 338-E7
NAREB ST
3200 SAC 95838 277-G4
NARI DR
- WSAC 95691 296-D4
NARRAGANSET WY
100 SaCo 95655 319-H2
NARROWGAUGE WY
6800 SAC 95823 338-B6
NARUTH WY
600 SAC 95838 277-H2
NARWAL PL
- SAC 95835 256-G5
NASCA WY
400 SAC 95831 336-G2
NASH AV
300 ANT 94509 (513-E4 See Page 493)
NASH WY
8600 SaCo 95828 338-F5
NASHONE VIEW LN
4200 EDCo 95630 202-J6
NASHUA CT
- RKLN 95765 200-C5
NASHUA WY
4700 SAC 95838 257-G7
NASHVILLE TR
- EDCo 95619 266-B7
- EDCo 95619 286-A2
NASREEN DR
9100 SaCo 95826 318-J2
NASSAU CT
- RKLN 95765 200-C6
NATALIE CT
12100 AUB 95603 162-D6
NATALINO CIR
100 SAC 95835 257-B5
NATCHEZ CT
14700 SaCo 95683 342-C4
NATHALIE CT
- PlaC 95747 239-B4
NATHAN CT
- SAC 95835 256-H6
3400 RKLN 95677 220-D2
NATHANIAL AV
500 GALT 95632 419-F5
NATION DR
100 PlaC 95603 162-F6
NATIONAL DR
- SaCo 95834 257-D7
1300 SaCo 95834 277-C2
NATIVE LN
3100 EDCo 95682 283-C2
NATIVE DANCER LN
9200 ELKG 95624 359-D5
NATIVE OAK LN
2300 SaCo 95825 278-D7
NATOMA AV
3800 SaCo 95628 280-B2
NATOMA ST
700 FOLS 95630 281-C3
3000 SAC 95833 277-F5
E NATOMA ST
- FOLS 95630 262-A5
- FOLS 95630 261-F3
300 FOLS 95671 261-F3
NATOMA WY
3600 SAC 95838 278-B3
NATOMA CANAL WY
- SaCo 95670 280-E5
NATOMAS BLVD
- SAC 95673 257-B5
4900 SAC 95834 257-B5
4900 SAC 95835 257-B5
E NATOMAS RD
- SaCo 95836 237-D2
- SuCo 95668 237-D2
1000 SuCo 95626 237-D2
NATOMAS CROSSING DR
- SAC 95834 276-H3
- SAC 95834 277-A3
NATOMAS PARK DR
2400 SAC 95833 277-B6
NATOMA STATION DR
- FOLS 95670 281-A2
2000 FOLS 95630 281-A2
NATTIER CT
- EDCo 95762 262-J4
NATURE TRWY
9600 ELKG 95757 357-E7
NATURES WY
3000 PLCR 95667 245-J5
NATURES INN CT
- EDCo 95667 266-E2
NATURE WALK CT
- EDCo 95762 282-D4
NATUREWOOD CT
4100 SaCo 95628 280-F2
NATUREWOOD RD
4000 EDCo 95630 202-J7
4000 EDCo 95630 222-J1
NAUTICA CT
- SAC 95833 276-H7
NAUTILUS CT
- SAC 95831 316-G6
NAVAHO DR
3400 SaCo 95843 238-G6
NAVAJO CT
- EDCo 95682 263-D3
NAVAJO DR
2600 RKLN 95765 200-C4
NAVARRE CT
6000 SaCo 95608 259-D7
NAVARRETIA CT
200 RSVL 95747 219-A6
NAVARRO CT
6900 CITH 95621 259-F4
NAVAS LN
2100 PlaC 95658 201-E2
NAVIGATION CT
5300 SaCo 95628 260-F6
NAVIGATOR DR
- LNCN 95648 179-F3
NAVION CT
3100 EDCo 95682 263-D5
NAVION DR
6200 CITH 95621 259-E1
6700 CITH 95621 239-F7
NAWAL DR
- EDCo 95762 262-F1
NAWI TR
- EDCo - 267-C7
NAXOS WY
9000 ELKG 95758 357-G4
NEAH CT
1100 ANT 94509 (513-F7 See Page 493)
NEAL RD
1000 SAC 95838 257-J6
1000 SAC 95838 258-A6
NEAL ST
7800 SaCo 95628 279-J3
NEASHAM CIR
1100 SAC 95814 297-B3
NEBBIOLO CT
- EDCo 95762 262-G4
- ELKG 95624 379-A2
NEBLINA CT
7300 SaCo 95683 342-C2
NEBRASKA LN
4800 SaCo 95628 279-H1
4800 SaCo 95628 259-H7
NEBRASKA RD
- SaCo 95742 280-J7
- SaCo 95742 281-A7
NEBULA CT
- RKLN 95677 220-H5
NEBULA WY
9900 RCCD 95827 299-D6
NECTAR CIR
5200 ELKG 95757 377-J2
5200 ELKG 95757 397-J2
NECTURINE DR
- FOLS 95630 261-D4
NEDRA CT
- SAC 95822 337-E3
NEEDLE CT
- RSVL 95678 219-F5
NEEDLES WY
200 FOLS 95630 261-C5
NEELY WY
3600 SaCo 95655 299-E6
NEFF LN
4500 EDCo 95682 264-C3
NEGLEY LN
4100 SaCo 95608 279-D3
NEGRARA WY
2400 RCCD 95670 299-G1
2400 RCCD 95670 279-G7
NEIGHBOR LN
3200 PlaC 95648 179-B2
NEIGHBORS LN
100 AUB 95603 182-E4
NEIHART AV
1500 SAC 95832 337-C4
NEIHI LN
1500 PlaC 95663 180-H7
1500 PlaC 95663 200-H1
NEIL CT
- SAC 95831 336-H2
NEILS RD
15200 PlaC 95602 162-J1
NEIRETTO CT
10400 RCCD 95670 299-F1
NEISA WY
8000 SaCo 95828 338-D5
NELDA LN
12500 SaCo 95638 (401-C7 See Page 381)
12500 SaCo 95638 421-C1
NELLE PL
5300 SaCo 95628 260-E6
NELLIS CT
- SAC 95835 257-D5
NELMARK ST
7300 SAC 95822 337-F2
NELROY WY
4700 SaCo 95608 279-A7
NELSON CT
- EDCo 95709 247-C1
NELSON DR
2900 RSVL 95661 240-E3
12400 PlaC 95603 162-C4
NELSON LN
- PlaC 95648 179-C3
7700 CITH 95610 259-J2
NELSON RD
- EDCo 95709 247-B1
NELSON ST
5200 SAC 95820 318-A4
NELSON CANYON RD
- EDCo 95634 225-F2
NEMEA WY
8600 ELKG 95624 358-F2
NEOPOLITAN WY
8500 SAC 95758 358-C2
NEOSHO DR
9200 ELKG 95758 357-H4
NEPHI WY
8500 SaCo 95628 280-D2
NEPONSET DR
8900 ELKG 95624 358-H4
NEPTUNE CT
- WSAC 95691 316-J1
5100 PlaC 95746 240-J4
NEPTUNE WY
1800 SaCo 95864 298-J1
NERISSA CT
- RSVL 95661 220-E6
NEROLY RD
4300 OAKL 94561 (514-A5 See Page 493)
NESBITT CT
100 FOLS 95630 261-C6
NESCLIFFE WY
5500 SaCo 95608 279-C4
NESMITH CT
- FOLS 95630 261-G7
NESS CT
- SAC 95826 298-F6
NESS RD
13000 SaCo 95638 420-D4
13100 SaCo 95632 420-D4
NESTANI WY
- ELKG 95758 357-E5
NESTING CIR
- ELKG 95757 357-F7
- ELKG 95757 377-F1
- ELKG 95757 397-F1
NESTING CT
- PLCR 95667 246-A6
8500 PlaC 95746 240-G2
NESTING PL
5300 RKLN 95677 220-G3
NESTING WY
- PLCR 95667 246-A6
NESTLE CT
3400 RKLN 95765 200-C7
NESTLENOOK CIR
100 SaCo 95655 319-H3
NET LN
12800 PlaC 95603 162-E4
NETA LN
1600 PlaC 95747 239-E4
NETHERDALE WY
- EDCo 95762 262-D3
NETHERLANDS AV
52000 YoCo 95612 356-G6
NETHERLANDS RD
36000 YoCo 95612 356-G7
36000 YoCo 95612 (376-G1 See Page 375)
S NETHERLANDS RD
50000 YoCo 95612 (376-B4 See Page 375)
NETTLE CT
8100 CITH 95610 260-B2
NEUBURGER LN
9100 SaCo 95662 260-G2
W NEUTRA CT
- ELKG 95758 357-E4
NEUTRA WY
- ELKG 95758 357-E4
E NEUTRA WY
- ELKG 95758 357-E4
NEVADA AV
100 RSVL 95678 239-J2
NEVADA CT
2600 EDCo 95667 245-A5
NEVADA LN
2600 ANT 94509 (513-A6 See Page 493)
NEVADA RD
- SaCo 95742 280-J7
- SaCo 95742 281-A7

STREET
Block City ZIP Pg-Grid

NEVADA ST
- SaCo 95742 300-H1
100 AUB 95603 182-C1
400 AUB 95603 162-D7
400 PlaC 95603 162-D6
3400 RKLN 95677 220-D2
NEVAR CT
14800 SaCo 95683 342-A1
NEVERS WY
10200 ELKG 95757 377-H2
10200 ELKG 95757 397-H2
NEVILLE CT
- LNCN 95648 179-E3
NEVILLE WY
- GALT 95632 419-H3
NEVINS WY
9300 SaCo 95662 260-H2
NEVIS CT
1200 SAC 95822 317-A4
NEW AGE CT
9000 ELKG 95758 358-C3
NEW AIRPORT RD
12200 PlaC 95603 162-C4
13300 PlaC 95602 162-D3
13500 AUB 95602 162-D3
NEW ALBION DR
11600 SaCo 95670 280-D5
NEWBERRY CT
2200 EDCo 95762 242-C5
NEWBERRY PL
9800 PlaC 95746 240-J6
NEWBERRY ST
- WSAC 95691 316-J1
NEWBOROUGH DR
1500 SAC 95833 277-C6
NEWBRIDGE CT
100 LNCN 95648 179-G5
NEWBRIDGE LN
600 LNCN 95648 179-G5
NEWBRIDGE WY
8200 CITH 95610 240-C6
NEW BRITTON CIR
5200 SaCo 95843 239-B6
NEWBURG WY
7900 SAC 95823 337-H5
NEWBURY AV
600 ANT 94509 (513-C6 See Page 493)
NEWBURY WY
100 FOLS 95630 261-G6
5600 SaCo 95608 299-C1
NEWBURY PARK CT
8200 SaCo 95828 338-G6
NEWBY WY
- ELKG 95624 338-D7
- ELKG 95624 358-D1
NEWCASTLE RD
600 PlaC 95658 181-G7
1600 PlaC 95658 201-H2
3000 PlaC 95658 202-A4
NEWCASTLE ST
4100 SAC 95838 277-G2
NEWCASTLE GAP DR
2200 SaCo 95670 280-B5
NEW CLASSIC CT
- ELKG 95758 358-C4
NEWCOMBE CT
700 RSVL 95661 240-E4
NEWCOME CT
5600 ELKG 95757 377-J2
5600 ELKG 95757 397-J2
NEWCOMERS LN
4000 EDCo 95682 283-J1
NEW COMMONS LN
8200 ELKG 95758 358-D6
NEWCOMS CT
2600 SAC 95826 298-D7
NEW COUNTRY CT
- ELKG 95758 358-C4
NEW CREEK LN
6900 CITH 95621 259-E2
NEW DAWN CT
8900 SaCo 95826 298-H7
NEW DAWN DR
8900 SaCo 95826 298-H7
NEW DOMAIN CT
8500 SaCo 95828 338-F7
NEWELL ST
4100 SaCo 95821 278-J3
NEW ENGLAND CT
1400 RSVL 95661 240-A6
NEW ENGLAND DR
1400 RSVL 95661 240-A6
NEW ENGLAND PL
11300 SaCo 95670 280-B5
NEW ERA CT
- ELKG 95758 358-D4
NEW EUREKA WY
2300 SaCo 95670 280-B6
NEWFIELD CIR
8300 SaCo 95828 338-D4
NEW FOREST WY
8500 SaCo 95828 338-F7
NEWFOUND WY
9300 ELKG 95758 357-H5
NEWGATE DR
7900 SAC 95823 337-J5
NEW GATEWAY LN
8200 ELKG 95758 358-D6
NEW GRAFTON CT
- SAC 95835 256-J3
NEWHALL DR
9000 SaCo 95826 318-J2
NEW HAMPSHIRE AV
- SaCo 95742 280-J7
NEW HAMPSHIRE WY
- SAC 95835 257-B5
NEW HARTFORD CT
5300 SaCo 95843 239-B7
NEWHAVEN LN
- LNCN 95648 180-A6
NEW HAVEN RD
2100 SAC 95815 278-B7
NEW HAVEN ST
- SaCo 95742 280-J7
- SaCo 95742 281-A7
NEW HELVETIA DR
- SaCo 95670 280-B4
NEW HILLS CT
8300 SaCo 95828 338-F7
NEW HOGAN PL
- WSAC 95691 316-D4
NEW HOME LN
8200 ELKG 95758 358-D6
NEW HOPE RD
100 GALT 95632 439-A1
3900 SaCo 95632 439-A1
7700 SaCo 95632 (438-G1 See Page 418)

NEW HOPE RD
7700 SaCo 95690 (438-C2 See Page 418)
N NEW HOPE RD
27000 SJCo 95686 (438-B2 See Page 418)
W NEW HOPE RD
8200 SJCo 95686 (438-B3 See Page 418)
NEWHOUSE RD
- EDCo 247-G1
NEWINGTON WY
100 FOLS 95630 261-H5
6600 ELKG 95758 358-B5
NEW ISLAND ST
- WSAC 95691 316-C2
NEW ISLAND WY
8500 SaCo 95828 338-F6
NEW JERSEY WY
3000 PLCR 95667 245-G4
NEWKIRK DR
6300 SAC 95824 318-C6
NEWLAND CT
- SAC 95823 357-J1
NEWLAND HEIGHTS CT
- RKLN 95765 200-D6
NEWLAND HEIGHTS DR
- RKLN 95765 200-D6
NEWMAN CT
5800 SaCo 95819 298-A5
NEWMARK WY
1100 FOLS 95630 281-F1
NEW MARKET DR
- SAC 95835 256-J7
2500 SAC 95835 257-A7
NEW MEADOW DR
- RSVL 95747 219-E2
NEW MEXICO AV
- SaCo 95742 300-G1
NEW MILLS CT
- ELKG 95624 358-F2
NEWMONT CT
11500 SaCo 95670 280-C4
NEW MOUNTAIN WY
8500 SaCo 95828 338-F7
NEW ORLEANS AV
- SaCo 95742 300-G1
NEW POINT DR
8200 SaCo 95828 338-F7
8300 ELKG 95624 338-F7
8300 ELKG 95828 338-F7
NEWPORT AV
1900 SAC 95822 337-C2
NEWPORT LN
7400 SaCo 95842 259-D1
NEWPORT WY
1100 RSVL 95661 240-A5
1100 RSVL 95661 239-J5
NEWPORT COVE WY
6800 SAC 95823 358-B2
NEWPORT PARK CT
8200 SaCo 95828 338-G6
NEWPORT WEST WY
9100 ELKG 95758 357-H4
NEW RIDGE CT
8500 SaCo 95828 338-E7
NEWRIVER CIR
11000 RCCD 95670 279-J6
NEWRY CT
8700 ELKG 95624 358-G2
NEW SACTO WY
7000 SAC 95824 318-B5
NEW SALEM CT
6300 SaCo 95608 279-E3
NEWSON CT
3400 SAC 95820 318-A2
NEW STAR CIR
8500 SaCo 95828 338-F7
NEWTON AV
- SaCo 95742 300-J1
NEWTON DR
- SaCo 95826 319-A4
- SaCo 95829 319-A4
NEWTON PL
- LNCN 95648 179-E1
NEWTON RD
4200 EDCo 266-H1
4200 EDCo 95667 266-H1
4500 EDCo 267-A1
5300 EDCo 95667 267-B3
NEWTON ST
9400 PlaC 95626 237-G1
NEWTON WY
10300 RCCD 95670 299-F2
NEWTOWN RD
2100 EDCo 95667 246-C5
4000 EDCo 246-G7
NEW TRADITION LN
9500 ELKG 95758 358-D6
NEW VALLEY WY
8500 SaCo 95828 338-F7
NEW VISTA CT
- RKLN 95765 200-A6
NEW VISTA DR
- RKLN 95765 200-A6
NEW WAGONRIDGE CT
- EDCo 95667 266-F1
NEW WAGONRIDGE RD
- EDCo 95667 266-F2
NEW WEST CT
8500 SaCo 95828 338-F7
NEW WILLOW CT
- SaCo 95828 338-B2
NEW YORK AV
3900 SaCo 95628 279-J3
NEW YORK RD
- SaCo 95742 280-E7
- SaCo 95742 281-B5
- SaCo 95742 300-G1
NEW YORK CREEK CT
2100 EDCo 95762 242-D7
2100 EDCo 95762 262-D1
NEYLAND CT
- SaCo 95829 338-J5
NEYLAND WY
7700 SaCo 95829 338-J5
NIAGARA WY
2500 SaCo 95826 298-J6
NIAGARA FALLS AV
- SaCo 95742 280-H7
- SaCo 95742 300-J1
NIANTIC WY
1800 SAC 95822 337-C2
NIBLICK DR
- RSVL 95678 219-F3
NIBLICK WY
4200 SaCo 95628 279-H2
15200 SaCo 95683 342-C3

NICANOR CT
10300 ELKG 95757 377-J3
10300 ELKG 95757 397-J3
NICE CT
7400 SaCo 95842 259-B1
NICHOLAS ST
7100 SaCo 95828 338-C1
E NICHOLS AV
4000 SaCo 95820 317-G3
W NICHOLS AV
- SaCo 95820 317-G3
NICHOLS CIR
- FOLS 95630 281-D1
NICHOLS CT
2800 WSAC 95691 316-F2
NICHOLS DR
2200 PlaC 95765 199-E7
NICHOLS LN
- SaCo 95683 (361-B1 See Page 341)
- SaCo 95693 (361-B1 See Page 341)
6300 SAC 95828 318-A7
N NICHOLS RD
3300 SJCo 95632 439-H1
26600 SJCo 95220 439-J3
NICHORA WY
5600 SaCo 95841 279-C1
5600 SaCo 95608 279-C1
NICK WY
- ELKG 95757 378-A2
NICKELS WY
4600 SaCo 95864 298-J2
4600 SaCo 95608 299-A2
4600 SaCo 95864 299-A2
NICKENS CT
8800 SaCo 95662 260-E2
NICKLAUS CT
2000 RSVL 95678 219-J6
NICKLAUS PL
3900 SaCo 95608 279-F3
NICKMAN WY
5300 SAC 95835 257-C5
NICKS LN
1200 PLCR 95667 245-J6
NICOLAUS RD
700 LNCN 95648 179-B2
2000 PlaC 95648 179-B2
NICOLE CT
- RKLN 95765 200-C5
NICOLE LN
- ELKG 95758 357-F6
NICOLETTE WY
3600 SaCo 95608 279-D4
NICOSIA CT
4300 ELKG 95758 357-G4
NIEBAUM CT
- SAC 95758 358-C1
NIEGEL ESTATES DR
3200 PlaC 95658 202-A4
NIELSEN WY
4000 SAC 95820 318-A2
NIEMANN LN
9400 ELKG 95624 359-B1
NIESSEN WY
8100 SaCo 95628 260-B5
NIGHTFALL CT
1200 RSVL 95661 240-A5
NIGHTFALL WY
8300 SAC 95823 337-J7
NIGHTHAWK CIR
1800 RSVL 95661 240-C4
NIGHTHAWK LN
- LNCN 95648 200-C1
NIGHT HAWK WY
2600 EDCo 95709 246-J2
NIGHTHAWK WY
1400 SAC 95833 277-D5
NIGHT HERON WY
9900 ELKG 95757 377-E1
9900 ELKG 95757 397-E1
NIGHTINGALE CT
6300 CITH 95610 259-J4
NIGHT RIDGE WY
- RKLN 95765 220-A2
NIGHTSHADE CT
8500 ELKG 95624 358-F1
NIGHT STAR CT
3300 SaCo 95843 238-G5
NIGHTWATCH DR
- RKLN 95677 220-G5
- RKLN 95746 220-G5
NIHOA CT
5100 SaCo 95628 260-C7
NIKE CT
3300 RCCD 95827 299-D6
NIKE RD
- RCCD 95742 300-G4
NIKKI CT
- SAC 95758 357-J2
NIKKI BEAU LN
3500 EDCo 95682 263-H5
NIKOL ST
3000 SaCo 95826 298-H7
NILE CT
4800 SaCo 95841 279-C1
NILE RIVER CT
11100 RCCD 95670 280-A5
NILES AV
400 RSVL 95678 239-H1
500 RSVL 95678 219-H7
NIMBUS CT
3400 RKLN 95765 200-C7
3400 RKLN 95765 220-C1
NIMBUS RD
- RCCD 95742 280-G4
- SaCo 95670 280-E4
- SaCo 95742 280-G4
- SaCo 95742 300-G2
NIMBUS RD Rt#-E3
- SaCo 95742 280-G4
NIMBUS WY
8800 SaCo 95662 260-E5
NIMITZ ST
100 SAC 95838 278-B2
NINA WY
2900 SAC 95826 318-E1
5700 SaCo 95824 317-J5
NIOBE CIR
4300 RCCD 95742 320-D2
NIPAWIN WY
8700 SaCo 95662 260-E1
NISEAN CT
2900 RKLN 95677 200-E6
NISENAN CT
7700 SaCo 95843 238-H7
NISENAN TR
- EDCo 247-C7

NISHIDA LN
52100 YoCo 95612 (376-F3 See Page 375)
NITEL CT
- SAC 95758 357-J2
NIVEN CT
- SaCo 95829 339-B6
NIXOS WY
7600 SAC 95823 337-G3
N LINCOLN WY
600 GALT 95632 419-F5
NOAH CT
- SAC 95831 316-H7
NOAH LN
3900 LMS 95650 200-J7
NOATAK RIVER CT
11100 RCCD 95670 280-A4
NOB CT
- SAC 95826 298-F6
NOBEL CREST LN
- RCCD 95670 280-C7
NOB HILL
100 AUB 95603 162-E6
NOB HILL CT
1100 RSVL 95661 239-J5
1100 RSVL 95661 240-A5
NOB HILL DR
6000 PlaC 95658 181-G7
6200 PlaC 95658 201-G1
7300 SaCo 95608 279-G4
NOB HILL LN
8400 PlaC 95746 221-F6
NOBLE CT
3900 SaCo 95821 278-H3
NOBLECREST LN
2900 EDCo 95682 263-G3
NOBLE FIR LN
- ELKG 95758 357-J2
NOBLE HOUSE CT
6400 ELKG 95758 358-A6
NOBLESSA WY
3400 RCCD 95670 299-J4
NOEL CT
3700 EDCo 95667 245-B4
NOEL DR
8400 SaCo 95662 260-C3
NOEMI LN
6500 SaCo 95662 260-H3
NOGAL CT
2800 ANT 94509 (513-J5 See Page 493)
NOGALERA WY
10900 RCCD 95670 299-J1
NOGALES ST
800 SAC 95838 277-J3
1200 SAC 95838 278-B3
NOHEA LN
8400 ELKG 95624 339-A7
8400 ELKG 95624 359-A1
NOIA AV
1400 ANT 94509 (513-E5 See Page 493)
NOLA PL
- SaCo 95662 260-G4
NOLAN ST
- ELKG 95758 357-F4
NOLANA CT
2900 SaCo 95843 238-E5
NOLAND LN
- SaCo 95628 280-E2
NOLDER LN
- EDCo 95667 266-J3
NOLDER WY
5600 SAC 95822 317-D4
NOLEN DR
- LNCN 95648 200-B2
NOMAD WY
7300 SaCo 95828 338-C1
NONA WY
5500 SaCo 95824 317-H5
NO NAME LN
4900 LMS 95650 200-H5
4900 PlaC 95650 200-H4
NONNIE AV
5400 SaCo 95608 259-C6
5400 SaCo 95841 259-C6
NOONAN DR
1200 SAC 95822 317-A4
NORA CT
600 SAC 95833 277-E4
NORA LN
2700 EDCo 95682 263-D2
NORA LEE CT
- ANT 94509 (513-E6 See Page 493)
NORBECK WY
7400 SAC 95824 318-C6
NORBERT WY
2400 SAC 95833 277-E6
NORBURY WY
- GALT 95632 419-G3
NORCADE CIR
2000 SaCo 95826 298-H7
NORCIA CT
600 SAC 95833 277-E5
NORCREST AV
5200 SaCo 95608 279-B2
NORCROFT WY
600 SAC 95833 277-E4
NORCROSS DR
2700 SAC 95833 277-E6
NORCROSS LN
100 OAKL 94561 (514-E6 See Page 493)
NORCUT CT
600 SAC 95833 277-E6
NORDELL WY
2600 SAC 95833 277-E6
NORDEN AV
- RCCD 95655 299-G6
- SaCo 95655 299-G6
NORDEN CT
- LNCN 95648 180-A7
NORDIC CT
6500 CITH 95610 259-H3
NORDIC WY
3500 EDCo 95667 245-D6
3500 PLCR 95667 245-D6
NORDLUND WY
2700 SAC 95833 277-E6
NORDMAN CT
9600 ELKG 95624 359-B7
NORDMAN WY
9500 ELKG 95624 359-A7
NORDYKE DR
3100 SaCo 95833 277-E5
NOREEN LN
2100 PlaC 95663 201-A2

NOREEN WY
7000 CITH 95621 259-G2
NORFOLK AV
1000 WSAC 95691 296-H4
NORFOLK ST
- SaCo 95742 300-G1
NORFOLK WY
1200 SAC 95831 317-A6
NORFORK CT
- RSVL 95678 219-G5
NORGARD CT
600 SAC 95833 277-E6
NORIKER DR
- ELKG 95757 357-H7
NORLAND DR
700 SAC 95833 277-E4
NORM CIR
4700 SAC 95822 317-A3
NORMA CT
600 SAC 95833 277-E4
NORMAN LN
9700 ELKG 95624 359-C1
11900 AUB 95603 182-C5
NORMAN ST
2900 PLCR 95667 245-G5
NORMAN WY
2900 EDCo 95709 247-B4
5600 SAC 95822 317-D4
NORMANDY LN
1300 SAC 95822 317-B3
NORMANDY ST
- RSVL 95661 240-E2
NORMANTON PL
1600 EDCo 95762 262-D4
NORMINGTON DR
2700 SAC 95833 277-E5
NORRIS AV
2900 SaCo 95821 278-H3
4600 SaCo 95841 278-H1
NORRIS CT
- LNCN 95648 179-E6
NORSEMAN CT
9200 SaCo 95829 338-J6
NORSID DR
9800 ELKG 95624 359-C3
NORSTROM WY
3200 SAC 95833 277-E5
NORTH AV
400 SAC 95838 278-A2
800 SAC 95838 277-J2
2400 SaCo 95838 278-D2
2600 SaCo 95652 278-D2
2600 SAC 95652 278-D2
4600 SaCo 95821 278-J5
4600 SaCo 95608 279-B5
4600 SaCo 95821 279-B5
NORTH BEND
4500 EDCo 95667 265-J2
NORTH PKWY
4900 SaCo 95823 317-H7
5400 SaCo 95823 337-J1
NORTH ST
- SaCo 95690 437-A1
6200 EDCo 95623 265-A4
6600 EDCo 95619 265-E3
NORTHAM DR
8200 SaCo 95843 238-G5
NORTHAM PL
11700 EDCo 95762 262-E4
NORTHAM WY
3400 EDCo 95762 262-D4
NORTHAMPTON DR
4400 SaCo 95608 279-F2
NORTHBEND RD
- EDCo 95667 265-J3
NORTHBOROUGH DR
- SAC 95673 257-A4
- SAC 95835 257-A4
NORTHBROOK AV
1800 RSVL 95661 240-B6
NORTHBROOK CT
500 ANT 94509 (513-E7 See Page 493)
NORTHBROOK WY
6400 SaCo 95628 259-E5
NORTH CIRCLE DR
500 EDCo 95619 265-E4
NORTHCLIFF DR
5300 RKLN 95765 200-C7
NORTHCLIFFE LN
- PlaC 95747 239-A4
NORTHCOTT WY
1000 RSVL 95746 240-G3
NORTH COUNTRY DR
3600 SaCo 95843 238-G7
7600 SaCo 95843 258-H1
NORTHCREEK CT
8400 SaCo 95843 238-H5
NORTHCREST CIR
6000 SaCo 95608 279-D1
NORTHEAST CIR
7600 CITH 95610 259-H6
NORTHERN LIGHTS RD
- EDCo 267-F4
- EDCo 95726 267-F4
NORTHERN LIGHTS WY
- RKLN 95765 220-A1
NORTHERN OAK CIR
- SaCo 95828 338-E6
NORTHEY DR
800 SAC 95833 277-E6
NORTH FALLS DR
100 FOLS 95630 241-A7
NORTHFIELD CT
- LNCN 95648 179-H5
NORTHFIELD DR
600 SAC 95833 277-E6
NORTHFIELD LN
- LNCN 95648 179-H5
NORTHGATE BLVD
2100 SAC 95833 277-F7
2100 SAC 95833 297-F1
3200 SAC 95834 277-F4
3900 SAC 95834 277-F2
4500 SaCo 95834 257-E7
NORTHGATE PL
200 OAKL 94561 (514-E6 See Page 493)
NORTHGLEN ST
2400 SAC 95833 277-E6
4500 PlaC 95746 240-G1
NORTHGROVE WY
5800 CITH 95610 259-H5
NORTHHAVEN DR
- RKLN 95677 200-F7
- RKLN 95677 220-F1
NORTH HILL WY
800 SAC 95838 257-J7

NORTHLAKE DR
200 FOLS 95630 241-B7
NORTHLAND DR
7600 SAC 95831 336-J3
NORTHLEA WY
7400 CITH 95610 259-H5
NORTHLITE CIR
- SAC 95831 316-H7
NORTHOLT CT
100 FOLS 95630 261-F7
NORTH PARK DR
2700 SaCo 95821 278-J6
NORTHPARK DR
- RSVL 95747 219-C1
NORTHPARK PL
3800 PlaC 95602 162-B1
NORTH POINT WY
6200 SAC 95831 316-F6
NORTHPORT CT
9700 RCCD 95827 299-C6
NORTHPORT DR
- WSAC 95691 296-E4
NORTHRANCH WY
3500 PlaC 95661 240-E6
NORTHRIDGE CT
- ANT 94509 (513-E7 See Page 493)
NORTH RIDGE DR
7600 CITH 95610 259-H5
NORTHRIDGE DR
1000 RSVL 95678 239-G4
2600 PLCR 95667 245-F4
NORTH RIVER WY
500 SaCo 95864 298-J4
NORTHROP AV
900 SaCo 95825 298-C4
2600 SaCo 95864 298-E3
NORTH SACRAMENTO FRWY
- SAC - 278-A7
- SAC - 297-F1
- SAC - 298-A1
NORTH SHINGLE RD
2400 EDCo 95682 244-A7
2400 EDCo 95682 264-A1
NORTHSHORE WY
6900 SAC 95831 316-G7
NORTH STAR CT
3800 EDCo 95682 264-B7
NORTHSTAR CT
- RSVL 95747 219-B3
NORTH STAR DR
4200 EDCo 95682 264-B7
NORTHSTAR LN
- RSVL 95747 219-B3
NORTH STAR ST
4400 RKLN 95677 220-C2
NORTH STAR WY
8400 SaCo 95662 260-C4
NORTHSTEAD DR
3000 SAC 95833 277-E4
NORTHVALE WY
8300 CITH 95610 240-C6
NORTHVIEW DR
700 SAC 95833 277-E5
NORTHWICH CT
- SaCo 95832 337-C4
NORTHWIND WY
8200 SaCo 95662 260-B3
NORTHWOOD DR
200 FOLS 95630 241-B7
3200 SaCo 95821 278-G5
NORTIC LN
2000 EDCo 95726 248-D4
NORTON CT
- RKLN 95677 220-E5
NORTON WY
2200 ANT 94509 (513-D6 See Page 493)
4000 SAC 95820 317-E3
NORVAL CT
600 SAC 95833 277-E4
NORWALK CIR
100 SaCo 95655 319-H3
NORWAY DR
5400 SaCo 95662 260-G6
NORWICH CT
600 SAC 95833 277-E5
1300 RSVL 95661 240-B5
NORWICH PL
2000 EDCo 95762 242-C5
NORWOOD AV
2500 SAC 95815 277-H5
3100 SAC 95838 277-H2
4200 SAC 95838 257-H7
NORWOOD BYPS
2500 SAC 95815 277-G6
NOSLER CT
3200 RCCD 95670 299-F4
NOSTAW ST
5600 SaCo 95628 260-E6
5600 SaCo 95662 260-E6
NOTRE DAME DR
2500 SAC 95826 298-E7
2800 SAC 95826 318-E1
NOTT CT
800 AUB 95603 182-C6
NOTT LN
- SaCo 95842 259-C1
NOTTA DR
3400 LMS 95650 201-B5
NOTTINGHAM CIR
4600 SaCo 95608 279-A7
4600 SaCo 95864 278-J7
4600 SaCo 95864 279-A7
NOTTINGHAM CT
1100 RSVL 95661 240-A5
NOTTINGHAM RD
4600 EDCo 95619 265-G5
NOUVEAU WY
3400 RCCD 95670 299-H4
NOVA PKWY
6900 SaCo 95823 317-J7
6900 SaCo 95823 337-H1
NOVARA WY
9800 ELKG 95757 378-A1
NOVARRA CT
- EDCo 95762 262-G6
NOVATO CT
7200 ELKG 95757 378-B3
NOVEMBER DR
9200 ELKG 95758 358-B5
NO WALK RD
- EDCo 95619 266-C7
NO WAY OUT CT
800 EDCo 95619 265-D7
N NOWELL RD
26400 SJCo 95686 (438-B3 See Page 418)

NOYACK WY
5200 SAC 95835 256-J4
NUEVA DR
15200 SaCo 95683 342-C2
NUGGET CT
600 RSVL 95678 219-J7
NUGGET DR
400 FOLS 95630 241-B7
3100 EDCo 95667 226-G3
NUGGET LN
3800 EDCo 95667 246-B7
NUGGET LP
- EDCo 95667 244-H2
NUGGET RD
5200 SaCo 95628 260-D6
NUGGET SQ
- EDCo 95667 265-H3
NUGGET CREEK CT
2100 SaCo 95670 280-D5
NUNES CT
- SAC 95823 337-J5
NUNEZ CT
2800 WSAC 95691 316-F2
NUNZIA CT
- RSVL 95661 240-D2
NUTE RD
6000 LMS 95650 221-A3
NUT HATCH CT
5800 SaCo 95628 260-B5
NUTMEG CT
2300 ANT 94509 (513-H6 See Page 493)
NUTMEG LN
- EDCo 95667 286-H3
NUT PLAINS DR
3400 RCCD 95827 299-E5
NUT TREE CT
9500 ELKG 95624 358-H6
NUT TREE LN
100 OAKL 94561 (514-B7 See Page 493)
NUTWOOD CIR
- SAC 95833 277-D5
NYGAARD LN
11100 SaCo 95693 (380-G7 See Page 379)
11100 SaCo 95693 (400-G1 See Page 379)
NYLA ST
- SAC 95835 257-C3
NYODA WY
5300 SaCo 95608 279-B4

O

O ST
100 ANT 94509 (513-C3 See Page 493)
100 LNCN 95648 179-G3
200 SAC 95814 297-B4
400 SAC 95673 257-H2
1000 SaCo 95673 258-A2
2000 SAC 95816 297-E5
5800 SAC 95819 298-A7
S O ST
100 LNCN 95648 179-G4
OAHU DR
8100 SaCo 95628 260-B7
OAK AV
100 GALT 95632 419-E7
5900 SaCo 95608 279-D7
6700 FOLS 95630 261-A3
7900 CITH 95610 260-A1
8000 PlaC 95747 239-D1
8400 CITH 95662 260-D1
8500 SaCo 95662 260-D1
OAK CT
4100 RKLN 95677 220-E3
N OAK CT
9900 ELKG 95624 378-H1
W OAK CT
6900 CITH 95610 259-J2
OAK LN
- EDCo 95633 205-A3
800 SaCo 95673 257-J2
6600 EDCo 95667 265-C1
OAK PL
- EDCo 95682 263-D2
OAK RD
11600 SaCo 95632 (399-H2 See Page 379)
OAK ST
- LMS 95650 201-A6
- PlaC 95626 237-E2
- SaCo 95690 437-A1
100 AUB 95603 182-E1
400 RSVL 95678 239-H2
800 WSAC 95605 296-G2
3700 LMS 95650 200-J6
3700 RKLN 95677 220-E3
6000 EDCo 95720 248-C1
7700 SaCo 95843 239-H2
W OAK ST
8400 SJCo 95686 (438-B3 See Page 418)
OAK TER
1700 PlaC 95658 201-H1
1800 PlaC 95658 181-H7
OAK VW
200 AUB 95603 182-C3
OAK ACORN CT
6400 CITH 95621 259-E5
OAK ARBOR CT
- SaCo 95628 260-D5
OAK AVENUE PKWY
100 FOLS 95630 261-A2
100 FOLS 95630 281-F2
9500 FOLS 95630 260-J2
9500 FOLS 95662 260-J2
9500 SaCo 95630 260-J2
9500 SaCo 95662 260-J2
OAKBANK DR
5000 SaCo 95842 259-B5
OAKBANK WY
7200 SaCo 95828 338-F2
OAKBARK CT
8200 ELKG 95758 358-D6
OAK BAY CIR
7700 SAC 95831 336-H4
OAK BEND WY
6500 CITH 95621 259-E2
OAKBERRY WY
7100 CITH 95621 239-F7
OAK BLUFF WY
1800 SAC 95833 277-B5
OAKBOROUGH AV
500 RSVL 95747 239-E1
OAKBOUGH WY
4700 SaCo 95608 279-F1

STREET
Block City ZIP Pg-Grid
OAKBOUGH WY
4700 SaCo 95628 279-F1
OAK BRANCH CT
6600 CITH 95621 259-F2
OAK BRIAR CIR
- ELKG 95758 358-D5
OAK BRIAR CT
200 FOLS 95630 281-A2
OAKBRIDGE CT
6000 CITH 95621 259-E5
OAKBRIDGE DR
6100 PlaC 95746 241-A6
OAKBROOK DR
5800 CITH 95621 259-E5
6400 CITH 95628 259-E5
6400 SaCo 95628 259-E5
OAKBROOKE CT
- PlaC 95746 240-J2
OAK BURL CT
8500 SaCo 95662 260-D3
OAK BUTTE CT
200 FOLS 95630 281-A3
OAK CANYON LN
5100 SaCo 95628 260-G7
OAK CANYON WY
100 FOLS 95630 260-J2
100 FOLS 95630 261-A2
OAK CLIFF CIR
3100 SaCo 95608 279-F5
OAK COVE CT
6400 SaCo 95662 260-D4
OAK CREEK CT
1300 EDCo 95762 242-D7
1700 RSVL 95661 240-B5
2700 EDCo 95682 263-C3
3200 PlaC 95603 161-H3
OAKCREEK DR
3300 RKLN 95677 220-E2
OAK CREEK PL
- PlaC 95746 240-J4
- PlaC 95746 241-A4
OAKCREEK WY
6200 CITH 95621 259-E5
OAKCREEK COVE WY
8500 SaCo 95662 260-D4
OAKCREST AV
6600 SaCo 95608 259-E7
OAK CREST CIR
700 PLCR 95667 245-E3
OAK CREST CT
1000 PLCR 95667 245-E3
OAK CREST DR
- RSVL 95661 220-E6
OAK DALE CT
2000 RSVL 95661 240-C5
OAKDALE CT
3700 RKLN 95677 200-E7
OAKDALE LN
3500 RKLN 95677 200-E7
OAKDALE ST
- FOLS 95630 261-B5
OAK DELL AV
3500 SaCo 95660 278-G1
OAKDELL DR
6400 EDCo 95623 265-C4
OAKEN AL
100 GALT 95632 419-E7
OAKEN BUCKET CT
9600 SaCo 95827 299-B6
OAKENSHAW WY
8200 SaCo 95662 260-B2
8200 SaCo 95610 260-B2
OAKENSHIELD CIR
8300 SaCo 95843 239-A5
OAK ESTATES LN
8400 SaCo 95828 338-E6
OAKFIELD CIR
4700 SaCo 95608 279-A5
OAKFIELD CT
1100 RSVL 95661 240-B4
OAK FLAT WY
8400 SaCo 95843 239-A5
OAK FORD WY
4600 SaCo 95842 259-A4
OAK FOREST AV
4500 OAKL 94561 (514-E7
See Page 493)
OAK FOREST CT
7800 CITH 95621 239-H7
OAK FRONT LN
8300 CITH 95610 240-C7
OAK GARDEN CT
5800 SaCo 95662 260-E5
OAK GLEN LN
7800 PlaC 95746 241-C1
OAK GLEN WY
4500 SaCo 95628 280-C2
OAKGLEN WY
- CITH 95621 259-G3
OAKGREEN CIR
6100 SaCo 95608 259-D7
6100 SaCo 95608 279-D1
OAK GROVE AV
7500 CITH 95610 239-H6
OAK GROVE DR
1400 RSVL 95747 219-E5
OAK HALL WY
1100 SAC 95822 317-A5
OAK HARBOUR CT
8500 SaCo 95628 260-D6
OAK HARBOUR DR
2300 SAC 95833 277-A7
OAKHAVEN CT
4800 SaCo 95608 279-D1
OAKHAVEN RD
600 PlaC 95603 162-G7
OAK HILL
- EDCo 95667 244-H2
OAK HILL CT
- RSVL 95661 240-D1
OAK HILL DR
5700 SaCo 95841 259-C4
6100 PlaC 95746 241-A6
6700 PlaC 95746 220-G7
OAK HILL RD
4600 EDCo 95619 266-A5
- EDCo 95619 265-J7
OAK HILL WY
- RSVL 95661 220-E7
- RSVL 95661 240-D1
700 RVIS 94571 454-F2
OAKHILL WY
200 PlaC 95603 162-F6
OAK HILLS CT
5500 SaCo 95608 279-C2
OAKHILLS LN
5800 EDCo 95630 222-A5
OAKHOLLOW CT
9100 PlaC 95746 241-A6

STREET
Block City ZIP Pg-Grid
OAKHOLLOW DR
4400 SaCo 95842 258-J5
4600 SaCo 95842 259-A4
OAK HOUSE CT
5800 SaCo 95662 260-D5
OAK HURST CIR
3900 SaCo 95628 279-J3
3900 SaCo 95628 280-A3
OAKHURST CT
- PlaC 95747 239-A2
OAKHURST TER
- AUB 95603 182-B6
OAKHURST WY
1400 SAC 95822 337-B1
6400 PlaC 95603 161-A7
6400 PlaC 95603 181-B1
6400 PlaC 95658 181-A1
OAK KNOLL CT
- FOLS 95630 261-G4
2000 EDCo 95667 245-A4
OAK KNOLL DR
4200 SaCo 95608 279-G3
4200 SaCo 95628 279-G3
8100 PlaC 95746 241-C2
OAK KNOLL LN
1600 PlaC 95658 180-J1
OAK KNOLL RD
1600 PlaC 95658 160-J7
2000 EDCo 95667 245-A4
2000 PLCR 95667 245-A4
OAK LAKES LN
6100 CITH 95621 259-D2
OAKLAND AV
500 RSVL 95678 239-G2
OAKLAND BAY DR
- WSAC 95691 316-C2
OAK LANDING CT
8100 SaCo 95828 338-D6
OAK LANE CT
6800 EDCo 95667 265-C1
OAK LANE DR
2400 EDCo 95672 263-G2
OAKLAWN WY
6700 SaCo 95628 259-F7
OAK LEAF AV
4900 SaCo 95608 299-A1
7700 SaCo 95628 279-J2
OAK LEAF CIR
- EDCo - 267-C6
OAK LEAF CT
- EDCo - 267-D7
12400 AUB 95603 162-D5
OAK LEAF DR
2700 EDCo 95682 263-C3
OAK LEAF WY
9000 PlaC 95746 241-B5
9300 RSVL 95746 241-B5
OAKLEY RD
2000 OAKL 94561 (514-A6
See Page 493)
2200 ANT 94509 (513-H6
See Page 493)
3000 ANT 94509 (514-A6
See Page 493)
OAKLEY WY
- ELKG 95624 359-A6
OAK MANOR WY
- SAC 95838 277-F3
OAK MARSH
- RVIS 94571 454-F1
OAKMEADOW CT
8000 CITH 95610 260-B3
OAK MEADOW RD
- EDCo 95667 243-H1
OAK MEADOWS RD
4200 EDCo 95667 243-H1
OAK MELLO CT
5000 ELKG 95758 357-H5
OAKMERE CT
- PlaC 95747 238-J2
100 FOLS 95630 241-A7
OAK MILL RD
100 FOLS 95630 261-G4
OAK MIST LN
12400 PlaC 95602 162-C1
OAKMONT DR
1400 RSVL 95661 240-B5
4100 RKLN 95677 220-E4
OAKMONT ST
2100 SAC 95815 277-H5
OAKMONT WY
2100 WSAC 95691 296-G4
OAKMORE WY
8900 SaCo 95662 260-F5
OAKMYRTLE WY
6900 CITH 95621 239-F6
OAK NOB WY
1300 SAC 95833 277-D5
OAK PARK CT
6200 SaCo 95608 259-E5
OAK PINE LN
7000 PlaC 95746 221-B7
OAK PLACE CT
- SaCo 95628 260-D5
OAKPLACE EAST
9800 FOLS 95630 261-B2
OAKPLACE WEST
9800 FOLS 95630 261-B2
OAK POINT WY
5000 SaCo 95628 259-J7
OAK POND LN
10600 ELKG 95624 359-G2
OAK RANCH CT
- SAC 95831 337-A4
OAK RANCH PL
9800 ELKG 95624 359-C4
OAK RAVINE CT
- RSVL 95661 220-E7
OAK RAVINE WY
100 FOLS 95630 261-A3
OAKRIDGE CT
5200 SaCo 95628 259-J7
OAK RIDGE DR
300 RSVL 95661 240-A3
6200 LMS 95650 221-A2
OAK RIDGE RD
5400 EDCo 95667 244-D6
OAKRIDGE ST
4100 RKLN 95677 220-E4
OAK RIDGE WY
1000 AUB 95603 162-D5
1200 PlaC 95603 162-D4
OAKRIDGE WY
- RVIS 94571 454-E1
5100 SaCo 95842 259-A3
6200 SAC 95831 317-A6
OAK RIM WY
100 FOLS 95630 261-A2
1800 SAC 95833 277-B5

STREET
Block City ZIP Pg-Grid
OAK RIVER CT
5500 SaCo 95841 259-C7
OAK ROCK CIR
100 FOLS 95630 260-J3
100 FOLS 95630 261-A3
W OAKS BLVD
- RKLN 95765 199-H7
- RKLN 95765 200-A5
OAK SHADE WY
5100 SaCo 95628 260-G7
OAKSHIRE CT
4700 SaCo 95608 279-A5
OAKSHORE DR
7700 SAC 95831 336-H4
OAKSIDE DR
6100 CITH 95621 259-E4
OAKSIDE LN
8000 CITH 95610 240-C7
OAK SPRING WY
6900 CITH 95621 239-F7
OAK STONE LN
5400 SaCo 95628 260-G6
OAK STREAM CT
3300 SaCo 95608 279-C5
OAK TERRACE CT
800 PLCR 95667 245-F4
1300 SaCo 95825 298-D2
OAK TERRACE DR
800 EDCo 95667 245-F4
800 PLCR 95667 245-F4
OAKTON WY
10700 RCCD 95670 279-H6
OAK TOP WY
7600 SaCo 95628 279-H3
OAK TRAIL CT
900 PLCR 95667 245-E4
4300 SaCo 95826 318-H3
OAK TREE CIR
1100 EDCo 95762 242-C7
OAK TREE DR
100 AUB 95603 162-E6
100 PlaC 95603 162-E6
1500 RSVL 95661 240-B3
OAK TREE LN
300 PlaC 95648 180-B4
300 LNCN 95648 180-B4
3600 LMS 95650 201-B7
3600 PlaC 95650 201-B7
9300 SaCo 95662 260-H3
OAK TWIG WY
4700 SaCo 95608 279-E1
OAKVALE CT
7400 SaCo 95660 258-G1
OAKVALE DR
2200 EDCo 95682 244-A6
OAK VALLEY DR
- LNCN 95648 199-J3
- LNCN 95648 200-A3
- PlaC 95602 161-C1
OAK VALLEY LN
6200 CITH 95621 259-D4
OAK VIEW CT
300 EDCo 95630 202-J2
OAKVIEW CT
4200 RKLN 95677 220-F4
OAK VIEW DR
4000 EDCo 95630 202-J2
5900 PlaC 95746 221-E5
OAKVIEW DR
1600 RSVL 95661 240-B4
4100 RKLN 95677 220-E3
OAK VIEW LN
8500 SaCo 95628 280-D2
OAKVIEW LN
3300 SaCo 95608 279-C5
OAK VIEW RD
100 PlaC 95658 180-J3
OAKVIEW TR
10900 AUB 95603 182-C5
OAK VILLA CIR
3900 SaCo 95608 279-B3
OAK VILLA DR
200 FOLS 95630 281-A2
OAK VILLAGE CT
8600 SaCo 95843 238-G5
OAK VILLAGE WY
- ELKG 95758 358-D5
OAK VISTA DR
4800 SaCo 95608 299-A3
OAK VISTA WY
3800 PlaC 95650 201-J7
OAKWILDE ST
100 GALT 95632 419-D7
OAKWIND CT
8400 SaCo 95662 260-D4
OAKWOOD CT
5200 RKLN 95677 220-F3
8500 SaCo 95628 280-D1
OAKWOOD DR
100 AUB 95603 182-D2
1700 RSVL 95661 240-B4
OAKWOOD LN
7600 CITH 95621 259-G1
7600 CITH 95621 239-G7
OAKWOOD RD
3000 EDCo 95682 263-C6
OAKWOOD ST
4200 RKLN 95677 220-E3
OAKWOOD WY
800 OAKL 94561 (514-D5
See Page 493)
OAKWOOD HILLS CIR
8000 CITH 95610 240-D6
OASIS CT
- SAC 95838 277-H1
OATES CT
- WSAC 95691 296-D7
OATES DR
9600 SaCo 95827 299-B5
OATES ST
- WSAC 95691 296-D7
- WSAC 95691 316-D1
OBEN FELL CT
5400 SaCo 95843 239-C5
OBERLIN CT
2900 SAC 95826 318-E1
OBERLIN WY
- GALT 95632 419-E6
OBERON AV
4100 SaCo 95660 258-H6
4200 SaCo 95842 258-H6
OBERON WY
- RSVL 95661 220-E6
OBERUN RIVER CT
11100 RCCD 95670 280-A5
OBESTER CT
3500 RCCD 95670 300-A5
OBRIEN CIR
- SaCo 95828 338-E2

STREET
Block City ZIP Pg-Grid
OBSERVATORY DR
2800 EDCo 95667 226-D7
2800 EDCo 95667 246-D1
OBSIDIAN WY
9900 SaCo 95829 339-C7
OBSIDIAN BAY CT
- SaCo 95829 338-H6
OBSIDIAN CLIFF CT
100 FOLS 95630 240-J7
OCASO CT
3600 EDCo 95682 263-B7
OCATILLO ST
- SaCo 95828 338-E3
OCCIDENTAL DR
2500 SAC 95826 298-E6
2900 SAC 95826 318-E1
OCEAN AV
- WSAC 95691 296-G7
OCEAN DR
- WSAC 95691 296-G7
OCEAN PL
- WSAC 95691 296-G6
OCEAN BREEZE CT
- ELKG 95758 357-J2
OCEAN DUNES CT
9900 SaCo 95829 339-D4
OCEAN FRONT CT
- SAC 95831 336-G2
OCEANIC WY
300 SAC 95831 336-G2
OCEANO CT
- SaCo 95843 239-A7
OCEAN PARK DR
- SaCo 95843 239-A7
OCEAN POINT WY
- ELKG 95758 357-D6
OCELOT CT
- SaCo 95829 338-H5
OCONEE CT
7200 CITH 95610 260-A2
OCONNELL CT
8700 ELKG 95624 358-G7
OCONNER WY
4200 SAC 95838 277-G2
OCOTILLO CT
- ELKG 95624 358-F1
OCTAGON PL
- EDCo 95672 243-E1
OCTAVIA WY
10200 RCCD 95670 299-E1
OCTOBER DR
9200 ELKG 95758 358-B5
OCTOBER HILL RD
5700 EDCo 95667 264-G1
ODD FELLOWS RD
4100 EDCo 95619 265-E3
ODEA DR
5600 SaCo 95824 317-G4
ODELL CIR
- SAC 95835 257-C4
ODEMIRA WY
10300 ELKG 95757 378-B3
ODESSA CT
4600 RKLN 95677 220-C1
ODIN CT
5100 RKLN 95765 199-J5
ODIN DR
- WSAC 95691 296-D5
ODOM CT
- SAC 95823 337-H5
ODONNELL AV
1000 SAC 95838 277-J2
1100 SAC 95838 278-A2
OESTE CT
- EDCo 95682 263-C4
OESTE LN
- EDCo 95682 263-C4
OFARRELL DR
3200 SAC 95815 278-B4
OFFHAM CT
4200 SaCo 95864 298-J4
OFFICE PARK CIR
9200 ELKG 95758 358-E5
OFFIELD CT
7200 SaCo 95842 259-C2
OFRIA DR
100 FOLS 95630 261-E3
OGDEN WY
2600 SaCo 95825 278-E7
OGDEN NASH WY
6000 SaCo 95842 259-A3
OGILBY WY
5400 SaCo 95608 259-E6
OGLETHORPE WY
9000 ELKG 95624 378-H2
OHANA PL
6900 SaCo 95662 260-J3
OHARA AV
100 OAKL 94561 (514-E6
See Page 493)
O'HARA LN
- LNCN 95648 179-E2
O'HARA PL
- LNCN 95648 179-F2
OHAVER LN
7500 PlaC 95650 201-D6
OHIO LN
3600 SaCo 95660 258-G7
OHIO ST
- SaCo 95742 300-D2
OHIO RIVER DR
2100 RCCD 95670 279-J5
OJAI
- PlaC 95746 240-J4
OJAI CT
7200 SaCo 95842 259-C2
OKEEFE CT
- SAC 95835 256-J3
OKEEFE ST
- OAKL 94561 (514-H6
See Page 493)
OKINAWA ST
- SAC 95828 318-E6
OKITA CT
2100 SAC 95822 337-D3
OKLAHOMA RD
- RCCD 95742 280-E7
- RCCD 95742 300-D2
- SaCo 95742 280-E7
- SaCo 95742 300-D2
OLANDER WY
8200 SaCo 95828 338-E7
OLBERDING WY
7800 SaCo 95843 239-A7
OLD AIRPORT RD
100 PlaC 95603 162-F3
1100 PlaC 95602 162-D2

STREET
Block City ZIP Pg-Grid
OLD ANTELOPE NORTH RD
- SaCo 95843 259-C1
5800 SaCo 95843 239-C7
OLD AUBURN RD
3100 PlaC 95661 240-D5
3100 RSVL 95661 240-D5
3200 CITH 95610 240-C7
3300 SaCo 95610 240-D5
3600 RSVL 95746 240-F5
7500 CITH 95610 259-H2
7700 CITH 95610 260-A1
OLD AUBURN FORESTHILL RD
200 PlaC 95603 162-H7
OLD BASS LAKE RD
1900 EDCo 95762 262-G7
2000 EDCo 95762 282-H1
OLD BLU CT
9100 SaCo 95662 260-G5
OLD BRIDLE CT
9600 SaCo 95827 299-B6
OLD CARSON RD
- EDCo 95726 248-G1
OLD COUNTRY CT
3500 PlaC 95661 240-E5
OLD COUNTRY LN
2500 SaCo 95608 279-D7
OLD COUNTRY RD
8800 PlaC 95661 240-E5
OLD CREEK DR
8900 ELKG 95758 357-J3
8900 ELKG 95758 358-A3
OLD CYPRESS LN
1500 PlaC 95603 181-H2
OLD DAIRY DR
4300 SaCo 95843 238-J5
OLD DEPOT RD
- EDCo 95667 265-D1
OLD DITCH DR
3300 EDCo 95667 246-D6
OLD DUDE RD
11000 PlaC 95603 182-B1
OLDENBURG WY
700 GALT 95632 419-E2
OLD ENGLAND CT
5400 SaCo 95843 239-B6
OLD EUREKA PL
- PlaC 95746 240-G3
OLD EUREKA WY
11700 SaCo 95670 280-D4
OLD FORESTHILL RD
- PlaC 95603 182-F1
OLD FORRESTHILL ST
- PlaC 95603 162-H6
- PlaC 95603 182-G1
OLD FRENCH TOWN RD
4700 EDCo 95682 264-E7
OLD GREEN VALLEY RD
5500 EDCo 95667 245-B6
OLDHAM LN
600 PlaC 95658 181-G6
5500 SaCo 95841 259-C5
OLD HART RANCH RD
1600 RSVL 95661 240-C6
OLD KENMARE RD
- LNCN 95648 200-B2
OLD KENT LN
4700 SaCo 95841 279-A2
OLD LEVEE RD
- SaCo 95690 436-J2
- SaCo 95690 437-A3
OLD MEDER RD
- EDCo 95672 263-E2
- EDCo 95682 263-E2
OLD MILL CIR
1000 RSVL 95747 219-F7
OLD MILL RD
3100 EDCo 95682 283-E3
OLD MILL WY
1000 SaCo 95626 237-J7
1000 SaCo 95626 238-A7
OLD MILL WY
7600 SaCo 95626 237-J7
OLD MOSS LN
5100 PlaC 95746 221-E3
OLD NAVE CT
7200 SaCo 95842 259-A2
OLD NEUMAN RD
- EDCo 95672 243-C3
OLD OAK CT
6700 CITH 95610 260-A3
OLD OAK RD
100 PlaC 95658 181-F4
OLD OAKEN PL
6400 SaCo 95662 260-D4
OLD OAK TREE WY
- RKLN 95765 200-C6
OLD ORCHARD LN
3200 PlaC 95650 201-G5
OLD ORCHARD WY
6200 SaCo 95662 260-F4
OLD OUTINGDALE RD
- EDCo 95684 286-H7
OLD OX RD
3700 EDCo 95682 283-H5
OLD PEAR HILL LN
- PlaC 95663 201-C2
OLD PLACERVILLE RD
9600 SaCo 95827 299-B7
9600 RCCD 95827 299-F6
10000 SaCo 95655 299-F6
10000 RCCD 95655 299-F6
OLD QUARRY CT
- PlaC 95650 221-H2
OLD RANCH RD
8200 CITH 95610 260-C2
8300 CITH 95662 260-C2
8300 SaCo 95662 260-C3
OLD RIVER RD
- WSAC 95605 276-E4
- YoCo 95605 255-G5
- YoCo 95605 256-A7
- YoCo 95605 276-B2
OLD SACRAMENTO AV
- SAC 95814 297-B3
OLD SAW MILL CT
- EDCo 95633 205-B1
OLD SAW MILL RD
- EDCo 95633 205-B1
OLD STAGE TR
- EDCo 95633 205-E5
OLD STATE HWY
- EDCo 95633 205-E4
8900 PlaC 95658 181-G6
OLD TIMER LN
5300 EDCo 95623 264-G6
OLD TOLL RD
2100 EDCo 95667 245-E2

STREET
Block City ZIP Pg-Grid
OLD VILLA CT
8600 SaCo 95628 260-D6
OLD VINE DR
- SaCo 95624 340-F3
OLD VINEYARD LN
2100 EDCo 95667 246-A2
OLD WALNUT GROVE RD
- SaCo 95690 436-J2
- SaCo 95690 437-A2
OLD WEST DR
1200 SAC 95834 277-D4
OLD WHITE ROCK RD
- RCCD 95742 300-D2
- SaCo 95742 300-F2
- SaCo 95742 301-B1
OLD WINDING WY
7900 SaCo 95628 280-A2
OLD WINERY PL
9800 RCCD 95827 299-C5
OLDWOODS WY
8600 SaCo 95828 338-F4
OLE CT
9400 SaCo 95826 319-A1
OLEAN ST
5000 SaCo 95628 260-F7
OLEANDER DR
4900 SaCo 95608 259-E7
4900 SaCo 95608 279-E1
OLEANDER LN
4000 EDCo 95667 244-A3
4000 EDCo 95667 243-J3
OLEANDER VIEW WY
- RCCD 95670 280-A6
OLEMA PL
400 LNCN 95648 180-A5
OLETA DR
2700 EDCo 95667 245-B4
OLGA LN
4200 SaCo 95628 279-J2
OLGA WY
- RSVL 95661 240-D5
OLIVA RD
- RSVL 95678 219-H2
OLIVE AV
5200 SaCo 95843 239-C6
8200 SaCo 95628 280-B3
OLIVE CT
700 GALT 95632 439-F1
2700 WSAC 95691 296-F7
OLIVE LN
1700 ANT 94509 (513-F5
See Page 493)
3800 SaCo 95608 279-D3
OLIVE PL
- PlaC 95746 240-J1
OLIVE ST
100 AUB 95603 182-E2
7700 SaCo 95628 279-J1
OLIVEBRANCH LN
3800 SaCo 95608 279-D3
OLIVE CANYON DR
800 GALT 95632 419-F2
OLIVEGATE DR
4500 SaCo 95628 279-G2
OLIVE GLEN CT
3000 SaCo 95821 278-H5
OLIVEGLEN CT
- RKLN 95677 220-F1
OLIVE GROVE DR
6900 SaCo 95662 260-G3
8000 PlaC 95746 240-H1
OLIVEHILL CT
8300 SaCo 95628 260-C4
OLIVEHURST WY
5100 ELKG 95758 357-J3
OLIVE LEAF LN
- PlaC 95746 240-J1
OLIVELEAF LN
8000 CITH 95610 240-C7
OLIVENE CT
500 PLCR 95667 245-E5
OLIVE OAK WY
4700 SaCo 95608 299-A2
OLIVE ORCHARD DR
400 AUB 95603 182-F1
OLIVE POINT WY
- RSVL 95678 219-J2
- RSVL 95678 220-A2
OLIVER
- EDCo 95682 244-C7
OLIVER CT
- SAC 95758 358-C1
OLIVERA WY
1000 SAC 95815 277-J6
OLIVE RANCH LN
8800 SaCo 95628 280-E1
OLIVE RANCH RD
4400 PlaC 95746 240-G1
7300 PlaC 95746 241-A1
OLIVE RIDGE RD
4100 EDCo 95667 244-A2
OLIVET CT
8400 SAC 95826 298-E7
OLIVE TREE CT
5300 PlaC 95746 240-H1
OLIVE TREE WY
6800 CITH 95610 260-A3
OLIVEVIEW AV
4000 SaCo 95821 278-H5
OLIVEWOOD CT
8600 SaCo 95628 280-D1
OLIVINE AV
8200 CITH 95610 260-C1
8300 CITH 95610 240-D7
OLLIE CT
- SAC 95758 358-C1
OLMSTEAD DR
- SAC 95838 277-G5
OLSON DR
10500 RCCD 95670 299-G2
OLSON LN
900 EDCo 95762 262-C5
OLY LN
9600 PlaC 95747 239-B5
OLYMPIA CT
4900 SaCo 95608 279-A3
OLYMPIA LN
2300 EDCo 95667 245-H2
OLYMPIAD WY
- SaCo 95826 318-J3
OLYMPIC
- PlaC 95746 240-J5
OLYMPIC CIR
- RKLN 95765 219-H1
OLYMPIC CT
900 EDCo 95762 262-D7
OLYMPIC DR
1000 RVIS 94571 454-F2

STREET
Block City ZIP Pg-Grid
OLYMPIC WY
- PlaC 95603 161-J4
- SaCo 95842 259-C3
3100 PlaC 95603 162-A3
7800 SaCo 95628 279-J1
OLYMPUS DR
1700 SaCo 95864 298-J2
3200 RSVL 95661 240-D2
6900 EDCo 95633 205-A6
OMAHA CT
- SAC 95823 338-A4
OMALLEY AV
- SaCo 95652 258-G6
OMALLEY WY
1000 SAC 95833 277-D6
OMAR CT
8800 ELKG 95624 358-G7
OMEARA WY
10100 SaCo 95829 339-E5
OMEC CIR
- RCCD 95670 300-B5
OMEC PARK DR
- RCCD 95670 300-B5
OMEGA CT
- SaCo 95660 258-G6
OMEGA DR
- LNCN 95648 200-B3
OMEGA LN
1000 EDCo 95630 202-H6
OMEGA WY
- LNCN 95648 200-B3
OMNI DR
5600 SaCo 95841 259-C7
ON CT
8000 ELKG 95624 358-G6
ONAWA CT
3900 SaCo 95843 238-H7
ONEDIA ST
- OAKL 94561 (514-C6
See Page 493)
ONE EYE CREEK CT
- EDCo 95667 226-E1
ONEIL CT
- OAKL 94561 (514-F7
See Page 493)
ONEIL WY
1800 SAC 95822 337-C2
ONEILL CT
- RSVL 95747 219-E6
100 FOLS 95630 261-F4
ONE WAY LN
- EDCo 95682 263-J6
- EDCo 95682 264-A6
ONG PL
- PlaC 95650 201-C6
ONTARIO ST
100 OAKL 94561 (514-C6
See Page 493)
5300 SAC 95820 318-C4
5300 SAC 95824 318-C4
ONYX DR
5600 RKLN 95677 220-B4
ONYX ST
2000 RSVL 95678 220-A6
ONYX TR
6400 EDCo 95726 248-E2
ONYX WY
4500 SaCo 95608 279-D2
ONYX PARK PL
9700 ELKG 95624 358-J7
OPAL CT
- RKLN 95677 220-B3
OPAL DR
1600 RSVL 95747 219-B1
3500 PlaC 95602 162-B3
OPAL LN
900 SAC 95815 277-J4
1100 SAC 95815 278-A4
3300 LMS 95650 200-G5
OPAL TR
3800 EDCo 95726 248-E2
OPAL CANYON CT
- SaCo 95829 338-H7
OPAL CREEK CT
5000 ELKG 95758 357-H3
OPAL CREST CT
9200 ELKG 95624 358-F4
OPAL RIDGE WY
11800 RCCD 95742 320-D1
OPEN RANGE LN
- RKLN 95765 199-J3
OPERATORS RD
- SaCo 95758 337-F7
- SaCo 95758 357-F1
OPHELIA CT
7700 CITH 95610 240-B7
OPHIR CT
2000 SaCo 95670 280-B4
OPHIR RD
10000 PlaC 95658 181-H5
10300 PlaC 95603 181-H5
10300 PlaC 95603 182-B3
10400 AUB 95603 182-B3
OPHIR HILL CT
2000 SaCo 95670 280-C4
OPP CT
8600 ELKG 95624 338-F7
OPPER AV
1700 SAC 95822 317-C4
OPPORTUNITY DR
2000 RSVL 95678 239-F3
OPPORTUNITY ST
100 SAC 95838 277-G2
OPTIMA DR
- RCCD 95670 300-A4
OPUS CIR
- SAC 95834 276-H3
OPUS CT
- RSVL 95661 239-J5
- SaCo 95621 239-E6
OPUS ONE CT
- EDCo 95630 222-G6
ORABELLE CT
7900 SaCo 95828 338-D5
ORACLE CT
- SaCo 95823 337-G4
ORANGE AV
5500 SaCo 95823 337-J2
5800 SaCo 95823 338-A2
7800 SaCo 95628 279-J2
7900 SaCo 95628 280-A2
ORANGE DR
2000 PlaC 95663 201-C2
7600 CITH 95610 239-H7
ORANGE RD
12800 SaCo 95693 360-J2
12800 SaCo 95693 (361-A2
See Page 341)

STREET Block City ZIP Pg-Grid

ORANGE RD
12900 SaCo 95683 (361-B3 See Page 341)
ORANGE ST
100 AUB 95603 182-E3
500 PlaC 95658 181-G6
ORANGE BLOSSOM CIR
100 FOLS 95630 281-B2
ORANGE COVE CT
8100 SaCo 95828 338-D6
ORANGE CREST CT
9200 ELKG 95624 358-E5
ORANGE GROVE AV
2900 SaCo 95660 278-E2
3900 SaCo 95841 278-H1
4600 SaCo 95841 279-A1
ORANGE GROVE WY
600 FOLS 95630 261-B5
ORANGE HILL LN
1300 PlaC 95663 181-D7
6400 SaCo 95608 279-E6
ORANGERIE WY
3600 SaCo 95608 279-F4
ORANGE TREE CT
8000 SaCo 95628 260-A7
ORANGEVALE AV
9100 SaCo 95662 260-G4
9100 FOLS 95662 260-G4
9500 FOLS 95630 260-J4
9500 SaCo 95630 260-J4
ORANGEVIEW
1100 FOLS 95630 260-J4
ORANGEWOOD DR
3900 SaCo 95628 279-J3
ORANMORE CT
8700 SaCo 95828 338-F7
ORBECK CT
- PlaC 95603 162-A5
ORBETELLO WY
- EDCo 95762 262-B2
ORBISON CT
- FOLS 95630 281-E2
ORBIT CT
10000 RCCD 95827 299-D6
ORCHARD CT
400 AUB 95603 182-F1
800 EDCo 95630 202-J3
ORCHARD DR
- FOLS 95630 261-D6
ORCHARD LN
900 ANT 94509 (513-E4 See Page 493)
2500 SAC 95833 276-J6
2700 SaCo 95833 276-H4
3000 PLCR 95667 245-J5
3700 SaCo 95821 278-G5
ORCHARD TRCT
1800 FOLS 95630 261-J5
ORCHARD WY
- WSAC 95691 296-H4
2700 EDCo 95667 245-B5
2700 PLCR 95667 245-B5
ORCHARD CREEK LN
- LNCN 95648 179-J6
ORCHARD CREEK WY
- ELKG 95624 338-D7
- ELKG 95624 358-D1
ORCHARD HILL WY
- ELKG 95757 357-J6
- ELKG 95757 358-A6
ORCHARD LOOP LN
8100 SaCo 95624 338-D7
ORCHARD OAKS CT
- OAKL 94561 (514-B7 See Page 493)
ORCHARD PARK CT
- LMS 95650 201-B4
ORCHARD PARK DR
- ELKG 95624 338-D7
4400 OAKL 94561 (514-F7 See Page 493)
ORCHARD PARK WY
- LMS 95650 201-B4
ORCHARD VIEW DR
- ELKG 95757 358-A7
ORCHARD VIEW RD
- RSVL 95747 219-A3
ORCHARD WOODS CIR
7800 SaCo 95828 338-C4
ORCHID CT
400 RSVL 95661 240-B5
ORCHID LN
- LNCN 95648 180-A4
ORCHID PL
- PlaC - 160-B2
ORCHID WY
4900 SaCo 95841 259-A7
ORCHID RANCH CT
5200 ELKG 95757 377-J1
5200 ELKG 95757 397-J1
ORCHID RANCH WY
5000 ELKG 95757 377-H1
5000 ELKG 95757 397-H1
ORCHID SHADE DR
- EDCo 95682 263-B5
ORCHID TREE WY
8100 SaCo 95843 238-E6
ORCUTT CIR
100 SAC 95834 276-J4
ORE ST
100 FOLS 95630 260-J4
OREANNA CT
- PlaC 95747 238-H3
ORE CART CT
- EDCo 95762 263-A6
OREGON CT
- EDCo 95619 266-A5
OREGON DR
1400 SAC 95822 317-B4
OREGON ST
- SaCo 95742 300-D2
OREGON BAR CT
11800 SaCo 95670 280-D5
OREILLY PL
8400 SaCo 95843 239-C5
ORELLE CREEK CT
8100 CITH 95610 240-C6
ORELLI CT
- SaCo 95828 338-F6
ORENZA WY
4500 SAC 95823 337-H5
OREO RANCH CIR
9300 ELKG 95624 379-A2
ORESTES WY
2000 SAC 95833 277-B6
ORIAL OAK WY
8400 CITH 95610 240-C6
ORIANA CT
7700 SaCo 95628 279-J3

ORIENTAL ST
4600 EDCo 95623 265-A4
4600 EDCo 95667 265-A4
ORILLA
6400 SaCo 95683 322-C7
ORINDA CIR
3500 EDCo 95682 263-F6
ORINDA PL
- WSAC 95691 316-J1
ORINDA WY
4400 SaCo 95820 317-H2
ORINO CT
9800 ELKG 95757 358-A7
ORIOLE CT
500 LNCN 95648 180-C7
1000 RSVL 95661 240-C4
ORIOLE WY
3200 PLCR 95667 245-H6
3200 SaCo 95843 238-F7
ORION DR
200 EDCo 95619 265-D5
ORION WY
- RKLN 95677 220-H5
1700 SaCo 95864 298-J1
ORISON CT
8600 ELKG 95624 358-H1
ORKNEY CT
- RSVL 95661 220-E7
8000 SaCo 95829 338-J6
ORLANDO AV
900 RSVL 95661 239-H5
ORLANDO WY
1500 SAC 95815 278-A6
ORLEANS WY
6600 SAC 95831 316-F7
ORLEANS RIVER CT
11000 RCCD 95670 279-J5
ORO CT
- EDCo - 247-C7
ORO LN
4100 EDCo 95623 265-B4
ORO WY
8900 SaCo 95662 260-F5
OROFINO DR
- EDCo 95762 282-E2
ORO GRANDE DR
- EDCo 95634 205-H2
ORO LOMA RD
1100 EDCo 95613 244-D1
ORONO CT
4700 SaCo 95628 279-F1
OROSCO DR
1000 EDCo 95762 242-F6
OROSCO WY
8400 ELKG 95624 358-E1
ORPHEUM WY
7600 SaCo 95843 238-J7
ORPINGTON PL
9700 ELKG 95624 359-A7
ORR RD
- SaCo 95632 419-A6
- GALT 95632 419-A6
8600 SaCo 95632 418-G6
8600 SaCo 95632 (438-G1 See Page 418)
ORR ST
100 AUB 95603 182-E1
ORRIN DR
100 AUB 95603 182-D4
ORRINGTON CIR
- SAC 95835 257-C6
ORSAGE CT
- ELKG 95624 338-D7
ORSAY WY
- EDCo 95762 262-H4
ORSI CIR
6100 SaCo 95608 259-D5
ORT WY
7600 SaCo 95843 238-G7
ORTEGA ST
4900 SAC 95820 318-A4
5600 SAC 95824 318-A5
ORTIZ CT
8400 SaCo 95662 260-C3
ORTON ST
8800 ELKG 95624 358-G6
ORVAL WY
3900 SaCo 95608 279-C3
ORVAL BECKETT CT
- EDCo 95667 226-E3
ORVIETTO DR
- RSVL 95661 240-D1
ORWELL CT
- SaCo 95829 339-B5
ORWELL DR
1400 RSVL 95747 219-E7
OSAGE AV
8900 SAC 95828 318-H5
8900 SAC 95829 318-H5
8900 SaCo 95828 318-H5
8900 SaCo 95829 318-H5
OSAGE LN
500 PlaC 95602 162-G2
OSBORNE CT
- FOLS 95630 261-J4
- RSVL 95746 240-G4
3200 SaCo 95608 279-B5
OSBORNE RD
2800 EDCo 95682 263-D6
OSCAR CIR
- ELKG 95757 378-A2
OSELOT WY
3200 RCCD 95670 300-A3
OSGOOD WY
- SaCo 95628 260-B7
OSLO CT
4200 SaCo 95843 238-J5
OSMER LN
3500 SAC 95838 278-A3
OSPREY CT
- RKLN 95765 219-H1
- RSVL 95747 219-A7
2000 FOLS 95630 282-B1
6600 SaCo 95660 259-A3
6600 SaCo 95842 259-A3
OSPREY DR
2100 FOLS 95630 282-B1
OSPREY POINT CIR
9800 ELKG 95757 377-E1
9800 ELKG 95757 397-E1
OSSMAN CT
9500 SaCo 95829 339-B6
OST PL
- SAC 95835 256-G7
OSTRANDER CT
- SaCo 95693 360-B6
OSULLIVAN
6200 SaCo 95842 259-A4

OSUNA WY
- SAC 95833 277-A4
OTAY ST
- WSAC 95691 316-E4
OTEROL CT
4200 SaCo 95821 278-H4
OTHEL CT
- SAC 95828 318-C7
OTHELLO DR
- RSVL 95747 219-A7
OTIS AV
3700 WSAC 95691 316-D3
OTIS CT
4400 SaCo 95608 279-D2
OTIUM CT
8100 SaCo 95843 239-A6
OTIUM WY
8000 SaCo 95843 239-A6
OTSEGO ST
500 WSAC 95691 296-H3
- OAKL 94561 (514-C8 See Page 493)
OTTAWA CT
- RKLN 95765 200-C5
OTTAWA WY
7000 SaCo 95843 238-H7
OTTER BAY CT
9700 ELKG 95757 358-A7
OTTER CREEK WY
9300 ELKG 95758 358-A5
OTTER GLEN CT
- RSVL 95661 220-D6
OTTER POND WY
5100 RCCD 95742 320-E4
OTTERVIEW CT
- ELKG 95757 377-J1
- ELKG 95757 397-J1
OTTO
- PlaC 95603 181-J3
OTTO CIR
100 SAC 95822 317-E6
OTTOBONN WY
10200 SaCo 95632 419-D2
OTTOMEYER CT
3900 SaCo 95660 258-H2
OTTOMON WY
9300 SaCo 95662 260-H2
OTTOWA ST
- OAKL 94561 (514-C6 See Page 493)
OTTUMNA DR
- SAC 95835 256-J6
OTTUMWA DR
- SAC 95835 256-J6
OUR WY
5800 CITH 95610 259-H5
OUTER BANKS PL
- SAC 95835 256-H4
OUTER LIMITS LN
3000 EDCo 95726 248-J1
OUTFALL CIR
5800 SAC 95828 318-F5
OUTINGDALE RD
4600 EDCo 95684 286-F6
OUTLOOK DR
- SaCo 95621 239-E6
3200 RKLN 95765 220-A1
6300 CITH 95621 239-E6
OUT OF THE WAY LN
900 PlaC 95603 162-E4
OUT OF THE WAY PL
12500 PlaC 95603 162-D4
OUTPOST CT
9200 SaCo 95628 260-G7
OUTRIDER WY
5600 EDCo 95667 244-F5
OUTRIGGER CT
400 RSVL 95661 240-D4
2000 EDCo 95762 242-A6
OUTRIGGER DR
1900 EDCo 95762 242-B6
OUTRIGGER WY
200 SAC 95831 316-F6
OVAR CT
7200 ELKG 95757 378-B3
OVERBROOK DR
100 FOLS 95630 241-B7
OVERBROOK WY
5200 SaCo 95841 259-B7
OVERHILL RD
5800 SaCo 95628 260-C5
OVERLAND CT
1500 WSAC 95691 296-D5
OVERLAND LN
- LNCN 95648 180-A4
OVERLAND WY
- EDCo - 267-J3
12100 SaCo 95693 360-F5
OVERLEAF WY
5600 SAC 95835 257-D4
OVERLOOK CT
1800 EDCo 95667 244-E3
OVERMILLER DR
3500 PlaC 95602 162-B3
OVERTON WY
8100 SaCo 95829 339-A6
OVERWOOD CT
6000 SaCo 95662 260-J5
OWEN CT
1300 PlaC 95663 180-J7
OWENCARROW LN
- LNCN 95648 200-B2
OWENS WY
3600 SaCo 95660 258-G2
OWEN THOMAS CT
- ELKG 95757 377-J3
- ELKG 95757 397-J3
OWL CT
- ELKG 95758 357-J2
OWLCREST CT
7300 SaCo 95660 258-H1
OWLET CT
8700 ELKG 95624 358-G1
OWL FEATHER CT
- RSVL 95747 219-C2
OWL MEADOW DR
2100 FOLS 95630 282-B1
OWL MEADOW ST
2000 FOLS 95630 282-B1
OWLS CLOVER WY
- RSVL 95747 219-A4
OWL TREE CT
4700 RCCD 95742 320-E3
OWNING LN
13200 SaCo 95632 419-B4
OXBOW DR
4500 SaCo 95864 278-J7
4600 SaCo 95608 279-A7
4600 SaCo 95864 279-A7
16500 SaCo 95641 456-B5

OXBOW DR
16800 SaCo 95641 455-J7
OX BOW LN
9300 PlaC 95650 201-H6
OXBOW CREEK PL
4500 SaCo 95628 280-C1
OXBOW MARINA LN
100 SaCo 95641 456-A6
OXBOW RIDGE PL
4500 SaCo 95628 280-C2
OXBOROUGH DR
100 FOLS 95630 261-B5
OXFORD CT
1800 RSVL 95661 240-C5
3300 EDCo 95682 263-F5
OXFORD RD
3100 EDCo 95682 263-E5
OXFORD ST
500 WSAC 95691 296-H3
1900 SAC 95815 297-H1
2000 SAC 95815 277-H7
OXFORD GLEN PL
5900 ELKG 95758 357-J3
5900 ELKG 95758 358-A3
OXFORD HILL CT
8500 SaCo 95828 338-F4
OXFORM LN
- SaCo 95829 339-C2
OXIDATION WY
- SaCo 95758 337-F7
OXLEIGH WY
- FOLS 95630 281-F2
OX TRAIL WY
1700 EDCo 95762 242-G7
OXWOOD DR
4200 SaCo 95826 319-A2
4400 SaCo 95827 319-A2
OZARK CIR
500 SAC 95834 277-F3
OZRO CT
4100 SaCo 95826 319-A2
OZZIE CT
3100 SaCo 95608 279-A5

P

P ST
200 SAC 95814 297-B4
300 LNCN 95648 179-F3
2000 SAC 95816 297-E5
3800 SAC 95819 297-H6
PAAVOLA CT
- FOLS 95630 261-H4
PAAVOLA WY
- FOLS 95630 260-J2
- FOLS 95630 261-A1
PABLO DR
5600 SaCo 95842 259-C2
PACE CT
2900 SAC 95826 318-E1
PACER CT
- ELKG 95624 358-J6
PACER PL
- PlaC 95603 162-C4
PACHBROOK LN
- RCCD 95670 280-A5
PACHECO CT
900 EDCo 95762 262-D4
PACHECO WY
6500 CITH 95610 260-A3
6600 CITH 95610 259-J3
PACHECO PASS WY
8900 ELKG 95624 378-H2
PACIFIC AV
- AUB 95603 182-D4
3600 SaCo 95668 236-J1
E PACIFIC AV
3700 SAC 95820 317-E2
W PACIFIC AV
3700 SAC 95820 317-E2
PACIFIC CT
10700 RCCD 95670 299-H1
PACIFIC DR
- WSAC 95691 296-F7
PACIFIC PL
- WSAC 95691 296-F7
PACIFIC ST
200 RSVL 95678 239-H1
800 PLCR 95667 245-G5
4000 LMS 95650 200-H7
4000 LMS 95677 200-H7
4000 RKLN 95677 200-H7
4000 RKLN 95677 220-F1
6100 RSVL 95678 220-C5
PACIFICA LN
- ELKG 95758 357-F7
PACIFIC BEACH CT
7800 SaCo 95828 338-E5
PACIFIC CREST CT
- EDCo - 267-F3
- EDCo 95726 267-F3
PACIFIC CREST TR
- EDCo - 267-F3
- EDCo 95726 267-F3
PACIFIC DUNES CT
7800 SaCo 95829 339-D4
PACIFIC GROVE CT
8300 SaCo 95828 338-E5
PACIFIC HILLS WY
8600 SaCo 95828 338-F4
PACIFIC OAK CT
200 FOLS 95630 281-A2
PACIFIC PALM CT
5300 SaCo 95628 259-F7
PACIFIC PARK WY
4700 SaCo 95843 239-A7
PACIFIC SHORE LN
- ELKG 95758 357-F6
PACKARD CT
4800 SaCo 95608 279-A4
PACKWOOD CT
4100 ELKG 95758 357-G5
PACKWOOD WY
4000 ELKG 95758 357-G5
PACO CT
6300 CITH 95621 239-E6
PADARO CT
4800 SaCo 95628 280-E1
PADBURY CT
900 GALT 95632 419-F3
PADDINGTON CIR
- GALT 95632 419-G5
PADDINGTON CT
- RSVL 95678 219-G3
PADDLE CT
- SAC 95833 277-C6
PADDLE PASS
- EDCo - 247-G1

PADDLE WHEEL CT
- SAC 95833 276-H7
PADDLEWHEEL CT
600 RSVL 95747 219-A4
PADDOCK CT
300 RSVL 95661 240-C3
9300 SaCo 95662 260-H4
PADDOCK LN
2000 PlaC 95658 201-J2
PADGETT CT
100 RSVL 95747 219-D7
PADOVA CT
8100 SaCo 95829 338-H6
PADRE CT
- PlaC 95746 241-C3
PADSIDE DR
- RSVL 95747 218-J5
PAGE CT
4700 EDCo 95623 265-B5
5600 SaCo 95841 259-B6
PAGE LN
6300 EDCo 95623 265-B5
PAGEANT DR
3400 SaCo 95826 [illegible]
3400 SaCo 95826 318-J1
PAGEL CT
5300 SaCo 95628 259-F7
PAIGE CT
4100 RKLN 95677 220-E4
PAIGE ST
9000 PlaC 95658 181-G5
PAINE CT
100 FOLS 95630 261-G5
PAINT DR
- PlaC 95603 161-J4
- PlaC 95603 162-A4
PAINT WY
8000 SaCo 95830 339-G6
PAINTED DESERT CT
- RSVL 95747 219-C3
PAINTED DESERT WY
- RSVL 95747 219-D3
PAINTED OCEAN PL
- SAC 95835 256-G5
PAINTED ROCK PL
- FOLS 95630 260-J1
- FOLS 95630 261-F1
PAINTER WY
4000 SaCo 95660 258-H2
PAINTROCK CT
3400 SaCo 95843 238-G5
PAIRBROOK CT
4600 RCCD 95742 320-E3
PAISAN CT
- SAC 95831 337-A3
PAISLEY CT
900 ANT 94509 (513-C7 See Page 493)
PAISLEY WY
4800 SaCo 95608 299-A4
PAIUTE CT
3200 EDCo 95682 263-C2
PAIUTE WY
10700 RCCD 95670 299-G3
PAIUTE POINT RD
- RSVL 95747 219-B3
PAIZANO CT
- RSVL 95661 240-D1
PAJARO CT
- AUB 95603 182-D6
500 SaCo 95864 298-G4
PALA WY
400 SAC 95819 297-J5
PALABRA CT
100 FOLS 95630 261-F3
PALACE CIR
7100 SaCo 95628 259-G7
PALACE LN
- EDCo 95667 266-F6
PALACIO WY
4300 SaCo 95628 280-F2
PALADENA ST
4800 SaCo 95841 278-J1
PALADIN WY
7100 SaCo 95673 257-G1
PALAFAXIA WY
- ELKG 95624 358-F1
PALATIA CT
100 RSVL 95661 240-D3
PALATIA DR
1600 RSVL 95661 240-D3
PALATINE PL
6800 SaCo 95842 259-C3
PALAVER CT
- PlaC 95747 238-H3
PALAZZO CT
- LNCN 95648 179-E3
9700 ELKG 95624 359-B7
PALAZZO PL
- SAC 95835 257-A3
PALEN CT
- SAC 95838 257-G7
PALERMO CT
- SAC 95828 318-B7
PALERMO WY
- EDCo 95762 262-F5
PALESTINE LN
3400 SaCo 95608 279-B4
PALESTRINA DR
- RSVL 95747 219-B1
PALIN AV
100 GALT 95632 419-F7
PALISADE CT
900 RSVL 95661 239-J5
PALISADE WY
7600 SaCo 95628 279-H2
PALISADES DR
- RVIS 94571 454-F1
PALLADAY RD
- PlaC 95626 238-A2
8300 SaCo 95626 237-J6
8500 SaCo 95626 238-A4
PALLAZZO WY
6300 ELKG 95757 358-A7
6300 ELKG 95757 378-A1
PALM AV
- SaCo 95632 419-F6
100 AUB 95603 182-D1
1200 RSVL 95661 240-A3
4000 SaCo 95660 258-H6
4100 SaCo 95842 258-H6
4700 SaCo 95842 259-A6
5000 SaCo 95841 259-A6
5700 SaCo 95608 259-E7
6700 SaCo 95628 259-F7
PALM CT
500 RSVL 95661 240-A3
PALM DR
3000 SaCo 95608 279-E5

PALM LN
4400 EDCo 95682 283-J2
PALM ST
- SaCo 95652 258-F6
- SaCo 95660 258-F6
PALMA PKWY
7700 SaCo 95823 337-H3
PALMAIRE WY
8400 SaCo 95662 260-C3
PALMARITAS CT
- SAC 95823 337-H5
PALMATE WY
3000 SAC 95834 276-J4
PALM BEACH DR
- SaCo 95829 339-F6
PALMCREST LN
1800 PlaC 95663 201-A1
PALMDALE WY
5500 SaCo 95842 258-H6
PALMDELL WY
6900 SaCo 95628 259-F7
PALMER CIR
- FOLS 95630 261-E7
PALMER DR
3400 EDCo 95682 263-F7
PALMER ST
3100 SAC 95815 278-A4
PALMERA LN
- SAC 95835 257-A4
PALMER HOUSE DR
7200 SaCo 95828 338-C2
PALMERSON DR
8000 SaCo 95843 238-J6
8400 SaCo 95843 239-A5
PALMERSTON LP
1200 RSVL 95678 219-F6
PALM ESTATES CT
2900 SaCo 95608 279-D6
PALMETTO ST
3900 SAC 95838 277-J2
PALMGATE CT
5600 SaCo 95841 259-A5
PALMGROVE DR
9900 RCCD 95827 299-D7
PALMIAS CT
8700 SaCo 95628 260-E7
PALM SPRINGS CT
5900 ELKG 95758 358-A3
PALMTREE CT
6700 SaCo 95628 259-F6
PALM VIEW LN
100 RCCD 95670 280-C7
PALMWOOD CT
2200 RCCD 95670 279-G7
PALMYRA DR
7700 SaCo 95628 259-J7
PALMYRA ST
100 AUB 95603 182-C4
PALOMA AV
4900 SaCo 95608 299-A2
PALOMA DR
3400 LMS 95650 200-H5
PALOMA RD
3500 EDCo 95709 246-H5
PALOMA BLANCA CT
7000 ELKG 95758 358-B4
PALOMAR AV
800 WSAC 95691 296-E4
PALOMAR CIR
1300 SAC 95831 337-B1
5700 RKLN 95677 220-B4
PALOMARES CT
- RSVL 95747 219-B2
PALOMARES WY
- RSVL 95747 219-B1
PALOMARIN CT
8200 SaCo 95828 338-D7
PALOMINO CT
- AUB 95603 182-C6
- EDCo 95762 262-B1
- RSVL 95678 219-H4
2100 FOLS 95630 282-B1
8700 PlaC 95746 241-B3
PALOMINO LN
4600 SaCo 95660 278-G1
PALORAN CT
3300 EDCo 95682 263-G5
PALORAN RD
3200 EDCo 95682 263-G5
PALOS VERDE CT
1500 EDCo 95762 262-C1
PALOS VERDES CT
1000 RSVL 95661 239-J5
PALO VERDE AV
1400 SAC 95815 278-A5
PALO VERDE WY
2900 ANT 94509 (513-B6 See Page 493)
PALO VISTA WY
2600 RCCD 95670 299-E2
PAMELA DR
3200 SAC 95815 278-A4
PAMELA LN
2300 SaCo 95825 278-D7
PAMLEE CT
4000 SaCo 95608 279-B3
PAMPAS WY
6900 SaCo 95628 259-F7
PANADERO DR
4000 EDCo 95682 264-A6
PANAMA AV
2900 SaCo 95608 279-D6
PANAMINT CT
- ELKG 95624 358-F3
PANARAMA CT
1200 RSVL 95661 240-A5
PANAY CT
2700 SaCo 95608 279-D6
PANDORA CT
9400 SaCo 95662 260-H7
P AND S LN
- PlaC 95658 181-J5
PANGA PL
- SaCo 95670 280-C6
PANNING WY
200 EDCo 95667 245-D4
PANNINI WY
- EDCo 95762 262-G3
PANORAMA CT
4500 EDCo 95667 265-A2
PANORAMA DR
6700 CITH 95621 259-D3
6700 CITH 95841 259-D3
PANORAMA RD
4300 EDCo 95667 265-A2
PANORAMA WY
3400 PlaC 95602 161-J3
PANOS CT
- SAC 95823 338-A5

PANSY AV
3600 SAC 95817 317-F2
PANTAGES CIR
2100 RCCD 95670 279-G6
PANTANO DR
6200 SAC 95824 318-B6
6300 SAC 95828 318-B6
PANTHER LN
4000 EDCo 95619 265-E3
PAPAGO WY
7900 SaCo 95843 238-F6
PAPAYA AL
- RSVL 95678 239-H1
PAPAYA DR
4700 SaCo 95628 279-F1
4800 SaCo 95628 259-F7
PAPOOSE CT
5900 CITH 95621 259-D3
PAPUSAS WY
- SAC 95835 256-H4
PAQUIN CT
6700 SaCo 95828 318-D7
PAR PKWY
7600 SaCo 95828 338-C3
PAR PL
2400 RKLN 95677 220-B3
PARACHUTE CT
9000 SaCo 95628 260-F7
PARADA CT
- PlaC 95747 238-J3
10100 ELKG 95757 378-B2
PARADE CT
- SAC 95817 317-J1
PARADISE CT
4700 PlaC 95677 220-G4
PARADISE DR
4200 SaCo 95608 279-F2
PARADISE LN
- EDCo 95667 267-B4
PARADISE WY
2700 WSAC 95691 316-G1
PARADISE BAY CT
7700 ELKG 95758 358-C4
PARADISE PINES
- RVIS 94571 454-E1
PARADISE RANCH RD
- EDCo 95684 286-H5
PARADISE VIEW CT
- RSVL 95678 219-G4
PARADISO CT
7200 ELKG 95757 358-B7
PARAGON CT
5400 RKLN 95677 220-C3
PARAGON LN
- LNCN 95648 179-J7
PARAGON ST
5200 RKLN 95677 220-C3
PARAGON WY
2900 SaCo 95608 279-B5
PARAMOUNT CIR
- SAC 95823 338-A5
5600 SAC 95823 337-J5
PARAMOUNT PASS
- EDCo - 267-B6
PARDAL CT
7700 CITH 95610 239-J7
PARDEE CT
3700 EDCo 95762 262-C4
PARDI WY
1000 PLCR 95667 245-G6
PARDILLO AV
8600 SaCo 95662 260-D1
PARDIS LN
7400 SaCo 95828 338-F3
PARDUCCI WY
9200 SaCo 95829 338-J7
PAREJO CT
- SAC 95835 256-J3
PARFAIT DR
9200 SaCo 95826 318-J1
9200 SaCo 95826 319-A1
PARGO PL
2300 SaCo 95670 280-B6
PARIS LN
1800 ANT 94509 (513-G5 See Page 493)
PARIS ST
6200 CITH 95621 259-F4
PARISH CT
5400 SAC 95822 317-B4
PARISH WY
7100 CITH 95621 239-F7
PARK AV
- YoCo 95612 356-J5
100 GALT 95632 419-F6
2700 PLCR 95667 245-J4
4100 SaCo 95628 280-B2
9400 PlaC 95658 181-G5
PARK BLVD
900 WSAC 95691 296-H5
PARK CIR
1100 WSAC 95691 296-J5
PARK CT
- ISLE 95641 455-G5
PARK DR
- RKLN 95677 200-E5
- RKLN 95765 200-D3
- RKLN 95765 219-J2
- RKLN 95765 220-A1
100 RSVL 95678 239-J2
3400 EDCo 95762 282-D1
3600 EDCo 95762 262-C7
3600 PlaC 95602 162-A2
7500 CITH 95610 259-H3
7900 SaCo 95628 280-A2
E PARK DR
9400 ELKG 95624 359-A6
N PARK DR
- SAC 95835 256-J6
- SAC 95835 257-A6
PARK LN
- ANT 94509 (513-D4 See Page 493)
3300 SaCo 95608 279-D4
PARK PL
- SAC 95831 336-H1
6800 PlaC 95746 241-B3
S PARK PL
3800 PlaC 95602 162-B1
PARK RD
- ELKG 95624 378-G1
- SaCo 95655 299-J7
- SaCo 95655 319-J1
800 SAC 95838 257-J7
3500 SAC 95821 278-G2
3500 SaCo 95821 278-G2
3600 SAC 95822 317-B2
3700 SAC 95841 278-G2
3700 SaCo 95841 278-G2

STREET Block City ZIP Pg-Grid

E PARK RD
- SAC 95822 317-B1
PARK ST
100 AUB 95603 182-D3
PARK WY
- FOLS 95630 261-A7
- FOLS 95630 281-A1
100 AUB 95603 182-F3
3300 ELKG 95624 378-G1
3300 SAC 95816 297-G4
PARK BROOK CT
- SAC 95822 317-B6
PARK CENTER DR
- SAC 95825 298-C5
PARK CIRCLE LN
3900 SaCo 95608 279-E3
PARK CITY CT
- RKLN 95765 219-J2
PARKCITY CT
- SAC 95831 337-A1
PARKCITY DR
7300 SAC 95831 337-A2
PARKCREEK CIR
6300 CITH 95621 259-E5
PARK CREEK RD
- EDCo 95726 248-G1
PARKCREST WY
- RSVL 95747 219-C1
6400 CITH 95621 259-E4
PARKDALE LN
3100 EDCo 95682 263-B2
PARKER AV
4400 SaCo 95820 317-H3
PARKER DR
300 FOLS 95630 281-A2
PARKER LN
500 ANT 94509 (513-E5 See Page 493)
PARKER ST
3400 RKLN 95765 220-B1
PARK ESTATES DR
2200 SaCo 95825 278-E7
PARKFAIR DR
300 SaCo 95864 298-G5
PARKFIELD CT
5500 SAC 95822 317-A4
PARKFORD CIR
5100 PlaC 95746 240-G6
PARK FRONT WY
- ELKG 95624 338-D7
- ELKG 95624 358-D1
PARKGATE WY
8000 SaCo 95828 338-E6
PARKGLEN CT
9900 ELKG 95624 378-H1
PARK GREEN CT
4400 SaCo 95821 278-J3
PARKGROVE CT
9900 ELKG 95624 378-H1
PARKHAVEN WY
700 SAC 95831 336-H1
800 SAC 95831 316-J7
PARK HEIGHTS DR
1100 GALT 95632 419-G2
PARK HILL DR
- EDCo - 267-E3
PARKHILL DR
2000 RSVL 95661 240-D4
PARK HILLS DR
2600 SaCo 95821 278-D6
PARKHURST CT
9900 ELKG 95624 378-H1
PARKINGTON CT
2200 SaCo 95825 298-C3
PARK LAKE CT
1100 PlaC 95658 181-B1
PARKLAKE WY
9800 ELKG 95624 378-H1
PARKLIN AV
700 SAC 95831 316-H6
PARKLITE CIR
- SAC 95831 316-J7
PARKMEAD WY
1600 SAC 95822 317-C3
PARK MEADOW CT
200 RSVL 95661 240-E4
PARK MEADOWS DR
8900 ELKG 95624 378-H1
PARK OAK DR
- RSVL 95661 220-D7
- RSVL 95661 240-D1
PARK OAK LN
- SaCo 95608 299-A2
PARKOAKS DR
5700 SaCo 95608 259-E5
5800 CITH 95621 259-E5
5800 SaCo 95621 259-E5
PARK PLACE DR
- SAC 95835 257-B7
1700 SaCo 95608 299-A1
PARK PLACE SOUTH DR
- SAC 95834 257-B7
PARK RANCH WY
900 SAC 95831 336-J1
PARK REGENCY DR
- RSVL 95747 219-B7
- RSVL 95747 239-B1
PARK RIDGE CT
2100 SaCo 95864 298-J1
PARKRIDGE RD
4400 SAC 95822 317-C3
PARK RIVER OAK CIR
7700 SAC 95831 336-G3
PARK RIVER OAK CT
- SAC 95831 336-G3
PARK RIVIERA WY
6400 SAC 95831 316-F7
PARKSHORE CIR
- SAC 95831 316-J7
- SAC 95831 336-J1
PARKSHORE DR
100 FOLS 95630 261-A7
100 FOLS 95630 281-A1
PARKSIDE CT
4000 SAC 95822 317-B2
PARKSIDE DR
- LNCN 95648 200-A2
- RSVL 95747 219-D2
3300 RKLN 95677 220-C3
PARKSIDE LN
8300 CITH 95610 240-C7
PARKSIDE TER
100 AUB 95603 182-E3
PARKSIDE WY
- RSVL 95747 219-C1
PARK SIERRA LN
- SaCo 95864 298-E5
PARKSTONE
600 FOLS 95630 241-B7
PARKSTONE CIR
- PlaC 95747 239-A4
PARKSTONE LN
- ELKG 95758 357-G7
PARK STREAM CT
900 GALT 95632 419-G2
PARK STREAM DR
900 GALT 95632 419-G2
PARK TERRACE CT
9900 ELKG 95624 378-G1
PARK TERRACE DR
1100 GALT 95632 419-G2
PARK TOWNE CIR
- SaCo 95825 278-F7
PARK TRAIL DR
9900 ELKG 95624 378-G2
PARK TREE CT
- SAC 95822 317-B5
PARKTREE WY
8900 ELKG 95624 358-G7
PARKVALE WY
6300 CITH 95621 259-D2
PARK VALLEY CT
1100 GALT 95632 419-G2
PARK VALLEY WY
1100 GALT 95632 419-G2
PARKVIEW DR
200 PLCR 95667 245-G5
1000 RSVL 95661 240-B4
PARKVIEW LN
3500 RKLN 95677 220-D2
PARKVIEW WY
6300 CITH 95621 259-E5
PARK VILLAGE ST
6300 SAC 95822 317-B5
PARKVILLE CT
5400 SaCo 95842 259-C2
PARK VISTA CIR
- SAC 95831 316-J7
PARK VISTA DR
8500 PlaC 95746 241-E3
PARKWAY BLVD
1400 WSAC 95691 296-E5
PARKWAY DR
- FOLS 95630 261-H4
2600 EDCo 95667 246-D4
3600 PlaC 95602 162-B1
PARKWAY LN
- FOLS 95630 261-B7
PARKWAY PL
3700 WSAC 95691 296-E5
3800 PlaC 95602 162-B1
PARK WEST CT
- SAC 95831 336-H1
PARKWIND LN
4100 ELKG 95758 357-G6
PARKWOOD CT
- PlaC 95747 239-A1
3000 SaCo 95608 279-E5
PARKWOOD DR
2300 SaCo 95825 278-E7
PARKWOOD WY
- PlaC 95747 239-A2
PARK WOODS DR
4200 EDCo 95726 248-E3
PARLEYS CANYON
3400 EDCo 95667 245-H1
PARLIAMENT CIR
1800 SaCo 95608 299-C1
PARMIS CT
7900 CITH 95610 239-H7
PARNEL WY
- GALT 95632 419-G3
PARNELL CT
- SAC 95835 256-G7
900 RSVL 95747 219-E6
PARNEVIK CT
10200 SaCo 95829 339-E4
PARODY WY
3000 SAC 95833 277-D4
PARQUE WY
3300 SAC 95835 256-H3
PARQUE DEL ROBLES CIR
- EDCo - 247-D6
- EDCo 95726 247-D6
PARQUE VISTA WY
5100 SaCo 95608 279-A7
PARROT ST
- SaCo 95826 319-A1
- SaCo 95827 319-A1
PARRY ST
- RSVL 95678 240-A1
PARSONS LN
- PlaC 95658 201-H5
1800 ANT 94509 (513-F5 See Page 493)
PARSONS WY
- FOLS 95630 281-G2
PARSONS LANDING ST
- ELKG 95624 358-J7
- ELKG 95624 359-A7
PARTRICKS LN
- CITH 95610 259-H1
PARTRIDGE AV
3300 WSAC 95691 316-F3
PARTRIDGE CT
200 RSVL 95661 240-C4
700 LNCN 95648 179-G2
PARTRIDGE DR
100 GALT 95632 419-D6
PARTRIDGE PL
1900 EDCo 95667 246-B4
PARUS WY
8100 PlaC 95746 221-E6
PASADA CT
2900 EDCo 95682 263-C5
PASADA RD
2900 EDCo 95682 263-C5
PASADENA AV
3800 SaCo 95821 278-H3
4500 SaCo 95608 279-A2
4500 SaCo 95821 279-A2
4600 SaCo 95841 278-H1
PASA ROBLES CT
- EDCo - 247-G6
- EDCo 95726 247-G6
PASA ROBLES DR
4800 SaCo 95841 278-J1
PASATIEMPO
2900 SAC 95833 276-J7
PASATIEMPO CIR
- PlaC 95747 239-B3
PASATIEMPO LN
2600 SaCo 95821 278-E5
PASCAL CT
9200 ELKG 95624 359-A7
PASCAL WY
9300 ELKG 95624 359-A7
PASCOE CT
100 FOLS 95630 261-F7
PASEO DR
2600 RCCD 95670 299-E3
PASEO DEL CAMPO
2500 SaCo 95821 278-D5
PASEO DEL SOL WY
6500 ELKG 95758 358-A4
PASEO GRANDE WY
9100 ELKG 95758 358-B4
PASEO NUEVO RD
- SAC 95838 277-H4
PASEO PENASCO
1800 RSVL 95747 219-C5
PASEO RIO WY
- SaCo 95827 299-C4
PASEO TRANQUILO
- LNCN 95648 180-E7
PASEO VILLENA
- PlaC 95746 221-F4
PASO CT
- EDCo - 267-A1
PASO WY
- EDCo - 247-A7
- EDCo - 267-A1
PASO DIABLO CT
- EDCo 95667 244-J3
PASO DIABLO RD
1400 EDCo 95667 244-J3
PASO FINO WY
9700 ELKG 95757 357-H7
PASO ROBLES WY
8900 ELKG 95758 358-A3
PASSAGE PL
- SAC 95835 256-H3
PASSALLIS LN
7500 SaCo 95829 338-J3
PASSARO WY
10100 ELKG 95757 378-B2
PASTOR DR
5100 PlaC 95746 240-H4
PASTORI WY
8400 SaCo 95828 338-E7
PASTURE CT
- SAC 95834 277-D4
PASTURE ROSE CT
9600 ELKG 95624 359-B6
PASTURE ROSE WY
9600 ELKG 95624 359-B6
PAT ST
- SAC 95838 277-G1
PATERO CIR
7300 SAC 95823 337-G2
PATHFINDER CT
8700 SaCo 95662 260-E4
PATHFINDER TR
- EDCo 95667 266-H7
PATHFINDER WY
6300 SaCo 95662 260-E4
PATHWAY CT
4900 SaCo 95628 260-A7
PATIENCE CT
7000 SaCo 95842 259-A2
PATINA CT
- RSVL 95747 199-B7
PATINA WY
8400 ELKG 95624 358-H1
PATIO AV
400 SAC 95834 277-F3
PATIO CT
- EDCo - 267-H3
- EDCo 95726 267-H3
PATKIRK CT
10600 RCCD 95670 279-G6
PATMON DR
- ELKG 95624 338-D7
PATMOS CT
- SAC 95823 337-G3
PATRIC WY
4900 SaCo 95608 279-A3
PATRICIA AV
2700 ANT 94509 (513-E6 See Page 493)
PATRICIA PL
12600 AUB 95603 162-E6
PATRICIA WY
600 RSVL 95678 219-G7
900 SaCo 95864 298-F3
PATRICK CIR
- FOLS 95630 281-E1
PATRICK LN
- EDCo 95726 248-A1
PATRICK SWELL CT
- ELKG 95624 358-F2
PATRIOT LN
11900 SaCo 95693 360-F3
PATROL RD
- SAC 95652 258-C5
- SaCo 95652 258-C5
- SaCo 95652 278-C1
- SaCo 95673 258-C5
PATS LN
2000 EDCo 95667 245-C1
PATTE WY
9500 SaCo 95662 260-J5
PATTERSON CT
100 EDCo 95619 265-D4
PATTERSON DR
2600 EDCo 95667 245-D4
4200 EDCo 95619 265-C3
PATTERSON LN
6100 CITH 95610 259-J5
PATTERSON WY
3300 EDCo 95762 262-C6
6300 SaCo 95828 318-A7
PATTI CT
2500 PLCR 95667 245-E4
PATTI WY
- ELKG 95757 378-A2
PATTI JO DR
5000 SaCo 95608 259-E7
PATTON AV
7800 CITH 95610 239-J7
PATTON CT
100 FOLS 95630 261-A2
PATTON DR
600 PlaC 95747 238-J4
PATTON WY
2600 SAC 95818 297-C6
PATTYCAKE CT
9800 ELKG 95624 359-A7
9800 ELKG 95624 379-A1
PATTYPEART WY
6200 SaCo 95608 279-D4
PAU HANA CIR
- CITH 95621 239-F6
PAUL AV
2200 SAC 95838 278-C2
PAUL CT
200 RSVL 95678 219-J6
1500 ANT 94509 (513-F7 See Page 493)
PAULA WY
4600 SaCo 95628 280-C1
PAUL BUNYON RD
2900 EDCo 95709 246-G4
PAUL CO MAR WY
6800 ELKG 95757 378-B3
PAUL COURTER WY
2000 SAC 95835 257-B4
PAULETTE WY
- ELKG 95757 378-A3
PAULHAUS WY
- ELKG 95758 358-D3
PAULINE CIR
- LMS 95650 200-J7
PAUMANOK WY
3200 SAC 95835 256-H4
PAVIA WY
8000 SAC 95823 337-J6
PAVICH LN
9900 ELKG 95624 359-D6
9900 SaCo 95624 359-D6
PAVILIONS LN
500 SaCo 95825 298-C4
PAVILLION CT
- SaCo 95817 317-J1
PAVILLION DR
9000 ELKG 95624 378-H1
PAVIN CT
7000 SaCo 95829 339-E5
PAVONIA CT
4600 EDCo 95682 263-B7
PAWDICK CT
2900 EDCo 95667 226-H3
PAWNEE WY
7800 SaCo 95843 238-G6
PAWTUCKET CT
100 FOLS 95630 261-H5
PAXTON CT
4700 SaCo 95608 279-E1
PAY DIRT CT
- PLCR 95667 246-A6
PAYDIRT CT
100 FOLS 95630 260-J4
PAY DIRT RD
3500 EDCo 95667 246-A6
3500 PLCR 95667 246-A6
PAYEN RD
- EDCo 95682 (302-E3 See Page 301)
- EDCo 95762 282-D7
- SaCo 95630 282-D6
- SaCo 95630 301-J7
- SaCo 95630 (302-E1 See Page 301)
- SaCo 95630 (321-H1 See Page 301)
PAYETTE DR
2700 SaCo 95826 298-J6
PAYNE WY
3600 SaCo 95660 258-G6
PAYNE RIVER CIR
- SAC 95831 336-G1
PAYTON ST
3800 SaCo 95821 278-J3
PEABODY CT
4400 SaCo 95842 258-J1
PEACE CT
3300 SaCo 95826 318-J1
PEACE TR
- EDCo 95619 266-B5
PEACEFUL GARDEN WY
2100 EDCo 95672 243-J7
2100 EDCo 95672 244-A6
2100 EDCo 95682 244-A6
PEACEFUL MOUNTAIN RD
- EDCo 95634 205-H1
PEACEKEEPER WY
- SaCo 95652 258-F7
- SaCo 95660 258-F7
PEACE SPRINGS RD
6100 PlaC 95650 221-D4
PEACE WATER CT
- RSVL 95747 219-D3
PEACH CIR
3700 PlaC 95650 201-H7
PEACH DR
3800 PlaC 95650 201-H7
PEACH LN
500 PlaC 95658 181-G6
11900 SaCo 95693 360-F3
PEACH BLOSSOM WY
8600 SaCo 95843 238-H5
PEACHDALE CT
12000 RCCD 95742 320-E4
PEACH LEAF CT
- SAC 95838 257-G7
PEACH LEAF WY
200 SAC 95838 257-G7
PEACH SPRUCE DR
- EDCo 95682 263-B5
- EDCo 95762 263-B5
PEACHTREE AV
7000 CITH 95621 259-G4
PEACH TREE LN
800 PlaC 95658 181-E6
800 PlaC 95663 181-E6
PEACHTREE LN
- RVIS 94571 454-F2
PEACHTREE ST
- WSAC 95691 316-J1
PEACHWOOD
3100 PlaC 95658 201-J4
PEACOCK LN
- PlaC 95626 237-G2
PEACOCK WY
6100 EDCo 95630 222-J3
7300 SAC 95820 318-C4
PEACOCK GAP CT
- SAC 95831 336-H1
PEAKVIEW AV
- SAC 95835 257-B4
PEAKVIEW CT
- LNCN 95648 179-J7
PEALE CT
2300 EDCo 95667 244-J4
2300 EDCo 95667 245-A4
PEALE DR
4700 SaCo 95842 259-A3
PEAR
- YoCo 95612 356-J5
PEAR DR
- PlaC 95603 162-B5
PEAR LN
10200 SaCo 95693 360-F2
PEAR RD
12700 SaCo 95693 360-J4
PEAR BLOSSOM CT
300 RSVL 95747 219-B5
PEAR BLOSSOM LN
1800 EDCo 95667 244-J4
PEARCE CT
- FOLS 95630 281-E1
PEAR HILL LN
13800 PlaC 95603 162-G3
PEARL DR
5700 RKLN 95677 220-B4
PEARL LN
2500 EDCo 95672 263-F1
PEARL PL
600 EDCo 95619 265-F2
PEARL RD
3800 EDCo 95726 248-F2
PEARL WY
- PlaC 95661 239-H6
8400 CITH 95610 239-H6
PEARL CREST CT
8500 ELKG 95624 358-F4
PEARL DROP CT
- SaCo 95843 238-H6
PEARLSTONE CT
- RSVL 95747 199-C7
PEARLSTONE DR
5400 SaCo 95843 239-C5
PEARL WOOD WY
4100 SaCo 95843 238-H5
PEAR ORCHARD CT
9000 SaCo 95662 260-F4
PEAR RIDGE RD
1100 EDCo 95667 245-A1
PEARSON AV
5700 LMS 95650 200-J5
PEARSON LN
6400 SaCo 95660 258-H3
PEAR TREE CT
10600 PlaC 95603 182-C7
10600 PlaC 95603 202-C1
PEBBLE CT
- PlaC 95603 162-F7
- SAC 95831 316-H6
PEBBLEBEACH CT
100 RSVL 95678 219-G5
PEBBLE BEACH DR
- RVIS 94571 454-E2
7900 CITH 95610 260-A6
PEBBLE BEACH RD
- RKLN 95765 200-C5
PEBBLEBROOK WY
6200 CITH 95621 259-E2
PEBBLE CANYON LN
9100 SaCo 95628 280-G1
PEBBLE CREEK DR
5900 RKLN 95765 220-A1
PEBBLE FIELD WY
- SaCo 95829 338-H6
PEBBLE OAKS CT
4100 SaCo 95843 238-H5
PEBBLE RIDGE CT
7900 SaCo 95828 338-D5
PEBBLE RIVER CIR
- SAC 95831 336-F1
PEBBLE RUN WY
4100 RCCD 95742 320-D1
PEBBLE SPRING CT
9000 SaCo 95829 338-H7
PEBBLESTONE LN
- LNCN 95648 200-A2
PEBBLESTONE WY
1400 SAC 95833 277-C5
PEBBLE TRAIL CT
- SaCo 95826 298-F6
PEBBLEWOOD DR
1100 SAC 95833 277-B5
PECAN AV
5600 SaCo 95662 260-F3
5600 SaCo 95628 260-F6
PECAN CT
1700 OAKL 94561 (514-D6 See Page 493)
2700 RKLN 95677 220-E1
PECAN LN
1600 OAKL 94561 (514-D6 See Page 493)
PECAN RD
- SaCo 95837 255-H2
PECAN ST
400 WSAC 95691 296-G3
PECAN GROVE WY
2300 RCCD 95670 279-G7
PECAN RANCH CT
8900 SaCo 95662 260-F3
PECANWOOD WY
8400 SaCo 95662 260-C4
PECK DR
6800 SaCo 95828 318-B7
6800 SaCo 95828 338-B1
PECKY CEDAR CT
3400 SaCo 95827 299-B7
PECOR WY
9000 SaCo 95662 260-G5
PECOS DR
7700 SaCo 95683 341-F2
PECOS RIVER CT
11200 RCCD 95670 280-A4
PEDDLERS LN
600 FOLS 95630 261-B5
PEDERSEN WY
4600 SaCo 95608 279-F1
4600 SaCo 95628 279-F1
PEDRA DR
3000 EDCo 95762 262-E5
PEDRA DO SOL CT
10200 ELKG 95757 378-B2
PEDRA DO SOL WY
10200 ELKG 95757 378-B2
PEDRICK ST
- SAC 95823 337-J5
PEDRO WY
10600 RCCD 95670 299-G1
PEER RD
2200 PlaC 95650 201-A2
2200 PlaC 95663 201-A2
PEERLESS AV
7700 SaCo 95662 240-G7
7700 SaCo 95662 260-G1
PEETS ST
- ELKG 95758 357-F4
PEEVEY CT
7000 SaCo 95823 317-H7
PEGASUS CT
- RKLN 95677 220-H5
PEGASUS TR
- EDCo 95726 248-D3
PEGASUS WY
3200 RCCD 95827 299-D5
PEGGY LN
2200 EDCo 95762 242-D7
5100 SaCo 95608 279-B6
PEGLER CT
2800 WSAC 95691 316-F2
PEGLER WY
8000 SAC 95823 337-J5
PEKIN CT
- RSVL 95747 219-E1
PEKINS CT
2800 WSAC 95691 316-F1
PEKOE WY
7600 SaCo 95828 338-F4
PELARA CT
10900 RCCD 95670 299-J4
PELARA WY
10900 RCCD 95670 299-J4
PELHAM CT
200 RSVL 95747 219-E6
PELHAM WY
9200 ELKG 95624 358-J5
PELICAN CT
- SAC 95833 277-E4
PELICAN WY
600 SAC 95833 277-E5
PELICAN BAY CIR
100 SAC 95833 256-J3
PELKIE LN
4400 EDCo 95682 283-J1
PELL CIR
100 SAC 95838 277-F2
PELL DR
4000 SAC 95838 277-F1
4100 SAC 95838 257-F7
PELLANDINI RD
12100 SaCo 95632 418-J2
PELLEGRINO CT
- LNCN 95648 179-G6
PELLIGRINI CT
- SaCo 95829 338-H7
PELLY WY
- ELKG 95758 358-C6
PELTON PL
11500 SaCo 95670 280-B3
PEMBERTON LN
300 FOLS 95630 281-A2
PEMBERTON WY
1400 EDCo 95762 262-D3
PEMBRIDGE DR
- ELKG 95624 378-H2
PEMBROKE WY
- RKLN 95677 220-F6
6800 CITH 95621 259-F3
PEMBURY WY
100 FOLS 95630 261-F7
PENARANDA DR
100 FOLS 95630 261-E5
PENASCO CT
- SAC 95833 277-E5
PENBRIDGE DR
- SaCo 95662 240-G6
9800 PlaC 95746 240-G6
PENBROOK CT
9300 ELKG 95758 357-J5
PENDER ISLAND ST
- WSAC 95691 316-C2
PENDLETON DR
2400 EDCo 95762 262-C1
8500 PlaC 95746 241-D3
PENDLETON ST
3100 SAC 95815 278-B4
6700 SAC 95822 317-D7
PENDOLA DR
8300 SaCo 95628 280-C1
PENELA WY
- EDCo 95762 262-E7
PENELOPE CT
- RSVL 95678 219-G4
PENHURST WY
1400 RSVL 95747 219-D7
PENINSULA DR
- RKLN 95765 199-J5
PENINSULA WY
6600 ELKG 95758 358-B3
PENN CT
2200 SaCo 95825 278-F7
PENN RD
4000 EDCo 95667 265-D1
PENNEFEATHER CT
- LNCN 95648 200-B3
PENNEFEATHER LN
- LNCN 95648 200-B3
PENNELL CT
100 RSVL 95747 239-C1
PENNELOPE CT
3200 SaCo 95826 299-A7
PENNEY WY
6600 SaCo 95608 259-E7
PENNIMAN DR
- EDCo 95762 262-H5
PENNINGTON WY
7400 CITH 95610 259-J1
PENNLAND DR
2400 SaCo 95825 278-E7
PENNOCK CT
100 FOLS 95630 261-F5
PENNSYLVANIA AV
200 WSAC 95691 296-H6
4000 SaCo 95628 279-J1
4800 SaCo 95628 259-J7
PENNSYLVANIA CT
2000 WSAC 95691 296-H6
PENNY DR
2800 PLCR 95667 245-H4
PENNY LN
1900 PLCR 95667 246-B5
2700 PlaC 95648 180-D5
4400 EDCo 95672 243-H7
9000 PlaC 95746 241-B4
PENNYFOOT CT
8700 SaCo 95828 338-G6
PENNY HILL PL
9700 ELKG 95624 358-J7
PENNYROYAL DR
5500 EDCo 95726 267-H2
PENNYROYAL WY
6300 SaCo 95608 259-E7
PENNYWOOD CT
- SAC 95823 337-F3
PENROD CT
- FOLS 95630 281-E2
PENROD WY
- FOLS 95630 281-F2
PENROSE CT
100 FOLS 95630 261-J6
PENROSE ST
- SAC 95838 278-B2
PENRY SQ
200 FOLS 95630 261-H6
PENRYN PZ
- PlaC 95663 201-C2
PENRYN RD
2700 PlaC 95663 201-C2
2900 PlaC 95650 201-C5
PENRYN ESTATES DR
7300 PlaC 95663 201-C3
PENSHURST CT
4300 SaCo 95864 298-J4
PENSTEMON WY
- SAC 95823 338-B6
PENSTOCK TR
10700 PlaC 95603 182-B2
PENSTONE LP
- RSVL 95747 218-J6
PENTLAND CT
- FOLS 95630 281-J2
PENWITH WY
4300 SaCo 95660 258-J3
PENWOOD LN
100 FOLS 95630 261-H7
PENWOOD WY
9500 PlaC 95746 240-H5
PEONY CT
7300 CITH 95621 259-F2
PEORIA DR
6000 CITH 95621 259-G5
PEPITO WY
100 FOLS 95630 261-F4
PEPITONE CT
7900 SaCo 95828 338-D5
PEPPER LN
2400 EDCo 95682 264-A1
4700 SaCo 95841 279-A1
PEPPERCRESS CT
6900 CITH 95621 239-F7
PEPPERGRASS WY
2900 ELKG 95757 357-F7
2900 ELKG 95757 377-F1
2900 ELKG 95757 397-F1
PEPPERMILL CT
5600 SaCo 95608 259-C6
5600 SaCo 95841 259-C6
PEPPERMINT CT
8000 CITH 95610 260-A3
PEPPER OAKS DR
2800 SaCo 95827 299-A5
PEPPERRIDGE DR
- RSVL 95678 219-J5
3000 SaCo 95843 238-F5
PEPPER TREE CT
- RSVL 95747 219-B7
PEPPERTREE CT
- WSAC 95691 316-J1
2400 ANT 94509 (513-B6 See Page 493)
PEPPERTREE RD
- WSAC 95691 316-J1
- WSAC 95691 317-A1
PEPPERTREE WY
2100 ANT 94509 (513-C5 See Page 493)
8000 CITH 95621 239-E6
PEPPERWOOD CIR
12300 PlaC 95603 162-D5
PEPPERWOOD WY
6600 SaCo 95608 259-F7
PEPPERWOOD KNOLL LN
7200 SaCo 95842 258-J2
7200 SaCo 95842 259-A1
PEQUENO CT
15100 SaCo 95683 342-C2
PERA DR
6700 SaCo 95683 322-A7
6700 SaCo 95683 342-A1
PERALTA AV
300 SAC 95833 277-F6
PERAZUL CIR
- SAC 95835 256-J4
PERAZZO CIR
- FOLS 95630 261-H5
PERCELL WY
8500 ELKG 95624 358-H1
PERCEPTIVE WY
4900 SaCo 95842 259-A1
PERCH CT
2600 SaCo 95826 298-G6
6100 EDCo 95726 248-B6
PERCHERON CT
5800 RKLN 95677 220-H5
PERCHERON DR
4600 ELKG 95757 357-H7
PERCIVAL DR
3100 SaCo 95826 298-J7
PERDETA LN
- SaCo 95670 280-B3
PERDEZ CT
7700 CITH 95610 239-J7
PERDITA LN
- LNCN 95648 179-J7
- LNCN 95648 199-J1
- LNCN 95648 200-A1
PEREGRINE CT
- RKLN 95765 219-H1
PEREGRINE WY
8200 CITH 95610 240-B6
12000 AUB 95603 182-D6
PEREGRINE VIEW CT
9700 ELKG 95757 357-E7
PEREL CT
11100 RCCD 95670 300-A4
PERERA CIR
7300 SAC 95831 336-H2
PEREZ CT
2800 WSAC 95691 316-F2
PERFORMANCE DR
3900 SAC 95838 277-G3
PERICLES DR
11900 RCCD 95742 320-E2
PERIDOT CT
- SAC 95834 277-B3
300 RSVL 95678 219-J6
PERIDOT DR
2700 EDCo 95672 263-C2
5500 RKLN 95677 220-B3
PERIDOT ST
2000 RSVL 95678 219-J6
2000 RSVL 95678 220-A6
PERINA WY
4800 SaCo 95660 278-H1
PERINO CT
- LNCN 95648 179-E3
PERIWINKLE CIR
8600 ELKG 95624 358-H2
PERIWINKLE LN
- LNCN 95648 180-A5
2300 EDCo 95667 245-A4

STREET
Block City ZIP Pg-Grid

PERKINS CT
900 EDCo 95762 262-C4
PERKINS WY
200 AUB 95603 182-D5
500 SAC 95818 297-D7
1200 SAC 95818 317-C1
PERKINS STATION WY
100 FOLS 95630 281-B1
PERKS CT
- PlaC 95648 160-D7
6800 EDCo 95667 245-C7
6800 EDCo 95667 265-C1
PERKTEL ST
2800 SAC 95815 277-J5
PERLETT DR
3100 EDCo 95682 263-E3
PERMAR ST
7400 SAC 95822 337-D2
PERMENTER CT
5800 SaCo 95662 260-F5
PERRARA CT
- RSVL 95747 199-B7
PERRAUD CT
100 FOLS 95630 261-D4
PERRAUD DR
100 FOLS 95630 261-D4
PERRETTI CT
[illegible]
PERRIN WY
6300 SaCo 95608 279-E1
PERRIS CT
- WSAC 95691 316-D4
PERRY AV
4300 SAC 95820 317-H3
4300 SaCo 95820 317-H3
PERRY CT
100 FOLS 95630 261-A4
PERRY CREEK CT
4100 SaCo 95843 238-H5
PERRY CREEK RD
5100 EDCo 95684 286-H7
PERRYDISE LN
7300 PlaC 95650 221-C2
PERRYHILL DR
- EDCo 95667 266-G3
PERRYMAN WY
3000 SAC 95820 318-A1
PERRY RANCH RD
200 AUB 95603 182-A5
200 PlaC 95603 182-A5
PERSEUS WY
4200 RCCD 95742 320-D1
PERSHING AV
8500 SaCo 95628 260-D6
8700 SaCo 95662 260-F5
PERSIFER ST
100 FOLS 95630 261-B5
PERSIMMON AV
7400 SaCo 95823 337-J3
PERSIMMON LN
1100 EDCo 95667 245-A2
2300 PlaC 95658 201-J2
2300 PlaC 95658 202-A2
PERSIMMON TER
12000 AUB 95603 182-D1
12000 AUB 95603 162-D7
PERTH CT
- RSVL 95747 239-B1
PERTH WY
3000 SaCo 95608 279-E5
PERTH GLEN DR
5100 SaCo 95843 239-B5
PERUVIAN WY
10500 SaCo 95830 339-G5
PESCADERO LN
- SAC 95835 257-A4
PESCADO CIR
6900 SaCo 95683 342-B1
PESCARA PL
- EDCo 95762 262-G4
PESTANA DR
600 GALT 95632 439-E1
PESTLE CT
100 FOLS 95630 261-E6
PETALUMA CT
5900 SaCo 95841 259-C5
PETAR PL
2800 ANT 94509 (513-A6 See Page 493)
PETE POPOVICH CT
- SAC 95835 257-B4
PETER AV
4600 SaCo 95628 279-G2
PETER A MCCUEN BLVD
- RCCD 95655 299-F5
PETER ISLAND RD
- WSAC 95691 316-D2
PETERSBOROUGH WY
- RSVL 95747 219-C4
PETERSBURG CT
9200 ELKG 95758 357-G4
PETERSEN CT
600 EDCo 95619 265-E3
PETERS RANCH WY
- ELKG 95757 357-H7
PETITE CREEK CT
3600 PlaC 95661 240-E5
PETITE CREEK DR
8700 PlaC 95661 240-E6
8700 SaCo 95662 240-E6
PETITE CREEK WY
3600 PlaC 95661 240-E6
PETITE SIRAH WY
9000 SaCo 95829 338-H5
PETIT VERDOT CT
8000 SaCo 95829 338-H5
PETREL CT
- SAC 95834 276-J2
PETRI LN
800 GALT 95632 419-F5
2000 EDCo 95667 245-A3
PETRILLI CIR
- SAC 95822 316-J5
- SAC 95822 317-A5
PET ROCK RD
1700 EDCo 95667 244-D2
PETROSYAN LN
2900 SaCo 95608 279-D6
PETRUCHIO WY
- RSVL 95661 220-D6
PETTIGREW RD
3800 PlaC - 218-B1
PETTY LN
3100 SaCo 95608 279-B5
PETUNIA WY
8500 ELKG 95624 358-F1
PEWTER CT
- SAC 95834 277-B3

PEYCOS DR
- EDCo 95667 226-G2
PEYTON CT
9400 ELKG 95758 357-G5
PEYTONA WY
7300 SAC 95831 336-G2
PEZ GALLO PL
- SaCo 95670 280-B6
PEZ VELA PL
- SaCo 95670 280-B6
PFE RD
1000 PlaC 95747 239-A4
1000 RSVL 95747 239-E4
3400 PlaC 95747 238-G4
PHASIS CT
8200 SaCo 95626 238-C5
PHEASANT DR
100 GALT 95632 419-D6
PHEASANT LN
- RKLN 95765 200-C7
100 FOLS 95630 260-J4
100 PlaC 95658 181-F4
1500 EDCo 95762 282-G2
PHEASANT RD
7100 SaCo 95628 259-G7
PHEASANT RUN
1800 [illegible]
PHEASANT TR
9100 PlaC 95650 201-G6
PHEASANT WY
- LNCN 95648 179-E5
- PlaC 95648 179-E5
PHEASANT CALL PL
- PlaC 95746 240-J1
PHEASANT CLUB CT
8600 SaCo 95662 260-D2
PHEASANT DOWN WY
7600 SaCo 95828 338-G3
PHEASANT HILL CT
8500 SaCo 95662 260-D2
PHEASANT HOLLOW DR
- WSAC 95691 316-G1
PHEASANT HOLLOW PL
7500 CITH 95610 260-B1
PHEASANT KNOLL CT
4000 PlaC 95602 161-J1
PHEASANT RUN CT
- SaCo 95690 436-J1
PHEASANT WALK LN
7500 CITH 95610 260-B1
PHEBE CT
- RSVL 95661 220-E6
PHELPS CT
3100 WSAC 95691 316-F2
4900 SaCo 95608 299-A3
PHILLIP CT
800 EDCo 95762 262-C5
PHILLIP RD
- RSVL - 218-E1
- RSVL 95747 218-J4
- RSVL 95747 219-A4
4400 PlaC - 218-B1
PHILLIP ISLAND RD
- WSAC 95691 316-C3
PHILLIPS CT
700 PLCR 95667 245-F6
3300 SAC 95838 277-G4
PHILLIPS LN
1800 ANT 94509 (513-J5 See Page 493)
PHILOMENE CT
1300 SaCo 95608 299-A3
PHINNEY DR
8100 SAC 95823 337-G6
PHLOX CT
5600 SaCo 95842 259-C2
PHOEBE CT
300 LNCN 95648 180-B7
PHOEBE WY
8000 CITH 95610 240-C7
PHOENICIAN WY
9900 SaCo 95829 339-D4
PHOENIX AV
8500 SaCo 95628 260-D7
PHOENIX CIR
- LNCN 95648 179-F3
PHOENIX DR
- SaCo 95683 (321-F7 See Page 301)
- SaCo 95683 341-F1
PHOENIX LN
7600 CITH 95610 259-J1
PHOENIX EAST CT
5100 SaCo 95628 260-F7
PHOENIX PARK DR
7400 SAC 95823 337-G2
PHOENIX RIDGE PL
5200 SaCo 95628 260-F7
PHYLLIS AV
2500 SAC 95820 317-E3
PHYLLIS DR
- CITH 95621 259-F4
PHYLLIS LN
1100 AUB 95603 162-D5
PIANELLA WY
- ELKG 95757 378-A1
PIAZZA CT
- EDCo 95726 248-B1
9000 ELKG 95624 358-H1
PIAZZA PL
- EDCo 95762 262-B2
PIBROCK LN
9800 SaCo 95693 (380-G1 See Page 379)
PICADILLY CIR
800 SaCo 95864 299-A3
PICARDY CT
600 RSVL 95661 240-E4
PICASSO CIR
- SAC 95835 256-J4
PICASSO DR
- OAKL 94561 (514-H6 See Page 493)
PICASSO WY
- EDCo 95762 262-H4
100 FOLS 95630 261-J3
PICCADILLY CIR
- EDCo 95726 247-G6
PICCOLO CT
6100 SaCo 95621 239-E6
PICKERING LN
- LNCN 95648 179-E6
PICKERING WY
- SAC 95833 276-J6
- SAC 95833 277-A6
PICKET CT
- SAC 95823 358-A1
PICKET FENCE LN
- LNCN 95648 199-J1

PICKET FENCE LN
- LNCN 95648 200-A1
PICKFORD PL
6100 ELKG 95758 358-A3
PICKNEY CT
- PlaC 95746 240-G5
PICK N SHOVEL CT
10900 AUB 95603 182-C5
PICKOI CIR
7600 SaCo 95828 338-C2
PICKWICK CT
3500 SaCo 95608 279-B4
PICNIC CT
7300 CITH 95621 239-F7
PICO WY
400 SAC 95819 297-J5
PICO RIVERA DR
- RSVL 95747 199-B7
PICTOR CT
8100 SaCo 95828 338-E6
PICTURE WY
3400 SaCo 95826 299-A7
3400 SaCo 95826 319-A1
PICTURE ROCK CT
11200 SaCo 95670 280-B4
PIEDMONT DR
[illegible]
1000 SAC 95822 317-A3
3200 EDCo 95709 246-G4
PIEDMONT WY
1700 RSVL 95661 240-C5
PIEDRA CT
4400 RKLN 95677 220-D2
PIEDRA WY
8700 SaCo 95628 260-E6
PIEDRA MONTANA RD
3500 EDCo 95762 242-F3
PIEDRA VERDE ST
2600 EDCo 95667 244-C5
PIER PL
2900 RKLN 95765 200-B6
PIERCE CT
1400 EDCo 95667 245-J3
3200 ANT 94509 (513-C7 See Page 493)
PIERCE ST
1000 WSAC 95605 296-J1
PIERCY WY
2300 SAC 95838 278-C3
PIERMONT CT
900 GALT 95632 419-G3
PIERMONT WY
900 GALT 95632 419-G3
PIER POINT CIR
100 FOLS 95630 261-C1
PIERRE AV
2200 SAC 95832 337-D3
PIERROZ RD
400 PLCR 95667 245-C4
PIERSON CT
2900 PLCR 95667 245-G4
PIETRO LN
4400 SaCo 95864 298-J3
PIGEON CT
- LNCN 95648 200-B3
PIKE AV
3500 SAC 95834 277-F3
PIKES PEAK CIR
6300 EDCo 95633 205-B7
6300 EDCo 95633 225-B1
PIKES PEAK CT
- EDCo 95633 225-B1
PIKES PEAK WY
5800 CITH 95621 259-D2
5800 SaCo 95621 259-D2
5800 SaCo 95842 259-D2
PILGRIM CT
3200 SAC 95815 278-B4
PILGRIMS DR
1300 RSVL 95747 239-E1
PILKERTON CT
7800 CITH 95610 260-A2
PILLSBURY RD
- WSAC 95691 316-D4
PILOT CREEK CT
2100 SaCo 95670 280-E5
PILOT HILL CT
2000 SaCo 95670 280-B4
PILOT HOUSE WY
- SAC 95833 276-G7
PILOT PEAK RD
5100 EDCo 95630 202-J6
5100 EDCo 95630 222-J1
PILOT POINT RD
- WSAC 95691 316-D2
PILOT VIEW CT
4000 EDCo 95630 202-J6
PILOT VIEW DR
4800 EDCo 95630 202-J6
PIMA ST
- RKLN 95765 199-J5
PIMA WY
3900 SaCo 95843 238-H6
PIMENTEL WY
400 SAC 95831 336-G2
PIMIENTA DR
7400 CITH 95621 259-G1
PIMLICO AV
5300 SaCo 95841 259-B7
PIMLICO CT
- LNCN 95648 200-B3
PIMLICO LN
2000 EDCo 95667 243-H1
PIMPERNEL CT
100 RSVL 95747 219-A5
PINA AV
3000 EDCo 95709 246-G4
PINA ST
- SaCo 95828 338-F3
PINACHE CT
- SAC 95838 257-G7
PINAFORE CT
6000 SaCo 95842 259-A4
PINATA WY
9000 SaCo 95826 298-H7
PINCHEM LN
1900 EDCo 95672 243-F2
PINCHEM CREEK DR
3000 EDCo 95672 243-F3
PINCKNEY WY
300 SaCo 95655 319-H2
PINDAR CT
500 RSVL 95661 240-E1
PINDER CT
- FOLS 95630 281-F2
PINE AV
800 WSAC 95691 296-F4
4100 EDCo 95667 265-H3

PINE DR
7700 CITH 95610 239-J6
PINE GDNS
2200 SaCo 95825 298-C4
PINE LN
100 FOLS 95630 261-B1
PINE ST
- SaCo 95690 437-A1
100 AUB 95603 182-D2
400 GALT 95632 419-F7
3700 RKLN 95677 220-E7
7800 SaCo 95843 239-C7
W PINE ST
8600 SJCo 95686 (438-A3 See Page 418)
PINE ACRE CT
9800 ELKG 95624 359-C4
PINEACRE LN
- RCCD 95670 280-C7
PINE BARRENS WY
7900 SaCo 95829 339-D5
PINE BLUFF CT
4000 EDCo 95667 265-B1
PINE BLUFF LN
4000 EDCo 95667 265-A1
PINEBROOK DR
100 FOLS 95630 241-B7
PINEBROOK WY
5000 SaCo 95842 259-B4
6400 RKLN 95677 220-D5
PINEBURR CT
6500 SaCo 95662 260-B4
PINE CABIN WY
- RSVL 95747 219-B6
PINECONE CT
- EDCo 95667 226-J3
5500 SaCo 95841 259-C6
PINE CONE DR
3900 EDCo 95672 243-E7
6900 EDCo 95726 248-D4
PINECONE LN
4800 RSVL 95747 219-A6
PINE CONE RD
6700 PlaC 95746 221-E6
PINE COVE CT
8100 SaCo 95828 338-D6
PINE CREEK CT
2800 EDCo 95682 263-C3
PINECREEK CT
- RSVL 95747 219-B5
PINECREEK WY
6100 CITH 95621 259-E1
PINE CREST AV
100 AUB 95603 182-E4
PINECREST CIR
6500 SaCo 95608 279-E2
PINE CREST CT
4100 RKLN 95677 220-E4
PINECREST CT
- RSVL 95678 219-G4
1200 PLCR 95667 245-H4
PINEDALE AV
100 SAC 95838 257-G7
1100 SAC 95838 258-A7
PINEDROPS CT
6900 SaCo 95628 259-F7
PINEFIELD DR
8100 SaCo 95843 238-F6
PINE FOREST DR
4300 EDCo 95726 248-D4
PINE GATE WY
7000 PlaC 95746 221-D6
PINE GROVE WY
7200 FOLS 95630 261-B2
PINEGROVE WY
7200 FOLS 95630 261-B2
PINE HAVEN DR
- EDCo 95726 247-J2
PINE HEARST CT
400 RSVL 95747 219-D7
PINE HILL RD
200 PlaC 95603 162-G4
1900 EDCo 95672 243-D6
PINEHILL WY
3400 SaCo 95843 238-G5
PINE HOLLOW WY
3500 SaCo 95843 238-G5
PINEHURST DR
- PlaC 95747 239-A4
- RVIS 94571 454-F3
PINEHURST WY
- ELKG 95758 357-H2
PINE KNOB
- EDCo 95667 244-H2
PINELL ST
3600 SAC 95838 278-C1
PINELLA WY
10900 RCCD 95670 299-J4
PINE MEADOW CT
3600 SaCo 95660 258-G1
PINENEEDLE CT
500 RSVL 95747 219-B4
PINENEEDLE LN
6100 EDCo 95667 226-H2
PINENUT CT
2200 ANT 94509 (513-H6 See Page 493)
PINE NUT WY
4900 SAC 95838 257-J7
PINENUT WY
2200 ANT 94509 (513-H6 See Page 493)
PINE OAKS CT
8100 SaCo 95828 338-E6
PINEOAKYO CT
3900 EDCo 95672 243-D7
PINEOAKYO RD
2300 EDCo 95672 243-E7
2300 EDCo 95672 263-E1
PINE RIDGE CT
- RSVL 95661 220-F6
4100 EDCo 95682 264-B7
PINE RIDGE LN
3400 PlaC 95603 161-G4
PINERIDGE LN
4900 SaCo 95628 259-H7
7500 SaCo 95628 279-H1
PINE RIVER WY
8400 SAC 95823 337-J7
8400 SAC 95823 357-J1
PINEROSE CT
500 RSVL 95747 219-A4
PINESCHI PL
7200 RSVL 95747 219-A4
PINE TREE CIR
100 EDCo 95630 202-H2
PINE TREE CT
4100 EDCo 95630 202-H1

PINETREE CT
2100 RCCD 95670 279-H6
PINE TREE DR
- EDCo 95726 248-A6
PINE TREE LN
4900 EDCo 95726 248-A7
N PINE TREE LN
- EDCo 95726 248-A5
S PINE TREE LN
- EDCo 95726 248-A6
PINE VALLEY CIR
1500 RSVL 95661 240-B6
PINE VALLEY DR
7600 SaCo 95828 338-F4
PINE VIEW DR
7000 FOLS 95630 261-B2
PINE VISTA WY
5900 ELKG 95758 358-A5
PINEWOOD CT
4400 SaCo 95864 278-J7
PINEWOOD ST
4200 RKLN 95677 220-F4
PINE ZETTE LN
- EDCo - 267-H3
- EDCo 95726 267-H3
PINFIELD CT
9000 ELKG 95758 357-H3
PINION DR
1700 RSVL 95747 239-D1
PINIOS RIVER CT
- SAC 95831 336-F2
PINNACLE CT
3000 EDCo 95682 264-D3
PINNACLE BUTTE CT
100 FOLS 95630 241-A7
PINNACLES CIR
- SAC 95835 257-B7
PINNACLES DR
2200 RKLN 95677 220-B4
PIN OAK CT
6900 SaCo 95628 259-F6
PINON RD
2200 EDCo 95672 243-J7
PINON WY
7500 SAC 95823 337-G3
PINO ROBLE DR
- EDCo 95667 226-D4
PINOT CT
4600 OAKL 94561 (514-D7 See Page 493)
PINOT WY
10500 RCCD 95670 279-G7
10500 RCCD 95670 299-G1
PINOT BLANC CT
9900 ELKG 95624 379-A2
PINOT GOLD PL
9900 ELKG 95624 379-A1
PINOT NOIR WY
8000 SaCo 95829 338-H5
PINO VISTA CT
800 PLCR 95667 245-F5
PINTA CT
- EDCo 95726 247-E5
PINTADO CT
6900 SaCo 95628 259-F7
PINTAIL CIR
- FOLS 95630 281-E1
7500 CITH 95621 259-D1
PINTAIL CT
- EDCo 95762 263-B5
2700 WSAC 95691 316-F1
PINTAIL LN
400 PLCR 95667 245-B5
6000 CITH 95621 259-D1
PINTAIL WY
- LNCN 95648 179-D1
E PINTAIL WY
3000 ELKG 95757 357-F7
3000 ELKG 95757 377-F1
3000 ELKG 95757 397-F1
W PINTAIL WY
2600 ELKG 95757 357-E7
2700 ELKG 95757 377-E1
2700 ELKG 95757 397-E1
PINTO CT
- AUB 95603 182-C6
- RSVL 95678 219-H4
8200 SaCo 95843 238-F6
PINTO CANYON WY
- RSVL 95747 219-C2
PINTO RANCH CT
10000 ELKG 95624 379-A2
PINTO TRAIL DR
1000 GALT 95632 419-E2
PINTURO WY
2300 RCCD 95670 279-H7
PINYON PINE PL
8400 SaCo 95843 239-C5
PIONEER CT
- RKLN 95765 200-E3
- OAKL 94561 (514-E7 See Page 493)
PIONEER DR
100 FOLS 95630 261-F5
PIONEER LN
9000 PlaC 95650 221-G1
PIONEER RD
- RSVL 95678 219-H5
PIONEER WY
- RKLN 95765 200-D3
5800 SaCo 95841 259-B5
PIONEER HILL RD
3100 EDCo 95709 246-G7
4700 EDCo - 246-G7
PIPER CT
3100 EDCo 95762 263-D5
6700 CITH 95621 259-F1
PIPER LN
- EDCo 95634 205-J2
5400 OAKL 94561 (514-D5 See Page 493)
PIPER GLEN WY
8300 SaCo 95843 239-B5
PIPESTONE LN
- RSVL 95747 218-H3
PIPING ROCK DR
- SaCo 95829 339-D4
PIPIT WY
8400 ELKG 95757 357-F7
PIPPIN WY
6800 CITH 95621 259-F2
PIRAIEUS CT
4300 ELKG 95758 357-G4
PIRATE POINT CT
6100 ELKG 95758 358-A6
PISCES DR
3400 RCCD 95827 299-D6
PISMO BEACH DR
4700 SaCo 95843 239-A7

PISTACHIO CT
2800 ANT 94509 (513-H6 See Page 493)
PISTACHIO LN
- EDCo 95667 286-H3
- EDCo 95684 286-H3
PISTACHIO WY
- RSVL 95747 218-J4
10300 RCCD 95827 299-E5
PIT RD
- RSVL 95678 239-G2
PITA CT
5000 OAKL 94561 (514-D6 See Page 493)
PITALO WY
8400 CITH 95610 240-C7
PITCAIRN CT
- SAC 95823 337-J6
PITCHER CT
500 RSVL 95747 219-A5
PITON WY
2800 RKLN 95677 220-B5
PIT RIVER CT
11100 RCCD 95670 280-A5
[illegible]
6400 SaCo 95842 259-B4
PITTMAN LN
8800 SaCo 95662 260-F3
PITTSBURG-ANTIOCH HWY
1600 ANT 94509 (513-A4 See Page 493)
PITTSBURGH LN
4900 SaCo 95660 258-C3
PITTSFIELD WY
100 SaCo 95655 319-H2
PITZER CIR
2800 WSAC 95691 316-F2
PIUTE WY
- RKLN 95765 200-A5
PIVOT CT
- SAC 95823 338-A5
PIXCROFT CT
7500 SaCo 95842 259-B1
PIXFORD PL
- SAC 95835 256-G6
PIXIE CT
5300 SaCo 95608 279-B5
PIXLEY WY
8100 SaCo 95828 338-D6
PLACER BLVD
900 PlaC 95765 199-F6
PLACER LN
10300 RCCD 95827 299-F4
PLACER ST
100 RSVL 95678 239-H1
300 AUB 95603 182-D2
E PLACER ST
100 AUB 95603 182-E2
PLACERADO AV
100 AUB 95603 182-F3
PLACER CANYON PKWY
9200 PlaC 95650 221-G2
PLACER CORPORATE DR
- PlaC 95765 199-F6
PLACERGOLD CT
1900 SaCo 95670 280-B3
PLACER MINE RD
100 FOLS 95630 260-J4
PLACERVILLE DR
- PLCR 95667 245-C5
- EDCo 95667 245-C5
PLACERVILLE RD
- FOLS 95630 281-J2
- SaCo 95630 281-J2
- SaCo 95630 282-A4
PLACER WEST DR
6000 RKLN 95677 220-C5
6000 RSVL 95678 220-C5
PLACID CT
- SAC 95838 257-G7
PLACID LN
7000 EDCo 95682 283-J7
PLACITAS DR
3900 EDCo 95682 263-C7
PLAID CIR
7600 SaCo 95843 238-E7
PLAINOAK WY
- ELKG 95758 358-D5
PLAINS CT
200 GALT 95632 419-D7
PLAINSFIELD WY
3900 SaCo 95821 278-J3
PLANET PKWY
5000 SAC 95823 317-J7
PLANETA WY
1400 EDCo 95762 242-B4
PLANO CT
14700 SaCo 95683 342-A1
PLANT DR
5500 EDCo 95667 264-G5
PLANTAIN CIR
5400 SaCo 95662 260-H6
PLANTATION DR
4300 SaCo 95628 279-G1
PLATEAU CIR
- EDCo 95682 263-C4
PLATER CT
7500 SaCo 95823 337-J3
7500 SaCo 95823 338-A3
PLATINA CT
5700 SaCo 95842 259-C2
PLATINUM CT
2900 RCCD 95670 299-H2
PLATO CT
- PlaC 95648 199-F3
PLATT CIR
600 EDCo 95762 262-C7
600 EDCo 95762 282-C1
N PLATTE WY
- SAC 95835 256-J6
PLATTE RIVER CT
11200 RCCD 95670 280-A4
PLAYA WY
2300 SaCo 95670 280-C6
PLAYA DEL REY
- SaCo 95683 322-C6
PLAYERS CT
8700 ELKG 95624 358-G4
PLAZA AV
600 SAC 95815 277-H6
PLAZA DR
- RKLN 95765 220-A2
- FOLS 95630 281-B1
- FOLS 95630 261-B7
2400 EDCo 95667 245-B7
PLAZA WY
2000 PlaC 95603 162-B3

PLAZA GOLDORADO
4000 EDCo 95682 263-F7
PLAZA PARK DR
8900 ELKG 95624 358-G7
PLEASANT AV
100 AUB 95603 182-D3
PLEASANT DR
5000 SAC 95822 317-B3
PLEASANT PL
100 ANT 94509 (513-E4 See Page 493)
PLEASANT ST
100 RSVL 95678 239-G1
2000 PLCR 95667 245-G4
PLEASANT CREEK DR
- RKLN 95765 200-D4
PLEASANTGLEN WY
5100 ELKG 95758 357-H3
PLEASANT GROVE BLVD
- PlaC 95747 218-H5
- RKLN 95765 219-J3
- RSVL 95747 218-H5
1200 RSVL 95678 219-J3
1300 [illegible]
PLEASANT GROVE RD
1000 SuCo 95626 237-D1
8100 PlaC 95626 237-D1
PLEASANT GROVE SCHOOL RD
9900 ELKG 95624 359-D3
PLEASANT HILL RD
4000 PlaC 95602 161-A3
5600 EDCo 95630 202-J6
PLEASANT HILLS LN
3700 SaCo 95742 301-D6
3700 SaCo 95742 (321-D1 See Page 301)
PLEASANT OAK CT
- EDCo - 267-C2
- PlaC 95650 201-E4
PLEASANT OAK RD
- EDCo - 267-C2
PLEASANT RANCH CT
1700 EDCo 95667 243-J1
PLEASANT RANCH RD
3900 EDCo 95667 243-J2
3900 EDCo 95667 244-A1
PLEASANT VALLEY CT
- EDCo - 267-C4
PLEASANT VALLEY RD
3000 EDCo 95619 265-F3
3000 EDCo 95667 265-F3
3300 EDCo 95619 266-F4
3300 EDCo 95667 266-F4
4200 EDCo 95667 267-A3
4500 EDCo 95619 267-A3
5800 EDCo 95623 264-H4
6000 EDCo 95623 265-A4
PLEASANT VALLEY GRANGE RD
4700 EDCo 95667 267-A3
PLEASANT VIEW DR
13600 CITH 95610 260-B2
PLEASANT VIEW LN
3400 EDCo 95682 263-G6
PLEASANT VISTA
13100 PlaC 95603 162-F7
PLEASANT VISTA LN
- PlaC 95603 162-F7
PLEASURE LN
6900 SAC 95823 337-F1
PLEIDES AV
7600 CITH 95610 259-J6
PLIO CT
- EDCo 95762 262-B4
PLOVER CT
400 LNCN 95648 180-C7
PLOVER ST
2600 SAC 95815 278-B6
PLUBELL DR
- EDCo - 247-F1
PLUM LN
9100 PlaC 95658 181-G6
12500 SaCo 95693 360-G2
PLUMA CT
10900 RCCD 95670 279-J6
PLUMAS CT
4200 SaCo 95820 317-G3
PLUMAS LN
500 RSVL 95747 219-A6
PLUMBAGO CT
2600 RKLN 95677 220-C2
PLUMBAGO PL
2600 RKLN 95677 220-C2
PLUMBER WY
1400 RSVL 95678 220-C5
7000 SaCo 95660 258-H2
PLUM BLOSSOM CT
9000 SaCo 95662 260-F4
PLUM CANYON LN
- RSVL 95747 219-B3
PLUM CREEK CT
500 FOLS 95630 262-A6
600 FOLS 95630 261-J6
PLUME WY
6900 ELKG 95758 358-B5
PLUMERIA AV
8100 SaCo 95628 280-A1
PLUMGROVE WY
9100 SaCo 95826 318-J2
PLUMLEIGH AV
2800 ANT 94509 (513-D7 See Page 493)
PLUMLEY CT
4300 EDCo 95762 262-B3
PLUMMER LN
100 FOLS 95630 261-H6
PLUM TREE CT
6700 CITH 95610 260-A3
PLUM TREE LN
1100 PlaC 95663 180-J7
PLUMWOOD CT
8300 SaCo 95662 260-C4
PLUTO WY
6400 SaCo 95864 298-J1
PLYMOUTH CT
1300 RSVL 95747 219-E7
PLYMOUTH DR
3600 SaCo 95660 258-G2
PLYMOUTH LN
1400 ANT 94509 (513-F5 See Page 493)
PLYMOUTH ROCK LN
6200 CITH 95621 259-D4
POACHING LN
3500 EDCo 95672 263-G2
POCA LN
- SaCo 95608 279-B4

STREET
Block City ZIP Pg-Grid

POCAHONTAS WY
2000 RSVL 95747 239-E1
POCA MONTOYA DR
6800 PlaC 95746 221-A6
POCKET RD
6600 SAC 95831 316-F7
6900 SAC 95831 336-F1
8400 SAC 95831 337-A3
8900 SAC 95832 337-A3
POCKET MINE RD
2000 EDCo 95667 245-G1
POCO LN
- OAKL 94561 (514-B7 See Page 493)
POCO WY
4800 EDCo 95667 244-A4
POCO LOCO LN
- EDCo 95633 205-E4
POCONO CT
4200 SaCo 95628 280-E2
POESIA CT
6700 ELKG 95758 358-B3
POET SMITH DR
200 AUB 95603 182-D5
POETT PL
- CITH 95621 239-G6
POINDEXTER PL
5700 PlaC 95650 221-D4
POINT ARENA CT
8200 SaCo 95828 338-D7
POINT EAST DR
11200 SaCo 95742 280-A7
POINTER CT
- SAC 95823 337-G5
POINT LOBO CT
4300 ELKG 95758 357-G6
POINT LOMA WY
8100 SaCo 95828 338-F6
POINT PACIFIC LN
- ELKG 95758 357-F6
POINT PLEASANT RD
3000 SaCo 95757 397-G9
POINT PRIM CT
5000 SaCo 95608 279-A5
POINT REYES WY
2600 SaCo 95826 298-H6
POINT ROCK WY
11800 SaCo 95670 280-D4
POINT VIEW DR
1700 PLCR 95667 246-B4
POINT WEST CT
3300 EDCo 95682 263-C5
POINT WEST WY
- SAC 95815 298-A1
POIRIER WY
7400 SAC 95822 337-D2
POKE CT
- EDCo 95667 226-E2
POKER LN
5200 SaCo 95843 239-A7
E POKER LN
7800 SaCo 95843 239-C7
POKER FLAT DR
11500 SaCo 95670 280-C5
POKO LN
12900 SaCo 95632 419-E3
POKO DOBI LN
6600 EDCo 95667 265-D2
POLAR BEAR CIR
800 GALT 95632 419-F3
POLARIS DR
3300 RCCD 95827 299-D6
POLARIS ST
2800 EDCo 95726 248-C1
POLAR STAR ST
2500 RKLN 95677 220-C2
POLHEMUS DR
8900 ELKG 95624 358-G5
POLK CT
3100 ANT 94509 (513-A7 See Page 493)
POLK ST
4900 SaCo 95660 258-G7
4900 SaCo 95660 278-G1
POLLARD AV
8100 SaCo 95628 280-B2
POLLARD LN
500 EDCo 95619 265-E4
POLLEN WY
6900 CITH 95610 259-H2
POLLEY DR
2000 RSVL 95661 240-C4
POLLOCK AV
6300 EDCo 95623 265-B5
6300 EDCo 95726 248-C1
POLLY AV
9000 SaCo 95662 260-F3
POLMONT WY
- SaCo 95829 338-J5
POLO CT
4800 SaCo 95628 280-C1
POLO CROSSE AV
8100 SaCo 95829 339-F6
8300 ELKG 95624 339-F7
8300 ELKG 95829 339-F7
POLO RANCH PL
- PlaC 95746 220-F7
POLVADERA CT
- SAC 95831 336-H1
POMBAL CT
10100 ELKG 95757 378-B2
POMEGRANATE AV
5000 SAC 95823 337-J3
5300 SaCo 95823 337-J3
5700 SaCo 95823 338-A3
POMEROL LN
7500 CITH 95621 259-F1
POMEROY WY
7800 CITH 95610 259-J2
POMINE CT
100 FOLS 95630 261-F3
POMO CIR
4400 SaCo 95628 280-F2
POMO CT
- WSAC 95691 316-H2
3200 EDCo 95682 263-C3
POMONA WY
8300 SaCo 95628 280-B1
POMPANO PL
- SAC 95835 256-G4
POMPEI CT
7700 CITH 95621 239-E7
PONCHO CONDE CIR
7200 SaCo 95683 342-A2
PONCIA CT
- SAC 95823 337-J6
POND LN
9400 SaCo 95693 360-E6

POND PL
3700 PlaC 95602 161-G3
POND BROOK WY
- ELKG 95758 358-D4
PONDERAY LN
4700 SaCo 95841 278-J1
PONDERHILL WY
1400 EDCo 95619 265-J4
PONDEROCHA PL
- PlaC - 160-F3
PONDEROSA CT
- EDCo 95709 247-C4
100 FOLS 95630 261-F4
600 RSVL 95747 219-B4
PONDEROSA DR
1600 OAKL 94561 (514-D7 See Page 493)
PONDEROSA LN
2900 SAC 95815 277-G5
PONDEROSA RD
2200 EDCo 95672 243-J6
2400 EDCo 95682 243-J7
2400 EDCo 95682 263-J1
3600 EDCo 95682 264-A6
PONDEROSA WY
1700 OAKL 94561 (514-D7 See Page 493)
3100 ANT 94509 (513-A7 See Page 493)
4300 EDCo 95709 247-C4
PONDEROSA GROVE DR
3400 EDCo 95667 226-H4
PONDORADO RD
3200 EDCo 95709 246-H4
POND VIEW DR
- FOLS 95630 261-G5
POND VIEW LN
100 PlaC 95658 181-F4
PONI CT
6600 SaCo 95662 260-G3
PONTA DELGADO CT
- EDCo 95762 262-E7
PONTA DO SOL WY
6600 ELKG 95757 378-A3
PONTIAC CT
6900 SaCo 95828 318-B7
PONTICELLI WY
8400 CITH 95610 240-D7
PONY CT
8000 SaCo 95830 339-G6
PONY BOB CT
100 RSVL 95747 219-B5
PONY BROWN RD
16000 SaCo 95683 342-G6
PONY EXPRESS CT
5600 EDCo 95726 247-J2
5600 EDCo 95726 248-A2
PONY EXPRESS DR
3300 SAC 95834 277-D4
3400 SAC 95833 277-D4
PONY EXPRESS TR
4200 EDCo 95709 247-E3
4300 EDCo - 247-E3
5400 EDCo 95726 247-E3
5600 EDCo 95726 248-A1
PONY TAIL LN
3900 EDCo 95682 263-J7
3900 EDCo 95682 264-A7
PONY TRAIL WY
6900 SAC 95828 318-C7
PONZI CT
3400 RCCD 95670 299-J4
POODLE LN
3400 EDCo 95667 244-G7
POOHS PTH
- EDCo 95633 205-C7
POOLE DR
2900 RCCD 95827 299-D4
POOLHOUSE RD
- EDCo 95726 248-B2
POOR HILL RD
3800 EDCo 95667 265-A1
POP BECKER ST
- SAC 95835 257-C4
POPE AV
2600 SaCo 95821 278-E4
POPE CT
- RSVL 95747 219-D5
POPE ST
- PlaC 95626 237-E1
POPE VALLEY WY
- SaCo 95829 338-H5
POPLAR AV
- CITH 95621 239-G7
- CITH 95621 259-G1
400 WSAC 95691 296-H3
POPLAR BLVD
5100 SaCo 95660 258-G6
POPLAR CT
- PlaC 95746 240-F3
POPLAR DR
2400 ANT 94509 (513-C6 See Page 493)
POPLAR LN
100 LNCN 95648 179-G4
2800 EDCo 95667 245-D4
2800 PLCR 95667 245-D4
POPLAR ST
400 GALT 95632 419-E6
POPLAR BLUFF WY
8700 PlaC 95747 238-G4
8700 SaCo 95843 238-G4
POPLAR HOLLOW LN
9000 ELKG 95624 359-A4
POPO LN
- EDCo 95667 226-E7
POPPINTREE CT
- LNCN 95648 200-B3
POPPINTREE LN
- LNCN 95648 200-C2
POPPLETON WY
4000 SaCo 95608 279-F3
POPPY CIR
- RKLN 95765 199-J6
POPPY CT
- GALT 95632 419-F3
POPPY DR
- RKLN 95765 199-J6
- RKLN 95765 200-A6
POPPY LN
900 RSVL 95678 239-J3
POPPY RD
5400 EDCo 95726 267-J1
POPPY ST
- WSAC 95691 316-F2
POPPY WY
1200 ANT 94509 (513-B4 See Page 493)
7600 CITH 95610 239-H7

POPPYFIELD CT
- LNCN 95648 179-H5
POPPY FIELD DR
- RSVL 95661 220-D7
POPPYFIELD WY
8100 CITH 95610 260-B2
POPPY HILL RD
4100 PlaC 95648 180-F5
POPPY HILL WY
- SAC 95834 276-H3
POPPY HOLLOW CT
200 FOLS 95630 282-B2
POPPY HOUSE RD
- RVIS 94571 454-H4
POPPY RIDGE CT
- LMS 95650 220-J3
POPPY RIDGE RD
7500 ELKG 95757 378-C2
POPPYSEED LN
8500 ELKG 95624 359-G1
POQUITA ST
2800 SAC 95815 277-J5
POQUITO CT
- RSVL 95747 219-B4
POROS CT
4400 ELKG 95758 357-H4
PORT CT
1400 OAKL 94561 (514-D7 See Page 493)
E PORT DR
7700 SAC 95831 336-J3
7700 SAC 95831 337-A3
PORT PL
2800 RKLN 95765 200-C6
PORT ST
2100 WSAC 95691 296-G4
PORT WY
1500 OAKL 94561 (514-D7 See Page 493)
PORTA BELLA CT
- RSVL 95747 219-B1
PORTAGE WY
3200 SAC 95835 256-H5
PORTAGE RIVER CT
11100 RCCD 95670 279-J5
11100 RCCD 95670 280-A5
PORTAL LN
- LNCN 95648 180-A6
PORTER ASHTON CT
900 GALT 95632 419-F3
PORTELLO WY
- LNCN 95648 179-E4
PORTER CT
500 FOLS 95630 282-B1
500 FOLS 95630 262-B7
PORTER DR
100 RSVL 95678 239-F2
300 RSVL 95678 219-F7
3500 RKLN 95677 220-D3
PORTER LN
100 PlaC 95602 162-H2
PORTER RD
400 FOLS 95630 282-B1
PORTER ST
5100 RKLN 95677 220-D3
PORTER WY
2100 SaCo 95825 278-D7
PORTER RANCH CT
- EDCo 95633 205-E3
PORTER RANCH RD
5100 EDCo 95633 205-E2
PORT GIBSON CT
6300 CITH 95621 259-E4
PORT HAYWOOD WY
8600 SAC 95823 358-B1
PORT HENLEY CT
- SAC 95835 257-A5
PORTIA CT
5000 SaCo 95608 279-A5
PORTIA WY
- RSVL 95661 220-E6
PORTILLO CT
3000 EDCo 95682 263-C4
PORTINAO CIR
- SAC 95831 336-F1
PORTLAND AV
100 AUB 95603 182-E4
PORTLAND LN
- GALT 95632 419-G4
PORTLAW WY
9400 ELKG 95758 358-B6
PORTMARNOCK WY
- RSVL 95678 219-J5
PORTO CT
- SuCo 95837 236-C1
PORTO DR
100 FOLS 95630 261-F3
PORTO BELLA WY
9200 ELKG 95624 358-J6
PORTOBELLO PL
4000 EDCo 95762 262-D2
PORTOFINO DR
8900 ELKG 95758 357-G3
PORTOFINO OAK LN
- SaCo 95628 279-J3
- SaCo 95628 280-A3
PORTOLA CIR
5400 RKLN 95677 220-B3
PORTOLA ST
- WSAC 95691 296-H7
PORTOLA WY
2100 SAC 95818 297-D7
2100 SAC 95818 317-D1
2700 SAC 95817 317-D1
PORTO MONIZ WY
10100 ELKG 95757 378-A3
PORTO PINO WY
4700 SaCo 95843 239-A6
PORTO ROSA DR
9100 ELKG 95624 358-J5
PORTO SANTO CT
- SAC 95831 336-F1
PORTO VISTA CT
9200 ELKG 95624 358-J6
PORT PACIFIC LN
- ELKG 95758 357-F6
PORTRAIT WY
3000 SaCo 95826 298-J7
PORT ROYALE WY
8100 SAC 95823 337-J6
PORTSIDE CIR
600 RSVL 95678 239-F5
PORTSIDE LN
9500 ELKG 95758 357-G6
PORTSMOUTH AV
1600 WSAC 95691 296-J3
PORTSMOUTH DR
1900 EDCo 95762 242-C5
2900 RCCD 95670 299-F4

PORTSMOUTH ST
3400 RKLN 95765 220-B1
PORTUGAL WY
700 SAC 95831 336-H2
PORTWOOD CT
4300 SaCo 95826 319-A2
POSADA WY
9000 SaCo 95826 298-H7
POSADERA AV
8600 SaCo 95662 260-D3
POSEIDON CT
7300 CITH 95621 259-G4
POSEIDON LN
8100 RSVL 95661 240-E1
POSSUM CREEK LN
- EDCo 95619 266-E7
- EDCo 95667 266-E7
POST CT
5000 EDCo 95762 282-E2
POST RD
8200 SaCo 95628 280-B2
POST ST
4500 EDCo 95762 282-E1
POSTEN LN
- EDCo 95619 266-A5
POSTEN WY
6600 CITH 95621 239-F7
POST OAK LN
2400 SaCo 95825 278-D7
POTOMAC AV
400 SAC 95833 277-E5
POTOMAC LN
4100 SaCo 95660 258-H7
POTOMAC RIVER CT
2100 RCCD 95670 279-H5
POTRERO WY
1400 SAC 95822 317-C3
POTTER LN
3200 SaCo 95821 278-F4
POTTS CT
8700 SaCo 95662 260-E3
POULSON ST
8000 CITH 95610 260-A2
POUNDS AV
3900 SaCo 95821 278-H4
POURNELLE CT
- SaCo 95829 339-A6
POURNELLE WY
- SaCo 95829 339-A6
POVERTY RD
15000 SaCo 95690 436-A7
15200 SaCo 95690 456-A1
POVERTY HILL DR
800 PLCR 95667 245-G3
POW WY
4300 SAC 95820 317-E3
POWDER CT
4700 ELKG 95758 357-H5
POWDERHORN WY
1300 SAC 95834 277-C3
POWDERLY CT
100 FOLS 95630 261-F3
POWDER PASS CT
- RKLN 95765 219-J2
POWDER PASS DR
- RKLN 95765 219-J2
POWDER RIDGE DR
- RKLN 95765 219-J2
POWDER RIVER CT
11200 RCCD 95670 280-A5
POWELL PL
- WSAC 95691 296-J7
POWER CENTER DR
- FOLS 95630 281-G1
POWERHOUSE RD
- PlaC 95603 202-A1
- PlaC 95658 202-A1
9100 PlaC 95658 181-G7
9400 PlaC 95658 201-J1
POWER INN RD
3000 SAC 95826 318-D3
5500 SAC 95820 318-D3
5500 SAC 95824 318-D3
6300 SAC 95828 318-C7
6800 SaCo 95828 338-D2
6900 SaCo 95828 318-C7
6900 SAC 95828 338-D2
7600 SaCo 95624 338-C6
7700 ELKG 95624 338-C6
8500 ELKG 95624 358-D1
POWER LINE RD
5300 SaCo 95834 256-D7
5300 SaCo 95834 276-D1
5500 SaCo 95835 256-D4
5700 SaCo 95837 256-D4
6500 SaCo 95836 236-D2
6500 SaCo 95836 256-D4
6700 SuCo 95659 236-D2
POWERS CT
3600 EDCo 95762 262-C7
POWERS DR
400 EDCo 95762 262-C4
POWFOOT PL
100 EDCo 95762 262-G4
POWFOOT WY
2000 EDCo 95762 262-G4
POWLES CT
9800 PlaC 95661 239-H5
PRADERA CT
100 FOLS 95630 261-E3
PRADERA MESA DR
6800 SAC 95824 318-B6
PRADO CT
- SAC 95833 277-B4
PRADO VISTA
- LNCN 95648 200-E2
- SaCo 95683 322-C6
PRADO VISTA CT
2500 EDCo 95667 245-C3
PRADO VISTA RD
2400 EDCo 95667 245-C3
2500 PLCR 95667 245-C3
PRAIA CT
10300 ELKG 95757 378-B3
PRAIRE WOODS WY
- RSVL 95747 219-C2
PRAIRIE CIR
100 SAC 95828 318-C6
PRAIRIE CT
700 GALT 95632 419-H2
6800 PlaC 95663 181-B7
PRAIRIE CITY RD
1900 FOLS 95630 261-C7
1900 FOLS 95630 281-E6
2500 FOLS 95630 281-E6
2500 SaCo 95742 281-E6
PRAIRIE CREEK WY
7800 SAC 95823 337-H4

PRAIRIE DAWN WY
5500 ELKG 95757 357-J7
PRAIRIE DUNES WY
9900 SaCo 95829 339-D4
PRAIRIE FALCON CT
- EDCo 95762 263-B5
PRAIRIE FALCON DR
- EDCo 95762 263-B5
PRAIRIE FIELD DR
- SaCo 95829 339-E5
PRAIRIE HILLS CT
8100 SaCo 95843 238-G6
PRAIRIE ROSE PL
2000 SaCo 95670 280-C4
PRAIRIE SMOKE CT
- ELKG 95624 358-F1
PRAIRIE STAR CT
8200 SaCo 95829 339-D7
PRAIRIE TRAIL WY
8900 SaCo 95826 318-H2
PRAIRIE VIEW CT
- LNCN 95648 200-B1
PRAIRIE VIEW LN
- LNCN 95648 200-A1
PRAIRIEWOODS DR
8600 SaCo 95828 338-F4
PRALINE WY
7700 SAC 95758 358-C2
PRANCER CT
- RSVL 95678 219-J5
PRARIE LP
5200 EDCo 95667 244-B5
PRATT AV
7400 CITH 95621 259-H1
7400 CITH 95610 259-H1
PRATT ST
- RSVL 95678 239-H2
PRATTON LN
12600 SaCo 95632 419-J1
PRAZZO WY
6900 ELKG 95757 378-B1
PREAKNESS WY
8100 SaCo 95843 238-F6
PRECIOUS LN
1000 FOLS 95630 261-B6
PREDIAL WY
7100 SaCo 95842 259-A2
PREGO WY
1000 SAC 95834 277-D4
PREMIER WY
9200 SaCo 95826 299-A7
PRENTICT CT
- FOLS 95630 261-J6
PRENTISS DR
1600 RSVL 95747 219-C5
6500 SaCo 95823 317-J7
PRESBURY WY
- GALT 95632 419-H3
PRESCOTT AV
2500 EDCo 95667 245-H3
2500 PLCR 95667 245-H3
PRESCOTT CT
200 RSVL 95746 240-G4
PRESCOTT WY
7600 SAC 95823 337-J3
PRESERVATION WY
- SaCo 95827 319-B1
PRESIDENT AV
4100 SaCo 95660 258-H6
4100 SaCo 95842 258-H6
PRESIDENTIAL LN
6200 SAC 95828 318-A7
PRESIDIO RD
- WSAC 95691 296-H7
PRESIDIO ST
3500 SAC 95838 278-B3
PRESIDIO WY
1600 RSVL 95661 240-B5
PRESLEY LN
4000 EDCo 95682 263-J7
4000 EDCo 95682 283-J1
PRESSAC DR
9900 ELKG 95624 379-A1
PRESTIGE LN
300 RCCD 95670 280-A6
PRESTON CIR
- RKLN 95765 199-J7
- RKLN 95765 219-J1
PRESTON WY
- EDCo 95762 262-J5
8200 SaCo 95828 338-D6
PRESTWICK CT
- SAC 95833 277-C6
PRESTWICK DR
2600 RSVL 95661 240-E4
5000 EDCo 95762 242-C6
PRETENSE CT
4000 SaCo 95628 280-E3
PRETENTIOUS WY
4600 SaCo 95842 259-A2
PRETTY BUSH CT
5900 CITH 95621 259-D3
PRETTY GIRL CT
6400 CITH 95621 259-D4
PRETTY GOOD RD
- EDCo 95667 266-B4
PREWETT DR
300 FOLS 95630 261-G5
PRICE AV
- SaCo 95652 258-F5
PRICE CT
800 SAC 95815 277-J5
PRICE WY
100 FOLS 95630 261-C5
PRIDES CRSG
- CITH 95621 239-D5
PRIM CT
5500 SaCo 95820 317-H4
PRIMA CT
- EDCo 95762 282-D3
PRIMA DR
- EDCo 95762 282-D3
PRIMARY RD
- SaCo 95758 337-F7
PRIMASING AV
100 SaCo 95615 (396-D3 See Page 375)
PRIMA VERA
7700 SaCo 95828 338-C4
PRIME WY
8200 CITH 95610 260-B2
PRIMERA CT
9200 ELKG 95758 358-A4
PRIMM VALLEY CT
7800 SaCo 95829 339-D5
PRIMO WY
2700 SAC 95833 277-B5
PRIMOAK WY
8000 ELKG 95758 358-D5

PRIMROSE AV
- PlaC 95603 162-C6
PRIMROSE DR
4900 SaCo 95628 259-J6
4900 SaCo 95628 260-A7
5300 CITH 95610 259-J5
5300 CITH 95628 259-J6
PRIMROSE LN
- LNCN 95648 179-E2
9300 PlaC 95661 240-F5
PRIMROSE PTH
- EDCo 95667 264-J3
PRIMROSE WY
- SAC 95819 297-J4
PRINCE ST
7400 CITH 95610 259-H2
PRINCE HENRY DR
3000 SAC 95833 277-D5
PRINCE MARK CT
- EDCo 95762 262-B1
PRINCESS CT
- RKLN 95765 219-J1
7200 CITH 95621 259-G2
PRINCESS HELEN CT
- EDCo 95762 262-B1
PRINCETON CT
300 RSVL 95661 240-D3
2900 EDCo 95682 263-C3
PRINCETON DR
12600 PlaC 95603 162-D4
PRINCETON LN
2600 ANT 94509 (513-A6 See Page 493)
PRINCETON RD
- WSAC 95691 316-J1
PRINCETON ST
2400 SAC 95815 278-A7
PRINCETON REACH WY
6000 PlaC 95746 241-A3
PRINCEVILLE CIR
- SAC 95831 336-H1
PRINGLE AV
400 GALT 95632 419-E5
9800 SaCo 95632 419-B5
PRIOR RDG
5100 PlaC 95746 240-H6
PRIOR WY
8000 SaCo 95843 238-G6
PRISCILLA LN
5000 SaCo 95820 318-C4
5400 SAC 95824 318-C4
PRISON RD
- FOLS 95671 261-D3
PRISSER WY
100 FOLS 95630 261-C6
PRITCHARD AV
- SaCo 95837 236-B6
- SaCo 95837 256-C1
PRITCHARD RD
7200 SaCo 95828 338-E2
PRIVET LN
5300 ELKG 95758 357-H2
PRIVETT CT
- RSVL 95747 219-B7
PRO-AM CT
2300 SAC 95833 276-J6
PROCTOR AV
1800 WSAC 95691 296-H4
PRODPERINE LN
4300 SaCo 95827 319-B2
PRODPERINE PL
4400 SaCo 95827 319-B2
PRODUCT DR
4100 EDCo 95682 283-H2
PRODUCTION DR
4600 EDCo 95667 264-G5
PROFESSIONAL DR
1700 SaCo 95825 298-F1
1700 SaCo 95864 298-F1
1900 RSVL 95661 240-D2
3100 PlaC 95603 162-B4
3200 PlaC 95602 162-B4
PROFESSOR LN
- SaCo 95834 257-D7
- SaCo 95834 277-D1
PROGRESS CT
10900 RCCD 95670 299-J1
PROMENADE CIR
- SAC 95834 277-C2
PROMENADE CT
- RSVL 95678 219-H5
PROMENADE DR
- SaCo 95823 337-G4
PROMENADE LN
3200 EDCo 95667 246-B7
PROMENADE ST
- WSAC 95691 296-D7
- WSAC 95691 316-D1
PROMISE WY
- SAC 95835 257-B5
PROMONTORY WY
9100 SaCo 95628 260-G7
PROMONTORY POINT CT
100 EDCo 95762 242-A5
PROMONTORY POINT LN
2000 SaCo 95670 280-B4
PROMONTORY POINT RD
1200 EDCo 95762 242-B5
PRONGHORN CT
8500 CITH 95621 239-F5
PROPELLER CT
9000 SaCo 95628 280-F1
PROPELLER WY
9000 SaCo 95628 280-F1
PROPER CT
4800 SaCo 95842 259-A2
PROPITIOUS CT
4800 SaCo 95842 259-A2
PROSPECT CT
- OAKL 94561 (514-B7 See Page 493)
7800 PlaC 95746 241-C1
PROSPECT DR
4100 SaCo 95608 279-F2
PROSPECT LN
- EDCo 95633 205-C3
PROSPECT HILL DR
11500 SaCo 95670 280-C5
PROSPECT MOUNTAIN WY
- RKLN 95765 220-A2
PROSPECTOR CT
100 FOLS 95630 260-J4
PROSPECTOR RD
4100 PlaC 95650 201-H7
4100 PlaC 95650 221-H1
PROSPECT PARK DR
2700 RCCD 95670 299-H2

PROSPECT POINT DR
2300 RSVL 95747 239-D1
PROSPECTS WY
100 ANT 94509 (513-C3 See Page 493)
PROSPER RD
- SAC 95834 277-A2
PROSPERITY CT
7400 SaCo 95828 338-D2
PROSSER ST
- WSAC 95691 316-E4
PROST CT
- ELKG 95758 358-C6
PROTEUS CT
- RSVL 95661 220-D6
E PROUTY RD
13500 SJCo 95638 421-F5
PROVENCE CT
1300 ANT 94509 (513-F7 See Page 493)
PROVENCE LN
300 FOLS 95630 261-H6
PROVENCIAL CT
9900 ELKG 95624 378-H1
PROVIDENCE LN
8800 PlaC 95746 241-B3
PROVIDENCE WY
1200 RSVL 95747 219-E7
1200 RSVL 95747 239-E1
6200 SaCo 95660 258-H4
PROVINCETOWN WY
100 SaCo 95655 319-H1
PROVO WY
2700 SAC 95822 337-E2
PROW CT
800 SAC 95822 316-J4
PRUDHOE CT
9100 SaCo 95829 338-J7
PRUITT LN
5500 SaCo 95843 239-C6
PRUNELLA CT
- LNCN 95648 180-A5
PRY CT
5600 SaCo 95841 259-B6
PUCKERBRASH
5900 EDCo 95623 265-B4
PUEBLA WY
1300 RSVL 95747 239-E2
PUEBLO CT
6500 PlaC 95746 241-B4
PUEBLO ST
4100 SaCo 95608 279-B3
PUENTE WY
4100 SaCo 95864 298-H3
PUERTA DEL SOL
- EDCo - 247-D6
- EDCo 95726 247-D6
PUERTO DR
6000 SaCo 95683 322-C6
PUERTO PK
- SaCo 95683 322-B7
PUERTO RICO RD
- WSAC 95691 316-D2
PUFFER WY
100 FOLS 95630 260-J3
100 FOLS 95630 261-A3
PUFFIN CIR
- OAKL 94561 (514-H7 See Page 493)
PUFFIN CT
- RKLN 95765 219-H1
- SAC 95834 276-J3
PUKA WY
8000 SAC 95823 337-G5
PULLEN ST
800 RSVL 95678 220-A7
PULLMAN CT
- RKLN 95765 199-J4
PULLMAN DR
3600 SaCo 95827 299-B7
3700 SaCo 95827 319-B1
PULSAR CIR
- SAC 95822 337-E1
PUMA WY
4900 SaCo 95608 299-A1
PUMICE CT
- SAC 95823 337-F2
PUMPHOUSE RD
- YoCo 95612 356-F2
PURDUE CT
8400 SAC 95826 298-E7
PURDY LN
9000 PlaC 95746 241-B4
PURINTON DR
2300 SaCo 95821 278-D6
PURPLE FINCH CT
- ELKG 95757 358-A6
PURPLE LEAF CT
3200 EDCo 95682 283-H5
PURPLE MARLIN CT
- RKLN 95765 219-J1
PURPLE MARTIN CT
- EDCo 95682 263-B5
PURPLE MARTIN RD
- EDCo 95682 263-B5
- EDCo 95762 263-B5
PURPLE MARTIN WY
8900 ELKG 95758 357-J3
PURPLE SKIES CT
- ELKG 95624 359-B4
PURRINGTON CT
9100 SaCo 95829 338-J6
PURSLANE WY
6800 CITH 95621 239-F7
6800 CITH 95621 259-F1
PURVIS RD
- SaCo 95638 421-A1
PUTCIE LN
8400 CITH 95610 240-A6
8400 PlaC 95661 240-A6
PUTNAM ST
200 ANT 94509 (513-C7 See Page 493)
PUTNAM WY
7300 SAC 95822 337-C2
PUTTER CT
2300 RKLN 95677 220-B2
PUZZLEWOOD LN
4000 PlaC 95602 161-C3
PYE LN
12000 PlaC 95602 162-B1
PYLOS WY
4100 RCCD 95742 320-D1
PYRACANTHA CT
8400 SaCo 95662 260-C2
PYRACANTHA DR
5400 EDCo 95682 283-H3
PYRAMID CT
- RKLN 95765 200-D5

STREET
Block City ZIP Pg-Grid

PYRAMID CT
7000 EDCo 95633 205-B6
9300 PlaC 95746 240-H4
PYRAMID PL
- WSAC 95691 316-C4
PYRAMID WY
2200 SaCo 95821 278-C6
PYRAMID PEAK DR
5300 EDCo 95623 264-G5
PYRAMID VIEW LN
- EDCo 95634 225-G1
PYRENEES CT
- ELKG 95624 358-F3
PYRITE LN
2000 PlaC 95603 181-H1
PYRITE ST
- RSVL 95747 219-A7
- RSVL 95747 239-A1
PYRITES CT
- SaCo 95670 280-B6
PYRITES WY
11300 SaCo 95670 280-C5
PYTHIAN CT
700 PLCR 95667 245-F5
PYXIS CIR
11800 RCCD 95742 320-D3

Q

Q ST
100 SaCo 95673 257-F1
200 SAC 95814 297-C4
400 LNCN 95648 179-F3
1000 SaCo 95673 258-A1
2000 SAC 95816 297-E5
2500 SaCo 95660 258-E1
4600 SAC 95819 297-H6
6700 SAC 95819 298-B7
6700 SAC 95819 318-B1
QUAD CT
4700 SaCo 95628 279-J1
QUAD LN
2700 EDCo 95682 263-D7
QUADRA AV
200 SaCo 95673 257-G3
QUAIL CIR
1500 RSVL 95661 240-B3
QUAIL CT
- WSAC 95691 296-J7
800 LNCN 95648 179-F2
QUAIL DR
3200 PLCR 95667 245-H6
QUAIL LN
8800 PlaC 95746 240-G3
QUAIL RD
- WSAC 95691 296-J7
- WSAC 95691 316-J1
1400 PlaC 95648 160-H7
1400 PlaC 95648 180-H1
1500 EDCo 95667 244-H3
7100 SaCo 95628 259-G7
QUAIL TR
5000 EDCo 95682 283-J5
QUAIL WY
5500 EDCo 95684 286-E7
QUAIL BAR CT
11700 SaCo 95670 280-D4
QUAIL BROOK CIR
- ELKG 95624 358-H4
QUAIL COVE DR
- ELKG 95624 358-H4
QUAIL COVEY CT
200 LNCN 95648 180-B7
QUAIL CREEK CT
8900 SaCo 95628 280-F1
QUAIL CREST WY
- ELKG 95624 358-H4
QUAIL CROSSING LN
6600 PlaC 95746 221-B7
QUAIL ESTATES LN
8400 SaCo 95828 338-E6
QUAIL FALLS WY
11900 RCCD 95742 320-E3
QUAIL FEATHER WY
- ELKG 95624 358-H4
QUAIL GLEN CT
800 AUB 95603 162-E5
8900 SaCo 95628 280-F1
QUAIL HAVEN LN
3400 SaCo 95608 279-F5
QUAIL HILL CT
700 AUB 95603 162-E6
QUAIL HILL DR
9900 PlaC 95658 181-J6
10000 PlaC 95658 182-A7
QUAIL HILL WY
8900 SaCo 95628 280-F1
QUAIL HOLLOW CT
600 AUB 95603 162-E6
4600 SaCo 95628 280-F1
QUAIL HOLLOW DR
100 GALT 95632 419-D6
12600 AUB 95603 162-E6
QUAIL KNOLL CT
- ELKG 95624 358-H4
QUAIL LAKE CT
9100 PlaC 95650 221-G1
QUAIL LAKE DR
4400 PlaC 95650 221-G1
QUAIL LEAF CT
- ELKG 95624 358-H4
QUAIL MEADOW DR
12500 PlaC 95603 162-E6
12500 AUB 95603 162-E6
QUAIL MEADOW WY
4700 SaCo 95628 280-F1
QUAIL NEST PL
7500 CITH 95610 260-B1
QUAIL OAK WY
8600 SaCo 95662 260-D5
QUAIL OAKS DR
8300 PlaC 95746 240-F2
QUAIL PARK WY
7800 SaCo 95843 238-F7
QUAIL PEAK CT
8300 ELKG 95758 358-E5
QUAIL POINT PL
- SaCo 95608 279-D7
QUAIL RANCH CT
2100 SaCo 95626 238-C6
QUAIL RIDGE CT
- RSVL 95678 219-G7
8100 SaCo 95828 338-E6
QUAIL RIDGE EAST LN
1000 RSVL 95678 219-G6
QUAIL RIDGE WEST LN
1800 RSVL 95678 219-G7
QUAIL RUN CT
4000 PlaC 95602 161-J1

QUAIL RUN LN
6600 ELKG 95757 378-B2
QUAIL RUN RD
4800 EDCo 95682 244-A7
QUAIL RUN WY
8900 SaCo 95628 280-F1
QUAILS NEST CT
- RSVL 95747 219-D1
QUAILS NEST ST
- RSVL 95747 219-D2
QUAIL SONG CT
- ELKG 95624 358-H4
QUAIL SPRINGS LN
2000 PlaC 95603 162-B6
QUAIL SPRINGS WY
8300 SaCo 95829 339-D7
QUAIL TERRACE WY
- ELKG 95624 358-H4
QUAIL TRACK DR
1100 EDCo 95672 243-B2
QUAIL TREE CT
- ELKG 95624 358-H4
QUAIL VALLEY RD
5200 EDCo 95682 264-E5
QUAIL VISTA LN
7400 CITH 95610 260-B1
QUAIL WALK PL
8100 CITH 95610 260-C1
QUAIL WALK WY
- RVIS 94571 454-G2
QUAIL WOOD CT
300 FOLS 95630 282-B1
QUAILWOOD WY
7200 CITH 95610 260-D2
7200 CITH 95662 260-D2
QUAKER CT
400 RSVL 95747 219-E7
QUAKER RIDGE WY
7900 SaCo 95829 339-D5
QUALITY DR
3300 RCCD 95670 299-H3
QUAMASH WY
2900 EDCo 95682 263-B4
QUANAH WY
6600 SaCo 95662 260-C3
QUANE CT
- RKLN 95765 200-B6
QUANE RD
- RKLN 95765 200-B6
QUANTIVA CT
6600 PlaC 95746 221-F6
QUARRY CT
- EDCo 95667 266-A4
2700 RCCD 95670 299-J1
2700 RCCD 95670 300-A1
4000 LMS 95650 200-J7
QUARRY LN
7200 PlaC 95663 201-C2
QUARRY RD
1400 EDCo 95667 265-J3
1500 EDCo 95667 266-A3
QUARRY ST
3700 RKLN 95677 220-D3
QUARRY BANK CT
- PlaC 95747 239-A2
QUARRY RIDGE WY
- SaCo 95829 338-H7
QUARTER LN
4500 OAKL 94561 (514-C7 See Page 493)
QUARTER HORSE CT
9500 ELKG 95624 358-J6
QUARTER RANCH CT
9300 ELKG 95624 379-A2
QUARTZ AL
3000 PLCR 95667 245-F5
QUARTZ CT
- SAC 95823 337-F2
3300 RKLN 95677 220-D1
QUARTZ DR
1300 PlaC 95602 162-A2
QUARTZ LN
900 RSVL 95678 239-F1
QUARTZ WY
- PlaC 95603 162-B3
QUARTZ CREEK LN
1900 EDCo 95667 244-C2
QUARTZ HILL PL
2000 SaCo 95670 280-B4
QUARTZ HILL RD
- EDCo 95667 226-B7
QUARTZITE CIR
8300 PlaC 95746 240-H3
QUARTZ MINE RD
600 PlaC 95658 181-F1
QUARTZ MOUNTAIN DR
- PLCR 95667 245-G4
QUASAR CIR
- SAC 95822 337-E1
QUATE CT
4100 SaCo 95843 238-H7
QUATTRO PL
10300 PlaC 95603 182-A5
QUAY CT
- SAC 95831 316-H6
QUAYMAS CT
9500 ELKG 95624 358-H6
QUEBEC WY
600 SaCo 95673 257-H2
QUEBEC RIVER CT
11100 RCCD 95670 280-A5
QUEEN CT
6100 SaCo 95660 258-H4
QUEEN ANN CT
900 EDCo 95762 262-C2
QUEEN ELAINE CT
- EDCo 95762 262-B1
QUEEN MARY CT
800 EDCo 95762 262-C3
QUEEN OAK CT
9400 ELKG 95624 358-F6
QUEENS CT
1800 RSVL 95661 240-C3
QUEENS ARBOR DR
10800 RCCD 95670 299-H5
QUEENSBURY CT
9400 ELKG 95758 358-A6
QUEENSIDE CT
3900 SaCo 95660 258-H7
QUEENSLAND CT
- SaCo 95829 339-F6
QUEENSTON CT
3900 SaCo 95608 279-E3
QUEEN VICTORIA CT
800 EDCo 95762 262-C2
QUEENWOOD DR
2400 RCCD 95670 279-H7
2600 RCCD 95670 299-J1

QUERCUS RD
- EDCo 95630 222-A5
QUESADA WY
9300 SaCo 95826 298-J7
9300 SaCo 95826 299-A7
QUESNEL CIR
9300 ELKG 95758 358-C5
QUEST CT
- EDCo 95682 283-H1
QUESTA CT
- SAC 95833 277-E5
QUESTA MIRADA CT
- EDCo 247-F6
QUICK CT
5100 ELKG 95757 377-H3
5100 ELKG 95757 397-H3
QUICKSILVER DR
- RCCD 95742 300-G6
QUIESCENCE LN
6400 SaCo 95608 279-E3
QUIET PL
- PlaC 95602 160-J2
QUIET WY
900 SaCo 95673 257-J1
QUIET DAWN CT
8600 ELKG 95624 358-H2
QUIET HAVEN CT
- SaCo 95830 339-G7
QUIET KNOLLS DR
8000 SaCo 95843 238-H6
QUIET MEADOW CT
4100 SaCo 95628 280-F2
QUIET OAK LN
7300 CITH 95610 260-B1
QUIET STAR CT
- RSVL 95747 219-D3
QUIGGLE RD
11500 SaCo 95632 420-B4
11500 SaCo 95638 420-B4
QUIGLEY CT
4400 RCCD 95742 320-E2
QUINBY WY
7600 SAC 95823 337-H3
QUINCE LN
12600 SaCo 95693 360-H1
QUINCEWOOD CIR
6100 CITH 95621 239-E7
QUINCY AV
2000 SAC 95822 337-C2
QUINLAN CT
8900 ELKG 95624 378-G1
QUINN AV
1100 SAC 95818 297-C6
QUINN PL
7200 PlaC 95650 221-C4
QUINN WY
700 AUB 95603 182-C5
3600 SaCo 95660 258-G1
QUINTA CT
- SAC 95823 338-B4
QUINTANNA CT
9300 ELKG 95758 358-B5
QUINTER WY
- SAC 95835 256-J6
QUONSET DR
4900 SAC 95820 318-C4

R

R ST
100 SAC 95814 297-C4
200 LNCN 95648 179-F3
2000 SAC 95816 297-E5
3900 SAC 95819 297-H6
S R ST
100 LNCN 95648 179-F4
RABBIT HOLLOW WY
- ELKG 95757 358-A6
RABEN WY
3200 EDCo 95682 263-F4
RABENECK WY
5100 SaCo 95628 260-F7
RACCOON RD
- EDCo 95619 286-C1
RACCOON TR
- EDCo 95726 248-C2
RACE TRACK CIR
4700 RKLN 95677 220-F3
RACE TRACK RD
- SaCo 95690 436-H3
4200 RKLN 95677 220-F3
RACE TRACK ST
100 AUB 95603 182-C3
RACHEL CT
- RKLN 95765 200-A7
3400 LMS 95650 201-A5
RACHEL DR
700 GALT 95632 419-F4
RACHEL LN
6100 LMS 95650 201-A5
RACHEL WY
2100 SaCo 95608 279-B7
2100 SaCo 95608 299-B1
RACOON RUN
3000 EDCo 95682 263-H4
RACOON HOLLOW LN
1700 PlaC 95603 182-B1
RACQUET CT
9500 ELKG 95758 358-A6
12600 PlaC 95603 162-E5
RACQUET WY
4200 EDCo 95619 265-F2
RACQUET CLUB DR
1000 AUB 95603 162-E5
1000 PlaC 95603 162-E5
RADALYAC CT
- SaCo 95673 257-J2
RADCLIFFE CT
2600 SAC 95826 298-E7
RADCLIFFE WY
1500 PlaC 95603 162-D4
RADFORD ST
8300 CITH 95621 239-F6
RADHA DR
- SAC 95828 318-B6
RADIANCE CIR
6900 CITH 95621 259-D2
RADMERE DR
- ELKG 95757 358-B7
RAEANNE LN
100 FOLS 95630 260-H4
RAEBURN WY
1300 RSVL 95747 239-C1
RAEJIM LN
4300 EDCo 95682 283-J2
RAFAEL DR
200 SaCo 95626 237-F5
RAFFERTY AV
5600 SaCo 95652 258-F5

RAFFIA CT
8300 SaCo 95843 238-F5
RAFTERS LN
- EDCo 95667 225-E6
RAGSDALE CT
300 LNCN 95648 179-E3
RAGTIME CIR
- RCCD 95670 299-G4
RAHERE CT
5200 SaCo 95842 259-B1
RAIL CT
- SAC 95820 317-H3
RAILROAD AV
- SaCo 95690 436-J2
- SaCo 95690 437-A1
100 ANT 94509 (513-D5 See Page 493)
4900 RKLN 95677 220-E3
E RAILROAD AV
4000 SAC 95826 318-C2
W RAILROAD AV
3900 SAC 95820 318-C2
RAILROAD DR
1900 SAC 95815 277-F7
1900 SAC 95833 277-F7
1900 SAC 95833 297-F1
1900 SAC 95815 297-F1
RAILROAD ST
9000 ELKG 95624 358-H6
RAILWAY CIR
2300 SaCo 95670 280-B5
RAIL YARD SQ
- SaCo 95758 357-G1
RAIMER WY
5400 SaCo 95608 299-B2
RAINBOW AV
2200 SaCo 95821 278-D5
RAINBOW LN
7600 PlaC 95663 201-D1
9700 SaCo 95693 359-H7
RAINBOW TR
4800 EDCo 95726 248-C6
RAINBOW CREEK WY
9200 ELKG 95624 359-A5
RAINBOW FALLS WY
9300 ELKG 95624 359-A5
RAINBOW LAKES CT
100 FOLS 95630 261-A1
RAINBOW MINE CT
2000 SaCo 95670 280-E4
RAINBOW RIVER CT
11000 RCCD 95670 279-J6
RAINBOW TROUT CT
- RSVL 95747 219-D1
RAINBOW TROUT ST
- RSVL 95747 219-D1
RAINBOW VALLEY LN
100 PlaC 95658 181-A3
RAINDANCE DR
- RSVL 95747 218-H4
RAINDROP CT
- SAC 95823 358-A1
RAINER DR
- EDCo 95633 205-A4
RAINIER AL
- RSVL 95678 239-H2
RAINIER AV
6000 RKLN 95677 220-C4
RAINIER CT
300 RVIS 94571 454-G5
6400 RKLN 95677 220-C5
RAIN MEADOW LN
6300 CITH 95621 259-D4
RAINSONG CIR
3500 RCCD 95670 299-H5
RAIN TREE CT
- PlaC 95602 161-J2
RAINTREE CT
- RKLN 95765 200-D4
1200 RSVL 95661 240-A5
RAINTREE DR
7000 CITH 95621 259-G2
RAINWOOD CT
- SAC 95823 358-A1
RAITT CT
- FOLS 95630 281-G2
RALDINA CT
6800 SaCo 95608 279-F5
RALEIGH CT
- RSVL 95678 219-G3
RALEIGH WY
2500 EDCo 95762 242-C6
5000 SaCo 95608 279-A3
RALEY BLVD
4000 SAC 95838 278-B1
4500 SAC 95838 258-B7
RALEY CT
4000 WSAC 95691 296-C5
RALSTON LN
400 PlaC 95658 181-F4
RALSTON RD
2200 SaCo 95821 278-C6
RALSTON WY
5500 EDCo 95667 264-F3
RAMA CT
8100 SaCo 95829 338-H6
RAMADA WY
3300 EDCo 95682 263-H5
6800 SAC 95823 337-F1
RAMBLEOAK CIR
- SAC 95831 336-J2
RAMBLER WY
5200 SaCo 95841 259-B5
RAMBLETON WY
8200 SaCo 95843 238-J6
8200 SaCo 95843 239-A6
RAMBLEWOOD WY
8000 CITH 95621 239-E7
RAMBLING
5000 EDCo 95619 265-J7
5000 EDCo 95619 266-A7
RAMBLING DR
100 FOLS 95630 261-G4
RAMBLING T TR
1700 EDCo 95762 242-F4
RAMCO ST
- WSAC 95691 296-F7
- WSAC 95691 316-D1
RAMEL WY
4000 SaCo 95864 298-H4
RAMO CT
2200 RCCD 95670 279-H6
RAMON CT
100 GALT 95632 419-E6
700 EDCo 95762 242-C4
RAMON DR
- GALT 95632 419-D6
2300 SaCo 95825 298-D3

RAMONA AV
3000 SAC 95826 318-C1
RAMONA CT
- RKLN 95677 220-J2
- WSAC 95691 296-J7
RAMONA LN
7500 CITH 95610 259-H1
RAMONA ST
4200 SaCo 95628 280-B2
RAMONA VISTA WY
5100 SaCo 95608 299-B1
RAMOS CIR
3200 RCCD 95827 299-E4
RAMOS DR
- WSAC 95691 316-C1
RAMOS RD
- EDCo 95709 247-D1
RAMP WY
- SAC 95818 297-A6
RAMPART CT
3100 EDCo 95726 248-D1
RAMPART DR
1400 RSVL 95661 240-A4
5900 SaCo 95608 279-D1
RAMPTON CT
9300 SaCo 95829 339-A6
RAMSDELL CT
- ELKG 95757 358-B6
RAMSEY DR
3800 SaCo 95660 258-H2
RAMSEY PL
- EDCo 95762 262-J5
RAMSEY WY
- EDCo 95762 262-H4
RAMSGATE DR
8000 PlaC 95746 240-G1
RAMSGATE WY
3000 RCCD 95670 299-E4
RAMSTAD AV
5100 SaCo 95628 260-F7
RAMWOOD WY
8100 SaCo 95662 260-B3
RANCH AV
7400 CITH 95610 259-H5
W RANCH DR
8800 SaCo 95662 240-F6
RANCH RD
- EDCo 95619 266-C7
- EDCo 95667 266-D7
900 GALT 95632 439-F1
RANCH BLUFF WY
- EDCo 95762 282-D4
RANCHERIA CT
3000 EDCo 95682 264-B2
RANCHERIA DR
9300 SaCo 95693 359-J6
RANCHERIA RD
2700 EDCo 95682 264-B2
RANCHERO WY
5600 SaCo 95608 279-C7
RANCH GATE DR
- RCCD 95742 320-E4
RANCH HAND WY
- CITH 95621 259-E3
RANCH HOUSE CT
- PlaC 95603 162-A5
RANCH HOUSE WY
- CITH 95621 259-E3
RANCHITA WY
8400 SaCo 95628 280-C2
RANCHITO
2200 RCCD 95670 279-H6
RANCHLAND CT
- RSVL 95747 218-H3
RANCHLAND WY
- RSVL 95747 218-H3
RANCHO CIR
100 AUB 95603 182-D5
RANCHO CT
3300 EDCo 95667 245-D7
RANCHO DR
200 AUB 95603 182-D4
9000 ELKG 95624 358-H5
RANCHO RD
4200 EDCo 95682 283-G2
RANCHO ADOBE DR
6400 SAC 95828 318-B6
RANCHO BARCELONA CT
200 RSVL 95747 219-C4
RANCHO CAMPO CT
- SAC 95828 318-B7
RANCHO GAVIOTA CT
800 RSVL 95747 219-C5
RANCHO GRANDE CT
8900 ELKG 95624 358-G5
RANCHO GRANDE WY
6600 SAC 95828 318-B7
RANCHO LAGUNA DR
6500 ELKG 95758 358-A5
RANCHO LOBO CT
- SAC 95828 318-B7
RANCHO LOMA CT
- SAC 95828 318-B6
RANCHO LOS PAVOS LN
6800 PlaC 95746 221-B7
RANCHO MADERA WY
6500 SAC 95828 318-B7
RANCHO MIRAGE CT
7000 CITH 95621 259-F3
RANCHO MONTES DR
- EDCo 95684 286-C6
RANCHO PICO WY
6600 SAC 95828 318-B6
RANCHO PLAZA DR
6700 SAC 95828 318-B7
RANCHO RIO WY
3400 SAC 95834 277-E4
RANCHO ROBLE WY
800 SAC 95834 277-E3
RANCHO RYAN RD
300 SaCo 95673 257-G4
RANCHO SIERRA RD
3600 PlaC 95602 161-J3
RANCHO SILVA DR
3100 SAC 95833 277-D4
RANCHO TIERRA CT
3300 EDCo 95682 263-C5
RANCHO TORRE CT
- SAC 95828 318-B7
RANCHO VERDE CT
- SAC 95828 318-B7
RANCHO VERDE LN
7100 PlaC 95650 201-C6
RANCHO VISTA LN
- PlaC 95658 201-G2
RANCHO VISTA RD
1300 EDCo 95667 244-D1
RANCHO VISTA WY
3500 SAC 95834 277-E3

RANCH PARK WY
8700 ELKG 95624 358-G5
RANCH RIVER DR
7600 SaCo 95626 238-C7
RANCHVIEW CT
9000 ELKG 95624 359-D4
RANCH VIEW DR
- RKLN 95765 199-H3
RANCHWOOD CT
3600 SaCo 95628 280-D1
RAND LN
4300 SaCo 95864 298-J3
RAND RD
3800 PlaC 95602 161-H2
RAND WY
1000 RSVL 95678 239-F1
RANDALL CT
100 FOLS 95630 261-F3
RANDALL DR
100 FOLS 95630 261-E3
RANDALL ISLAND RD
11600 SaCo 95615 (396-G1 See Page 375)
RANDHURST WY
4200 SaCo 95628 280-D2
RANDOLPH AV
2700 SaCo 95608 279-D6
RANDOLPH CT
2100 ANT 94509 (513-A7 See Page 493)
RANDOLPH RD
- WSAC 95691 296-J6
11200 SaCo 95693 360-A6
RANDOM LN
3700 SaCo 95864 298-G1
RANDOM OAKS LN
4300 PlaC 95650 221-G1
RANDY ST
6400 SaCo 95673 257-G3
RANELLS CT
2300 SaCo 95608 279-D7
RANFORD CT
- GALT 95632 419-G3
RANFURLY DR
- ELKG 95758 358-C4
RANGE WY
800 GALT 95632 419-D7
RANGER WY
5900 SaCo 95608 279-D1
RANGEVIEW LN
- SaCo 95828 338-C5
RANGEVIEW RD
7500 SaCo 95828 338-C5
RANIER WY
6200 SaCo 95842 259-B4
RANKEN PL
3100 EDCo 95762 262-D3
RANSOM AV
2300 SaCo 95825 298-C3
RAPALLO PL
- EDCo 95762 262-G5
RAPHAEL DR
- EDCo 95762 262-G3
RAPID CT
5600 SaCo 95841 259-B6
RAPID RIVER CT
- SAC 95831 336-G2
RAPOZO CT
8400 SaCo 95843 238-G5
RAPP LN
5500 SaCo 95843 239-C6
RAPPAHANNOCK WY
6700 SaCo 95608 279-E2
RASCOMMON WY
2800 SaCo 95827 299-B5
RASHA CT
- SAC 95831 336-G3
RASHAWN DR
2400 RCCD 95670 279-J7
RASMUSSEN CIR
8300 SaCo 95626 238-D5
RASMUSSEN RD
7600 PlaC 95650 201-D6
RASPBERRY WY
- ELKG 95624 358-G1
RASSY WY
2100 SaCo 95821 278-C6
RATHBONE CIR
- FOLS 95630 281-F1
RATHMORE CT
7000 ELKG 95758 358-B6
RATTAN WY
8100 CITH 95621 239-F7
RATTLESNAKE RD
2600 PlaC 95603 202-A2
2800 PlaC 95658 202-A4
RATTLESNAKE BAR RD
4300 EDCo 95630 202-H3
4600 EDCo 95630 222-D4
5600 EDCo 95630 221-J7
RATY LN
- EDCo 95633 205-D1
RAU RD
10600 SaCo 95757 378-D5
RAVEN LN
- EDCo 95667 266-D3
RAVEN BROOK DR
1000 GALT 95632 439-E2
RAVENCREST WY
8000 CITH 95621 239-E6
RAVENDALE DR
- ELKG 95758 358-C5
RAVEN HILL WY
8700 SaCo 95843 238-F4
RAVENNA CT
- ELKG 95757 378-A1
RAVENNA WY
- RSVL 95747 199-B7
- RSVL 95747 219-B1
- EDCo 95762 242-A4
RAVENS WY
5700 RCCD 95670 299-D3
RAVENSHOE WY
1100 EDCo 95762 262-D4
RAVENSTONE WY
4700 SaCo 95842 259-A4
RAVENSWOOD CT
- OAKL 94561 (514-D5 See Page 493)
RAVENSWOOD LN
5700 SaCo 95608 279-C1
RAVENSWORTH PL
- PlaC 95747 239-A3
RAVENSWORTH WY
7700 SaCo 95843 239-C7
7700 SaCo 95843 259-C1
RAVENVIEW CT
- RKLN 95677 220-F1

RAVENWOOD AV
4300 SaCo 95821 278-J6
4400 SaCo 95608 279-A6
4400 SaCo 95821 279-A6
RAVENWOOD CT
- RSVL 95746 240-F5
900 ANT 94509 (513-C7 See Page 493)
RAVENWOOD LN
3500 EDCo 95682 283-B6
RAVINE CIR
300 RCCD 95670 280-C7
RAVINE CT
6700 PlaC 95658 181-C4
N RAVINE LN
5100 SaCo 95628 260-H7
S RAVINE LN
9200 SaCo 95628 260-H7
RAVINE CREEK WY
5400 ELKG 95758 357-J4
RAVINE VIEW DR
1100 RSVL 95661 240-A4
RAVINE VIEW LN
5300 SaCo 95628 260-G7
RAVINIA CT
8000 SaCo 95628 280-A3
RAWHIDE CT
3500 RKLN 95677 200-E6
RAWHIDE LN
8600 SaCo 95693 360-H1
9300 PlaC 95747 239-B4
RAWHIDE RD
3800 RKLN 95677 200-E7
4100 RKLN 95677 220-D1
RAWHIDE WY
9000 SaCo 95826 298-H6
RAWLEY WY
- ELKG 95757 358-B6
RAWLINGS CT
100 FOLS 95630 261-F4
RAWLINGS LN
- LNCN 95648 179-F6
N RAY RD
22500 SJCo 95242 (438-G7 See Page 418)
RAY ST
2300 SAC 95815 278-B7
RAYALL CT
3200 PlaC 95650 201-F5
RAYBEL AV
5700 SaCo 95841 259-C6
RAYCROFT WY
- ELKG 95757 358-B7
RAYFEN LN
9600 PlaC 95658 201-H2
RAY LAWYER DR
2800 PLCR 95667 245-C5
RAYMAR CT
- SAC 95835 257-B5
RAYMAR WY
- SAC 95835 257-B5
RAYMOND CT
5600 EDCo 95682 283-G5
RAYMOND LN
200 FOLS 95630 261-B1
RAYMOND WY
5800 SAC 95820 317-J2
5800 SAC 95820 318-A2
RAYMUS ST
- SaCo 95758 358-C1
RAYNEAL WY
4800 SaCo 95843 239-A5
RAYWOOD CT
6600 CITH 95610 259-H3
RE CIR
- SaCo 95758 337-F7
READING ST
- FOLS 95630 261-A5
READING WY
- RKLN 95765 200-B7
- RKLN 95765 220-B1
REAGAN CT
2800 ANT 94509 (513-A7 See Page 493)
REALI WY
- SaCo 95824 318-B6
REAMER ST
100 AUB 95603 182-E2
REAMS RD
400 PlaC 95658 181-E3
REARDON CT
600 RSVL 95678 239-F1
REARES LN
3000 SAC 95817 317-E1
REBA CT
6500 PlaC 95746 241-B1
10100 RCCD 95827 299-E5
REBA DR
5900 PlaC 95746 240-J1
5900 PlaC 95746 241-A1
REBA RD
12300 PlaC 95603 162-C4
REBANO CT
7300 SaCo 95683 342-C2
REBECCA CT
- RKLN 95765 200-D3
2000 RSVL 95661 240-C5
REBECCA WY
100 FOLS 95630 261-E4
3200 SaCo 95821 278-J5
REBEKAH CT
8200 SaCo 95829 338-J6
REBEL CIR
6200 CITH 95621 259-D4
REBEL RIDGE LN
- EDCo 95667 266-H2
RECREATION DR
100 AUB 95603 182-D4
RECTOR ST
700 PLCR 95667 245-F5
RECYCLE RD
- RCCD 95655 300-B5
- RCCD 95670 300-B5
RED RD
- EDCo 95633 205-D1
REDBAND PL
- SaCo 95829 339-F5
REDBANK WY
8300 SaCo 95829 339-A7
RED BARN CT
3400 SaCo 95827 299-B7
RED BERRY HILL LN
- EDCo 95633 205-E5
W RED BERRY HILL LN
- EDCo 95633 205-E5
RED BIRCH WY
6100 ELKG 95758 358-A3
RED BLOOM WY
- RSVL 95747 218-H4

STREET Block City ZIP Pg-Grid

RED BRICK LN
2400 EDCo 95667 245-E3
REDBRIDGE WY
1700 SAC 95832 337-C4
RED BROOK WY
2100 RCCD 95670 279-F7
REDBUD DR
2600 RKLN 95677 220-F2
RED BUD LN
7500 SaCo 95828 338-C3
REDBUD LN
4500 EDCo 95672 243-G5
REDBUD RD
7400 PlaC 95746 241-D3
REDBUD GROVE LN
5100 RSVL 95747 219-A5
REDBURN LN
10500 RCCD 95670 299-G2
RED CEDAR CIR
9700 RCCD 95827 299-C6
REDCLIFF DR
6200 SaCo 95841 259-C4
REDCLIFFE CT
- LNCN 95648 179-F7
- PlaC 95648 179-F7
REDCLIFFE LN
- LNCN 95648 179-F7
RED CLOUD LN
4000 EDCo 95630 202-J5
RED CLOVER WY
- LNCN 95648 179-D1
8600 ELKG 95624 358-E1
REDCOAT LN
3100 RCCD 95827 299-D5
RED CRESTED CT
- RSVL 95747 219-E2
RED CURRENT WY
9600 ELKG 95757 358-A6
RED DEER CT
3000 PlaC 95602 162-C1
RED DEER WY
4100 SAC 95823 337-G4
REDDICK CT
3400 EDCo 95762 262-C6
REDDICK WY
700 EDCo 95762 262-C6
REDDING AV
1800 SAC 95819 318-B2
2000 SAC 95820 318-B2
REDDING RD
- WSAC 95691 296-J7
REDDINGTON CT
100 FOLS 95630 281-C1
RED DOG LN
1200 AUB 95603 182-C6
RED DOG CREEK DR
9000 ELKG 95758 357-J3
RED EAGLE CT
3700 SaCo 95843 238-G7
RED ELK DR
9500 ELKG 95758 358-D5
RED FERN CT
- SaCo 95843 239-B6
REDFORD WY
- SaCo 95829 338-J6
RED FOX
1600 EDCo 95667 244-A1
RED FOX CT
- PlaC 95602 162-A1
RED FOX ST
- RSVL 95747 219-D1
RED FOX WY
8200 ELKG 95758 358-E5
REDGOLD WY
3500 SaCo 95826 299-A7
3500 SaCo 95826 319-A1
RED GULCH CT
11600 SaCo 95670 280-D4
RED HAWK CT
- RKLN 95765 200-D4
REDHAWK CT
- PlaC 95602 161-J2
RED HAWK LN
- AUB 95603 182-C1
RED HAWK WY
2900 SAC 95833 277-C5
REDHEAD CT
- RSVL 95747 219-E2
REDHEAD WY
4600 SaCo 95842 258-J2
4600 SaCo 95842 259-A2
RED HILL CT
11700 SaCo 95670 280-D4
RED JASPER WY
5500 SaCo 95843 239-C5
REDLANDS WY
8600 SaCo 95828 338-F4
RED LEAF CT
200 RSVL 95747 239-D1
RED LEAF WY
1200 LNCN 95648 180-A2
8900 SaCo 95826 318-H1
RED MAPLE WY
6800 CITH 95610 260-A3
REDMIRE WY
- RSVL 95747 218-H5
REDMONT
- RVIS 94571 454-F1
RED MOUNTAIN RD
1600 EDCo 95762 242-F6
RED OAK CT
- RSVL 95678 219-H5
200 FOLS 95630 281-A3
RED OAKS CT
8000 CITH 95621 239-G7
REDONDO AV
- SAC 95815 277-G5
REDONDO DR
- EDCo 95762 262-E6
REDONDO RD
- WSAC 95691 316-H1
RED PINE CT
8000 CITH 95610 260-A3
RED RAVINE RD
1100 PlaC 95658 181-F7
RED RIDGE CT
100 FOLS 95630 241-A7
RED RIVER CT
- SAC 95831 336-J1
RED ROBIN CT
- EDCo 95726 267-J3
RED ROBIN LN
- SAC 95821 278-C6
2100 SaCo 95821 278-C6
RED ROBIN RD
- EDCo - 267-H3
- EDCo 95726 267-H2
REDROCK CT
100 FOLS 95630 261-B3

RED ROCK LN
3200 EDCo 95682 264-B5
RED ROCK RD
- LNCN 95648 199-H1
RED RUBY WY
- SaCo 95843 238-H6
RED SATYR CT
8800 ELKG 95624 358-F3
RED SETTER CT
- RKLN 95765 199-J4
RED SETTER RD
- RKLN 95765 199-J4
RED SHACK LN
- EDCo 95667 245-B1
RED SHALE CT
100 FOLS 95630 240-J7
RED SHERRY LN
8100 SaCo 95628 260-C6
REDSKIN CT
6000 CITH 95621 259-D3
RED SPRUCE WY
9300 ELKG 95624 359-A7
RED SQUIRREL ST
- RSVL 95747 219-D1
RED STAR CT
2000 SaCo 95670 280-E4
REDSTONE CT
- PlaC 95746 240-G4
- RSVL 95746 240-G4
REDSTONE DR
9900 RCCD 95827 299-D6
REDWATER DR
8500 SaCo 95843 238-G5
RED WILLOW LN
5600 RSVL 95747 219-B5
RED WILLOW ST
7400 SAC 95832 337-C3
7500 SAC 95832 337-C3
REDWING CT
7300 SaCo 95662 260-E1
RED WOLF WY
- SaCo 95829 338-H5
REDWOOD AV
- SAC 95815 277-G6
2900 WSAC 95691 316-J1
REDWOOD DR
- RKLN 95765 219-G2
4300 OAKL 94561 (514-D7
See Page 493)
REDWOOD LN
- FOLS 95630 261-B1
800 EDCo 95762 262-C7
800 EDCo 95762 282-D1
8100 PlaC 95746 241-B2
REDWOOD WY
100 PlaC 95603 162-F7
REDWOOD BURL WY
5500 SaCo 95843 239-C5
REDWOOD GROVE WY
- ELKG 95624 358-G2
REECEMAR AV
8000 SaCo 95662 260-D5
REED AV
1600 WSAC 95605 296-F2
REED CT
8300 SAC 95826 298-E7
REED LN
800 PlaC 95602 162-G1
REEDLY WY
8100 SaCo 95828 338-D6
REEDSPORT CT
3600 SaCo 95826 319-A1
REEF CT
- SAC 95831 316-H7
1100 RSVL 95661 239-J4
REEL CIR
3500 SAC 95832 337-F4
REEM CT
- EDCo 95762 262-E1
REENEL WY
7700 SAC 95832 337-B4
REESE RD
7200 SaCo 95828 338-E2
REETEY AV
8600 SaCo 95662 260-D4
REEVES CT
300 LNCN 95648 179-E3
REEVES WY
100 FOLS 95630 261-H6
REFINED CT
7000 SaCo 95842 259-A2
REFINEMENT RD
- RCCD 95670 300-C5
REFLECTION RD
3500 EDCo 95682 263-J1
REFUGE HOLLOW WY
- SaCo 95830 339-G7
REGAL CT
- RKLN 95765 200-C6
4300 OAKL 94561 (514-A7
See Page 493)
7200 SaCo 95828 338-F2
REGAN CT
7000 CITH 95621 259-F2
REGAN HALL LN
5700 SaCo 95608 279-C1
REGARD WY
7100 SaCo 95842 259-A2
REGATTA DR
600 SAC 95833 277-E5
REGENCY CIR
600 SaCo 95864 299-A4
REGENCY CT
4800 EDCo 95762 242-C6
REGENCY DR
5000 RKLN 95677 220-H4
7200 CITH 95621 259-G4
REGENCY WY
1100 RSVL 95661 239-J4
REGENCY PARK CIR
- SaCo 95835 257-C4
REGENCY WOODS WY
7800 SaCo 95843 238-J7
REGENT CIR
- LNCN 95648 179-F6
REGENT RD
3800 SaCo 95821 278-G4
REGENT ST
300 WSAC 95691 296-H5
REGGIE WY
4000 SaCo 95608 279-B3
REGGINALD WY
600 SAC 95838 277-H2
REGINA ST
- RKLN 95765 199-J5
REGINA WY
2700 SAC 95818 297-C7
REGIS DR
500 SAC 95838 257-H7

REGLI WOODS CT
8500 CITH 95621 239-F5
REICHMUTH WY
6900 SAC 95831 317-A7
6900 SAC 95831 337-A1
7100 SAC 95831 336-J1
REID CT
- EDCo 95682 283-A1
REID WY
4800 SAC 95819 297-J4
4900 SAC 95819 298-A4
REIGL RD
10100 SaCo 95693 (380-D2
See Page 379)
REILLY CT
800 RSVL 95747 219-E6
REIMAN WY
- FOLS 95630 261-J7
REIMS WY
5200 SaCo 95842 259-B1
REINA CT
6300 CITH 95621 239-E7
REINDEER WY
7900 SAC 95823 337-G5
REINECKE CT
- LNCN 95648 200-C1
REINER WY
2500 SAC 95833 277-D6
REINHOLD ST
5600 SaCo 95628 260-B6
REINO
- SaCo 95683 322-C6
REINO PK
- SaCo 95683 322-C6
REISLING CT
- OAKL 94561 (514-D7
See Page 493)
REISLING WY
5400 CITH 95610 260-A6
REITH CT
- SaCo 95826 318-G1
REJECT RD
6100 EDCo 95623 264-J6
RELIABLE CT
5200 SaCo 95842 259-B2
RELIANCE CT
- SaCo 95829 339-F6
RELVAS CT
- FOLS 95630 261-J5
REMBRANDT CT
- EDCo 95762 262-J4
- OAKL 94561 (514-H7
See Page 493)
REMBRANT CT
8800 ELKG 95624 358-G3
REMINGTON AV
6000 SaCo 95608 259-D5
REMINGTON CT
300 RSVL 95661 240-C3
REMINGTON DR
100 FOLS 95630 261-E5
REMO WY
7000 SAC 95822 337-D1
REMUDA CT
- PlaC 95746 220-F6
5100 EDCo 95682 283-J2
RENAISSANCE CT
7600 CITH 95610 259-H2
RENAISSANCE WY
- EDCo 95762 262-J4
RENDHAM WY
- SaCo 95829 338-J7
RENDON CT
- ELKG 95624 358-D1
RENE AV
1300 SAC 95838 278-A2
2100 SAC 95652 278-C2
RENEE CT
2900 WSAC 95691 316-E1
RENEE ANN ST
9100 SaCo 95662 260-G5
RENFREW CT
7700 CITH 95610 259-J1
RENICK WY
3900 SaCo 95660 258-H7
RENISON LN
- LNCN 95648 179-F6
RENKE RD
13200 SaCo 95632 420-B5
RENNER ST
3900 SaCo 95608 279-G3
RENO LN
7600 CITH 95610 239-J7
RENOIR CT
- EDCo 95762 262-J4
- OAKL 94561 (514-H7
See Page 493)
8900 SaCo 95628 280-F2
RENOIR LN
- FOLS 95630 261-J3
RENPOINT CT
- RSVL 95661 220-F7
RENPOINT WY
- RSVL 95661 220-E7
1600 FOLS 95630 281-H1
RENSSELAER WY
8200 SAC 95826 318-D1
RENTON WY
7700 SaCo 95828 338-C3
RENWICK AV
2800 ELKG 95758 357-E4
RENWICK LN
2100 ANT 94509 (513-F6
See Page 493)
REPRESENTATIVE LN
6700 SAC 95828 318-A7
REPUBLIC CT
4000 SaCo 95660 258-H2
REQUA WY
6300 SaCo 95823 338-A2
RESCUE CT
5100 SaCo 95841 259-B6
RESCUE DR
800 EDCo 95672 243-C1
800 EDCo 95667 243-D1
RESCUE RD
700 EDCo 95672 243-E2
RESEARCH DR
3900 SAC 95838 277-G2
RESERVATION CT
5100 EDCo 95682 264-E2
RESERVATION RD
4700 EDCo 95682 264-E1
5100 EDCo 95667 264-E2
RESERVE DR
- RCCD 95670 299-G4
- RSVL 95678 220-A6
RESERVOIR CT
6100 PlaC 95746 241-A6

RESERVOIR DR
6300 PlaC 95746 241-A6
RESERVOIR RD
7600 SaCo 95837 255-J1
7600 SaCo 95837 256-A1
7600 SaCo 95837 235-H7
RESERVOIR ST
800 PLCR 95667 245-G5
RESLER WY
3300 EDCo 95682 263-H5
RESNICK WY
- SaCo 95829 339-A6
RESPETO CT
7300 SaCo 95683 342-C2
RESPONSE RD
1300 SAC 95815 298-A1
RESSWOODS CT
7700 SaCo 95828 338-C4
REST LN
3000 EDCo 95623 265-C4
RESTORATION CT
- SAC 95823 337-G2
RETA AV
7000 SAC 95820 318-B2
RETIREMENT LN
2500 EDCo 95667 245-A4
RETREAT LN
- EDCo 95726 248-D5
RETREAT WY
1300 RSVL 95747 219-D6
5300 SaCo 95608 280-B1
RETRIEVER WY
800 GALT 95632 419-D7
800 GALT 95632 439-D1
REUTER DR
700 WSAC 95605 297-A2
REUTER RANCH RD
- RSVL 95661 239-J4
REVEIL LN
4300 SaCo 95827 319-B2
REVEIL PL
4400 SaCo 95827 319-B2
REVELSTOK DR
5600 SaCo 95842 258-J5
5700 SaCo 95842 259-A5
REVELSTOKE CT
7000 EDCo 95633 205-A7
REVERE DR
1600 RSVL 95747 219-E7
REVERE ST
- SAC 95818 297-B6
REVOLUTION LN
6000 CITH 95621 259-D4
REX CT
- EDCo 95667 226-C1
4700 SAC 95822 317-A3
REXFORD CT
6200 PlaC 95746 241-A1
REXFORD WY
6400 SaCo 95608 259-E6
REXLEIGH CT
- SAC 95823 357-J1
REXLEIGH DR
- SAC 95823 357-J1
REYCRAFT DR
4500 SaCo 95841 278-H1
REYES CT
- SAC 95831 316-G6
REYMAN LN
3300 LMS 95650 200-H5
REYMOUTH AV
10400 RCCD 95670 299-F4
REYN OAKS WY
7100 SaCo 95842 259-B2
REYNOLDS LN
- EDCo 95709 247-C5
REYNOLDS WY
1700 SAC 95652 278-B1
1700 SAC 95838 278-B1
1700 SaCo 95652 278-B1
REYNOSA DR
14700 SaCo 95683 342-C2
REZZANO CT
- RSVL 95747 199-B7
REZZANO DR
- RSVL 95747 199-B7
RHAPSODY CT
3900 SaCo 95843 238-H6
RHINE CT
- OAKL 94561 (514-D7
See Page 493)
RHINE WY
900 OAKL 94561 (514-D7
See Page 493)
2400 SaCo 95626 238-D6
RHINE RIVER CT
11100 RCCD 95670 280-A5
RHINO RIDGE RD
3500 EDCo 95630 202-G6
RHOADES WY
100 FOLS 95630 261-F4
RHODA WY
2200 RCCD 95670 299-E1
RHODE ISLAND DR
5000 SaCo 95841 259-C7
RHODES AV
6700 EDCo 95667 265-B2
RHODES DR
100 PlaC 95603 162-G4
RHODIN LN
700 SAC 95814 297-C5
RHODORA CT
8200 SaCo 95662 260-C3
RHONDA WY
2800 SaCo 95821 278-F6
RHONE CT
4300 PlaC 95650 221-J1
RHONE RIVER DR
- ELKG 95624 379-A1
RHONE VALLEY WY
- ELKG 95624 379-A1
RIALTO CT
- EDCo 95762 262-J5
- SAC 95823 337-J7
RIATA CT
2400 EDCo 95682 263-B7
RIBBON LN
- EDCo 95667 265-B1
RIBIER WY
- EDCo 95682 263-E3
2500 RCCD 95670 299-G2
RICE AV
2500 WSAC 95691 296-G3
RICE CT
3100 PLCR 95667 245-H6
RICE LN
1300 RSVL 95678 219-G7
RICH LN
5500 SaCo 95843 239-C6

RICH ST
1000 WSAC 95605 296-J2
RICHARD AV
6400 EDCo 95667 244-G3
RICHARD CT
- EDCo 95762 282-D4
1700 LNCN 95648 179-F3
RICHARDS AV
- SaCo 95690 (416-E2
See Page 415)
RICHARDS BLVD
200 SAC 95814 297-C1
RICHARDS DR
- RSVL 95678 219-F6
RICHARDS LN
13500 PlaC 95603 162-F3
RICHARDSON CIR
3000 EDCo 95762 262-C3
RICHARDSON DR
2700 PlaC 95603 162-A5
2900 PlaC 95602 162-A1
RICH BAR CT
300 RSVL 95747 239-D1
RICHBOROUGH WY
9000 ELKG 95624 378-H2
RICH CREEK CT
8500 SaCo 95828 338-F4
RICHDALE WY
9500 SaCo 95662 260-J7
RICHER CT
700 EDCo 95619 265-F4
RICHERT LN
10800 ELKG 95624 339-H7
10800 ELKG 95624 359-H1
10800 SaCo 95624 359-H1
RICHEVE WY
6900 SaCo 95828 318-B7
6900 SaCo 95828 338-B1
RICHFIELD WY
1900 SAC 95832 337-D4
RICHFORD LN
- PlaC 95746 240-G5
RICH HILL DR
5800 SaCo 95662 260-G5
RICHION DR
7800 SAC 95823 338-A5
RICHLAND RD
- PlaC - 159-H4
RICHLANDS WY
6600 SAC 95823 358-B1
RICHLYN WY
- ELKG 95757 358-B6
RICHMAN WY
6900 SaCo 95828 318-B7
6900 SaCo 95828 338-B1
RICHMOND AV
- SaCo 95742 281-B4
RICHMOND ST
1700 SaCo 95825 298-F1
1700 SaCo 95864 298-F1
2000 SaCo 95825 278-F7
RICHON VISTA CT
5100 SaCo 95608 279-B3
RICHWOOD CT
4900 SaCo 95628 260-B7
RICKENBACKER ST
- SaCo 95655 299-E6
RICKENBACKER WY
2300 AUB 95602 162-D2
RICKETY RACK RD
5800 LMS 95650 221-B4
5800 PlaC 95650 221-B4
RICKEY DR
5600 SAC 95822 317-C5
RICKEY DICK LN
6500 SaCo 95608 279-E5
RICK HEINRICH CIR
100 SAC 95835 257-C4
RICK MARY CT
8400 SaCo 95628 260-C6
RICO CT
8900 SaCo 95662 260-F5
RIDDIO ST
5800 CITH 95610 259-J5
RIDDLE CT
2300 SaCo 95825 298-C3
RIDER CT
100 RSVL 95678 219-G7
W RIDGE
5000 SaCo 95660 258-F4
RIDGE CT
3100 PLCR 95667 245-H5
RIDGE DR
4000 PlaC 95650 201-E7
4500 EDCo 95682 264-D6
RIDGE RD
100 PlaC 95658 181-B3
RIDGE ST
3900 SaCo 95628 280-A3
RIDGE WY
100 AUB 95603 182-F3
8800 PlaC 95746 241-D3
RIDGE CREEK CT
- RSVL 95661 240-D1
6100 ELKG 95758 358-A3
RIDGE CREEK WY
- RSVL 95661 240-D1
RIDGECREST CT
2600 PLCR 95667 245-C4
7300 SaCo 95608 279-G4
RIDGECREST WY
1200 RSVL 95661 240-D5
9800 PlaC 95650 201-J7
RIDGEDALE CT
1300 RSVL 95661 240-D5
RIDGEFIELD AV
5300 SaCo 95608 279-B2
RIDGE GATE CT
- RKLN 95765 200-A6
RIDGEGATE WY
5100 SaCo 95628 260-A7
RIDGEGLEN WY
8000 SaCo 95628 260-A7
RIDGEGROVE WY
8000 SaCo 95628 260-A7
RIDGE HILL CT
8800 SaCo 95662 260-E4
RIDGELINE DR
3100 EDCo 95672 243-B7
RIDGELINE LN
4900 SaCo 95628 280-G1
4900 SaCo 95628 260-G7
RIDGELY CT
7900 SaCo 95628 260-A7
RIDGEMARK CT
- SAC 95831 336-H1
RIDGEMERE CIR
- RSVL 95747 218-J4

RIDGEMONT DR
7900 SaCo 95628 260-A7
RIDGEMORE CT
5800 SaCo 95662 260-H5
RIDGEPARK CT
4300 SaCo 95628 279-H2
RIDGE PARK DR
5500 LMS 95650 220-J5
5900 LMS 95650 221-A5
RIDGEPASS DR
2900 EDCo 95682 283-D1
RIDGEPOINT DR
5500 SaCo 95843 239-C5
RIDGE RIM CT
3400 SaCo 95843 238-G5
RIDGEROCK DR
9600 ELKG 95624 359-B7
RIDGERUN DR
1300 RSVL 95747 239-E1
RIDGESIDE CT
2400 RSVL 95661 240-E5
RIDGESIDE LN
9300 SaCo 95662 260-H5
RIDGE TOP CT
8100 SaCo 95628 260-B7
RIDGE TOP LN
- LNCN 95648 180-B7
- LNCN 95648 200-B1
RIDGETOP LN
- EDCo 95726 248-D1
RIDGEVALE WY
5200 SaCo 95628 260-A6
RIDGE VIEW CIR
100 RKLN 95677 220-E4
RIDGEVIEW CIR
1400 AUB 95603 182-B7
RIDGEVIEW CT
200 EDCo 95762 262-C5
6000 CITH 95621 259-E5
RIDGE VIEW DR
1800 RSVL 95661 240-C5
RIDGEVIEW DR
2900 EDCo 95762 262-C4
RIDGEVIEW LN
7300 PlaC 95663 181-C6
RIDGEVINE WY
5100 SaCo 95628 260-A7
RIDGE VISTA CT
5200 SaCo 95628 260-A7
RIDGEWAY CT
- EDCo - 247-H3
RIDGEWAY DR
1200 SAC 95822 317-B3
4200 EDCo 95726 248-D1
4900 EDCo - 247-J2
4900 EDCo 95726 247-J2
RIDGE WILLOW CT
7400 SaCo 95828 338-B3
RIDGEWOOD CT
2400 RKLN 95677 220-D5
3800 EDCo 95672 243-D3
RIDGEWOOD DR
1300 EDCo 95672 243-D3
3500 PlaC 95650 201-E5
E RIDGEWOOD DR
- EDCo 95667 266-F2
W RIDGEWOOD DR
- EDCo 95667 266-E2
RIDGEWOOD WY
3500 SaCo 95821 278-H4
RIDING CLUB LN
4000 SaCo 95864 298-H1
RIDING TRAIL DR
12700 SaCo 95693 360-H6
RIDLEY WY
6500 SaCo 95660 258-G3
RIEGO RD
- SuCo 95837 236-C1
2900 SuCo 95659 236-C1
2900 SuCo 95668 236-G1
3000 SuCo 95626 237-D1
3000 SuCo 95668 237-B1
RIESLING CT
- EDCo 95672 263-E2
RIESLING DR
100 RSVL 95747 239-F2
RIESLING WY
- EDCo 95667 266-E6
- EDCo 95672 263-E2
2500 RCCD 95670 299-H1
RIFFLE CT
2600 EDCo 95667 226-E3
RIFFLES LN
5000 EDCo 95726 248-C7
RIFLE CT
900 SaCo 95608 299-B3
RIFLE RIDGE DR
8200 SaCo 95626 238-C5
RIFTON CT
9400 ELKG 95758 358-C5
RIGADOON LN
3800 EDCo 95667 244-J7
3800 EDCo 95667 264-J1
RIGBY CT
600 RSVL 95747 219-E6
RIGEL CT
4500 EDCo 95682 264-B7
RIGGING CT
7500 CITH 95621 259-D1
RIGGINS CT
100 FOLS 95630 261-H3
RIGGS AV
- SAC 95835 257-B6
RIGHTWOOD WY
5500 SAC 95823 357-J1
5500 SAC 95823 337-J7
5600 SAC 95823 338-A7
RIGLER ST
4600 SaCo 95628 280-F1
RIGNEY CT
100 FOLS 95630 281-B1
RILEY CT
100 FOLS 95630 261-E7
RILEY LN
- LNCN 95648 179-F6
RILEY RD
10800 SaCo 95693 379-F5
11200 SaCo 95693 (399-F1
See Page 379)
11200 SaCo 95632 (399-F2
See Page 379)
RILEY ST
200 FOLS 95630 261-B5
RILEY ANTON WY
3900 RCCD 95742 300-E7
RILL CT
3300 RKLN 95765 220-B1
RIMFIRE DR
12700 SaCo 95693 360-J5

RIMFIRE DR
12900 SaCo 95693 (361-A5
See Page 341)
RIMINI CT
- ELKG 95757 378-A1
RIMINI WY
- EDCo 95762 262-G5
RIMMA WY
- RSVL 95661 240-C5
RIMMER AV
500 SAC 95834 277-F4
RIM ROCK CIR
- PlaC 95650 221-J2
RIMROCK CT
- EDCo 95619 266-D7
RIMROCK DR
7100 SaCo 95828 338-B1
RIMROCK RD
- EDCo 95619 266-D7
- EDCo 95667 266-E7
RIMSTONE PL
8400 SaCo 95843 239-B5
RIM VIEW CIR
10500 PlaC 95603 202-B1
RIMWOOD DR
4900 SaCo 95628 260-A7
RINALDO WY
900 SAC 95833 277-E5
RINCONADA DR
6500 CITH 95610 259-J3
RINCON VILLA
7600 SaCo 95828 338-C4
RINDA DR
10100 RCCD 95670 299-E1
RINETTI WY
- SaCo 95673 257-G3
RING DR
6200 SAC 95824 318-B6
6200 SAC 95828 318-B6
RING DOVE CT
8700 ELKG 95624 358-G2
RINGE CIR
9400 ELKG 95624 358-J5
RINGFORD CT
9500 SaCo 95829 339-A6
RINGGOLD ST
2600 SAC 95818 297-B6
RINGNECK CT
- RSVL 95747 219-E2
4600 SaCo 95842 259-A2
4700 EDCo 95682 283-H7
RINGNECK DR
- RSVL 95747 219-E2
RINGOLD RD
4500 EDCo 95619 265-G4
RINGTAIL LN
- EDCo 95667 244-F7
RINGWOOD RD
11800 SaCo 95693 360-D7
RIO CIR
15000 SaCo 95683 322-B7
RIO CT
3200 RKLN 95677 220-E2
7100 SaCo 95683 342-B1
RIO LN
1000 SAC 95822 317-A3
RIO ADELANTO CT
- SAC 95834 277-D3
RIO ALTA WY
- SAC 95834 277-D3
RIO BARCO WY
7700 SAC 95831 336-J4
7700 SAC 95831 337-A4
RIO BLANCO DR
6300 SaCo 95683 322-B7
RIO BONITO DR
6200 SaCo 95608 279-D7
RIO BRAVO CIR
2400 SaCo 95826 299-A5
2500 SaCo 95826 298-J5
RIO BRAZOS WY
9700 SuCo 95837 236-B2
RIO CAMINO
- SAC 95834 277-D3
RIO CAMINO ST
100 AUB 95603 182-F3
RIO CAMPO CT
- SAC 95834 277-D3
RIO CAVADO WY
6800 ELKG 95757 378-B3
RIO CIDADE WY
1000 SAC 95831 336-J4
1000 SAC 95831 337-A3
RIO COSUMNES CIR
9900 ELKG 95624 378-H1
RIO CRESTA WY
1200 SAC 95834 277-D3
RIO CUARTO CT
7000 CITH 95621 259-F3
RIO DEL ORO LN
200 SaCo 95825 298-D5
RIO DEL RAY
- AUB 95603 182-E3
RIO DE ONAR WY
6300 ELKG 95757 378-A3
RIO DE ORO
2500 SAC 95826 298-E7
RIO ENCANTO CT
100 RSVL 95747 219-C4
RIO ESTRADA WY
7700 SAC 95831 336-J4
7700 SAC 95831 337-A4
RIO GRANDE CT
1200 ANT 94509 (513-B7
See Page 493)
9800 SuCo 95837 236-B2
RIO GRANDE DR
2000 ANT 94509 (513-B6
See Page 493)
5600 SuCo 95837 236-B2
RIO GRANDE WY
9000 SaCo 95826 298-J6
RIOJO WY
3500 RCCD 95670 299-J5
RIO LARGO WY
- SAC 95834 277-D3
RIO LINDA BLVD
800 SAC 95815 277-J6
3200 SAC 95838 277-J2
4600 SAC 95838 257-H6
5100 SaCo 95673 257-H4
5200 SaCo 95838 257-H4
7300 SaCo 95673 237-G7
7400 SaCo 95626 237-F4
RIO LOMA WY
3500 SAC 95834 277-D3
RIOLO RANCH WY
- SaCo 95843 239-C6

STREET Block City ZIP Pg-Grid

RIO MESA CT
200 GALT 95632 419-D7
RIO MESA WY
100 GALT 95632 419-D7
RIO MONDEGO DR
7500 SAC 95831 336-J2
7500 SAC 95831 337-A3
RIO MONTE CT
4200 SaCo 95608 279-F2
RIO NORTE WY
1000 SAC 95834 277-D3
RIO OSO DR
6300 SaCo 95683 322-C7
RIO PACIFICA WY
3500 SAC 95834 277-D3
RIO PORTO CT
- SAC 95831 337-A4
RIO RAMAZA DR
9700 SuCo 95659 236-B2
9700 SuCo 95837 236-B2
RIO ROCA CT
3300 SaCo 95843 238-F5
RIO ROSA WY
3500 SAC 95834 277-D3
RIO ROYAL WY
1100 SAC 95834 277-D3
RIO TAMEGA DR
7000 ELKG 95757 378-B3
RIO TEJO WY
6600 ELKG 95757 378-A3
RIO TIERRA AV
600 SAC 95833 277-E4
RIO TIERRA CT
1300 EDCo 95667 244-A2
RIO TINTO AV
4200 SaCo 95821 278-J3
RIO VERDE WY
5600 SaCo 95660 258-H5
RIO VISTA AV
4300 SaCo 95821 278-J3
RIO VISTA BRDG Rt#-12
- SaCo - 454-J5
RIO VISTA CT
9900 SuCo 95837 236-C1
RIO VISTA DR
300 PlaC 95603 162-F5
9700 SuCo 95837 236-B2
RIO VISTA WY
- EDCo 95667 226-F6
RIPARIAN DR
- ELKG 95757 357-E6
RIPLEY ST
3600 SAC 95838 278-C4
RIPON CT
2700 SAC 95826 298-E7
RIPPEY RD
2200 PlaC 95650 201-B3
2200 PlaC 95663 201-C2
2900 LMS 95650 201-A4
RIPPLE CT
- SAC 95831 316-G6
RIPPLEWOOD CT
7500 CITH 95621 259-H1
RIPPLING WY
6400 RKLN 95677 220-C5
RIPTIDE WY
6600 SAC 95831 316-G7
RIQUEZA CT
- ELKG 95757 378-B2
RISATA WY
6700 ELKG 95758 358-B3
RISING RD
- SaCo 95693 381-B1
11600 SaCo 95693 (380-D1 See Page 379)
RISING CREEK WY
9200 ELKG 95624 359-A5
RISING HILL CT
3000 EDCo 95667 245-A4
RISING HILL RD
2200 EDCo 95667 245-A4
2400 EDCo 95667 244-J3
W RISING HILL RD
1200 EDCo 95667 245-A4
RISING MIST WY
- RSVL 95747 219-D3
RISING OAKS CT
4100 SaCo 95628 280-F3
RISING STAR PL
11600 SaCo 95670 280-C5
RISING SUN WY
11900 SaCo 95670 280-E4
RISKE LN
800 WSAC 95691 297-A4
RISLEY CT
5000 SaCo 95842 259-B2
RISLEY PL
8800 PlaC 95746 241-A3
RITA AV
5200 SaCo 95608 279-B4
RITA LOU WY
6100 CITH 95610 259-H4
RITCHIE ST
2100 FOLS 95630 262-A6
RITTER CT
4700 SaCo 95608 279-E1
RITZ RD
5700 EDCo 95726 248-A2
N RITZ RD
26200 SJCo 95220 439-F3
RITZ WY
5500 SaCo 95628 260-D6
RIVA DR
- WSAC 95691 297-A7
RIVAGE CIR
100 FOLS 95630 261-H3
RIVAGE WY
9600 ELKG 95624 359-B7
RIVALO WY
8200 SaCo 95829 339-A7
RIVARA CIR
1100 SaCo 95864 298-E3
RIVA RIDGE CT
1000 RSVL 95661 240-A5
RIVA RIDGE DR
3800 SaCo 95628 280-E2
RIVENDALE RD
- EDCo - 267-F4
- EDCo 95726 267-F3
RIVENDELL LN
400 PlaC 95603 182-B2
8700 SaCo 95628 280-E1
RIVER DR
3900 SaCo 95628 279-J3
3900 SaCo 95628 280-A3
W RIVER DR
- SAC 95833 296-G1
3600 SAC 95833 276-H6

RIVER RD
- SaCo 95615 (396-C4 See Page 375)
- SaCo 95615 (416-D1 See Page 415)
- SaCo 95690 (416-G3 See Page 415)
RIVER RD Rt#-E13
13500 SaCo 95690 (416-H5 See Page 415)
13500 SaCo 95690 417-A6
13700 SaCo 95690 437-A1
RIVER RD Rt#-J11
- SaCo 95690 436-J2
- SaCo 95690 437-A1
RIVER RD Rt#-84
- RVIS 94571 455-A7
- RVIS 94571 454-J5
RIVER RD Rt#-160
- SaCo 95615 (376-J5 See Page 375)
- SaCo 95615 (396-G1 See Page 375)
- SaCo 95639 357-A6
- SaCo 95639 (376-J3 See Page 375)
- SaCo 95639 377-A2
- SaCo 95639 397-A2
- SaCo 95832 337-C7
- SaCo 95832 356-H3
- SaCo 95832 357-A3
S RIVER RD
4300 WSAC 95691 316-E7
4900 YoCo 95612 336-H4
4900 YoCo 95691 316-E7
4900 YoCo 95691 336-F2
12600 YoCo 95612 337-A4
S RIVER RD Rt#-E9
28800 YoCo 95612 337-B7
28800 YoCo 95612 356-H3
28800 YoCo 95612 357-B2
42900 YoCo 95612 (376-J2 See Page 375)
42900 YoCo 95612 377-A2
42900 YoCo 95612 397-A2
50200 YoCo 95612 (396-F1 See Page 375)
RIVER WY
900 FOLS 95630 261-A5
RIVERA DR
900 SAC 95838 277-J4
1200 SAC 95838 278-A4
RIVER ACRES DR
- SAC 95831 336-F1
RIVER BANK CT
- PlaC 95747 239-B4
RIVERBANK PL
- SaCo 95608 279-D7
RIVERBANK RD
1000 WSAC 95605 276-H7
1000 WSAC 95605 296-G1
RIVERBELLE CT
6200 SaCo 95673 257-H4
RIVER BEND CIR
300 SAC 95818 297-A7
RIVER BEND CT
1100 FOLS 95630 260-J4
RIVERBEND DR
- EDCo 95667 225-C5
RIVER BIRCH PL
5700 SaCo 95843 239-C5
RIVER BLUFF LN
- SaCo 95608 279-D7
RIVERBOAT WY
6900 SAC 95831 316-G7
7000 SAC 95831 336-G1
RIVERBREA CT
- SAC 95831 336-J1
RIVER BROOK CT
3400 SaCo 95827 299-B6
RIVERBROOK WY
200 SAC 95831 316-F7
RIVER CHASE CIR
100 SAC 95864 298-D6
RIVER CITY WY
1600 SAC 95833 277-C5
RIVER CLIFF DR
- RVIS 94571 454-E1
RIVER COLLEGE DR
4600 SaCo 95841 279-A1
RIVERCOVE WY
7000 SAC 95831 336-F1
RIVER CREST DR
600 WSAC 95605 276-J7
600 WSAC 95605 277-A7
600 WSAC 95605 297-A1
RIVERCREST DR
500 SAC 95831 316-H6
RIVERDALE WY
3400 SaCo 95608 279-F4
RIVER DOLPHIN CT
9700 ELKG 95757 358-A7
RIVER EDGE CT
- WSAC 95605 297-A1
RIVER EDGE WY
2200 RCCD 95670 279-F7
RIVER ESTATES DR
7800 SAC 95831 336-G3
RIVER FALLS CT
9400 ELKG 95624 359-A4
RIVER FRONT LN
8100 SaCo 95628 280-B3
RIVER GARDEN CT
- SAC 95831 337-A4
RIVERGATE DR
- WSAC 95605 297-A1
RIVERGATE WY
300 SAC 95831 336-F1
RIVERGLADE CT
- SAC 95831 336-J1
RIVER GLEN CT
5900 SaCo 95608 299-C1
RIVERGREEN DR
8000 SaCo 95626 238-C6
RIVER GROVE CIR
7700 SAC 95831 336-G3
RIVERHURST CT
7800 SaCo 95828 338-D4
RIVER ISLE WY
300 SAC 95831 336-F2
RIVERKNOLL PL
- SaCo 95608 279-D7
RIVERLAKE WY
600 SAC 95831 316-G5
RIVER LANDING DR
7700 SAC 95831 336-G4
RIVERLITE CT
11100 RCCD 95670 279-J5
11100 RCCD 95670 280-A5

RIVER LOOK LN
9100 SaCo 95628 280-G1
RIVER MEAD CT
- SAC 95831 336-G1
RIVER MIST LN
- EDCo 95684 286-F6
RIVER MIST WY
9900 RCCD 95670 299-D3
RIVERMONT CT
- SAC 95833 277-E6
RIVERMONT ST
- WSAC 95691 316-F3
RIVER MOOR CT
- SAC 95831 336-F1
RIVER OAK WY
1500 RSVL 95747 219-E5
5600 SaCo 95608 299-C1
RIVER OAKS LN
9300 SaCo 95662 260-H5
RIVER OTTER WY
7700 ELKG 95758 358-C4
RIVER PARK DR
- SAC 95815 297-J1
- SAC 95815 298-A1
RIVER PEBBLE WY
- SAC 95833 276-H6
RIVERPINE CT
2600 SaCo 95608 279-D6
RIVER PLACE WY
7200 SAC 95831 336-F2
RIVER PLAZA DR
2100 SAC 95833 277-A7
2400 SAC 95833 276-J7
RIVERPOINT CIR
800 WSAC 95605 296-F2
RIVERPOINT DR
700 WSAC 95605 296-G2
RIVER POINT LN
- ELKG 95758 357-G6
RIVERPORT CIR
- SAC 95831 336-J1
RIVER RAFT CT
- SAC 95823 358-A1
RIVER RANCH WY
7500 SAC 95831 337-A3
RIVER RIDGE CT
- SAC 95831 336-G2
100 FOLS 95630 261-A2
RIVER RIDGE DR
- WSAC 95605 297-A1
RIVER RIDGE WY
100 FOLS 95630 261-A2
RIVER ROCK DR
1100 FOLS 95630 260-J4
RIVER ROCK LN
- LNCN 95648 179-J4
- LNCN 95648 180-A4
RIVER ROSE WY
9500 SaCo 95827 299-B7
RIVER RUN CIR
100 SAC 95833 277-D5
5700 RKLN 95765 220-B1
RIVER SANDS CT
- WSAC 95605 297-A1
RIVERSBEND CT
9400 ELKG 95624 359-B6
RIVERSCAPE CT
- SAC 95833 276-H7
RIVER SHOAL AV
- SAC 95833 276-G7
RIVERSHORE CT
- SAC 95831 336-J4
RIVERSIDE AV
- SaCo 95615 (396-D3 See Page 375)
100 RSVL 95678 239-H4
900 RSVL 95661 239-H4
RIVERSIDE BLVD
2300 SAC 95818 297-B7
3000 SAC 95818 317-B1
3500 SAC 95822 317-A3
5400 SAC 95822 316-J5
5700 SAC 95831 316-J5
7000 SAC 95831 336-F1
RIVERSIDE PKWY
800 WSAC 95605 296-E2
RIVER SPRINGS WY
9400 ELKG 95624 359-A4
RIVERSTAR CIR
- SAC 95831 336-J1
RIVERSTONE LN
- ELKG 95758 357-G7
RIVER SWAN LN
- SAC 95834 276-H1
RIVER THREAD CT
9600 ELKG 95624 359-B5
RIVER THREAD DR
9600 ELKG 95624 359-B5
RIVERTHREAD WY
- ELKG 95624 359-B5
RIVERTON WY
6100 SAC 95831 316-H5
RIVERTRAILS CIR
2200 RCCD 95670 279-F7
2200 RCCD 95670 299-F1
RIVERTREE WY
200 SAC 95831 336-F1
RIVERVIEW CT
800 SAC 95822 316-J3
RIVERVIEW DR
200 AUB 95603 182-E5
RIVERVIEW DR Rt#-E9
- YoCo 95612 356-H5
RIVERVIEW ST
200 RVIS 94571 454-H6
RIVER VILLAGE CT
- SAC 95831 336-G3
RIVER VILLAGE DR
- SAC 95831 336-G3
RIVER VISTA WY
2100 RCCD 95670 279-F7
RIVER WALK WY
6500 SaCo 95608 299-B3
RIVER WIND WY
7200 SAC 95831 336-F1
RIVERWOOD CT
5500 RKLN 95677 220-C4
RIVERWOOD LN
- RVIS 94571 454-F1
RIVERWOOD WY
10400 RCCD 95670 279-F7
RIVER WOODS DR
4000 PlaC 95602 162-A1
4000 PlaC 95602 161-J1
RIVIERA
- PlaC 95746 240-J5
RIVIERA CIR
1000 EDCo 95762 262-C2

RIVIERA LN
3800 ELKG 95758 357-G6
RIVIERA POINT LN
- ELKG 95758 357-G7
RIVULET CT
- SAC 95833 276-G7
RIZA AV
5900 SAC 95823 318-A7
RIZA RD
- SaCo 95683 (361-C2 See Page 341)
RIZES WY
- ELKG 95758 357-E4
RIZZO CT
3800 SaCo 95824 317-G4
ROADHOUSE CT
- RSVL 95747 219-B2
ROADRUNNER CT
- RSVL 95747 219-B7
ROADRUNNER DR
- RSVL 95747 219-B7
ROAD RUNNER LN
4000 EDCo 95667 226-G7
4000 EDCo 95667 246-G1
4000 EDCo 95709 246-G1
ROADS END PL
9500 SaCo 95827 299-B6
ROAN CT
400 RSVL 95747 219-B4
3100 SaCo 95843 238-F6
ROAN FIELDS PL
- ELKG 95624 359-B6
ROANOAKE AV
1500 SAC 95838 278-A3
ROANOKE AV
900 SAC 95838 277-J3
1200 SAC 95838 278-B3
ROANOKE RIVER CT
11000 RCCD 95670 279-J5
ROAN RANCH CIR
9300 ELKG 95624 379-A1
ROANWOOD CT
800 ANT 94509 (513-F7 See Page 493)
ROARING CAMP DR
2000 SaCo 95670 280-C4
ROARING CREEK ST
- WSAC 95691 297-A7
ROBALO CT
2300 SaCo 95670 280-B5
ROBANDER ST
5000 SaCo 95608 259-E7
ROBB CT
- RSVL 95678 219-F2
ROBBINS RD
8900 SaCo 95829 338-H7
ROBERT CT
8200 PlaC 95746 241-D2
ROBERT RD
5200 EDCo - 247-H2
ROBERT ST
200 ANT 94509 (513-D7 See Page 493)
ROBERT WY
2000 SaCo 95825 278-C7
5100 OAKL 94561 (514-D6 See Page 493)
ROBERTA CT
2000 RSVL 95678 219-G6
ROBERTA LN
7600 SaCo 95843 238-G7
7600 SaCo 95843 258-F1
ROBERT CREEK CT
8100 CITH 95610 240-C6
ROBERT FROST WY
4700 SaCo 95842 259-A4
ROBERT J MATHEWS PKWY
- EDCo 95762 282-F5
ROBERTS DR
7600 CITH 95610 239-J6
ROBERTS PL
- RSVL 95661 220-E7
ROBERTS RD
7400 FOLS 95630 261-B1
ROBERTSON AV
3500 SaCo 95821 278-G5
4600 SaCo 95608 279-A5
4600 SaCo 95821 279-A5
ROBERTSON WY
600 SAC 95818 297-B7
ROBERTS RIVER WY
7700 SAC 95831 336-G3
ROBIE DR
100 AUB 95603 182-F3
200 PlaC 95603 182-F3
ROBIE WY
8400 CITH 95610 239-J6
8400 PlaC 95661 239-J6
ROBIELEE WY
3800 SaCo 95821 278-H3
ROBIN CT
100 GALT 95632 419-D6
900 PLCR 95667 245-F4
4700 PlaC 95677 220-G4
ROBIN LN
200 FOLS 95630 261-C1
300 GALT 95632 419-D6
3400 SaCo 95864 298-J4
3400 EDCo 95682 283-F1
9300 PlaC 95658 201-H4
ROBIN RD
100 PlaC 95603 162-F4
7000 SaCo 95628 259-G7
ROBINA CT
8300 SaCo 95662 260-C3
ROBIN BROOK WY
- RSVL 95661 220-E7
ROBINDALE CT
- EDCo 95709 246-H4
ROBINDALE DR
- EDCo 95709 246-H3
ROBINETTE RD
7700 SaCo 95828 338-C4
ROBIN HILL WY
8600 SaCo 95662 260-E5
ROBIN HOOD CT
1600 SAC 95815 278-B7
ROBINHOOD LN
- EDCo - 247-H1
- EDCo 95726 247-H1
ROBIN HOOD WY
7000 PlaC 95746 241-C2
ROBINRIDGE WY
3700 SAC 95823 337-G3
ROBINSON CT
- RSVL 95747 219-C4
ROBINSON DR
- RSVL 95747 219-C4

ROBINSON WY
4300 RKLN 95677 220-F3
ROBINSONS CREEK LN
2700 ELKG 95758 357-E5
ROBLE CT
3600 EDCo 95762 262-C7
ROBLE WY
4100 RKLN 95677 220-E1
6800 SaCo 95842 259-C2
ROBLEDO DR
- EDCo 95667 266-F5
ROBLES CT
3100 EDCo 95682 263-C4
ROBLES ST
- SaCo 95828 338-F3
ROBLES GRANDES DR
15000 SaCo 95683 322-C7
ROBLIN CT
9500 ELKG 95758 358-C6
ROBMAR CT
7400 CITH 95610 259-H1
ROBOLA CT
10700 RCCD 95670 299-H5
ROBOLA WY
10700 RCCD 95670 299-H5
ROB RIVER WY
7100 SAC 95831 336-G1
ROB ROY LN
8000 PlaC 95746 241-B1
ROBSHELL CT
7300 SaCo 95828 338-D2
ROBSON RD
9300 SaCo 95632 418-H4
9400 SaCo 95632 419-A4
ROBUR WY
8000 CITH 95610 240-B6
ROBUST WY
11000 RCCD 95670 300-A4
ROC RD
- EDCo 95667 266-E3
ROCA ST
2400 ANT 94509 (513-H6 See Page 493)
ROCA WY
7000 SaCo 95842 259-C1
ROCHAMPTON PL
1700 EDCo 95762 262-D4
ROCHDALE DR
3900 SaCo 95608 279-B3
ROCHELLE CT
200 RSVL 95661 240-E2
ROCHELLE WY
7300 SaCo 95628 259-G7
ROCHON WY
2600 SAC 95818 297-E7
ROCK CT
6600 PlaC 95746 221-F5
9500 SaCo 95662 260-J5
ROCK LN
100 EDCo 95762 242-A5
ROCKAWAY LN
- SAC 95835 256-J3
2700 SAC 95835 257-A3
ROCK BARN RD
4700 EDCo 95682 264-C5
ROCKBOLT CIR
100 FOLS 95630 261-B6
ROCK BOUND CT
8400 SaCo 95843 238-G5
ROCKBRIDGE RD
1900 SAC 95815 298-B1
1900 SAC 95825 298-B1
2100 SAC 95815 278-B7
ROCKBURY WY
8100 SaCo 95843 238-J6
ROCK CANYON CT
100 FOLS 95630 261-A2
ROCK CANYON WY
9200 SaCo 95662 260-G5
ROCKCLIFF CT
- RSVL 95747 218-H3
ROCK CREEK CT
- RSVL 95747 219-D1
ROCK CREEK LN
- LNCN 95648 180-A6
ROCK CREEK RD
2300 EDCo 95667 226-F1
11100 EDCo 95634 225-G6
11100 EDCo 95667 225-E6
11300 EDCo 95634 226-A3
12100 PlaC 95602 162-B3
ROCK CREEK WY
- RSVL 95747 219-C1
7000 SAC 95824 318-B6
ROCK CREST LN
6800 CITH 95621 259-E3
ROCK CREST PL
7500 PlaC 95650 221-D6
ROCK DOVE WY
2400 ELKG 95757 357-E7
ROCKET CIR
- SaCo 95742 280-G4
ROCK FIELD CT
- RKLN 95765 200-A6
ROCKFIELD CT
8100 SaCo 95628 260-B7
ROCKFORD AV
- SaCo 95742 281-B4
ROCKFORD CT
3400 RKLN 95765 220-B2
ROCKFORD WY
3000 SAC 95833 277-C5
ROCKGLEN RD
100 FOLS 95630 241-B7
ROCKHAMPTON DR
3100 SAC 95833 277-D4
ROCK HILL CT
- SAC 95833 277-C5
ROCK HILL RD
3900 EDCo 95682 264-A1
ROCK HOUSE CIR N
- SAC 95835 257-B4
ROCK HOUSE CIR S
100 SAC 95835 257-B4
ROCKHURST WY
6100 PlaC 95746 241-A2
7800 SaCo 95828 338-C2
ROCKINGHAM DR
1100 RSVL 95661 240-D4
10100 RCCD 95827 299-E5
10400 RCCD 95670 299-F5
ROCKING HORSE LN
4900 EDCo 95682 264-D6
ROCKINGHORSE WY
1100 SAC 95834 277-D3
ROCK ISLAND DR
3700 SaCo 95827 299-B7
3700 SaCo 95827 319-B1

ROCKLAND WY
4800 SaCo 95628 279-F1
ROCKLEDGE CIR
6800 ELKG 95758 358-B5
ROCKLIN RD
- LMS 95650 220-G3
- LMS 95650 221-C3
3400 RKLN 95677 220-E3
5600 RKLN 95650 220-G3
5800 PlaC 95650 221-C3
ROCKLIN MANOR DR
5400 RKLN 95677 220-H3
ROCKLIN RANCH CT
- RKLN 95765 219-J2
ROCKLIN RANCH WY
- RKLN 95765 219-H2
ROCKMONT CIR
- SAC 95835 256-J4
- SAC 95835 257-A4
ROCKMOOR DR
5500 RKLN 95677 220-G4
ROCK OAK LN
9200 SaCo 95628 260-G7
ROCKPORT CIR
400 FOLS 95630 261-H6
ROCKPORTE CT
- PlaC 95747 238-J2
ROCK RANCH DR
6800 SaCo 95662 260-J3
ROCK RAVINE CT
100 FOLS 95630 261-A3
ROCKROSE CIR
- RSVL 95747 218-J4
ROCKROSE CT
- SAC 95834 277-B3
ROCKROSE RD
1400 WSAC 95691 296-H3
ROCK SPRING CT
7800 SaCo 95828 338-D5
ROCK SPRINGS RD
7600 PlaC 95663 201-D2
7900 PlaC 95658 201-G3
8100 PlaC 95650 201-E3
ROCK VIEW CT
10500 PlaC 95602 161-H2
ROCKWALL PL
9700 ELKG 95624 359-A7
ROCKWELL DR
5300 SaCo 95660 258-G6
ROCKWELL LN
3400 PlaC 95648 179-B3
ROCKWOOD DR
- EDCo 95667 266-A3
1800 SaCo 95864 298-G1
ROCKWOOD ST
4100 RKLN 95677 220-F4
ROCK WREN CT
5600 ELKG 95758 357-J3
ROCKY LN
9300 SaCo 95662 260-H3
ROCKY RD
- EDCo 95726 248-E1
800 ANT 94509 (513-C6 See Page 493)
ROCKY BEND DR
1600 SAC 95833 277-C5
ROCKYBROOK WY
9500 ELKG 95624 359-B5
ROCKY COVE CT
100 FOLS 95630 261-F3
ROCKY CREEK CT
8900 ELKG 95758 357-J3
ROCKY FALLS CT
9200 ELKG 95624 359-B5
ROCKY HILL CT
3200 PlaC 95650 201-D5
ROCKY HILLS LN
200 RCCD 95670 280-A6
ROCKY MEADOW WY
8400 SaCo 95843 239-A5
ROCKY PASS WY
5000 SaCo 95843 239-A5
ROCKY POINT CT
7900 CITH 95610 260-A6
ROCKY POINTE
400 RSVL 95678 240-A1
ROCKY RIDGE DR
1200 RSVL 95661 240-C1
ROCKY RIDGE LN
8300 PlaC 95746 240-J2
ROCKY RIDGE RD
5100 EDCo 95619 265-J7
5100 EDCo 95619 266-A7
5100 EDCo 95619 286-A1
ROCKY RIDGE WY
- LNCN 95648 180-B6
3500 EDCo 95762 262-C6
ROCKY RIVER CT
- SAC 95831 336-G2
ROCKY SPRINGS CT
1700 EDCo 95762 242-F7
ROCKY SPRINGS RD
1900 EDCo 95762 242-F7
ROCKY TRAIL WY
9000 SaCo 95826 318-H3
RODANTE WY
500 SaCo 95864 298-G4
ROD BEAUDRY DR
2600 RCCD 95670 299-D3
2700 RCCD 95827 299-D3
RODDAN CT
900 PLCR 95667 245-G3
RODEO CT
400 FOLS 95630 282-A1
RODEO DR
100 SAC 95823 337-F2
RODEO PL
5800 RKLN 95677 220-H4
RODEO RD
3000 EDCo 95682 263-F7
3000 EDCo 95682 283-F1
RODEO WY
1000 SAC 95819 297-J6
RODIN CT
100 FOLS 95630 261-H3
RODNEY CT
6600 SaCo 95828 318-B7
6600 SaCo 95828 338-B1
RODOLFO CT
6600 SaCo 95823 317-G7
RODRIQUEZ CIR
7800 SaCo 95829 339-E4
ROE CT
5400 SAC 95822 316-J4
ROEDELL CT
9700 ELKG 95624 359-A7
ROEDELL WY
9700 ELKG 95624 359-A7

ROEDER WY
900 SAC 95822 316-J3
ROEDIGER LN
8800 SaCo 95628 260-F7
ROELLING LN
300 ANT 94509 (513-E5 See Page 493)
ROEMER LN
5000 SAC 95820 317-H3
ROESBORO CIR
7800 SaCo 95828 338-D5
ROGART WY
- RSVL 95747 239-B1
ROGER WY
5300 SAC 95819 298-A4
ROGERS CIR
- FOLS 95630 261-E7
ROGERS LN
100 AUB 95603 182-B4
100 PlaC 95603 182-B4
ROGERS RD
9500 SaCo 95829 339-A5
ROGERS ST
1000 WSAC 95605 296-J1
ROGUE CT
8100 SaCo 95828 338-F6
ROGUE WY
- RSVL 95747 219-C1
ROGUE RIVER CIR
- WSAC 95691 316-H1
ROGUE RIVER CT
- WSAC 95691 316-H1
ROGUE RIVER DR
2200 SaCo 95826 298-H6
ROJELIO CT
10000 ELKG 95757 378-B2
ROLAND CT
3100 EDCo 95726 248-D1
ROLAND RD
2400 SaCo 95821 278-D4
ROLLESTON PL
1600 EDCo 95762 262-D4
ROLLING PL
- RVIS 94571 454-G4
ROLLING WY
6400 SaCo 95608 279-E2
ROLLING ACRES CT
9300 SaCo 95662 260-H2
ROLLINGBROOK CIR
- SAC 95833 277-B5
ROLLING CREEK WY
8400 SaCo 95628 260-C7
ROLLING FIELD CT
5100 SaCo 95843 239-B6
ROLLING GLEN CT
9300 SaCo 95662 260-H6
ROLLING GREEN DR
700 WSAC 95605 297-A1
700 RVIS 94571 454-H4
ROLLING GREEN WY
8500 SaCo 95628 280-D2
ROLLING GREENS TER
9000 PlaC 95746 240-J4
ROLLING HILLS DR
1300 RSVL 95661 240-A5
ROLLING HILLS LN
5400 PlaC 95658 180-J4
ROLLING HILLS RD
1700 SaCo 95864 298-H1
ROLLING OAK DR
5600 SaCo 95841 259-C7
5600 SaCo 95841 279-C1
ROLLING OAKS CT
3900 PlaC 95602 161-J2
ROLLING OAKS DR
4200 PlaC 95746 240-F2
ROLLING RANCH RD
2500 EDCo 95682 243-H7
2500 EDCo 95682 263-H1
2500 EDCo 95672 243-H7
2500 EDCo 95672 263-H1
ROLLING RIVER LN
100 RCCD 95670 280-C7
ROLLINGROCK
5400 EDCo 95667 264-E1
ROLLING ROCK RD
5300 EDCo 95667 264-E2
ROLLINGROCK WY
4400 SaCo 95608 279-D2
ROLLINGSIDE CT
7100 CITH 95621 259-E2
ROLLING TREE LN
9100 SaCo 95628 260-G6
ROLLINGWOOD BLVD
7000 CITH 95621 239-F7
7400 CITH 95610 239-F7
ROLLINS CT
- WSAC 95691 316-D4
100 AUB 95603 182-E3
ROLLINS WY
3600 SaCo 95843 238-G6
ROLLO RD
- EDCo 95619 266-A5
ROLLS CT
2800 EDCo 95682 263-C3
ROLLS DR
3200 EDCo 95682 263-C3
ROLLS WY
1900 SaCo 95608 299-C1
ROLOFF WY
6000 SaCo 95662 260-E5
ROLPH WY
3400 EDCo 95762 262-C6
ROMA CT
- WSAC 95691 316-J1
- SAC 95831 337-A5
1900 SAC 95833 277-B4
ROMACK CIR
6400 SaCo 95822 317-D6
ROMAN CT
3000 SaCo 95826 298-H7
ROMANO CT
3300 RCCD 95670 299-J4
ROMAN OAK WY
7600 SAC 95831 337-A4
ROMANY RD
2500 SaCo 95821 278-D6
ROMANZO WY
6500 ELKG 95758 358-B4
ROMBIOLO CT
9800 ELKG 95757 358-A7
ROMERO WY
5000 SaCo 95628 259-J7
ROMFORD WY
3300 RCCD 95827 299-D5
ROMULAN CT
5100 SaCo 95823 317-J7
RON WY
500 GALT 95632 419-F5

SACRAMENTO COUNTY STREET INDEX

STREET Block City ZIP Pg-Grid

RONALD LP
1600 PLCR 95667 246-A4
RONAN CT
9200 ELKG 95624 358-J5
RONK WY
3500 SaCo 95821 278-H4
RONNIE CT
4600 RKLN 95677 220-C2
RONNIE LN
7300 PlaC 95650 201-C5
RONNIE ST
5300 SaCo 95628 259-G7
ROOD AV
800 SAC 95838 257-J6
1000 SAC 95838 258-A6
ROOK DR
8000 PlaC 95746 240-J1
ROOKERY PL
2200 EDCo 95762 262-D1
ROOSEVELT AV
3900 EDCo 95709 247-B4
4300 SaCo 95820 317-H3
4400 SaCo 95820 317-H3
ROOSEVELT CT
2700 ANT 94509 (513-E7 See Page 493)
ROOSEVELT LN
2700 ANT 94509 (513-E6 See Page 493)
ROOSEVELT ST
3100 PLCR 95667 245-G5
ROOSTER WY
8700 SaCo 95828 338-G3
ROOSTERFISH WY
7600 SaCo 95828 338-G4
ROOT AV
2700 SaCo 95608 279-A6
ROPER AV
5300 SaCo 95628 260-D6
ROSA CT
- SAC 95822 317-A5
ROSA LN
4300 EDCo 95682 263-J1
ROSA PL
- LNCN 95648 179-E6
ROSA DEL RIO WY
- SAC 95822 316-J4
- SAC 95822 317-A4
ROSADO DR
- EDCo 95762 262-E5
ROSADO WY
2300 RCCD 95670 279-H7
ROSALES ST
2500 EDCo 95682 263-B7
ROSALIND ST
1500 SaCo 95838 278-B4
ROSALIND WY
- RSVL 95747 219-B7
ROSANNA DR
9800 ELKG 95757 358-A7
9800 ELKG 95757 378-B1
ROSARIO BLVD
5600 SaCo 95660 258-G5
ROSA VISTA AV
6900 CITH 95610 259-J2
ROSA VISTA LN
6800 CITH 95610 259-J3
ROSCOE WY
4300 RCCD 95742 320-E2
ROSCOMARE CT
8900 ELKG 95624 358-G3
ROSE AV
4400 OAKL 94561 (514-F7 See Page 493)
ROSE CT
1100 WSAC 95691 296-J4
2500 SaCo 95608 279-A7
5900 PlaC 95746 221-A7
5900 PlaC 95746 241-A1
ROSE LN
1500 EDCo 95667 245-J1
1500 EDCo 95667 246-A1
3500 LMS 95650 200-G6
ROSE RD
53900 YoCo 95612 356-H1
ROSE ST
- SaCo 95673 257-J5
- SaCo 95838 257-J5
3800 SAC 95838 277-J1
5000 SAC 95838 257-J6
ROSE ACRES RD
6600 SaCo 95662 260-G3
ROSEANA CT
5200 SaCo 95628 259-G7
ROSE ARBOR DR
- SAC 95835 257-B3
ROSEAU WY
- SAC 95833 276-J5
- SAC 95833 277-A5
ROSE BAY LN
5300 ELKG 95758 357-H2
ROSEBERY CT
8000 SaCo 95829 338-J6
ROSE BLOSSOM PL
- ELKG 95757 377-J1
- ELKG 95757 397-J1
ROSE BOUQUET DR
- LNCN 95648 199-J1
- LNCN 95648 200-A1
ROSEBRIAR CT
- SAC 95835 257-B5
ROSE BRIDGE CT
- RSVL 95678 220-A3
ROSE BRIDGE DR
- RSVL 95678 219-J3
- RSVL 95678 220-A3
ROSE BROOK WY
4100 SaCo 95826 319-A2
ROSEBUD DR
3300 EDCo 95682 263-G5
ROSEBUD LN
5800 SaCo 95621 259-C5
5800 SaCo 95841 259-C5
ROSEBURG CT
9400 SaCo 95826 319-A1
ROSEBURY DELL PL
5100 SaCo 95843 239-B5
ROSE CANYON CT
5200 RCCD 95742 320-E4
ROSECLIFF CIR
100 SaCo 95655 319-H2
ROSE CLOVER WY
9900 SaCo 95632 419-C5
ROSE CREEK CT
200 RSVL 95747 219-B5
ROSECREEK CT
4300 SaCo 95826 319-A2
ROSE CREEK RD
- RSVL 95747 219-B5

ROSECREST WY
4200 SaCo 95826 319-B2
ROSECUT CT
9200 SaCo 95829 338-J7
ROSEDALE WY
5600 SAC 95822 317-A4
ROSEFIELD WY
4200 SaCo 95826 319-A2
ROSE GARDEN LN
6000 RSVL 95747 219-B4
ROSE GLEN DR
- RSVL 95661 220-D6
ROSEGOLD PL
1000 FOLS 95630 261-B6
ROSEHALL DR
- RSVL 95678 219-H3
ROSEHALL WY
1900 SAC 95832 337-C5
ROSEHILL CT
10400 RCCD 95670 279-G7
ROSELAKE AV
- SaCo 95825 298-C3
ROSELEE WY
2200 SaCo 95825 298-C3
ROSELIN WY
4800 ELKG 95758 357-H5
ROSE MARIE DR
- SaCo 95632 419-D2
ROSEMARY CIR
3900 SaCo 95821 278-H4
ROSEMARY CT
- RSVL 95678 219-G3
ROSEMARY DR
11000 AUB 95603 182-D6
ROSEMARY LN
900 OAKL 94561 (514-F7 See Page 493)
ROSE MEAD CIR
- SAC 95831 337-B1
ROSE MIST CT
5600 ELKG 95757 357-J7
ROSEMONT DR
2900 SaCo 95826 299-A7
2900 SaCo 95827 299-A7
3100 SaCo 95826 298-J7
3300 SaCo 95826 318-H1
ROSEMONT LN
1800 PlaC 95663 201-A1
ROSENE CT
900 PlaC 95603 162-E5
ROSENE WY
12900 PlaC 95603 162-E5
ROSENSTOCK WY
4300 RCCD 95742 320-E2
ROSE PARADE WY
9100 SaCo 95826 318-J2
ROSE PETAL WY
7700 SaCo 95828 338-G4
ROSE POINT CT
- ELKG 95624 359-A6
ROSEPORT WY
9400 SaCo 95826 319-A2
9400 SaCo 95827 319-A2
ROSE RIVER CT
- SAC 95831 336-H1
ROSE RIVER WY
9400 SaCo 95826 319-A2
ROSE SPRINGS CT
3700 EDCo 95672 244-A7
3700 EDCo 95682 244-A7
ROSE SPRINGS LN
2400 EDCo 95672 243-J7
2400 EDCo 95672 244-A7
2400 EDCo 95682 244-A7
7500 PlaC 95746 220-J7
7500 PlaC 95746 240-J1
ROSESTONE CT
- RSVL 95747 219-B3
ROSESTONE LN
- RSVL 95747 219-A3
ROSE TREE WY
1100 SAC 95831 337-A3
ROSETTA CIR
8900 SaCo 95826 318-H2
ROSE VALLEY WY
4200 SaCo 95826 319-A2
ROSEVIEW WY
7900 SaCo 95828 338-C5
ROSEVILLE BYPS Rt#-65
- RKLN 95677 220-C5
- RSVL 95678 220-A4
ROSEVILLE FRWY I-80
- CITH - 239-F6
- CITH - 259-D2
- SaCo - 259-D2
ROSEVILLE PKWY
900 RSVL 95678 219-G3
1100 RSVL 95678 220-A5
E ROSEVILLE PKWY
- PlaC 95746 241-A5
700 RSVL 95661 220-C7
700 RSVL 95661 240-D2
1200 RSVL 95678 220-C7
1500 RSVL 95746 240-G5
1700 PlaC 95746 240-G5
ROSEVILLE RD
400 RSVL 95678 239-E6
400 RSVL 95747 239-E6
3100 SAC 95821 278-C4
3600 SAC 95660 278-E2
3600 SaCo 95660 278-E2
4400 SaCo 95660 258-F7
5300 SaCo 95842 258-H5
6000 SaCo 95842 259-C1
7000 SaCo 95842 239-F6
7800 SaCo 95621 239-E6
8300 CITH 95621 239-E6
ROSEVILLE RDG
500 PlaC 95661 239-H5
ROSEVILLE ST
100 RSVL 95678 239-H1
ROSE VINE LN
8100 SaCo 95628 260-C6
ROSE VISTA CT
9500 SaCo 95827 299-B7
ROSE VISTA WY
9500 SaCo 95827 299-B7
ROSEWALK WY
9900 ELKG 95757 377-H1
9900 ELKG 95757 397-H1
ROSEWHIT DR
5800 PlaC 95650 200-J3
ROSE WIND CT
11700 RCCD 95742 320-D2
ROSEWOOD CT
400 RSVL 95747 239-D1
1500 OAKL 94561 (514-D7 See Page 493)

ROSEWOOD DR
100 PlaC 95603 162-F6
8900 SaCo 95826 318-H1
ROSEY WY
3800 EDCo 95667 265-C1
ROSIER CIR
- SAC 95833 276-J5
- SAC 95833 277-A5
ROSIER ST
1200 PLCR 95667 245-H4
ROSIN CT
3700 SAC 95834 277-F3
ROSITA WY
5200 SAC 95822 317-C4
ROSLYN WY
2400 SaCo 95864 278-H7
2600 SaCo 95821 278-H7
ROSS AV
300 ANT 94509 (513-E5 See Page 493)
6200 SaCo 95608 279-D3
ROSS CT
- EDCo 95682 263-F6
1200 RSVL 95678 219-F7
ROSS LN
- EDCo 95619 265-E2
ROSS WY
300 SaCo 95864 298-F5
ROSSBURN WY
900 GALT 95632 419-F3
ROSSI AV
- ANT 94509 (513-D6 See Page 493)
ROSSI DR
- GALT 95632 419-D6
ROSSI LN
- LNCN 95648 200-C1
ROSSIGNOL CIR
- SAC 95833 277-A5
- SAC 95833 276-J5
ROSSLARE CT
8900 ELKG 95624 378-G1
ROSSLER RD
4200 EDCo 95667 243-J1
ROSSMERE CT
- LNCN 95648 179-F6
ROSSMERE LN
- LNCN 95648 179-F6
ROSSMOOR DR
1900 RCCD 95670 279-G5
ROSSPORT WY
- ELKG 95624 359-A6
ROSSWOOD DR
7800 CITH 95621 239-G7
ROSTO CT
- SAC 95823 337-G5
ROSWELL CT
6800 SaCo 95828 318-B7
ROSWITHA CT
6000 SaCo 95608 279-D4
ROSWITHA WY
5900 SaCo 95608 279-D4
ROTELLA DR
5900 SAC 95824 318-B5
ROTHBURY WY
8100 SaCo 95829 338-J6
ROTHENBURG CT
8600 SaCo 95828 338-F7
ROTHERFIELD CT
7100 SaCo 95662 260-H2
ROTHERFIELD WY
7200 SaCo 95662 260-H2
ROTHERHAM DR
900 ANT 94509 (513-C6 See Page 493)
ROTHERTON WY
7600 SAC 95823 338-A4
ROTHGARDEN CT
3600 EDCo 95667 264-G1
ROTHSAY WY
9100 SaCo 95829 338-J6
ROTTERDAM DR
2400 SaCo 95626 238-D6
ROUGH GOLD CIR
2000 SaCo 95670 280-E4
ROUGH RIDER CT
1100 AUB 95603 182-C5
ROUGHRIDER CT
3000 EDCo 95667 244-A5
ROUGH RIDGE RD
2500 EDCo 95672 243-A6
ROUGH SAND CT
1000 WSAC 95605 296-J2
ROUGHWOOD RD
3200 EDCo 95682 264-B4
ROUNDABOUT CT
8900 ELKG 95624 358-G3
ROUNDHILL CIR
2400 EDCo 95667 244-C4
ROUND HILL CT
5300 SaCo 95628 260-A6
ROUNDHILL CT
- WSAC 95691 316-J1
300 RSVL 95747 219-A6
2900 EDCo 95667 244-B4
ROUND HOUSE CT
11400 SaCo 95670 280-C4
ROUNDSTONE DR
900 GALT 95632 419-G5
ROUNDTABLE CT
8800 SaCo 95628 280-E3
ROUNDTREE CT
100 SAC 95831 316-G7
ROUNDUP CT
8100 SaCo 95662 260-B3
ROUSTON WY
3200 PLCR 95667 246-B5
ROUTIER RD
2900 RCCD 95827 299-E6
3500 RCCD 95655 299-E6
ROUTY LN
2800 EDCo 95709 247-C4
ROVANA CIR
- SAC 95828 318-E7
ROVEN CT
2700 WSAC 95691 316-F1
ROVONOC LN
3700 EDCo 95667 245-A7
ROWAN ST
- RSVL 95678 219-G7
ROWAN WY
6000 CITH 95621 259-G5
ROWBERRY DR
- FOLS 95630 281-G2
ROWENA WY
1300 SaCo 95864 298-E2
ROWLAND CT
100 GALT 95632 419-D7

ROWLAND ST
1000 PLCR 95667 245-H6
ROWLANDS CT
500 FOLS 95630 261-E7
ROWLEY CT
700 RSVL 95747 239-C1
ROWSER WY
5400 ELKG 95757 377-J3
5400 ELKG 95757 397-J3
ROXANA ST
2400 EDCo 95667 245-D3
ROXANNE CT
2800 SAC 95826 298-F7
ROXBURGH LN
2800 SaCo 95864 298-E3
ROXBURY CT
800 ANT 94509 (513-F7 See Page 493)
5300 SaCo 95608 299-B1
ROXBY WY
- RSVL 95747 218-H4
ROXHEIM CT
9200 SaCo 95829 338-J5
ROXIE CT
1200 PLCR 95667 245-H4
ROXIE WY
2300 SaCo 95608 279-A7
ROY AV
1800 SAC 95815 278-B7
ROYAL CT
- LNCN 95648 179-E1
- GALT 95632 419-D6
ROYAL DR
2900 EDCo 95682 263-D7
ROYAL RD
- RKLN 95765 200-C6
ROYAL ABBY CT
8500 ELKG 95624 358-F6
ROYAL COACH LN
3900 SaCo 95660 258-F4
ROYAL CREST CIR
300 RCCD 95670 280-A6
ROYAL CREST CT
- PlaC 95746 240-J4
ROYAL DOWN CIR
- SaCo 95829 339-D4
ROYALE RD
- SAC 95815 278-A7
ROYAL ENFIELD CT
2100 SaCo 95626 238-C6
ROYAL ESTATES WY
8600 SaCo 95628 260-D7
ROYAL GARDEN AV
700 SAC 95831 316-H6
ROYAL GATE WY
8900 ELKG 95624 358-G4
ROYALGLEN WY
8600 SAC 95826 298-F6
ROYAL GREEN AV
800 SAC 95831 316-J6
ROYAL HEIGHTS CT
9100 ELKG 95624 358-J1
ROYALL OAKS DR
8200 PlaC 95746 241-A2
ROYAL OAK CT
- RSVL 95661 220-D7
ROYAL OAKS DR
300 WSAC 95605 277-H7
300 WSAC 95605 297-A1
1900 SAC 95815 297-H1
1900 SAC 95815 277-H7
ROYAL PALM WY
2700 SaCo 95608 279-D6
ROYAL PARK CT
2900 EDCo 95682 263-D3
ROYAL PARK DR
2500 EDCo 95682 263-C4
ROYAL STATE CT
7600 SaCo 95628 279-H1
ROYAL SUNSET CT
8600 ELKG 95624 358-F1
ROYAL TERN CT
- RKLN 95765 219-J1
ROYALTON CIR
100 FOLS 95630 281-C1
ROYAL TROON DR
3900 EDCo 95762 262-G4
ROYAL TROON PL
800 EDCo 95762 262-H4
ROYALTY
- SAC 95838 257-H7
ROYAL VIEW CT
8800 ELKG 95624 358-H2
ROYAL VIEW DR
1900 EDCo 95667 245-D1
ROYALWOOD LN
100 RCCD 95670 280-C7
ROYCE CT
3500 EDCo 95672 263-C1
ROYCE DR
2800 EDCo 95672 263-D1
ROYCE WY
2900 SaCo 95864 298-E5
ROYCROFT DR
- RSVL 95678 219-J2
ROYER ST
500 RSVL 95678 239-H2
ROY ROGERS PL
7400 CITH 95610 260-C1
ROYSTER CT
8700 ELKG 95624 358-G3
ROYSTON CT
- PlaC 95746 240-H5
ROYSTON WY
9500 ELKG 95758 358-C6
ROZAN CT
- RSVL 95678 239-F2
R R RANCH RD
5000 PlaC 95602 160-H1
RUAN CT
1800 FOLS 95630 281-J1
RUA PERA
1500 OAKL 94561 (514-D6 See Page 493)
RUBELLITE CT
9600 ELKG 95624 359-B7
RUBENS PKWY
7500 SAC 95823 337-H3
7500 SaCo 95823 337-H3
RUBENS WY
- OAKL 94561 (514-H7 See Page 493)
RUBI LN
9900 PlaC 95658 202-A5
RUBIA DR
8700 ELKG 95624 358-J1
RUBICON LN
2200 LNCN 95648 200-B2

RUBICON WY
2700 SaCo 95821 278-E5
2900 WSAC 95691 316-H1
RUBIER WY
- RVIS 94571 454-H3
RUBILITE WY
11800 RCCD 95742 320-D2
RUBIO WY
9900 SaCo 95829 339-C7
RUBION CIR
5500 CITH 95610 260-A6
RUBY CT
- EDCo 95726 248-E2
- PLCR 95667 245-F4
400 RSVL 95678 220-A6
2100 SAC 95821 278-C5
2500 RKLN 95677 220-C2
RUBY LN
5600 EDCo 95667 264-H3
RUBY ST
100 AUB 95603 182-E1
E RUBY ST
100 OAKL 94561 (514-E7 See Page 493)
W RUBY ST
100 OAKL 94561 (514-E6 See Page 493)
RUBY CREST CT
8600 ELKG 95624 358-F4
RUBYE DR
1900 ANT 94509 (513-E5 See Page 493)
RUBY LANDING WY
4400 RCCD 95742 320-D3
RUBY MERLOT PL
9900 ELKG 95624 379-A1
RUBYSTONE CT
8700 ELKG 95624 358-G7
RUDAT CIR
2300 RCCD 95670 279-G7
RUDDY CT
4500 SaCo 95842 258-J2
RUDDY DUCK CT
- LNCN 95648 200-B1
RUDDY DUCK WY
9700 ELKG 95757 357-D7
RUDGER WY
1100 SAC 95833 277-D5
RUDGWICK DR
- RSVL 95747 239-B1
RUDWAY CT
9600 SaCo 95827 299-B5
RUDYARD CIR
7700 SaCo 95843 238-F7
RUE DE LAC DR
2100 EDCo 95667 244-C6
RUE ESPERANZA
- LNCN 95648 200-E1
RUFFY LN
4400 EDCo 95623 264-J3
RUGBY CT
10400 RCCD 95670 279-G7
RUGE CT
8300 SaCo 95843 238-G5
RUGER CT
4900 SaCo 95842 259-A3
RUGGED LN
3100 EDCo 95667 246-F4
RUGGLES CT
8400 SaCo 95628 280-C1
RUGOSA DR
100 FOLS 95630 261-D4
RUHKALA RD
5400 RKLN 95677 220-E4
RUIZ CT
- SAC 95823 337-G5
RULA CT
4600 SaCo 95660 278-H1
RULANDER WY
3500 RCCD 95670 299-H5
RUMFORD AV
6100 CITH 95621 239-D7
RUMSEY PL
- WSAC 95691 316-H1
RUMSEY ST
- WSAC 95691 316-H2
RUMSEY WY
800 FOLS 95630 261-C5
RUNAWAY BAY PL
- SAC 95835 256-G5
RUNDEL WY
1500 RSVL 95747 239-C1
RUNDELAY WY
9100 SaCo 95826 298-J7
RUNDGREN WY
- FOLS 95630 281-G1
RUNNERS PL
3400 PlaC 95650 201-F5
RUNNING BEAR WY
3900 SaCo 95843 238-H7
RUNNING DEER RD
2400 EDCo 95682 264-A1
RUNNING QUAIL CT
3100 EDCo 95667 226-H2
RUNNING SPRING LN
- EDCo 95633 225-E2
- EDCo 95634 225-E2
RUNNING WATER CT
5900 CITH 95621 259-D3
RUNNING WOLF CT
- RSVL 95747 219-C2
RUNNING WOLF WY
- RSVL 95747 219-C2
RUNNYMEADE CT
6600 EDCo 95667 265-A1
RUNNYMEADE DR
6400 EDCo 95667 265-A1
RUNSWICK CT
12000 RCCD 95742 320-E4
RUNWAY DR
4800 SaCo 95628 280-F1
4900 SaCo 95628 260-F7
RUNYON CT
8100 CITH 95610 240-B7
RURAL LN
2000 EDCo 95682 264-A1
RURAL ESTATES LN
8200 SaCo 95828 338-E6
RUSANDRA RD
- EDCo 95633 205-F4
RUSCADA CT
- PlaC 95650 221-D5
RUSCAL WY
5100 SaCo 95628 260-E7
RUSCELLO CT
- EDCo 95762 262-G5
RUSCH DR
7300 CITH 95621 239-G6

RUSERT RD
4700 PlaC 95663 200-G3
RUSHCLIFFE CT
200 EDCo 95762 242-C6
RUSH CREEK CT
9400 ELKG 95624 359-B6
RUSHDEN DR
1200 SaCo 95864 298-F2
RUSHFORD CT
- RSVL 95747 218-G4
RUSHING CREEK WY
9200 ELKG 95624 359-A5
RUSHING RIVER CT
2000 SaCo 95626 238-C6
RUSHMORE DR
6100 SaCo 95842 259-B4
RUSHMORE WY
- EDCo 95762 282-D4
RUSH RIVER DR
- SAC 95831 336-G1
7800 SAC 95831 337-A3
RUSHWOOD DR
- EDCo 95762 282-D3
RUSKIN CT
4500 SaCo 95842 258-J5
4500 SaCo 95842 259-A5
RUSKUT WY
6900 SaCo 95823 337-G1
6900 SaCo 95823 317-G7
RUSSELL DR
- ANT 94509 (513-C5 See Page 493)
RUSSELL LP
100 PlaC 95603 162-F7
RUSSELL RD
- PlaC 95603 162-E7
- AUB 95603 162-F7
100 SaCo 95615 (396-J5 See Page 375)
RUSSELL WY
1600 RSVL 95661 240-B3
RUSSELL HOLLOW RD
5400 EDCo 95630 202-G5
RUSSI CT
300 FOLS 95630 261-E7
RUSSI RD
- FOLS 95630 261-C7
- FOLS 95630 281-D1
RUSSIAN RIVER CT
11200 RCCD 95670 280-A4
RUSSI RANCH DR
- EDCo 95762 262-F7
RUSSLER LN
100 FOLS 95630 261-E6
RUSSVILLE CT
100 FOLS 95630 261-A1
RUSTIC LN
2300 PlaC 95603 180-D2
8100 PlaC 95746 241-B2
RUSTIC RD
3800 EDCo 95682 263-D7
3800 EDCo 95682 283-E1
4300 SaCo 95608 279-F2
4700 SaCo 95628 279-F2
RUSTIC CREEK LN
1100 EDCo 95672 243-A3
RUSTIC HILLS DR
6000 RKLN 95677 220-E4
RUSTIC OAK CT
2600 RKLN 95677 220-C4
RUSTIC OAK WY
4700 SaCo 95608 279-E1
RUSTIC RANCH CT
- LNCN 95648 179-J4
RUSTIC RANCH LN
- LNCN 95648 179-H4
RUSTIC RIDGE DR
2100 FOLS 95630 282-B2
RUSTICWOOD WY
3200 RCCD 95827 299-C5
RUSTIC WOODS CT
- PlaC 95650 201-E4
RUSTIC WOODS WY
- PlaC 95650 201-E5
RUSTLING PINES RD
4200 EDCo 95682 264-B6
RUSTY SPRING CT
- EDCo 95709 226-H7
RUTGERS CT
1500 PlaC 95603 162-D4
RUTGERS LN
2600 ANT 94509 (513-B6 See Page 493)
RUTGERS WY
4400 SaCo 95821 278-J2
RUTH CT
100 SAC 95819 298-A4
100 FOLS 95630 261-E4
2800 EDCo 95682 263-C3
RUTHAVEN CT
1300 PLCR 95667 245-J5
RUTHERFORD CT
4900 PlaC 95746 240-G1
RUTHERFORD LN
1300 OAKL 94561 (514-D5 See Page 493)
RUTHERFORD WY
7300 SaCo 95660 258-G1
RUTHERFORD CANYON RD
- LMS 95650 221-A3
- PlaC 95650 221-A3
RUTHWOOD WY
8000 SaCo 95662 260-B3
RUTLAN CT
- RKLN 95677 220-E5
RUTLAN WY
- RKLN 95677 220-E5
RUTLAND DR
- RVIS 94571 454-G2
6000 SaCo 95608 259-D6
RUTLEDGE WY
4100 SaCo 95608 279-E3
RUTSEY CT
- FOLS 95630 281-G1
RUTTER CT
7300 SaCo 95828 338-D2
RUXTON CT
8000 SaCo 95828 338-G5
RYAN CT
1100 LNCN 95648 179-J2
2500 EDCo 95667 265-C3
4600 RKLN 95677 220-C2
RYAN DR
3500 EDCo 95667 265-C3
RYAN LN
5500 SaCo 95608 279-C3
RYAN RANCH CT
5200 EDCo 95762 282-J6
5200 EDCo 95762 283-A6
RYAN RANCH RD
6400 EDCo 95762 282-J5
6500 EDCo 95762 (302-J1 See Page 301)
6500 EDCo 95762 283-A5
RYAN TAYLOR DR
- RKLN 95677 220-H4
RYAN TAYLOR WY
- CITH 95621 259-G3
- RSVL 95747 219-C4
RYDE CT
3000 RCCD 95670 299-F4
RYE CT
- RSVL 95747 219-D6
3800 EDCo 95762 263-A6
5500 RKLN 95765 220-A1
RYE WY
5900 SaCo 95608 279-D1
RYECROFT CT
9200 SaCo 95829 338-J6
RYEDALE LN
2100 SAC 95835 257-A3
RYEGATE DR
- ELKG 95758 358-C5
RYER AV Rt#-84
41000 SolC 94571 (395-F5 See Page 375)
41000 YoCo 95612 (395-F1 See Page 375)
42000 SolC 94571 415-F1
44000 SolC 95690 415-F1
RYER RD E
3000 SolC 95690 415-F1
3400 SolC 95690 455-E1
3500 SolC 95690 (435-J1 See Page 415)
RYER ISLAND ST
- WSAC 95691 316-E2
RYLAN CT
- SaCo 95843 239-C6
RYLAND CT
200 RSVL 95747 239-C1
7500 ELKG 95758 358-C5
RYTON CT
9500 SaCo 95829 339-B6

S

S ST
- SaCo 95673 258-B1
200 SAC 95814 297-B5
600 SaCo 95673 257-H1
1800 SAC 95819 297-G6
2000 SAC 95816 297-E6
6300 SAC 95819 298-A7
6300 SAC 95819 318-B1
SABALO CT
11300 SaCo 95670 280-B6
SABALO WY
2300 SaCo 95670 280-B6
SABANA DR
3400 EDCo 95682 263-F7
SABBATINI CT
10200 SaCo 95829 339-E4
SABERTON CT
- RKLN 95765 200-E3
SABINE WY
2300 RCCD 95670 279-H7
SABLE CT
- SAC 95864 298-D5
3900 EDCo 95630 222-H2
SABLE RIVER CT
11100 RCCD 95670 280-A5
SABO DR
6400 SAC 95820 318-A4
SABRE CT
- SAC 95835 257-C7
3000 EDCo 95682 244-A7
SABRINA LN
9500 ELKG 95758 358-E6
SACHI WY
7400 SaCo 95823 338-A3
SACRAMENTO AV
100 WSAC 95605 297-A2
900 WSAC 95605 296-G2
N SACRAMENTO BLVD
26400 SJCo 95686 (438-A3 See Page 418)
N SACRAMENTO FRWY
- SAC - 278-A7
SACRAMENTO RD
- SaCo 95742 281-B5
SACRAMENTO ST
- RVIS 94571 454-H5
100 AUB 95603 182-D3
3000 PLCR 95667 245-F5
8000 SaCo 95628 280-A2
10500 SaCo 95632 (399-F3 See Page 379)
10700 SaCo 95632 (400-A3 See Page 379)
48000 YoCo 95612 356-H5
SACRAMENTO INN WY
1600 SAC 95815 278-A7
1600 SAC 95815 298-A1
SADDLE CT
100 GALT 95632 419-D7
200 FOLS 95630 261-D4
1200 PlaC 95603 162-B5
SADDLE DR
2900 OAKL 94561 (514-B7 See Page 493)
SADDLE LN
5300 SaCo 95628 260-G7
SADDLEBACK CT
4000 EDCo 95667 243-J1
SADDLEBACK DR
3500 EDCo 95762 263-A6
SADDLEBACK LN
- LNCN 95648 179-J4
SADDLEBACK WY
5900 SaCo 95823 338-A4
SADDLEBAG CT
200 RSVL 95747 219-B5
SADDLEBRED CT
9700 SaCo 95693 360-H7
SADDLEBROOK CT
8100 SaCo 95828 338-D6
SADDLEBROOK WY
6500 RKLN 95677 220-G5
SADDLE CREEK DR
- SaCo 95829 339-E6
SADDLE CREST CIR
3000 SaCo 95632 419-C3
SADDLEHILL CT
- EDCo 95667 266-G5

STREET
Block City ZIP Pg-Grid

SADDLEHILL RD
- EDCo 95667 266-G5
SADDLEHORN CT
4000 EDCo 95682 283-D7
8800 ELKG 95624 359-H3
SADDLEHORN LP
- LNCN 95648 179-J4
SADDLEHORN RD
5500 EDCo 95682 283-D7
SADDLEHORN WY
1100 SAC 95834 277-D3
SADDLE HORSE WY
- CITH 95621 259-F3
SADDLEPEAK CT
- RKLN 95765 200-E3
SADDLE RIDGE WY
9100 SaCo 95628 260-G7
SADDLE ROCK CT
- RSVL 95747 218-J4
SADDLEROCK WY
4900 SaCo 95841 259-A7
SADDLESPUR WY
9100 PlaC 95746 241-A4
SADDLETREE LN
2600 RKLN 95677 220-C4
SADDLE VIEW CT
4000 PlaC 95602 162-B1
SADDLEWOOD ST
5000 SaCo 95841 259-B7
SADEK WY
4100 SaCo 95628 279-H3
SADIE CT
8500 SaCo 95843 238-E5
SADRO ST
7500 CITH 95621 259-H1
SAFARI CT
1600 SaCo 95608 299-A2
SAFARI TR
3100 EDCo 95630 202-G6
3200 EDCo 95630 222-H1
SAFFLOWER PL
400 WSAC 95691 316-G1
400 WSAC 95691 296-F7
SAFFRON LN
2200 EDCo 95630 202-H7
SAFFRON WY
7200 CITH 95621 259-G6
SAGA WY
7200 SaCo 95828 338-C2
SAGAMORE WY
900 SAC 95822 316-J3
1000 SAC 95822 317-A4
SAGAN CT
- EDCo 95682 283-B1
SAGAR AV
4600 SaCo 95821 278-J3
4600 SaCo 95821 279-A3
SAGE CT
- RKLN 95765 200-A6
SAGE DR
- RKLN 95765 199-J6
- RKLN 95765 200-A6
3300 EDCo 95682 263-E5
SAGE LN
2800 PlaC 95648 180-E4
SAGE ST
100 CITH 95621 239-G6
SAGE WY
800 AUB 95603 182-C5
SAGEBERRY CT
9600 SaCo 95693 360-F7
SAGEBRUSH WY
6300 SaCo 95842 259-B4
SAGE CANYON CT
8400 SaCo 95843 238-H5
SAGE CREEK CT
9400 ELKG 95624 359-B6
SAGE FLAT CT
100 FOLS 95630 260-H1
SAGE GLEN WY
- ELKG 95758 357-J4
SAGE GROUSE CT
- SAC 95834 276-H1
SAGEHEN CT
- LMS 95650 200-J7
SAGEHEN WY
3400 SAC 95834 277-C3
SAGE HILL LN
- LNCN 95648 200-B2
SAGE HILL PL
- LNCN 95648 200-B2
SAGEL CT
5200 SaCo 95608 299-B1
SAGE MEADOWS DR
- RVIS 94571 454-F1
SAGEMILL WY
2800 SAC 95833 277-C5
SAGEMONT WY
7400 CITH 95610 260-A1
SAGEMOOR CT
- RSVL 95678 220-A3
SAGEMOOR DR
- RSVL 95678 220-A3
SAGE OAK CT
7300 CITH 95621 259-E2
SAGE RANCH CT
9500 ELKG 95624 359-B6
SAGE RIVER CIR
- SAC 95831 336-G1
SAGE ROSE LN
3300 EDCo 95682 245-E6
SAGE THRASHER CIR
9700 ELKG 95757 357-E7
SAGEVIEW DR
- SAC 95673 257-C3
- SAC 95835 257-C3
SAGE WAGON WY
12000 RCCD 95742 320-E3
SAGEWOOD CT
3200 RCCD 95827 299-E4
SAGEWOOD DR
100 RSVL 95747 239-D1
SAG HARBOR PL
- SAC 95835 256-G4
SAGINAW CIR
- SAC 95833 277-C4
SAGINAW ST
- WSAC 95691 316-E2
SAGINAW WY
7400 CITH 95610 260-A1
SAGITARIUS WY
5400 CITH 95610 259-H6
SAGPOND WY
5500 SAC 95835 256-H4
SAGUARO WY
2400 RKLN 95677 220-B4
SAHARA CT
7300 SaCo 95828 338-B2

SAIL CT
- SAC 95831 316-H6
SAILBOAT WY
6800 SAC 95831 316-G7
SAILFISH WY
7500 SAC 95831 336-G3
SAILFISH BAY CIR
8800 SaCo 95828 338-G4
SAILOR CLAIM WY
3000 SaCo 95670 280-D4
SAILOR CREEK CT
11900 SaCo 95670 280-E5
SAILOR CREEK RD
- EDCo 95633 205-A4
SAILORS CREEK RD
- EDCo 95633 205-A4
SAILORS RAVINE RD
3100 PlaC 95603 161-D3
SAILSBURY DR
2200 EDCo 95762 242-C6
SAIL VIEW DR
1500 EDCo 95762 242-F7
SAILWIND WY
- SAC 95831 336-G1
SAINT ALBANS CT
7300 CITH 95621 239-G5
SAINT ANDRE LN
7500 SaCo 95828 338-D3
SAINT ANDREWS AV
4100 SaCo 95821 278-H4
SAINT ANDREWS DR
- RKLN 95765 200-C5
- RSVL 95678 219-H7
1000 RVIS 94571 454-F2
2200 EDCo 95762 262-D3
2300 LNCN 95648 179-D2
SAINT ANN CT
1800 SaCo 95608 299-A1
SAINT ANNES PL
200 RSVL 95678 219-G6
SAINT ANSELN CT
4100 SaCo 95628 279-J2
SAINT ANTHONY CT
8800 ELKG 95624 358-J2
SAINT ANTHONY LN
- RSVL 95747 219-A7
SAINT ANTON CT
5400 SaCo 95608 279-B7
SAINT ARVANT CT
8400 ELKG 95624 358-F3
SAINT AUGUSTINE DR
4800 ELKG 95758 357-H5
SAINT BASIL CIR
- RSVL 95747 219-A7
SAINT BASIL CT
- RSVL 95747 219-A7
SAINT BEDE WY
7500 SaCo 95842 259-B1
SAINT BOSWELL PL
300 EDCo 95762 262-G4
SAINT BRENDAN CT
- RSVL 95747 219-C4
SAINT BRENDAN PL
8100 SaCo 95829 338-H6
SAINT CHARLES CT
300 RSVL 95661 240-D4
SAINT CHARLES DR
5500 SaCo 95608 259-E6
SAINT CHARLES WY
- RKLN 95765 220-B1
SAINT CLAIRE DR
1200 ANT 94509 (513-G5 See Page 493)
1200 CCCo 94509 (513-G5 See Page 493)
SAINT CLAIRE WY
5600 CITH 95621 259-G6
SAINT CROIX CT
- LNCN 95648 179-D3
SAINT CROIX RD
- WSAC 95691 316-D2
SAINT DIXIER CT
5000 SaCo 95842 259-B2
SAINT EDWARDS WY
5100 ELKG 95758 357-H4
SAINT FRANCES DR
900 ANT 94509 (513-B6 See Page 493)
SAINT FRANCES WY
5000 RKLN 95677 220-H4
SAINT FRANCIS CIR E
5500 LMS 95650 220-J4
SAINT FRANCIS CIR W
5500 LMS 95650 220-J4
SAINT FRANCIS CT
5800 LMS 95650 220-J4
SAINT FRANCIS DR
2300 SaCo 95821 278-D6
SAINT FRANCIS WY
100 RVIS 94571 454-H5
SAINT GEORGE DR
3500 SaCo 95821 278-G4
SAINT GERMAINE CT
- PlaC 95747 239-B2
SAINT GERTRUDE AV
100 RVIS 94571 454-H6
SAINT GREGORY WY
8800 ELKG 95624 358-G4
SAINT HELENA CT
8000 SaCo 95829 338-J5
SAINT IVES CT
3300 EDCo 95682 263-J6
SAINT IVES WY
6500 CITH 95621 259-E3
SAINT JAMES CT
- GALT 95632 419-E2
1100 LNCN 95648 179-G4
SAINT JAMES DR
6200 SaCo 95608 259-D7
6500 SaCo 95628 259-E7
SAINT JAMES LN
10900 SaCo 95693 359-H6
SAINT JAMES WY
- RKLN 95765 220-B1
SAINT JEANNE PL
- CITH 95610 260-C1
SAINT JOHN RD
- EDCo 95726 248-B3
- WSAC 95691 316-D3
SAINT JOHN WY
7300 SaCo 95662 260-H2
SAINT JONES CT
4300 ELKG 95758 357-G5
SAINT JOSEPH CT
- RSVL 95747 219-A6
SAINT JOSEPH ST
200 RVIS 94571 454-H6
SAINT JOSEPHS DR
3000 SAC 95820 317-E4

SAINT JOSEPHS DR
3000 SAC 95824 317-E4
SAINT JUDE CT
8800 ELKG 95624 358-J2
SAINT JULIEN WY
- PlaC 95747 239-B3
SAINT LO CT
5100 SaCo 95842 259-B1
SAINT LOUIS WY
9400 SaCo 95827 299-A5
SAINT LUCIA PL
- WSAC 95691 316-D2
SAINT LUCIA WY
- LNCN 95648 179-D3
SAINT LUKES WY
7500 SAC 95822 337-J3
SAINT LUZ CT
7000 SaCo 95842 259-B2
SAINT LYNN WY
2200 SaCo 95608 279-A7
SAINT MARIE CIR
- SAC 95823 337-H3
SAINT MARKS WY
2100 SaCo 95864 278-G7
SAINT MARTIN CT
4400 SaCo 95864 298-J4
SAINT MATHEWS DR
3200 SaCo 95821 278-F6
3200 SaCo 95825 278-F6
SAINT MORITZ CT
- LNCN 95648 179-D3
5200 SaCo 95842 259-B1
SAINT PATRICK CT
6800 CITH 95621 259-F1
SAINT PATRICK LN
- RSVL 95747 219-A7
1500 PlaC 95603 181-H2
1500 PlaC 95658 181-H2
SAINT PETER CT
- SAC 95823 337-H3
SAINT PHILOMENA WY
7400 CITH 95610 260-B1
SAINT RAPHAEL CT
4100 ELKG 95758 357-G3
SAINT RUBEN CT
2100 SaCo 95608 279-B7
SAINTS WY
8700 SaCo 95826 298-G7
SAINTSBURY CT
10100 ELKG 95624 378-H2
SAINTSBURY DR
- SAC 95834 276-J2
SAINT SIMONS CT
8300 ELKG 95758 358-D5
SAINT STORY CT
7500 SaCo 95842 259-B1
SAINT THOMAS CT
- LNCN 95648 179-D3
SAINT THOMAS DR
4800 SaCo 95628 280-D1
4800 SaCo 95628 260-D7
SAINT TROPEZ LN
- LNCN 95648 179-D4
SAINT TROPEZ WY
7400 SaCo 95842 259-B1
SAKO CT
4900 SaCo 95842 259-A3
SAKURA CT
7300 SaCo 95828 338-C2
SAKURA LN
2300 SAC 95818 297-D7
SALADO CT
9300 ELKG 95758 357-H5
SALAS RD
- SaCo 95693 (380-A6 See Page 379)
10600 SaCo 95693 379-F6
SALAZAR DR
7200 SaCo 95660 258-H1
SALDANA CT
12200 SaCo 95693 360-F6
SALEM WY
- RKLN 95765 200-A7
4800 SaCo 95608 279-A3
SALERNO CT
8300 SaCo 95829 339-E7
SALEWSKY CT
- ELKG 95757 378-B1
SALFORD ST
7400 SAC 95822 337-F2
SALGADO AV
4200 OAKL 94561 (514-E7 See Page 493)
SALIDA CT
3100 EDCo 95682 263-D4
SALIDA ST
100 SAC 95838 277-G2
SALIDA WY
3100 EDCo 95682 263-D5
6500 SaCo 95660 258-H3
SALINA WY
- SaCo 95827 299-A5
SALINGER CT
7700 SaCo 95828 338-D4
SALISBURY CT
300 RSVL 95661 240-E3
SALISBURY RD
2500 RCCD 95742 280-B7
2500 RCCD 95742 300-B2
SALISHAN CT
9400 SaCo 95826 319-A1
SALIX WY
2400 SaCo 95825 298-D2
SALIZAR WY
- SAC 95835 257-C4
SALLY CT
10200 RCCD 95670 299-E1
SALLY LN
1600 EDCo 95667 244-H3
SALLY WY
2000 RSVL 95661 240-C5
SALMAAN DR
4100 SaCo 95608 279-D2
SALMON DR
1000 RSVL 95661 239-J4
SALMON WY
6100 EDCo 95726 248-B6
SALMON CREEK DR
9200 ELKG 95624 359-B5
SALMON FALLS DR
8800 SaCo 95826 298-G6
SALMON FALLS RD
700 EDCo 95630 242-D1
700 EDCo 95762 242-F3
4900 EDCo 95630 222-J5
5700 EDCo 95672 222-H7
5800 EDCo 95762 222-H7
SALMON RIVER DR
7000 SaCo 95842 259-C2

SALONIKA CT
4300 ELKG 95758 357-G4
SALT CT
- SaCo 95823 337-G2
SALTANA WY
10500 RCCD 95670 299-F2
SALTERS LN
- SAC 95835 256-G6
SALTGRASS WY
7200 ELKG 95758 358-B5
SALTON SEA WY
7400 SAC 95831 336-G2
SALT RIVER CT
3300 SaCo 95843 238-G5
SALT WASH WY
- EDCo 95762 263-B6
SALVATERRA CIR
- ELKG 95757 378-B2
SALVATOR WY
5400 SAC 95822 317-C4
SAM AV
- SAC 95822 337-E1
SAMANTHA WY
7600 SaCo 95828 338-C1
SAM HILL RANCH RD
- EDCo 95667 266-C4
SAMMY CT
2400 EDCo 95672 243-J7
SAMMY WY
- RKLN 95765 199-J7
- RKLN 95765 219-J1
SAMOA WY
1200 RSVL 95661 240-C4
6200 SaCo 95608 279-D4
W SAMOHA CT
8400 SJCo 95686 (438-B4 See Page 418)
SAMOS WY
3700 SAC 95823 337-G3
SAMPOLO CT
7800 CITH 95610 259-J2
7800 CITH 95610 260-A2
SAMPSON BLVD
5300 SAC 95820 317-H4
5300 SAC 95824 317-H4
5600 SaCo 95824 317-H5
6200 SaCo 95823 317-H6
SAMUEL DR
- PlaC 95650 200-G3
SAMUEL WY
- EDCo 95682 263-A6
- EDCo 95762 263-A6
500 SAC 95838 277-H2
SAMURAI CT
5100 EDCo 95623 265-A7
SAMWELL CT
2200 FOLS 95630 281-F1
SAMWOOD CT
8300 SaCo 95829 339-D7
SANA CT
- SAC 95758 357-J2
SAN ALTOS CIR
7000 CITH 95621 259-G4
SAN AMADEO CT
500 RSVL 95747 219-C5
SAN ANGELO CT
6900 CITH 95621 259-F3
SAN ANSELMO LN
- SAC 95835 257-A4
SAN ANTONIO LN
- RSVL 95747 219-A7
- RSVL 95747 239-A1
SAN ANTONIO WY
100 SAC 95819 297-H4
600 SAC 95816 297-H5
SAN ARDO WY
5700 SaCo 95660 258-H5
SAN AUGUSTINE WY
1300 SAC 95831 337-A1
SAN BADGER WY
8800 ELKG 95624 358-G4
SAN BENITO WY
6300 CITH 95610 259-H4
SANBORN CT
100 FOLS 95630 261-F3
SANBORN LN
7300 SaCo 95823 338-A2
SAN BRISTOL CT
6100 SaCo 95823 338-A3
SAN BUENAVENTURA ST
- RSVL 95747 239-A1
SANBURY CIR
3200 RCCD 95670 299-F4
SAN CARLOS CIR
- RSVL 95747 219-A7
SAN CARLOS CT
- WSAC 95691 316-H1
SAN CARLOS DR
900 ANT 94509 (513-B6 See Page 493)
SAN CARLOS WY
- RKLN 95765 200-B6
3000 SAC 95817 317-G2
3700 SAC 95820 317-G2
SANCHEZ DR
- EDCo 95726 248-D1
SAN CLEMENTE WY
1300 SAC 95831 317-A7
SAN COSME DR
7900 CITH 95610 260-A2
SAND CIR
1000 WSAC 95605 296-H2
SAND CT
- SAC 95831 316-H6
1000 WSAC 95605 296-H2
SAND PL
1000 WSAC 95605 296-H2
SAND ST
3400 RKLN 95765 220-C1
SANDAGE AV
9500 ELKG 95624 359-B3
SANDALS PL
7800 SaCo 95829 339-D5
SANDALWOOD DR
7300 CITH 95621 239-G6
7400 CITH 95610 239-G6
SANDALWOOD RD
3300 RKLN 95765 220-A1
SANDAY CT
9100 SaCo 95829 338-J6
SAND BAR CIR
900 SaCo 95608 299-B3
SANDBROOK CT
2800 SaCo 95826 298-F7
SANDBURG CT
100 RSVL 95747 219-C6
SANDBURG DR
- SAC 95819 298-A4

SANDCASTLE WY
2100 SAC 95833 277-D6
SAND CITY DR
- SaCo 95843 239-A7
SANDCREST CT
7900 SaCo 95628 260-A7
SAND DOLLAR WY
2800 SaCo 95821 278-E4
SANDEMARA ST
900 SAC 95838 277-J1
SANDERLING CT
- RKLN 95765 219-J1
- SAC 95833 276-H7
SANDERS DR
- EDCo 95726 248-B1
11300 RCCD 95742 300-A3
11300 SaCo 95742 300-A3
SANDERSON CT
8200 SaCo 95843 238-H6
SAND FIELD CT
- SaCo 95829 338-H6
SANDGATE LN
- ELKG 95758 357-G6
SAND HARBOUR LN
4000 ELKG 95758 357-G5
SANDHILL CT
- SAC 95831 316-G5
SANDHILL DR
- RKLN 95765 219-H1
SANDHILL CRANE CT
- OAKL 94561 (514-H7 See Page 493)
SAND HILLS DR
- RVIS 94571 454-F1
SAND HOLLOW WY
9700 ELKG 95757 357-J7
SANDHURST CT
- RKLN 95677 220-F5
2900 SaCo 95821 278-J5
3200 EDCo 95682 263-C4
SANDHURST DR
2700 EDCo 95682 263-C4
SANDHURST WY
- RKLN 95677 220-F6
SANDI CT
9600 SaCo 95662 260-J5
SAN DIEGO CIR
- RSVL 95747 239-A1
SAN DIEGO WY
3000 SAC 95820 317-H1
SANDILANDS WY
7800 SaCo 95828 338-D4
SAN DIMAS CT
6800 CITH 95621 259-F4
SANDLEWOOD LN
3600 EDCo 95682 263-H7
SANDLEWOOD WY
5700 RSVL 95747 219-B4
SANDLIN WY
6000 SAC 95819 298-A7
SANDMARK DR
- SAC 95835 257-C3
SANDMONT CT
1500 RSVL 95661 240-C6
SANDMONT DR
1800 RSVL 95661 240-C6
SAND PEBBLE CT
- SAC 95831 336-G5
SANDPIPER CT
- RKLN 95765 200-A7
6300 CITH 95610 259-J4
SANDPIPER DR
100 GALT 95632 419-D6
SANDPIPER LN
- WSAC 95691 316-G1
SANDPIPER WY
2400 EDCo 95682 263-B2
3100 SAC 95835 256-H5
SANDPOINTE CT
- SAC 95831 336-J2
SANDRA CIR
1200 PLCR 95667 245-H4
SANDRA CT
300 LNCN 95648 179-F3
3800 SaCo 95821 278-F3
SANDRA WY
800 GALT 95632 419-F5
SAND RIDGE RD
1000 EDCo 95619 286-E4
1000 EDCo 95667 286-E4
2100 EDCo 95684 286-A6
4600 EDCo 286-E4
SANDRIDGE WY
7900 CITH 95621 239-E7
SANDRINE CT
9100 SaCo 95829 338-J7
SANDRINGHAM DR
1000 RSVL 95661 240-A5
SANDRINGHAM RD
2400 SaCo 95825 278-E7
SAND RIVER CT
- SAC 95831 337-A3
SANDROCK WY
6800 SaCo 95828 338-B2
SANDS CT
300 WSAC 95605 276-J7
SANDS RD
2500 EDCo 95672 243-A6
SANDS WY
- FOLS 95630 261-C7
SANDSPRIT CT
7900 SaCo 95828 338-D5
SANDSTONE CT
- RKLN 95677 220-G4
- RSVL 95747 199-C7
100 FOLS 95630 261-B3
8500 PlaC 95746 241-D3
SANDSTONE DR
- EDCo 95762 282-D4
SANDSTONE ST
5200 SaCo 95608 259-E7
SANDSTONE SEA WY
- SaCo 95829 338-H7
SANDWICK WY
- FOLS 95630 261-J5
- FOLS 95630 262-A5
SANDWOOD CT
6100 CITH 95621 239-D7
SANDY CT
200 EDCo 95619 265-D4
1500 ANT 94509 (513-G5 See Page 493)
SANDY LN
5000 OAKL 94561 (514-B5 See Page 493)
SANDY RD
5500 PlaC 95650 200-J3
5500 PlaC 95650 201-A3

SANDY WY
1500 ANT 94509 (513-G5 See Page 493)
SANDY BAR CT
11600 SaCo 95670 280-C4
SANDY BAY CT
8600 SaCo 95828 338-F2
SANDY BEACH WY
2300 ELKG 95758 357-E6
SANDY COVE LN
6400 SaCo 95608 279-E3
SANDY CREEK CT
6900 PlaC 95746 241-C1
SANDY CREEK DR
1100 FOLS 95630 201-A2
SANDY HOOK PL
- SAC 95835 256-H5
SANDY KNOLL CT
11800 RCCD 95742 320-D1
SANDYLEE WY
6600 SaCo 95828 338-B2
SANDYPOINT CT
- WSAC 95691 316-J1
SANDYPOINT RD
- WSAC 95691 296-J7
- WSAC 95691 316-J1
SANDY SOUZA WY
7000 ELKG 95758 358-B4
SANDY TRAIL WY
- RKLN 95765 219-J2
- RKLN 95765 220-A2
SANDYWOOD CT
5300 SaCo 95608 299-B2
SAN ESTEBAN CIR
- RSVL 95747 219-B1
SAN FELICE CIR
7500 SAC 95822 337-E3
SAN FELIPE CT
7000 CITH 95621 259-F3
SAN FERNANDO DR
- RSVL 95747 238-J1
- RSVL 95747 239-A1
SAN FERNANDO WY
2500 SAC 95817 297-E7
2500 SAC 95818 297-E7
SANFORD CT
2300 EDCo 95672 243-C7
SANFORD DR
2300 EDCo 95672 243-C6
SANFORD ST
4800 SaCo 95628 280-E1
SAN FRANCISCO BLVD
4900 SAC 95820 317-H2
SAN FRANCISCO CT
4800 RKLN 95677 220-E3
SAN GABRIEL CT
5700 SaCo 95842 259-C2
SAN GABRIEL ST
- RSVL 95747 219-A7
SANGAMON ST
4000 SaCo 95608 279-E3
SANGIOVESE DR
- EDCo 95762 262-E2
SANGIOVESE LN
- SaCo 95615 (396-J4 See Page 375)
- SaCo 95615 397-A11
SAN GORGONIO CT
- EDCo 95633 205-B6
SANGRIA WY
8700 ELKG 95624 358-G5
SANIBEL WY
11800 RCCD 95742 320-D2
SANICLE WY
5100 SaCo 95628 260-G7
SAN IGNACIO WY
1100 SAC 95833 277-D5
SAN JACINTO CT
7000 CITH 95621 259-G3
SAN JOAQUIN AV
200 ANT 94509 (513-D6 See Page 493)
SAN JOAQUIN ST
2500 SAC 95817 297-G7
6500 SaCo 95820 318-B1
SAN JOAQUIN HARBOR RD
- CCCo 94509 (514-A3 See Page 493)
SAN JOSE DR
1100 ANT 94509 (513-A5 See Page 493)
SAN JOSE WY
- RSVL 95747 239-A1
2400 SAC 95817 297-G7
2600 SAC 95817 317-G1
SAN JUAN AV
100 RSVL 95678 239-H1
3700 SaCo 95628 279-G3
4400 SaCo 95608 279-G3
4800 SaCo 95628 259-G6
5400 CITH 95610 259-G6
5400 CITH 95628 259-G6
SAN JUAN CT
3100 ANT 94509 (513-B7 See Page 493)
SAN JUAN RD
- SAC 95838 277-E4
200 SAC 95834 277-E4
800 SAC 95833 277-A4
2300 SAC 95833 276-H4
2600 SAC 95833 276-F4
SAN JUAN BAUTISTA CT
- RSVL 95747 239-A1
SAN LORENZO WY
2800 SaCo 95608 279-E5
SAN LUCAS CIR
- PlaC 95747 239-B3
SAN LUCAS WY
3500 SaCo 95864 298-G4
SAN LUIS CT
2700 SAC 95818 297-B7
SAN MARCO PL
- EDCo 95762 262-J5
SAN MARCO ST
- WSAC 95691 297-A7
SAN MARCOS CT
- RKLN 95765 200-B6
SAN MARCOS WY
5700 SaCo 95660 258-G5
SAN MARIN LN
- SAC 95835 256-J3
2500 SAC 95835 257-A3
SAN MARINO CT
- EDCo 95762 282-D2
4300 ELKG 95758 357-G4
SAN MARQUE CIR
4900 SaCo 95608 299-A1

SAN MARTIN ST
6200 SaCo 95660 258-G4
SAN MATEO CT
- SAC 95822 317-B2
SAN MATEO WY
1000 SAC 95822 317-B1
SAN MIGUEL CT
- RKLN 95765 200-D6
600 RSVL 95747 219-C5
SAN MIGUEL ST
- WSAC 95691 316-E2
SAN MIGUEL WY
200 SAC 95819 297-H4
600 SAC 95816 297-H5
SANNAM WY
- SaCo 95828 338-D5
SAN NICOLAS RD
- WSAC 95691 316-E1
SAN NITA WY
7400 SaCo 95628 279-H1
SAN NOVADO WY
3800 SaCo 95660 258-G5
SAN PABLO DR
- CITH 95610 259-J4
SAN PACIFIC CT
7400 SaCo 95673 257-H1
SAN PAULO CIR
9400 ELKG 95624 358-J6
SAN PEDRO WY
8700 ELKG 95624 378-G1
SAN RAFAEL WY
3000 SAC 95817 317-G1
SAN RAMON WY
700 SaCo 95864 298-G3
SAN REMO CT
- WSAC 95691 316-J1
SAN REMO WY
5500 SAC 95823 337-J6
SAN ROGUE CT
- SAC 95823 337-H5
SAN SALVADOR ST
- WSAC 95691 316-C2
SAN SEBASTIAN WY
4400 SAC 95823 337-H5
SAN SIMEON DR
1200 RSVL 95661 239-J5
7600 CITH 95610 259-H4
SANSOME ST
- WSAC 95691 296-J7
SAN STEFANO ST
6400 CITH 95610 259-J4
SANTA ANA AV
400 SAC 95838 257-H7
1200 SAC 95838 258-A7
SANTA ANITA DR
2300 SaCo 95825 278-D7
SANTA BARBARA CT
1000 SAC 95816 297-G5
SANTA BARBARA ST
- WSAC 95691 316-E2
SANTA BUENA WY
2800 SAC 95818 297-A7
3600 SAC 95818 317-B1
SANTA CATARINA WY
6300 CITH 95610 259-J4
SANTA CLARA AV
200 RVIS 94571 454-G6
SANTA CLARA DR
1600 RSVL 95661 240-B2
SANTA CLARA WY
- LNCN 95648 179-D3
2700 SAC 95817 317-G1
SANTA CRUZ
500 EDCo 95762 262-C7
500 EDCo 95762 282-C1
SANTA CRUZ CT
900 RSVL 95661 239-J4
SANTA CRUZ RD
- WSAC 95691 316-E2
SANTA CRUZ ST
- SAC 95828 318-D6
SANTA CRUZ WY
2500 SAC 95817 297-G7
2600 SAC 95817 317-G2
SANTA DOMINGO CT
- SAC 95833 277-D5
SANTA FE AV
1800 CCCo 94509 (513-H4 See Page 493)
SANTA FE CIR
1400 RSVL 95678 239-F2
SANTA FE CT
800 OAKL 94561 (514-D6 See Page 493)
SANTA FE ST
1800 OAKL 94561 (514-C6 See Page 493)
SANTA FE WY
- RKLN 95765 200-B7
3800 SaCo 95660 258-H5
SANTA INES ST
- RSVL 95747 219-A7
- RSVL 95747 239-A1
SANTA JUANITA AV
6600 SaCo 95630 260-J1
6600 SaCo 95662 260-J1
7500 FOLS 95630 260-J1
7500 FOLS 95662 260-J1
7600 FOLS 95662 240-J7
7600 FOLS 95630 241-A7
7600 SaCo 95630 240-J7
SANTA LUCIA WY
2000 SaCo 95608 299-A1
SANTA MARGARITA CT
700 RSVL 95747 219-C5
SANTA MARIA WY
1700 EDCo 95762 262-C7
1900 SAC 95864 298-D6
SANTA MONICA AV
4400 SaCo 95824 317-H5
SANTANA WY
100 FOLS 95630 261-F3
SANTA PAULA CT
2800 SaCo 95821 278-E6
SANTAREM CT
7000 ELKG 95757 378-B2
SANTA RIDGE CIR
9500 ELKG 95624 358-G7
SANTA RITA WY
700 SaCo 95864 298-G4
SANTA ROSA AV
4100 SAC 95817 317-G1
SANTA ROSA CT
900 RSVL 95661 239-J4
SANTA SUSANA WY
7400 SaCo 95628 279-G3
SANTA TERESA WY
7200 SAC 95831 336-H1

STREET
Block City ZIP Pg-Grid

SANTA YNEZ WY
300 SAC 95816 297-G4
SANTEE DR
4800 SaCo 95628 279-H1
SANTENAY WY
9200 SaCo 95829 338-J6
SANTIAGO AV
- SAC 95815 277-G6
SANTIAGO CIR
- PlaC 95747 239-B2
SANTIAGO CT
1600 ANT 94509 (513-A7 See Page 493)
SANTIAM ST
- WSAC 95691 316-H1
SANTIAM RIVER CT
11000 RCCD 95670 279-J5
SANTINA WY
2400 SaCo 95626 238-D6
SANTINI LN
7800 PlaC 95658 181-E1
SANTO CT
10300 ELKG 95757 378-B3
SAN TOMAS DR
6800 CITH 95621 259-F3
SANTORINI DR
9000 ELKG 95758 357-H4
SANTORINI LN
900 LNCN 95648 179-J2
SANTOS CIR
3300 EDCo 95682 263-F6
SANTOS CT
3400 EDCo 95682 263-F6
SANTOS RD
7800 PlaC 95658 181-D3
SANTUCK LN
- SAC 95835 256-G6
SAN VICENTE RD
- WSAC 95691 316-D4
SAN VINCENTE WY
5600 SaCo 95660 258-H5
SANWOOD CT
8200 SaCo 95662 260-C3
SAN YSIDRO WY
3500 SaCo 95864 298-G3
SAO JORGE WY
700 SAC 95831 336-H2
SAO TIAGO WY
6600 ELKG 95757 378-A3
SAPPHIRE CT
200 RSVL 95678 219-J6
8700 ELKG 95624 358-G7
SAPPHIRE DR
3400 RKLN 95677 220-A3
3500 PlaC 95602 162-A2
SAPPHIRE WY
1800 EDCo 95762 262-C4
SAPPORO WY
4200 SaCo 95843 238-J5
SAPUNOR WY
5500 SaCo 95608 259-D6
SARA DR
- SaCo 95821 278-E6
SARA LN
4200 EDCo 95667 246-D6
SARA ST
8900 ELKG 95624 358-H5
SARABANDE DR
3300 SaCo 95826 318-H1
SARABEC CT
- RSVL 95747 219-D5
SARADALE LN
14000 SaCo 95632 439-C1
SARAH CT
5900 SaCo 95608 279-C7
5900 SaCo 95608 299-D1
SARAH ROYCE CT
11400 SaCo 95670 280-B5
SARA LYNN WY
7500 CITH 95621 259-H1
SARAMENT CT
3600 RCCD 95827 299-D6
SARASOTA CT
8100 SaCo 95828 338-D6
SARATOGA CIR
- SAC 95864 298-E5
SARATOGA LN
3200 EDCo 95682 283-F1
SARATOGA WY
1000 EDCo 95762 282-D1
SARAYAH LN
- SaCo 95638 420-D2
SARAZEN AV
2100 SAC 95822 317-D7
SARDA WY
2500 RCCD 95670 299-G1
SARDANIA CT
- SAC 95831 337-A3
SARDEN DR
2800 PLCR 95667 245-G2
SARDINIA CT
4100 ELKG 95758 357-G3
SARDONYX CT
4200 RCCD 95742 320-E1
SARDONYX WY
4200 RCCD 95742 320-E1
SARECO CT
3600 SaCo 95608 279-C4
SAREN CT
9600 ELKG 95624 359-B7
SARGENT AV
13300 SaCo 95632 419-C6
13800 SaCo 95632 439-C1
SARGES WY
10300 ELKG 95757 378-A3
SARINA CT
2800 SAC 95826 298-F7
SARNOFF RD
- SaCo 95632 (399-E7 See Page 379)
SARTE CT
3000 SaCo 95826 298-J7
SARTO CT
- EDCo 95762 262-J4
SASHA ROSE
200 GALT 95632 419-D7
SASPARILLA CT
2500 RKLN 95765 200-E5
SASSY CT
5900 CITH 95621 259-D2
SASSY TREE CT
- SaCo 95829 339-D6
SATELLITE PKWY
5200 SaCo 95823 337-J1
SATILLIA CT
4300 ELKG 95758 357-G5
SATIN BELLS WY
- SaCo 95624 358-F1
SATIN SPAR WY
- SaCo 95829 339-D6
SATINWOOD WY
4500 SaCo 95842 258-J2
SATOW DR
10100 RCCD 95827 299-E5
SATTLEY PL
9800 PlaC 95746 240-J6
SATURN DR
3200 RCCD 95827 299-D5
SAUK RIVER CT
11200 RCCD 95670 280-A5
SAUL CT
4100 ELKG 95758 357-G5
SAUL WY
3900 ELKG 95758 357-G5
SAUNDERS AV
4700 LMS 95650 200-G6
SAUNDERS CT
1100 GALT 95632 419-G2
SAUSALITO CT
- SAC 95823 338-B5
SAUSALITO RD
- WSAC 95691 296-J7
SAUTERNE WY
1800 OAKL 94561 (514-C7 See Page 493)
9400 ELKG 95624 379-A1
SAUVIGNON CT
8000 SaCo 95829 338-H5
SAVAGE RD
- EDCo 95667 266-H3
SAVANNAH CT
300 RSVL 95747 219-B5
SAVANNAH DR
- LNCN 95648 179-E3
SAVANNAH LN
4000 SAC 95823 337-G3
SAVANT DR
4800 SaCo 95842 259-A2
SAVERIEN DR
700 SaCo 95864 298-J3
SAVIN PL
9300 ELKG 95624 358-J5
SAVINGS PL
- SaCo 95828 318-A7
- SaCo 95828 338-A1
SAVOIE CT
4200 PlaC 95650 221-J1
SAVOIE WY
- SAC 95835 256-G7
SAVONA DR
10100 SaCo 95829 339-E6
W SAVONA DR
- SaCo 95829 339-D6
SAVONNA CT
- ELKG 95757 357-J7
- RSVL 95747 219-B2
SAVOY AV
300 SaCo 95673 257-G1
SAWBILLS CT
2800 WSAC 95691 316-F1
SAWGRASS CIR
8000 CITH 95610 260-A5
SAWKA DR
- AUB 95603 182-B6
SAWMILL CT
- LNCN 95648 179-J4
SAWMILL LN
- LNCN 95648 180-A4
- LNCN 95648 179-J3
SAW MILL RD
- EDCo 95619 266-A6
SAWMILL WY
- SaCo 95670 280-B4
SAWTELL RD
300 RSVL 95678 219-G7
SAWTELLE WY
8800 SaCo 95826 298-H6
SAWTOOTH CT
5400 SaCo 95842 259-C2
SAWYER CIR
5900 SAC 95823 357-J1
5900 SAC 95823 358-A1
SAWYER CT
700 RSVL 95747 219-E6
3600 EDCo 95667 265-C4
SAWYER ST
200 AUB 95603 182-D2
SAXON WY
7400 SaCo 95842 259-B1
SAXONVILLE WY
3200 SaCo 95843 238-F6
SAXONY CT
- RSVL 95678 219-G3
SAXONY DR
- RKLN 95677 220-F4
SAXTON CIR
100 CITH 95621 239-G6
SAYBROOK DR
7400 CITH 95621 259-E1
7700 CITH 95621 239-D7
SAYERS CT
- ELKG 95757 377-H2
- ELKG 95757 397-H2
SAYOMA LN
4000 EDCo 95667 264-J1
SAYONARA DR
6500 CITH 95610 259-J4
7800 CITH 95610 260-A3
SCALA PL
- LNCN 95648 179-F6
SCALFORD CT
8100 SaCo 95829 339-A7
SCALLOP CT
3700 SaCo 95660 258-G7
SCAMPI CT
9000 ELKG 95758 357-H3
SCANDIA WY
2800 SaCo 95608 279-D6
SCARBOROUGH DR
- RKLN 95677 220-F6
- RKLN 95746 220-F6
- RSVL 95661 220-E6
SCARBOROUGH WY
4700 SAC 95823 337-J4
SCARLET CT
8500 SaCo 95843 238-E5
SCARLET OAK CIR
8200 CITH 95610 240-C7
SCARLET OAK CT
- LNCN 95648 180-A1
SCARLET SAGE WY
8600 ELKG 95624 358-F1
SCARLETWOOD CT
900 GALT 95632 419-F2
SCARSDALE CT
3600 RCCD 95827 299-C7
SCAUP LN
7500 CITH 95621 259-D1
SCENIC CIR
2700 EDCo 95709 246-J3
2700 EDCo 95709 247-A3
SCENIC CT
2400 RKLN 95765 200-D6
3800 EDCo 95762 282-D1
7600 SaCo 95628 279-H2
SCENIC DR
4500 EDCo 95682 264-C6
4500 RKLN 95765 200-C6
SCENIC ELK CT
8800 ELKG 95624 358-H2
SCENIC HEIGHTS WY
3000 SaCo 95608 279-E5
SCENIC HILLS WY
8100 SaCo 95828 338-D6
SCENIC OAK CT
6400 SaCo 95608 279-E1
SCENIC TRAILS WY
8100 SaCo 95829 339-D6
SCENIC VIEW DR
- EDCo 95667 266-F2
SCENIC VISTA WY
- SaCo 95628 260-C7
SCENIC WOODS LN
- ELKG 95758 358-D6
SCEPTOR CT
- RSVL 95747 219-B7
SCEPTRE CT
8600 SaCo 95828 338-F2
SCEPTRE DR
- RKLN 95765 200-C6
SCHANDONEY AV
- SaCo 95836 237-D4
SCHATZ LN
5500 RKLN 95677 220-H4
SCHAUER CT
- SaCo 95690 436-J1
SCHEIDEGGER CIR
- FOLS 95630 261-H4
SCHEIDLER WY
7800 SaCo 95843 239-B7
SCHELIN CT
4000 EDCo 95682 263-C5
SCHELLBACH DR
- LNCN 95648 179-F3
SCHELLER WY
300 EDCo 95667 245-E3
SCHEUREBE PL
9300 ELKG 95624 379-A1
SCHILLERS CT
1600 FOLS 95630 261-H7
SCHINDLER RD
- PlaC 95603 161-B7
SCHIRO CT
1100 SAC 95822 317-A3
SCHIRRA AV
- RCCD 95655 299-G5
SCHMIDTS LN
3000 SaCo 95758 397-E10
3300 SaCo 95757 397-F10
SCHMUCKLEY DR
- SaCo 95826 318-J2
SCHNELL CT
2100 SaCo 95670 280-D5
SCHNELL SCHOOL RD
2800 PLCR 95667 245-J4
SCHOEFFLER RD
12600 SaCo 95693 361-A1
12600 SaCo 95693 (361-A1 See Page 341)
SCHOFIELD WY
4100 SaCo 95660 258-H2
SCHOLAR WY
100 FOLS 95630 261-G7
SCHOOL RD
- SaCo 95655 319-J2
SCHOOL ST
- YoCo 95612 356-H5
200 ISLE 95641 455-H5
800 FOLS 95630 261-C5
1100 PLCR 95667 245-H4
2900 EDCo 95726 248-C1
9100 ELKG 95624 358-H6
SCHOOL HOUSE CT
- RSVL 95747 219-B3
SCHOOL HOUSE LN
7200 RSVL 95747 219-A3
SCHOOL HOUSE RD
5300 SaCo 95837 255-J3
SCHOONER DR
1100 RSVL 95661 240-A5
1800 EDCo 95762 242-C6
SCHOONER WY
7100 CITH 95621 259-D2
SCHOONOVER DR
8100 SaCo 95626 238-D6
SCHRAMSBERG CT
- SAC 95758 358-C1
SCHREINER ST
7400 SAC 95822 337-B3
SCHRIEVER AV
- RCCD 95655 299-F5
SCHUBERT CT
- ELKG 95624 358-F1
SCHULER RANCH RD
- ELKG 95757 378-B2
SCHULZ RD
12100 SaCo 95638 420-E1
SCHUMAN LN
6200 CITH 95610 259-H4
SCHUTT WY
3700 SAC 95838 278-C3
SCHUYLER DR
4800 SaCo 95608 279-D1
4900 SaCo 95608 259-D7
SCOBEE WY
3300 SAC 95838 277-H4
SCOFIELD WY
11200 PlaC 95603 162-A5
SCOLES CT
- SAC 95838 277-F5
SCONCE WY
100 SAC 95838 277-G5
SCORPIO DR
3500 RCCD 95827 299-D6
SCOTCH CT
4800 SaCo 95608 279-D1
SCOTCH BROOM LN
- EDCo 95633 205-B2
SCOTCH PINE LN
- EDCo 95619 266-A5
SCOTER WY
6800 SaCo 95842 258-J3
SCOTIA WY
6200 SaCo 95660 258-H4
SCOTLAND DR
3000 SaCo 95843 238-E7
3500 SaCo 95843 258-G1
E SCOTLAND DR
3400 SaCo 95843 238-F7
SCOTSMAN WY
10800 RCCD 95670 299-H1
SCOTS PINE CT
8600 ELKG 95624 358-H2
SCOTSWOOD WY
8400 SaCo 95843 239-B5
SCOTT CT
- FOLS 95630 261-B1
SCOTT RD
- EDCo - 267-J3
- EDCo 95726 267-J3
200 SaCo 95630 281-J5
300 SaCo 95630 301-F1
4000 SaCo 95630 (321-H1 See Page 301)
4600 SaCo 95630 322-A3
5000 SaCo 95683 322-A5
10100 PlaC 95658 202-A4
SCOTT ST
200 FOLS 95630 261-B5
1000 RVIS 94571 454-H4
SCOTTSBORO DR
3600 SaCo 95826 318-J1
SCOTTS CREEK RD
4100 EDCo 95630 202-J5
SCOTTSDALE DR
7700 SaCo 95828 338-C2
SCOTTS MILL CT
400 RSVL 95661 240-D4
SCOTTSVIEW CT
9300 ELKG 95758 358-B5
SCOTTY WY
3900 SaCo 95821 278-J3
3900 SaCo 95821 279-A3
3900 SaCo 95608 279-A3
SCOWERS CT
- EDCo 95762 262-D6
SCRANTON CIR
4100 SaCo 95608 279-C2
SCREECH OWL WY
2600 SAC 95834 276-J3
SCREECH OWL CREEK RD
4300 EDCo 95762 282-G2
SCRIBNER AV
7600 CITH 95610 239-H7
SCRIBNER RD
1000 SaCo 95639 357-A6
1000 SaCo 95832 357-A6
SCRIPPS DR
- SAC 95825 298-C5
SCRUB OAK CT
200 RSVL 95747 239-E1
SCRUB OAK WY
8200 SaCo 95843 238-H5
SCRUGGS CT
9100 ELKG 95758 357-G4
SEA CT
- SAC 95831 316-H6
SEA ANCHOR CT
- SAC 95838 257-H7
SEABISCUIT LN
9200 ELKG 95624 359-D5
SEABLER PL
2300 SaCo 95608 279-C7
SEABORG WY
3300 RCCD 95827 299-D6
SEABOUGH CT
900 FOLS 95630 281-E2
SEABOURNE CT
1100 ANT 94509 (513-F7 See Page 493)
SEA BREEZE WY
- RCCD 95670 280-C7
SEABROOK CT
500 WSAC 95691 296-J3
SEABROOK ST
- SaCo 95828 338-F3
SEABURY CT
9700 ELKG 95624 359-A7
SEA CLIFF CT
9600 ELKG 95758 357-E5
SEA CLIFF WY
9400 ELKG 95758 357-D6
SEACREST CT
- SAC 95835 257-A5
SEA DRIFT WY
4100 SAC 95823 337-G5
SEADUCK CT
6900 SaCo 95842 259-A2
SEAFARER CT
100 FOLS 95630 261-F3
SEA FOAM CT
- SAC 95831 336-G2
SEAFORD DR
8600 SAC 95823 358-B1
SEA FOREST WY
3800 SAC 95823 337-G6
SEAFORTH CT
- LNCN 95648 179-G7
SEAGATE PL
- ELKG 95758 357-G6
SEAGLENN WY
- SAC 95835 257-A5
SEA GULL CT
1000 RSVL 95661 240-C3
SEAGULL WY
400 SAC 95831 336-G2
SEA HAWK PL
- SAC 95835 256-G4
SEA ISLAND CT
4800 ELKG 95758 358-E5
SEA ISLAND WY
8300 ELKG 95758 358-E5
SEAL CT
3200 RCCD 95827 299-C6
SEA LION CT
- SAC 95831 336-G3
SEAL ROCK WY
7400 SAC 95831 336-F2
SEAMAS AV
800 SAC 95822 316-J4
1100 SAC 95822 317-A4
SEA MEADOW WY
4100 SAC 95823 337-G5
SEAMIST DR
2400 SAC 95833 277-D6
SEAN CT
- RSVL 95678 219-G5
SEAN DR
1400 PLCR 95667 245-J6
3600 SaCo 95821 278-G4
SEAN PATRICK DR
4600 SAC 95838 277-H1
SEANSHELLY LN
3500 EDCo 95672 243-C5
SEAPORT BLVD
1900 WSAC 95691 296-D6
SEA RIDGE CT
9100 SaCo 95829 338-H7
SEARSPORT CT
1000 ANT 94509 (513-F7 See Page 493)
SEA SCAPE CT
5600 CITH 95610 260-A6
SEA SHELL CT
6000 CITH 95621 259-F5
SEASIDE CT
- SAC 95831 336-G2
SEASONS CT
- EDCo 95762 282-D4
SEASONS DR
6500 ELKG 95758 358-B5
SEASTONE WY
6300 SAC 95831 316-G6
SEATON DR
- FOLS 95630 281-B1
SEATTLE SLEW LN
10000 ELKG 95624 359-D4
SEATUCK CT
- SAC 95835 256-H4
SEAVEY CIR
- SAC 95818 297-A6
SEAVEY LN
8900 PlaC 95650 201-G4
9200 PlaC 95658 201-G4
SEAVIEW CT
- SAC 95831 336-G3
SEAWAY AV
- WSAC 95691 296-G7
SEAWAY CT
- WSAC 95691 296-G7
SEAWAY PL
- WSAC 95691 296-G7
SEAWELL CT
400 RSVL 95747 219-A6
SEAWIND DR
4500 SAC 95838 277-H1
SEAY LN
7000 PlaC 95663 201-C1
SEBASTIAN CT
- RSVL 95661 220-E6
3600 EDCo 95682 242-C6
SEBASTIAN WY
- RSVL 95661 220-D6
1300 SaCo 95864 298-F2
SEBASTIANI WY
9100 SaCo 95829 338-J7
SEBRELL WY
8600 SAC 95823 358-A1
SEBRING CT
4800 ELKG 95758 357-H6
SECKEL CT
8700 ELKG 95624 358-G6
SECLUDED CT
- AUB 95603 182-B7
- PlaC 95603 182-B7
SECLUDED OAKS LN
- SaCo 95608 259-D7
- SaCo 95608 279-D1
SECLUSION LN
- EDCo - 267-C1
SECO CT
- SAC 95823 338-A4
SECOND PKWY
7000 SaCo 95823 317-H7
7000 SaCo 95823 337-H1
SECRET CT
4100 RKLN 95677 220-E5
SECRETARIAT LN
9300 ELKG 95624 359-D5
SECRET CANYON CT
100 FOLS 95630 260-H1
SECRET GARDEN LP
7100 RSVL 95747 219-B4
SECRET LAKE LP
- LNCN 95648 179-J6
SECRET PLACE RD
2400 EDCo 95667 245-D3
SECRET RAVINE PKWY
- RSVL 95661 220-D6
SECRET RAVINE RD
7300 PlaC 95650 201-C5
SECRET RAVINE WY
4100 RKLN 95677 220-E5
SECRET RIVER DR
900 SAC 95831 336-J1
SECRET TOWN CT
11400 SaCo 95670 280-B5
SECURITY LN
- SaCo 95828 338-G3
SECURITY PARK DR
- RCCD 95742 300-G6
SEDGE CT
2800 ELKG 95757 357-E7
SEDGEFORD CT
100 FOLS 95630 261-F7
SEDGEFORD WY
100 FOLS 95630 261-F7
SEDGEWICK CT
8900 ELKG 95624 358-G3
SEDLEY CT
- SAC 95823 358-A1
SEDONA CT
- RKLN 95765 199-J5
5300 SaCo 95608 279-B2
SEDONA ST
- RKLN 95765 199-J5
SEEBLICK CT
2000 EDCo 95762 242-F3
SEEBOLD WY
2200 RSVL 95747 239-D1
SEEFOREVER CT
- EDCo 95667 226-B7
SEENO AV
8100 PlaC 95746 240-G2
SEERGREEN WY
100 FOLS 95630 261-D6
SEESCAPE
3000 EDCo 95667 264-G1
SEE VIEW CT
3400 EDCo 95672 243-F5
SEGO CT
- SAC 95835 256-H6
SEGO LN
1300 PlaC 95648 180-C1
SEGOLILY CT
100 LNCN 95648 179-J5
SEGOLILY LN
1100 LNCN 95648 179-J5
1100 LNCN 95648 180-A5
SEGOVIA WY
10700 RCCD 95670 279-H7
SEGURIDAD DR
15000 SaCo 95683 342-B2
SEINE CT
- SAC 95826 298-E7
SEIWELL CT
- FOLS 95630 281-G2
SELBOME CT
7900 SaCo 95829 338-J5
SELBY LN
- CITH 95621 239-G5
SELBY RANCH RD
200 SaCo 95864 298-G5
SELF ESTEEM LN
10100 SaCo 95632 419-D3
SELKIRK WY
4700 SaCo 95628 279-F1
SELLERS AV
6300 OAKL 94561 (514-J6 See Page 493)
SELLERS WY
2400 WSAC 95691 296-G4
SELMA ST
2300 SAC 95815 277-J6
SELSEY CT
700 SaCo 95864 299-A4
SELVA WY
9700 ELKG 95757 357-E7
9800 ELKG 95757 377-E1
9800 ELKG 95757 397-E1
SELWAY CT
4700 ELKG 95758 357-H5
SEMILLION WY
10500 RCCD 95670 279-G7
10500 RCCD 95670 299-H1
SEMINOLE CT
- RVIS 94571 454-F3
SEMINOLE WY
2900 SAC 95833 277-E5
SENATE AV
3900 SaCo 95660 258-H6
SENATOR AV
500 SAC 95833 277-F5
SENATOR CT
800 EDCo 95762 262-C4
SENATOR LN
6400 SAC 95828 318-A6
SENDA ROBLE
- LNCN 95648 200-E1
SENDERO ST
3300 SAC 95838 277-J4
SENECA WY
7800 SaCo 95843 238-F6
SENIDA WY
1200 SAC 95833 277-D4
SENIOR WY
800 SAC 95831 316-H7
SENN LN
8300 SaCo 95683 341-B7
8300 SaCo 95683 (361-B1 See Page 341)
8300 SaCo 95693 (361-B1 See Page 341)
SENTIDO CT
- SAC 95823 337-G2
SENTINEL CIR
4600 RKLN 95677 220-G5
SENTINEL ST
8100 SaCo 95628 280-B2
SEOUL CT
8600 SaCo 95843 238-H5
SEPALO CT
- SAC 95823 337-G2
SEPTAGE WY
- SaCo 95758 337-F7
SEPTER
- RCCD 95827 299-E4
SEPULTRA CT
- RSVL 95747 219-B1
N SEQUA LN
- SJCo 95220 439-C6
SEQUEIRA CT
7900 SaCo 95828 338-D5
SEQUOIA CIR
5500 CITH 95610 260-B6
5500 CITH 95628 260-B6
SEQUOIA CT
100 RVIS 94571 454-G5
900 EDCo 95762 262-C7
5800 RKLN 95677 220-D4
SEQUOIA DR
- PlaC 95650 221-G2
2300 ANT 94509 (513-A7 See Page 493)
4300 OAKL 94561 (514-D7 See Page 493)
SEQUOIA LN
6000 EDCo 95623 264-J5
SEQUOIA ST
100 RSVL 95678 239-J1
300 RSVL 95678 219-J7
SEQUOIA WY
3900 SAC 95823 337-G3
SEQUOIA PACIFIC BLVD
400 SAC 95814 297-C1
SEQUOIA WOOD CT
8400 ELKG 95624 358-G2
SERAFINO CT
- ELKG 95624 338-J7
SERANO CT
3100 EDCo 95709 246-G4
SERENA CT
4800 SaCo 95608 279-A6
SERENADE LN
8200 SaCo 95828 338-D3
SERENATA CT
- SAC 95835 257-A5
SERENATA WY
- SAC 95835 257-A5
SERENDIPITY LN
6500 EDCo 95667 265-A2
SERENE CT
600 RSVL 95678 219-J6
SERENE LAKE PL
- SAC 95835 257-A3
SERENITY DR
- EDCo 95667 266-E2
E SERENITY DR
6800 SAC 95823 337-F1
W SERENITY DR
6800 SAC 95823 337-F1
SERENITY LN
9100 SaCo 95662 260-G2
SERGIO WY
7800 SaCo 95829 339-E5
SERGIS CT
- LNCN 95648 179-E3
SERINITY LN
3100 EDCo 95667 244-H1
SERIO WY
- SAC 95758 338-C7
- SAC 95758 358-C1
SERNA CT
3500 EDCo 95682 263-B6
SERPA WY
- FOLS 95630 282-A2
300 FOLS 95630 281-J1
500 FOLS 95630 261-J7
SERPENTINE CT
11200 SaCo 95670 280-B4
SERPENTINE DR
3300 ANT 94509 (513-F7 See Page 493)
SERPENTINE WY
12200 PlaC 95602 162-B1
SERRA WY
3100 SAC 95816 297-F6
SERRA BELLA CT
6600 ELKG 95758 358-A4
SERRANO CT
7800 CITH 95621 239-E7
SERRANO PKWY
4500 EDCo 95762 262-E6
SERRANOS CT
- RSVL 95747 219-B1
SERRAVILLA WY
- ELKG 95758 358-B3
SERTA CT
7200 ELKG 95757 378-B3
SERVICE CT
- EDCo 95619 265-F2
SERVICE DR
- EDCo 95619 265-F2
SERVICE RD
- ANT 94509 (513-D5 See Page 493)
SESAME ST
3000 EDCo 95726 248-D1
4100 SaCo 95821 278-J3
SETINA LN
9500 SaCo 95827 319-B2
SETINA PL
9500 SaCo 95827 319-B2
SETON CT
- EDCo 95682 263-F4
SETON HILL CT
2800 SAC 95826 298-F7
SETTLERS CT
- FOLS 95630 261-H5
SETTLERS TR
6800 EDCo 95682 (302-J6 See Page 301)
SEVEN CEDARS PL
6000 PlaC 95746 241-A4
SEVEN OAKS CT
2200 EDCo 95762 262-C1
SEVEN OAKS LN
900 SaCo 95864 298-J4
SEVEN RIDGES CT
- EDCo 95709 247-C4
SEVEN RIDGES RD
- EDCo 95709 247-C5
SEVEN SPRINGS RD
2900 EDCo 95667 246-B4
2900 PLCR 95667 246-B4
SEVILLA DR
- RSVL 95747 199-B7
- RSVL 95747 219-B1
SEVILLE
500 EDCo 95762 262-C7
SEVILLE CIR
2800 ANT 94509 (513-A6 See Page 493)
8700 PlaC 95746 221-E4
SEVILLE CIR E
- PlaC 95746 221-F5
SEVILLE WY
1200 SAC 95816 297-G5
SEWAN AV
6200 SaCo 95841 259-D4
SEWARD CT
5600 SAC 95819 298-B4
SEWELL CT
7900 SaCo 95828 338-D5
SEXTANT WY
400 SAC 95838 257-H7
SEYFERTH WY
5500 SAC 95823 337-J4
5500 SAC 95823 338-A4
SEYMOUR AV
3400 WSAC 95691 316-E3
SEYMOUR CIR
- LNCN 95648 179-F7
SEYMOUR CT
- WSAC 95691 316-E2
SEYMOUR PL
4100 PlaC 95746 240-F2
SHAD CT
2600 SaCo 95826 298-G6
SHAD WY
6100 EDCo 95726 248-B6
SHADA WY
8100 SaCo 95828 338-D4
SHADDICK DR
400 ANT 94509 (513-E7 See Page 493)
SHADE TREE WY
4600 SaCo 95843 239-A5
SHADLE WY
5600 SaCo 95628 260-D6
SHADMOOR PL
- SAC 95835 256-H4
SHADOW CT
2800 EDCo 95726 247-J2
SHADOW LN
1700 ANT 94509 (513-D5 See Page 493)
3200 EDCo 95667 245-D7
6000 CITH 95621 259-D5
SHADOWBROOK DR
100 FOLS 95630 241-B7
6100 PlaC 95746 241-A6
SHADOWBROOK LN
1100 EDCo 95762 242-E3
SHADOW BROOK PL
6100 PlaC 95746 241-A4
SHADOWBROOK WY
5700 SaCo 95628 259-E5
5800 SaCo 95621 259-E5
5800 CITH 95621 259-E5
5800 CITH 95628 259-E5
SHADOW CREEK DR
5400 SaCo 95608 259-C6
5400 SaCo 95841 259-C6
SHADOWCREEK DR
6200 SaCo 95608 259-D7
SHADOW CREEK WY
- RVIS 94571 454-E1

STREET
Block City ZIP Pg-Grid

SHADOW CREST CIR
8500 SaCo 95843 238-G5
SHADOWFAX CT
1100 EDCo 95762 261-J2
1100 EDCo 95762 262-A2
SHADOWFAX LN
1100 EDCo 95762 261-J2
1100 EDCo 95762 262-A2
SHADOW GLEN CT
- RSVL 95661 239-J4
SHADOW GLEN LN
- LNCN 95648 180-A7
SHADOWGLEN RD
1100 SaCo 95864 298-F3
SHADOW HAWK DR
6500 CITH 95621 259-D3
SHADOW LAKE CT
- LNCN 95648 179-H5
SHADOW LAKE LN
- LNCN 95648 179-H5
SHADOW LAKE PL
- LNCN 95648 179-H5
SHADOW MOUNTAIN CT
- PlaC 95602 162-G1
SHADOW MOUNTAIN WY
1200 PlaC 95602 162-F1
SHADOW OAK DR
5900 CITH 95621 259-F5
SHADOW OAKS LN
7500 PlaC 95746 220-H7
7500 PlaC 95746 240-H1
S SHADOW OAKS LN
7800 PlaC 95746 240-H1
SHADOWOOD CT
8000 PlaC 95746 241-D2
SHADOWOOD WY
5000 SaCo 95628 260-B7
SHADOW PINE CT
1400 RSVL 95661 240-A5
SHADOW RANCH RD
2000 EDCo 95667 246-C3
SHADOWRIDGE
300 RSVL 95678 240-A1
SHADOW ROCK DR
700 PlaC 95602 162-G1
SHADOW RUN RD
2000 EDCo 95667 246-B1
SHADOW TREE DR
- SAC 95833 277-B4
3300 SAC 95834 277-B4
SHADY CT
3700 EDCo 95667 245-A7
SHADY GN
100 AUB 95603 182-F2
SHADY LN
- EDCo 95726 247-J1
- SAC 95821 278-C5
100 ANT 94509 (513-D4
See Page 493)
3400 SaCo 95821 278-F4
6600 SaCo 95608 279-E4
6900 EDCo 95667 245-A7
8300 PlaC 95746 240-H2
SHADY RUN
- AUB 95603 182-D6
SHADY ACRES DR
- EDCo 267-J3
SHADY ARBOR DR
- SAC 95833 276-G7
SHADYBROOK CT
- PlaC 95746 240-G3
SHADY CREEK LN
1400 EDCo 95667 244-D2
5000 PlaC 95746 220-G7
SHADY CREEK RD
2100 FOLS 95630 282-B1
SHADY CREST WY
8300 CITH 95621 239-G6
SHADYDALE CT
2200 SaCo 95825 298-C3
SHADY ELM LN
- SaCo 95662 260-E2
SHADY FIR LN
- RSVL 95747 219-A5
SHADY GLEN RD
2000 EDCo 95682 263-B6
SHADY GROVE CT
6700 CITH 95610 260-A3
SHADY HOLLOW WY
9000 SaCo 95628 260-G7
SHADY LAKE CT
- SAC 95834 277-E3
SHADY LAKE LN
6600 PlaC 95746 221-D6
SHADYLANE CT
100 RSVL 95747 219-B4
SHADYLANE WY
7200 RSVL 95747 219-B4
SHADY LEAF WY
4900 SAC 95838 257-G7
SHADY OAK DR
- FOLS 95630 261-B1
SHADY OAK LN
500 EDCo 95619 265-E4
SHADY OAK WY
4400 SaCo 95628 279-J2
SHADY OAKS LN
500 PlaC 95658 181-A2
SHADY PARK CT
- SAC 95822 317-B5
SHADY PINE LN
4800 SaCo 95628 280-B1
SHADY RIVER CIR
- SAC 95831 336-J1
SHADY SLOPE LN
- SaCo 95828 338-B3
SHADY SPRINGS WY
6300 CITH 95621 259-E2
SHADY TRAIL LN
- RKLN 95765 200-C5
SHADY TREE CT
9200 SaCo 95628 260-G7
SHADY VALLEY CT
200 SaCo 95673 257-G2
SHADY VIEW CT
10000 ELKG 95624 378-H2
SHADY VISTA CT
8900 ELKG 95624 378-H1
SHADY WILLOW CT
6900 SaCo 95673 257-G2
SHADY WOODS WY
6800 SaCo 95673 257-G2
SHAE CT
4900 SaCo 95841 259-A6
SHAFTESBURY CT
4600 SaCo 95608 279-B1
4600 SaCo 95841 279-B1

SHAHAN CT
100 ANT 94509 (513-E7
See Page 493)
SHAKESPEARE CT
700 RSVL 95747 219-C5
SHALDON LN
- RSVL 95747 218-J5
SHALE CT
9600 ELKG 95624 359-B7
SHALE DR
- EDCo 95667 226-E4
SHALE RIDGE LN
12100 PlaC 95602 162-B2
12200 AUB 95602 162-B2
SHALE ROCK CT
6000 ELKG 95758 358-A3
SHALFORD WY
- GALT 95632 419-G3
SHALIMAR WY
6700 CITH 95621 259-F4
SHALLOW WY
4600 SAC 95820 317-E3
SHALLOW CREEK RD
3500 PlaC 95650 201-E5
SHALOHM WY
- EDCo 95667 266-G3
SHALOM CT
- PlaC 95602 161-J1
SHAMBAUGH LN
5700 LMS 95650 220-J5
5700 LMS 95650 221-A4
SHAMIM LN
12100 SaCo 95632 420-E4
SHAMROCK CT
1600 LNCN 95648 179-F3
SHAMROCK DR
4800 SaCo 95628 280-C1
4900 SaCo 95628 260-C7
SHAMUS CT
6600 CITH 95621 259-D3
SHANA WY
- ELKG 95757 377-J2
- ELKG 95757 378-A2
- ELKG 95757 397-J2
SHANDONY AV
- SaCo 95626 237-E4
SHANDWICK DR
4100 SaCo 95843 238-J6
SHANE LN
8100 CITH 95610 260-B1
SHANGHAI WY
300 EDCo 95667 245-E3
SHANGRAL AL
5300 EDCo - 247-H2
SHANGRI LN
600 SaCo 95825 298-C4
SHANGRI LA CT
- EDCo - 267-C5
SHANGRILA DR
8100 SaCo 95628 280-B1
SHANGRI LA LN
- EDCo - 267-B5
- EDCo 95667 267-B5
SHANK CT
8000 SAC 95826 318-E4
SHANLEY CT
- RSVL 95747 219-C4
SHANLEY LN
9400 PlaC 95603 161-G5
SHANLEY RD
2500 PlaC 95603 161-H6
SHANNON ST
3400 SaCo 95821 278-J4
SHANNON WY
400 RSVL 95678 239-G5
SHANNON BAY DR
5700 RKLN 95677 220-C4
SHANNONDALE CT
- SAC 95835 256-J6
SHANNON OAK LN
8100 ELKG 95758 358-D6
SHAOOW LN
2800 EDCo 95726 247-J2
SHAREEN WY
7800 CITH 95610 239-J7
SHARI WY
- PlaC 95746 240-G6
SHARIAN ST
900 WSAC 95605 296-J1
SHARIDGE CT
5200 SaCo 95628 259-J7
SHARIFA WY
- RSVL 95747 219-A7
SHARK WY
- SaCo 95828 338-G4
SHARKEY AV
8900 ELKG 95624 358-G5
SHARLO CT
- SAC 95758 358-C1
SHARMEAD WY
8700 SaCo 95628 280-E2
SHARON CT
100 FOLS 95630 261-E4
2900 WSAC 95691 296-E7
2900 WSAC 95691 316-F1
SHARON LN
- EDCo 95667 266-C5
SHARON WY
- RVIS 94571 454-H3
100 RSVL 95678 239-J1
200 RSVL 95678 240-A2
1300 SAC 95831 337-B3
SHARON BEE LN
12500 SaCo 95638 (401-D7
See Page 381)
12500 SaCo 95638 421-D1
SHARP CIR
200 RSVL 95678 240-A1
SHARP CT
6400 EDCo 95667 265-A2
SHARP LN
6400 EDCo 95667 265-A2
SHARPES LN
- SaCo 95690 436-J2
SHARPS CIR
5800 SaCo 95608 259-D5
SHARRMONT CT
11200 SaCo 95693 (400-E1
See Page 379)
SHARWOOD WY
4100 SaCo 95608 279-B3
SHASTA AV
- SAC 95758 338-B7
SHASTA CIR
200 EDCo 95762 262-D7
SHASTA CT
100 ANT 94509 (513-D7
See Page 493)

SHASTA DR
- RVIS 94571 454-G5
SHASTA RD
6000 EDCo 95633 205-B6
SHASTA ST
700 RSVL 95678 219-J7
900 RSVL 95678 239-J1
SHASTA WY
2900 WSAC 95691 316-H2
3000 SaCo 95821 278-E5
SHASTA CREEK WY
6300 ELKG 95758 358-A4
SHASTA DAISY CT
8300 CITH 95610 260-C1
SHASTA LILY DR
8700 ELKG 95624 358-F1
SHASTA OAKS CIR
- RSVL 95678 219-J7
SHASTA OAKS CT
- RSVL 95678 219-J7
SHAUNSETTA CT
12300 PlaC 95603 162-C5
SHAVER CT
- WSAC 95691 316-D4
5500 SaCo 95841 259-B6
SHAW DR
- WSAC 95691 296-G3
SHAW ST
2200 SaCo 95821 278-C6
SHAWHAN LN
- SaCo 95608 279-B4
SHAW MINE RD
100 EDCo 95619 265-D5
SHAWMUTT CT
- SaCo 95662 260-G4
SHAWN LN
11700 SaCo 95693 (380-C1
See Page 379)
SHAWN WY
2900 RCCD 95670 299-G3
3800 LMS 95650 200-J7
SHAWNDA CT
6000 CITH 95621 259-D2
SHAWNEE AV
8500 SaCo 95628 280-D1
SHAWNEE CT
3100 EDCo 95682 263-B2
SHAWNEE RD
2500 PlaC 95603 161-H6
SHAWNTEL WY
8400 SaCo 95843 239-A5
SHAW RIVER WY
500 SAC 95831 336-G1
SHAYLYNN CT
23900 SJCo 95220 439-J6
SHAYLYNN LN
- SaCo 95638 420-D2
SHEARER ST
800 RSVL 95678 239-J1
800 RSVL 95678 240-A1
SHEARWATER CT
- LNCN 95648 200-B3
100 SAC 95833 276-H7
SHEARWATER DR
- SAC 95833 276-H7
SHEARWATER WY
- OAKL 94561 (514-H7
See Page 493)
SHEAVES CT
5800 ELKG 95758 357-J4
SHEBA CT
- PlaC 95746 240-J2
SHEEDY CT
3800 SaCo 95843 238-G5
SHEEHAN WY
8000 SaCo 95843 238-G6
SHEEN CT
- SAC 95835 256-J4
SHEEPHERDER RIDGE RD
- EDCo 95634 225-B4
SHEFFIELD DR
2100 EDCo 95762 242-C5
SHEFFIELD LN
600 LNCN 95648 179-G5
SHEFFIELD WY
1200 RSVL 95661 240-B5
SHEFFIELD OAK DR
10100 ELKG 95624 378-H2
SHEHY GLEN PL
- LNCN 95648 200-B2
SHELATO WY
5200 SaCo 95608 299-B3
SHELBORN CT
8700 SaCo 95628 260-E7
SHELBORNE DR
7300 PlaC 95746 221-C7
7700 PlaC 95746 241-C1
SHELBY CIR
2000 EDCo 95762 262-C4
SHELBY CT
- RKLN 95765 200-C6
1900 EDCo 95762 262-C4
SHELBY ST
7500 SAC 95758 358-C1
SHELBY RANCH CT
- RSVL 95678 219-H5
SHELBY RANCH LN
- RSVL 95678 219-H5
SHELDON RD
7600 ELKG 95758 358-B2
8200 ELKG 95624 358-E2
8500 ELKG 95624 359-A2
SHELDON ST
3300 SaCo 95838 278-B3
SHELDON CREEK DR
8600 ELKG 95624 358-F2
SHELDON LAKE DR
11700 SaCo 95624 340-D3
SHELDON NORTH DR
8400 ELKG 95624 338-F7
8400 ELKG 95624 358-F1
SHELDON OAKS LN
8800 ELKG 95624 359-F3
SHELDON PARK WY
10500 ELKG 95624 359-G2
SHELDON PLACE DR
8200 ELKG 95624 358-D1
SHELDON WOODS WY
10600 ELKG 95624 359-G3
SHELDUCK CT
200 GALT 95632 419-D6
SHELDUCK LN
300 GALT 95632 419-D6
SHELFIELD DR
1800 SaCo 95608 299-C1
2200 SaCo 95608 279-C7
SHELFORD PL
8500 SaCo 95843 238-H5

SHELL LN
- EDCo 267-E4
SHELL ST
4900 SaCo 95660 258-G7
SHELL BANKS PL
- SaCo 95835 256-H5
SHELL BEACH DR
7800 SaCo 95843 239-A7
SHELLBROOK CT
7800 SaCo 95828 338-D4
SHELLDRAKE CT
5800 SaCo 95628 260-B5
SHELLEY CT
100 FOLS 95630 261-E4
200 RSVL 95747 219-C5
SHELLEY WY
5400 SaCo 95608 299-B2
SHELLWOOD WY
900 SAC 95831 336-J2
SHELTER BAY LN
- ELKG 95758 357-F7
SHELTER COVE CT
- RKLN 95765 220-A2
SHELTER COVE DR
3400 LMS 95650 201-A5
SHELTER COVE LN
- ELKG 95758 357-F6
SHELTER POINT CT
- SAC 95831 316-H6
SHELTON ST
- RKLN 95765 200-B6
SHENANDOAH DR
5800 SaCo 95841 259-B4
SHENANDOAH RD
- RKLN 95765 200-C6
SHENANGO WY
4400 ELKG 95758 357-H4
SHENENCOCK CT
800 RSVL 95747 219-D7
SHENENCOCK WY
900 RSVL 95747 219-D7
SHENNECOCK WY
5300 SAC 95835 256-H4
SHENSTONE WY
- SAC 95833 277-A6
SHEPARD AV
5300 SAC 95819 298-A4
SHEPHERD LN
3000 EDCo 95667 245-A3
SHEPHERDS CT
- LNCN 95648 199-J1
SHEPPARDS TR
- EDCo 95633 205-D1
SHER CT
3200 SAC 95820 318-B1
SHERATON DR
8500 SaCo 95628 260-D6
SHERBORNE CT
- GALT 95632 419-H5
SHERBOURG DR
- RSVL 95678 219-G3
SHERBOURNE LN
500 LNCN 95648 179-F4
SHERBROOK WY
5200 SaCo 95843 239-B6
SHERBURN AV
1100 SAC 95822 317-B2
SHEREEN CT
5200 SaCo 95841 259-C7
SHERICE CT
900 SAC 95831 336-J1
SHERIDAN AV
1200 RSVL 95661 240-C5
1600 CITH 95610 240-C5
SHERIDAN CT
4000 PlaC 95602 161-G3
SHERIDAN RD
3600 EDCo 95682 263-B6
SHERIDAN ST
3000 PLCR 95667 245-H5
SHERIDAN WY
2600 SaCo 95821 278-J6
SHERINGTON WY
- SAC 95835 257-B5
SHERI RIDGE WY
- RCCD 95670 280-C7
SHERLOCK WY
- CITH 95610 239-H7
4800 SaCo 95608 299-A4
SHERMAN LN
9500 SaCo 95693 360-A7
9700 SaCo 95693 379-J1
9700 SaCo 95693 (380-A1
See Page 379)
SHERMAN ST
1100 PLCR 95667 245-H5
SHERMAN WY
3600 SAC 95817 297-G7
SHERMAN ISLAND RD
- WSAC 95691 316-E2
3700 SaCo 94571 (494-C1
See Page 493)
4300 SaCo 94571 493-J3
19500 SaCo 94571 (514-C1
See Page 493)
SHERMAN ISLAND EAST LEVEE RD
17400 SaCo 94571 474-G6
17900 SaCo 94571 (494-H1
See Page 493)
20000 SaCo 94571 (514-D1
See Page 493)
SHERMAN OAKS CT
10300 ELKG 95624 359-F4
SHERRILEE WY
9100 SaCo 95662 260-G5
SHERRY CIR
1900 OAKL 94561 (514-C7
See Page 493)
SHERRY DR
8700 SaCo 95662 260-E5
SHERRY RIDGE LN
2100 EDCo 95667 246-A2
SHERWILL CT
- SAC 95823 357-J1
SHERWOOD AV
1400 SAC 95822 317-B3
SHERWOOD CT
3500 LMS 95650 201-A5
SHERWOOD LN
1100 EDCo 95619 265-H4
SHERWOOD PL
4100 PlaC 95602 162-A1
SHERWOOD WY
11400 PlaC 95602 161-J1
11400 PlaC 95602 162-A1
SHETLAND CT
- EDCo 95762 262-E1
- LNCN 95648 179-E3

SHETLAND CT
1400 RSVL 95661 240-B5
9000 ELKG 95624 358-H6
SHETLAND WY
1100 EDCo 95762 262-E1
SHIELAH WY
2100 SAC 95822 317-C3
SHIELDS AV
100 AUB 95603 182-E2
SHIELDS CT
2700 SaCo 95864 298-E5
SHIELE LN
8400 SaCo 95828 338-E7
SHILLING CT
8300 PlaC 95746 240-G2
SHILO DR
2600 EDCo 95667 226-E3
SHILOH CT
1600 EDCo 95667 225-C7
SHILOH WY
6200 SaCo 95841 259-C4
SHIMMER RIVER LN
7800 CITH 95610 240-B7
SHINER CT
8800 ELKG 95624 358-G4
S SHINGLE RD
4400 EDCo 95682 283-J4
7900 EDCo 95682 322-H2
8300 SaCo 95630 322-H2
SHINGLE CREEK CT
- PlaC 95747 239-A3
SHINGLE LIME MINE RD
4100 EDCo 95682 283-H2
SHINGLE SPRINGS DR
2200 EDCo 95682 244-C7
2400 EDCo 95682 264-C1
SHINGLE WOOD WY
7100 SaCo 95673 257-J2
SHINING STAR DR
3600 SAC 95823 337-G2
SHINN RANCH RD
- EDCo 95623 264-H6
SHIPMAN CT
- SAC 95823 358-B1
SHIPTON CT
- RSVL 95747 218-J5
SHIPTON DR
- RSVL 95747 218-J6
SHIPTON PL
11500 SaCo 95670 280-C5
SHIRAZ WY
9900 ELKG 95624 379-A1
SHIRE CT
- LNCN 95648 180-A6
- RSVL 95678 219-H4
5400 SaCo 95628 260-B6
SHIRE HORSE CT
- RKLN 95765 200-E4
SHIRE OAKS LN
9100 ELKG 95624 359-D4
SHIRLAND PARK PL
2300 PlaC 95603 182-C7
2300 PlaC 95603 202-C1
SHIRLAND TRACT RD
900 AUB 95603 182-D6
900 PlaC 95603 182-D7
1900 PlaC 95603 202-B1
SHIRLEY AV
5900 SaCo 95608 279-D4
SHIRLEY DR
1400 SAC 95822 317-B4
SHIRLEY ST
100 AUB 95603 182-D2
2900 WSAC 95691 316-E1
SHIRLEY WY
1200 LNCN 95648 179-G4
SHIVA CT
- SAC 95838 277-G3
SHIVELEY CT
400 RSVL 95747 219-C6
SHOAL CT
- SAC 95831 316-G6
SHOAL CREEK CT
7900 SaCo 95829 339-D5
SHOBAR AV
1200 SAC 95815 278-A6
SHOCKLEY CT
12700 AUB 95603 162-E7
SHOCKLEY RD
200 AUB 95603 162-E6
200 PlaC 95603 162-E5
SHOCKLEY WOODS CT
12700 AUB 95603 162-E6
12700 PlaC 95603 162-E6
SHOECH CT
10300 ELKG 95757 377-H3
10300 ELKG 95757 397-H3
SHOECH WY
10200 ELKG 95757 377-H3
10200 ELKG 95757 397-H3
SHOEMAKER WY
8400 CITH 95610 240-C6
SHOOFLY CT
8300 ELKG 95624 358-E2
SHOO FLY RD
5800 EDCo 95634 225-F1
6300 EDCo 95633 205-F6
6300 EDCo 95634 205-F6
SHOOTING STAR RD
4800 EDCo 95726 247-G7
4800 EDCo 95726 267-G1
SHOP ST
- SaCo 95690 436-J1
SHORE CT
- FOLS 95630 281-A1
E SHORE DR
7700 SAC 95831 336-J3
W SHORE DR
7700 SAC 95831 336-H4
SHORE ST
1300 WSAC 95691 296-G5
SHOREBIRD CT
- SAC 95833 276-H7
2300 ELKG 95757 377-E1
2300 ELKG 95757 397-E1
SHOREBIRD DR
- SAC 95833 276-H7
SHOREBIRD WY
2400 ELKG 95757 377-E1
2400 ELKG 95757 397-E1
SHORE BREEZE DR
800 SAC 95831 336-H4
SHORECLIFF CT
- SAC 95831 336-J4
SHOREHAM CT
- SaCo 95655 319-J2
SHORELAKE DR
- ELKG 95758 357-F7

SHORELINE CIR
- SAC 95831 316-H6
SHORELINE POINTE
500 EDCo 95762 242-C3
SHORE PINE CT
8600 ELKG 95624 358-H2
SHORESIDE CT
7100 PlaC 95746 241-C4
SHORESIDE DR
- SAC 95831 316-G6
SHORE STONE CT
- SAC 95831 336-J4
SHORE VIEW DR
7700 SAC 95831 336-J3
SHOREVIEW DR
1000 EDCo 95762 242-C3
SHOREWOOD ST
2300 SaCo 95608 279-D7
SHORT LN
2400 PlaC 95603 162-C4
SHORT RD
500 EDCo 95619 265-E3
8200 SaCo 95828 338-E7
8200 ELKG 95624 338-E7
SHORT ST
600 WSAC 95605 296-G1
SHORT BRANCH CT
- SAC 95834 277-C3
SHORT HILLS RD
1700 SaCo 95864 298-H2
SHORTHORN RD
4300 EDCo 95672 243-J6
12500 SaCo 95693 360-F5
SHORTLIDGE CT
2300 EDCo 95762 242-D7
2300 EDCo 95762 262-D1
SHORTLINE LN
8800 ELKG 95624 358-F4
SHORT OAK WY
7000 SaCo 95662 260-B2
SHORTWAY DR
5200 SAC 95823 337-J7
SHOSHONE WY
8700 SaCo 95662 260-E1
SHOVELER CT
2700 WSAC 95691 316-F1
SHOVELERS LN
5900 CITH 95621 259-D1
SHOWERS CT
100 FOLS 95630 261-G3
SHOW JUMPER CT
9600 SaCo 95693 360-J7
SHRADER CIR
7700 SAC 95832 337-F4
SHREWSBURY AV
7900 SaCo 95628 280-A1
SHRIKE CIR
100 SAC 95834 276-H4
SHRINE
- RCCD 95827 299-E4
SHROPSHIRE ST
- RSVL 95747 219-B7
- RSVL 95747 239-A1
SHUMWAY DR
9400 SaCo 95662 260-H6
SHUPE DR
6000 CITH 95621 259-G4
SHURWIN LN
3900 SaCo 95608 279-E5
SHYLA WY
- RCCD 95827 299-C7
SIBLEY ST
400 FOLS 95630 261-A5
SICKLE CT
5600 ELKG 95758 357-J4
SIDE PORCH LN
4200 EDCo 95682 264-A6
SIDE SADDLE DR
9400 SaCo 95693 360-J6
9400 SaCo 95693 (361-A6
See Page 341)
SIDESADDLE WY
1900 RSVL 95661 240-C3
SIDNEY AV
500 ANT 94509 (513-E5
See Page 493)
6000 SAC 95823 338-A7
SIDNEY DR
7300 CITH 95610 259-H1
SIEFKER CT
10400 ELKG 95624 359-F3
SIEGFRIED CT
5400 SaCo 95823 337-J3
SIENA AV
- SAC 95828 318-D5
SIENA PL
- RVIS 94571 454-G6
SIENNA CT
- ELKG 95757 377-J1
- ELKG 95757 397-J1
SIENNA LN
- SAC 95835 256-G6
- SaCo 95864 298-E3
SIENNA LP
- RSVL 95678 219-H2
SIENNA TR
- EDCo - 247-G3
SIENNA FELL CT
8500 SaCo 95843 239-B5
SIENNA HILLS WY
5500 SaCo 95843 239-C5
SIENNA RIVER CT
- RSVL 95747 199-B7
SIERRA AV
- RVIS 94571 454-G5
SIERRA BLVD
100 RSVL 95678 239-J1
400 RSVL 95678 219-J7
2200 SaCo 95825 298-D4
2500 SaCo 95864 298-E4
SIERRA CIR
1000 WSAC 95605 296-H2
SIERRA CT
1000 WSAC 95605 296-H2
SIERRA DR
- PLCR 95667 245-F6
7200 PlaC 95746 241-D3
SIERRA LN
400 SaCo 95864 298-E5
SIERRA PL
1000 WSAC 95605 296-H2
SIERRA RD
- WSAC 95691 316-H2
SIERRA ST
1300 WSAC 95605 296-H2
8000 SaCo 95628 280-A2
8900 ELKG 95624 358-G6
SIERRA TR
13100 PlaC 95603 162-F5

SIERRA WY
200 PlaC 95603 162-G6
9300 ELKG 95624 359-A5
SIERRA BLANCA DR
3100 EDCo 95709 246-G4
SIERRA BONITA WY
6900 SAC 95831 317-A7
SIERRA BROOK CT
8500 ELKG 95624 358-F2
SIERRA COLLEGE BLVD
- PlaC 95648 180-E4
800 PlaC 95663 180-F6
1600 PlaC 95650 200-F2
1600 PlaC 95663 200-G1
2200 RKLN 95650 200-G1
3000 LMS 95650 200-G6
SIERRA COLLEGE BLVD Rt#-E3
3900 LMS 95650 200-H7
4000 RKLN 95677 220-H3
4000 LMS 95650 220-H3
4000 LMS 95677 220-H3
5400 RKLN 95650 220-H3
6000 RKLN 95746 220-G6
6000 PlaC 95746 220-G6
6400 RSVL 95661 220-F7
6400 RSVL 95746 220-G6
6500 RSVL 95661 240-F3
6500 PlaC 95746 240-F6
8200 RSVL 95746 240-F3
8200 SaCo 95662 240-F6
8200 PlaC 95661 240-F3
SIERRA CREEK DR
9400 ELKG 95624 359-B6
SIERRA CREEK LN
- SaCo 95864 298-E3
SIERRA CREST WY
10400 RCCD 95670 299-G4
SIERRA EXPRESS DR
- EDCo - 247-C1
- EDCo 95709 247-C1
SIERRA FLAT DR
2100 SaCo 95670 280-C5
SIERRA GARDENS DR
1500 RSVL 95661 240-B2
SIERRA GATE PZ
- RSVL 95678 240-A1
SIERRA GLEN WY
10000 RCCD 95827 299-D3
SIERRA GOLD DR
- SaCo 95843 238-H6
SIERRAMA DR
2900 EDCo 95682 263-H3
SIERRA MADRE CT
2300 RCCD 95670 299-F1
SIERRA MADRE DR
4300 SaCo 95864 298-J2
SIERRA MEADOW CT
- ELKG 95758 357-F5
SIERRA MEADOWS DR
2200 RKLN 95677 220-F2
SIERRA MESA CT
- PlaC 95603 162-F6
SIERRA MESA PL
100 PlaC 95603 162-G6
SIERRA MILLS LN
2800 SaCo 95864 298-E3
SIERRA NEVADA WY
- ELKG 95624 358-F3
SIERRA OAK CT
200 FOLS 95630 281-A2
SIERRA OAKS CIR
1200 PlaC 95658 181-H7
SIERRA OAKS CT
100 RSVL 95678 219-J6
6000 EDCo 95623 264-J6
SIERRA OAKS DR
3000 SaCo 95864 298-F5
5000 EDCo 95623 264-J6
SIERRA OAKS VISTA LN
- SaCo 95864 298-E4
SIERRA PARK LN
- SaCo 95864 298-E3
SIERRA POINT DR
- SaCo 95834 277-C2
SIERRA PONDS LN
7000 PlaC 95746 221-C7
SIERRARAMA RD
2900 EDCo 95682 263-H4
SIERRA REAL
5500 EDCo 95623 265-B7
SIERRA RIVER DR
9200 ELKG 95624 359-A5
SIERRA ROCK RD
5100 EDCo 95667 244-A3
SIERRA SHADOWS PL
- PlaC 95603 162-C4
SIERRA SPRING WY
- ELKG 95624 359-B5
SIERRA SPRINGS CT
- PlaC 95650 201-D4
SIERRA SPRINGS DR
4000 EDCo 95726 247-H7
4000 EDCo 95726 267-G1
4800 EDCo 95726 248-A7
SIERRA SUNRISE TR
- EDCo - 267-C1
SIERRA SUNRISE WY
- PlaC 95603 162-G5
SIERRA SUNSET DR
8300 SaCo 95828 338-E5
SIERRAVALE WY
6000 CITH 95621 259-D2
SIERRA VALLEY LN
9000 PlaC 95650 221-G2
SIERRA VIEW CIR
- LNCN 95648 179-F6
800 PlaC 95603 162-E5
SIERRAVIEW DR
- RSVL 95678 219-J7
SIERRA VIEW LN
- LNCN 95648 179-F5
3300 SaCo 95821 278-F4
SIERRA VIEW PL
7100 PlaC 95650 221-C5
SIERRA VIEW TR
2600 SaCo 95608 279-E6
SIERRA VIEW WY
4400 SaCo 95628 280-B2
5500 SAC 95820 317-J2
SIERRA VISTA AV
3900 SAC 95820 317-G3
3900 SaCo 95820 317-G3
SIERRA VISTA CT
800 AUB 95603 182-B6
SIERRA VISTA DR
300 RCCD 95670 280-C7
2400 EDCo 95672 262-G2

STREET Block City ZIP Pg-Grid

SIERRAWOODS CIR
100 FOLS 95630 261-D4
SIESTA LN
4600 SaCo 95628 280-C1
5600 EDCo 95684 286-E7
SIGGENS CT
100 RSVL 95747 219-A6
SIGNAC CT
- SAC 95835 256-J4
SIGNAL CT
8100 SAC 95824 318-D6
9500 SaCo 95827 319-B1
SIGNET WY
200 SAC 95838 277-G3
SIGWART DR
- EDCo 95667 266-H3
SIKES CT
- SAC 95835 257-C4
SILBERHORN DR
100 FOLS 95630 261-H5
SILENT WINGS WY
- SaCo 95830 339-G7
SILICA AV
1300 SAC 95815 278-A7
1900 SAC 95825 278-B7
SILK CT
2900 SAC 95822 337-F2
SILK OAK CT
6400 CITH 95621 259-E1
SILK TREE WY
8200 SaCo 95843 238-F5
SILKWOOD DR
- AUB 95603 162-D6
SILKWOOD PL
3800 EDCo 95762 262-D2
SILK WOOD WY
6400 CITH 95621 259-E2
SILKWOOD WY
- RSVL 95746 240-F5
SILKY CT
7500 SaCo 95823 337-J3
SILLIMAN WY
700 SAC 95831 336-H2
SILMARK CT
- SAC 95831 336-G5
SILOUETTE CT
5300 ELKG 95757 377-J2
5300 ELKG 95757 397-J2
SILVA CT
100 FOLS 95630 261-A3
SILVANER CT
- EDCo 95762 262-G4
SILVANO ST
800 SAC 95838 277-J4
SILVA RANCH WY
7700 SAC 95831 336-J4
SILVA VALLEY PKWY
2200 EDCo 95762 262-D1
2200 EDCo 95762 242-D7
SILVA VALLEY RD
- EDCo 95762 262-F7
- EDCo 95762 282-F1
SILVEIRA WY
6300 SAC 95831 316-F6
SILVER CT
2000 SAC 95821 278-C5
SILVER DR
4200 EDCo 95619 265-E3
7800 CITH 95610 239-H7
SILVER ST
4000 RKLN 95677 200-E7
4000 RKLN 95677 220-D1
SILVERADO CIR
100 RSVL 95678 219-G5
SILVERADO DR
2700 OAKL 94561 (514-B7
See Page 493)
SILVERADO ST
- WSAC 95691 296-J7
- WSAC 95691 316-J1
4800 SaCo 95628 279-J1
SILVERADO WY
100 GALT 95632 439-E1
SILVER ASPEN CT
100 GALT 95632 419-C7
SILVER BAY CT
8900 SaCo 95829 338-H7
SILVER BAY WY
8900 SaCo 95829 338-H7
SILVERBEND LN
9200 ELKG 95624 359-C5
SILVER BEND WY
200 PlaC 95603 162-F6
SILVERBERRY AV
8700 ELKG 95624 358-G1
SILVER BIRCH PL
7400 CITH 95610 260-C1
SILVER BRIDLE WY
9400 ELKG 95758 357-H5
SILVERBROOK LN
9100 SaCo 95662 260-G2
SILVER CAVE WY
8300 SaCo 95829 338-H7
SILVER CLIFF WY
11800 SaCo 95670 280-E4
SILVERCOVE LN
9200 ELKG 95624 359-C5
SILVER CREEK LN
100 FOLS 95630 260-J4
2200 RSVL 95747 239-D1
SILVER CREST AV
4100 SaCo 95821 278-H5
SILVER CREST CIR
400 SaCo 95673 257-H1
SILVERCREST ST
2800 PLCR 95667 245-F4
SILVER CROWN CT
- ELKG 95624 358-F1
SILVER CYPRESS CT
100 GALT 95632 419-C7
SILVERDALE CT
- SaCo 95829 338-J7
SILVER DOLLAR CT
11300 SaCo 95693 360-B7
SILVER DOVE WY
4100 EDCo 95762 262-H7
SILVER EAGLE DR
- LNCN 95648 179-E3
SILVER EAGLE RD
- SAC 95838 277-G4
W SILVER EAGLE RD
400 SAC 95834 277-F4
SILVER FERN DR
2900 SaCo 95843 238-E6
SILVERFIELD WY
- RSVL 95747 219-C4
SILVER FORK CT
- LNCN 95648 179-J6
SILVER FOX WY
9400 ELKG 95758 358-D5
SILVERGATE LN
9700 ELKG 95624 359-B5
SILVER GLEN WY
7000 SaCo 95673 257-H2
SILVER GULCH CT
- RKLN 95765 200-A4
SILVER HARBOR DR
- ELKG 95624 358-J7
- ELKG 95624 359-A7
SILVER HAWK CT
6500 ELKG 95758 358-A3
SILVERHAWK CT
- PlaC 95602 161-J2
SILVER HAWK WY
6400 ELKG 95758 358-A3
SILVERHAWK WY
- PlaC 95602 161-J2
SILVER HILL CT
- LNCN 95648 180-B6
SILVERHOLLOW LN
9300 ELKG 95624 359-C5
SILVERHORN CT
- RSVL 95678 219-G3
SILVERHORN DR
- RSVL 95678 219-G3
SILVERHORSE CT
- SAC 95834 276-H1
SILVER KNOLL ST
7000 SaCo 95673 257-H2
SILVER LAKE DR
1000 SAC 95831 316-J6
1000 SAC 95831 317-A6
SILVERLEAF WY
8000 SaCo 95829 338-H6
SILVER LEGEND DR
8300 SaCo 95829 339-D7
SILVER LODE CT
3000 EDCo 95667 264-H2
SILVER LODE DR
5300 EDCo 95667 264-G3
SILVER MAPLE LN
8500 SaCo 95662 260-D3
SILVER MEADOW CT
- SaCo 95829 339-D6
SILVER MEADOW WY
8200 SaCo 95829 339-D6
SILVER MILL WY
- RSVL 95678 220-A2
SILVER MOON WY
8300 SaCo 95829 338-H7
SILVER MOUNTAIN CT
- RKLN 95765 219-J2
SILVER OAK CT
500 RSVL 95678 219-J7
SILVER OAK WY
1200 SAC 95831 337-A2
SILVEROD PL
- SaCo 95829 339-C6
SILVER PARK AV
400 SaCo 95673 257-H1
SILVER PEAK LN
- RKLN 95677 200-D7
- RKLN 95765 200-D7
SILVER PINE CT
100 GALT 95632 419-C7
SILVER PLUME DR
- FOLS 95630 260-J1
- FOLS 95630 261-F1
SILVER POINT LN
- SaCo 95670 280-F4
SILVER POPLAR CT
- RSVL 95678 219-J5
SILVER POPLAR LN
5300 ELKG 95758 357-J2
SILVER RANCH AV
3500 LMS 95650 201-B5
SILVER RANCH WY
4900 SaCo 95608 279-A5
SILVER RIDGE CT
- EDCo - 267-C5
SILVER RIDGE LN
- EDCo - 267-B6
- EDCo 95667 267-B6
SILVER RIDGE WY
1100 SAC 95831 337-A2
SILVER ROCK CT
8400 CITH 95610 240-C6
SILVER RUN WY
8400 SaCo 95843 238-G5
SILVER SADDLE LN
- RKLN 95765 199-J4
- RKLN 95765 200-A4
SILVERSADDLE WY
- CITH 95621 259-E3
SILVER SAGE CT
3500 SaCo 95843 238-G6
SILVER SEA CT
8900 SaCo 95829 338-H7
SILVER SHADOW CIR
5900 SAC 95823 357-J1
5900 SAC 95823 358-A1
SILVERSIDE DR
8200 SaCo 95843 238-H6
SILVER SKY CT
500 SaCo 95673 257-H2
SILVER SPRINGS LN
6600 CITH 95621 259-E3
SILVER SPRUCE CT
100 GALT 95632 419-D7
SILVER SPUR CIR
1300 LNCN 95648 179-J1
SILVER SPUR CT
- RKLN 95677 200-D6
- RKLN 95765 200-D6
200 FOLS 95630 261-D4
SILVER SPUR WY
3800 SaCo 95841 278-G2
SILVER STAR CT
- RKLN 95765 200-E5
SILVERSTONE CT
- RSVL 95747 199-D7
SILVERSTONE LN
9300 ELKG 95624 359-C5
SILVER STRAND WY
5300 SaCo 95841 259-B4
SILVER STRIKE CT
- RSVL 95747 219-A5
SILVERTHORNE CIR
6600 SaCo 95842 259-B3
SILVERTON CIR
900 LNCN 95648 179-G5
SILVERTON WY
4400 SAC 95838 277-F1
6100 SaCo 95608 259-E7
SILVERTRAIL LN
9700 ELKG 95624 359-B5
SILVER TREE CT
500 SaCo 95673 257-H2
SILVER TREE PL
7200 PlaC 95746 241-C3
SILVER VIEW WY
7300 SaCo 95673 257-H1
SILVER WATER WY
4200 RCCD 95742 320-D1
SILVER WILLOW CT
100 GALT 95632 419-C7
SILVER WINGS ST
- RCCD 95655 299-F6
- SaCo 95655 299-F6
SILVERWOOD CT
- LNCN 95648 180-A4
- PlaC 95746 240-H4
SILVERWOOD RD
- WSAC 95691 316-C4
SILVERWOOD WY
10500 RCCD 95670 299-G3
SILVERY BLUE WY
8800 ELKG 95624 358-F3
SILVEY CT
- ELKG 95624 358-D1
SILVIES WY
4400 ELKG 95758 357-H5
SIMAK CT
- SaCo 95829 339-B6
SIMAS WY
900 PLCR 95667 245-F4
SIMCOE CT
- SAC 95823 337-J5
SIMI CT
8100 SaCo 95828 338-F6
SIMI VALLEY WY
3900 SaCo 95843 238-H5
SIMKO RANCH LN
- SaCo 95632 419-B7
- SaCo 95632 439-B1
SIMMER WY
- RVIS 94571 454-H3
SIMMERHORN RD
3000 SaCo 95632 419-G6
6500 GALT 95632 419-G6
11100 SaCo 95632 420-A6
12900 SaCo 95638 421-A6
12900 SaCo 95632 421-A6
SIMMERHORN RD Rt#-J10
900 GALT 95632 419-F5
SIMMONS ST
1200 ANT 94509 (513-F4
See Page 493)
SIMMONS WY
100 FOLS 95630 261-B2
SIMOES CT
5100 ELKG 95757 377-H3
5100 ELKG 95757 397-H3
SIMON DR
1000 PLCR 95667 245-G5
SIMON ST
7200 SaCo 95828 338-E1
SIMON TER
900 WSAC 95605 296-J2
SIMONE PL
5200 SaCo 95628 260-F7
SIMONICH WY
- ELKG 95757 377-H3
- ELKG 95757 397-H3
SIMONS ST
600 GALT 95632 419-E6
SIMOTAS CT
- SAC 95820 318-C3
SIMPLICITY WY
- SaCo 95826 318-J3
SIMPSON CT
7100 SaCo 95828 338-B1
SIMPSON RANCH CT
12500 SaCo 95683 340-J6
12500 SaCo 95683 341-A7
12500 SaCo 95693 341-A7
SIMS RD
- SaCo 95758 337-F7
6500 ELKG 95758 357-G2
6500 SaCo 95758 357-G2
N SIMS WY
5100 SaCo 95628 259-F7
SIMUNICH CT
6000 EDCo 95630 222-G3
SINBAD CT
7800 SaCo 95828 338-E4
SINCLAIR DR
- EDCo 95682 263-F3
SINCLAIR RD
- SAC 95819 298-B6
SINCLAIR WY
1100 RSVL 95747 219-E6
SINGER LN
100 FOLS 95630 261-G3
SINGER PL
- LNCN 95648 179-D4
SINGING TREE WY
4100 SaCo 95843 238-H5
SINGINGWOOD RD
900 SaCo 95864 298-F3
SINGLE WY
7300 CITH 95610 260-B2
SINGLETERRY WY
8000 SaCo 95843 238-F6
SINGLETON CT
3800 SaCo 95843 238-G5
SINGLETREE CT
- RKLN 95765 219-J2
700 GALT 95632 439-F1
SINSKEY CT
- SAC 95758 358-C1
SIOUX CT
3600 SaCo 95843 238-G6
SIPLER WY
- ELKG 95758 357-E4
SIPPOLA RANCH RD
7200 PlaC 95746 221-G3
SIRANI CT
8300 SaCo 95828 338-E7
SIR BRADLEY WY
- SAC 95838 257-H6
SIRBUCK WY
5200 SaCo 95608 279-B5
SIR EDWARDS CT
4900 SaCo 95628 260-D7
4900 SaCo 95628 280-D1
SIR HENRY CT
4900 SaCo 95628 260-E7
4900 SaCo 95628 280-E1
SIRL WY
5900 SaCo 95662 260-H5
SIR LANCELOT LN
5200 SaCo 95628 260-C7
SIROCCO CT
8300 ELKG 95758 358-E5
SIROCCO WY
8300 ELKG 95758 358-E5
SIR ROBERT CT
- EDCo 95762 262-B1
SISKIN CT
4800 SaCo 95842 259-A3
SISKIYOU AV
4800 SaCo 95820 317-G3
SISLEY RD
1200 PlaC 95663 181-D7
1500 PlaC 95663 201-D1
SITA CT
8100 SaCo 95829 338-H6
SITKA CT
- RKLN 95765 200-D5
5400 ELKG 95758 357-J3
SITKA DR
- RKLN 95765 200-D5
SITKA ST
300 SAC 95814 297-E2
SITTA LN
6500 PlaC 95746 221-E6
SITTING BULL WY
3900 SaCo 95843 238-H7
SITTON WY
5100 SaCo 95823 317-J6
SIX RIVERS CIR
- SAC 95831 336-J1
SIXTH PKWY
7000 SaCo 95823 337-J1
SIZEMORE LN
6100 SaCo 95608 279-D4
SKAGIT RIVER CT
11200 RCCD 95670 280-A5
SKAGWAY CT
7100 SaCo 95673 257-H1
SKANDER WY
7300 SaCo 95828 338-C3
SKARDA CT
- SAC 95835 256-H4
SKEENA CIR
- RSVL 95747 219-C2
SKELLIG ROCK WY
5000 EDCo 95762 262-H4
SKELTON WY
7500 SAC 95822 337-D3
SKI CT
8700 ELKG 95624 358-G6
SKI RUN
- EDCo 95726 248-A4
SKIDMORE CT
100 FOLS 95630 261-G3
SKINNER LN
2200 EDCo 95672 243-J7
SKI PARK CT
6000 SaCo 95673 257-J4
6000 SaCo 95673 258-A5
SKIPJACK WY
8800 SaCo 95828 338-G4
SKIPPER CIR
700 SAC 95822 316-J4
SKIPPER CV
100 PlaC 95603 162-F5
SKIPPEREEN WY
9100 SaCo 95829 338-H6
SKIPTON CT
2800 ANT 94509 (513-C6
See Page 493)
SKIROS WY
7600 SAC 95823 337-F3
SKIS RD
3700 EDCo 95667 245-A7
3700 EDCo 95667 265-A1
SKOKIE PL
7000 SaCo 95621 259-D2
SKOPAS CT
200 RSVL 95661 240-E1
SKUBE LN
200 SaCo 95825 298-D5
SKUNK LN
- EDCo 95633 205-C1
SKVARLA AV
- SaCo 95652 258-F5
- SaCo 95660 258-F5
SKY CT
3000 EDCo 95667 265-C1
3200 EDCo 95682 263-E5
SKY LN
3300 EDCo 95682 263-G5
SKY PKWY
4900 SaCo 95823 317-H7
5000 SaCo 95823 337-J1
5400 SaCo 95823 318-A7
5400 SaCo 95823 338-A1
SKY WY
7900 PlaC 95746 241-E3
SKYBROOK LN
- SaCo 95828 338-F3
SKY CREEK DR
6100 SAC 95828 318-F6
SKYCREST CT
5400 EDCo 95623 264-G6
7400 CITH 95610 259-H5
SKYCREST DR
5300 EDCo 95623 264-G6
SKYDOME CT
9400 ELKG 95624 358-G5
SKYE CT
9400 PlaC 95746 241-A5
SKY HAWK RD
6200 EDCo 95630 222-J2
SKYKING RD Rt#-E14
4700 SaCo 95835 256-D3
SKYLAKE WY
700 SAC 95831 336-H1
700 SAC 95831 316-H7
SKYLANE DR
6500 CITH 95621 259-F1
SKYLARK CT
7400 CITH 95610 259-H5
SKYLARK DR
- RSVL 95747 219-B7
SKYLARK LN
2500 EDCo 95709 246-J2
SKYLES CT
8800 SaCo 95828 338-G3
SKYLES WY
8800 SaCo 95828 338-G3
SKYLINE CT
600 EDCo 95667 245-E6
600 PLCR 95667 245-E6
7500 CITH 95610 259-H5
SKYLINE DR
400 PLCR 95667 245-E5
400 EDCo 95667 245-E5
1000 PlaC 95602 162-F3
SKYMASTER WY
- SaCo 95655 299-E7
SKY RANCH CT
- EDCo 95709 226-J7
SKY RANCH LN
- EDCo 95709 226-H7
2400 EDCo 95709 246-J1
SKY RIDGE CT
100 RSVL 95678 219-F6
SKYRIDGE DR
100 AUB 95603 182-D4
- SaCo 95662 260-G6
SKY RIDGE RD
4600 EDCo 95619 265-H5
SKYSAIL CT
- SAC 95831 316-H6
SKYVIEW DR
6500 SaCo 95662 260-B3
SKY VIEW LN
9000 PlaC 95746 240-H4
SKYVIEW LN
6500 EDCo 95667 244-H2
24700 SJCo 95220 439-H6
SKY VIEW WY
400 PlaC 95658 181-E5
SKY VISTA CT
6300 CITH 95621 259-E1
SKYWALKER CT
8300 SaCo 95828 338-E5
SKYWARD CT
3400 RCCD 95827 299-E6
SKYWARD LN
3800 EDCo 95667 265-C1
SKYWAY DR
4800 SaCo 95628 260-F7
4800 SaCo 95628 280-F1
SKYWIND CT
- SAC 95831 336-J2
SKYWOODS WY
7900 SaCo 95828 338-C4
SLAB CREEK CT
7200 EDCo 95667 226-J4
SLAB CREEK RD
- EDCo 95667 226-J6
- EDCo 95667 246-H1
- EDCo 95709 226-J6
SLADE LN
1100 PlaC 95603 162-D5
1100 AUB 95603 162-D5
SLALOM LN
- EDCo 95726 247-J5
SLATE CT
- RSVL 95678 219-H5
4600 RKLN 95677 220-B2
SLATE WY
6100 SaCo 95608 279-D2
SLATE CREEK CT
100 FOLS 95630 260-J4
SLATE CREEK RD
4800 EDCo 95623 264-J5
SLATE FALLS WY
11800 RCCD 95742 320-D1
SLATER WY
- FOLS 95630 260-J3
SLATE RIDGE CT
- EDCo 95762 282-D4
SLATE RIVER WY
6900 SAC 95831 316-G7
6900 SAC 95831 336-G1
SLAWSON LN
- LNCN 95648 180-B6
SLAYBACK CT
600 FOLS 95630 262-A5
SLEEPY CREEK LN
4100 EDCo 95682 264-C5
SLEEPY HOLLOW CT
2800 PLCR 95667 245-D4
SLEEPY HOLLOW DR
2200 EDCo 95682 264-B1
2400 EDCo 95682 244-B6
SLEEPY HOLLOW LN
8500 ELKG 95624 359-F2
SLEEPY HOLLOW RD
4900 EDCo 95682 283-F3
SLEEPY HOLLOW WY
1200 RSVL 95661 240-A5
SLEEPY RIVER WY
7700 SAC 95831 337-A4
SLIDELL PARK CT
1100 GALT 95632 419-G2
SLIGO CT
6200 SaCo 95662 260-C4
SLIPPERY CREEK LN
6300 CITH 95621 259-D4
SLOAN DR
4200 SaCo 95660 258-H2
SLOAT WY
2000 SAC 95818 297-D7
SLOBE AV
400 SAC 95815 297-G1
SLOCUM CT
7300 SAC 95822 337-C2
SLOCUM DR
400 FOLS 95630 281-A2
SLODUSTY RD
4200 EDCo 95633 205-D1
SLOOP CT
7500 CITH 95621 259-D1
SLOUGHHOUSE RD
7100 SaCo 95624 340-F4
SLOW DOWN RD
400 PlaC 95658 181-G4
SLUICE ST
- EDCo 95667 226-E2
SLUICE BOX CIR
10900 AUB 95603 182-C6
SLUICE BOX RD
3500 EDCo 95667 245-H6
SLUMBER CT
3400 EDCo 95667 245-G7
SLY PARK RD Rt#-E16
3000 EDCo 95726 248-D1
5000 EDCo - 248-D3
5900 EDCo - 267-D4
SLYVANER DR
- RCCD 95670 300-A3
SMALL HILL CT
5900 CITH 95621 259-D4
SMALLWOOD LN
4000 SaCo 95628 280-B2
SMATHERS WY
3200 SaCo 95608 279-A5
SMILAX AV
500 WSAC 95605 296-H1
SMILAX WY
3400 SAC 95834 277-D4
SMITH CT
100 AUB 95603 182-D5
SMITH LN
1100 RSVL 95661 239-J3
1100 RSVL 95661 240-A3
SMITH WY
- FOLS 95630 261-J5
SMITHART ST
6600 SaCo 95662 260-C3
SMITH FARM CT
- SaCo 95628 260-B7
SMITHFIELD WY
3900 SaCo 95826 318-H2
SMITH FLAT RD
1600 PLCR 95667 246-A4
1900 EDCo 95667 246-C4
SMITH FLAT CEMETERY RD
1900 EDCo 95667 246-C4
SMITH FLAT SCHOOL RD
2800 EDCo 95667 246-C4
SMITHLEE DR
3200 RCCD 95827 299-E5
SMOKE RIVER WY
1100 SAC 95831 337-A3
SMOKESTACK WY
2100 SAC 95833 276-G7
SMOKE TREE CT
6600 CITH 95610 260-A3
SMOKETREE DR
1900 SAC 95833 277-B4
1900 SAC 95834 277-B4
SMOKETREE ST
2700 ANT 94509 (513-J5
See Page 493)
SMOKE WOOD CT
6100 LMS 95650 201-A5
SMOKEWOOD CT
5200 SaCo 95628 260-G7
SMOKEY LN
- EDCo 95726 267-J3
SMOKEY GROVE CT
- RSVL 95661 239-J5
SMOKEY LEAF CT
- SAC 95838 257-H7
SMOKEY MOUNTAIN CIR
3300 EDCo 95762 262-D7
SMOKY CT
3100 SaCo 95826 298-J7
SMOLEY WY
7700 CITH 95610 240-B7
7700 CITH 95610 260-B1
SMUD DR
4900 SaCo 95842 259-A2
SNAFFLE BIT CT
4400 SaCo 95843 238-J5
SNAPDRAGON CIR
- WSAC 95691 296-G7
SNAPDRAGON CT
8600 ELKG 95624 358-F1
SNAPDRAGON LN
- LNCN 95648 180-A5
- RSVL 95747 219-D6
SNAPDRAGON PL
- LNCN 95648 180-A4
SNAPDRAGON ST
- WSAC 95691 296-F7
SNEAD WY
7800 SaCo 95829 339-E5
SNELLING LN
- SAC 95835 256-G6
SNIPES BLVD
5600 SaCo 95662 260-J6
SNOOPY CT
6800 EDCo 95623 265-C5
SNOOPY RD
6400 EDCo 95623 265-C5
SNOW BAR CT
100 FOLS 95630 261-F4
SNOWBERRY CIR
- WSAC 95691 296-G7
SNOWBERRY WY
9600 SaCo 95662 260-J5
SNOWBIRD WY
9300 SaCo 95826 299-A7
SNOW BREEZE CT
- RSVL 95747 219-D3
SNOW CAP CT
5300 EDCo 95623 264-G5
SNOWCAP VIEW CIR
3500 PlaC 95602 162-A2
SNOWDEN CT
- PlaC 95746 240-G4
SNOWDOWN CT
- LNCN 95648 179-F7
SNOWDROP LN
- EDCo 95726 247-H7
SNOWDROP PL
300 LNCN 95648 180-A5
SNOW FALL WY
- EDCo 95762 282-D3
SNOW FIRE CT
8600 ELKG 95624 338-F7
SNOWFLOWER LN
- EDCo - 247-B7
SNOW GOOSE LN
7500 CITH 95621 259-D1
SNOW GOOSE WY
- RSVL 95747 239-B1
SNOWHAVEN CT
- RKLN 95765 219-J2
SNOW LAKE PL
- ELKG 95758 357-E5
SNOW LEOPARD CIR
5900 ELKG 95757 358-A7
SNOW LILY AV
900 GALT 95632 419-F2
SNOW LILY CT
900 GALT 95632 419-F2
SNOWMASS LN
2300 RKLN 95677 220-B5
SNOW RIVER WY
7100 SAC 95831 336-G1
SNOWROSE LN
- EDCo 95709 247-C6
SNOWS CT
- EDCo - 267-C1
SNOWS RD
3000 EDCo 95709 247-B4
3800 EDCo - 247-B4
3800 EDCo - 267-C1
SNOW SPRING PL
5400 SaCo 95843 239-C6
SNOW WHISPER CT
- RSVL 95747 219-C3
SNOWY BIRCH WY
7100 SAC 95823 338-B6
SNOWY EGRET BLVD
- SAC 95834 276-J1
SNOWY EGRET CT
- OAKL 94561 (514-H7
See Page 493)
- RSVL 95661 220-E7
2400 ELKG 95757 377-E1
2400 ELKG 95757 397-E1
SNOWY EGRET WY
- OAKL 94561 (514-H6
See Page 493)
2400 ELKG 95757 377-E1
2400 ELKG 95757 397-E1
SNOWY OWL CT
10000 AUB 95603 182-E6
SNOWY OWL WY
10000 AUB 95603 182-D6
SNOWY RANGE CT
- FOLS 95630 261-A2
SNOWY RIVER CT
- RSVL 95747 219-B3
SNOWY SPRINGS CIR
- ELKG 95758 358-E6
SOAP PLANT LN
3500 EDCo 95682 263-H6
SOARING HAWK CT
- LNCN 95648 199-J3
- LNCN 95648 200-A3
SOARING HAWK LN
- LNCN 95648 199-J3
- LNCN 95648 200-A3
SOARING HAWK PL
- LNCN 95648 200-A3
SOARING OAKS DR
9300 ELKG 95758 358-B5
SOAVE CT
11100 RCCD 95670 300-A4
SOBRANTE WY
2600 RCCD 95670 299-E3
SOCORRO WY
1000 SAC 95833 277-D5
SODA ROCK RD
500 OAKL 94561 (514-E6
See Page 493)
SODA SPRINGS WY
11500 SaCo 95670 280-C5
SOFAR RD
4200 EDCo 95667 265-H1
SOFTWOOD CT
6100 CITH 95621 239-D7
SOHAIR CT
3700 EDCo 95762 262-E1
SOL WY
6400 CITH 95621 259-G4
SOLA CT
- SAC 95835 256-H3
SOLANO AV
47500 SolC 94571 (395-H6
See Page 375)
48900 SolC 94571 (396-A6
See Page 375)
SOLANO RD
2500 EDCo 95682 263-C7
SOLANO ST
600 WSAC 95605 296-G1
SOLANO WY
4600 SaCo 95628 279-G1
SOLAR WY
3500 RCCD 95827 299-D6
SOLAR HILL DR
- EDCo - 247-F2
SOLARI CT
- EDCo 95762 282-E3
SOLARI WY
3400 SaCo 95821 278-J4
SOLEDAD AV
4100 SaCo 95820 317-G4
4400 SAC 95820 317-G4
SOLEDAD CT
- RSVL 95747 219-A7
SOLEDAD DR
- RSVL 95747 219-A7
- RSVL 95747 239-A1
SOLERA DR
10900 RCCD 95670 299-J5
SOLIDAY CT
100 FOLS 95630 261-G4
SOLITARY LN
6400 SaCo 95608 279-E3
SOLITUDE CT
- RKLN 95765 220-A2
8400 SaCo 95843 239-B5
SOLITUDE WY
- RKLN 95765 219-J1
- RKLN 95765 220-A1
SOLOMON ISLAND RD
- WSAC 95691 316-C2
SOLORA WY
- SAC 95828 318-C7
- SAC 95828 338-C1
SOLSTICE CIR
400 EDCo 95619 265-C5
SOLSTICE CT
100 EDCo 95619 265-C5
SOMBRA CT
3500 EDCo 95682 263-C7
SOMBRERO CT
- PlaC 95603 162-A5
SOMBRERO WY
100 FOLS 95630 261-E3
SOMERDALE CIR
1900 RSVL 95661 240-E3
SOMER RIDGE DR
- RSVL 95661 239-J4
SOMERSBY WY
900 SaCo 95864 298-J3
SOMERSET CT
1200 RSVL 95661 240-A5
SOMERSET DR
1300 WSAC 95605 296-H2
SOMERSET LP
- EDCo - 267-C5
SOMERSET PL
1600 ANT 94509 (513-F5
See Page 493)
SOMERSET RD
3100 SaCo 95864 298-F2
SOMERSET WY
3000 RKLN 95677 220-D5
SOMERSHIRE WY
8800 SaCo 95828 338-G6
SOMERSVILLE RD
1100 ANT 94509 (513-B4
See Page 493)
SOMERSWORTH DR
6700 CITH 95621 259-F3
SOMERSWORTH LN
- LNCN 95648 179-F7
SOMERTON WY
7300 SAC 95828 318-B7

STREET Block City ZIP Pg-Grid

SOMERVILLE WY
6800 SaCo 95628 259-F7
SOMIS WY
6400 SAC 95828 318-C6
SOMMER STAR CT N
- EDCo - 267-B1
SOMMER STAR RD
- EDCo - 267-B1
SOMMER STAR RD N
- EDCo - 247-C7
- EDCo - 267-B1
SONATA DR
2300 RCCD 95670 279-H7
W SONDIESA CT
- ELKG 95758 357-F5
SONDIESA WY
9300 ELKG 95758 357-F5
SONGBIRD CT
- SAC 95823 358-A1
SONGBIRD LN
300 EDCo 95619 265-D6
SONGBIRD WY
- RSVL 95747 218-H4
SONG SPARROW LN
2200 LNCN 95648 180-B7
SONG SPARROW WY
8900 ELKG 95758 358-C3
SONIA AV
8500 SaCo 95662 260-D5
SONJA CT
4400 EDCo 95667 264-H3
SONOMA AV
600 SAC 95815 277-H5
1100 SAC 95815 278-A5
SONOMA CT
100 RSVL 95747 219-A5
SONOMA LN
2500 ANT 94509 (513-A6 See Page 493)
SONOMA WY
900 SAC 95819 297-H5
SONOMA CREEK DR
- ELKG 95624 379-A2
SONOMA HILLS WY
8100 SaCo 95828 338-F6
SONOMA VALLEY WY
8800 SaCo 95829 338-H5
SONORA AV
1300 WSAC 95691 296-H4
SONORA CT
2500 EDCo 95762 262-C1
SONORA DR
2400 EDCo 95762 262-D1
7200 SaCo 95683 342-A2
SONORA WY
5200 SaCo 95608 259-E7
SONORAN WY
8800 ELKG 95624 358-F2
SONORA PASS WY
- RKLN 95765 219-J1
SONTERRA WY
- SAC 95835 257-C5
SOPHIA CT
- SAC 95831 337-A3
SOPHIA PKWY
- EDCo 95762 262-A3
- FOLS 95630 262-A3
SOPHIA WY
3500 SAC 95820 317-J2
SOPHISTRY DR
4200 RCCD 95742 320-E2
SOPHOCLES DR
- RCCD 95742 320-D2
SOPHYS CT
- RSVL 95747 219-A7
SOQUEL WY
7500 CITH 95610 260-A1
SORA WY
3300 SAC 95833 276-J4
3300 SAC 95834 276-J4
SORBELL CT
- SAC 95823 357-J1
SORENSON DR
- LNCN 95648 179-E1
SORENSON WY
5100 SaCo 95843 239-B7
SORENSTAM DR
10100 SaCo 95829 339-E5
SORENTO RD
4800 SaCo 95835 257-E4
4900 SaCo 95834 257-E6
4900 SAC 95835 257-E4
5400 SaCo 95673 257-E1
7700 SaCo 95626 237-E5
SORNEY LOOP RD
2600 EDCo 95672 263-F1
SORRBENTO CT
- RSVL 95747 219-B1
SORREL LN
3100 EDCo 95667 244-G6
SORRELL CIR
- RKLN 95765 199-J5
SORRELL CT
- RKLN 95765 199-J5
6300 CITH 95621 239-E7
SORRENA WY
9700 ELKG 95757 357-H7
SORRENTINO WY
- ELKG 95757 358-A7
- ELKG 95757 378-A1
SORRENTO PKWY
- LNCN 95648 179-E5
SORTWELL CT
- EDCo 95762 262-F6
SOTANO DR
600 SAC 95833 277-E5
SOTHEBY CT
8700 SaCo 95628 280-E1
SOTNIP RD
- SAC 95834 257-E7
- SAC 95835 257-E7
- SaCo 95834 257-E7
SOTO WY
- FOLS 95630 261-F4
SOUCRAN CT
8300 SaCo 95829 338-J7
SOUKUP CT
100 FOLS 95630 261-E6
SOULE ST
900 WSAC 95691 296-J4
900 WSAC 95691 297-A4
SOULES WY
7500 SaCo 95823 337-J3
SOURDOUGH CT
100 FOLS 95630 260-J4
6500 EDCo 95667 244-J1
SOURDOUGH LN
- EDCo 95667 244-H1
SOURDOUGH TR
- EDCo 95634 225-B3
SOUTH AV
- SAC 95838 277-H3
1300 SAC 95838 278-A3
SOUTH CT
- EDCo 95623 265-B4
SOUTH DR
2200 PlaC 95603 162-B4
SOUTH PKWY
7500 SaCo 95823 337-H3
SOUTH ST
6100 EDCo 95623 265-A5
SOUTHAMPTON WY
6900 SaCo 95823 317-G7
6900 SaCo 95823 337-G1
SOUTH BLUFF DR
1000 RSVL 95678 219-F6
SOUTHBREEZE DR
7600 SaCo 95828 338-G4
SOUTHBRIDGE CIR
900 LNCN 95648 179-G4
SOUTHBROOK WY
5700 SaCo 95608 259-E5
SOUTHBURY CT
- SAC 95835 256-J5
SOUTHBURY WY
- SAC 95835 256-J5
- SAC 95835 257-A5
SOUTHCLIFF DR
7600 SaCo 95628 279-H3
SOUTH COAST LN
9500 ELKG 95758 358-D6
SOUTHCOUNTRY WY
8200 SaCo 95828 338-D4
SOUTHCREEK CIR
100 FOLS 95630 241-B7
SOUTHCREEK DR
2600 LNCN 95648 200-A3
SOUTHCREST CT
- SAC 95831 336-J4
SOUTHDALE CT
800 GALT 95632 439-F1
SOUTHEAST PKWY
4900 SaCo 95823 337-H2
SOUTHERLAND RD
- WSAC 95691 316-D4
SOUTHERN CROSS CT
- RSVL 95747 219-B3
SOUTHERNESS DR
6000 EDCo 95762 262-G4
SOUTHERN HILLS DR
- RVIS 94571 454-E1
SOUTHERN PINE LN
- SaCo 95842 259-A1
SOUTHFIELDS CIR
8300 SaCo 95828 338-D3
E SOUTHGATE DR
- SaCo 95823 337-J2
- SaCo 95823 338-A1
SOUTHGATE RD
- SAC 95815 277-H7
SOUTHGLEN CT
5000 ELKG 95758 357-H3
SOUTHGROVE DR
5600 CITH 95610 259-H6
SOUTHLAND CT
7700 SaCo 95828 338-F4
SOUTHLAND WY
7700 SaCo 95828 338-F4
SOUTHLIGHT LN
- LNCN 95648 200-C1
SOUTHLITE CIR
- SAC 95831 316-H7
- SAC 95831 336-J1
SOUTH LOOP RD
- PlaC 95765 199-F7
SOUTHMONT WY
7200 SAC 95822 337-B1
SOUTH OAK WY
7600 SAC 95831 337-A4
SOUTHOLM CT
5400 SaCo 95628 260-F6
SOUTH PARK DR
4300 SaCo 95821 278-J6
4600 SaCo 95608 279-A6
4600 SaCo 95821 279-A6
SOUTH POINT RD
4500 EDCo 95619 265-E4
SOUTH PORT DR
3300 SaCo 95826 318-J1
SOUTHPORT PKWY
- WSAC 95691 296-E7
- WSAC 95691 316-D2
SOUTHPORT PKWY NW
- WSAC 95691 296-F7
SOUTHRIDGE CT
1500 EDCo 95762 262-C7
SOUTHRIDGE DR
900 AUB 95603 182-C6
SOUTH RIVER RD
- WSAC 95691 296-J6
- WSAC 95691 297-A4
800 WSAC 95691 317-A2
2000 WSAC 95691 316-H3
SOUTH SHINGLE RD
4200 EDCo 95682 264-A7
SOUTHSIDE AV
8800 ELKG 95624 358-G7
SOUTHSIDE RANCH RD
5000 RKLN 95677 220-G4
5100 RKLN 95650 220-G4
SOUTHVIEW CT
- PLCR 95667 245-F6
5700 CITH 95610 259-H5
SOUTHWEST AV
5100 SaCo 95824 317-J5
SOUTHWICK LN
1100 LNCN 95648 179-G5
SOUTHWICK WY
- SaCo 95864 298-J4
SOUTHWIND CIR
3300 RKLN 95765 200-C7
SOUTHWIND DR
100 SaCo 95823 337-F1
SOUTHWOOD CIR
500 FOLS 95630 241-B7
SOUTHWOOD WY
1400 RSVL 95747 219-E5
6800 SaCo 95828 338-B1
SOUVERAIN CT
800 OAKL 94561 (514-D5 See Page 493)
SOUZA CIR
7300 SAC 95831 336-H2
SOUZA DR
- EDCo 95762 262-E6
SOUZA WY
- FOLS 95630 261-H4
SOVEREIGN CT
7300 CITH 95621 259-G1
N SOWLES RD
22800 SJCo 95220 (440-J5 See Page 420)
27000 SJCo 95632 (440-J5 See Page 420)
SPAANS DR
400 GALT 95632 419-E5
SPAATZ WY
- SaCo 95655 299-E7
SPACE CT
- SAC 95831 316-J7
SPAHN RANCH RD
3100 PlaC 95661 240-D6
3100 RSVL 95661 240-D6
SPALDING CT
- WSAC 95691 316-D4
- SAC 95832 337-C4
SPALETTA WY
1800 SAC 95835 257-C5
SPANISH TR
- RKLN 95765 219-J2
- RKLN 95765 220-A2
SPANISH BAR CT
2000 SaCo 95670 280-D4
SPANISH BAY CT
500 RSVL 95747 219-D7
SPANISH BAY WY
1400 RSVL 95747 219-D7
SPANISH CORRAL LN
2000 PlaC 95603 181-H1
SPANISH FLAT RD
5500 EDCo 95633 205-E7
5500 EDCo 95634 205-E7
SPANISH GRANT RD
10800 ELKG 95624 359-H2
SPANISH OAKS LN
7100 PlaC 95746 220-H7
SPANISH RAVINE RD
3000 PLCR 95667 245-H5
SPANISH WELLS CT
8100 SaCo 95828 338-D6
SPANNA CT
3300 RCCD 95670 300-A4
SPANOS CT
1900 SaCo 95825 298-C4
SPANOS ST
2100 ANT 94509 (513-B5 See Page 493)
SPAR CT
800 SAC 95822 316-J4
SPARAS ST
5500 LMS 95650 200-J4
SPARKS WY
9300 SaCo 95827 299-A5
SPARROW CT
5000 SaCo 95608 279-A5
SPARROW DR
- SaCo 95632 419-D6
100 GALT 95632 419-D6
3000 SaCo 95834 276-J3
SPARROW COVE PL
- SaCo 95829 339-E5
SPARROW HAWK CT
5800 ELKG 95758 357-J5
SPARROWOOD WY
3700 SaCo 95823 337-G3
SPARTA LN
- SaCo 95683 (361-C2 See Page 341)
900 LNCN 95648 179-J2
SPARTAN LN
4200 EDCo 95682 264-A7
SPARTAN WY
- ANT 94509 (513-C7 See Page 493)
100 SAC 95838 257-G7
3400 SaCo 95826 299-A7
SPAULDING DR
- RSVL 95678 219-G3
SPAULDING WY
10400 RCCD 95670 299-F3
SPEAKERS CT
- GALT 95632 419-G5
SPEAR ST
2700 PLCR 95667 245-E4
SPEARBERRY WY
8000 SaCo 95828 338-E6
SPEARMENT LN
3500 EDCo 95682 263-H6
SPECIALTY CIR
- SAC 95828 318-E7
- SAC 95828 338-E1
SPECKLE WY
6700 SaCo 95842 259-A3
SPECKLED RD
6000 EDCo 95726 248-B6
SPECTRUM WY
4000 EDCo 95682 283-J6
SPEILBERG WY
8100 SaCo 95828 338-D5
SPELLBINDER CT
4400 SaCo 95826 318-J3
SPENCE RD
3200 PlaC 95650 201-B5
SPENCER LN
100 RSVL 95746 240-G6
7700 CITH 95610 259-J1
SPENCER ST
200 FOLS 95630 261-D4
SPENCER WY
3800 SaCo 95821 278-H3
N SPENCERS RD
- EDCo - 247-F3
S SPENCERS RD
- EDCo - 247-E4
SPENGLER DR
8000 SaCo 95828 338-E7
SPENLOW WY
5700 SAC 95835 257-C4
SPERRY DR
5500 CITH 95621 259-G5
5900 CITH 95610 259-G5
SPICA PKWY
4900 SaCo 95823 317-H7
5000 SaCo 95823 337-H1
SPICE WY
8200 SAC 95823 337-J6
SPICEBERRY CT
- ELKG 95624 358-F1
SPICEBERRY WY
- ELKG 95624 358-F1
SPICER DR
7000 SaCo 95628 259-G5
7100 CITH 95621 259-G5
7100 SaCo 95621 259-G5
7200 CITH 95610 259-G5
SPICEWOOD DR
7400 SAC 95831 336-G2
E SPIESS RD
2200 SJCo 95220 439-G3
SPIKE CT
- SAC 95823 337-G4
SPIKE RUSH CT
7900 ELKG 95758 358-C4
SPILL WY
3100 EDCo 95682 263-D4
SPILLANE CT
900 RSVL 95747 219-C6
SPILMAN AV
5300 SAC 95819 298-A4
SPILSBY CT
- SaCo 95829 338-J7
SPIN ACRES LN
3900 EDCo 95682 263-J2
SPINAKER CT
- EDCo - 267-C1
SPINDRIFT LN
5600 SaCo 95662 260-J6
SPINDRIFTER LN
- ELKG 95758 357-G6
SPINEL CIR
- SAC 95834 277-B3
3800 EDCo 95672 263-C2
SPINEL CT
- RSVL 95747 219-A7
SPINNAKER WY
300 SAC 95831 336-G1
SPINNER POINT CT
- SAC 95831 336-J3
SPINNING ROD CT
- SAC 95833 276-H6
SPINNING ROD WY
- SAC 95833 276-H6
SPINNING WHEEL CT
- EDCo 95762 263-A6
SPIRIT LN
- EDCo 95726 248-C2
SPIRITS REST CT
3500 EDCo 95672 263-H3
SPIVA CT
- FOLS 95630 261-C6
SPIVA RD
10400 SaCo 95829 339-F5
10400 SaCo 95830 339-F5
SPLENDER WY
9700 SaCo 95829 339-C5
SPLENDID WY
7500 SAC 95758 358-C2
SPLENDIDO WY
6600 ELKG 95758 358-B4
SPLENDOR LN
8300 ELKG 95624 358-D1
SPLIT BEND RD
6900 EDCo 95726 248-E1
SPLIT RAIL WY
- SaCo 95829 339-D6
SPLITROCK CT
11500 SaCo 95670 280-C4
SPOERRIWOOD CT
6600 SAC 95828 318-A7
SPOKANE RD
- WSAC 95691 316-H1
SPOONBILL LN
200 GALT 95632 419-D6
SPOONER CT
8700 PlaC 95746 241-D3
SPOONWOOD WY
3000 SAC 95833 276-J4
3100 SAC 95833 277-A4
SPORTS DR
1500 SaCo 95834 277-C1
SPORTS PKWY
- SAC 95834 257-A7
- SAC 95834 256-J7
- SAC 95834 276-J1
- SAC 95834 277-A1
SPORTS CLUB DR
- EDCo 95682 264-A6
SPORTSMAN CT
10300 RCCD 95670 279-F7
SPOTO DR
- RCCD 95670 299-J5
SPOTTED FAWN WY
4100 RKLN 95677 220-D1
- RSVL 95747 219-D2
SPOTTED PONY CT
- RKLN 95765 199-H5
SPOTTED PONY LN
- RKLN 95765 199-H5
SPRAY CT
- SAC 95831 316-G6
SPREADING OAK CT
5600 SaCo 95842 259-C2
SPREADING OAK LN
300 RCCD 95670 280-C7
6000 EDCo 95623 264-J6
SPREE CT
100 GALT 95632 419-E6
SPRENITZ ST
200 FOLS 95630 282-A2
SPRIG CIR
- FOLS 95630 281-F1
SPRIG CT
- RSVL 95678 219-G6
SPRIG DR
6700 SaCo 95842 259-A3
6700 SaCo 95842 258-J2
SPRIG OAKS CT
7300 CITH 95621 239-G7
SPRING CIR
5300 EDCo 95667 244-C6
SPRING CT
- RKLN 95765 200-E5
4100 EDCo 95630 202-H2
SPRING LN
100 PlaC 95658 181-C5
SPRING ST
800 PLCR 95667 245-F5
9700 SaCo 95632 419-B3
SPRING VWY
- ELKG 95757 357-H7
9800 ELKG 95757 377-H1
9800 ELKG 95757 397-H1
SPRINGARDEN WY
7900 SaCo 95828 338-D5
SPRING AZURE WY
8000 ELKG 95624 358-F3
SPRING BLOSSOM PL
9800 ELKG 95757 377-J1
9800 ELKG 95757 397-J1
SPRING BREEZE CT
- ELKG 95757 358-A6
SPRINGBROOK CIR
- SAC 95831 316-H6
SPRINGBROOK CT
- RSVL 95747 199-D7
2000 OAKL 94561 (514-C6 See Page 493)
SPRINGBURN WY
2800 EDCo 95762 262-D3
SPRING CREEK DR
- RKLN 95765 199-J4
SPRING CREEK WY
3300 ELKG 95758 357-J4
SPRINGCREST CT
6600 ELKG 95758 358-A3
SPRINGDALE WY
1100 RSVL 95661 240-A5
SPRINGER RD
2900 EDCo 95667 266-F5
SPRING FALLS CT
5500 ELKG 95757 357-J7
SPRINGFIELD CIR
600 RSVL 95678 219-G7
SPRINGFIELD DR
- RKLN 95765 200-D6
1400 RSVL 95678 219-F7
SPRINGFIELD WY
4900 SaCo 95841 259-A6
SPRING FLOWER DR
- ELKG 95757 358-A7
5400 ELKG 95757 357-J7
SPRING GLEN DR
5800 SaCo 95628 260-B5
SPRING GROVE DR
- RSVL 95747 218-H4
SPRINGHAVEN
6000 SaCo 95842 258-J4
SPRINGHAVEN CIR
6000 SaCo 95842 258-J4
SPRING HAVEN LN
7100 EDCo 95630 222-H3
SPRINGHILL DR
- PlaC 95747 238-J2
- PlaC 95747 239-A2
SPRINGHILLS WY
8700 SaCo 95662 260-E4
SPRING HOUSE WY
8600 ELKG 95624 358-G1
SPRINGHURST DR
8700 ELKG 95624 358-G2
SPRINGLEAF CT
7200 CITH 95621 259-E2
SPRINGMAN ST
7300 SAC 95822 337-E2
SPRING MEADOW DR
12900 SaCo 95632 419-C3
SPRING MEADOW RD
4200 EDCo 95682 283-F2
SPRINGMIST CT
- SAC 95831 336-J2
SPRINGMONT DR
6800 ELKG 95758 358-B5
SPRING OAK CT
200 FOLS 95630 281-A2
SPRING PARK DR
1800 SAC 95834 277-C4
SPRING RAIN WY
6400 SaCo 95662 260-B4
SPRINGRIDGE WY
- ELKG 95758 358-B3
SPRING RIVER WY
9500 ELKG 95624 359-B5
SPRING ROSE WY
3400 SaCo 95827 299-B7
SPRING TIME LN
12900 SaCo 95632 419-D3
SPRINGVALE LN
- LNCN 95648 200-A2
SPRINGVALE RD
1000 EDCo 95667 244-A1
SPRINGVALE WY
7400 CITH 95621 259-D1
SPRING VALLEY AV
7700 CITH 95610 259-J3
SPRING VALLEY DR
1400 RSVL 95661 240-D5
SPRING VALLEY PKWY
- LNCN 95648 180-B6
- LNCN 95648 200-A1
SPRING VALLEY RD
4100 RKLN 95677 220-D1
SPRINGVIEW DR
5700 RKLN 95677 220-B5
SPRING VIEW LN
2900 PLCR 95667 245-C4
SPRINGVIEW MEADOWS DR
3000 RKLN 95677 220-C5
SPRING WALK WY
11800 RCCD 95742 320-D1
SPRING WATER WY
100 FOLS 95630 261-A3
100 FOLS 95630 260-J3
SPRINGWOOD CT
- RSVL 95678 219-J5
SPRINGWOOD DR
6800 SaCo 95842 259-C3
SPRINGWOOD WY
1700 ANT 94509 (513-B5 See Page 493)
SPROULE AV
1400 SAC 95814 297-E2
SPRUCE AV
100 GALT 95632 419-E7
6100 EDCo 95726 248-C1
6100 SaCo 95841 259-C4
SPRUCE CT
- LNCN 95648 179-J1
1600 PlaC 95603 162-C5
SPRUCE WY
2900 WSAC 95691 316-J2
SPRUCE HILL CT
3100 SaCo 95843 238-F4
SPRUCE MEADOW LN
- PlaC 95746 240-H1
SPRUCE PINE LN
- SaCo 95842 259-A1
SPRUCE RIDGE WY
8600 SaCo 95843 238-F4
SPRUCE TREE CIR
1100 SAC 95831 337-A2
SPRUCEWOOD CT
4500 SaCo 95823 317-H7
SPUMANTE CT
- EDCo 95762 262-A3
8000 SaCo 95829 338-J6
SPUR LN
- PlaC 95603 162-A4
SPUR RD
- EDCo 95682 263-E3
SPUR WY
800 GALT 95632 419-E7
800 GALT 95632 439-E1
SPURLOCK CT
200 RSVL 95661 240-C3
SPURLOCK WY
6600 SAC 95831 316-F7
SPUR OAK LN
5200 SaCo 95628 260-G7
SPYGLASS CT
- RSVL 95678 219-J7
- RVIS 94571 454-E1
900 LNCN 95648 179-D2
SPYGLASS DR
- RVIS 94571 454-E2
SPYGLASS LN
2000 EDCo 95762 242-G6
5700 CITH 95610 260-A6
SPYGLASS HILL
- RSVL 95678 219-J7
SQUADRON CT
4800 SaCo 95628 280-F1
SQUANAN RIVER CT
11100 RCCD 95670 280-A5
SQUATTERS LN
3800 EDCo 95682 283-J1
SQUAW CT
- WSAC 95691 316-D4
SQUAW RD
- WSAC 95691 316-D4
SQUAW-HOLLOW
1600 EDCo 95619 265-J6
1600 EDCo 95619 266-A6
SQUAW VALLEY WY
2600 SaCo 95826 298-H6
SQUIRE CT
1200 RSVL 95661 240-A4
SQUIRE LN
100 PlaC 95603 162-D4
3400 EDCo 95667 246-E6
SQUIRES CT
5100 SAC 95822 317-A4
SQUIREWOOD CT
8000 SaCo 95828 338-F6
SQUIRREL CREEK RD
1100 PlaC 95602 162-F1
SQUIRRELVIEW CT
- ELKG 95757 377-J1
- ELKG 95757 397-J1
SREIA DR
- WSAC 95691 296-D4
W SST RD
- SaCo 95758 337-F7
- SaCo 95758 357-F1
S SST WY
- SaCo 95758 357-F1
STABLE DR
- WSAC 95691 316-E2
STABLEFORD WY
7400 SaCo 95683 342-D3
STABLEGATE RD
9200 SaCo 95693 360-H6
9800 SaCo 95693 (361-A6 See Page 341)
STABLER CT
7700 SaCo 95828 338-D4
STACEY HILLS DR
8100 CITH 95610 260-B2
8100 CITH 95662 260-B2
STACIA WY
2100 SAC 95822 317-C3
STACY AV
6400 SaCo 95823 338-A3
STACY LN
- OAKL 94561 (514-B6 See Page 493)
STADIUM DR
- SAC 95819 298-B7
W STADIUM LN
600 SaCo 95834 277-E1
STADIUM WY
100 AUB 95603 182-E3
STAFFORD LN
3600 PlaC 95648 160-E7
STAFFORD ST
300 FOLS 95630 261-C4
STAFFORD WY
2800 SaCo 95821 278-F6
STAFFORDSHIRE CT
- ELKG 95624 358-F3
STAGE CT
4000 EDCo 95619 265-E2
4000 EDCo 95667 265-E2
STAGECOACH CIR
- RSVL 95747 219-B2
STAGECOACH CT
4000 EDCo 95667 244-D5
STAGECOACH DR
6200 SaCo 95842 258-J4
STAGECOACH LN
200 PlaC 95648 180-D4
STAGECOACH RD
1800 EDCo 95667 244-E4
STAGECOACH TR
3300 PlaC 95650 201-F5
STAGELINE CIR
- RKLN 95765 199-J3
STAGELINE CT
9100 SaCo 95628 260-G7
STAGE STOP CT
- EDCo 95762 242-B7
STAGGS WY
4600 SAC 95822 317-D3
STAGGS LEAP CT
- OAKL 94561 (514-D5 See Page 493)
STAGHORN CT
8400 SaCo 95843 238-G5
STAGHORN WY
- RSVL 95747 218-J3
STAGS LEAP CT
8000 SaCo 95829 338-J6
STAGS LEAP LN
- LNCN 95648 179-J4
- LNCN 95648 180-A4
STAHL CT
2300 SaCo 95670 280-C6
STAINES CT
400 RSVL 95661 240-D4
STALLINGS DR
7500 SAC 95824 318-C6
STALLION WY
8000 SaCo 95830 339-G6
STALLON WY
5800 SaCo 95823 338-A3
STAMAS LN
4900 SaCo 95628 259-H7
4900 SaCo 95628 279-H1
STAMM DR
2700 ANT 94509 (513-E6 See Page 493)
STAMOS CT
200 RSVL 95747 219-A5
STAMPEDE CT
- RKLN 95765 200-D6
- SAC 95834 277-D4
STAMPEDE LN
5200 EDCo 95682 283-J6
STAMPEDE TR
- GALT 95632 439-F1
STAMPER WY
6900 SaCo 95828 318-C7
6900 SaCo 95828 338-C1
STAMP MILL CT
5700 SaCo 95608 279-C6
STANDISH CIR
- LNCN 95648 179-F7
STANDISH RD
5100 SAC 95820 318-C4
5300 SAC 95824 318-C4
STANDRICH ST
4400 SAC 95838 277-G1
STANFEL PL
- EDCo 95762 262-H5
STANFIELD CT
7400 SaCo 95828 338-D3
STANFORD AV
100 SAC 95815 277-G7
400 RSVL 95678 239-H1
7900 CITH 95610 240-A6
STANFORD LN
2700 EDCo 95762 262-C3
STANFORD COURT LN
- SaCo 95670 280-B5
STANFORD OAK DR
6900 SaCo 95842 259-C2
STANFORD RANCH RD
- RKLN 95765 199-J6
5800 RKLN 95765 220-B2
5900 RKLN 95765 200-C7
6700 RKLN 95677 220-A3
6700 RSVL 95678 220-A3
W STANFORD RANCH RD
- RKLN 95765 199-J6
STANFORD VILLAGE CT
3300 RKLN 95765 220-B1
STANHOPE WY
3000 SAC 95833 277-D5
STANISLAUS CIR
- SAC 95831 336-G2
STANLEY AV
3100 SaCo 95608 279-D5
STANMARK LN
- LNCN 95648 179-G6
STANMORE WY
5600 ELKG 95758 357-J5
STANPHYL LN
3900 EDCo 95682 263-J2
3900 EDCo 95682 264-A2
STANSBERRY WY
2400 SaCo 95826 298-H6
STANSBURY CIR
- LNCN 95648 179-F7
STANSBURY LN
- LNCN 95648 179-F7
STANTON CIR
3000 SaCo 95608 279-C5
STANTON CT
- LNCN 95648 179-F7
100 FOLS 95630 261-F5
STANWELL WY
- ELKG 95624 378-H1
STANWOOD WY
7200 SAC 95831 337-B1
STAPLEHURST WY
- ELKG 95624 358-F2
STAPLETON DR
- SaCo 95828 338-F2
STAR CT
3000 SaCo 95864 298-E2
STAR LN
1100 PlaC 95603 162-D5
5500 EDCo 95623 265-B5
STAR RD
4700 SaCo 95628 279-H1
STAR ST
100 OAKL 94561 (514-E7 See Page 493)
STAR BIRD CT
6500 ELKG 95758 358-A2
STARBOARD DR
3200 WSAC 95691 296-F4
STARBOARD WY
2000 RSVL 95678 239-F5
6700 SAC 95831 316-G7
STARBOTTLE CT
11600 SaCo 95670 280-C5
STAR BRIGHT CT
8500 SaCo 95843 238-J5
STARBROOK DR
1000 GALT 95632 419-G3
STARBUCK RD
1600 EDCo 95672 243-C6
1900 EDCo 95672 263-C1
2500 EDCo 95682 263-C1
STARBUCK WY
- RSVL 95747 219-D4
STARBURST LN
- EDCo 95684 286-D6
8100 ELKG 95758 358-D6
STARBURST WY
- SAC 95823 358-A1
STARDUST LN
100 PlaC 95648 180-D4
STARDUST ST
3100 RKLN 95677 220-C1
STARDUST WY
9600 SaCo 95827 299-B7
STARFALL WY
8800 ELKG 95624 358-G2
STARFIRE DR
3000 SaCo 95826 298-J7
STARFISH WY
9100 ELKG 95758 358-C4
STARFLOWER DR
7200 CITH 95621 259-E2
STARGAZER LN
1100 EDCo 95667 246-C6
STARGLOW CIR
- SAC 95831 316-J7
STARGLOW PL
1000 FOLS 95630 261-B6
STAR HAVEN DR
3000 EDCo 95667 245-E6
STAR HAWK CT
6500 ELKG 95758 358-A2
STARINA WY
9100 SaCo 95826 298-J7
STARKES GRADE RD
4000 EDCo - 267-C2

STREET
Block City ZIP Pg-Grid

STARKES GRADE RD
4500 EDCo - 247-G7
5100 EDCo 95726 247-G7
6000 EDCo 95726 248-A4
STARKEY WY
- FOLS 95630 281-G2
STARKVIEW PL
7100 PlaC 95650 221-C5
STAR LIGHT CT
4700 EDCo 95682 264-A1
STARLIGHT LN
2400 ANT 94509 (513-B5 See Page 493)
4000 LMS 95650 200-H7
STARLIGHT WY
4200 SaCo 95628 279-H2
STARLILY CT
- ELKG 95758 358-E6
STARLING CT
5300 EDCo 95630 202-H4
6700 CITH 95621 239-F6
STARLING LN
- WSAC 95691 316-G1
500 EDCo 95630 202-H4
STARLIT CIR
- SAC 95831 316-J6
STARMOUNT WY
2400 EDCo 95762 262-C2
STARR CT
- LNCN 95648 179-E2
STARRLYN WY
2100 RCCD 95670 279-F7
STARSTONE WY
3700 SAC 95823 337-F2
STARTHISTLE
100 EDCo 95667 265-C2
STAR THISTLE LN
- PlaC 95603 182-A2
STAR THISTLE WY
8300 SAC 95823 337-J7
STARTING GATE CT
9300 SaCo 95693 360-J5
STARVIEW
3200 EDCo 95667 226-G7
STAR VIEW CT
3500 EDCo 95682 283-J6
STARVIEW CT
- SAC 95823 358-A1
STARVIEW DR
- EDCo 95667 226-G7
STARVIEW LN
- LNCN 95648 180-A6
STAR VISTA LN
- RKLN 95677 220-G5
STARWIZARD LN
- EDCo 95684 286-H7
STARWOOD CT
- RSVL 95747 219-C1
6100 CITH 95621 239-E6
STATE AV
5300 SAC 95819 298-A4
STATE FRWY I-80
- SaCo - 258-J7
- SaCo - 259-A6
- SaCo - 278-H1
STATE LN
6500 SAC 95828 318-A7
STATELY OAK LN
5500 SaCo 95608 279-B2
N STATEN ISLAND RD
18500 SJCo 95686 437-B6
STATE UNIVERSITY DR
- SAC 95819 298-B6
STATE UNIVERSITY DR E
- SAC 95819 298-B6
- SAC 95819 318-B1
- SAC 95826 298-B6
- SAC 95826 318-B1
STATE UNIVERSITY DR N
- SAC 95819 298-A6
STATE UNIVERSITY DR S
- SAC 95819 298-B7
- SAC 95826 298-B7
STATE UNIVERSITY DR W
- SAC 95819 298-A6
STATHOS DR
10100 ELKG 95757 378-B2
STATION CT
300 RSVL 95747 219-A5
STATION ST
3700 SaCo 95827 299-B7
3700 SaCo 95827 319-B1
STATIONERS WY
5400 SaCo 95842 259-C1
STATION INN PL
- SAC 95835 257-A4
STATIRA CT
8800 ELKG 95624 358-F3
STATLER CT
5500 SaCo 95628 260-D6
STATTON HOUSE LN
- RKLN 95765 199-J5
STATUE WY
8600 SAC 95758 358-C2
STAUSS CT
3700 SaCo 95843 238-G6
STAVROS CT
- RSVL 95678 239-H4
STAXTON CIR
- RSVL 95747 318-H4
STAYNER CT
- SAC 95828 318-F7
STAYSAIL ST
3000 SAC 95833 276-J4
3000 SAC 95833 277-A4
STAYTON WY
- ELKG 95624 378-H2
STEADMAN PL
6000 ELKG 95758 358-A2
STEAM CT
3600 SaCo 95827 299-B7
STEAMBOAT LN
- RSVL 95747 219-B2
STEAMBOAT WY
6700 SAC 95831 316-G7
STEAMER WY
7500 SaCo 95823 338-A3
STEARMAN WY
7400 CITH 95621 259-E1
STEBBING CT
- RKLN 95677 220-F5
STEBBING DR
- RSVL 95747 239-B1
STECCATO DR
4200 RCCD 95742 320-D1

STEDWAY CT
3900 SaCo 95827 319-B1
STEED WY
8000 SaCo 95830 339-G6
STEELE WY
- GALT 95632 419-G3
4800 SaCo 95628 260-D7
4800 SaCo 95628 280-D1
STEELE OAK LN
6700 SaCo 95608 279-F4
STEELHEAD LN
4900 EDCo 95726 248-B6
STEELMAN CIR
7100 SaCo 95828 338-C1
STEEN CT
- FOLS 95630 281-E2
STEEPLE CHASE CT
- EDCo 95682 283-G5
STEEPLE CHASE DR
7000 EDCo 95682 283-F5
STEEPLECHASE DR
100 FOLS 95630 261-D6
STEEP ROCK CT
700 GALT 95632 419-F4
STEFANIE CT
- RKLN 95765 200-A5
STEFANIE DR
- RKLN 95765 200-D5
STEFANI RANCH CT
- SAC 95826 298-G7
STEFFANO CT
6500 CITH 95621 239-E4
STEHLIN AV
8600 SaCo 95662 260-D5
STEINBECK DR
1500 RSVL 95747 219-B6
STEINBECK WY
8100 SaCo 95828 338-D4
STEINBRENNER CT
3100 SaCo 95608 279-A5
STEINER DR
5100 SaCo 95823 317-J7
STEINER RD
13400 SaCo 95632 419-G5
STEINER MARKS
12600 SaCo 95693 340-J7
12600 SaCo 95693 341-A7
12600 SaCo 95693 (361-A1 See Page 341)
STELLA LN
- SaCo 95608 279-F3
STELLA WY
7400 SAC 95822 337-B2
STELLAR WY
3700 SaCo 95827 319-B1
STEM CT
6900 CITH 95610 259-H2
STEMMLER DR
- SAC 95834 276-H2
STENCAR DR
4200 SaCo 95628 279-H2
STENTON CT
900 GALT 95632 419-G4
STENTON WY
900 GALT 95632 419-G4
STEPHANIE AV
1300 SAC 95838 278-A2
STEPHANIE CT
400 LNCN 95648 179-G3
STEPHEN DR
3600 SaCo 95660 258-G4
STEPHENS AV
100 AUB 95603 182-E1
STEPHENS CT
- RSVL 95678 219-G6
STEPHENS LN
2800 EDCo 95762 262-C3
STEPHINA CT
10000 RCCD 95827 299-D6
STEPPING STONE LN
- LNCN 95648 200-A1
STERLING AV
100 AUB 95603 182-D2
STERLING CIR
- FOLS 95630 281-E1
STERLING CT
700 EDCo 95762 282-D3
1700 RSVL 95661 240-C3
STERLING DR
- RKLN 95765 200-D3
2500 EDCo 95672 263-D1
STERLING PKWY
- LNCN 95648 179-G6
STERLING ST
1400 SAC 95822 317-B5
STERLING WY
2600 EDCo 95682 263-C2
STERLING GROVE DR
100 GALT 95632 419-D6
STERLING OAK DR
100 GALT 95632 419-D6
STERLING POINT CT
9400 PlaC 95650 221-J1
STERLING STONE PL
- FOLS 95630 261-B7
STERLING WOOD WY
10700 RCCD 95670 299-H2
STERN CIR
900 SAC 95822 316-J4
STERNSBURG WY
5800 SAC 95823 358-A1
5800 SAC 95823 357-J1
STERNWHEELER WY
2100 SAC 95833 276-G7
STETSON CT
400 FOLS 95630 282-A1
2000 SaCo 95626 238-C6
STETSON WY
800 GALT 95632 419-E7
STEVE WY
8700 SaCo 95628 260-E6
8700 SaCo 95662 260-E6
STEVEN AV
8700 SaCo 95662 240-E7
STEVEN RD
- SaCo 95638 421-C2
STEVENS CT
4300 EDCo 95667 264-J3
STEVENS RD
- SaCo 95828 338-C4
STEVENSON AV
7700 SaCo 95828 338-C5
STEVES WY
6600 EDCo 95762 242-F7
STEWART LN
1800 CCCo 94509 (513-H5 See Page 493)
STEWART RD
1000 SaCo 95864 298-J3

STEWART ST
- FOLS 95630 281-D1
STEWART WY
- RVIS 94571 454-H4
STEWART MINE RD
- EDCo 95634 225-C3
- EDCo 95667 225-B5
STEWARTON CT
9400 SaCo 95829 339-A6
STICKLES LN
8100 PlaC 95747 239-C1
STILL BAY CT
- SAC 95831 336-J3
STILL BEACH CT
- SAC 95831 336-J3
STILL BREEZE WY
700 SAC 95831 336-J3
STILL HARBOR CT
- SAC 95831 336-J3
STILLMAN PARK CIR
3800 SaCo 95824 317-G6
STILL MEADOW CT
3200 EDCo 95667 246-F4
STILL MEADOW RD
3100 EDCo 95709 246-E4
3100 EDCo 95667 246-F4
STILLMEADOW WY
4100 SaCo 95821 279-A3
4100 SaCo 95608 279-A3
STILL REEF CT
- SAC 95831 336-J3
STILL RIVER WY
7600 SAC 95831 336-J3
STILL SHORE CT
- SAC 95831 336-J3
STILLWATER CT
- LNCN 95648 180-A7
7100 PlaC 95746 241-C4
STILLWATER PL
- LNCN 95648 180-A7
STILLWATER RD
900 WSAC 95605 296-E3
STILLWATER WY
6900 SaCo 95828 318-B7
6900 SaCo 95828 338-B1
STILLWELL CIR
- ANT 94509 (513-C6 See Page 493)
STILLWELL CT
400 SAC 95838 278-B2
STILLWIND LN
2200 RCCD 95670 279-J6
STILLWOOD CT
1800 FOLS 95630 262-A7
STILL WOODS CT
8500 SaCo 95828 338-F3
STILT CT
- SAC 95834 276-J4
STINGRAY CT
2600 SaCo 95826 298-G6
STINNET WY
- FOLS 95630 281-F2
STINSON CT
- RSVL 95746 240-F4
STINSON WY
7300 CITH 95621 259-E1
STINSON BEACH WY
9000 ELKG 95758 357-H4
STIRLING CT
- SaCo 95843 239-C5
STIRLING ST
4500 PlaC 95746 240-H1
STIRLING PARK DR
9900 RCCD 95827 299-D4
STIRRUP CT
- EDCo 95667 266-G5
STIRRUP DR
2800 OAKL 94561 (514-B7 See Page 493)
STIRUP CT
100 GALT 95632 419-D7
400 RSVL 95661 240-C3
STITES WY
- SaCo 95608 279-B5
STIZZO CT
4300 RCCD 95742 320-E2
STOCKBRIDGE AV
4300 SaCo 95842 258-J6
STOCKDALE ST
7300 SAC 95822 337-D2
STOCKER WY
7000 SaCo 95828 338-B1
STOCKHORSE LN
9000 PlaC 95746 240-H4
STOCKMAN CIR
1900 FOLS 95630 282-A1
STOCKMAN LN
- LNCN 95648 179-H4
STOCKMEN WY
10200 ELKG 95757 377-H3
10200 ELKG 95757 397-H3
STOCK RANCH RD
- CITH 95610 259-G3
- CITH 95621 259-G3
STOCKTON BLVD
1600 SAC 95816 297-G7
1900 SAC 95817 297-G7
2500 SAC 95817 317-H1
2900 SAC 95820 317-J4
3900 SaCo 95820 317-H1
5000 SAC 95824 317-J4
5600 SaCo 95824 317-J4
6100 SAC 95824 318-A6
6200 SAC 95828 318-A6
6200 SAC 95823 318-A6
6500 SaCo 95828 318-A6
6800 SaCo 95828 338-B2
6800 SaCo 95823 318-A6
6800 SaCo 95823 338-B2
7600 SAC 95823 338-B2
12200 GALT 95632 419-E3
12800 SaCo 95632 419-E3
E STOCKTON BLVD
- SaCo 95828 338-C6
8500 ELKG 95624 338-C6
8500 ELKG 95624 358-D1
9300 ELKG 95624 378-G3
12300 SaCo 95632 (399-D6 See Page 379)
- SaCo 95632 419-D1
W STOCKTON BLVD
8200 ELKG 95758 358-D2
8300 SAC 95758 338-C7
8500 SAC 95758 358-D1
8500 ELKG 95757 358-E6
9900 ELKG 95757 378-H3
10400 ELKG 95757 378-H3
10400 SaCo 95757 379-A5

W STOCKTON BLVD
12000 SaCo 95757 (399-C4 See Page 379)
12600 SaCo 95757 419-D1
STOCKTON ST
10500 SaCo 95632 (399-F3 See Page 379)
10700 SaCo 95632 (400-A3 See Page 379)
W STOCKTON ST
8300 SJCo 95686 (438-A4 See Page 418)
STOCKWOOD CT
3700 EDCo 95762 262-D2
STOCKWOOD DR
2600 RSVL 95661 240-E4
STOCKWOOD WY
3500 EDCo 95762 262-D2
STODDARD LN
7500 CITH 95610 259-H4
STODDARD ST
1400 SAC 95822 317-B5
STODDARD WY
300 PlaC 95603 162-E6
STODICK LN
- EDCo 95667 286-G4
- EDCo 95684 286-G4
STOECKER CT
10300 ELKG 95757 377-H3
10300 ELKG 95757 397-H3
STOECKER WY
10200 ELKG 95757 377-H3
10200 ELKG 95757 397-H3
STOFFELS CT
900 RSVL 95747 239-D1
STOFFELS WY
2200 RSVL 95747 239-D1
STOFFER WY
6100 SaCo 95662 260-E5
STOKE CT
3000 RCCD 95670 299-F4
STOKELY CT
5600 SaCo 95662 260-G6
STOKEWOOD WY
2400 RCCD 95670 279-J7
STOLLWOOD CT
9200 PlaC 95746 240-H4
STOLLWOOD DR
4200 SaCo 95608 279-F2
STONE BLVD
100 WSAC 95691 296-F5
STONE CT
2000 WSAC 95691 296-H6
4100 SaCo 95821 278-H3
STONE LN
2600 EDCo 95667 245-D3
2800 PLCR 95667 245-D4
STONE RD
5600 LMS 95650 200-J7
STONE WY
1300 AUB 95603 182-D6
STONE BAY CT
9000 SaCo 95829 338-H7
STONEBRIAR CT
4500 EDCo 95762 282-C3
4500 SaCo 95843 238-J7
4500 SaCo 95843 239-A7
STONEBRIAR DR
- EDCo 95762 282-C3
STONEBRIDGE ST
800 EDCo 95762 282-D2
STONEBRIDGE WY
1300 RSVL 95661 240-A5
STONEBROOK CT
- PlaC 95603 162-A5
STONEBROOK DR
- ELKG 95624 359-A5
- PlaC 95603 162-B5
200 FOLS 95630 241-B7
STONE CANYON CIR
7900 CITH 95610 260-A2
STONE CANYON DR
- RSVL 95661 220-D7
STONE CLIFF WY
- SaCo 95829 338-H7
STONE CORRAL PL
11400 SaCo 95670 280-C4
STONECREEK DR
2600 SAC 95833 277-C5
STONECREEK WY
5300 RKLN 95677 220-E4
STONECREST AV
1300 SAC 95832 337-C5
STONECREST CT
2700 EDCo 95667 245-J3
2700 PLCR 95667 245-J3
STONECREST DR
- RSVL 95747 219-A7
STONECREST LN
- LNCN 95648 200-A1
STONECREST RD
1500 EDCo 95667 245-J4
1500 PLCR 95667 245-J4
1600 PLCR 95667 246-A4
1600 EDCo 95667 246-A4
STONECROP CT
6800 CITH 95621 239-F6
STONECUTTER WY
4100 SaCo 95660 258-H1
STONEFIELD CT
- SAC 95831 336-J3
STONEFLOWER WY
8500 ELKG 95624 358-E2
STONEGATE AV
- WSAC 95691 316-H2
STONEGATE CIR
800 OAKL 94561 (514-D5 See Page 493)
STONEGATE CT
3900 LMS 95650 200-J7
STONEGATE DR
- ELKG 95758 357-H5
- RKLN 95765 200-B4
- WSAC 95691 296-H7
- WSAC 95691 316-H1
STONEGLEN WY
5100 ELKG 95758 357-H3
STONEHAND AV
6000 CITH 95621 239-D7
STONEHAVEN DR
2500 SaCo 95827 299-B5
STONEHAVEN LN
5600 PlaC 95746 240-J1
STONE HEARTH LN
- LNCN 95648 199-J1
- LNCN 95648 200-A1
STONEHEDGE CT
6600 PlaC 95746 221-F5

STONEHEDGE DR
200 FOLS 95630 281-E2
STONEHEDGE WY
4300 SaCo 95823 337-G1
4400 SaCo 95823 317-H7
STONEHILL CT
7300 SaCo 95660 258-H1
STONEHILL DR
6100 PlaC 95677 220-G5
STONE HILL RD
1900 EDCo 95762 262-J6
STONE HOLLOW WY
11800 RCCD 95742 320-D1
STONE HOUSE CIR
- LNCN 95648 180-A5
STONEHOUSE CT
100 RSVL 95678 220-C5
500 PlaC 95603 182-B2
STONE HOUSE LN
- LNCN 95648 180-A5
STONE HOUSE RD
6900 SaCo 95683 322-A7
7100 SaCo 95683 342-A1
STONEHOUSE RD
100 PlaC 95603 182-B2
STONEHURST CT
3100 EDCo 95762 262-E5
STONEHURST DR
2200 EDCo 95762 262-E5
STONEHURST WY
4700 SaCo 95842 259-A5
STONE LAKE RD
10800 SaCo 95758 377-D7
10800 SaCo 95758 397-D7
STONELAKE CLUB DR
- ELKG 95757 357-F7
STONELEIGH CT
- PlaC 95747 239-A2
STONEMAN DR
6400 SaCo 95660 258-H2
STONEMAN WY
800 EDCo 95762 262-C3
STONE MILL DR
- FOLS 95630 262-A6
STONE MOUNTAIN RD
3300 EDCo 95667 244-F7
STONE OAK WY
9000 ELKG 95624 378-H1
STONEPINE CT
- SAC 95834 277-B3
STONE PINE LN
- LNCN 95648 179-J6
STONE POINT DR
- RSVL 95661 220-C7
- RSVL 95661 240-C1
STONER DR
5000 SAC 95820 318-A4
STONERIDGE BLVD
- LNCN 95648 180-B6
STONERIDGE LN
- LNCN 95648 180-A6
STONE RIDGE SQ
100 FOLS 95630 261-J6
STONE RIDGE WY
7500 CITH 95621 259-E1
STONE RIVER CT
2300 SaCo 95670 280-B6
STONESIFER CT
3900 SaCo 95821 278-H5
STONE SPRINGS DR
9300 ELKG 95624 359-A5
STONES THROW RD
5200 EDCo 95682 264-D1
STONE TEMPLE CT
- RKLN 95765 200-E4
STONE VALLEY CIR
- SAC 95823 337-H3
STONE VALLEY CT
- SAC 95823 337-H3
STONEVIEW CT
- ELKG 95757 377-J1
- ELKG 95757 397-J1
STONE WALK CT
3700 SaCo 95843 238-G5
STONEWALL DR
4400 SaCo 95628 279-G2
STONEWOOD CT
4900 SaCo 95628 280-C1
7600 PlaC 95746 241-D1
STONEWOOD RD
700 PlaC 95658 180-J2
700 PlaC 95658 181-A2
STONEWORK CT
300 RSVL 95747 219-A6
STONEY RD
3400 RKLN 95765 220-B2
STONEY WY
4500 SaCo 95608 279-D2
STONEYBECK CIR
- SaCo 95828 338-E6
STONEYBROKE CT
5500 SaCo 95628 260-F6
E STONEY CREEK CIR
2400 SJCo 95220 439-G4
STONEY CREEK WY
5200 ELKG 95758 357-J2
STONEY CROSS LN
- LNCN 95648 179-F7
STONEY END CT
5300 SaCo 95660 258-J6
STONEYGATE CT
600 GALT 95632 419-G4
STONEYGATE DR
500 GALT 95632 419-G5
STONEY HILL CIR
200 OAKL 94561 (514-E6 See Page 493)
STONEY HILL CT
- OAKL 94561 (514-E6 See Page 493)
STONEY HILL DR
100 FOLS 95630 261-G4
STONEY HILL PL
- OAKL 94561 (514-E6 See Page 493)
STONEY OAKS CT
11800 RCCD 95742 320-D4
STONEY POINT CT
- LNCN 95648 179-F6
STONEY POINT WY
1200 RSVL 95661 240-D4
STONEY RIDGE RD
9600 PlaC 95603 161-H6
STONEY RIDGE WY
11800 RCCD 95742 320-D2
STONEY WOOD WY
1400 PlaC 95663 180-J7
STONINGTON WY
100 FOLS 95630 261-G5

STONY BAR WY
2100 SaCo 95670 280-D4
STONYFORD LN
5800 SaCo 95842 259-D1
STONY HILL PL
- SaCo 95835 256-G4
STOPE CT
7000 EDCo 95667 226-H3
STOPE DR
3000 EDCo 95667 226-J1
STOREYFIELD LN
1500 LNCN 95648 179-F4
STORIA WY
6700 ELKG 95758 358-B4
STORMS CT
100 FOLS 95630 261-C6
STORMWOOD AV
1100 GALT 95632 419-G2
STORMY CT
3400 RKLN 95765 200-C7
STORNOWAY CT
8100 SaCo 95829 338-J6
STORROW WY
4600 SaCo 95842 259-A1
N STORY LN
- EDCo 95667 226-B4
S STORY LN
- EDCo 95667 226-B4
STORY WY
4500 ELKG 95758 357-H3
STORYBOOK LN
2300 EDCo 95667 245-A4
STORY RIDGE WY
8300 SaCo 95843 238-H5
STORZ RD
- SAC 95823 337-F2
STOUGHTON WY
2600 SaCo 95827 299-B5
STOUT CT
3000 PLCR 95667 245-H5
STOVER WY
2000 SAC 95822 317-C4
STOWE WY
4000 SaCo 95864 298-H5
STRABANE WY
- FOLS 95630 261-H7
STRADER AV
1500 SAC 95815 278-A4
STRAIGHT RD
5400 PlaC 95747 238-F3
STRAND RD
3100 RKLN 95765 220-A1
STRAND ST
7200 SaCo 95828 338-C1
STRASBOURG LN
1800 ANT 94509 (513-G5 See Page 493)
STRASBOURG WY
5000 SaCo 95842 259-A1
STRATFORD CIR
2500 EDCo 95762 242-C5
STRATFORD CT
100 RSVL 95661 240-E5
STRATFORD PL
- SaCo 95842 259-A1
STRATFORD ST
7300 SAC 95822 337-C2
STRATHAVEN WY
800 GALT 95632 419-F3
STRATHMORE WY
4100 SaCo 95660 258-H1
STRATTON AV
6600 CITH 95621 259-F5
STRATTON CT
- RKLN 95765 200-B5
STRATTON LN
- SolC 94571 493-A1
STRATTON WY
- AUB 95603 182-F1
STRATUS DR
8500 SaCo 95662 260-D4
STRAUCH DR
1600 RSVL 95661 240-C2
STRAUGH RD
700 SaCo 95673 257-E1
STRAUS DR
4400 SAC 95838 278-B1
STRAWBERRY LN
5100 SAC 95820 317-F4
STRAWBERRY STATION LP
- RSVL 95747 219-B3
STRAWBRIDGE DR
8900 SaCo 95829 338-H6
STREAM CT
2700 RKLN 95765 200-A7
STREAM VWY
- SAC 95826 298-F6
STREAM WY
5500 EDCo 95684 286-E6
STREAMBED LN
600 EDCo 95619 265-E1
STREAMSIDE CT
- PlaC 95746 240-F3
3300 EDCo 95667 245-A6
STREET A
- RSVL 95747 219-A2
STREET JUDES HILL RD
- EDCo - 267-D2
STRENG AV
8200 CITH 95610 260-B2
8300 SaCo 95610 260-B2
STRESA WY
- EDCo 95762 262-G5
STRETTO CT
8000 SaCo 95843 238-H4
STREVEL WY
3200 SaCo 95825 278-F7
STRICKLAND MINE CT
4200 EDCo 95667 264-J2
STRICKLAND MINE RD
4000 EDCo 95667 264-H2
STRIKER AV
- SAC 95834 277-D1
700 SaCo 95834 277-D1
STRIKER CT
100 RSVL 95747 239-D1
STRIPED MOSS CT
- RSVL 95678 219-G4
STRIPED MOSS ST
- RSVL 95678 219-G4
STROER LN
1800 ANT 94509 (513-J5 See Page 493)
STROLLING HILLS CT
- LNCN 95648 179-J6
STROLLING HILLS LN
- LNCN 95648 179-J6

STROLLING HILLS RD
2900 EDCo 95682 283-D1
3600 EDCo 95682 263-F7
STROMAN LN
- SaCo 95835 256-G6
STROMFORD WY
100 SaCo 95655 319-H1
STRONG AV
8500 SaCo 95662 260-D3
STRONGBOX CT
200 RSVL 95747 219-B6
STRONSERY CT
- FOLS 95630 281-J1
STROUP LN
100 FOLS 95630 260-J4
100 FOLS 95662 260-J4
STROUSE CT
100 FOLS 95630 261-F3
STRUOD CT
5800 SaCo 95843 239-D5
STUART CT
- EDCo 95672 263-C1
800 WSAC 95605 296-H2
STUART PL
- RKLN 95765 200-C5
STUART ST
- RKLN 95765 200-C5
STUART ISLAND ST
- WSAC 95691 316-C2
STUBBLEFIELD WY
5800 SAC 95823 338-A7
STUBEN CT
4600 ELKG 95758 357-H5
STUBEN WY
4500 ELKG 95758 357-H5
STUCKEY LN
12000 SaCo 95693 (380-F1 See Page 379)
STUDARAS DR
- RCCD 95670 279-G7
STUDEBAKER PL
1900 SaCo 95670 280-B3
STUDEBAKER RD
4500 EDCo 95667 264-E4
N STUDEBAKER RD
4100 EDCo 95667 264-E3
STUDIO CT
- ELKG 95758 358-E5
STUPPI WY
4200 SaCo 95864 278-H7
STURBRIDGE CT
5800 SaCo 95842 258-J5
STURBRIDGE DR
- FOLS 95630 261-J6
- FOLS 95630 262-A6
STURCH DR
4400 EDCo 95682 283-J2
STURGEON WY
8700 SaCo 95826 298-G6
STURGES CT
100 FOLS 95630 261-A1
STURM LN
8100 PlaC 95746 241-B2
STUTZ CT
8000 SaCo 95828 338-G5
SUANNE CT
6800 SaCo 95828 338-B1
SUBARU CT
3000 SaCo 95826 299-A6
SUBURBAN CT
- SAC 95820 318-A3
SUDBURY CT
3600 EDCo 95682 263-F6
SUDBURY RD
3000 EDCo 95682 263-E5
SUDBURY WY
4900 SaCo 95608 299-A2
SUDDEN WIND CT
6500 CITH 95621 259-D3
SUDOR LN
3500 PlaC 95650 201-G6
SUEDA RANCH RD
10000 PlaC 95603 181-J2
SUEDE HILL CT
9200 SaCo 95662 260-G5
SUE PAM DR
3400 SaCo 95608 279-C4
SUFFEX CT
4700 SaCo 95842 259-A1
SUFFOLK CT
5000 PlaC 95746 240-J5
SUFFOLK WY
1800 SaCo 95608 299-C1
4300 EDCo 95762 262-B2
SUFFOLK HILLS PL
- SAC 95835 256-H5
SUGAR LN
5000 SaCo 95608 279-A4
SUGARHOUSE LN
- LNCN 95648 200-B3
SUGAR LOAF CT
2100 SaCo 95670 280-B5
SUGARLOAF CT
100 RSVL 95747 219-B5
SUGARLOAF MOUNTAIN RD
3200 PlaC 95650 201-E4
SUGAR MAPLE WY
6700 CITH 95610 260-A3
SUGARNOTCH CT
8700 ELKG 95758 357-H2
SUGAR PINE CT
1900 ANT 94509 (513-J5 See Page 493)
5400 SaCo 95841 259-C6
SUGAR PINE DR
4100 EDCo 95726 248-E3
SUGAR PINE LP
- RSVL 95747 219-B5
SUGAR PINE ST
2000 ANT 94509 (513-J5 See Page 493)
SUGAR SHACK LN
- EDCo 95667 266-D3
SUGARWOOD CT
600 GALT 95632 419-F4
SUISUN BAY RD
- WSAC 95691 316-E2
SULLIVAN CT
1200 WSAC 95605 296-H1
SULLIVAN DR
2500 PlaC 95603 162-C3
7600 SaCo 95843 238-F7
7600 SaCo 95843 258-F1
SULLIVAN LN
1100 EDCo 95667 244-J1
SULLIVAN ST
- RVIS 94571 454-H4

573 SULLY ST
SACRAMENTO COUNTY STREET INDEX
SWETZER CT
SACRAMENTO CO.

STREET Block City ZIP Pg-Grid

SULLY ST
4800 SAC 95838 257-H7
SULTANA CT
- EDCo 95682 263-E3
SUMAC LN
3900 SAC 95820 317-F2
SUMATRA DR
200 SAC 95838 257-G7
SUMATRA ST
- WSAC 95691 316-D2
SUMERLIN CT
9200 ELKG 95624 358-F5
SUMMER AV
7400 CITH 95621 239-G7
SUMMER CT
- EDCo 95682 263-C5
SUMMER DR
- EDCo 95682 263-B6
- EDCo 95762 263-A5
SUMMER PL
1200 PlaC 95603 162-D5
SUMMER WY
6600 EDCo 95684 286-F7
SUMMERBREEZE CT
2300 RCCD 95670 279-J7
SUMMERBROOK WY
5200 SAC 95823 337-J4
SUMMER CLOUD CT
1700 FOLS 95630 261-J7
SUMMER CLOUD DR
- RKLN 95765 220-A1
SUMMER CREEK CT
4600 EDCo 95682 283-D7
8300 SaCo 95828 338-E5
SUMMER CREEK RD
4600 EDCo 95682 283-D7
SUMMER CREST CT
8500 ELKG 95624 358-F1
SUMMER DAWN CT
6000 SaCo 95628 260-B5
SUMMER FALLS CIR
8200 SaCo 95828 338-D5
SUMMERFIELD CT
- EDCo 95762 282-D2
2300 LNCN 95648 179-E1
2300 RCCD 95670 279-J6
2800 WSAC 95691 316-F1
E SUMMERFIELD CT
1900 OAKL 94561 (514-C5 See Page 493)
W SUMMERFIELD CT
1800 OAKL 94561 (514-D6 See Page 493)
SUMMERFIELD DR
2600 WSAC 95691 316-F1
2600 WSAC 95691 296-F7
5600 RKLN 95677 220-A3
SUMMERFIELD WY
- EDCo 95762 282-C2
SUMMER GARDEN WY
300 SAC 95833 277-F4
SUMMERGATE CT
- SAC 95823 337-J5
SUMMER GLEN WY
9700 ELKG 95757 357-J7
SUMMERGROVE CIR
200 RSVL 95678 219-G5
SUMMERHAVEN WY
7800 SAC 95823 337-J4
SUMMERHILL CT
1800 RSVL 95661 240-C6
SUMMERHILL DR
1700 RSVL 95661 240-C6
SUMMERHILL LN
- LNCN 95648 179-J6
- LNCN 95648 180-A6
10000 PlaC 95658 202-A2
SUMMERHILL RD
- EDCo 95684 286-G6
SUMMER HOLLOW DR
- RCCD 95742 320-E4
SUMMER KNOLL WY
8500 ELKG 95624 358-F2
SUMMERLAND WY
- RSVL 95747 218-H3
SUMMER MIST CT
7800 SaCo 95828 338-D5
SUMMER OAK CT
4700 SaCo 95843 239-A5
SUMMER PARK DR
3300 SAC 95833 277-C4
3300 SAC 95834 277-C4
SUMMERPLACE DR
7800 CITH 95621 239-E6
SUMMER POINTE DR
8600 ELKG 95624 358-F2
SUMMER POND CT
9200 ELKG 95624 358-J4
SUMMER RAIN WY
6600 CITH 95621 259-F4
SUMMER RIDGE DR
12000 PlaC 95603 162-D6
SUMMER RIM CIR
- SAC 95823 338-A7
100 SAC 95823 358-A1
SUMMER SANDS CT
7900 SaCo 95828 338-D5
SUMMERSDALE DR
- SAC 95823 337-J4
SUMMERSET CT
9800 PlaC 95746 240-G6
SUMMERSET DR
500 RVIS 94571 454-E1
SUMMERSET LN
6100 CITH 95621 259-E3
SUMMER SHADE CT
100 FOLS 95630 261-A1
SUMMER SKY DR
8300 SaCo 95828 338-E5
SUMMER STAR WY
- PlaC 95658 181-D5
SUMMER STREAM LN
4500 EDCo 95667 244-A3
SUMMER STROLL
- SAC 95823 337-G4
SUMMER SUN WY
8600 ELKG 95624 358-G1
SUMMER SUNSET DR
8100 SaCo 95828 338-D5
SUMMER TEA WY
9200 ELKG 95624 358-J4
SUMMERTIDE WY
6300 SAC 95823 338-A7
SUMMERTIME LN
- RSVL 95747 219-B3
SUMMERTREE CT
4900 SaCo 95841 259-C7
SUMMERVIEW
7800 SAC 95823 337-J5
SUMMER VISTA CT
8500 ELKG 95624 358-F2
SUMMERWIND WY
7400 SAC 95831 336-H3
SUMMERWOOD CIR
4900 SaCo 95841 259-A6
SUMMERWOOD CT
7100 PlaC 95746 241-C1
SUMMIT DR
5600 RKLN 95765 220-B2
SUMMIT ST
100 AUB 95603 182-D2
9400 ELKG 95624 358-H6
SUMMIT WY
4500 SaCo 95820 317-H3
SUMMIT BROOK CT
8500 ELKG 95624 358-F2
SUMMIT LAKES CT
600 GALT 95632 419-F4
SUMMIT LAKES WY
600 GALT 95632 419-F4
SUMMIT MINE CT
2000 SaCo 95670 280-E4
SUMMIT VIEW CT
4900 EDCo 95623 264-G6
SUMMIT VIEW DR
4800 EDCo 95623 264-G5
SUMMIT VIEW LN
4900 SaCo 95628 280-G1
SUMNER LN
4000 SaCo 95608 279-F3
SUMO CT
- SAC 95828 318-B7
SUMTER DR
4200 SaCo 95628 279-G2
SUN AV
7500 CITH 95610 239-H6
SUN ACER WY
6700 SaCo 95673 257-G2
SUNAMBER LN
7100 SaCo 95828 338-B4
SUNBEAM AV
500 SAC 95814 297-E2
SUNBEAM WY
- RCCD 95670 280-C7
SUNBIRD WY
- SAC 95823 338-A7
SUNBLAZE WY
6100 SAC 95823 358-A1
6200 SAC 95823 338-A7
SUN BLOSSOM CT
- RSVL 95678 219-J3
- RSVL 95678 220-A3
SUN BONNET CT
- RKLN 95765 199-J4
SUNBONNET DR
8100 SaCo 95628 260-B5
SUNBORG CT
- SAC 95838 277-G1
SUNBOROUGH LN
7400 SaCo 95828 338-C4
SUN BRAE CT
6700 SaCo 95673 257-G2
SUNBREEZE LN
7100 SaCo 95828 338-B3
SUNBRIDGE LN
7600 SaCo 95828 338-B3
SUNBROOK LN
7800 RCCD 95670 279-J6
SUNBURST CT
- RKLN 95765 219-J2
8100 SaCo 95843 239-B6
SUNBURST WY
6900 CITH 95621 259-E2
SUNBURY CT
400 RSVL 95661 240-D3
SUNCAST LN
1000 EDCo 95762 282-D4
SUN CASTLE LN
7400 SAC 95823 337-H3
SUN CENTER DR
10900 RCCD 95670 299-J2
11000 RCCD 95670 300-A2
11200 SaCo 95670 300-A2
SUN CHASER WY
5200 SAC 95835 256-J5
SUN CITY BLVD
- LNCN 95648 179-J4
- LNCN 95648 180-A5
4400 RSVL 95747 219-A5
E SUN CITY BLVD
4000 RSVL 95747 219-B6
W SUN CITY BLVD
4000 RSVL 95747 219-B6
SUN CITY LN
- LNCN 95648 180-A6
SUNCLOUD CT
- SAC 95823 358-A1
SUNCO DR
- SaCo 95742 280-A7
- SaCo 95742 300-A1
SUNCOUNTRY LN
7500 SaCo 95828 338-B4
SUN COVE LN
7600 SaCo 95828 338-B3
SUNCREEK WY
7200 SaCo 95662 260-D2
SUNCREST DR
3300 EDCo 95667 245-B6
SUNCREST WY
4800 SaCo 95628 280-A1
SUNDALE CT
- EDCo 95762 262-E5
SUNDALE DR
2200 RCCD 95670 279-J6
SUNDALE WY
6000 SaCo 95628 260-B4
SUN DANCE CT
300 RSVL 95661 240-C3
SUNDANCE CT
3500 EDCo 95667 245-A7
SUNDANCE DR
8100 SaCo 95662 260-B3
SUNDANCE LN
8300 ELKG 95624 358-D2
SUNDANCE TR
3100 EDCo 95667 244-H7
3500 EDCo 95667 245-A7
SUNDANCE WY
- SaCo 95628 260-B4
SUNDAY DR
6100 SaCo 95660 258-H4
SUNDIAL CT
- LNCN 95648 200-A1
SUN DIAL WY
6300 SAC 95823 358-A1
SUNDOWN CT
1800 EDCo 95667 245-B1
6700 SaCo 95608 279-E2
SUNDOWN DR
6900 SAC 95823 337-F1
N SUNDOWN DR
6800 SAC 95823 337-F1
SUNDOWN TR
1800 EDCo 95667 245-B2
SUNDOWN WY
1100 RSVL 95661 240-A4
SUNDOWNER CT
7900 SaCo 95828 338-F5
SUNDRIFT LN
7600 SaCo 95828 338-B4
SUNDROP WY
7400 SaCo 95843 239-C5
SUN FAIRE LN
7500 SaCo 95828 338-C4
SUNFAIRE LN
2900 EDCo 95682 263-G3
SUNFIELD LN
7500 SaCo 95828 338-C4
SUNFIRE WY
9100 SaCo 95826 318-J2
SUNFISH CT
2600 SaCo 95826 298-G6
SUN FLARE CT
- LNCN 95648 180-A6
SUN FLORIN DR
8500 SaCo 95828 338-E2
SUNFLOWER CT
5700 RKLN 95677 220-C5
SUNFLOWER DR
2800 ANT 94531 (513-G7 See Page 493)
SUNFLOWER LN
4000 EDCo 95682 283-J1
SUNFLOWER RD
9400 SaCo 95693 360-C6
SUNGARDEN DR
7800 CITH 95610 259-J2
7800 CITH 95610 260-A2
SUNGATE LN
7400 SaCo 95828 338-C4
SUNGLOW CT
- EDCo 95762 282-E4
6000 SaCo 95608 279-D5
SUNGOLD WY
9200 SaCo 95826 298-J7
9200 SaCo 95826 299-A7
SUN HILL DR
7700 CITH 95610 260-A4
7700 CITH 95610 259-J4
SUN KNOLL DR
3500 LMS 95650 201-A6
SUN KOSI WY
9700 ELKG 95757 357-E7
SUNLAND CT
8200 CITH 95610 240-B7
SUNLAND VISTA AV
1200 SAC 95831 337-A2
SUNLEAF LN
7300 SaCo 95828 338-B4
SUNLIGHT DR
200 EDCo 95619 265-C6
SUNLIGHT LN
9500 ELKG 95758 358-D6
SUNLIT CIR
- SAC 95831 316-J6
SUN MAIDEN WY
3500 SaCo 95843 238-G7
SUNMEADOW CT
- SAC 95823 337-G3
SUNMEADOW DR
4100 SAC 95823 337-G3
SUNMILL LN
7400 SaCo 95828 338-C4
SUNMIST WY
6200 CITH 95621 259-E2
SUNMORE LN
7500 SaCo 95828 338-B3
SUNNINGDALE CT
400 RSVL 95747 219-D6
SUNNINGDALE DR
1600 RSVL 95747 219-D5
SUNNY LN
1700 ANT 94509 (513-B5 See Page 493)
6600 SaCo 95608 279-E4
SUNNYBANK LN
3300 SaCo 95608 279-F5
SUNNYBRAE DR
6300 SAC 95823 338-A7
6300 SAC 95823 358-A1
SUNNY BREEZE WY
8700 SaCo 95828 338-G4
SUNNYBROOK CT
1500 PlaC 95663 180-J7
SUNNYBROOK LN
8700 SaCo 95628 260-E6
SUNNY CREEK WY
8200 SAC 95823 338-B6
SUNNYCREST CT
8700 ELKG 95624 358-G2
SUNNYDALE LN
2400 PlaC 95663 201-D2
SUNNYFIELD WY
6400 SAC 95823 358-A1
SUNNY GLADE CT
9300 ELKG 95758 358-A5
SUNNYGLEN WY
2400 SaCo 95826 298-F6
SUNNY HILL RD
- EDCo 95672 263-D1
2400 EDCo 95672 243-D7
SUNNYHILL RD
12100 PlaC 95602 162-B1
SUNNY HILLS DR
200 RCCD 95670 280-C7
SUNNY HOLLOW CT
- SAC 95823 338-A7
SUNNY LAKE WY
6300 SAC 95823 338-A7
6300 SAC 95823 358-A1
SUNNY MEADOWS LN
7400 SaCo 95828 338-C4
SUNNY OAK DR
2100 AUB 95602 162-E1
2100 PlaC 95602 162-E1
SUNNYSIDE CT
- LNCN 95648 200-A2
SUNNYSIDE WY
7900 SaCo 95828 338-F5
SUNNYSLOPE DR
6600 SaCo 95828 338-B1
SUNNYSLOPE WY
- AUB 95603 182-A6
SUNNYVALE AV
3700 SaCo 95821 278-G3
SUNNYWOOD LN
9800 FOLS 95630 261-B2
SUN OAK LN
5300 SaCo 95628 260-G7
SUNOL WY
10200 RCCD 95827 299-E5
SUNPACE LN
7600 SaCo 95828 338-B3
SUN PARK LN
- LNCN 95648 179-J6
SUN PASSAGE LN
- SAC 95823 337-G3
SUN PEAK PL
- SaCo 95829 339-E5
SUN PEARL CT
6000 SaCo 95628 260-B5
SUN POINT LN
7400 SaCo 95828 338-C4
SUN POPPY WY
- EDCo 95762 282-D4
SUN RANCH DR
6400 SAC 95823 358-A1
SUN RAY CT
800 SaCo 95673 257-J1
SUNRAY RIDGE DR
- ELKG 95757 377-H1
- ELKG 95757 397-H1
SUN REIGN LN
- SAC 95823 337-H3
SUNREY RD
- EDCo - 267-B5
SUNRIDGE CT
7900 SaCo 95628 260-A6
SUNRIDGE RD
1100 EDCo 95619 265-H6
SUNRISE AV
100 AUB 95603 182-E3
SUNRISE AV Rt#-E2
100 RSVL 95661 240-A4
8400 CITH 95610 240-A4
8400 PlaC 95661 240-A4
N SUNRISE AV
100 RSVL 95661 240-A2
800 RSVL 95661 220-C7
SUNRISE BLVD Rt#-E2
900 RCCD 95742 280-A6
2000 RCCD 95670 280-A6
2000 SaCo 95628 280-A3
2000 SaCo 95670 280-A3
2500 SaCo 95742 280-A6
2600 RCCD 95670 300-C6
2600 RCCD 95670 280-A6
2700 SaCo 95670 300-A2
2700 SaCo 95742 300-A2
4100 RCCD 95742 320-D3
5000 SaCo 95628 260-A5
5400 CITH 95610 260-A3
5400 CITH 95628 260-A3
6500 SaCo 95830 320-D6
7200 SaCo 95830 340-D2
7200 SaCo 95624 340-D2
7900 CITH 95610 240-A7
SUNRISE DR
4200 EDCo 95619 265-D3
SUNRISE LN
6900 EDCo 95667 244-J5
SUNRISE MALL
- CITH 95610 260-A5
SUNRISE CREEK CT
7700 CITH 95610 259-J4
SUNRISE EAST WY
8000 CITH 95610 260-A5
8000 CITH 95628 260-A5
8100 SaCo 95628 260-A5
SUNRISE GOLD CIR
11200 SaCo 95742 300-A1
11400 RCCD 95742 300-A1
SUNRISE GREENS DR
7800 SaCo 95828 338-E4
SUNRISE HILLS DR
5000 SaCo 95628 259-J7
SUNRISE MEADOWS LN
5300 OAKL 94561 (514-D5 See Page 493)
SUNRISE MIST WY
7800 SaCo 95828 338-E5
SUNRISE PARK DR
11200 RCCD 95742 300-A2
11200 SaCo 95742 300-A2
SUNRISE PINES DR
3500 RCCD 95827 299-D6
SUNRISE RIDGE CIR
10600 AUB 95603 182-B6
SUNRISE RIDGE DR
7900 SaCo 95628 260-A7
SUNRISE RIDGE RD
4200 EDCo 95682 264-B7
10600 AUB 95603 182-B6
SUNRISE SOUTH DR
6200 SAC 95824 318-C6
6300 SAC 95828 318-C6
SUNRISE TERRACE LN
7800 CITH 95610 260-A2
SUNRISE VISTA
- AUB 95603 182-A6
SUNRISE VISTA DR
6100 CITH 95610 260-A5
SUNRISE WOODS WY
8300 SaCo 95828 338-E4
SUN RIVER DR
6200 SAC 95824 318-C6
6300 SAC 95828 318-C7
SUNROCK DR
100 FOLS 95630 261-B3
SUN RUN LN
4700 SaCo 95628 280-G1
SUNSEASON LN
7300 SaCo 95828 338-C4
SUNSET AV
600 WSAC 95605 296-G2
7100 SaCo 95628 279-G1
7900 SaCo 95628 280-A1
SUNSET BLVD
300 RKLN 95765 199-G6
1000 RKLN 95765 219-J1
1000 RKLN 95765 220-B3
1500 RKLN 95677 220-B3
W SUNSET BLVD
1100 PlaC 95765 199-F6
SUNSET BLVD W
4400 PlaC 95747 199-A5
SUNSET CT
- RVIS 94571 454-F1
1600 EDCo 95667 245-B1
SUNSET DR
- ANT 94509 (513-D6 See Page 493)
100 AUB 95603 182-E1
400 GALT 95632 419-F6
1000 RSVL 95678 239-J3
1700 PlaC 95658 181-G7
1800 PlaC 95658 201-G1
4600 SAC 95822 317-B3
SUNSET LN
- SaCo 95693 360-H1
1100 PlaC 95658 181-H3
2700 ANT 94509 (513-D6 See Page 493)
3900 EDCo 95682 264-B6
SUNSET LNDG
- RVIS 94571 454-F1
SUNSET TER
3200 PlaC 95602 161-J3
3200 PlaC 95602 162-A3
SUNSET BAY CT
7800 SaCo 95828 338-E4
SUNSET BLUFFS ST
- SAC 95758 358-A2
SUNSET DOWNS DR
8100 SaCo 95828 338-D5
SUNSET HILL CT
3200 RKLN 95677 220-D2
SUNSET HILL RD
3000 RKLN 95677 220-D2
SUNSET HILLS LN
- SaCo 95843 239-C7
SUNSET MEADOWS LN
5400 OAKL 94561 (514-D5 See Page 493)
SUNSET OAK
5500 SaCo 95842 259-C2
SUNSET PLACE LN
4800 SaCo 95628 280-G1
SUNSET POINT LN
- ELKG 95758 357-F6
SUNSET TERRACE LN
7900 SaCo 95628 280-A1
SUN SHADOW LN
3700 SaCo 95821 278-H3
SUNSHINE CT
- GALT 95632 419-D6
3800 EDCo 95667 264-J1
SUNSHINE DR
- GALT 95632 419-D6
SUNSHINE LN
3700 EDCo 95667 265-A1
3800 EDCo 95667 264-J1
4900 SaCo 95841 259-A7
SUNSHINE WY
3400 PlaC 95602 161-J3
SUNSHIRE LN
7300 SaCo 95828 338-B3
SUN SHOWER CIR
- SAC 95823 337-G4
SUNSILVER LN
7300 SaCo 95828 338-C4
SUNSPARK LN
7400 SaCo 95828 338-C4
SUNSPRING LN
7500 SaCo 95828 338-C5
SUN SPRITE CT
8500 ELKG 95624 358-F1
SUN SPRITE WY
8500 ELKG 95624 358-F1
SUNSTAR LN
7600 SaCo 95828 338-B3
SUNSTONE CIR
- SAC 95834 277-B2
SUNSTONE DR
- RSVL 95747 219-A7
- RSVL 95747 239-A1
SUNSTREAM CT
7800 SaCo 95828 338-D5
SUNSTREAM WY
7200 RSVL 95747 219-A4
SUNSWEET LN
7100 SaCo 95828 338-B3
SUN TERRACE WY
7800 CITH 95610 240-C7
7800 CITH 95610 260-C1
SUNTRAIL CIR
- SAC 95823 338-A7
SUN TRAIL LN
- LNCN 95648 179-J7
- RSVL 95747 219-D1
SUN TREE CT
500 RSVL 95661 240-A5
SUN TREE DR
500 RSVL 95661 240-A5
SUN TREE LN
8100 SaCo 95628 260-B5
SUN VALLEY LP
- LNCN 95648 180-A6
SUNVALLEY PL
11500 AUB 95603 182-C6
SUN VALLEY WY
5800 SAC 95823 338-A6
SUNVAUGHT LN
7500 SaCo 95828 338-B3
SUNVIEW AV
3100 SaCo 95825 278-F7
SUNVIEW WY
6500 SaCo 95673 257-G3
SUN VISTA CT
800 SaCo 95673 257-J1
SUNWAY LN
7300 SaCo 95828 338-C4
SUNWEST LN
7500 SaCo 95828 338-C3
SUN WILLOW LN
7500 SAC 95823 337-G4
SUNWIND WY
800 SAC 95831 336-J3
SUNWISPER LN
7600 SaCo 95828 338-C3
E SUNWOOD CT
5400 RKLN 95677 220-C4
W SUNWOOD CT
5500 RKLN 95677 220-C4
SUNWOOD WY
900 SAC 95831 336-J2
7200 CITH 95621 259-E2
SUPERB CIR
8700 ELKG 95624 358-G6
SUPERFORTRESS AV
- SaCo 95655 299-F6
SUPERIOR DR
4500 EDCo - 247-D3
6700 SaCo 95660 258-H2
SUPREME CT
800 AUB 95603 182-C5
1400 RSVL 95678 219-F7
9500 ELKG 95624 358-G6
SURBAUGH SQ
100 FOLS 95630 261-H6
SURETTE LN
7200 PlaC 95650 201-C7
7200 PlaC 95650 221-C1
SURF WY
5600 SAC 95822 316-J4
SURFBIRD LN
- RKLN 95765 219-J1
SURFSIDE WY
6200 SAC 95831 316-F6
SURF WATER CT
- SAC 95831 336-H3
SURITA ST
4200 SaCo 95864 298-J2
SURLE CT
5000 SaCo 95842 259-B1
SURLINGHAM CT
9200 SaCo 95829 338-J4
SURLYN CT
15400 SaCo 95683 342-D3
SUR MER DR
5400 EDCo 95762 262-E2
SURREY CT
3400 RKLN 95677 220-F2
SURREY RD
2100 SAC 95815 278-B7
2100 SAC 95825 278-B7
SURREYGLEN WY
5100 ELKG 95758 357-J3
SURREY PARK CT
8200 SaCo 95828 338-G6
SURREYTOP LN
200 LNCN 95648 179-J4
SURREYWOOD WY
7100 SAC 95823 338-B6
SURRITT WY
9500 ELKG 95624 359-B7
SURRY LN
3400 EDCo 95682 263-C6
SURVEY RD
9200 ELKG 95624 378-J4
SUSAN CIR
1300 RSVL 95661 240-A3
SUSAN CT
300 LNCN 95648 179-F3
3000 WSAC 95691 316-F2
SUSAN LN
- EDCo 95672 243-H6
SUSAN WY
5500 SaCo 95608 299-C2
SUSAN HOLLOW CT
4900 SaCo 95628 260-F7
SUSANNA CT
6800 CITH 95621 259-G3
SUSAN OAK DR
5000 SaCo 95628 260-F7
SUSSEX CT
1400 RSVL 95661 240-B5
1900 SAC 95815 298-B1
SUTCLIFFE CIR
100 FOLS 95630 281-C1
SUTHERLAND DR
- PlaC 95603 162-F6
SUTHERLAND WY
7000 ELKG 95758 358-B6
SUTHERLAND RANCH RD
- RSVL 95678 219-H5
SUTLEY CIR
- SAC 95835 256-G6
SUTLEY TAYLOR LN
9900 PlaC 95603 202-A1
9900 PlaC 95658 202-A1
SUTRO CT
6900 CITH 95621 259-G2
SUTTER AV
100 RSVL 95678 239-J2
5600 SaCo 95608 279-C3
SUTTER RD
47900 YoCo 95612 (395-J3 See Page 375)
47900 YoCo 95612 (396-A3 See Page 375)
SUTTER ST
- OAKL 94561 (514-B7 See Page 493)
100 AUB 95603 182-D2
300 FOLS 95630 261-A5
500 WSAC 95691 296-F3
SUTTER BUTTES DR
- RSVL 95747 199-C7
- RSVL 95747 219-C1
SUTTER BUTTES WY
8300 SaCo 95828 338-E5
SUTTER CREEK CT
1600 EDCo 95762 262-C1
SUTTER CREEK DR
1100 EDCo 95762 242-C7
1100 EDCo 95762 262-C1
SUTTER CREEK WY
8500 SaCo 95843 238-H5
SUTTER HILL LN
3700 SaCo 95608 279-E4
SUTTER ISLAND RD
12000 SaCo 95615 (396-C6 See Page 375)
12000 SaCo 95615 (416-B1 See Page 415)
12400 SaCo 95615 (395-J7 See Page 375)
12400 SaCo 95615 415-J1
SUTTER ISLAND CROSS RD
700 SaCo 95615 (395-J7 See Page 375)
700 SaCo 95615 (396-A7 See Page 375)
700 SaCo 95615 (416-A1 See Page 415)
SUTTER ISLAND UPPER CROSS RD
15600 SaCo 95615 (395-J6 See Page 375)
15600 SaCo 95615 (396-C3 See Page 375)
SUTTER OAK CT
7000 SaCo 95842 259-C2
SUTTERS FORT WY
11300 SaCo 95670 280-B4
SUTTERS GOLD DR
8900 SaCo 95826 318-H1
SUTTER SLOUGH BRIDGE RD Rt#-E9
- YoCo 95612 (396-E1 See Page 375)
11900 SaCo 95615 (396-C3 See Page 375)
SUTTERS MILL CIR
11300 SaCo 95670 280-B4
SUTTER VIEW LN
- LNCN 95648 200-B1
SUTTERVILLE BYPS
2300 SAC 95818 317-E2
2300 SAC 95820 317-E2
2300 SAC 95822 317-D2
SUTTERVILLE RD
800 SAC 95822 317-B2
2300 SAC 95820 317-D2
SUTTERWOODS WY
3600 SaCo 95827 299-B7
SUTTON PL
400 AUB 95603 182-D5
SUTTON WY
9100 SaCo 95662 260-G6
SUTTON POINTE CT
- ELKG 95757 358-A7
SUWANNEE CT
4300 ELKG 95758 357-G5
SUZETTE CT
9100 SaCo 95662 260-G5
SUZUKI LN
7500 PlaC 95650 221-D1
SWADLY WY
- SAC 95835 257-A4
SWAIM CT
3300 SAC 95838 277-G4
SWAIN SQ
100 FOLS 95630 261-H6
SWAINSON WY
- SAC 95833 276-H7
SWAINSON HAWK DR
9800 ELKG 95757 357-F7
9800 ELKG 95757 377-F1
9800 ELKG 95757 397-F1
SWALE CT
100 SAC 95834 277-D4
SWALE RIVER WY
7200 SAC 95831 336-H1
SWALLOW WY
1500 RSVL 95661 240-B3
8800 SaCo 95628 280-E2
SWALLOW RIDGE WY
- RSVL 95661 220-E7
SWALLOWS NEST DR
2300 SAC 95833 276-H7
SWALLOWS NEST LN
- SAC 95833 276-H7
SWALLOWSVIEW CT
- RKLN 95677 220-G5
SWALLOWVIEW CT
- LNCN 95648 179-D1
SWALLOWVIEW DR
- LNCN 95648 179-D1
SWAMPY LN
7600 PlaC 95650 221-D3
SWAN CT
- PlaC 95746 240-G4
- RKLN 95765 219-H1
SWAN LN
4000 EDCo 95667 264-H3
SWANBROOK CT
9500 ELKG 95758 358-E6
SWAN FALLS WY
- RSVL 95661 220-D7
SWAN ISLAND ST
- WSAC 95691 316-D2
SWAN LAKE DR
9500 PlaC 95746 240-H5
SWANN WY
10100 ELKG 95757 377-J2
10100 ELKG 95757 397-J2
SWAN RIVER CT
- SAC 95831 336-G1
SWANSBORO RD
1600 EDCo 95667 226-C1
SWANSEA WY
3000 RCCD 95670 299-F3
SWANSON LN
2200 LNCN 95648 200-B2
SWANSTON DR
500 SAC 95818 297-B7
SWARTHMORE DR
2200 SAC 95825 298-C6
SWAZEY CT
200 RSVL 95747 219-A5
SWEENEY RD
300 ANT 94509 (513-E6 See Page 493)
SWEET WY
2800 SaCo 95821 278-E6
SWEET BIRCH CT
5200 SaCo 95842 259-B2
SWEET BIRCH DR
5300 SaCo 95842 259-B2
SWEET BIRCH LN
- EDCo - 247-G2
SWEETBRIAR CT
- PlaC 95603 162-F7
SWEETBRIAR LN
- EDCo 95633 205-G3
SWEETBRIER WY
7700 SAC 95832 337-D4
SWEET CREEK LN
2500 EDCo 95672 243-F4
SWEETDALE CT
- SAC 95829 338-J7
SWEETFERN WY
7500 SAC 95822 337-E3
SWEET GRASS CT
6400 RKLN 95677 220-G5
SWEETGRASS LN
- LNCN 95648 179-D1
SWEET GUM CT
6600 CITH 95610 260-A3
SWEET JULIET LN
- LNCN 95648 179-J7
- LNCN 95648 180-A7
- LNCN 95648 200-A1
SWEET MAPLE WY
- SAC 95833 276-H6
SWEET PEA WY
- SAC 95833 276-H7
SWEET VALLEY RD
1800 EDCo 95762 242-H6
SWEETWATER AV
4100 SaCo 95820 317-G4
SWEETWATER CT
4000 RKLN 95677 220-F1
SWEETWATER DR
3700 RKLN 95677 220-E2
SWEETWATER LN
4100 EDCo 95672 243-G5
SWEETWOOD CT
7100 CITH 95621 239-F7
SWENSON CT
200 AUB 95603 162-E7
SWENSON WY
6600 SAC 95831 317-A7
SWETZER CT
2600 LMS 95650 201-A5
2900 LMS 95650 200-J5

© 2007 Rand McNally & Company

SWETZER RD — SACRAMENTO COUNTY STREET INDEX — THATCHER CIR 574

© 2007 Rand McNally & Company

SACRAMENTO CO.

STREET Block City ZIP Pg-Grid

SWETZER RD
2100 PlaC 95650 201-A3
2100 PlaC 95663 201-B2
2900 LMS 95650 201-A3
SWIFT CT
- LNCN 95648 179-F7
SWIFT ST
- WSAC 95691 316-J1
SWIFT WY
2800 SAC 95822 337-E2
SWIFT FOX WY
8400 ELKG 95758 358-E5
SWIFT RIVER DR
100 FOLS 95630 261-A1
SWIFT WATER CT
4100 SaCo 95608 279-D3
SWINDON CT
- RKLN 95765 200-B6
SWINDON RD
- RKLN 95765 200-B6
SWINDON WY
4500 SaCo 95843 238-J6
4500 SaCo 95843 239-A6
SWINGING BRIDGE CT
- SAC 95833 276-H6
SWINTON DR
- FOLS 95630 261-J5
- FOLS 95630 262-A5
SWISS CT
4300 ELKG 95758 357-G6
SWITCHMAN DR
1400 RSVL 95678 239-F1
SYBIL WY
2900 SaCo 95608 279-D5
SYCAMORE AV
800 WSAC 95691 296-H4
4300 SaCo 95841 279-A2
SYCAMORE DR
- SaCo 95690 455-E4
1100 ANT 94509 (513-A5 See Page 493)
7500 CITH 95610 259-H1
W SYCAMORE DR
7400 CITH 95610 259-H1
7400 CITH 95621 259-H1
SYCAMORE PL
- EDCo 95682 263-D2
4600 PlaC 95677 220-F4
SYCAMORE GLEN WY
8600 SaCo 95843 238-G5
SYCAMORE HILL RD
5800 PlaC 95658 181-A3
SYDLING CT
500 SaCo 95864 298-H4
SYLMAR LN
7400 SaCo 95842 259-D1
SYLVAN CT
- RKLN 95765 200-D4
SYLVAN DR
- RKLN 95765 200-D5
SYLVAN LN
3300 EDCo 95667 244-G7
3400 EDCo 95667 264-F1
SYLVAN RD
6400 CITH 95610 259-H2
SYLVAN CREEK CT
7500 CITH 95610 259-H3
SYLVAN GLEN LN
- RSVL 95747 219-B6
SYLVAN GLEN PL
1000 PlaC 95603 162-G5
SYLVAN GLEN WY
6900 CITH 95610 259-H3
SYLVAN GROVE WY
7200 CITH 95610 259-H2
SYLVAN MEADOW CT
- CITH 95610 259-H3
SYLVAN OAK WY
7900 CITH 95610 240-B7
SYLVAN VALLEY WY
- CITH 95610 259-H3
SYLVAN VISTA DR
- PlaC 95603 162-G5
SYLVESTER WY
6100 SaCo 95608 259-D5
SYLVIA LN
3700 PlaC 95602 161-H2
SYLVIA WY
7400 SAC 95822 337-C2
SYMINGTON WY
7900 SaCo 95829 338-J5
SYMPHONY CT
2800 SAC 95826 298-F7
SYNTHIA CT
- SAC 95823 337-G2
SYRACUSE WY
1100 SAC 95833 277-D4
SYRAH CT
- EDCo 95762 262-G4
- ELKG 95624 379-A2
SYSTEMS PKWY
10100 RCCD 95655 299-E6
10100 RCCD 95827 299-E6

T

T ST
200 SAC 95818 297-C5
2700 SAC 95817 297-G7
3000 SAC 95816 297-E6
4000 SAC 95819 297-G7
5800 SAC 95817 298-A7
6000 SAC 95817 318-A1
TAAJANAR CT
8700 SaCo 95662 260-E2
TAB CT
2400 SaCo 95825 298-D2
TABARE CT
7800 CITH 95621 239-F7
TABARI CT
2200 EDCo 95762 262-C4
TABER ST
1000 WSAC 95605 296-J1
TABLE ROCK CT
100 FOLS 95630 241-A7
TABORA DR
3100 ANT 94509 (513-C7 See Page 493)
TACANA DR
100 FOLS 95630 261-E3
TACK CT
9700 SaCo 95693 360-H7
TACOMA NARROWS ST
- WSAC 95691 316-D2
TACOMIC DR
4700 SaCo 95842 259-A3
TAD LN
7600 CITH 95610 260-A1
TADWORTH WY
- RKLN 95677 220-G6
TAFT CT
- RKLN 95765 219-H2
1700 ANT 94509 (513-A7 See Page 493)
TAFT DR
- RKLN 95765 219-H1
TAFT ST
2500 SAC 95815 278-A5
TAGGART CT
1000 GALT 95632 419-G4
TAGGERT CT
400 RSVL 95678 239-F1
TAHAMA ST
5600 SaCo 95841 259-B6
TAHAN LN
8800 SaCo 95628 280-E1
TAHITI ST
8800 SaCo 95662 260-F2
TAH-NEE WY
3400 EDCo 95762 262-D4
TAHOE AV
100 RSVL 95678 239-J1
TAHOE CT
3300 ANT 94509 (513-E7 See Page 493)
TAHOE DR
100 RVIS 94571 454-G5
TAHOE ST
- WSAC 95691 316-D4
11000 PlaC 95602 161-J3
TAHOE WY
5900 SAC 95817 318-A1
TAHOE STAR CT
- RKLN 95677 200-D6
TAHOE VIEW CT
- SAC 95835 257-B7
TAHOE VISTA CT
- RKLN 95677 200-E5
- RKLN 95765 200-E5
TAHOE VISTA DR
- RKLN 95677 200-E6
- RKLN 95765 200-D6
TAHOE WOODS CT
8500 SaCo 95828 338-F4
TAHOMA LN
1300 LNCN 95648 180-B7
TAILINGS DR
- RCCD 95742 300-G6
TAIL RACE CT
- RSVL 95747 219-C3
TAIL RACE DR
- RSVL 95747 219-C3
TAILRACE DR
- SaCo 95670 280-B4
TAILWIND DR
600 SAC 95838 277-H1
TAISLEY DR
3000 RCCD 95670 299-F3
TAJERO CT
- SAC 95838 257-G7
TAJO CT
- SAC 95835 256-H4
TAKAMI CT
900 SaCo 95673 257-J1
TAKEOFF CT
9000 SaCo 95628 260-F7
TALBOT WY
3100 ANT 94509 (513-F7 See Page 493)
7900 CITH 95610 240-C6
TALEGA CT
- RSVL 95747 219-B1
TALENT ST
3900 SAC 95838 278-D3
TALGARTH CT
- RSVL 95661 220-E7
7900 SaCo 95829 338-J5
TALGARTH WY
- RSVL 95661 220-E7
TALISMAN DR
200 FOLS 95630 261-D4
8900 SaCo 95826 298-H7
9000 SaCo 95826 318-J1
TALLAC LN
1300 LNCN 95648 180-B7
TALLAC ST
2200 SaCo 95821 278-C6
TALL BRAVE CT
6000 CITH 95621 259-D3
TALLEGA CT
600 GALT 95632 419-G4
TALLEYVILLE WY
100 FOLS 95630 261-G6
TALL GRASS CT
300 FOLS 95630 281-J1
TALL GRASS WY
- ELKG 95758 357-J2
TALL OAK LN
5300 SaCo 95628 260-G7
TALLON WY
8000 SaCo 95843 239-A6
TALLOW TREE LN
- SaCo 95662 260-E3
TALLOW WOOD WY
8300 CITH 95621 239-G6
TALL PINE CT
- ELKG 95757 358-A6
TALL PINE LN
7500 PlaC 95746 221-A7
7500 PlaC 95746 241-A1
TALL RIVER DR
7700 CITH 95610 259-J3
7800 CITH 95610 260-A3
TALL TREE CIR
6400 CITH 95621 259-D4
TALL TREE LN
- EDCo 95667 266-B2
TALLWOOD CIR
- CITH 95621 239-D5
TALLYHO DR
3700 SaCo 95826 318-J2
4200 SaCo 95826 319-A2
TALMAGE CT
3900 SaCo 95827 319-B1
TALMONT CIR
- RSVL 95678 219-H4
TALON RD
1800 RKLN 95765 200-A5
TALON WY
- AUB 95603 182-D6
TALON REACH CT
- RSVL 95747 219-C2
TALUS WY
4700 SaCo 95608 279-D1
TAMALPAIS RD
6800 EDCo 95633 205-A7
TAMALPAIS WY
3000 SaCo 95821 278-E4
TAMANGO WY
3000 SaCo 95826 298-J7
TAMARA DR
7800 SaCo 95628 259-J7
TAMARACK CT
1000 RSVL 95661 240-A4
2400 RKLN 95677 220-F2
TAMARACK DR
2600 RKLN 95677 220-F2
TAMARACK RD
1500 WSAC 95691 316-J2
TAMARACK WY
2200 SaCo 95821 278-C6
2200 SaCo 95825 278-C6
TAMARA JEAN RD
9200 SaCo 95662 260-G5
TAMARIND CT
2900 SaCo 95843 238-E6
TAMARINDO LN
5300 ELKG 95758 357-J2
TAMARINDO WY
- RSVL 95678 219-H5
TAMARINDO BAY DR
7600 SaCo 95828 338-G3
TAMARISK CT
5000 SaCo 95842 259-B4
TAMBOR WY
- SAC 95758 358-C1
TAMERTON WY
- SaCo 95829 338-J7
TAMI WY
4100 SaCo 95608 279-D3
TAMMY LN
4000 EDCo 95682 283-J2
TAM O SHANTER DR
- EDCo 95762 262-D2
TAM-O-SHANTER LN
12400 PlaC 95603 162-D5
TAMOSHANTER WY
7000 SAC 95822 337-D1
7500 SAC 95832 337-D3
TAMPICO CT
8300 SaCo 95628 260-C7
TAMSEN CT
5200 SaCo 95608 299-B2
TAMWOOD CT
11400 PlaC 95602 161-J1
11400 PlaC 95602 162-A1
TAMWORTH WY
3000 SAC 95833 277-C5
TANA CT
5100 ELKG 95758 357-H2
TANAGER CT
- RSVL 95747 219-B7
TANAGER LN
2400 EDCo 95709 246-H1
TANAGER WY
- RKLN 95765 219-H1
- RSVL 95747 219-B7
- RSVL 95747 239-B1
4700 SaCo 95842 259-A3
TANAKA CT
5000 SaCo 95628 259-J7
TANANA RIVER CT
7900 CITH 95610 240-B7
TANANGER CT
- SAC 95833 277-D4
TANBARK CT
6300 CITH 95621 259-E1
TANBARK OAK CT
600 EDCo 95762 262-A1
TANDEM CT
7000 CITH 95621 259-G2
TANDY DR
3900 SAC 95834 277-F2
TANDY LN
6800 CITH 95621 259-D3
TANFIELD CT
- SAC 95833 277-C4
TANFORAN CT
5900 SaCo 95628 260-C5
TANGANYIKA CIR
200 ANT 94509 (513-C7 See Page 493)
TANGERINE AV
4800 SAC 95823 337-J3
5300 SaCo 95823 337-J3
5600 SaCo 95823 338-A3
5600 SAC 95823 338-A3
TANGLEWOOD CIR
9600 SaCo 95826 260-J5
TANGLEWOOD DR
11000 AUB 95603 182-D6
TANGLEWOOD LN
1700 RSVL 95661 240-B3
TANGLEWOOD WY
9100 PlaC 95650 221-G1
TANGO ST
3000 SaCo 95826 298-H7
3100 SaCo 95826 318-H1
TANGORS WY
7900 CITH 95610 260-A3
TANIN CT
3400 RCCD 95670 300-A5
TANNAT WY
2500 RCCD 95670 299-F2
TANNENBAUM CT
4700 EDCo 95619 265-J5
TANNER CT
- FOLS 95630 281-E1
400 RSVL 95678 219-G7
TANNER LN
9900 SaCo 95693 379-H1
TAN OAK WY
8200 CITH 95621 239-F6
TANOAK WY
1400 AUB 95603 182-D6
TANOWA CT
8200 SaCo 95828 338-D7
TANSY CT
8600 SaCo 95843 238-H5
TANTURA WY
- SAC 95832 337-C4
TANUS CIR
- RKLN 95677 220-H4
TAN WOOD RD
9000 PlaC 95626 238-D4
9000 SaCo 95626 238-D4
TANYA CT
3000 SaCo 95826 298-J6
TANYA LN
8200 SaCo 95828 338-D3
TANYA WY
- RSVL 95661 240-D5
TANZANIA DR
1000 RSVL 95661 239-J5
TANZANITE AV
- SAC 95834 277-B3
TAPADERAS LP
- PlaC 95747 238-J2
TAPESTRY WY
3100 SaCo 95826 299-A7
TAPLEY RD
2500 WSAC 95691 316-F3
TAPLIN WY
- GALT 95632 419-G3
TAPO CT
6400 SAC 95828 318-C6
TAPPER LN
9100 SaCo 95662 260-G2
TARA CT
- PlaC 95765 199-F6
TARA LN
3600 SaCo 95821 278-G4
TARA BELLA DR
- LNCN 95648 179-E5
TARA BELLA PL
- LNCN 95648 179-E4
TARAMORE CT
8400 SaCo 95662 260-C3
TARANTO CT
6600 ELKG 95757 378-B1
TARAPIN LN
- LNCN 95648 180-A4
TARATA PL
8600 ELKG 95624 358-H2
TARAYA CT
- EDCo 95682 283-B1
TARBERT DR
9500 ELKG 95758 358-B6
TARBOLTON CIR
- FOLS 95630 262-A5
TARBORO LN
- SAC 95835 256-G5
TARES CIR
5400 ELKG 95757 377-J1
5400 ELKG 95757 397-J1
TAREYTON WY
6700 CITH 95621 259-F2
TARGA CIR
8000 CITH 95610 260-B5
TARKENTON CT
- ELKG 95757 377-J2
- ELKG 95757 397-J2
TARKINGTON CT
300 RSVL 95747 219-C6
TARLETON DR
4500 SaCo 95842 258-J5
TARMAC CT
9000 SaCo 95628 260-G7
TARMAC WY
9000 SaCo 95628 260-F7
TARMIGAN DR
3800 SaCo 95843 238-H6
TAROCCO WY
6900 CITH 95610 260-A3
E TARON DR
9900 ELKG 95757 377-E1
9900 ELKG 95757 397-E1
10000 ELKG 95757 357-F7
W TARON DR
9700 ELKG 95757 357-E7
9800 ELKG 95757 377-E1
9800 ELKG 95757 397-E1
TARPAN CT
- ELKG 95757 377-H1
- ELKG 95757 397-H1
TARQUINA CT
- EDCo 95762 262-G4
TARRAGON WY
- SAC 95831 336-G2
TARRANT CT
- RSVL 95747 239-C1
TARRO WY
3500 SaCo 95608 279-C4
TARRYTON CT
1300 ANT 94509 (513-F7 See Page 493)
TARSHES DR
6300 SaCo 95608 279-E6
TARTAN CT
- LNCN 95648 179-D2
TARTAN DR
7600 SaCo 95843 238-F7
7600 SaCo 95843 258-F1
TARTAN LN
- LNCN 95648 179-D2
TARTAN TR
3300 EDCo 95762 242-F7
TARTANILLA CIR
7300 CITH 95621 259-H2
TARVISIO WY
- EDCo 95762 262-G5
TARWOOD WY
5600 SaCo 95842 259-C2
TARZO WY
9800 ELKG 95757 378-B1
TASH CT
- SAC 95831 336-H2
TASMAN CT
8100 SaCo 95828 338-F6
TATE LN
400 OAKL 94561 (514-B7 See Page 493)
TATE ST
3900 SAC 95838 278-D3
TATIANA CT
- RSVL 95747 219-B7
TATIANA ST
- RSVL 95747 219-A7
TATTERSHALL WY
7600 SAC 95823 337-J3
TATTINGER CT
- EDCo 95762 262-B2
TATUM CT
- SAC 95835 257-D7
TAUNTON WY
100 FOLS 95630 261-G6
TAUPIN CT
- FOLS 95630 281-G1
TAURUS CT
7600 CITH 95610 259-J6
TAVARES CT
- RVIS 94571 454-H5
TAVERNOR RD
8600 SaCo 95693 360-H4
9600 SaCo 95693 (380-E1 See Page 379)
TAVERNOR TRAIL LN
12200 SaCo 95693 (380-F1 See Page 379)
TAVI AV
3800 SaCo 95660 258-G7
TAVIRA CT
7200 ELKG 95757 378-B3
TAVISTOCK LN
- LNCN 95648 179-G7
TAWNY CT
4800 OAKL 94561 (514-D7 See Page 493)
8400 SaCo 95828 338-E6
TAWNY MEADOW WY
3900 SaCo 95843 238-H6
TAXI LN
- EDCo 95619 266-D5
TAY WY
8500 SAC 95826 298-F7
TAYLOR LN
1200 PlaC 95603 162-D5
TAYLOR RD
100 PlaC 95658 181-F6
1500 PlaC 95663 181-E7
1500 PlaC 95663 201-D1
2000 RSVL 95678 220-B7
2400 PlaC 95650 201-D1
2500 RSVL 95661 220-B7
2900 LMS 95650 201-A4
3400 LMS 95650 200-H7
TAYLOR ST
- FOLS 95630 281-C1
100 RSVL 95678 239-H2
3300 SAC 95838 277-H2
4700 SAC 95838 257-H7
TAYLOR WY
- EDCo 95762 282-E6
- SAC 95819 297-J4
TAYLOR MORGAN WY
700 SAC 95838 277-J1
TEA LN
- AUB 95603 182-B6
TEA BERRY WY
7600 SaCo 95828 338-F3
TEA CART CT
8600 SaCo 95828 338-F4
TEA CART WY
8600 SaCo 95828 338-F4
TEA GARDEN CT
8600 SaCo 95828 338-F4
TEAGUE LN
6100 PlaC 95746 241-A1
TEAK CT
1200 RSVL 95661 239-J5
7500 SAC 95823 337-G3
TEAK WY
7500 SAC 95823 337-G3
TEAKWOOD CT
4500 OAKL 94561 (514-D7 See Page 493)
9000 SaCo 95826 318-H1
TEAKWOOD DR
4700 OAKL 94561 (514-D6 See Page 493)
TEAL CT
- RKLN 95765 219-J1
1000 AUB 95603 162-E5
1400 OAKL 94561 (514-D7 See Page 493)
TEAL DR
2600 WSAC 95691 316-F1
TEAL LN
- EDCo 95726 248-C1
100 GALT 95632 419-D6
TEAL WY
6400 SaCo 95608 259-E7
TEA LEAF CT
8600 SaCo 95828 338-F3
TEAL HOLLOW DR N
- LNCN 95648 179-D1
TEAL HOLLOW DR S
900 LNCN 95648 179-D2
TEALLY PL
1300 EDCo 95762 262-D3
TEAL POND CT
1500 EDCo 95667 245-C1
TEAL POND RD
1600 EDCo 95667 245-C1
TEAMTRACK RD
100 AUB 95603 182-E1
TEA ROSE CT
4000 EDCo 95762 263-B4
TEA ROSE DR
3200 EDCo 95762 263-B4
TEARPAK CT
- SAC 95823 337-J7
- SAC 95823 338-A7
TEASEL CT
8200 SaCo 95829 339-D6
TEATER CT
7700 CITH 95610 240-B7
7700 CITH 95610 260-B1
TECEIRA WY
100 FOLS 95630 261-E7
TECH CENTER DR
9300 SaCo 95826 299-A6
9300 SaCo 95827 299-A6
TECHNOLOGY WY
- PlaC 95765 199-F6
TECK ST
5700 SaCo 95628 260-B6
TECOLOTE DR
- EDCo 95667 266-A2
TECOPA WY
8100 SaCo 95828 338-E6
TEDDINGTON WY
9000 ELKG 95624 378-H2
TED FORD CT
100 FOLS 95630 281-B2
TEEKAY WY
7500 SAC 95832 337-E4
TEGAN RD
4500 ELKG 95758 357-H4
TEGEA WY
8600 ELKG 95624 358-F1
TEICHERT AV
5000 SAC 95819 297-J3
5000 SAC 95819 298-A4
TEIXEIRA WY
5000 OAKL 94561 (514-D6 See Page 493)
TEJON AV
200 SaCo 95673 257-G1
TELEGRAPH AV
7400 SaCo 95662 260-H1
7700 SaCo 95662 240-H7
TELEGRAPH HILL
2200 EDCo 95762 242-C7
2200 EDCo 95762 262-C1
TELEGRAPH HILL DR
- RKLN 95765 199-J3
TELEMARK CT
2800 EDCo 95667 245-A5
TELESCO WY
5900 SaCo 95608 259-D7
TELEVISION CIR
300 SAC 95814 297-D3
TELFER WY
7500 SAC 95823 338-A4
7600 SAC 95823 338-A4
TELL CT
5700 SaCo 95660 258-H5
TEMBLOR CT
- SAC 95838 257-G7
TEMBROOK DR
3300 SaCo 95864 298-F3
TEMESCAL ST
4100 SaCo 95628 280-A3
TEMPERENCE RIVER CT
100 FOLS 95630 241-A7
TEMPEST CT
3300 RKLN 95765 200-C7
TEMPLE
- RCCD 95827 299-E4
TEMPLE AV
3400 SAC 95820 317-F2
TEMPLE DR
13200 PlaC 95603 162-G7
TEMPLE LN
7800 CITH 95610 259-J6
TEMPLE PARK RD
8000 SaCo 95628 260-A7
TEMPLETON CT
300 RSVL 95746 240-F5
TEMPLETON DR
2500 EDCo 95762 242-B6
6100 SaCo 95608 259-D6
TEMPRANILLO CT
- SAC 95833 276-J5
TEMS CT
2800 RKLN 95765 200-A7
2800 RKLN 95765 220-A1
TEMWOODS WY
7700 SaCo 95828 338-C4
TENABO CT
9300 SaCo 95827 299-A5
TENAYA AV
400 SAC 95833 277-E5
TENBURY CT
- RKLN 95677 220-F5
TENBURY LN
- RKLN 95677 220-G5
TENBY CT
200 RSVL 95747 219-D5
TENDER TR
- EDCo - 247-B7
TENDERFOOT DR
11600 SaCo 95670 280-D5
TENEIGHTH WY
1000 SAC 95818 317-B1
TENNESSEE AV
- SaCo 95742 281-C3
TENNESSEE DR
4200 EDCo 95682 264-B3
TENNIS CT
7700 SaCo 95843 239-B7
TENNIS WY
100 AUB 95603 182-E2
TENNIS CLUB CT
8600 ELKG 95624 358-F2
TENNY CT
6200 SaCo 95608 279-D1
TENNYSON CT
500 RSVL 95747 219-C5
TENNYSON WY
- SaCo 95608 299-A3
TENWOODS CT
3100 RCCD 95827 299-D5
TERALBA WY
1600 SaCo 95833 277-C4
TERBEKAH WY
- EDCo - 267-H3
TERESA CT
800 PlaC 95603 162-C6
5200 OAKL 94561 (514-D6 See Page 493)
TERESA LN
1900 OAKL 94561 (514-C6 See Page 493)
2800 WSAC 95691 316-F1
TERESA WY
8700 ELKG 95624 378-F1
TERESTIA CT
7400 SaCo 95828 338-B2
TERILYN ST
2900 SAC 95826 298-F7
2900 SAC 95826 318-F1
TERKEN PL
300 PlaC 95603 162-E6
TERMINAL ST
1200 WSAC 95691 296-G5
TERMINAL WY
1100 SAC 95814 297-D3
TERMINOUS RD
16000 ISLE 95641 455-G6
16000 SaCo 95641 455-G6
16600 SaCo 95641 (475-J1 See Page 456)
16600 SaCo 95641 (476-A2 See Page 456)
TERMON DR
- ELKG 95758 358-B6
TERN CT
- SAC 95831 316-H7
TERNHAVEN WY
3400 SAC 95835 256-H4
TERRA LN
- LNCN 95648 180-A5
TERRA WY
1100 RSVL 95661 240-B4
6400 CITH 95610 259-J4
TERRA ALTA CT
- SAC 95831 336-J2
TERRA BELLA LN
5300 EDCo 95623 265-B7
TERRA BLANCA WY
11000 RCCD 95670 300-A4
TERRACE CT
- AUB 95603 182-F3
TERRACE DR
1900 ANT 94509 (513-F5 See Page 493)
1900 SaCo 95825 298-F1
1900 SaCo 95825 278-F7
5600 RKLN 95765 220-B1
6500 PlaC 95658 201-F1
TERRACE LN
800 GALT 95632 419-F6
TERRACE PL
3400 RKLN 95765 220-B1
TERRACE ST
100 AUB 95603 182-E3
TERRACE COVE CT
1800 FOLS 95630 261-J6
TERRACE DOWNS WY
4500 SAC 95842 258-J6
TERRACE OAK CIR
5300 SaCo 95628 260-A7
TERRACE PARK WY
5700 LMS 95650 200-J4
TERRACE VIEW AV
2800 ANT 94531 (513-G7 See Page 493)
TERRACINA CT
- PlaC 95650 221-D5
TERRACINA DR
- EDCo 95762 262-F5
4400 SAC 95834 257-B7
4400 SAC 95834 277-C1
TERRACINA LN
- PlaC 95650 221-C5
TERRACOTTA CT
8400 ELKG 95624 358-H1
TERRALAND CT
8200 CITH 95610 240-B7
TERRA LINDA DR
9200 ELKG 95624 358-G4
TERRA LOMA DR
- RCCD 95670 299-D3
- RCCD 95827 299-D4
TERRAMORE DR
9000 SaCo 95662 260-F5
TERRANOVA DR
- ANT 94509 (513-D7 See Page 493)
TERRAPIN CT
- ELKG 95757 358-A7
TERRA SERENA DR
- EDCo 95667 266-F5
TERRA VERDE LN
2900 OAKL 94561 (514-B7 See Page 493)
TERRA VISTA WY
3800 SaCo 95821 278-J3
TERRAZA CT
6400 ELKG 95758 358-A4
TERRAZA ST
3200 EDCo 95682 263-B7
TERRAZO CT
- RSVL 95747 219-B1
TERRAZZO DR
- ELKG 95757 378-B1
TERRCINA CIR
- RSVL 95747 219-B1
TERRELL DR
6100 CITH 95621 259-G5
TERRENO DR
6700 SaCo 95683 342-B1
TERRETORIAL WY
8600 ELKG 95624 358-F2
TERRI LN
600 EDCo 95619 265-E1
TERRIER WY
10000 RCCD 95827 299-D6
TERRITORIAL WY
8600 ELKG 95624 358-E1
TERRY LN
100 PlaC 95603 162-F5
TERRY ST
100 GALT 95632 439-D1
100 SaCo 95632 439-D1
TERRY WY
3100 SaCo 95608 279-B5
TERSK WY
5300 ELKG 95757 357-J7
TESLA WY
2500 SaCo 95825 298-D1
TESORO LN
- SAC 95835 257-A4
TESORO WY
- EDCo 95762 262-G6
TESSA AV
1500 SAC 95815 278-A5
TESSARA CT
9600 ELKG 95624 359-B6
TESTAROSSA CT
- RSVL 95747 219-B1
TESTAROSSA WY
- RSVL 95747 219-B1
TESTERMAN WY
9000 ELKG 95758 357-G3
TETLOW CT
- SAC 95823 337-J7
TETON WY
7800 SaCo 95843 238-G7
TETOTOM PARK WY
8000 SaCo 95843 239-B6
TETWORTH WY
100 FOLS 95630 261-F6
TEVERE PL
- EDCo 95762 262-B3
TEVERSHAM DR
- RSVL 95747 239-B1
TEVIS RD
2100 SaCo 95825 278-D7
TEVRIN WY
8100 SaCo 95828 338-G7
TEXAS AV
- SaCo 95742 281-D4
TEXAS ST
- ANT 94509 (513-C6 See Page 493)
TEXAS BAR CT
2000 SaCo 95670 280-D4
TEXAS CANYON RD
- EDCo 95667 225-D5
TEXAS CANYON RD E
- EDCo 95634 225-E4
- EDCo 95667 225-E4
TEXAS HILL RD
2600 EDCo 95667 246-C6
TEXAS RIVER CT
11100 RCCD 95670 280-A5
TEXERNA CT
3000 EDCo 95667 246-B5
3000 PLCR 95667 246-B5
THACKERAY CT
600 RSVL 95747 219-C5
THADDEUS CT
6700 ELKG 95758 358-B5
THALASSA CT
- EDCo 95762 262-C3
THALIA CT
7400 CITH 95621 259-G4
THALIA DR
- EDCo 95762 262-A2
THALIA WY
4200 RCCD 95742 320-D1
6500 CITH 95621 259-G3
THAMES WY
5700 SaCo 95608 299-C1
THATCHER CIR
- SAC 95823 337-J4

STREET Block City ZIP Pg-Grid

THAYER WY
- SaCo 95662 260-E3
THE CT
4400 SaCo 95821 278-J3
THEATER ST
- SaCo 95690 437-A1
THELEN CT
8600 SaCo 95662 260-E5
THELMA AV
3300 SAC 95833 277-D6
THEO WY
1100 SAC 95822 317-A3
THEODORE AV
8500 SaCo 95828 338-F3
THEONA WY
- RKLN 95765 200-B7
THERESA CT
10300 RCCD 95670 299-F3
THERESA LN
800 LNCN 95648 179-J2
800 PlaC 95648 179-J2
THEREZA WY
700 RVIS 94571 454-H4
THESEUS WY
4200 RCCD 95742 320-D1
THETFORD CT
9300 ELKG 95624 358-F5
THETHYS WY
8400 CITH 95610 240-C7
THICKET CT
6200 ELKG 95758 358-A5
THIERY RD
1400 SAC 95822 317-B6
THILOW CT
9000 SaCo 95826 298-H7
THILOW DR
9000 SaCo 95826 298-J7
9200 SaCo 95826 299-A7
THIRA CT
- ELKG 95758 357-H4
THIRA WY
4500 ELKG 95758 357-H4
THIRD PKWY
5200 SaCo 95823 317-J7
5200 SaCo 95823 337-H1
THIRZA CT
100 AUB 95603 182-F1
THIS WY
8100 CITH 95610 239-H6
THISTLE CT
- RKLN 95765 200-C7
- SAC 95823 337-G2
THISTLE LN
1600 PlaC 95658 201-F1
THISTLE WY
2300 LNCN 95648 179-D1
THISTLEDOWN DR
2300 RSVL 95661 240-D4
4100 SaCo 95628 280-E2
THISTLEDOWN PL
- PlaC 95603 162-F7
THISTLELOOP CT
6700 SaCo 95842 259-A3
THISTLEPATCH
2200 PlaC 95658 201-H2
THISTLEWOOD WY
1400 SaCo 95608 299-B3
THODE WY
3800 SaCo 95821 278-G3
THOM WY
3100 SaCo 95826 298-J7
THOMAS CT
100 FOLS 95630 261-E4
1000 ANT 94509 (513-F7
See Page 493)
2100 OAKL 94561 (514-B7
See Page 493)
THOMAS DR
4700 OAKL 94561 (514-B7
See Page 493)
6400 SaCo 95660 258-G2
THOMAS LN
2400 SaCo 95608 279-A7
THOMAS PL
- WSAC 95691 296-E7
THOMAS ST
100 RSVL 95678 239-J1
THOMASINO WY
5200 SaCo 95843 259-B1
5300 SaCo 95843 239-B7
THOMPI LN
3800 EDCo 95667 264-J1
THOMPSON CIR
900 FOLS 95630 281-E2
THOMPSON WY
900 PLCR 95667 245-G5
2300 SAC 95822 317-D6
THOMSEN WY
- LNCN 95648 179-E3
THOR CT
5100 RKLN 95765 199-J5
THOR DR
- WSAC 95691 296-D4
THOR WY
4400 SaCo 95864 298-J1
4600 SaCo 95608 299-A1
4600 SaCo 95864 299-A1
THOREAU CT
900 RSVL 95747 219-E6
THOREAU DR
- EDCo 95682 283-B1
THOREAU LN
100 FOLS 95630 261-H6
THORES ST
2300 RCCD 95670 299-E2
THORESON CT
8700 SaCo 95662 260-E3
THORNBRIDGE DR
1000 GALT 95632 419-F2
THORNBURY DR
8400 SaCo 95843 238-G5
THORNDIKE WY
100 FOLS 95630 261-G6
THORNE CT
100 FOLS 95630 261-E4
THORNECROFT LN
- RSVL 95747 218-J6
THORNFIELD DR
8400 SaCo 95828 338-E6
THORNHILL CT
3400 EDCo 95762 263-B6
THORNHILL DR
1000 RSVL 95746 240-F4
3300 EDCo 95762 263-A5
3600 SaCo 95826 318-H2
THORNHILL LN
- LNCN 95648 179-F7
THORNLEY WY
400 SaCo 95864 298-H4

THORNTON AV
1600 SAC 95814 297-E2
THORNTON RD Rt#-J8
- SaCo 95690 417-J6
N THORNTON RD Rt#-J8
22000 SJCo 95242 (438-C6
See Page 418)
22000 SJCo 95686 (438-A1
See Page 418)
28500 SJCo 95686 417-J7
28500 SJCo 95686 418-A7
THORNWOOD DR
3600 SaCo 95821 278-G5
6000 LMS 95650 201-A5
THOROE CT
5100 ELKG 95758 357-H2
THOROUGHBRED CT
- PlaC 95658 181-G7
5800 RKLN 95677 220-H5
THOROUGHBRED WY
9200 ELKG 95624 358-J6
THORP RD
- WSAC 95691 296-E7
THORPE WY
7500 SAC 95822 337-D3
THORSON DR
- EDCo 95667 266-J3
- EDCo 95667 267-A3
THOUSAND OAKS CT
4800 SaCo 95841 259-C7
4800 SaCo 95841 279-C1
THRACIAN CT
8600 ELKG 95624 358-F2
THRASHER CT
2900 EDCo 95682 263-B3
THREE SISTERS CT
7200 CITH 95621 259-G2
THRELKEL ST
400 PlaC 95658 181-G5
THRESHER CT
6300 ELKG 95758 358-A5
THRIFTY WY
7600 SaCo 95843 238-F7
THROWITA WY
4000 EDCo 95619 265-E2
THRUSH CT
- RSVL 95747 219-B7
7700 CITH 95610 259-J5
THRUSH LN
2500 EDCo 95709 246-H2
THUNDER WY
4300 SaCo 95826 318-J3
THUNDERBIRD CT
600 RSVL 95747 219-D7
7700 SaCo 95628 279-J1
THUNDERBIRD LN
4000 EDCo 95672 243-E6
THUNDERCLOUD LN
- EDCo - 247-C7
THUNDERHEAD CIR
6600 SaCo 95662 260-B3
THUNDER HEAD CT
5000 EDCo 95667 265-A2
THUNDER HEAD LN
6500 EDCo 95667 265-A1
THUNDER RIDGE CIR
5300 RKLN 95765 200-C7
5300 RKLN 95765 220-C1
THUNDER VALLEY CT
3100 PlaC 95648 199-F4
THURMAN WY
- FOLS 95630 261-H4
5000 SaCo 95824 317-J5
THURTON DR
2200 RSVL 95747 239-E1
THYS CT
8500 SAC 95828 318-F5
TIANT WY
7000 ELKG 95758 358-B4
TIARA WY
7400 CITH 95610 260-A1
TIBER DR
2700 SaCo 95826 298-J6
2700 SaCo 95826 299-A6
TIBER RIVER DR
2100 RCCD 95670 279-J5
TIBESSART CT
1600 FOLS 95630 281-H1
TIBURON WY
5300 SaCo 95841 259-B5
TICKERHOOF WY
3400 SaCo 95608 279-D4
TICONDEROGA LN
4200 SaCo 95660 258-H7
TIDE CT
- SAC 95833 277-D6
TIDEPOOL CT
100 FOLS 95630 261-F3
TIDES EDGE PL
- SAC 95835 256-H5
TIDEWATER CT
- SAC 95831 336-G3
TIDEWIND DR
4500 SAC 95838 277-H1
TIEMANN CT
- RSVL 95678 239-G4
TIEMPO CT
100 FOLS 95630 261-E3
TIERRA PL
200 PlaC 95603 162-F6
TIERRA WY
100 PlaC 95603 162-F7
7400 SaCo 95628 279-H2
TIERRA ARBOR WY
7600 SAC 95828 318-C7
TIERRA BUENA CT
- SAC 95823 337-H5
TIERRA CREEK DR
1000 GALT 95632 419-G2
TIERRA DE DIOS DR
3000 EDCo 95762 283-A1
TIERRA DEL LAGO PL
10100 PlaC 95658 202-A5
TIERRA EAST WY
7600 SAC 95828 338-C1
TIERRA GLEN WY
7600 SAC 95828 338-C1
TIERRA GRANDE CIR
2600 RCCD 95827 299-D3
TIERRA GREEN WY
6900 SAC 95828 318-C7
TIERRA LAWN CT
7600 SAC 95828 318-C7
TIERRA NUEVO RD
- SAC 95838 277-H4
TIERRA OAKS LN
2400 SaCo 95608 279-B7

TIERRAS
- SaCo 95683 322-B6
TIERRA VERDE WY
7700 SaCo 95828 338-C4
TIERRA VISTA WY
5300 SaCo 95843 239-B7
TIERRA WOOD WY
7500 SAC 95828 318-C7
TIFFANY CIR
1400 RSVL 95661 240-A3
TIFFANY CT
2400 RKLN 95677 220-F2
E TIFFANY LN
2700 RCCD 95670 299-D3
2700 RCCD 95827 299-D3
TIFFANY PT
5000 PlaC 95746 240-H5
TIFFANY WY
4800 SaCo 95628 280-B1
TIFFANY HILL DR
- EDCo 95672 243-G5
TIFFANY WEST WY
2800 RCCD 95827 299-D4
TIGER WY
- RSVL 95678 220-A7
- RSVL 95678 240-A1
500 RSVL 95678 239-J1
TIGERLILY CT
8300 ELKG 95624 358-E1
TIGER LILY LN
- EDCo 95726 267-J1
1000 LNCN 95648 180-A5
1200 LNCN 95648 179-J5
TIGER LILY RD
- EDCo 95630 202-G4
TIGERS EYE RD
- EDCo 95684 286-J4
TIGERWOOD DR
7700 SaCo 95829 339-E5
TIKI LN
8200 SaCo 95828 338-D3
TILBURY CT
- RSVL 95661 220-E6
TILBURY WY
- RSVL 95661 220-F6
TILDEN DR
2900 RSVL 95661 240-E4
3800 EDCo 95762 262-E5
TILDEN WY
4600 SaCo 95842 259-A1
TILLAMOOK WY
3900 SaCo 95826 319-A1
TILLANDER WY
9000 ELKG 95624 358-H1
TILLER CT
- ELKG 95758 357-F7
TILLMAN CIR
- SAC 95823 337-H4
TILTON WY
9300 SaCo 95662 260-H3
TIMBER CT
8600 SaCo 95662 260-D5
TIMBER LN
- EDCo 95726 267-G3
- RVIS 94571 454-F1
TIMBER COVE WY
8200 SaCo 95828 338-D7
TIMBERCREEK WY
4900 SaCo 95841 259-A5
TIMBERLAKE WY
7500 SAC 95823 338-C5
TIMBERLAND CT
- LNCN 95648 180-A4
TIMBERLAND DR
- RCCD 95742 300-F7
- RCCD 95742 320-F1
TIMBERLAND LN
- LNCN 95648 180-A4
TIMBERLANE CT
300 AUB 95603 182-D3
TIMBERLANE PL
3100 SaCo 95843 238-F6
TIMBERLEAF WY
6000 SaCo 95662 260-D5
TIMBERLINE DR
1700 EDCo 95762 242-D7
1700 EDCo 95762 262-D1
TIMBERLINE LN
100 AUB 95603 182-D3
TIMBERLINE WY
- RKLN 95765 219-J2
TIMBERLINE RIDGE CT
2200 EDCo 95762 242-D7
2200 EDCo 95762 262-D1
TIMBERLINE RIDGE DR
2300 EDCo 95762 242-D7
TIMBERLODGE CT
- RSVL 95747 219-A5
TIMBERLODGE LN
- RSVL 95747 219-A5
TIMBER RIVER WY
9400 ELKG 95624 359-A5
TIMBERROSE WY
7000 RSVL 95747 219-A3
TIMBER TRAIL LP
- EDCo 95762 282-D5
TIMBERTREE LN
- ELKG 95758 358-D6
TIMBERVIEW CT
- ELKG 95757 377-J1
- ELKG 95757 397-J1
TIMBER VIEW DR
1800 EDCo 95667 244-D2
TIMBERWOOD CT
- SAC 95833 277-C6
TIME CT
5600 SAC 95824 318-B5
TIMKIR WY
- ELKG 95757 378-A2
TIMM AV
8800 SaCo 95628 280-E1
TIMMCO CT
3600 SaCo 95608 279-C4
TIMMERMAN WY
5600 CITH 95621 259-G6
TIMMS MINE RD
- EDCo 95633 205-G6
- EDCo 95634 205-G6
TIMOTHY LN
4200 RKLN 95677 220-F2
TIMOTHY WY
4800 SaCo 95628 260-B7
4800 SaCo 95628 280-B1
TIMPANI CT
4000 SaCo 95843 238-H6
TIMS LN
- PlaC 95626 237-E2
- SuCo 95626 237-E2

TIMS MINE RD
- EDCo 95633 205-H6
- EDCo 95634 205-H6
TIMSON CT
100 FOLS 95630 261-D6
TIMSON DR
100 FOLS 95630 261-D6
TINA CT
6300 SaCo 95608 259-E5
TINA WY
900 RSVL 95661 239-J4
TINA LAKE LN
14100 SaCo 95690 436-D1
TINDAL WY
- FOLS 95630 261-E7
TINKER RD
1200 PlaC 95765 199-F7
TINKER WY
- SAC 95838 278-B2
TINNEIL CT
- SAC 95833 277-C5
TINOS WY
9100 ELKG 95758 357-H4
TINTA FINA DR
11000 RCCD 95670 299-J5
11000 RCCD 95670 300-A4
TINTORERA WY
3000 SAC 95833 276-J4
TINY LN
2100 EDCo 95667 244-C7
TINY WY
3000 PlaC 95747 239-C2
TIOGA CT
- LNCN 95648 179-H6
TIOGA LN
- LNCN 95648 179-H5
5200 EDCo 95623 265-A6
TIOGA WY
2600 SaCo 95821 278-E5
TIOGAWOODS DR
- SaCo 95829 338-G4
8500 SaCo 95828 338-F4
TIPPENS WY
- FOLS 95630 281-G1
TIPPERARY WY
7500 CITH 95610 259-H5
TIPPWOOD WY
4500 SaCo 95842 258-J1
4600 SaCo 95842 259-A1
TIPTOE CT
1000 SaCo 95825 298-C3
TIPTON CT
8600 ELKG 95624 358-F6
TISDALE WY
4800 SaCo 95841 279-B1
TISHIMINGO CT
- SAC 95831 336-H2
TITAN RD
9400 ELKG 95624 359-C6
TITAN RIDGE CT
5400 SaCo 95628 259-F6
TITIAN PKWY
7500 SAC 95823 337-H3
7500 SaCo 95823 337-H3
TITLEIST WY
- EDCo 95762 262-G4
TITTLE WY
- ELKG 95757 377-H2
- ELKG 95757 397-H2
TIVERTON AV
1400 SAC 95822 337-B1
TIVERTON CT
- RKLN 95677 220-G5
TIVERTON LN
- LNCN 95648 179-F7
TIVOLI WY
100 SAC 95819 297-H3
TOAD HOLLOW DR
- LNCN 95648 179-E5
TOAD HOLLOW WY
8200 ELKG 95624 358-D1
TOBAGO CT
- WSAC 95691 316-D2
TOBAGO ST
- WSAC 95691 316-D2
TOBARI CT
3200 SaCo 95821 278-H5
TOBIA WY
7600 SaCo 95628 279-J3
TOBIANO DR
- SaCo 95829 339-F6
TOBIAS LN
- EDCo 95634 225-D3
TOBOGGAN RD
6100 EDCo 95682 283-F6
TOBRURRY WY
300 FOLS 95630 281-J1
300 FOLS 95630 282-A1
TOBY DR
- EDCo 95762 262-E6
TOCCATA WY
8000 SaCo 95843 238-H4
TODD CT
6600 SaCo 95842 259-B3
TODD LN
- LNCN 95648 179-J1
- LNCN 95648 180-A1
TODD RD
3800 PlaC 95602 161-A4
TODHUNTER AV
400 WSAC 95605 296-H1
TODROB LN
- EDCo 95667 266-J5
TOIYABE LN
3900 EDCo 95682 263-J3
TOKAY AV
7100 SaCo 95828 338-E1
TOKAY DR
4500 OAKL 94561 (514-F7
See Page 493)
TOKAY LN
8900 SaCo 95829 318-H7
9200 SaCo 95829 319-A7
TOLAMA PL
- SaCo 95829 339-D6
TOLAND LN
1800 SolC 94571 474-A6
1800 SolC 94571 (494-A1
See Page 493)
TOLEDO ST
- SaCo 95742 281-D4
TOLEDO WY
4000 SaCo 95821 278-E4
TOLENAS CT
3600 SaCo 95864 298-G4
TOLKIEN AV
8000 SAC 95758 358-D1
TOLLERTON WY
9200 SaCo 95829 338-J5

TOLMAN LN
2900 SaCo 95843 238-F5
TOLOWA TR
- EDCo - 267-E6
TOLUCA LN
6900 CITH 95621 259-F4
TOLWORTH CT
500 RSVL 95661 [illegible]
TOM ST
2000 EDCo 95667 245-C1
TOM WY
- ELKG 95757 377-J2
- ELKG 95757 378-A2
- ELKG 95757 397-J2
TOM AND JERRY LN
4100 PlaC 95602 162-B1
TOMASINI WY
4800 SAC 95823 337-J5
TOMATO PATCH LN
- SaCo 95833 276-G5
TOMBSTONE CT
800 EDCo 95619 265-D6
TOMIES OAKWOOD CT
- LNCN 95648 200-B2
TOMKI WY
7900 CITH 95610 260-A1
TOMLINSON DR
100 FOLS 95630 261-A1
100 FOLS 95630 241-A7
TOMMAR DR
4800 SaCo 95628 280-B1
4900 SaCo 95628 260-B7
TOMMY CIR
8100 SaCo 95828 338-D2
TOMMY CT
4300 EDCo 95672 243-J7
TOM THUMB CT
8700 ELKG 95624 358-G4
TONDELA WY
8700 SaCo 95628 260-E7
TONEY CT
100 FOLS 95630 261-F4
TONG RD
1300 EDCo 95762 262-F7
TONGA CT
- SAC 95758 358-C1
TONI CT
100 GALT 95632 419-D7
TONI LN
- EDCo 95667 245-D7
TONKIN DR
9400 SaCo 95662 260-H5
TONO WY
4800 SaCo 95841 279-B1
TONY CT
- SAC 95831 336-H2
TONYA WY
5000 SaCo 95608 259-E7
TOOMBS ST
5400 SaCo 95628 259-F6
TOPAM CT
- SAC 95833 277-C4
TOPANGA LN
- LNCN 95648 180-A4
7300 SaCo 95842 259-C1
TOPAZ AV
4800 RKLN 95677 220-C3
TOPAZ CT
1000 RSVL 95661 239-J5
4800 RKLN 95677 220-C2
TOPAZ DR
6300 EDCo 95726 248-D2
TOPAZ LN
3200 EDCo 95682 263-E7
TOPAZ RD
- WSAC 95691 316-C4
TOPAZ WY
1300 SaCo 95864 298-E2
TOPAZ CREEK WY
- ELKG 95758 357-J3
TOPAZ HILLS CT
2600 RCCD 95827 299-D3
TOPAZ VALLEY WY
4200 RCCD 95742 320-D1
TOP CASTLE DR
- ELKG 95758 357-F7
TOPEKA WY
2600 SaCo 95827 299-A5
TOPHAM CT
100 FOLS 95630 281-F1
TOPP CT
5800 SaCo 95608 279-C6
TOP RAIL CT
6100 EDCo 95682 283-F6
TOP RAIL LN
5800 EDCo 95682 283-F6
TOPSAIL CT
- SAC 95831 316-G7
TOPSIDE DR
2400 PlaC 95603 161-J6
TOPSPIN WY
15500 SaCo 95683 342-E3
TORCHY CT
9400 SaCo 95826 319-A1
TORC MOUNTAIN LN
- LNCN 95648 200-B2
TORERO WY
500 EDCo 95762 242-C4
TORINO ST
- WSAC 95691 296-J7
- WSAC 95691 297-A7
TORINO WY
- EDCo 95762 262-H4
9100 SaCo 95829 338-H7
TORK CT
- FOLS 95630 281-G2
TORLAND ST
3000 SAC 95833 276-J4
TORMOLO WY
2500 RCCD 95670 299-F2
TORO CT
1500 EDCo 95762 242-C4
1800 RCCD 95670 299-E3
TORONJA WY
2700 SAC 95833 276-J7
TORONTO RD
3800 EDCo 95682 263-E6
TORONTO WY
4800 SAC 95820 318-C3
TORQUAY PL
- SaCo 95843 239-C5
TORRANCE AV
2900 SAC 95822 337-E2
TORRAZZO WY
- EDCo 95762 262-G5
TORRENTE WY
4500 SAC 95823 337-H5

TORRE RAMEL LN
3000 OAKL 94561 (514-A7
See Page 493)
TORREY WY
8700 ELKG 95624 358-G4
TORREY PINES CT
5200 SaCo 95608 299-B1
TORRINGTON LN
- LNCN 95648 179-F7
TORRINGTON PL
- SaCo 95842 259-A1
TORTOLA RD
- WSAC 95691 316-D2
TORTOLA WY
6700 SAC 95828 318-B7
TORY LN
3100 RCCD 95827 299-D4
TORY DALE CT
- RSVL 95747 219-C1
TOSCA CT
5500 EDCo 95667 [illegible]
TOSCANA LP
- EDCo 95762 262-B2
TOSCANA PL
- PlaC 95603 202-B1
TOSCANO CT
- RSVL 95661 240-D2
TOSCANO DR
- ELKG 95757 358-B7
TOTEM DR
- SaCo 95690 455-E4
TOTEM RD
6800 EDCo 95667 265-C2
TOTTENHAM CT
600 GALT 95632 419-G4
TOTTENHAM DR
1100 GALT 95632 419-H4
TOUCHMAN ST
3000 SaCo 95833 276-J4
TOUCHSTONE CT
100 WSAC 95691 296-G7
9200 PlaC 95746 221-G3
TOUCHSTONE PL
100 WSAC 95691 296-G7
100 WSAC 95691 316-G1
TOULON LN
7400 SaCo 95828 338-F2
TOURBROOK WY
- SAC 95833 277-A4
2800 SaCo 95833 276-J4
TOURMALINE CT
3600 EDCo 95672 263-C2
TOURMALINE WY
2800 SaCo 95843 238-E5
3300 EDCo 95672 263-C2
TOURNEY WY
1600 SAC 95833 277-C5
TOWER AV
2300 SaCo 95825 298-D1
TOWER CT
700 WSAC 95691 297-A3
8200 PlaC 95746 240-H2
TOWER LN
2000 EDCo 95667 245-A4
N TOWER RD
26100 SJCo 95686 (438-A3
See Page 418)
TOWER ST
100 WSAC 95691 297-A4
TOWER BRIDGE GATEWAY
- WSAC 95691 296-J4
- WSAC 95691 297-A3
TOWERING OAKS CT
200 FOLS 95630 281-A3
TOWER ROCK CT
100 FOLS 95630 240-J7
TOWHEE LN
3300 EDCo 95667 245-G6
TOWHEE WY
5500 SaCo 95842 258-J6
TOWLE CT
- LNCN 95648 179-D4
TOWN CIR
2400 SaCo 95821 278-D5
TOWN CT
3500 PlaC 95602 162-B3
TOWN CENTER BLVD
4200 EDCo 95762 282-D2
TOWN CENTER DR
- SAC 95834 257-A7
- SAC 95835 257-A7
TOWN CENTER PZ
- WSAC 95691 296-H7
- WSAC 95691 316-H1
TOWNHALL WY
7200 SaCo 95828 338-D2
TOWNSEND CT
- RSVL 95678 219-G5
2600 SaCo 95864 298-E5
TOWN VIEW DR
12500 AUB 95603 162-E5
TOY AV
2600 SAC 95822 317-E7
TOYAN CT
600 EDCo 95619 265-F3
TOYAN DR
4200 EDCo 95619 265-E3
TOYAN ST
- EDCo 95762 242-C5
TOYON AV
8100 SaCo 95628 280-B2
TOYON CIR
1100 LNCN 95648 179-D2
TOYON DR
100 AUB 95603 182-F1
TOYON WY
300 RSVL 95678 239-J3
TOYON BAY CT
- ELKG 95624 359-A7
TRABERT CT
7000 SaCo 95608 279-F2
TRACTION AV
2200 SAC 95815 277-G7
TRACY CT
2000 FOLS 95630 262-A7
5000 SaCo 95842 259-A5
TRACY LN
- EDCo 95633 205-E1
1700 PlaC 95603 162-C5
2800 PlaC 95650 200-J3
TRACY TER
8500 PlaC 95746 241-D2
TRADE WY
- EDCo 95682 283-H1
TRADE CENTER DR
10900 RCCD 95670 299-J2
11000 RCCD 95670 300-A1
11200 RCCD 95742 300-A1

TRADE CENTER DR
11200 SaCo 95742 300-A1
11200 SaCo 95742 280-A7
TRADEPOST TR
- GALT 95632 439-G1
TRADERS LN
700 FOLS 95630 261-B6
TRADE WIND AV
1800 SaCo 95825 298-D1
TRADEWINDS AV
1400 SAC 95822 317-B4
TRADEWINDS CIR
1400 WSAC 95691 296-G5
TRADEWINDS DR
- RSVL 95747 219-C1
TRADING POST CT
2000 SaCo 95626 238-C7
TRAFALGAR CIR
- GALT 95632 419-G5
TRAFFIC WY
4100 SaCo 95827 319-B2
TRAFTON CT
10100 ELKG 95757 377-H2
10100 ELKG 95757 397-H2
TRAGUS WY
8400 ELKG 95624 358-E2
TRAILEE CT
2000 RSVL 95747 219-C7
TRAIL END WY
1300 SAC 95834 277-D3
TRAIL GULCH
7100 EDCo 95667 226-C3
TRAILHEAD CT
9800 SaCo 95693 360-J7
TRAILING VINE CT
- SaCo 95829 339-D6
TRAIL OF TEARS
- EDCo 95667 286-G3
TRAILRIDE WY
- CITH 95621 259-F3
TRAILS CT
2200 RCCD 95670 279-F7
TRAILS END RD
4800 EDCo 95682 283-F3
TRAILSIDE DR
7600 SaCo 95628 279-H2
TRAIL WOODS DR
8000 SaCo 95828 338-D4
TRAINOR WY
- ELKG 95758 357-E4
TRAJAN DR
5900 SaCo 95628 260-C5
6200 SaCo 95662 260-C4
TRAKHANER CT
700 GALT 95632 419-F2
TRALEE WY
9700 ELKG 95624 358-G7
9700 ELKG 95624 378-H1
TRAMEZZO WY
- EDCo 95762 262-H5
TRAMINER WY
8000 SaCo 95829 338-J6
TRAMMEL WY
600 GALT 95632 419-G4
8400 SAC 95823 337-J7
8400 SAC 95823 357-J1
TRAMONTI CT
- SAC 95835 257-B5
TRANQUIL LN
800 GALT 95632 419-F4
TRANQUIL GLEN CT
- SaCo 95829 339-E6
TRANQUILITY DR
6900 SAC 95823 337-F1
N TRANQUILITY DR
6800 SAC 95823 337-F1
TRANQUILITY RDG
3500 EDCo 95682 283-B7
TRANQUILLITY LN
- EDCo 95633 205-E1
TRANSITION WY
7700 ELKG 95758 358-C4
TRAPANI CT
- ELKG 95757 377-J1
- ELKG 95757 397-J1
TRAPANI WY
- ELKG 95757 377-J1
- ELKG 95757 378-A1
- ELKG 95757 397-J1
TRAPPER CT
3700 SaCo 95843 238-G6
TRAP ROCK WY
2900 SAC 95835 256-J6
TRAVARY WY
8500 SaCo 95843 239-A5
TRAVER CT
8100 SaCo 95828 338-D6
TRAVERS ST
- AUB 95603 182-F3
TRAVERSE CT
- EDCo 95633 205-H2
- EDCo 95634 205-H2
TRAVERSE CREEK RD
- EDCo 95634 205-G4
5800 EDCo 95633 205-E4
TRAVERTINE CIR
4900 SaCo 95841 259-A7
TRAVIS CT
200 RSVL 95747 219-D6
TRAVIS LN
- SaCo 95825 298-C1
TRAVIS ST
- FOLS 95630 261-D7
TRAVO WY
- ELKG 95757 358-A7
- ELKG 95757 378-A1
TRAVOIS CIR
- EDCo 95672 263-A2
TRAVOIS CT
- EDCo 95672 263-A2
TRAWANGAN CT
- ELKG 95758 357-E5
TRAWLER WY
5900 CITH 95621 259-D1
TRAYLEN CT
100 FOLS 95630 261-F7
TRAYNOR WY
8500 SaCo 95828 338-F7
TRAZIEL CT
1600 FOLS 95630 281-H1
TRAZIEL WY
1700 FOLS 95630 281-J1
TREASURE DR
- RKLN 95765 199-J5
TREASURE LN
1000 RSVL 95678 239-G1
5600 EDCo 95667 244-E7
5600 EDCo 95667 264-E1

STREET Block City ZIP Pg-Grid

TREASURE WY
6900 SAC 95831 316-G7
6900 SAC 95831 336-G1
TREASURE HILL CT
11400 SaCo 95670 280-B4
TREASURE ISLAND RD
- WSAC 95691 316-D2
TREASURE ROCK LN
- EDCo - 267-C1
TREBBIANO CIR
9300 ELKG 95624 379-A1
TREE CT
4200 SaCo 95628 280-B2
TREEBINE AV
6800 CITH 95621 239-F6
TREECREST AV
8000 CITH 95610 260-B6
8000 CITH 95628 260-B6
8100 SaCo 95628 260-B6
TREECREST CT
- RSVL 95678 219-H5
TREE FROG LN
- EDCo 95619 286-C5
TREE HILL CT
5800 CITH 95841 259-D3
TREE HOUSE LN
700 SaCo 95864 298-H4
TREELAKE RD
9400 PlaC 95746 240-G5
TREELARK WY
6800 CITH 95621 239-F7
TREELEAF WY
- EDCo 95762 282-D4
8200 CITH 95621 239-F6
TREE LINE CT
6000 SaCo 95662 260-H5
TREELINE CT
7100 PlaC 95746 241-C2
TREELINE WY
- EDCo 95762 282-D3
TREEN CT
2900 RCCD 95670 299-G3
TREEPOND CT
5200 SaCo 95843 239-B7
TREESE WY
600 RSVL 95678 219-J7
600 RSVL 95678 220-A6
TREE SHADOW PL
4700 SaCo 95628 280-G1
TREE SIDE DR
1800 SaCo 95608 299-B1
TREESIDE LN
- EDCo 95633 205-C3
TREE SWALLOW CIR
2800 ELKG 95757 357-F7
TREESWIFT CT
- LNCN 95648 200-B3
TREETOP CT
7100 CITH 95621 259-E2
TREE TOP LN
200 PlaC 95603 162-G6
TREE VIEW LN
2900 PLCR 95667 245-C4
TREE VIEW RD
5900 SaCo 95830 319-J6
TREFETHEN CT
3300 RCCD 95670 299-J4
TREFETHEN WY
- SAC 95834 276-J3
TREFOIL CT
8100 CITH 95621 239-F6
TREFTON CT
100 FOLS 95630 261-H5
E TREGALLAS RD
- ANT 94509 (513-E6 See Page 493)
W TREGALLAS RD
300 ANT 94509 (513-C6 See Page 493)
TREHOWELL CT
- RSVL 95678 219-G5
TREHOWELL DR
- RSVL 95678 219-H5
TREJO WY
- FOLS 95630 261-B6
TRELEAVEN CT
3500 SaCo 95843 238-G7
TRELLIS CT
- LNCN 95648 200-A2
TRELLIS LN
600 GALT 95632 419-F5
TRELLIS TR
- EDCo 95709 246-G6
TRELLIUM CT
8300 CITH 95610 260-C1
TREMAIN DR
6100 CITH 95621 259-F4
TREMBATH CT
1700 ANT 94509 (513-G5 See Page 493)
TREMBATH LN
1300 ANT 94509 (513-G5 See Page 493)
1400 CCCo 94509 (513-G5 See Page 493)
TREMBATH ST
1800 ANT 94509 (513-G5 See Page 493)
TREMEZZO WY
9800 ELKG 95757 378-B1
TREMOLO CT
8000 SaCo 95843 238-H6
TREMONT CT
800 ANT 94509 (513-F7 See Page 493)
9500 SaCo 95662 260-J7
TREMONT DR
5000 EDCo 95619 265-C6
TREMWELL CT
5800 CITH 95610 259-J5
TRENARY CT
9300 ELKG 95624 358-J5
TRENHOLM DR
9200 ELKG 95758 358-C4
TRENT CT
- GALT 95632 419-D6
TRENT DR
- GALT 95632 419-E6
TRENTON CT
100 RSVL 95661 240-D5
TRENTON ST
- SaCo 95742 281-D5
4800 OAKL 94561 (514-C6 See Page 493)
TRENTON WY
3500 EDCo 95762 242-D6
6300 CITH 95621 259-E3
TRENTWICK CT
2600 SaCo 95608 279-C6

TRENTWOOD WY
2900 SAC 95822 337-E3
TRESLER AV
4000 SaCo 95660 258-H7
4100 SaCo 95842 258-H7
TRES PIEZAS WY
5700 SAC 95835 256-H4
TRESTLE DR
200 RSVL 95678 219-G4
TRESTLE GLEN CT
3800 EDCo 95682 263-D5
TRESTLE GLEN WY
900 SAC 95831 316-J7
TREVA ANN DR
4400 EDCo 95619 265-H3
TREVI WY
- EDCo 95762 262-B2
TREVISO CT
- RSVL 95747 219-B2
TREVOR CT
1300 RSVL 95678 239-F2
TREVOR WY
1400 RSVL 95678 239-F2
TRI LN
2700 EDCo 95682 263-D7
TRIAD CIR
8300 SaCo 95828 338-E6
TRIANGLE CT
- WSAC 95605 296-J2
TRIATHLON LN
- ELKG 95758 357-E5
TRIBUTARY LN
12100 SaCo 95670 280-F4
TRIBUTARY CROSSING DR
- SaCo 95670 280-F4
TRIBUTARY POINT DR
2000 SaCo 95670 280-F4
TRIBUTE CT
- AUB 95603 182-B6
TRIBUTE RD
900 SAC 95815 297-J1
1600 SAC 95815 298-A2
TRICIA WY
3900 SaCo 95660 258-H7
3900 SaCo 95660 278-H1
TRIESTE CT
8200 SaCo 95843 239-A6
TRIESTE WY
- EDCo 95762 262-G6
TRI FAMILY RD
3500 EDCo 95630 202-H7
TRIFF CT
100 FOLS 95630 261-C6
TRIGO WY
2700 SAC 95833 276-J7
TRILBY CT
6600 CITH 95610 259-H3
TRILLIUM CT
5500 SaCo 95662 260-H6
TRIMBLE WY
800 RSVL 95661 240-A4
1900 SaCo 95825 298-F1
1900 SaCo 95825 278-F7
TRIMMER WY
8300 SaCo 95828 338-E6
TRIMOTOR CT
5300 SaCo 95628 260-F7
TRIMSTONE CT
- RSVL 95747 218-J4
TRIMSTONE WY
- RSVL 95747 218-J4
TRINIDAD CT
14800 SaCo 95683 342-B1
14800 SaCo 95683 322-B7
TRINIDAD DR
4100 EDCo 95682 283-B1
14900 SaCo 95683 322-B7
TRINIDAD RD
- WSAC 95691 316-D3
TRINITY CT
200 RVIS 94571 454-G5
1800 ANT 94509 (513-F5 See Page 493)
4800 SaCo 95820 317-G3
E TRINITY LN
8300 SaCo 95628 260-C7
TRINITY WY
1700 WSAC 95691 316-H1
2400 RKLN 95677 220-B3
6500 EDCo 95667 265-B1
TRINITY RIVER DR
11100 RCCD 95670 280-A5
TRIPLE CROWN CT
8800 SaCo 95628 280-E3
TRIPLE OAK CT
100 RSVL 95747 239-E1
TRIPLE R RD
- EDCo 95667 226-E5
TRIPLETT CT
4000 SaCo 95608 279-C3
TRIPP CT
- RKLN 95765 200-A7
TRIPP WY
- RKLN 95765 200-A7
TRISH LN
5100 EDCo 95633 205-B3
TRISTAN CIR
- SAC 95823 337-J3
TRISTAN DR
- SaCo 95608 279-C6
TRITON CT
- SAC 95823 337-G2
TRITONIA CT
8700 ELKG 95624 358-F2
TRIUNFADOR LN
1900 EDCo 95672 243-E5
TROLIO WY
9400 ELKG 95624 359-A5
TROLLEYBELL CT
300 RSVL 95747 219-B5
TROLLEYBELL LN
200 RSVL 95747 219-B6
TRONA WY
4800 SaCo 95628 279-G1
TRONERO WY
2500 RCCD 95670 299-F2
TRONZANO WY
6600 ELKG 95757 378-A1
TROON CT
700 RSVL 95747 219-D7
TROON WY
7400 SAC 95822 337-D2
TROPHY CT
300 WSAC 95605 277-A7
TROPICANA CT
3300 SaCo 95826 299-A7
TROTTER CT
- SAC 95831 336-G3

TROUBLEMAKER CT
- EDCo 95619 266-D7
TROUT CT
8800 ELKG 95624 358-G5
TROUT WY
9200 ELKG 95624 358-G4
TROUT CREEK CT
7800 SaCo 95828 338-D5
TROUTDALE WY
5300 SAC 95823 337-J7
TROUVILLE LN
- SAC 95835 256-H6
TROVILLION ST
5900 CITH 95621 259-F5
TROVITA WY
6800 CITH 95610 260-A3
TROWBRIDGE CT
- PlaC 95746 240-G4
TROWBRIDGE LN
400 FOLS 95630 261-J5
TROWER CT
2200 FOLS 95630 281-F1
TROY CT
10600 RCCD 95670 279-H7
TROY WY
9300 PlaC 95746 241-B5
TROY CREEK LN
- SaCo 95662 260-E5
TRUAX CT
3100 SaCo 95821 278-C5
TRUCHARD LN
- LNCN 95648 179-J4
- LNCN 95648 180-A4
TRUCK ST
700 EDCo 95619 265-E2
TRUCKEE WY
3300 SAC 95817 297-F6
TRUCKEE RIVER DR
- RCCD 95670 279-J6
TRUDY WY
100 GALT 95632 419-E6
6600 SAC 95831 316-F7
TRUE CT
10300 RCCD 95670 299-F3
TRUEMPER WY
- SaCo 95655 299-E7
TRUFFLE CT
7700 SaCo 95843 239-A7
TRUJILLO WY
8900 SaCo 95826 298-H7
TRUMAN CT
- RKLN 95765 219-H2
TRUMAN ST
8900 ELKG 95624 358-H6
TRUMBAUER WY
- ELKG 95758 357-E4
TRUMPETER CT
4400 SaCo 95826 318-J3
TRUSCOT CT
- EDCo 95623 265-C6
TRUSCOT LN
5000 EDCo 95623 265-B5
TRUSCOTT CT
1600 RSVL 95661 240-B3
TRUSSEL WY
- SaCo 95864 298-F2
TRUXEL RD
- SAC 95834 257-B7
- SAC 95834 277-B1
2500 SAC 95833 277-C7
TRYON CT
100 SaCo 95864 298-F5
TSA LA GI RD
- EDCo 95667 266-D5
TUALATIN WY
3300 RCCD 95670 300-A4
TUCKAWAY LN
2200 EDCo 95667 246-B1
TUCKER WY
- EDCo 95762 262-B6
- FOLS 95630 262-B6
8000 SaCo 95828 338-F5
TUCKERMAN WY
- SAC 95835 257-C5
TUCSON CIR
5200 SaCo 95628 260-F7
TUCUMCARI CT
- RSVL 95678 219-G5
TUCUMCARI WY
9300 SaCo 95827 299-A5
TUDOR CT
1900 SaCo 95608 299-C1
2600 EDCo 95672 263-C1
TUDOR ST
800 GALT 95632 439-D2
TUDOR WY
5600 LMS 95650 200-J7
TUDSBURY RD
8500 PlaC 95650 201-F7
8500 PlaC 95650 221-F1
TUFTS ST
4900 SaCo 95841 259-B7
TUGGLE WY
1300 SAC 95831 317-A7
TULA CT
8300 SaCo 95628 280-C1
TULANE CT
4700 SaCo 95841 279-A1
TULARE CT
8700 ELKG 95624 358-F5
TULE CT
9300 ELKG 95758 358-A5
TULE LN
2500 RKLN 95677 220-B5
TULE RD
- YoCo 95612 356-E7
TULE ST
- WSAC 95691 316-D4
TULIP CIR
1500 PlaC 95603 162-D5
TULIP CT
- EDCo 95667 266-D3
TULIP DR
1200 ANT 94509 (513-B4 See Page 493)
TULIP WY
2200 SaCo 95821 278-C5
TULIP PARK WY
4100 RCCD 95742 320-D1
TULIP TREE CIR
- SAC 95834 277-B2
TULIPTREE WY
8300 SaCo 95843 239-C5
TULLAMORE CT
9100 SaCo 95829 338-J6
TULLE LN
4600 EDCo 95682 264-C7
TULLIA PL
8500 SaCo 95843 239-B5

TULLIS MINE RD
4200 EDCo 95619 265-D4
TULLOCH CT
100 RSVL 95747 239-B1
TULSA ST
- SaCo 95742 281-D5
TUMBLE LN
6900 PlaC 95650 201-B4
TUMBLEWEED CT
3400 RKLN 95677 200-D7
TUMBLEWEED WY
1300 SAC 95833 277-C4
1300 SAC 95834 277-C4
TUMBLEWOOD CT
6000 SaCo 95662 260-D5
TUMBRIDGE WY
5600 SaCo 95608 299-C1
TUMELI DR
7100 EDCo 95667 226-G4
TUNDRA WY
- SAC 95834 277-D4
TUNDRA SWAN CIR
9700 ELKG 95757 357-E7
TUNGSTEN WY
7900 SAC 95832 337-C4
TUNIS RD
4800 SAC 95834 257-E6
4800 SAC 95835 257-E6
TUNNEL CT
2700 PLCR 95667 245-F4
TUNNEL ST
- PlaC 95658 181-H5
2700 PLCR 95667 245-F4
TUNNEL HILL WY
11300 SaCo 95670 280-B4
TUOLUMNE DR
8900 SaCo 95826 298-H6
TUOLUMNE LN
- LNCN 95648 179-F6
TUPACK CT
2000 EDCo 95667 245-B1
TUPELO DR
5500 SaCo 95842 259-C1
5800 SaCo 95621 259-D1
5900 CITH 95621 259-D1
6400 CITH 95621 239-E7
TURACO CT
- LNCN 95648 200-B3
TURAN CT
3300 RCCD 95670 299-J4
TURBO CT
8400 SaCo 95828 338-E5
TURBO LN
4200 EDCo 95667 265-C3
TURIN CT
- ELKG 95757 378-A1
TURKEY CREEK CIR
- PlaC 95648 180-B3
TURKEY FEATHER TR
1800 EDCo 95619 266-A7
5200 EDCo 95619 286-A1
TURKEY TRACK RD
5000 EDCo 95667 264-E1
TURLOCK ST
- WSAC 95691 316-D4
TURLOCK WY
8100 SaCo 95828 338-D6
TURNACE CT
100 GALT 95632 439-D1
TURNBERRY CT
100 RSVL 95747 219-D7
TURNBERRY LN
1200 RSVL 95747 219-C7
TURNBERRY TER
- RVIS 94571 454-F2
TURNBRIDGE DR
4000 SaCo 95823 317-G7
4000 SaCo 95823 337-G1
TURNBRIDGE RD
3300 SAC 95823 337-F1
TURNBUCKLE CIR
- ELKG 95758 357-E6
TURNBULL CIR
5500 SaCo 95628 260-D6
TURNBURY DR
8200 SaCo 95828 338-D5
TURNER CIR
3300 EDCo 95682 263-C5
TURNER CT
1100 PLCR 95667 245-H5
3000 EDCo 95682 263-D5
TURNER DR
3600 SaCo 95660 258-G2
7000 PlaC 95746 221-E7
TURNER PL
- LNCN 95648 179-E1
TURNER RD
6200 SAC 95829 318-H6
6200 SaCo 95829 318-H6
TURNER ST
3100 PLCR 95667 245-H5
TURNESA AV
2300 SaCo 95822 317-D6
TURN PIKE DR
100 FOLS 95630 281-B2
TURNSBERRY CT
5100 ELKG 95758 357-H5
TURNSTONE DR
600 SaCo 95834 277-E3
TURNSTONE WY
- RKLN 95765 219-H1
TURNSWORTH CT
4300 SaCo 95842 258-J6
TURQUOISE DR
6000 RKLN 95677 220-B3
TURQUOISE WY
- ELKG 95624 339-D7
- ELKG 95829 339-D7
- SaCo 95829 339-D7
1100 EDCo 95762 262-C4
TURRET CT
- RSVL 95678 219-H5
5200 SaCo 95842 259-B1
TURTLE PTH
5000 EDCo 95667 264-F5
TURTLE COVE WY
7600 ELKG 95758 358-C4
TURTLE CREEK LN
9100 SaCo 95628 260-G7
TURTLE DOVE CT
9800 ELKG 95624 378-H1
TURTLEDOVE CT
100 LNCN 95648 180-B7
TURTLEVIEW CT
- ELKG 95757 357-J7
TUSCAN LN
- SaCo 95864 298-J4
TUSCAN GROVE CIR
- RSVL 95747 219-B2

TUSCAN GROVE CT
- RSVL 95747 219-B2
TUSCANO CT
2400 RCCD 95670 279-G7
TUSCAN RIVER CT
- RSVL 95747 219-B2
TUSCAN RIVER WY
- RSVL 95747 219-B2
TUSCANY CT
- SAC 95831 337-A3
100 RSVL 95661 240-E2
6500 SaCo 95673 257-G3
TUSCANY ST
2300 RSVL 95661 240-E2
TUSCANY WY
- EDCo 95762 262-F6
- RVIS 94571 454-G6
TUSCANY OAKS CT
- PlaC 95746 240-J4
TUSKET RIVER DR
11100 RCCD 95670 280-A5
TUSTIN CT
- SAC 95823 338-A4
TUTTLE AV
100 AUB 95603 182-E2
TUTTLE DR
4500 RKLN 95677 220-F2
TUXFORD CT
9100 ELKG 95624 358-J5
TUZZA CT
- ELKG 95757 378-B2
TWAIN CT
500 RSVL 95747 219-E6
7700 SaCo 95828 338-D4
TWAIN HARTE CT
2500 EDCo 95762 262-D1
TWEDE WY
2300 SaCo 95626 238-D5
TWEED CT
5100 SaCo 95843 259-B1
TWEEDSMUIR DR
5800 RKLN 95677 220-C4
TWELVE BRIDGES RD
- LNCN 95648 180-C7
- LNCN 95648 199-G2
- LNCN 95648 200-A2
- PlaC 95648 180-D7
- PlaC 95648 199-G2
TWELVE OAKS CT
3000 EDCo 95667 245-D6
TWELVE OAKS DR
2700 PlaC 95663 201-D3
TWELVE OAKS LN
3000 EDCo 95667 245-D6
TWIG CT
7400 PlaC 95746 241-D2
TWILANE RD
- EDCo 95619 286-E4
TWILIGHT DR
7500 SAC 95822 337-E3
TWILIGHT LN
3700 EDCo 95682 283-H6
TWILIGHTSKY DR
- EDCo 95667 266-E4
TWILLEY DR
2900 RCCD 95827 299-D4
TWILLINGATE CT
8700 ELKG 95624 358-G2
TWIN CT
2400 RCCD 95670 279-J7
TWINBERRY WY
- ELKG 95624 358-G1
TWIN BROOK CT
7100 CITH 95621 259-E2
TWIN BUTTES DR
- FOLS 95630 260-J1
- FOLS 95630 261-F1
TWIN CEDARS CT
- EDCo - 267-J3
TWIN CEDARS DR
- EDCo - 267-J3
TWIN CITIES RD
- SaCo 95632 419-B2
TWIN CITIES RD Rt#-E13
1000 SaCo 95690 (416-J3 See Page 415)
1000 SaCo 95690 417-A3
1000 SaCo 95758 417-G2
4900 SaCo 95757 417-G2
5800 SaCo 95690 418-A2
5800 SaCo 95757 418-A2
8200 SaCo 95632 418-G2
9400 SaCo 95757 419-A2
9400 SaCo 95632 419-A2
TWIN CITIES RD Rt#-104
10100 SaCo 95757 419-F2
10100 GALT 95632 419-F2
10100 SaCo 95632 419-F2
11100 SaCo 95632 420-A2
11400 SaCo 95638 420-A2
11700 SaCo 95638 (400-J4 See Page 379)
12700 SaCo 95638 (401-J1 See Page 381)
13800 SaCo 95638 381-G7
14400 SaCo 95638 (382-J3 See Page 381)
16100 AmCo 95638 (382-J3 See Page 381)
TWIN CREEKS CT
5900 CITH 95621 259-E5
TWIN CREEKS LN
2900 RKLN 95677 220-C5
TWIN FALLS DR
8900 SaCo 95826 298-H6
TWIN GARDENS DR
5800 SaCo 95608 279-C7
TWIN HILLS DR
800 GALT 95632 419-E3
TWINING WY
6600 CITH 95621 239-E6
TWIN LAKES AV
9300 SaCo 95662 260-H6
TWIN LAKES DR
3300 PlaC 95650 201-G5
TWIN LAKES LN
- RVIS 94571 454-F2
TWIN LEAF CT
- SAC 95838 257-G7
TWIN OAKS AV
7500 CITH 95610 239-H6
7800 CITH 95610 240-A6
TWIN OAKS RD
2900 EDCo 95682 263-D7
TWIN PALMS LN
3900 LMS 95650 201-B7

TWIN PARK DR
6500 CITH 95621 259-E2
TWIN PINES DR
- RVIS 94571 454-F2
TWIN PINES LP
- EDCo 95633 205-C1
TWIN PINES TR
1100 PlaC 95602 162-F2
TWIN PONDS LN
100 PlaC 95648 180-F4
TWIN RIVER WY
400 SAC 95831 316-G7
400 SAC 95831 336-G1
TWIN ROCKS RD
7800 PlaC 95746 221-E6
TWIN SCHOOLS RD
9100 PlaC 95746 240-H4
TWIN TRAILS DR
8400 SaCo 95843 238-J5
TWINWOOD LP
- RSVL 95678 219-H5
TWIN WOOD WY
6300 CITH 95621 259-E2
TWISTING TR
4600 EDCo 95633 205-G6
TWISTING TRAILS RD
- EDCo 95633 205-G5
- EDCo 95634 205-G6
TWITCHELL RD
1800 EDCo 95619 265-J6
1800 EDCo 95619 266-A6
TWITCHELL ISLAND RD
1500 SaCo 95641 474-J3
1500 SaCo 95641 (475-A3 See Page 456)
TWITCHELL ISLAND ST
- WSAC 95691 316-F2
TWO EAGLE LN
1600 EDCo 95762 242-F6
TWO HARBORS CT
- ELKG 95624 359-A6
TWO HARBORS DR
- ELKG 95624 359-A7
TWO PINE CT
5000 EDCo 95682 264-D4
TWO POND RD
- EDCo - 267-G4
TWO RIVERS CT
- SAC 95833 276-H6
TWO RIVERS DR
- SAC 95833 276-H6
TWO TOWERS CT
- RKLN 95765 219-J2
TWO TOWERS WY
- RKLN 95765 219-J1
TWYLA LN
2000 PlaC 95658 201-G1
TY CT
5100 RKLN 95765 199-J5
TYA LN
- EDCo 95667 266-G3
TYEE AV
6200 SaCo 95841 259-D4
TYLER CT
2200 ANT 94509 (513-A7 See Page 493)
TYLER DR
- AUB 95603 182-B7
TYLER ST
- SaCo 95690 437-A1
4800 SaCo 95841 258-J7
4800 SaCo 95841 278-J1
5100 SaCo 95841 259-A7
5300 SaCo 95842 258-J6
TYLER WY
2600 WSAC 95691 316-F1
TYLER ISLAND RD
14700 SaCo 95690 436-G6
14900 SaCo 95690 456-F1
15100 SaCo 95641 456-B3
17000 SaCo 95641 (476-B1 See Page 456)
17500 SaCo 95690 (476-D1 See Page 456)
TYLER ISLAND BRIDGE RD
700 SaCo 95641 455-J4
700 SaCo 95641 456-A4
700 ISLE 95641 455-J4
700 ISLE 95641 456-A4
TYLER RIVER CT
10000 RCCD 95670 279-H6
TYNDALL CT
- SAC 95823 337-H6
TYNDRUM LN
- FOLS 95630 262-A5
TYNEBOURNE ST
4500 SAC 95834 256-H7
4500 SAC 95834 276-H1
TYNE FELL CT
8000 SaCo 95843 239-C6
TYOSA ST
5200 SaCo 95628 260-E7
TYRELL CT
100 FOLS 95630 261-F7
TYROLEAN CT
400 RSVL 95661 240-D4
TYROLEAN WY
2300 SaCo 95821 278-D6
TYRONE WY
4100 SaCo 95608 279-B3
TYRREL LN
2100 EDCo 95667 225-C7
2100 EDCo 95667 245-C1
TYSON CT
8000 SaCo 95843 238-H6
TYWOOD CT
9800 RCCD 95827 299-C5

U

U ST
100 SAC 95818 297-B5
100 SAC 95673 237-G7
700 SaCo 95673 238-A7
2000 SAC 95817 297-F6
2500 SaCo 95660 258-F1
2500 SaCo 95673 258-F1
2600 SaCo 95843 258-F1
5800 SAC 95817 298-A7
5900 SAC 95817 318-A1
UCCELLO WY
- SAC 95835 256-J4
UDINE WY
- EDCo 95762 262-G5
UKIAH LN
- ELKG 95758 357-F5
ULANI WY
7900 SaCo 95828 338-E5

ULENKAMP RD
2300 EDCo 95672 263-F1
2300 EDCo 95672 243-F7
ULRICH WY
4300 SAC 95822 317-A3
ULTRA CT
9200 SaCo 95662 260-H5
ULYSSES DR
4300 SaCo 95864 298-J1
4600 SaCo 95608 299-A1
4600 SaCo 95864 299-A1
UMBRIA AV
- SAC 95828 318-D5
UN RD
- EDCo 95633 205-B6
UNA PL
- SAC 95835 256-G6
UNCLE JOES LN
100 PlaC 95658 181-E4
UNDERHILL DR
8500 SaCo 95828 338-F7
UNDERWOOD LN
- LNCN 95648 179-F7
E UNDERWOOD RD
9300 SJCo 95220 (440-G6 See Page 420)
UNDERWOOD WY
4500 SaCo 95823 317-H7
UNICORN LN
4100 EDCo 95726 248-D3
UNION CT
- RSVL 95678 239-F1
UNION ST
100 ISLE 95641 455-H5
200 RSVL 95678 239-F2
200 AUB 95603 182-D2
800 SAC 95838 277-J4
1300 PLCR 95667 245-G5
3000 RKLN 95677 220-D2
UNION CREEK WY
8200 SaCo 95828 338-D5
UNION FLAT LN
- EDCo 95633 205-F5
UNION HOUSE WY
8200 SAC 95823 338-A6
UNION MILL WY
11600 SaCo 95670 280-C5
UNION MINE RD
4700 EDCo 95623 265-B6
UNION PARK WY
9000 ELKG 95624 378-H3
UNION RIDGE CT
2300 EDCo 95667 246-B2
UNION RIDGE RD
1700 EDCo 95667 246-A1
UNION SPRINGS WY
3300 RCCD 95827 299-C6
UNION SQUARE RD
- WSAC 95691 296-J7
UNITED CT
4200 SaCo 95660 258-J2
UNITED DR
3200 EDCo 95682 263-D4
UNITY CIR
100 SAC 95833 276-J6
UNITY CT
400 RSVL 95678 239-G5
UNITY PARK ST
- SAC 95833 276-J6
UNITY POINTE AV
2700 SAC 95833 276-J6
UNIVERSAL CT
- SAC 95826 318-G4
UNIVERSITY AV
- SaCo 95825 298-C6
- SAC 95825 298-C6
1600 SAC 95864 298-C6
UNIVERSITY PARK DR
1900 SAC 95825 298-D6
1900 SAC 95864 298-D6
UN RD A
- EDCo 95633 205-D3
UN RD D
- EDCo 95633 205-A3
UN RD E
- EDCo 95633 205-E4
UNSER WY
- ELKG 95758 358-C6
UNSWORTH AV
8500 SAC 95828 318-F5
UP CT
7700 CITH 95610 259-J6
UP CHICK ST
- EDCo - 267-H3
- EDCo 95726 267-H3
UPHAM CT
2400 SaCo 95608 279-A7
UPHILL WY
3000 SaCo 95843 238-F4
UPLAND CT
6600 RKLN 95677 220-G5
UPLAND DR
- RSVL 95747 218-J6
UPLAND ST
100 AUB 95603 182-F3
UPLANDS DR
1000 EDCo 95762 242-D7
UPLANDS WY
7700 CITH 95610 259-J6
7700 CITH 95628 259-J6
7800 CITH 95610 260-A6
UPPER LN
2700 EDCo 95682 264-A1
UPPER AUBURN HTS
100 PlaC 95603 162-F6
UPPER HOMESTEAD WY
- EDCo - 267-J4
UPPER LAKEVIEW
- EDCo 95667 244-H3
UPPER MEADOW DR
11400 SaCo 95670 280-C4
UPSHAW WY
10000 ELKG 95757 377-J2
10000 ELKG 95757 397-J2
UPSON DOWNS RD
4400 PlaC 95658 180-G3
UPTON CT
10300 ELKG 95624 359-E4
URANUS PKWY
7000 SaCo 95823 337-H1
URBANA WY
1700 SAC 95833 277-B4
URSA PKWY
7000 SaCo 95823 337-H1
URSULA WY
- RSVL 95661 220-E6
UTAH AV
- SaCo 95742 281-D5
2600 SAC 95822 337-E2

STREET Block City ZIP Pg-Grid

UTE WY
3800 SaCo 95843 238-G6
UTE RIVER CT
- SAC 95831 336-G1
UTICA AV
- SaCo 95742 281-D4
UTICA CT
9700 RCCD 95827 299-C6
UTICA MINE CT
11800 SaCo 95670 280-D4
UTOPIA RIVER CT
11100 RCCD 95670 280-A5

V

V ST
- SAC 95818 297-B5
3200 SAC 95817 297-F7
VACATION BLVD
5600 EDCo 95684 286-E7
VADA RANCH RD
1900 PlaC 95603 161-J7
1900 PlaC 95603 162-A7
1900 PlaC 95603 182-A1
VAGABOND WY
2200 SaCo 95825 298-C2
VAIL CT
- RKLN 95765 220-A2
N VAIL RD
26200 SJCo 95686 437-F1
28500 SJCo 95686 417-F7
VALASSTRADA CT
3000 SaCo 95608 279-B5
VALDERAMA CT
9900 SaCo 95829 339-D5
VALDERAMA WY
9900 SaCo 95829 339-D5
VALDEZ AV
- SAC 95828 318-D5
VALE DR
5100 SaCo 95608 279-B7
VALE RD
200 EDCo 95667 265-D2
VALENCIA AV
100 RSVL 95678 239-H1
VALENCIA PL
2800 ANT 94509 (513-A6 See Page 493)
VALENCIA WY
3100 SaCo 95825 278-F7
VALENDA CT
6400 ELKG 95757 378-A3
VALENSIN RD
10900 SaCo 95632 (399-F4 See Page 379)
10900 SaCo 95632 (400-A4 See Page 379)
N VALENSIN RD
11700 SaCo 95632 (400-C4 See Page 379)
VALENSIN RANCH RD
11600 SaCo 95632 (399-C3 See Page 379)
VALENTINE CT
600 GALT 95632 419-E2
VALERIAN LN
- LNCN 95648 180-A5
VALERIANA AV
7000 CITH 95621 259-F1
VALERIE CT
- SaCo 95841 259-C6
VALERIO DR
3600 EDCo 95682 263-F6
VALEWOOD CT
8200 SaCo 95662 260-B3
VALGRANDE WY
9800 ELKG 95757 358-B7
9800 ELKG 95757 378-B1
VALHALLA DR
5200 SaCo 95608 279-B2
VALIANT WY
4100 SaCo 95608 279-E3
VALIM WY
500 SAC 95831 336-G1
VALINE CT
- SAC 95831 316-J5
VALKO AV
2200 SAC 95822 337-D3
VALKYRIE WY
3000 SaCo 95821 278-G5
VALL CT
5600 SaCo 95608 279-C2
VALLARTA CIR
1600 SAC 95834 277-C4
VALLE CT
200 LNCN 95648 180-C7
VALLECITO RD
7100 EDCo 95633 205-E4
VALLECITOS WY
7500 SAC 95828 318-C7
VALLEJO AV
100 RSVL 95678 239-G1
400 RSVL 95678 219-G7
VALLEJO DR
9200 SaCo 95662 260-H3
VALLEJO WY
1900 SAC 95818 297-A6
VALLERO WY
14700 SaCo 95683 342-C4
VALLETTA CT
- RSVL 95747 199-B7
VALLETTA WY
4800 SAC 95820 317-J3
4800 SAC 95820 318-A3
VALLE VISTA CT
- PlaC 95603 181-J1
- PlaC 95603 182-A1
5800 PlaC 95746 221-F4
VALLE VISTA RD
3800 SaCo 95608 279-E3
VALLEY CT
1800 PLCR 95667 246-B5
E VALLEY DR
8900 ELKG 95624 378-H2
VALLEY RD
2400 SaCo 95821 278-D5
VALLEY ST
8100 SaCo 95628 280-B2
VALLEY BROOK AV
1300 SAC 95831 337-B2
VALLEY CREST CT
- SAC 95823 337-H4
VALLEY FALLS PL
- FOLS 95630 260-J1
- FOLS 95630 261-F1
VALLEY FORGE LN
- SaCo 95842 258-H7
4800 SaCo 95660 258-H7

VALLEY FORGE WY
2300 RSVL 95661 240-D5
VALLEY GLEN DR
1400 RSVL 95747 219-E4
VALLEY GLEN WY
5800 SAC 95823 338-A6
VALLEY GREEN DR
5200 SAC 95823 337-J6
7800 SAC 95823 338-A5
VALLEY HI DR
- SAC 95823 337-G5
5600 SAC 95823 338-A5
VALLEY LARK DR
8300 SAC 95823 337-J7
VALLEY OAK CT
100 FOLS 95630 261-B3
VALLEY OAK DR
100 RSVL 95678 239-H4
VALLEY OAK LN
8700 ELKG 95624 358-F7
VALLEY OAKS CT
5600 EDCo 95667 244-E6
VALLEY PARK CT
7400 SaCo 95828 338-D2
VALLEY PINES DR
9800 FOLS 95630 261-B2
VALLEY QUAIL CT
7800 SaCo 95843 238-F7
VALLEY QUAIL DR
3800 PlaC 95650 201-F7
VALLEY QUAIL LN
1200 PlaC 95602 162-F1
VALLEY RIDGE CT
500 PlaC 95603 182-B2
VALLEY RIDGE WY
- RSVL 95678 219-F6
VALLEY RIM WY
8600 SaCo 95843 238-J5
VALLEY SPRINGS RD
1900 PlaC 95658 201-E1
VALLEY SPRINGS WY
5800 ELKG 95758 357-J4
5800 ELKG 95758 358-A4
VALLEY TREE RD
- SaCo 95632 418-J6
- SaCo 95632 (438-J1 See Page 418)
VALLEY VALE WY
5600 SAC 95823 337-J6
5600 SAC 95823 338-A6
VALLEY VIEW CT
- EDCo 95726 267-J2
1600 RSVL 95661 240-C6
3900 SaCo 95628 279-J4
VALLEY VIEW DR
- EDCo - 267-J3
- EDCo 95726 267-J3
100 AUB 95603 182-D5
8900 PlaC 95658 181-G6
10600 RCCD 95670 279-G6
VALLEY VIEW PKWY
- EDCo 95762 282-F2
VALLEY VIEW RD
3100 EDCo 95672 263-E2
VALLEY VISTA DR
- EDCo 95709 247-B5
VALLEY VISTA LN
1500 PlaC 95603 162-B6
VALLEY VISTA RD
4500 EDCo 95682 283-E3
VALLEY WILLOW WY
4900 ELKG 95758 357-H5
VALLEY WIND WY
7600 SAC 95823 337-G3
VALLEY WOOD DR
7600 SaCo 95828 338-F4
VALLEYWOOD WY
100 RSVL 95678 219-G5
VALMAR CT
5100 ELKG 95758 357-H5
VALMONTE DR
4300 SaCo 95864 298-J2
4500 SaCo 95608 299-A2
4500 SaCo 95864 299-A2
VALONIA ST
5200 SaCo 95628 260-D7
VALOR WY
6200 SaCo 95608 279-D2
VALPARAISO CIR
5300 SaCo 95841 259-B4
VALTARA RD
4200 EDCo 95682 263-B7
VAL VERDE CT
3500 PlaC 95650 221-C3
VAL VERDE RD
3600 PlaC 95650 201-D7
4000 PlaC 95650 221-D3
VALVERDE WY
4400 SAC 95823 337-H5
VALVISTA WY
800 AUB 95603 182-B6
VALWOOD CT
3500 SaCo 95821 278-J4
VAN ALSTINE AV
5900 SaCo 95608 279-D7
VANBRO CT
5300 SaCo 95842 259-B1
VAN BROCKLIN WY
- ELKG 95757 377-H2
- ELKG 95757 397-H2
VAN BUREN CT
3000 ANT 94509 (513-A7 See Page 493)
VAN BUREN DR
3000 ANT 94509 (513-A7 See Page 493)
VAN BUREN PL
3100 ANT 94509 (513-A7 See Page 493)
VAN BUREN WY
- RKLN 95765 219-H2
- SAC 95835 257-C7
VANCE LN
9900 FOLS 95630 261-B3
VAN CORTLANDT CT
- EDCo 95762 262-D6
VANCOUVER DR
9100 SaCo 95826 298-J6
VANDENBERG CIR
100 PlaC 95747 239-A4
100 PlaC 95747 238-J4
VANDENBERG DR
7200 SAC 95820 318-C4
VANDER WY
4600 SaCo 95821 278-J3
VANDERBILT CT
- EDCo 95762 262-J5
VANDERBILT WY
900 SAC 95825 298-C6

VANDUZEN CT
600 GALT 95632 419-F4
VANDYCE WY
4400 SaCo 95628 280-C2
VANE CT
8500 PlaC 95746 241-D3
VAN ELGORT CT
100 FOLS 95630 261-B3
VANETTE LN
7100 SAC 95823 337-F1
VAN EYCK WY
5700 SAC 95835 256-J4
VAN GOGH CIR
8900 SaCo 95628 280-F2
VAN GOGH DR
- EDCo 95762 262-H4
VANGUARD DR
9900 RCCD 95827 299-D6
VAN HORN CT
- SAC 95832 337-C4
VANIER CT
9200 SaCo 95826 318-J1
VANISHING WY
1800 EDCo 95672 243-F3
VANITA WY
7200 SaCo 95828 338-C2
VAN MAREN LN
6200 CITH 95621 259-F4
7600 CITH 95621 239-F7
VAN MOORE LN
8000 SaCo 95829 338-H6
VAN NESS DR
2100 RSVL 95661 240-C4
VAN NESS ST
1500 SAC 95815 278-A6
VAN NUYS WY
2000 RCCD 95670 279-G6
VAN OWEN ST
3600 SaCo 95660 258-G3
VAN PARKER LN
10100 SaCo 95632 419-D2
VAN PELT LN
- OAKL 94561 (514-H7 See Page 493)
VAN RIPER LN
10000 PlaC 95658 202-A2
VAN RUITEN LN
9900 ELKG 95624 359-D5
VAN STEYN CT
4800 ELKG 95757 377-H2
4800 ELKG 95757 397-H2
VANSTOM CT
800 GALT 95632 419-F3
VANSTON WY
1000 RSVL 95747 239-C1
VAN STRALEN WY
10600 RCCD 95670 279-G6
VAN UFFORD LN
2200 SaCo 95608 279-C7
VAN VLECK RD
7700 SaCo 95683 342-C5
VAN WINKLE CT
100 FOLS 95630 261-B2
VAQUERO VISTA DR
- PlaC 95603 162-A5
VARDON AV
2300 SAC 95822 317-D7
VARESE CT
9900 ELKG 95757 378-A1
VARGAS LN
8100 PlaC 95746 241-C2
VARICK DR
- RSVL 95747 219-C7
VARIO CT
- SAC 95828 318-B7
VARNEY AV
8400 SaCo 95828 338-E1
VARNUM WY
6500 SaCo 95660 258-G3
VARSITY CT
4500 SaCo 95841 278-J2
VASCONCELOS CT
- SAC 95833 277-D5
VASOS WY
7600 SaCo 95628 279-H2
VASQUEZ CIR
9800 PlaC 95650 201-J6
VASSAR WY
4400 SaCo 95841 278-J2
VATEN DR
- WSAC 95691 296-D4
VAUGHN WY
- FOLS 95630 281-G2
VAUX AV
- ELKG 95758 357-E4
VAUXHALL AV
- GALT 95632 419-G5
VECINO DR
2900 SAC 95833 277-E5
VEGA CT
5600 SaCo 95608 279-C4
VEGA LP
4000 EDCo 95682 264-B7
VEGA DEL RIO DR
4500 SaCo 95628 280-G2
VEHICLE DR
- RCCD 95670 279-J6
- RCCD 95670 280-A6
VELAGA CT
7600 SaCo 95828 338-C4
VELARDE CT
- SAC 95831 336-J3
VELD WY
3200 EDCo 95682 263-F5
VELLA CIR
- OAKL 94561 (514-H7 See Page 493)
VELLIA LN
7000 PlaC 95663 201-C2
VELMA WY
5600 SaCo 95824 317-J4
VELOZ CT
- SAC 95823 337-G5
VELVET AV
- SaCo 95615 (396-D3 See Page 375)
VELVET BLOOM CT
- LNCN 95648 180-A1
VELVET GLEN CT
8000 SaCo 95843 239-C6
VELVET HORN LN
1500 EDCo 95672 243-B7
1500 EDCo 95672 263-B1
VENADITO LN
- SaCo 95632 439-C2
VENADO DR
14900 SaCo 95683 322-B6
VENADO WY
2600 EDCo 95672 243-A6

VENETIAN CT
6700 ELKG 95758 358-B4
VENETO CT
- EDCo 95762 262-F5
VENETO WY
- ELKG 95757 378-A1
VENEZIA CT
- SAC 95831 337-A3
VENEZIA DR
- EDCo 95762 262-A2
VENEZIAN CT
- RSVL 95661 240-D2
VENICE CT
4100 ELKG 95758 357-G3
VENICE LN
1800 ANT 94509 (513-G5 See Page 493)
VENICE ST
- WSAC 95691 316-E2
VENN CT
8100 SaCo 95828 338-D2
VENTANA DR
6600 SaCo 95683 322-B7
VENTANA LN
- EDCo 95682 263-C4
VENTANA PL
5400 CITH 95610 260-A6
5400 CITH 95628 260-A6
VENTNOR CT
8000 SaCo 95829 338-H6
VENTNOR LN
2200 OAKL 94561 (514-C6 See Page 493)
VENTO CT
- RSVL 95678 219-H2
VENTRY CT
9400 ELKG 95758 358-A5
VENTURA CT
- EDCo 95762 282-E2
2900 ANT 94509 (513-B7 See Page 493)
VENTURA ST
6100 SAC 95822 317-E6
VENTURA WY
- EDCo 95762 282-E2
VENTURA WEST CT
4600 ELKG 95758 357-H4
VENTURE CT
900 SaCo 95825 298-C3
VENTURE DR
1900 LNCN 95648 179-C1
VENTURE LN
3000 EDCo 95667 264-H4
VENTURE OAKS WY
2500 SAC 95833 277-A6
VENTURE VALLEY RD
5600 EDCo 95682 283-B7
VENUS DR
1800 SaCo 95864 298-J1
2100 SaCo 95864 278-J7
VENUTO WY
4900 SaCo 95841 259-A6
VERA CT
700 EDCo 95762 242-C4
VERACRUZ CT
6900 CITH 95621 259-F3
VERALEE LN
4100 SAC 95838 278-C2
VERANDAH CT
6600 ELKG 95758 358-A3
VERANO CT
3200 EDCo 95682 263-E5
VERANO ST
1800 SAC 95838 278-B4
2100 SAC 95815 278-B4
VERANO WY
2900 RKLN 95677 220-E1
3200 EDCo 95682 263-E5
VERBANIA CT
9900 ELKG 95757 378-A1
VERBENA CT
400 RSVL 95747 219-C4
6800 CITH 95621 259-F1
VERBENA WY
1400 RSVL 95747 219-C4
VERDANT LN
1700 PlaC 95603 202-A1
4000 SaCo 95608 279-A3
VERDECA WY
3300 RCCD 95670 299-H4
VERDE CRUZ WY
5700 SaCo 95841 279-C1
5800 SaCo 95608 279-C1
VERDELLO WY
2600 RCCD 95670 299-F2
VERDE OAK CT
5500 SaCo 95842 259-C2
VERDE ROBLES CT
3000 EDCo 95667 246-F5
VERDE ROBLES DR
3100 EDCo 95709 246-G5
3100 EDCo 95667 246-G5
VERDE VALLEY LN
3100 EDCo 95762 242-G7
3100 EDCo 95762 262-G1
VERDIS LN
1900 EDCo 95667 265-C1
VERDUGO WY
7300 SaCo 95842 259-B1
VERDURE WY
6900 ELKG 95758 358-B5
VERENA CT
3800 PlaC 95602 161-H3
VERENA LN
- SAC 95835 256-G6
VERHOVEN CT
6600 CITH 95610 259-J3
VERLA ST
3400 SaCo 95608 279-D4
VERMONT AV
1500 WSAC 95691 296-J6
VERMONT LN
1800 ANT 94509 (513-B6 See Page 493)
VERN ST
3600 SAC 95838 277-H3
VERNA WY
2400 SaCo 95864 278-H7
2500 SaCo 95821 278-H6
VERNACCIA CIR
2500 RCCD 95670 299-G1
VERNACE WY
6500 SaCo 95823 317-J7
VERNAL CT
- LNCN 95648 200-B1
VERNAL WY
6100 SaCo 95608 279-D1
VERNA MAE AV
7600 SaCo 95828 338-C1

VERNER AV
5100 SaCo 95841 259-C3
6300 CITH 95621 259-D2
6300 CITH 95841 259-D2
6300 SaCo 95621 259-D2
VERNER OAK CT
5600 SaCo 95841 259-C5
VERNE ROBERTS CIR
1300 ANT 94509 (513-A4 See Page 493)
VERNETTA WY
9100 ELKG 95624 358-J7
VERNON ST
- RSVL 95678 239-G4
VERNON WY
6200 SaCo 95608 279-D6
VERNON OAKS DR
100 CITH 95621 239-F5
100 RSVL 95678 239-F5
VERONA AV
2000 OAKL 94561 (514-C7 See Page 493)
VERONA CT
2000 OAKL 94561 (514-C7 See Page 493)
VERONA DR
7400 SaCo 95683 342-D3
VERONICA CT
1300 ANT 94509 (513-G5 See Page 493)
VERRAZANO DR
- RSVL 95747 199-B7
- RSVL 95747 219-B1
VERSAILLES WY
7400 SaCo 95842 259-B1
VESPAS WY
10100 ELKG 95757 378-A2
VESTA WY
1800 SaCo 95864 298-J1
VESTRY CT
- SAC 95835 257-B6
VETCH WY
- SAC 95834 277-D3
VETERANS LN
7300 CITH 95610 259-J2
VIA CT
9300 ELKG 95624 358-G5
VIA ALICANTE CT
6000 PlaC 95746 221-G5
VIA ALTA WY
8600 ELKG 95624 378-F1
8700 ELKG 95624 358-G7
VIA AVION
5600 PlaC 95746 221-G3
VIA CAMINO AV
2300 SaCo 95608 279-A7
VIA CASITAS
5900 SaCo 95608 259-D6
VIA DE LA ROSA
- PlaC 95746 220-J7
- PlaC 95746 221-A7
VIA DEL CERRITO
6400 SaCo 95683 322-C7
VIA DEL GATOS
4000 EDCo 95682 263-H7
4000 EDCo 95682 283-H1
VIA DE PALMAS LN
8000 SaCo 95628 280-A2
VIADER WY
- SAC 95834 276-H3
VIA DE ROBLES DR
6500 SaCo 95683 322-B7
VIA DIABLO
- LNCN 95648 200-D2
VIA FIORI
- EDCo 95762 262-B6
VIA FRANCESCO CT
- LMS 95650 220-J4
- LMS 95650 221-A4
VIA GRANDE
3200 SaCo 95825 298-F1
VIA GWYNN WY
8500 SaCo 95628 260-D7
VIA INVIERNO
1800 RSVL 95747 219-C5
VIA LA LUNA
7600 SaCo 95828 338-C4
VIA LINDA CT
2200 SaCo 95608 279-B7
VIA MADRID
5900 PlaC 95746 221-F5
VIA MEDIA WY
8700 ELKG 95624 358-G7
VIA MILANO CT
- PlaC 95746 240-J2
VIA MONTANOSA RD
- EDCo 95667 245-F6
- PLCR 95667 245-F6
VIA MONTECITO CT
5700 PlaC 95746 221-G4
VIANI WY
10600 RCCD 95670 279-G7
VIANO CT
10900 RCCD 95670 299-J4
VIANSA WY
11000 RCCD 95670 299-J5
11000 RCCD 95670 300-A5
VIA PALAGIO LN
- SaCo 95628 280-D2
VIA RIATA
1700 RSVL 95747 219-C5
VIA ROMA DR
7900 SaCo 95628 279-J1
7900 SaCo 95628 280-A1
VIA SERENO
6500 SaCo 95683 322-C7
VIA TREVISO
1100 EDCo 95762 262-B7
VIA VISTOSO
- LNCN 95648 200-E1
VICEROY WY
6000 CITH 95610 259-J4
VICHY CIR
5300 SaCo 95843 259-B1
VICINI DR
- PLCR 95667 245-C5
VICINO DR
9000 ELKG 95758 358-B3
VICK CT
12600 AUB 95603 162-E7
VICKREY CT
1100 SaCo 95673 258-A2
VICKSBURG LN
4100 SaCo 95660 258-H7
VICO WY
4400 SaCo 95864 298-J2
VICTOR LN
900 PLCR 95667 245-G5

VICTOR WY
9000 ELKG 95624 358-H7
9000 ELKG 95624 378-H1
VICTORIA CT
300 RSVL 95678 219-H6
VICTORIA DR
3000 SaCo 95821 278-E4
VICTORIA LN
5600 CITH 95610 259-J6
VICTORIA WY
2600 WSAC 95691 316-F1
VICTORIA ISLAND CT
- WSAC 95691 316-C2
VICTORIAN PARK DR
600 GALT 95632 419-E6
VICTORY AV
7800 SaCo 95828 338-C5
VICTORY DR
3200 RKLN 95765 200-C6
VICTORY HWY
19000 SaCo 94571 (494-C5 See Page 493)
19200 SaCo 94571 (514-B1 See Page 493)
VICTORY LN
5300 RKLN 95765 200-C7
VICTORY WY
8400 CITH 95610 240-A6
8400 PlaC 95661 240-A6
VICTORY MINE RD
- EDCo 95619 266-B6
VIDAL LN
12900 AUB 95603 162-E7
VIDMAR CT
- SAC 95823 337-G5
VIEIR ST
- RVIS 94571 454-H3
VIENNA AV
3300 SaCo 95608 279-F5
VIENTO CT
100 FOLS 95630 261-E3
VIERA AV
1400 CCCo 94509 (513-H4 See Page 493)
2100 ANT 94509 (513-H5 See Page 493)
VIERA CT
2100 ANT 94509 (513-H6 See Page 493)
VIERNA
6600 CITH 95621 259-F4
VIERRA CIR
100 FOLS 95630 261-C7
VIERRA CT
- SAC 95831 336-J2
VIEW CT
1800 RSVL 95661 240-B4
7600 SaCo 95628 279-H4
VIEW DR
3000 ANT 94509 (513-C7 See Page 493)
W VIEW DR
- EDCo 95709 247-C3
- PlaC 95658 181-D4
VIEWCREST CT
- AUB 95603 182-B6
VIEWOODS CT
10000 RCCD 95827 299-D5
VIEW POINT DR
- EDCo - 267-D4
VIGNOLA CT
- OAKL 94561 (514-H7 See Page 493)
VIGNOLIA CT
- RSVL 95747 199-B7
VIKING DR
3300 RCCD 95827 299-C6
VIKING PL
9200 PlaC 95747 239-D4
VILA FLOR PL
- EDCo 95762 262-E6
VILAMOURA WY
6200 ELKG 95757 378-A2
VILANDRY PL
8600 SaCo 95828 338-F7
VILA REAL WY
10300 ELKG 95757 378-B3
VILLA CT
4000 SaCo 95628 280-A3
VILLA DR
6300 SaCo 95842 259-A3
VILLA ALTA WY
- PlaC 95746 240-H4
VILLA BELLA LN
9300 SaCo 95662 260-H5
VILLA CAMPO WY
8800 SaCo 95628 260-E7
VILLA CAPRI CT
6100 SaCo 95608 279-D4
VILLA CAPRI LN
- PlaC 95746 240-G6
VILLA DEL MAR DR
- SaCo 95683 342-A2
VILLA DEL SOL
700 EDCo 95762 242-D4
VILLA DEL SOL LN
7200 CITH 95610 259-G5
7200 CITH 95621 259-G5
VILLA FLORENCE LN
- PlaC 95746 240-G5
VILLAFONT WY
2200 SaCo 95825 298-C2
VILLA FRANCISO LN
- PlaC 95746 240-G5
VILLA GARDENS CT
- RSVL 95678 219-H4
VILLAGE CIR
- GALT 95632 419-E2
- SAC 95838 278-B2
VILLAGE CT
3300 EDCo 95682 263-C3
VILLAGE DR
- GALT 95632 419-E2
1900 RSVL 95661 240-E3
VILLAGE LN
- RCCD 95670 299-G2
100 AUB 95603 182-D1
1200 PLCR 95667 245-H4
3500 SaCo 95864 298-G1
VILLAGE PKWY
- WSAC 95691 296-J7
- WSAC 95691 297-A7
- WSAC 95691 316-J2
- WSAC 95691 317-A1
VILLAGE WY
5400 CITH 95610 259-J6
5400 CITH 95628 259-J6
VILLAGE BROOK WY
8100 ELKG 95758 358-D6

VILLAGE CENTER DR
- RSVL 95747 218-H5
700 EDCo 95762 242-C7
9700 PlaC 95746 240-G6
VILLAGE CENTRE DR
6400 SAC 95823 338-A4
VILLAGE CREEK WY
8200 SAC 95823 337-J6
VILLAGE ELM DR
5100 SAC 95823 337-J7
VILLAGE ESTATES LN
8000 SaCo 95628 260-B7
VILLAGE GLEN CT
- SAC 95823 337-J6
VILLAGE GREEN DR
- EDCo 95762 262-F6
- RSVL 95747 218-J5
- RSVL 95747 219-A5
- SAC 95838 278-B2
VILLAGE GRN WY
9300 SaCo 95662 260-H3
VILLAGE MILL WY
4600 RCCD 95742 320-E3
VILLAGE OAK CT
5600 SaCo 95842 259-C2
VILLAGE OAKS DR
4900 RKLN 95677 220-C2
VILLAGE PARK CT
8600 SaCo 95662 260-E5
VILLAGE PARK DR
- RSVL 95747 218-H5
VILLAGE PLAZA DR
- RSVL 95747 218-H5
VILLAGE POND WY
11700 RCCD 95742 300-D7
VILLAGE RIDGE WY
5600 SAC 95823 337-J7
5700 SAC 95823 338-A7
VILLAGE RUN DR
800 GALT 95632 419-D7
800 GALT 95632 439-D1
VILLAGE STAR DR
4900 SAC 95823 337-J7
VILLAGE TREE DR
9400 ELKG 95758 358-D5
VILLAGE WOOD DR
4900 SAC 95823 337-J7
VILLAGIO DR
- EDCo 95762 262-G5
VILLA GRANITO LN
- PlaC 95746 240-G5
VILLAJOY WY
7400 SAC 95823 337-G2
VILLA JUAREZ CIR
6600 SAC 95828 318-B6
VILLANELLA CT
- PlaC 95603 162-B6
VILLANOVA CIR
2300 SaCo 95825 298-D3
VILLA OAK DR
8100 CITH 95610 260-B1
VILLA PALAZZO DR
7100 SAC 95831 337-A3
VILLA ROSA WY
6000 ELKG 95758 357-J3
6000 ELKG 95758 358-A3
VILLA ROYALE WY
4700 SAC 95823 337-J6
VILLA SERENA CIR
- RKLN 95765 200-B7
VILLA SERENA DR
- ELKG 95624 358-E1
VILLAVIEW DR
8200 CITH 95621 239-E6
VILLA VISTA WY
2800 SaCo 95821 278-H6
VILLENEUVE DR
8400 ELKG 95624 358-E2
VILLEROY CT
- RSVL 95746 240-G5
VILLETTE CT
9900 ELKG 95757 378-A1
VINCENT AV
8900 SaCo 95628 260-F7
VINCENT CT
- RKLN 95765 200-D3
VINCI AV
900 SAC 95838 257-J6
900 SAC 95838 258-A6
1500 SAC 95652 258-A6
VINE AV
500 RSVL 95678 239-H3
VINE CIR
- RKLN 95765 199-J7
- RKLN 95765 200-A7
- RKLN 95765 219-J1
- RKLN 95765 220-A1
VINE LN
1900 CCCo 94509 (513-H5 See Page 493)
VINE ST
- EDCo 95762 282-E1
1000 SAC 95814 297-E1
VINE WY
500 RSVL 95678 239-H3
VINECREST DR
5500 SaCo 95628 260-B6
VINE GROVE LN
8100 SaCo 95628 260-C6
VINE HILL CT
- WSAC 95691 316-J1
VINEHILL RD
2800 OAKL 94561 (514-A7 See Page 493)
VINEWOOD AV
700 RSVL 95678 239-J3
VINEYARD DR
- PlaC 95603 162-A6
1600 ANT 94509 (513-J5 See Page 493)
VINEYARD LN
8300 PlaC 95747 239-A2
VINEYARD RD
- PlaC 95747 238-J2
200 RSVL 95678 239-F2
300 PlaC 95747 239-B2
600 RSVL 95747 239-F2
7600 SaCo 95829 339-E4
8300 ELKG 95624 339-D7
8300 ELKG 95829 339-D7
VINEYARD HILL DR
800 PlaC 95658 181-C1
VINEYARD HILLS DR
12200 SaCo 95624 340-F3
VINEYARDS CT
600 GALT 95632 439-E1
VINICOLA CT
- EDCo 95762 262-B2

STREET Block City ZIP Pg-Grid

VINMAR CT
1400 RSVL 95661 240-A4
VIN ROSE CT
5400 CITH 95610 260-A6
VINTAGE CT
1000 RVIS 94571 454-E2
VINTAGE DR
- RVIS 94571 454-F2
VINTAGE LN
- EDCo 95667 265-J2
- EDCo 95667 266-A1
VINTAGE PKWY
800 OAKL 94561 (514-C5 See Page 493)
VINTAGE WY
1200 AUB 95603 182-C7
1300 PlaC 95603 182-C7
7900 SaCo 95628 260-A7
VINTAGE OAK AV
600 GALT 95632 419-F4
VINTAGE OAK LN
4300 SaCo 95628 280-A2
VINTAGE PARK DR
8300 ELKG 95624 338-G7
8300 ELKG 95828 338-G7
8300 SaCo 95828 338-G6
8700 SaCo 95829 338-H6
8900 SaCo 95829 339-A6
VINTON CT
- SAC 95823 358-B1
VIOLA DR
3700 SaCo 95660 278-G1
VIOLA WY
- RSVL 95661 220-D6
VIOLA VIEW CT
- LNCN 95648 200-A2
VIOLET CT
2800 ANT 94531 (513-G7 See Page 493)
VIOLET DR
- EDCo 95630 202-H4
2900 WSAC 95691 316-F2
VIOLET LN
400 LNCN 95648 180-A5
500 LNCN 95648 179-J5
VIOLET ST
2100 SaCo 95825 278-C7
VIOLET RIDGE CT
5800 ELKG 95757 357-J7
5800 ELKG 95757 358-A7
VIONA RD
- EDCo - 247-H2
VIRADA RD
3400 EDCo 95682 263-E4
VIREO CT
6400 PlaC 95746 221-E6
VIREO WY
6400 PlaC 95746 221-E5
VIRGIL CT
1000 SAC 95833 277-D6
VIRGINIA AV
- SaCo 95742 281-C6
1000 WSAC 95691 296-J4
VIRGINIA LN
1100 PlaC 95658 180-J1
VIRGINIA ST
200 AUB 95603 182-E3
VIRGINIA WY
600 RVIS 94571 454-H4
4900 SAC 95822 317-C3
VIRGINIA DENISE LN
- SaCo 95673 258-C2
VIRGINIA FIFE WY
8900 ELKG 95624 358-H4
VIRGINIATOWN RD
300 LNCN 95648 179-J2
500 LNCN 95648 180-A2
700 PlaC 95648 180-E2
4600 PlaC 95658 180-H2
6300 PlaC 95658 181-A2
VIRGO ST
3300 RCCD 95827 299-C6
VIRGUSELL CIR
4300 SaCo 95608 279-B2
VIRIDIAN WY
9300 ELKG 95624 359-A7
VIRLIN CT
9600 SaCo 95662 260-J5
VIR MAR ST
4900 SaCo 95628 259-H7
4900 SaCo 95628 279-H1
VISAGE CIR
8900 SaCo 95825 280-F3
VISALIA WY
8100 SaCo 95828 338-D6
VISCONTI CT
9900 ELKG 95757 378-A1
VISCOUNT WY
6500 CITH 95621 239-E6
VISTA AV
5600 SaCo 95824 317-H5
6200 SaCo 95823 317-H6
VISTA CT
9100 PlaC 95650 201-G7
S VISTA CT
2700 ANT 94509 (513-B6 See Page 493)
VISTA DR
4000 PlaC 95650 201-D7
4000 PlaC 95650 221-D1
VISTA LN
3300 EDCo 95667 244-J6
VISTA PL
2900 ANT 94509 (513-B7 See Page 493)
VISTA WY
2800 ANT 94509 (513-B6 See Page 493)
W VISTA WY
7600 SAC 95831 336-H3
VISTA ALEGRE CT
- SAC 95831 336-J2
VISTA AMADO CT
- PlaC 95658 181-J7
- PlaC 95658 182-A7
VISTA BONITA CT
6900 PlaC 95650 201-B3
VISTA BROOK DR
8400 ELKG 95624 358-E2
VISTA CAMPO WY
8900 ELKG 95758 358-B3
VISTA CIELO DR
- PlaC 95658 182-A7
- PlaC 95658 201-J1
- PlaC 95658 202-A1
VISTA COVE CIR
- SAC 95835 256-G6
VISTA COVE PL
4700 PlaC 95650 221-G2
VISTA CREEK CIR
- SAC 95835 256-G6
VISTA CREEK DR
1400 RSVL 95661 240-B5
VISTA CREEK WY
- ELKG 95758 358-D3
VISTA DE LAGO CT
8800 PlaC 95746 221-F5
VISTA DE LAGO WY
4200 SaCo 95628 280-G2
VISTA DEL HUERTO DR
- EDCo 95633 205-A2
VISTA DEL LAGO
1800 AUB 95603 182-E6
VISTA DEL LAGO CT
- EDCo 95630 222-F2
VISTA DEL MONTE
1600 AUB 95603 182-E5
VISTA DEL MONTE DR
4000 EDCo 95682 264-A6
VISTA DEL MUNDO
3200 EDCo 95709 246-H4
VISTA DEL ORO
5000 SaCo 95628 260-G7
VISTA DEL ORO CT
6900 PlaC 95650 201-B3
VISTA DEL RIO AV
9000 SaCo 95628 280-G2
VISTA DEL SIERRA CT
6300 EDCo 95630 222-G3
VISTA DEL SOL
- PlaC 95603 162-B6
VISTA DE MADERA
- LNCN 95648 200-E2
VISTA DOME CT
9100 SaCo 95628 260-G6
VISTA GRANDE DR
3500 EDCo 95682 263-G4
VISTA GRANDE WY
9800 ELKG 95624 358-G7
9800 ELKG 95624 378-G1
VISTA LE FONTI
- EDCo 95762 262-B5
VISTA MAR DR
1900 EDCo 95762 242-B6
VISTA NUEVO WY
- SAC 95838 277-H4
VISTA OAK DR
100 FOLS 95630 261-B3
VISTA OAK WY
5600 SaCo 95842 259-C2
VISTA PARK CT
- SaCo 95834 277-D2
VISTA POINT LN
7700 SaCo 95843 238-G7
VISTA RAVINE CT
9200 PlaC 95650 221-G2
VISTA RIDGE CT
- RSVL 95661 240-D1
VISTA RIDGE DR
7800 CITH 95610 259-J1
7800 CITH 95610 260-A1
VISTA RIDGE WY
- RSVL 95661 240-D1
VISTA ROBLE LN
2700 PlaC 95603 161-J5
VISTA SIERRA DR
5100 SaCo 95843 239-B6
VISTA TIERRA DR
3000 EDCo 95709 246-H4
VISTA VERDE
7600 SaCo 95828 338-C4
VISTA VERDE DR
2800 EDCo 95682 263-C5
VISTAWOOD CT
- SAC 95831 336-J2
VITA GRANDE CT
- EDCo - 247-D5
- EDCo 95726 247-D5
VITALE ST
500 RSVL 95678 239-H3
VITIS CT
11000 RCCD 95670 300-A4
VITRUVIUS CT
- OAKL 94561 (514-H7 See Page 493)
VIVIAN CT
800 PLCR 95667 245-F4
8100 SaCo 95828 338-D2
VIVIAN LN
- SaCo 95673 257-H3
VIVIEN WY
- RKLN 95765 200-D7
VIVIENDA LN
6700 CITH 95621 259-F3
VOELKE CT
3500 SaCo 95608 279-D4
VOGELSANG DR
4800 SaCo 95842 259-A5
VOGELSANG LN
- EDCo - 267-E5
VOGEL VALLEY RD
7000 PlaC 95746 221-E7
VOGT PL
- LNCN 95648 179-E1
VOGUE CT
3400 SaCo 95826 318-J1
VOLCANO CT
11300 SaCo 95670 280-B4
VOLCANO RDG
- PlaC 95746 240-J5
VOLEYN ST
3600 SaCo 95608 279-F4
VOLGA WY
2600 SaCo 95826 298-J5
VOLLAN WY
2100 SAC 95822 337-D2
VOLO MINE RD
4500 EDCo 95619 265-D5
VOLTA WY
7200 CITH 95621 259-G1
VOLTAIRE CT
- EDCo 95682 283-B1
VOLTAIRE DR
- EDCo 95682 283-C1
1400 RSVL 95747 219-C5
VOLTI WY
1800 SAC 95833 277-B5
VOLUNTEER LN
8900 SaCo 95826 298-G7
VOLZ DR
1100 SAC 95822 317-A2
VOLZ LN
- EDCo 95667 226-B7
VON WY
5100 SaCo 95608 279-B5
VON BAUER WY
3400 SaCo 95821 278-H4
VONDA ST
2300 SaCo 95608 279-B7
VON KARMAN ST
- RCCD 95655 299-G5
- SaCo 95655 299-G5
VONNIE CT
100 FOLS 95630 281-B2
VOOS CT
9100 ELKG 95624 358-H6
VORDEN RD
500 SaCo 95690 (416-J2 See Page 415)
500 SaCo 95690 417-A2
VORTOLK AV
1200 WSAC 95691 296-H4
VOSBURG ST
4000 SaCo 95826 319-A2
VOSSPARK WY
1600 SAC 95835 257-C3
VOUGHT DR
5200 SaCo 95628 260-F7
VOULA LN
8800 SaCo 95693 (361-B3 See Page 341)
VOUVRAY LN
- SaCo 95615 (396-J6 See Page 375)
VOYAGER WY
1900 EDCo 95682 283-J7
7400 CITH 95621 259-E1
VOYIATZES RD
10500 PlaC 95603 182-B2
VULCAN DR
4300 SaCo 95864 298-J1
VYTINA DR
- ELKG 95624 358-F2

W

W ST
300 SAC 95818 297-C5
3100 SAC 95817 297-F7
WABASH CT
1000 RSVL 95678 239-F2
WABASH WY
1400 RSVL 95678 239-F2
WABASH RIVER CT
11000 RCCD 95670 279-J5
WABASSOL
4300 EDCo 95633 205-E2
WACHTEL WY
7400 CITH 95610 260-D1
7400 CITH 95662 260-D1
7400 SaCo 95610 260-D1
7400 SaCo 95662 260-D1
7700 CITH 95610 240-D7
7700 SaCo 95610 240-D7
WACKER WY
1400 SAC 95822 337-B2
WADDELL LN
7000 RSVL 95747 219-A4
9300 ELKG 95624 359-A1
WADE CT
4000 EDCo 95667 265-C3
8400 SaCo 95662 260-D3
WADE DR
- RSVL 95661 240-E3
WADENA WY
9400 ELKG 95758 358-C5
WADKINS CT
15400 SaCo 95683 342-D3
WADSWORTH CT
- ELKG 95624 358-F2
- SAC 95835 257-A5
WADSWORTH WY
- SAC 95835 257-A5
WAGNER CT
8000 SaCo 95843 238-G6
WAGON LP
6300 EDCo 95667 244-G5
WAGON TR
- EDCo - 267-G4
WAGON WY
100 GALT 95632 419-E7
5200 SaCo 95628 260-F7
8800 PlaC 95746 241-A3
WAGONMASTER CT
- RSVL 95747 219-B4
WAGONMASTER LN
- RSVL 95747 219-B4
WAGON MASTER RD
- EDCo 95619 266-B7
- EDCo 95619 286-A1
WAGON TRAIL WY
8000 SAC 95828 338-C1
WAGON WHEEL DR
300 FOLS 95630 282-B2
WAGON WHEEL LN
600 LNCN 95648 179-J4
800 LNCN 95648 180-A3
WAGON WHEEL WY
6900 SAC 95828 318-C7
6900 SAC 95828 338-C1
WAH AV
2500 SAC 95822 317-E7
WAHOO CT
8800 SaCo 95826 338-G4
WAIKIKI DR
8100 SaCo 95628 260-B6
WAILEA CT
200 RSVL 95747 219-D7
WAILEA PL
2300 SAC 95833 276-J7
WAILEA WY
1000 RSVL 95747 219-D7
WAIMEA LN
- ELKG 95624 359-D5
WAINFLEET CT
900 ANT 94509 (513-C7 See Page 493)
WAINWRIGHT CT
200 SAC 95838 278-B1
WAINWRIGHT ST
100 SAC 95838 278-B2
WAITSFIELD CIR
100 SaCo 95655 319-H3
WAKE
- SAC 95828 318-E4
WAKEFIELD PL
- EDCo 95633 205-A1
WAKEFIELD WY
1500 SAC 95822 337-C1
WAKE FOREST LN
6900 CITH 95621 259-E2
WAKEHURST CT
- PlaC 95747 239-A2
WAKE ISLAND CT
- WSAC 95691 316-D2
WALALI WY
4400 SaCo 95628 280-F2
WALBRIDGE WY
- ELKG 95758 358-B3
WALBROOK CT
- SAC 95833 277-C4
WALDEN CT
7900 SaCo 95828 338-F5
WALDEN DR
- FOLS 95630 281-G1
WALDEN LN
5400 PlaC 95746 221-G4
WALDEN VIEW CT
- LNCN 95648 200-C1
WALDEN VIEW LN
- LNCN 95648 180-B7
- LNCN 95648 200-C1
WALDEN WOODS WY
8100 PlaC 95746 221-E5
WALDIE CT
- ELKG 95758 357-E5
WALDIE PZ
100 ANT 94509 (513-C3 See Page 493)
WALDO RD
12500 SaCo 95632 (399-H6 See Page 379)
12500 SaCo 95632 419-H1
WALDORF CT
6600 SaCo 95828 338-B1
WALDRON ST
5400 SaCo 95628 260-E6
WALDWICK CIR
3600 EDCo 95762 263-A5
WALDWICK CT
3900 EDCo 95762 263-A5
WALERGA RD
5500 SaCo 95842 259-A5
5700 SaCo 95842 258-J4
6100 SaCo 95660 258-J4
7500 SaCo 95843 238-J7
7500 SaCo 95843 258-J2
8800 PlaC 95747 238-J3
WALES DR
200 FOLS 95630 261-C4
S WALES WY
9400 ELKG 95758 357-J6
WALK ABOUT WY
3000 EDCo 95667 246-E4
3100 EDCo 95709 246-E4
WALKER DR
- RSVL 95747 239-F3
100 AUB 95603 182-E1
500 EDCo 95619 265-E4
WALKER RD
- WSAC 95691 316-D4
WALKER LANDING RD
100 SaCo 95690 436-B5
800 SaCo 95690 (435-J5 See Page 415)
WALKER PARK DR
3600 EDCo 95762 262-E5
WALKERVILLE RD
12100 SaCo 95638 420-E1
WALKING STICK CT
5900 CITH 95621 259-D3
WALL ST
500 AUB 95603 182-D1
5200 SaCo 95841 259-A7
WALLABY WY
5300 SaCo 95660 258-H6
WALLACE AV
4900 SAC 95838 257-H7
5600 SAC 95824 318-C5
WALLACE RD
1000 EDCo 95667 244-J1
1000 EDCo 95667 245-A1
WALLACE ST
- RVIS 94571 454-H3
WALLINGFORD LN
500 FOLS 95630 261-H7
WALLINGTON DR
1000 GALT 95632 419-G5
WALLS WY
- EDCo 95667 266-H2
WALLWOOD CT
6100 CITH 95621 239-E7
WALLY ALLEN RD
3600 PlaC 95648 160-H3
WALMORT RD
10800 SaCo 95693 379-G3
11000 SaCo 95693 (380-A3 See Page 379)
WALNUT AV
- SaCo 95690 (416-J7 See Page 415)
800 WSAC 95691 296-G1
1500 CCCo 94509 (513-H4 See Page 493)
1800 SaCo 95608 299-B1
2000 SaCo 95608 279-B3
5000 SaCo 95841 259-B5
5000 SaCo 95841 279-B1
5500 SaCo 95662 260-H2
9600 ELKG 95624 358-H6
10200 SaCo 95632 419-D3
10400 GALT 95632 419-F3
WALNUT CT
2000 EDCo 95672 263-F2
2200 WSAC 95691 296-G4
WALNUT DR
600 OAKL 94561 (514-F7 See Page 493)
3500 EDCo 95672 263-E2
7500 CITH 95610 239-H6
WALNUT PL
- EDCo 95682 263-B3
WALNUT RD
7200 SaCo 95628 279-H2
7200 SaCo 95608 279-G2
7300 SaCo 95837 255-H2
7300 SaCo 95837 235-J7
7300 SaCo 95837 236-A7
WALNUT ST
200 RSVL 95678 239-J1
400 WSAC 95691 296-G3
5900 LMS 95650 200-J6
6000 LMS 95650 201-A6
S WALNUT ST
- LMS 95650 200-J7
4500 LMS 95650 201-A6
WALNUT BAY CT
- SAC 95831 336-H4
WALNUT FAIR CIR
5800 SaCo 95628 260-B5
WALNUT GARDEN CT
5100 SaCo 95608 279-B5
WALNUT GLEN CT
700 SaCo 95864 298-H4
WALNUT GROVE BRDG
- SaCo - 436-J1
- SaCo - 437-A1
W WALNUT GROVE RD
15400 SJCo 95686 437-A4
W WALNUT GROVE RD Rt#-J8
8600 SJCo 95686 (438-A3 See Page 418)
W WALNUT GROVE RD Rt#-J11
9000 SJCo 95686 (438-A3 See Page 418)
9200 SJCo 95686 437-F3
WALNUT GROVE WY
2300 RCCD 95670 279-F7
WALNUT GROVE THRNTN RD Rt#-J11
- SaCo 95690 436-J2
- SaCo 95690 437-A3
WALNUT HAVEN WY
5100 SaCo 95608 279-B5
WALNUT HILLS WY
8100 SaCo 95628 260-B5
WALNUT MEADOWS CT
100 OAKL 94561 (514-E6 See Page 493)
WALNUT MEADOWS DR
1200 OAKL 94561 (514-D5 See Page 493)
WALNUT OAKS LN
2400 SaCo 95608 279-B7
WALNUT PLACE LN
5100 SaCo 95608 279-B4
WALNUT POINTE LN
5100 SaCo 95608 279-B3
WALNUT RANCH WY
700 OAKL 94561 (514-D5 See Page 493)
WALNUT RIDGE WY
8600 SaCo 95828 338-F3
WALNUT VILLA WY
8100 SaCo 95628 260-B5
WALNUTWOOD WY
10800 RCCD 95670 279-H7
WALSH ST
200 AUB 95603 182-E2
WALSH WY
7600 SAC 95832 337-D4
WALSHFORD PL
- SAC 95835 257-A3
WALTER AV
6900 SaCo 95828 338-B3
WALTER WY
- ANT 94509 (513-D5 See Page 493)
WALTERS ST
- AUB 95603 182-D2
WALTERS RANCH RD
- PlaC 95648 180-G4
WALTON LN
1200 ANT 94509 (513-D7 See Page 493)
WALTON PL
2800 EDCo 95762 262-D1
WALTON WY
200 RSVL 95678 219-J7
2700 SaCo 95821 278-F6
WALWORTH DR
500 GALT 95632 419-H5
WAMEGO RD
3500 EDCo 95667 245-C7
WAMSLEY CT
200 GALT 95632 419-D7
WANDA WY
400 SAC 95819 298-A5
WANDA LEE CT
1100 RSVL 95661 239-J4
WANDERING WY
- EDCo - 247-F2
- PlaC - 160-E5
- PlaC 95648 160-E5
WANDERLUST LP
4400 RSVL 95747 219-A6
WAPELLO CIR
100 SAC 95835 256-J6
WAPITI PL
7900 CITH 95610 260-A1
WARBLER CT
3300 EDCo 95709 246-H1
WARBLER LN
2600 LNCN 95648 180-C7
WARBLER WY
6900 SAC 95831 316-F7
6900 SAC 95831 336-F1
WAR BRIDAL LN
8000 SaCo 95626 237-E5
WARD AV
3900 SaCo 95660 258-H7
WARD LN
5100 RKLN 95677 220-F3
7600 SaCo 95628 279-H1
WARD WY
700 FOLS 95630 261-C6
WARDELL WY
5500 SAC 95823 337-J3
5600 SAC 95823 338-A3
WAREHOUSE CT
3000 SaCo 95660 278-F1
WAREHOUSE WY
4900 SAC 95826 318-F4
WARHOL WY
- OAKL 94561 (514-H7 See Page 493)
WAR HORSE CT
8200 SaCo 95662 260-B3
WARMERDAM CT
4900 ELKG 95757 377-H3
4900 ELKG 95757 397-H3
WARMERDAM WY
- ELKG 95757 377-H3
- ELKG 95757 397-H3
WARM HEARTH LN
- RSVL 95747 218-H3
WARM SPRINGS DR
- RSVL 95678 219-G4
WARMSPRINGS ST
8900 ELKG 95758 357-G4
WARMUTH CT
8100 SaCo 95843 238-G6
WARMWOOD CT
1100 GALT 95632 419-H2
WARNER ST
700 SAC 95818 297-B6
WARREGO WY
2500 SaCo 95826 298-H6
WARREN AV
4000 SAC 95822 317-B2
4800 SAC 95838 257-H7
WARREN CT
1800 PLCR 95667 246-B5
8000 PlaC 95746 221-E7
8000 PlaC 95746 241-E1
WARREN DR
- RKLN 95677 220-G2
WARREN LN
1800 PLCR 95667 246-B5
2900 EDCo 95762 262-C3
WARREN WY
700 PlaC 95603 182-A2
WARRENTON DR
2200 RCCD 95670 279-G7
WARRINGTON CT
- SaCo 95829 338-J7
WARWICK AV
4800 SAC 95820 317-G4
WARWICK CT
- RSVL 95746 240-F4
WARWICK PL
1800 EDCo 95762 242-C5
WASATCH RD
3200 EDCo 95667 245-H1
WASATCH WY
6200 SaCo 95842 259-B4
WASHBOARD
4500 EDCo 95667 265-J2
WASHBOURNE WY
- RSVL 95747 218-H5
WASHBURN WY
7200 SaCo 95660 258-H1
WASHFORD CT
9300 SaCo 95829 339-A6
WASHINGTON AV
400 WSAC 95691 296-H3
3900 SAC 95820 317-G2
11800 SaCo 95615 (396-D3 See Page 375)
WASHINGTON BLVD
100 RSVL 95678 239-H1
600 RSVL 95678 219-G4
WASHINGTON ST
200 AUB 95603 182-D3
3000 PLCR 95667 245-H5
E WASHINGTON ST
100 RSVL 95678 239-H1
W WASHINGTON ST
100 RSVL 95678 239-J2
WASHINGTON WY
2200 ANT 94509 (513-A7 See Page 493)
WASHOE CT
- WSAC 95691 316-H2
500 RSVL 95747 219-A5
WASHOE ST
- SAC 95835 256-J5
WASHOE WY
500 RSVL 95747 219-A5
WASSON LN
6100 SaCo 95841 259-C4
WATAUGA WY
4500 ELKG 95758 357-H5
WATCO CT
3800 SaCo 95608 278-J3
3800 SaCo 95608 279-A3
WATER ST
300 SAC 95814 297-C2
600 WSAC 95605 296-G1
WATERASH WY
5900 SAC 95823 338-A3
WATER BAY CT
- SAC 95831 336-H3
WATERBORO SQ
100 FOLS 95630 261-H6
WATERBROOK WY
10800 RCCD 95670 299-H4
WATERBUCK CT
- SaCo 95843 239-B7
WATERBURY WY
4800 PlaC 95746 240-G6
5000 SaCo 95628 259-G7
WATERCOLOR LN
- WSAC 95605 297-A2
WATERCOURSE LN
- WSAC 95605 297-A1
WATERCOURSE WY
- SAC 95833 276-H6
WATERCREST CT
- SAC 95831 336-H3
WATERFALL CT
6400 SaCo 95662 260-B4
WATERFIELD CT
- LNCN 95648 179-H5
WATERFIELD DR
10000 ELKG 95757 377-H2
10000 ELKG 95757 397-H2
WATERFIELD WY
- RSVL 95678 219-H5
WATERFORD CT
400 OAKL 94561 (514-G7 See Page 493)
WATERFORD DR
- PlaC 95746 240-H2
1000 WSAC 95605 296-J1
WATERFORD RD
1900 SAC 95815 298-B1
1900 SAC 95825 298-B1
2000 SAC 95815 278-B7
WATERFORD WY
4500 OAKL 94561 (514-G7 See Page 493)
WATERFORD GLEN CIR
2500 RSVL 95747 219-C1
WATERFOWL DR
9700 ELKG 95757 357-E7
WATERFRONT CT
- SAC 95831 336-G2
WATERGLEN CIR
- SAC 95826 298-F6
WATER LILLY CT
9200 ELKG 95624 358-J4
WATER LILY CT
- PlaC 95747 239-C5
WATERLILY CT
- RSVL 95747 218-J4
WATERLOO CT
600 GALT 95632 419-H4
WATERMAN CT
3000 EDCo 95762 262-C3
WATERMAN RD
- SaCo 95624 378-J2
7900 SaCo 95829 338-J6
8300 SaCo 95624 338-J6
8400 ELKG 95624 338-J6
8400 ELKG 95624 358-J1
9900 ELKG 95624 378-J2
WATER POPPY WY
8400 ELKG 95624 338-F7
8400 ELKG 95624 358-F1
WATER REEF CT
- SAC 95831 336-H3
WATERS COVE CT
- SAC 95831 336-F2
WATERS EDGE WY
- SAC 95833 276-H6
WATERSHORE CIR
- SAC 95831 336-H3
WATERSIDE ST
- RSVL 95747 219-D2
WATERSONG CIR
- RSVL 95747 219-C3
WATERSONG LN
12100 SaCo 95693 360-F6
WATERSTONE DR
- PlaC 95747 238-J3
- PlaC 95747 239-A3
WATERTHRUSH CT
- SAC 95831 316-G5
WATERTON WY
2500 SaCo 95826 298-H6
WATERTREE WY
2600 SaCo 95826 298-H6
WATER VIEW WY
100 FOLS 95630 261-A3
WATERVIEW WY
6800 SAC 95831 316-G7
6900 SAC 95831 336-H1
WATERVILLE WY
5300 SAC 95835 256-H4
WATERWHEEL DR
1500 SAC 95833 277-C6
WATERWHEEL LN
- LNCN 95648 179-J4
- LNCN 95648 180-A4
WATERWILLOW DR
7500 SaCo 95828 338-B3
WATERWILLOW LN
- EDCo 95633 205-B5
7500 SaCo 95828 338-B3
WATERWIND WY
- SAC 95831 336-J3
WATERWOOD CT
1100 GALT 95632 419-G2
WATERWOOD DR
- RVIS 94571 454-E2
WATKINS CT
7300 SaCo 95828 338-D2
WATKINS DR
4200 SaCo 95628 280-A2
WATROUS AV
4200 SaCo 95842 258-H6
WATSAM LN
2800 SaCo 95821 278-E6
WATSEKA WY
- SAC 95835 256-J6
WATSON ST
2400 SaCo 95864 278-H6
2500 SaCo 95821 278-H6
WATSON WY
7500 CITH 95610 239-H7
7800 CITH 95610 240-A7
WATSON HOLLOW DR
- RVIS 94571 454-E1
WATSONIA GLEN DR
3900 EDCo 95762 263-B4
WATT AV
400 SaCo 95864 298-F4
2100 SaCo 95864 278-G7
2300 SaCo 95825 278-G7
2500 SaCo 95821 278-G4
3500 SAC 95660 278-G1
3500 SaCo 95660 278-G1
3900 SAC 95821 278-G1
4700 SaCo 95660 258-G3
7500 SaCo 95843 238-F6
7500 SaCo 95843 258-G3
8600 PlaC 95747 238-F4
S WATT AV
2200 SAC 95826 298-G6
2200 SaCo 95826 298-G6
3100 SaCo 95826 318-G1
4200 SAC 95826 318-H3
5400 SAC 95829 318-H3
5400 SaCo 95829 318-H3
6600 SaCo 95829 338-G1
WAUKEENA RD
39000 YoCo 95612 (376-E4 See Page 375)
40000 YoCo 95612 (396-C1 See Page 375)
41000 SolC 94571 (396-A5 See Page 375)
WAUNITA WY
200 SAC 95838 277-G1
WAUSAU WY
9200 SaCo 95826 298-J5
9200 SaCo 95826 299-A5
WAVECREST WY
6800 SAC 95831 316-G7
6900 SAC 95831 336-G1
WAVERLY CT
5000 PlaC 95746 240-H6
6600 SaCo 95842 259-C3
WAVERLY DR
- LNCN 95648 179-D2
2700 EDCo 95682 263-C3
WAVERLY ST
2200 SaCo 95825 298-C3
WAVERTON LN
- LNCN 95648 179-F7
WAWONA CIR
4500 SaCo 95628 280-F2
WAXBILL LN
- LNCN 95648 200-A3
WAXWING LN
2400 EDCo 95709 246-H1
WAXWING WY
6700 SaCo 95842 259-A3
WAYLAND AV
1000 SaCo 95825 298-D2
WAYLAND RD
7800 PlaC 95650 221-C1
WAYMAR CT
4200 SaCo 95608 279-B2
WAYNART CT
3600 SaCo 95608 279-F4
WAYNE CT
9000 SAC 95829 318-H5
WAYNE DR
1100 RSVL 95678 239-J2
1100 RSVL 95678 240-A3
WAYNESBURGH LN
3600 SaCo 95660 258-C3
WAYSIDE LN
1500 RSVL 95661 240-C5
1800 SaCo 95864 298-H1
3900 SaCo 95608 279-D3

STREET Block City ZIP Pg-Grid

WAYSTIER LN
- LNCN 95648 179-E2

WEALD WY
- SAC 95833 277-A5

WEATHERBY CT
8900 PlaC 95746 241-C3

WEATHERBY WY
6600 SaCo 95842 259-A3

WEATHERFORD WY
6200 SaCo 95823 338-A6

WEATHERGLASS CT
6200 SaCo 95662 260-D4

WEATHERVANE CT
4200 EDCo 95762 242-C7

WEAVER WY
600 PLCR 95667 245-F4
3400 SaCo 95821 278-J4

WEBB ST
5700 LMS 95650 200-J5
6000 LMS 95650 201-A6
9600 ELKG 95624 358-J6

WEBB WY
500 FOLS 95630 261-C6

WEBBER LN
100 PlaC 95603 182-A4

WEBBERTOWN RD
- EDCo 95667 265-F1

WEBER RD
3000 EDCo - 246-H7
3000 EDCo 95709 246-H7
3100 EDCo 95709 247-B6

WEBER WY
1100 SAC 95822 317-A3

WEBER CREEK DR
3900 EDCo 95619 265-G2

WEBSTER LN
1800 EDCo 95667 244-B1
6200 CITH 95621 259-D4

WEBSTER ST
300 WSAC 95691 296-J4

WEBSTERS CT
400 RSVL 95747 219-A3

WEB WOB LN
3300 EDCo 95682 264-B5

WEDDELL CT
8400 CITH 95610 240-C6

WEDDIGEN WY
6800 SaCo 95660 258-J2

WEDDINGTON CIR
9700 PlaC 95746 240-H5

WEDDINGTON CT
- RKLN 95765 200-D4

WEDGE CIR
5300 SaCo 95628 259-H6

WEDGE WY
- RKLN 95765 200-D6

WEDGEFIELD WY
6200 SaCo 95662 260-C4

WEDGE HILL CT
4100 EDCo 95667 265-D2

WEDGE HILL RD
3400 EDCo 95667 265-D2

WEDGESTONE CT
8500 SaCo 95843 238-G5

WEDGEWOOD AV
5900 SaCo 95608 279-C7

WEDGEWOOD CT
800 WSAC 95605 296-J1
800 WSAC 95605 297-A1

WEDGEWOOD DR
5800 PlaC 95746 241-A6
5800 PlaC 95746 240-J6

WEDGEWOOD PL
9700 PlaC 95746 240-J6

WEDGEWOOD WY
- RKLN 95765 200-C7

WEDMORE CT
300 RSVL 95747 239-C1

WEEBEELEE LN
- EDCo 95667 286-H4

WEEPING BIRCH LN
- ELKG 95758 357-H2

WEEPING FIG WY
8900 ELKG 95758 357-J4

WEEPING WILLOW CT
5300 EDCo 95682 283-J3

WEGAT LN
- SaCo 95841 259-C4

WEIBEL CIR
900 OAKL 94561 (514-D5 See Page 493)

WEIBEL CT
9100 SaCo 95829 338-J5

WEIDER CT
- FOLS 95630 281-G1

WEIKERT DR
2900 RCCD 95827 299-D4

WEINREICH CT
- FOLS 95630 261-H4

WEISEL CT
- SAC 95831 336-J2

WELCH CT
3500 SaCo 95821 278-J4

WELCH RD
11900 SaCo 95693 360-F7

WELCHS WY
400 FOLS 95630 261-C5

WELCOME LN
7000 EDCo 95633 205-A5

WELCOME RD
100 PlaC 95658 181-C3

WELDON WY
2100 SaCo 95825 278-E7

WELERA WY
- ELKG 95757 377-H1
- ELKG 95757 397-H1

WELFORD CT
9200 SaCo 95829 338-J6

WELKER LN
3900 EDCo 95682 263-J4

WELLAND WY
600 WSAC 95605 297-A2

WELLBROOK PL
- PlaC 95747 238-J1

WELLER WY
1200 SAC 95818 297-C7
1200 SAC 95818 317-C1

WELLESLEY PL
2000 EDCo 95762 242-B6

WELLESLY WY
4500 SaCo 95841 278-J2

WELLFLEET CIR
100 FOLS 95630 261-G6

WELLINGTON DR
300 RSVL 95661 240-D4
3300 SaCo 95864 298-F3

WELLINGTON WY
9200 PlaC 95746 240-G5

WELLS AV
5900 LMS 95650 220-J4
5900 LMS 95650 221-A4
7000 PlaC 95650 221-C4
7400 CITH 95610 259-H6

WELLSBORO WY
6600 CITH 95621 259-E3

WELLSLEY CT
- FOLS 95630 281-B1

WELLSPRING CT
- RSVL 95747 218-H4

WELLWORTH LN
1000 SaCo 95864 298-J3

WELSFORD CT
- LNCN 95648 179-F7

WELSH WY
- ELKG 95757 357-H7

WELTY LN
11200 AUB 95603 182-C3
11200 PlaC 95603 182-C3

WELTY WY
6100 SaCo 95824 317-H6
6200 SaCo 95823 317-H6

WELWYN DR
- ELKG 95758 357-E5

WEMBERLEY DR
3100 SaCo 95864 298-F3

WEMBERLY DR
600 RSVL 95678 239-G3

WEMBLEY CT
100 FOLS 95630 261-F7

WEMBLY CT
- RKLN 95677 220-J2

WENATCHEE CT
4200 SaCo 95628 279-J2

WENDAL LN
6000 SaCo 95841 259-C4

WENDI LEE CT
2900 SaCo 95608 279-D6

WENDOVER CT
4300 SaCo 95628 280-D6

WENDSAN LN
- EDCo 95667 264-E4

WENDY CT
1300 RSVL 95661 240-A4
4900 SaCo 95608 279-A3

WENDY WY
1800 PlaC 95658 201-G1

WENDY HOPE DR
800 GALT 95632 419-F6

WENHAM WY
500 FOLS 95630 261-H7

WENLOCK CT
9200 SaCo 95829 338-J6

WENSLEY PL
- SAC 95835 257-A3

WENTE CT
4600 OAKL 94561 (514-D7 See Page 493)

WENTE WY
7900 SaCo 95829 338-J5

WENTWORTH AV
1400 SAC 95822 317-B3

WENTWORTH CT
- PlaC 95747 238-J3
600 PLCR 95667 245-F5

WENTWORTH RD
2600 EDCo 95682 263-D7

WENTWORTH WY
- PlaC 95747 238-J3

WEOTT CT
- SAC 95823 337-J5

WERBE LN
- SaCo 95608 279-A7

WERNER RD
- AUB 95603 182-B4
10400 PlaC 95603 182-A4

WERRE CT
4900 ELKG 95757 377-H3
4900 ELKG 95757 397-H3

WES WY
7600 CITH 95610 259-H2

WESCOTT CT
100 AUB 95603 182-E3

WESLEY AV
6500 SaCo 95823 317-G7

WESLEY CT
- RKLN 95765 200-A6
200 RSVL 95661 240-E4

WESLEY DR
- FOLS 95630 262-A5

WESLEY LN
1100 PlaC 95603 162-D5
7400 CITH 95610 260-A1

WESLEY RD
- RKLN 95765 200-A6

WESLEYAN WY
100 FOLS 95630 261-G5

WESMEAD CT
1500 SAC 95822 317-C3

WESSEX WY
100 FOLS 95630 261-F7

WEST CT
6600 PlaC 95658 181-C3

WEST LN
7000 PlaC 95746 221-D7
12600 SaCo 95638 420-C3

WEST PKWY
7300 SaCo 95823 337-H2

WEST ST
500 WSAC 95605 296-J3

WEST WY
3500 SaCo 95821 278-G4

WESTACRE RD
- EDCo 95619 266-E7
400 WSAC 95691 296-J3

WESTBANK CT
7800 SaCo 95828 338-D5

WESTBORO WY
7900 SaCo 95823 338-B5

WESTBOURNE DR
3100 ANT 94509 (513-F7 See Page 493)

WESTBOURNE WY
- SaCo 95843 239-B7
9800 PlaC 95746 240-H6

WESTBREEZE AV
7600 SaCo 95828 338-G4

WESTBROOK DR
6000 CITH 95621 259-E3

WESTBURY CIR
100 FOLS 95630 261-H5
5000 PlaC 95746 240-H6

WESTCAMP RD
8000 SaCo 95628 260-A7

WESTCHESTER CT
600 FOLS 95630 261-J7

WESTCHESTER DR
- PlaC 95747 239-B2
600 FOLS 95630 261-J7

WESTCHESTER PL
- PlaC 95747 239-B3

WESTCHESTER WY
6800 CITH 95621 259-F2

WESTCLIFF LN
9100 SaCo 95628 280-G1

WESTCOTT WY
100 SaCo 95864 298-E6

WESTERBERG WY
4900 SaCo 95608 259-E7

WESTERIA WY
9000 SaCo 95662 260-F5

WESTERLY DR
100 SaCo 95655 319-H3

WESTERN AV
- SAC 95815 277-G6
3100 SAC 95838 277-F3

WESTERN CT
- RKLN 95765 200-C6

WESTERN DR
3100 EDCo 95682 263-D5

WESTERN LN
700 PlaC 95603 162-F3
3300 PlaC 95640 160-E6

WESTERN WY
- RKLN 95765 200-C6

WESTERN HILLS DR
- RVIS 94571 454-F2

WESTERN LARK WY
- ELKG 95758 358-C4

WESTERN PORT WY
7800 SaCo 95828 338-E5

WESTERN SIERRA WY
- EDCo 95762 262-E2

WESTERN SUN WY
8600 SaCo 95828 338-F4

WESTFALEN WY
9700 ELKG 95757 357-H7

WESTFIELD ST
5800 SaCo 95608 259-D5

WESTGATE DR
7400 CITH 95610 259-H5

WESTHAM WY
4900 SAC 95758 357-J1

WESTHAMPTON WY
5400 SAC 95835 256-H4

WESTHAMPTON BAY WY
- SAC 95835 256-G4

WESTHAVEN DR
8600 SaCo 95662 260-E4

WEST HILL CT
1100 GALT 95632 419-G2

WESTHILLS DR
- RSVL 95747 218-J7
- RSVL 95747 219-A7

WESTHOLME WY
6100 SaCo 95823 338-A5

WESTIN LN
- SaCo 95662 260-E2

WESTKNOLL AV
8700 ELKG 95624 358-G2

WESTLAKE CT
- RSVL 95747 219-A7
- RSVL 95747 239-A1

WESTLAKE DR
- RSVL 95747 218-J7
- RSVL 95747 219-A7
300 WSAC 95605 276-J7
300 WSAC 95605 296-J1

WESTLAKE PKWY
- SAC 95835 256-G6

WESTLEY RD
- EDCo 95667 266-B5

WESTLITE CIR
700 SAC 95831 316-H7
700 SAC 95831 336-H1

WESTLITE CT
- SAC 95831 316-H7

WESTLYNN WY
1100 SAC 95831 317-A6

WESTMAN CT
- SAC 95838 277-G1

WESTMINISTER CT
- RSVL 95678 219-G4

WESTMINSTER CT
1800 SaCo 95608 299-B1

WESTMONT WY
5000 SaCo 95608 279-A6

WESTMORE WY
6800 SaCo 95608 279-F2

WESTMORELAND WY
6800 SAC 95831 316-J7
6800 SAC 95831 317-A7
6900 SAC 95831 336-J1

WESTON LN
6200 PlaC 95650 201-A3

WESTON WY
2900 RCCD 95670 299-G2
5100 RSVL 95746 240-F6

WESTOVER CT
300 RSVL 95661 240-E4
7500 SaCo 95628 279-H1

WESTPARK DR
5200 RSVL 95747 218-H3
8900 ELKG 95624 378-H2

WEST POINT LN
4100 SaCo 95660 258-H7

WESTPORT CIR
8200 SaCo 95828 338-G6

WESTPORTER DR
3800 SaCo 95826 318-J2
4100 SaCo 95826 319-A2

WESTRAY DR
8100 SaCo 95829 338-J6

WESTREE CT
- LNCN 95648 179-F7

WESTRIDGE DR
2500 EDCo 95682 263-B6

WEST RIVER DR
2400 SAC 95833 276-J6

WEST SACRAMENTO FRWY I-80
- WSAC - 296-D4
- YoCo - 296-D4

WEST SIDE FRWY I-5
- ELKG - 357-D4
- ELKG - 377-D1
- ELKG - 397-D1
- SAC - 256-F5
- SAC - 276-J1
- SAC - 277-A3
- SAC - 297-B1
- SAC - 316-J6
- SAC - 317-A3
- SAC - 317-A7
- SAC - 337-B4
- SaCo - 255-H5
- SaCo - 256-C5
- SaCo - 256-F5
- SaCo - 337-B4
- SaCo - 357-C1
- SaCo - 357-D4
- SaCo - 377-D1
- SaCo - 397-D1
- SaCo - 397-F8
- SaCo - 417-G3
- SJCo - 417-G3
- SJCo - 437-H1
- SJCo - (438-A3 See Page 418)
- YoCo - 255-H5

WESTSIDE WY
6100 ELKG 95758 358-A2

WEST VIEW CT
700 EDCo 95619 265-F4

WESTVIEW DR
- LNCN 95648 199-H3

WESTVIEW WY
6100 SaCo 95831 316-H5

WESTWARD WY
1000 SAC 95833 277-D4

WEST WIND CT
- SAC 95823 338-A7

WESTWOOD CIR
1700 WSAC 95691 296-H5

WEST WOOD CT
10300 RCCD 95670 299-G1

WESTWOOD CT
1000 EDCo 95762 262-C2

WESTWOOD DR
2600 EDCo 95667 245-D4
2600 PLCR 95667 245-D4
3100 RKLN 95677 220-D5
12000 AUB 95603 162-D6

WESTWOOD LN
2800 SaCo 95608 279-A6

WESWIN CT
2900 PLCR 95667 245-G4

WETHERLY CT
8800 ELKG 95624 358-G3

WETHERSFIELD DR
100 SaCo 95655 319-H2

WETLAND WY
9900 ELKG 95757 377-E1
9900 ELKG 95757 397-E1

WETSEL-OVIATT RD
- EDCo 95762 282-F7
- EDCo 95762 (302-H1 See Page 301)

WETZEL CT
7800 CITH 95610 240-C7

WEXFORD CIR
6300 CITH 95621 259-E4
9600 PlaC 95746 240-H6

WEXFORD CT
500 RSVL 95661 240-E3

WEXTED WY
- ELKG 95757 378-B1

WEYAND AV
8500 SaCo 95828 338-F1

WEYBRIDGE CT
500 RSVL 95661 240-E3

WEYBRIDGE WY
3900 SaCo 95843 238-G5

WEYBURN WY
8200 SaCo 95828 338-D4

WEYMOUTH LN
4000 SAC 95823 337-G3

WEYMOUTH WY
3100 EDCo 95672 263-B2

WHALER CT
5900 CITH 95621 259-D1

WHALERS COVE CT
5900 ELKG 95758 357-J5
5900 ELKG 95758 358-A5

WHALEWOOD LN
- SaCo 95828 338-F5

WHARFDALE PL
5800 SaCo 95835 257-A3

WHARTON WY
- ELKG 95624 358-H1

WHEAT ST
4100 SaCo 95821 278-J3

WHEAT FIELD CT
- RSVL 95747 219-D1

WHEATFIELD WY
8200 SaCo 95828 338-D4

WHEATLAND DR
8300 SaCo 95828 338-E6

WHEATLAND WY
8400 SaCo 95828 338-E6

WHEATLEY CIR
4100 SaCo 95838 278-A2

WHEATLEY LN
500 LNCN 95648 179-G4

WHEATON CT
6400 SaCo 95608 279-E5

WHEATSHEAF LN
- SAC 95835 256-J3

WHEELER CT
4300 ELKG 95758 357-G4

WHEELER PEAK DR
- SaCo 95829 339-E6

WHEELHOUSE AV
- SAC 95833 296-G1
3400 SAC 95833 276-G7

WHEELMAN CT
3700 SaCo 95843 238-G6

WHELAN CT
100 FOLS 95630 261-F3

WHETSTONE CT
- RSVL 95746 240-G5

WHICKHAM CT
100 RSVL 95661 240-E4

WHIMBREL CT
- RKLN 95765 219-H1

WHIMBRELL CT
4500 SaCo 95843 238-J5

WHIPPOORWILL CT
200 LNCN 95648 180-C7

WHIPPOORWILL LN
2100 SaCo 95821 278-C6

WHIRLAWAY LN
9900 ELKG 95624 359-D4

WHISKEY BAR RD
9200 PlaC 95650 201-H6

WHISKEY CREEK DR
- ELKG 95758 357-J3

WHISKEY DRIFT DR
- EDCo 95762 263-A6

WHISKEY FLAT RD
6000 EDCo 95667 245-A7

WHISKEY HILL RD
3600 PlaC 95650 201-H6

WHISPER LN
4900 SaCo 95841 259-A6

WHISPER WY
5000 PlaC 95746 240-G1

WHISPER HOLLOW CT
- ELKG 95624 339-E7
- ELKG 95624 359-E1

WHISPERING OAK LN
8400 SaCo 95662 260-C4

WHISPERING OAKS CIR
4200 PlaC 95746 240-F1

WHISPERING PALMS DR
7700 SaCo 95823 338-B3

WHISPERING PINES CT
3800 EDCo 95682 263-J6

WHISPERING PINES DR
100 RCCD 95670 280-A6

WHISPERING PINES LN
3700 EDCo 95682 263-J6

WHISPERING WATERS LN
6200 PlaC 95650 201-A3

WHISPERING WIND DR
1700 EDCo 95667 246-A3
2400 EDCo 95667 245-J3

WHISPERLODGE CT
- RSVL 95747 219-A5

WHISPERLODGE WY
- RSVL 95747 219-A5

WHISPER OAKS LN
5100 SaCo 95608 279-B7

WHISPER RIDGE RD
3700 EDCo 95667 245-H6
3700 PLCR 95667 245-H6

WHISPERWILLOW DR
7400 SaCo 95828 338-B3

WHISPER WINDS CT
2000 SaCo 95626 238-C6

WHISPER WOOD WY
7800 SAC 95823 337-H4

WHISTLER CT
- LNCN 95648 200-C3

WHISTLER WY
2200 RCCD 95670 279-H7

WHISTLERS BEND WY
- EDCo 95682 263-A6
- EDCo 95762 263-A6

WHISTLE STOP WY
- FOLS 95630 281-B1

WHISTLESTOP WY
- RSVL 95747 219-A3

WHISTLE WOOD CT
4700 SaCo 95843 239-A5

WHISTLING STRAITS WY
- RVIS 94571 454-E2

WHITBY CT
8500 SaCo 95828 338-F5

WHITCOMB WY
- EDCo 95667 264-J3

WHITE CT
4900 SAC 95820 318-A4

WHITE LN
6800 LMS 95650 221-B1

WHITE ST
- AUB 95603 182-D2

WHITE ASTER PL
- ELKG 95757 377-J1
- ELKG 95757 397-J1

WHITE BIRCH CT
- RSVL 95678 219-H5
8000 CITH 95610 260-A3

WHITE CANYON WY
3100 SaCo 95843 238-F4

WHITECAP CT
- SAC 95833 277-D6

WHITE CASTLE WY
8000 SaCo 95828 338-F5

WHITE CEDAR LN
8700 ELKG 95758 357-J2

WHITECHAPEL DR
600 GALT 95632 419-G4

WHITE CHAPEL WY
- RKLN 95677 220-J2

WHITECLIFF WY
6200 SaCo 95660 258-J4

WHITE CLOUD CT
6000 CITH 95621 259-D3

WHITE CLOUD RD
- EDCo 95634 225-F2

WHITECLOVER LN
5000 RSVL 95747 219-A6

WHITE DOE CT
- PlaC 95602 162-A2

WHITE EAGLE LN
- SAC 95834 276-H1

WHITE FEATHER CT
- RSVL 95747 218-J3

N WHITE FENCE CT
25300 SJCo 95220 439-H5

WHITE FIR WY
5500 SaCo 95841 259-C6

WHITE FISH BAY ST
- WSAC 95691 316-E3

WHITE GOLD CT
- SaCo 95843 238-H6

WHITEHALL LN
- LNCN 95648 179-J4
- LNCN 95648 180-A4

WHITEHALL WY
600 SaCo 95864 299-A4

WHITEHAVEN CT
800 ANT 94509 (513-C7 See Page 493)

WHITEHAVEN WY
5300 SaCo 95843 239-C6

WHITEHAWK CT
8500 SaCo 95628 260-D5

WHITEHEAD ST
- RCCD 95655 299-G5
- SaCo 95655 299-G5

WHITE HORSE WY
- ELKG 95624 359-B6

WHITE HOUSE RD
- ELKG 95758 358-C2
- SAC 95758 358-C2

WHITE LILY CT
- SAC 95833 276-H6

WHITELOCK PKWY
- ELKG 95757 377-H1
- ELKG 95757 397-H1
6400 ELKG 95757 378-A1

WHITE LOTUS WY
5100 ELKG 95757 377-H2
5100 ELKG 95757 397-H2

WHITE MILL CRESCENT RD
- PlaC 95747 238-J2
- PlaC 95747 239-A2

WHITE MOUNTAIN RANCH RD
- EDCo - 247-F1

WHITE OAK CT
200 FOLS 95630 281-A3
3300 SaCo 95864 298-F5
4400 RKLN 95677 220-E2

WHITEOAK DR
7300 EDCo 95667 226-H5

WHITE OAK RD
2500 EDCo 95672 263-G1
7300 EDCo 95667 244-J7

WHITE OWL CT
8600 SaCo 95662 260-D2

WHITE PEACOCK CT
8800 ELKG 95624 358-F3

WHITE PEACOCK WY
8700 ELKG 95624 358-F3

WHITE PINE WY
9700 ELKG 95624 359-A7

WHITEPLAINS CT
8400 CITH 95621 239-G6

WHITE RABBIT CT
- RSVL 95747 219-D1

WHITE RAIN WY
11800 RCCD 95742 300-D7

WHITERIVER LN
7300 SaCo 95842 259-D1

WHITE ROCK RD
400 SaCo 95630 282-A5
700 EDCo 95762 282-F1
1500 EDCo 95762 262-G7
10300 RCCD 95670 299-F3
11000 RCCD 95670 300-A2
11200 RCCD 95742 300-A2
11200 SaCo 95742 300-E2
11500 SaCo 95742 301-B1
11800 SaCo 95742 281-C7
11900 SaCo 95630 281-G6

S WHITE ROCK RD
10200 RCCD 95670 299-G4
10300 RCCD 95655 299-G4

WHITE ROSE CT
8700 SaCo 95828 338-G4

WHITEROSE CT
300 RSVL 95747 219-A4

WHITE ROSE LN
- EDCo 95667 266-F3

WHITE SANDS WY
8200 SaCo 95828 338-D2

WHITES LANDING CT
- ELKG 95624 359-A7

WHITE SPRUCE WY
8300 SaCo 95843 239-D5

WHITE STAG WY
7800 SAC 95823 337-G5

WHITE STAR WY
8900 ELKG 95758 358-A3

WHITE STONE CT
- SAC 95758 358-A2

WHITETAIL DR
3000 EDCo 95672 263-B1

WHITE TAIL WY
7800 SAC 95823 337-H4

WHITETAIL RUN WY
5200 SaCo 95843 239-B7

WHITEWATER WY
2500 SaCo 95826 298-J5

WHITEWILLOW DR
- SaCo 95828 338-B3

WHITEWOOD DR
2900 SaCo 95608 279-C5

WHITFIELD LN
600 LNCN 95648 179-F5

WHITFIELD WY
5500 SaCo 95608 279-C4

WHITFORD CT
900 GALT 95632 419-G3

WHITHORN CT
9400 ELKG 95758 358-A6

WHITING WY
100 FOLS 95630 261-C6

WHITLAND CT
- RKLN 95677 220-F6

WHITLOCK LN
3300 EDCo 95667 245-E6

WHITLOW WY
- SaCo 95828 338-F6

WHITMAN CT
- EDCo 95682 283-B1

WHITMAN WY
1900 SAC 95822 337-C2

WHITMORE PL
3700 EDCo 95762 242-D6

WHITMORE ST
7500 SAC 95758 358-C1

WHITNEY AV
2900 SaCo 95821 278-F4
4600 SaCo 95608 279-A4
4600 SaCo 95821 279-A4

WHITNEY BLVD
- RKLN 95765 220-C2
4600 RKLN 95677 220-C2

S WHITNEY BLVD
2100 RKLN 95677 220-B4

WHITNEY CT
5400 EDCo 95633 205-A4

WHITNEY OAKS DR
- RKLN 95765 200-D4

WHITNEY RANCH BLVD
4600 RKLN 95765 199-G4

WHITNEY RANCH PKWY
- LNCN 95648 200-A4
- RKLN 95765 200-A4
4600 RKLN 95765 199-G4

WHITNOR CT
3400 SaCo 95821 278-H4

WHITSETT DR
6500 SaCo 95660 258-H3

WHITSTABLE DR
- RSVL 95747 219-B7
- RSVL 95747 239-B1

WHITTEMORE CT
- GALT 95632 419-F4

WHITTEMORE DR
9200 ELKG 95624 358-H4

WHITTIER DR
4900 SAC 95820 318-B4

WHITTINGTON DR
- PlaC 95658 181-B4

WHITTNEY AV
1200 SAC 95814 297-C5

WHIZNAN ST
3800 SaCo 95821 278-J3

WHYSE LN
- SaCo 95690 437-A1

WHYTE AV
- RSVL 95661 239-H5
200 RSVL 95661 239-H5
1200 RSVL 95678 239-G5
6700 CITH 95621 239-F5

WICKENBY CT
- RSVL 95661 220-F6

WICKENBY WY
- RSVL 95661 220-F6

WICKER WY
700 GALT 95632 419-F4

WICKERSHAM CT
8800 ELKG 95624 358-G2

WICKFORD WY
100 SaCo 95655 319-H2

WICKHAM DR
7500 CITH 95610 259-J1

WICKHAM WY
4000 EDCo 95762 262-D2

WICKLOW CT
- RSVL 95747 219-C1

WICKLOW ST
3600 SaCo 95821 278-J4

WIDENER WY
7300 SaCo 95842 258-J1

WIDGEON CT
- FOLS 95630 281-F1
- LNCN 95648 179-D1
600 RSVL 95661 240-B3

WIDGEON RD
40000 YoCo 95612 375-G6
40000 YoCo 95612 (395-G1 See Page 375)

WIDGEON WY
7500 SaCo 95628 279-H1

WIEDMAN WY
4800 SaCo 95608 279-D1

WIESE WY
2800 SAC 95833 277-D5

WIGAN CT
3200 RCCD 95670 299-F3

WIGEON CT
4000 EDCo 95682 263-H5

WIGHILL CIR
- RSVL 95747 218-H4

WIGHTMAN AV
8200 SaCo 95628 260-B6

WIGHTMAN CT
- ANT 94509 (513-D6 See Page 493)

WIGHTMAN LN
- ANT 94509 (513-J5 See Page 493)

WIGMORE CT
- ELKG 95624 378-H1

WIGWAM DR
6400 SaCo 95662 260-C4

WILBUR AV
- ANT 94509 (513-D4 See Page 493)
600 CCCo 94509 (513-H4 See Page 493)
3300 ANT 94509 (514-A4 See Page 493)
3300 CCCo 94509 (514-A4 See Page 493)

WILBUR LN
1400 ANT 94509 (513-H4 See Page 493)
1400 CCCo 94509 (513-H4 See Page 493)

WILBUR WY
2300 AUB 95602 162-C2
7600 SaCo 95828 338-E4

WILCOX PL
7100 PlaC 95746 241-C2

WILD WY
4200 SaCo 95608 279-B2

WILD BERRY LN
- RKLN 95765 199-J4

WILDBERRY LN
2200 PlaC 95603 162-B5

WILDBRIAR LN
4200 SaCo 95628 280-C2

WILDBROOK CT
- GALT 95632 419-F2

WILDCAT CT
1400 OAKL 94561 (514-D6 See Page 493)

WILDCAT WY
1400 OAKL 94561 (514-D6 See Page 493)

WILD CHAPARRAL DR
3800 EDCo 95682 263-H7
4000 EDCo 95682 264-A7

WILD CHERRY CT
- ELKG 95757 358-A6

WILD CREEK RD
2500 PlaC 95663 201-E3
2600 PlaC 95658 201-E3

WILDCREST RD
5500 EDCo 95623 264-G7

WILD DEW CT
- EDCo 95619 265-F4

WILD DUCK CT
8700 ELKG 95624 358-G1

WILD EAGLE CT
- ELKG 95757 358-A7

WILDER LN
2300 EDCo 95667 245-H2

WILDERNESS CT
- EDCo 95619 266-C5

WILDERNESS RD
- RCCD 95670 280-A6

WILDERNESS WY
- EDCo 95619 266-C5
- EDCo 95667 266-C5

WILDER SPARLING LN
2500 PlaC 95603 161-G6

WILDFIRE LN
8200 SaCo 95828 338-D3

WILD FLOWER CIR
5400 SaCo 95608 279-B2

WILDFLOWER CT
- EDCo 95667 226-J2
7600 PlaC 95746 241-A1

WILDFLOWER DR
- RSVL 95678 219-G4
- GALT 95632 419-D6
2600 ANT 94531 (513-G7 See Page 493)

WILDFLOWER LN
4700 RKLN 95677 220-G3

WILD FOX CT
- ELKG 95757 358-A6

WILDGINGER CT
900 GALT 95632 419-F2

WILDGINGER ST
- WSAC 95691 296-G7

WILD GOOSE CANYON — SACRAMENTO COUNTY STREET INDEX — WOOD DUCK WY 580

SACRAMENTO CO.

STREET Block City ZIP Pg-Grid

WILD GOOSE CANYON RD
2000 EDCo 95667 245-G2
N WILD HARE LN
- SJCo 95220 439-B5
WILDHAWK DR
10300 SaCo 95829 339-E5
WILDHAWK TR
- EDCo 95726 267-G2
WILDHAWK WEST DR
9900 SaCo 95829 339-D5
WILD HORSE CT
- RKLN 95765 199-J5
6800 SaCo 95662 260-E3
WILDLIFE WY
1400 EDCo 95667 245-J4
1400 PLCR 95667 245-J4
WILD MEADOW PL
5100 ELKG 95757 377-H1
5100 ELKG 95757 397-H1
WILD OAK CT
- LNCN 95648 200-A3
WILD OAK DR
- LNCN 95648 200-A3
WILDOAK DR
7500 CITH 95621 259-E1
WILD OAT CT
300 RSVL 95747 219-B6
WILD OAT WY
300 RSVL 95747 219-B5
WILDOMAR LN
- LNCN 95648 180-B6
WILDOMAR WY
6200 SaCo 95608 259-E6
WILD ORCHID WY
10000 ELKG 95757 377-H1
10000 ELKG 95757 397-H1
WILD PLAINS CIR
- RKLN 95765 199-J4
WILD PLAINS CT
- RKLN 95765 199-J4
WILD PLUM CT
8700 ELKG 95624 358-G1
WILD POPPY CT
1100 GALT 95632 419-F2
WILDRIDGE DR
2000 EDCo 95762 242-B6
7800 SaCo 95628 259-J7
7800 SaCo 95628 260-A7
WILD RIVER LN
100 FOLS 95630 260-J4
WILD ROSE CT
- GALT 95632 419-E2
WILD ROSE DR
2300 LNCN 95648 179-D1
WILDROSE WY
3700 SaCo 95826 318-H2
WILD SIENNA CT
5300 ELKG 95757 377-J1
5300 ELKG 95757 397-J1
WILD TEAK CT
9700 ELKG 95757 357-J7
WILD TREE PL
8200 CITH 95610 260-B1
WILD TURKEY RD
- EDCo 95634 225-B3
1400 PlaC 95648 180-B2
WILD WATER CT
- ELKG 95757 358-A7
WILD WAY CT
100 FOLS 95630 261-E3
WILDWIND CT
3400 RCCD 95827 299-E6
WILDWOOD
3500 EDCo 95667 244-E7
WILDWOOD CT
400 LNCN 95648 179-F3
7000 PlaC 95746 241-C1
WILDWOOD DR
11100 AUB 95603 182-D6
WILDWOOD PL
7000 PlaC 95746 241-C1
WILDWOOD WY
1800 RSVL 95661 240-C5
4100 EDCo 95682 264-A2
5400 CITH 95610 259-J6
WILD YAK CT
- SaCo 95829 338-H5
WILHAGGIN DR
300 SaCo 95864 298-H5
WILHAGGIN PARK LN
1000 SaCo 95864 298-J3
WILHERT CT
8600 SaCo 95828 338-F7
WILHOFF LN
5900 PlaC 95746 220-J7
5900 PlaC 95746 221-A7
WILKES BARRE ST
- SaCo 95742 281-C5
WILKINS WY
- CITH 95610 259-H5
3000 SaCo 95608 279-E5
WILKINSON CT
1200 EDCo 95667 245-B1
WILKINSON RD
2800 EDCo 95682 263-B4
WILKINSON ST
5600 SAC 95824 318-C5
WILL RD
- EDCo 95634 225-G2
WILLARA WY
4300 SaCo 95821 278-J5
WILLARD AV
4900 SAC 95838 257-H7
WILLARD DR
- FOLS 95630 281-C1
WILLARD PKWY
- ELKG 95757 377-H3
- ELKG 95757 397-H3
- SaCo 95757 377-H3
- SaCo 95757 397-H3
WILLARD WY
3500 RKLN 95677 220-D4
WILLENHALL WY
- RSVL 95661 220-F7
WILLETT CT
3400 SaCo 95825 298-F1
3400 SaCo 95864 298-F1
WILLEY CT
9900 PlaC 95746 241-B6
WILLEY WY
7100 SaCo 95608 279-G1
7100 SaCo 95628 279-G1
WILLIAM ST
600 WSAC 95605 297-A2
WILLIAM WY
1100 RSVL 95678 239-G1
3500 SaCo 95821 278-G4
4000 EDCo 95709 247-B4

WILLIAM BIRD AV
- SAC 95835 257-C4
WILLIAMETTE WY
9400 SaCo 95826 319-A1
WILLIAM FIFE DR
- ELKG 95624 358-H4
WILLIAM REED DR
200 ANT 94509 (513-C5 See Page 493)
WILLIAMS AV
- SAC 95838 277-H2
WILLIAMS LN
5800 LMS 95650 200-J5
WILLIAMS ST
- FOLS 95630 281-D1
WILLIAMS WY
8800 PlaC 95658 181-G2
WILLIAMSBOROUGH DR
4000 SaCo 95823 337-G1
WILLIAMSBURG LN
5000 SaCo 95660 258-F4
WILLIAMSON CT
9000 SaCo 95826 318-H2
WILLIAMSON DR
8700 ELKG 95624 358-G6
WILLIAMSPOND LN
3500 LMS 95650 200-J5
WILLINGS WY
8500 SaCo 95628 280-D3
WILLIS AV
200 SaCo 95673 257-F4
WILLISTON WY
3100 EDCo 95762 262-D4
WILLITS DR
6900 SaCo 95683 341-H1
WILLIWAW LN
6900 SaCo 95828 338-B3
WILLOW AV
- YoCo 95612 356-H4
100 RSVL 95678 239-H3
1700 WSAC 95691 296-H4
2100 ANT 94509 (513-H5 See Page 493)
WILLOW LN
7300 PlaC 95746 241-D1
WILLOW RD
8400 SolC 94571 (435-B5 See Page 415)
WILLOW ST
- SJCo 95686 437-J3
- SJCo 95686 (438-A3 See Page 418)
2800 PLCR 95667 245-H4
3700 SAC 95838 278-B3
4600 EDCo 95623 265-B5
WILLOW WY
- RKLN 95677 220-D5
2500 SaCo 95608 279-D6
7500 CITH 95610 259-H1
WILLOWBANK WY
7200 SaCo 95608 279-G3
WILLOW BAR CT
2000 SaCo 95670 280-D4
WILLOW BAY LN
2800 ELKG 95758 357-E6
WILLOW BEND PL
3700 SaCo 95843 238-G5
WILLOW BEND RD
1500 FOLS 95630 261-G5
WILLOWBERRY WY
8200 ELKG 95758 358-D3
WILLOWBRAE WY
6600 SAC 95831 317-A7
WILLOW BRIDGE CT
- PlaC 95747 239-B4
WILLOWBROOK DR
4700 SaCo 95842 258-J5
4700 SaCo 95842 259-A5
WILLOWBROOK LN
1800 PlaC 95663 200-H1
WILLOW COVE CT
- SAC 95831 336-H4
WILLOW CREEK DR
- PlaC 95603 162-B4
100 FOLS 95630 261-E4
WILLOWCREEK DR
- EDCo 95667 266-H3
WILLOWCREST DR
7400 CITH 95610 259-H6
WILLOWCREST WY
7800 SaCo 95628 260-A7
WILLOWDALE DR
1000 EDCo 95762 262-C2
WILLOWDALE WY
8300 SaCo 95628 260-C7
WILLOW FALLS CIR
9200 ELKG 95624 359-A4
WILLOW GATE CT
- PlaC 95746 240-H1
WILLOW GLEN CT
8000 CITH 95610 260-B3
WILLOW GLEN DR
- RSVL 95678 219-G4
WILLOW GLEN RD
- EDCo 95619 286-B6
- EDCo 95684 286-B6
WILLOWGLEN WY
4300 RKLN 95677 220-D2
WILLOWGREEN CIR
600 GALT 95632 419-E3
WILLOW GROVE LN
- LNCN 95648 200-A1
WILLOW GROVE WY
8600 SaCo 95828 338-F6
WILLOWHOLLOW LN
8400 ELKG 95624 359-E1
WILLOW LAKE WY
7300 SAC 95831 337-A2
WILLOWLEAF DR
6500 CITH 95621 259-F1
WILLOWMERE DR
200 FOLS 95630 261-E5
WILLOW MIST WY
- RSVL 95678 220-A3
WILLOWMONT CIR
6100 SaCo 95842 258-J4
WILLOW OAK WY
5500 SaCo 95628 259-F6
WILLOWOOD WY
300 FOLS 95630 241-B7
WILLOW PARK CT
5200 SaCo 95608 279-B7
WILLOW PASS LN
9300 SaCo 95693 360-F6
WILLOW POINT RD
49400 YoCo 95612 356-B3
WILLOW POINT WY
7700 SAC 95831 336-J4
WILLOW POND CIR
9300 ELKG 95624 359-A5

WILLOWRIDGE CT
7900 SaCo 95628 259-J7
7900 SaCo 95628 260-C7
WILLOWRIVER CT
7200 SaCo 95828 338-B3
WILLOW ROCK WY
4900 SaCo 95841 259-A6
WILLOWSIDE CIR
- SAC 95823 337-F4
WILLOWSPRING CT
8900 ELKG 95758 358-A3
WILLOW TREE CT
5000 SaCo 95608 259-D7
WILLOW TREE WY
8300 CITH 95621 239-F6
WILLOW VALE WY
4900 ELKG 95758 357-H5
WILLOW VALLEY PL
8300 PlaC 95746 221-F3
WILLOWVIEW CT
7500 SaCo 95628 279-H3
WILLOW VISTA CT
8600 SaCo 95843 238-G5
WILLOWWARD CIR
4600 SaCo 95842 258-J4
WILLOW WATER PL
11400 SaCo 95670 280-B4
WILLOWWEST CT
7200 SaCo 95828 338-B3
WILLOWWICK WY
7300 SAC 95822 337-D2
WILLOW WIND CT
7200 SaCo 95828 338-B3
WILLOWWOOD WY
6800 SAC 95831 316-J7
WILLOWYND CT
5400 RKLN 95677 220-C4
WILLOWYND DR
5900 RKLN 95677 220-C4
WILL ROGERS DR
6700 SaCo 95628 279-F1
6700 SaCo 95628 259-F7
WILLS RD
100 RSVL 95678 220-B7
WILLSBORO CT
500 FOLS 95630 261-H7
WILLYS CT
8000 SaCo 95828 338-G5
WILMA CT
8600 SaCo 95628 260-D7
WILMARTH WY
- ELKG 95624 358-D1
WILMER ST
4700 SaCo 95608 279-E1
WILMINGTON AV
2400 SAC 95820 317-E2
WILMINGTON CT
100 FOLS 95630 261-G6
WILMINGTON LN
- RVIS 94571 454-F2
WILMINGTON ST
- SaCo 95742 281-D6
WILMOT CT
8600 ELKG 95624 358-F3
WILSALL CT
7400 ELKG 95758 358-C5
WILSEY WY
5500 SaCo 95608 259-D6
WILSHIRE AV
100 SAC 95823 337-F2
WILSHIRE CIR
7000 SAC 95822 337-B1
WILSON AV
300 SAC 95833 277-E6
900 LNCN 95648 179-J2
WILSON BLVD
500 EDCo 95762 262-D6
700 EDCo 95762 282-C1
WILSON CT
- ANT 94509 (513-J5 See Page 493)
100 FOLS 95630 261-E4
WILSON DR
3100 PlaC 95603 162-A3
WILSON LP
- EDCo 95667 266-H3
WILSON RD
12000 SaCo 95615 (396-H2 See Page 375)
WILSON ST
2100 ANT 94509 (513-J5 See Page 493)
4900 SAC 95838 257-H7
WILSON WY
4000 PlaC 95602 160-H1
WILTON RD
10400 ELKG 95624 359-F4
10400 SaCo 95624 359-F4
10900 SaCo 95693 359-H6
10900 SaCo 95693 360-A7
10900 SaCo 95693 (380-B1 See Page 379)
WILTON WY
1500 SaCo 95864 298-F2
WILTON OAKS CT
10000 ELKG 95624 359-D2
WILTON SOUTH RD
- SaCo 95693 379-J2
WILTSE CT
1300 PLCR 95667 245-J5
WILTSE RD
3000 PLCR 95667 245-J5
3100 PLCR 95667 246-A5
WILTSHIRE WY
- SaCo 95662 260-H2
WILUNA PL
1400 EDCo 95762 262-D3
WIMBLEDON CT
800 SaCo 95864 299-A3
WIMBLEDON DR
- EDCo 95619 265-F2
1300 PlaC 95603 162-E5
WIMBLEY CT
9000 ELKG 95624 358-G3
WINAFRED ST
2100 SaCo 95825 278-C7
WINAMAC DR
- SAC 95835 256-J6
WINCHESTER CT
- RKLN 95765 200-E4
100 FOLS 95630 261-F4
500 RSVL 95661 240-C3
WINCHESTER DR
2900 EDCo 95672 263-C1
WINCHESTER WY
1600 RSVL 95661 240-C3
2900 RCCD 95670 299-F3
WIND WY
7700 CITH 95610 259-J6

WINDANCE CT
- SAC 95823 358-A1
WINDBREAKER WY
6000 SAC 95823 358-A1
WINDBRIDGE DR
7300 SAC 95831 336-J2
WINDBROOK CT
- SAC 95823 358-A1
WINDCATCHER CT
- SAC 95834 276-H2
WINDCHIME CT
- SAC 95823 358-A1
WINDCHIME WY
7000 RSVL 95747 219-A5
WINDCLOUD AV
4400 SAC 95838 277-H1
WINDCOVE CT
9300 SaCo 95628 280-F1
WIND CREEK DR
4800 SAC 95838 257-J7
WINDEMERE CT
1300 WSAC 95605 296-H2
WINDEMERE LN
1900 SaCo 95864 298-H1
WINDERMERE AV
1000 RSVL 95678 239-G4
WINDFALL WY
7300 CITH 95621 239-G6
WINDFIELD WY
1100 EDCo 95762 282-D3
WIND FLOWER WY
8300 SaCo 95843 239-E5
WINDFORD WY
8400 SaCo 95843 239-B5
8500 PlaC 95747 239-B5
WINDGATE CT
7900 SaCo 95828 338-C5
WINDGATE WY
7900 SaCo 95828 338-C5
WINDHAM WY
- RKLN 95765 200-B5
11800 RCCD 95742 320-D2
WINDHAVEN LN
- EDCo 95633 205-H3
- EDCo 95634 205-H3
2200 RCCD 95670 279-J6
WINDING LN
- EDCo 95709 247-B1
3900 RKLN 95677 220-E4
WINDING WY
- LNCN 95648 180-A6
4100 SAC 95821 278-J2
4100 SAC 95841 278-J2
4100 SaCo 95821 278-J2
4100 SaCo 95841 278-J2
4600 SAC 95821 279-B2
4600 SAC 95841 279-B2
5000 SaCo 95608 279-E1
7000 SaCo 95628 279-H2
7900 SaCo 95628 280-A2
N WINDING WY
8700 SaCo 95628 280-E2
WINDING BLUFF LN
4100 SaCo 95821 278-J2
WINDING BROOK WY
9200 ELKG 95624 359-B5
WINDING CANYON LN
100 FOLS 95630 260-J4
100 FOLS 95630 261-A4
WINDING CREEK RD
- RSVL 95678 219-E2
3500 SaCo 95864 278-G7
3500 SaCo 95864 298-G1
WINDING CREEK WY
- RSVL 95678 219-E1
WINDING HILL WY
4300 SaCo 95628 280-D2
WINDING OAK DR
5000 SaCo 95628 260-G7
5000 SaCo 95662 260-G7
WINDING OAK LN
1500 EDCo 95762 242-F5
WINDING RIDGE CT
- SaCo 95821 279-A2
WINDING RIVER WY
9400 ELKG 95624 359-A5
WINDING WOODS WY
4200 SaCo 95628 280-D2
WINDJAMMER WY
7200 CITH 95621 259-D2
WINDLASS CT
6000 CITH 95621 259-D1
WINDMILL CT
- LNCN 95648 179-J4
WINDMILL WY
5700 SaCo 95608 279-C1
12500 PlaC 95603 162-D5
WINDMILL OAKS PL
8200 SaCo 95843 239-C6
WINDMOOR CT
5400 RCCD 95742 320-E4
WINDORAH WY
6200 SaCo 95662 260-D4
WINDOW LN
4600 PlaC 95648 180-G1
WINDPLAY DR
4800 EDCo 95762 282-D3
WINDRIFT LN
9400 ELKG 95758 357-G5
E WINDRIM CT
- ELKG 95758 357-E4
W WINDRIM CT
- ELKG 95758 357-E4
WINDRIM WY
- ELKG 95758 357-E4
WIND RIVER CT
11200 RCCD 95670 280-A4
WINDROSE LN
- PlaC 95746 240-G5
WINDROSE PL
3900 SaCo 95843 238-H5
WINDROW LN
- RKLN 95765 199-J4
WINDRUNNER LN
9400 ELKG 95758 357-G6
WINDRUSH LN
- RSVL 95747 239-A1
WINDSHIRE LN
- SaCo 95662 260-E5
WINDSOCK AV
9000 SaCo 95628 260-G7
WINDSONG CT
- RKLN 95765 200-A7
9100 SaCo 95826 318-H2
12900 PlaC 95602 162-C1
WINDSONG LN
- EDCo 95633 205-D3
2800 PLCR 95667 245-J4
2800 PLCR 95667 246-A4

WINDSONG PL
2200 PlaC 95602 162-C1
WINDSONG ST
- SAC 95834 276-H1
WINDSONG WY
4800 EDCo 95682 283-D7
WINDSONG HILL LN
- EDCo 95633 205-D3
WINDSOR CT
500 OAKL 94561 (514-C6 See Page 493)
2900 EDCo 95672 263-C1
WINDSOR DR
600 RSVL 95678 239-G4
2700 ANT 94509 (513-F6 See Page 493)
3100 SaCo 95864 298-F3
WINDSOR LN
2200 OAKL 94561 (514-C6 See Page 493)
7800 CITH 95610 259-J6
WINDSOR POINT PL
4000 EDCo 95762 242-C6
WINDSOR POINT WY
- ELKG 95624 358-F1
WINDSOR POINTE WY
8500 ELKG 95624 358-F1
WINDSOR VILLAGE LN
- SaCo 95628 259-J7
4900 SaCo 95628 260-A7
WINDSPUN ST
8800 ELKG 95624 358-G3
WINDSTAR CIR
100 FOLS 95630 261-E2
WINDSTONE CT
- SAC 95831 336-J2
WIND STREAM WY
- SaCo 95828 338-D5
WINDSWEPT CT
8300 ELKG 95758 358-E5
WINDUBEY CIR
- SAC 95831 336-F2
WINDWARD CIR
1400 WSAC 95691 296-G5
WINDWARD LN
2200 RCCD 95670 279-J6
WINDWARD WY
200 RSVL 95678 239-G5
300 SAC 95831 316-G7
6300 EDCo 95623 265-B6
WINDWOOD WY
8300 ELKG 95758 358-E5
WINDY WY
4300 SaCo 95826 318-H2
WINDY COVE DR
- ELKG 95758 357-G6
WINDY FEN CT
6000 ELKG 95758 358-A5
WINDY PEAK CT
100 FOLS 95630 260-H1
WINDY POINT PL
9400 ELKG 95758 357-G5
WINDY RIVER LN
- ELKG 95758 357-G6
WINE WY
3600 LMS 95650 200-H6
WINEWOOD CIR
- ELKG 95758 358-D5
WINFIELD CT
400 RSVL 95747 219-C7
WINFIELD WY
5300 SaCo 95841 259-C6
WINFIN WY
3400 SaCo 95608 279-A4
W WING DR
- ELKG 95758 358-C2
8300 SAC 95758 358-C2
WINGATE CT
7800 PlaC 95746 241-C1
WINGATE DR
3700 SaCo 95608 279-A4
WINGED FOOT
- PlaC 95746 240-J5
WINGED FOOT DR
- SaCo 95829 339-D5
WINGFIELD WY
1900 SaCo 95608 299-C1
WINGINA CT
- SAC 95823 357-J1
WINGS WY
3600 SaCo 95660 258-G6
WINGTIP CT
9000 SaCo 95628 260-F7
WINIFRED CT
- ANT 94509 (513-E4 See Page 493)
WINJE DR
4100 SaCo 95843 238-J7
4500 SaCo 95843 239-A7
WINKLER WY
8200 SaCo 95828 338-D5
WINKLEY WY
7400 SAC 95822 337-D2
WINLOCK AV
6800 CITH 95621 259-F2
WINLOCK WY
- RSVL 95746 240-F4
3700 EDCo 95762 262-D2
WINN DR
700 GALT 95632 419-F4
WINNABO LN
- PlaC 95746 241-E3
WINNERS CIR
4400 RKLN 95677 220-F2
WINNETICA CT
5800 SaCo 95621 259-D1
5800 SaCo 95842 259-D1
WINNETT WY
7300 SAC 95823 337-G2
WINNIE ST
- SaCo 95690 437-A1
WINNING WY
3000 SAC 95823 337-F1
S WINNING WY
3500 SAC 95823 337-F1
WINNINGHAM CT
- ELKG 95758 357-F5
WINNIPEG ST
2300 SAC 95815 277-H7
WINOCO CT
- SAC 95823 337-J7
WINONA WY
3200 SaCo 95660 278-F1
WINSFORD LN
2500 SaCo 95608 279-C7
WINSLOW CT
3900 SaCo 95821 278-G5
WINSLOW DR
100 RSVL 95678 219-G5

WINSOME LN
3300 SaCo 95608 279-C5
WINSTON WY
3500 SaCo 95608 279-A4
WINTER CT
2800 EDCo 95667 245-C5
WINTER LN
3300 LMS 95650 200-F5
7400 EDCo 95667 245-C6
7400 PLCR 95667 245-C6
WINTER WY
5600 EDCo 95684 286-E7
WINTERBERRY DR
8400 ELKG 95624 338-F7
8400 ELKG 95624 358-F1
WINTERBROOK WY
9500 SaCo 95662 260-H7
WINTERCREST LN
4000 EDCo 95682 264-A4
WINTER DAWN PL
3800 SaCo 95843 238-G5
WINTERFEST CT
8600 ELKG 95624 358-G2
WINTERFIELD DR
- EDCo 95762 282-C2
WINTER GARDEN AV
300 SAC 95833 277-F4
WINTERGARDEN RD
- EDCo 95667 266-A4
WINTERGLEN CT
- ELKG 95758 357-H2
WINTERGREEN DR
7700 CITH 95610 240-C7
7700 CITH 95610 260-C1
WINTERHAM WY
5900 SAC 95823 358-A1
WINTERHAVEN AV
400 SAC 95833 277-F4
WINTERHAVEN CIR
- EDCo 95682 263-C2
WINTERHAVEN CT
- EDCo 95682 263-D2
WINTERHAVEN DR
- EDCo 95672 263-C2
- EDCo 95682 263-C2
WINTER HAVEN WY
4800 RSVL 95747 219-A6
WINTERHAWK LN
8000 PlaC 95746 240-H1
WINTERHILL DR
- EDCo 95667 266-F4
WINTERMIST CT
- SAC 95831 336-J2
WINTER OAK WY
4500 SaCo 95843 239-A5
WINTER PARK DR
3300 SAC 95833 277-B4
3300 SAC 95834 277-B4
WINTER RUSH DR
- RKLN 95677 220-F5
WINTERS ST
- SaCo 95652 258-D7
2300 SAC 95838 278-D2
4000 SAC 95652 278-D2
4000 SaCo 95652 278-D1
4000 SaCo 95838 278-D2
WINTER SNOW CT
7700 PlaC 95658 181-D5
WINTERSTEIN DR
100 FOLS 95630 261-G4
WINTERTREE CT
4900 SaCo 95841 259-C7
4900 SaCo 95841 279-C1
WINTERUSH LN
2300 LNCN 95648 179-D1
WINTERWILLOW CT
7200 SaCo 95828 338-B3
WINTERWIND LN
11000 RCCD 95670 279-J6
WINTERWOOD CT
7000 PlaC 95746 241-C1
WINTERWOOD WY
9800 RCCD 95827 299-C6
WINTHROP CT
3600 SaCo 95660 258-G1
4400 EDCo 95682 265-B2
WINTHROP RD
4200 EDCo 95667 265-B2
WINTUN CT
- EDCo 95633 205-D1
WINTUN DR
- SaCo 95608 279-D4
WIRE DR
5500 SaCo 95823 317-J7
WISAM CT
7400 SaCo 95628 279-H2
WISCONSIN AV
500 SAC 95833 277-F5
WISCONSIN DR
7400 CITH 95610 259-H5
WISCONSIN ST
- SaCo 95742 281-C6
WISE CT
- SaCo 95608 279-F2
WISE RD
1600 PlaC 95648 159-A5
2100 LNCN 95648 159-A5
3700 PlaC 95648 160-C5
4200 PlaC - 160-G5
5600 PlaC 95603 160-J4
5900 PlaC 95603 161-A5
8400 PlaC 95603 181-G1
8800 PlaC 95658 181-H2
10200 PlaC 95603 182-B3
10400 AUB 95603 182-B3
WISHING STAR LN
- LNCN 95648 200-B3
WISHING WELL WY
6500 LMS 95650 221-B1
WISNER DR
1300 ANT 94509 (513-E5 See Page 493)
WISP CT
- RKLN 95765 219-J2
WISSEMANN DR
2700 SAC 95826 298-F7
3000 SAC 95826 318-G1
WISTERIA CT
- LNCN 95648 199-J2
- OAKL 94561 (514-C7 See Page 493)
200 RSVL 95678 219-F6
WISTERIA LN
3900 SaCo 95608 279-G3
WISTERIA RD
5400 EDCo 95726 267-H2
WISTERIA WY
11200 PlaC 95603 182-D7

WITBURN WY
- FOLS 95630 261-J3
WITCHINGHOUR CT
7100 CITH 95621 259-G2
WITHERS CT
- FOLS 95630 281-F2
WITHINGTON AV
100 SaCo 95673 257-G3
WITHROW CT
8000 SaCo 95628 280-A1
WITMER DR
100 FOLS 95630 261-G4
WITT CT
- ELKG 95757 357-J7
WITT WY
- ELKG 95757 357-J7
- ELKG 95757 358-A7
WITTENHAM WY
6200 SaCo 95662 260-C4
W WITTER WY
3300 SAC 95833 276-H3
3300 SAC 95834 276-H2
WITTKOP WY
2300 SaCo 95825 298-D2
2500 SaCo 95864 298-D2
WITTS WY
- PlaC 95650 221-C3
WIXFORD WY
800 SaCo 95864 298-J3
800 SaCo 95864 299-A4
WOBURN CT
- RSVL 95746 240-G5
WOCHANGA WY
- EDCo 95667 266-E1
WOEDEE DR
3200 EDCo 95762 262-D5
WOLCOT CT
100 FOLS 95630 261-H6
WOLF CT
- AUB 95603 182-B7
WOLFBORO CT
8500 SaCo 95828 338-F5
WOLF CREEK CT
6100 ELKG 95758 358-A4
WOLF CREEK RD
1100 EDCo 95762 242-D6
WOLFE CT
3000 SaCo 95843 238-F6
WOLFGRAM WY
6900 SaCo 95828 338-B2
WOLFHAN RD
- EDCo - 267-J3
WOLF POINT CT
100 FOLS 95630 241-A7
WOLF RIVER CT
- RSVL 95661 220-D6
WOLLASTON WY
9100 ELKG 95624 358-J4
WOMACK WY
1300 PLCR 95667 245-J5
WONDER ST
7800 CITH 95610 240-A7
WONNER WY
7000 CITH 95621 259-E2
WOOD LN
3300 EDCo 95682 263-E5
WOOD ST
2900 PLCR 95667 245-F5
WOODACRE CT
- LNCN 95648 180-C7
1700 SaCo 95608 299-B2
WOODACRE LN
- LNCN 95648 180-C6
WOODACRE WY
1800 RSVL 95661 240-C5
WOODARD LN
100 FOLS 95630 261-G3
WOODBERRY CT
1100 RSVL 95661 240-B4
WOODBERRY WY
2700 RCCD 95670 299-G2
WOODBINE AV
6400 SAC 95822 317-E7
6800 SAC 95822 337-E1
WOODBOROUGH DR
7500 PlaC 95746 241-D1
WOODBOROUGH WY
8300 SaCo 95628 280-C1
WOODBRIAR WY
5900 CITH 95621 239-D7
WOODBRIDGE CT
5500 RKLN 95677 220-C4
WOODBRIDGE LN
- LNCN 95648 199-J1
WOODBRIDGE WY
5900 RKLN 95677 220-C4
10400 RCCD 95670 279-G7
10400 RCCD 95670 299-F1
WOODBROOK CT
5800 CITH 95841 259-D3
WOODBURN
- SAC 95823 337-G4
WOODBURY CT
3200 LMS 95650 200-J4
WOODCHASE DR
6700 PlaC 95746 241-B5
WOODCHUCK WY
7600 CITH 95610 240-B7
7600 CITH 95610 260-B1
WOODCLIFF WY
2200 RCCD 95670 279-F7
WOODCOCK DR
- ELKG 95758 358-D6
WOODCREEK DR
6200 CITH 95621 259-E5
WOODCREEK OAKS BLVD
1000 RSVL 95747 239-C1
1000 RSVL 95747 219-D1
10500 RSVL 95747 199-D7
WOODCREST CT
1000 RSVL 95661 240-B4
6600 RKLN 95677 220-D5
WOODCREST RD
3600 SaCo 95821 278-G5
WOODCREST WY
100 AUB 95603 182-E3
WOODDALE WY
7500 CITH 95610 260-B1
7700 CITH 95610 240-B7
WOOD DUCK CT
- LNCN 95648 200-B1
WOOD DUCK LN
- YoCo 95612 356-F6
WOODDUCK LN
7400 CITH 95621 259-D1
7600 CITH 95621 239-D7
WOOD DUCK WY
- EDCo 95684 286-G6

STREET	Block	City	ZIP	Pg-Grid
WOODED WY	12800	AUB	95603	162-E7
WOODED BROOK DR	-	ELKG	95758	358-D3
WOODED CREEK WY	6500	SaCo	95662	260-D3
WOODED GLEN PL	5400	SaCo	95843	239-C6
WOODENDALE CT	6600	CITH	95841	259-C3
WOODENFIELD CT	6600	CITH	95841	259-C3
WOOD ESTATES CT	4300	SaCo	95628	279-G2
WOODFAIR WY	4500	SaCo	95608	279-E2
WOOD FALLS CT	-	RSVL	95678	220-A3
WOODFIELD AV	1200	SAC	95831	337-A1
WOODFIELD CT	-	RSVL	95747	218-H4
WOODFIELD WY	-	RSVL	95747	218-H4
WOODFLOWER CT	1100	GALT	95632	419-G2
WOODFORD LN	-	LNCN	95648	179-F7
WOODFORD WY	3500	SaCo	95821	278-H4
WOODFOREST DR	5500	SaCo	95842	259-C3
WOODGATE CIR	-	PlaC	95650	221-J1
WOOD GATE WY	-	SaCo	95841	278-J1
	4900	SaCo	95841	258-J7
WOODGATE WY	-	RSVL	95747	218-H4
WOODGLADE AV	5900	CITH	95621	239-D7
WOODGLADE CT	3500	RKLN	95677	220-D5
WOOD GLEN CT	3400	RKLN	95677	200-E6
WOODGLEN CT	1100	RSVL	95661	240-B4
WOODGLEN DR	1000	RSVL	95661	240-B4
	1800	FOLS	95630	261-J7
	7600	SaCo	95628	279-H2
WOODGREEN CT	8300	SaCo	95843	238-G6
WOODGROVE LN	-	SAC	95823	337-G4
WOODGROVE WY	-	PlaC	95746	240-D1
	-	RSVL	95661	240-D1
WOODHALL WY	2800	ANT	94509	(513-B7 See Page 493)
WOODHAVEN AV	6000	SaCo	95608	279-D1
WOODHAVEN CIR	-	RSVL	95747	219-D1
WOODHAVEN PL	300	WSAC	95605	277-A7
	300	WSAC	95605	297-A1
WOODHAWK WY	-	SaCo	95843	259-A1
	4400	SaCo	95843	238-J7
	4400	SaCo	95843	239-A7
WOODHEAD ST	2100	FOLS	95630	262-B6
WOODHILL DR	1600	RSVL	95661	240-D3
WOODHILLS WY	6400	CITH	95621	259-E5
WOODHOLLOW WY	9700	RCCD	95827	299-C6
WOODHOUSE CT	-	RKLN	95765	200-D4
WOODHUE WY	3800	SaCo	95660	258-H7
WOODHURST CT	6500	CITH	95621	259-E4
WOODKIRK CT	11100	RCCD	95670	280-A7
	11100	RCCD	95670	279-J7
WOODKNOLL WY	7000	SaCo	95608	279-F2
WOODLAKE DR	400	SAC	95815	277-H7
WOODLAKE LN	200	PlaC	95658	181-C5
	900	RSVL	95661	240-B3
WOODLAKE HILLS DR	7100	CITH	95610	260-A4
	7100	CITH	95662	260-B4
	8100	SaCo	95662	260-B4
WOODLAND CT	-	EDCo	95667	266-C2
WOODLAND DR	1800	ANT	94509	(513-E5 See Page 493)
	4200	EDCo	95667	266-D2
WOODLAND LN	7600	SaCo	95628	279-H3
WOODLAND RD	200	PlaC	95603	162-F6
WOODLAND OAKS WY	1400	SAC	95833	277-C5
WOODLAWN DR	2100	RCCD	95670	279-H6
WOODLEAF CIR	-	RSVL	95747	219-D1
WOODLEAF DR	8100	SaCo	95628	260-B7
WOODLEIGH CT	3000	EDCo	95682	263-B4
WOODLEIGH DR	5400	SaCo	95608	259-D6
	5900	CITH	95608	259-D6
WOODLEIGH LN	2700	EDCo	95682	263-B3
WOOD LILY WY	-	ELKG	95757	357-H7
	-	ELKG	95757	377-H1
	-	ELKG	95757	397-H1
WOODLOCK WY	6800	CITH	95621	259-F5
WOODMAN CIR	1400	PLCR	95667	245-J4
WOODMAN LN	8100	PlaC	95658	181-E2
WOODMAN WY	8700	SaCo	95826	298-G6
WOODMAR DR	1900	EDCo	95762	242-C6
WOODMARK CT	3100	SaCo	95821	278-H5
WOODMERE RD	100	FOLS	95630	261-A7
	100	FOLS	95630	281-A1
WOOD MILL PL	8100	SaCo	95843	238-H6
WOODMINSTER CIR	-	SaCo	95662	260-J5
WOODMONT CT	4500	SaCo	95628	279-J2
WOODMORE DR	8300	SaCo	95662	260-C3
WOODMORE OAKS DR	7000	SaCo	95662	260-B2
	7000	CITH	95610	260-A2
	7000	CITH	95662	260-B2
WOODMOSS CT	4300	SaCo	95826	319-A2
WOOD OAK CT	1200	RSVL	95747	219-E5
WOODOAKS CT	6100	CITH	95621	259-E4
WOODPARK WY	6500	CITH	95621	259-E5
WOODPECKER CT	900	PLCR	95667	245-F4
WOODPOINTE CIR	3900	SaCo	95821	278-G3
WOOD RANCH RD	-	EDCo	95667	243-H2
WOODRICK WY	7000	SaCo	95842	259-C2
WOODRIDGE CT	2600	PLCR	95667	245-D4
	6400	CITH	95621	259-E5
WOODRIDGE RD	-	EDCo	95667	225-A6
WOODRIDGE WY	7600	PlaC	95746	241-D2
WOODRIDGE OAK WY	1500	SAC	95833	277-C5
WOODRING DR	-	SaCo	95655	320-A2
	100	SaCo	95655	319-H2
WOODRIVER CT	-	SAC	95831	336-J1
WOODROCK WY	8600	PlaC	95746	221-E5
WOODROSE CT	8200	SaCo	95828	338-D7
WOODROW WY	9200	ELKG	95758	357-G4
WOODRUFF WY	7300	CITH	95621	239-G6
WOODS CT	100	FOLS	95630	261-H4
WOODS DR	-	LMS	95650	220-J3
WOODS RD	11700	SaCo	95693	(380-C7 See Page 379)
WOODS CREEK CT	2100	SaCo	95670	280-D5
WOODSDALE CT	1400	PlaC	95663	180-G7
WOODS EDGE LN	8200	ELKG	95758	358-D6
WOODSHIRE WY	900	SAC	95822	316-J5
	1000	SAC	95822	317-A5
WOODSIDE DR	300	WSAC	95605	297-A1
	5700	RKLN	95677	220-D5
	6800	SaCo	95842	259-C2
	7300	CITH	95610	259-G3
	7300	CITH	95621	259-G3
WOODSIDE LN	-	EDCo	95667	225-A6
	2200	SaCo	95825	298-C4
WOODSIDE LN E	-	SaCo	95825	298-D4
WOODSIDE WY	600	PlaC	95663	162-J2
WOODSIDE GLEN WY	1200	SAC	95833	277-D5
WOODSIDE OAKS	500	SaCo	95825	298-D4
WOODSIDE SIERRA	600	SaCo	95825	298-D4
WOODSMAN CT	1800	EDCo	95667	244-D3
WOODSMAN LP	4600	EDCo	95667	244-D3
WOODSMAN RD	-	EDCo	95672	243-E1
WOODSMOKE WY	100	FOLS	95630	261-E6
WOODSON AV	4400	SaCo	95821	278-J4
E WOODSON RD	2300	SJCo	95220	439-H6
	3400	SJCo	95220	(440-A7 See Page 420)
WOOD SORREL WY	5200	SaCo	95843	239-B6
WOODSPICE WY	4100	RCCD	95742	300-D7
	4100	RCCD	95742	320-D1
WOODSPRING CT	-	PlaC	95746	240-F3
WOODSTOCK LN	6800	EDCo	95623	265-C5
WOODSTOCK WY	1900	SaCo	95825	298-D1
WOODSTONE PL	5300	SaCo	95843	239-B5
WOODSTREAM LN	2600	RKLN	95677	220-B5
WOODTHRUSH DR	4400	EDCo	95762	262-E5
WOOD THRUSH WY	4200	PlaC	95746	240-F2
WOODVALE WY	5200	SaCo	95608	279-B2
WOODVIEW CT	100	FOLS	95630	261-B2
WOODVIEW DR	100	FOLS	95630	261-B2
WOODVIEW ST	4400	SaCo	95608	279-F2
WOODVILLE LN	-	SaCo	95842	259-A1
WOOD VIOLET WY	2600	SAC	95822	337-E2
WOODWARD WY	8900	SaCo	95662	260-F4
WOODWELL CT	5200	SaCo	95843	239-B7
WOODWILLOW LN	-	ELKG	95758	357-G6
WOODWORTH AV	6300	SaCo	95608	279-E1
WOODWRIGHT WY	1100	SaCo	95673	257-J2
	1100	SaCo	95673	258-A2
WOODWYNN CT	5400	SaCo	95628	260-F6
WOODY CT	-	SAC	95831	336-H2
WOODYARD WY	8200	CITH	95621	239-E6
WOODY CREEK CT	2000	EDCo	95682	263-D3
WOOL ST	200	FOLS	95630	261-B5
WOOLLEY WY	1700	SAC	95815	278-B7
WOOLWICH CIR	100	SaCo	95655	319-H1
WORCESTER ST	-	SaCo	95742	281-C5
WORCESTER WY	4300	EDCo	95667	264-J3
	5100	ELKG	95758	357-H5
WORDSWORTH CT	300	RSVL	95747	219-C5
WORLINTON WY	-	RSVL	95747	218-H4
WORRELL RD	-	ANT	94509	(513-D7 See Page 493)
WORSHAM AV	2300	SAC	95822	317-D7
WORTELL DR	-	LNCN	95648	179-E1
WORTHINGTON CT	1000	ANT	94509	(513-F7 See Page 493)
WORTHINGTON DR	4100	SaCo	95660	258-J1
WOSIQUA LN	2300	PlaC	95650	200-J2
	2300	PlaC	95663	200-J2
WRANGLER CT	500	RSVL	95661	240-C3
WRANGLER DR	10200	ELKG	95624	359-E5
WRANGLER PL	2600	EDCo	95762	262-D1
WRANGLER RD	4200	EDCo	95619	265-D3
WREN CIR	8600	ELKG	95624	358-F4
WREN CT	200	GALT	95632	419-D6
	600	RSVL	95661	240-C4
	900	PLCR	95667	245-F4
	3500	EDCo	95709	246-H2
WREN DR	200	GALT	95632	419-D6
WREN LN	7800	CITH	95610	259-J6
WRENDALE WY	2600	SaCo	95821	278-J6
	2800	SaCo	95821	279-A6
	4600	SaCo	95608	279-A6
WRENFORD WY	4500	SaCo	95842	258-J1
	4500	SaCo	95842	259-A1
WRENTHAN ST	100	FOLS	95630	261-G5
WRENWOOD DR	7500	SAC	95823	337-G3
WREYFORD CT	4700	SaCo	95842	259-A1
WRIGHT RD	13700	PlaC	95602	162-E1
WRIGHT ST	1700	SaCo	95825	298-D1
WRIGLEY CIR	3700	SaCo	95660	258-G1
WRINGER DR	2500	RSVL	95661	240-E4
WRISTEN WY	800	GALT	95632	419-D7
WULFF LN	2400	SaCo	95821	278-D6
WUNSCHEL LN	4500	EDCo	95667	244-A5
WURTH CT	2400	SaCo	95825	298-D1
WYALONG WY	4000	SaCo	95826	318-H2
WYANDOTTE CT	-	ELKG	95624	358-D1
WYANT WY	1300	SaCo	95864	298-E2
WYATT CT	-	LNCN	95648	179-E3
	2700	RKLN	95765	200-E5
WYATT LN	6700	SaCo	95662	260-J3
WYATT RANCH WY	7800	SaCo	95829	339-D5
WYCKFORD BLVD	-	RKLN	95765	200-B5
WYCKFORD CT	2600	RKLN	95765	200-B5
WYCLIFFE WY	6100	SAC	95822	317-A5
WYCOMBE DR	3900	SaCo	95864	298-H4
WYDA WY	2000	SaCo	95825	298-C1
WYLAND DR	9600	ELKG	95624	359-A7
	9600	ELKG	95624	379-A1
WYLIE DR	-	ELKG	95758	357-G5
WYMAN DR	4400	SaCo	95821	278-J5
	4500	SaCo	95608	279-A5
	4500	SaCo	95821	279-A5
WYMARK DR	7900	ELKG	95758	358-C6
WYMORE WY	1200	ANT	94509	(513-H5 See Page 493)
	1200	CCCo	94509	(513-G5 See Page 493)
	5800	SAC	95822	317-B5
WYNDBROOK ST	100	SaCo	95828	338-F3
WYNDGATE RD	300	SaCo	95864	298-G5
WYNDHAM DR	6500	SAC	95823	338-B5
WYNDHAM LN	-	LNCN	95648	179-F7
WYNDHAM PL	1400	EDCo	95762	262-D3
WYNDHAM WY	1600	EDCo	95762	262-D3
WYNDHAM HILL	8000	PlaC	95746	240-G1
WYNDHAM HILL CT	5500	SaCo	95608	279-C7
WYNDHAM OAKS LN	5200	SaCo	95608	279-B7
WYNDRUSH WY	-	EDCo	95762	282-D3
WYNDVIEW WY	-	SAC	95834	256-G7
	-	SAC	95835	256-G7
WYNDWILLOW WY	-	ELKG	95758	358-D3
WYNDEL WY	7400	ELKG	95758	358-C5
WYNNEWOOD CT	6000	SAC	95823	358-A1
WYNNEWOOD WY	8300	SAC	95823	358-A1
WYTHE CT	4300	SaCo	95820	317-H4
X				
X ST	400	SAC	95818	297-B5
	2700	SAC	95817	297-F7
XANDRIA DR	1200	SAC	95838	278-A2
XAVIER CT	4700	SaCo	95841	279-A1
XAVIER LN	-	RSVL	95747	218-J6
Y				
Y ST	3100	SAC	95817	297-F7
YACABUCCI CT	-	SAC	95815	278-A6
YACHT CT	800	SAC	95822	316-J3
YAGER DR	100	FOLS	95630	261-F4
YAHI CT	-	SAC	95833	277-D4
YAKIMA RIVER CT	11000	RCCD	95670	279-J5
YALE CT	1600	PlaC	95603	162-D4
YALE DR	400	RSVL	95678	219-G3
YALE ST	-	RKLN	95765	200-B5
	1000	SAC	95818	297-C6
YAMASAKI WY	-	PlaC	95603	162-C4
YAMPA CIR	300	SAC	95838	277-G2
YANCEY DR	7900	PlaC	95603	161-D3
YANCY CT	5000	SaCo	95842	259-A5
YANKEE HILL RD	4100	RKLN	95677	200-F7
	4100	RKLN	95677	220-F1
YANKEE JOHN CT	6500	EDCo	95667	226-G2
YANKS STATION CT	-	RSVL	95747	219-B4
YANKTON ST	100	FOLS	95630	281-B2
YARDGATE WY	8200	CITH	95621	239-E6
YARDIS CT	-	SAC	95833	277-B4
YARDLEY PL	2800	EDCo	95762	242-C5
YARDLEY WY	8400	CITH	95621	239-E6
YARMOUTH CT	8800	ELKG	95624	358-G3
YARNELL WY	-	ELKG	95758	357-D5
YARROW CT	-	RKLN	95677	220-F5
	5000	SaCo	95628	260-H7
YARROW DR	-	EDCo	95726	267-G1
YARROW WY	-	RKLN	95677	220-F5
	7000	CITH	95610	260-B2
YARWOOD WY	2900	SAC	95833	277-B5
YAWL WY	5900	CITH	95621	259-D2
YDRA CT	5400	SaCo	95628	260-F6
YEAGER WY	7900	SaCo	95828	338-D5
YEARLING CT	12800	SaCo	95693	360-J6
YEARLING TR	-	EDCo	95619	286-A6
YEARLING WY	-	PlaC	95747	239-B4
YEATES CT	4400	RCCD	95742	320-E2
YEFIM WY	-	RSVL	95661	240-C5
YEGO ST	2100	PlaC	95663	201-C1
YELLOW ASTER CT	2000	SaCo	95670	280-B4
YELLOW BRICK RD	4200	EDCo	95682	264-D5
YELLOWBRICK RD	-	EDCo	95633	205-D6
YELLOW FLOWER PL	9100	SaCo	95628	280-G1
YELLOW HAMMER CT	3100	SaCo	95843	238-F7
YELLOW PINE DR	3800	EDCo	95672	263-G1
YELLOW PINE WY	5400	SaCo	95841	259-C6
YELLOW ROSE CT	8700	SaCo	95828	338-G4
YELLOWSTONE CT	-	RKLN	95765	219-H2
	1900	ANT	94509	(513-G5 See Page 493)
	3800	EDCo	95762	282-D1
YELLOWSTONE DR	1400	ANT	94509	(513-F5 See Page 493)
YELLOWSTONE LN	2900	SaCo	95821	278-D5
	3800	EDCo	95762	282-D1
YELLOWTAIL WY	8500	SaCo	95843	238-G5
YEOMAN DR	-	RSVL	95747	239-A1
YEOMAN WY	5800	CITH	95610	259-J5
YERBA CT	-	SAC	95833	277-E5
YERBA WY	1800	LNCN	95648	180-C7
	1800	LNCN	95648	200-D1
YERINGTON CT	-	LNCN	95648	180-A6
YERINGTON LN	-	LNCN	95648	180-A6
YERINGTON PL	-	LNCN	95648	180-A5
YERMO WY	8300	SaCo	95828	338-E6
YEW WOODS WY	-	EDCo	-	247-F2
YGNACIO DR	5300	SaCo	95842	259-B2
YOKOLI LN	7000	EDCo	95633	205-E4
YOLO ST	500	WSAC	95605	296-H1
YOLOY WY	4600	SaCo	95628	280-F1
YONDER HILL RD	6300	EDCo	95667	265-A2
YORBA LINDA CT	5400	SaCo	95843	239-C7
YORK CT	-	EDCo	95726	248-C1
	200	RSVL	95661	240-C4
	500	LNCN	95648	179-G4
YORK ST	500	SAC	95815	277-H7
YORK COVE WY	8100	SaCo	95828	338-G6
YORK GLEN WY	5900	SaCo	95842	259-A4
YORKSHIP CT	9200	ELKG	95758	357-F5
YORKSHIRE RD	2100	SaCo	95815	278-B7
YORKSHIRE WY	4700	PlaC	95746	240-G2
YORKTON WY	-	SaCo	95829	338-J7
YORKTOWN AV	2500	SaCo	95821	278-F6
	2500	SaCo	95825	278-F6
YORKTOWN PL	-	SaCo	95842	259-A1
YORKVILLE PL	5200	SaCo	95608	299-B3
YOSEMITE AV	4700	SaCo	95820	317-H3
YOSEMITE CT	-	LNCN	95648	179-J5
	-	RKLN	95765	219-H2
YOSEMITE DR	-	RVIS	94571	454-G5
	1400	ANT	94509	(513-F6 See Page 493)
YOSEMITE LN	-	LNCN	95648	179-J5
	800	EDCo	95762	262-C7
YOSEMITE PL	-	EDCo	95667	286-H2
YOSEMITE ST	-	RSVL	95678	239-J1
	400	RSVL	95678	219-J7
YOSEMITE PARK WY	-	ELKG	95758	357-F5
YOST CT	100	FOLS	95630	261-G3
YOTON CT	400	RSVL	95661	240-A5
YOU BET CT	-	EDCo	-	247-C7
YOU BET PL	1200	AUB	95603	182-C6
YOUNG CT	-	GALT	95632	419-E2
YOUNG ST	5100	SaCo	95824	317-J4
	5100	SAC	95824	317-J4
YOUNG WY	600	RSVL	95678	220-A7
YOUNGER WY	4200	SaCo	95608	279-C2
YOUNGER CREEK DR	8500	SAC	95828	318-F5
YOUNGHEART LN	-	SaCo	95628	280-A1
YOUNG OAK CT	6500	SaCo	95662	260-D3
YOUNGS AV	1300	SAC	95838	278-A2
YOUNGS CT	3000	EDCo	95762	262-C3
YOUNGS WY	-	EDCo	95667	266-G4
YOUNGSTOWN AV	-	SaCo	95742	281-C6
YOUNGSTOWN LN	2900	SaCo	95821	278-D5
YOUNG WO CIR	-	FOLS	95630	261-A5
YOUNT CT	9100	ELKG	95624	358-H6
YOUTH CENTER CT	-	SaCo	95827	319-B2
YREKA AV	2500	SAC	95822	337-E1
YUBA CT	4900	SaCo	95841	279-C1
YUBA CANAL DR	-	SaCo	95670	280-D5
YUBA RIVER CIR	-	SAC	95831	336-G1
YUCCA WY	4800	SaCo	95660	278-H1
	4900	SaCo	95660	258-H7
YUCATAN AV	6200	CITH	95841	259-D4
	6200	SaCo	95841	259-D4
YUHRE CT	9000	ELKG	95758	357-H4
YUKON CT	7100	SaCo	95673	257-H1
YUKON RIVER WY	10000	RCCD	95670	279-H5
YUMA CIR	2600	SaCo	95827	299-A5
YUMA CT	2700	EDCo	95682	263-D3
YURA WY	100	RSVL	95661	240-D5
YUROK PL	-	WSAC	95691	316-H1
YVETTE WY	5300	SaCo	95823	337-J6
YVONNE WY	4900	SAC	95823	337-J6
	8300	SaCo	95628	260-C7
Z				
ZACCORO WY	-	ELKG	95758	357-G3
ZACHARY CT	100	RSVL	95747	219-D6
ZACHARY WY	4500	SaCo	95842	258-J6
ZACHIS WY	8300	SaCo	95843	239-A5
ZACHMAN WY	2700	SaCo	95608	279-C6
ZAGOS CT	2400	RCCD	95670	299-H1
ZALEMA CT	-	SAC	95834	276-H4
ZALEMA WY	-	SAC	95834	276-H4
ZAMBRA WY	9300	SaCo	95826	299-A7
ZAMORA DR	6300	EDCo	95667	265-C2
ZAMZOW CT	400	RSVL	95747	219-C5
ZANCADA CT	7300	SaCo	95683	342-C2
ZANCANARO CT	8300	CITH	95610	260-C1
ZANDONNELLA RD	1200	EDCo	95619	265-H3
ZANE GREY DR	-	RSVL	95747	219-E6
ZANETTA CT	100	FOLS	95630	261-F3
ZAPATA DR	1500	EDCo	95762	242-B4
ZARAHEMLA RD	5600	EDCo	95667	264-G1
ZARTOP ST	100	OAKL	94561	(514-C6 See Page 493)
ZEBRA CT	4400	EDCo	95630	222-J1
ZEELAND DR	6900	CITH	95621	259-F1
ZELDA WY	1500	SAC	95822	317-B5
ZELINDA DR	7100	SaCo	95608	279-G1
	7100	SaCo	95628	279-G1
ZELLER CT	4100	EDCo	95619	265-F3
ZELLER PL	-	SAC	95835	256-G5
ZELLERBACH DR	-	SaCo	95670	280-C4
ZENITH DR	7800	CITH	95621	239-E7
ZENOBIA WY	3300	SAC	95833	277-E4
	3300	SAC	95834	277-E4
ZEPHYR CT	1000	RSVL	95678	239-F2
ZEPHYR CV	-	RKLN	95677	220-B3
ZEPHYR WY	4100	SaCo	95821	278-H2
ZEPHYR COVE CIR	-	SAC	95831	336-G1
ZEPHYR CREEK CT	8300	CITH	95610	240-B6
ZEPHYR HILLS WY	7600	SaCo	95843	238-H7
	7600	SaCo	95843	258-H1
ZEPHYR RANCH DR	300	SAC	95831	336-F1
ZERLANG CT	-	FOLS	95630	261-H4
ZET CT	-	SAC	95824	318-C6
ZEUS CT	9900	RCCD	95827	299-D6
ZEUS LN	-	RSVL	95661	240-F1
ZIA RD	1700	EDCo	95667	245-C1
ZIANA RD	3800	EDCo	95682	263-B6
ZIBIBBA WY	10500	RCCD	95670	299-G1
ZIEBELL CT	7700	CITH	95610	240-B7
	7700	CITH	95610	260-B1
ZIEGLER CT	8400	CITH	95610	240-C7
ZIEN CT	1900	RSVL	95661	240-A3
ZIGGY RD	4200	EDCo	95619	265-G3
ZIG ZAG LN	-	EDCo	-	247-C7
ZIMMERMAN CT	5700	SaCo	95628	260-D5
ZINC DR	3000	EDCo	95726	248-D2
ZINFANDEL CT	1300	RSVL	95747	239-E2
ZINFANDEL DR	-	RCCD	95670	300-A5
	100	RCCD	95670	280-A6
	900	RCCD	95670	279-H7
	1200	RSVL	95747	239-F2
	2300	RCCD	95670	299-H3
	4300	OAKL	94561	(514-D7 See Page 493)
ZINNIA RD	-	EDCo	95726	267-J1
ZINNIA WY	1400	RSVL	95747	219-C4
	8500	ELKG	95624	358-F1
ZION CT	5800	RKLN	95677	220-C4
ZION WY	9900	RCCD	95827	299-D6
ZIRCON CT	4300	ELKG	95758	357-G6
ZIRCON DR	-	EDCo	95726	248-C2
	3300	RKLN	95677	220-B4
ZIRCON CREST CT	8600	ELKG	95624	358-F5
ZIRONE WY	10900	RCCD	95670	299-J5
ZITTLE DR	2200	FOLS	95630	282-B1
ZLATA CT	-	SaCo	95828	338-C4
Z LINE RD	35000	YoCo	95612	356-A4
	35000	YoCo	95612	375-H1
	35000	YoCo	95612	(395-F1 See Page 375)
ZODIAC CT	10000	RCCD	95827	299-D6
ZOE ANN DR	500	LNCN	95648	179-F3
ZOLA AV	100	RSVL	95678	239-J2
	300	RSVL	95678	240-A1
ZOLLER CT	-	ELKG	95757	357-J7
ZOOLANDER CT	-	SAC	95822	317-B6
	-	SAC	95831	317-B6
ZOOT ALLURES RD	2500	EDCo	95667	246-B2
ZORAM CT	5600	SaCo	95841	259-C7
ZORINA WY	3300	SaCo	95826	299-A7
ZUBE CT	4800	SaCo	95608	279-A4
ZUEGER CT	10700	RCCD	95670	279-H6
ZUIDER ZEE CIR	2500	SaCo	95626	238-D6
ZUMWALT AV	8700	SaCo	95662	260-E3
ZURLO WY	1700	SAC	95835	257-B3
#				
1 PK	-	SaCo	95683	322-C7
	-	SaCo	95683	342-C1
1ST AV	400	SAC	95818	297-B6
	1200	SaCo	95690	(416-J7 See Page 415)
	1200	SaCo	95690	417-A7
	2600	SAC	95817	297-E7
	6000	SAC	95817	318-A1
	9500	ELKG	95624	358-H6
1ST ST	-	PlaC	95648	179-E3
	100	ISLE	95641	455-H5
	100	ISLE	95690	455-H5
	200	LNCN	95648	179-E3
	500	GALT	95632	439-E1
	500	GALT	95632	419-E7
	700	ANT	94509	(513-C3 See Page 493)
	2800	PlaC	95603	162-A3
	3300	WSAC	95691	296-F3
2 PK	-	SaCo	95683	342-C1
2ND AV	1100	SaCo	95690	(416-J7 See Page 415)
	1100	SaCo	95690	417-A7
	1100	SAC	95818	297-C6
	1100	SaCo	95690	437-A1
	2800	SAC	95817	297-F7
	3700	SAC	95817	317-G1
	5800	SAC	95817	318-A1
	8500	CITH	95621	239-F5
	8900	ELKG	95624	358-G6
2ND CT	1100	ANT	94509	(513-C3 See Page 493)
2ND ST	-	RVIS	94571	454-H6
	100	GALT	95632	419-E7
	100	ISLE	95641	455-H5
	100	WSAC	95605	297-B2
	100	OAKL	94561	(514-E6 See Page 493)
	100	RSVL	95678	239-H2
	300	ANT	94509	(513-C3 See Page 493)
	400	LNCN	95648	179-G3
	500	PlaC	95658	181-G6
	900	SAC	95814	297-B3
	2700	PlaC	95603	162-A4
	4100	EDCo	95709	247-B4
	4800	RKLN	95677	220-E2
	4900	SaCo	95660	258-G7
	5600	SaCo	95673	257-G2
	5600	SaCo	95838	257-G5
	7100	SaCo	95673	237-G7
W 2ND ST	5800	SaCo	95673	257-G2
	5800	SaCo	95838	257-G5
	7500	SaCo	95673	237-G7
3 PK	-	SaCo	95683	342-C1
3RD AV	-	ELKG	95624	358-H6
	-	ISLE	95641	455-G5
	-	SaCo	95690	(416-J7 See Page 415)
	-	SaCo	95690	436-J1
	-	SaCo	95690	437-A1
	600	SAC	95818	297-B7
	2700	SAC	95817	297-E7
	3500	SAC	95817	317-G1
	6000	SAC	95817	318-A1
3RD ST	-	PlaC	95648	179-D3
	-	PlaC	95658	181-G5
	-	SaCo	95639	(376-J5 See Page 375)
	-	GALT	95632	419-E7
	100	WSAC	95605	297-B3
	100	RSVL	95678	239-H3
	100	RVIS	94571	454-H6
	200	OAKL	94561	(514-E6 See Page 493)

STREET Block	City	ZIP	Pg-Grid
3RD ST			
200	ANT	94509	(513-C4
	See Page		493)
400	ISLE	95641	455-H5
400	LNCN	95648	179-D3
500	GALT	95632	439-E1
800	WSAC	95691	297-B3
900	SAC	95814	297-B5
1900	SAC	95818	297-A6
2700	PlaC	95603	162-A4
4100	EDCo	95709	247-B4
4600	RKLN	95677	220-E2
5000	SaCo	95660	258-G7
N 3RD ST			
400	SAC	95814	297-C1
4TH AV			
-	ISLE	95641	455-G5
-	SaCo	95690	436-J1
-	SaCo	95690	437-A1
500	SAC	95818	297-B7
2700	SAC	95817	297-F7
3200	SAC	95817	317-F1
5900	SAC	95817	318-A1
6500	SAC	95820	318-B1
6600	SaCo	95673	257-H3
4TH ST			
-	SaCo	95639	377-A4
-	SaCo	95639	397-A4
-	RVIS	94571	454-H6
100	GALT	95632	419-E7
100	RSVL	95678	239-G3
100	WSAC	95605	297-B2
[illegible]			
	See Page		493)
200	ISLE	95641	455-H5
600	GALT	95632	439-E1
800	LNCN	95648	179-F3
1000	SAC	95814	297-C3
1900	SAC	95818	297-B5
5000	SaCo	95660	258-G7
5000	RKLN	95677	220-D3
5600	SaCo	95673	257-H5
W 4TH ST			
100	ANT	94509	(513-B4
	See Page		493)
5700	SaCo	95673	257-F2
5700	SaCo	95838	257-F5
7100	SaCo	95673	237-F7
5 PK			
-	SaCo	95683	342-D1
5 MILE RD			
2900	EDCo	95667	246-G4
2900	EDCo	95709	246-G4
5TH AV			
500	SAC	95818	297-B7
1700	SAC	95818	317-D1
2700	SAC	95817	317-E1
6600	SaCo	95673	257-H1
5TH ST			
-	ISLE	95641	455-H5
-	SaCo	95639	377-A5
-	SaCo	95639	397-A5
-	WSAC	95691	297-A4
-	RVIS	94571	454-H5
-	WSAC	95605	297-A4
100	GALT	95632	419-E7
100	RSVL	95678	239-G3
200	LNCN	95648	179-E3
200	ANT	94509	(513-B4
	See Page		493)
400	OAKL	94561	(514-F6
	See Page		493)
600	SAC	95814	297-A4
1900	SAC	95818	297-B5
4500	RKLN	95677	220-D3
4900	SaCo	95838	257-H7
5000	SaCo	95660	258-G7
6600	SaCo	95673	257-H3
E 5TH ST			
1200	LNCN	95648	179-J3
1200	PlaC	95648	179-J3
N 5TH ST			
200	SAC	95814	297-C1
6TH AV			
500	SAC	95818	297-B7
2100	SAC	95818	317-D1
2600	SAC	95817	317-F1
4400	SAC	95820	317-H1
6600	SaCo	95673	257-H3
6TH ST			
-	SaCo	95639	377-A5
-	SaCo	95639	397-A5
-	ANT	94509	(513-B4
	See Page		493)
-	LNCN	95648	179-F3
-	RVIS	94571	454-H5
-	WSAC	95605	297-A2
100	ISLE	95641	455-H5
100	RSVL	95678	239-G3
100	GALT	95632	419-F7
800	SAC	95814	297-C3
1900	SAC	95818	297-B5
5000	SaCo	95660	258-G7
6400	SaCo	95673	257-H1
7400	SaCo	95673	237-H7
E 6TH ST			
100	LNCN	95648	179-J3
W 6TH ST			
5600	SaCo	95673	257-F1
5600	SaCo	95838	257-F5
7300	SaCo	95673	237-F7
7 PK			
-	SaCo	95683	322-B7
-	SaCo	95683	342-B1
7TH AV			
700	SAC	95818	297-B7
700	SAC	95818	317-B1
2600	SAC	95817	317-F1
4400	SAC	95820	317-H1
5800	SAC	95820	318-A1
6700	SaCo	95673	257-J2
7TH ST			
-	ANT	94509	(513-B4
	See Page		493)
-	LNCN	95648	179-J3
-	RVIS	94571	454-G5
100	GALT	95632	419-F7
400	OAKL	94561	(514-F7
	See Page		493)
400	SAC	95814	297-C3
1900	SAC	95818	297-C5
5000	SaCo	95660	258-G7
6600	SaCo	95673	257-H1
E 7TH ST			
200	LNCN	95648	179-J3
N 7TH ST			
200	SAC	95814	297-D2
8 PK			
6900	SaCo	95683	342-B1
8TH AV			
700	SAC	95818	317-B1
3000	SAC	95817	317-E1
4300	SAC	95820	317-H1
5700	SAC	95820	318-A1
6800	SaCo	95673	257-J2
8TH ST			
-	SaCo	95639	377-A5
-	SaCo	95639	397-A5
-	ANT	94509	(513-B4
	See Page		493)
-	LNCN	95648	179-G2
-	WSAC	95605	297-A2
400	SAC	95814	297-C3
1900	SAC	95818	297-C5
6700	SaCo	95673	257-J1
7300	SaCo	95673	237-J7
7900	SaCo	95626	237-J6
E 8TH ST			
100	LNCN	95648	179-J2
200	PlaC	95648	179-J2
9TH AV			
800	SAC	95818	317-B1
2600	SAC	95817	317-F2
4500	SAC	95820	317-H2
5800	SAC	95820	318-A2
6800	SaCo	95673	257-J2
9TH ST			
-	LNCN	95648	179-G2
200	ANT	94509	(513-B4
	See Page		493)
600	SAC	95814	297-C4
[illegible]			
6800	SaCo	95673	257-J2
7800	SaCo	95626	237-J7
7800	SaCo	95673	237-J7
E 9TH ST			
100	LNCN	95648	179-J2
500	PlaC	95648	179-J2
700	LNCN	95648	180-A2
700	PlaC	95648	180-A2
10TH AV			
800	SAC	95818	317-B1
2800	SAC	95817	317-E2
4400	SAC	95820	317-H2
10TH ST			
-	ANT	94509	(513-B4
	See Page		493)
100	LNCN	95648	179-J2
100	WSAC	95691	296-J4
400	SAC	95814	297-C4
700	LNCN	95648	180-A2
1100	CCCo	94509	(513-C4
	See Page		493)
1100	SaCo	95673	257-J2
1100	SaCo	95673	258-A3
1900	SAC	95818	297-C5
7400	SaCo	95673	237-J7
7600	SaCo	95626	237-J7
N 10TH ST			
200	SAC	95814	297-D2
11TH AV			
900	SAC	95818	317-B1
900	SAC	95822	317-B1
2900	SAC	95817	317-E2
4300	SAC	95820	317-H2
5800	SAC	95820	318-A2
11TH ST			
100	LNCN	95648	179-J2
200	WSAC	95691	296-J4
300	SAC	95814	297-E1
400	ANT	94509	(513-C4
	See Page		493)
1900	SAC	95818	297-C5
3300	SAC	95818	317-B1
N 11TH ST			
300	SAC	95814	297-D2
12TH AV			
-	SAC	95822	317-B1
1500	SAC	95818	317-C1
2900	SAC	95820	317-F2
5800	SAC	95820	318-A2
12TH ST			
100	LNCN	95648	179-J2
300	WSAC	95691	297-D4
400	ANT	94509	(513-C4
	See Page		493)
1900	SAC	95818	297-C5
3800	SAC	95822	317-B2
E 12TH ST			
100	LNCN	95648	179-J2
N 12TH ST			
400	SAC	95814	297-E2
13TH AV			
-	SAC	95818	317-C1
1100	SAC	95822	317-B1
2900	SAC	95820	317-E2
5800	SAC	95820	318-A2
13TH ST			
-	WSAC	95691	296-J5
200	SAC	95814	297-D3
300	ANT	94509	(513-C5
	See Page		493)
1900	SAC	95818	297-C6
3300	SAC	95818	317-B1
3500	SAC	95822	317-B2
6100	SAC	95831	317-A7
6700	SAC	95831	337-A1
E 13TH ST			
-	ANT	94509	(513-E4
	See Page		493)
14TH AV			
1100	SAC	95822	317-B2
2800	SAC	95820	317-E2
4000	SaCo	95820	317-G2
5800	SAC	95820	318-A2
7800	SAC	95828	318-C1
14TH AV N			
2400	SAC	95822	317-D2
14TH ST			
200	SAC	95814	297-D3
1900	SAC	95818	297-C6
5800	SAC	95822	317-B5
6200	SAC	95831	317-B7
6400	SaCo	95673	258-A1
7300	SaCo	95673	238-A7
E 14TH ST			
100	SAC	95814	297-E2
400	ANT	94509	(513-E5
	See Page		493)
W 14TH ST			
500	ANT	94509	(513-C5
	See Page		493)
15TH AV			
2000	SAC	95822	317-B2
2700	SAC	95820	317-E2
4100	SaCo	95820	317-G2
5800	SAC	95820	318-A2
15TH ST			
300	SAC	95814	297-E3
400	WSAC	95691	296-J5
500	ANT	94509	(513-C5
	See Page		493)
1300	WSAC	95691	297-D5
1900	SAC	95818	297-D5
7200	SAC	95822	337-B2
E 15TH ST			
-	ANT	94509	(513-D5
	See Page		493)
W 15TH ST			
-	ANT	94509	(513-D5
	See Page		493)
16TH AV			
2000	SAC	95822	317-C2
2700	SAC	95820	317-E2
4000	SaCo	95820	317-G2
6000	SAC	95820	318-A2
16TH ST			
-	ANT	94509	(513-C5
	See Page		493)
-	WSAC	95691	296-H5
100	SAC	95814	297-D6
1600	SaCo	95626	238-B5
1600	SaCo	95673	238-B7
1900	SAC	95818	297-D6
2200	SaCo	95673	258-B1
3100	SAC	95818	317-C1
5700	SaCo	95838	258-B5
7000	SAC	95822	337-C1
7300	PlaC	95626	238-D5
[illegible]			
-	ANT	94509	(513-D5
	See Page		493)
N 16TH ST			
100	SAC	95814	297-E2
17TH AV			
2000	SAC	95822	317-C2
2700	SAC	95820	317-E2
4700	SaCo	95820	317-H3
5800	SAC	95820	318-A3
17TH ST			
-	ANT	94509	(513-C5
	See Page		493)
-	WSAC	95691	296-H5
300	SAC	95814	297-E3
1900	SAC	95818	297-D6
3000	SAC	95818	317-C1
3700	SAC	95818	317-C1
7100	SAC	95822	337-C1
E 17TH ST			
-	SAC	95814	297-E2
18TH AV			
2000	SAC	95822	317-D3
2400	SAC	95820	317-E3
4000	SaCo	95820	317-G3
5900	SAC	95820	318-A3
8000	SAC	95826	318-C3
18TH ST			
100	WSAC	95691	296-H5
200	SAC	95814	297-E3
1900	SAC	95818	297-D6
3500	SAC	95818	317-C2
3600	SAC	95822	317-C2
6400	SaCo	95673	258-B1
7400	SAC	95822	337-C3
7500	SaCo	95673	238-B7
7600	SAC	95832	337-C4
E 18TH ST			
-	ANT	94509	(513-D5
	See Page		493)
1400	CCCo	94509	(513-G5
	See Page		493)
3200	ANT	94509	(514-A5
	See Page		493)
W 18TH ST			
-	ANT	94509	(513-A4
	See Page		493)
19TH AV			
2100	SAC	95822	317-D3
2500	SAC	95820	317-E3
5800	SAC	95820	318-A3
8000	SAC	95826	318-C3
19TH ST			
-	WSAC	95691	296-H5
300	SAC	95814	297-E4
1900	SAC	95818	297-D6
2900	SAC	95818	317-D1
3600	SAC	95822	317-D1
7300	SAC	95822	337-C2
7600	SAC	95832	337-C4
E 19TH ST			
-	ANT	94509	(513-D5
	See Page		493)
S 19TH ST			
3700	SAC	95822	317-C2
W 19TH ST			
100	ANT	94509	(513-C5
	See Page		493)
20TH AV			
2000	SAC	95822	317-D3
3100	SAC	95820	317-F3
4000	SaCo	95820	317-G3
5800	SAC	95820	318-A3
8000	SAC	95826	318-C3
20TH ST			
-	SaCo	95673	238-C7
200	SAC	95814	297-E4
1700	SaCo	95838	258-C7
1900	SAC	95818	297-D6
5600	SaCo	95673	258-C1
5600	SaCo	95838	258-C3
7000	SAC	95822	337-D1
W 20TH ST			
-	ANT	94509	(513-C5
	See Page		493)
21ST AV			
2500	SAC	95820	317-E3
4400	SAC	95820	318-B3
8100	SAC	95826	318-D3
21ST ST			
200	SAC	95816	297-E4
1900	SAC	95818	297-D7
4000	SAC	95822	317-D3
6700	SAC	95822	337-D1
7400	SAC	95832	337-C3
22ND AV			
2100	SAC	95822	317-D3
3100	SAC	95820	317-F3
3800	SAC	95820	317-G3
22ND ST			
200	SAC	95816	297-E5
1900	SAC	95818	297-E6
2900	SAC	95818	317-D2
4000	SAC	95822	317-D2
5900	SaCo	95673	258-C2
7300	SAC	95822	337-D2
7600	SAC	95832	337-D4
23RD AV			
-	SAC	95826	318-F3
2100	SAC	95822	317-D3
2500	SAC	95820	317-E3
3800	SaCo	95820	317-G3
23RD ST			
200	SAC	95816	297-E5
1900	SAC	95818	297-E6
2900	SAC	95818	317-D2
4000	SAC	95822	317-D3
6800	SAC	95822	337-D1
7600	SAC	95832	337-D3
24TH AV			
2200	SAC	95822	317-D3
2500	SAC	95820	317-E3
8300	SAC	95826	318-E4
24TH ST			
200	SAC	95816	297-E4
1900	SAC	95818	297-E6
2900	SAC	95818	317-E1
3600	SAC	95820	317-E1
3900	SAC	95822	317-E5
5800	SaCo	95673	258-D2
6900	SAC	95822	337-E1
7500	SAC	95832	337-E3
24TH STREET BYPS			
7300	SAC	95822	337-D2
25TH AV			
1100	SAC	95822	317-A3
2600	SAC	95820	317-E3
4300	SaCo	95820	317-F3
5000	SAC	95820	318-A4
[illegible]			
200	SAC	95816	297-E5
1900	SAC	95818	297-E6
2900	SAC	95818	317-E1
5100	SAC	95822	317-E4
6700	SAC	95822	337-E1
7600	SAC	95832	337-E4
26TH AV			
1100	SAC	95822	317-A3
2500	SAC	95820	317-E4
3900	SaCo	95820	317-G4
6000	SAC	95820	318-A4
26TH ST			
200	SAC	95816	297-F4
1900	SAC	95818	297-E6
2500	SAC	95820	317-E4
2900	SAC	95818	317-E1
5700	SaCo	95673	258-D2
5900	SAC	95822	317-E5
5900	SaCo	95652	258-D2
26TH WY			
4900	SAC	95820	317-E4
27TH AV			
1100	SAC	95822	317-A4
3200	SAC	95820	317-F4
5800	SAC	95820	318-A4
27TH ST			
200	SAC	95816	297-F5
1900	SAC	95818	297-E6
2900	SAC	95818	317-E1
6100	SAC	95822	317-E6
6900	SAC	95822	337-E1
28TH AV			
1100	SAC	95822	317-A3
3400	SAC	95820	317-F4
4300	SaCo	95820	317-H4
6200	SAC	95820	318-A4
28TH ST			
100	SAC	95816	297-F4
1900	SAC	95817	297-F6
2100	SAC	95818	297-F6
3900	SAC	95820	317-E2
5200	SAC	95824	317-E4
6600	SaCo	95652	258-E3
6700	SaCo	95660	258-E2
7600	SaCo	95843	238-E7
7600	SaCo	95843	258-E2
29TH AV			
2700	SAC	95820	317-E4
29TH ST			
200	SAC	95816	297-F6
1900	SAC	95817	297-F6
2100	SAC	95818	297-F6
7200	SAC	95822	337-E2
7500	SAC	95832	337-E2
30TH ST			
-	SaCo	95652	258-E4
200	SAC	95816	297-F5
1900	SAC	95817	297-E7
2700	SAC	95822	317-E7
3700	SAC	95820	317-F2
7000	SaCo	95660	258-E2
31ST ST			
2900	SAC	95817	297-E7
2900	SAC	95817	317-F2
32ND AV			
1400	SAC	95822	317-B4
2700	SAC	95824	317-E4
3800	SaCo	95824	317-F4
5900	SAC	95824	318-C4
32ND ST			
200	SAC	95816	297-G4
1900	SAC	95817	297-F7
2900	SAC	95817	317-F1
3700	SAC	95820	317-F2
5800	SaCo	95652	258-F5
6000	SaCo	95660	258-F2
7400	SAC	95822	337-F3
7500	SaCo	95843	238-F7
7500	SaCo	95843	258-F2
33RD AV			
2400	SAC	95822	317-E4
2700	SAC	95824	317-E4
3400	SaCo	95824	317-H4
3000	SAC	95824	318-A4
33RD ST			
100	SAC	95816	297-G4
2100	SAC	95817	297-F6
2800	SAC	95817	317-F1
3600	SAC	95820	317-F2
34TH AV			
1100	SAC	95822	317-A4
2700	SAC	95824	317-J4
3900	SaCo	95824	317-G5
5600	SAC	95824	318-A4
34TH ST			
300	SAC	95816	297-G4
1900	SAC	95817	297-F7
2800	SAC	95817	317-F1
3600	SAC	95820	317-F3
5500	SAC	95824	317-F4
6000	SaCo	95660	258-F2
35TH AV			
900	SAC	95822	316-J4
900	SAC	95822	317-A4
2700	SAC	95824	317-J4
3800	SaCo	95824	317-G5
5600	SAC	95824	318-A4
35TH ST			
300	SAC	95816	297-G4
1900	SAC	95817	297-G6
2800	SAC	95817	317-F1
3500	SAC	95820	317-F2
5600	SAC	95824	317-F4
5600	SaCo	95824	317-F4
36TH AV			
2400	SAC	95822	317-E5
2800	SAC	95824	317-E5
4900	SaCo	95824	317-H5
5500	SAC	95824	318-A5
36TH ST			
300	SAC	95816	297-H4
2000	SAC	95817	297-F7
2700	SAC	95817	317-F1
3400	SAC	95820	317-F2
36TH WY			
200	SAC	95819	297-H4
300	SAC	95816	297-H4
37TH AV			
2400	SAC	95822	317-E5
2800	SAC	95824	317-E5
3900	SaCo	95824	317-G5
5500	SAC	95824	318-A5
8800	SAC	95828	318-G5
37TH ST			
300	SAC	95816	297-H4
1900	SAC	95817	297-G7
2700	SAC	95817	317-F1
[illegible]			
6000	SaCo	95824	317-F6
38TH AV			
1400	SAC	95822	317-B5
2700	SAC	95824	317-E5
4100	SaCo	95824	317-G5
5500	SAC	95824	318-A5
38TH ST			
400	SAC	95816	297-G5
2800	SAC	95817	317-F1
3400	SAC	95820	317-F2
39TH AV			
2400	SAC	95822	317-E5
3900	SaCo	95824	317-G5
5500	SaCo	95824	317-G5
5500	SAC	95824	318-A5
39TH ST			
200	SAC	95819	297-H4
200	SAC	95816	297-H5
1900	SAC	95817	297-G7
2700	SAC	95817	317-G1
3700	SAC	95820	317-G2
5700	SaCo	95824	317-G5
40TH AV			
1200	SAC	95822	317-A5
3700	SaCo	95824	317-F5
5500	SAC	95824	317-H5
5500	SAC	95824	318-A5
40TH ST			
100	SAC	95819	297-H4
500	SAC	95816	297-H5
3000	SAC	95817	317-G2
3500	SAC	95820	317-G2
5800	SaCo	95824	317-G5
41ST AV			
1200	SAC	95822	317-A5
3500	SaCo	95824	317-F5
41ST ST			
-	SAC	95819	297-H5
2400	SAC	95817	297-G7
2400	SAC	95817	317-G1
3900	SAC	95820	317-G2
5800	SaCo	95824	317-G6
42ND AV			
1200	SAC	95822	317-A5
3600	SaCo	95824	317-F6
42ND ST			
400	SAC	95819	297-H5
1900	SAC	95817	297-G7
2700	SAC	95817	317-G2
3600	SAC	95820	317-G2
3900	SaCo	95820	317-G4
5600	SaCo	95824	317-G5
6600	SaCo	95823	317-G7
43RD AV			
900	SAC	95831	316-J5
900	SAC	95822	316-J5
900	SAC	95822	317-A5
3600	SaCo	95824	317-F6
7700	SAC	95824	318-C6
8800	SAC	95828	318-H6
8800	SAC	95829	318-H6
43RD ST			
-	SAC	95819	297-J4
2600	SAC	95817	297-G7
2600	SAC	95817	317-G2
3500	SAC	95820	317-G2
3900	SaCo	95820	317-G3
5800	SaCo	95824	317-G5
44TH AV			
3600	SaCo	95824	317-F6
44TH ST			
100	SAC	95819	297-J4
2900	SAC	95817	317-H2
3000	SAC	95820	317-H2
3900	SaCo	95820	317-H3
5500	SaCo	95824	317-H5
6300	SaCo	95823	317-H7
45TH AV			
2400	SAC	95822	317-E6
3600	SaCo	95824	317-F6
45TH ST			
-	SAC	95819	297-J5
1800	SAC	95817	297-H7
3300	SAC	95820	317-H2
3900	SaCo	95820	317-H2
4400	SAC	95817	317-H1
6200	SaCo	95823	317-H6
6200	SaCo	95824	317-H6
46TH AV			
3600	SaCo	95824	317-F6
46TH ST			
-	SAC	95819	297-J4
1800	SAC	95817	297-H7
3700	SAC	95820	317-H2
3900	SaCo	95820	317-H2
6400	SaCo	95823	317-H7
47TH AV			
1200	SAC	95831	317-B6
1400	SAC	95822	317-B6
2700	SAC	95823	317-E6
3100	SaCo	95823	317-E6
5800	SaCo	95823	318-A6
5800	SaCo	95823	318-A6
47TH ST			
600	SAC	95819	297-J5
1900	SAC	95817	297-H7
3700	SAC	95820	317-H2
4000	SaCo	95820	317-H3
6600	SaCo	95823	317-H6
48TH AV			
2000	SAC	95822	317-E6
3700	SaCo	95823	317-J6
6100	SAC	95828	318-A6
48TH ST			
600	SAC	95819	297-J6
1900	SAC	95817	297-H7
2400	SAC	95817	317-H3
4300	SaCo	95820	317-H3
4700	SAC	95820	317-H3
5000	SAC	95824	317-H3
49ER TR			
3900	EDCo	95667	246-A7
49TH AV			
2400	SAC	95822	317-E6
3800	SaCo	95823	317-G7
49TH ST			
-	SAC	95819	297-J5
-	SAC	95819	298-A4
2200	SAC	95817	297-H7
2300	SAC	95817	317-H1
2600	SAC	95820	317-H3
4400	SaCo	95820	317-H3
5000	SAC	95824	317-H3
5600	SaCo	95824	317-J4
50TH AV			
2100	SAC	95822	317-D7
4700	SaCo	95823	317-H7
[illegible]			
50TH ST			
-	SAC	95819	298-A4
600	SAC	95819	297-J5
2200	SAC	95817	297-J7
2900	SAC	95817	317-H1
2900	SAC	95820	317-H2
6600	SaCo	95823	317-H7
51ST AV			
2000	SAC	95822	317-D7
3500	SaCo	95823	317-F7
7500	SAC	95828	318-C7
51ST ST			
-	SAC	95819	298-A4
600	SAC	95819	297-J5
2000	SAC	95817	297-J7
2500	SAC	95817	317-J1
4000	SAC	95820	317-H3
6600	SaCo	95823	317-J7
52ND AV			
2300	SAC	95822	317-D7
3000	SaCo	95823	317-F7
3000	SaCo	95823	317-F7
7500	SAC	95828	318-C7
52ND ST			
-	SAC	95819	298-A4
600	SAC	95819	297-J5
2300	SAC	95817	297-J7
2300	SAC	95817	317-J1
3400	SAC	95820	317-J2
6700	SaCo	95823	317-J7
53RD AV			
2000	SAC	95822	317-D7
5000	SaCo	95823	317-J7
6500	SaCo	95828	318-B7
7000	SAC	95828	318-C7
53RD ST			
600	SAC	95819	298-A5
900	SAC	95819	297-J6
1900	SAC	95817	297-J7
2600	SAC	95817	317-J1
3000	SAC	95820	317-J2
5600	SAC	95824	317-J4
6600	SaCo	95823	317-J7
54TH AV			
2100	SAC	95822	317-D7
54TH ST			
500	SAC	95819	298-A5
1100	SAC	95819	297-J6
2600	SAC	95817	297-J7
2600	SAC	95817	317-J1
4000	SAC	95820	317-J3
6400	SaCo	95823	317-J6
55TH AV			
2100	SAC	95822	317-D7
55TH ST			
500	SAC	95819	298-A6
1200	SAC	95819	297-J7
1900	SAC	95817	297-J7
2200	SAC	95817	317-J1
3000	SAC	95820	317-J1
5300	SAC	95824	317-J5
7200	SaCo	95823	337-J1
56TH AV			
1100	SAC	95831	317-A7
2000	SAC	95822	337-D1
56TH ST			
700	SAC	95819	298-A6
1100	SAC	95819	297-J7
2000	SAC	95817	297-J7
2200	SAC	95817	317-J1
3000	SAC	95820	317-J2
5300	SAC	95824	317-J4
57TH AV			
2100	SAC	95822	337-D1
57TH ST			
700	SAC	95819	298-A6
2000	SAC	95817	297-J7
2100	SAC	95817	317-J1
2800	SAC	95820	317-J2
5300	SAC	95824	317-J4
58TH AV			
1100	SAC	95831	337-A1
58TH ST			
1000	SAC	95819	298-A7
2000	SAC	95817	297-J7
2100	SAC	95817	317-J1
2700	SAC	95820	317-J2
5100	SAC	95824	317-J4
59TH AV			
1600	SAC	95822	337-C1
59TH ST			
1700	SAC	95819	298-A7
1900	SAC	95817	298-A7
2000	SAC	95817	318-A1
2900	SAC	95820	318-A2
6300	SAC	95824	318-A5
60TH AV			
1400	SAC	95822	337-C1
60TH ST			
1200	SAC	95819	298-A7
2200	SAC	95817	298-A7
2300	SAC	95817	318-A1
3000	SAC	95820	318-A1
5500	SAC	95824	318-A5
61ST ST			
1200	SAC	95819	298-A7
2000	SAC	95817	318-A1
2900	SAC	95820	318-A2
5200	SAC	95824	318-A5
62ND AV			
2100	SAC	95822	337-D1
62ND ST			
1200	SAC	95819	298-A7
2000	SAC	95817	318-A1
3000	SAC	95820	318-A3
5300	SAC	95824	318-A5
63RD AV			
1400	SAC	95822	337-C1
63RD ST			
1400	SAC	95819	298-A7
1900	SAC	95817	318-A1
2900	SAC	95820	318-A2
5400	SAC	95824	318-A5
6100	SAC	95828	318-A7
64TH AV			
1400	SAC	95822	337-B2
64TH ST			
1300	SAC	95819	298-A7
2700	SAC	95817	318-A1
2800	SAC	95820	318-A2
5200	SAC	95824	318-B5
65TH AV			
1400	SAC	95822	337-D1
65TH ST			
1000	SAC	95819	298-B7
1800	SAC	95819	318-B2
2000	SAC	95817	318-D2
[illegible]			
5700	SAC	95824	318-B5
65TH STXP			
3900	SAC	95820	318-B4
4700	SAC	95824	318-B4
6100	SAC	95828	318-A7
6600	SaCo	95828	318-A7
6700	SaCo	95828	338-A1
7000	SaCo	95823	337-J1
7000	SaCo	95823	338-A1
66TH AV			
1400	SAC	95822	337-B2
5500	SaCo	95823	337-J2
5700	SaCo	95823	338-A2
66TH ST			
1400	SAC	95819	298-B7
3400	SAC	95820	318-B2
5600	SAC	95824	318-B5
67TH AV			
1700	SAC	95822	337-C2
67TH ST			
3400	SAC	95820	318-B3
5900	SAC	95824	318-B5
68TH AV			
1400	SAC	95822	337-B2
7800	SaCo	95828	338-C2
68TH ST			
5900	SAC	95824	318-B5
69TH AV			
1400	SAC	95822	337-B2
69TH ST			
1700	SAC	95819	298-B7
1700	SAC	95819	318-B3
4000	SAC	95820	318-B3
5800	SAC	95824	318-B5
70TH ST			
5300	SAC	95820	318-B4
5300	SAC	95824	318-B4
71ST AV			
1500	SAC	95832	337-C4
71ST ST			
3900	SAC	95820	318-B3
5400	SAC	95824	318-B5
73RD ST			
3900	SAC	95820	318-B3
5300	SAC	95824	318-B4
75TH ST			
6400	SAC	95828	318-C7
6800	SaCo	95828	318-C7
76TH ST			
4200	SAC	95820	318-C3
77TH ST			
4200	SAC	95820	318-C3
78TH ST			
4300	SAC	95820	318-C3
5200	SAC	95824	318-C4
79TH ST			
4300	SAC	95820	318-C3
5400	SAC	95824	318-C5
6400	SAC	95828	318-C6
80TH ST			
5000	SAC	95820	318-C4
82ND ST			
3900	SAC	95826	318-D3
83RD ST			
4800	SAC	95826	318-E4
5000	SAC	95828	318-E4
84TH ST			
5000	SAC	95826	318-E4
5000	SAC	95828	318-E4
88TH ST			
5700	SAC	95828	318-G5
I-5 WEST SIDE FRWY			
-	ELKG	-	357-D4
-	ELKG	-	377-D1
-	ELKG	-	397-D1
-	SAC	-	256-F5
-	SAC	-	276-J1
-	SAC	-	277-A3
-	SAC	-	297-B1
-	SAC	-	316-J6
-	SAC	-	317-A3
-	SAC	-	317-A7
-	SAC	-	337-B4
-	SaCo	-	[illegible]
-	SaCo	-	256-C5
-	SaCo	-	256-F5
-	SaCo	-	337-B4
-	SaCo	-	357-C1
-	SaCo	-	357-D4
-	SaCo	-	377-D1
-	SaCo	-	397-D1
-	SaCo	-	397-F8
-	SaCo	-	417-G3
-	SJCo	-	417-G3
-	SJCo	-	437-H1
-	SJCo	-	(438-A3
	See Page		418)
-	YoCo	-	255-H5
I-80 ALAN S HART FRWY			
-	AUB	-	162-F7
-	AUB	-	182-A5
-	LMS	-	200-J7
-	LMS	-	201-B6
-	LMS	-	220-C6
-	PlaC	-	162-F7

STREET Block	City	ZIP	Pg-Grid
I-80 ALAN S HART FRWY			
-	PlaC	-	181-G7
-	PlaC	-	182-A5
-	PlaC	-	201-B6
-	PlaC	-	201-G1
-	RKLN	-	200-J7
-	RKLN	-	220-C6
-	RSVL	-	220-C6
-	RSVL	-	239-J4
-	RSVL	-	240-A2
I-80 CAPITAL CITY FRWY			
-	SAC	-	278-C3
-	SAC	-	297-G3
-	SAC	-	298-A1
-	SaCo	-	278-C5
I-80 FRWY			
-	SAC	-	276-J5
-	SAC	-	277-B4
-	SAC	-	277-F2
-	SAC	-	278-A2
-	SAC	-	278-F2
-	SAC	-	296-G1
-	SaCo	-	276-J5
-	SaCo	-	277-E2
-	SaCo	-	278-H1
-	SaCo	-	296-G1
-	WSAC	-	296-F3
-	WSAC	-	296-G1
I-80 ROSEVILLE FRWY			
-	CITH	-	239-F6
-	CITH	-	259-D2
-	SaCo	-	259-D2
I-80 STATE FRWY			
-	SaCo	-	258-J7
-	SaCo	-	259-A6
-	SaCo	-	278-H1
I-80 WEST SACRAMENTO FRWY			
-	WSAC	-	296-D4
-	YoCo	-	296-D4
Rt#-E2 GRANT LINE RD			
6600	SaCo	95624	340-A6
7400	SaCo	95624	339-J7
7900	ELKG	95624	339-J7
8000	ELKG	95624	359-G2
8000	SaCo	95624	359-G2
9500	ELKG	95624	379-B1
9500	SaCo	95624	379-B1
10100	ELKG	95757	378-J3
10400	SaCo	95624	378-J3
10500	ELKG	95624	378-J3
Rt#-E2 SUNRISE AV			
100	RSVL	95661	240-A4
8400	CITH	95610	240-A4
8400	PlaC	95661	240-A4
Rt#-E2 SUNRISE BLVD			
900	RCCD	95742	280-A6
2000	RCCD	95670	280-A6
2000	SaCo	95628	280-A3
2000	SaCo	95670	280-A3
2500	SaCo	95742	280-A6
2600	RCCD	95742	300-C6
2600	RCCD	95670	300-A2
2700	SaCo	95670	300-A2
2700	SaCo	95742	300-A2
4100	RCCD	95742	320-D3
5000	SaCo	95628	260-A5
5400	CITH	95610	260-A3
5400	CITH	95628	260-A5
6500	SaCo	95830	320-D6
7200	SaCo	95830	340-D2
7200	SaCo	95624	340-D2
7900	CITH	95610	240-A7
Rt#-E3 HAZEL AV			
1900	SaCo	95628	280-F2
1900	SaCo	95670	280-F3
4900	SaCo	95628	260-F7
5600	SaCo	95662	260-F3
7500	SaCo	95662	240-F7
Rt#-E3 NIMBUS RD			
-	SaCo	95742	280-G4
Rt#-E3 SIERRA COLLEGE BLVD			
3900	LMS	95650	200-H7
4000	RKLN	95677	220-H3
4000	LMS	95650	220-H3
4000	LMS	95677	220-H3
5400	RKLN	95650	220-H3
6000	RKLN	95746	220-G6
6000	PlaC	95746	220-G6
6400	RSVL	95661	220-F7
6400	RSVL	95746	220-G6
6500	RSVL	95661	240-F3
6500	PlaC	95746	240-F6
8200	RSVL	95746	240-F3
8200	SaCo	95662	240-F6
8200	PlaC	95661	240-F3
Rt#-E9 FREEPORT BRDG			
-	SaCo	-	337-B7
-	YoCo	-	337-B7
Rt#-E9 RIVERVIEW DR			
-	YoCo	95612	356-H5
Rt#-E9 S RIVER RD			
28800	YoCo	95612	337-B7
28800	YoCo	95612	356-H3
28800	YoCo	95612	357-B2
42900	YoCo	95612	(376-J2 See Page 375)
42900	YoCo	95612	377-A2
42900	YoCo	95612	397-A2
50200	YoCo	95612	(396-F1 See Page 375)
Rt#-E9 SUTTER SLOUGH BRDG RD			
-	YoCo	95612	(396-E1 See Page 375)
11900	SaCo	95615	(396-C3 See Page 375)
Rt#-E12 ELK GROVE BLVD			
-	SaCo	95758	357-E6
2800	ELKG	95757	357-F7
2800	ELKG	95758	357-E6
5700	ELKG	95757	358-A6
5700	ELKG	95758	358-A6
8400	ELKG	95624	358-F6
9300	ELKG	95624	359-C6
9900	SaCo	95624	359-C6
Rt#-E13 RIVER RD			
13500	SaCo	95690	(416-H5 See Page 415)
13500	SaCo	95690	417-A6
13700	SaCo	95690	437-A1
Rt#-E13 TWIN CITIES RD			
1000	SaCo	95690	(416-J3 See Page 415)
1000	SaCo	95690	417-A3
1000	SaCo	95758	417-G2
4900	SaCo	95757	417-G2
5800	SaCo	95690	418-A2
5800	SaCo	95757	418-A2
8200	SaCo	95632	418-G2
9400	SaCo	95757	419-A2
9400	SaCo	95632	419-A2
Rt#-E14 ELKHORN BLVD			
100	SaCo	95673	257-A3
1100	SaCo	95673	258-A3
2400	SaCo	95652	258-E2
2800	SaCo	95660	258-E2
3000	SAC	95835	256-J3
3000	SaCo	95835	256-F3
3800	SAC	95673	257-A3
4100	SaCo	95835	257-A3
4100	SAC	95835	257-A3
4200	SaCo	95842	258-J2
4500	SaCo	95842	259-B3
Rt#-E14 GREENBACK LN			
-	CITH	95628	260-A4
5700	SaCo	95841	259-F4
5800	CITH	95621	259-F4
5800	CITH	95841	259-F4
7100	CITH	95610	259-F4
7800	CITH	95610	260-A4
8100	SaCo	95628	260-A4
8100	SaCo	95662	260-H4
9400	FOLS	95630	260-H4
9400	FOLS	95662	260-H4
9400	SaCo	95630	260-H4
Rt#-E14 SKYKING RD			
4700	SaCo	95835	256-D3
Rt#-E16 MOUNT AUKUM RD			
3800	EDCo	-	267-C5
5300	EDCo	95684	286-J5
Rt#-E16 SLY PARK RD			
3000	EDCo	95726	248-D1
5000	EDCo	-	248-D3
5900	EDCo	-	267-D4
Rt#-E19 CLARKSBURG AV			
48000	YoCo	95612	356-H5
Rt#-E19 CLARKSBURG RD			
48000	YoCo	95612	356-B5
Rt#-J5 N ELLIOT RD			
27000	SJCo	95638	421-B7
29200	SaCo	95638	421-B7
Rt#-J8 FRANKLIN BLVD			
2600	SAC	95817	297-E7
2900	SAC	95817	317-E3
3600	SAC	95820	317-E3
5400	SAC	95824	317-E3
5500	SaCo	95824	317-E3
6300	SaCo	95823	317-G7
6800	SaCo	95823	337-H6
6800	SAC	95823	337-G1
8300	SaCo	95823	357-H2
8300	SAC	95823	357-H2
8500	SaCo	95758	357-H2
8500	SAC	95758	357-H2
8600	ELKG	95758	357-H2
9600	ELKG	95757	357-H7
9900	ELKG	95757	377-G3
9900	ELKG	95757	397-G3
9900	SaCo	95757	377-G3
9900	SaCo	95757	397-G3
12500	SaCo	95757	417-J2
12800	SaCo	95690	417-J2
Rt#-J8 N THORNTON RD			
22000	SJCo	95242	(438-C6 See Page 418)
22000	SJCo	95686	(438-A1 See Page 418)
28500	SJCo	95686	417-J7
28500	SJCo	95686	418-A7
Rt#-J8 THORNTON RD			
-	SaCo	95690	417-J6
Rt#-J8 W WALNUT GROVE RD			
8600	SJCo	95686	(438-A3 See Page 418)
Rt#-J10 LINCOLN WY			
100	GALT	95632	419-F6
800	GALT	95632	439-F1
900	SaCo	95632	439-F1
Rt#-J10 N LOWER SACRAMENTO RD			
22500	SJCo	95220	439-F6
Rt#-J10 SIMMERHORN RD			
900	GALT	95632	419-F5
Rt#-J11 RIVER RD			
-	SaCo	95690	436-J2
-	SaCo	95690	437-A1
Rt#-J11 W WALNUT GROVE RD			
9000	SJCo	95686	(438-A3 See Page 418)
9200	SJCo	95686	437-F3
Rt#-J11 WALNUT GRV THRNTN RD			
-	SaCo	95690	436-J2
-	SaCo	95690	437-A3
Rt#-4 CALIFORNIA DELTA HWY			
-	ANT	-	(513-F6 See Page 493)
-	ANT	-	(514-A7 See Page 493)
600	OAKL	94561	(514-B5 See Page 493)
900	OAKL	94509	(514-A5 See Page 493)
Rt#-4 MAIN ST			
600	OAKL	94561	(514-B5 See Page 493)
900	ANT	94509	(514-A5 See Page 493)
900	OAKL	94509	(514-A5 See Page 493)
Rt#-12 HIGHWAY			
-	RVIS	94571	454-D2
-	SaCo	95641	454-J5
-	SaCo	95641	455-A6
-	SaCo	95641	(475-E1 See Page 456)
-	SaCo	95641	(476-A2 See Page 456)
-	SolC	94571	454-A2
Rt#-12 KETTLEMAN LN			
-	SaCo	95641	(476-B3 See Page 456)
14900	SJCo	95242	(476-B3 See Page 456)
Rt#-12 RIO VISTA BRDG			
-	SaCo	-	454-J5
Rt#-16 FOLSOM BLVD			
8000	SAC	95826	318-D1
Rt#-16 HOWE AV			
1500	SAC	95826	298-D7
2200	SAC	95826	318-D1
Rt#-16 JACKSON RD			
8300	SAC	95826	318-E1
9000	SaCo	95826	318-H3
9200	SaCo	95826	319-A3
9200	SaCo	95827	319-F5
9800	SaCo	95829	319-F5
9800	SaCo	95830	319-F5
10700	SaCo	95830	320-A6
11000	SaCo	95624	340-F1
11000	SaCo	95830	340-F1
12200	SaCo	95624	341-A2
12800	SaCo	95683	341-J1
14500	SaCo	95683	342-B2
16000	AmCo	95683	342-J4
Rt#-49 GOLDEN CHAIN HWY			
-	EDCo	95630	162-H7
-	EDCo	95630	182-J1
100	AUB	95603	182-D1
100	PLCR	95667	245-D1
200	PlaC	95603	182-F2
400	PlaC	95603	162-D7
600	AUB	95603	162-D7
1500	EDCo	95667	245-D1
2600	EDCo	95667	225-A7
3800	EDCo	95619	265-E2
4600	EDCo	95623	265-B4
4700	EDCo	95667	265-E2
Rt#-49 GRASS VALLEY HWY			
800	PlaC	95603	162-B2
3000	PlaC	95602	162-B2
Rt#-65 G ST			
-	PlaC	95648	179-F1
100	LNCN	95648	179-H2
Rt#-65 S G ST			
-	LNCN	95648	179-H4
Rt#-65 HAROLD T JOHNSON EXWY			
-	PlaC	-	199-G5
-	RKLN	-	199-G5
-	RKLN	-	199-G5
-	RKLN	-	199-G5
-	RKLN	-	219-G1
-	RSVL	-	199-G5
-	RSVL	-	219-G1
-	RSVL	-	220-A4
-	LNCN	-	179-G7
Rt#-65 HIGHWAY			
600	PlaC	-	159-A1
1400	PlaC	95648	159-C5
1600	LNCN	95648	159-E7
2700	LNCN	95648	179-H4
Rt#-65 ROSEVILLE BYPS			
-	RKLN	95677	220-C5
-	RSVL	95678	220-A4
Rt#-84 COURTLAND RD			
48000	YoCo	95612	(395-F1 See Page 375)
48000	YoCo	95612	(396-A1 See Page 375)
Rt#-84 HIGHWAY			
-	RVIS	94571	455-A3
-	SolC	94571	455-B1
3300	SolC	95690	415-F1
3300	SolC	95690	455-C1
3500	SolC	95690	(435-C1 See Page 415)
Rt#-84 JEFFERSON BLVD			
29700	WSAC	95691	316-C7
29700	YoCo	95612	336-C7
29700	YoCo	95612	356-B7
29700	YoCo	95691	316-C7
29700	YoCo	95691	336-C3
36500	YoCo	95612	(376-B1 See Page 375)
38600	YoCo	95612	(396-B1 See Page 375)
Rt#-84 RIVER RD			
-	RVIS	94571	455-A3
-	RVIS	94571	454-J5
Rt#-84 RYER AV			
41000	SolC	94571	(395-F5 See Page 375)
41000	YoCo	95612	(395-F1 See Page 375)
42000	SolC	94571	415-F1
44000	SolC	95690	415-F1
Rt#-88 HIGHWAY			
-	SJCo	95638	422-J5
Rt#-99 EL CENTRO BLVD			
2900	SuCo	95659	236-H2
2900	SuCo	95668	236-H2
4300	SaCo	95836	236-H2
Rt#-99 EL CENTRO RD			
-	SaCo	95835	256-H2
2200	SaCo	95836	236-H6
2200	SaCo	95836	256-H2
Rt#-99 GOLDEN STATE HWY			
-	ELKG	-	358-D1
-	ELKG	-	378-G2
-	ELKG	-	379-A5
-	ELKG	-	358-D1
-	ELKG	-	378-G2
-	ELKG	-	358-D1
-	GALT	-	419-E2
-	GALT	-	439-H2
-	SAC	-	338-A3
-	SAC	-	358-D1
-	SAC	-	338-A3
-	SAC	-	358-D1
-	SAC	-	297-F6
-	SAC	-	317-F3
-	SAC	-	317-F3
-	SAC	-	338-A3
-	SAC	-	317-F3
-	SAC	-	338-A3
-	SaCo	-	338-A3
-	SaCo	-	378-G2
-	SaCo	-	379-A5
-	SaCo	-	(399-C3 See Page 379)
-	SaCo	-	419-E2
-	SaCo	-	379-B7
-	SaCo	-	(399-B1 See Page 379)
-	SaCo	-	378-G2
-	SaCo	-	379-A5
-	SaCo	-	(399-B1 See Page 379)
-	SaCo	-	419-E2
-	SaCo	-	317-F3
-	SaCo	-	337-J1
-	SaCo	-	338-A3
-	SaCo	-	317-F3
-	SaCo	-	338-A3
-	SJCo	-	439-H2
-	SJCo	-	(440-A6 See Page 420)
-	SJCo	-	439-H2
Rt#-104 TWIN CITIES RD			
10100	SaCo	95757	419-F2
10100	GALT	95632	419-F2
10100	SaCo	95632	419-F2
11100	SaCo	95632	420-A2
11400	SaCo	95638	420-A2
11700	SaCo	95638	(400-J4 See Page 379)
12700	SaCo	95638	(401-J1 See Page 381)
13800	SaCo	95638	381-G7
14400	SaCo	95638	(382-J3 See Page 381)
16100	AmCo	95638	(382-J3 See Page 381)
Rt#-160 FRWY			
-	ANT	-	(514-A4 See Page 493)
-	CCCo	-	(514-A4 See Page 493)
-	OAKL	-	(514-A4 See Page 493)
Rt#-160 HIGHWAY			
-	CCCo	94509	(514-A3 See Page 493)
-	ISLE	95641	455-J4
-	OAKL	94509	(514-A3 See Page 493)
-	SaCo	95641	455-B3
-	SaCo	95641	456-A4
-	SaCo	95680	436-F1
-	SaCo	95690	455-D4
-	SaCo	95690	456-D1
6800	SaCo	94571	(494-F1 See Page 493)
12000	SaCo	95615	(396-C4 See Page 375)
12400	SaCo	95690	(396-C6 See Page 375)
12400	SaCo	95690	(416-D1 See Page 415)
13400	SaCo	95690	417-A6
13700	SaCo	95690	437-A1
13700	SaCo	95690	436-J1
16700	SaCo	95641	454-J6
16700	SaCo	95641	474-J1
16800	SaCo	94571	474-H3
18100	SaCo	94571	(514-A1 See Page 493)
Rt#-160 RIVER RD			
-	SaCo	95615	(376-J5 See Page 375)
-	SaCo	95615	(396-G1 See Page 375)
-	SaCo	95639	357-A6
-	SaCo	95639	(376-J3 See Page 375)
-	SaCo	95639	377-A2
-	SaCo	95639	397-A2
-	SaCo	95832	337-C7
-	SaCo	95832	356-H3
-	SaCo	95832	357-A3
Rt#-193 GEORGETOWN RD			
1700	EDCo	95667	245-E1
1700	PLCR	95667	245-E1
1700	EDCo	95667	225-D5
7300	EDCo	95633	205-E5
9300	EDCo	95633	225-E1
9300	EDCo	95634	225-E1
Rt#-193 HIGHWAY			
7900	PlaC	95658	181-H5
Rt#-193 LINCOLN NEWCASTLE HWY			
1200	PlaC	95648	179-J3
1200	PlaC	95648	180-A3
1200	LNCN	95648	179-J3
1200	LNCN	95648	180-A3
4900	PlaC	95658	180-F4
6300	PlaC	95658	181-B3
Rt#-193 MCBEAN PARK DR			
-	LNCN	95648	179-H3
Rt#-220 GRAND ISLAND RD			
-	SaCo	95690	(435-J2 See Page 415)
Rt#-220 HIGHWAY			
-	SaCo	95690	(435-J2 See Page 415)
100	SaCo	95680	436-D1
100	SaCo	95690	436-D1
1000	SolC	95690	(435-C1 See Page 415)
Rt#-275 CAPITOL MALL			
-	WSAC	95691	297-B3
-	SAC	95814	297-B3
U.S.-50 CAPITAL CITY FRWY			
-	SAC	-	297-A4
-	WSAC	-	296-F4
-	WSAC	-	297-A4
U.S.-50 EL DORADO FRWY			
-	EDCo	-	245-C7
-	EDCo	-	246-A4
-	EDCo	-	262-F7
-	EDCo	-	263-H7
-	EDCo	-	264-B6
-	EDCo	-	264-E3
-	EDCo	-	265-A1
-	EDCo	-	282-G1
-	EDCo	-	283-A1
-	FOLS	-	280-F4
-	FOLS	-	281-B2
-	FOLS	-	281-F2
-	FOLS	-	282-A2
-	PLCR	-	245-C7
-	PLCR	-	246-A4
-	RCCD	-	279-J7
-	RCCD	-	280-B7
-	RCCD	-	299-J1
-	SaCo	-	280-F4
-	SaCo	-	281-B2
-	SaCo	-	282-A2
U.S.-50 FRWY			
-	EDCo	-	247-D3
-	EDCo	-	247-J2
-	RCCD	-	299-F4
-	RCCD	-	299-J1
-	SAC	-	297-F6
-	SAC	-	297-G6
-	SAC	-	298-A7
-	SAC	-	298-G7
-	SAC	-	318-A1
-	SAC	-	318-B1
-	SAC	-	318-C1
-	SaCo	-	298-J6
-	SaCo	-	299-A6
-	SaCo	-	299-C6
-	EDCo	-	248-F1
U.S.-50 HIGHWAY			
-	EDCo	95667	246-E4
-	EDCo	95709	246-J3
-	EDCo	95709	247-A4

AIRPORTS

FEATURE NAME / Address City, ZIP Code	PAGE-GRID
AUBURN MUNICIPAL NEW AIRPORT RD, AUB, 95602	162 - D1
BORGES CLARKSBURG S RIVER RD, YoCo, 95612	357 - A1
CAMERON PK UNITED DR & BOEING RD, EDCo, 95682	263 - E4
FRANKLIN FIELD 12480 BRUCEVILLE RD, SaCo, 95757	397 - J14
LINCOLN REGIONAL 1480 FLIGHTLINE DR, LNCN, 95648	179 - A1
LODI 23987 N HWY 99, SJCo, 95220	439 - H7
MATHER 3745 WHITEHEAD ST, SaCo, 95655	299 - F6
MCCLELLAN 3331 PEACEKEEPER WY, SaCo, 95652	258 - D5
PLACERVILLE 3501 AIRPORT RD, EDCo, 95667	246 - B6
RANCHO MURIETA 7443 MURIETA DR, SaCo, 95683	342 - A2
RIO LINDA 930 E ST, SaCo, 95673	257 - J5
RIO VISTA MUNICIPAL 6000 AIRPORT RD, RVIS, 94571	454 - G1
SACRAMENTO EXECUTIVE 6151 FREEPORT BLVD, SAC, 95822	317 - D6
SACRAMENTO INTL 6900 AIRPORT BLVD, SaCo, 95837	256 - C1
SUNSET SKYRANCH GRANT LINE RD & BRADSHAW RD, SaCo, 95624	379 - C1
VAN VLECK VAN VLECK RD, SaCo, 95683	342 - D6
WALNUT GROVE ANDRUS ISLAND RD, SaCo, 95690	436 - F5

BEACHES, HARBORS & WATER REC

FEATURE NAME / Address City, ZIP Code	PAGE-GRID
BIG BREAK MARINA (SEE PAGE 493) BIG BREAK RD, OAKL, 94561	514 - C4
DELTA MARINA YACHT HARBOR 100 MARINA, RVIS, 94571	454 - H7
DRIFTWOOD MARINA (SEE PAGE 493) BRIDGEHEAD RD, OAKL, 94561	514 - A4
GEORGIANA SLOUGH FISHING ACCESS ANDRUS ISLAND RD, SaCo, 95690	436 - G5
JENKINSON LAKE SLY PARK & MORMON EMIGRANT, EDCo, 95726	248 - E6
LAURITZEN YACHT HARBOR- (SEE PAGE 493) 115 LAURITZEN LN, OAKL, 94561	514 - B3
LLOYDS HOLIDAY HARBOR (SEE PAGE 493) 415 FLEMING LN, CCCo, 94509	514 - A4
NEW BRIDGE MARINA (SEE PAGE 493) 6325 BRIDGEHEAD RD, CCCo, 94509	514 - A4
PARADISE BEACH CARLSON DR & SANDBURG DR, SAC, 95819	298 - B3

BUILDINGS

FEATURE NAME / Address City, ZIP Code	PAGE-GRID
DOWNTOWN BUILDINGS SEE PAGE F	-
CAR RENTAL AGENCIES AVIATION DR & MCNAIR CIR, SaCo, 95837	256 - B3
CITY WATER TREATMENT PLANT RANDELL DR, FOLS, 95630	261 - E3
E A FAIRBAIRN TREATMENT PLANT COLLEGE TOWN DR & JED SMITH DR, SAC, 95826	298 - C7
SCOTTISH RITE TEMPLE 6151 H ST, SAC, 95819	298 - B5

BUILDINGS - GOVERNMENTAL

FEATURE NAME / Address City, ZIP Code	PAGE-GRID
CALIFORNIA DEPARTMENT OF FORESTRY MOTHER LODE DR & PLEASANT VLY, EDCo, 95623	264 - H5
CALIFORNIA HIGHWAY PATROL ACADEMY 3500 REED AV, WSAC, 95605	296 - F1
CALTRANS TEST CTR REED AV, WSAC, 95605	296 - D1
CHILDRENS RECEIVNG HOME OF SAC 3555 AUBURN BLVD, SAC, 95821	278 - G3
COURTHOUSE 101 MAPLE ST, AUB, 95603	182 - D3
CYA RECEPTION CTR & CLINIC 3001 RAMONA AV, SAC, 95826	318 - C1
EL DORADO COUNTY SUPERIOR COURT 495 MAIN ST, PLCR, 95667	245 - G5
FEDERAL AVIATION AGENCY FLIGHTLINE CIR, SaCo, 95837	256 - B3
FEDERAL BLDG 2800 COTTAGE WY, SaCo, 95825	298 - E1
FEDERAL BLDG & POST OFFICE 801 I ST, SAC, 95814	297 - C3
FEDERAL COURTHOUSE 501 I ST, SAC, 95814	297 - C3
FEDERAL COURTHOUSE BLDG 650 CAPITOL MALL, SAC, 95814	297 - C4
FOLSOM STATE PRISON 300 PRISON RD, FOLS, 95671	261 - C3
MUNICIPAL COURT 1319 BROADWAY, PLCR, 95667	245 - J4
PLACER COUNTY ADMIN 2956 RICHARDSON DR, PlaC, 95603	162 - A4
PRISON INDUSTRIES 560 NATOMA, FOLS, 95671	261 - E3
SACRAMENTO CHILDRENS HOME 2750 SUTTERVILLE RD, SAC, 95820	317 - E2
SACRAMENTO CO OFFICE OF EDUCATION 9738 LINCOLN VILLAGE DR, RCCD, 95827	299 - C6
SACRAMENTO COUNTY ADMIN 700 H ST, SAC, 95814	297 - C3
SACRAMENTO COUNTY COURTHOUSE 720 9TH ST, SAC, 95814	297 - C3
SECRETARY OF STATE BLDG 1500 11TH ST, SAC, 95814	297 - C4
STATE ARCHIVES BLDG 1020 O ST, SAC, 95814	297 - D4
STATE AUTOMOTIVE SHOPS STOCKTON BL & 34TH ST, SAC, 95816	297 - F6
STATE BOARD OF EQUALIZATION 450 N ST, SAC, 95814	297 - C4
STATE CAPITOL 10TH ST & L ST, SAC, 95814	297 - D4
STATE DEPARTMENT OF EMPLOYMENT 800 CAPITOL MALL, SAC, 95814	297 - C4
STATE DEPARTMENT OF FINANCE 9TH ST & L ST, SAC, 95814	297 - C4
STATE EDUCATION DEPARTMENT 1430 N ST, SAC, 95814	297 - D4
STATE FOOD & AGRICULTURE 1220 N ST, SAC, 95814	297 - D4
STATE OF CALIFORNIA R T C E NATOMA ST, FOLS, 95671	261 - E2
STATE OFFICE BLDG NO 1 915 CAPITOL MALL, SAC, 95814	297 - C4
STATE OFFICE BLDG NO 8 714 P ST, SAC, 95814	297 - C4
STATE OFFICE BLDG NO 9 Q ST & 8TH ST, SAC, 95814	297 - C4
STATE OFFICE CIVIL DEFENSE 2800 MEADOWVIEW RD, SAC, 95832	337 - E3
STATE PRINTING PLANT 344 N 7TH ST, SAC, 95814	297 - D1
STATE RESOURCE BLDG 1416 9TH ST, SAC, 95814	297 - C4

CASINOS

FEATURE NAME / Address City, ZIP Code	PAGE-GRID
THUNDER VALLEY CASINO 1200 ATHENS AV, PlaC, 95648	199 - E3

CEMETERIES

FEATURE NAME / Address City, ZIP Code	PAGE-GRID
ARLINGTON MEM CEM ELDER CREEK RD, SaCo, 95829	319 - D6
CALVARY CEM 7101 VERNER AV, CITH, 95621	259 - E2
CAMELLIA MEM LAWN CEM 10221 JACKSON RD, SaCo, 95827	319 - E4
CITY CEM 10TH & BROADWAY, SAC, 95818	297 - B6
CITY CEM RECTOR ST & CHAMBERLAIN ST, PLCR, 95667	245 - F5
EAST LAWN MEM CEM 43RD ST & FOLSOM BLVD, SAC, 95819	297 - H6
EAST LAWN SIERRA HILLS MEM PK 5757 GREENBACK LN, SaCo, 95841	259 - C4
ELDER CREEK CEM ELDER CK RD & SUNRISE SOUTH DR, SAC, 95824	318 - C6
FAIR OAKS CEM 7780 OLIVE ST, SaCo, 95628	279 - J1
FRANKLIN CEM HOOD FRANKLIN RD & FRANKLIN BL, SaCo, 95757	377 - G3
FRANKLIN CEM HOOD FRANKLIN RD & FRANKLIN BL, SaCo, 95757	397 - G3
GALT ARNO CEM 14180 JOY DR, GALT, 95632	439 - F1
HICKSVILLE CEM (SEE PAGE 379) ARNO RD, SaCo, 95693	399 - D4
HOLY CROSS CEM (SEE PAGE 493) 2200 E 18TH ST, CCCo, 94509	513 - H5
JAYHAWK CEM DEER VALLEY RD & REDBUD LN, EDCo, 95672	243 - G4
LAKESIDE MEM LAWN CEM FOLSOM BLVD & NATOMA ST, FOLS, 95630	261 - A5
LINCOLN CEM 1445 1ST ST, LNCN, 95648	179 - G4
MASONIC LAWN CEM 2700 RIVERSIDE BLVD, SAC, 95818	297 - B6
MATHEW KILGORE CEM KILGORE RD, RCCD, 95670	300 - A1
MOUNT VERNON MEM CEM 8201 GREENBACK LN, SaCo, 95610	260 - B4
OAK VIEW MEM PK CEM (SEE PAGE 493) 2500 E 18TH ST, ANT, 94509	513 - H5
ODD FELLOWS LAWN CEM 2720 RIVERSIDE BLVD, SAC, 95818	297 - B6
PLACERVILLE UNION CEM BEE ST, PLCR, 95667	245 - F5
ROCKLIN CEM 4090 KANNASTO ST, RKLN, 95677	220 - E4
ROSEVILLE CEM 95678 BERRY ST, RSVL, 95678	220 - A7
SACRAMENTO COUNTY CEM 21ST AV, SAC, 95820	318 - B4
SACRAMENTO MEM LAWN CEM 6100 STOCKTON BLVD, SAC, 95824	317 - J6
SAINT JOSEPH CEM MAIN ST & HWY 12, RVIS, 94571	454 - G5
SAINT JOSEPHS CEM 2615 21ST ST, SAC, 95818	297 - D7
SAINT MARYS CEM 6700 21ST AV, SAC, 95820	318 - B4
SAINT ROSE CATHOLIC CEM FRANKLIN BLVD, SAC, 95824	317 - F5
SAN JOAQUIN CEM 9189 STOCKTON BLVD, SAC, 95758	358 - D2
SOUTH EAST LAWN MEM PK 9189 E STOCKTON BLVD, ELKG, 95624	358 - E3
SUNSET LAWN CEM 4701 MARYSVILLE BLVD, SAC, 95838	277 - J1
SYLVAN CEM RAMONA LN & AUBURN BL, CITH, 95621	259 - G1
WEST SACRAMENTO MEM PK ALABAMA AV & REGENT ST, WSAC, 95691	296 - H5
WESTWOOD HILLS MEM CEM COLD SPRINGS RD & ANDLER RD, PLCR, 95667	245 - C4

CITY HALLS

FEATURE NAME / Address City, ZIP Code	PAGE-GRID
ANTIOCH (SEE PAGE 493) 3RD ST & H ST, ANT, 94509	513 - C4
AUBURN 1225 LINCOLN WY, AUB, 95603	182 - D2
CITRUS HEIGHTS 6237 FOUNTAIN SQUARE DR, CITH, 95621	259 - G4
ELK GROVE 8400 LAGUNA PALMS WY, ELKG, 95758	358 - E5
FOLSOM 50 NATOMA ST, FOLS, 95630	261 - C4
GALT 380 CIVIC DR, GALT, 95632	419 - F7
ISLETON 100 2ND ST, ISLE, 95641	455 - H5
LINCOLN 640 5TH ST, LNCN, 95648	179 - H3
LOOMIS 6140 HORSESHOE BAR RD, LMS, 95650	201 - A6
OAKLEY (SEE PAGE 493) 3633 MAIN ST, OAKL, 94561	514 - E6
PLACERVILLE 487 MAIN ST, PLCR, 95667	245 - G5
RANCHO CORDOVA 3121 GOLD CANAL DR, RCCD, 95670	300 - A2
RIO VISTA 1 MAIN ST, RVIS, 94571	454 - H6
ROCKLIN 3980 ROCKLIN RD, RKLN, 95677	220 - E3
ROSEVILLE 311 VERNON ST, RSVL, 95678	239 - H2
SACRAMENTO 915 I ST, SAC, 95814	297 - D3
WEST SACRAMENTO 1110 W CAPITAL AV, WSAC, 95691	296 - J3

COLLEGES & UNIVERSITIES

FEATURE NAME / Address City, ZIP Code	PAGE-GRID
AMERICAN RIVER COLLEGE 4700 COLLEGE OAK DR, SaCo, 95841	279 - B1
CALIFORNIA STATE UNIV SACRAMENTO 6000 J ST, SAC, 95819	298 - B7
COSUMNES RIVER COLLEGE 8401 CENTER PKWY, SAC, 95823	338 - B7
EL DORADO CTR 6699 CAMPUS DR, EDCo, 95667	244 - H6
FOLSOM LAKE COMM COLLEGE 100 SCHOLAR WY, FOLS, 95630	261 - H7
MCGEORGE SCHOOL OF LAW 3200 5TH AV, SAC, 95817	317 - F1
MOUNT SAINT JOSEPH SEMINARY RICKETY RACK RD, LMS, 95650	221 - A4
SACRAMENTO CITY COLLEGE 3835 FREEPORT BLVD, SAC, 95822	317 - D2
SIERRA COMM COLLEGE 5000 ROCKLIN RD, RKLN, 95677	220 - G3
UNIV OF CALIFORNIA-UNIVERSITY EXT 2901 K ST, SAC, 95816	297 - F5
UNIV OF NORTHERN CALIFORNIA 1012 J ST, SAC, 95814	297 - D4
UNIV OF PHOENIX, SACRAMENTO 1760 CREEKSIDE OAKS DR, SAC, 95833	277 - C7
UNIV OF SAN FRANCISCO-SACRAMENTO 1485 RESPONSE RD, SAC, 95815	297 - J1
WILLIAM JESSUP UNIV 333 SUNSET BLVD, RKLN, 95765	199 - H6

ENTERTAINMENT & SPORTS

FEATURE NAME / Address City, ZIP Code	PAGE-GRID
ARCO ARENA 1 SPORTS PKWY, SAC, 95834	277 - A1
AUBURN FAIR GROUNDS AUBURN-FOLSOM RD & FAIRGATE DR, AUB, 95603	182 - D3
CALIFORNIA EXPO & FAIR 1600 EXPOSITION BLVD, SAC, 95815	297 - J2
CONTRA COSTA FAIR GROUNDS- (SEE PAGE 493) 1201 10TH ST, CCCo, 94509	513 - B5
CONVENTION CTR 1400 J ST, SAC, 95814	297 - D4
EL DORADO COUNTY FAIRGROUNDS 100 PLACERVILLE DR, PLCR, 95667	245 - C5
FAIRY TALE TOWN 3901 LAND PARK DR, SAC, 95822	317 - C2
HORSE RACE TRACK EXPOSITION BL & ETHAN WY, SAC, 95815	298 - B2
HUGHES STADIUM 3835 FREEPORT BLVD, SAC, 95822	317 - D2
ORCHARD PARK SKATEPARK BERGAMO WY & WEST RIVER DR, SAC, 95833	276 - J6
PLACER COUNTY FAIRGROUNDS 800 ALL AMERICA BLVD, RSVL, 95678	219 - G7
RALEY FIELD 400 BALLPARK DR, WSAC, 95691	297 - A4
RIO VISTA SKATEPARK POPPY HOUSE RD, RVIS, 94571	454 - J4
SKATE SACRAMENTO 28TH ST & C ST, SAC, 95816	297 - F3
WATERWORLD USA 1600 EXPOSITION BLVD, SAC, 95815	298 - A2

GOLF COURSES

FEATURE NAME / Address City, ZIP Code	PAGE-GRID
ANTELOPE GREENS GC 2721 ELVERTA RD, SaCo, 95843	238 - E5
APPLE MTN GOLF RESORT 3455 CARSON RD, EDCo, 95667	246 - G2
BASS LAKE GC 3000 ALEXANDRITE DR, EDCo, 95672	263 - B1
BLACK OAK GC 2455 BLACK OAK RD, PlaC, 95602	162 - E1
BRADSHAW RANCH GC 7350 BRADSHAW RD, SaCo, 95829	339 - B2
CAMERON PK CC 3201 ROYALE DR, EDCo, 95682	263 - D5
CAMPUS COMMONS GC 2 CADILLAC DR, SAC, 95825	298 - B4
CATTA VERDERA CC 1111 CATTA VERDERA DR, LNCN, 95648	180 - D7
CAVANAUGH, BARTLEY GC 8301 FREEPORT BLVD, SaCo, 95832	337 - C7
CHAMPIONS GOLF LINKS 8915 GERBER RD, SaCo, 95829	338 - H3
CHERRY ISLAND GC 2360 ELVERTA RD, SaCo, 95626	238 - D7
COLD SPRINGS GOLF & CC 6500 CLUBHOUSE DR, EDCo, 95667	244 - G2
CORDOVA RECREATION GC 9425 JACKSON RD, SaCo, 95826	319 - A2
COURSE AT RASPBERRY HILL 14500 MUSSO RD, PlaC, 95602	162 - H2
DEL PASO CC 3333 MARCONI AV, SaCo, 95821	278 - F5
DIAMOND OAKS MUN GC 349 DIAMOND OAKS RD, RSVL, 95678	219 - H6
DRY CREEK RANCH GC 809 CRYSTAL WY, GALT, 95632	439 - G1
EL DORADO HILLS GC 3775 EL DORADO HILLS BLVD, EDCo, 95762	262 - D7
EMERALD LAKES GC 10651 E STOCKTON BLVD, ELKG, 95624	378 - J5
EMPIRE RANCH GC 1620 E NATOMA ST, FOLS, 95630	261 - J4
FOOTHILL GC 7000 VERNER AV, CITH, 95621	259 - D2
FOREST LAKE GC 2450 E WOODSON RD, SJCo, 95220	439 - G5
GRANITE BAY GC 9600 GOLF CLUB DR, PlaC, 95746	240 - J5
HAGGIN OAKS MUNICIPAL GC NORTH 3645 FULTON AV, SAC, 95821	278 - E3
HOFFMAN, ANCIL PK GC 6700 TARSHES DR, SaCo, 95608	279 - E7
INDIAN CREEK CC 4487 BARTON RD, LMS, 95650	221 - A1
LAND, WILLIAM GC 1701 SUTTERVILLE RD, SAC, 95822	317 - C2
LAWRENCE LINKS GC 3825 BLACKFOOT WY, SaCo, 95843	238 - G7
LINCOLN HILLS GC 1005 SUN CITY LN, LNCN, 95648	179 - J6
MALONEY, BING GC 6801 FREEPORT BLVD, SAC, 95822	317 - C7
MATHER GC 4103 EAGLES NEST RD, SaCo, 95655	300 - B7
MORGAN CREEK GOLF & CC 8791 MORGAN CREEK LN, PlaC, 95747	239 - A3
NORTHRIDGE CC 7600 MADISON AV, SaCo, 95628	259 - H7
RANCHO MURIETA GC & CC 7000 ALAMEDA DR, SaCo, 95683	322 - B7
RANCHO MURIETA GC & CC 7000 ALAMEDA DR, SaCo, 95683	342 - D2
RIDGE GC 2020 GOLF COURSE RD, PlaC, 95602	162 - D3
RIO VISTA GC 1000 SUMMERSET DR, RVIS, 94571	454 - F1
ROSEVILLE ROLLING GREENS GC 5572 EUREKA RD, PlaC, 95746	240 - J4
SERRANO CC 5005 SERRANO PKWY, EDCo, 95762	262 - G4
SIERRA GC 1822 COUNTRY CLUB DR, PLCR, 95667	246 - A6
SIERRA VIEW CC 105 ALTA VISTA AV, RSVL, 95678	219 - H6
SUN CITY ROSEVILLE GC 7050 DEL WEBB BLVD, RSVL, 95747	219 - A5
SUNSET WHITNEY CC 4201 MIDAS AV, RKLN, 95677	220 - C1
TEAL BEND GC 7200 GARDEN HWY, SaCo, 95837	235 - H7
TURKEY CREEK GC 1525 HWY 193, PlaC, 95648	180 - B2

FEATURE NAME	Address City, ZIP Code	PAGE-GRID
VALLEY-HI GC & CC	9595 FRANKLIN BLVD, ELKG, 95758	357 - J5
WHITNEY OAKS GC	2305 CLUBHOUSE DR, RKLN, 95765	200 - D5
WILDHAWK GC	7713 VINEYARD RD, SaCo, 95829	339 - E4
WOODCREEK GC	5880 WOODCREEK OAKS BLVD, RSVL, 95747	219 - D5

HOSPITALS

FEATURE NAME	Address City, ZIP Code	PAGE-GRID
KAISER FOUNDATION HOSP	2025 MORSE AV, SaCo, 95825	298 - E1
KAISER FOUNDATION HOSP SOUTH	6600 BRUCEVILLE RD, SAC, 95823	338 - B5
KAISER MED CTR	10725 INTERNATIONAL DR, RCCD, 95670	299 - G4
KAISER PERMANENTE HOSP	1600 EUREKA RD, RSVL, 95661	240 - C2
KINDRED HOSP	223 FARGO WY, FOLS, 95630	261 - D4
MARSHALL HOSP	1100 MARSHALL WY, PLCR, 95667	245 - G5
MERCY GENERAL HOSP	4001 J ST, SAC, 95816	297 - H5
MERCY HOSP OF FOLSOM	1650 CREEKSIDE DR, FOLS, 95630	261 - E6
MERCY SAN JUAN HOSP	6501 COYLE AV, SaCo, 95608	259 - E6
METHODIST HOSP OF SACRAMENTO	7500 HOSPITAL DR, SAC, 95823	338 - C6
SHRINERS HOSP FOR CHILDREN	2425 STOCKTON BLVD, SAC, 95817	297 - H7
SUTTER AUBURN FAITH COMM HOSP	11815 EDUCATION ST, PlaC, 95602	162 - A3
SUTTER GENERAL HOSP	2801 L ST, SAC, 95816	297 - F5
SUTTER MEM HOSP	5151 F ST, SAC, 95819	297 - J5
SUTTER ROSEVILLE MED CTR	ONE MEDICAL PLAZA DR, RSVL, 95661	220 - C6
UC DAVIS MED CTR	2315 STOCKTON BLVD, SAC, 95817	297 - H7

HOTELS

FEATURE NAME	Address City, ZIP Code	PAGE-GRID
BEST INN & SUITES	1875 AUBURN RAVINE RD, PlaC, 95603	162 - F6
BEST WESTERN CAMERON PK INN	3361 COACH LN, EDCo, 95682	283 - F1
BEST WESTERN HERITAGE INN	11269 POINT EAST DR, SaCo, 95742	280 - A7
BEST WESTERN PLACERVILLE	6850 GREENLEAF DR, EDCo, 95667	265 - C1
BEST WESTERN ROSEVILLE INN	220 HARDING BLVD, RSVL, 95678	240 - A2
BEST WESTERN SANDMAN MOTEL	236 JIBBOOM ST, SAC, 95814	297 - B1
BEST WESTERN SUTTER HOUSE	1100 H ST, SAC, 95814	297 - D3
CANTERBURY INN	1900 CANTERBURY RD, SAC, 95815	277 - G7
CLARION HOTEL	700 16TH ST, SAC, 95814	297 - E3
COURTYARD BY MARRIOTT-NATOMAS	2101 RIVER PLAZA DR, SAC, 95833	277 - B7
COURTYARD BY MARRIOTT-RANCHO CORDOVA	10683 WHITE ROCK RD, RCCD, 95670	299 - G3
COURTYARD BY MARRIOTT SAC CAL EXPO	1781 TRIBUTE RD, SAC, 95815	297 - H1
COURTYARD BY MARRIOTT SAC MIDTOWN	4422 Y ST, SAC, 95817	297 - H7
DAYS INN - DISCOVERY PK	350 BERCUT DR, SAC, 95814	297 - C1
DELTA KING RIVER BOAT HOTEL	1000 FRONT ST, SAC, 95814	297 - B3
DOUBLETREE HOTEL	2001 POINT WEST WY, SAC, 95815	298 - A1
EMBASSY SUITES SACRAMENTO	100 CAPITOL MALL, SAC, 95814	297 - B4
FAIRFIELD INN BY MARRIOTT	10713 WHITE ROCK RD, RCCD, 95670	299 - H3
FIRST CHOICE INN	4420 ROCKLIN RD, RKLN, 95677	220 - F3
GOVERNORS INN	210 RICHARDS BLVD, SAC, 95814	297 - C1
HALLMARK SUITES	11260 POINT EAST DR, SaCo, 95742	280 - A7
HAWTHORNE SUITES SACRAMENTO	321 BERCUT DR, SAC, 95814	297 - C1
HERITAGE HOTEL	1780 TRIBUTE RD, SAC, 95815	297 - J1
HERITAGE INN	204 HARDING BLVD, RSVL, 95678	240 - A2
HILTON GARDEN INN	1951 TAYLOR RD, RSVL, 95661	220 - C7
HILTON GARDEN INN	2540 VENTURE OAKS WY, SAC, 95833	277 - A6
HILTON GARDEN INN-FOLSOM	221 IRON POINT RD, FOLS, 95630	281 - A2
HILTON SACRAMENTO ARDEN WEST	2200 HARVARD ST, SAC, 95815	278 - A7
HOLIDAY INN-AUBURN	120 GRASS VALLEY HWY, AUB, 95603	182 - D2
HOLIDAY INN-CAPITOL PLAZA	300 J ST, SAC, 95814	297 - C3
HOLIDAY INN NORTH EAST	5321 DATE AV, SaCo, 95841	259 - A6
HOLIDAY INN RANCHO CORDOVA	11131 FOLSOM BLVD, RCCD, 95670	280 - A7
HOMESTEAD VILLAGE	2800 GATEWAY OAKS DR, SAC, 95833	277 - A5
HOST HOTEL	6945 AIRPORT BLVD, SaCo, 95837	256 - B2
HOWARD JOHNSON HOTEL	3343 BRADSHAW RD, SaCo, 95827	299 - B6
HYATT REGENCY	1209 L ST, SAC, 95814	297 - D4
INN AT LAKE NATOMA	702 GOLD LAKE DR, FOLS, 95630	261 - B4
INNS OF AMERICA	12249 FOLSOM BLVD, SaCo, 95742	280 - F4
INNS OF AMERICA	25 HOWE AV, SAC, 95826	318 - D1
LA QUINTA INN	200 JIBBOOM ST, SAC, 95814	297 - B2
LA QUINTA INN	4604 MADISON AV, SaCo, 95841	259 - A7
MARRIOTT RESIDENCE INN	1530 HOWE AV, SaCo, 95825	298 - C2
MARRIOTT SACRAMENTO	11211 POINT EAST DR, SaCo, 95742	280 - A7
RADISSON HOTEL SACRAMENTO	500 LEISURE LN, SAC, 95815	297 - H1
RAMADA INN	2600 AUBURN BLVD, SaCo, 95821	278 - E4
RED LION HOTEL SACRAMENTO	1401 ARDEN WY, SAC, 95815	298 - A1
RED ROOF INN	3796 NORTHGATE BLVD, SAC, 95834	277 - E3
RESIDENCE INN BY MARRIOTT SOUTH-NATOMAS	2410 W EL CAMINO AV, SAC, 95833	277 - A6
SACRAMENTO HILTON INN	2200 HARVARD ST, SAC, 95815	278 - A7
SHERATON GRAND SACRAMENTO HOTEL	1230 J ST, SAC, 95814	297 - D4
SUPER 8 LODGE	4317 MADISON AV, SaCo, 95842	258 - J7
VAGABOND INN	909 3RD ST, SAC, 95814	297 - C3

LAW ENFORCEMENT

FEATURE NAME	Address City, ZIP Code	PAGE-GRID
ANTIOCH POLICE STA (SEE PAGE 493)	300 L ST, ANT, 94509	513 - C4
AUBURN POLICE STA	1225 LINCOLN WY, AUB, 95603	182 - D2
CALIFORNIA HIGHWAY PATROL	9440 INDIAN HILL RD, PlaC, 95658	181 - H6
CITRUS HEIGHTS POLICE DEPT	6237 FOUNTAIN SQUARE DR, CITH, 95621	259 - G4
ELK GROVE POLICE DEPARTMENT	8380 LAGUNA PALMS WY, ELKG, 95758	358 - E5
FOLSOM POLICE STA	50 NATOMA ST, FOLS, 95630	261 - C4
GALT POLICE STA	380 CIVIC DR, GALT, 95632	419 - E5
HIGHWAY PATROL HDQTRS	2555 1ST AV, SAC, 95818	297 - E7
ISLETON POLICE STA	210 JACKSON BLVD, ISLE, 95641	455 - H5
LINCOLN POLICE STA	472 E ST, LNCN, 95648	179 - H3
N SACRAMENTO CALIFORNIA HWY PATROL	5109 TYLER ST, SaCo, 95841	258 - J7
PLACERVILLE POLICE STA	730 MAIN ST, PLCR, 95667	245 - H5
POLICE STA	3550 MARYSVILLE BLVD, SAC, 95838	278 - B3
POLICE STA	5303 FRANKLIN BLVD, SAC, 95820	317 - F4
POLICE STA	JEFFERSON BL & TRIANGLE CT, WSAC, 95605	296 - J3
RIO VISTA POLICE DEPARTMENT	POPPY HOUSE RD, RVIS, 94571	454 - H4
ROCKLIN POLICE STA	4060 ROCKLIN RD, RKLN, 95677	220 - E3
ROSEVILLE POLICE STA	1051 JUNCTION BLVD, RSVL, 95678	219 - G7
SACRAMENTO CITY POLICE DEPARTMENT HQ	900 8TH ST, SAC, 95814	297 - C3
SACRAMENTO COUNTY SHERIFFS DEPT	711 G ST, SAC, 95814	297 - C3
SHERIFF STA	5510 GARFIELD AV, SaCo, 95841	259 - C6
SHERIFF STA	FAIR LN, PLCR, 95667	245 - D5
SOUTH SACRAMENTO CALIFORNIA HWY-PATROL	6 MASSIE CT, SAC, 95823	338 - B4
VALLEY DIVISION CHP	11336 TRADE CENTER DR, SaCo, 95742	280 - B7

LIBRARIES

FEATURE NAME	Address City, ZIP Code	PAGE-GRID
ANTIOCH (SEE PAGE 493)	501 W 18TH ST, ANT, 94509	513 - D5
ARCADE	2443 MARCONI AV, SaCo, 95821	278 - D5
ARDEN-DIMICK	891 WATT AV, SaCo, 95864	298 - F4
AUBURN-PLACER COUNTY	350 NEVADA ST, AUB, 95603	182 - D1
BELLE COOLEDGE	5600 S LAND PARK DR, SAC, 95822	317 - A4
CAMERON PK BRANCH	2500 COUNTRY CLUB DR, EDCo, 95682	263 - B7
CARMICHAEL	5605 MARCONI AV, SaCo, 95608	279 - C6
CENTRAL	828 I ST, SAC, 95814	297 - C3
COLONIAL HEIGHTS	4799 STOCKTON BLVD, SAC, 95820	317 - J3
COURTLAND (SEE PAGE 375)	170 PRIMASING AV, SaCo, 95615	396 - D3
DEL PASO HEIGHTS	920 GRAND AV, SAC, 95838	277 - J3
EL DORADO COUNTY	345 FAIR LN, PLCR, 95667	245 - D5
ELK GROVE	8962 ELK GROVE BLVD, ELKG, 95624	358 - H6
FAIR OAKS	11601 FAIR OAKS BLVD, SaCo, 95628	260 - B6
FOLSOM	300 PERSIFER ST, FOLS, 95630	261 - C5
FRANKLIN BRANCH	10055 FRANKLIN HIGH RD, ELKG, 95757	378 - A1
GALT-MARIAN O LAWRENCE	1000 CAROLINE AV, GALT, 95632	419 - F7
GRANITE BAY BRANCH	6475 DOUGLAS BLVD, PlaC, 95746	241 - B2
ISELTON	412 UNION ST, ISLE, 95641	455 - H5
KING JR, MARTIN LUTHER	7340 24TH ST BYPS, SAC, 95822	337 - E2
LINCOLN	590 5TH ST, LNCN, 95648	179 - H3
LOOMIS BRANCH	6050 LIBRARY DR, LMS, 95650	201 - A6
MAIDU BRANCH	1530 MAIDU DR, RSVL, 95661	240 - C4
MCCLATCHY	2112 22ND ST, SAC, 95818	297 - E6
MCKINLEY	601 ALHAMBRA BLVD, SAC, 95816	297 - G4
NORTH HIGHLANDS-ANTELOPE	4235 ANTELOPE RD, SaCo, 95843	258 - J1
NORTH HIGHLANDS BRANCH	3601 PLYMOUTH DR, SaCo, 95660	258 - G2
NORTH NATOMAS BRANCH	2500 NEW MARKET DR, SAC, 95835	257 - A7
N SACRAMENTO/HAGGINWOOD	2109 DEL PASO BLVD, SAC, 95815	277 - H6
OAK RIDGE BRANCH	1120 HARVARD WY, EDCo, 95762	262 - D4
ORANGEVALE	8820 GREENBACK LN, SaCo, 95662	260 - E4
PENRYN BRANCH	2215 RIPPEY RD, PlaC, 95663	201 - C2
POLLOCK PINES	6210 PONY EXPRESS TR, EDCo, 95726	248 - C1
RANCHO CORDOVA	9845 FOLSOM BLVD, SaCo, 95827	299 - C4
RIO LINDA	902 OAK LN, SaCo, 95673	257 - J2
RIO VISTA	44 SECOND ST, RVIS, 94571	454 - H6
ROCKLIN BRANCH	5460 5TH ST, RKLN, 95677	220 - D3
ROSEVILLE MAIN	225 TAYLOR ST, RSVL, 95678	239 - H2
SOUTHGATE	6132 66TH AV, SaCo, 95823	338 - A2
SOUTH NATOMAS	2901 TRUXEL RD, SAC, 95833	277 - C5
STATE	914 CAPITOL MALL, SAC, 95814	297 - C4
SYLVAN OAKS	6700 AUBURN BLVD, CITH, 95621	259 - F3
THORNTON BRANCH (SEE PAGE 418)	26341 N THORNTON RD, SJCo, 95686	438 - A3
TURNER, AF BRANCH	1212 MERKLEY AV, WSAC, 95691	296 - J3
VALLEY HI-NORTH LAGUNA	6351 MACK RD, SAC, 95823	338 - A4
WALNUT GROVE	14177 MARKET ST, SaCo, 95690	437 - A1

MILITARY INSTALLATIONS

FEATURE NAME	Address City, ZIP Code	PAGE-GRID
ARMY NATL GUARD	FEMOYER AV & STRATOTANKER AV, SaCo, 95655	299 - G6
NATL GUARD ARMORY	1013 58TH ST, SAC, 95819	298 - A6
UNITED STATES COAST GUARD RESV	BEACH DR, SolC, 94571	454 - H7

MUSEUMS

FEATURE NAME	Address City, ZIP Code	PAGE-GRID
BERNHARD MUS COMPLEX	291 AUBURN-FOLSOM RD, AUB, 95603	182 - D3
CALIFORNIA MILITARY MUS	1119 2ND ST, SAC, 95814	297 - B3
CALIFORNIA MUS FOR HIST, WOMEN, ARTS	1020 O ST, SAC, 95814	297 - C4
CALIFORNIA STATE RAILROAD MUS	125 I ST, SAC, 95814	297 - B3
CROCKER ART MUS	216 O ST, SAC, 95814	297 - B4
DISCOVERY MUS	101 I ST, SAC, 95814	297 - B3
DISCOVERY MUS LEARNING CTR	3615 AUBURN BLVD, SAC, 95821	278 - G3
EL DORADO COUNTY MUS	104 PLACERVILLE DR, PLCR, 95667	245 - C6
FOLSOM HIST MUS	823 SUTTER ST, FOLS, 95630	261 - B5
FOLSOM PRISON MUS	NATOMA ST & GREEN VALLEY RD, FOLS, 95671	261 - E3
GOLD COUNTRY MUS	1273 HIGH ST, AUB, 95603	182 - D3
GRIFFITH QUARRY MUS	7504 ROCK SPRINGS RD, PlaC, 95663	201 - D2
HIST POWERHOUSE MUS	LEIDESDORF ST & RILEY ST, FOLS, 95630	261 - B4
MCCLELLAN AVIATION MUS	3200 FREEDOM PARK DR, SaCo, 95652	258 - F5
PLACER COUNTY MUS	101 MAPLE ST, AUB, 95603	182 - D3
RIO VISTA MUS	16 N FRONT ST, RVIS, 94571	454 - H5
SACRAMENTO ARCHIVES & MUS COLLECTION	551 SEQUOIA PACIFIC BLVD, SAC, 95814	297 - C1
STATE CAPITOL MUS	10TH & L ST, SAC, 95814	297 - D4
STATE INDIAN MUS	2618 K ST, SAC, 95816	297 - F5
TOWE AUTO MUS	2200 FRONT ST, SAC, 95818	297 - A5
WELLS FARGO HIST MUS	400 CAPITOL MALL, SAC, 95814	297 C4

OPEN SPACE PRESERVES

FEATURE NAME	Address City, ZIP Code	PAGE-GRID
COSUMNES RIVER PRESERVE	FRANKLIN BLVD & DESMOND RD, SaCo, 95690	417 - H4
DOW WETLANDS PRESERVE (SEE PAGE 493)	PITTSBURG-ANTIOCH HWY, ANT, 94509	513 - B3
EDGECLIFF COURT OPEN SPACE	8233 NEWBRIDGE, CITH, 95610	240 - C6
HAZELWOOD GREENS OPEN SPACE	HAZELWOOD AV & WRENDALE WY, SaCo, 95821	278 - J6
HINKLE CREEK NATURE AREA	710 BALDWIN DAM RD, FOLS, 95630	261 - A3
INDIAN RIVER DRIVE OPEN SPACE	INDAIN RIVER DR & BROKEN BOW, CITH, 95621	259 - D4
LA SIERRA OPEN SPACE	GIBBONS DR & OAK VILLA CIR, SaCo, 95608	279 - B3
MANANA OPEN SPACE	MANANA WY & AQUADUCT DR, SaCo, 95628	260 - C5
MATHENY OPEN SPACE	MATHENY WY & MI CT, CITH, 95621	259 - D4
MINERS RAVINE NATURE RESERVE	7530 AUBURN-FOLSOM RD, PlaC, 95746	241 - C1
NORTH LAGUNA CREEK WILDLIFE AREA	SHELDON RD & CENTER PKWY, SAC, 95758	357 - J1
OLIVINE AV OPEN SPACE	OLIVINE AV, CITH, 95610	240 - C7
OPEN SPACE (SEE PAGE 493)	MARSH CREEK REGIONAL TR, CCCo, 94561	514 - F5
STOCK RANCH OPEN SPACE	AUBURN BLVD, CITH, 95621	259 - G3
TRAYLOR RANCH NATURE RESERVE	ENGLISH COLONY WY & HMPHREY RD, PlaC, 95663	200 - H1
WOODSIDE OAKS OPEN SPACE	WACHTEL WY & PITALO WY, CITH, 95610	240 - C7

PARK & RIDE

FEATURE NAME	Address City, ZIP Code	PAGE-GRID
PARK & RIDE	47TH AV & 27TH ST, SAC, 95822	317 - E6
PARK & RIDE	99 FRWY & HWY 104, GALT, 95632	419 - E2
PARK & RIDE	ARDEN WY & DEL PASO BLVD, SAC, 95815	277 - G7
PARK & RIDE	BELL RD & BOWMAN RD, PlaC, 95603	162 - G3
PARK & RIDE	BOWMAN RD & BELL RD, PlaC, 95602	162 - G3
PARK & RIDE	BUTTERFIELD WY & MAYHEW RD, SaCo, 95827	299 - B6
PARK & RIDE	CAMBRIDGE RD & 50 FRWY, EDCo, 95682	263 - C7
PARK & RIDE	CAMERON PARK DR & HWY 50, EDCo, 95682	263 - F7
PARK & RIDE	CIRBY WY & ORLANDO AV, RSVL, 95661	239 - J4
PARK & RIDE	DIXIEANNE AV & SELMA ST, SAC, 95815	277 - J7
PARK & RIDE	DOUGLAS BL & BULJAN DR, RSVL, 95678	239 - J2
PARK & RIDE	DRY CREEK RD & LAKE ARTHUR RD, PlaC, 95602	162 - J1
PARK & RIDE	ELKHORN BL & EL CENTRO RD, SaCo, 95835	256 - G3
PARK & RIDE	ENTERPRISE BL & 80 FRWY, WSAC, 95691	296 - C4
PARK & RIDE	E STOCKTON BL & ELK GROVE BLVD, ELKG, 95624	358 - F6
PARK & RIDE	E STOCKTON BL & OLD CALVINE RD, ELKG, 95624	338 - D7
PARK & RIDE	12500 FOLSOM BLVD, SaCo, 95742	280 - G4

FEATURE NAME Address City, ZIP Code	PAGE-GRID
PARK & RIDE FOLSOM BLVD & IRON POINT RD, FOLS, 95630	280 - J2
PARK & RIDE FOLSOM BLVD & SUNRISE BLVD, SaCo, 95742	280 - A7
PARK & RIDE 1025 GLENN DR, FOLS, 95630	261 - A6
PARK & RIDE GRASS VALLEY HWY & ATWOOD RD, PlaC, 95603	162 - B4
PARK & RIDE GRASSY RUN CT & GREENSTONE RD, EDCo, 95667	264 - F2
PARK & RIDE HAZEL AV & GOLD COUNTRY BL, SaCo, 95670	280 - F3
PARK & RIDE (SEE PAGE 493) HILLCREST AV & 4 FRWY, ANT, 94509	513 - G6
PARK & RIDE HORSESHOE BAR RD & 80 FRWY, LMS, 95650	201 - A7
PARK & RIDE 150 IRON POINT RD, FOLS, 95630	281 - A2
PARK & RIDE INDIAN HILL RD & NEWCASTLE RD, PlaC, 95658	181 - G6
PARK & RIDE JACKSON RD & SUNRISE BLVD, SaCo, 95830	320 - C7
PARK & RIDE LEIDESDORFF ST, FOLS, 95630	261 - B5
PARK & RIDE LIME KILN RD & DIAMOND RD, EDCo, 95619	265 - E2
PARK & RIDE LINCOLN WY & BOWMAN UC RD, PlaC, 95603	162 - G4
PARK & RIDE LNCN NWCSTLE HWY & SIERRA COL, PlaC, 95648	180 - D4
PARK & RIDE MARCONI AV & ARCADE BLVD, SAC, 95815	278 - B5
PARK & RIDE MATHER FIELD RD & MILLS STA, RCCD, 95827	299 - E3
PARK & RIDE MEADOWVIEW RD, SAC, 95822	337 - F3
PARK & RIDE MISSOURI FLAT & MOTHER LODE DR, EDCo, 95667	245 - B7
PARK & RIDE NEWCASTLE RD & 80 FWY, PlaC, 95658	181 - G6
PARK & RIDE OPHIR RD & HWY 193, PlaC, 95658	181 - H5
PARK & RIDE PENRYN RD & 80 FWY, PlaC, 95663	201 - C4
PARK & RIDE PONDEROSA RD & NORTH SHINGLE, EDCo, 95682	264 - A7
PARK & RIDE POWER INN RD & CUCAMONGA AV, SAC, 95826	318 - D1
PARK & RIDE ROCK BARN RD & SHINGLE SPRINGS, EDCo, 95682	264 - C4
PARK & RIDE ROCKY RIDGE DR & MAIDU DR, RSVL, 95661	240 - C3
PARK & RIDE ROSEVILLE RD & LONGVIEW DR, SAC, 95660	278 - E2
PARK & RIDE SHELDON RD & 99 FRWY, ELKG, 95624	358 - D2
PARK & RIDE SIERRA COLLEGE BL & I-80 FRWY, RKLN, 95677	220 - H1
PARK & RIDE S SHINGLE RD & DUROCK RD, EDCo, 95682	264 - A7
PARK & RIDE SUNSET BL & PEBBLE CREEK DR, RKLN, 95765	220 - B2
PARK & RIDE TAYLOR RD & 1-80 FRWY, RSVL, 95661	220 - B7
PARK & RIDE WATT AV & HWY 80 WEST, SaCo, 95660	278 - G2
PARK & RIDE WATT AV & I-80, SaCo, 95660	278 - F2
PARK & RIDE WATT AV & MANLOVE RD, SaCo, 95826	298 - H7
PARK & RIDE WHITE ROCK RD & LATROBE RD, EDCo, 95762	282 - E2
PARK & RIDE WILD CHAPARRAL DR & PONDEROSA, EDCo, 95682	264 - A7

PARKS & RECREATION

FEATURE NAME Address City, ZIP Code	PAGE-GRID
4TH AV PK, SAC	317 - G1
21ST AV PKWY, SAC	317 - J3
24TH STREET BYPASS PK, SAC	337 - E2
AHLSTRON PK, RCCD	299 - H1
AHNER, EUGENE H PK, SaCo	259 - C6
ALI, BEN PK, SAC	278 - B6
ALMOND PK, SaCo	260 - D5
ALMONDRIDGE PK, ANT (SEE PAGE 493)	513 - J6
AMERICAN LAKES PK, SAC	277 - D5
AMERICAN RIVER PARKWAY, SAC	277 - E7
AMUNDSON PK, ELKG	358 - H1
ANTELOPE COMM PK, SaCo	238 - J6
ANTELOPE CREEK PK, RKLN	220 - C3
ANTELOPE STA PK, SaCo	239 - E6
ANTHONY PK, SAC	337 - F4
ANTHONY, SUSAN B PK, SAC	337 - F5
ANTIOCH/OAKLEY REGL SHORELINE, OAKL- (SEE PAGE 493)	514 - A3
ANTIOCH YOUTH SPORTS COMPLEX, ANT- (SEE PAGE 493)	513 - F4
ARCADE CREEK NATURE AREA, SaCo	259 - B7
ARCADE CREEK PK, SaCo	259 - C7
ARCADE CREEK PK RESERVE, CITH	259 - J4
ARCHERY RANGE, EDCo	262 - D5
ARCOHE PK, SaCo	420 - C1
ARGONAUT PK, SAC	317 - B5
ASHFORD PK, AUB	162 - F7
ASHTON PK, SaCo	298 - H4
AUBURN DIST REGL PK, PlaC	162 - A2
AUBURN STATE REC AREA, EDCo	202 - H1
AUTUMN MEADOW PK, SAC	257 - A4
AZEVEDO, MARGARET COMM PK, RKLN	199 - J6
BABCOCK PK, SAC	278 - B7
BACKER RANCH PK, ELKG	358 - B7
BAER, MAX PK, SAC	318 - C5
BAHNFLETH PK, SAC	316 - J4
BAKER PK, ELKG	358 - G7
BANNISTER PK, SaCo	279 - H3
BANNON CREEK PARKWAY, SAC	277 - B6
BARANDAS PK, SAC	276 - J6
BARTHOLOMEW PK, ELKG	357 - F4
BARTHOLOMEW SPORTS PK, ELKG	378 - A2
BATEY PK, ELKG	358 - B5
BEACON HILL PK, FOLS	261 - H6
BEAN, BILL C PK, SAC	318 - C3
BEAR FLAG PK, SAC	316 - J6
BECERRA, ADAM PK, RSVL	219 - C3
BEEMAN PK, ELKG	358 - G6
BELL AVENUE PK, SAC	278 - C2
BELLVIEW PK, SaCo	278 - C6
BENNETT PK, PLCR	245 - E4
BERENS PK, ELKG	379 - A2
BESANA, SYLVIA PK, RSVL	219 - H5
BEST, BABE PK, SaCo	237 - J7
BETSCHART PK, ELKG	357 - J3
BICENTENNIAL PK, AUB	182 - D3
BIDWELL PK, SAC	337 - C2
BIRD TRACK PK, SaCo	259 - G7
BIRNEY PK, SAC	317 - B6
BLUE OAK PK, SaCo	238 - J7
BLUE OAK PK, SAC	257 - A5
BLUE OAKS PK, RSVL	219 - C3
BOHEMIAN PK, SaCo	278 - D5
BOWLING GREEN PK, SaCo	317 - G7
BRADFORD PK, ELKG	377 - H1

FEATURE NAME Address City, ZIP Code	PAGE-GRID
BRANNAN ISLAND STATE REC AREA, SaCo	474 - H4
BRANNAN PK, SAC	317 - A4
BREEN PK, RKLN	200 - B6
BRIDGEWAY ISLAND PK, WSAC	316 - D2
BRIGGS, ELVIE PERAZZO PK, FOLS	261 - H3
BROCK PK, SaCo	258 - H1
BROCKWAY PK, SAC	317 - D1
BROOKTREE PK, CITH	259 - F5
BROWN, VENCIL PK, RSVL	219 - G4
BRUNAVISTA PK, RVIS	454 - G5
BRYTE, ALYCE NORMAN PLAYFIELD, WSAC	296 - H1
BRYTE PK, WSAC	296 - H1
BULJAN PK, RSVL	219 - G5
BURBANK PK, SAC	337 - F2
BURBERRY PK, SAC	257 - A5
CABRILLO PK, SAC	337 - C2
CALIFORNIA HILLS NEIGHBORHOOD PK, FOLS	261 - C6
CALIFORNIA LILAC PK, SAC	257 - C5
CALIFORNIA PK, SAC	297 - C7
CALVINE STA PK, SaCo	338 - F7
CAMDEN PK, ELKG	358 - F4
CAMELLIA PK, SAC	318 - B7
CANAL PK, ANT (SEE PAGE 493)	513 - A7
CANYON CREEK PK, GALT	419 - F4
CAPEHART YOUTH CTR, SaCo	238 - G6
CAPITOL MALL PK, SAC	297 - C4
CAPITOL PK, SAC	297 - D4
CARDINAL OAKS PK, SaCo	279 - B6
CARMICHAEL PK, SaCo	279 - C4
CASE PK, ELKG	357 - J3
CASTELLO PK, ELKG	358 - G4
CASTORI PK, SAC	278 - B3
CATERINO, MICHAEL PK, ELKG	357 - G6
CATLIN, AMOS P PK, FOLS	261 - D7
CAYMUS PK, SaCo	338 - H6
C-BAR-C PK, CITH	260 - B1
CENTRAL PK HORSE ARENA, SaCo	257 - J3
CHABOLLA PK, GALT	419 - F7
CHARDONAY PK, SaCo	259 - B1
CHARTER POINTE PK, SAC	336 - G3
CHAVEZ, CEASAR E PK, SAC	297 - C3
CHERRY CREEK PK (SITE), CITH	259 - G5
CHERRY ISLAND SOCCER COMPLEX, SaCo	238 - D7
CHORLEY PK, SAC	337 - C1
CHRISTIAN VALLEY PK, PlaC	162 - H1
CHUCKWAGON PK, SAC	277 - D4
CHURCHILL DOWNS COMM PK, SaCo	338 - J6
CIRBY CREEK PK, RSVL	239 - H4
CIRCLE PK, WSAC	296 - J5
CITY PK, ANT (SEE PAGE 493)	513 - D4
CITY PK, PLCR	245 - G5
CITY PK, RVIS	454 - H5
CITY PK, LNCN	200 - A2
CLAREMONT PK, OAKL (SEE PAGE 493)	514 - G7
CLARKE DOMINGUEZ PK, RKLN	200 - D7
CLARKSBURG RIVER ACCESS, YoCo- (SEE PAGE 375)	376 - J2
CLIFF HOUSE FISHING ACCESS, SaCo	455 - B3
CLOVER VALLEY PK, RKLN	220 - D1
COCHRAN PK, SaCo	338 - J6
COHN, PHILLIP C PK, FOLS	261 - H5
COLEMAN PK, SaCo	260 - E3
COLLIN, ILLA PK, SaCo	338 - G7
COLLINS, BT PK, FOLS	261 - F4
COLOMA PK, SAC	297 - H7
COLONIAL PK, SAC	317 - J3
COLTON PK, ELKG	358 - E5
COMBS, SAM PK, WSAC	296 - J6
COMM PK II, RCCD	279 - H6
CONLIN, BILL YOUTH SPORTS COMPLEX, SAC	337 - B4
CONTRA LOMA PK, ANT (SEE PAGE 493)	513 - B6
COOLEDGE, BELLE PK, SAC	317 - A4
COOLEDGE PK, SAC	317 - B4
CORRAL-ALVIS NEIGHBORHOOD PK, RKLN	220 - F4
COSUMNES RIVER PARKWAY, SaCo	342 - B2
COSUMNES PK, SAC	338 - B7
COTTAGE PK, SaCo	278 - F7
COTTONWOOD PK, SAC	257 - C7
COTTONWOOD PK, SaCo	338 - F6
COUNTRYSIDE COMM PK, SaCo	338 - D6
COUNTRYSIDE PK, RCCD	299 - E5
COWAN PK, SAC	278 - H4
CRABTREE PK, SaCo	298 - F3
CREEKSIDE PK, SaCo	278 - E6
CRESCENT PK, RVIS	454 - H5
CRESCENT PK, SAC	297 - G6
CRESTA PK, SaCo	298 - H2
CRESTHAVEN PK, RSVL	239 - G5
CRESTMONT PK, RSVL	240 - C5
CROCKER PK, SAC	297 - B4
CROFOOT PK (CIRCLE PARK), SaCo	337 - J1
CROSSWOODS PK, CITH	259 - F3
CUMMINGS FAMILY PK, FOLS	261 - F5
CURTIS PK, SAC	317 - E1
DANBURY PARKWAY, SaCo	338 - F7
DARLING PK, FOLS	261 - J4
DAVID, JIM PK, SaCo	280 - F1
DA VINCI PK, SAC	317 - D3
DAVIS, JACK PK, SaCo	317 - G2
DAVIS, LEONARD DUKE PK, RSVL	219 - C1
DAVIS, WALT PK, ELKG	358 - A3
DEL CAMPO PK, SaCo	259 - E7
DEL MEYER PK, ELKG	358 - H4
DEL PASO HEIGHTS PK, SAC	277 - H3
DEL PASO MANOR PK, SaCo	278 - H6
DEL PASO PK, SAC	278 - F2
DEPOT PK, SaCo	257 - J3
DETERDING PK, SaCo	298 - F2
DIAMOND OAKS PK, RSVL	219 - J6
DIDION PK, SAC	316 - F6
DIETRICH, WILLARD PK, RSVL	240 - D4
DISCOVERY PK, SAC	277 - C7
DIXIANNE TOT LOT, SAC	277 - H6
DIXIE-ANNE PK, SAC	277 - J6
DOS RIOS PK, SAC	297 - E1
DOUGLAS RANCH PK, PlaC	240 - H1
DOYLE RANCH PK, PlaC	238 - H3
DOYLE, ROBERT PK, RSVL	219 - C5
DROUIN PK, RVIS	454 - G5
DRY CREEK PARKWAY, SaCo	238 - D7
DUTRA PK, SAC	316 - G7
EAST DRAINAGE PARKWAY, SAC	277 - B1
EASTERN OAK PK, SaCo	278 - H5
EAST LAWN CHILDRENS PK, SAC	297 - H6
EAST PORTAL PK, SAC	297 - J6
EASTWOOD PK, RSVL	239 - J4
EGBERT FIELD, RVIS	454 - J5
EGLOFF FAMILY PK, FOLS	261 - B1
EGRET PK, SAC	256 - G6
EHRHARDT OAKS PK, ELKG	357 - H7
ELDORADO NATL FOREST, EDCo	247 - G3
ELK GROVE REGL PK, ELKG	378 - G1
ELKHORN BOAT ACCESS, SaCo	255 - H5
ELKHORN PK, WSAC	296 - J1
ELKHORN PK, YoCo	255 - J6
ELKHORN STAGING AREA, SaCo	257 - E3
ELLIOTT, H C PK, RSVL	219 - B7
EMERALD VISTA PK, GALT	419 - E4
ERVEN, MELBA & WILLIAM PK, RSVL	220 - A4
FAIR OAKS PK, SaCo	260 - A7
FAIR PK, AUB	182 - D3
FAIRVIEW PK, ANT (SEE PAGE 493)	513 - B4

FEATURE NAME Address City, ZIP Code	PAGE-GRID
FALES PK, ELKG	338 - D7
FEDERSPIEL PK, RCCD	299 - G1
FEICKERT PK, ELKG	358 - F5
FERRETTI PK, RSVL	239 - G1
FIRESTONE PK, SaCo	239 - B7
FISHING ACCESS PK, RVIS	454 - H5
FITE PK, ELKG	357 - G3
FLORIN CREEK PK, SaCo	337 - J2
FLORIN RESERVOIR PK, SAC	318 - C7
FOLSOM CITY PK, FOLS	261 - C4
FOLSOM KIDS PLAY PK, FOLS	261 - G5
FOLSOM LAKE STATE REC AREA, EDCo	222 - F5
FOOTHILL COMM PK, SaCo	259 - C3
FOULKS PK, ELKG	358 - C5
FOUNTAIN PLAZA PK, SaCo	317 - J6
FRANKLIN VILLA PK, SAC	337 - H3
FREEDOM PK, SaCo	258 - F5
FREEPORT PK, SAC	337 - C3
FREEPORT SCHOOL PK, SAC	337 - C3
FREMONT PK, SAC	297 - D5
FROST, ROBERT PK, SaCo	259 - A4
FRUITRIDGE COMM PK, SaCo	317 - G4
FUMASI GROVE, GALT	419 - D7
FUNDERLAND PK, SAC	297 - D5
GAGE PK, ELKG	358 - G1
GALT COMM PK, GALT	419 - G3
GARBOLINO PK, RSVL	239 - J3
GARCIA BEND PK, SAC	336 - G3
GARDEN HIGHWAY PARKWAY, SAC	277 - B7
GARDENLAND PK, SAC	277 - F5
GARDEN PK, FOLS	261 - B5
GARDEN VALLEY PK, SAC	277 - E3
GATES PK, ELKG	359 - A7
GATEWAY PK, WSAC	296 - J7
GATEWAY PK, SAC	277 - H4
GENTRY TOWN PK, ANT (SEE PAGE 493)	513 - A7
GIBBONS PK, SaCo	279 - A3
GIBSON RANCH CO PK, SaCo	238 - E5
GLANCY OAKS PK, SaCo	279 - B7
GLENBROOK PK, SAC	298 - F7
GLEN HALL PK, SAC	298 - B4
GLENWOOD PK, SAC	277 - G2
GOETHE PK, RCCD	299 - D1
GOETHE PK, SAC	337 - D2
GOLD BUG PK, PLCR	245 - G3
GOLD RIVER PK, SaCo	280 - C4
GOLD STA PK, SaCo	280 - B6
GRANITE BAY COMM PK, PlaC	241 - A3
GRANITE PK, FOLS	261 - B5
GRANITE REGL PK, SAC	318 - E2
GRANT PK, SAC	297 - F3
GREENBACK WOODS PK, CITH	259 - D3
GREENFAIR PK, SAC	317 - J1
GREER BASIN PK, GALT	419 - D7
GREER PK, SaCo	298 - D2
GRIFFITH QUARRY PK, PlaC	201 - D2
HAGAN COMM PK, RCCD	279 - F7
HAGGINWOOD PK, SAC	278 - A4
HALL, JAMES A PK, RSVL	239 - D1
HAMILTON STREET PK, SaCo	278 - H1
HAMPTON PK, SaCo	338 - A2
HANDY FAMILY PK, FOLS	281 - J1
HANNAFORD FAMILY PK, FOLS	261 - B1
HANSEN RANCH PK, SAC	257 - F5
HARBOUR PK, ANT (SEE PAGE 493)	513 - E7
HARDESTER PK, SaCo	338 - F7
HARVEY PK, GALT	419 - E7
HAWKINS PK, ELKG	357 - D4
HAYER, ROY E PK, SaCo	257 - J4
HEARST PK, SAC	298 - A7
HENDERSON PK, ELKG	377 - E1
HENSCHEL PK, SAC	297 - J4
HERBURGER PK, ELKG	358 - B3
HERON PK, SAC	257 - B5
HIGHLAND COMM SPORTS COMPLEX, SaCo	258 - G4
HILLCREST PK, ANT (SEE PAGE 493)	513 - G7
HILL PK, ELKG	358 - J5
HILLSBOROUGH PK, RSVL	240 - F4
HITE PK, SAC	337 - J5
HOFFMAN, ANCIL PK, SaCo	279 - E6
HOLLYWOOD PK, SAC	317 - D3
HOLYOKE NATURE AREA, SaCo	259 - B7
HOME COMING PK, RVIS	454 - H3
HOPKINS PK, SAC	337 - D2
HOUDE PK, ELKG	357 - E7
HOWE PK, SaCo	278 - C7
HREPICH PK, ELKG	358 - G1
HUDSON, SALLY PK, SAC	276 - J7
HUGHES, WILLIAM PK, RSVL	219 - C2
HUMMINGBIRD PK, SAC	276 - J3
HUNTINGTON PK, SAC	317 - E5
INDEPENDENCE PK, SaCo	319 - J2
INDIAN STONE CORRAL, SaCo	240 - H6
JACINTO CREEK PK, SAC	358 - D1
JACINTO CREEK PARKWAY, SAC	358 - B2
JACOBSEN PK, ANT (SEE PAGE 493)	513 - F5
JEFFERSON PK, SAC	277 - B5
JEFFERSON PK, SAC	298 - E7
JEFFERSON SCHOOL PK, SAC	277 - B5
JENSEN, CHARLES C BOTANICAL PK, SaCo	279 - F3
JIBBOOM STREET PK, SAC	297 - B2
JOHN PICHES PK, RSVL	240 - D1
JOHNSON, NEELY PK, SAC	297 - D3
JOHNSON PK, ELKG	357 - F6
JOHNSON SPRINGVIEW PK, RKLN	220 - D3
JOHNSON, TOBY PK, SaCo	338 - E6
JOHNSTON PK, SAC	277 - G5
JOHNSTON PK, ELKG	378 - B1
JOINER PK, LNCN	179 - F2
JONES PK, ELKG	358 - G1
JONES, STEVE PK, SAC	337 - E3
JUNGKEIT PK, ELKG	357 - J7
KASEBERG PK, RSVL	239 - F1
KEEMA PK, ELKG	357 - J7
KEMBLE PK, SAC	337 - E3
KEMP, JOHN COMM PK, FOLS	281 - G1
KENNEDY PK, SaCo	338 - C1
KENNEDY PK, SAC	316 - H7
KENTFIELD PK, FOLS	261 - F7
KENWOOD OAKS AT JOHN MACKEY PK, SAC	278 - B4
KENWOOD OAKS PK, RSVL	239 - J5
KING JR, MARTIN LUTHER PK, SAC	337 - E2
KING PK, ELKG	357 - E5
KLOSS PK, ELKG	357 - J5
KOKOMO PK, SAC	256 - J6
KRAMER PK, ELKG	358 - A7
LAGUNA COMM PK, ELKG	358 - B3
LAGUNA STONELAKE COMM PK, ELKG	377 - F1
LAKE CANYON PK, GALT	419 - F2
LAND, WILLIAM PK, SAC	317 - B1
LARCHMONT COMM PK, SaCo	298 - J5
LARCHMONT PK, SaCo	258 - G3
LARCHMONT-ROSSMOOR PK, RCCD	279 - G6
LARKSPUR, JONAS PK, SaCo	298 - E3
LAS LERRA PK, SaCo	298 - H3
LAWRENCE PK, SAC	317 - H4
LAWRENCE PK, ELKG	357 - G5
LAWSON, GARY PK, ELKG	357 - E4
LEIMBACH PK, SAC	338 - B6
LEIVA PK, SAC	297 - B5
LEMBI PK, FOLS	261 - D6
LEW HOWARD PK, FOLS	261 - A2

FEATURE NAME Address City, ZIP Code	PAGE-GRID
LEWIS PK, ELKG	359 - A6
LEWIS PK, SAC	316 - F6
LICHTENBERGER PK, ELKG	358 - A6
LINCOLN ESTATES PK, RSVL	240 - A1
LINCOLN VILLAGE COMM PK, RCCD	299 - D6
LINDA CREEK PK, SaCo	258 - A4
LINDEN PK, SAC	277 - B2
LINDEN PK, WSAC	296 - F7
LIONS OAK PK, GALT	419 - E6
LIONS PK, PLCR	245 - J6
LIPPINCOTT PK, ELKG	357 - F4
LITTLE LEAGUE PK, ELKG	317 - E6
LITTLE PHOENIX PK, SaCo	260 - F7
LIVERMORE COMM PK, FOLS	261 - E7
LOCKRIDGE, RAY E PK, RSVL	240 - E3
LOMBARDI PK, ELKG	358 - E2
LONE OAK PK, SaCo	238 - G6
LONETREE PK, RKLN	199 - H7
LOOMIS REG PK NORTH, PlaC	201 - B5
LOOMIS REG PK SOUTH, PlaC	201 - B5
LUBIN PK, SAC	297 - G5
LUMSDEN PK, PLCR	245 - J5
MACDONALD, EDIE PK, ELKG	358 - F3
MACHADO PK, LNCN	179 - E5
MACK PK, SAC	337 - J3
MADDOX PK, SaCo	299 - A1
MADERA PK, CITH	240 - A6
MAHANY PK, RSVL	219 - C6
MAIDU REGL PK, RSVL	240 - D4
MAIN AVENUE PK, SAC	258 - A7
MANGAN, JAMES PK, SAC	317 - D5
MANLOVE PK, SaCo	298 - J7
MANN PK, FOLS	281 - B2
MANOR PK, SAC	277 - G4
MANSION OAKS PK, RKLN	200 - C5
MAPLE PK, SAC	317 - F5
MARCO DOG PK, RSVL	240 - B2
MARKHAM RAVINE PK, LNCN	179 - D2
MARKS, MAMA PK, SAC	277 - J3
MARRIOTT PK, SAC	337 - A4
MARSHALL PK, SAC	297 - F4
MASON, WILLIAM T PK, SaCo	259 - C2
MATHER REGL PK, SaCo	299 - J7
MATHER SPORTS COMPLEX, RCCD	299 - F5
MCBEAN MEM PK, LNCN	179 - H3
MCCAFFREY SPORTS PK, GALT	419 - G2
MCCLATCHY, JAMES PK, SAC	317 - F1
MCCLATCHY PK, SAC	317 - C1
MCCONNELL, JENNIE PK, ELKG	378 - H2
MCDONALD FIELD PK, CITH	240 - A7
MCFARLAND, HAZEL PK, FOLS	261 - J4
MCKINLEY PK, SAC	297 - G4
MEADOW BROOK PK, ANT- (SEE PAGE 493)	513 - G6
MEADOWDALE PK, WSAC	296 - E4
MEADOWVIEW PK, SAC	337 - E4
MEADOWVIEW PK, GALT	439 - E2
MEMORIAL PK, SaCo	258 - H1
MEMORIAL PK, ANT (SEE PAGE 493)	513 - C7
MENDOZA PK, ELKG	358 - H5
MESA GRANDE PK, SAC	337 - H5
MILES PK, ELKG	359 - B7
MILLER PK, SAC	297 - A6
MILLER PK, SaCo	280 - C1
MIRA VISTA PK, ANT (SEE PAGE 493)	513 - B7
MISSION NORTH PK, SaCo	279 - A4
MISTY WOOD PK, RSVL	219 - E5
MITCHELL, ED PK, FOLS	261 - E5
MIWOK PK, ELKG	358 - D5
MIX PK, ELKG	358 - G3
MONTE VISTA PK, RKLN	220 - G4
MONTVIEW PK, SaCo	279 - H2
MONUMENT NEIGHBORHOOD PK, RKLN	200 - D5
MORSE PK, ELKG	357 - J7
MORSE SCHOOL PK, SAC	337 - C1
MOUNTAIRE PK, ANT (SEE PAGE 493)	513 - E7
MUIR PK, SAC	297 - E3
NATOMAS OAKS PK, SAC	277 - A7
NATOMAS REGL PK, SAC	256 - J6
NATOMA STA NEIGHBORHOOD PK, FOLS	281 - B1
NATOMA STA MINI PK A, FOLS	281 - C1
NATOMA STA MINI PK B, FOLS	281 - B2
NELSON, RUBE PK, RSVL	219 - F6
NICHOLAS PK, SaCo	317 - H7
NIELSEN PK, SAC	337 - J3
NIGHT RIDGE PK, RKLN	220 - A2
NINOS PARKWAY, SAC	277 - E6
NISENAN COMM PK, FOLS	261 - J7
NORTH AVENUE PK, SAC	278 - A2
NORTHBOROUGH PK, SAC	257 - A5
NORTHBROOK PK, SaCo	238 - E5
NORTHGATE PK, SAC	277 - D5
NORTH LAGUNA CREEK PK, SAC	358 - A1
NORTH NATOMAS COMM PK, SAC	257 - C5
NORTH NATOMAS PK NATURE CTR, SAC	257 - B5
NORTH PK, PlaC	162 - B1
NORTH POINT PK, SAC	257 - G7
NORTH VETERANS MEM PK, RSVL	219 - B2
NORTHWOODS PK, CITH	260 - C2
NUEVO PK, SAC	277 - H4
OAKDALE PK, SaCo	278 - G1
OAKLEY PK, OAKL (SEE PAGE 493)	514 - E7
OAK MEADOW PK, SaCo	298 - E6
OAK PK COMM CTR, SAC	317 - G2
OHARA PK, OAKL (SEE PAGE 493)	514 - E7
OKI PK, SAC	298 - F7
OLDE FLORINTOWN PK, SaCo	338 - E1
OLYMPUS PK, RSVL	240 - E2
ONEIL PK, SAC	297 - B5
ONETO PK, ELKG	358 - D6
ORANGEVALE COMM CTR & PK, SaCo	260 - F3
ORANGEVALE PK, SaCo	260 - F2
ORANGEVALE YOUTH CTR PK, SaCo	260 - F3
ORCHARD HILL PK, PLCR	245 - B5
ORCHARD PK, SAC	276 - J6
PALISADES PK, SaCo	260 - J5
PANNEL, SAMUEL COMM CTR, SAC	337 - E3
PARK OAKS PARK, SaCo	259 - E5
PARK PLAZA, SAC	277 - C6
PARKWAY OAKS PARK, SAC	336 - J2
PATRIOT PK, OAKL (SEE PAGE 493)	514 - E6
PAUL J DUGAN PARK, DR, RSVL	219 - D1
PEBBLE CREEK PK, RKLN	220 - B1
PECAN PK, SaCo	260 - F5
PEDERSEN PK, ELKG	357 - J5
PENNSYLVANIA PK, WSAC	296 - H5
PEREGRINE PK, SAC	276 - J4
PEREZ PK, ELKG	357 - E6
PERRY, JOSEPH PK, ELKG	358 - J1
PHILLIPS PK, SAC	317 - E3
PHOENIX PK, SaCo	280 - F1
PINKERTON PK, ELKG	358 - C3
PIONEER PK, SaCo	259 - B5
PLANEHAVEN PK, SaCo	258 - G6
PLAZA CERVANTES PK, SAC	317 - D2
PLAZA PK, SaCo	280 - A2
PLEASANT VALLEY CREEK PK, RKLN	200 - C3
POCKET CANAL PARKWAY, SAC	316 - G7
POKELMA PK, SAC	238 - H6
POLLOCK RANCH PK, SAC	337 - F3
PONDEROSA FARM COMM PK, SaCo	237 - F5
POND, WILLIAM REC AREA, SaCo	299 - C3

FEATURE NAME Address City, ZIP Code	PAGE-GRID
PONY EXPRESS PK, SAC	317 - A7
PORTUGUESE COMM PK, SAC	336 - H2
PRAIRIE CITY OFF HIGHWAY VEHICLE PK, - SaCo	281 - D7
PRAIRIE PK, SAC	337 - J5
PRICE, BARBARA MARINA PK, ANT- (SEE PAGE 493)	513 - C3
PRIMROSE PK, SaCo	318 - J3
PROSPECT HILL PK, SaCo	280 - C5
PROSSERVILLE PK, ANT- (SEE PAGE 493)	513 B4
QUAIL PK, SAC	256 - H7
QUARRY PK, RKLN	220 - E3
RAINBOW MINI PK, SaCo	317 - G5
RANCHO SECO PK, SaCo- (SEE PAGE 381)	402 - B2
RAU PK, ELKG	358 - H2
REA PK, SAC	277 - G6
RECREATION PK, AUB	182 - D4
REDBUD PK, SAC	256 - J5
REDDING PK, SAC	277 - J3
REDTAIL HAWK PK, SAC	276 - J4
REDWOOD PK, SAC	277 - G6
REDWOOD PK, WSAC	316 - J2
REGENCY COMM PK, SAC	257 - C4
REICHMUTH PK, SAC	317 - A6
REITH PK, SAC	337 - J7
RENFREE PK, SAC	278 - G2
RENFREE PK, SAC	336 - G2
RICHARDSON VILLAGE PK, SAC	277 - H5
RIDGEPOINT PK, SaCo	258 - J1
RIO TIERRA PK, SAC	277 - E4
RIVER OTTER PK, SAC	276 - H6
RIVER PK, SAC	297 - H3
RIVERSIDE PK, SAC	297 - B7
RIVER VIEW PK, SAC	276 - G4
RIVER WALK PK, WSAC	297 - B3
RIVIERA EAST PK, SaCo	299 - B4
RIZAL COMM CTR, SaCo	338 - A2
ROBERTSON PK, SAC	277 - G3
ROBLA COMM PK, SAC	277 - H1
RODEO NEIGHBORHOOD PK, FOLS	261 - C4
RONALD L FEIST PK, PlaC	240 - G4
ROOSEVELT PK, SAC	297 - C4
ROSARIO, KARL PK, SaCo	258 - G5
ROSEMONT COMM PK, SaCo	319 - A1
ROSEMONT NORTH PK, SaCo	299 - A7
ROSE PK, ELKG	357 - J2
ROSEVIEW PK, SaCo	239 - D6
ROSSWOOD PK, SaCo	319 - A2
ROTARY PK, PLCR	245 - G5
ROYAL PK, SaCo	337 - H2
ROYER PK, RSVL	239 - J2
RUHKALA PK, RKLN	219 - J1
RUSCH COMM PK, CITH	239 - G7
RUSHMORE-JEANINE PK, SaCo	259 - B4
RUSSELL PK, ELKG	358 - J6
RUTH, BABE BASEBALL FIELD, ANT- (SEE PAGE 493)	513 - B4
RUTTER PK, SaCo	338 - C2
SABRE CITY REC PK, PlaC	238 - J4
SACRAMENTO PK, SAC	297 - F7
SACRAMENTO NORTHERN PARKWAY, SAC	297 - F1
SACRAMENTO RIVER PARKWAY, SAC	316 - J5
SACRAMENTO SOFTBALL COMPLEX, SAC	278 - F3
SAINT ROSE OF LIMA PK, SAC	297 - C3
SAND COVE PK, SAC	276 - G7
SANDY BEACH PK, SolC	454 - G7
SANDY BEACH PK, SaCo	493 - G5
SAN JUAN PK, CITH	259 - H6
SAN JUAN RESERVOIR PK, SAC	276 - H3
SANTA ANITA PK, SaCo	278 - D7
SARAH CT PK, SaCo	299 - D1
SASAKI PK, RKLN	220 - G4
SAUGSTAD PK, RSVL	239 - H3
SCHOOL HOUSE PK, RSVL	219 - A3
SCULPTURE PK, RSVL	240 - B1
SEELY PK, SaCo	278 - E5
SEYMOUR PK, SAC	316 - H5
SHADOWCREEK PK, CITH	259 - D5
SHEFFIELD PK, LNCN	179 - G5
SHELDON PK, SaCo	338 - A2
SHELFIELD PK, SaCo	299 - C1
SHOREBIRD PK, SAC	276 - H7
SHORE PK, SAC	336 - H4
SHORES MINI PARK, THE, FOLS	261 - D6
SIERRA 2 PK, SAC	297 - E7
SIERRA CREEK PK, SaCo	238 - F7
SIERRA GARDENS PK, RSVL	240 - B3
SIERRA MEADOWS PK, RKLN	220 - F2
SIERRA OAKS PK, SaCo	298 - E5
SIERRA PK, RVIS	454 - H5
SIERRA VISTA PK, SAC	297 - H7
SILBERHORN PK, FOLS	261 - J5
SILVA, MANUAL PK, SAC	337 - E3
SILVERADO OAKS PK, RSVL	219 - E7
SILVER LEAF PK, SaCo	339 - D6
SIM PK, SAC	318 - C6
SIMPSON PK, ELKG	359 - B5
SKY PK, SaCo	317 - J7
SKYRIDGE PK, AUB	182 - D5
SLOAT SCHOOL PK, SAC	337 - C3
SMEDBERG PK, ELKG	378 - H1
SMITH PK, SAC	297 - B6
SMUD PK, GALT	419 - F7
SNIPES-PERSHING PK, SaCo	260 - J6
SOJOURNER TRUTH PK, SAC	336 - H1
SONOMA PK, RCCD	299 - H5
SONORA PK, RKLN	219 - J2
SOUTH NATOMAS COMM PK, SAC	277 - C5
SOUTHSIDE PK, SAC	297 - B5
SOUTHWOODS PK, SaCo	338 - F4
SPARROW PK, SAC	256 - H6
S P PK, GALT	419 - E7
SPRING MEADOWS PK, PlaC	162 - D5
STANFORD PK, SAC	297 - F3
STEEPLECHASE MINI PK, FOLS	261 - C7
STERLING POINTE PK, PlaC	221 - H2
STILL SCHOOL PK, SAC	337 - D4
STONE CREEK COMM PK, RCCD	319 - B5
STRAUCH PK, SAC	277 - E5
STRIZEK PK, SaCo	258 - G4
STRONG PK, ELKG	359 - A6
SUMMERHILL PK, RSVL	219 - G3
SUNDANCE PK, SAC	276 - H2
SUNDANCE PK, SaCo	260 - B3
SUNRISE FLORIN PK, SaCo	338 - F2
SUNRISE-LOOMIS PK, LMS	200 - J4
SUNRISE OAKS PK, CITH	260 - A2
SUN RIVER PK, RCCD	279 - J5
SUNSET EAST RIVERWOOD PK, RKLN	220 - C4
SUNSET PK, SAC	297 - G7
SUTTER PK, SaCo	279 - F3
SUTTERS LANDING REGL PK, SAC	297 - H3
SUTTERVILLE PK, SAC	317 - C4
SWANSTON PK, SaCo	298 - D4
SYCAMORE PK, SAC	257 - B5
TAHOE PK, SAC	318 - A2
TAHOE TALLAC PK, SAC	318 - B1
TANZANITE COMM PK, SAC	277 - B3
TAYLOR PK, RCCD	299 - D2
TAYLOR STREET PK, SAC	277 - H1

FEATURE NAME Address City, ZIP Code	PAGE-GRID
TAYLOR, WILLIAM L PK, RSVL	240 - A1
TEMPLE AV PK, SAC	317 - F2
TEMPO PK, CITH	260 - A3
TETOTOM PK, SaCo	239 - B6
TILLOTSON PARKWAY, SaCo	339 - A6
TISCORNIA PK, SAC	297 - B1
TOUCHSTONE LAKE PK, WSAC	296 - G7
TOWN HALL PK, ELKG	357 - F4
TREELAKE PK, PlaC	240 - H6
TRIANGLE PK, SAC	277 - H6
TUPELO PK, SaCo	259 - D1
TUSCANY PK, RCCD	299 - J4
TWAIN PK, SAC	317 - J3
TWELVE BRIDGES PK, LNCN	199 - H2
TWIN OAKS PK, RKLN	200 - B7
TWINWOOD PK, RSVL	219 - H5
TWO RIVERS PK, SAC	276 - H6
UEDA PARKWAY, SAC	277 - F4
UNION PK, SAC	337 - G4
UNIVERSITY PK, SAC	298 - D6
URIBE, DAVID PK, RSVL	220 - F6
VAL DEFLORES PK, RVIS	454 - H4
VALLEY HI PK, SAC	338 - A6
VALLEY OAK PK, SaCo	298 - J3
VALLEY SCHOOL PK, SAC	338 - A7
VAN DOREN PK, ELKG	358 - H5
VAN MAREN PK, CITH	259 - G3
VERANO CREEK PK, SAC	278 - B2
VETERANS PK, SaCo	319 - H2
VETERANS MEM PK, RSVL	219 - B2
VILLAGE EAST PK, ANT- (SEE PAGE 493)	513 - A6
VILLAGE PK, SaCo	280 - A2
VINEYARD PK, SaCo	338 - J7
VINTAGE PK, SaCo	338 - G6
VINTAGE PKWAY PARK, OAKL- (SEE PAGE 493)	514 - E5
VISTA GRANDE PK, RKLN	220 - B4
WACKMAN PK, ELKG	357 - J4
WALERGA PK, SaCo	259 - A6
WANISH PK, RSVL	219 - E7
WARREN PK, SAC	318 - B4
WARREN, EARL PK, SAC	318 - C4
WASHINGTON PK, SAC	297 - E3
WATERS, NORMAN PK, SaCo	338 - E4
WATT AV PK, SaCo	298 - G6
W C FIELD DEWITT PK, PlaC	162 - A4
WEBER PK, RSVL	239 - H1
WELCOME RIO LINDA PK, SaCo	258 - B2
WENZEL PK, SAC	316 - J7
WESLEY PK, RKLN	200 - A6
WESTACRE PK, WSAC	296 - H4
WESTFIELD PLAYSITE, WSAC	296 - H3
WESTLAKE COMM PK, SAC	256 - G7
WEST SACRAMENTO SUMMERFIELD PK, WSAC	316 - E1
WESTSIDE PK, SAC	257 - F3
WESTWOOD PK, CITH	239 - F6
WHITE ALDER PK, SAC	257 - C3
WHITE, MARK PK, RSVL	239 - G3
WHITE ROCK COMM PK, RCCD	299 - F3
WILDHAWK EAST PK, SaCo	339 - E5
WILLARD PK, ELKG	358 - A7
WILLOW BEND PK, FOLS	261 - H4
WILLOWOOD PK, SaCo	338 - D5
WILLOW PK, SAC	257 - A3
WILLOW RANCHO PK, SAC	337 - B1
WILSON PK, ISLE	455 - G5
WINDEMERE PK, SaCo	298 - H1
WINDSOR PK, FOLS	261 - F7
WINN PK, SAC	297 - F5
WINTERSTIEN PK, SaCo	298 - F3
WITTER RANCH PK, SAC	276 - J2
WOMACK PK, ELKG	357 - G5
WOOD PK, SAC	318 - A5
WOOD PK, SAC	338 - B5
WOODBINE PK, SAC	317 - E7
WOODBRIDGE PK, RSVL	219 - J7
WOODLAKE PK, SAC	277 - H7
WOODS, CARLISLE PK, SaCo	338 - H5
WOODSIDE PK, RKLN	220 - D5
WRIGHT, ORVILLE PK, SaCo	278 - G7
ZAPATA PK, SAC	297 - D3
ZBERG PK, SAC	337 - B2
ZEHNDER PK, ELKG	357 - G4
ZIMBELMAN PK, ELKG	358 - C4

PERFORMING ARTS

FEATURE NAME Address City, ZIP Code	PAGE-GRID
MEMORIAL AUDITORIUM 1515 J ST, SAC, 95814	297 - D4
SACRAMENTO THEATRE COMPANY 1419 H ST, SAC, 95814	297 - D3

POINTS OF INTEREST

FEATURE NAME Address City, ZIP Code	PAGE-GRID
BLUE DIAMOND GROWERS VISITORS CTR 1701 C ST, SAC, 95814	297 - E3
FOLSOM ZOO NATOMA ST & STAFFORD ST, FOLS, 95630	261 - C4
INTL WORLD PEACE ROSE GARDENS N ST & 15TH ST, SAC, 95814	297 - D4
SACRAMENTO ZOO 3930 LAND PARK DR, SAC, 95822	317 - B2
SHEPARD GARDEN ART CTR 3330 MCKINLEY BLVD, SAC, 95816	297 - G4
YEAW, EFFIE NATURE CTR 2850 SAN LORENZO WY, SaCo, 95608	279 - F6

POINTS OF INTEREST - HISTORIC

FEATURE NAME Address City, ZIP Code	PAGE-GRID
CALIFORNIA VIETNAM VETERANS MEM 15TH ST & CAPITOL AV, SAC, 95814	297 - D4
GOLD BUG MINE 2635 GOLD BUG LN, PLCR, 95667	245 - G3
HIST GOVERNORS MANSION 16TH ST & H ST, SAC, 95814	297 - D4
LELAND STANFORD HIST MANSION 8TH ST & N ST, SAC, 95814	297 - C4
MARSHALLS BLACKSMITH SHOP ROCK CREEK RD, EDCo, 95667	225 - G6
OLD SACRAMENTO ST HIST PK FRONT ST, SAC, 95814	297 - B3
SUTTERS FORT STATE HIST PK 2701 L ST, SAC, 95816	297 - F4
WITTER RANCH HIST FARM 3480 W WITTER WY, SAC, 95834	276 - H3

SCHOOLS - PRIVATE ELEMENTARY

FEATURE NAME Address City, ZIP Code	PAGE-GRID
ALICANTE NORTH 5325 ENGLE RD, SaCo, 95608	279 - B4
ALL HALLOWS 5700 13TH AV, SAC, 95820	317 - J2
AMERICAN CHRISTIAN ACADEMY 7412 HOLLYHOCK CT, CITH, 95621	259 - F1
ANTELOPE CHRISTIAN ACADEMY 4533 ANTELOPE RD, SaCo, 95843	258 - J1
AUBURN DISCOVERY MONTESSORI 1273 HIGH ST, AUB, 95603	182 - D3
BRADSHAW CHRISTIAN 8324 BRADSHAW RD, SaCo, 95829	339 - B7

SCHOOLS - PRIVATE ELEMENTARY

FEATURE NAME Address City, ZIP Code	PAGE-GRID
BROOKFIELD 3600 RIVERSIDE BLVD, SAC, 95818	317 - B1
CALIFORNIA MONTESSORI PROJECT 8828 ELK GROVE BLVD, ELKG, 95624	358 - G6
CALVARY 2727 DEL PASO BLVD, SAC, 95815	277 - J6
CALVARY CHAPEL CHRISTIAN 202 DAIRY RD, AUB, 95603	162 - E7
CALVARY CHRISTIAN 5051 47TH AV, SaCo, 95824	317 - H6
CAMERON PARK MONTESSORI 4645 BUCKEYE RD, EDCo, 95682	264 - C6
CAPITAL CHRISTIAN 7520 STOCKTON BLVD, SaCo, 95823	338 - B3
CAPITAL CHRISTIAN 9470 MICRON AV, SaCo, 95827	299 - A6
CAPITOL MONTESSORI 2700 L ST, SAC, 95816	297 - F5
CARDEN -SACTO 3020 MARCONI AV, SaCo, 95821	278 - E6
CARDEN SUNRISE 7723 OLD AUBURN RD, CITH, 95610	259 - J1
CEDAR SPRINGS WALDORF 6029 GOLD MEADOWS RD, EDCo, 95667	264 - J3
CITADEL CHRISTIAN 5230 EHRHARDT AV, SAC, 95823	337 - J6
CORNERSTONE CHRISTIAN 143 CLINTON AV, RSVL, 95678	239 - H3
COURTYARD 2324 L ST, SAC, 95816	297 - E5
CREATIVE FRONTIERS 6446 SYLVAN RD, CITH, 95610	259 - H4
DEI, GLORIA LUTHERAN 4910 LEMON HILL AV, SaCo, 95824	317 - H6
EL DORADO JUNIOR ACADEMY 1900 BROADWAY, PLCR, 95667	246 - B5
EL RANCHO 5636 EL CAMINO AV, SaCo, 95608	279 - C7
FAITH CHRISTIAN ACADEMY 7737 HIGHLAND AV, CITH, 95610	259 - J3
FAITH LUTHERAN 4000 SAN JUAN AV, SaCo, 95628	279 - H3
FAMILY CHRISTIAN ACADEMY 6521 HAZEL AV, SaCo, 95662	260 - F3
FREEDOM CHRISTIAN 7736 SUNSET AV, SaCo, 95628	279 - J1
GATEWAY CHRISTIAN LIFE 4148 SAN JUAN AV, SaCo, 95628	279 - H3
GOLDEN HILLS 1060 SUNCAST LN, EDCo, 95762	282 - D3
GRANITE BAY HOUSE 8265 SIERRA COLLEGE BLVD, PlaC, 95746	240 - F2
HILLTOP CHRISTIAN (SEE PAGE 493) 320 WORRELL RD, ANT, 94509	513 - E7
HOLY CROSS 800 TODHUNTER AV, WSAC, 95605	296 - H1
HOLY FAMILY 7817 OLD AUBURN RD, CITH, 95610	259 - J1
HOLY ROSARY (SEE PAGE 493) 25 E 15TH ST, ANT, 94509	513 - D5
HOLY SPIRIT 3920 W LAND PARK DR, SAC, 95822	317 - B2
IMMACULATE CONCEPTION 3263 1ST AV, SAC, 95817	297 - F7
KWEST ACADEMY 7221 SUNCREEK WY, SaCo, 95662	260 - D1
LIBERTY TOWERS CHRISTIAN 5132 ELKHORN BLVD, SaCo, 95842	259 - B3
MERRYHILL COUNTRY 2565 MILLCREEK DR, SAC, 95833	277 - C6
MERRYHILL COUNTRY 9036 CALVINE RD, SaCo, 95829	338 - H7
MERRYHILL COUNTRY 1622 SIERRA GARDENS DR, RSVL, 95661	240 - B3
MERRYHILL COUNTRY 2730 EASTERN AV, SaCo, 95821	278 - H6
MERRYHILL COUNTRY 7276 FRENCH RD, SaCo, 95828	338 - E2
MERRYHILL COUNTRY 7450 POCKET RD, SAC, 95831	336 - F2
MERRYHILL COUNTRY NATIONAL 2401 NORTHVIEW DR, SAC, 95833	277 - E6
MORNING STAR CHRISTIAN 4837 MARCONI AV, SaCo, 95608	279 - A5
OUR LADY OF ASSUMPTION 5055 COTTAGE WY, SaCo, 95608	299 - A1
OUR LADY OF GRACE 1990 LINDEN RD, WSAC, 95691	316 - H1
OUR SAVIOR LUTHERAN 5461 44TH ST, SaCo, 95820	317 - H4
PHOENIX SCHOOLS 650 WILLARD DR, FOLS, 95630	281 - C1
PINE HILLS ADVENTIST 13500 RICHARDS LN, PlaC, 95603	162 - F3
PLACERVILLE CHRISTIAN 4657 MISSOURI FLAT RD, EDCo, 95667	265 - D3
PRESENTATION 3100 NORRIS AV, SaCo, 95821	278 - H5
SACRAMENTO ADVENTIST ACADEMY 5601 WINDING WY, SaCo, 95608	279 - C1
SACRAMENTO CHRISTIAN SCHOOLS 7361 24TH ST, SAC, 95822	337 - E2
SACRAMENTO COUNTRY DAY 2636 LATHAM DR, SAC, 95864	298 - E5
SACRAMENTO WALDORF 3750 BANNISTER RD, SaCo, 95628	279 - H4
SACRED HEART 3933 I ST, SAC, 95816	297 - H5
SAINT ALBANS COUNTRY DAY 2312 VERNON ST, RSVL, 95678	239 - G5
SAINT ANNES 7720 24TH ST, SAC, 95832	337 - E4
SAINT CHARLES BORROMEO 7580 CENTER PKWY, SAC, 95823	337 - J3
SAINT ELIZABETH ANN SETON 9539 RACQUET CT, ELKG, 95758	358 - B6
SAINT FRANCIS OF ASSISI 2500 K ST, SAC, 95816	297 - F5
SAINT IGNATIUS 3245 ARDEN WY, SaCo, 95825	298 - F1
SAINT JOHN EVANGELIST 5701 LOCUST AV, SaCo, 95608	279 - C2
SAINT JOHNS-NOTRE DAME 309 MONTROSE DR, FOLS, 95630	261 - D4
SAINT JOHN VIANNEY 10499 COLOMA RD, RCCD, 95670	299 - F1
SAINT JOSEPH PARISH 1718 EL MONTE AV, SaCo, 95815	277 - H7
SAINT JOSEPH PARISH 11610 ATWOOD RD, PlaC, 95603	162 - B4
SAINT LAWRENCE 4325 DON JULIO BLVD, SaCo, 95660	258 - J3
SAINT MARKS LUTHERAN 7869 KINGSWOOD DR, CITH, 95610	260 - A6
SAINT MARYS 5815 N ST, SAC, 95819	298 - A6
SAINT MELS PAROCHIAL 4745 PENNSYLVANIA AV, SaCo, 95628	279 - J1
SAINT MICHAELS EPISCOPAL DAY 2140 MISSION AV, SaCo, 95608	279 - A7
SAINT PATRICK 5945 FRANKLIN BLVD, SAC, 95824	317 - F5
SAINT PETERS 6200 MCMAHON DR, SAC, 95824	318 - A5
SAINT PETERS LUTHERAN 8701 ELK GROVE FLORIN RD, ELKG, 95624	358 - H2
SAINT PHILOMENE 2320 EL CAMINO AV, SAC, 95825	278 - D7
SAINT ROBERT 2251 IRVIN WY, SAC, 95822	317 - D3
SAINT ROSE 633 VINE AV, RSVL, 95678	239 - H3
SHALOM 2351 WYDA WY, SaCo, 95825	298 - D1
SIERRA CHRISTIAN ACADEMY 6900 DESTINY DR, RKLN, 95677	220 - B5
SOUTH LAND PARK MONTESSORI 6400 FREEPORT BLVD, SAC, 95822	317 - B6
TOWN & COUNTRY LUTHERAN 4049 MARCONI AV, SaCo, 95821	278 - H6
TRINITY CHRISTIAN 5225 HILLSDALE BLVD, SaCo, 95660	258 - J6
VALLEY CHRISTIAN ACADEMY 301 WHYTE AV, RSVL, 95678	239 - G5
VICTORY CHRISTIAN 3045 GARFIELD AV, SaCo, 95608	279 - C5
VICTORY CHRISTIAN 5010 HAZEL AV, SaCo, 95628	260 - F7
WALDORF, CAMELLIA 5701 FREEPORT BLVD, SAC, 95822	317 - C5
WIGGINS SAINT LUKE CHRISTIAN 7595 CENTER PKWY, SAC, 95823	337 - J3
WILTON CHRISTIAN 9697 DILLARD RD, SaCo, 95693	360 - B7

SCHOOLS - PRIVATE HIGH

FEATURE NAME Address City, ZIP Code	PAGE-GRID
ALICANTE NORTH 5325 ENGLE RD, SaCo, 95608	279 - B3
AMERICAN CHRISTIAN ACADEMY 7412 HOLLYHOCK CT, CITH, 95621	259 - F1
CALVARY CHRISTIAN 5051 47TH AV, SaCo, 95824	317 - H6
CAPITAL CHRISTIAN 9470 MICRON AV, SaCo, 95827	299 - B6
CHRISTIAN BROTHERS 4315 MARTIN LUTHER KING JR. BL, SAC, 95820	317 - G3
CITADEL CHRISTIAN 5320 EHRHARDT AV, SAC, 95823	337 - J6
CORNERSTONE CHRISTIAN 143 CLINTON AV, RSVL, 95678	239 - H3
DELTA CHRISTIAN (SEE PAGE 493) 625 W 4TH ST, ANT, 94509	513 - C4
EL DORADO JUNIOR ACADEMY 1900 BROADWAY, PLCR, 95667	246 - B5
FAMILY CHRISTIAN ACADEMY 6521 HAZEL AV, SaCo, 95662	260 - E3
FREEDOM CHRISTIAN 7736 SUNSET AV, SaCo, 95628	279 - J1
GATEWAY CHRISTIAN LIFE 4148 SAN JUAN AV, SaCo, 95628	279 - H3
JESUIT 1200 JACOB LN, SaCo, 95608	299 - A3
KWEST ACADEMY 7221 SUNCREEK WY, SaCo, 95662	260 - D2
LORETTO 2360 EL CAMINO AV, SaCo, 95825	278 - D7
SACRAMENTO ADVENTIST ACADEMY 5601 WINDING WY, SaCo, 95608	279 - C1
SACRAMENTO COUNTRY DAY 2636 LATHAM DR, SAC, 95864	298 - E5
SACRAMENTO LUTHERAN 2331 SAINT MARKS WY, SaCo, 95864	278 - G7
SACRAMENTO WALDORF 3750 BANNISTER RD, SaCo, 95628	279 - H4
SAINT FRANCIS GIRLS 6051 M ST, SAC, 95819	298 - A6
VALLEY CHRISTIAN ACADEMY 301 WHYTE AV, RSVL, 95678	239 - G5
VICTORY CHRISTIAN 3045 GARFIELD AV, SaCo, 95608	279 - B5
WILTON CHRISTIAN 9697 DILLARD RD, SaCo, 95693	360 - B7

SCHOOLS - PUBLIC ELEMENTARY

FEATURE NAME Address City, ZIP Code	PAGE-GRID
ADREANI, ARNOLD 9927 WILDHAWK WEST DR, SaCo, 95829	339 - D5
AERO-HAVEN 5450 GEORGIA DR, SaCo, 95660	258 - G6
ALLISON, WARREN A 4315 DON JULIO BLVD, SaCo, 95660	258 - J3
ALTA VISTA 173 OAK ST, AUB, 95603	182 - F1
AMERICAN LAKES 2800 STONECREEK DR, SAC, 95833	277 - D5
ANDERSON, MARIAN 2850 49TH ST, SAC, 95817	317 - H1
ANTELOPE CREEK 6185 SPRINGVIEW DR, RKLN, 95677	220 - B5
ANTELOPE MEADOWS 8343 PALMERSON DR, SaCo, 95843	238 - J5
ANTELOPE VIEW CHARTER 8725 WATT AV, SaCo, 95843	238 - F4
ANTHONY, SUSAN B 7864 DETROIT BLVD, SAC, 95832	337 - F4
ARCOHE 11755 IVIE RD, SaCo, 95638	420 - C1
ARLINGTON HEIGHTS 6401 TRENTON WY, CITH, 95621	259 - E3
AUBURN 11400 LARIAT LN, PlaC, 95603	162 - A5
BABCOCK, DW 2400 CORMORANT WY, SAC, 95815	278 - B7
BAKER, ETHEL I 5717 LAURINE WY, SaCo, 95824	317 - H5
BAKER, JESSIE 8850 SOUTHSIDE AV, ELKG, 95624	358 - G7
BANCROFT, HUBERT H 2929 BELMAR ST, SAC, 95826	290 - F7
DANNON CREEK 2775 MILLCREEK DR, SAC, 95833	277 - C6
BATES (SEE PAGE 375) 180 PRIMASING AV, SaCo, 95615	396 - D3
BATEY, EDNA 9421 STONEBROOK DR, ELKG, 95624	359 - A5
BEAR FLAG 6620 GLORIA DR, SAC, 95831	316 - J6
BEITZEL, MAEOLA 8140 CAYMUS DR, SaCo, 95829	338 - H6
BELL AVENUE 1900 BELL AV, SAC, 95838	278 - C1
BELSHAW (SEE PAGE 493) 2801 ROOSEVELT LN, ANT, 94509	513 - E6
BEN ALI CHILDRENS CTR 2625 PLOVER ST, SAC, 95815	278 - B6
BIDWELL (SEE PAGE 493) 800 GARY AV, ANT, 94509	513 - F6
BIDWELL, JOHN 1730 65TH AV, SAC, 95822	337 - C2
BIRNEY, ALICE 6251 13TH ST, SAC, 95831	317 - B6
BLUE OAK 2391 MERRYCHASE DR, EDCo, 95682	263 - B7
BLUE OAKS 8150 HORNCASTLE AV, RSVL, 95747	219 - C3
BONNHEIM, JOSEPH 7300 MARIN AV, SAC, 95820	318 - C3
BOWLING GREEN 4211 TURNBRIDGE DR, SaCo, 95823	317 - G7
BOWMAN 13777 BOWMAN RD, PlaC, 95603	162 - F4
BREEN 2751 BREEN DR, RKLN, 95765	200 - B6
BRIDGEWAY ISLAND 3255 HALF MOON BAY CIR, WSAC, 95691	316 - D2
BROOKS, WILLIAM 3610 PARK DR, EDCo, 95762	262 - C7
BROWN, CHARLES F 6520 OAKDELL DR, EDCo, 95623	265 - C5
BROWN, VINCIL 250 TRESTLE DR, RSVL, 95678	219 - G4
BRYTE 637 TODHUNTER AV, WSAC, 95605	296 - H1
BUCKEYE 4561 BUCKEYE RD, EDCo, 95682	264 - C6
BURNETT, PETER 6032 36TH AV, SAC, 95824	318 - A5
BUTLER, ARTHUR C 9180 BROWN RD, ELKG, 95624	358 - J1
CABRILLO, JOHN 1141 SEAMAS AV, SAC, 95822	317 - A4
CAMBRIDGE HEIGHTS 5555 FLEETWOOD DR, CITH, 95621	259 - G6
CAMELLIA BASIC 6600 COUGAR DR, SAC, 95828	318 - B7
CAMERON RANCH 4333 HACKBERRY LN, SaCo, 95608	279 - C2
CAPITAL CITY-INDEP STUDY 7000 FRANKLIN BLVD STE 1230, SAC, 95823	337 - G1
CARMICHAEL 6141 SUTTER AV, SaCo, 95608	279 - D3
CARRIAGE DRIVE 7519 CARRIAGE DR, CITH, 95621	259 - G1
CASE, RAYMOND 8565 SHASTA LILY DR, ELKG, 95624	358 - F2
CASTELLO, HELEN CARR 9850 FIRE POPPY DR, ELKG, 95757	357 - J7
CASTORI, MICHAEL J 1801 SOUTH AV, SAC, 95838	278 - B3
CHAN, OAK 101 PREWETT DR, FOLS, 95630	261 - G5
CHAVEZ, CESAR 7500 32ND ST, SAC, 95822	337 - F2
CIRBY 814 DARLING WY, RSVL, 95678	239 - J3
CITRUS HEIGHTS 7085 AUBURN BLVD, CITH, 95621	259 - G2
CLARKSBURG 52870 NETHERLANDS AV, YoCo, 95612	356 - H5
COBBLESTONE 5740 COBBLESTONE DR, RKLN, 95765	220 - B1
COHEN, ISADOR 9025 SALMON FALLS DR, SaCo, 95826	298 - H6
COLEMAN, THOMAS W 6545 BEECH AV, SaCo, 95662	260 - E3
COPPIN, CARLIN C 150 12TH ST, LNCN, 95648	179 - J2
CORDOVA GARDENS 2400 DAWES ST, RCCD, 95670	299 - E2
CORDOVA LANE 2460 CORDOVA LN, RCCD, 95670	279 - H7
CORDOVA MEADOWS 2550 LA LOMA DR, RCCD, 95670	299 - E2
CORDOVA VILLA 10359 S WHITE ROCK RD, RCCD, 95670	299 - G4
COSUMNES RIVER 13580 JACKSON RD, SaCo, 95683	341 - D2
COTTAGE 2221 MORSE AV, SaCo, 95825	278 - E7
COWAN, JAMES R FUNDAMENTAL 3350 BECERRA WY, SaCo, 95821	278 - H4
COYLE AVENUE 6330 COYLE AV, SaCo, 95608	259 - E6
COYOTE RIDGE 1751 MORNINGSTAR DR, RSVL, 95747	219 - A7
CREEKSIDE 2641 KENT DR, SaCo, 95821	278 - E6
CREEKSIDE OAKS 2030 1ST ST, LNCN, 95648	179 - E3
CRESTMONT 1501 SHERIDAN AV, RSVL, 95661	240 - C5
CROCKER/RIVERSIDE 2970 RIVERSIDE BLVD, SAC, 95818	297 - B7
DA VINCI, LEONARDO 4701 JOAQUIN WY, SAC, 95822	317 - D3
DEL DAYO 1301 MCCLAREN DR, SaCo, 95608	299 - B3
DEL PASO HEIGHTS 590 MOREY AV, SAC, 95838	277 - H3
DEL PASO MANOR 2700 MARYAL DR, SaCo, 95821	278 - H6
DETERDING, MARY A 6000 STANLEY AV, SaCo, 95608	279 - D5
DEWEY, HARRY 7025 FALCON RD, SaCo, 95628	279 - G1
DIAMOND CREEK 3151 HOPSCOTCH WY, RSVL, 95747	219 - C1
DIDION, GENEVIEVE 6490 HARMON DR, SAC, 95831	316 - F6
DILLARD 9721 DILLARD RD, SaCo, 95693	360 - C7
DONNER, ELITHA 9461 SOARING OAKS DR, ELKG, 95758	358 - C5
DOS RIOS 700 DOS RIOS ST, SAC, 95814	297 - E1
DRY CREEK 1230 G ST, SaCo, 95673	258 - A4
DRY CREEK 2955 PFE RD, PlaC, 95747	239 - C4
DUDLEY, ARTHUR 8000 AZTEC WY, SaCo, 95843	238 - G6
DYER-KELLY 2236 EDISON AV, SaCo, 95821	278 - D5
EDISON, THOMAS A 1500 DOM WY, SaCo, 95864	298 - F2
EHRHARDT, JOHN 8900 OLD CREEK DR, ELKG, 95758	358 - A3
ELDER CREEK 7934 LEMON HILL AV, SAC, 95824	318 - C6
ELK GROVE CHARTER 5900 BAMFORD DR, SAC, 95823	338 - A5
ELK GROVE 9373 CROWELL DR, ELKG, 95624	358 - H5
ELKHORN VILLAGE 750 CUMMINS WY, WSAC, 95605	297 - A1
ELLIOTT RANCH 10000 S TARON DR, ELKG, 95757	377 - E1
ELVERTA 7900 ELOISE AV, SaCo, 95626	237 - G6
EMPIRE OAKS 1830 BONHILL DR, FOLS, 95630	261 - J5
ERLEWINE, O W 2441 STANSBERRY WY, SaCo, 95826	298 - J5
EUREKA UNION 5477 EUREKA RD, PlaC, 95746	240 - J3

FEATURE NAME	Address City, ZIP Code	PAGE-GRID
EXCELSIOR	2701 EUREKA RD, RSVL, 95661	240 - F3
FAIRBANKS	227 FAIRBANKS AV, SAC, 95838	277 - G4
FAIR OAKS	10700 FAIR OAKS BLVD, SaCo, 95628	280 - B2
FAIRSITE	902 CAROLINE AV, GALT, 95632	419 - F7
FEICKERT	9351 FEICKERT DR, ELKG, 95624	358 - F5
FIRST STREET	1400 1ST ST, LNCN, 95648	179 - G4
FITE , ROBERT	9561 FITE SCHOOL DR, SaCo, 95829	339 - B5
FLORIN	7300 KARA DR, SaCo, 95828	338 - D2
FOLSOM HILLS	106 MANSEAU DR, FOLS, 95630	261 - G3
FOOTHILL OAKS	5520 LANCELOT DR, SaCo, 95842	259 - C2
FOULKS RANCH	6211 LAGUNA PARK DR, ELKG, 95758	358 - A5
FRANKLIN	4011 HOOD-FRANKLIN RD, SaCo, 95757	377 - G4
FRANKLIN	7050 FRANKLIN SCHOOL RD, PlaC, 95650	221 - C3
FREEPORT	2118 MEADOWVIEW RD, SAC, 95832	337 - C3
FREMONT (SEE PAGE 493)	1413 F ST, ANT, 94509	513 - D5
FRONTIER	6691 SILVERTHORNE CIR, SaCo, 95842	259 - B4
FRUIT RIDGE	4625 44TH ST, SAC, 95820	317 - H3
GALLARDO, SANDRA	755 RUSSI RD, FOLS, 95630	281 - D1
GARDEN VALLEY	3601 LARCHWOOD DR, SAC, 95834	277 - E3
GARFIELD	3700 GARFIELD AV, SaCo, 95608	279 - B3
GATES, CATHERYN	1051 TREHOWELL DR, RSVL, 95678	219 - J5
GLENWOOD	201 JESSIE AV, SAC, 95838	277 - G2
GOLDEN EMPIRE	9045 CANBERRA DR, SaCo, 95826	318 - H2
GOLDEN VALLEY CHARTER	7833 HIGHLAND AV, CITH, 95610	259 - J3
GOLD RIDGE	735 HALIDON WY, FOLS, 95630	281 - G1
GOLD RIVER DISCOVERY CTR	2220 ROARING CAMP DR, SaCo, 95670	280 - C4
GRAND OAKS	7901 ROSSWOOD DR, CITH, 95621	239 - F7
GREENHILLS	8200 GREENHILLS WY, PlaC, 95746	240 - G1
GREEN OAKS FUNDAMENTAL	7145 FILBERT AV, SaCo, 95662	260 - G2
GREEN VALLEY	2380 BASS LAKE RD, EDCo, 95672	263 - B2
GREENWOOD, CALEB	5457 CARLSON DR, SAC, 95819	298 - A4
GREER	2301 HURLEY WY, SaCo, 95825	298 - D2
HAGGINWOOD	1418 PALO VERDE AV, SAC, 95815	278 - A5
HARKNESS, H W	2147 54TH AV, SAC, 95822	317 - D7
HARTE, BRET	2751 9TH AV, SAC, 95818	317 - E1
HEARST, PHOEBE APPERSN	1410 60TH ST, SAC, 95819	298 - A7
HEIN, ARLENE	6820 BELLATERRA DR, ELKG, 95757	378 - B1
HERBURGER, ROY	8565 SHASTA LILY DR, ELKG, 95624	358 - E2
HERITAGE OAK	2271 AMERICANA DR, RSVL, 95747	219 - E7
HILLSDALE	6469 GUTHRIE WY, SaCo, 95660	259 - A3
HOLLYWOOD PK	4915 HARTE WY, SAC, 95822	317 - D3
HOLMES, OLIVER WENDALL	7201 ARUTAS DR, SaCo, 95660	258 - H1
HOLST, JOHN	4501 BANNISTER RD, SaCo, 95628	279 - H2
HOPKINS, MARK	2221 MATSON DR, SAC, 95822	337 - D2
HORIZON INSTRUCTIONAL SYSTEMS	1530 3RD ST, LNCN, 95648	179 - G3
HOWE AVENUE	2404 HOWE AV, SaCo, 95825	278 - C7
HUNTINGTON, COLLIS P	5921 26TH ST, SAC, 95822	317 - E5
INDIAN CREEK	6701 GREEN VALLEY RD, EDCo, 95667	244 - H6
ISLETON	412 UNION ST, ISLE, 95641	455 - H5
JACKSON	2561 FRANCISCO DR, EDCo, 95762	262 - C1
JACKSON, ISABELLE	8351 CUTLER WY, SaCo, 95828	338 - E6
JEFFERSON	2001 PEBBLEWOOD DR, SAC, 95833	277 - B5
JEFFERSON, THOMAS	2635 CHESTNUT HILL DR, SAC, 95826	298 - E7
JEFFERSON, THOMAS	750 CENTRAL PARK ST, RSVL, 95678	219 - J3
JOHNSON, HARMON	2591 EDGEWATER RD, SAC, 95815	277 - G6
JOYCE, FREDERICK C	6050 WATT AV, SaCo, 95660	258 - G4
JUDAH, THEODORE	101 DEAN WY, FOLS, 95630	261 - C5
JUDAH, THEODORE	3919 MCKINLEY BLVD, SAC, 95819	297 - H4
KASEBERG	1040 MAIN ST, RSVL, 95678	239 - F1
KELLY, THOMAS	6301 MORAGA DR, SaCo, 95608	279 - E1
KEMBLE, EDWARD	7495 29TH ST, SAC, 95822	337 - E2
KENNEDY, SAMUEL	7037 BRIGGS DR, SaCo, 95828	338 - C1
KENNETH AVENUE	4825 KENNETH AV, SaCo, 95608	279 - A6
KENNY, KEITH B	3525 MARTIN LUTHER KING JR BLV, SAC, 95817	317 - G2
KIMBALL (SEE PAGE 493)	1310 AUGUST WY, ANT, 94509	513 - E5
KING JR, MARTIN LUTHER	480 LITTLE RIVER WY, SAC, 95831	336 - G2
KING, STARR	4848 COTTAGE WY, SaCo, 95608	299 - A1
KINGSWOOD	5700 PRIMROSE DR, CITH, 95610	259 - J5
KIRCHGATER, ANNA	8141 STEVENSON AV, SaCo, 95828	338 - D5
KOHLER	4004 BRUCE WY, SaCo, 95660	258 - J4
LAKE CANYON	800 LAKE CANYON BLVD, GALT, 95632	419 - F2

FEATURE NAME	Address City, ZIP Code	PAGE-GRID
LAKE FOREST	2240 SALISBURY DR, EDCo, 95762	242 - C6
LAND, WILLIAM	2120 12TH ST, SAC, 95818	297 - C5
LARCHMONT	6560 MELROSE DR, SaCo, 95660	258 - H3
LEARNER-CENTERED CHARTER- (SEE PAGE 493)	1201 10TH ST, ANT, 94509	513 - C4
LEGETTE, EARL	4623 KENNETH AV, SaCo, 95628	280 - D1
LEIMBACH, HERMAN	8101 GRANDSTAFF DR, SAC, 95823	338 - B6
LICHEN	8319 LICHEN DR, CITH, 95621	239 - F6
LINCOLN, ABRAHAM	3324 GLENMOOR DR, RCCD, 95827	299 - E5
LISBON	7555 S LAND PARK DR, SAC, 95831	336 - J2
LITTLEJOHN, LEIGHTON	6838 KERMIT LN, SaCo, 95628	259 - F6
LOOMIS	3505 TAYLOR RD, LMS, 95650	201 - A5
LUBIN, DAVID	3535 M ST, SAC, 95816	297 - G5
MACK, CHARLES E	4701 BROOKFIELD DR, SAC, 95823	337 - H3
MADISON	5241 HARRISON ST, SaCo, 95660	258 - H6
MAIDU	1950 JOHNSON RANCH DR, RSVL, 95661	240 - C3
MAIN AVENUE	1400 MAIN AV, SAC, 95838	258 - A7
MAPLE	3301 37TH AV, SAC, 95824	317 - E5
MARENGO RANCH	1000 ELK HILLS DR, GALT, 95632	419 - G3
MARIEMONT	1401 CORTA WY, SaCo, 95864	298 - H2
MARIPOSA AVENUE	7940 MARIPOSA AV, CITH, 95610	239 - J7
MARKOFER, FLORENCE M	9759 TRALEE WY, ELKG, 95624	378 - H1
MARSHALL, JAMES W	9525 GOETHE RD, SaCo, 95827	299 - B7
MARSHALL, MARVIN	5309 KENNETH AV, SaCo, 95608	279 - B6
MARSH (SEE PAGE 493)	2304 G ST, ANT, 94509	513 - C6
MATHER HEIGHTS	4379 SCHOOL RD, SaCo, 95655	319 - J2
MATSUYAMA	7680 WINDBRIDGE DR, SAC, 95831	336 - H3
MCKEE, JAMES A	8701 HALVERSON DR, ELKG, 95624	358 G5
MISSION AVENUE	2925 MISSION AV, SaCo, 95821	279 - A5
MISSION (SEE PAGE 493)	1711 MISSION DR, ANT, 94509	513 - A6
MITCHELL, BILLY	4425 LAURELWOOD WY, SaCo, 95864	278 - J7
MORSE, BARBARA COMSTOCK	7000 CRANLEIGH AV, SAC, 95823	358 - B1
NATOMAS CHARTER	3710 DEL PASO RD, SAC, 95834	256 - G7
NATOMAS CHARTER	4600 BLACKROCK DR, SAC, 95835	257 - D7
NATOMAS PARK	4700 CREST DR, SAC, 95835	257 - C6
NATOMA STATION	500 TURN PIKE DR, FOLS, 95630	281 - B1
NEWCASTLE	8951 VALLEY VIEW DR, PlaC, 95658	181 - G6
NEWCOMER CENTER	5201 STRAWBERRY LN, SAC, 95820	317 - F4
NEW HOPE (SEE PAGE 418)	26675 N SACRAMENTO BLVD, SJCo, 95686	438 - A3
NICHOLAS	6601 STEINER DR, SaCo, 95823	317 - J6
NORALTO	477 LAS PALMAS AV, SAC, 95815	277 - H5
NORMAN, ALYCE	1200 ANNA ST, WSAC, 95605	296 - J1
NORTH AVENUE	1281 NORTH AV, SAC, 95838	278 - A2
NORTH COUNTY	3901 LITTLE ROCK DR, SaCo, 95843	238 - H7
NORTHRIDGE	5150 COCOA PALM WY, SaCo, 95628	260 - B7
NORTHWOOD	2630 TAFT ST, SAC, 95815	278 - A6
OAKDALE	3708 MYRTLE AV, SaCo, 95660	278 - G1
OAK HILL	3909 N LOOP BLVD, SaCo, 95843	238 - H5
OAKHILLS	9233 TWIN SCHOOLS RD, PlaC, 95746	240 - H4
OAKLEY (SEE PAGE 493)	501 NORCROSS LN, OAKL, 94561	514 - E7
OAK MEADOW	7701 SILVA VALLEY PKWY, EDCo, 95762	262 - F7
OAK RIDGE	4501 MARTIN LUTHER KING JR BLV, SAC, 95820	317 - G3
OAKVIEW COMM	7229 BEECH AV, SaCo, 95662	260 - E2
OAK VIEW (SEE PAGE 420)	7474 E COLLIER RD, SJCo, 95220	440 - E5
OLIVE GROVE	7926 FIRESTONE WY, SaCo, 95843	[illegible]
OPHIR	1373 LOZANOS RD, PlaC, 95658	181 - H3
ORANGEVALE OPEN STRUCTURE	6550 FILBERT AV, SaCo, 95662	260 - G3
ORCHARD	1040 Q ST, SaCo, 95673	257 - J1
OTTOMON WAY	9460 OTTOMON WY, SaCo, 95662	260 - J2
PACIFIC	6201 41ST ST, SAC, 95824	317 - G6
PALISADES	9601 LAKE NATOMA DR, SaCo, 95662	260 - J5
PARKWAY	4720 FOREST PKWY, SaCo, 95823	337 - H2
PASADENA AVENUE	4330 PASADENA AV, SaCo, 95821	278 - J3
PECK, CHARLES	6230 RUTLAND DR, SaCo, 95608	259 - E7
PENRYN	6885 ENGLISH COLONY WY, PlaC, 95663	201 - B1
PERSHING	9010 PERSHING AV, SaCo, 95662	260 - F6
PHILLIPS, ETHEL	2930 21ST AV, SAC, 95820	317 - E3
PIONEER	5816 PIONEER WY, SaCo, 95841	259 - B5
PLACER	8650 HORSESHOE BAR RD, PlaC, 95650	221 - F1
PLEASANT GROVE	10160 PLEASANT GRV SCH RD, ELKG, 95624	359 - E3
PONY EXPRESS	1250 56TH AV, SAC, 95831	317 - A7

FEATURE NAME	Address City, ZIP Code	PAGE-GRID
POWERS, CLARKE H	3296 HUMPHREY RD, LMS, 95650	200 - J4
PRAIRIE	5251 VALLEY HI DR, SAC, 95823	337 - J5
QUAIL GLEN	1250 CANEVARI DR, RSVL, 95747	219 - C5
RANCHO CORDOVA	2562 CHASSELLA WY, RCCD, 95670	299 - G1
REESE, DAVID	7600 LINDALE DR, SaCo, 95828	338 - B2
REGENCY PARK	5901 BRIDGECROSS DR, SAC, 95835	257 - C4
REITH, JOHN	8401 VALLEY LARK DR, SAC, 95823	337 - J7
RESCUE	3880 GREEN VALLEY RD, EDCo, 95672	263 - G1
RIDGEPOINT	4680 MONUMENT DR, SaCo, 95842	259 - A1
RIO LINDA	631 L ST, SaCo, 95673	257 - H2
RIVER OAKS	905 VINTAGE OAK AV, GALT, 95632	419 - F4
RIVERVIEW	10700 AMBASSADOR DR, RCCD, 95670	279 - G6
ROBERTS	5630 ILLINOIS AV, SaCo, 95628	260 - E6
ROBLA	5200 MARYSVILLE BLVD, SAC, 95838	257 - J6
ROCK CREEK	2140 COLLET QUARRY DR, RKLN, 95765	219 - J2
ROCK CREEK	3050 BELL RD, PlaC, 95602	162 - B3
ROCKLIN ACADEMY	2996 CREST DR, RKLN, 95765	200 - D7
ROCKLIN	5025 MEYERS ST, RKLN, 95677	220 - F3
RUHKALA	6530 TURNSTONE WY, RKLN, 95765	219 - H1
SARGEANT	1200 RIDGECREST WY, RSVL, 95661	240 - D4
SCHNELL, LOUISIANA	2871 SCHNELL SCHOOL RD, PLCR, 95667	245 - J4
SCHWEITZER, ALBERT	4350 GLENRIDGE DR, SaCo, 95608	279 - G2
SEQUOIA	3333 ROSEMONT DR, SaCo, 95826	318 - H1
SHIELDS, PETER J	10434 GEORGETOWN DR, RCCD, 95670	279 - F7
SIERRA ACCELERATED	1100 THOMPSON WY, PLCR, 95667	245 - G5
SIERRA	6811 CAMBONE WY, RKLN, 95677	220 - G5
SIERRA ENTERPRISE	9115 FRUITRIDGE RD, SaCo, 95826	318 - J4
SIERRA GARDENS	711 OAK RIDGE DR, RSVL, 95661	240 - A3
SIERRA OAKS	171 MILLS RD, SaCo, 95864	298 - E5
SIERRA VIEW	3638 BAINBRIDGE DR, SaCo, 95660	258 - G1
SILVA VALLEY	3001 GOLDEN EAGLE LN, EDCo, 95762	262 - E5
SIMS, JOSEPH	3033 BUCKMINSTER DR, ELKG, 95758	357 - F5
SKYCREST	5641 MARIPOSA AV, CITH, 95610	259 - H6
SKYRIDGE	800 PERKINS WY, AUB, 95603	182 - D6
SLOAT, JOHN D	7525 CANDLEWOOD WY, SAC, 95822	337 - C3
SMITH, JEDEDIAH	401 MCCLATCHY WY, SAC, 95818	297 - A6
SMYTHE, ALETHEA B	2781 NORTHGATE BLVD, SAC, 95833	277 - E6
SOUTHPORT	2747 LINDEN RD, WSAC, 95691	296 - G7
SPANGER, FERRIS	699 SHASTA ST, RSVL, 95678	219 - J7
SPINELLI, CYRIL	3401 E SCOTLAND DR, SaCo, 95843	238 - F7
SPRENTZ, BLANCHE	249 FLOWER DR, FOLS, 95630	261 - E4
STILL, JOHN H	2250 JOHN STILL DR, SAC, 95832	337 - D4
STONE LAKE	9673 LAKEPOINT DR, ELKG, 95758	357 - G6
STONERIDGE	2501 ALEXANDRA DR, RSVL, 95661	220 - E7
STRAUCH, HAZEL	3141 NORTHSTEAD DR, SAC, 95833	277 - E4
SUNDAHL, CARL H	9932 INWOOD RD, FOLS, 95630	261 - B1
SUNRISE	7322 SUNRISE BLVD, CITH, 95610	260 - A1
SUTTERVILLE	4967 MONTEREY WY, SAC, 95822	317 - C4
TAHOE	3110 60TH ST, SAC, 95820	318 - A1
TAYLOR STREET	4350 TAYLOR ST, SAC, 95838	277 - H1
TRAJAN	6601 TRAJAN DR, SaCo, 95662	260 - C3
TSUKAMOTO, MARY	8737 BRITTANY PARK DR, SaCo, 95828	338 - G6
TWAIN, MARK	4914 58TH ST, SAC, 95820	317 - J3
TWELVE BRIDGES	[illegible]	200 - A2
TWIN LAKES	5515 MAIN AV, SaCo, 95662	260 - H6
TWIN OAKS	2835 CLUB DR, RKLN, 95765	200 - A7
TWO RIVERS	3201 W RIVER DR, SAC, 95833	276 - H6
UNION HOUSE	7850 DEER CREEK DR, SAC, 95823	337 - G4
VALLEY OAKS	21 C ST, GALT, 95632	419 - E7
VALLEY VIEW	3000 CREST DR, RKLN, 95765	200 - D7
VILLAGE	6845 LARCHMONT DR, SaCo, 95660	258 - H2
VINELAND	6450 20TH ST, SaCo, 95673	258 - C3
VINTAGE PARKWAY (SEE PAGE 493)	1000 VINTAGE PKWY, OAKL, 94561	514 - E5
WALNUT GROVE	14181 GROVE ST, SaCo, 95690	437 - A1
WARREN, EARL	5420 LOWELL ST, SAC, 95820	318 - C4
WASHINGTON	520 18TH ST, SAC, 95814	297 - E3
WENZEL, CAROLINE	6870 GREENHAVEN DR, SAC, 95831	316 - J7
WESTFIELD VILLAGE	508 POPLAR ST, WSAC, 95691	296 - H3
WEST, IRENE B	SERIO WY, SAC, 95758	358 - C1
WESTMORE OAKS	1504 FALLBROOK ST, WSAC, 95691	296 - H5
WESTSIDE	6537 W 2ND ST, SaCo, 95673	257 - G3

FEATURE NAME	Address City, ZIP Code	PAGE-GRID
WHITE, DH	500 ELM WY, RVIS, 94571	454 - H4
WHITE ROCK	10487 WHITE ROCK RD, RCCD, 95670	299 - F3
WHITNEY AVENUE	4248 WHITNEY AV, SaCo, 95821	278 - H4
WHITNEY, PARKER	5145 TOPAZ AV, RKLN, 95677	220 - C3
WILLIAMSON	2275 BENITA DR, RCCD, 95670	279 - H6
WINN, AM	3351 EXPLORER DR, RCCD, 95827	299 - D6
WIRE, CLAYTON B	5100 EL PARAISO AV, SaCo, 95824	317 - H6
WITTER RANCH	3790 POPPY HILL WY, SAC, 95834	276 - H3
WOODBINE	2500 52ND AV, SAC, 95822	317 - E7
WOODBRIDGE	515 NILES AV, RSVL, 95678	239 - H1
WOODLAKE	700 SOUTHGATE RD, SAC, 95815	277 - H7
WOODRIDGE	5761 BRETT DR, SaCo, 95842	259 - A5
WOODSIDE	8248 VILLA OAK DR, CITH, 95610	260 - B1

SCHOOLS - PUBLIC HIGH

FEATURE NAME	Address City, ZIP Code	PAGE-GRID
ADELANTE	350 ATLANTIC ST, RSVL, 95678	239 - J1
AMERICAN LEGION	3801 BROADWAY, SAC, 95817	317 - G1
ANTELOPE VIEW CHARTER	8725 WATT AV, SaCo, 95843	238 - F4
ANTIOCH (SEE PAGE 493)	700 W 18TH ST, ANT, 94509	513 - C5
BELLA VISTA	8301 MADISON AV, SaCo, 95628	260 - C6
BURBANK, LUTHER	3500 FLORIN RD, SAC, 95823	337 - F1
CALVINE	8333 VINTAGE PARK DR, SaCo, 95828	338 - G7
CASA ROBLE FUNDAMENTAL	9151 OAK AV, SaCo, 95662	260 - G1
CENTER	3243 CENTER COURT LN, SaCo, 95843	238 - F5
CHANA CONT	3775 RICHARDSON DR, PlaC, 95602	162 - A2
CHARTER COMM	6262 GREEN VALLEY RD, EDCo, 95667	244 - H6
CORDOVA	2239 CHASE DR, RCCD, 95670	299 - F1
DAYLOR, WILLIAM	6131 ORANGE AV, SaCo, 95823	338 - A2
DEL CAMPO	4925 DEWEY DR, SaCo, 95628	279 - E1
DEL ORO	3301 TAYLOR RD, LMS, 95650	201 - A4
DELTA	52810 NETHERLANDS AV, YoCo, 95612	356 - H5
DISCOVERY	3401 ROSIN BLVD, SAC, 95834	277 - C3
EL CAMINO	4300 EL CAMINO AV, SaCo, 95864	278 - J7
EL CENTRO JR-SR	9601 KIEFER BLVD, SaCo, 95827	319 - B1
EL DORADO	561 CANAL ST, PLCR, 95667	245 - E4
ELK GROVE	9800 ELK GROVE FLORIN RD, ELKG, 95624	358 - G7
EL SERENO ALTERNATIVE EDUCATION	8301 MADISON AV, SaCo, 95628	260 - C6
ENCINA	1400 BELL ST, SaCo, 95825	298 - D2
ESTRELLITA	117 CAMELLIA WY, GALT, 95632	419 - F6
FLORIN	7956 COTTONWOOD LN, SaCo, 95828	338 - E5
FOLSOM	1655 IRON POINT RD, FOLS, 95630	281 - D2
FOLSOM LAKE	955 RILEY, FOLS, 95630	261 - C5
FOOTHILL	5000 MCCLOUD DR, SaCo, 95842	259 - A4
FORTY NINER R O P	360 NEVADA ST, AUB, 95603	182 - C2
FRANKLIN	6400 WHITELOCK PKWY, ELKG, 95757	378 - A1
GALT	145 LINCOLN WY, GALT, 95632	419 - F6
GENESIS	5601 47TH AV, SAC, 95824	317 - J6
GRANITE BAY	1 GRIZZLY WY, PlaC, 95746	240 - G4
GRANT UNION	1400 GRAND AV, SAC, 95838	278 - A3
GRANT WEST	1220 SOUTH AV, SAC, 95838	278 - A3
HIGHLANDS	6601 GUTHRIE ST, SaCo, 95660	258 - J3
HORIZON INSTRUCTIONAL SYSTEMS	1530 3RD ST, LNCN, 95648	179 - F3
INDEPENDENCE	2227 PLEASANT VALLEY RD, EDCo, 95667	265 - D3
INDERKUM	2500 NEW MARKET DR, SAC, 95835	257 - A7
JOHNSON, HIRAM	6879 14TH AV, SAC, 95820	318 - B2
JOHNSON, HIRAM WEST CAMPUS	5022 58TH ST, SAC, 95820	317 - J4
KENNEDY, JOHN F	6715 GLORIA DR, SAC, 95831	316 - H7
KINNEY	2710 KILGORE RD, RCCD, 95670	299 - J1
LA ENTRADA	5320 HEMLOCK ST, SaCo, 95841	259 - B6
LAGUNA CREEK	9050 VICINO DR, ELKG, 95758	358 - A3
LAS FLORES	5900 BAMFORD DR, SAC, 95823	338 - A5
LA VISTA	5843 ALMOND AV, SaCo, 95662	260 - D5
LINCOLN	790 J ST, LNCN, 95648	179 - G2
LIVE OAK (SEE PAGE 493)	1708 F ST, ANT, 94509	513 - C5
MAIDU	3775 RICHARDSON DR, PlaC, 95602	162 - A2
MCCLATCHY, CK	3066 FREEPORT BLVD, SAC, 95818	317 - D1
MESA VERDE	7501 CARRIAGE DR, CITH, 95621	259 - G1
MIRA LOMA	4000 EDISON AV, SaCo, 95821	278 - H3
MONTEREY TRAIL	8661 POWER HILL RD, ELKG, 95624	358 - E1
NATOMAS CHARTER	4600 BLACKROCK DR, SAC, 95835	257 - D7
NATOMAS	3301 ROSIN BLVD, SAC, 95834	277 - C4
OAKMONT	1710 CIRBY WY, RSVL, 95661	240 - B5
OAK RIDGE	1120 HARVARD WY, EDCo, 95762	262 - D4
PACIFIC	3800 BOLIVAR AV, SaCo, 95660	258 - G4
PACIFIC WEST	2035 NORTH AV, SAC, 95838	278 - C2
PALMITER, LEO A	10170 MISSILE WY, SaCo, 95655	299 - E7
PALOS VERDE CONT	7501 CARRIAGE DR, CITH, 95621	259 - G1
PLACER	275 ORANGE ST, AUB, 95603	182 - E3
PLEASANT GROVE	9531 BOND RD, ELKG, 95624	359 - A4
PONDEROSA	3661 PONDEROSA RD, EDCo, 95682	263 - J5
PROSPECTS (SEE PAGE 493)	820 W 2ND ST, ANT, 94509	513 - C3
RIO AMERICANO	4540 AMERICAN RIVER DR, SaCo, 95864	298 - J4
RIO CAZADERO	7025 GRANDSTAFF DR, SAC, 95823	338 - A5
RIO LINDA	6309 DRY CREEK RD, SaCo, 95673	258 - A3
RIO VISTA	410 4TH ST, RVIS, 94571	454 - G6
RIVER CITY	1100 CLARENDON ST, WSAC, 95691	296 - H4
ROCKLIN	5301 VICTORY LN, RKLN, 95765	200 - C7
ROSEMONT	9594 KEIFER BLVD, SaCo, 95827	319 - B2
ROSEVILLE	1 TIGER WY, RSVL, 95678	219 - J7
SACRAMENTO CHARTER	2315 34TH ST, SAC, 95817	297 - F7
SACRAMENTO NEW TECHNOLOGY	1400 DICKSON ST, SAC, 95822	317 - B5
SAN JUAN	7551 GREENBACK LN, CITH, 95610	259 - H4
SHELDON	8333 KINGSBRIDGE DR, SaCo, 95829	339 - A7
UNION MINE	6530 KOKI LN, EDCo, 95623	265 - C4
VALLEY	6300 EHRHARDT AV, SAC, 95823	338 - A7
VIA DEL CAMPO	4925 DEWEY DR, SaCo, 95628	279 - E1
VICTORY HIGH CONT	3250 VICTORY DR, RKLN, 95765	200 - C6
WALDORF, JOHN MORSE	1901 60TH AV, SAC, 95822	337 - C1
WHITNEY	701 LIBERTY PKWY, RKLN, 95765	199 - H3
WOODCREEK	2551 WOODCREEK OAKS BLVD, RSVL, 95747	219 - C7

SCHOOLS - PUBLIC INTERMEDIATE

FEATURE NAME	Address City, ZIP Code	PAGE-GRID
ALPHA	8920 ELWYN AV, SaCo, 95626	237 - G4
ARCADE FUNDAMENTAL	3500 EDISON AV, SaCo, 95821	278 - G3
CAMPOS VEREDE ALTERNATIVE MAGNET	3701 STEPHEN DR, SaCo, 95660	258 - G4
EICH, WARREN T	1509 SIERRA GARDENS DR, RSVL, 95661	240 - B3
MARINA VILLAGE	1901 FRANCISCO DR, EDCo, 95762	242 - C6
RIDGEVIEW	9177 TWIN SCHOOLS RD, PlaC, 95746	240 - H4

SCHOOLS - PUBLIC JUNIOR HIGH

FEATURE NAME	Address City, ZIP Code	PAGE-GRID
CAVITT, WILLMA E	7200 FULLER DR, PlaC, 95746	241 - C3
CENTER	3111 CENTER COURT LN, SaCo, 95843	238 - F5
DON JULIO	6444 WALERGA RD, SaCo, 95660	258 - J3
FOOTHILL FARMS	5001 DIABLO DR, SaCo, 95842	259 - B4
KING, MARTIN LUTHER JR	3051 FAIRFIELD ST, SAC, 95815	277 - H5
NORWOOD	4601 NORWOOD AV, SAC, 95838	277 - H1
OLYMPUS	2625 LA CROIX DR, RSVL, 95661	240 - E2
RIO LINDA	1101 G ST, SaCo, 95673	257 - J4
RIO TIERRA FUNDAMENTAL	3201 NORTHSTEAD DR, SAC, 95833	277 - E4

SCHOOLS - PUBLIC MIDDLE

FEATURE NAME	Address City, ZIP Code	PAGE-GRID
ALBIANI, KATHERINE L	9140 BRADSHAW RD, ELKG, 95624	339 - D4
ANTELOPE CROSSING	9200 PALMERSON DR, SaCo, 95843	239 - B6
ANTIOCH (SEE PAGE 493)	1500 D ST, ANT, 94509	513 - D5
ARDEN	1640 WATT AV, SaCo, 95864	298 - G2
BACON, FERN	4140 CUNY AV, SaCo, 95823	317 - G7
BARRETT, JOHN	4243 BARRETT RD, SaCo, 95608	279 - E2
BRANNAN, SAM	5301 ELMER WY, SAC, 95822	317 - A4
BULJAN, GEORGE MIDDLE	100 HALLISSY DR, RSVL, 95678	219 - G4
CAIN, E V	150 PALM AV, AUB, 95603	182 - D1
CALIFORNIA	1600 VALLEJO WY, SAC, 95818	297 - C7
CAMERADO SPRINGS	2480 MERRYCHASE DR, EDCo, 95682	263 - C7
CARNEGIE, ANDREW	5820 ILLINOIS AV, SaCo, 95662	260 - E5
CARSON, KIT	5301 N ST, SAC, 95819	297 - J6
CHURCHILL, WINSTON	4900 WHITNEY AV, SaCo, 95608	279 - A4
COOLEY, ROBERT C	9300 PRAIRIE WOODS WY, RSVL, 95747	219 - C2
DELTA VISTA (SEE PAGE 493)	4901 FRANK HENGEL WY, OAKL, 94561	514 - H7
EDDY, HARRIET	9329 SOARING OAKS DR, ELKG, 95758	358 - C5
EDWARD HARRIS	POWER INN RD, ELKG, 95624	358 - E1
EDWARDS, GLEN	204 L ST, LNCN, 95648	179 - G3
EINSTEIN, ALBERT	9325 MIRANDY DR, SaCo, 95826	319 - A1
FOLSOM	500 BLUE RAVINE RD, FOLS, 95630	261 - E5
GOETHE, CHARLES M	2250 68TH AV, SAC, 95822	337 - D2
GOLDEN STATE	1100 CARRIE ST, WSAC, 95605	296 - J1
GRANITE OAKS	2600 WYCKFORD BLVD, RKLN, 95765	200 - C6
GREENE, LEROY F	2950 W RIVER DR, SAC, 95833	276 - J6
GREEN, HERBERT C	3781 FORNI RD, EDCo, 95667	265 - C1
GREER, VERON E	248 W A ST, GALT, 95632	419 - D7
JACKMAN, SAMUEL	7925 KENTWAL DR, SAC, 95823	337 - J5
KERR, JOSEPH	8865 ELK GROVE BLVD, ELKG, 95624	358 - G6
KING, STARR	4848 COTTAGE WY, SaCo, 95608	299 - A1
MARKHAM, EDWIN	2800 MOULTON DR, PLCR, 95667	245 - E4
MCCAFFREY, ROBERT L	997 PARK TERRACE DR, GALT, 95632	419 - G3
MILLS	10439 COLOMA RD, RCCD, 95670	299 - F1
MITCHELL, W E MIDDLE	2100 ZINFANDEL DR, RCCD, 95670	279 - J7
NATOMAS	3700 DEL PASO RD, SAC, 95834	256 - G7
PARK (SEE PAGE 493)	1 SPARTAN WY, ANT, 94509	513 - C7
PASTEUR, LOUIS	8935 ELM AV, SaCo, 95662	260 - F2
PLEASANT GROVE	2540 GREEN VALLEY RD, EDCo, 95672	263 - A2
RIVERVIEW	525 S 2ND ST, RVIS, 94571	454 - H6
ROGERS, WILL	4924 DEWEY DR, SaCo, 95628	279 - F1
ROLLING HILLS	7141 SILVA VALLEY PKWY, EDCo, 95762	262 - E4
RUTTER, JAMES	7350 PALMER HOUSE DR, SaCo, 95828	338 - C2
SALK, JONAS ALTERNATIVE	2950 HURLEY WY, SaCo, 95864	298 - E3
SILVERADO	2525 COUNTRY CLUB DR, RSVL, 95747	219 - D7
SMEDBERG, T R	8239 KINGSBRIDGE DR, SaCo, 95829	339 - A7
SPRING VIEW	5040 5TH ST, RKLN, 95677	220 - D2
STILL, JOHN H	2250 JOHN STILL DR, SAC, 95832	337 - D4
SUTTER	3150 I ST, SAC, 95816	297 - G5
SUTTER	715 RILEY ST, FOLS, 95630	261 - C5
SYLVAN	7137 AUBURN BLVD, CITH, 95621	259 - H2
TOBY JOHNSON	10099 FRANKLIN HIGH RD, ELKG, 95757	378 - A2
TWELVE BRIDGES	770 WESTVIEW DR, LNCN, 95648	199 - H2
WOOD, WILL C	6201 LEMON HILL AV, SAC, 95824	318 - A5

SHOPPING - REGIONAL

FEATURE NAME	Address City, ZIP Code	PAGE-GRID
ARDEN FAIR	1689 ARDEN WY, SAC, 95815	278 - A7
BROADSTONE MALL	E BIDWELL ST & BROADSTONE PKWY, FOLS, 95630	281 - H1
COUNTRY CLUB CENTRE	3382 EL CAMINO AV, SaCo, 95825	278 - F7
COUNTRY CLUB PLAZA	2401 BUTANO DR, SaCo, 95825	278 - G7
ELK GROVE PROMENADE	HWY 99 & GRANT LINE RD, ELKG, 95757	378 - H4
FLORIN MALL	6117 FLORIN RD, SaCo, 95823	337 - J1
FOLSOM PREMIUM OUTLETS	FOLSOM BLVD & IRON POINT RD, FOLS, 95630	280 - J2
LAGUNA CROSSROADS CTR	LAGUNA BLVD & BRUCEVILLE RD, ELKG, 95758	358 - C4
MARKETPLACE-99	HWY 99 & STOCKTON BLVD, ELKG, 95624	358 - E4
NATOMAS MARKETPLACE	I-80 & TRUXEL RD, SAC, 95834	277 - B3
PARK PLACE	NATOMAS BLVD & DEL PASO RD, SAC, 95835	257 - B7
PROMENADE AT NATOMAS	I-80 & TRUXEL RD, SAC, 95834	277 - C2
RANCHO CORDOVA TOWN CTR	ZINFANDEL DR & OLSON DR, RCCD, 95670	299 - H2
ROSEVILLE CTR	DOUGLAS BL & ROCKY RIDGE DR, RSVL, 95661	240 - B2
SOMERSVILLE TOWNE CTR (SEE PAGE 493)	2556 SOMERSVILLE RD, ANT, 94509	513 - A5
SOUTHGATE PLAZA	446 FLORIN RD, SaCo, 95823	337 - G1
SUNRISE MALL	6041 SUNRISE BLVD, CITH, 95610	260 - A5
WAL-MART CENTRAL	RILEY ST & GLENN DR, FOLS, 95630	261 - C6
WESTFIELD SHOPPINGTOWN DOWNTOWN PLAZA	547 L ST, SAC, 95814	297 - C3
WESTFIELD SHOPPINGTOWN GALLERIA	1151 GALLERIA BLVD, RSVL, 95678	220 - A5
ZINFANDEL SQUARE	10971 OLSON DR, RCCD, 95670	299 - H2

TRANSPORTATION

FEATURE NAME	Address City, ZIP Code	PAGE-GRID
AMTRAK SACRAMENTO STA	401 I ST, SAC, 95814	297 - C3
AMTRAK STA	201 PACIFIC ST, RSVL, 95678	239 - H1
AMTRAK STA	277 NEVADA ST, AUB, 95603	182 - C1
AMTRAK STA	ROCKLIN RD, RKLN, 95677	220 - E3
BNSF STA (SEE PAGE 493)	1ST ST & I ST, ANT, 94509	513 - C3
BUS TRANSIT CTR	ARCADIA DR & GREENBACK LN, CITH, 95610	260 - A4
BUS TRANSIT CTR	ARDEN WY, SAC, 95815	298 - B1
BUS TRANSIT CTR	COSUMNES RIVER COLLEGE, SAC, 95823	338 - B7
BUS TRANSIT CTR	CSU SACRAMENTO, SAC, 95819	298 - B6
BUS TRANSIT CTR	FLORIN MALL, SaCo, 95823	338 - A1
GREYHOUND BUS DEPOT	10369 FOLSOM BLVD, RCCD, 95670	299 - F3
GREYHOUND BUS DEPOT	1924 EL CAMINO AV, SAC, 95815	278 - B6
GREYHOUND BUS DEPOT	201 PACIFIC ST, RSVL, 95678	239 - H1
GREYHOUND BUS DEPOT	2426 MARCONI AV, SaCo, 95821	278 - D5
GREYHOUND BUS DEPOT	715 L ST, SAC, 95814	297 - C4
GREYHOUND BUS DEPOT	MOSQUITO RD & CLAY ST, PLCR, 95667	245 - H4

FEATURE NAME Address City, ZIP Code	PAGE-GRID
LIGHT RAIL STA 1025 GLENN DR, FOLS, 95630	**261 - A7**
LIGHT RAIL STA 12500 FOLSOM BLVD, SaCo, 95742	**280 - G4**
LIGHT RAIL STA 150 IRON POINT RD, FOLS, 95630	**280 - J2**
LIGHT RAIL STA 930 LEIDESDORFF ST, FOLS, 95630	**261 - B5**
LIGHT RAIL STA 11TH ST, SAC, 95814	**297 - D4**
LIGHT RAIL STA 21ST ST & FREEPORT BLVD, SAC, 95818	**297 - D7**
LIGHT RAIL STA 24TH ST & R ST, SAC, 95816	**297 - E5**
LIGHT RAIL STA 39TH ST & R ST, SAC, 95819	**297 - G6**
LIGHT RAIL STA 47TH AV & 27TH ST, SAC, 95822	**317 - E6**
LIGHT RAIL STA 48TH ST & Q ST, SAC, 95819	**297 - H7**
LIGHT RAIL STA 59TH ST, SAC, 95819	**298 - A7**
LIGHT RAIL STA 5TH ST & H ST, SAC, 95814	**297 - C3**
LIGHT RAIL STA 7TH ST & CAPITOL MALL, SAC, 95814	**297 - C4**
LIGHT RAIL STA 7TH ST & I ST, SAC, 95814	**297 - C3**
LIGHT RAIL STA 7TH ST, SAC, 95814	**297 - C3**
LIGHT RAIL STA 8TH ST & CAPITOL MALL, SAC, 95814	**297 - C4**
LIGHT RAIL STA 8TH ST & MERCHANT ST, SAC, 95814	**297 - C3**
LIGHT RAIL STA 8TH ST, SAC, 95814	**297 - C4**
LIGHT RAIL STA ARCHIVES PLAZA, 11TH ST & O ST, SAC, 95814	**297 - C4**
LIGHT RAIL STA ARDEN WY & BOXWOOD ST, SAC, 95815	**277 - J7**
LIGHT RAIL STA ARDEN WY & OXFORD ST, SAC, 95815	**277 - H7**
LIGHT RAIL STA AUBURN BLVD & ARCADE BLVD, SAC, 95815	**278 - B5**
LIGHT RAIL STA BROADWAY & FREEPORT BLVD, SAC, 95818	**297 - D6**
LIGHT RAIL STA CAPITAL CITY FRWY AT R ST, SAC, 95816	**297 - F6**
LIGHT RAIL STA CAPITAL MALL & 8TH ST, SAC, 95814	**297 - C4**
LIGHT RAIL STA DEL PASO BLVD & BAXTER AV, SAC, 95815	**277 - G7**
LIGHT RAIL STA E ST & 12TH ST, SAC, 95814	**297 - D3**
LIGHT RAIL STA FLORIN RD & 29TH ST, SAC, 95822	**337 - F1**
LIGHT RAIL STA FOLSOM BLVD & BUTTERFIELD WY, SaCo, 95827	**299 - A6**
LIGHT RAIL STA FOLSOM BLVD & MATHER FIELD RD, RCCD, 95827	**299 - E3**
LIGHT RAIL STA FOLSOM BLVD & OLSON DR, RCCD, 95670	**299 - H1**
LIGHT RAIL STA FOLSOM BLVD & STARFIRE DR, SaCo, 95826	**298 - J7**
LIGHT RAIL STA FOLSOM BLVD & SUNRISE BLVD, SaCo, 95742	**280 - A7**
LIGHT RAIL STA FOLSOM BLVD & TIBER DR, SaCo, 95826	**299 - A6**
LIGHT RAIL STA FOLSOM BLVD & WATT AV, SaCo, 95826	**298 - G7**
LIGHT RAIL STA FOLSOM BLVD & ZINFANDEL DR, RCCD, 95670	**299 - H2**
LIGHT RAIL STA FOLSOM BLVD, SAC, 95826	**318 - E1**
LIGHT RAIL STA FRUITRIDGE RD & 24TH ST, SAC, 95822	**317 - E4**
LIGHT RAIL STA H ST & 12TH ST, SAC, 95814	**297 - D3**
LIGHT RAIL STA I-80 FRWY & WATT AV, SaCo, 95660	**278 - G2**
LIGHT RAIL STA I80 FRWY, SAC, 95660	**278 - D3**
LIGHT RAIL STA I-80 FRWY, SaCo, 95660	**278 - F2**
LIGHT RAIL STA MEADOWVIEW RD, SAC, 95822	**337 - F3**
LIGHT RAIL STA O ST & 7TH ST, SAC, 95814	**297 - C4**
LIGHT RAIL STA O ST & 9TH ST, SAC, 95814	**297 - C4**
LIGHT RAIL STA POWER INN RD, SAC, 95826	**318 - D1**
LIGHT RAIL STA Q ST & 15TH ST, SAC, 95814	**297 - D5**
LIGHT RAIL STA Q ST & 65TH ST, SAC, 95819	**298 - B7**
LIGHT RAIL STA SACRAMENTO CITY COLLEGE, SAC, 95822	**317 - D2**
LIGHT RAIL STA SELMA ST, SAC, 95815	**277 - J7**

VISITOR INFORMATION

FEATURE NAME Address City, ZIP Code	PAGE-GRID
OLD SACRAMENTO VIS CTR K ST & 2ND ST, SAC, 95814	**297 - B3**
PLACER COUNTY VIS BUREAU 661 NEWCASTLE RD, PlaC, 95658	**181 - G6**
PLACER CO VISITOR INFO CTR NEWCASTLE RD, PlaC, 95658	**201 - H1**
SACRAMENTO CONV & VISITORS BUREAU 16TH ST & I ST, SAC, 95814	**297 - E4**

CUT ALONG DOTTED LINE

The Thomas Guide®

Thank you for purchasing this Rand McNally Thomas Guide!
We value your comments and suggestions.

Please help us serve you better by completing this postage-paid reply card.
This information is for internal use ONLY and will not be distributed or sold to any external third party.

Missing pages? Maybe not... Please refer to the "Using Your Street Guide" page for further explanation.

Thomas Guide Title: Sacramento County **ISBN-13# 978-0-5288-5977-9** **MKT: SAC**

Today's Date: ________ Gender: ☐M ☐F Age Group: ☐18-24 ☐25-31 ☐32-40 ☐41-50 ☐51-64 ☐65+

1. What type of industry do you work in?
   ☐Real Estate ☐Trucking ☐Delivery ☐Construction ☐Utilities ☐Government
   ☐Retail ☐Sales ☐Transportation ☐Landscape ☐Service & Repair
   ☐Courier ☐Automotive ☐Insurance ☐Medical ☐Police/Fire/First Response
   ☐Other, please specify: ________
2. What type of job do you have in this industry? ________
3. Where did you purchase this Thomas Guide? (store name & city) ________
4. Why did you purchase this Thomas Guide? ________
5. How often do you purchase an updated Thomas Guide? ☐Annually ☐2 yrs. ☐3-5 yrs. ☐Other: ________
6. Where do you use it? ☐Primarily in the car ☐Primarily in the office ☐Primarily at home ☐Other: ________
7. How do you use it? ☐Exclusively for business ☐Primarily for business but also for personal or leisure use
   ☐Both work and personal evenly ☐Primarily for personal use ☐Exclusively for personal use
8. What do you use your Thomas Guide for?
   ☐Find Addresses ☐In-route navigation ☐Planning routes ☐Other: ________
   Find points of interest: ☐Schools ☐Parks ☐Buildings ☐Shopping Centers ☐Other: ________
9. How often do you use it? ☐Daily ☐Weekly ☐Monthly ☐Other: ________
10. Do you use the internet for maps and/or directions? ☐Yes ☐No
11. How often do you use the internet for directions? ☐Daily ☐Weekly ☐Monthly ☐Other: ________
12. Do you use any of the following mapping products in addition to your Thomas Guide?
    ☐Folded paper maps ☐Folded laminated maps ☐Wall maps ☐GPS ☐PDA ☐In-car navigation ☐Phone maps
13. What features, if any, would you like to see added to your Thomas Guide? ________
14. What features or information do you find most useful in your Rand McNally Thomas Guide? (please specify) ________
15. Please provide any additional comments or suggestions you have. ________

We strive to provide you with the most current updated information available if you know of a map correction, please notify us here.

Where is the correction? Map Page #: ________ Grid #: ________ Index Page #: ________

Nature of the correction: ☐Street name missing ☐Street name misspelled ☐Street information incorrect
☐Incorrect location for point of interest ☐Index error ☐Other: ________

Detail: ________

I would like to receive information about updated editions and special offers from Rand McNally
☐via e-mail E-mail address: ________
☐via postal mail
Your Name: ________ Company (if used for work): ________
Address: ________ City/State/ZIP: ________

Thank you for your time and help. We are working to serve you better.
This information is for internal use ONLY and will not be distributed or sold to any external third party.

CUT ALONG DOTTED LINE

TG-noCD.06

TAPE SHUT

TAPE SHUT

get directions at

randmcnally.com

CUT ALONG DOTTED LINE

2ND FOLD LINE

NO POSTAGE
NECESSARY
IF MAILED
IN THE
UNITED STATES

BUSINESS REPLY MAIL

FIRST-CLASS MAIL PERMIT NO. 388 CHICAGO IL

POSTAGE WILL BE PAID BY ADDRESSEE

RAND MCNALLY
CONSUMER AFFAIRS
PO BOX 7600
CHICAGO IL 60680-9915

1ST FOLD LINE

CUT ALONG DOTTED LINE

The Thomas Guide®

Solano County
street guide

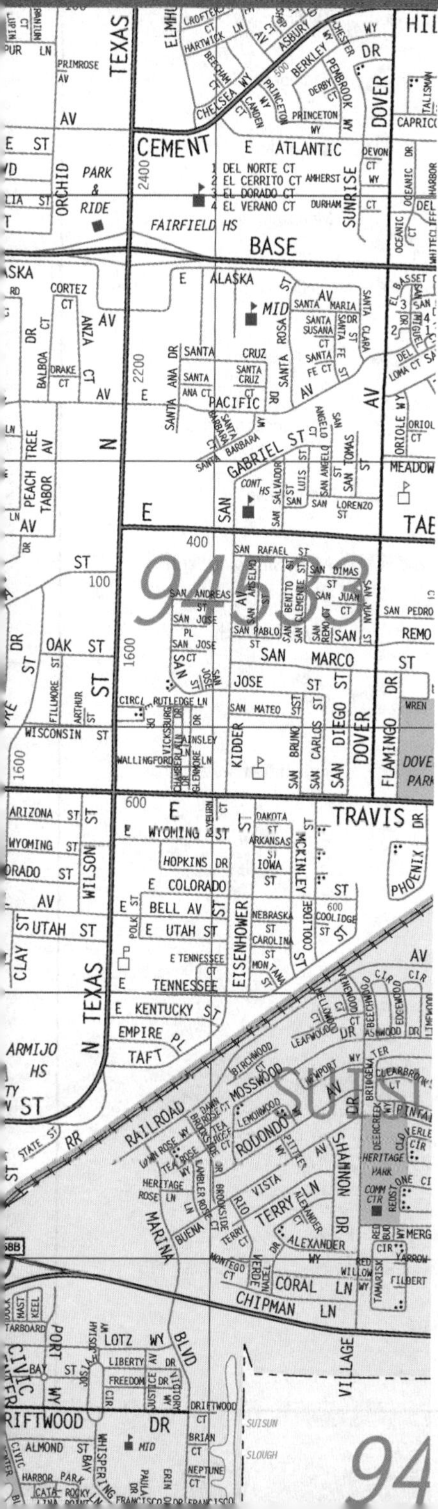

TELL US WHAT YOU THINK
comment card on last page

Contents

PageFinder™ Map U.S. Patent No. 5,419,586
Canadian Patent No. 2,116,425
Patente Mexicana No. 188186

RAND McNALLY
Rand McNally Consumer Affairs
P.O. Box 7600
Chicago, IL 60680-9915
randmcnally.com
For comments or suggestions, please call
(800) 777-MAPS (-6277)
or email us at:
consumeraffairs@randmcnally.com

Legend

- Freeway
- Interchange/ramp
- Highway
- Primary road
- Secondary road
- Minor road
- Restricted road
- Alley
- Unpaved road
- Tunnel
- Toll road
- High occupancy vehicle lane
- Stacked multiple roadways
- Proposed road
- Proposed freeway
- Freeway under construction
- One-way road
- Two-way road
- Trail, walkway
- Stairs
- Railroad
- Rapid transit
- Rapid transit, underground

- Ferry
- City boundary
- County boundary
- State boundary
- International boundary
- Military base, Indian reservation
- Township, range, rancho
- River, creek, shoreline
- 98607 ZIP code boundary, ZIP code
- 5 Interstate
- 5 Interstate (Business)
- 3 U.S. highway
- 1 4 8 9 State highways
- Carpool lane
- A Street list marker
- Street name continuation
- Street name change
- Station (train, bus)
- Building (see List of Abbreviations page)
- Building footprint
- Public elementary school
- Public high school

- Private elementary school
- Private high school
- Fire station
- Library
- Mission
- Campground
- H Hospital
- Mountain
- Section corner
- Boat launch
- Gate, locks, barricades
- Lighthouse
- Major shopping center
- Dry lake, beach
- Dam
- Intermittent lake, marsh
- 29 Exit number

Sacramento International Airport

Sacramento International Airport is conveniently close to surrounding communities of Auburn, Chico, Davis, Fairfield, Folsom, Lincoln, Lodi, Marysville, Oroville, Placerville, Roseville, Stockton, Vacaville, Woodland, Yuba City and Napa. There are over 20,000 public parking spaces at the airport, and four parking lots: Terminals A and B have Hourly and Daily lots, plus Economy parking. The maximum daily rates are $7.00 a day in the Economy lot, $12.00 a day for Daily lots and $26.00 a day for the close-in Hourly lots. The first 30 minutes are free in the hourly lots. The per hour rates for all lots are the same — $1.00 for the first hour and $2.00 for each additional hour or portion thereof. Parking rates are subject to change. Use the Hourly lots for pickup, drop-off, or quick visits to the airport. The hourly lots are located directly across the street from each terminal within easy walking distance. For more information visit www.sacairports.org.

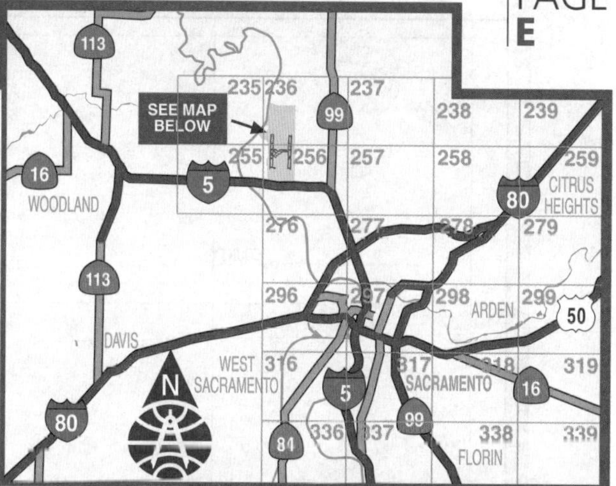

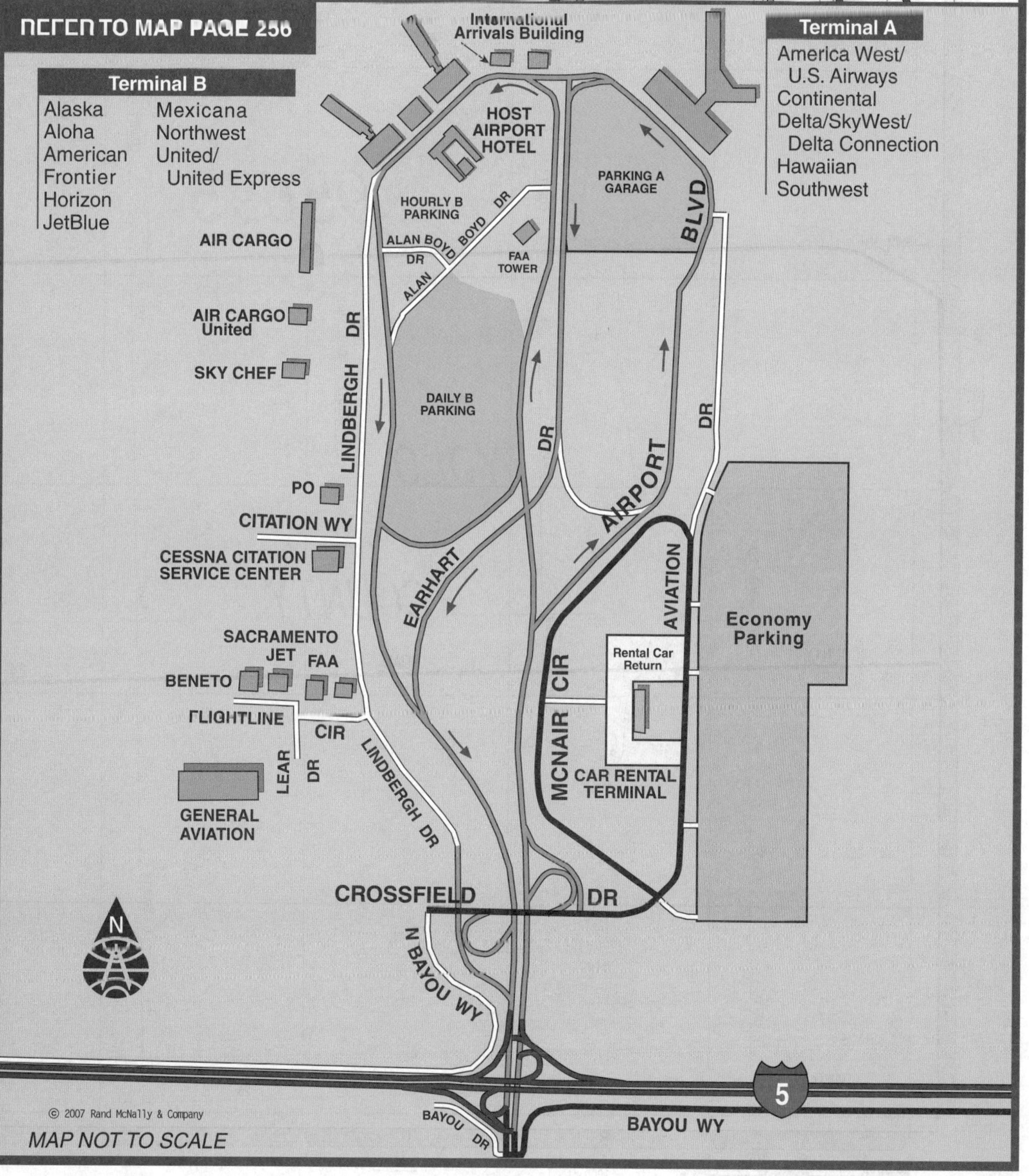

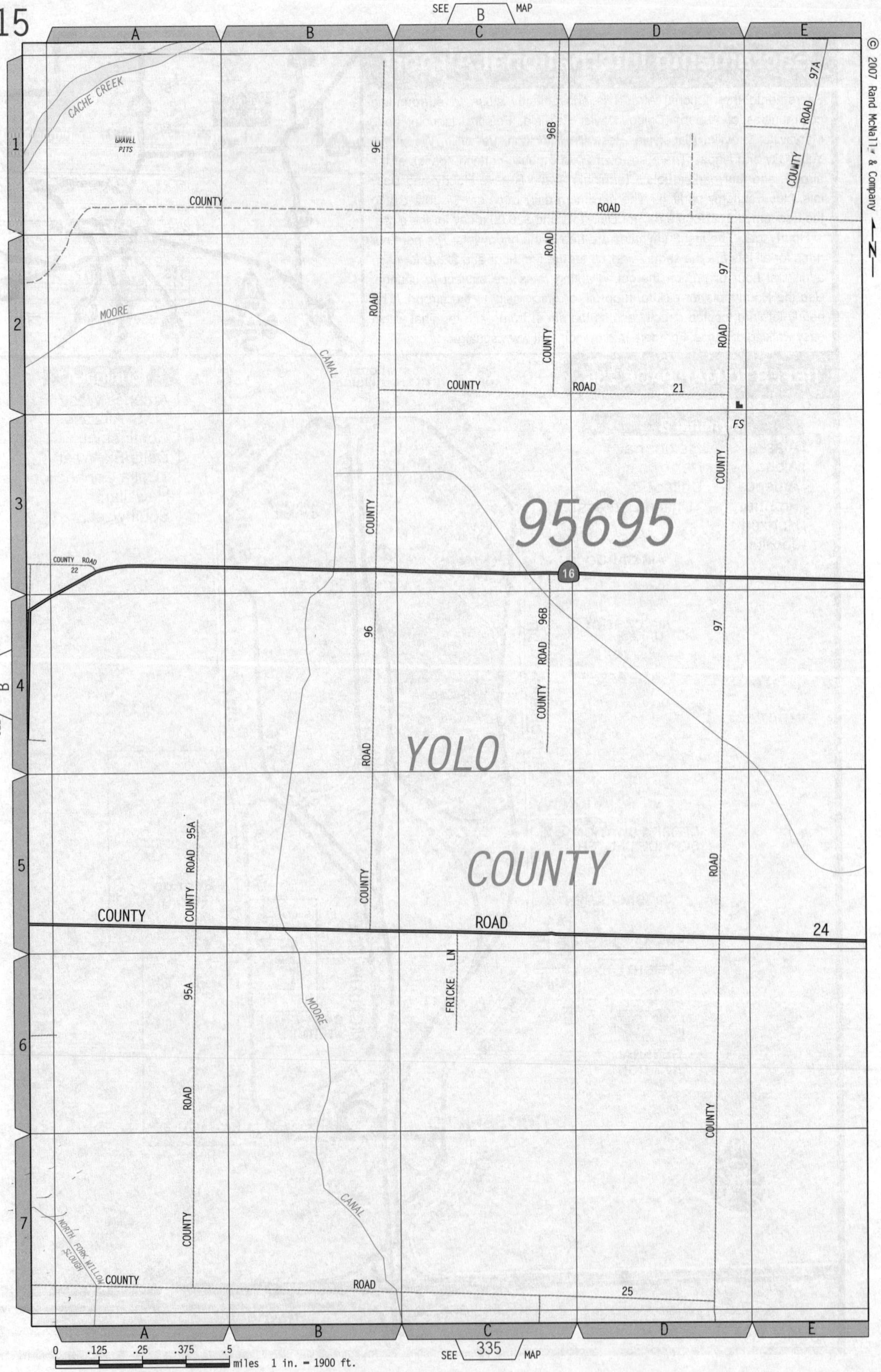
SEE B MAP
A
B
C
D
E
1
2
3
4
5
6
7
CACHE CREEK
GRAVEL PITS
COUNTY
ROAD
9E
96B
COUNTY ROAD
97A
MOORE
CANAL
COUNTY
ROAD
21
FS
97
95695
COUNTY ROAD 22
16
96
YOLO
COUNTY
95A
COUNTY
ROAD
24
FRICKE LN
NORTH FORK WILLOW SLOUGH
25
SEE B MAP
SEE 335 MAP
0 .125 .25 .375 .5
miles 1 in. = 1900 ft.
SOLANO CO.

SEE B MAP

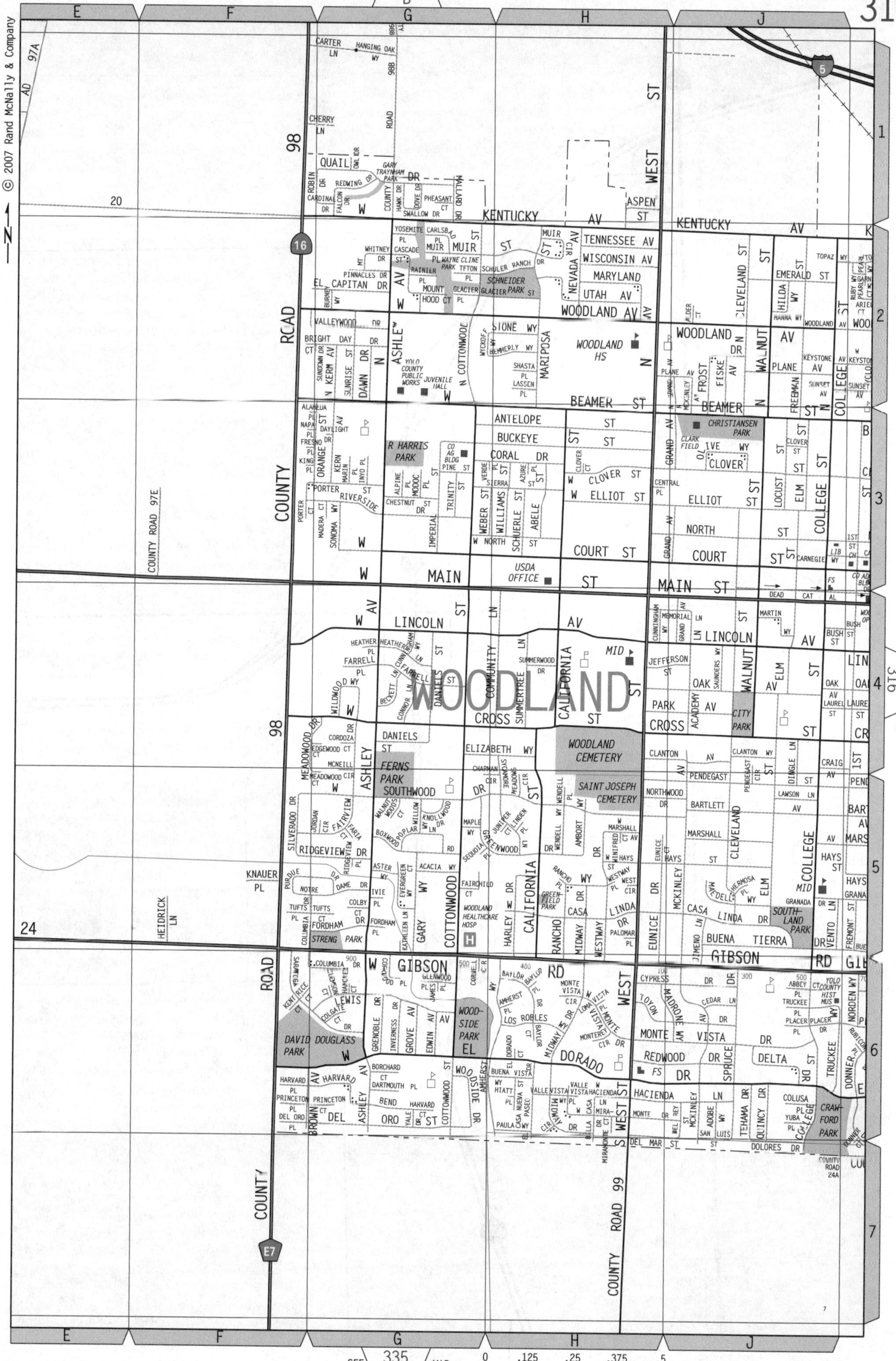

E
F
G
H
J
1
2
3
4
5
6
7
WOODLAND
COUNTY ROAD 98
COUNTY ROAD 99
COUNTY ROAD 97E
COUNTY ROAD 24A
16
E7
5
20
24
97A
CARTER LN
HANGING OAK WY
CHERRY LN
QUAIL DR
GARY TRAYNHAM PARK
REDWING DR
ROBIN
CARDINAL
FALCON DR
PHEASANT CT
SWALLOW DR
MALLARD DR
KENTUCKY AV
ASPEN ST
WEST ST
YOSEMITE
CARLSBAD
MUIR ST
TENNESSEE AV
WISCONSIN AV
MARYLAND
UTAH AV
WAYNE CLINE PARK
SCHNEIDER GLACIER PARK
SCHULER RANCH DR
NEVADA AV
EL CAPITAN DR
WOODLAND AV
VALLEYWOOD DR
BRIGHT DAY DR
ASHLEY AV
N COTTONWOOD ST
STONE WY
SHASTA PL
LASSEN PL
MARIPOSA
WOODLAND HS
YOLO COUNTY PUBLIC WORKS
JUVENILE HALL
BEAMER ST
CLEVELAND ST
EMERALD ST
TOPAZ WY
HILDA WY
WALNUT ST
PLANE AV
FROST
FISKE
BEAMER
FREEMAN
COLLEGE ST
KEYSTONE AV
SUNSET AV
ANTELOPE ST
BUCKEYE ST
CORAL DR
R HARRIS PARK
CO AG BLDG
CHRISTIANSEN PARK
CLARK FIELD
CLOVER ST
ELLIOT ST
NORTH ST
COURT ST
GRAND AV
CARNEGIE WY
RIVERSIDE ST
PORTER CT
SONOMA WY
ORANGE ST
KERN
MODOC
TRINITY ST
IMPERIAL
WEBER ST
WILLIAMS ST
SCHUERLE ST
ABELE
W NORTH ST
MAIN ST
USDA OFFICE
DEAD CAT AL
LINCOLN AV
HEATHER
FARRELL PL
WILDWOOD DR
DANIELS ST
COMMUNITY LN
SUMMERTREE LN
SUMMERWOOD DR
CALIFORNIA ST
JEFFERSON ST
OAK AV
PARK AV
ACADEMY
CITY PARK
CROSS ST
ELM AV
LAUREL ST
MEMORIAL LN
CUNNINGHAM WY
MARTIN WY
BUSH ST
MEADOWOOD DR
CORDOZA
ELIZABETH WY
WOODLAND CEMETERY
SAINT JOSEPH CEMETERY
FERNS PARK
SOUTHWOOD DR
CLANTON AV
PENDEGAST
NORTHWOOD DR
BARTLETT
MARSHALL
DINGLE LN
LAWSON LN
CRAIG AV
1ST ST
SILVERADO DR
FAIRVIEW
RIDGEVIEW DR
KNAUER PL
HEIDRICK LN
STRENG PARK
FORDHAM
GARY WY
COTTONWOOD ST
WOODLAND HEALTHCARE HOSP
HARLEY DR
GREENWOOD
GREEN FIELD PARK
RANCHO
MIDWAY
WESTWAY
CASA LINDA DR
EUNICE
MCKINLEY
HAYS ST
SOUTH LAND PARK
BUENA TIERRA
GIBSON RD
CYPRESS DR
MADRONE
TOYON
CEDAR LN
MONTE VISTA DR
LEWIS
DAVID DOUGLASS PARK
WOODSIDE PARK
LOS ROBLES
DORADO
REDWOOD DR
SPRUCE
DELTA DR
TRUCKEE
PLACER
YOLO COUNTY HIST MUS
ABBEY CT
NORDEN WY
DONNER
HARVARD AV
PRINCETON
DEL ORO ST
BROWN
ASHLEY
BEND
WOODSIDE DR
BUENA VISTA
VALLE VISTA
HACIENDA LN
ADOBE
TEHAMA DR
QUINCY DR
COLUSA
YUBA
CRAWFORD PARK
DEL MAR ST
DOLORES DR
SAN LUIS
0
.125
.25
.375
.5
miles 1 in. = 1900 ft.

SEE 316 MAP

SEE 335 MAP

SEE B MAP
SEE 315 MAP
SEE 336 MAP
A
B
C
D
E
1
2
3
4
5
6
7
95695
95776
DUBACH PARK
CHURCHILL DOWNS AV
COUNTY ROAD 101
SANTA ANITA DR
SANTA ANITA CT
TANFORAN AV
PIONEER AV
CFNR
BEST WESTERN SHADOW INN
HARTER AV
KENTUCKY AV
E KENTUCKY AV
PADDOCK PL
STABLE CT
FORTNA AV
BLUEGRASS PL
COMMERCE AV
HARTER
EAST ST
WOODLAND AV
COLLEGE ST
PALM AV
BEAMER PARK
HOLLISTER
KEYSTONE
SUTTER ST
BEAMER ST
E BEAMER ST
WILSON WY
DONNELLY CIR
YOLANO VILLAGE (CO HOUSING PROJECT)
GONZALEZ PARK
YOLANO DR
LEMEN AV
MATMOR RD
CANNERY RD
INDUSTRIAL WY
DEANER AV
DOCTOR CLASSEN WY
TIDE CT
CASE PL
CLOVER ST
GRAFTON ST
ELLIOT ST
NORTH ST
COURT ST
FREEMAN PARK
MAIN ST
E MAIN ST
SNR
DEPOT ST
WOODLAND OPERA HOUSE
LINCOLN AV
ALICE ST
JOHNSON ST
COLFAX DR
OAK AV
CROSS ST
PENDEGAST
BARTLETT AV
GUM AV
MARSHALL AV
HAYS ST
EVERMAN PARK
CAMPBELL PARK
MOLLY AV
BETTY AV
THOMAS
HELEN WY
BARBARA WY
DENISE DR
DODDS DR
CRYSTAL
SPRINGS DR
SPRINGCREEK DR
LAUGENOUR DR
ELSTON
HOMESTEAD WY
FARNHAM
KLENHARD PARK
HAYS ANTIQUE TRUCK MUSEUM
BLOWERS
HECKE DR
KINCHELOE
SAIPAN DR
ADAK
KISKA
MAUI
PRATHER
WOODARD DR
ATWELL
CLARK
MAXWELL
E GUM AV
LEO WY
ELWOOD ST
STETSON
WESTLAND
BRIDLE LN
PRAIRIE PARK
TOWSE
SUN VALLEY DR
BOURN
DUNCAN
SANTONI
ANDERSON AV
LOSOYA DR
HUNTER
PIONEER PARK
BRANIGAN
YOLO COUNTY FAIRGROUNDS
LEISUREVILLE CIR
HOMEWOOD
ROSEWOOD WY
D GIBSON RD
E GIBSON RD
GIBSON RD
(COUNTY ROAD 24)
MORRIS CIR
COUNTY FAIR MALL
ROOSEVELT
COOLIDGE
GARFIELD
HOOVER
TYLER
MONROE
WASHINGTON DR
YOLO COUNTY HIST MUS
NORDEN WY
CAMINO
PLACER DR
ARCHER DR
6TH ST
EL DORADO DR
TRUCKEE
DONNER
CRAWFORD PARK
TREDWAY PARK
AMADOR WY
PIONEER HS
PIONEER AV
WOODLAND COMMUNITY COLLEGE
SHERIFF
YOLO COUNTY JAIL
COUNTY ROAD 24A
COUNTY ROAD 24C
VIC FAZIO HWY
COUNTY ROAD
FARMERS
CENTRAL RD
BRUBAKER
FLORES
ARMUS PL
ORTIZ
DELGADO
GALVIN WY
ACKLEY PL
MCNARY WY
MIEKLE
BRISCOE PL
SHINN PL
CAMPOS
HOLLAND WY
NAKAGAKI WY
ROHWER WY
NICOLSON
ALLEN CIR
113
5
538
537
37
36
101
0 .125 .25 .375 .5
miles 1 in. = 1900 ft.

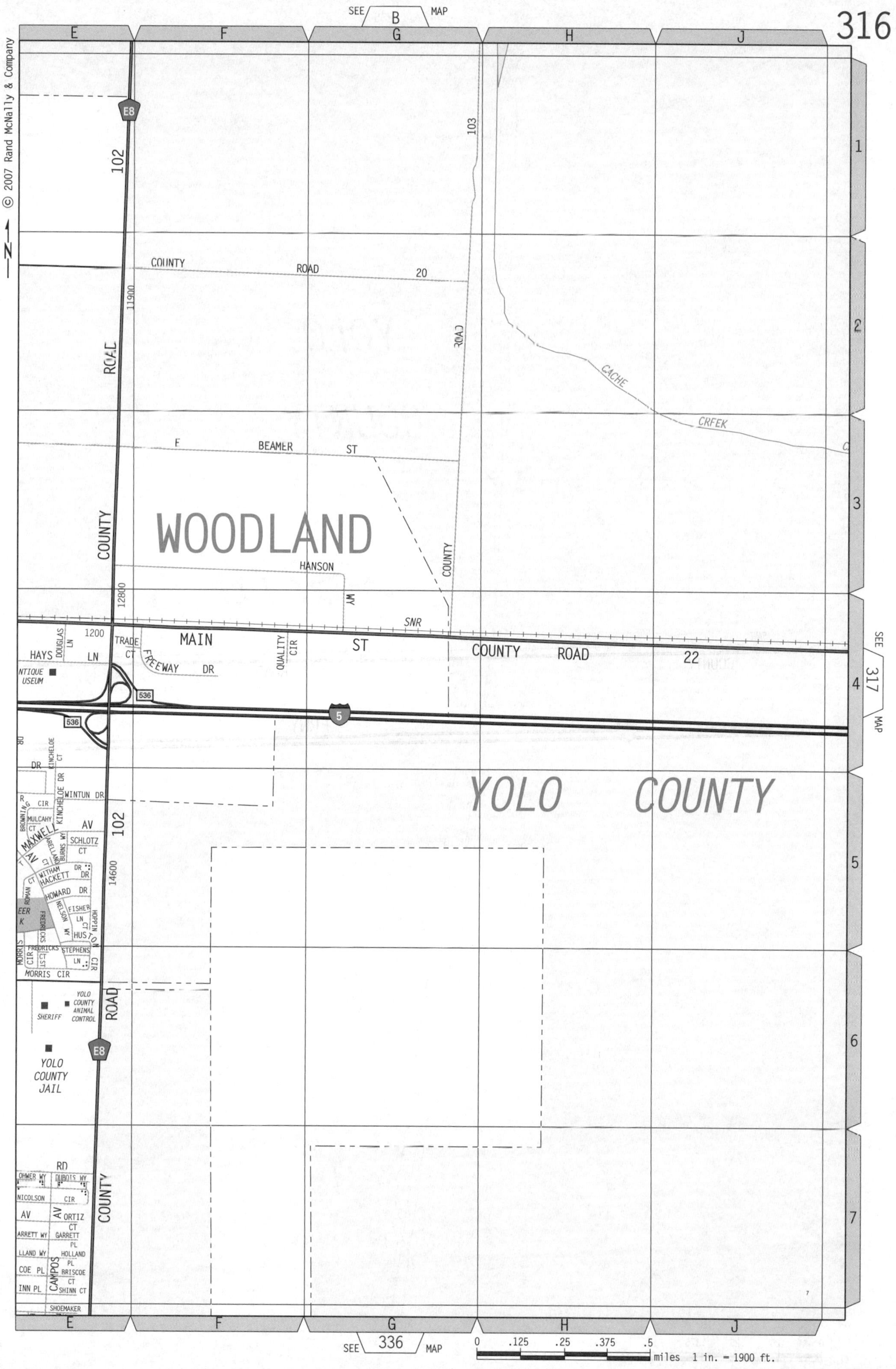
SEE B MAP
E
F
G
H
J
1
2
3
4
5
6
7
E8
102
103
COUNTY
ROAD
20
11900
ROAD
CACHE
CREEK
F
BEAMER
ST
WOODLAND
HANSON
WY
COUNTY
ROAD
12800
SNR
1200
HAYS
DOUGLAS LN
LN
TRADE CT
MAIN
ST
QUALITY CIR
COUNTY
ROAD
22
FREEWAY
DR
ANTIQUE MUSEUM
536
5
SEE 317 MAP
DR
KINCHELOE CT
KINCHELOE DR
WINTUN DR
CIR
BROWNING
MULCAHY CT
MAXWELL AV
AV
SCHLOTZ CT
BURNS WY
ARELLANO
WITHAM
HACKETT
DR
ROMAN CT
HOWARD DR
FISHER LN
NELSON WY
FREDRICKS
HOPPIN
CT
HUSTON
FREDRICKS
STEPHENS LN
MORRIS
CIR
MORRIS CIR
YOLO COUNTY
102
14600
SHERIFF
YOLO COUNTY ANIMAL CONTROL
ROAD
E8
YOLO COUNTY JAIL
RD
DUBOIS WY
NICOLSON
CIR
AV
AV
ORTIZ CT
GARRETT PL
HOLLAND PL
CAMPOS
BRISCOE CT
SHINN CT
COE PL
INN PL
SHOEMAKER
COUNTY
SEE 336 MAP
0
.125
.25
.375
.5
miles 1 in. = 1900 ft.

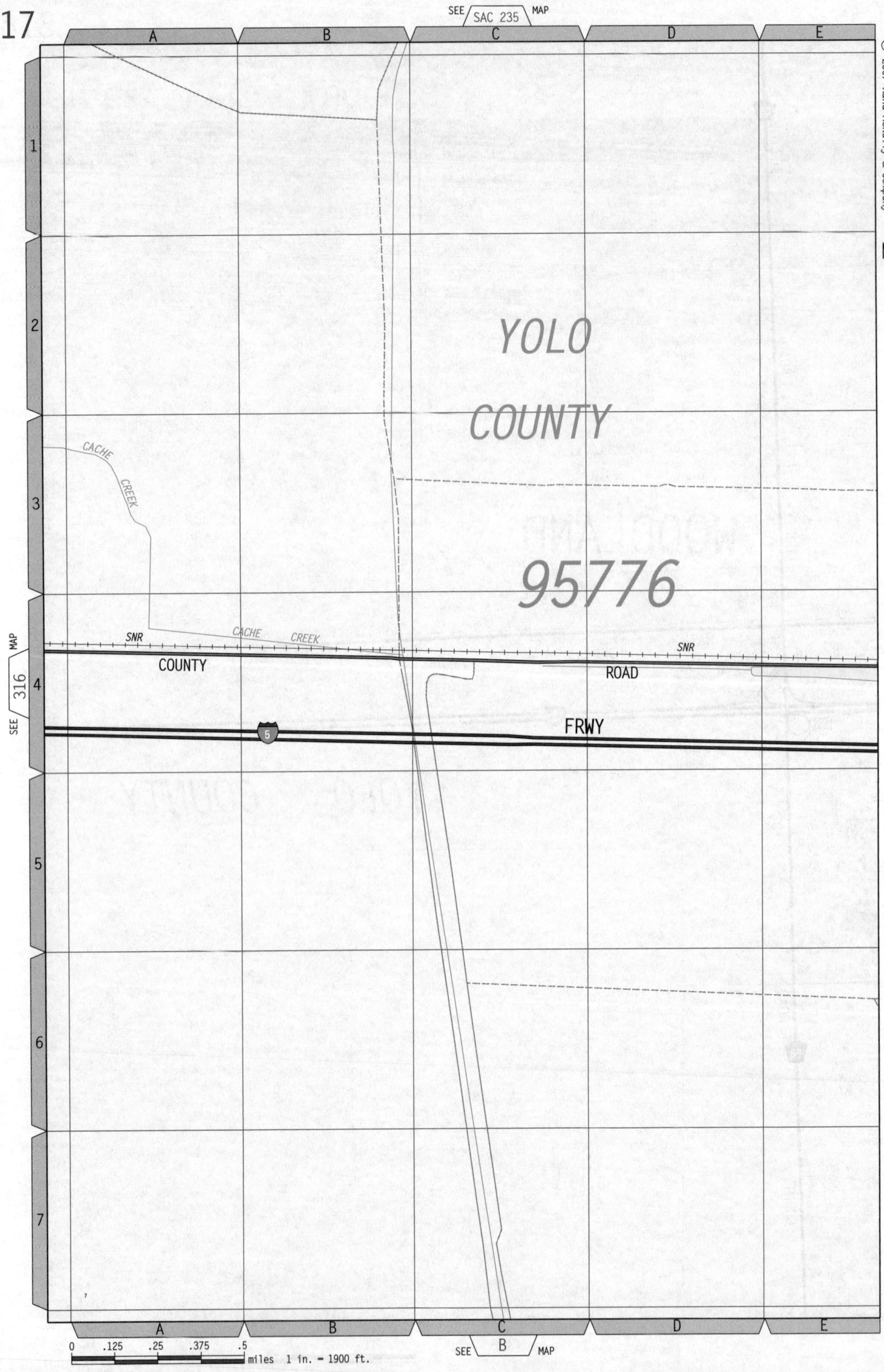
SEE SAC 235 MAP
A
B
C
D
E
1
2
3
4
5
6
7
YOLO
COUNTY
95776
CACHE
CREEK
CACHE
CREEK
SNR
SNR
COUNTY
ROAD
5
FRWY
SEE 316 MAP
SEE B MAP
0
.125
.25
.375
.5
miles 1 in. = 1900 ft.

SEE SAC 235 MAP

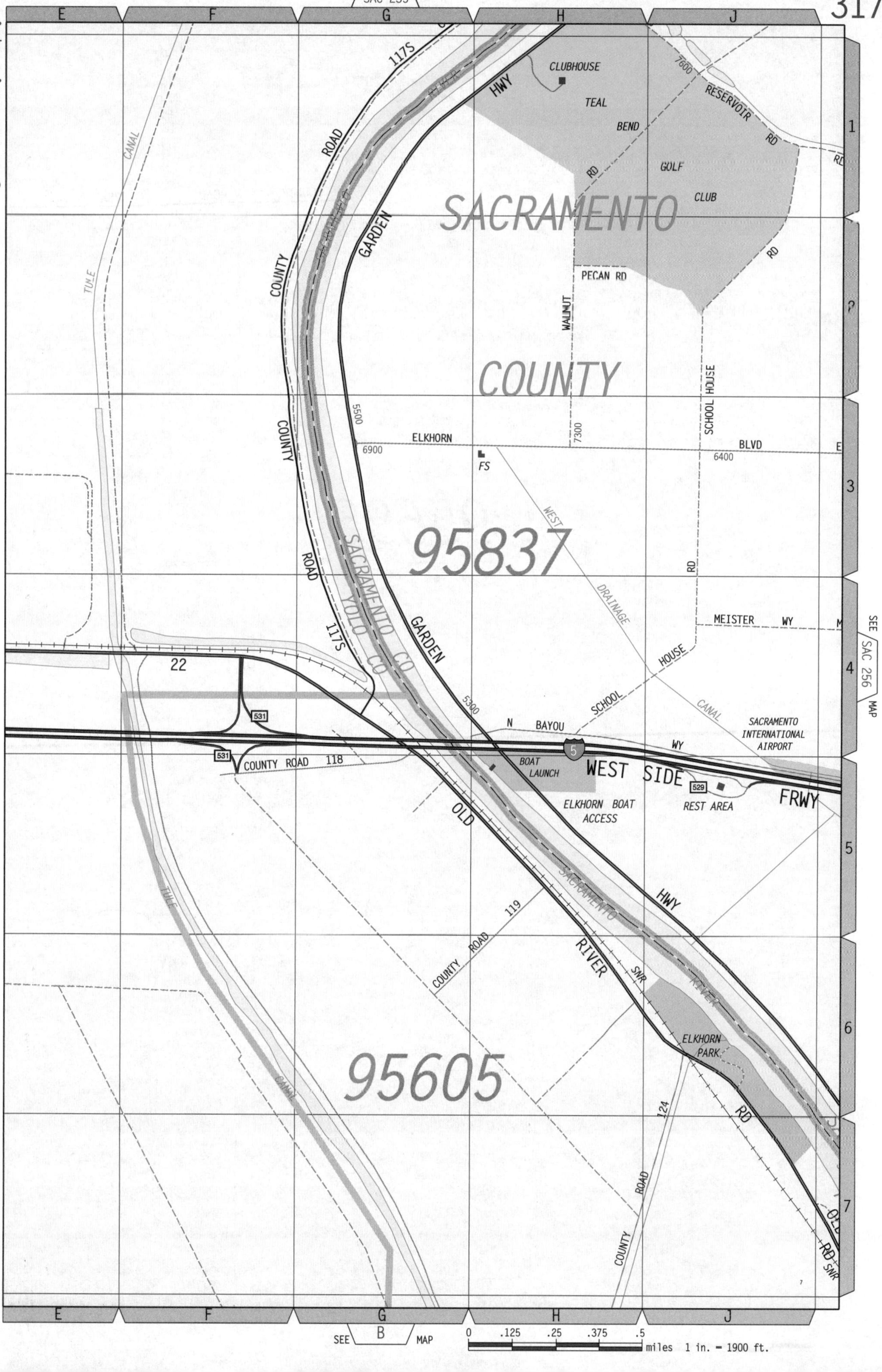

E F G H J
1 2 3 4 5 6 7
SOLANO CO.
SACRAMENTO COUNTY
95837
95605
CLUBHOUSE
TEAL BEND GOLF CLUB
RESERVOIR RD
7600
PECAN RD
WALNUT RD
SCHOOL HOUSE RD
ELKHORN BLVD
6900
7300
6400
5500
5300
FS
WEST DRAINAGE CANAL
MEISTER WY
COUNTY ROAD 117S
GARDEN HWY
SACRAMENTO RIVER
SACRAMENTO CO
YOLO CO
TULE CANAL
22
531
COUNTY ROAD 118
N BAYOU WY
5
BOAT LAUNCH
WEST SIDE FRWY
529
REST AREA
ELKHORN BOAT ACCESS
SACRAMENTO INTERNATIONAL AIRPORT
OLD RIVER RD
SNR
COUNTY ROAD 119
ELKHORN PARK
COUNTY ROAD 124
0 .125 .25 .375 .5 miles 1 in. = 1900 ft.

SEE SAC 256 MAP

SEE B MAP

SEE 315 MAP

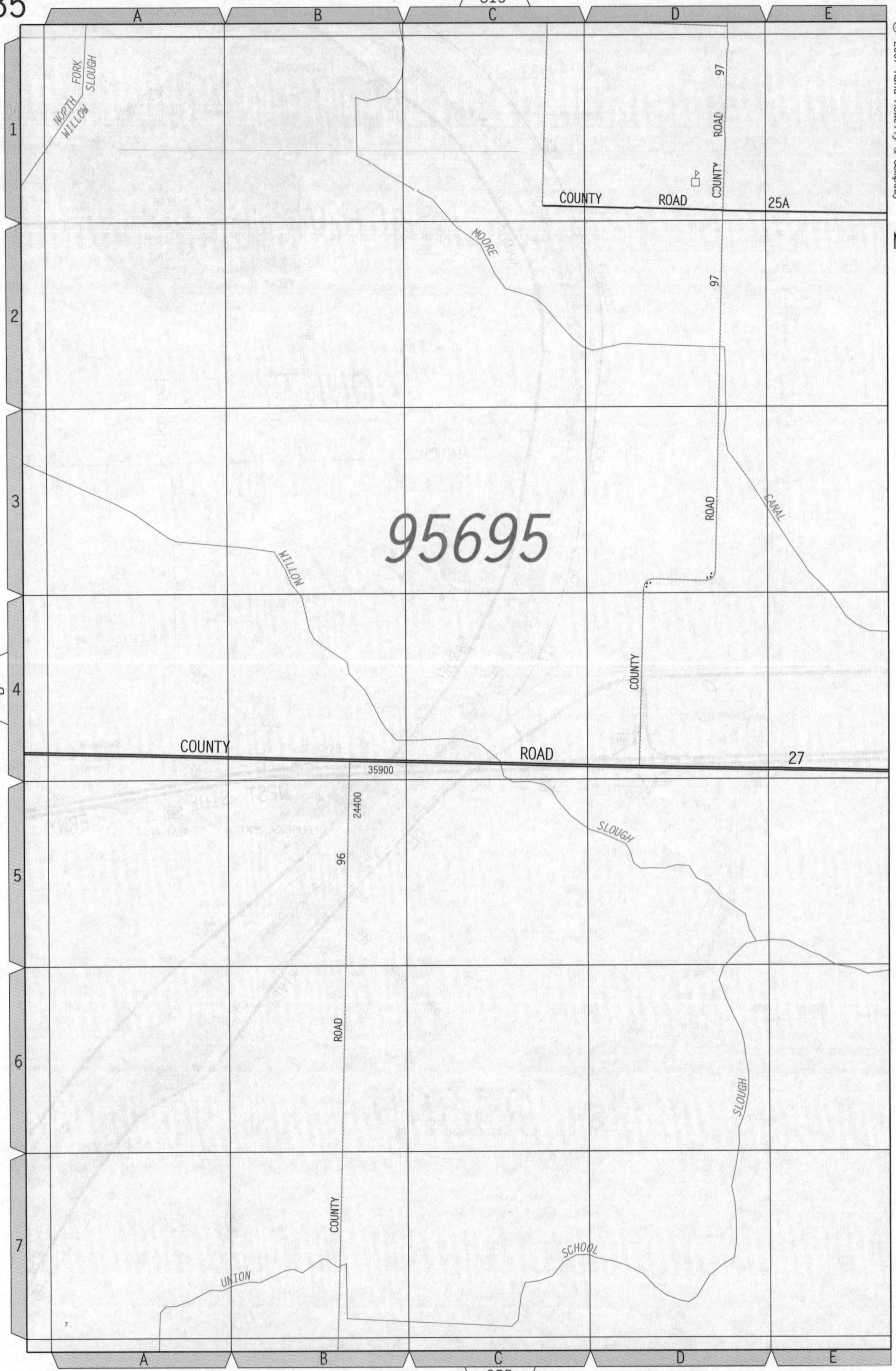

SEE B MAP

SEE 355 MAP

0 .125 .25 .375 .5 miles 1 in. = 1900 ft.

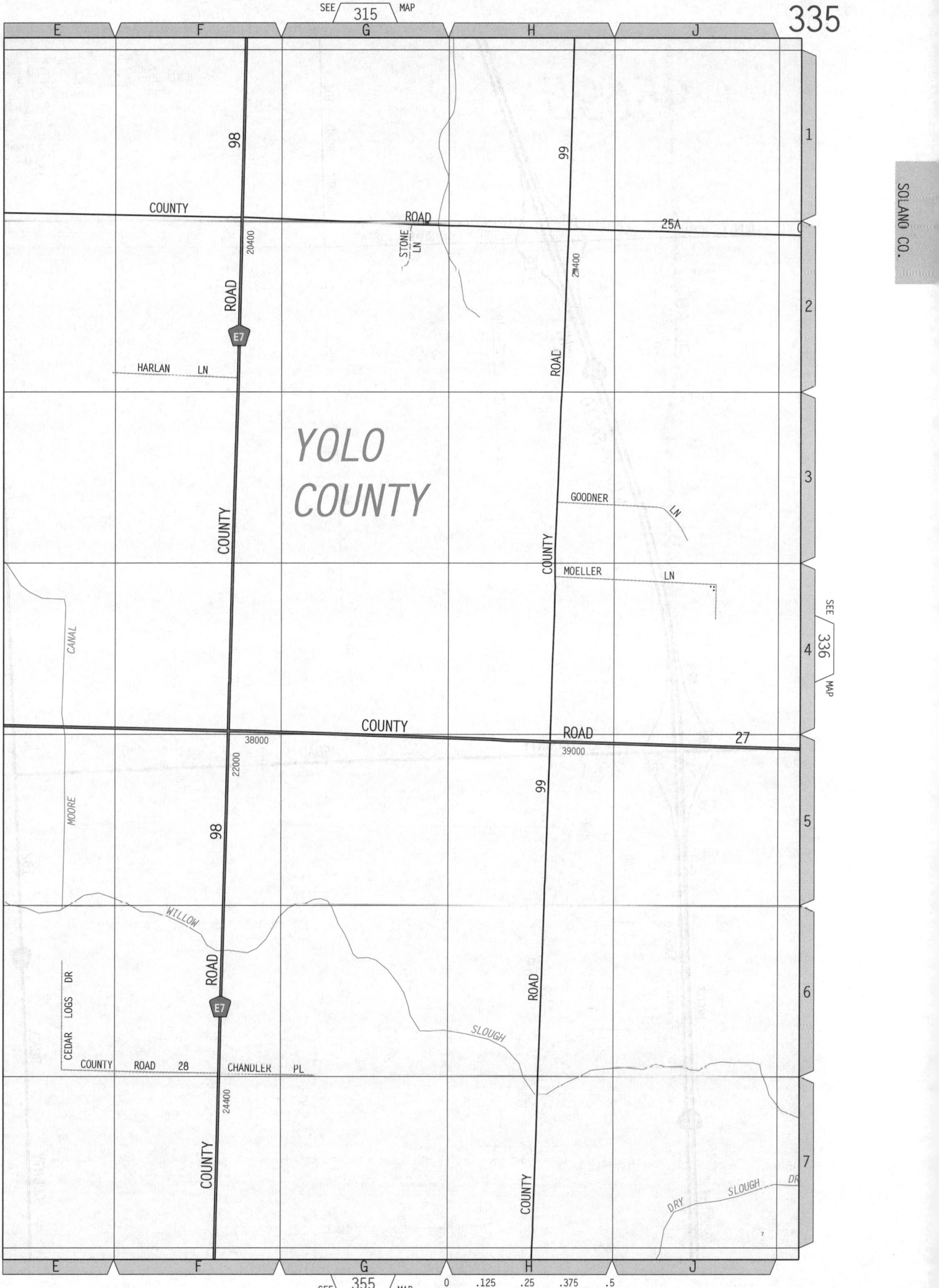
SEE 315 MAP
E
F
G
H
J
1
2
3
4
5
6
7
COUNTY ROAD 25A
STONE LN
20400
COUNTY ROAD 98
E7
HARLAN LN
COUNTY ROAD 99
YOLO
COUNTY
GOODNER LN
MOELLER LN
SEE 336 MAP
CANAL
COUNTY ROAD 27
38000
39000
22000
MOORE
WILLOW SLOUGH
CEDAR LOGS DR
COUNTY ROAD 28
CHANDLER PL
24400
DRY SLOUGH
SOLANO CO.
SEE 355 MAP
0 .125 .25 .375 .5 miles 1 in. = 1900 ft.

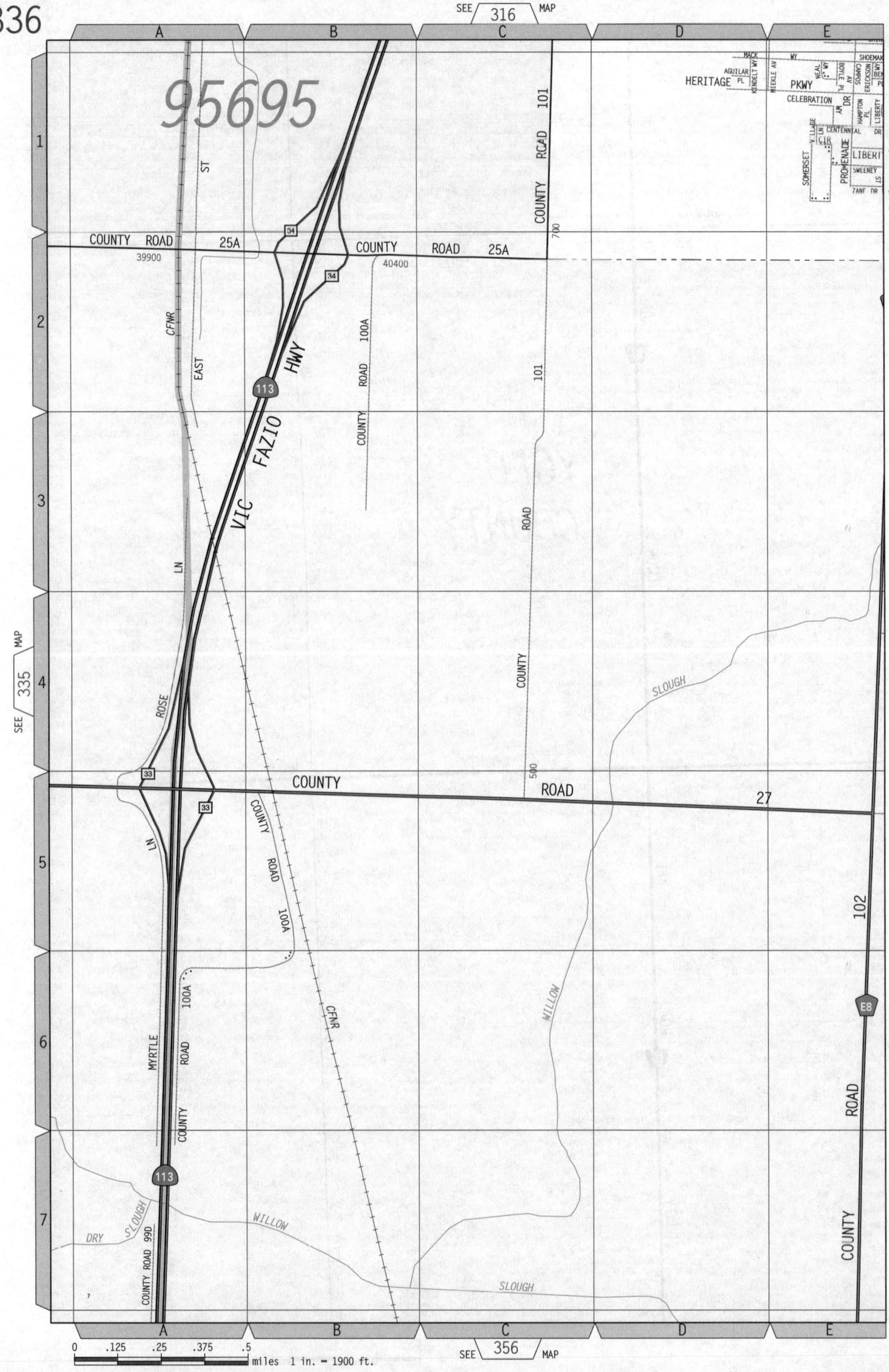
SEE 316 MAP
SEE 335 MAP
SEE 356 MAP
95695
COUNTY ROAD 25A
39900
40400
COUNTY ROAD 101
700
500
COUNTY ROAD 100A
VIC FAZIO HWY
113
34
33
CFNR
EAST ST
ROSE LN
MYRTLE LN
COUNTY ROAD 27
COUNTY ROAD 99D
COUNTY ROAD 102
E8
WILLOW SLOUGH
DRY SLOUGH
HERITAGE PKWY
MACK WY
AGUILAR PL
KINDELT WY
MIEKLE AV
NEAL WY
BOYLE PL
CAMPOS AV
ERICKSON WY
SHOEMAKER
CELEBRATION DR
HAMPTON PL
LIBERTY
CENTENNIAL DR
VILLAGE CIR
SOMERSET LN
PROMENADE
SWEENEY ST
ZANE DR
0 .125 .25 .375 .5 miles 1 in. = 1900 ft.

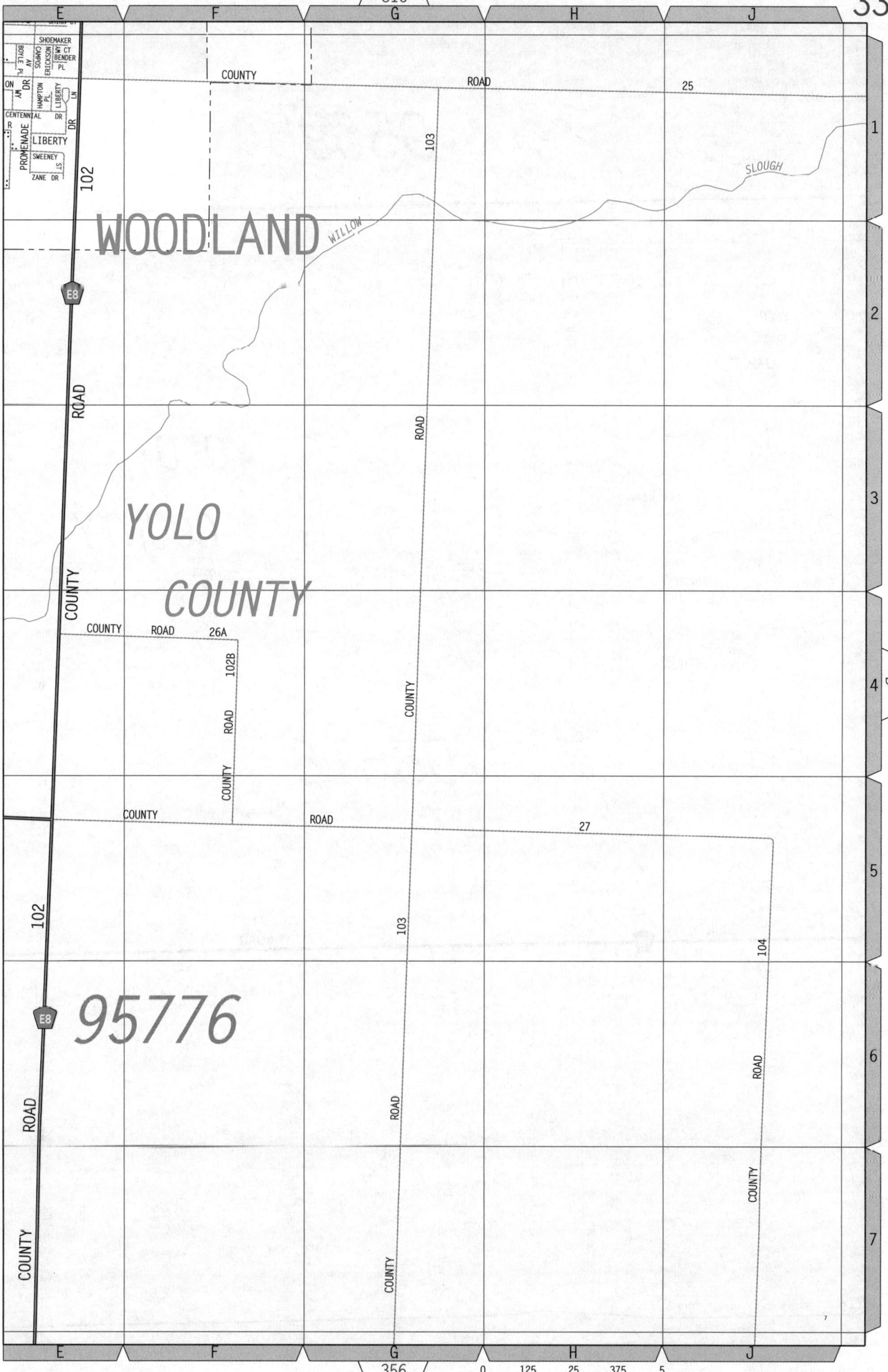
SEE 316 MAP
E
F
G
H
J
SHOEMAKER
BOYLE PL
CAMPOS AV
ERICKSON WY
CT
BENDER PL
HAMPTON PL
LIBERTY LN
CENTENNIAL DR
LIBERTY DR
PROMENADE
SWEENEY ST
ZANE DR
COUNTY ROAD 25
102
103
SLOUGH
WILLOW
WOODLAND
E8
ROAD
YOLO
COUNTY
COUNTY ROAD 26A
102B
COUNTY ROAD
COUNTY ROAD 27
103
104
102
95776
COUNTY ROAD
COUNTY
ROAD
1
2
3
4
5
6
7
SEE B MAP
SOLANO CO.
SEE 356 MAP
0 .125 .25 .375 .5
miles 1 in. = 1900 ft.

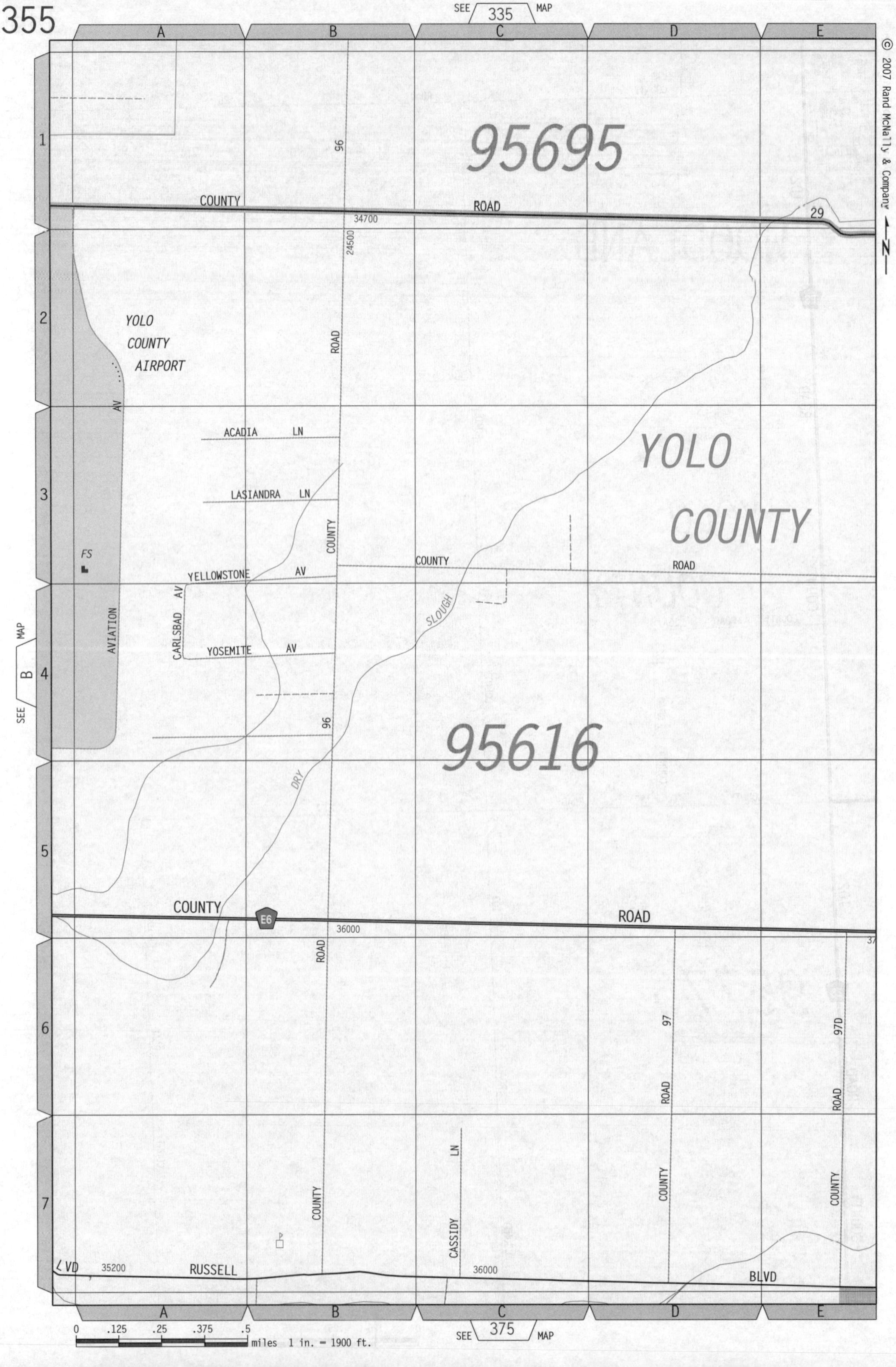
SEE 335 MAP
A
B
C
D
E
1
2
3
4
5
6
7
95695
COUNTY
ROAD
34700
29
96
24500
ROAD
YOLO
COUNTY
AIRPORT
AV
ACADIA
LN
LASIANDRA
LN
COUNTY
YOLO
COUNTY
FS
YELLOWSTONE
AV
COUNTY
ROAD
CARLSBAD
AV
SLOUGH
AVIATION
YOSEMITE
AV
SEE B MAP
96
95616
DRY
COUNTY
E6
ROAD
36000
ROAD
97
97D
ROAD
ROAD
LN
COUNTY
COUNTY
COUNTY
CASSIDY
LVD
35200
RUSSELL
36000
BLVD
SEE 375 MAP
0
.125
.25
.375
.5
miles 1 in. = 1900 ft.
SOLANO CO.

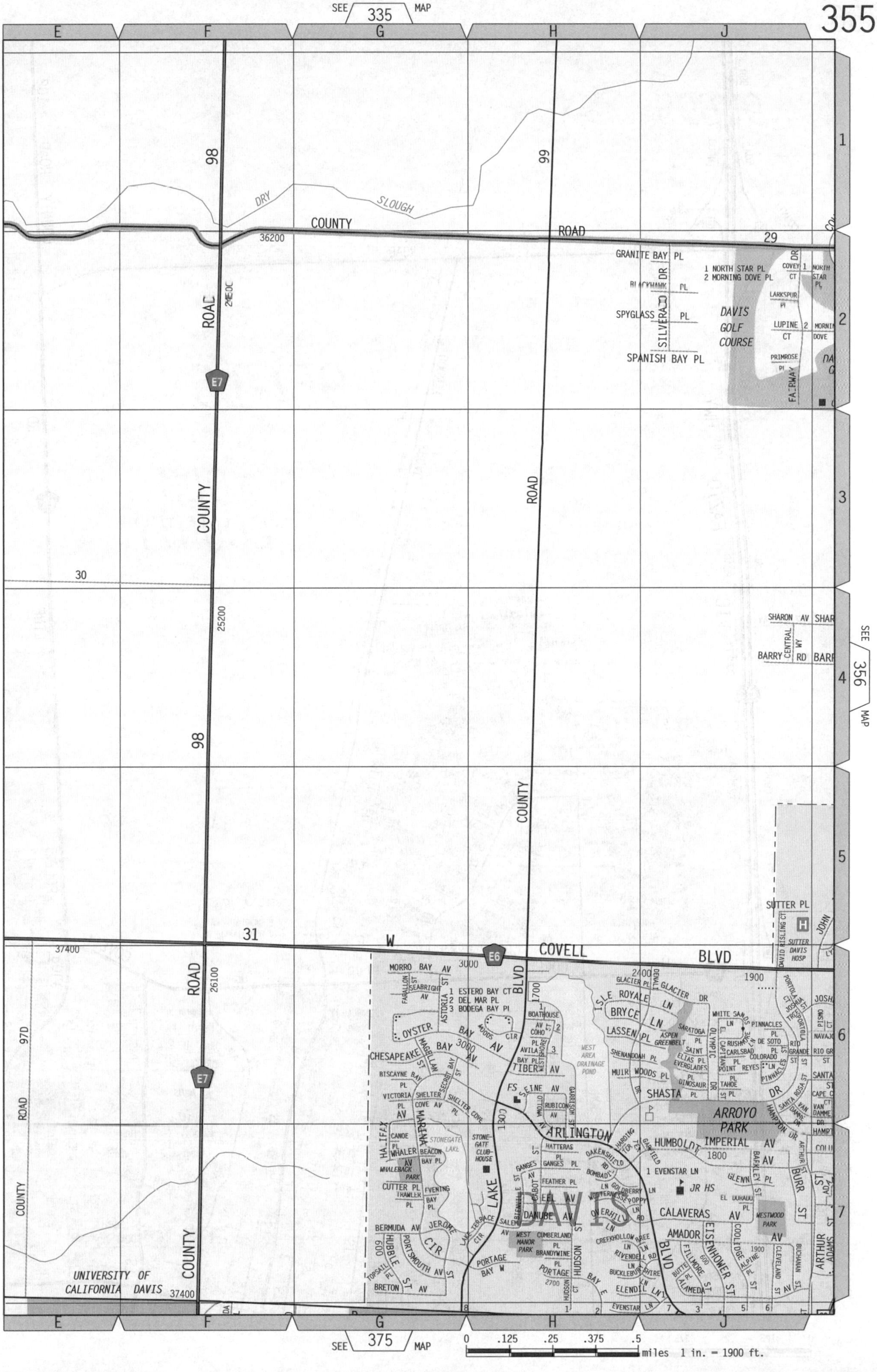
SEE 335 MAP
E
F
G
H
J
1
2
3
4
5
6
7
SOLANO CO.
SEE 356 MAP
SEE 375 MAP
DRY SLOUGH
COUNTY ROAD 29
36200
COUNTY ROAD 98
COUNTY ROAD 99
E7
E6
GRANITE BAY PL
BLACKHAWK PL
SPYGLASS PL
SILVERADO DR
SPANISH BAY PL
1 NORTH STAR PL
2 MORNING DOVE PL
COVEY CT
NORTH STAR PL
LARKSPUR PL
LUPINE CT
MORNING DOVE
PRIMROSE PL
FAIRWAY DR
DAVIS GOLF COURSE
30
25200
SHARON AV
CENTRAL WY
BARRY RD
SUTTER PL
DAVID RISLING CT
SUTTER DAVIS HOSP
JOHN
31
37400
W COVELL BLVD
3000
2400
1900
26100
97D
COUNTY ROAD
MORRO BAY AV
FARALLON ST
SEABRIGHT AV
ASTORIA ST
1 ESTERO BAY CT
2 DEL MAR PL
3 BODEGA BAY PL
LAKE BLVD
1700
BOATHOUSE
COHO
AVILA
OYSTER BAY AV
WOODS CIR
CHESAPEAKE BAY AV
MAGELLAN ST
SECRET BAY
TIBER AV
BISCAYNE BAY PL
VICTORIA AV
SHELTER COVE
MARINA CIR
FS
SEINE AV
RUBICON
GARRISON ST
WEST AREA DRAINAGE POND
ISLE ROYALE LN
GLACIER DR
DENALI
BRYCE LN
LASSEN PL
ASPEN GREENBELT
SHENANDOAH PL
MUIR WOODS PL
EVERGLADES
DINOSAUR PL
SHASTA DR
WHITE SANDS
SARATOGA
OLYMPIC
SAINT ELIAS PL
EL CAPITAN
RUSHMORE
CARLSBAD
POINT REYES
TAHOE PL
DE SOTO
COLORADO
PINNACLES
PORTOLA
JOSHUA TREE
RIO GRANDE
NAVAJO
PISMO
SANTA ROSA ST
HAMPTON DR
VAN DAMME
ARROYO PARK
HALIFAX
CANOE PL
WHALER AV
BEACON BAY PL
WHALEBACK PARK
STONEGATE LAKE
STONEGATE CLUBHOUSE
1300
ARLINGTON
HATTERAS
GANGES PL
OAKENSHIELD RD
HUMBOLDT AV
IMPERIAL AV
1800
BARKLEY PL
BURR ST
1 EVENSTAR LN
JR HS
GLENN PL
CUTTER PL
TRAWLER PL
EVENING BAY PL
FEATHER PL
EEL AV
DANUBE AV
DAVIS
POPPY LN
OVERHILL RD
CALAVERAS AV
EL DORADO PL
WESTWOOD PARK
ARTHUR ST
ADAMS ST
BERMUDA AV
JEROME CIR
HUBBLE ST
PORTSMOUTH AV
LAKE TERRACE CIR
SALEM
WEST MANOR PARK
CUMBERLAND PL
BRANDYWINE PL
PORTAGE BAY W
PORTAGE BAY E
HUDSON ST
CREEKHOLLOW LN
RIVENDELL
BUCKLEBURY
AMADOR AV
FILLMORE
EISENHOWER ST
COOLIDGE
ALPINE
CLEVELAND ST
BUCHANAN ST
ALAMEDA
ELENDIL LN
EVENSTAR LN
600
1900
2700
TOPSAIL PL
BRETON AV
UNIVERSITY OF CALIFORNIA DAVIS
37400
0 .125 .25 .375 .5 miles 1 in. = 1900 ft.

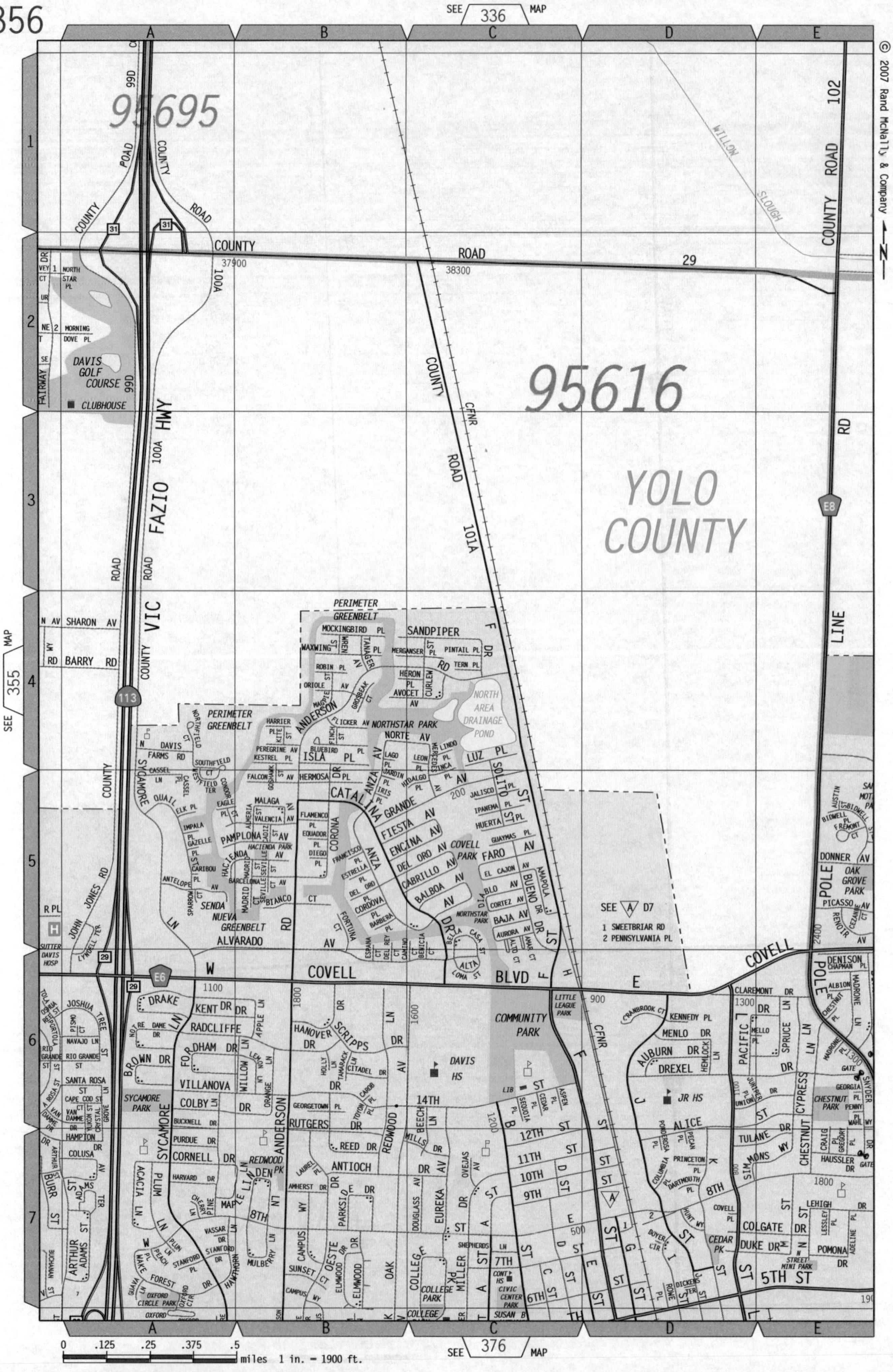
SEE 336 MAP
A
B
C
D
E
1
2
3
4
5
6
7
95695
95616
YOLO
COUNTY
COUNTY ROAD 29
37900
38300
COUNTY ROAD 102
COUNTY ROAD 99D
COUNTY ROAD 100A
COUNTY ROAD 101A
CFNR
WILLOW SLOUGH
DAVIS GOLF COURSE
CLUBHOUSE
NORTH STAR PL
MORNING DOVE PL
FAIRWAY
FAZIO HWY
VIC FAZIO HWY
113
31
29
E6
E8
SHARON AV
BARRY RD
SEE 355 MAP
POLE LINE RD
PERIMETER GREENBELT
SANDPIPER
MOCKINGBIRD PL
NORTHSTAR PARK
NORTH AREA DRAINAGE POND
CATALINA
ANZA
FIESTA AV
ENCINA AV
DEL ORO AV
CABRILLO AV
BALBOA AV
COVELL PARK
SENDA NUEVA GREENBELT
ALVARADO AV
SUTTER DAVIS HOSP
JOHN JONES RD
SEE A D7
1 SWEETBRIAR RD
2 PENNSYLVANIA PL
W COVELL BLVD
E COVELL BLVD
1100
900
LITTLE LEAGUE PARK
COMMUNITY PARK
DAVIS HS
JR HS
SYCAMORE PARK
REDWOOD PK
CEDAR PK
CHESTNUT PARK
OAK GROVE PARK
COLLEGE PARK
CIVIC CENTER PARK
OXFORD CIRCLE PARK
STREET MINI PARK
5TH ST
SEE 376 MAP
0 .125 .25 .375 .5 miles 1 in. = 1900 ft.

SEE 336 MAP

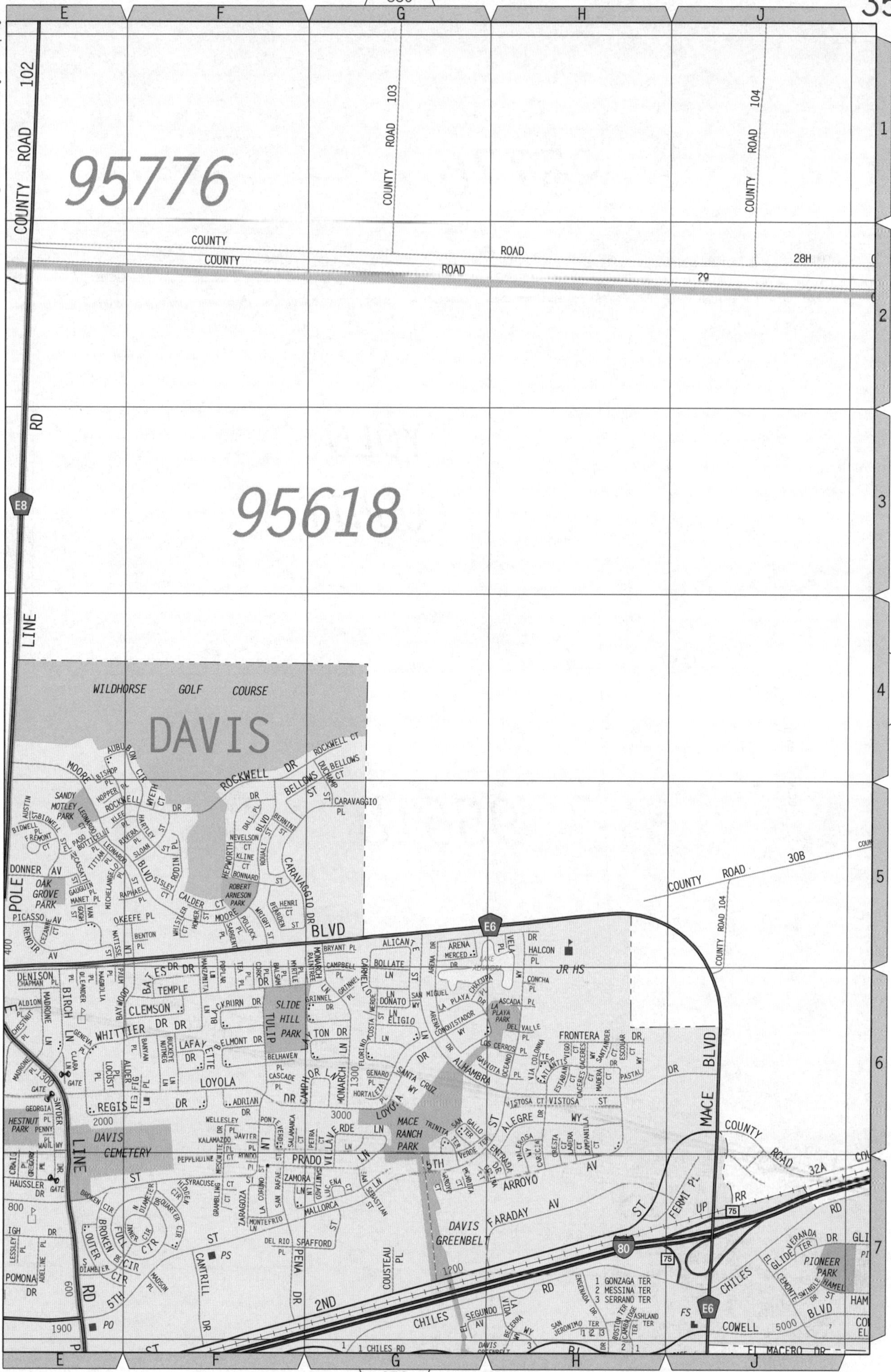

SEE 357 MAP

SEE 376 MAP

0 .125 .25 .375 .5 miles 1 in. = 1900 ft.

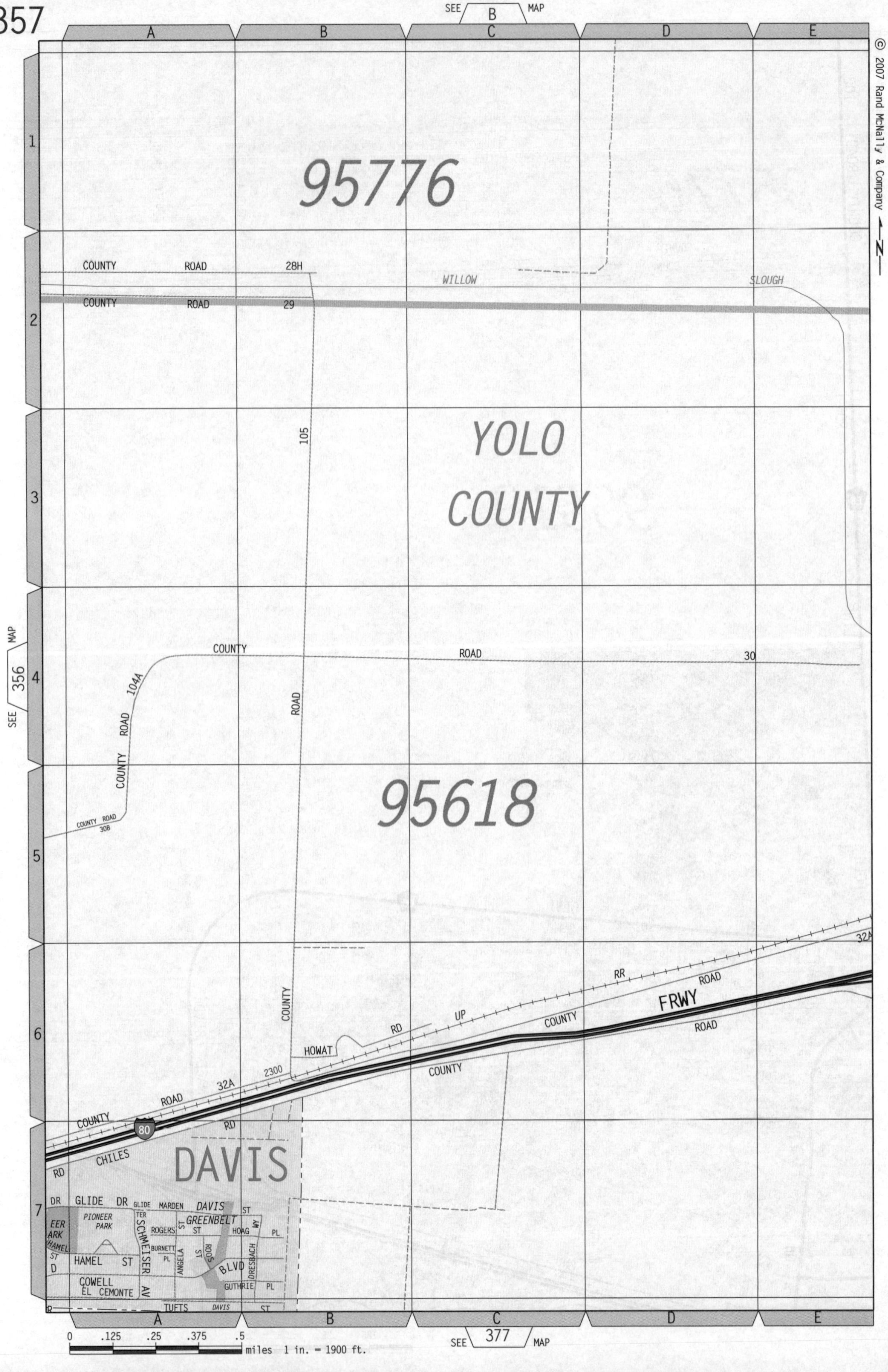
SEE B MAP
A
B
C
D
E
1
2
3
4
5
6
7
95776
COUNTY ROAD 28H
COUNTY ROAD 29
WILLOW SLOUGH
105
YOLO
COUNTY
SEE 356 MAP
COUNTY ROAD 30
COUNTY ROAD 104A
COUNTY ROAD 30B
COUNTY ROAD
95618
RR
UP
32A
COUNTY ROAD
FRWY
COUNTY
HOWAT
RD
2300
ROAD
32A
COUNTY
80
CHILES
RD
DAVIS
DR
GLIDE DR
GLIDE
MARDEN
DAVIS
GREENBELT
PIONEER
PARK
TER
SCHMEISER AV
ROGERS
ST
HOAG
WY
PL
BURNETT
PL
ANGELA
ST
ROOS
BLVD
DRESBACH
HAMEL
ST
HAMEL ST
COWELL
EL CEMONTE
GUTHRIE
PL
TUFTS
DAVIS
ST
SEE 377 MAP
0 .125 .25 .375 .5
miles 1 in. = 1900 ft.

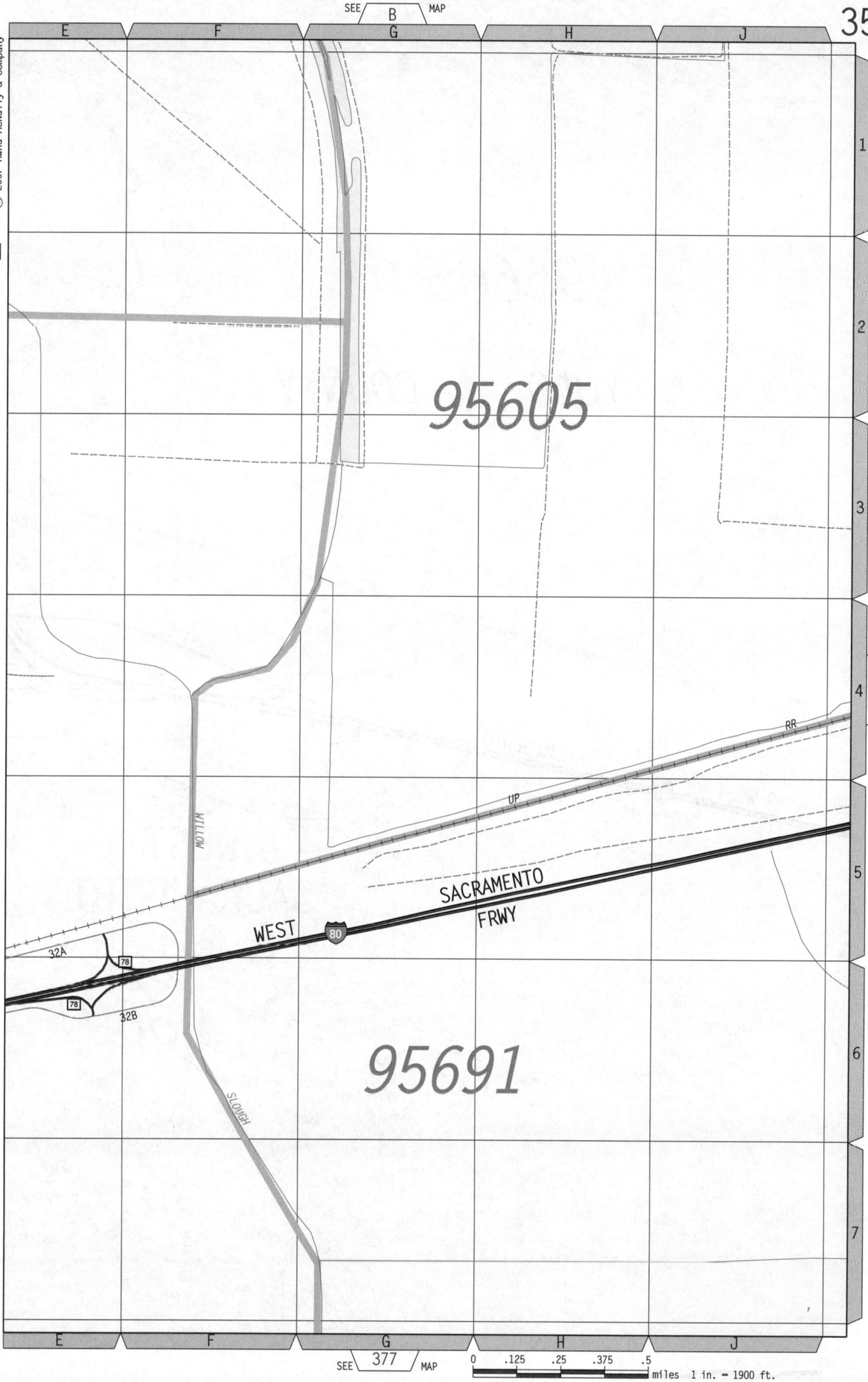
SEE B MAP
E
F
G
H
J
1
2
3
4
5
6
7
SEE 358 MAP
SEE 377 MAP
95605
95691
WILLOW
SLOUGH
UP
RR
WEST
SACRAMENTO
FRWY
80
78
32A
32B
0 .125 .25 .375 .5
miles 1 in. = 1900 ft.

SOLANO CO.

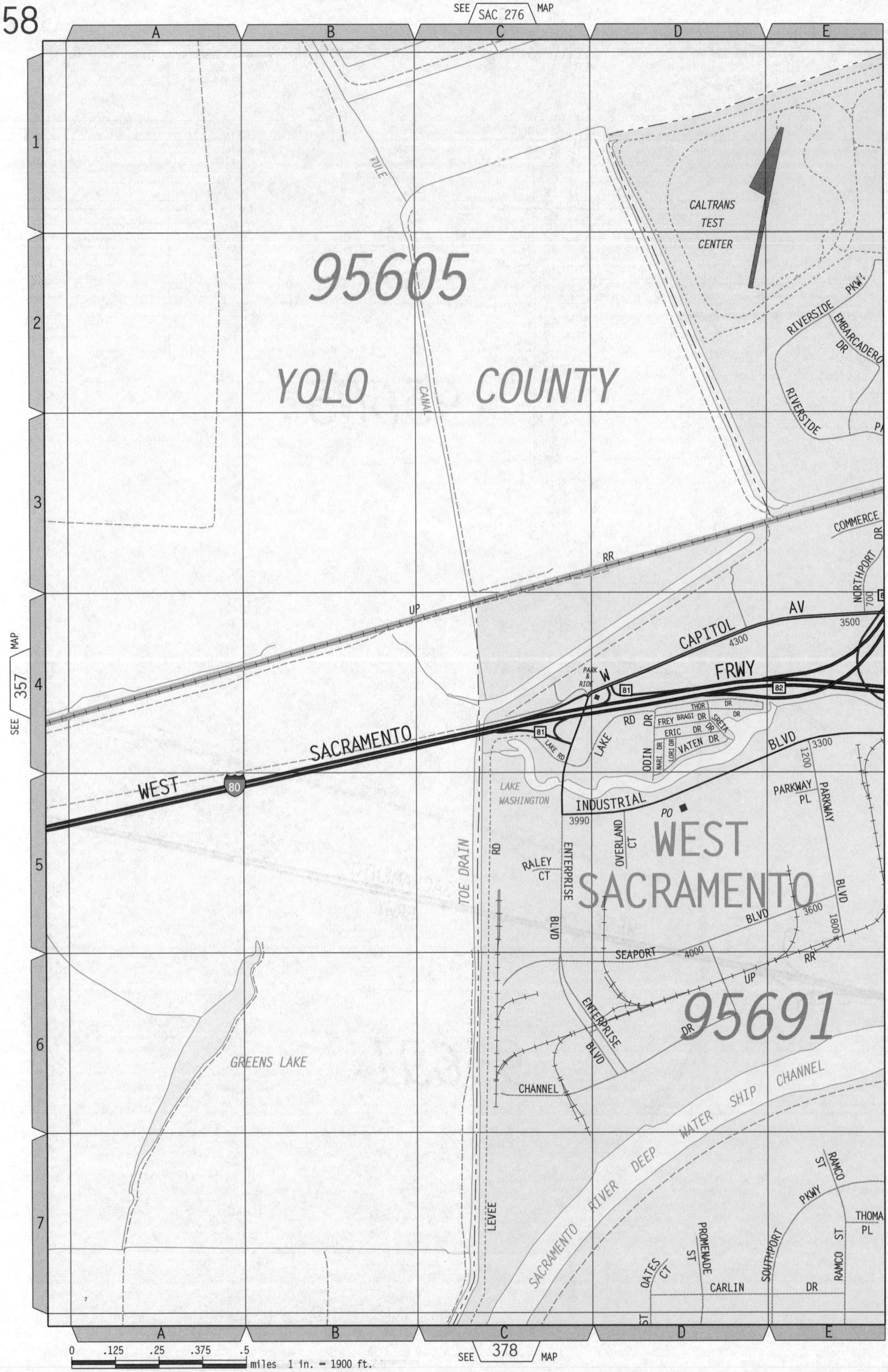
SEE SAC 276 MAP
SEE 357 MAP
SEE 378 MAP
SOLANO CO.
A
B
C
D
E
1
2
3
4
5
6
7
95605
YOLO COUNTY
TULE
CANAL
CALTRANS
TEST
CENTER
RIVERSIDE PKWY
EMBARCADERO DR
RIVERSIDE
COMMERCE DR
NORTHPORT
700
RR
UP
CAPITOL AV
4300
3500
W
FRWY
PARK & RIDE
81
82
WEST SACRAMENTO
80
LAKE RD
THOR DR
FREY BRAGI DR
SRETA DR
ERIC DR
LORI DR
NARI DR
VATEN DR
ODIN DR
BLVD
3300
1200
PARKWAY PL
PARKWAY
LAKE WASHINGTON
INDUSTRIAL
3990
PO
WEST
SACRAMENTO
OVERLAND CT
RALEY CT
ENTERPRISE BLVD
RD
TOE DRAIN
BLVD
3600
1800
SEAPORT
4000
UP
RR
95691
DR
ENTERPRISE BLVD
GREENS LAKE
CHANNEL
SACRAMENTO RIVER DEEP WATER SHIP CHANNEL
LEVEE
RAMCO ST
PKWY
THOMA PL
PROMENADE ST
OATES CT
SOUTHPORT
RAMCO ST
CARLIN DR
ST
0 .125 .25 .375 .5 miles 1 in. = 1900 ft.

SEE SAC 276 MAP

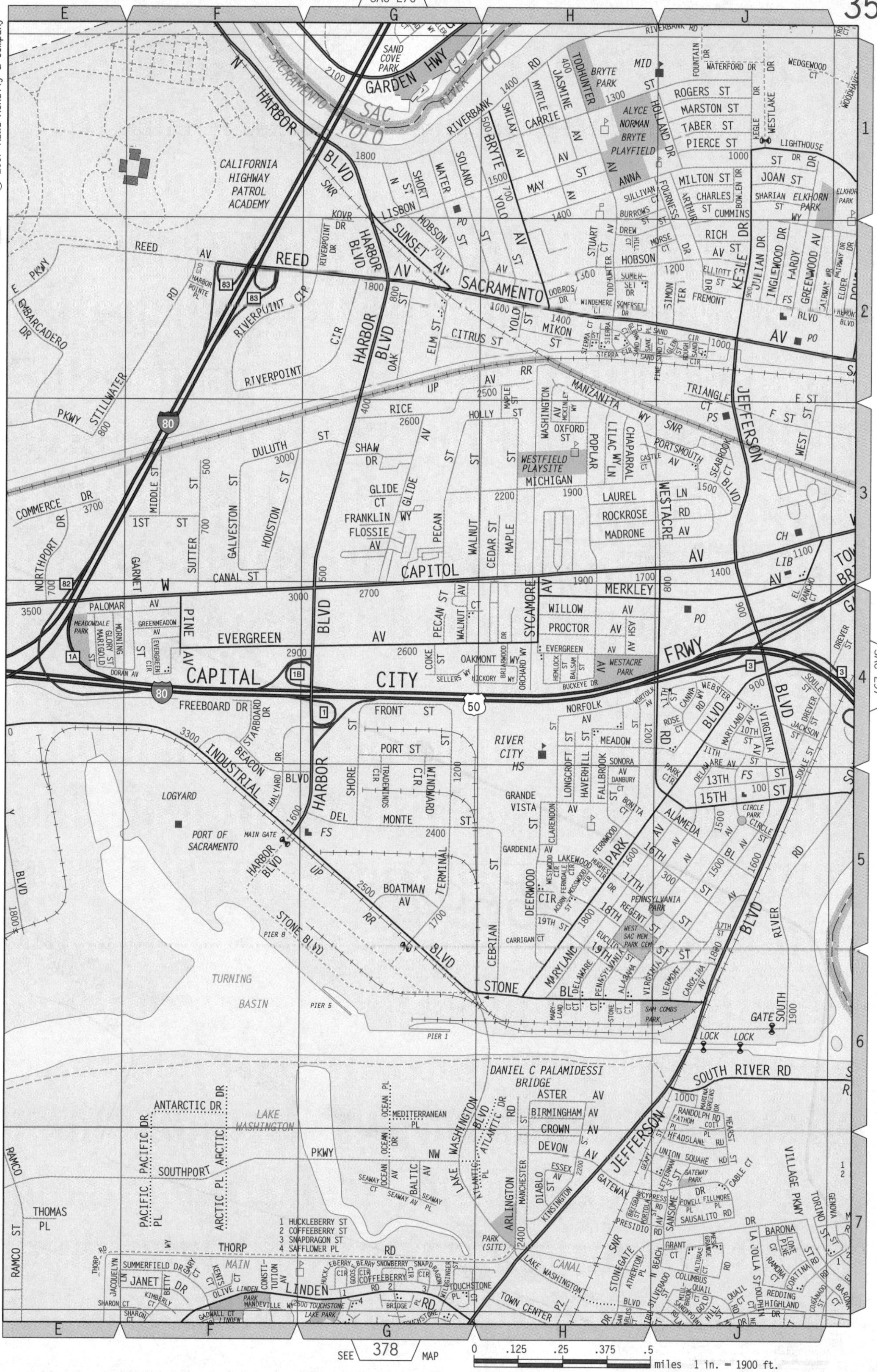

SEE SAC 297 MAP

SEE 378 MAP

0 .125 .25 .375 .5 miles 1 in. = 1900 ft.

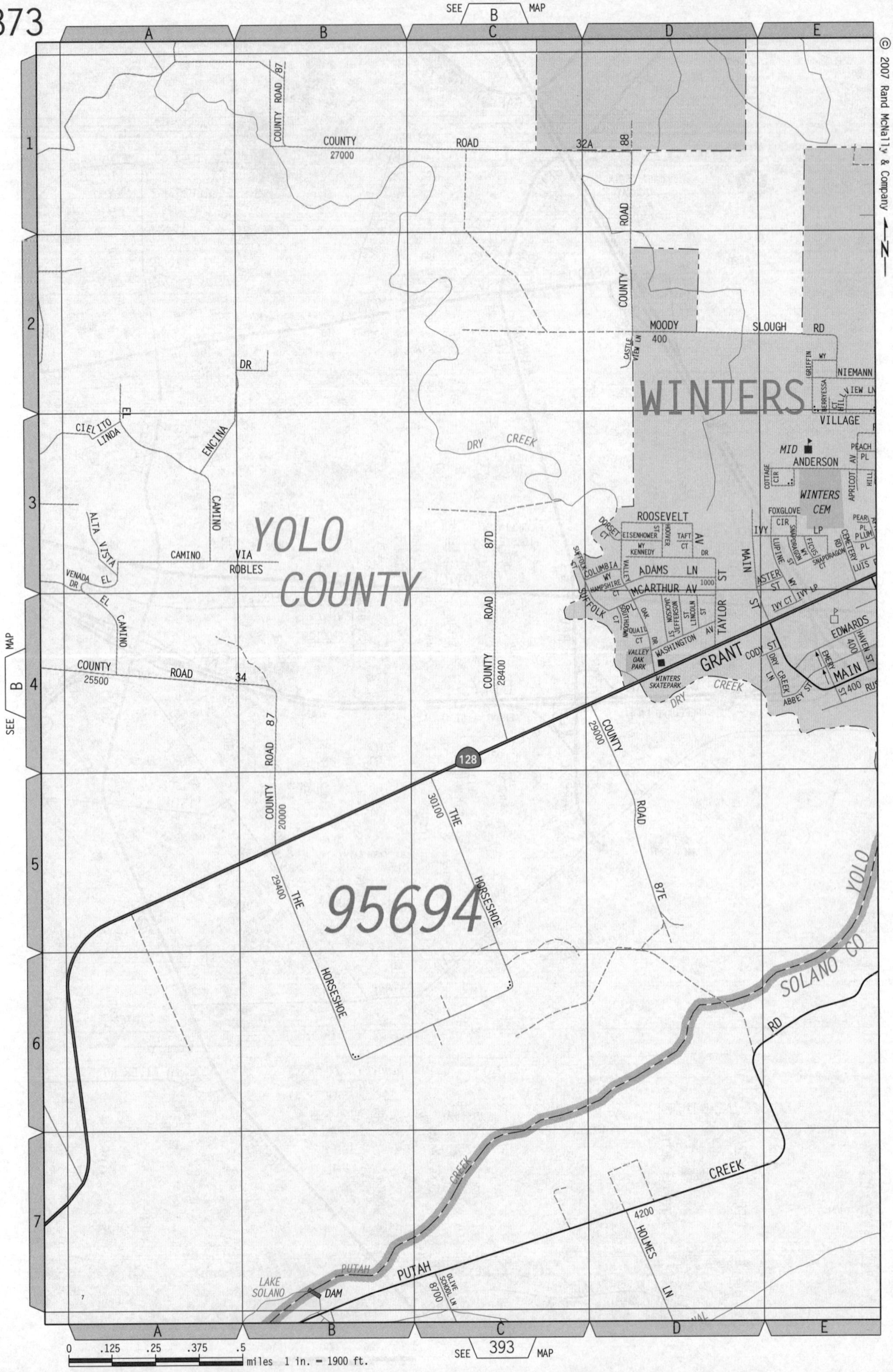
SEE B MAP
YOLO COUNTY
95694
WINTERS
COUNTY ROAD 27000
COUNTY ROAD 87
32A
88
COUNTY ROAD
MOODY 400
SLOUGH RD
CASTLE VIEW LN
DR
GRIFFIN WY
NIEMANN
BERRYESSA CT
HILL
VIEW LN
VILLAGE
CIELITO LINDA
EL ENCINA
CAMINO
DRY CREEK
MID
ANDERSON
PEACH PL
APRICOT AV
COTTAGE CIR
WINTERS CEM
ALTA VISTA
CAMINO VIA ROBLES
VENADA DR
EL CAMINO
COUNTY ROAD 87D
ROOSEVELT
DORSET CT
EISENHOWER
HOOVER
TAFT CT
KENNEDY WY
AV
DR
COLUMBIA WY
ADAMS LN
1000
HAMPSHIRE CT
VALLEY
MCARTHUR AV
SUFFOLK
MAIN ST
FOXGLOVE CIR
LUPINE ST
IVY
LP
PEAR PL
PLUM PL
CEMETERY RD
SNAPDRAGON CT
FICUS WY
LUIS
ASTER ST
IVY CT
IVY LP
TAYLOR ST
JACKSON ST
JEFFERSON
LINCOLN ST
QUAIL CT
OAK DR
WASHINGTON AV
VALLEY OAK PARK
WINTERS SKATEPARK
GRANT
CODY ST
DRY CREEK LN
ABBEY ST
EDWARDS
HAVEN ST
400
EMERY
MAIN
ST 400
RUS
COUNTY 25500 ROAD 34
COUNTY ROAD 28400
128
COUNTY ROAD 29000
COUNTY ROAD 20000
30100 THE HORSESHOE
29400 THE HORSESHOE
87E
YOLO
SOLANO CO
RD
CREEK
CREEK
4200 HOLMES LN
PUTAH
PUTAH
LAKE SOLANO
DAM
OLIVE SCHOOL LN 8700
SEE B MAP
SEE 393 MAP
SOLANO CO.
0 .125 .25 .375 .5 miles 1 in. = 1900 ft.

SEE B MAP

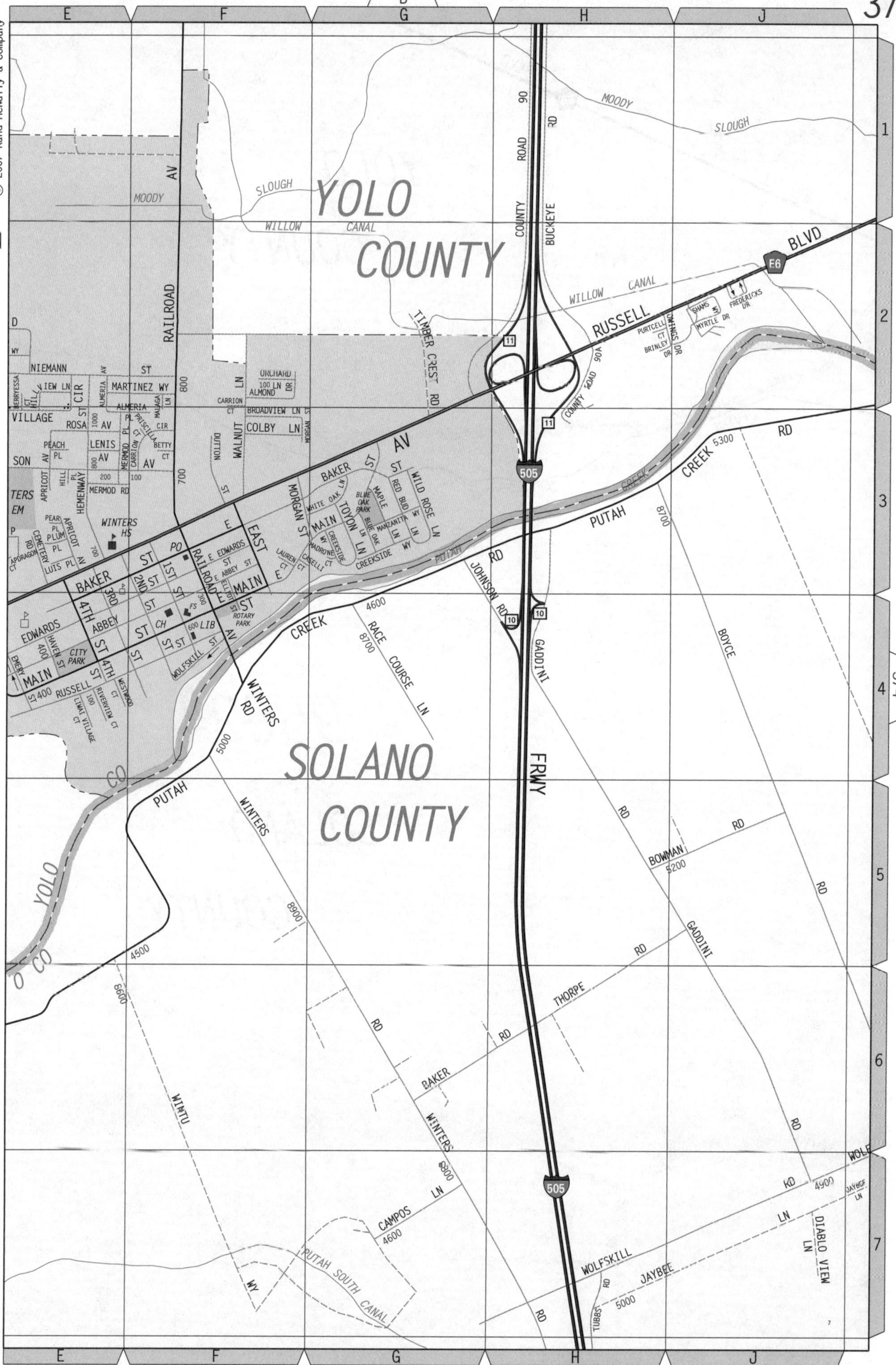

SEE 374 MAP
SEE 393 MAP

0 .125 .25 .375 .5 miles 1 in. = 1900 ft.

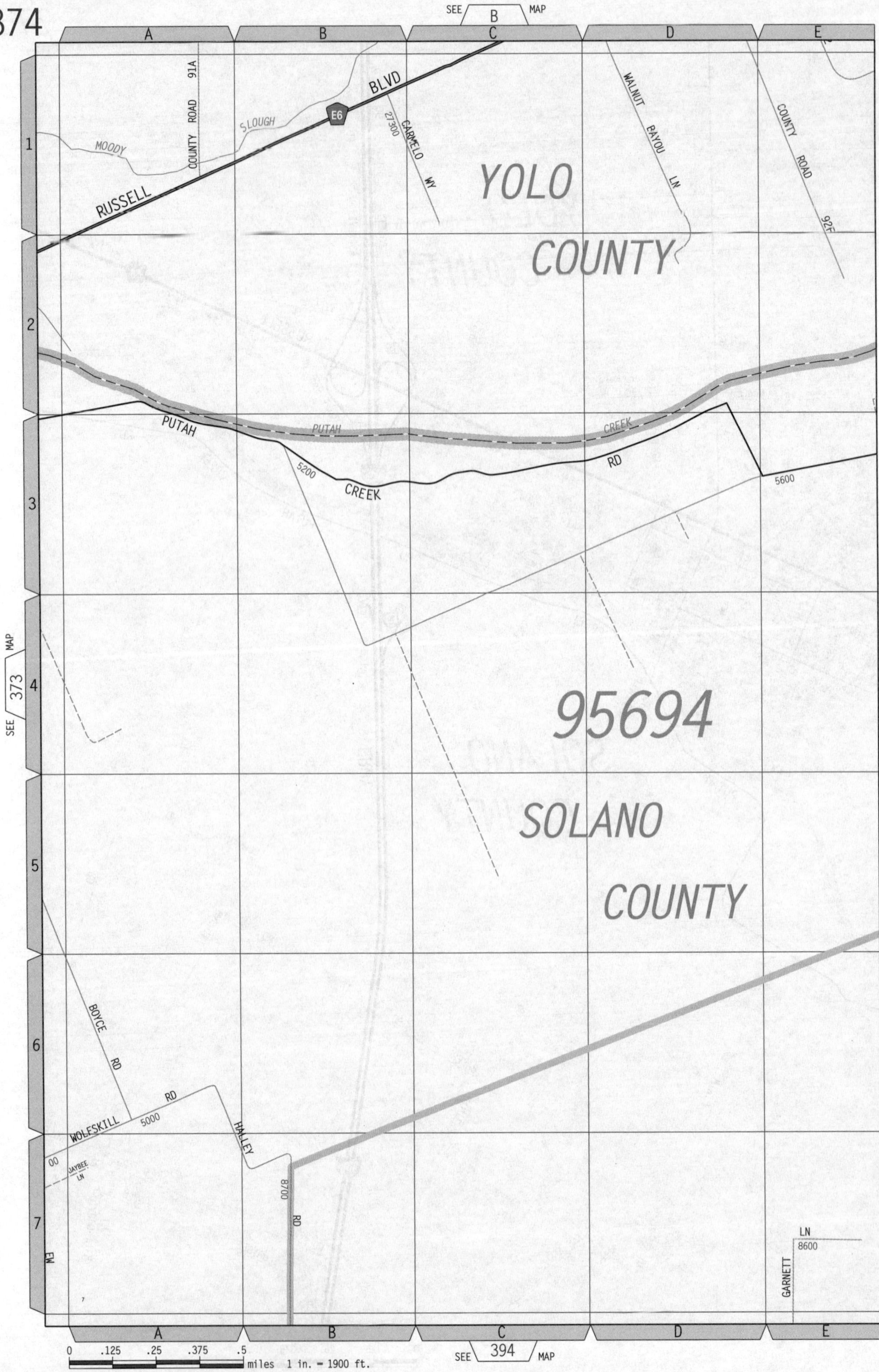
SEE B MAP
A
B
C
D
E
1
2
3
4
5
6
7
RUSSELL BLVD
E6
MOODY SLOUGH
COUNTY ROAD 91A
27300
CARMELO WY
WALNUT BAYOU LN
COUNTY ROAD 92F
YOLO COUNTY
PUTAH CREEK
PUTAH CREEK RD
5200
5600
SEE 373 MAP
95694
SOLANO COUNTY
BOYCE RD
WOLFSKILL RD
5000
HALLEY RD
8700
JAYBEE LN
EW
GARNETT LN
8600
SEE 394 MAP
0 .125 .25 .375 .5
miles 1 in. = 1900 ft.

SEE B MAP
E
F
G
H
J
COUNTY ROAD 32
KINSELLA LN
COUNTY ROAD 95A
95616
YOLO CO
SOLANO CO
CREEKSEDGE RD
PUTAH CREEK
PUTAH CREEK RD
5400
MCNEILL LN
CAMPBELL RD
STEVENSON
SEE 375 MAP
CAMPBELL RD
9000
RD
RANCH RD
SPARKS
BRIDGE RD
STEVENSON
8800
95620
1
2
3
4
5
6
7
SEE 394 MAP
0 .125 .25 .375 .5 miles 1 in. = 1900 ft.

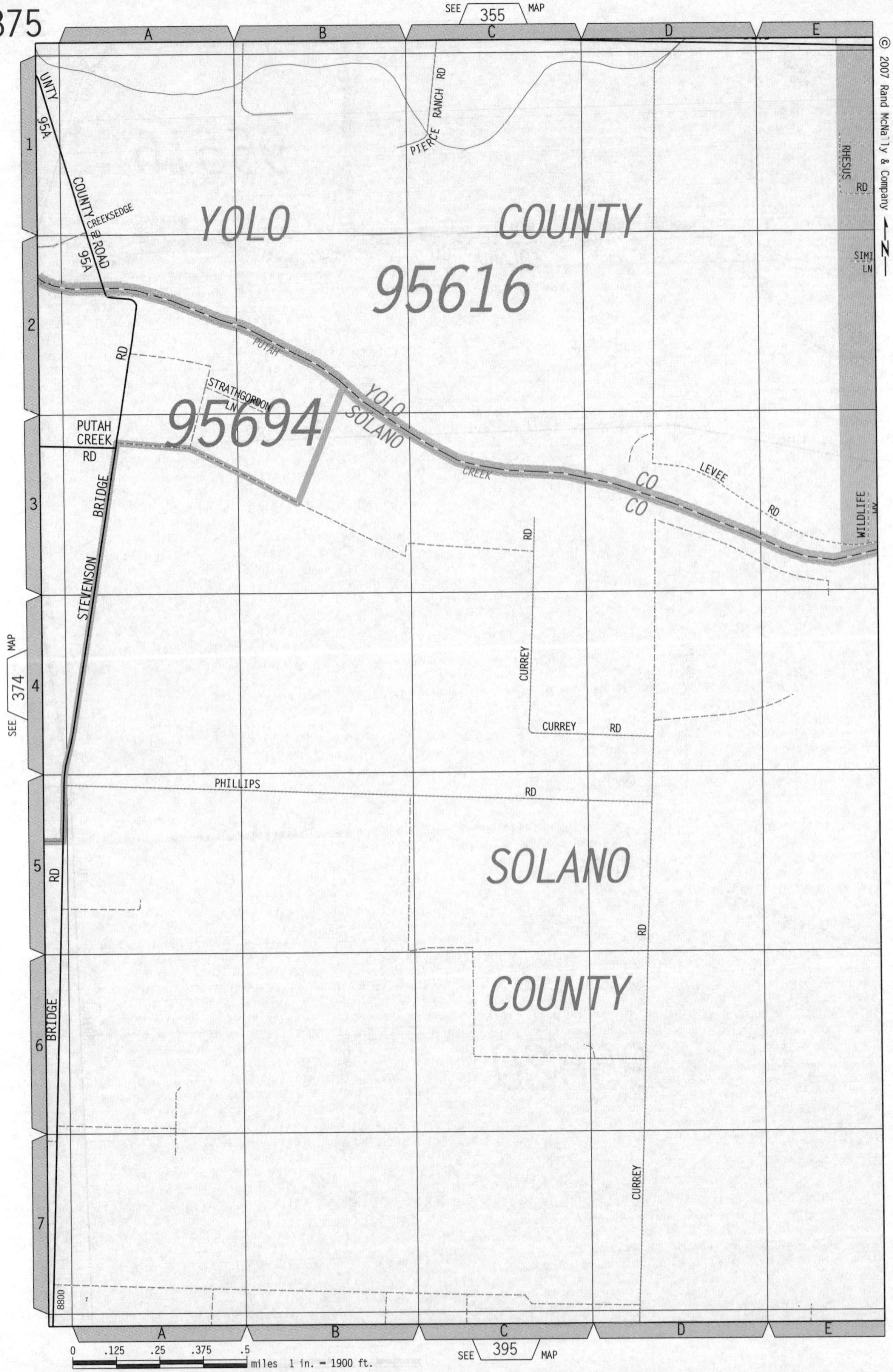
SEE 355 MAP
SEE 374 MAP
SEE 395 MAP
SOLANO CO.
A
B
C
D
E
1
2
3
4
5
6
7
YOLO COUNTY
95616
95694
SOLANO COUNTY
COUNTY ROAD 95A
95A
UNTY
CREEKSEDGE RD
PIERCE RANCH RD
RHESUS RD
SIMI LN
PUTAH CREEK
YOLO SOLANO CO CO
STRATHGORDON LN
PUTAH CREEK RD
RD
LEVEE RD
WILDLIFE
CURREY RD
CURREY RD
CURREY
RD
STEVENSON BRIDGE RD
BRIDGE
RD
PHILLIPS RD
8800
0 .125 .25 .375 .5
miles 1 in. = 1900 ft.
© 2007 Rand McNally & Company
N

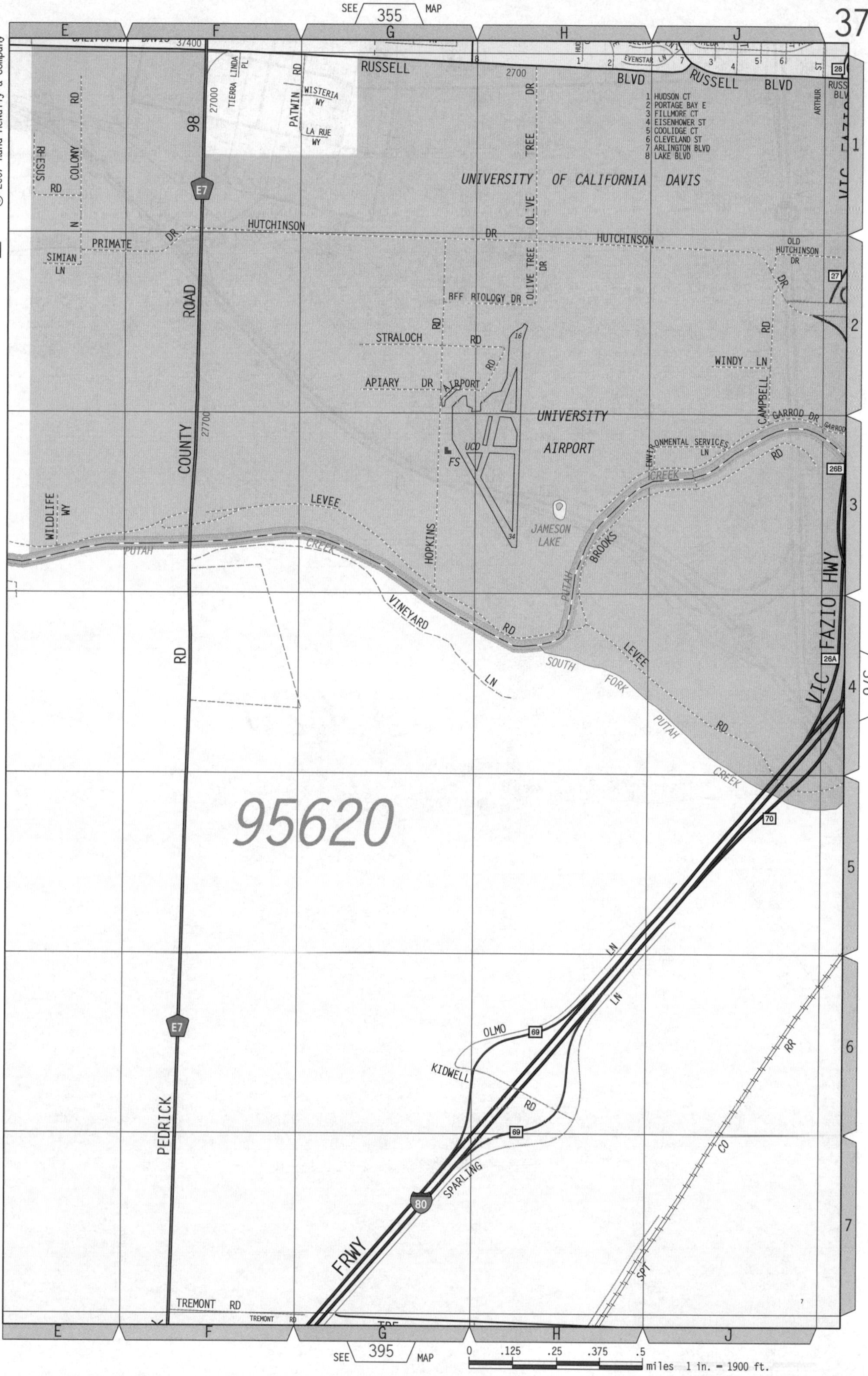
SEE 355 MAP
E
F
G
H
J
RUSSELL
BLVD
RUSSELL BLVD
EVENSTAR LN
TIERRA LINDA PL
PATWIN RD
WISTERIA WY
LA RUE WY
27000
2700
37400
98
E7
1 HUDSON CT
2 PORTAGE BAY E
3 FILLMORE CT
4 EISENHOWER ST
5 COOLIDGE CT
6 CLEVELAND ST
7 ARLINGTON BLVD
8 LAKE BLVD
ARTHUR ST
28
UNIVERSITY OF CALIFORNIA DAVIS
OLIVE TREE DR
RHESUS RD
COLONY RD
SIMIAN LN
PRIMATE DR
HUTCHINSON DR
OLD HUTCHINSON DR
27
BFF BIOLOGY DR
STRALOCH RD
APIARY DR
AIRPORT RD
WINDY LN
CAMPBELL RD
GARROD DR
UNIVERSITY AIRPORT
UCD
FS
ENVIRONMENTAL SERVICES LN
COUNTY ROAD
27700
26B
LEVEE RD
WILDLIFE WY
JAMESON LAKE
HOPKINS RD
BROOKS
PUTAH CREEK
VINEYARD RD
SOUTH FORK PUTAH CREEK
LN
VIC FAZIO HWY
26A
SEE 376 MAP
70
95620
OLMO LN
69
KIDWELL RD
SPARLING
80
FRWY
CO RR
SPT
PEDRICK RD
TREMONT RD
1
2
3
4
5
6
7
SEE 395 MAP
0 .125 .25 .375 .5
miles 1 in. = 1900 ft.

SOLANO CO.

SEE 356 MAP

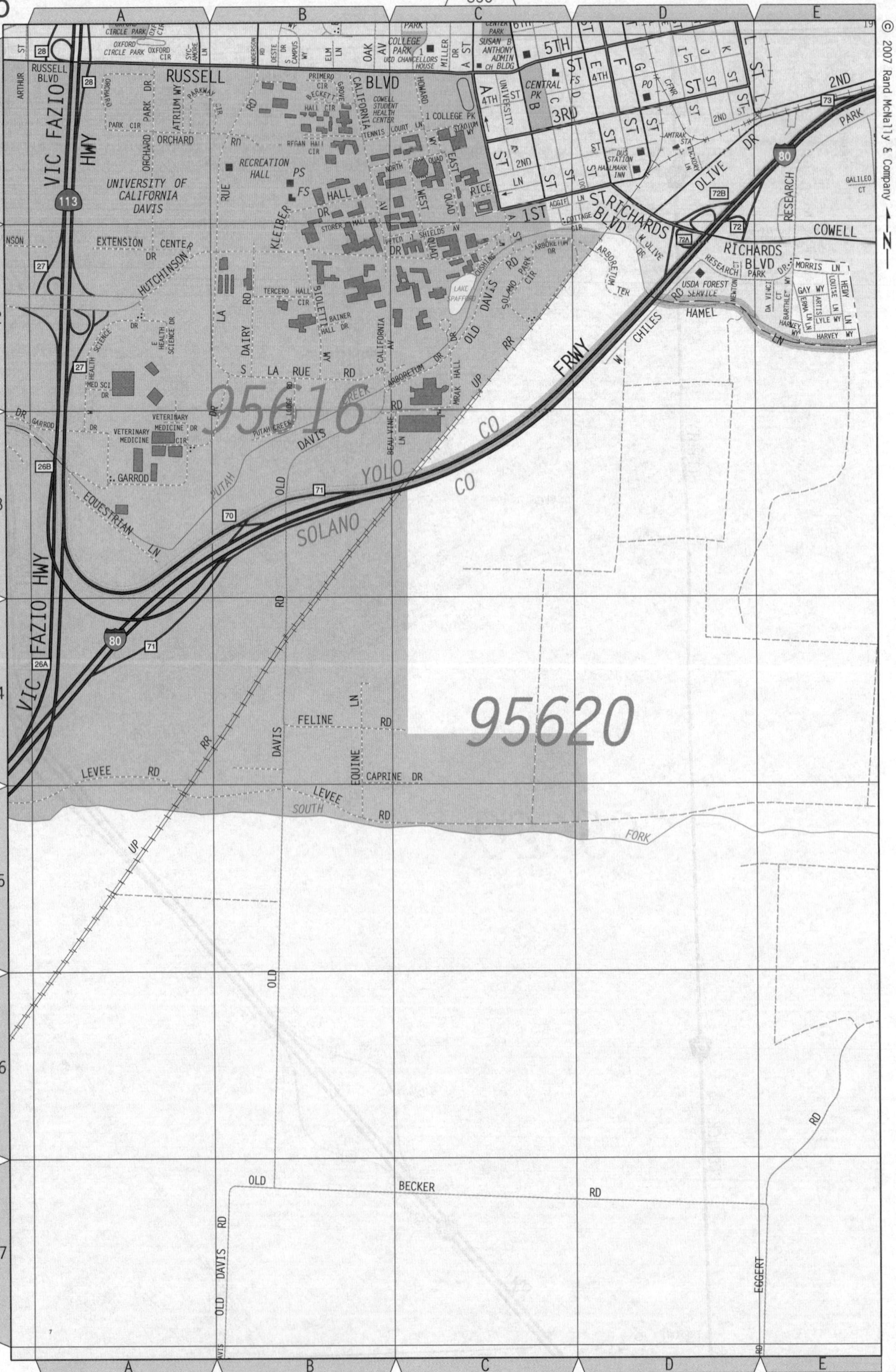

SEE 375 MAP

SEE B MAP

0 .125 .25 .375 .5 miles 1 in. = 1900 ft.

SEE 356 MAP
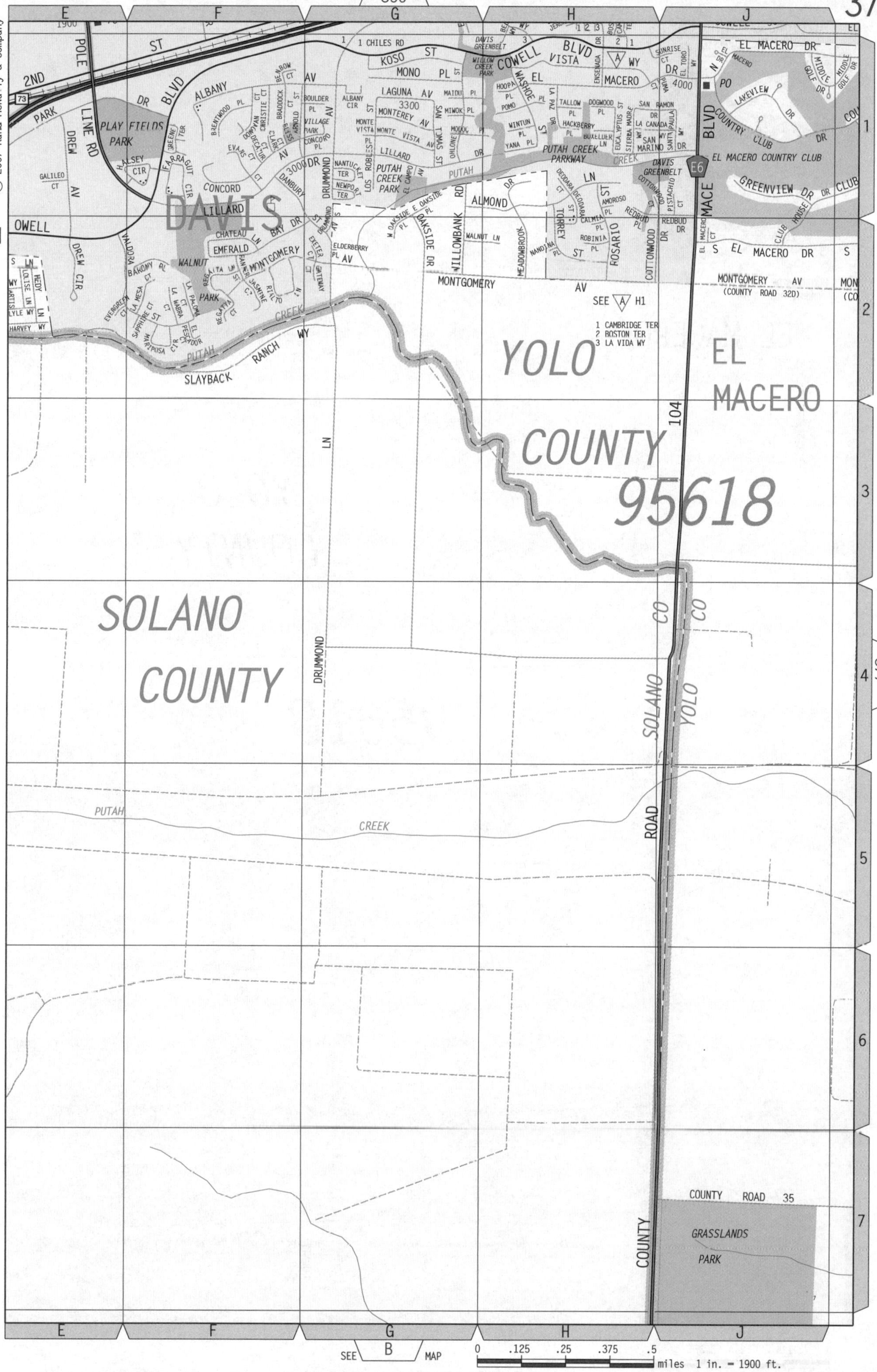

SEE 377 MAP
SEE B MAP
0 .125 .25 .375 .5 miles 1 in. = 1900 ft.

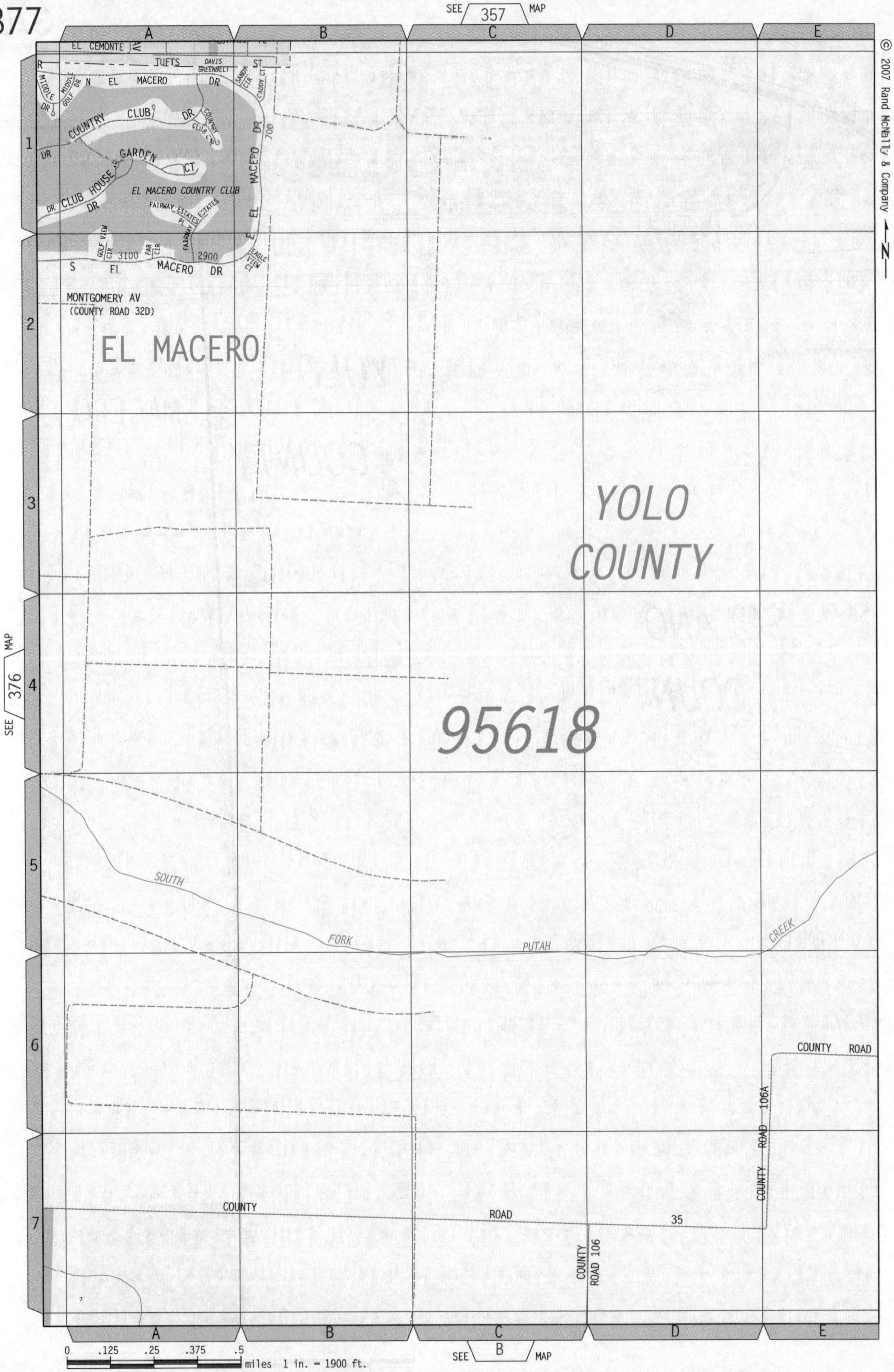
SEE 357 MAP
A
B
C
D
E
EL CEMONTE AV
TUFTS
DAVIS GREENBELT
ST
MIDDLE DR
MIDDLE GOLF DR
N EL MACERO DR
SANDY CIR
CADDY CT
COUNTRY CLUB DR
COUNTRY CLUB CT
DR
GARDEN CT
EL MACERO DR
700
EL MACERO COUNTRY CLUB
DR CLUB HOUSE DR
FAIRWAY ESTATES PL
FAIRWAY ESTATES
E
GOLF VIEW CIR
3100
PAR CIR
2900
EAGLE VIEW CT
S EL MACERO DR
MONTGOMERY AV
(COUNTY ROAD 32D)
EL MACERO
YOLO COUNTY
95618
SEE 376 MAP
1
2
3
4
5
6
7
SOUTH FORK PUTAH CREEK
COUNTY ROAD
COUNTY ROAD 106A
COUNTY ROAD 35
COUNTY ROAD 106
SEE B MAP
0 .125 .25 .375 .5
miles 1 in. = 1900 ft.

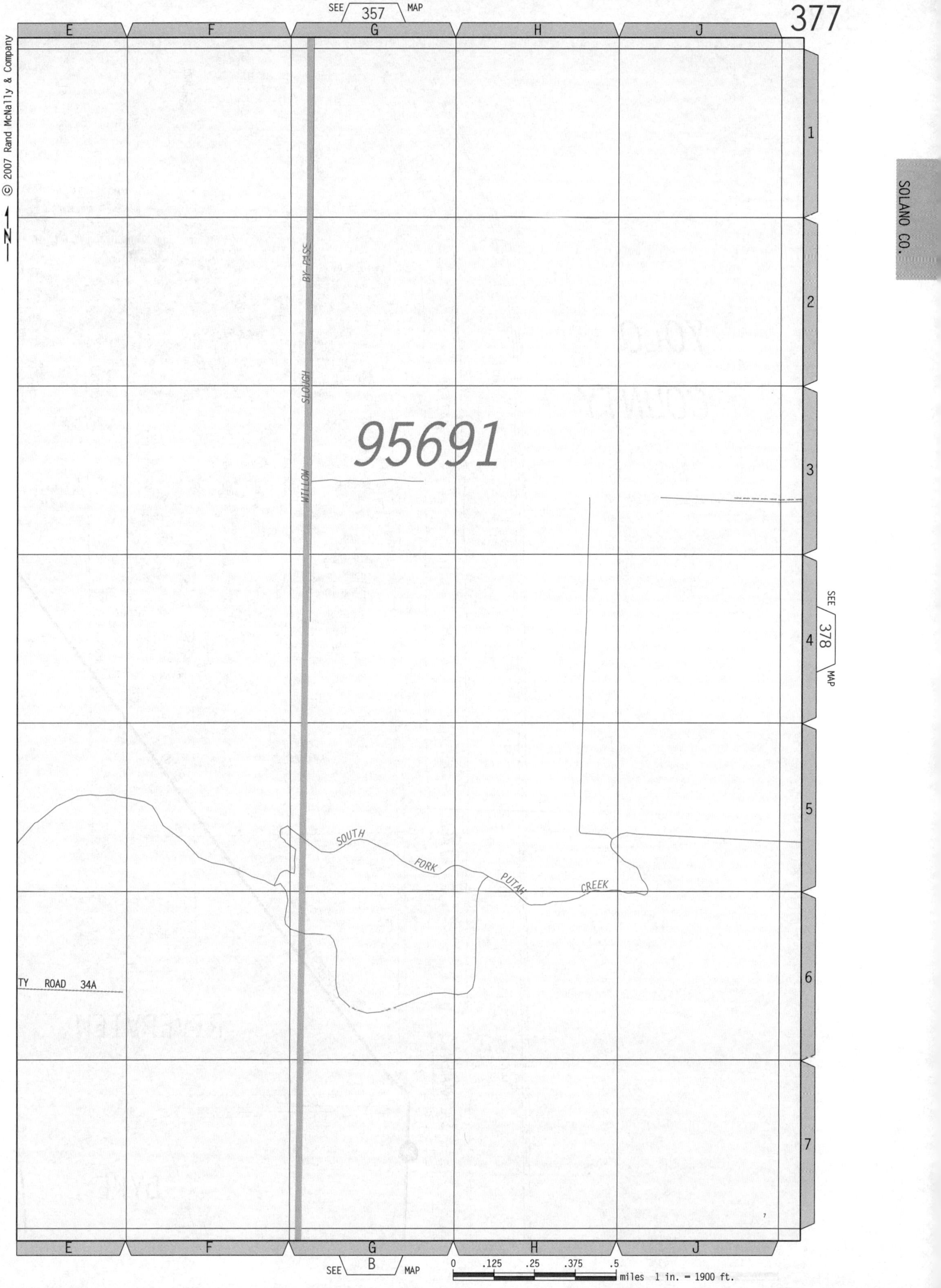
SEE 357 MAP
E
F
G
H
J
1
2
3
4
5
6
7
SOLANO CO.
SEE 378 MAP
95691
WILLOW SLOUGH BY-PASS
SOUTH FORK PUTAH CREEK
TY ROAD 34A
SEE B MAP
0 .125 .25 .375 .5 miles 1 in. = 1900 ft.
N

SOLANO CO.

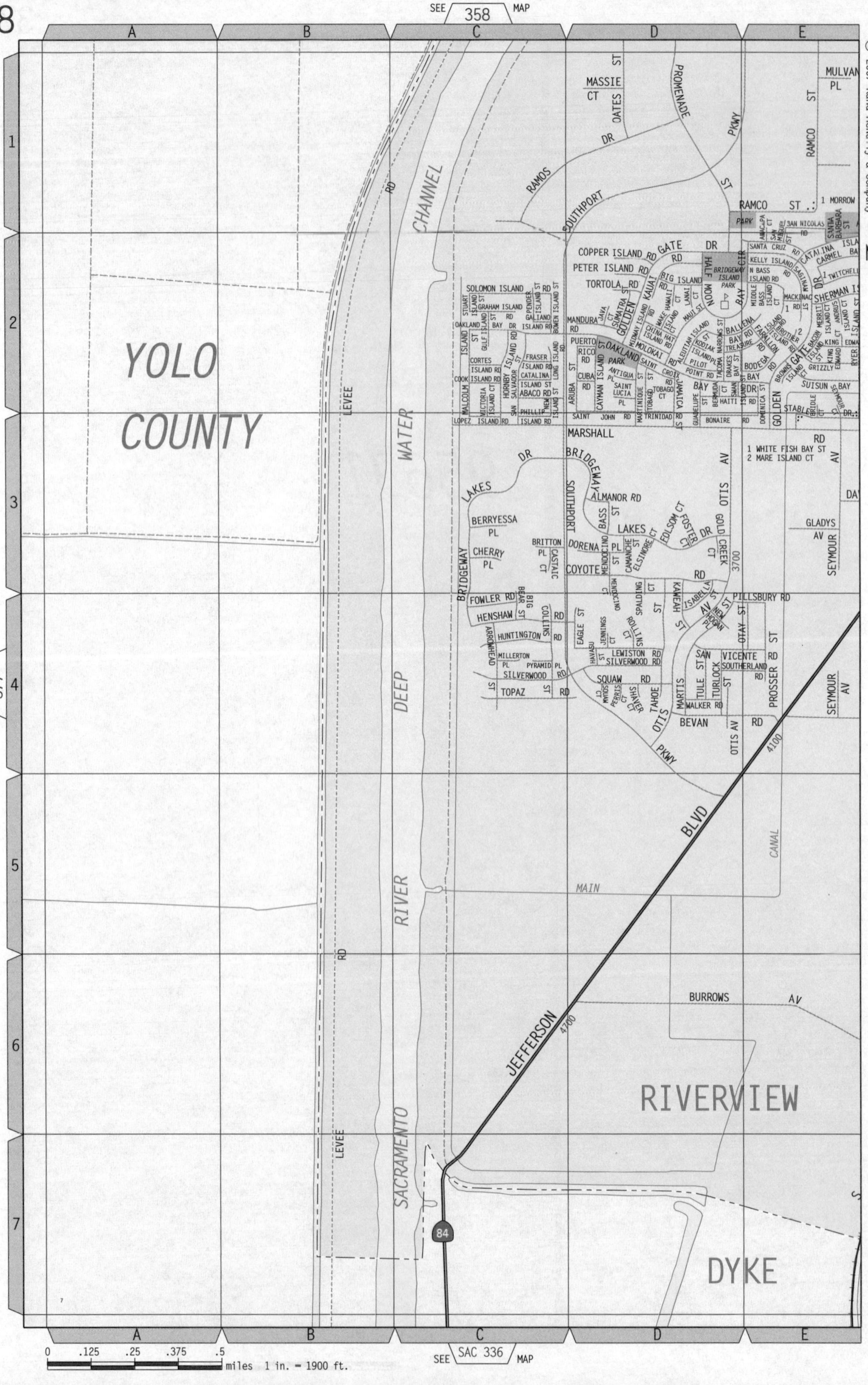
SEE 358 MAP
A
B
C
D
E
1
2
3
4
5
6
7
SEE 377 MAP
YOLO COUNTY
LEVEE RD
DEEP WATER CHANNEL
SACRAMENTO RIVER
MASSIE CT
OATES ST
PROMENADE PKWY
RAMOS DR
SOUTHPORT
RAMCO ST
MULVANEY PL
1 MORROW
PARK
SAN NICOLAS RD
SANTA BARBARA ST
COPPER ISLAND RD
GATE DR
PETER ISLAND RD
TORTOLA RD
HALF MOON BAY CIR
BRIDGEWAY ISLAND PARK
SANTA CRUZ RD
KELLY ISLAND
CATALINA ISLAND
CARMEL BAY
TWITCHELL
SHERMAN IS
SOLOMON ISLAND RD
GRAHAM ISLAND
OAKLAND BAY DR
MANDURA RD
GOLDEN GATE
BIG ISLAND
KAUAI
MOLOKAI
SUMATRA
JAVA
PUERTO RICO RD
OAKLAND PARK
ANTIGUA PL
SAINT CROIX
SAINT LUCIA PL
CORTES ISLAND RD
COOK ISLAND RD
FRASER ISLAND RD
CATALINA ISLAND ST
ABACO RD
ARUBA ST
CUBA RD
CAYMAN ISLAND ST
TOBAGO CT
JAMAICA ST
TRINIDAD RD
BONAIRE RD
BAY DR
BODEGA BAY
SUISUN BAY
GRIZZLY
LOPEZ ISLAND RD
PHILLIP ISLAND RD
SAINT JOHN RD
MARSHALL RD
1 WHITE FISH BAY ST
2 MARE ISLAND CT
BRIDGEWAY LAKES DR
ALMANOR RD
BASS ST
LAKES DR
EDLSOM CT
FOSTER CT
GOLD CREEK CT
OTIS AV
GLADYS AV
SEYMOUR AV
BERRYESSA PL
CHERRY PL
BRITTON PL
CASTAIC CT
DORENA PL
COYOTE ST
MENDOCINO
CAMANCHE ST
ELSINORE CT
SPALDING ST
KAWEAH ST
ISABELLA
PILLSBURY RD
FOWLER RD
BIG BEAR CT
HENSHAW ST
COLLINS RD
HUNTINGTON RD
ARROWHEAD
EAGLE ST
JENNINGS CT
HAVASU ST
ROLLINS CT
NEW HOGAN
OTAY ST
MILLERTON PL
PYRAMID PL
SILVERWOOD CT
TOPAZ ST
LEWISTON RD
SILVERWOOD RD
SAN VICENTE RD
SOUTHERLAND RD
SQUAW CT
PERRIS CT
SHAVER CT
TAHOE CT
MARTIS CT
TULE ST
TURLOCK ST
PROSSER ST
WALKER RD
BEVAN RD
OTIS PKWY
OTIS AV
3700
4100
JEFFERSON BLVD
4700
CANAL
MAIN
BURROWS AV
RIVERVIEW
DYKE
84
SEE SAC 336 MAP
0 .125 .25 .375 .5
miles 1 in. = 1900 ft.

SEE 358 MAP

E
F
G
H
J
1
2
3
4
5
6
7
95691
WEST SACRAMENTO
95822
95831
SACRAMENTO
GREENHAVEN
YOLO CO
SACRAMENTO CO
SACRAMENTO RIVER
SOLANO CO.
JEFFERSON BLVD
LINDEN RD
SOUTH RIVER RD
DAVIS RD
GREGORY AV
ANTIOCH AV
PARTRIDGE AV
HARMON RD
FRENCH
HILARY AV
MILLER CT
TAPLEY RD
BEVAN RD
SEYMOUR AV
GLADYS AV
ALLAN AV
RIVER RD
BURROWS AV
SWR
FS
WEST SACRAMENTO SUMMERFIELD PARK
SANTA BARBARA ST PARK
REDWOOD PARK
BAHNFLETH PARK
RIVERSIDE BL
WEST SIDE FRWY
43RD AV
35TH AV
GREENHAVEN DR
FLORIN RD
SEYMOUR PARK
GREENHAVEN LAKE
BEAR FLAG SCHOOL PARK
DIDION SCHOOL PARK
LEWIS PARK
JOHN F KENNEDY HS
KENNEDY SCHOOL PARK
WENZEL SCHOOL PARK
SACRAMENTO RIVER PARKWAY
SEE A F7
1 SANDHILL CT
2 WATERTHRUSH CT
3 CHICKADEE CT
4 KINGBIRD CT
1 SEASTONE WY
2 MARYMANUEL CIR
SEE SAC 317 MAP
SEE SAC 336 MAP
0 .125 .25 .375 .5
miles 1 in. = 1900 ft.

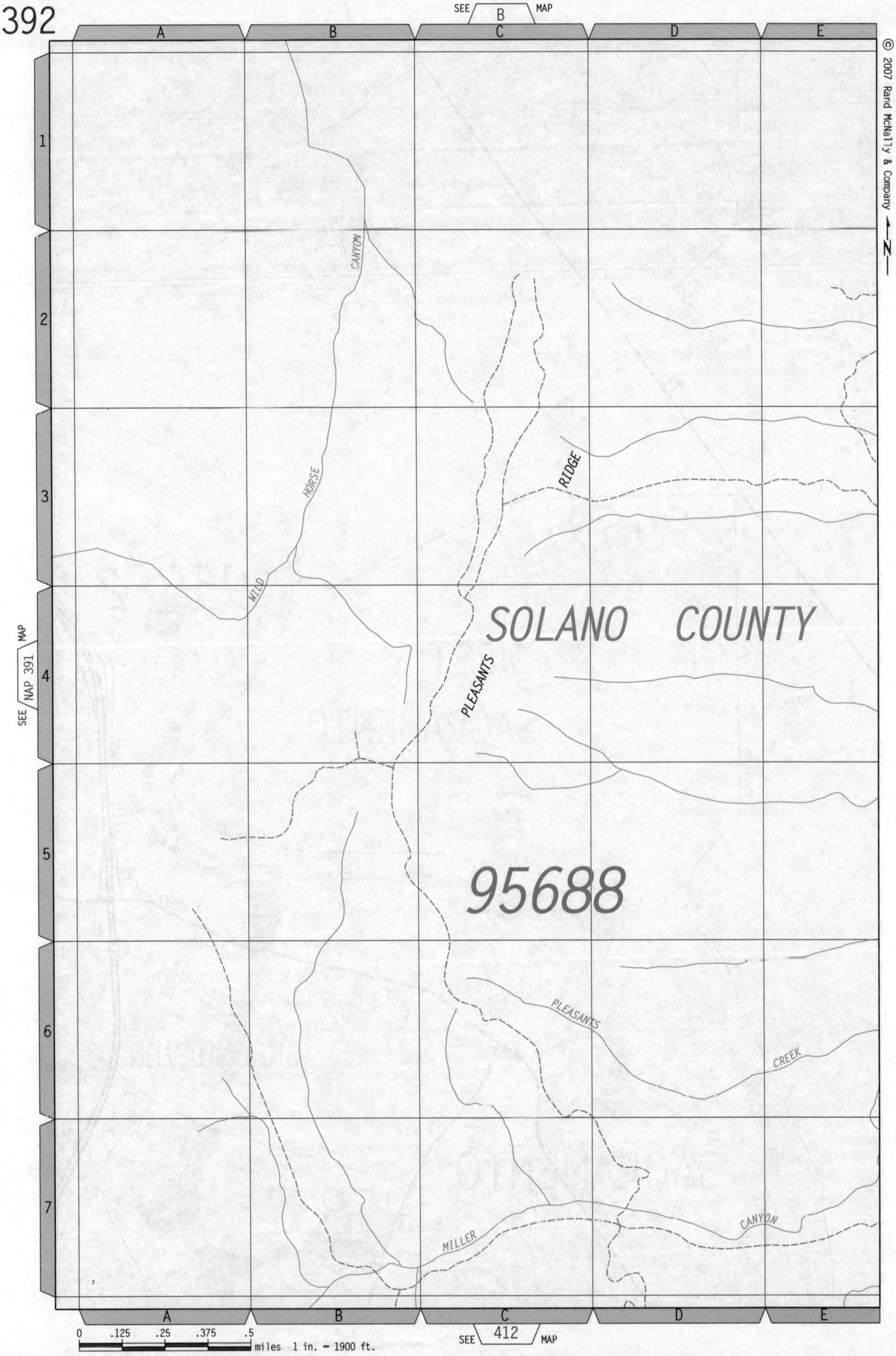
SEE B MAP
A
B
C
D
E
1
2
3
4
5
6
7
SEE NAP 391 MAP
CANYON
HORSE
WILD
RIDGE
PLEASANTS
SOLANO COUNTY
95688
PLEASANTS
CREEK
MILLER
CANYON
SEE 412 MAP
0 .125 .25 .375 .5 miles 1 in. = 1900 ft.

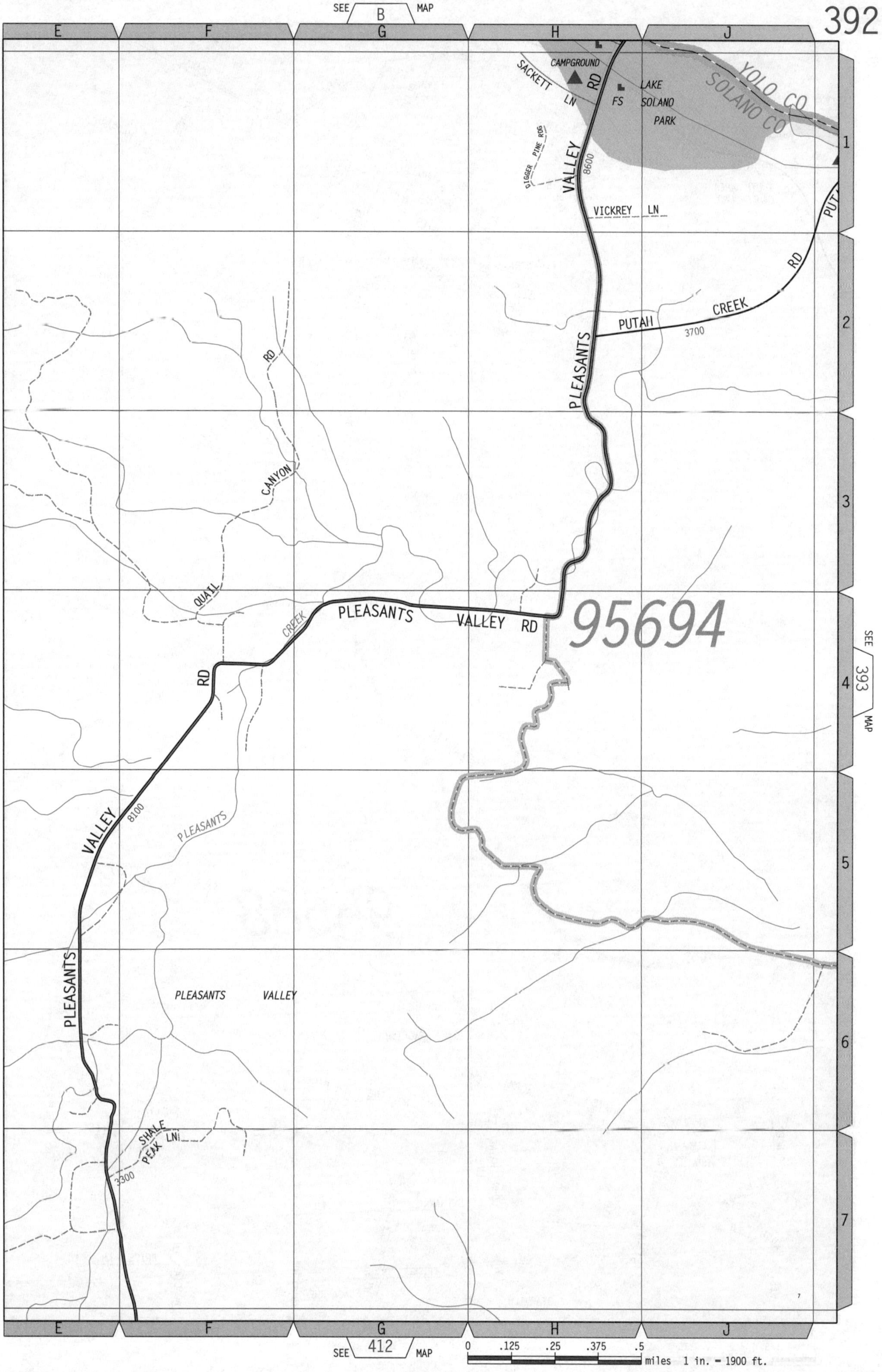
SEE B MAP
E
F
G
H
J
1
2
3
4
5
6
7
CAMPGROUND
SACKETT LN
RD
LAKE
SOLANO
PARK
FS
YOLO CO
SOLANO CO
DIGGER PINE RDG
VALLEY
8600
VICKREY LN
PUTAH
RD
PUTAH CREEK RD
3700
PLEASANTS
RD
CANYON
QUAIL
CREEK
PLEASANTS VALLEY RD
95694
SEE 393 MAP
RD
VALLEY
8100
PLEASANTS
PLEASANTS
PLEASANTS VALLEY
SHALE PEAK LN
3300
SEE 412 MAP
0 .125 .25 .375 .5
miles 1 in. = 1900 ft.

SOLANO CO.

SEE 373 MAP

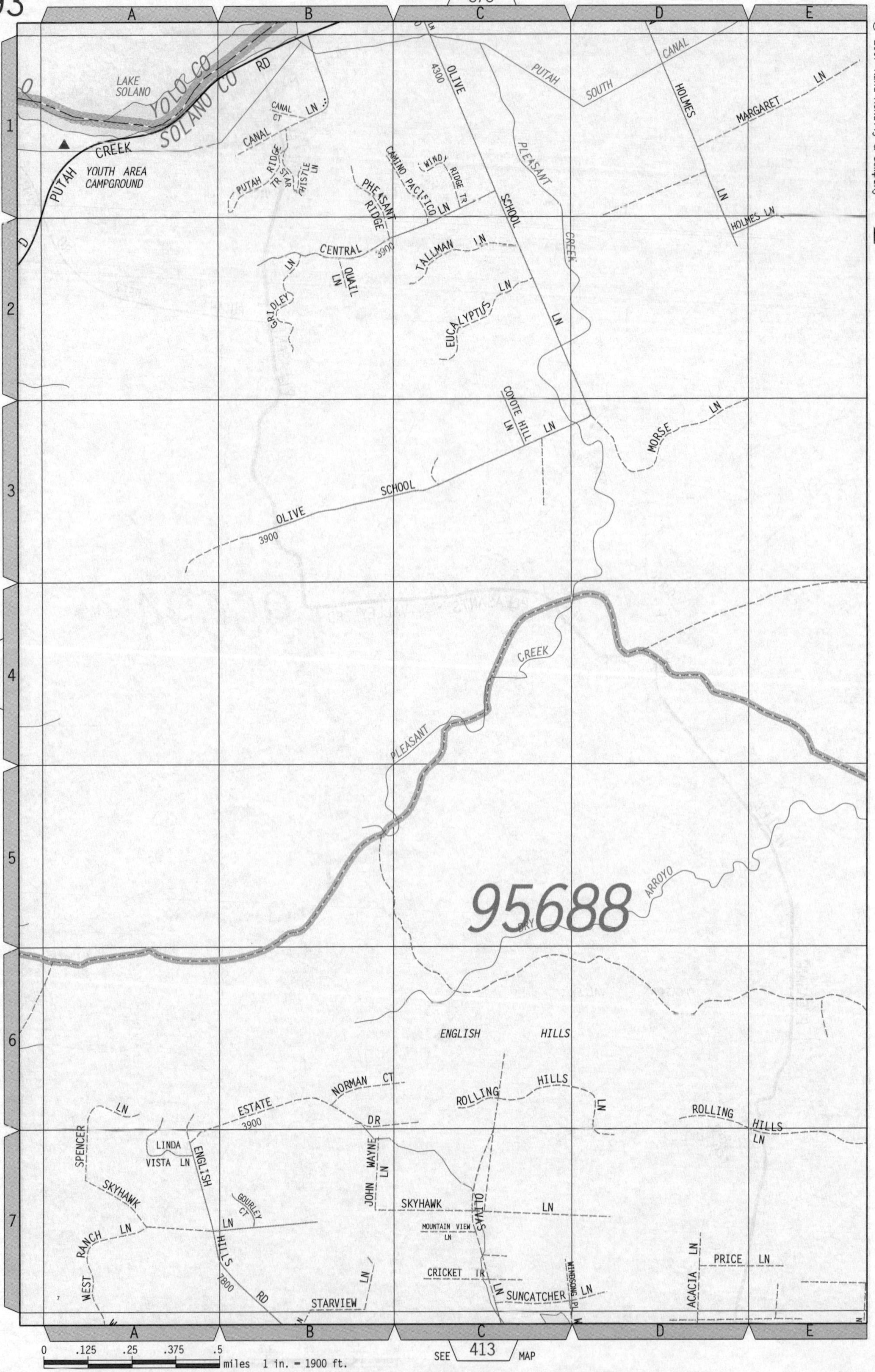
A
B
C
D
E
1
2
3
4
5
6
7
LAKE SOLANO
YOLO CO
SOLANO CO RD
PUTAH CREEK
YOUTH AREA CAMPGROUND
CANAL CT
CANAL LN
PUTAH RIDGE TR
STAR THISTLE LN
PHEASANT RIDGE
CAMINO PACIFICO LN
WIND RIDGE TR
4300
OLIVE SCHOOL LN
PLEASANT CREEK
PUTAH SOUTH CANAL
HOLMES LN
MARGARET LN
HOLMES LN
CENTRAL
3900
GRIDLEY LN
QUAIL LN
TALLMAN LN
EUCALYPTUS LN
COYOTE HILL LN
MORSE LN
OLIVE SCHOOL
3900
PLEASANT CREEK
95688
DRY ARROYO
ENGLISH HILLS
NORMAN CT
ESTATE DR
3900
ROLLING HILLS LN
ROLLING HILLS LN
SPENCER LN
LINDA VISTA LN
ENGLISH HILLS RD
2800
SKYHAWK
GOURLEY CT
WEST RANCH LN
JOHN WAYNE LN
SKYHAWK LN
OLIVAS
MOUNTAIN VIEW LN
CRICKET TR
SUNCATCHER LN
WINDSONG PL
STARVIEW
ACACIA LN
PRICE LN
0 .125 .25 .375 .5
miles 1 in. = 1900 ft.

SEE 392 MAP

SEE 413 MAP

SOLANO CO.

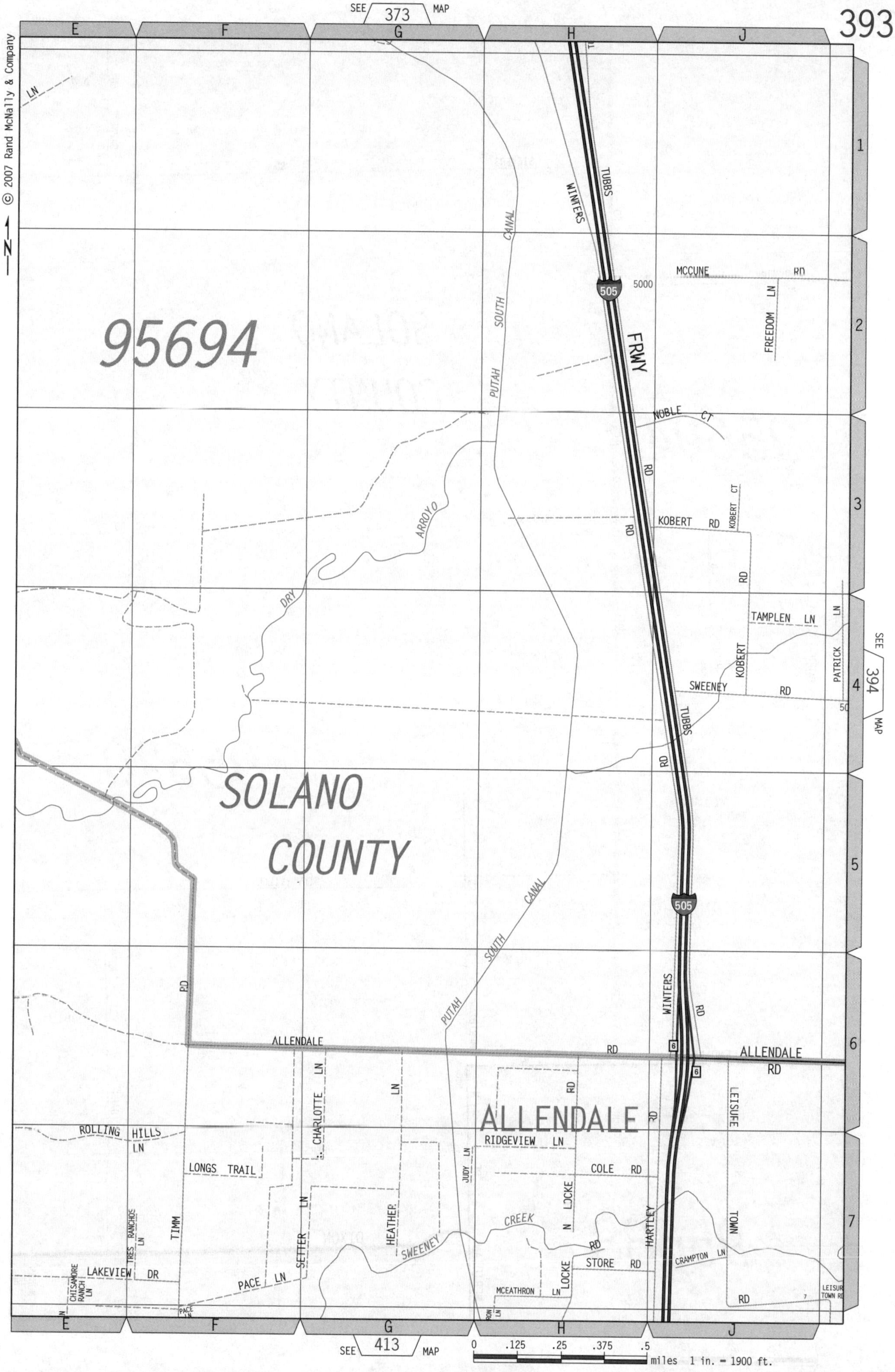
SEE 373 MAP
E
F
G
H
J
1
2
3
4
5
6
7
95694
SOLANO
COUNTY
ALLENDALE
LN
TUBBS
WINTERS
SOUTH
PUTAH
CANAL
505
5000
MCCUNE
RD
FREEDOM LN
FRWY
NOBLE CT
RD
KOBERT RD
KOBERT CT
ARROYO
DRY
TAMPLEN LN
LN
KOBERT
SWEENEY RD
PATRICK
SEE 394 MAP
TUBBS RD
RD
WINTERS RD
6
ALLENDALE RD
ALLENDALE RD
CHARLOTTE LN
LN
RD
LEISURE
ROLLING HILLS LN
LONGS TRAIL
RIDGEVIEW LN
JUDY LN
COLE RD
TIMM
TRES RANCHOS LN
LN
SETTER
HEATHER
SWEENEY CREEK
N LOCKE
RD
HARTLEY
TOWN
STORE RD
CRAMPTON LN
LAKEVIEW DR
CHISAMORE RANCH LN
PACE LN
PACE LN
MCEATHRON LN
LOCKE
LEISURE TOWN RD
RD
RON LN
N
SEE 413 MAP
0 .125 .25 .375 .5
miles 1 in. = 1900 ft.

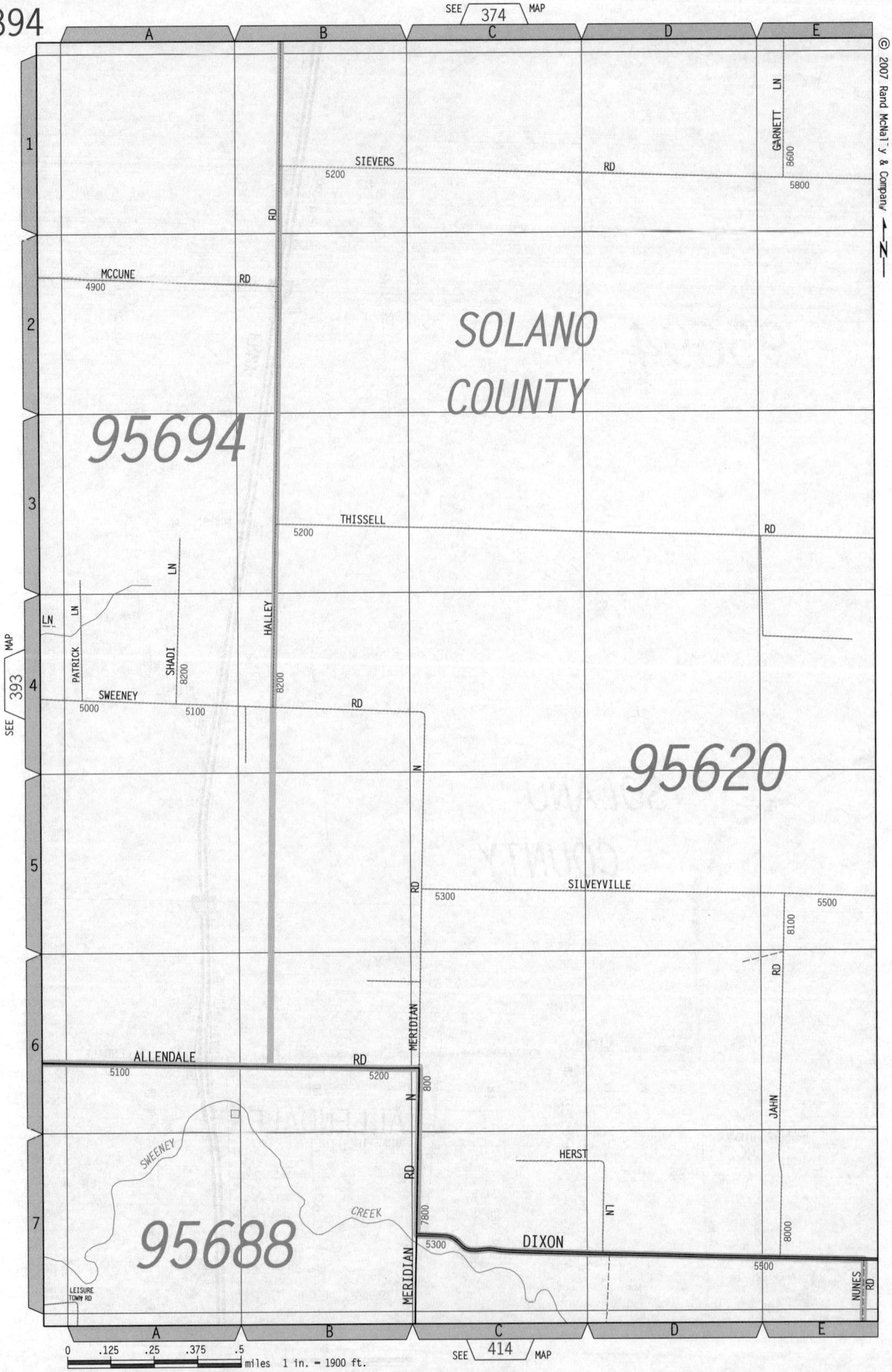
SEE 374 MAP
A
B
C
D
E
1
2
3
4
5
6
7
SEE 393 MAP
SOLANO COUNTY
95694
95620
95688
SIEVERS RD
5200
5800
GARNETT LN
8600
MCCUNE RD
4900
HALLEY RD
8200
THISSELL RD
5200
LN
PATRICK LN
SHADI LN
SWEENEY RD
5000
5100
MERIDIAN RD N
SILVEYVILLE
5300
5500
JAHN RD
8100
8000
ALLENDALE RD
5100
5200
800
SWEENEY CREEK
HERST LN
7800
DIXON
5300
5500
NUNES RD
LEISURE TOWN RD
SEE 414 MAP
0 .125 .25 .375 .5 miles 1 in. = 1900 ft.

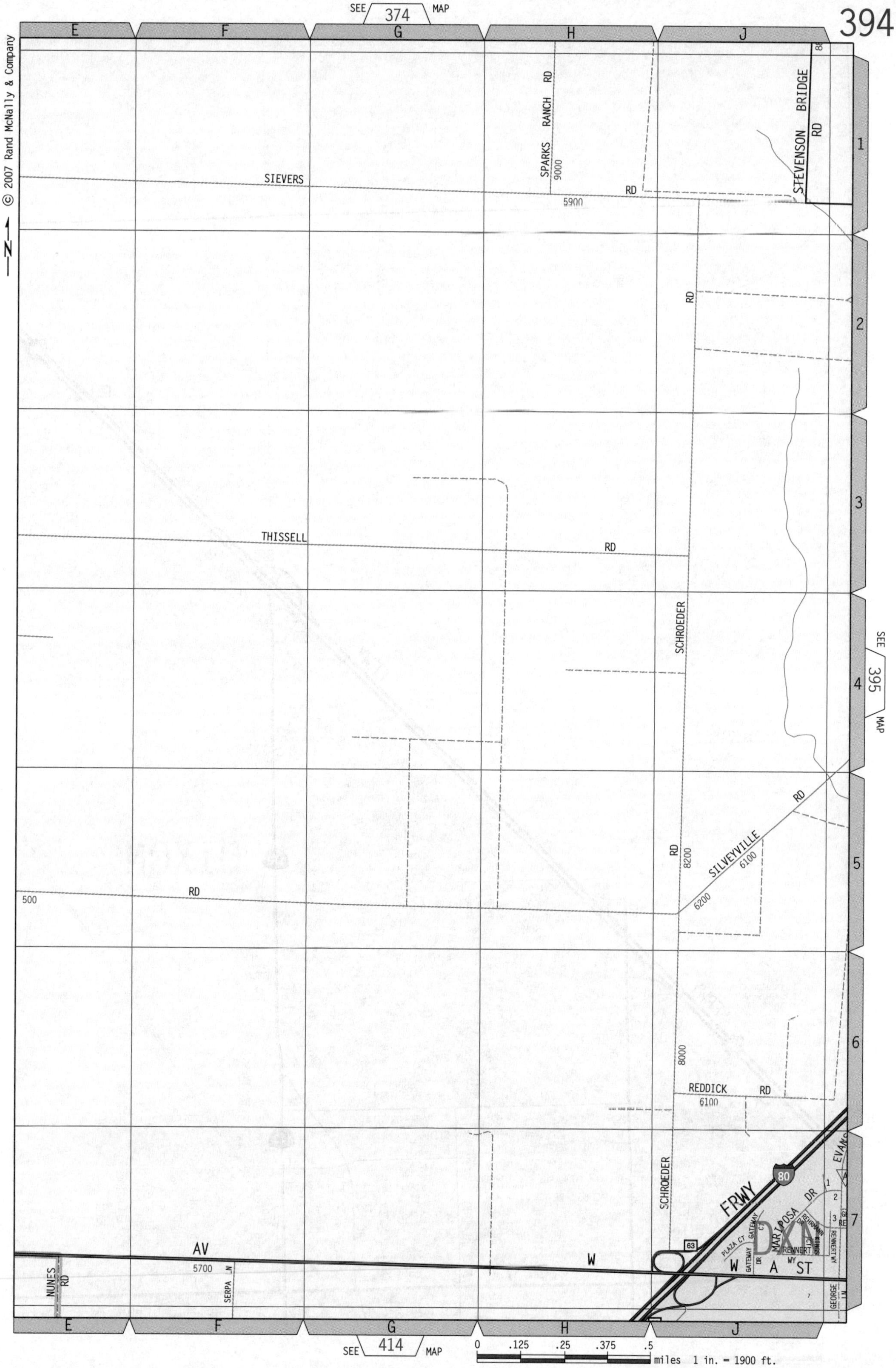
SEE 374 MAP
E
F
G
H
J
1
2
3
4
5
6
7
SPARKS RANCH RD
9000
STEVENSON BRIDGE RD
SIEVERS
RD
5900
RD
THISSELL
RD
SCHROEDER
SEE 395 MAP
RD
SILVEYVILLE
6100
RD
8200
6200
500
RD
8000
REDDICK
RD
6100
SCHROEDER
FRWY
80
EVANS
MARIPOSA
DR
GATEWAY CT
PLAZA CT
GATEWAY DR
REHRMANN DR
RENNERT WY
RENNERT CT
DXN
63
AV
5700
W
W
A
ST
NUNES RD
SERPA LN
GEORGE LN
SEE 414 MAP
0 .125 .25 .375 .5
miles 1 in. = 1900 ft.

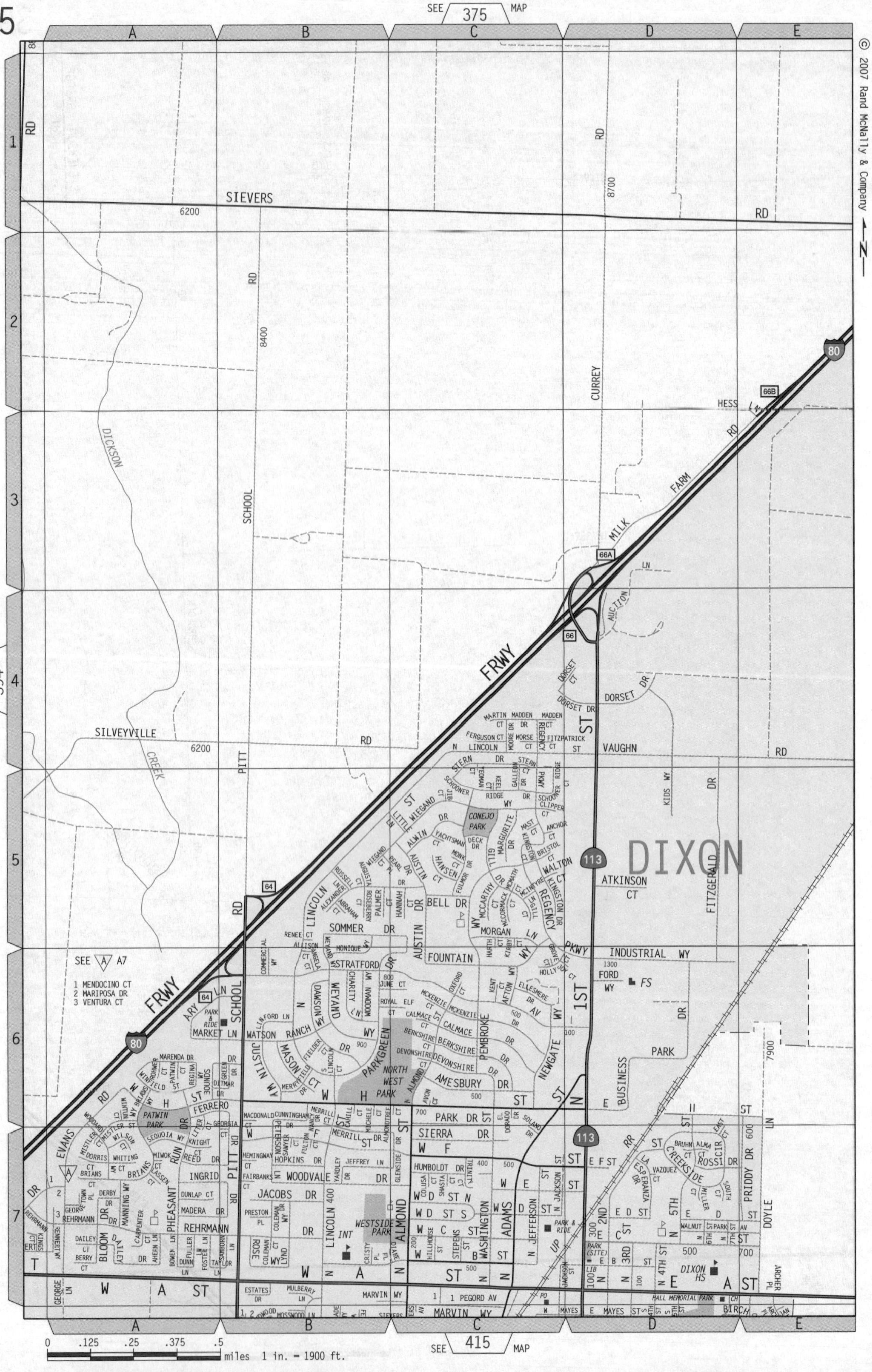
SEE 375 MAP
A
B
C
D
E
1
2
3
4
5
6
7
SEE 394 MAP
SEE 415 MAP
SIEVERS
6200
RD
CURREY
RD
8700
SCHOOL
RD
8400
PITT
DICKSON
CREEK
SILVEYVILLE
6200
RD
VAUGHN
RD
80
66B
HESS
LN
MILK
FARM
RD
66A
66
AUCTION
LN
FRWY
DORSET CT
DORSET DR
DORSET DR
DIXON
ATKINSON CT
FITZGERALD
KIDS WY
DR
INDUSTRIAL WY
FORD WY
FS
1300
BUSINESS
PARK
DR
7900
113
1ST
ST
N
PKWY
REGENCY
LINCOLN
FOUNTAIN
SOMMER DR
STRATFORD
BELL DR
MORGAN LN
CONEJO PARK
NORTH WEST PARK
PARKGREEN
PATWIN PARK
WESTSIDE PARK
64
FRWY
80
SEE A A7
1 MENDOCINO CT
2 MARIPOSA DR
3 VENTURA CT
MARKET LN
PARK & RIDE
WATSON RANCH
JUSTIN
MASON CT
WEYAND
DAWSON WY
AMESBURY DR
PEMBROKE
NEWGATE
W H ST
PARK DR
SIERRA DR
W F
WOODVALE
JACOBS DR
REHRMANN
PHEASANT
RUN DR
INGRID
MADERA
DUNLAP CT
EVANS RD
BRIANS
WHITING
SEQUOIA WY
FERRERO
ALMOND ST
WASHINGTON
ADAMS
JEFFERSON
JACKSON
2ND
3RD
5TH
CREEKSIDE CIR
ROSSI
PRIDDY DR
DOYLE
W A ST
N A ST
E A ST
MARVIN WY
PEGORD AV
MAYES
BIRCH
HALL MEMORIAL PARK
DIXON HS
LIB
PO
PARK (SITE)
PARK & RIDE
UP RR
INT
ESTATES DR
MULBERRY LN
GEORGE LN
0 .125 .25 .375 .5 miles 1 in. = 1900 ft.

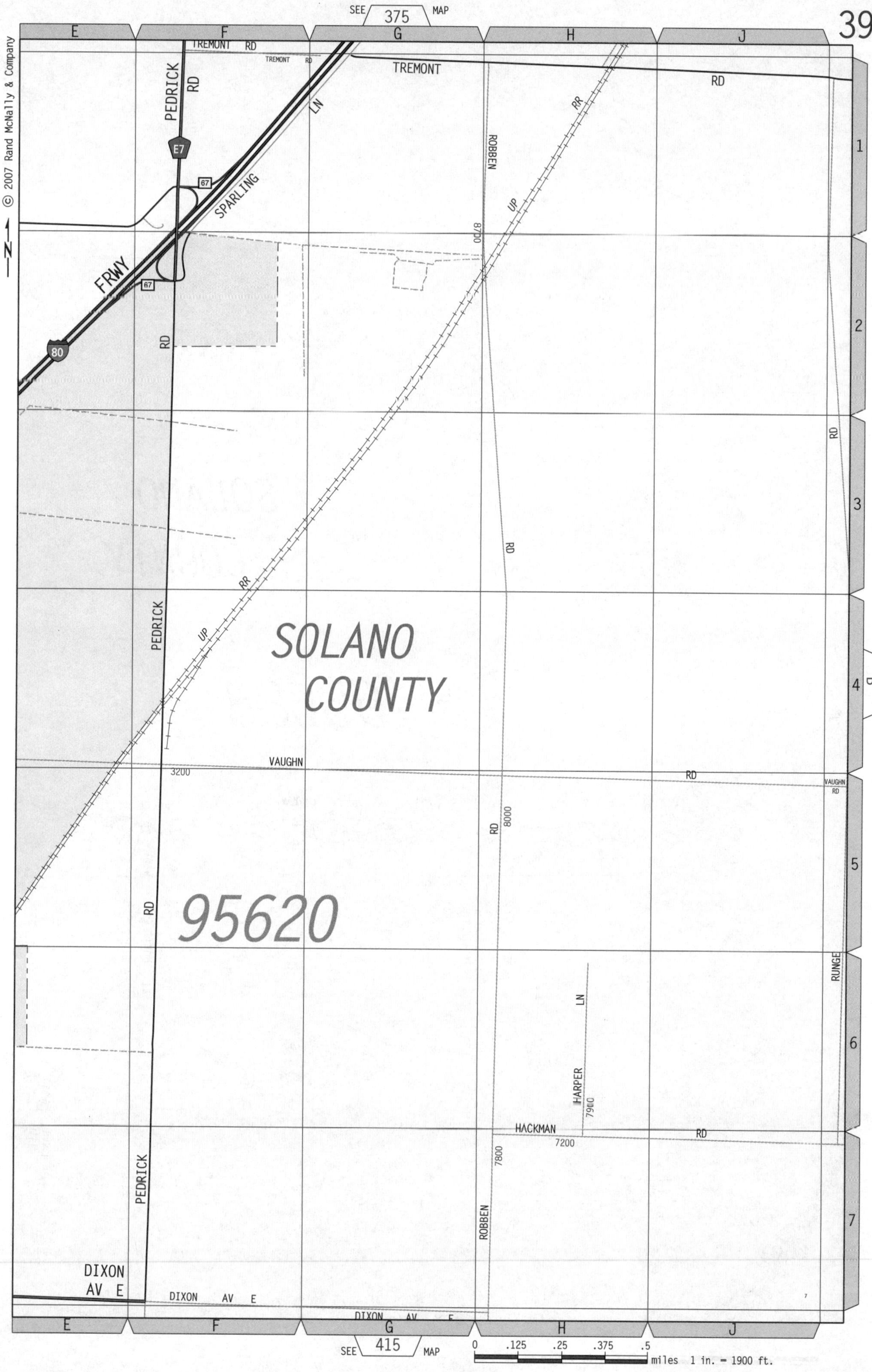
SEE 375 MAP
E
F
G
H
J
TREMONT RD
TREMONT RD
TREMONT
RD
PEDRICK RD
E7
LN
SPARLING
67
67
FRWY
80
ROBBEN
8700
UP
RR
RD
RD
1
2
3
4
5
6
7
SEE B MAP
SOLANO COUNTY
95620
PEDRICK
UP
RR
VAUGHN
3200
RD
VAUGHN RD
RD
8000
RD
RUNGE
LN
HARPER
7900
HACKMAN
7200
RD
7800
ROBBEN
PEDRICK
DIXON AV E
DIXON AV E
DIXON AV E
SEE 415 MAP
0 .125 .25 .375 .5
miles 1 in. = 1900 ft.

SEE 392 MAP

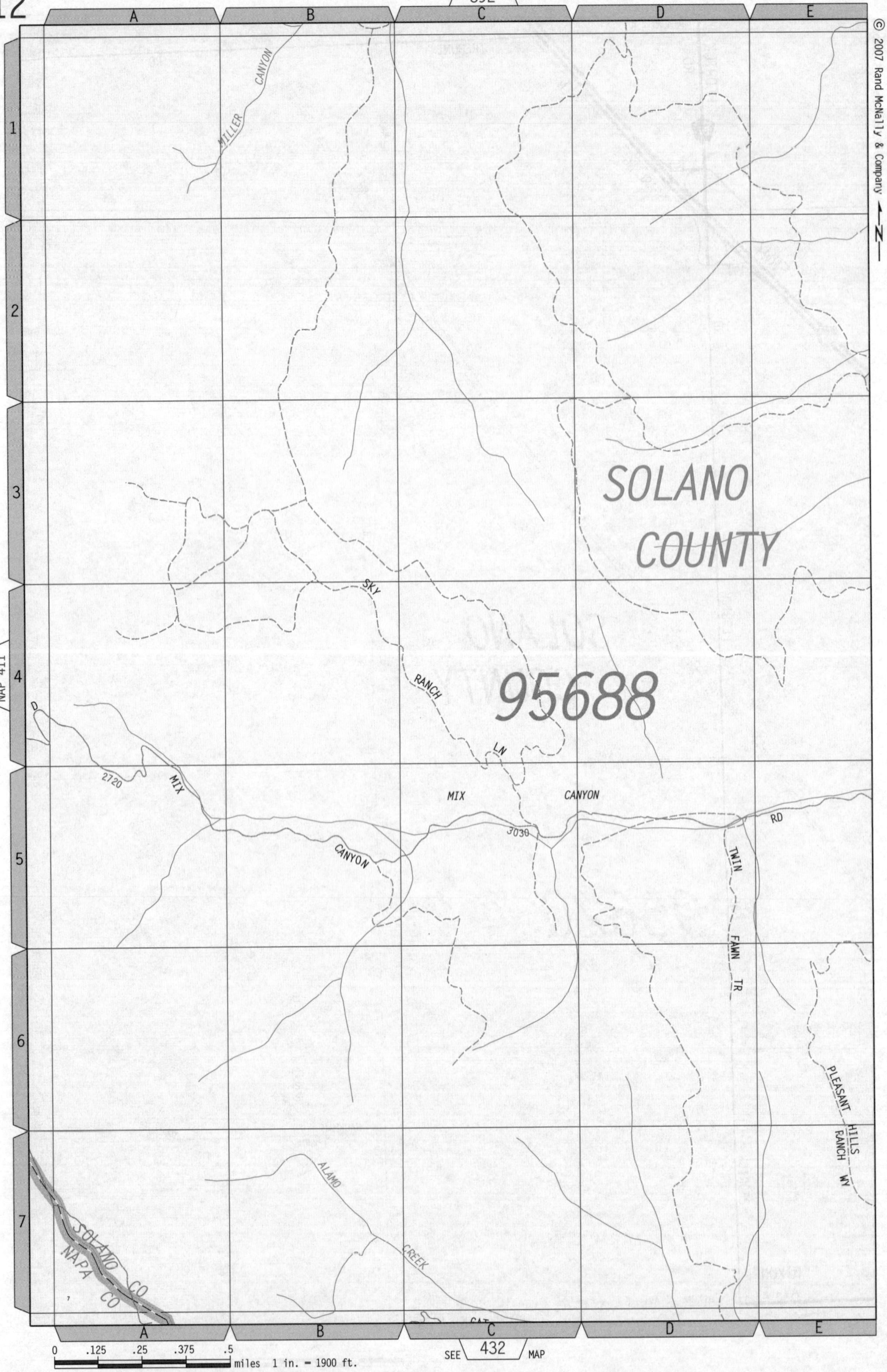
A
B
C
D
E
1
2
3
4
5
6
7
MILLER CANYON
SOLANO
COUNTY
SKY RANCH LN
95688
D
2720
MIX CANYON
MIX CANYON RD
3030
TWIN FAWN TR
PLEASANT HILLS RANCH WY
ALAMO CREEK
SOLANO CO
NAPA CO
0 .125 .25 .375 .5 miles 1 in. = 1900 ft.

SEE NAP 411 MAP

SEE 432 MAP

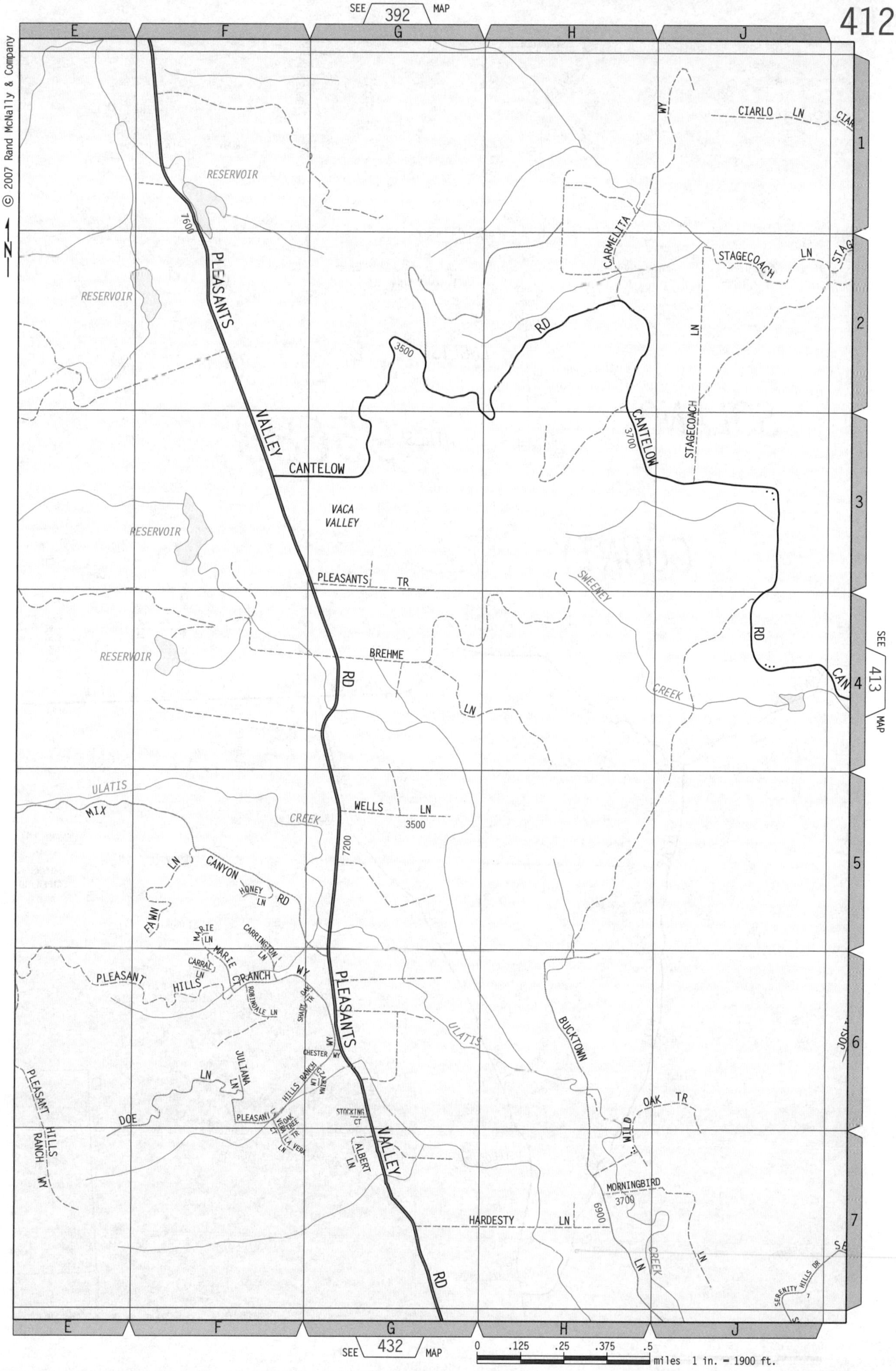
SEE 392 MAP
E
F
G
H
J
1
2
3
4
5
6
7
SOLANO CO.
SEE 413 MAP
SEE 432 MAP
0 .125 .25 .375 .5
miles 1 in. = 1900 ft.
RESERVOIR
RESERVOIR
RESERVOIR
RESERVOIR
7600
PLEASANTS
VALLEY
RD
CANTELOW
3500
VACA VALLEY
PLEASANTS TR
BREHME
LN
CARMELITA
WY
CIARLO LN
STAGECOACH LN
STAGECOACH LN
CANTELOW RD
3700
SWEENEY CREEK
ULATIS
MIX CANYON RD
CREEK
WELLS LN
3500
7200
FAWN LN
HONEY LN
MARIE LN
MARIE CT
CARRAL LN
CARRINGTON LN
RANCH WY
PLEASANT HILLS
ROBINDALE LN
SHADY OAK TR
PLEASANTS
CHESTER WY
ULATIS
BUCKTOWN
JULIANA LN
LN
DOE
HILLS RANCH
ZARINA LN
PLEASANT
OAK TR
VERA LN
STOCKING CT
VALLEY
ALBERT LN
WILD OAK TR
PLEASANT HILLS RANCH WY
MORNINGBIRD
3700
6900
HARDESTY LN
LN
CREEK
LN
RD
SERENITY HILLS DR

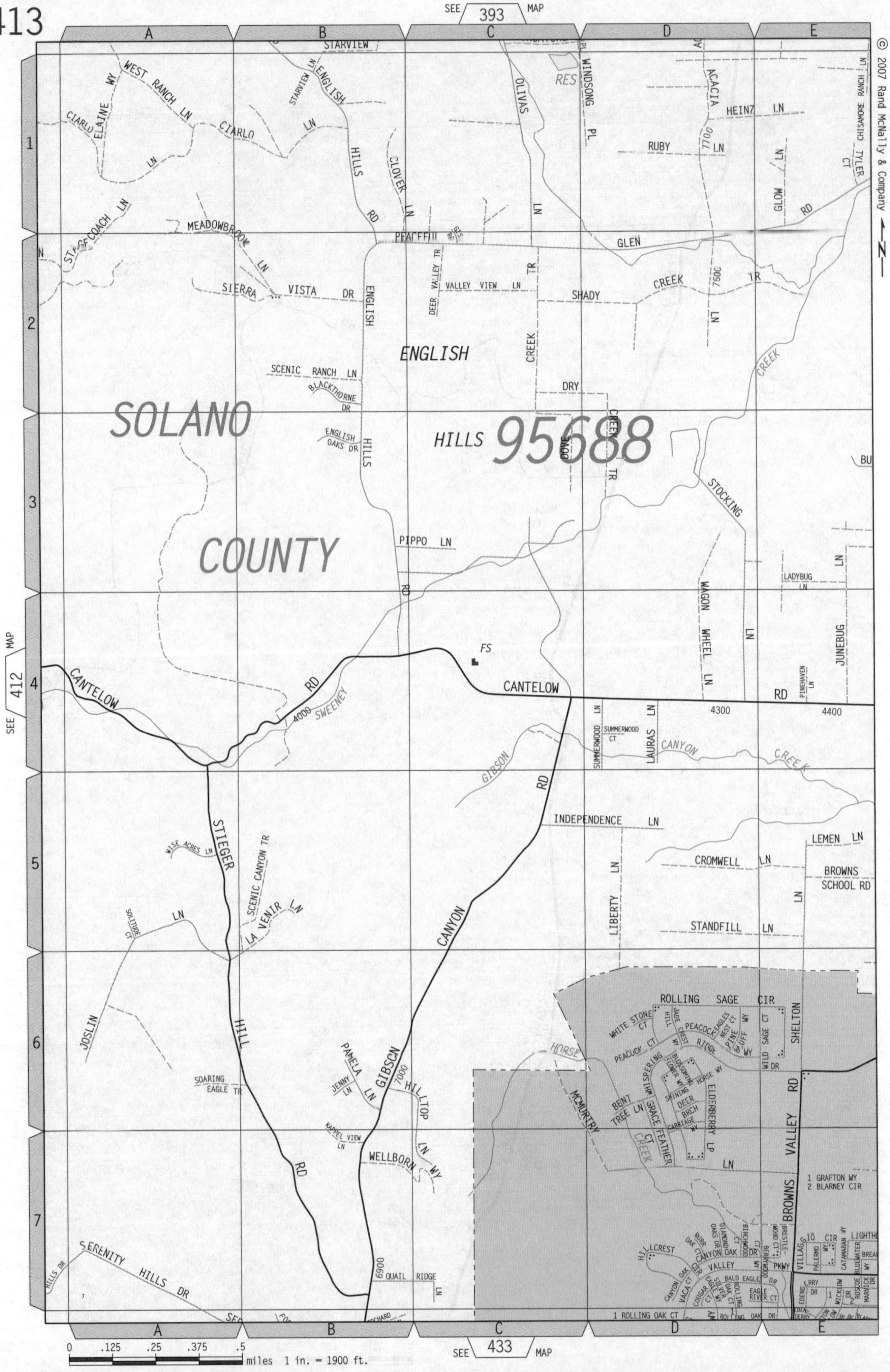
SEE 393 MAP
SEE 412 MAP
SEE 433 MAP
A
B
C
D
E
1
2
3
4
5
6
7
SOLANO
COUNTY
ENGLISH
HILLS
95688
STARVIEW
STARVIEW LN
ENGLISH
WEST RANCH LN
ELAINE WY
CIARLO
CIARLO
LN
LN
HILLS
RD
CLOVER LN
OLIVAS
RES
WINDSONG PL
ACACIA
7700
HEINZ LN
RUBY LN
GLOW LN
CHISAMORE RANCH LN
TYLER CT
RD
LN
STAGECOACH LN
MEADOWBROOK
LN
PEACEFUL
GLEN
SIERRA
VISTA DR
ENGLISH
DEER VALLEY TR
VALLEY VIEW LN
TR
SHADY
CREEK
TR
7900
LN
CREEK
SCENIC RANCH LN
BLACKTHORNE DR
CREEK
DRY
ENGLISH OAKS DR
HILLS
DOVE
CREEK TR
STOCKING
BU
PIPPO LN
RD
LADYBUG LN
LN
WAGON WHEEL LN
LN
JUNEBUG
PINEHAVEN LN
FS
CANTELOW
RD
4000
SWEENEY
CANTELOW
RD
4300
4400
SUMMERWOOD LN
SUMMERWOOD CT
LAURAS LN
CANYON
CREEK
GIBSON
RD
INDEPENDENCE LN
LEMEN LN
CROMWELL LN
BROWNS SCHOOL RD
LN
STIEGER
WISE ACRES LN
SCENIC CANYON TR
LA VENIR LN
SOLITUDE CT
LN
CANYON
LIBERTY LN
STANDFILL LN
ROLLING SAGE CIR
WHITE STONE CT
JADE HILL
PEACOCK CT
WEST CT
EAGLES
CREST
PINE
BLUFF
WY
WILD SAGE CT
SHELTON
DR
RIDGE
WY
WHISPERING
FLOWER WY
SHINING
HORSE WY
BLOSSOMING
DEER
BRCH
CARRIAGE
WY
ELDERBERRY LP
GRACE
FEATHER
BENT TREE LN
CT
CREEK
HORSE
MCMURTRY
LN
JOSLIN
HILL
PAMELA LN
JENNY LN
GIBSON
7000
HILLTOP
LN
SOARING EAGLE TR
KAPPEL VIEW LN
WELLBORN
WY
RD
VALLEY
RD
BROWNS
1 GRAFTON WY
2 BLARNEY CIR
HILLCREST
CANYON OAK
VALLEY
PKWY
BALD EAGLE
EAGLE RIVER CT
CIR
LIGHTHO
VILLAGE
PALERMO
CATAMARAN WY
BLUEWATER
BREAK
1 ROLLING OAK CT
ROLLING OAK DR
SERENITY
HILLS DR
HILLS DR
6900
QUAIL RIDGE
LN
ORCHARD
A
B
C
D
E

0 .125 .25 .375 .5 miles 1 in. = 1900 ft.

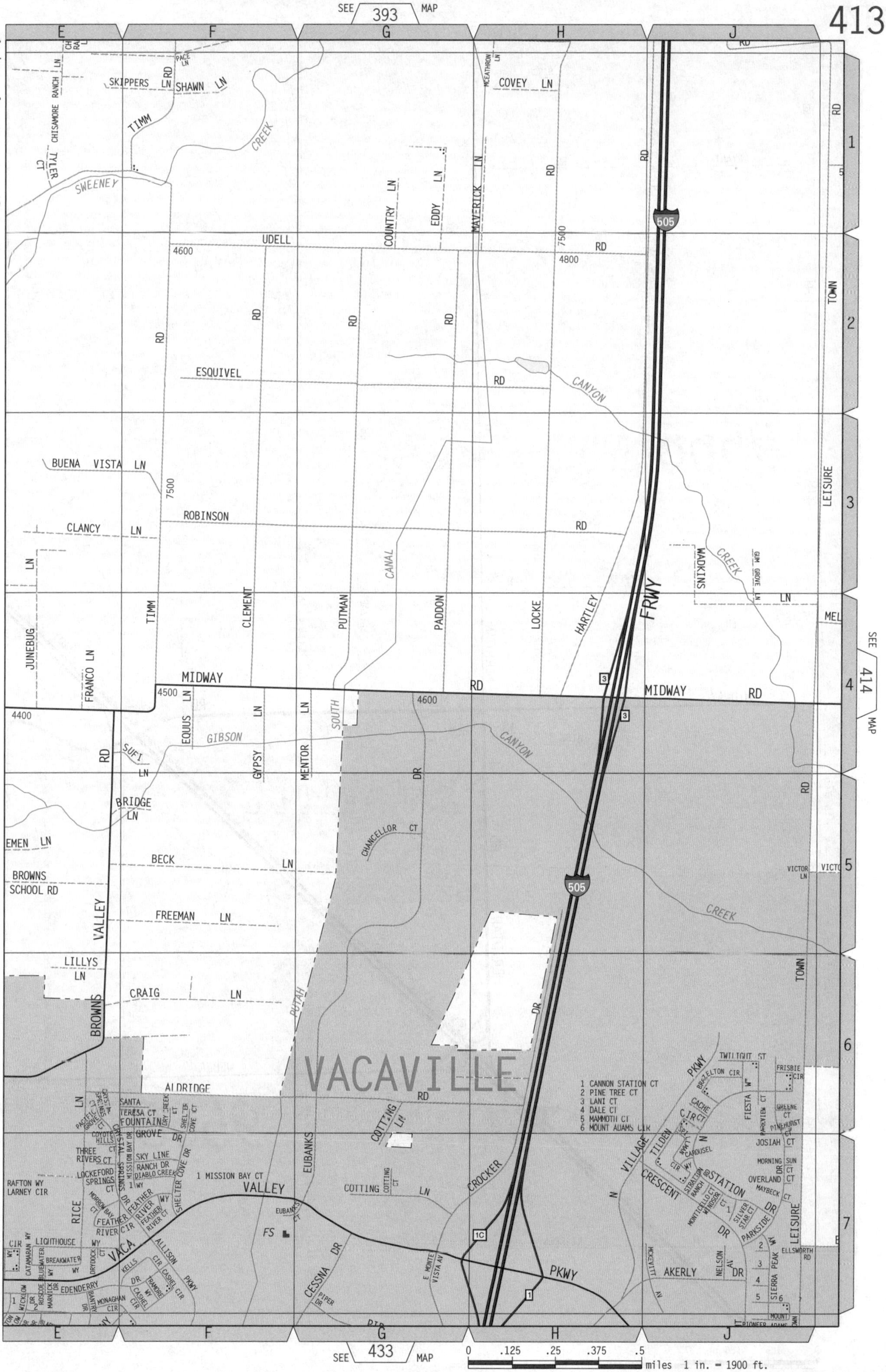
SEE 393 MAP
SEE 414 MAP
SEE 433 MAP
SOLANO CO.
VACAVILLE
MIDWAY RD
UDELL RD
ROBINSON RD
ESQUIVEL RD
CANYON CREEK
GIBSON CANYON CREEK
SWEENEY CREEK
PUTAH SOUTH CANAL
FRWY
505
BUENA VISTA LN
CLANCY LN
JUNEBUG LN
FRANCO LN
TIMM RD
CLEMENT RD
PUTMAN RD
PADDON RD
LOCKE RD
HARTLEY
COUNTRY LN
EDDY LN
MAVERICK LN
MCEATHRON LN
COVEY LN
SKIPPERS LN
SHAWN LN
PACE LN
CHISAMORE RANCH LN
TYLER CT
EQUUS LN
GYPSY LN
MENTOR LN
SUFI LN
BRIDGE LN
BECK LN
FREEMAN LN
LILLYS LN
CRAIG LN
BROWNS SCHOOL RD
BROWNS VALLEY RD
CHANCELLOR CT
ALDRIDGE RD
COTTING LN
EUBANKS
CROCKER DR
VACA VALLEY PKWY
CESSNA DR
PIPER DR
WADKINS LN
GUM GROVE LN
LEISURE TOWN RD
VICTOR LN
1 CANNON STATION CT
2 PINE TREE CT
3 LANI CT
4 DALE CT
5 MAMMOTH CT
6 MOUNT ADAMS CIR
1 MISSION BAY CT
N VILLAGE PKWY
CRESCENT DR
STATION DR
TILDEN CIR
AKERLY DR
NELSON AV
MCKEVITT AV
TWILIGHT ST
FIESTA WY
JOSIAH CT
OVERLAND CT
ELLSWORTH RD
SIERRA PEAK WY
FOUNTAIN GROVE DR
SKY LINE RANCH DR
FEATHER RIVER CIR
ALLISON PKWY
RICE LN
miles 1 in. = 1900 ft.
0 .125 .25 .375 .5

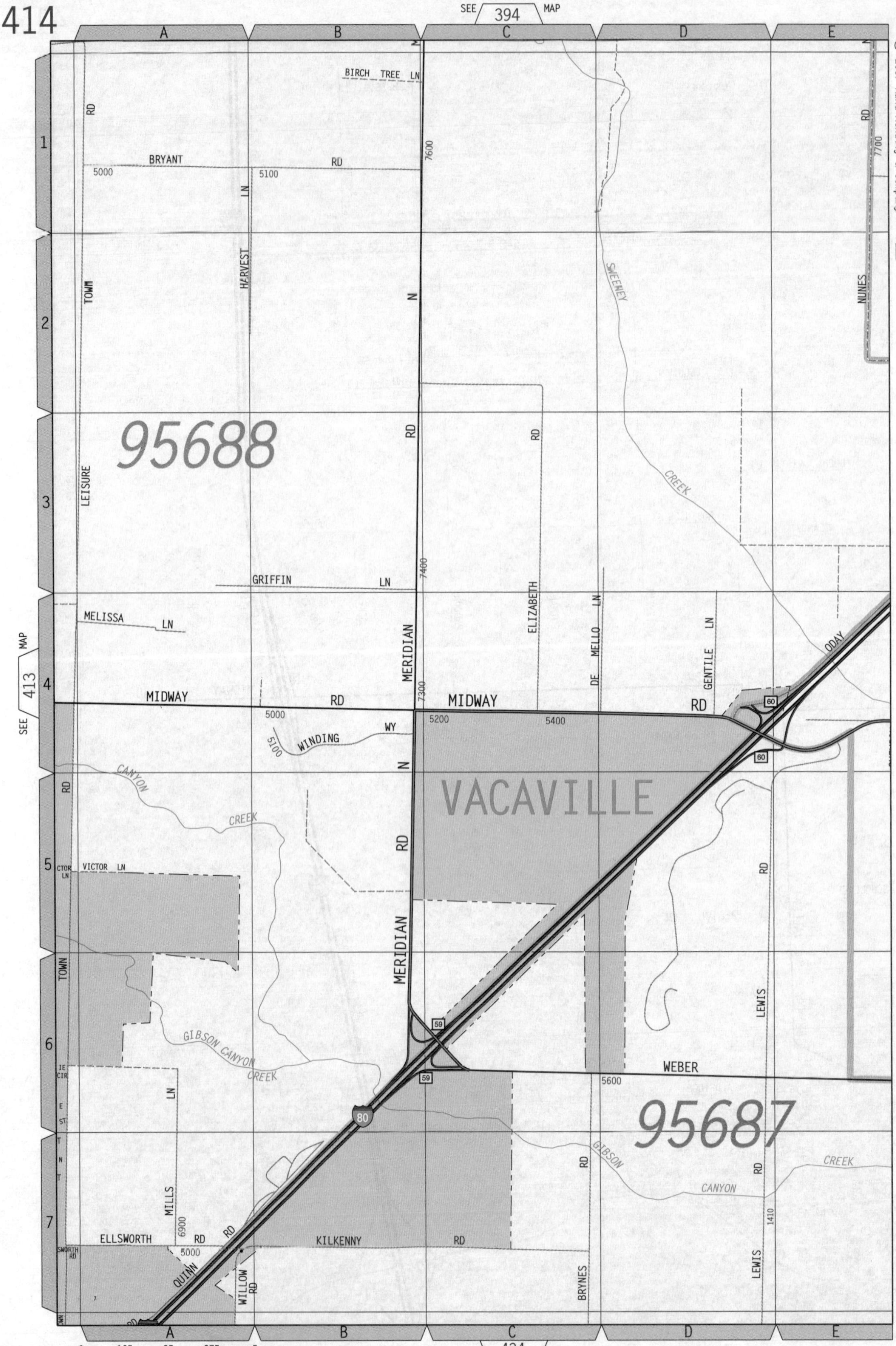
SEE 394 MAP
A
B
C
D
E
1
2
3
4
5
6
7
BIRCH TREE LN
BRYANT RD
5000
5100
7600
7700
NUNES RD
TOWN RD
HARVEST LN
SWEENEY CREEK
95688
LEISURE
GRIFFIN LN
7400
MELISSA LN
ELIZABETH RD
DE MELLO LN
GENTILE LN
ODAY
MERIDIAN RD
SEE 413 MAP
MIDWAY RD
MIDWAY RD
7300
5000
5200
5400
60
WINDING WY
5100
CANYON CREEK
VACAVILLE
VICTOR LN
59
GIBSON CANYON CREEK
WEBER
5600
80
95687
LEWIS RD
MILLS LN
6900
ELLSWORTH RD
5000
QUINN RD
WILLOW RD
KILKENNY RD
BRYNES RD
GIBSON CANYON CREEK
1410
SEE 434 MAP
0 .125 .25 .375 .5
miles 1 in. = 1900 ft.

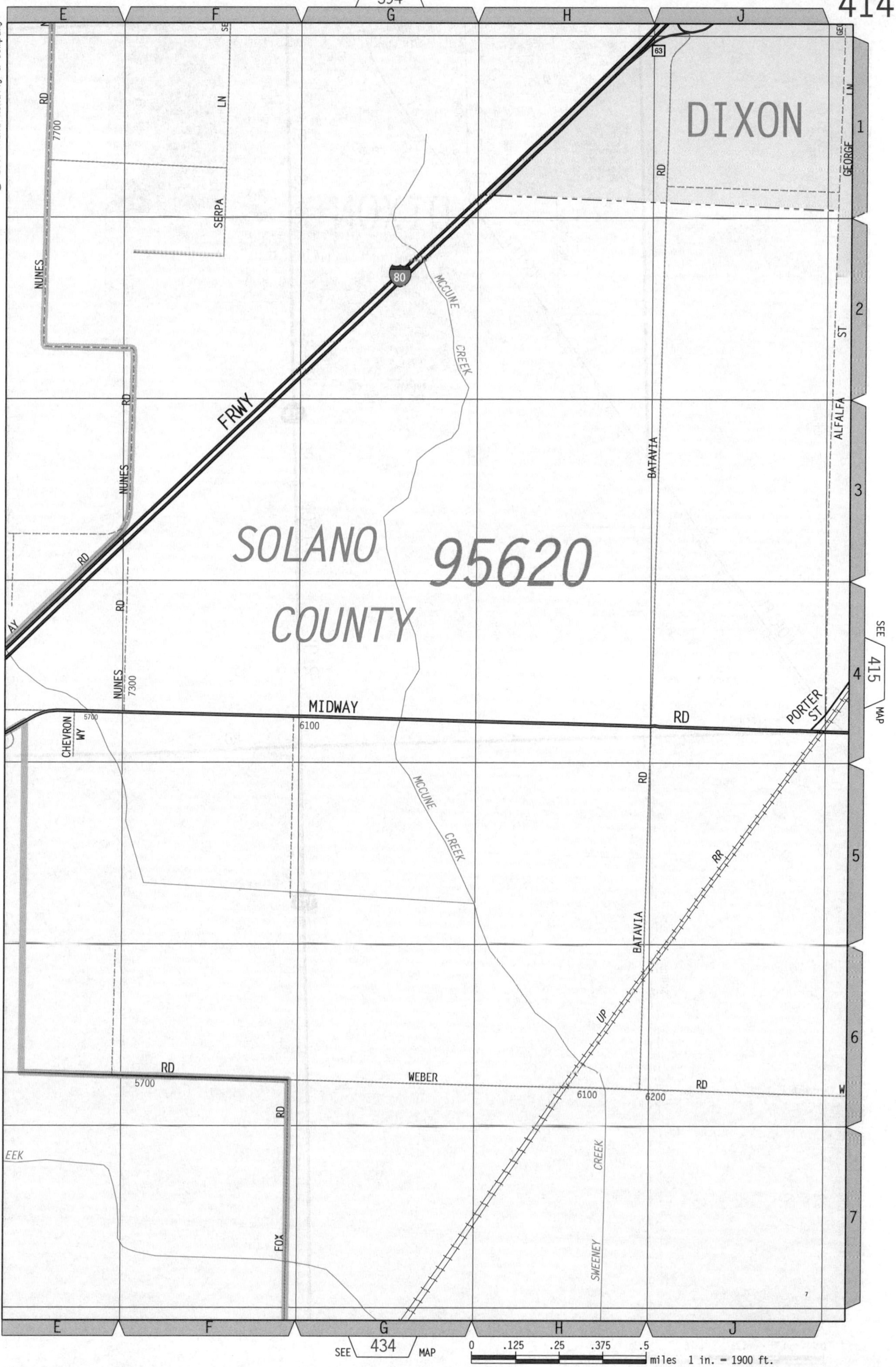
SEE 394 MAP
E
F
G
H
J
DIXON
SOLANO CO.
SOLANO COUNTY
95620
FRWY
80
63
MCCUNE CREEK
NUNES RD
7700
SERPA LN
GEORGE LN
BATAVIA RD
ALFALFA ST
MIDWAY RD
6100
5700
7300
CHEVRON WY
PORTER ST
SEE 415 MAP
UP RR
WEBER RD
6200
FOX RD
SWEENEY CREEK
EEK
1
2
3
4
5
6
7
SEE 434 MAP
0 .125 .25 .375 .5
miles 1 in. = 1900 ft.

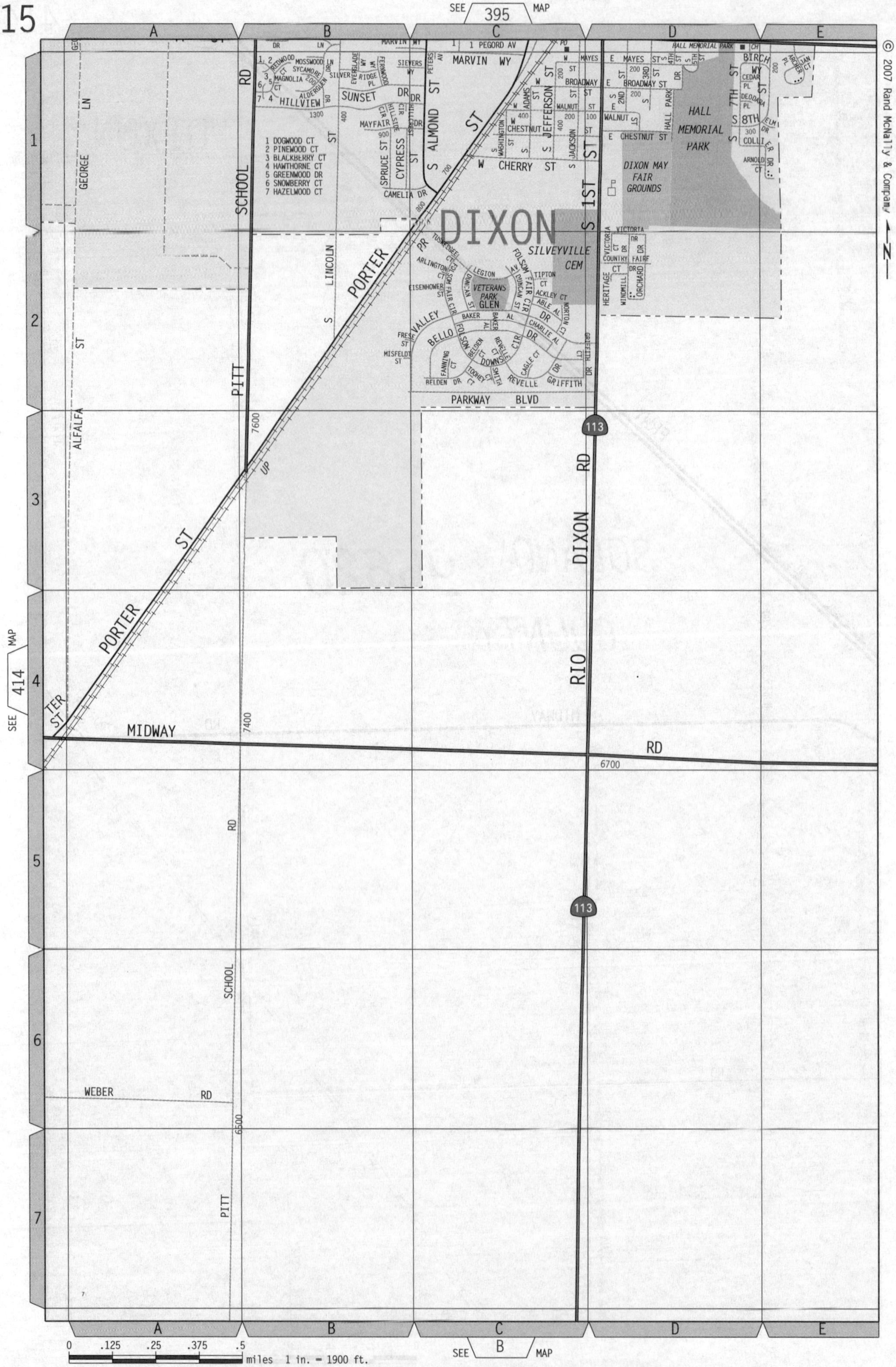
SEE 395 MAP
SEE 414 MAP
SEE B MAP
SOLANO CO.
© 2007 Rand McNally & Company
DIXON
SILVEYVILLE CEM
DIXON MAY FAIR GROUNDS
HALL MEMORIAL PARK
VETERANS PARK GLEN
1 DOGWOOD CT
2 PINEWOOD CT
3 BLACKBERRY CT
4 HAWTHORNE CT
5 GREENWOOD DR
6 SNOWBERRY CT
7 HAZELWOOD CT
MARVIN WY
PEGORD AV
HILLVIEW
SUNSET DR
MAYFAIR
CYPRESS ST
SPRUCE ST
CAMELIA DR
S ALMOND ST
W CHERRY ST
W CHESTNUT
JEFFERSON ST
JACKSON
S 1ST ST
E MAYES ST
BROADWAY
WALNUT
E CHESTNUT ST
HALL PARK DR
S 7TH ST
S 8TH
BIRCH WY
VICTORIA
COUNTRY CT
FAIRF DR
ORCHARD DR
WINDMILL
HERITAGE CT
TUSKEGEE CT
ARLINGTON CT
LEGION
EISENHOWER CT
FOLSOM FAIR CIR
DUNCAN ST
TIPTON CT
ACKLEY CT
ABLE AL
NORTON CT
BAKER AL
CHARLIE AL
VALLEY PR
BELLO
FOLSOM
BELDEN DR
FANNING CT
MISFELDT ST
DOWNS CIR
CAGLE CT
REVELLE
GRIFFITH DR
PARKWAY BLVD
GEORGE LN
ALFALFA ST
SCHOOL RD
PITT
PORTER ST
LINCOLN
UP
TER ST
MIDWAY RD
DIXON RIO RD
113
WEBER RD
PITT SCHOOL RD
7600
7400
6700
6500
A B C D E
1 2 3 4 5 6 7
0 .125 .25 .375 .5 miles 1 in. = 1900 ft.

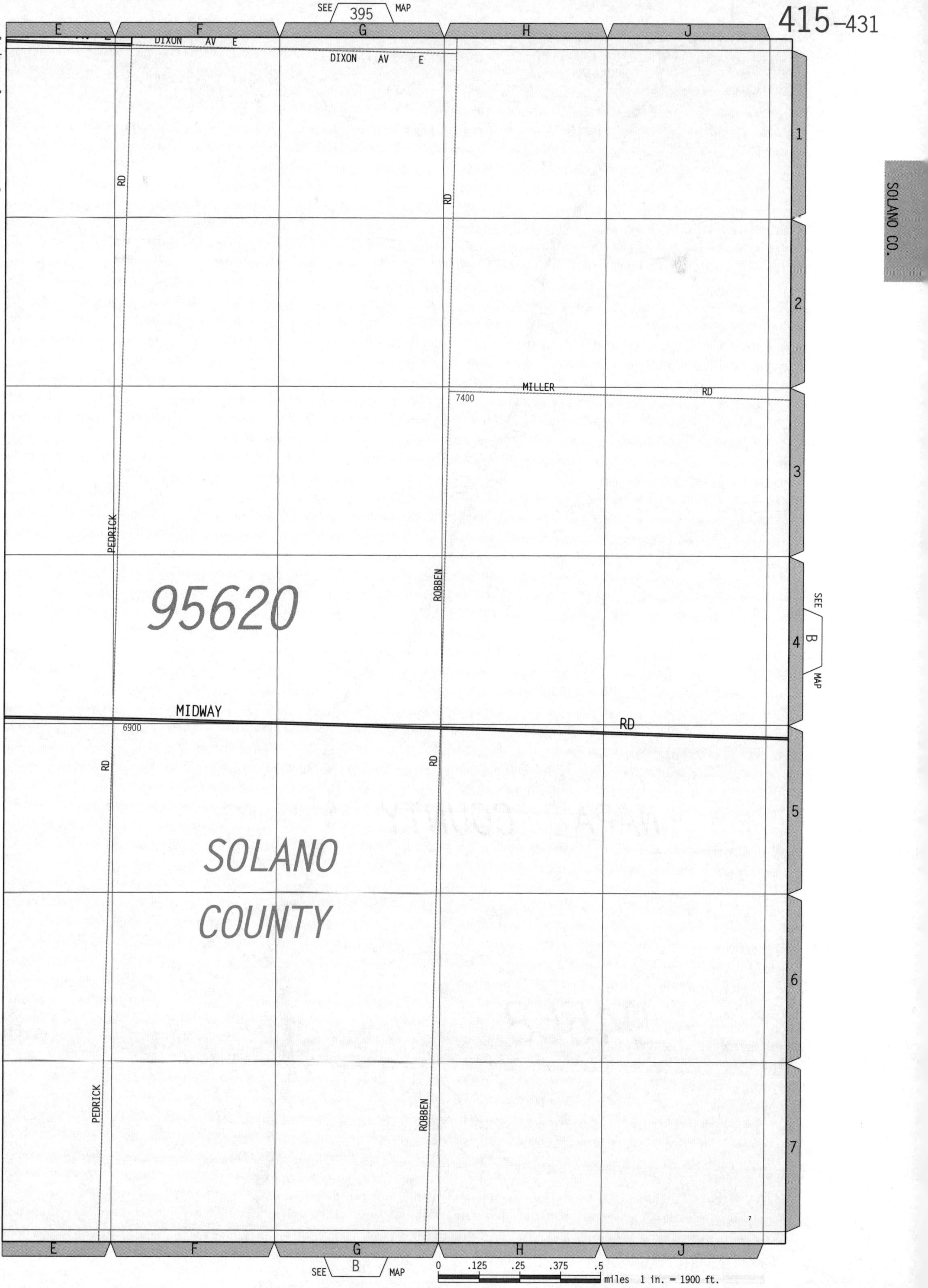
SEE 395 MAP
E
F
G
H
J
DIXON AV E
DIXON AV E
1
2
3
4
5
6
7
SOLANO CO.
RD
RD
MILLER RD
7400
PEDRICK
ROBBEN
95620
SEE B MAP
MIDWAY RD
6900
RD
RD
SOLANO
COUNTY
PEDRICK
ROBBEN
SEE B MAP
0 .125 .25 .375 .5
miles 1 in. = 1900 ft.

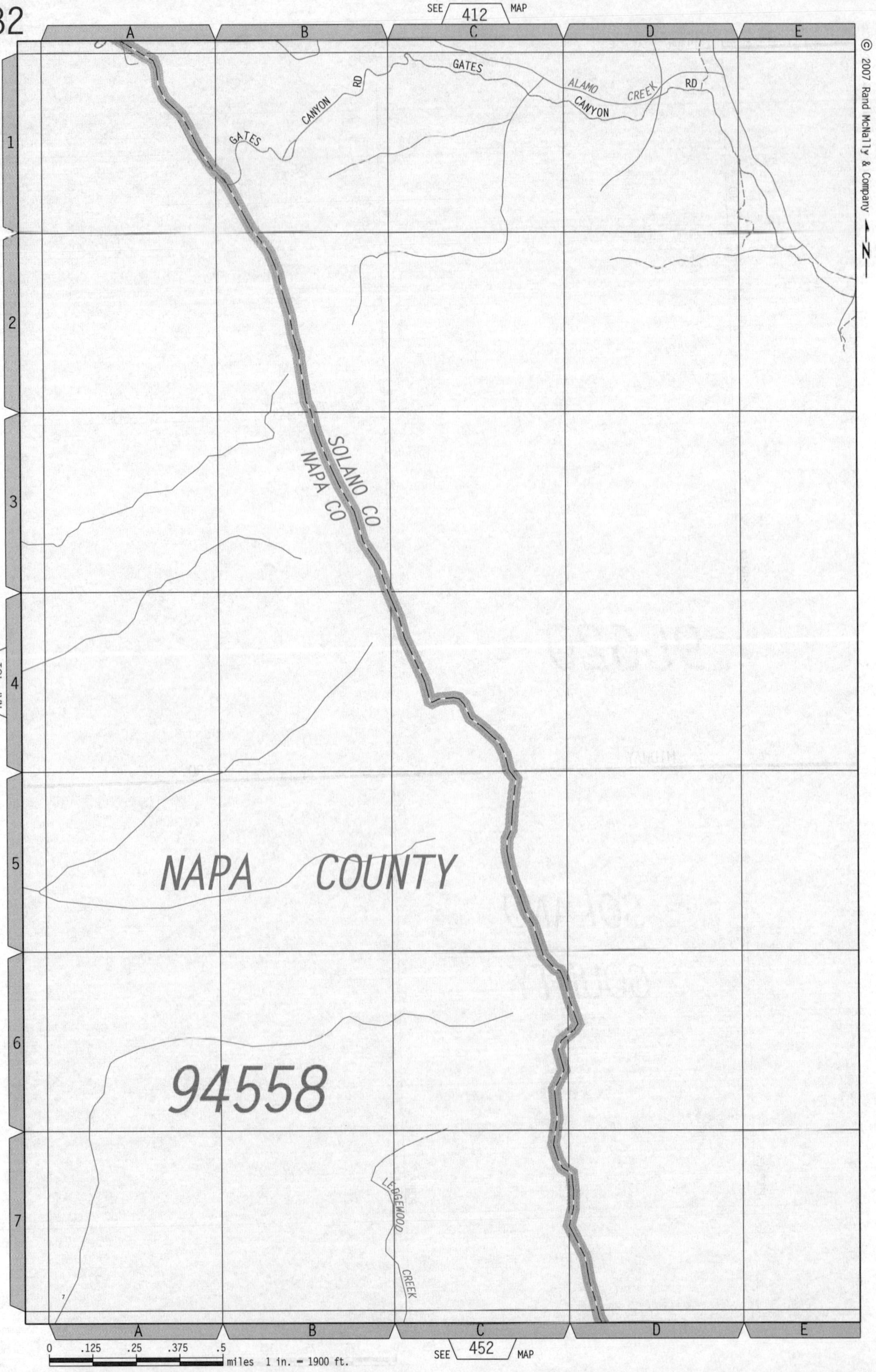
SEE 412 MAP
A
B
C
D
E
1
2
3
4
5
6
7
GATES CANYON RD
GATES
ALAMO CREEK RD
CANYON
SOLANO CO
NAPA CO
NAPA COUNTY
94558
LEDGEWOOD CREEK
SEE NAP 431 MAP
SOLANO CO.
© 2007 Rand McNally & Company
N
SEE 452 MAP
0 .125 .25 .375 .5 miles 1 in. = 1900 ft.

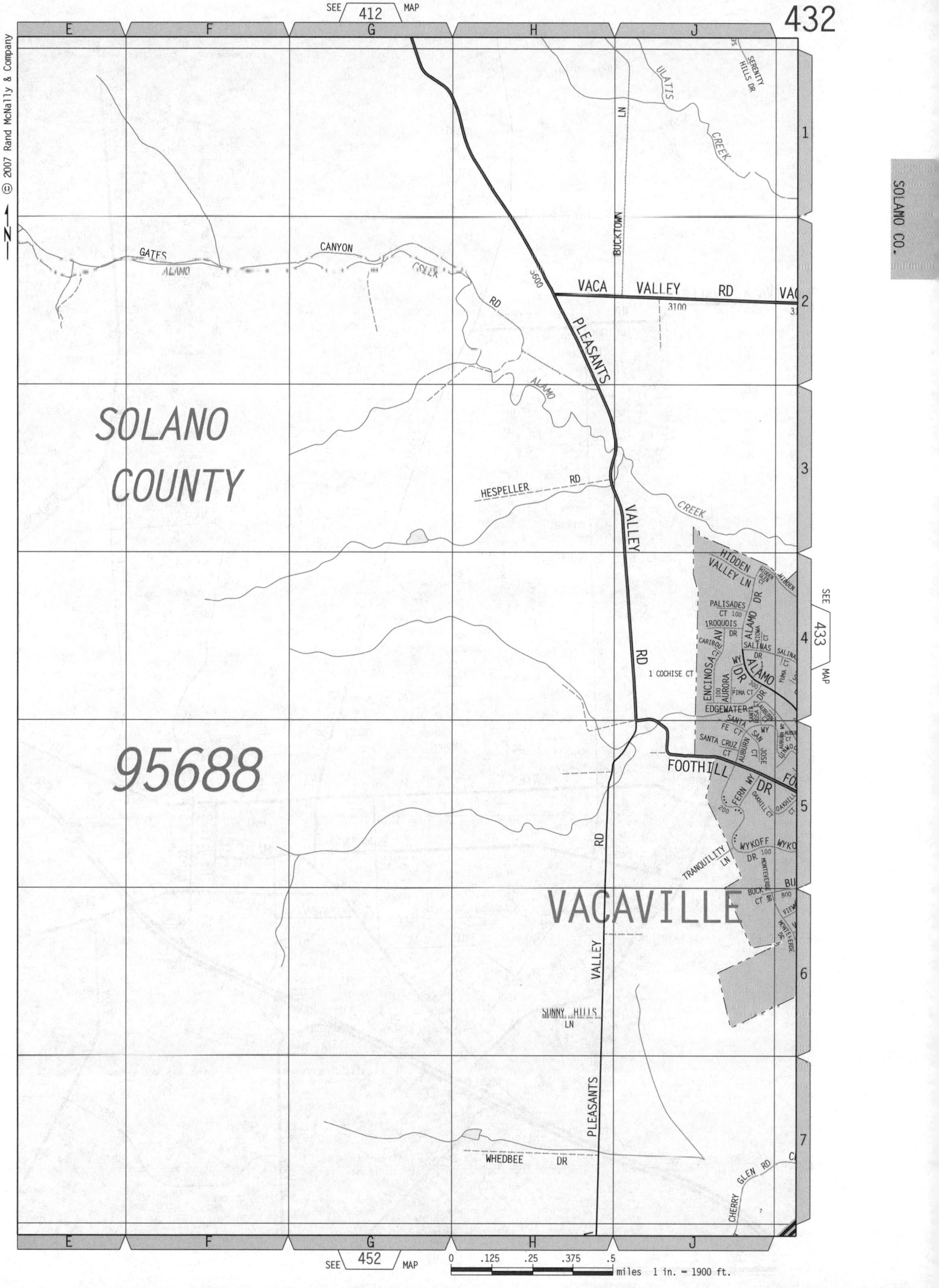
SEE 412 MAP
E
F
G
H
J
SOLANO CO.
© 2007 Rand McNally & Company
1
2
3
4
5
6
7
SERENITY HILLS DR
ULATIS
CREEK
BUCKTOWN LN
GATES
CANYON
ALAMO
CREEK
RD
3600
VACA VALLEY RD
3100
PLEASANTS
ALAMO
SOLANO COUNTY
HESPELLER RD
VALLEY
CREEK
HIDDEN VALLEY LN
HIDDEN BLFF CT
PALISADES CT 100
IROQUOIS DR
ALAMO DR
CARIBOU CT
AV
SALINAS DR
ENCINOSA
WY
DR
ALAMO
1 COCHISE CT
AURORA
PIMA CT
EDGEWATER
SANTA FE CT
SANTA CRUZ CT
AUBURN
SAN JOSE CT
FOOTHILL DR
95688
FERN WY
OAKHILL CT
WYKOFF DR
TRANQUILITY LN
BUCK CT
MONTEVERDE DR
VACAVILLE
RD
VALLEY
SUNNY HILLS LN
PLEASANTS
WHEDBEE DR
CHERRY GLEN RD
SEE 433 MAP
SEE 452 MAP
0 .125 .25 .375 .5
miles 1 in. = 1900 ft.

SEE 413 MAP

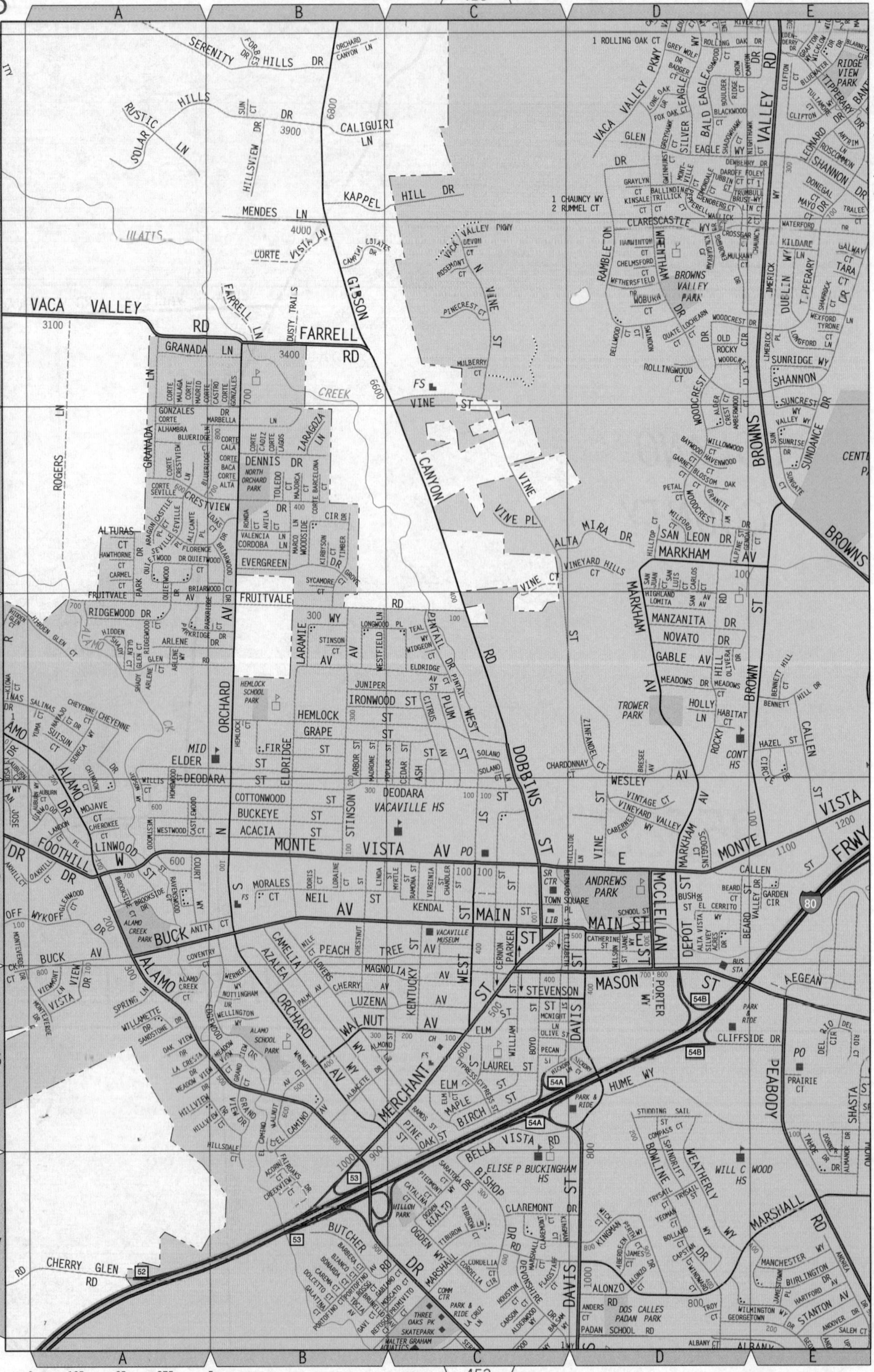

SEE 432 MAP

SEE 453 MAP

0 .125 .25 .375 .5 miles 1 in. = 1900 ft.

SEE 413 MAP

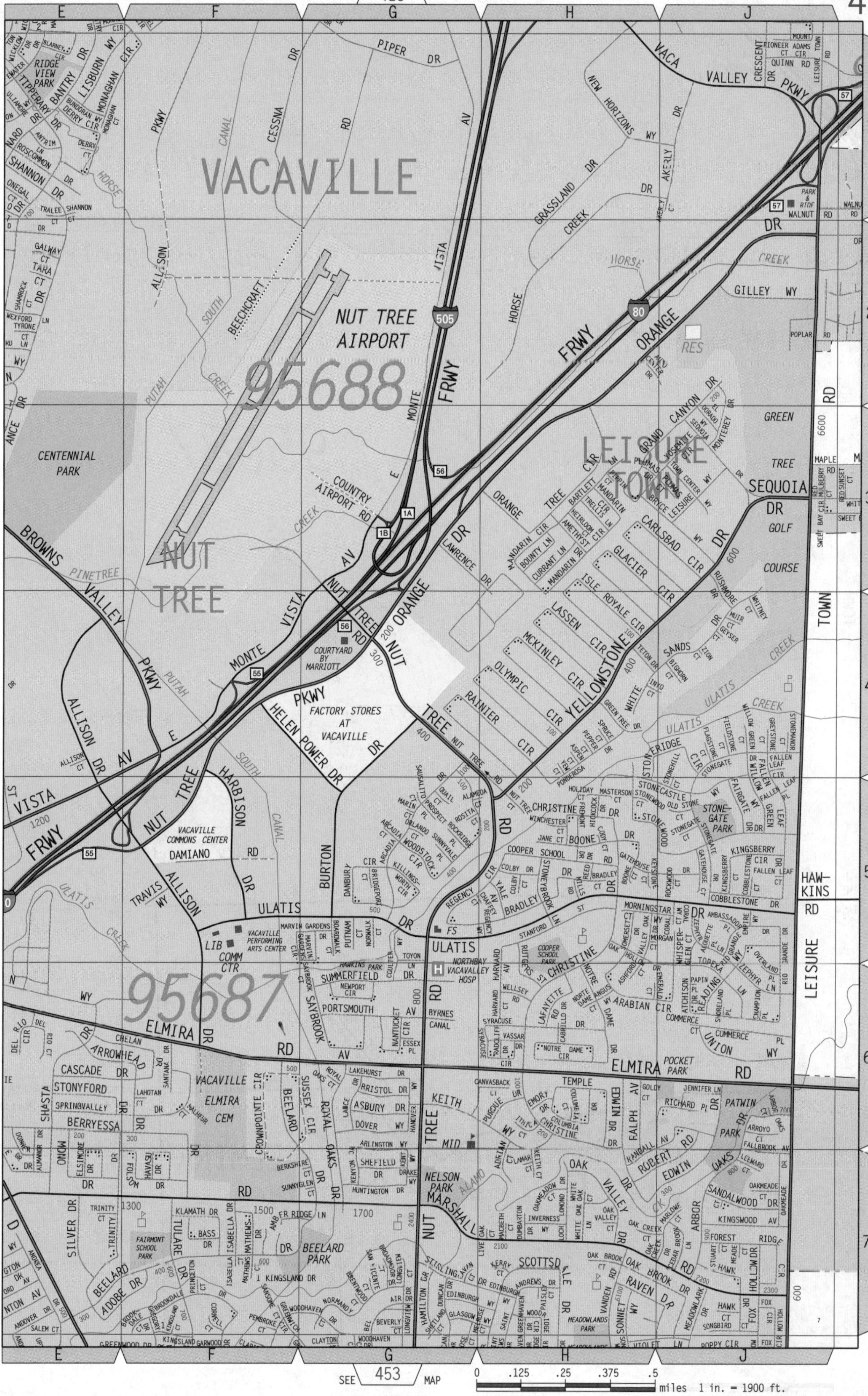

SEE 434 MAP

SEE 453 MAP

0 .125 .25 .375 .5 miles 1 in. = 1900 ft.

SOLANO CO.

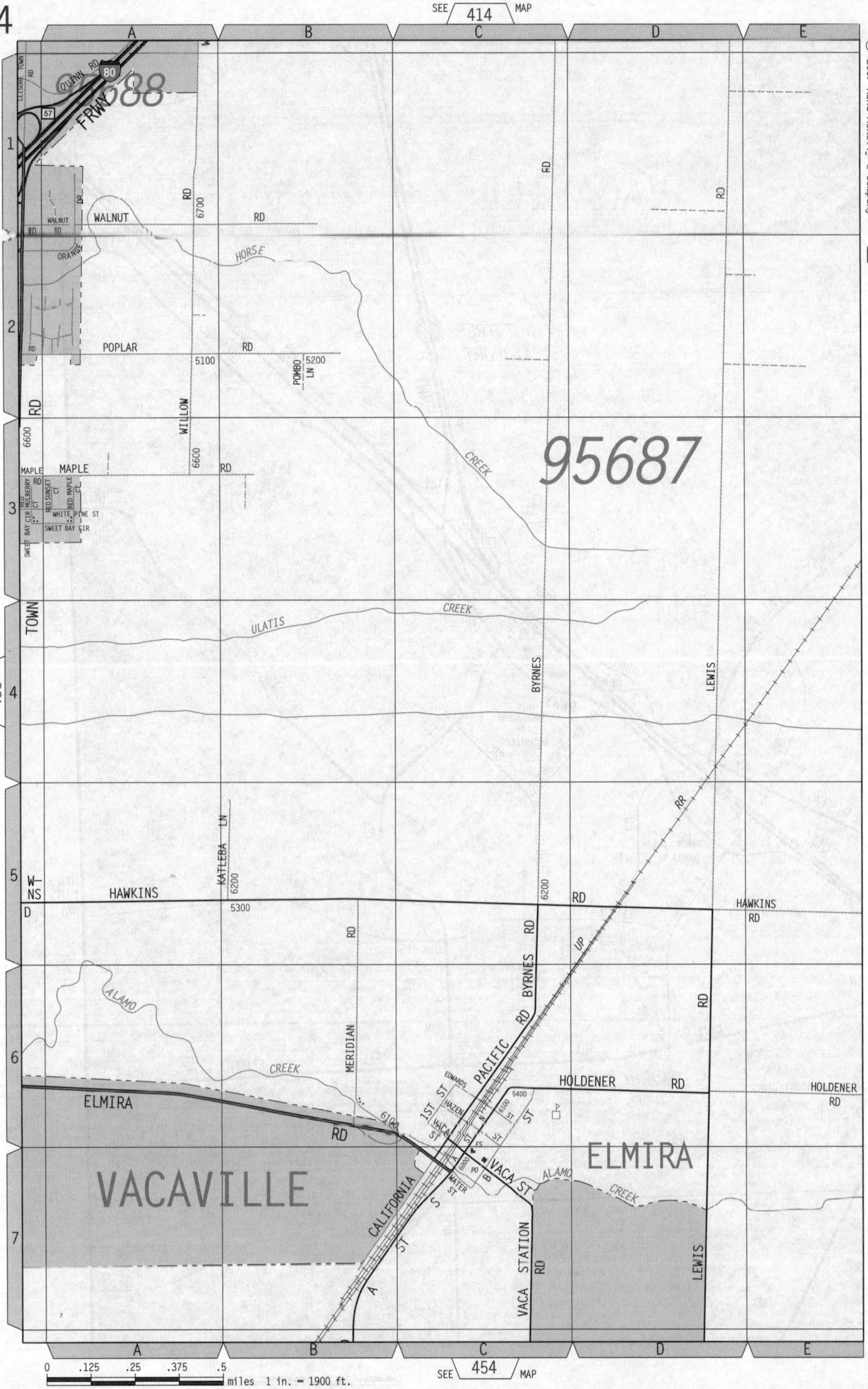
SEE 414 MAP
SEE 454 MAP
SEE 433 MAP
SOLANO CO.
95688
95687
80
57
QUINN RD
LEISURE TOWN RD
FRWY
WALNUT RD
WALNUT
ORANGE
DR
HORSE CREEK
POPLAR RD
5100
5200
POMBO LN
WILLOW
6700
6600
RD
MAPLE RD
MAPLE
MULBERRY
RED SUNSET CT
RED MAPLE CT
WHITE PINE ST
SWEET BAY CIR
TOWN
ULATIS CREEK
BYRNES
LEWIS
RR
UP
KATLEBA LN
6200
HAWKINS RD
5300
MERIDIAN RD
BYRNES RD
PACIFIC RD
ALAMO CREEK
ELMIRA RD
6100
EDWARDS
1ST ST
HAZEN
VACA ST
HOLDENER RD
5400
6000
PO
WATER ST
CALIFORNIA ST
VACA STATION RD
VACAVILLE
ELMIRA
A ST
W-NS
D

0 .125 .25 .375 .5 miles 1 in. = 1900 ft.

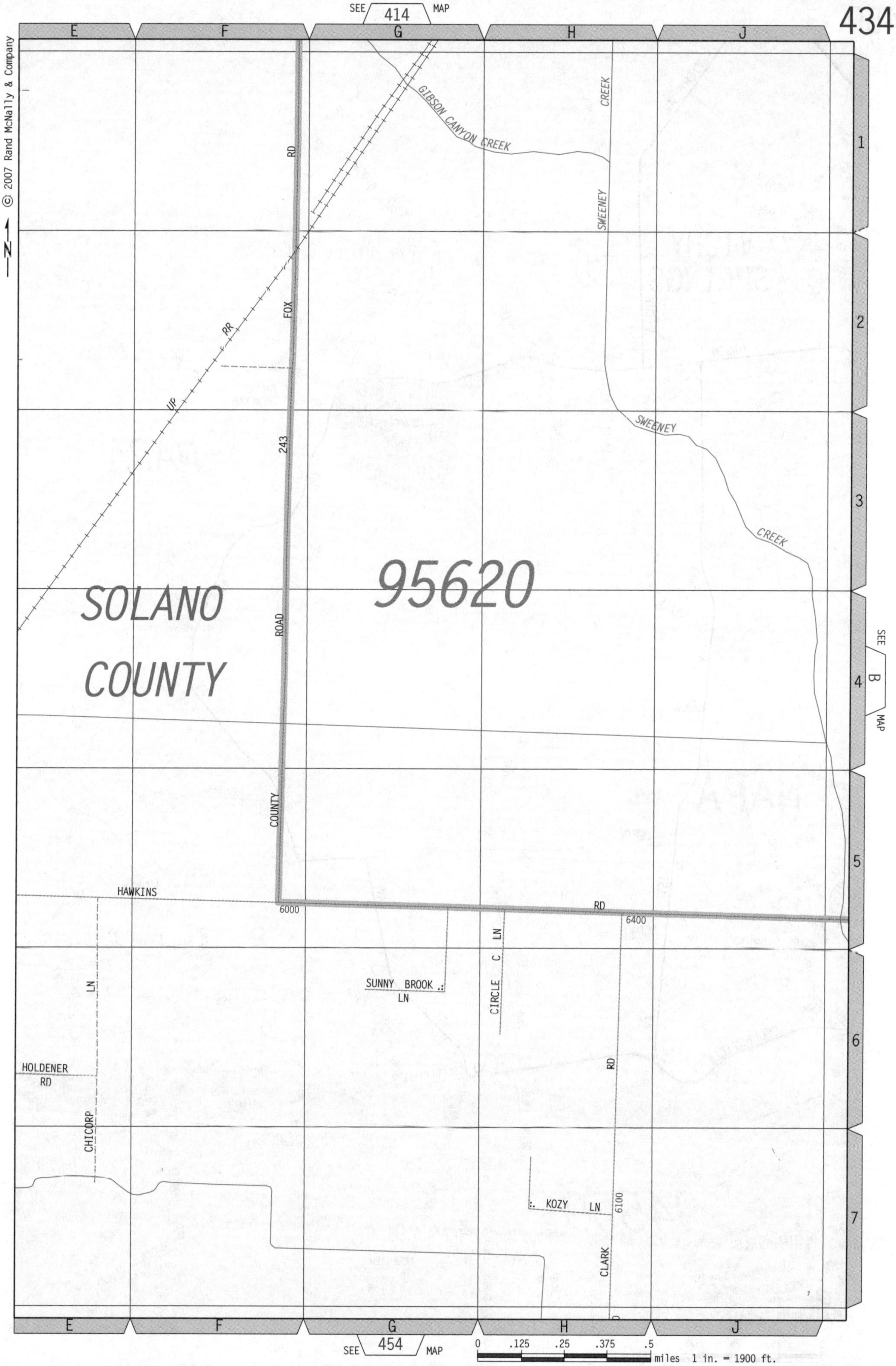
SEE 414 MAP
E
F
G
H
J
1
2
3
4
5
6
7
SEE B MAP
GIBSON CANYON CREEK
SWEENEY CREEK
SWEENEY CREEK
UP RR
FOX RD
COUNTY ROAD 243
95620
SOLANO
COUNTY
HAWKINS RD
6000
6400
SUNNY BROOK LN
CIRCLE C LN
LN
HOLDENER RD
CHICORP
KOZY LN
CLARK RD
6100
SEE 454 MAP
0 .125 .25 .375 .5
miles 1 in. = 1900 ft.

SEE NAP 430 MAP

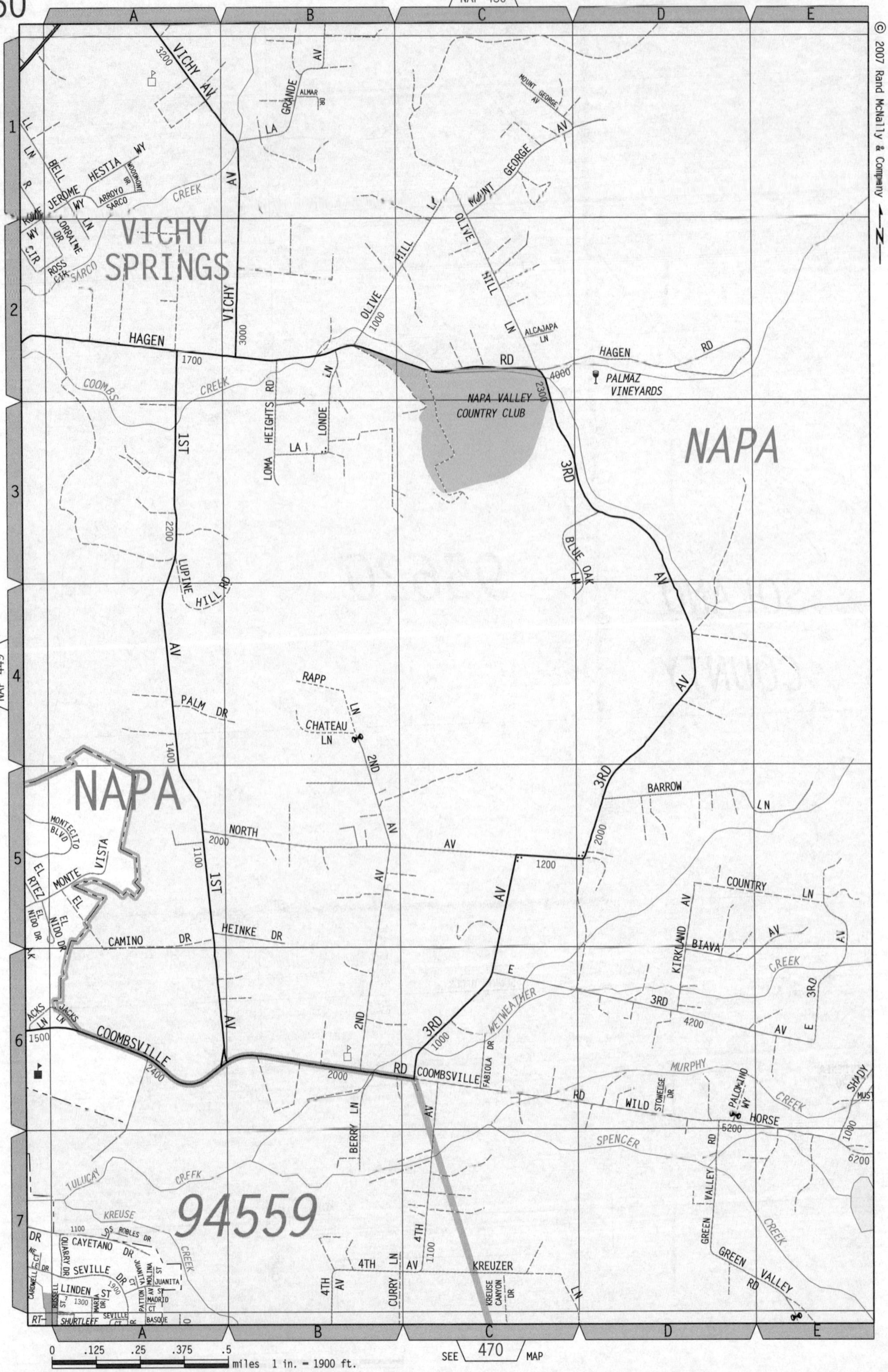
VICHY SPRINGS
NAPA
NAPA
94559
VICHY AV
3200
3000
LA GRANDE AV
ALMAR DR
MOUNT GEORGE AV
MOUNT GEORGE
HESTIA WY
BELL
JERDOME WY
ARROYO SARCO
LORRAINE DR
ROSS CIR
SARCO
CREEK
OLIVE HILL LN
1000
ALCAJAPA LN
HAGEN RD
HAGEN
1700
4000
2300
PALMAZ VINEYARDS
NAPA VALLEY COUNTRY CLUB
COOMBS CREEK
LOMA HEIGHTS RD
LONDE LN
LA
1ST AV
2200
LUPINE HILL RD
3RD AV
BLUE OAK LN
PALM DR
RAPP LN
CHATEAU LN
2ND AV
1400
BARROW LN
NORTH AV
2000
1100
1200
MONTECITO BLVD
MONTE VISTA
EL RTEZ
EL NIDO DR
CAMINO DR
HEINKE DR
COUNTRY LN
KIRKLAND AV
BIAVA AV
E
3RD
4200
JACKS LN
1500
COOMBSVILLE RD
2400
WETWEATHER CREEK
FABIOLA DR
COOMBSVILLE
WILD HORSE
STONEDGE DR
PALOMINO WY
MURPHY CREEK
5200
6200
SHADY
BERRY LN
SPENCER
TULUCAY CREEK
KREUSE CREEK
GREEN VALLEY RD
CAYETANO DR
DOS ROBLES DR
QUARRY DR
SEVILLE DR
LINDEN ST
RUSSELL ST
1300
1900
JUANITA
MOLINA
MADRID
MARIA DR
PATTON
SHURTLEFF
BASQUE
CARDWELL
4TH AV
4TH
CURRY LN
KREUZER LN
KREUSE CANYON DR
0 .125 .25 .375 .5 miles 1 in. = 1900 ft.
SOLANO CO.

SEE NAP 449 MAP

SEE 470 MAP

SEE NAP 430 MAP

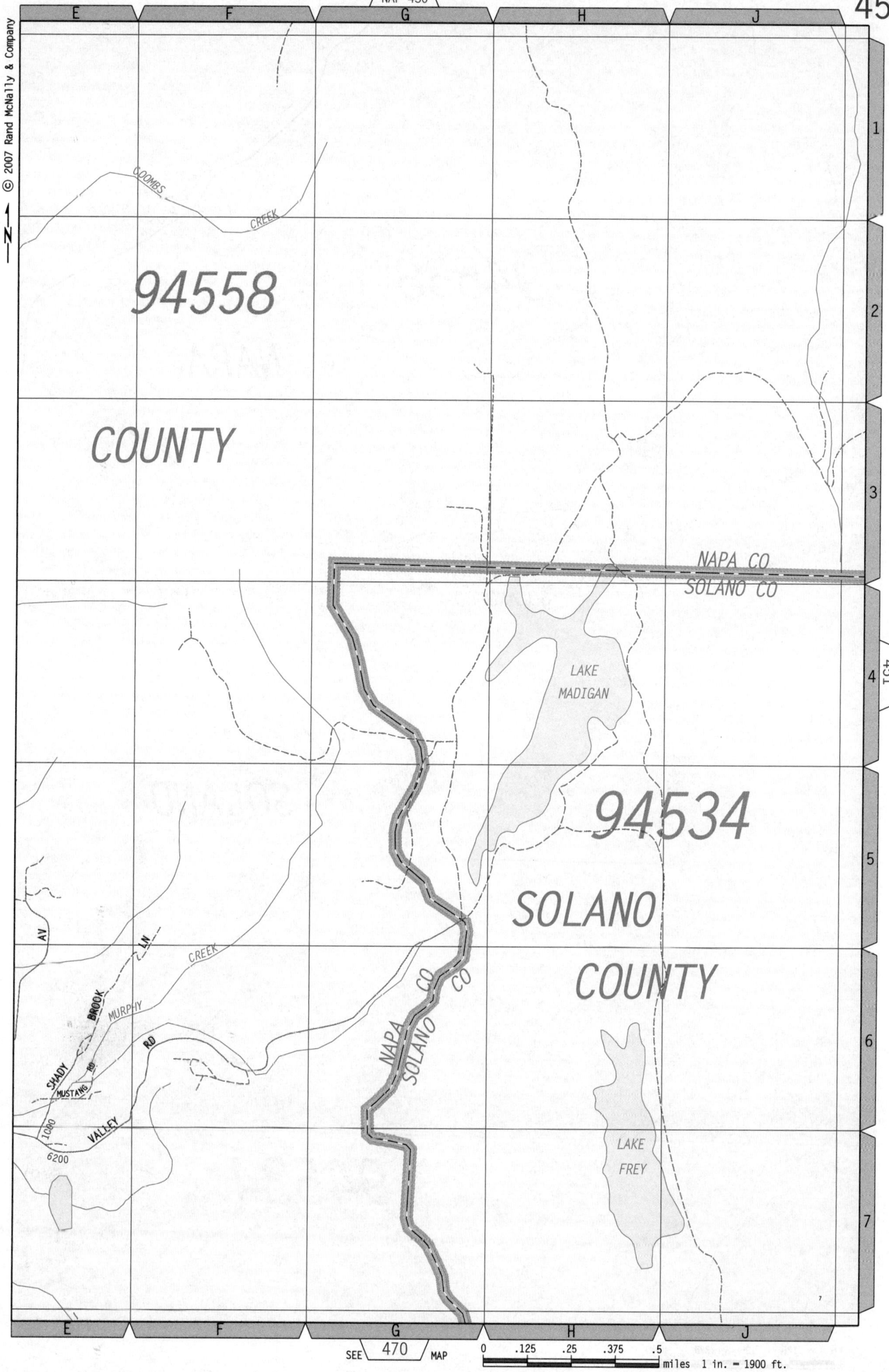
E
F
G
H
J
1
2
3
4
5
6
7
COOMBS
CREEK
94558
COUNTY
NAPA CO
SOLANO CO
LAKE
MADIGAN
94534
SOLANO
COUNTY
NAPA
SOLANO
CO
CO
AV
LN
CREEK
BROOK
MURPHY
SHADY
RD
RD
MUSTANG
1080
VALLEY
6200
LAKE
FREY
0
.125
.25
.375
.5
miles 1 in. = 1900 ft.

SEE 451 MAP

SEE 470 MAP

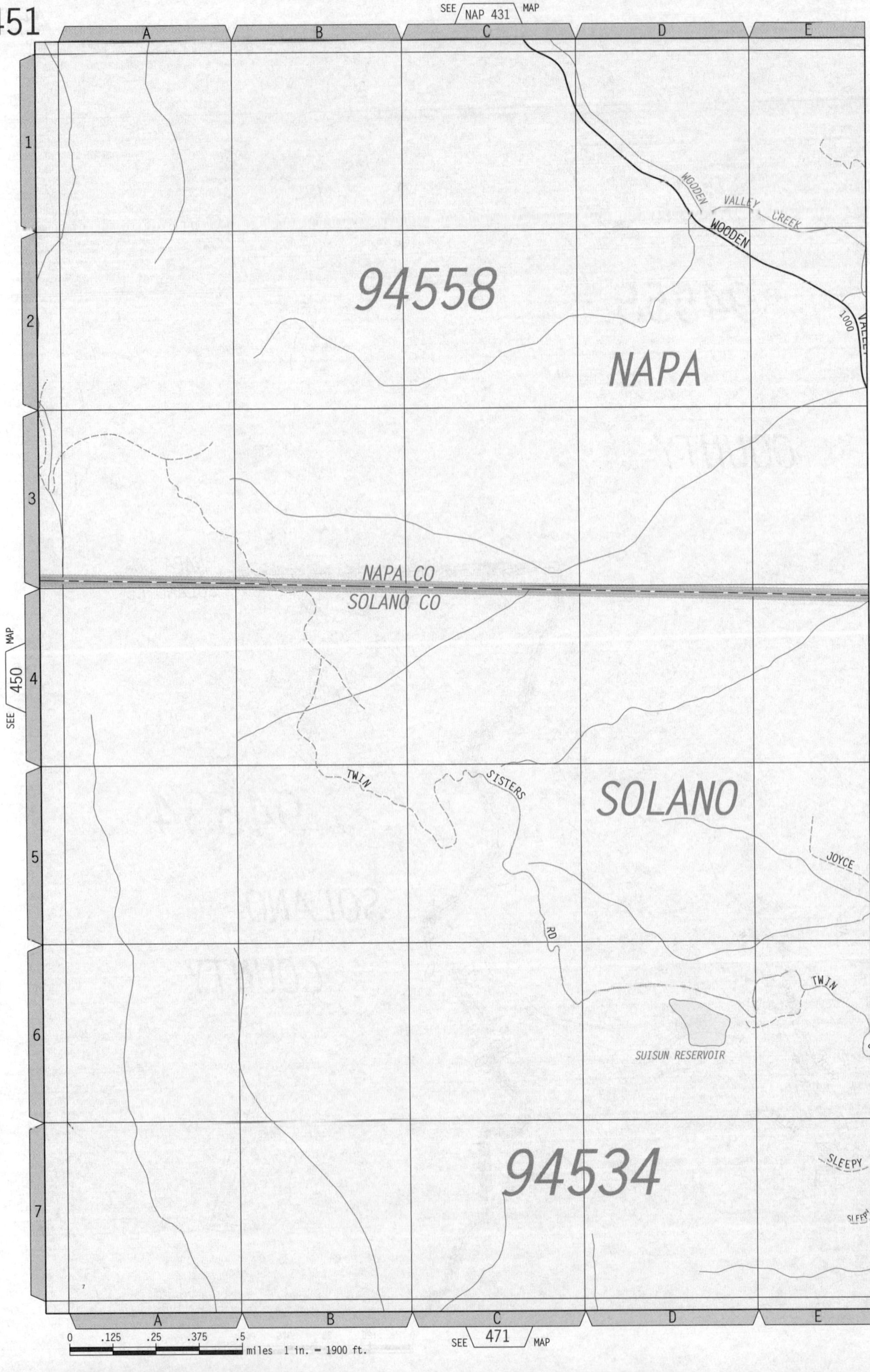
SEE NAP 431 MAP
A
B
C
D
E
1
2
3
4
5
6
7
WOODEN
VALLEY
CREEK
WOODEN
1000
VALLEY
94558
NAPA
NAPA CO
SOLANO CO
SEE 450 MAP
TWIN
SISTERS
RD
SOLANO
JOYCE
TWIN
SUISUN RESERVOIR
94534
SLEEPY
SLEEPY
0
.125
.25
.375
.5
miles 1 in. = 1900 ft.
SEE 471 MAP

SEE NAP 431 MAP

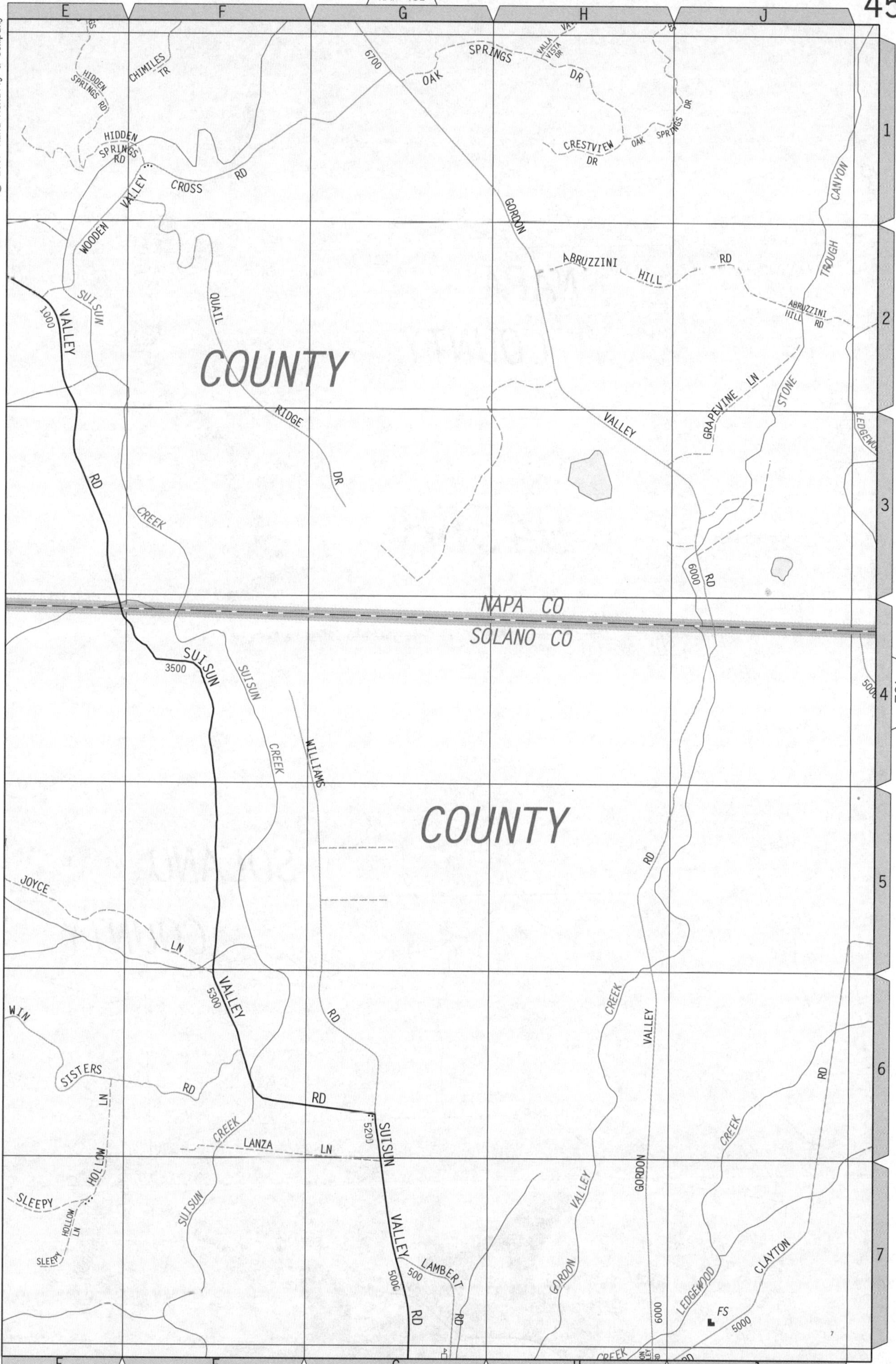

SEE 452 MAP

SEE 471 MAP

0 .125 .25 .375 .5 miles 1 in. = 1900 ft.

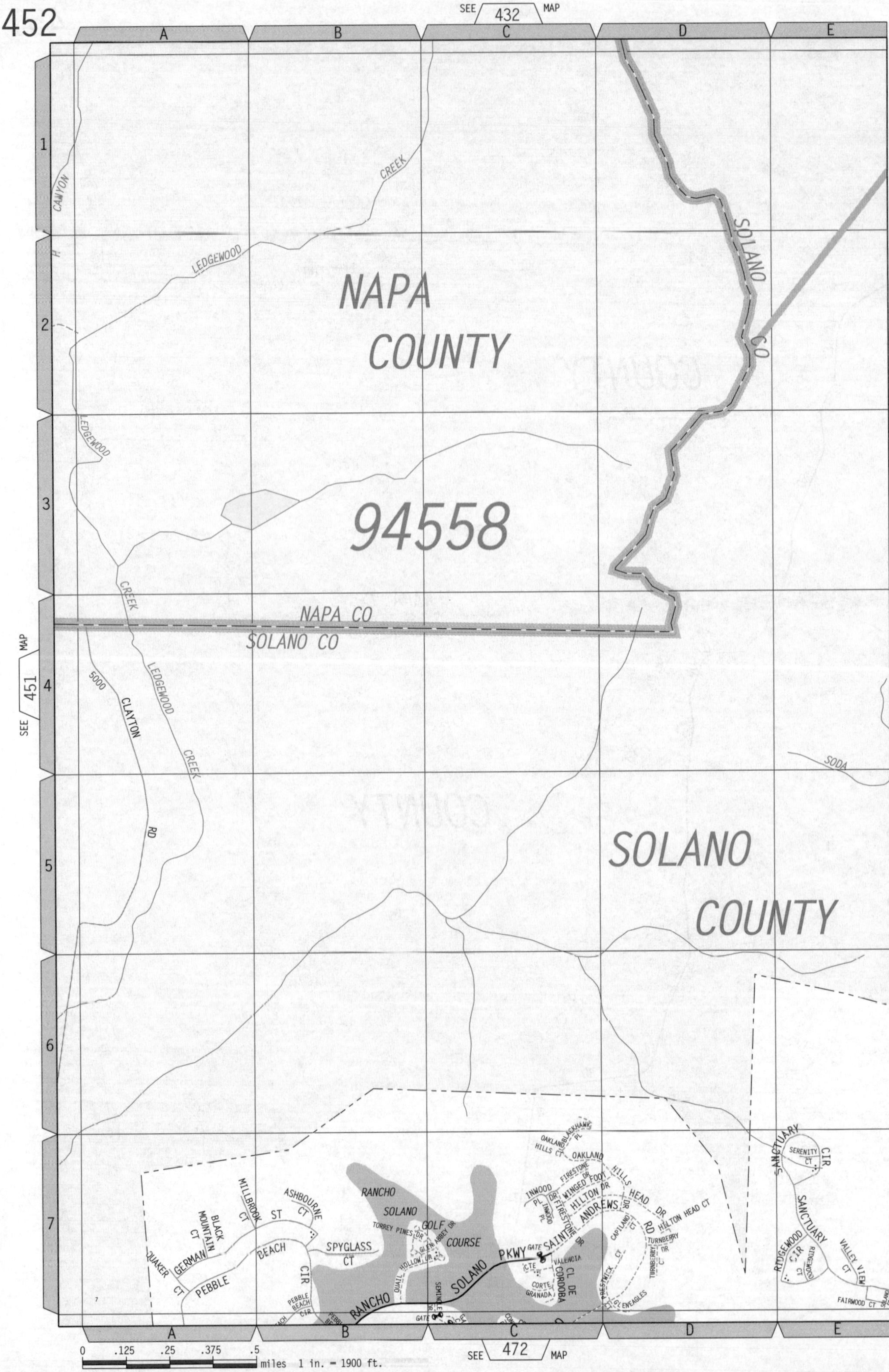
SEE 432 MAP
SEE 451 MAP
SEE 472 MAP
A
B
C
D
E
1
2
3
4
5
6
7
NAPA
COUNTY
94558
SOLANO
COUNTY
NAPA CO
SOLANO CO
SOLANO
CO
CANYON
LEDGEWOOD
CREEK
LEDGEWOOD
CREEK
5000
CLAYTON
RD
LEDGEWOOD
CREEK
SODA
RANCHO
SOLANO
GOLF
COURSE
RANCHO
SOLANO
PKWY
GATE
SAINT
ANDREWS
RD
MILLBROOK
CT
ST
ASHBOURNE
CT
BLACK
MOUNTAIN
CT
GERMAN
QUAKER
CT
PEBBLE
BEACH
CIR
SPYGLASS
CT
PEBBLE
BEACH
CIR
TORREY PINES DR
GLEN ABBEY DR
QUAIL HOLLOW DR
SEMINOLE DR
GATE
OAKLAND HILLS CT
BLACKHAWK PL
OAKLAND
HILLS
HEAD
DR
HILTON HEAD CT
FIRESTONE DR
WINGED FOOT DR
HILTON DR
INWOOD PL
INWOOD PL
FIRESTONE DR
VALENCIA
CTE
CORTE GRANADA
CL DE CORDOBA
CAPILANO CT
TURNBERRY DR
TURNBERRY CT
PRESTWICK CT
GLENEAGLES
SANCTUARY
CIR
SERENITY CT
SANCTUARY
RIDGEWOOD CIR
RIDGEWOOD CT
VALLEY VIEW CT
FAIRWOOD CT
SOLANO FOOT
0 .125 .25 .375 .5
miles 1 in. = 1900 ft.

SEE 432 MAP

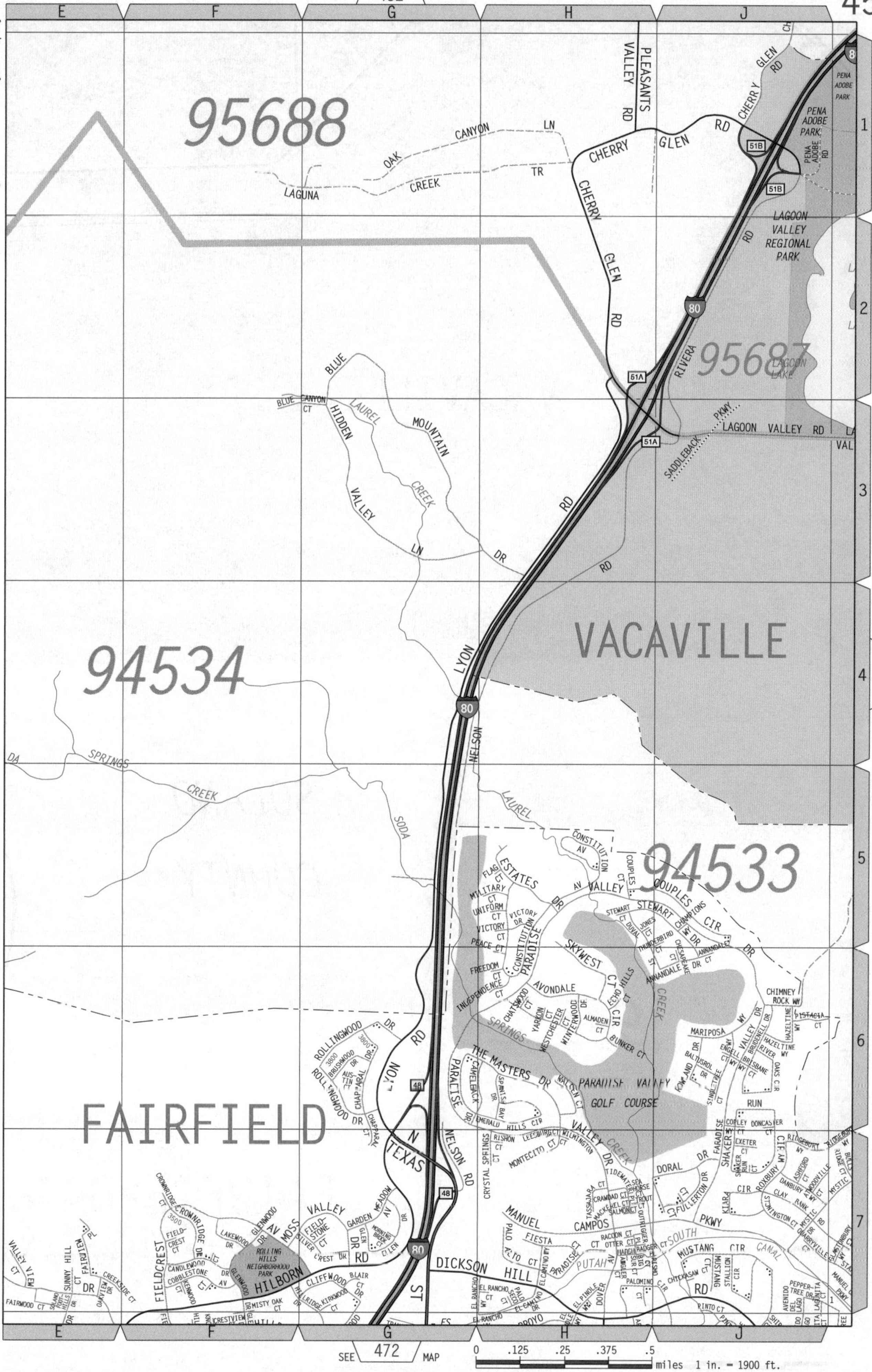

SEE 453 MAP

SEE 472 MAP

0 .125 .25 .375 .5 miles 1 in. = 1900 ft.

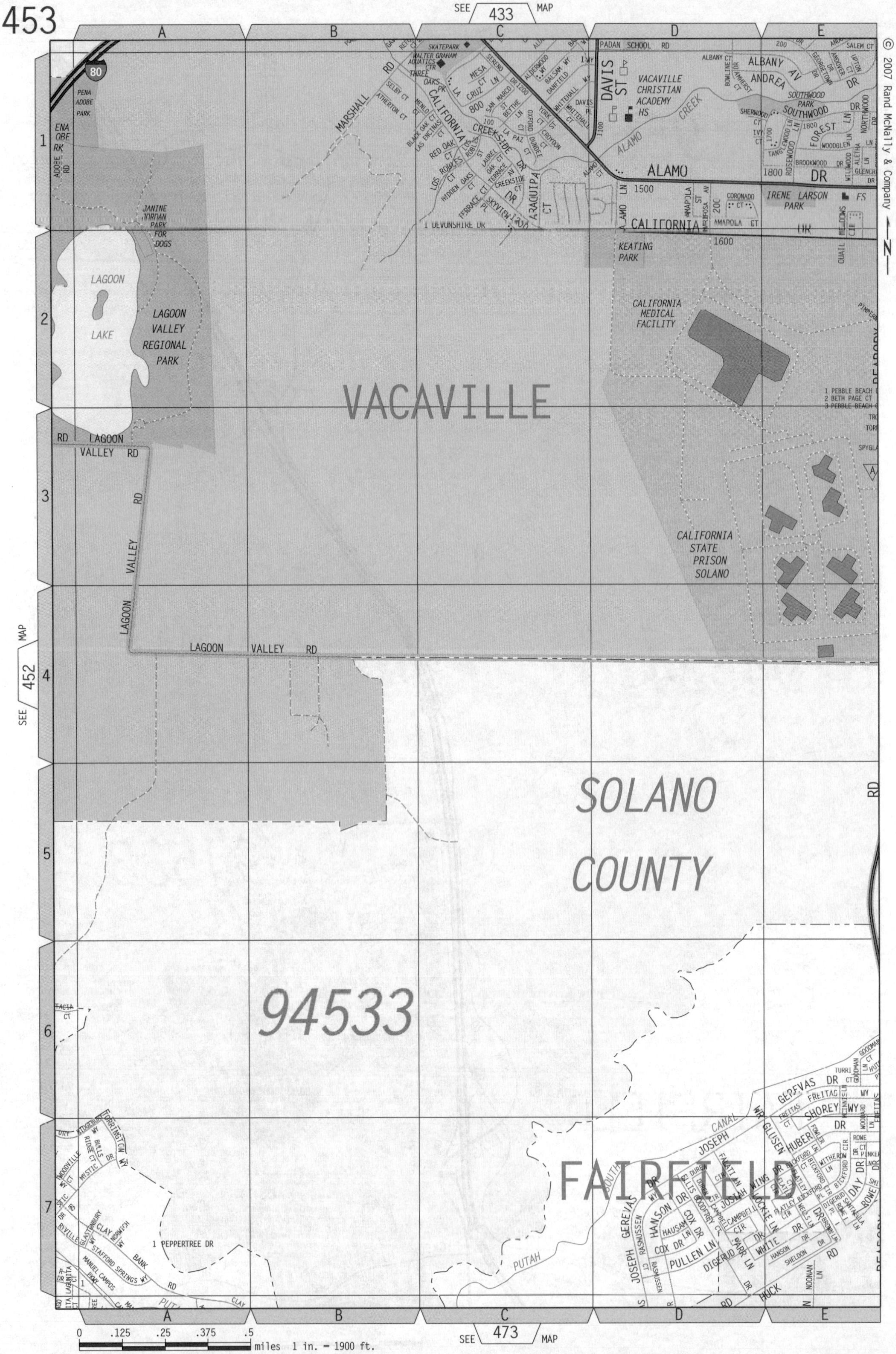
SEE 433 MAP
SEE 452 MAP
SEE 473 MAP
A
B
C
D
E
1
2
3
4
5
6
7
VACAVILLE
SOLANO
COUNTY
FAIRFIELD
94533
80
PENA ADOBE PARK
JANINE JORDAN PARK FOR DOGS
LAGOON
LAKE
LAGOON VALLEY REGIONAL PARK
LAGOON VALLEY RD
MARSHALL RD
CALIFORNIA
CREEKSIDE DR
ARAQUIPA CT
ALAMO DR
ALAMO CREEK
DAVIS ST
PADAN SCHOOL RD
VACAVILLE CHRISTIAN ACADEMY HS
ALBANY AV
ANDREA
SOUTHWOOD DR
SOUTHWOOD PARK
FOREST LN
BROOKWOOD DR
IRENE LARSON PARK
KEATING PARK
CALIFORNIA MEDICAL FACILITY
CALIFORNIA STATE PRISON SOLANO
SKATEPARK
WALTER GRAHAM AQUATICS CTR
THREE OAKS PK
1 DEVONSHIRE DR
1 PEBBLE BEACH CT
2 BETH PAGE CT
3 PEBBLE BEACH CT
GEREVAS DR
FREITAG WY
SHOREY WY
JOSEPH
GLUSEN
HUBER
HANSON DR
COX DR
PULLEN LN
DIGERUD
HUCK
NOONAN LN
PUTAH
SOUTH
CANAL
1 PEPPERTREE DR
STAFFORD SPRINGS WY
MANUEL CAMPOS PKY
BANK
CLAY
0
.125
.25
.375
.5
miles 1 in. = 1900 ft.

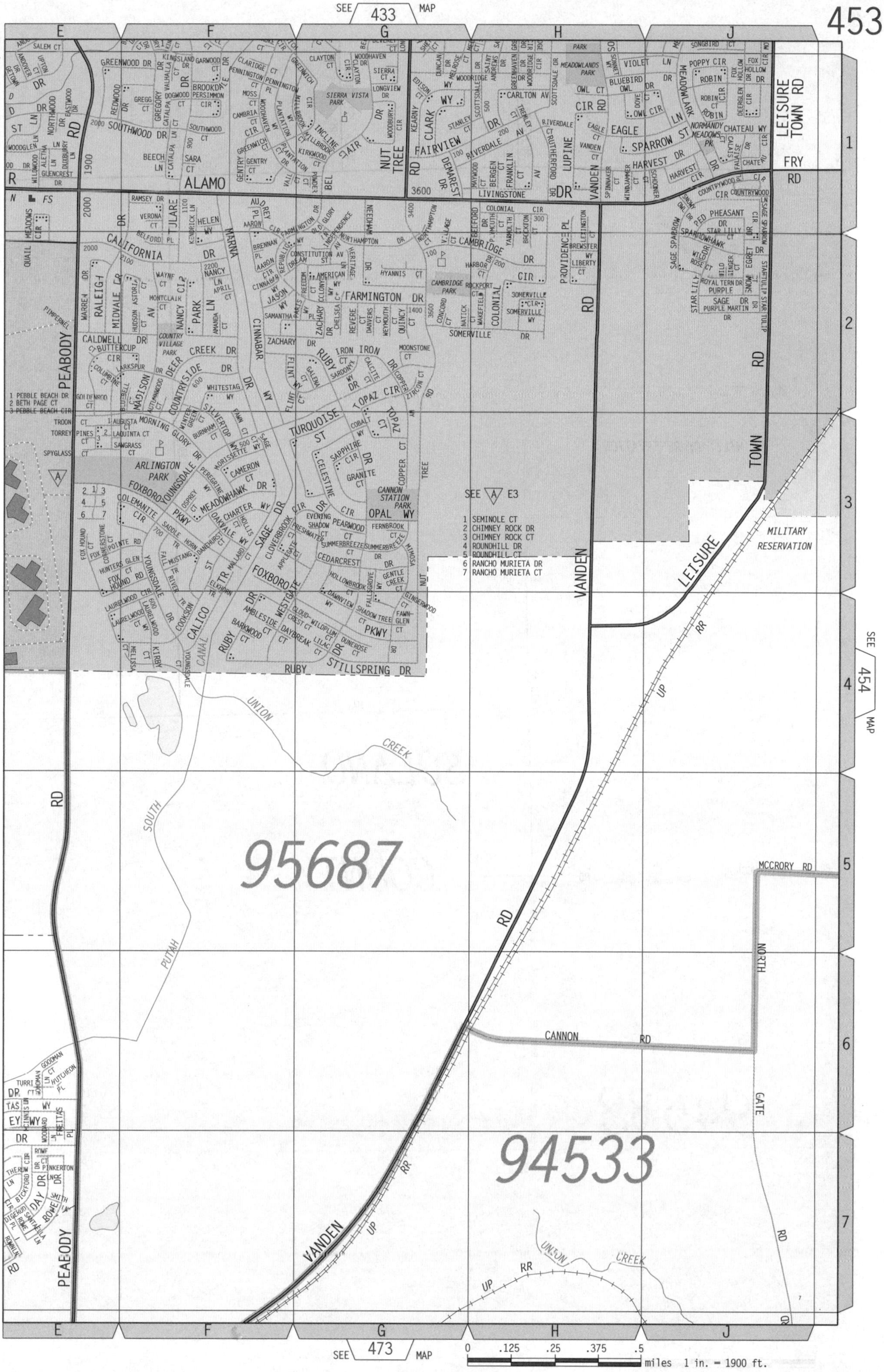

SEE 433 MAP
SEE 454 MAP
SEE 473 MAP
SOLANO CO.
E
F
G
H
J
1
2
3
4
5
6
7
ALAMO DR
LEISURE TOWN RD
FRY RD
PEABODY RD
VANDEN RD
CALIFORNIA DR
FARMINGTON DR
CAMBRIDGE DR
LIVINGSTONE DR
NUT TREE RD
SOUTHWOOD DR
FAIRVIEW DR
RIVERDALE AV
SPARROW ST
EAGLE
HARVEST DR
CINNABAR DR
MARNA DR
TURQUOISE ST
TOPAZ CIR
YOUNGSDALE DR
FOXBORO PKWY
STILLSPRING DR
RUBY DR
SIERRA VISTA PARK
CAMBRIDGE PARK
COUNTRY VILLAGE PARK
ARLINGTON PARK
CANNON STATION PARK
MEADOWLANDS PARK
NORMANDY MEADOWS PK
SEE A E3
1 SEMINOLE CT
2 CHIMNEY ROCK DR
3 CHIMNEY ROCK CT
4 ROUNDHILL DR
5 ROUNDHILL CT
6 RANCHO MURIETA DR
7 RANCHO MURIETA CT
1 PEBBLE BEACH DR
2 BETH PAGE CT
3 PEBBLE BEACH CIR
MILITARY RESERVATION
UNION CREEK
SOUTH PUTAH CANAL
UP RR
95687
94533
MCCRORY RD
NORTH GATE RD
CANNON RD
0 .125 .25 .375 .5
miles 1 in. = 1900 ft.

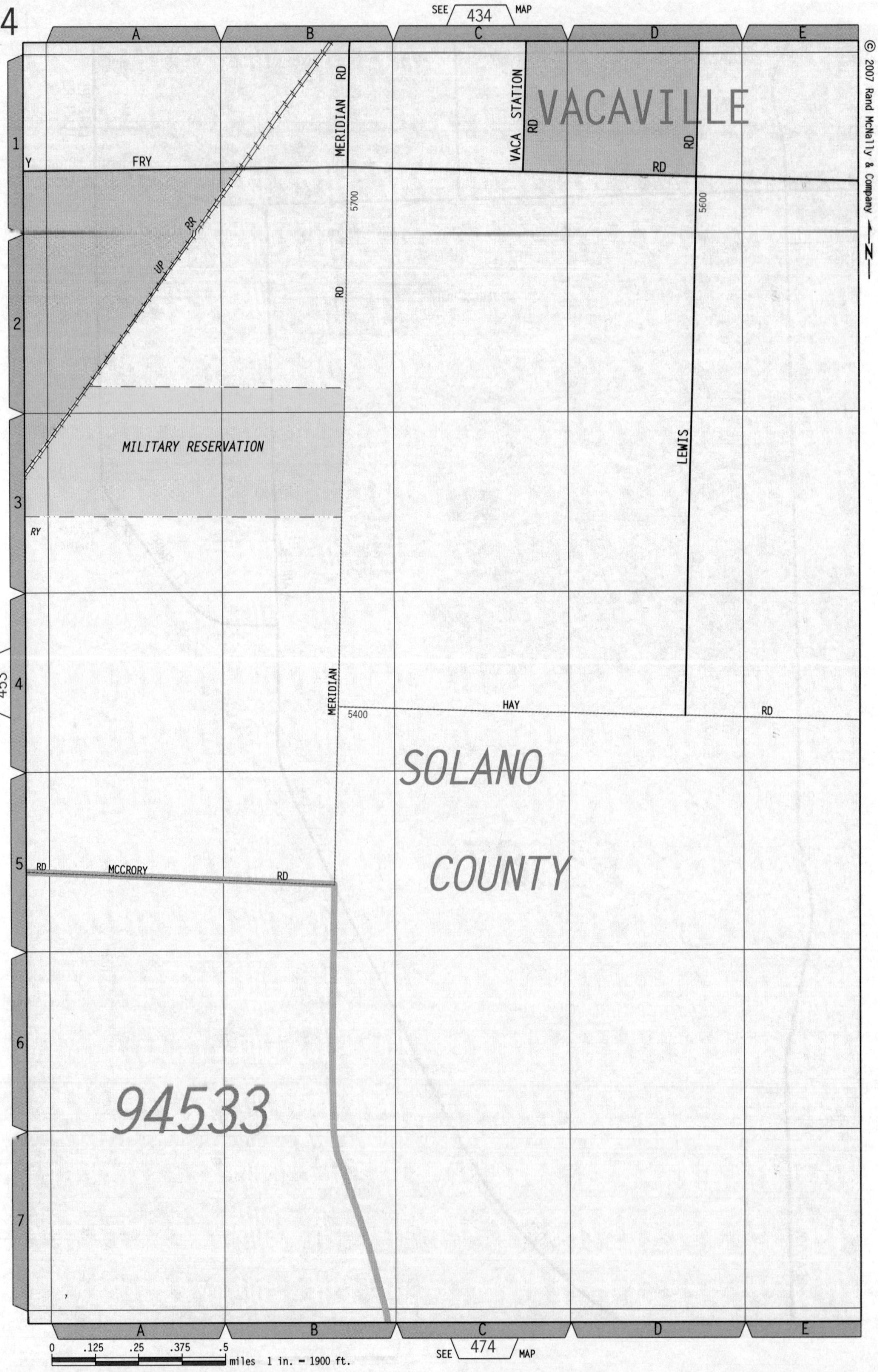
SEE 434 MAP
A
B
C
D
E
1
2
3
4
5
6
7
VACAVILLE
FRY
RD
MERIDIAN RD
VACA STATION RD
RD
5700
5600
UP RR
MILITARY RESERVATION
LEWIS
RY
SEE 453 MAP
MERIDIAN
5400
HAY
RD
SOLANO
COUNTY
MCCRORY
RD
94533
SEE 474 MAP
0 .125 .25 .375 .5
miles 1 in. = 1900 ft.

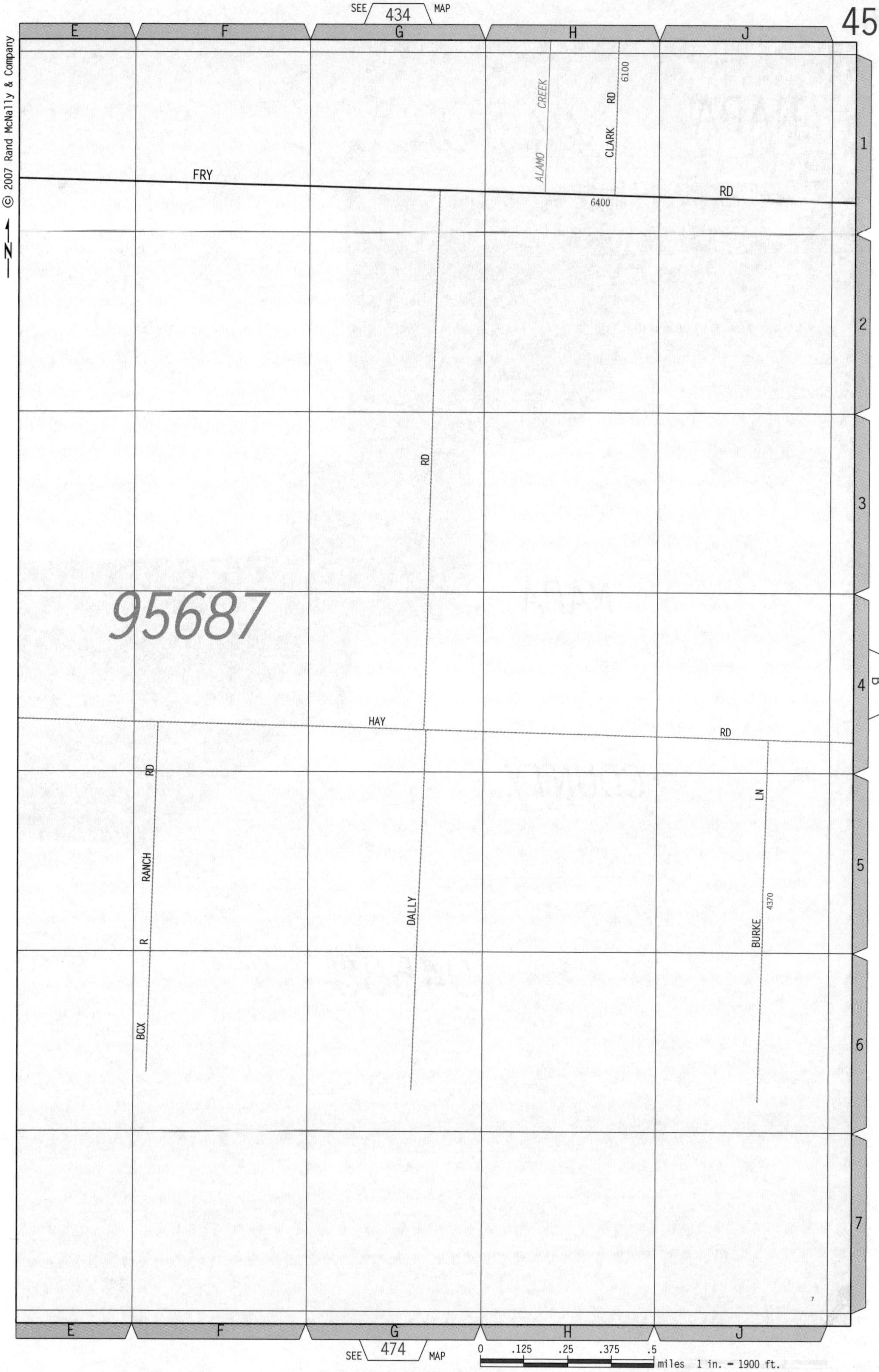
SEE 434 MAP
E
F
G
H
J
1
2
3
4
5
6
7
FRY RD
6400
ALAMO CREEK
CLARK RD
6100
95687
HAY RD
DALLY RD
BCX R RANCH RD
BURKE LN
4370
SEE B MAP
SEE 474 MAP
0 .125 .25 .375 .5 miles 1 in. = 1900 ft.

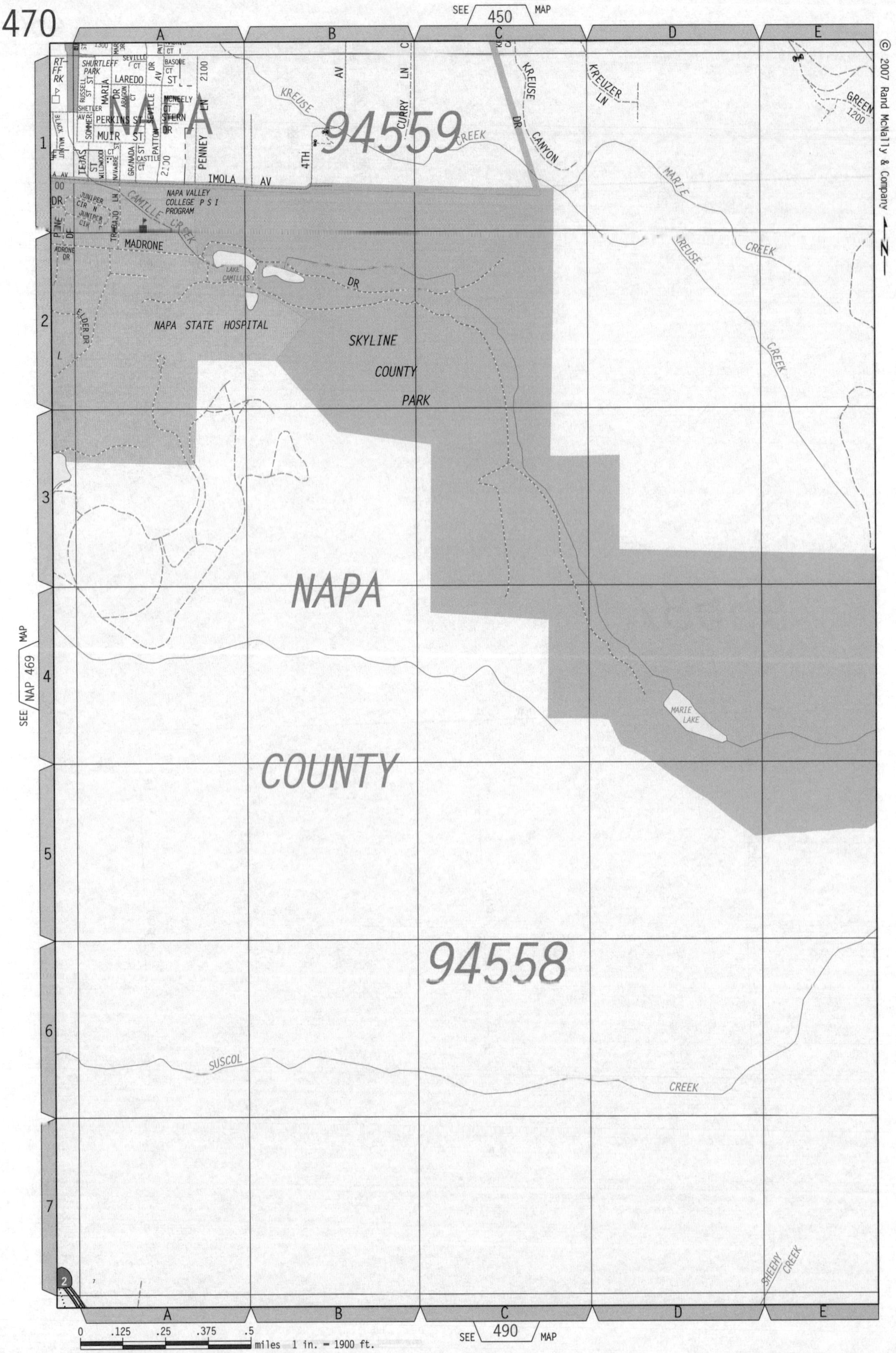
SEE 450 MAP
NAPA
94559
SHURTLEFF PARK
LAREDO
MARIA
PERKINS ST
MUIR ST
SHETLER AV
SOMMER
TEJAS ST
GRANADA
PATTON
CASTILLE
NAVARRE ST
SEVILLE
BASQUE CT
ST
MCNEELY
STERN DR
PENNEY LN
2100
2200
BLACK WALNUT
IMOLA AV
4TH
AV
CURRY LN
KREUSE
KREUSE DR
KREUZER LN
CANYON
CREEK
GREEN
1200
JUNIPER CIR N
JUNIPER CIR
CAMILLE CREEK
NAPA VALLEY COLLEGE P S I PROGRAM
MADRONE
MADRONE DR
PINE DR
LAKE CAMILLE
DR
ELDER DR
NAPA STATE HOSPITAL
SKYLINE COUNTY PARK
MARIE CREEK
KREUSE CREEK
NAPA
COUNTY
MARIE LAKE
SEE NAP 469 MAP
94558
SUSCOL CREEK
SHEEHY CREEK
A B C D E
1 2 3 4 5 6 7
0 .125 .25 .375 .5 miles 1 in. = 1900 ft.
SEE 490 MAP
© 2007 Rand McNally & Company

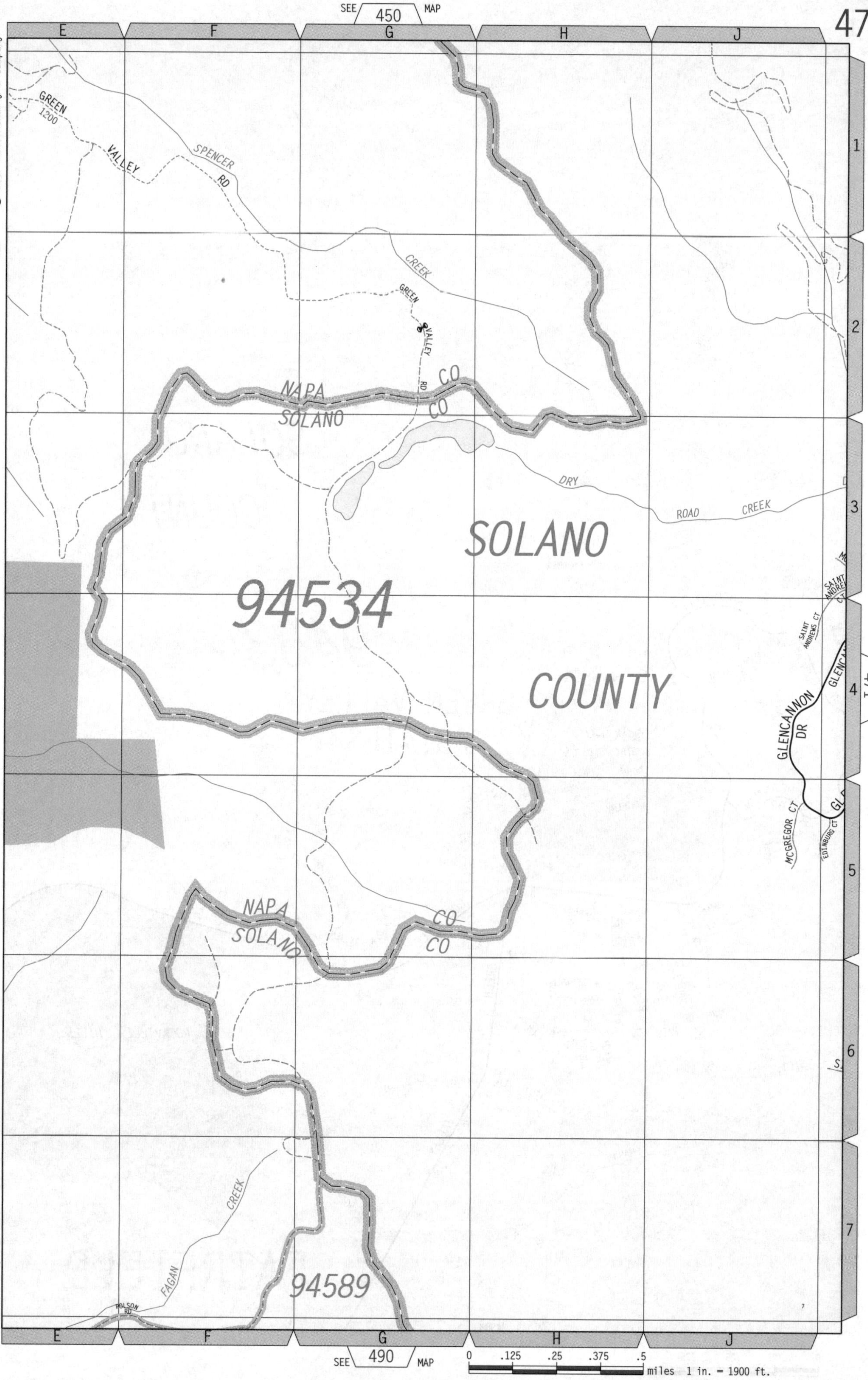
SEE 450 MAP
E
F
G
H
J
1
2
3
4
5
6
7
GREEN VALLEY
1200
SPENCER RD
CREEK
GREEN VALLEY RD
NAPA CO
SOLANO CO
DRY ROAD CREEK
SOLANO COUNTY
94534
SAINT ANDREWS CT
GLENCANNON DR
SEE 471 MAP
MCGREGOR CT
EDINBURG CT
NAPA CO
SOLANO CO
CREEK
FAGAN
94589
FOLSOM RD
SEE 490 MAP
0 .125 .25 .375 .5
miles 1 in. = 1900 ft.

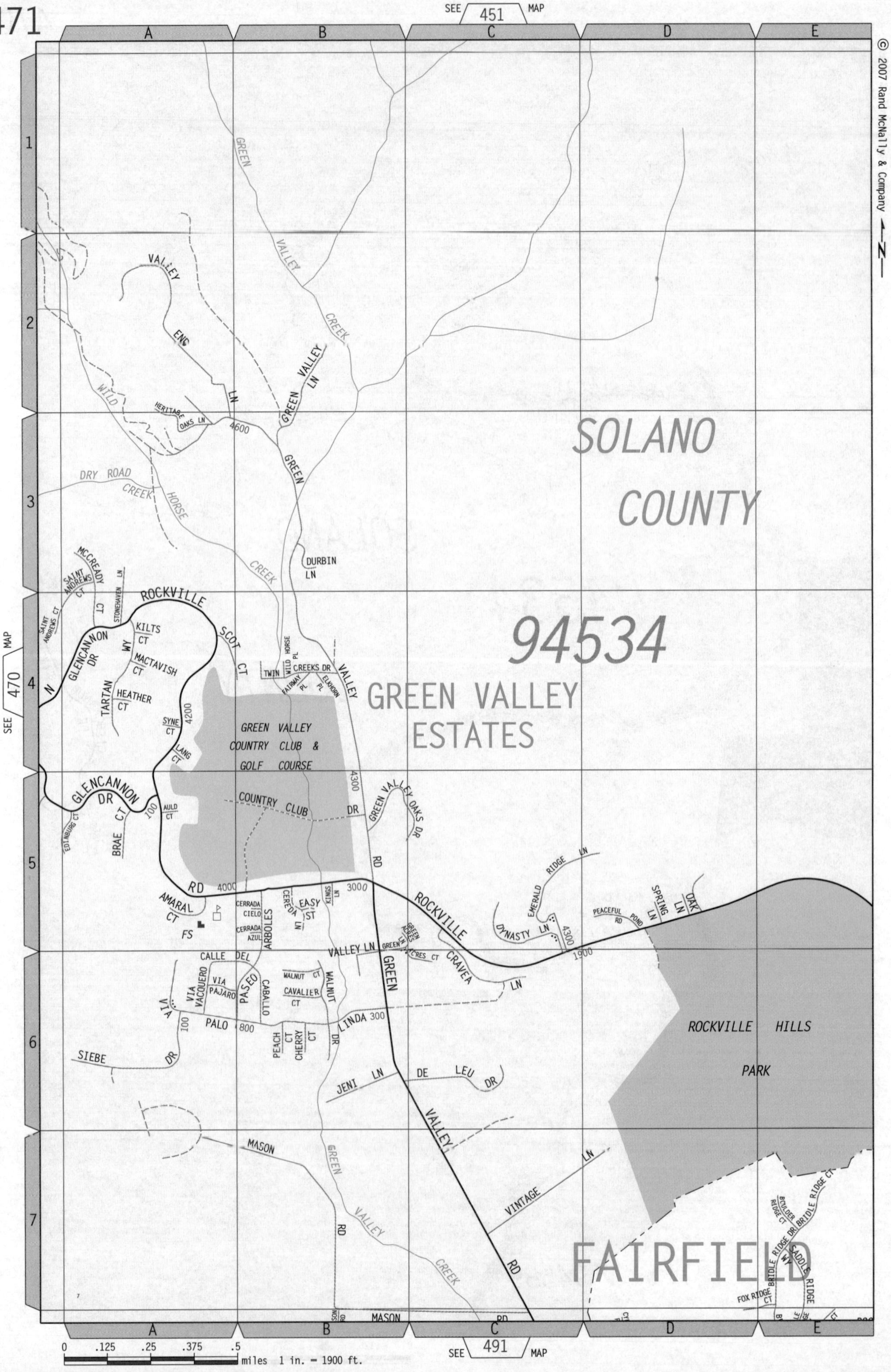
SEE 451 MAP
A
B
C
D
E
1
2
3
4
5
6
7
SEE 470 MAP
SEE 491 MAP
SOLANO
COUNTY
94534
GREEN VALLEY
ESTATES
GREEN VALLEY
COUNTRY CLUB &
GOLF COURSE
ROCKVILLE HILLS
PARK
FAIRFIELD
GREEN VALLEY CREEK
WILD HORSE CREEK
DRY ROAD CREEK
VALLEY ENS LN
GREEN VALLEY LN
HERITAGE OAKS LN
4600
GREEN VALLEY RD
DURBIN LN
MCCREADY CT
SAINT ANDREWS CT
STONEHAVEN LN
ROCKVILLE RD
SCOT CT
N GLENCANNON DR
KILTS CT
MACTAVISH CT
TARTAN CT
HEATHER CT
SYNE CT
LANG CT
4200
TWIN CREEKS DR
WILD HORSE PL
FAIRWAY PL
ELKHORN PL
GLENCANNON DR
EDINBURG CT
BRAE CT
AULD CT
100
COUNTRY CLUB DR
4300
GREEN VALLEY OAKS DR
4000
3000
AMARAL CT
FS
CERRADA CIELO
CERRADA AZUL
ARBOLES
CEREDA LN
EASY ST
EMERALD RIDGE LN
DYNASTY LN
PEACEFUL POND RD
SPRING LN
OAK LN
1900
VALLEY LN
GREEN ACRES CT
CRAVEA LN
CALLE DEL
VIA VACQUERO
VIA PAJARO
PASEO CABALLO
WALNUT CT
CAVALIER CT
WALNUT DR
LINDA 300
VIA PALO 800
PEACH CT
CHERRY CT
SIEBE DR
JENI LN
DE LEU DR
MASON
VINTAGE LN
FOX RIDGE CT
BRIDLE RIDGE DR
BOULDER RIDGE CT
BRIDLE RIDGE CT
SADDLE RIDGE WY
MASON RD
0 .125 .25 .375 .5
miles 1 in. = 1900 ft.
© 2007 Rand McNally & Company
N

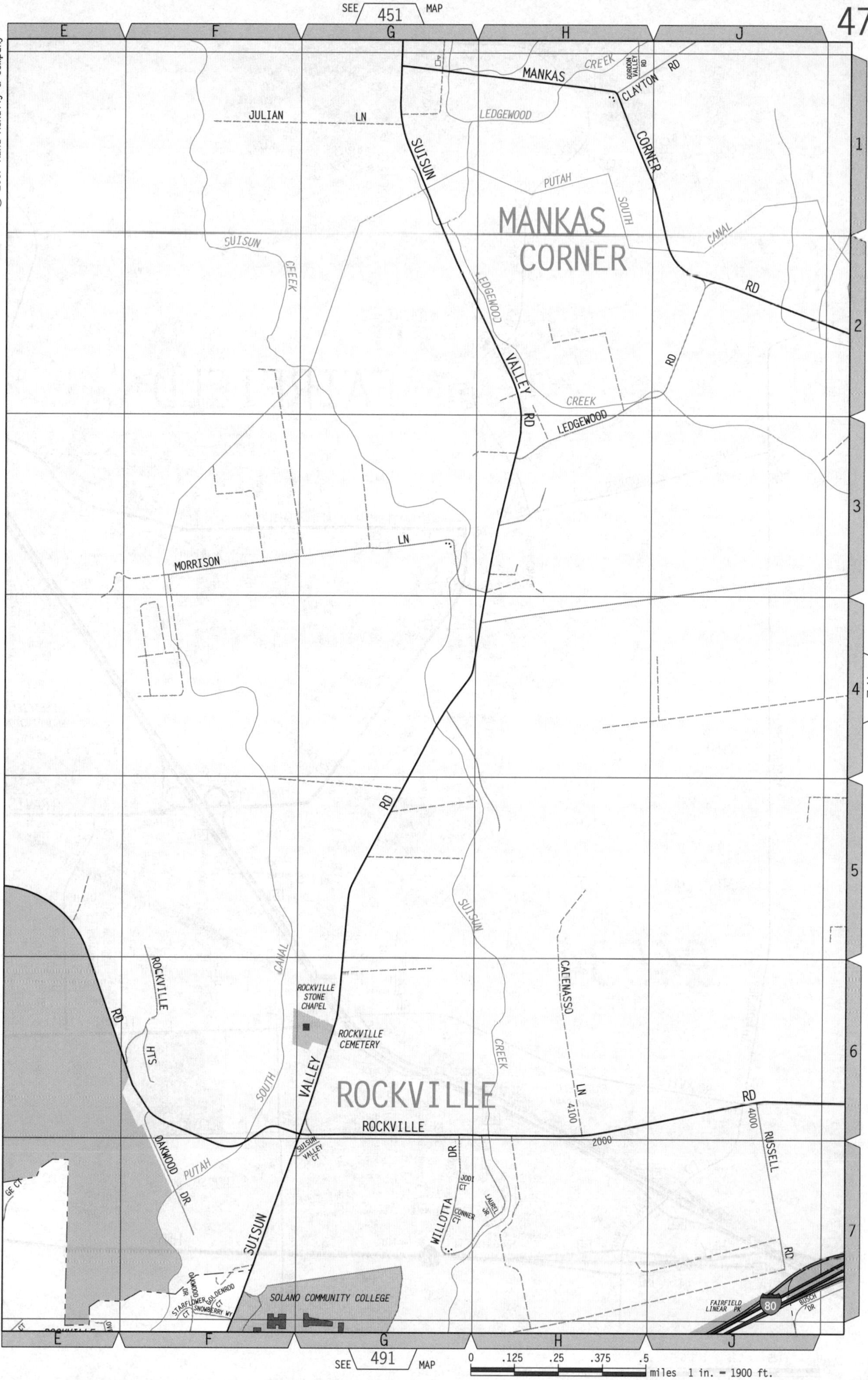

SEE 451 MAP
E
F
G
H
J
1
2
3
4
5
6
7
SEE 472 MAP
SEE 491 MAP
N
MANKAS CORNER
ROCKVILLE
MANKAS
CREEK
GORDON VALLEY RD
CLAYTON RD
CORNER
RD
JULIAN
LN
LEDGEWOOD
SUISUN
VALLEY
RD
PUTAH
SOUTH
CANAL
SUISUN
CREEK
LEDGEWOOD
CREEK
LEDGEWOOD
MORRISON
LN
SUISUN
CANAL
ROCKVILLE
HTS
RD
ROCKVILLE STONE CHAPEL
ROCKVILLE CEMETERY
SOUTH
PUTAH
CAENASSO
LN
4100
2000
ROCKVILLE
RD
4000
RUSSELL
RD
OAKWOOD
DR
SUISUN VALLEY CT
DR
WILLOTTA
JODI CT
CONNER CT
LAUREL DR
SUISUN
GOLDENROD CT
STARFLOWER CT
SNOWBERRY WY
OAKWOOD DR
SOLANO COMMUNITY COLLEGE
FAIRFIELD LINEAR PK
80
BUSCH DR
GE CT
CT
0
.125
.25
.375
.5
miles 1 in. = 1900 ft.

SEE 452 MAP

SOLANO CO.

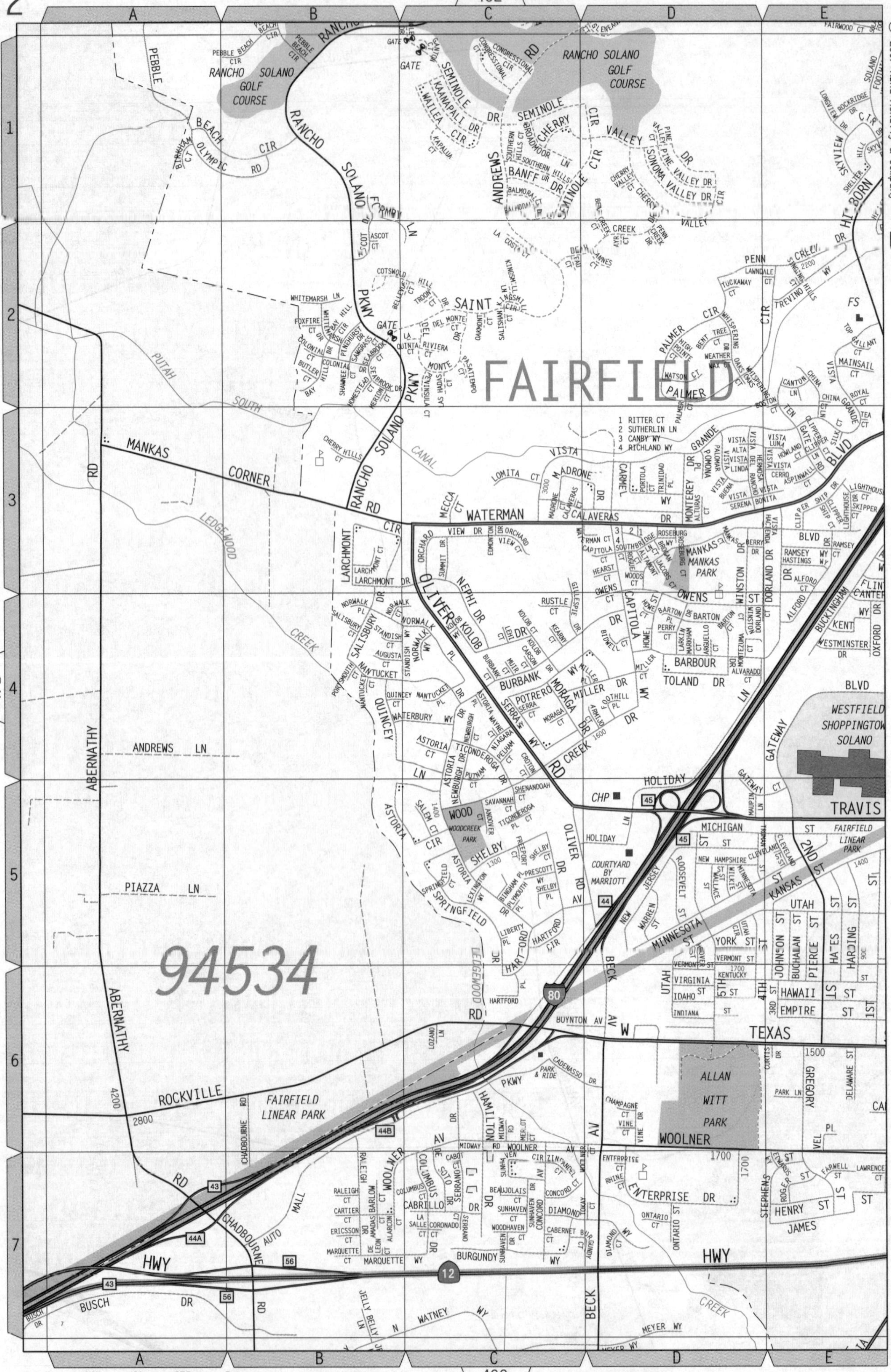

0 .125 .25 .375 .5 miles 1 in. = 1900 ft.

SEE 492 MAP

SEE 452 MAP

SEE 473 MAP

SEE 492 MAP

0 .125 .25 .375 .5 miles 1 in. = 1900 ft.

SEE 453 MAP

SOLANO CO.

SEE 472 MAP

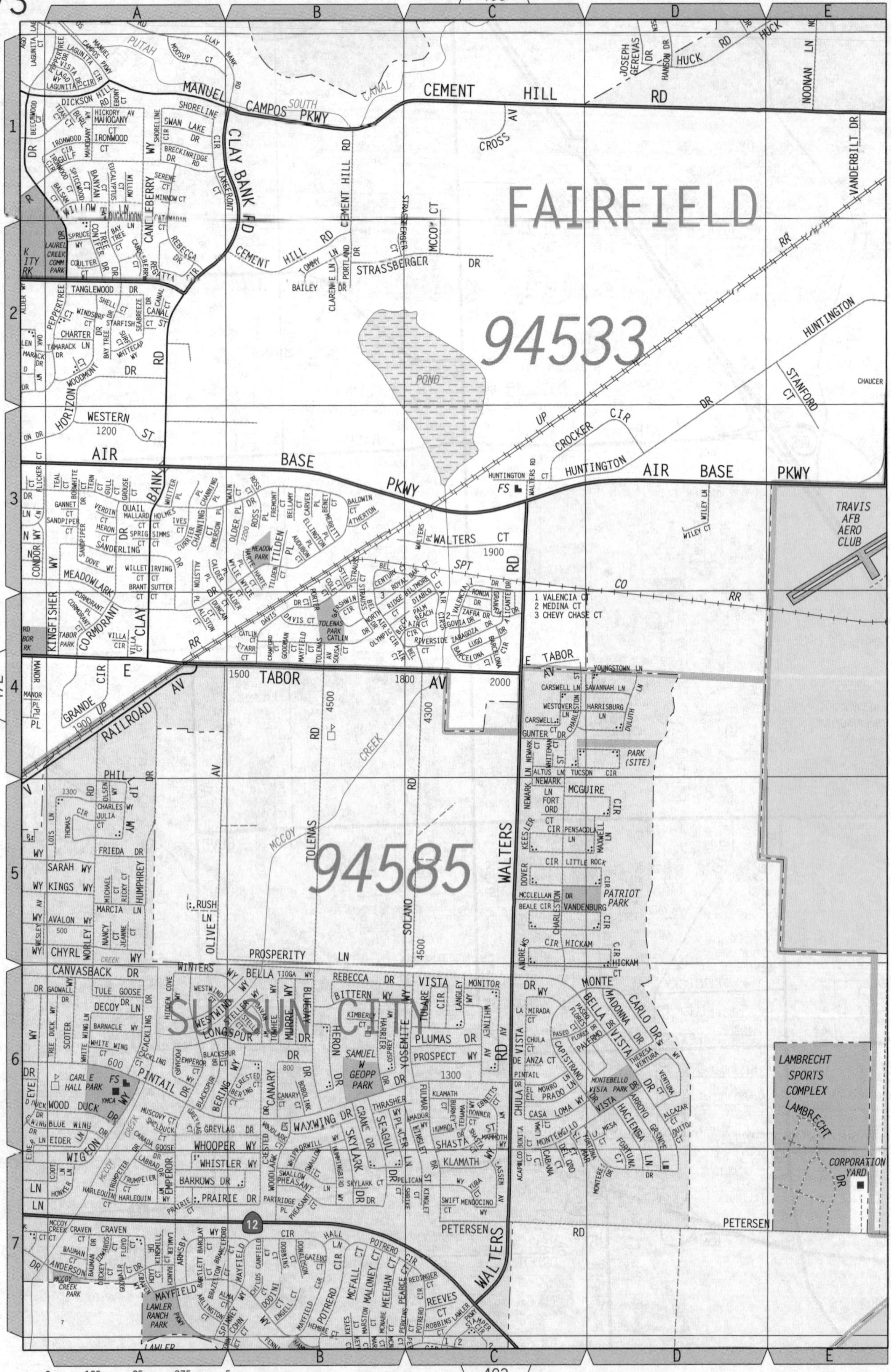

0 .125 .25 .375 .5 miles 1 in. = 1900 ft.

SEE 493 MAP

SEE 453 MAP

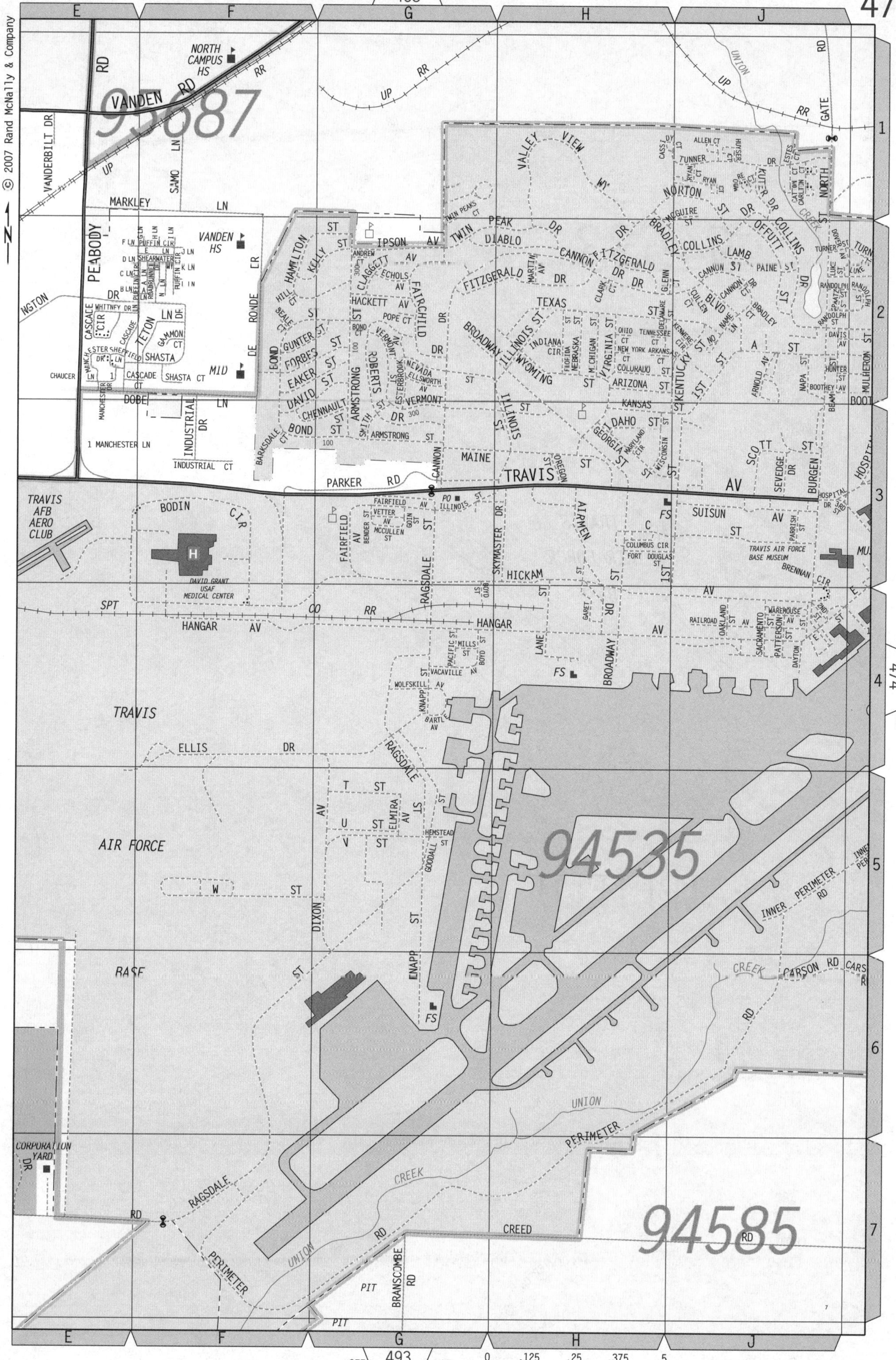

SEE 493 MAP

0 .125 .25 .375 .5 miles 1 in. = 1900 ft.

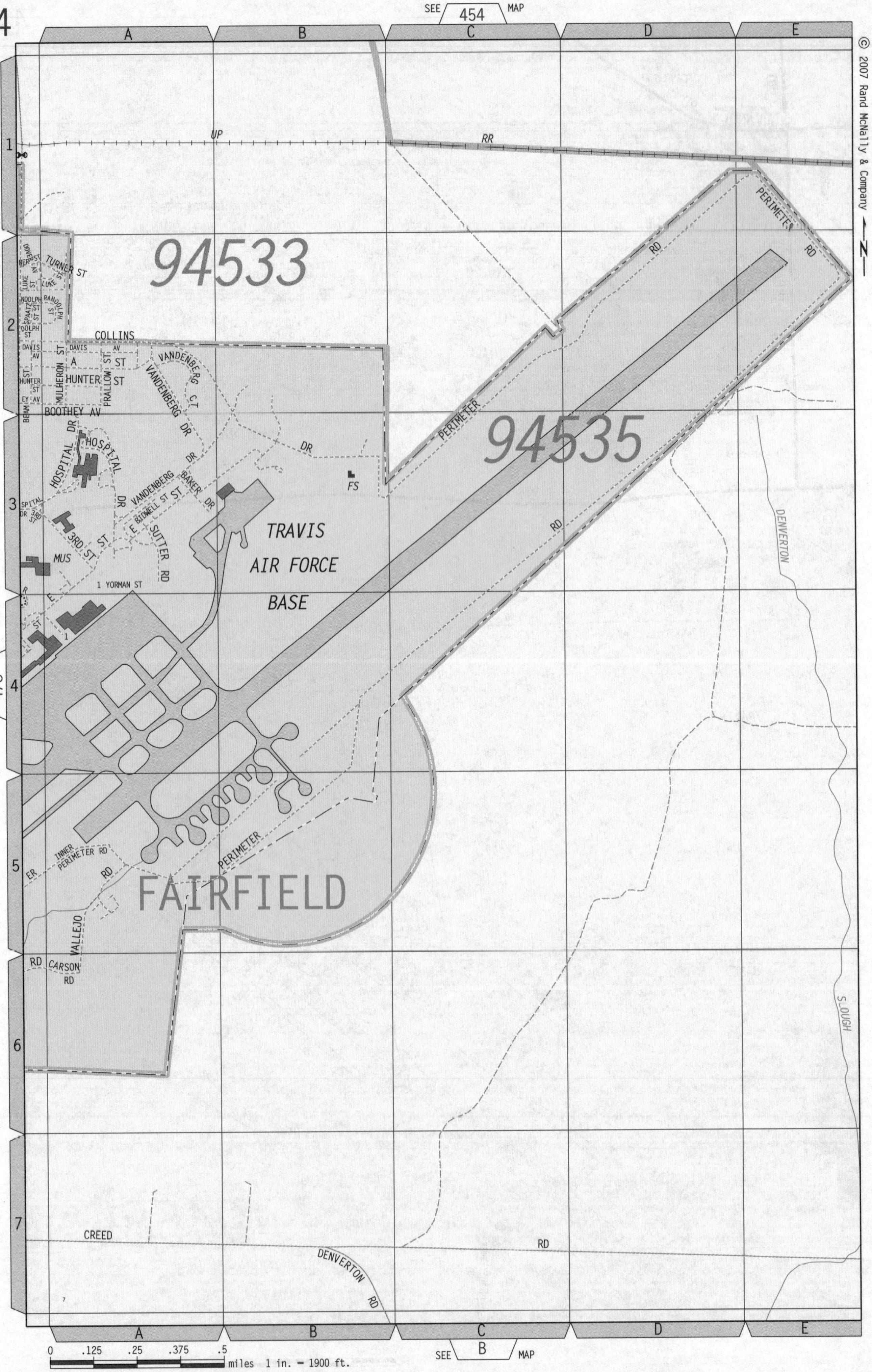
SEE 454 MAP
A
B
C
D
E
1
2
3
4
5
6
7
UP
RR
94533
94535
TURNER ST
LUKE ST
RANDOLPH ST
DAVIS AV
COLLINS
A ST
HUNTER ST
MULHERON ST
PRALLOW ST
BOOTHEY AV
VANDENBERG CT
VANDENBERG DR
HOSPITAL DR
3RD ST
E BIDWELL ST
BAKER DR
SUTTER RD
MUS
1 YORMAN ST
FS
TRAVIS
AIR FORCE
BASE
PERIMETER RD
INNER PERIMETER RD
VALLEJO RD
CARSON RD
FAIRFIELD
DENVERTON
SLOUGH
CREED RD
DENVERTON RD
SEE 473 MAP
SEE B MAP
0 .125 .25 .375 .5 miles 1 in. = 1900 ft.

SEE 454 MAP
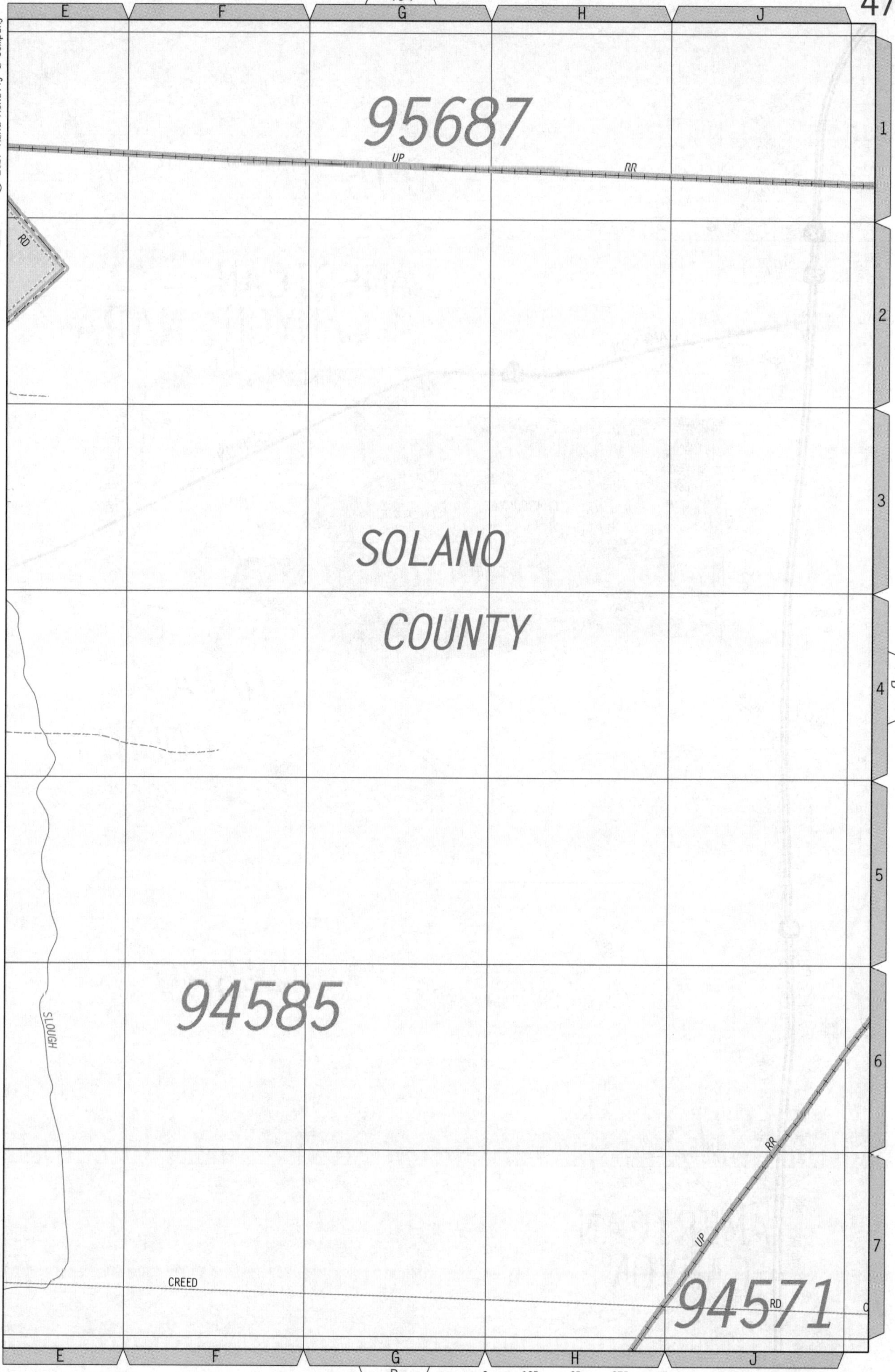
E
F
G
H
J
1
2
3
4
5
6
7
95687
UP
RR
RD
SOLANO
COUNTY
94585
SLOUGH
CREED
RD
UP
RR
94571
0 .125 .25 .375 .5
miles 1 in. = 1900 ft.
SEE B MAP
SEE B MAP

SEE 470 MAP

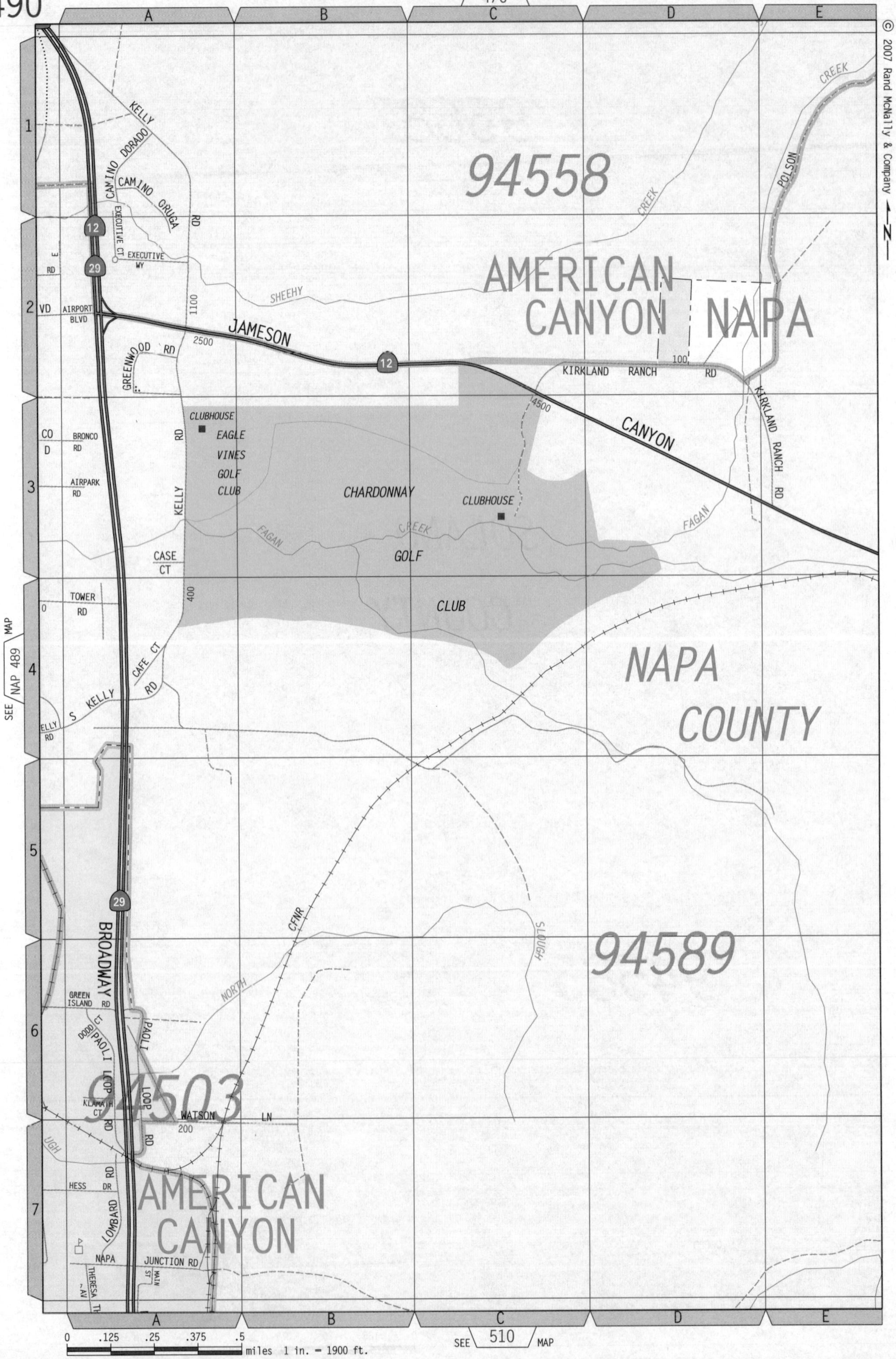

A
B
C
D
E
1
2
3
4
5
6
7
SOLANO CO.
94558
AMERICAN CANYON
NAPA
KELLY
CAMINO DORADO
CAMINO ORUGA
RD
12
29
EXECUTIVE CT
EXECUTIVE WY
SHEEHY
CREEK
POLSON
1100
AIRPORT BLVD
JAMESON
2500
GREENWOOD RD
KIRKLAND RANCH RD
100
4500
CANYON
CLUBHOUSE
EAGLE VINES GOLF CLUB
CHARDONNAY GOLF CLUB
BRONCO RD
AIRPARK RD
KELLY RD
FAGAN CREEK
CASE CT
400
TOWER RD
CAFE CT
S KELLY RD
NAPA COUNTY
BROADWAY
CFNR
NORTH
SLOUGH
94589
GREEN ISLAND RD
DODD CT
PAOLI LOOP RD
94503
KLAMATH
WATSON LN
200
HESS DR
LOMBARD RD
AMERICAN CANYON
NAPA JUNCTION RD
MAIN ST
THERESA AV
0
.125
.25
.375
.5
miles 1 in. = 1900 ft.

SEE NAP 489 MAP

SEE 510 MAP

SEE 470 MAP

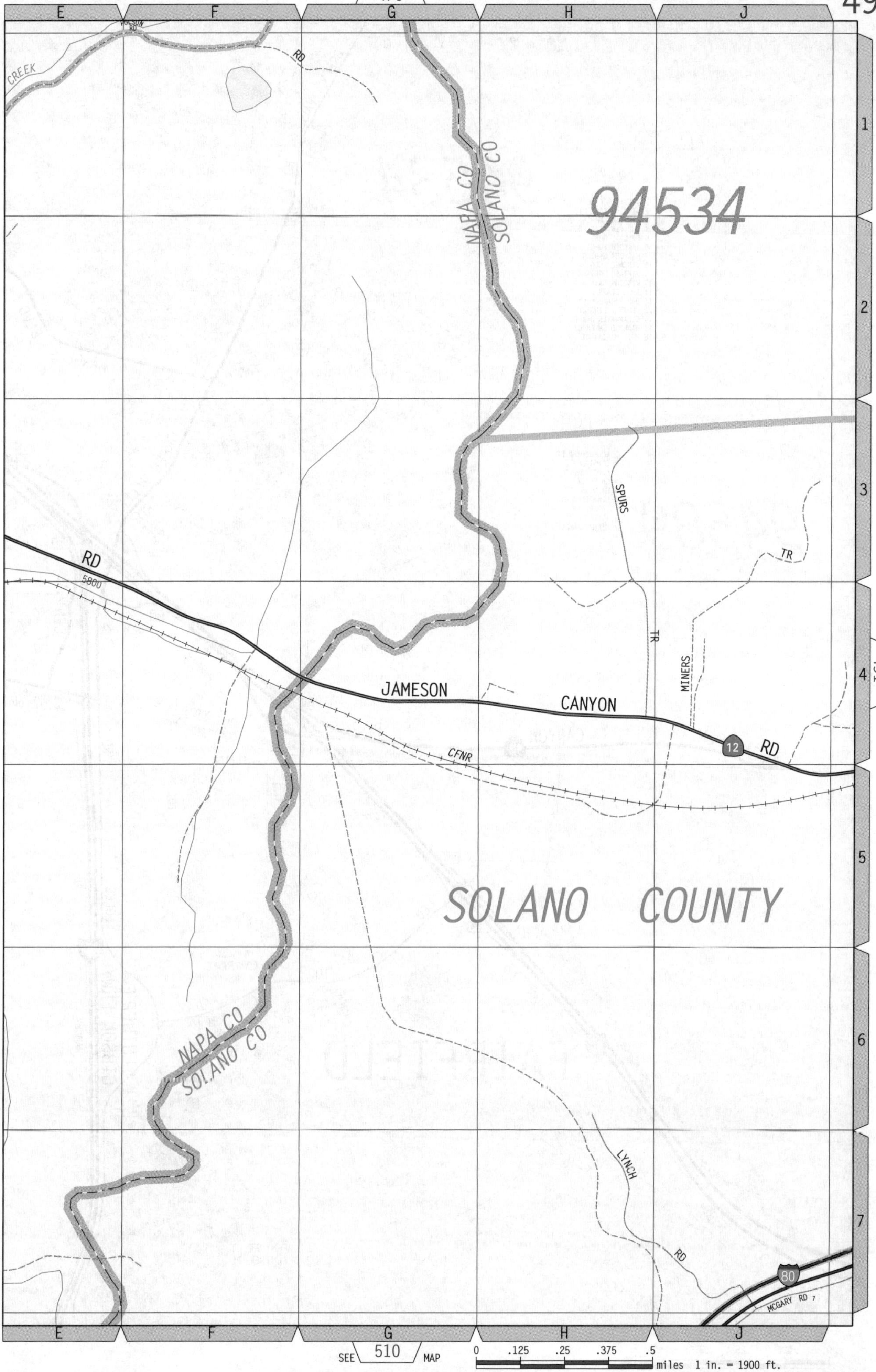

SEE 491 MAP
SEE 510 MAP

0 .125 .25 .375 .5 miles 1 in. = 1900 ft.

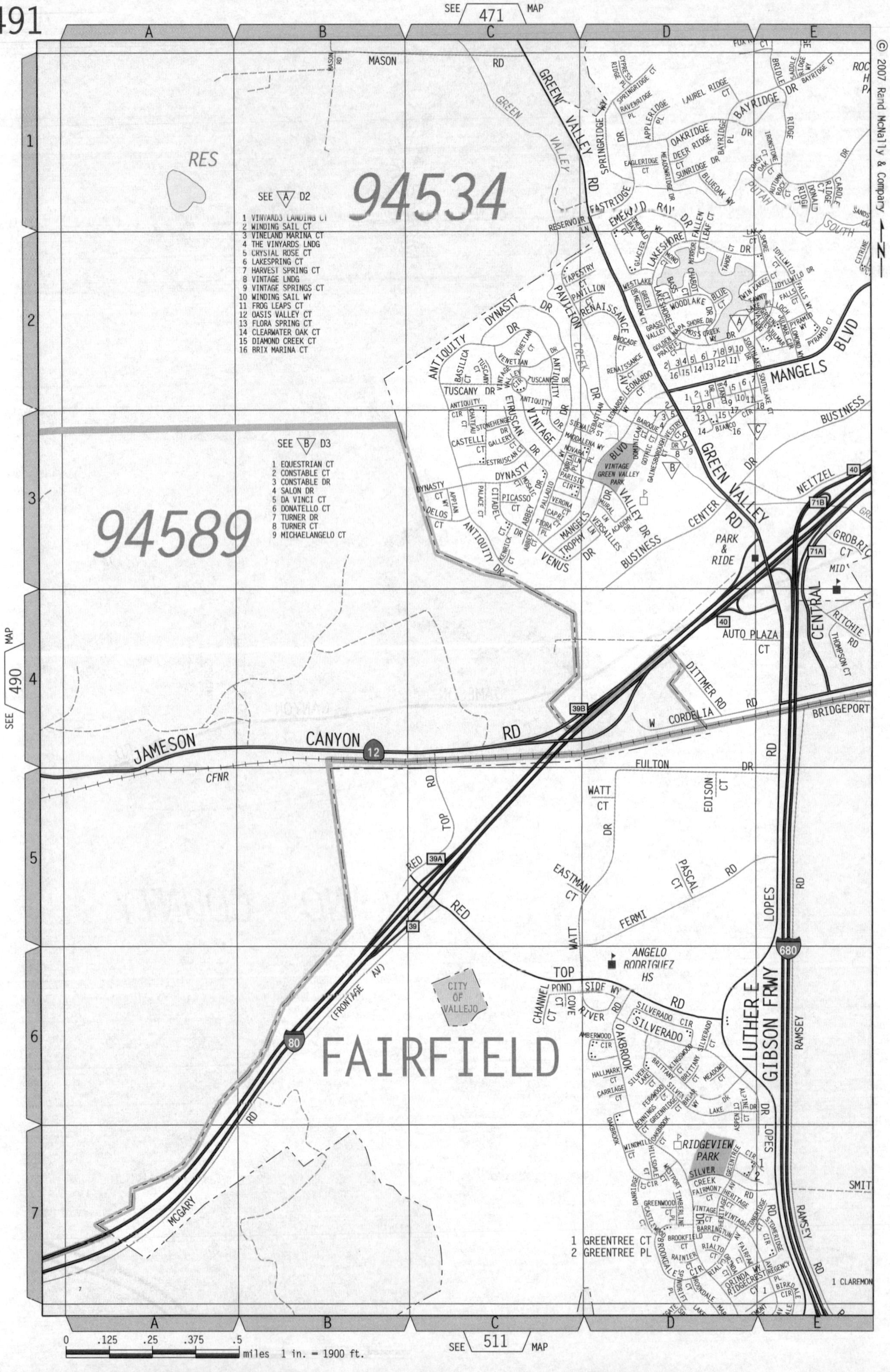
SEE 471 MAP
SEE 490 MAP
SEE 511 MAP
A
B
C
D
E
1
2
3
4
5
6
7
94534
94589
FAIRFIELD
RES
SEE A D2
1 VINYARDS LANDING CT
2 WINDING SAIL CT
3 VINELAND MARINA CT
4 THE VINYARDS LNDG
5 CRYSTAL ROSE CT
6 LAKESPRING CT
7 HARVEST SPRING CT
8 VINTAGE LNDG
9 VINTAGE SPRINGS CT
10 WINDING SAIL WY
11 FROG LEAPS CT
12 OASIS VALLEY CT
13 FLORA SPRING CT
14 CLEARWATER OAK CT
15 DIAMOND CREEK CT
16 BRIX MARINA CT
SEE B D3
1 EQUESTRIAN CT
2 CONSTABLE CT
3 CONSTABLE DR
4 SALON DR
5 DA VINCI CT
6 DONATELLO CT
7 TURNER DR
8 TURNER CT
9 MICHAELANGELO CT
1 GREENTREE CT
2 GREENTREE PL
1 CLAREMONT
MASON RD
GREEN VALLEY RD
MANGELS BLVD
BUSINESS CENTER DR
JAMESON CANYON RD
CFNR
W CORDELIA RD
BRIDGEPORT
FULTON DR
DITTMER RD
AUTO PLAZA CT
CENTRAL
NEITZEL
PARK & RIDE
VINTAGE GREEN VALLEY PARK
ANGELO RODRIGUEZ HS
RIDGEVIEW PARK
CITY OF VALLEJO
LUTHER E GIBSON FRWY
RED TOP RD
TOP POND SIDE WY
(FRONTAGE AV)
MCGARY RD
LOPES RD
RAMSEY RD
FERMI
PASCAL CT
EASTMAN CT
WATT DR
EDISON CT
SILVERADO CIR
OAKBROOK
12
80
680
39
39A
39B
40
71A
71B
0 .125 .25 .375 .5 miles 1 in. = 1900 ft.

SEE 471 MAP

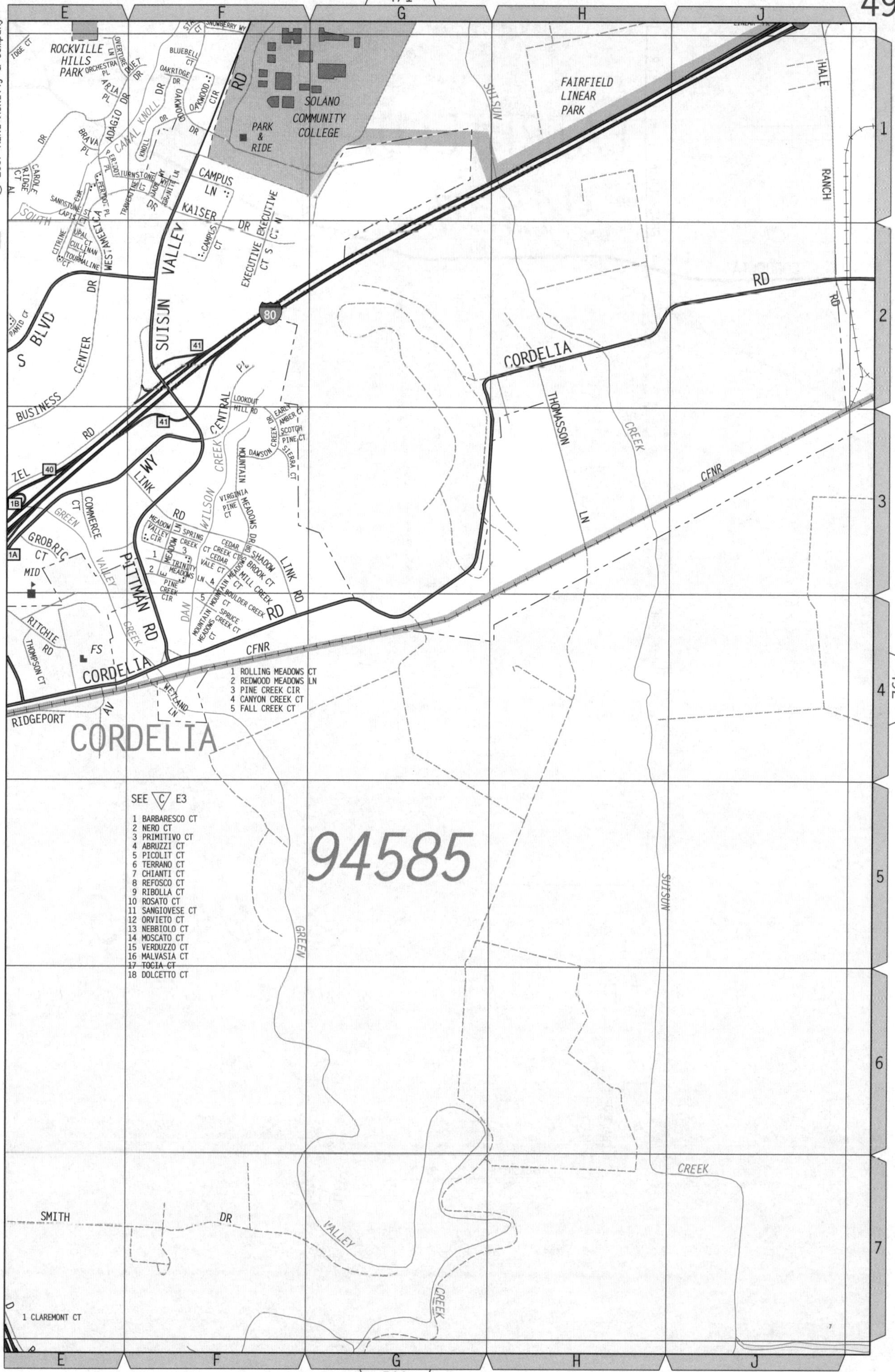

E F G H J
1 2 3 4 5 6 7
ROCKVILLE HILLS PARK
SOLANO COMMUNITY COLLEGE
PARK & RIDE
FAIRFIELD LINEAR PARK
SUISUN VALLEY RD
BUSINESS CENTER DR
CORDELIA RD
THOMASSON LN
RANCH RD
HALE RANCH RD
CFNR
PITTMAN RD
LINK RD
CENTRAL PL
GREEN VALLEY CREEK
SUISUN CREEK
WILSON CREEK
MOUNTAIN MEADOWS DR
RIDGEPORT AV
WETLAND LN
CORDELIA
94585
SMITH DR
1 ROLLING MEADOWS CT
2 REDWOOD MEADOWS LN
3 PINE CREEK CIR
4 CANYON CREEK CT
5 FALL CREEK CT
SEE C E3
1 BARBARESCO CT
2 NERO CT
3 PRIMITIVO CT
4 ABRUZZI CT
5 PICOLIT CT
6 TERRANO CT
7 CHIANTI CT
8 REFOSCO CT
9 RIBOLLA CT
10 ROSATO CT
11 SANGIOVESE CT
12 ORVIETO CT
13 NEBBIOLO CT
14 MOSCATO CT
15 VERDUZZO CT
16 MALVASIA CT
17 TOCIA CT
18 DOLCETTO CT
1 CLAREMONT CT
0 .125 .25 .375 .5 miles 1 in. = 1900 ft.

SOLANO CO.

SEE 492 MAP

SEE 511 MAP

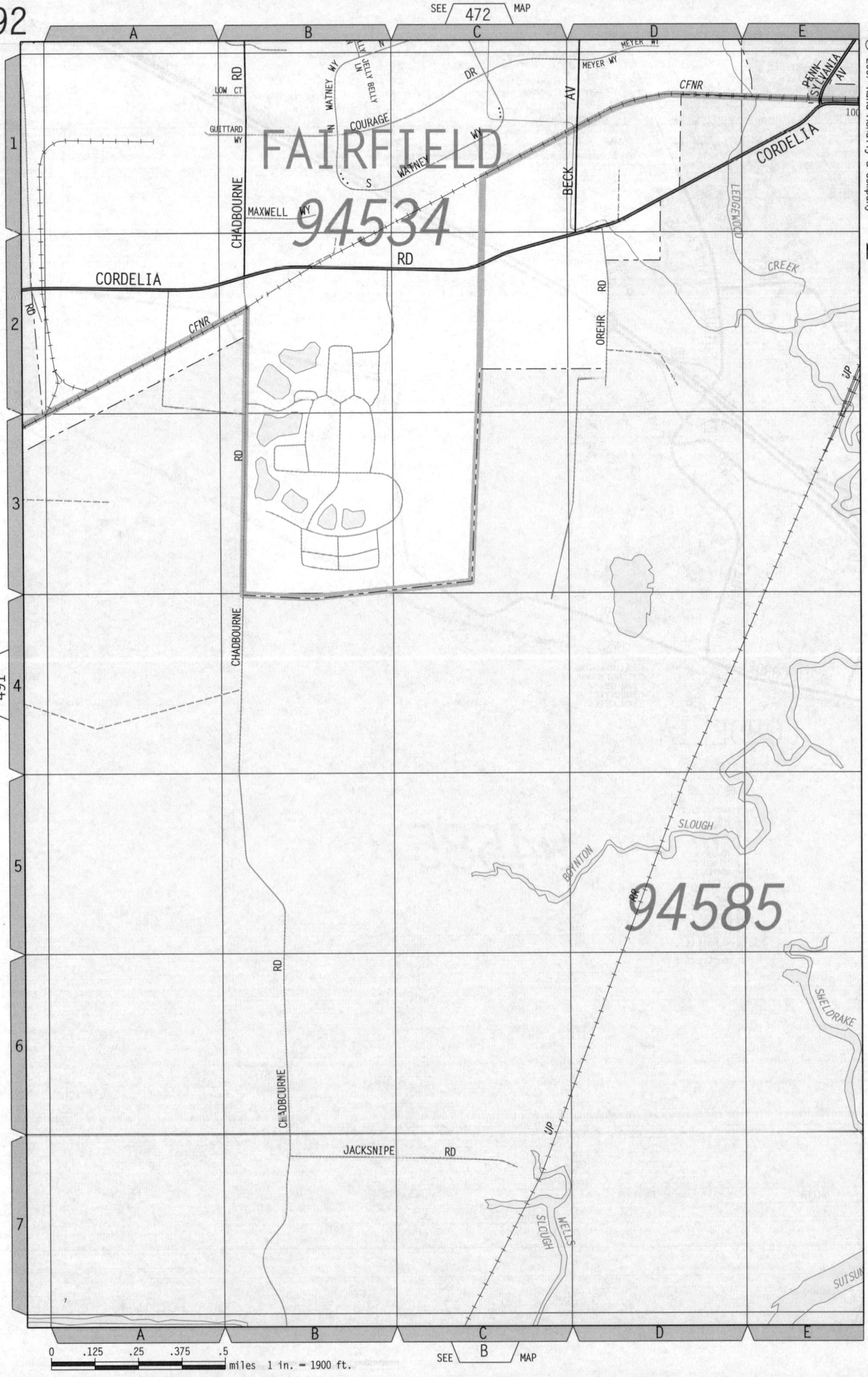
SEE 472 MAP
A
B
C
D
E
1
2
3
4
5
6
7
FAIRFIELD
94534
94585
CORDELIA
RD
CORDELIA RD
CFNR
CHADBOURNE RD
LOW CT
GUITTARD WY
MAXWELL WY
N WATNEY WY
S WATNEY WY
JELLY BELLY LN
COURAGE DR
MEYER WY
BECK AV
OREHR RD
LEDGEWOOD
CREEK
PENNSYLVANIA AV
100
UP
RR
SLOUGH
BOYNTON
SHELDRAKE
JACKSNIPE RD
CHADBOURNE
WELLS
SLOUGH
SUISUN
SEE 491 MAP
SEE B MAP
0 .125 .25 .375 .5
miles 1 in. = 1900 ft.

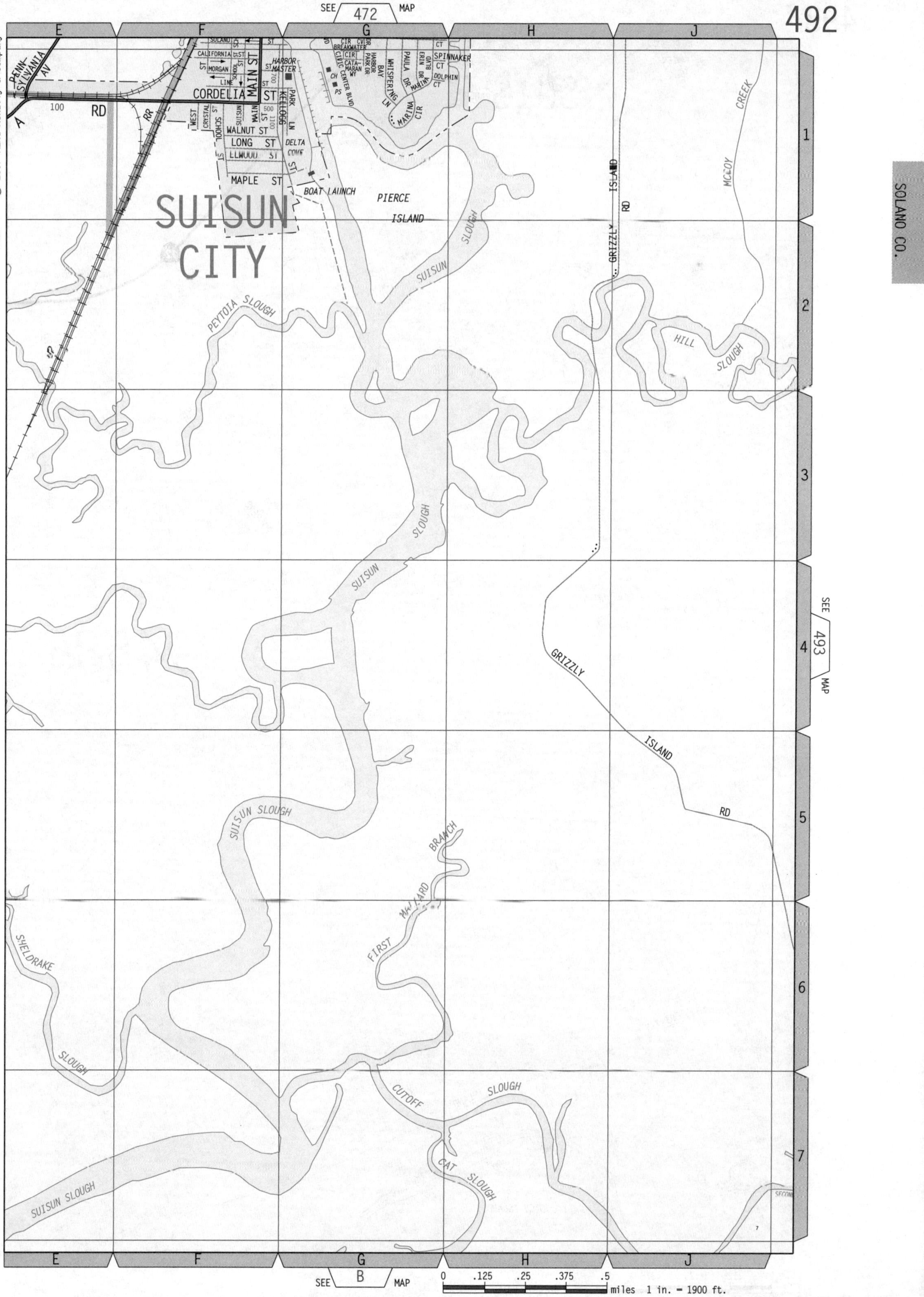
SEE 472 MAP
E
F
G
H
J
PENN-SYLVANIA AV
A
100
RD
CORDELIA ST
RR
SOLANO
CALIFORNIA ST
MORGAN
LINE
MAIN ST
SCHOOL ST
WEST
CRYSTAL ST
SUISUN ST
MAIN ST
WALNUT ST
LONG ST
ELLWOOD ST
MAPLE ST
KELLOGG
PARK LN
HARBOR MASTER
DELTA COVE
ST
BOAT LAUNCH
CIR
BREAKWATER
CATA-MARAN WY
CIVIC CENTER BLVD
CH
PS
HARBOR PARK DR
BAY
WHISPERING LN
PAULA DR
ERIN DR
MARINA CIR
SPINNAKER CT
CT
DOLPHIN CT
SUISUN CITY
PIERCE ISLAND
SUISUN SLOUGH
PEYTOIA SLOUGH
GRIZZLY ISLAND RD
MCCOY CREEK
HILL SLOUGH
SUISUN SLOUGH
SUISUN
GRIZZLY ISLAND RD
SUISUN SLOUGH
BRANCH
FIRST MALLARD
SHELDRAKE SLOUGH
CUTOFF SLOUGH
CAT SLOUGH
SUISUN SLOUGH
1
2
3
4
5
6
7
SEE 493 MAP
SOLANO CO.
SEE B MAP
0 .125 .25 .375 .5
miles 1 in. = 1900 ft.

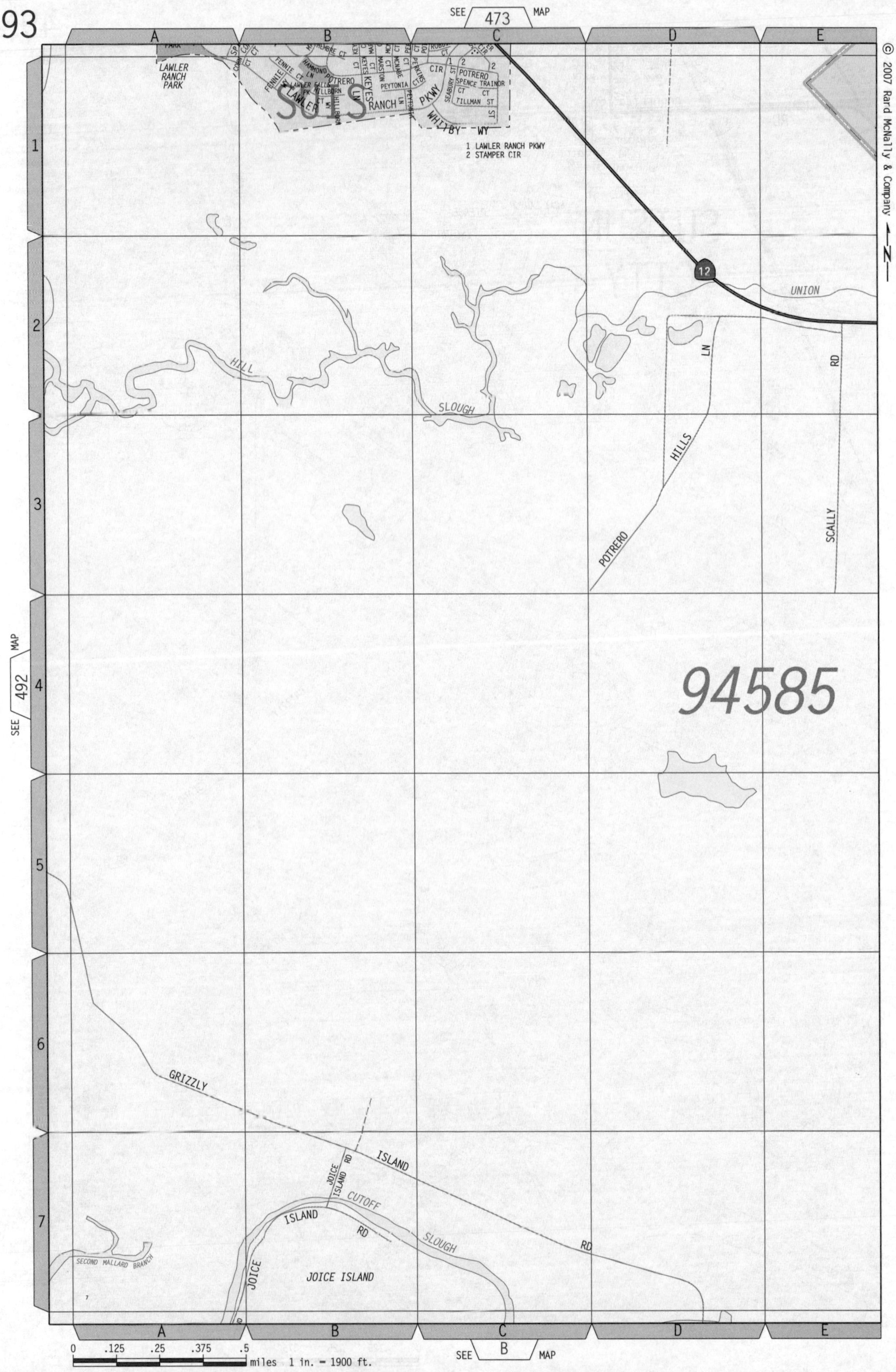
SEE 473 MAP
A
B
C
D
E
1
2
3
4
5
6
7
LAWLER RANCH PARK
FENNIE CT
HAMMOND LN
POTRERO
LAWLER FALLS PK
HILLBORN
LAWLER RANCH PKWY
KEYES
MARSTON CT
MCNABE CT
PEYTONIA
PERKINS CT
CIR
SEABURY ST
POTRERO
SPENCE CT
TRAINOR CT
TILLMAN ST
WHITBY WY
SUIS
1 LAWLER RANCH PKWY
2 STAMPER CIR
12
UNION
HILL SLOUGH
LN
HILLS
POTRERO
RD
SCALLY
94585
SEE 492 MAP
GRIZZLY ISLAND RD
JOICE ISLAND RD
CUTOFF SLOUGH
ISLAND RD
JOICE
JOICE ISLAND
SECOND MALLARD BRANCH
SEE B MAP
0 .125 .25 .375 .5 miles 1 in. = 1900 ft.

SOLANO CO.

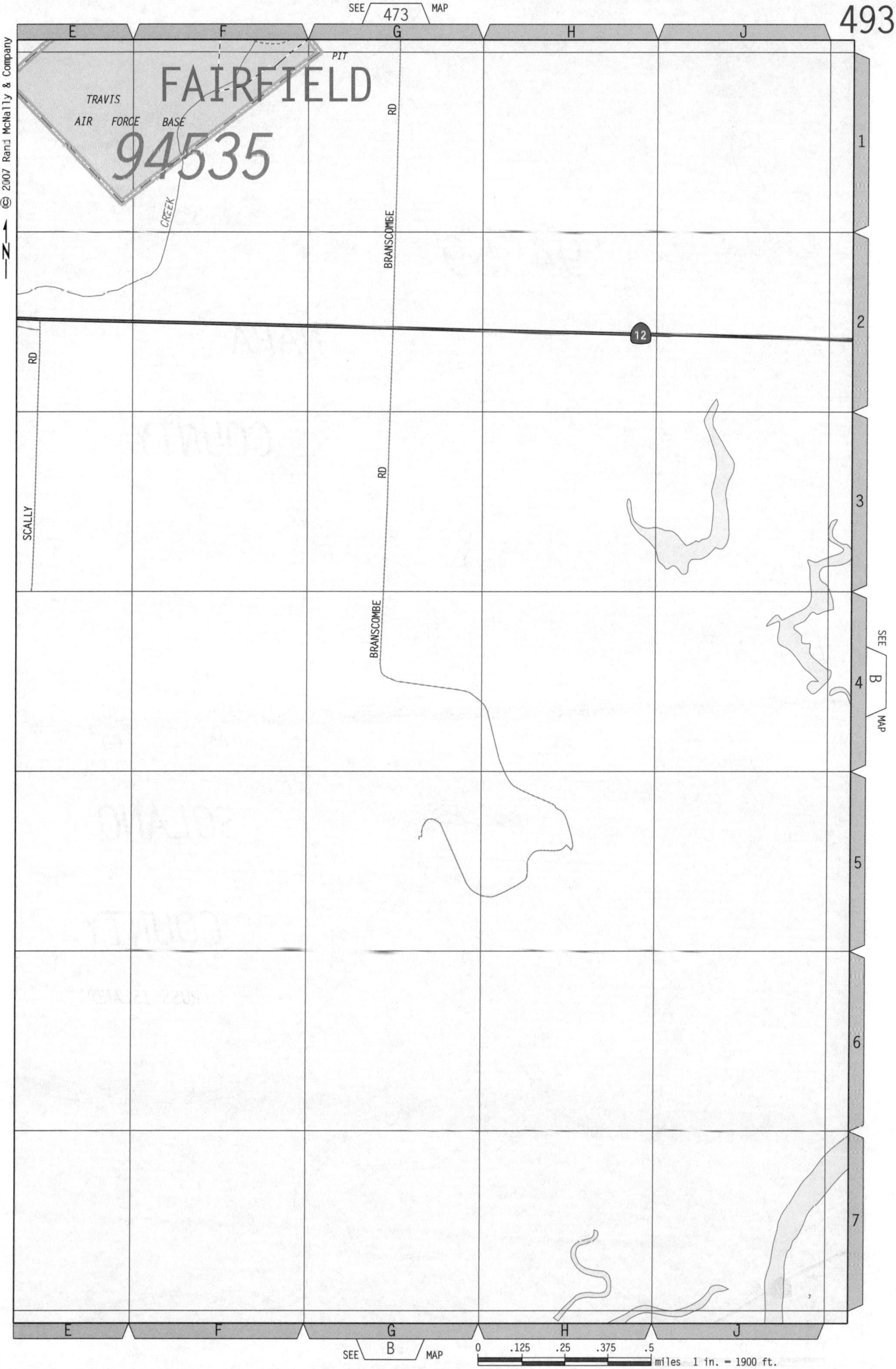
SEE 473 MAP
E
F
G
H
J
1
2
3
4
5
6
7
FAIRFIELD
94535
TRAVIS
AIR FORCE BASE
PIT
CREEK
BRANSCOMBE RD
SCALLY RD
12
SEE B MAP
0 .125 .25 .375 .5 miles 1 in. = 1900 ft.

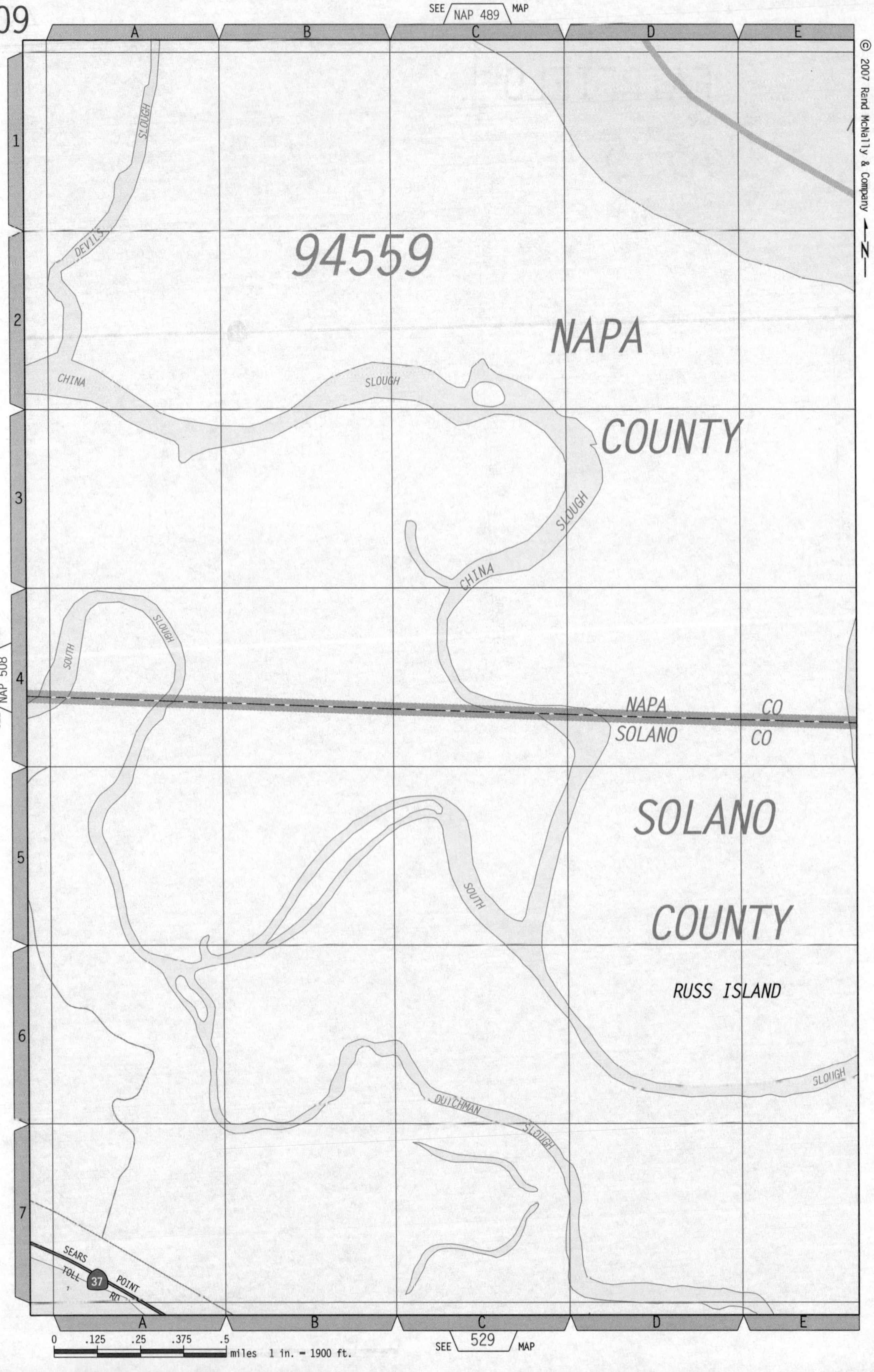
SEE NAP 489 MAP
A
B
C
D
E
1
2
3
4
5
6
7
94559
NAPA
COUNTY
DEVILS SLOUGH
CHINA SLOUGH
SLOUGH
CHINA
SOUTH SLOUGH
SEE NAP 508 MAP
NAPA CO
SOLANO CO
SOLANO
COUNTY
SOUTH
RUSS ISLAND
SLOUGH
DUTCHMAN SLOUGH
SEARS POINT TOLL RD
37
SEE 529 MAP
0 .125 .25 .375 .5
miles 1 in. = 1900 ft.
N

SEE NAP 489 MAP

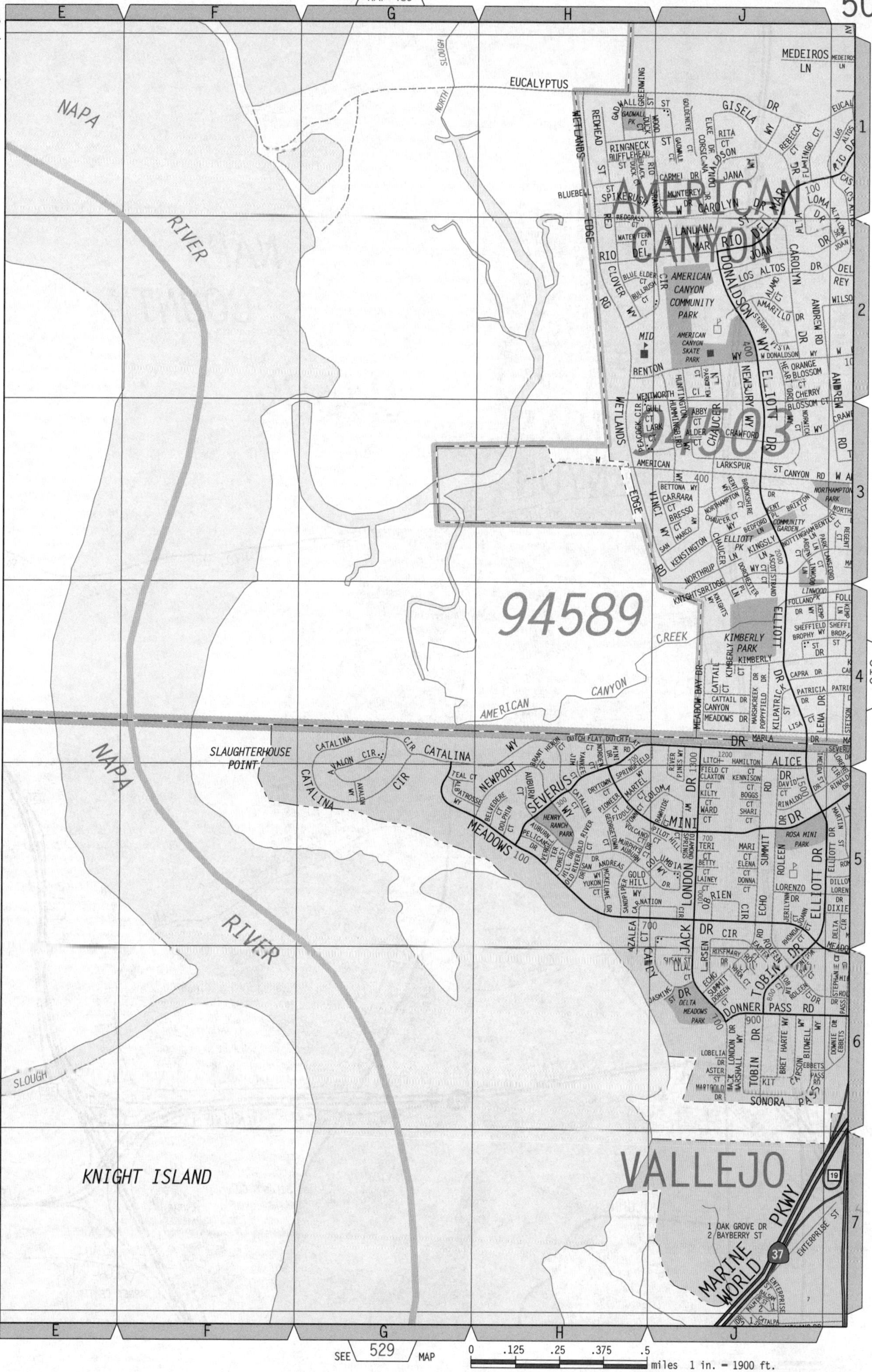

SEE 510 MAP

SEE 529 MAP

0 .125 .25 .375 .5 miles 1 in. = 1900 ft.

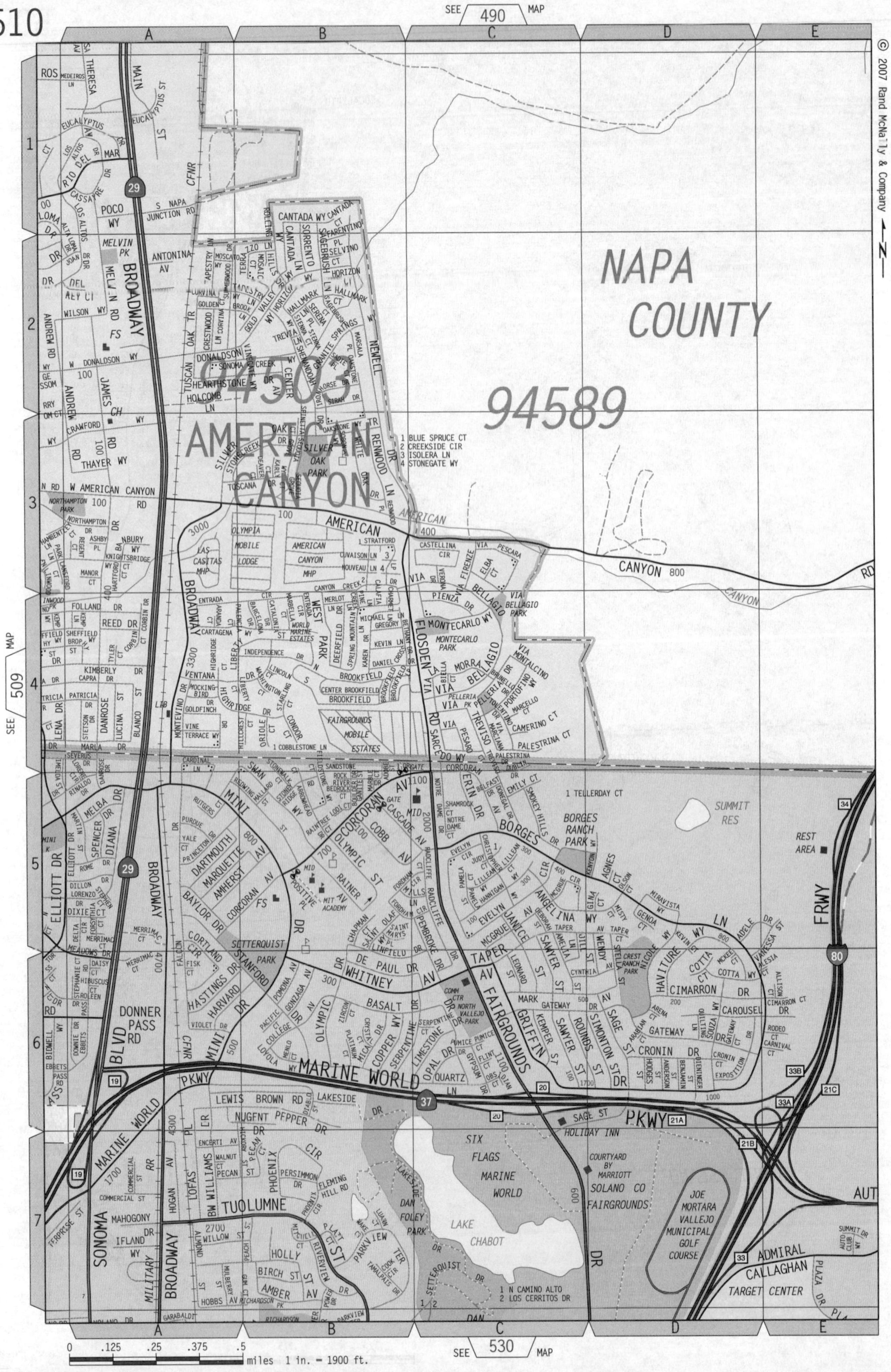
SEE 490 MAP
SEE 509 MAP
SEE 530 MAP
SOLANO CO.
NAPA COUNTY
94503
94589
AMERICAN CANYON
BROADWAY
W AMERICAN CANYON RD
AMERICAN CANYON RD
CANYON
MELVIN PK
NORTHAMPTON PARK
LAS CASITAS MHP
OLYMPIA MOBILE LODGE
AMERICAN CANYON MHP
SILVER OAK PARK
VIA BELLAGIO PARK
MONTECARLO PARK
FAIRGROUNDS MOBILE ESTATES
WORLD MARINE ESTATES
BORGES RANCH PARK
SUMMIT RES
REST AREA
SETTERQUIST PARK
MIT ACADEMY
COMM CTR
NORTH VALLEJO PARK
CREST RANCH PARK
MARINE WORLD PKWY
DONNER PASS RD
SIX FLAGS MARINE WORLD
LAKE CHABOT
DAN FOLEY PARK
HOLIDAY INN
COURTYARD BY MARRIOTT
SOLANO CO FAIRGROUNDS
JOE MORTARA VALLEJO MUNICIPAL GOLF COURSE
TARGET CENTER
AUTO CLUB
FLOSDEN RD
FAIRGROUNDS DR
TUOLUMNE
SONOMA
ADMIRAL CALLAGHAN
FRWY
1 BLUE SPRUCE CT
2 CREEKSIDE CIR
3 ISOLERA LN
4 STONEGATE WY
1 STRATFORD
1 TELLERDAY CT
1 COBBLESTONE LN
1 N CAMINO ALTO
2 LOS CERRITOS DR
0 .125 .25 .375 .5
miles 1 in. = 1900 ft.

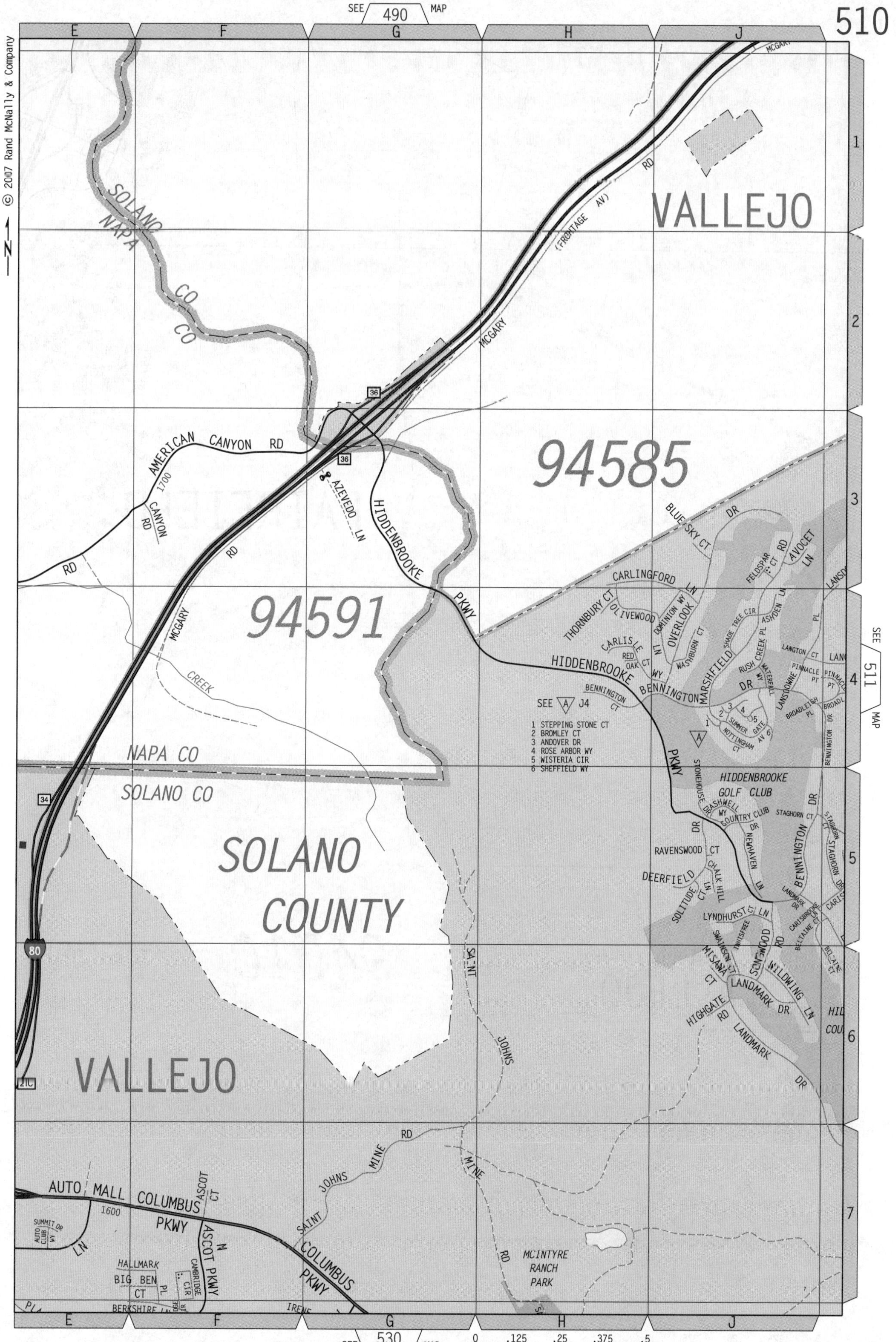
SEE 490 MAP
E
F
G
H
J
1
2
3
4
5
6
7
VALLEJO
SOLANO
NAPA
CO
CO
MCGARY
RD
(FRONTAGE AV)
MCGARY
36
AMERICAN CANYON RD
1700
CANYON RD
RD
AZEVEDO LN
HIDDENBROOKE PKWY
94585
94591
MCGARY
CREEK
BLUE SKY CT
DR
CARLINGFORD LN
FELDSPAR CT
AVOCET LN
THORNBURY CT
OLIVEWOOD LN
DOMINION WY
OVERLOOK
CARLISLE
RED OAK CT
WY
WASHBURN CT
MARSHFIELD
SHADE TREE CIR
RUSH CREEK PL
ASHDEN LN
LANSDOWNE
HIDDENBROOKE
BENNINGTON
BENNINGTON CT
DR
WATERFALL
LANGTON CT
PINNACLE PT
BROADLEIGH PL
SEE A J4
1 STEPPING STONE CT
2 BROMLEY CT
3 ANDOVER DR
4 ROSE ARBOR WY
5 WISTERIA CIR
6 SHEFFIELD WY
SUMMER GATE
NOTTINGHAM AV
CT
NAPA CO
SOLANO CO
34
PKWY
STONEHOUSE DR
HIDDENBROOKE GOLF CLUB
BASHWELL WY
COUNTRY CLUB DR
STAGHORN CT
NEWHAVEN LN
BENNINGTON DR
STAGHORN DR
SOLANO COUNTY
RAVENSWOOD CT
DEERFIELD
CHALK HILL LN
SOLITUDE CT
LYNDHURST CT
LN
SWANSON CT
INNISFREE
STONEWOOD RD
LANDMARK DR
CARISBROOKE CT
BELTAINE CT
80
SAINT
MISANA CT
WILDWING LN
LANDMARK DR
HIGHGATE RD
LANDMARK DR
JOHNS
VALLEJO
21C
RD
MINE
JOHNS
SAINT
MINE
AUTO MALL COLUMBUS PKWY
1600
ASCOT CT
SUMMIT AUTO CLUB WY
LN
ASCOT PKWY
COLUMBUS PKWY
HALLMARK
BIG BEN CT
PL
CAMBRIDGE CIR
BERKSHIRE LN
IRENE
RD
MCINTYRE RANCH PARK
SEE 511 MAP
SEE 530 MAP
0 .125 .25 .375 .5
miles 1 in. = 1900 ft.

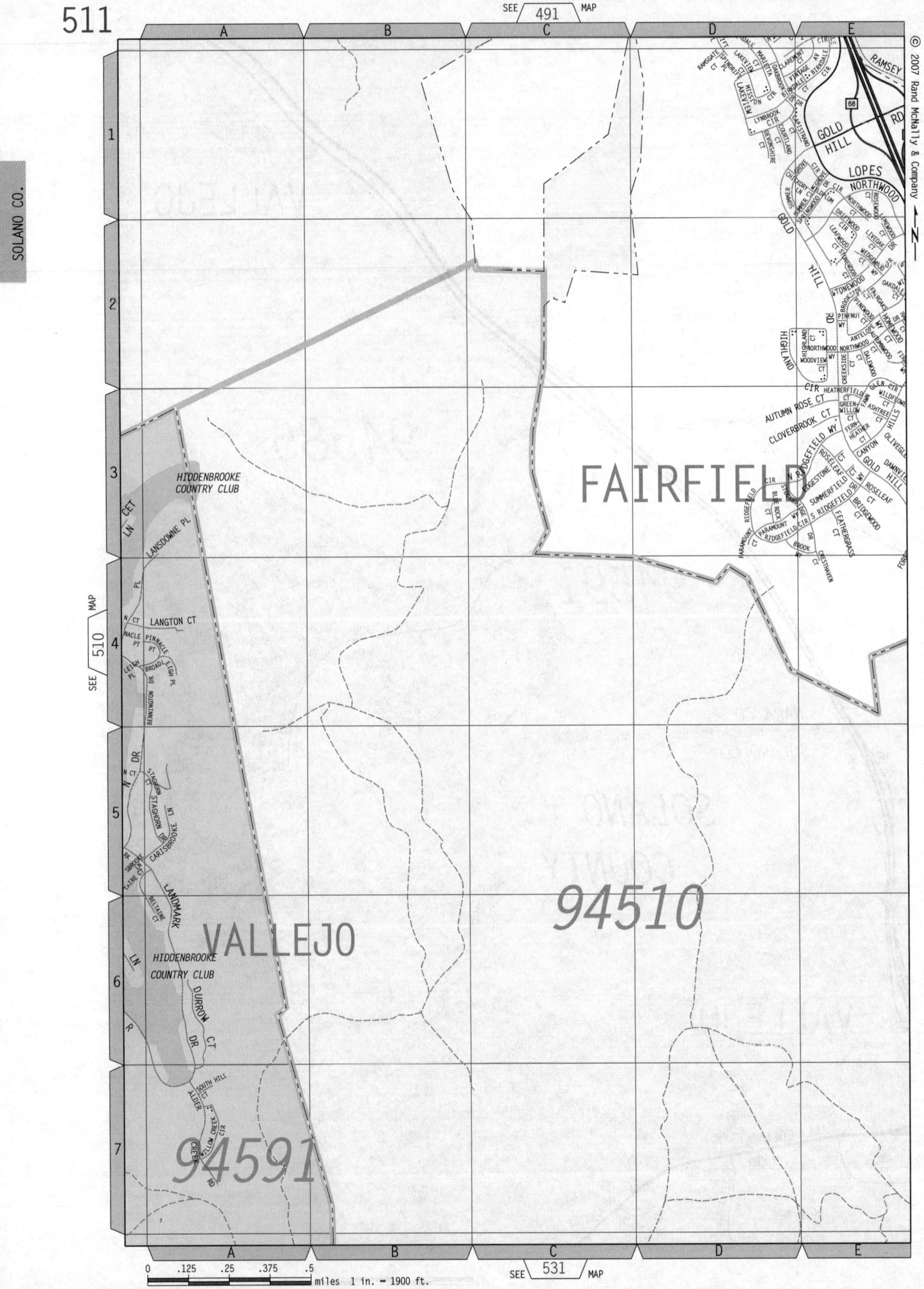
SEE 491 MAP
SEE 510 MAP
SEE 531 MAP
SOLANO CO.
FAIRFIELD
VALLEJO
94510
94591
HIDDENBROOKE COUNTRY CLUB
HIDDENBROOKE COUNTRY CLUB
LANSDOWNE PL
LANGTON CT
PINNACLE PT
BROADLEIGH PL
BENNINGTON DR
STAGHORN DR
CARISBROOKE
BELTAINE CT
LANDMARK
DURROW CT
DR
SOUTH HILL CT
ALDER
WILLOW CREEK CIR
CREEK RD
RAMSEY
68
GOLD HILL RD
LOPES
NORTHWOOD
GOLD HILL RD
HIGHLAND
WOODVIEW CT
NORTHWOOD CT
CREEKSIDE
AUTUMN ROSE CT
CLOVERBROOK CT
RIDGEFIELD WY
N RIDGEFIELD CIR
S RIDGEFIELD CIR
EDGESTONE
ROSELEAF
SUMMERFIELD DR
FEATHERGRASS CT
BRIDGEWOOD CT
PARAMOUNT CT
BLUE ROCK CT
CRESTHAVEN CT
BROOK WY
CANYON
GOLD HILL
OLIVEGLEN
ASHTREE
WILDFLOWER
HEATHERFIELD
GREENWILLOW
FERN
HEATHER CT
LAKEVIEW
MISSION
LYNBROOK CTR
DEVONSHIRE CT
COURTLAND CT
CAPISTRANO
MARIETTA CT
OAKBROOK CT
VINTAGE AV
BIRKDALE CIR
CLAREMONT
RAMSGATE CT
SPINDRIFT PL
STONEWOOD
PINENUT CT
ANTELOPE CT
HOMEWOOD
MEADOWOOD
LIVEOAK
ROSEWOOD
DRIFTWOOD
LEAFWOOD
OAKDALE
DAWNVIEW
0 .125 .25 .375 .5 miles 1 in. = 1900 ft.
© 2007 Rand McNally & Company

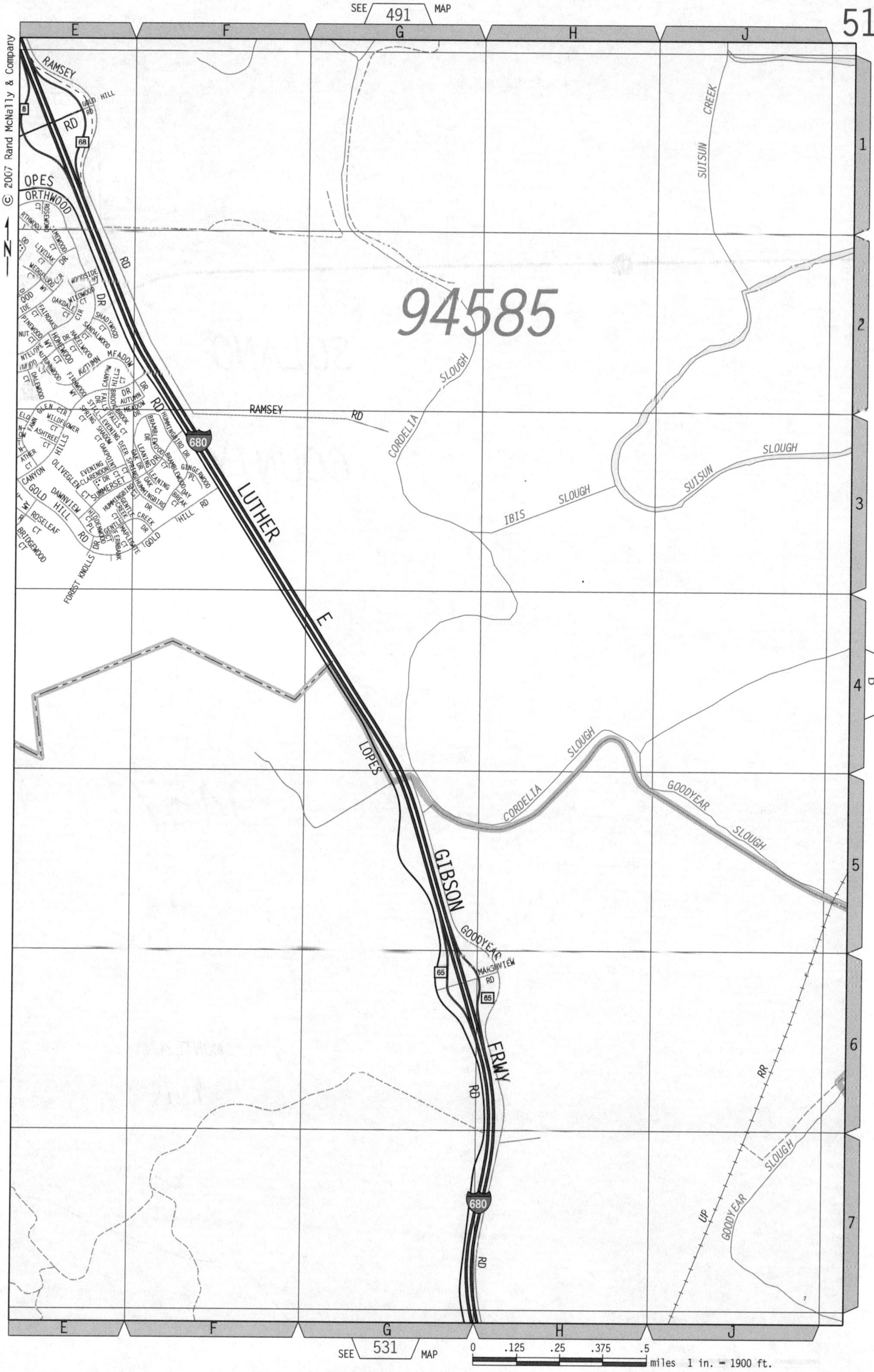
SEE 491 MAP
E
F
G
H
J
1
2
3
4
5
6
7
SEE B MAP
94585
RAMSEY
GOLD HILL RD
RD
68
8
OPES
ORTHWOOD
RD
DR
MEADOW
RD
RAMSEY RD
680
LUTHER
E
LOPES
GIBSON
FRWY
RD
RD
680
GOODYEAR
MARSHVIEW RD
65
65
CORDELIA SLOUGH
CORDELIA
SLOUGH
CORDELIA
IBIS SLOUGH
SUISUN SLOUGH
SUISUN CREEK
GOODYEAR SLOUGH
GOODYEAR SLOUGH
UP
RR
CANYON
GOLD HILL
DAWNVIEW
ROSELEAF CT
BRIDGEWOOD CT
FOREST KNOLLS DR
GOLD HILL RD
HUMMINGBIRD DR
GINGERWOOD
SUMMERSET
OLIVEGLEN CT
SEE 531 MAP
0 .125 .25 .375 .5
miles 1 in. = 1900 ft.

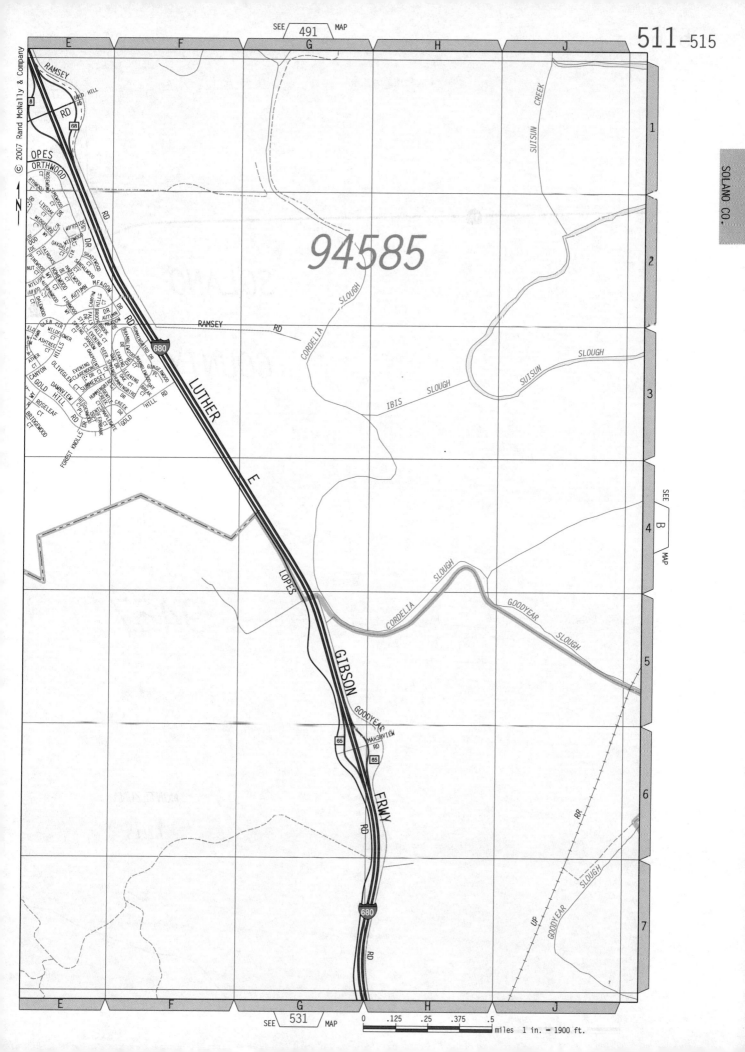

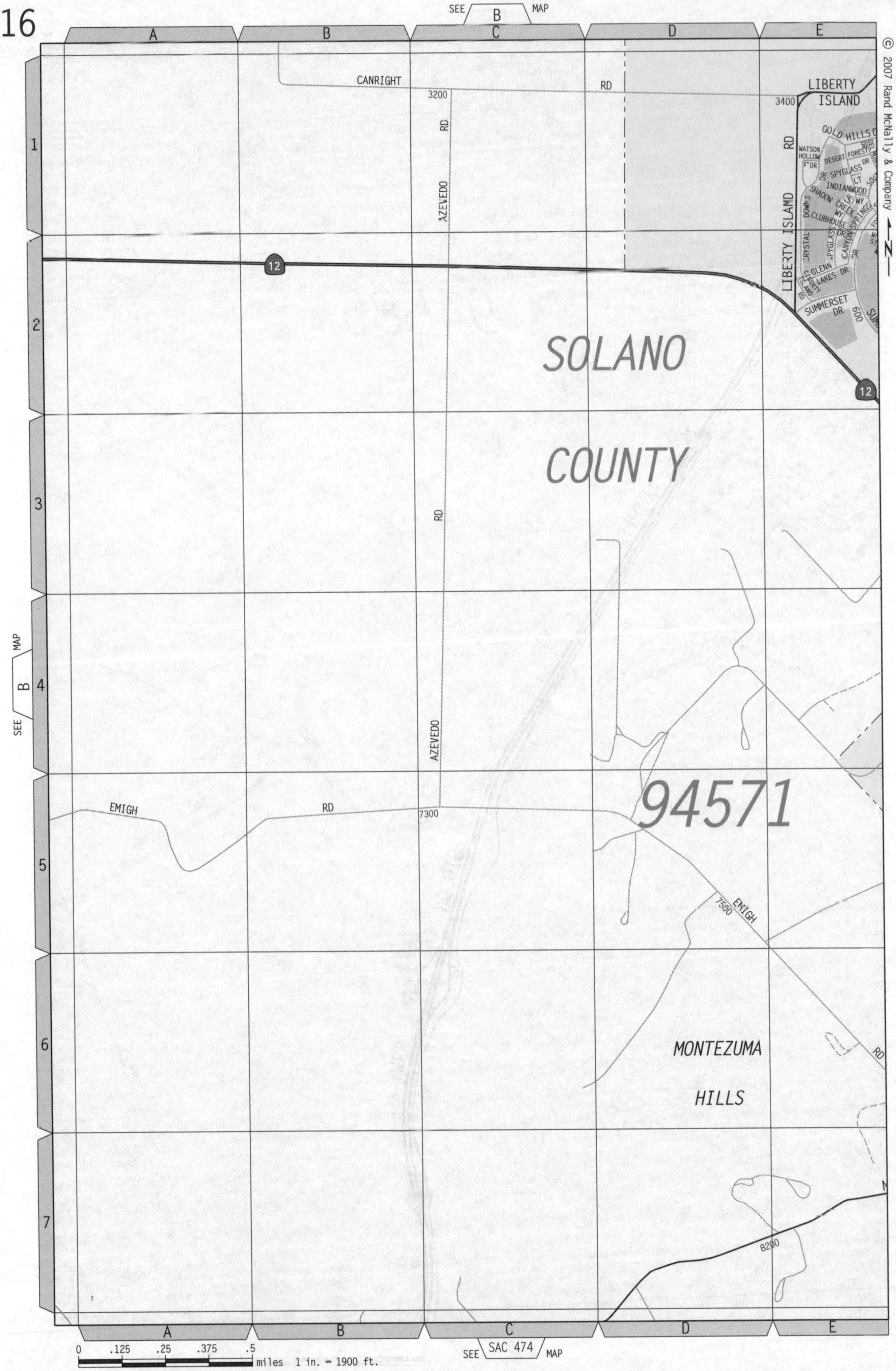
SEE B MAP
A
B
C
D
E
1
2
3
4
5
6
7
CANRIGHT
RD
3200
AZEVEDO
RD
LIBERTY ISLAND
3400
LIBERTY ISLAND
RD
GOLD HILLS
WATSON HOLLOW DR
DESERT
FOREST
SPYGLASS DR
INDIANWOOD
LT
SHADOW CREEK WY
DOWNS
CLUBHOUSE
CRYSTAL
SPYGLASS DR
CANYON SPRINGS
GLENN
LAKES DR
SUMMERSET DR
600
12
SOLANO
COUNTY
94571
EMIGH
7300
7500
MONTEZUMA
HILLS
8200
SEE B MAP
SEE SAC 474 MAP
0
.125
.25
.375
.5
miles 1 in. = 1900 ft.

SEE B MAP

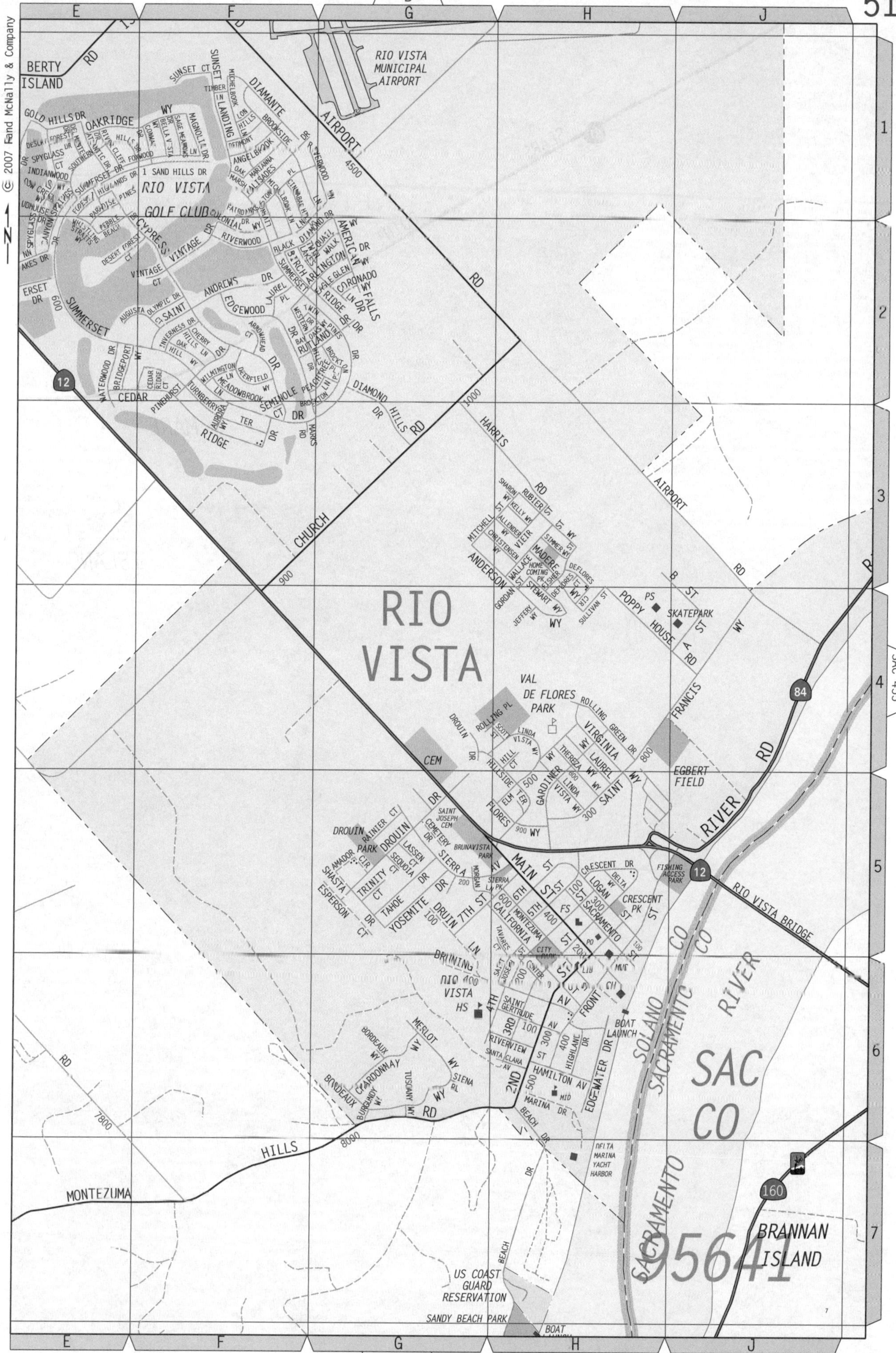

SEE SAC 455 MAP

SEE SAC 474 MAP

0 .125 .25 .375 .5 miles 1 in. = 1900 ft.

SEE 509 MAP

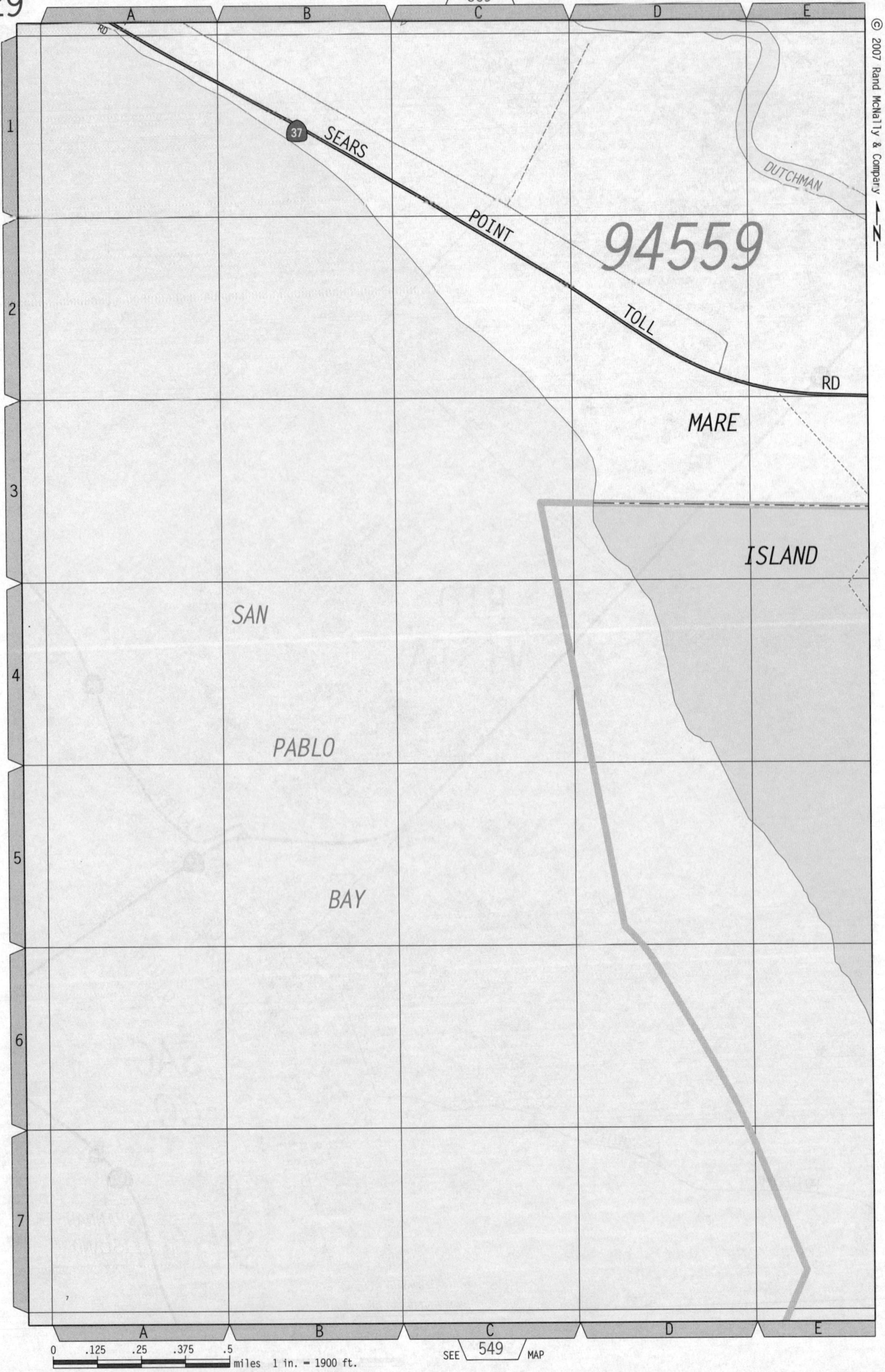
SOLANO CO.
A
B
C
D
E
1
2
3
4
5
6
7
RD
37
SEARS POINT TOLL RD
DUTCHMAN
94559
MARE
ISLAND
SAN
PABLO
BAY
0 .125 .25 .375 .5
miles 1 in. = 1900 ft.
N

SEE 549 MAP

SEE 509 MAP

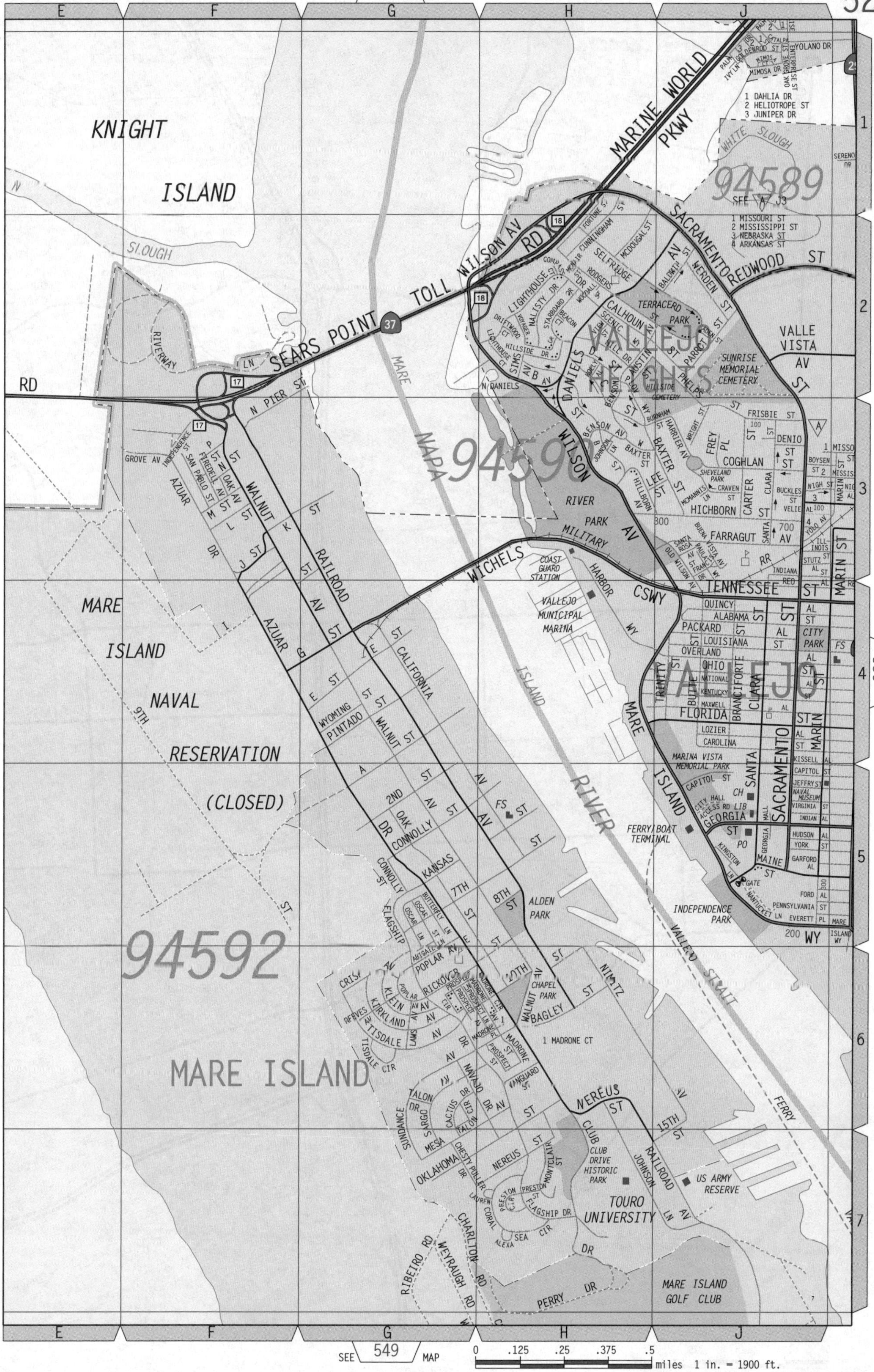

SEE 530 MAP

SOLANO CO.

SEE 549 MAP

0 .125 .25 .375 .5 miles 1 in. = 1900 ft.

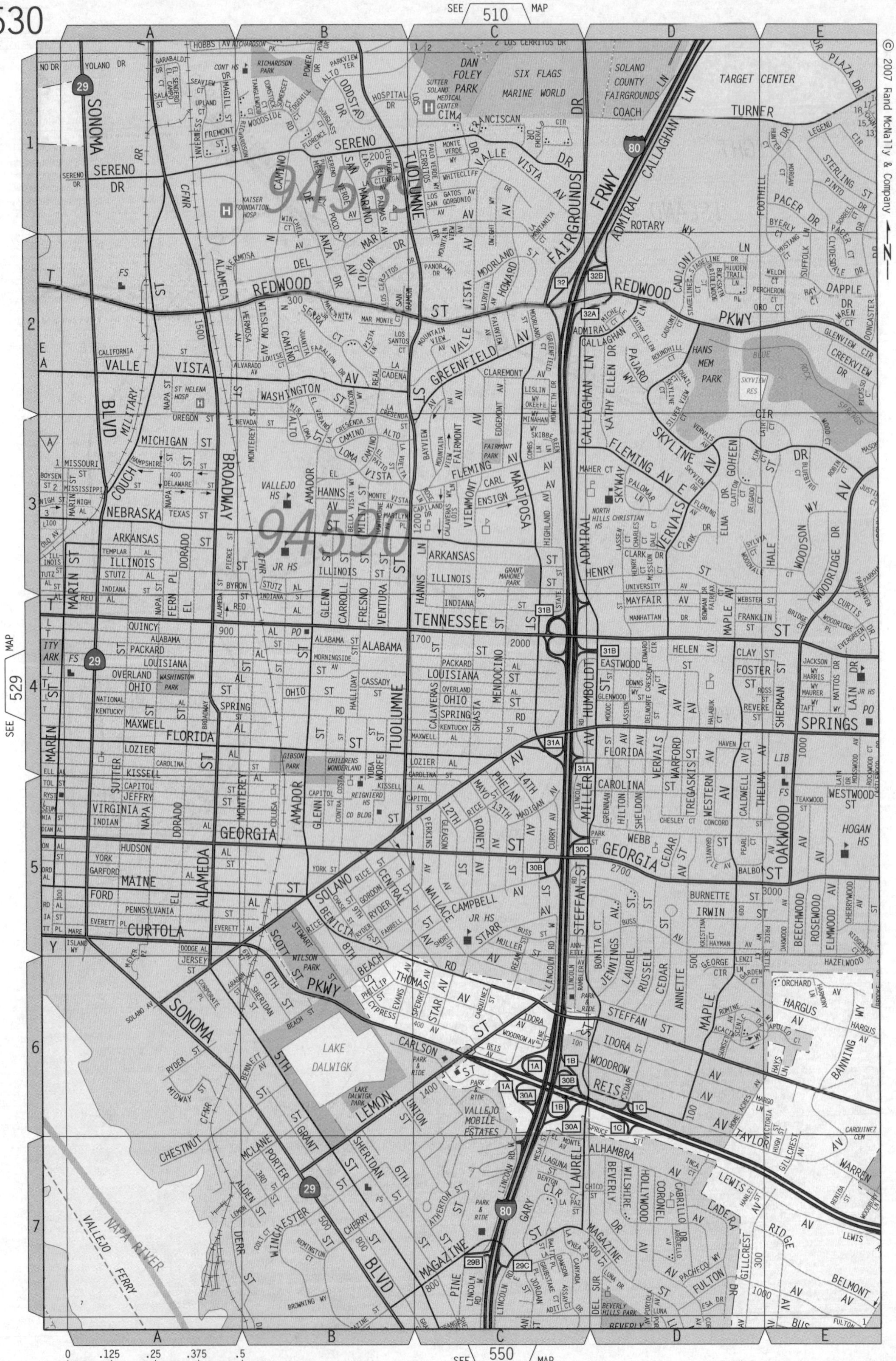
SEE 510 MAP
SEE 550 MAP
SEE 529 MAP
SOLANO CO.
© 2007 Rand McNally & Company
A
B
C
D
E
1
2
3
4
5
6
7
94589
94590
SONOMA BLVD
SERENO DR
REDWOOD ST
REDWOOD PKWY
VALLE VISTA
BROADWAY
TUOLUMNE ST
FAIRGROUNDS DR
ADMIRAL CALLAGHAN LN
FRWY
DAN FOLEY PARK
SIX FLAGS MARINE WORLD
SOLANO COUNTY FAIRGROUNDS
TARGET CENTER
TURNER
SUTTER SOLANO MEDICAL CENTER
KAISER FOUNDATION HOSP
ST HELENA HOSP
VALLEJO HS
JR HS
HANS MEM PARK
SKYLINE AV
FLEMING AV E
NORTH HILLS CHRISTIAN HS
GRANT MAHONEY PARK
TENNESSEE ST
WASHINGTON PARK
SPRINGS
HOGAN HS
GEORGIA ST
CURTOLA
SOLANO AV
BENICIA RD
CHILDRENS WONDERLAND
GIBSON PARK
CO BLDG
STARR JR HS
WILSON PARK
LAKE DALWIGK
LAKE DALWIGK PARK
SONOMA
LEMON
VALLEJO MOBILE ESTATES
STEFFAN ST
MAGAZINE ST
NAPA RIVER
VALLEJO FERRY
0 .125 .25 .375 .5 miles 1 in. = 1900 ft.

SEE 510 MAP

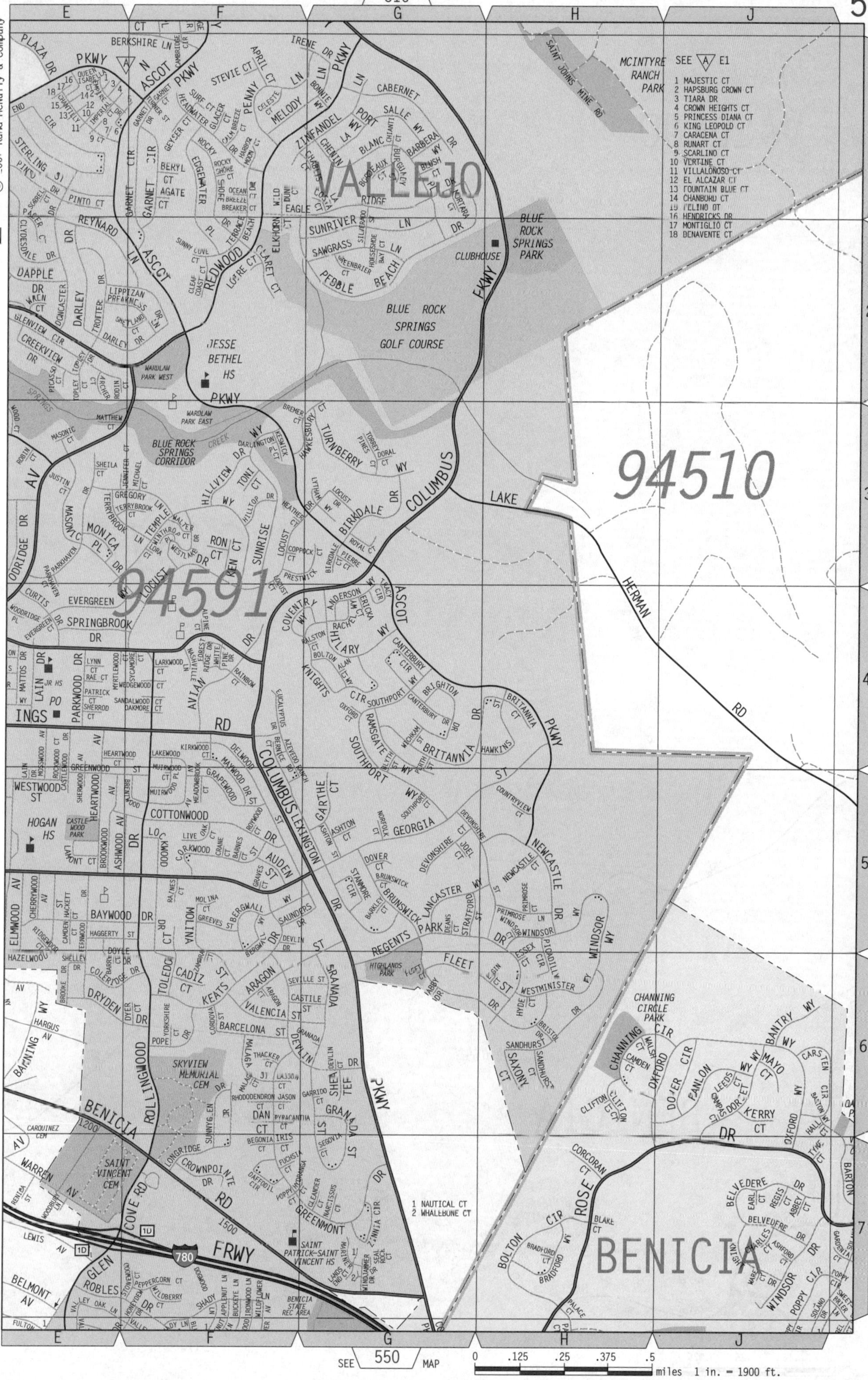

SEE 531 MAP

SOLANO CO.

SEE 550 MAP

0 .125 .25 .375 .5 miles 1 in. = 1900 ft.

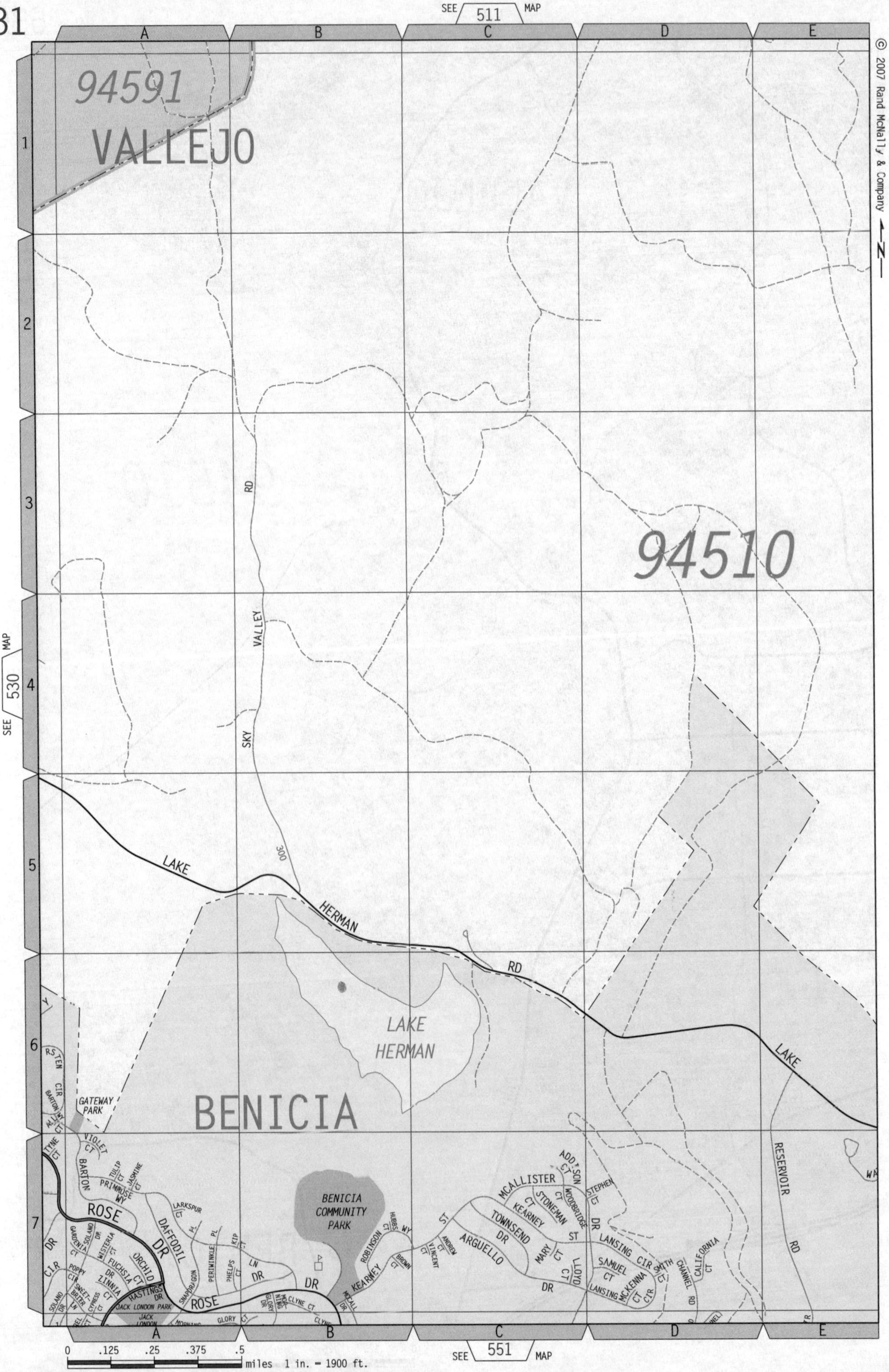
SEE 511 MAP
SEE 551 MAP
SEE 530 MAP
A
B
C
D
E
1
2
3
4
5
6
7
94591
VALLEJO
94510
BENICIA
SKY VALLEY RD
300
LAKE HERMAN RD
LAKE
LAKE HERMAN
GATEWAY PARK
BENICIA COMMUNITY PARK
ROSE DR
DAFFODIL DR
ORCHID CT
HASTINGS DR
JACK LONDON PARK
PRIMROSE WY
VIOLET CT
BARTON
TULIP CT
JASMINE CT
LARKSPUR CT
PERIWINKLE PL
KIP CT
PHELPS CT
SNAPDRAGON
FUCHSIA CT
ZINNIA CT
WISTERIA DR
GARDENIA CT
SOLANO DR
POPPY CIR
CYPRESS CT
TYNE CT
CLYNE CT
GLORY CT
MORNING
ROBINSON CT
KEARNEY
HIBBS WY
BROWN CT
VINCENT CT
ANDREW CT
ARGUELLO DR
TOWNSEND DR
KEARNEY CT
MCALLISTER CT
STONEMAN CT
WOODBRIDGE DR
ADDISON CT
STEPHEN CT
MARY CT
LLOYD CT
SAMUEL CT
MCKENNA CT
LANSING CIR
SMITH CT
CHANNEL RD
CALIFORNIA CT
RESERVOIR RD
0 .125 .25 .375 .5 miles 1 in. = 1900 ft.

SEE 511 MAP

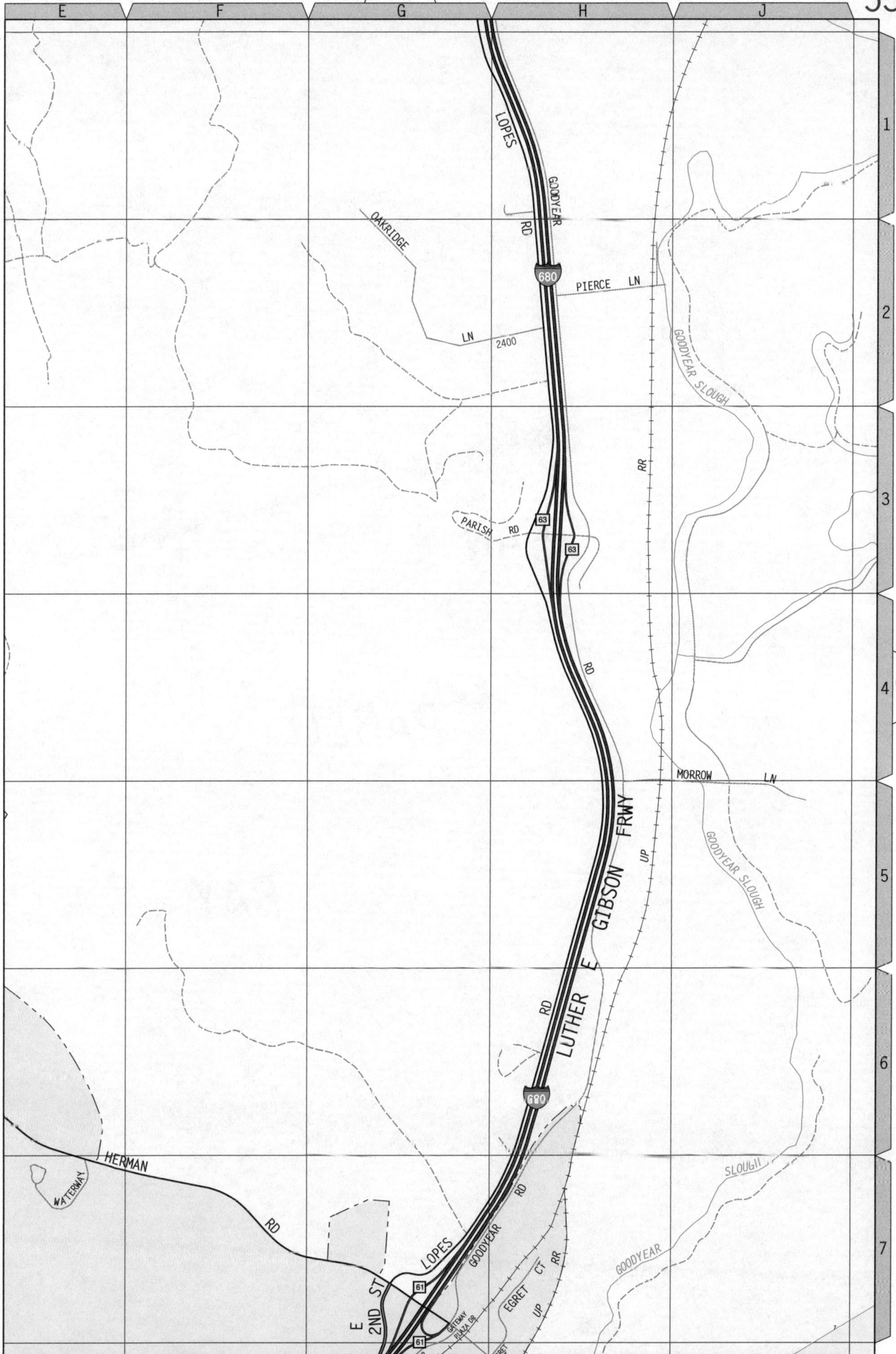

SEE B MAP

SEE 551 MAP

0 .125 .25 .375 .5 miles 1 in. = 1900 ft.

SEE 529 MAP

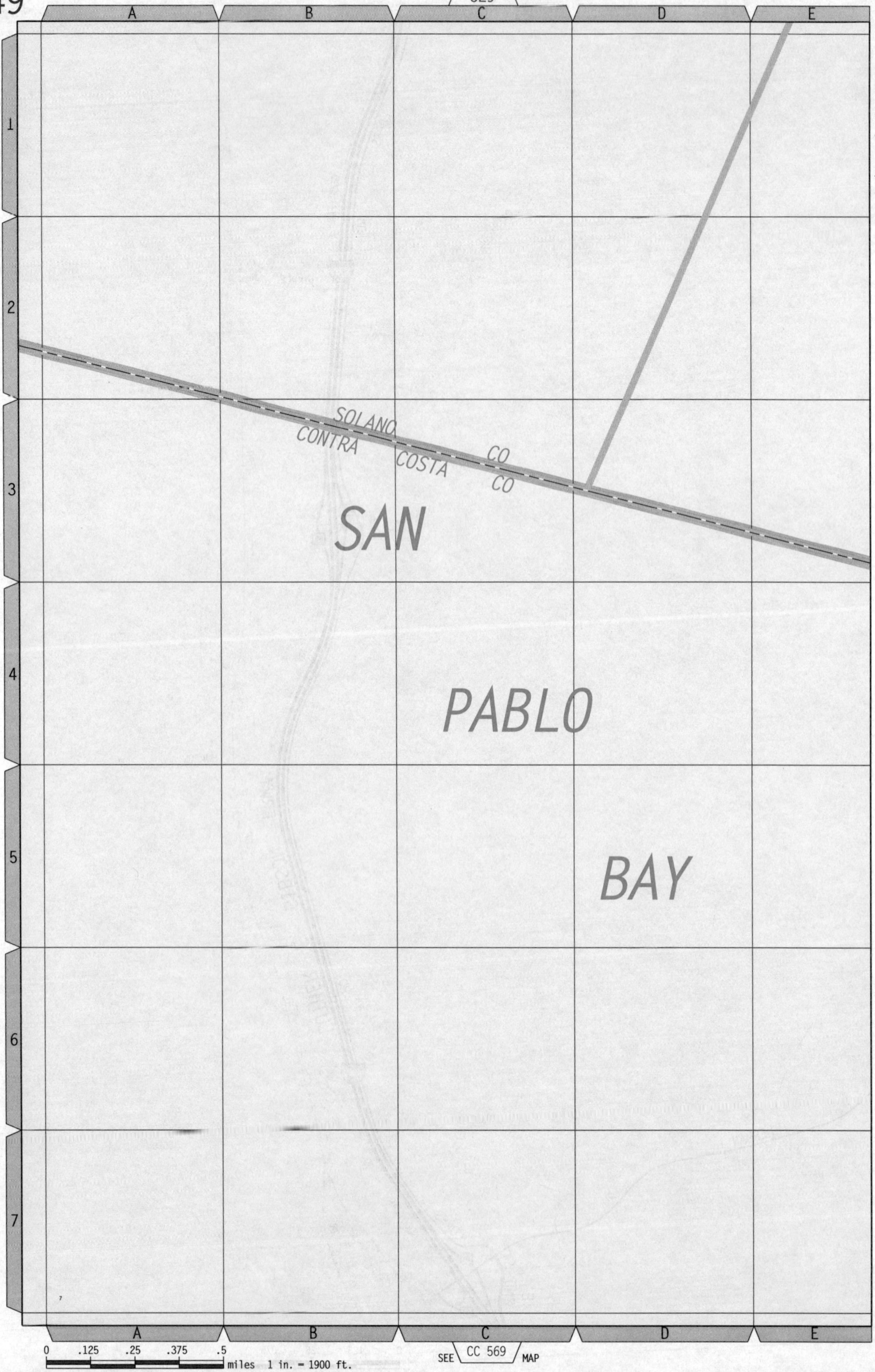
A
B
C
D
E
1
2
3
4
5
6
7
SOLANO
CONTRA
COSTA
CO
CO
SAN
PABLO
BAY
SOLANO CO.
0
.125
.25
.375
.5
miles 1 in. = 1900 ft.

SEE CC 569 MAP

SEE 529 MAP

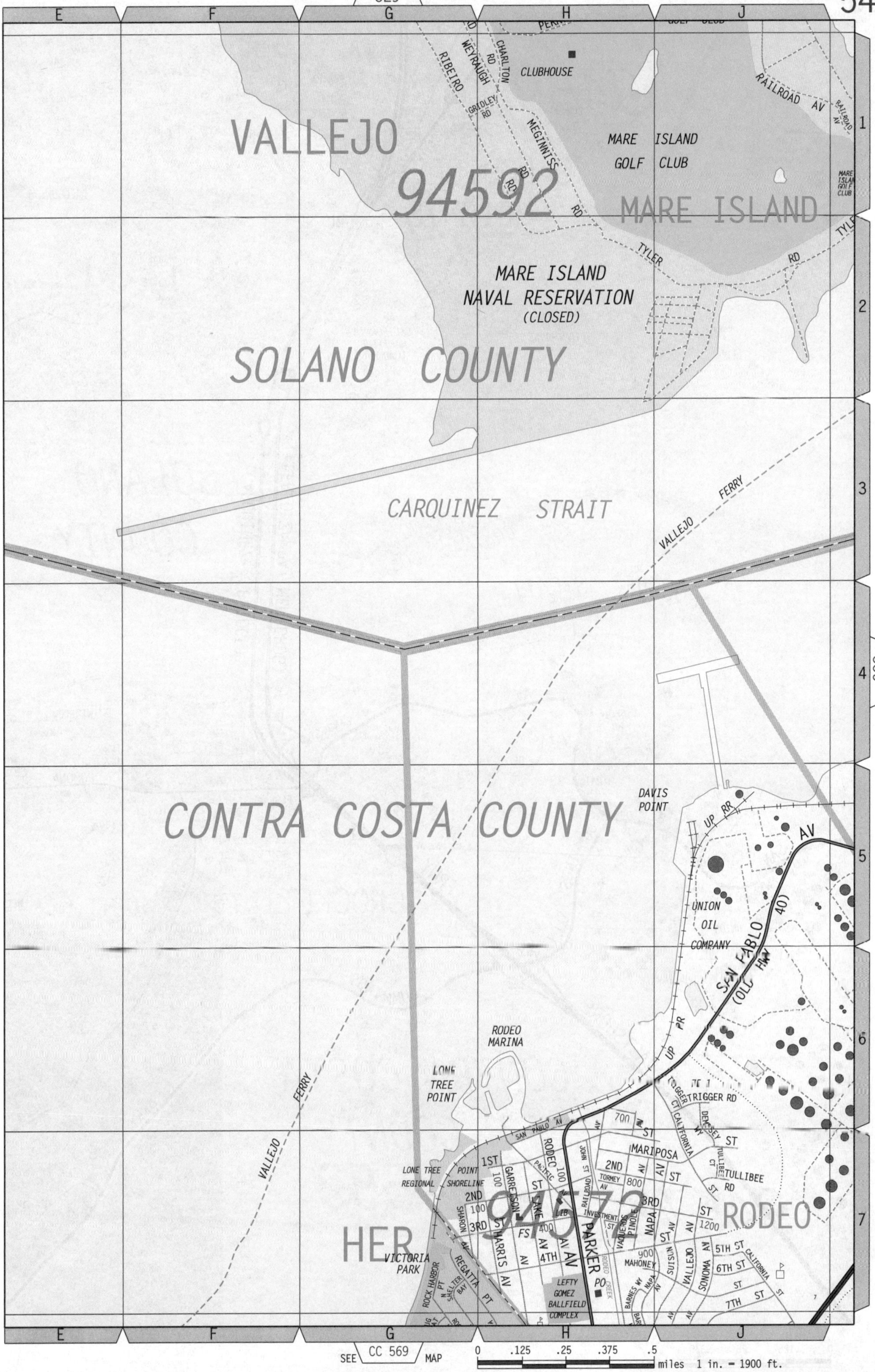

SEE 550 MAP

SEE CC 569 MAP

0 .125 .25 .375 .5 miles 1 in. = 1900 ft.

SOLANO CO.

SEE 530 MAP

SOLANO CO.

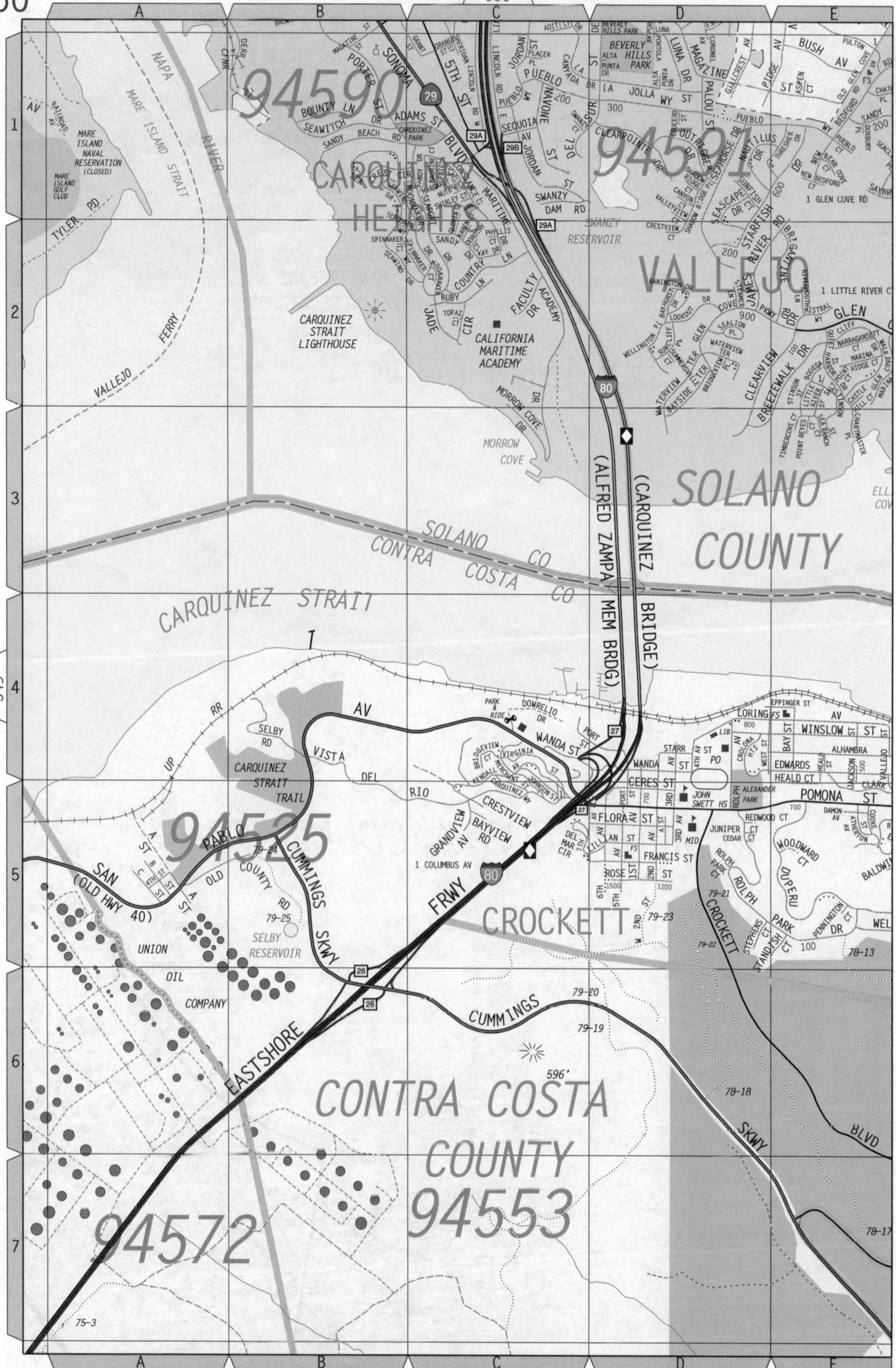

SEE 549 MAP

SEE CC 570 MAP

0 .125 .25 .375 .5 miles 1 in. = 1900 ft.

SEE 530 MAP

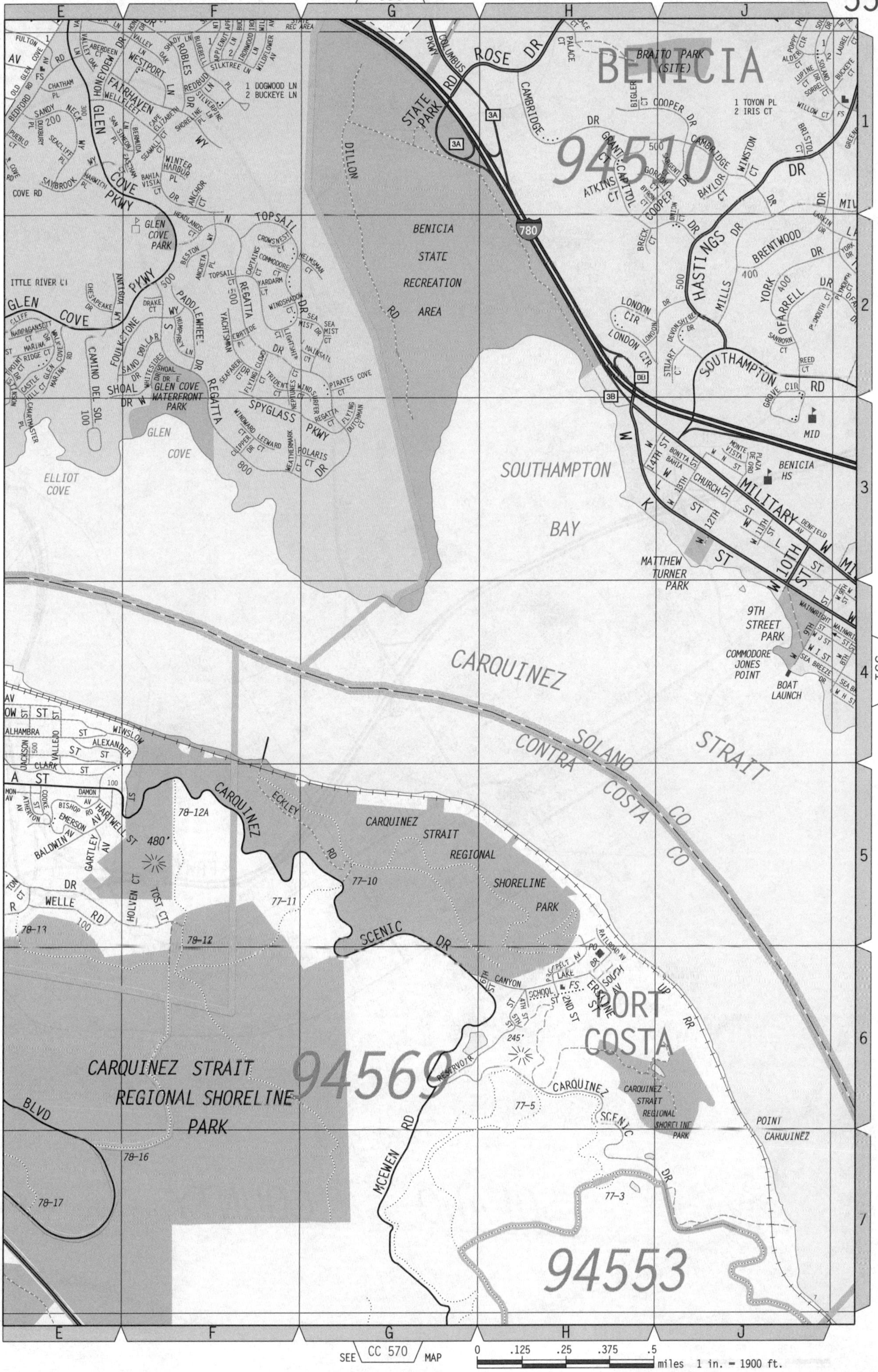

SEE CC 570 MAP

0 .125 .25 .375 .5 miles 1 in. = 1900 ft.

SEE 531 MAP

0 .125 .25 .375 .5 miles 1 in. = 1900 ft.

SEE 550 MAP

SEE CC 571 MAP

SEE 531 MAP

SEE CC 552 MAP

SEE CC 571 MAP

0 .125 .25 .375 .5 miles 1 in. = 1900 ft.

SOLANO CO.

Cities and Communities

Community Name	Abbr.	County	ZIP Code	Map Page
Allendale		SolC	95688	393
* American Canyon	AMCN	NaCo	94503	509
* Benicia	BEN	SolC	94510	551
Carquinez Heights		SolC	94590	550
Cordelia		SolC	94585	491
* Davis	DVS	YoCo	95616	356
* Dixon	DXN	SolC	95620	395
Dyke		YoCo	95691	378
El Macero		YoCo	95616	376
Elmira		SolC	95687	434
* Fairfield	FRFD	SolC	94533	472
Green Valley Estates		SolC	94585	471
Leisure Town		SolC	95687	433
Mankas Corner		SolC	94585	471
Mare Island		SolC	94592	529
-- Napa County	NaCo			
Nut Tree		SolC	95688	433
* Rio Vista	RVIS	SolC	94571	516
Riverview		YoCo	95691	378
Rockville		SolC	94585	471
-- Solano County	SolC			
* Suisun City	SUIS	SolC	94585	472
Travis Air Force Base		SolC	94535	473
* Vacaville	VAC	SolC	95688	433
* Vallejo	VAL	SolC	94590	530
Vallejo Heights		SolC	94590	529
* West Sacramento	WSAC	YoCo	95691	378
* Winters	WIN	YoCo	95694	373
* Woodland	WDLD	YoCo	95695	315
-- Yolo County	YoCo			

*Indicates incorporated city

List of Abbreviations

PREFIXES AND SUFFIXES

AL	ALLEY
ARC	ARCADE
AV, AVE	AVENUE
AVCT	AVENUE COURT
AVD	AVENIDA
AVD D LA	AVENIDA DE LA
AVD D LOS	AVENIDA DE LOS
AVD DE	AVENIDA DE
AVD DE LAS	AVENIDA DE LAS
AVD DEL	AVENIDA DEL
AVDR	AVENUE DRIVE
AVEX	AVENUE EXTENSION
AV OF	AVENUE OF
AV OF THE	AVENUE OF THE
AVPL	AVENUE PLACE
BAY	BAY
BEND	BEND
BL, BLVD	BOULEVARD
BLCT	BOULEVARD COURT
BLEX	BOULEVARD EXTENSION
BRCH	BRANCH
BRDG	BRIDGE
BYPS	BYPASS
BYWY	BYWAY
CIDR	CIRCLE DRIVE
CIR	CIRCLE
CL	CALLE
CL DE	CALLE DE
CL DL	CALLE DEL
CL D LA	CALLE DE LA
CL D LAS	CALLE DE LAS
CL D LOS	CALLE DE LOS
CL EL	CALLE EL
CLJ	CALLEJON
CL LA	CALLE LA
CL LAS	CALLE LAS
CL LOS	CALLE LOS
CLTR	CLUSTER
CM	CAMINO
CM DE	CAMINO DE
CM DL	CAMINO DEL
CM D LA	CAMINO DE LA
CM D LAS	CAMINO DE LAS
CM D LOS	CAMINO DE LOS
CMTO	CAMINITO
CMTO DEL	CAMINITO DEL
CMTO D LA	CAMINITO DE LA
CMTO D LAS	CAMINITO DE LAS
CMTO D LOS	CAMINITO DE LOS
CNDR	CENTER DRIVE
COM	COMMON
COMS	COMMONS
CORR	CORRIDOR
CRES	CRESCENT
CRLO	CIRCULO
CRSG	CROSSING
CST	CIRCLE STREET
CSWY	CAUSEWAY
CT	COURT
CTAV	COURT AVENUE
CTE	CORTE
CTE D	CORTE DE
CTE DEL	CORTE DEL
CTE D LAS	CORTE DE LAS
CTO	CUT OFF
CTR	CENTER
CTST	COURT STREET
CUR	CURVE
CV	COVE
DE	DE
DIAG	DIAGONAL
DR	DRIVE
DRAV	DRIVE AVENUE
DRCT	DRIVE COURT
DRLP	DRIVE LOOP
DVDR	DIVISION DR
EXAV	EXTENSION AVENUE
EXBL	EXTENSION BOULEVARD
EXRD	EXTENSION ROAD
EXST	EXTENSION STREET
EXT	EXTENSION
EXWY	EXPRESSWAY
FOREST RT	FOREST ROUTE
FRWY	FREEWAY
FRY	FERRY
GDNS	GARDENS
GN, GLN	GLEN
GRN	GREEN
GRV	GROVE
HTS	HEIGHTS
HWY	HIGHWAY
ISL	ISLE
JCT	JUNCTION
LN	LANE
LNCR	LANE CIRCLE
LNDG	LANDING
LNDR	LAND DRIVE
LNLP	LANE LOOP
LP	LOOP
MNR	MANOR
MT	MOUNT
MTWY	MOTORWAY
MWCR	MEWS COURT
MWLN	MEWS LANE
NFD	NAT'L FOREST DEV
NK	NOOK
OH	OUTER HIGHWAY
OVL	OVAL
OVLK	OVERLOOK
OVPS	OVERPASS
PAS	PASEO
PAS DE	PASEO DE
PAS DE LA	PASEO DE LA
PAS DE LAS	PASEO DE LAS
PAS DE LOS	PASEO DE LOS
PAS DL	PASEO DEL
PASG	PASSAGE
PAS LA	PASEO LA
PAS LOS	PASEO LOS
PASS	PASS
PIKE	PIKE
PK	PARK
PKDR	PARK DRIVE
PKWY, PKY	PARKWAY
PL	PLACE
PLWY	PLACE WAY
PLZ, PZ	PLAZA
PT	POINT
PTAV	POINT AVENUE
PTH	PATH
PZ DE	PLAZA DE
PZ DEL	PLAZA DEL
PZ D LA	PLAZA DE LA
PZ D LAS	PLAZA DE LAS
PZWY	PLAZA WAY
RAMP	RAMP
RD	ROAD
RDAV	ROAD AVENUE
RDBP	ROAD BYPASS
RDCT	ROAD COURT
RDEX	ROAD EXTENSION
RDG	RIDGE
RDSP	ROAD SPUR
RDWY	ROAD WAY
RR	RAILROAD
RUE	RUE
RUE D	RUE D
RW	ROW
RY	RAILWAY
SKWY	SKYWAY
SQ	SQUARE
ST	STREET
STAV	STREET AVENUE
STCT	STREET COURT
STDR	STREET DRIVE
STEX	STREET EXTENSION
STLN	STREET LANE
STLP	STREET LOOP
ST OF	STREET OF
ST OF THE	STREET OF THE
STOV	STREET OVERPASS
STPL	STREET PLACE
STPM	STREET PROMENADE
STWY	STREET WAY
STXP	STREET EXPRESSWAY
TER	TERRACE
TFWY	TRAFFICWAY
THWY	THROUGHWAY
TKTR	TRUCK TRAIL
TPKE	TURNPIKE
TRC	TRACE
TRCT	TERRACE COURT
TR, TRL	TRAIL
TRWY	TRAIL WAY
TTSP	TRUCK TRAIL SPUR
TUN	TUNNEL
UNPS	UNDERPASS
VIA D	VIA DE
VIA DL	VIA DEL
VIA D LA	VIA DE LA
VIA D LAS	VIA DE LAS
VIA D LOS	VIA DE LOS
VIA LA	VIA LA
VW	VIEW
VWY	VIEW WAY
VIS	VISTA
VIS D	VISTA DE
VIS D L	VISTA DE LA
VIS D LAS	VISTA DE LAS
VIS DEL	VISTA DEL
WK	WALK
WY	WAY
WYCR	WAY CIRCLE
WYDR	WAY DRIVE
WYLN	WAY LANE
WYPL	WAY PLACE

DIRECTIONS

E	EAST
KPN	KEY PENINSULA NORTH
KPS	KEY PENINSULA SOUTH
N	NORTH
NE	NORTHEAST
NW	NORTHWEST
S	SOUTH
SE	SOUTHEAST
SW	SOUTHWEST
W	WEST

BUILDINGS

CH	CITY HALL
CHP	CALIFORNIA HIGHWAY PATROL
COMM CTR	COMMUNITY CENTER
CON CTR	CONVENTION CENTER
CONT HS	CONTINUATION HIGH SCHOOL
CTH	COURTHOUSE
FAA	FEDERAL AVIATION ADMIN
FS	FIRE STATION
HOSP	HOSPITAL
HS	HIGH SCHOOL
INT	INTERMEDIATE SCHOOL
JR HS	JUNIOR HIGH SCHOOL
LIB	LIBRARY
MID	MIDDLE SCHOOL
MUS	MUSEUM
PO	POST OFFICE
PS	POLICE STATION
SR CIT CTR	SENIOR CITIZENS CENTER
STA	STATION
THTR	THEATER
VIS BUR	VISITORS BUREAU

OTHER ABBREVIATIONS

BCH	BEACH
BLDG	BUILDING
CEM	CEMETERY
CK	CREEK
CO	COUNTY
COMM	COMMUNITY
CTR	CENTER
EST	ESTATE
HIST	HISTORIC
HTS	HEIGHTS
LK	LAKE
MDW	MEADOW
MED	MEDICAL
MEM	MEMORIAL
MHP	MOBILE HOME PARK
MT	MOUNT
MTN	MOUNTAIN
NATL	NATIONAL
PKG	PARKING
PLGD	PLAYGROUND
RCH	RANCH
RCHO	RANCHO
REC	RECREATION
RES	RESERVOIR
RIV	RIVER
RR	RAILROAD
SPG	SPRING
STA	SANTA
VLG	VILLAGE
VLY	VALLEY
VW	VIEW

STREET Name City ZIP Pg-Grid

A

A LN
FRFD 94533 473-F2
A ST
CCCo 94525 550-A5
DVS 95616 356-C7
DVS 95616 376-C1
FRFD 94535 473-J2
FRFD 94535 474-A2
RVIS 94571 516-J4
VAL 94592 529-G5
WDLD 95776 316-A3
YoCo 95616 376-C1
E A ST
DXN 95620 395-D7
W A ST
DXN 95620 394-J7
DXN 95620 395-A7
A ST N
SolC 95687 434-C7
A ST S
SolC 95687 434-B7
AARON CIR
VAC 95687 453-F1
ABACO RD
WSAC 95691 378-C2
ABBEY CT
BEN 94510 530-J7
FRFD 94534 491-C3
WDLD 95695 315-J6
ABBEY DR
FRFD 94534 491-C3
ABBEY PL
WDLD 95695 315-J6
ABBEY ST
WIN 95694 373-E4
E ABBEY ST
WIN 95694 373-F3
ABBY CT
AMCN 94503 509-J3
ABBY DR
VAL 94591 530-G6
ABELE ST
WDLD 95695 315-H3
ABERDEEN CT
VAL 94591 550-E1
ABERDEEN WY
VAC 95687 433-D7
ABERNATHY RD
SolC 94534 472-A5
ABIGAIL LN
VAL 94592 529-G6
ABLE AL
DXN 95620 415-C2
ABRAHAM CT
DXN 95620 395-B5
ABRUZZI CT
FRFD 94534 491-F5
ABRUZZINI HILL RD
NaCo 94558 451-H2
NaCo 94558 452-A2
ACACIA LN
DVS 95616 356-A7
SolC 95688 393-D7
SolC 95688 413-D1
ACACIA ST
FRFD 94533 472-G4
VAC 95688 433-B5
ACACIA WY
VAL 94591 530-D6
WDLD 95695 315-G5
ACADEMY DR
FRFD 94534 491-D3
ACADEMY LN
WDLD 95695 315-J4
ACADIA LN
YoCo 95616 355-A3
ACAPULCO CT
SUIS 94585 473-C7
ACKLEY CT
DXN 95620 415-C2
ACKLEY PL
WDLD 95776 316-D7
ACORN CT
VAC 95688 433-B7
ACORN ST
WSAC 95691 358-H5
ADAGIO DR
FRFD 94534 491-E1
ADAK DR
WDLD 95776 316-C5
ADAMS CT
WDLD 95776 316-B6
ADAMS LN
WIN 95694 373-D3
ADAMS ST
BEN 94510 551-D6
DVS 95616 356-A7
FRFD 94533 472-F5
VAL 94590 550-B1
N ADAMS ST
DXN 95620 395-C7
S ADAMS ST
DXN 95620 415-C1
ADAMS TER
DVS 95616 356-A7
ADDISON CT
BEN 94510 531-C7
ADELE DR
VAL 94589 510-D5
ADELINE PL
DVS 95616 356-E7
ADEN ST
VAL 94590 529-J2
ADIT CT
VAL 94591 530-C7
ADMIRAL CALLAGHAN LN
VAL 94591 510-E7
VAL 94591 530-C2
ADOBE DR
VAC 95687 433-E7
ADOBE ST
VAL 94589 510-B5
ADOBE WY
WDLD 95695 315-J6
ADRIAN CT
VAC 95687 433-H7
ADRIAN DR
DVS 95618 356-F6
AEGEAN WY
VAC 95687 433-E6
AFTON WY
DXN 95620 395-C6
AGATE CT
VAL 94591 530-F1
AGGIE LN
DVS 95616 376-C1
AGNES CT
VAL 94589 510-D5
AGUILAR PL
WDLD 95776 336-D1
AHERN LN
DXN 95620 395-A7
AINSLEY LN
FRFD 94533 472-G5
AIR BASE PKWY
FRFD 94533 472-F3
FRFD 94533 473-A3
FRFD 94535 473-D3
SolC 94535 473-D3
AIRMEN DR
FRFD 94535 473-H3
AIRONS CT
WSAC 95691 378-F1
AIRPARK RD
NaCo 94589 490-A3
AIRPORT BLVD
NaCo 94589 490-A2
AIRPORT RD
RVIS 94571 516-G1
SolC 94571 516-H3
YoCo 95616 375-G2
AKERLY CT
VAC 95688 433-J1
AKERLY DR
VAC 95688 413-J7
VAC 95688 433-J1
ALABAMA AV
WSAC 95691 358-H6
ALABAMA CT
WSAC 95691 358-H6
ALABAMA ST
VAL 94590 529-J4
VAL 94590 530-A4
ALAMEDA AV
DVS 95616 355-J7
ALAMEDA BLVD
WSAC 95691 358-J5
ALAMEDA CT
VAC 95687 433-G5
ALAMEDA PL
WDLD 95695 315-F3
ALAMEDA ST
VAL 94589 530-A2
VAL 94590 530-A4
ALAMO CT
AMCN 94503 509-J2
VAC 95687 453-C1
ALAMO DR
VAC 95687 433-A6
VAC 95687 453-D1
VAC 95688 432-J4
VAC 95688 433-A4
ALAMO LN
VAC 95687 453-D2
ALAMO PL
WSAC 95691 378-J1
ALAMO CREEK CT
VAC 95688 433-A6
ALAN CT
VAL 94591 530-G4
ALARCON CT
FRFD 94533 472-B7
ALASKA AV
FRFD 94533 472-F3
E ALASKA AV
FRFD 94533 472-G3
ALBACETE DR
VAC 95688 433-B6
ALBANY AV
DVS 95618 376-F1
VAC 95687 453-D1
ALBANY CIR
DVS 95618 376-G1
ALBANY CT
VAC 95687 453-D1
ALBATROSSE WY
VAL 94589 509-G5
ALBERT LN
SolC 95688 412-G7
ALBION PL
DVS 95618 356-E6
ALCAJAPA LN
NaCo 94558 450-C2
ALCAZAR CT
SUIS 94585 473-D6
ALDEN ST
VAL 94590 530-A7
ALDER CT
AMCN 94503 509-J3
BEN 94510 550-J1
WDLD 95695 315-J2
ALDER PL
DVS 95618 356-F6
ALDER WY
WSAC 95691 378-J2
ALDER CREEK RD
VAL 94591 511-A7
ALDER CREST CT
VAC 95688 433-D3
ALDERGLEN DR
DXN 95620 395-B7
DXN 95620 415-B1
ALDERWOOD WY
VAC 95687 433-C7
VAC 95687 453-C1
ALDRIDGE RD
SolC 95688 413-F6
VAC 95688 413-F6
ALEGRE WY
DVS 95618 356-H6
ALESIA CT
VAL 94589 510-E6
ALETHA LN
VAC 95687 453-E1
ALEUTIAN ISLAND ST
WSAC 95691 378-D2
ALEXA
VAL 94592 529-H7
ALEXANDER CT
SUIS 94585 472-H6
ALEXANDER DR
DXN 95620 395-B5
ALEXANDER ST
CCCo 94525 550-E4
ALEXANDER WY
SUIS 94585 472-H6
ALFALFA ST
SolC 95620 415-A3
ALFORD CT
FRFD 94534 472-E3
ALFORD DR
FRFD 94534 472-E4
ALHAMBRA AV
VAL 94591 530-D7
ALHAMBRA DR
DVS 95618 356-G6
ALHAMBRA ST
CCCo 94525 550-E4
ALICANTE DR
FRFD 94533 473-C4
ALICANTE PL
VAC 95688 433-A3
ALICANTE ST
DVS 95618 356-G5
ALICE DR
VAL 94589 509-J4
ALICE ST
DVS 95616 356-D7
WDLD 95776 316-A4
ALLAN AV
WSAC 95691 378-F1
ALLEN CIR
WDLD 95776 316-E7
ALLEN CT
FRFD 94535 473-J1
ALLEN WY
BEN 94510 551-C2
ALLENDALE RD
SolC 95620 394-A6
SolC 95688 393-F6
SolC 95688 413-F1
SolC 95694 393-F6
ALLENDALE RD
SolC 95694 394-A6
ALLENDER WY
RVIS 94571 516-H3
ALLENPORT WY
SAC 95831 378-H6
ALLISON CT
DXN 95620 395-B5
VAC 95688 433-E4
VAL 94589 510-E6
ALLISON DR
VAC 95687 433-F5
VAC 95688 433-E4
ALLISON PKWY
VAC 95688 413-F7
VAC 95688 433-F2
ALLSTON CT
FRFD 94533 473-A4
ALLSTON PL
FRFD 94533 473-A3
ALMA CT
DXN 95620 395-D7
SUIS 94585 473-A7
ALMADEN CT
FRFD 94533 452-H6
ALMANOR DR
VAC 95687 433-E7
ALMANOR RD
WSAC 95691 378-D3
ALMAR DR
NaCo 94558 450-B1
ALMERIA AV
WIN 95694 373-E3
ALMERIA PL
WIN 95694 373-E3
ALMERIA ST
DVS 95616 356-B5
ALMOND DR
WIN 95694 373-F2
ALMOND LN
DVS 95618 376-G1
YoCo 95618 376-G1
ALMOND ST
SUIS 94585 472-G7
VAC 95688 433-B6
VAL 94589 510-A7
WSAC 95691 378-J1
N ALMOND ST
DXN 95620 395-C6
S ALMOND ST
DXN 95620 395-C7
DXN 95620 415-C1
ALMONDTREE CT
DXN 95620 395-B7
ALMONDWOOD WY
FRFD 94534 472-F1
ALONZO CT
VAC 95687 433-D7
ALONZO RD
VAC 95687 433-D7
ALOUETTE PL
VAC 95687 433-J5
ALPINE CT
FRFD 94585 491-D6
VAL 94591 530-F4
ALPINE PL
DVS 95616 355-J7
WDLD 95695 315-G3
ALPINE ST
VAC 95688 433-D3
ALTA LOMA
BEN 94510 551-A4
ALTA LOMA DR
AMCN 94503 509-J2
AMCN 94503 510-A1
ALTA LOMA ST
DVS 95616 356-C6
ALTA MIRA DR
VAC 95688 433-C3
ALTAMONT CT
FRFD 94534 472-D3
ALTA PUNTA DR
VAL 94591 550-D1
ALTA VISTA
YoCo 95694 373-A3
ALTA VISTA DR
VAC 95688 433-D5
ALTO CT
DVS 95616 356-C5
ALTURAS CT
FRFD 94534 472-D3
VAC 95688 433-A3
WSAC 95691 358-J7
ALTUS LN
SUIS 94585 473-C4
ALVARADO AV
DVS 95616 356-A5
VAL 94590 530-B2
ALVARADO CT
FRFD 94534 472-D4
ALWIN DR
DXN 95620 395-C5
AMADAS CT
FRFD 94533 472-B7
AMADOR AV
DVS 95616 355-J7
AMADOR CIR
RVIS 94571 516-G5
AMADOR ST
VAL 94590 530-B3
AMADOR WY
SUIS 94585 473-C6
WDLD 95695 316-A6
AMANDA CT
VAC 95687 453-F2
AMAPOLA DR
DVS 95616 356-C5
AMAPOLA ST
VAC 95687 453-D1
AMAR CT
DVS 95616 356-C5
AMARAL CT
SolC 94534 471-A5
AMARILLO DR
AMCN 94503 509-J2
AMBASSADOR PL
VAC 95687 433-J5
AMBER AV
VAL 94589 510-B7
AMBER DR
SUIS 94585 472-J5
AMBER RIDGE LN
VAC 95687 433-F7
AMBERWOOD CIR
FRFD 94585 491-D6
AMBERWOOD CT
VAC 95688 433-D3
AMBLESIDE CT
VAC 95687 453-F4
AMBORT WY
WDLD 95695 315-H5
AMELIA ST
VAL 94589 510-C5
AMERICAN WY
VAC 95687 453-G2
AMERICAN CANYON RD
AMCN 94503 510-B3
NaCo 94589 510-F3
VAL 94585 510-F3
VAL 94589 510-F3
W AMERICAN CANYON RD
AMCN 94503 509-H3
W AMERICAN CANYON RD
AMCN 94503 510-A3
NaCo 94503 509-H3
AMERICAN FALLS DR
RVIS 94571 516-G2
AMERICANO CT
FRFD 94533 472-H1
AMERICANO WY
FRFD 94533 472-H1
AMESBURY DR
DXN 95620 395-C6
AMETHYST DR
VAC 95687 433-H3
AMHERST AV
VAL 94589 510-A5
AMHERST CT
VAC 95687 453-D1
AMHERST DR
DVS 95616 356-B7
AMHERST PL
WDLD 95695 315-H6
AMHERST WY
FRFD 94533 472-H2
WDLD 95695 315-G6
AMMONS ST
WDLD 95776 316-C5
AMOROSO PL
DVS 95618 376-H1
ANACAPA CT
WSAC 95691 378-E2
ANCHETA PL
VAL 94591 550-F2
ANCHOR
SUIS 94585 472-G7
ANCHOR CT
DXN 95620 395-C5
VAL 94591 550-F1
ANDERS CT
VAC 95687 433-D7
ANDERSON AV
WIN 95694 373-E3
ANDERSON CIR
WDLD 95776 316-D5
ANDERSON DR
SUIS 94585 472-J7
SUIS 94585 473-A7
ANDERSON LN
BEN 94510 551-B5
ANDERSON RD
DVS 95616 356-B4
DVS 95616 376-B1
ANDERSON ST
VAL 94589 510-D6
ANDERSON WY
RVIS 94571 516-G3
VAL 94591 530-G4
ANDOVER CT
FRFD 94534 472-C5
ANDOVER DR
VAC 95687 433-E7
VAC 95687 453-E1
VAL 94591 510-H4
ANDREA DR
VAC 95687 433-E7
VAC 95687 453-D1
ANDREW CT
BEN 94510 531-C7
FRFD 94535 473-G2
ANDREW RD
AMCN 94503 509-J2
AMCN 94503 510-A2
ANDREWS CIR
SUIS 94585 473-C6
ANDREWS LN
SolC 94534 472-A4
ANDRUS ISLAND CT
WSAC 95691 378-E2
ANGEL CT
WSAC 95691 378-E1
ANGELA CT
DXN 95620 395-B6
ANGELA ST
DVS 95618 357-A7
DVS 95618 377-A1
ANGELBROOK
RVIS 94571 516-F1
ANGELINA WY
VAL 94589 510-C5
ANGLER CT
FRFD 94533 452-H7
ANGUS WY
VAC 95687 433-H6
ANITA CIR
BEN 94510 551-A3
ANITA CT
VAC 95688 433-A5
ANN CT
VAL 94590 550-C1
ANNA ST
WSAC 95605 358-H1
ANNANDALE CT
FRFD 94533 452-J6
ANNANDALE DR
FRFD 94533 452-H6
ANNETTE AV
VAL 94591 530-D6
ANTARCTIC DR
WSAC 95691 358-F6
ANTELOPE AV
DVS 95616 356-A5
ANTELOPE CIR
FRFD 94585 511-E2
ANTELOPE ST
WDLD 95695 315-H3
ANTIGUA PL
WSAC 95691 378-D2
ANTIGUA WY
SAC 95831 378-F7
VAL 94591 550-E2
ANTIOCH AV
WSAC 95691 378-G4
ANTIOCH DR
DVS 95616 356-B7
ANTIQUITY CIR
FRFD 94534 491-C2
ANTIQUITY CT
FRFD 94534 491-C2
ANTIQUITY DR
FRFD 94534 491-C2
ANTOINETTE WY
WDLD 95776 316-B4
ANTONINA AV
AMCN 94503 510-A2
ANTRIM LN
VAC 95688 433-E1
ANZA AV
DVS 95616 356-B5
ANZA CT
FRFD 94533 472-G3
APACHE ST
WSAC 95691 378-H2
APIARY DR
YoCo 95616 375-G2
APOLLO CT
VAL 94591 530-E6
APPALOOSA CT
FRFD 94533 472-H1
APPALOOSA WY
FRFD 94533 472-H1
APPIAN WY
FRFD 94534 491-C3
APPLE CT
WDLD 95776 316-B5
APPLE LN
DVS 95616 356-B6
APPLEGATE CT
VAC 95687 453-F3
APPLENUT LN
VAL 94591 530-F7
VAL 94591 550-F1
APPLERIDGE PL
FRFD 94534 491-D1
APPLE TREE LN
FRFD 94533 472-G4
APPLEWOOD DR
FRFD 94534 472-F1
APPOLLO WY
SAC 95822 378-J3
APRICOT AV
WIN 95694 373-E3
APRIL CT
VAC 95687 453-F2
VAL 94591 530-F1
ARABELLA WY
SAC 95831 378-F7
ARABIAN CIR
VAC 95687 433-H6
ARABIAN CT
VAL 94589 510-D6
ARAGON CT
NAP 94559 470-A1
VAL 94591 530-F6
ARAGON PL
VAC 95688 433-A3
ARAGON ST
VAL 94590 530-A6
VAL 94591 530-F6
ARANDA CT
AMCN 94503 510-A4
ARAQUIPA CT
VAC 95687 453-C1
ARARAT CT
SAC 95831 378-H7
ARBOR CT
BEN 94510 551-B3
ARBOR ST
VAC 95688 433-B4
ARBORETUM DR
YoCo 95616 376-B2
ARBORETUM TER
DVS 95616 376-D2
ARBOR OAKS CT
VAC 95687 433-J6
ARBOR OAKS DR
VAC 95687 433-J7
ARCADIA CT
VAC 95687 433-G5
ARCADIA DR
VAC 95687 433-G5
ARCATA BAY RD
WSAC 95691 378-E2
ARCHER CT
VAL 94591 530-E2
ARCHER DR
WDLD 95695 316-A6
ARCHER PL
DXN 95620 395-E7
DXN 95620 415-E1
WDLD 95695 316-A6
ARCTIC DR
WSAC 95691 358-F7
ARCTIC PL
WSAC 95691 358-F7
ARDEN CT
AMCN 94503 509-J3
ARDMORE CT
BEN 94510 551-B3
ARDMORE WY
BEN 94510 551-B3
ARELLANO CT
WDLD 95776 316-E5
ARENA CT
VAL 94589 510-D6
ARENA DR
DVS 95618 356-G5
ARGUELLO AV
VAL 94591 530-D7
ARGUELLO CT
FRFD 94534 472-D4
ARGUELLO DR
BEN 94510 531-C7
ARIA PL
FRFD 94534 491-E1
ARIEL CT
WDLD 95695 316-A2
ARIEL WY
WDLD 95695 316-A2
ARIZONA ST
FRFD 94533 472-G5
FRFD 94535 473-H2
ARK WY
SAC 95831 378-H7
ARKANSAS CT
FRFD 94535 473-H2
ARKANSAS ST
FRFD 94533 472-H5
VAL 94590 529-J3
VAL 94590 530-A3
ARLENE CT
VAC 95688 433-A4
ARLENE DR
VAC 95688 433-A4
ARLENE WY
VAC 95688 433-A4
ARLINGTON BLVD
DVS 95616 355-H7
DVS 95616 375-J1
ARLINGTON CIR
FRFD 94533 472-G1
WDLD 95695 316-A2
ARLINGTON CT
DXN 95620 415-C2
SUIS 94585 473-A7
ARLINGTON DR
RVIS 94571 516-F2
ARLINGTON RD
WSAC 95691 358-H7
ARLINGTON WY
VAC 95687 433-G6
ARMFIELD AV
WDLD 95776 316-A4
ARMIJO CT
FRFD 94534 472-D4
ARMSBY WY
SUIS 94585 473-A7
ARMSTRONG ST
FRFD 94533 473-G3
FRFD 94535 473-G3
ARMUS PL
WDLD 95776 316-D7
ARMUS ST
WDLD 95776 316-D7
ARNOLD AV
FRFD 94535 473-J2
ARNOLD CT
DXN 95620 415-D1
ARNOLD ST
DVS 95618 376-F1
ARROWHEAD CT
RVIS 94571 516-F2
VAL 94589 510-B5
ARROWHEAD DR
VAC 95687 433-E6
VAL 94589 510-B5
ARROWHEAD ST
WSAC 95691 378-C4
ARROYO AV
DVS 95618 356-H7
ARROYO CT
DVS 95618 356-G7
FRFD 94533 472-H1
VAC 95687 433-J6
ARROYO DR
FRFD 94533 472-H1
ARROYO GRANDE LN
SUIS 94585 473-D6
ARROYO SARCO
NaCo 94558 450-A1
ARTHUR DR
WSAC 95605 358-J1
ARTHUR ST
DVS 95616 355-J7
DVS 95616 356-A7
DVS 95616 375-J1
FRFD 94533 472-G4
ARTIS LN
YoCo 95618 376-E2
ARUBA ST
WSAC 95691 378-D2
ARY LN
DXN 95620 395-A6
ASBURY DR
VAC 95687 433-G6
ASBURY LN
FRFD 94533 472-H2
ASCADA PL
DVS 95618 356-H6
ASCOT CT
AMCN 94503 509-J3
FRFD 94534 472-B2
VAL 94591 510-F7
ASCOT DR
FRFD 94534 472-B2
ASCOT PKWY
VAL 94591 530-F2
N ASCOT PKWY
VAL 94591 510-F7
VAL 94591 530-F1
ASH AV
WSAC 95691 358-H4
ASH CT
FRFD 94533 472-J2
ASH DR
WDLD 95776 316-C5
ASH ST
VAC 95688 433-C4
ASHBOURNE CT
FRFD 94534 452-B7
ASHBY PL
AMCN 94503 510-A3
ASHDEN LN
VAL 94591 510-J4
ASHFORD CT
BEN 94510 530-J7
FRFD 94533 452-J7
VAC 95687 433-H6
ASHLAND TER
DVS 95618 356-H7
ASHLEY AV
WDLD 95695 315-G5
N ASHLEY AV
WDLD 95695 315-G2
ASHORE WY
SAC 95831 378-G7
ASHTON CT
VAL 94591 530-G5
ASHTON ST
VAL 94591 530-G5
ASHTREE CT
FRFD 94585 511-E3
ASHWELL WY
VAL 94591 510-J5
ASHWOOD AV
VAL 94591 530-E5
ASHWOOD CT
VAC 95688 433-D1
ASHWOOD DR
SUIS 94585 472-H6
ASPEN
BEN 94510 551-B5
ASPEN CT
FRFD 94585 491-D7
SolC 94591 550-E1
VAC 95687 433-H4
ASPEN PL
DVS 95616 356-C6
ASPEN ST
YoCo 95695 315-H1
ASPINWALL CT
FRFD 94534 472-E3
ASPINWALL DR
BEN 94510 551-C1
ASSAY CT
VAL 94591 530-C7
ASTER AV
WSAC 95691 358-H6
ASTER ST
VAL 94589 509-J6
WIN 95694 373-E3
ASTER WY
WDLD 95695 315-G5
ASTORIA CIR
FRFD 94534 472-B5
ASTORIA CT
FRFD 94534 472-C4
VAC 95687 453-F2
ASTORIA DR
FRFD 94534 472-C5
ASTORIA PL
FRFD 94534 472-C4
ASTORIA ST
DVS 95616 355-G6
ASTRO CT
SAC 95831 378-J6
ATCHISON DR
VAC 95687 433-J6
ATHERTON AV
CCCo 94525 550-E5
ATHERTON CT
FRFD 94533 473-B3
VAC 95687 453-B1
ATHERTON PL
WSAC 95691 358-H7
ATHERTON ST
VAL 94590 530-C7
ATKINS CT
BEN 94510 550-H1
ATKINSON CT
DXN 95620 395-D5
ATLANTIC AV
FRFD 94533 472-F2
E ATLANTIC AV
FRFD 94533 472-H2
E ATLANTIC CT
FRFD 94533 472-J2
ATLANTIC DR
RVIS 94571 516-E1
WSAC 95691 358-H7
ATLANTIC PL
WSAC 95691 358-H7
ATLANTIS DR
DVS 95618 356-H6
ATRIUM WY
YoCo 95616 376-A1
ATWELL CIR
WDLD 95776 316-D5
ATWOODVILLE CT
FRFD 94533 452-J7
AUBUBON CIR
DVS 95618 356-E4
AUBURN CT
VAC 95688 432-J4
VAC 95688 433-A5
VAL 94589 509-H5
AUBURN DR
DVS 95616 356-D6
VAL 94589 509-H5
AUBURN WY
VAC 95688 432-J5
VAC 95688 433-A5
WDLD 95695 316-A6
AUCTION LN
DXN 95620 395-D4
AUDEN ST
VAL 94591 530-F5
AUDREY CT
BEN 94510 551-B3
AUDREY PL
VAC 95687 453-F1
AUDUBON CT
FRFD 94533 473-B3
AUGUSTA CT
DXN 95620 395-B5
FRFD 94534 472-B4
RVIS 94571 516-E2
VAC 95687 453-E3
AULD CT
SolC 94534 471-A5
AURORA AV
DVS 95616 356-C5
AURORA WY
RVIS 94571 516-F3
VAC 95688 432-J4
AUSTIN CT
FRFD 94534 452-G6
AUSTIN DR
DXN 95620 395-C5
AUSTIN ST
DVS 95618 356-E5
VAL 94590 529-H2
AUTO CENTER DR
VAC 95687 433-H2
AUTO CLUB WY
VAL 94591 510-E7
AUTO MALL PKWY
FRFD 94533 472-B7
AUTO MALL COLUMBUS PKWY
VAL 94591 510-E7
AUTO PLAZA CT
FRFD 94534 491-D4
AUTUMN MEADOW DR
FRFD 94585 511-E2
AUTUMN ROCK CT
FRFD 94534 491-E1
AUTUMN ROSE CT
FRFD 94585 511-D3
AUTUMNWOOD CT
FRFD 94585 511-E2
VAC 95687 453-F2
AVALON CIR
VAL 94589 509-G5
AVALON WY
SUIS 94585 472-J5
SUIS 94585 473-A5
VAL 94589 509-G5
AVENIDO DEL LAGO
FRFD 94533 452-J7
FRFD 94533 472-J1
AVIAN DR
VAL 94591 530-F4
AVILA CT
VAC 95688 433-B3
AVILA BAY PL
DVS 95616 355-H6
AVOCET AV
DVS 95616 356-B4
AVOCET LN
VAL 94591 510-J3
AVON CT
DXN 95620 395-C6
AVON WY
FRFD 94533 472-E3
AVONDALE CIR
FRFD 94533 452-H6
AYLESBURY CT
WSAC 95691 378-F1
AYR CT
FRFD 94534 472-D2
AZALEA CT
VAL 94589 509-H5
AZALEA DR
FRFD 94533 472-G2
AZALEA PL
WSAC 95691 378-F2
AZALEA WY
VAC 95688 433-B5
AZEVEDO LN
NaCo 94591 510-G3
AZEVEDO RD
SolC 94571 516-C1
AZEVEDO RANCH RD
VAL 94591 530-F4
AZUAR DR
VAL 94592 529-F3
AZURE PL
WDLD 95695 315-H3

B

B LN
FRFD 94533 473-E2
B ST
CCCo 94525 550-A5
DVS 95616 356-C7
DVS 95616 376-C1
RVIS 94571 516-H3
SolC 95687 434-C7
VAL 94590 529-H2
WDLD 95776 316-B3
E B ST
BEN 94510 551-B6
DXN 95620 395-D7
W B ST
DXN 95620 395-C7
BACON ISLAND ST
WSAC 95691 378-E2
BADGER CT
FRFD 94533 452-H7
VAC 95688 433-D1
BAGLEY ST
VAL 94592 529-H6
BAHIA VISTA CT
VAL 94591 550-F1
BAILEY DR
FRFD 94533 473-B2
BAINER HALL DR
YoCo 95616 376-B2
BAIRD CT
WDLD 95776 316-D6
BAJA AV
DVS 95616 356-C5
BAJIA CT
SAC 95831 378-F6
BAKER AL
DXN 95620 415-C2
BAKER CT
BEN 94510 551-A2

STREET Name	City	ZIP	Pg-Grid
BAKER DR	FRFD	94535	474-A3
BAKER RD	SolC	95694	373-G6
BAKER ST	BEN	94510	551-A2
	WIN	95694	373-E3
E BAKER ST	WIN	95694	373-G3
BALBOA AV	DVS	95616	356-C5
	VAL	94591	530-D5
BALBOA CT	FRFD	94533	472-G3
BALD EAGLE DR	VAC	95688	413-D7
	VAC	95688	433-D1
BALDPATE CT	WSAC	95691	378-F1
BALD PATE DR	SUIS	94585	472-J6
BALDWIN AV	CCCo	94525	550-E5
BALDWIN CT	FRFD	94533	473-B3
BALDWIN ST	VAL	94589	529-J2
	VAL	94590	529-J2
BALLENA BAY RD	WSAC	95691	378-D2
BALLINDINE DR	VAC	95688	433-D1
BALMORAL CT	FRFD	94534	472-C1
BALMORAL DR	FRFD	94534	472-C1
BALSAM CT	FRFD	94533	473-A1
BALSAM PL	DVS	95618	356-F6
BALSAM ST	VAL	94589	509-J7
	WSAC	95691	358-H4
BALSAM WY	VAC	95687	433-C7
	VAC	95687	453-C1
BALTIC AV	WSAC	95691	358-G7
BALTIC CT	FRFD	94533	472-J3
BALTIC DR	FRFD	94533	472-J2
BALTIC ST	VAL	94591	530-C7
BALTUSROL DR	FRFD	94533	452-J6
BANBURY CT	BEN	94510	551-B2
BANBURY WY	AMCN	94503	510-A3
	BEN	94510	551-B2
BANDALIN CT	WSAC	95691	378-F1
BANFF DR	FRFD	94534	472-C1
BANINGTON DR	VAL	94591	550-D2
BANNING WY	SolC	94591	530-E6
BANTRY DR	VAC	95688	413-E7
	VAC	95688	433-E1
BANTRY WY	BEN	94510	530-J6
BANYAN CT	FRFD	94533	473-A1
BANYAN PL	DVS	95618	356-F6
BARBARA WY	WDLD	95776	316-B5
BARBARESCO CT	FRFD	94534	491-F5
BARBERA CT	VAC	95687	433-B7
BARBERA PL	DVS	95616	356-B5
BARBERA WY	VAL	94591	530-G1
BARBERRY PL	WSAC	95691	378-E2
BARBOUR DR	FRFD	94534	472-D4
BARCELONA AV	DVS	95616	356-A5
BARCELONA CIR	FRFD	94533	473-C4
BARCELONA CT	FRFD	94533	473-C4
BARCELONA DR	AMCN	94503	510-B4
BARCELONA ST	VAL	94591	530-F6
BARCLAY CT	SUIS	94585	473-A7
BARKLEY CT	VAL	94591	530-G5
BARKLEY ST	DVS	95616	355-J7
BARKSDALE CT	FRFD	94535	473-F3
BARKWOOD CT	VAC	95687	453-F4
BARLOW CT	FRFD	94533	472-D7
BARNACLE WY	SUIS	94585	473-A6
BARNES CIR	WDLD	95776	316-D6
BARNES CT	VAL	94591	530-F5
BARNES WY	CCCo	94572	549-H7
BARONA ST	WSAC	95691	358-J7
BARONY PL	DVS	95618	376-F2
BAROQUE DR	FRFD	94534	491-D3
BARRINGTON CT	FRFD	94585	491-D7
BARROW LN	NaCo	94558	450-D5
BARROWS DR	SUIS	94585	473-A7
BARRY CT	VAL	94591	530-E6
BARRY RD	YoCo	95616	355-J4
	YoCo	95616	356-A4
BARTH CT	WDLD	95776	316-E5
BARTHLEY WY	DVS	95618	376-E2
	YoCo	95618	376-E2
BARTLE AV	FRFD	94535	473-G4
BARTLETT AV	WDLD	95695	315-J5
	WDLD	95695	316-A5
BARTLETT CT	SUIS	94585	473-A7
BARTLETT LN	VAC	95687	433-H3
BARTON CT	FRFD	94534	472-D4
BARTON DR	FRFD	94534	472-D4
BARTON PL	FRFD	94534	472-D4
BARTON WY	BEN	94510	530-J6
	BEN	94510	531-A7
BASALT DR	VAL	94589	510-B6
BASILICA CT	FRFD	94534	491-C2
BASQUE CT	NAP	94559	470-A1
BASS CT	FRFD	94534	491-D2
BASS DR	VAC	95687	433-F7
BASS ST	WSAC	95691	378-D3
N BASS ISLAND RD	WSAC	95691	378-E2
BASTONE CT	WSAC	95691	378-J2
BATAVIA RD	DXN	95620	394-J7
	DXN	95620	414-J3
	SolC	95620	414-J3
BATES DR	DVS	95618	356-F6
BAUMAN CT	SUIS	94585	473-A7
BAUMAN DR	SUIS	94585	473-A7
BAXTER ST	VAL	94590	529-H3
W BAXTER ST	VAL	94590	529-H3
BAY CT	VAL	94591	530-E2
BAY ST	CCCo	94525	550-E4
	SUIS	94585	472-G7
BAYBERRY CT	VAL	94589	509-J7
	WSAC	95691	358-J7
	WSAC	95691	378-J1
BAY HILL CIR	FRFD	94534	472-B2
BAY HILL DR	FRFD	94534	472-B2
BAYHURST DR	VAL	94591	550-D2
BAYLOR CT	BEN	94510	550-J1
	WDLD	95695	315-H6
BAYLOR DR	VAL	94589	510-A5
	WDLD	95695	315-H6
BAYLOR PL	WDLD	95695	315-H6
BAY OAKS WY	RVIS	94571	516-G2
BAYOU CT	SAC	95831	378-G7
N BAYOU WY	SaCo	95837	317-H4
BAYRIDGE CT	FRFD	94534	491-E1
BAYRIDGE DR	FRFD	94534	491-D1
BAYRIDGE PL	FRFD	94534	491-D1
BAYSHORE RD	BEN	94510	551-E3
BAYSIDE TER	VAL	94591	550-D3
BAY TREE CT	FRFD	94533	473-A2
BAY TREE DR	FRFD	94533	473-A1
BAYVIEW AV	VAL	94590	530-C3
BAYVIEW CIR	BEN	94510	551-C4
BAYVIEW RD	CCCo	94525	550-C5
BAY VISTA CT	BEN	94510	551-E3
BAYWOOD CT	VAC	95688	433-D3
BAYWOOD DR	VAL	94591	530-E5
BAYWOOD LN	DVS	95618	356-E6
N BEACH AV	WSAC	95691	358-J7
BEACH DR	RVIS	94571	516-H6
	SolC	94571	516-H7
BEACH ST	SolC	94590	530-B6
	VAL	94590	530-B6
BEACON BLVD	WSAC	95691	358-F4
BEACON CT	VAL	94590	529-H2
BEACON BAY PL	DVS	95616	355-G7
BEALE CIR	SUIS	94585	473-C5
BEALE CT	FRFD	94535	473-F2
BEAM ST	FRFD	94535	473-J3
BEAMER ST	WDLD	95695	315-J3
	WDLD	95695	316-A3
	WDLD	95776	316-A3
E BEAMER ST	WDLD	95776	316-D3
	YoCo	95776	316-F3
W BEAMER ST	WDLD	95695	315-H3
BEAR COVE CT	VAL	94591	550-E1
BEAR CREEK CT	FRFD	94534	472-D1
BEAR CREEK DR	FRFD	94534	472-C2
BEARD CT	VAC	95688	433-D5
BEARD ST	VAC	95688	433-E5
BEARDEN ST	DVS	95618	356-F5
BEAUFORD CT	FRFD	94533	472-J2
BEAUFORD DR	FRFD	94533	472-J3
BEAUJOLAIS CT	FRFD	94533	472-C7
BEAU VINE LN	YoCo	95616	376-C3
BECERRA WY	DVS	95618	356-H7
	DVS	95618	376-H1
BECK AV	FRFD	94533	472-D5
	FRFD	94534	472-D7
	FRFD	94534	492-D1
	FRFD	94585	492-D1
BECK LN	SolC	95688	413-F5
BECKETT LN	WDLD	95695	315-G4
BECKETT HALL CIR	YoCo	95616	376-B1
BEDFORD DR	VAC	95687	453-H1
BEDFORD LN	AMCN	94503	509-J3
BEDROCK CT	VAL	94589	510-B5
BEE BIOLOGY DR	YoCo	95616	375-G2
BEECH LN	DVS	95616	356-C6
	VAC	95687	453-F1
BEECHAM CT	FRFD	94533	472-G2
BEECHCRAFT RD	VAC	95688	433-F2
BEECHWOOD AV	VAL	94591	530-E5
BEECHWOOD CIR	SUIS	94585	472-H6
BEECHWOOD CT	FRFD	94533	472-J1
	FRFD	94533	473-A1
BEE JAY WY	WDLD	95776	316-B3
BEELARD DR	VAC	95687	433-F6
BEGONIA BLVD	FRFD	94533	472-F2
BEGONIA CT	VAL	94591	530-F7
BEL AIR CIR	FRFD	94533	473-B3
BEL AIR CT	FRFD	94533	473-B4
BEL AIR DR	VAC	95687	433-G7
	VAC	95687	453-G1
BELDEN CT	DXN	95620	415-C2
BELDEN DR	DXN	95620	415-C2
BELFAST DR	VAL	94589	510-C5
BELFORD PL	VAC	95687	453-F2
BELHAVEN PL	DVS	95618	356-F6
BELL AV	FRFD	94533	472-G5
E BELL AV	FRFD	94533	472-G5
BELL DR	DXN	95620	395-C5
	WDLD	95776	316-D5
BELL LN	NaCo	94558	450-A1
BELLA CASA DR	WDLD	95695	315-H6
BELLA CASA ST	DVS	95616	356-C5
BELL AIR DR	SAC	95822	378-J4
BELLAMY CT	FRFD	94533	473-B3
BELLA VISTA DR	SolC	94585	473-B6
	SUIS	94585	473-B6
BELLA VISTA RD	VAC	95687	433-C7
BELLA VISTA WY	RVIS	94571	516-F1
	VAL	94590	530-B3
BELLEVUE CT	FRFD	94534	472-B2
BELLO DR	DXN	95620	415-C2
BELLO RIO WY	SAC	95831	378-F6
BELLOWS CT	DVS	95618	356-G4
BELLOWS ST	DVS	95618	356-F5
BELMONT AV	SolC	94591	530-E7
BELMONT DR	DVS	95618	356-F6
BELTAINE CT	VAL	94591	510-J6
	VAL	94591	511-A6
BELVEDERE CT	VAL	94589	509-H5
BELVEDERE DR	BEN	94510	530-J7
BEMMERLY WY	WDLD	95695	315-G2
BENAVENTE CT	VAL	94591	530-J2
BENBOW CT	DVS	95618	376-F1
BENDER PL	WDLD	95776	336-E1
BENDER ST	FRFD	94535	473-G3
BENDITA CT	DVS	95618	356-G7
BENET CT	FRFD	94533	473-B3
BENHAM WY	SAC	95831	378-F7
BENICIA CT	DVS	95616	356-C6
BENICIA RD	SolC	94590	530-B5
	SolC	94591	530-B5
	VAL	94590	530-B5
	VAL	94591	530-E6
BENICIA-MARTINEZ BRDG I-680	BEN	-	551-F7
	MRTZ	-	551-F7
	SolC	-	551-F7
BENJAMIN ST	VAL	94589	510-D6
BENNETT AV	VAL	94590	530-B6
BENNETT HILL CT	VAC	95688	433-E4
BENNETT HILL DR	VAC	95688	433-E4
BENNINGTON CT	VAL	94591	510-H4
BENNINGTON DR	VAL	94591	510-H4
	VAL	94591	511-A4
BENSON AV	VAL	94590	529-H3
BENTLEY CT	AMCN	94503	509-J3
	AMCN	94503	510-A3
BENTON CT	SUIS	94585	472-F7
BENTON PL	DVS	95618	356-F5
	WSAC	95691	378-H1
BENTON ST	WSAC	95691	378-H2
BENTON WY	AMCN	94503	509-H2
BENT TREE CT	FRFD	94534	472-D2
BENT TREE LN	VAC	95688	413-D6
BERGEN CT	VAC	95687	453-H1
BERGWALL WY	VAL	94591	530-F5
BERING CT	SUIS	94585	473-B6
BERING WY	SUIS	94585	473-A6
BERKLEY WY	FRFD	94533	472-H2
BERKSHIRE CT	DXN	95620	395-C6
	VAC	95687	433-F7
BERKSHIRE DR	DXN	95620	395-C6
BERKSHIRE LN	VAL	94591	530-E1
BERMUDA AV	DVS	95616	355-G7
BERMUDA CT	WSAC	95691	378-D2
BERMUDA LN	VAL	94591	550-F1
BERNADETTE WY	WDLD	95776	316-B4
BERNARD ST	VAC	95688	433-C5
BERNICE CT	VAL	94591	530-F4
BERNINI ST	DVS	95618	356-F5
BERRY CT	DXN	95620	395-A7
BERRY DR	FRFD	94534	472-D3
BERRY LN	NaCo	94559	450-B7
BERRYESSA CT	WIN	95694	373-E2
BERRYESSA DR	VAC	95687	433-E6
BERRYESSA PL	WSAC	95691	378-C3
BERRYWOOD CT	VAC	95688	413-E7
BERRYWOOD WY	VAC	95688	413-D7
BERYL CT	VAL	94591	530-F1
BESTON WY	VAL	94591	550-F2
BETHANY DR	AMCN	94503	510-B4
BETHEL WY	WSAC	95691	378-F1
BETH PAGE CT	VAC	95687	453-E2
BETTONA WY	AMCN	94503	509-J3
BETTY AV	WDLD	95776	316-B5
BETTY CT	VAL	94589	509-J5
	WIN	95694	373-F3
BETTY WY	WSAC	95691	358-F7
	WSAC	95691	378-F1
BEVAN RD	WSAC	95691	378-D4
BEVERLY CT	VAC	95687	433-G7
BEVERLY DR	VAL	94591	530-D7
BEYTHE LN	VAC	95687	453-C1
B GALE WILSON BLVD	FRFD	94533	472-E4
BIANCO CIR	FRFD	94534	491-D3
BIANCO CT	DVS	95616	356-B5
	VAC	95687	433-B7
BIANCO DR	FRFD	94534	491-D2
BIAVA AV	NaCo	94558	450-D6
BICKFORD CIR	FRFD	94533	453-E7
BICKFORD CT	FRFD	94533	453-E7
BICKFORD PL	FRFD	94533	453-E7
BIDWELL CT	FRFD	94534	472-D4
BIDWELL PL	DVS	95618	356-E5
	WDLD	95695	316-A6
BIDWELL ST	DVS	95618	356-E5
	FRFD	94535	474-A3
BIDWELL WY	VAL	94589	509-J6
BIELLA CT	AMCN	94503	510-C4
BIENVILLE ST	DVS	95616	355-H7
BIG BEAR ST	WSAC	95691	378-C4
BIG BEN CT	VAL	94591	510-E7
BIGHORN CT	VAC	95687	433-J4
BIG ISLAND RD	WSAC	95691	378-D2
BIGLER CT	BEN	94510	550-H1
BIG SUR CT	FRFD	94533	452-H7
BILTMORE CT	FRFD	94533	472-C4
BINGHAM PL	FRFD	94534	472-C5
BIOLETTI WY	YoCo	95616	376-B2
BIRCH	BEN	94510	551-B5
BIRCH AV	WSAC	95691	378-J2
BIRCH CT	FRFD	94533	472-J1
BIRCH LN	DVS	95618	356-E6
BIRCH RD	BEN	94510	551-D5
BIRCH ST	VAC	95688	433-C6
	VAL	94589	510-B7
BIRCH WY	DXN	95620	415-D1
BIRCH RIDGE DR	RVIS	94571	516-F2
BIRCH TREE LN	SolC	95688	414-B1
BIRCHWOOD CT	SUIS	94585	472-H6
	VAC	95688	413-D7
BIRKDALE CIR	FRFD	94585	491-E7
	FRFD	94585	511-E1
BIRKDALE CT	FRFD	94585	511-D1
	VAL	94591	530-G3
BIRKDALE DR	VAL	94591	530-G3
BIRKHAM CT	FRFD	94534	472-A1
BIRMINGHAM AV	WSAC	95691	358-H6
BISCAYNE BAY PL	DVS	95616	355-G6
BISHOP CT	FRFD	94533	472-H2
BISHOP DR	VAC	95687	433-C7
BISHOP PL	DVS	95618	356-E6
BISHOP RD	CCCo	94525	550-E6
BITTERN WY	SUIS	94585	473-B6
BLACKBERRY CT	DXN	95620	415-B1
BLACKBIRD LN	SAC	95831	378-F7
BLACKBURN DR	DVS	95618	356-F6
BLACK DIAMOND DR	RVIS	94571	516-F2
BLACK DUCK CT	AMCN	94503	509-H1
BLACKER RD	WSAC	95691	378-F2
BLACKFOOT CT	WSAC	95691	378-H2
BLACKFOOT RD	WSAC	95691	378-H2
BLACKHAWK PL	FRFD	94534	452-C7
	YoCo	95616	355-H2
BLACK MOUNTAIN CT	FRFD	94534	452-A7
BLACK OAK CT	VAC	95687	453-B1
BLACKSPUR CT	SUIS	94585	473-A6
BLACKSPUR DR	SUIS	94585	473-A6
BLACKTHORNE DR	SolC	95688	413-B2
BLACKWELL CT	FRFD	94533	472-H1
BLACKWOOD CT	VAC	95688	433-D1
BLAIR CT	FRFD	94534	452-G7
BLAKE CT	BEN	94510	530-H7
BLAKEMORE CT	FRFD	94533	472-G2
BLANCHARD LN	BEN	94510	551-B3
BLANCO ST	AMCN	94503	510-A4
BLARNEY CIR	VAC	95688	413-E7
	VAC	95688	433-E1
BLISS AV	WDLD	95695	316-A3
BLISS CT	DVS	95618	376-F1
BLOOM DR	DXN	95620	395-A7
BLOOMFIELD CT	FRFD	94533	472-H2
BLOSSOM AV	FRFD	94533	472-J5
BLOSSOM CT	FRFD	94533	472-J4
BLOSSOM RD	SolC	94585	472-J6
	SUIS	94585	472-J6
BLOSSOMING FLOWER WY	VAC	95688	413-D6
BLOSSOM OAK CT	VAC	95688	433-D3
BLOWERS DR	WDLD	95776	316-D4
BLUE CT	FRFD	94534	491-D2
BLUEBELL CT	FRFD	94534	491-E1
	VAC	95687	453-F2
BLUEBELL PL	VAL	94591	550-F1
BLUEBELL ST	AMCN	94503	509-H1
BLUE BILL WY	SUIS	94585	472-J6
BLUEBIRD CT	VAL	94591	530-E3
BLUEBIRD DR	VAC	95687	453-H1
BLUEBIRD PL	DVS	95616	356-B4
BLUEBIRD WY	FRFD	94533	472-J3
BLUE BONNET CT	FRFD	94533	472-F2
BLUE CANYON CT	SolC	94534	452-F3
BLUE ELDER CT	AMCN	94503	509-H2
BLUEGRASS PL	WDLD	95776	316-B2
BLUEJAY DR	SUIS	94585	473-B6
BLUE MOUNTAIN DR	SolC	94534	452-G2
BLUE OAK LN	NaCo	94558	450-C3
	WIN	95694	373-G3
BLUEOAK WY	FRFD	94534	491-D1
BLUERIDGE CT	VAC	95688	433-A3
BLUERIDGE LN	VAC	95688	433-A3
BLUE ROCK CT	FRFD	94585	511-D3
BLUE SKY CT	VAL	94591	510-J3
BLUE SPRUCE CT	AMCN	94503	510-B3
BLUEWATER DR	VAC	95688	413-E7
	VAC	95688	433-E1
BLUEWATER WY	VAC	95688	413-E7
BLUE WING DR	SUIS	94585	472-J6
	SUIS	94585	473-A6
BLUSH CT	VAL	94591	530-G1
BLYTH ST	VAL	94591	530-G4
BOARDWALK CT	VAC	95687	433-G5
BOATHOUSE AV	DVS	95616	355-H6
BOATMAN AV	WSAC	95691	358-G5
BOBOLINK CT	SUIS	94585	473-B6
BOBOLINK WY	SAC	95831	378-F7
BOBWHITE CT	FRFD	94533	473-A3
BODEGA ST	VAL	94591	550-E2
BODEGA BAY PL	DVS	95616	355-G6
BODEGA BAY RD	WSAC	95691	378-E2
BODIN CIR	FRFD	94535	473-F3
BOGGS CT	VAL	94589	509-J5
BOLLARD CT	VAC	95687	433-D7
BOLLATE LN	DVS	95618	356-G5
BOLTON CIR	BEN	94510	530-H7
BOLTON WY	VAL	94591	530-G4
BOMBADIL LN	DVS	95616	355-H7
BONAIRE RD	WSAC	95691	378-D3
BONARDA CT	VAC	95687	433-B7
BOND CT	FRFD	94535	473-G2
BOND ST	FRFD	94535	473-F2
BONITA CT	SUIS	94585	473-C6
	VAL	94591	530-D6
	WSAC	95691	358-H5
BONITA BAHIA	BEN	94510	550-J3
BONNARD ST	DVS	95618	356-F5
BONNIE WY	VAL	94591	530-G1
BOONE CT	VAC	95687	433-H5
BOONE DR	VAC	95687	433-H5
BOOTHEY AV	FRFD	94535	473-J2
	FRFD	94535	474-A3
BORCHARD CT	WDLD	95695	315-G6
BORDEAUX CT	VAL	94591	530-G1
BORDEAUX WY	RVIS	94571	516-G6
BORGES LN	VAL	94589	510-C5
BOSTON CT	FRFD	94534	472-D3
BOSTON TER	DVS	95618	356-H7
	DVS	95618	376-H2
BOTTICELLI PL	DVS	95618	356-E5
BOTTLEBRUSH CT	SUIS	94585	472-J5
BOULDER DR	VAL	94589	510-B5
BOULDER PL	DVS	95618	376-G1
BOULDER CREEK CT	FRFD	94534	491-F3
BOULDER RIDGE CT	FRFD	94534	471-E7
	VAC	95688	433-D1
BOUNDS DR	DXN	95620	395-A6
BOUNTY LN	VAC	95687	433-H3
	VAL	94590	550-B1
BOURN CT	WDLD	95776	316-C4
BOURN DR	WDLD	95776	316-C5
BOWEN LN	DXN	95620	395-A7
BOWEN ISLAND ST	WSAC	95691	378-C2
BOWLEN DR	WSAC	95605	358-J1
BOWLINE DR	VAC	95687	433-D7
	VAC	95687	453-D1
BOWMAN DR	VAL	94591	530-D4
BOWMAN RD	SolC	95694	373-H5
BOXELDER LN	DVS	95618	376-H1
BOX R RANCH RD	SolC	95687	454-F6
BOXWOOD LN	FRFD	94533	472-J2
BOXWOOD RD	WDLD	95695	315-G5
BOYCE RD	SolC	95694	373-J4
	SolC	95694	374-A6
BOYD ST	FRFD	94535	473-G4
	VAC	95688	433-C6
BOYER CIR	DVS	95616	356-D7
BOYLE PL	WDLD	95776	336-E1
BOYNTON AV	FRFD	94533	472-C6
BOYSEN ST	VAL	94590	529-J3
	VAL	94590	530-A3
BRADBURY WY	FRFD	94534	472-F3
BRADDOCK CT	DVS	95618	376-F1
BRADFORD CT	BEN	94510	530-H7
BRADFORD WY	BEN	94510	530-H7
	WSAC	95691	378-F1
BRADLEY BLVD	FRFD	94535	473-H2
BRADLEY CT	FRFD	94535	473-J2
	VAC	95687	433-H5
BRADLEY DR	VAC	95687	433-H5
BRAE CT	SolC	94534	471-A5
BRAEMER CT	BEN	94510	551-B3
BRAGI DR	WSAC	95691	358-D4
BRAMBLEWOOD CT	FRFD	94585	511-F3
BRAMBLEWOOD DR	FRFD	94585	511-F3
BRANCEFORD CT	SUIS	94585	473-A7
BRANCIFORTE ST	VAL	94590	529-J4
BRANDON PL	BEN	94510	551-C4
BRANDON WY	FRFD	94533	472-J4
BRANDYWINE PL	DVS	95616	355-H7
BRANIGAN AV	WDLD	95776	316-D5
BRANNAN WY	WSAC	95691	378-F1
BRANSCOMBE RD	SolC	94585	473-G7
	SolC	94585	493-G2
BRANSFORD CT	FRFD	94533	472-F4
BRANT CT	FRFD	94533	473-A3
	VAL	94589	509-H4
BRAVA PL	FRFD	94534	491-E1
BRAZELTON CIR	VAC	95688	413-J6
BRAZELTON CT	SUIS	94585	473-A7
BREAKER CT	VAL	94591	530-F1
BREAKWATER CIR	SUIS	94585	492-G1
BREAKWATER WY	SAC	95831	378-G7
	VAC	95688	413-E7
BRECK CT	BEN	94510	550-H2
BRECKINRIDGE RD	FRFD	94533	473-A1
BREE LN	DVS	95616	355-J7
BREEZEWALK DR	VAL	94591	550-D3
BREHME LN	SolC	95688	412-G4
BREMER CT	VAL	94591	530-F3
BRENDA WY	WSAC	95691	378-E2
BRENNAN CIR	FRFD	94535	473-J3
BRENNAN PL	VAC	95687	453-F2
BRENNEN DR	WDLD	95776	316-D5
BRENTWOOD AV	VAL	94591	530-F5
BRENTWOOD CT	VAC	95687	433-G7
BRENTWOOD DR	BEN	94510	550-J2
BRENTWOOD PL	DVS	95618	376-F1
BRESEE AV	VAC	95688	433-D4
BRESSO CT	AMCN	94503	509-J3
BRET HARTE WY	VAL	94589	509-J6
BRETON AV	DVS	95616	355-G7
BRETON DR	FRFD	94533	472-F3
BREWSTER AV	SAC	95831	378-F7
BREWSTER WY	VAC	95687	453-H2
BRIAN CT	SUIS	94585	472-G7
BRIANS CT	DXN	95620	395-A7
BRIANS WY	DXN	95620	395-A6
BRIAR WY	FRFD	94585	491-D6
BRIARCREST WY	SAC	95831	378-J6
BRIARWOOD CT	FRFD	94533	472-J2
	VAC	95688	433-A3
BRIARWOOD DR	VAC	95688	433-B3
	WSAC	95691	358-H4
BRICKYARD DR	SAC	95831	378-G5
BRIDGE CT	VAL	94591	530-E4
BRIDGE LN	SolC	95688	413-F5
BRIDGE PL	WSAC	95691	358-G7
	WSAC	95691	378-G1
BRIDGEHEAD RD	MRTZ	94553	551-F7
BRIDGEPORT AV	FRFD	94585	491-E4
	SolC	94534	491-E4
	SolC	94585	491-E4
BRIDGEPORT CT	VAC	95687	433-G5
BRIDGEPORT WY	RVIS	94571	516-E2
BRIDGEVIEW CT	BEN	94510	551-B4
	CCCo	94525	550-C4
BRIDGEVIEW PL	VAL	94591	550-D2
BRIDGEVIEW HEIGHTS PL	BEN	94510	551-B4
BRIDGEWATER CIR	SUIS	94585	472-H6
BRIDGEWAY LAKES DR	WSAC	95691	378-C3
BRIDGEWOOD CT	FRFD	94585	511-E3
BRIDLE CT	WSAC	95691	378-E2
BRIDLE LN	WDLD	95776	316-C5
BRIDLE RIDGE CT	FRFD	94534	471-E7
BRIDLE RIDGE DR	FRFD	94534	471-E7
	FRFD	94534	491-E1
BRIDLEWOOD CT	VAL	94591	530-D2
BRIGANTINE RD	VAL	94591	550-E2
BRIGHT DAY CT	WDLD	95695	315-F2
BRIGHT DAY DR	WDLD	95695	315-F2
BRIGHTON CT	FRFD	94533	472-F3
BRIGHTON DR	FRFD	94533	472-F3
	VAL	94591	530-G4
BRINLEY DR	YoCo	95694	373-H2
BRISBANE CT	FRFD	94533	452-J6

STREET
Name City ZIP Pg-Grid

BRISBANE ST
WSAC 95691 358-H7
BRISBANE WY
FRFD 94533 452-J6
BRISCOE CT
WDLD 95776 316-E7
BRISCOE PL
WDLD 95776 316-E7
BRISTLEWOOD CT
VAC 95688 413-E7
BRISTOL CT
BEN 94510 550-J1
DXN 95620 395-C5
BRISTOL DR
VAC 95687 433-G6
VAL 94591 530-H6
BRISTOL LN
FRFD 94533 472-F4
BRISTOL WY
DXN 95620 395-C5
BRITANNIA CT
VAL 94591 530-H4
BRITANNIA DR
VAL 94591 530-G4
BRITTANY CT
FRFD 94585 491-D6
BRITTANY DR
FRFD 94585 491-D6
BRITTON PL
WSAC 95691 378-C3
BRIX MARINA CT
FRFD 94534 491-B2
BRIXTON CT
AMCN 94503 509-J3
BROADLEIGH PL
VAL 94591 510-J4
VAL 94591 511-A4
BROADMOOR CT
VAC 95687 433-G7
BROADMOOR LN
FRFD 94534 472-C1
BROADVIEW LN
WIN 95694 373-F3
BROADWAY
AMCN 94503 510-A3
VAL 94589 510-A5
VAL 94589 530-A3
VAL 94590 530-A3
BROADWAY RT#-29
AMCN 94503 490-A5
AMCN 94503 510-A2
NaCo 94589 490-A5
BROADWAY ST
FRFD 94533 472-F6
FRFD 94535 473-G2
E BROADWAY ST
DXN 95620 415-D1
W BROADWAY ST
DXN 95620 415-C1
BROCADE CT
FRFD 94534 491-D2
BROCK CT
WSAC 95691 378-F2
BROCKTON CT
VAC 95687 453-H2
BROCKTON PL
FRFD 94533 472-J2
RVIS 94571 516-G2
BROGAN CT
FRFD 94534 472-D3
BROKEN CIR
DVS 95618 356-E7
BROMLEY CT
VAL 94591 510-H4
BRONCO RD
NaCo 94589 490-A3
BROOK WY
FRFD 94585 511-D3
BROOKDALE CIR
FRFD 94585 491-D7
BROOKDALE CT
FRFD 94585 491-D7
VAC 95687 433-F7
BROOKDALE DR
VAC 95687 433-F7
VAC 95687 453-F1
BROOKE DR
VAL 94591 530-E6
BROOK FALLS CT
FRFD 94585 511-E3
BROOK FALLS DR
FRFD 94585 511-E2
N BROOKFIELD
AMCN 94503 510-B4
S BROOKFIELD
AMCN 94503 510-B4
BROOKFIELD CT
FRFD 94585 491-D7
BROOKFIELD LP
AMCN 94503 510-B4
BROOKFIELD CROSS
AMCN 94503 510-B4
BROOKS RD
SolC 95620 375-H3
BROOKSHIRE CT
AMCN 94503 509-J3
BROOKSIDE CIR
FRFD 94585 511-E2
BROOKSIDE CT
SUIS 94585 472-H6
VAC 95688 433-A5
BROOKSIDE DR
SUIS 94585 472-G6
VAC 95688 433-A5
WDLD 95776 316-C5
BROOKSIDE LN
RVIS 94571 516-F1
BROOKWOOD AV
VAL 94591 530-E5
BROOKWOOD DR
VAC 95687 453-E1
BROPHY ST
AMCN 94503 509-J4
AMCN 94503 510-A4
BROTHER ISLAND RD
WSAC 95691 378-E2
BROWN AV
WDLD 95695 315-G6
BROWN CT
BEN 94510 531-B7
BROWN DR
DVS 95616 356-A6
BROWN LN
FRFD 94533 453-E7
SolC 94533 453-E7
BROWN ST
VAC 95688 433-E4
BROWNING CIR
WDLD 95776 316-E5
BROWNING WY
VAL 94590 530-B7
BROWNS ISLAND CT
WSAC 95691 378-E2
BROWNS SCHOOL RD
SolC 95688 413-E5
BROWNS VALLEY PKWY
VAC 95688 433-E3
BROWNS VALLEY RD
SolC 95688 413-E6
VAC 95688 413-E6
VAC 95688 433-E3
BRUBAKER ST
WDLD 95776 316-D7

BRUDENELL DR
FRFD 94533 452-J6
BRUHN CT
DXN 95620 395-D7
BRUNELLO AV
VAC 95687 433-B7
BRUNELLO DR
AMCN 94503 510-C4
BRUNING AV
RVIS 94571 516-G6
BRUNSWICK CT
VAL 94591 530-G5
BRUNSWICK DR
VAL 94591 530-G5
BRUSHWOOD DR
FRFD 94534 452-G6
BRUSTLIN CT
VAC 95688 433-D1
BRUTON LN
WDLD 95695 316-A2
BRYANT PL
DVS 95618 356-G5
BRYANT RD
SolC 95688 414-A1
BRYCE LN
DVS 95616 355-H6
BRYCE WY
VAC 95687 433-H3
BRYNES RD
SolC 95687 414-C7
SolC 95687 434-C1
BRYTE AV
WSAC 95605 358-H1
BUCHANAN ST
BEN 94510 551-D5
DVS 95616 355-J7
FRFD 94533 472-E6
BUCK AV
VAC 95688 432-J6
VAC 95688 433-A5
BUCK CT
VAC 95688 432-J6
BUCKEYE CT
BEN 94510 550-J1
BEN 94510 551-A1
BUCKEYE DR
WSAC 95691 358-H4
BUCKEYE LN
DVS 95618 356-F6
VAL 94591 530-F7
VAL 94591 550-F1
BUCKEYE RD
YoCo 95694 373-H2
BUCKEYE ST
VAC 95688 433-B5
WDLD 95695 315-H3
BUCKINGHAM DR
FRFD 94533 472-E4
BUCKLEBURY RD
DVS 95616 355-H7
BUCKLES ST
VAL 94590 529-J3
BUCKNELL DR
DVS 95616 356-A6
BUCKSKIN PL
VAL 94591 530-D2
BUCKTHORN LN
FRFD 94533 473-A1
BUCKTOWN LN
SolC 95688 412-H6
SolC 95688 432-J2
BUDDY DR
WDLD 95776 316-B5
BUENA TIERRA DR
WDLD 95695 315-J5
WDLD 95695 316-A5
BUENA TIERRA ST
BEN 94510 551-D5
BUENA VISTA
BEN 94510 551-A3
BUENA VISTA AV
SUIS 94585 472-G6
VAL 94590 529-J3
BUENA VISTA LN
SolC 95688 413-E3
BUENA VISTA WY
WDLD 95695 315-H6
BUENO DR
DVS 95616 356-C5
BUFFLEHEAD ST
AMCN 94503 509-H1
BULLRUSH CT
AMCN 94503 509-H2
BULLS RIDGE CT
FRFD 94533 453-A7
BUNDORAN WY
VAC 95688 433-E1
BUNKER CT
FRFD 94533 452-H6
BUNKHOUSE WY
SAC 95831 378-G6
BUOY WY
SAC 95831 378-F7
BURBANK CT
FRFD 94534 472-C4
BURBANK DR
FRFD 94534 472-C4
BURGEN ST
FRFD 94535 473-J3
SolC 94533 473-J3
BURGUNDY CT
FRFD 94533 472-C7
VAL 94591 530-G1
BURGUNDY WY
FRFD 94533 472-C7
RVIS 94571 516-G6
BURKE LN
SolC 95687 454-J5
BURL CT
FRFD 94533 473-A1
BURLINGTON DR
VAC 95687 433-E7
BURNETT PL
DVS 95618 357-A7
BURNETTE ST
VAL 94591 530-D5
BURNEY CT
SUIS 94585 473-C6
BURNEY WY
WDLD 95695 315-G2
BURNHAM CT
VAC 95687 453-F3
BURNHAM ST
VAL 94590 529-H3
BURNS WY
WDLD 95776 316-E5
BURR ST
DVS 95616 355-J7
DVS 95616 356-A7
BURRELL DR
FRFD 94533 472-J2
BURR OAK CT
VAC 95688 413-D7
BURROWS AV
WSAC 95691 378-D6
BURROWS ST
WSAC 95605 358-H1
BURTON DR
VAC 95687 433-G5
BUSCH DR
FRFD 94534 471-J7
FRFD 94534 472-A7

BUSH AV
SolC 94591 550-E1
BUSH ST
VAC 95688 433-D5
WDLD 95695 315-J4
WDLD 95695 316-A4
BUSINESS CENTER DR
FRFD 94534 491-D3
BUSINESS PARK DR
DXN 95620 395-D6
BUSS AV
VAL 94591 530-D5
BUSS ST
VAL 94590 530-C5
BUTCHER RD
VAC 95687 433-B7
BUTLER CT
FRFD 94534 472-B2
WSAC 95691 378-F1
BUTTE PL
DVS 95616 355-J7
BUTTE ST
VAL 94590 529-J4
BUTTERCUP CIR
VAC 95687 453-E2
BUTTERFLY LN
VAL 94592 529-G5
BUTTERNUT CT
FRFD 94533 472-J3
BW WILLIAMS DR
VAL 94589 510-A7
BYERLY CT
VAL 94591 530-E1
BYRNES RD
SolC 95687 434-C4
BYRNES CANAL
VAC 95687 433-G6
BYRON CT
BEN 94510 550-H1
BYRON ST
VAL 94590 530-A3

C

C LN
FRFD 94533 473-E2
C ST
CCCo 94525 550-A5
DVS 95616 356-C7
DVS 95616 376-C1
FRFD 94535 473-H3
VAL 94590 529-H2
WDLD 95776 316-B3
E C ST
DXN 95620 395-D7
W C ST
BEN 94510 551-B6
DXN 95620 395-C7
CABANA CT
SUIS 94585 473-C7
CABERNET CT
FRFD 94533 472-C7
VAC 95688 433-D5
CABERNET DR
VAL 94591 530-G1
CABLE CT
WSAC 95691 358-J7
CABOT CT
FRFD 94533 472-C7
CABOT ST
DVS 95616 355-H7
CABRILLO AV
DVS 95616 356-C5
CABRILLO DR
FRFD 94533 472-C7
VAC 95687 433-H6
VAL 94591 530-D7
CACERES CT
DVS 95618 356-H6
CACERES WY
DVS 95618 356-H6
CACHE CT
VAC 95688 413-J6
CACKLING CT
SUIS 94585 473-A6
CACKLING DR
SUIS 94585 473-A6
CACTUS DR
VAL 94592 529-G6
CADDY CT
YoCo 95618 377-B1
CADENASSO DR
FRFD 94533 472-C6
CADENASSO LN
SolC 94534 471-H6
CADIZ CT
VAL 94591 530-F6
CADIZ ST
DVS 95616 356-B5
CADLONI CT
VAL 94591 530-D2
CADLONI LN
VAL 94591 530-D2
CAFE CT
NaCo 94589 490-A4
CAGLE CT
DXN 95620 415-C2
CAHILL CT
DXN 95620 395-B6
CALAFIA LN
AMCN 94503 510-B3
CALAIS CT
VAC 95687 453-J1
CALAVERAS AV
DVS 95616 355-J7
CALAVERAS CT
FRFD 94534 472-C3
CALAVERAS DR
FRFD 94534 472-C3
CALAVERAS ST
VAL 94590 530-C4
CALAVERAS WY
VAL 94590 530-C3
CALCITE CT
VAC 95687 453-G2
CALDER CT
DVS 95618 356-F5
FRFD 94533 473-A3
CALDER PL
FRFD 94533 473-A3
CALDWELL AV
VAL 94591 530-D5
CALDWELL DR
VAC 95687 453-E2
WDLD 95776 316-D4
CALHOUN ST
VAL 94590 529-H2
CALICO TR
VAC 95687 453-F4
CALIFORNIA AV
VAL 94592 529-G4
YoCo 95616 376-B1
S CALIFORNIA AV
YoCo 95616 376-B2
CALIFORNIA CT
BEN 94510 531-D7
CALIFORNIA DR
VAC 95687 453-C1
CALIFORNIA ST
CCCo 94572 549-A6
RVIS 94571 516-H5
SUIS 94585 492-F1
VAL 94590 530-A2

CALIFORNIA ST
WDLD 95695 315-H4
CALIFORNIA PACIFIC RD
SolC 95687 434-B7
VAC 95687 434-B7
CALIGUIRI LN
SolC 95688 433-B1
CALL CT
WSAC 95691 378-F2
CALLE DE CORDOBA
FRFD 94534 452-C7
CALLE DEL CABALLO
SolC 94534 471-B6
CALLEN ST
VAC 95688 433-E4
CALMACE CT
DXN 95620 395-C6
CALMACE DR
DXN 95620 395-C6
CALM BREEZE CT
VAL 94591 530-F1
CALMIA PL
DVS 95618 376-H2
CAMACHO WY
WDLD 95776 316-E7
CAMANCHE ST
WSAC 95691 378-D3
CAMBRIA CT
VAC 95687 453-F1
CAMBRIDGE CIR
VAL 94591 510-F7
VAL 94591 530-F1
CAMBRIDGE DR
BEN 94510 550-H1
FRFD 94533 472-F4
VAC 95687 453-G2
CAMBRIDGE ST
FRFD 94533 472-F4
CAMBRIDGE TER
DVS 95618 356-H7
DVS 95618 376-H2
CAMDEN CT
BEN 94510 530-H6
FRFD 94533 472-H2
VAL 94591 530-E5
CAMEL RD
BEN 94510 551-D5
CAMELBACK DR
FRFD 94533 452-G6
CAMELIA DR
DXN 95620 415-B1
CAMELIA WY
VAC 95688 433-B5
CAMELLIA CT
BEN 94510 551-A1
SUIS 94585 472-J5
CAMELLIA LN
SUIS 94585 472-J5
CAMELLIA ST
FRFD 94533 472-G3
CAMERINO CT
AMCN 94503 510-C4
CAMERON CT
VAC 95687 453-F3
CAMINO CT
DVS 95616 356-B6
CAMINO WY
WDLD 95695 316-A6
CAMINO ALTO
VAL 94590 530-B3
N CAMINO ALTO
VAL 94589 510-C7
VAL 94589 530-B1
VAL 94590 530-B3
CAMINO DEL SOL
VAL 94591 550-E3
CAMINO DORADO
NaCo 94558 490-A1
CAMINO ORUGA
NaCo 94558 490-A1
CAMINO PACIFICO
SolC 95694 393-C1
CAMPANILLA CT
DVS 95618 356-H6
CAMPAS CT
BEN 94510 530-J6
CAMPBELL AV
VAL 94590 530-C5
CAMPBELL CIR
FRFD 94533 453-D7
SolC 94533 453-D7
CAMPBELL CT
FRFD 94533 453-D7
CAMPBELL PL
DVS 95618 356-G6
CAMPBELL RD
SolC 95620 374-F5
SolC 95694 374-F4
YoCo 95616 375-J3
CAMPELL CIR
WDLD 95776 316-D5
CAMPHOR DR
WDLD 95776 316-B6
CAMPHOR LN
DVS 95618 356-G6
CAMPINI ESTATES DR
SolC 95688 433-B2
CAMPOS AV
WDLD 95776 316-E7
WDLD 95776 336-E1
CAMPOS LN
SolC 95694 373-G7
CAMPUS CT
FRFD 94534 491-F2
CAMPUS LN
FRFD 94534 491-F1
CAMPUS WY
DVS 95616 356-B7
S CAMPUS WY
DVS 95616 356-B7
DVS 95616 376-B1
CAMROSE AV
FRFD 94533 472-H2
CANADA GOOSE DR
SUIS 94585 473-A6
CANAL CT
FRFD 94533 473-A2
SolC 95694 393-B1
CANAL LN
SolC 95694 393-B1
CANAL ST
FRFD 94533 473-A2
WSAC 95691 358-F4
CANARY CT
SUIS 94585 473-B6
CANARY DR
SUIS 94585 473-B6
CANBY WY
FRFD 94534 472-D3
CANDLEBERRY CT
FRFD 94533 473-A2
CANDLEBERRY WY
FRFD 94533 473-A2
CANDLEWOOD CT
FRFD 94534 452-F7
CANDLEWOOD DR
FRFD 94534 452-F7
CANDY DR
VAL 94589 509-H6
CANFIELD CT
SUIS 94585 473-B7

CANNA WY
WSAC 95691 358-J4
CANNERY RD
WDLD 95776 316-B3
CANNES CT
FRFD 94534 472-D2
CANNON CT
FRFD 94535 473-J2
CANNON DR
FRFD 94535 473-H2
CANNON RD
SolC 94533 453-H6
SolC 95687 453-H6
CANNON STATION CT
VAC 95688 413-H6
CANOE PL
DVS 95616 355-G7
CANOVA LN
FRFD 94533 472-E6
CANRIGHT RD
RVIS 94571 516-B1
SolC 94571 516-B1
CANTADA CT
AMCN 94503 510-B1
CANTADA WY
AMCN 94503 510-B1
CANTELOW RD
SolC 95688 412-F3
SolC 95688 413-A4
CANTERBURY CIR
VAL 94591 530-G4
CANTERBURY DR
FRFD 94533 472-E4
VAL 94591 530-G4
CANTON LN
FRFD 94534 472-E2
CANTRILL DR
DVS 95618 356-F7
DVS 95618 376-F1
CANVASBACK CT
VAC 95687 433-H6
CANVASBACK DR
SUIS 94585 472-J6
SUIS 94585 473-A6
CANVASBACK WY
WSAC 95691 378-F2
CANYON CT
BEN 94510 551-B3
VAL 94591 550-D1
CANYON RD
NaCo 94589 510-F3
CANYON CREEK CT
FRFD 94534 491-F4
CANYON CREEK DR
AMCN 94503 510-B3
CANYON HILLS CT
FRFD 94585 511-E2
CANYON HILLS DR
FRFD 94585 511-E3
CANYON LAKE DR
CCCo 94569 550-H6
CANYON MEADOWS DR
AMCN 94503 509-J4
CANYON OAK CT
VAC 95688 413-D7
CANYON OAK DR
VAC 95688 413-D7
CANYON SPRINGS DR
RVIS 94571 516-E2
CAPAY VALLEY DR
WDLD 95776 316-C5
CAPE COD CT
DVS 95616 356-A6
CAPE COD ST
DVS 95616 356-A6
CAPE ELIZABETH CT
VAL 94591 550-F1
CAPILAND DR
VAL 94590 530-C3
CAPILANO CT
FRFD 94534 452-D7
CAPISTRANO CT
FRFD 94585 511-D1
CAPISTRANO DR
SUIS 94585 473-C6
CAPITAL CITY FRWY U.S.-50
WSAC - 358-F4
W CAPITOL AV
WSAC 95691 358-D4
CAPITOL DR
BEN 94510 550-H1
CAPITOL ST
VAL 94590 529-J5
VAL 94590 530-A5
CAPITOLA CT
FRFD 94534 472-D3
CAPITOLA WY
FRFD 94534 472-D4
CAPRA DR
AMCN 94503 509-J4
AMCN 94503 510-A4
CAPRI CT
FRFD 94534 491-C3
CAPRICORN CIR
FRFD 94533 472-H2
CAPRINE DR
SolC 95620 376-B4
CAPSTAN CT
VAC 95687 433-D7
CAPSTAN WY
SAC 95822 378-J4
CAPTAIN CT
SAC 95831 378-G7
CAPTAINS CT
VAL 94591 550-F2
CARACENA CT
VAL 94591 530-J1
CARAVAGGIO DR
DVS 95618 356-F5
CARAVAGGIO PL
DVS 95618 356-G5
CARDINAL DR
WDLD 95695 315-F1
CARDINAL LN
VAL 94589 510-A4
CARDINAL WY
FRFD 94533 472-H3
CAREMA CT
VAC 95687 433-B7
CARIBOU CT
VAC 95688 432-J4
CARIBOU PL
DVS 95616 356-A5
CARICIA DR
DVS 95618 356-H7
CARISBROOKE LN
VAL 94591 510-J5
VAL 94591 511-A5
CARL AV
VAL 94590 530-C3
CARLIN DR
WSAC 95691 358-D7
CARLINGFORD LN
VAL 94591 510-H3
CARLISLE CT
BEN 94510 551-C2
CARLISLE PL
BEN 94510 551-B2
CARLISLE WY
BEN 94510 551-A2
VAL 94591 510-H4

CARLSBAD AV
YoCo 95616 355-A4
CARLSBAD CIR
VAC 95687 433-H3
CARLSBAD PL
DVS 95616 355-J6
WDLD 95695 315-G2
CARLSON ST
SolC 94590 530-B6
VAL 94590 530-B6
CARLTON AV
VAC 95687 453-H1
CARLTON CT
FRFD 94535 473-J1
CARMEL CT
VAC 95688 433-A3
WSAC 95691 378-H1
CARMEL DR
AMCN 94503 509-J1
CARMEL WY
FRFD 94534 472-D3
CARMEL BAY RD
WSAC 95691 378-E2
CARMELITA WY
SolC 95688 412-H2
CARMELLO LN
DVS 95618 356-G5
CARMELO WY
YoCo 95694 374-B1
CARMEL VALLEY DR
WDLD 95776 316-C5
CARNATION CT
VAL 94589 509-H5
CARNATION DR
FRFD 94533 472-F2
CARNEGIE WY
WDLD 95695 315-J3
WDLD 95695 316-A3
CARNELIAN CT
WDLD 95695 316-A6
CARNIVAL CT
VAL 94589 510-E6
CAROB PL
DVS 95616 356-B6
CAROB WY
WDLD 95776 316-D5
CAROLE RIDGE CT
FRFD 94534 491-E1
CAROLINA AV
WSAC 95691 358-J6
CAROLINA DR
BEN 94510 551-A4
CAROLINA ST
FRFD 94533 472-H5
VAL 94590 529-J4
VAL 94590 530-A4
VAL 94591 530-D5
CAROLYN DR
AMCN 94503 509-J2
W CAROLYN DR
AMCN 94503 509-J1
CAROUSEL DR
VAL 94589 510-D6
CAROUSEL WY
VAC 95688 413-J7
CARPENTER CT
DXN 95620 395-A7
CARPENTER ST
FRFD 94533 472-F5
CARQUINEZ CIR
BEN 94510 551-A3
CARQUINEZ CT
BEN 94510 551-B4
CARQUINEZ ST
SolC 94590 530-C6
CARQUINEZ WY
CCCo 94525 550-C5
CARQUINEZ SCENIC DR
CCCo 94525 550-F5
CCCo 94553 550-H6
CCCo 94569 550-H6
CARRAL LN
SolC 95688 412-F6
CARRARA CT
AMCN 94503 509-J3
CARRIAGE CT
FRFD 94585 491-D6
CARRIAGE DR
WDLD 95776 316-B6
CARRIAGE WY
VAC 95688 413-D7
CARRIE ST
WSAC 95605 358-H1
CARRIGAN CT
WSAC 95691 358-H5
CARRINGTON LN
SolC 95688 412-F5
CARRION CIR
WIN 95694 373-F3
CARRION CT
WIN 95694 373-F2
CARROLL ST
VAL 94590 530-B4
CARSON CT
FRFD 94534 472-C4
VAC 95687 433-C7
CARSON RD
FRFD 94535 473-J6
FRFD 94535 474-A6
CARSON ST
WDLD 95695 316-A6
CARSTEN CIR
BEN 94510 530-J6
CARSWELL CT
SUIS 94585 473-C4
CARSWELL LN
SUIS 94585 473-C4
CARTAGENA WY
AMCN 94503 510-A4
CARTER LN
YoCo 95695 315-F1
CARTER ST
VAL 94590 529-J3
CARTIER CT
FRFD 94533 472-B7
CARVER PL
FRFD 94533 473-B3
CASA GRANDE PL
BEN 94510 551-D4
CASA GRANDE ST
BEN 94510 551-D5
CASA LINDA DR
WDLD 95695 315-J5
W CASA LINDA DR
WDLD 95695 315-H5
CASA LOMA WY
SUIS 94585 473-C6
CASA NUEVA ST
WDLD 95695 315-H6
CASCADE AV
VAL 94589 510-B5
CASCADE CIR
FRFD 94533 473-E2
CASCADE CT
FRFD 94533 473-E2
CASCADE DR
VAC 95687 433-E6
CASCADE LN
FRFD 94533 473-E2
FRFD 94535 473-E2
CASCADE PL
DVS 95618 356-F6

CASCADE ST
WDLD 95695 315-G2
WSAC 95691 378-H1
CASE CT
NaCo 94589 490-A3
CASE PL
WDLD 95776 316-C4
CASELLI CT
WIN 95694 373-F3
CASEY CT
BEN 94510 551-C1
CASHEL CIR
VAC 95688 413-F7
CASHEW CT
FRFD 94533 472-J1
CASILADA WY
SAC 95822 378-J3
CASSADY ST
VAL 94590 530-B4
CASSATT ST
DVS 95618 356-E5
CASSAYRE DR
AMCN 94503 510-A1
CASSEL LN
DVS 95616 356-A5
CASSEL PL
DVS 95616 356-A5
CASSIDY CT
FRFD 94535 473-H1
CASSIDY LN
YoCo 95616 355-C7
CASTAIC CT
WSAC 95691 378-C3
CASTELLI CT
FRFD 94534 491-C3
CASTELLINA CIR
AMCN 94503 510-C3
CASTILE CT
NAP 94559 470-A1
VAC 95688 433-A3
CASTILE ST
VAL 94591 530-F6
CASTLE CT
WSAC 95691 358-H3
CASTLE HILL CT
VAL 94591 550-E2
CASTLE VIEW LN
WIN 95694 373-D2
YoCo 95694 373-D2
CASTLEWOOD
VAC 95688 433-A5
CASTLEWOOD CT
FRFD 94585 491-D7
CASTLEWOOD DR
VAL 94591 530-E5
CATALINA CIR
SUIS 94585 472-G7
VAL 94589 509-G4
CATALINA CT
VAC 95687 433-C7
VAL 94589 509-H5
CATALINA DR
DVS 95616 356-B5
CATALINA WY
VAL 94589 509-G4
CATALINA ISLAND RD
WSAC 95691 378-C2
CATALONIA DR
AMCN 94503 510-B4
CATALPA CT
VAC 95687 453-F1
CATALPA LN
VAC 95687 453-F1
CATALPA ST
VAL 94589 509-J7
VAL 94589 529-J1
CATAMARAN CT
FRFD 94533 473-A1
CATAMARAN WY
SUIS 94585 492-G1
VAC 95688 413-E7
CATHERINE ST
VAC 95688 433-D5
CATLIN CT
FRFD 94533 473-B4
CATLIN DR
FRFD 94533 473-B4
CATTAIL CT
AMCN 94503 509-J4
CATTAIL DR
AMCN 94503 509-J4
CATTON CT
FRFD 94535 473-J1
CAVALCADE CIR
SAC 95831 378-H7
CAVALIER CT
SolC 94534 471-B6
CAVAN CT
VAC 95687 433-G7
CAYETANO DR
NaCo 94559 450-A7
NAP 94559 450-A7
CAYMAN ISLAND ST
WSAC 95691 378-D2
CEBRIAN ST
WSAC 95691 358-H6
CEDAR CT
CCCo 94525 550-D5
WSAC 95691 378-J2
CEDAR LN
WDLD 95695 315-J6
CEDAR PL
DVS 95616 356-C6
DXN 95620 415-D1
CEDAR ST
VAC 95688 433-C5
VAL 94591 530-D5
WSAC 95691 358-H3
CEDARBROOK CT
FRFD 94534 472-F2
CEDARBROOK DR
FRFD 94534 472-F2
CEDAR BROOK LN
VAC 95687 433-J7
CEDARBROOK RD
WSAC 95691 378-J1
CEDAR CREEK CT
FRFD 94534 491-F3
CEDARCREST DR
VAC 95687 453-G3
CEDAR LOGS DR
YoCo 95695 335-E6
CEDAR RIDGE CT
RVIS 94571 516-F2
CEDAR RIDGE DR
RVIS 94571 516-E3
CEDAR RIVER WY
SAC 95831 378-F7
CEDAR VALE CT
FRFD 94534 491-F3
CELEBRATION WY
WDLD 95776 336-E1
CELESTE CT
VAL 94591 530-F1
CELESTINE CIR
VAC 95687 453-G3
CEMENT HILL RD
FRFD 94533 472-G2
FRFD 94533 473-C1
SolC 94533 473-C1
CEMETERY DR
RVIS 94571 516-G5

CEMETERY RD
SOLANO COUNTY STREET INDEX
COUNTY ROAD 29 557

SOLANO CO.

STREET Name City ZIP Pg-Grid
CEMETERY RD
WIN 95694 373-E3
CENTENNIAL DR
WDLD 95776 336-E1
CENTER AV
AMCN 94503 510-B2
CENTER ST
RVIS 94571 516-H6
CENTER BROOKFIELD
AMCN 94503 510-B4
CENTRAL AV
VAL 94590 530-B3
CENTRAL LN
SolC 95694 393-B2
CENTRAL PL
FRFD 94534 491-F3
WDLD 95695 315-H3
CENTRAL WY
FRFD 94534 491-E4
SolC 94534 491-E4
YoCo 95616 355-J4
CENTURY CT
FRFD 94533 473-B3
CEREBA LN
SolC 94534 471-B5
CERES ST
CCCo 94525 550-D5
CERNON ST
VAC 95688 433-C6
CERRADA AZUL
SolC 94534 471-B5
CERRADA CIELO
SolC 94534 471-B5
CESSNA DR
VAC 95688 413-G7
VAC 95688 433-F1
CEZANNE CT
DVS 95618 356-E5
CHABLIS CT
VAL 94591 530-F1
CHABOT CT
FRFD 94534 491-D2
CHADBOURNE RD
FRFD 94533 472-A7
FRFD 94534 472-A7
FRFD 94534 492-B2
FRFD 94585 492-B2
SolC 94534 472-B7
SolC 94534 492-B2
SolC 94585 492-B4
CHADWICK CT
BEN 94510 551-A2
CHAFFEY CT
VAC 95687 433-H5
CHALICE CT
FRFD 94533 472-J2
CHALK HILL LN
VAL 94591 510-J5
CHALUPA PL
DVS 95618 356-G6
CHAMBERLAIN DR
FRFD 94533 472-G5
CHAMISE CT
FRFD 94533 472-G2
CHAMPAGNE CT
FRFD 94533 472-D6
CHAMPION PL
VAC 95687 433-J6
CHAMPIONS WY
FRFD 94533 452-J5
CHANBORD CT
VAL 94591 530-J1
CHANCELLOR CT
VAC 95688 413-G5
CHANDLER CT
WDLD 95695 316-A2
CHANDLER PL
YoCo 95695 335-F6
CHANDLER ST
VAC 95688 433-C5
CHANNEL CT
BEN 94510 551-D1
FRFD 94585 491-C6
CHANNEL DR
WSAC 95691 358-C6
CHANNEL RD
BEN 94510 531-D7
BEN 94510 551-D1
CHANNING CIR
BEN 94510 530-H6
CHANNING CT
FRFD 94533 473-A3
CHANNING PL
FRFD 94533 473-A3
CHANTILLY CT
VAL 94591 530-E1
CHAPARRAL WY
WSAC 95691 358-H3
CHAPMAN CIR
WDLD 95695 315-G5
CHAPMAN CT
VAL 94589 510-B5
CHAPMAN PL
DVS 95618 356-E6
CHAPPARAL CT
FRFD 94534 452-G6
CHAPPARAL DR
FRFD 94534 452-G6
CHARDONNAY CT
VAC 95688 433-C4
CHARDONNAY WY
RVIS 94571 516-G6
CHARITY LN
DXN 95620 395-B6
CHARLES CT
BEN 94510 530-J7
VAL 94591 530-D3
CHARLES ST
WSAC 95605 358-J1
CHARLEE WY
SUIS 94585 473-A5
CHARLESTON ST
FRFD 94533 473-C4
SUIS 94585 473-C4
CHARLIE AL
DXN 95620 415-C2
CHARLOTTE LN
SolC 95688 393-G7
CHARLTON RD
VAL 94592 529-G7
VAL 94592 549-H1
CHARMET LN
AMCN 94503 510-B3
CHARMIAN CT
BEN 94510 551-A3
CHARTER LN
FRFD 94533 473-A2
CHARTER WY
VAC 95687 453-F3
CHARTMASTER PL
VAL 94591 550-E3
CHASE ST
VAL 94590 530-B5
CHATEAU CIR
VAC 95687 453-J1
CHATEAU CT
FRFD 94534 491-C3
CHATEAU LN
DVS 95618 376-F2
NaCo 94558 450-B4
CHATEAU WY
VAC 95687 453-J1
CHATHAM PL
VAL 94591 550-E1
CHATSWOOD CT
FRFD 94533 452-H6
CHAUCER CT
AMCN 94503 509-J3
CHAUCER LN
AMCN 94503 509-J3
FRFD 94533 473-F7
CHAUNCY CT
VAC 95688 433-E2
CHAUNCY WY
VAC 95688 433-C1
CHELAN DR
VAC 95687 433-E6
CHELAN RD
WSAC 95691 378-J1
CHELMSFORD CT
VAC 95688 433-D2
CHELSEA CT
VAC 95687 453-G2
CHELSEA WY
FRFD 94533 472-G2
CHELSEA HILLS DR
BEN 94510 551-B2
CHENIN BLANC PL
VAL 94591 530-G1
CHENNAULT ST
FRFD 94535 473-F3
CHEROKEE CT
VAC 95688 433-A5
CHEROKEE RD
WSAC 95691 378-H2
CHERRY AV
VAC 95688 433-B6
CHERRY CT
SolC 94534 471-B6
CHERRY LN
DVS 95616 356-A7
YoCo 95695 315-F1
CHERRY PL
WSAC 95691 378-C3
CHERRY ST
VAL 94590 530-B7
W CHERRY ST
DXN 95620 415-C1
CHERRY BLOSSOM CT
AMCN 94503 509-J2
CHERRY GLEN RD
SolC 94534 452-H1
SolC 95688 432-J7
SolC 95688 433-A7
SolC 95688 452-H1
VAC 94533 452-H1
VAC 94534 452-H1
VAC 95687 452-H1
VAC 95688 433-A7
VAC 95688 452-H1
CHERRY HILLS CT
FRFD 94534 472-B3
CHERRY HILLS LN
RVIS 94571 516-F2
CHERRY VALLEY CIR
FRFD 94534 472-D1
CHERRY VALLEY CT
FRFD 94534 472-D1
CHERRY VALLEY DR
FRFD 94534 472-C1
CHERRYWOOD AV
VAL 94591 530-E5
CHERYL DR
BEN 94510 551-A3
CHESAPEAKE CT
FRFD 94533 452-J5
CHESAPEAKE DR
VAL 94591 550-E2
CHESAPEAKE BAY AV
DVS 95616 355-G6
CHESLEY CT
VAL 94591 530-D5
CHESTER WY
FRFD 94533 472-H2
SolC 95688 412-G6
CHESTNUT CT
FRFD 94533 472-H1
CHESTNUT DR
FRFD 94533 472-H1
CHESTNUT LN
DVS 95616 356-E7
CHESTNUT PL
DVS 95618 356-E6
CHESTNUT ST
VAC 95688 433-B5
VAL 94590 530-A7
WDLD 95695 315-G3
E CHESTNUT ST
DXN 95620 415-D1
W CHESTNUT ST
DXN 95620 415-C1
CHESTY PULLER DR
VAL 94592 529-G7
CHEVRON WY
SolC 95620 414-E4
CHEVY CHASE CT
FRFD 94533 473-C4
CHEYENNE CT
VAC 95688 433-A4
CHEYENNE DR
VAC 95688 433-A4
CHIANTI CT
FRFD 94534 491-F5
VAL 94591 530-G1
CHICKADEE CT
SAC 95831 378-G5
CHICKASAW CT
FRFD 94533 452-J7
CHICKORY LN
FRFD 94585 511-D1
CHICO ST
VAL 94591 530-D7
CHICORD LN
SolC 95687 434-E7
CHILDS CT
SUIS 94585 473-B7
CHILES RD
DVS 95618 356-G7
DVS 95618 357-A7
DVS 95618 376-G1
SolC 95620 376-G1
YoCo 95618 356-J7
YoCo 95618 357-A7
W CHILES RD
DVS 95618 376-D2
SolC 95620 376-D2
CHIMILES TR
NaCo 94558 451-F1
CHIMNEY ROCK CT
VAC 95687 453-H3
CHIMNEY ROCK DR
VAC 95687 453-H3
CHIMNEY ROCK WY
FRFD 94533 452-J6
SolC 94533 452-J6
CHINA CT
FRFD 94534 472-E2
CHINA LN
FRFD 94534 472-E2
CHINA HAT ISLAND RD
WSAC 95691 378-D2
CHINOOK CT
VAC 95688 433-A4
CHINOOK RD
WSAC 95691 378-H1
CHIPMAN LN
SUIS 94585 472-H7
CHISAMORE RANCH LN
SolC 95688 393-E7
SolC 95688 413-E1
CHRISTENSEN WY
RVIS 94571 516-G3
CHRISTIE CT
DVS 95618 376-F1
CHRISTINE DR
VAC 95687 433-H5
CHRISTOPHER WY
VAL 94589 510-C5
CHULA CT
SUIS 94585 473-C6
CHULA VISTA WY
SUIS 94585 473-C6
CHURCH RD
RVIS 94571 516-F3
CHURCH ST
BEN 94510 550-J3
CHURCHILL DR
FRFD 94533 472-F4
CHURCHILL DOWNS AV
WDLD 95776 316-B1
YoCo 95776 316-B1
CHYRL WY
SUIS 94585 472-J5
SUIS 94585 473-A5
CIARLO LN
SolC 95688 412-J1
SolC 95688 413-A1
CIELITO LINDA
YoCo 95694 373-A3
CIMA DR
VAL 94589 530-C1
CIMARRON CT
VAL 94589 510-E6
CIMARRON DR
VAL 94589 510-D6
CINDER CT
SAC 95831 378-J7
CINNABAR WY
VAC 95687 453-F2
CINNABAR HILLS
RVIS 94571 516-F1
CINNAMON WY
SUIS 94585 472-J6
CIRCLE DR
FRFD 94533 472-G4
VAC 95688 433-E4
CIRCLE ST
WSAC 95691 358-J5
CIRCLE C LN
SolC 95687 434-H6
CITADEL CT
FRFD 94534 491-C3
CITADEL DR
DVS 95616 356-B6
FRFD 94534 491-C3
CITRINE CIR
FRFD 94534 491-E2
CITRUS AV
VAC 95688 433-C4
CITRUS ST
WSAC 95605 358-G2
CITY HALL ACCESS RD
VAL 94590 529-J5
CIVIC CENTER BLVD
SUIS 94585 472-G7
SUIS 94585 492-G1
CIVIC CENTER DR
FRFD 94533 472-E5
CLAGGETT AV
FRFD 94535 473-G2
CLAIBORNE WY
SAC 95831 378-F7
CLANCY LN
SolC 95688 413-E3
CLANTON AV
WDLD 95695 315-H4
CLANTON WY
WDLD 95695 315-J4
CLARA LN
DVS 95618 356-E6
CLAREMONT AV
VAL 94590 530-C2
CLAREMONT CT
FRFD 94585 491-E7
FRFD 94585 511-D1
VAC 95687 433-C7
CLAREMONT DR
DVS 95616 356-D6
VAC 95687 433-C7
CLARENCE LN
FRFD 94533 473-B2
CLARENDON ST
WSAC 95691 358-H5
CLARESCASTLE WY
VAC 95688 433-D2
CLARET CT
VAL 94591 530-F2
CLARIDGE CT
VAC 95687 453-F1
CLARK CT
DVS 95618 376-F1
FRFD 94535 473-H2
WDLD 95776 316-E5
CLARK DR
VAL 94591 530-D3
CLARK RD
SolC 95687 434-H7
SolC 95687 454-H1
CLARK ST
CCCo 94525 550-E5
CLARK WY
VAC 95687 453-G1
CLATTON CT
VAL 94591 530-D3
CLAUDIA CT
WSAC 95691 378-E1
CLAVERIE WY
BEN 94510 551-A4
CLAXTON CT
VAL 94589 509-J5
CLAY ST
FRFD 94533 472-G5
VAL 94591 530-D4
CLAY BANK RD
FRFD 94533 452-J7
FRFD 94533 453-A7
FRFD 94533 473-A1
CLAYTON CIR
VAC 95687 433-G7
VAC 95687 453-G1
CLAYTON CT
VAC 95687 453-G1
CLAYTON RD
SolC 94534 451-J7
SolC 94534 452-A4
SolC 94534 471-H1
CLEARBROOK CT
SUIS 94585 472-H6
CLEAR COAST CT
VAL 94591 530-F2
CLEARPOINTE DR
VAL 94591 550-D1
CLEAR VIEW CIR
BEN 94510 551-B3
CLEARVIEW DR
VAL 94591 550-D2
CLEARWATER WY
WDLD 95776 316-C5
CLEARWATER OAK CT
FRFD 94534 491-B2
CLEMENT RD
SolC 95688 413-F4
CLEMSON CT
WDLD 95695 315-G6
CLEMSON DR
DVS 95618 356-F6
CLEVELAND ST
DVS 95616 355-J7
DVS 95616 375-H1
FRFD 94533 472-E5
WDLD 95695 315-J5
N CLEVELAND ST
WDLD 95695 315-J2
CLICKER CT
WSAC 95691 378-F1
CLIFFSIDE DR
VAC 95687 433-D6
CLIFF WALK DR
VAL 94591 550-E2
CLIFFWOOD DR
FRFD 94534 452-G7
FRFD 94534 472-G1
CLIFTON CT
BEN 94510 530-H6
VAC 95688 433-E1
CLIFTON WY
VAC 95688 433-E1
CLIPPER CT
DXN 95620 395-C5
FRFD 94534 472-E3
CLIPPER DR
VAL 94591 550-F3
CLIPPER LN
FRFD 94534 472-E3
CLIPPER WY
SAC 95831 378-H5
CLIPPER BAY LN
BEN 94510 551-A4
CLIPPER SHIP CT
FRFD 94534 472-E3
CLIPPER SHIP DR
FRFD 94534 472-E3
CLOS DUVALL
BEN 94510 551-D5
CLOUDCREST CT
VAC 95687 453-F4
CLOVER CT
WDLD 95695 315-H3
CLOVER LN
SolC 95688 413-B1
CLOVER ST
WDLD 95695 315-J3
WDLD 95695 316-A3
WDLD 95776 316-A3
W CLOVER ST
WDLD 95695 315-H3
CLOVERBROOK CIR
VAC 95687 453-F3
CLOVERBROOK CT
FRFD 94585 511-D3
CLOVERDALE RD
WSAC 95691 378-G2
CLOVERLEAF CIR
SUIS 94585 472-H6
CLUB DR
VAL 94592 529-H6
CLUB HOUSE DR
YoCo 95618 376-J2
YoCo 95618 377-A1
CLUBHOUSE DR
RVIS 94571 516-E1
CLYDESDALE DR
VAL 94591 530-E2
CLYDESDALE WY
FRFD 94533 472-J1
CLYNE CT
BEN 94510 531-B7
BEN 94510 551-B1
COACH LN
VAL 94589 530-D1
COACHLITE WY
SAC 95831 378-H7
COAST OAK CT
FRFD 94534 491-E1
COBALT WY
VAC 95687 453-G3
COBB AV
VAL 94589 510-B5
COBBLESTONE AV
FRFD 94534 452-F7
COBBLESTONE CT
FRFD 94534 452-F7
VAC 95687 433-J5
COBBLESTONE DR
VAC 95687 433-J5
COBBLESTONE LN
VAL 94589 510-B4
COCHISE CT
VAC 95688 432-J4
CODY CT
VAC 95687 433-H5
CODY ST
WIN 95694 373-D4
COFFEEBERRY RD
WSAC 95691 358-G7
COFFEEBERRY ST
WSAC 95691 358-F7
COGHLAN ST
VAL 94590 529-J3
COHN CT
SUIS 94585 473-B7
SUIS 94585 493-A1
COHO PL
DVS 95616 355-H6
COIT PL
WSAC 95691 358-J6
COKE ST
WSAC 95691 358-G4
COLBY CT
VAC 95687 433-H5
WDLD 95695 315-G5
COLBY DR
DVS 95616 356-A6
VAC 95687 433-H5
COLBY LN
WIN 95694 373-F3
COLE CT
FRFD 94533 473-B3
WDLD 95695 316-A2
COLE RD
SolC 95688 393-H7
COLEMAN CT
DXN 95620 395-B7
COLEMAN DR
DXN 95620 395-B7
COLEMANITE CIR
VAC 95687 453-E3
COLERIDGE DR
VAL 94591 530-E6
COLETTE WY
WDLD 95776 316-B4
COLFAX DR
WDLD 95776 316-B4
COLFAX PL
WDLD 95776 316-B4
COLGATE CT
WDLD 95695 315-G6
COLGATE DR
DVS 95616 356-D7
COLINA CT
DVS 95618 356-G7
COLLEEN CT
WSAC 95691 378-F1
COLLEGE AV
VAL 94589 510-B6
COLLEGE PK
DVS 95616 356-C7
DVS 95616 376-C1
COLLEGE ST
WDLD 95695 315-J5
N COLLEGE ST
WDLD 95695 315-J3
COLLIER DR
DXN 95620 415-D1
COLLINS DR
FRFD 94535 473-J2
FRFD 94535 474-A2
SolC 94533 474-A2
COLLINS PL
WDLD 95776 316-D5
COLLINS ST
WSAC 95691 378-C4
COLOMA WY
VAL 94589 509-J5
WDLD 95695 316-A6
COLONIAL CIR
VAC 95687 453-H1
COLONIAL CT
FRFD 94534 472-B2
COLONIAL DR
FRFD 94534 472-B2
COLONIAL WY
RVIS 94571 516-F1
N COLONY RD
YoCo 95616 375-E1
COLONY WY
VAC 95687 453-G2
COLORADO LN
DVS 95616 355-J6
COLORADO ST
FRFD 94533 472-G5
FRFD 94535 473-H2
E COLORADO ST
FRFD 94533 472-G5
COLT CT
VAL 94590 530-B7
COLUMBIA CIR
BEN 94510 551-C1
COLUMBIA CT
VAC 95687 433-H6
COLUMBIA DR
VAC 95687 433-H6
WDLD 95695 315-F5
COLUMBIA PL
DVS 95616 356-D7
COLUMBIA WY
VAL 94589 509-J5
WIN 95694 373-D3
COLUMBINE CT
VAC 95687 453-E2
COLUMBUS AV
CCCo 94525 550-C5
COLUMBUS CIR
FRFD 94535 473-H3
COLUMBUS CT
FRFD 94533 472-B7
COLUMBUS DR
FRFD 94533 472-C7
COLUMBUS PKWY
BEN 94510 550-G1
BEN 94591 530-F4
BEN 94591 550-G1
SolC 94591 530-F4
SolC 94591 550-G1
VAL 94591 510-F7
VAL 94591 530-G3
COLUMBUS RD
WSAC 95691 358-J7
COLUSA AV
DVS 95616 355-J7
DVS 95616 356-A7
COLUSA CT
DXN 95620 395-C7
COLUSA PL
WDLD 95695 315-J6
COLUSA RD
WSAC 95691 378-H2
COLUSA ST
VAL 94590 530-B5
COMBS LN
VAL 94590 530-C3
COMMANDANTS LN
BEN 94510 551-E6
COMMERCE AV
WDLD 95776 316-B2
COMMERCE CT
FRFD 94534 491-E3
VAC 95687 433-J6
COMMERCE DR
WSAC 95691 358-E3
COMMERCE PL
VAC 95687 433-J6
COMMERCIAL ST
VAL 94589 510-A7
COMMERCIAL WY
DXN 95620 395-B6
COMMODORE CT
VAL 94591 550-F2
COMMON ST
SUIS 94585 472-F7
COMMUNITY LN
WDLD 95695 315-H4
COMPASS CT
VAC 95687 433-D6
VAL 94590 529-H2
COMSTOCK CT
VAL 94589 530-B1
CONCHA PL
DVS 95618 356-H6
CONCORD AV
DVS 95618 376-F1
FRFD 94533 472-C7
CONCORD CT
FRFD 94533 472-C7
VAC 95687 453-G2
CONCORD PL
DVS 95618 376-G1
CONCORD ST
VAL 94591 530-D5
CONDOR CT
AMCN 94503 510-B4
DVS 95616 356-A5
CONDOR WY
FRFD 94533 472-J3
CONGRESSIONAL CIR
FRFD 94534 472-C1
CONGRESSIONAL CT
FRFD 94534 472-C1
CONIFER DR
FRFD 94533 473-A2
CONNECTICUT ST
FRFD 94533 472-E6
CONNER CT
SolC 94534 471-G7
CONNOLLY ST
VAL 94592 529-G5
CONNOR LN
WDLD 95695 315-G4
CONQUISTADOR WY
DVS 95618 356-G6
CONSTABLE CT
FRFD 94534 491-B3
CONSTABLE DR
FRFD 94534 491-B3
CONSTANCE DR
VAL 94590 550-C1
CONSTITUTION AV
FRFD 94533 452-H5
VAC 95687 453-F2
WSAC 95691 358-F7
WSAC 95691 378-F1
CONTRA COSTA ST
VAL 94590 530-B5
CONWAY DR
RVIS 94571 516-F1
COOK CIR
VAL 94589 510-B7
COOKE ST
CCCo 94525 550-E5
COOK ISLAND RD
WSAC 95691 378-C2
COOKSON ST
VAC 95687 453-F4
COOLIDGE CT
DVS 95616 355-J7
DVS 95616 375-H1
COOLIDGE DR
WDLD 95776 316-B6
COOLIDGE PL
WDLD 95776 316-B6
COOLIDGE ST
DVS 95616 355-J7
FRFD 94533 472-H5
COOMBSVILLE RD
NaCo 94558 450-A6
NaCo 94559 450-A6
NAP 94559 450-A6
COOPER DR
BEN 94510 550-H1
COOPER SCHOOL RD
VAC 95687 433-H5
COOT LN
SUIS 94585 472-J7
SUIS 94585 473-A7
COPLEY CT
FRFD 94533 452-J7
COPLEY WY
FRFD 94533 452-J6
COPPER CT
VAC 95687 453-G3
COPPER WY
VAC 95687 453-G2
VAL 94589 510-B6
COPPER ISLAND RD
WSAC 95691 378-D2
COPPOCK CT
VAL 94591 530-F3
CORAL CT
VAC 95687 433-J5
CORAL DR
WDLD 95695 315-H3
CORAL LN
SUIS 94585 472-H7
CORAL WY
VAC 95687 433-J5
CORAL SEA CIR
VAL 94592 529-H7
CORANADO ST
WSAC 95691 358-J7
WSAC 95691 378-J1
CORBIN CT
AMCN 94503 510-A4
CORBIN DR
AMCN 94503 510-A4
CORCORAN AV
VAL 94589 510-A5
CORCORAN CT
BEN 94510 530-H7
CORDELIA CIR
VAC 95687 433-C7
CORDELIA CT
VAC 95687 433-C7
CORDELIA RD
FRFD 94534 491-H2
FRFD 94534 492-A2
FRFD 94585 492-E1
SolC 94534 491-H2
SolC 94534 492-E1
SolC 94585 492-E1
SUIS 94534 492-E1
SUIS 94585 492-E1
W CORDELIA RD
FRFD 94534 491-D4
SolC 94534 491-D4
SolC 94589 491-D4
CORDELIA ST
SolC 94585 492-F1
SUIS 94585 492-F1
CORDOBA LN
VAC 95688 433-B3
CORDOVA PL
DVS 95616 356-B5
CORDOVA ST
VAL 94591 530-F6
CORDOZA CT
WDLD 95695 315-G4
CORK PL
DVS 95618 356-F5
CORKWOOD PL
WDLD 95695 315-G6
CORKWOOD ST
VAL 94591 530-F5
CORMORANT CT
FRFD 94533 473-A4
CORMORANT DR
FRFD 94533 473-A4
CORMORANT PL
FRFD 94533 473-A4
CORNELL CIR
WDLD 95695 315-G6
CORNELL CT
VAC 95687 433-F7
CORNELL DR
DVS 95616 356-A7
CORNERSTONE CT
VAC 95687 453-E3
CORONA DR
DVS 95616 356-B5
CORONADO CT
FRFD 94533 472-C7
VAC 95687 453-D1
CORONADO WY
RVIS 94571 516-G2
CORONEL AV
VAL 94591 530-D7
VAL 94591 550-D1
CORPORATE PL
VAL 94590 530-A6
CORRIGAN CT
BEN 94510 551-A3
CORSICANA DR
AMCN 94503 509-J1
CORTE ALHAMBRA
VAC 95688 433-A3
CORTE ALTA
VAC 95688 433-B3
CORTE BACA
VAC 95688 433-B3
CORTE BARCELONA CT
VAC 95688 433-B3
CORTE CADIZ
VAC 95688 433-B3
CORTE CALA
VAC 95688 433-B3
CORTE CASTRO
VAC 95688 433-B2
CORTE CRESTVIEW
VAC 95688 433-A3
CORTE DEL SOL
BEN 94510 551-C4
CORTE DORADO
BEN 94510 551-D4
CORTE GONZALES
VAC 95688 433-B2
CORTE GRANADA
FRFD 94534 452-C7
CORTE LAGOS
VAC 95688 433-B3
CORTE MADRID
VAC 95688 433-A3
CORTE MALAGA
VAC 95688 433-A2
CORTE SEVILLE
VAC 95688 433-A3
CORTES ISLAND RD
WSAC 95691 378-C2
CORTE VALENCIA
FRFD 94534 452-C7
CORTE VISTA LN
SolC 95688 433-B2
CORTEZ AV
DVS 95616 356-C5
CORTEZ CT
FRFD 94533 472-G3
CORTINA RD
WSAC 95691 358-J7
CORTLAND CIR
VAL 94589 510-A5
CORVINA CT
AMCN 94503 510-A2
CORVINA WY
AMCN 94503 510-A2
COSTA CT
WSAC 95691 378-F2
COSTA VERDE ST
DVS 95618 356-G6
COTSWOLD HILL DR
FRFD 94534 472-B2
COTTA CT
VAL 94589 510-D6
COTTA WY
VAL 94589 510-D6
COTTAGE CIR
DVS 95616 376-C2
WIN 95694 373-E3
COTTAGE DR
WDLD 95695 316-A5
COTTING CT
VAC 95688 413-G7
COTTING LN
VAC 95688 413-G7
COTTONWOOD
BEN 94510 551-B6
COTTONWOOD CT
DVS 95618 376-H1
FRFD 94533 472-G4
COTTONWOOD DR
DVS 95618 376-H2
FRFD 94533 472-F4
VAL 94591 530-F5
YoCo 95618 376-H2
COTTONWOOD ST
VAC 95688 433-B5
WDLD 95695 315-G5
N COTTONWOOD ST
WDLD 95695 315-G2
COUCH ST
VAL 94589 530-A3
VAL 94590 530-A3
COUGAR CT
VAC 95688 413-D7
COULTER CT
FRFD 94533 473-A2
COULTER WY
VAC 95687 433-G6
COUNTRY LN
NaCo 94558 450-D5
SolC 95688 413-G2
VAL 94590 550-C2
COUNTRY PL
SAC 95831 378-H7
COUNTRY AIRPORT RD
VAC 95688 433-G3
COUNTRY CLUB CIR
YoCo 95618 377-A1
COUNTRY CLUB DR
SolC 94534 471-B5
VAL 94591 510-J5
YoCo 95618 376-J1
YoCo 95618 377-A1
COUNTRY FAIRE DR
DXN 95620 415-D2
COUNTRYSIDE DR
VAC 95687 453-F2
COUNTRYVIEW CT
VAL 94591 530-H5
COUNTRYWOOD CIR
VAC 95687 453-J1
COUNTRYWOOD LN
VAC 95687 453-J1
COUNTRYWOOD PL
VAC 95687 453-J1
COUNTY ROAD 20
YoCo 95695 315-A1
YoCo 95776 316-F2
COUNTY ROAD 21
YoCo 95695 315-C2
COUNTY ROAD 22
YoCo 95605 317-A4
YoCo 95695 315-A3
YoCo 95776 316-G4
YoCo 95776 317-A4
COUNTY ROAD 24
YoCo 95695 315-A5
COUNTY ROAD 24A
WDLD 95695 315-J7
WDLD 95695 316-A7
WDLD 95776 316-A7
YoCo 95695 315-J7
YoCo 95695 316-A7
YoCo 95776 316-A7
COUNTY ROAD 24C
WDLD 95776 316-A7
YoCo 95776 316-A7
COUNTY ROAD 25
WDLD 95776 336-F1
YoCo 95695 315-A7
YoCo 95776 336-F1
COUNTY ROAD 25A
YoCo 95695 335-C1
YoCo 95695 336-A2
YoCo 95776 336-B2
COUNTY ROAD 26A
YoCo 95776 336-E4
COUNTY ROAD 27
YoCo 95695 335-A4
YoCo 95695 336-A5
YoCo 95776 336-B5
COUNTY ROAD 28
YoCo 95695 335-E6
COUNTY ROAD 28H
YoCo 95776 356-F2
YoCo 95776 357-A2
COUNTY ROAD 29
YoCo 95616 355-A1
YoCo 95616 356-A2
YoCo 95695 355-A1
YoCo 95695 356-A2
YoCo 95776 356-A2

STREET Name City ZIP Pg-Grid

COUNTY ROAD 29
YoCo 95776 357-A2
COUNTY ROAD 30
YoCo 95616 355-B3
YoCo 95618 357-A4
COUNTY ROAD 30B
YoCo 95618 356-J5
YoCo 95618 357-A5
COUNTY ROAD 31
Rt#-E6
DVS 95616 355-A5
YoCo 95616 355-A5
COUNTY ROAD 32
YoCo 95694 374-E1
COUNTY ROAD 32A
DVS 95618 356-J6
YoCo 95618 356-J6
YoCo 95618 357-C6
YoCo 95694 373-B1
COUNTY ROAD 32B
DVS 95618 357-C6
YoCo 95618 357-C6
COUNTY ROAD 32D
YoCo 95618 376-J2
YoCo 95618 377-A2
COUNTY ROAD 34
YoCo 95694 373-A4
COUNTY ROAD 34A
YoCo 95618 377-E6
COUNTY ROAD 35
YoCo 95618 376-J7
YoCo 95618 377-A7
COUNTY ROAD 87
YoCo 95694 373-B1
COUNTY ROAD 87D
YoCo 95694 373-C4
COUNTY ROAD 87E
YoCo 95694 373-D4
COUNTY ROAD 88
WIN 95694 373-D2
YoCo 95694 373-D2
COUNTY ROAD 90
WIN 95694 373-H2
YoCo 95694 373-H2
COUNTY ROAD 90A
YoCo 95694 373-H3
COUNTY ROAD 91A
YoCo 95694 374-A1
COUNTY ROAD 92F
YoCo 95694 374-E1
COUNTY ROAD 95A
YoCo 95616 374-J1
YoCo 95616 375-A1
YoCo 95695 315-A5
COUNTY ROAD 96
YoCo 95616 355-B3
YoCo 95695 315-B3
YoCo 95695 335-B7
YoCo 95695 355-B3
COUNTY ROAD 96B
YoCo 95695 315-C2
COUNTY ROAD 97
YoCo 95616 355-D7
YoCo 95695 315-D3
YoCo 95695 335-D1
COUNTY ROAD 97A
YoCo 95695 315-E1
COUNTY ROAD 97D
YoCo 95616 355-E7
COUNTY ROAD 97E
YoCo 95695 315-F3
COUNTY ROAD 98
Rt#-E7
WDLD 95695 315-F7
YoCo 95616 355-F3
YoCo 95616 375-F3
YoCo 95695 315-F7
YoCo 95695 335-F3
YoCo 95695 355-F3
COUNTY ROAD 98
Rt#-16
WDLD 95695 315-F3
YoCo 95695 315-F3
COUNTY ROAD 98B
WDLD 95695 315-G1
YoCo 95695 315-G1
COUNTY ROAD 99
WDLD 95695 315-H7
YoCo 95616 355-H5
YoCo 95695 315-H7
YoCo 95695 335-H4
YoCo 95695 355-H5
COUNTY ROAD 99D
DVS 95616 356-A5
YoCo 95616 356-A5
YoCo 95695 336-A7
YoCo 95695 356-A1
COUNTY ROAD 100A
DVS 95616 356-A4
YoCo 95616 356-A4
YoCo 95776 336-B3
YoCo 95776 356-A1
COUNTY ROAD 101
WDLD 95776 316-C7
WDLD 95776 336-C1
YoCo 95776 316-C1
YoCo 95776 336-C1
COUNTY ROAD 101A
DVS 95616 356-C2
YoCo 95616 356-C2
COUNTY ROAD 102
Rt#-E8
WDLD 95776 316-E3
WDLD 95776 336-E4
YoCo 95616 356-E2
YoCo 95618 356-E2
YoCo 95776 316-E3
YoCo 95776 336-E4
YoCo 95776 356-E2
COUNTY ROAD 102B
YoCo 95776 336-F5
COUNTY ROAD 103
YoCo 95776 316-G3
YoCo 95776 336-G4
YoCo 95776 356-G1
COUNTY ROAD 104
SolC 95620 370-H7
YoCo 95618 356-J5
YoCo 95618 376-H7
YoCo 95776 336-J7
YoCo 95776 356-J1
COUNTY ROAD 104A
YoCo 95618 357-A5
COUNTY ROAD 105
YoCo 95618 357-B6
YoCo 95776 357-B6
COUNTY ROAD 106
YoCo 95618 377-C7
COUNTY ROAD 106A
YoCo 95618 377-E7
COUNTY ROAD 117S
YoCo 95605 317-F3
YoCo 95776 317-F2
COUNTY ROAD 118
YoCo 95605 317-F5
COUNTY ROAD 119
YoCo 95605 317-G6
COUNTY ROAD 124
YoCo 95605 317-H7
COUNTY ROAD 243
SolC 95620 434-F5
SolC 95687 434-F5

COUPLES CIR
FRFD 94533 452-H5
COUPLES CT
FRFD 94533 452-H5
COURAGE DR
FRFD 94534 492-B1
COURT ST
WDLD 95695 315-J3
WDLD 95695 316-A3
WDLD 95776 316-A3
W COURT ST
WDLD 95695 315-H3
COURT WY
VAC 95688 433-A5
COURTLAND CT
FRFD 94585 511-D1
COUSTEAU PL
DVS 95618 356-G7
COVE CT
FRFD 94585 491-C6
SAC 95831 378-H7
COVE WY
BEN 94510 551-A4
E COVELL BLVD
Rt#-E6
DVS 95616 356-D6
DVS 95618 356-D6
YoCo 95616 356-D6
YoCo 95618 356-D6
W COVELL BLVD
Rt#-E6
DVS 95616 355-H6
DVS 95616 356-B6
YoCo 95616 355-H6
COVELL PL
DVS 95616 356-D7
COVENTRY CT
VAC 95688 433-A5
COVENTRY LN
FRFD 94533 472-F4
COVENTRY WY
VAL 94591 530-F4
COVEY CT
YoCo 95616 355-J2
COVEY LN
SolC 95688 413-H1
COWELL BLVD
DVS 95618 356-J7
DVS 95618 357-A7
DVS 95618 376-H1
COX DR
FRFD 94533 453-D7
COYOTE RD
WSAC 95691 378-C3
COYOTE HILL LN
SolC 95694 393-C2
COYOTE HILLS CT
VAC 95688 413-E7
CRAFT DR
WDLD 95776 316-C5
CRAIG AV
WDLD 95695 315-J4
WDLD 95695 316-A4
CRAIG LN
SolC 95688 413-F6
CRAIG PL
DVS 95616 356-E7
CRAMPTON LN
SolC 95688 393-J7
CRANBROOK CT
DVS 95616 356-D6
CRANE CT
VAL 94591 530-F5
CRANE DR
SUIS 94585 473-B6
CRANSTON DR
WDLD 95776 316-E5
CRAVEA LN
SolC 94534 471-C6
CRAVEN CT
SUIS 94585 473-A7
CRAVEN DR
SUIS 94585 473-A7
CRAVEN ST
VAL 94590 529-J3
CRAVEN WY
SUIS 94585 473-A7
CRAWDAD CT
FRFD 94533 452-H7
CRAWFORD CT
FRFD 94533 473-B4
CRAWFORD WY
AMCN 94503 509-J3
AMCN 94503 510-A3
CREED RD
FRFD 94535 473-H7
SolC 94571 474-F7
SolC 94585 473-H7
SolC 94585 474-A7
CREEKHOLLOW LN
DVS 95616 355-H7
CREEKSEDGE RD
YoCo 95616 374-J1
YoCo 95616 375-A1
CREEKSIDE CIR
AMCN 94503 510-B3
DXN 95620 395-D7
CREEKSIDE CT
FRFD 94534 452-E7
FRFD 94585 511-E2
VAC 95687 453-C1
CREEKSIDE DR
VAC 95687 453-C1
CREEKSIDE WY
WIN 95694 373-G3
CREEKVIEW CT
VAC 95688 433-B7
CREEKVIEW DR
VAL 94591 530-E2
CRESCENT CT
VAL 94591 530-D4
CRESCENT DR
RVIS 94571 516-H5
VAC 95688 413-H7
VAC 95688 433-J1
CRESTA CT
DVS 95618 356-H7
CRESTED CT
SUIS 94585 473-B6
CRESTED DR
SUIS 94585 473-B7
CRESTHAVEN CT
FRFD 94585 511-E3
CRESTVIEW
CCCo 94525 550-C5
CRESTVIEW CT
FRFD 94534 472-F1
VAL 94591 550-D2
CRESTVIEW DR
NaCo 94558 451-H1
VAC 95688 433-A3
CRESTWATER LN
SAC 95831 378-G6
CRESTWOOD LN
AMCN 94503 510-A2
CRICKET TR
SolC 95688 393-C7
CRISP AV
VAL 94592 529-G6
CRISTY PL
DXN 95620 395-B7
CROCKER CIR
FRFD 94533 473-C3

CROCKER DR
VAC 95688 413-H7
CROCKETT BLVD
CCCo 94525 550-D5
CCCo 94553 550-D5
CCCo 94569 550-D5
CROFTERS CT
FRFD 94533 472-G2
CROLONA HTS
CCCo 94525 550-D4
CROMWELL LN
SolC 95688 413-D5
CRONIN CT
VAL 94589 510-D6
CRONIN DR
VAL 94589 510-D6
CROSS AV
FRFD 94533 473-C1
CROSS ST
WDLD 95695 315-H4
WDLD 95695 316-A4
WDLD 95776 316-A4
W CROSS ST
WDLD 95695 315-G4
CROSSGAR CT
VAC 95688 433-D2
CROTON CT
FRFD 94534 472-C4
CROW CANYON
VAC 95688 433-D1
CROWLEY LN
FRFD 94533 472-E6
CROWN AV
WSAC 95691 358-H7
CROWN HEIGHTS CT
VAL 94591 530-J1
CROWNPOINTE CIR
VAC 95687 433-F7
CROWNPOINTE DR
VAL 94591 530-F7
CROWNRIDGE CT
FRFD 94534 452-F7
CROWNRIDGE DR
FRFD 94534 452-F7
CROWSNEST CT
VAL 94591 550-F2
CROYDON CT
VAC 95687 453-C1
CRUCERO ST
VAL 94591 550-D1
CRUISE WY
SAC 95831 378-F6
CRYSTAL CT
VAL 94589 510-B6
WDLD 95776 316-C4
WSAC 95691 378-G1
CRYSTAL ST
SUIS 94585 492-F1
CRYSTAL DOWNS DR
RVIS 94571 516-E2
CRYSTAL GROVE LN
DVS 95616 356-A7
CRYSTAL ROSE CT
FRFD 94534 491-B2
CRYSTAL SPRINGS CT
FRFD 94533 452-H7
VAC 95688 413-E6
CRYSTAL SPRINGS DR
VAC 95688 413-E6
WDLD 95776 316-C4
CUBA RD
WSAC 95691 378-D2
CULLEN CT
FRFD 94535 473-J2
CULLINAN CT
FRFD 94534 491-E2
CUMBERLAND PL
DVS 95616 355-H7
CUMMINGS SKWY
CCCo 94525 550-B5
CCCo 94553 550-C6
CCCo 94569 550-C6
CUMMINS WY
WSAC 95605 358-J1
CUNNINGHAM DR
DXN 95620 395-B6
FRFD 94533 472-F3
CUNNINGHAM ST
VAL 94589 529-H2
VAL 94590 529-H2
CUNNINGHAM WY
WDLD 95695 315-G4
CURLEW ST
DVS 95616 356-C4
CURRANT LN
VAC 95687 433-H3
CURREY CT
BEN 94510 551-C1
CURREY RD
SolC 95620 375-C4
SolC 95620 395-D2
CURRIER PL
FRFD 94533 473-A3
CURRY AV
VAL 94590 530-C5
CURRY LN
NaCo 94559 450-B7
NaCo 94559 470-B1
CURTIS DR
FRFD 94533 472-E6
VAL 94591 530-E4
CURTOLA PKWY
SolC 94590 530-A5
VAL 94590 530-A5
CUSHING WY
YoCo 95616 376-C2
CUTTER PL
DVS 95616 355-G7
CUVAISON LN
AMCN 94503 510-B3
CYNTHIA AV
VAL 94589 510-C6
CYPRESS AV
SolC 94590 530-B6
CYPRESS CIR
FRFD 94533 472-H2
CYPRESS CT
BEN 94510 531-A7
BEN 94510 551-A1
VAC 95688 433-C6
WSAC 95691 378-J1
CYPRESS DR
RVIS 94571 516-F2
WDLD 95695 315-H6
CYPRESS LN
DVS 95616 356-E6
CYPRESS RD
WSAC 95691 358-H7
CYPRESS ST
DXN 95620 415-B1
VAC 95688 433-C6
CYPRESS WY
FRFD 94533 472-H2
CYPRESS RIDGE PL
FRFD 94534 491-D1
CZARINA LN
SolC 95688 412-G6

D

D LN
FRFD 94533 473-E2
D ST
BEN 94510 551-B6
DVS 95616 356-C7
DVS 95616 376-D1
VAL 94590 529-H2
WDLD 95776 316-B3
E D ST
BEN 94510 531-B6
DXN 95620 395-D7
SolC 95620 395-D7
W D ST
BEN 94510 551-B5
DXN 95620 395-C7
W D ST N
DXN 95620 395-C7
W D ST S
DXN 95620 395-C7
DAFFODIL CIR
VAL 94591 530-F7
DAFFODIL DR
BEN 94510 531-A7
FRFD 94533 472-G1
DAHLIA CT
FRFD 94533 472-F3
DAHLIA DR
VAL 94589 529-J1
DAHLIA ST
FRFD 94533 472-F3
DAILEY CT
DXN 95620 395-A7
DAILEY DR
DXN 95620 395-A7
DAIRY CT
SAC 95831 378-F6
DAIRY RD
YoCo 95616 376-B2
DAISY CT
VAL 94589 510-A6
DAKOTA ST
FRFD 94533 472-H5
DALE CT
BEN 94510 551-B3
VAC 95688 413-H6
VAL 94591 530-D3
DALEWOOD CT
FRFD 94585 511-E2
DALI CT
FRFD 94534 472-F2
DALI PL
DVS 95618 356-F5
DALLY RD
SolC 95687 454-G5
DALTON CT
BEN 94510 551-A2
DAMIANO RD
VAC 95687 433-F5
DAMON AV
CCCo 94525 550-E5
DAN CT
VAL 94591 530-F6
DANA DR
FRFD 94533 472-E5
DANBURY CIR
VAC 95687 433-G5
DANBURY CT
WSAC 95691 358-H5
DANBURY ST
DVS 95618 376-F1
YoCo 95618 376-F1
DANBURY WY
FRFD 94533 452-J7
DANEHURST CT
VAC 95687 453-F3
DANFIELD WY
VAC 95687 453-C1
DANIEL CT
FRFD 94533 472-J4
DANIEL DR
AMCN 94503 510-B4
DANIEL ST
FRFD 94533 472-J5
DANIEL HILLS CT
BEN 94510 551-A4
DANIELS AV
VAL 94590 529-H2
N DANIELS AV
VAL 94590 529-H2
DANIELS ST
WDLD 95695 315-G4
DANRIDGE CT
FRFD 94585 491-D7
DANROSE DR
AMCN 94503 510-A4
VAL 94589 510-A5
DANUBE AV
DVS 95616 355-H7
DANUBE CT
FRFD 94533 472-J3
DANVERS CT
VAC 95687 453-G2
DAPHNE DR
FRFD 94533 472-G1
DAPPLE DR
VAL 94591 530-E2
DARBY CT
WDLD 95776 316-E5
DARLEY DR
VAL 94591 530-E2
DARLINGTON PL
VAL 94591 530-F3
DAROFF CT
VAC 95688 433-D1
DARTMOUTH
VAL 94589 510-A5
DARTMOUTH PL
BEN 94510 551-B3
DVS 95616 356-D7
WDLD 95695 315-G6
DAVID CT
VAL 94589 509-J5
DAVID ST
FRFD 94535 473-F3
DAVID RISLING CT
DVS 95616 356-J6
DA VINCI CT
DVS 95618 376-E2
FRFD 94534 491-B3
DAVIS AV
FRFD 94535 473-J2
FRFD 94535 474-A2
DAVIS CT
FRFD 94533 473-B4
DAVIS DR
FRFD 94533 473-B4
DAVIS PL
VAC 95687 453-C1
DAVIS RD
WSAC 95691 378-E3
DAVIS ST
VAC 95687 433-D7
VAC 95687 453-D1
VAC 95688 433-D6
N DAVIS FARMS RD
DVS 95616 356-A4
DAWN DR
WDLD 95695 315-G2
DAWN WY
FRFD 94533 472-J3
DAWN ROSE CT
SUIS 94585 472-G6
DAWN ROSE WY
SUIS 94585 472-G6

DAWNVIEW PL
FRFD 94585 511-E3
DAWNVIEW WY
VAC 95687 453-G4
DAWSON DR
DXN 95620 395-B6
DAWSON PL
VAL 94591 530-C7
DAWSON CREEK DR
FRFD 94534 491-F3
DAY DR
FRFD 94533 453-E7
DAY BREAK CT
FRFD 94585 511-F3
DAYBREAK CT
VAC 95687 453-F4
DAYLIGHT DR
WDLD 95695 315-G3
DAYTON ST
FRFD 94535 473-J4
DEAD CAT AL
WDLD 95695 315-J4
WDLD 95695 316-A4
DEANER AV
WDLD 95776 316-C3
DEANS CT
VAL 94591 530-G5
DE ANZA CT
SUIS 94585 473-C6
DE ANZA DR
VAL 94589 530-B1
DEAVER CT
AMCN 94503 510-B3
DE BENEDETTI CT
BEN 94510 551-B4
DEBORAH ST
VAL 94589 510-C5
WDLD 95776 316-B5
DECATUR CT
DVS 95618 376-F1
DECK DR
DXN 95620 395-C5
DECKER WY
WSAC 95691 378-F1
DECOY LN
SUIS 94585 473-A6
DEER BRCH
VAC 95688 413-D6
DEER CREEK DR
VAC 95687 453-F2
DEERCREEK WY
SUIS 94585 472-H6
DEERFIELD DR
AMCN 94503 510-B4
VAL 94591 510-H5
DEERFIELD PL
FRFD 94533 472-J2
DEERFIELD WY
RVIS 94571 516-F2
DEERGLEN CIR
VAC 95687 453-J1
DEER RIDGE CT
FRFD 94534 491-D1
DEER RIVER WY
SAC 95831 378-F7
DEER SPRING CT
FRFD 94585 511-E3
DEER VALLEY TR
SolC 95688 413-C2
DEERWOOD CIR
WSAC 95691 358-H5
DEERWOOD ST
WSAC 95691 358-H5
DEFLORES CIR
RVIS 94571 516-H3
DEFLORES CT
RVIS 94571 516-H4
DELAWARE AV
WSAC 95691 358-J5
DELAWARE CT
WSAC 95691 358-H6
DELAWARE ST
FRFD 94533 472-E6
FRFD 94535 473-H2
VAL 94590 530-A3
DEL CENTRO
BEN 94510 551-D4
DE LEON CT
FRFD 94533 472-B7
DE LEU DR
SolC 94534 471-C6
DELGADO CT
VAL 94591 530-D3
DELGADO PL
WDLD 95776 316-D7
DEL LOMA CT
FRFD 94533 472-H3
DEL LUZ CT
FRFD 94533 472-J3
DELLWOOD CT
VAC 95688 433-D2
DEL MAR AV
VAL 94589 530-B2
DEL MAR CIR
CCCo 94525 550-C5
DEL MAR PL
DVS 95616 355-G6
DEL MAR ST
FRFD 94533 472-H3
WDLD 95695 315-H7
DEL MONTE CT
FRFD 94534 472-C2
DEL MONTE DR
FRFD 94534 472-C2
RVIS 94571 516-E1
DEL MONTE ST
WSAC 95691 358-G5
DEL NORTE CT
FRFD 94533 472-H2
DELNORTE ST
VAL 94591 530-D4
DEL ORO AV
DVS 95616 356-D5
DEL ORO CT
SUIS 94585 473-C6
DEL ORO PL
DVS 95616 356-B5
WDLD 95695 315-F6
DEL ORO ST
WDLD 95695 315-G6
DELOS CT
FRFD 94534 491-C3
DEL PASO CT
FRFD 94533 472-H3
DEL PRADO CIR
FRFD 94533 472-E3
DEL REY CT
AMCN 94503 510-A2
DVS 95616 356-B6
FRFD 94533 472-H3
DEL REY ST
WDLD 95695 315-J6
DEL RIO CIR
VAC 95687 433-E6
DEL RIO CT
VAC 95687 433-E6
DEL RIO PL
DVS 95618 356-F7
DEL SUR CT
FRFD 94533 472-J3
DEL SUR ST
VAL 94591 530-D7
VAL 94591 550-C1

DELTA CIR
VAL 94589 510-A5
DELTA DR
WDLD 95695 315-J6
DELTA WY
RVIS 94571 516-H5
DEL VALLE PL
DVS 95618 356-H6
DELWOOD ST
VAL 94591 530-F4
DEMAREST DR
VAC 95687 453-G1
DE MELLO LN
SolC 95688 414-C4
DEMPSEY WY
CCCo 94572 549-J6
DENALI DR
DVS 95616 355-J6
DENFIELD AV
BEN 94510 550-J3
DENIO ST
VAL 94590 529-J3
DENISE CT
WSAC 95691 378-E1
DENISE DR
WDLD 95776 316-B4
DENISON DR
DVS 95618 356-E6
DENNIS DR
VAC 95688 433-B3
DENTON CT
FRFD 94533 472-J2
VAL 94591 530-C7
DENVERTON RD
SolC 94585 474-B7
DEODARA CT
DVS 95618 376-H1
DEODARA PL
DXN 95620 415-D1
DEODARA ST
DVS 95618 376-H1
VAC 95688 433-A5
DE PAUL DR
VAL 94589 510-B6
DEPOT ST
VAC 95688 433-D5
WDLD 95776 316-A4
DERBY CT
FRFD 94533 472-H2
DERBY DR
DXN 95620 395-A7
DE RONDE DR
FRFD 94533 473-F2
FRFD 94535 473-F2
SolC 94533 473-F2
DERR ST
SolC 94590 550-B1
VAL 94590 530-A7
VAL 94590 550-B1
DERRY CIR
VAC 95688 433-E1
DERRY CT
VAC 95688 433-E1
DESERT FOREST CT
RVIS 94571 516-E2
DESERT FOREST DR
RVIS 94571 516-E1
DE SOTO DR
FRFD 94533 472-C7
DE SOTO PL
DVS 95616 355-J6
DEVLIN CT
VAL 94591 530-G6
DEVLIN DR
VAL 94591 530-F5
DEVON AV
WSAC 95691 358-H7
DEVON CT
FRFD 94533 472-H2
VAC 95688 433-C2
DEVONSHIRE CT
DXN 95620 395-C6
FRFD 94585 511-D1
VAL 94591 530-G5
DEVONSHIRE DR
BEN 94510 550-J2
DXN 95620 395-C6
VAC 95687 433-C7
VAC 95687 453-C1
DEVONSHIRE ST
VAL 94591 530-G5
DEWBERRY DR
VAC 95688 433-D1
DIABLO AV
DVS 95616 356-C5
DIABLO CT
FRFD 94533 473-C4
DIABLO DR
FRFD 94535 473-G2
DIABLO ST
VAL 94589 510-B6
WSAC 95691 358-H7
DIABLO CREEK WY
VAC 95688 413-F7
DIABLO VIEW LN
SolC 95694 373-J7
DIAMANTE
RVIS 94571 516-F1
N DIAMETER DR
DVS 95618 356-F7
S DIAMETER DR
DVS 95618 356-E7
DIAMOND CT
FRFD 94533 472-D7
DIAMOND WY
FRFD 94533 472-C7
DIAMOND CREEK CT
FRFD 94534 491-B2
DIAMOND HILLS DR
RVIS 94571 516-G2
DIAMOND OAKS DR
VAC 95688 413-D7
DIAMOND SPRINGS CT
VAL 94589 509-J5
DIANA DR
VAL 94589 510-A5
DIANE DR
WSAC 95691 378-E1
DIANE PL
DXN 95620 395-C7
DICKENS TER
DVS 95616 356-D7
DICKEY CT
SUIS 94585 473-A7
DICKSON HILL RD
FRFD 94533 452-G7
FRFD 94533 472-J1
FRFD 94533 473-A1
DIEGO PL
DVS 95616 356-B5
DIENINGER ST
VAL 94589 510-D6
DIGERUD DR
FRFD 94533 453-E7
SolC 94533 453-D7
DIGGER PINE RDG
SolC 95688 392-H1
DILLON DR
VAL 94589 509-J5
VAL 94589 510-A5
DILLON RD
BEN 94510 550-G1

DINGLE LN
WDLD 95695 315-J5
DINOSAUR PL
DVS 95616 355-J6
DINSDALE CIR
WDLD 95776 316-E5
DITMAR DR
DXN 95620 395-A6
DITTMER RD
FRFD 94534 491-D4
DIXIE CT
VAL 94589 509-J5
VAL 94589 510-A5
DIXON AV
FRFD 94535 473-G5
DIXON AV E
DXN 95620 395-E7
SolC 95620 395-E7
SolC 95620 415-G1
DIXON AV W
DXN 95620 394-C7
SolC 95620 394-C7
SolC 95688 394-C7
DOBBINS CT
SUIS 94585 473-B7
DOBBINS ST
VAC 95688 433-C4
DOBE LN
FRFD 94533 473-E3
FRFD 94535 473-E3
DOBROS DR
WSAC 95605 358-H2
DOCK
SUIS 94585 472-G7
DOCTOR CLAASSEN WY
WDLD 95776 316-C3
DODD CT
AMCN 94503 490-A6
DODDS CT
WDLD 95776 316-B4
DODDS DR
WDLD 95776 316-B4
DODGE AL
VAL 94590 530-A5
DODINI CT
SUIS 94585 473-B7
DOE LN
SolC 95688 412-E6
DOGWOOD
BEN 94510 551-B6
DOGWOOD CIR
FRFD 94533 472-H1
DOGWOOD CT
DXN 95620 415-B1
FRFD 94533 472-J1
VAC 95687 453-F1
DOGWOOD DR
FRFD 94533 472-H1
DOGWOOD LN
VAL 94591 530-F7
VAL 94591 550-F1
DOGWOOD PL
DVS 95618 376-H1
DOLCETTO CT
FRFD 94534 491-F6
VAC 95687 433-B7
DOLORES DR
WDLD 95695 315-J7
DOLPHIN CT
SUIS 94585 492-G1
VAL 94589 509-H5
WSAC 95691 358-J7
DOMINIC CT
BEN 94510 551-A4
DOMINICA ST
WSAC 95691 378-E3
DOMINICAN CT
FRFD 94534 491-D3
DOMINION WY
VAL 94591 510-J4
DONALD RIDGE CT
FRFD 94534 491-E1
DONALDSON CT
SUIS 94585 473-B7
DONALDSON WY
AMCN 94503 509-J1
AMCN 94503 510-A2
W DONALDSON WY
AMCN 94503 509-J2
AMCN 94503 510-A2
DONATELLO CT
FRFD 94534 491-B3
DONATO LN
DVS 95618 356-G6
DONCASTER CT
FRFD 94533 452-J6
DONCASTER DR
VAL 94591 530-E2
DONEGAL CT
VAC 95688 433-E1
DONEGAL DR
VAL 94589 510-C5
DONNA CT
VAL 94589 509-J5
DONNELLY CIR
WDLD 95776 316-B3
DONNER AV
DVS 95618 356-E5
DONNER CT
SUIS 94585 473-C6
WDLD 95695 316-A7
DONNER DR
VAC 95687 433-E6
DONNER RD
WSAC 95691 378-H2
DONNER WY
WDLD 95695 316-A6
DONNER PASS RD
VAL 94589 509-J6
VAL 94589 510-A6
DONOVAN CT
DVS 95618 376-F1
DORAL CT
FRFD 94533 452-J7
VAL 94591 530-G3
DORAL DR
FRFD 94533 452-J7
DORAN AV
WSAC 95691 358-E4
DORCHESTER PL
AMCN 94503 509-J3
DOREEN CT
VAL 94589 509-J6
DORENA PL
WSAC 95691 378-D3
DORIA PL
FRFD 94534 491-C3
DORIS CT
VAC 95688 433-B5
DORLAND CT
FRFD 94534 472-D4
DORLAND DR
FRFD 94534 472-E4
DOROTHY CT
VAL 94590 550-C2
DORRIS CT
DXN 95620 395-A7
DORSET CT
DXN 95620 395-C4
WIN 95694 373-D3
DORSET DR
DXN 95620 395-C4

STREET Name	City	ZIP	Pg-Grid
DORSET WY			
	BEN	94510	530-J6
	SAC	95822	378-J4
DOUGLAS LN			
	WDLD	95776	316-E4
DOUGLASS AV			
	DVS	95616	356-C7
DOUGLASS CT			
	VAL	94589	530-B1
DOVE CT			
	VAC	95687	453-H1
DOVE DR			
	WDLD	95695	315-G1
DOVE WY			
	FRFD	94533	473-A3
DOVE CREEK TR			
	SolC	95688	413-C3
DOVER AV			
	FRFD	94533	452-H7
	FRFD	94533	472-H2
	FRFD	94535	473-J2
	FRFD	94535	474-A2
DOVER CIR			
	BEN	94510	530-J6
	SUIS	94585	473-C5
DOVER CT			
	VAL	94591	530-G5
DOVER WY			
	VAC	95687	433-G6
DOWNIE DR			
	VAL	94589	510-A6
DOWNING CT			
	FRFD	94533	472-F4
DOWNS WY			
	VAL	94591	530-D4
DOWRELIO DR			
	CCCo	94525	550-C4
DOYLE DR			
	VAL	94591	530-E6
DOYLE LN			
	DXN	95620	395-E7
	SolC	95620	395-E7
DRAKE CT			
	BEN	94510	551-A2
	FRFD	94533	472-G3
	VAL	94591	550-F2
DRAKE DR			
	DVS	95616	356-A6
DRAKE WY			
	VAC	95687	433-G7
DRAKES BAY ST			
	WSAC	95691	378-D2
DREAM ST			
	VAC	95687	453-F2
DRESBACH WY			
	DVS	95618	357-B7
	DVS	95618	377-B1
DREVER ST			
	WSAC	95691	358-J4
DREW AV			
	DVS	95618	376-E1
DREW CIR			
	DVS	95618	376-E2
DREW ST			
	WSAC	95605	358-H2
DREXEL DR			
	DVS	95616	356-D6
DRIFTWOOD CIR			
	FRFD	94585	511-E1
DRIFTWOOD CT			
	SUIS	94585	472-G7
	VAL	94590	529-H2
	WSAC	95691	378-G1
DRIFTWOOD DR			
	SUIS	94585	472-F7
DRIFTWOOD ST			
	SAC	95831	378-F6
DROLETTE WY			
	BEN	94510	551-A3
DROUIN DR			
	RVIS	94571	516-G4
DRUIN LN			
	RVIS	94571	516-G5
DRUMMOND AV			
	DVS	95618	376-G1
	SolC	95620	376-G1
	YoCo	95618	376-G1
DRUMMOND AV S			
	DVS	95618	376-G2
	YoCo	95618	376-G2
DRUMMOND LN			
	SolC	95620	376-G4
DRY CREEK CT			
	VAC	95688	413-F6
DRY CREEK LN			
	WIN	95694	373-E4
DRY CREEK ST			
	WSAC	95691	378-G2
DRY CREEK TR			
	SolC	95688	413-C2
DRYDEN DR			
	VAL	94591	530-E6
DRYDOCK CT			
	VAC	95688	413-E7
DRYTOWN CT			
	VAL	94589	509-H5
DUAL WIDE DR			
	WDLD	95776	316-B5
DUBLIN DR			
	VAL	94589	510-C4
DUBLIN WY			
	VAC	95688	433-E2
DUBOIS WY			
	WDLD	95776	316-E7
DUCHAMP ST			
	DVS	95618	356-G4
DUET DR			
	FRFD	94534	491-E1
	WSAC	95691	378-G1
DUKE DR			
	DVS	95616	356-D7
DULUTH LN			
	SUIS	94585	473-D4
DULUTH ST			
	WSAC	95691	358-F3
DUMBARTON DR			
	VAC	95687	433-H7
DUNCAN CIR			
	WDLD	95776	316-C5
DUNCAN CT			
	FRFD	94533	473-A4
DUNCAN DR			
	VAC	95687	433-G7
	VAC	95687	453-G1
DUNCAN ST			
	DXN	95620	415-C2
DUNDEE CT			
	VAC	95687	453-C1
DUNDEE WY			
	BEN	94510	551-A2
DUNEROSE CT			
	VAC	95687	453-G4
DUNLAP CT			
	DXN	95620	395-A7
DUNN LN			
	DXN	95620	395-A7
DUPERU DR			
	CCCo	94525	550-E5
DURBIN LN			
	SolC	94534	471-B3
DUREN CIR			
	FRFD	94533	453-D7
DURHAM CT			
	BEN	94510	551-A2
	FRFD	94533	472-H3
DURROW CT			
	VAL	94591	511-A6
DUSTIN WY			
	FRFD	94533	472-J4
DUSTY TRAILS			
	SolC	95688	433-B2
DUTCH FLAT CT			
	VAL	94589	509-H4
DUTCH FLAT RD			
	VAL	94589	509-H4
DUTTON ST			
	WIN	95694	373-F3
DUVAL ST			
	FRFD	94533	452-H5
DUVALL CT			
	BEN	94510	531-A1
DUXBURRY LN			
	VAC	95687	453-E1
DUXBURY PL			
	VAL	94591	550-E1
DWIGHT WY			
	VAL	94589	530-C2
DYER CT			
	VAL	94591	530-F6
DYNASTY CT			
	FRFD	94534	491-C3
DYNASTY DR			
	FRFD	94534	491-C2
DYNASTY LN			
	SolC	94534	471-C5

E

STREET Name	City	ZIP	Pg-Grid
E LN			
	FRFD	94533	473-F2
E ST			
	DVS	95616	356-D7
	DVS	95616	376-D1
	FRFD	94535	473-J4
	FRFD	94535	474-A3
	VAL	94592	529-G4
	WDLD	95776	316-B4
	WSAC	95605	358-J3
E E ST			
	BEN	94510	551-B5
W E ST			
	BEN	94510	551-B5
	DXN	95620	395-C7
EAGLE CT			
	VAC	95687	453-H1
EAGLE LN			
	VAC	95687	453-H1
EAGLE PL			
	DVS	95616	356-A5
EAGLE ST			
	WSAC	95691	378-D4
EAGLE WY			
	FRFD	94533	472-J3
EAGLE GLEN WY			
	RVIS	94571	516-G2
EAGLERIDGE CT			
	FRFD	94534	491-D1
EAGLE RIDGE DR			
	VAL	94591	530-F1
EAGLE RIVER CT			
	VAC	95688	413-D7
EAGLE ROCK PL			
	WDLD	95776	316-B4
EAGLES NEST CT			
	VAC	95688	413-D6
EAGLE VIEW CT			
	YoCo	95618	377-B2
EAKER ST			
	FRFD	94535	473-F2
EAKLE LN			
	WDLD	95776	316-D4
EARL CT			
	BEN	94510	530-J7
EARLY AMBER CT			
	FRFD	94534	491-F3
EASSON CT			
	VAL	94591	530-F6
EAST			
	WIN	95694	373-F3
EAST CT			
	DXN	95620	395-D7
EAST ST			
	WDLD	95776	316-A5
	YoCo	95776	316-A7
	YoCo	95776	336-A2
EAST ST Rt#-113			
	WDLD	95776	316-B3
EASTER CT			
	VAL	94589	509-J5
EASTHAM CT			
	VAL	94591	550-F1
EASTMAN CT			
	FRFD	94585	491-C5
EAST QUAD			
	YoCo	95616	376-C1
EASTRIDGE DR			
	FRFD	94534	491-D1
EASTSHORE FRWY I-80			
	CCCo	-	549-J7
	CCCo	-	550-B6
EASTWOOD DR			
	VAC	95687	453-E1
EASTWOOD ST			
	VAL	94591	530-D4
EASY ST			
	SolC	94534	471-B5
EATON CT			
	BEN	94510	551-B2
	WDLD	95776	316-E5
EBBETS PASS RD			
	VAL	94589	509-J6
	VAL	94589	510-A6
EBBETTS CT			
	SUIS	94585	473-C6
EBBTIDE CT			
	SAC	95831	378-G7
EBBTIDE PL			
	VAL	94591	550-F2
EBONY CT			
	FRFD	94533	473-A1
ECHO PL			
	WDLD	95776	316-B4
ECHO HILLS CT			
	FRFD	94533	452-H6
ECHOLS AV			
	FRFD	94535	473-G2
ECHO SUMMIT RD			
	VAL	94589	509-J5
ECKLEY RD			
	CCCo	94569	550-F5
EDDY LN			
	SolC	95688	413-G1
EDENDERRY DR			
	VAC	95688	413-E7
	VAC	95688	433-E1
EDGEHILL CT			
	VAL	94589	530-B1
EDGEMONT AV			
	VAL	94590	530-C3
EDGESTONE CT			
	FRFD	94585	511-E3
EDGEWATER DR			
	RVIS	94571	516-H6
	VAC	95688	432-J4
EDGEWATER PL			
	VAL	94591	530-F1
EDGEWOOD CIR			
	SUIS	94585	472-H6
EDGEWOOD CT			
	WDLD	95695	315-G4
EDGEWOOD DR			
	RVIS	94571	516-F2
	VAC	95688	433-A6
EDINBURG CT			
	SolC	94534	470-J5
	SolC	94534	471-A5
EDINBURGH WY			
	VAC	95687	433-G7
EDISON CT			
	FRFD	94585	491-D5
	VAC	95687	453-G1
EDMOND CT			
	FRFD	94534	472-E1
EDMONDALE CT			
	VAC	95688	433-D1
EDMONTON DR			
	FRFD	94534	472-C3
EDNA CT			
	BEN	94510	551-B3
EDWARD CIR			
	VAL	94591	530-D4
EDWARDS CIR			
	WDLD	95776	316-C4
EDWARDS CT			
	SUIS	94585	473-A7
EDWARDS ST			
	CCCo	94525	550-E4
	SolC	95687	434-C6
	WIN	95694	373-E4
E EDWARDS ST			
	WIN	95694	373-F3
EDWARDS WY			
	FRFD	94533	472-F7
EDWIN AV			
	WDLD	95695	315-G6
EDWIN DR			
	VAC	95687	433-H6
EEL AV			
	DVS	95616	355-H7
EGGERT RD			
	SolC	95620	376-E7
EGRET CT			
	BEN	94510	531-H7
	BEN	94510	551-H1
EIDER LN			
	SUIS	94585	472-J7
	SUIS	94585	473-A6
EISENHOWER DR			
	WDLD	95776	316-B6
EISENHOWER ST			
	DVS	95616	355-J7
	DVS	95616	375-H1
	DXN	95620	415-B2
	FRFD	94533	472-H5
EISENHOWER WY			
	WIN	95694	373-D3
ELAINE WY			
	SolC	95688	413-A1
EL ALCAZAR CT			
	VAL	94591	530-J1
ELANE WY			
	BEN	94510	551-A4
ELBA CT			
	AMCN	94503	510-C3
EL BASSET CT			
	FRFD	94533	472-H3
EL BONITO WY			
	BEN	94510	551-C4
EL CAJON AV			
	DVS	95616	356-C5
EL CAMINO			
	YoCo	95694	373-A2
EL CAMINO AV			
	VAC	95688	433-B6
EL CAMINO CT			
	VAC	95688	433-B7
EL CAMINO DR			
	FRFD	94533	452-H7
	NaCo	94558	450-A5
	NAP	94559	450-A5
EL CAMINO WY			
	FRFD	94533	452-H7
EL CAMINO REAL			
	VAL	94590	530-B3
EL CAMPO AV			
	DVS	95618	376-G1
EL CAMPO CT			
	VAL	94589	530-A1
EL CAPITAN DR			
	WDLD	95695	315-G2
EL CAPITAN ST			
	DVS	95616	355-J6
EL CEMONTE			
	DVS	95618	356-J7
	DVS	95618	357-A7
EL CERRITO CT			
	FRFD	94533	472-H2
EL CERRITO WY			
	VAC	95688	433-D5
ELDER DR			
	NaCo	94558	470-A2
ELDER ST			
	VAC	95688	433-A4
ELDERBERRY CT			
	FRFD	94533	472-J2
ELDERBERRY LP			
	VAC	95688	413-D6
ELDERBERRY PL			
	YoCo	95618	376-G2
EL DORADO CT			
	FRFD	94533	472-H3
	WDLD	95695	315-H6
EL DORADO DR			
	DXN	95620	395-C6
	WDLD	95695	315-J6
	WDLD	95695	316-A6
W EL DORADO DR			
	WDLD	95695	315-G6
EL DORADO PL			
	DVS	95616	355-J7
EL DORADO ST			
	VAL	94590	530-A4
EL DORADO WY			
	VAC	95687	433-J3
ELDRIDGE AV			
	VAC	95688	433-C4
ELENA CT			
	VAL	94589	509-J5
ELENDIL LN			
	DVS	95616	355-H7
	DVS	95616	375-J1
ELGIN CT			
	VAL	94591	530-H6
ELIGIO LN			
	DVS	95618	356-G6
ELIZABETH RD			
	SolC	95688	414-C4
ELIZABETH ST			
	VAC	95688	433-C5
ELIZABETH WY			
	WDLD	95695	315-G4
ELK PL			
	DVS	95616	356-A5
ELKE DR			
	AMCN	94503	509-J1
ELKHORN BLVD			
	SaCo	95837	317-G3
ELKHORN CT			
	VAL	94591	530-F2
ELKHORN PL			
	SolC	94534	471-B4
ELKHORN TR			
	VAC	95687	453-F3
ELLEN CT			
	FRFD	94533	472-G3
ELLEN ROSE CT			
	SAC	95831	378-G7
ELLESMERE DR			
	DXN	95620	395-C6
ELLIE CT			
	BEN	94510	551-B4
ELLINGTON PL			
	FRFD	94533	473-B3
ELLIOT ST			
	WDLD	95695	315-J3
	WDLD	95695	316-A3
	WDLD	95776	316-A3
	WIN	95694	373-F3
W ELLIOT ST			
	WDLD	95695	315-H3
ELLIOTT DR			
	AMCN	94503	509-J2
	VAL	94589	509-J5
	VAL	94589	510-A5
ELLIOTT ST			
	WSAC	95605	358-J2
ELLIS DR			
	FRFD	94535	473-F4
ELLIS GOODFREY DR			
	FRFD	94533	453-D7
	SolC	94533	453-D7
	SolC	94533	473-D1
ELLSWORTH AV			
	FRFD	94535	473-G2
ELLSWORTH RD			
	SolC	95688	413-J7
	SolC	95688	414-A7
	VAC	95688	413-J7
	VAC	95688	414-A7
ELM			
	BEN	94510	551-B6
ELM CT			
	VAC	95688	433-C6
ELM DR			
	DXN	95620	415-E1
ELM LN			
	DVS	95616	376-B1
ELM ST			
	BEN	94510	551-D5
	FRFD	94533	472-G4
	VAC	95688	433-C6
	WDLD	95695	315-J3
	WSAC	95605	358-G2
ELM WY			
	RVIS	94571	516-H5
EL MACERO CT			
	YoCo	95618	376-J2
EL MACERO DR			
	DVS	95618	376-H1
	YoCo	95618	376-J1
E EL MACERO DR			
	YoCo	95618	377-B1
N EL MACERO DR			
	YoCo	95618	376-J1
	YoCo	95618	377-A1
S EL MACERO DR			
	YoCo	95618	376-J2
	YoCo	95618	377-A2
EL MAR CT			
	SUIS	94585	473-C6
ELMHURST CIR			
	FRFD	94533	472-G2
ELMIRA AV			
	FRFD	94535	473-G5
ELMIRA RD			
	SolC	95687	434-A6
	VAC	95687	433-F6
	VAC	95687	434-A6
EL MONTE AV			
	VAL	94591	530-C7
EL MORRO LN			
	SUIS	94585	473-C6
ELMWOOD AV			
	VAL	94591	530-E5
ELMWOOD DR			
	DVS	95616	356-B7
	DVS	95616	376-B1
ELNA DR			
	VAL	94591	530-D3
EL NIDO DR			
	NAP	94559	450-A5
EL PASEO			
	BEN	94510	551-A4
EL PASEO DR			
	WDLD	95695	315-H6
EL PASO AV			
	DVS	95618	356-E5
EL PATIO			
	VAL	94590	530-B3
EL PESCADOR CT			
	DVS	95618	376-F2
EL PINOLE WY			
	FRFD	94533	452-H7
	FRFD	94533	472-H1
EL POCO PL			
	VAL	94589	530-B1
EL PRADO LN			
	SUIS	94585	473-C6
EL RANCHO CT			
	FRFD	94533	452-H7
	WSAC	95691	358-J4
EL RANCHO WY			
	FRFD	94533	452-G7
	FRFD	94533	472-G1
EL SEGUNDO AV			
	DVS	95618	356-G7
EL SENDERO			
	VAL	94589	530-A1
ELSINORE CT			
	WSAC	95691	378-D3
ELSINORE DR			
	VAC	95687	433-E7
ELSTON CIR			
	WDLD	95776	316-D4
EL TORO WY			
	DVS	95618	376-J1
EL VERANO			
	VAL	94590	530-B2
EL VERANO CT			
	FRFD	94533	472-H3
ELWOOD ST			
	SUIS	94585	492-F1
	WDLD	95776	316-B5
EMBARCADERO DR			
	WSAC	95605	358-E2
EMBASSY DR			
	WDLD	95776	316-B5
EMERALD CIR			
	VAL	94589	530-C1
EMERALD CT			
	VAC	95687	433-J6
EMERALD ST			
	WDLD	95695	315-J2
EMERALD BAY CT			
	FRFD	94534	491-D1
EMERALD BAY DR			
	DVS	95618	376-F2
	FRFD	94534	491-D1
EMERALD HILLS CIR			
	FRFD	94533	452-H6
EMERALD RIDGE LN			
	SolC	94534	471-C5
EMERSON AV			
	CCCo	94525	550-E5
EMERSON PL			
	FRFD	94533	473-A3
EMERY ST			
	WIN	95694	373-E4
EMIGH RD			
	SolC	94571	516-A5
EMILY CT			
	VAL	94589	510-C5
EMORY DR			
	VAC	95687	433-H6
EMPEROR CT			
	SUIS	94585	473-A6
EMPEROR DR			
	SUIS	94585	473-A7
EMPIRE DR			
	VAL	94591	530-E1
EMPIRE PL			
	FRFD	94533	472-G6
EMPIRE ST			
	FRFD	94533	472-E6
EMPIRE WY			
	VAC	95687	433-J5
ENCERTI AV			
	VAL	94589	510-A7
ENCINA AV			
	DVS	95616	356-B5
ENCINA DR			
	YoCo	95694	373-A3
ENCINOSA AV			
	VAC	95688	432-J4
ENDBERG CT			
	VAC	95688	433-D1
ENDBERG DR			
	VAC	95688	433-D2
ENGELL CT			
	FRFD	94533	452-J6
	SUIS	94585	473-B7
ENGELL WY			
	FRFD	94533	452-J6
ENGLISH HILLS RD			
	SolC	95688	393-A7
	SolC	95688	413-B1
ENGLISH OAKS DR			
	SolC	95688	413-B3
ENSENADA DR			
	DVS	95618	356-H7
	DVS	95618	376-H1
ENSIGN AV			
	VAL	94590	530-C3
ENTERPRISE BLVD			
	WSAC	95691	358-C5
ENTERPRISE CT			
	FRFD	94533	472-D7
ENTERPRISE DR			
	FRFD	94533	472-D7
ENTERPRISE ST			
	VAL	94589	509-J7
	VAL	94589	510-A7
	VAL	94589	529-J1
ENTRADA CIR			
	AMCN	94503	510-A4
ENTRADA DR			
	DVS	95618	356-H6
ENVIRONMENTAL SERVICES LN			
	YoCo	95616	375-J3
EPPERSON CT			
	WDLD	95776	316-D5
EPPINGER ST			
	CCCo	94525	550-D4
EQUADOR PL			
	DVS	95616	356-B5
EQUESTRIAN CT			
	FRFD	94534	491-B3
EQUESTRIAN LN			
	YoCo	95616	376-A3
EQUINE LN			
	SolC	95620	376-B5
EQUUS LN			
	SolC	95688	413-F4
ERIC DR			
	WSAC	95691	358-D4
ERICKA CT			
	VAL	94591	530-G4
ERICKSON WY			
	WDLD	95776	336-E1
ERICSSON CT			
	FRFD	94533	472-B7
ERIN DR			
	SUIS	94585	472-G7
	SUIS	94585	492-G1
	VAL	94589	510-C5
ERMA LN			
	YoCo	95618	376-E2
ERSKINE ST			
	CCCo	94569	550-H6
ESA DR			
	VAL	94591	530-D7
ESCOLAR CT			
	DVS	95618	356-H6
ESPANA CT			
	DVS	95616	356-B6
ESPERSON CT			
	RVIS	94571	516-G5
ESQUIVEL RD			
	SolC	95688	413-F2
ESSEX AV			
	WSAC	95691	358-H7
ESSEX CT			
	BEN	94510	551-B2
	VAL	94591	530-H6
ESSEX DR			
	FRFD	94533	472-E3
ESSEX PL			
	VAC	95687	433-G6
ESSEX WY			
	BEN	94510	551-B2
ESTABAN CT			
	DVS	95618	356-H6
ESTATE DR			
	SolC	95688	393-B6
ESTATES DR			
	DXN	95620	395-B7
	FRFD	94533	452-H5
ESTERBROOK AV			
	FRFD	94535	473-G2
ESTERO BAY CT			
	DVS	95616	355-G6
ESTES CT			
	FRFD	94535	473-J1
	SolC	94533	473-J1
	SolC	94535	473-J1
ESTRELLA PL			
	DVS	95616	356-B5
ESTRUSCAN CT			
	FRFD	94534	491-C3
ETON CT			
	FRFD	94533	472-F3
ETRUSCAN DR			
	FRFD	94534	491-C2
EUBANKS CT			
	VAC	95688	413-F7
EUBANKS DR			
	VAC	95688	413-G7
EUCALYPTUS CT			
	FRFD	94533	473-A1
EUCALYPTUS DR			
	AMCN	94503	509-H1
	AMCN	94503	510-A1
	NaCo	94589	509-H1
	VAL	94591	530-F4
EUCALYPTUS LN			
	SolC	95694	393-C2
EUCALYPTUS ST			
	AMCN	94503	510-A1
	DVS	95618	376-H1
EUCLID ST			
	WSAC	95691	358-H5
EUNICE CT			
	WDLD	95695	315-H5
EUNICE DR			
	WDLD	95695	315-H5
EUREKA AV			
	DVS	95616	356-C7
EVANS AV			
	SolC	94590	530-B6
EVANS CT			
	DVS	95618	376-F1
EVANS RD			
	DXN	95620	395-A7
EVELYN CIR			
	VAL	94589	510-C5
EVENING BAY PL			
	DVS	95616	355-G7
EVENING CLARENDON DR			
	FRFD	94585	511-E3
EVENING SHADOW CT			
	FRFD	94585	511-E3
	VAC	95687	453-G3
EVENSTAR LN			
	DVS	95616	355-J7
	DVS	95616	375-H1
EVERETT AL			
	VAL	94590	530-A5
EVERETT PL			
	VAL	94590	529-J5
	VAL	94590	530-A5
EVERGLADE WY			
	DXN	95620	415-B1
EVERGLADES PL			
	DVS	95616	355-J6
EVERGREEN AV			
	WSAC	95691	358-F4
EVERGREEN CIR			
	WSAC	95691	358-F4
EVERGREEN CT			
	DVS	95618	376-E2
	FRFD	94533	472-J1
	VAL	94591	530-E4
	WDLD	95695	315-G5
EVERGREEN DR			
	FRFD	94533	472-J1
	VAC	95688	433-B3
EVERGREEN WY			
	VAL	94591	530-E4
	WDLD	95695	315-G5
EXECUTIVE CT			
	NaCo	94558	490-A1
EXECUTIVE CT N			
	FRFD	94534	491-F2
EXECUTIVE CT S			
	FRFD	94534	491-F2
EXECUTIVE WY			
	NaCo	94558	490-A2
EXETER CT			
	DVS	95618	376-G2
	FRFD	94533	452-J7
EXPOSITION DR			
	VAL	94589	510-D6
EXTENSION CENTER DR			
	YoCo	95616	376-A2

F

STREET Name	City	ZIP	Pg-Grid
F LN			
	FRFD	94533	473-E2
F ST			
	BEN	94510	551-B5
	DVS	95616	356-C4
	DVS	95616	376-D1
	WSAC	95605	358-J3
E F ST			
	BEN	94510	551-B5
	DXN	95620	395-D7
W F ST			
	BEN	94510	551-B5
	DXN	95620	395-B7
FABIOLA DR			
	NaCo	94558	450-C6
FACULTY DR			
	VAL	94590	550-C2
FAIRBANKS CT			
	DXN	95620	395-B7
FAIRBANKS DR			
	RVIS	94571	516-F1
FAIRBROOK CT			
	SUIS	94585	472-H6
FAIRCHILD CT			
	WDLD	95695	315-G5
FAIRCHILD DR			
	FRFD	94535	473-G2
FAIRFAX CT			
	FRFD	94585	491-D7
	VAL	94591	530-D4
FAIRFIELD AV			
	FRFD	94533	472-F5
	FRFD	94535	473-G3
FAIRGATE DR			
	VAC	95687	433-J5
FAIRGROUNDS DR			
	VAL	94589	510-C6
	VAL	94589	530-C2
FAIRHAVEN WY			
	VAL	94591	550-E1
FAIRMONT AV			
	VAL	94590	530-C3
FAIRMONT CT			
	FRFD	94585	491-D7
FAIROAKS CT			
	FRFD	94585	511-E2
FAIROAKS DR			
	VAC	95688	433-B7
FAIRVIEW AV			
	VAL	94589	530-C2
	VAL	94590	530-C2
FAIRVIEW DR			
	VAC	95687	453-G1
	WDLD	95695	315-G5
FAIRVIEW PL			
	FRFD	94534	452-E7
FAIRWAY DR			
	WSAC	95605	358-J2
	YoCo	95616	355-J2
FAIRWAY PL			
	SolC	94534	471-B4
FAIRWAY ESTATES			
	YoCo	95618	377-A2
FAIRWAY ESTATES PL			
	YoCo	95618	377-A1
FAIRWOOD CT			
	FRFD	94534	452-E7
FALAISE DR			
	VAC	95687	453-J1
FALATI LN			
	FRFD	94533	453-D7
FALCON AV			
	DVS	95616	356-B5
FALCON CT			
	FRFD	94533	472-J4
FALCON DR			
	FRFD	94533	472-J4
	VAL	94589	510-A6
	WDLD	95695	315-G1
FALLBROOK AV			
	VAC	95687	433-J6
FALLBROOK ST			
	WSAC	95691	358-H5
FALL CREEK CT			
	FRFD	94534	491-F4
FALLEN LEAF CIR			
	VAC	95687	433-J4
FALLEN LEAF CT			
	FRFD	94534	491-D7
	VAC	95687	433-J5
FALLEN LEAF DR			
	VAC	95687	433-J4
FALLEN LEAF PL			
	VAC	95687	433-J5
FALL RIVER TR			
	VAC	95687	453-F3
FALLS CT			
	FRFD	94534	491-E2
FALLS WY			
	FRFD	94534	491-E2
FALLSGROVE WY			
	VAC	95687	453-G4
FANNING CT			
	DXN	95620	415-C2
FARADAY AV			
	DVS	95618	356-H7
FARALLON DR			
	VAL	94590	530-B2
FARALLON RD			
	WSAC	95691	378-E2
FARALLON ST			
	DVS	95616	355-G6
FARENTINO PL			
	AMCN	94503	510-B2
FARIA CT			
	WDLD	95695	315-G5
FARMERS CENTRAL RD			
	WDLD	95776	316 D7
FARMINGTON DR			
	VAC	95687	453-F2
FARNHAM AV			
	WDLD	95776	316-D4
FARO AV			
	DVS	95616	356-C5
FARRAGUT AV			
	VAL	94590	529-J3
FARRAGUT CIR			
	DVS	95618	376-F1
FARRELL LN			
	SolC	95688	433-B2
FARRELL PL			
	WDLD	95695	315-G4
FARRELL RD			
	SolC	95688	433-B2
	VAC	95688	433-B2
FARRELL ST			
	VAL	94590	530-B5
	WDLD	95695	315-G4
FARWELL ST			
	FRFD	94533	472-E7
FATHOM PL			
	WSAC	95691	358-J6
FAUSTINO WY			
	SAC	95831	378-G6
FAWN CT			
	VAC	95687	453-F3
FAWN LN			
	SolC	95688	412-F5
FAWN GLEN CIR			
	FRFD	94585	511-E3
FAWNGLEN CT			
	VAC	95687	453-G4
FEATHER PL			
	DVS	95616	355-H7
FEATHERGRASS CT			
	FRFD	94585	511-E3
FEATHER RIVER CIR			
	VAC	95688	413-E7
FEATHER RIVER CT			
	VAC	95688	413-F7
FEATHER RIVER WY			
	VAC	95688	413-F7
FELDSPAR CT			
	VAL	94591	510-J3
FELINE RD			
	SolC	95620	376-B4
FELINO CT			
	VAL	94591	530-J1
FENNIE CT			
	SUIS	94585	493-B1
FENNIE WY			
	SUIS	94585	493-B1
FENNWOOD CT			
	SAC	95831	378-J5
FERGUSON CT			
	DXN	95620	395-C4
FERMI PL			
	DVS	95618	356-J7
FERMI RD			
	FRFD	94585	491-D5
FERN PL			
	VAL	94590	530-A4
FERN WY			
	VAC	95688	432-J5
FERNBANK CT			
	FRFD	94585	511-E3
FERNBROOK CT			
	VAC	95687	453-G3
FERNDALE CIR			
	WSAC	95691	358-H5
FERNHEATHER CT			
	FRFD	94585	511-E3
FERNWOOD CT			
	FRFD	94585	491-D6
FERNWOOD DR			
	VAL	94591	530-E5
FERNWOOD ST			
	WSAC	95691	358-H5
FERNWOOD WY			
	DXN	95620	415-B1
FERRERO DR			
	DXN	95620	395-A6
FICUS WY			
	WIN	95694	373-E3
FIDDLE TOWN CT			
	VAL	94589	509-H5
FIELDCREST AV			
	FRFD	94534	452-F7
	FRFD	94534	472-F1
FIELDCREST CT			
	FRFD	94534	452-F7
FIELDER CT			
	DXN	95620	395-B6
FIELDSTONE CT			
	FRFD	94534	452-G7
	VAC	95687	433-J4
	VAL	94589	510-B4
FIELDSTONE WY			
	VAL	94589	510-B4
FIESTA AV			
	DVS	95616	356-B5
FIESTA CT			
	FRFD	94533	452-H7
FIESTA WY			
	VAC	95688	413-J6
FIG LN			
	DVS	95618	356-F6

© 2007 Rand McNally & Company

SOLANO CO.

STREET Name City ZIP Pg-Grid

FIG PL DVS 95618 356-F6
FILBERT CT SUIS 94585 472-H7
FILLMORE CT DVS 95616 355-J7; DVS 95616 375-H1
FILLMORE PL WSAC 95691 358-J7
FILLMORE ST DVS 95616 355-J7; FRFD 94533 472-G4
FINCH ST DVS 95616 356-D4
FINCH WY FRFD 94533 472-J4
FINE SAND CT WSAC 95605 358-J2
FIORA PL FRFD 94534 491-C3
FIR RD BEN 94510 551-D5
FIR ST VAC 95688 433-B4
FIREDELL AV VAL 94592 529-F3
FIRESTONE DR FRFD 94534 452-C7
FIRNWOOD WY FRFD 94585 511-E2
FISHER LN WDLD 95776 316-E5
FISHER ST RVIS 94571 516-H3
FISK CT VAL 94589 510-A6
FISKE AV WDLD 95695 315-J2
FITZGERALD DR DXN 95620 395-D5; FRFD 94535 473-G2
FITZPATRICK CT DXN 95620 395-C4
FLAG CT FRFD 94533 452-H5
FLAGSHIP DR VAL 94592 529-G5
FLAGSTAFF CT VAC 95687 433-C7
FLAGSTONE CIR SUIS 94585 472-H6
FLAGSTONE CT VAC 95687 433-J4
FLAMENCO PL DVS 95616 356-B5
FLAMINGO CT AMCN 94503 509-J1
FLAMINGO DR FRFD 94533 472-H5
FLATLEY CIR FRFD 94533 453-E7
FLATLEY CT FRFD 94533 453-E7
FLEET CT VAL 94591 530-G6
FLEET ST VAL 94591 530-G6
FLEMING AV VAL 94590 530-C3; VAL 94591 530-D3
FLEMING AV E VAL 94591 530-D3
FLEMING HILL RD VAL 94589 510-B7
FLICKER AV DVS 95616 356-B4
FLICKER CT FRFD 94533 472-J3
FLICKER LN FRFD 94533 472-J3
FLINT CT VAC 95687 453-F2; VAL 94589 510-C6
FLINT WY FRFD 94533 472-E3; VAC 95687 453-F2
FLINTWOOD WY SAC 95831 378-J7
FLORA ST CCCo 94525 550-D5
FLORA SPRING CT FRFD 94534 491-B2
FLORENCE CT VAL 94589 530-B1
FLORENCE DR VAC 95688 433-A3
FLORES CT FRFD 94533 472-G3
FLORES WY RVIS 94571 516-G5; WDLD 95776 316-D7
FLORIDA ST FRFD 94535 473-H2; VAL 94590 529-J4; VAL 94590 530-A4; VAL 94591 530-D4
FLORIN RD SAC 95831 378-G6
FLORINDA LN DVS 95618 356-G6
FLOSDEN RD AMCN 94503 510-C4
FLOSSIE AV WSAC 95691 358-G3
FLOYD CT SUIS 94585 473-A7
FLYING CLOUD CT VAL 94591 550-F2
FLYING DUTCHMAN CT VAL 94591 550-G3
FOLEY CT VAC 95688 433-E1
FOLLAND DR AMCN 94503 509-J4; AMCN 94503 510-A4
FOLSOM CT WSAC 95691 378-D3
FOLSOM DR VAC 95687 433-F7
FOLSOM DOWNS CIR DXN 95620 415-C2
FOLSOM FAIR CIR DXN 95620 415-C2
FOOTHILL DR SolC 95688 432-J5; VAC 95688 432-J5; VAC 95688 433-A5; VAL 94591 530-E1
FOOTHILL PL FRFD 94534 472-D4
FORBES DR SolC 95688 433-B1
FORBES ST FRFD 94535 473-F2
FORD AL VAL 94590 529-J5; VAL 94590 530-A5
FORD WY DXN 95620 395-D6
FORDHAM CIR VAL 94589 510-B5
FORDHAM DR DVS 95616 356-A6; WDLD 95695 315-G5
FORDHAM PL WDLD 95695 315-G5
FOREST LN VAC 95687 453-E1
FOREST HIGHLANDS DR RVIS 94571 516-E1
FOREST HILL DR VAL 94589 509-H5
FOREST KNOLLS DR FRFD 94585 511-E4
FOREST RIDGE CIR VAC 95687 433-J7
FOREST RIDGE DR VAL 94591 530-F4
FORMBY LN FRFD 94534 472-B1
FORSYTHIA CT VAL 94589 510-A5
FORTADO CIR SAC 95831 378-J6
FORT DOUGLAS ST FRFD 94535 473-H3
FORTNA AV WDLD 95776 316-A2
FORT ORD CT SUIS 94585 473-C5
FORTUNA CT DVS 95616 356-B5; SUIS 94585 473-D6
FORTUNA DR SUIS 94585 473-C6
FORTUNE ST VAL 94590 529-H2
FOSTER CT WSAC 95691 378-D3
FOSTER LN DXN 95620 395-A7
FOSTER ST VAL 94591 530-D4
FOULKSTONE WY VAL 94591 550-E2
FOUNTAIN DR WSAC 95605 358-J1
FOUNTAIN WY DXN 95620 395-C6
FOUNTAIN BLUE CT VAL 94591 530-J1
FOUNTAIN GROVE DR VAC 95688 413-F6
FOURNESS DR WSAC 95605 358-J1
FOWLER LN FRFD 94533 453-F7
FOWLER RD WSAC 95691 378-C4
FOX RD SolC 95620 414-F7; SolC 95620 434-F2; SolC 95687 414-F7; SolC 95687 434-F2
FOXBORO PKWY VAC 95687 453-F3
FOXFIRE CT FRFD 94534 472-B2
FOX GLEN DR FRFD 94534 472-F1
FOXGLOVE CIR WIN 95694 373-E3
FOX HOLLOW CIR VAC 95687 433-J7; VAC 95687 453-J1
FOX HOLLOW DR VAC 95687 433-J7; VAC 95687 453-J1
FOX HOUND CT VAC 95687 453-E3
FOX HOUND RD VAC 95687 453-E3
FOX OAK CT VAC 95688 433-D1
FOX POINTE RD VAC 95687 453-E3
FOX RIDGE CT FRFD 94534 471-D7; FRFD 94534 491-D1
FOXWOOD LN RVIS 94571 516-E1
FRANCIS ST CCCo 94525 550-D5
FRANCISCA CT BEN 94510 551-C4
FRANCISCAN DR VAL 94589 530-C1
FRANCISCO CT SUIS 94585 472-G7
FRANCISCO DR SUIS 94585 472-G7
FRANCISCO PL DVS 95616 356-B5
FRANCO LN SolC 95688 413-E4
FRANKLIN CT VAC 95687 453-H1
FRANKLIN ST VAL 94591 530-D4
FRANKLIN WY WSAC 95691 358-G3
FRASER ISLAND RD WSAC 95691 378-C2
FRATES WY SAC 95831 378-G6
FREDERICKS DR YoCo 95694 373-J2
FREDRICKS CT WDLD 95776 316-E6
FREDRICKS ST WDLD 95776 316-E5
FREEBOARD DR WSAC 95691 358-F4
FREEDOM CT FRFD 94533 452-G6; VAC 95687 453-G2
FREEDOM DR SUIS 94585 472-G7
FREEDOM LN SolC 95694 393-J2
FREEMAN LN SolC 95688 413-F5
FREEMAN ST WDLD 95695 315-J3
FREEPORT CT FRFD 94534 472-C5
FRWY I-5 SAC - 378-J4; WDLD - 316-A1; YoCo - 315-J1; YoCo - 316-A1; YoCo - 316-G4; YoCo - 317-A4; YoCo - 317-F4
FRWY I-80 CCCo - 550-D3; DVS - 356-J7; DVS - 376-F1; DXN - 394-J7; DXN - 395-F1; DXN - 414-J1; DXN - 415-A1; FRFD - 452-G6; FRFD - 471-J7; FRFD - 472-G1; FRFD - 491-C4; NaCo - 510-G3; SAC - 358-G1; SaCo - 358-G1; SolC - 375-J4; SolC - 376-D2; SolC - 394-J7; SolC - 395-G1; SolC - 414-B6; SolC - 433-A7; SolC - 452-G4; SolC - 453-A1; SolC - 471-J7; SolC - 472-A7; SolC - 490-J7; SolC - 491-C4; SolC - 510-J1; SolC - 530-C6; SolC - 550-D3; VAC - 414-D4; VAC - 414-E4; VAC - 433-J1; VAC - 434-A1; VAC - 452-H3; VAC - 453-A1; VAL - 510-E3; VAL - 530-C2; VAL - 550-C1; WSAC - 358-F3; YoCo - 356-J7; YoCo - 357-E6; YoCo - 376-D2
FRWY I-505 SolC - 373-H3; SolC - 393-H1; SolC - 413-J1; VAC - 413-H4; VAC - 433-G3; WIN - 373-H3; YoCo - 373-H1
FRWY I-680 BEN - 551-E5; FRFD - 491-E3; MRTZ - 551-F7; SolC - 551-E6
FRWY I-780 BEN - 530-G7; BEN - 550-G1; BEN - 551-A3; SolC - 530-C6; VAL - 530-C6
FRWY Rt#-113 SolC - 376-A3; YoCo - 376-B3
FREEWAY DR WDLD 95776 316-F4
FREITAS CT FRFD 94533 453-E7
FREITAS PL FRFD 94533 453-E7
FREITAS WY FRFD 94533 453-E6
FREMONT BLVD WSAC 95605 358-J2
FREMONT CT DVS 95618 356-E5; FRFD 94533 473-B3
FREMONT DR VAC 95687 433-H5
FREMONT ST VAL 94589 530-A1; WDLD 95695 316-A5
FRENCH AV WSAC 95691 378-F3
FRESE ST DXN 95620 415-B2
FRESHWATER CT VAC 95687 453-F3
FRESNO PL WDLD 95695 315-F3
FRESNO ST VAL 94590 530-B4
FREY DR WSAC 95691 358-D4
FREY PL VAL 94590 529-J3
FRICKE LN YoCo 95695 315-C6
FRIEDA CT VAL 94590 550-C1
FRIEDA DR SUIS 94585 473-A5
FRISBIE CIR VAC 95688 413-J6
FRISBIE ST VAL 94590 529-J3
FROG LEAPS CT FRFD 94534 491-B2
FRONT ST RVIS 94571 516-H6; WSAC 95691 358-G4
FRONTAGE AV FRFD 94585 491-B6; NaCo 94591 510-H2; SolC 94585 490-J7; SolC 94585 491-B6; SolC 94585 510-H2; VAL 94585 510-H2
FRONTERA DR DVS 95618 356-H6
FROST DR WDLD 95695 315-J2
FROST PL FRFD 94533 472-J4
FRUITVALE AV SolC 95688 433-A4; VAC 95688 433-A4
FRUITVALE RD SolC 95688 433-B4; VAC 95688 433-B4
FRY CT BEN 94510 551-A3
FRY RD SolC 95687 453-J1; SolC 95687 454-A1; VAC 95687 453-J1; VAC 95687 454-A1
FUCHSIA CT VAL 94591 530-F7
FUCHSIA DR BEN 94510 531-A7
FUCHSIA ST FRFD 94533 472-F2
FULL CIR DVS 95618 356-E7
FULLER LN DXN 95620 395-A7
FULLERTON CT FRFD 94533 452-J7
FULLERTON DR FRFD 94533 452-J7
FULMAR DR SUIS 94585 473-C6
FULMOR DR DXN 95620 395-C5
FULTON AV SolC 94591 530-D7; SolC 94591 550-E1; VAL 94591 530-D7; VAL 94591 550-E1
FULTON CT DXN 95620 395-B7
FULTON DR FRFD 94585 491-D5

G

G LN FRFD 94533 473-F2
G ST BEN 94510 551-B5; DVS 95616 356-D7; DVS 95616 376-D1; VAL 94592 529-F4
E G ST BEN 94510 551-B5
W G ST BEN 94510 551-B5
GABIANO CT VAC 95687 433-B7
GABLE AV VAC 95688 433-D4
GABLE DR WDLD 95776 316-D4
GADDINI RD SolC 95694 373-H4
GADWALL CT AMCN 94503 509-J1; WSAC 95691 378-F1
GADWALL DR SUIS 94585 472-J6; SUIS 94585 473-A6
GADWALL ST AMCN 94503 509-H1
GAINESBOROUGH CT FRFD 94534 491-D3
GALATINA CT VAC 95687 433-B7
GALENA CT VAC 95687 453-G2
GALIANO ISLAND RD WSAC 95691 378-C2
GALILEO CT DVS 95618 376-E1
GALLAGHER DR BEN 94510 551-B1
GALLEON DR DXN 95620 395-C5
GALLERY CT FRFD 94534 491-C3
GALLERY WY SAC 95831 378-J7
GALLEY CT SAC 95831 378-G6
GALVESTON ST WSAC 95691 358-F3
GALVIN WY WDLD 95776 316-D7
GALWAY CT VAC 95688 433-E2
GAMMON CT FRFD 94533 473-F2
GANGES AV DVS 95616 355-H7
GANGES PL DVS 95616 355-H7
GANITE ST VAL 94589 510-B5
GANNET CT FRFD 94533 473-A3
GANTON CT FRFD 94534 472-C1
GARABALDI DR VAL 94589 530-A1
GARCIA CT SAC 95831 378-E7
GARCIA DR WDLD 95776 316-D5
GARDEN CIR VAC 95688 433-E5
GARDEN CT VAL 94591 530-D6; YoCo 95618 377-A1
GARDEN HWY SAC 95833 358-G1; SaCo 95833 358-G1; SaCo 95837 317-G2
GARDENIA AV WSAC 95691 358-H5
GARDENIA CIR FRFD 94533 472-F2
GARDENIA CT BEN 94510 531-A7
GARDEN MEADOW AV FRFD 94534 452-G7
GARDINER WY RVIS 94571 516-H5
GARET ST FRFD 94535 473-H4
GARFIELD CT WDLD 95776 316-C6
GARFIELD DR WDLD 95776 316-B6
GARFIELD PL WDLD 95776 316-B6
GARFIELD ST FRFD 94533 472-F5
GARFIELD TER DVS 95616 355-J7
GARFORD AL VAL 94590 529-J5; VAL 94590 530-A5
GARNET CIR VAL 94591 530-F1
GARNET CT VAC 95688 433-D3; VAL 94591 530-F1
GARNET DR VAL 94591 530-F1
GARNET ST WSAC 95691 358-F3
GARNET WY WDLD 95695 316-A2
GARNETT LN SolC 95620 374-E7; SolC 95620 394-E1
GARRETSON AV CCCo 94572 549-H7
GARRETT PL WDLD 95776 316-E7
GARRETT WY WDLD 95776 316-E7
GARRIDO CT VAL 94591 530-G6
GARRISON ST DVS 95616 355-H6
GARROD DR YoCo 95616 375-J3; YoCo 95616 376-A3
GARTHE CT VAL 94591 530-G5
GARTLEY AV CCCo 94525 550-E5
GARWOOD CT VAC 95687 453-F1
GARY CIR VAL 94591 530-C7
GARY CT WSAC 95691 358-F7
GARY WY WDLD 95695 315-G5
GATEHOUSE CT VAC 95687 433-J5
GATEHOUSE DR VAC 95687 433-H5
GATES CANYON RD NaCo 94558 432-B1; SolC 95688 432-B1
GATEWAY BLVD FRFD 94533 472-E4
GATEWAY CT DVS 95618 376-G2; DXN 95620 394-J7; FRFD 94533 472-D4; VAL 94589 510-D6
GATEWAY DR DXN 95620 394-J7; VAL 94589 510-C6; WSAC 95691 358-H7
GATEWAY RD E NaCo 94589 490-A2
GATEWAY PLAZA DR BEN 94510 531-G7; BEN 94510 551-G1
GAUGUIN PL DVS 95618 356-E5
GAVI CT VAC 95687 433-B7
GAVIOTA PL DVS 95618 356-G6
GAY WY YoCo 95618 376-E2
GAZEBO CT SUIS 94585 473-B7
GAZELLE PL DVS 95616 356-A5
GEARY ST WSAC 95691 358-H7
GENARO PL DVS 95618 356-G6
GENEVA PL DVS 95618 356-E6
GENOA CT VAC 95688 433-E3; VAL 94589 510-D5
GENTILE LN SolC 95688 414-D4
GENTLE CREEK CT FRFD 94585 511-E3; VAC 95687 453-G3
GENTLE CREEK DR FRFD 94585 511-E3
GENTRY CIR VAC 95687 453-F1
GENTRY CT VAC 95687 453-F1
GEOFFREY ST WDLD 95776 316-B4
GEORGE CIR VAL 94591 530-D6
GEORGE CT BEN 94510 551-A3
GEORGE LN DXN 95620 395-A7; DXN 95620 415-A1; SolC 95620 415-A1
GEORGE MILLER JR MEMORIAL BRDG BEN - 551-E6; MRTZ - 551-F7; SolC - 551-E6
GEORGETOWN CT VAL 94589 509-H5
GEORGETOWN DR VAC 95687 433-D7; VAC 95687 453-E1
GEORGETOWN PL DVS 95616 356-B6; DXN 95620 395-A7
GEORGIA CT DXN 95620 395-A6
GEORGIA MALL VAL 94590 529-J5
GEORGIA PL DVS 95616 356-E6
GEORGIA ST FRFD 94535 473-H3; VAL 94590 529-J5; VAL 94590 530-A5; VAL 94591 530-D5
GEORGIA WY FRFD 94533 472-F5
GERALD CT BEN 94510 551-A1
GERANIUM CT FRFD 94533 472-G2
GERMAN ST FRFD 94534 452-A7
GERSHWIN CIR FRFD 94533 473-B4
GETTY CT BEN 94510 551-E1
GEYSER CT VAC 95687 433-J4; VAL 94591 530-F1
GIBSON RD WDLD 95695 315-J6; WDLD 95695 316-A6; WDLD 95776 316-B6
E GIBSON RD WDLD 95776 316-D6; YoCo 95776 316-B6
W GIBSON RD WDLD 95695 315-G6
GIBSON CANYON RD SolC 95688 413-B6; SolC 95688 433-B2; VAC 95688 433-B2
GIGEY DR BEN 94510 551-A4
GILL CT BEN 94510 551-B2; DXN 95620 395-C5
GILL DR DXN 95620 395-C5
GILL WY BEN 94510 551-B2
GILLCREST AV SolC 94591 530-D7; SolC 94591 550-D1; VAL 94591 550-D1
GILLESPIE DR FRFD 94534 472-C3
GILLETTE DR WDLD 95776 316-C5
GILLEY WY VAC 95687 433-J2
GINA CT VAL 94589 510-D5
GINGERWOOD CT VAC 95687 453-G4
GINGERWOOD PL FRFD 94585 511-F3
GISELA DR AMCN 94503 509-J1
GISH RD SolC 95688 413-C1
GLACER CT VAL 94591 530-F1
GLACIER CIR VAC 95687 433-H3
GLACIER DR DVS 95616 355-J6
GLACIER PL DVS 95616 355-H6; WDLD 95695 315-G2
GLACIER ST WDLD 95695 315-G2
GLACIER WY FRFD 94534 491-D2
GLADYS AV WSAC 95691 378-E3
GLASGOW WY VAC 95687 433-G7
GLASTONBURY WY FRFD 94533 453-A7
GLEASON AV VAL 94590 530-C5
GLEN ST WSAC 95605 358-J2
GLEN ABBEY DR FRFD 94534 452-B7
GLENCANNON DR SolC 94534 470-J4; SolC 94534 471-A4
GLEN COVE PKWY VAL 94591 550-E1
GLEN COVE RD SolC 94591 530-E7; SolC 94591 550-E1; VAL 94591 530-E7; VAL 94591 550-E1
GLEN COVE MARINA RD VAL 94591 550-E2
GLENCREST DR VAC 95687 453-E1
GLEN EAGLE WY VAC 95688 433-D1
GLENEAGLES CT FRFD 94534 452-D7; FRFD 94534 472-D1
GLEN ELLEN DR FRFD 94534 452-G7
GLENMORE DR FRFD 94533 472-G5
GLENN CT FRFD 94535 473-H2; WSAC 95605 358-H2
GLENN PL DVS 95616 355-J7
GLENN ST VAL 94590 530-B4
GLENN LAKES DR RVIS 94571 516-E2
GLENSIDE DR DXN 95620 395-C7
GLENVIEW CIR VAL 94591 530-E2
GLENWOOD CT VAC 95688 433-A5
GLENWOOD DR FRFD 94534 452-F7; FRFD 94534 472-F1
GLENWOOD PL WDLD 95695 315-G6
GLENWOOD ST VAL 94591 530-D4; WSAC 95691 378-J1
GLIDE AV WSAC 95691 358-G3
GLIDE CT WSAC 95691 358-G3
GLIDE DR DVS 95618 356-J7; DVS 95618 357-A7
GLIDE TER DVS 95618 357-A7
GLORIA CT VAL 94590 550-C2
GLORIA DR SAC 95831 378-G7
GLORIA WY BEN 94510 551-A4
GLOW CT SAC 95831 378-J6
GLOW LN SolC 95688 413-E1
GOETTEL CT BEN 94510 551-A3
GOHEEN CIR VAL 94591 530-D3
GOIN ST FRFD 94535 473-G3
GOLDBERRY LN DVS 95616 355-H7
GOLD COAST CT FRFD 94533 472-J3
GOLD COAST DR FRFD 94533 472-H3
GOLD CREEK CT WSAC 95691 378-D3
GOLDEN BROOK LN AMCN 94503 510-A2
GOLDENEYE CT AMCN 94503 509-J1; WSAC 95691 378-F1
GOLDEN EYE WY SUIS 94585 472-J7
GOLDEN GATE DR WSAC 95691 378-D2
GOLDENHILL WY BEN 94510 551-C4
GOLDEN PRAIRIE CT FRFD 94534 491-D2
GOLDENROD CT FRFD 94534 471-F7; VAC 95687 453-E2
GOLDENROD ST SolC 94589 529-J1; VAL 94589 529-J1
GOLDEN SLOPES CT BEN 94510 551-C4
GOLDFINCH DR AMCN 94503 510-A4
GOLD HILL RD FRFD 94585 511-E1; SolC 94585 511-E1
GOLD HILL ST WSAC 95691 358-J7; WSAC 95691 378-J1
GOLD HILL WY VAL 94589 509-H5
GOLD HILLS DR RVIS 94571 516-E1
GOLD VALLEY WY AMCN 94503 510-B2
GOLDY CT VAC 95687 433-H6
GOLF VIEW CIR YoCo 95618 377-A2
GONDOLA CT SAC 95831 378-G7
GONZAGA AV VAL 94589 510-B6
GONZAGA TER DVS 95618 356-H7
GONZALES DR VAC 95688 433-A3
GOODAIR CT SUIS 94585 473-A7
GOODALL ST FRFD 94535 473-G5
GOODMAN CT FRFD 94533 453-E6; FRFD 94533 473-B4
GOODMAN LN FRFD 94533 453-E6
GOODNER LN YoCo 95695 335-H3
GOODYEAR RD BEN 94510 531-G7; SolC 94510 511-G5; SolC 94510 531-H1
GOOSEBERRY CIR WSAC 95691 358-G7
GORDAN ST RVIS 94571 516-H4
GORDON CT BEN 94510 550-H1
GORDON ST VAL 94590 530-B5
GORDON VALLEY RD NaCo 94558 451-H1; SolC 94534 451-H7; SolC 94534 471-H1
GOSHAWK ST DVS 95616 356-B5
GOTHIC CT FRFD 94534 491-D3
GOURLEY CT SolC 95688 393-B7
GOYA DR FRFD 94534 472-E2
GRACE FEATHER CT VAC 95688 413-D6
GRAFTON ST WDLD 95695 316-A3
GRAFTON WY VAC 95688 413-E7; VAC 95688 433-E1
GRAHAM ISLAND RD WSAC 95691 378-C2
GRAMBLING CT DVS 95618 356-F7
GRANADA VAL 94591 530-F6
GRANADA DR FRFD 94533 473-C4; WDLD 95695 315-J5; WDLD 95695 316-A5
GRANADA LN SolC 95688 433-A2; VAC 95688 433-A2
GRANADA ST NAP 94559 470-A1; VAL 94591 530-G6
GRAND AV WDLD 95695 315-J3
N GRAND AV WDLD 95695 315-J2
GRAND CANYON DR VAC 95687 433-H3
GRANDE AV BEN 94510 551-C4; DVS 95616 356-B5
GRANDE CIR FRFD 94533 473-A4
GRANDE VISTA AV WSAC 95691 358-H5
GRANDVIEW AV CCCo 94525 550-C5
GRAND VIEW CT VAC 95688 433-B6
GRAND VIEW DR VAC 95688 433-B6
GRANGERS DAIRY DR SAC 95831 378-G6
GRANITE CT VAC 95687 453-G3
GRANITE LN FRFD 94534 491-F1; SolC 94534 491-F1
GRANITE WY VAC 95688 433-D3
GRANITE BAY PL YoCo 95616 355-H2
GRANITE SPRINGS WY AMCN 94503 510-B2
GRANT AV Rt#-128 WIN 95694 373-D4; YoCo 95694 373-D4
GRANT CT BEN 94510 550-H1; FRFD 94533 472-E5; WSAC 95691 358-J7
GRANT ST BEN 94510 551-D6; FRFD 94533 472-E5; VAL 94590 530-B6; VAL 94590 550-C1
GRANVILLE AV VAL 94591 530-D5
GRAPE ST VAC 95688 433-B4
GRAPEVINE LN NaCo 94558 451-J3
GRAPEWOOD ST VAL 94591 530-F5
GRASSLAND DR VAC 95688 433-H2
GRASS VALLEY CT FRFD 94534 491-D2
GRASS VALLEY DR WDLD 95776 316-C5
GRAVES CT VAL 94591 530-F5
GRAVINK CT WDLD 95776 316-B5
GRAY CT BEN 94510 551-B1
GRAY HAWK LN SUIS 94585 472-J7
GRAYLYN CT VAC 95688 433-D1
GREAT JONES ST FRFD 94533 472-F6
GREEN DR DXN 95620 395-B6
GREEN ACRES CT SolC 94534 471-B5
GREEN ACRES LN SolC 94534 471-C5
GREENBRIER CT BEN 94510 551-A1; VAL 94591 530-G2
GREENBRIER RD WSAC 95691 378-J1
GREENE CT VAC 95688 413-J6
GREENE TER DVS 95618 376-F1
GREENFIELD AV VAL 94590 530-C2
GREENFIELD CT VAL 94590 530-C2
GREENFIELD DR FRFD 94534 472-F2
GREENHAVEN DR SAC 95831 378-J6; VAC 95687 433-H7; VAC 95687 453-H1
GREENHEAD WY SUIS 94585 472-J6
GREENHURST WY SAC 95831 378-J7
GREEN ISLAND RD AMCN 94503 490-A6
GREENMEADOW AV WSAC 95691 358-F4
GREEN MEADOW CT FRFD 94534 491-D2
GREENMONT DR VAL 94591 530-G7

STREET Name City ZIP Pg-Grid

GREENRIDGE CT
FRFD 94585 491-D6
GREENSTAR WY
SAC 95831 378-J7
GREENTREE CIR
FRFD 94585 491-D7
GREENTREE CT
FRFD 94585 491-D7
GREEN TREE DR
VAC 95687 433-H4
GREENTREE PL
FRFD 94585 491-D7
GREEN VALLEY CT
WDLD 95776 316-C5
GREEN VALLEY LN
SolC 94534 471-B3
GREEN VALLEY LNDG
FRFD 94534 491-[illegible]
GREEN VALLEY RD
FRFD 94534 491-D3
NaCo 94558 450-D7
NaCo 94558 470-E1
SolC 94534 471-B3
SolC 94534 491-C1
GREEN VALLEY OAKS DR
SolC 94534 471-B5
GREENVIEW DR
YoCo 95618 376-J1
GREENWAY CIR
SAC 95831 378-J7
GREENWICH CIR
VAC 95687 433-F7
VAC 95687 453-F1
GREENWICH CT
VAC 95687 453-F1
GREENWILLOW CT
FRFD 94585 511-E3
GREEN WING DR
SUIS 94585 472-J6
GREENWING ST
AMCN 94503 509-H1
GREENWOOD AV
WSAC 95605 358-J2
GREENWOOD CT
FRFD 94585 491-D7
GREENWOOD DR
DXN 95620 415-B1
VAC 95687 453-E1
WDLD 95695 315-G5
GREENWOOD RD
NaCo 94589 490-A2
GREENWOOD ST
VAL 94591 530-E5
GREEVES ST
VAL 94591 530-F5
GREGG CT
VAC 95687 453-F1
GREGORY AV
WSAC 95691 378-F5
GREGORY DR
VAC 95687 433-F7
VAC 95687 453-F1
GREGORY LN
AMCN 94503 510-B4
VAL 94591 530-E3
GREGORY PL
DVS 95616 356-E7
GREGORY ST
FRFD 94533 472-E6
GRENNAN ST
VAL 94591 530-D5
GRENOBLE DR
WDLD 95695 315-G6
GREYCALLS CT
WSAC 95691 378-F1
GREY FOX LN
FRFD 94534 472-F1
GREYHAWK CT
VAC 95688 433-D1
GREYLAG CT
SUIS 94585 473-A6
GREYLAG DR
SUIS 94585 473-A6
GREYSTONE CT
VAC 95687 433-J4
GREY WOLF DR
VAC 95688 433-D1
GRIDLEY LN
SolC 95694 393-B2
GRIDLEY RD
VAL 94592 549-H1
GRIFFIN DR
VAL 94589 510-C6
GRIFFIN LN
SolC 95688 414-B3
GRIFFIN WY
WIN 95694 373-E2
GRIFFITH CT
DXN 95620 415-C2
GRIFFITH DR
DXN 95620 415-C2
GRINNEL DR
DVS 95618 356-G6
GRINNEL PL
DVS 95618 356-G6
GRIZZLY BAY RD
WSAC 95691 378-E2
GRIZZLY ISLAND RD
SolC 94585 472-J7
SolC 94585 492-J2
SolC 94585 493-A6
SUIS 94585 472-J7
GROBRIC CT
FRFD 94534 491-[illegible]
GROSBEAK CT
DVS 95616 356-B4
GROUSE CT
FRFD 94533 473-A3
GROVE AV
VAL 94592 529-F3
WDLD 95695 315-G6
GROVE CIR
BEN 94510 550-J3
GROVE CT
DXN 95620 395-C6
VAC 95688 433-B3
GRUBSTAKE PL
VAL 94591 530-C7
GUADELUPE ST
WSAC 95691 378-D3
GUAVA LN
DVS 95616 356-A7
GUAYMAS PL
DVS 95616 356-C5
GUERRERO LN
WDLD 95776 316-E6
GUITTARD WY
FRFD 94534 492-A1
GULF CT
FRFD 94533 472-J2
GULF DR
FRFD 94533 472-J2
FRFD 94533 473-A1
GULF ISLAND ST
WSAC 95691 378-C2
GULL CT
AMCN 94503 509-H3
FRFD 94533 473-A3
GULL POINT CT
BEN 94510 551-A5
GUM AV
WDLD 95695 316-A5
WDLD 95776 316-A5
E GUM AV
WDLD 95776 316-B5
GUM CT
VAL 94589 510-A7
GUM GROVE LN
SolC 95688 413-J3
GUNTER DR
SUIS 94585 473-C4
GUNTER ST
FRFD 94535 473-F2
GUTHRIE PL
DVS 95618 357-A7
GWINHURST CT
VAC 95688 433-D1
GWINN CT
WDLD 95776 316-D4
GYPSUM DR
VAL 94589 510-C6
GYPSY LN
SolC 95688 413-F5

H

H LN
FRFD 94533 473-F2
H ST
BEN 94510 551-C6
DVS 95616 356-C6
E H ST
BEN 94510 551-C5
DXN 95620 395-D6
SolC 95620 395-D6
W H ST
BEN 94510 550-J4
BEN 94510 551-A4
DXN 95620 395-A6
HABITAT CT
VAC 95688 433-D4
HACIENDA AV
DVS 95616 356-A5
HACIENDA LN
SUIS 94585 473-D6
WDLD 95695 315-H6
W HACIENDA LN
WDLD 95695 315-H6
HACKBERRY PL
DVS 95618 376-H1
HACKETT AV
FRFD 94535 473-G2
HACKETT CT
VAL 94591 530-E5
HACKETT DR
WDLD 95776 316-E5
HACKMAN RD
SolC 95620 395-H7
HAGEN RD
NaCo 94558 450-A2
HAGGERTY ST
VAL 94591 530-E5
HAITI RD
WSAC 95691 378-D2
HALABUK CT
VAL 94591 530-D4
HALCON PL
DVS 95618 356-H5
HALE ST
VAL 94591 530-E3
HALE RANCH RD
FRFD 94534 471-J7
FRFD 94534 491-J1
SolC 94534 491-J1
HALF MOON BAY CIR
WSAC 95691 378-D2
HALIFAX AV
DVS 95616 355-G7
HALL CT
BEN 94510 530-J6
HALL LN
SUIS 94585 473-B7
HALLEY RD
SolC 95620 374-A6
SolC 95620 394-B4
SolC 95694 374-A6
SolC 95694 394-B4
HALLIDAY ST
VAL 94590 530-B4
HALLMARK CT
AMCN 94503 510-B2
FRFD 94585 491-D6
HALLMARK LN
AMCN 94503 510-B2
HALLMARK PL
VAL 94591 510-E7
VAL 94591 530-F1
HALL PARK DR
DXN 95620 415-D1
HALSEY CIR
DVS 95618 376-E1
HALYARD DR
WSAC 95691 358-F5
HAMEL LN
DVS 95618 376-D2
SolC 95620 376-D2
YoCo 95618 376-D2
HAMEL ST
DVS 95618 356-J7
DVS 95618 357-A7
HAMILTON AV
RVIS 94571 516-H6
HAMILTON CT
VAL 94589 509-J4
HAMILTON DR
FRFD 94533 472-C6
SolC 94533 472-C6
VAC 95687 433-G7
VAC 95687 453-G1
HAMILTON ST
FRFD 94535 473-F2
HAMMOND LN
SUIS 94585 473-B7
SUIS 94585 493-B1
HAMPSHIRE CT
WIN 95694 373-D4
HAMPSHIRE ST
VAL 94590 530-A3
HAMPTON DR
DVS 95616 355-J6
DVS 95616 356-A7
HAMPTON PL
FRFD 94533 472-F4
WDLD 95776 336-E1
HAMPTON ST
WSAC 95691 378-J1
HANFORD CT
FRFD 94533 472-H1
HANGAR AV
FRFD 94535 473-F4
HANGING OAK WY
YoCo 95695 315-G1
HANLEY ST
SolC 94591 530-D7
HANLON WY
BEN 94510 530-J6
HANNA WY
WDLD 95695 315-J2
HANNAH CT
DXN 95620 395-C5
HANNIGAN WY
VAL 94589 510-C5
HANNS AV
VAL 94590 530-B3
HANNS LN
VAL 94590 530-C4
HANOVER CT
WDLD 95695 315-G6
HANOVER DR
DVS 95616 356-B6
HANOVER WY
VAC 95687 433-G6
HANSEN CT
DXN 95620 [illegible]
HANSON DR
FRFD 94533 453-D7
FRFD 94533 473-D1
SolC 94533 453-E7
SolC 94533 473-D1
HANSON WY
WDLD 95776 316-F3
HAPSBURG CROWN CT
VAL 94591 530-J1
HARBISON DR
VAC 95687 433-F4
HARBOR BLVD
WSAC 95605 358-G2
WSAC 95691 358-F5
N HARBOR BLVD
WSAC 95605 [illegible]
HARBOR CT
FRFD 94533 472-H2
VAC 95687 453-G2
HARBOR CTR
SUIS 94585 472-G7
HARBOR WY
VAL 94590 529-H3
HARBOR MOON CT
VAL 94591 530-F1
HARBOR PARK DR
SUIS 94585 472-G7
SUIS 94585 492-G1
HARBOR POINTE PL
WSAC 95605 358-F2
HARBOR VISTA CT
BEN 94510 551-C4
HARDESTY LN
SolC 95688 412-G7
HARDING ST
FRFD 94533 472-E5
HARDING TER
DVS 95616 355-H7
HARDY DR
WDLD 95776 316-D4
WSAC 95605 358-J2
HARGUS AV
SolC 94591 530-E6
VAL 94591 530-E6
HARLAN LN
YoCo 95695 335-F2
HARLEQUIN CT
SUIS 94585 473-A7
HARLEQUIN WY
SUIS 94585 473-A7
HARLEY DR
WDLD 95695 315-H5
HARMON DR
SAC 95831 378-F7
HARMON RD
WSAC 95691 378-G2
HARMONY LN
SolC 94591 530-E6
HARPER LN
SolC 95620 395-H6
HARRIER AV
VAL 94590 529-J3
HARRIER DR
SUIS 94585 473-B6
HARRIER PL
DVS 95616 356-B4
HARRIS AV
CCCo 94572 549-H7
HARRIS RD
RVIS 94571 516-G3
HARRIS WY
VAL 94591 530-E4
HARRISBURG LN
SUIS 94585 473-D4
HARRISON ST
FRFD 94533 472-F5
HART AV
WSAC 95691 378-F1
HARTE CT
FRFD 94533 473-B3
HARTE PL
FRFD 94533 473-B3
HARTER AV
WDLD 95776 316-A1
HARTFORD AV
FRFD 94534 472-C6
VAC 95687 433-E7
HARTFORD CIR
FRFD 94534 472-C5
HARTFORD CT
AMCN 94503 510-A3
HARTFORD PL
FRFD 94534 472-C6
HARTH CT
DXN 95620 395-C6
HARTLEY RD
SolC 95688 393-J7
SolC 95688 413-H4
VAC 95688 413-H4
HARTLEY ST
DVS 95618 356-F5
HARTWELL ST
CCCo 94525 550-E5
HARTWICK LN
FRFD 94533 472-G2
HARVARD
VAL 94590 510-A6
HARVARD AV
VAC 95687 433-H6
HARVARD BEND
WDLD 95695 315-G6
HARVARD CT
VAC 95687 433-H6
WDLD 95695 315-G6
HARVARD DR
DVS 95616 356-A7
WDLD 95695 315-G4
HARVARD PL
WDLD 95695 315-F6
HARVEST CIR
VAC 95687 453-J1
HARVEST DR
VAC 95687 453-H1
HARVEST LN
SolC 95688 414-A2
HARVEST SPRING CT
FRFD 94534 491-B2
HARVEY WY
YoCo 95618 376-E2
HARWICH PL
VAL 94591 550-E1
HARWINTON CT
VAC 95688 433-D2
HASTINGS DR
BEN 94510 531-A7
BEN 94510 550-J2
BEN 94510 551-A1
VAL 94589 510-A6
HASTINGS WY
FRFD 94534 472-E3
HATCHER DR
WDLD 95776 316-D5
HATTERAS PL
DVS 95616 355-H7
HAUSAM LN
FRFD 94533 453-D7
HAUSSLER DR
DVS 95616 356-E7
HAVASU DR
VAC 95687 433-F7
HAVASU ST
WSAC 95691 378-D4
HAVEN CT
SAC 95831 378-J7
VAL 94591 [illegible]
HAVEN ST
WIN 95694 373-E4
HAVENHILL DR
BEN 94510 551-B3
HAVENHURST DR
SAC 95831 378-J7
HAVENSIDE DR
SAC 95831 378-H6
HAVENWOOD CIR
SAC 95831 378-H7
HAVENWOOD CT
VAC 95688 433-D3
HAVERHILL ST
WSAC 95691 358-H5
HAVITURE WY
VAL 94589 [illegible]
HAWAII CT
WSAC 95691 378-D2
HAWAII ST
FRFD 94533 472-E6
HAWK CT
VAC 95687 433-J7
HAWK DR
VAC 95687 433-J7
WDLD 95695 315-G1
HAWK LN
FRFD 94533 472-J3
HAWKESBURY CT
VAL 94591 530-G3
HAWKINS RD
SolC 95620 434-E5
SolC 95687 433-J5
SolC 95687 434-A5
VAC 95687 433-J5
HAWKINS ST
VAL 94591 530-H4
HAWTHORN DR
FRFD 94533 472-G2
HAWTHORN LN
DVS 95616 356-A7
HAWTHORNE AV
VAL 94590 530-B3
HAWTHORNE CT
DXN 95620 415-B1
VAC 95688 433-A3
HAWTHORNE LN
BEN 94510 551-A1
HAY RD
SolC 95687 454-C4
HAYES ST
BEN 94510 551-D6
FRFD 94533 472-E5
HAYMAN AV
VAL 94591 530-D5
HAYS LN
SolC 94591 530-E6
VAL 94591 530-E6
WDLD 95776 316-E4
HAYS ST
WDLD 95695 315-H5
WDLD 95695 316-A5
W HAYS ST
WDLD 95695 315-H5
HAZEL ST
VAC 95688 433-E4
HAZELTINE WY
FRFD 94533 452-J6
HAZELWOOD CT
DXN 95620 415-B1
FRFD 94585 511-E2
HAZELWOOD ST
VAL 94591 530-E6
HAZEMAN CT
WDLD 95776 316-D5
HAZEN ST
SolC 95687 434-C6
HEADLANDS CT
VAL 94591 550-F2
HEADSLANE RD
WSAC 95691 358-J7
HEADWATER DR
VAL 94591 530-F1
HEALD CT
CCCo 94525 550-E4
HEALD ST
CCCo 94525 550-E4
E HEALTH SCIENCE DR
YoCo 95616 376-A2
W HEALTH SCIENCE DR
YoCo 95616 376-A2
HEARST CT
FRFD 94534 472-D3
HEARST ST
WSAC 95691 358-J6
HEARTFORD WY
AMCN 94503 509-J2
HEARTHSTONE DR
AMCN 94503 510-A2
HEARTWOOD AV
VAL 94591 530-E5
HEARTWOOD CT
VAL 94591 530-E4
HEATH CT
FRFD 94533 472-F3
HEATH DR
FRFD 94533 472-F3
HEATHER CT
BEN 94510 551-A1
SolC 94534 471-A4
VAL 94591 530-F3
HEATHER DR
FRFD 94533 472-F3
HEATHER LN
SolC 95688 393-G7
WDLD 95695 315-G4
HEATHER PL
WDLD 95695 315-G4
HEATHERFIELD CT
FRFD 94585 511-E3
HECKE DR
WDLD 95776 316-E5
HEDY LN
YoCo 95618 376-E2
HEIDRICK LN
YoCo 95695 315-F5
HEINKE DR
NaCo 94558 450-A5
HEINZ LN
SolC 95688 413-D1
HEIRLOOM CT
VAC 95687 433-H3
HELANE CT
BEN 94510 551-B3
HELEN AV
VAL 94591 530-D4
HELEN WY
VAC 95687 453-F1
WDLD 95776 316-B5
HELEN POWER DR
VAC 95687 433-F4
HELIOTROPE ST
VAL 94589 529-J1
HELMSMAN CT
VAL 94591 550-G2
HEMBRE CT
SUIS 94585 473-B7
SUIS 94585 493-B1
HEMENWAY ST
WIN 95694 373-E3
HEMINGWAY CT
DXN 95620 395-B7
HEMLOCK CT
VAC 95688 433-B4
HEMLOCK LN
DVS 95616 356-D6
HEMLOCK ST
FRFD 94533 472-G4
VAC 95688 433-B4
WSAC 95691 358-H4
HEMSTEAD ST
FRFD 94535 473-G5
HENDERSON WY
WDLD 95776 316-B5
HENDRICKS DR
VAL 94591 530-J2
HENRI CT
DVS 95618 356-F6
HENRY CT
VAL 94591 530-D3
HENRY ST
FRFD 94533 472-E7
VAL 94591 530-D3
HENSHAW RD
WSAC 95691 378-C4
HEPWORTH DR
DVS 95618 356-F5
HERITAGE AV
FRFD 94585 491-D7
HERITAGE CT
DXN 95620 415-D2
FRFD 94585 491-D7
HERITAGE LN
VAC 95687 453-G2
HERITAGE PKWY
WDLD 95776 336-D1
HERITAGE OAKS LN
SolC 94534 471-A2
HERITAGE ROSE LN
SUIS 94585 472-G6
HERMOSA AV
VAL 94589 530-A2
VAL 94590 530-B2
HERMOSA PL
DVS 95616 356-B5
WDLD 95695 315-J5
HERON CT
FRFD 94533 473-A3
VAL 94589 509-H4
HERON DR
SUIS 94585 473-B6
HERON PL
DVS 95616 356-B4
HERSHEY DR
WDLD 95776 316-E4
HERST LN
SolC 95620 394-C7
HESPELLER RD
SolC 95688 432-H3
HESS DR
AMCN 94503 490-A7
HESS LN
SolC 95620 395-D2
HESTIA WY
NaCo 94558 450-A1
HIATT PL
WDLD 95695 315-H6
HIBISCUS LN
SUIS 94585 472-J5
HIBISCUS CT
VAL 94589 510-A6
HICHBORN ST
VAL 94590 529-J3
HICKAM AV
FRFD 94535 473-H3
HICKAM CIR
SUIS 94585 473-C5
HICKAM CT
SUIS 94585 473-D6
HICKCOCK DR
VAC 95687 433-H5
HICKORY AV
FRFD 94533 472-J1
FRFD 94533 473-A1
HICKORY CT
FRFD 94533 472-J1
VAC 95688 433-D6
HICKORY LN
DVS 95616 376-D1
VAC 95688 433-C6
HICKORY ST
VAL 94589 510-A7
HICKORY WY
WSAC 95691 358-G4
HIDALGO PL
DVS 95616 356-B5
HIDDEN CIR
DVS 95618 356-F7
HIDDENBROOKE PKWY
NaCo 94591 510-G3
SolC 94505 510-G3
VAL 94585 510-G3
VAL 94591 510-H4
HIDDEN COVE WY
SUIS 94585 473-A6
HIDDEN GLEN CT
VAC 95688 432-J4
VAC 95688 433-A4
HIDDEN OAKS CT
VAC 95687 453-C1
HIDDEN SPRINGS RD
NaCo 94558 451-E1
HIDDEN TRAIL LN
VAL 94591 530-D2
HIDDEN VALLEY LN
SolC 94534 452-G3
VAC 95688 432-J4
HIDDENWOOD CT
FRFD 94585 511-E3
HIDEOUT CT
SAC 95831 378-H6
HIGGINS RD
WSAC 95691 378-F1
HIGHGATE RD
VAL 94591 510-J6
HIGHLAND AV
VAC 95688 433-D4
VAL 94590 530-C3
HIGHLAND CIR
YoCo 95695 315-F5
HIGHLAND CT
FRFD 94585 511-D2
FRFD 94585 511-E2
HIGHLAND DR
RVIS 94571 516-H6
WSAC 95691 358-J7
WSAC 95691 378-J1
HIGH POINTE CT
FRFD 94534 472-D2
HIGHRIDGE CT
AMCN 94503 510-A4
HIGHRIDGE DR
AMCN 94503 510-A4
HIGHWAY Rt#-12
FRFD 94533 472-A7
FRFD 94534 471-J7
FRFD 94534 472-A7
HIGHWAY Rt#-12
RVIS 94571 516-D2
SaCo 95641 516-J5
SolC 94533 472-E7
SolC 94534 471-J7
SolC 94534 472-A7
SolC 94534 491-J1
SolC 94571 516-A2
SolC 94585 493-C1
SUIS 94533 472-F7
SUIS 94534 472-F7
SUIS 94585 472-G7
SUIS 94585 473-A7
SUIS 94585 493-C1
HIGHWAY Rt#-16
YoCo 95695 315-A3
HIGHWAY Rt#-29
AMCN 94503 490-A6
AMCN 94503 510-A3
NaCo 94558 490-A1
NaCo 94589 490-A1
HIGHWAY Rt#-113
DXN 95620 395-D2
SolC 95620 395-D2
SolC 95620 415-D4
HIGHWAY Rt#-128
WIN 95694 373-D4
YoCo 95694 373-D4
HIGHWAY Rt#-160
SaCo 95641 516-J6
HILARY AV
WSAC 95691 378-G3
HILARY WY
VAL 94591 530-G4
HILBORN RD
FRFD 94534 452-F7
FRFD 94534 472-E2
HILDA WY
WDLD 95695 315-J2
HILDEBRAND CT
WDLD 95776 316-E5
HILL CT
FRFD 94535 473-F2
RVIS 94571 516-H4
WSAC 95605 358-H2
HILL DR
VAL 94590 529-H2
HILL PL
WIN 95694 373-E3
HILLBORN AV
VAL 94590 529-H3
HILLBORN CT
SUIS 94585 493-B1
HILLBORN WY
SUIS 94585 493-B1
HILLCREST AV
BEN 94510 551-C4
HILLCREST CIR
DXN 95620 415-B1
VAC 95688 413-D7
HILLCREST CT
AMCN 94503 510-B4
FRFD 94533 472-F4
HILLER CT
WDLD 95776 316-D5
HILL GLEN DR
FRFD 94534 472-E1
HILLHOUSE ST
DXN 95620 395-C7
HILLRIDGE CT
FRFD 94534 472-F1
HILLRIDGE DR
FRFD 94534 452-F7
FRFD 94534 472-F1
HILLSDALE CT
FRFD 94585 491-D7
VAC 95688 433-B6
HILLSIDE CIR
DXN 95620 415-B1
HILLSIDE CT
FRFD 94533 472-H1
HILLSIDE DR
FRFD 94533 472-H1
VAL 94590 529-H2
HILLSIDE LN
VAC 95688 433-D5
HILLSIDE TER
RVIS 94571 516-G4
HILLSVIEW DR
SolC 95688 433-B1
HILLTOP CT
VAC 95688 433-D3
HILLTOP DR
VAL 94591 530-F3
HILLTOP LN
SolC 95688 413-B6
HILLVIEW CT
FRFD 94534 472-E1
VAC 95688 433-A6
HILLVIEW DR
DXN 95620 415-B1
FRFD 94534 472-E1
VAC 95688 433-A6
VAL 94591 530-F3
HILLVIEW LN
WIN 95694 373-E2
HILTON AV
VAL 94591 530-D5
HILTON HEAD CT
FRFD 94534 452-D7
HILTON HEAD DR
FRFD 94534 452-C7
HOAG PL
DVS 95618 357-A7
HOBBS AV
VAL 94589 510-A7
HOBSON AV
WSAC 95605 358-H2
N HOBSON AV
WSAC 95605 358-G2
HODGES ST
VAL 94589 510-D6
HOGAN AV
VAL 94589 510-A7
HOLCOMB LN
AMCN 94503 510-A2
HOLDENER RD
SolC 95687 434-C6
HOLIDAY CT
VAC 95687 433-H5
HOLIDAY LN
FRFD 94534 472-D5
HOLIDAY COVE CT
SAC 95831 378-H6
HOLLAND DR
WSAC 95605 358-H1
HOLLAND PL
WDLD 95776 316-E7
HOLLAND WY
WDLD 95776 316-E7
HOLLIS CT
VAC 95687 453-F3
HOLLISTER RD
WDLD 95695 316-A2
HOLLOWBROOK CT
VAC 95687 453-G3
HOLLY AL
VAL 94590 529-H2
HOLLY CT
DXN 95620 395-C6
HOLLY DR
FRFD 94533 472-G1
HOLLY LN
DVS 95616 356-B6
VAC 95688 433-D4
HOLLY ST
VAL 94589 510-B7
WSAC 95691 358-G3
HOLLYWOOD AV
VAL 94591 530-D7
HOLMES CT
FRFD 94533 473-A3
HOLMES LN
SolC 95694 373-D7
SolC 95694 393-D1
[illegible] CT
CCCo 94525 [illegible]
HOME ACRES AV
SolC 94591 530-D6
VAL 94591 530-D6
HOMER ST
DVS 95618 356-F5
HOMESTEAD CT
FRFD 94534 472-B2
HOMESTEAD WY
WDLD 95776 316-D4
HOMEWOOD CT
FRFD 94585 511-E2
HOMEWOOD DR
WDLD 95695 316-A5
HOMEWOOD ST
VAC 95688 433-A5
HOMEWOOD WY
FRFD 94585 511-E2
HONEY LN
SolC 95688 412-F5
HONEYDEW DR
VAL 94591 530-F7
VAL 94591 550-E1
HONEYSUCKLE DR
FRFD 94533 472-F2
HONKER LN
SUIS 94585 472-J7
SUIS 94585 473-A7
HOOPA PL
DVS 95618 376-H1
HOOPA RD
WSAC 95691 378-H2
HOOVER CT
WDLD 95776 316-C6
HOOVER DR
WDLD 95776 316-B6
HOOVER PL
WDLD 95776 316-B6
HOOVER ST
FRFD 94533 472-D5
WIN 95694 373-D3
HOPKINS DR
DXN 95620 395-B7
FRFD 94533 472-G5
HOPKINS RD
YoCo 95616 375-G3
HOPLAND ST
WSAC 95691 378-H2
HOPPER PL
DVS 95618 356-E5
HOPPIN CT
WDLD 95776 316-E5
HORIZON CT
AMCN 94503 510-B2
HORIZON DR
FRFD 94533 472-J3
FRFD 94533 473-A3
HORIZON WY
AMCN 94503 510-B2
HORNBY ISLAND RD
WSAC 95691 378-C2
HORSE CREEK DR
VAC 95688 433-H2
HORSESHOE BAY CT
VAL 94591 530-G2
HORTALEZA PL
DVS 95618 356-G6
HOSPITAL DR
FRFD 94535 473-J3
FRFD 94535 474-A3
VAL 94589 530-B1
HOSPITAL RD
BEN 94510 551-D5
HOUSTON CT
VAC 95687 433-C7
HOUSTON ST
WSAC 95691 358-F3
HOWARD AV
VAL 94589 530-C2
VAL 94590 530-C2
HOWARD DR
WDLD 95776 316-E5
HOWARD WY
YoCo 95616 376-C1
HOWAT RD
YoCo 95618 357-B6
HOWE CT
FRFD 94534 472-D4
HOWE ST
FRFD 94534 472-D4
HOWLAND CT
FRFD 94534 472-E3
HOYT CT
SUIS 94585 473-A7
HUBBLE ST
DVS 95616 355-G7
HUBBS CT
BEN 94510 531-B7
HUBER DR
FRFD 94533 453-E7
HUCK RD
FRFD 94533 473-D1
SolC 94533 453-E7
SolC 94533 473-D1
HUCKLEBERRY CIR
WSAC 95691 358-G7
HUCKLEBERRY ST
WSAC 95691 358-F7
HUDSON AL
VAL 94590 529-J5
VAL 94590 530-A5
HUDSON CT
DVS 95616 355-H7
DVS 95616 375-H1
VAC 95687 453-F2
HUDSON ST
DVS 95616 355-H7
HUERTA PL
DVS 95616 356-C5
HUGH CT
BEN 94510 551-C1
HUGH ST
SolC 94591 530-E7
HUGHES CIR
WSAC 95691 358-H5
HUMBOLDT AV
DVS 95616 355-J7
HUMBOLDT DR
DXN 95620 395-C7
HUMBOLDT ST
VAL 94591 530-D4
HUMBOLT DR
SUIS 94585 473-C6
HUME WY
VAC 95687 433-D6
HUMMINGBIRD CT
FRFD 94585 511-E3
HUMMINGBIRD DR
FRFD 94585 511-F3

STREET Name	City	ZIP	Pg-Grid
HUMMINGBIRD WY	AMCN	94503	509-J2
	SUIS	94585	473-B6
HUMPHREY DR	SUIS	94585	473-A5
HUMPHREY LN	VAL	94591	550-F2
HUNT WY	DVS	95616	356-D7
HUNTER CT	VAL	94591	530-F1
HUNTER LN	WDLD	95776	316-D5
HUNTER ST	FRFD	94533	473-J2
	FRFD	94535	474-A2
HUNTERS GLEN CT	VAC	95687	453-E3
HUNTINGTON CT	FRFD	94533	473-C3
HUNTINGTON DR	FRFD	94533	473-E2
	VAC	95687	433-G7
HUNTINGTON RD	WSAC	95691	378-C4
HUNTINGTON WY	AMCN	94503	509-J2
HUSTON CIR	WDLD	95776	316-E5
HUTCHEON PL	FRFD	94533	453-E6
HUTCHINSON DR	YoCo	95616	375-F1
	YoCo	95616	376-A2
HUYSER CT	FRFD	94535	473-J1
HYANNIS CT	VAC	95687	453-G2
HYDE CT	VAL	94591	530-H6
HYDRANGA CT	VAL	94591	530-F7
I			
I LN	FRFD	94533	473-F2
I ST	DVS	95616	356-D7
	DVS	95616	376-D1
	VAL	94592	529-F4
E I ST	BEN	94510	551-B5
W I ST	BEN	94510	550-J4
	BEN	94510	551-A4
IDAHO ST	FRFD	94533	472-D6
	FRFD	94535	473-H3
IDORA AV	SolC	94590	530-C6
	VAL	94591	530-D6
IDYLLWILD CT	FRFD	94534	491-E2
IDYLLWILD DR	FRFD	94534	491-E2
IFLAND WY	VAL	94589	510-A7
ILLINOIS ST	FRFD	94533	472-F7
	FRFD	94535	473-H2
	SUIS	94533	472-F7
	VAL	94590	529-J3
	VAL	94590	530-A3
IMELDA ST	VAL	94589	509-J4
	VAL	94589	510-A5
IMOLA AV	NaCo	94558	470-A1
	NaCo	94559	470-A1
	NAP	94559	470-A1
IMPALA PL	DVS	95616	356-A5
IMPERIAL AV	DVS	95616	355-J7
IMPERIAL CT	VAL	94591	530-E1
IMPERIAL ST	WDLD	95695	315-G3
INCA CT	VAL	94591	530-D7
INCA PL	DVS	95616	356-C4
INCLINE CT	VAC	95687	453-G1
INCLINE PL	BEN	94510	551-B4
INDEPENDENCE AV	VAC	95687	453-G2
	WSAC	95691	358-G7
	WSAC	95691	378-F1
INDEPENDENCE CT	FRFD	94533	452-G6
INDEPENDENCE DR	AMCN	94503	510-B4
INDEPENDENCE LN	SolC	95688	413-C5
INDEPENDENCE ST	VAL	94592	529-F3
INDIAN AL	VAL	94590	529-J5
	VAL	94590	530-A5
INDIANA CIR	FRFD	94535	473-H2
INDIANA ST	BEN	94510	551-E2
	FRFD	94533	472-D6
	FRFD	94535	473-F6
	VAL	94590	529-J3
	VAL	94590	530-A3
INDIANWOOD WY	RVIS	94571	516-E1
INDUSTRIAL BLVD	WSAC	95691	358-F4
INDUSTRIAL CT	BEN	94510	551-E2
	FRFD	94535	473-F3
INDUSTRIAL DR	FRFD	94535	473-F3
INDUSTRIAL WY	BEN	94510	551-E1
	DXN	95620	395-D6
	WDLD	95776	316-C4
INEZ WY	SAC	95822	378-J3
INGLEWOOD DR	WSAC	95605	358-J2
INGRID DR	DXN	95620	395-A7
INNER CIR	DVS	95618	356-F7
INNER PERIMETER RD	FRFD	94535	473-J5
	FRFD	94535	474-A5
INNISFREE CT	VAL	94591	510-J6
INVERNESS CT	BEN	94510	551-B3
	FRFD	94533	472-F3
INVERNESS DR	RVIS	94571	516-F2
	VAL	94589	530-A1
	WDLD	95695	315-G6
INVERNESS WY	VAC	95687	433-H7
INVESTMENT ST	CCCo	94572	549-H7
INWOOD DR	FRFD	94534	452-C7
INWOOD PL	FRFD	94534	452-C7
INYO CT	VAC	95687	433-H4
INYO PL	WDLD	95695	315-G3
IOWA ST	BEN	94510	551-E2
	FRFD	94533	472-H5
IPANEMA PL	DVS	95616	356-C5
IPSON AV	FRFD	94535	473-G2
IRENE DR	VAL	94591	530-F1
	WDLD	95776	316-B5
IRIS CT	BEN	94510	550-J1
	FRFD	94533	472-G2
	VAL	94591	530-F7
IRIS PL	DVS	95616	356-B5
	WSAC	95691	378-E2
IRON CT	VAC	95687	453-G2
IRON DR	VAC	95687	453-G2
IRONHORSE DR	AMCN	94503	510-B2
IRONSTONE CT	FRFD	94534	491-E1
IRONWOOD CIR	FRFD	94533	472-J1
	FRFD	94533	473-A1
IRONWOOD CT	FRFD	94533	473-A1
IRONWOOD LN	VAL	94591	530-F7
	VAL	94591	550-F1
IRONWOOD ST	VAC	95688	433-B4
IRONWOOD WY	SAC	95831	378-G5
	WSAC	95691	378-J2
IROQUOIS DR	VAC	95688	432-J4
IRVING CT	FRFD	94533	473-A3
IRWIN ST	VAL	94591	530-D5
ISABELLA CT	VAC	95687	433-F7
ISABELLA DR	VAC	95687	433-F7
ISABELLA ST	WSAC	95691	378-D4
ISABELLA WY	FRFD	94533	472-H1
ISLA PL	DVS	95616	356-B4
ISLE ROYALE CIR	VAC	95687	433-H3
ISLE ROYALE LN	DVS	95616	355-H6
ISOLERA LN	AMCN	94503	510-B3
ITHICA CT	VAC	95687	433-H6
IVES CT	FRFD	94533	473-A3
IVIE PL	WDLD	95695	315-G5
IVY CT	VAC	95687	453-D1
	WIN	95694	373-E4
IVY LN	SolC	94589	529-J1
IVY LP	WIN	95694	373-D3
IVY WY	WDLD	95776	316-D5
J			
J LN	FRFD	94533	473-F2
J ST	BEN	94510	551-C6
	DVS	95616	356-D6
	DVS	95616	376-D1
	VAL	94592	529-F3
E J ST	BEN	94510	551-B5
W J ST	BEN	94510	550-J4
	BEN	94510	551-A4
JACARANDA DR	SUIS	94585	472-J5
JACK LONDON DR	VAL	94589	509-J5
JACKS LN	NaCo	94558	450-A6
	NAP	94559	450-A6
JACKSNIPE RD	SolC	94585	492-B7
JACKSON ST	BEN	94510	551-D6
	CCCo	94525	550-E5
	DXN	95620	395-D7
	FRFD	94533	472-F6
	WDLD	95695	316-A3
	WIN	95694	373-D4
	WSAC	95691	358-J4
N JACKSON ST	DXN	95620	395-C7
S JACKSON ST	DXN	95620	395-C7
	DXN	95620	415-C1
JACKSON WY	VAL	94591	530-E4
JACOBS CT	FRFD	94534	472-D3
JACOBS DR	DXN	95620	395-B7
JACQUELYN LN	WSAC	95691	358-E7
JADE CIR	VAL	94590	550-C2
JADE WY	FRFD	94534	491-F1
	SolC	94534	491-F1
JADE CREST HILL WY	VAC	95688	413-D6
JAHN RD	SolC	95620	394-E6
JALISCO PL	DVS	95616	356-C5
JAMAICA ST	WSAC	95691	378-D2
JAMES CT	BEN	94510	551-A2
	VAC	95687	433-D7
JAMES PL	WDLD	95695	315-G6
JAMES RD	AMCN	94503	510-A2
JAMES ST	FRFD	94533	472-E7
JAMESON CANYON RD Rt#-12	FRFD	94533	491-A4
	FRFD	94589	491-A4
	NaCo	94558	490-A2
	NaCo	94589	490-A2
	SolC	94534	491-A4
	SolC	94589	490-G4
	SolC	94589	491-A4
JAMES RIVER RD	VAL	94591	550-D2
JAMESTOWN PL	VAC	95687	433-E7
JAN CT	DXN	95620	415-E1
JANA WY	AMCN	94503	509-J1
JANE CT	VAC	95687	433-H5
JANE WY	VAC	95688	433-D5
JANET CT	BEN	94510	551-B4
JANET DR	WSAC	95691	358-F7
JANICE ST	VAL	94589	510-C5
JARDIN PL	DVS	95616	356-B5
JASMINE AV	WSAC	95605	358-H1
JASMINE CT	BEN	94510	531-A7
	DVS	95618	376-F2
JASMINE ST	FRFD	94533	472-G2
	VAL	94589	509-J6
JASON CT	VAL	94591	530-F6
JASON WY	VAC	95687	453-F2
JASPER CT	BEN	94510	551-B1
JAVA CT	WSAC	95691	378-D2
JAVAN WY	SUIS	94585	473-B6
JAVIER PL	DVS	95618	356-F6
JAYBEE LN	SolC	95694	373-H7
	SolC	95694	374-A7
JEANNE CT	SUIS	94585	473-A5
JEFFERSON BLVD	WSAC	95605	358-J2
	WSAC	95691	358-H7
	WSAC	95691	378-F3
JEFFERSON BLVD Rt#-84	WSAC	95691	378-C7
	YoCo	95691	378-C7
JEFFERSON ST	BEN	94510	551-D5
	FRFD	94533	472-F5
	WDLD	95695	315-H4
	WIN	95694	373-D4
N JEFFERSON ST	DXN	95620	395-C7
S JEFFERSON ST	DXN	95620	415-C1
JEFFERY WY	RVIS	94571	516-H4
JEFFREY LN	DXN	95620	395-B7
JEFFRY ST	VAL	94590	529-J5
	VAL	94590	530-A5
JELLY BELLY LN	FRFD	94534	472-B7
	FRFD	94534	492-B1
JENI LN	SolC	94534	471-B6
JENNIFER CT	VAL	94591	530-F3
JENNIFER LN	VAC	95687	433-J6
JENNINGS AV	VAL	94591	530-D6
JENNINGS CT	FRFD	94585	491-D7
	WSAC	95691	378-D4
JENNY LN	SolC	95688	413-B6
JEPSON WY	VAC	95688	433-A4
JERILYNN CT	VAL	94589	509-J5
JEROME ST	DVS	95616	355-G7
JEROME WY	NaCo	94558	450-A1
JERSEY ST	VAL	94590	530-A6
JIB CT	DXN	95620	395-C5
	SAC	95831	378-H7
JILL LN	VAL	94589	510-C5
JIMENO LN	WDLD	95695	315-J6
JOAN DR	AMCN	94503	509-J2
	AMCN	94503	510-A2
JOAN ST	WSAC	95605	358-J1
JOANN CT	VAL	94589	509-J5
JODI CT	SolC	94534	471-G7
JOEL CT	VAL	94591	530-G5
JOHANSEN PL	BEN	94510	551-B4
JOHN ST	CCCo	94572	549-H7
JOHNFER WY	SAC	95831	378-J3
JOHN JONES RD	DVS	95616	356-A5
JOHNS PL	BEN	94510	551-A4
JOHNSON LN	VAL	94592	529-H3
	VAL	94592	529-H7
JOHNSON RD	SolC	95694	373-G3
JOHNSON ST	CCCo	94525	550-C5
	FRFD	94533	472-E6
	WDLD	95776	316-B4
JOHN WAYNE LN	SolC	95688	393-B7
JOICE ISLAND RD	SolC	94585	493-B7
JONES CT	FRFD	94533	452-H5
JORDAN CIR	WDLD	95695	315-G5
JORDAN ST	VAL	94591	530-C7
	VAL	94591	550-C1
JOSEPH GEREVAS DR	FRFD	94533	453-D7
	FRFD	94533	473-D1
JOSHUA TREE ST	DVS	95616	355-J6
	DVS	95616	356-A6
JOSIAH CIR	SUIS	94585	472-G7
JOSIAH CT	VAC	95688	413-J7
JOSIAH WY	SUIS	94585	472-G7
JOSIAH WING DR	FRFD	94533	453-D7
JOSLIN LN	SolC	95688	413-A6
JOY CT	DXN	95620	395-C6
JOYCE CT	WDLD	95776	316-D5
JOYCE LN	SolC	94534	451-E5
JUANITA CT	NAP	94559	450-A7
	VAL	94590	530-B2
JUANITA ST	NAP	94559	450-A7
JUDY CT	VAL	94591	530-F3
JUDY LN	SolC	95688	393-G7
JULIA CT	SUIS	94585	473-A5
JULIAN DR	WSAC	95605	358-J2
JULIAN LN	SolC	94534	471-F1
JULIANA LN	SolC	95688	412-F6
JULIE CT	FRFD	94533	472-F4
JULMAR CIR	FRFD	94534	491-E2
JULMAR CT	FRFD	94534	491-E2
JUNE CT	DXN	95620	395-B6
JUNEBUG LN	SolC	95688	413-E4
JUNIPER	BEN	94510	551-C6
JUNIPER CIR N	NaCo	94558	470-A1
JUNIPER CIR S	NaCo	94558	470-A1
JUNIPER CT	CCCo	94525	550-D5
	FRFD	94533	472-H1
	WDLD	95695	315-H5
JUNIPER DR	VAL	94589	529-J1
JUNIPER PL	DVS	95616	356-D6
JUNIPER ST	FRFD	94533	472-H1
	VAC	95688	433-B4
JUSTICE AV	SUIS	94585	472-G7
JUSTIN CT	VAL	94591	530-E3
JUSTIN WY	DXN	95620	395-B6
K			
K LN	FRFD	94533	473-F2
K ST	BEN	94510	551-D6
	DVS	95616	356-D7
	DVS	95616	376-D1
	VAL	94592	529-F3
E K ST	BEN	94510	551-C5
W K ST	BEN	94510	550-H3
	BEN	94510	551-A4
KAANAPALI DR	FRFD	94534	472-C1
KAISER DR	FRFD	94534	491-F1
KALAMAZOO PL	DVS	95618	356-F6
KANSAS ST	FRFD	94533	472-E5
	FRFD	94535	473-H3
	VAL	94592	529-G5
KAPALUA CT	FRFD	94534	472-C1
KAPPEL HILL DR	SolC	95688	433-B1
	VAC	95688	433-B1
KAPPEL VIEW LN	SolC	95688	413-B6
KAREN CT	VAL	94590	550-C2
KAREN DR	AMCN	94503	510-B4
	BEN	94510	551-A4
KARLY CT	AMCN	94503	510-B3
KATE LN	WDLD	95776	316-C5
KATHLEEN LN	WDLD	95695	315-G5
KATHY CIR	WSAC	95691	378-F2
KATHY CT	SAC	95831	378-G6
KATHY ELLEN CT	VAL	94591	530-D2
KATHY ELLEN DR	VAL	94591	530-D3
KATLEBA LN	SolC	95687	434-B5
KATZ AV	SAC	95831	378-J7
KAUAI RD	WSAC	95691	378-D2
KAWEAH ST	WSAC	95691	378-D3
KAY DR	VAL	94590	550-C2
KEARNEY ST	BEN	94510	531-B7
KEARNY CT	FRFD	94534	472-C4
KEARNY WY	VAC	95687	453-G1
KEATS DR	VAL	94591	530-F6
KEEL	SUIS	94585	472-G7
KEEL CT	DXN	95620	395-C5
	SAC	95831	378-H7
KEESLER CIR	SUIS	94585	473-C5
KEGLE DR	WSAC	95605	358-J1
KEITH CT	VAC	95687	433-H7
KEITH WY	VAC	95687	433-G6
KELLOGG ST	SUIS	94585	472-F7
	SUIS	94585	492-F1
KELLS CIR	VAC	95688	413-F7
KELLY RD	NaCo	94558	490-A1
	NaCo	94589	490-A3
S KELLY RD	NaCo	94589	490-A4
KELLY ST	FRFD	94535	473-F2
KELLY WY	RVIS	94571	516-H3
KELLY ISLAND RD	WSAC	95691	378-E2
KELLYN CT	BEN	94510	551-C1
KEMP LN	AMCN	94503	510-A4
KEMP WY	AMCN	94503	509-J4
KEMPER ST	VAL	94589	510-C6
KEN CT	VAL	94591	530-F3
KENDAL ST	VAC	95687	433-C5
KENDALL AV	CCCo	94525	550-C5
KENDRICK LN	VAC	95687	453-F2
KENNEDY CT	FRFD	94533	472-F5
KENNEDY DR	WIN	95694	373-D3
KENNEDY PL	DVS	95616	356-D6
KENNISON CT	VAL	94589	509-J5
KENRICK CT	FRFD	94534	491-C3
KENSINGTON DR	FRFD	94533	472-E4
KENSINGTON WY	AMCN	94503	509-J3
KENT CT	DXN	95620	395-C6
	WDLD	95695	315-F6
KENT DR	DVS	95616	356-A6
KENT PL	AMCN	94503	509-J3
KENT WY	AMCN	94503	509-J3
	FRFD	94533	472-E4
	VAC	95687	433-G7
KENTS CT	WSAC	95691	358-F7
KENTUCKY AV	WDLD	95695	315-J2
	WDLD	95695	316-A2
	WDLD	95776	316-A2
	YoCo	95695	315-J2
	YoCo	95695	316-A2
	YoCo	95776	316-A2
E KENTUCKY AV	WDLD	95776	316-C2
	YoCo	95776	316-C2
W KENTUCKY AV	WDLD	95695	315-G1
	YoCo	95695	315-G1
KENTUCKY ST	FRFD	94533	472-D6
	FRFD	94535	473-J2
	VAC	95688	433-C6
	VAL	94590	529-J4
	VAL	94590	530-A4
E KENTUCKY ST	FRFD	94533	472-G6
KENWERE CIR	FRFD	94535	473-J2
KENWOOD CT	FRFD	94534	452-F7
KENYON DR	VAC	95687	433-G7
KENYON WY	VAL	94589	510-D5
KERN AV	WDLD	95695	315-G3
N KERN AV	WDLD	95695	315-G2
KERRY CT	BEN	94510	530-J6
	VAC	95687	433-H7
KESTREL PL	DVS	95616	356-B4
KESWICK CT	VAL	94591	530-F3
KEVIN CT	VAL	94589	510-D5
KEVIN LN	AMCN	94503	510-B4
KEYES CT	SUIS	94585	473-B7
	SUIS	94585	493-B1
KEYES LN	SUIS	94585	493-B1
E KEYSTONE AV	WDLD	95695	316-A2
W KEYSTONE AV	WDLD	95695	315-J2
	WDLD	95695	316-A2
KEYSTONE CT	VAC	95687	433-H5
KIARA CIR	FRFD	94533	452-J7
KIDDER AV	FRFD	94533	472-H5
KIDS WY	DXN	95620	395-D5
KIDWELL RD	SolC	95620	375-G6
KILDARE LN	VAC	95688	433-E2
KILGARVAN CT	VAC	95688	433-D2
KILKENNY RD	SolC	95687	414-B7
	VAC	95687	414-B7
KILLINGSWORTH CIR	VAC	95687	433-G5
KILPATRICK ST	AMCN	94503	509-J4
KILTS CT	SolC	94534	471-A4
KILTY CT	VAL	94589	509-J5
KIM CT	BEN	94510	551-D4
	VAL	94591	530-D3
KIMBERLY CT	AMCN	94503	509-J4
	SUIS	94585	473-B6
	WSAC	95691	358-F7
	WSAC	95691	378-F1
KIMBERLY DR	AMCN	94503	509-J4
	AMCN	94503	510-A4
KIMMIE CT	SAC	95831	378-J7
KINCHELOE CT	WDLD	95776	316-E4
KINCHELOE DR	WDLD	95776	316-E5
KINDELT WY	WDLD	95776	336-D1
KING PL	WDLD	95695	315-F3
KINGBIRD CT	SAC	95831	378-G5
KING EDWARD CT	WSAC	95691	378-E2
KING EDWARD RD	WSAC	95691	378-E2
KINGFISHER WY	FRFD	94533	473-A4
KING LEOPOLD CT	VAL	94591	530-J1
KINGLET CT	SUIS	94585	473-C7
KINGLET ST	SUIS	94585	473-C6
KINGMAN CT	VAC	95687	433-C7
KINGMAN DR	VAC	95687	433-D7
KINGS CT	DXN	95620	394-J7
KINGS LN	SolC	94534	471-B5
KINGS WY	SUIS	94585	472-J5
	SUIS	94585	473-A5
KINGSBERRY CIR	VAC	95687	433-J5
KINGSBERRY CT	VAC	95687	433-J5
KINGSLAND CT	VAC	95687	433-F7
KINGSLAND DR	VAC	95687	433-F7
	VAC	95687	453-F1
KINGSLY LN	AMCN	94503	509-J3
KINGSMILL CIR	FRFD	94534	472-C2
KINGSMILL LN	FRFD	94534	472-C2
KINGSTON CT	DXN	95620	395-C5
	FRFD	94533	472-H2
KINGSTON DR	DXN	95620	395-C5
KINGSTON LN	VAL	94590	529-J5
KINGSWOOD AV	VAC	95687	433-J7
KINGSWOOD CT	FRFD	94585	491-D6
KINSALE CT	VAC	95688	433-D1
KINSELLA LN	YoCo	95616	374-H1
	YoCo	95694	374-H1
KINSINGTON ST	WSAC	95691	358-H7
KINSMILL CT	SUIS	94585	473-A7
KIOWA CT	VAC	95688	432-J4
KIP CT	BEN	94510	531-A7
KIRBY CT	DXN	95620	395-C6
	VAC	95687	453-F4
KIRBYSON CT	VAC	95688	433-B3
KIRKLAND AV	NaCo	94558	450-D6
	VAL	94592	529-G6
KIRKLAND RANCH RD	AMCN	94558	490-D2
	NaCo	94558	490-C2
	NaCo	94589	490-C2
	NAP	94558	490-D2
	NAP	94589	490-D2
KIRKWOOD CT	FRFD	94534	452-G7
	FRFD	94534	472-G1
	VAC	95687	453-G1
	VAL	94591	530-F4
KISKA DR	WDLD	95776	316-C5
KISSELL AL	VAL	94590	529-J4
	VAL	94590	530-A5
KIT CARSON WY	VAL	94589	509-J6
KITE ST	DVS	95616	356-B4
KLAMATH CT	AMCN	94503	490-A6
	FRFD	94533	452-J7
KLAMATH DR	FRFD	94533	472-J1
	VAC	95687	433-F7
KLAMATH RD	WSAC	95691	378-H1
KLAMATH WY	SUIS	94585	473-C6
KLEE PL	DVS	95618	356-E5
KLEIBER HALL DR	YoCo	95616	376-B2
KLEIN AV	VAL	94592	529-G6
KLINE CT	DVS	95618	356-F5
KNAPP ST	FRFD	94535	473-G4
KNAUER PL	YoCo	95695	315-F5
KNIGHT CT	DXN	95620	395-A7
KNIGHT DR	BEN	94510	530-J7
KNIGHTS CIR	VAL	94591	530-F4
KNIGHTS WY	AMCN	94503	509-J4
KNIGHTSBRIDGE CT	AMCN	94503	510-A3
KNIGHTSBRIDGE WY	AMCN	94503	509-J4
	AMCN	94503	510-A3
KNOLL DR	FRFD	94534	491-F1
	SolC	94534	491-F1
KNOLLWOOD CT	FRFD	94534	472-F1
KNOLLWOOD DR	WDLD	95695	315-G5
KOBERT CT	SolC	95694	393-J3
KOBERT RD	SolC	95694	393-J3
KODIAK DR	WDLD	95776	316-C5
KODIAK ISLAND PL	WSAC	95691	378-D2
KOLOB CT	FRFD	94534	472-C4
KOLOB DR	FRFD	94534	472-C4
KOLOB WY	FRFD	94534	472-C4
KOSO ST	DVS	95618	376-G1
KOVR DR	WSAC	95605	358-G2
KOZY LN	SolC	95687	434-H7
KREUSE CANYON DR	NaCo	94558	450-C7
	NaCo	94558	470-C1
KREUZER LN	NaCo	94558	450-C7
	NaCo	94558	470-D1
	NaCo	94559	450-C7
KRISTINA CT	VAL	94591	530-D5
KUTER DR	FRFD	94535	473-J1
L			
L LN	FRFD	94533	473-F2
L ST	DVS	95616	356-D6
	DVS	95616	376-D1
	VAL	94592	529-F3
E L ST	BEN	94510	551-C5
W L ST	BEN	94510	550-J3
	BEN	94510	551-A4
LABRADOR LN	BEN	94510	551-B4
LABRADOR WY	BEN	94510	551-B4
	SUIS	94585	473-A7
LA BREA ST	VAL	94591	530-C7
LA CADENA	VAL	94590	530-B2
LA CANADA WY	DVS	95618	376-H1
LA CANYADA DR	VAL	94591	530-C7
	VAL	94591	550-C1
LA CIENEGA AV	VAL	94589	530-B1
LA CIENEGA PL	VAL	94589	530-B1
LA CORUNO ST	DVS	95618	356-F7
LA COSTA CT	FRFD	94534	472-C2
	VAL	94591	530-G1
LA CRESENDA ST	VAL	94590	530-B3
LA CRESTA DR	VAC	95688	433-A6
LA CRUZ AV	BEN	94510	551-C4
LA CRUZ LN	VAC	95687	433-C7
	VAC	95687	453-C1
LADERA CT	DVS	95618	356-H7
LADERA DR	VAL	94591	530-D7
	VAL	94591	550-D1
LADYBUG LN	SolC	95688	413-E3
LA ESPERANZA DR	DXN	95620	395-D7
LAFAYETTE DR	DVS	95618	356-F6
LAFAYETTE RD	VAC	95687	433-H6
LAGO PL	DVS	95616	356-B4
LAGOON LN	WSAC	95691	378-G1
LAGOON VALLEY RD	VAC	94533	452-J3
	VAC	94533	453-A4
	VAC	95687	452-J3
	VAC	95687	453-A3
LA GRANDE AV	NaCo	94558	450-B1
LAGUNA AV	DVS	95618	376-G1
LAGUNA CT	FRFD	94533	472-J2
LAGUNA ST	VAL	94591	530-C7
LAGUNA CREEK TR	SolC	95688	452-F1
LAGUNITA CIR	FRFD	94533	472-J1
	FRFD	94533	473-A1
LAGUNITA CT	FRFD	94533	452-J7
	FRFD	94533	472-J1
LA HABRA CT	DVS	95618	376-F2
LAHOTAN CT	VAC	95687	433-F6
LAIN DR	VAL	94591	530-E4
LAINEY CT	VAL	94589	509-J5
LAIR CT	VAL	94591	530-E3
LA JOLLA ST	VAL	94591	550-D1
	WSAC	95691	358-J7
LAKE AV	CCCo	94572	549-H7
LAKE BLVD	DVS	95616	355-H7
	DVS	95616	375-J1
LAKE RD	WSAC	95691	358-C4
LAKEFRONT CT	FRFD	94533	473-A1
LAKE GLEN WY	SAC	95822	378-J5
LAKE HERMAN RD	BEN	94510	531-E6
	BEN	94510	551-H1
	SolC	94510	530-H3
	SolC	94510	531-A5
	SolC	94510	551-H1
	VAL	94510	530-H3
	VAL	94591	530-H3
LAKEHURST CT	FRFD	94533	472-H1
LAKEHURST DR	VAC	95687	433-G6
LAKE PARK DR	SAC	95831	378-J6
LAKESHORE CIR	SAC	95831	378-H6
LAKESHORE CT	FRFD	94534	491-D2
LAKESHORE DR	FRFD	94534	491-D2
LAKESIDE DR	VAL	94589	510-B6
LAKESPRING CT	FRFD	94534	491-B2

SOLANO CO.

STREET Name City ZIP Pg-Grid

LAKE TERRACE CIR
DVS 95616 355-G7
LAKEVIEW CIR
FRFD 94585 511-D1
LAKEVIEW CT
FRFD 94585 511-D1
LAKEVIEW DR
SolC 95688 393-F7
YoCo 95618 376-J1
LAKE VISTA CT
SAC 95831 378-H6
LAKE WASHINGTON BLVD
WSAC 95691 358-G7
WSAC 95691 378-J1
LAKEWOOD AV
VAL 94591 530-F4
LAKEWOOD DR
FRFD 94534 452-F7
WSAC 95691 358-H5
LA LONDE LN
NaCo 94558 450-B3
LAMAR CT
VAC 95687 433-H7
LAMB ST
FRFD 94535 473-J2
LAMBERT RD
SolC 94534 451-G7
SolC 94534 471-G1
LAMBRECHT DR
FRFD 94585 473-E6
LA MESA CT
DVS 95618 376-F2
SUIS 94585 473-D6
LA MIRADA CT
SUIS 94585 473-C6
LAMONT CT
VAL 94591 530-E5
LA MONTANITA CT
VAL 94589 530-C1
LANAI CT
WSAC 95691 378-D2
LANCASTER WY
VAL 94591 530-G5
LANCE DR
VAC 95687 433-G6
LANDAHL CT
BEN 94510 551-A3
LANDANA ST
AMCN 94503 509-J2
LANDMARK DR
VAL 94591 510-J5
VAL 94591 511-A5
LANDON CT
VAC 95688 433-A5
LANDS END CT
VAL 94591 530-G7
LANE ST
FRFD 94535 473-H4
LANG CT
SolC 94534 471-A4
LANGLEY WY
SUIS 94585 473-C6
LANGRELL WY
SAC 95831 378-F7
LANGSTON WY
SAC 95831 378-F7
LANGTON CT
VAL 94591 510-J4
VAL 94591 511-A4
LANI CT
VAC 95688 413-H6
LANSDOWNE PL
VAL 94591 510-J4
VAL 94591 511-A3
LANSFORD CT
AMCN 94503 509-J3
LANSING CIR
BEN 94510 531-D7
LANTANA PL
FRFD 94533 472-H1
LANZA LN
SolC 94534 451-F6
LA PALOMA CT
DVS 95618 376-F2
LA PAZ DR
DVS 95618 376-H1
LA PAZ ST
VAC 95687 453-C1
VAL 94591 530-C7
LAPIS CT
FRFD 94534 491-E1
LA PLAYA DR
DVS 95618 356-G6
LA PRENDA AV
BEN 94510 551-D4
LA QUINTA CT
FRFD 94534 472-C2
LAQUINTA CT
VAC 95687 453-E3
LARAMIE WY
VAC 95688 433-B4
LARCHMONT CIR
FRFD 94534 472-B3
LARCHMONT CT
FRFD 94534 472-B3
LARCHMONT DR
FRFD 94534 472-B3
LAREDO ST
NAP 94559 470-A1
LARGO CT
FRFD 94533 472-J2
LARK CIR
SUIS 94585 472-J6
LARK CT
AMCN 94503 509-H3
LARKIN CT
BEN 94510 551-A2
LARKIN DR
BEN 94510 550-J2
BEN 94510 551-A2
FRFD 94534 472-D4
LARKSPUR CT
BEN 94510 531-A7
LARKSPUR DR
VAC 95687 453-F2
LARKSPUR LN
FRFD 94533 472-G2
LARKSPUR PL
YoCo 95616 355-J2
LARKSPUR ST
AMCN 94503 509-J3
LARKWOOD CT
VAL 94591 530-F4
LARSEN CIR
VAL 94589 509-J6
LA RUE RD
YoCo 95616 376-B2
S LA RUE RD
YoCo 95616 376-B2
LA RUE WY
YoCo 95616 375-G1
LA SALLE CT
FRFD 94533 472-C7
LA SALLE WY
VAL 94591 530-G1
LAS ENCINAS CT
VAC 95687 453-C1
LAS HADAS CT
FRFD 94534 472-C2
LASIANDRA LN
YoCo 95616 355-A3

LAS PALMAS AV
VAL 94589 530-B1
LASSEN AV
SUIS 94585 473-C7
LASSEN CIR
VAC 95687 433-H4
LASSEN CT
DXN 95620 395-A7
RVIS 94571 516-G5
VAL 94591 530-D3
WSAC 95691 378-H2
LASSEN PL
DVS 95616 355-H6
WDLD 95695 315-H2
LASSEN ST
VAL 94591 530-D4
WSAC 95691 378-H2
LASSIK ST
WSAC 95691 378-H2
LAUGENOUR CT
WDLD 95776 316-D5
LAUGENOUR DR
WDLD 95776 316-C4
LAURAL DR
WDLD 95776 316-C5
LAURAS LN
SolC 95688 413-D4
LAUREL CT
BEN 94510 551-A1
LAUREL DR
FRFD 94533 472-F2
SolC 94534 471-H7
LAUREL LN
WSAC 95691 358-H3
LAUREL PL
DVS 95616 356-B7
RVIS 94571 516-F2
LAUREL ST
SolC 94591 530-D6
VAC 95688 433-C6
VAL 94591 530-D6
WDLD 95695 315-J4
WDLD 95695 316-A4
LAUREL WY
RVIS 94571 516-H4
LAUREL CREEK WY
FRFD 94533 472-J2
LAUREL OAK CT
VAC 95687 453-C1
LAUREL RIDGE CT
FRFD 94534 491-D1
LAURELWOOD CIR
VAC 95687 453-E4
LAURELWOOD CT
VAC 95687 453-E4
LAURELWOOD WY
VAC 95687 453-F4
LAUREN
VAL 94592 529-G7
LAUREN CT
WIN 95694 373-F3
LA VENIR LN
SolC 95688 413-B5
LA VERA CT
SolC 95688 412-F6
LA VERA LN
SolC 95688 412-F7
LA VIDA WY
DVS 95618 356-H7
DVS 95618 376-H2
LA VUELTA ST
VAL 94590 530-B3
LAWLER CENTER DR
SUIS 94585 472-J7
LAWLER RANCH PKWY
SUIS 94585 473-A7
SUIS 94585 493-B1
LAWNDALE CT
FRFD 94534 472-D2
LAWRENCE CT
FRFD 94533 472-E7
LAWRENCE DR
VAC 95687 433-G3
LAWRENCE ST
FRFD 94533 472-E7
LAWS AV
VAL 94592 529-G6
LAWSON LN
WDLD 95695 315-J5
LAYTON DR
DVS 95618 356-G6
LEAF AV
SAC 95831 378-J6
LEAFWOOD CT
FRFD 94585 511-E2
SUIS 94585 472-H6
LEAKE CIR
WDLD 95776 316-E6
LEANING OAK CT
FRFD 94585 511-F3
LEANING OAK DR
FRFD 94585 511-F3
LEDGEWOOD RD
SolC 94534 471-H3
LEE CT
WDLD 95776 316-D4
LEE DR
WDLD 95776 316-D4
LEE ST
VAL 94590 529-H3
LEEDS CT
BEN 94510 530-J6
LEESBURG CT
FRFD 94533 452-H7
LEEWARD CT
VAC 95687 433-J7
VAL 94591 550-F3
LEEWARD WY
SAC 95831 378-G7
LEGEND CIR
VAL 94591 530-E1
LEGION AV
DXN 95620 415-C2
LEHI CT
FRFD 94534 472-C4
LEHIGH DR
DVS 95616 356-E7
LEISURE WY
VAC 95687 433-J3
LEISURE TOWN RD
SolC 95687 433-J6
SolC 95687 453-J1
SolC 95688 393-J6
SolC 95688 394-A7
SolC 95688 413-J7
SolC 95688 414-A3
VAC 95687 433-J1
VAC 95687 453-J1
VAC 95688 413-J7
VAC 95688 433-J1
LEISUREVILLE CIR
WDLD 95776 316-B5
LEISUREVILLE DR
WDLD 95776 316-B6
LELAND HAVEN WY
SAC 95831 378-G6
LEMEN AV
WDLD 95776 316-B3
LEMEN LN
SolC 95688 413-E5
LEMON LN
DVS 95616 356-B6

LEMON ST
SolC 94590 530-B6
VAL 94590 530-B6
LEMONTREE RD
WSAC 95691 378-J1
LEMONWOOD WY
SUIS 94585 472-H6
LENA DR
AMCN 94503 509-J4
LENIJ AV
WIN 95694 373-E3
LENZI LN
VAL 94591 530-D6
LEO WY
WDLD 95776 316-B5
LEON PL
DVS 95616 356-C4
LEONARD DR
VAC 95688 433-E1
LEONARD ST
VAL 94589 510-C6
LEONARDO CT
DVS 95618 356-F5
FRFD 94534 491-D2
LEONARDO ST
DVS 95618 356-F5
LEONARDO WY
FRFD 94534 491-D3
LESLIE LN
WSAC 95691 378-E1
LESSLEY PL
DVS 95616 356-E7
LETTERMAN ST
WSAC 95691 358-J7
LEVEE RD
SolC 95620 375-H4
SolC 95620 376-A4
WSAC 95691 358-C7
WSAC 95691 378-B2
YoCo 95616 375-D3
YoCo 95691 378-B7
LEWIS AV
SolC 94591 530-D7
VAL 94591 530-D7
WDLD 95695 315-G6
LEWIS CT
FRFD 94533 472-F3
LEWIS RD
SolC 95687 414-D6
SolC 95687 434-D4
SolC 95687 454-D3
VAC 95687 434-D7
VAC 95687 454-D3
LEWIS BROWN RD
VAL 94589 510-A6
LEWISTON RD
WSAC 95691 378-D4
LEXINGTON CT
VAC 95687 453-H2
WDLD 95695 316-A2
LEXINGTON DR
VAL 94591 530-F5
LEXINGTON WY
FRFD 94534 472-C5
WDLD 95695 316-A2
LIBERTY CT
AMCN 94503 510-B4
VAC 95687 453-H2
LIBERTY DR
SUIS 94585 472-G7
WDLD 95776 336-E1
LIBERTY LN
SolC 95688 413-D5
VAC 95688 413-D5
WDLD 95776 336-E1
LIBERTY PL
FRFD 94534 472-C5
LIBERTY ST
AMCN 94503 510-A4
LIBERTY ISLAND RD
RVIS 94571 516-E2
LIGHTHOUSE CT
FRFD 94534 472-E3
VAL 94590 529-H2
LIGHTHOUSE DR
FRFD 94534 472-E3
VAL 94590 529-H2
WSAC 95605 358-J1
LIGHTHOUSE WY
VAC 95688 413-E7
LIGHTSHIP CT
VAL 94591 550-F2
LILAC CT
BEN 94510 551-A1
VAC 95687 453-G4
VAL 94589 509-J6
LILAC LN
WSAC 95691 358-H3
LILAC ST
FRFD 94533 472-F2
LILLARD DR
DVS 95618 376-F1
LILLEAN CT
VAL 94589 510-C5
LILLEAN WY
VAL 94589 510-C5
LILLIAN ST
CCCo 94525 550-D5
LILLYS LN
SolC 95688 413-E6
LILY PL
WSAC 95691 378-E2
LILY ST
FRFD 94533 472-F2
LIMERICK PL
VAC 95688 433-E2
LIMERICK WY
VAC 95688 433-E2
LIMESTONE DR
VAL 94589 510-C6
LIMEWOOD CT
FRFD 94585 511-E2
LIMEWOOD RD
WSAC 95691 378-J1
LIMEWOOD ST
SUIS 94585 472-H6
LINCOLN AV
WDLD 95695 315-J4
WDLD 95695 316-A4
W LINCOLN AV
WDLD 95695 315-G4
LINCOLN CT
AMCN 94503 510-B4
S LINCOLN CT
DXN 95620 395-B6
LINCOLN RD
SolC 94591 530-C6
VAL 94591 530-C5
LINCOLN RD E
VAL 94591 530-C7
VAL 94591 550-C1
LINCOLN RD W
SolC 94590 530-C6
VAL 94590 530-C6
VAL 94590 550-C1
LINCOLN ST
BEN 94510 551-D6
FRFD 94533 472-F5
WIN 95694 373-D4
N LINCOLN ST
DXN 95620 395-C4
S LINCOLN ST
DXN 95620 395-B7

S LINCOLN ST
DXN 95620 415-B2
SolC 95620 415-B2
LINDA ST
VAC 95688 433-B5
LINDA VISTA AV
BEN 94510 551-D4
LINDA VISTA LN
SolC 95688 393-A7
LINDA VISTA WY
RVIS 94571 516-H4
LINDEN AV
FRFD 94533 472-J1
LINDEN CT
FRFD 94533 472-J1
LINDEN LN
DVS 95616 356-B7
LINDEN PL
WDLD 95695 315-H5
LINDEN RD
WSAC 95691 358-F7
WSAC 95691 378-H1
LINDEN ST
NAP 94559 450-A7
LINDO PL
DVS 95616 356-C4
LINDO ST
BEN 94510 551-D5
LINE ST
SUIS 94585 492-F1
LINFIELD DR
VAL 94589 510-B6
LINFORD LN
DXN 95620 395-B6
LINK RD
FRFD 94534 491-F3
LINVALE CT
SAC 95822 378-J3
LINWOOD LN
AMCN 94503 509-J7
LINWOOD PL
VAC 95688 433-A5
LINWOOD ST
VAC 95688 433-A5
LIPPIZAN DR
VAL 94591 530-E2
LISA CT
AMCN 94503 509-J4
LISBON AV
WSAC 95605 358-G1
LISBURN WY
VAC 95688 413-F7
VAC 95688 433-E1
LISLIN WY
VAL 94590 530-C2
LITCHFIELD CT
VAL 94589 509-J4
LITER CT
DXN 95620 395-A7
LITTLE LN
DXN 95620 395-C5
LITTLE RIVER CT
VAL 94591 550-E2
LITTLE RIVER ST
VAL 94591 550-E2
LITTLE ROCK CIR
SUIS 94585 473-C5
LIVE OAK CT
VAC 95687 433-H7
VAL 94591 530-F5
LIVEOAK CT
FRFD 94585 511-E2
LIVINGSTON PL
RVIS 94571 516-F2
LIVINGSTONE AV
VAC 95687 453-H1
LIWAI VILLAGE CT
WIN 95694 373-E4
LLOYD CT
BEN 94510 531-C7
LOBELIA DR
VAL 94589 509-J6
LOCHEARN CT
VAC 95688 433-D2
LOCH LOMOND DR
VAC 95687 433-H7
LOCH LOMOND WY
FRFD 94534 491-E2
LOCKE RD
SolC 95688 393-H7
SolC 95688 413-H4
N LOCKE RD
SolC 95688 393-H7
LOCKEFORD SPRINGS CT
VAC 95688 413-E7
LOCKIE LN
FRFD 94533 453-D7
SolC 94533 453-D7
LOCKWOOD DR
VAL 94591 530-F5
LOCUST CT
VAL 94591 530-F3
LOCUST DR
VAL 94591 530-F3
LOCUST PL
DVS 95618 356-E6
LOCUST ST
FRFD 94533 472-J1
WDLD 95695 315-J3
LOCUST WY
WDLD 95776 316-C5
LODI CT
VAL 94589 510-B5
LOFAS PL
VAL 94589 510-A7
LOGAN ST
RVIS 94571 516-H5
LOIRE CT
VAL 94591 530-F2
LOIS LN
SUIS 94585 473-A5
VAL 94590 530-C3
LOJAS CT
VAC 95688 433-B3
LOLA DR
WDLD 95776 316-B4
LOMA CT
SUIS 94585 473-C6
LOMA HEIGHTS RD
NaCo 94558 450-B3
LOMA VISTA
VAL 94590 530-B3
LOMA VISTA PL
WDLD 95695 315-H6
LOMBARD RD
AMCN 94503 490-A7
LOMITA AV
VAC 95688 433-D4
LOMITA CT
FRFD 94534 472-C3
LONDON CIR
BEN 94510 550-H2
LONDON CT
FRFD 94533 472-F4
LONDON DR
BEN 94510 550-H2
LONDON LN
FRFD 94533 472-F4
LONE OAK DR
VAC 95688 433-D1
LONE PINE CT
WSAC 95691 358-J7

LONG ST
SUIS 94585 492-F1
LONGCROFT ST
WSAC 95691 358-H5
LONGFORD LN
VAC 95688 433-E2
LONG ISLAND RD
WSAC 95691 378-C2
LONGRIDGE DR
VAL 94591 530-F7
LONGS TR
SolC 95688 393-F7
LONGSPUR DR
SUIS 94585 473-A6
LONGVIEW CT
VAC 95687 433-G7
LONGVIEW DR
FRFD 94534 472-E1
VAC 95687 433-G7
VAC 95687 453-G1
LONGWOOD PL
VAC 95688 433-B4
LON HILLS
RVIS 94571 516-F1
LOOKOUT CT
SAC 95831 378-G6
LOOKOUT DR
VAL 94591 550-D2
LOOKOUT HILL RD
FRFD 94534 491-F2
LOPES CT
WDLD 95776 316-B5
LOPES RD
FRFD 94534 491-E5
FRFD 94585 491-E5
FRFD 94585 511-E1
SolC 94510 511-G4
SolC 94510 531-H1
SolC 94585 511-G4
LOPEZ ISLAND RD
WSAC 95691 378-C3
LORA CT
VAL 94591 530-F3
LORAINE CT
VAC 95688 433-B5
LORENE CIR
VAL 94589 510-A4
LORENZO DR
VAL 94589 509-J5
VAL 94589 510-A5
LORI DR
BEN 94510 551-A3
WSAC 95691 358-D4
LORING AV
CCCo 94525 550-D4
LORRAINE DR
NaCo 94558 450-A1
LOS ALTOS DR
AMCN 94503 509-J2
AMCN 94503 510-A1
LOS CERRITOS DR
VAL 94589 510-C7
VAL 94589 530-C1
LOS CERROS PL
DVS 95618 356-G6
LOS GATOS AV
VAL 94589 530-C1
LOSOYA DR
WDLD 95776 316-D5
LOS ROBLES CT
VAC 95687 453-C1
LOS ROBLES DR
NaCo 94559 450-A7
LOS ROBLES ST
DVS 95618 376-G1
VAC 95687 453-C1
LOS ROBLES WY
WDLD 95695 315-H6
LOS SANTOS CT
VAL 94590 530-B2
LOTZ WY
SUIS 94585 472-F7
LOUISE CT
VAL 94590 530-B2
LOUISE LN
YoCo 95618 376-E2
LOUISIANA ST
VAL 94590 529-J4
VAL 94590 530-A4
LOVERS LN
VAC 95688 433-B6
LOW CT
FRFD 94534 492-B1
LOWE DR
WDLD 95776 316-D5
LOYOLA DR
DVS 95618 356-F6
LOYOLA WY
VAL 94589 510-B6
LOZANO LN
SolC 94534 472-C6
LOZIER AL
VAL 94590 529-J4
VAL 94590 530-A4
LUANN CT
VAL 94589 510-B7
LUCENA CT
DVS 95618 356-G7
LUCERO PL
WDLD 95776 316-C5
LUCINA ST
AMCN 94503 510-A4
LUGO DR
FRFD 94533 473-C4
LUIS PL
WIN 95694 373-E3
LUKE ST
FRFD 94535 473-J2
FRFD 94535 474-A2
LUNA DR
VAL 94591 530-D7
VAL 94591 550-D1
LUPIN CT
FRFD 94533 472-G2
LUPINE CIR
VAC 95687 453-H1
LUPINE CT
BEN 94510 550-J1
YoCo 95616 355-J2
LUPINE WY
WIN 95694 373-E3
LUPINE HILL RD
NaCo 94558 450-A3
LUSK DR
WDLD 95776 316-D5
LUTHER E GIBSON FRWY I-680
BEN - 531-H6
BEN - 551-E5
FRFD - 491-E6
FRFD - 511-F3
SolC - 491-E6
SolC - 511-F3
SolC - 531-H6
LUZ PL
DVS 95616 356-C4
LUZENA AV
VAC 95688 433-B6
LYLE WY
YoCo 95618 376-E2
LYNBROOK DR
FRFD 94585 511-D1

LYNCH PL
BEN 94510 551-C1
LYNCH RD
SolC 94585 490-H7
SolC 94589 490-H7
LYND WY
DXN 95620 395-B7
LYNDELL TER
DVS 95616 356-A6
LYNDHURST LN
VAL 94591 510-J5
LYNN CT
VAL 94591 530-E4
LYON CT
BEN 94510 551-A1
LYON RD
FRFD 94534 452-G6
SolC 94534 452-G4
LYTHAM WY
VAL 94591 530-G3

M

M ST
DVS 95616 356-E7
VAL 94592 529-F3
W M ST
BEN 94510 551-B4
MACBETH CT
VAC 95687 433-H7
MACDONALD CT
DXN 95620 395-B6
MACE BLVD Rt#-E6
DVS 95618 356-J6
DVS 95618 376-J1
YoCo 95618 356-J6
YoCo 95618 376-J1
MACHADO WY
SAC 95822 378-J5
MACK PL
WDLD 95776 336-D1
MACK WY
WDLD 95776 336-D1
MACKEREL CT
FRFD 94533 452-H7
MACKINAC RD
WSAC 95691 378-E2
MACTAVISH CT
SolC 94534 471-A4
MADDALENA PL
FRFD 94534 491-D3
MADDALENA WY
FRFD 94534 491-C3
MADDEN CT
DXN 95620 395-C4
MADDEN DR
DXN 95620 395-C4
MADERA CT
DVS 95618 356-H6
WDLD 95695 315-G3
MADERA DR
DXN 95620 395-A7
MADERE WY
RVIS 94571 516-H3
MADIGAN AV
VAL 94590 530-C5
MADISON AV
VAC 95687 453-F2
MADISON PL
WDLD 95776 316-B6
MADISON ST
BEN 94510 551-E6
FRFD 94533 472-F6
MADONNA DR
SUIS 94585 473-D6
MADRID CT
DVS 95616 356-B5
NAP 94559 450-A7
MADRID ST
DVS 95616 356-B5
MADRONE AV
VAL 94592 529-G6
WSAC 95691 358-H3
MADRONE CIR
VAL 94592 529-H6
MADRONE CT
FRFD 94534 472-C3
VAL 94592 529-H6
WIN 95694 373-G3
MADRONE DR
FRFD 94534 472-C3
NaCo 94558 470-A2
MADRONE LN
DVS 95618 356-E6
MADRONE PL
DVS 95616 356-E6
VAL 94592 529-H6
MADRONE ST
VAC 95688 433-B4
VAL 94592 529-H6
MADRONE WY
WDLD 95695 315-H6
MADSON PL
DVS 95618 356-F7
MAEDELL WY
WDLD 95695 315-J5
MAGAZINE ST
SolC 94591 550-D1
VAL 94590 530-C7
VAL 94590 550-B1
VAL 94591 530-D7
VAL 94591 550-D1
MAGELLAN ST
DVS 95616 355-G6
MAGILL ST
VAL 94589 530-A1
MAGNOLIA AV
VAC 95688 433-B6
MAGNOLIA CT
DXN 95620 415-B1
FRFD 94533 472-H1
MAGNOLIA DR
RVIS 94571 516-F1
MAGNOLIA PL
DVS 95618 356-E6
MAGPIE ST
DVS 95616 356-B4
MAHER CT
VAL 94591 530-C3
MAHOGANY CT
FRFD 94533 473-A1
MAHOGANY WY
FRFD 94533 473-A1
MAHOGONY DR
VAL 94589 510-A7
MAHONEY ST
CCCo 94572 549-H7
MAIDU PL
DVS 95616 376-G1
MAIN ST
AMCN 94503 490-A7
AMCN 94503 510-A1
RVIS 94571 516-H5
SUIS 94585 472-F7
SUIS 94585 492-F1
VAC 95688 433-C5
WDLD 95695 315-H4
WDLD 95695 316-A4
WDLD 95776 316-A4
WIN 95694 373-D3
E MAIN ST
WDLD 95776 316-B4
WIN 95694 373-G3

E MAIN ST
YoCo 95776 316-F4
W MAIN ST
WDLD 95695 315-G3
MAIN ST E
VAC 95688 433-D5
MAINE ST
FRFD 94535 473-G3
VAL 94590 529-J5
VAL 94590 530-A5
MAIN GATE TER
BEN 94510 551-D5
MAINSAIL CT
FRFD 94534 472-E2
VAL 94591 550-G2
MAJESTIC CT
VAL 94591 530-J1
MAJORCA CT
VAC 95688 433-B3
MALAGA AV
DVS 95616 356-B5
MALAGA CT
VAL 94591 530-F6
MALAGA LN
WIN 95694 373-F3
MALAGA ST
VAL 94591 530-F6
MALCOLM ISLAND ST
WSAC 95691 378-C2
MALIBUR CT
VAC 95687 433-H6
MALIBU CT
FRFD 94533 472-J3
WSAC 95691 378-H1
MALLARD CT
FRFD 94533 473-A3
VAC 95687 453-F3
MALLARD DR
BEN 94510 551-F3
WDLD 95695 315-G1
YoCo 95695 315-G1
MALLARD ST
VAL 94589 510-B5
MALLORCA LN
DVS 95618 356-F7
MALONEY CT
SUIS 94585 473-B7
MALVASIA CT
FRFD 94534 491-F5
MAMMOTH CT
VAC 95688 413-H6
MAMMOTH WY
SUIS 94585 473-C6
MANCHESTER DR
FRFD 94533 473-E2
FRFD 94535 473-E3
MANCHESTER LN
FRFD 94533 473-E3
MANCHESTER ST
WSAC 95691 358-H7
MANCHESTER WY
VAC 95687 433-E7
MANDARIN CIR
VAC 95687 433-H3
MANDARIN CT
WSAC 95691 378-F1
MANDEVILLE WY
WSAC 95691 358-F7
WSAC 95691 378-F1
MANDURA RD
WSAC 95691 378-D2
MANET PL
DVS 95618 356-E5
MANGELS BLVD
FRFD 94534 491-E2
MANHATTAN DR
VAL 94591 530-D4
MANKAS BLVD
FRFD 94534 472-D3
MANKAS CT
FRFD 94534 472-D3
MANKAS CORNER RD
FRFD 94534 472-A3
SolC 94534 471-H1
SolC 94534 472-A3
MANNING WY
DXN 95620 395-A7
MANOR CT
AMCN 94503 510-A3
MANOR PL
FRFD 94533 472-J4
MANUEL CAMPOS PKWY
FRFD 94533 452-H7
FRFD 94533 453-A7
FRFD 94533 473-A1
MANZANITA AV
FRFD 94533 472-F2
MANZANITA DR
VAC 95688 433-D4
VAL 94591 530-B2
MANZANITA LN
DVS 95618 356-F5
MANZANITA WY
WIN 95694 373-G3
WSAC 95691 358-H2
MAPLE
BEN 94510 551-B6
MAPLE AV
VAL 94591 530-D4
MAPLE LN
DVS 95616 356-A7
WIN 95694 373-G3
MAPLE RD
SolC 95687 433-J3
SolC 95687 434-A3
VAC 95687 433-J3
MAPLE ST
SUIS 94585 492-F1
VAC 95688 433-C6
WSAC 95691 358-H3
MAPLE WY
WDLD 95695 315-G5
MAPLEGATE CT
FRFD 94585 511-E3
MARBELLA CT
AMCN 94503 510-B4
MARBELLA LN
VAC 95688 433-B3
MARBLE CT
VAL 94589 510-B5
MARBURY CT
FRFD 94533 472-H1
MARCELLO CT
AMCN 94503 510-C4
MARCIA LN
SUIS 94585 473-A5
MARCO LN
VAC 95688 433-B3
MARDEN ST
DVS 95618 357-A7
MARECA WY
WSAC 95691 378-F1
MARE ISLAND CT
WSAC 95691 378-E3
MARE ISLAND WY
VAL 94590 529-H4
VAL 94590 530-A5
MARENDA DR
DXN 95620 395-A6
MARGARET CT
VAL 94590 550-C1
MARGARET LN
SolC 95694 393-D1

564 MARGO LN
SOLANO COUNTY STREET INDEX
MUSCOVY CT

SOLANO CO.

STREET Name City ZIP Pg-Grid

MARGO LN
SolC 94591 530-D6
MARGURITE DR
DXN 95620 395-C5
MARI CT
VAL 94589 509-J5
MARIA DR
NAP 94559 450-A7
NAP 94559 470-A1
MARIANNA
RVIS 94571 516-F1
MARIE CT
SolC 95688 412-F6
MARIE LN
SolC 95688 412-F5
MARIETTA CT
FRFD 94585 491-D7
FRFD 94585 511-D1
MARIGOLD CT
FRFD 94533 472-F2
MARIGOLD DR
FRFD 94533 472-H1
VAL 94589 509-J6
MARIGOLD ST
WSAC 95691 358-E4
MARILYN PL
VAL 94590 530-B3
MARIN CT
VAC 95687 433-G5
MARIN PL
WDLD 95695 315-G3
MARIN ST
VAL 94590 529-J4
VAL 94590 530-A3
MARINA BLVD
SUIS 94585 472-G6
SUIS 94585 492-G1
MARINA CIR
DVS 95616 355-G6
SUIS 94585 492-G1
MARINA DR
RVIS 94571 516-H6
MARINA PL
BEN 94510 551-A4
MARINA GREENS DR
WSAC 95691 358-J6
MARINA RIDGE CT
VAL 94591 550-E2
MARINA VILLAGE WY
BEN 94510 551-B6
MARINER DR
VAL 94591 530-G7
MARINE WORLD PKWY
VAL 94589 509-J7
VAL 94589 510-A7
MARINE WORLD PKWY Rt#-37
SolC 94589 509-J7
SolC 94589 529-H1
VAL 94589 509-J7
VAL 94589 510-B6
VAL 94589 529-H1
VAL 94590 529-H1
MARIPOSA AV
VAC 95687 453-D1
MARIPOSA CIR
DVS 95618 376-F2
MARIPOSA DR
DXN 95620 394-J7
DXN 95620 395-A6
MARIPOSA ST
CCCo 94572 549-H7
VAL 94590 530-C3
WDLD 95695 315-H2
MARIPOSA WY
FRFD 94533 452-J6
MARITIME ACADEMY DR
VAL 94590 550-C1
MARK AV
VAL 94589 510-C6
MARKET LN
DXN 95620 395-A6
MARKHAM AV
VAC 95688 433-D3
MARKHAM CT
FRFD 94534 472-D4
MARKLEY LN
FRFD 94533 473-E1
SolC 94533 473-E1
MARKS RD
RVIS 94571 516-F3
MARLA DR
AMCN 94503 509-J4
AMCN 94503 510-A4
MARLOWE CT
VAC 95687 433-J7
MAR MONTE CT
VAL 94590 530-B2
MARNA DR
VAC 95687 453-F2
MARQUETTE
VAL 94589 510-A5
MARQUETTE CT
FRFD 94533 472-B7
MARQUETTE WY
FRFD 94533 472-B7
MARSALA PL
AMCN 94503 510-B2
MARSH 34
FRFD 94533 452-H7
MARSHALL AV
WDLD 95695 315-J5
WDLD 95695 316-A5
W MARSHALL AV
WDLD 95695 315-H5
MARSHALL CT
VAC 95687 433-C7
MARSHALL RD
VAC 95687 433-C7
VAC 95687 453-B1
WSAC 95691 378-D3
MARSHALL WY
VAL 94589 509-J6
MARSHCREEK DR
AMCN 94503 509-J4
MARSHFIELD RD
VAL 94591 510 J4
MARSHVIEW RD
SolC 94510 511-H6
MARSTON CT
SUIS 94585 473-B7
SUIS 94585 493-B1
MARSTON ST
WSAC 95605 358-J1
MARTEL CT
VAL 94589 509-H5
MARTIN AV
FRFD 94535 473-H2
MARTIN CT
BEN 94510 551-B2
DXN 95620 395-C4
MARTIN RD
FRFD 94534 472-E1
MARTIN ST
VAL 94589 510-A5
MARTIN WY
WDLD 95695 315-J4
MARTINEZ WY
WIN 95694 373-E2
MARTINIQUE ST
WSAC 95691 378-D3
MARTIS ST
WSAC 95691 378-D4

MARVIN WY
DXN 95620 395-B7
DXN 95620 415-C1
MARVIN GARDENS CIR
VAC 95687 433-G5
MARVIN GARDENS DR
VAC 95687 433-F5
MARY CT
BEN 94510 531-C7
MARYLAND AV
WDLD 95695 315-H2
WSAC 95691 358-J4
MARYLAND CIR
FRFD 94535 473-H3
MARYLAND CT
WSAC 95691 358-H6
MARYLAND ST
FRFD 94533 472-F5
MARYMANUEL CIR
SAC 95831 378-G6
MASON CT
DXN 95620 395-B6
MASON RD
SolC 94534 471-B7
SolC 94534 491-B1
MASON ST
VAC 95687 433-D6
VAC 95688 433-D6
MASONIC CT
VAL 94591 530-E3
MASONIC DR
VAL 94591 530-E3
MASSIE CT
WSAC 95691 378-D1
MAST
SUIS 94585 472-G7
MAST CT
DXN 95620 395-C5
SAC 95831 378-H7
WDLD 95776 316-D5
MASTERSON CT
VAC 95687 433-H5
MATHEWS CT
VAC 95687 433-F7
MATHEWS DR
VAC 95687 433-F7
MATISSE ST
DVS 95618 356-E5
MATMOR RD
WDLD 95776 316-B3
MATTHEW CT
FRFD 94533 472-J5
VAL 94591 530-E3
MATTHEW DR
FRFD 94533 472-J5
MATTOS DR
VAL 94591 530-E4
MAUI DR
WDLD 95776 316-C5
MAUI ST
WSAC 95691 378-D2
MAUPIN LN
FRFD 94533 472-D5
MAURER WY
VAL 94591 530-E4
MAURINE CT
VAL 94590 550-C1
MAVERICK LN
SolC 95688 413-H1
MAXWELL AL
VAL 94590 529-J4
VAL 94590 530-A4
MAXWELL AV
WDLD 95776 316-E5
MAXWELL LN
SUIS 94585 473-D5
MAXWELL WY
FRFD 94534 492-B1
MAY ST
WSAC 95605 358-H1
MAYBECK CT
VAC 95688 413-J7
MAYBERRY CT
FRFD 94533 472-F5
E MAYES ST
DXN 95620 415-D1
W MAYES ST
DXN 95620 415-C1
MAYFAIR AV
VAL 94591 530-D4
MAYFAIR DR
DXN 95620 415-B1
MAYFIELD CIR
SUIS 94585 473-B7
MAYFIELD CT
FRFD 94533 473-B4
MAYFIELD WY
SUIS 94585 473-A7
MAYO AV
VAL 94590 530-C5
MAYO CT
BEN 94510 530-J6
VAC 95688 433-E1
MAYWOOD CT
VAC 95687 453-H1
MAYWOOD DR
VAL 94591 530-F4
MAYWOOD WY
FRFD 94533 472-H1
MCALLISTER DR
BEN 94510 531-C7
BEN 94510 551-C1
MCARTHUR AV
WIN 95694 373-D4
MCCALL DR
BEN 94510 531-B7
BEN 94510 551-B1
MCCARTHY CT
DXN 95620 395-C5
MCCLELLAN DR
SUIS 94585 473-C5
MCCLELLAN ST
VAC 95688 433-D5
MCCORMACK CT
DXN 95620 395-C5
MCCOY CT
FRFD 94533 473-C2
MCCOY CREEK CIR
SUIS 94585 472-J7
MCCOY CREEK CT
SUIS 94585 472-J7
SUIS 94585 473-A7
MCCOY CREEK WY
SUIS 94585 472-J7
MCCREADY CT
SolC 94534 471-A3
MCCRORY RD
SolC 94533 454-A5
SolC 95687 453-J5
SolC 95687 454-A5
MCCULLEN ST
FRFD 94535 473-G3
MCCUNE RD
SolC 95694 393-J2
SolC 95694 394-A2
MCDOUGAL ST
VAL 94590 529-H2
MCEATHRON LN
SolC 95688 393-H7
SolC 95688 413-H1
MCEWEN RD
CCCo 94569 550-G7

MCFALL CT
SUIS 94585 473-B7
MCGARY RD
FRFD 94585 491-A7
NaCo 94591 510-F4
SolC 94585 490-J7
SolC 94585 491-A7
SolC 94585 510-H2
VAL 94585 510-H2
MCGREGOR CT
SolC 94534 470-J5
MCGRUE AV
VAL 94589 510-C5
MCGRUE CIR
VAL 94589 510-C5
MCGUIRE CIR
SUIS 94585 473-C5
MCGUIRE ST
FRFD 94535 473-H1
MCINNIS LN
FRFD 94533 453-E7
MCINTYRE LN
DXN 95620 395-C5
MCKAY WY
BEN 94510 551-A4
MCKEE CT
VAL 94589 510-D6
MCKELUME DR
VAL 94589 509-H5
MCKENNA CT
BEN 94510 531-D7
MCKENZIE CT
DXN 95620 395-C6
MCKENZIE DR
DXN 95620 395-C6
MCKEVITT AV
VAC 95688 413-J7
MCKINLEY AV
WDLD 95695 315-J5
N MCKINLEY AV
WDLD 95695 315-J3
MCKINLEY CIR
VAC 95687 433-H4
MCKINLEY ST
FRFD 94533 472-H5
MCKINLEY WY
WSAC 95691 358-H3
MCLANE ST
VAL 94590 530-B7
MCMANNIS LN
VAL 94590 529-J3
MCMATH CT
DXN 95620 395-C5
MCMURTRY LN
SolC 95688 413-C6
VAC 95688 413-C6
MCNABE CT
SUIS 94585 473-B7
SUIS 94585 493-B1
MCNAIR ST
VAL 94590 529-H2
MCNARY WY
WDLD 95776 316-D7
MCNEELY CT
NAP 94559 470-A1
MCNEILL CIR
WDLD 95695 315-G4
MCNEILL LN
SolC 95694 374-E4
MCNIGHT LN
VAC 95688 433-C6
MEADE CT
VAC 95687 433-J7
E MEADOW LN
FRFD 94534 491-F3
MEADOW RD
WSAC 95691 358-H4
MEADOW BAY DR
AMCN 94503 509-J4
MEADOWBROOK CT
VAL 94591 530-F5
MEADOWBROOK DR
YoCo 95618 376-H2
MEADOWBROOK LN
RVIS 94571 516-F2
SolC 95688 413-A1
MEADOW GLEN CT
FRFD 94533 472-J2
MEADOWHAWK DR
VAC 95687 453-F3
MEADOWLARK CIR
WSAC 95691 378-G1
MEADOWLARK DR
FRFD 94533 472-J3
FRFD 94533 473-A3
VAC 95687 433-J7
VAC 95687 453-J1
MEADOWOOD CT
WDLD 95695 315-G5
MEADOWOOD DR
WDLD 95695 315-F5
MEADOWRIDGE DR
FRFD 94534 491-D1
MEADOWS CIR
WDLD 95695 315-H5
MEADOWS CT
FRFD 94585 491-D6
VAC 95688 433-D4
MEADOWS DR
VAC 95688 433-D4
VAL 94589 509-G5
VAL 94589 510-A5
MEADOW VALLEY CIR
FRFD 94534 491-F3
MEADOW VIEW CT
VAC 95688 433-B6
MEADOW VIEW DR
VAC 95688 433-A6
MECCA CT
FRFD 94534 472-C3
MEDEIROS LN
AMCN 94503 509-J1
AMCN 94503 510-A1
MEDINA CT
FRFD 94533 473-C4
MEDITERRANEAN PL
WSAC 95691 358-G6
MED SCI DR
YoCo 95616 376-A2
MEEHAN CT
SUIS 94585 473-B7
MEGINNISS RD
VAL 94592 549-H1
MEISTER WY
SaCo 95837 317-J4
MELBA DR
VAL 94589 510-A5
MELISSA CT
VAC 95687 453-F4
MELISSA LN
SolC 95688 413-J4
SolC 95688 414-A4
MELLO PL
DVS 95616 356-D6
MELLOWOOD CT
SUIS 94585 472-H6
MELODY LN
VAL 94591 530-F1
MELROSE CT
VAC 95687 433-H7
VAC 95687 453-G1
MELVIN RD
AMCN 94503 510-A2

MEMORIAL LN
WDLD 95695 315-H4
MENDES LN
SolC 95688 433-B1
MENDOCINO CT
DXN 95620 394-J7
DXN 95620 395-A6
WSAC 95691 378-D3
MENDOCINO ST
VAL 94590 530-C4
WSAC 95691 378-D3
MENDOCINO WY
SUIS 94585 473-C7
MENLO CT
VAC 95687 453-C1
VAL 94589 510-B6
MENLO DR
DVS 95616 356-D6
MENTOR LN
SolC 95688 413-G5
MERCED DR
DVS 95618 356-G5
MERCED WY
WSAC 95691 378-H1
MERCEDES AV
DVS 95616 356-C4
MERCHANT ST
CCCo 94525 550-C4
VAC 95688 433-C6
MERGANSER DR
SUIS 94585 472-H6
MERGANSER PL
DVS 95616 356-B4
MERGANSERS CT
WSAC 95691 378-F1
MERIDIAN RD
SolC 95687 434-B6
SolC 95687 454-B4
VAC 95687 434-B6
MERIDIAN RD N
SolC 95620 394-C6
SolC 95687 414-B6
SolC 95688 394-C7
SolC 95688 414-B4
VAC 95687 414-B6
VAC 95688 414-B4
MERION CT
FRFD 94534 472-B2
MERKLEY AV
WSAC 95691 358-H4
MERLIN CT
BEN 94510 551-A2
MERLOT CT
FRFD 94533 472-C6
MERLOT LN
AMCN 94503 510-B4
MERLOT WY
RVIS 94571 516-G6
MERMOD PL
WIN 95694 373-E3
MERMOD RD
WIN 95694 373-E3
MERRILL CT
DXN 95620 395-B6
MERRILL DR
DXN 95620 395-B7
MERRIMAC CT
VAL 94589 510-A5
MERRIT ISLAND CT
WSAC 95691 378-E2
MERRITT CIR
WDLD 95776 316-D4
MERRITT PL
FRFD 94533 473-B3
MERRYFIELD DR
DXN 95620 395-B6
MESA AV
VAL 94592 529-G7
MESA CT
VAC 95687 453-C1
MESA ST
VAL 94591 530-C7
MESA GRANDE
WSAC 95691 358-J7
MESA VERDE AV
VAL 94589 530-B1
MESQUITE DR
DVS 95618 356-F7
MESSINA TER
DVS 95618 356-H7
MEYER PZ
VAL 94590 530-A6
MEYER WY
FRFD 94534 472-D7
FRFD 94534 492-D1
MICA DR
VAL 94589 510-B6
MICHAEL CT
SUIS 94585 473-A5
VAL 94591 530-F3
MICHAEL LN
AMCN 94503 510-B4
MICHAELANGELO CT
FRFD 94534 491-B3
MICHELANGELO PL
DVS 95618 356-E5
MICHELBOOK LN
RVIS 94571 516-F1
MICHELE CT
DXN 95620 395-B7
VAL 94591 530-D2
MICHIGAN BLVD
WSAC 95691 358-H3
MICHIGAN ST
FRFD 94533 472-D5
FRFD 94535 473-H2
VAL 94590 530-A3
MIDDLE ST
WSAC 95691 358-F3
MIDDLE BASS ISLAND CT
WSAC 95691 378-E2
MIDDLE GOLF DR
YoCo 95618 376-J1
YoCo 95618 377-A1
MIDVALE DR
VAC 95687 453-E2
MIDWAY CIR
WDLD 95695 315-H6
MIDWAY DR
WDLD 95695 315-H5
MIDWAY RD
FRFD 94533 472-C6
SolC 94533 472-C6
SolC 95620 414-G4
SolC 95620 415-A4
SolC 95687 414-C4
SolC 95688 413-F4
SolC 95688 414-A4
VAC 95620 414-C4
VAC 95687 414-C4
VAC 95688 413-F4
VAC 95688 414-A4
MIDWAY ST
VAL 94590 530-A6
MIDWAY ISLAND RD
WSAC 95691 378-D2
MIEKLE AV
WDLD 95776 316-E7
WDLD 95776 336-E1
MIELKE AV
WDLD 95776 316-E7

MIKON ST
WSAC 95605 358-H2
MILANO DR
WSAC 95691 358-J7
MILFORD CT
VAC 95688 433-D3
MILITA ST
VAL 94590 530-B3
MILITARY E
BEN 94510 551-C5
MILITARY W
BEN 94510 550-J3
BEN 94510 551-A3
MILITARY CT
FRFD 94533 452-G5
MILK FARM RD
SolC 95620 395-D3
MILLBROOK CT
FRFD 94534 452-A7
VAC 95687 453-G1
WSAC 95691 358-J7
MILLBROOK WY
VAC 95687 453-F1
MILL CREEK CT
FRFD 94534 491-F3
MILLER AV
VAL 94591 530-D5
MILLER CT
DXN 95620 395-D7
FRFD 94534 472-D4
WSAC 95691 378-F3
MILLER DR
DVS 95616 356-C7
DVS 95616 376-C1
FRFD 94534 472-C4
MILLER PL
FRFD 94534 472-C4
MILLER RD
SaCo 95833 358-G1
SolC 95620 415-H3
MILLERTON PL
WSAC 95691 378-C4
MILLS CT
BEN 94510 551-A1
MILLS DR
BEN 94510 550-J2
BEN 94510 551-A1
DVS 95616 356-C7
MILLS LN
SolC 95688 414-A7
VAL 94589 510-B5
MILLS RD
VAC 95687 433-H5
MILLS ST
FRFD 94535 473-G4
MILTON ST
WSAC 95605 358-J1
MIMOSA CT
VAL 94589 529-J1
MIMOSA DR
SolC 94589 529-J1
VAC 95687 453-G3
VAL 94589 529-J1
MINAHAN WY
VAL 94590 530-C3
MINERS TR
SolC 94589 490-J4
MINI DR
VAL 94589 509-H4
VAL 94589 510-A5
MINNESOTA ST
FRFD 94533 472-D5
MINNOW CT
FRFD 94533 473-A1
MIRA LOMA
VAL 94590 530-B2
MIRA LOMA CT
WSAC 95691 378-J1
MIRAMAR CT
FRFD 94533 472-H3
MIRAMONTE CT
WDLD 95695 315-H7
W MIRAMONTE DR
WDLD 95695 315-H6
MIRAVISTA WY
VAL 94589 510-D5
MIRROR CT
FRFD 94534 491-D2
MISAWA CT
VAL 94591 510-J6
MISFELDT ST
DXN 95620 415-B2
MISSION CIR
FRFD 94585 511-D1
MISSION CT
VAL 94591 530-D3
MISSION BAY CT
VAC 95688 413-F7
MISSION BAY DR
VAC 95688 413-F7
MISSISSIPPI ST
VAL 94590 529-J3
VAL 94590 530-A3
MISSOURI ST
FRFD 94533 472-F6
VAL 94590 529-J3
VAL 94590 530-A3
MISTLER CT
DXN 95620 395-A7
MISTLER ST
DXN 95620 395-A7
MISTRAL WY
VAL 94591 550-E2
MISTY CT
VAL 94589 510-D5
MISTY OAK CT
FRFD 94534 452-F7
FRFD 94534 472-F1
MITCHELL CT
VAL 94589 510-B7
MITCHELL ST
RVIS 94571 516-G3
MIWOK CT
DXN 95620 395-A7
MIWOK PL
DVS 95618 376-G1
MIX CANYON RD
SolC 95688 412-A5
MIZNER CT
BEN 94510 551-B1
MOCKINGBIRD CT
FRFD 94533 472-J4
MOCKINGBIRD DR
AMCN 94503 510-A4
MOCKINGBIRD LN
FRFD 94533 472-J4
MOCKINGBIRD PL
DVS 95616 356-B4
MOCOCO RD
MRTZ 94553 551-G7
MODOC CT
WSAC 95691 378-H2
MODOC PL
DVS 95618 376-G1
WDLD 95695 315-G3
MODOC ST
VAL 94591 530-D4
MOELLER LN
YoCo 95695 335-H4
MOJAVE CT
VAC 95688 433-A5
MOJAVE DR
WSAC 95691 378-H1

MOLINA CT
VAL 94591 530-F5
MOLINA ST
NAP 94559 450-A7
VAL 94591 530-F5
MOLLY AV
WDLD 95776 316-B5
MOLOKAI RD
WSAC 95691 378-D2
MONAGHAN CIR
VAC 95688 413-E7
VAC 95688 433-E1
MONAGHAN CT
VAC 95688 433-E1
MONARCH LN
DVS 95618 356-G5
MONICA PL
VAL 94591 530-E3
MONIQUE WY
DXN 95620 395-B6
MONITOR AV
SUIS 94585 473-C6
MONITOR PASS CT
VAL 94589 509-J6
MONK CT
DXN 95620 395-C5
MONO CT
FRFD 94534 491-D2
MONO DR
VAC 95687 433-E6
MONO PL
DVS 95618 376-G1
MONROE CT
WDLD 95776 316-B6
MONROE ST
FRFD 94533 472-F5
MONTANA ST
FRFD 94533 472-H5
MONTCLAIR CT
FRFD 94534 472-F1
VAC 95687 453-F2
MONTCLAIR ST
VAL 94592 529-H7
MONTCLAIR WY
FRFD 94534 472-F2
MONTEBELLO VISTA DR
SUIS 94585 473-C6
MONTE CARLO DR
SUIS 94585 473-C6
MONTECARLO WY
AMCN 94503 510-C4
MONTECITO BLVD
NAP 94559 450-A5
MONTECITO CT
FRFD 94533 452-H7
MONTEFRIO LN
DVS 95618 356-F7
MONTEGO CT
SUIS 94585 472-H7
MONTEITH DR
VAL 94590 530-C3
MONTEREY AV
DVS 95618 376-G1
MONTEREY CIR
WDLD 95695 315-H6
MONTEREY CT
WSAC 95691 378-J1
MONTEREY DR
AMCN 94503 509-J1
FRFD 94534 472-D3
SUIS 94585 473-D7
VAC 95687 433-J3
MONTEREY ST
VAL 94590 530-B3
MONTEVERDE DR
VAC 95688 432-J5
VAC 95688 433-A6
MONTE VERDE WY
VAL 94589 530-C1
MONTEVINO DR
AMCN 94503 510-A4
MONTE VISTA
BEN 94510 550-J3
NAP 94559 450-A5
MONTE VISTA AV
DVS 95618 376-G1
VAL 94590 530-B3
E MONTE VISTA AV
VAC 95688 413-G7
VAC 95688 433-G3
W MONTE VISTA AV
VAC 95688 433-B5
MONTE VISTA CIR
WDLD 95695 315-H6
MONTE VISTA CT
WSAC 95691 378-J1
MONTE VISTA DR
WDLD 95695 315-H6
W MONTE VISTA DR
WDLD 95695 315-H6
MONTE VISTA PL
DVS 95618 376-G1
MONTE VISTA ST
WSAC 95691 378-J1
MONTEZUMA CT
FRFD 94534 472-D4
MONTEZUMA ST
RVIS 94571 516-H5
MONTEZUMA HILLS RD
RVIS 94571 516-E7
SolC 94571 516-E7
MONTGOMERY AV
DVS 95618 376-F2
YoCo 95618 376-G2
YoCo 95618 377-A2
MONTGOMERY PL
WDLD 95776 316-B5
MONTICELLO CT
VAC 95688 413-J7
MONTICELLO RD Rt#-121
NaCo 94558 450-A1
MONTIGLIO CT
VAL 94591 530-J2
MONTVILLE CT
VAC 95688 433-D1
MOODY SLOUGH RD
WIN 95694 373-D2
YoCo 95694 373-D2
MOONLIT CIR
SAC 95831 378-J6
MOONRAKER CT
VAL 94590 550-C2
MOONRAKER DR
VAL 94590 550-C1
MOONSTONE CT
VAC 95687 453-G2
MOORE BLVD
DVS 95618 356-E4
MOORE CT
FRFD 94535 473-J1
MOORE DR
DXN 95620 395-C4
MOORLAND ST
VAL 94589 530-C2
VAL 94590 530-C2
MOOSUP CT
FRFD 94533 473-A1
MORAGA CT
FRFD 94534 472-C4
MORAGA DR
FRFD 94534 472-C4

MORALES CT
VAC 95688 433-B5
MORGAN CT
VAC 95687 433-H5
VAL 94591 530-E1
MORGAN LN
DXN 95620 395-C5
RVIS 94571 516-G5
MORGAN ST
SUIS 94585 492-F1
WIN 95694 373-F3
MORISSETTE WY
VAC 95687 453-F3
MORNINGBIRD LN
SolC 95688 412-H7
MORNING BROOK CT
FRFD 94534 452-G7
MORNING DOVE PL
YoCo 95616 355-J2
YoCo 95616 356-A2
MORNING GLORY DR
BEN 94510 531-B7
BEN 94510 551-A1
VAC 95687 453-F3
MORNING GLORY ST
WSAC 95691 358-E4
MORNINGSIDE AV
VAL 94590 530-B4
MORNINGSTAR CT
VAC 95687 433-H5
MORNINGSTAR WY
VAC 95687 433-H5
MORNING SUN CT
VAC 95688 413-J7
MORRIS CIR
WDLD 95776 316-E6
MORRIS LN
YoCo 95618 376-E2
MORRISON LN
SolC 94534 471-F3
MORRO BAY AV
DVS 95616 355-G6
MORROW LN
SolC 94510 531-J4
MORROW BAY CT
VAC 95688 413-E7
MORROW BAY ST
WSAC 95691 378-E1
MORROW COVE DR
VAL 94590 550-C2
MORSE CT
DXN 95620 395-C4
WSAC 95605 358-H2
MORSE LN
SolC 95694 393-D3
MORTARA CT
VAL 94591 530-G1
MORTON RD
WSAC 95691 378-F2
MOSAIC CT
AMCN 94503 510-B2
FRFD 94534 491-C3
MOSCATO CT
FRFD 94534 491-F5
VAC 95687 433-B7
MOSCATO WY
AMCN 94503 510-A2
MOSS CT
VAC 95687 453-F1
MOSS CREEK WY
FRFD 94534 491-D2
MOSS VALLEY DR
FRFD 94534 452-F7
MOSSWOOD AV
VAL 94591 530-E5
MOSSWOOD CIR
WSAC 95691 358-H5
MOSSWOOD DR
SUIS 94585 472-H6
MOSSWOOD LN
DXN 95620 415-B1
MOTTA ST
WDLD 95776 316-D7
MOUNT ADAMS CIR
VAC 95688 413-H6
VAC 95688 433-J1
MOUNTAIN MEADOWS CT
FRFD 94534 491-F4
MOUNTAIN MEADOWS DR
FRFD 94534 491-F3
MOUNTAIN VIEW AV
VAL 94589 530-C2
VAL 94590 530-C2
MOUNTAIN VIEW CT
FRFD 94534 472-E1
MOUNTAIN VIEW LN
SolC 95688 393-C7
MOUNTAIN VIEW TER
BEN 94510 551-B4
MOUNT GEORGE AV
NaCo 94558 450-C1
MOUNT HOOD CT
WDLD 95695 315-G2
MOUNT WHITNEY DR
WDLD 95695 315-G2
MRAK HALL DR
YoCo 95616 376-C2
MUIR CIR
WDLD 95695 315-H2
MUIR CT
FRFD 94534 472-C4
VAC 95687 433-J4
MUIR PL
WDLD 95695 315-G2
MUIR ST
NAP 94559 470-A1
WDLD 95695 315-G2
MUIRWOOD CT
VAL 94591 530-F5
MUIRWOOD PL
VAL 94591 530-F5
MUIR WOODS PL
DVS 95616 355-H6
MULBERRY CT
VAC 95688 433-C2
MULBERRY LN
DVS 95616 356-B7
DXN 95620 395-B7
MULBERRY ST
VAL 94589 510-A7
MULCAHY CT
WDLD 95776 316-E5
MULHERON ST
FRFD 94535 474-A2
MULLBERRY DR
WDLD 95776 316-C5
MULLBERRY WY
WDLD 95776 316-C5
MULLER ST
VAL 94590 530-C5
MULRANY CT
VAC 95688 433-D2
MULVANY PL
WSAC 95691 378-E1
MURAL LN
FRFD 94534 491-D3
MURPHYS CT
VAL 94589 509-H5
MURRE WY
SUIS 94585 473-B6
MUSCOVY CT
SUIS 94585 473-A6

MUSTANG CIR SOLANO COUNTY STREET INDEX PATRICK LN 565

STREET Name City ZIP Pg-Grid

MUSTANG CIR
FRFD 94533 452-J7
FRFD 94533 472-J1
MUSTANG CT
FRFD 94533 452-J7
FRFD 94533 472-J1
VAL 94591 530-E2
MUSTANG RD
NaCo 94558 450-E6
MUSTANG TR
VAC 95687 453-F3
MYRTLE AV
WSAC 95605 358-H1
MYRTLE CT
BEN 94510 551-A1
FRFD 94533 472-F2
MYRTLE DR
YoCo 95694 373-J2
MYRTLE LN
YoCo 95695 336-A6
MYRTLE PL
DVS 95618 356-F5
MYRTLE ST
VAC 95688 433-C5
MYRTLEWOOD CT
VAL 94591 530-E4
MYSTIC DR
FRFD 94533 452-J7
FRFD 94533 453-A7

N

N LN
FRFD 94533 473-F2
N ST
BEN 94510 551-B4
DVS 95616 356-E7
VAL 94592 529-F3
E N ST
BEN 94510 551-C5
W N ST
BEN 94510 550-J3
NADEL DR
SUIS 94585 472-H7
NAKAGAKI WY
WDLD 95776 316-E7
NALISTY DR
VAL 94590 529-H2
NANCY CIR
VAC 95687 453-F2
NANCY CT
SUIS 94585 473-A5
NANCY DR
DXN 95620 395-B7
NANCY LN
VAC 95687 453-F2
WSAC 95691 378-E2
NANDINA PL
DVS 95618 376-H2
NANTUCKET CIR
VAC 95687 433-G6
NANTUCKET CT
FRFD 94534 472-B4
NANTUCKET DR
FRFD 94534 472-B4
NANTUCKET LN
VAL 94590 529-J5
NANTUCKET PL
FRFD 94534 472-C4
NANTUCKET TER
DVS 95618 376-G1
NAPA AV
CCCo 94572 549-H7
NAPA PL
WDLD 95695 315-F3
NAPA ST
FRFD 94535 473-J2
VAL 94590 530-A2
NAPA JUNCTION RD
AMCN 94503 490-A7
S NAPA JUNCTION RD
AMCN 94503 510-A1
NAPA SHORE DR
FRFD 94534 491-D2
NARCISSUS CT
VAL 94591 530-G7
NARI DR
WSAC 95691 358-D4
NARRAGANSETT CT
VAL 94591 550-E2
NASHVILLE LN
VAL 94591 530-F4
NATICK CT
VAC 95687 453-G2
NATIONAL AL
VAL 94590 529-J4
VAL 94590 530-A4
NAUTICAL CT
VAL 94591 530-G7
NAUTILUS CT
SAC 95831 378-G6
NAUTILUS DR
VAL 94591 550-D1
NAVAJO CT
VAC 95688 433-A4
NAVAJO DR
VAL 94592 529-G6
NAVAJO LN
DVS 95616 355-J6
DVS 95616 356-A6
NAVARRE ST
NAP 94559 470-A1
NAVONE ST
VAL 94591 550-C1
NEAL WY
WDLD 95776 336-E1
NEBBIOLO CT
FRFD 94534 491-F5
NEBRASKA ST
FRFD 94533 472-H5
FRFD 94535 473-H2
VAL 94590 529-J3
VAL 94590 530-A3
NEEDHAM DR
VAC 95687 453-G1
NEIL ST
VAC 95688 433-B5
NEITZEL RD
FRFD 94534 491-E3
NELSON AV
VAC 95688 413-J7
NELSON RD
FRFD 94533 452-G7
SolC 94533 452-G7
VAC 94533 452-G4
NELSON WY
WDLD 95776 316-E5
NEPHI DR
FRFD 94534 472-C3
NEPTUNE CT
SUIS 94585 472-G7
WSAC 95691 378-J1
NEPTUNES CT
VAL 94591 550-F3
NEREUS ST
VAL 94592 529-H6
NERO CT
FRFD 94534 491-F5
NEVADA AV
WDLD 95695 315-H2
NEVADA ST
BEN 94510 551-E2
FRFD 94533 472-F5
FRFD 94535 473-G2
VAL 94590 530-B3
NEVELSON CT
DVS 95618 356-F5
NEWARK CT
SUIS 94585 473-C4
NEWARK LN
SUIS 94585 473-B3
NEW BEDFORD CT
VAL 94591 550-E1
NEW BEDFORD PL
FRFD 94533 472-J2
NEW BEDFORD RD
VAL 94591 530-E1
NEWBERRY ST
WSAC 95691 378-J1
NEWBURGH CT
FRFD 94534 472-C4
NEWBURGH DR
FRFD 94534 472-C5
NEWBURY WY
AMCN 94503 509-J2
NEWCASTLE CT
FRFD 94533 472-F3
VAL 94591 530-H5
NEWCASTLE DR
VAL 94591 530-H5
NEWELL DR
AMCN 94503 510-B2
NEWGATE WY
DXN 95620 395-C6
NEW HAMPSHIRE ST
FRFD 94533 472-D5
NEWHAVEN LN
VAL 94591 510-J5
NEW HOGAN PL
WSAC 95691 378-D4
NEW HORIZONS WY
VAC 95687 413-H7
VAC 95688 433-H1
NEW ISLAND ST
WSAC 95691 378-C2
NEW JERSEY ST
FRFD 94533 472-D5
NEWPORT CIR
VAC 95687 433-G6
NEWPORT TER
DVS 95618 376-G1
NEWPORT WY
SUIS 94585 472-H6
VAL 94589 509-H5
NEWTON CT
DVS 95618 376-D2
NEW YORK CT
FRFD 94535 473-H2
NIAGARA WY
FRFD 94534 472-C4
NICHOLS CT
WSAC 95691 378-F2
NICOLE WY
VAL 94589 510-D6
NICOLSON CIR
WDLD 95776 316-E7
NIEMANN ST
WIN 95694 373-E2
NIGH AL
VAL 94590 530-A3
NIGH ST
VAL 94590 529-J3
VAL 94590 530-A3
NIGHTHAWK CT
VAC 95688 433-E1
NIGHTINGALE CT
FRFD 94533 472-J3
NIGHTINGALE DR
FRFD 94533 472-H3
NILE CT
VAC 95688 433-B5
NIMITZ AV
VAL 94592 529-H6
NOAH CT
SAC 95831 378-H7
NOBLE CT
SolC 95694 393-J3
NO NAME LN
FRFD 94535 473-J2
NOONAN LN
FRFD 94533 473-E1
SolC 94533 453-E7
SolC 94533 473-E1
NORDEN CT
VAL 94589 509-H4
NORDEN WY
WDLD 95695 316-A6
NORFOLK AV
WSAC 95691 358-H4
NORFOLK CT
VAL 94591 530-G5
NORMAN CT
SolC 95688 393-B6
NORMANDY CT
FRFD 94533 472-J2
VAC 95687 433-G7
NORMANDY DR
VAC 95687 433-G7
NORTE AV
DVS 95616 356-B4
NORTE DAME CT
VAC 95687 433-H6
NORTH AV
NaCo 94558 450-B5
NORTH ST
WDLD 95695 315-J3
WDLD 95695 316-A3
WDLD 95776 316-A3
W NORTH ST
WDLD 95695 315-G3
NORTHAMPTON CT
VAC 95687 453-G2
NORTHAMPTON DR
AMCN 94503 509-J3
AMCN 94503 510-A3
VAC 95687 453-G2
NORTHFIELD CT
DVS 95616 356-A4
NORTH GATE RD
FRFD 94533 473-J1
FRFD 94535 473-J1
SolC 94533 473-J1
SolC 94533 473-J1
SolC 95687 453-J5
NORTHLITE CIR
SAC 95831 378-H7
NORTH POINT WY
SAC 95831 378-F6
NORTHPORT DR
WSAC 95691 358-E4
NORTH QUAD
YoCo 95616 376-C1
NORTH RIDGE CT
FRFD 94533 473-B4
NORTHRUP LN
AMCN 94503 509-J3
NORTHSHORE WY
SAC 95831 378-G7
NORTH STAR PL
YoCo 95616 355-J2
YoCo 95616 356-A2
NORTHWOOD CT
FRFD 94585 511-E1
NORTHWOOD DR
FRFD 94585 511-E1
VAC 95687 453-E1
WDLD 95695 315-H5
NORTHWOOD WY
FRFD 94585 511-E2
NORTON CT
DXN 95620 415-C2
NORTON ST
FRFD 94535 473-H1
NORWALK CT
FRFD 94534 472-B4
VAC 95687 433-G5
NORWALK PL
FRFD 94534 472-B4
NORWALK WY
FRFD 94534 472-C4
NORWICH WY
FRFD 94533 453-A7
NORWICK CT
AMCN 94503 509-J3
NOTA CT
VAL 94590 550-C1
NOTRE DAME CIR
VAC 95687 433-H6
NOTRE DAME CT
VAL 94589 510-C5
NOTRE DAME DR
DVS 95616 356-A6
VAC 95687 433-H6
VAL 94589 510-C5
WDLD 95695 315-F5
NOTTINGHAM CT
VAL 94591 510-J4
NOTTINGHAM DR
FRFD 94533 472-F3
VAC 95688 433-B6
NOTTINGHAM LN
AMCN 94503 509-J3
NOUVEAU LN
AMCN 94503 510-B3
NOVARA LN
FRFD 94534 491-C3
NOVATO DR
VAC 95688 433-D4
NOYES CT
BEN 94510 551-E3
NUGENT DR
VAL 94589 510-A6
NUNES RD
SolC 95620 394-E7
SolC 95620 414-E4
SolC 95688 394-E7
SolC 95688 414-E2
NUNEZ CT
WSAC 95691 378-F2
NUTMEG LN
DVS 95618 356-F6
NUT TREE CT
VAC 95687 433-H5
NUT TREE PKWY
VAC 95687 433-F5
NUT TREE RD
VAC 95687 433-G4
VAC 95687 453-G1
VAC 95688 433-G3
NYACK PL
WDLD 95776 316-B4

O

O ST
BEN 94510 551-C4
E O ST
BEN 94510 551-C5
OAK
BEN 94510 551-C6
OAK AV
DVS 95616 356-B7
DVS 95616 376-B1
VAL 94592 529-F3
WDLD 95695 315-J4
WDLD 95695 316-A4
WDLD 95776 316-A4
E OAK AV
WDLD 95776 316-B4
OAK DR
WDLD 95776 316-D5
OAK LN
SolC 94534 471-D5
OAK RD
BEN 94510 551-E5
OAK ST
FRFD 94533 472-G4
VAC 95688 433-C6
VAL 94592 529-G5
WSAC 95605 358-G2
OAKBROOK CIR
FRFD 94585 491-D6
OAK BROOK CT
VAC 95687 433-H7
OAKBROOK CT
FRFD 94585 491-D7
OAK BROOK DR
VAC 95687 433-H7
VAC 95687 453-J1
OAKBROOK DR
FRFD 94585 491-D7
FRFD 94585 511-D1
OAK CANYON LN
SolC 95688 452-G1
OAK CREEK CT
VAC 95687 433-H7
OAK CREEK DR
VAC 95687 433-H7
OAKDALE CT
FRFD 94585 511-E2
OAKENSHIELD RD
DVS 95616 355-H7
OAK GROVE DR
VAL 94589 509-J7
OAK GROVE ST
VAL 94589 529-J1
OAKHILL CT
VAC 95688 432-J5
VAC 95688 433-A5
OAK HILL WY
RVIS 94571 516-F2
OAK HOLLOW DR
VAC 95687 433-H5
OAKLAND ST
FRFD 94535 473-J4
OAKLAND BAY DR
WSAC 95691 378-C2
OAKLAND HILLS CT
FRFD 94534 452-C7
OAKLAND HILLS DR
FRFD 94534 452-C7
OAK MARSH
RVIS 94571 516-F1
OAKMEADE CT
VAC 95687 433-J7
OAKMEADE DR
VAC 95687 433-J7
OAKMEADOW CT
VAC 95687 433-H7
OAKMONT CT
FRFD 94534 472-C2
OAKMONT WY
WSAC 95691 358-G4
OAKMORE CT
VAL 94591 530-F4
OAKPOINT CT
FRFD 94585 511-E3
OAKRIDGE DR
FRFD 94534 491-D1
OAKRIDGE LN
SolC 94510 531-G2
OAKRIDGE WY
RVIS 94571 516-E1
OAKSIDE DR
YoCo 95618 376-G2
E OAKSIDE PL
YoCo 95618 376-G1
W OAKSIDE PL
YoCo 95618 376-G2
OAK SPRINGS DR
NaCo 94558 451-G1
OAKSTONE CT
AMCN 94503 510-B2
OAKSTONE WY
AMCN 94503 510-B3
OAK TREE TR
SolC 95688 412-F6
OAKVALE WY
VAC 95687 453-F3
OAK VALLEY CT
VAC 95687 433-H7
OAK VALLEY DR
VAC 95687 433-H7
OAK VIEW DR
VAC 95688 433-A6
OAKVIEW DR
FRFD 94534 452-E7
OAKWOOD AV
VAL 94591 530-E5
OAKWOOD CIR
FRFD 94534 491-F1
OAKWOOD DR
FRFD 94534 471-F7
FRFD 94534 491-F1
SolC 94534 471-F7
SolC 94534 491-F1
OASIS VALLEY CT
FRFD 94534 491-B2
OATES CT
WSAC 95691 358-D7
OATES ST
WSAC 95691 358-D7
WSAC 95691 378-D1
OBRIEN CIR
VAL 94589 509-J5
OBSIDIAN CT
VAL 94589 510-C6
OCEAN AV
WSAC 95691 358-G7
OCEAN DR
WSAC 95691 358-G7
OCEAN PL
WSAC 95691 358-G6
OCEAN BREEZE CT
VAL 94591 530-F1
OCEANIC CT
FRFD 94533 472-H3
OCEANIC DR
FRFD 94533 472-H3
OCEANO WY
DVS 95618 356-H6
ODAY RD
SolC 95620 414-E4
SolC 95688 414-E4
VAC 95620 414-E4
VAC 95688 414-E4
ODDSTAD DR
VAL 94589 530-B1
ODIN DR
WSAC 95691 358-D5
OESTE DR
DVS 95616 356-B7
DVS 95616 376-B1
OFARRELL DR
BEN 94510 550-J2
BEN 94510 551-A2
OFFUTT ST
FRFD 94535 473-J2
OGDEN ST
WDLD 95776 316-E6
OGDEN WY
VAC 95687 433-C7
OHARE DR
BEN 94510 551-B4
OHIO CT
FRFD 94535 473-H2
OHIO ST
FRFD 94533 472-F7
SUIS 94533 472-F7
VAL 94590 529-J4
VAL 94590 530-A4
OHLONE ST
DVS 95616 376-G1
OKEEFE PL
DVS 95618 356-E5
OKEEFE WY
VAL 94590 530-C2
OKLAHOMA ST
VAL 94592 529-G7
OLD BECKER RD
SolC 95620 376-B7
OLD COUNTY RD
CCCo 94525 550-A5
OLD DAVIS RD
SolC 95620 376-B6
YoCo 95616 376-C2
OLDER PL
FRFD 94533 473-B3
OLD GLEN COVE RD
SolC 94591 550-E1
VAL 94591 550-E1
OLD GLORY LN
VAC 95687 453-G2
OLD HUTCHINSON DR
YoCo 95616 375-J2
YoCo 95616 376-A2
OLD HWY 40
CCCo 94525 550-A5
CCCo 94572 549-J6
CCCo 94572 550-A5
OLD RIVER CT
VAL 94589 509-H5
OLD RIVER DR
VAL 94589 509-H5
OLD RIVER RD
YoCo 95605 317-G5
OLD ROCKY CIR
VAC 95688 433-D2
OLD STONE CT
VAC 95687 433-J5
OLD SUISUN RD
BEN 94510 551-C3
OLD WILSON AV
VAL 94590 529-J3
OLEANDER CT
VAL 94591 530-G7
OLEANDER PL
DVS 95618 356-E6
OLIVAS LN
SolC 95688 393-C7
SolC 95688 413-C1
OLIVE AV
SolC 94585 473-A5
SUIS 94585 473-A5
OLIVE CT
WSAC 95691 358-F7
OLIVE DR
DVS 95616 376-D1
W OLIVE DR
DVS 95616 376-D2
OLIVE ST
VAC 95688 433-C6
OLIVE WY
WDLD 95695 315-J3
OLIVE BRANCH CT
BEN 94510 551-C3
OLIVEGLEN CT
FRFD 94585 511-E3
OLIVE HILL LN
NaCo 94558 450-C1
OLIVER RD
FRFD 94534 472-C3
OLIVERA DR
VAC 95688 433-D4
OLIVE SCHOOL LN
SolC 95694 373-C7
SolC 95694 393-C1
OLIVE TREE DR
YoCo 95616 375-H1
OLIVEWOOD LN
VAL 94591 510-H4
OLMO LN
SolC 95620 375-H6
OLSEN WY
SUIS 94585 473-A5
OLSON CT
VAL 94589 510-D5
OLVERA CT
WDLD 95776 316-D5
OLVERA DR
WDLD 95776 316-D5
OLYMPIC CIR
VAC 95687 433-H4
OLYMPIC CT
FRFD 94533 473-B4
OLYMPIC DR
DVS 95616 355-J6
RVIS 94571 516-F2
VAL 94589 510-B6
OLYMPIC RD
FRFD 94534 472-A1
OLYMPIC ST
VAL 94589 510-B5
ONTARIO CT
FRFD 94533 472-D7
ONTARIO ST
FRFD 94533 472-D7
OPAL CT
FRFD 94534 491-E2
OPAL DR
VAL 94589 510-C6
OPAL WY
VAC 95687 453-G3
ORANGE DR
VAC 95687 433-H2
VAC 95687 434-A2
ORANGE LN
DVS 95616 356-B6
ORANGE ST
VAL 94590 550-C1
WDLD 95695 315-G3
ORANGE BLOSSOM CT
AMCN 94503 509-J2
ORANGE TREE CIR
VAC 95687 433-H3
ORANGE TREE WY
FRFD 94533 472-G4
ORCHARD AV
SolC 94591 530-E6
VAL 94591 530-E6
N ORCHARD AV
SolC 95688 433-B4
VAC 95688 433-B4
S ORCHARD AV
VAC 95688 433-B6
ORCHARD DR
DXN 95620 415-D2
ORCHARD LN
WIN 95694 373-F2
ORCHARD RD
YoCo 95616 376-A1
ORCHARD WY
WSAC 95691 358-H4
ORCHARD CANYON LN
SolC 95688 433-B1
ORCHARD PARK CIR
YoCo 95616 376-A1
ORCHARD PARK DR
YoCo 95616 376-A1
ORCHARD VIEW CT
FRFD 94534 472-C3
ORCHARD VIEW DR
FRFD 94534 472-C3
ORCHESTRA PL
FRFD 94534 491-E1
ORCHID CT
BEN 94510 531-A7
ORCHID ST
FRFD 94533 472-G3
OREGON ST
BEN 94510 551-E2
FRFD 94533 472-F5
FRFD 94535 473-H3
VAL 94590 530-A3
OREHR RD
FRFD 94585 492-D2
SolC 94585 492-D2
ORINDA CT
FRFD 94585 491-D7
ORINDA PL
WSAC 95691 378-J1
ORINDA WY
FRFD 94585 491-D7
ORIOLE AV
DVS 95616 356-B4
ORIOLE CT
AMCN 94503 510-B4
FRFD 94533 472-H3
ORIOLE WY
FRFD 94533 472-H3
ORLANDO CT
VAC 95687 433-G5
ORLEANS WY
SAC 95831 378-F7
ORO CT
VAL 94591 530-D2
ORTIZ AV
WDLD 95776 316-D7
ORTIZ CT
WDLD 95776 316-E7
ORVIETO CT
FRFD 94534 491-F5
OSCAR LN
VAL 94592 529-G5
OSCAR ST
VAL 94592 529-G5
OSPREY CT
VAC 95687 453-F3
OSPREY WY
SUIS 94585 473-B6
OTAY ST
WSAC 95691 378-E4
OTIS AV
WSAC 95691 378-D3
OTTER CT
FRFD 94533 452-H7
OTTOWA AV
DVS 95616 355-H6
OUTER CIR
DVS 95618 356-E7
OUTRIGGER DR
VAL 94591 550-D1
OUTRIGGER PL
FRFD 94533 452-H7
OUTRIGGER WY
SAC 95831 378-F6
OVEJAS AV
DVS 95616 356-C7
OVERHILL LN
DVS 95616 355-H7
OVERLAND AL
VAL 94590 529-J4
VAL 94590 530-A4
OVERLAND CT
VAC 95688 413-J7
WSAC 95691 358-D5
OVERLAND PL
VAC 95687 433-J5
OVERLOOK DR
VAL 94591 510-J4
OVERTURE LN
FRFD 94534 491-E1
OWENS CT
FRFD 94534 472-D4
OWENS ST
FRFD 94534 472-D4
OWENS VALLEY DR
WDLD 95776 316-C5
OWINGS DR
YoCo 95694 373-H2
OWL CIR
VAC 95687 453-H1
OWL CT
VAC 95687 453-H1
OWL DR
VAC 95687 453-H1
WDLD 95695 315-G1
OXFORD CIR
DVS 95616 356-A7
DVS 95616 376-A1
OXFORD CT
DXN 95620 395-C6
VAC 95687 453-C1
VAL 94591 530-G4
OXFORD DR
FRFD 94533 472-E4
OXFORD ST
WSAC 95691 358-H3
OXFORD WY
BEN 94510 530-J6
OYSTER BAY AV
DVS 95616 355-G6

P

P ST
BEN 94510 551-B4
VAL 94592 529-F3
PACE LN
SolC 95688 393-F7
SolC 95688 413-F1
PACER CT
VAL 94591 530-E1
PACER DR
VAL 94591 530-E1
PACHECO WY
VAL 94591 530-D7
PACIFIC AV
CCCo 94572 549-H7
FRFD 94533 472-F3
E PACIFIC AV
FRFD 94533 472-G3
PACIFIC CT
VAL 94589 510-B6
PACIFIC DR
DVS 95616 356-D6
WSAC 95691 358-F7
PACIFIC PL
WSAC 95691 358-F7
PACIFIC ST
FRFD 94535 473-G4
WDLD 95695 316-A5
PACIFICA CT
BEN 94510 551-C4
PACIFIC GROVE CT
VAC 95688 413-E6
PACKARD AL
VAL 94590 529-J4
VAL 94590 530-A4
PADAN SCHOOL RD
VAC 95687 433-D7
PADDLEWHEEL DR
VAL 94591 550-F2
PADDOCK PL
WDLD 95776 316-B2
PADDON RD
SolC 95688 413-G4
PAINE ST
FRFD 94535 473-J2
PAISLEY CT
VAC 95687 433-H7
PAJARO WY
VAL 94591 530-D2
PALACE CT
BEN 94510 530-H7
BEN 94510 550-H1
FRFD 94534 491-C3
PALENCIA CT
AMCN 94503 510-A4
PALERMO DR
SUIS 94585 473-C6
PALERMO WY
VAC 95688 413-E7
PALESTRINA CT
AMCN 94503 510-C4
PALESTRINA DR
AMCN 94503 510-C4
PALISADES CT
VAC 95688 432-J4
PALISADES DR
RVIS 94571 516-F1
PALLADIO WY
FRFD 94534 491-C3
PALM
BEN 94510 551-C5
PALM AV
VAC 95688 433-B6
WDLD 95695 316-A2
PALM DR
NaCo 94558 450-A4
VAL 94589 509-J7
VAL 94589 529-J1
PALM PL
DVS 95618 356-E6
PALM WY
WDLD 95776 316-D5
PALM BEACH CT
FRFD 94533 473-C4
PALMER CIR
FRFD 94534 472-D2
PALMER CT
DXN 95620 395-B5
FRFD 94534 472-D3
PALO ALTO CT
FRFD 94533 452-H7
PALOMAR AV
WSAC 95691 358-E4
PALOMAR LN
VAL 94591 530-D3
PALOMAR PL
WDLD 95695 315-H5
PALOMINO CIR
FRFD 94533 452-H7
FRFD 94533 472-H1
PALOMINO CT
FRFD 94533 452-H7
PALOMINO WY
NaCo 94558 450-D6
PALO SECO CT
FRFD 94533 452-H7
PALOU ST
VAL 94591 550-D1
PALO VERDE WY
VAL 94589 530-C1
PAMELA CT
VAL 94589 510-C5
PAMELA LN
SolC 95688 413-B6
PAMELA ST
VAL 94589 510-C5
PAMPLONA AV
DVS 95616 356-A5
PANORAMA CT
BEN 94510 551-A2
PANORAMA DR
BEN 94510 551-B1
VAL 94589 530-C2
PAOLI LOOP RD
AMCN 94503 490-A6
NaCo 94589 490-A6
PAPIN PL
VAC 95687 433-J6
PAR CIR
YoCo 95616 377-A7
PARADISE CT
FRFD 94533 452-H7
PARADISE WY
WSAC 95691 378-G1
PARADISE PINES
RVIS 94571 516-E1
PARADISE VALLEY DR
FRFD 94533 452-G6
WDLD 95776 316-C5
PARAMOUNT CT
FRFD 94585 511-D3
PARAMOUNT WY
FRFD 94585 511-D3
PARIS WY
VAC 95687 453-G2
PARISH RD
SolC 94510 531-G3
PARISIO CIR
FRFD 94534 491-C3
W PARK
AMCN 94503 510-B4
PARK AV
WDLD 95695 315-H4
PARK BLVD
WSAC 95691 358-H5
PARK CIR
WSAC 95691 358-J5
PARK DR
DXN 95620 395-C6
VAC 95688 433-A3
PARK LN
AMCN 94503 509-J3
FRFD 94533 472-E6
SUIS 94585 492-G1
VAC 95687 453-F2
PARK RD
BEN 94510 551-F1
PARK ST
VAL 94591 530-D5
PARKER AV
CCCo 94572 549-H7
PARKER RD
FRFD 94535 473-G3
PARKER ST
VAC 95688 433-C5
PARKFIELD CT
FRFD 94533 472-H1
PARKFIELD DR
FRFD 94533 472-H1
PARKGREEN DR
DXN 95620 395-B6
PARKHAVEN CT
VAL 94591 530-E3
PARKHAVEN DR
VAL 94591 530-E3
PARKHAVEN WY
SAC 95831 378-J7
PARKLIN AV
SAC 95831 378-H6
PARKLITE CIR
SAC 95831 378-J7
PARKRIDGE CT
VAC 95688 433-B4
PARKRIDGE DR
VAC 95688 433-A4
PARK RIVIERA WY
SAC 95831 378-F7
PARKSHORE CIR
SAC 95831 378-J7
PARKSIDE DR
DVS 95616 356-B7
SUIS 94585 472-H6
VAC 95688 413-J7
PARKVIEW CT
AMCN 94503 509-J2
VAC 95688 413-J7
WDLD 95776 316-B4
PARKVIEW DR
WDLD 95776 316-B4
PARKVIEW TER
FRFD 94534 472-E2
VAL 94589 510-B7
VAL 94589 530-B1
PARK VISTA CIR
SAC 95831 378-J7
PARKWAY BLVD
DXN 95620 415-C2
WSAC 95691 358-E5
PARKWAY CIR
YoCo 95616 376-A1
PARKWAY PL
WSAC 95691 358-E5
PARKWOOD DR
VAL 94591 530-E4
PARR LN
SolC 94533 453-D7
PARRISH ST
FRFD 94535 473-J3
PARROT ST
VAL 94590 529-J2
PARTRIDGE AV
WSAC 95691 378-F3
PARTRIDGE PL
SUIS 94585 473-B7
PASATIEMPO CT
FRFD 94534 472-C2
PASCAL CT
FRFD 94585 491-D5
PASEO ARBOLES
SolC 94534 471-B5
PASEO FLORES CT
SUIS 94585 473-C6
PASEO FLORES DR
SUIS 94585 473-C6
PASTAL WY
DVS 95618 356-H6
PATRICIA DR
AMCN 94503 509-J4
AMCN 94503 510-A4
PATRICK CT
VAL 94591 530-E4
PATRICK LN
SolC 95694 394-A4

SOLANO CO.

STREET
Name City ZIP Pg-Grid

PATTERSON ST
FRFD 94535 473-J4
PATTON AV
NAP 94559 450-A7
NAP 94559 470-A1
PATWIN CT
DXN 95620 395-A6
PATWIN PL
FRFD 94534 472-E1
PATWIN RD
YoCo 95616 375-F1
PAU CT
FRFD 94534 472-C2
PAUL CT
BEN 94510 551-C1
PAULA DR
SUIS 94585 472-G7
SUIS 94585 492-G1
PAULA WY
VAL 94590 529-J3
WDLD 95695 315-H6
PAVILION CT
FRFD 94534 491-C2
PAVILION DR
FRFD 94534 491-C2
PEABODY RD
FRFD 94533 453-E7
FRFD 94533 473-E2
FRFD 94535 473-E2
FRFD 95687 473-E2
SolC 94533 453-E7
SolC 94533 473-E2
SolC 95687 453-E2
SolC 95687 473-E2
VAC 95687 433-E6
VAC 95687 453-E2
PEACE CT
FRFD 94533 452-G5
PEACEFUL GLEN RD
SolC 95688 413-B2
PEACEFUL POND RD
SolC 94534 471-D5
PEACH CT
SolC 94534 471-B6
PEACH PL
DVS 95616 356-A7
WIN 95694 373-E3
PEACH ST
VAL 94589 510-B7
PEACH TREE AV
VAC 95688 433-B5
PEACH TREE CT
FRFD 94533 472-G3
PEACH TREE DR
FRFD 94533 472-F3
PEACHTREE LN
RVIS 94571 516-F2
PEACHTREE ST
WSAC 95691 378-J1
PEACOCK CIR
AMCN 94503 509-H3
PEACOCK CT
VAC 95688 413-D6
PEACOCK WY
VAC 95688 413-D6
PEAR PL
WDLD 95776 316-B5
WIN 95694 373-E3
PEARCE CT
SUIS 94585 473-B7
PEARL CT
VAL 94591 530-D5
PEARL PL
DXN 95620 395-B5
PEARL WY
WDLD 95695 316-A2
PEAR TREE LN
FRFD 94533 472-G3
PEARWOOD CT
VAC 95687 453-G3
PEBBLE CT
SAC 95831 378-H6
PEBBLE BEACH CIR
FRFD 94534 452-A7
FRFD 94534 472-A1
SolC 94534 472-A1
VAC 95687 453-E3
PEBBLE BEACH DR
RVIS 94571 516-E2
VAC 95687 453-E2
VAL 94591 530-G2
PECAN CIR
FRFD 94533 472-J1
PECAN CT
VAL 94589 510-B7
PECAN PL
DVS 95616 356-D7
PECAN RD
SaCo 95837 317-H2
PECAN ST
VAC 95688 433-C6
VAL 94589 510-A7
WSAC 95691 358-G3
PEDRICK RD
DXN 95620 395-F4
SolC 95620 395-F7
SolC 95620 415-F3
PEDRICK RD Rt#-E7
SolC 95620 375-F7
SolC 95620 395-F1
PEGLER CT
WSAC 95691 378-F2
PEGORD AV
DXN 95620 395-C7
DXN 95620 415-C1
PEKINS CT
WSAC 95691 378-F1
PELHAM CT
FRFD 94534 472-C4
PELICAN DR
VAL 94589 509-H5
PELICAN WY
SUIS 94585 473-B7
PELLERIA DR
AMCN 94503 510-C4
PEMBROKE CT
VAC 95687 433-F7
PEMBROKE DR
VAL 94589 510-C5
PEMBROKE WY
DXN 95620 395-C6
PEMBROOK WY
FRFD 94533 472-H2
PENA DR
DVS 95618 356-F7
PENA ADOBE RD
VAC 95687 452-J1
PENDEGAST CIR
WDLD 95695 315-J5
PENDEGAST ST
WDLD 95695 315-J5
WDLD 95695 316-A5
WDLD 95776 316-A5
PENDER ISLAND ST
WSAC 95691 378-C2
PENINSULA CT
FRFD 94534 472-C2
PENN CREEK DR
FRFD 94534 472-D1
PENNEY LN
NaCo 94559 470-A1
NAP 94559 470-A1

PENNINGTON CT
CCCo 94525 550-E5
VAC 95687 453-F1
PENNINGTON PL
VAC 95687 453-F1
PENNSYLVANIA AV
FRFD 94533 472-E6
FRFD 94533 472-E7
SolC 94534 472-E7
SolC 94534 492-E1
SolC 94585 492-E1
SUIS 94534 492-E1
SUIS 94585 492-E1
WSAC 95691 358-H6
PENNSYLVANIA CT
WSAC 95691 358-H6
PENNSYLVANIA PL
DVS 95616 356-D5
PENNSYLVANIA ST
VAL 94590 529-J5
VAL 94590 530-A5
PENNY LN
VAL 94591 530-F1
PENNY PL
DVS 95616 356-E6
PENSACOLA LN
SUIS 94585 473-C5
PEPPER CT
VAC 95687 433-H4
PEPPER DR
VAL 94589 510-B6
PEPPERCORN CT
VAL 94591 530-F7
PEPPERDINE CT
DVS 95618 356-F7
PEPPERELL CT
VAC 95688 433-D1
PEPPERTREE CT
FRFD 94533 473-A2
WSAC 95691 378-J1
PEPPERTREE DR
FRFD 94533 452-J7
FRFD 94533 453-A7
FRFD 94533 472-J1
FRFD 94533 473-A1
PEPPERTREE RD
WSAC 95691 378-J1
PEPPERWOOD ST
SUIS 94585 472-H6
PERCHERON CT
VAL 94591 530-D2
PEREGRINE AV
DVS 95616 356-B4
PEREGRINE WY
VAC 95687 453-F3
PEREZ CT
WSAC 95691 378-F2
PERIDOT PL
FRFD 94534 491-E1
PERIMETER RD
FRFD 94535 473-F7
FRFD 94535 474-E1
SolC 94535 474-B5
PERIWINKLE PL
BEN 94510 531-A7
PERKINS AV
VAL 94590 530-C5
PERKINS CT
SUIS 94585 473-B7
SUIS 94585 493-C1
PERKINS ST
NAP 94559 470-A1
PERRIS CT
WSAC 95691 378-D4
PERRY CT
FRFD 94534 472-D4
PERRY DR
VAL 94592 529-H7
VAL 94592 549-H1
PERSHING AV
WDLD 95695 316-A3
PERSIMMON CIR
VAC 95687 453-F1
PERSIMMON DR
VAL 94589 510-B7
PERSIMMON PL
FRFD 94533 472-J1
PERTH CT
VAC 95687 433-D7
PERTH ST
VAL 94591 530-G5
PERTH WY
BEN 94510 551-B2
PETAL CT
VAC 95688 433-D3
PETER ISLAND RD
WSAC 95691 378-D2
PETER J SHIELDS AV
YoCo 95616 376-B2
PETERS AV
DXN 95620 395-C7
DXN 95620 415-C1
PETERSEN RD
FRFD 94535 473-D7
FRFD 94585 473-D7
SolC 94535 473-D7
SolC 94585 473-D7
SUIS 94585 473-C7
PETERSON LN
DXN 95620 395-B6
PETRA CT
DVS 95618 356-G6
PETRILLI CIR
SAC 95822 378-J5
PEYTONIA CT
SUIS 94585 493-B1
PEYTONIA LN
SUIS 94585 493-B1
PHEASANT CT
SUIS 94585 473-B7
WDLD 95695 315-G1
PHEASANT DR
SUIS 94585 473-B7
PHEASANT RDG
SolC 95694 393-B1
PHEASANT HOLLOW DR
WSAC 95691 378-G1
PHEASANT RUN DR
DXN 95620 395-A7
PHELAN AV
VAL 94590 530-C5
PHELPS CT
BEN 94510 531-A7
WSAC 95691 378-F2
PHELPS ST
VAL 94590 529-J2
PHILLIP ST
SolC 94590 530-B6
PHILLIP WY
SUIS 94585 473-A5
PHILLIP ISLAND RD
WSAC 95691 378-C3
PHILLIPS RD
SolC 95620 374-J5
SolC 95620 375-A5
PHOENIX CIR
VAL 94589 510-B7
PHOENIX DR
FRFD 94533 472-H5
PHYLLIS CT
VAL 94590 550-C2
PIAZZA LN
SolC 94534 472-A5

PICADILLY CIR
VAL 94591 530-H5
PICASSO AV
DVS 95618 356-E5
PICASSO CT
FRFD 94534 491-C3
VAL 94591 530-E2
PICOLIT CT
FRFD 94534 491-F5
PIEDMONT CT
VAC 95687 433-C7
PIEDMONT DR
SAC 95822 378-J3
PIENZA DR
AMCN 94503 510-C4
N PIER ST
SolC 94592 529-F3
VAL 94592 529-F3
PIERCE LN
SolC 94510 531-H2
PIERCE ST
FRFD 94533 472-E6
VAL 94590 530-A3
WSAC 95605 358-J1
PIERCE RANCH RD
YoCo 95616 355-C7
YoCo 95616 375-C1
PIERRE CT
VAL 94591 530-G3
PILLSBURY RD
WSAC 95691 378-D4
PILOT HILL CT
VAL 94589 509-J5
PILOT POINT RD
WSAC 95691 378-D2
PIMA CT
VAC 95688 432-J4
PIMPERNEL CT
VAC 95687 453-E2
PINE AV
WSAC 95691 358-F4
PINE LN
DVS 95616 356-A7
PINE ST
SolC 94590 530-C6
VAC 95688 433-C6
VAL 94590 530-B7
VAL 94590 550-C1
WDLD 95695 315-G3
PINE BLUFF WY
VAC 95688 413-D6
PINE CREEK CIR
FRFD 94534 491-F3
PINE CREEK LN
AMCN 94503 510-B3
PINECREST CT
VAC 95688 433-C2
PINEHAVEN LN
SolC 95688 413-E4
PINEHURST CT
VAC 95688 413-J6
PINEHURST DR
FRFD 94534 472-B2
RVIS 94571 516-F3
PINENUT WY
FRFD 94585 511-E2
PINE TREE CT
VAC 95688 413-H6
PINE VALLEY CT
FRFD 94534 472-D1
PINE VALLEY DR
FRFD 94534 472-D1
PINEWOOD CT
DXN 95620 415-B1
FRFD 94585 511-E2
PINKERTON LN
FRFD 94533 453-E7
PINNACLE PT
VAL 94591 510-J4
VAL 94591 511-A4
PINNACLES DR
WDLD 95695 315-G2
PINNACLES PL
DVS 95616 355-J6
PINNACLES ST
DVS 95616 355-J6
PINOLE AV
CCCo 94572 549-H7
PINTADO ST
VAL 94592 529-G4
PINTAIL CT
VAC 95688 433-C4
WSAC 95691 378-F1
PINTAIL DR
SUIS 94585 472-H6
SUIS 94585 473-A6
VAC 95688 433-C4
PINTAIL PL
DVS 95616 356-C4
PINTO CT
FRFD 94533 452-J7
FRFD 94533 472-J1
VAL 94591 530-E1
PINTO DR
VAL 94591 530-E1
PINYON CT
FRFD 94533 472-J1
PIONEER AV
WDLD 95776 316-C3
N PIONEER AV
WDLD 95776 316-C1
PIONEER CT
VAC 95688 433-J1
VAL 94589 509-H5
PIPER DR
VAC 95688 413-G7
VAC 95688 433-G1
PIPPIN CT
VAC 95687 433-H3
PIPPO LN
SolC 95688 413-B3
PIRATES COVE CT
VAL 94591 550-G2
PISMO CT
DVS 95616 356-A6
FRFD 94533 452-H7
PISTACHIO CT
DVS 95618 376-J1
PISTACIA CT
FRFD 94533 452-J6
PITTIER WY
SUIS 94585 472-H6
PITTMAN RD
FRFD 94534 491-E3
SolC 94534 491-E3
PITT SCHOOL RD
DXN 95620 395-B7
DXN 95620 415-B2
SolC 95620 395-B4
SolC 95620 415-B2
PITZER CIR
WSAC 95691 378-F2
PLACER DR
WDLD 95695 315-J6
WDLD 95695 316-A6
PLACER LN
SUIS 94585 473-B6
PLACER PL
VAL 94591 550-C1
WDLD 95695 315-J6
PLANE AV
WDLD 95695 315-H2

PLANTATION CT
VAC 95687 453-F1
PLANTATION WY
VAC 95687 453-F1
PLATINUM CT
VAL 94589 510-B6
PLATT CT
VAL 94589 510-B7
PLAZA CT
DXN 95620 394-J7
PLAZA DR
VAL 94591 510-E7
VAL 94591 530-E1
PLAZA DE ORO
BEN 94510 550-J3
PLEASANT HILLS RANCH WY
SolC 95688 412-E6
PLEASANTS TR
SolC 95688 412-G3
PLEASANTS VALLEY RD
SolC 95688 392-H2
SolC 95688 412-F2
SolC 95688 432-H2
SolC 95688 452-H1
SolC 95694 392-H2
PLOV WY
VAL 94590 529-H2
PLUM LN
DVS 95616 356-A7
PLUM PL
WIN 95694 373-E3
PLUM ST
VAC 95688 433-C4
PLUMAS CT
VAC 95687 433-J3
PLUMAS DR
SUIS 94585 473-C6
VAC 95687 433-H3
PLUM TREE WY
FRFD 94533 472-G4
PLYMOUTH CT
BEN 94510 550-J2
BEN 94510 551-A2
VAC 95687 453-H2
PLYMOUTH PL
FRFD 94534 472-C5
POCHARD WY
SUIS 94585 473-A6
POCKET RD
SAC 95831 378-F7
POCO WY
AMCN 94503 510-A1
POINT BENICIA CIR
BEN 94510 551-A3
POINT BENICIA WY
BEN 94510 551-B6
POINT REYES CT
VAL 94591 550-E3
POINT REYES PL
DVS 95616 355-J6
POLARIS CT
VAL 94591 550-G3
POLE LINE RD
DVS 95616 356-E6
DVS 95616 376-E1
DVS 95618 356-E6
DVS 95618 376-E1
POLE LINE RD Rt#-E8
DVS 95618 356-E5
YoCo 95616 356-E5
YoCo 95618 356-E5
POLK ST
BEN 94510 551-D6
FRFD 94533 472-G5
POLLOCK PL
DVS 95618 356-F5
POLSON RD
NaCo 94558 470-F7
NaCo 94558 490-E1
NaCo 94559 470-F7
NaCo 94559 490-E1
NAP 94558 490-E1
POMBO LN
SolC 95687 434-B2
POMO CT
WSAC 95691 378-H2
POMO PL
DVS 95618 376-H1
POMONA AV
VAL 94589 510-B6
POMONA DR
DVS 95616 356-E7
POMONA PL
FRFD 94534 472-D3
POMONA ST
CCCo 94525 550-E5
PONDEROSA CT
FRFD 94533 472-H1
PONDEROSA DR
VAC 95687 433-H5
PONDEROSA PL
DVS 95616 356-D6
POND SIDE WY
FRFD 94585 491-C6
PONTEVERDE LN
DVS 95618 356-F6
POPE CT
FRFD 94535 473-G2
POPE DR
VAL 94591 530-F6
POPLAR AV
VAL 94592 529-G6
WSAC 95691 358-H3
POPLAR AV E
VAL 94592 529-G6
POPLAR CT
FRFD 94533 472-J1
POPLAR LN
DVS 95618 356-F5
WDLD 95695 315-G5
POPLAR RD
SolC 95687 433-J2
SolC 95687 434-A2
VAC 95687 433-J2
VAC 95687 434-A2
POPLAR ST
VAC 95688 433-C4
POPPY CIR
BEN 94510 530-J7
BEN 94510 531-A7
BEN 94510 550-J1
VAC 95687 453-J1
POPPY CT
VAL 94591 530-F7
POPPY LN
DVS 95616 355-H7
POPPY ST
WSAC 95691 378-F2
POPPYFIELD DR
AMCN 94503 509-J4
POPPY HOUSE RD
RVIS 94571 516-H4
PORT ST
CCCo 94575 [illegible]
WSAC 95691 358-G4
PORT WY
SUIS 94585 472-G7
VAL 94591 530-G1
PORTAGE BAY E
DVS 95616 355-H7
DVS 95616 375-H1

PORTAGE BAY W
DVS 95616 355-H7
PORTER CT
FRFD 94533 473-B3
WDLD 95695 315-F3
PORTER ST
DXN 95620 395-C7
DXN 95620 415-B2
SolC 95620 414-J4
SolC 95620 415-B2
VAL 94590 530-B7
VAL 94590 550-B1
WDLD 95695 315-G3
PORTER WY
VAC 95688 433-D6
PORTLAND DR
FRFD 94533 473-B2
PORTOFINO AV
VAC 95687 433-B7
PORTOFINO CT
VAC 95687 433-B7
PORTOFINO WY
AMCN 94503 510-C4
PORTOLA AV
VAL 94591 530-D7
VAL 94591 550-D1
PORTOLA CT
DVS 95616 355-J6
FRFD 94534 472-D3
PORTOLA ST
DVS 95616 355-J6
WSAC 95691 358-H7
PORTSMOUTH AV
DVS 95616 355-G7
VAC 95687 433-G6
WSAC 95691 358-J3
PORTSMOUTH CT
FRFD 94534 472-B4
POSITIVE PL
VAL 94589 510-B5
POTRERO CIR
SUIS 94585 473-B7
SUIS 94585 493-B1
POTRERO ST
SUIS 94585 493-C1
POTRERO WY
FRFD 94534 472-C4
POTRERO HILLS LN
SolC 94585 493-D3
POWDER CT
VAC 95687 453-G1
POWELL PL
WSAC 95691 358-J7
POWER DR
VAL 94589 510-B7
VAL 94589 530-B1
POWERS CIR
WDLD 95776 316-C6
PRADO LN
DVS 95618 356-F7
PRAIRIE CT
SUIS 94585 473-A7
VAC 95687 433-E6
PRAIRIE DR
SUIS 94585 473-A7
PRALLOW ST
FRFD 94535 474-A2
PRATHER CT
WDLD 95776 316-C5
PREAKNESS LN
VAL 94591 530-E2
PRESCOTT WY
FRFD 94534 472-C5
PRESIDIO RD
WSAC 95691 358-H7
PRESTON CIR
VAL 94592 529-H7
PRESTON PL
DXN 95620 395-B7
PRESTON ST
VAL 94592 529-H7
PRESTWICK CT
FRFD 94534 452-D7
VAL 94591 530-F3
PRICE LN
SolC 95688 393-D7
PRICE WY
VAL 94591 530-E5
PRIDDY DR
DXN 95620 395-E7
PRIMATE DR
YoCo 95616 375-E2
PRIMERO GROVE CIR
YoCo 95616 376-B1
PRIMITIVO CT
FRFD 94534 491-F5
PRIMIVITO CT
VAC 95687 433-C7
PRIMROSE AV
FRFD 94533 472-G2
PRIMROSE CT
VAL 94591 530-H5
PRIMROSE LN
BEN 94510 531-A7
VAL 94591 530-H5
PRIMROSE PL
YoCo 95616 355-J2
PRINCESS DIANA CT
VAL 94591 530-J1
PRINCETON
VAL 94589 510-A5
PRINCETON CT
VAC 95687 433-F7
WDLD 95695 315-G6
PRINCETON PL
DVS 95616 356-D7
WDLD 95695 315-F6
PRINCETON RD
WSAC 95691 378-J1
PRINCETON WY
FRFD 94533 472-H2
PRISCILLA CT
WIN 95694 373-F3
PROCTOR AV
WSAC 95691 358-H4
PROCTOR CT
WDLD 95695 316-A6
PROMENADE CIR
SUIS 94585 472-H6
PROMENADE DR
WDLD 95776 336-E1
PROMENADE ST
WSAC 95691 358-D7
WSAC 95691 378-D1
PROSPECT AV
CCCo 94569 550-H6
VAL 94592 529-G6
PROSPECT CIR
VAL 94592 529-G6
PROSPECT LN
VAL 94592 529-G6
PROSPECT PL
VAC 95687 433-G5
PROSPECT ST
VAL 94592 529-H6
PROSPECT WY
VAC 95687 473-C6
PROSPERITY LN
SUIS 94585 473-B5
PROSSER ST
WSAC 95691 378-E4
PROVIDENCE PL
VAC 95687 453-H2

PROW CT
SAC 95822 378-J4
PUEBLO CT
VAL 94591 550-E1
PUEBLO WY
VAL 94591 550-C1
PUERTO RICO RD
WSAC 95691 378-D2
PUFFIN CIR
FRFD 94533 473-F2
PULLEN LN
FRFD 94533 453-D7
SolC 94533 453-D7
PUMA CT
DVS 95618 376-J1
PUMICE CT
VAL 94589 510-C6
PUMICE DR
VAL 94589 510-C6
PURDUE DR
DVS 95616 356-A7
VAC 95687 433-H6
VAL 94589 510-A5
WDLD 95695 315-F5
PURPLE MARTIN DR
VAC 95687 453-J2
PURPLE SAGE DR
VAC 95687 453-J2
PURTCELL CT
YoCo 95694 373-H2
PUTAH CREEK RD
SolC 95694 373-H3
SolC 95694 374-A3
SolC 95694 375-A3
SolC 95694 392-H2
SolC 95694 393-A1
PUTAH CREEK LODGE RD
YoCo 95616 376-B3
PUTAH RIDGE TR
SolC 95694 393-B1
PUTMAN RD
SolC 95688 413-G4
PUTNAM CT
FRFD 94534 472-C4
VAC 95687 433-G5
PYRACANTHA CT
VAL 94591 530-F6
PYRAMID CT
FRFD 94534 491-E2
PYRAMID PL
WSAC 95691 378-C4
PYRAMID WY
FRFD 94534 491-E2

Q

QUAIL CT
FRFD 94533 472-J3
VAC 95687 433-G5
VAL 94591 530-D2
WIN 95694 373-D4
WSAC 95691 358-J7
QUAIL DR
FRFD 94533 472-J3
FRFD 94533 473-A3
WDLD 95695 315-G1
QUAIL LN
SolC 95694 393-B2
QUAIL RD
WSAC 95691 358-J7
WSAC 95691 378-J1
QUAIL ST
DVS 95616 356-A5
QUAIL CANYON RD
SolC 95688 392-F4
QUAIL HOLLOW DR
FRFD 94534 452-B7
QUAIL MEADOWS CIR
VAC 95687 453-E2
QUAIL RIDGE DR
NaCo 94558 451-F2
QUAIL RIDGE LN
SolC 95688 413-B7
QUAIL WALK WY
RVIS 94571 516-G2
QUAKER CT
FRFD 94534 452-A7
QUALITY CIR
WDLD 95776 316-F4
QUARRY DR
NAP 94559 450-A7
QUARRYVILLE CT
FRFD 94533 452-J7
FRFD 94533 453-A7
QUARTER CIR
DVS 95618 356-F7
QUARTZ LN
VAL 94589 510-C6
QUATE CT
VAC 95688 433-D2
QUAY CT
SAC 95831 378-H6
QUEEN ISABELLA CT
VAL 94591 530-E1
QUIET HARBOR DR
VAL 94591 550-E2
QUIETWOOD CT
VAC 95688 433-A3
QUIETWOOD DR
VAC 95688 433-A3
QUILTING LN
VAL 94589 510-D6
QUINCEY CT
FRFD 94534 472-B4
QUINCEY LN
FRFD 94534 472-B4
QUINCY AL
VAL 94590 529-J4
VAL 94590 530-A4
QUINCY CT
VAC 95687 453-G2
QUINCY DR
WDLD 95695 315-J6
QUINN RD
SolC 95688 414-A7
VAC 95688 414-A7
VAC 95688 433-J1
VAC 95688 434-A1
QUITO CT
SUIS 94585 473-D6

R

RACE COURSE LN
SolC 95694 373-G4
RACHEL WY
VAL 94591 530-G4
RACOON CT
FRFD 94533 452-H7
RADCLIFF DR
VAC 95687 433-H6
RADCLIFFE CT
VAL 94589 510-C5
RADCLIFFE DR
DVS 95616 356-A6
VAL 94589 510-C5
RADNOR CT
BEN 94510 551-B2
RAE CT
VAL 94591 530-E4
RAGSDALE ST
FRFD 94535 473-G4

RAGSDALE ST
SolC 94535 473-F7
RAILROAD AV
CCCo 94569 550-H5
CCCo 94572 549-H7
FRFD 94535 473-J4
SolC 94585 472-J5
SUIS 94585 472-J5
SUIS 94585 473-A4
VAL 94592 529-G3
VAL 94592 549-J1
VAL 94592 550-A1
WIN 95694 373-F2
YoCo 95694 373-F2
RAILROAD ST
WDLD 95776 316-A3
RAINBOW CT
VAL 94591 530-F4
RAINER AV
VAL 94589 510-B5
RAINES CT
VAL 94591 530-F5
RAINIER CIR
VAC 95687 433-G4
RAINIER CT
FRFD 94585 491-D7
RVIS 94571 516-G5
RAINIER PL
WDLD 95695 315-G2
RAINTREE CT
VAL 94589 510-B5
RAINTREE PL
DVS 95618 356-G5
RALEIGH CT
FRFD 94533 472-B7
RALEIGH DR
FRFD 94533 472-B7
VAC 95687 453-E2
RALEY CT
WSAC 95691 358-C5
RALPH AV
VAC 95687 433-H6
RALSTON CT
VAL 94591 530-G4
RAMBLER AL
SolC 94591 530-C6
VAL 94591 530-C6
RAMBLER ROSE LN
SUIS 94585 472-G6
RAMBLETON DR
VAC 95688 433-D2
RAMCO ST
WSAC 95691 358-E7
WSAC 95691 378-D1
RAMONA CT
WSAC 95691 358-J7
RAMONA ST
VAC 95688 433-C5
RAMOS DR
WSAC 95691 378-C1
RAMOS ST
VAC 95688 433-C6
RAMSEY CT
FRFD 94534 472-E3
RAMSEY DR
VAC 95687 453-F1
RAMSEY RD
SolC 94585 491-E6
SolC 94585 511-E1
RAMSEY WY
FRFD 94534 472-E3
RAMSGATE CT
FRFD 94585 511-D1
RAMSGATE WY
VAL 94591 530-G4
RANCHO PL
WDLD 95695 315-H5
RANCHO WY
WDLD 95695 315-H5
RANCHO MURIETA CT
VAC 95687 453-H3
RANCHO MURIETA DR
VAC 95687 453-H3
RANCHO SOLANO PKWY
FRFD 94534 452-B7
FRFD 94534 472-B1
RANDALL AV
VAC 95687 433-H7
RANDOLPH RD
WSAC 95691 358-J6
RANDOLPH ST
FRFD 94535 473-J2
FRFD 94535 474-A2
RANIER ST
DVS 95618 376-F2
RANKIN WY
BEN 94510 551-C4
RAPHAEL PL
DVS 95618 356-E5
RAPP LN
NaCo 94558 450-B4
RASMUSSEN CT
FRFD 94533 453-D7
RASMUSSEN WY
FRFD 94533 453-D7
RAVEN CT
FRFD 94533 472-J3
RAVEN DR
VAC 95687 433-H7
VAC 95687 453-J1
RAVENRIDGE PL
FRFD 94534 491-D1
RAVENSWOOD CT
VAC 95688 433-A5
VAL 94591 510-J5
RAWHIDE CT
VAL 94589 509-J5
RAYBURN CT
FRFD 94533 472-H3
RAYMOND DR
BEN 94510 551-A4
READING WY
VAC 95687 433-J6
REAM ST
SolC 94590 530-C6
VAL 94590 530-C6
REBECCA CT
AMCN 94503 509-J1
REBECCA DR
FRFD 94533 473-A2
SUIS 94585 473-B6
REDBUD DR
DVS 95618 376-J2
RED BUD LN
WIN 95694 373-G3
REDBUD LN
VAL 94591 550-F1
REDBUD PL
DVS 95618 376-H1
RED BUD WY
SUIS 94585 472-H6
RED CLOVER WY
AMCN 94503 509-H1
REDDICK RD
SolC 95620 394-J6
REDDING RD
WSAC 95691 358-J7
REDGRASS CT
AMCN 94503 509-H2
REDHEAD ST
AMCN 94503 509-H1
REDHEAD WY
SUIS 94585 472-J6

REDINGER CT — SOLANO COUNTY STREET INDEX — SANTA MARIA DR 567

(c) 2007 Rand McNally & Company

SOLANO CO.

STREET Name City ZIP Pg-Grid

REDINGER CT
SUIS 94585 473-C7
RED MAPLE CT
VAC 95687 434-A3
REDMONT
RVIS 94571 516-F1
RED MULBERRY CT
VAC 95687 433-J3
RED OAK CT
VAC 95687 453-C1
VAL 94591 510-H4
REDONDO RD
WSAC 95691 378-H1
RED PHEASANT DR
VAC 95687 453-J1
REDSTONE CIR
SUIS 94585 472-H6
RED SUNSET CT
VAC 95687 434-A3
RED TOP RD
FRFD 94585 491-C5
SolC 94585 491-C5
SolC 94589 491-C5
RED WILLOW WY
SUIS 94585 472-H7
REDWING DR
WDLD 95695 315-G1
REDWING ST
VAL 94589 510-A5
REDWOOD
BEN 94510 551-C6
REDWOOD AV
WSAC 95691 378-J1
REDWOOD CT
CCCo 94525 550-D5
DXN 95620 415-B1
FRFD 94533 472-J1
REDWOOD DR
FRFD 94533 452-J7
FRFD 94533 472-J1
VAC 95687 453-E1
WDLD 95695 315-H6
REDWOOD LN
DVS 95616 356-B7
REDWOOD PKWY
VAL 94589 530-D2
VAL 94590 530-D2
VAL 94591 530-D2
REDWOOD ST
VAL 94589 529-J2
VAL 94589 530-B2
VAL 94590 529-J2
VAL 94590 530-B2
REDWOOD MEADOWS LN
FRFD 94534 491-F4
REED AV
WSAC 95605 358-F2
REED CT
BEN 94510 550-J2
REED DR
AMCN 94503 510-A4
DVS 95616 356-B7
DXN 95620 395-A7
VAC 95687 433-H5
REEF CT
SAC 95831 378-H7
REEVES AV
VAL 94592 529-G6
REEVES CT
SUIS 94585 473-C7
REFOSCO CT
FRFD 94534 491-F5
VAC 95687 433-B7
REGAN HALL CIR
YoCo 95616 376-B1
REGATTA CIR
FRFD 94533 473-A2
REGATTA CT
DVS 95618 376-F2
VAL 94591 550-G3
N REGATTA DR
VAL 94591 550-F2
S REGATTA DR
VAL 94591 550-F2
REGATTA LN
DVS 95618 376-F2
REGATTA PT
HER 94547 549-G7
REGENCY CIR
VAC 95687 433-G5
REGENCY PKWY
DXN 95620 395-C4
REGENCY PL
FRFD 94585 491-E7
REGENCY WY
VAC 95687 433-H5
REGENT CT
AMCN 94503 510-A3
REGENT ST
WSAC 95691 358-H5
REGENTS PARK DR
VAL 94591 530-G6
REGINA WY
DXN 95620 395-A6
REGIS CT
BEN 94510 530-J7
REGIS DR
DVS 95618 356-E6
REHRMANN DR
DXN 95620 394-J7
DXN 95620 395-A7
REIFF PL
WDLD 95776 316-F5
REIS AV
SolC 94590 530-C6
SolC 94591 530-D6
VAL 94591 530-D6
REMINGTON CT
VAL 94590 530-B7
RENAISSANCE AV
FRFD 94534 491-D2
RENAISSANCE CT
FRFD 94534 491-D2
RENEE CT
DXN 95620 395-B5
WSAC 95691 378-E1
RENIDA ST
SolC 94591 530-E7
RENNERT WY
DXN 95620 394-J7
DXN 95620 395-A7
RENOIR AV
DVS 95618 356-E5
RENWOOD LN
AMCN 94503 510-B3
RENWOOD PL
AMCN 94503 510-B3
REO AL
VAL 94590 529-J4
VAL 94590 530-A4
REPUBLIC WY
VAC 95687 453-F2
RESEARCH PARK DR
DVS 95618 376-D2
YoCo 95618 376-E2
RESERVOIR LN
SolC 94534 491-C2
RESERVOIR RD
BEN 94510 531-E7
BEN 94510 551-E1
SaCo 95837 317-J1
RESERVOIR ST
CCCo 94569 550-G6

REVELLE CT
DXN 95620 415-C2
REVELLE DR
DXN 95620 415-C2
REVERE CT
VAC 95687 453-G2
REVERE ST
VAL 94591 530-D4
REYES CT
SAC 95831 378-G6
REYNARD LN
VAL 94591 530-E2
RHEA CT
VAL 94589 509-J6
RHESUS RD
YoCo 95616 375-E1
RHINE CT
FRFD 94533 472-D7
RHODODENDRON CT
VAL 94591 530-F6
RHONDA CT
VAL 94589 509-J5
RIALTO AV
FRFD 94585 491-D7
RIALTO CT
FRFD 94585 491-D7
RIALTO DR
VAC 95687 433-C7
RIALTO LN
DVS 95618 376-F2
RIBEIRO RD
VAL 94592 529-G7
VAL 94592 549-H1
RIBOLLA CT
FRFD 94534 491-F5
RICE AV
WSAC 95691 358-G3
RICE CT
WDLD 95695 315-F6
RICE LN
DVS 95616 376-C1
VAC 95688 413-E7
YoCo 95616 376-C1
RICE ST
VAL 94590 530-B5
RICH ST
WSAC 95605 358-J2
RICHARD PL
VAC 95687 433-J6
RICHARDS BLVD
DVS 95616 376-D1
DVS 95618 376-D2
RICHARDS CT
FRFD 94533 472-F5
RICHARDSON DR
VAL 94589 530-B1
RICHLAND WY
FRFD 94534 472-D3
RICKOVER ST
VAL 94592 529-G6
RICKY CT
SUIS 94585 473-A5
RIDGE AV
SolC 94591 530-E7
SolC 94591 550-D1
RIDGE CIR
BEN 94510 551-A4
RIDGEBURY WY
FRFD 94533 452-J7
FRFD 94533 453-A7
RIDGECREST CIR
SUIS 94585 472-H6
RIDGECREST CT
FRFD 94585 491-D7
RIDGEFIELD CIR
FRFD 94585 511-D3
N RIDGEFIELD WY
FRFD 94585 511-E3
S RIDGEFIELD WY
FRFD 94585 511-E3
RIDGEVIEW DR
WDLD 95695 315-F5
RIDGEVIEW LN
SolC 95688 393-H7
RIDGEVIEW PL
WDLD 95695 315-G5
RIDGEWOOD CIR
FRFD 94534 452-E7
RIDGEWOOD CT
FRFD 94534 452-E7
VAC 95688 433-A4
VAL 94591 530-E5
RIDGEWOOD DR
VAC 95688 433-A4
RINALDO DR
VAL 94589 509-J5
VAL 94589 510-A5
RINCON WY
VAL 94590 530-B2
RINCONADA CT
BEN 94510 551-C5
RING NECK CT
SUIS 94585 472-J6
RING NECK LN
SUIS 94585 472-J6
RINGNECK ST
AMCN 94503 509-H1
RIO DEL MAR
AMCN 94503 509-H2
AMCN 94503 510-A1
RIO DIXON RD Rt#-113
DXN 95620 415-C4
SolC 95620 415-C4
RIO GRANDE DR
AMCN 94503 509-H1
VAC 95687 433-J6
RIO GRANDE ST
DVS 95616 355-J6
DVS 95616 356-A6
RIO VERDE
SUIS 94585 472-H6
RIO VISTA BRDG Rt#-12
SaCo 95641 516-J5
RIPPLE CT
SAC 95831 378-G6
RIPTIDE WY
SAC 95831 378-G7
RISHON CT
FRFD 94533 452-H7
RITA CT
AMCN 94503 509-J1
RITCHIE RD
SolC 94534 491-E4
RITTER CT
FRFD 94534 472-D3
RIVENDELL LN
DVS 95616 355-H7
W RIVER DR
SAC 95833 358-G1
RIVER RD
FRFD 94585 491-C6
RIVER RD Rt#-84
RVIS 94571 516-J5
S RIVER RD
WSAC 95691 378-E7
YoCo 95691 378-E7
RIVERA PL
DVS 95618 356-E5
RIVERA RD
VAC 95687 452-J2

RIVERBANK RD
WSAC 95605 358-G1
RIVERBOAT WY
SAC 95831 378-G7
RIVERBROOK WY
SAC 95831 378-F7
RIVER CLIFF DR
RVIS 94571 516-E1
RIVERCREST DR
SAC 95831 378-H6
RIVERDALE AV
VAC 95687 453-G1
RIVERDALE CT
VAC 95687 453-H1
RIVERHILL DR
BEN 94510 551-C4
RIVERLAKE WY
SAC 95831 378-G5
RIVERMONT ST
WSAC 95691 378-F3
RIVERMOUTH LN
VAL 94591 550-F2
RIVER OAKS CIR
FRFD 94533 452-J6
RIVER PINES WY
VAL 94589 509-J5
RIVERPOINT CIR
WSAC 95605 358-F2
RIVERPOINT DR
WSAC 95605 358-G2
RIVERSIDE BLVD
SAC 95822 378-J5
SAC 95831 378-J5
RIVERSIDE CT
FRFD 94533 473-C4
RIVERSIDE DR
WDLD 95695 315-G7
RIVERSIDE PKWY
WSAC 95605 358-E2
RIVERTON WY
SAC 95831 378-H5
RIVERVIEW CT
SAC 95822 378-J3
WIN 95694 373-E4
RIVERVIEW DR
VAL 94589 510-B7
RIVERVIEW ST
RVIS 94571 516-H6
RIVERVIEW TER
BEN 94510 551-B4
RIVERWAY LN
SolC 94559 529-F2
VAL 94592 529-F2
RIVERWOOD LN
RVIS 94571 516-F1
RIVIERA CT
FRFD 94534 472-C2
ROADRUNNER DR
FRFD 94533 473-F2
ROBBEN RD
SolC 95620 395-H1
SolC 95620 415-G4
ROBBINS CT
SUIS 94585 473-C7
ROBERT RD
VAC 95687 433-H7
ROBERTS DR
FRFD 94535 473-G2
ROBIN CIR
FRFD 94533 472-D5
ROBIN CT
VAC 95687 453-J1
VAL 94591 530-E3
ROBIN DR
VAC 95687 453-J1
WDLD 95695 315-F1
ROBIN PL
DVS 95616 356-B4
ROBIN WY
FRFD 94533 472-H3
ROBINDALE LN
SolC 95688 412-F6
ROBINIA PL
DVS 95618 376-H2
ROBINSON RD
SolC 95688 413-F3
ROBINSON WY
BEN 94510 531-B7
ROBLES DR
VAL 94591 530-E7
VAL 94591 550-F1
ROCK HARBOR PT
HER 94547 549-G7
ROCKHURST CT
FRFD 94533 472-G1
ROCKPORT CT
VAC 95687 453-G2
ROCKRIDGE DR
FRFD 94534 472-E1
ROCKRIDGE PL
VAC 95687 433-G5
ROCK RIVER DR
VAL 94589 510-B6
ROCKROSE RD
WSAC 95691 358-H3
ROCKVILLE HTS
SolC 94534 471-F6
ROCKVILLE RD
FRFD 94534 472-A6
SolC 94534 471-J6
SolC 94534 472-A6
ROCKWELL CT
DVS 95618 356-G4
ROCKWELL DR
DVS 95618 356-E5
ROCKWOOD CT
VAC 95687 433-J5
VAL 94591 530-E5
ROCKY HILL RD
VAC 95688 433-D4
ROCKY POINT CV
SUIS 94585 472-G7
ROCKY SHORE CT
VAL 94591 530-F1
ROCKY SHORE DR
VAL 94591 530-F1
RODEO AV
CCCo 94572 549-H7
RODEO CT
VAL 94589 510-E6
RODGERS ST
VAL 94590 529-H2
RODIN CT
VAL 94591 530-E2
RODIN PL
DVS 95618 356-F5
RODONDO AV
SUIS 94585 472-H6
ROE CT
SAC 95822 378-J4
ROEDER WY
SAC 95822 378-J3
ROGER ST
FRFD 94533 472-E7
ROGERS LN
SolC 95688 433-A3
ROGERS ST
DVS 95618 357-A7
WSAC 95605 358-J1
ROGUE CT
FRFD 94534 472-D3
ROGUE RIVER CIR
WSAC 95691 378-H1

ROGUE RIVER CT
WSAC 95691 378-H1
ROHWER CT
DXN 95620 395-A6
ROHWER WY
WDLD 95776 316-E7
ROLEEN CT
VAL 94589 509-J6
ROLEEN DR
VAL 94589 509-J6
VAL 94589 510-A6
ROLLING PL
RVIS 94571 516-G4
ROLLING GREEN DR
RVIS 94571 516-H4
ROLLING HILLS DR
AMCN 94503 510-B1
ROLLING HILLS LN
SolC 95688 393-C6
ROLLING MEADOWS CT
FRFD 94534 491-F4
ROLLING OAK CT
VAC 95688 413-D7
VAC 95688 433-D1
ROLLING OAK DR
VAC 95688 433-D1
ROLLING SAGE CIR
VAC 95688 413-D6
ROLLINGWOOD CT
VAC 95688 433-D2
ROLLINGWOOD DR
FRFD 94534 452-G6
VAL 94591 530-F6
ROLLINS CT
WSAC 95691 378-D4
ROLPH AV
CCCo 94525 550-D5
ROLPH PARK CT
CCCo 94525 550-D5
ROLPH PARK DR
CCCo 94525 550-D5
ROMA CT
WSAC 95691 378-J1
ROMAN CT
WDLD 95776 316-E5
ROME DR
VAL 94589 510-A5
ROMINE WY
VAL 94591 530-D6
RON CT
VAL 94591 530-F3
RONDA CT
VAC 95688 433-B3
RONDA DR
FRFD 94533 473-C4
RONDO PL
DVS 95618 356-F7
RONEY AV
VAL 94590 530-C5
ROOS ST
DVS 95618 357-A7
ROOSEVELT AV
WIN 95694 373-D3
ROOSEVELT DR
WDLD 95776 316-B6
ROOSEVELT PL
WDLD 95776 316-B6
ROOSEVELT ST
FRFD 94533 472-D5
ROSA AV
WIN 95694 373-E3
ROSA DEL RIO WY
SAC 95822 378-J4
ROSARIO ST
DVS 95618 376-H2
ROSATO CT
FRFD 94534 491-F5
ROSCOE MARVICK DR
VAC 95688 413-E7
ROSCOMMON DR
VAC 95688 433-E1
ROSE CT
FRFD 94533 472-G2
VAL 94589 509-J6
WSAC 95691 358-J4
ROSE DR
BEN 94510 530-H7
BEN 94510 531-A7
BEN 94510 550-G1
BEN 94510 551-B1
ROSE LN
VAL 94590 530-C3
YoCo 95695 336-A4
YoCo 95776 336-A4
ROSE ST
CCCo 94525 550-D5
ROSE WY
DXN 95620 395-B7
ROSE ARBOR WY
VAL 94591 510-H4
ROSEBERRY CT
DXN 95620 395-B5
ROSEBURG CT
FRFD 94534 472-D3
ROSEBURG WY
FRFD 94534 472-D3
ROSELEAF CT
FRFD 94585 511-E3
ROSELEAF DR
FRFD 94585 511-E3
ROSEMARY CT
FRFD 94533 472-H1
ROSEMARY DR
VAL 94589 509-J6
ROSEMONT CT
VAC 95688 433-C2
ROSEWOOD AV
VAL 94591 530-E5
ROSEWOOD CT
FRFD 94585 511-E1
ROSEWOOD LN
VAC 95687 453-E1
ROSEWOOD WY
WDLD 95695 316-A5
ROSITA CT
VAC 95687 433-G5
ROSS CIR
NaCo 94558 450-A2
ROSS CT
FRFD 94533 473-B3
ROSS DR
WDLD 95776 316-D5
ROSS PL
FRFD 94533 473-B3
ROSS ST
VAL 94591 530-D4
ROSSI DR
DXN 95620 395-D7
ROSSO CT
VAC 95687 433-B7
ROTARY WY
VAL 94591 530-D1
ROUALT ST
DVS 95618 356-F5
ROUGH SAND CT
WSAC 95605 358-J2
ROUNDHILL CT
VAC 95687 453-H3
VAL 94591 530-D2
WSAC 95691 378-J1
ROUNDHILL DR
VAC 95687 453-H3

ROUNDS ST
VAL 94589 510-C6
ROUNDTREE CT
SAC 95831 378-G7
ROVEN CT
WSAC 95691 378-F1
ROWE CT
FRFD 94533 453-E7
ROWE DR
FRFD 94533 453-E7
SolC 94533 453-F7
ROWE PL
DVS 95616 356-D7
DVS 95616 376-D1
FRFD 94533 453-E7
SolC 94533 453-E7
ROWLAND DR
FRFD 94533 452-J6
ROXBURY WY
FRFD 94533 452-J7
ROYAL CT
FRFD 94534 472-E2
VAL 94591 530-G3
ROYAL ELF CT
DXN 95620 395-B6
ROYAL GARDEN AV
SAC 95831 378-H6
ROYAL GREEN AV
SAC 95831 378-J6
ROYAL OAK CT
FRFD 94533 473-B3
ROYAL OAKS CT
VAC 95687 433-G6
ROYAL OAKS DR
VAC 95687 433-G6
ROYAL TERN DR
VAC 95687 453-J2
ROYWOOD CT
VAL 94591 530-F5
RUBICON AV
DVS 95616 355-H6
RUBICON PL
WDLD 95695 316-A6
RUBICON WY
WSAC 95691 378-H1
RUBIER WY
RVIS 94571 516-H3
RUBY DR
VAC 95687 453-G2
RUBY LN
SolC 95688 413-D1
VAL 94590 550-C2
RUBY WY
WDLD 95695 316-A2
RUDDY LN
SUIS 94585 472-J6
RUMMEL CT
VAC 95688 433-C1
RUMSEY PL
WSAC 95691 378-H1
RUMSEY ST
WSAC 95691 378-H2
RUNART CT
VAL 94591 530-J1
RUSH LN
SolC 94585 473-A5
RUSH CREEK PL
VAL 94591 510-J4
RUSHMORE DR
VAC 95687 433-J3
RUSHMORE LN
DVS 95616 355-J6
RUSSELL BLVD
DVS 95616 375-J1
DVS 95616 376-A1
YoCo 95616 355-A7
YoCo 95616 375-G1
YoCo 95616 376-A1
RUSSELL BLVD Rt#-E6
YoCo 95694 373-H2
YoCo 95694 374-A1
RUSSELL LN
DXN 95620 395-B5
RUSSELL RD
SolC 94534 471-J6
RUSSELL ST
NAP 94559 450-A7
NAP 94559 470-A1
VAL 94591 530-D6
WIN 95694 373-E4
RUSTIC LN
SolC 95688 433-A1
RUSTLE CT
FRFD 94534 472-C4
RUTGERS CT
VAL 94589 510-A5
RUTGERS DR
DVS 95616 356-B6
RUTGERS ST
VAC 95687 433-H5
RUTHERFORD DR
VAC 95687 453-H1
RUTLAND DR
RVIS 94571 516-G2
RUTLEDGE LN
FRFD 94533 472-H4
RYAN CT
FRFD 94535 473-J1
RYDER ST
VAL 94590 530-B5
RYER ISLAND ST
WSAC 95691 378-E2

S

S ST
BEN 94510 551-C4
SACKETT LN
SolC 95688 392-H1
SACRAMENTO AV
WSAC 95605 358-G2
SACRAMENTO ST
FRFD 94535 473-J4
RVIS 94571 516-H5
SUIS 94585 472-F7
VAL 94589 529-J2
VAL 94590 529-J5
SADDLE PL
WDLD 95776 316-C5
SADDLEBACK PKWY
VAC 94533 452-J3
VAC 95687 452-J3
SADDLE HORN TR
VAC 95687 453-F3
SADDLE RIDGE WY
FRFD 94534 471-E7
FRFD 94534 491-E1
SADIE PL
AMCN 94503 510-B2
SAFFLOWER PL
WSAC 95691 358-F7
WSAC 95691 378-G1
SAGAMORE WY
SAC 95822 378-J3
SAGE CT
BEN 94510 551-A1
FRFD 94533 472-G1
VAC 95687 453-F3
SAGE DR
VAC 95687 453-F3
SAGE ST
VAL 94589 510-C6

SAGEBRUSH CT
AMCN 94503 510-B2
SAGEBRUSH LN
AMCN 94503 510-B2
SAGE MEADOWS DR
RVIS 94571 516-F1
SAGE SPARROW CIR
VAC 95687 453-J1
SAGINAW ST
WSAC 95691 378-E2
SAIL CT
SAC 95831 378-H6
SAILBOAT WY
SAC 95831 378-G7
SAINT ANDREWS CT
SolC 94534 470-J4
SolC 94534 471-A3
SAINT ANDREWS DR
RVIS 94571 516-F2
VAC 95687 433-H7
VAC 95687 453-H1
SAINT ANDREWS RD
FRFD 94534 452-C7
FRFD 94534 472-C2
SAINT AUGUSTINE CT
BEN 94510 551-C4
SAINT AUGUSTINE DR
BEN 94510 551-C4
SAINT CATHERINES LN
BEN 94510 551-B4
SAINT CATHERINES SQ
BEN 94510 551-B4
SAINT CROIX RD
WSAC 95691 378-D2
SAINT ELIAS PL
DVS 95616 355-J6
SAINT FRANCIS CT
BEN 94510 551-C4
SAINT FRANCIS DR
VAL 94590 529-J3
SAINT FRANCIS WY
RVIS 94571 516-H5
SAINT GERTRUDE AV
RVIS 94571 516-H6
SAINT JOHN RD
WSAC 95691 378-D3
SAINT JOHNS MINE RD
VAL 94591 510-G6
VAL 94591 530-H1
SAINT JOSEPH ST
RVIS 94571 516-H6
SAINT LUCIA PL
WSAC 95691 378-D2
SAINT MARYS PL
VAL 94589 510-B5
SAINT OLAF WY
VAL 94589 510-B5
SAIPAN DR
WDLD 95776 316-C5
SALA ST
VAL 94589 530-A1
SALAMANCA CT
DVS 95618 356-F6
SALEM AV
DVS 95616 355-H7
SALEM CT
FRFD 94534 472-C5
VAC 95687 433-E7
SALINAS DR
VAC 95688 432-J4
VAC 95688 433-A4
SALISBURY CT
FRFD 94534 472-B4
SALISBURY DR
FRFD 94534 472-B4
SALISHAN CT
FRFD 94534 472-C2
SALMON CT
FRFD 94533 452-H7
SALON DR
FRFD 94534 491-B3
SALT POINT CT
VAL 94591 550-E2
SAMANTHA PL
VAC 95687 453-F2
SAMO LN
SolC 94533 473-F1
SAMUEL CT
BEN 94510 531-D7
SAN ANDREAS ST
FRFD 94533 472-G4
SAN ANDREAS WY
VAL 94589 509-H5
SAN ANGELO CT
FRFD 94533 472-H3
SAN ANGELO ST
FRFD 94533 472-H4
SAN ANSELMO ST
FRFD 94533 472-H4
SAN ANTONIO CT
FRFD 94533 472-H1
SAN BENITO ST
FRFD 94533 472-H4
SANBORN CT
BEN 94510 550-J2
SANBORN LN
DXN 95620 395-B7
SAN BRUNO ST
FRFD 94533 472-H5
SAN CARLOS CT
VAC 95688 433-D4
WSAC 95691 378-H1
SAN CARLOS ST
FRFD 94533 472-H5
SAN CLEMENTE ST
FRFD 94533 472-H4
SANCTUARY CIR
FRFD 94534 452-E7
SANCTUARY DR
FRFD 94534 452-E7
FRFD 94534 472-F1
SAND CIR
WSAC 95605 358-H2
SAND CT
SAC 95831 378-H6
WSAC 95605 358-H2
SAND PL
WSAC 95605 358-H2
SANDALWOOD CT
FRFD 94585 511-E2
VAC 95687 433-J7
VAL 94591 530-E4
SANDALWOOD DR
VAC 95687 433-J7
SAND DOLLAR DR
VAL 94591 550-E2
SANDERLING DR
FRFD 94533 473-A3
SANDHILL CT
SAC 95831 378-G5
SAND HILLS DR
RVIS 94571 516-F1
SANDHURST CT
VAL 94591 530-H6
SANDHURST DR
VAL 94591 530-H6
SAN DIEGO ST
FRFD 94533 472-H5
SAN DIMAS ST
FRFD 94533 472-H4
SANDPIPER CT
FRFD 94533 473-A3

SANDPIPER DR
DVS 95616 356-C4
FRFD 94533 473-A3
VAL 94589 509-H5
SANDPIPER LN
WSAC 95691 378-G1
SAND POINT DR
WDLD 95776 316-B5
SANDSTONE DR
VAC 95688 433-A6
VAL 94589 510-B4
SANDSTONE ST
FRFD 94534 491-E1
SANDY CIR
YoCo 95618 377-B1
SANDY DR
VAL 94590 550-C1
SANDY LN
SUIS 94585 472-J6
SANDY WY
BEN 94510 551-B3
SANDY BEACH RD
VAL 94590 550-B1
SANDY NECK WY
VAL 94591 550-E1
SANDYPOINT CT
WSAC 95691 378-J1
SANDYPOINT RD
WSAC 95691 358-J7
WSAC 95691 378-J1
SAN GABRIEL ST
FRFD 94533 472-H4
SAN GALLO TER
DVS 95618 356-G6
SANGIOVESE CT
FRFD 94534 491-F5
SAN GORGONIO AV
VAL 94589 530-C1
SAN JERONIMO TER
DVS 95618 356-H7
SAN JOSE CT
FRFD 94533 472-G4
VAC 95688 432-J5
SAN JOSE PL
FRFD 94533 472-G4
SAN JOSE ST
FRFD 94533 472-G4
SAN JUAN CT
FRFD 94533 472-H4
VAC 95688 433-D3
SAN JUAN ST
FRFD 94533 472-H4
SAN LEON DR
VAC 95688 433-D3
SAN LORENZO ST
FRFD 94533 472-H4
SAN LUCAS DR
FRFD 94533 472-H3
SAN LUIS CT
VAC 95688 433-D3
SAN LUIS ST
FRFD 94533 472-H4
WDLD 95695 315-J6
SAN MARCO ST
FRFD 94533 472-H4
VAC 95687 453-C1
SAN MARCO WY
AMCN 94503 509-J3
SAN MARINO AV
VAL 94589 530-B1
SAN MARINO DR
DVS 95618 376-H1
SAN MATEO ST
FRFD 94533 472-H4
SAN MIGUEL DR
FRFD 94533 472-H3
SAN MIGUEL ST
WSAC 95691 378-E2
SAN MIGUEL WY
DVS 95618 356-G6
SAN NICOLAS RD
WSAC 95691 378-E1
SAN PABLO AV
CCCo 94525 550-A5
CCCo 94572 549-J6
CCCo 94572 550-A5
SAN PABLO ST
FRFD 94533 472-H4
VAL 94592 529-F3
SAN PEDRO CT
FRFD 94533 472-H4
SAN PEDRO ST
FRFD 94533 472-H4
SAN RAFAEL ST
DVS 95618 356-F7
FRFD 94533 472-H4
SAN RAMON
VAL 94589 530-B2
SAN RAMON DR
DVS 95618 376-H1
SAN REMO CT
FRFD 94533 472-H4
WSAC 95691 378-J1
SAN REMO ST
FRFD 94533 472-H4
SAN SALVADOR ST
FRFD 94533 472-H4
WSAC 95691 378-C2
SAN SEBASTIAN ST
DVS 95618 356-G7
SAN SIMEON PL
VAL 94591 550-E1
SANSOME CT
VAC 95687 433-F7
SANSOME ST
WSAC 95691 358-J7
SANTA ANA CT
FRFD 94533 472-G3
SANTA ANA DR
FRFD 94533 472-G3
SANTA ANITA CT
WDLD 95776 316-B1
SANTA ANITA DR
WDLD 95776 316-B1
SANTA BARBARA CT
FRFD 94533 472-H3
SANTA BARBARA ST
WSAC 95691 378-E2
SANTA BARBARA WY
FRFD 94533 472-G4
SANTA CLARA AV
RVIS 94571 516-G6
SANTA CLARA ST
FRFD 94533 472-H3
VAL 94590 529-J3
SANTA CRUZ CT
FRFD 94533 472-H3
VAC 95688 432-J5
SANTA CRUZ DR
FRFD 94533 472-G3
SANTA CRUZ RD
WSAC 95691 378-E2
SANTA CRUZ WY
DVS 95618 356-G6
SANTAELLA LN
FRFD 94533 453-E7
SANTA FE CT
FRFD 94533 472-H3
VAC 95688 432-J4
SANTA FE ST
FRFD 94533 472-H3
SANTA MARIA DR
FRFD 94533 472-H3

568 SANTA MONICA CT — SOLANO COUNTY STREET INDEX — STAGELINE DR

SOLANO CO.

© 2007 Rand McNally & Company

STREET Name City ZIP Pg-Grid

SANTA MONICA CT FRFD 94533 472-H4
SANTA MONICA ST FRFD 94533 472-H4
SANTANA DR VAC 95687 433-F6
SANTANDER CT DVS 95618 356-H6
SANTA PAULA WY DVS 95618 376-J1
SANTA ROSA AV VAL 94590 529-J3
SANTA ROSA CT VAC 95688 432-J4
SANTA ROSA ST DVS 95616 355-J6; DVS 95616 356-A6; FRFD 94533 472-H3
SANTA SUSANA CT FRFD 94533 472-H3
SANTA TERESA CT VAC 95688 413-F6
SANTIAGO LN DVS 95618 356-G7
SANTIAM ST WSAC 95691 378-H1
SAN TOMAS ST DVS 95618 376-G1; FRFD 94533 472-H4
SANTONI LN WDLD 95776 316-C5
SAN VICENTE CT VAC 95687 433-G7
SAN VICENTE RD WSAC 95691 378-D4
SAPPHIRE CIR VAC 95687 453-G3
SAPPHIRE CT DVS 95618 376-F2
SARA CT VAC 95687 453-F1
SARAH WY SUIS 94585 472-J5; SUIS 94585 473-A5
SARATOGA CT VAC 95687 433-C7
SARATOGA DR WDLD 95695 315-F6
SARATOGA PL DVS 95616 355-J6
SARCEDO WY AMCN 94503 510-C4
SARDONYX WY VAC 95687 453-G2
SARGENT CT BEN 94510 550-J1
SARGENT PL DVS 95618 356-F5
SARGO AV VAL 94592 529-G7
SAUNDERS DR VAL 94591 530-F5
SAUNDERS WY WDLD 95695 315-J4
SAUSALITO CT VAC 95687 433-G4
SAUSALITO RD WSAC 95691 358-J7
SAVANNAH CT FRFD 94534 472-C5
SAVANNAH LN SUIS 94585 473-C4
SAWBILLS CT WSAC 95691 378-F1
SAWGRASS CT FRFD 94534 472-B2; VAC 95687 453-E3
SAWGRASS LN VAL 94591 530-G2
SAWYER CT DXN 95620 395-B7
SAWYER ST VAL 94589 510-C5
SAXONY CT VAL 94591 530-H6
SAYBROOK AV VAC 95687 433-G6
SAYBROOK CT VAC 95687 433-G5
SAYBROOK WY VAL 94591 550-E1
SCALLY RD SolC 94585 493-E3
SCARLINO CT VAL 94591 530-J1
SCAUP LN SUIS 94585 472-J6
SCENIC DR VAL 94591 530-D6
SCENIC WY VAL 94590 529-H2
SCENIC CANYON TR SolC 95688 413-B5
SCENIC RANCH LN SolC 95688 413-B2
SCHLOTZ CT WDLD 95776 316-E5
SCHMEISER AV DVS 95618 357-A7
SCHOOL ST CCCo 94569 550-H6; SUIS 94585 472-F7; SUIS 94585 492-F1; VAC 95688 433-D5
SCHOOL HOUSE RD SaCo 95837 317-J3
SCHOONER CT VAC 95687 453-J1
SCHOONER WY VAL 94590 550-B1
SCHOONER RIDGE CT DXN 95620 395-C5
SCHOONER RIDGE DR DXN 95620 395-C5
SCHROEDER RD SolC 95620 394-J4
SCHUERLE ST WDLD 95695 315-H3
SCHULER RANCH DR WDLD 95695 315-G2
SCOGGINS CT VAC 95688 433-D5
SCOT CT SolC 94534 471-A4
SCOTCH PINE CT FRFD 94534 491-F3
SCOTER WY SUIS 94585 473-A6
SCOTT ST FRFD 94533 472-J5; FRFD 94535 473-J3; RVIS 94571 516-H4; VAL 94590 530-B5
SCOTTSDALE DR VAC 95687 433-H7; VAC 95687 453-H1
SCRIPPS DR DVS 95616 356-B6
SEA CT SAC 95831 378-H6
SEA BREEZE DR BEN 94510 550-J4; BEN 94510 551-A4
SEABREEZE DR FRFD 94533 473-A2
SEABRIGHT AV DVS 95616 355-G6
SEABROOK CT FRFD 94534 472-B2; WSAC 95691 358-J3
SEABROOK DR FRFD 94534 472-B2
SEABURY ST SUIS 94585 493-C1
SEACLIFF PL VAL 94591 550-E1
SEA CREST CIR VAL 94590 550-B1
SEAFARER CT VAL 94591 550-F2
SEAGULL DR SUIS 94585 473-B6
SEA HORSE CT FRFD 94533 452-H7
SEAHORSE DR VAL 94591 550-D1
SEALION PL VAL 94591 550-D1
SEAL ROCK CT VAL 94591 530-G7
SEAMAS AV SAC 95822 378-J4
SEA MIST CT VAL 94591 550-G2
SEA MIST DR VAL 94591 550-G2
SEAPORT BLVD WSAC 95691 358-D6
SEAPORT DR VAL 94590 550-C1
SEA RANCH CT VAL 94591 550-E3
SEARS POINT TOLL RD Rt#-37 SolC 94559 509-A7; SolC 94559 529-F2; SolC 94589 529-F2; SolC 94590 529-F2; SolC 94592 529-F2; VAL 94590 529-F2; VAL 94592 529-F2
SEASCAPE DR VAL 94591 550-D1
SEASTONE WY SAC 95831 378-G6
SEAVIEW CT VAL 94589 530-A1
SEAVIEW DR BEN 94510 551-B3
SEAWALL CT VAL 94591 550-F1
SEAWAY AV WSAC 95691 358-G7
SEAWAY CT WSAC 95691 358-G7
SEAWAY PL WSAC 95691 358-G7
SEAWIND DR VAL 94590 550-B1
SEAWITCH DR VAL 94590 550-B1
SEBASTIAN PL FRFD 94534 491-D3
SECRET BAY ST DVS 95616 355-G6
SEGOVIA CT VAL 94591 530-G7
SEGOVIA DR FRFD 94533 473-C4
SEINE AV DVS 95616 355-H6
SELBY CT VAC 95687 453-B1
SELBY RD CCCo 94525 550-B4
SELFRIDGE RD VAL 94590 529-H2
SELLERS WY WSAC 95691 358-G4
SELVINO CT AMCN 94503 510-B2
SEMINOLE CIR FRFD 94534 472-C1
SEMINOLE CT RVIS 94571 516-F3; VAC 95687 453-H3
SEMINOLE DR FRFD 94534 452-C7; FRFD 94534 472-C1
SEMPLE CRSG BEN 94510 551-B5
SEMPLE CT BEN 94510 551-B5
SENECA WY VAC 95688 433-A4
SENIOR WY SAC 95831 378-H7
SEQUOIA AV VAL 94591 550-C1
SEQUOIA CT FRFD 94533 472-H2; RVIS 94571 516-G5
SEQUOIA DR FRFD 94533 472-H2; VAC 95687 433-J3
SEQUOIA PL DVS 95616 356-C6; FRFD 94533 472-J2; WDLD 95695 315-G5
SEQUOIA WY DXN 95620 395-A7
SEQUOIA GROVE CT AMCN 94503 510-B3
SEQUOIA GROVE WY AMCN 94503 510-B3
SERENA PL AMCN 94503 510-B2
SERENE CT FRFD 94533 473-A1
SERENITY CT FRFD 94534 452-E7
SERENITY HILLS DR SolC 95688 412-J7; SolC 95688 413-A7; SolC 95688 432-J1; SolC 95688 433-A1
SERENO DR VAC 95687 453-C1; VAL 94589 530-A1
SERENO PL VAL 94589 530-B1
SERPA LN SolC 95620 394-F7; SolC 95620 414-F2
SERPENTINE CT VAL 94589 510-C6
SERPENTINE DR VAL 94589 510-B6
SERRA CT FRFD 94534 472-C4; VAL 94590 530-B2
SERRA WY FRFD 94534 472-C4
SERRANO CT FRFD 94533 472-C7
SERRANO DR FRFD 94533 472-C7
SERRANO TER DVS 95618 356-H7
SETTER LN SolC 95688 393-G7
SETTERQUIST DR VAL 94589 510-C7
SETTLE CT VAL 94591 530-E6
SEVEDGE DR FRFD 94535 473-J3
SEVERUS DR VAL 94589 509-H5; VAL 94589 510-A4
SEVILLE CT DVS 95616 356-B5; NAP 94559 470-A1
SEVILLE DR NAP 94559 450-A7; NAP 94559 470-A1
SEVILLE LN VAC 95688 433-A3
SEVILLE PL VAC 95688 433-A3
SEVILLE ST DVS 95616 356-B5; VAL 94591 530-F6
SEYMOUR AV WSAC 95691 378-E3
SEYMOUR CT WSAC 95691 378-E2
SHADE TREE CIR VAL 94591 510-J4
SHADI LN SolC 95694 394-A4
SHADOW BROOK CT FRFD 94534 491-F3
SHADOW CREEK WY RVIS 94571 516-E1
SHADOWHAWK CT VAC 95688 433-D1
SHADOW RIDGE CT VAL 94591 550-D1
SHADOW RIDGE PL VAL 94591 550-D2
SHADOW TREE CT VAC 95687 453-G4
SHADY LN VAL 94591 530-F7; VAL 94591 550-F1
SHADY BROOK LN NaCo 94558 450-E6
SHADY CREEK TR SolC 95688 413-C2
SHADY GLEN CT VAC 95688 433-A4
SHADY GLEN RD VAC 95688 433-A4
SHADY OAK TR SolC 95688 412-F6
SHADYWOOD CIR SUIS 94585 472-H5
SHADYWOOD CT FRFD 94585 511-E2
SHAKER RUN CIR FRFD 94533 452-J7
SHAKER RUN CT FRFD 94533 452-J7
SHALE PEAK LN SolC 95688 392-F7
SHAMROCK CT FRFD 94533 472-H1; VAC 95688 433-E2; VAL 94589 510-C5
SHAMS WY YoCo 95694 373-J2
SHANNON CT BEN 94510 551-B4; VAC 95688 433-E1
SHANNON DR SUIS 94585 472-H6; VAC 95688 433-E1
SHARI CT VAL 94589 509-J5
SHARIAN ST WSAC 95605 358-J1
SHARON AV CCCo 94572 549-G7; YoCo 95616 355-J4; YoCo 95616 356-A4
SHARON CT WSAC 95691 358-E7; WSAC 95691 378-F1
SHARON WY RVIS 94571 516-H3
SHASTA CT DXN 95620 395-C7; FRFD 94533 473-F2; SUIS 94585 473-C6
SHASTA DR DVS 95616 355-J6; FRFD 94533 473-F2; RVIS 94571 516-G5; VAC 95687 433-E6
SHASTA PL WDLD 95695 315-H2
SHASTA ST SUIS 94585 473-C6; VAL 94590 530-C4
SHASTA WY WSAC 95691 378-H2
SHAVER CT WSAC 95691 378-D4
SHAW DR WSAC 95691 358-G3
SHAWN LN SolC 95688 413-F1
SHAWNEE CT FRFD 94534 472-B2
SHEA TER VAL 94591 530-G6
SHEARWATER WY FRFD 94533 473-E2
SHEFFIELD LN FRFD 94533 473-E2
SHEFFIELD WY AMCN 94503 509-J4; AMCN 94503 510-A4; VAL 94591 510-H5
SHEFIELD DR VAC 95687 433-G7
SHEILA CT VAL 94591 530-E3
SHELBY CT FRFD 94534 472-C5
SHELBY DR FRFD 94534 472-C5
SHELBY PL FRFD 94534 472-C5
SHELDON AV VAL 94591 530-D5
SHELDON DR SolC 94533 453-E7
SHELDUCK CT SUIS 94585 473-A6
SHELL CT FRFD 94533 473-A2
SHELLEY DR VAL 94591 530-E6
N SHELTER BAY HER 94547 549-G7
SHELTER COVE AV DVS 95616 355-G6
SHELTER COVE CT VAC 95688 413-F6
SHELTER COVE DR VAC 95688 413-F7
SHELTER COVE PL DVS 95616 355-G6
SHELTER HILL DR FRFD 94534 472-E1
SHELTER POINT CT SAC 95831 378-H6
SHELTON LN SolC 95688 413-E5; VAC 95688 413-E5
SHENANDOAH CT FRFD 94534 472-C5
SHENANDOAH DR AMCN 94503 510-B2
SHENANDOAH PL DVS 95616 355-H6
SHEPHERDS LN DVS 95616 356-C7
SHERIDAN ST VAL 94590 530-B6; VAL 94590 550-C1
SHERMAN DR BEN 94510 551-B4
SHERMAN ST VAL 94591 530-E4; WDLD 95695 316-A6
SHERMAN ISLAND RD WSAC 95691 378-E2
SHERROD CT VAL 94591 530-E4
SHERWOOD AV VAL 94591 530-E5
SHERWOOD CT FRFD 94533 472-G4; VAC 95687 453-D1
SHETLAND CT FRFD 94533 472-H1; VAC 95687 433-G7; VAC 95687 453-G1; VAL 94591 530-E2
SHETLER AV NAP 94559 470-A1
SHILOH CT WDLD 95695 316-A2
SHINING HORSE WY VAC 95688 413-D6
SHINN CT WDLD 95776 316-E7
SHINN PL WDLD 95776 316-E7
SHIRE CT FRFD 94533 472-J1
SHIRE LN DVS 95616 355-J7
SHIRLEY CT VAL 94590 550-C1
SHIRLEY DR BEN 94510 551-B4
SHIRLEY ST WSAC 95691 378-E1
SHOAL CT SAC 95831 378-G6
SHOAL DR E VAL 94591 550-F2
SHOAL DR W VAL 94591 550-E2
SHOEMAKER CT WDLD 95776 336-E1
SHORE ST WSAC 95691 358-G5
SHORELAND PL VAC 95687 433-J6
SHORELINE CIR FRFD 94533 473-A1; SAC 95831 378-H6
SHORELINE PL VAL 94591 550-F1
SHORESIDE DR SAC 95831 378-G6
SHOREY WY FRFD 94533 453-E7
SHORT ST VAL 94590 530-C5; WSAC 95605 358-G1
SHOVELER CT WSAC 95691 378-F1
SHOVELLER DR SUIS 94585 472-J6
SHRIKE CT SUIS 94585 473-C7
SIEBE DR SolC 94534 471-A6
SIENA PL RVIS 94571 516-G6
SIENA ST FRFD 94534 491-C3
SIENNA CT AMCN 94503 510-B2
SIENNA WY AMCN 94503 510-B2
SIERRA AV RVIS 94571 516-G5
SIERRA CIR WSAC 95605 358-H2
SIERRA CT FRFD 94534 491-F3; VAC 95687 453-G1; WSAC 95605 358-H2
SIERRA DR DXN 95620 395-C7
SIERRA PL WSAC 95605 358-H2
SIERRA RD WSAC 95691 378-H2
SIERRA ST WDLD 95695 315-G3; WSAC 95605 358-H2
SIERRA MADRE WY DVS 95618 376-H1
SIERRA PEAK WY VAC 95688 413-J7; VAC 95688 433-J1
SIERRA VISTA AMCN 94503 509-J2
SIERRA VISTA DR SolC 95688 413-A2
SIEVERS RD SolC 95620 394-B1; SolC 95620 395-B1
SIEVERS WY DXN 95620 415-B1
SIGNATURE DR WDLD 95776 316-B5
SILAS CT BEN 94510 551-C1
SILBERSTEIN PL WDLD 95776 316-C5
SILK CT FRFD 94534 472-F3
SILK OAK CT SUIS 94585 472-J5
SILK OAK DR SUIS 94585 472-J5
SILKTREE LN VAL 94591 550-F1
SILVEIRA WY SAC 95831 378-F6
SILVER DR VAC 95687 433-E7
SILVERADO CIR FRFD 94585 491-D6
SILVERADO CT FRFD 94585 491-D6
SILVERADO DR FRFD 94585 491-D6; WDLD 95695 315-F5; YoCo 95616 355-J2
SILVERADO ST VAL 94591 530-G2; WSAC 95691 358-J7; WSAC 95691 378-J1
SILVER CREEK RD FRFD 94585 491-D7
SILVER CREST DR FRFD 94534 452-F7
SILVER EAGLE WY VAC 95688 413-D7; VAC 95688 433-D1
SILVER FOX CIR FRFD 94534 472-E1
SILVER LAKE CT FRFD 94585 491-D6
SILVER LAKE DR FRFD 94585 491-D6; SAC 95831 378-J6
SILVER OAK TR AMCN 94503 510-A3
SILVERPINE LN VAL 94591 550-F1
SILVER RIDGE PL DXN 95620 415-B1
SILVER STAR CT VAC 95688 413-J7
SILVERTOP WY VAC 95687 453-F2
SILVER VIEW CT VAL 94591 530-D3
SILVERWOOD RD WSAC 95691 378-C4
SILVEY ACRES DR VAC 95688 433-D5
SILVEYVILLE RD SolC 95620 394-C5; SolC 95620 395-A4
SIMIAN LN YoCo 95616 375-E2
SIMMER WY RVIS 94571 516-H3
SIMMONS WY DVS 95616 356-D7
SIMMS CT FRFD 94533 473-A3
SIMON TER WSAC 95605 358-J2
SIMONTON ST VAL 94589 510-D6
SIMS AV VAL 94590 529-H2
SINGING HILLS CT FRFD 94534 472-E2
SINGLETREE CT FRFD 94533 452-J6
SINGLETREE WY FRFD 94533 452-J6
SIRAH DR AMCN 94503 510-B2
SISLEY CT DVS 95618 356-F5
SKIBBEREEN LN VAL 94590 530-C3
SKIPPER CIR SAC 95822 378-J4
SKIPPER CT FRFD 94534 472-E3
SKIPPERS LN SolC 95688 413-E1
SKYHAWK LN SolC 95688 393-A7
SKYLARK WY SAC 95831 378-H7
SKYLARK CT SUIS 94585 473-B7
SKYLARK DR SUIS 94585 473-B6
SKYLINE CT VAL 94591 530-D2
SKYLINE DR VAL 94591 530-D3
SKY LINE RANCH DR VAC 95688 413-F7
SKYMASTER DR FRFD 94535 473-H3
SKY RANCH LN SolC 95688 412-B4
SKYSAIL CT SAC 95831 378-H6
SKY VALLEY RD SolC 94510 531-B4
SKYVIEW CIR FRFD 94534 472-E1
SKYVIEW DR VAL 94591 530-D3
SKYVIEW PL FRFD 94534 472-E1; VAC 95687 453-C1
SKYWAY VAL 94591 530-D3
SKYWEST CT FRFD 94533 452-H5
SLATE RIVER WY SAC 95831 378-G7
SLAYBACK RANCH WY DVS 95618 376-F2; SolC 95620 376-F2
SLEEPY HOLLOW LN SolC 94534 451-E7
SLOAN ST DVS 95618 356-F5
SMILAX AV WSAC 95605 358-H1
SMITH CT BEN 94510 531-D7; DXN 95620 415-C2
SMITH DR SolC 94585 491-E7
SMITH LN FRFD 94533 453-E7
SMITH ST FRFD 94535 473-G3
SMOKEY HILLS DR VAL 94589 510-C5
SNAPDRAGON CIR WSAC 95691 358-G7
SNAPDRAGON CT WIN 95694 373-E3
SNAPDRAGON PL BEN 94510 531-A7; BEN 94510 551-A1
SNAPDRAGON ST WIN 95694 373-E3; WSAC 95691 358-F7
SNOW DR SUIS 94585 472-J7
SNOWBERRY CIR WSAC 95691 358-G7
SNOWBERRY CT DXN 95620 415-B1
SNOWBERRY WY FRFD 94534 471-F7
SNOW EGRET DR VAC 95687 453-J2
SNOWY OWL DR VAC 95687 453-J1
SNYDER DR DVS 95616 356-E6
SOARING EAGLE TR SolC 95688 413-A6
SOBON WY AMCN 94503 510-B3
SOLANO AV VAL 94590 530-B5; VAL 94591 530-B5
SOLANO CT VAC 95688 433-C4
SOLANO DR BEN 94510 530-J7; BEN 94510 531-A7; BEN 94510 550-J1; BEN 94510 551-A1; DXN 95620 395-C6
SOLANO LN VAC 95688 433-C4
SOLANO RD SolC 94585 473-C5
SOLANO ST SUIS 94585 472-F7; WSAC 95605 358-G1
SOLANO FOOTHILLS DR FRFD 94534 452-E7; FRFD 94534 472-E1
SOLANO PARK CIR YoCo 95616 376-C2
SOLAR HILLS DR SolC 95688 433-A1
SOLITO ST DVS 95616 356-C4
SOLITUDE CT SolC 95688 413-A5; VAL 94591 510-J5
SOLOMON ISLAND RD WSAC 95691 378-C2
SOMERSET CIR WDLD 95776 336-E1
SOMERSET CT VAL 94589 530-B1
SOMERSET DR VAC 95687 433-H5; WSAC 95605 358-H2
SOMERVILLE CIR VAC 95687 453-H2
SOMERVILLE DR VAC 95687 453-G2
SOMERVILLE WY VAC 95687 453-H2
SOMMER DR DXN 95620 395-B5
SOMMER ST NAP 94559 450-A7; NAP 94559 470-A1
SONGBIRD CT VAC 95687 433-J7
SONGWOOD RD VAL 94591 510-J6
SONNET WY VAC 95687 433-H7; VAC 95687 453-H1
SONOMA AV CCCo 94572 549-J7
SONOMA BLVD Rt#-29 AMCN 94503 510-A7; SolC 94589 530-A1; VAL 94589 510-A7; VAL 94589 530-A1; VAL 94590 530-A6; VAL 94590 550-B1
SONOMA WY WDLD 95695 315-G3
SONOMA CREEK WY AMCN 94503 510-A2
SONOMA VALLEY DR FRFD 94534 472-D1
SONORA AV WSAC 95691 358-H4
SONORA PASS VAL 94589 509-J6
SONORA PL WDLD 95695 316-A6
SORREL CT BEN 94510 550-J1; VAL 94591 530-E1
SORRENTO LN AMCN 94503 510-B1
SOULE ST WSAC 95691 358-J4
SOUSA CT FRFD 94533 473-B4
SOUTH AV CCCo 94569 550-H6
SOUTH CT DXN 95620 395-D7
SOUTHAMPTON RD BEN 94510 550-J2; BEN 94510 551-A3
SOUTHBRIDGE LN FRFD 94534 472-D3
SOUTHDOWN CT WIN 95694 373-D4
SOUTHERLAND RD WSAC 95691 378-D4
SOUTHERN HILLS CT FRFD 94534 472-C1
SOUTHERN HILLS DR FRFD 94534 472-C1; RVIS 94571 516-E1
SOUTHFIELD CT DVS 95616 356-A4
SOUTH HILL CT VAL 94591 511-A7
SOUTHLAKE CT FRFD 94534 491-E2
SOUTHLAKE DR FRFD 94534 491-D2
SOUTHLITE CIR SAC 95831 378-H7
SOUTHPORT CT VAL 94591 530-G5
SOUTHPORT PKWY WSAC 95691 358-E7; WSAC 95691 378-D2
SOUTHPORT PKWY NW WSAC 95691 358-F7
SOUTHPORT WY VAL 94591 530-G4
SOUTH RIVER RD WSAC 95691 358-J6; WSAC 95691 378-H3
SOUTHWOOD CT VAC 95687 453-F1
SOUTHWOOD DR VAC 95687 453-E1
W SOUTHWOOD DR WDLD 95695 315-G5
SOUZA WY VAL 94589 510-D6
SPAATZ ST FRFD 94535 473-J2
SPACE CT SAC 95831 378-J7
SPAFFORD ST DVS 95618 356-F7
SPALDING CT WSAC 95691 378-D4
SPANISH BAY DR FRFD 94533 452-H6
SPANISH BAY PL YoCo 95616 355-H2
SPAR CT SAC 95822 378-J4
SPARKS RANCH RD SolC 95620 374-H7; SolC 95620 394-H1
SPARLING LN DXN 95620 395-F1; SolC 95620 375-G7; SolC 95620 395-F1
SPARROW CT DVS 95616 356-A5
SPARROW LN FRFD 94533 472-J3
SPARROW ST VAC 95687 453-H1
SPARROWHAWK DR VAC 95687 453-J2
SPENCE CT SUIS 94585 493-C1
SPENCER VAL 94589 510-A5
SPENCER LN SolC 95688 393-A7
SPERRY AV SolC 94590 530-C6
SPICEWOOD CT FRFD 94533 473-A1
SPIKERUSH CIR AMCN 94503 509-H1
SPILLMAN CIR VAC 95688 413-J6
SPINDRIFT PL FRFD 94585 491-D7; FRFD 94585 511-D1
SPINDRIFT WY VAC 95687 433-D6
SPINETTA CT AMCN 94503 510-B2
SPINNAKER CT SUIS 94585 492-G1; VAC 95687 453-H1; VAL 94590 550-B2
SPINNAKER WY VAL 94590 550-C2
SPINNEY WY SUIS 94585 473-A7; SUIS 94585 493-A1
SPOKANE RD WSAC 95691 378-H1
SPOONBILL LN SUIS 94585 472-J6
SPRAY CT SAC 95831 378-G6
SPRIG CT FRFD 94533 473-A3
SPRIG DR BEN 94510 551-F3
SPRING CT WDLD 95776 316-C4
SPRING LN SolC 94534 471-D5; VAC 95688 433-A6
SPRINGBROOK CIR SAC 95831 378-H6
SPRINGBROOK DR VAL 94591 530-E4
SPRING CREEK CT FRFD 94534 491-F3
SPRINGCREEK DR WDLD 95776 316-B4
SPRINGDALE DR WDLD 95776 316-B5
SPRINGFIELD CT FRFD 94534 472-C5
SPRINGFIELD DR FRFD 94534 472-C5
SPRINGFIELD WY VAL 94589 509-H5
SPRINGLAKE CT WDLD 95776 316-C4
SPRING MOUNTAIN LN AMCN 94503 510-B4
SPRINGRIDGE CT FRFD 94534 491-D1
SPRINGRIDGE WY FRFD 94534 491-D1
SPRINGS RD VAL 94590 530-A4; VAL 94591 530-E4
SPRINGS ST SUIS 94585 472-F7
SPRINGVALLEY DR VAC 95687 433-E6
SPRINGWOOD CIR FRFD 94585 511-E2
SPRUCE CT VAC 95687 433-H4
SPRUCE DR WDLD 95695 315-J6
SPRUCE LN DVS 95616 356-E6
SPRUCE ST DXN 95620 415-B1; SolC 94591 530-C6; VAL 94591 530-C6
SPRUCE WY FRFD 94533 473-A2; WSAC 95691 378-J2
SPRUCE CREEK CT FRFD 94534 491-F4
SPURLOCK WY SAC 95831 378-F7
SPURS TR SolC 94534 490-H3; SolC 94589 490-H3
SPYGLASS CT FRFD 94534 452-B7; RVIS 94571 516-E1; VAC 95687 453-E3
SPYGLASS DR RVIS 94571 516-E2
SPYGLASS PKWY VAL 94591 550-F3
SPYGLASS PL YoCo 95616 355-H2
SQUAW CT WSAC 95691 378-D4
SQUAW RD WSAC 95691 378-D4
SQUAW VALLEY DR WDLD 95776 316-C5
SREIA DR WSAC 95691 358-D4
STABLE CT WDLD 95776 316-C2
STABLE DR WSAC 95691 378-E2
STADIUM WY YoCo 95616 376-C1
STAFFORD SPRINGS WY FRFD 94533 453-A7
STAGECOACH LN SolC 95688 412-J2; SolC 95688 413-A2
STAGELINE CT VAL 94591 530-D2
STAGELINE DR VAL 94591 530-D2

570 TROON CT — SOLANO COUNTY STREET INDEX — WHITEMARSH LN

SOLANO CO.

STREET Name City ZIP Pg-Grid

TROON CT FRFD 94534 472-C2; VAC 95687 453-E3
TROPHY DR FRFD 94534 491-C3
TROTTER DR VAL 94591 530-E2
TROUT CT FRFD 94533 452-H7
TROY CT VAC 95687 433-D7
TRUCKEE PL WDLD 95695 315-J6
TRUCKEE WY WDLD 95695 315-J6
TRUDY WY SAC 95831 378-F7
TRUMAN ST FRFD 94533 472-D5
TRUMBULL WY VAC 95688 433-D1
TRUMPETER CT SUIS 94585 473-A7
TRUMPETER DR SUIS 94585 473-A7
TRYSAIL CT VAC 95687 433-D7
TRYSAIL ST VAC 95687 433-D7
TUBBIN CT VAC 95688 433-D1
TUBBS RD SolC 95694 373-H7; SolC 95694 393-H1
TUCKAWAY CT FRFD 94534 472-D2
TUCSON CIR SUIS 94585 473-C4
TUFTS CT WDLD 95695 315-G5
TUFTS PL WDLD 95695 315-F5
TUFTS ST DVS 95618 377-A1
TULANE DR DVS 95616 356-D7
TULARE CIR SUIS 94585 473-C6
TULARE DR VAC 95687 433-F7; VAC 95687 453-F1
TULE ST WSAC 95691 378-D4
TULE GOOSE DR SUIS 94585 473-A6
TULIAMORE CT VAC 95688 433-E1
TULIP CT BEN 94510 531-A7
TULIP LN DVS 95618 356-F6
TULIP ST FRFD 94533 472-F3
TULLIBEE CT CCCo 94572 549-J7
TULLIBEE RD CCCo 94572 549-J7
TUNNER DR FRFD 94535 473-J1
TUOLUMNE ST VAL 94589 510-A7; VAL 94589 530-B1; VAL 94590 530-B4
TURLOCK ST WSAC 95691 378-D4
TURNBERRY CT FRFD 94534 452-D7
TURNBERRY DR FRFD 94534 452-D7
TURNBERRY TER RVIS 94571 516-F2
TURNBERRY WY VAL 94591 530-G3
TURNER CT FRFD 94534 491-B3
TURNER DR BEN 94510 551-A2; FRFD 94534 491-B3
TURNER PKWY VAL 94591 530-D1
TURNER ST FRFD 94535 473-J2; FRFD 94535 474-A2; VAL 94591 530-F1
TURNSTONE WY FRFD 94534 491-E1
TURQUOISE ST VAC 95687 453-F3
TURRI CT FRFD 94533 453-E6
TUSCAN OAK TR AMCN 94503 510-A2
TUSCANY CT FRFD 94534 491-C2
TUSCANY DR FRFD 94534 491-C2
TUSCANY WY RVIS 94571 516-G6
TUSKEEGEE CT DXN 95620 415-C2
TUSTIN CT BEN 94510 551-B1
TWAIN CT FRFD 94533 473-B3
TWILIGHT ST VAC 95688 413-J6
TWIN CREEKS DR SolC 94534 471-B4
TWIN FAWN TR SolC 95688 412-D5
TWIN LAKES CT FRFD 94534 491-D2
TWIN LAKES LN RVIS 94571 516-F2
TWIN PEAK DR FRFD 94535 473-G2
TWIN PEAKS CT FRFD 94533 473-G2; FRFD 94535 473-G2; SolC 94533 473-G2
TWIN PINES DR RVIS 94571 516-F2
TWIN RIVER WY SAC 95831 378-G7
TWIN SISTERS RD SolC 94534 451-B5
TWITCHELL ISLAND ST WSAC 95691 378-E2
TYLER CT AMCN 94503 510-A4; SolC 95688 413-E1; WDLD 95776 316-B6
TYLER DR WDLD 95776 316-B6
TYLER PL WDLD 95776 316-C6
TYLER RD VAL 94592 549-H2; VAL 94592 550-A2
TYLER ST BEN 94510 551-D6; FRFD 94533 472-E5
TYLER WY WSAC 95691 378-F1
TYNE CT BEN 94510 530-J7
TYRONE CT VAC 95688 433-E2

U

U ST FRFD 94535 473-G5
UDELL RD SolC 95688 413-F2
ULATIS DR VAC 95687 433-F5
UNIFORM CT FRFD 94533 452-H5
UNION AV FRFD 94533 472-F4; SUIS 94533 472-F6
UNION CT BEN 94510 550-J2
UNION DR DVS 95616 356-D6
UNION ST VAL 94590 530-B6
UNION WY VAC 95687 433-J6
UNION SQUARE RD WSAC 95691 358-J7
UNIVERSITY AV DVS 95616 376-C1; VAL 94591 530-D3
UPLAND CT VAL 94589 530-A1
UPTON CT VAC 95687 453-E1
UTAH AV WDLD 95695 315-H2
UTAH CIR FRFD 94533 472-D5
UTAH ST FRFD 94533 472-E5
E UTAH ST FRFD 94533 472-G5

V

V ST FRFD 94535 473-G5
VACA ST SolC 95687 434-C6
VACA STATION RD SolC 95687 434-C7; VAC 95687 434-C7; VAC 95687 454-C1
VACA VALLEY PKWY VAC 95688 413-D7; VAC 95688 433-D1
VACA VALLEY RD SolC 95688 432-H2; SolC 95688 433-A2; VAC 95688 433-A2
VACAVILLE AV FRFD 94535 473-G4
VAIL CT VAC 95687 453-F1
VALDORA ST DVS 95618 376-E2
VALENCIA AV DVS 95616 356-B5
VALENCIA CT FRFD 94533 473-C4
VALENCIA DR FRFD 94533 473-C4
VALENCIA LN VAC 95688 433-B3
VALENCIA ST VAL 94591 530-F6
VALERIE CT BEN 94510 551-B3
VALEROSA WY DVS 95618 356-H7
VALHALLA CT VAC 95687 453-F1
VALINE CT SAC 95831 378-J5
VALLA VISTA DR NaCo 94558 451-H1
VALLEJO AV CCCo 94572 549-J7
VALLEJO RD FRFD 94535 474-A5
VALLEJO ST CCCo 94525 550-E4
VALLEJO FERRY CCCo 94572 549-J3; HER 94547 549-F7; VAL 94590 529-J5; VAL 94592 529-J5; VAL 94592 530-A7; VAL 94592 549-J3; VAL 94592 550-A2
VALLE VISTA AV VAL 94589 530-C1; VAL 94590 529-J2; VAL 94590 530-A2
VALLE VISTA PL WDLD 95695 315-H6
VALLE VISTA WY WDLD 95695 315-H6
VALLEY DR VAC 95688 433-E5
VALLEY LN SolC 94534 471-B6
VALLEY END LN SolC 94534 471-A2
VALLEY GLEN DR DXN 95620 415-C2
VALLEY OAK DR VAC 95687 433-H5; WIN 95694 373-D3
VALLEY OAK LN VAL 94591 530-E7; VAL 94591 550-E1
VALLEY OAK WY FRFD 94533 472-J2
VALLEY VIEW CT FRFD 94534 452-E7
VALLEYVIEW CT VAL 94591 550-D1
VALLEY VIEW LN SolC 95688 413-C2
VALLEY VIEW WY FRFD 94535 473-H1
VALLEYWOOD DR WDLD 95695 315-F2
VAN BUREN PL WDLD 95776 316-B6
VAN BUREN ST FRFD 94533 472-E3
VAN DAMME DR DVS 95616 355-J6; DVS 95616 356-A6
VANDEN CT VAC 95687 453-H1
VANDEN RD SolC 94533 453-G7; SolC 94533 473-E1; SolC 95687 453-H4; SolC 95687 473-E1; VAC 95687 433-H7; VAC 95687 453-H1
VANDENBERG CT FRFD 94535 474-A2
VANDENBERG DR FRFD 94535 474-A2
VANDENBURG CIR SUIS 94585 473-C5
VANDERBILT DR FRFD 94533 473-E1; SolC 94533 473-E1
VANESSA ST VAL 94589 510-E6
VAN GOGH ST DVS 95618 356-E5
VANGUARD ST VAL 94592 529-H6
VAQUEROS AV CCCo 94572 549-H7
VARNI CT BEN 94510 551-C4
VASSAR DR DVS 95616 356-A7; VAC 95687 433-H6
VATEN DR WSAC 95691 358-D4
VAUGHN RD DXN 95620 395-D4; SolC 95620 395-F4
VAZQUEZ CT DXN 95620 395-D7
VECINO ST BEN 94510 551-D5
VEL PL FRFD 94533 472-E6
VELA PL DVS 95618 356-H5
VELIE AL VAL 94590 529-J3; VAL 94590 530-A3
VENADA DR YoCo 95694 373-A3
VENETIAN CT FRFD 94534 491-C2
VENETIAN DR FRFD 94534 491-C2
VENICE ST WSAC 95691 378-E2
VENTANA DR AMCN 94503 510-A4
VENTO LN WDLD 95695 315-J5
VENTURA CT DXN 95620 395-A6; SUIS 94585 473-D6
VENTURA ST VAL 94590 530-B4
VENTURA WY SUIS 94585 473-D6
VENUS DR FRFD 94534 491-C3
VERANDA TER DVS 95618 356-J7
VERDE PL WDLD 95695 315-G3
VERDE TER DVS 95618 356-G7
VERDIN CT FRFD 94533 473-A3
VERDUZZO CT FRFD 94534 491-F5
VERGEL TER VAL 94589 509-H5
VERMONT AV WSAC 95691 358-J6
VERMONT ST FRFD 94533 472-D5; FRFD 94535 473-G2
VERONA CT FRFD 94534 491-C3; VAC 95687 453-F1
VERONA DR AMCN 94503 510-C3
VERSAILLES LN FRFD 94534 491-D3
VERTINE CT VAL 94591 530-J1
VERVAIS AV VAL 94591 530-D3
VESTRY CT FRFD 94534 491-D3
VETERINARY MEDICINE CIR YoCo 95616 376-A3
VETERINARY MEDICINE DR YoCo 95616 376-A3
VETTER AV FRFD 94535 473-G3
VIA ALTA BEN 94510 551-D4
VIA BELLAGIO AMCN 94503 510-C4
VIA COLONNA TER DVS 95618 356-H6
VIA FIRENZE AMCN 94503 510-C3
VIA LA MORRA AMCN 94503 510-C4
VIA MARCIANA AMCN 94503 510-C4
VIA MEDIA BEN 94510 551-D4
VIA MONTALCINO AMCN 94503 510-C4
VIA PAJARO SolC 94534 471-A6
VIA PALO LINDA SolC 94534 471-A6
VIA PESARO AMCN 94503 510-C4
VIA PESCARA AMCN 94503 510-C3
VIA ROBLES YoCo 95694 373-A3
VIA TREVISO AMCN 94503 510-C4
VIA VACQUERO SolC 94534 471-A6
VIC FAZIO HWY Rt#-113 DVS 95616 356-A4; DVS 95616 376-A1; SolC 95620 375-J4; SolC 95620 376-A3; WDLD 95776 316-B7; YoCo 95616 356-A4; YoCo 95616 376-A1; YoCo 95695 336-A3; YoCo 95695 356-A4; YoCo 95776 316-B7; YoCo 95776 336-A3; YoCo 95776 356-A4
VICHY AV NaCo 94558 450-A1
VICKREY LN SolC 95694 392-H1
VICKSBURG DR FRFD 94533 472-G5
VICTOR LN SolC 95688 413-J5; SolC 95688 414-A5
VICTORIA CT DXN 95620 415-D2; FRFD 94533 472-F4
VICTORIA DR DXN 95620 415-D2
VICTORIA PL DVS 95616 355-G6
VICTORIA ST SolC 94591 530-E7
VICTORIA WY WSAC 95691 378-F1
VICTORIA ISLAND CT WSAC 95691 378-C2
VICTORIAN CT BEN 94510 551-D5
VICTORY CT FRFD 94533 452-H5
VICTORY DR FRFD 94533 452-H5
VICTORY WY SUIS 94585 472-G7; WDLD 95695 316-A3
VIEIR ST RVIS 94571 516-H3
VIENNA CT FRFD 94533 472-F3
VIEW ST VAL 94590 529-H2
VIEWMONT AV VAL 94590 530-C3
VIEWMONT LN VAC 95688 433-A6
VIEWMONT ST BEN 94510 551-C4
VIGO CT DVS 95618 356-H6
VILLA CIR FRFD 94533 473-A4
VILLA CT FRFD 94533 473-A4
VILLAGE CIR WIN 95694 373-E3
VILLAGE CT VAC 95687 453-G2
VILLAGE DR SUIS 94585 472-H7
VILLAGE LN BEN 94510 551-D5; WDLD 95776 336-E1
VILLAGE PKWY WSAC 95691 358-J7; WSAC 95691 378-J2
N VILLAGE PKWY VAC 95688 413-H7
VILLAGGIO CIR VAC 95688 413-E7
VILLALONOSO CT VAL 94591 530-J1
VILLANOVA DR DVS 95616 356-A6
VILLAVERDE LN DVS 95618 356-G7
VINCENT CT BEN 94510 531-C7
VINCI WY AMCN 94503 509-H3
VINE CT FRFD 94533 472-D6; SolC 95688 433-C3; VAC 95688 433-C3
VINE DR FRFD 94533 472-D6
VINE PL VAC 95688 433-C3
VINE ST SolC 95688 433-C3; VAC 95688 433-C3
N VINE ST VAC 95688 433-C2
VINEGATE WY AMCN 94503 510-B2
VINE HILL CT WSAC 95691 378-J1
VINELAND MARINA CT FRFD 94534 491-B2
VINE TERRACE WY AMCN 94503 510-A4
VINEWOOD CT SUIS 94585 472-H5
VINEYARD LN SolC 95620 375-G4
VINEYARD HILLS CT VAC 95688 433-C3
VINEYARD VALLEY WY VAC 95688 433-D5
VINTAGE AV FRFD 94585 491-D7; FRFD 94585 511-D1
VINTAGE CT FRFD 94585 491-D7; RVIS 94571 516-E2; VAC 95688 433-D5
VINTAGE DR RVIS 94571 516-F2
VINTAGE LN SolC 94534 471-C7
VINTAGE LNDG FRFD 94534 491-B2
VINTAGE SPRINGS CT FRFD 94534 491-B2
VINTAGE VALLEY CIR FRFD 94534 491-C2
VINTAGE VALLEY DR FRFD 94534 491-C3
VINYARDS LANDING CT FRFD 94534 491-B1
VIOLET AV FRFD 94533 472-F2
VIOLET CT BEN 94510 531-A7; FRFD 94533 472-F2
VIOLET DR VAL 94589 510-A6; WSAC 95691 378-F2
VIOLET LN VAC 95687 453-H1
VIRGINIA AV WSAC 95691 358-J4
VIRGINIA ST CCCo 94525 550-C4; FRFD 94533 472-D6; FRFD 94535 473-H2; VAC 95688 433-C5; VAL 94590 529-J5; VAL 94590 530-A5
VIRGINIA WY RVIS 94571 516-H4
VIRGINIA PINE CT FRFD 94534 491-F3
VISTA CT BEN 94510 551-B4
VISTA LN VAL 94590 530-B2
VISTA WY DVS 95618 376-H1
VISTA ALTA FRFD 94534 472-D3
VISTA BONITA FRFD 94534 472-D3
VISTA BUENA FRFD 94534 472-D3
VISTA CERRO FRFD 94534 472-E3
VISTA DEL LAGO WY FRFD 94533 473-A1
VISTA DEL RANCHO FRFD 94534 472-D3
VISTA DEL RIO CCCo 94525 550-B5
VISTA GRANDE FRFD 94534 472-E2
VISTA HACIENDA FRFD 94534 472-E3
VISTA HERMOSA FRFD 94534 472-D3
VISTA LINDA FRFD 94534 472-D3
VISTA LUNA FRFD 94534 472-E3
VISTA PALOMAR FRFD 94534 472-D3
VISTA SERENA FRFD 94534 472-D3
VISTA VIEW DR VAC 95688 433-A6
VISTOSA CT DVS 95618 356-H6
VISTOSA ST DVS 95618 356-H6
VOLCANO CT VAL 94589 509-H5
VORTOLK AV WSAC 95691 358-H4
VOYAGER DR VAL 94590 529-H2

W

W ST BEN 94510 551-D4; FRFD 94535 473-F5
WADKINS LN SolC 95688 413-J3
WAGNER ST BEN 94510 551-F1
WAGON WHEEL LN SolC 95688 413-D3
WAHL WY DVS 95616 356-E6
WAILEA CIR FRFD 94534 472-C1
WAINWRIGHT ST BEN 94510 550-J4; BEN 94510 551-A4
WAKE CT VAL 94589 510-B7
WAKEFIELD DR VAC 95687 453-H2
WAKE FOREST DR DVS 95616 356-A7
WAKE ISLAND CT WSAC 95691 378-D2
WALDEN CT FRFD 94533 452-H6
WALKER PL WDLD 95776 316-E5
WALKER RD WSAC 95691 378-D4
WALKER ST WDLD 95776 316-D5
WALLACE AV VAL 94590 530-C5
WALLACE DR WDLD 95776 316-D5
WALLACE ST FRFD 94533 472-D5; RVIS 94571 516-H3
WALLICK CT VAC 95688 433-D1
WALLINGFORD LN FRFD 94533 472-G5
WALNUT BEN 94510 551-B6
WALNUT AV VAC 95688 433-B6; VAL 94592 529-F3; WSAC 95691 358-G4
WALNUT CT SolC 94534 471-B6; VAC 95688 433-B6; VAL 94589 510-A7; WSAC 95691 358-G4
WALNUT DR SolC 94534 471-B6
WALNUT LN WIN 95694 373-F3; YoCo 95618 376-G2; YoCo 95694 373-F3
WALNUT RD SaCo 95837 317-H2; SolC 95687 434-A1; VAC 95687 433-J1; VAC 95687 434-A1
WALNUT ST SUIS 94585 492-F1; WDLD 95695 315-J4; WSAC 95691 358-G3
E WALNUT ST DXN 95620 415-D1
N WALNUT ST WDLD 95695 315-J2
W WALNUT ST DXN 95620 415-C1
WALNUT PARK AV DXN 95620 395-D7; SolC 95620 395-D7
WALNUT WOODS CT WDLD 95695 315-G5
WALSH CT BEN 94510 530-H6
WALTER CT VAL 94591 530-F3
WALTERS CT FRFD 94533 473-C3
WALTERS PL FRFD 94533 473-C3
WALTERS RD FRFD 94533 473-C3; SolC 94533 473-C3; SolC 94585 473-C5; SUIS 94533 473-C3; SUIS 94585 473-C7
WALTON CT DXN 95620 395-C5
WANDA ST CCCo 94525 550-C4
WARBLER WY FRFD 94533 472-J4; SAC 95831 378-F7
WARD CT VAL 94589 509-J5
WARE CT BEN 94510 530-J7
WAREHOUSE AV FRFD 94535 473-J4
WARFORD AV VAL 94591 530-D4
WARING PL FRFD 94533 472-G1
WARREN AV SolC 94591 530-E7; VAL 94591 530-E7
WARREN DR VAC 95687 453-E2
WARREN ST FRFD 94533 472-D5
WARWICK DR BEN 94510 551-B3
WASHBURN CT VAL 94591 510-J4
WASHINGTON AV WIN 95694 373-D4; WSAC 95691 358-H3
WASHINGTON CT AMCN 94503 510-B4
WASHINGTON DR WDLD 95776 316-B6
WASHINGTON ST BEN 94510 551-E6; FRFD 94533 472-G6; VAL 94590 530-B2
N WASHINGTON ST DXN 95620 395-C7
S WASHINGTON ST DXN 95620 415-C1
WASHOE CT WSAC 95691 378-H2
WASHOE ST DVS 95618 376-H1
WATER ST SolC 95687 434-C7; WSAC 95605 358-G1
WATERBURY WY FRFD 94534 472-B4
WATERFALL WY VAL 94591 510-J4
WATER FERN CT AMCN 94503 509-H2
WATERFORD DR VAC 95688 433-E2; WSAC 95605 358-J1
WATERMAN BLVD FRFD 94533 472-C3; FRFD 94534 472-C3
WATERMAN CT FRFD 94534 472-C3
WATERTHRUSH CT SAC 95831 378-G5
WATERVIEW TER VAL 94591 550-D2
WATERVIEW WY SAC 95831 378-G7
WATERWAY BEN 94510 531-E7
WATERWOOD DR RVIS 94571 516-E2
N WATNEY WY FRFD 94534 472-C7; FRFD 94534 492-B1
S WATNEY WY FRFD 94534 492-C1
WATSON CT BEN 94510 551-B1; FRFD 94534 472-D2
WATSON LN AMCN 94503 490-A6; NaCo 94589 490-A6
WATSON HOLLOW DR RVIS 94571 516-E1
WATSON RANCH WY DXN 95620 395-B6
WATT CT FRFD 94585 491-D5
WATT DR FRFD 94585 491-C5
WAVECREST WY SAC 95831 378-G7
WAVERLY WY FRFD 94533 472-H2
WAXWING DR SUIS 94585 473-B6
WAXWING PL DVS 95616 356-B4
WAYNE CT FRFD 94534 472-C4; VAC 95687 453-F2
WEATHERLY WY VAC 95687 433-D7
WEATHERMARK CT VAL 94591 550-F3
WEATHER WAX CT FRFD 94534 472-D2
WEBB ST VAL 94591 530-D5
WEBER RD SolC 95620 414-G6; SolC 95620 415-A6; SolC 95687 414-D6; VAC 95687 414-D6
WEBER ST WDLD 95695 315-G3
WEBSTER ST FRFD 94533 472-F5; VAL 94591 530-D4; WSAC 95691 358-J4
WEDGEWOOD CT FRFD 94585 511-E2; VAL 94591 530-E4; WSAC 95605 358-J1
WEDGEWOOD WY FRFD 94585 511-E2
WELCH CT VAL 94591 530-E2
WELDON CT BEN 94510 551-A2
WELLBORN WY SolC 95688 413-B7
WELLE RD CCCo 94525 550-E5
WELLESLEY PL DVS 95618 356-F6
WELLFLEET DR VAL 94591 550-E1
WELLINGTON PL VAL 94591 550-D2
WELLINGTON WY VAC 95688 433-B6
WELLS LN FRFD 94533 453-E7; SolC 95688 412-G5
WELLSEY RD VAC 95687 433-H6
WENDELL PL WDLD 95695 315-H5
WENDELL WY WDLD 95695 315-H5
WENDY ST VAL 94589 510-D5
WENTWORTH CT AMCN 94503 509-H2
WERDEN ST VAL 94590 529-J2
WERNER WY VAC 95688 433-B6
WESLEY AV SUIS 94585 472-J5; VAC 95688 433-D5
WEST CIR WDLD 95695 315-H5
WEST ST CCCo 94525 550-D4; SUIS 94585 472-F7; SUIS 94585 492-F1; VAC 95688 433-C4; WDLD 95695 315-H6; WSAC 95605 358-J3
N WEST ST WDLD 95695 315-H1; YoCo 95695 315-H1
S WEST ST WDLD 95695 315-H6
WESTACRE RD WSAC 95691 358-J3
WESTAMERICA DR FRFD 94534 491-E2
WESTCHESTER CT FRFD 94533 452-H6
WESTERN AV VAL 94591 530-D5
WESTERN ST FRFD 94533 473-A3
WESTERNESSE RD DVS 95616 355-H7
WESTERN HILLS DR RVIS 94571 516-F2
WESTFIELD LN VAC 95688 433-B4
WESTFIELD TER DVS 95616 356-A4
WESTGATE DR VAC 95687 453-F4
WESTLAKE DR FRFD 94534 491-D2; VAL 94591 530-F3; WSAC 95605 358-J1
WESTLAND RANCH DR WDLD 95776 316-C5
WESTLITE CIR SAC 95831 378-H7
WESTLITE CT SAC 95831 378-H7
WESTMINSTER WY VAL 94591 530-H6
WESTMINSTER DR FRFD 94533 472-E4
WESTMORELAND WY SAC 95831 378-J7
WESTOVER LN SUIS 94585 473-C4
WESTPORT CT FRFD 94585 491-D7
WESTPORT LN VAL 94591 550-F1
WEST QUAD YoCo 95616 376-C1
WEST RANCH LN SolC 95688 393-A7; SolC 95688 413-A1
WEST SACRAMENTO FRWY I-80 WSAC 358-D4; YoCo 357-F5; YoCo 358-D4
WESTSHORE ST DVS 95616 355-H6
WEST SIDE FRWY I-5 SAC 378-J6; SaCo 317-H5; YoCo 317-H5
WESTVIEW WY SAC 95831 378-H5
WESTWAY DR WDLD 95695 315-H5
WESTWAY PL WDLD 95695 315-H5
WESTWIND CT SUIS 94585 473-A6
WESTWIND WY SUIS 94585 473-A6
WESTWOOD CIR WSAC 95691 358-H5
WESTWOOD CT VAC 95688 433-A5; WIN 95694 373-E4
WESTWOOD ST VAC 95688 433-A5; VAL 94591 530-E5
WESTWOOD WY WDLD 95695 316-A5
WETHERSFIELD DR VAC 95688 433-D2
WETLAND LN FRFD 94534 491-F4; FRFD 94585 491-F4; SolC 94585 491-F4
WETLANDS EDGE RD AMCN 94503 509-H2
WEXFORD LN VAC 95688 433-E2
WEYAND WY DXN 95620 395-B5
WEYMOUTH CT VAC 95687 453-G2
WEYRAUGH RD VAL 94592 529-G7; VAL 94592 549-H1
WHALEBONE CT VAL 94591 530-G7
WHALER AV DVS 95616 355-G7
WHEDBEE DR SolC 95688 432-H7
WHEELHOUSE AV SAC 95833 358-G1
WHIPPORWILL WY SUIS 94585 473-B7
WHISPERGLEN CT VAC 95687 433-J5
WHISPERING BAY LN SUIS 94585 472-G7; SUIS 94585 492-G1
WHISPERING OAKS CT FRFD 94534 472-D2
WHISPERING OAKS DR FRFD 94534 472-D2
WHISPERING RIDGE DR VAC 95688 413-D6
WHISTLER CT DVS 95618 356-F5
WHISTLER WY SUIS 94585 473-A7
WHISTLING STRAITS WY RVIS 94571 516-E2
WHITBY WY SUIS 94585 493-C1
WHITE DR FRFD 94533 453-D7; SolC 94533 453-D7
WHITE ALDER WY FRFD 94533 472-J2
WHITECAP WY FRFD 94533 473-A2
WHITE CHAPEL DR BEN 94510 551-B3
WHITECLIFF CT FRFD 94533 472-H3
WHITECLIFF DR VAL 94589 530-C1
WHITE FISH BAY ST WSAC 95691 378-E3
WHITEHALL CIR FRFD 94533 472-F4
WHITEHALL CT VAC 95687 453-C1
WHITEHALL WY VAC 95687 453-D1
WHITEMAN CT SUIS 94585 473-C4
WHITEMARSH DR FRFD 94534 472-B2
WHITEMARSH LN FRFD 94534 472-B2

WHITE OAK CT SOLANO COUNTY STREET INDEX U.S.-50 CAPITAL 571

© 2007 Rand McNally & Company

STREET Name City ZIP Pg-Grid

WHITE OAK CT VAC 95687 433-H7
WHITE OAK DR AMCN 94503 510-B3
WHITE OAK LN VAC 95687 433-H7; WIN 95694 373-G3
WHITE PINE DR VAL 94591 530-F4
WHITE PINE ST VAC 95687 433-J3; VAC 95687 434-A3
WHITE SANDS DR VAC 95687 433-H4
WHITE SANDS LN DVS 95616 355-J6
WHITESIDES DR VAL 94591 550-F2
WHITESTAG WY VAC 95687 453-F2
WHITE STONE CT VAC 95688 413-D6
WHITE WING CT SUIS 94585 473-A6
WHITE WING LN SUIS 94585 473-A6
WHITING CT DXN 95620 395-A7
WHITNEY AV SUIS 94585 473-C6; VAL 94589 510-B6
WHITNEY CT VAC 95687 433-J4
WHITNEY DR FRFD 94533 473-E2
WHITTER PL FRFD 94533 473-A3
WHITTIER DR DVS 95618 356-E6
WHOOPER WY SUIS 94585 473-A6
WICHELS CSWY VAL 94590 529-G4; VAL 94592 529-G4
WICHKAM ST VAL 94591 530-G4
WICK CT VAC 95687 433-D7
WICKLOW DR VAC 95688 413-E7; VAC 95688 433-E1
WIDGEON CT VAC 95688 433-C4
WIEGAND CT DXN 95620 395-B5
WIEGAND WY DXN 95620 395-B5
WIGEON WY SUIS 94585 472-J6; SUIS 94585 473-A7
WILDBERRY CT VAL 94591 530-F7
WILD DUNE CT VAL 94591 530-F1
WILDFLOWER AV VAL 94591 530-F7; VAL 94591 550-F1
WILDFLOWER CT FRFD 94585 511-E3
WILD GINGER CT VAC 95687 453-J2
WILDGINGER ST WSAC 95691 358-G7
WILD HORSE PL SolC 94534 471-B4
WILD HORSE VALLEY RD NaCo 94558 450-D6
WILDLIFE WY YoCo 95616 375-E3
WILD OAK TR SolC 95688 412-H7
WILDPLUM CT FRFD 94585 511-E1; VAC 95687 453-G4
WILD ROSE CT VAC 95687 453-J2
WILD ROSE LN WIN 95694 373-G3
WILD SAGE CT VAC 95688 413-E6
WILDWING LN VAL 94591 510-J6
WILDWOOD NaCo 94559 470-A1; NAP 94559 470-A1
WILDWOOD CT FRFD 94585 511-E2; NAP 94559 470-A1
WILDWOOD LN VAC 95687 453-E1
WILDWOOD WY WDLD 95695 315-G4
WILEY CT SolC 94533 473-D3
WILEY LN SolC 94533 473-D3
WILKIE ST FRFD 94533 472-D5
WILLAMETTE DR VAC 95688 433-A6
WILLET CT FRFD 94533 473-A3
WILLIAM ST VAC 95688 433-C6
WILLIAMS RD SolC 94534 451-F4
WILLIAMS ST WDLD 95695 315-H3
WILLIS CT VAC 95688 433-A5
WILLOTTA DR SolC 94534 471-G7
WILLOW AV WSAC 95691 358-H4
WILLOW CT BEN 94510 550-J1; BEN 94510 551-A1; FRFD 94533 473-A1; SUIS 94585 472-J5
WILLOW LN DVS 95616 356-B6; FRFD 94533 473-A1
WILLOW RD SolC 95687 414-A7; SolC 95687 434-A3; VAC 95687 414-A7; VAC 95687 434-A3
WILLOW ST VAL 94589 510-A7
WILLOW WY WDLD 95695 315-G5
WILLOWBANK RD YoCo 95618 376-G2
WILLOW CREEK CIR VAL 94591 511-A7
WILLOW GREEN CT VAC 95687 433-J4
WILLOW GREEN WY VAC 95687 433-J4
WILLOW SPRINGS DR WDLD 95776 316-B5
WILLOWWOOD CT VAC 95688 433-D3
WILLOWWOOD WY SAC 95831 378-J7
WILMINGTON CT FRFD 94533 452-H7
WILMINGTON LN RVIS 94571 516-F2
WILMINGTON WY VAC 95687 433-D7
WILSHIRE AV VAL 94591 530-D7
WILSON AV SolC 94589 529-H3; SolC 94590 529-H3; VAL 94590 529-H3
WILSON CT DXN 95620 395-A7
WILSON ST FRFD 94533 472-G5; VAC 95688 433-D6
WILSON WY AMCN 94503 509-J2; AMCN 94503 510-A2; WDLD 95776 316-B3
WINCHELL CT VAL 94589 530-B1
WINCHESTER CT FRFD 94533 472-F4; VAC 95687 433-H5
WINCHESTER PL FRFD 94533 472-F4
WINCHESTER ST VAL 94590 530-B7
WINDEMERE CT WSAC 95605 358-H2
WINDING WY SolC 95688 414-B4
WINDING SAIL CT FRFD 94534 491-B1
WINDING SAIL WY FRFD 94534 491-B2
WINDJAMMER CT VAC 95687 453-H1
WINDJAMMER DR VAL 94591 530-G7
WINDMILL CT FRFD 94585 491-D7
WINDMILL DR DXN 95620 415-D2
WINDSHADOW CT VAL 94591 550-F2
WINDSONG PL SolC 95688 393-C7; SolC 95688 413-D1
WINDSOR CT VAC 95688 413-J7; VAL 94591 530-H5
WINDSOR DR BEN 94510 530-J7
WINDSOR PL FRFD 94533 472-F4
WINDSOR WY VAL 94591 530-H5
WINDSURF CT FRFD 94533 473-A2
WINDSURFER CT VAL 94591 550-G2
WINDWARD CIR WSAC 95691 358-G5
WINDWARD CT VAC 95687 433-D7; VAL 94591 550-F3
WINDWARD WY SAC 95831 378-G7
WINDY LN YoCo 95616 375-J2
WINDY RIDGE TR SolC 95694 393-C1
WINFIELD ST DXN 95620 395-A6
WINGED FOOT DR FRFD 94534 452-C7
WINGFIELD WY BEN 94510 551-C5
WINIFRED CT WDLD 95695 315-H5
WINSLOW AV VAL 94590 530-B2
WINSLOW ST CCCo 94525 550-E4
WINSTON CT BEN 94510 550-J1; FRFD 94534 472-D4
WINSTON DR FRFD 94534 472-D4
WINTERGREEN CT VAC 95687 453-F3
WINTER HARBOR PL VAL 94591 550-F1
WINTERS RD SolC 95694 373-F4; SolC 95694 393-H1; WIN 95694 373-F4
WINTERS WY SUIS 94585 473-A6
WINTERWOOD DR FRFD 94533 452-H6
WINTHROP PL VAL 94591 530-F3
WINTU WY SolC 95694 373-F6
WINTUN CT DXN 95620 395-A6
WINTUN DR WDLD 95776 316-E5
WINTUN PL DVS 95618 376-H1
WISCONSIN AV WDLD 95695 315-H2
WISCONSIN ST FRFD 94533 472-G5; FRFD 94535 473-H3
WISE ACRES LN SolC 95688 413-A5
WISTERIA CIR VAL 94591 510-H4
WISTERIA CT BEN 94510 531-A7
WISTERIA WY YoCo 95616 375-G1
WITHAM DR WDLD 95776 316-E5
WITHEROW LN FRFD 94533 453-E7
WOBURN CT VAC 95688 433-D2
WOLF GLEN PL FRFD 94534 472-E1
WOLFSKILL AV FRFD 94535 473-G4
WOLFSKILL RD SolC 95694 373-H7; SolC 95694 374-A7
WOLFSKILL ST WIN 95694 373-F4
WOOD CT VAL 94591 530-E3
WOODALL ST VAL 94590 529-H2
WOODARD DR WDLD 95776 316-C4
WOODARD LN FRFD 94533 453-E7
WOODARD WY DXN 95620 395-A6
WOODBRIDGE CT BEN 94510 531-C7
WOODBURY CIR VAC 95687 453-G1
WOODBURY LN SolC 94591 530-E7; VAL 94591 530-E7
WOOD CREEK DR FRFD 94534 472-C5
WOODCREST CT VAC 95688 433-D2
WOODCREST DR VAC 95688 433-D2
WOOD DUCK CT AMCN 94503 509-H1
WOOD DUCK DR SUIS 94585 472-J6; SUIS 94585 473-A6
WOODEN VALLEY RD NaCo 94558 451-D1
WOODEN VALLEY CROSS RD NaCo 94558 451-E2
WOODGLEN LN VAC 95687 453-E1
WOODGREEN WY BEN 94510 551-B3
WOODHAVEN CT FRFD 94533 472-C7
WOODHAVEN DR VAC 95687 433-F7; VAC 95687 453-F1
WOOD HOLLOW CIR FRFD 94533 472-J2
WOOD HOLLOW CT FRFD 94533 472-J2
WOODLAKE DR FRFD 94534 491-D2
WOODLAND AV WDLD 95695 315-J2; WDLD 95695 316-A2
W WOODLAND AV WDLD 95695 315-G2
WOODLARK CT SUIS 94585 473-B6
WOODLARK DR SUIS 94585 473-B6
WOODMAN WY DXN 95620 395-B6
WOODMONT CT FRFD 94533 473-A2
WOODMONT DR FRFD 94533 473-A2; NaCo 94558 450-A1
WOODRIDGE CIR VAC 95687 433-H7; VAC 95687 453-H1
WOODRIDGE DR VAC 95687 453-G1; VAL 94591 530-E4
WOODRIDGE PL VAL 94591 530-E4
WOODROW AV SolC 94590 530-C6; VAL 94591 530-D6
WOODS CIR DVS 95616 355-H6
WOODS CT FRFD 94534 472-D3
WOODSHIRE WY SAC 95822 378-J5
WOODSIDE CIR VAC 95688 433-B3
WOODSIDE DR WDLD 95695 315-G6
WOODSIDE RD VAL 94589 530-B1
WOODSIDE WY FRFD 94585 511-E2
WOODSON WY VAL 94591 530-E3
WOODSTOCK CIR VAC 95687 433-G5
WOODSTOCK CT BEN 94510 551-B3
WOODVALE CT VAL 94591 530-D3
WOODVALE DR DXN 95620 395-B7
WOODVIEW CT FRFD 94585 511-E2
WOODWARD CT CCCo 94525 550-E5
WOOL CT BEN 94510 551-C1
WOOLNER AV FRFD 94533 472-C6
WOOLNER CT FRFD 94533 472-C7
WORFE ST VAL 94590 530-B4
WORLEY RD SUIS 94585 473-A5
WREN CT FRFD 94533 472-H4; VAL 94591 530-E2
WREN ST DVS 95616 356-B4
WRENTHAM DR VAC 95688 433-D2
WR GLUSJEN DR FRFD 94533 453-D6; SolC 94533 453-D6
WRIGHT ST DVS 95618 356-F5; VAL 94590 529-J3
WYCKOFF WY WDLD 95695 315-G2
WYETH CT DVS 95618 356-F5
WYKOFF DR VAC 95688 432-J5; VAC 95688 433-A5
WYLIE CT FRFD 94533 473-B3
WYLIE PL FRFD 94533 473-B3
WYOMING ST FRFD 94533 472-G5; FRFD 94535 473-H2; VAL 94592 529-G4
E WYOMING ST FRFD 94533 472-G5

Y

YACHT CT SAC 95822 378-J3
YACHTSMAN CT DXN 95620 395-C5
YACHTSMAN DR VAL 94591 550-F2
YALE AV VAC 95687 433-H5
YALE CT VAL 94589 510-A5
YALE DR WDLD 95695 315-G6
YANA PL DVS 95618 376-H1
YANKEE JIM CT VAL 94589 509-H4
YARDARM CT VAL 94591 550-F2
YARDLEY DR DXN 95620 395-B7
YARROW CT FRFD 94533 452-H6
YARMOUTH CT VAC 95687 453-H2
YARROW CT SUIS 94585 472-H7
YELLOWSTONE AV DVS 95616 355-A3
YELLOWSTONE DR VAC 95687 433-H4
YEOMAN CT DXN 95620 395-C4; VAC 95687 433-D7
YEW CT VAC 95687 433-H4
YOLANO DR VAL 94589 529-J1; VAL 94589 530-A1; WDLD 95776 316-D3
YOLO AV VAL 94590 529-J3; VAL 94590 530-A3
YOLO ST WDLD 95695 316-A2; WSAC 95605 358-H1
YORK CT VAC 95687 453-C1
YORK DR BEN 94510 550-J2; BEN 94510 551-A2
YORK ST FRFD 94533 472-D5; VAL 94590 529-J5; VAL 94590 530-A5
YORKSHIRE CT VAL 94591 530-F6
YORMAN ST FRFD 94535 473-J4; FRFD 94535 474-A3
YOSEMITE AV YoCo 95616 355-A4
YOSEMITE CIR VAC 95687 433-J3
YOSEMITE DR RVIS 94571 516-G5
YOSEMITE PL WDLD 95695 315-G2
YOSEMITE WY SUIS 94585 473-C6
YOUNGSDALE CT VAC 95687 453-F4
YOUNGSDALE DR VAC 95687 453-F3
YOUNGSTOWN LN SUIS 94585 473-D4
YUBA CT SUIS 94585 473-C7
YUBA PL WDLD 95695 315-J6
YUBA ST VAL 94590 530-B4
YUKON CT VAL 94589 509-H5
YUKON ST DVS 95616 356-A7
YUMA CT VAC 95688 433-A4
YUROK PL WSAC 95691 378-H1

Z

ZACHARY DR VAC 95687 453-F2
ZAFRA DR FRFD 94533 473-C4
ZAMORA CT VAL 94591 530-F6
ZAMORA LN DVS 95618 356-F7
ZANE DR WDLD 95776 336-E1
ZARAGOZA DR FRFD 94533 473-C4
ZARAGOZA LN VAC 95688 433-B3
ZARAGOZA ST DVS 95618 356-F7
ZEPHYR LN VAC 95687 433-J5
ZINFANDEL CT FRFD 94533 472-C7; VAC 95688 433-D4
ZINFANDEL LN VAL 94591 530-F1
ZINNIA CT FRFD 94533 472-G1
ZINNIA CIR VAL 94591 530-G7
ZINNIA CT BEN 94510 531-A7
ZION CT VAC 95687 433-J4
ZIRCON CT VAC 95687 453-G2; VAL 94589 510-B6

#

1ST AV CCCo 94525 550-D5; NaCo 94558 450-A3
1ST ST BEN 94510 551-C3; CCCo 94572 549-H7; DVS 95616 376-C1; FRFD 94533 472-E6; FRFD 94535 473-J2; SolC 95687 434-C6; WDLD 95695 315-J3; WDLD 95695 316-A3; WIN 95694 373-F3; WSAC 95691 358-F3; YoCo 95616 376-C1
N 1ST ST Rt#-113 DXN 95620 395-D6
S 1ST ST Rt#-113 DXN 95620 395-D7; DXN 95620 415-D1
2ND AV CCCo 94525 550-D5; NaCo 94558 450-B4
2ND ST CCCo 94569 550-H6; CCCo 94572 549-G7; DVS 95616 376-C1; DVS 95618 356-G7; DVS 95618 376-E1; FRFD 94533 472-E5; FRFD 94535 473-J4; RVIS 94571 516-H6; VAL 94592 529-G5; WDLD 95695 316-A3; WIN 95694 373-F3
E 2ND ST BEN 94510 531-G7; BEN 94510 551-F1
N 2ND ST DXN 95620 395-D7
S 2ND ST DXN 95620 395-D7; DXN 95620 415-D1
W 2ND ST BEN 94510 551-B5
3RD AV CCCo 94525 550-D5; NaCo 94558 450-C3
E 3RD AV NaCo 94558 450-D6
3RD ST BEN 94510 551-C4; CCCo 94572 549-G7; DVS 95616 376-C1; FRFD 94533 472-E6; FRFD 94535 473-J3; FRFD 94535 474-A3; HFR 94547 549-G7; RVIS 94571 516-H6; VAL 94590 530-B7; WDLD 95695 316-A3; WIN 95694 373-E4
E 3RD ST BEN 94510 551-C4
N 3RD ST DXN 95620 395-D7
S 3RD ST DXN 95620 395-D7; DXN 95620 415-D1
W 3RD ST BEN 94510 551-B5
4TH AV CCCo 94525 550-D4; NaCo 94558 450-A4; NaCo 94559 450-B7; NaCo 94559 470-B1
4TH ST CCCo 94525 550-A5; CCCo 94569 550-H6; CCCo 94572 549-H7; DVS 95616 376-C1; FRFD 94533 472-E6; RVIS 94571 516-H6; WDLD 95695 316-A5; WIN 95694 373-E4
E 4TH ST BEN 94510 551-C5
N 4TH ST DXN 95620 395-D7
S 4TH ST DXN 95620 395-D7; DXN 95620 415-D1
W 4TH ST BEN 94510 551-B4
5TH AV CCCo 94525 550-D5
5TH ST CCCo 94569 550-H6; CCCo 94572 549-J7; DVS 95616 356-E7; DVS 95616 376-C1; DVS 95618 356-E7; FRFD 94533 472-D6; RVIS 94571 516-H5; VAL 94590 530-B6; VAL 94590 550-C1; WDLD 95695 316-A3
E 5TH ST BEN 94510 551-C5
N 5TH ST DXN 95620 395-D7
S 5TH ST DXN 95620 395-D7; DXN 95620 415-D1
W 5TH ST BEN 94510 551-A4
6TH AV CCCo 94525 550-D5
6TH ST CCCo 94569 550-H6; CCCo 94572 549-J7; DVS 95616 356-C7; RVIS 94571 516-H5; VAL 94590 530-B5; WDLD 95695 316-A4
E 6TH ST BEN 94510 551-C6
N 6TH ST DXN 95620 395-D7
W 6TH ST BEN 94510 551-A4
7TH AV CCCo 94525 550-C5
7TH ST CCCo 94572 549-J7; DVS 95616 356-C7; RVIS 94571 516-G5; VAL 94592 529-G5
E 7TH ST BEN 94510 551-C6
N 7TH ST DXN 95620 395-D7
S 7TH ST DXN 95620 395-D7; DXN 95620 415-D1
W 7TH ST BEN 94510 551-A4
8TH ST SolC 94590 530-B5; VAL 94590 530-B5
E 8TH ST DVS 95616 356-D7; DVS 95618 356-D7
S 8TH ST DXN 95620 395-E7; DXN 95620 415-D1
W 8TH ST BEN 94510 550-J4; BEN 94510 551-A4; DVS 95616 356-B7
9TH ST DVS 95616 356-C7; VAL 94590 530-B5; VAL 94592 529-F4
W 9TH ST BEN 94510 550-J4; BEN 94510 551-A4
10TH ST DVS 95616 356-C7; VAL 94592 529-H6; WSAC 95691 358-J4
W 10TH ST BEN 94510 550-J3
11TH ST DVS 95616 356-C7; WSAC 95691 358-J4
W 11TH ST BEN 94510 550-J3
12TH ST DVS 95616 356-C7; VAL 94590 530-C5
W 12TH ST BEN 94510 550-J3
13TH ST VAL 94590 530-C5; WSAC 95691 358-J5
W 13TH ST BEN 94510 550-J3
14TH ST DVS 95616 356-C6; VAL 94590 530-C5
W 14TH ST BEN 94510 550-H3
15TH ST VAL 94592 529-J6; WSAC 95691 358-J5
16TH ST WSAC 95691 358-H5
17TH ST WSAC 95691 358-H5
18TH ST WSAC 95691 358-H5
19TH ST WSAC 95691 358-H5
35TH AV SAC 95822 378-J4
43RD AV SAC 95822 378-J5; SAC 95831 378-J5
I-5 FRWY SAC - 378-J4; WDLD - 316-A1; YoCo - 315-J1; YoCo - 316-A1; YoCo - 316-G4; YoCo - 317-A4; YoCo - 317-F4
I-5 WEST SIDE FRWY SAC - 378-J6; SaCo - 317-H5; YoCo - 317-H5
I-80 EASTSHORE FRWY CCCo - 549-J7; CCCo - 550-B6
I-80 FRWY CCCo - 550-D3; DVS - 356-J7; DVS - 376-F1; DXN - 394-J7; DXN - 395-F1; DXN - 414-J1; FRFD - 452-G6; FRFD - 471-J7; FRFD - 472-G1; FRFD - 491-C4; NaCo - 510-G3; SAC - 358-G1; SaCo - 358-G1; SolC - 375-J4; SolC - 376-D2; SolC - 394-J7; SolC - 395-G1; SolC - 414-B6; SolC - 433-A7; SolC - 452-G4; SolC - 453-A1; SolC - 471-J7; SolC - 472-A7; SolC - 490-J7; SolC - 491-C4; SolC - 510-J1; SolC - 530-C6; SolC - 550-D3; VAC - 414-D4; VAC - 433-J1; VAC - 434-A1; VAC - 452-H3; VAC - 453-A1; VAL - 510-E5; VAL - 530-C2; VAL - 550-C1; WSAC - 358-F3; YoCo - 356-J7; YoCo - 357-C5; YoCo - 376-D2
I-80 WEST SACRAMENTO FRWY WSAC - 358-D4; YoCo - 357-F5; YoCo - 358-D4
I-505 FRWY SolC - 373-H3; SolC - 393-H1; SolC - 413-J1; VAC - 413-H4; VAC - 433-G3; WIN - 373-H3; YoCo - 373-H1
I-680 BENICIA-MRTNZ BRDG BEN - 551-F7; MRTZ - 551-F7; SolC - 551-F7
I-680 FRWY BEN - 551-E5; FRFD - 491-E3; MRTZ - 551-F7; SolC - 551-E6
I-680 G MILLER JR MEM BRDG BEN - 551-E6; MRTZ - 551-F7; SolC - 551-E6
I-680 LUTHER E GIBSON FRWY BEN - 531-H6; BEN - 551-E5; FRFD - 491-E6; FRFD - 511-F3; SolC - 491-E6; SolC - 511-F3; SolC - 531-H6
I-780 FRWY BEN - 530-G7; BEN - 550-G1; BEN - 551-A3; SolC - 530-C6; VAL - 530-C6
Rt#-E6 COUNTY ROAD 31 DVS 95616 355-A5; YoCo 95616 355-A5
Rt#-E6 E COVELL BLVD DVS 95616 356-D6; DVS 95618 356-D6; YoCo 95616 356-D6; YoCo 95618 356-D6
Rt#-E6 W COVELL BLVD DVS 95616 355-H6; DVS 95616 356-B6; YoCo 95616 355-H6
Rt#-E6 MACE BLVD DVS 95618 356-J6; DVS 95618 376-J1; YoCo 95618 356-J6; YoCo 95618 376-J1
Rt#-E6 RUSSELL BLVD YoCo 95694 373-H2; YoCo 95694 374-A1
Rt#-E7 COUNTY ROAD 98 WDLD 95695 315-F7; YoCo 95616 355-F3; YoCo 95616 375-F3; YoCo 95695 315-F7; YoCo 95695 335-F3; YoCo 95695 355-F3
Rt#-E7 PEDRICK RD SolC 95620 375-F7; SolC 95620 395-F1
Rt#-E8 COUNTY ROAD 102 WDLD 95776 316-E3; WDLD 95776 336-E4; YoCo 95616 356-E2; YoCo 95618 356-E2; YoCo 95776 316-E3; YoCo 95776 336-E4; YoCo 95776 356-E2
Rt#-E8 POLE LINE RD DVS 95618 356-E5; YoCo 95616 356-E5; YoCo 95618 356-E5
Rt#-12 HIGHWAY FRFD 94533 472-A7; FRFD 94534 471-J7; FRFD 94534 472-A7; RVIS 94571 516-D2; SaCo 95641 516-J5; SolC 94533 472-E7; SolC 94534 471-J7; SolC 94534 472-A7; SolC 94534 491-J1; SolC 94571 516-A2; SolC 94585 493-C1; SUIS 94533 472-F7; SUIS 94534 472-F7; SUIS 94585 472-G7; SUIS 94585 473-A7; SUIS 94585 493-C1
Rt#-12 JAMESON CANYON RD FRFD 94534 491-A4; FRFD 94589 491-A4; NaCo 94558 490-A2; NaCo 94589 490-A2; SolC 94534 491-A4; SolC 94589 490-G4; SolC 94589 491-A4
Rt#-12 RIO VISTA BRDG SaCo 95641 516-J5
Rt#-16 COUNTY ROAD 98 WDLD 95695 315-F3; YoCo 95695 315-F3
Rt#-16 HIGHWAY YoCo 95695 315-A3
Rt#-29 BROADWAY AMCN 94503 490-A5; AMCN 94503 510-A2; NaCo 94589 490-A5
Rt#-29 HIGHWAY AMCN 94503 490-A6; AMCN 94503 510-A3; NaCo 94558 490-A1; NaCo 94589 490-A1
Rt#-29 SONOMA BLVD AMCN 94503 510-A7; SolC 94589 530-A1; VAL 94589 510-A7; VAL 94589 530-A1; VAL 94590 530-A6; VAL 94590 550-B1
Rt#-37 MARINE WORLD PKWY SolC 94589 509-J7; SolC 94589 529-H1; VAL 94589 509-J7; VAL 94589 510-B6; VAL 94589 529-H1; VAL 94590 529-H1
Rt#-37 SEARS POINT TOLL RD SolC 94559 509-A7; SolC 94559 529-F2; SolC 94589 529-F2; SolC 94590 529-F2; SolC 94592 529-F2; VAL 94590 529-F2; VAL 94592 529-F2
Rt#-84 JEFFERSON BLVD WSAC 95691 378-C7; YoCo 95691 378-C7
Rt#-84 RIVER RD RVIS 94571 516-J5
Rt#-113 EAST ST WDLD 95776 316-B3
Rt#-113 FRWY SolC - 376-A3; YoCo - 376-B3
Rt#-113 HIGHWAY DXN 95620 395-D3; SolC 95620 395-D3; SolC 95620 415-D4
Rt#-113 N 1ST ST DXN 95620 395-D6
Rt#-113 RIO DIXON RD DXN 95620 415-C4; SolC 95620 415-C4
Rt#-113 S 1ST ST DXN 95620 395-D7; DXN 95620 415-D1
Rt#-113 W C FATIO HWY DVS 95616 356-A4; DVS 95616 376-A1; SolC 95620 375-J4; SolC 95620 376-A3; WDLD 95776 316-B7; YoCo 95616 356-A4; YoCo 95616 376-A1; YoCo 95695 336-A3; YoCo 95695 356-A4; YoCo 95776 316-B7; YoCo 95776 336-A3; YoCo 95776 356-A4
Rt#-121 MONTICELLO RD NaCo 94558 450-A1
Rt#-128 GRANT AV WIN 95694 373-D4; YoCo 95694 373-D4
Rt#-128 HIGHWAY WIN 95694 373-D4; YoCo 95694 373-D4
Rt#-160 HIGHWAY SaCo 95641 516-J6
U.S.-50 CAPITAL CITY FRWY WSAC - 358-F4

SOLANO CO.

FEATURE NAME / Address City, ZIP Code — PAGE-GRID

AIRPORTS

NUT TREE 433 - F2
301 COUNTY AIRPORT RD, VAC, 95688
RIO VISTA MUNICIPAL 516 - G1
6000 AIRPORT RD, RVIS, 94571
SACRAMENTO INTL 317 - J4
6900 AIRPORT BLVD, SaCo, 95837
UNIVERSITY 375 - H3
AIRPORT RD, YoCo, 95616
YOLO COUNTY 355 - A2
AVIATION AV & COUNTY RD 29, YoCo, 95616

BEACHES, HARBORS & WATER REC

VALLEJO MUNICIPAL MARINA 529 - H4
42 HARBOR WY, VAL, 94590

BUILDINGS - GOVERNMENTAL

CALIFORNIA HIGHWAY PATROL ACADEMY 358 - F1
3500 REED AV, WSAC, 95605
CALIFORNIA STATE PRISON SOLANO 453 - D3
2100 PEABODY RD, VAC, 95687
CALTRANS TEST CTR 358 - D1
REED AV, WSAC, 95605
COUNTY ADMIN 472 - G6
580 TEXAS ST, FRFD, 94533
COUNTY AGRICULTURAL BLDG 315 - G3
70 COTTONWOOD ST, WDLD, 95695
FAIRFIELD COURT HOUSE 472 - F6
530 UNION AV, FRFD, 94533
JUVENILE HALL 315 - G2
238 W BEAMER ST, WDLD, 95695
LAW AND JUSTICE CTR 472 - F6
600 UNION AV, FRFD, 94533
SOLANO COUNTY BLDG 530 - B5
321 TUOLUMNE ST, VAL, 94590
SUSAN B ANTHONY ADMIN BLDG 376 - C1
526 B ST, DVS, 95616
USDA FOREST SERVICE 376 - D2
1100 W CHILES RD, DVS, 95618
USDA OFFICE 315 - H3
194 AVD D LOS MAIN ST, WDLD, 95695
YOLO COUNTY ADMIN BLDG 316 - A3
625 COURT ST, WDLD, 95695
YOLO COUNTY COURTHOUSE 316 - A3
725 COURT ST, WDLD, 95695
YOLO COUNTY JAIL 316 - E6
2500 AVD GIBSON RD, WDLD, 95776
YOLO COUNTY PUB WORKS 315 - G2
292 W BEAMER ST, WDLD, 95695

CEMETERIES

CARQUINEZ CEM 530 - E6
BENICIA RD & RENIDA ST, VAL, 94591
DAVIS CEM 356 - E6
820 POLE LINE, DVS, 95618
FAIRMONT MEM PK 472 - F4
1901 UNION, FRFD, 94533
HANS MEM PK 530 - D2
SKYLINE & REDWOOD, VAL, 94591
HILLSIDE CEM 529 - H2
PHELPS ST, VAL, 94590
MILITARY CEM 551 - D5
BIRCH RD, BEN, 94510
ROCKVILLE CEM 471 - G6
4219 SUISIN VALLEY RD, SolC, 94534
SAINT DOMINICS CEM 551 - D4
5TH ST & HILLCREST AV, BEN, 94510
SAINT JOSEPH CEM 315 - H5
503 CALIFORNIA, WDLD, 95695
SAINT JOSEPH CEM 516 - G5
MAIN ST & HWY 12, RVIS, 94571
SAINT VINCENT CEM 530 - E7
BENICIA RD & GLEN COVE RD, VAL, 94591
SILVEYVILLE CEM 415 - C2
7661 RIO DIXON RD, DXN, 95620
SKYVIEW MEM CEM 530 - F6
ROLLINGWOOD DR & BENICIA RD, VAL, 94591
SUNRISE MEM CEM 529 - J2
SACRAMENTO ST & VALLE VISTA AV, VAL, 94590
VACAVILLE ELMIRA CEM 433 - F6
ELMIRA RD, VAC, 95687
WEST SACRAMENTO MEM PK 358 - H5
ALABAMA AV & REGENT ST, WSAC, 95691
WINTERS CEM 373 - E3
CEMETERY RD, WIN, 95694
WOODLAND CEM 315 - H4
800 WEST ST, WDLD, 95695

CITY HALLS

AMERICAN CANYON 510 - A3
300 CRAWFORD WY, AMCN, 94503
BENICIA 551 - C5
250 E L ST, BEN, 94510
DAVIS 376 - C1
23 RUSSELL BLVD, DVS, 95616
DIXON 395 - D7
600 E A ST, DXN, 95620
FAIRFIELD 472 - F6
1000 WEBSTER ST, FRFD, 94533
RIO VISTA 516 - H6
1 MAIN ST, RVIS, 94571
SUISUN 492 - G1
701 CIVIC CENTER BLVD, SUIS, 94585
VACAVILLE 433 - C6
650 MERCHANT ST, VAC, 95688
VALLEJO 529 - J5
555 SANTA CLARA ST, VAL, 94590
WEST SACRAMENTO 358 - J3
1110 W CAPITAL AV, WSAC, 95691
WINTERS 373 - F4
318 1ST ST, WIN, 95694
WOODLAND 316 - A3
300 1ST ST, WDLD, 95695

COLLEGES & UNIVERSITIES

CALIFORNIA MARITIME ACADEMY 550 - C2
200 MARITIME ACADEMY DR, VAL, 94590
SOLANO COMM COLLEGE 491 - G1
4000 SUISUN VALLEY RD, SolC, 94534
TOURO UNIV 529 - H7
1310 JOHNSON LN, VAL, 94592
UNIV OF CALIFORNIA DAVIS 376 - A1
RUSSELL BLVD, YoCo, 95616
WOODLAND COMM COLLEGE 316 - D6
41605 GIBSON RD, WDLD, 95776

ENTERTAINMENT & SPORTS

AMERICAN CANYON SKATE PK 509 - J2
100 BENTON WY, AMCN, 94503
DIXON MAY FAIR GROUNDS 415 - D1
655 S 1ST ST, DXN, 95620
RIO VISTA SKATEPARK 516 - J4
POPPY HOUSE RD, RVIS, 94571
SIX FLAGS MARINE WORLD 510 - C7
2001 MARINE WORLD PKWY, VAL, 94589
SOLANO COUNTY FAIRGROUNDS 510 - D7
900 FAIRGROUNDS DR, VAL, 94589
VACAVILLE SKATEPARK 433 - C7
1201 ALAMO DR, VAC, 95687
WINTERS SKATEPARK 373 - D4
VALLEY OAK DR & GRANT AV, WIN, 95694
YOLO COUNTY FAIRGROUNDS 316 - A5
1125 EAST ST, YoCo, 95776

GOLF COURSES

BLUE ROCK SPRINGS GC 530 - G2
655 COLUMBUS PKWY, VAL, 94591
CHARDONNAY GC 490 - B3
2555 JAMESON CANYON RD, NaCo, 94589
DAVIS GC 355 - J2
24439 FAIRWAY DR, YoCo, 95616
EAGLE VINES GC 490 - A3
580 S KELLY RD, NaCo, 94589
EL MACERO CC 376 - J1
44571 CLUB HOUSE DR, YoCo, 95618
GREEN TREE GC 433 - J3
999 LEISURE TOWN RD, VAC, 95687
GREEN VALLEY CC & GC 471 - B4
35 COUNTRY CLUB DR, SolC, 94534
HIDDENBROOKE GC 510 - J5
1095 HIDDENBROOKE PKWY, VAL, 94591
MARE ISLAND GC 529 - J7
1800 CLUB DR, VAL, 94592
MONTARA, JOE VALLEJO MUNICIPAL GC 510 - D7
900 FAIRGROUNDS DR, VAL, 94589
NAPA VALLEY CC 450 - C3
3385 HAGEN RD, NaCo, 94558
PARADISE VALLEY GC 452 - H6
3950 PARADISE VALLEY DR, FRFD, 94533
RANCHO SOLANO GC 472 - C1
3250 RANCHO SOLANO PKWY, FRFD, 94534
RIO VISTA GC 516 - F1
1000 SUMMERSET DR, RVIS, 94571
TEAL BEND GC 317 - H1
7200 GARDEN HWY, SaCo, 95837
WILDHORSE GC 356 - E4
2323 ROCKWELL DR, DVS, 95618

HOSPITALS

CALIFORNIA MED FACILITY 453 - D2
1600 CALIFORNIA DR, VAC, 95687
GRANT, DAVID USAF MED CTR 473 - F3
101 BODIN CIR, FRFD, 94535
KAISER FOUNDATION HOSP 530 - B1
975 SERENO DR, VAL, 94589
NAPA STATE HOSP 470 - A2
2100 NAPA-VALLEJO HWY, NaCo, 94558
NORTHBAY MED CTR 472 - F4
1200 B GALE WILSON BLVD, FRFD, 94533
NORTHBAY VACAVALLEY HOSP 433 - G6
1000 NUT TREE RD, VAC, 95687
SAINT HELENA HOSP 530 - A2
525 OREGON ST, VAL, 94590
SUTTER DAVIS HOSP 355 - J5
2000 SUTTER PL, DVS, 95616
SUTTER SOLANO MED CTR 530 - C1
300 HOSPITAL DR, VAL, 94589
WOODLAND HEALTHCARE 315 - G5
1325 COTTONWOOD ST, WDLD, 95695

HOTELS

BEST WESTERN HERITAGE INN 551 - C4
1955 E 2ND ST, BEN, 94510
BEST WESTERN INN 395 - B6
1345 COMMERCIAL WY, DXN, 95620
BEST WESTERN SHADOW INN 316 - B1
584 EAST ST, WDLD, 95776
COURTYARD BY MARRIOTT 433 - G4
120 NUT TREE PKWY, VAC, 95687
COURTYARD BY MARRIOTT 472 - D5
1350 HOLIDAY LN, FRFD, 94534
COURTYARD BY MARRIOTT VALLEJO 510 - D7
1000 FAIRGROUNDS DR, VAL, 94589
HALLMARK INN 376 - D1
110 F ST, DVS, 95616
HOLIDAY INN NAPA GATEWAY 510 - C7
1000 FAIRGROUNDS DR, VAL, 94589
HOLIDAY INN SELECT 472 - D5
1350 HOLIDAY LN, FRFD, 94534

LIBRARIES

AMERICAN CANYON 510 - A4
3421 BROADWAY, AMCN, 94503
BENICIA 551 - C5
150 E L ST, BEN, 94510
CROCKETT 550 - D4
991 LORING AV, CCCo, 94525
DAVIS BRANCH 356 - C6
315 E 14TH ST, DVS, 95616
DIXON 395 - D7
230 N 1ST ST, DXN, 95620
FAIRFIELD-SUISUN COMM 472 - F6
1150 KENTUCKY ST, FRFD, 94533
KENNEDY, JOHN F 529 - J5
505 SANTA CLARA ST, VAL, 94590
RIO VISTA 516 - H6
44 SECOND ST, RVIS, 94571
RODEO 549 - H7
220 PACIFIC AV, CCCo, 94572
SPRINGSTOWNE 530 - E4
1003 OAKWOOD AV, VAL, 94591
SUISUN CITY 472 - J6
333 SUNSET AV, SUIS, 94585
TURNER, AF BRANCH 358 - J3
1212 MERKLEY AV, WSAC, 95691
VACAVILLE 433 - F5
1020 ULATIS DR, VAC, 95687
VACAVILLE TOWN SQUARE 433 - C5
1 TOWN SQUARE PL, VAC, 95688
WINTERS BRANCH 373 - F4
201 1ST ST, WIN, 95694
WOODLAND 315 - J3
250 1ST ST, WDLD, 95695

MILITARY INSTALLATIONS

COAST GUARD STA CARQUINEZ 529 - H3
WICHELS CSWY & HARBOR WY, VAL, 94590
MARE ISLAND NAVAL RESV (CLOSED) 529 - E4
MARE ISLAND, VAL, 94592
MILITARY RESV 453 - J3
MERIDIAN RD, SolC, 95687
TRAVIS AIR FORCE BASE 473 - E4
AIR BASE PKWY, FRFD, 94535
UNITED STATES COAST GUARD RESV 516 - H7
BEACH DR, SolC, 94571
US ARMY RESERVE 529 - J7
1481 RAILROAD AV, VAL, 94592

MUSEUMS

BENICIA HIST MUS 551 - E5
2060 CAMEL RD, BEN, 94510
HAYS ANTIQUE TRUCK MUS 316 - E4
2000 E MAIN ST, WDLD, 95776
RIO VISTA MUS 516 - H5
16 N FRONT ST, RVIS, 94571
TRAVIS AFB MUS 473 - J3
661 E ST, FRFD, 94535
VACAVILLE MUS 433 - C5
213 BUCK AV, VAC, 95688
VALLEJO NAVAL & HIST MUS 529 - J5
734 MARIN ST, VAL, 94590
YOLO COUNTY HIST MUS 315 - J6
512 GIBSON RD, WDLD, 95695

OPEN SPACE PRESERVES

LONE TREE POINT REGL SHORELINE 549 - G7
PACIFIC AV & SAN PABLO AV, CCCo, 94572

PARK & RIDE

PARK & RIDE 433 - C7
ALAMO DR & MARSHALL RD, VAC, 95687
PARK & RIDE 433 - D6
BELLA VISTA RD & I-80, VAC, 95687
PARK & RIDE 530 - C6
BENICIA RD & LINCOLN RD, VAL, 94591
PARK & RIDE 433 - D6
CLIFFSIDE DR & I-80, VAC, 95687
PARK & RIDE 530 - C6
CURTOLA PKWY & LEMON ST, SolC, 94590
PARK & RIDE 358 - C4
ENTERPRISE BL & 80 FRWY, WSAC, 95691
PARK & RIDE 491 - D3
GREEN VALLEY RD & I-80, FRFD, 94534
PARK & RIDE 551 - C4
I-780 & S ST, BEN, 94510
PARK & RIDE 530 - C7
I-80 & MAGAZINE ST, VAL, 94590
PARK & RIDE 472 - C6
I-80 AT W TEXAS ST, FRFD, 94533
PARK & RIDE 433 - J1
LEISURE TOWN RD & ORANGE DR, VAC, 95687
PARK & RIDE 395 - A6
MARKET LN & PITT SCHOOL RD, DXN, 95620
PARK & RIDE 472 - G2
N TEXAS ST & AIR BASE HWY, FRFD, 94533
PARK & RIDE 472 - G7
RTE 12 AT MAIN ST, SUIS, 94585
PARK & RIDE 550 - C4
SAN PABLO AV & WANDA ST, CCCo, 94525
PARK & RIDE 491 - F1
SOLANO COMMUNITY COLLEGE, SolC, 94534
PARK & RIDE 395 - C7
W B ST & N JEFFERSON ST, DXN, 95620

PARKS & RECREATION

9TH STREET PK, BEN 550 - J4
ALAMO CREEK PK, VAC 433 - A5
ALAMO PK, VAC 433 - B6
ALDEN PK, VAL 529 - H5
ALEXANDER PK, CCCo 550 - D5
AMERICAN CANYON COMM PK, AMCN 509 - J2
ANDREWS PK, VAC 433 - D5
ARLINGTON PK, VAC 453 - F3
ARROYO PK, DVS 355 - J6
ASPEN GREENBELT, DVS 355 - J6
BAHNFLETH PK, SAC 378 - J4
BEAMER CIRCLE PK, WDLD 316 - A2
BEAMER PK, WDLD 316 - A2
BEAR FLAG PK, SAC 378 - J6
BEELARD PK, VAC 433 - G7
BELL, LEE PK, FRFD 472 - F5
BENICIA COMM PK, BEN 531 - B7
BENICIA STATE REC AREA, BEN 530 - F7
BEVERLY HILLS PK, VAL 530 - D7
BLUE OAK PK, WIN 373 - G3
BLUE ROCK SPRINGS CORRIDOR, VAL 530 - F3
BLUE ROCK SPRINGS PK, VAL 530 - H2
BORGES RANCH PK, VAL 510 - C5
BRIDGEVIEW PK, BEN 551 - B4
BRIDGEWAY ISLAND PK, WSAC 378 - D2
BROWNS VALLEY PK, VAC 433 - D2
BRUNAVISTA PK, RVIS 516 - G5
BRYTE, ALYCE NORMAN PLAYFIELD, WSAC 358 - H1
BRYTE PK, WSAC 358 - H1
CAMBRIDGE PK, VAC 453 - G2
CAMPBELL PK, WDLD 316 - B5
CANNON STA PK, VAC 453 - G3
CARQUINEZ PK, VAL 550 - B1
CARQUINEZ STRAIT REGL SHORELINE PK, CCCo 550 - G5
CASTLEWOOD PK, VAL 530 - E5
CEDAR PK, DVS 356 - D7
CENTENNIAL PK, VAC 433 - E3
CENTRAL PK, DVS 376 - C1
CHANNING CIRCLE PK, BEN 530 - H6
CHAPEL PK, VAL 529 - H6
CHESTNUT PK, DVS 356 - E6
CHILDRENS WONDERLAND, VAL 530 - B4
CHRISTIANSEN PK, WDLD 315 - J3
CIRCLE PK, WSAC 358 - J5
CITY PK, WIN 373 - E4
CITY PK, BEN 551 - B5
CITY PK, RVIS 516 - H5
CITY PK, VAL 529 - J4
CITY PK, WDLD 315 - J4
CIVIC CTR PK, DVS 356 - C7
CIVIC CTR PK, BEN 551 - B5
CLUB DRIVE HIST PK, VAL 529 - H7
COLLEGE PK, DVS 356 - C7
COMBS, SAM PK, WSAC 358 - J6
COMM GARDEN, AMCN 509 - J3
COMM PK, DVS 356 - C6
CONEJO PK, DXN 395 - C5
COOPER PK, VAC 433 - H5
COUNTRY VILLAGE PK, VAC 453 - F2
COVELL PK, DVS 356 - C5
CRAWFORD PK, WDLD 315 - J6
CRESCENT PK, RVIS 516 - H5
CREST RANCH PK, VAL 510 - D6
DAVID DOUGLASS PK, WDLD 315 - F6
DAVIS GREENBELT, DVS 356 - G7
DAY PK, SUIS 472 - G7
DELTA MEADOWS PK, VAL 509 - J6
DIDION PK, SAC 378 - F6
DOS CALLES PADAN PK, VAC 433 - D7
DOVER PK, FRFD 472 - H5
DROUIN PK, RVIS 516 - G5
DUBACH PK, WDLD 316 - A1
DUTRA PK, SAC 378 - G7
EGBERT FIELD, RVIS 516 - J5
ELKHORN BOAT ACCESS, SaCo 317 - H5
ELKHORN PK, WSAC 358 - J1

FEATURE NAME Address City, ZIP Code	PAGE-GRID
ELKHORN PK, YoCo	317 - J6
ELLIOTT PK, AMCN	509 - J3
EVERMAN PK, WDLD	316 - A5
FAIRFIELD LINEAR PK, FRFD	472 - E5
FAIRMONT PK, VAL	530 - C3
FAIRMONT PK, VAC	433 - F7
FERNS PK, WDLD	315 - G5
FISHING ACCESS PK, RVIS	516 - H5
FITZGERALD FIELD, BEN	551 - B5
FOLEY, DAN PK, VAL	510 - B7
FRANCESCA TERRACE PK, BEN	551 - D4
FREEMAN PK, WDLD	316 - A3
GADWALL PK, AMCN	509 - H1
GARY TRAYNHAM PK, WDLD	315 - G1
GATEWAY PK, BEN	531 - A6
GATEWAY PK, WSAC	358 - J7
GEOPP, SAMUEL W PK, SUIS	473 - B6
GIBSON PK, VAL	530 - B4
GLEN COVE PK, VAL	550 - F2
GLEN COVE WATERFRONT PK, VAL	550 - F2
GOMEZ, LEFTY BALLFIELD COMPLEX, CCCo	549 - H7
GONZALEZ PK, WDLD	316 - B3
GRAHAM, DUNCAN PK, BEN	551 - C4
GRANT MAHONEY PK, VAL	530 - C3
GRASSLANDS PK, YoCo	376 - J7
GREENFIELD PK, WDLD	315 - H5
HACIENDA PK, DVS	356 - B5
HALL, CARL E PK, SUIS	473 - A6
HALL MEM PK, DXN	395 - D7
HARRIS, R PK, WDLD	315 - G3
HAWKINS PK, VAC	433 - G6
HEMLOCK PK, VAC	433 - B4
HENRY RANCH PK, VAL	509 - H5
HERITAGE PK, SUIS	472 - H6
HIGHLANDS PK, VAL	530 - G6
HILLVIEW PK, FRFD	472 - F2
HOME COMING PK, RVIS	516 - H3
INDEPENDENCE PK, VAL	529 - J5
IRENE LARSON PK, VAC	453 - E1
JORDAN, JANINE PK FOR DOGS, VAC	453 - A1
KEATING PK, VAC	453 - D2
KENNEDY PK, SAC	378 - H7
KIMBERLY PK, AMCN	509 - J4
KLENHARD PK, WDLD	316 - D5
LAGOON VALLEY REGL PK, VAC	452 - J2
LAKE DALWIGK PK, VAL	530 - B6
LAKE SOLANO PK, SolC	392 - J1
LAMBRECHT SPORTS COMPLEX, FRFD	473 - E6
LA PLAYA PK, DVS	356 - H6
LAUREL CREEK COMM PK, FRFD	472 - J2
LAWLER FALLS PK, SUIS	473 - B7
LAWLER RANCH PK, SUIS	473 - A7
LEWIS PK, SAC	378 - F6
LINDEN PK, WSAC	358 - F7
LINWOOD PK, AMCN	509 - J4
LITTLE LEAGUE FIELD PK, BEN	551 - C5
LITTLE LEAGUE PK, DVS	356 - C6
LONDON, JACK PK, BEN	531 - A7
MACE RANCH PK, DVS	356 - G6
MANKAS PK, FRFD	472 - D3
MARINA VISTA MEM PK, VAL	529 - J4
MCCOY CREEK PK, SUIS	473 - A7
MCINTYRE RANCH PK, VAL	510 - H7
MEADOWDALE PK, WSAC	358 - E4
MEADOWLANDS PK, VAC	433 - H7
MEADOW PK, FRFD	473 - B3
MELVIN PK, AMCN	510 - A2
MINI, ROSA PK, VAL	509 - J5
MONTEBELLO VISTA PK, SUIS	473 - D6
MONTECARLO PK, AMCN	510 - C4
MOTLEY, SANDY PK, DVS	356 - E5
NELSON PK, VAC	433 - G7
NORMANDY MEADOWS PK, VAC	453 - J1
NORTHAMPTON PK, AMCN	509 - J3
NORTH ORCHARD PK, VAC	433 - B3
NORTHSTAR PK, DVS	356 - B4
NORTH VALLEJO PK, VAL	510 - C6
NORTH WEST PK, DXN	395 - B6
N STREET MINI PK, DVS	356 - E7
OAK GROVE PK, DVS	356 - E5
OVERLOOK PK, BEN	551 - C3
OXFORD CIRCLE PK, DVS	356 - A7
PATRIOT PK, SUIS	473 - D5
PATWIN PK, VAC	433 - J6
PATWIN PK, DXN	395 - A6
PELLERIA PK, AMCN	510 - C4
PENA ADOBE PK, VAC	452 - J1
PENNSYLVANIA PK, WSAC	358 - H5
PERIMETER GREENBELT, DVS	356 - B4
PIONEER PK, WDLD	316 - E5
PIONEER PK, DVS	356 - J7
PLAY FIELDS PK, DVS	376 - E1
POCKET CANAL PARKWAY, SAC	[illegible]
POCKET PK, VAC	433 - J6
PRAIRIE PK, WDLD	316 - B5
PUTAH CREEK PK, DVS	376 - G1
PUTAH CREEK PARKWAY, DVS	376 - H1
REDWOOD PK, DVS	356 - B7
REDWOOD PK, WSAC	378 - J2
RICHARDSON PK, VAL	510 - B7
RIDGE VIEW PK, VAC	433 - E1
RIDGEVIEW PK, FRFD	491 - D7
RIVER PK, VAL	529 - H3
ROBERT ARNESON PK, DVS	356 - F5
ROCKVILLE HILLS PK, SolC	471 - D6
ROLLING HILLS NEIGHBORHOOD PK, FRFD	452 - F7
ROTARY PK, WIN	373 - F4
SACRAMENTO RIVER PARKWAY, SAC	378 - J5
SAND COVE PK, SAC	358 - G1
SANDY BEACH PK, SolC	516 - G7
SARAIVA, ETHEREE PK, BEN	551 - C5
SCHNEIDER PK, WDLD	315 - G2
SENDA NUEVA GREENBELT, DVS	356 - A5
SETTERQUIST PK, VAL	510 - A5
SEYMOUR PK, SAC	378 - H5
SHEVELAND PK, VAL	529 - J3
SHURTLEFF PK, NAP	450 - A7
SIERRA PK, RVIS	516 - H5
SIERRA VISTA PK, VAC	453 - G1
SILVER OAK PK, AMCN	510 - B3
SKILMAN, FRANK PK, BEN	551 - B1
SKYLINE COUNTY PK, NaCo	470 - B2
SLIDE HILL PK, DVS	356 - F6
SOUTHAMPTON PK, BEN	551 - B2
SOUTHLAND PK, WDLD	315 - J5
SOUTHWOOD PK, VAC	453 - E1
STONEGATE PK, VAC	433 - J5
STRENG PK, WDLD	315 - G5
SUNRISE PK, FRFD	472 - H1
SYCAMORE PK, DVS	356 - A6
TABOR PK, FRFD	472 - J4
TERRACE PK, VAL	529 - H2
THREE OAKS PK, VAC	433 - C7
TOLENAS PK, FRFD	473 - B4
TOUCHSTONE LAKE PK, WSAC	358 - G7
TREDWAY PK, WDLD	316 - A6
TROWER PK, VAC	433 - D4
TURNBULL PK, BEN	551 - B6
TURNER, MATTHEW PK, BEN	550 - J3
VAL DE FLORES PK, RVIS	516 - H4
VALLEY OAK PK, WIN	373 - D4
VETERANS PK, FRFD	472 - F3
VETERANS PK, DXN	415 - C2
VIA BELLAGIO PK, AMCN	510 - C4
VICTORIA PK, HER	549 - G7
VILLAGE PK, DVS	376 - G1
VINTAGE GREEN VALLEY PK, FRFD	491 - D3
WALNUT PK, DVS	376 - F2
WARDLAW PK EAST, VAL	530 - F3
WARDLAW PK WEST, VAL	530 - F2
WASHINGTON PK, VAL	530 - A4
WAYNE CLINE PK, WDLD	315 - G2
WENZEL PK, SAC	378 - J7
WESTACRE PK, WSAC	358 - H4
WESTFIELD PLAYSITE, WSAC	358 - H3
WEST MANOR PK, DVS	355 - H7
WEST SACRAMENTO SUMMERFIELD PK, WSAC	378 - E1
WESTSIDE PK, DXN	395 - B7
WESTWOOD PK, DVS	355 - J7
WHALEBACK PK, DVS	355 - G7
WILLOW CREEK PK, DVS	376 - G1
WILLOW GLEN PK, BEN	551 - A4
WILLOW PK, VAC	433 - C7
WILSON PK, VAL	530 - B6
WITT, ALLAN PK, FRFD	472 - D6
WOODCREEK PK, FRFD	472 - C5
WOODSIDE PK, WDLD	315 - G6

PERFORMING ARTS

FEATURE NAME Address City, ZIP Code	PAGE-GRID
FAIRFIELD CTR FOR CREATIVE ARTS 1035 TEXAS ST, FRFD, 94533	472 - F6
VACAVILLE PERF ARTS CTR 1010 ULATIS DR, VAC, 95687	433 - F5
WOODLAND OPERA HOUSE 340 2ND ST, WDLD, 95695	316 - A4

POINTS OF INTEREST

FEATURE NAME Address City, ZIP Code	PAGE-GRID
CARQUINEZ STRAIT LIGHTHOUSE SEAWIND DR, VAL, 94590	550 - B2
CLARK FIELD BEAMER ST & GRAND AV, WDLD, 95695	315 - J3
CLOCKTOWER 1189 WASHINGTON ST, BEN, 94510	551 - E6
GRAHAM, WALTER AQUATICS CTR 1100 ALAMO DR, VAC, 95687	453 - C1
SUISUN CITY HARBOR MASTER KELLOGG ST & LINE ST, SUIS, 94585	492 - G1

POINTS OF INTEREST - HISTORIC

FEATURE NAME Address City, ZIP Code	PAGE-GRID
BENICIA CAPITOL STATE HIST PK 1ST ST & H ST, BEN, 94510	551 - B5
ROCKVILLE STONE CHAPEL OFF SUISUN VALLEY RD, SolC, 94534	471 - G6

SCHOOLS - PRIVATE ELEMENTARY

FEATURE NAME Address City, ZIP Code	PAGE-GRID
DAVIS WALDORF 3100 SYCAMORE LN, DVS, 95616	356 - A4
HILLTOP CHRISTIAN 210 LOCUST DR, VAL, 94591	530 - F4
HOLY CROSS 800 TODHUNTER AV, WSAC, 95605	358 - H1
HOLY ROSARY CATHOLIC 505 CALIFORNIA ST, WDLD, 95695	315 - H4
HOLY SPIRIT 1050 N TEXAS ST, FRFD, 94533	472 - G5
MILTON JOHN L 6391 LEISURE TOWN RD, VAC, 95687	433 - J4
NEIGHBORHOOD CHRISTIAN 655 S 1ST ST, DXN, 95620	415 - D1
NORTH HILLS CHRISTIAN 200 ADMIRAL CALLAGHAN LN, VAL, 94591	530 - D3
NOTRE DAME 1781 MARSHALL RD, VAC, 95687	433 - G7
OUR LADY OF GRACE 1990 LINDEN RD, WSAC, 95691	378 - H1
REIGNIERD 380 CONTRA COSTA ST, VAL, 94590	530 - B5
SAINT BASIL CATHOLIC 1230 NEBRASKA ST, VAL, 94590	530 - C3
SAINT CATHERINE OF SIENA 3460 TENNESSEE ST, VAL, 94591	530 - F4
SAINT DOMINICS CATHOLIC 935 5TH ST, BEN, 94510	551 - C5
SAINT JAMES CATHOLIC 1215 B ST, DVS, 95616	356 - C7
SAINT VINCENT FERRER 420 FLORIDA ST, VAL, 94590	529 - J4
SOLANO CHRISTIAN ACADAMY 2000 FAIRFIELD AV, FRFD, 94533	472 - F3
VACAVILLE CHRISTIAN ACADEMY 1117 DAVIS ST, VAC, 95687	453 - D1
WOODLAND CHRISTIAN 1616 WEST ST, WDLD, 95695	[illegible]

SCHOOLS - PRIVATE HIGH

FEATURE NAME Address City, ZIP Code	PAGE-GRID
NORTH HILLS CHRISTIAN 200 ADMIRAL CALLAGHAN LN, VAL, 94591	530 - D3
REIGNIERD 380 CONTRA COSTA ST, VAL, 94590	530 - B5
SAINT PATRICK-SAINT VINCENT 1500 BENICIA RD, VAL, 94591	530 - G7
VACAVILLE CHRISTIAN ACADEMY 1117 DAVIS ST, VAC, 95687	453 - D1

SCHOOLS - PUBLIC ELEMENTARY

FEATURE NAME Address City, ZIP Code	PAGE-GRID
ALAMO 500 S ORCHARD AV, VAC, 95688	433 - B6
ANDERSON, LINFORD 415 E C ST, DXN, 95620	395 - D7
BEAMER 525 E BEAMER ST, WDLD, 95695	316 - A2
BEAR FLAG 6620 GLORIA DR, SAC, 95831	378 - J6
BEVERLY HILLS 1450 CORONEL AV, VAL, 94591	530 - D7
BIRCH LANE 1600 BIRCH LN, DVS, 95618	356 - E6
BLANC, AMY 230 ATLANTIC AV, FRFD, 94533	472 - G2
BRANSFORD 900 TRAVIS BLVD, FRFD, 94533	472 - F5
BRIDGEWAY ISLAND 3255 HALF MOON BAY CIR, WSAC, 95691	378 - D2
BROWNS VALLEY 333 WRENTHAM DR, VAC, 95688	433 - D2
BRYTE 637 TODHUNTER AV, WSAC, 95605	358 - H1
BUCKINGHAM, ELISE P CHARTER 188 BELLA VISTA RD, VAC, 95687	433 - C7
CALLISON, JEAN 6261 VANDEN RD, VAC, 95687	433 - H7
CAMBRIDGE 100 CAMBRIDGE DR, VAC, 95687	453 - G2
CANYON OAKS SILVER OAK TR & WHITE OAK DR, AMCN, 94503	510 - B3
CAVE, ELMER 770 TREGASKIS AV, VAL, 94591	530 - D4
CENTER 2900 ARMSTRONG ST, FRFD, 94533	473 - G2
CHAVEZ, CESAR 1221 ANDERSON RD, DVS, 95616	356 - B7
CLAYTON, JOHN KINDER 200 BAKER ST, WIN, 95694	373 - E3
COOPER 750 CHRISTINE DR, VAC, 95687	433 - H5
COOPER, JOHNSTON 612 DEL MAR AV, VAL, 94589	530 - B1
CRESCENT 1001 ANDERSON DR, SUIS, 94585	472 - J7
DAVIDSON, JOHN 436 DEL SUR ST, VAL, 94591	530 - D7
DIDION, GENEVIEVE 6490 HARMON DR, SAC, 95831	378 - F6
DINGLE 625 ELM ST, WDLD, 95695	315 - J4
DONALDSON WAY 430 DONALDSON WY, AMCN, 94503	509 - J2
ELM 129 ELM ST, VAC, 95688	433 - C6
ELMIRA 5416 HOLDENER RD, SolC, 95687	434 - C6
FAIRFIELD 26960 COUNTY RD 96, YoCo, 95616	355 - B7
FAIRMONT 1355 MARSHALL RD, VAC, 95687	433 - F7
FAIRVIEW 830 1ST ST, FRFD, 94533	472 - E6
FALLS 1634 ROCKVILLE RD, SolC, 94534	471 - A5
FARMAR, MARY 901 MILITARY W, BEN, 94510	551 - A3
FARRAGUT, ADMIRAL DAVID G 301 FARRAGUT AV, VAL, 94590	529 - J3
FEDERAL TERRACE 415 DANIELS AV, VAL, 94590	529 - H2
FOXBORO 600 MORNING GLORY DR, VAC, 95687	453 - F3
FREEMAN 126 N WEST ST, WDLD, 95695	315 - H2
GIBSON 312 GIBSON RD, WDLD, 95695	315 - J6
GLEN COVE 501 GLEN COVE PKWY, VAL, 94591	550 - F2
GORDON, CLEO 1950 DOVER AV, FRFD, 94533	472 - H4
HEMLOCK 400 HEMLOCK ST, VAC, 95688	433 - B4
HENDERSON, JOE 650 HASTINGS DR, BEN, 94510	551 - A1
HIGGINS, GRETCHEN 1525 PEMBROKE WY, DXN, 95620	395 - C5
HIGHLAND 1309 ENSIGN AV, VAL, 94590	530 - C3
HILLCREST 601 CALIFORNIA ST, CCCo, 94572	549 - J7
JONES, K I 2001 WINSTON DR, FRFD, 94534	472 - D3
KYLE, ANNA 1600 KIDDER AV, FRFD, 94533	472 - H5
LAUREL CREEK 2900 GULF DR, FRFD, 94533	472 - J2
LINCOLN 620 CAROLINA ST, VAL, 94590	530 - A4
LOMA VISTA 146 RAINIER AV, VAL, 94589	510 - B5
MARE ISLAND 400 RICKOVER ST, VAL, 94592	529 - G6
MARKHAM, EDWIN 101 MARKHAM AV, VAC, 95688	433 - D4
MAXWELL, RHODA 50 ASHLEY AV, WDLD, 95695	315 - G3
MILLS 401 E K ST, BEN, 94510	551 - C5
MINI, DAN 1530 LORENZO DR, VAL, 94589	509 - J5
MONTGOMERY, MARGUERITE 1441 DANBURY ST, DVS, 95618	376 - F1
MT GEORGE 1019 2ND AV, NaCo, 94558	450 - B6
MUNDY, NELDA 570 VINTAGE VALLEY DR, FRFD, 94534	491 - D3
NAPA JUNCTION 300 NAPA JUNCTION RD, AMCN, 94503	490 - A7
NORMAN, ALYCE 1200 ANNA ST, WSAC, 95605	358 - J1
NORTH DAVIS 555 E 14TH ST, DVS, 95616	356 - C6
OAKBROOK 700 OAKBROOK DR, FRFD, 94585	491 - D7
ORCHARD 805 N ORCHARD AV, VAC, [illegible]	433 - B2
PADAN, EUGENE 200 PADAN SCHOOL RD, VAC, 95687	[illegible] - D1
PATTERSON, GRACE 1080 PORTER ST, VAL, 94590	550 - B1
PATWIN 2222 SHASTA DR, DVS, 95616	355 - J6
PENNYCOOK ANNIE 3620 FERNWOOD DR, VAL, 94591	530 - E5
PLAINFIELD 20450 COUNTY ROAD 97, YoCo, 95695	335 - D1
PUBLIC COLUSA ST & KISSELL AL, VAL, 94590	530 - B5
RICHARDSON, H GLENN 1069 MEADOWLARK DR, FRFD, 94533	472 - J3
ROOT, DAN O II 820 HARRIER DR, SUIS, 94585	473 - D6
SCANDIA 100 BROADWAY ST, FRFD, 94535	473 - H3
SEMPLE, ROBERT 2015 E 3RD ST, BEN, 94510	551 - C4
SHELDON, RUTH E 1901 WOOLNER AV, FRFD, 94533	472 - D7
SIERRA VISTA 301 BEL AIR DR, VAC, 95687	453 - G1
SILVEYVILLE PRIMARY 355 N ALMOND ST, DXN, 95620	395 - B7
SOUTHPORT 2747 LINDEN RD, WSAC, 95691	358 - G7
STEFFAN MANOR 815 CEDAR ST, VAL, 94591	530 - D5
SUISUN 725 GOLDEN EYE WY, SUIS, 94585	473 - A6
SUISUN VALLEY 4985 LAMBERT RD, SolC, 94534	471 - G1
TAFOYA, RAMON HOMESTED WY & GUM AV, WDLD, 95776	316 - D5
TOLENAS 4500 TOLENAS RD, SolC, 94585	473 - B4
TRAVIS 100 HICKAM AV, FRFD, 94535	473 - G3
TREMONT 355 PHEASANT RUN DR, DXN, 95620	395 - A7

FEATURE NAME Address City, ZIP Code	PAGE-GRID
TURNER, MATTHEW 540 ROSE DR, BEN, 94510	531 - B7
ULATIS 100 MCCLELLAN ST, VAC, 95688	433 - D5
VALLEY OAK 1400 E 8TH ST, DVS, 95616	356 - E7
VICHY 3261 VICHY AV, NaCo, 94558	450 - A1
WAGGONER 500 EDWARDS ST, WIN, 95694	373 - E4
WARDLAW JOSEPH H 1698 OAKWOOD AV, VAL, 94591	530 - F3
WEIR, DAVID A 1975 PENNSYLVANIA AV, FRFD, 94533	472 - E4
WENZEL, CAROLINE 6870 GREENHAVEN DR, SAC, 95831	378 - J7
WESTFIELD VILLAGE 508 POPLAR ST, WSAC, 95691	358 - H3
WESTMORE OAKS 1504 FALLBROOK ST, WSAC, 95691	358 - H5
WHITE, D H 500 ELM WY, RVIS, 94571	516 - H4
WHITEHEAD, T L 624 W SOUTHWOOD DR, WDLD, 95695	315 - G5
WIDENMANN, ELSA 100 WHITNEY AV, VAL, 94589	510 - B5
WILLETT, ROBERT 1207 SYCAMORE LN, DVS, 95616	356 - A7
WILLOW SPRING 1585 GIBSON RD, WDLD, 95776	316 - C6
WILSON, B GALE 3301 CHERRY HILLS CT, FRFD, 94534	472 - B3
WOODLAND PRAIRIE 1444 STETSON ST, WDLD, 95776	316 - C5
ZAMORA 1716 COTTONWOOD ST, WDLD, 95695	315 - G6

SCHOOLS - PUBLIC HIGH

FEATURE NAME Address City, ZIP Code	PAGE-GRID
ARMIJO 824 WASHINGTON ST, FRFD, 94533	472 - G6
BENICIA 1101 MILITARY W, BEN, 94510	550 - J3
BETHEL, JESSE 1800 ASCOT PKWY, VAL, 94591	530 - F2
BIRD, MARY 420 E TABOR AV, FRFD, 94533	472 - H4
BUCKINGHAM, ELISE P CHARTER 188 BELLA VISTA RD, VAC, 95687	433 - C7
COUNTRY CONT 343 BROWN ST, VAC, 95688	433 - D4
DAVIS 315 W 14TH ST, DVS, 95616	356 - C6
DIXON 455 E A ST, DXN, 95620	395 - D7
FAIRFIELD 205 E ATLANTIC AV, FRFD, 94533	472 - G2
HOGAN 850 ROSEWOOD AV, VAL, 94591	530 - E5
KENNEDY, JOHN F 6715 GLORIA DR, SAC, 95831	378 - H7
KING, MARTIN LUTHER CONT 635 B ST, DVS, 95616	356 - C7
LIBERTY 350 K ST, BEN, 94510	551 - C5
MARE ISLAND TECHNOLOGY ACADEMY 2 POSITIVE PL, VAL, 94589	510 - B5
NORTH CAMPUS 5011 VANDEN RD, SolC, 95687	473 - F1
PEOPLES CONT 233 HOBBS AV, VAL, 94589	530 - B1
PIONEER 1400 PIONEER AV, WDLD, 95776	316 - D6
RIO VISTA 410 4TH ST, RVIS, 94571	516 - G6
RIVER CITY 1100 CLARENDON ST, WSAC, 95691	358 - H4
RODRIGUEZ, ANGELO 5000 RED TOP RD, FRFD, 94585	491 - D6
SWETT, JOHN 1098 POMONA ST, CCCo, 94525	550 - D5
VACAVILLE 100 MONTE VISTA AV, VAC, 95688	433 - C5
VALLEJO 840 NEBRASKA ST, VAL, 94590	530 - B3
VANDEN 2951 MARKLEY LN, FRFD, 94533	473 - F2
WINTERS 101 GRANT AV, WIN, 95694	373 - E3
WOODLAND 21 N WEST ST, WDLD, 95695	315 - H2
WOOD, WILL C 998 MARSHALL RD, VAC, 95687	433 - E7
YETO, SAM CONT 421 MADISON ST, FRFD, 94533	472 - F7

SCHOOLS - PUBLIC INTERMEDIATE

FEATURE NAME Address City, ZIP Code	PAGE-GRID
JACOB, C A 200 N LINCOLN ST, DXN, 95620	395 - B7

SCHOOLS - PUBLIC JUNIOR HIGH

FEATURE NAME Address City, ZIP Code	PAGE-GRID
EMERSON, RALPH WALDO 2121 CALAVERAS AV, DVS, 95616	355 - J7
FRANKLIN 501 STARR AV, VAL, 94590	530 - C5
HARPER 43555 E COVELL BLVD, DVS, 95618	356 - H5
HOLMES, OLIVER WENDELL 1229 DREXEL DR, DVS, 95616	356 - D6
SPRINGSTOWNE 2833 TENNESSEE ST, VAL, 94591	530 - E4
VALLEJO 1347 AMADOR ST, VAL, 94590	530 - B3

SCHOOLS - PUBLIC MIDDLE

FEATURE NAME Address City, ZIP Code	PAGE-GRID
AMERICAN CANYON 300 BENTON WY, AMCN, 94503	509 - H2
BENICIA 1100 SOUTHAMPTON RD, BEN, 94510	550 - J3
CARQUINEZ 1099 POMONA ST, CCCo, 94525	550 - D5
CRYSTAL 400 WHISPERING BAY LN, SUIS, 94585	472 - G7
DOUGLASS 525 GRANADA DR, WDLD, 95695	315 - J5
DOVER 301 E ALASKA AV, FRFD, 94533	472 - H3
GOLDEN STATE 1100 CARRIE ST, WSAC, 95605	358 - J1
GOLDEN WEST 2651 DE RONDE DR, FRFD, 94533	473 - F2
GRANGE 1975 BLOSSOM AV, FRFD, 94533	472 - J4
GREEN VALLEY 3630 RITCHIE RD, FRFD, 94534	491 - E3
JEPSON, WILLIS 580 ELDER ST, VAC, 95688	433 - B4
LEE 520 WEST ST, WDLD, 95695	315 - H4
MARE ISLAND TECHNOLOGY ACADEMY 2 POSITIVE PL, VAL, 94589	510 - B5
RIVERVIEW 525 S 2ND ST, RVIS, 94571	516 - H6
SOLANO 1025 CORCORAN AV, VAL, 94589	510 - C5
SULLIVAN, CHARLES L 2195 UNION AV, FRFD, 94533	472 - F3
VACA PENA 200 KEITH WY, VAC, 95687	433 - G6
WINTERS 425 ANDERSON AV, WIN, 95694	373 - E3

SHOPPING - REGIONAL

FEATURE NAME Address City, ZIP Code	PAGE-GRID
COUNTY FAIR MALL 1264 E GIBSON RD, WDLD, 95776	316 - A6
FACTORY STORES AT VACAVILLE 326 NUT TREE RD, VAC, 95687	433 - G4
TARGET CTR 900 ADMIRAL CALLAGHAN LN, VAL, 94591	510 - D7
TARGET CTR 900 ADMIRAL CALLAGHAN LN, VAL, 94591	530 - D1
VACAVILLE COMMONS CTR HARBISON DR & NUT TREE PKWY, VAC, 95687	433 - F5
WESTFIELD SHOPPINGTOWN SOLANO 1350 TRAVIS BLVD, FRFD, 94533	472 - E4

TRANSPORTATION

FEATURE NAME Address City, ZIP Code	PAGE-GRID
AMTRAK DAVIS STA 840 2ND ST, DVS, 95616	376 - D1
AMTRAK SUISUN FAIRFIELD STA 177 MAIN ST, SUIS, 94585	472 - F7
FERRY TERMINAL 289 MARE ISLAND WY, VAL, 94590	529 - J5
GREYHOUND BUS STA 826 2ND ST, DVS, 95616	376 - D1
GREYHOUND VACAVILLE BUS TERMINAL 1040 MASON ST, VAC, 95688	433 - D6

FEATURE NAME Address City, ZIP Code	PAGE-GRID

CUT ALONG DOTTED LINE

The Thomas Guide®

Thank you for purchasing this Rand McNally Thomas Guide! We value your comments and suggestions.

Please help us serve you better by completing this postage-paid reply card.
This information is for internal use ONLY and will not be distributed or sold to any external third party.

Missing pages? Maybe not... Please refer to the "Using Your Street Guide" page for further explanation.

Thomas Guide Title: Solano County **MKT: SAC**

Today's Date: ____________ Gender: ☐M ☐F Age Group: ☐18-24 ☐25-31 ☐32-40 ☐41-50 ☐51-64 ☐65+

1. What type of industry do you work in?
   ☐Real Estate ☐Trucking ☐Delivery ☐Construction ☐Utilities ☐Government
   ☐Retail ☐Sales ☐Transportation ☐Landscape ☐Service & Repair
   ☐Courier ☐Automotive ☐Insurance ☐Medical ☐Police/Fire/First Response
   ☐Other, please specify: ____________
2. What type of job do you have in this industry? ____________
3. Where did you purchase this Thomas Guide? (store name & city) ____________
4. Why did you purchase this Thomas Guide? ____________
5. How often do you purchase an updated Thomas Guide? ☐Annually ☐2 yrs. ☐3-5 yrs. ☐Other: ____________
6. Where do you use it? ☐Primarily in the car ☐Primarily in the office ☐Primarily at home ☐Other: ____________
7. How do you use it? ☐Exclusively for business ☐Primarily for business but also for personal or leisure use
   ☐Both work and personal evenly ☐Primarily for personal use ☐Exclusively for personal use
8. What do you use your Thomas Guide for?
   ☐Find Addresses ☐In-route navigation ☐Planning routes ☐Other: ____________
   Find points of interest: ☐Schools ☐Parks ☐Buildings ☐Shopping Centers ☐Other: ____________
9. How often do you use it? ☐Daily ☐Weekly ☐Monthly ☐Other: ____________
10. Do you use the internet for maps and/or directions? ☐Yes ☐No
11. How often do you use the internet for directions? ☐Daily ☐Weekly ☐Monthly ☐Other: ____________
12. Do you use any of the following mapping products in addition to your Thomas Guide?
    ☐Folded paper maps ☐Folded laminated maps ☐Wall maps ☐GPS ☐PDA ☐In-car navigation ☐Phone maps
13. What features, if any, would you like to see added to your Thomas Guide? ____________
14. What features or information do you find most useful in your Rand McNally Thomas Guide? (please specify)
    ____
15. Please provide any additional comments or suggestions you have. ____________

We strive to provide you with the most current updated information available if you know of a map correction, please notify us here.

Where is the correction? Map Page #: ________ Grid #: ________ Index Page #: ________

Nature of the correction: ☐Street name missing ☐Street name misspelled ☐Street information incorrect
☐Incorrect location for point of interest ☐Index error ☐Other: ____________

Detail: ____________

I would like to receive information about updated editions and special offers from Rand McNally

☐via e-mail E-mail address: ____________
☐via postal mail
Your Name: ____________ Company (if used for work): ____________
Address: ____________ City/State/ZIP: ____________

Thank you for your time and help. We are working to serve you better.

This information is for internal use ONLY and will not be distributed or sold to any external third party.

CUT ALONG DOTTED LINE

TG-noCD.06

TAPE SHUT TAPE SHUT

get directions at

randmcnally.com

CUT ALONG DOTTED LINE

2ND FOLD LINE

NO POSTAGE
NECESSARY
IF MAILED
IN THE
UNITED STATES

BUSINESS REPLY MAIL

FIRST-CLASS MAIL PERMIT NO. 388 CHICAGO IL

POSTAGE WILL BE PAID BY ADDRESSEE

RAND MCNALLY
CONSUMER AFFAIRS
PO BOX 7600
CHICAGO IL 60680-9915

1ST FOLD LINE

RAND McNALLY

The most trusted name on the map.

You'll never need to ask for directions again with these Rand McNally products!

- EasyFinder® Laminated Maps
- Folded Maps
- Street Guides
- Wall Maps
- CustomView Wall Maps
- Road Atlases
- Motor Carriers' Road Atlases

CUT ALONG DOTTED LINE